Official 1998 National Football League Record & Fact Book

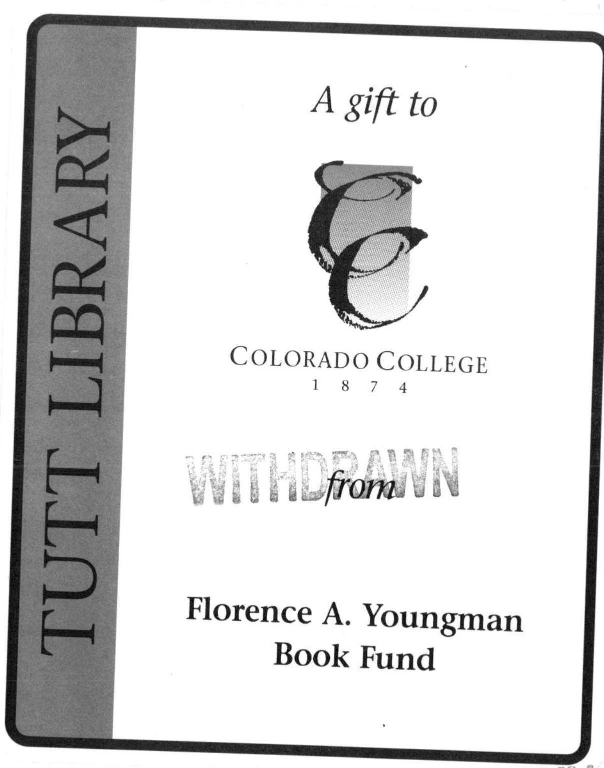

A National Football League Book.
Workman Publishing Co., New York.

NATIONAL FOOTBALL LEAGUE
280 Park Avenue, New York, N.Y. 10017 (212) 450-2000. NFL Internet Address: http://nfl.com

Printed in the United States of America.

A National Football League Book.

Compiled by the NFL Communications Department and Seymour Siwoff, Elias Sports Bureau.

Edited by Chris McCloskey, NFL Communications Department, and Matt Marini, NFLP Publishing. Layout by William Tham. Proofread by Joe Velazquez and Chip Namias. Print managing by Dick Falk and Tina Dahl. Cover layout by Helen Choy Whang and Tania Baban. Typesetting by Cynthia Jolissaint, Dawn Dellamano, Jill Franks, and Laura Basile-Dowell.
Statistics by Elias Sports Bureau.
Produced by NFL Properties, Inc., Publishing Group, Los Angeles.

Cover photograph by E.B. Graphics.

Workman Publishing Co.
708 Broadway, New York, N.Y. 10003
Manufactured in the United States of America.
First printing, July 1998.
10 9 8 7 6 5 4 3 2 1

INDEX

1998 SCHEDULE AND NOTE CALENDAR

(All times local except American Bowl games, which are EDT.)
Nationally televised games in parentheses.

PRESEASON/FIRST WEEK

Friday, July 31	Seattle ____ at Dallas ____	8:00
Saturday, August 1	Pro Football Hall of Fame Game at Canton, Ohio	
	Pittsburgh ____ vs. Tampa Bay____ (ABC)	7:00
	American Bowl at Tokyo, Japan	
	Green Bay ____ vs. Kansas City ____ (ESPN)	10:15
Sunday, August 2	New England____at San Francisco____	3:00
Thursday, August 6	New York Jets ____ at Philadelphia ____	8:00
Friday, August 7	Arizona ____ at Detroit ____	7:00
	Tennessee ____ at Atlanta ____	7:30
Saturday, August 8	Buffalo ____ at Pittsburgh ____	7:30
	Chicago ____ at Baltimore ____	7:30
	Cincinnati ____ at New York Giants ____	8:00
	Denver ____ at St. Louis ____	7:00
	Indianapolis ____ at Seattle ____	7:00
	Jacksonville ____ at Carolina ____	7:30
	Kansas City ____ vs. Tampa Bay ____ at Norman, Oklahoma	7:00
	Miami ____ at Washington ____	7:30
	New Orleans ____ at Green Bay ____	7:00
	Oakland ____ at Dallas ____	8:00
	San Francisco ____ at San Diego ____	7:00
Sunday, August 9	Minnesota ____ at New England ____	7:30

PRESEASON/SECOND WEEK

Thursday, August 13	Tampa Bay ____ at Miami ____	(ESPN) 8:20
Friday, August 14	Atlanta ____ at Detroit ____	7:00
	Carolina ____ at Buffalo ____	7:30
	Chicago ____ at Arizona ____	7:00
	New Orleans ____ at Denver ____	7:00
	New York Giants ____ at Jacksonville ____	8:00
	Pittsburgh ____ at Philadelphia ____	8:00
Saturday, August 15	American Bowl at Vancouver, Canada	
	San Francisco ____ vs. Seattle ____	(CBS) 8:00
	Baltimore ____ at New York Jets ____	5:00
	Kansas City ____ at Minnesota ____	7:00
	St. Louis ____ at San Diego ____	8:00
	Washington ____ at Tennessee ____	1:00
Sunday, August 16	Oakland ____ at Green Bay ____	(FOX) 3:00
Monday, August 17	American Bowl at Mexico City, Mexico	
	Dallas ____ vs. New England ____	(ABC) 8:00
	Indianapolis ____ at Cincinnati ____	7:30

PRESEASON/THIRD WEEK

Thursday, August 20	New York Giants ____ at New York Jets ____	(ESPN) 8:20
Friday, August 21	Buffalo ____ at Chicago ____	7:00
Saturday, August 22	Atlanta ____ vs. Pittsburgh ____ at Morgantown, West Virginia	6:00
	Dallas ____ at St. Louis ____	7:00
	Detroit ____ at Cincinnati ____	7:30
	Jacksonville ____ at Kansas City ____	7:00
	Minnesota ____ at Carolina ____	7:30
	New England ____ at Washington ____	7:30
	San Diego ____ at Indianapolis ____	7:00
	Seattle ____ at Arizona ____	7:00
	Tennessee ____ at New Orleans ____	7:00
Sunday, August 23	Miami ____ at San Francisco ____	(FOX) 1:00
Monday, August 24	Green Bay ____ at Denver ____	(ABC) 6:00
	Philadelphia ____ at Baltimore ____	7:30
	Tampa Bay ____ at Oakland ____	6:00

PRESEASON/FOURTH WEEK	**Thursday, August 27**	Dallas ____ at Jacksonville ____	(CBS) 8:00
		Detroit ____ at Indianapolis ____	7:30
	Friday, August 28	Baltimore ____ at New York Giants ____	8:00
		Cincinnati ____ at Atlanta ____	7:30
		Green Bay ____ at Miami ____	7:00
		New York Jets ____ at Chicago ____	7:00
		St. Louis ____ at Kansas City ____	7:00
		San Diego ____ at Minnesota ____	7:00
		San Francisco ____ at Seattle ____	7:00
		Tampa Bay ____ at New Orleans ____	7:30
		Washington ____ at Buffalo ____	7:00
	Saturday, August 29	Arizona ____ at Oakland ____	1:00
		Carolina ____ at Pittsburgh ____	(ESPN) 8:20
		Denver ____ at Tennessee ____	1:00
		Philadelphia ____ at New England ____	8:00
KICKOFF WEEKEND	**Sunday, September 6** **(CBS-TV National Weekend)**	Arizona ____ at Dallas ____	3:05
		Atlanta ____ at Carolina ____	1:01
		Buffalo ____ at San Diego ____	1:15
		Detroit ____ at Green Bay ____	12:01
		Jacksonville ____ at Chicago ____	12:01
		Miami ____ at Indianapolis ____	3:15
		New Orleans ____ at St. Louis ____	12:01
		New York Jets ____ at San Francisco ____	1:15
		Pittsburgh ____ at Baltimore ____	1:01
		Seattle ____ at Philadelphia ____	1:01
		Tampa Bay ____ at Minnesota ____	12:01
		Tennessee ____ at Cincinnati ____	1:01
		Washington ____ at New York Giants ____	1:01
		Oakland ____ at Kansas City ____	(ESPN) 7:20
	Monday, September 7	New England ____ at Denver ____	(ABC) 6:20
SECOND WEEK	**Sunday, September 13** **(FOX-TV National Weekend)**	Arizona ____ at Seattle ____	1:15
		Baltimore ____ at New York Jets ____	1:01
		Buffalo ____ at Miami ____	1:01
		Carolina ____ at New Orleans ____	12:01
		Chicago ____ at Pittsburgh ____	1:01
		Cincinnati ____ at Detroit ____	1:01
		Dallas ____ at Denver ____	2:15
		Kansas City ____ at Jacksonville ____	1:01
		Minnesota ____ at St. Louis ____	12:01
		New York Giants ____ at Oakland ____	1:15
		Philadelphia ____ at Atlanta ____	1:01
		San Diego ____ at Tennessee ____	12:01
		Tampa Bay ____ at Green Bay ____	12:01
		Indianapolis ____ at New England ____	(ESPN) 8:20
	Monday, September 14	San Francisco ____ at Washington ____	(ABC) 8:20
THIRD WEEK **Open Dates:** **Atlanta, Carolina,** **New Orleans, San Francisco**	**Sunday, September 20** **(CBS-TV National Weekend)**	Baltimore ____ at Jacksonville ____	4:15
		Chicago ____ at Tampa Bay ____	4:05
		Denver ____ at Oakland ____	1:15
		Detroit ____ at Minnesota ____	12:01
		Green Bay ____ at Cincinnati ____	1:01
		Indianapolis ____ at New York Jets ____	1:01
		Pittsburgh ____ at Miami ____	1:01
		St. Louis ____ at Buffalo ____	1:01
		San Diego ____ at Kansas City ____	12:01
		Tennessee ____ at New England ____	1:01
		Washington ____ at Seattle ____	1:05
		Philadelphia ____ at Arizona ____	(ESPN) 5:20
	Monday, September 21	Dallas ____ at New York Giants ____	(ABC) 8:20

1998 SCHEDULE AND NOTE CALENDAR

FOURTH WEEK	**Sunday, September 27**	Arizona ____ at St. Louis ____	12:01
Open Dates:	**(FOX-TV National Weekend)**	Atlanta ____ at San Francisco ____	1:15
Buffalo, Miami,		Denver ____ at Washington ____	1:01
New England, New York Jets		Green Bay ____ at Carolina ____	1:01
		Jacksonville ____ at Tennessee ____	12:01
		Kansas City ____ at Philadelphia ____	1:01
		Minnesota ____ at Chicago ____	3:15
		New Orleans ____ at Indianapolis ____	12:01
		New York Giants ____ at San Diego ____	1:15
		Oakland ____ at Dallas ____	12:01
		Seattle ____ at Pittsburgh ____	4:05
		Cincinnati ____ at Baltimore ____	(ESPN) 8:20
	Monday, September 28	Tampa Bay ____ at Detroit ____	(ABC) 8:20

FIFTH WEEK	**Sunday, October 4**	Carolina ____ at Atlanta ____	1:01
Open Dates:	**(FOX-TV National Weekend)**	Dallas ____ at Washington ____	1:01
Baltimore, Cincinnati,		Detroit ____ at Chicago ____	12:01
Jacksonville, Pittsburgh,		Miami ____ at New York Jets ____	1:01
St. Louis, Tennessee		New England ____ at New Orleans ____	12:01
		New York Giants ____ at Tampa Bay ____	4:15
		Oakland ____ at Arizona ____	1:05
		Philadelphia ____ at Denver ____	2:15
		San Diego ____ at Indianapolis ____	12:01
		San Francisco ____ at Buffalo ____	1:01
		Seattle ____ at Kansas City ____	(ESPN) 7:20
	Monday, October 5	Minnesota ____ at Green Bay ____	(ABC) 7:20

SIXTH WEEK	**Sunday, October 11**	Buffalo ____ at Indianapolis ____	12:01
Open Dates:	**(CBS-TV National Weekend)**	Carolina ____ at Dallas ____	12:01
Detroit, Green Bay,		Chicago ____ at Arizona ____	1:05
Minnesota, Tampa Bay		Denver ____ at Seattle ____	1:15
		Kansas City ____ at New England ____	1:01
		New York Jets ____ at St. Louis ____	3:15
		Pittsburgh ____ at Cincinnati ____	1:01
		San Diego ____ at Oakland ____	1:15
		San Francisco ____ at New Orleans ____	12:01
		Tennessee ____ at Baltimore ____	1:01
		Washington ____ at Philadelphia ____	1:01
		Atlanta ____ at New York Giants ____	(ESPN) 8:20
	Monday, October 12	Miami ____ at Jacksonville ____	(ABC) 8:20

SEVENTH WEEK	**Thursday, October 15**	Green Bay ____ at Detroit ____	(ESPN) 8:20
Open Dates:	**Sunday, October 18**	Arizona ____ at New York Giants ____	1:01
Denver, Kansas City	**(FOX-TV National Weekend)**	Baltimore ____ at Pittsburgh ____	1:01
Oakland, Seattle		Carolina ____ at Tampa Bay ____	1:01
		Cincinnati ____ at Tennessee ____	12:01
		Dallas ____ at Chicago ____	3:15
		Indianapolis ____ at San Francisco ____	1:05
		Jacksonville ____ at Buffalo ____	1:01
		New Orleans ____ at Atlanta ____	1:01
		Philadelphia ____ at San Diego ____	1:15
		St. Louis ____ at Miami ____	4:15
		Washington ____ at Minnesota ____	12:01
	Monday, October 19	New York Jets ____ at New England ____	(ABC) 8:20

EIGHTH WEEK **Open Dates:** **Arizona, Dallas, Indianapolis, New York Giants, Philadelphia, Washington**	**Sunday, October 25** **(CBS-TV National Weekend)**	Atlanta _____ at New York Jets _____	1:01
		Baltimore _____ at Green Bay _____	12:01
		Chicago _____ at Tennessee _____	3:05
		Cincinnati _____ at Oakland _____	1:15
		Jacksonville _____ at Denver _____	2:15
		Minnesota _____ at Detroit _____	1:01
		New England _____ at Miami _____	1:01
		San Francisco _____ at St. Louis _____	12:01
		Seattle _____ at San Diego _____	1:15
		Tampa Bay _____ at New Orleans _____	12:01
		Buffalo _____ at Carolina _____	(ESPN) 8:20
	Monday, October 26	Pittsburgh _____ at Kansas City _____	(ABC) 7:20
NINTH WEEK **Open Dates:** **Chicago, San Diego**	**Sunday, November 1** **(FOX-TV National Weekend)**	Arizona _____ at Detroit _____	1:01
		Denver _____ at Cincinnati _____	1:01
		Jacksonville _____ at Baltimore _____	1:01
		Miami _____ at Buffalo _____	1:01
		Minnesota _____ at Tampa Bay _____	1:01
		New England _____ at Indianapolis _____	1:01
		New Orleans _____ at Carolina _____	1:01
		New York Giants _____ at Washington _____	1:01
		New York Jets _____ at Kansas City _____	3:05
		St. Louis _____ at Atlanta _____	1:01
		San Francisco _____ at Green Bay _____	3:15
		Tennessee _____ at Pittsburgh _____	1:01
		Oakland _____ at Seattle _____	(ESPN) 5:20
	Monday, November 2	Dallas _____ at Philadelphia _____	(ABC) 8:20
TENTH WEEK	**Sunday, November 8** **(CBS-TV National Weekend)**	Atlanta _____ at New England _____	1:01
		Buffalo _____ at New York Jets _____	4:15
		Carolina _____ at San Francisco _____	1:01
		Cincinnati _____ at Jacksonville _____	1:01
		Detroit _____ at Philadelphia _____	1:01
		Indianapolis _____ at Miami _____	1:01
		Kansas City _____ at Seattle _____	1:15
		New Orleans _____ at Minnesota _____	12:01
		New York Giants _____ at Dallas _____	12:01
		Oakland _____ at Baltimore _____	1:01
		St. Louis _____ at Chicago _____	12:01
		San Diego _____ at Denver _____	2:15
		Washington _____ at Arizona _____	2:05
		Tennessee _____ at Tampa Bay _____	(ESPN) 8:20
	Monday, November 9	Green Bay _____ at Pittsburgh _____	(ABC) 8:20
ELEVENTH WEEK	**Sunday, November 15** **(FOX-TV National Weekend)**	Baltimore _____ at San Diego _____	1:05
		Cincinnati _____ at Minnesota _____	12:01
		Dallas _____ at Arizona _____	2:15
		Green Bay _____ at New York Giants _____	4:15
		Miami _____ at Carolina _____	1:01
		New England _____ at Buffalo _____	1:01
		New York Jets _____ at Indianapolis _____	1:01
		Philadelphia _____ at Washington _____	1:01
		Pittsburgh _____ at Tennessee _____	12:01
		St. Louis _____ at New Orleans _____	12:01
		San Francisco _____ at Atlanta _____	1:01
		Seattle _____ at Oakland _____	1:05
		Tampa Bay _____ at Jacksonville _____	4:15
		Chicago _____ at Detroit _____	(ESPN) 8:20
	Monday, November 16	Denver _____ at Kansas City _____	(ABC) 7:20

1998 SCHEDULE AND NOTE CALENDAR

TWELFTH WEEK	**Sunday, November 22**	Arizona ____ at Washington ____	1:01
	(CBS-TV National Weekend)	Baltimore ____ at Cincinnati ____	4:15
		Carolina ____ at St. Louis ____	3:05
		Chicago ____ at Atlanta ____	1:01
		Detroit ____ at Tampa Bay ____	1:01
		Green Bay ____ at Minnesota ____	12:01
		Indianapolis ____ at Buffalo ____	1:01
		Jacksonville ____ at Pittsburgh ____	1:01
		Kansas City ____ at San Diego ____	1:15
		New York Jets ____ at Tennessee ____	3:15
		Oakland ____ at Denver ____	2:15
		Philadelphia ____ at New York Giants ____	1:01
		Seattle ____ at Dallas ____	12:01
		New Orleans ____ at San Francisco ____	(ESPN) 5:20
	Monday, November 23	Miami ____ at New England ____	(ABC) 8:20
THIRTEENTH WEEK	**Thursday, November 26**	Minnesota ____ at Dallas ____	(FOX) 3:05
		Pittsburgh ____ at Detroit ____	(CBS) 12:35
	Sunday, November 29	Arizona ____ at Kansas City ____	12:01
	(FOX-TV National Weekend)	Atlanta ____ at St. Louis ____	12:01
		Buffalo ____ at New England ____	4:05
		Carolina ____ at New York Jets ____	1:01
		Indianapolis ____ at Baltimore ____	1:01
		Jacksonville ____ at Cincinnati ____	1:01
		New Orleans ____ at Miami ____	1:01
		Philadelphia ____ at Green Bay ____	3:15
		Tampa Bay ____ at Chicago ____	12:01
		Tennessee ____ at Seattle ____	1:05
		Washington ____ at Oakland ____	1:15
		Denver ____ at San Diego ____	(ESPN) 5:20
	Monday, November 30	New York Giants ____ at San Francisco ____	(ABC) 5:20
FOURTEENTH WEEK	**Thursday, December 3**	St. Louis ____ at Philadelphia ____	(ESPN) 8:20
	Sunday, December 6	Baltimore ____ at Tennessee ____	3:15
	(CBS-TV National Weekend)	Buffalo ____ at Cincinnati ____	1:01
		Dallas ____ at New Orleans ____	12:01
		Detroit ____ at Jacksonville ____	1:01
		Indianapolis ____ at Atlanta ____	1:01
		Kansas City ____ at Denver ____	2:15
		Miami ____ at Oakland ____	1:15
		New England ____ at Pittsburgh ____	1:01
		New York Giants ____ at Arizona ____	2:05
		San Diego ____ at Washington ____	1:01
		San Francisco ____ at Carolina ____	1:01
		Seattle ____ at New York Jets ____	1:01
		Chicago ____ at Minnesota ____	(ESPN) 7:20
	Monday, December 7	Green Bay ____ at Tampa Bay ____	(ABC) 8:20
FIFTEENTH WEEK	**Sunday, December 13**	Arizona ____ at Philadelphia ____	1:01
	(FOX-TV National Weekend)	Atlanta ____ at New Orleans ____	12:01
		Chicago ____ at Green Bay ____	12:01
		Cincinnati ____ at Indianapolis ____	1:01
		Dallas ____ at Kansas City ____	3:15
		Denver ____ at New York Giants ____	1:01
		Minnesota ____ at Baltimore ____	4:15
		New England ____ at St. Louis ____	12:01
		Oakland ____ at Buffalo ____	1:01
		Pittsburgh ____ at Tampa Bay ____	1:01
		San Diego ____ at Seattle ____	1:05
		Tennessee ____ at Jacksonville ____	1:01
		Washington ____ at Carolina ____	1:01
		New York Jets ____ at Miami ____	(ESPN) 8:20
	Monday, December 14	Detroit ____ at San Francisco ____	(ABC) 5:20

SIXTEENTH WEEK

Saturday, December 19	New York Jets ____ at Buffalo ____	(CBS) 12:35
	Tampa Bay ____ at Washington ____	(FOX) 4:05
Sunday, December 20	Atlanta ____ at Detroit ____	1:01
(FOX-TV National Weekend)	Baltimore ____ at Chicago ____	12:01
	Cincinnati ____ at Pittsburgh ____	1:01
	Indianapolis ____ at Seattle ____	1:05
	Kansas City ____ at New York Giants ____	1:01
	New Orleans ____ at Arizona ____	2:15
	Oakland ____ at San Diego ____	1:05
	Philadelphia ____ at Dallas ____	3:15
	St. Louis ____ at Carolina ____	1:01
	San Francisco ____ at New England ____	1:01
	Tennessee ____ at Green Bay ____	12:01
	Jacksonville ____ at Minnesota ____	(ESPN) 7:20
Monday, December 21	Denver ____ at Miami ____	(ABC) 8:20

SEVENTEENTH WEEK

Saturday, December 26	Kansas City ____ at Oakland ____	(CBS) 1:05
	Minnesota ____ at Tennessee ____	(FOX) 11:35A.M.
Sunday, December 27	Buffalo ____ at New Orleans ____	12:01
(CBS-TV National Weekend)	Carolina ____ at Indianapolis ____	1:01
	Detroit ____ at Baltimore ____	1:01
	Green Bay ____ at Chicago ____	12:01
	Miami ____ at Atlanta ____	1:01
	New England ____ at New York Jets ____	1:01
	New York Giants ____ at Philadelphia ____	4:05
	St. Louis ____ at San Francisco ____	1:05
	San Diego ____ at Arizona ____	2:15
	Seattle ____ at Denver ____	2:15
	Tampa Bay ____ at Cincinnati ____	1:01
	Washington ____ at Dallas ____	(ESPN) 7:20
Monday, December 28	Pittsburgh ____ at Jacksonville ____	(ABC) 8:20

Wild Card Playoff Games
Site Priorities
Three Wild Card teams (division non-champions with best three records) from each conference and the division champion with the third-best record in each conference will enter the first round of the playoffs. The division champion with the third-best record will play host to the Wild Card team with the third-best record. The Wild Card team with the best record will play host to the Wild Card team with the second-best record. There are no restrictions on intra-division games.

Saturday, January 2, 1999
American Football Conference
__________ at __________ (ABC)
National Football Conference
__________ at __________ (ABC)

Sunday, January 3, 1999
American Football Conference
__________ at __________ (CBS)
National Football Conference
__________ at __________ (FOX)

Divisional Playoff Games
Site Priorities
In each conference, the two division champions with the highest won-lost-tied percentage during the regular season will play host to the Wild Card winners. The division champion with the best record in each conference is assured of playing the lowest seeded Wild Card survivor. There are no restrictions on intra-division games.

Saturday, January 9, 1999
American Football Conference
__________ at __________ (CBS)
National Football Conference
__________ at __________ (FOX)

Sunday, January 10, 1999
American Football Conference
__________ at __________ (CBS)
National Football Conference
__________ at __________ (FOX)

1998 SCHEDULE AND NOTE CALENDAR

Championship Games **Site Priorities for Championship Games** The home teams will be the surviving playoff winners with the best won-lost-tied percentage during the regular season. A Wild Card team cannot play host unless two Wild Card teams are in the game, in which case the Wild Card team that was seeded highest in the first round of the playoffs will be the home team.	**Sunday, January 17, 1999**	American Football Conference __________ at __________ (CBS) National Football Conference __________ at __________ (FOX)
Super Bowl XXXIII	**Sunday, January 31, 1999**	Super Bowl XXXIII at Pro Player Stadium, Miami, Florida __________ vs. __________(FOX)
AFC-NFC Pro Bowl	**Sunday, February 7, 1999**	AFC-NFC Pro Bowl at Honolulu, Hawaii AFC __________ vs. NFC __________(ABC)

POSTSEASON AND NATIONALLY TELEVISED GAMES

POSTSEASON GAMES

Saturday, January 2	AFC and NFC Wild Card Playoffs (ABC)
Sunday, January 3	AFC and NFC Wild Card Playoffs (CBS and FOX)
Saturday, January 9	AFC and NFC Divisional Playoffs (CBS and FOX)
Sunday, January 10	AFC and NFC Divisional Playoffs (CBS and FOX)
Sunday, January 17	AFC and NFC Championship Games (CBS and FOX)
Sunday, January 31	Super Bowl XXXIII at Pro Player Stadium in Miami, Florida (FOX)
Sunday, February 7	AFC-NFC Pro Bowl in Honolulu, Hawaii (ABC)

1998 NATIONALLY TELEVISED GAMES

Regular Season

Sunday, September 6	New York Jets at San Francisco (day, CBS)
	Oakland at Kansas City (night, ESPN)
Monday, September 7	New England at Denver (night, ABC)
Sunday, September 13	Dallas at Denver (day, FOX)
	Indianapolis at New England (night, ESPN)
Monday, September 14	San Francisco at Washington (night, ABC)
Sunday, September 20	Denver at Oakland (day, CBS)
	Philadelphia at Arizona (night, ESPN)
Monday, September 21	Dallas at New York Giants (night, ABC)
Sunday, September 27	Minnesota at Chicago (day, FOX)
	Cincinnati at Baltimore (night, ESPN)
Monday, September 28	Tampa Bay at Detroit (night, ABC)
Sunday, October 4	Philadelphia at Denver (day, FOX)
	Seattle at Kansas City (night, ESPN)
Monday, October 5	Minnesota at Green Bay (night, ABC)
Sunday, October 11	Denver at Seattle (day, CBS)
	Atlanta at New York Giants (night, ESPN)
Monday, October 12	Miami at Jacksonville (night, ABC)
Thursday, October 15	Green Bay at Detroit (night, ESPN)
Sunday, October 18	Dallas at Chicago (day, FOX)
Monday, October 19	New York Jets at New England (night, ABC)
Sunday, October 25	Jacksonville at Denver (day, CBS)
	Buffalo at Carolina (night, ESPN)
Monday, October 26	Pittsburgh at Kansas City (night, ABC)
Sunday, November 1	San Francisco at Green Bay (day, FOX)
	Oakland at Seattle (night, ESPN)
Monday, November 2	Dallas at Philadelphia (night, ABC)
Sunday, November 8	San Diego at Denver (day, CBS)
	Tennessee at Tampa Bay (night, ESPN)
Monday, November 9	Green Bay at Pittsburgh (night, ABC)
Sunday, November 15	Green Bay at New York Giants (day, FOX)
	Chicago at Detroit (night, ESPN)
Monday, November 16	Denver at Kansas City (night, ABC)
Sunday, November 22	Oakland at Denver (day, CBS)
	New Orleans at San Francisco (night, ESPN)
Monday, November 23	Miami at New England (night, ABC)
Thursday, November 26	Pittsburgh at Detroit (day, CBS)
	Minnesota at Dallas (day, FOX)
Sunday, November 29	Philadelphia at Green Bay (day, FOX)
	Denver at San Diego (night, ESPN)
Monday, November 30	New York Giants at San Francisco (night, ABC)
Thursday, December 3	St. Louis at Philadelphia (night, ESPN)
Sunday, December 6	Kansas City at Denver (day, CBS)
	Chicago at Minnesota (night, ESPN)
Monday, December 7	Green Bay at Tampa Bay (night, ABC)
Sunday, December 13	Dallas at Kansas City (day, FOX)
	New York Jets at Miami (night, ESPN)
Monday, December 14	Detroit at San Francisco (night, ABC)
Saturday, December 19	New York Jets at Buffalo (day, CBS)
	Tampa Bay at Washington (day, FOX)
Sunday, December 20	Philadelphia at Dallas (day, FOX)
	Jacksonville at Minnesota (night, ESPN)
Monday, December 21	Denver at Miami (night, ABC)
Saturday, December 26	Minnesota at Tennessee (day, FOX)
	Kansas City at Oakland (day, CBS)
Sunday, December 27	Seattle at Denver (day, CBS)
	Washington at Dallas (night, ESPN)
Monday, December 28	Pittsburgh at Jacksonville (night, ABC)

NATIONAL PRIMETIME TELEVISION GAMES AT A GLANCE

(All times local; Sunday and Thursday on ESPN, Monday on ABC; all on CBS radio)

Sunday, September 6	Oakland at Kansas City (ESPN)	7:20
Monday, September 7	New England at Denver (ABC)	6:20
Sunday, September 13	Indianapolis at New England (ESPN)	8:20
Monday, September 14	San Francisco at Washington (ABC)	8:20
Sunday, September 20	Philadelphia at Arizona (ESPN)	6:20
Monday, September 21	Dallas at New York Giants (ABC)	8:20
Sunday, September 27	Cincinnati at Baltimore (ESPN)	8:20
Monday, September 28	Tampa Bay at Detroit (ABC)	8:20
Sunday, October 4	Seattle at Kansas City (ESPN)	7:20
Monday, October 5	Minnesota at Green Bay (ABC)	7:20
Sunday, October 11	Atlanta at New York Giants (ESPN)	8:20
Monday, October 12	Miami at Jacksonville (ABC)	8:20
Thursday, October 15	Green Bay at Detroit (ESPN)	8:20
Monday, October 19	New York Jets at New England (ABC)	8:20
Sunday, October 25	Buffalo at Carolina (ESPN)	8:20
Monday, October 26	Pittsburgh at Kansas City (ABC)	7:20
Sunday, November 1	Oakland at Seattle (ESPN)	5:20
Monday, November 2	Dallas at Philadelphia (ABC)	8:20
Sunday, November 8	Tennessee at Tampa Bay (ESPN)	8:20
Monday, November 9	Green Bay at Pittsburgh (ABC)	8:20
Sunday, November 15	Chicago at Detroit (ESPN)	8:20
Monday, November 16	Denver at Kansas City (ABC)	7:20
Sunday, November 22	New Orleans at San Francisco (ESPN)	5:20
Monday, November 23	Miami at New England (ABC)	8:20
Sunday, November 29	Denver at San Diego (ESPN)	5:20
Monday, November 30	New York Giants at San Francisco (ABC)	5:20
Thursday, December 3	St. Louis at Philadelphia (ESPN)	8:20
Sunday, December 6	Chicago at Minnesota (ESPN)	7:20
Monday, December 7	Green Bay at Tampa Bay (ABC)	8:20
Sunday, December 13	New York Jets at Miami (ESPN)	8:20
Monday, December 14	Detroit at San Francisco (ABC)	5:20
Sunday, December 20	Jacksonville at Minnesota (ESPN)	7:20
Monday, December 21	Denver at Miami (ABC)	8:20
Sunday, December 27	Washington at Dallas (ESPN)	7:20
Monday, December 28	Pittsburgh at Jacksonville (ABC)	8:20

IMPORTANT DATES

1998

July 7	Claiming period of 24 hours begins in waiver system. All waiver requests for the rest of the year are no-recall and no-withdrawal.
Mid-July	Training camps open. Veteran players cannot be required to report earlier than 15 days prior to club's first preseason game or July 15, whichever is later.
July 15	Signing period ends at 4 P.M., Eastern Time, for Unrestricted Free Agents to whom June 1 tender was made by Old Club, and for Transition Players, and Franchise Players who are eligible to recieve Offer Sheets. After this date and through 4 P.M., Eastern Time, on November 10, Old Club has exclusive negotiating rights to these players.
August 1	Hall of Fame Game, Canton, Ohio: Pittsburgh vs. Tampa Bay.
August 1	American Bowl, Tokyo, Japan: Green Bay vs. Kansas City.
August 7	If a drafted rookie has not signed with his club by this date, he may not be traded to any other club in 1998.
August 7	Deadline for players under contract to report in order to earn a season of free agency credit.
August 15	American Bowl, Vancouver, Canada: San Francisco vs. Seattle.
August 17	American Bowl, Mexico City, Mexico: Dallas vs. New England.
August 25	Roster cutdown to maximum of 60 players on Active List by 4 P.M., Eastern Time.
August 30	Roster cutdown to maximum of 53 players on Active/Inactive List by 4 P.M., Eastern Time. Clubs may dress minimum of 42 and maximum of 45 players and third quarterback for each regular-season and postseason game.
August 31	After 4 P.M., Eastern Time, clubs may establish a Practice Squad of five players by signing free agents who do not have an accrued season of free-agency credit or who were on the Active/Inactive List for less than nine regular season games during their only Accrued Season(s).
September 4	All clubs are required to identify their 49-player Active List by 7:00 P.M., Eastern Time, on this Friday and thereafter on each Friday before a regular-season Sunday game. No later than one hour and 30 minutes prior to kickoff, clubs must identify their 45-player Active List and third quarterback, if any.
September 6-7	Regular season opens.
September 22	Priority on multiple waiver claims is now based on the current season's standing.
October 13	All trading ends at 4 P.M., Eastern Time.
October 14	Players with at least four previous pension-credited seasons are subject to the waiver system for the remainder of the regular season and postseason.
October 27-28	NFL Fall Meeting, Kansas City, Missouri.
November 10	Deadline for clubs to sign by 4 P.M., Eastern Time, their Franchise and Transition players. If still unsigned after this date, such players are prohibited from playing in NFL in 1998.
November 10	Deadline for clubs to sign by 4 P.M., Eastern Time, their Unrestricted and Restricted Free Agents to whom June 1 tender was made. If still unsigned after this date, such players are prohibited from playing in NFL in 1998.
November 10	Deadline for clubs to sign drafted players by 4 P.M., Eastern Time. If such players remain unsigned, they are prohibited from playing in NFL in 1998.
November 28	Deadline for reinstatement of players in Reserve List categories of Retired, Did Not Report, Exclusive Rights, and of players who were placed on Reserve/Left Squad in a previous season.
December 25	Deadline for waiver requests in 1998, except for "special waiver requests" which have a 10-day claiming period, with termination or assignment delayed until after the Super Bowl.
December 29	Clubs may begin signing free-agent players for the 1999 season.

1999

January 2-3	Wild-Card Playoff Games.
January 9-10	Divisional Playoff Games.
January 17	AFC and NFC Championship Games.
January 31	Super Bowl XXXIII, Pro Player Stadium, Miami, Florida.
February 7	AFC-NFC Pro Bowl, Honolulu, Hawaii.
February 8	Waiver system begins for 1999. Players with at least four previous pension-credited seasons that a club desires to terminate are not subject to the waiver system until after the trading deadline.
February 11	Deadline for clubs to designate Franchise and Transition Players.
February 11	Expiration date of all player contracts due to expire in 1999.
February 12	Free Agency period begins.
February 12	Trading period begins for 1999 after expiration of all 1998 contracts.
February 18-22	Combine Timing and Testing, RCA Dome, Indianapolis, Indiana.
March 14-18	NFL Annual Meeting, Phoenix, Arizona.
*April 12	Deadline for signing of Offer Sheets by Restricted Free Agents.
*April 17-18	Annual player selection meeting, New York, New York.
May 25-28	NFL Spring Meeting, Atlanta, Georgia.
*June 1	Deadline for Old Club to send tender to its unsigned Restricted Free Agents or to extend Qualifying Offer, whichever is greater, in order to retain rights.
*June 1	Deadline for Old Club to send tender to its unsigned Unrestricted Free Agents to retain rights if player is not signed by another club by July 15.
*July 31	Hall of Fame Game, Canton, Ohio.
*September 12-13	Regular season opens.

2000

*January 8-9	Wild-Card Playoff Games.
*January 15-16	Divisional Playoff Games.
*January 23	AFC and NFC Championship Games.
*January 30	Super Bowl XXXIV, Georgia Dome, Atlanta, Georgia.

2001

*January 28	Super Bowl XXXV, Tampa, Florida.

**Tentatively scheduled.*

The NFL is online to provide fans and media quick and easy access to all the latest professional football information.

NFL.COM—(http://nfl.com)

NFL.com, the league's year-round home page on the Internet, enters its fourth season in cyberspace. The site continues to provide NFL information during the regular season, postseason, and offseason, including:

NEWS/STATS: Up-to-the-minute news from around the league, plus game previews, injury reports, and player and team stats.

TEAM AREAS: Customized areas for all 31 clubs featuring updated rosters, depth carts, and all the latest news from the teams.

GAMEDAY COVERAGE: Live game coverage with play-by-play, scores, and statistics, including graphical drive charts and comprehensive Java scoreboard that does not require reloading to get the latest information. Also includes "Player Tracker," which instantaneously updates individual player statistics.

VIDEO HIGHLIGHTS: The site will showcase NFL Films video highlights of the previous week's games as well as upcoming matchups. Video will also support feature stories and team highlight clips from every game last season.

PLAY FOOTBALL: An interactive area dedicated to the league's younger fans featuring educational and interactive games and activities, plus information on players and teams.

SUPERBOWL.COM—(http://superbowl.com)

Look for superbowl.com in late December for complete coverage of the playoffs and Super Bowl XXXIII. The multimedia site follows all postseason action and features audio and video clips of past Super Bowls.

During the week leading up to Super Bowl XXXIII, the site will go 'live' from south Florida, providing coverage of events, press conferences, and chats with Super Bowl players.

On Super Bowl Sunday, superbowl.com will showcase a live Internet cybercast, complete with online commentators calling the action. The site also features digital photos from the game, live public address audio and press-box announcements, and live audio from foreign broadcasts.

NFLeurope.COM—(http://nfleurope.com)

The official site of NFL Europe League provides in-depth information on the six teams and their players, streaming video of one game each weekend, live audio broadcasts of all games, and weekly video highlights of game action. In addition, the site includes collectible online player trading cards of the league's Players of the Week, weekly player diaries from NFL allocated players, as well as a complete league stats package.

NFL PLAYER SITES

Following are addresses for some current and former NFL players who have their own websites:

Darren Bennett, Chargers (www.nflaussie.com)
Doug Brien, Saints (www.kicking.com)
Robert Brooks, Packers (www.robertbrooks.com)
Toi Cook, Panthers (www.bltpro.com/cookbook/)
Brett Favre, Packers (www.favre4.com)
Jim Flanigan, Bears (www.jimflanigan.com)
Jim Kelly, Bills (www.jimkelly.com)
Jerry Rice, 49ers (www.sportsline.com/u/jrice/)
Reggie Rivers, Broncos (http://www.reggierivers.com)
Junior Seau, Chargers (www.juniorseau.org/)
Fran Tarkenton, Vikings-Giants (www.tarkenton.com)
Mike Utley, Lions (www.imageone.com/mikeutley/)

OFFICIAL NFL TEAM SITES

In addition to a dedicated area on NFL.COM, several teams have created their own Web sites, which have separate URLs, and are hot linked from NFL.COM.

Atlanta Falcons (www.atlantafalcons.com)
Buffalo Bills (www.buffalobills.com)
Cleveland Browns (www.clevelandbrowns.com)
Dallas Cowboys (www.dallascowboys.com)
Denver Broncos (www.denverbroncos.com)
Detroit Lions (www.detroitlions.com)
Green Bay Packers (www.packers.com)
Jacksonville Jaguars (www.jaguarsnfl.com)
Indianapolis Colts (www.colts.com)
Kansas City Chiefs (www.kcchiefs.com)
Miami Dolphins (www.pwr.com/dolphins)
New England Patriots (www.patriots.com)
New York Giants (www.giants.com)
New York Jets (www.newyorkjets.com)
Oakland Raiders (www.raiders.com)
Philadelphia Eagles (www.eaglesnet.com)
St. Louis Rams (www.stlouisrams.com)
San Francisco 49ers (www.sf49ers.com)
Seattle Seahawks (www.seahawks.com)

1998 SCHEDULING FORMULA

Each 1998 team schedule is based on a "common-opponent" formula initiated for the 1978 season and most recently modified in 1995. Under the common-opponent format, all teams in a division play at least 11 of their 16 games the following season against common opponents. It is not a position scheduling format in which the strong play the strong and the weak play the weak.

In creating a schedule, the NFL seeks an easily understood and balanced formula that provides both competitive equality and a variety of opponents. Under the rotation scheduling system in effect from 1970-77, non-division opponents were determined by a pre-set formula. This often resulted in competitive imbalances.

With common opponents as the basis for scheduling, a more competitive and equitable method of determining division champions and postseason playoff representatives has developed. Teams battling for a division title are playing more than two-thirds of their games against common opponents.

In 1987, NFL owners passed a bylaw proposal designed to modify the common-opponent scheduling format and create greater equity. And in 1995, with the addition of two expansion teams, the 1987 changes were modified to include fifth-place teams in the common-opponent scheduling format for each division. The following chart shows a history of the pairings in non-division games within the conference since the change to a common-opponent format in 1978:

Prior Year's Finish in Division	Current Pairings in Non-Division Games Within Conference	Previous Pairings 1987-94	Previous Pairings 1978-86
1	1-1-2-3	1-1-2-3	1-1-4-4
2	1-2-2-4	1-2-2-4	2-2-3-3
3	1-3-3-5	1-3-3-4	2-2-3-3
4	2-4-4-5	2-3-4-4	1-1-4-4
5	3-4-5-5		

Under the common-opponent format, schedules of all NFL teams are figured according to the following formula. (The reference point for the figuring is the team's final division standing. Ties in divisions are broken according to the tie-breaking procedures outlined on page 15.)

1. Home-and-away round-robin **within the division** (8 games).
2. In the **interconference games,** each team plays four teams in a division of the other conference (4 games). In 1998, the AFC East plays the NFC West, the AFC Central plays the NFC Central, and the AFC West plays the NFC East.
   Individual interconference matchups for the 1998 season are a reflection of a rotation of interconference games put in place prior to the 1995 seaon.
3. **Within the conference,** the first-place team plays the first-place teams in the other divisions plus a second- and third-place team in the conference. The second-place team plays the second-place teams in the other divisions plus a first- and fourth-place team in the conference. The third-place team plays the third-place teams in the other divisions plus a first- and fifth-place team in the conference. The fourth-place team plays the fourth-place teams in the other divisions plus a second- and fifth-place team in the conference. The fifth-place team plays the fifth-place teams in the other divisions plus a third- and fourth-place team in the conference (4 games, see chart).

This completes the 16-game schedule.

With the addition of Cleveland as the NFL's 31st franchise, scheduling formulas (both intra-conference and inter-conference) for the 1999 season and beyond will be distributed during the 1998 season.

NOTES

The following procedures will be used to break standings ties for postseason playoffs and to determine regular-season schedules. NOTE: Tie games count as one-half win and one-half loss for both clubs.

TO BREAK A TIE WITHIN A DIVISION

If, at the end of the regular season, two or more clubs in the same division finish with identical won-lost-tied percentages, the following steps will be taken until a champion is determined.

TWO CLUBS

1. Head-to-head (best won-lost-tied percentage in games between the clubs).
2. Best won-lost-tied percentage in games played within the division.
3. Best won-lost-tied percentage in games played within the conference.
4. Best won-lost-tied percentage in common games, if applicable.
5. Best net points in division games.
6. Best net points in all games.
7. Strength of schedule.
8. Best net touchdowns in all games.
9. Coin toss.

THREE OR MORE CLUBS

(Note: If two clubs remain tied after third or other clubs are eliminated during any step, tie breaker reverts to step 1 of the two-club format).

1. Head-to-head (best won-lost-tied percentage in games among the clubs).
2. Best won-lost-tied percentage in games played within the division.
3. Best won-lost-tied percentage in games played within the conference.
4. Best won-lost-tied percentage in common games.
5. Best net points in division games.
6. Best net points in all games.
7. Strength of schedule.
8. Best net touchdowns in all games.
9. Coin toss.

TO BREAK A TIE FOR THE WILD-CARD TEAM

If it is necessary to break ties to determine the three Wild-Card clubs from each conference, the following steps will be taken.

1. If the tied clubs are from the same division, apply division tie breaker.
2. If the tied clubs are from different divisions, apply the following steps.

TWO CLUBS

1. Head-to-head, if applicable.
2. Best won-lost-tied percentage in games played within the conference.
3. Best won-lost-tied percentage in common games, minimum of four.
4. Best net points in conference games.
5. Best net points in all games.
6. Strength of schedule.
7. Best net touchdowns in all games.
8. Coin toss.

THREE OR MORE CLUBS

(Note: If two clubs remain tied after third or other clubs are eliminated, tie breaker reverts to step 1 of applicable two-club format.)

1. Apply division tie breaker to eliminate all but the highest ranked club in each division prior to proceeding to step 2. The original seeding within a division upon application of the division tie breaker remains the same for all subsequent applications of the procedure that are necessary to identify the three Wild-Card participants.
2. Head-to-head sweep. (Applicable only if one club has defeated each of the others or if one club has lost to each of the others.)
3. Best won-lost-tied percentage in games played within the conference.
4. Best won-lost-tied percentage in common games, minimum of four.
5. Best net points in conference games.
6. Best net points in all games.
7. Strength of schedule.
8. Best net touchdowns in all games.
9. Coin toss.

When the first Wild-Card team has been identified, the procedure is repeated to name the second Wild-Card, i.e., eliminate all but the highest-ranked club in each division prior to proceeding to step 2, and repeated a third time, if necessary, to identify the third Wild Card. In situations where three or more teams from the same division are involved in the procedure, the original seeding of the teams remains the same for subsequent applications of the tie breaker if the top-ranked team in that division qualifies for a Wild-Card berth.

OTHER TIE-BREAKING PROCEDURES

1. Only one club advances to the playoffs in any tie-breaking step. Remaining tied clubs revert to the first step of the applicable division or Wild-Card tie breakers. As an example, if two clubs remain tied in any tie-breaker step after all other clubs have been eliminated, the procedure reverts to step one of the two-club format to determine the winner. When one club wins the tie breaker, all other clubs revert to step 1 of the applicable two-club or three-club format.
2. In comparing division and conference records or records against common opponents among tied teams, the best won-lost-tied percentage is the deciding factor since teams may have played an unequal number of games.
3. To determine home-field priority among division titlists, apply Wild-Card tie breakers.
4. To determine home-field priority for Wild-Card qualifiers, apply division tie breakers (if teams are from the same division) or Wild-Card tie breakers (if teams are from different divisions).

TIE-BREAKING PROCEDURE FOR SELECTION MEETING

If two or more clubs are tied in the selection order, the strength-of-schedule tie breaker is applied, subject to the following exceptions for playoff clubs:

1. The Super Bowl winner is last and the Super Bowl loser next-to-last.
2. Any non-Super Bowl playoff club involved in a tie shall be assigned priority within its segment below that of non-playoff clubs and in the order that the playoff clubs exited from the playoffs. Thus, within a tied segment a playoff club that loses in the Wild-Card game will have priority over a playoff club that loses in the Divisional playoff game, which in turn will have priority over a club that loses in the Conference Championship game. If two tied clubs exited the playoffs in the same round, the tie is broken by strength of schedule.

If any ties cannot be broken by strength of schedule, the divisional or conference tie breakers, whichever are applicable, are applied. Any ties that still exist are broken by a coin flip.

NFL PASSER RATING SYSTEM

The NFL rates its passers for statistical purposes against a fixed performance standard based on statistical achievements of all qualified pro passers since 1960. The current system replaced one that rated passers in relation to their position in a total group based on various criteria. The current system, which was adopted in 1973, removes inequities that existed in the former method and, at the same time, provides a means of comparing passing performances from one season to the next.

It is important to remember that the system is used to rate **passers,** not **quarterbacks.** Statistics do not reflect leadership, play-calling, and other intangible factors that go into making a successful professional quarterback. Four categories are used as a basis for compiling a rating:

—Percentage of completions per attempt
—Average yards gained per attempt
—Percentage of touchdown passes per attempt
—Percentage of interceptions per attempt

The **average** standard, is 1.000. The bottom is .000. To earn a 2.000 rating, a passer must perform at exceptional levels, i.e., 70 percent in completions, 10 percent in touchdowns, 1.5 percent in interceptions, and 11 yards average gain per pass attempt. The **maximum** a passer can receive in any category is 2.375.

For example, to gain a 2.375 in completion percentage, a passer would have to complete 77.5 percent of his passes. The NFL record is 70.55 by Ken Anderson (Cincinnati, 1982). To earn a 2.375 in percentage of touchdowns, a passer would have to achieve a percentage of 11.9. The record is 13.9 by Sid Luckman (Chicago, 1943). To gain 2.375 in percentage of interceptions, a passer would have to go the entire season without an interception. The 2.375 figure in average yards is 12.50, compared with the NFL record of 11.17 by Tommy O'Connell (Cleveland, 1957).

In order to make the rating more understandable, the point rating is then converted into a scale of 100. In rare cases, where statistical performance has been superior, it is possible for a passer to surpass a 100 rating. For example, take Steve Young's record-setting season in 1994 when he completed 324 of 461 passes for 3,969 yards, 35 touchdowns, and 10 interceptions. The four calculations would be:

—**Percentage of Completions**—324 of 461 is 70.28 percent. Subtract 30 from the completion percentage (40.28) and multiply the result by 0.05. The result is a point rating of **2.014**.
Note: If the result is less than zero (Comp. Pct. less than 30.0), award zero points. If the results are greater than 2.375 (Comp. Pct. greater than 77.5), award 2.375.

—**Average Yards Gained Per Attempt**—3,969 yards divided by 461 attempts is 8.61. Subtract three yards from yards-per-attempt (5.61) and multiply the result by 0.25. The result is **1.403**.
Note: If the result is less than zero (yards per attempt less than 3.0), award zero points. If the result is greater than 2.375 (yards per attempt greater than 12.5), award 2.375 points.

—**Percentage of Touchdown Passes**—35 touchdowns in 461 attempts is 7.59 percent. Multiply the touchdown percentage by 0.2. The result is **1.518**.
Note: If the result is greater than 2.375 (touchdown percentage greater than 11.875), award 2.375.

—**Percentage of Interceptions**—10 interceptions in 461 attempts is 2.17 percent. Multiply the interception percentage by 0.25 (0.542) and subtract the number from 2.375. The result is **1.833**.
Note: If the result is less than zero (interception percentage greater than 9.5), award zero points.

The sum of the four steps is (2.014 + 1.403 + 1.518 + 1.833) **6.768**. The sum is then divided by six (1.128) and multiplied by 100. In this case, the result is **112.8**. This same formula can be used to determine a passer rating for any player who attempts at least one pass.

The following is a list of qualifying passers who had a single-season passer rating of 100 or higher:

Player, Team	Season	Rating	Att.	Comp.	Pct.	Yds.	Avg.	TD	TD Pct.	Int.	Int. Pct.
Steve Young, San Francisco	1994	112.8	461	324	70.2	3,969	8.61	35	7.6	10	2.2
Joe Montana, San Francisco	1989	112.4	386	271	70.2	3,521	9.12	26	6.7	8	2.1
Milt Plum, Cleveland	1960	110.4	250	151	60.4	2,297	9.19	21	8.4	5	2.0
Sammy Baugh, Washington	1945	109.9	182	128	70.3	1,669	9.17	11	6.0	4	2.2
Dan Marino, Miami	1984	108.9	564	362	64.2	5,084	9.01	48	8.5	17	3.0
Sid Luckman, Chicago Bears	1943	107.5	202	110	54.5	2,194	10.86	28	13.9	12	5.9
Steve Young, San Francisco	1992	107.0	402	268	66.7	3,465	8.62	25	6.2	7	1.7
Bart Starr, Green Bay	1966	105.0	251	156	62.2	2,257	8.99	14	5.6	3	1.2
Roger Staubach, Dallas	1971	104.8	211	126	59.7	1,882	8.92	15	7.1	4	1.9
Y.A. Tittle, N.Y. Giants	1963	104.8	367	221	60.2	3,145	8.57	36	9.8	14	3.8
Steve Young, San Francisco	1997	104.7	356	241	67.7	3,029	8.51	19	5.3	6	1.7
Bart Starr, Green Bay	1968	104.3	171	109	63.7	1,617	9.46	15	8.8	8	4.7
Ken Stabler, Oakland	1976	103.4	291	194	66.7	2,737	9.41	27	9.3	17	5.8
Joe Montana, San Francisco	1984	102.9	432	279	64.6	3,630	8.40	28	6.5	10	2.3
Charlie Conerly, N.Y. Giants	1959	102.7	194	113	58.2	1,706	8.79	14	7.2	4	2.1
Bert Jones, Baltimore	1976	102.5	343	207	60.3	3,104	9.05	24	7.0	9	2.6
Joe Montana, San Francisco	1987	102.1	398	266	66.8	3,054	7.67	31	7.8	13	3.3
Steve Young, San Francisco	1991	101.8	279	180	64.5	2,517	9.02	17	6.1	8	2.9
Len Dawson, Kansas City	1966	101.7	284	159	56.0	2,527	8.90	26	9.2	10	3.5
Steve Young, San Francisco	1993	101.5	462	314	68.0	4,023	8.71	29	6.3	16	3.5
Jim Kelly, Buffalo	1990	101.2	346	219	63.3	2,829	8.18	24	6.9	9	2.6

WAIVERS

The waiver system is a procedure by which player contracts or NFL rights to players are made available by a club to other clubs in the League. During the procedure, the 29 other clubs either file claims to obtain the players or waive the opportunity to do so—thus the term "waiver." Claiming clubs are assigned players on a priority based on the inverse of won-and-lost standing. The claiming period is three business days from the beginning of the League Year through April 30, 10 days from May 1 through the last business day before July 4, and 24 hours after July 4 through the conclusion of the regular season. If a player passes through waivers unclaimed, he becomes a free agent. All waivers are no recall and no withdrawal. Under the Collective Bargaining Agreement, from the beginning of the waiver system each year through the trading deadline (October 13, 1998), any veteran who has acquired four years of pension credit is not subject to the waiver system if the club desires to release him. After the trading deadline, such players are subject to the waiver system.

ACTIVE/INACTIVE LIST

The Active/Inactive List is the principal status for players participating for a club. It consists of all players under contract who are eligible for preseason, regular-season, and postseason games. Teams are permitted to open training camp with no more than 80 players under contract and thereafter must meet two mandatory roster reductions prior to the season opener. Teams will be permitted an Active List of 45 players and an Inactive List of eight players for each regular-season and postseason game. Provided that a club has two quarterbacks on its 45-player Active List, a third quarterback from its Inactive List is permitted to dress for the game, but if he enters the game during the first three quarters, the other two quarterbacks are thereafter prohibited from playing. Teams also are permitted to establish Practice Squads of up to five players who are eligible to participate in practice, but these players remain free agents and are eligible to sign with any other team in the league.

August 25 ....Roster reduction to 60 players
August 30 ....Roster reduction to 53 players
August 31 ....Teams establish a Practice Squad of up to five players

In addition to the squad limits described above, the overall roster limit of 80 players remains in effect throughout the regular season and postseason. The overall limit is applicable to players on a team's Active, Inactive, and Exempt Lists, players on the Practice Squad, and players on the Reserve List as Injured, Physically Unable to Perform, Non-Football Illness/Injury, and Suspended by Club.

RESERVE LIST

The Reserve List is a status for players who, for reasons of injury, retirement, military service, or other circumstances, are not immediately available for participation with a club. Players on Reserve/Injured are not eligible to practice or return to the Active/Inactive List in the same season that they are placed on Reserve. Players in the category of Reserve/Retired, Reserve/Did Not Report, Reserve/Exclusive Rights, and players who were placed in the category of Reserve/Left Squad in a previous season may not be reinstated during the period from 30 days before the end of the regular season through the postseason.

TRADES

Unrestricted trading between the AFC and NFC is allowed in 1998 through October 13, after which trading will end until 1999.

ANNUAL ACTIVE PLAYER LIMITS

NFL

Year(s)	Limit
1991-98	45**
1985-90	45
1983-84	49
1982	45†-49
1978-81	45
1975-77	43
1974	47
1964-73	40
1963	37
1961-62	36
1960	38
1959	36
1957-58	35
1951-56	33
1949-50	32
1948	35
1947	35*-34
1945-46	33
1943-44	28
1940-42	33
1938-39	30
1936-37	25
1935	24
1930-34	20
1926-29	18
1925	16

**45 plus a third quarterback
† 45 for first two games
* 35 for first three games

AFL

Year(s)	Limit
1966-69	40
1965	38
1964	34
1962-63	33
1960-61	35

NFL FREE AGENCY MOVEMENT

The following chart details veteran free agents who signed with new teams:

	1993	1994	1995	1996	1997
Unrestricted	108	121	171	99	85
Restricted	8	7	6	4	2
Transition	4	4	2	2	2
Franchise	1	0	0	0	0
TOTALS	121	132	179	105	89

NFL ACTIVE STATISTICAL LEADERS

TOP ACTIVE PASSERS

1,000 or more attempts

	Yrs.	Att.	Comp.	Pct. Comp.	Yards	TD	Pct. TD	Had Int.	Pct. Int.	Rating Pts.
1.Steve Young, S.F.	13	3,548	2,300	64.8	28,508	193	5.4	91	2.6	97.0
2.Brett Favre, G.B.	7	3,206	1,971	61.5	22,591	182	5.7	95	3.0	89.3
3.Dan Marino, Miami	15	7,452	4,453	59.8	55,416	385	5.2	220	3.0	87.8
4.Mark Brunell, Jax.	4	1,365	830	60.8	9,911	52	3.8	34	2.5	85.3
5.Troy Aikman, Dall.	9	3,696	2,292	62.0	26,016	129	3.5	110	3.0	82.3
6.Dave Krieg, Tenn.	18	5,290	3,093	58.5	37,948	261	4.9	199	3.8	81.5
7.Warren Moon, Sea.	14	6,528	3,827	58.6	47,465	279	4.3	224	3.4	81.2
8.Jeff Hostetler, Wash.	12	2,338	1,357	58.0	16,430	94	4.0	71	3.0	80.5
9.Neil O'Donnell, NYJ	7	2,519	1,438	57.1	16,810	89	3.5	53	2.1	80.5
10.Scott Mitchell, Det.	7	2,016	1,146	56.8	14,000	90	4.5	63	3.1	80.2
11.Jeff George, Oak.	8	3,233	1,878	58.1	22,043	120	3.7	87	2.7	80.1
12.Jeff Blake, Cin.	5	1,748	978	55.9	11,765	74	4.2	48	2.7	79.4
13.Jim Harbaugh, Balt.	11	2,989	1,769	59.2	20,272	99	3.3	82	2.7	79.3
14.John Elway, Den.	15	6,894	3,913	56.8	48,669	278	4.0	216	3.1	79.2
15.Mark Rypien, Atl.	10	2,604	1,461	56.1	18,416	115	4.4	88	3.4	78.9
16.Jim Everett, *	12	4,923	2,841	57.7	34,837	203	4.1	175	3.6	78.6
17.Randall Cunningham, Minn.	12	3,450	1,918	55.6	23,378	156	4.5	109	3.2	78.6
18.Erik Kramer, Chi.	8	1,908	1,088	57.0	12,726	81	4.2	62	3.2	78.0
19.Chris Chandler, Atl.	10	2,260	1,304	57.7	15,372	94	4.2	78	3.5	78.0
20.Steve Bono, St.L.	12	1,564	865	55.3	9,632	57	3.6	38	2.4	75.9
21.Wade Wilson, *	16	2,340	1,339	57.2	16,715	92	3.9	98	4.2	75.2
22.Steve Beuerlein, Car.	9	1,701	910	53.5	11,953	67	3.9	57	3.4	75.1
23.Drew Bledsoe, N.E.	5	2,901	1,624	56.0	18,348	108	3.7	88	3.0	74.9
24.Rich Gannon, K.C.	9	1,404	794	56.6	8,853	56	4.0	48	3.4	74.5
25.Craig Erickson, Miami	6	1,092	591	54.1	7,625	41	3.8	38	3.5	74.3
26.Gus Frerotte, Wash.	4	1,368	719	52.6	9,486	47	3.4	41	3.0	73.7
27.Rodney Peete, Phil.	9	1,808	1,037	57.4	12,821	57	3.2	73	4.0	73.1
28.Vinny Testaverde, Balt.	11	4,177	2,300	55.1	29,223	175	4.2	183	4.4	72.8
29.John Friesz, Sea.	7	1,294	705	54.5	8,224	43	3.3	39	3.0	72.5
30.Bubby Brister, Den.	11	2,041	1,107	54.2	13,290	71	3.5	71	3.5	71.5

TOP ACTIVE SCORERS

(number in parentheses represents 2-point conversions scored)

	Yrs.	TD	FG	PAT	TP
1. Gary Anderson, Minn.	16	0	385	526	1,681
2. Morten Andersen, Atl.	16	0	378	507	1,641
3. Norm Johnson, Pitt.	16	0	322	592	1,558
4. Eddie Murray, *	17	0	337	521	1,532
5. Al Del Greco, Tenn.	14	0	263	435	1,224
6. Kevin Butler, *	13	0	265	413	1,208
7. Jerry Rice, S.F.	13	166	0	(2)	1,000
8. Pete Stoyanovich, K.C.	9	0	219	315	972
9. Jeff Jaeger, Chi.	10	0	206	287	905
10. Greg Davis, *	11	0	207	259	880
11. Chris Jacke, Wash.	8	0	173	306	825
12. Steve Christie, Buff.	8	0	188	253	817
13. John Carney, S.D.	10	0	188	231	795
14. Emmitt Smith, Dall.	8	119	0	(1)	716
15. John Kasay, Car.	7	0	167	181	682
16. Matt Stover, Balt.	7	0	153	222	681
17. Jason Hanson, Det.	6	0	139	220	637
18. Barry Sanders, Det.	9	105	0	0	630
19. Jason Elam, Den.	5	0	134	201	603
20. Cris Carter, Minn.	11	90	0	(5)	550
21. Herschel Walker, Dall.	12	84	0	0	504
22. Doug Pelfrey, Cin.	5	0	116	153	501
23. Thurman Thomas, Buff.	10	83	0	0	498
24. Andre Reed, Buff.	13	81	0	0	486
25. Cary Blanchard, Ind.	4	0	120	121	481
26. Irving Fryar, Phil.	14	79	0	(2)	478
27. Chris Boniol, Phil.	4	0	103	151	460
28. Andre Rison, K.C.	9	73	0	(1)	440
29. Henry Ellard, *	15	69	0	0	414
30. Michael Husted, T.B.	5	0	96	122	410

TOP ACTIVE INTERCEPTORS

	Yrs.	No.	Yards	TD
1.Eugene Robinson, Atl.	13	49	719	0
2.Darrell Green, Wash.	15	44	517	6
3.Rod Woodson, Balt.	11	41	860	5
4.Albert Lewis, Oak.	15	40	329	0
5.Eric Allen, Oak.	10	39	570	5
6.Kevin Ross, K.C.	14	38	654	2
Aeneas Williams, Ariz.	7	38	531	6
Eugene Daniel, *	14	38	483	3
9.Lionel Washington, *	15	37	418	4
10.Deion Sanders, Dall.	9	36	941	7
Donnell Woolford, *	9	36	303	1
12.Tyrone Braxton, Den.	11	35	545	4
Cris Dishman, Wash.	10	35	395	2
14.Terry McDaniel, Oak.	10	34	624	5
Tim McDonald, S.F.	11	34	600	4
Mike Prior, G.B.	12	34	440	1
17.Tim McKyer, Den.	12	33	235	2
18.LeRoy Butler, G.B.	8	31	505	1
19.Darren Perry, Pitt.	6	30	505	1
James Hasty, K.C.	10	30	362	2
21.Merton Hanks, S.F.	7	27	343	2
22.Mark Collins, Sea.	12	26	343	2
Greg Jackson, S.D.	9	26	279	2
24.Mark Carrier, Det.	8	25	291	1
25.Eric Turner, Oak.	7	24	318	2
Seth Joyner, G.B.	12	24	307	2
Ray Crockett, Den.	9	24	302	1
28.Darryll Lewis, Tenn.	7	23	500	5
Steve Atwater, Den.	9	23	404	1
Dwayne Harper, S.D.	10	23	325	0

TOP ACTIVE RUSHERS

	Yrs.	Att.	Yards	TD
1. Barry Sanders, Det.	9	2,719	13,778	95
2. Thurman Thomas, Buff.	10	2,720	11,405	63
3. Emmitt Smith, Dall.	8	2,595	11,234	112
4. Herschel Walker, Dall.	12	1,954	8,225	61
5. Rodney Hampton, *	8	1,824	6,897	49
6. Chris Warren, Dall.	8	1,559	6,706	44
7. Ricky Watters, Sea.	6	1,628	6,634	56
8. Jerome Bettis, Pitt.	5	1,491	6,187	31
9. Terry Allen, Wash.	6	1,536	6,181	58
10. Randall Cunningham, Minn.	12	696	4,609	32
11. Terrell Davis, Den.	3	951	4,405	35
12. Harold Green, Atl.	8	1,131	4,328	13
13. Craig Heyward, St.L.	10	1,025	4,286	30
14. Natrone Means, S.D.	5	1,085	4,055	36
15. Marshall Faulk, Ind.	4	1,065	4,001	36
16. Curtis Martin, NYJ	3	958	3,799	32
17. Steve Young, S.F.	13	641	3,728	37
18. Harvey Williams, Oak.	7	893	3,456	18
19. Adrian Murrell, Ariz.	5	860	3,447	15
20. Erric Pegram, NYG	7	855	3,398	13
21. Garrison Hearst, S.F.	5	856	3,369	7
22. Edgar Bennett, Chi.	5	936	3,353	19
23. John Elway, Den.	15	737	3,313	32
24. Robert Smith, Minn.	5	646	3,095	17
25. Keith Byars, NYJ	12	861	3,075	23
26. Gary Brown, NYG	6	730	3,060	16
27. Derrick Fenner, *	9	804	2,996	32
28. Leroy Hoard, Minn.	8	755	2,930	17
29. Bam Morris, *	4	722	2,906	24
30. Errict Rhett, Balt.	4	823	2,853	24

TOP ACTIVE PASS RECEIVERS

	Yrs.	No.	Yards	TD
1.Jerry Rice, S.F.	13	1,057	16,455	155
2.Andre Reed, Buff.	13	826	11,764	80
3.Henry Ellard, *	15	807	13,662	65
4.Cris Carter, Minn.	11	756	9,436	89
5.Irving Fryar, Phil.	14	736	11,427	75
6.Michael Irvin, Dall.	10	666	10,680	61
7.Andre Rison, K.C.	9	641	8,839	73
8.Tim Brown, Oak.	10	599	8,588	60
9.Anthony Miller, *	10	595	9,148	63
10.Keith Byars, NYJ	12	584	5,403	29
11.Ronnie Harmon, Chi.	12	582	6,076	24
12.Brian Blades, Sea.	10	566	7,436	34
13.Webster Slaughter, S.D.	11	555	8,018	44
14.Mark Carrier, Car.	11	550	8,462	46
15.Herman Moore, Det.	7	528	7,484	52
16.Brett Perriman, *	10	525	6,589	30
17.Rob Moore, Ariz.	8	524	7,765	39
18.Herschel Walker, Dall.	12	512	4,859	21
19.Eric Metcalf, Ariz.	9	495	5,096	31
20.Larry Centers, Ariz.	8	466	3,980	17
21.Shannon Sharpe, Den.	8	465	5,991	34
22.Quinn Early, Buff.	10	435	6,148	39
23.Michael Haynes, *	10	428	6,588	47
24.Thurman Thomas, Buff.	10	427	4,084	20
25.Terance Mathis, Atl.	8	413	5,196	37
26.Tony Martin, S.D.	8	397	5,906	42
27.Carl Pickens, Cin.	6	391	5,127	52
Ben Coates, N.E.	7	391	4,433	42
29.Emmitt Smith, Dall.	8	388	2,434	7
30.Ricky Proehl, St.L.	8	373	4,931	30

TOP ACTIVE PUNT RETURNERS

40 or more punt returns

	Yrs.	No.	Yards	Avg.	TD
1.Karl Williams, T.B.	2	59	871	14.8	2
2.Darrien Gordon, Den.	4	143	1,950	13.6	6
3.Leon Johnson, NYJ	1	51	619	12.1	1
4.Jermaine Lewis, Balt.	2	64	776	12.1	2
5.Desmond Howard, Oak.	6	119	1,440	12.1	4
6.Amani Toomer, NYG	2	65	753	11.6	3
7.Brian Mitchell, Wash.	8	233	2,638	11.3	7
8.Henry Ellard, *	15	135	1,527	11.3	4
9.Darrell Green, Wash.	15	51	576	11.3	0
10.Mel Gray, *	12	252	2,753	10.9	3
11.Winslow Oliver, Car.	2	66	709	10.7	1
12.David Palmer, Minn.	4	112	1,195	10.7	2
13.David Meggett, *	9	344	3,668	10.7	7
14.Eddie Kennison, St.L.	2	63	670	10.6	2
15.Eric Metcalf, Ariz.	9	238	2,509	10.5	9
16.Jeff Burris, Ind.	4	100	1,045	10.5	0
17.Tim Brown, Oak.	10	301	3,083	10.2	2
18.Kevin Williams, Buff.	5	135	1,375	10.2	3
19.Joey Galloway, Sea.	3	51	518	10.2	2
20.Charles Jordan, Miami	4	48	486	10.1	0
21.Tamarick Vanover, K.C.	3	103	1,039	10.1	2
22.Irving Fryar, Phil.	14	206	2,055	10.0	3
23.Deion Sanders, Dall.	9	128	1,254	9.8	3
24.Glyn Milburn, G.B.	5	193	1,875	9.7	0
25.Eric Guliford, N.O.	4	124	1,199	9.7	1
26.Corey Sawyer, Cin.	4	50	482	9.6	1
27.Dale Carter, K.C.	6	83	787	9.5	2
28.Anthony Parker, T.B.	8	46	431	9.4	0
29.Mark Seay, Phil.	5	51	477	9.4	0
30.Todd Kinchen, Atl.	6	158	1,455	9.2	2

TOP ACTIVE KICKOFF RETURNERS

40 or more kickoff returns

	Yrs.	No.	Yards	Avg.	TD
1.Tamarick Vanover, K.C.	3	127	3,257	25.6	4
2.Eric Guliford, N.O.	4	48	1,229	25.6	1
3.Anthony Miller, *	10	50	1,269	25.4	2
4.Tim Brown, Oak.	10	49	1,235	25.2	1
5.Tyrone Hughes, *	5	272	6,725	24.7	3
6.Byron Hanspard, Atl.	1	40	987	24.7	2
7.Michael Bates, Car.	5	145	3,566	24.6	1
8.Mel Gray, *	12	421	10,250	24.3	6
9.Robert Brooks, G.B.	6	51	1,237	24.3	2
10.Duce Staley, Phil.	1	47	1,139	24.2	0
11.Glyn Milburn, G.B.	5	215	5,192	24.1	0
12.Kevin Williams, Buff.	5	203	4,874	24.0	1
13.Napoleon Kaufman, Oak.	3	47	1,120	23.8	1
14.Derrick Witherspoon, *	3	80	1,901	23.8	3
15.Herschel Walker, Dall.	12	215	5,084	23.6	2
16.Aaron Glenn, NYJ	4	57	1,341	23.5	1
17.Thomas Lewis, Chi.	4	53	1,237	23.3	1
18.Andre Coleman, Pitt.	4	193	4,466	23.1	4
19.Irving Spikes, *	4	89	2,058	23.1	0
20.Vaughn Hebron, Den.	4	112	2,586	23.1	0
21.Brian Mitchell, Wash.	8	319	7,356	23.1	1
22.Aaron Bailey, Ind.	4	119	2,742	23.0	2
23.Deion Sanders, Dall.	9	149	3,421	23.0	3
24.O.J. McDuffie, Miami	5	91	2,086	22.9	0
25.Ernie Mills, Dall.	7	80	1,818	22.7	0
26.David Dunn, Cin.	3	104	2,361	22.7	1
27.David Thompson, St.L.	1	49	1,110	22.7	0
28.Steve Broussard, Sea.	8	146	3,279	22.5	0
29.Corey Harris, Miami	6	115	2,578	22.4	0
30.Eric Moulds, Buff.	2	95	2,126	22.4	1

TOP ACTIVE QUARTERBACK SACKERS (since 1982)

	Yrs.	No.
1.Reggie White, G.B.	13	176.5
2.Bruce Smith, Buff.	13	154.0
3.Richard Dent, *	15	137.5
4.Kevin Greene, Car.	13	133.0
5.Chris Doleman. S.F.	13	127.5
6.Leslie O'Neal, K.C.	11	122.5
7.Greg Townsend, *	13	109.5
8.Clyde Simmons, Cin.	12	109.0
9.Derrick Thomas, K.C.	9	107.5
10.William Fuller, S.D.	12	97.5
11.Neil Smith, Den.	10	94.0
12.Ken Harvey, Wash.	10	87.0
13.John Randle, Minn.	8	85.5
14.Henry Thomas, N.E.	11	79.5
15.Wayne Martin, N.O.	9	75.0
16.Bryce Paup, Jax.	8	65.5
17.Tony Bennett, Ind.	8	64.5
18.Trace Armstrong, Miami	9	64.0
19.Cornelius Bennett, Atl.	11	62.5
20.Jumpy Geathers, *	13	62.0
21.Michael Dean Perry, *	10	61.0
22.Tony Tolbert, Dall.	9	59.0
23.Anthony Smith, Oak.	7	57.5
24.Greg Lloyd, Pitt.	10	53.5
25.Alfred Williams, Den.	7	52.5
26.Seth Joyner, G.B.	12	52.0
27.Danny Stubbs, Miami	9	51.5
28.Cortez Kennedy, Sea.	8	48.5
29.Rob Burnett, Balt.	8	47.5
Broderick Thomas, Dall.	9	47.5

TOP ACTIVE PUNTERS

50 or more punts

	Yrs.	No.	Avg.	LG
1.Darren Bennett, S.D.	3	248	45.0	66
2.Leo Araguz, Oak.	2	106	44.6	63
3.Matt Turk, Wash.	3	233	44.3	63
4.Sean Landeta, G.B.	13	861	43.6	74
5.Greg Montgomery, Balt.	9	524	43.6	77
6.Reggie Roby, *	15	932	43.4	77
7.Rick Tuten, St.L.	9	614	43.4	73
8.Rohn Stark, *	16	1,141	43.4	72
9.Tom Tupa, N.E.	9	292	43.3	73
10.Tom Rouen, Den.	5	320	43.1	62
11.Tommy Barnhardt, T.B.	11	648	42.8	65
12.Craig Hentrich, Tenn.	4	289	42.8	70
13.Tom Hutton, Phil.	3	245	42.6	63
14.Lee Johnson, Cin.	13	915	42.4	70
15.Bryan Barker, Jax.	8	555	42.4	67
16.Ken Walter, Car.	1	85	42.4	62
17.Brian Hansen, NYJ	13	1,017	42.4	73
18.Mike Horan, *	13	913	42.3	75
19.Todd Sauerbrun, Chi.	3	228	42.2	72
20.Mark Royals, N.O.	9	640	42.1	69
21.John Jett, Det.	5	337	42.0	60
22.Chris Gardocki, Ind.	7	433	41.9	72
23.Josh Miller, Pitt.	2	119	41.9	72
24.Tommy Thompson, S.F.	3	208	41.9	65
25.Toby Gowin, Dall.	1	86	41.8	72
26.John Kidd, *	14	916	41.5	67
27.Jeff Feagles, Sea.	10	815	41.5	77
28.Louie Aguiar, K.C.	7	556	41.4	71
29.Mitch Berger, Minn.	3	186	41.4	65
30.Chris Mohr, Buff.	8	616	40.8	80

** Free agent; subject to developments.*

COACHES RECORDS

ACTIVE COACHES' CAREER RECORDS (Order Based on Career Victories)

Start of 1998 Season

Coach	Team(s)	Regular Season Yrs.	Won	Lost	Tied	Pct.	Postseason Won	Lost	Tied	Pct.	Career Won	Lost	Tied	Pct.
Dan Reeves	Denver Broncos, New York Giants, Atlanta Falcons	17	148	115	1	.563	8	7	0	.533	156	122	1	.561
Marty Schottenheimer	Cleveland Browns, Kansas City Chiefs	14	138	76	1	.644	5	11	0	.313	143	87	1	.621
Bill Parcells	New York Giants, New England Patriots New York Jets	13	118	88	1	.573	10	5	0	.667	128	93	1	.579
Mike Ditka	Chicago Bears, New Orleans Saints	12	112	72	0	.609	6	6	0	.500	118	78	0	.602
Jim Mora	New Orleans Saints, Indianapolis Colts	11	93	74	0	.557	0	4	0	.000	93	78	0	.544
Ted Marchibroda	Baltimore-Indianapolis Colts, Baltimore Ravens	11	81	88	1	.479	2	4	0	.333	83	92	1	.474
Mike Holmgren	Green Bay Packers	6	64	32	0	.667	9	4	0	.692	73	36	0	.670
Bill Cowher	Pittsburgh Steelers	6	64	32	0	.667	5	6	0	.455	69	38	0	.645
Jimmy Johnson	Dallas Cowboys, Miami Dolphins	7	61	51	0	.545	7	2	0	.778	68	53	0	.562
Dick Vermeil	Philadelphia Eagles, St. Louis Rams	8	59	58	0	.504	3	4	0	.429	62	62	0	.500
Bobby Ross	San Diego Chargers, Detroit Lions	6	56	40	0	.583	3	4	0	.429	59	44	0	.573
Dennis Green	Minnesota Vikings	6	56	40	0	.583	1	5	0	.167	57	45	0	.559
Mike Shanahan	Los Angeles Raiders, Denver Broncos	5	41	27	0	.603	4	1	0	.800	45	28	0	.616
Bruce Coslet	New York Jets, Cincinnati Bengals	6	40	49	0	.449	0	1	0	.000	40	50	0	.444
Dave Wannstedt	Chicago Bears	5	36	44	0	.450	1	1	0	.500	37	45	0	.451
Dom Capers	Carolina Panthers	3	26	22	0	.542	1	1	0	.500	27	23	0	.540
Ray Rhodes	Philadelphia Eagles	3	26	21	1	.552	1	2	0	.333	27	23	1	.539
Tom Coughlin	Jacksonville Jaguars	3	24	24	0	.500	2	2	0	.500	26	26	0	.500
Norv Turner	Washington Redskins	4	26	37	1	.414	0	0	0	.000	26	37	1	.414
Jeff Fisher	Tennessee Oilers	3	24	30	0	.444	0	0	0	.000	24	30	0	.444
Dennis Erickson	Seattle Seahawks	3	23	25	0	.479	0	0	0	.000	23	25	0	.479
Pete Carroll	New York Jets, New England Patriots	2	16	16	0	.500	1	1	0	.500	17	17	0	.500
Tony Dungy	Tampa Bay Buccaneers	2	16	16	0	.500	1	1	0	.500	17	17	0	.500
Wade Phillips	Denver Broncos, Buffalo Bills	2	16	16	0	.500	0	1	0	.000	16	17	0	.485
Vince Tobin	Arizona Cardinals	2	11	21	0	.334	0	0	0	.000	11	21	0	.334
Steve Mariucci	San Francisco 49ers	1	13	3	0	.813	1	1	0	.500	14	4	0	.777
Jim Fassel	New York Giants	1	10	5	1	.656	0	1	0	.000	10	6	1	.618
Kevin Gilbride	San Diego Chargers	1	4	12	0	.250	0	0	0	.000	4	12	0	.250
Chan Gailey	Dallas Cowboys	0	0	0	0	.000	0	0	0	.000	0	0	0	.000
Jon Gruden	Oakland Raiders	0	0	0	0	.000	0	0	0	.000	0	0	0	.000

COACHES WITH 100 CAREER VICTORIES (Order Based on Career Victories)

Start of 1998 Season

Coach	Team(s)	Regular Season Yrs.	Won	Lost	Tied	Pct.	Postseason Won	Lost	Tied	Pct.	Career Won	Lost	Tied	Pct.
Don Shula	Baltimore Colts, Miami Dolphins	33	328	156	6	.676	19	17	0	.528	347	173	6	.665
George Halas	Chicago Bears	40	318	148	31	.671	6	3	0	.667	324	151	31	.671
Tom Landry	Dallas Cowboys	29	250	162	6	.605	20	16	0	.556	270	178	6	.601
Earl (Curly) Lambeau	Green Bay Packers, Chicago Cardinals, Washington Redskins	33	226	132	22	.624	3	2	0	.600	229	134	22	.623
Chuck Noll	Pittsburgh Steelers	23	193	148	1	.566	16	8	0	.667	209	156	1	.572
Chuck Knox	Los Angeles Rams, Buffalo Bills, Seattle Seahawks	22	186	147	1	.558	7	11	0	.389	193	158	1	.550
Paul Brown	Cleveland Browns, Cincinnati Bengals	21	166	100	6	.621	4	8	0	.333	170	108	6	.609
Bud Grant	Minnesota Vikings	18	158	96	5	.620	10	12	0	.455	168	108	5	.607
Dan Reeves	Denver Broncos, New York Giants, Atlanta Falcons	17	148	115	1	.563	8	7	0	.533	156	122	1	.561
Marv Levy	Kansas City Chiefs, Buffalo Bills	17	143	102	0	.584	11	8	0	.579	154	120	0	.562
Steve Owen	New York Giants	23	151	100	17	.595	2	8	0	.200	153	108	17	.581
Marty Schottenheimer	Cleveland Browns, Kansas City Chiefs	14	138	76	1	.644	5	11	0	.313	143	87	1	.621
Joe Gibbs	Washington Redskins	12	124	60	0	.674	16	5	0	.762	140	65	0	.683
Hank Stram	Kansas City Chiefs, New Orleans Saints	17	131	97	10	.571	5	3	0	.625	136	100	10	.573
Weeb Ewbank	Baltimore Colts, New York Jets	20	130	129	7	.502	4	1	0	.800	134	130	7	.507
Bill Parcells	New York Giants, New England Patriots New York Jets	13	118	88	1	.573	10	5	0	.667	128	93	1	.579
Sid Gillman	Los Angeles Rams, Los Angeles-San Diego Chargers, Houston Oilers	18	122	99	7	.550	1	5	0	.167	123	104	7	.541
George Allen	Los Angeles Rams, Washington Redskins	12	116	47	5	.705	2	7	0	.222	118	54	5	.681
Mike Ditka	Chicago Bears, New Orleans Saints	12	112	72	0	.609	6	6	0	.500	118	78	0	.602
Don Coryell	St. Louis Cardinals, San Diego Chargers	14	111	83	1	.572	3	6	0	.333	114	89	1	.561
John Madden	Oakland Raiders	10	103	32	7	.750	9	7	0	.563	112	39	7	.731
George Seifert	San Francisco 49ers	8	98	30	0	.766	10	5	0	.667	108	35	0	.755
Ray (Buddy) Parker	Chicago Cardinals, Detroit Lions, Pittsburgh Steelers	15	104	75	9	.577	3	1	0	.750	107	76	9	.581
Vince Lombardi	Green Bay Packers, Washington Redskins	10	96	34	6	.728	9	1	0	.900	105	35	6	.740
Tom Flores	Oakland-Los Angeles Raiders, Seattle Seahawks	12	97	87	0	.527	8	3	0	.727	105	90	0	.538
Bill Walsh	San Francisco 49ers	10	92	59	1	.609	10	4	0	.714	102	63	1	.617

Active coaches in bold.

The **New Orleans Saints** need one sack in each of their first 12 games to pass the Washington Redskins (60) for most consecutive games with a sack. The Saints have had a sack in 49 straight games.

The **New York Giants** will play their 1,000th regular-season game in Week 16, their 15th game of the 1998 season.

Head coach **Jim Mora**, Indianapolis, needs seven victories to become only the fifth active coach and 27th all-time to reach 100 career.

Head coach **Marty Schottenheimer**, Kansas City, needs seven victories to become only the second active and 12th all-time to reach 150 career.

John Elway, Denver, needs 1,331 yards passing to become the second player all-time to reach 50,000. Elway has 48,669 yards in 15 seasons.

Elway needs 3,000 yards passing to set the all-time record with 13 3,000-yard seasons (see Marino note).

He also needs two touchdown passes to pass Warren Moon (279) and 13 to pass Johnny Unitas (290) for fourth and third place all-time respectively. Elway needs 22 to reach 300 career (see Moon note).

Brett Favre, Green Bay, needs 2,128 yards passing to become the Packers' all-time leader, surpassing Bart Starr (24,718). Favre has thrown for 22,591 yards in six seasons.

Favre needs 30 touchdown passes to break a tie with Dan Marino and become the first player in NFL history with five 30-TD pass seasons.

Favre (1995-97) can join Johnny Unitas (1957-60) and Len Dawson (1962-63, 1965-66) as the only players in league history to lead the league in touchdown passes four times.

He can also join Dan Marino (9) and John Elway (7) as the only players in league history with seven consecutive 3,000-yard passing seasons.

Dan Marino, Miami, needs 15 touchdown passes to become the first player in NFL history to throw 400. He has thrown 385 touchdown passes in 15 seasons.

Marino needs 3,000 yards passing to set the all-time record with 13 3,000-yard seasons (see Elway note).

Warren Moon, Seattle, needs 12 touchdown passes to pass Johnny Unitas (290) and move into third place on the all-time list. He has 279 TD passes in 14 seasons. Moon needs 21 for 300 career (see Elway note).

Moon needs 2,535 yards passing to become the second player all-time to reach 50,000. He has 47,465 yards in 14 seasons.

Cris Carter, Minnesota, needs 64 receptions to move into fourth place all-time, passing James Lofton (764), Henry Ellard (807) and Steve Largent (819). Carter has 756 receptions in 11 seasons.

Carter needs 12 receiving touchdowns to move into second place all-time, passing Don Hutson (99) and Steve Largent (100). He has 89 touchdowns in 11 seasons.

Irving Fryar, Philadelphia, needs 64 receptions to become the sixth player in NFL history to record 800 career. He also needs 573 receiving yards to become the seventh player to record 12,000 career yards. Fryar has 736 catches and 11,427 receiving yards in 14 seasons.

Michael Irvin, Dallas, needs 34 receptions to become the 10th player in league history to record 700 career catches. Irvin has 666 receptions in 10 seasons.

Keenan McCardell and **Jimmy Smith**, Jacksonville, need 1,000 receiving yards each to become only the second duo in league history to record three straight 1,000-yard seasons.

Jerry Rice, San Francisco, needs a reception in each of his first seven games to become the NFL's all-time leader in consecutive games with a reception, surpassing Art Monk (183). Rice has recorded a reception in 177 consecutive games.

Rice and quarterback **Steve Young** need to connect for five touchdown passes to become the all-time leading QB-receiver duo, surpassing Dan Marino and Mark Clayton (79). Rice and Young have connected for 75 TD passes.

Rice needs 9 total touchdowns to become the first player in league history with 175.

Young needs to lead the league in passing to break a tie with Sammy Baugh for most seasons leading the league with seven.

Shannon Sharpe, Denver, needs 79 receptions to pass Lionel Taylor (543) as the Broncos' all-time leader. Sharpe has 465 receptions in eight seasons.

Marshall Faulk, Indianapolis, needs a reception in each of his first two games to pass Jessie Hester (62) for most consecutive games with a reception in Colts history.

Barry Sanders, Detroit, needs 222 rushing yards to join Walter Payton (16,726) as the only players in league history with 14,000. Sanders has 13,778 yards in nine seasons.

Sanders needs five rushing touchdowns to become the sixth player in NFL history with 100 career.

He can also extend his NFL record of nine straight 1,000-yard rushing seasons to 10.

Emmitt Smith, Dallas, needs 12 rushing touchdowns to become the NFL's all-time leader, passing Marcus Allen (123). Smith has 112 rushing touchdowns in eight seasons.

Smith needs 1,079 rushing yards to move into fifth place all-time, passing O.J. Simpson (11,236), John Riggins (11,352), Thurman Thomas (11,405), Franco Harris (12,120), Marcus Allen (12,243) and Jim Brown (12,312). Smith has 11,234 yards in eight seasons (see Thomas note).

He can also become the third player in NFL history to rush for eight straight 1,000-yard seasons.

Thurman Thomas, Buffalo, needs 908 rushing yards to move into fifth place all-time, passing Franco Harris (12,120), Marcus Allen (12,243), and Jim Brown (12,312). Thomas has 11,405 yards in 10 seasons (see Emmitt Smith note).

Chris Doleman, San Francisco, needs 2.5 sacks to become the sixth player all-time with 130. Doleman has 127.5 sacks in 13 seasons (see O'Neal note).

Kevin Greene, Carolina, needs seven sacks to become only the third player in NFL history with 140. Greene has 133 sacks in 13 seasons.

Leslie O'Neal, Kansas City, needs 7.5 sacks to become the sixth player all-time with 130. O'Neal has 122.5 sacks in 11 seasons (see Doleman note).

John Randle, Minnesota, needs 10 sacks to tie Lawrence Taylor for second-most consecutive 10-sack seasons all-time with seven. Randle has had at least 10 sacks in each of the previous six seasons (see Bruce Smith note).

Clyde Simmons, Cincinnati, needs one sack to pass Greg Townsend (109.5) for 10th place all-time and 4.5 sacks to pass Sean Jones (113.0) for ninth place. Simmons has 109 sacks in 12 seasons.

Bruce Smith, Buffalo, needs 10 sacks to tie Lawrence Taylor for second-most consecutive 10-sack seasons all-time with seven. Smith has had at least 10 sacks in each of the previous six seasons (see Randle note).

Reggie White, Green Bay, needs three sacks to become the Packers' all-time leader, passing Tim Harris (55). White has 52.5 sacks in five seasons with the Packers.

Eugene Robinson, Atlanta, needs one interception to become the 27th player in league history with 50. He leads all active players with 49 interceptions in 13 seasons.

Darrell Green, Washington, will enter his 16th season as a Redskin which ties him with Sammy Baugh and Monte Coleman for the most in team history.

Morten Andersen, Atlanta, needs six field goals to pass Nick Lowery (383) and move into second place all-time. Andersen has 378 field goals in 16 seasons.

Gary Anderson, Minnesota, needs 31 points to move into second place on the all-time list, passing Jan Stenerud (1,699) and Nick Lowery (1,711). Anderson has 1,681 points in 16 seasons.

Anderson needs 15 field goals to become the first player in league history with 400.

DRAFT LIST FOR 1998

63rd Annual NFL Draft, April 18-19, 1998
*Denotes Compensatory Selection

ARIZONA CARDINALS
1. Choice to San Diego
   Andre Wadsworth—3, DE, Florida State, from San Diego
2. Corey Chavous—33, DB, Vanderbilt, from San Diego
   Anthony Clement—36, T, Southwestern Louisiana
3. Choice to St. Louis through New York Jets
4. Michael Pittman—95, RB, Fresno State
5. Terry Hardy—125, TE, Southern Mississippi
6. Zack Walz—158, LB, Dartmouth
7. Phil Savoy—193, WR, Colorado
   Jomo Cousins—209, DE, Florida A&M, from New York Jets
   *Pat Tillman—226, DB, Arizona State
   *Ron Janes—233, RB, Missouri

ATLANTA FALCONS
1. Keith Brooking—12, LB, Georgia Tech
2. Choice to Tampa Bay
   Bob Hallen—53, C, Kent State, from Tampa Bay
3. Jammi German—74, WR, Miami
4. Omar Brown—103, DB, North Carolina
   Tim Dwight—114, WR, Iowa, from Tampa Bay
5. Choice to Pittsburgh
6. Elijah Williams—166, DB, Florida
7. Ephraim Salaam—199, T, San Diego State, from Baltimore through Pittsburgh
   Ken Oxendine—201, RB, Virginia Tech
   Henry Slay—203, DT, West Virginia, from Carolina through Pittsburgh

BALTIMORE RAVENS
1. Duane Starks—10, DB, Miami
2. Pat Johnson—42, WR, Oregon
3. Choice to Indianapolis
4. Choice to Tampa Bay
5. Martin Chase—124, DT, Oklahoma, from Indianapolis
   Ryan Sutter—133, DB, Colorado
6. Ron Rogers—154, LB, Georgia Tech, from Indianapolis
   Sammy Williams—164, T, Oklahoma
7. Choice to Atlanta through Pittsburgh
   *Cam Quayle—241, TE, Weber State

BUFFALO BILLS
1. Choice to Jacksonville
2. Sam Cowart—39, LB, Florida State
3. Robert Hicks—68, T, Mississippi State
4. Choice to Jacksonville
5. Jonathan Linton—131, RB, North Carolina
6. Fred Coleman—160, WR, Washington
7. Victor Allotey—198, G, Indiana
   *Kamil Loud—238, WR, Cal Poly-San Luis Obispo

CAROLINA PANTHERS
1. Jason Peter—14, DT, Nebraska
2. Choice to Miami
3. Chuck Wiley—62, DE, Louisiana State, from Indianapolis
   Mitch Marrow—73, DE, Pennsylvania
4. Donald Hayes—106, WR, Wisconsin
5. Jerry Jensen—136, LB, Washington
6. Damien Richardson—165, DB, Arizona State
7. Viliami Maumau—196, DT, Colorado, from New Orleans
   Choice to Atlanta through Pittsburgh
   *Jim Turner—228, WR, Syracuse

CHICAGO BEARS
1. Curtis Enis—5, RB, Penn State
2. Tony Parrish—35, DB, Washington
3. Olin Kreutz—64, C, Washington
4. Alonzo Mayes—94, TE, Oklahoma State
5. Choice to Kansas City
6. Chris Draft—157, LB, Stanford
   *Patrick Mannelly—189, T, Duke
7. Choice to Jacksonville
   Chad Overhauser—217, T, UCLA, from San Francisco
   *Moses Moreno—232, QB, Colorado State

CINCINNATI BENGALS
1. Takeo Spikes—13, LB, Auburn
   Brian Simmons—17, LB, North Carolina, from Washington
2. Artrell Hawkins—43, DB, Cincinnati
3. Steve Foley—75, LB, Northeast Louisiana
   Mike Goff—78, G, Iowa, from Washington
4. Glen Steele—105, DT, Michigan
5. Choice to Indianapolis
6. Jason Tucker—167, WR, Texas Christian
7. Marcus Parker—202, RB, Virginia Tech
   *Damian Vaughn—222, TE, Miami, Ohio

DALLAS COWBOYS
1. Greg Ellis—8, DE, North Carolina
2. Flozell Adams—38, T, Michigan State
3. Choice to New York Giants through Philadelphia
4. Michael Myers—100, DT, Alabama
5. Darren Hambrick—130, LB, South Carolina
   Oliver Ross—138, T, Iowa State, from Seattle
6. Choice to Seattle
   *Izell Reese—188, DB, Alabama-Birmingham
7. Choice to Seattle
   *Tarik Smith—223, RB, California
   *Antonio Fleming—227, G, Georgia
   *Rodrick Monroe—237, TE, Cincinnati

DENVER BRONCOS
1. Marcus Nash—30, WR, Tennessee
2. Eric Brown—61, DB, Mississippi State
3. Brian Griese—91, QB, Michigan
4. Curtis Alexander—122, RB, Alabama
5. Chris Howard—153, RB, Michigan
6. Choice to New York Jets
7. Trey Teague—200, T, Tennessee, from Philadelphia
   Nate Wayne—219, LB, Mississippi

DETROIT LIONS
1. Terry Fair—20, DB, Tennessee
2. Germane Crowell—50, WR, Virginia
   Charlie Batch—60, QB, Eastern Michigan, from Green Bay through Miami
3. Choice to Miami
4. Choice to Washington through Oakland
5. Choice to Miami
6. Choice to Miami
   *Jamaal Alexander—185, DB, Southern Mississippi
7. Chris Liwienski—207, T, Indiana

GREEN BAY PACKERS
1. Vonnie Holliday—19, DT, North Carolina, from Miami
   Choice to Miami
2. Choice to Detroit through Miami
3. Jonathan Brown—90, DE, Tennessee
4. Roosevelt Blackmon—121, DB, Morris Brown
5. Corey Bradford—150, WR, Jackson State, from Kansas City
   Choice to Oakland
6. Scott McGarrahan—156, DB, New Mexico, from Oakland
   Choice to Jacksonville
   *Matt Hasselbeck—187, QB, Boston College
7. Edwin Watson—218, RB, Purdue

INDIANAPOLIS COLTS
1. Peyton Manning—1, QB, Tennessee
2. Jerome Pathon—32, WR, Washington
3. Choice to Carolina
   E.G. Green—71, WR, Florida State, from Baltimore
4. Steve McKinney—93, G, Texas A&M
5. Choice to Baltimore
   Antony Jordon—135, LB, Vanderbilt, from Cincinnati
6. Choice to Baltimore
7. Aaron Taylor—190, G, Nebraska
   *Corey Gaines—231, DB, Tennessee

JACKSONVILLE JAGUARS
1. Fred Taylor—9, RB, Florida, from Buffalo
   Donovin Darius—25, DB, Syracuse
2. Cordell Taylor—57, DB, Hampton
3. Jonathan Quinn—86, QB, Middle Tennessee State
4. Tavian Banks—101, RB, Iowa, from Buffalo
   Harry Deligianis—118, DT, Youngstown State
5. John Wade—148, C, Marshall
6. Lamanzer Williams—179, DE, Minnesota
   Kevin McLeod—182, RB, Auburn, from Green Bay
7. Alvis Whitted—192, WR, North Carolina State, from Chicago
   Brandon Tolbert—214, LB, Georgia

KANSAS CITY CHIEFS
1. Victor Riley—27, T, Auburn
2. Choice to San Diego through Oakland and Tampa Bay
3. Rashaan Shehee—88, RB, Washington
4. Greg Favors—120, LB, Mississippi State
5. Robert Williams—128, DB, North Carolina, from Chicago
   Choice to Green Bay
6. Derrick Ransom—181, DT, Cincinnati
7. Eric Warfield—216, DB, Nebraska
   *Ernest Blackwell—224, RB, Missouri

MIAMI DOLPHINS
1. Choice to Green Bay
   John Avery—29, RB, Mississippi, from Green Bay
2. Patrick Surtain—44, DB, Southern Mississippi, from Carolina
   Kenny Mixon—49, DE, Louisiana State
3. Brad Jackson—79, LB, Cincinnati, from Detroit
   Larry Shannon—82, WR, East Carolina
4. Lorenzo Bromell—102, DE, Clemson, from Philadelphia
   Choice to Philadelphia
5. Choice to Philadelphia
   Scott Shaw—143, G, Michigan State, from Detroit
6. Nathan Strikwerda—171, C, Northwestern
   John Dutton—172, QB, Nevada, from Detroit
7. Jim Bundren—210, G, Clemson

MINNESOTA VIKINGS
1. Randy Moss—21, WR, Marshall
2. Kailee Wong—51, LB, Stanford
3. Ramos McDonald—80, DB, New Mexico
4. Kivuusama Mays—110, LB, North Carolina
5. Kerry Cooks—144, DB, Iowa
6. Matt Birk—173, T, Harvard
7. Chester Burnett—208, LB, Arizona
   *Tony Darden—225, DB, Texas Tech

NEW ENGLAND PATRIOTS
1. Robert Edwards—18, RB, Georgia, from New York Jets
   Tebucky Jones—22, DB, Syracuse
2. Tony Simmons—52, WR, Wisconsin, from New York Jets
   Rod Rutledge—54, TE, Alabama
3. Chris Floyd—81, RB, Michigan, from New York Jets
   Greg Spires—83, DE, Florida State
4. Leonta Rheams—115, DT, Houston
5. Ron Merkerson—145, LB, Colorado
6. Harold Shaw—176, RB, Southern Mississippi
7. Jason Andersen—211, C, Brigham Young

NEW ORLEANS SAINTS
1. Kyle Turley—7, T, San Diego State
2. Cameron Cleeland—40, TE, Washington
3. Choice to Washington
4. Fred Weary—97, DB, Florida, from Oakland
   Julian Pittman—99, DE, Florida State
5. Wilmont Perry—132, RB, Livingstone College
6. Chris Bordano—161, LB, Southern Methodist
7. Choice to Carolina
   Andy McCullough—204, WR, Tennessee, from Seattle
   *Ron Warner—239, LB, Kansas

NEW YORK GIANTS
1. Shaun Williams—24, DB, UCLA
2. Joe Jurevicius—55, WR, Penn State
3. Brian Alford—70, WR, Purdue, from Dallas through Phiadelphia
   Choice to Philadelphia
4. Choice to Philadelphia
5. Toby Myles—147, T, Jackson State
6. Todd Pollack—177, TE, Boston College
7. Ben Fricke—213, C, Houston

NEW YORK JETS
1. Choice to New England
2. Choice to New England
   Dorian Boose—56, DE, Washington State, from Philadelphia
3. Scott Frost—67, DB, Nebraska, from St. Louis
   Choice to New England
   Kevin Williams—87, DB, Oklahoma State, from Pittsburgh
4. Jason Fabini—111, T, Cincinnati
5. Casey Dailey—134, LB, Northwestern, from Philadelphia
   Doug Karczewski—141, G, Virginia
   Blake Spence—146, TE, Oregon, from Tampa Bay
   Eric Bateman—149, T, Brigham Young, from Pittsburgh
6. Eric Ogbogu—163, DE, Maryland, from Philadelphia
   Chris Brazzell—174, WR, Angelo State
   Dustin Johnson—183, RB, Brigham Young, from Denver
7. Lawrence Hart—195, TE, Southern, from St. Louis
   Choice to Arizona

OAKLAND RAIDERS
1. Charles Woodson—4, DB, Michigan
   Mo Collins—23, T, Florida, from Tampa Bay
2. *Leon Bender—31, DT, Washington State
   Choice to Tampa Bay
3. Jon Ritchie—63, RB, Stanford
4. Choice to New Orleans
   Gennaro DiNapoli—109, G, Virginia Tech, from Washington
5. Jeremy Brigham—127, TE, Washington
   Travian Smith—152, LB, Oklahoma, from Green Bay
6. Choice to Green Bay
7. Choice to Washington
   *Vince Amey—230, DE, Arizona State
   *David Sanders—235, DE, Arkansas

PHILADELPHIA EAGLES
1. Tra Thomas—11, T, Florida State
2. Choice to Pittsburgh through New York Jets
3. Jeremiah Trotter—72, LB, Stephen F. Austin
   Allen Rossum—85, DB, Notre Dame, from New York Giants
4. Choice to Miami
   Brandon Whiting—112, DT, California, from Miami
   Clarence Love—116, DB, Toledo, from New York Giants
5. Choice to New York Jets
   Ike Reese—142, LB, Michigan State, from Miami
6. Choice to New York Jets
7. Choice to Denver
   *Chris Akins—220, DT, Texas
   *Melvin Thomas—240, G, Colorado

PITTSBURGH STEELERS
1. Alan Faneca—26, G, Louisiana State
2. Jeremy Staat—41, DE, Arizona State, from Philadelphia through New York Jets
   Choice to New York Jets
3. Chris Conrad—66, T, Fresno State, from San Diego
   Choice to New York Jets
   *Hines Ward—92, WR, Georgia
4. Deshea Townsend—117, DB, Alabama
   *Carlos King—123, RB, North Carolina State
5. Jason Simmons—137, DB, Arizona State, from Atlanta
   Choice to New York Jets
6. Chris Fuamatu-Ma'afala—178, RB, Utah
   *Ryan Olson—186, LB, Colorado
7. Choice to San Francisco through Atlanta
   *Angel Rubio—221, DE, Southeast Missouri State

ST. LOUIS RAMS
1. Grant Wistrom—6, DE, Nebraska
2. Robert Holcombe—37, RB, Illinois
3. Leonard Little—65, LB, Tennessee, from Arizona through New York Jets
   Choice to New York Jets
4. Az-Zahir Hakim—96, WR, San Diego State, from San Diego
   Roland Williams—98, TE, Syracuse
5. Raymond Priester—129, RB, Clemson
6. Glenn Rountree—159, G, Clemson
7. Choice to New York Jets
   *Jason Chorak—236, DE, Washington

SAN DIEGO CHARGERS
1. Ryan Leaf—2, QB, Washington State, from Arizona
   Choice to Arizona
2. Choice to Arizona
   Mikhael Ricks—59, WR, Stephen F. Austin, from Kansas City through Oakland and Tampa Bay
3. Choice to Pittsburgh
4. Choice to St. Louis
5. Cedric Harden—126, DE, Florida A&M
6. Clifford Ivory—155, DB, Troy State
7. Jon Haskins—194, LB, Stanford
   *Kio Sanford—234, WR, Kentucky

SAN FRANCISCO 49ERS
1. R.W. McQuarters—28, DB, Oklahoma State
2. Jeremy Newberry—58, C, California
3. Chris Ruhman—89, T, Texas A&M
4. Lance Schulters—119, DB, Hofstra
5. Phil Ostrowski—151, G, Penn State
6. Fred Beasley—180, RB, Auburn
7. Ryan Thelwell—215, WR, Minnesota, from Pittsburgh through Atlanta
   Choice to Chicago

SEATTLE SEAHAWKS
1. Anthony Simmons—15, LB, Clemson
2. Todd Weiner—47, T, Kansas State
3. Ahman Green—76, RB, Nebraska
4. DeShone Myles—108, LB, Nevada
5. Choice to Dallas
6. Carl Hansen—162, DE, Stanford, from Dallas
   Bobby Shaw—169, WR, California
7. Jason McEndoo—197, C, Washington State, from Dallas
   Choice to New Orleans

TAMPA BAY BUCCANEERS
1. Choice to Oakland
2. Jacquez Green—34, WR, Florida, from Oakland
   Brian Kelly—45, DB, Southern California, from Atlanta
   Choice to Atlanta
3. Jamie Duncan—84, LB, Vanderbilt
4. Todd Washington—104, C, Virginia Tech, from Baltimore
   Choice to Atlanta
5. Choice to New York Jets
6. James Cannida—175, DT, Nevada
   *Shevin Smith—184, DB, Florida State
7. Chance McCarty—212, DE, Texas Christian

TENNESSEE OILERS
1. Kevin Dyson—16, WR, Utah
2. Samari Rolle—46, DB, Florida State
3. Dainon Sidney—77, DB, Alabama-Birmingham
4. Joe Salave'a—107, DT, Arizona
5. Benji Olson—139, G, Washington
6. Lee Wiggins—168, DB, South Carolina
7. Jimmy Sprotte—205, LB, Arizona
   *Kevin Long—229, C, Florida State

WASHINGTON REDSKINS
1. Choice to Cincinnati
2. Stephen Alexander—48, TE, Oklahoma
3. Skip Hicks—69, RB, UCLA, from New Orleans
   Choice to Cincinnati
4. Choice to Oakland
   Shawn Barber—113, LB, Richmond, from Detroit through Oakland
5. Mark Fischer—140, C, Purdue
6. Patrick Palmer—170, WR, Northwestern State, La.
7. David Terrell—191, DB, Texas-El Paso, from Oakland
   Antwaune Ponds—206, LB, Syracuse

DRAFT LIST

NUMBER OF PLAYERS DRAFTED—1998

BY POSITION:

Defensive Backs	43
Linebackers	34
Wide Receivers	31
Running Backs	29
Defensive Ends	22
Tackles	21
Defensive Tackles	15
Guards	14
Tight Ends	13
Centers	11
Quarterbacks	8

BY COLLEGE:

Washington	10
Florida State	9
Tennessee	8
North Carolina	7
Colorado	6
Nebraska	6
Arizona State	5
Cincinnati	5
Clemson	5
Florida	5
Michigan	5
Stanford	5
Syracuse	5
Alabama	4
Auburn	4
California	4
Georgia	4
Iowa	4
Oklahoma	4
Southern Mississippi	4
Virginia Tech	4
Washington State	4
Arizona	3
Brigham Young	3
Louisiana State	3
Michigan State	3
Mississippi	3
Nevada	3
Oklahoma State	3
Penn State	3
Purdue	3
San Diego State	3
UCLA	3
Vanderbilt	3
Alabama-Birmingham	2
Boston College	2
Florida A&M	2
Fresno State	2
Georgia Tech	2
Houston	2
Indiana	2
Jackson State	2
Marshall	2
Miami	2
Minnesota	2
Mississippi	2
Missouri	2
New Mexico	2
North Carolina State	2
Northwestern	2
Oregon	2
South Carolina	2
Stephen F. Austin	2
Texas A&M	2
Texas Christian	2
Utah	2
Virginia	2
Wisconsin	2
Angelo State	1
Arkansas	1
Cal Poly-San Luis Obispo	1
Colorado State	1
Dartmouth	1
Duke	1
East Carolina	1
Eastern Michigan	1
Hampton	1
Harvard	1
Hofstra	1
Illinois	1
Iowa State	1
Kansas	1
Kansas State	1
Kent	1
Kentucky	1
Livingstone College	1
Maryland	1
Miami, Ohio	1
Middle Tennessee State	1
Morris Brown	1
Northeast Louisiana	1
Northwestern State, La.	1
Notre Dame	1
Pennsylvania	1
Richmond	1
Southeast Missouri State	1
Southern	1
Southern California	1
Southern Methodist	1
Southwestern Louisiana	1
Texas	1
Texas-El Paso	1
Texas Tech	1
Toledo	1
Troy State	1
Weber State	1
West Virginia	1
Youngstown State	1

BY CONFERENCE:

SEC	40
Pac 10	37
ACC	29
Big 12	28
Big 10	27
WAC	17
Big East	14
Conference USA	12
Independent	7
MAC	6
Southland	4
Big West	3
Ivy	3
MEAC	3
Ohio Valley	2
Southern	2
SWAC	2
Atlantic 10	1
Big Sky	1
Gateway	1
Lone Star	1
Southern Intercollegiate	1

UNDERCLASSMEN AND THE DRAFT

Year	Entered	Drafted	In Top 10
1989	25	12	3
1990	38	18	5
1991	33	22	2
1992	48	25	5
1993	46	24	5
1994	42	26	6
1995	42	22	2
1996	47	21	4
1997	44	27	7
1998	41	20	3

The AFC

BALTIMORE RAVENS

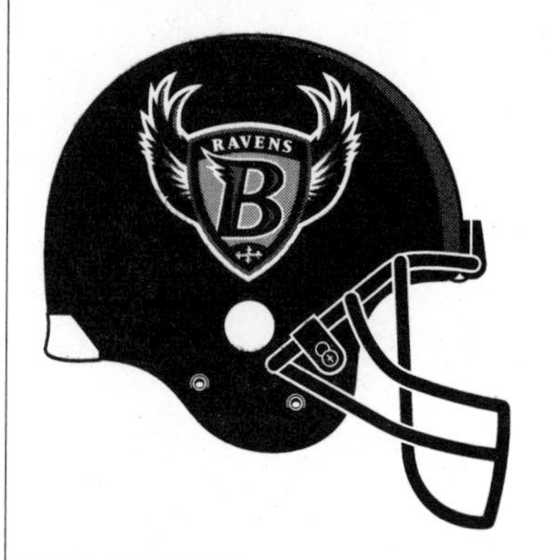

American Football Conference
Central Division
Team Colors: Black, Purple, and Metallic Gold
11001 Owings Mills Boulevard
Owings Mills, Maryland 21117
Telephone: (410) 654-6200

CLUB OFFICIALS

President and Owner: Arthur B. Modell
Executive Vice President/Legal and Administration: Jim Bailey
Executive Vice President/Assistant to the President: David Modell
Vice President/Public Relations: Kevin Byrne
Vice President/Sales and Marketing: David Cope
Vice President/Player Personnel: Ozzie Newsome
Vice President/Administration: Pat Moriarty
Treasurer: Luis Perez
Director of Ticket Operations: Roy Sommerhof
Director of Operations/Information: Bob Eller
Director of Publications/Assistant Director of Public Relations: Francine Lubera
Director of Player Development: Earnest Byner
Director of Broadcasting: Lisa Bercu
Director of Pro Personnel: James Harris
Director of College Scouting: Phil Savage
Assistant Director of Pro Personnel and College Scouting: John Wooten
Scouts: Eric DeCosta, George Kokinis, Ron Marciniak, Terry McDonough, Vince Newsome, Art Perkins, Ernie Plank, Ellis Rainsberger
Head Trainer: Bill Tessendorf
Facilities Manager: Chuck Cusick
Equipment Manager: Ed Carroll
Video Director: Jon Dube
Stadium: Ravens Stadium At Camden Yards
•**Capacity:** 68,400
1101 Russell Street
Baltimore, Maryland 21230
Playing Surface: SportGrass
Training Camp: Western Maryland College
2 College Hill
Westminster, Maryland 21157

RECORD HOLDERS

INDIVIDUAL RECORDS—CAREER

Category	Name	Performance
Rushing (Yds.)	Byron (Bam) Morris, 1996-97	1,511
Passing (Yds.)	Vinny Testaverde, 1996-97	7,148
Passing (TDs)	Vinny Testaverde, 1996-97	51
Receiving (No.)	Michael Jackson, 1996-97	145
Receiving (Yds.)	Michael Jackson, 1996-97	2,119
Interceptions	Antonio Langham, 1996-97	5
	Eric Turner, 1996	5
Punting (Avg.)	Greg Montgomery, 1996-97	43.2
Punt Return (Avg.)	Jermaine Lewis, 1996-97	12.1
Kickoff Return (Avg.)	Jermaine Lewis, 1996-97	21.8
Field Goals	Matt Stover, 1996-97	45
Touchdowns (Tot.)	Michael Jackson, 1996-97	18
Points	Matt Stover, 1996-97	201

INDIVIDUAL RECORDS—SINGLE SEASON

Category	Name	Performance
Rushing (Yds.)	Byron (Bam) Morris, 1997	774
Passing (Yds.)	Vinny Testaverde, 1996	4,177
Passing (TDs)	Vinny Testaverde, 1996	33
Receiving (No.)	Michael Jackson, 1996	76
Receiving (Yds.)	Michael Jackson, 1996	1,201
Interceptions	Antonio Langham, 1996	5
	Eric Turner, 1996	5
Punting (Avg.)	Greg Montgomery, 1996	43.8
Punt Return (Avg.)	Jermaine Lewis, 1997	15.6
Kickoff Return (Avg.)	Jermaine Lewis, 1997	22.1
Field Goals	Matt Stover, 1997	26
Touchdowns (Tot.)	Michael Jackson, 1996	14
Points	Matt Stover, 1997	110

INDIVIDUAL RECORDS—SINGLE GAME

Category	Name	Performance
Rushing (Yds.)	Byron (Bam) Morris, 10-26-97	176
Passing (Yds.)	Vinny Testaverde, 10-27-96	429
Passing (TDs)	Vinny Testaverde, 10-20-96	4
Receiving (No.)	Many times	9
	Last time by Eric Green, 11-2-97	
Receiving (Yds.)	Derrick Alexander, 12-1-96	198
Interceptions	Many times	2
	Last time by Ralph Staten, 12-7-97	
Field Goals	Matt Stover, 11-24-96	4
Touchdowns (Tot.)	Michael Jackson, 12-22-96	3
	Jermaine Lewis, 12-7-97	
Points	Michael Jackson, 12-22-96	18
	Jermaine Lewis, 12-7-97	

1998 SCHEDULE

PRESEASON

Aug. 8	**Chicago**	7:30
Aug. 15	at New York Jets	5:00
Aug. 24	**Philadelphia**	7:30
Aug. 28	at New York Giants	8:00

REGULAR SEASON

Sept. 6	**Pittsburgh**	1:01
Sept. 13	at New York Jets	1:01
Sept. 20	at Jacksonville	4:15
Sept. 27	**Cincinnati**	8:20
Oct. 4	Open Date	
Oct. 11	**Tennessee**	1:01
Oct. 18	at Pittsburgh	1:01
Oct. 25	at Green Bay	12:01
Nov. 1	**Jacksonville**	1:01
Nov. 8	**Oakland**	1:01
Nov. 15	at San Diego	1:05
Nov. 22	at Cincinnati	4:15
Nov. 29	**Indianapolis**	1:01
Dec. 6	at Tennessee	3:15
Dec. 13	**Minnesota**	4:15
Dec. 20	at Chicago	12:01
Dec. 27	**Detroit**	1:01

COACHING HISTORY

(10-21-1)

1996-97	Ted Marchibroda	10-21-1

RAVENS STADIUM AT CAMDEN YARDS

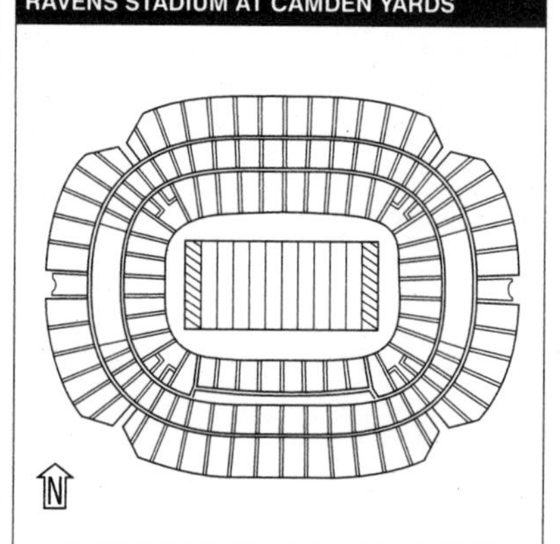

1997 TEAM RECORD

PRESEASON (0-4)

Date	Result		Opponent
8/2	L	20-21	New York Giants
8/8	L	29-39	at New York Jets
8/16	L	13-24	at Philadelphia
8/22	L	28-31	Buffalo

REGULAR SEASON (6-9-1)

Date	Result		Opponent	Att.
8/31	L	27-28	Jacksonville	61,018
9/7	W	23-0	Cincinnati	52,968
9/14	W	24-23	at New York Giants	69,768
9/21	W	36-10	at Tennessee	17,737
9/28	L	17-21	at San Diego	54,094
10/5	L	34-42	Pittsburgh	64,421
10/19	L	13-24	Miami	64,354
10/26	W	20-17	at Washington	75,067
11/2	L	16-19	at New York Jets (OT)	59,524
11/9	L	0-37	at Pittsburgh	56,669
11/16	T	10-10	Philadelphia (OT)	63,546
11/23	L	13-16	Arizona	53,976
11/30	L	27-29	at Jacksonville	63,712
12/7	W	31-24	Seattle	54,395
12/14	W	21-19	Tennessee	60,558
12/21	L	14-16	at Cincinnati	50,917

(OT) Overtime

SCORE BY PERIODS

Ravens	67	98	58	103	0	—	326
Opponents	89	92	81	80	3	—	345

ATTENDANCE

Home 475,236 Away 447,488 Total 922,724
Single-game home record, 64,421 (10/5/97)
Single-season home record, 475,236 (1997)

1997 TEAM STATISTICS

	Ravens	Opp.
Total First Downs	292	306
Rushing	114	109
Rushing	99	101
Passing	176	180
Penalty	17	25
Third Down: Made/Att	82/227	94/233
Third Down Pct.	36.1	40.3
Fourth Down: Made/Att	12/21	7/14
Fourth Down Pct.	57.1	50.0
Total Net Yards	5,291	5,363
Avg. Per Game	330.7	335.2
Total Plays	1,043	1,068
Avg. Per Play	5.1	5.0
Net Yards Rushing	1,589	1,690
Avg. Per Game	99.3	105.6
Total Rushes	420	470
Net Yards Passing	3,702	3,673
Avg. Per Game	231.4	229.6
Sacked/Yards Lost	37/227	42/293
Gross Yards	3,929	3,966
Att./Completions	586/338	556/332
Completion Pct.	57.7	59.7
Had Intercepted	16	17
Punts/Average	83/42.7	82/44.0
Net Punting Avg.	83/36.6	82/35.5
Penalties/Yards Lost	101/777	106/828
Fumbles/Ball Lost	37/17	23/11
Touchdowns	35	39
Rushing	7	17
Passing	25	20
Returns	3	2
Avg. Time of Possession	28:30	31:30

1997 INDIVIDUAL STATISTICS

PASSING	Att.	Comp.	Yds.	Pct.	TD	Int.	Tkld.	Rating
Testaverde	470	271	2,971	57.7	18	15	20/129	75.9
Zeier	116	67	958	57.8	7	1	17/98	101.1
Ravens	586	338	3,929	57.7	25	16	37/227	80.9
Opponents	556	332	3,966	59.7	20	17	42/293	80.8

SCORING	TD R	TD P	TD Rt	PAT	FG	Saf	PTS
Stover	0	0	0	32/32	26/34	0	110
Alexander	0	9	0	0/0	0/0	0	54
J. Lewis	0	6	2	0/0	0/0	0	48
Green	0	5	0	0/0	0/0	0	30
Jackson	0	4	0	0/0	0/0	0	26
Morris	4	0	0	0/0	0/0	0	24
Graham	2	0	0	0/0	0/0	0	12
Cotton	1	0	0	0/0	0/0	0	6
Kinchen	0	1	0	0/0	0/0	0	6
Langham	0	0	1	0/0	0/0	0	6
Byner	0	0	0	0/0	0/0	0	2
Ravens	7	25	3	32/32	26/34	1	326
Opponents	17	20	2	33/35	24/34	1	345

2-Point conversions: Byner, Jackson.
Team 2-3, Opponents: 2-4.

RUSHING	Att.	Yds.	Avg.	LG	TD
Morris	204	774	3.8	25	4
Byner	84	313	3.7	19	0
Graham	81	299	3.7	19	2
Testaverde	34	138	4.1	16	0
J. Lewis	3	35	11.7	24	0
Zeier	10	17	1.7	12	0
Montgomery	1	11	11.0	11	0
Cotton	2	2	1.0	1t	1
Alexander	1	0	0.0	0	0
Ravens	420	1,589	3.8	25	7
Opponents	470	1,690	3.6	74t	17

RECEIVING	No.	Yds.	Avg.	LG	TD
Jackson	69	918	13.3	54t	4
Alexander	65	1,009	15.5	92	9
Green	65	601	9.2	37t	5
J. Lewis	42	648	15.4	42t	6
Morris	29	176	6.1	15	0
Byner	21	128	6.1	17	0
Yarborough	16	183	11.4	26	0
Graham	12	51	4.3	19	0
Kinchen	11	95	8.6	24t	1
Roe	7	124	17.7	29	0
Testaverde	1	-4	-4.0	-4	0
Ravens	338	3,929	11.6	92	25
Opponents	332	3,966	11.9	77t	20

INTERCEPTIONS	No.	Yds.	Avg.	LG	TD
Moore	4	56	14.0	38	0
Daniel	3	60	20.0	43	0
Langham	3	40	13.3	40t	1
Staten	2	12	6.0	9	0
C. Brown	1	21	21.0	21	0
R. Lewis	1	18	18.0	18	0
Jenkins	1	15	15.0	15	0
R. Jones	1	15	15.0	15	0
Sharper	1	4	4.0	4	0
Ravens	17	241	14.2	43	1
Opponents	16	118	7.4	42	0

PUNTING	No.	Yds.	Avg.	In 20	LG
Montgomery	83	3,540	42.7	24	60
Ravens	83	3,540	42.7	24	60
Opponents	82	3,611	44.0	24	63

PUNT RETURNS	No.	FC	Yds.	Avg.	LG	TD
J. Lewis	28	13	437	15.6	89t	2
Roe	8	0	72	9.0	14	0
Ethridge	5	1	21	4.2	16	0
Alexander	1	0	34	34.0	34	0
Ravens	42	14	564	13.4	89t	2
Opponents	53	11	460	8.7	60	0

KICKOFF RETURNS	No.	Yds.	Avg.	LG	TD
J. Lewis	41	905	22.1	51	0
Roe	9	189	21.0	33	0
Graham	6	115	19.2	24	0
Brew	5	88	17.6	24	0
Singleton	4	64	16.0	19	0
Ethridge	2	37	18.5	22	0
Byner	1	0	0.0	0	0
Holmes	1	14	14.0	14	0
McCloud	1	0	0.0	0	0
Morris	1	23	23.0	23	0
Ravens	71	1,435	20.2	51	0
Opponents	58	1,323	22.8	97t	1

FIELD GOALS	1-19	20-29	30-39	40-49	50+
Stover	0/0	8/9	12/12	6/11	0/2
Ravens	0/0	8/9	12/12	6/11	0/2
Opponents	0/0	10/10	6/6	7/16	1/2

SACKS	No.
Boulware	11.5
McCrary	9.0
J. Jones	6.0
Burnett	4.0
R.Lewis	4.0
Sharper	3.0
Washington	2.0
Herring	1.0
Langham	1.0
C. Brown	0.5
Ravens	42.0
Opponents	37.0

1998 DRAFT CHOICES

Round	Name	Pos.	College
1	Duane Starks	DB	Miami
2	Pat Johnson	WR	Oregon
5	Martin Chase	DT	Oklahoma
	Ryan Sutter	DB	Colorado
6	Ron Rogers	LB	Georgia Tech
	Sammy Williams	T	Oklahoma
7	Cam Quayle	TE	Weber State

BALTIMORE RAVENS

1998 VETERAN ROSTER

No.	Name	Pos.	Ht.	Wt.	Birthdate	NFL Exp.	College	Hometown	How Acq.	'97 Games/ Starts
82	Anderson, Stevie	WR	6-6	216	5/12/70	4	Grambling	Jonesboro, La.	FA-'98	0*
74	Atkins, James	C-G-T	6-6	306	1/28/70	5	Southwestern Louisiana	Amite, La.	FA-'98	13/3*
69	Blackshear, Jeff	G	6-6	323	3/29/69	6	Northeast Louisiana	Fort Pierce, Fla.	T(Sea)-'96	16/16
58	Boulware, Peter	LB	6-4	255	2/18/74	2	Florida State	Columbia, S.C.	D1-'97	16/16
24	Brady, Donny	DB	6-2	195	11/24/73	3	Wisconsin	North Bellmore, N.Y.	FA-'95	16/5
51	Brown, Cornell	LB	6-0	240	3/15/75	2	Virginia Tech	Lynchburg, Va.	D6-'97	16/1
77	Brown, Orlando	T	6-7	350	11/12/70	6	South Carolina State	Washington, D.C.	FA-'93	16/16
90	Burnett, Rob	DE	6-4	280	8/27/67	9	Syracuse	Coram, N.Y.	D5-'90	15/15
65	Cavil, Ben	G	6-2	310	1/31/72	2	Oklahoma	Lamarque, Tex.	T(Phil)-'97	15/8
23	Cotton, Kenyon	RB	6-0	255	2/23/74	2	Southwestern Louisiana	Minden, La.	FA-'97	15/0
71	Folau, Spencer	T	6-5	300	4/5/73	2	Idaho	Sequoia, Calif.	FA-'96	10/0
94	† Frederick, Mike	DE	6-5	280	8/6/72	4	Virginia	Neshaminy, Pa.	D3b-'95	16/1
34	Graham, Jay	RB	5-11	220	7/14/75	2	Tennessee	Concord, N.C.	D3-'97	13/3
86	Green, Eric	TE	6-5	285	6/22/67	9	Liberty	Savannah, Ga.	FA-'96	16/15
4	Harbaugh, Jim	QB	6-3	215	12/23/63	12	Michigan	Ann Arbor, Mich.	T(Ind)-'98	12/11*
20	Herring, Kim	S	5-11	210	9/10/75	2	Penn State	Solon, Ohio	D2b-'97	15/4
33	Holmes, Priest	RB	5-9	205	10/7/73	2	Texas	San Antonio, Tex.	FA-'97	7/0
64	Isaia, Sale	C-G-T	6-5	315	6/13/72	4	UCLA	Oceanside, Calif.	FA-'95	0*
21	Jackson, Alfred	CB-S	6-0	183	7/10/67	7	San Diego State	Tulare, Calif.	FA-'98	0*
81	Jackson, Michael	WR	6-4	195	4/12/69	8	Southern Mississippi	Kentwood, La.	D6-'91	16/15
25	Jenkins, De Ron	CB	5-11	190	11/14/73	3	Tennessee	St. Louis, Mo.	D2-'96	16/6
97	Jones, James	DT	6-2	290	2/6/69	8	Northern Iowa	Davenport, Iowa	FA-'96	16/16
31	Jones, Rondell	S	6-2	210	5/7/71	6	North Carolina	Sunderland, Md.	UFA(Sea)-'97	14/12
88	Kinchen, Brian	TE	6-2	240	8/6/65	11	Louisiana State	Baton Rouge, La.	FA-'91	16/7
84	Lewis, Jermaine	WR-KR	5-7	172	10/16/74	3	Maryland	Lanham, Md.	D5-'96	14/7
52	Lewis, Ray	LB	6-1	240	5/15/75	3	Miami	Lakeland, Fla.	D1b-'96	16/16
29	Lyons, Lamar	S	6-3	210	3/25/73	2	Washington	Santa Monica, Calif.	FA-'97	1/0
54	McCloud, Tyrus	LB	6-1	250	11/23/74	2	Louisville	Pompano Beach, Fla.	D4b-'97	16/0
99	McCrary, Michael	DE	6-4	270	7/7/70	6	Wake Forest	Vienna, Va.	UFA(Sea)-'97	15/15
60	Mitchell, Jeff	C	6-4	300	1/29/74	2	Florida	Clearwater, Fla.	D5-'97	0*
9	Montgomery, Greg	P	6-4	215	10/29/64	10	Michigan State	Little Silver, N.J.	FA-'96	16/0
27	Moore, Stevon	S	5-11	210	2/9/67	10	Mississippi	Wiggins, Miss.	PB(Mia)-'92	13/13
89	Ofodile, A.J.	TE	6-6	260	10/10/73	3	Missouri	Detroit, Mich.	FA-'96	12/0
75	Ogden, Jonathan	C-G-T	6-8	318	7/31/74	3	UCLA	Washington, D.C.	D1a-'96	16/16
53	Peters, Tyrell	LB	6-0	230	8/4/74	2	Oklahoma	Norman, Okla.	FA-'97	4/0
42	Potts, Roosevelt	RB	6-0	250	1/8/71	5	Northeast Louisiana	Rayville, La.	UFA(Mia)-'98	8/1*
32	t- Rhett, Errict	RB	5-11	210	12/11/70	4	Florida	Hollywood, Fla.	T(TB)-'98	11/0*
14	Richardson, Wally	QB	6-4	225	2/11/74	2	Penn State	Sumter, S.C.	D7b-'97	0*
83	Roe, James	WR	6-1	187	8/23/73	3	Norfolk State	Richmond, Va.	D6b-'96	12/4
55	Sharper, Jamie	LB	6-3	240	11/23/74	2	Virginia	Glen Allen, Va.	D2a-'97	16/15
98	Siragusa, Tony	DT	6-3	320	5/14/67	9	Pittsburgh	Kenilworth, N.J.	UFA(Ind)-'97	14/13
41	Staten, Ralph	S	6-3	205	12/3/74	2	Alabama	Montgomery, Ala.	D7c-'97	10/3
3	Stover, Matt	K	5-11	178	1/27/68	9	Louisiana Tech	Dallas, Tex.	PB(NYG)-'91	16/0
12	Testaverde, Vinny	QB	6-5	238	11/13/63	12	Miami	Floral Park, N.Y.	UFA(TB)-'93	13/3
37	Thompson, Bennie	S	6-0	214	2/10/63	9	Grambling	New Orleans, La.	UFA(NO)-'94	16/0
44	Vinson, Tony	RB	6-1	229	3/13/71	2	Towson State	Newport News, Va.	FA-'97	13/0
95	Ward, Chris	DE	6-3	275	2/4/74	2	Kentucky	Decatur, Ga.	D7a-'97	5/0
93	Washington, Keith	DE	6-4	270	12/18/72	4	Nevada-Las Vegas	Dallas, Tex.	FA-'97	10/1
79	Webster, Larry	DE-DT	6-5	288	1/18/69	6	Maryland	Elkton, Md.	FA-'95	16/3
63	Williams, Wally	G-C	6-2	305	3/19/71	6	Florida A&M	Tallahassee, Fla.	FA-'93	10/10
26	Woodson, Rod	CB	6-0	200	3/10/65	12	Purdue	Fort Wayne, Ind.	FA-'98	14/14*
80	Yarborough, Ryan	WR	6-2	195	4/26/71	4	Wyoming	Park Forest, Ill.	W(GB)-'97	16/3
10	Zeier, Eric	QB	6-1	205	9/6/72	4	Georgia	Marietta, Ga.	D3a-'95	5/3

* Anderson last active with Arizona in '96; Atkins played 13 games with Seattle in '97; Harbaugh played 12 games with Indianapolis; Isaia and Mitchell missed '97 season because of injury; A. Jackson last active with Minnesota in '96; Potts played 2 games with Indianapolis, 6 with Miami; Rhett played 11 games with Tampa Bay; Richardson inactive for 16 games; Woodson played 14 games with San Francisco.

† Restricted free agent; subject to developments.

t- Ravens traded for Rhett (Tampa Bay).

Retired—Earnest Byner, 14-year running back, 16 games in '97.

Players lost through free agency (3): WR Derrick Alexander (KC; 15 games in '97), CB Antonio Langham (SF; 16), C Quentin Neujahr (Jax; 9).

Also played with Ravens in '97—CB Dorian Brew (3 games), G Bernard Dafney (1), CB Eugene Daniel (9), WR Ray Ethridge (2), G Leo Goeas (11), RB Byron (Bam) Morris (11), WR Nate Singleton (4), DT Leland Taylor (1), CB John Williams (4).

COACHING STAFF

Head Coach, Ted Marchibroda

Pro Career: Ted Marchibroda enters his third year at the helm of the Baltimore Ravens (10-21-1). The '97 Ravens (6-9-1) were 4-7 in games decided by a touchdown or less and 3-5-1 in games decided by a field goal or less. Baltimore's final three losses were by a combined total of seven points. Six games were decided in the final seconds of the games (1-4-1). While the Ravens showed a two-victory, one-tie improvement over the '96 season, the biggest gains, according to Marchibroda, were made in strengthening the team's depth: "We're going to be a better football team in 1998 because of all the young players we played last season. That means we're going to have solid competition for positions." Prior to his return to Baltimore, Marchibroda coached the Indianapolis Colts from 1992-94 (32-35). His 1995 Colts came within one "Hail Mary" pass of going to Super Bowl XXX in the thrilling 20-16 loss to the Pittsburgh Steelers at Three Rivers Stadium. Twice in his career he has improved his team by a margin of eight victories. Inheriting a 2-12 Baltimore Colts' team when he was named head coach in 1975, he led Baltimore to a 10-4 record and the AFC East title and was named NFL Coach of the Year. The Colts followed with two more division titles, earning 11-3 and 10-4 records in 1976 and 1977. Those are the most titles won by any coach in Colts' history. From October 26, 1975, through November 20, 1977, Marchibroda's Colts won 29 of 33 regular-season games. Marchibroda (41-36) left the Colts following the 1979 season and was rehired as Indianapolis' team boss on January 28, 1992. Marchibroda achieved the eight-game swing the second time in 1992, taking Indianapolis to a 9-7 mark after the team finished 1-15 in 1991. He began his career as backfield coach with the Washington Redskins in 1961. Marchibroda joined George Allen's staff with the Los Angeles Rams in 1966 and moved with Allen to the Washington Redskins in 1971, where he served as offensive coordinator through the 1974 season. Marchibroda served as quarterback coach with the Chicago Bears in 1981, then moved on to Detroit as offensive coordinator with the Lions from 1982-83. He served in that same role with the Philadelphia Eagles from 1984-85 prior to joining Buffalo in 1987. Marchibroda was the first draft pick of the Pittsburgh Steelers in 1953 and played one year before serving in the Army. He returned to Pittsburgh for the 1955-56 seasons. His top season was 1956, when he completed 124 of 275 passes for 1,585 yards and 12 touchdowns. His playing career ended with the Chicago Cardinals in 1957. Career record: 83-92-1.

Background: Quarterback at St. Bonaventure 1950-51 and University of Detroit 1952. Led nation in total offense at Detroit. He was a football, basketball (all-state selection), and baseball player at Franklin (Pa.) High School.

Personal: Born March 15, 1931, Franklin, Pa. Ted and his wife Ann reside in Timonium, Md. They have two daughters, Jodi and Lonni and two sons, Ted Jr. and Robert.

ASSISTANT COACHES

Maxie Baughan, linebackers; born August 3, 1938, Forkland, Ala., lives in Reisterstown, Md. Center-linebacker Georgia Tech 1957-60. Pro linebacker Philadelphia Eagles 1960-65, Los Angeles Rams 1966-70, Washington Redskins 1971, 1974. College coach: Georgia Tech 1972-73, Cornell 1983-88 (head coach). Pro coach: Baltimore Colts 1975-79, Detroit Lions 1980-82, Minnesota Vikings 1990-91, Tampa Bay Buccaneers, 1992-95, joined Ravens in 1996.

Jacob Burney, defensive line; born January 24, 1959, Chattanooga, Tenn., lives in Reisterstown, Md. Defensive tackle Tennessee-Chattanooga 1977-80. No pro playing experience. College coach: New Mexico 1983-86, Tulsa 1987, Mississippi State 1988, Wisconsin 1989, UCLA 1990-92, Tennessee 1993. Pro coach: Joined Ravens/Browns in 1994.

Kirk Ferentz, assistant head coach-offense; born August 1, 1955, Royal Oak, Mich., lives in Baldwin, Md. Linebacker Connecticut 1973-76. No pro playing experience. College coach: Connecticut 1977, Pittsburgh 1980, Iowa 1981-89, Maine 1990-92 (head coach). Pro coach: Joined Ravens/Browns in 1993.

Al Lavan, running backs; born September 13, 1946, Pierce, Fla., lives in Reisterstown, Md. Defensive back Colorado State 1965-67. Pro defensive back Philadelphia Eagles 1968, Atlanta Falcons 1969-70. College coach: Colorado State 1972, Louisville 1973, Iowa State 1974, Georgia Tech 1977-78, Stanford 1979, Washington 1992-95. Pro coach: Atlanta Falcons 1975-76, Dallas Cowboys 1980-88, San Francisco 49ers 1989-90, joined Ravens in 1996.

Marvin Lewis, defensive coordinator; born September 23, 1958, McDonald, Pa., lives in Finksburg, Md. Linebacker Idaho State 1977-80. No pro playing experience. College coach: Idaho State 1981-84, Long Beach State 1985-86, New Mexico, 1987-89, Pittsburgh 1990-91. Pro coach: Pittsburgh Steelers, 1992-95, joined Ravens in 1996.

Richard Mann, receivers; born April 20, 1947, Aliquippa, Pa., lives in Owings Mills, Md. Wide receiver Arizona State 1966-68. No pro playing experience. College coach: Arizona State 1974-79, Louisville 1980-81. Pro coach: Baltimore/Indianapolis Colts 1982-84, Cleveland Browns 1985-93, New York Jets 1994-96, joined Ravens in 1997.

Scott O'Brien, special teams; born June 25, 1957, Superior, Wis., lives in Reisterstown, Md. Defensive end Wisconsin-Superior 1975-78. Pro defensive end Green Bay Packers 1979, Toronto Argonauts (CFL) 1979. College coach: Wisconsin-Superior 1980-82, Nevada-Las Vegas 1983-85, Rice 1986, Pittsburgh 1987-90. Pro coach: Joined Ravens/Browns in 1991.

Alvin Reynolds, secondary; born June 24, 1959, Pineville, La., lives in Owings Mills, Md. Safety Indiana State 1978-81. No pro playing experience. College coach: Indiana State 1982-92. Pro coach: Denver Broncos 1993-95, joined Ravens in 1996.

Jerry Simmons, strength and conditioning; born June 15, 1954, Elkhart, Kan., lives in Reisterstown, Md. Linebacker Fort Hays State 1976-77. No pro playing experience. College coach: Fort Hays State 1978, Clemson 1980, Rice 1981-82, Southern California 1983-87. Pro coach: New England Patriots 1988-90, joined Ravens/Browns in 1991.

Don Strock, quarterbacks; born November 27, 1950, Pottstown, Pa., lives in Pikesville, Md. Quarterback Virginia Tech 1970-72. Pro quarterback Miami 1973-87, Cleveland 1988, Indianapolis 1989. Pro coach: Miami (Arena Football League) 1993 (head coach), Mass Marauders (Arena Football League) 1994 (head coach), Rhein Fire (World League) 1995, joined Ravens in 1996.

Ken Whisenhunt, tight ends; born February 28, 1962, Atlanta, Ga., lives in Reisterstown, Md. End Georgia Tech 1980-1984. Pro tight end Atlanta Falcons 1985-1988, Washington Redskins 1989-1990, New York Jets 1991-1993. College coach: Vanderbilt 1995-1996. Pro coach: Joined Ravens in 1997.

1998 FIRST-YEAR ROSTER

Name	Pos.	Ht.	Wt.	Birthdate	College	Hometown	How Acq.
Abdul-Majid, Shabaka	T	6-6	320	9/24/75	Florida A&M	Detroit, Mich.	FA
Bernstein, Alex (1)	C-G-T	6-3	325	8/11/75	Amherst	Aspen, Co.	FA-'97
Buxton, Chris	LB	6-2	225	12/21/74	Georgetown, Ky.	Alexandria, Va.	FA
Campbell, Marcus	CB	6-0	184	2/13/75	Arkansas	N. Little Rock, Ark.	FA
Chase, Martin	DT	6-2	295	12/19/74	Oklahoma	Lawton, Okla.	D5a
Coley, Greg	T	6-6	320	10/3/75	North Carolina A&T	Wilson, N.C.	FA
Dalton, Lional	DT	6-1	320	2/21/75	Eastern Michigan	Detroit, Mich.	FA
Darby, Chatric	DT	6-0	250	10/22/75	South Carolina State	North, S.C.	FA
Dyson, Brandon	C-G-T	6-4	290	5/31/76	Utah State	Bountiful, Utah	FA
Fitzpatrick, Larry	DT	6-4	275	8/17/76	Illinois State	Detroit, Mich.	FA
Flynn, Mike (1)	C-G-T	6-3	295	6/15/74	Maine	Agawam, Mass.	FA-'97
Garner, Nelson	K-P	6-0	180	2/23/76	James Madison	Burlington, N.C.	FA
Gregory, Duane	WR	6-1	195	6/24/76	New Mexico State	Waller, Tex.	FA
Hankerson, Mario	LB	5-8	225	10/23/75	East Tennessee State	Montezume, Ga.	FA
Hernandez, Adam	C-G-T	6-5	280	11/14/76	Yale	Potomac, Md.	FA
Johnson, Mac Arthur	WR	6-0	190	7/16/75	Howard	Jacksonville, Fla.	FA
Johnson, Patrick	WR	5-10	180	8/10/76	Oregon	Redlands, Calif.	D2
Kish, Bryan	WR	6-1	190	4/19/75	Hofstra	Allentown, Pa.	FA
Mack, Rebert	CB	6-1	195	10/17/72	West Texas A&M	Galveston, Tex.	FA
Newhouse, Roddrick	RB	5-10	205	5/21/75	Rice	Dallas, Tex.	FA
Quayle, Cam	TE	6-7	255	9/24/72	Weber State	Ogden, Utah	D7
Richard, Donald (1)	WR	6-0	180	11/18/72	Southwestern Louisiana	Kaplan, La.	FA-'97
Richards, Scott (1)	TE	6-4	244	1/7/74	East Carolina	North Augusta, S.C.	FA
Robertson, Rob	RB	5-11	223	11/6/75	Northwestern State (La.)	Baton Rouge, La.	FA
Robinson, Kareem	DE	6-4	250	7/1/76	Tennessee-Chattanooga	Nashville, Tenn.	FA
Rogers, Ron	LB	6-0	245	4/20/75	Georgia Tech	Dublin, Ga.	D6a
Saturday, Jeff	C-G-T	6-2	292	6/8/75	North Carolina	Tucker, Ga.	FA
Snell, Ben	RB	6-2	225	7/24/76	Ohio Northern	Canton, Ohio	FA
Starks, Duane	CB	5-10	170	5/23/74	Miami	Miami Beach, Fla.	D1
Sutter, Ryan	S	6-1	203	9/14/74	Colorado	Ft. Collins, Colo.	D5b
Ward, Bill	QB	6-3	215	10/25/75	Georgetown	Montvale, N.J.	FA
Williams, John (1)	CB-S	5-7	180	7/26/74	Southern	Hammond, Va.	FA-'97
Williams, Sammy	T	6-5	318	12/14/74	Oklahoma	Harvey, Ill.	D6b

The term NFL Rookie is defined as a player who is in his first season of professional football and has not been on the roster of another professional football team for any regular-season or postseason games. A Rookie is designated by an "R" on NFL rosters. Players who have been active in another professional football league or players who have NFL experience, including either preseason training camp or being on an Active List or Inactive List, or on Reserve/Injured or Reserve/Physically Unable to Perform for fewer than six regular-season games, are termed NFL First-Year Players. An NFL First-Year Player is designated by a "1" on NFL rosters. Thereafter, a player is credited with an additional year of experience for each season in which he accumulates six games on the Active List or Inactive List, or on Reserve/Injured or Reserve/Physically Unable to Perform.

NOTES

BUFFALO BILLS

American Football Conference
Eastern Division
Team Colors: Royal Blue, Scarlet Red, and White
One Bills Drive
Orchard Park, New York 14127-2296
Telephone: (716) 648-1800

CLUB OFFICIALS

President: Ralph C. Wilson, Jr.
Exec. V.P./General Manager: John Butler
Corporate V.P.: Linda Bogdan
Treasurer: Jeffrey C. Littmann
Vice President/Administration: Jim Miller
Director of Ticket Sales: Jerry Foran
Vice President/Business Operations: Bill Munson
Director of Business Operations: Jim Overdorf
Executive Director of Marketing and Business Development: Russ Brandon
Assistant Director of Marketing Communications: Marc Honan
Assistant Director of Marketing Partnerships: Brett Reynolds
Director of Merchandising: Christy Wilson Hofmann
Director of Player Personnel: Dwight Adams
Director of Pro Personnel: A.J. Smith
Director of Player/Alumni Relations: Jerry Butler
Director of Public/Community Relations: Denny Lynch
Director of Media Relations: Scott Berchtold
Asst. Director of Media Relations: Mark Dalton
Director of Stadium Operations: George Koch
Engineering and Operations Manager: Joseph Frandina
Director of Security: Bill Bambach
Ticket Director: June Foran
Equipment Manager: Dave Hojnowski
Asst. Equipment Manager: Randy Ribbeck
Strength/Conditioning Coordinator: Rusty Jones
Conditioning Assistant: Rich Gray
Trainers: Bud Carpenter, Melvin Lewis, Greg McMillen
Video Director: Henry Kunttu
Video Assistant: Matt Werder
Scouts: Brad Forsyth, Tom Gibbons, Joe Haering, Doug Majeski, Buddy Nix, Bob Ryan, George (Chink) Sengel, Jim Shofner, David G. Smith, David W. Smith, Bob Williams
Stadium: Rich Stadium • **Capacity:** 80,024
One Bills Drive
Orchard Park, New York 14127-2296
Playing Surface: AstroTurf
Training Camp: Fredonia State University
Fredonia, New York 14063

1998 SCHEDULE

PRESEASON

Aug. 8	at Pittsburgh	7:30
Aug. 14	**Carolina**	7:30
Aug. 22	at Chicago	7:00
Aug. 28	**Washington**	7:00

REGULAR SEASON

Sept. 6	at San Diego	1:15
Sept. 13	at Miami	1:01
Sept. 20	**St. Louis**	1:01
Sept. 27	Open Date	
Oct. 4	**San Francisco**	1:01
Oct. 11	at Indianapolis	12:01
Oct. 18	**Jacksonville**	1:01
Oct. 25	at Carolina	8:20
Nov. 1	**Miami**	1:01
Nov. 8	at New York Jets	4:15
Nov. 15	**New England**	1:01
Nov. 22	**Indianapolis**	1:01
Nov. 29	at New England	4:05
Dec. 6	at Cincinnati	1:01
Dec. 13	**Oakland**	1:01
Dec. 19	**New York Jets** (Sat.)	12:35
Dec. 27	at New Orleans	12:01

RECORD HOLDERS

INDIVIDUAL RECORDS—CAREER

Category	Name	Performance
Rushing (Yds.)	Thurman Thomas, 1988-1997	11,405
Passing (Yds.)	Jim Kelly, 1986-1996	35,467
Passing (TDs)	Jim Kelly, 1986-1996	237
Receiving (No.)	Andre Reed, 1985-1997	826
Receiving (Yds.)	Andre Reed, 1985-1997	11,764
Interceptions	George (Butch) Byrd, 1964-1970	40
Punting (Avg.)	Paul Maguire, 1964-1970	42.1
Punt Return (Avg.)	Clifford Hicks, 1990-92	12.2
Kickoff Return (Avg.)	O.J. Simpson, 1969-1977	30.0
Field Goals	Scott Norwood, 1985-1991	133
Touchdowns (Tot.)	Thurman Thomas, 1988-1997	83
Points	Scott Norwood, 1985-1991	670

INDIVIDUAL RECORDS—SINGLE SEASON

Category	Name	Performance
Rushing (Yds.)	O.J. Simpson, 1973	2,003
Passing (Yds.)	Jim Kelly, 1991	3,844
Passing (TDs)	Jim Kelly, 1991	33
Receiving (No.)	Andre Reed, 1994	90
Receiving (Yds.)	Andre Reed, 1989	1,312
Interceptions	Billy Atkins, 1961	10
	Tom Janik, 1967	10
Punting (Avg.)	Billy Atkins, 1961	44.5
Punt Return (Avg.)	Keith Moody, 1977	13.1
Kickoff Return (Avg.)	Ed Rutkowski, 1963	30.2
Field Goals	Scott Norwood, 1988	32
Touchdowns (Tot.)	O.J. Simpson, 1975	23
Points	O.J. Simpson, 1975	138

INDIVIDUAL RECORDS—SINGLE GAME

Category	Name	Performance
Rushing (Yds.)	O.J. Simpson, 11-25-76	273
Passing (Yds.)	Joe Ferguson, 10-9-83	419
Passing (TDs)	Jim Kelly, 9-8-91	6
Receiving (No.)	Andre Reed, 11-20-94	15
Receiving (Yds.)	Jerry Butler, 9-23-79	255
Interceptions	Many Times	3
	Last time by Jeff Nixon, 9-7-80	
Field Goals	Steve Christie, 10-20-96	6
Touchdowns (Tot.)	Cookie Gilchrist, 12-8-63	5
Points	Cookie Gilchrist, 12-8-63	30

COACHING HISTORY

(281-302-8)

1960-61	Buster Ramsey	11-16-1
1962-65	Lou Saban	38-18-3
1966-68	Joe Collier*	13-17-1
1968	Harvey Johnson	1-10-1
1969-70	John Rauch	7-20-1
1971	Harvey Johnson	1-13-0
1972-76	Lou Saban**	32-29-1
1976-77	Jim Ringo	3-20-0
1978-82	Chuck Knox	38-38-0
1983-85	Kay Stephenson***	10-26-0
1985-86	Hank Bullough****	4-17-0
1986-97	Marv Levy	123-78-0

*Released after two games in 1968
**Resigned after five games in 1976
***Released after four games in 1985
****Released after nine games in 1986

RICH STADIUM

1997 TEAM RECORD

PRESEASON (2-3)

Date	Result		Opponents
7/26	L	10-31	at Denver
8/2	L	17-20	Chicago (OT)
8/8	W	19-3	Minnesota
8/16	L	3-35	vs. Green Bay at Toronto, Canada
8/22	W	31-28	at Baltimore

REGULAR SEASON (6-10)

Date	Result		Opponent	Att.
8/31	L	13-34	Minnesota	79,139
9/7	W	28-22	at New York Jets	72,988
9/14	L	16-22	at Kansas City	78,169
9/21	W	37-35	Indianapolis	55,340
10/5	W	22-13	Detroit	78,025
10/12	L	6-33	at New England	59,802
10/20	W	9-6	at Indianapolis	61,139
10/26	L	20-23	Denver (OT)	78,458
11/2	W	9-6	Miami	78,011
11/9	L	10-31	New England	65,783
11/17	L	13-30	at Miami	74,155
11/23	L	14-31	at Tennessee	23,571
11/30	W	20-10	New York Jets	47,776
12/7	L	3-20	at Chicago	39,784
12/14	L	14-20	Jacksonville	41,231
12/20	L	21-31	at Green Bay	60,108

(OT) Overtime

SCORE BY PERIODS

Bills	19	66	45	125	0	—	255
Opponents	78	118	68	100	3	—	367

ATTENDANCE

Home 523,768 Away 469,716 Total 993,484
Single-game home record, 80,368 (10/4/92)
Single-season home record, 635,889 (1991)

1997 TEAM STATISTICS

	Bills	Opp.
Total First Downs	268	265
Rushing	128	94
Rushing	98	85
Passing	144	160
Penalty	26	20
Third Down: Made/Att	53/212	85/240
Third Down Pct.	25.0	35.4
Fourth Down: Made/Att	11/29	7/16
Fourth Down Pct.	37.9	43.8
Total Net Yards	4,657	4,853
Avg. Per Game	291.1	303.3
Total Plays	1,014	1,041
Avg. Per Play	4.6	4.7
Net Yards Rushing	1,782	1,792
Avg. Per Game	111.4	112.0
Total Rushes	422	493
Net Yards Passing	2,875	3,061
Avg. Per Game	179.7	191.3
Sacked/Yards Lost	46/338	46/344
Gross Yards	3,213	3,405
Att./Completions	546/293	502/287
Completion Pct.	53.7	57.2
Had Intercepted	25	15
Punts/Average	91/41.4	86/42.0
Net Punting Avg.	91/36.0	86/36.1
Penalties/Yards Lost	92/742	98/992
Fumbles/Ball Lost	39/17	23/7
Touchdowns	26	37
Rushing	12	11
Passing	14	17
Returns	0	9
Avg. Time of Possession	27:59	32:01

1997 INDIVIDUAL STATISTICS

PASSING	Att.	Comp.	Yds.	Pct.	TD	Int.	Tkld.	Rating
Collins	391	215	2,367	55.0	12	13	39/278	69.5
Van Pelt	124	60	684	48.4	2	10	4/33	37.2
Hobert	30	17	133	56.7	0	2	2/7	40.0
Mohr	1	1	29	100.0	0	0	0/0	118.8
Reed	0	0	0	—	0	0	1/20	—
Bills	546	293	3,213	53.7	14	25	46/338	60.8
Opponents	502	287	3,405	57.2	17	15	46/344	76.8

SCORING	TD R	TD P	TD Rt	PAT	FG	Saf	PTS
Christie	0	0	0	21/21	24/30	0	93
A. Smith	8	0	0	0/0	0/0	0	48
Early	0	5	0	0/0	0/0	0	30
Reed	0	5	0	0/0	0/0	0	30
Riemersma	0	2	0	0/0	0/0	0	14
Holmes	2	0	0	0/0	0/0	0	12
Johnson	0	2	0	0/0	0/0	0	12
Thomas	1	0	0	0/0	0/0	0	6
Van Pelt	1	0	0	0/0	0/0	0	6
Hansen	0	0	0	0/0	0/0	1	2
Moulds	0	0	0	0/0	0/0	0	2
Bills	12	14	0	21/21	24/30	1	255
Opponents	11	17	9	34/35	37/46	0	367

2-Point conversions: Moulds, Riemersma.
Team 2-5, Opponents: 0-2.

RUSHING	Att.	Yds.	Avg.	LG	TD
A. Smith	194	840	4.3	56t	8
Thomas	154	643	4.2	24	1
Holmes	22	106	4.8	19	2
Collins	30	77	2.6	11	0
Moulds	4	59	14.8	29	0
Van Pelt	11	33	3.0	9	1
Reed	3	11	3.7	9	0
Hobert	2	7	3.5	7	0
Johnson	1	6	6.0	6	0
Mohr	1	0	0.0	0	0
Bills	422	1,782	4.2	56t	12
Opponents	493	1,792	3.6	78t	11

RECEIVING	No.	Yds.	Avg.	LG	TD
Reed	60	880	14.7	77t	5
Early	60	853	14.2	45	5
Johnson	41	340	8.3	62t	2
Thomas	30	208	6.9	30	0
Moulds	29	294	10.1	32	0
A. Smith	28	177	6.3	19	0
Riemersma	26	208	8.0	22	2
Holmes	13	106	8.2	22	0
Tindale	4	105	26.3	45	0
Cline	1	29	29.0	29	0
Reese	1	13	13.0	13	0
Bills	293	3,213	11.0	77t	14
Opponents	287	3,405	11.9	60	17

INTERCEPTIONS	No.	Yds.	Avg.	LG	TD
Irvin	2	28	14.0	28	0
Schulz	2	23	11.5	21	0
Kerner	2	20	10.0	20	0
Burris	2	19	9.5	10	0
Moran	2	12	6.0	12	0
Maddox	1	25	25.0	25	0
Martin	1	12	12.0	12	0
Spielman	1	8	8.0	8	0
Covington	1	6	6.0	6	0
Perry	1	4	4.0	4	0
Bills	15	157	10.5	28	0
Opponents	25	359	14.4	62t	3

PUNTING	No.	Yds.	Avg.	In 20	LG
Mohr	90	3,764	41.8	24	59
Bills	91	3,764	41.4	24	59
Opponents	86	3,608	42.0	33	65

PUNT RETURNS	No.	FC	Yds.	Avg.	LG	TD
Burris	21	8	198	9.4	32	0
Tasker	12	9	113	9.4	47	0
Galloway	2	2	15	7.5	15	0
Moulds	2	0	20	10.0	10	0
Jackson	1	0	0	0.0	0	0
Jones	1	0	0	0.0	0	0
Bills	39	19	346	8.9	47	0
Opponents	44	24	366	8.3	29	0

KICKOFF RETURNS	No.	Yds.	Avg.	LG	TD
Moulds	43	921	21.4	53	0
Holmes	23	430	18.7	36	0
Galloway	6	130	21.7	30	0
Burris	1	10	10.0	10	0
Cline	1	0	0.0	0	0
Coons	1	12	12.0	12	0
Pike	1	11	11.0	11	0
Tasker	1	12	12.0	12	0
Wiley	1	12	12.0	12	0
Bills	78	1,538	19.7	53	0
Opponents	55	1,385	25.2	96t	3

FIELD GOALS	1-19	20-29	30-39	40-49	50+
Christie	0/0	6/6	9/12	8/10	1/2
Bills	0/0	6/6	9/12	8/10	1/2
Opponents	2/2	11/11	12/15	9/13	3/5

SACKS	No.
B. Smith	14.0
Paup	9.5
Hansen	6.0
Moran	4.5
Washington	4.0
Rogers	3.5
Jones	2.0
Holecek	1.5
Covington	0.5
Jeffcoat	0.5
Bills	46.0
Opponents	46.0

1998 DRAFT CHOICES

Round	Name	Pos.	College
2	Sam Cowart	LB	Florida State
3	Robert Hicks	T	Mississippi State
5	Jonathan Linton	RB	North Carolina
6	Fred Coleman	WR	Washington
7	Victor Allotey	G	Indiana
	Kamil Loud	WR	Cal Poly-San Luis Obispo

BUFFALO BILLS

1998 VETERAN ROSTER

No.	Name	Pos.	Ht.	Wt.	Birthdate	NFL Exp.	College	Hometown	How Acq.	'97 Games/ Starts
76	Albright, Ethan	C-G-T	6-5	283	5/1/71	4	North Carolina	Greensboro, N.C.	FA-'96	16/0
13	Ballard, Jim	QB	6-3	223	4/16/72	2	Mount Union	Cuyahoga, Ohio	FA-'97	0*
96	Brandenburg, Dan	LB	6-3	240	2/16/73	2	Indiana State	Renssalaer, Ind.	D7a-'96	12/0
79	Brown, Ruben	G	6-3	304	2/13/72	4	Pittsburgh	Lynchburg, Va.	D1-'95	16/16
2	Christie, Steve	K	6-0	185	11/13/67	9	William & Mary	Oakville, Canada	PB(TB)-'92	16/0
15	Collins, Todd	QB	6-4	224	11/5/71	4	Michigan	Walpole, Mass.	D2-'95	14/13
51	Cummings, Joe	LB	6-2	242	6/8/74	2	Wyoming	Mizzoula, Mont.	FA-'98	0*
88	Early, Quinn	WR	6-0	190	4/13/65	11	Iowa	West Hempstead, N.Y.	UFA(NO)-'96	16/16
70	Fina, John	T	6-4	300	3/11/69	7	Arizona	Tucson, Ariz.	D1-'92	16/16
48	Fitzgerald, Pat	TE	6-2	228	12/4/74	2	Texas	Van Nuys, Calif.	D7-'97	0*
7	Flutie, Doug	QB	5-10	175	10/23/62	5	Boston College	Natick, Mass.	FA-'98	0*
33	Gash, Sam	RB	6-0	235	3/7/69	7	Penn State	Hendersonville, N.C.	UFA(NE)-'98	16/5*
90	Hansen, Phil	DE	6-5	278	5/20/68	8	North Dakota State	Ellendale, N.D.	D2-'91	16/16
52	Holecek, John	LB	6-2	242	5/7/72	4	Illinois	Steger, Ill.	D5-'95	14/8
44	Holmes, Darick	RB	6-0	226	7/1/71	4	Portland State	Pasadena, Calif.	D7b-'95	13/0
25	Ingoglia, Rene	RB	5-10	202	5/23/72	2	Massachusetts	Rochester, N.Y.	FA-'97	0*
27	Irvin, Ken	CB	5-10	186	7/11/72	4	Memphis	Rome, Ga.	D4a-'95	16/0
31	Jackson, Raymond	CB-S	5-10	189	2/17/73	3	Colorado State	Denver, Colo.	D5-'96	9/0
84	Johnson, Lonnie	TE	6-3	240	2/14/71	5	Florida State	Miami, Fla.	D2b-'94	16/16
11	t- Johnson, Rob	QB	6-4	214	3/18/73	4	Southern California	Newport Beach, Calif.	T(Jax)-'98	5/1*
20	Jones, Henry	S	5-11	197	12/29/67	8	Illinois	St. Louis, Mo.	D1-'91	15/15
46	† Kerner, Marlon	CB	5-10	187	3/18/73	4	Ohio State	Columbus, Ohio	D3a-'96	13/2
21	Martin, Manny	S	5-11	184	7/31/69	3	Alabama State	Miami, Fla.	FA-'96	16/1
9	Mohr, Chris	P	6-5	215	5/11/66	9	Alabama	Thompson, Ga.	FA-'91	16/0
98	Moran, Sean	DE	6-3	275	6/5/73	3	Colorado State	Aurora, Colo.	D4-'96	16/7
80	Moulds, Eric	WR	6-0	204	7/17/73	3	Mississippi State	Lucedale, Miss.	D1-'96	16/8
74	Nails, Jamie	T	6-6	354	6/3/75	2	Florida A&M	Baxley, Ga.	D4-'97	2/0
99	Northern, Gabe	LB	6-2	240	6/8/74	3	Louisiana State	Baton Rouge, La.	D2-'96	16/1
60	Otroski, Jerry	G	6-4	310	7/12/70	4	Tulsa	Collegeville, Pa.	FA-'93	16/16
72	Panos, Joe	G	6-2	293	1/24/71	5	Wisconsin	Brookfield, Ill.	UFA(Phil)-'98	13/13*
58	Perry, Marlo	LB	6-4	250	8/25/72	5	Jackson State	Forest, Miss.	D3a-'94	13/0
94	Pike, Mark	LB	6-4	272	12/27/63	13	Georgia Tech	Villa Hills, Ky.	D7b-'86	15/0
91	Price, Shawn	DE	6-5	285	3/28/70	6	Pacific	Woodland Hills, Calif.	FA-'96	10/0
83	Reed, Andre	WR	6-2	190	1/29/64	14	Kutztown	Allentown, Pa.	D4a-'85	15/15
81	Reese, Jerry	WR-KR	5-11	190	3/18/73	2	San Jose State	Pittsburg, Calif.	FA-'97	5/0
85	Riemersma, Jay	TE	6-5	254	5/17/73	2	Michigan	Leeland, Mich.	D7b-'96	16/8
59	Rogers, Sam	LB	6-3	245	5/30/70	5	Colorado	Pontiac, Mich.	D2c-'94	15/15
95	Sabb, Dwayne	LB	6-4	248	10/9/69	7	New Hampshire	Jersey City, N.J.	FA-'98	0*
24	Schulz, Kurt	S	6-1	208	12/12/68	7	Eastern Washington	Yakima, Wash.	D7-'92	15/15
40	Smedley, Eric	CB-S	5-11	199	7/23/73	3	Indiana	Charleston, W. Va.	D7c-'96	13/1
23	Smith, Antowain	RB	6-2	224	3/14/72	2	Houston	Montgomery, Ala.	D1-'97	16/0
78	Smith, Bruce	DE	6-4	273	6/18/63	14	Virginia Tech	Norfolk, Va.	D1a-'85	16/16
28	Smith, Thomas	CB	5-11	188	12/5/70	6	North Carolina	Gates, N.C.	D1-'93	16/16
54	Spielman, Chris	LB	6-0	247	10/11/65	11	Ohio State	Massillon, Ohio	UFA(Det)-'96	8/8
69	Spriggs, Marcus	T	6-3	295	5/17/74	2	Houston	Hattiesburg, Miss.	D6-'97	2/0
34	Thomas, Thurman	RB	5-10	198	5/16/66	11	Oklahoma State	Missouri City, Tex.	D2-'88	16/16
10	Van Pelt, Alex	QB	6-0	220	5/1/70	4	Pittsburgh	Pittsburgh, Pa.	FA-'94	6/3
92	Washington, Ted	NT	6-4	325	4/13/68	8	Louisville	Tampa, Fla.	UFA(Den)-'95	16/16
75	Wiley, Marcellus	DE	6-5	271	11/30/74	2	Columbia	Los Angeles, Calif.	D2-'97	16/0
82	Williams, Kevin	WR-KR	5-9	195	1/25/71	6	Miami	Nashville, Tenn.	UFA(Ariz)-'98	16/0*
93	Williams, Pat	DT	6-3	270	10/24/72	2	Texas A&M	Monroe, La.	FA-'97	1/0
37	Woodson, Sean	S	6-0	214	8/27/74	2	Jackson State	Jackson, Miss.	D5-'97	0*
87	Young, Duane	TE	6-3	270	5/29/68	6	Michigan State	Kalamazoo, Mich.	FA-'98	0*
61	Zeigler, Dusty	C-G	6-5	298	9/27/73	3	Notre Dame	Rincon, Ga.	D6b-'96	13/13

* Ballard inactive for 10 games in '97; Cummings last active with San Diego in '96; Fitzgerald missed '97 season because of injury; Flutie last active with New England in '89; Gash played 16 games with New England; Ingoglia and Woodson inactive for 6 games; R. Johnson played 5 games with Jacksonville; Panos played 13 games with Philadelphia; Sabb last active with New England in '96; K. Williams played 16 games with Arizona; Young last active with San Diego in '95.

† Restricted free agent; subject to developments.

t - Bills traded for R. Johnson (Jacksonville).

Retired—Jim Jeffcoat, 15-year defensive end, 7 games in '97; Steve Tasker, 13-year wide receiver, 14 games.

Players lost through free agency (5): CB Jeff Burris (Ind; 14 games in '97), G Corbin Lacina (Car; 16), T Corey Louchiey (Atl; 16), LB Mark Maddox (Ariz; 8), LB Bryce Paup (Jax; 16).

Also played with Bills in '97—TE Tony Cline (10 games), TE Robert Coons (12), LB Damien Covington (8), QB Billy Joe Hobert (2), RB Tim Tindale (7).

COACHING STAFF

Head Coach,
Wade Phillips

Pro Career: Became the eleventh head coach in Bills history on January 5, 1998, after having served as the club's defensive coordinator since 1995. Has been a NFL coach for 22 years, which includes a two-year stint as the head coach of the Denver Broncos in 1993-94. He led them to a wild-card playoff spot in 1993. Began his pro coaching career in 1976 with the Houston Oilers, where he remained until 1980. Then accepted the position of defensive coordinator for the New Orleans Saints (1981-85) and served as the head coach for the final four games of the 1985 season. Served as the defensive coordinator for the Philadelphia Eagles (1986-88) before joining the Broncos staff in 1989 and serving as the defensive coordinator through the 1992 season. During the 1990 preseason, Phillips assumed the capacity of interim head coach. No pro playing experience. Career record: 16-17.
Background: Linebacker at Houston 1966-68. Coached at his alma mater in 1969. Served as the head coach at Orange (Texas) High in 1970-72. Moved to Oklahoma State as an assistant in 1973-74. Later served as an assistant at Kansas in 1975.
Personal: Born June 21, 1947. Is the son of former NFL coaching legend O.A. (Bum) Phillips. Has two children, daughter Tracy and a son Wesley, who plays quarterback at UTEP. He and his wife, Laurie, reside in East Amherst, New York.

ASSISTANT COACHES

Max Bowman, Assistant to the head coach-tight ends; born September 18, 1945, Colorado Springs, Colo., lives in East Amherst, N.Y. No college or pro playing experience. College coach: Westchester C.C. 1972-79, Lees McRae College 1979, Boston College 1980, Kent State 1981, Texas-El Paso 1982-85, Greenville College 1986-93. Pro coach: West Virginia Rockets (AFL) 1981, joined Bills in 1998.
Bill Bradley, defensive backs; born January 14, 1947, Paletine, Texas, lives in Orchard Park, N.Y. Quarterback-defensive back-punter-kicker-returner-holder Texas 1966-68. Pro safety-punter-returner-holder Philadelphia Eagles 1969-77, St. Louis Cardinals 1978. College coach: Texas 1987. Pro Coach: San Antonio Gunslingers (USFL) 1983-84, Memphis Showboats (USFL) 1985, Calgary Stampeders (CFL) 1988-90, San Antonio Riders (WLAF) 1991-92, Sacramento Gold Miners (CFL) 1993-94, San Antonio Texans (CFL) 1995, Toronto Argonauts (CFL) 1996-97, joined Bills in 1998.
Ted Cottrell, defensive coordinator; born June 13, 1947, Chester, Pa., lives in Orchard Park, N.Y. Linebacker Delaware Valley College 1966-68. Pro linebacker Atlanta Falcons 1969-70, Winnipeg Blue Bombers (CFL) 1971. College coach: Rutgers 1973-80, 1983. Pro coach: Kansas City Chiefs 1981-82, New Jersey Generals (USFL) 1983-84, Buffalo Bills 1986-89, Arizona Cardinals 1990-94, rejoined Bills in 1995.
Bruce DeHaven, special teams; born September 6, 1952, Trousdale, Kan., lives in East Aurora, N.Y. No college or pro playing experience. College coach: Kansas 1979-81, New Mexico State 1982. Pro coach: New Jersey Generals (USFL) 1983, Pittsburgh Maulers (USFL) 1984, Orlando Renegades (USFL) 1985, joined Bills in 1987.
Chris Dickson, offensive quality control; born June 29, 1971, North Bay, N.Y., lives in Orchard Park, N.Y. Defensive back Cortland State 1990-93. No pro playing experience. Pro coach: Joined Bills in 1995.
Bishop Harris, running backs; born November 23, 1941, Phoenix City, Ala., lives in Buffalo. Running back-defensive back North Carolina College 1960-63. No pro playing experience. College coach: Duke 1972-75, North Carolina State 1977-79, Louisiana State 1980-83, Notre Dame 1984-85, Minnesota 1986-90, North Carolina Central 1991-92 (head coach). Pro coach: Denver Broncos 1993-94, Oakland Raiders 1995, joined Bills in 1998.
Charlie Joiner, receivers; born October 14, 1947, Many, La., lives in Orchard Park, N.Y. Wide receiver Grambling 1965-68. Pro defensive back-wide receiver Houston Oilers 1969-72, Cincinnati Bengals 1972-75, San Diego Chargers 1976-86. Inducted into Pro Football Hall of Fame 1996. Pro coach: San Diego Chargers 1987-91, joined Bills in 1992.
Rusty Jones, strength and conditioning; born August 14, 1953, Berwick, Maine, lives in Hamburg, N.Y. No college or pro playing experience. College coach: Springfield 1978-79. Pro coach: Pittsburgh Maulers (USFL) 1983-84, joined Bills in 1985.
Chuck Lester, assistant linebackers; born May 18, 1955, Chicago, lives in Orchard Park, N.Y. Linebacker Oklahoma 1974. No pro playing experience. College coach: Iowa State 1980-81, Oklahoma 1982-84. Pro coach: Kansas City Chiefs 1984-86 (scout), joined Bills in 1987.
John Levra, defensive line; born October 2, 1937, Arma, Kan., lives in Hamburg, N.Y. Guard-linebacker Pittsburg State 1963-65. No pro playing experience. College coach: New Mexico Highlands 1966-70, Stephen F. Austin 1971-74, Kansas 1975-78, North Texas State 1979. Pro coach: British Columbia Lions (CFL) 1980, New Orleans Saints 1981-85, Chicago Bears 1986-92, Denver Broncos 1993-94, Minnesota Vikings 1995, joined Bills in 1998.
Carl Mauck, offensive line; born July 7, 1947, McLeansboro, Ill., lives in Orchard Park, N.Y. Linebacker-center Southern Illinois 1966-68. Pro center Baltimore Colts 1969, Miami Dolphins 1970, San Diego Chargers 1971-74, Houston Oilers 1975-81. Pro coach: New Orleans Saints 1982-85, Kansas City Chiefs 1986-88, Tampa Bay Buccaneers 1991, San Diego Chargers 1992-95, Arizona Cardinals 1996-97, joined Bills in 1998.
Joe Pendry, offensive coordinator; born August 5, 1947. Matheny, W.V., lives in Orchard Park, N.Y. Tight end West Virginia 1966-67. No pro playing experience. College coach: West Virginia 1967-74, 1976-77, Kansas State 1975, Pittsburgh 1978-79, Michigan State 1980-81. Pro coach: Philadelphia Stars (USFL) 1983, Pittsburgh Maulers (USFL) 1984 (head coach), Cleveland Browns 1985-88, Kansas City Chiefs 1989-92, Chicago Bears 1993-94, Carolina Panthers 1995-97, joined Bills in 1998.
Elijah Pitts, assistant head coach-running backs (medical leave); born February 3, 1938, Mayflower, Ark., lives in Orchard Park, N.Y. Running back Philander Smith 1957-60. Pro running back Green Bay Packers 1961-69, 1971, Los Angeles Rams 1970, Chicago Bears 1970, New Orleans Saints 1970. Pro coach: Los Angeles Rams 1974-77, Buffalo Bills 1978-80, Houston Oilers 1981-83, Hamilton Tiger Cats (CFL) 1984, rejoined Bills in 1985.
Turk Schonert, quarterbacks; born January 15, 1957, Torrance, Calif., lives in Lancaster, N.Y. Quarterback Stanford 1975-79. Pro quarterback Cincinnati Bengals 1980-85, Atlanta Falcons 1986, Cincinnati Bengals 1987-89. Pro coach: Tampa Bay Buccaneers 1992-95, joined Bills in 1998.

1998 FIRST-YEAR ROSTER

Name	Pos.	Ht.	Wt.	Birthdate	College	Hometown	How Acq.
Allotey, Victor	G	6-3	325	4/8/75	Indiana	Brooklyn, N.Y.	D7a
Carlson, Gerald (1)	P	6-0	195	7/26/74	Buffalo	Randolph, N.Y.	FA
Coleman, Fred	WR	6-1	190	1/31/75	Washington	Tyler, Tex.	D6
Cowart, Sam	LB	6-2	239	2/26/75	Florida State	Jacksonville, Fla.	D2
Crebo, Jason	LB	6-1	220	2/7/75	Montana	Helena, Mont.	FA
Doyle, Shane	DE	6-2	265	5/13/75	Washington State	Spokane, Wash.	FA
Grier, James	DT	6-4	327	12/20/74	Mississippi State	Macon, Ga.	FA
Hicks, Robert	DT	6-7	338	11/17/74	Mississippi State	Atlanta, Ga.	D3
Hill, Raymond	CB-S	6-0	182	8/7/75	Michigan State	Detroit, Mich.	FA
Howard, Herb	DT	6-3	318	4/15/75	Virginia State	Petersburg, Va.	FA
Kollar, Todd	T	6-4	294	8/6/76	Youngstown State	North Lima, Ohio	FA
Linton, Jonathan	RB	6-0	248	10/7/74	North Carolina	Catasauqua, Pa.	D5
Loud, Kamil	WR	6-0	190	6/25/76	Cal Poly-SLO	El Cerrito, Calif.	D7b
McCullough, Carl	RB	6-1	226	11/14/73	Wisconsin	St. Paul, Minn.	FA
Mitchell, Hardy	DT	6-4	298	6/29/75	Buffalo	Pelzer, S.C.	FA
Mudge, David	T	6-7	293	10/22/74	Michigan State	Whitby, Canada	FA
Nohra, Mark	RB	5-11	228	10/23/73	British Columbia	Toronto, Canada	FA
Phair, John (1)	K	6-8	235	2/23/71	Fort Lewis	San Ramon, Calif.	FA
Ross, Jerry	TE	6-4	248	9/11/74	Pittsburg State	Cherokee, Kan.	FA
Shamsid-Deen, Hassan	CB-S	5-9	174	1/21/76	North Carolina State	Atlanta, Ga.	FA
Stewart, Duane	CB-S	6-2	219	5/18/75	Washington State	Ontario, Calif.	FA
Turner, Paul	WR	5-8	194	4/27/75	Colorado State	San Diego, Calif.	FA
Williams, Clarence	RB	6-1	286	1/20/75	Florida State	Crescent City, Calif.	FA
Williams, Dan	C	6-2	336	11/18/75	Wofford	Cincinnati, Ohio	FA
Williams, Undre	WR	5-9	165	2/11/75	Florida A&M	Macon, Ga.	FA

The term NFL Rookie is defined as a player who is in his first season of professional football and has not been on the roster of another professional football team for any regular-season or postseason games. A Rookie is designated by an "R" on NFL rosters. Players who have been active in another professional football league or players who have NFL experience, including either preseason training camp or being on an Active List or Inactive List, or on Reserve/Injured or Reserve/Physically Unable to Perform for fewer than six regular-season games, are termed NFL First-Year Players. An NFL First-Year Player is designated by a "1" on NFL rosters. Thereafter, a player is credited with an additional year of experience for each season in which he accumulates six games on the Active List or Inactive List, or on Reserve/Injured or Reserve/Physically Unable to Perform.

NOTES

CINCINNATI BENGALS

American Football Conference
Central Division
Team Colors: Black, Orange, and White
One Bengals Drive
Cincinnati, Ohio 45204
Telephone: (513) 621-3550

CLUB OFFICIALS

President/General Manager: Michael Brown
Chairman of the Board: Austin E. Knowlton
Vice President: John Sawyer
Assistant General Manager/Director of Player Personnel: Pete Brown
General Counsel/Corporate Secretary: Katherine Blackburn
Director of Stadium Development: Troy Blackburn
Scouting/Player Personnel: Paul H. Brown
Business Manager: Bill Connelly
Director of Community Affairs/Premium Seat Sales: Jeff Berding
Stadium Sales/Marketing: Jennifer L. McNally
Stadium Construction Manager: Eric J. Brown
Director of Pro Personnel/Scouting: Jim Lippincott
Director of Finance: Bill Scanlon
Controller: Johanna Kappner
Public Relations Director: Jack Brennan
Assistant Public Relations Director: Patrick J. Combs
Director of Marketing: Mike Hoffbauer
Director of Events: Dave Slyby
Director of Group Sales/Corporate Entertainment: Michael Alford
Ticket Manager: Paul Kelly
Athletic Trainer: Paul Sparling
Assistant Athletic Trainers: Billy Brooks, Rob Recker
Equipment Manager: Tom Gray
Video Director: Travis Brammer
Assistant Video Director: Andy Fineberg
Stadium: Cinergy Field • **Capacity:** 60,389
200 Cinergy Field
Cincinnati, Ohio 45202
Playing Surface: AstroTurf-8
Training Camp: Georgetown College
Georgetown, Kentucky 40324

1998 SCHEDULE

PRESEASON

Aug. 8	at N.Y. Giants	8:00
Aug. 17	**Indianapolis**	7:30
Aug. 22	**Detroit**	7:30
Aug. 28	at Atlanta	7:30

REGULAR SEASON

Sept. 6	**Tennessee**	1:01
Sept. 13	at Detroit	1:01
Sept. 20	**Green Bay**	1:01
Sept. 27	at Baltimore	8:20
Oct. 4	Open Date	
Oct. 11	**Pittsburgh**	1:01
Oct. 18	at Tennessee	12:01
Oct. 25	at Oakland	1:15
Nov. 1	**Denver**	1:01
Nov. 8	at Jacksonville	1:01
Nov. 15	at Minnesota	12:01
Nov. 22	**Baltimore**	4:15
Nov. 29	**Jacksonville**	1:01
Dec. 6	**Buffalo**	1:01
Dec. 13	at Indianapolis	1:01
Dec. 20	at Pittsburgh	1:01
Dec. 27	**Tampa Bay**	1:01

RECORD HOLDERS

INDIVIDUAL RECORDS—CAREER

Category	Name	Performance
Rushing (Yds.)	James Brooks, 1984-1991	6,447
Passing (Yds.)	Ken Anderson, 1971-1986	32,838
Passing (TDs)	Ken Anderson, 1971-1986	197
Receiving (No.)	Cris Collinsworth, 1981-88	417
Receiving (Yds.)	Isaac Curtis, 1973-1984	7,101
Interceptions	Ken Riley, 1969-1983	65
Punting (Avg.)	Dave Lewis, 1970-73	43.9
Punt Return (Avg.)	Mitchell Price, 1990-92	10.4
Kickoff Return (Avg.)	Lemar Parrish, 1970-77	24.7
Field Goals	Jim Breech, 1980-1992	225
Touchdowns (Tot.)	Pete Johnson, 1977-1983	70
Points	Jim Breech, 1980-1992	1,151

INDIVIDUAL RECORDS—SINGLE SEASON

Category	Name	Performance
Rushing (Yds.)	James Brooks, 1989	1,239
Passing (Yds.)	Boomer Esiason, 1986	3,959
Passing (TDs)	Ken Anderson, 1981	29
Receiving (No.)	Carl Pickens, 1996	100
Receiving (Yds.)	Eddie Brown, 1988	1,273
Interceptions	Ken Riley, 1976	9
Punting (Avg.)	Dave Lewis, 1970	46.2
Punt Return (Avg.)	Mike Martin, 1984	15.7
Kickoff Return (Avg.)	Lemar Parrish, 1970	30.2
Field Goals	Doug Pelfrey, 1995	29
Touchdowns (Tot.)	Carl Pickens, 1995	17
Points	Doug Pelfrey, 1995	121

INDIVIDUAL RECORDS—SINGLE GAME

Category	Name	Performance
Rushing (Yds.)	Corey Dillon, 12-4-97	246
Passing (Yds.)	Boomer Esiason, 10-7-90	490
Passing (TDs)	Boomer Esiason, 12-21-86	5
	Boomer Esiason, 10-29-89	5
Receiving (No.)	James Brooks, 12-25-89	12
	Carl Pickens, 11-10-96	12
Receiving (Yds.)	Eddie Brown, 11-6-88	216
Interceptions	Many times	3
	Last time by David Fulcher, 12-17-89	
Field Goals	Doug Pelfrey, 11-6-94	6
Touchdowns (Tot.)	Larry Kinnebrew, 10-28-84	4
	Corey Dillon, 12-4-97	4
Points	Larry Kinnebrew, 10-28-84	24
	Corey Dillon, 12-4-97	24

COACHING HISTORY

(212-251-1)

1968-75	Paul Brown	55-59-1
1976-78	Bill Johnson*	18-15-0
1978-79	Homer Rice	8-19-0
1980-83	Forrest Gregg	34-27-0
1984-91	Sam Wyche	64-68-0
1992-96	Dave Shula**	19-52-0
1996-97	Bruce Coslet	14-11-0

* Resigned after five games in 1978
** Released after seven games in 1996

CINERGY FIELD

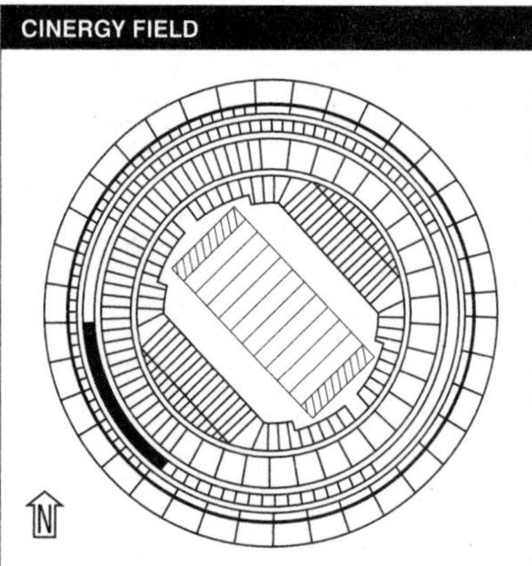

1997 TEAM RECORD

PRESEASON (2-2)

Date	Result		Opponent
8/1	L	16-20	at Indianapolis
8/8	W	27-23	at Detroit
8/16	W	37-13	Minnesota
8/22	L	28-31	Seattle

REGULAR SEASON (7-9)

Date	Result		Opponent	Att.
8/31	W	24-21	Arizona	53,644
9/7	L	10-23	at Baltimore	52,968
9/21	L	20-38	at Denver	73,871
9/28	L	14-31	New York Jets	57,209
10/05	L	13-21	at Jacksonville	67,128
10/12	L	7-30	at Tennessee	17,071
10/19	L	10-26	Pittsburgh	60,020
10/26	L	27-29	at New York Giants	72,584
11/02	W	38-31	San Diego	53,754
11/09	W	28-13	at Indianapolis	58,473
11/16	L	3-20	at Pittsburgh	55,226
11/23	W	31-26	Jacksonville	55,158
11/30	L	42-44	at Philadelphia	66,623
12/4	W	41-14	Tennessee	49,086
12/14	W	31-24	Dallas	60,043
12/21	W	16-14	Baltimore	50,917

SCORE BY PERIODS

Bengals	77	110	80	88	—	355
Opponents	65	108	90	142	—	405

ATTENDANCE

Home 439,831 Away 463,944 Total 903,775
Single-game home record, 60,284 (10/17/71)
Single-season home record, 473,288 (1990)

1997 TEAM STATISTICS

	Bengals	Opp.
Total First Downs	310	351
Rushing	104	141
Passing	171	188
Penalty	35	22
3rd Down: Made/Att	88/214	102/227
3rd Down Pct.	41.1	44.9
4th Down: Made/Att	10/20	11/16
4th Down Pct.	50.0	68.8
Total Net Yards	5,282	5,682
Avg. Per Game	330.1	355.1
Total Plays	1,002	1091
Avg. Per Play	5.3	5.2
Net Yards Rushing	1,966	2,223
Avg. Per Game	122.9	138.9
Total Rushes	452	514
Net Yards Passing	3,316	3,459
Avg. Per Game	207.3	216.2
Sacked/Yards Lost	46/287	35/209
Gross Yards	3,603	3,668
Att./Completions	504/302	542/309
Completion Pct.	59.9	57.0
Had Intercepted	9	13
Punts/Average	81/42.9	69/44.7
Net Punting Avg.	81/35.9	69/40.3
Penalties/Yards Lost	98/877	107/951
Fumbles/Ball Lost	25/13	23/10
Touchdowns	46	48
Rushing	23	15
Passing	21	30
Returns	2	3
Avg. Time of Possession	27:56	32:04

1997 INDIVIDUAL STATISTICS

PASSING	Att.	Comp.	Yds.	Pct.	TD	Int.	Tkld.	Rate
Blake	317	184	2,125	58.0	8	7	39/244	77.6
Esiason	186	118	1,478	63.4	13	2	7/43	106.9
Carter	1	0	0	0.0	0	0	0/0	39.6
Bengals	504	302	3,603	59.9	21	9	46/287	88.3
Opponents	542	309	3,668	57.0	30	13	35/209	86.2

SCORING	TD R	TD P	TD Rt	PAT	FG	Saf	PTS
Pelfrey	0	0	0	41/43	12/16	0	77
Dillon	10	0	0	0/0	0/0	0	60
Carter	7	0	0	0/0	0/0	0	42
McGee	0	6	0	0/0	0/0	0	38
Pickens	0	5	0	0/0	0/0	0	30
Scott	0	5	0	0/0	0/0	0	30
Blake	3	0	0	0/0	0/0	0	18
Bieniemy	1	0	1	0/0	0/0	0	12
Dunn	0	2	0	0/0	0/0	0	12
Hundon	0	2	0	0/0	0/0	0	12
Milne	2	0	0	0/0	0/0	0	12
Battaglia	0	1	0	0/0	0/0	0	6
Copeland	0	0	1	0/0	0/0	0	6
Bengals	23	21	2	41/43	12/16	0	355
Opponents	15	30	3	45/45	24/29	0	405

2-Point conversions: McGee.
Team 1-3, Opponents 0-3.

RUSHING	Att.	Yds.	Avg.	LG	TD
Dillon	233	1,129	4.8	71t	10
Carter	128	464	3.6	79t	7
Blake	45	234	5.2	16	3
Bieniemy	21	97	4.6	20t	1
Milne	13	32	2.5	5	2
Esiason	8	11	1.4	8	0
Scott	1	6	6.0	6	0
Johnson	1	0	0.0	0	0
Graham	1	-1	-1.0	-1	0
Pickens	1	-6	-6.0	-6	0
Bengals	452	1,966	4.3	79t	23
Opponents	514	2,223	4.3	50t	15

RECEIVING	No.	Yds.	Avg.	LG	TD
Scott	54	797	14.8	77t	5
Pickens	52	695	13.4	50t	5
McGee	34	414	12.2	37	6
Bieniemy	31	249	8.0	21	0
Dunn	27	414	15.3	39t	2
Dillon	27	259	9.6	28	0
Milne	23	138	6.0	20	0
Carter	21	157	7.5	35	0
Hundon	16	285	17.8	61	2
Battaglia	12	149	12.4	34	1
Twyner	4	45	11.3	16	0
Graham	1	1	1.0	1	0
Bengals	302	3,603	11.9	77t	21
Opponents	309	3,668	11.9	83t	30

INTERCEPTIONS	No.	Yds.	Avg.	LG	TD
Sawyer	4	44	11.0	37	0
Ambrose	3	56	18.7	29	0
Mack	1	29	29.0	29	0
Myers	1	25	25.0	25	0
Shade	1	21	21.0	21	0
Francis	1	7	7.0	7	0
Orlando	1	3	3.0	3	0
Spencer	1	-2	-2.0	-2	0
Bengals	13	183	14.1	37	0
Opponents	9	26	2.9	18	0

PUNTING	No.	Yds.	Avg.	In 20	LG
Johnson	81	3,471	42.9	27	66
Bengals	81	3,471	42.9	27	66
Opponents	69	3,082	44.7	21	59

PUNT RETURNS	No.	FC	Yds.	Avg.	LG	TD
Myers	26	19	201	7.7	18	0
Bengals	26	19	201	7.7	18	0
Opponents	35	10	407	11.6	85t	2

KICKOFF RETURNS	No.	Yds.	Avg.	LG	TD
Bieniemy	34	789	23.2	102t	1
Dunn	19	487	25.6	85	0
Hundon	10	169	16.9	28	0
Dillon	6	182	30.3	58	0
Twyner	4	72	18.0	24	0
Carter	1	9	9.0	9	0
Bengals	74	1,708	23.1	102t	1
Opponents	67	1,406	21.0	45	0

FIELD GOALS	1-19	20-29	30-39	40-49	50+
Pelfrey	0/0	4/4	3/3	5/7	0/2
Bengals	0/0	4/4	3/3	5/7	0/2
Opponents	1/1	7/8	8/10	8/10	0/0

SACKS	No.
Dixon	8.5
Wilkinson	5.0
Shade	4.0
Francis	3.5
Collins	3.0
Copeland	3.0
Wilson	3.0
Ambrose	1.0
Langford	1.0
McDonald	1.0
Orlando	1.0
Tumulty	1.0
Bengals	35.0
Opponents	46.0

1998 DRAFT CHOICES

Round	Name	Pos.	College
1	Takeo Spikes	LB	Auburn
	Brian Simmons	LB	North Carolina
2	Artrell Hawkins	DB	Cincinnati
3	Steve Foley	LB	Northeast Louisiana
	Mike Goff	G	Iowa
4	Glen Steele	DT	Michigan
6	Jason Tucker	WR	Texas Christian
7	Marcus Parker	RB	Virginia Tech
	Damian Vaughn	TE	Miami, Ohio

CINCINNATI BENGALS

1998 VETERAN ROSTER

No.	Name	Pos.	Ht.	Wt.	Birthdate	NFL Exp.	College	Hometown	How Acq.	'97 Games/ Starts
33	Ambrose, Ashley	CB	5-10	185	9/17/70	7	Mississippi Valley State	New Orleans, La.	UFA(Ind)-'96	16/16
71	Anderson, Willie	T	6-5	335	7/11/75	3	Auburn	Mobile, Ala.	D1-'96	16/16
90	Bankston, Michael	DE	6-4	287	3/12/70	7	Sam Houston State	Elm Grove, Tex.	UFA(Ariz)-'98	16/16*
89	Battaglia, Marco	TE	6-3	250	1/25/73	3	Rutgers	Howard Beach, N.Y.	D2-'96	16/0
21	Bieniemy, Eric	RB	5-7	205	8/15/69	8	Colorado	New Orleans, La.	UFA(SD)-'95	16/0
66	Blackman, Ken	G	6-6	315	11/8/72	3	Illinois	Abilene, Tex.	D3-'96	13/13
8	Blake, Jeff	QB	6-0	205	12/4/70	7	East Carolina	Sanford, Fla.	W(NYJ)-'94	11/11
74	Braham, Rich	G	6-4	302	11/6/70	5	West Virginia	Morgantown, W. Va.	W(Ariz)-'94	16/16
65	Brilz, Darrick	C	6-3	295	2/14/64	12	Oregon State	Pinole Valley, Calif.	UFA(Sea)-'94	16/16
75	Brown, Anthony	G-T	6-5	315	11/6/72	4	Utah	Salt Lake City, Utah	FA-'95	6/0
72	Brumfield, Scott	G	6-8	325	8/19/70	6	Brigham Young	Spanish Fork, Utah	FA-'94	15/3
88	Bush, Steve	TE	6-3	258	7/4/74	2	Arizona State	Phoenix, Ariz.	FA-'97	16/0
32	Carter, Ki-Jana	RB	5-10	222	9/12/73	4	Penn State	Westerville, Ohio	D1-'95	15/10
92	Copeland, John	DE	6-3	280	9/20/70	6	Alabama	Lanett, Ala.	D1-'93	15/15
98	Curtis, Canute	LB	6-2	256	8/4/74	2	West Virginia	Amityville, N.Y.	FA-'97	3/0
28	Dillon, Corey	RB	6-1	220	10/24/75	2	Washington	Seattle, Wash.	D2-'97	16/6
80	Dunn, David	WR	6-3	220	6/10/72	4	Fresno State	San Diego, Calif.	D5-'95	14/5
50	Francis, James	LB	6-5	257	8/4/68	9	Baylor	Houston, Tex.	D1-'90	16/16
91	Granville, Billy	LB	6-3	252	3/11/74	2	Duke	Lawrenceville, N.J.	FA-'97	12/4
62	Gutierrez, Brock	C	6-3	304	9/25/73	3	Central Michigan	Charlotte, Mich.	FA-'96	5/0
85	Hundon, James	WR	6-1	173	4/9/71	2	Portland State	Daly City, Calif.	FA-'96	16/0
11	Johnson, Lee	P-K	6-2	200	11/27/61	14	Brigham Young	Conroe, Tex.	W(Clev)-'88	16/0
60	Jones, Rod	G-T	6-4	320	1/11/74	3	Kansas	Detroit, Mich.	D7-'96	13/8
10	t- Justin, Paul	QB	6-4	211	5/19/68	4	Arizona State	Schaumburg, Ill.	T(Ind)-'98	8/4*
94	Langford, Jevon	DE	6-3	276	2/16/74	3	Oklahoma State	Washington, D.C.	D4-'96	14/0
34	Mack, Tremain	S	6-0	193	11/21/74	2	Miami	Tyler, Tex.	D4-'97	4/4
12	May, Chad	QB	6-1	219	9/28/71	3	Kansas State	West Covina, Calif.	FA-'98	0*
82	McGee, Tony	TE	6-3	246	4/21/71	6	Michigan	Terre Haute, Ind.	D2-'93	16/16
44	Milne, Brian	RB	6-3	254	1/7/73	3	Penn State	Waterford, Pa.	W(Ind)-'96	16/16
31	Myers, Greg	S	6-1	202	9/30/72	3	Colorado State	Windsor, Colo.	D5-'96	16/14
95	Olsavsky, Jerry	LB	6-1	224	3/29/67	10	Pittsburgh	Youngstown, Ohio	FA-'98	16/0*
64	Payne, Rod	C	6-4	295	6/14/74	2	Michigan	Miami, Fla.	D3-'97	0*
9	Pelfrey, Doug	K	5-11	185	9/25/70	6	Kentucky	Fort Thomas, Ky.	D8-'93	16/0
81	Pickens, Carl	WR	6-2	206	3/23/70	7	Tennessee	Murphy, N.C.	D2-'92	12/12
97	Purvis, Andre	DE-NT	6-4	304	7/14/73	2	North Carolina	Jacksonville, N.C.	D5-'97	7/1
20	Randolph, Thomas	CB	5-9	185	10/5/70	5	Kansas State	Norfolk, Va.	UFA(NYG)-'98	16/4*
77	Sargent, Kevin	T	6-6	295	3/31/69	7	Eastern Washington	Bremerton, Wash.	FA-'92	10/8
23	Sawyer, Corey	CB	5-11	177	10/4/71	5	Florida State	Key West, Fla.	D4-'94	15/2
86	Scott, Darnay	WR	6-1	180	7/7/72	5	San Diego State	St. Louis, Mo.	D2-'94	16/15
99	Seals, Ray	DE	6-3	306	6/17/65	11	No College	Syracuse, N.Y.	FA-'98	14/7*
35	† Shade, Sam	S	6-1	201	6/14/73	4	Alabama	Birmingham, Ala.	D4-'95	16/12
96	Simmons, Clyde	DE	6-6	281	8/4/64	13	Western Carolina	Lanes, S.C.	FA-'98	16/13*
22	Spencer, Jimmy	CB	5-10	185	3/29/69	7	Florida	South Bay, Fla.	UFA(NO)-'96	16/9
79	Stallings, Ramondo	DE	6-7	290	11/21/71	5	San Diego State	Winston-Salem, N.C.	D7-'94	6/0
52	Terry, Tim	LB	6-3	248	7/26/74	2	Temple	Hempstead, N.Y.	FA-'97	5/0
93	Thompson, Mike	NT	6-4	290	12/22/71	2	Wisconsin	Portage, Wis.	FA-'97	0*
58	Tovar, Steve	LB	6-3	244	4/25/70	6	Ohio State	Elyria, Ohio	D3-'93	14/5
59	Truitt, Greg	LS	6-0	235	12/8/65	5	Penn State	Sarasota, Fla.	FA-'94	16/0
53	Tumulty, Tom	LB	6-3	247	2/11/73	3	Pittsburgh	Penn Hills, Pa.	D6-'96	11/11
67	Von Oelhoffen, Kimo	NT	6-4	305	1/30/71	5	Boise State	Molokai, Hawaii	D6-'94	13/13
57	Wilson, Reinard	LB	6-2	251	12/17/73	2	Florida State	Lake City, Fla.	D1-'97	16/3
42	Wright, Lawrence	S	6-1	211	9/6/73	2	Florida	Miami, Fla.	FA-'97	4/0

* Bankston played 16 games with Arizona in '97; Justin played 8 games with Indianapolis; May last active with Arizona in '96; Olsavsky played 16 games with Pittsburgh; Payne inactive for 16 games; Randolph played 16 games with N.Y. Giants; Seals played 14 games with Carolina; Simmons played 16 games with Jacksonville; Thompson inactive for 1 game.

† Restricted free agent; subject to developments.

Traded—DE Dan Wilkinson (15 games in '97) to Washington.

t- Bengals traded for Justin (Indianapolis).

Retired—Boomer Esiason, 14-year quarterback, 7 games in '97.

Players lost through free agency (4): DE Brentson Buckner (SF; 14 games in '97), LB Andre Collins (Chi; 16), LB Gerald Dixon (SD; 15), LB Ricardo McDonald (Chi; 13).

Also played with the Bengals in '97—RB Ty Douthard (1 game), CB Cory Gilliard (1), RB Scottie Graham (5), WR Mike Jenkins (4), CB Anthone Lott (5), S Bo Orlando (16), CB Tito Paul (14), WR Gunnard Twyner (2), T Joe Walter (5).

COACHING STAFF

Head Coach,
Bruce Coslet

Pro Career: Coslet is entering his second full season as head coach of the Cincinnati Bengals. He was named the team's seventh head coach seven games into the 1996 season, leading the team to an impressive 7-2 record over the final nine games after its 1-6 start. The Bengals started slow again in 1997 with a 1-7 record, but again rebounded strongly under Coslet's leadership to finish 7-9. With a 14-11 record at Cincinnati, Coslet enters the 1998 season with the highest winning percentage (.560) of any head coach in team history. This is the second head coaching position held by Coslet, who was head coach of the New York Jets for four seasons from 1990-93. Coslet began his coaching career as an assistant coach with the San Francisco 49ers in 1980. He joined the Bengals as an assistant coach in 1981. Coslet coached with Cincinnati for nine seasons from 1981-89, including four as offensive coordinator from 1986-89, before becoming head coach of the Jets. After four seasons with the Jets, he again returned to Cincinnati as offensive coordinator in 1994, and retained that position until his promotion to head coach in 1996. Coslet played tight end for the Bengals for eight seasons from 1969-76. Career record: 40-50.

Background: Coslet is a native of Oakdale, Calif., and played football for Joint H.S. He was a tight end for the University of the Pacific from 1965-67.

Personal: Born August 5, 1946, Coslet and his wife, Kathy, live in Cincinnati and have two children, son J.J., and daughter Amy.

ASSISTANT COACHES

Paul Alexander, offensive line; born February 12, 1960, Rochester, N.Y., lives in Cincinnati. Tackle Cortland State 1979-81. No pro playing experience. College coach: Penn State 1982-84, Michigan 1985-86, Central Michigan 1987-91. Pro coach: New York Jets 1992-93, joined Bengals in 1994.

Jim Anderson, running backs; born March 27, 1948, Harrisburg, Pa., lives in Cincinnati. Linebacker-defensive end Cal Western 1967-70. No pro playing experience. College coach: Cal Western 1970-71, Scottsdale (Ariz.) Community College 1973, Nevada-Las Vegas 1974-75, Southern Methodist 1976-80, Stanford 1981-83. Pro coach: Joined Bengals in 1984.

Ken Anderson, offensive coordinator; born February 15, 1949, Batavia, Ill., lives in Highland Heights, Ky. Quarterback Augustana (Ill.) 1967-70. Pro quarterback Cincinnati Bengals 1971-86. Pro coach: Joined Bengals in 1992.

Louie Cioffi, defensive staff assistant; born September 21, 1973, Greenlawn, N.Y., lives in Cincinnati. Attended SUNY-Stony Brook 1991-95. No college or pro playing experience. College coach: C.W. Post 1995-96. Pro coach: New York Jets 1993-94, joined Bengals in 1997.

Mark Duffner, linebackers; born July 19, 1953, Annandale, Va., lives in Cincinnati. Defensive lineman William & Mary 1973-74. No pro playing experience. College coach: Ohio State 1975-76, Cincinnati 1977-80, Holy Cross 1981-91 (head coach 1986-91), Maryland 1992-96 (head coach). Pro coach: Joined Bengals in 1997.

John Garrett, offensive staff assistant; born March 2, 1965, Danville, Pa., lives in Cincinnati. Wide receiver Columbia 1983-84, Princeton 1987. Pro wide receiver Cincinnati Bengals 1989, San Antonio Riders (World League) 1991. Pro coach: Joined Bengals in 1995.

Ray Horton, defensive backs; born April 12, 1960, Tacoma, Wash., lives in Cincinnati. Defensive back Washington 1979-82. Pro defensive back Cincinnati Bengals 1983-88, Dallas Cowboys 1989-92. Pro coach: Washington Redskins 1994-96, joined Bengals in 1997.

Tim Krumrie, defensive line; born May 20, 1960, Menomonie, Wis., lives in Cincinnati. Defensive tackle Wisconsin 1979-82. Pro defensive tackle Cincinnati Bengals 1983-94. Pro coach: Joined Bengals in 1995.

Dick LeBeau, assistant head coach-defensive coordinator; born September 9, 1937, London, Ohio, lives in Cincinnati. Offensive-defensive back Ohio State 1954-57. Pro cornerback Detroit Lions 1959-72. Pro coach: Philadelphia Eagles 1973-75, Green Bay Packers 1976-79, Cincinnati Bengals 1980-91, Pittsburgh Steelers 1992-96, rejoined Bengals in 1997.

Al Roberts, special teams; born January 6, 1944, Fresno, Calif., lives in Cincinnati. Running back Washington 1964-65, Puget Sound 1967-68. No pro playing experience. College coach: Washington 1977-82, 1996, Purdue 1986-87. Pro coach: Los Angeles Express (USFL) 1983-84, Houston Oilers 1984-85, Philadelphia Eagles 1988-90, New York Jets 1991-93, Arizona Cardinals 1994-95, joined Bengals in 1997.

Kim Wood, strength; born July 12, 1945, Barrington, Ill., lives in Cincinnati. Running back Wisconsin 1965-68. No pro playing experience. Pro coach: Joined Bengals in 1975.

Bob Wylie, tight ends; born February 16, 1951, West Warwick, R.I., lives in Cincinnati. Linebacker Colorado 1969-71. No pro playing experience. College coach: Brown 1980-82, Holy Cross 1983-84, Ohio University 1985-87, Colorado State 1988-89, Cincinnati 1996. Pro coach: New York Jets 1990-91, Tampa Bay Buccaneers 1992-95, joined Bengals in 1997.

1998 FIRST-YEAR ROSTER

Name	Pos.	Ht.	Wt.	Birthdate	College	Hometown	How Acq.
Bennett, Brandon (1)	RB	5-11	223	2/3/73	South Carolina	Greer, S.C.	FA
Clayton, Alonzo	WR	6-1	194	10/5/74	Northern Iowa	Fort Dodge, Iowa	FA
Costello, Brad	P	6-0	230	12/12/74	Boston University	Moorestown, N.J.	FA
Davis, Joel (1)	G	6-5	310	4/6/73	Army	Binghamton, N.Y	FA-'97
Doering, Chris (1)	WR	6-4	195	5/19/73	Florida	Gainesville, Fla.	FA-'97
Doughty, Mike	T	6-7	315	2/18/75	Notre Dame	Lakeville, Minn.	FA
Douthard, Ty (1)	RB	6-1	214	5/27/73	Illinois	Cincinnati, Ohio	FA-'97
Foley, Steve	LB	6-4	270	9/9/75	Northeast Louisiana	Little Rock, Ark.	D3a
Gibson, Damon	WR	5-9	184	2/25/75	Iowa	Houston, Tex.	FA
Gilliard, Cory (1)	S	6-0	210	10/10/74	Ball State	Bronx, N.Y.	FA-'97
Goff, Mike	G	6-5	311	1/6/76	Iowa	Peru, Ill.	D3b
Hawkins, Artrell	CB	5-10	190	11/24/75	Cincinnati	Johnstown, Pa.	D2
Heidelburg, Daryle	WR	5-11	180	1/29/75	Jackson State	Miami, Fla.	FA
Jenkins, Mike (1)	WR	6-3	191	8/25/74	Hampton	Portsmouth, Va.	FA-'97
Kirchoff, Jay (1)	K	6-5	205	5/28/70	Arizona	San Diego, Calif.	FA
Kresser, Eric (1)	QB	6-2	223	2/6/73	Marshall	Palm Beach Gardens, Fla.	FA-'97
Kushner, Bill (1)	P	6-0	203	1/13/70	Boston College	San Diego, Calif.	FA-'97
Leonard, Jeff	DE-DT	6-2	285	9/14/75	Wyoming	San Ramon, Calif.	FA
Levake, Derrick	T	6-5	305	5/31/72	Wisconsin-Whitewater	Westallis, Wis.	FA
Luster, Adrian	DE-DT	6-1	308	11/2/75	Citadel	Laurens, S.C.	FA
Mathias, Ric	CB-S	5-9	180	12/10/75	Wisconsin-LaCrosse	Monroe, Wis.	FA
Moore, Jason	CB-S	5-10	185	1/15/76	San Diego State	San Bernardino, Calif.	FA
Moore, Kelvin	CB-S	6-0	203	3/7/75	Morgan State	Los Angeles, Calif.	FA
Parker, Marcus	RB	5-10	221	11/12/76	Virginia Tech	Roanoke, Va.	D7a
Rodgers, Buddy	RB	5-10	230	8/5/76	Maryland	East Providence, R.I.	FA
Ross, Adrian	LB	6-3	244	2/19/75	Colorado State	Elk Grove, Calif.	FA
Simmons, Brian	LB	6-3	233	6/21/75	North Carolina	New Bern, N.C.	D1b
Spikes, Takeo	LB	6-2	221	12/17/76	Auburn	Sandersville, Ga.	D1a
Steele, Glen	DE-DT	6-4	295	10/4/74	Michigan	Ligonier, Ind.	D4
Storz, Erik	LB	6-2	234	6/24/75	Boston College	Rockaway, N.J.	FA
Tucker, Jason	WR	6-1	182	6/24/76	Texas Christian	Waco, Tex.	D6
Vaughn, Damian	TE	6-4	247	6/14/75	Miami, Ohio	Orrville, Ohio	D7b

The term NFL Rookie is defined as a player who is in his first season of professional football and has not been on the roster of another professional football team for any regular-season or postseason games. A Rookie is designated by an "R" on NFL rosters. Players who have been active in another professional football league or players who have NFL experience, including either preseason training camp or being on an Active List or Inactive List, or on Reserve/Injured or Reserve/Physically Unable to Perform for fewer than six regular-season games, are termed NFL First-Year Players. An NFL First-Year Player is designated by a "1" on NFL rosters. Thereafter, a player is credited with an additional year of experience for each season in which he accumulates six games on the Active List or Inactive List, or on Reserve/Injured or Reserve/Physically Unable to Perform.

NOTES

CLEVELAND BROWNS TRUST

Team Colors: Brown, Orange, and White
80 First Avenue
Berea, Ohio 44017
Telephone: (440) 891-5000

TRUST OFFICIALS

President: William F. Futterer, III
Director of Player Personnel: Joe Mack
Director of College Scouting: Phil Neri
Personnel Administrative Assistant: Stella Harhay
Communications, Marketing and Broadcast Manager: Laura Paquelet
Communications & Broadcast Coordinator: Jason Ferrante
Community Relations Manager: Ella Fong
Customer Relations Manager: Mike Patton
Customer Relations Coordinators: Monica Donahue, Kerry Sayers, Paul Yappel
Director of Stadium Development: Dave Hamill
Facilities Manager: Dean Phillips
Facilities Administrative Assistant: Carla Farison
Facilities Assistant: Greg Hipp
Grounds Assistant: Tyler Good
Human Resources Manager: Vicki Dansby
Office Manager: Theresa Kempf
Accounting & Research Coordinator: Janet Mackin
General Sales Manager: Mike Dolan
Sales Associate: Dino Lucarelli
Receptionist: Carol Meier
Stadium: New Cleveland Stadium
•**Capacity:** 72,000
West 3rd Street
Cleveland, Ohio 44114
Playing Surface: Grass
Headquarters/Training Camp: 80 First Avenue
Berea, Ohio 44017

HALL OF FAMERS

Jim Brown	RB	Inducted 1971
Paul Brown	Coach	Inducted 1967
Len Ford	DE	Inducted 1976
Frank Gatski	C	Inducted 1985
Otto Graham	QB	Inducted 1965
Lou Groza	T-K	Inducted 1974
Leroy Kelly	RB	Inducted 1994
Dante Lavelli	E	Inducted 1975
Mike McCormack	T	Inducted 1984
Bobby Mitchell	RB	Inducted 1983
Marion Motley	RB	Inducted 1968
Paul Warfield	WR	Inducted 1983
Bill Willis	G	Inducted 1977

RECORD HOLDERS

INDIVIDUAL RECORDS—CAREER

Category	Name	Performance
Rushing (Yds.)	Jim Brown, 1957-1965	12,312
Passing (Yds.)	Brian Sipe, 1974-1983	23,713
Passing (TDs)	Brian Sipe, 1974-1983	154
Receiving (No.)	Ozzie Newsome, 1978-1990	662
Receiving (Yds.)	Ozzie Newsome, 1978-1990	7,980
Interceptions	Thom Darden, 1972-74, 1976-1981	45
Punting (Avg.)	Horace Gillom, 1950-56	43.8
Punt Return (Avg.)	Greg Pruitt, 1973-1981	11.8
Kickoff Return (Avg.)	Greg Pruitt, 1973-1981	26.3
Field Goals	Lou Groza, 1950-59, 1961-67	234
Touchdowns (Tot.)	Jim Brown, 1957-1965	126
Points	Lou Groza, 1950-59, 1961-67	1,349

INDIVIDUAL RECORDS—SINGLE SEASON

Category	Name	Performance
Rushing (Yds.)	Jim Brown, 1963	1,863
Passing (Yds.)	Brian Sipe, 1980	4,132
Passing (TDs)	Brian Sipe, 1980	30
Receiving (No.)	Ozzie Newsome, 1983	89
	Ozzie Newsome, 1984	89
Receiving (Yds.)	Webster Slaughter, 1989	1,236
Interceptions	Thom Darden, 1978	10
Punting (Avg.)	Gary Collins, 1965	46.7
Punt Return (Avg.)	Leroy Kelly, 1965	15.6
Kickoff Return (Avg.)	Billy Reynolds, 1954	29.5
Field Goals	Matt Stover, 1995	29
Touchdowns (Tot.)	Jim Brown, 1965	21
Points	Jim Brown, 1965	126

INDIVIDUAL RECORDS—SINGLE GAME

Category	Name	Performance
Rushing (Yds.)	Jim Brown, 11-24-57	237
	Jim Brown, 11-19-61	237
Passing (Yds.)	Bernie Kosar, 1-3-87	489
Passing (TDs)	Frank Ryan, 12-12-64	5
	Bill Nelsen, 11-2-69	5
	Brian Sipe, 10-7-79	5
Receiving (No.)	Ozzie Newsome, 10-14-84	14
Receiving (Yds.)	Ozzie Newsome, 10-14-84	191
Interceptions	Many times	3
	Last time by Frank Minnifield, 11-22-87	
Field Goals	Don Cockroft, 10-19-75	5
Touchdowns (Tot.)	Dub Jones, 11-25-51	*6
Points	Dub Jones, 11-25-51	36

*NFL Record

COACHING HISTORY

(385-285-10)

1950-62	Paul Brown	115-49-5
1963-70	Blanton Collier	79-38-2
1971-74	Nick Skorich	30-26-2
1975-77	Forrest Gregg*	18-23-0
1977	Dick Modzelewski	0-1-0
1978-84	Sam Rutigliano**	47-52-0
1984-88	Marty Schottenheimer	46-31-0
1989-90	Bud Carson***	12-14-1
1990	Jim Shofner	1-6-0
1991-95	Bill Belichick	37-45-0

*Resigned after 13 games in 1977
**Released after eight games in 1984
***Released after nine games in 1990

CLEVELAND STADIUM

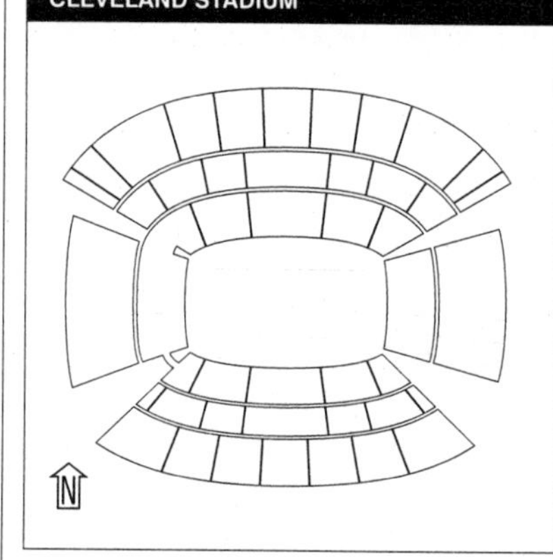

AGREEMENT BETWEEN THE NFL AND THE CITY OF CLEVELAND

The 1996 agreement between the city of Cleveland and the NFL guarantees the Browns franchise will return to Cleveland in a new state-of-the-art stadium in 1999.

The Cleveland Browns operate as a franchise front office that actively participates in broadcast network operations, special events, charitable work, alumni and fan relations, and facilities management.

The next Cleveland Browns preseason home game is currently scheduled for August 21, 1999.

The agreement includes the following key points:

- **Cleveland Browns Franchise:** The Browns franchise will remain in Cleveland and is scheduled to resume play in 1999. This team will be an expansion franchise.
- **Cleveland Browns' History:** The tradition and records, including the Browns' name, trademarks, colors, history, playing records, trophies, and memorabilia, will remain in Cleveland as property of the Cleveland Browns franchise.
- **New Cleveland Stadium:** The new stadium will be owned by the city of Cleveland and will have a 30-year lease with the Browns.

CHRONOLOGY OF BROWNS RETURN

June 12, 1996
The city of Cleveland and the NFL announce the terms of historic public-private partnership that continues the Browns franchise in Cleveland and guarantees a new state-of-the-art stadium in Cleveland in 1999.

July 1, 1996
Bill Futterer is introduced as President of the Cleveland Browns Trust. Operating from the Cleveland Browns Training Facility in Berea, Ohio, the Browns begin operating as a front office overseeing the return of the Browns.

October 8, 1996
NFL Commissioner Paul Tagliabue and members of the Browns staff join Cleveland Mayor Michael R. White to kickoff the sale of the 110 luxury suites in the New Cleveland Stadium.

November 25, 1996
On the same day demolition begins at Municipal Stadium, the Cleveland Browns begin "Countdown to '99" with a celebration marking 999 days until the team returns to the field.

January 21, 1997
The city of Cleveland announces it has met and exceeded the suite and club seat sales goals required by the agreement between the city of Cleveland and the National Football League.

March 14, 1997
The private sale of Permanent Seat Licenses begins to 1995 season ticket holders, who are rewarded with PSL discounts of 10-50 percent.

May 15, 1997
At the site of the new Cleveland Stadium, NFL President Neil Austrian and Cleveland Mayor Michael R. White, and local officials officially break ground for the new home of the Browns.

July 1997
The private sale of PSLs concludes, with more than 23,000 PSLs sold to 1995 season ticket holders.

August 21, 1997
Browns fans crowd Tower City on the Avenue in Cleveland to celebrate the 2-year countdown until the team returns to the field.

August 31, 1997
Countdown to '99, the official radio and television network of the Cleveland Browns, has its debut throughout Ohio and western Pennsylvania.

September 11, 1997
The "Wall of Memories," one of the largest pieces of outdoor art in Ohio, featuring Hall of Fame inductees Lou Groza, Otto Graham, Paul Warfield, and Jim Brown, is unveiled during the announcement for the beginning of the public PSL sale.

October 6, 1997
Public PSL sale concludes with 17,000 new season ticket holders.

October 12, 1997
The team announces 52,449 season ticket applications have been received for the 1999 season, including the 1995 season ticket holders sale. The world famous Dawg Pound is virtually sold out, as are club seats.

March 23, 1998
At a league meeting in Orlando, NFL owners agree that the Cleveland Browns will be an expansion team in 1999. Veteran NFL executive Joe Mack is named Player Personnel Director.

ALL-TIME LEADERS

PASSER RATING (minimum 1000 attempts)	Att.	Comp.	Yds.	TD	Int.	Rating
Plum, Milt	1,083	627	8,914	66	39	89.9
Kosar, Bernie	3,150	1,853	21,904	116	81	81.6
Ryan, Frank	1,755	907	13,361	134	88	81.4
Graham, Otto	1,565	872	13,499	88	94	78.2
Sipe, Brian	3,439	1,944	23,713	154	149	74.8
Nelsen, Bill	1,314	689	9,725	71	71	72.1
Phipps, Mike	1,317	633	7,700	40	81	51.0

SCORING	Pts.
Groza, Lou	1,349
Cockroft, Don	1,080
Brown, Jim	756
Bahr, Matt	677
Kelly, Leroy	540
Stover, Matt	480
Collins, Gary	420
Renfro, Ray	330
Mack, Kevin	324
Warfield, Paul	318

RUSHING	Att.	Yds.	TD
Brown, Jim	2,359	12,312	106
Kelly, Leroy	1,727	7,274	74
Pruitt, Mike	1,593	6,540	47
Pruitt, Greg	1,158	5,496	25
Mack, Kevin	1,291	5,123	46
Byner, Earnest	862	3,364	27
Green, Ernie	668	3,204	15
Mitchell, Bobby	423	2,297	16
Miller, Cleo	546	2,286	16
Metcalf, Eric	592	2,229	11

RECEIVING	No.	Yds.	TD
Newsome, Ozzie	662	7,980	47
Collins, Gary	331	5,299	70
Pruitt, Greg	323	3,022	17
Brennan, Brian	315	4,148	19
Rucker, Reggie	310	4,953	32
Slaughter, Webster	305	4,834	27
Metcalf, Eric	297	2,732	15
Renfro, Ray	281	5,508	50
Byner, Earnest	276	2,630	10
Morin, Milt	271	4,208	16
Warfield, Paul	271	5,210	52

RECEIVING YARDAGE	Yds.	No.	TD
Newsome, Ozzie	7,980	662	47
Renfro, Ray	5,508	281	50
Collins, Gary	5,299	331	70
Warfield, Paul	5,210	271	52
Rucker, Reggie	4,953	310	32
Slaughter, Webster	4,834	305	27
Logan, Dave	4,247	262	24
Morin, Milt	4,208	271	16
Brennan, Brian	4,148	315	19
Lavelli, Dante	3,908	244	33

INTERCEPTIONS	No.	Yds.	TD
Darden, Thom	45	820	2
Lahr, Warren	40	530	5
Scott, Clarence	39	407	2
Konz, Ken	30	392	4
Parrish, Bernie	29	557	3
Fichtner, Ross	27	581	3
Howell, Mike	27	252	0
Dixon, Hanford	26	225	0
James, Tommy	26	208	0
Wright, Felix	26	469	2

PUNT RETURNS (minimum 50 returns)	No.	Yds.	Avg.	TD
Pruitt, Greg	56	659	11.8	0
Mitchell, Bobby	54	607	11.2	3
Metcalf, Eric	127	1,341	10.6	5
Kelly, Leroy	94	990	10.5	3
McNeil, Gerald	161	1,545	9.6	1
Konz, Ken	68	556	8.2	1
Hall, Dino	111	901	8.1	0
Brennan, Brian	55	435	7.9	1
Wright, Keith	78	467	6.0	0
Reynolds, Billy	67	363	5.4	0

KICKOFF RETURNS (minimum 50 returns)	No.	Yds.	Avg.	TD
Pruitt, Greg	58	1,523	26.3	1
Roberts, Walt	62	1,608	25.9	0
Wright, Keith	70	1,767	25.2	0
Mitchell, Bobby	62	1,550	25.0	3
Lefear, Billy	60	1,461	24.4	0
Young, Glen	87	2,079	23.9	0
Kelly, Leroy	76	1,784	23.5	0
Baldwin, Randy	82	1,872	22.8	1
Hall, Dino	151	3,185	21.1	0
McNeil, Gerald	64	1,301	20.3	1

DENVER BRONCOS

American Football Conference
Western Division
Team Colors: Orange, Broncos Navy Blue, and White
13655 Broncos Parkway
Englewood, Colorado 80112
Telephone: (303) 649-9000

CLUB OFFICIALS

President-Chief Executive Officer: Pat Bowlen
General Manager: John Beake
Vice President of Business Operations: David Wass
Director of Player Personnel: Neal Dahlen
Chief Financial Officer: Allen Fears
Director of Ticket Operations/Business Development: Rick Nichols
Executive Assistant to the President: Yolanda Saltus
Senior Director of Media Relations: Jim Saccomano
Director of Stadium Operations: Gail Stuckey
Director of Operations: Bill Harpole
Director of Marketing: Sara Gilbertson
Assistant to the General Manager/Community Relations: Fred Fleming
Director of Player Relations: Bill Thompson
Community Relations Coordinator: Steve Sewell
Trainer: Steve Antonopulos
Equipment Manager: Doug West
Video Director: Kent Erickson
Stadium: Denver Mile High Stadium
•**Capacity:** 76,082
1900 West Eliot
Denver, Colorado 80204
Playing Surface: Grass (PAT)
Training Camp: University of Northern Colorado
Greeley, Colorado 80639

1998 SCHEDULE

PRESEASON

Aug. 8	at St. Louis	7:00
Aug. 14	**New Orleans**	7:00
Aug. 24	**Green Bay**	6:00
Aug. 29	at Tennessee	1:00

REGULAR SEASON

Sept. 7	**New England** (Mon.)	6:20
Sept. 13	**Dallas**	2:15
Sept. 20	at Oakland	1:15
Sept. 27	at Washington	1:01
Oct. 4	**Philadelphia**	2:15
Oct. 11	at Seattle	1:15
Oct. 18	Open Date	
Oct. 25	**Jacksonville**	2:15
Nov. 1	at Cincinnati	1:01
Nov. 8	**San Diego**	2:15
Nov. 16	at Kansas City (Mon.)	7:20
Nov. 22	**Oakland**	2:15
Nov. 29	at San Diego	5:20
Dec. 6	**Kansas City**	2:15
Dec. 13	at New York Giants	1:01
Dec. 21	at Miami (Mon.)	8:20
Dec. 27	**Seattle**	2:15

RECORD HOLDERS

INDIVIDUAL RECORDS—CAREER

Category	Name	Performance
Rushing (Yds.)	Floyd Little, 1967-1975	6,323
Passing (Yds.)	John Elway, 1983-1997	48,669
Passing (TDs)	John Elway, 1983-1997	278
Receiving (No.)	Lionel Taylor, 1960-66	543
Receiving (Yds.)	Lionel Taylor, 1960-66	6,872
Interceptions	Steve Foley, 1976-1986	44
Punting (Avg.)	Jim Fraser, 1962-64	45.2
Punt Return (Avg.)	Darrien Gordon, 1997	13.6
Kickoff Return (Avg.)	Abner Haynes, 1965-66	26.3
Field Goals	Jim Turner, 1971-79	151
Touchdowns (Tot.)	Floyd Little, 1967-1975	54
Points	Jim Turner, 1971-79	742

INDIVIDUAL RECORDS—SINGLE SEASON

Category	Name	Performance
Rushing (Yds.)	Terrell Davis, 1997	1,750
Passing (Yds.)	John Elway, 1993	4,030
Passing (TDs)	John Elway, 1997	27
Receiving (No.)	Lionel Taylor, 1961	100
Receiving (Yds.)	Steve Watson, 1981	1,244
Interceptions	Goose Gonsoulin, 1960	11
Punting (Avg.)	Jim Fraser, 1963	46.1
Punt Return (Avg.)	Floyd Little, 1967	16.9
Kickoff Return (Avg.)	Bill Thompson, 1969	28.5
Field Goals	Jason Elam, 1995	31
Touchdowns (Tot.)	Terrell Davis, 1996, 1997	15
Points	Gene Mingo, 1962	137

INDIVIDUAL RECORDS—SINGLE GAME

Category	Name	Performance
Rushing (Yds.)	Terrell Davis, 9-21-97	215
Passing (Yds.)	Frank Tripucka, 9-15-62	447
Passing (TDs)	Frank Tripucka, 10-28-62	5
	John Elway, 11-18-84	5
Receiving (No.)	Lionel Taylor, 11-29-64	13
	Bobby Anderson, 9-30-73	13
Receiving (Yds.)	Lionel Taylor, 11-27-60	199
Interceptions	Goose Gonsoulin, 9-18-60	*4
	Willie Brown, 11-15-64	*4
Field Goals	Gene Mingo, 10-6-63	5
	Rich Karlis, 11-20-83	5
	Jason Elam, 9-3-95	5
Touchdowns (Tot.)	Many times	3
	Last time by Terrell Davis, 11-24-97	
Points	Gene Mingo, 12-10-60	21

*NFL Record

COACHING HISTORY

(294-284-10)

1960-61	Frank Filchock	7-20-1
1962-64	Jack Faulkner*	9-22-1
1964-66	Mac Speedie**	6-19-1
1966	Ray Malavasi	4-8-0
1967-71	Lou Saban***	20-42-3
1971	Jerry Smith	2-3-0
1972-76	John Ralston	34-33-3
1977-80	Robert (Red) Miller	42-25-0
1981-92	Dan Reeves	117-79-1
1993-94	Wade Phillips	16-17-0
1995-97	Mike Shanahan	37-16-0

*Released after four games in 1964
**Resigned after two games in 1966
***Resigned after nine games in 1971

DENVER MILE HIGH STADIUM

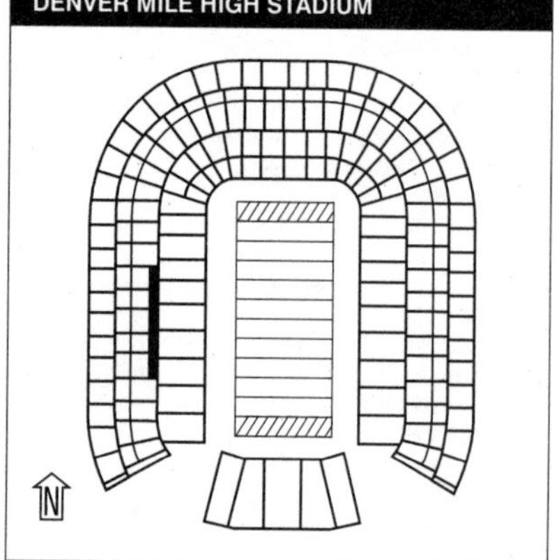

1997 TEAM RECORD

PRESEASON (3-2)

Date	Result		Opponent
7/26	W	31-10	Buffalo
8/4	L	19-38	vs. Miami at Mexico City, Mexico
8/9	W	23-13	at Carolina
8/17	L	21-31	at New England
8/23	W	31-17	San Francisco

REGULAR SEASON (12-4)

Date	Result		Opponent	Att.
8/31	W	19-3	Kansas City	75,600
9/7	W	35-14	at Seattle	55,859
9/14	W	35-14	St. Louis	74,338
9/21	W	38-20	Cincinnati	73,871
9/28	W	29-21	at Atlanta	48,211
10/6	W	34-13	New England	75,821
10/19	L	25-28	at Oakland	57,006
10/26	W	23-20	at Buffalo (OT)	78,458
11/2	W	30-27	Seattle	74,212
11/9	W	34-0	Carolina	71,408
11/16	L	22-24	at Kansas City	77,963
11/24	W	31-3	Oakland	75,307
11/30	W	38-28	at San Diego	54,245
12/7	L	24-35	at Pittsburgh	59,739
12/15	L	17-34	at San Francisco	68,461
12/21	W	38-3	San Diego	69,632

POSTSEASON (4-0)

Date	Result		Opponent	Att.
12/27	W	42-17	Jacksonville	74,481
1/4	W	14-10	at Kansas City	76,965
1/11	W	24-21	at Pittsburgh	61,382
1/25	W	31-24	vs. Green Bay	68,912

(OT) Overtime

SCORE BY PERIODS

Broncos	107	140	137	85	3	—	472
Opponents	34	100	68	85	0	—	287

ATTENDANCE

Home 590,189 Away 499,942 Total 1,090,131
Single-game home record, 76,089 (10/26/86)
Single-season home record, 598,224 (1981)

1997 TEAM STATISTICS

	Broncos	Opp.
Total First Downs	340	258
Rushing	138	83
Passing	172	145
Penalty	30	30
Third Down: Made/Att	92/217	65/207
Third Down Pct.	42.4	31.4
Fourth Down: Made/Att	7/16	8/19
Fourth Down Pct.	43.8	42.1
Total Net Yards	5,872	4,671
Avg. Per Game	367.0	291.9
Total Plays	1,068	951
Avg. Per Play	5.5	4.9
Net Yards Rushing	2,378	1,803
Avg. Per Game	148.6	112.7
Total Rushes	520	381
Net Yards Passing	3,494	2,868
Avg. Per Game	218.4	179.3
Sacked/Yards Lost	35/210	44/298
Gross Yards	3,704	3,166
Att./Completions	513/287	526/290
Completion Pct.	55.9	55.1
Had Intercepted	11	18
Punts/Average	60/43.3	94/43.5
Net Punting Avg.	60/38.1	94/35.7
Penalties/Yards Lost	116/1,006	130/1,118
Fumbles/Ball Lost	25/10	27/13
Touchdowns	55	35
Rushing	18	10
Passing	27	20
Returns	10	5
Avg. Time of Possession	32:07	27:53

1997 INDIVIDUAL STATISTICS

PASSING	Att.	Comp.	Yds.	Pct.	TD	Int.	Tkld.	Rating
Elway	502	280	3,635	55.8	27	11	34/203	87.5
Brister	9	6	48	66.7	0	0	0/0	79.9
Lewis	2	1	21	50	0	0	1/7	87.5
Broncos	513	287	3,704	55.9	27	11	35/210	87.4
Opponents	526	290	3,166	55.1	20	18	44/298	71.5

SCORING	TD R	TD P	TD Rt	PAT	FG	Saf	PTS
Elam	0	0	0	46/46	26/36	0	124
Davis	15	0	0	0/0	0/0	0	96
R. Smith	0	12	0	0/0	0/0	0	72
McCaffrey	0	8	0	0/0	0/0	0	48
Gordon	0	0	4	0/0	0/0	0	24
Sharpe	0	3	0	0/0	0/0	0	20
Green	0	2	0	0/0	0/0	0	12
Bentley	0	0	0	4/4	2/3	0	10
Atwater	0	0	1	0/0	0/0	0	6
Braxton	0	0	1	0/0	0/0	0	6
Carswell	0	1	0	0/0	0/0	0	6
Elway	1	0	0	0/0	0/0	0	6
Hebron	1	0	0	0/0	0/0	0	6
Johnson	0	0	1	0/0	0/0	0	6
Loville	1	0	0	0/0	0/0	0	6
Mobley	0	0	1	0/0	0/0	0	6
D. Smith	0	1	0	0/0	0/0	0	6
Traylor	0	0	1	0/0	0/0	0	6
Williams	0	0	1	0/0	0/0	0	6
Broncos	18	27	10	50/50	28/39	0	472
Opponents	10	20	5	35/35	14/19	0	287

2-Point conversions: Davis 3, Sharpe. Team 4-5, Opponents: 0-0.

RUSHING	Att.	Yds.	Avg.	LG	TD
Davis	369	1,750	4.7	50t	15
Hebron	49	222	4.5	46	1
Elway	50	218	4.4	23	1
Loville	25	124	5.0	17	1
Griffith	9	34	3.8	9	0
R. Smith	5	16	3.2	21	0
D. Smith	4	10	2.5	11	0
Brister	4	2	0.5	2	0
Lewis	5	2	0.4	5	0
Broncos	520	2,378	4.6	50t	18
Opponents	381	1,803	4.7	83t	10

RECEIVING	No.	Yds.	Avg.	LG	TD
Sharpe	72	1,107	15.4	68t	3
R. Smith	70	1,180	16.9	78	12
McCaffrey	45	590	13.1	35	8
Davis	42	287	6.8	25	0
Green	19	240	12.6	31	2
Carswell	12	96	8.0	24t	1
Griffith	11	55	5.0	20	0
D. Smith	4	41	10.3	17t	1
Hebron	3	36	12.0	21	0
Jeffers	3	24	8.0	10	0
Chamberlain	2	18	9.0	9	0
Loville	2	10	5.0	7	0
Lynn	1	21	21.0	21	0
Nalen	1	-1	-1.0	-1	0
Broncos	287	3,704	12.9	78	27
Opponents	290	3,166	10.9	69t	20

INTERCEPTIONS	No.	Yds.	Avg.	LG	TD
Braxton	4	113	28.3	43	1
Gordon	4	64	16.0	32t	1
Crockett	4	18	4.5	10	0
Atwater	2	42	21.0	22t	1
Traylor	1	62	62.0	62t	1
Mobley	1	13	13.0	13t	1
Romanowski	1	7	7.0	7	0
McKyer	1	0	0.0	0	0
Broncos	18	319	17.7	62t	5
Opponents	11	193	17.5	55t	1

PUNTING	No.	Yds.	Avg.	In 20	LG
Rouen	60	2,598	43.3	22	57
Broncos	60	2,598	43.3	22	57
Opponents	94	4,091	43.5	16	73

PUNT RETURNS	No.	FC	Yds.	Avg.	LG	TD
Gordon	40	22	543	13.6	94t	3
R. Smith	1	0	12	12.0	12	0
Broncos	41	22	555	13.5	94t	3
Opponents	26	17	235	9.0	83t	1

KICKOFF RETURNS	No.	Yds.	Avg.	LG	TD
Hebron	43	1,009	23.5	46	0
Loville	5	136	27.2	61	0
Burns	4	45	11.3	18	0
Chamberlain	1	13	13.0	13	0
D. Smith	1	0	0.0	0	0
Broncos	54	1,203	22.3	61	0
Opponents	89	1,827	20.5	77	0

FIELD GOALS	1-19	20-29	30-39	40-49	50+
Elam	0/0	10/11	10/12	3/8	3/5
Bentley	0/0	1/1	1/1	0/1	0/0
Broncos	0/0	11/12	11/13	3/9	3/5
Opponents	0/0	4/4	3/5	4/4	3/6

SACKS	No.
N. Smith	8.5
Tanuvasa	8.5
Williams	8.5
Mobley	4.0
Gordon	2.0
Pryce	2.0
Romanowski	2.0
Traylor	2.0
Hasselbach	1.5
Atwater	1.0
Lodish	1.0
McKyer	1.0
Braxton	0.5
Richie	0.5
Broncos	44.0
Opponents	35.0

1998 DRAFT CHOICES

Round	Name	Pos.	College
1	Marcus Nash	WR	Tennessee
2	Eric Brown	DB	Mississippi State
3	Brian Griese	QB	Michigan
4	Curtis Alexander	RB	Alabama
5	Chris Howard	RB	Michigan
7	Trey Teague	T	Tennessee
	Nate Wayne	LB	Mississippi

DENVER BRONCOS

1998 VETERAN ROSTER

No.	Name	Pos.	Ht.	Wt.	Birthdate	NFL Exp.	College	Hometown	How Acq.	'97 Games/ Starts
83	Armour, Justin	WR	6-4	209	1/1/73	4	Stanford	Colorado Springs, Colo.	FA-'98	1/0*
27	Atwater, Steve	S	6-3	217	10/28/66	10	Arkansas	Chicago, Ill.	D1-'89	15/15
28	Barnes, Tomur	DB	5-10	188	9/8/70	3	North Texas	Houston, Tex.	FA-'98	3/0*
34	Braxton, Tyrone	S	5-11	185	12/17/64	12	North Dakota State	Madison, Wis.	FA-'95	16/16
6	Brister, Bubby	QB	6-3	207	8/15/62	12	Northeast Louisiana	Monroe, La.	FA-'97	1/0
56	Burns, Keith	LB	6-2	245	5/16/72	5	Oklahoma State	Greeleyville, S.C.	D7a-'94	16/0
59	Cadrez, Glenn	LB	6-3	245	1/2/70	7	Houston	El Centro, Calif.	FA-'95	16/0
89	Carswell, Dwayne	TE	6-3	261	1/18/72	4	Liberty	Jacksonville, Fla.	FA-'94	16/3
86	Chamberlain, Byron	TE	6-1	240	10/17/71	3	Wayne State	Fort Worth, Tex.	D7b-'95	10/0
36	Christopherson, Ryan	RB	5-11	246	7/26/72	3	Wyoming	Sioux Falls, S.D.	FA-'98	0*
48	Coghill, George	S	6-0	211	3/30/70	2	Wake Forest	Fredricksburg, Va.	FA-'98	0*
39	Crockett, Ray	CB	5-10	185	1/5/67	10	Baylor	Dallas, Tex.	UFA(Det)-'94	16/16
30	Davis, Terrell	RB	5-11	200	10/28/72	4	Georgia	San Diego, Calif.	D6b-'95	15/15
63	Diaz-Infante, David	G	6-3	292	3/31/64	3	San Jose State	San Jose, Calif.	FA-'95	16/7
33	Dodge, Dedrick	S	6-2	184	6/14/67	7	Florida State	Neptune, N.J.	FA-'97	16/1
1	Elam, Jason	K	5-11	192	3/8/70	6	Hawaii	Ft. Walton Beach, Fla.	D3b-'93	15/0
7	Elway, John	QB	6-3	215	6/28/60	16	Stanford	Port Angeles, Wash.	T(Balt)-'83	16/16
82	Gamble, David	WR	6-1	190	6/14/71	2	New Hampshire	San Antonio, Tex.	FA-'98	2/0
21	Gordon, Darrien	CB	5-11	182	11/14/70	6	Stanford	Shawnee, Okla.	UFA(SD)-'97	16/16
85	Green, Willie	WR	6-4	188	4/2/66	9	Mississippi	Athens, Ga.	UFA(Car)-'97	16/1
29	Griffith, Howard	RB	6-0	240	11/17/67	6	Illinois	Chicago, Ill.	UFA(Car)-'97	15/13
61	Hall, Courtney	C	6-1	281	8/26/68	9	Rice	Los Angeles, Calif.	FA-'98	0*
78	Harrison, Martin	DE	6-5	265	9/20/67	8	Washington	Livermore, Calif.	FA-'98	8/0*
96	Hasselbach, Harald	DE	6-6	280	9/22/67	5	Washington	Amsterdam, Holland	FA-'94	16/3
22	Hebron, Vaughn	RB	5-8	195	10/7/70	6	Virginia Tech	Baltimore, Md.	FA-'96	16/1
23	Hilliard, Randy	CB	5-11	165	2/6/67	9	Northwestern State, La.	Metairie, La.	FA-'94	14/0
20	James, Tory	CB	6-1	188	5/18/73	3	Louisiana State	New Orleans, La.	D2-'96	0*
81	Jeffers, Patrick	WR	6-3	217	2/2/73	3	Virginia	Fort Campbell, Ky.	D5-'96	10/0
76	Jeffries, Damien	DE-DT	6-4	277	5/7/73	2	Alabama	Sylacauga, Ala.	FA-'98	0*
25	Johnson, Darrius	CB	5-9	175	9/17/72	3	Oklahoma	Terrell, Tex.	D4b-'96	16/0
72	Jones, Ernest	DE	6-2	255	4/1/71	4	Oregon	Utica, N.Y.	FA-'96	1/0
60	Jones, K.C.	C	6-1	260	3/28/74	2	Miami	Midland, Tex.	RFA-'97	0*
47	Jones, Selwyn	CB	6-0	185	5/13/70	7	Colorado State	Houston, Tex.	FA-'97	0*
77	Jones, Tony	T	6-5	295	5/24/66	11	Western Carolina	Royston, Ga.	T(Balt)-'97	16/16
11	Jordan, Kevin	WR	6-2	197	12/14/72	2	UCLA	Beltsville, Md.	FA-'98	0*
43	Joseph, Vance	CB	6-0	202	9/20/72	4	Colorado	Marrero, La.	FA-'97	0*
46	Kidd, Carl	CB	6-1	200	6/10/73	3	Arkansas	Pine Bluff, Ark.	FA-'98	0*
8	Lewis, Jeff	QB	6-2	217	4/17/73	3	Northern Arizona	Columbus, Ohio	D4a-'96	3/0
31	# Loville, Derek	RB	5-10	205	7/4/68	8	Oregon	San Francisco, Calif.	UFA(SF)-'97	16/0
37	Lynn, Anthony	RB	6-3	230	12/21/68	5	Texas Tech	McKinney, Tex.	UFA(SF)-'97	16/0
87	McCaffrey, Ed	WR	6-5	215	8/17/68	8	Stanford	Allentown, Pa.	UFA(SF)-'95	15/15
51	Mobley, John	LB	6-1	230	10/10/73	3	Kutztown	Chester, Pa.	D1-'96	16/16
66	Nalen, Tom	C	6-2	280	5/13/71	5	Boston College	Foxboro, Mass.	D7c-'94	16/16
62	Neil, Dan	C-G	6-2	281	10/21/73	2	Texas	Cypress Creek, Tex.	D3-'97	3/0
64	Novitsky, Craig	T	6-5	295	5/12/71	4	UCLA	Washington, D.C.	FA-'98	0*
13	Nussmeier, Doug	QB	6-3	211	12/11/70	5	Idaho	Portland, Ore.	FA-'98	5/2*
10	Paul, Tito	CB	6-0	195	5/24/72	4	Ohio State	Osceola, Fla.	FA-'98	15/5*
93	Pryce, Trevor	DT	6-5	284	8/3/75	2	Clemson	Winter Park, Fla.	D1-'97	8/3
24	Ray, Terry	CB	6-1	205	10/12/69	6	Oklahoma	Killeen, Tex.	FA-'98	0*
53	Romanowski, Bill	LB	6-4	241	4/2/66	11	Boston College	Vernon, Conn.	UFA(Phil)-'96	16/16
16	Rouen, Tom	P	6-3	215	6/9/68	6	Colorado	Hindsdale, Ill.	FA-'93	16/0
69	Schlereth, Mark	G	6-3	278	1/25/66	10	Idaho	Anchorage, Alaska	UFA(Wash)-'95	11/11
84	Sharpe, Shannon	TE	6-2	230	6/26/68	9	Savannah State	Glennville, Ga.	D7-'90	16/16
42	Smith, Detron	RB	5-9	231	2/25/74	3	Texas A&M	Dallas, Tex.	D3a-'96	16/0
99	Smith, Neil	DE	6-4	273	4/10/66	11	Nebraska	New Orleans, La.	UFA(KC)-'97	14/13
80	Smith, Rod	WR	6-0	195	5/15/70	4	Missouri Southern	Texarkana, Ark.	FA-'95	16/16
74	Swayne, Harry	T	6-5	295	2/2/65	12	Rutgers	Philadelphia, Pa.	UFA(SD)-'97	7/0
98	Tanuvasa, Maa	DT	6-2	277	11/6/70	5	Hawaii	Mililani, Hawaii	FA-'95	15/5
94	Traylor, Keith	DT	6-2	315	9/3/69	7	Central State, Oklahoma	Little Rock, Ark.	UFA(KC)-'97	16/16
71	Tuten, Melvin	T	6-6	305	11/11/71	3	Syracuse	Washington, D.C.	FA-'98	0*
95	Washington, Marvin	DE	6-6	285	10/22/65	10	Idaho	Dallas, Tex.	UFA(SF)-'98	10/1*
68	Watkins, Kendall	G	6-1	282	3/8/73	3	Mississippi State	Jackson, Miss.	FA-'98	0*
91	Williams, Alfred	DE	6-6	265	11/6/68	8	Colorado	Houston, Tex.	UFA(SF)-'96	16/16
65	Zimmerman, Gary	T	6-6	294	12/13/61	13	Oregon	Walnut, Calif.	T(Minn)-'94	14/14

* Armour played 1 game with Philadelphia in '97; Barnes played 3 games with Tennessee; Christopherson last active with Arizona in '96; Coghill last active with New Orleans in '94; Hall last active with San Diego in '96; Harrison played 8 games with Seattle; James, K. Jones and S. Jones missed '97 season because of injury; Jeffries last active with New Orleans in '95; Jordan and Tuten last active with Cincinnati in '96; Joseph last active with Indianapolis in '96; Kidd last active with Oakland in '96; Novitsky last active with New Orleans in '96; Nussmeier played 5 games with New Orleans; Paul played 14 games with Cincinnati and 1 game with Arizona; Ray last active with New England in '96; Washington played in 10 games with San Francisco; Watkins last active with Dallas in '96.

\# Unresticted free agent, subject to developments.

Traded—T Jamie Brown (11 games in '97) to San Francisco.

Players lost through free agency (2): LB Allen Aldridge (Det; 16 games in '97), G Brian Habib (Sea; 14).

Also played with Broncos in '97—WR Flipper Anderson (4 games), K Scott Bentley (1), CB Tim McKyer (16), DT Michael Dean Perry (9), DT David Richie (2).

COACHING STAFF

Head Coach,
Mike Shanahan

Pro Career: Became the eleventh head coach in Broncos history on January 31, 1995, coming to Denver from the 1994 world champion San Francisco 49ers, where he served as offensive coordinator from 1992-94. Mike Shanahan led the Broncos to their first World Championiship last year, becoming just the second coach ever to win four postseason games in a single season, culminating with the 31-24 victory over the Green Bay Packers in Super Bowl XXXII. His 1997 Broncos become just the second Wild Card team to win the Super Bowl, and they became the first AFC team to capture the NFL crown in 14 years. In 1996 Shanahan led the Broncos to a 13-3 record and the AFC Western Division title, tying the club record for wins in a season and leading the NFL in total offense. In 1995 he improved the Broncos to an 8-8 mark while stamping the Denver offense with his signature as the most productive unit in the AFC, finishing third in the NFL. The three seasons under Shanahan have produced the most prolific three-year total offensive statistics in Broncos history. San Francisco's three-year average under Shanahan's direction was the most-productive offense in the history of pro football. During his NFL career, Shanahan has been a part of teams that have played in eight AFC or NFC Championship Games, in addition to his five Super Bowl appearances, four with Denver and Super Bowl XXIX with San Francisco. In his 23 seasons coaching in the NFL and at the college level, Shanahan's teams have participated in postseason playoffs or bowl games 17 times. A driving force behind the Broncos' offense for all three of the team's Super Bowl appearances in the 1980's (following the '86, '87, and '89 seasons), he first came to Denver in 1984 as wide receivers coach. Shanahan was Broncos' offensive coordinator from 1985-87, and returned to Denver as quarterbacks coach on October 16, 1989, after serving as head coach of the Los Angeles Raiders in 1988 and through the first four games of the 1989 season. His record with the Raiders was 8-12. Career record: 45-28.

Background: Shanahan began his coaching career at Oklahoma in 1975-76, also coaching at Northern Arizona (1977), Eastern Illinois (1978), and Minnesota (1979), before moving on to Florida (1980-83), where he led the Gators to an NCAA-record 4,540 yards as assistant head coach in 1983. During his tenure on the college level, Shanahan's teams had a combined record of 77-29-3 (.720), including national championship seasons at Oklahoma in 1975 and at Eastern Illinois in 1978.

Personal: Shanahan was born in Oak Park, Illinois, on August 24, 1952. He attended East Leyden High School in Franklin Park and was a wishbone quarterback/defensive back at Eastern Illinois, graduating in 1974 with a degree in physical education and a master's degree in 1975. Mike and his wife, Peggy, have two children, son Kyle and daughter Krystal.

ASSISTANT COACHES

Frank Bush, linebackers; born January 10, 1963, Athens, Ga., lives in Englewood, Colo. Linebacker North Carolina State 1981-84. Pro linebacker Houston Oilers 1985-86. Pro coach: Houston Oilers 1992-94, joined Broncos in 1995.

Barney Chavous, assistant offensive line-assistant strength and conditioning; born March 22, 1951, Aiken, S.C., lives in Englewood, Colo. Defensive end South Carolina State 1969-72. Pro defensive end Denver Broncos 1973-85. Pro coach: Joined Broncos in 1989.

Rick Dennison, special teams; born June 22, 1958, in Kalispell, Mont., lives in Englewood, Colo. Tight end Colorado State 1976-79. Pro linebacker Denver Broncos 1982-90. Pro coach: Joined Broncos in 1995.

Ed Donatell, defensive backs; born February 4, 1957, Akron, Ohio, lives in Littleton, Colo. Safety Glenville State 1975-78. No pro playing experience. College coach: Kent State 1979-80, Washington 1981-82, Pacific 1983-85, Idaho 1986-88, Cal State-Fullerton 1989. Pro coach: New York Jets 1990-94, joined Broncos in 1995.

George Dyer, defensive line; born May 4, 1940, Alhambra, Calif., lives in Aurora, Colo. Center-linebacker U.C. Santa Barbara 1961-63. No pro playing experience. College coach: Humboldt State 1964-66, Coalinga (Calif.) J.C. 1967 (head coach), Portland State 1968-71, Idaho 1972, San Jose State 1973, Michigan State 1977-79, Arizona State 1980-81. Pro coach: Winnipeg Blue Bombers (CFL) 1974-76, Buffalo Bills 1982, Seattle Seahawks 1983-91, Los Angeles Rams 1992-94, joined Broncos in 1995.

Alex Gibbs, assistant head coach-offensive line; born February 11, 1941, Morganton, N.C., lives in Greenwood Village, Colo. Running back-defensive back Davidson College 1959-63. No pro playing experience. College coach: Duke 1969-70, Kentucky 1971-72, West Virginia 1973-74, Ohio State 1975-78, Auburn 1979-81, Georgia 1982-83. Pro coach: Denver Broncos 1984-87, Los Angeles Raiders 1988-89, San Diego Chargers 1990-91, Indianapolis Colts 1992, Kansas City Chiefs 1993-94, rejoined Broncos in 1995.

Mike Heimerdinger, wide receivers; born October 13, 1952, DeKalb, Ill., lives in Englewood, Colo. Wide receiver Eastern Illinois 1970-74. No pro playing experience. College coach: Florida 1980, Air Force 1981, North Texas State 1982, Florida 1983-87, Cal State-Fullerton 1988, Rice 1989-93, Duke 1994. Pro coach: Joined Broncos in 1995.

Gary Kubiak, offensive coordinator-quarterbacks; born August 15, 1961, Houston, Tex., lives in Englewood, Colo. Quarterback Texas A&M 1979-82. Pro quarterback Denver Broncos 1983-91. College coach: Texas A&M 1992-93. Pro coach: San Francisco 49ers 1994, joined Broncos in 1995.

Pat McPherson, defensive assistant; born April 15, 1969, Santa Clara, Calif., live in Englewood, Colo. Linebacker Santa Clara 1991-92. No pro playing experience. Pro coach: Joined Broncos in 1998.

Brian Pariani, tight ends; born July 2, 1965, San Francisco, Calif., lives in Castle Pines, Colo. No college or pro playing experience. College coach: UCLA 1989. Pro coach: San Francisco 49ers 1991-94, joined Broncos in 1995.

Ricky Porter, offensive assistant; born January 14, 1960, Sylacaga, Ala., lives in Englewood, Colo. Running back Slippery Rock 1978-81. Pro running back Detroit Lions 1982, Baltimore Colts 1983, Memphis Showboats (USFL) 1985, Montreal Alouettes (CFL) 1986-87, Buffalo Bills 1987. College coach: Slippery Rock 1990-91, Kent 1992-93. Pro coach: Tampa Bay Buccaneers 1996, joined Broncos in 1997.

Greg Robinson, defensive coordinator; born October 9, 1951, Los Angeles, Calif., lives in Aurora, Colo. Linebacker-tight end Pacific 1972-74. No pro playing experience. College coach: Pacific 1975-76, Cal State-Fullerton 1977-79, North Carolina State 1980-81, UCLA 1982-89. Pro coach: New York Jets 1990-94, joined Broncos in 1995.

Greg Saporta, assistant strength and conditioning; born February 2, 1957, New York, N.Y., lives in Englewood, Colo. Wide receiver Buffalo State 1977-79. No pro playing experience. College coach: Florida 1981-88, 1993-94, North Carolina 1989-92. Pro coach: Joined Broncos in 1995.

Rick Smith, defensive assistant; born September 3, 1969, Petersburg, Va., lives in Aurora, Colo. Safety Purdue 1987-91. No pro playing experience. College coach: Purdue 1992-95. Pro coach: Joined Broncos in 1996.

John Teerlinck, pass rush specialist; born April 9, 1951, Rochester, N.Y., lives in Englewood, Colo. Defensive lineman Western Illinois 1970-73. Pro defensive tackle San Diego Chargers 1974-76. College coach: Iowa Lakes J.C. 1977, Eastern Illinois 1978-79, Illinois 1980-82. Pro coach: Chicago Blitz (USFL) 1983, Arizona Wranglers/Outlaws (USFL) 1984-85, Cleveland Browns 1989-90, Los Angeles Rams 1991, Minnesota Vikings 1992-94, Detroit Lions 1995-96, joined Broncos in 1997.

Bobby Turner, running backs; born May 6, 1949, East Chicago, Ind., lives in Englewood, Colo. Defensive back Indiana State 1968-71. No pro playing experience. College coach: Indiana State 1975-82, Fresno State 1983-88, Ohio State 1989-90, Purdue 1991-94. Pro coach: Joined Broncos in 1995.

Rich Tuten, strength and conditioning; born December 30, 1953, Columbia, S.C., lives in Englewood, Colo. Nose guard Clemson 1976-78. No pro playing experience. College coach: Florida 1979-88, 1993-94, North Carolina 1989-92. Pro coach: Joined Broncos in 1995.

1998 FIRST-YEAR ROSTER

Name	Pos.	Ht.	Wt.	Birthdate	College	Hometown	How Acq.
Ashman, Duane (1)	DE-DT	6-3	276	12/29/73	Virginia	Washington, D.C.	FA
Alexander, Curtis	RB	6-0	204	6/1/74	Alabama	Memphis, Tenn.	D4
Banks, Chris (1)	G	6-1	304	4/4/73	Kansas	Lexington, Miss.	FA
Branch, Darrick (1)	WR	6-0	196	2/10/70	Hawaii	Dallas, Tex.	FA
Brown, Cyron	DE	6-5	241	6/28/75	Western Illinois	Chicago, Ill.	FA
Brown, Eric	S	6-0	203	3/20/75	Mississippi State	San Antonio, Tex.	D2
Burkett, Jeremy (1)	TE	6-1	215	4/15/73	Colorado State	Denver, Colo.	FA
Butler, Hillary (1)	LB	6-2	244	1/5/71	Washington	Tacoma, Wash.	FA
Cooper, Andre (1)	WR	6-2	195	6/21/75	Florida State	Plantation, Fla.	FA
Gizzi, Chris	LB	6-0	230	3/8/75	Air Force	Brunswick, Ohio	FA
Griese, Brian	QB	6-3	215	3/18/75	Michigan	Miami, Fla.	D3
Herrin, Errick (1)	LB	6-1	235	4/3/69	Southern California	Akron, Ohio	FA
Howard, Chris	RB	5-10	223	5/5/75	Michigan	River Ridge, La.	D5
Ivey, Pat (1)	DE	6-4	247	12/27/72	Missouri	St. Louis, Mo.	FA
Kaiser, Jason	CB	6-0	190	11/9/73	Culver-Stockton	Canton, Mo.	FA
LaRocca, Josh (1)	QB	6-1	210	3/9/73	Rice	Charleston, S.C.	FA
McCoy, Ryan (1)	LB	6-2	237	3/13/72	Houston	Beaumont, Tex.	FA
Nash, Marcus	WR	6-3	195	2/1/76	Tennessee	Tulsa, Okla.	D1
Noel, Tori	CB-S	6-0	200	2/17/75	Tennessee	Memphis, Tenn.	FA
Panasuk, Mike (1)	P-K	5-11	198	12/1/68	Ferris State	Southfield, Mich.	FA
Teague, Trey	T	6-5	307	12/27/74	Tennessee	Jackson, Miss.	D7a
Wayne, Nate	LB	6-0	229	1/12/75	Mississippi	Macon, Miss.	D7b

The term NFL Rookie is defined as a player who is in his first season of professional football and has not been on the roster of another professional football team for any regular-season or postseason games. A Rookie is designated by an "R" on NFL rosters. Players who have been active in another professional football league or players who have NFL experience, including either preseason training camp or being on an Active List or Inactive List, or on Reserve/Injured or Reserve/Physically Unable to Perform for fewer than six regular-season games, are termed NFL First-Year Players. An NFL First-Year Player is designated by a "1" on NFL rosters. Thereafter, a player is credited with an additional year of experience for each season in which he accumulates six games on the Active List or Inactive List, or on Reserve/Injured or Reserve/Physically Unable to Perform.

NOTES

INDIANAPOLIS COLTS

American Football Conference
Eastern Division
Team Colors: Royal Blue and White
P.O. Box 535000
Indianapolis, Indiana 46253
Telephone: (317) 297-2658

CLUB OFFICIALS

Owner and CEO: James Irsay
President: Bill Polian
Vice-Chairman: Michael G. Chernoff
Vice President: Bob Terpening
Vice President-Administration: Pete Ward
Executive Director-Business Development: Ray Compton
Director of Football Operations: Dom Anile
Director of Pro Player Personnel: Clyde Powers
Director of College Player Personnel: George Boone
Controller: Kurt Humphrey
Director of Public Relations: Craig Kelley
Director of Player Development: Steve Champlin
Director of Marketing: Patrick Coyle
Director of Ticket Operations: Larry Hall
Director of Corporate Sales: Rene Longoria
Director of Ticket Sales: Greg Hylton
Asst. Director of Public Relations: Todd Stewart
Purchasing Administrator: David Filar
Equipment Manager: Jon Scott
Assistant Equipment Manager: Mike Mays
Video Director: Marty Heckscher
Assistant Video Director: John Starliper
Head Trainer: Hunter Smith
Assistant Trainer: Dave Hammer
Team Physician and Orthopedic Surgeon: K. Donald Shelbourne
Orthopedic Surgeon: Arthur C. Rettig
Physician: Douglas Robertson
Stadium: RCA Dome • **Capacity:** 60,567
100 South Capitol Avenue
Indianapolis, Indiana 46225
Playing Surface: AstroTurf
Training Camp: Anderson University
Anderson, Indiana 46011

1998 SCHEDULE

PRESEASON

Aug. 8	at Seattle	7:00
Aug. 17	at Cincinnati	7:30
Aug. 22	**San Diego**	7:00
Aug. 27	**Detroit**	7:30

REGULAR SEASON

Sept. 6	**Miami**	3:15
Sept. 13	at New England	8:20
Sept. 20	at New York Jets	1:01
Sept. 27	**New Orleans**	12:01
Oct. 4	**San Diego**	12:01
Oct. 11	**Buffalo**	12:01
Oct. 18	at San Francisco	1:05
Oct. 25	Open Date	
Nov. 1	**New England**	1:01
Nov. 8	at Miami	1:01
Nov. 15	**New York Jets**	1:01
Nov. 22	at Buffalo	1:01
Nov. 29	at Baltimore	1:01
Dec. 6	at Atlanta	1:01
Dec. 13	**Cincinnati**	1:01
Dec. 20	at Seattle	1:05
Dec. 27	**Carolina**	1:01

RECORD HOLDERS

INDIVIDUAL RECORDS—CAREER

Category	Name	Performance
Rushing (Yds.)	Lydell Mitchell, 1972-77	5,487
Passing (Yds.)	Johnny Unitas, 1956-1972	39,768
Passing (TDs)	Johnny Unitas, 1956-1972	287
Receiving (No.)	Raymond Berry, 1955-1967	631
Receiving (Yds.)	Raymond Berry, 1955-1967	9,275
Interceptions	Bob Boyd, 1960-68	57
Punting (Avg.)	Rohn Stark, 1982-1994	43.8
Punt Return (Avg.)	Ron Gardin, 1970-71	13.5
Kickoff Return (Avg.)	Jim Duncan, 1969-1971	32.5
Field Goals	Dean Biasucci 1984, 1986-1994	176
Touchdowns (Tot.)	Lenny Moore, 1956-1967	113
Points	Dean Biasucci, 1984, 1986-1994	783

INDIVIDUAL RECORDS—SINGLE SEASON

Category	Name	Performance
Rushing (Yds.)	Eric Dickerson, 1988	1,659
Passing (Yds.)	Johnny Unitas, 1963	3,481
Passing (TDs)	Johnny Unitas, 1959	32
Receiving (No.)	Reggie Langhorne, 1993	85
Receiving (Yds.)	Raymond Berry, 1960	1,298
Interceptions	Tom Keane, 1953	11
Punting (Avg.)	Rohn Stark, 1985	45.9
Punt Return (Avg.)	Clarence Verdin, 1989	12.9
Kickoff Return (Avg.)	Jim Duncan, 1970	35.4
Field Goals	Cary Blanchard, 1996	36
Touchdowns (Tot.)	Lenny Moore, 1964	20
Points	Cary Blanchard, 1996	135

INDIVIDUAL RECORDS—SINGLE GAME

Category	Name	Performance
Rushing (Yds.)	Norm Bulaich, 9-19-71	198
Passing (Yds.)	Johnny Unitas, 9-17-67	401
Passing (TDs)	Gary Cuozzo, 11-14-65	5
	Gary Hogeboom, 10-4-87	5
Receiving (No.)	Lydell Mitchell, 12-15-74	13
	Joe Washington, 9-2-79	13
Receiving (Yds.)	Raymond Berry, 11-10-57	224
Interceptions	Many times	3
	Last time by Mike Prior, 12-20-92	
Field Goals	Many times	5
	Last time by Cary Blanchard, 9-21-97	
Touchdowns (Tot.)	Many times	4
	Last time by Eric Dickerson, 10-31-88	
Points	Many times	24
	Last time by Eric Dickerson, 10-31-88	

COACHING HISTORY

BALTIMORE 1953-1983
(320-338-7)

1953	Keith Molesworth	3-9-0
1954-62	Weeb Ewbank	61-52-1
1963-69	Don Shula	73-26-4
1970-72	Don McCafferty*	26-11-1
1972	John Sandusky	4-5-0
1973-74	Howard Schnellenberger**	4-13-0
1974	Joe Thomas	2-9-0
1975-79	Ted Marchibroda	41-36-0
1980-81	Mike McCormack	9-23-0
1982-84	Frank Kush***	11-28-1
1984	Hal Hunter	0-1-0
1985-86	Rod Dowhower****	5-24-0
1986-91	Ron Meyer#	36-36-0
1991	Rick Venturi	1-10-0
1992-95	Ted Marchibroda	32-35-0
1996-97	Lindy Infante	12-21-0

*Released after five games in 1972
**Released after three games in 1974
***Resigned after 15 games in 1984
****Released after 13 games in 1986
#Released after five games in 1991

RCA DOME

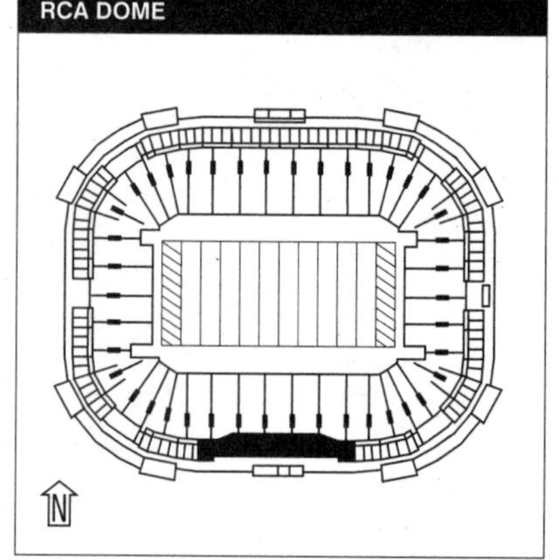

1997 TEAM RECORD

PRESEASON (2-2)

Date	Result		Opponent
8/1	W	20-16	Cincinnati
8/9	L	17-23	at San Diego
8/16	L	3-45	at Seattle
8/21	W	16-3	Detroit

REGULAR SEASON (3-13)

Date	Result		Opponent	Att.
8/31	L	10-16	at Miami	70,813
9/7	L	6-31	New England	53,632
9/14	L	3-31	Seattle	49,194
9/21	L	35-37	at Buffalo	55,340
10/5	L	12-16	New York Jets	48,295
10/12	L	22-24	at Pittsburgh	57,925
10/20	L	6-9	Buffalo	61,139
10/26	L	19-35	at San Diego	63,177
11/2	L	28-31	Tampa Bay	58,512
11/9	L	13-28	Cincinnati	58,473
11/16	W	41-38	Green Bay	60,928
11/23	L	10-32	at Detroit	62,803
11/30	L	17-20	at New England	58,507
12/7	W	22-14	at New York Jets	61,168
12/14	W	41-0	Miami	61,282
12/21	L	28-39	at Minnesota	54,107

SCORE BY PERIODS

Colts	62	103	50	98	0	—	313
Opponents	74	141	65	121	0	—	401

ATTENDANCE

Home 451,455 Away 483,840 Total 935,295
Single-game home record, 61,139 (10/20/97)
Single-season home record, 481,305 (1984)

1997 TEAM STATISTICS

	Colts	Opp.
Total First Downs	301	280
Rushing	109	95
Passing	171	163
Penalty	21	22
Third Down: Made/Att	83/219	83/199
Third Down Pct.	37.9	41.7
Fourth Down: Made/Att	10/20	4/14
Fourth Down Pct.	50.0	28.6
Total Net Yards	4,869	4,854
Avg. Per Game	304.3	303.4
Total Plays	1,035	928
Avg. Per Play	4.7	5.2
Net Yards Rushing	1,727	2,034
Avg. Per Game	107.9	127.1
Total Rushes	450	438
Net Yards Passing	3,142	2,820
Avg. Per Game	196.4	176.3
Sacked/Yards Lost	62/418	37/247
Gross Yards	3,560	3,067
Att./Completions	523/317	453/261
Completion Pct.	60.6	57.6
Had Intercepted	17	12
Punts/Average	67/45.3	64/46.1
Net Punting Avg.	67/36.2	64/39.1
Penalties/Yards Lost	106/880	102/861
Fumbles/Ball Lost	23/11	23/13
Touchdowns	31	46
Rushing	10	18
Passing	16	26
Returns	5	2
Avg. Time of Possession	32:56	27:04

1997 INDIVIDUAL STATISTICS

PASSING	Att.	Comp.	Yds.	Pct.	TD	Int.	Tkld.	Rating
Harbaugh	309	189	2,060	61.2	10	4	41/256	86.2
Justin	140	83	1,046	59.3	5	5	10/86	79.6
Holcomb	73	45	454	61.6	14	8	11/76	44.3
Warren	1	0	0	0	0	0	0/0	39.6
Colts	523	317	3,560	60.6	16	17	62/418	77.6
Opponents	453	261	3,067	57.6	26	12	37/247	86.4

SCORING	TD R	TD P	TD Rt	PAT	FG	Saf	PTS
Blanchard	0	0	0	21/21	32/41	0	117
Faulk	7	1	0	0/0	0/0	0	48
Harrison	0	6	0	0/0	0/0	0	40
Bailey	0	3	0	0/0	0/0	0	18
Dilger	0	3	0	0/0	0/0	0	18
Dawkins	0	2	0	0/0	0/0	0	12
Warren	2	0	0	0/0	0/0	0	12
Stablein	0	1	0	0/0	0/0	0	8
Alexander	0	0	1	0/0	0/0	0	6
Belser	0	0	1	0/0	0/0	0	6
Blackmon	0	0	1	0/0	0/0	0	6
Crockett	1	0	0	0/0	0/0	0	6
Fontenot	0	0	1	0/0	0/0	0	6
McElroy	0	0	1	0/0	0/0	0	6
Pollard	0	0	0	0/0	0/0	0	2
Harbaugh	0	0	0	0/0	0/0	0	0
Colts	10	16	5	21/21	32/41	1	313
Opponents	18	26	2	42/44	27/31	1	401

2-Point conversions: Harrison 2, Pollard, Stablein. Team 4-10, Opponents: 0-2.

RUSHING	Att.	Yds.	Avg.	LG	TD
Faulk	264	1,054	4.0	45	7
Crockett	95	300	3.2	20	1
Harbaugh	36	206	5.7	18	0
Warren	28	80	2.9	11	2
Groce	10	66	6.6	29	0
Bailey	3	20	6.7	18	0
Holcomb	5	5	1.0	3	0
Justin	6	2	0.3	3	0
Potts	1	1	1.0	1	0
Harrison	2	-7	-3.5	0	0
Colts	450	1,727	3.8	45	10
Opponents	438	2,034	4.6	80t	18

RECEIVING	No.	Yds.	Avg.	LG	TD
Harrison	73	866	11.9	44	6
Dawkins	68	804	11.8	51	2
Faulk	47	471	10.0	58	1
Dilger	27	380	14.1	43	3
Bailey	26	329	12.7	22	3
Stablein	25	253	10.1	30	1
Warren	20	192	9.6	31	0
Crockett	15	112	7.5	19	0
Pollard	10	116	11.6	28	0
Slutzker	3	22	7.3	11	0
Doering	2	12	6.0	8	0
Glenn	1	3	3.0	3	0
Colts	317	3,560	11.2	58	16
Opponents	261	3,067	11.8	74	26

INTERCEPTIONS	No.	Yds.	Avg.	LG	TD
Belser	2	121	60.5	50t	1
Coryatt	2	3	1.5	3	0
C. Gray	2	0	0.0	0	0
Alexander	1	43	43.0	43t	1
Mathis	1	31	31.0	31	0
E. Johnson	1	18	18.0	18	0
Clark	1	14	14.0	14	0
Blackmon	1	2	2.0	2	0
Morrison	1	2	2.0	2	0
Team	12	234	19.5	52t	2
Opponents	17	285	16.8	43	0

PUNTING	No.	Yds.	Avg.	In 20	LG
Gardocki	67	3,034	45.3	18	72
Colts	67	3,034	45.3	18	72
Opponents	64	2,948	46.1	14	65

PUNT RETURNS	No.	FC	Yds.	Avg.	LG	TD
Stablein	17	9	133	7.8	20	0
Jacquet	13	0	96	7.4	17	0
Bailey	1	0	19	19.0	19	0
Harrison	0	1	0	—	—	0
Team	31	10	248	8.0	20	0
Opponents	43	8	491	11.4	63	0

KICKOFF RETURNS	No.	Yds.	Avg.	LG	TD
Bailey	55	1,206	21.9	61	0
Jacquet	8	156	19.5	27	0
Hetherington	2	23	11.5	23	0
Groce	1	15	15.0	15	0
Neal	1	23	23.0	23	0
Warren	1	19	19.0	19	0
Team	68	1,442	21.2	61	0
Opponents	64	1,544	24.1	53	1

FIELD GOALS	1-19	20-29	30-39	40-49	50+
Blanchard	0/0	9/9	12/14	10/15	1/3
Team	0/0	9/9	12/14	10/15	1/3
Opponents	2/2	10/10	8/9	4/6	3/4

SACKS	No.
Footman	10.5
Fontenot	4.5
E. Johnson	4.5
Bennett	3.0
Blackmon	3.0
McCoy	2.5
Coryatt	2.0
Alexander	1.0
Belser	1.0
Burroughs	1.0
Montgomery	1.0
Morrison	1.0
Shello	1.0
Team	37.0
Opponents	62.0

1998 DRAFT CHOICES

Round	Name	Pos.	College
1	Peyton Manning	QB	Tennessee
2	Jerome Pathon	WR	Washington
3	E.G. Green	WR	Florida State
4	Steve McKinney	G	Texas A&M
5	Antony Jordan	LB	Vanderbilt
7	Aaron Taylor	G	Nebraska
	Corey Gaines	DB	Tennessee

INDIANAPOLIS COLTS

1998 VETERAN ROSTER

No.		Name	Pos.	Ht.	Wt.	Birthdate	NFL Exp.	College	Hometown	How Acq.	'97 Games/ Starts
50		Alexander, Elijah	LB	6-2	237	8/2/70	7	Kansas State	Fort Worth, Tex.	UFA-'96	13/11
80		Bailey, Aaron	WR	5-10	185	10/24/71	5	Louisville	Ann Arbor, Mich.	FA-'94	13/4
94		Baker, Myron	LB	6-1	232	1/6/71	5	Louisiana Tech	Haughton, La.	UFA(Car)-'98	2/0*
83		Banta, Bradford	TE	6-6	260	12/14/70	5	Southern California	Baton Rouge, La.	D4-'94	15/0
29		Belser, Jason	CB-S	5-9	188	5/28/70	7	Oklahoma	Kansas City, Mo.	D8a-'92	16/16
56	#	Bennett, Tony	LB	6-2	250	7/1/67	9	Mississippi	Alligator, Miss.	UFA-'94	6/6
57		Berry, Bert	LB	6-2	248	8/15/75	2	Notre Dame	Houston, Tex.	D3-'97	10/1
25		Blackmon, Robert	CB-S	6-0	208	5/12/67	9	Baylor	Van Vleck, Tex.	UFA-'97	14/14
14		Blanchard, Cary	K	6-1	227	11/5/68	6	Oklahoma State	Hurst, Tex.	FA-'95	16/0
20		Burris, Jeff	CB-S	6-0	204	6/7/72	5	Notre Dame	Rock Hill, S.C.	UFA(Buff)-'98	14/14*
53		Burroughs, Sammie	LB	6-0	227	6/21/73	3	Portland State	Pomona, Calif.	FA-'96	16/1
55		Coryatt, Quentin	LB	6-3	250	8/1/70	7	Texas A&M	St. Croix, Virgin Islands	D1b-'92	15/15
32	†	Crockett, Zack	RB	6-2	246	12/2/72	4	Florida State	Pompano Beach, Fla.	D3-'95	16/11
85		Dilger, Ken	TE	6-5	259	2/2/71	4	Illinois	Mariah Hill, Ind.	D2-'95	14/14
23		Elias, Keith	RB	5-9	203	2/3/72	4	Princeton	Virginia Beach, Va.	FA-'98	0*
28		Faulk, Marshall	RB	5-10	211	2/26/73	5	San Diego State	New Orleans, La.	D1a-'94	16/16
99		Fontenot, Al	DE	6-4	287	9/17/70	6	Baylor	Houston, Tex.	UFA(Chi)-'97	16/16
98		Footman, Dan	DE-DT	6-5	290	1/13/69	6	Florida State	Tampa, Fla.	FA-'97	16/10
17		Gardocki, Chris	P	6-1	200	2/7/70	8	Clemson	Stone Mountain, Ga.	UFA(Chi)-'95	16/0
78		Glenn, Tarik	T	6-5	335	5/25/76	2	California	Oakland, Calif.	D1-'97	16/16
26		Gray, Carlton	CB-S	6-0	200	6/26/71	6	UCLA	Cincinnati, Ohio	UFA(Sea)-'97	15/13
33	†	Groce, Clif	RB	5-11	245	7/30/72	3	Texas A&M	College Station, Tex.	FA-'95	7/0
66		Hardin, Steve	G	6-6	334	12/30/71	2	Oregon	Snohomish, Wash.	FA-'98	1/0
88		Harrison, Marvin	WR	6-0	181	8/25/72	3	Syracuse	Philadelphia, Pa.	D1-'96	16/15
63		Hayes, Brandon	G	6-2	305	3/11/73	3	Central State, Ohio	Muncie, Ind.	FA-'98	0/0
54		Herrod, Jeff	LB	6-0	249	9/29/66	11	Mississippi	Birmingham, Ala.	UFA(Phil)-'98	10/2*
44	†	Hetherington, Chris	RB	6-3	236	11/27/72	3	Yale	North Branford, Conn.	FA-'96	16/0
13	†	Holcomb, Kelly	QB	6-2	212	7/9/73	2	Middle Tennessee State	Fayetteville, Tenn.	FA-'96	5/1
86		Jacquet, Nate	WR	6-0	173	9/2/75	2	San Diego State	San Diego, Calif.	D5a-'97	5/0
62		Johnson, Ellis	DE-DT	6-2	292	10/30/73	4	Florida	Wildwood, Fla.	D1-'95	15/15
58		Leeuwenburg, Jay	C-G	6-3	290	6/18/69	7	Colorado	St. Louis, Mo.	UFA(Chi)-'96	16/16
65		Mahlum, Eric	G	6-4	302	12/6/70	4	California	San Diego, Calif.	D2-'94	0/0
79		Mandarich, Tony	G-T-C	6-5	324	9/23/66	7	Michigan State	Ontario, Canada	FA-'96	16/16
59		Marshall, Whit	LB	6-2	245	1/6/73	2	Georgia	Atlanta, Ga.	FA-'98	0*
90		Martin, Steve	DT	6-4	303	5/31/74	3	Missouri	Jefferson City, Mo.	D5-'96	12/0
61		McCoy, Tony	DT	6-0	282	6/10/69	7	Florida	Orlando, Fla.	D4b-'92	16/11
39		McDaniel, Emmanuel	CB-S	5-9	180	7/27/72	3	East Carolina	Charlotte, N.C.	FA-'97	3/0
40		McElroy, Ray	CB-S	5-11	207	7/31/72	4	Eastern Illinois	Bellwood, Ill.	D4-'95	16/4
73		Meadows, Adam	G-T-C	6-5	292	1/25/74	2	Georgia	Powder Springs, Ga.	D2-'97	16/16
34		Montgomery, Monty	CB-S	5-11	189	12/8/73	2	Houston	Gladewater, Tex.	D4-'97	16/3
52		Morrison, Steve	LB	6-3	246	12/28/71	4	Michigan	Birmingham, Mich.	FA-'95	16/9
3		Musgrave, Bill	QB	6-3	220	11/11/67	7	Oregon	Grand Junction, Colo.	FA-'98	0*
67		Myslinski, Tom	G-T-C	6-3	287	12/7/68	7	Tennessee	Rome, N.Y.	UFA(Pitt)-'98	16/7*
81		Pollard, Marcus	TE	6-4	257	2/8/72	4	Bradley	Valley, Ala.	FA-'95	16/6
92		Powell, Carl	DE	6-3	265	1/4/74	2	Louisville	Detroit, Mich.	D5b-'97	11/0
15		Scott, Freddie	WR	5-11	188	8/26/74	3	Penn State	Miami Beach, Fla.	FA-'98	2/0*
97	†	Shello, Kendel	DE-DT	6-3	301	11/24/73	3	Southern	New Iberia, La.	FA-'96	6/0
87		Small, Torrance	WR	6-3	209	9/4/70	7	Alcorn State	Tampa, Fla.	UFA(StL)-'98	13/7*
84		Slutzker, Scott	TE	6-4	250	12/20/72	3	Iowa	Hasbrouck Heights, N.J.	D3-'96	12/2
49	#	Tate, David	CB-S	6-1	210	11/22/64	11	Colorado	Denver, Colo.	FA-'94	8/2
71		Vickers, Kipp	G-T-C	6-2	303	8/27/69	4	Miami	Tarpon Springs, Fla.	FA-'94	9/0
51		Von Der Ahe, Scott	LB	5-11	242	10/12/75	2	Arizona State	Lancaster, Calif.	D6-'97	9/2
21		Warren, Lamont	RB	5-11	214	1/4/73	5	Colorado	Los Angeles, Calif.	D6-'94	13/0
72	†	West, Derek	T	6-8	312	3/28/72	4	Colorado	Denver, Colo.	D5-'95	1/0
95		Whittington, Bernard	DE	6-6	280	8/20/71	5	Indiana	St. Louis, Mo.	FA-'94	15/6

* Baker played 2 games with Carolina in '97; Burris played 14 games with Buffalo; Elias last active with N.Y. Giants in '96; Herrod played 10 games with Philadelphia; Marshall last active with Philadelphia in '96; Musgrave last active with Denver in '96; Myslinski played 16 games with Pittsburgh; Scott played 2 games with Atlanta; Small played 13 games with St. Louis.

\# Unrestricted free agent; subject to developments.

† Restricted free agent; subject to developments.

t- Traded—QB Paul Justin (8 games in '97) to Cincinnati.

Players lost through free agency (4): WR Sean Dawkins (NO; 14 games in '97), CB-S Derwin Gray (Car; 11), T Jason Mathews (TB; 16), WR Brian Stablein (NE; 16).

Also played with Colts in '97—G-T-C Eugene Chung (10 games), WR Chris Doering (2), LB Stephen Grant (9), QB Jim Harbaugh (12), CB-S Dedric Mathis (13), RB Leon Neal (1), CB-S Damon Watts (8), G-T-C Derek West (1), G-T-C Doug Widell (16).

COACHING STAFF

Head Coach,
Jim Mora

Pro Career: Jim Mora joined the Colts as head coach on January 12, 1998. Mora spent 1986-96 as head coach at New Orleans, amassing a 93-74 regular-season record and four playoff appearances. In 1996, Mora stood as the most tenured coach with the same team in all of professional sports, and he had won more games than the previous nine Saints coaches combined. Mora is one of only 19 head coaches in NFL history who had 10 or more consecutive seasons of service with the same team. Mora produced 91 victories during his first 10 seasons, a total exceeded by only eight other coaches in NFL history. Mora's 93 career wins rank fifth among active coaches, and he stands to become the 27th overall coach to produce 100 career victories. His 1991 Saints squad went 11-5, earning the only division title in club history. Prior to his stint with New Orleans, Mora directed the Philadelphia/Baltimore Stars of the USFL from 1983-85. Mora forged a 48-13-1 record and led the Stars to two titles in three league championship game appearances. Mora began his pro coaching career in 1978 as defensive line coach with Seattle. In 1982, he was defensive coordinator at New England.

Background: Played tight end and defensive end at Occidental College. Assistant coach at Occidental from 1960-63 and head coach from 1964-66. Linebacker coach at Stanford in 1967. Defensive assistant at Colorado from 1968-73. Linebacker coach at UCLA in 1974. Defensive coordinator at Washington from 1975-77. Received bachelor's degree in physical education from Occidental in 1957. Also holds master's degree in education from Southern California.

Personal: Born May 24, 1935, in Glendale, Calif. Jim and his wife, Connie, live in Indianapolis, Ind., and have three sons—Michael, Stephen and Jim (defensive backs coach with San Francisco 49ers).

ASSISTANT COACHES

Bruce Arians, quarterbacks; born October 3, 1952, Paterson, N.J., lives in Indianapolis. Quarterback Virginia Tech 1971-74. No pro playing experience. College coach: Virginia Tech 1975-77, Mississippi State 1978-80, 1993-95, Alabama 1981-82, 1997, Temple 1983-88 (head coach). Pro coach: Kansas City Chiefs 1989-92, New Orleans Saints 1996, joined Colts in 1998.

Greg Blache, defensive line; born March 9, 1949, New Orleans, lives in Indianapolis. Attended Notre Dame. No college or pro playing experience. College coach: Notre Dame 1973-75, 1981-83, Tulane 1976-80, Southern 1986, Kansas 1987. Pro coach: Jacksonville Bulls (USFL) 1984-85, Green Bay Packers 1988-93, joined Colts in 1994.

George Catavolos, assistant head coach-defensive backs; born May 8, 1945, Chicago, lives in Indianapolis. Defensive back Purdue 1964-67. No pro playing experience. College coach: Purdue 1967-68, 1971-76, Middle Tennessee State 1969, Louisville 1970, Kentucky 1977-81, Tennessee 1982-83. Pro coach: Indianapolis Colts 1984-93, Carolina Panthers 1995-97, rejoined Colts in 1998.

Gene Huey, running backs; born July 20, 1947, Uniontown, Pa., lives in Indianapolis. Defensive back/wide receiver Wyoming 1966-1969. No pro playing experience. College coach: Wyoming 1970-74, New Mexico 1975-77, Nebraska 1978-86, Arizona State 1987, Ohio State 1988-91. Pro coach: Joined Colts in 1992.

Tony Marciano, tight ends; born June 14, 1956, Scranton, Pa., lives in Indianapolis. Attended Indiana (Pennsylvania). No college or pro playing experience. College coach: Texas Christian 1978-80, Southern Methodist 1981-87, Brown 1987-88, Richmond 1989-90, Kent State 1991-92. Pro coach: Toronto Argonauts (CFL) 1994, Calgary Stampeders (CFL) 1995-97, joined Colts in 1998.

Tom Moore, offensive coordinator; born November 7, 1938, Owatanna, Minn., lives in Indianapolis. Quarterback Iowa 1957-60. No pro playing experience. College coach: Iowa 1961-62, Dayton 1965-68, Wake Forest 1969, Georgia Tech 1970-71, Minnesota 1972-73, 1975-76. Pro coach: New York Stars (WFL) 1974, Pittsburgh Steelers 1977-89, Minnesota Vikings 1990-93, Detroit Lions 1994-96, New Orleans Saints 1997, joined Colts in 1998.

Howard Mudd, offensive line; born February 10, 1942, Midland, Mich., lives in Indianapolis. Guard Hillsdale (Mich.) College 1960-63. Pro offensive lineman San Francisco 49ers 1964-69, Chicago Bears 1969-70. College coach: California 1972-73. Pro coach: San Diego Chargers 1974-76, San Francisco 49ers 1977, Seattle Seahawks 1978-82, 1993-97, Cleveland Browns 1983-88, Kansas City Chiefs 1989-92, joined Colts in 1998.

Mike Murphy, linebackers; born September 25, 1944, New York, N.Y., lives in Indianapolis. Guard-linebacker Huron (S.D.) 1963-66. No pro playing experience. College coach: Vermont 1970-73, Idaho State 1974-76, Western Illinois 1977-78. Pro coach: Saskatchewan Roughriders (CFL) 1979-83, Chicago Blitz (USFL) 1984, Detroit Lions 1985-89, Phoenix Cardinals 1990-93, Seattle Seahawks 1995-97, joined Colts in 1998.

Jay Norvell, receivers; born March 28, 1963, Madison, Wis., lives in Indianapolis. Defensive back Iowa 1982-85. Pro defensive back Chicago Bears 1987. College coach: Iowa 1986, Northern Iowa 1988, Wisconsin 1989-93, Iowa State 1995-97. Pro coach: Joined Colts in 1998.

John Pagano, defensive assistant; born March 30, 1967, Boulder, Colo., lives in Indianapolis. Linebacker Mesa State College 1985-88. No pro playing experience. College coach: Mesa State College 1989, Nevada-Las Vegas 1990-91, Louisiana Tech 1994, Mississippi 1995. Pro coach: New Orleans Saints 1996-97, joined Colts in 1998.

Kevin Spencer, special teams; born November 2, 1953, Queens, N.Y, lives in Indianapolis. Attended Springfield (Mass.) College. No college or pro playing experience. College coach: SUNY 1975-76, Cornell 1979-80, Ithaca 1981-86, Wesleyan 1987-90. Pro coach: Cleveland Browns 1991-94, Oakland Raiders 1995-97, joined Colts in 1998.

Rusty Tillman, defensive coordinator; born February 27, 1946, Beloit, Wis., lives in Indianapolis. Tight end-defensive end-linebacker Northern Arizona 1966-69. Pro linebacker Washington Redskins 1970-77. Pro coach: Seattle Seahawks 1979-94, Tampa Bay Buccaneers 1995, Oakland Raiders 1996-97, joined Colts in 1998.

Jon Torine, conditioning; born November 16, 1973, Livingston, N.J., lives in Indianapolis. Linebacker Springfield (Mass.) College 1991. No pro playing experience. Pro coach: Buffalo Bills 1995-97, joined Colts in 1998.

Tom Zupancic, strength; born September 14, 1955, Indianapolis, lives in Indianapolis. Defensive tackle-offensive tackle Indiana Central 1975-78. Pro coach: Joined Colts in 1984.

1998 FIRST-YEAR ROSTER

Name	Pos.	Ht.	Wt.	Birthdate	College	Hometown	How Acq.
Carr, William (1)	DT	6-1	314	1/13/75	Michigan	Dallas, Tex.	FA
Chester, Larry	DT	6-2	305	10/17/75	Temple	Hammond, La.	FA
Ekiyor, Emil	DE	6-4	265	12/25/73	Central Florida	Daytona Beach, Fla.	FA
Embra, Donnie (1)	DE	6-3	286	8/26/74	Baylor	Kalamazoo, Mich.	FA
Evans, Marlon (1)	WR	5-11	185	2/25/75	Stanford	Gaithersburg, Md.	FA
Gaines, Cory	CB-S	5-11	195	5/9/76	Tennessee	Baton Rouge, La.	D7b
Green, E.G.	WR	5-11	187	6/28/75	Florida State	Ft. Walton Beach, Fla.	D3
Jackson, Je'ney	CB-S	5-8	181	7/8/75	Wyoming	Guernsey, Wyo.	FA
Jackson, Waverly (1)	T	6-2	310	12/19/72	Virginia Tech	South Hill, Va.	FA
Johnson, Garrett	DB	5-11	188	2/22/74	Southwestern Louisiana	Baton Rouge, La.	FA
Johnson, Jason (1)	C	6-3	290	2/6/74	Kansas State	Gladstone, Mo.	FA
Jordan, Anthony	LB	6-2	234	12/19/74	Vanderbilt	Sewell, N.J.	D5b
Jurewicz, Bryan (1)	TE	6-5	302	2/23/74	Wisconsin	Brookfield, Wis.	FA
Kirby, Charles	RB	6-1	247	11/27/74	Virginia	Fayetteville, N.C.	FA
Kubiak, Jim	QB	6-2	215	5/12/72	Navy	Buffalo, N.Y.	FA
Manning, Peyton	QB	6-5	230	3/24/76	Tennessee	New Orleans, La.	D1
McFadden, Peter	WR	5-9	197	6/7/75	Liberty	Olanta, S.C.	FA
McKinney, Steve	C-G-T	6-4	297	10/15/75	Texas A&M	Houston, Tex.	D4
Moore, Larry (1)	G	6-3	301	6/1/75	Brigham Young	San Diego, Calif.	FA
Pathon, Jerome	WR	6-0	187	12/16/75	Washington	Capetown, South Africa	D2
Pearsall, Melvin	TE	6-1	247	2/3/75	Florida State	Lake Wales, Fla.	FA
Reddick, Nakia (1)	CB-S	5-11	211	9/29/74	Central Florida	Miami, Fla.	FA
Rosga, Steve (1)	CB-S	6-1	205	7/10/74	Colorado	St. Paul, Minn.	FA
Running, Mitchell (1)	WR	5-11	185	9/7/72	Kansas State	Decorah, Iowa	FA
Sartin, Trey	T	6-7	322	3/19/75	Liberty	Charlotte, N.C.	FA
Shamburger, Clifton (1)	CB-S	5-9	190	7/22/74	Troy State	Cleveland, Ohio	FA
Shields, Brian	T	6-6	308	1/9/75	California	San Diego, Calif.	FA
Taylor, Aaron	C-G-T	6-1	320	1/21/75	Nebraska	Wichita Falls, Tex.	D7a
Vanderjagt, Mike (1)	P-K	6-5	210	3/24/70	West Virginia	Oakville, Canada	FA

The term NFL Rookie is defined as a player who is in his first season of professional football and has not been on the roster of another professional football team for any regular-season or postseason games. A Rookie is designated by an "R" on NFL rosters. Players who have been active in another professional football league or players who have NFL experience, including either preseason training camp or being on an Active List or Inactive List, or on Reserve/Injured or Reserve/Physically Unable to Perform for fewer than six regular-season games, are termed NFL First-Year Players. An NFL First-Year Player is designated by a "1" on NFL rosters. Thereafter, a player is credited with an additional year of experience for each season in which he accumulates six games on the Active List or Inactive List, or on Reserve/Injured or Reserve/Physically Unable to Perform.

NOTES

JACKSONVILLE JAGUARS

American Football Conference
Central Division
Team Colors: Teal, Black, and Gold
ALLTEL Stadium
One ALLTEL Stadium Place
Jacksonville, Florida 32202
Telephone: (904) 633-6000

CLUB OFFICIALS

Chairman, President and Chief Executive Officer: Wayne Weaver
Senior Vice President/Football Operations: Michael Huyghue
Senior Vice President/Marketing: Dan Connell
Chief Financial Officer/Vice President: Bill Prescott
General Counsel/Vice President, Administration: Paul Vance
Executive Director of Communications: Dan Edwards
Director of Player Personnel: Rick Reiprish
Director of Pro Scouting: Fran Foley
Director of College Scouting: Rick Mueller
Director of Finance: Kim Dodson
Director of Facilities: Jeff Cannon
Director of Security: Skip Richardson
Director of Information Systems: Bruce Swindell
Director of Broadcasting: Jennifer Kumik
Director of Corporate Sponsorship: Macky Weaver
Director of Special Events: Roddy White
Director of Player Development/Staff Counsel: Quentin Williams
Director of Football Administration/Staff Counsel: Ryan Smith
Head Athletic Trainer: Michael Ryan
Video Director: Mike Perkins
Equipment Manager: Bob Monica

Chair & Chief Executive Officer, Jaguars Foundation: Delores Barr Weaver
President, Jaguars Foundation: Dr. Gregory Gross
Stadium: ALLTEL Stadium • **Capacity:** 73,000
One ALLTEL Stadium Place
Jacksonville, Florida 32202
Playing Surface: Grass
Training Camp: ALLTEL Stadium
One ALLTEL Stadium Place
Jacksonville, Florida 32202

RECORD HOLDERS

INDIVIDUAL RECORDS—CAREER

Category	Name	Performance
Rushing (Yds.)	James Stewart, 1995-97	1,803
Passing (Yds.)	Mark Brunell, 1995-97	9,816
Passing (TDs)	Mark Brunell, 1995-97	52
Receiving (No.)	Jimmy Smith, 1995-97	187
Receiving (Yds.)	Jimmy Smith, 1995-97	2,856
Interceptions	Deon Figures, 1997	5
	Chris Hudson 1996-97	5
Punting (Avg.)	Bryan Barker, 1995-97	44.1
Punt Return (Avg.)	Reggie Barlow, 1997	11.4
Kickoff Return (Avg.)	Jimmy Smith, 1995-97	22.7
Field Goals	Mike Hollis, 1995-97	81
Touchdowns (Tot.)	James Stewart, 1995-97	22
Points	Mike Hollis, 1995-97	338

INDIVIDUAL RECORDS—SINGLE SEASON

Category	Name	Performance
Rushing (Yds.)	Natrone Means, 1997	823
Passing (Yds.)	Mark Brunell, 1996	4,367
Passing (TDs)	Mark Brunell, 1996	19
Receiving (No.)	Keenan McCardell, 1996 & 1997	85
Receiving (Yds.)	Jimmy Smith, 1997	1,324
Interceptions	Deon Figures, 1997	5
Punting (Avg.)	Bryan Barker, 1997	44.9
Punt Return (Avg.)	Reggie Barlow, 1997	11.4
Kickoff Return (Avg.)	Bucky Brooks, 1996	24.2
Field Goals	Mike Hollis, 1997	31
Touchdowns (Tot.)	James Stewart, 1996	10
Points	Mike Hollis, 1997	134

INDIVIDUAL RECORDS—SINGLE GAME

Category	Name	Performance
Rushing (Yds.)	James Stewart, 10-20-96	112
Passing (Yds.)	Mark Brunell, 9-22-96	432
Passing (TDs)	Mark Brunell, 10-15-95, 12-10-95, 9-22-96,10-5-97,10-19-97	3
Receiving (No.)	Keenan McCardell, 10-20-96	16
Receiving (Yds.)	Keenan McCardell, 10-20-96	232
Interceptions	Deon Figures, 8-31-97	2
Field Goals	Mike Hollis, 12-1-96, 11-30-97	5
Touchdowns (Tot.)	James Stewart, 10-12-97	5
Points	James Stewart, 10-12-97	30

1998 SCHEDULE

PRESEASON

Aug. 8	at Carolina	7:30
Aug. 14	**New York Giants**	8:00
Aug. 22	at Kansas City	7:00
Aug. 27	**Dallas**	8:00

REGULAR SEASON

Sept. 6	at Chicago	12:01
Sept. 13	**Kansas City**	1:01
Sept. 20	**Baltimore**	4:15
Sept. 27	at Tennessee	12:01
Oct. 4	Open Date	
Oct. 12	**Miami** (Mon.)	8:20
Oct. 18	at Buffalo	1:01
Oct. 25	at Denver	2:15
Nov. 1	at Baltimore	1:01
Nov. 8	**Cincinnati**	1:01
Nov. 15	**Tampa Bay**	4:15
Nov. 22	at Pittsburgh	1:01
Nov. 29	at Cincinnati	1:01
Dec. 6	**Detroit**	1:01
Dec. 13	**Tennessee**	1:01
Dec. 20	at Minnesota	7:20
Dec. 28	**Pittsburgh** (Mon.)	8:20

COACHING HISTORY

(26-26-0)

1995-97	Tom Coughlin	26-26-0

ALLTEL STADIUM

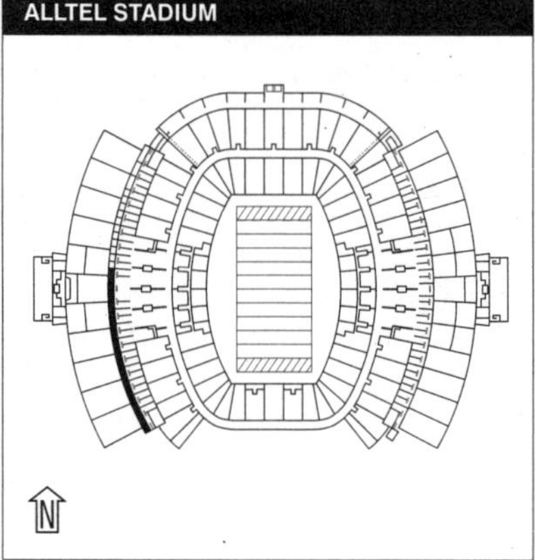

1997 TEAM RECORD

PRESEASON (4-0)

Date	Result		Opponent
8/3	W	23-9	Carolina
8/9	W	38-16	at New York Giants
8/18	W	28-20	at San Francisco
8/22	W	26-17	Atlanta

REGULAR SEASON (11-5)

Date	Result		Opponent	Att.
8/31	W	28-27	at Baltimore	61,018
9/7	W	40-13	New York Giants	70,581
9/22	W	30-21	Pittsburgh	73,016
9/28	L	12-24	at Washington	74,421
10/5	W	21-13	Cincinnati	67,128
10/12	W	38-21	Philadelphia	69,150
10/19	L	22-26	at Dallas	64,464
10/26	L	17-23	at Pittsburgh (OT)	57,011
11/2	W	30-24	at Tennessee	27,208
11/9	W	24-10	Kansas City	70,444
11/16	W	17-9	Tennessee	70,070
11/23	L	26-31	at Cincinnati	55,158
11/30	W	29-27	Baltimore	63,712
12/7	L	20-26	New England	73,446
12/14	W	20-14	at Buffalo	41,231
12/21	W	20-9	at Oakland	40,032

POSTSEASON (0-1)

12/27	L	17-42	at Denver	74,481

(OT) Overtime

SCORE BY PERIODS

Jaguars	117	111	66	100	0	—	394
Opponents	65	91	58	98	6	—	318

ATTENDANCE

Home 557,547 Away 420,543 Total 978,090
Single-game home record, 73,446 (12/7/98)
Single-season home record, 557,547 (1997)

1997 TEAM STATISTICS

	Jaguars	Opp.
Total First Downs	308	318
Rushing	103	107
Passing	187	190
Penalty	18	21
Third Down: Made/Att	82/209	102/226
Third Down Pct.	39.2	45.1
Fourth Down: Made/Att	5/12	12/23
Fourth Down Pct.	41.7	52.2
Total Net Yards	5,424	5,238
Avg. Per Game	339.0	327.4
Total Plays	998	1,035
Avg. Per Play	5.4	5.1
Net Yards Rushing	1,720	1,734
Avg. Per Game	107.5	108.4
Total Rushes	454	455
Net Yards Passing	3,704	3,504
Avg. Per Game	231.5	219.0
Sacked/Yards Lost	40/218	48/331
Gross Yards	3,922	3,835
Att./Completions	504/313	532/320
Completion Pct.	62.1	60.2
Had Intercepted	9	14
Punts/Average	66/44.9	73/41.9
Net Punting Avg.	66/38.8	73/34.4
Penalties/Yards Lost	110/914	90/800
Fumbles/Ball Lost	17/11	26/15
Touchdowns	43	39
Rushing	20	12
Passing	20	24
Returns	3	3
Avg. Time of Possession	29:40	30:20

1997 INDIVIDUAL STATISTICS

PASSING	Att.	Comp.	Yds.	Pct.	TD	Int.	Tkld.	Rating
Brunell	435	264	3,281	60.7	18	7	33/189	91.2
Matthews	40	26	275	65.0	0	0	1/0	84.9
Johnson	28	22	344	78.6	2	2	6/29	111.9
Barker	1	1	22	100.0	0	0	0/0	118.8
Jaguars	504	313	3,922	62.1	20	9	40/218	92
Opponents	532	320	3,835	60.2	24	14	48/331	86.3

SCORING	TD R	TD P	TD Rt	PAT	FG	Saf	PTS
Hollis	0	0	0	41/41	31/36	0	134
Means	9	0	0	0/0	0/0	0	54
Stewart	8	1	0	0/0	0/0	0	54
McCardell	0	5	0	0/0	0/0	0	30
Mitchell	0	4	0	0/0	0/0	0	24
Smith	0	4	0	0/0	0/0	0	24
Jackson	0	2	0	0/0	0/0	0	14
Brunell	2	0	0	0/0	0/0	0	12
Hudson	0	0	2	0/0	0/0	0	12
Jones	0	2	0	0/0	0/0	0	12
Barlow	0	0	1	0/0	0/0	0	6
Brown	0	1	0	0/0	0/0	0	6
Hallock	0	1	0	0/0	0/0	0	6
Johnson	1	0	0	0/0	0/0	0	6
Jaguars	20	20	3	41/41	31/36	0	394
Opponents	12	24	3	31/32	17/25	0	318

2-Point conversions: Jackson.
Team 1-2, Opponents: 1-6.

RUSHING	Att.	Yds.	Avg.	LG	TD
Means	244	823	3.4	20	9
Stewart	136	555	4.1	33	8
Brunell	48	257	5.4	15	2
Johnson	10	34	3.4	25t	1
Hallock	4	21	5.3	11	0
Jackson	3	14	4.7	13	0
Matthews	1	10	10.0	10	0
Shelton	6	4	0.7	2	0
Jordan	1	2	2.0	2	0
Barker	1	0	0.0	0	0
Jaguars	454	1,720	3.8	33	20
Opponents	455	1,734	3.8	30	12

RECEIVING	No.	Yds.	Avg.	LG	TD
McCardell	85	1,164	13.7	60	5
Smith	82	1,324	16.1	75	4
Stewart	41	336	8.2	40	1
Mitchell	35	380	10.9	33	4
Hallock	18	131	7.3	23	1
Jackson	17	206	12.1	45	2
Means	15	104	6.9	21	0
Brown	8	84	10.5	21	1
Jones	5	87	17.4	26t	2
Barlow	5	74	14.8	29	0
Hall	1	22	22.0	22	0
Moore	1	10	10.0	10	0
Jaguars	313	3,922	12.5	75	20
Opponents	320	3,835	12.0	64t	24

INTERCEPTIONS	No.	Yds.	Avg.	LG	TD
Figures	5	48	9.6	32	0
Hudson	3	26	8.7	23	0
Thomas	2	34	17.0	23	0
Davis	1	23	23.0	23	0
Kopp	1	9	9.0	9	0
Beasley	1	5	5.0	5	0
Robinson	1	0	0.0	0	0
Jaguars	14	145	10.4	32	0
Opponents	9	184	20.4	47t	2

PUNTING	No.	Yds.	Avg.	In 20	LG
Barker	66	2,964	44.9	27	64
Jaguars	66	2,964	44.9	27	64
Opponents	73	3,060	41.9	20	72

PUNT RETURNS	No.	FC	Yds.	Avg.	LG	TD
Barlow	36	16	412	11.4	52	0
Jaguars	36	16	412	11.4	52	0
Opponents	29	7	241	8.3	25	0

KICKOFF RETURNS	No.	Yds.	Avg.	LG	TD
Jackson	32	653	20.4	38	0
Barlow	10	267	26.7	92t	1
Logan	10	236	23.6	39	0
Mitchell	2	17	8.5	12	0
Davis	1	9	9.0	9	0
Hallock	1	6	6.0	6	0
Moore	1	36	36.0	36	0
C. Parker	1	9	9.0	9	0
Jaguars	58	1,233	21.3	92t	1
Opponents	77	1,730	22.5	85	0

FIELD GOALS	1-19	20-29	30-39	40-49	50+
Hollis	2/2	12/14	8/9	7/9	2/2
Jaguars	2/2	12/14	8/9	7/9	2/2
Opponents	1/1	3/3	9/12	4/8	0/1

SACKS	No.
Simmons	8.5
Brackens	7.0
Smeenge	6.5
Lageman	5.0
Davey	3.0
Pritchett	3.0
Hardy	2.5
Wynn	2.5
Davis	2.0
Robinson	2.0
Boyer	1.5
Hamilton	1.0
Kopp	1.0
Tuaolo	1.0
Schwartz	0.5
Jaguars	*48.0
Opponents	40.0

**Jaguars credited with 1 team sack.*

1998 DRAFT CHOICES

Round	Name	Pos.	College
1	Fred Taylor	RB	Florida
	Donovin Darius	DB	Syracuse
2	Cordell Taylor	DB	Hampton
3	Jonathan Quinn	QB	Middle Tennessee State
4	Tavian Banks	RB	Iowa
	Harry Deligianis	DT	Youngstown State
5	John Wade	C	Marshall
6	Lamanzer Williams	DE	Minnesota
	Kevin McLeod	RB	Auburn
7	Alvis Whitted	WR	North Carolina State
	Brandon Tolbert	LB	Georgia

JACKSONVILLE JAGUARS

1998 VETERAN ROSTER

No.	Name	Pos.	Ht.	Wt.	Birthdate	NFL Exp.	College	Hometown	How Acq.	'97 Games/ Starts
25	Anderson, Curtis	CB	6-0	203	9/29/73	2	Pittsburgh	Lynchburg, Va.	FA-'97	9/0
4	Barker, Bryan	P	6-2	200	6/28/64	9	Santa Clara	Orlinda, Calif.	UFA(Phil)-'95	16/0
84	Barlow, Reggie	WR-PR	6-0	191	1/22/73	3	Alabama State	Montgomery, Ala.	D4-'96	16/0
21	Beasley, Aaron	CB	6-0	196	7/7/73	3	West Virginia	Pottstown, Pa.	D3-'96	9/7
71	Boselli, Tony	T	6-7	322	4/17/72	4	Southern California	Boulder, Colo.	D1a-'95	12/12
52	Boyer, Brant	LB	6-1	230	6/27/71	5	Arizona	Hooper, Utah	FA-'96	16/2
90	Brackens, Tony	DE	6-4	258	12/26/74	3	Texas	Fairfield, Tex.	D2a-96	15/3
8	Brunell, Mark	QB	6-1	214	9/17/70	6	Washington	Santa Maria, Calif.	T(GB)-'95	14/14
63	Cheever, Michael	C	6-4	295	6/24/73	3	Georgia Tech	Newnan, Ga.	D2b-'96	6/4
62	Coleman, Ben	G-T	6-5	327	5/18/71	6	Wake Forest	South Hill, Va.	W(Ariz)-'95	16/16
92	Davey, Don	DT	6-4	270	4/8/68	8	Wisconsin	Manitowoc, Wis.	UFA(GB)-'95	10/10
45	† Davis, Travis	S	6-0	204	1/10/73	4	Notre Dame	Carson, Calif.	FA-'95	16/16
73	DeMarco, Brian	G-T	6-7	329	4/9/72	4	Michigan State	Lorain, Ohio	D2a-'95	14/5
26	Devine, Kevin	CB	5-9	177	12/11/74	2	California	West Covina, Calif.	FA-'97	12/0
27	Figures, Deon	CB	6-0	195	1/20/70	6	Colorado	Bellflower, Calif.	UFA(Pitt)-'97	16/12
78	Fordham, Todd	G-T	6-5	303	10/9/73	2	Florida State	Tifton, Ga.	FA-'97	1/0
85	Griffith, Rich	TE	6-5	280	7/31/69	5	Arizona	Tucson, Ariz.	FA-'95	16/1
54	Hamilton, James	LB	6-5	238	4/17/74	2	North Carolina	Hamlet, N.C.	D3-'97	9/0
51	Hardy, Kevin	LB	6-4	249	7/24/73	3	Illinois	Evansville, Ind.	D1-'96	13/11
1	Hollis, Mike	K	5-7	178	5/5/72	4	Idaho	Spokane, Wash.	FA-'95	16/0
37	† Hudson, Chris	S	5-10	204	10/6/71	4	Colorado	Houston, Tex.	D3-'95	16/16
80	Jackson, Willie	WR-KR	6-1	204	8/16/71	5	Florida	Gainesville, Fla.	ED11(Dall)-'95	16/1
86	Jones, Damon	TE	6-5	272	9/18/74	2	Southern Illinois	Evanston, Ill.	D5-'97	11/3
64	Jurkovic, John	DT	6-2	306	8/16/67	7	Eastern Illinois	Calumet City, Ill.	UFA(GB)-'96	3/3
57	Kopp, Jeff	LB	6-3	245	7/8/71	4	Southern California	Danville, Calif.	FA-'96	16/3
68	Lageman, Jeff	DE	6-6	265	7/18/67	10	Virginia	Sterling, Va.	UFA(NYJ)-'95	16/16
32	Logan, Mike	S	6-0	206	9/15/74	2	West Virginia	McKeesport, Pa.	D2-'97	11/0
10	Martin, Jamie	QB	6-2	210	2/8/70	4	Weber State	Arroyo Grande, Calif.	FA-'98	0*
16	Matthews, Steve	QB	6-3	227	10/13/70	3	Memphis	Tullahorne, Tenn.	W(KC)-'97	2/1
67	McCardell, Keenan	WR	6-1	184	1/6/70	7	Nevada-Las Vegas	Houston, Tex.	UFA(Balt)-'96	16/16
55	McManus, Tom	LB	6-2	255	7/30/70	4	Boston College	Edgewater, Fla.	FA-'95	0*
83	Mitchell, Pete	TE	6-2	238	10/9/71	4	Boston College	Birmingham, Mich.	T(Mia)-'95	16/12
81	Moore, Wes	WR	6-1	185	2/21/70	3	Texas Southern	Dallas, Tex.	FA-'97	11/0
65	Neujahr, Quentin	C	6-4	305	1/30/71	4	Kansas State	Ulysses, Neb.	RFA(Balt)-'98	9/7*
67	Novak, Jeff	G-T	6-6	292	7/27/67	5	Southwest Texas State	Arlington Heights, Ill.	ED3(Mia)-'95	7/2
39	Parker, Chris	RB	5-11	213	12/31/72	2	Marshall	Lynchburg, Va.	FA-'97	1/0
29	Parker, Ricky	DB	6-1	209	12/4/74	2	San Diego State	Sacramento, Calif.	FA-'97	12/0
95	Paup, Bryce	LB	6-5	247	2/29/68	9	Northern Iowa	Jefferson, Iowa	UFA(Buff)-'98	16/16*
91	Payne, Seth	DT	6-4	292	2/12/75	2	Cornell	Victor, N.Y.	D4-'97	12/5
94	Pritchett, Kelvin	DT	6-3	300	10/24/69	8	Mississippi	Atlanta, Ga.	UFA(Det)-'95	8/5
50	Robinson, Eddie	LB	6-1	233	4/13/70	7	Alabama State	New Orleans, La.	UFA(Hou)-'96	16/13
19	Ross, Jermaine	WR	6-0	191	4/27/71	3	Purdue	Jeffersonville, Ind.	FA-'98	4/0*
56	Schwartz, Bryan	LB	6-4	251	12/6/71	4	Augustana, S.D.	St. Lawrence, S.D.	D2b-'95	16/16
72	Searcy, Leon	T	6-4	316	12/21/69	7	Miami	Washington, D.C.	UFA(Pitt)-'96	16/16
31	Shelton, Daimon	RB	6-0	251	9/15/72	2	Sacramento State	Fresno, Calif.	D6-'97	13/0
99	Smeenge, Joel	DE-LB	6-6	270	4/1/68	9	Western Michigan	Grand Rapids, Mich.	UFA(NO)-'95	16/0
62	Smith, Jimmy	WR	6-1	205	2/9/69	6	Jackson State	Jackson, Miss.	FA-'95	16/16
33	Stewart, James	WR	6-1	224	12/27/71	4	Tennessee	Morristown, Tenn.	D1b-'95	16/5
41	Thomas, Dave	CB	6-3	214	8/25/68	6	Tennessee	Miami, Fla.	ED16(Dall)-'95	16/16
98	Threats, Jabbar	DE	6-5	264	4/26/75	2	Michigan State	Springfield, Ohio	FA-'97	2/0
76	Tylski, Rich	C-G	6-5	306	2/27/71	3	Utah State	San Diego, Calif.	W(NE)-'95	13/13
93	White, Jose	DT	6-3	274	3/2/73	2	Howard	Washington, D.C.	FA-'97	3/0
97	Wynn, Renaldo	DT	6-3	290	9/3/74	2	Notre Dame	Chicago, Ill.	D1-'97	16/8

* Martin last active with St. Louis in '96; McManus missed '97 season because of injury; Neujahr played 9 games with Baltimore; Paup played 16 games with Buffalo; Ross played 4 games with St. Louis.

† Restricted free agent; subject to developments.

Traded—QB Rob Johnson (5 games in '97) to Buffalo.

Players lost through free agency (5): TE Derek Brown (Oak; 13 games in '97), RB Ty Hallock (Chi; 15), RB Natrone Means (SD; 14), DT Esera Tuaolo (Atl;6), C Dave Widell (Atl;16).

Also played with Jaguars in '97—CB Bucky Brooks (3 games), S Dana Hall (16), RB Randy Jordan (7), DE Clyde Simmons (16).

COACHING STAFF

Head Coach,
Tom Coughlin

Pro Career: Under Tom Coughlin, the Jaguars became the only expansion team in NFL history to advance to the playoffs twice in its first three seasons. After a 4-12 inaugural season, Coughlin's team went 9-7 in year two on the way to the AFC Championship Game, and 11-5, and into the playoffs again last year. En route to the 1996 AFC Championship Game, the Jaguars became the first visiting team to win a playoff game at Buffalo's Rich Stadium, and only the second to win a playoff game at Denver's Mile High Stadium. Coughlin became the first head coach of the NFL's newest franchise on February 21, 1994, following a successful three seasons as head coach at Boston College. A veteran of 28 years in coaching, including 17 at the collegiate level and seven as an NFL assistant, Coughlin previously coached wide receivers for the Philadelphia Eagles (1984-85), Green Bay Packers (1986-87), and New York Giants (1988-1990). He was a member of the Giants' Super Bowl XXV champion coaching staff prior to being named head coach at Boston College in 1991. In three seasons at Boston College, he turned a struggling program into a top-20 team, posting a 21-13-1 record. His final season at Boston College was highlighted by eight consecutive wins, including a 41-39 victory over top-ranked Notre Dame, and a 9-3 finish. Despite an 0-2 start to the season, Boston College ranked thirteenth in the *Associated Press* poll and twelfth in the *USA Today/CNN* coaches poll at the end of the 1993 season. Coughlin's previous 14 seasons as a college coach were at Rochester Institute of Technology 1970-73 (head coach), Syracuse 1974-80, and Boston College 1981-83. No pro playing experience. Career record: 26-26.

Background: Played wingback for Syracuse from 1965-67 under legendary coach Ben Schwartzwalder, along with teammates Larry Csonka and Floyd Little. Received Syracuse 1967 Orange Key Award as outstanding scholar athlete, and graduated in 1968 with bachelor's degree in education. Received master's degree in education from Syracuse in 1969.

Personal: Born August 31, 1947, Waterloo, N.Y. Was standout scholastic star for Waterloo Central High School. Tom and his wife, Judy, reside in Jacksonville. They have two daughters, Keli and Katie, and two sons, Tim and Brian.

ASSISTANT COACHES

Joe Baker, assistant special teams; born June 29, 1969, Glen Ridge, N.J., lives in Jacksonville. Wide receiver Princeton 1987-90. No pro playing experience. College coach: Samford 1993. Pro coach: Joined Jaguars in 1995.

Pete Carmichael, wide receivers; born March 4, 1941, North Plainfield, N.J., lives in Jacksonville. Quarterback Dayton 1961, Montclair State College 1962-63. No pro playing experience. College coach: Virginia Military 1965-66, New Hampshire 1967, Boston College 1968-72, 1981-93, Trenton State College 1973 (head coach), Columbia 1974-77, Merchant Marine Academy 1977-80 (head coach). Pro coach: Joined Jaguars in 1995.

Perry Fewell, secondary; born November 7, 1962, Gastonia, N.C., lives in Jacksonville. Defensive back Lenoir-Rhyne 1981-84. No pro playing experience. College coach: Army 1987, 1992-94, Kent State 1988-91, Vanderbilt 1995-97. Pro coach: Joined Jaguars in 1998.

Greg Finnegan, assistant strength and conditioning; born February 21, 1969, Toledo, Ohio, lives in Jacksonville. Center Cornell 1988-92. No pro playing experience. College coach: Kansas State 1993, Boston College 1994-97. Pro coach: Joined Jaguars in 1998.

Fred Hoaglin, tight ends; born January 28, 1944, Alliance, Ohio, lives in Jacksonville. Center Pittsburgh 1962-65. Pro center Cleveland Browns 1966-72, Baltimore Colts 1973, Houston Oilers 1974-75, Seattle Seahawks 1976. Pro coach: Detroit Lions 1978-84, New York Giants 1985-92, New England Patriots 1993-96, joined Jaguars in 1997.

Jerald Ingram, running backs; born December 24, 1960, Beaver, Pa., lives in Jacksonville. Fullback Michigan 1979-84. No pro playing experience. College coach: Ball State 1985-90, Boston College 1991-93. Pro coach: Joined Jaguars in 1995.

Dick Jauron, defensive coordinator; born October 7, 1950, Peoria, Ill., lives in Jacksonville. Running back Yale 1970-72. Pro defensive back Detroit Lions 1973-77, Cincinnati Bengals 1978-80. Pro coach: Buffalo Bills 1985, Green Bay Packers 1986-94, joined Jaguars in 1995.

Mike Maser, offensive line; born March 2, 1947, Clayton, N.Y., lives in Jacksonville. Guard Buffalo 1967-70. No pro playing experience. College coach: Marshall 1973, Bluefield State College 1974-78, Maine 1979-80, Boston College 1981-93. Pro coach: Joined Jaguars in 1995.

John McNulty, quality control; born May 29, 1968, Scranton, Pa., lives in Jacksonville. Safety Penn State 1987-90. No pro playing experience. College coach: Michigan 1991-94, Connecticut 1995-97. Pro coach: Joined Jaguars in 1998.

Chris Palmer, offensive coordinator; born September 23, 1949, Mt. Kisco, N.Y., lives in Jacksonville. Quarterback Southern Connecticut State 1968-71. No pro playing experience. College coach: Connecticut 1972-74, Lehigh 1975, Colgate 1976-82, New Haven 1986-87 (head coach), Boston University 1988-89 (head coach). Pro coach: Montreal Concordes (CFL) 1983, New Jersey Generals (USFL) 1984-85, Houston Oilers 1990-92, New England Patriots 1993-96, joined Jaguars in 1997.

Jerry Palmieri, strength and conditioning; born October 30, 1958, Englewood, N.J., lives in Jacksonville. No college or pro playing experience. College coach: Oklahoma State 1984-87, Kansas State 1988-92, Boston College 1993-94. Pro coach: Joined Jaguars in 1995.

Larry Pasquale, special teams coordinator; born April 21, 1941, Brooklyn, N.Y., lives in Jacksonville. Quarterback Bridgeport 1961-63. No pro playing experience. College coach: Slippery Rock State 1967, Boston University 1968, Navy 1969-70, Massachusetts 1971-75, Idaho State 1976. Pro coach: Montreal Alouettes (CFL) 1977-78, Detroit Lions 1979, New York Jets 1980-89, San Diego Chargers 1990-91, Philadelphia Eagles 1992-94, joined Jaguars in 1995.

John Pease, defensive line; born October 14, 1943, Pittsburgh, Pa., lives in Jacksonville. Wingback Utah 1963-64. No pro playing experience. College coach: Fullerton, Calif., J.C. 1970-73, Long Beach State 1974-76, Utah 1977, Washington 1978-83. Pro coach: Philadelphia/Baltimore Stars (USFL) 1983-85, New Orleans Saints 1986-94, joined Jaguars in 1995.

Lucious Selmon, outside linebackers; born March 15, 1951, Muskogee, Okla., lives in Jacksonville. Defensive tackle Oklahoma 1970-73. Pro defensive tackle Memphis Southmen (WFL) 1974-75. College coach: Oklahoma 1976-94. Pro Coach: Joined Jaguars in 1995.

Steve Szabo, inside linebackers; born September 11, 1943, Chicago, Ill., lives in Jacksonville. Halfback/defensive back Navy 1961-64. No pro playing experience. College coach: Johns Hopkins 1969, Toledo 1970, Iowa 1971-73, Syracuse 1974-76, Iowa State 1977-78, Ohio State 1979-81, Western Michigan 1982-84, Edinboro 1985-87 (head coach), Northern Iowa 1988, Colorado State 1989-90, Boston College 1991-93. Pro coach: Joined Jaguars in 1995.

1998 FIRST-YEAR ROSTER

Name	Pos.	Ht.	Wt.	Birthdate	College	Hometown	How Acq.
Baker, Jason	T	6-6	342	2/6/75	Montana	Coos Bay, Ore.	FA
Banks, Tavian	RB	5-10	198	2/17/74	Iowa	Bettendorf, Iowa	D4a
Brillant, Pierre	T	6-7	328	8/10/73	Cincinnati	Garnerville, N.Y.	FA
Clyburn, James	DT	6-2	325	8/17/74	North Carolina A&T	Winston-Salem, N.C.	FA
Curtis, Isaac (1)	TE	6-3	245	1/30/74	Kentucky	Cincinnati, Ohio	FA-97
Darius, Donovin	S	6-1	213	8/12/75	Syracuse	Camden, N.J.	D1b
Deligianis, Harry	DT	6-4	302	8/4/75	Youngstown State	Ashtabula, Ohio	D4b
Dunn, Damon	WR	5-9	179	3/15/76	Stanford	Arlington, Texas	FA
Floyd, Todd	WR	6-3	188	5/24/74	Nevada-Las Vegas	Reno, Nev.	FA
Garnett, Winfield	DT	6-6	324	7/24/76	Ohio State	Chicago, Ill.	FA
Harrison, Ronald	CB	5-10	179	5/10/76	William & Mary	Silver Spring, Md.	FA
Hines, Tyrone (1)	LB	6-1	244	3/14/73	Tennessee	Brownsville, Tenn.	FA
Lawson, Jason	RB	6-1	251	8/19/75	South Carolina	Union, S.C.	FA
McLeod, Kevin	RB	6-0	242	10/17/74	Auburn	Clarkston, Ga.	D6b
Nori, Mark (1)	G	6-4	307	1/1/74	Boston College	Germantown, Pa.	FA
O'Neal, Heron	CB	6-2	192	2/9/75	Western Michigan	Chicago, Ill.	FA
Quinn, Jonathan	QB	6-5	242	2/27/75	Middle Tenn. State	Nashville, Tenn.	D3
Robinson, Dwaine (1)	DT	6-4	290	8/26/75	Virginia Union	Newton, Va.	FA
Skinner, Justin	K	6-2	173	7/31/75	Citadel	Charleston, S.C.	FA
Strey, Derek	LB	6-2	247	10/26/74	Eastern Washington	Port Orchard, Wash.	FA
Swinton, Reginald	WR	5-11	175	7/24/75	Murray State	Little Rock, Ark.	FA
Taylor, Cordell	CB	5-11	191	12/22/73	Hampton	Norfolk, Va.	D2
Taylor, Fred	RB	6-0	228	6/27/76	Florida	Belle Glade, Fla.	D1a
Thomas, Malcom (1)	RB	5-7	202	5/15/74	Syracuse	Jacksonville, Fla.	FA
Thomas, Mark	TE	6-4	247	4/26/75	North Carolina State	Smithfield, N.C.	FA
Thomas, Tre (1)	S	6-1	211	9/12/75	Texas	Sugar Land, Texas	FA
Tolbert, Brandon	LB	6-4	225	4/6/75	Georgia	Villa Rica, Ga.	D7b
Wade, John	C-G	6-5	293	1/25/75	Marshall	Harrisonburg, Va.	D5
Whitted, Alvis	WR	5-11	187	9/4/74	North Carolina State	Hillsborough, N.C.	D7a
Williams, Lamanzer	DE	6-4	276	11/17/74	Minnesota	Ypsilanti, Mich.	D6a
Zahursky, Steve	T	6-6	310	9/2/76	Kent State	Euclid, Ohio	FA

The term NFL Rookie is defined as a player who is in his first season of professional football and has not been on the roster of another professional football team for any regular-season or postseason games. A Rookie is designated by an "R" on NFL rosters. Players who have been active in another professional football league or players who have NFL experience, including either preseason training camp or being on an Active List or Inactive List, or on Reserve/Injured or Reserve/Physically Unable to Perform for fewer than six regular-season games, are termed NFL First-Year Players. An NFL First-Year Player is designated by a "1" on NFL rosters. Thereafter, a player is credited with an additional year of experience for each season in which he accumulates six games on the Active List or Inactive List, or on Reserve/Injured or Reserve/Physically Unable to Perform.

NOTES

KANSAS CITY CHIEFS

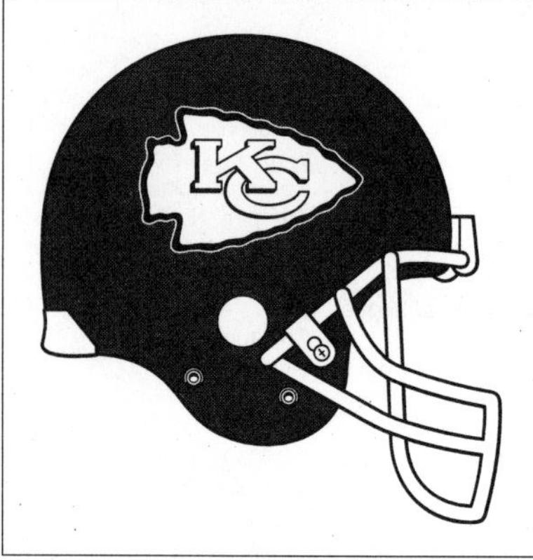

American Football Conference
Western Division
Team Colors: Red, Gold, and White
One Arrowhead Drive
Kansas City, Missouri 64129
Telephone: (816) 924-9300

CLUB OFFICIALS

Founder: Lamar Hunt
Chairman of the Board: Jack Steadman
President/General Manager and Chief Executive Officer: Carl Peterson
Executive Vice President, Assistant General Manager: Dennis Thum
Vice President of Administration: Dennis Watley
Secretary: Jim Seigfreid
Director of Finance/Treasurer: Dale Young
Director of Public Relations: Bob Moore
Director of Sales and Marketing: Wallace Bennett
Director of Player Personnel: Terry Bradway
Director of Pro Personnel: John Schneider
Director of College Scouting: Chuck Cook
Director of Operations: Steve Schneider
Director of Development: Ken Blume
Assistant Director of Public Relations: Jim Carr
Director of Corporate Sponsorships: Anita Bailey
Community Relations Manager: Brenda Sniezek
Director of Ticket Operations: Doug Hopkins
Equipment Manager: Mike Davidson
Asst. Equipment Managers: Allen Wright, Chris Shropshire
Trainer: Dave Kendall
Assistant Trainer: Bud Epps
Director of Video Operations: John Wuehrmann
Manager of Video Operations: Mike Kirk
Stadium: Arrowhead Stadium • **Capacity:** 79,409
One Arrowhead Drive
Kansas City, Missouri 64129
Playing Surface: Grass
Training Camp: University of Wisconsin-River Falls
River Falls, Wisconsin 54022

1998 SCHEDULE

PRESEASON

Aug. 1	vs. Green Bay at Tokyo, Japan	9:15
Aug. 8	vs. Tampa Bay at Norman, Okla.	7:00
Aug. 15	at Minnesota	7:00
Aug. 22	**Jacksonville**	7:00
Aug. 28	**St. Louis**	7:00

REGULAR SEASON

Sept. 6	**Oakland**	7:20
Sept. 13	at Jacksonville	1:01
Sept. 20	**San Diego**	12:01
Sept. 27	at Philadelphia	1:01
Oct. 4	**Seattle**	7:20
Oct. 11	at New England	1:01
Oct. 18	Open Date	
Oct. 26	**Pittsburgh** (Mon.)	7:20
Nov. 1	**New York Jets**	3:05
Nov. 8	at Seattle	1:15
Nov. 16	**Denver** (Mon.)	7:20
Nov. 22	at San Diego	1:15
Nov. 29	**Arizona**	12:01
Dec. 6	at Denver	2:15
Dec. 13	**Dallas**	3:15
Dec. 20	at N. Y. Giants	1:01
Dec. 26	at Oakland (Sat.)	1:05

RECORD HOLDERS

INDIVIDUAL RECORDS—CAREER

Category	Name	Performance
Rushing (Yds.)	Christian Okoye, 1987-1992	4,897
Passing (Yds.)	Len Dawson, 1962-1975	28,507
Passing (TDs)	Len Dawson, 1962-1975	237
Receiving (No.)	Henry Marshall, 1976-1987	416
Receiving (Yds.)	Otis Taylor, 1965-1975	7,306
Interceptions	Emmitt Thomas, 1966-1978	58
Punting (Avg.)	Jerrel Wilson, 1963-1977	43.5
Punt Return (Avg.)	J.T. Smith, 1979-1984	10.6
Kickoff Return (Avg.)	Noland Smith, 1967-69	26.8
Field Goals	Nick Lowery, 1980-1993	329
Touchdowns (Tot.)	Otis Taylor, 1965-1975	60
Points	Nick Lowery, 1980-1993	1,466

INDIVIDUAL RECORDS—SINGLE SEASON

Category	Name	Performance
Rushing (Yds.)	Christian Okoye, 1989	1,480
Passing (Yds.)	Bill Kenney, 1983	4,348
Passing (TDs)	Len Dawson, 1964	30
Receiving (No.)	Carlos Carson, 1983	80
Receiving (Yds.)	Carlos Carson, 1983	1,351
Interceptions	Emmitt Thomas, 1974	12
Punting (Avg.)	Jerrel Wilson, 1965	46.0
Punt Return (Avg.)	Abner Haynes, 1960	15.4
Kickoff Return (Avg.)	Dave Grayson, 1962	29.7
Field Goals	Nick Lowery, 1990	34
Touchdowns (Tot.)	Abner Haynes, 1962	19
Points	Nick Lowery, 1990	139

INDIVIDUAL RECORDS—SINGLE GAME

Category	Name	Performance
Rushing (Yds.)	Barry Word, 10-14-90	200
Passing (Yds.)	Len Dawson, 11-1-64	435
Passing (TDs)	Len Dawson, 11-1-64	6
Receiving (No.)	Ed Podolak, 10-7-73	12
Receiving (Yds.)	Stephone Paige, 12-22-85	309
Interceptions	Bobby Ply, 12-16-62	*4
	Bobby Hunt, 12-4-64	*4
	Deron Cherry, 9-29-85	*4
Field Goals	Many times	5
	Last time by Nick Lowery, 9-20-93	
Touchdowns (Tot.)	Abner Haynes, 11-26-61	5
Points	Abner Haynes, 11-26-61	30

*NFL Record

COACHING HISTORY

DALLAS TEXANS 1960-62
(307-264-12)

1960-74	Hank Stram	129-79-10
1975-77	Paul Wiggin*	11-24-0
1977	Tom Bettis	1-6-0
1978-82	Marv Levy	31-42-0
1983-86	John Mackovic	30-35-0
1987-88	Frank Gansz	8-22-1
1989-97	Marty Schottenheimer	97-56-1

*Released after seven games in 1977

ARROWHEAD STADIUM

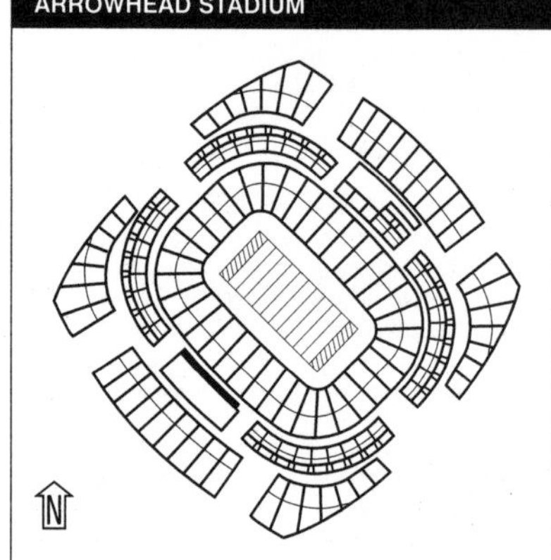

1997 TEAM RECORD

PRESEASON (1-3)

Date	Result		Opponent
8/2	L	14-28	Pittsburgh
8/9	L	7-26	at New Orleans
8/14	W	30-10	Carolina
8/22	L	13-14	at St. Louis

REGULAR SEASON (13-3)

Date	Result		Opponent	Att.
8/31	L	3-19	at Denver	75,600
9/8	W	28-27	at Oakland	61,523
9/14	W	22-16	Buffalo	78,169
9/21	W	35-14	at Carolina	67,402
9/28	W	20-17	Seattle (OT)	77,877
10/5	L	14-17	at Miami	71,794
10/16	W	31-3	San Diego	77,196
10/26	W	28-20	at St. Louis	64,864
11/3	W	13-10	Pittsburgh	78,301
11/09	L	10-24	at Jacksonville	70,444
11/16	W	24-22	Denver	77,963
11/23	W	19-14	at Seattle	66,264
11/30	W	44-9	San Francisco	77,535
12/7	W	30-0	Oakland	76,379
12/14	W	29-7	at San Diego	54,594
12/21	W	25-13	New Orleans	66,772

POSTSEASON (0-1)

Date	Result		Opponent	Att.
1/4	L	10-14	Denver	76,965

(OT) Overtime

SCORE BY PERIODS

Chiefs	63	149	59	101	3	—	375
Opponents	61	80	47	44	0	—	232

ATTENDANCE

Home 610,192 Away 532,485 Total 1,142,677

Single-game home record, 82,094 (11/5/72)

Single-season home record, 620,180 (1995)

1997 TEAM STATISTICS

	Chiefs	Opp.
Total First Downs	315	278
Rushing	129	94
Passing	163	158
Penalty	23	26
Third Down: Made/Att	93/225	65/206
Third Down Pct.	41.3	31.6
Fourth Down: Made/Att	5/16	4/13
Fourth Down Pct.	31.3	30.8
Total Net Yards	5,064	4,880
Avg. Per Game	316.5	305.0
Total Plays	1,054	974
Avg. Per Play	4.8	5.0
Net Yards Rushing	2,171	1,621
Avg. Per Game	135.7	101.3
Total Rushes	529	413
Net Yards Passing	2,893	3,259
Avg. Per Game	180.8	203.7
Sacked/Yards Lost	32/236	54/359
Gross Yards	3,129	3,618
Att./Completions	493/281	507/271
Completion Pct.	57.0	53.5
Had Intercepted	10	21
Punts/Average	83/42.0	84/41.3
Net Punting Avg.	83/38.0	84/33.9
Penalties/Yards Lost	121/1,035	113/977
Fumbles/Ball Lost	21/10	30/13
Touchdowns	42	23
Rushing	15	8
Passing	20	15
Returns	7	0
Avg. Time of Possession	31:16	28:44

1997 INDIVIDUAL STATISTICS

PASSING	Att.	Comp.	Yds.	Pct.	TD	Int.	Tkld.	Rating
Grbac	314	179	1,943	57.0	11	6	19/150	79.1
Gannon	175	98	1,144	56.0	7	4	13/86	79.8
Tolliver	1	1	-8	100.0	0	0	0/0	79.2
Allen	2	2	15	100.0	2	0	0/0	137.5
Aguiar	1	1	35	100.0	0	0	0/0	118.8
Chiefs	493	281	3,129	57.0	20	10	32/236	81.1
Opponents	507	271	3,618	53.5	15	21	54/359	69.0

SCORING	TD R	TD P	TD Rt	PAT	FG	Saf	PTS
Stoyanovich	0	0	0	35/36	26/27	0	113
Allen	11	0	0	0/0	0/0	0	66
Rison	0	7	0	0/0	0/0	0	42
Hughes	0	2	1	0/0	0/0	0	18
McMillian	0	0	3	0/0	0/0	0	18
Richardson	0	3	0	0/0	0/0	0	18
Gonzalez	0	2	0	0/0	0/0	0	14
Vanover	0	0	2	0/0	0/0	0	14
Anders	0	2	0	0/0	0/0	0	12
Dawson	0	2	0	0/0	0/0	0	12
Gannon	2	0	0	0/0	0/0	0	12
Popson	0	2	0	0/0	0/0	0	12
Anderson	0	0	1	0/0	0/0	0	6
Bennett	1	0	0	0/0	0/0	0	6
Grbac	1	0	0	0/0	0/0	0	6
Phillips	0	0	0	0/0	0/0	1	2
Thomas	0	0	0	0/0	0/0	1	2
Chiefs	15	20	7	35/36	26/27	3	375
Opponents	8	15	0	22/22	24/33	0	232

2-Point conversions: Gonzalez, Vanover. Team 2-6, Opponents: 0-1.

RUSHING	Att.	Yds.	Avg.	LG	TD
Hill	157	550	3.5	38	0
Allen	124	505	4.1	30	11
Anders	79	397	5.0	43	0
Bennett	94	369	3.9	14	1
Grbac	30	168	5.6	20	1
Gannon	33	109	3.3	13	2
Vanover	5	50	10.0	17	0
Aguiar	2	11	5.5	6	0
Richardson	2	11	5.5	6	0
Tolliver	2	-1	-0.5	0	0
Rison	1	2	2.0	2	0
Chiefs	529	2,171	4.1	43	15
Opponents	413	1,621	3.9	45	8

RECEIVING	No.	Yds.	Avg.	LG	TD
Rison	72	1,092	15.2	45	7
Anders	59	453	7.7	55t	2
Popson	35	320	9.1	21	2
Gonzalez	33	368	11.2	30	2
Dawson	21	273	13.0	27	2
Hill	12	126	10.5	39	0
Allen	11	86	7.8	18	0
Vanover	7	92	13.1	42	0
Hughes	7	65	9.3	14t	2
Bennett	7	5	0.7	4	0
Perriman	6	83	13.8	27	0
Walker	5	60	12.0	22	0
Richardson	3	6	2.0	3t	3
Horn	2	65	32.5	47	0
Lockett	1	35	35.0	35	0
Chiefs	281	3,129	11.1	55t	20
Opponents	271	3,618	13.4	78	15

INTERCEPTIONS	No.	Yds.	Avg.	LG	TD
McMillian	8	274	34.3	87t	3
Woods	4	57	14.3	27	0
Hasty	3	22	7.3	19	0
Edwards	2	15	7.5	12	0
Carter	2	9	4.5	9	0
Anderson	1	55	55.0	55t	1
Tongue	1	0	0.0	0	0
Chiefs	21	432	20.6	87t	4
Opponents	10	148	14.8	43	0

PUNTING	No.	Yds.	Avg.	In 20	LG
Aguiar	82	3,465	42.3	28	65
Stoyanovich	1	24	24.0	1	24
Chiefs	83	3,489	42.0	29	65
Opponents	84	3,468	41.3	25	65

PUNT RETURNS	No.	FC	Yds.	Avg.	LG	TD
Vanover	35	14	383	10.9	82t	1
Chiefs	35	14	383	10.9	82t	1
Opponents	39	16	255	6.5	25	0

KICKOFF RETURNS	No.	Yds.	Avg.	LG	TD
Vanover	51	1,308	25.6	94t	1
Anders	1	0	0.0	0	0
Hughes	1	21	21.0	21	0
Manusky	1	16	16.0	16	0
Horn	0	0	—	—	0
Chiefs	54	1,345	24.9	94t	1
Opponents	80	1,672	20.9	50	0

FIELD GOALS	1-19	20-29	30-39	40-49	50+
Stoyanovich	0/0	9/9	3/3	12/13	2/2
Chiefs	0/0	9/9	3/3	12/13	2/2
Opponents	0/0	7/7	11/13	4/7	2/6

SACKS	No.
Williams	10.5
Thomas	9.5
Booker	4.0
Browning	4.0
Davis	3.5
McDaniels	3.5
Simmons	3.5
Edwards	2.5
Tongue	2.5
Anderson	2.0
Barndt	2.0
Hasty	2.0
Wooden	2.0
Dumas	1.0
Woods	1.0
Phillips	0.5
Chiefs	54.0
Opponents	32.0

1998 DRAFT CHOICES

Round	Name	Pos.	College
1	Victor Riley	T	Auburn
3	Rashaan Shehee	RB	Washington
4	Greg Favors	LB	Mississippi State
5	Robert Williams	DB	North Carolina
6	Derrick Ransom	DT	Cincinnati
7	Eric Warfield	DB	Nebraska
	Ernest Blackwell	RB	Missouri

KANSAS CITY CHIEFS

1998 VETERAN ROSTER

No.	Name	Pos.	Ht.	Wt.	Birthdate	NFL Exp.	College	Hometown	How Acq.	'97 Games/ Starts
26	Adams, Vashone	S	5-10	196	9/12/73	3	Eastern Michigan	Aurora, Colo.	FA-'98	5/4*
5	Aguiar, Louie	P	6-2	218	6/30/66	8	Utah State	Livermore, Calif.	FA-'94	16/0
82	Alexander, Derrick	WR	6-2	195	11/6/71	5	Michigan	Detroit, Mich.	UFA(Balt)-'98	15/13*
38	Anders, Kimble	RB	5-11	230	9/10/66	8	Houston	Galveston, Tex.	FA-'91	15/14
71	Barndt, Tom	DT	6-3	301	3/14/72	3	Pittsburgh	Mentor, Ohio	D6b-'95	16/1
17	Barnes, Pat	QB	6-3	215	2/23/75	2	California	Trabuco Hills, Calif.	D4-'97	0*
30	Bennett, Donnell	RB	6-0	232	9/14/72	5	Miami	Ft. Lauderdale, Fla.	D2-'94	14/1
27	Bostic, James	RB	5-11	225	3/13/72	3	Auburn	Ft. Lauderdale, Fla.	FA-'98	0*
45	Brooks, Bucky	CB	6-0	201	1/22/71	4	North Carolina	Raleigh, N.C.	FA-'97	3/0
93	Browning, John	DE	6-4	290	9/30/73	3	West Virginia	Miami, Fla.	D3-'96	14/13
34	Carter, Dale	CB	6-1	188	11/28/69	7	Tennessee	Covington, Ga.	D1-'92	16/15
57	Clark, Reggie	LB	6-2	240	10/17/67	3	North Carolina	Charlotte, N.C.	FA-'98	0*
69	Criswell, Jeff	T	6-7	294	3/7/64	11	Graceland College	Searsboro, Iowa	UFA(NYJ)-'95	16/16
50	Davis, Anthony	LB	6-0	235	3/7/69	5	Utah	Pasco, Wash.	FA-'94	15/15
23	Dorsett, Matt	CB	5-11	190	8/23/73	3	Southern	New Orleans, La.	FA-'98	0*
85	Dowdell, Marcus	WR	5-10	179	5/22/70	4	Tennessee State	Birmingham, Ala.	FA-'98	0*
59	Edwards, Donnie	LB	6-2	236	4/6/73	3	UCLA	Chula Vista, Calif.	D4-'96	16/16
22	Ellis, Kwame	CB	5-10	188	2/27/74	2	Stanford	Oakland, Calif.	FA-'98	0*
60	El-Mashtoub, Hicham	C	6-2	300	5/11/72	3	Arizona	Montreal, Canada	FA-'98	0*
12	Gannon, Rich	QB	6-3	210	12/20/65	11	Delaware	Philadelphia, Pa.	FA-'95	9/6
55	George, Ron	LB	6-2	236	3/20/70	6	Stanford	Heidelberg, Germany	FA-'98	16/0*
88	Gonzalez, Tony	TE	6-4	244	2/27/76	2	California	Huntington Beach, Calif.	D1-'97	16/0
11	Grbac, Elvis	QB	6-5	232	8/13/70	6	Michigan	Cleveland, Ohio	UFA(SF)-'97	10/10
61	Grunhard, Tim	C	6-2	307	5/17/68	9	Notre Dame	Chicago, Ill.	D2-'90	16/16
40	Hasty, James	CB	6-0	208	5/23/65	11	Washington State	Seattle, Wash.	UFA(NYJ)-'95	16/15
99	t- Holland, Darius	DT	6-5	320	11/10/73	4	Colorado	Las Cruces, N.M.	T(GB)-'98	12/1*
84	Horn, Joe	WR	6-1	199	1/16/72	3	Itawamba J.C.	Fayetteville, N.C.	D5-'96	8/0
83	Hughes, Danan	WR	6-2	211	12/11/70	6	Iowa	Bayonne, N.J.	D7-'93	16/1
35	t- Johnson, Melvin	S	6-0	198	4/15/72	4	Kentucky	Cincinnati, Ohio	T(TB)-'98	16/7*
9	Jones, Reggie	WR	6-0	191	5/5/71	3	Louisiana State	Kansas City, Mo.	FA-'97	0*
81	Lockett, Kevin	WR	6-0	177	9/8/74	2	Kansas State	Tulsa, Okla.	D2-'97	9/0
95	Manuel, Sean	TE	6-2	245	12/1/73	2	New Mexico State	El Sobrante, Calif.	FA-'98	0*
51	Manusky, Greg	LB	6-1	234	8/12/66	11	Colgate	Dallas, Pa.	FA-'94	16/1
77	McDaniels, Pellom	DE	6-3	285	2/21/68	6	Oregon State	San Jose, Calif.	FA-'93	16/6
75	McGlockton, Chester	DT	6-4	320	9/16/69	7	Clemson	Whiteville, N.C.	RFA(Oak)-'98	16/16*
29	McMillian, Mark	CB	5-7	148	4/29/70	7	Alabama	Los Angeles, Calif.	FA-'97	16/2
91	O'Neal, Leslie	DE	6-4	270	5/7/64	13	Oklahoma State	Little Rock, Ark.	FA-'98	15/14*
62	Parker, Glenn	T	6-5	305	4/22/66	9	Arizona	Huntington Beach, Calif.	FA-'97	15/15
72	Parks, Nathan	T	6-5	303	10/24/74	2	Stanford	Durham, Calif.	D7-'97	0*
97	Parten, Ty	DT	6-5	295	10/13/69	3	Arizona	Scottsdale, Ariz.	FA-'97	2/0
48	Popson, Ted	TE	6-4	250	9/10/66	5	Portland State	Truckee, Calif.	FA-'97	13/12
41	Prior, Anthony	CB	5-11	186	3/27/70	5	Washington State	Riverside, Calif.	FA-'98	12/0*
49	Richardson, Tony	RB	6-1	237	12/17/71	4	Auburn	Daleville, Ala.	FA-'95	14/0
89	Rison, Andre	WR	6-1	188	3/18/67	10	Michigan State	Flint, Mich.	FA-'97	16/16
43	Robinson, Greg	RB	5-10	205	8/8/69	5	Northeast Louisiana	Grenada, Miss.	FA-'98	0*
31	Ross, Kevin	S	5-9	185	1/16/62	15	Temple	Paulsboro, N.J.	FA-'97	5/0
68	Shields, Will	G	6-3	305	9/15/71	6	Nebraska	Lawton, Okla.	D3-'93	16/16
56	Simmons, Wayne	LB	6-2	250	12/15/69	6	Clemson	Hilton Head, S.C.	T(GB)-'97	16/14*
65	Smith, Jeff	C	6-3	322	5/25/73	3	Tennessee	Deactur, Tenn.	D7b-96	3/0
70	Spears, Marcus	T	6-4	305	9/28/71	5	Northwestern State, La.	Scotlandville, La.	FA-'97	4/0
10	Stoyanovich, Pete	K	5-11	195	4/28/67	10	Indiana	Dearborn Heights, Mich.	T(Mia)-'96	16/0
79	Szott, Dave	G	6-4	293	12/12/67	9	Penn State	Clifton, N.J.	D7-'90	16/16
58	Thomas, Derrick	LB	6-3	247	1/1/67	10	Alabama	Miami, Fla.	D1-'89	12/10
8	Tolliver, Billy Joe	QB	6-1	217	2/7/66	9	Texas Tech	Boyd, Tex.	FA-'97	9/2*
25	Tongue, Reggie	S	6-0	201	4/11/73	3	Oregon State	Fairbanks, Alaska	D2-'96	16/16
87	Vanover, Tamarick	RB-WR	5-11	218	2/25/74	4	Florida State	Tallahassee, Fla.	D3a-'95	16/0
92	Williams, Dan	DE	6-4	290	12/15/69	6	Toledo	Ypsilanti, Mich.	FA-'97	15/6
90	Wooden, Terry	LB	6-3	239	1/14/67	9	Syracuse	Farmington, Conn.	UFA(Sea)-'97	15/8
21	Woods, Jerome	S	6-2	200	3/17/73	3	Memphis	Memphis, Tenn.	D1-'96	16/16

* Adams played 4 games with New Orleans in '97; Alexander played in 15 games with Baltimore; Barnes inactive for 15 games; Bostic last active with St. Louis in '94; Clark last active with Jacksonville in '96; Dorsett last active with Green Bay in '95; Dowdell last active with Arizona in '96; Ellis last active with the N.Y. Jets in '96; El-Mashtoub last active with Tennessee in '96; George played 16 games with Minnesota; Holland played 12 games with Green Bay; Johnson played 16 games with Tampa Bay; Jones missed '97 season because of injury; Manuel last active with San Francisco in '96; McGlockton played 16 games with Oakland; O'Neal played 15 games with St. Louis; Parks inactive for 16 games; Prior played 12 games with Minnesota; Robinson last active with St. Louis in '96; Simmons played 6 games with Green Bay; Tolliver played 6 games with Atlanta.

Traded—DE Vaughn Booker (13 games in '97) to Green Bay.

t- Chiefs traded for Holland (Green Bay) and Johnson (Tampa Bay).

Retired—Marcus Allen, 16-year running back, 16 games in '97.

Also played with Chiefs in '97—CB Darren Anderson (11 games), DT Shannon Clavelle (1), WR Lake Dawson (11), LB Troy Dumas (8), DT Kerry Hicks (2), RB Greg Hill (16), LB Bobby Houston (5), T Trezelle Jenkins (2), S Clyde Johnson (15), DT Dexter Nottage (1), WR Brett Perriman (5), DT Michael Dean Perry (1), DT Joe Phillips (15), TE Alfred Pupunu (1), S Todd Scott (10), LB Tracy Simien (16), G Ralph Tamm (16), TE Derrick Walker (16), T Steve Wallace (10).

COACHING STAFF

Head Coach,
Marty Schottenheimer

Pro Career: In nine seasons as head coach of the Kansas City Chiefs, Schottenheimer has established the highest regular-season winning percentage in franchise history (.656). His .644 career regular-season winning percentage is the highest among active NFL coaches with 100 or more games. Since 1985, he has led all NFL coaches with 134 victories. He is also the only NFL coach that has taken his team to the playoffs 11 times since 1985. Since 1960, the only coaches who have taken their teams to the playoffs as many times as Schottenheimer are Don Shula (19), Tom Landry (18), Chuck Noll (12), Bud Grant (12), and Chuck Knox (11). He has directed his teams to four-year playoff streaks with both the Chiefs and the Cleveland Browns, making him the only coach in NFL history to do that with two different franchises. He won division titles with the Browns from 1985-87 and with the Chiefs in 1993, 1995, and again last year. His first coaching job came as an assistant coach with the Portland Storm (WFL) in 1974. With the New York Giants, he was linebackers coach and later defensive coordinator from 1975-77. He moved to the Detroit Lions in 1978 and then became defensive coordinator with the Browns in 1980 before ascending to the head coaching position during the 1984 season. A seventh-round draft choice of the Buffalo Bills in 1965, he played linebacker with the Bills until 1968 and finished his pro playing career with the Boston Patriots in 1969-70. Career record: 143-87-1.

Background: Schottenheimer was an All-America linebacker at the University of Pittsburgh from 1962-64. Following his retirement from pro football, he worked as a real estate developer in both Miami and Denver from 1971-74.

Personal: Born September 23, 1943, Canonsburg, Pa. Marty and his wife, Patricia, live in Overland Park, Kan., and have one daughter, Kristen, and one son, Brian, who is an offensive assistant quality control coach with the Chiefs.

1998 FIRST-YEAR ROSTER

Name	Pos.	Ht.	Wt.	Birthdate	College	Hometown	How Acq.
Blackwell, Ernest	RB	6-3	250	8/7/75	Missouri	Eureka, Mo.	D7b
Closs, Tavarr	T	6-5	299	9/17/74	Connecticut	Hartford, Conn.	FA
Coleman, Herb	DE	6-4	285	9/4/72	Trinity	Country Club Hills, Ill.	FA
Cotton, Kotto	WR	6-0	182	4/17/73	Arkansas	North Little Rock, Ark.	FA-'97
Favors, Greg	LB	6-1	236	9/30/74	Mississippi State	Atlanta, Ga.	D4
Flick, Chad	TE	6-5	255	2/9/73	San Diego State	Vista, Calif.	FA
Gaine, Brian	TE	6-5	255	4/20/73	Maine	Ramsey, N.J.	FA
Haynes, Jesse	RB	5-9	210	8/8/72	Northwest Missouri St.	Fort Worth, Tex.	FA-'97
Heimsoth, Jay	DT	6-3	285	4/4/74	Northern Iowa	LeMars, La.	FA
Hicks, Eric	DE	6-6	261	6/17/76	Maryland	Erie, Pa.	FA
Huntley, Kevin	WR	6-1	207	7/31/76	Wisconsin	Fremont, Ohio	FA
Johnson, Damien	TE	6-3	242	1/31/75	Northwestern State	New Orleans, La.	FA
Kubik, Brad	G	6-4	292	3/31/75	Southwest Missouri State	Springfield, Mo.	FA
McWashington, Shawn	WR	5-9	180	1/24/75	Washington State	Seattle, Wash.	FA
Moore, Brandon	LB	5-11	220	11/13/75	Washington State	Carson, Calif.	FA
Moore, Jim	TE	6-3	262	4/29/73	Kansas	Garden City, Kan.	FA
Ortiz, Chris	WR	6-2	202	9/25/74	Southern Connecticut St.	Waterbury, Conn.	FA
Ransom, Derrick	DT	6-3	286	9/13/76	Cincinnati	Indianapolis, Ind.	D6
Reed, Kavis	CB	6-0	175	2/24/73	Furman	Georgetown, S.C.	FA
Rice-Locket, Terry	LB	6-3	244	3/15/75	Louisville	St. Louis, Mo.	FA
Riley, Victor	T	6-5	321	11/4/74	Auburn	Swansea, S.C.	D1
Shehee, Rashaan	RB	5-10	207	6/20/75	Washington	Bakersfield, Calif.	D3
Smith, Mark	LB	6-3	242	1/27/74	Arkansas	Webb City, Mo.	FA-'97
Swanson, Pete	T	6-5	307	3/26/74	Stanford	Hollister, Cal.	FA-'97
Thomas, Rod	CB	6-0	195	8/19/75	Southern Mississippi	Madison, Miss.	FA
Warfield, Eric	CB	6-0	192	3/3/76	Nebraska	Texarkana, Ark.	D7a
Washington, Vann	S	6-0	212	5/18/74	West Virginia	Monticello, Fla.	FA
Waterman, Toussaint	WR	6-0	207	12/5/74	Northwestern	Detroit,Mich.	FA
Williams, Robert	CB	5-10	172	5/29/77	North Carolina	Shelby, N.C.	D5

The term NFL Rookie is defined as a player who is in his first season of professional football and has not been on the roster of another professional football team for any regular-season or postseason games. A Rookie is designated by an "R" on NFL rosters. Players who have been active in another professional football league or players who have NFL experience, including either preseason training camp or being on an Active List or Inactive List, or on Reserve/Injured or Reserve/Physically Unable to Perform for fewer than six regular-season games, are termed NFL First-Year Players. An NFL First-Year Player is designated by a "1" on NFL rosters. Thereafter, a player is credited with an additional year of experience for each season in which he accumulates six games on the Active List or Inactive List, or on Reserve/Injured or Reserve/Physically Unable to Perform.

NOTES

ASSISTANT COACHES

Russ Ball, administrative assistant to the head coach; born August 28, 1959, Moberly, Mo., lives in Shawnee Mission, Kan. Center Central Missouri State 1977-80. No pro playing experience. College coach: Missouri 1981-88. Pro coach: Joined Chiefs in 1989.

Gunther Cunningham, defensive coordinator; born December 6, 1944, Munich, Germany, lives in Leawood, Kan. Linebacker-placekicker Oregon 1966-68. No pro playing experience. College coach: Oregon 1969-71, Arkansas 1972, Stanford 1973-76, California 1977-80. Pro coach: Hamilton Tiger-Cats (CFL) 1981, Baltimore-Indianapolis Colts 1982-84, San Diego Chargers 1985-90, Los Angeles Raiders 1991-94, joined Chiefs in 1995.

Jim Erkenbeck, tight ends-offensive assistant; born September 10, 1933, Los Angeles, Calif., lives in Kansas City, Mo. Linebacker-end San Diego State 1949-51. No pro playing experience. College coach: San Diego State 1961-63, Grossmont (Calif.) J.C. 1964-67 (head coach), Utah State 1968, Washington State 1969-71, California 1972-76. Pro coach: Winnepeg Blue Bombers (CFL) 1977, Montreal Alouettes (CFL) 1978-81, Calgary Stampeders (CFL) 1982, Philadelphia/Baltimore Stars (USFL) 1983-85, New Orleans Saints 1986, Dallas Cowboys 1987-88, Kansas City Chiefs 1989-91, Los Angeles Rams 1992-94, rejoined Chiefs in 1995.

Jeff Hurd, strength and conditioning; born April 24, 1958, Pomona, Calif., lives in Overland Park, Kan. Attended Fort Hays State. No college or pro playing experience. College coach: Fort Hays State 1984, Delta State 1985, Clemson 1986, Western Michigan 1987-93, Tulsa 1994. Pro coach: Jacksonville Jaguars 1995-97, joined Chiefs in 1998.

Lionel James, running backs; born May 25, 1962, Albany, Ga., lives in Kansas City, Mo. Running back Auburn 1980-83. Pro running back San Diego Chargers 1984-88. College coach: Appalachian State 1995, Auburn 1996-97. Pro coach: Joined Chiefs in 1998.

Bob Karmelowicz, defensive line; born July 22, 1949, New Britain, Conn., lives in Lenexa, Kan. Nose tackle Bridgeport 1968-71. No pro playing experience. College coach: Arizona State 1974-78, Massachusetts 1979-80, Texas-El Paso 1980-81, Illinois 1982-86, Washington State 1987-88, Miami 1989-91. Pro coach: Cincinnati Bengals 1992-93, Washington Redskins 1994-96, joined Chiefs in 1997.

Woodrow Lowe, linebackers; born June 9, 1954, Columbus, Ga., lives in Lenexa, Kan. Linebacker Alabama 1973-75. Pro linebacker San Diego Chargers 1976-86. Pro coach: Joined Chiefs in 1995.

Mike McCarthy, quarterbacks; born November 10, 1963, Pittsburgh, Pa., lives in Lenexa, Kan. Tight end Baker University 1985-86. No pro playing experience. College coach: Fort Hays State 1987-88, Pittsburgh 1989-92. Pro coach: Joined Chiefs in 1993.

Roberto Parker, asst. strength and conditioning; born September 10, 1956, Omaha, Neb., lives in Blue Springs, Mo. Defensive lineman South Dakota State 1976-79. No pro playing experience. College coach: Nebraska-Omaha 1981-82, Oklahoma State 1982-84, 1995-96, Fresno State 1984-95. Pro coach: Joined Chiefs in 1997.

Jimmy Raye, offensive coordinator; born March 26, 1946, Fayetteville, N.C., lives in Kansas City, Mo. Quarterback Michigan State 1965-67. Pro defensive back Philadelphia Eagles 1969. College coach: Michigan State 1971-75, Wyoming 1976. Pro coach: San Francisco 49ers 1977, Detroit Lions 1978-79, Atlanta Falcons 1980-82, 1987-89, Los Angeles Rams 1983-84, 1991, Tampa Bay Buccaneers 1985-86, New England Patriots 1990, joined Chiefs in 1992.

Al Saunders, assistant head coach-receivers; born February 1, 1947, London, England, lives in Overland Park, Kan. Defensive back San Jose State 1966-68. No pro playing experience. College coach: Southern California 1970-71, Missouri 1972, Utah State 1973-75, California 1976-81, Tennessee 1982. Pro coach: San Diego Chargers 1983-88 (head coach 1986-88), joined Chiefs in 1989.

Brian Schottenheimer, offensive assistant-quality control; born October 16, 1973, Denver, lives in Overland Park, Kan. Quarterback Kansas 1992, Florida 1993-96. No pro playing experience. Pro coach: St. Louis Rams 1997, joined Chiefs in 1998.

Kurt Schottenheimer, defensive backs; born October 1, 1949, McDonald, Pa., lives in Leawood, Kan. Defensive back Miami 1969-70. No pro playing experience. College coach: William Patterson 1974, Michigan State 1978-82, Tulane 1983, Louisiana State 1984-85, Notre Dame 1986. Pro coach: Cleveland Browns 1987-88, joined Chiefs in 1989.

Mike Solari, offensive line; born January 16, 1955, Daly City, Calif., lives in Leawood, Kan. Offensive lineman San Diego State 1975-76. No pro playing experience. College coach: Mira Vista (Calif.) J.C. 1977-78, U.S. International 1979, Boise State 1980, Cincinnati 1990-91. Pro coach: Dallas Cowboys 1987-88, Phoenix Cardinals 1989, San Francisco 49ers 1992-96, joined Chiefs in 1997.

Mike Stock, special teams; born September 29, 1939, Barberton, Ohio, lives in Overland Park, Kan. Fullback Northwestern 1957-60. Pro running back Saskatchewan Roughriders (CFL) 1961. College coach: Northwestern 1961, Buffalo 1966-67, Navy 1968, Notre Dame 1969-74, Wisconsin 1975-78, Eastern Michigan 1979-83 (head coach), Notre Dame 1984-86, Ohio State 1992-94. Pro coach: Cincinnati Bengals 1987-91, joined Chiefs in 1995.

Darvin Wallis, special assistant-quality control; born February 14, 1949, Ft. Branch, Ind., lives in Overland Park, Kan. Defensive end Arizona 1970-71. No pro playing experience. College coach: Adams State 1976-77, Tulane 1978-79, Mississippi 1980-81. Pro coach: Cleveland Browns 1982-88, joined Chiefs in 1989.

MIAMI DOLPHINS

American Football Conference
Eastern Division
Team Colors: Aqua, Coral, Blue, and White
7500 S.W. 30th Street
Davie, Florida 33314
Telephone: (954) 452-7000

CLUB OFFICIALS

Owner/Chairman of the Board: H. Wayne Huizenga
President/Chief Operating Officer: Eddie J. Jones
General Manager/Head Coach: Jimmy Johnson
Vice President-Administration: Bryan Wiedmeier
Vice President-Finance: Jill R. Strafaci
Director of Football Operations: Bob Ackles
Director of Pro Personnel: Tom Heckert
Director of College Scouting: Tom Braatz
Vice President-Media Relations: Harvey Greene
Media Relations Coordinator: Neal Gulkis
Director of Publications: Scott Stone
Senior Director-Marketing: David Evans
Senior Director-Information Systems: Burt Gilner
Community Relations Director: Fudge Browne
Vice President-Ticket Sales: Bill Galante
Head Athletic Trainer: Kevin O'Neill
Equipment Manager: Tony Egues
Stadium: Pro Player Stadium • **Capacity:** 75,192
2269 N.W. 199th Street
Miami, Florida 33056
Playing Surface: Grass (PAT)
Training Camp: Nova University
7500 S.W. 30th Street
Davie, Florida 33314

1998 SCHEDULE

PRESEASON

Aug. 8	at Washington	7:30
Aug. 13	**Tampa Bay**	8:20
Aug. 23	at San Francisco	1:00
Aug. 28	**Green Bay**	7:00

REGULAR SEASON

Sept. 6	at Indianapolis	3:15
Sept. 13	**Buffalo**	1:01
Sept. 20	**Pittsburgh**	1:01
Sept. 27	Open Date	
Oct. 4	at New York Jets	1:01
Oct. 12	at Jacksonville (Mon.)	8:20
Oct. 18	**St. Louis**	4:15
Oct. 25	**New England**	1:01
Nov. 1	at Buffalo	1:01
Nov. 8	**Indianapolis**	1:01
Nov. 15	at Carolina	1:01
Nov. 23	at New England (Mon.)	8:20
Nov. 29	**New Orleans**	1:01
Dec. 6	at Oakland	1:15
Dec. 13	**New York Jets**	8:20
Dec. 21	**Denver** (Mon.)	8:20
Dec. 27	at Atlanta	1:01

RECORD HOLDERS

INDIVIDUAL RECORDS—CAREER

Category	Name	Performance
Rushing (Yds.)	Larry Csonka, 1968-1974, 1979	6,737
Passing (Yds.)	Dan Marino, 1983-1997	*55,416
Passing (TDs)	Dan Marino, 1983-1997	*385
Receiving (No.)	Mark Clayton, 1983-1992	550
Receiving (Yds.)	Mark Duper, 1982-1992	8,869
Interceptions	Jake Scott, 1970-75	35
Punting (Avg.)	John Kidd, 1994-97	44.2
Punt Return (Avg.)	Freddie Solomon, 1975-77	11.4
Kickoff Return (Avg.)	Mercury Morris, 1969-1975	26.5
Field Goals	Pete Stoyanovich, 1989-1995	176
Touchdowns (Tot.)	Mark Clayton, 1983-1992	82
Points	Garo Yepremian, 1970-78	830

INDIVIDUAL RECORDS—SINGLE SEASON

Category	Name	Performance
Rushing (Yds.)	Delvin Williams, 1978	1,258
Passing (Yds.)	Dan Marino, 1984	*5,084
Passing (TDs)	Dan Marino, 1984	*48
Receiving (No.)	Mark Clayton, 1988	86
Receiving (Yds.)	Mark Clayton, 1984	1,389
Interceptions	Dick Westmoreland, 1967	10
Punting (Avg.)	John Kidd, 1996	46.3
Punt Return (Avg.)	Freddie Solomon, 1975	12.3
Kickoff Return (Avg.)	Duriel Harris, 1976	32.9
Field Goals	Pete Stoyanovich, 1991	31
Touchdowns (Tot.)	Mark Clayton, 1984	18
Points	Pete Stoyanovich, 1992	124

INDIVIDUAL RECORDS—SINGLE GAME

Category	Name	Performance
Rushing (Yds.)	Mercury Morris, 9-30-73	197
Passing (Yds.)	Dan Marino, 10-23-88	521
Passing (TDs)	Bob Griese, 11-24-77	6
	Dan Marino, 9-21-86	6
Receiving (No.)	Jim Jensen, 11-6-88	12
Receiving (Yds.)	Mark Duper, 11-10-85	217
Interceptions	Dick Anderson, 12-3-73	*4
Field Goals	Garo Yepremian, 9-26-71	5
Touchdowns (Tot.)	Paul Warfield, 12-15-73	4
	Mark Ingram, 11-27-94	4
Points	Paul Warfield, 12-15-73	24
	Mark Ingram, 11-27-94	24

*NFL Record

COACHING HISTORY

(306-202-4)

1966-69	George Wilson	15-39-2
1970-95	Don Shula	274-147-2
1996-97	Jimmy Johnson	17-16-0

PRO PLAYER STADIUM

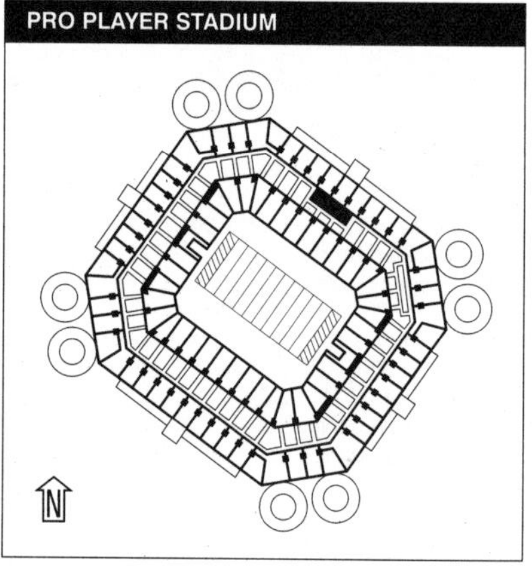

1997 TEAM RECORD

PRESEASON (3-2)

Date	Result		Opponent
7/26	L	0-20	at Green Bay
8/4	W	38-19	vs. Denver at Mexico City, Mexico
8/10	W	21-14	Chicago
8/16	L	10-24	at Tampa Bay
8/21	W	28-7	Washington

REGULAR SEASON (9-7)

Date	Result		Opponent	Att.
8/31	W	16-10	Indianapolis	70,813
9/7	W	16-13	Tennessee (OT)	64,439
9/14	L	18-23	at Green Bay	60,075
9/21	L	21-31	at Tampa Bay	73,314
10/5	W	17-14	Kansas City	71,794
10/12	W	31-20	at New York Jets	75,601
10/19	W	24-13	at Baltimore	64,354
10/27	L	33-36	Chicago (OT)	73,156
11/2	L	6-9	at Buffalo	78,011
11/9	W	24-17	New York Jets	73,809
11/17	W	30-13	Buffalo	74,155
11/23	L	24-27	at New England	59,002
11/30	W	34-16	at Oakland	50,569
12/7	W	33-30	Detroit	72,266
12/14	L	0-41	at Indianapolis	61,282
12/22	L	12-14	New England	74,379

POSTSEASON (0-1)

12/28	L	3-17	at New England	60,041

(OT) Overtime

SCORE BY PERIODS

Dolphins	67	103	49	117	3	—	339
Opponents	43	135	51	95	3	—	327

ATTENDANCE

Home 574,811 Away 522,208 Total 1,097,019
Single-game home record, 75,283 (10/27/96)
Single-season home record, 574,811(1997)

1997 TEAM STATISTICS

	Dolphins	Opp.
Total First Downs	311	299
Rushing	87	106
Passing	199	176
Penalty	25	17
Third Down: Made/Att.	82/217	92/215
Third Down Pct.	37.8	42.8
Fourth Down: Made/Att.	13/23	7/18
Fourth Down Pct.	56.5	38.9
Total Net Yards	5,135	5,364
Avg. Per Game	320.9	335.3
Total Plays	1,028	1,004
Avg. Per Play	5.0	5.3
Net Yards Rushing	1,343	1,813
Avg. Per Game	83.9	113.3
Total Rushes	430	443
Net Yards Passing	3,792	3,551
Avg. Per Game	237.0	221.9
Sacked/Yards Lost	22/153	31/231
Gross Yards	3,945	3,782
Att./Completions	576/332	530/329
Completion Pct.	57.6	62.1
Had Intercepted	12	10
Punts/Average	68/43.6	63/42.5
Net Punting Avg.	68/37.0	63/35.9
Penalties/Yards Lost	93/783	92/892
Fumbles/Ball Lost	23/8	31/17
Touchdowns	37	36
Rushing	18	9
Passing	16	23
Returns	3	4
Avg. Time of Possession	30:29	29:31

1997 INDIVIDUAL STATISTICS

PASSING	Att.	Comp.	Yds.	Pct.	TD	Int.	Tkld.	Rating
Marino	548	319	3,780	58.2	16	11	20/132	80.7
Erickson	28	13	165	46.4	0	1	2/21	50.4
Dolphins	576	332	3,945	57.6	16	12	22/153	79.2
Opponents	530	329	3,782	62.1	23	10	31/231	90.1

SCORING	TD R	TD P	TD Rt	PAT	FG	Saf	PTS
Mare	0	0	0	33/33	28/36	0	117
Abdul-Jabbar	15	1	0	0/0	0/0	0	96
Drayton	0	4	0	0/0	0/0	0	24
Jordan	0	3	0	0/0	0/0	0	18
McDuffie	0	1	1	0/0	0/0	0	12
McPhail	1	1	0	0/0	0/0	0	12
Spikes	2	0	0	0/0	0/0	0	12
L. Thomas	0	2	0	0/0	0/0	0	12
Barnett	0	1	0	0/0	0/0	0	6
Bowens	0	0	1	0/0	0/0	0	6
Buckley	0	0	1	0/0	0/0	0	6
Parmalee	0	1	0	0/0	0/0	0	6
Perriman	0	1	0	0/0	0/0	0	6
Perry	0	1	0	0/0	0/0	0	6
Dolphins	18	16	3	33/33	28/36	0	339
Opponents	9	23	4	30/32	25/35	1	327

2-Point conversions: Team 0-4, Opponents: 2-4.

RUSHING	Att.	Yds.	Avg.	LG	TD
Abdul-Jabbar	283	892	3.2	22	15
Spikes	63	180	2.9	14	2
McPhail	17	146	8.6	71t	1
Parmalee	18	59	3.3	12	0
Phillips	18	44	2.4	8	0
Jordan	3	12	4.0	16	0
Erickson	4	8	2.0	4	0
Pritchett	3	7	2.3	4	0
Kidd	1	4	4.0	4	0
Potts	1	3	3.0	3	0
Nealy	1	2	2.0	2	0
Marino	18	-14	-0.8	1	0
Dolphins	430	1,343	3.1	71t	18
Opponents	443	1,813	4.1	43t	9

RECEIVING	No.	Yds.	Avg.	LG	TD
McDuffie	76	943	12.4	55	1
Drayton	39	558	14.3	30t	4
McPhail	34	262	7.7	19	1
Abdul-Jabbar	29	261	9.0	36t	1
L. Thomas	28	402	14.4	26	2
Parmalee	28	301	10.8	29	1
Jordan	27	471	17.4	44t	3
Perriman	19	309	16.3	26	1
Barnett	17	166	9.8	20	1
Perry	11	45	4.1	10	1
Manning	7	85	12.1	21	0
Spikes	7	70	10.0	24	0
Pritchett	5	35	7.0	17	0
Potts	3	27	9.0	13	0
Dotson	1	4	4.0	4	0
Phillips	1	6	6.0	6	0
Dolphins	332	3,945	11.9	55	16
Opponents	329	3,782	11.5	70	23

INTERCEPTIONS	No.	Yds.	Avg.	LG	TD
Buckley	4	26	6.5	12	0
Teague	2	25	12.5	23	0
Wooden	2	10	5.0	10	0
Madison	1	21	21.0	21	0
Z. Thomas	1	10	10.0	10	0
Dolphins	10	92	9.2	23	0
Opponents	12	307	25.6	100t	4

PUNTING	No.	Yds.	Avg.	In 20	LG
Kidd	52	2,247	43.2	13	58
Richardson	11	480	43.6	0	54
Mare	5	235	47.0	2	53
Dolphins	68	2,962	43.6	15	58
Opponents	63	2,679	42.5	19	65

PUNT RETURNS	No.	FC	Yds.	Avg.	LG	TD
Jordan	26	15	273	10.5	38	0
Buckley	4	0	58	14.5	26	0
McDuffie	2	1	4	2.0	3	0
Dolphins	32	16	335	10.5	38	0
Opponents	43	3	323	7.5	25	0

KICKOFF RETURNS	No.	Yds.	Avg.	LG	TD
Spikes	24	565	23.5	48	0
McPhail	15	314	20.9	39	0
C. Harris	11	224	20.4	34	0
Ismail	8	166	20.8	27	0
A. Harris	1	0	0.0	0	0
Hollier	1	0	0.0	0	0
Jordan	1	6	6.0	6	0
Perry	1	7	7.0	7	0
Potts	1	16	16.0	16	0
Wooden	0	0	—	—	0
Dolphins	63	1,298	20.6	48	0
Opponents	53	1,018	19.2	40	0

FIELD GOALS	1-19	20-29	30-39	40-49	50+
Mare	2/2	14/15	8/10	3/6	1/3
Dolphins	2/2	14/15	8/10	3/6	1/3
Opponents	0/0	11/11	9/12	4/9	1/3

SACKS	No.
Armstrong	5.5
Bowens	5.0
Rodgers	5.0
Taylor	5.0
Burton	4.0
Wilson	2.0
Gardener	1.5
A. Harris	1.0
Stubbs	1.0
Jackson	0.5
Z. Thomas	0.5
Dolphins	31.0
Opponents	22.0

1998 DRAFT CHOICES

Round	Name	Pos.	College
1	John Avery	RB	Mississippi
2	Patrick Surtain	DB	Southern Mississippi
	Kenny Mixon	DE	Louisiana State
3	Brad Jackson	LB	Cincinnati
	Larry Shannon	WR	East Carolina
4	Lorenzo Bromell	DE	Clemson
5	Scott Shaw	G	Michigan State
6	Nathan Strikwerda	C	Northwestern
	John Dutton	QB	Nevada
7	Jim Bundren	G	Clemson

MIAMI DOLPHINS

1998 VETERAN ROSTER

No.	Name	Pos.	Ht.	Wt.	Birthdate	NFL Exp.	College	Hometown	How Acq.	'97 Games/ Starts
33	Abdul-Jabbar, Karim	RB	5-10	197	6/28/74	3	UCLA	Los Angeles, Calif.	D3b-'96	16/14
86	Alexander, Kevin	WR	5-9	185	1/10/74	3	Utah State	Valencia, Calif.	FA(NYG)-'98	14/8*
71	Anderson, Dunstan	DE	6-4	270	12/31/70	2	Tulsa	Ft. Worth, Tex.	FA-'98	9/1
93	Armstrong, Trace	DE	6-4	270	10/5/65	10	Florida	Birmingham, Ala.	T(Chi)-'95	16/16
60	Bock, John	G	6-3	290	2/11/71	4	Indiana State	Crystal Lake, Ill.	FA-'96	14/3
95	Bowens, Tim	DT	6-4	315	2/7/73	5	Mississippi	Okolona, Miss.	D1-'94	16/16
57	Brigance, O.J.	LB	6-0	231	9/29/69	3	Rice	Sugarland, Tex.	FA-'96	16/0
76	Brown, James	T	6-6	329	11/30/70	6	Virginia State	Philadelphia, Pa.	T(NYJ)-'96	16/16
77	Buckey, Jeff	G	6-5	303	8/7/74	3	Stanford	Bakersfield, Calif.	D7a-'96	16/12
27	Buckley, Terrell	CB	5-9	182	6/7/71	7	Florida State	Pascagoula, Miss.	T(GB)-'95	16/16
75	Burton, Shane	DT	6-6	302	1/18/74	3	Tennessee	Catawba, N.C.	D5b-'96	16/4
70	Chalenski, Mike	DE	6-5	278	1/28/70	6	UCLA	Kenilworth, N.J.	FA-'97	8/0
56	Crawford, Mike	LB	6-1	245	10/29/74	2	Nevada	Zephyr Cover, Nev.	D6c-'97	7/0
15	Dar Dar, Kirby	WR	5-9	178	3/27/72	3	Syracuse	Tampa, Fla.	FA-'95	0*
65	Donnalley, Kevin	G	6-5	305	6/10/68	8	North Carolina	Raleigh, N.C.	UFA(Tenn)-'98	16/16*
84	Drayton, Troy	TE	6-3	265	6/29/70	6	Penn State	Steelton, Pa.	T(StL)-'96	16/15
7	Erickson, Craig	QB	6-2	213	5/17/69	7	Miami	West Palm Beach, Fla.	FA-'96	2/0
92	Gardener, Daryl	DT	6-6	315	2/25/73	3	Baylor	Lawton, Okla.	D1-'96	16/16
87	Green, Yatil	WR	6-2	206	11/25/73	2	Miami	Lake City, Fla.	D1-'97	0*
51	Harris, Anthony	LB	6-1	231	1/25/73	3	Auburn	Fort Pierce, Fla.	FA-'96	16/16
25	Harris, Corey	CB	5-11	196	10/25/69	7	Vanderbilt	Indianapolis, Ind.	UFA(Sea)-'97	16/7
50	Hollier, Dwight	LB	6-2	242	4/21/69	7	North Carolina	Hampton, Va.	D4-'92	16/3
11	Huard, Damon	QB	6-3	215	7/9/73	2	Washington	Puyallup, Wash.	FA-'97	0*
53	Izzo, Larry	LB	5-10	236	9/26/74	3	Rice	Houston, Tex.	FA-'96	0*
38	Jackson, Calvin	CB	5-9	201	10/28/72	4	Auburn	Ft. Lauderdale, Fla.	FA-'95	16/16
34	Jacobs, Tim	CB	5-10	185	4/5/70	6	Delaware	Greenbelt, Md.	FA-'96	16/1
43	Jones, Larry	RB	6-0	257	2/16/71	2	Miami	Gainesville, Fla.	FA-'98	0*
88	Jordan, Charles	WR	5-11	184	10/9/69	6	Long Beach City College	Inglewood, Calif.	RFA(GB)-'96	14/1
17	# Kidd, John	P	6-3	215	8/22/61	15	Northwestern	Findlay, Ohio	FA-'94	13/0
48	Kitts, Jim	RB	6-2	244	12/28/72	2	Ferrum College	Chesapeake, Va.	FA-'97	10/0
29	Madison, Sam	CB	5-11	179	4/23/74	2	Louisville	Monticello, Fla.	D2-'97	14/3
83	Manning, Brian	WR	5-11	187	4/22/75	2	Stanford	Kansas City, Mo.	D6b-'97	7/0
10	Mare, Olindo	K	5-10	183	6/6/73	2	Syracuse	Cooper City, Fla.	FA-'97	16/0
13	Marino, Dan	QB	6-4	229	9/15/61	16	Pittsburgh	Pittsburgh, Pa.	D1-'83	16/16
31	Marion, Brock	S	5-11	197	6/11/70	6	Nevada	Bakersfield, Calif.	UFA(Dall)-'98	16/16*
81	McDuffie, O.J.	WR	5-10	184	12/2/69	6	Penn State	Gate Mills, Ohio	D1-'93	16/16
18	McPhail, Jerris	WR	5-11	201	6/26/72	3	East Carolina	Clinton, N.C.	D5a-'96	14/1
30	Parmalee, Bernie	RB	5-11	205	9/16/67	7	Ball State	Jersey City, N.J.	FA-'92	16/4
89	Perry, Ed	TE	6-4	250	9/1/74	2	James Madison	Richmond, Va.	D6d-'97	16/4
21	Phillips, Lawrence	RB	6-0	231	5/12/75	3	Nebraska	Baldwin Park, Calif.	FA-'97	12/9*
36	Pritchett, Stanley	RB	6-1	245	12/12/73	3	South Carolina	College Park, Ga.	D4b-'96	6/5
59	Rodgers, Derrick	LB	6-1	215	10/14/71	2	Arizona State	New Orleans, La.	D3b-'97	15/14
61	Ruddy, Tim	C	6-3	290	4/27/72	5	Notre Dame	Dunmore, Pa.	D2b-'94	15/15
68	Sheldon, Mike	T	6-4	306	6/8/73	2	Grand Valley State	Villa Park, Ill.	FA-'97	11/0
74	Smith, Brent	G	6-5	309	11/21/73	2	Mississippi State	Pontotoc, Miss.	D3d-'97	0*
96	Stubbs, Daniel	DE	6-4	266	1/3/65	10	Miami	Red Bank, N.J.	UFA(Phil)-'96	1/0
72	Tanner, Barron	DT	6-3	310	9/14/73	2	Oklahoma	Athens, Tex.	D5a-'97	16/0
99	Taylor, Jason	DE	6-6	240	9/1/74	2	Akron	Woodland Hills, Pa.	D3a-'97	13/11
85	Thomas, Lamar	WR	6-1	165	2/12/70	6	Miami	Gainesville, Fla.	FA-'96	12/6
54	Thomas, Zach	LB	5-11	235	9/1/73	3	Texas Tech	Pampa, Tex.	D5c-'96	15/15
46	Tucker, Syii	TE	6-4	236	7/31/73	2	Miami	Oklahoma City, Okla.	FA-'98	0*
82	Wainright, Frank	TE	6-3	246	10/10/67	8	Northern Colorado	Arvada, Colo.	FA-'95	9/0
26	Walker, Bracey	S	6-0	200	10/28/70	5	North Carolina	Fayetteville, N.C.	W(Cin)-'97	12/0
45	Walker, Brian	S	6-1	191	5/31/72	3	Washington State	Colorado Springs, Colo.	FA-'97	5/0*
55	Ward, Ronnie	LB	6-0	223	2/11/74	2	Kansas	St. Louis, Mo.	D3c-'97	4/0
78	Webb, Richmond	T	6-6	318	1/11/67	9	Texas A&M	Dallas, Tex.	D1-'90	16/16
14	White, Stan	QB	6-2	209	8/14/71	4	Auburn	Birmingham, Ala.	FA-'98	0*
8	Wilmsmeyer, Klaus	P	6-2	210	12/4/67	6	Louisville	Mississauga, Canada	FA-'98	0*
24	Wilson, Jerry	CB	5-10	188	7/17/73	4	Southern	Lake Charles, La.	FA-'96	16/0
22	Wooden, Shawn	S	5-11	195	10/23/73	3	Notre Dame	Abington, Pa.	D6-'96	16/15

* Alexander played 14 games with N.Y. Giants in '97; Dar Dar, Green, and Izzo missed '97 season because of injury; Donnalley played 16 games with Tennessee; Huard inactive for 15 games; Jones last active with Washington in '95; Marion played 16 games with Dallas; Phillips played 10 games with St. Louis; Smith inactive for 16 games; Tucker last active with Carolina in '96; Brian Walker played 5 games with Washington; White last active with N.Y. Giants in '96; Wilmsmeyer last active with New Orleans in '96.

Unrestricted free agent; subject to developments.

Players lost through free agency (2): G Everett McIver (Dall; 14 games in '97), RB Roosevelt Potts (Balt; 6).

Also played with the Dolphins in '97—WR Fred Barnett (6 games), RB Dewayne Dotson (10), WR Qadry Ismail (3), RB Ray Nealy (1), P Kyle Richardson (3), G Keith Sims (8), RB Irving Spikes (12), S George Teague (15).

COACHING STAFF

Head Coach,
Jimmy Johnson

Pro Career: Begins his eighth season as an NFL head coach and his third with the Miami Dolphins. He has led the Dolphins to a 17-15 regular-season record in his previous two seasons, including a playoff appearance in 1997. Named general manager/head coach of the Dolphins on January 11, 1996, becoming the third head coach in club history. Became the first, and one of only two head coaches ever in football history, to win both a Super Bowl title (Dallas Cowboys - 1992 and 1993) and a national collegiate championship (University of Miami - 1987). Served as head coach of the Cowboys from 1989 through 1993. Became only the third man in NFL history to coach consecutive Super Bowl winners, winning Super Bowl XXVII in 1992 and following that with a victory in Super Bowl XXVIII in 1993. In his five years in Dallas, Johnson led the Cowboys to two NFL championships, with their first title in 1992 coming just three years after the franchise produced a 1-15 mark in 1989. In addition, Johnson's postseason winning percentage of .778 (7-2 record) is the second best in NFL history among coaches with five of more postseason wins, behind only Vince Lombardi's mark of .900 (9-1). Career record: 68-53.

Background: At the University of Miami (1984-88), Johnson led the Hurricanes to a 52-9 (.853) record, including a 44-4 mark over the final four seasons. His Hurricane teams also captured two Orange Bowl titles, a national championship in 1987, and two number two finishes (1986, 1988). In his first head coaching job, Johnson took over a losing program at Oklahoma State in 1979 and brought it to national prominence, compiling a 29-25 record in five seasons, including two bowl appearances. Johnson was named Big Eight Coach of the Year following his first season. Served as assistant head coach/defensive coordinator at Pittsburgh (1977-78), defensive coordinator at Arkansas (1973-76), defensive line coach at Oklahoma (1970-72), defensive coordinator at Iowa State (1968-69), assistant coach at Wichita State (1967), and defensive line coach at Louisiana Tech (1965). Before beginning his coaching career, Johnson was an All-Southwest Conference defensive lineman at Arkansas and helped lead the Razorbacks to the 1964 national championship. A three-year letterman, Johnson was named to Arkansas' All-Decade Team of the 1960s.

Personal: Born July 16, 1943, in Port Arthur, Texas. Lives in Miami. He has two sons, Brent and Chad.

ASSISTANT COACHES

Larry Beightol, offensive line; born November 21, 1942, Morrisville, Pa., lives in Plantation, Fla. Guard-linebacker Catawba College 1961-63. No pro playing experience. College coach: William & Mary 1968-71, North Carolina State 1972-75, Auburn 1976, Arkansas 1977-78, 1980-82, Louisiana Tech 1979 (head coach), Missouri 1983-84. Pro coach: Atlanta Falcons 1985-86, Tampa Bay Buccaneers 1987-88, San Diego Chargers 1989, New York Jets 1990-94, Houston Oilers 1995, joined Dolphins in 1996.

Doug Blevins, kicking; born August 3, 1963, Abingdon, Va., lives in Vero Beach, Fla. No college or pro playing experience. College coach: Tennessee 1982-83, Emory & Henry College 1984-85, East Tennessee State 1986-87. Pro coach: World League kicking coordinator 1995-97, joined Dolphins in 1997.

Kippy Brown, offensive coordinator; born March 6, 1955, Sweetwater, Tenn., lives in Plantation, Fla. Quarterback Memphis State 1974-77. No pro playing experience. College coach: Memphis State 1978-80, Louisville 1982, Tennessee 1983-89, 1993-94. Pro coach: New York Jets 1990-92, Tampa Bay Buccaneers 1995, joined Dolphins in 1996.

Joel Collier, running backs; born December 25, 1963, Buffalo, N.Y., lives in Plantation, Fla. Linebacker Northern Colorado 1984-87. No pro playing experience. College coach: Syracuse 1988-89. Pro coach: Tampa Bay Buccaneers 1990, New England Patriots 1991-93, joined Dolphins in 1994.

Robert Ford, wide receivers; born June 21, 1951, Belton, Texas, lives in Miami. Wide receiver Houston 1970-72. No pro playing experience. College coach: Western Illinois 1974-76, New Mexico 1977-79, Oregon State 1980-81, Mississippi State 1982-83, Kansas 1986, Texas Tech 1987-88, Texas A&M 1989-90. Pro coach: Houston Gamblers (USFL) 1985, Dallas Cowboys 1991-97, joined Dolphins in 1998.

John Gamble, strength and conditioning; born June 26, 1957, Richmond, Va., lives in Weston, Fla. Linebacker Hampton Institute 1975-78. No pro playing experience. College coach: Virginia 1982-93. Pro coach: Joined Dolphins in 1994.

Cary Godette, defensive line; born March 20, 1954, New Bern, N.C., lives in Plantation, Fla. Defensive end East Carolina 1973-76. No pro playing experience. College coach: East Carolina 1977-79, 1990-91, Wyoming 1980-82, Cincinnati 1983-88, Georgia Tech 1992-93, North Carolina State 1994. Pro coach: Carolina Panthers 1995, joined Dolphins in 1996.

George Hill, defensive coordinator-linebackers; born April 28, 1933, Bay Village, Ohio, lives in Plantation, Fla. Tackle-fullback Denison 1954-57. No pro playing experience. College coach: Findlay 1959, Denison 1960-64, Cornell 1965, Duke 1966-70, Ohio State 1971-78. Pro coach: Philadelphia Eagles 1979-84, Indianapolis Colts 1985-88, joined Dolphins in 1989.

Pat Jones, tight ends; born November 4, 1947, Memphis, Tenn., lives in Ft. Lauderdale, Fla. Nose guard Arkansas Tech 1965, linebacker-nose guard Arkansas 1966-67. No pro playing experience. College coach: Arkansas 1974-75, Southern Methodist 1976-77, Pittsburgh 1978, Oklahoma State 1979-94 (1984-94 head coach). Pro coach: Joined Dolphins in 1996.

Bill Lewis, defensive nickel package; born August 5, 1941, Bristol, Pa., lives in Ft. Lauderdale, Fla. Quarterback East Stroudsburg State 1959-62. No pro playing experience. College coach: East Stroudsburg State 1963-65, Pittsburgh 1966-68, Wake Forest 1969-70, Georgia Tech 1971-72, 1992-94 (head coach), Arkansas 1973-76, Wyoming 1977-79, Georgia 1980-88, East Carolina 1989-91 (head coach). Pro coach: Joined Dolphins in 1996.

Rich McGeorge, assistant offensive line; born September 14, 1948, Roanoke, Va., lives in Plantation, Fla. Tight end Elon College 1966-69. Pro tight end Green Bay Packers 1970-78. College coach: Duke 1981-82, 1987-89, Florida 1990-92. Pro coach: Birmingham Stallions (USFL) 1983-84, Tampa Bay Bandits (USFL) 1985, joined Dolphins in 1993.

Mel Phillips, secondary; born January 6, 1942, Shelby, N.C., lives in Miami Lakes, Fla. Defensive back-running back North Carolina A&T 1964-65. Pro defensive back San Francisco 49ers 1966-77. Pro coach: Detroit Lions 1980-84, joined Dolphins in 1985.

Brad Roll, assistant strength and conditioning; born July 4, 1958, Houston, Tex., lives in Ft. Lauderdale, Fla. Center Blinn (Tex.) J.C. 1976-77, Stephen F. Austin 1978-79. No pro playing experience. College coach: Stephen F. Austin 1980, Southwestern Louisiana 1981-86, Kansas 1987-88, Miami 1989-92. Pro coach: Tampa Bay Buccaneers 1993-95, joined Dolphins in 1996.

Larry Seiple, quarterbacks; born February 14, 1945, Allentown, Pa., lives in Pembroke Pines, Fla. Running back-receiver-punter Kentucky 1964-66. Pro punter-tight end-receiver-running back Miami Dolphins 1966-77. College coach: Miami 1978-79. Pro coach: Detroit Lions 1980-84, Tampa Bay Buccaneers 1985-86, joined Dolphins in 1988.

Randy Shannon, defensive assistant; born February 24, 1966, Miami, lives in Miami. Linebacker Miami 1985-88. Pro linebacker Dallas Cowboys 1989-90. College coach: Miami 1991-97. Pro coach: Joined Dolphins in 1998.

Mike Westhoff, special teams; born January 10, 1948, Pittsburgh, Pa., lives in Plantation, Fla. Center-linebacker Wichita State 1967-69. No pro playing experience. College coach: Indiana 1974-75, Dayton 1976, Indiana State 1977, Northwestern 1978-80, Texas Christian 1981. Pro coach: Baltimore/Indianapolis Colts 1982-84, Arizona Outlaws (USFL) 1985, joined Dolphins in 1986.

1998 FIRST-YEAR ROSTER

Name	Pos.	Ht.	Wt.	Birthdate	College	Hometown	How Acq.
Avery, John	RB	5-9	184	1/11/76	Mississippi	Asheville, N.C.	D1
Baker, Jon (1)	K	6-1	170	8/13/72	Arizona State	Bakersfield, Calif.	FA
Bromell, Lorenzo	DE	6-6	265	9/23/75	Clemson	Chopee, S.C.	D4
Bundren, Jim	G	6-3	303	10/6/74	Clemson	Wilmington, Del.	D7
Celaj, Ken	G	6-4	317	9/7/74	Georgia Tech	Westchester, N.Y.	FA
Cochran, Nate (1)	P	6-5	215	4/26/75	Pittsburgh	Greenville, S.C.	FA
Dixon, Mark (1)	T	6-4	285	11/6/70	Virginia	Jamestown, N.C.	FA
Dutton, John	QB	6-4	219	9/20/75	Nevada	Fallbrook, Calif.	D6b
Fontenot, Chris	TE	6-3	247	7/11/74	McNeese State	Iota, La.	FA
Jackson, Brad	LB	6-0	220	1/11/75	Cincinnati	Akron, Ohio	D3a
Miller, Selvesta	LB	6-2	259	7/7/75	South Carolina	Columbia, S.C.	FA
Mixon, Kenny	DE	6-4	270	5/31/75	Louisiana State	Pineville, La.	D2b
Mosley, Denorse (1)	CB	6-0	177	2/15/75	Edinboro	Pahokee, Fla.	FA-'97
Nealy, Ray (1)	RB	5-11	230	4/30/75	Arkansas-Pine Bluff	Little Rock, Ark.	FA-'97
Shannon, Larry	WR	6-4	220	2/2/75	East Carolina	Starke, Fla.	D3b
Shaw, Scott	G	6-3	303	6/2/74	Michigan State	Sterling Heights, Mich.	D5
Shepard, Derrick	DT	6-2	292	5/29/75	Georgia Tech	Dayton, Ohio	FA
Simpson, Antoine	DT	6-2	307	12/7/76	Houston	LaPorte, Texas	FA
Smith, Landon	RB	5-11	245	8/16/76	Cincinnati	Madison, Miss.	FA
Steagall, Derrick	WR	6-0	207	1/21/74	Georgia Tech	Newnan, Ga.	FA
Stokes, Barry (1)	T	6-4	312	12/20/73	Eastern Michigan	Davison, Mich.	FA
Strikwerda, Nathan	C	6-3	295	8/20/75	Northwestern	Madison, Wis.	D6a
Surtain, Patrick	CB	5-11	195	5/19/76	Southern Mississippi	New Orleans, La.	D2a
Turner, Geoff	WR	5-8	190	9/12/74	Colorado State	Urbandale, Iowa	FA
Wheeler, Randy (1)	G	6-2	320	5/4/75	South Carolina	Hartsville, S.C.	FA
White, Raymond	DT	6-2	285	10/19/74	Clemson	Clinton, Miss.	FA

The term NFL Rookie is defined as a player who is in his first season of professional football and has not been on the roster of another professional football team for any regular-season or postseason games. A Rookie is designated by an "R" on NFL rosters. Players who have been active in another professional football league or players who have NFL experience, including either preseason training camp or being on an Active List or Inactive List, or on Reserve/Injured or Reserve/Physically Unable to Perform for fewer than six regular-season games, are termed NFL First-Year Players. An NFL First-Year Player is designated by a "1" on NFL rosters. Thereafter, a player is credited with an additional year of experience for each season in which he accumulates six games on the Active List or Inactive List, or on Reserve/Injured or Reserve/Physically Unable to Perform.

NOTES

NEW ENGLAND PATRIOTS

American Football Conference
Eastern Division
Team Colors: Blue, Red, Silver, and White
Foxboro Stadium
60 Washington Street
Foxboro, Massachusetts 02035
Telephone: (508) 543-8200

CLUB OFFICIALS

Owner/Chief Executive Officer: Robert K. Kraft
Vice President-Owner's Representative: Jonathan A. Kraft
Vice President-Business Operations: Andrew Wasynczuk
Vice President of Player Personnel: Bobby Grier
Vice President of Marketing and Broadcast Sales: Daniel A. Kraft
Vice President-Finance: James Hausmann
Vice President of Player Develoment and Community Affairs: Donald Lowery
Dir. of Marketing & Special Events: Lou Imbriano
Director of Media Relations: Stacey James
Director of Football Operations: Ken Deininger
Controller: Jim Nolan
Director of Pro Scouting: Dave Uyrus
Director of Ticketing: Mike Nichols
General Manager of Foxboro Stadium: Dan Murphy
Building Services Manager: Bernie Reinhart
Head Trainer: Ron O'Neil
Equipment Manager: Don Brocher
Video Director: Jimmy Dee
Stadium: Foxboro Stadium • **Capacity:** 60,292
60 Washington Street
Foxboro, Massachusetts 02035
Playing Surface: Grass
Training Camp: Bryant College
Route 7
Smithfield, Rhode Island 02917

1998 SCHEDULE

PRESEASON

Aug. 2	at San Francisco	3:00
Aug. 9	**Minnesota**	7:30
Aug. 17	vs. Dallas at Mexico City, Mexico	8:00
Aug. 22	at Washington	7:30
Aug. 29	**Philadelphia**	8:00

REGULAR SEASON

Sept. 7	at Denver (Mon.)	6:20
Sept. 13	**Indianapolis**	8:20
Sept. 20	**Tennessee**	1:01
Sept. 27	Open Date	
Oct. 4	at New Orleans	12:01
Oct. 11	**Kansas City**	1:01
Oct. 19	**New York Jets** (Mon.)	8:20
Oct. 25	at Miami	1:01
Nov. 1	at Indianapolis	1:01
Nov. 8	**Atlanta**	1:01
Nov. 15	at Buffalo	1:01
Nov. 23	**Miami** (Mon.)	8:20
Nov. 29	**Buffalo**	4:05
Dec. 6	at Pittsburgh	1:01
Dec. 13	at St. Louis	12:01
Dec. 20	**San Francisco**	1:01
Dec. 27	at New York Jets	1:01

RECORD HOLDERS

INDIVIDUAL RECORDS—CAREER

Category	Name	Performance
Rushing (Yds.)	Sam Cunningham, 1973-79, 1981-82	5,453
Passing (Yds.)	Steve Grogan, 1975-1990	26,886
Passing (TDs)	Steve Grogan, 1975-1990	182
Receiving (No.)	Stanley Morgan, 1977-1989	534
Receiving (Yds.)	Stanley Morgan, 1977-1989	10,352
Interceptions	Raymond Clayborn, 1977-1989	36
Punting (Avg.)	Tom Tupa, 1996-97	44.7
Punt Return (Avg.)	Mack Herron, 1973-75	12.0
Kickoff Return (Avg.)	Allen Carter, 1975-76	27.2
Field Goals	Gino Cappelletti, 1960-1970	176
Touchdowns (Tot.)	Stanley Morgan, 1977-1989	68
Points	Gino Cappelletti, 1960-1970	1,130

INDIVIDUAL RECORDS—SINGLE SEASON

Category	Name	Performance
Rushing (Yds.)	Curtis Martin, 1995	1,487
Passing (Yds.)	Drew Bledsoe, 1994	4,555
Passing (TDs)	Vito (Babe) Parilli, 1964	31
Receiving (No.)	Ben Coates, 1994	96
Receiving (Yds.)	Stanley Morgan, 1986	1,491
Interceptions	Ron Hall, 1964	11
Punting (Avg.)	Tom Tupa, 1997	45.8
Punt Return (Avg.)	Mack Herron, 1974	14.8
Kickoff Return (Avg.)	Raymond Clayborn, 1977	31.0
Field Goals	Tony Franklin, 1986	32
Touchdowns (Tot.)	Curtis Martin, 1996	17
Points	Gino Cappelletti, 1964	155

INDIVIDUAL RECORDS—SINGLE GAME

Category	Name	Performance
Rushing (Yds.)	Tony Collins, 9-18-83	212
Passing (Yds.)	Drew Bledsoe, 11-13-94	426
Passing (TDs)	Vito (Babe) Parilli, 11-15-64	5
	Vito (Babe) Parilli, 10-15-67	5
	Steve Grogan, 9-9-79	5
Receiving (No.)	Ben Coates, 11-27-94	12
Receiving (Yds.)	Stanley Morgan, 11-8-81	182
Interceptions	Many times	3
	Last time by Roland James, 10-23-83	
Field Goals	Gino Cappelletti, 10-4-64	6
Touchdowns (Tot.)	Many times	3
	Last time by Curtis Martin, 11-3-96	
Points	Gino Cappelletti, 12-18-65	28

COACHING HISTORY

BOSTON 1960-1970
(265-306-9)

1960-61	Lou Saban*	7-12-0
1961-68	Mike Holovak	53-47-9
1969-70	Clive Rush**	5-16-0
1970-72	John Mazur***	9-21-0
1972	Phil Bengtson	1-4-0
1973-78	Chuck Fairbanks****	46-41-0
1978	Hank Bullough-Ron Erhardt#	0-1-0
1979-81	Ron Erhardt	21-27-0
1982-84	Ron Meyer##	18-16-0
1984-89	Raymond Berry	51-41-0
1990	Rod Rust	1-15-0
1991-92	Dick MacPherson	8-24-0
1993-96	Bill Parcells	34-34-0
1997	Pete Carroll	11-7-0

*Released after five games in 1961
**Released after seven games in 1970
***Resigned after nine games in 1972
****Suspended for final regular-season game in 1978
#Co-coaches
##Released after eight games in 1984

FOXBORO STADIUM

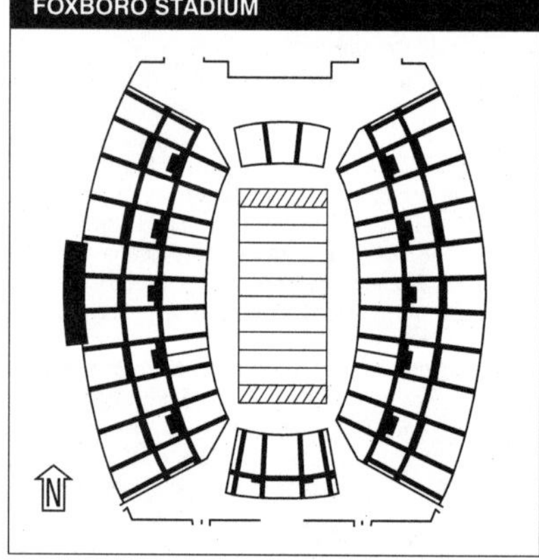

1997 TEAM RECORD

PRESEASON (3-1)

Date	Result		Opponents
7/31	L	3-7	at Green Bay
8/8	W	16-10	Dallas
8/17	W	31-21	Denver
8/21	W	23-14	at Philadelphia

REGULAR SEASON (10-6)

Date	Result		Opponent	Att.
8/31	W	41-7	San Diego	60,190
9/7	W	31-6	at Indianapolis	53,632
9/14	W	27-24	New York Jets (OT)	60,072
9/21	W	31-3	Chicago	59,873
10/6	L	13-34	at Denver	75,821
10/12	W	33-6	Buffalo	59,802
10/19	L	19-24	at New York Jets	71,061
10/27	L	10-28	Green Bay	59,972
11/2	L	18-23	at Minnesota	62,917
11/9	W	31-10	at Buffalo	65,783
11/16	L	7-27	at Tampa Bay	70,479
11/23	W	27-24	Miami	59,002
11/30	W	20-17	Indianapolis	58,507
12/7	W	26-20	at Jacksonville	73,446
12/13	L	21-24	Pittsburgh (OT)	60,013
12/22	W	14-12	at Miami	74,379

POSTSEASON (1-1)

Date	Result		Opponent	Att.
12/28	W	17-3	Miami	60,041
1/3	L	6-7	at Pittsburgh	61,228

(OT) Overtime

SCORE BY PERIODS

Patriots	82	126	61	97	3	— 369
Opponents	60	39	89	98	3	— 289

ATTENDANCE

Home 477,431 Away 547,518 Total 1,024,949

Single-game home record, 61,457 (12/5/71)

Single-season home record, 482,572 (1986)

1997 TEAM STATISTICS

	Patriots	Opp.
Total First Downs	267	322
Rushing	71	114
Passing	173	183
Penalty	23	25
Third Down: Made/Att	88/218	90/233
Third Down Pct.	40.4	38.6
Fourth Down: Made/Att	3/13	16/30
Fourth Down Pct.	23.1	53.3
Total Net Yards	5,014	5,085
Avg. Per Game	313.4	317.8
Total Plays	960	1,100
Avg. Per Play	5.2	4.6
Net Yards Rushing	1,464	1,616
Avg. Per Game	91.5	101.0
Total Rushes	398	436
Net Yards Passing	3,550	3,469
Avg. Per Game	221.9	216.8
Sacked/Yards Lost	30/258	45/303
Gross Yards	3,808	3,772
Att./Completions	532/321	619/368
Completion Pct.	60.3	59.5
Had Intercepted	15	19
Punts/Average	79/45.2	74/44.4
Net Punting Avg.	79/36.1	74/36.5
Penalties/Yards Lost	99/845	106/763
Fumbles/Ball Lost	17/7	29/13
Touchdowns	42	33
Rushing	6	16
Passing	31	14
Returns	5	3
Avg. Time of Possession	28:08	31:52

1997 INDIVIDUAL STATISTICS

PASSING	Att.	Comp.	Yds.	Pct.	TD	Int.	Tkld.	Rating
Bledsoe	522	314	3,706	60.2	28	15	30/258	87.7
Zolak	9	6	67	66.7	2	0	0/0	128.2
Meggett	1	1	35	100.0	1	0	0/0	158.3
Patriots	532	321	3,808	60.3	31	15	30/258	89.9
Opponents	619	368	3,772	59.5	14	19	45/303	71.8

SCORING	TD R	TD P	TD Rt	PAT	FG	Saf	PTS
Vinatieri	0	0	0	40/40	25/29	0	115
Coates	0	8	0	0/0	0/0	0	48
T. Brown	0	6	0	0/0	0/0	0	36
Martin	4	1	0	0/0	0/0	0	30
Byars	0	3	0	0/0	0/0	0	18
Gash	0	3	0	0/0	0/0	0	18
Purnell	0	3	0	0/0	0/0	0	18
Brisby	0	2	0	0/0	0/0	0	12
Glenn	0	2	0	0/0	0/0	0	12
Jefferson	0	2	0	0/0	0/0	0	12
Meggett	1	1	0	0/0	0/0	0	12
Clay	0	0	1	0/0	0/0	0	6
Cullors	0	0	1	0/0	0/0	0	6
Grier	1	0	0	0/0	0/0	0	6
Hitchcock	0	0	1	0/0	0/0	0	6
Slade	0	0	1	0/0	0/0	0	6
Whigham	0	0	1	0/0	0/0	0	6
Patriots	6	31	5	40/40	25/29	1	369
Opponents	16	14	3	29/29	20/29	0	289

2-Point conversions: Team 0-2, Opponents: 1-4.

RUSHING	Att.	Yds.	Avg.	LG	TD
Martin	274	1,160	4.2	70t	4
Cullors	22	101	4.6	24	0
Grier	33	75	2.3	12	1
Meggett	20	60	3.0	10	1
Bledsoe	28	55	2.0	8	0
Byars	11	24	2.2	5	0
Gash	6	10	1.7	4	0
Zolak	3	-3	-1.0	-1	0
T. Brown	1	-18	-18.0	-18	0
Patriots	398	1,464	3.7	70t	6
Opponents	436	1,616	3.7	34	16

RECEIVING	No.	Yds.	Avg.	LG	TD
Coates	66	737	11.2	35	8
Jefferson	54	841	15.6	76	2
T. Brown	41	607	14.8	67	6
Martin	41	296	7.2	22	1
Glenn	27	431	16.0	50	2
Brisby	23	276	12.0	31	2
Gash	22	154	7.0	19	3
Byars	20	189	9.5	51	3
Meggett	19	203	10.7	49t	1
Purnell	5	57	11.4	20t	3
Cullors	2	8	4.0	6	0
Jells	1	9	9.0	9	0
Patriots	321	3,808	11.9	76	31
Opponents	368	3,772	10.3	51	14

INTERCEPTIONS	No.	Yds.	Avg.	LG	TD
Clay	6	109	18.2	53t	1
Law	3	70	23.3	40	0
Milloy	3	15	5.0	15	0
Hitchcock	2	104	52.0	100t	1
Whigham	2	60	30.0	60t	1
Moore	2	7	3.5	7	0
Slade	1	1	1.0	1t	1
Patriots	19	366	19.3	100t	4
Opponents	15	213	14.2	45	2

PUNTING	No.	Yds.	Avg.	In 20	LG
Tupa	78	3,569	45.8	24	73
Patriots	79	3,569	45.2	24	73
Opponents	74	3,288	44.4	17	66

PUNT RETURNS	No.	FC	Yds.	Avg.	LG	TD
Meggett	45	8	467	10.4	47	0
Patriots	45	8	467	10.4	47	0
Opponents	38	11	437	11.5	26	0

KICKOFF RETURNS	No.	Yds.	Avg.	LG	TD
Meggett	33	816	24.7	61	0
Cullors	15	386	25.7	86t	1
Canty	4	115	28.8	63	0
Coates	1	20	20.0	20	0
Patriots	53	1,337	25.2	86t	1
Opponents	75	1,651	22.0	92t	1

FIELD GOALS	1-19	20-29	30-39	40-49	50+
Vinatieri	0/0	11/11	7/9	6/8	1/1
Patriots	0/0	11/11	7/9	6/8	1/1
Opponents	0/0	7/8	7/10	5/8	1/3

SACKS	No.
Slade	9.0
Thomas	7.0
Bruschi	4.0
Johnson	4.0
Jones	4.0
Wheeler	4.0
Canty	2.0
McGinest	2.0
Whigham	2.0
Collins	1.5
Collons	1.0
Eaton	1.0
Israel	1.0
McGruder	1.0
Law	0.5
Patriots	45.0
Opponents	30.0

1998 DRAFT CHOICES

Round	Name	Pos.	College
1	Robert Edwards	RB	Georgia
	Tebucky Jones	DB	Syracuse
2	Tony Simmons	WR	Wisconsin
	Rod Rutledge	TE	Alabama
3	Chris Floyd	RB	Michigan
	Greg Spires	DE	Florida State
4	Leonta Rheams	DT	Houston
5	Ron Merkerson	LB	Colorado
6	Harold Shaw	RB	Southern Mississippi
7	Jason Andersen	C	Brigham Young

NEW ENGLAND PATRIOTS

1998 VETERAN ROSTER

No.	Name	Pos.	Ht.	Wt.	Birthdate	NFL Exp.	College	Hometown	How Acq.	'97 Games/ Starts
78	Armstrong, Bruce	T	6-4	295	9/7/65	12	Louisville	Miami, Fla.	D1-'87	16/16
86	Bartrum, Mike	TE	6-5	245	6/23/70	5	Marshall	Pomeroy, Ohio	T(GB)-'95	9/0
11	Bledsoe, Drew	QB	6-0	233	2/14/72	6	Washington State	Walla Walla, Wash.	D1-'93	16/16
82	Brisby, Vincent	WR	6-3	193	1/25/71	6	Northeast Louisiana	Lake Charles, La.	D2c-'93	16/4
80	Brown, Troy	WR	5-10	190	7/2/71	6	Marshall	Blackville, S.C.	D8-'93	16/6
54	Bruschi, Tedy	LB	6-1	245	6/9/73	3	Arizona	Roseville, Calif.	D3-'96	16/1
26	Canty, Chris	CB	5-9	185	3/30/76	2	Kansas State	Voorhees, N.J.	D1-'97	16/1
42	Carter, Chris	S	6-1	201	9/27/74	2	Texas	Tyler, Tex.	D3b-'97	16/0
30	Carter, Tony	RB	5-11	236	8/23/72	4	Minnesota	Columbus, Ohio	UFA(Chi)-'98	16/10*
32	Clay, Willie	S	5-10	200	9/5/70	7	Georgia Tech	Pittsburgh, Pa.	UFA-'96	16/16
87	Coates, Ben	TE	6-5	245	8/16/69	8	Livingstone College	Greenwood, S.C.	D5b-'91	16/16
59	Collins, Todd	LB	6-2	248	5/27/70	6	Carson-Newman	New Market, Tenn.	D3a-'92	15/15
92	Collons, Ferric	DE	6-6	285	12/4/69	5	California	Sacramento, Calif.	T(GB)-'95	5/5
99	Crawford, Vernon	LB	6-3	245	6/25/74	2	Florida State	Texas City, Tex.	D5-'97	16/0
29	Cullors, Derrick	RB	5-11	205	12/26/72	2	Murray State	Dallas, Tex.	FA-'97	15/1
61	Denson, Damon	G	6-3	305	2/8/75	2	Michigan	Pittsburgh, Pa.	D4a-'97	1/0
90	Eaton, Chad	DT	6-5	300	4/6/72	2	Washington State	Puyallup, Wash.	FA-'96	16/1
66	Ellis, Ed	T	6-7	340	10/13/75	2	Buffalo	Hamden, Conn.	D4b-'97	1/0
88	Glenn, Terry	WR	5-11	185	7/23/74	3	Ohio State	Columbus, Ohio	D1-'96	9/9
35	Grier, Marrio	RB	5-10	229	12/5/71	3	Tennessee-Chattanooga	Charlotte, N.C.	D6b-'96	16/0
63	Irwin, Heath	G	6-4	300	6/27/73	3	Colorado	Boulder, Colo.	D4a-'96	16/1
21	Israel, Steve	CB	5-11	194	3/16/69	7	Pittsburgh	Haddon Heights, N.J.	UFA(SF)-'97	5/0
84	Jefferson, Shawn	WR	5-11	180	2/22/69	8	Central Florida	Jacksonville, Fla.	FA-'96	16/14
83	Jells, Dietrich	WR	5-10	186	4/11/72	3	Pittsburgh	Erie, Pa.	W(KC)-'96	11/0
52	Johnson, Ted	LB	6-3	240	12/4/72	4	Colorado	Carlsbad, Calif.	D2-'95	16/16
96	Jones, Mike	DE-DT	6-4	280	8/25/69	8	North Carolina State	Columbus, Ohio	FA-'94	16/7
68	Lane, Max	G	6-6	305	2/22/71	5	Navy	Norborne, Mo.	D6b-'94	16/16
24	Law, Ty	CB	5-11	200	2/10/74	4	Michigan	Aliquippa, Pa.	D1-'95	16/16
38	Lofton, Steve	CB	5-9	177	11/26/68	7	Texas A&M	Jacksonville, Fla.	FA-'97	4/0
55	McGinest, Willie	DE	6-5	255	12/11/71	5	Southern Cal	Long Beach, Calif.	D1-'94	11/11
36	Milloy, Lawyer	S	6-1	208	11/14/73	3	Washington	Tacoma, Wash.	D2-'96	16/16
98	Mitchell, Brandon	DE	6-3	289	6/19/75	2	Texas A&M	Abbeville, La.	D2-'97	12/0
58	Moore, Marty	LB	6-1	244	3/19/71	5	Kentucky	Fort Thomas, Ky.	D7b-'94	16/0
77	Moss, Zefross	T	6-6	325	8/17/66	10	Alabama	Holt, Ala.	UFA(Det)-'97	15/15
85	Purnell, Lovett	TE	6-3	245	4/7/72	3	West Virginia	Seaford, Del.	D7a-'96	16/2
60	Rehberg, Scott	T	6-8	336	11/17/73	2	Central Michigan	Kalamazoo, Mich.	D7-'97	6/0
71	Rucci, Todd	G	6-5	296	7/14/70	6	Penn State	Upper Darby, Pa.	D2b-'93	16/16
23	Shaw, Sedrick	RB	6-1	214	11/16/73	2	Iowa	Austin, Tex.	D3a-'97	1/0
53	Slade, Chris	LB	6-5	245	1/30/71	6	Virginia	Newport News, Va.	D2a-'93	16/16
70	Smith, Artie	DT	6-5	305	5/15/70	5	Louisiana Tech	Stillwater, Okla.	FA-'98	0*
81	Stablein, Brian	WR	6-1	193	4/14/70	5	Ohio State	Erie, Pa.	UFA(Ind)-'98	16/0*
74	Sullivan, Chris	DE	6-4	279	3/14/73	3	Boston College	North Attleboro, Mass.	D4b-'96	16/10
95	Thomas, Henry	DT	6-2	277	1/12/65	12	Louisiana State	Houston, Tex.	FA-'97	16/16
19	Tupa, Tom	P-QB	6-4	220	2/6/66	10	Ohio State	Cleveland, Ohio	UFA(Balt)-'96	16/0
4	Vinatieri, Adam	K	6-0	200	12/28/72	3	South Dakota State	Rapid City, S.D.	FA-'96	16/0
97	Wheeler, Mark	DT	6-3	285	4/1/70	7	Texas A&M	San Marcos, Tex.	UFA(TB)-'96	14/14
25	Whigham, Larry	S	6-2	205	6/23/72	5	Northeast Louisiana	Hattiesburg, Miss.	FA-'94	16/0
64	Wohlabaugh, Dave	C	6-3	292	4/13/72	4	Syracuse	Hamburg, N.Y.	D4-'95	14/14
72	Wyman, Devin	DT	6-7	290	8/29/73	3	Kentucky State	East Palo Alto, Calif.	D6c-'96	6/0
16	Zolak, Scott	QB	6-5	235	12/13/67	8	Maryland	Monongahela, Pa.	D4-'91	4/0

* T. Carter played 16 games with Chicago in '97; Smith last active with Cincinnati in '96; Stablein played 16 games with Indianapolis.

Traded—CB Jimmy Hitchcock (15 games in '97) to Minnesota.

Players lost to free agency (4): RB Keith Byars (NYJ; 16 games), RB Sam Gash (Buff; 16), C Mike Gisler (NYJ; 16), RB Curtis Martin (NYJ; 13).

Also played with Patriots in '97—CB Mike McGruder (3 games), RB David Meggett (16), C Danny Villa (7).

COACHING STAFF

Head Coach,
Pete Carroll

Pro Career: Pete Carroll was named the thirteenth head coach in franchise history on February 3, 1997. In his first season at the helm, the Patriots repeated as division champions and fell just two points shy of hosting their second consecutive AFC Championship Game. The Patriots had a 17-3 victory over Miami in the first round of the playoffs, but were eliminated from playoff contention the following week at Pittsburgh, 7-6. Prior to joining the Patriots, Carroll served two seasons as the defensive coordinator for the San Francisco 49ers. Under Carroll's guidance, the 1995 49ers defense ranked first in the league in total defense, rushing defense, and scoring defense and were credited with a league-leading 26 interceptions. Carroll joined the 49ers after five seasons with the New York Jets. His tenure in New York began in 1990 when he was named defensive coordinator. In 1994, the Jets named Carroll as their ninth head coach in franchise history. That year, the Jets were in contention for the AFC East title through the first 11 games of the season. Despite the early success the Jets enjoyed that year, Carroll was relieved of his duties after just one rebuilding season. He began his NFL coaching career in 1984 with the Buffalo Bills. The following year, he joined Bud Grant's staff in Minnesota and spent the next five seasons (1985-89) as the defensive backs coach for the Vikings. Career record: 17-17.

Background: Carroll began his coaching career at Pacific in 1974 at the age of 22. He coached three seasons at Pacific before moving on, gaining coaching experience at Arkansas (1977), Iowa State (1978), and Ohio State (1979) before settling in at North Carolina State in 1980. For the next three seasons (1980-82), Carroll directed the Wolfpack's defense before returning to his alma mater for one year as the assistant head coach in 1983.

Personal: Carroll was born September 15, 1951, in San Francisco. He was a football standout at Redwood High School prior to attending the University of Pacific, where he twice earned All-Pacific Coast Conference honors as a defensive back. He had a tryout with the Hawaiians of the World Football League before pursuing a coaching career. He and his wife, Glena, live in Medfield, Mass., and have two sons, Brennan and Nathan, and a daughter, Jaime.

ASSISTANT COACHES

Paul Boudreau, offensive line; born December 30, 1949, Arlington, Mass., lives in Wrentham, Mass. Guard Boston College 1971-73. No pro playing experience. College coach: Boston College 1975-76, Maine 1977-79, Dartmouth 1980-82, Navy 1983. Pro coach: Edmonton Eskimos (CFL) 1983-86, New Orleans Saints 1987-93, Detroit Lions 1994-96, joined Patriots in 1997.

Jeff Davidson, offensive assistant-offensive line; born October 3, 1967, Akron, Ohio, lives in Franklin, Mass. Offensive lineman Ohio State 1986-89. Pro offensive lineman Denver Broncos 1990-92, New Orleans Saints 1994. Pro coach: New Orleans Saints 1995-96, joined Patriots in 1997.

Ray Hamilton, defensive line; born January 20, 1951, Omaha, Neb., lives in Sharon, Mass. Nose tackle Oklahoma 1969-72. Pro nose tackle-defensive end New England Patriots 1973-81. College coach: Tennessee 1992. Pro coach: New England Patriots 1985-89, Tampa Bay Buccaneers 1991, Los Angeles Raiders 1993-94, New York Jets 1995-96, rejoined Patriots in 1997.

Ron Lynn, defensive backs; born December 6, 1944, Youngstown, Ohio, lives in Dover, Mass. Quarterback-defensive back Mt. Union (Ohio) 1962-65. No pro playing experience. College coach: Toledo 1966, Mt. Union (Ohio) 1967-73, Kent State 1974-76, San Jose State 1977-78, Pacific 1979, California 1980-82. Pro coach: Oakland Invaders (USFL) 1983-85, San Diego Chargers 1986-91, Cincinnati Bengals 1992-93, Washington Redskins 1994-96, joined Patriots in 1997.

1998 FIRST-YEAR ROSTER

Name	Pos.	Ht.	Wt.	Birthdate	College	Hometown	How Acq.
Andersen, Jason	C	6-6	312	9/3/75	Brigham Young	San Jose, Calif.	D7
Beveridge, Bob	T	6-6	308	6/1/73	British Columbia	London, Canada	FA
Billups, Terry	CB	5-9	179	2/9/75	North Carolina	Orlando, Fla.	FA
Byrd, Rodney (1)	RB	6-2	245	4/28/74	Illinois	East St. Louis, Ill.	FA
Compas, Jeff	S	5-10	213	7/28/76	Harvard	Great Neck, N.Y.	FA
Cottrell, Dana (1)	LB	6-3	244	1/11/74	Syracuse	Billerica, Mass.	FA
Cox, Matt	G	6-6	305	2/25/73	Brigham Young	Walpole, Mass.	FA
Doxzon, Todd (1)	WR	6-1	186	3/28/75	Iowa State	Omaha, Neb.	FA
Dragos, Scott	TE	6-2	255	10/28/75	Boston College	Rochester, Mass.	FA
Edwards, Robert	RB	5-11	218	10/2/74	Georgia	Tennille, Ga.	D1a
Floyd, Chris	RB	6-1	231	6/23/75	Michigan	Detroit, Mich.	D3a
Gaiter, Tony (1)	WR	5-8	170	7/15/74	Miami	Miami, Fla.	D6-'97
Geter, Mike	RB	5-10	215	4/13/75	North Carolina	Arlington, Va.	FA
Irwin, Blake	LB	6-1	231	4/20/75	New Mexico	Boulder, Colo.	FA
Jones, Tebucky	CB	6-2	216	10/6/74	Syracuse	New Britian, Conn.	D1b
Ladd, Anthony (1)	WR	6-1	193	12/23/73	Cincinnati	Homestead, Fla.	FA
Lee, Brian	S	6-2	195	1/23/75	Wyoming	Denver, Colo.	FA
McGee, Curtis (1)	G-T	6-4	285	3/28/74	Georgia Tech	Marshville, N.C.	FA
Merkerson, Ron	LB	6-2	247	8/30/75	Colorado	Las Vegas, Nev.	D5
Montana, Denis (1)	WR	6-1	200	1/6/72	Concordia, Canada	St. Jean, Canada	FA
Murphy, Jim	QB	6-3	230	2/23/75	Northeastern	Reading, Mass.	FA
Porter, Juan (1)	C	6-3	295	11/26/73	Ohio State	Cleveland, Ohio	FA
Rheams, Leonta	DT	6-2	280	8/1/76	Houston	Tyler, Tex.	D4
Russ, Bernard (1)	LB	6-1	225	11/4/73	West Virginia	Utica, N.Y.	FA
Rutledge, Rod	TE	6-5	262	8/12/75	Alabama	Birmingham, Ala.	D2b
Serwanga, Kato	CB	5-11	192	7/23/76	California	Sacramento, Calif.	FA
Shaw, Harold	RB	6-1	228	9/3/74	Southern Mississippi	Magee, Miss.	D6
Simmons, Tony	WR	6-1	206	12/8/74	Wisconsin	Chicago, Ill.	D2a
Spires, Greg	DE	6-1	260	8/12/74	Florida State	Cape Coral, Fla.	D3b
Tate, Mark (1)	CB	6-1	185	3/20/74	Penn State	Erie, Pa.	FA
Turner, Shawn (1)	WR	6-1	200	5/18/73	Utah State	Nampa, Idaho	FA
Warren, Brent	T	6-5	338	2/10/75	Syracuse	Brockton, Mass.	FA

The term NFL Rookie is defined as a player who is in his first season of professional football and has not been on the roster of another professional football team for any regular-season or postseason games. A Rookie is designated by an "R" on NFL rosters. Players who have been active in another professional football league or players who have NFL experience, including either preseason training camp or being on an Active List or Inactive List, or on Reserve/Injured or Reserve/Physically Unable to Perform for fewer than six regular-season games, are termed NFL First-Year Players. An NFL First-Year Player is designated by a "1" on NFL rosters. Thereafter, a player is credited with an additional year of experience for each season in which he accumulates six games on the Active List or Inactive List, or on Reserve/Injured or Reserve/Physically Unable to Perform.

Johnny Parker, strength and conditioning; born February 1, 1947, Greenville, S.C., lives in Foxboro, Mass. Attended Mississippi. No college or pro playing experience. College coach: South Carolina 1974-76, Indiana 1977-79, Louisiana State 1980, Mississippi 1981-83. Pro coach: New York Giants 1984-92, joined Patriots in 1993.

Bo Pelini, linebackers; born December 13, 1967, Youngstown, Ohio, lives in Attleboro, Mass. Defensive back Ohio State 1986-90. No pro playing experience. College coach: Iowa 1991-92. Pro coach: San Francisco 49ers 1994-96, joined Patriots in 1997.

Jack Reilly, quarterbacks; born May 22, 1945, Boston, Mass., lives in Foxboro, Mass. Quarterback Washington State 1963, Santa Monica (Calif.) J.C. 1964, Long Beach State 1965-66. No pro playing experience. College coach: El Camino (Calif.) J.C. 1980-84 (head coach 1981-84), Utah 1985-89. Pro coach: San Diego Chargers 1990-93, Los Angeles Raiders 1994, St. Louis Rams 1995-96, Dallas Cowboys 1997, joined Patriots in 1998.

Dante Scarnecchia, special teams; born February 15, 1948, Los Angeles, lives in Wrentham, Mass. Center-guard California Western 1968-70. No pro playing experience. College coach: California Western (now U.S. International) 1970-72, Iowa State 1973, Southern Methodist 1975-76, 1980-81, Pacific 1977-78, Northern Arizona 1979. Pro coach: New England Patriots 1982-89, Indianapolis Colts 1990, rejoined Patriots in 1991.

Steve Sidwell, defensive coordinator; born August 30, 1944, Winfield, Kan., lives in Wrentham, Mass. Linebacker Colorado 1962-65. No pro playing experience. College coach: Colorado 1966-73, Nevada-Las Vegas 1974-75, Southern Methodist 1976-81. Pro coach: New England Patriots 1982-84, Indianapolis Colts 1985, New Orleans Saints 1986-94, Houston Oilers 1995-96, rejoined Patriots in 1997.

Carl Smith, tight ends, born April 26, 1948, Wasco, Calif., lives in Franklin, Mass. Defensive back Cal Poly-SLO 1968-70. No pro playing experience. College coach: Cal Poly-SLO 1974-78, Lamar 1979-81, North Carolina State 1982. Pro coach: Philadelphia/Baltimore Stars (USFL) 1983-85, New Orleans Saints 1986-96, joined Patriots in 1997.

DeWayne Walker, defensive assistant-secondary; born December 3, 1960, Los Angeles, lives in Foxboro, Mass. Cornerback Pasadena C.C. 1978-79, Minnesota 1980-81. Pro cornerback Edmonton Eskimos (CFL) 1982, Oakland Invaders (USFL) 1984, Arizona Outlaws (USFL) 1985. College coach: Mt. San Antonio J.C. 1988-92, Utah State 1993, Brigham Young 1994, Oklahoma State 1995, California 1996-97. Pro coach: Joined Patriots in 1998.

Steve Walters, wide receivers; born June 16, 1948, Jonesboro, Ark., lives in North Attleboro, Mass. Quarterback-defensive back Arkansas 1967-70. No pro playing experience. College coach: Tampa 1973, Northeastern Louisiana 1974-75, Morehead State 1976, Tulsa 1977-78, Memphis State 1979, Southern Methodist 1980-81, Alabama 1985. Pro coach: New England Patriots 1982-84, New Orleans Saints 1986-96, rejoined Patriots in 1997.

Kirby Wilson, running backs; born August 24, 1961, Los Angeles, lives in Franklin, Mass. Running back-wide receiver Pasadena C.C. 1979-80, wide receiver-kick returner Illinois 1981-82. Pro defensive back-kick returner Winnipeg (CFL) 1983, Toronto (CFL) 1984. College coach: Pasadena C.C. 1985, L.A. Southwest C.C. 1989-90, Southern Illinois 1991-92, Wyoming 1993-94, Iowa State 1995-96. Pro coach: Joined Patriots in 1997.

Ernie Zampese, offensive coordinator; born March 12, 1936, Santa Barbara, Calif., lives in Foxboro, Mass. Halfback Southern California 1956-58. No pro playing experience. College coach: Hancock (Calif.) J.C. 1962-65, Cal Poly-SLO 1966, San Diego State 1967-75. Pro coach: San Diego Chargers 1976, 1979-86, Los Angeles Rams 1987-93, Dallas Cowboys 1994-97, joined Patriots in 1998.

NEW YORK JETS

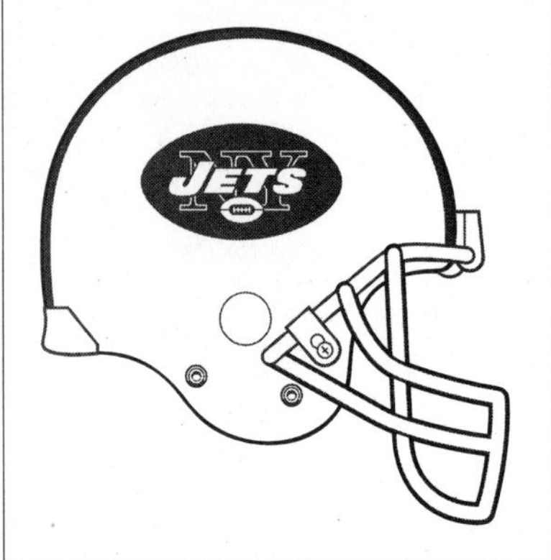

American Football Conference
Eastern Division
Team Colors: Green and White
1000 Fulton Avenue
Hempstead, New York 11550
Telephone: (516) 560-8100

CLUB OFFICIALS

Chairman of the Board: Leon Hess
President: Steve Gutman
Head Coach and Chief Football Operations Officer: Bill Parcells
Director of Player Personnel: Dick Haley
Director of Pro Personnel: Scott Pioli
Director of Player Contract Negotiations: Mike Tannenbaum
Director of Player Development: Carl Banks
Director of Public Relations: Frank Ramos
Treasurer & C.F.O.: Mike Gerstle
Director of Operations: Mike Kensil
Executive Director of Business Operations: Bob Parente
Talent Scouts: Joey Clinkscales, Michael Davis, Sid Hall, Jesse Kaye, Bob Schmitz, Lionel Vital
Director of Team Travel: Kevin Coyle
College Scouting Coordinator: John Griffin
Asst. Director of Public Relations: Doug Miller
Public Relations Assistants: Sharon Czark, Danny Ferrauiola, Berj Najarian
Coordinator of Special Projects: Ken Ilchuk
Controller: Mike Minarczyk
Director of Marketing: Mark Riccio
Senior Marketing Manager: Beth Conroy
Director of Ticket Operations: John Buschhorn
Computer Ticket Operations Manager: Carol Anne Coppola
Director of Computer Technology: Hal Masure
Football Video Director: Jim Pons
Video Director: John Seiter
Head Trainer: David Price
Assistant Head Trainer: John Mellody
Equipment Manager: Bill Hampton
Equipment Director: Clay Hampton
Stadium: Giants Stadium • **Capacity:** 78,739
East Rutherford, New Jersey 07073
Playing Surface: AstroTurf
Training Center: 1000 Fulton Avenue
Hempstead, New York 11550

1998 SCHEDULE

PRESEASON

Aug. 6	at Philadelphia	8:00
Aug. 15	**Baltimore**	5:00
Aug. 20	**New York Giants**	8:20
Aug. 28	at Chicago	7:00

REGULAR SEASON

Sept. 6	at San Francisco	1:15
Sept. 13	**Baltimore**	1:01
Sept. 20	**Indianapolis**	1:01
Sept. 27	Open Date	
Oct. 4	**Miami**	1:01
Oct. 11	at St. Louis	3:15
Oct. 19	at New England (Mon.)	8:20
Oct. 25	**Atlanta**	1:01
Nov. 1	at Kansas City	3:05
Nov. 8	**Buffalo**	4:15
Nov. 15	at Indianapolis	1:01
Nov. 22	at Tennessee	3:15
Nov. 29	**Carolina**	1:01
Dec. 6	**Seattle**	1:01
Dec. 13	at Miami	8:20
Dec. 19	at Buffalo (Sat.)	12:35
Dec. 27	**New England**	1:01

RECORD HOLDERS

INDIVIDUAL RECORDS—CAREER

Category	Name	Performance
Rushing (Yds.)	Freeman McNeil, 1981-1992	8,074
Passing (Yds.)	Joe Namath, 1965-1976	27,057
Passing (TDs)	Joe Namath, 1965-1976	170
Receiving (No.)	Don Maynard, 1960-1972	627
Receiving (Yds.)	Don Maynard, 1960-1972	11,732
Interceptions	Bill Baird, 1963-69	34
Punting (Avg.)	Curley Johnson, 1961-68	42.8
Punt Return (Avg.)	Dick Christy, 1961-63	16.2
Kickoff Return (Avg.)	Bobby Humphery, 1984-89	22.8
Field Goals	Pat Leahy, 1974-1991	304
Touchdowns (Tot.)	Don Maynard, 1960-1972	88
Points	Pat Leahy, 1974-1991	1,470

INDIVIDUAL RECORDS—SINGLE SEASON

Category	Name	Performance
Rushing (Yds.)	Freeman McNeil, 1985	1,331
Passing (Yds.)	Joe Namath, 1967	4,007
Passing (TDs)	Al Dorow, 1960	26
	Joe Namath, 1967	26
Receiving (No.)	Al Toon, 1988	93
Receiving (Yds.)	Don Maynard, 1967	1,434
Interceptions	Dainard Paulson, 1964	12
Punting (Avg.)	Curley Johnson, 1965	45.3
Punt Return (Avg.)	Dick Christy, 1961	21.3
Kickoff Return (Avg.)	Bobby Humphery, 1984	30.7
Field Goals	Jim Turner, 1968	34
Touchdowns (Tot.)	Art Powell, 1960	14
	Don Maynard, 1965	14
	Emerson Boozer, 1972	14
Points	Jim Turner, 1968	145

INDIVIDUAL RECORDS—SINGLE GAME

Category	Name	Performance
Rushing (Yds.)	Adrian Murrell, 10-27-96	199
Passing (Yds.)	Joe Namath, 9-24-72	496
Passing (TDs)	Joe Namath, 9-24-72	6
Receiving (No.)	Clark Gaines, 9-21-80	17
Receiving (Yds.)	Don Maynard, 11-17-68	228
Interceptions	Many times	3
	Last time by Marcus Turner, 11-20-94	
Field Goals	Jim Turner, 11-3-68	6
	Bobby Howfield, 12-3-72	6
Touchdowns (Tot.)	Wesley Walker, 9-21-86	4
Points	Wesley Walker, 9-21-86	24

COACHING HISTORY

New York Titans 1960-62
(245-322-8)

1960-61	Sammy Baugh	14-14-0
1962	Clyde (Bulldog) Turner	5-9-0
1963-73	Weeb Ewbank	73-78-6
1974-75	Charley Winner*	9-14-0
1975	Ken Shipp	1-4-0
1976	Lou Holtz**	3-10-0
1976	Mike Holovak	0-1-0
1977-82	Walt Michaels	41-49-1
1983-89	Joe Walton	54-59-1
1990-93	Bruce Coslet	26-39-0
1994	Pete Carroll	6-10-0
1995-96	Rich Kotite	4-28-0
1997	Bill Parcells	9-7-0

*Released after nine games in 1975
**Resigned after 13 games in 1976

GIANTS STADIUM

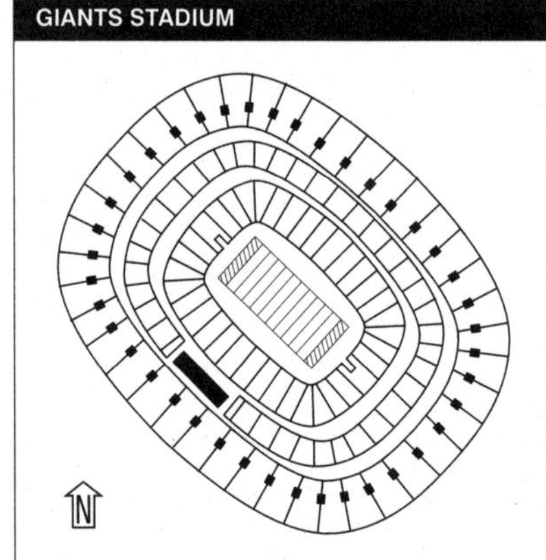

1997 TEAM RECORD

PRESEASON (4-0)

Date	Result		Opponent
8/2	W	31-17	vs. Houston
8/8	W	39-29	at Philadelphia
8/16	W	27-17	N.Y. Giants
8/22	W	15-9	vs. Tampa Bay at Orlando, Fla. (OT)

REGULAR SEASON (9-7)

Date	Result		Opponent	Att.
8/31	W	41-3	at Seattle	53,893
9/7	L	22-28	Buffalo	53,632
9/14	L	24-27	at New England (OT)	60,072
9/21	W	23-22	Oakland	72,586
9/28	W	31-14	at Cincinnati	57,209
10/5	W	16-12	at Indianapolis	48,295
10/12	L	20-31	Miami	75,601
10/19	W	24-19	New England	71,061
11/2	W	19-16	Baltimore (OT)	59,524
11/9	L	17-24	at Miami	73,809
11/16	W	23-15	at Chicago	45,642
11/23	W	23-21	Minnesota	70,131
11/30	L	10-20	at Buffalo	47,776
12/7	L	14-22	Indianapolis	61,168
12/14	W	31-0	Tampa Bay	60,122
12/21	L	10-13	at Detroit	77,624

(OT) Overtime

SCORE BY PERIODS

Jets	91	116	74	64	3	—	348
Opponents	40	97	47	100	3	—	287

ATTENDANCE

Home 523,285 Away 464,320 Total 987,605

Single-game home record, 75,606 (11/27/94)

Single-season home record, 541,832 (1985)

1997 TEAM STATISTICS

	Jets	Opp.
Total First Downs	291	301
Rushing	97	103
Passing	173	177
Penalty	21	21
Third Down: Made/Att	91/238	72/228
Third Down Pct.	38.2	31.6
Fourth Down: Made/Att	12/21	8/21
Fourth Down Pct.	57.1	38.1
Total Net Yards	4,727	5,320
Avg. Per Game	295.4	332.5
Total Plays	1,043	1,057
Avg. Per Play	4.5	5.0
Net Yards Rushing	1,485	1,899
Avg. Per Game	92.8	118.7
Total Rushes	431	470
Net Yards Passing	3,242	3,421
Avg. Per Game	202.6	213.8
Sacked/Yards Lost	48/313	29/242
Gross Yards	3,555	3,663
Att./Completions	564/319	558/304
Completion Pct.	56.6	54.5
Had Intercepted	10	18
Punts/Average	75/42.8	92/42.0
Net Punting Avg.	75/35.4	92/32.7
Penalties/YardsLost	83/678	99/832
Fumbles/Ball Lost	27/12	27/7
Touchdowns	38	33
Rushing	10	9
Passing	20	23
Returns	8	1
Avg. Time of Possesion	29:42	30:18

1997 INDIVIDUAL STATISTICS

PASSING	Att.	Comp.	Yds.	Pct.	TD	Int.	Tkld.	Rate
O'Donnell	460	259	2,796	56.3	17	7	45/289	80.3
Foley	97	56	705	57.7	3	1	3/24	86.5
Lucas	4	3	28	75.0	0	1	0/0	54.2
L. Johnson	2	0	0	0.0	0	1	0/0	0.0
Hansen	1	1	26	100.0	0	0	0/0	118.8
Jets	564	319	3,555	56.6	20	10	48/313	79.9
Opponents	558	304	3,663	54.5	23	18	29/242	75.1

SCORING	TD R	TD P	TD Rt	PAT	FG	Saf	PTS
Hall	0	0	0	36/36	28/41	0	120
Murrell	7	0	0	0/0	0/0	0	42
K. Johnson	0	5	0	0/0	0/0	0	30
L. Johnson	2	0	2	0/0	0/0	0	24
Baxter	0	3	0	0/0	0/0	0	18
Chrebet	0	3	0	0/0	0/0	0	18
Smith	0	0	3	0/0	0/0	0	18
Brady	0	2	0	0/0	0/0	0	12
Graham	0	2	0	0/0	0/0	0	12
Van Dyke	0	2	0	0/0	0/0	0	12
Anderson	0	1	0	0/0	0/0	0	6
Glenn	0	0	1	0/0	0/0	0	6
Lewis	0	0	1	0/0	0/0	0	6
Mickens	0	0	1	0/0	0/0	0	6
Neal	0	1	0	0/0	0/0	0	6
O'Donnell	1	0	0	0/0	0/0	0	6
Ward	0	1	0	0/0	0/0	0	6
Jets	10	20	8	36/36	28/41	0	348
Opponents	9	23	1	27/28	18/27	2	287

2-Point conversions: Team: 0-2, Opponents: 2-5.

RUSHING	Att.	Yds.	Avg.	LG	TD
Murrell	300	1,086	3.6	43t	7
L. Johnson	48	158	3.3	20	2
Anderson	21	70	3.3	19	0
Lucas	6	55	9.2	17	0
O'Donnell	32	36	1.1	19	1
Sowell	7	35	5.0	10	0
Neal	10	28	2.8	8	0
Ward	2	25	12.5	21	0
Clements	2	-3	-1.5	-1	0
Foley	3	-5	-1.7	-1	0
Jets	431	1,485	3.4	43t	10
Opponents	470	1,899	4.0	53	9

RECEIVING	No.	Yds.	Avg.	LG	TD
K. Johnson	70	963	13.8	39	5
Chrebet	58	799	13.8	70	3
Graham	42	542	12.9	47t	2
Baxter	27	276	10.2	37	3
Murrell	27	106	3.9	23	0
Anderson	26	150	5.8	19	1
Brady	22	238	10.8	24	2
Ward	18	212	11.8	33	1
L. Johnson	16	142	8.9	20	0
Neal	8	40	5.0	14	1
Van Dyke	3	53	17.7	18t	2
Brown	1	26	26.0	26	0
Sowell	1	8	8.0	8	0
Jets	319	3,555	11.1	70	20
Opponents	304	3,663	12.0	67	23

INTERCEPTIONS	No.	Yds.	Avg.	LG	TD
Smith	6	158	26.3	51t	3
Mickens	4	2	0.5	2	0
Green	3	89	29.7	39	0
Henderson	1	45	45.0	45	0
Lewis	1	43	43.0	43t	1
Coleman	1	24	24.0	24	0
P. Johnson	1	13	13.0	13	0
Glenn	1	5	5.0	5	0
Jets	18	379	21.1	51t	4
Opponents	10	100	10.0	23	0

PUNTING	No.	Yds.	Avg.	In 20	LG
Hansen	71	3,068	43.2	20	58
Hall	3	144	48.0	0	57
Jets	75	3,212	42.8	20	58
Opponents	92	3,862	42.0	17	74

PUNT RETURNS	No.	FC	Yds.	Avg.	LG	TD
L. Johnson	51	6	619	12.1	66t	1
Ward	8	2	55	6.9	12	0
Jets	59	8	674	11.4	66t	1
Opponents	47	13	459	9.8	47	0

KICKOFF RETURNS	No.	Yds.	Avg.	LG	TD
Glenn	28	741	26.5	96t	1
L. Johnson	12	319	26.6	101t	1
Van Dyke	6	138	23.0	30	0
Neal	2	22	11.0	22	0
Ward	2	10	5.0	11	0
Baxter	1	0	0.0	0	0
Chrebet	1	5	5.0	5	0
Ferguson	1	1	1.0	1	0
Hamilton	1	0	0.0	0	0
Jets	54	1236	22.9	101t	2
Opponents	54	1134	21.0	63	0

FIELD GOALS	1-19	20-29	30-39	40-49	50+
Hall	1/1	10/11	11/17	2/6	4/6
Jets	1/1	10/11	11/17	2/6	4/6
Opponents	0/0	7/8	5/9	6/9	0/1

SACKS	No.
Lewis	8.0
Douglas	4.0
Ferguson	3.5
M. Jones	3.0
Lyle	3.0
Terry	2.0
Farrior	1.5
Gordon	1.0
Green	1.0
Hamilton	1.0
Mickens	1.0
Jets	29.0
Opponents	48.0

1998 DRAFT CHOICES

Round	Name	Pos.	College
2	Dorian Boose	DE	Washington State
3	Scott Frost	DB	Nebraska
	Kevin Williams	DB	Oklahoma State
4	Jason Fabini	T	Cincinnati
5	Casey Dailey	LB	Northwestern
	Doug Karczewski	G	Virginia
	Blake Spence	TE	Oregon
	Eric Bateman	T	Brigham Young
6	Eric Ogbogu	DE	Maryland
	Chris Brazzell	WR	Angelo State
	Dustin Johnson	RB	Brigham Young
7	Lawrence Hart	TE	Southern

NEW YORK JETS

1998 VETERAN ROSTER

No.	Name	Pos.	Ht.	Wt.	Birthdate	NFL Exp.	College	Hometown	How Acq.	'97 Games/ Starts
20	Anderson, Richie	RB	6-2	225	9/13/71	6	Penn State	Sandy Spring, Md.	D6-'93	16/3
25	Austin, Raymond	S-CB	5-11	190	12/21/74	2	Tennessee	Lawton, Okla.	D5b-'97	16/0
84	Baxter, Fred	TE	6-3	265	6/14/71	6	Auburn	Brundidge, Ala.	D5a-'93	16/9
88	Brady, Kyle	TE	6-6	268	1/14/72	4	Penn State	New Cumberland, Pa.	D1a-'95	16/14
44	Brown, Corwin	S	6-1	200	4/25/70	6	Michigan	Chicago, Ill.	FA-'97	16/0
62	Burger, Todd	G	6-3	303	3/20/70	5	Penn State	Clark, N.J.	UFA(Chi)-'98	15/15*
63	Burns, Lamont	G-C	6-4	300	3/16/74	2	East Carolina	Greensboro, N.C.	D5a-'97	4/3
41	Byars, Keith	RB	6-1	255	10/14/63	13	Ohio State	Dayton, Ohio	UFA(NE)-'98	16/7*
53	Cascadden, Chad	LB	6-1	240	5/14/72	4	Wisconsin	Chippewa Falls, Wis.	FA-'95	15/0
80	Chrebet, Wayne	WR	5-10	185	8/14/73	4	Hofstra	Garfield, N.J.	FA-'95	15/1
7	Clements, Chuck	QB	6-3	214	9/29/73	2	Houston	Huntsville, Tex.	D6b-'97	1/0
42	Coleman, Marcus	CB-S	6-2	210	5/24/74	3	Texas Tech	Dallas, Tex.	D5-'96	16/2
64	Conrad, J.R.	C-T-G	6-4	300	2/2/74	2	Oklahoma	Fairland, Okla.	FA-'97	12/1
78	Day, Terry	DE	6-4	280	9/18/74	2	Mississippi State	Pickens, Miss.	D4a-'97	1/0
91	Dixon, Ronnie	DT	6-3	310	5/10/71	5	Cincinnati	Clinton, N.C.	FA-'97	5/3
76	Elliott, John	T	6-7	308	4/1/65	11	Michigan	Lake Ronkonkoma, N.Y.	UFA(NYG)-'96	13/13
58	Farrior, James	LB	6-2	240	1/6/75	2	Virginia	Ettrick, Va.	D1-'97	16/15
72	Ferguson, Jason	DT	6-3	300	11/28/74	2	Georgia	Nettleton, Miss.	D7b-'97	13/1
51	Finkes, Matt	LB	6-3	260	2/12/75	2	Ohio State	Piqua, Ohio	W(Car)-'97	8/0
4	Foley, Glenn	QB	6-2	210	10/10/70	5	Boston College	Cherry Hill, N.J.	D7-'94	6/2
67	Gisler, Mike	C-G	6-4	295	8/26/69	6	Houston	Runge, Tex.	UFA(NE)-'98	16/2*
31	Glenn, Aaron	CB-KR	5-9	185	7/16/72	5	Texas A&M	Aldine, Tex.	D1-'94	16/16
54	Gordon, Dwayne	LB	6-1	240	11/2/69	6	New Hampshire	LaGrangeville, N.Y.	FA-'97	16/8
21	Green, Victor	S	5-11	205	12/8/69	6	Akron	Americus, Ga.	FA-'93	16/16
77	Hagood, Jay	T	6-4	306	8/9/73	2	Virginia Tech	Easley, S.C.	FA-'97	2/0
9	Hall, John	K	6-3	223	3/17/74	2	Wisconsin	Port Charlotte, Fla.	FA-'97	16/0
92	Hamilton, Bobby	DE	6-5	280	1/7/71	3	Southern Mississippi	Columbia, Miss.	FA-'96	16/0
11	Hansen, Brian	P	6-4	215	10/26/60	14	Sioux Falls	Hawarden, Iowa	FA-'97	15/0
30	Hayes, Chris	S	6-0	200	5/7/72	2	Washington State	San Bernadino, Calif.	T(GB)-'97	16/0
26	Henderson, Jerome	S-CB	5-10	200	8/8/69	8	Clemson	Statesville, N.C.	UFA(NE)-'97	16/14
65	Hudson, John	C-G	6-2	270	1/29/68	9	Auburn	Paris, Tenn.	UFA(Phil)-'96	16/0
19	Johnson, Keyshawn	WR	6-3	210	7/22/72	3	Southern California	Los Angeles, Calif.	D1-'96	16/16
32	Johnson, Leon	RB-KR	6-0	215	7/13/74	2	North Carolina	Morganton, N.C.	D4b-'97	16/1
52	Johnson, Pepper	LB	6-3	259	7/29/64	13	Ohio State	Detroit, Mich.	UFA(Det)-'97	8/8
55	Jones, Marvin	LB	6-2	244	6/28/72	6	Florida State	Miami, Fla.	D1-'93	16/16
57	Lewis, Mo	LB	6-3	258	10/21/69	8	Georgia	Peachtree, Ga.	D3-'91	16/16
93	Logan, Ernie	DT-DE	6-3	290	5/18/68	7	East Carolina	Fayetteville, N.C.	UFA(Jax)-'97	15/14
95	Lyle, Rick	DE-DT	6-5	285	2/26/71	5	Missouri	Hickman Hills, Mo.	FA-'97	16/16
75	Malamala, Siupeli	T-G	6-5	305	1/15/69	7	Washington	Kalaheo, Hawaii	D3-'92	10/5
36	Marshall, Anthony	S	6-1	212	9/16/70	4	Louisiana State	Mobile, Ala.	W(Chi)-'97	0*
28	Martin, Curtis	RB	5-11	203	5/1/73	4	Pittsburgh	Pittsburgh, Pa.	RFA(NE)-'98	13/13*
68	Mawae, Kevin	C	6-4	305	1/23/71	5	Louisiana State	Leesville, La.	UFA(Sea)-'98	16/16*
24	Mickens, Ray	CB-KR	5-8	180	1/4/73	3	Texas A&M	El Paso, Tex.	D3-'96	16/0
14	O'Donnell, Neil	QB	6-3	228	7/3/66	9	Maryland	Madison, N.J.	UFA(Pitt)-'96	15/14
70	O'Dwyer, Matt	G	6-5	300	9/1/72	4	Northwestern	Lincolnshire, Ill.	D2-'95	16/16
66	Palelei, Lonnie	G-T	6-3	315	10/15/70	5	Nevada-Las Vegas	Blue Springs, Mo.	FA-'97	15/14
98	Pleasant, Anthony	DE	6-5	280	1/27/68	9	Tennessee State	Century, Fla.	FA-'98	11/0*
45	Smith, Otis	CB	5-11	190	10/22/65	9	Missouri	New Orleans, La.	UFA(NE)-'97	16/16
33	Sowell, Jerald	RB	6-0	248	1/21/74	2	Tulane	Baker, La.	W(GB)-'97	9/0
94	Terry, Rick	DT-DE	6-4	302	4/5/74	2	North Carolina	Lexington, N.C.	D2-'97	14/0
86	Van Dyke, Alex	WR-KR	6-0	200	7/24/74	3	Nevada	Sacramento, Calif.	D2-'96	5/0
89	Ward, Dedric	WR-KR	5-9	180	9/29/74	2	Northern Iowa	Cedar Rapids, Iowa	D3-'97	11/0
73	Williams, David	T	6-5	300	6/21/66	10	Florida	Lakeland, Fla.	FA-'96	12/11

* Burger played 15 games with Chicago in '97; Byars and Gisler played 16 games with New England; Marshall inactive for 2 games; Martin played 13 games with New England; Mawae played 16 games with Seattle; Pleasant played 11 games with Atlanta.

Traded—DE Hugh Douglas (15 games in '97) to Philadelphia; WR Jeff Graham (16) to Philadelphia; RB Adrian Murrell (16) to Arizona; RB Lorenzo Neal (16) to Tampa Bay.

Retired—William Roberts, 14-year guard, 12 games in '97.

Players lost through free agency (2): C Roger Duffy (Pitt; 15 games in '97), TE John Burke (SD; 7).

Also played for Jets in '97—G-T Casey Wiegmann (3 games), LB Chris Wing (2).

COACHING STAFF

Head Coach,
Bill Parcells

Pro Career: On February 11, 1997, Parcells was named the Jets' eleventh full-time head coach. He went 9-7 and came up just shy of the playoffs in his first season with the Jets. The eight-game improvement from 1996 to 1997 equalled the second best of all time. Parcells came to the Jets after having led the New England Patriots to the 1996 AFC Championship and an appearance in Super Bowl XXXI versus the Green Bay Packers. In New England, Parcells inherited a team that went 2-14 in 1992 and began the rebuilding process with a 6-10 campaign in 1993. In just his second year at the helm, Parcells steered the Patriots into the playoffs on the heels of a franchise record seven consecutive victories and a wild-card matchup versus the Cleveland Browns. Over the course of his four year Patriots career, Parcells had a 34-34 record, including 2-2 in the postseason. Parcells made his NFL coaching debut with the Patriots as linebackers coach on Ron Erhardt's staff in 1980. He accepted the same position on the New York Giants staff in 1981 and was named the Giants' head coach in 1983. In eight seasons at the helm of the Giants, Parcells led his teams to two Super Bowl championships. His first title came in 1986, with a 39-20 win over the Denver Broncos. Four years later, the Giants claimed another victory over the Buffalo Bills. On May 15, 1991 Parcells resigned from the Giants due to health reasons. During his two years away from coaching, Parcells served as a studio analyst in 1991 and as a color commentator in 1992 for NBC Sports. Career record: 128-93-1.
Background: Linebacker at Wichita State 1961-63. College assistant Hastings (Neb.) 1964, Wichita State 1965, Army 1966-69, Florida State 1970-72, Vanderbilt 1973-74, Texas Tech 1975-77, Air Force 1978 (head coach).
Personal: Born August 22, 1941, Englewood, N.J. Bill and his wife, Judy, live in Sea Girt, N.J., and have three daughters—Suzy, Jill, and Dallas.

ASSISTANT COACHES

Bill Belichick, assistant head coach-defensive backs; born April 16, 1952, Nashville, Tenn., lives on Long Island, N.Y. Center/tight end Wesleyan 1971-74. No pro playing experience. Pro coach: Baltimore Colts 1975, Detroit Lions 1976-77, Denver Broncos 1978, New York Giants 1979-90, Cleveland Browns 1991-95 (head coach), New England Patriots 1996, joined Jets in 1997.
Maurice Carthon, running backs; born April 24, 1961, Chicago, Ill., lives on Long Island, N.Y. Running back Arkansas State 1979-82. Pro running back New Jersey Generals (USFL) 1983-85, New York Giants 1985-91, Indianapolis Colts 1992. Pro coach: New England Patriots 1994-96, joined Jets in 1997.
Romeo Crennel, defensive line; born June 18, 1947, Lynchburgh, Va., lives on Long Island, N.Y. Defensive-offensive tackle, linebacker Western Kentucky 1966-69. No pro playing experience. College coach: Western Kentucky 1970-74, Texas Tech 1975-77, Mississippi 1978-79, Georgia Tech 1980. Pro coach: New York Giants 1981-92, New England Patriots 1993-96, joined Jets in 1997.
Al Groh, linebackers; born July 13, 1944, New York, N.Y., lives on Long Island, N.Y. Defensive end Virginia 1964-67. No pro playing experience. College coach: Army 1968-69, Virginia 1970-72, North Carolina 1973-77, Air Force 1978-79, Texas Tech 1980, Wake Forest 1981-86 (head coach), South Carolina 1988. Pro coach: Atlanta Falcons 1987, New York Giants 1989-91, Cleveland Browns 1992, New England Patriots 1993-96, joined Jets in 1997.
Todd Haley, offensive assistant-quality control; born February 28, 1967, Atlanta, Ga., lives on Long Island, N.Y. Attended Florida and Miami. No college or pro playing experience. Pro coach: Joined Jets in 1997.
Dan Henning, quarterbacks; born June 21, 1942, Bronx, N.Y., lives on Long Island, N.Y. Quarterback William & Mary 1962-64. Pro quarterback San Diego Chargers 1964, 1966-67. College coach: Florida State 1968-70, 1974, Virginia Tech 1971, 1973, Boston College 1994-96 (head coach). Pro coach: Houston Oilers 1972, New York Jets 1976-78, Miami Dolphins 1979-80, Washington Redskins 1981-82, 1987-88, Atlanta Falcons 1983-86 (head coach), San Diego Chargers 1989-91 (head coach), Detroit Lions 1992-93, Buffalo Bills 1997, rejoined Jets in 1998.
Pat Hodgson, tight ends; born January 30, 1944, Columbus, Ga., lives on Long Island, N.Y. Tight end Georgia 1963-65. Pro tight end Washington Redskins 1966, Minnesota Vikings 1967. College coach: Georgia 1968-70, 1972-77, Florida State 1971, Texas Tech 1978. Pro coach: San Diego Chargers 1978, New York Giants 1979-87, Pittsburgh Steelers 1992-95, joined Jets in 1996.
John Lott, strength and conditioning; born May 9, 1964 in Denton, Tex., lives on Long Island, N.Y. Offensive lineman North Texas State 1983-86. Offensive lineman Pittsburgh Steelers 1987. College coach: North Texas State 1989, Houston 1990-96. Pro coach: Joined Jets in 1997.
Eric Mangini, defensive assistant-quality control; born January 19, 1971, Hartford, Conn., lives on Long Island, N.Y. Defensive tackle Wesleyan 1990-93. No pro playing experience. Pro coach: Baltimore Ravens 1996, joined Jets in 1997.
Bill Muir, offensive line; born October 26, 1942, Pittsburgh, Pa., lives on Long Island, N.Y. Tackle Susquehanna 1962-64. No pro playing experience. College coach: Susquehanna 1965, Delaware Valley 1966-67, Rhode Island 1970-71, Idaho State 1972-73, Southern Methodist 1976-77. Pro coach: Orlando (Continental Football League) 1968-69, Houston-Shreveport Steamer (WFL) 1975, New England Patriots 1982-88, Indianapolis Colts 1989-91, Philadelphia Eagles 1992-94, joined Jets in 1995.
Mike Sweatman, special teams; born October 23, 1947, Kansas City, Mo., lives on Long Island, N.Y. Linebacker Kansas 1964-67. No pro playing experience. College coach: Kansas 1973-74, 1979-82, Tulsa 1977-78, Tennessee 1983. Pro coach: Minnesota Vikings 1984, New York Giants 1985-92, New England Patriots 1993-96, joined Jets in 1997.
Charlie Weis, offensive coordinator- receivers; born March 30, 1956, Trenton, N.J., lives on Long Island, N.Y. Attended Notre Dame. No college or pro playing experience. College coach: South Carolina 1985-88. Pro coach: New York Giants 1990-92, New England Patriots 1993-96, joined Jets in 1997.

1998 FIRST-YEAR ROSTER

Name	Pos.	Ht.	Wt.	Birthdate	College	Hometown	How Acq.
Bateman, Eric	T	6-7	319	12/28/73	Brigham Young	Camarillo, Calif.	D5d
Bell, Geno	DT	6-3	290	6/3/75	Arkansas	Columbia, S.C.	FA
Boose, Dorian	DE	6-5	283	1/29/74	Washington State	Tacoma, Wash.	D2
Brazzell, Chris	WR	6-2	182	5/22/76	Angelo State	Alice, Tex.	D6b
Brown, Shannon (1)	DT	6-5	290	5/23/72	Alabama	Millbrook, Ala.	FA
Dailey, Casey	LB	6-3	249	6/11/75	Northwestern	Covina, Calif.	D5a
Deignan, Robert (1)	P	6-5	230	1/8/74	Purdue	Ft. Lauderdale Fla.	FA
Donaldson, Cedric	CB	5-9	180	2/12/76	Louisiana State	Jackson, Miss.	FA
Fabini, Jason	T	6-7	318	8/25/74	Cincinnati	Ft. Wayne, Ind.	D4
Farmer, Robert (1)	RB	5-11	217	3/4/74	Notre Dame	Bolingbrook, Ill.	FA-'97
Frost, Scott	S	6-3	219	1/4/75	Nebraska	Lincoln, Neb.	D3a
Gallery, Nick (1)	P	6-4	239	2/15/75	Iowa	Manchester, Iowa	FA-'97
Gibson, Ed	CB	5-10	180	1/18/75	Iowa	Davenport, Iowa	FA
Guest, Craig (1)	LB	6-1	242	12/10/75	Buffalo	North Haven, Conn.	FA-'97
Hart, Lawrence	TE	6-4	261	9/19/76	Southern	Shreveport, La.	D7
Holmes, Bernard (1)	WR	5-11	178	5/13/73	Texas A&M-Kingsville	Houston, Tex.	FA-'97
Jenkins, Nakia	WR	6-1	215	6/29/75	Utah State	Belle Glade, Fla.	FA
Johnson, Alonzo (1)	WR-KR	5-11	186	4/18/73	Central State, Ohio	Tuscaloosa, Ala.	FA-'97
Johnson, Dustin	RB	6-2	236	8/5/73	Brigham Young	Eagar, Ariz.	D6c
Karczewski, Doug	G	6-5	298	2/6/75	Virginia	Gaithersburg, Md.	D5b
Keneley, Matt (1)	DT	6-4	295	12/1/73	Southern California	Mission Viejo, Calif.	FA-'97
Lozowski, Keith	RB	6-2	245	2/22/75	Northwestern	Palatine, Ill.	FA
Munch, John	LB	6-1	235	1/7/76	Illinois-Wesleyan	Sycamore, Ill.	FA
Musso, Brian	WR-KR	6-0	190	9/11/75	Northwestern	Hinsdale, Ill.	FA
Ogbogu, Eric	DE	6-4	266	7/18/75	Maryland	Irvington, N.Y.	D6a
Spence, Blake	TE	6-4	249	6/20/75	Oregon	San Juan Capistrano, Calif.	D5c
Thorp, Deron (1)	T	6-8	330	8/31/73	Nevada	Santa Clara, Calif.	FA-'97
Viger, David	DT	6-4	280	5/13/75	Navy	Vista, Calif.	FA
Williams, Kevin	CB-S	6-0	190	8/4/75	Oklahoma State	Pine Bluff, Ark.	D3b
Wing, Chris (1)	LB	6-2	240	5/28/71	Boise State	Redmond, Wash.	FA-'97

The term NFL Rookie is defined as a player who is in his first season of professional football and has not been on the roster of another professional football team for any regular-season or postseason games. A Rookie is designated by an "R" on NFL rosters. Players who have been active in another professional football league or players who have NFL experience, including either preseason training camp or being on an Active List or Inactive List, or on Reserve/Injured or Reserve/Physically Unable to Perform for fewer than six regular-season games, are termed NFL First-Year Players. An NFL First-Year Player is designated by a "1" on NFL rosters. Thereafter, a player is credited with an additional year of experience for each season in which he accumulates six games on the Active List or Inactive List, or on Reserve/Injured or Reserve/Physically Unable to Perform.

NOTES

OAKLAND RAIDERS

American Football Conference
Western Division
Team Colors: Silver and Black
1220 Harbor Bay Parkway
Alameda, California 94502
Telephone: (510) 864-5000

CLUB OFFICIALS

President of the General Partner: Al Davis
Chief Executive: Amy Trask
Executive Assistant: Al LoCasale
Senior Assistant: Bruce Allen
Pro Football Scout: George Karras
Personnel Executive: Ken Herock
Legal Affairs: Jeff Birren, Roxanne Kosarzycki
Finance: Marc Badain, Tom Blanda, Derek Person
Senior Administrator: Morris Bradshaw
Senior Executive: John Herrera
Public Relations: Mike Taylor
Public Relations Assistants: Mario Perez, Marc McKinney
Special Projects: Jim Otto
Ticket Operations: Peter Eiges
Trainers: H. Rod Martin, Jonathan Jones, Scott Touchet
Equipment Manager: Bob Romanski
Video Director: Dave Nash
Stadium: Oakland-Alameda County Coliseum
•**Capacity:** 63,263
Playing Surface: Grass
Training Camp: Napa Valley Marriott
Napa, California 94558

1998 SCHEDULE

PRESEASON

Aug. 8	at Dallas	8:00
Aug. 16	at Green Bay	3:00
Aug. 24	**Tampa Bay**	6:00
Aug. 29	**Arizona**	1:00

REGULAR SEASON

Sept. 6	at Kansas City	7:20
Sept. 13	**New York Giants**	1:15
Sept. 20	**Denver**	1:15
Sept. 27	at Dallas	12:01
Oct. 4	at Arizona	1:05
Oct. 11	**San Diego**	1:15
Oct. 18	Open Date	
Oct. 25	**Cincinnati**	1:15
Nov. 1	at Seattle	5:20
Nov. 8	at Baltimore	1:01
Nov. 15	**Seattle**	1:05
Nov. 22	at Denver	2:15
Nov. 29	**Washington**	1:15
Dec. 6	**Miami**	1:15
Dec. 13	at Buffalo	1:01
Dec. 20	at San Diego	1:05
Dec. 26	**Kansas City** (Sat.)	1:05

RECORD HOLDERS

INDIVIDUAL RECORDS—CAREER

Category	Name	Performance
Rushing (Yds.)	Marcus Allen, 1982-1992	8,545
Passing (Yds.)	Ken Stabler, 1970-79	19,078
Passing (TDs)	Ken Stabler, 1970-79	150
Receiving (No.)	Tim Brown, 1988-1997	599
Receiving (Yds.)	Fred Biletnikoff, 1965-1978	8,974
Interceptions	Willie Brown, 1967-1978	39
	Lester Hayes, 1977-1986	39
Punting (Avg.)	Leo Araguz, 1996-97	44.5
Punt Return (Avg.)	Claude Gibson, 1963-65	12.6
Kickoff Return (Avg.)	Jack Larscheid, 1960-61	28.4
Field Goals	Chris Bahr, 1980-88	162
Touchdowns (Tot.)	Marcus Allen, 1982-1992	98
Points	George Blanda, 1967-1975	863

INDIVIDUAL RECORDS—SINGLE SEASON

Category	Name	Performance
Rushing (Yds.)	Marcus Allen, 1985	1,759
Passing (Yds.)	Jeff George, 1997	3,917
Passing (TDs)	Daryle Lamonica, 1969	34
Receiving (No.)	Tim Brown 1997	104
Receiving (Yds.)	Tim Brown, 1997	1,408
Interceptions	Lester Hayes, 1980	13
Punting (Avg.)	Ray Guy, 1973	45.3
Punt Return (Avg.)	Claude Gibson, 1964	14.4
Kickoff Return (Avg.)	Harold Hart, 1975	30.5
Field Goals	Jeff Jaeger, 1993	35
Touchdowns (Tot.)	Marcus Allen, 1984	18
Points	Jeff Jaeger, 1993	132

INDIVIDUAL RECORDS—SINGLE GAME

Category	Name	Performance
Rushing (Yds.)	Napoleon Kaufman, 10-19-97	227
Passing (Yds.)	Jeff Hostetler, 10-31-93	424
Passing (TDs)	Tom Flores, 12-22-63	6
	Daryle Lamonica, 10-19-69	6
Receiving (No.)	Tim Brown, 12-21-97	14
Receiving (Yds.)	Art Powell, 12-22-63	247
Interceptions	Many times	3
	Last time by Terry McDaniel, 10-9-94	
Field Goals	Jeff Jaeger, 12-11-94	5
Touchdowns (Tot.)	Art Powell, 12-22-63	4
	Marcus Allen, 9-24-84	4
	Harvey Williams, 11-16-97	4
Points	Art Powell, 12-22-63	24
	Marcus Allen, 9-24-84	24
	Harvey Williams, 11-16-97	24

COACHING HISTORY

OAKLAND 1960-1981
LOS ANGELES 1982-1994
(353-236-11)

1960-61	Eddie Erdelatz*	6-10-0
1961-62	Marty Feldman**	2-15-0
1962	Red Conkright	1-8-0
1963-65	Al Davis	23-16-3
1966-68	John Rauch	35-10-1
1969-78	John Madden	112-39-7
1979-87	Tom Flores	91-56-0
1988-89	Mike Shanahan***	8-12-0
1989-94	Art Shell	56-41-0
1995-96	Mike White	15-17-0
1997	Joe Bugel	4-12-0

*Released after two games in 1961
**Released after five games in 1962
***Released after four games in 1989

OAKLAND-ALAMEDA COUNTY COLISEUM

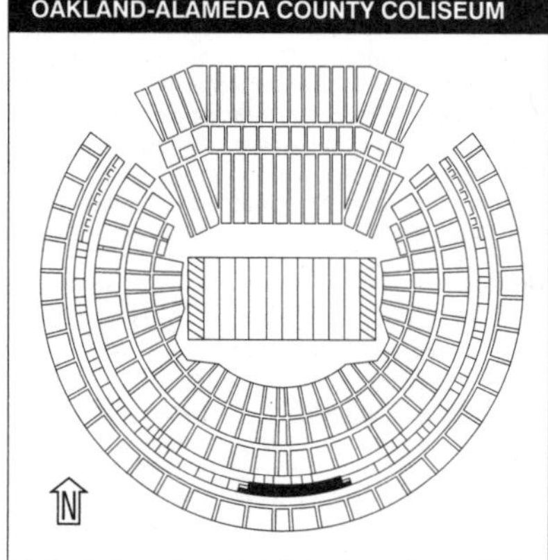

1997 TEAM RECORD

PRESEASON (2-2)

Date	Result		Opponent
8/3	W	34-27	at Dallas
8/8	L	24-37	Green Bay
8/16	W	18-16	New Orleans
8/22	L	13-15	at Arizona

REGULAR SEASON (4-12)

Date	Result		Opponent	Att.
8/31	L	21-24	at Tennessee (OT)	30,171
9/8	L	27-28	Kansas City	61,523
9/14	W	36-31	at Atlanta	47,922
9/21	L	22-23	at New York Jets	72,586
9/28	W	35-17	St. Louis	42,506
10/5	L	10-25	San Diego	43,648
10/19	W	28-25	Denver	57,006
10/26	L	34-45	at Seattle	66,264
11/2	L	14-38	at Carolina	71,064
11/9	L	10-13	New Orleans	40,091
11/16	W	38-13	at San Diego	65,714
11/24	L	3-31	at Denver	75,307
11/30	L	16-34	Miami	50,569
12/7	L	0-30	at Kansas City	76,379
12/14	L	21-22	Seattle	40,124
12/21	L	9-20	Jacksonville	40,032

(OT) Overtime

SCORE BY PERIODS

Raiders	69	100	113	42	0	—	324
Opponents	87	123	102	104	3	—	419

ATTENDANCE

Home 335,467 Away 505,407 Total 840,874

Single-game home record, 61,523 (9/8/97)

Single-season home record, 398,915 (1996)

1997 TEAM STATISTICS

	Raiders	Opp.
Total First Downs	263	345
Rushing	74	121
Passing	170	199
Penalty	19	25
Third Down: Made/Att	65/204	92/236
Third Down Pct.	31.9	39.0
Fourth Down: Made/Att	5/18	7/14
Fourth Down Pct.	27.8	50.0
Total Net Yards	5,102	6116
Avg. Per Game	318.9	382.3
Total Plays	947	1,108
Avg. Per Play	5.4	5.5
Net Yards Rushing	1,588	2,246
Avg. Per Game	99.3	140.4
Total Rushes	360	525
Net Yards Passing	3,514	3,870
Avg. Per Game	219.6	241.9
Sacked/Yards Lost	58/430	31/239
Gross Yards	3,944	4,109
Att./Completions	529/294	552/324
Completion Pct.	55.6	58.7
Had Intercepted	10	10
Punts/Avg.	93/45.0	77/39.4
Net Punting Avg.	93/39.1	77/35.6
Penalties/Yards Lost	117/976	117/977
Fumbles/Ball Lost	25/14	26/12
Touchdowns	41	44
Rushing	9	19
Passing	29	21
Returns	3	4
Avg. Time of Possession	26:24	33:36

1997 INDIVIDUAL STATISTICS

PASSING	Att.	Comp.	Yds.	Pct.	TD	Int.	Tkld.	Rate
George	521	290	3,917	55.7	29	9	58/430	91.2
Klingler	7	4	27	57.1	0	1	0/0	26.2
Kaufman	1	0	0	0.0	0	0	0/0	39.6
Raiders	529	294	3,944	55.6	29	10	58/430	89.9
Opponents	552	324	4,109	58.7	21	10	31/239	87.1

SCORING	TD R	TD P	TD Rt	PAT	FG	Saf	PTS
Ford	0	0	0	33/35	13/22	0	72
Jett	0	12	0	0/0	0/0	0	72
Kaufman	6	2	0	0/0	0/0	0	48
Dudley	0	7	0	0/0	0/0	0	42
T. Brown	0	5	0	0/0	0/0	0	32
Williams	3	2	0	0/0	0/0	0	32
Shedd	0	0	1	0/0	0/0	0	6
Truitt	0	1	0	0/0	0/0	0	6
Turner	0	0	1	0/0	0/0	0	6
Washington	0	0	1	0/0	0/0	0	6
Smith	0	0	0	0/0	0/0	1	2
Raiders	9	29	3	33/35	13/22	1	324
Opponents	19	21	4	37/37	38/43	0	419

2-Pt. Conversions: T. Brown, Williams.
Team 2-6, Opponents 2-7.

RUSHING	Att.	Yds.	Avg.	LG	TD
Kaufman	272	1,294	4.8	83t	6
Hall	23	120	5.2	15	0
Williams	18	70	3.9	13	3
George	17	44	2.6	12	0
Fenner	7	24	3.4	7	0
T. Brown	5	19	3.8	12	0
Aska	12	10	0.8	4	0
Davison	2	4	2.0	5	0
Levitt	2	3	1.5	2	0
Araguz	1	0	0.0	0	0
Klingler	1	0	0.0	0	0
Raiders	360	1,588	4.4	83t	9
Opponents	525	2,246	4.3	77	19

RECEIVING	No.	Yds.	Avg.	LG	TD
T. Brown	104	1,408	13.5	59t	5
Dudley	48	787	16.4	76	7
Jett	46	804	17.5	56t	12
Kaufman	40	403	10.1	70t	2
Williams	16	147	9.2	32t	2
Fenner	14	92	6.6	13	0
Shedd	10	115	11.5	19	0
Truitt	7	91	13.0	19t	1
Howard	4	30	7.5	9	0
Davison	2	34	17.0	25	0
Levitt	2	24	12.0	22	0
Hall	1	9	9.0	9	0
Raiders	294	3,944	13.4	76	29
Opponents	324	4,109	12.7	61	21

INTERCEPTIONS	No.	Yds.	Avg.	LG	TD
Turner	2	45	22.5	29	0
Washington	2	44	22.0	44t	1
Trapp	2	24	12.0	25	0
Lynch	2	6	3.0	6	0
McDaniel	1	17	17.0	17	0
Land	1	13	13.0	13	0
Raiders	10	149	14.9	44t	1
Opponents	10	192	19.2	55t	2

PUNTING	No.	Yds.	Avg.	In 20	LG
Araguz	93	4,189	45.0	28	63
Raiders	93	4,189	45.0	28	63
Opponents	77	3,035	39.4	27	65

PUNT RETURNS	No.	FC	Yds.	Avg.	LG	TD
Howard	27	20	210	7.8	31	0
Raiders	27	20	210	7.8	31	0
Opponents	52	26	431	8.3	32	0

KICKOFF RETURNS	No.	Yds.	Avg.	LG	TD
Howard	61	1,318	21.6	45	0
Hall	9	182	20.2	34	0
Aska	2	46	23.0	26	0
Shedd	2	38	19.0	23	0
Truitt	2	51	25.5	30	0
Biekert	1	16	16.0	16	0
T. Brown	1	7	7.0	7	0
Holmberg	1	15	15.0	15	0
Levitt	1	12	12.0	12	0
Morton	1	14	14.0	14	0
Raiders	81	1,699	21.0	45	0
Opponents	48	1,124	23.4	42	0

SACKS	No.
Smith	6.5
Maryland	4.5
McGlockton	4.5
Johnstone	3.5
Russell	3.5
Biekert	2.5
Fredrickson	2.0
Lewis	2.0
Bruce	1.0
Lynch	1.0
Raiders	31.0
Opponents	58.0

FIELD GOALS	1-19	20-29	30-39	40-49	50+
Ford	0/0	3/5	4/6	5/10	1/1
Raiders	0/0	3/5	4/6	5/10	1/1
Opponents	1/1	13/14	11/12	11/14	2/2

1998 DRAFT CHOICES

Round	Name	Pos.	College
1	Charles Woodson	DB	Michigan
	Mo Collins	T	Florida
2	Leon Bender	DT	Washington State
3	Jon Ritchie	RB	Stanford
4	Gennaro DiNapoli	G	Virginia Tech
5	Jeremy Brigham	TE	Washington
	Travian Smith	LB	Oklahoma
7	Vince Amey	DE	Arizona State
	David Sanders	DE	Arkansas

OAKLAND RAIDERS

1998 VETERAN ROSTER

No.		Name	Pos.	Ht.	Wt.	Birthdate	NFL Exp.	College	Hometown	How Acq.	'97 Games/ Starts
21	t-	Allen, Eric	CB	5-10	180	11/22/65	11	Arizona State	San Diego, Calif.	T(NO)-'98	16/16*
2		Araguz, Leo	P	5-11	190	1/18/70	2	Stephen F. Austin	Harlington, Tex.	FA-'97	16/0
73		Ashmore, Darryl	T	6-7	310	11/1/69	7	Northwestern	Peoria, Ill.	UFA(Wash)-'98	12/2*
35		Aska, Joe	RB	5-11	240	7/14/72	4	Central Oklahoma	Putnam City, Okla.	D3-'95	7/0
43		Bates, Patrick	S	6-3	220	11/27/70	4	Texas A&M	Galveston, Tex.	FA-'98	0*
54		Biekert, Greg	LB	6-2	240	3/14/69	6	Colorado	Longmont, Colo.	D7-'93	16/16
27		Branch, Calvin	S	5-11	195	5/8/74	2	Colorado State	Spring, Tex.	D6-'97	6/0
86		Brown, Derek	TE	6-6	265	3/31/70	7	Notre Dame	Fairfax, Va.	UFA(Jax)-'98	13/8*
24		Brown, Larry	CB	5-11	185	11/30/69	8	Texas Christian	Los Angeles, Calif.	UFA(Dall)-'96	4/0
81		Brown, Tim	WR	6-0	195	7/22/66	11	Notre Dame	Dallas, Tex.	D1-88	16/16
20		Carter, Perry	CB	6-0	200	8/5/71	2	Southern Mississippi	Magnolia, Miss.	FA-'96	16/7
68		Cunningham, Rick	G-T	6-7	315	1/4/69	8	Texas A&M	Beverly Hills, Calif.	FA-'96	7/0
83		Dudley, Ricky	TE	6-6	250	7/15/72	3	Ohio State	Hendersonville, Tex.	D1-'96	16/16
95		Faumui, Ta'ase	DT	6-3	285	3/19/71	3	Hawaii	Honolulu, Hawaii	FA-'97	0*
34	#	Fenner, Derrick	RB	6-3	240	4/6/67	10	North Carolina	Oxen Hill, Md.	FA-'97	9/7
55		Folston, James	LB	6-3	235	8/14/71	5	Northeast Louisiana	Cocoa, Fla.	D2-'94	16/7
5		Ford, Cole	K	6-2	205	12/31/72	4	Southern California	Tucson, Ariz.	FA-'95	16/0
3		George, Jeff	QB	6-4	210	12/8/67	8	Illinois	Indianapolis, Ind.	FA-'97	16/16
45		Hall, Tim	RB	5-11	215	2/15/74	3	Robert Morris	Kansas City, Mo.	D6-'96	16/0
77		Harlow, Pat	T	6-6	295	3/16/69	8	Southern California	Norco, Calif.	T(NE)-'96	16/16
93		Harris, James	DE	6-6	300	5/13/68	5	Temple	East St. Louis, Ill.	FA-'98	0*
12		Hollas, Don	QB	6-3	210	11/22/67	6	Rice	Rosenberg, Tex.	FA-'97	0*
57		Holmberg, Rob	LB	6-3	230	5/6/71	5	Penn State	Mt. Pleasant, Pa.	D7-'94	16/0
80		Howard, Desmond	WR-KR	5-10	185	5/15/70	7	Michigan	Cleveland, Ohio	UFA(GB)-'97	15/0
90		Jackson, Grady	DT	6-2	325	1/21/73	2	Knoxville	Greensboro, Ala.	D6-'97	5/0
82		Jett, James	WR	5-10	165	12/28/70	6	West Virginia	Kearneysville, W. Va.	FA-'93	16/16
51		Johnstone, Lance	DE	6-4	245	6/11/73	3	Temple	Philadelphia, Pa.	D2-'96	14/6
26		Kaufman, Napoleon	RB	5-9	180	6/7/73	4	Washington	Lompoc, Calif.	D1-'95	16/16
72		Kennedy, Lincoln	T	6-6	340	2/12/71	6	Washington	San Diego, Calif.	T(Atl)-'96	16/16
72		Kohn, Tim	G-T	6-5	305	12/6/73	2	Iowa State	Wadsworth, Ill.	D3-'97	0*
25		Land, Dan	S	6-0	200	7/3/65	10	Albany State	Donalsonville, Ga.	FA-'89	16/0
31		Levitt, Chad	RB	6-1	235	11/21/75	2	Cornell	Melrose Park, Pa.	D4-'97	10/2
29		Lewis, Albert	CB	6-2	205	10/6/60	16	Grambling	Mansfield, La.	UFA(KC)-'94	14/11
43	#	Lynch, Lorenzo	S	5-11	200	4/6/63	12	Cal State-Sacramento	Oakland, Calif.	FA-'97	15/0
67		Maryland, Russell	DT	6-1	300	3/22/69	8	Miami	Chicago, Ill.	UFA(Dall)-'96	16/16
36		McDaniel, Terry	CB	5-10	180	2/8/65	11	Tennessee	Saginaw, Mich.	D1-'88	13/12
85		Mickens, Terry	WR	6-0	195	2/21/71	5	Florida A&M	Tallahassee, Fla.	UFA(GB)-'98	11/0*
56		Mills, John Henry	LB	6-0	230	10/31/69	6	Wake Forest	Jacksonville, Fla.	UFA(Hou)-'97	16/0
50		Morton, Mike	LB	6-4	235	3/28/72	4	North Carolina	Kannapolis, N.C.	D4-'95	11/11
30		Newman, Anthony	S	6-0	200	11/21/65	11	Oregon	Beaverton, Ore.	UFA(NO)-'98	12/12*
41		Riddick, Louis	S	6-2	215	3/15/69	6	Pittsburgh	Quakertown, Pa.	FA-'98	11/0*
63		Robbins, Barret	C	6-3	320	8/26/73	4	Texas Christian	Houston, Tex.	D2-'95	16/16
96		Russell, Darrell	DT	6-5	325	5/27/76	2	Southern California	San Diego, Calif.	D1-'97	16/10
84		Shedd, Kenny	WR	5-10	165	2/14/71	4	Northern Iowa	Davenport, Iowa	FA-'96	16/0
94	#	Smith, Anthony	DE	6-3	265	6/28/67	9	Arizona	Elizabeth City, N.C.	D1-'90	13/13
37		Trapp, James	S	6-0	195	12/28/69	6	Clemson	Lawton, Okla.	D3-'93	16/16
62		Treu, Adam	G-T	6-5	300	6/24/74	2	Nebraska	Lincoln, Neb.	D3-'97	16/0
88		Truitt, Olanda	WR	6-0	190	1/4/71	6	Mississippi State	Birmingham, Ala.	FA-'96	14/0
42		Turner, Eric	S	6-1	210	9/20/68	8	UCLA	Ventura, Calif.	FA-'97	16/15
38		Walker, Marquis	CB	5-10	175	7/6/72	3	Southeast Missouri	St. Louis, Mo.	FA-'98	11/0*
59		Wallace, Aaron	LB	6-3	245	4/17/67	8	Texas A&M	Dallas, Tex.	FA-'97	5/0
23	#	Washington, Lionel	CB	6-0	185	10/21/60	14	Tulane	New Orleans, La.	FA-'97	9/3
66		Whitley, Curtis	C	6-1	295	5/10/69	7	Clemson	Southfield, N.C.	FA-'97	15/1
78		Whittaker, Scott	G	6-7	305	6/7/74	2	Kansas	Alto Loma, Calif.	FA-'97	0*
22		Williams, Harvey	RB	6-2	220	4/22/67	8	Louisiana State	Hempstead, Tex.	UFA(KC)-'94	14/6
76		Wisniewski, Steve	G	6-4	300	4/7/76	10	Penn State	Houston, Tex.	D2-'89	16/16

* Allen played 16 games with New Orleans in '97; Ashmore played 12 games with Washington; Bates last active with Atlanta in '96; Brown played 13 games for-Jacksonville; Faumui inactive for 1 game; Harris last active with St. Louis in '96; Hollas and Kohn inactive for 16 games; Mickens played 11 games with Green Bay; Newman played 12 games with New Orleans; Riddick last active with Atlanta in '96; Walker played 11 games with St. Louis; Whittaker inactive for 14 games.

Unrestricted free agent: subject to developments.

t- Raiders traded for Allen (New Orleans).

Traded—LB Rob Fredrickson (16 games in '97) to Detroit.

Players lost through free agency (1): DT Chester McGlockton (KC; 16 games in '97).

Also played with Raiders in '97—S Eddie Anderson (11 games), DE Aundray Bruce (10), RB Jerone Davison (8), G Lester Holmes (15), DT Kevin Johnson (15), QB David Klingler (1), TE Bob Rosenstiel (4), DE Greg Townsend (4).

COACHING STAFF

Head Coach,
Jon Gruden

Pro career: Became the twelfth head coach in Raiders history on January 22, 1998, after seven years as an assistant coach in the National Football League. Gruden's teams reached the postseason five times during his assistant coaching tenure. Spent the last three years as offensive coordinator for the Philadelphia Eagles on Ray Rhodes's staff. The Eagles were 26-21-1 during this 1995-97 period, including playoff appearances after both the 1995 and 1996 seasons. In '97, the Eagles ranked second in passing, fifth in rushing and third in total offense in the NFC. In '96, they led the NFC in passing, were second in rushing and led the NFC in total offense. In '95—his first season as an NFL offensive coordinator—the Eagles finished fourth in the league in rushing. He served as an offensive assistant to Green Bay Packers head coach Mike Holmgren in 1992, then spent the 1993 and 1994 campaigns as Green Bay's receivers coach. The Packers had a 27-21 record those three seasons and were a playoff team in two of those years. Gruden spent the 1991 season as wide receivers coach at the University of Pittsburgh under coach Paul Hackett. In 1990, he was an offensive assistant to head coach George Seifert with the San Francisco 49ers, working with offensive coordinator Holmgren. The 49ers were an NFL best 14-2 that season and reached the NFC Championship Game.

Background: Quarterback at the University of Dayton, 1983-85, while earning bachelor's degree in communications. Won the prestigious Lt. Andy Zulli Memorial Award given annually "to the senior player who best exemplifies the qualities of sportsmanship and character." Dayton had a 24-7 record in Gruden's three varsity seasons there.

Personal: Born August 17, 1963 in Sandusky, Ohio. Gruden and his wife Cindy have two sons, Jon II, 4, and Michael, 1. His father, Jim, is a regional scout for the San Francisco 49ers and formerly served as an assistant coach under John McKay with the Tampa Bay Buccaneers from 1982-83. His brother Jay, who played in the Arena Football League, served as offensive coordinator of that league's Nashville team and is presently offensive coordinator of the Arena League's Orlando Predators.

1998 FIRST-YEAR ROSTER

Name	Pos.	Ht.	Wt.	Birthdate	College	Hometown	How Acq.
Amey, Vince	DE	6-2	300	2/9/75	Arizona State	Los Angeles, Calif.	D7a
Benjamin, Na'il (1)	WR	5-10	190	11/20/74	California	Los Angeles, Calif.	FA
Bobo, Phillip (1)	WR	5-9	180	12/6/71	Washington State	Moreno Valley, Calif.	FA
Branscomb, Kenyon (1)	WR	6-2	205	6/13/70	Oregon State	Beaverton, Ore.	FA
Brigham, Jeremy	TE	6-4	250	3/22/75	Washington	Scottsdale, Ariz.	D5a
Carey, Tim	QB	6-4	190	2/20/75	Hawaii	Seal Beach, Calif.	FA
Collins, Mo	T	6-4	335	9/22/76	Florida	Charlotte, N.C.	D1b
Davis, Jason (1)	QB	6-4	220	1/11/73	Western State	Eager, Ariz.	FA
Dawson, Phil	K	5-11	190	1/23/75	Texas	Dallas, Tex.	FA
DiNapoli, Gennaro	G	6-3	295	5/25/75	Virginia Tech	Cazenovia, N.Y.	D4
Franklin, Kevin	CB	5-9	170	9/28/74	Southern	Baton Rouge, La.	FA
Muirbrook, Shay (1)	LB	6-0	230	11/15/73	Brigham Young	Norco, Calif.	FA-'97
Nartey, Kofi	WR	6-1	195	7/21/75	California	Los Angeles, Calif.	FA
Ritchie, Jon	RB	6-2	245	9/4/74	Stanford	Mechanicsburg, Pa.	D3
Robinson, Derrick	LB	6-2	245	5/9/74	Southern	Benham Springs, La.	FA
Rosenstiel, Bob (1)	TE	6-3	240	2/7/74	Eastern Illinois	Junction City, Ore.	FA-'97
Sanders, David	DE	6-4	305	7/25/75	Arkansas	Jackson, Miss.	D7b
Sargeant, Shatony (1)	DE	6-5	280	9/27/75	Fresno State	Long Beach, Calif.	FA
Smith, Myron	LB	6-1	225	3/28/75	Louisiana Tech	Corsicana, Tex.	FA
Smith, Travian	LB	6-4	240	8/26/75	Oklahoma	Tatum, Okla.	D5b
Williams, Jermaine (1)	RB	6-0	230	7/3/72	Houston	Greenville, N.C.	FA
Williams, Rodney	WR	6-0	190	8/15/73	Arizona	Santa Monica, Calif.	FA
Woodson, Charles	CB	6-1	200	10/7/76	Michigan	Fremont, Ohio	D1a

The term NFL Rookie is defined as a player who is in his first season of professional football and has not been on the roster of another professional football team for any regular-season or postseason games. A Rookie is designated by an "R" on NFL rosters. Players who have been active in another professional football league or players who have NFL experience, including either preseason training camp or being on an Active List or Inactive List, or on Reserve/Injured or Reserve/Physically Unable to Perform for fewer than six regular-season games, are termed NFL First-Year Players. An NFL First-Year Player is designated by a "1" on NFL rosters. Thereafter, a player is credited with an additional year of experience for each season in which he accumulates six games on the Active List or Inactive List, or on Reserve/Injured or Reserve/Physically Unable to Perform.

NOTES

ASSISTANT COACHES

Dave Adolph, linebackers; born June 6, 1937, Akron, Ohio, lives in Alameda, Calif. Guard-linebacker Akron 1955-58. No pro playing experience. College coach: Akron 1963-64, Connecticut 1965-68, Kentucky 1969-72, Illinois 1973-76, Ohio State 1977-78. Pro coach: Cleveland Browns 1979-84, 1986-88, San Diego Chargers 1985, 1995-96, Los Angeles Raiders 1989-91, Kansas City Chiefs 1992-94, rejoined Raiders in 1997.

Fred Biletnikoff, wide receivers; born February 23, 1943, Erie, Pa., lives in Danville, Calif. Wide receiver Florida State 1962-64. Pro wide receiver Oakland Raiders 1965-78, Montreal Alouettes (CFL) 1980. College coach: Palomar (Calif.) J.C. 1983, Diablo Valley (Calif.) J.C. 1984, 1986. Pro coach: Oakland Invaders (USFL) 1985, Calgary Stampeders (CFL) 1987-88, joined Raiders in 1989.

Chuck Bresnahan, defensive backs; born September 8, 1960, Springfield, Mass., lives in Alameda, Calif. Linebacker Navy 1979-82. No pro playing experience. College coach: Navy 1983, 1986, Georgia Tech 1987-91, Maine 1992-93. Pro coach: Cleveland Browns 1994-95, Indianapolis Colts 1996-97, joined Raiders in 1998.

Willie Brown, squad development; born December 2, 1940, Yazoo City, Miss., lives in San Ramon, Calif. Defensive back Grambling 1959-62. Pro defensive back Denver Broncos 1963-66, Oakland Raiders 1967-78. College coach: Long Beach State 1990-91 (head coach 1991). Pro coach: Oakland/Los Angeles Raiders 1979-88, rejoined Raiders in 1995.

Bill Callahan, offensive coordinator and tight ends; born July 31, 1956, Chicago, lives in Danville, Calif. Quarterback Illinois-Benedictine 1975-77. No pro playing experience. College coach: Illinois 1980-86, Northern Arizona 1987-88, Southern Illinois 1989, Wisconsin 1990-94. Pro coach: Philadelphia Eagles 1995-97, joined Raiders in 1998.

Frank Gansz, Jr., special teams; born August 8, 1962, Greenville, S.C, lives Alameda, Calif. Defensive back The Citadel 1981-84. No pro playing experience. College coach: Kansas 1987, Pittsburgh 1988-89, Army 1990-91, Houston 1993-97. Pro coach: New York-New Jersey Knights (WLAF) 1992, joined Raiders in 1998.

Garrett Giemont, strength and conditioning; born August 31, 1957, Fullerton, Calif., lives in Alameda, Calif. Attended Fullerton College. No college or pro playing experience. Pro coach: Los Angeles Rams 1990-91, joined Raiders in 1995.

Robert Jenkins, offensive assistant; born December 30, 1963, San Francisco, lives in San Ramon, Calif. Tackle UCLA 1984-85. Pro tackle Los Angeles Rams 1986-93, Los Angeles Raiders 1994, Oakland Raiders 1995-96. Pro coach: Joined Raiders in 1997.

Don Martin, quality control-defense; born September 17, 1949, Carrollton, Mo., lives in Alameda, Calif. Running back Yale 1968-70. Pro defensive back New England Patriots 1973, Kansas City Chiefs 1975, Tampa Bay Buccaneers 1976. College coach: Yale 1981-96. Pro coach: Joined Raiders in 1998.

John Morton, offensive assistant; born September 24, 1969, Pontiac, Mich., lives in Castro Valley, Calif. Wide receiver Western Michigan 1991-92, Grand Rapids C.C. 1989-90. Pro wide receiver Los Angeles Raiders 1993-94, Toronto Argonauts (CFL) 1995-96, Frankfurt Galaxy (WLAF) 1997. Pro coach: Joined Raiders in 1998.

Skip Peete, running backs; born January 30, 1963, Mesa, Ariz., lives in Alameda, Calif. Wide receiver Arizona 1981-82, Kansas 1984-85. Pro wide receiver New York Jets 1987. College coach: Pittsburgh 1988-92, Michigan State 1993-94, Rutgers 1995, UCLA 1996-97. Pro coach: joined Raiders in 1998.

Keith Rowen, offensive line; born September 2, 1952, New York, N.Y., lives in San Ramon, Calif. Offensive tackle Stanford 1972-74. No pro playing experience. College coach: Stanford 1975-76, Long Beach State 1977-78, Arizona 1979-82. Pro coach: Boston/New Orleans Breakers (USFL) 1983-84, Cleveland Browns 1984, Indianapolis Colts 1985-88, New England Patriots 1989, Atlanta Falcons 1990-93, Minnesota Vikings 1994-96, joined Raiders in 1997.

David Shaw, quality control-offense; born July 31, 1972, San Diego, lives in Alameda, Calif. Wide receiver Stanford 1990-94. No pro playing experience. College coach: Western Washington 1995-96. Pro coach: Philadelphia Eagles 1997, joined Raiders in 1998.

Willie Shaw, defensive coordinator; born January 11, 1944, Glenmora, La., lives in Union City, Calif. Cornerback New Mexico 1966-68. No pro playing experience. College coach: San Diego C.C. 1970-73, Stanford 1974-76, 1989-91, Long Beach State 1977-78, Oregon 1979, Arizona State 1980-84. Pro coach: Detroit Lions 1985-88, Minnesota Vikings 1992-93, San Diego Chargers 1994, St. Louis Rams 1995-96, New Orleans Saints 1997, joined Raiders in 1998.

Gary Stevens, quarterbacks; born March 19, 1943, Cleveland, lives in Alameda, Calif. Running back John Carroll 1963-65. No pro playing experience. College coach: Louisville 1971-74, Kent State 1975, West Virginia 1976-79, Miami 1980-88. Pro coach: Miami Dolphins 1989-97, joined Raiders in 1998.

Mike Waufle, defensive line; born June 27, 1954, Hornell, N.Y., lives in Oakland. Defensive lineman Bakersfield J.C. 1975-76, Utah State 1977-78. No pro playing experience. College coach: Alfred 1979, Utah State 1980-84, Fresno State 1985-88, UCLA 1989, Oregon State 1990-91, California 1992-97. Pro coach: Joined Raiders in 1998.

PITTSBURGH STEELERS

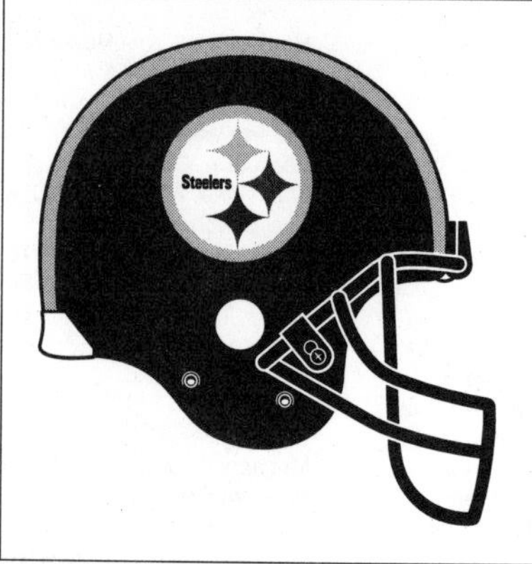

American Football Conference
Central Division
Team Colors: Black and Gold
Three Rivers Stadium
300 Stadium Circle
Pittsburgh, Pennsylvania 15212
Telephone: (412) 323-0300

CLUB OFFICIALS

President: Daniel M. Rooney
Vice President: John R. McGinley
Vice President: Arthur J. Rooney, Jr.
Vice President/General Counsel: Arthur J. Rooney II
Administration Advisor: Charles H. Noll
Director of Marketing: Mark Fuhrman
Communications Coordinator: Ron Wahl
Public Relations Manager: David Lockett
Director of Business: Mark Hart
Business Relations Coordinator: Dan Ferens
Business Accounting Coordinator: Jim Ellenberger
Director of Football Operations: Tom Donahoe
Pro Personnel Coordinator: Charles Bailey
College Scouts: Mark Gorscak, Phil Kreidler, Bob Lane, Max McCartney, Dan Rooney
Office/Ticket Coordinator: Geraldine R. Glenn
Ticket Manager: Brian Bonihate
Player Development Coordinator: Anthony Griggs
Trainers: John Norwig, Rick Burkholder
Equipment Manager: Rodgers Freyvogel
Stadium: Three Rivers Stadium • **Capacity:** 59,600
300 Stadium Circle
Pittsburgh, Pennsylvania 15212
Playing Surface: AstroTurf
Training Camp: St. Vincent College
Latrobe, Pennsylvania 15650

1998 SCHEDULE

PRESEASON

Aug. 1	vs. Tampa Bay at Canton, Ohio	7:00
Aug. 8	**Buffalo**	7:30
Aug. 14	at Philadelphia	8:00
Aug. 22	vs. Atlanta at Morgantown, W. Va.	6:00
Aug. 29	**Carolina**	8:20

REGULAR SEASON

Sept. 6	at Baltimore	1:01
Sept. 13	**Chicago**	1:01
Sept. 20	at Miami	1:01
Sept. 27	**Seattle**	4:05
Oct. 4	Open Date	
Oct. 11	at Cincinnati	1:01
Oct. 18	**Baltimore**	1:01
Oct. 26	at Kansas City (Mon.)	7:20
Nov. 1	**Tennessee**	1:01
Nov. 9	**Green Bay** (Mon.)	8:20
Nov. 15	at Tennessee	12:01
Nov. 22	**Jacksonville**	1:01
Nov. 26	at Detroit (Thurs.)	12:35
Dec. 6	**New England**	1:01
Dec. 13	at Tampa Bay	1:01
Dec. 20	**Cincinnati**	1:01
Dec. 28	at Jacksonville (Mon.)	8:20

RECORD HOLDERS

INDIVIDUAL RECORDS—CAREER

Category	Name	Performance
Rushing (Yds.)	Franco Harris, 1972-1983	11,950
Passing (Yds.)	Terry Bradshaw, 1970-1983	27,989
Passing (TDs)	Terry Bradshaw, 1970-1983	212
Receiving (No.)	John Stallworth, 1974-1987	537
Receiving (Yds.)	John Stallworth, 1974-1987	8,723
Interceptions	Mel Blount, 1970-1983	57
Punting (Avg.)	Bobby Joe Green, 1960-61	45.7
Punt Return (Avg.)	Bobby Gage, 1949-1950	14.9
Kickoff Return (Avg.)	Lynn Chandnois, 1950-56	29.6
Field Goals	Gary Anderson, 1982-1994	309
Touchdowns (Tot.)	Franco Harris, 1972-1983	100
Points	Gary Anderson, 1982-1994	1,343

INDIVIDUAL RECORDS—SINGLE SEASON

Category	Name	Performance
Rushing (Yds.)	Barry Foster, 1992	1,690
Passing (Yds.)	Terry Bradshaw, 1979	3,724
Passing (TDs)	Terry Bradshaw, 1978	28
Receiving (No.)	Yancey Thigpen, 1995	85
Receiving (Yds.)	Yancey Thigpen, 1997	1,398
Interceptions	Mel Blount, 1975	11
Punting (Avg.)	Bobby Joe Green, 1961	47.0
Punt Return (Avg.)	Bobby Gage, 1949	16.0
Kickoff Return (Avg.)	Lynn Chandnois, 1952	35.2
Field Goals	Norm Johnson, 1995	34
Touchdowns (Tot.)	Louis Lipps, 1985	15
Points	Norm Johnson, 1995	141

INDIVIDUAL RECORDS—SINGLE GAME

Category	Name	Performance
Rushing (Yds.)	John Fuqua, 12-20-70	218
Passing (Yds.)	Bobby Layne, 12-3-58	409
Passing (TDs)	Terry Bradshaw, 11-15-81	5
	Mark Malone, 9-8-85	5
Receiving (No.)	J.R. Wilburn, 10-22-67	12
Receiving (Yds.)	Buddy Dial, 10-22-61	235
Interceptions	Jack Butler, 12-13-53	*4
Field Goals	Gary Anderson, 10-23-88	6
Touchdowns (Tot.)	Ray Mathews, 10-17-54	4
	Roy Jefferson, 11-3-68	4
Points	Ray Mathews, 10-17-54	24
	Roy Jefferson, 11-3-68	24

*NFL Record

COACHING HISTORY

Pittsburgh Pirates 1933-1940
(439-450-20)

1933	Forrest (Jap) Douds	3-6-2
1934	Luby DiMelio	2-10-0
1935-36	Joe Bach	10-14-0
1937-39	Johnny (Blood) McNally*	6-19-0
1939-40	Walt Kiesling	3-13-3
1941	Bert Bell**	0-2-0
	Aldo (Buff) Donelli***	0-5-0
1941-44	Walt Kiesling****	13-20-2
1945	Jim Leonard	2-8-0
1946-47	Jock Sutherland	13-10-1
1948-51	Johnny Michelosen	20-26-2
1952-53	Joe Bach	11-13-0
1954-56	Walt Kiesling	14-22-0
1957-64	Raymond (Buddy) Parker	51-48-6
1965	Mike Nixon	2-12-0
1966-68	Bill Austin	11-28-3
1969-91	Chuck Noll	209-156-1
1992-97	Bill Cowher	69-38-0

*Released after three games in 1939
**Resigned after two games in 1941
***Released after five games in 1941
****Co-coach with Earle (Greasy) Neale in Philadelphia-Pittsburgh merger in 1943 and with Phil Handler in Chicago Cardinals-Pittsburgh merger in 1944

THREE RIVERS STADIUM

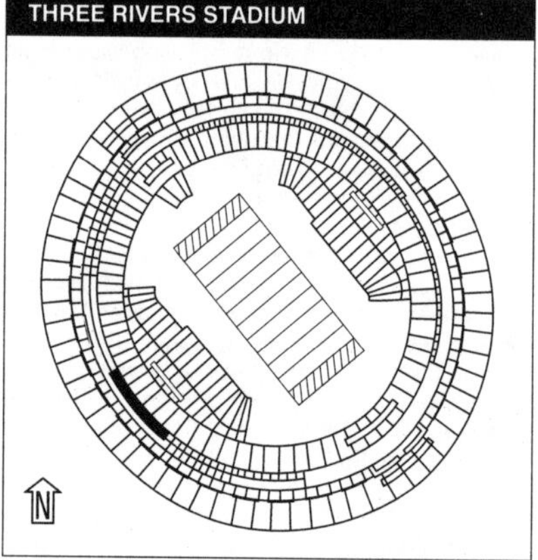

PITTSBURGH STEELERS

1997 TEAM RECORD

PRESEASON (5-0)

Date	Result		Opponents
7/27	W	30-17	vs. Chicago at Dublin, Ireland
8/2	W	28-14	at Kansas City
8/11	W	42-26	Philadelphia
8/17	W	28-20	Detroit
8/22	W	27-19	at Carolina

REGULAR SEASON (11-5)

Date	Result		Opponents	Att.
8/31	L	7-37	Dallas	60,396
9/7	W	14-13	Washington	58,059
9/22	L	21-30	at Jacksonville	73,016
9/28	W	37-24	Tennessee	57,507
10/5	W	42-34	at Baltimore	64,421
10/12	W	24-22	Indianapolis	57,925
10/19	W	26-10	at Cincinnati	60,020
10/26	W	23-17	Jacksonville (OT)	57,011
11/3	L	10-13	at Kansas City	78,301
11/9	W	37-0	Baltimore	56,669
11/16	W	20-3	Cincinnati	55,226
11/23	L	20-23	at Philadelphia	67,166
11/30	W	26-20	at Arizona (OT)	66,341
12/7	W	35-24	Denver	59,739
12/13	W	24-21	at New England (OT)	60,013
12/21	L	6-16	at Tennessee	50,677

POSTSEASON (1-1)

1/3	W	7-6	New England	61,228
1/11	L	21-24	Denver	61,382

(OT) Overtime

SCORE BY PERIODS

Steelers	67	98	86	106	15	— 372
Opponents	69	106	65	67	0	— 307

ATTENDANCE

Home 462,532 Away 519,955 Total 982,487
Single-game home record, 60,608 (12/18/94)
Single-season home record, 466,944 (1996)

1997 TEAM STATISTICS

	Steelers	Opp.
Total First Downs	326	285
Rushing	154	82
Passing	157	177
Penalty	15	26
Third Down: Made/Att	98/219	102/228
Third Down Pct.	44.7	44.7
Fourth Down: Made/Att	11/18	7/13
Fourth Down Pct.	61.1	53.8
Total Net Yards	5,542	4,705
Avg. Per Game	346.4	294.1
Total Plays	1,058	1,005
Avg. Per Play	5.2	4.7
Net Yards Rushing	2,479	1,318
Avg. Per Game	154.9	82.4
Total Rushes	572	403
Net Yards Passing	3,063	3,387
Avg. Per Game	191.4	211.7
Sacked/Yards Lost	20/152	48/294
Gross Yards	3,215	3,681
Att./Completions	466/253	554/295
Completion Pct.	54.3	53.2
Had Intercepted	19	20
Punts/Avg.	64/42.6	66/42.5
Net Punting Avg.	64/35.0	66/37.9
Penalties/Yards Lost	95/861	90/708
Fumbles/Ball Lost	25/14	26/14
Touchdowns	44	31
Rushing	19	5
Passing	22	24
Returns	3	2
Avg. Time of Possession	32:05	27:55

1997 INDIVIDUAL STATISTICS

PASSING	Att.	Comp.	Yds.	Pct.	TD	Int.	Tkld.	Rate
Stewart	440	236	3,020	53.6	21	17	20/152	75.2
Tomczak	24	16	185	66.7	1	2	0/0	68.9
Quinn	2	1	10	50	0	0	0/0	64.6
Steelers	466	253	3,215	54.3	22	19	20/152	74.8
Opponents	554	295	3,681	53.2	24	20	48/294	73.5

SCORING	TD R	TD P	TD Rt	PAT	FG	Saf	PTS
N. Johnson	0	0	0	40/40	22/25	0	106
Stewart	11	0	0	0/0	0/0	0	66
Bettis	7	2	0	0/0	0/0	0	54
Thigpen	0	7	0	0/0	0/0	0	44
Bruener	0	6	0	0/0	0/0	0	36
Hawkins	0	3	0	0/0	0/0	0	18
Blackwell	0	1	1	0/0	0/0	0	12
C. Johnson	0	2	0	0/0	0/0	0	12
G. Jones	1	1	0	0/0	0/0	0	12
Gildon	0	0	1	0/0	0/0	0	6
Lake	0	0	1	0/0	0/0	0	6
Steelers	19	22	3	40/40	22/25	0	372
Opponents	5	24	2	28/28	29/35	1	307

2-Point conversions: Thigpen.
Team 1-2, Opponents 2-3.

RUSHING	Att.	Yds.	Avg.	LG	TD
Bettis	375	1,665	4.4	34	7
Stewart	88	476	5.4	74t	11
G. Jones	72	235	3.3	32	1
McAfee	13	41	3.2	9	0
Hawkins	5	17	3.4	11	0
Blackwell	2	14	7.0	11	0
Tomczak	7	13	1.9	17	0
Witman	5	11	2.2	4	0
Lester	2	9	4.5	6	0
Thigpen	1	3	3.0	3	0
Marsh	1	2	2.0	2	0
Jo. Miller	1	-7	-7.0	-7	0
Steelers	572	2,479	4.3	74t	19
Opponents	403	1,318	3.3	47	5

RECEIVING	No.	Yds.	Avg.	LG	TD
Thigpen	79	1,398	17.7	69t	7
C. Johnson	46	568	12.3	49	2
Hawkins	45	555	12.3	44t	3
Bruener	18	117	6.5	18t	6
G. Jones	16	96	6.0	25	1
Bettis	15	110	7.3	19t	2
Blackwell	12	168	14.0	46	1
Lester	10	51	5.1	14	0
Lyons	4	29	7.3	13	0
McAfee	2	44	22.0	30	0
Marsh	2	14	7.0	8	0
Adams	1	39	39.0	39	0
Sadowski	1	12	12.0	12	0
Botkin	1	11	11.0	11	0
Witman	1	3	3.0	3	0
Steelers	253	3,215	12.7	69t	22
Opponents	295	3,681	12.5	55	24

INTERCEPTIONS	No.	Yds.	Avg.	LG	TD
Woolford	4	91	22.8	34	0
Perry	4	77	19.3	42	0
Lake	3	16	5.3	11	0
Oldham	2	16	8.0	8	0
Kirkland	2	14	7.0	11	0
Scott	2	-4	-2.0	0	0
Henry	1	36	36.0	36	0
Bell	1	10	10.0	7	0
Conley	1	-3	-3.0	-3	0
Steelers	20	253	12.7	42	0
Opponents	19	270	14.2	43	0

PUNTING	No.	Yds.	Avg.	In 20	LG
Jo. Miller	64	2,729	42.6	17	72
Steelers	64	2,729	42.6	17	72
Opponents	66	2,804	42.5	17	59

PUNT RETURNS	No.	FC	Yds.	Avg.	LG	TD
Blackwell	23	6	149	6.5	15	0
Coleman	5	2	5	1.0	5	0
Hawkins	4	2	68	17.0	30	0
Steelers	32	10	222	6.9	30	0
Opponents	23	6	271	11.8	38	0

KICKOFF RETURNS	No.	Yds.	Avg.	LG	TD
Blackwell	32	791	24.7	97t	1
Coleman	24	487	20.3	28	0
Adams	10	215	21.5	31	0
Vrabel	1	0	0.0	0	0
Steelers	67	1,493	22.3	97t	1
Opponents	74	1,556	21.0	97t	1

FIELD GOALS	1-19	20-29	30-39	40-49	50+
N. Johnson	1/1	6/6	8/8	6/8	1/2
Steelers	1/1	6/6	8/8	6/8	1/2
Opponents	1/1	13/14	11/12	3/6	1/2

SACKS	No.
Lake	6.0
Gildon	5.0
Kirkland	5.0
Henry	4.5
Conley	4.0
Harrison	4.0
Holmes	4.0
Oldham	4.0
Lloyd	3.5
Bell	1.5
Vrabel	1.5
Fuller	1.0
Gibson	1.0
Perry	1.0
Roye	1.0
Steed	1.0
Steelers	48.0
Opponents	20.0

1998 DRAFT CHOICES

Round	Name	Pos.	College
1	Alan Faneca	G	Louisiana State
2	Jeremy Staat	DE	Arizona State
3	Chris Conrad	T	Fresno State
	Hines Ward	WR	Georgia
4	Deshea Townsend	DB	Alabama
	Carlos King	RB	North Carolina State
5	Jason Simmons	DB	Arizona State
6	Chris Fuamatu-Ma'afala	RB	Utah
	Ryan Olson	WR	Colorado
7	Angel Rubio	DE	Southeast Missouri State

PITTSBURGH STEELERS

1998 VETERAN ROSTER

No.	Name	Pos.	Ht.	Wt.	Birthdate	NFL Exp.	College	Hometown	How Acq.	'97 Games/ Starts
86	Adams, Mike	WR	5-11	184	3/25/74	2	Texas	Arlington, Tex.	D7-'97	6/0
80	Arnold, Jahine	WR	6-0	187	6/19/73	3	Fresno State	Cupertino, Calif.	D4b-'96	0*
82	Bailey, Henry	WR	5-8	176	2/28/73	3	Nevada-Las Vegas	Chicago, Ill.	FA-'97	0*
36	Bettis, Jerome	RB	5-11	243	2/16/72	6	Notre Dame	Detroit, Mich.	T(StL)-'96	15/15
89	Blackwell, Will	WR	6-0	184	7/9/75	2	San Diego State	Capitol Heights, Md.	D2-'97	14/0
84	† Botkin, Kirk	TE	6-3	245	3/19/71	4	Arkansas	Baytown, Tex.	FA-'96	13/1
27	Brown, J.B.	CB	6-0	191	1/5/67	10	Maryland	Washington, D.C.	FA-'97	13/0
29	Brown, Lance	CB-S	6-2	200	2/2/72	3	Indiana	Jacksonville, Fla.	FA-'97	0*
87	Bruener, Mark	TE	6-4	258	9/16/72	4	Washington	Aberdeen, Wash.	D1-'95	16/16
19	Coleman, Andre	WR	5-9	165	9/19/72	5	Kansas	Hermitage, Pa.	FA-'97	8/0
53	Conley, Steven	LB	6-5	235	1/18/72	3	Arkansas	Chicago, Ill.	D3-'96	16/0
63	Dawson, Dermontti	C	6-2	288	6/17/65	11	Kentucky	Lexington, Ky.	D2-'88	16/16
62	Duffy, Roger	G	6-3	305	7/16/67	9	Penn State	Canton, Ohio	UFA(NYJ)-'98	15/15*
51	Emmons, Carlos	LB	6-5	246	9/3/73	3	Arkansas State	Greenwood, Miss.	D7-'97	5/0
41	† Flowers, Lethon	CB-S	6-0	213	1/14/73	4	Georgia Tech	Spring Valley, N.C.	D5a-'95	10/0
98	† Gibson, Oliver	DE-DT	6-3	298	3/15/72	4	Notre Dame	Romeoville, Ill.	D4a-'95	16/0
92	Gildon, Jason	LB	6-3	245	7/31/72	5	Oklahoma State	Altus, Okla.	D3a-'94	16/16
74	Harrison, Nolan	DE	6-5	280	1/25/69	8	Indiana	Chicago, Ill.	FA-'97	16/16
88	Hawkins, Courtney	WR	5-9	183	12/12/69	7	Michigan State	Flint, Mich.	UFA(TB)-'97	15/3
76	Henry, Kevin	DE	6-4	282	10/23/68	6	Mississippi State	Mound Bayou, Miss.	D4-'93	16/16
83	Holliday, Corey	WR	6-2	208	1/31/71	3	North Carolina	Richmond, Va.	FA-'95	2/0
50	Holmes, Earl	LB	6-2	246	4/28/73	3	Florida A&M	Tallahassee, Fla.	D4a-'96	16/16
33	Huntley, Richard	RB	5-11	224	9/18/72	2	Winston-Salem State	Monroe, N.C.	FA-'98	0*
81	Johnson, Charles	WR	6-0	195	1/3/72	5	Colorado	San Bernardino, Calif.	D1-'94	13/11
9	Johnson, Norm	K	6-2	202	5/31/60	17	UCLA	Garden Grove, Calif.	FA-'97	16/0
54	† Jones, Donta	LB	6-2	234	8/27/72	4	Nebraska	Pomfret, Md.	D4b-'95	16/4
43	Jones, George	RB	5-9	204	12/31/73	2	San Diego State	Greenville, S.C.	D5b-'97	16/0
99	Kirkland, Levon	LB	6-1	274	2/17/69	7	Clemson	Lamar, S.C.	D2-'92	16/16
37	Lake, Carnell	S	6-1	210	7/15/67	10	UCLA	Inglewood, Calif.	D2-'89	16/16
34	Lester, Tim	RB	5-10	238	6/5/68	7	Eastern Kentucky	Miami, Fla.	FA-'95	16/13
95	Lloyd, Greg	LB	6-2	235	5/26/65	12	Fort Valley State	Fort Valley, Ga.	D6b-'87	12/12
85	Lyons, Mitch	TE	6-5	265	5/13/70	6	Michigan State	Grand Rapids, Mich.	UFA(Atl)-'97	10/3
97	Manuel, Rod	DE	6-5	290	10/8/74	2	Oklahoma	Fort Worth, Tex.	D6b-'97	1/0
17	Marsh, Curtis	WR	6-2	206	11/24/70	4	Utah	Simi Valley, Calif.	FA-'97	5/0
25	McAfee, Fred	RB	5-10	198	6/20/68	8	Mississippi College	Philadelphia, Miss.	FA-'94	14/0
4	Miller, Josh	P	6-3	215	7/14/70	3	Arizona	East Brunswick, N.J.	FA-'96	16/0
24	Oldham, Chris	CB	5-9	200	10/20/68	8	Oregon	Sacramento, Calif.	UFA(Ariz)-'95	16/0
39	Perry, Darren	S	5-11	196	12/29/68	7	Penn State	Deep Creek, Va.	D8-'92	16/16
11	Quinn, Mike	QB	6-3	220	4/15/74	2	Stephen F. Austin	Houston, Tex.	FA-'97	1/0
44	Ravotti, Eric	LB	6-2	250	3/16/71	4	Penn State	Freeport, Pa.	FA-'98	0*
71	Roye, Orpheus	DE	6-4	290	1/21/74	3	Florida State	Miami Springs, Fla.	D6a-'96	16/0
46	Sadowski, Troy	TE	6-5	252	12/8/65	9	Georgia	Woodstock, Ga.	FA-'97	6/0
30	Scott, Chad	CB-S	6-1	203	9/6/74	2	Maryland	Capitol Heights, Md.	D1-'97	13/9
68	† Stai, Brenden	G	6-4	305	3/30/72	4	Nebraska	Anaheim, Calif.	D3-'95	11/9
93	Steed, Joel	NT	6-2	310	2/17/69	7	Colorado	Denver, Colo.	D3-'92	16/16
67	Stephens, Jamain	T	6-6	336	1/9/74	3	North Carolina A&T	Lumberton, N.C.	D1-'96	8/1
10	Stewart, Kordell	QB	6-1	212	10/16/72	4	Colorado	Marrero, La.	D2-'95	16/16
73	Strzelczyk, Justin	G-T	6-6	305	8/18/68	9	Maine	Seneca, N.Y.	D11-'90	14/14
66	Sweeney, Jim	C-G	6-4	298	8/8/62	15	Pittsburgh	Pittsburgh, Pa.	FA-'96	16/1
18	Tomczak, Mike	QB	6-1	207	10/23/62	14	Ohio State	Calumet City, Ill.	UFA(Clev)-'93	16/0
96	Vrabel, Mike	DE	6-4	275	8/14/75	2	Ohio State	Stow, Ohio	D3b-'97	15/0
20	Washington, Dewayne	CB	6-0	190	12/27/72	5	North Carolina State	Durham, N.C.	UFA(Minn)-'98	16/16*
79	Wiggins, Paul	G-T	6-3	307	8/17/73	2	Oregon	Portland, Ore.	D3a-'97	1/0
38	Witman, Jon	RB	6-1	240	6/1/72	3	Penn State	Wrightsville, Pa.	D3b-'96	16/2
77	Wolford, Will	G-T	6-5	300	5/18/64	13	Vanderbilt	Louisville, Ky.	UFA(Ind)-'96	16/16
21	Woolford, Donnell	CB	5-9	200	1/6/66	10	Clemson	Byrd, N.C.	UFA(Chi)-'97	15/2

* Arnold and Bailey missed '97 season because of injury; L. Brown last active with N.Y. Jets in '96; Duffy played 15 games with N.Y. Jets in '97; Huntley last active with Atlanta in '96; Ravotti last active with Pittsburgh in '96; Washington played 16 games with Minnesota.

† Restricted free agent; subject to developments.

Players lost through free agency (4); CB Randy Fuller (Atl; 12 games in '97), T John Jackson (SD; 16), G Tom Myslinski (Ind; 16), WR Yancey Thigpen (Tenn; 16).

Also played with Steelers in '97—S Myron Bell (16 games), LB Jerry Olsavsky (16).

COACHING STAFF

Head Coach,
Bill Cowher

Pro Career: Begins his seventh season as the fifteenth head coach in Steelers' history, replacing Chuck Noll on January 21, 1992. Cowher led the Steelers to an 11-5 regular-season record in 1997. In 1995, at age 38, he became the youngest coach to lead his team to a Super Bowl. Cowher is only the second coach in NFL history to lead his team to the playoffs during his first six seasons as head coach, the other coach is Pro Football Hall of Fame member Paul Brown. During Cowher's 13-year coaching career, teams he has been associated with have made the postseason 12 times. Began his NFL career as a free-agent linebacker with the Philadelphia Eagles in 1979, and then signed with the Cleveland Browns the following year. Cowher played three seasons (1980-82) in Cleveland before being traded back to the Eagles, where he played two more years (1983-84). Cowher began his coaching career in 1985 at age 28 under Marty Schottenheimer with the Browns. He was the Browns' special teams coach in 1985-86 and secondary coach in 1987-88 before following Schottenheimer to the Kansas City Chiefs in 1989 as defensive coordinator. Career record: 69-38.
Background: Excelled in football, basketball, and track for Carlynton High in Crafton, Pa. Was a three-year starter at linebacker for North Carolina State, serving as captain and earning team MVP honors as a senior. Graduated in 1979 with education degree.
Personal: Born in Pittsburgh, Pa., on May 8, 1957. His wife Kaye, also a North Carolina State graduate, played professional basketball for the New York Stars of the Women's Professional Basketball League with twin sister Faye. Bill and Kaye live in Pittsburgh and have three daughters—Meagan Lyn, Lauren Marie, and Lindsay Morgan.

ASSISTANT COACHES

Mike Archer, linebackers; born July 26, 1953, State College, Pa., lives in Pittsburgh. Safety/punter Miami 1972-75. No pro playing experience. College coach: Miami 1978-83, Louisiana State 1984-90 (head coach 1987-90), Virginia 1991-92, Kentucky 1993-95. Pro coach: Joined the Steelers in 1996.
Dave Culley, receivers; born September 17, 1955, Sparta, Tenn., lives in Pittsburgh. Quarterback Vanderbilt 1973-77. No pro playing experience. College coach: Austin Peay 1978, Vanderbilt 1979-81, Middle Tennessee State 1982, Tennessee-Chattanooga 1983, Western Kentucky 1984, Southwestern Louisiana 1985-88, Texas-El Paso 1989-90, Texas A&M 1991-93. Pro coach: Tampa Bay Buccaneers 1994-95, joined Steelers in 1996.
Jim Haslett, defensive coordinator; born December 9, 1955, Pittsburgh, Pa., lives in Pittsburgh. Defensive end Indiana University (Pa.) 1975-78. Linebacker Buffalo Bills 1979-86, New York Jets 1987. College coach: Buffalo 1988-90. Pro coach: Sacramento Surge (World League) 1991-92, Los Angeles Raiders 1993-94, New Orleans Saints 1995-96, joined Steelers in 1997.
Dick Hoak, running backs; born December 8, 1939, Jeannette, Pa., lives in Greensburg, Pa. Halfback-quarterback Penn State 1958-60. Pro running back Pittsburgh Steelers 1961-70. Pro coach: Joined Steelers in 1972.
Tim Lewis, defensive backs; born December 18, 1961, Quakertown, Pa., lives in Pittsburgh. Defensive back Pittsburgh 1979-82. Pro cornerback Green Bay Packers 1983-86. College coach: Texas A&M 1987-88, Southern Methodist 1989-92, Pittsburgh 1993-94. Pro coach: Joined Steelers in 1995.
John Mitchell, defensive line; born October 14, 1951, Mobile, Ala., lives in Pittsburgh. Defensive end Eastern Arizona J.C. 1969-70, Alabama 1971-72. No pro playing experience. College coach: Alabama 1973-76, Arkansas 1977-82, Temple 1986, Louisiana State 1987-90. Pro coach: Birmingham Stallions (USFL) 1983-85, Cleveland Browns 1991-93, joined Steelers in 1994.
Mike Mularkey, tight ends; born November 19, 1961, Ft. Lauderdale, Fla., lives in Pittsburgh. Tight end Florida 1979-82. Pro tight end Minnesota Vikings 1983-88, Pittsburgh Steelers 1989-91. College coach: Concordia 1993. Pro coach: Tampa Bay Buccaneers 1994-95, joined Steelers in 1996.
Ray Sherman, offensive coordinator; born November 17, 1951, Berkeley, Calif., lives in Pittsburgh. Wide receiver Lancey (Calif.) J.C. 1969-1970, Fresno State 1971-72. Pro defensive back Green Bay Packers 1973. College coach: San Jose State 1974, California 1975, 1981, Michigan State 1976-77, Wake Forest 1978-80, Purdue 1982-84, Georgia 1986-87. Pro coach: Houson Oilers 1988-89, San Francisco 49ers 1991-93, New York Jets 1994, Minnesota Vikings 1995-97, joined Steelers in 1998.
Kent Stephenson, offensive line; born February 4, 1942, Anita, Iowa, lives in Pittsburgh. Guard-nose tackle Northern Iowa 1962-64. No pro playing experience. College coach: Wayne State 1965-68, North Dakota 1969-71, Southern Methodist 1972-73, Iowa 1974-76, Oklahoma State 1977-78, Kansas 1979-82. Pro coach: Michigan Panthers (USFL) 1983-84, Seattle Seahawks 1985-91, joined Steelers in 1992.
Ron Zook, special teams; born April 28, 1954, Ashland, Ohio, lives in Pittsburgh. Defensive back Miami (Ohio) 1972-75. No pro playing experience. College coach: Murray State 1978-80, Cincinnati 1981-82, Kansas 1983, Tennessee 1984-86, Virginia Tech 1987, Ohio State 1988-90, Florida 1991-95. Pro coach: Joined Steelers in 1996.

1998 FIRST-YEAR ROSTER

Name	Pos.	Ht.	Wt.	Birthdate	College	Hometown	How Acq.
Brown, DeAuntae (1)	CB-S	5-10	195	4/28/74	Central State, Ohio	Detroit, Mich.	FA
Brown, Morocco	LB	6-0	230	2/9/76	North Carolina State	Hampton, Va.	FA
Conrad, Chris	T	6-6	301	5/27/75	Fresno State	Fullerton, Calif	D3a
Cushing, Matt	TE	6-3	260	7/2/75	Illinois	Chicago, Ill.	FA
DeLaTorre, Aaron	NT	6-1	296	5/6/75	Stephen F. Austin	Irving, Tex.	FA
Evans, Mike	T	6-4	315	7/28/73	Mercyhurst	Pittsburgh, Pa.	FA
Faneca, Alan	G	6-4	322	12/7/76	Louisiana State	New Orleans, La.	D1
Fiala, John (1)	LB	6-2	235	11/25/73	Washington	Kirkland, Wash.	FA
Fuamatu-Ma'afala, Chris	RB	5-11	252	3/4/77	Utah	Honolulu, Hawaii	D6a
George, Matt	P-K	5-11	190	1/13/75	Chapman	Canyon Country, Calif.	FA
Gonzalez, Pete	QB	6-1	216	7/4/74	Pittsburgh	Miami, Fla.	FA
Harper, Matt	DE	6-4	275	4/28/74	Texas Christian	Richmond, Tex.	FA
Henne, Aaron (1)	G	6-5	299	3/2/74	Maryland	Allison Park, Pa.	FA
Huntley, Richard (1)	RB	5-11	224	9/18/72	Winston-Salem State	Monroe, N.C.	FA
Jenkins, John	CB-S	6-0	188	5/11/75	Pittsburgh	East McKeesport, Pa.	FA
King, Carlos	RB	6-0	235	11/27/73	North Carolina State	Booneville, N.C.	D4b
McCann, David (1)	RB	5-11	220	7/27/75	Murray State	Elizabethtown, Ky.	FA
Murphy Seamus	C	6-5	290	9/23/76	North Carolina State	Pittsburgh, Pa.	FA
Olson, Ryan	LB	6-2	275	6/27/75	Colorado	Lakewood, Calif.	D6b
Rubio, Angel	DE	6-2	300	4/12/75	Southeast Missouri State	Modesto, Calif.	D7
Simmons, Jason	CB	5-8	188	3/30/76	Arizona State	Inglewood, Calif.	D5
Staat, Jeremy	DE	6-5	300	10/10/76	Arizona State	Bakersfield, Calif.	D2
Townsend, Deshea	CB	5-10	180	9/8/75	Alabama	Batesville, Miss.	D4a
Ward, Hines	WR	6-0	194	3/8/76	Georgia	Rex, Ga.	D3b

The term NFL Rookie is defined as a player who is in his first season of professional football and has not been on the roster of another professional football team for any regular-season or postseason games. A Rookie is designated by an "R" on NFL rosters. Players who have been active in another professional football league or players who have NFL experience, including either preseason training camp or being on an Active List or Inactive List, or on Reserve/Injured or Reserve/Physically Unable to Perform for fewer than six regular-season games, are termed NFL First-Year Players. An NFL First-Year Player is designated by a "1" on NFL rosters. Thereafter, a player is credited with an additional year of experience for each season in which he accumulates six games on the Active List or Inactive List, or on Reserve/Injured or Reserve/Physically Unable to Perform.

NOTES

SAN DIEGO CHARGERS

American Football Conference
Western Division
Team Colors: Navy Blue, White, and Gold
Qualcomm Stadium
P.O. Box 609609
San Diego, California 92160-9609
Telephone: (619) 874-4500

CLUB OFFICIALS

Chairman of the Board: Alex G. Spanos
President-Vice Chairman: Dean A. Spanos
Executive Vice President: Michael A. Spanos
General Manager: Bobby Beathard
Vice President-Finance: Jeremiah T. Murphy
Chief Financial and Administrative Officer: Jeanne Bonk
Director of Player Personnel: Billy Devaney
Director of Pro Personnel: Greg Gaines
Coordinator of Football Operations: Ed McGuire
Director of Sales & Marketing: Lynn Abramson
Business Manager: John Hinek
Director of Public Relations: Bill Johnston
Director of Business & Community Affairs: Richard Ledford
Director of Ticket Operations: Ron Tuck
Director of Video Operations: Brian Duddy
Head Trainer: Keoki Kamau
Equipment Manager: Sid Brooks
Stadium: Qualcomm Stadium • **Capacity:** 71,000
9449 Friars Road
San Diego, California 92108
Playing Surface: Grass
Training Camp: University of California-San Diego
Third College
La Jolla, California 92037

1998 SCHEDULE

PRESEASON

Aug. 8	**San Francisco**	7:00
Aug. 15	**St. Louis**	8:00
Aug. 22	at Indianapolis	7:00
Aug. 28	at Minnesota	7:00

REGULAR SEASON

Sept. 6	**Buffalo**	1:15
Sept. 13	at Tennessee	12:01
Sept. 20	at Kansas City	12:01
Sept. 27	**New York Giants**	1:15
Oct. 4	at Indianapolis	12:01
Oct. 11	at Oakland	1:15
Oct. 18	**Philadelphia**	1:15
Oct. 25	**Seattle**	1:15
Nov. 1	Open Date	
Nov. 8	at Denver	2:15
Nov. 15	**Baltimore**	1:05
Nov. 22	**Kansas City**	1:15
Nov. 29	**Denver**	5:20
Dec. 6	at Washington	1:01
Dec. 13	at Seattle	1:05
Dec. 20	**Oakland**	1:05
Dec. 27	at Arizona	2:15

RECORD HOLDERS

INDIVIDUAL RECORDS—CAREER

Category	Name	Performance
Rushing (Yds.)	Paul Lowe, 1960-67	4,963
Passing (Yds.)	Dan Fouts, 1973-1987	43,040
Passing (TDs)	Dan Fouts, 1973-1987	254
Receiving (No.)	Charlie Joiner, 1976-1986	586
Receiving (Yds.)	Lance Alworth, 1962-1970	9,585
Interceptions	Gill Byrd, 1983-1992	42
Punting (Avg.)	Darren Bennett, 1995-97	45.2
Punt Return (Avg.)	Darrien Gordon, 1993-96	13.6
Kickoff Return (Avg.)	Leslie (Speedy) Duncan, 1964-1970	25.3
Field Goals	John Carney, 1990-97	186
Touchdowns (Tot.)	Lance Alworth, 1962-1970	83
Points	John Carney, 1990-97	783

INDIVIDUAL RECORDS—SINGLE SEASON

Category	Name	Performance
Rushing (Yds.)	Natrone Means, 1994	1,350
Passing (Yds.)	Dan Fouts, 1981	4,802
Passing (TDs)	Dan Fouts, 1981	33
Receiving (No.)	Tony Martin, 1995	90
Receiving (Yds.)	Lance Alworth, 1965	1,602
Interceptions	Charlie McNeil, 1961	9
Punting (Avg.)	Darren Bennett, 1996	45.6
Punt Return (Avg.)	Leslie (Speedy) Duncan, 1965	15.5
Kickoff Return (Avg.)	Keith Lincoln, 1962	28.4
Field Goals	John Carney, 1994	34
Touchdowns (Tot.)	Chuck Muncie, 1981	19
Points	John Carney, 1994	135

INDIVIDUAL RECORDS—SINGLE GAME

Category	Name	Performance
Rushing (Yds.)	Gary Anderson, 12-18-88	217
Passing (Yds.)	Dan Fouts, 10-19-80, 12-11-82	444
Passing (TDs)	Dan Fouts, 11-22-81	6
Receiving (No.)	Kellen Winslow, 10-7-84	15
Receiving (Yds.)	Wes Chandler, 12-20-82	260
Interceptions	Many times	3
	Last time by Dwayne Harper, 11-27-95	
Field Goals	John Carney, 9-5-93, 9-18-93	6
	Greg Davis, 10-5-97	6
Touchdowns (Tot.)	Kellen Winslow, 11-22-81	5
Points	Kellen Winslow, 11-22-81	30

COACHING HISTORY

Los Angeles 1960
(284-287-11)

1960-69	Sid Gillman*	83-51-6
1969-70	Charlie Waller	9-7-3
1971	Sid Gillman**	4-6-0
1971-73	Harland Svare***	7-17-2
1973	Ron Waller	1-5-0
1974-78	Tommy Prothro****	21-39-0
1978-86	Don Coryell#	72-60-0
1986-88	Al Saunders	17-22-0
1989-91	Dan Henning	16-32-0
1992-96	Bobby Ross	50-36-0
1997	Kevin Gilbride	4-12-0

*Retired after nine games in 1969
**Resigned after 10 games in 1971
***Resigned after eight games in 1973
****Resigned after four games in 1978
#Resigned after eight games in 1986

QUALCOMM STADIUM

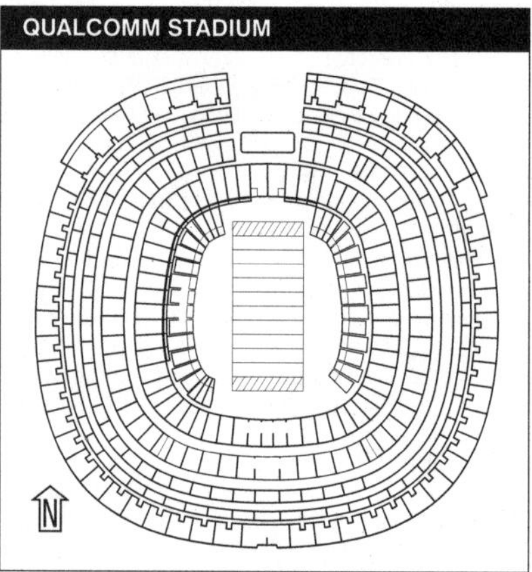

1997 TEAM RECORD

PRESEASON (3-1)

Date	Result		Opponent
8/2	W	20-13	San Francisco
8/9	W	23-17	Indianapolis
8/16	W	21-7	at Tennessee
8/22	L	22-28	at Minnesota

REGULAR SEASON (4-12)

Date	Result		Opponent	Att.
8/31	L	7-41	at New England	60,190
9/7	W	20-6	at New Orleans	65,760
9/14	L	7-26	Carolina	63,149
9/21	L	22-26	at Seattle	51,110
9/28	W	21-17	Baltimore	54,094
10/5	W	25-10	at Oakland	43,648
10/16	L	3-31	at Kansas City	77,196
10/26	W	35-19	Indianapolis	63,177
11/2	L	31-38	at Cincinnati	53,754
11/9	L	31-37	Seattle	64,616
11/16	L	13-38	Oakland	65,714
11/23	L	10-17	at San Francisco	61,195
11/30	L	28-38	Denver	54,245
12/7	L	3-14	Atlanta	46,317
12/14	L	7-29	Kansas City	54,594
12/21	L	3-38	at Denver	69,632

SCORE BY PERIODS

Chargers	61	71	71	63	—	266
Opponents	64	170	98	93	—	425

ATTENDANCE

Home 465,906 Away 482,485 Total 948,391
Single-game home record, 65,714 (11/16/97)
Single-season home record, 479,842 (1994)

1997 TEAM STATISTICS

	Chargers	Opp.
Total First Downs	251	308
Rushing	70	92
Passing	160	181
Penalty	21	35
Third Down: Made/Att	78/237	85/221
Third Down Pct.	32.9	38.5
Fourth Down: Made/Att	8/21	7/18
Fourth Down Pct.	38.1	38.9
Total Net Yards	4,505	5,166
Avg. Per Game	281.6	322.9
Total Plays	1,025	1,048
Avg. Per Play	4.4	4.9
Net Yards Rushing	1,416	1,698
Avg. Per Game	88.5	106.1
Total Rushes	409	453
Net Yards Passing	3,089	3,468
Avg. Per Game	193.1	216.8
Sacked/Yards Lost	51/386	27/164
Gross Yards	3,475	3,632
Att./Completions	565/291	568/297
Completion Pct.	51.5	52.3
Had Intercepted	21	15
Punts/Avg.	90/44.1	85/43.6
Net Punting Avg.	90/37.7	85/35.4
Penalties/Yards Lost	129/1,101	101/784
Fumbles/Ball Lost	30/14	21/11
Touchdowns	27	50
Rushing	5	12
Passing	12	31
Returns	10	7
Avg. Time of Possession	29:22	30:38

1997 INDIVIDUAL STATISTICS

PASSING	Att.	Comp.	Yds.	Pct.	TD	Int.	Tkld.	Rate
Whelihan	237	118	1,357	49.8	6	10	21/168	58.3
Humphries	225	121	1,488	53.8	5	6	18/144	70.8
Everett	75	36	457	48	1	4	4/30	49.7
Philcox	28	16	173	57.1	0	1	8/44	60.6
Team	565	291	3,475	51.5	12	21	51/386	62.2
Opponents	568	297	3,632	52.3	31	15	27/164	79.5

SCORING	TD R	TD P	TD Rt	PAT	FG	Saf	PTS
G. Davis	0	0	0	21/22	19/24	0	78
Martin	0	6	0	0/0	0/0	0	36
Metcalf	0	2	3	0/0	0/0	0	30
Carney	0	0	0	5/5	7/7	0	26
Brown	4	0	0	0/0	0/0	0	24
Harrison	0	0	3	0/0	0/0	0	18
Bradford	0	0	2	0/0	0/0	0	12
Jackson	0	0	2	0/0	0/0	0	12
F. Jones	0	2	0	0/0	0/0	0	12
Hartley	0	1	0	0/0	0/0	0	6
C. Jones	0	1	0	0/0	0/0	0	6
Pegram	1	0	0	0/0	0/0	0	6
Chargers	5	12	10	26/27	26/31	0	266
Opponents	12	31	7	46/46	25/26	1	425

2-Point conversions: Chargers: 0-1, Opponents 0-3.

RUSHING	Att.	Yds.	Avg.	LG	TD
Brown	253	945	3.7	32	4
Fletcher	51	161	3.2	13	0
Bynum	30	97	3.2	19	0
Craver	20	71	3.6	22	0
C. Jones	4	42	10.5	17	0
Whelihan	13	29	2.2	7	0
Humphries	13	24	1.8	11	0
Pegram	9	23	2.6	6t	1
Gardner	7	20	2.9	5	0
Everett	5	6	1.2	6	0
Philcox	1	3	3.0	3	0
Metcalf	3	-5	-1.7	2	0
Chargers	409	1,416	3.5	32	5
Opponents	453	1,698	3.7	71t	12

RECEIVING	No.	Yds.	Avg.	LG	TD
Martin	63	904	14.3	72t	6
F. Jones	41	505	12.3	62	2
Metcalf	40	576	14.4	62	2
Fletcher	39	292	7.5	25	0
C. Jones	32	423	13.2	44t	1
Still	24	324	13.5	39	0
Brown	21	137	6.5	27	0
Hartley	19	246	12.9	35	1
Craver	4	26	6.5	20	0
Gardner	2	10	5.0	8	0
Pegram	2	7	3.5	4	0
Bynum	2	4	2.0	3	0
Mitchell	1	14	14.0	14	0
Pupunu	1	7	7.0	7	0
Chargers	291	3,475	11.9	72t	12
Opponents	297	3,632	12.2	70t	31

INTERCEPTIONS	No.	Yds.	Avg.	LG	TD
Harrison	2	75	37.5	75t	1
Bradford	2	56	28.0	56t	1
Harper	2	43	21.5	43	0
Jackson	2	37	18.5	36t	1
Seau	2	33	16.5	26	0
Shaw	1	11	11.0	11	0
Coleman	1	2	2.0	2	0
Dumas	1	0	0.0	0	0
Fuller	1	0	0.0	0	0
Gouveia	1	0	0.0	0	0
Chargers	15	257	17.1	75t	3
Opponents	21	387	18.4	87t	3

PUNTING	No.	Yds.	Avg.	In 20	LG
Bennett	89	3,972	44.6	26	66
Chargers	90	3,972	44.1	26	66
Opponents	85	3,702	43.6	27	72

PUNT RETURNS	No.	FC	Yds.	Avg.	LG	TD
Metcalf	45	8	489	10.9	85t	3
Harrison	1	0	0	0.0	0	0
Jackson	1	0	0	0.0	0	0
Chargers	47	8	489	10.4	85t	3
Opponents	39	20	416	10.7	35	0

KICKOFF RETURNS	No.	Yds.	Avg.	LG	TD
Bynum	38	814	21.4	57	0
Metcalf	16	355	22.2	63	0
Rachal	15	336	22.4	30	0
Craver	3	68	22.7	27	0
Bordelon	2	0	0.0	0	0
Harrison	1	40	40.0	40t	1
Chargers	75	1,613	21.5	63	1
Opponents	63	1,517	24.1	99t	1

FIELD GOALS	1-19	20-29	30-39	40-49	50+
G. Davis	0/0	4/5	10/10	5/9	0/0
Carney	0/0	3/3	2/2	2/2	0/0
Chargers	0/0	7/8	12/12	7/11	0/0
Opponents	0/0	13/13	7/8	5/5	0/0

SACKS	No.
Seau	7.0
Harrison	4.0
Parrella	3.5
Fuller	3.0
Lee	3.0
Johnson	2.5
Coleman	2.0
Dumas	1.0
Hand	1.0
Chargers	27.0
Opponents	51.0

1998 DRAFT CHOICES

Round	Name	Pos.	College
1	Ryan Leaf	QB	Washington State
2	Mikheal Ricks	WR	Stephen F. Austin
5	Cedric Harden	DE	Florida A&M
6	Clifford Ivory	DB	Troy State
7	Jon Haskins	LB	Stanford
	Kio Sanford	WR	Kentucky

SAN DIEGO CHARGERS

1998 VETERAN ROSTER

No.	Name	Pos.	Ht.	Wt.	Birthdate	NFL Exp.	College	Hometown	How Acq.	'97 Games/ Starts
2	Bennett, Darren	P	6-5	235	1/9/65	3	No College	Western, Australia	FA-'95	16/0
75	Berti, Tony	G-T	6-6	300	6/21/72	4	Colorado	Thornton, Colo.	D6d-'95	16/16
50	Binn, David	LS	6-3	240	2/6/72	5	California	San Mateo, Calif.	FA-'94	16/0
69	Bordelon, Ben	T	6-4	291	4/9/74	2	Louisiana State	Mathews, La.	FA-'97	16/2
25	Bradford, Paul	CB	5-8	185	4/20/74	2	Portland State	Palo Alto, Calif.	D5b-'97	15/4
22	Brew, Dorian	CB	5-10	182	7/19/74	3	Kansas	St. Louis, Mo.	FA-'97	6/0
85	Brown, Tyrone	WR	5-11	168	1/3/73	3	Toledo	Cincinnati, Ohio	FA-'98	0*
52	Burgess, James	LB	5-11	230	3/31/74	2	Miami	Homestead, Fla.	FA-'97	15/4
83	Burke, John	TE	6-3	248	9/7/71	5	Virginia Tech	Elizabeth, N.J.	FA-'98	7/1*
58	Bush, Lew	LB	6-2	245	12/2/69	6	Washington State	Tacoma, Wash.	D4b-'93	14/13
43	Bynum, Kenny	RB	5-11	191	5/29/74	2	South Carolina State	Gainesville, Fla.	D5a-'97	13/0
3	Carney, John	K	5-11	170	4/20/64	9	Notre Dame	West Palm Beach, Fla.	FA-'90	4/0
32	Chancey, Robert	RB	6-0	258	9/7/72	2	None	Millbrook, Ala.	FA-'97	6/0
68	# Cocozzo, Joe	G	6-4	300	8/7/70	6	Michigan	Mechanicville, N.Y.	D3-'93	16/12
90	Coleman, Marco	DE	6-3	267	12/18/69	7	Georgia Tech	Dayton, Ohio	UFA(Mia)-'96	16/16
93	Davis, Reuben	DT	6-5	320	5/7/65	11	North Carolina	Greensboro, N.C.	UFA(Ariz)-'94	0*
51	Dixon, Gerald	LB	6-3	250	6/20/69	7	South Carolina	Rock Hill, S.C.	UFA(Cin)-'98	15/13*
20	Dumas, Michael	S	6-0	198	3/18/69	7	Indiana	Lowell, Mich.	FA-'97	16/15
60	Engel, Greg	C	6-3	285	1/18/71	5	Illinois	Bloomington, Ill.	FA-'94	9/0
41	† Fletcher, Terrell	RB	5-8	196	9/14/73	4	Wisconsin	St. Louis, Mo.	D2b-'95	13/1
67	Fortin, Roman	C-G	6-5	297	2/26/67	9	San Diego State	Ventura, Calif.	FA-'98	3/3
95	Fuller, William	DE	6-3	280	3/8/62	13	North Carolina	Chesapeake, Va.	UFA(Phil)-'97	16/16
54	Gouveia, Kurt	LB	6-1	240	9/14/64	13	Brigham Young	Honolulu, Hawaii	UFA(Phil)-'96	7/6
53	Hamilton, Michael	LB	6-1	244	12/3/73	2	North Carolina A&T	Greenville, S.C.	D3-'97	6/0
96	† Hand, Norman	DT	6-3	313	9/4/72	4	Mississippi	Walterboro, S.C.	W(Mia)-'97	15/1
28	Harper, Dwayne	CB	5-11	175	3/29/66	11	South Carolina State	Orangeburg, S.C.	UFA(Sea)-'94	12/12
37	Harrison, Rodney	S	6-0	201	12/15/72	5	Western Illinois	Chicago Heights, Ill.	D5b-'94	16/16
89	Hartley, Frank	TE	6-2	268	12/15/67	5	Illinois	Chicago, Ill.	FA-'97	16/16
42	# Jackson, Greg	S	6-1	205	8/20/66	10	Louisiana State	Miami, Fla.	UFA(NO)-'97	13/0
65	Jackson, John	T	6-6	297	1/4/65	11	Eastern Kentucky	Cincinnati, Ohio	UFA(Pitt)-'98	16/16*
59	James, Toran	LB	6-3	247	3/8/74	2	North Carolina A&T	Ahoskie, N.C.	D7a-'97	14/0
99	Johnson, Raylee	DE	6-3	265	6/1/70	6	Arkansas	Fordyce, Ark.	D4a-'93	16/0
82	Jones, Charlie	WR	5-8	175	12/1/72	3	Fresno State	Hanford, Calif.	D4-'96	16/11
88	Jones, Freddie	TE	6-4	260	9/16/74	2	North Carolina	Landover, Md.	D2-'97	13/8
63	McKenzie, Raleigh	C-G	6-2	283	2/8/63	14	Tennessee	Knoxville, Tenn.	UFA(Phil)-'97	16/16
	Means, Natrone	RB	5-10	245	4/26/72	6	North Carolina	Harrisburg, N.C.	UFA(Jax)-'98	14/11*
66	Mills, Jim	G-T	6-4	290	3/30/73	3	Idaho	Marysville, Wash.	D6a-'96	1/0
40	Montreuil, Mark	CB	6-1	200	12/29/71	4	Concordia, Canada	Montreal, Canada	D7-'95	6/1
70	Parker, Vaughn	T	6-3	296	6/5/71	5	UCLA	Buffalo, N.Y.	D2b-'94	16/16
97	Parrella, John	DT	6-3	290	11/22/69	6	Nebraska	Topeka, Kan.	FA-'94	16/16
79	Price, Marcus	G-T	6-6	321	3/3/72	2	Louisiana State	Port Arthur, Tex.	FA-'97	2/0
85	Rachal, Latario	WR	5-11	183	1/31/73	2	Fresno State	Los Angeles, Calif.	FA-'97	14/0
87	Roche, Brian	TE	6-4	255	5/5/73	3	San Jose State	LaVerne, Calif.	D3-'96	5/0
74	Roundtree, Raleigh	T	6-4	295	8/31/75	2	South Carolina State	Augusta, Georgia	D4-'97	0*
55	Seau, Junior	LB	6-3	250	1/19/69	9	Southern California	Oceanside, Calif.	D1-'90	15/15
29	Shaw, Terrance	CB	5-11	190	11/11/73	4	Stephen F. Austin	Marshall, Tex.	D2a-'95	16/16
72	† Sienkiewicz, Troy	G-T	6-5	310	5/27/72	4	New Mexico State	Alamogordo, N.M.	D6a-'95	14/6
84	Slaughter, Webster	WR	6-1	175	10/19/64	12	San Diego State	Stockton, Calif.	FA-'98	0*
80	Still, Bryan	WR	5-11	174	6/3/74	3	Virginia Tech	Richmond, Va.	D2a-'96	15/4
73	Taylor, Aaron	G	6-4	305	11/14/72	5	Notre Dame	Concord, Calif.	UFA(GB)-'98	14/14*
47	Thomas, Johnny	CB	5-9	191	8/3/64	11	Baylor	Houston, Tex.	UFA (Phil)-'97	0*
91	Tuinei, Van	DE	6-3	266	2/16/71	2	Arizona	Westminster, Calif.	FA-'97	3/0
8	Weldon, Casey	QB	6-1	206	2/3/69	7	Florida State	Tallahassee, Fla.	FA-'97	0*
5	Whelihan, Craig	QB	6-5	204	4/15/71	4	Pacific	San Jose, Calif.	D6c-'95	9/7
23	Williams, Gerome	S	6-2	210	7/9/73	2	Houston	Houston, Tex.	FA-'97	6/0

* Brown last active with Atlanta in '96; Burke played in 7 games with N.Y. Jets in '97; Davis missed '97 season because of injury; Dixon played 15 games with Cincinnati; Fortin played 3 games with Atlanta; Jackson played 16 games with Pittsburgh; Means played 14 games with Jacksonville; Roundtree and Thomas inactive for 16 games; Slaughter last active with N.Y. Jets in '96; Taylor played 14 games with Green Bay; Weldon inactive for 6 games.

Unrestricted free agents; subject to developments.

† Restricted free agent; subject to developments.

Traded—DT Shawn Lee (16 games in '97) to Chicago; WR Tony Martin (16) to Atlanta; RB Eric Metcalf (16) and LB Patrick Sapp (16) to Arizona.

Retired—Stan Humphries, 9-year quarterback, 8 games in '97.

Players lost through free agency (2): RB Gary Brown (NYG; 15 games in '97), RB Aaron Craver (NO; 15).

Also played with the Chargers in '97—WR Ray Crittenden (2), K Greg Davis (12), G Isaac Davis (12), QB Jim Everett (4), RB Carwell Gardner (5), S David Hendrix (4), LB Bobby Houston (2), TE Shannon Mitchell (4), RB Erric Pegram (4), QB Todd Philcox (2), TE Al Pupunu (8), CB Michael Swift (12).

COACHING STAFF

Head Coach,
Kevin Gilbride

Pro Career: Begins his second year as head coach of the San Diego Chargers after spending eight seasons as an NFL assistant. Named the tenth head coach in team history on January 19, 1997. Spent two seasons (1995-96) as the offensive coordinator for the Jacksonville Jaguars. In 1996, Gilbride led Jacksonville to the NFL's number-one ranked pass offense (256.9 yards per game). Jacksonville also ranked second overall in the league in total offense by averaging 360.2 yards per game in 1996. A veteran of 24 years in coaching, Gilbride's first professional coaching job began with the Ottawa Rough Riders of the Canadian Football League. He served as the quarterback/receivers coach in 1985 and offensive coordinator in 1986. Gilbride began his NFL coaching career in Houston as quarterbacks coach in 1989, before being named the Oilers' offensive coordinator in 1990. Remained Oilers' offensive coordinator through 1993 before spending the 1994 season as the team's assistant head coach/offense. Under Gilbride's direction, the Oilers' offense ranked first in the NFL in passing yards from 1990 through 1992 and ranked third in 1993. For four consecutive seasons (1990-93), the Oilers ranked among the NFL's top three teams in total offense, including a number-one ranking in 1990. Career record: 4-12.

Background: Played quarterback and tight end for Southern Connecticut State from 1970-73. Began coaching career at Idaho State in 1974. After two seasons at Idaho State, Gilbride was the linebackers coach for two seasons at Tufts University (1976-77) and the defensive coordinator for two years (1978-79) at American International. Spent five seasons (1980-84) as head coach at Southern Connecticut State, compiling a career collegiate head coaching record of 35-14-2. During his tenure as Southern Connecticut State's head coach, Gilbride was named New England Coach of the Year and the NCAA Division II Coach of the Year by various groups, including the ECAC Officials, the Walter Camp Foundation, and the New Haven Gridiron Club. After two years in the Canadian Football League, Gilbride coached for two years (1987-88) at East Carolina, the first season as passing game coordinator and second as offensive coordinator.

Personal: Born August 27, 1951, in New Haven, Conn. Kevin and his wife, Deborah, have three children—Kelly, Kristen, and Kevin.

ASSISTANT COACHES

Joe Bugel, offensive line; born March 10, 1940, Pittsburgh, lives in San Diego. Guard-linebacker Western Kentucky 1960-63. No pro playing experience. College coach: Western Kentucky 1964-68, United States Naval Academy 1969-72, Iowa State 1973, Ohio State 1974. Pro coach: Detriot Lions 1975-76, Houston Oilers 1977-80, Washington Redskins 1981-89, Phoenix Cardinals (head coach) 1990-93, Oakland Raiders 1995-97 (head coach 1997), joined Chargers in 1998.

June Jones, quarterbacks; born February 19, 1953, Portland, Ore., lives in San Diego. Quarterback Hawaii 1973-74, Portland State 1975-76. Pro quarterback Atlanta Falcons 1977-81, Toronto Argonauts (CFL) 1982. College coach: Hawaii 1983. Pro coach: Houston Gamblers (USFL) 1984, Denver Gold (USFL) 1985, Ottawa Rough Riders (CFL) 1986, Houston Oilers 1987-88, Detriot Lions 1989-90, Atlanta Falcons 1991-96 (head coach 1994-96), joined Chargers in 1998.

Bill Macdermott, tight ends; born May 14, 1936, Providence, R.I., lives in San Diego. Guard-tackle Trinity (Conn.) College 1955, 1957-59. No pro playing experience. College coach: Wesleyan University 1966-86 (head coach 1971-86), Cal Poly-San Luis Obispo 1987-89. Pro coach: Montreal Alouettes (CFL) 1987, Toronto Argonauts (CFL) 1990, Orlando Thunder (World League) 1991-92, Edmonton Eskimos (CFL) 1992-96, Winnipeg Blue Bombers (CFL) 1997, joined Chargers in 1997.

1998 FIRST-YEAR ROSTER

Name	Pos.	Ht.	Wt.	Birthdate	College	Hometown	How Acq.
Baker, Jeff	QB	6-3	215	3/2/75	Wisconsin-La Crosse	West Bend, Wisc.	FA
Bradley, Marcus	S	5-11	195	10/20/76	Western Carolina	Gaffney, S.C.	FA
Buzzard, Jim	G	6-3	294	1/25/75	Eastern Washington	Centralia, Wash.	FA
Conley, Bart	LB	6-4	230	11/1/73	Findlay	Cincinnati, Ohio	FA
Davis, Wendell	TE	6-2	246	10/24/75	Temple	Escatawpa, Miss.	FA
Downey, Patrick	C	6-2	302	6/21/74	New Hampshire	Beverly, Mass.	FA
Earp, Jeremy	WR	6-1	208	7/23/74	Wisconsin-La Crosse	La Crosse, Wis.	FA
Filer, Rodney (1)	RB	6-1	235	6/14/74	Iowa	Waco, Tex.	FA-'97
Gmelin, Dan	WR	5-11	187	1/18/76	Albany State, N.Y.	Bedford Hills, N.Y.	FA
Graham, DeMingo	T	6-2	310	9/10/73	Hofstra	Newark, N.J.	FA
Hall, Carlton	LB	6-0	234	10/5/75	Vanderbilt	Midwest City, Okla.	FA
Harden, Cedric	DE	6-6	260	10/19/74	Florida A&M	Atlanta, Ga.	D5
Harris, Dayroni	DE	6-5	285	7/15/76	Central Arkansas	Los Angeles, Calif.	FA
Haskins, Jon	LB	6-2	245	10/6/75	Stanford	Sarasota, Fla.	D7a
Ivory, Clifford	CB	5-11	183	8/1/75	Troy State	Quitman, Ga.	D6
Jackson, Marlyn	CB	5-8	177	12/9/74	Fresno State	Fresno, Calif.	FA
Jacox, Kendyl	C	6-2	330	6/10/75	Kansas State	Dallas, Tex.	FA
Jones, LaJhon	LB	6-3	260	9/16/75	Rhode Island	Warwick, R.I.	FA
Joseph, Terrance	S	6-2	210	2/14/75	Tulsa	Midwest City, Okla.	FA
Leaf, Ryan	QB	6-5	240	5/15/76	Washington State	Great Falls, Mont.	D1
Lee, Gregory	S	6-3	203	6/23/75	Fort Valley State	Decatur, Ga.	FA
Lee, Lloyd	S	6-2	215	8/10/76	Dartmouth	Bloomington, Minn.	FA
Palmer, Daniel (1)	T	6-4	290	8/24/73	Air Force	Anderson, S.C.	D6-'97
Ricks, Mikhael	WR	6-5	237	11/14/74	Stephen F. Austin	Anahuac, Tex.	D2
Rodgers, Anthony (1)	WR	6-3	190	12/11/73	Cal State-Northridge	Los Angeles, Calif.	FA-'97
Roth, Tim	K-P	6-2	202	1/23/75	University of San Diego	Pleasant Valley, Calif.	FA
Sanford, Kio	WR	5-10	180	1/8/75	Kentucky	Lexington, Ky.	D7b
Smith, Eric	TE	6-6	255	10/12/74	Millikin	Findlay, Ill.	FA
Stallworth, Jay	DE	6-2	275	4/6/75	Vanderbilt	Marshall, Tex.	FA
Stephens, Tremayne	RB	5-11	205	4/16/76	North Carolina State	Greer, S.C.	FA
Suttle, Jason	DB	5-11	185	12/2/74	Wisconsin	Burnsville, Minn.	FA
Taylor, Henry	DT	6-2	295	11/29/75	South Carolina	Barnwell, S.C.	FA
Taylor, Tyrone	WR	5-9	175	9/29/76	Cal State-Sacramento	Pittsburg, Calif.	FA
Traylor, Champ	TE	6-3	265	9/9/74	Stephen F. Austin	Pasadena, Tex.	FA
Watson, Justin	RB	6-1	227	1/7/75	San Diego State	Pasadena, Calif.	FA
Watts, Quincy	CB	6-2	217	6/19/71	Southern California	Taft, Calif.	FA

The term NFL Rookie is defined as a player who is in his first season of professional football and has not been on the roster of another professional football team for any regular-season or postseason games. A Rookie is designated by an "R" on NFL rosters. Players who have been active in another professional football league or players who have NFL experience, including either preseason training camp or being on an Active List or Inactive List, or on Reserve/Injured or Reserve/Physically Unable to Perform for fewer than six regular-season games, are termed NFL First-Year Players. An NFL First-Year Player is designated by a "1" on NFL rosters. Thereafter, a player is credited with an additional year of experience for each season in which he accumulates six games on the Active List or Inactive List, or on Reserve/Injured or Reserve/Physically Unable to Perform.

Nick Nicolau, assistant head coach; born May 5, 1933, New York, N.Y., lives in San Diego. Running back Southern Connecticut State 1957-59. No pro playing experience. College coach: Southern Connecticut State 1960, Springfield 1961, Bridgeport 1962-69 (head coach 1965-69), Massachusetts 1970, Connecticut 1971-72, Kentucky 1973-75, Kent State 1976. Pro coach: Hamilton Tiger-Cats (CFL) 1977, Montreal Alouettes (CFL) 1978-79, New Orleans Saints 1980, Denver Broncos 1981-87, Los Angeles Raiders 1988, Buffalo Bills 1989-91, Indianapolis Colts 1992-94, Jacksonville Jaguars 1995-96, joined Chargers in 1997.

Frank Novak, special teams; born May 18, 1938, Leominster, Mass., lives in San Diego. Quarterback Northern Michigan 1959-61. No pro playing experience. College coach: Northern Michigan 1966-72, East Carolina 1973, Virginia 1974-75, Western Illinois 1976-77, Holy Cross 1978-83, Massachusetts 1986, Missouri 1988. Pro coach: Oklahoma Outlaws (USFL) 1984, Birmingham Stallions (USFL) 1985, Houston Oilers 1989-94, Detroit Lions 1995-96, joined Chargers in 1997.

Wayne Nunnely, defensive line; born March 29, 1952, Los Angeles, Calif., lives in San Diego. Fullback Nevada-Las Vegas 1972-75. No pro playing experience. College coach: Nevada-Las Vegas 1976, 1982-89 (head coach 1986-89), Cal Poly-Pomona 1977-78, Cal State-Fullerton 1979, Pacific 1980-81, Southern California 1991-92, UCLA 1993-94. Pro coach: New Orleans Saints 1995-96, joined Chargers in 1997.

Joe Pascale, defensive coordinator; born April 4, 1946, New York, N.Y., lives in San Diego. Linebacker Connecticut 1963-66. No pro playing experience. College coach: Connecticut 1967-68, Rhode Island 1969-73, Idaho State 1974-76 (head coach 1976), Princeton 1977-79. Pro coach: Montreal Alouettes (CFL) 1980-81, Ottawa Rough Riders (CFL) 1982-83, New Jersey Generals (USFL) 1984-85, St. Louis/Phoenix Cardinals 1986-93, Cincinnati Bengals 1994-96, joined Chargers in 1997.

Rod Perry, defensive backs; born September 11, 1953, Fresno, Calif., lives in San Diego. Defensive back Colorado 1972-74. Pro cornerback Los Angeles Rams 1975-82, Cleveland Browns 1983-84. College coach: Columbia 1985, Fresno City College 1986, Fresno State 1987-88. Pro coach: Seattle Seahawks 1989-91, Los Angeles Rams 1992-94, Houston Oilers 1995-96, joined Chargers in 1997.

Mike Sheppard, offensive coordinator; born October 29, 1951, Tulsa, Okla., lives in San Diego. Wide receiver Cal Lutheran 1969-72. No pro playing experience. College coach: Cal Lutheran 1974-76, Brigham Young 1977-78, U.S. International 1979, Idaho State 1980-81, Long Beach State 1982, 1984-86 (head coach), Kansas 1983, New Mexico 1987-91 (head coach), California 1992. Pro coach: Cleveland Browns 1993-95/Baltimore Ravens 1996, joined Chargers in 1997.

Jim Vechiarella, linebackers; born February 20, 1937, Youngstown, Ohio, lives in San Diego. Linebacker Youngstown State 1955-57. No pro playing experience. College coach: Youngstown State 1964-74, Southern Illinois 1976-77, Tulane 1978-80. Pro coach: Charlotte Hornets (WFL) 1975, Los Angeles Rams 1981-82, Kansas City Chiefs 1983-85, New York Jets 1986-89, 1995-96, Cleveland Browns 1990, Philadelphia Eagles 1991-94, joined Chargers in 1997.

Ollie Wilson, running backs; born March 3, 1951, Worcester, Mass., lives in San Diego. Wide receiver Springfield 1971-73. No pro playing experience. College coach: Springfield 1975, Northeastern 1976-82, California 1983-90. Pro coach: Atlanta Falcons 1991-96, joined Chargers in 1997.

SEATTLE SEAHAWKS

American Football Conference
Western Division
Team Colors: Blue, Green, and Silver
11220 N.E. 53rd Street
Kirkland, Washington 98033
Telephone: (425) 827-9777

CLUB OFFICIALS

Chairman: Paul Allen
Vice Chair: Bert Kolde
President: Bob Whitsitt
Sr. V.P./Marketing Ops: Harry Hutt
V.P./Football Operations: Randy Mueller
V.P./CFO: Nathaniel (Buster) Brown
V.P./General Counsel: Richard Leigh
V.P./Community Outreach & Info Systems: Mike Flood
V.P./Communications: Gary Wright
V.P./Ticket Sales & Service: Duane McLean
V.P./Corporate Sales: Scott Patrick
Public Relations Director: Dave Pearson
Asst. Public Relations Dir.: Steve Wright
Community Outreach Dir.: Sandy Gregory
Publications Director: Vernon Cheek
Player Relations Director: Nesby Glasgow
College Scouting Director: Pat Mondock
Pro Scouting Director: Bill Quinter
Ticket Ops/Customer Service: Chuck Arnold
Season Ticket Sales Director: Donn Bagnall
Corporate Sales Director: Kevin Williams
Trainer: Jim Whitesel
Equipment Manager: Erik Kennedy
Stadium: Kingdome • **Capacity:** 66,400
201 South King Street
Seattle, Washington 98104
Playing Surface: AstroTurf
Training Camp: Eastern Washington University
Cheney, Washington 99004

1998 SCHEDULE

PRESEASON

July 31	at Dallas	8:00
Aug. 8	**Indianapolis**	7:00
Aug. 15	vs. San Francisco at Vancouver, Canada	5:00
Aug. 22	at Arizona	7:00
Aug. 28	**San Francisco**	7:00

REGULAR SEASON

Sept. 6	at Philadelphia	1:01
Sept. 13	**Arizona**	1:15
Sept. 20	**Washington**	1:05
Sept. 27	at Pittsburgh	4:05
Oct. 4	at Kansas City	7:20
Oct. 11	**Denver**	1:15
Oct. 18	Open Date	
Oct. 25	at San Diego	1:15
Nov. 1	**Oakland**	5:20
Nov. 8	**Kansas City**	1:15
Nov. 15	at Oakland	1:05
Nov. 22	at Dallas	12:01
Nov. 29	**Tennessee**	1:05
Dec. 6	at New York Jets	1:01
Dec. 13	**San Diego**	1:05
Dec. 20	**Indianapolis**	1:05
Dec. 27	at Denver	2:15

RECORD HOLDERS

INDIVIDUAL RECORDS—CAREER

Category	Name	Performance
Rushing (Yds.)	Chris Warren, 1990-97	6,706
Passing (Yds.)	Dave Krieg, 1980-1991	26,132
Passing (TDs)	Dave Krieg, 1980-1991	195
Receiving (No.)	Steve Largent, 1976-1989	819
Receiving (Yds.)	Steve Largent, 1976-1989	13,089
Interceptions	Dave Brown, 1976-1986	50
Punting (Avg.)	Rick Tuten, 1991-97	43.8
Punt Return (Avg.)	Paul Johns, 1981-84	11.4
Kickoff Return (Avg.)	Steve Broussard, 1995-97	22.9
Field Goals	Norm Johnson, 1982-1990	159
Touchdowns (Tot.)	Steve Largent, 1976-1989	101
Points	Norm Johnson, 1982-1990	810

INDIVIDUAL RECORDS—SINGLE SEASON

Category	Name	Performance
Rushing (Yds.)	Chris Warren, 1994	1,545
Passing (Yds.)	Warren Moon, 1997	3,678
Passing (TDs)	Dave Krieg, 1984	32
Receiving (No.)	Brian Blades, 1994	81
Receiving (Yds.)	Steve Largent, 1985	1,287
Interceptions	John Harris, 1981	10
	Kenny Easley, 1984	10
Punting (Avg.)	Rick Tuten, 1995	45.0
Punt Return (Avg.)	Bobby Joe Edmonds, 1987	12.6
Kickoff Return (Avg.)	Steve Broussard, 1995	24.7
Field Goals	Todd Peterson, 1996	28
Touchdowns (Tot.)	Chris Warren, 1995	16
Points	Todd Peterson, 1996	111

INDIVIDUAL RECORDS—SINGLE GAME

Category	Name	Performance
Rushing (Yds.)	Curt Warner, 11-27-83	207
Passing (Yds.)	Dave Krieg, 11-20-83	418
Passing (TDs)	Dave Krieg, 12-2-84, 9-15-85, 11-28-88	5
	Warren Moon, 10-26-97	5
Receiving (No.)	Steve Largent, 10-18-87	15
Receiving (Yds.)	Steve Largent, 10-18-87	261
Interceptions	Kenny Easley, 9-3-84	3
	Eugene Robinson, 12-6-92	3
	Darryl Williams, 9-21-97	3
Field Goals	Norm Johnson, 9-20-87, 12-18-88	5
Touchdowns (Tot.)	Daryl Turner, 9-15-85	4
	Curt Warner, 12-11-88	4
Points	Daryl Turner, 9-15-85	24

COACHING HISTORY

(159-188-0)

1976-82	Jack Patera*	35-59-0
1982	Mike McCormack	4-3-0
1983-91	Chuck Knox	83-67-0
1992-94	Tom Flores	14-34-0
1995-97	Dennis Erickson	23-25-0

*Released after two games in 1982

KINGDOME

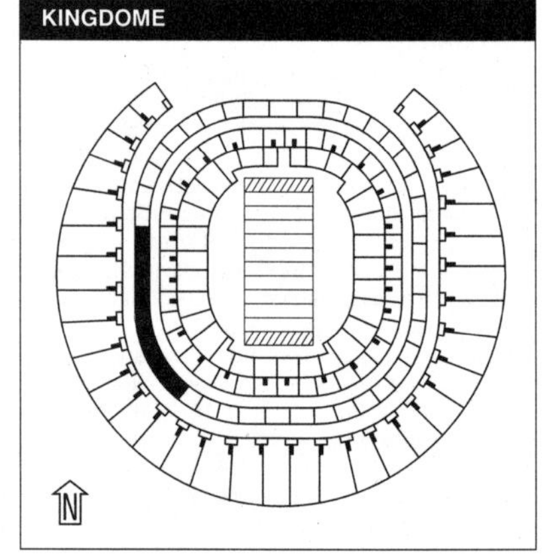

1997 TEAM RECORD

PRESEASON (3-2)

Date	Result		Opponent
7/26	L	26-28	vs. Minnesota at Canton, Ohio
8/2	W	34-6	Arizona
8/9	L	17-21	at San Francisco
8/16	W	45-3	Indianapolis
8/22	W	31-28	at Cincinnati

REGULAR SEASON (8-8)

Date	Result		Opponent	Att.
8/31	L	3-41	New York Jets	53,893
9/7	L	14-35	Denver	55,859
9/14	W	31-3	at Indianapolis	49,194
9/21	W	26-22	San Diego	51,110
9/28	L	17-20	at Kansas City (OT)	77,877
10/5	W	16-13	Tennessee	49,897
10/19	W	17-9	at St. Louis	64,819
10/26	W	45-34	Oakland	66,264
11/2	L	27-30	at Denver	74,212
11/9	W	37-31	at San Diego	64,616
11/16	L	17-20	at New Orleans (OT)	50,493
11/23	L	14-19	Kansas City	66,264
11/30	L	17-24	Atlanta	52,584
12/7	L	24-31	at Baltimore	54,395
12/14	W	22-21	at Oakland	40,124
12/21	W	38-9	San Francisco	66,253

(OT) Overtime

SCORE BY PERIODS

Seahawks	44	126	92	103	0	—	365
Opponents	101	111	93	51	6	—	362

ATTENDANCE

Home 462,124 Away 475,730 Total 937,854

Single-game home record, 66,264 (10/26/97, 11/23/97)

Single-season home record, 514,984 (1992)

1997 TEAM STATISTICS

	Seahawks	Opp.
Total First Downs	331	286
Rushing	98	96
Passing	207	166
Penalty	26	24
Third Down: Made/Att	91/224	66/198
Third Down Pct.	40.6	33.3
Fourth Down: Made/Att	8/16	8/16
Fourth Down Pct.	50.0	50.0
Total Net Yards	5,759	4,849
Avg. Per Game	359.9	303.1
Total Plays	1,049	959
Avg. Per Play	5.5	5.1
Net Yards Rushing	1,800	1,731
Avg. Per Game	112.5	108.2
Total Rushes	404	455
Net Yards Passing	3,959	3,118
Avg. Per Game	247.4	194.9
Sacked/Yards Lost	36/228	42/238
Gross Yards	4,187	3,356
Att./Completions	609/359	462/276
Completion Pct.	58.9	59.7
Had Intercepted	21	13
Punts/Avg.	78/40.3	74/42.0
Net Punting Avg.	78/32.3	74/36.8
Penalties/Yards Lost	109/911	100/820
Fumbles/Ball Lost	26/11	33/16
Touchdowns	43	38
Rushing	13	10
Passing	26	19
Returns	4	9
Avg. Time of Possession	30:47	29:13

1997 INDIVIDUAL STATISTICS

PASSING	Att.	Comp.	Yds.	Pct.	TD	Int.	Tkld.	Rating
Moon	528	313	3,678	59.3	25	16	30/192	83.7
Kitna	45	31	371	68.9	1	2	3/10	82.7
Friesz	36	15	138	41.7	0	3	2/11	18.1
Galloway	0	0	0	—	0	0	1/15	—
Seahawks	609	359	4,187	58.9	26	21	36/228	79.7
Opponents	462	276	3,356	59.7	19	13	42/238	84.1

SCORING	TD R	TD P	TD Rt	PAT	FG	Saf	PTS
Peterson	0	0	0	37/37	22/28	0	103
Galloway	0	12	0	0/0	0/0	0	72
Broussard	5	1	0	0/0	0/0	0	36
McKnight	0	6	0	0/0	0/0	0	36
Warren	4	0	0	0/0	0/0	0	24
Smith	2	0	0	0/0	0/0	0	14
Br. Blades	0	2	0	0/0	0/0	0	12
C. Brown	0	0	2	0/0	0/0	0	12
Pritchard	0	2	0	0/0	0/0	0	12
Strong	0	2	0	0/0	0/0	0	12
Crumpler	0	1	0	0/0	0/0	0	6
Kitna	1	0	0	0/0	0/0	0	6
Moon	1	0	0	0/0	0/0	0	6
Sinclair	0	0	1	0/0	0/0	0	6
D. Williams	0	0	1	0/0	0/0	0	6
Saleaumua	0	0	0	0/0	0/0	1	2
Seahawks	13	26	4	37/37	22/28	1	365
Opponents	10	19	9	35/35	31/34	1	362

2-Pt. Conversions: Smith.
Seahawks 1-6, Opponents 2-3.

RUSHING	Att.	Yds.	Avg.	LG	TD
Warren	200	847	4.2	36t	4
Broussard	70	418	6.0	77t	5
Smith	91	392	4.3	35	2
Galloway	9	72	8.0	44	0
Moon	17	40	2.4	17	1
Pritchard	1	14	14.0	14	0
Kitna	10	9	0.9	8	1
Strong	4	8	2.0	6	0
Friesz	1	0	0.0	0	0
K. Richardson	1	0	0.0	0	0
Seahawks	404	1,800	4.5	77t	13
Opponents	455	1,731	3.8	55t	10

RECEIVING	No.	Yds.	Avg.	LG	TD
Galloway	72	1,049	14.6	53t	12
Pritchard	64	843	13.2	61	2
Warren	45	257	5.7	20	0
McKnight	34	637	18.7	60t	6
Crumpler	31	361	11.6	30	1
Br. Blades	30	319	10.6	27	2
Broussard	24	143	6.0	20t	1
Smith	23	183	8.0	22	0
Strong	13	91	7.0	20	2
Fauria	10	110	11.0	25	0
Hobbs	5	44	8.8	21	0
Harris	4	81	20.3	34	0
Davis	2	48	24.0	37	0
May	2	21	10.5	11	0
Seahawks	359	4,187	11.7	61	26
Opponents	276	3,356	12.2	92	19

INTERCEPTIONS	No.	Yds.	Avg.	LG	TD
D. Williams	8	172	21.5	44t	1
Be. Blades	2	11	5.5	11	0
Bellamy	1	13	13.0	13	0
Springs	1	0	0.0	0	0
W. Williams	1	0	0.0	0	0
Seahawks	13	196	15.1	44t	1
Opponents	21	372	17.7	75t	4

PUNTING	No.	Yds.	Avg.	In 20	LG
Tuten	48	2,007	41.8	15	65
Stark	20	813	40.7	7	52
K. Richardson	8	324	40.5	2	52
Seahawks	78	3,144	40.3	24	65
Opponents	74	3,111	42.0	21	66

PUNT RETURNS	No.	FC	Yds.	Avg.	LG	TD
Harris	21	12	144	6.9	19	0
Davis	16	6	104	6.5	28	0
Seahawks	37	18	248	6.7	28	0
Opponents	38	14	463	12.2	89t	2

KICKOFF RETURNS	No.	Yds.	Avg.	LG	TD
Broussard	50	1,076	21.5	43	0
Harris	14	318	22.7	34	0
Coleman	3	65	21.7	29	0
Davis	2	25	12.5	23	0
Beede	1	0	0.0	0	0
R. Brown	1	16	16.0	16	0
Daniels	1	-2	-2.0	-2	0
May	1	8	8.0	8	0
McKnight	1	14	14.0	14	0
Smith	1	14	14.0	14	0
Strong	1	16	16.0	16	0
Seahawks	76	1,550	20.4	43	0
Opponents	77	1,779	23.1	93t	1

FIELD GOALS	1-19	20-29	30-39	40-49	50+
Peterson	0/0	9/9	7/10	5/7	1/2
Seahawks	0/0	9/9	7/10	5/7	1/2
Opponents	2/2	12/13	5/5	8/10	4/4

SACKS	No.
Sinclair	12.0
Adams	7.0
C. Brown	6.5
Daniels	4.0
Saleaumua	3.5
LaBounty	3.0
Bellamy	2.0
Kennedy	2.0
Be.Blades	1.0
Wells	1.0
Seahawks	42.0
Opponents	36.0

1998 DRAFT CHOICES

Round	Name	Pos.	College
1	Anthony Simmons	LB	Clemson
2	Todd Weiner	T	Kansas State
3	Ahman Green	RB	Nebraska
4	DeShone Myles	LB	Nevada
6	Carl Hansen	DE	Stanford
	Bobby Shaw	WR	California
7	Jason McEndoo	C	Washington State

SEATTLE SEAHAWKS

1998 VETERAN ROSTER

No.	Name	Pos.	Ht.	Wt.	Birthdate	NFL Exp.	College	Hometown	How Acq.	'97 Games/ Starts
98	Adams, Sam	DT	6-3	297	6/13/73	5	Texas A&M	Houston, Tex.	D1-'94	16/15
75	Ballard, Howard	T	6-6	325	11/3/63	11	Alabama A&M	Ashland, Ala.	UFA(Buff)-'94	10/10
54	† Barber, Michael	LB	6-1	246	11/9/71	4	Clemson	Edgemore, SC.	FA-'95	8/2
63	Beede, Frank	G	6-4	296	5/1/73	3	Panhandle State	Antioch, Calif.	FA-'96	16/6
20	Bellamy, Jay	S	5-11	199	7/8/72	5	Rutgers	Aberdeen, N.J.	FA-'94	16/7
36	Blades, Bennie	S	6-1	221	9/3/66	11	Miami	Ft. Lauderdale, Fla.	UFA(Det)-'97	10/9
89	Blades, Brian	WR	5-11	190	7/24/65	11	Miami	Ft. Lauderdale, Fla.	D2-'88	11/3
60	Bloedorn, Greg	G	6-6	278	11/15/72	2	Cornell	Glen Ellyn, Ill.	FA-'96	2/0
31	Broussard, Steve	RB	5-7	201	2/22/67	9	Washington State	Los Angeles, Calif.	FA-'95	16/1
94	Brown, Chad	LB	6-2	240	7/12/70	6	Colorado	Altadena, Calif.	UFA(Pitt)-'97	15/15
34	Brown, Reggie	RB	6-0	244	6/26/73	3	Fresno State	Detroit, Mich.	D3b-'96	11/0
28	Burton, James	CB	5-9	184	4/27/71	5	Fresno State	Long Beach, Calif.	FA-'98	5/1*
59	Cain, Joe	LB	6-1	242	6/11/65	10	Oregon Tech	Compton, Calif.	UFA(Chi)-'97	11/0
25	Collins, Mark	S	5-10	196	1/16/64	13	California State-Fullerton	San Bernardino, Calif.	UFA(GB)-'98	1/0*
87	Crumpler, Carlester	TE	6-6	260	9/5/71	5	East Carolina	Greenville, N.C.	D7-'94	15/12
30	Cunningham, T.J.	S	6-0	197	10/24/72	2	Colorado	Aurora, Colo.	D6b-'96	0*
93	Daniels, Phillip	DE	6-5	263	3/4/73	3	Georgia	Donalsonville, Ga.	D4a-'96	13/10
83	Davis, Tyree	WR	5-9	175	9/23/70	3	Central Arkansas	Altheimer, Ark.	FA-'97	13/1
86	Fauria, Christian	TE	6-4	245	9/22/71	4	Colorado	Encino, Calif.	D2-'95	16/3
10	Feagles, Jeff	P	6-1	207	8/7/66	11	Miami	Anaheim, Calif.	UFA(Ariz)-'98	16/0*
17	Friesz, John	QB	6-4	223	5/19/67	9	Idaho	Coeur d'Alene, Idaho	UFA(Wash)-'95	2/1
84	Galloway, Joey	WR	5-11	188	11/20/71	4	Ohio State	Bellaire, Ohio	D1-'95	15/15
53	Glover, Kevin	C	6-2	282	6/17/63	14	Maryland	Columbia, Md.	UFA(Det)-'98	16/16*
77	# Graham, Derrick	G	6-4	315	3/18/67	9	Appalachian State	Groveland, Fla.	FA-'96	9/9
62	Gray, Chris	G	6-4	305	6/19/70	6	Auburn	Birmingham, Ala.	UFA(Chi)-'98	8/2*
35	Gray, Oscar	RB	6-1	255	8/7/72	2	Arkansas	Houston, Tex.	FA-'96	0*
72	Greene, Andrew	G	6-3	304	9/24/69	2	Indiana	Ontario, Canada	FA-'97	0*
68	Habib, Brian	G	6-7	299	12/2/64	11	Washington	Ellensburg, Wash.	UFA(Den)-'98	14/14*
58	Hardy, Darryl	LB	6-2	230	11/22/68	3	Tennessee	Cincinnati, Ohio	W(Dall)-'97	14/0*
81	Harris, Ronnie	WR	5-11	179	6/4/70	5	Oregon	San Jose, Calif.	FA-'94	13/0
71	Jones, Walter	T	6-5	300	1/19/74	2	Florida State	Aliceville, Ala.	D1b-'97	12/12
66	Kendall, Pete	G	6-5	292	7/9/73	3	Boston College	Weymouth, Mass.	D1-'96	16/16
96	Kennedy, Cortez	DT	6-3	306	8/23/68	9	Miami	Wilson, Ark.	D1a-'90	8/8
7	Kitna, Jon	QB	6-2	217	9/21/72	2	Central Washington	Tacoma, Wash.	FA-'96	3/1
57	Kyle, Jason	LB	6-3	242	5/12/72	4	Arizona State	Tempe, Ariz.	D4b-'95	0*
99	LaBounty, Matt	DE	6-4	275	1/3/69	6	Oregon	Novato, Calif.	T(GB)-'96	16/6
56	Logan, James	LB	6-2	225	12/6/72	4	Memphis	Opp, Ala.	W(Cin)-'95	14/1
88	May, Deems	TE	6-4	263	3/6/69	7	North Carolina	Lexington, N.C.	UFA(SD)-'97	16/0
82	McKnight, James	WR	6-1	198	6/17/72	4	Liberty	Apopka, Fla.	FA-'94	12/6
49	Mili, Itula	TE	6-4	265	4/20/73	2	Brigham Young	Laie, Hawaii	D6-'97	0*
1	Moon, Warren	QB	6-3	213	11/18/56	15	Washington	Los Angeles, Calif.	FA-'97	15/14
76	Parker, Riddick	DT	6-3	274	11/20/72	2	North Carolina	Southampton, Va.	FA-'96	12/0
2	† Peterson, Todd	K	5-10	171	2/4/70	4	Georgia	Valdosta, Ga.	FA-'95	16/0
85	Pritchard, Mike	WR	5-10	193	10/26/69	8	Colorado	Las Vegas, Nev.	FA-'96	16/15
21	Rusk, Reggie	CB	5-10	190	10/19/72	2	Kentucky	Texas City, Tex.	FA-'97	2/0
97	Saleaumua, Dan	DT	6-0	315	11/25/64	12	Arizona State	National City, Calif.	FA-'97	16/9
70	Sinclair, Michael	DE	6-4	267	1/31/68	8	Eastern New Mexico	Beaumont, Tex.	D6-'91	16/16
50	Smith, Darrin	LB	6-1	230	4/15/70	6	Miami	Miami, Fla.	UFA(Phil)-'98	7/7*
24	Springs, Shawn	CB	6-0	195	3/11/75	2	Ohio State	Silver Springs, Md.	D1a-'97	10/10
37	Stokes, Eric	S	5-11	201	12/18/73	2	Nebraska	Lincoln, Neb.	D5-'97	7/0
38	Strong, Mack	RB	6-0	235	9/11/71	5	Georgia	Columbus, Ga.	FA-'93	16/9
22	Thomas, Fred	CB	5-9	172	9/11/73	3	Tennessee-Martin	Bruce, Miss.	D2-'96	16/3
32	Watters, Ricky	RB	6-1	217	4/7/69	8	Notre Dame	Harrisburg, Pa.	UFA(Phil)-'98	16/16*
95	Wells, Dean	LB	6-3	248	7/20/70	6	Kentucky	Louisville, Ky.	D4-'93	16/16
33	Williams, Darryl	S	6-0	202	1/8/70	7	Miami	Hialeah, Fla.	UFA(Cin)-'96	16/16
69	Williams, Grant	T	6-7	323	5/10/74	3	Louisiana Tech	Clinton, Miss.	FA-'96	16/8
27	Williams, Willie	CB	5-9	180	12/26/70	6	Western Carolina	Columbia, S.C.	UFA(Pitt)-'97	16/16
19	Wilson, Robert	WR	5-11	176	6/23/74	2	Florida A&M	Monticello, Fla.	FA-'97	0*

* Burton played 5 games with Chicago in '97; Collins played 1 game with Green Bay; Cunningham, Kyle, and Mili missed '97 season because of injury; Feagles played 16 games with Arizona; Glover played 16 games with Detroit; C. Gray played 8 games with Chicago; O. Gray inactive 2 games; Greene last active with Miami in '95; Habib played 14 games with Denver; Hardy played 12 games with Dallas; Smith played 7 games with Philadelphia; Watters played 16 games with Philadelphia; Wilson inactive for 1 game.

\# Unrestricted free agent; subject to developments.

† Restricted free agent; subject to developments.

Retired—Winston Moss, 11-year linebacker, 14 games in '97.

Players lost through free agency (3): C Kevin Mawae (NYJ; 16 games in '97), RB Lamar Smith (NO; 12), P Rick Tuten (StL; 11).

Also played with Seattle in '97—G-T James Atkins (13 games), WR-KR Andre Coleman (2), DE Antonio Edwards (1), DE Martin Harrison (8), S Tim Hauck (16), WR Daryl Hobbs (10), CB Jeremy Lincoln (12), CB Dexter Seigler (2), P Rohn Stark (4), LB Eric Unverzagt (1), RB Chris Warren (15).

COACHING STAFF

Head Coach,
Dennis Erickson

Pro Career: Named the fifth head coach in franchise history on January 12, 1995. Career record: 23-25.

Background: Started his coaching career at Montana State as a graduate assistant in 1969. Also served as a graduate assistant at Washington State in 1970. Was an assistant at Montana State, Idaho, and Fresno State before becoming the head coach at Idaho in 1982. Twice advanced to NCAA I-AA playoffs and was a two-time All-Big Sky Conference coach of the year. Head coach one season (1986) at Wyoming before moving to Washington State in 1987. Took Cougars to their first bowl game since 1981 and posted their first bowl game win in 72 years in 1988. Finished the season with a national ranking of sixteenth, the school's best ever. Spent 1989-94 at the University of Miami, where he won national championships in 1989 (his first season) and in 1991, compiling an undefeated (12-0) record. Played in six New Year's Day bowl games, including five with national championship implications. Twice finished third in the country and once sixth in addition to the two national titles. Posted a then NCAA-best 63-9 record during tenure at Miami and reached 100 career wins in just 137 games, the fourth fastest among Division I coaches active in 1994. Was 35-2 at the Orange Bowl, including being part of a then NCAA-record 58-game winning streak. Played quarterback collegiately at Montana State from 1966-68. Collegiate career record: 137-40-1.

Personal: Born March 24, 1947, in Everett, Washington. Graduated from Montana State with a bachelor of arts degree in Physical Education. Dennis and his wife, Marilyn, have two sons, Bryce and Ryan, and live in Redmond, Washington.

ASSISTANT COACHES

Tommy Brasher, defensive line; born December 30, 1940, El Dorado, Ark., lives in Redmond, Wash. Linebacker Arkansas 1962-63. No pro playing experience. College coach: Arkansas 1970, Virginia Tech 1971, Northeast Louisiana 1974, 1976, Southern Methodist 1977-81. Pro coach: Shreveport Steamer (WFL) 1975, New England Patriots 1982-84, Philadelphia Eagles 1985, Atlanta Falcons 1986-89, Tampa Bay Buccaneers 1990, joined Seahawks in 1992.

Bob Bratkowski, offensive coordinator; born December 2, 1955, San Angelo, Tex., lives in Redmond, Wash. Wide receiver Washington State 1974, 1976-77. No pro playing experience. College coach: Missouri 1978-80, Weber State 1981-85, Wyoming 1986, Washington State 1987-88, Miami 1989-91. Pro coach: Joined Seahawks in 1992.

Dave Brown, defensive assistant; born January 16, 1953, Akron, Ohio, lives in Woodinville, Wash. Defensive back Michigan 1972-74. Pro defensive back Pittsburgh Steelers 1975, Seattle Seahawks 1976-86, Green Bay Packers 1987-90. Pro coach: Joined Seahawks in 1992.

Keith Gilbertson, tight ends; born May 15, 1948, Snohomish, Wash., lives in Kirkland, Wash. Lineman Hawaii 1969-70. No pro playing experience. College coach: Idaho State 1971-73, Western Washington 1974, Washington 1976, 1989-91, Utah State 1977-81, Idaho 1982, 1985-88 (head coach 1986-88), California 1992-95 (head coach). Pro coach: Joined Seahawks in 1996.

Milt Jackson, wide recievers; born October 16, 1943, Groesbeck, Tex., lives in Bellevue, Wash. Defensive back Tulsa 1965-66. Pro defensive back San Francisco 49ers 1967. College coach: Oregon State 1973, Rice 1974, California 1975-76, Oregon 1977-78, UCLA 1979. Pro coach: San Francisco 49ers 1980-82, Buffalo Bills 1983-84, Philadelphia Eagles 1985, Houston Oilers 1986-88, Indianapolis Colts 1989-91, Los Angeles Rams 1992-93, Atlanta Falcons 1994-96, New York Giants 1997, joined Seahawks in 1998.

Jim Johnson, linebackers; born May 26, 1941, Maywood, Ill., lives in Bellevue, Wash. Quarterback Missouri 1959-62. Pro tight end Buffalo Bills 1963-64. College coach: Missouri Southern 1967-68 (head coach), Drake 1969-72, Indiana 1973-76, Notre Dame 1977-80. Pro coach: Oklahoma Outlaws (USFL) 1984, Jacksonville Bulls (USFL) 1985, Phoenix Cardinals 1986-93, Indianapolis Colts 1994-97, joined Seahawks in 1998.

Darren Krein, assistant strength and conditioning; born July 7, 1971, Aurora, Colo., lives in Kirkland, Wash. Linebacker/defensive end Miami 1989-93. Pro defensive end San Diego Chargers 1994, Barcelona Dragons (World League) 1996. Pro coach: Joined Seahawks in 1997.

Tim Lappano, running backs; born October 14, 1956, Spokane, Wash., lives in Bellevue, Wash. Running back Idaho 1975-79. No pro playing experience. College coach: Idaho 1982-85, Wyoming 1986, 1996, Washington State 1987-91, California 1992-95, Purdue 1997. Pro coach: Joined Seahawks in 1998.

Dana LeDuc, strength and conditioning; born March 22, 1953, Tacoma, Wash., lives in Bellevue, Wash. No college or pro playing experience. College coach: Texas 1977-92, Miami 1993-94. Pro coach: Joined Seahawks in 1995.

Greg McMakin, defensive coordinator; born April 24, 1947, Springfield, Ore., lives in Redmond, Wash. Defensive back Southern Oregon 1964-68. No pro playing experience. College coach: Arizona 1968-69, Western Oregon State 1973-76, Idaho 1976-78, San Jose State 1978-83, Stanford 1984-85, Oregon Tech 1986-90, Utah 1990-92, Miami 1993-94. Pro coach: Denver Gold (USFL) 1985-86, joined Seahawks in 1995.

Bill Meyers, assistant offensive line; born October 8, 1946, Chippewa Falls, Wis., lives in Bellevue, Wash. Tackle Stanford 1970-71. No pro playing experience. College coach: California 1972-73, 1977-78, Santa Clara 1974-76, Notre Dame 1979-81, Missouri 1985-86, Pittsburgh 1987-92. Pro coach: Green Bay Packers 1982-83, Pittsburgh Steelers 1984, Oakland Raiders 1993, joined Seahawks in 1998.

Rich Olson, quarterbacks; born July 7, 1948, Wilmington, Calif., lives in Bellevue, Wash. Quarterback-free safety Washington State 1968-69. No pro playing experience. College coach: Washington State 1970, Fresno State 1976, Southern California 1977, Southern Methodist 1978-80, Arkansas 1981-83, Fresno State 1984-91, Miami 1992-94. Pro coach: Joined Seahawks in 1995.

Willy Robinson, defensive backs; born February 10, 1956, Fort Carson, Colo., lives in Bellevue, Wash. No college or pro playing experience. College coach: Fresno State 1978, 1980-93, San Jose State 1979, Miami 1994. Pro coach: Joined Seahawks in 1995.

Pete Rodriguez, assistant head coach-special teams; born July 25, 1940, Chicago, lives in Kirkland, Wash. Guard-linebacker Denver 1959-60, Western State (Colo.) 1961-63. No pro playing experience. College coach: Western State (Colo.) 1964, Arizona 1968-69, Western Illinois 1970-73, 1979-82 (head coach), Florida State 1974-75, Iowa State 1976-78, Northern Iowa 1986. Pro coach: Michigan Panthers (USFL) 1983-84, Denver Gold (USFL) 1985, Jacksonville Bulls (USFL) 1986, Ottawa Rough Riders (CFL) 1987, Los Angeles Raiders 1988-89, Phoenix Cardinals 1990-93, Washington Redskins 1994-1997, joined Seahawks in 1998.

Gregg Smith, offensive line; born October 28, 1946, Oklahoma City, Okla., lives in Bellevue, Wash. Tight end Idaho 1965-66. No pro playing experience. College coach: Idaho 1967-68, 1982-85, Wyoming 1986, Washington State 1987-88, Miami 1989-94. Pro coach: Joined Seahawks in 1995.

Eric Yarber, offensive quality control; born September 22, 1963, Los Angeles, lives in Bellevue, Wash. Wide receiver Idaho 1984-85. Pro wide receiver Washington Redskins 1986-87. College coach: Idaho 1996, UNLV 1997. Pro coach: Joined Seahawks in 1998.

1998 FIRST-YEAR ROSTER

Name	Pos.	Ht.	Wt.	Birthdate	College	Hometown	How Acq.
Arellanes, Jim (1)	QB	6-3	217	1/30/74	Fresno State	Pico Rivera, Calif.	FA-'97
Black, Michael	RB	5-11	206	5/3/74	Washington State	Los Angeles, Calif.	FA
Brown, Chris	C	6-3	320	2/10/75	Illinois	Kansas City, Mo.	FA
Brymer, Chris	G	6-2	311	11/29/74	Southern California	Apple Valley, Calif.	FA
Crosland, Ben	DE	6-4	277	4/29/74	Utah State	Kemmerer, Wyo.	FA
Eloms, Joey	CB	5-10	183	4/4/76	Indiana	Ft. Wayne, Ind.	FA
Finneran, Brian	WR	6-5	196	1/31/76	Villanova	Mission Viejo, Calif.	FA
Galick, Curtis	S	6-0	207	7/5/74	British Columbia	Burnaby, Canada	FA
Green, Ahman	RB	6-0	213	2/16/77	Nebraska	Omaha, Neb.	D3
Hankton, Furnell	TE	6-5	260	1/8/74	Louisiana State	New Orleans, La.	FA
Hansen, Carl	DT	6-5	280	1/25/76	Stanford	Houston, Tex.	D6
Hanson, Stuart	DE	6-3	265	10/21/74	Wyoming	Lisbon, N.D.	FA
Jackson, Chris	WR	6-1	203	2/26/75	Washington State	Santa Ana, Calif.	FA
Jackson, Stanley	WR	6-1	215	3/24/75	Ohio State	Paterson, N.J.	FA
Jackson, Vershan	RB	6-0	236	2/27/75	Nebraska	Omaha, Neb.	FA
Johnson, Dirk	P	6-0	233	6/1/75	Northern Colorado	Montrose, Colo.	FA
Jones, Carlos (1)	CB	5-10	180	8/31/73	Miami	Marrero, La.	FA
Loggins, Jarrett	DT	6-2	295	1/4/75	Northern Arizona	San Diego, Calif.	FA
Lowe, Reggie	DE	6-2	250	6/14/75	Troy State	Phenix City, Ala.	FA
McEndoo, Jason	C	6-5	315	2/25/75	Washington State	Cosmopolis, Wash.	D7
Myles, DeShone	LB	6-2	235	10/31/74	Nevada	Las Vegas, Nev.	D4
Richey, Wade	K	6-4	200	5/17/76	Louisiana State	Lafayette, La.	FA
Rommel, Mark	T	6-5	296	5/6/76	Utah State	Orange, Calif.	FA
Sadler, Jason	T	6-5	296	7/1/75	Nevada	Palm Springs, Calif.	FA
Shaw, Bobby	WR	6-0	186	4/23/75	California	San Francisco, Calif.	D6b
Simmons, Anthony	LB	6-0	230	6/7/76	Clemson	Spartanburg, S.C.	D1
Spicer, Paul	DE	6-4	256	8/18/75	Saginaw Valley State	Indianapolis, Ind.	FA
Weiner, Todd	T	6-4	300	9/16/75	Kansas State	Coral Springs, Fla.	D2
Williams, Tashe (1)	T	6-4	300	9/23/72	Northern Colorado	Colorado Springs, Colo.	FA-'97

The term NFL Rookie is defined as a player who is in his first season of professional football and has not been on the roster of another professional football team for any regular-season or postseason games. A Rookie is designated by an "R" on NFL rosters. Players who have been active in another professional football league or players who have NFL experience, including either preseason training camp or being on an Active List or Inactive List, or on Reserve/Injured or Reserve/Physically Unable to Perform for fewer than six regular-season games, are termed NFL First-Year Players. An NFL First-Year Player is designated by a "1" on NFL rosters. Thereafter, a player is credited with an additional year of experience for each season in which he accumulates six games on the Active List or Inactive List, or on Reserve/Injured or Reserve/Physically Unable to Perform.

NOTES

TENNESSEE OILERS

American Football Conference
Central Division
Team Colors: Columbia Blue, Scarlet, and White
Baptist Sports Park
7640 Hwy 70 South
Nashville, Tennessee 37221
Telephone: (615) 673-1500

CLUB OFFICIALS

President: K.S. (Bud) Adams, Jr.
Executive Assistant to President: Thomas S. Smith
Executive V.P./General Manager: Floyd Reese
Executive V.P./Marketing, Broadcasting,& Ticketing: Don MacLachlan
Executive V.P./Governmental Relations & Stadium Affairs: Mike McClure
Vice President/General Counsel: Steve Underwood
Asst. General Counsel Elza Bullock
Vice President/Director of Regional Scouting: Mike Holovak
Vice President/Finance: Jackie Curley
Vice President/Community Affairs: Bob Hyde
Director of Player Personnel: Rich Snead
Director of College Scouting: Glenn Cumbee
Director of Sales and Operations: Stuart Spears
Asst. Dir. Of Sales and Operations: Chad Bottorff
Director of Broadcasting: Mike Keith
Director of Marketing: Ralph Ockenfels
Director of Media Relations: Tony Wyllie
Asst. Dir. of Media Relations: Robbie Bohren
Director of Security: Steve Berk
Director of Ticket Operations: Marty Collins
Director of Player Programs: Al Smith
Head Trainer: Brad Brown
Assistant Trainers: Don Moseley, Geoff Kaplan
Equipment Manager: Paul Noska
Video Coordinator: Ken Sparacino
Stadium: Vanderbilt Stadium • **Capacity:** 41,600
Natchez Trace & Jess Neeley Drive
Nashville, Tennessee 37212
Playing Surface: Astroturf
Training Camp: Hale Hall
Tennessee State University
Nashville, Tennessee 37209-1561

1998 SCHEDULE

PRESEASON

Aug. 7	at Atlanta	7:30
Aug. 15	**Washington**	1:00
Aug. 22	at New Orleans	7:00
Aug. 29	**Denver**	1:00

REGULAR SEASON

Sept. 6	at Cincinnati	1:01
Sept. 13	**San Diego**	12:01
Sept. 20	at New England	1:01
Sept. 27	**Jacksonville**	12:01
Oct. 4	Open Date	
Oct. 11	at Baltimore	1:01
Oct. 18	**Cincinnati**	12:01
Oct. 25	**Chicago**	3:05
Nov. 1	at Pittsburgh	1:01
Nov. 8	at Tampa Bay	8:20

RECORD HOLDERS

INDIVIDUAL RECORDS—CAREER

Category	Name	Performance
Rushing (Yds.)	Earl Campbell, 1978-1984	8,574
Passing (Yds.)	Warren Moon, 1984-1993	33,685
Passing (TDs)	Warren Moon, 1984-1993	196
Receiving (No.)	Ernest Givins, 1986-1994	542
Receiving (Yds.)	Ernest Givins, 1986-1994	7,935
Interceptions	Jim Norton, 1960-68	45
Punting (Avg.)	Greg Montgomery, 1988-1993	43.6
Punt Return (Avg.)	Billy Johnson, 1974-1980	13.2
Kickoff Return (Avg.)	Bobby Jancik, 1962-67	26.5
Field Goals	Al Del Greco, 1991-97	162
Touchdowns (Tot.)	Earl Campbell, 1978-1984	73
Points	George Blanda, 1960-66	596

INDIVIDUAL RECORDS—SINGLE SEASON

Category	Name	Performance
Rushing (Yds.)	Earl Campbell, 1980	1,934
Passing (Yds.)	Warren Moon, 1991	4,690
Passing (TDs)	George Blanda, 1961	36
Receiving (No.)	Charlie Hennigan, 1964	101
Receiving (Yds.)	Charlie Hennigan, 1961	1,746
Interceptions	Fred Glick, 1963	12
	Mike Reinfeldt, 1979	12
Punting (Avg.)	Greg Montgomery, 1992	46.9
Punt Return (Avg.)	Billy Johnson, 1977	15.4
Kickoff Return (Avg.)	Ken Hall, 1960	31.3
Field Goals	Al Del Greco, 1996	32
Touchdowns (Tot.)	Earl Campbell, 1979	19
Points	Al Del Greco, 1996	131

INDIVIDUAL RECORDS—SINGLE GAME

Category	Name	Performance
Rushing (Yds.)	Billy Cannon, 12-10-61	216
	Eddie George, 8-31-97	216
Passing (Yds.)	Warren Moon, 12-16-90	527
Passing (TDs)	George Blanda, 11-19-61	*7
Receiving (No.)	Charlie Hennigan, 10-13-61	13
	Haywood Jeffires, 10-13-91	13
Receiving (Yds.)	Charlie Hennigan, 10-13-61	272
Interceptions	Many times	3
	Last time by Marcus Robertson, 11-21-93	
Field Goals	Roy Gerela, 9-28-69	5
Touchdowns (Tot.)	Billy Cannon, 12-10-61	5
Points	Billy Cannon, 12-10-61	30

*NFL Record

Nov. 15	**Pittsburgh**	12:01
Nov. 22	**New York Jets**	3:15
Nov. 29	at Seattle	1:05
Dec. 6	**Baltimore**	3:15
Dec. 13	at Jacksonville	1:01
Dec. 20	at Green Bay	12:01
Dec. 26	**Minnesota** (Sat.)	11:35 A.M.

COACHING HISTORY

HOUSTON 1960-1996
(268-312-6)

1960-61	Lou Rymkus*	12-7-1
1961	Wally Lemm	10-0-0
1962-63	Frank (Pop) Ivy	17-12-0
1964	Sammy Baugh	4-10-0
1965	Hugh Taylor	4-10-0
1966-70	Wally Lemm	28-40-4
1971	Ed Hughes	4-9-1
1972-73	Bill Peterson**	1-18-0
1973-74	Sid Gillman	8-15-0
1975-80	O.A. (Bum) Phillips	59-38-0
1981-83	Ed Biles***	8-23-0
1983	Chuck Studley	2-8-0
1984-85	Hugh Campbell****	8-22-0
1985-89	Jerry Glanville	35-35-0
1990-94	Jack Pardee#	44-35-0
1994-97	Jeff Fisher	24-30-0

* Released after five games in 1961
** Released after five games in 1973
*** Resigned after six games in 1983
**** Released after 14 games in 1985
# Released after 10 games in 1994

VANDERBILT STADIUM

N

1997 TEAM RECORD

PRESEASON (0-4)

Date	Result		Opponent
8/2	L	12-21	vs. New Orleans at Memphis, Tenn.
8/9	L	12-18	Washington
8/16	L	7-21	San Diego
8/22	L	10-34	at Dallas

REGULAR SEASON (8-8)

Date	Result		Opponent	Att.
8/31	W	24-21	Oakland (OT)	30,171
9/7	L	13-16	at Miami (OT)	64,439
9/21	L	10-36	Baltimore	17,737
9/28	L	24-37	at Pittsburgh	57,507
10/5	L	13-16	at Seattle	49,897
10/12	W	30-7	Cincinnati	17,071
10/19	W	28-14	Washington	31,042
10/26	W	41-14	at Arizona	44,030
11/2	L	24-30	Jacksonville	27,208
11/9	W	10-6	New York Giants	26,744
11/16	L	9-17	at Jacksonville	70,070
11/23	W	31-14	Buffalo	23,571
11/27	W	27-14	at Dallas	63,421
12/4	L	14-41	at Cincinnati	49,096
12/14	L	19-21	at Baltimore	60,558
12/21	W	16-6	Pittsburgh	50,677

(OT) Overtime

SCORE BY PERIODS

Oilers	74	107	55	94	3	— 333
Opponents	54	93	77	83	3	— 310

ATTENDANCE

Home 224,221 Away 459,008 Total 683,229
Single-game home record, 50,677 (12/21/97)
Single-season home record, 224,211 (1997)

1997 TEAM STATISTICS

	Oilers	Opp.
Total First Downs	288	292
Rushing	130	79
Passing	136	193
Penalty	22	20
Third Down: Made/Att	92/219	80/205
Third Down Pct.	42.0	39.0
Fourth Down: Made/Att	9/14	9/20
Fourth Down Pct.	64.3	45.0
Total Net Yards	4,919	5,231
Avg. Per Game	307.4	326.9
Total Plays	993	992
Avg. Per Play	5.0	5.3
Net Yards Rushing	2,414	1,573
Avg. Per Game	150.9	98.3
Total Rushes	541	414
Net Yards Passing	2,505	3,658
Avg. Per Game	156.6	228.6
Sacked/Yards Lost	32/199	35/240
Gross Yards	2,704	3,898
Att./Completions	420/220	543/321
Completion Pct.	52.4	59.1
Had Intercepted	13	14
Punts/Average	74/41.6	69/43.6
Net Punting Avg.	74/35.3	69/38.0
Penalties/Yards Lost	103/814	94/830
Fumbles/Ball Lost	31/13	32/18
Touchdowns	36	35
Rushing	17	12
Passing	15	21
Returns	4	2
Avg. Time of Possession	31:27	28:33

1997 INDIVIDUAL STATISTICS

PASSING	Att.	Comp.	Yds.	Pct.	TD	Int.	Tkld.	Rate
McNair	415	216	2,665	52.0	14	13	31/190	70.4
Krieg	2	1	2	50.0	0	0	0/0	56.3
Ritchey	2	2	15	100.0	0	0	1/9	97.9
Davis	1	1	22	100.0	1	0	0/0	158.3
Oilers	420	220	2,704	52.4	15	13	32/199	71.6
Opponents	543	321	3,898	59.1	21	14	35/240	83.4

SCORING	TD R	TD P	TD Rt	PAT	FG	Saf	PTS
Del Greco	0	0	0	32/32	27/35	0	113
McNair	8	0	0	0/0	0/0	0	48
E. George	6	1	0	0/0	0/0	0	44
Wycheck	0	4	0	0/0	0/0	0	26
Davis	0	4	0	0/0	0/0	0	24
Sanders	0	3	0	0/0	0/0	0	18
Thomas	3	0	0	0/0	0/0	0	18
Robertson	0	0	2	0/0	0/0	0	12
Kent	0	1	0	0/0	0/0	0	6
D. Lewis	0	0	1	0/0	0/0	0	6
Norgard	0	1	0	0/0	0/0	0	6
Russell	0	1	0	0/0	0/0	0	6
D. Walker	0	0	1	0/0	0/0	0	6
Oilers	17	15	4	32/32	27/35	0	333
Opponents	12	21	2	34/34	22/30	0	310

2-Pt. Conversions: E. George, Wycheck.
Oilers 2-4, Opponents 0-1.

RUSHING	Att.	Yds.	Avg.	LG	TD
E. George	357	1,399	3.9	30	6
McNair	101	674	6.7	47	8
Thomas	67	310	4.6	25t	3
Harmon	8	30	3.8	14	0
Roby	1	12	12.0	12	0
Ritchey	1	6	6.0	6	0
Krieg	4	-2	-.5	0	0
Mason	1	-7	-7.0	-7	0
Sanders	1	-8	-8.0	-8	0
Oilers	541	2,414	4.5	47	17
Opponents	414	1,573	3.8	77t	12

RECEIVING	No.	Yds.	Avg.	LG	TD
Wycheck	63	748	11.9	42	4
Davis	43	564	13.1	46	4
Sanders	31	498	16.1	55t	3
Harmon	16	189	11.8	27	0
Mason	14	186	13.3	38	0
Thomas	14	111	7.9	22	0
Roan	12	159	13.3	26	0
Russell	12	141	11.8	23	1
E. George	7	44	6.3	15	1
Kent	6	55	9.2	19	1
R. Lewis	1	7	7.0	7	0
Norgard	1	2	2.0	2t	1
Oilers	220	2,704	12.3	55t	15
Opponents	321	3,898	12.1	59t	21

INTERCEPTIONS	No.	Yds.	Avg.	LG	TD
Robertson	5	127	25.4	48	0
D. Lewis	5	115	23.0	47t	1
D. Walker	2	53	26.5	39t	1
R. Jones	1	24	24.0	24	0
Bowden	1	9	9.0	9	0
Bishop	0	0	—	0	0
Oilers	14	328	23.4	48	2
Opponents	13	48	3.7	24	0

PUNTING	No.	Yds.	Avg.	In 20	LG
Roby	73	3,049	41.8	25	59
Del Greco	1	32	32.0	0	32
Oilers	74	3,081	41.6	25	59
Opponents	69	3,007	43.6	22	64

PUNT RETURNS	No.	FC	Yds.	Avg.	LG	TD
Gray	17	10	144	8.5	30	0
Mason	13	3	95	7.3	29	0
Archie	1	0	5	5.0	5	0
Robertson	1	0	0	0.0	0	0
Oilers	32	13	244	7.6	30	0
Opponents	36	23	430	11.9	52	0

KICKOFF RETURNS	No.	Yds.	Avg.	LG	TD
Mason	26	551	21.2	54	0
Thomas	17	346	20.4	33	0
Gray	8	185	23.1	33	0
Archie	2	24	12.0	15	0
Roan	2	20	10.0	12	0
Harmon	1	16	16.0	16	0
Layman	1	5	5.0	5	0
Wycheck	1	3	3.0	3	0
Robertson	0	0	—	—	0
Oilers	58	1,150	19.8	54	0
Opponents	71	1,528	21.5	51	0

FIELD GOALS	1-19	20-29	30-39	40-49	50+
Del Greco	2/2	6/6	10/11	7/14	2/2
Oilers	2/2	6/6	10/11	7/14	2/2
Opponents	0/0	7/9	8/9	7/11	0/1

SACKS	No.
Holmes	7.0
G. Walker	7.0
Ford	5.0
Bowden	2.5
Lyons	2.5
Evans	2.0
Hall	2.0
Roberson	2.0
Bishop	1.5
S. Jackson	1.0
L. Jones	1.0
Marts	1.0
Stewart	0.5
Oilers	35.0
Opponents	32.0

1998 DRAFT CHOICES

Round	Name	Pos.	College
1	Kevin Dyson	WR	Utah
2	Samari Rolle	DB	Florida State
3	Dainon Sidney	DB	Alabama-Birmingham
4	Joe Salave'a	DT	Arizona
5	Benji Olson	G	Washington
6	Lee Wiggins	DB	South Carolina
7	Jimmy Sprotte	LB	Arizona
	Kevin Long	C	Florida State

TENNESSEE OILERS

1998 VETERAN ROSTER

No.	Name	Pos.	Ht.	Wt.	Birthdate	NFL Exp.	College	Hometown	How Acq.	'97 Games/ Starts
22	Archie, Mike	RB	5-8	211	10/14/72	3	Penn State	Sharon, Pa.	D7-'96	5/0
23	Bishop, Blaine	S	5-9	193	7/24/70	6	Ball State	Indianapolis, Ind.	D8-'93	14/14
58	Bowden, Joe	LB	5-11	224	2/25/70	7	Oklahoma	Mesquite, Tex.	D5-'92	16/16
94	Burton, Kendrick	DE	6-5	288	9/7/73	2	Alabama	Hartselle, Ala.	D4-'96	0*
83	Byrd, Isaac	WR	6-1	173	11/16/74	2	Kansas	St. Louis, Mo.	FA-'97	2/0
78	Cook, Anthony	DE-DT	6-3	290	5/30/72	4	South Carolina State	Bennettsville, S.C.	D2-'95	16/16
84	Davis, Willie	WR	6-0	182	10/10/67	7	Central Arkansas	Little Rock, Ark.	UFA(KC)-'96	16/15
3	Del Greco, Al	K	5-10	202	3/2/62	15	Auburn	Coral Gables, Fla.	FA-'91	16/0
33	Dorsett, Anthony	CB	5-11	203	9/14/73	3	Pittsburgh	Dallas, Tex.	D6-'96	16/0
68	† England, Eric	DE	6-3	276	4/25/71	4	Texas A&M	Houston, Tex.	FA-'97	0*
91	† Evans, Josh	DE-DT	6-0	275	9/6/72	4	Alabama-Birmingham	West Shawmut, Ala.	FA-'95	15/0
92	Ford, Henry	DE-DT	6-3	292	10/30/71	5	Arkansas	Ft. Worth, Tex.	D1-'94	16/16
27	George, Eddie	RB	6-3	238	9/24/73	3	Ohio State	Philadelphia, Pa.	D1-'96	16/16
93	Halapin, Mike	DT	6-4	283	7/1/73	3	Pittsburgh	Apollo, Pa.	FA-'96	3/1
51	Hall, Lemanski	LB	6-0	230	11/24/70	4	Alabama	Valley, Ala.	D7-'94	16/2
88	Harris, Jackie	TE	6-4	254	1/4/68	9	Northeast Louisiana	Pine Bluff, Ark.	UFA(TB)-'98	12/11*
71	† Hayes, Melvin	T	6-6	328	4/28/73	4	Mississippi State	New Orleans, La.	FA-'96	1/0
15	Hentrich, Craig	P-K	6-3	200	5/18/71	5	Notre Dame	Alton, Ill.	UFA(GB)-'98	16/0*
99	Holmes, Kenny	DE	6-4	270	10/24/73	2	Miami	Vero Beach, Fla.	D1-'97	16/5
72	Hopkins, Brad	T	6-3	295	9/5/70	6	Illinois	Moline, Ill.	D1-'93	16/16
24	Jackson, Steve	CB	5-8	188	4/8/69	8	Purdue	Houston, Tex.	D3a-'91	12/5
57	Jones, Lenoy	LB	6-1	230	9/25/74	3	Texas Christian	Groesbeck, Tex.	FA-'96	16/0
86	Kent, Joey	WR	6-1	186	4/23/74	2	Tennessee	Huntsville, Ala.	D2-'97	12/0
50	Killens, Terry	LB	6-1	227	3/24/74	3	Penn State	Cincinnati, Ohio	D3-'96	16/0
17	Krieg, Dave	QB	6-1	202	10/20/58	19	Milton College	Schofield, Wis.	UFA(Chi)-'97	8/0
66	Layman, Jason	G-T	6-5	311	7/29/73	3	Tennessee	Sevierville, Tenn.	D2b-'96	14/0
29	Lewis, Darryll	CB	5-9	186	12/16/68	8	Arizona	La Puente, Calif.	D2b-'91	16/16
98	Lyons, Pratt	DE-DT	6-5	281	9/17/74	2	Troy State	Ft. Worth, Tex.	D4b-'97	16/0
56	Marts, Lonnie	LB	6-2	241	11/10/68	9	Tulane	New Orleans, La.	UFA(TB)-'97	14/14
85	Mason, Derrick	WR	5-10	190	1/17/74	2	Michigan State	Detroit, Mich.	D4a-'97	16/2
74	Matthews, Bruce	G-C	6-5	309	8/8/61	16	Southern California	Arcadia, Calif.	D1-'83	16/16
87	McKeehan, James	TE	6-3	251	8/9/73	3	Texas A&M	Willis, Tex.	FA-'97	10/0
9	McNair, Steve	QB	6-2	229	2/14/73	4	Alcorn State	Mt. Olive, Miss.	D1-'95	16/16
97	Mix, Bryant	DE-DT	6-3	293	7/28/72	3	Alcorn State	Water Valley, Miss.	D2a-'96	1/0
64	Norgard, Erik	G-C	6-1	289	11/4/65	10	Colorado	Arlington, Wash.	FA-'90	16/0
16	Ritchey, James	QB	6-2	210	7/10/73	3	Stephen F. Austin	Copperas Cove, Tex.	FA-'96	1/0
80	Roan, Michael	TE	6-3	242	8/29/72	4	Wisconsin	Iowa City, Iowa	D4-'95	14/13
90	Roberson, James	DE	6-3	275	5/3/71	3	Florida State	Lake Wales, Fla.	FA-'96	15/11
31	Robertson, Marcus	S	5-11	202	10/2/69	8	Iowa State	Pasadena, Calif.	D4b-'91	14/14
69	Runyan, Jon	T	6-7	316	11/27/73	3	Michigan	Flint, Mich.	D4b-'96	16/16
81	Sanders, Chris	WR	6-1	180	5/8/72	4	Ohio State	Denver, Colo.	D3a-'95	15/14
73	Sanderson, Scott	T	6-6	278	7/25/74	2	Washington State	Concord, Calif.	D3b-'97	10/0
59	Stallings, Dennis	LB	6-0	234	5/25/74	2	Illinois	East St. Louis, Ill.	D6-'97	13/0
53	Stepnoski, Mark	C	6-2	263	1/20/67	10	Pittsburgh	Erie, Pa.	UFA(Dall)-'95	16/16
26	Stewart, Rayna	CB-S	5-10	198	6/18/73	3	Northern Arizona	Chatsworth, Calif.	D5-'96	16/4
82	Thigpen, Yancey	WR	6-1	206	8/15/69	7	Winston-Salem State	Rocky Mount, N.C.	UFA(Pitt)-'98	16/15*
20	† Thomas, Rodney	RB	5-10	213	3/30/73	4	Texas A&M	Groveton, Tex.	D3b-'95	16/1
25	Walker, Denard	CB	6-1	192	8/9/73	2	Louisiana State	Garland, Tex.	D3a-'97	15/11
96	† Walker, Gary	DE-DT	6-2	288	2/28/73	4	Auburn	Lavonia, Ga.	D5-'95	15/15
32	Whittle, Ricky	RB	5-9	200	12/21/71	2	Oregon	Fresno, Calif.	FA-'98	0*
42	Williams, Armon	S-LB	6-0	215	8/13/73	2	Arizona	Tempe, Ariz.	D7-'97	6/0
52	Wortham, Barron	LB	5-11	240	11/1/69	5	Texas-El Paso	Everman, Tex.	D6b-'94	16/16
89	Wycheck, Frank	TE	6-3	248	10/14/71	6	Maryland	Philadelphia, Pa.	W(Wash)-'95	16/16

* Burton last active with Houston in '96; England inactive 5 games; Harris played 12 games with Tampa Bay in '97; Hentrich played 16 games with Green Bay; Thigpen played 16 games with Pittsburgh; Whittle last active with New Orleans in '96.

† Restricted free agent; subject to developments.

Players lost through free agency (1): T Kevin Donnalley (Mia; 16 games in '97).

Also played with Oilers in '97—CB Tomur Barnes (3 games), RB Spencer George (5), WR-KR Mel Gray (11), RB Ronnie Harmon (11), CB Roger Jones (2), TE Roderick Lewis (10), RB George McCullough (2), S Rafael Robinson (3), P Reggie Roby (16), WR Derek Russell (11).

COACHING STAFF

Head Coach,
Jeff Fisher

Pro Career: Officially named as Oilers' fifteenth head coach on January 5, 1995. The Oilers missed the playoffs by just one game in 1996, his second full season as head coach. Was elevated to head coach-defensive coordinator on November 14, 1994, after head coach Jack Pardee and assistant head coach-offense Kevin Gilbride were relieved of their duties. Took over a 1-9 team and guided them through the final six games of the season, picking up his first victory against the New York Jets in the season finale. Originally joined the Oilers on February 9, 1994, as defensive coordinator after spending two seasons as defensive backs coach for the San Francisco 49ers (1992-93). Prior to stint with the 49ers, worked as defensive coordinator for the Los Angeles Rams (1991). From 1986-1990, was an assistant for Buddy Ryan's Philadelphia Eagles, serving as defensive backs coach from 1986-88 before becoming the NFL's youngest defensive coordinator in 1989. Drafted by Chicago in seventh round in 1981, spent five seasons as a cornerback and kick returner for the Bears (1981-85). Did not play in Bears' 1985 Super Bowl championship season after being placed on injured reserve with an ankle injury. That season he assisted defensive coordinator Buddy Ryan. Career record: 24-30.

Background: Played at Southern California (1977-1980) for John Robinson in a star-studded defensive backfield that included Ronnie Lott, Dennis Smith, and Joey Browner. Member of the USC team that won the national championship in 1978. Also served as the Trojans' backup placekicker and was a Pac-10 All-Academic selection in 1980.

Personal: Born February 25, 1958, in Culver City, Calif. Jeff and his wife, Juli, have three children, sons Brandon and Trenton, and daughter Tara. The family resides in Franklin, Tenn.

ASSISTANT COACHES

Bart Andrus, offensive assistant-quality control; born March 30, 1958, Logan, Utah, lives in Franklin, Tenn. Quarterback Montana 1978-81. No pro playing experience. College coach: Humboldt State 1986-89, Montana State 1990-91, Southern Utah 1993-95, Rocky Mountain College 1996 (head coach). Pro coach: Joined Oilers in 1997.

Greg Brown, defensive backs; born October 10, 1957, Denver, Colo., lives in Nashville. Defensive back Texas-El Paso 1978-79. No pro playing experience. College coach: Wyoming 1987-88, Purdue 1989-90, Colorado 1991-93. Pro coach: Denver Gold (USFL) 1983-84, Tampa Bay Buccaneers 1984-86, Atlanta Falcons 1994, San Diego Chargers 1995-96, joined Oilers in 1997.

O'Neill Gilbert, linebackers; born March 29, 1965, Monroe, La., lives in Franklin, Tenn. Linebacker Texas A&M 1985-88. Pro linebacker San Francisco 49ers 1990, Montreal Machine (WFL) 1991. College coach: Navarro (Tex.) J.C. 1991, Nevada-Las Vegas 1992-94, Illinois 1995-96. Pro coach: Joined Oilers in 1997.

Jerry Gray, defensive assistant-quality control; born December 16, 1962, Lubbock, Tex., lives in Franklin, Tenn. Defensive back Texas 1981-84. Pro safety-cornerback Los Angeles Rams 1985-91, Houston Oilers 1992, Tampa Bay Buccaneers 1993. College coach: Southern Methodist 1995-96. Pro coach: Joined Oilers in 1997.

George Henshaw, offensive line-tight ends; born January 22, 1948, Richmond, Va., lives in Nashville. Defensive tackle West Virginia 1967-69. No pro playing experience. College coach: West Virginia 1970-75, Florida State 1976-82, Alabama 1983-86, Tulsa 1987 (head coach). Pro coach: Denver Broncos 1988-92, New York Giants 1993-96, joined Oilers in 1997.

Alan Lowry, wide receivers; born November 21, 1950, Miami, Okla., lives in Franklin, Tenn. Defensive back-quarterback Texas 1970-72. No pro playing experience. College coach: Virginia Tech 1974, Wyoming 1975, Texas 1977-81. Pro coach: Dallas Cowboys 1982-90, Tampa Bay Buccaneers 1991, San Francisco 49ers 1992-95, joined Oilers in 1996.

Mike Munchak, offensive line; born March 5, 1960, Scranton, Pa., lives in Brentwood, Tenn. Guard-tackle Penn State 1979-81. Pro guard Houston Oilers 1982-93. Pro coach: Joined Oilers in 1994.

Rex Norris, defensive line; born December 10, 1939, Tipton, Ind., lives in Nashville. Linebacker San Angelo (Tex.) J.C. 1959-60, East Texas State 1961-62. No pro playing experience. College coach: Navarro (Tex.) J.C. 1970-71, Texas A&M 1972, Oklahoma 1973-83, Arizona State 1984, Florida 1988-89, Tennessee 1990-91, Texas 1992-93. Pro coach: Detroit Lions 1985-87, Denver Broncos 1994, joined Oilers in 1995.

Russ Purnell, special teams; born June 12, 1948, Chicago, Ill., lives in Brentwood, Tenn. Center Orange Coast (Calif.) J.C. 1966-67, Whittier College 1968-69. No pro playing experience. College coach: Whittier College 1970-71, Southern California 1982-84. Pro coach: Seattle Seahawks 1986-94, joined Oilers in 1995.

Sherman Smith, running backs; born November 1, 1954, Youngstown, Ohio, lives in Franklin, Tenn. Quarterback Miami (Ohio) 1972-75. Pro running back Seattle Seahawks 1976-82, San Diego Chargers 1983-84. College coach: Miami (Ohio) 1990-91, Illinois 1992-94. Pro coach: Joined Oilers in 1995.

Les Steckel, offensive coordinator-quarterbacks; born July 1, 1946, North Hampton, Pa., lives in Brentwood, Tenn. Running back Kansas 1964-68. No pro playing experience. College coach: Colorado 1972-76, 1991-92, Navy 1977, Brown 1989. Pro coach: San Francisco 49ers 1978, Minnesota Vikings 1979-84 (head coach 1984), New England Patriots 1985-88, Denver Broncos 1993-94, joined Oilers in 1995.

Steve Watterson, strength and rehabilitation; born November 27, 1956, Newport, R.I., lives in Brentwood, Tenn. Attended Rhode Island. No college or pro playing experience. Pro coach: Philadelphia Eagles 1984-85, joined Oilers in 1986.

Gregg Williams, defensive coordinator; born July 15, 1958 in Excelsior Springs, Mo., lives in Franklin, Tenn. Quarterback Northeast Missouri State 1976-79. No pro playing experience. College coach: Houston 1988-89. Pro coach: Joined Oilers in 1990.

1998 FIRST-YEAR ROSTER

Name	Pos.	Ht.	Wt.	Birthdate	College	Hometown	How Acq.
Adams, Louis (1)	LB	6-1	231	7/8/74	Oklahoma State	Pontiac, Mich.	FA-'97
Bradley, Josh	TE	6-6	271	3/27/74	Louisiana Tech	Oak Grove, La.	FA
Bryant, Maurice	WR	6-0	195	10/8/73	Houston	Houston, Tex.	FA
Dyson, Kevin	WR	6-1	199	6/23/75	Utah	Clearfield, Utah	D1
George, Spencer (1)	RB	5-9	202	10/28/73	Rice	Beaumont, Tex.	FA-'97
Gilbert, Lonnie	G	6-2	287	8/27/75	North Carolina State	Miami, Fla.	FA-'98
Lewis, Derrick	CB	5-10	178	11/15/74	Jackson State	Louisville, Miss.	FA
Long, Kevin	C	6-5	296	5/2/75	Florida State	Summerville, S.C.	D7
McCullough, George	CB	5-10	187	2/18/75	Baylor	Galveston, Tex.	D5-'97
Mustafa, Isaiah (1)	WR	6-2	204	2/11/74	Arizona State	Oxnard, Calif.	FA-'97
Norman, Steven	TE	6-2	222	7/9/75	Texas A&M-Kingsville	El Campo, Tex.	FA
Olson, Benji	C-G-T	6-3	313	6/5/75	Washington	Port Orchard, Wash.	D5
Parker, Mike	LB	6-1	220	7/12/75	Houston	Houston, Tex.	FA
Phenix, Perry	S	5-11	195	11/14/74	Southern Mississippi	Dallas, Tex.	FA
Powlus, Ron	QB	6-1	219	7/16/74	Notre Dame	Berwick, Pa.	FA
Richards, Jason	DT	6-3	275	11/17/75	Toledo	Ellwood City, Pa.	FA
Rolle, Samari	CB	6-0	175	8/10/76	Florida State	Miami, Fla.	D2
Salave'a, Joe	DT	6-3	285	3/23/75	Arizona	San Diego, Calif.	D4
Sidney, Dainon	CB	6-0	186	5/30/75	Alabama-Birmingham	Atlanta, Ga.	D3
Sprotte, Jimmy	LB	6-3	245	10/2/74	Arizona	Lakeside, Ariz.	D7
Sutton, Mike	DE	6-4	272	4/21/75	Louisiana	Fliell, La.	FA
Washington, T.J. (1)	C-G-T	6-4	335	7/1/74	Virginia Tech	Melfa, Va.	FA-'97
Wiggins, Lee	CB	5-11	187	4/27/75	South Carolina	Hartsville, S.C.	D6

The term NFL Rookie is defined as a player who is in his first season of professional football and has not been on the roster of another professional football team for any regular-season or postseason games. A Rookie is designated by an "R" on NFL rosters. Players who have been active in another professional football league or players who have NFL experience, including either preseason training camp or being on an Active List or Inactive List, or on Reserve/Injured or Reserve/Physically Unable to Perform for fewer than six regular-season games, are termed NFL First-Year Players. An NFL First-Year Player is designated by a "1" on NFL rosters. Thereafter, a player is credited with an additional year of experience for each season in which he accumulates six games on the Active List or Inactive List, or on Reserve/Injured or Reserve/Physically Unable to Perform.

NOTES

The NFC

ARIZONA CARDINALS

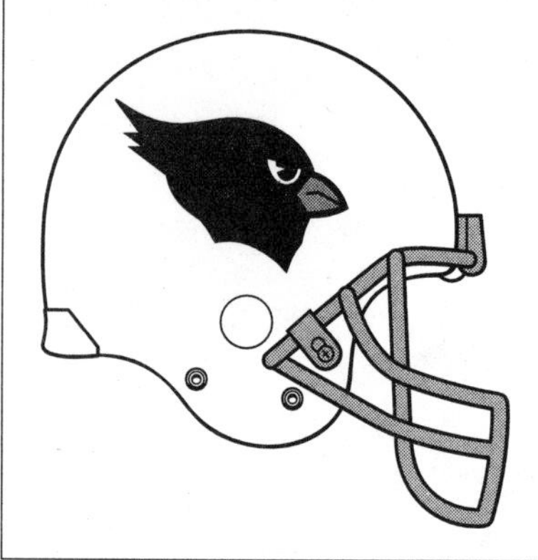

National Football Conference
Eastern Division
Team Colors: Cardinal Red, Black, and White
P.O. Box 888
Phoenix, Arizona 85001-0888
Telephone: (602) 379-0101

CLUB OFFICIALS

President: William V. Bidwill
Vice President: Larry Wilson
Vice President of Sales and Marketing: John Shean
Vice Chairman: Thomas J. Guilfoil
Treasurer and Chief Financial Officer: Charley Schlegel
Vice President: William V. Bidwill, Jr.
Vice President/General Counsel: Michael Bidwill
Vice President-Player Personnel: Bob Ferguson
Assistant to the President: Rod Graves
Public Relations Director: Paul Jensen
Media Coordinator: Greg Gladysiewski
Publications/Internet Coordinator: Luke Sacks
Director-NFL Programs & Community Outreach: Garth Jax
Director of Players Programs: Earl Edwards
Director of Community Relations: Adele Harris
Director of Marketing: Joe Castor
Business Manager: Steve Walsh
Ticket Manager: Steve Bomar
Trainer: John Omohundro
Assistant Trainers: Jim Shearer, Jeff Herndon
Equipment Manager: Mark Ahlemeier
Assistant Equipment Manager: Steve Christensen
Stadium: Sun Devil Stadium •**Capacity:** 73,273
Fifth Street
Tempe, Arizona 85287
Playing Surface: Grass
Training Camp: Northern Arizona University
Flagstaff, Arizona 86011

1998 SCHEDULE

PRESEASON

Aug. 7	at Detroit	7:00
Aug. 14	**Chicago**	7:00
Aug. 22	**Seattle**	7:00
Aug. 29	at Oakland	1:00

REGULAR SEASON

Sept. 6	at Dallas	3:05
Sept. 13	at Seattle	1:15
Sept. 20	**Philadelphia**	5:20
Sept. 27	at St. Louis	12:01
Oct. 4	**Oakland**	1:05
Oct. 11	**Chicago**	1:05
Oct. 18	at New York Giants	1:01
Oct. 25	Open Date	
Nov. 1	at Detroit	1:01
Nov. 8	**Washington**	2:05
Nov. 15	**Dallas**	2:15
Nov. 22	at Washington	1:01
Nov. 29	at Kansas City	12:01
Dec. 6	**New York Giants**	2:05
Dec. 13	at Philadelphia	1:01
Dec. 20	**New Orleans**	2:15
Dec. 27	**San Diego**	2:15

RECORD HOLDERS

INDIVIDUAL RECORDS—CAREER

Category	Name	Performance
Rushing (Yds.)	Ottis Anderson, 1979-1986	7,999
Passing (Yds.)	Jim Hart, 1966-1983	34,639
Passing (TDs)	Jim Hart, 1966-1983	209
Receiving (No.)	Roy Green, 1979-1990	522
Receiving (Yds.)	Roy Green, 1979-1990	8,497
Interceptions	Larry Wilson, 1960-1972	52
Punting (Avg.)	Jerry Norton, 1959-1961	44.9
Punt Return (Avg.)	Charley Trippi, 1947-1955	13.7
Kickoff Return (Avg.)	Ollie Matson, 1952, 1954-58	28.5
Field Goals	Jim Bakken, 1962-1978	282
Touchdowns (Tot.)	Roy Green, 1979-1990	70
Points	Jim Bakken, 1962-1978	1,380

INDIVIDUAL RECORDS—SINGLE SEASON

Category	Name	Performance
Rushing (Yds.)	Ottis Anderson, 1979	1,605
Passing (Yds.)	Neil Lomax, 1984	4,614
Passing (TDs)	Charley Johnson, 1963	28
	Neil Lomax, 1984	28
Receiving (No.)	Larry Centers, 1995	101
Receiving (Yds.)	Rob Moore, 1997	1,584
Interceptions	Bob Nussbaumer, 1949	12
Punting (Avg.)	Jerry Norton, 1960	45.6
Punt Return (Avg.)	John (Red) Cochran, 1949	20.9
Kickoff Return (Avg.)	Ollie Matson, 1958	35.5
Field Goals	Greg Davis, 1995	30
Touchdowns (Tot.)	John David Crow, 1962	17
Points	Jim Bakken, 1967	117
	Neil O'Donoghue, 1984	117

INDIVIDUAL RECORDS—SINGLE GAME

Category	Name	Performance
Rushing (Yds.)	LeShon Johnson, 9-22-96	214
Passing (Yds.)	Boomer Esiason, 11-10-96 (OT)	522
Passing (TDs)	Jim Hardy, 10-2-50	6
	Charley Johnson, 9-26-65, 11-2-69	6
Receiving (No.)	Sonny Randle, 11-4-62	16
Receiving (Yds.)	Sonny Randle, 11-4-62	256
Interceptions	Bob Nussbaumer, 11-13-49	*4
	Jerry Norton, 11-20-60	*4
Field Goals	Jim Bakken, 9-24-67	*7
Touchdowns (Tot.)	Ernie Nevers, 11-28-29	*6
Points	Ernie Nevers, 11-28-29	*40

*NFL Record

COACHING HISTORY

Chicago 1920-1959, St. Louis 1960-1987
(409-567-39)

1920-22	John (Paddy) Driscoll	17-8-4
1923-24	Arnold Horween	13-8-1
1925-26	Norman Barry	16-8-2
1927	Guy Chamberlin	3-7-1
1928	Fred Gillies	1-5-0
1929	Dewey Scanlon	6-6-1
1930	Ernie Nevers	5-6-2
1931	LeRoy Andrews*	0-1-0
1931	Ernie Nevers	5-3-0
1932	Jack Chevigny	2-6-2
1933-34	Paul Schissler	6-15-1
1935-38	Milan Creighton	16-26-4
1939	Ernie Nevers	1-10-0
1940-42	Jimmy Conzelman	8-22-3
1943-45	Phil Handler**	1-29-0
1946-48	Jimmy Conzelman	27-10-0
1949	Phil Handler-Buddy Parker***	2-4-0
1949	Raymond (Buddy) Parker	4-1-1
1950-51	Earl (Curly) Lambeau****	7-15-0
1951	Phil Handler-Cecil Isbell#	1-1-0
1952	Joe Kuharich	4-8-0
1953-54	Joe Stydahar	3-20-1
1955-57	Ray Richards	14-21-1
1958-61	Frank (Pop) Ivy##	17-29-2
1961	Chuck Drulis-Ray Prochaska-Ray Willsey###	2-0-0
1962-65	Wally Lemm	27-26-3
1966-70	Charley Winner	35-30-5
1971-72	Bob Hollway	8-18-2
1973-77	Don Coryell	42-29-1
1978-79	Bud Wilkinson####	9-20-0
1979	Larry Wilson	2-1-0
1980-85	Jim Hanifan	39-50-1
1986-89	Gene Stallings@	23-34-1
1989	Hank Kuhlmann	0-5-0
1990-93	Joe Bugel	20-44-0
1994-95	Buddy Ryan	12-20-0
1996-97	Vince Tobin	11-21-0

* Resigned after one game in 1931
** Co-coach with Walt Kiesling in Chicago Cardinals-Pittsburgh merger in 1944
*** Co-coaches for first six games in 1949
**** Resigned after 10 games in 1951
\# Co-coaches
\## Resigned after 12 games in 1961
\### Co-coaches
\#### Released after 13 games in 1979
@ Released after 11 games in 1989

SUN DEVIL STADIUM

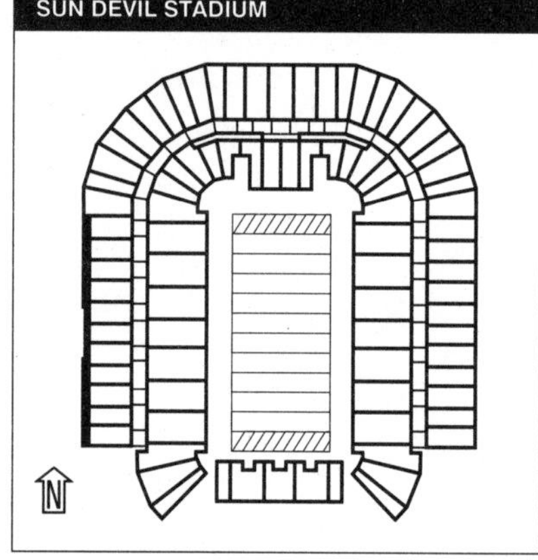

1997 TEAM RECORD

PRESEASON (1-3)

Date	Result		Opponent
8/2	L	6-34	at Seattle
8/10	L	0-12	at St. Louis
8/17	L	10-22	at Chicago
8/23	W	15-13	Oakland

REGULAR SEASON (4-12)

Date	Result		Opponent	Att.
8/31	L	21-24	at Cincinnati	53,644
9/7	W	25-22	Dallas (OT)	71,578
9/14	L	13-19	at Washington (OT)	78,270
9/28	L	18-19	at Tampa Bay	53,804
10/5	L	19-20	Minnesota	45,550
10/12	L	13-27	New York Giants	38,959
10/19	L	10-13	at Philadelphia (OT)	66,860
10/26	L	14-41	Tennessee	44,030
11/2	W	31-21	Philadelphia	39,549
11/9	L	6-24	at Dallas	64,302
11/16	L	10-19	at New York Giants	68,316
11/23	W	16-13	at Baltimore	53,976
11/30	L	20-26	Pittsburgh (OT)	66,341
12/7	L	28-38	Washington	41,537
12/14	L	10-27	at New Orleans	45,517
12/21	W	29-26	Atlanta	32,003

(OT) Overtime

SCORE BY PERIODS

Cardinals	44	67	85	84	3	—	283
Opponents	63	101	83	117	15	—	379

ATTENDANCE

Home 379,547 Away 484,689 Total 864,236
Single-game home record, 73,025 (9/19/93)
Single-season home record, 497,330 (1994)

1997 TEAM STATISTICS

	Cardinals	Opp.
Total First Downs	295	298
Rushing	79	112
Passing	186	167
Penalty	30	19
Third Down: Made/Att	85/242	76/222
Third Down Pct.	35.1	34.2
Fourth Down: Made/Att	11/22	6/11
Fourth Down Pct.	50.0	54.5
Total Net Yards	4,713	5,426
Avg. Per Game	294.6	339.1
Total Plays	1,075	1,049
Avg. Per Play	4.4	5.2
Net Yards Rushing	1,255	2,180
Avg. Per Game	78.4	136.3
Total Rushes	395	524
Net Yards Passing	3,458	3,246
Avg. Per Game	216.1	202.9
Sacked/Yards Lost	78/495	34/215
Gross Yards	3,953	3,461
Att./Completions	602/317	491/279
Completion Pct.	52.7	56.8
Had Intercepted	22	15
Punts/Avg.	92/43.8	94/43.9
Net Punting Avg.	92/36.8	94/35.6
Penalties/Yards Lost	93/775	113/981
Fumbles/Ball Lost	27/20	16/5
Touchdowns	32	42
Rushing	9	13
Passing	19	23
Returns	4	6
Avg. Time of Possession	29:02	30:58

1997 INDIVIDUAL STATISTICS

Passing	Att.	Comp.	Yds.	Pct.	TD	Int.	Tkld.	Rating
Plummer	296	157	2,203	53.0	15	15	52/291	73.1
K. Graham	250	130	1,408	52.0	4	5	16/115	65.9
Case	55	29	316	52.7	0	2	10/89	54.8
Sanders	1	1	26	100.0	0	0	0/0	118.8
Cardinals	602	317	3,953	52.7	19	22	78/495	68.6
Opponents	491	279	3,461	56.8	23	15	34/215	81.7

SCORING	TD R	TD P	TD Rt	PAT	FG	Saf	PTS
Nedney	0	0	0	19/19	11/17	0	52
Rob Moore	0	8	0	0/0	0/0	0	50
Butler	0	0	0	9/10	8/12	0	33
Sanders	0	4	0	0/0	0/0	0	26
Gedney	0	4	0	0/0	0/0	0	24
Plummer	2	0	0	0/0	0/0	0	14
Centers	1	1	0	0/0	0/0	0	12
K. Graham	2	0	0	0/0	0/0	0	12
McElroy	2	0	0	0/0	0/0	0	12
A. Williams	0	0	2	0/0	0/0	0	12
Bennett	0	0	1	0/0	0/0	0	6
Carter	0	1	0	0/0	0/0	0	6
Case	1	0	0	0/0	0/0	0	6
C. Smith	1	0	0	0/0	0/0	0	6
K. Williams	0	1	0	0/0	0/0	0	6
Wilson	0	0	1	0/0	0/0	0	6
Cardinals	9	19	4	28/29	19/29	0	283
Opponents	13	23	6	35/37	30/35	0	379

2-Pt. Conversions: Rob Moore, Plummer, Sanders. Team 3-3, Opponents 1-3.

RUSHING	Att.	Yds.	Avg.	LG	TD
McElroy	135	424	3.1	18	2
Centers	101	276	2.7	14	1
Plummer	39	216	5.5	31	2
Ron. Moore	57	175	3.1	16	0
Johnson	23	81	3.5	11	0
Bouie	11	26	2.4	6	0
K. Graham	13	23	1.8	10	2
Gedney	1	15	15.0	—	0
Case	7	8	1.1	3	1
Sanders	1	5	5.0	5	0
C. Smith	4	5	1.3	2	1
McKinnon	1	3	3.0	3	0
Feagles	0	0	—	—	0
Swann	1	0	0.0	0	0
K. Williams	1	-2	-2.0	-2	0
Team	395	1,255	3.2	31	9
Opponents	524	2,180	4.2	44	13

RECEIVING	No.	Yds.	Avg.	LG	TD
Rob Moore	97	1,584	16.3	47t	8
Sanders	75	1,017	13.6	70t	4
Centers	54	409	7.6	29	1
Gedney	23	261	11.3	37t	4
K. Williams	20	273	13.7	31t	1
Edwards	20	203	10.2	33	0
McWilliams	7	75	10.7	15	0
Carter	7	44	6.3	15	1
McElroy	7	32	4.6	17	0
Johnson	3	4	1.3	7	0
C. Smith	2	20	10.0	18	0
Brock	1	29	29.0	29	0
Plummer	1	2	2.0	2	0
Wilson	0	0	—	—	0
Cardinals	317	3,953	12.5	70t	19
Opponents	279	3,461	12.4	69	23

INTERCEPTIONS	No.	Yds.	Avg.	LG	TD
A. Williams	6	95	15.8	42t	2
McKinnon	3	40	13.3	17	0
Wilson	1	66	66.0	66t	1
McCleskey	1	15	15.0	15	0
Lassiter	1	10	10.0	10	0
Caldwell	1	5	5.0	5	0
Bennett	1	0	0.0	0	0
Rice	1	0	0.0	0	0
Cardinals	15	231	15.4	66t	3
Opponents	22	289	13.1	41	2

PUNTING	No.	Yds.	Avg.	In 20	LG
Feagles	91	4,028	44.3	24	62
Cardinals	92	4,028	43.8	24	62
Opponents	94	4,130	43.9	26	66

PUNT RETURNS	No.	FC	Yds.	Avg.	LG	TD
K. Williams	40	15	462	11.6	50	0
Edwards	1	1	-1	-1.0	-1	0
Cardinals	41	16	461	11.2	50	0
Opponents	40	27	441	11.0	63t	1

KICKOFF RETURNS	No.	Yds.	Avg.	LG	TD
K. Williams	59	1,458	24.7	63	0
Bouie	6	136	22.7	27	0
C. Smith	3	50	16.7	21	0
Gedney	2	26	13.0	16	0
Johnson	0	26	—	26	0
Cardinals	70	1,696	24.2	63	0
Opponents	42	945	22.5	42	1

FIELD GOALS	1-19	20-29	30-39	40-49	50+
Nedney	1/1	3/3	4/4	3/7	0/2
Butler	0/0	4/4	2/4	2/4	0/0
Cardinals	1/1	7/7	6/8	5/11	0/2
Opponents	1/1	9/9	12/13	7/9	1/3

SACKS	No.
Swann	7.5
M. Smith	6.0
Miller	5.5
Rice	5.0
Lassiter	3.0
Bankston	2.0
Caldwell	2.0
Howard	1.0
McCleskey	1.0
McKinnon	1.0
Cardinals	34.0
Opponents	78.0

1998 DRAFT CHOICES

Round	Name	Pos.	College
1	Andre Wadsworth	DE	Florida State
2	Corey Chavous	DB	Vanderbilt
	Anthony Clement	T	Southwestern Louisiana
4	Michael Pittman	RB	Fresno State
5	Terry Hardy	TE	Southern Mississippi
6	Zack Walz	LB	Dartmouth
7	Phil Savoy	WR	Colorado
	Jomo Cousins	DE	Florida A&M
	Pat Tillman	DB	Arizona State
	Ron Janes	RB	Missouri

ARIZONA CARDINALS

1998 VETERAN ROSTER

No.		Name	Pos.	Ht.	Wt.	Birthdate	NFL Exp.	College	Hometown	How Acq.	'97 Games/ Starts
24		Bates, Mario	RB	6-1	217	1/16/73	5	Arizona State	Tucson, Ariz.	UFA(NO)-'98	12/7*
28		Bennett, Tommy	S	6-2	219	2/19/73	3	UCLA	San Diego, Calif.	FA-'96	13/7
89		Brock, Fred	WR	5-11	181	11/15/74	2	Southern Mississippi	Mongomery, Ala.	FA-'96	2/0
17		Brown, Dave	QB	6-5	230	2/25/70	7	Duke	Summit, N.J.	FA-'98	7/6*
75		Brown, Lomas	T	6-4	290	3/30/63	14	Florida	Miami, Fla.	UFA(Det)-'96	14/14
15		Case, Stoney	QB	6-3	201	7/7/72	4	New Mexico	Odessa, Tex.	D3-'95	3/1
37		Centers, Larry	RB	6-0	225	6/1/68	9	Stephen F. Austin	Tatum, Tex.	D5-'90	15/14
79		Clark, Jon	T	6-6	345	4/11/73	3	Temple	Philadelphia, Pa.	FA-'98	1/0*
51		Cobbins, Lyron	LB	6-0	250	9/17/74	2	Notre Dame	Kansas City, Kan.	FA-'97	6/0
62		Devlin, Mike	C	6-2	318	11/16/69	6	Iowa	Blacksburg, Va.	UFA(Buff)-'96	15/13
64		Dexter, James	T	6-7	319	3/3/73	3	South Carolina	Springfield, Va.	D5-'96	10/9
67		Dishman, Chris	G	6-3	320	2/27/74	2	Nebraska	Cozad, Neb.	D4-'97	8/0
76		Drake, Jerry	DT	6-5	310	7/9/69	3	Hastings College, Neb.	Kingston, N.Y.	FA-'95	0*
83		Edwards, Anthony	WR	5-10	197	5/26/66	10	New Mexico Highlands	Casa Grande, Ariz.	FA-'91	16/1
84		Gedney, Chris	TE	6-5	250	8/9/70	6	Syracuse	Liverpool. N.Y.	UFA(Chi)-'97	16/3
54		Graham, Aaron	C	6-4	293	5/22/73	3	Nebraska	Denton, Tex.	D4-'96	16/4
71		Guynes, Thomas	T	6-5	330	9/9/74	2	Michigan	Kankakee, Ill.	FA-'97	4/0
38		Harris, Kenny	S	6-1	203	4/27/75	2	North Carolina State	Durham, N.C.	FA-'96	11/0
70		Holmes, Lester	G	6-4	315	9/27/69	6	Jackson State	Tylertown, Miss.	FA-'98	16/15*
29		Howard, Ty	CB	5-9	185	11/30/73	2	Ohio State	Columbus, Ohio	D3-'97	15/2
56		Irving, Terry	LB	6-2	236	7/3/71	5	McNeese State	Galveston, Tex.	D4c-'94	16/6
73		Joyce, Matt	G	6-7	313	3/30/72	3	Richmond	St. Petersburg, Fla.	FA-'96	9/6
86		Junkin, Trey	TE	6-2	258	1/23/61	16	Louisiana Tech	North Little Rock, Ark.	W(Oak)-'96	16/0
22		Knight, Tom	CB	5-11	196	12/29/74	2	Iowa	Marlton, N.J.	D1-'97	15/14
42		Lassiter, Kwamie	S	6-0	202	12/3/69	4	Kansas	Newport News, Va.	FA-'95	16/1
53		Maddox, Mark	LB	6-1	233	3/23/68	8	Northern Michigan	Milwaukee, Wis.	UFA(Buff)-'98	8/1*
39		Malone, Van	S	5-11	186	7/1/70	5	Texas	Houston, Tex.	UFA(Det)-'98	8/4*
44		McCleskey, J.J.	CB	5-8	184	4/10/70	5	Tennessee	Knoxville, Tenn.	W(NO)-'96	13/0
50		McCombs, Tony	LB	6-2	246	8/24/74	2	Eastern Kentucky	Hopkinsville, Ky.	D6b-'97	12/0
30		McElroy, Leeland	RB	5-9	212	6/25/74	3	Texas A&M	Beaumont, Tex.	D2-'96	14/8
23		McGee, Dell	CB	5-8	185	9/7/73	2	Auburn	Columbus, Ga.	D5c-'96	0*
57		McKinnon, Ronald	LB	6-0	240	9/20/73	3	North Alabama	Elba, Ala.	FA-'96	16/16
87		McWilliams, Johnny	TE	6-4	271	12/14/72	3	Southern California	Ontario, Calif.	D3-'96	16/7
21	t-	Metcalf, Eric	WR	5-10	188	1/23/68	10	Texas	Seattle, Wash.	T(SD)-'98	16/1*
95		Miller, Jamir	LB	6-5	266	11/19/73	5	UCLA	Oakland, Calif.	D1-'94	16/16
85		Moore, Rob	WR	6-3	203	9/27/68	9	Syracuse	Hempstead, N.Y.	T(NYJ)-'95	16/16
20		Moore, Ronald	RB	5-10	220	1/26/70	6	Pittsburg State	Spencer, Okla.	FA-'97	13/4*
27	t-	Murrell, Adrian	RB	5-11	214	10/16/70	6	West Virginia	Wahaiwa, Hawaii	T(NYJ)-'98	16/16*
6		Nedney, Joe	K	6-4	215	3/22/73	3	San Jose State	San Jose, Calif.	FA-'97	10/0
96		Ottis, Brad	DT	6-5	281	8/2/72	5	Wayne State	Fremont, Neb.	FA-'96	16/4
16		Plummer, Jake	QB	6-2	197	12/19/74	2	Arizona State	Boise, Idaho	D2-'97	10/9
60	#	Redmon, Anthony	G	6-5	308	4/9/71	5	Auburn	Brewton, Ala.	D5b-'94	16/16
97		Rice, Simeon	DE	6-5	260	2/24/74	3	Illinois	Chicago, Ill.	D1-'96	16/15
81		Sanders, Frank	WR	6-2	197	2/17/73	4	Auburn	Fort Lauderdale, Fla.	D2-'95	16/16
55	t-	Sapp, Patrick	LB	6-4	258	5/11/73	3	Clemson	Jacksonville, Fla.	T(SD)-'98	16/9*
74	#	Selby, Rob	G	6-4	290	10/11/67	8	Auburn	Birmingham, Ala.	FA-'95	10/9
45		Smith, Cedric	RB	5-11	250	5/27/68	7	Florida	Enterprise, Ala.	FA-'96	16/3
93		Smith, Mark	DE	6-4	290	8/28/74	2	Auburn	Vicksburg, Miss.	D7-'97	16/4
98		Swann, Eric	DT	6-5	313	8/16/70	8	No College	Swann Station, N.C.	D1-'91	13/13
35		Williams, Aeneas	CB	5-11	202	1/29/68	8	Southern	New Orleans, La.	D3-'90	16/16
94		Wilson, Bernard	DT	6-3	318	8/17/70	6	Tennessee State	Nashville, Tenn.	W(TB)-'94	16/14
68	#	Wolf, Joe	C-G-T	6-6	297	12/28/66	10	Boston College	Allentown, Pa.	D1b-'89	15/9

* Bates played 12 games with New Orleans in '97; Brown played 7 games with N.Y. Giants; Clark played 1 game with Chicago; Drake and McGee missed '97 season because of injury; Holmes played 15 games with Oakland; Maddox played 8 games with Buffalo; Malone played 8 games with Detroit; Metcalf and Sapp played 16 games with San Diego; Ronald Moore played 7 games with St. Louis; Murrell played 16 games with N.Y. Jets.

Unrestricted free agent; subject to developments.

t- traded for Metcalf and Sapp (San Diego), Murrell (N.Y. Jets).

Players lost through free agency (8): S Brent Alexander (Car; 16 games in '97), DE Micheal Bankston (Cin; 16), LB Mike Caldwell (Phil; 16), P Jeff Feagles (Sea; 16), QB Kent Graham (NYG; 8), LB Eric Hill (StL; 11), RB Leshon Johnson (NYG; 14), WR Kevin Williams (Buff; 16).

Also played with Cardinals in '97—RB Kevin Bouie (5 games), K Kevin Butler (6), DT Mark Campbell (4), TE Pat Carter (16), S Matt Darby (11), CB-S Kevin Miniefield (3), CB-S Tito Paul (1).

COACHING STAFF

Head Coach,
Vince Tobin

Pro Career: Named Cardinals' head coach on February 7, 1996. Became thirty-third coach in the history of the franchise dating back to 1920. In his first season, Arizona rebounded from an 0-3 start to claim a 7-4 record in final 11 games and remain in playoff contention until the final week of the season. Arizona improved from twenty-fourth (1995) to twelfth in offense, from twenty-sixth (1995) to twenty-first in defense, and forged the club's first winning November (3-1) since 1987. As a defensive coordinator of the Indianapolis Colts from 1994-95, oversaw a defense that was a principal reason Indianapolis finished 9-7 during the 1995 regular season before defeating San Diego (35-10) and Kansas City (10-7) in the first two rounds of postseason play. Tobin earned credit for rebuilding a Colts defense he inherited that ranked last in overall defense in 1993. Tobin's first unit improved to twentieth in 1994 and tied for seventh with Carolina in 1995 at 314.2 yards per game. In four seasons prior to Tobin's arrival, the Colts' defense finished twenty-fourth or lower against the run. In 1994, Tobin's first Indianapolis defense ranked twelfth against the rush, then improved to sixth in 1995 at 91.1 yards per game, the second lowest figure in team history. It also was just the third time in Colts history the opposition averaged less than 100 yards per game on the ground. Over the past two seasons, Tobin's defensive unit did not allow an individual to rush for 100 yards in 24 consecutive games (final 13 games in 1994, first 11 games in 1995). His 1994 Colts' defense also boasted the lowest red-zone touchdown percentage (40) in the NFL and did not allow a touchdown at home in the final 12 quarters of the season. Tobin previously served as defensive coordinator of the Chicago Bears (1986-1992), tutoring a Bears' defense that set an NFL record for fewest points allowed in a 16-game season (187 in 1986). His 1986 Chicago unit topped the league by allowing just 258 yards per contest. The 1987 Bears surrendered the league's fewest points (215) and sported the best rushing defense (82.9). Tobin also earned victories over Tampa Bay and Washington as Chicago's interim head coach for Mike Ditka. Tobin's other coaching stops have been with the USFL Philadelphia/Baltimore Stars (1983-85), the CFL British Columbia Lions (1977-1982), and his alma mater, the University of Missouri (1967-1976). Tobin's defensive units in the CFL ranked second overall during his six seasons, while his defensive schemes in the USFL helped the Stars rank first defensively in 1983 and 1984 and second in 1985 while allowing the fewest points all three seasons. The Stars reached the league championship game each season, winning the final two times. Career record: 11-21.

Background: Tobin played defensive back at Missouri from 1961-64. He joined the Missouri coaching staff as a defensive assistant from 1967-1976, serving the final six years as defensive coordinator. Tobin owns a bachelor's degree in education and a master's degree in guidance and counseling.

Personal: Born September 29, 1943, in Burlington Junction, Missouri. He and his wife, Kathy, have two children—son Ryan and daughter Shannon.

ASSISTANT COACHES

George (Geep) Chryst, quarterbacks; born June 25, 1962, Madison, Wis., lives in Phoenix. Linebacker Princeton 1981-84. Pro linebacker Orlando Thunder (World League) 1991. College coach: Wisconsin-Platteville 1987, Wisconsin 1988-90. Pro coach: Orlando Thunder (World League) 1991, Chicago Bears 1991-95, joined Cardinals in 1996.

Alan Everest, special teams; born August 22, 1950, Santa Barbara, Calif., lives in Phoenix. Safety Southern Methodist 1970-71. No pro playing experience. College coach: Southern Methodist 1972, North Texas State 1973-74, Cameron (Okla.) 1974-75, U.S. International 1981-87. Pro coach: Arkansas Miners (PSFL) 1991-92, Birmingham Barracudas (CFL) 1995, joined Cardinals in 1996.

Joe Greene, defensive line; born September 24, 1946, Temple, Tex., lives in Phoenix. Defensive tackle North Texas State 1966-68. Pro defensive tackle Pittsburgh Steelers 1969-81. Inducted into Pro Football Hall of Fame in 1987. Pro coach: Pittsburgh Steelers 1987-91, Miami Dolphins 1992-95, joined Cardinals in 1996.

Hank Kuhlmann, tight ends; born October 6, 1937, Webster Groves, Mo., lives in Phoenix. Running back Missouri 1956-59. No pro playing experience. College coach: Missouri 1962-71, Notre Dame 1975-77. Pro coach: Green Bay Packers 1972-74, Chicago Bears 1978-82, Birmingham Stallions (USFL) 1983-85, St.Louis/Phoenix Cardinals 1986-89, Tampa Bay Buccaneers 1991, Indianapolis Colts 1994-97, rejoined Cardinals in 1998.

Larry Marmie, defensive backs; born October 17, 1942, Barnesville, Ohio, lives in Phoenix. Quarterback Eastern Kentucky 1962-65. No pro playing experience. College coach: Eastern Kentucky 1967-68, 1972-76, Morehead State 1968-71, Tulsa 1977-78, North Carolina 1979-82, Tennessee 1983-84, 1992-94, Arizona State 1988-91 (head coach), UCLA 1995. Pro coach: Joined Cardinals in 1996.

Dave McGinnis, defensive coordinator; born August 7, 1951, Independence, Kan., lives in Phoenix. Defensive back Texas Christian 1970-72. No pro playing experience. College coach: Texas Christian 1973-74, 1982, Missouri 1975-77, Indiana State 1978-81, Kansas State 1983-85. Pro coach: Chicago Bears 1986-95, joined Cardinals in 1996.

Glenn Pires, linebackers; born September 13, 1958, New Bedford, Mass., lives in Phoenix. Linebacker Springfield College 1978-80. No pro playing experience. College coach: Syracuse 1983-84, Dartmouth 1985-88, Michigan State 1989-95. Pro coach: Joined Cardinals in 1996.

Vic Rapp, wide receivers; born December 23, 1935, Marionville, Mo., lives in Phoenix. Running back Southwest Missouri State 1954-57. No pro playing experience. Pro coach: Edmonton Eskimos (CFL) 1972-76, British Columbia Lions (CFL) 1977-82 (head coach), Houston Oilers 1983, Los Angeles Rams 1984, Tampa Bay Buccaneers 1985-86, Detroit Lions 1987, Chicago Bears 1989-92, joined Cardinals in 1996.

Bob Rogucki, strength and conditioning; born September 27, 1953, Clarksburg, W.Va., lives in Phoenix. No college or pro playing experience. College coach: Penn State 1981, Weber State 1982, Army 1983-89. Pro coach: Joined Cardinals in 1990.

Johnny Roland, running backs; born May 21, 1943, Corpus Christi, Tex., lives in Phoenix. Running back Missouri 1961-65. Pro running back St. Louis Cardinals 1966-72, New York Giants 1973. College coach: Notre Dame 1975. Pro coach: Green Bay Packers 1974, Philadelphia Eagles 1976-78, Chicago Bears 1983-92, New York Jets 1993-94, St. Louis Rams 1995-96, joined Cardinals in 1997.

Marc Trestman, offensive coordinator; born January 15, 1956, Minneapolis, Minn., lives in Phoenix. Quarterback Minnesota 1975-77, Moorhead (Minn.) State 1978. Pro quarterback Minnesota Vikings 1979. College coach: Miami (Fla.) 1981-84. Pro coach: Minnesota Vikings 1985-86, 1990-91, Tampa Bay Buccaneers 1987, Cleveland Browns 1988-89, San Francisco 49ers 1995-96, Detroit Lions 1997, joined Cardinals in 1998.

George Warhop, offensive line; born September 19, 1961, Riverside, Calif., lives in Phoenix. Guard Mt. San Jacinto (Calif.) J.C. 1979-80. Pro center Cincinnati Bengals 1981-82. College coach: Cincinnati 1983, Kansas 1984-86, Vanderbilt 1987-89, New Mexico 1990, Southern Methodist 1993, Boston College 1994-95. Pro coach: London Monarchs (World League) 1991-92, St. Louis Rams 1996-97, joined Cardinals in 1998.

1998 FIRST-YEAR ROSTER

Name	Pos.	Ht.	Wt.	Birthdate	College	Hometown	How Acq.
Brown, Rod (1)	RB	5-11	247	2/28/74	North Carolina State	Lithonia, Ga.	D6a-'97
Burnstein, Brent (1)	DE-DT	6-7	268	11/21/73	Arizona State	Glendale, Ariz.	FA
Carpenter, Chad (1)	WR	5-11	198	7/17/73	Washington State	Ontario, Ore.	D5-'97
Chavous, Corey	CB-S	6-0	204	1/15/76	Vanderbilt	Aiken, S.C.	D2a
Clement, Anthony	T	6-7	355	4/10/76	Southwestern Louisiana	Lafayette, La.	D2b
Collins, Aaron	LB	6-0	237	7/19/75	Penn State	Cinnaminson, N.J.	FA
Cousins, Jomo	DE	6-5	277	9/2/74	Florida A&M	Seneca Valley, Calif.	D7a
Daniels, Jerome (1)	C-G-T	6-5	350	9/13/74	Northeastern	Hartford, Conn.	FA-'97
DeGraffenreid, Allen (1)	C-G-T	6-4	293	6/3/74	Vanderbilt	Kansas City, Mo.	FA-'97
Drake, Kevin	WR	6-3	187	1/2/75	Alabama-Birmingham	Gardendale, Ala.	FA
Hardy, Terry	TE	6-4	266	5/31/76	Southern Mississippi	Montgomery, Ala.	D5
Himebauch, Jonathan	C	6-3	287	8/13/75	Southern California	San Dimas, Calif.	FA
Janes, Ron	RB	6-1	276	2/14/75	Missouri	Clarence, Mo.	D7c
Kenney, Marchant	LB	6-1	232	11/17/74	Southern Mississippi	New Orleans, La.	FA
Lake, Jeff	WR	6-4	206	9/6/74	Nebraska	Columbus, Neb.	FA
Perry, George	DE	6-4	275	7/27/75	Southern California	San Bernardino, Calif.	FA
Pittman, Michael	RB	6-0	214	8/14/75	Fresno State	San Diego, Calif.	D4
Player, Scott	P	6-0	220	12/17/69	Florida State	St. Augustine, Fla.	FA
Reader, Jamie	RB	5-11	233	5/4/74	Akron	Monessen, Pa.	FA
Sauter, Cory	QB	6-4	218	11/21/74	Minnesota	Hutchinson, Minn.	FA
Savoy, Phil	WR	6-2	195	2/16/75	Colorado	Washington, D.C.	FA
Swinger, Rashod (1)	DT	6-2	286	11/17/74	Rutgers	Manalapan, N.J.	FA-'97
Thomas, Danny	CB	5-10	192	9/17/76	Eastern Kentucky	Winchester, Ky.	FA
Tillman, Pat	CB-S	5-11	204	11/6/76	Arizona State	San Jose, Calif.	D7b
Turner, Lamont	T	6-6	316	11/23/75	Hampton	Richmond, Va.	FA
Volz, Pascal	WR	5-10	191	8/7/76	New Mexico	Tempe, Ariz.	FA
Wadsworth, Andre	DE	6-4	278	10/19/74	Florida State	Miami, Fla.	D1
Walz, Zack	LB	6-4	228	2/13/76	Dartmouth	San Jose, Calif.	D6
Wedel, Cory	K	5-8	180	12/12/74	Wyoming	Burlington, Colo.	FA
Wilkerson, Terry	DE	6-3	290	8/19/76	Alcorn State	Cedar Grove, Ga.	FA
Williams, Marcus	P	6-1	225	11/23/74	Arizona State	Tempe, Ariz.	FA
Workman, Eli	TE	6-3	261	6/17/74	Colorado State	Billings, Mont.	FA
Zatechka, Jon	G	6-2	306	11/10/75	Nebraska	Lincoln, Neb.	FA

The term NFL Rookie is defined as a player who is in his first season of professional football and has not been on the roster of another professional football team for any regular-season or postseason games. A Rookie is designated by an "R" on NFL rosters. Players who have been active in another professional football league or players who have NFL experience, including either preseason training camp or being on an Active List or Inactive List, or on Reserve/Injured or Reserve/Physically Unable to Perform for fewer than six regular-season games, are termed NFL First-Year Players. An NFL First-Year Player is designated by a "1" on NFL rosters. Thereafter, a player is credited with an additional year of experience for each season in which he accumulates six games on the Active List or Inactive List, or on Reserve/Injured or Reserve/Physically Unable to Perform.

ATLANTA FALCONS

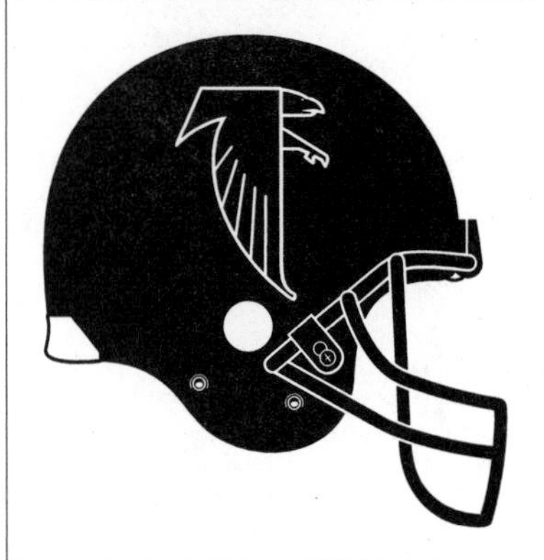

National Football Conference
Western Division
Team Colors: Black, Red, Silver, and White
One Falcon Place
Suwanee, Georgia 30024
Telephone: (770) 945-1111

CLUB OFFICIALS

President: Taylor Smith
Executive Vice President/Football Operations & Head Coach: Dan Reeves
Executive Vice President of Administration: Jim Hay
General Manager: Harold Richardson
Vice President of Football Operations: Ron Hill
Vice President of Finance, CFO: Kevin Anthony
Vice President of Corporate Development: Tommy Nobis
Controller: Wallace Norman
Administrative Asst./Finance: John Knox
Vice President of Administration: Rob Jackson
Sales & Marketing: Todd Marble, Jan Zeller
Special Events: Spencer Treadwell
Director of Public Relations: Charlie Taylor
Asst. Director of Public Relations: Frank Kleha
Director of Ticket Operations: Jack Ragsdale
Asst. Director of Ticket Operations: Mike Jennings
Director of Community Relations: Carol Breeding
Player Programs Coordinator: Billy (White Shoes) Johnson
Director of Information Systems: Randy Kopp
Special Assistant to President: Jerry Rhea
Director of Player Personnel/Pro: Chuck Connor
Director of Player Personnel/College: Reed Johnson
Area Scouts: Ken Blair, Melvin Bratton, Dick Corrick, Boyd Dowler, Elbert Dubenion, Bill Groman, Bob Harrison
National Scout: Mike Hagen
Assistant to Vice President of Football Operations: Les Snead
Head Trainer: Ron Medlin
Assistant Trainers: Matt Smith, Harold King
Video Director: Tom Atcheson
Equipment Manager: Brian Boigner
Senior Director/Gameday Coordinator: Horace Daniel
Stadium: Georgia Dome • **Capacity:** 71,228
One Georgia Dome Drive
Atlanta, Georgia 30313
Playing Surface: Artificial turf
Training Camp: One Falcon Place
Suwanee, Georgia 30024

1998 SCHEDULE

PRESEASON

Aug. 7	**Tennessee**	7:30
Aug. 14	at Detroit	7:00
Aug. 22	vs. Pittsburgh at Morgantown, W., Va.	6:00
Aug. 28	**Cincinnati**	7:30

REGULAR SEASON

Sept. 6	at Carolina	1:01
Sept. 13	**Philadelphia**	1:01
Sept. 20	Open Date	
Sept. 27	at San Francisco	1:15
Oct. 4	**Carolina**	1:01
Oct. 11	at New York Giants	8:20
Oct. 18	**New Orleans**	1:01
Oct. 25	at New York Jets	1:01
Nov. 1	**St. Louis**	1:01
Nov. 8	at New England	1:01
Nov. 15	**San Francisco**	1:01
Nov. 22	**Chicago**	1:01
Nov. 29	at St. Louis	12:01
Dec. 6	**Indianapolis**	1:01
Dec. 13	at New Orleans	12:01
Dec. 20	at Detroit	1:01
Dec. 27	**Miami**	1:01

RECORD HOLDERS

INDIVIDUAL RECORDS—CAREER

Category	Name	Performance
Rushing (Yds.)	Gerald Riggs, 1982-88	6,631
Passing (Yds.)	Steve Bartkowski, 1975-1985	23,468
Passing (TDs)	Steve Bartkowski, 1975-1985	154
Receiving (No.)	Andre Rison, 1990-94	423
Receiving (Yds.)	Alfred Jenkins, 1975-1983	6,257
Interceptions	Rolland Lawrence, 1973-1980	39
Punting (Avg.)	Rick Donnelly, 1985-89	42.6
Punt Return (Avg.)	Al Dodd, 1973-74	11.8
Kickoff Return (Avg.)	Tony Smith, 1992-94	24.9
Field Goals	Mick Luckhurst, 1981-87	115
Touchdowns (Tot.)	Andre Rison, 1990-94	56
Points	Mick Luckhurst, 1981-87	558

INDIVIDUAL RECORDS—SINGLE SEASON

Category	Name	Performance
Rushing (Yds.)	Gerald Riggs, 1985	1,719
Passing (Yds.)	Jeff George, 1995	4,143
Passing (TDs)	Steve Bartkowski, 1980	31
Receiving (No.)	Terance Mathis, 1994	111
Receiving (Yds.)	Alfred Jenkins, 1981	1,358
Interceptions	Scott Case, 1988	10
Punting (Avg.)	Billy Lothridge, 1968	44.3
Punt Return (Avg.)	Al Dodd, 1974	12.7
Kickoff Return (Avg.)	Sylvester Stamps, 1987	27.5
Field Goals	Morten Andersen, 1995	31
Touchdowns (Tot.)	Andre Rison, 1993	15
Points	Morten Andersen, 1995	122

INDIVIDUAL RECORDS—SINGLE GAME

Category	Name	Performance
Rushing (Yds.)	Gerald Riggs, 9-2-84	202
Passing (Yds.)	Steve Bartkowski, 11-15-81	416
Passing (TDs)	Wade Wilson, 12-13-92	5
Receiving (No.)	William Andrews, 11-15-81	15
Receiving (Yds.)	Alfred Jackson, 12-2-84	193
	Andre Rison, 9-4-94	193
Interceptions	Many times	2
	Last time by Ray Buchanan, 12-7-97	
Field Goals	Norm Johnson, 11-13-94	6
Touchdowns (Tot.)	Many times	3
	Last time by Terance Mathis, 11-19-95	
Points	Norm Johnson, 11-13-94	20

COACHING HISTORY

(184-298-5)

1966-68	Norb Hecker*	4-26-1
1968-74	Norm Van Brocklin**	37-49-3
1974-76	Marion Campbell***	6-19-0
1976	Pat Peppler	3-6-0
1977-82	Leeman Bennett	47-44-0
1983-86	Dan Henning	22-41-1
1987-89	Marion Campbell****	11-32-0
1989	Jim Hanifan	0-4-0
1990-93	Jerry Glanville	28-38-0
1994-96	June Jones	19-30-0
1997	Dan Reeves	7-9-0

*Released after three games in 1968
**Released after eight games in 1974
***Released after five games in 1976
****Retired after 12 games in 1989

GEORGIA DOME

1997 TEAM RECORD

PRESEASON (1-3)

Date	Result		Opponent
8/1	L	17-20	at Detroit
8/9	W	17-12	Tampa Bay
8/16	L	31-35	Washington
8/22	L	17-26	at Jacksonville

REGULAR SEASON (7-9)

Date	Result		Opponent	Att.
8/31	L	17-28	at Detroit	61,244
9/7	L	6-9	Carolina	51,829
9/14	L	31-36	Oakland	47,922
9/21	L	7-34	at San Francisco	60,404
9/28	L	21-29	Denver	48,211
10/12	W	23-17	at New Orleans	65,619
10/19	L	28-35	San Francisco	53,378
10/26	L	12-21	at Carolina	54,675
11/2	W	34-31	St. Louis	36,583
11/9	L	10-31	Tampa Bay	46,018
11/16	W	27-21	at St. Louis	64,299
11/23	W	20-3	New Orleans	48,620
11/30	W	24-17	at Seattle	52,584
12/7	W	14-3	at San Diego	46,317
12/14	W	20-17	Philadelphia	42,866
12/21	L	26-29	at Arizona	32,003

SCORE BY PERIODS

Falcons	58	97	99	66	—	320
Opponents	70	118	72	101	—	361

ATTENDANCE

Home 375,427 Away 437,145 Total 812,572
Single-game home record, 70,089 (10/29/95)
Single-season home record, 553,979 (1992)

1997 TEAM STATISTICS

	Falcons	Opp.
Total First Downs	281	274
Rushing	88	76
Passing	168	180
Penalty	25	18
Third Down: Made/Att	74/210	78/213
Third Down Pct.	39.5	42.2
Fourth Down: Made/Att	35.2	36.6
Fourth Down Pct.	61.5	83.3
Total Net Yards	4,716	5,106
Avg. Per Game	294.8	319.1
Total Plays	980	960
Avg. Per Play	4.8	5.3
Net Yards Rushing	1,643	1,666
Avg. Per Game	102.7	104.1
Total Rushes	442	409
Net Yards Passing	3,073	3,440
Avg. Per Game	192.1	215.0
Sacked/Yards Lost	54/372	55/354
Gross Yards	3,445	3,794
Att./Completions	484/273	496/275
Completion Pct.	56.4	55.4
Had Intercepted	11	18
Punts/Avg.	89/39.3	90/42.6
Net Punting Avg.	89/36.7	90/35.9
Penalties/Yards Lost	101/773	115/872
Fumbles/Ball Lost	34/13	27/10
Touchdowns	36	45
Rushing	8	18
Passing	26	24
Returns	2	3
Avg. Time of Possession	31:29	28:31

1997 INDIVIDUAL STATISTICS

Passing	Att.	Comp.	Yds.	Pct.	TD	Int.	Tkld.	Rate
Chandler	342	202	2,692	59.1	20	7	39/261	95.1
Tolliver	115	63	685	54.8	5	1	14/104	83.4
Graziani	23	7	41	30.4	0	2	1/7	3.7
Anderson	4	1	27	25.0	1	1	0/0	55.2
Falcons	484	273	3,445	56.4	26	11	54/372	87.2
Opponents	496	275	3,794	55.4	24	18	55/354	81.2

SCORING	TD R	TD P	TD Rt	PAT	FG	Saf	PTS
Andersen	0	0	0	35/35	23/27	0	104
Anderson	7	3	0	0/0	0/0	0	60
Emanuel	0	9	0	0/0	0/0	0	54
Mathis	0	6	0	0/0	0/0	0	36
Hanspard	0	1	2	0/0	0/0	0	18
Santiago	0	2	0	0/0	0/0	0	12
Christian	0	1	0	0/0	0/0	0	6
Green	1	0	0	0/0	0/0	0	6
Haynes	0	1	0	0/0	0/0	0	6
Kinchen	0	1	0	0/0	0/0	0	6
Kozlowski	0	1	0	0/0	0/0	0	6
West	0	1	0	0/0	0/0	0	6
Tolliver	0	0	0	0/0	0/0	0	0
Falcons	8	26	2	35/35	23/27	0	320
Opponents	18	24	3	39/39	14/20	1	361

2-Point conversions: Team 0-1, Opponents 4-6.

RUSHING	Att.	Yds.	Avg.	LG	TD
Anderson	290	1,002	3.5	39	7
Hanspard	53	335	6.3	77	0
Chandler	43	158	3.7	19	0
Green	36	78	2.2	22	1
Mathis	3	35	11.7	16	0
Graziani	3	19	6.3	10	0
Christian	7	8	1.1	3	0
Tolliver	7	8	1.1	12	0
Falcons	442	1,643	3.7	77	8
Opponents	409	1,666	4.1	61t	18

RECEIVING	No.	Yds.	Avg.	LG	TD
Emanuel	65	991	15.2	56	9
Mathis	62	802	12.9	49	6
Green	29	360	12.4	47	0
Anderson	29	284	9.8	47t	3
Christian	22	154	7.0	19	1
Santiago	17	217	12.8	30	2
Kinchen	16	266	16.6	53t	1
Haynes	12	154	12.8	24t	1
Kozlowski	7	99	14.1	29	1
West	7	63	9.0	23	1
Hanspard	6	53	8.8	21	1
E. Smith	1	2	2.0	2	0
Falcons	273	3,445	12.6	56	26
Opponents	275	3,794	13.8	82	24

INTERCEPTIONS	No.	Yds.	Avg.	LG	TD
Buchanan	5	49	9.8	31	0
Bradford	4	9	2.3	9	0
Booker	3	16	5.3	10	0
Owens	1	14	14.0	14	0
White	1	11	11.0	11	0
McGill	1	7	7.0	7	0
Bush	1	4	4.0	4	0
C. Smith	1	4	4.0	4	0
Archambeau	1	0	0.0	0	0
Falcons	18	114	6.3	31	0
Opponents	11	124	11.3	38t	1

PUNTING	No.	Yds.	Avg.	In 20	LG
Stryzinski	89	3,498	39.3	20	57
Falcons	89	3,498	39.3	20	57
Opponents	90	3,835	42.6	25	59

PUNT RETURNS	No.	FC	Yds.	Avg.	LG	TD
Kinchen	52	13	446	8.6	38	0
Buchanan	0	1	37	—	37	0
Falcons	52	14	483	9.3	38	0
Opponents	21	45	55	2.6	24	0

KICKOFF RETURNS	No.	Yds.	Avg.	LG	TD
Hanspard	40	987	24.7	99t	2
Bolden	5	106	21.2	34	0
Kozlowski	2	49	24.5	26	0
Burrough	1	6	6.0	6	0
Green	1	23	23.0	23	0
Kinchen	1	18	18.0	18	0
Owens	1	9	9.0	9	0
Falcons	51	1,198	23.5	99t	2
Opponents	52	1,167	22.4	43	0

FIELD GOALS	1-19	20-29	30-39	40-49	50+
Andersen	1/1	10/10	7/7	3/6	2/3
Falcons	1/1	10/10	7/7	3/6	2/3
Opponents	0/0	2/3	10/10	1/5	1/2

SACKS	No.
C. Smith	12.0
Hall	10.5
Archambeau	8.5
Owens	8.0
Bennett	7.0
Dronett	3.0
Crockett	2.0
Tuggle	1.5
Brandon	1.0
Burrough	1.0
Pleasant	0.5
Falcons	55.0
Opponents	54.0

1998 DRAFT CHOICES

Round	Name	Pos.	College
1	Keith Brooking	LB	Georgia Tech
2	Bob Hallen	C	Kent State
3	Jammi German	WR	Miami
4	Omar Brown	DB	North Carolina
	Tim Dwight	WR	Iowa
6	Elijah Williams	DB	Florida
7	Ephraim Salaam	T	San Diego State
	Ken Oxendine	RB	Virgina Tech
	Henry Slay	DT	West Virginia

1998 VETERAN ROSTER

No.	Name	Pos.	Ht.	Wt.	Birthdate	NFL Exp.	College	Hometown	How Acq.	'97 Games/ Starts
71	Adams, Scott	G-T	6-6	315	9/28/66	7	Georgia	Lake City, Fla.	FA-'97	6/0
5	Andersen, Morten	K	6-2	225	8/19/60	17	Michigan State	Struer, Denmark	FA-'95	16/0
32	Anderson, Jamal	RB	5-11	234	9/30/72	5	Utah	El Camino, Calif.	D7-'94	16/15
92	Archambeau, Lester	DE	6-5	275	6/27/67	9	Stanford	Montville, N.J.	T(GB)-'93	16/16
47	Bayne, Chris	S	6-1	205	3/22/76	2	Fresno State	Riverside, Calif.	D7-'97	13/0
97	Bennett, Cornelius	LB	6-2	240	8/25/65	12	Alabama	Birmingham, Ala.	UFA(Buff)-'96	16/16
43	Bolden, Juran	CB	6-2	201	6/27/74	3	Mississippi Delta	Tampa, Fla.	D4-'96	14/1
20	Booker, Michael	CB	6-2	203	4/27/75	2	Nebraska	Oceanside, Calif.	D1-'97	15/3
23	Bradford, Ronnie	CB	5-10	188	10/1/70	6	Colorado	Minot, N.D.	UFA(Ariz)-'97	16/14
51	Brandon, David	LB	6-4	238	2/9/65	12	Memphis	Memphis, Tenn.	UFA(SD)-'96	4/4
34	Buchanan, Ray	CB	5-9	195	9/29/71	6	Louisville	Chicago, Ill.	UFA(Ind)-97	16/16
91	Burrough, John	DE	6-5	275	5/17/72	4	Wyoming	Pinedale, Wyo.	D7-'95	16/1
25	Bush, Devin	S	5-11	210	7/3/73	4	Florida State	Miami, Fla.	D1-'95	16/16
12	Chandler, Chris	QB	6-4	225	10/12/65	11	Washington	Everett, Wash.	T(Hou)-'97	14/14
44	Christian, Bob	RB	5-11	230	11/14/68	5	Northwestern	Florissant, Mo.	UFA(Car)-'97	16/12
68	Collins, Calvin	C-G	6-2	307	1/5/74	2	Texas A&M	Beaumont, Tex.	D6-'97	15/13
82	Crawford, Keith	WR	6-2	195	11/21/70	5	Howard Payne, Tex.	Palestine, Tex.	UFA(StL)-'98	15/2*
94	Crockett, Henri	LB	6-2	251	10/28/74	2	Florida State	Whittier, Calif.	D4-'97	16/10
99	Davis, Nathan	DT	6-5	312	2/6/74	2	Indiana	Richmond, Ind.	D2-'97	2/0
45	Downs, Gary	RB	6-1	212	6/6/72	5	North Carolina State	Columbus, Ga.	FA-'97	16/0
75	Dronett, Shane	DT	6-8	288	1/12/71	7	Texas	Orange, Tex.	FA-'97	16/1
53	Elliott, Matt	C-G	6-3	295	10/1/68	6	Michigan	Carmel, Ind.	UFA(Car)-'98	16/6*
29	Fuller, Randy	CB	5-10	175	6/2/70	5	Tennessee State	Columbus, Ga.	UFA(Pitt)-'98	12/3*
19	Graziani, Tony	QB	6-2	195	12/23/73	2	Oregon	Modesto, Calif.	D7-'97	3/1
28	Green, Harold	RB	6-2	222	1/29/68	9	South Carolina	Goose Creek, S.C.	UFA(StL)-'97	16/1
98	Hall, Travis	DT	6-5	288	8/3/72	4	Brigham Young	Kenai, Alaska	D6-'95	16/16
54	Hamilton, Ruffin	LB	6-1	238	3/2/71	3	Tulane	Zachary, La.	FA-'97	12/0
24	Hanspard, Byron	RB	5-10	198	1/23/76	2	Texas Tech	DeSoto, Tex.	D2b-'97	16/0
84	Hayes, Mercury	WR	5-11	195	1/1/73	3	Michigan	Houston, Tex.	FA-'97	2/0
89	Kinchen, Todd	WR	5-11	187	1/7/69	7	Louisiana State	Baton Rouge, La.	UFA(Den)-'97	16/0
85	Kozlowski, Brian	TE	6-3	255	10/4/70	5	Connecticut	Rochester, N.Y.	FA-'97	16/5
75	Louichiey, Corey	T	6-8	305	10/10/71	5	South Carolina	Greenville, S.C.	UFA(Buff)-'98	16/6*
t-	Martin, Tony	WR	6-0	181	9/5/65	9	Mesa, Colo.	Miami, Fla.	T(SD)-'98	16/16*
81	Mathis, Terance	WR	5-10	185	6/7/67	9	New Mexico	Stone Mountain, Ga.	UFA(NYJ)-'94	16/16
22	McGill, Lenny	CB	6-1	202	5/31/71	5	Arizona State	Escondido, Calif.	T(GB)-'96	15/0
55	Miller, Nate	G	6-3	310	10/8/71	2	Louisiana State	Tuscaloosa, Ala.	FA-'95	13/0
73	Mitchell, Barry	DE	6-3	268	3/18/74	1	Idaho	Aurora, Colo.	FA-'97	0*
41	Robinson, Eugene	S	6-1	197	5/28/63	14	Colgate	Hartford, Conn.	UFA(GB)-'98	16/16
11	Rypien, Mark	QB	6-4	225	10/2/62	13	Washington State	Spokane, Wash.	UFA(StL)-'98	5/0*
88	Santiago, O.J.	TE	6-7	267	4/4/74	2	Kent State	Whitby, Canada	D3-'97	11/11
52	Sauer, Craig	LB	6-1	240	12/13/72	3	Minnesota	Sartell, Minn.	D6-'96	16/1
49	Sexton, Brian	TE	6-6	268	3/13/72	2	Boston College	Whippany, N.J.	FA-'97	3/0
67	Schreiber, Adam	C-G	6-4	298	2/20/62	14	Texas	Galveston, Tex.	UFA(NYG)-'97	16/0
90	Smith, Chuck	DE	6-2	265	12/21/69	7	Tennessee	Athens, Ga.	D2-'92	16/15
4	Stryzinski, Dan	P	6-2	200	5/15/65	9	Indiana	Vincennes, Ind.	UFA(TB)-'95	16/0
50	Sutter, Eddie	LB	6-3	239	10/3/69	6	Northwestern	Peoria, Ill.	FA-'97	16/0
59	Talley, Ben	LB	6-3	248	7/14/72	3	Tennessee	Griffin, Ga.	FA-'98	0*
61	Tobeck, Robert	G	6-4	300	3/6/70	5	Washington State	Tarpon Springs, Fla.	FA-'93	16/15
58	Tuggle, Jessie	LB	5-11	230	4/4/66	12	Valdosta State	Griffin, Ga.	FA-'87	16/15
35	White, William	S	5-10	205	2/19/66	11	Ohio State	Lima, Ohio	FA-'97	16/16
70	Whitfield, Bob	T	6-5	310	10/18/71	7	Stanford	Carson, Calif.	D1a-'92	16/16
69	Williams, Gene	G	6-2	315	10/14/68	8	Iowa State	Omaha, Neb.	T(Clev)-'95	15/15
48	Wimberly, Marcus	S	5-11	192	7/8/74	2	Miami	Memphis, Tenn.	D5-'97	6/0

* Crawford played 15 games with St. Louis in '97; Elliott played 16 games with Carolina; Fuller played 12 games with Pittsburgh, Louichiey played 16 games with Buffalo; Martin played 16 games with San Diego; Mitchell inactive for 16 games; Rypien played 5 games with St. Louis; Talley last active with N.Y. Giants in '96.

Players lost to free agency (3): WR Bert Emanuel (TB; 16 games in '97), QB Jim Miller (Det; 0), DE Dan Owens (Det; 15).

t- Falcons traded for Martin (San Diego).

Also played with Falcons in '97—K Scott Bentley (2 games), T Antone Davis (3), G Scott Davis (2), LB Jamal Fountaine (3), CB Donovan Greer (1), WR Michael Haynes (12), DE Anthony Pleasant (11), WR Freddie Scott (2), CB Chris Shelling (2), QB Billy Joe Tolliver (6), TE Ed West (12), T Matt Willig (16).

COACHING STAFF

Head Coach,
Dan Reeves

Pro Career: Named the eighth coach in Falcons history on January 20, 1997. Reeves enters the 1998 season as the NFL's winningest active coach with a career record of 156-122-1 in 17 years, ranking ninth on the league's all-time list. Reeves led the Falcons to a 6-2 finish in his first season in '97. Reeves had been the head coach of the New York Giants from 1993-96. Prior to that, he compiled a 117-79-1 record as head coach of the Denver Broncos from 1981-92, earning NFL Coach of the Year honors in 1982, 1988, and 1991. He led the Broncos to three Super Bowl berths, four AFC Championship games, five AFC West Division titles, and eight winning seasons. In his first year in New York, he earned NFL Coach of the Year honors for a fourth time, taking the Giants from 6-10 to an 11-5 mark, including a wild-card playoff victory. Overall, Reeves has accumulated ten winning seasons as head coach, participated in 45 playoff games and eight Super Bowls as an NFL player, assistant coach, and head coach. He was the only NFL coach in the 1980's to take his team to back-to-back Super Bowls. Reeves, whose teams have won at least 10 games eight different times, was very successful at Mile High Stadium, where he compiled a 72-21 (.774) record. His Broncos teams finished in first place five times and in second place three times in the AFC West. In 1984, Denver set a team record with 10 straight wins en route to a franchise-best 13-win season. The following season (1985), the Broncos set a team record for total offense and points scored. In 1986, they started out 6-0 and established thirty-five team and individual club marks. Career record: 149-113-1.
Background: Prior to obtaining his first NFL head coaching job in 1981, Reeves had been a member of the Dallas Cowboys coaching staff since 1970, spending a total of 16 years under Tom Landry as a player and coach. In 1977 he was named offensive coordinator of Landry's staff. Reeves began his pro career as a free agent running back for Dallas in 1965. Prior to that he was a quarterback at South Carolina from 1962-64, passing for 2,561 yards and 16 TD's. He totaled 3,376 yards during his career with the Gamecocks, leading to his induction into the school's hall of fame in 1978. Reeves later was inducted into the state of Georgia Sports Hall of Fame.
Personal: Born January 19, 1944, Americus, Ga. Dan and his wife, Pam, live in Atlanta, and have three children—Dana, Laura, and Lee.

ASSISTANT COACHES

Marvin Bass, assistant to head coach-pro personnel; born August 28, 1919, Norfolk, Va., lives in Suwanee, Ga. Tackle William & Mary 1940-42. No pro playing experience. College coach: William & Mary 1944-48, 1950-51 (head coach), North Carolina 1949, 1953-55, South Carolina 1956-59, 1961-65, Georgia Tech 1960, Richmond 1963. Pro coach: Washington Redskins 1952, Montreal Beavers (Continental League) 1966-67, Montreal Alouettes (CFL) 1968, Buffalo Bills 1969-71, Birmingham Americans (WFL) 1974-75, Denver Broncos 1982-92. Joined Falcons in 1997.
Don Blackmon, linebackers; born March 14, 1958, Pompano Beach, Fla., lives in Suwanee, Ga. Linebacker Tulsa 1977-80. Pro linebacker New England Patriots 1981-87. Pro coach: New England Patriots 1988-90, Cleveland Browns 1991-92, New York Giants 1993-96, joined Falcons in 1997.
Rich Brooks, assistant head coach-defensive coordinator; born August 10, 1941, Forest, Calif., lives in Duluth, Ga. Tailback, defensive back, and quarterback Oregon State 1959-62. No pro playing experience. College coach: Oregon State 1965-69, 1973, UCLA 1970, 1976, Oregon 1977-94 (head coach). Pro coach: Los Angeles Rams 1971-72, San Francisco 49ers 1974-75, St. Louis Rams 1995-96 (head coach), joined Falcons in 1997.
Jack Burns, quarterbacks, born January 3, 1949, Tampa, Fla., lives in Suwanee, Ga. Safety Florida, 1967-70. No pro playing experience. College coach: Florida 1971-73, 1975, Louisville 1974, 1985-88, Texas 1976, Vanderbilt 1977-78, Auburn 1979-80. Pro coach: Tampa Bay Bandits (USFL) 1983, Washington Redskins 1989-91, Minnesota Vikings 1992-93, joined Falcons in 1997.
James Daniel, tight ends; born January 17, 1953, Wetumpka, Ala., lives in Suwanee, Ga. Offensive guard Alabama State 1970-73. No pro playing experience. College coach: Auburn 1981-92. Pro coach: New York Giants 1993-96, joined Falcons in 1997.
Joe DeCamillis, special teams; born June 29, 1965, Arvada, Colo., lives in Alpharetta, Ga. No college or pro playing experience. College coach: Wyoming 1988. Pro coach: Denver Broncos 1989, Miami Dolphins 1990, New York Giants 1993-96, joined Falcons in 1997.
Tim Jorgensen, assistant strength and conditioning; born April 21, 1955, St. Louis, Mo., lives in Snellville, Ga. Guard Southwest Missouri State 1974-76. No pro playing experience. College coach: Southwest Missouri State 1977-78, Alabama 1979, Louisiana State 1980-83. Pro coach: Philadelphia Eagles 1984-86, joined Falcons in 1987.
Bill Kollar, defensive line; born November 27, 1952, Warren, Ohio, lives in Duluth, Ga. Defensive end Montana State 1971-74. Pro defensive end Cincinnati Bengals 1974-76, Tampa Bay Buccaneers 1977-81. College coach: Illinois 1985-87, Purdue 1988-89. Pro coach: Tampa Bay Buccaneers 1984, joined Falcons in 1990.
Ron Meeks, secondary; born August 27, 1954, Jacksonville, Fla., lives in Suwanee, Ga. Defensive back Arkansas State 1975-76. Pro defensive back Hamilton Tiger-Cats (CFL) 1977-79, Ottawa Rough Riders (CFL) 1979, Toronto Argonauts (CFL) 1980-81. College coach: Arkansas State 1984-85, Miami 1986-87, New Mexico State 1988, Fresno State 1989-90. Pro coach: Dallas Cowboys 1991, Cincinnati Bengals 1992-96, joined Falcons in 1997.
Al Miller, strength and conditioning; born August 29, 1947, El Dorado, Ark., lives in Alpharetta, Ga. Wide receiver Northeast Louisiana 1965-69. No pro playing experience. College coach: Northwestern State (La.) 1974-78, Mississippi State 1980, Northeast Louisiana 1981, Alabama 1982-84. Pro coach: Denver Broncos 1987-92, New York Giants 1993-96, joined Falcons in 1997.
George Sefcik, offensive coordinator-running backs; born December 27, 1939, Cleveland, Ohio, lives in Suwanee, Ga. Halfback Notre Dame 1959-61. No pro playing experience. College coach: Notre Dame 1963-68, Kentucky 1969-72. Pro coach: Baltimore Colts 1973-74, Cleveland Browns 1975-77, 1989-90, Cincinnati Bengals 1978-83, Green Bay Packers 1984-87, Kansas City Chiefs 1988, New York Giants 1991-96, joined Falcons in 1997.
Art Shell, offensive line; born November 26, 1946, Charleston, S.C., lives in Lawrenceville, Ga. Offensive-defensive tackle Maryland State 1965-67. Pro offensive tackle Oakland/Los Angeles Raiders 1968-82. Inducted into Pro Football Hall of Fame 1989. Pro coach: Los Angeles Raiders 1983-94 (head coach 1989-94), Kansas City Chiefs 1995-96, joined Falcons in 1997.
Warren "Rennie" Simmons, wide receivers; born February 25, 1942, Poughkeepsie, N.Y., lives in Gainesville, Ga. Center San Diego State 1961-65. No pro playing experience. College coach: Cal State-Fullerton 1974-78, Cerritos (Calif.) J.C. 1978-80, Vanderbilt 1995. Pro coach: Washington Redskins 1981-93, Los Angeles Rams 1994, Houston Oilers 1996, joined Falcons in 1997.
Ed West, offensive quality control; born August 2, 1961, Leighton, Ala., lives in Woodstock, Ga. Tight end Auburn 1980-83. Pro tight end Green Bay Packers 1984-94, Philadelphia Eagles 1995-96, Atlanta Falcons 1997. Pro coach: Joined Falcons in 1998.
Brian Xanders, defensive quality control; born April 10, 1971, East Stroudsburg, Pa., lives in Atlanta. Linebacker Florida State 1989-92. No pro playing experience. Pro coach: Joined Falcons in 1997.

1998 FIRST-YEAR ROSTER

Name	Pos.	Ht.	Wt.	Birthdate	College	Hometown	How Acq.
Akers, David	K	5-10	180	12/9/74	Louisville	Lexington, Ky.	FA
Akers, Jeremy	T	6-5	304	1/9/74	Notre Dame	Washington, D.C.	FA
Allen, Corey	WR	6-1	199	4/10/76	Georgia	Riverdale, Ga.	FA
Barnes, Octavus	WR	6-2	200	11/1/74	North Carolina	Wilson, N.C.	FA
Brennan, Brian	QB	6-5	225	11/5/74	Idaho	Lacey, Wash.	FA
Brooking, Keith	LB	6-2	244	10/30/75	Georgia Tech	Senoia, Ga.	D1
Brown, Omar	S	5-10	200	3/28/75	North Carolina	York, Pa.	D4a
Dwight, Tim	WR-KR	5-8	184	7/13/75	Iowa	Iowa City, Iowa	D4b
Edwards, Michael	T	6-6	290	7/11/75	Nevada	Auburn, Calif.	FA
Evans, Jason	DT	6-4	290	9/1/75	Southern Methodist	Mansfield, Tex.	FA
Fisk, Darren	RB	6-1	230	5/14/74	Colorado	Los Gatos, Calif.	FA
Freeman, Schad	DE	6-3	235	6/17/75	Valdosta State	Fernandina Beach, Fla.	FA
German, Jammi	WR	6-1	187	7/4/74	Miami	Ft. Meyers, Fla.	D3
Grenier, Geoff	RB	6-2	240	1/25/73	Oklahoma State	Fullerton, Calif.	FA
Hallen, Bob	C-T	6-4	292	3/9/75	Kent State	Cleveland, Ohio	D2
Huff, Ben	DT	6-4	275	2/21/75	Michigan	Charlotte, N.C.	FA
Johnson, Kevin	LB	6-2	230	12/27/73	Ohio State	Athens, Ga.	FA
Johnson, Van	WR	6-1	200	8/19/74	Temple	Washington, D.C.	FA
Littleton, Jody	LB	6-1	235	10/23/74	Baylor	Brighton, Colo.	FA
Mitchell, Barry	DE	6-3	268	3/18/74	Idaho	Aurora, Colo.	FA
Oxendine, Ken	RB	6-1	228	10/4/75	Virginia Tech	Chester, Va.	D7b
Portilla, Jose	T	6-6	320	9/11/72	Arizona	Houston, Tex.	FA
Salaam, Ephraim	T	6-7	290	6/19/76	San Diego State	Sacramento, Calif.	D7a
Slay, Henry	DT	6-2	290	4/28/75	West Virginia	Cleveland, Ohio	D7c
Swayda, Shawn	DE	6-5	280	9/4/74	Arizona State	Phoenix, Ariz.	FA
Thornal, Kevin	WR	6-2	186	11/28/74	Southern Methodist	Desoto, Tex.	FA
Trout, Brad	S	6-2	209	1/22/75	Valdosta State	Miami, Fla.	FA
Williams, Clay	DT	6-6	310	5/6/73	Indiana	Toboso, Ohio	FA
Williams, Elijah	CB	5-10	181	8/20/75	Florida	Milton, Fla.	D6

The term NFL Rookie is defined as a player who is in his first season of professional football and has not been on the roster of another professional football team for any regular-season or postseason games. A Rookie is designated by an "R" on NFL rosters. Players who have been active in another professional football league or players who have NFL experience, including either preseason training camp or being on an Active List or Inactive List, or on Reserve/Injured or Reserve/Physically Unable to Perform for fewer than six regular-season games, are termed NFL First-Year Players. An NFL First-Year Player is designated by a "1" on NFL rosters. Thereafter, a player is credited with an additional year of experience for each season in which he accumulates six games on the Active List or Inactive List, or on Reserve/Injured or Reserve/Physically Unable to Perform.

NOTES

CAROLINA PANTHERS

National Football Conference
Western Division
Team Colors: Black, Panther Blue, and Silver
800 South Mint Street
Charlotte, North Carolina 28202-1502
Telephone: (704) 358-7000

CLUB OFFICIALS

Founder/Owner: Jerry Richardson
President: Mark Richardson
President Carolina Stadium Corp.: Jon Richardson
Director of Player Personnel: Jack Bushofsky
Director of Football Administration: Marty Hurney
Director of Marketing and Sponsorships: Charles Waddell
Counsel: Richard Thigpen, Jr.
Chief Financial Officer: Dave Olsen
Controller: Lisa Garber
Pro Scouts: Hal Hunter, Sam Mills
College Scouts: Hal Athon, Joe Bushofsky, Bob Guarini, Ralph Hawkins, Tony Softli
Director of Communications: Charlie Dayton
Media Relations Assistant: Lex Sant
Communications and Marketing Assistant: Bruce Speight
Director of Ticket Sales: Phil Youtsey
Assistant Ticket Manager: Kati Hynes
Director of Player Relations: Donnie Shell
Director of Community Relations/Family Programs: B.J. Harrison Waymer
Director of Special Events: Leslie Matz
Director of Information Systems: Roger Goss
Football Systems: Rob Rogers
Programmer: Troy Bigelow
Video Director: Dave Sutherby
Assistant Video Director: Mark Hobbs
Head Trainer: John Kasik
Assistant Trainers: Al Shuford, Dan Ruiz
Head Equipment Manager: Jackie Miles
Assistant Equipment Manager: Don Toner
Director of Football Stadium Security: Gene Brown
Manager of Football Administration: Mark Koncz
Director of Facilities: Tom Fellows
Stadium Operations Manager: Rick Skaar
Office Manager: Jackie Jeffries
Stadium: Ericsson Stadium • **Capacity:** 73,250
Charlotte, North Carolina 28202-1502
Playing Surface: Grass
Training Camp: Wofford College
Spartanburg, South Carolina
29303

RECORD HOLDERS

INDIVIDUAL RECORDS—CAREER

Category	Name	Performance
Rushing (Yds.)	Anthony Johnson, 1995-97	1,588
Passing (Yds.)	Kerry Collins, 1995-97	7,295
Passing (TDs)	Kerry Collins, 1995-97	39
Receiving (No.)	Mark Carrier, 1995-97	157
Receiving (Yds.)	Mark Carrier, 1995-97	2,246
Interceptions	Eric Davis, 1996-97	10
Punting (Avg.)	Ken Walter, 1997	42.4
Punt Return (Avg.)	Winslow Oliver, 1996-97	11.5
Kickoff Return (Avg.)	Michael Bates, 1996-97	28.5
Field Goals	John Kasay, 1995-97	85
Touchdowns (Tot.)	Wesley Walls, 1996-97	16
Points	John Kasay, 1995-97	341

INDIVIDUAL RECORDS—SINGLE SEASON

Category	Name	Performance
Rushing (Yds.)	Anthony Johnson, 1996	1,120
Passing (Yds.)	Kerry Collins, 1995	2,717
Passing (TDs)	Kerry Collins 1995, 1996	14
Receiving (No.)	Mark Carrier, 1995	66
Receiving (Yds.)	Mark Carrier, 1995	1,002
Interceptions	Brett Maxie, 1995	6
Punting (Avg.)	Ken Walter, 1997	42.4
Punt Return (Avg.)	Winslow Oliver, 1996	11.5
Kickoff Return (Avg.)	Michael Bates, 1996	30.2
Field Goals	John Kasay, 1996	37
Touchdowns (Tot.)	Wesley Walls, 1996	10
Points	John Kasay, 1996	145

INDIVIDUAL RECORDS—SINGLE GAME

Category	Name	Performance
Rushing (Yds.)	Fred Lane, 11-2-97	147
Passing (Yds.)	Kerry Collins, 11-26-95	335
Passing (TDs)	Kerry Collins, 11-26-95, 10-13-96, 12-8-96	3
	Steve Beuerlein, 11-24-96	3
Receiving (No.)	Willie Green, 11-3-96	9
Receiving (Yds.)	Willie Green, 11-12-95, 12-8-96	157
Interceptions	Brett Maxie, 10-22-95	2
	Pat Terrell, 11-10-96	2
	Eric Davis, 10-19-97	2
Field Goals	John Kasay, 9-1-96, 9-8-96	5
Touchdowns (Tot.)	Fred Lane, 11-2-97	3
Points	Fred Lane, 11-2-97	18

1998 SCHEDULE

PRESEASON

Aug. 8	**Jacksonville**	7:30
Aug. 14	at Buffalo	7:30
Aug. 22	**Minnesota**	7:30
Aug. 29	at Pittsburgh	8:20

REGULAR SEASON

Sept. 6	**Atlanta**	1:01
Sept. 13	at New Orleans	12:01
Sept. 20	Open Date	
Sept. 27	**Green Bay**	1:01
Oct. 4	at Atlanta	1:01
Oct. 11	at Dallas	12:01
Oct. 18	at Tampa Bay	1:01
Oct. 25	**Buffalo**	8:20
Nov. 1	**New Orleans**	1:01
Nov. 8	at San Francisco	1:01
Nov. 15	**Miami**	1:01
Nov. 22	at St. Louis	3:05
Nov. 29	at New York Jets	1:01
Dec. 6	**San Francisco**	1:01
Dec. 13	**Washington**	1:01
Dec. 20	**St. Louis**	1:01
Dec. 27	at Indianapolis	1:01

ERICSSON STADIUM

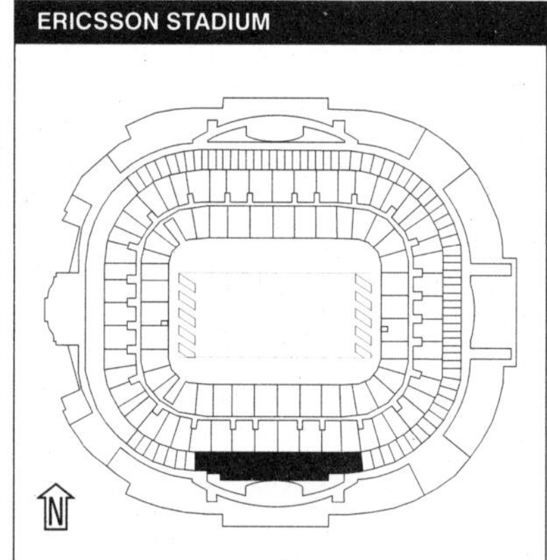

COACHING HISTORY

(27-23-0)

1995-97 Dom Capers 27-23-0

1997 TEAM RECORD

PRESEASON (0-4)

Date	Result		Opponent
8/3	L	9-23	at Jacksonville
8/9	L	13-23	Denver
8/14	L	10-30	at Kansas City
8/22	L	19-27	Pittsburgh

REGULAR SEASON (7-9)

Date	Result		Opponent	Att.
8/31	L	10-24	Washington	72,633
9/7	W	9-6	at Atlanta	51,829
9/14	W	26-7	at San Diego	63,149
9/21	L	14-35	Kansas City	67,402
9/29	L	21-34	San Francisco	70,972
10/12	L	14-21	at Minnesota	62,625
10/19	W	13-0	at New Orleans	50,963
10/26	W	21-12	Atlanta	54,675
11/2	W	38-14	Oakland	71,064
11/9	L	0-34	at Denver	71,408
11/16	L	19-27	at San Francisco	61,500
11/23	W	16-10	at St. Louis	64,609
11/30	L	13-16	New Orleans	57,957
12/8	W	23-13	at Dallas	63,251
12/14	L	10-31	Green Bay	70,887
12/20	L	18-30	St. Louis	58,101

SCORE BY PERIODS

Panthers	54	70	37	104	—	265
Opponents	62	102	61	89	—	314

ATTENDANCE

Home 523,691 Away 489,334 Total 1,013,025
Single-game home record, 73,025 (9/19/93)
Single-season home record, 553,382 (1996)

1997 TEAM STATISTICS

	Panthers	Opp.
Total First Downs	284	290
Rushing	91	112
Passing	170	163
Penalty	23	15
Third Down: Made/Att	99/225	82/222
Third Down Pct.	44.0	36.9
Fourth Down: Made/Att	3/9	6/18
Fourth Down Pct.	33.3	33.3
Total Net Yards	4615	4980
Avg. Per Game	288.4	311.3
Total Plays	1019	1023
Avg. Per Play	4.5	4.9
Net Yards Rushing	1770	1973
Avg. Per Game	110.6	123.3
Total Rushes	441	497
Net Yards Passing	2845	3007
Avg. Per Game	177.8	187.9
Sacked/Yards Lost	44/311	36/246
Gross Yards	3156	3253
Att./Completions	534/289	490/260
Completion Pct.	54.1	53.1
Had Intercepted	24	11
Punts/Avg.	85/42.4	88/42.7
Net Punting Avg.	85/36.4	88/37.1
Penalties/Yards Lost	94/763	97/757
Fumbles/Ball Lost	30/15	26/11
Touchdowns	28	36
Rushing	11	12
Passing	17	17
Returns	0	7
Avg. Time of Possession	29:43	30:17

1997 INDIVIDUAL STATISTICS

Passing	Att.	Comp.	Yds.	Pct.	TD	Int.	Tkld.	Rate
Collins	381	200	2,124	52.5	11	21	27/200	55.7
Beuerlein	153	89	1,032	58.2	6	3	17/111	83.6
Panthers	534	289	3,156	54.1	17	24	44/311	63.7
Opponents	490	260	3,253	53.1	17	11	36/246	76.2

SCORING	TD R	TD P	TD Rt	PAT	FG	Saf	PTS
Kasay	0	0	0	25/25	22/26	0	91
Lane	7	0	0	0/0	0/0	0	42
Walls	0	6	0	0/0	0/0	0	36
Carruth	0	4	0	0/0	0/0	0	24
Biakabutuka	2	0	0	0/0	0/0	0	12
Carrier	0	2	0	0/0	0/0	0	12
S. Greene	1	1	0	0/0	0/0	0	12
Ismail	0	2	0	0/0	0/0	0	12
Johnson	0	1	0	0/0	0/0	0	8
Collins	1	0	0	0/0	0/0	0	6
E. Mills	0	1	0	0/0	0/0	0	6
Muhammad	0	0	0	0/0	0/0	0	2
Stone	0	0	0	0/0	0/0	1	2
Panthers	11	17	0	25/25	22/26	1	265
Opponents	12	17	7	35/35	21/25	0	314

2-Point conversions: Johnson, Muhammad. Team 2-3, Opponents 0-1.

RUSHING	Att.	Yds.	Avg.	LG	TD
Lane	182	809	4.4	50	7
Johnson	97	358	3.7	20	0
Biakabutuka	75	299	4.0	26t	2
S. Greene	45	157	3.5	10t	1
Collins	26	65	2.5	21	1
Beuerlein	4	32	8.0	20	0
Ismail	4	32	8.0	18	0
Carruth	6	23	3.8	6	0
Oliver	1	0	0.0	0	0
Walter	1	-5	-5.0	-5	0
Panthers	441	1,770	4.0	50	11
Opponents	497	1,973	4.0	26	12

RECEIVING	No.	Yds.	Avg.	LG	TD
Walls	58	746	12.9	52	6
Carruth	44	545	12.4	52	4
S. Greene	40	277	6.9	25	1
Ismail	36	419	11.6	59t	2
Carrier	33	436	13.2	36	2
Muhammad	27	317	11.7	38	0
Johnson	21	158	7.5	25	1
E. Mills	11	127	11.5	37	1
Lane	8	27	3.4	7	0
Oliver	6	47	7.8	11	0
Mangum	4	56	14.0	22	0
Rasby	1	1	1.0	1	0
Panthers	289	3,156	10.9	59t	17
Opponents	260	3,253	12.5	59	17

INTERCEPTIONS	No.	Yds.	Avg.	LG	TD
Davis	5	25	5.0	17	0
Cota	2	28	14.0	15	0
Poole	2	0	0.0	0	0
S. Mills	1	18	18.0	18	0
Lathon	1	1	1.0	1	0
Panthers	11	72	6.5	18	0
Opponents	24	265	11.0	62t	2

PUNTING	No.	Yds.	Avg.	In 20	LG
Walter	85	3,604	42.4	29	62
Panthers	85	3,604	42.4	29	62
Opponents	88	3,756	42.7	25	60

PUNT RETURNS	No.	FC	Yds.	Avg.	LG	TD
Poole	26	18	191	7.3	40	0
Oliver	14	5	111	7.9	26	0
Bates	1	0	8	8.0	8	0
Panthers	41	23	310	7.6	40	0
Opponents	38	25	428	11.3	82t	2

KICKOFF RETURNS	No.	Yds.	Avg.	LG	TD
Bates	47	1,281	27.3	56	0
E. Mills	4	65	16.3	33	0
S. Greene	3	18	6.0	8	0
Rasby	3	32	10.7	12	0
Stone	3	76	25.3	37	0
S. Mills	2	12	6.0	12	0
Garcia	1	11	11.0	11	0
Poole	1	5	5.0	5	0
Panthers	64	1,500	23.4	56	0
Opponents	55	1,276	23.2	101t	1

FIELD GOALS	1-19	20-29	30-39	40-49	50+
Kasay	1/1	6/7	8/8	4/4	3/6
Panthers	1/1	6/7	8/8	4/4	3/6
Opponents	0/0	6/6	4/4	8/12	3/3

SACKS	No.
Barrow	8.5
Miller	5.5
Royal	5.0
Minter	3.5
King	2.0
Kragen	2.0
Lathon	2.0
Cook	1.0
Cota	1.0
Poole	1.0
Saleh	1.0
Seals	1.0
Turnbull	1.0
Raybon	0.5
Panthers	36.0
Opponents	44.0

1998 DRAFT CHOICES

Round	Name	Pos.	College
1	Jason Peter	DT	Nebraska
3	Chuck Wiley	DE	Louisiana State
	Mitch Marrow	DE	Pennsylvania
4	Donald Hayes	WR	Wisconsin
5	Jerry Jensen	LB	Washington
6	Damien Richardson	DB	Arizona State
7	Viliami Maumau	DT	Colorado
	Jim Turner	WR	Syracuse

CAROLINA PANTHERS

1998 VETERAN ROSTER

No.	Name	Pos.	Ht.	Wt.	Birthdate	NFL Exp.	College	Hometown	How Acq.	'97 Games/ Starts
46	Alexander, Brent	S	5-11	196	7/10/71	5	Tennessee State	Gallatin, Tenn.	UFA(Ariz)-'98	16/15*
54	# Bailey, Carlton	LB	6-3	242	12/15/64	11	North Carolina	Baltimore, Md.	FA-'97	8/0
56	Barrow, Micheal	LB	6-2	236	4/19/70	6	Miami	Homestead, Fla.	UFA(Hou)-'97	16/16
82	Bates, Michael	WR	5-10	189	12/19/69	6	Arizona	Tucson, Ariz.	FA-'96	16/0
7	Beuerlein, Steve	QB	6-3	220	3/7/65	12	Notre Dame	Anaheim, Calif.	UFA(Jax)-'96	7/3
21	Biakabutuka, Tshimanga	RB	6-0	210	1/24/74	3	Michigan	Lonqueuil, Canada	D1-'96	8/2
52	Brady, Jeff	LB	6-1	243	11/9/68	8	Kentucky	Newport, Ky.	FA-'98	15/14*
78	Brockermeyer, Blake	T	6-4	300	4/11/73	4	Texas	Fort Worth, Tex.	D1c-'95	16/13
88	Broughton, Luther	TE	6-2	248	11/30/74	2	Furman	Huger, S.C.	FA-'97	0*
66	Campbell, Mathew	T	6-4	300	7/14/72	4	South Carolina	North Augusta, S.C.	FA-'95	16/14
83	Carrier, Mark	WR	6-0	186	10/28/65	12	Nicholls State	Church Point, La.	FA-'97	9/6
89	Carruth, Rae	WR	5-11	194	1/20/74	2	Colorado	Sacramento, Calif.	D1-'97	15/14
12	† Collins, Kerry	QB	6-5	240	12/30/72	4	Penn State	Lebanon, Pa.	D1a-'95	13/13
41	# Cook, Toi	CB	5-11	188	12/3/64	12	Stanford	Van Nuys, Calif.	FA-'96	16/0
72	Dafney, Bernard	G-T	6-5	329	11/1/68	7	Tennessee	Los Angeles, Calif.	FA-'98	1/0*
76	Davidds-Garrido, Norberto	T	6-6	313	10/4/72	3	Southern California	La Puente, Calif.	D4a-'96	15/15
25	Davis, Eric	CB	5-11	185	1/26/68	9	Jacksonville State	Anniston, Ala.	UFA(SF)-'96	14/14
59	Dixon, Ernest	LB	6-1	240	10/17/71	5	South Carolina	Fort Mill, S.C.	UFA(NO)-'98	15/0*
34	Dulaney, Mike	RB	6-0	245	9/9/70	3	North Carolina	Kingsport, Tenn.	FA-'98	7/0*
33	Evans, Doug	CB	6-1	190	5/13/70	6	Louisiana Tech	Haynesville, La.	UFA(GB)-'98	15/15*
40	Floyd, William	RB	6-1	230	2/17/72	5	Florida State	St. Petersburg, Fla.	UFA(SF)-'98	15/15*
93	Fox, Mike	DE	6-8	295	8/5/67	9	West Virginia	Akron, Ohio	UFA(NYG)-'95	11/9
65	Garcia, Frank	G	6-1	295	1/28/72	4	Washington	Phoenix, Ariz.	D4-'95	16/16
55	Gaskins, Percell	LB	6-0	230	4/25/72	3	Kansas State	Daytona, Fla.	W(StL)-'97	12/0
94	Gilbert, Sean	DE	6-5	318	4/10/70	6	Pittsburgh	Aliquippa, Pa.	FA-'98	0*
44	Gray, Derwin	CB-S	5-11	210	4/9/71	6	Brigham Young	San Antonio, Tex.	UFA(Ind)-'98	11/0*
60	† Greeley, Bucky	C-G	6-2	285	7/30/72	3	Penn State	Wilkes-Barre, Pa.	FA-'96	6/0
91	Greene, Kevin	LB	6-3	247	7/31/62	14	Auburn	Granite City, Ill.	FA-'98	14/4*
43	Greene, Scott	RB	5-11	225	6/1/72	3	Michigan State	Canandaigua, N.Y.	D6-'96	16/14
61	Hannah, Shane	G	6-5	320	10/21/71	2	Michigan State	Germantown, Ohio	FA-'98	0*
81	# Ismail, Raghib	WR	5-11	175	11/18/69	6	Notre Dame	Wilkes Barre, Pa.	T(Oak)-'96	13/2
23	Johnson, Anthony	RB	6-0	225	10/25/67	9	Notre Dame	South Bend, Ind.	W(Chi)-'95	16/7
4	Kasay, John	K	5-10	198	10/27/69	8	Georgia	Athens, Ga.	UFA(Sea)-'95	16/0
96	King, Shawn	DE	6-3	278	6/24/72	4	Northeast Louisiana	Monroe, La.	D2-'95	9/2
64	Lacina, Corbin	G	6-4	297	11/2/70	5	Augustana	Woodbury, Minn.	UFA(Buff)-'98	16/13*
32	Lane, Fred	RB	5-10	205	9/6/75	2	Lane College	Franklin, Tenn.	FA-'97	13/7
57	Lathon, Lamar	LB	6-3	260	12/23/67	9	Houston	Wharton, Tex.	UFA(Hou)-'95	15/15
58	Mason, Eddie	LB	5-11	245	1/9/72	3	North Carolina	Siler City, N.C.	FA-'98	0*
9	Matthews, Shane	QB	6-3	196	6/1/70	5	Florida	Pascagoula, Miss.	FA-'97	0*
69	Miller, Les	DE	6-7	305	3/1/65	11	Fort Hayes State	Arkansas City, Kan.	FA-'96	16/11
30	Minter, Mike	S	5-10	188	1/15/74	2	Nebraska	Lawton, Okla.	D2-'97	16/11
95	Morabito, Tim	NT	6-3	296	10/12/73	3	Boston College	Garnerville, N.Y.	W(Cin)-'97	8/0
87	Muhammad, Muhsin	WR	6-2	217	5/5/73	3	Michigan State	Lansing, Mich.	D2-'96	13/5
20	Oliver, Winslow	RB	5-7	180	3/3/73	3	New Mexico	Houston, Tex.	D3a-'96	6/0
27	† Pieri, Damon	S	6-0	186	9/25/70	4	San Diego State	Phoenix, Ariz.	FA-'96	16/0
38	Poole, Tyrone	CB	5-8	188	2/3/72	4	Fort Valley State	LaGrange, Ga.	D1b-'95	16/16
63	Rodenhauser, Mark	C	6-5	280	6/1/61	11	Illinois State	Addison, Ill.	ED17(Det)-'95	16/0
92	Saleh, Tarek	LB	6-1	240	11/7/74	2	Wisconsin	Woodbridge, Conn.	D4-'97	3/0
98	Sasa, Don	DE	6-3	303	9/16/72	3	Washington State	Long Beach, Calif.	FA-'97	0*
75	Skrepenak, Greg	G	6-7	325	1/31/70	7	Michigan	Wilkes-Barre, Pa.	UFA(Oak)-'96	16/16
22	Smith, Marquette	RB	5-7	190	7/14/72	3	Central Florida	Lake Howell, Fla.	D5-'96	0*
31	Smith, Rod	CB	5-11	194	3/12/70	7	Notre Dame	St. Paul, Minn.	FA-'96	16/2
80	Stone, Dwight	WR	6-0	195	1/28/64	12	Middle Tennessee State	Florala, Ala.	UFA(Pitt)-'95	16/0
50	Tatum, Kinnon	LB	6-0	222	7/19/75	2	Notre Dame	Fayetteville, N.C.	D3-'97	16/0
85	Walls, Wesley	TE	6-5	250	2/26/66	10	Mississippi	Pontotoc, Miss.	UFA(NO)-'96	15/15
13	Walter, Ken	P	6-1	195	8/15/72	2	Kent State	Euclid, Ohio	FA-'96	16/0
37	Wheeler, Leonard	CB	6-0	198	1/15/69	7	Troy State	Toccoa, Ga.	UFA(Minn)-'98	15/0*
73	Wilson, Jamie	G-T	6-7	283	6/6/73	2	Marshall	Gloucester, Va.	FA-'97	0*

* Alexander played 16 games with Arizona in '97; Brady played 15 games with Minnesota; Broughton inactive for 1 game; Dafney played 1 game with Baltimore; Dixon played 15 games with New Orleans; Dulaney played 7 games with Chicago; Evans played 15 games with Green Bay; Floyd played 15 games with San Francisco; Gilbert last active with Washington in '96; Gray played 11 games with Indianapolis; Greene played 14 games with San Francisco; Hannah last active with Dallas in '95; Lacina played 16 games with Buffalo; Mason last active with N.Y. Jets in '96; Matthews inactive for 11 games; Sasa inactive for 1 game; M. Smith missed the '97 season because of injury; Wheeler played 15 games with Minnesota; Wilson inactive for 16 games.

\# Unrestricted free agent, subject to developments.

† Restricted free agent; subject to developments.

Retired—Greg Kragen, 13-year nose tackle, 16 games in '97; Sam Mills, 12-year linebacker, 16 games.

Players lost through free agency (6): LB Myron Baker (Ind; 2 games in '97), S Chad Cota (NO; 16), G Matt Elliott (Atl; 16), TE Walter Rasby (Det; 14), LB Andre Royal (NO; 16), S Pat Terrell (GB; 16).

Also played with Panthers in '97—CB Clifton Abraham (1 game), TE Kris Mangum (2), WR Ernie Mills (10), DE Ray Seals (14), DE Renaldo Turnbull (16), DE Gerald Williams (5).

COACHING STAFF

Head Coach,
Dom Capers

Pro Career: Enters his fourth season as head coach of the Carolina Panthers after being named the first head coach in the team's history on January 23, 1995. He earned NFL Coach of the Year honors from *AP, UPI,* PFWA and *The Sporting News* among others in 1996 after directing the Panthers to 12-4-regular season record, NFC Western Division championship, and a berth in the NFC Championship Game in only the franchise's second season. Led team that yielded only 56 second-half points to set an NFL record, and the team established another league mark by posting fewer penalty yards than its opponents in 20 consecutive games. Guided team from an 0-5 start to a 7-9 finish in 1995, the best expansion record in NFL history. Capers also directed the Panthers to other expansion records including the first to win four consecutive games, the first to defeat the reigning world champions, the first to win four games in a row at home, the first to win two straight on the road, and the first team to post a winning record at home (5-3). Also, the Panthers were just the third team in NFL history to begin the season 0-5 and win their next four games. Capers joined Carolina after spending three seasons as defensive coordinator for the Pittsburgh Steelers where he oversaw a unit that allowed the fewest points in the league from 1992-94. His 1994 defense was the best overall in the AFC, for the second consecutive year, and led the league in sacks. In addition to leading the league in overall defense in 1993, Capers' unit led all teams in forced fumbles, while the 1992 Steelers' defense led the NFL in takeaways, fumble recoveries, and tied for the league lead in touchdowns allowed. Capers entered the professional coaching ranks in 1984 as an assistant under Jim Mora with the USFL Baltimore/Philadephia Stars where he helped them earn championships in 1984 and 1985. He then moved with Mora to the New Orleans Saints where he coached the secondary from 1986-1991. Career record: 27-23.

Background: Capers played defensive back for Mount Union College. He was a graduate assistant at Kent State (1972-74) and served full-time coaching stints at Hawaii (1975-76), San Jose State (1977), California (1978-79), Tennessee (1980-81), and Ohio State (1982-83).

Personal: Born August 5, 1950, in Cambridge, Ohio. Capers and his wife, Karen, were married in June, 1994. They live in Davidson, N.C.

ASSISTANT COACHES

Don Breaux, tight ends; born August 3, 1940, Jennings, La., lives in Charlotte, N.C. Quarterback McNeese State 1959-61. Pro quarterback Denver Broncos 1963, San Diego Chargers 1964-65. College coach: Florida State 1966-67, Arkansas 1968-71, 1977-80, Florida 1973-74, Texas 1975-76. Pro coach: Houston Oilers 1972, Washington Redskins 1981-1993, New York Jets 1994, joined Panthers in 1995.

Billy Davis, outside linebackers; born November 5, 1965, Youngstown, Ohio, lives in Charlotte, N.C. Quarterback Cincinnati 1984-88. No pro playing experience. College coach: Michigan State 1990-91. Pro coach: Pittsburgh Steelers 1992-94, joined Panthers in 1995.

Vic Fangio, defensive coordinator; born August 22, 1958, Dunmore, Pa., lives in Charlotte, N.C. Attended East Stroudsburg State. No college or pro playing experience. College coach: North Carolina 1983. Pro coach: Philadelphia/Baltimore Stars (USFL) 1984-85, New Orleans Saints 1986-94, joined Panthers in 1995.

Ted Gill, defensive line; born October 3, 1948, Washington, D.C., lives in Charlotte, N.C. Defensive tackle Idaho State. No pro playing experience. College coach: Utah 1974-76, New Mexico State 1977, Ball State 1978-81, Cornell 1982, Army 1983, North Carolina 1984-87, Rice 1988-89, Iowa 1990-94, Oklahoma State 1995. Pro coach: Joined Panthers in 1996.

Gill Haskell, offensive coordinator; born September 24, 1943, San Francisco, lives in Charlotte, N.C. Defensive back San Francisco State 1961, 1963-65. No pro playing experience. College coach: Southern California 1978-82. Pro coach: Los Angeles Rams 1983-91, Green Bay Packers 1992-97, joined Panthers in 1998.

Chick Harris, running backs; born September 21, 1945, Durham, N.C., lives in Charlotte, N.C. Running back Northern Arizona 1966-69. No pro playing experience. College coach: Colorado State 1970-72, Long Beach State 1973-74, Washington 1975-80. Pro coach: Buffalo Bills 1981-82, Seattle Seahawks 1983-91, Los Angeles Rams 1992-94, joined Panthers in 1995.

Brett Maxie, defensive assistant; born January 13, 1962, Dallas, lives in Charlotte, N.C. Defensive back-quarterback Texas Southern 1981-84. Pro safety New Orleans Saints 1985-93, Atlanta Falcons 1994, Carolina Panthers 1995-96, San Francisco 49ers 1997. No college coaching experience. Pro coach: Joined Panthers in 1998.

Jim McNally, offensive line; born December 13, 1943, Buffalo, lives in Charlotte, N.C. Guard Buffalo 1961-65. No pro playing experience. College coach: Buffalo 1966-70, Marshall 1971-74, Boston College 1975-77, Wake Forest 1978-79. Pro coach: Cincinnati Bengals 1980-94, joined Panthers in 1995.

Chip Morton, strength and conditioning; born November 27, 1962, Hamden, Conn., lives in Charlotte, N.C. No college or pro playing experience. College coach: Ohio State 1985-86, Penn State 1987-91. Pro coach: San Diego Chargers 1992-94, joined Panthers in 1995.

Brad Seely, special teams; born September 6, 1956, Vinton, Iowa, lives in Charlotte, N.C. Tackle-guard South Dakota State 1974-77. No pro playing experience. College coach: Colorado State 1980, Southern Methodist 1981, North Carolina State 1982, Pacific 1983, Oklahoma State 1984-88. Pro coach: Indianapolis Colts 1989-93, New York Jets 1994, joined Panthers in 1995.

Steve Shafer, defensive backs, born December 8, 1940, Glendale, Calif., lives in Charlotte, N.C. Quarterback-defensive back Utah State 1961-62. Pro defensive back British Columbia Lions (CFL) 1963-67. College coach: San Mateo (Calif.) J.C. 1968-74 (head coach 1973-74), San Diego State 1975-82, 1994. Pro coach: Los Angeles Rams 1983-90, Tampa Bay Buccaneers 1991-93, Oakland Raiders 1995-97, joined Panthers in 1998.

John Shoop, quarterbacks; born August 1, 1969, Pittsburgh, lives in Charlotte, N.C. Quarterback University of the South 1987-91. No pro playing experience. College coach: Dartmouth 1991, Vanderbilt 1992-94. Pro coach: Joined Panthers in 1995.

Kevin Steele, linebackers; born March 17, 1958, La Jolla, Calif., lives in Matthews, N.C. Linebacker Tennessee 1976-79. No pro playing experience. College coach: Tennessee 1981-82, 1987-88, New Mexico State 1983, Oklahoma State 1984-86, Nebraska, 1989-94. Pro coach: Joined Panthers in 1995.

Richard Williamson, wide receivers; born April 13, 1941, Ft. Deposit, Ala., lives in Charlotte, N.C. Receiver Alabama 1961-62. No pro playing experience. College coach: Alabama 1963-67, 1970-71, Arkansas 1968-69, 1972-74, Memphis State 1975-80 (head coach). Pro coach: Kansas City Chiefs 1983-86, Tampa Bay Buccaneers 1987-91 (interim head coach final three games of 1990 season, head coach 1991), Cincinnati Bengals 1992-94, joined Panthers in 1995.

1998 FIRST-YEAR ROSTER

Name	Pos.	Ht.	Wt.	Birthdate	College	Hometown	How Acq.
Bohlinger, Rob	C-G-T	6-9	282	6/14/75	Wyoming	Maple Grove, Minn.	FA
Calicchio, Lonnie (1)	P	6-2	237	10/14/72	Mississippi	Plantation, Fla.	FA
Clark, Derrik	LB	6-3	242	4/6/75	Iowa State	Livermore, Iowa	FA
Craig, Dameyune	QB	6-1	200	4/19/74	Auburn	Pritchard, Ala.	FA
Davis, Thabiti	WR	6-3	211	3/24/75	Wake Forest	Charlotte, N.C.	FA
Edmonds, Brian	RB	5-10	235	6/14/74	Virginia Tech	Blackstone, Va.	FA
Hayes, Donald	WR	6-5	210	7/13/75	Wisconsin	Madison, Wis.	D4
Jackson, Ray	S	6-1	207	1/15/75	Washington State	Santa Anna, Calif.	FA
Janus, Paul	C-G-T	6-4	294	3/17/75	Northwestern	Edgerton, Wis.	FA
Jensen, Jerry	LB	6-0	235	2/26/75	Washington	Everett, Wash.	D5
Mangum, Kris (1)	TE	6-4	249	8/15/73	Mississippi	Magee, Miss.	D7-'97
Marrow, Mitch	DE-DT	6-4	280	7/16/75	Pennsylvania	Harrison, N.Y.	D3b
Maumau, Viliami	NT	6-2	302	4/3/75	Colorado	Honolulu, Hawaii	D7a
Peter, Jason	DE	6-5	288	9/13/74	Nebraska	Locust, N.J.	D1
Reid, Spencer	LB	6-1	247	2/8/76	Brigham Young	Pago Pago, Amer. Samoa	FA
Richardson, Damien	S	6-2	210	4/3/76	Arizona State	Fresno, Calif.	D6
Smith, Ryan (1)	DE	6-4	263	10/7/72	Idaho	Grants Pass, Ore.	FA
Stewart, Todd (1)	T	6-6	290	9/30/74	California	Vallejo, Calif.	FA
Thomas, Seth	TE	6-4	260	7/25/75	SUNY-Albany	Canandaigua, N.Y.	FA
Turner, Jim	WR	6-4	212	11/13/75	Syracuse	Jacksonville, Fla.	D7b
Wiggins, Brian (1)	WR	5-11	187	6/14/68	Texas Southern	San Antonio, Tex.	FA
Wiley, Chuck	DE-DT	6-4	275	7/16/75	Louisiana State	Baton Rouge, La.	D3a
Williams, Shaun	CB	6-0	182	6/11/75	Ohio	Cleveland, Ohio	FA

The term NFL Rookie is defined as a player who is in his first season of professional football and has not been on the roster of another professional football team for any regular-season or postseason games. A Rookie is designated by an "R" on NFL rosters. Players who have been active in another professional football league or players who have NFL experience, including either preseason training camp or being on an Active List or Inactive List, or on Reserve/Injured or Reserve/Physically Unable to Perform for fewer than six regular-season games, are termed NFL First-Year Players. An NFL First-Year Player is designated by a "1" on NFL rosters. Thereafter, a player is credited with an additional year of experience for each season in which he accumulates six games on the Active List or Inactive List, or on Reserve/Injured or Reserve/Physically Unable to Perform.

NOTES

CHICAGO BEARS

National Football Conference
Central Division
Team Colors: Navy Blue, Orange, and White
Halas Hall at Conway Park
1000 Football Drive
Lake Forest, Illinois 60045
Telephone: (847) 295-6600

CLUB OFFICIALS

Chairman of the Board: Edward W. McCaskey
President and CEO: Michael B. McCaskey
Secretary: Virginia H. McCaskey
Vice President: Tim McCaskey
Vice President of Operations: Ted Phillips
Director of Pro Personnel: Rick Spielman
Director of College Scouting: Bill Rees
Vice President of Player Personnel: Mark Hatley
Director of Administration: Bill McGrane
Ticket Manager: George McCaskey
Director of Community Relations: Pat McCaskey
Player Liaison: Brian McCaskey
Director of Marketing/Communications: Ken Valdiserri
Manager of Promotions: John Bostrom
Manager of Sales: Jack Trompeter
Director of Public Relations: Bryan Harlan
Asst. Directors of Public Relations: Phil Handler, Scott Hagel
Computer Systems: Greg Gershuny
Controller: Kris Voska
Video Director: Dean Pope
Head Athletic Trainer: Tim Bream
Assistant Trainers: Eric Sugarman, Jimmy Jordan
Physical Development Coordinator: Russ Riederer
Assistant Physical Development Coordinator: Steve Little
Head Equipment Manager: Tony Medlin
Quality Control: Eric Studesville, Ron Rivera
Assistant Equipment Managers: Randy Knowles, Carl Piekarski
Scouts: Marty Barrett, Charles Garcia, Bobby Riggle, Jeff Shiver
Stadium: Soldier Field • **Capacity:** 66,944
425 McFetridge Place
Chicago, Illinois 60605
Playing Surface: Grass
Training Camp: University of Wisconsin-Platteville
Platteville, Wisconsin 53818

1998 SCHEDULE

PRESEASON

Aug. 8	at Baltimore	7:30
Aug. 14	at Arizona	7:00
Aug. 21	**Buffalo**	7:00
Aug. 28	**New York Jets**	7:00

REGULAR SEASON

Sept. 6	**Jacksonville**	12:01
Sept. 13	at Pittsburgh	1:01
Sept. 20	at Tampa Bay	4:05
Sept. 27	**Minnesota**	3:15
Oct. 4	**Detroit**	12:01
Oct. 11	at Arizona	1:05
Oct. 18	**Dallas**	3:15
Oct. 25	at Tennessee	3:05
Nov. 1	Open Date	
Nov. 8	**St. Louis**	12:01
Nov. 15	at Detroit	8:20
Nov. 22	at Atlanta	1:01
Nov. 29	**Tampa Bay**	12:01
Dec. 6	at Minnesota	7:20
Dec. 13	at Green Bay	12:01
Dec. 20	**Baltimore**	12:01
Dec. 27	**Green Bay**	12:01

RECORD HOLDERS

INDIVIDUAL RECORDS—CAREER

Category	Name	Performance
Rushing (Yds.)	Walter Payton, 1975-1987	*16,726
Passing (Yds.)	Sid Luckman, 1939-1950	14,686
Passing (TDs)	Sid Luckman, 1939-1950	137
Receiving (No.)	Walter Payton, 1975-1987	492
Receiving (Yds.)	Johnny Morris, 1958-1967	5,059
Interceptions	Gary Fencik, 1976-1987	38
Punting (Avg.)	George Gulyanics, 1947-1952	44.5
Punt Return (Avg.)	Ray (Scooter) McLean, 1940-47	14.8
Kickoff Return (Avg.)	Gale Sayers, 1965-1971	30.6
Field Goals	Kevin Butler, 1985-1995	243
Touchdowns (Tot.)	Walter Payton, 1975-1987	125
Points	Kevin Butler, 1985-1995	1,116

INDIVIDUAL RECORDS—SINGLE SEASON

Category	Name	Performance
Rushing (Yds.)	Walter Payton, 1977	1,852
Passing (Yds.)	Erik Kramer, 1995	3,838
Passing (TDs)	Erik Kramer, 1995	29
Receiving (No.)	Johnny Morris, 1964	93
Receiving (Yds.)	Jeff Graham, 1995	1,301
Interceptions	Mark Carrier, 1990	10
Punting (Avg.)	Bobby Joe Green, 1963	46.5
Punt Return (Avg.)	Harry Clark, 1943	15.8
Kickoff Return (Avg.)	Gale Sayers, 1967	37.7
Field Goals	Kevin Butler, 1985	31
Touchdowns (Tot.)	Gale Sayers, 1965	22
Points	Kevin Butler, 1985	144

INDIVIDUAL RECORDS—SINGLE GAME

Category	Name	Performance
Rushing (Yds.)	Walter Payton, 11-20-77	*275
Passing (Yds.)	Johnny Lujack, 12-11-49	468
Passing (TDs)	Sid Luckman, 11-14-43	*7
Receiving (No.)	Jim Keane, 10-23-49	14
Receiving (Yds.)	Harlon Hill, 10-31-54	214
Interceptions	Many times	3
	Last time by Mark Carrier, 12-9-90	
Field Goals	Roger LeClerc, 12-3-61	5
	Mac Percival, 10-20-68	5
Touchdowns (Tot.)	Gale Sayers, 12-12-65	*6
Points	Gale Sayers, 12-12-65	36

*NFL Record

COACHING HISTORY

Decatur Staleys 1920,
Chicago Staleys 1921
(616-420-42)

1920-29	George Halas	84-31-19
1930-32	Ralph Jones	24-10-7
1933-42	George Halas*	88-24-4
1942-45	Hunk Anderson-Luke Johnsos**	24-12-2
1946-55	George Halas	76-43-2
1956-57	John (Paddy) Driscoll	14-10-1
1958-67	George Halas	76-53-6
1968-71	Jim Dooley	20-36-0
1972-74	Abe Gibron	11-30-1
1975-77	Jack Pardee	20-23-0
1978-81	Neill Armstrong	30-35-0
1982-92	Mike Ditka	112-68-0
1993-97	Dave Wannstedt	37-45-0

*Retired after five games to enter U.S. Navy
**Co-coaches

SOLDIER FIELD

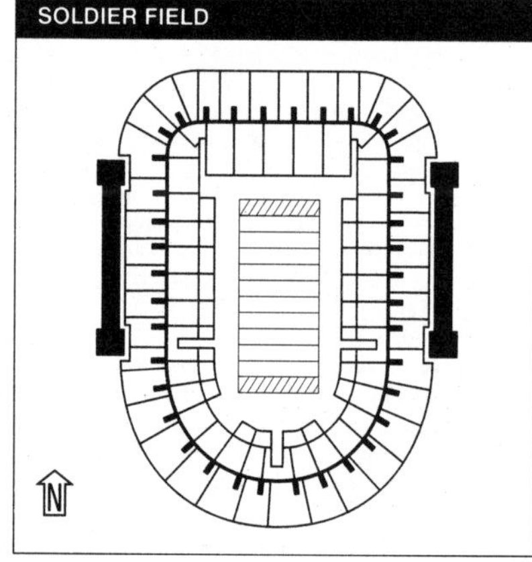

CHICAGO BEARS

1997 TEAM RECORD

PRESEASON (2-3)

Date	Result		Opponent
7/27	L	17-30	vs. Pittsburgh at Dublin, Ireland
8/2	W	20-17	at Buffalo (OT)
8/10	L	14-21	at Miami
8/16	W	22-10	Arizona
8/22	L	7-13	New Orleans

REGULAR SEASON (4-12)

Date	Result		Opponent	Att.
9/1	L	24-38	at Green Bay	60,766
9/7	L	24-27	Minnesota	59,263
9/14	L	7-32	Detroit	59,147
9/21	L	3-31	at New England	59,873
9/28	L	3-27	at Dallas	64,082
10/05	L	17-20	New Orleans	58,865
10/12	L	23-24	Green Bay	62,212
10/27	W	36-33	at Miami (OT)	73,156
11/2	L	8-31	Washington	53,032
11/9	L	22-29	at Minnesota	63,443
11/16	L	15-23	New York Jets	45,642
11/23	W	13-7	Tampa Bay	43,955
11/27	L	20-55	at Detroit	77,904
12/7	W	20-3	Buffalo	39,784
12/14	W	13-10	at St. Louis	66,030
12/21	L	15-31	at Tampa Bay	70,930

(OT) Overtime

SCORE BY PERIODS

Bears	61	72	36	91	3	—	263
Opponents	78	123	107	113	0	—	421

ATTENDANCE

Home 421,900 Away 536,184 Total 958,084
Single-game home record, 66,900 (9/5/93)
Single-season home record, 495,484 (1986)

1997 TEAM STATISTICS

	Bears	Opp.
Total First Downs	305	281
Rushing	94	97
Passing	188	156
Penalty	23	28
Third Down: Made/Att	91/253	60/189
Third Down Pct.	36.0	31.7
Fourth Down: Made/Att.	14/27	3/9
Fourth Down Pct.	51.9	33.3
Total Net Yards	4,990	4,888
Avg. Per Game	311.9	305.5
Total Plays	1,128	935
Avg. Per Play	4.4	5.2
Net Yards Rushing	1,461	2,041
Avg. Per Game	91.3	127.6
Total Rushes	329	473
Net Yards Passing	1,746	1,858
Avg. Per Game	109.1	116.1
Sacked/Yards Lost	43/257	38/259
Gross Yards	3,501	3,289
Att./Completions	595/336	476/273
Completion Pct.	56.5	57.4
Had Intercepted	22	13
Punts/Avg.	96/42.5	81/43.5
Net Punting Avg.	96/32.6	81/36.6
Penalties/Yards Lost	96/32.6	81/36.6
Fumbles/Ball Lost	33/19	25/17
Touchdowns	28	50
Rushing	14	18
Passing	14	25
Returns	0	7
Avg. Time of Possession	33:08	26:52

1997 INDIVIDUAL STATISTICS

Passing	Att.	Comp.	Yds.	Pct.	TD	Int.	Tkld.	Rate
Kramer	477	275	3,011	57.7	14	14	25/149	74.0
Mirer	103	53	420	51.5	0	6	16/89	37.7
Stenstrom	14	8	70	57.1	0	2	2/19	31.0
Conway	1	0	0	0.0	0	0	0/0	39.6
Bears	595	336	3,501	56.5	14	22	43/257	66.1
Opponents	476	273	3,289	57.4	25	13	38/259	84.8

SCORING	TD R	TD P	TD Rt	PAT	FG	Saf	PTS
Jaeger	0	0	0	20/20	21/26	0	83
R. Harris	10	0	0	0/0	0/0	0	60
Proehl	0	7	0	0/0	0/0	0	44
Penn	0	3	0	0/0	0/0	0	18
Engram	0	2	0	0/0	0/0	0	14
Kramer	2	0	0	0/0	0/0	0	12
Autry	1	0	0	0/0	0/0	0	8
Mirer	1	0	0	0/0	0/0	0	8
Conway	0	1	0	0/0	0/0	0	6
Wetnight	0	1	0	0/0	0/0	0	6
Flanigan	0	0	0	0/0	0/0	0	2
Bears	14	14	0	20/20	21/26	1	263
Opponents	18	25	7	45/45	24/32	0	421

2-Point conversions: Autry, Engram, Flanigan, Mirer, Proehl.
Team 5-8, Opponents 2-5.

RUSHING	Att.	Yds.	Avg.	LG	TD
R. Harris	275	1,033	3.8	68t	10
Autry	112	319	2.8	17	1
Salaam	31	112	3.6	17	0
Kramer	27	83	3.1	31	2
Mirer	20	78	3.9	20	1
Ton. Carter	9	56	6.2	16	0
Conway	3	17	5.7	10	0
Hicks	4	14	3.5	8	0
Smith	1	12	12.0	12	0
Sauerbrun	2	8	4.0	8	0
Stenstrom	1	6	6.0	6	0
Harmon	2	6	3.0	4	0
Hughes	1	3	3.0	3	0
LeBel	1	0	0.0	0	0
Penn	1	-1	-1.0	-1	0
Bears	490	1,746	3.6	68t	14
Opponents	421	1,858	4.4	76	18

RECEIVING	No.	Yds.	Avg.	LG	TD
Proehl	58	753	13.0	78t	7
Penn	47	576	12.3	33	3
Wetnight	46	464	10.1	34	1
Engram	45	399	8.9	23	2
Conway	30	476	15.9	55t	1
R. Harris	28	115	4.1	16	0
Ton. Carter	24	152	6.3	19	0
Jennings	14	164	11.7	23	0
Bownes	12	146	12.2	21	0
Autry	9	59	6.6	14	0
Allred	8	70	8.8	18	0
Hughes	8	68	8.5	16	0
Smith	2	22	11.0	12	0
Salaam	2	20	10.0	18	0
Harmon	2	8	4.0	6	0
T. Allen	1	9	9.0	9	0
Bears	336	3,501	10.4	78t	14
Opponents	273	3,289	12.0	89t	25

INTERCEPTIONS	No.	Yds.	Avg.	LG	TD
W. Harris	5	30	6.0	12	0
Tom Carter	3	12	4.0	12	0
Mangum	2	4	2.0	4	0
Marshall	2	0	0.0	0	0
M. Carter	1	14	14.0	14	0
Bears	13	60	4.6	14	0
Opponents	22	328	14.9	38t	1

PUNTING	No.	Yds.	Avg.	In 20	LG
Sauerbrun	95	4,059	42.7	26	67
Jaeger	1	18	18.0	0	18
Bears	96	4,077	42.5	26	67
Opponents	81	3,526	43.5	28	72

PUNT RETURNS	No.	FC	Yds.	Avg.	LG	TD
Hughes	36	7	258	7.2	19	0
Proehl	8	1	59	7.4	14	0
Dulaney	1	0	0	0.0	0	0
Engram	1	0	4	4.0	4	0
Bears	46	8	321	7.0	19	0
Opponents	52	16	727	14.0	83t	2

KICKOFF RETURNS	No.	Yds.	Avg.	LG	TD
Hughes	43	1,008	23.4	58	0
Bownes	19	396	20.8	36	0
Smith	10	196	19.6	28	0
Allred	2	21	10.5	11	0
Ton. Carter	2	34	17.0	19	0
Engram	2	27	13.5	20	0
Wetnight	1	9	9.0	9	0
Marshall	0	3	—	3	0
Bears	79	1,694	21.4	58	0
Opponents	52	1,237	23.8	69	0

FIELD GOALS	1-19	20-29	30-39	40-49	50+
Jaeger	0/0	8/9	8/10	4/6	1/1
Bears	0/0	8/9	8/10	4/6	1/1
Opponents	0/0	9/9	12/12	3/9	0/2

SACKS	No.
Flanigan	6.0
Minter	6.0
B. Cox	5.0
Simpson	4.5
Thomas	4.5
Marshall	3.0
Thierry	3.0
Spellman	2.0
M. Carter	1.0
R. Cox	1.0
Mangum	1.0
Grasmanis	0.5
Reeves	0.5
Bears	38.0
Opponents	43.0

1998 DRAFT CHOICES

Round	Name	Pos.	College
1	Curtis Enis	RB	Penn State
2	Tony Parrish	DB	Washington
3	Olin Kreutz	C	Washington
4	Alonzo Mayes	TE	Oklahoma State
6	Chris Draft	LB	Stanford
	Patrick Mannelly	T	Duke
7	Chad Overhauser	T	UCLA
	Moses Moreno	QB	Colorado State

CHICAGO BEARS

1998 VETERAN ROSTER

No.		Name	Pos.	Ht.	Wt.	Birthdate	NFL Exp.	College	Hometown	How Acq.	'97 Games/ Starts
85	#	Allen, Tremayne	TE	6-2	234	8/9/74	2	Florida	Nashville, Tenn.	FA-'97	2/0
84		Allred, John	TE	6-4	246	9/9/74	2	Southern California	Del Mar, Calif.	D2-'97	15/4
21		Autry, Darnell	RB	5-10	210	6/19/76	2	Northwestern	Tempe, Ariz.	D4a-'97	13/3
30		Bell, Ricky	CB	5-10	188	10/2/74	2	North Carolina State	Columbia, S.C.	FA-'97	5/0
32		Bennett, Edgar	RB	6-0	215	2/15/69	7	Florida State	Jacksonville, Fla.	UFA(GB)-'98	0*
82		Bownes, Fabien	WR	5-11	186	2/29/72	2	Western Illinois	Auruza, Ill.	FA-'95	16/0
23		Carter, Marty	S	6-1	212	12/17/69	8	Middle Tennessee State	LaGrange, Ga.	UFA(TB)-'95	15/15
25		Carter, Tom	CB	6-0	187	9/5/72	6	Notre Dame	St. Petersburg, Fla.	RFA(Wash)-'97	16/16
80		Conway, Curtis	WR	6-0	194	3/13/71	6	Southern California	Hawthorne, Calif.	D1-'93	7/7
24	#	Cousin, Terry	CB	5-9	176	4/11/75	2	South Carolina	Miami Beach, Fla.	FA-'97	6/0
54	#	Cox, Ron	LB	6-2	235	2/27/68	9	Fresno State	Fresno, Calif.	UFA(GB)-'97	15/13
81		Engram, Bobby	WR	5-10	192	1/7/73	3	Penn State	Camden, S.C.	D2-'96	11/11
99		Flanigan, Jim	DT	6-2	286	8/27/71	5	Notre Dame	Green Bay, Wis.	D3-'94	16/16
46	†	Forbes, Marlon	S	6-1	205	12/25/71	3	Penn State	Long Island, N.Y.	FA-'95	16/1
93		Grasmanis, Paul	DT	6-2	298	8/2/74	3	Notre Dame	Jenison, Mich.	D4-'96	16/1
49		Hallock, Ty	RB	6-2	256	4/30/71	5	Michigan State	Grand Rapids, Mich.	UFA(Jax)-'98	15/7*
22		Harmon, Ronnie	RB	5-11	192	5/7/64	13	Iowa	Queens, N.Y.	FA-'97	1/0
29	#	Harris, Raymont	RB	6-0	225	12/23/70	5	Ohio State	Lorain, Ohio	D4-'94	13/13
57	†	Harris, Sean	LB	6-3	245	2/25/72	4	Arizona	Magnet, Ariz.	D3a-'95	11/1
27		Harris, Walt	CB	5-11	194	8/10/74	3	Mississippi State	LaGrange, Ga.	D1-'96	16/16
64		Heck, Andy	T	6-6	298	1/1/67	10	Notre Dame	Fairfax, Va.	RFA(Sea)-'94	16/16
74		Herndon, Jimmy	T	6-8	313	8/30/73	3	Houston	Baytown, Tex.	T(Jax)-'97	7/0
48		Hiles, Van	S	6-0	195	11/1/75	2	Kentucky	Baton Rouge, La.	D5-'97	16/1
67		Huntington, Greg	G	6-3	278	9/22/70	5	Penn State	Cincinnati, Ohio	FA-'97	1/0
1		Jaeger, Jeff	K	5-11	190	11/26/64	12	Washington	Kent, Wash.	FA-'96	16/0
35		Johnson, Clyde	S	5-9	191	5/22/70	2	Kansas State	Austin, Tex.	W(KC)-'97	15/0*
12		Kramer, Erik	QB	6-1	200	11/6/64	10	North Carolina State	Burbank, Calif.	UFA(Det)-'94	15/13
88	#	LeBel, Harper	TE	6-4	250	7/14/63	10	Colorado State	Sherman Oaks, Calif.	FA(GB)-'97	16/0
	t-	Lee, Shawn	DT	6-2	300	10/24/66	11	North Alabama	Brooklyn, N.Y.	T(SD)-'98	16/15*
87		Lewis, Thomas	WR	6-1	195	1/10/72	5	Indiana	Akron, Ohio	UFA(NYG)-'98	4/2*
53	†	Lowery, Michael	LB	6-0	224	2/14/74	3	Mississippi	McComb, Miss.	FA-'96	16/0
26		Mangum, John	S	5-10	190	3/16/67	9	Alabama	Magee, Miss.	D7-'90	16/16
		Mathis, Dedric	CB	5-10	188	9/26/73	3	Houston	Cuero, Tex.	W(Ind)-'98	13/5*
92		Minter, Barry	LB	6-2	242	1/28/70	6	Tulsa	Mt. Pleasant, Tex.	T(Dall)-'93	16/16
13		Mirer, Rick	QB	6-2	214	3/19/70	6	Notre Dame	Goshen, Ind.	T(Sea)-'96	7/3
86		Penn, Chris	WR	6-0	198	4/20/71	5	Tulsa	Lenapah, Okla.	T(KC)-'97	14/4
75		Perry, Todd	G	6-5	312	11/28/70	6	Kentucky	Elizabethtown, Ky.	D4a-'93	11/11
68		Reeves, Carl	DE	6-4	265	12/17/71	4	North Carolina State	Durham, N.C.	D6b-'95	15/10
31		Salaam, Rashaan	RB	6-1	224	10/8/74	4	Colorado	LaJolla, Calif.	D1-'95	3/3
16	†	Sauerbrun, Todd	P-K	5-10	209	1/4/73	4	West Virginia	Setanket, N.Y.	D2b-'95	16/0
98		Simpson, Carl	DT	6-2	292	4/18/70	6	Florida State	Baxley, Ga.	D2-'93	16/16
83		Smith, Eric	WR	5-11	183	9/15/71	2	Louisiana State	Vero Beach, Fla.	FA-'97	7/0
90		Spellman, Alonzo	DE	6-4	292	9/27/71	7	Ohio State	Rancocas, N.J.	D1-'92	7/5
45	#	Stargell, Tony	CB	5-11	192	8/7/66	8	Tennessee State	LaGrange, Ga.	FA-'97	1/0
18	†	Stenstrom, Steve	QB	6-1	202	12/23/71	4	Stanford	El Toro, Calif.	W(KC)-'95	3/0
94		Thierry, John	DE	6-4	265	9/4/71	5	Alcorn State	Opelousas, La.	D1-'94	9/9
95		Thomas, Mark	DE	6-5	280	5/6/69	7	North Carolina State	Liburn, Ga.	UFA(Car)-'97	16/7
58		Villarrial, Chris	C-G	6-4	305	6/9/73	3	Indiana, Pa.	Hershey, Pa.	D5-'96	11/1
97		Wells, Mike	DT	6-3	287	1/6/71	5	Iowa	Arnold, Mo.	UFA(Det)-'98	16/16*
89		Wetnight, Ryan	TE	6-2	235	11/5/70	6	Stanford	Fresno, Calif.	FA-'93	16/3
60		Wiegmann, Casey	C	6-3	290	7/20/75	3	Iowa	Parkersburg, Iowa	W(NYJ)-'97	1/0
71		Williams, James	T	6-7	340	3/29/68	8	Cheyney State, Pa.	Allerdice, Pa.	FA-'91	16/16
96		Williams, Tyrone	DT	6-4	282	10/22/72	2	Wyoming	Papillion, Neb.	FA-'97	3/0
		Zandofsky, Mike	G	6-2	308	11/30/65	10	Washington	Corvallis, Ore.	FA-'98	5/2*

* Bennett missed '97 season with Green Bay because of injury; Hallock played 15 games for Jacksonville; Johnson played 15 games for Kansas City; Lee played 16 games for San Diego; Mathis played 13 games for Indianapolis; Wells played 16 games for Detroit; Zandofsky played 5 games for Philadelphia.

\# Unrestricted free agent; subject to developments.

† Restricted free agent; subject to developments.

Traded- LB Anthony Peterson (16 games) to San Francisco.

t- Bears traded for Lee (San Diego).

Players lost through free agency (5); G Todd Burger (NYJ; 15 games in '97), RB Tony Carter (NE; 16), G Chris Gray (Sea; 8), WR Ricky Proehl (StL; 15).

Also played with Bears in '97—CB James Burton (5), LB Daryl Carter (1), T Jon Clark (1), LB Bryan Cox (16), CB Corey Dowden (2), RB Mike Dulaney (7), KR Tyrone Hughes (14), TE Keith Jennings (12), S Anthony Marshall (14), G Evan Pilgrim (13), G Bill Schultz (8), DT Chris Zorich (3).

COACHING STAFF

Head Coach,
Dave Wannstedt

Pro Career: Has guided Bears to a 36-44 regular season record, 1-1 in the playoffs, since being named Chicago's head coach on January 19, 1993. He was an integral part of one of the most successful turnarounds in NFL history, helping to turn the 1989 Dallas Cowboys, which finished the season 1-15, into Super Bowl champions four years later. In January, 1992, he was named Dallas's assistant head coach and defensive coordinator. He was the defensive coordinator for the Cowboys in 1989. Selected by the Green Bay Packers in the fifteenth round of the 1974 draft, but spent the entire season on injured reserve. Career record: 37-45.
Background: Played offensive tackle at the University of Pittsburgh from 1970-73. Began coaching career at Pittsburgh in 1975 and was part of the staff that led the Panthers to a 12-0 record and the NCAA championship in 1976. In 1979, he took a job with Jimmy Johnson at Oklahoma State as defensive line coach. After two seasons, he was promoted to defensive coordinator. In 1983, Wannstedt was the defensive line coach for Southern California before rejoining Johnson at the University of Miami as the Hurricanes' defensive coordinator. In his first year (1986), Miami went 11-0 before losing to Penn State in the Fiesta Bowl. The following season Miami was crowned NCAA champion with a perfect 12-0 record.
Personal: Born May 21, 1952, Pittsburgh, Pa. Dave and his wife, Jan, live in Lake Forest, Ill. and have two children—Keri and Jami.

ASSISTANT COACHES

Keith Armstrong, special teams; born December 15, 1963, Trenton, N.J., lives in Lake Forest, Ill. Running back-defensive back Temple 1983-86. No pro playing experience. College coach: Temple 1986, Miami 1987-88, Akron 1989, Oklahoma State 1990-92, Notre Dame 1993. Pro coach: Atlanta Falcons 1994-96, joined Bears in 1997.
Joe Brodsky, running backs; born June 9, 1934, Miami, lives in Lake Forest, Ill. Fullback-linebacker Florida 1953-56. No pro playing experience. College coach: Miami 1978-88. Pro coach: Dallas Cowboys 1989-97, joined Bears in 1998.
Clarence Brooks, defensive line; born May 20, 1951, New York, N.Y., lives in Lake Forest, Ill. Guard Massachusetts 1970-73. No pro playing experience. College coach: Massachusetts 1976-80, Syracuse 1981-89, Arizona 1990-92. Pro coach: Joined Bears in 1993.
Matt Cavanaugh, offensive coordinator-quarterbacks; born October 27, 1956, Youngstown, Ohio, lives in Riverwoods, Ill. Quarterback Pittsburgh 1974-77. Pro quarterback New England Patriots 1978-82, San Francisco 49ers 1983-85, Philadelphia Eagles 1986-89, New York Giants 1990-91. College coach: Pittsburgh 1993. Pro coach: Arizona Cardinals 1994-95, San Francisco 49ers 1996, joined Bears in 1997.
Ivan Fears, wide receivers; born November 15, 1954, Portsmouth, Va., lives in Lake Forest, Ill. Running back William & Mary 1973-75. No pro playing experience. College coach: William & Mary 1977-80, Syracuse 1981-90. Pro coach: New England Patriots 1991-92, joined Bears in 1993.
Carlos Mainord, linebackers; born August 26, 1944, Greenville, Tex., lives in Lake Forest, Ill. Linebacker Navarro (Tex.) Junior College 1962-63, McMurry College 1964-65. No pro playing experience. College coach: McMurry College 1966-68, Texas Tech 1969, 1983-85, 1987-92, Ranger (Tex.) Junior College 1970-71, 1972-77 (head coach), Rice 1978-82, Miami 1986. Pro coach: Joined Bears in 1993.
Tom Rossley, tight ends; born August 9, 1946, Painesville, Ohio, lives in Lake Forest, Ill. Wide receiver Cincinnati 1966-68. No pro playing experience. College coach: Cincinnati 1977, Rice 1978-81, Holy Cross 1986-87, Southern Methodist 1988-89, 1991-96 (head coach). Pro coach: Montreal Concorde (CFL) 1982-84, San Antonio Gunslingers (USFL) 1985, Atlanta Falcons 1990, joined Bears in 1998.
Greg Schiano, defensive backs; born June 1, 1966, Paterson, N.J., lives in Lake Forest, Ill. Linebacker Bucknell 1984-88. No pro playing experience. College coach: Rutgers 1989, Penn State 1990-95. Pro coach: Joined Bears in 1996.
Bob Slowik, defensive coordinator-nickel package; born May 16, 1954, Pittsburgh, lives in Lake Forest, Ill. Cornerback Delaware 1973-76. No pro playing experience. College coach: Delaware 1977, Florida 1978-81, Drake 1982, Rutgers 1983, East Carolina 1984-91. Pro coach: Dallas Cowboys 1992, joined Bears in 1993.
Tony Wise, assistant head coach-offensive line; born December 28, 1951, Albany, N.Y., lives in Lake Forest, Ill. Offensive lineman Ithaca College 1971-72. No pro playing experience. College coach: Albany State 1973, Bridgeport 1974, Central Connecticut State 1975, Washington State 1976, Pittsburgh 1977-78, Oklahoma State 1979-83, Syracuse 1984, Miami 1985-88. Pro coach: Dallas Cowboys 1989-92, joined Bears in 1993.

1998 FIRST-YEAR ROSTER

Name	Pos.	Ht.	Wt.	Birthdate	College	Hometown	How Acq.
Allen, James (1)	RB	5-10	212	3/28/75	Oklahoma	Wynnewood, Okla.	FA
Anderson, Ken	DT	6-3	306	10/4/75	Arkansas	Shreveport, La.	FA
Bookman, Anthony	RB	5-6	185	1/11/76	Stanford	Grand Prairie, Tex.	FA
Brown, Mike	TE	6-3	252	10/21/74	Texas Christian	Del Rio, Tex.	FA
Cantelupe, Jim	CB-S	6-0	210	3/12/74	Army	Garfield Heights, Ohio	FA
Carter, Daryl (1)	LB	6-2	222	2/24/75	Wisconsin	Milwaukee, Wis.	FA-'97
Coleman, Quincy	CB-S	5-10	182	7/23/75	Jackson State	Birmingham, Ala.	FA
Crowley, Brad	CB-S	6-4	275	9/8/74	Texas A&M	Corpus Christi, Tex.	FA
Draft, Chris	LB	5-11	222	2/26/76	Stanford	Placentia, Calif.	D6a
DuBose, KeJaun	DT	6-2	285	4/1/75	Northwestern	Jennings, Mo.	FA
Enis, Curtis	RB	6-0	242	6/15/76	Penn State	Union City, Ohio	D1
Farrell, Jim	WR	6-1	203	3/6/76	Western Illinois	Palatine, Ill.	FA
Ford, Chester	RB	5-11	238	1/16/74	Tennessee	Danville, Ky.	FA
Hogans, Richard (1)	LB	6-2	249	7/8/75	Memphis	Columbus, Ga.	D6b-'97
Kanner, Aaron (1)	P	6-1	220	9/25/70	Catawba College	Manalapan, N.J.	FA
Knight, Carlos	RB	5-10	230	11/15/74	Jackson State	Jackson, Miss.	FA
Korth, Jay	G	6-3	294	8/1/74	Wyoming	Battle Creek, Nev.	FA
Kreutz, Olin	C	6-2	300	6/9/77	Washington	Honolulu, Hawaii	D3
Lee, Mark (1)	DE	6-4	270	6/4/72	Western State, Colo.	Colorado Springs, Colo.	FA
Mannelly, Pat	T	6-5	285	4/18/75	Duke	Atlanta, Ga.	D6b
Mayes, Alonzo	TE	6-4	259	6/4/75	Oklahoma State	Oklahoma City, Okla.	D4
McCullough, Saladin	RB	5-10	190	7/17/75	Oregon	Pasadena, Calif.	FA
McElroy, Jim	WR	5-10	155	9/15/76	UCLA	Los Angeles, Calif.	FA
Miller, Chris (1)	WR	5-10	192	7/10/73	Southern California	Los Angeles, Calif.	FA
Moreno, Moses	QB	6-1	205	9/5/75	Colorado State	Chula Vista, Calif.	D7b
Overhauser, Chad	T	6-4	316	6/17/75	UCLA	Sacramento, Calif.	D7a
Parrish, Tony	S	5-10	206	11/23/75	Washington	Huntington Beach, Calif.	D2
Peoples, Shont'e (1)	LB	6-2	249	8/30/72	Michigan	Saginaw, Mich.	FA
Robinson, Marcus (1)	WR	6-3	213	2/27/75	South Carolina	Ft. Valley, Ga.	D4b-'97
Serwanga, Wasswa	CB-S	5-11	194	7/23/76	UCLA	Sacramento, Calif.	FA
Williams, Greg	S	5-10	191	3/12/76	North Carolina	Bolingbrook, Ill.	FA
Williams, Tyrone (1)	DT	6-4	292	10/22/72	Wyoming	Papillion, Nev.	FA
Zitelli, Emmett (1)	C	6-3	295	3/13/74	Purdue	McKees Rocks, Pa.	FA

The term NFL Rookie is defined as a player who is in his first season of professional football and has not been on the roster of another professional football team for any regular-season or postseason games. A Rookie is designated by an "R" on NFL rosters. Players who have been active in another professional football league or players who have NFL experience, including either preseason training camp or being on an Active List or Inactive List, or on Reserve/Injured or Reserve/Physically Unable to Perform for fewer than six regular-season games, are termed NFL First-Year Players. An NFL First-Year Player is designated by a "1" on NFL rosters. Thereafter, a player is credited with an additional year of experience for each season in which he accumulates six games on the Active List or Inactive List, or on Reserve/Injured or Reserve/Physically Unable to Perform.

NOTES

DALLAS COWBOYS

National Football Conference
Eastern Division
Team Colors: Royal Blue, Metallic Silver Blue, and White
Cowboys Center
One Cowboys Parkway
Irving, Texas 75063
Telephone: (972) 556-9900

CLUB OFFICIALS

Owner/President/General Manager: Jerry Jones
Executive Vice President-Player Personnel: Stephen Jones
Vice President/Marketing: George Hays
Vice President/Director of Marketing and Special Events: Charlotte Anderson
Vice President/Legal Operations: Jerry Jones, Jr.
Public Relations Director: Rich Dalrymple
Assistant Director of Public Relations: Brett Daniels
Director of College and Pro Scouting: Larry Lacewell
Director of Operations: Bruce Mays
Director of Human Resources: Debbie Ross
Treasurer: Robert Nunez
Ticket Manager: Carol Padgett
Trainer: Jim Maurer
Equipment Manager: Mike McCord
Video Director: Robert Blackwell
Cheerleader Director: Kelli Finglass
Stadium: Texas Stadium • **Capacity:** 65,675 Irving, Texas 75062
Playing Surface: Sportfield Turf
Training Camp: Midwestern State University Wichita Falls, Texas 76308

1998 SCHEDULE

PRESEASON

July 31	**Seattle**	8:00
Aug. 8	**Oakland**	8:00
Aug. 17	vs. New England at Mexico City, Mexico	6:00
Aug. 22	at St. Louis	7:00
Aug. 27	at Jacksonville	8:00

REGULAR SEASON

Sept. 6	**Arizona**	3:05
Sept. 13	at Denver	2:15
Sept. 21	at New York Giants (Mon)	8:20
Sept. 27	**Oakland**	12:01
Oct. 4	at Washington	1:01
Oct. 11	**Carolina**	12:01
Oct. 18	at Chicago	3:15
Oct. 25	Open Date	
Nov. 2	at Philadelphia (Mon.)	8:20
Nov. 8	**New York Giants**	12:01
Nov. 15	at Arizona	2:15
Nov. 22	**Seattle**	12:01
Nov. 26	**Minnesota** (Thurs.)	3:05
Dec. 6	at New Orleans	12:01
Dec. 13	at Kansas City	3:15
Dec. 20	**Philadelphia**	3:15
Dec. 27	**Washington**	7:20

RECORD HOLDERS

INDIVIDUAL RECORDS—CAREER

Category	Name	Performance
Rushing (Yds.)	Tony Dorsett, 1977-1987	12,036
Passing (Yds.)	Troy Aikman, 1989-1997	26,016
Passing (TDs)	Danny White, 1976-1988	155
Receiving (No.)	Michael Irvin, 1988-1997	666
Receiving (Yds.)	Michael Irvin, 1988-1997	10,680
Interceptions	Mel Renfro, 1964-1977	52
Punting (Avg.)	Mike Saxon, 1985-1992	41.5
Punt Return (Avg.)	Bob Hayes, 1965-1974	11.1
Kickoff Return (Avg.)	Mel Renfro, 1964-1977	26.4
Field Goals	Rafael Septien, 1978-1986	162
Touchdowns (Tot.)	Emmitt Smith, 1990-97	119
Points	Rafael Septien, 1978-1986	874

INDIVIDUAL RECORDS—SINGLE SEASON

Category	Name	Performance
Rushing (Yds.)	Emmitt Smith, 1995	1,773
Passing (Yds.)	Danny White, 1983	3,980
Passing (TDs)	Danny White, 1983	29
Receiving (No.)	Michael Irvin, 1995	111
Receiving (Yds.)	Michael Irvin, 1995	1,603
Interceptions	Everson Walls, 1981	11
Punting (Avg.)	Sam Baker, 1962	45.4
Punt Return (Avg.)	Bob Hayes, 1968	20.8
Kickoff Return (Avg.)	Mel Renfro, 1965	30.0
Field Goals	Richie Cunningham, 1997	34
Touchdowns (Tot.)	Emmitt Smith, 1995	*25
Points	Emmitt Smith, 1995	150

INDIVIDUAL RECORDS—SINGLE GAME

Category	Name	Performance
Rushing (Yds.)	Emmitt Smith, 10-31-93	237
Passing (Yds.)	Don Meredith, 11-10-63	460
Passing (TDs)	Many times	5
	Last time by Danny White, 10-30-83	
Receiving (No.)	Lance Rentzel, 11-19-67	13
Receiving (Yds.)	Bob Hayes, 11-13-66	246
Interceptions	Herb Adderley, 9-26-71	3
	Lee Roy Jordan, 11-4-73	3
	Dennis Thurman, 12-13-81	3
Field Goals	Chris Boniol, 11-18-96	*7
Touchdowns (Tot.)	Many times	4
	Last time by Emmitt Smith, 9-4-95	
Points	Many times	24
	Last time by Emmitt Smith, 9-4-95	

*NFL Record

COACHING HISTORY

(366-241-6)

1960-88	Tom Landry	270-178-6
1989-93	Jimmy Johnson	51-37-0
1994-97	Barry Switzer	45-26-0

TEXAS STADIUM

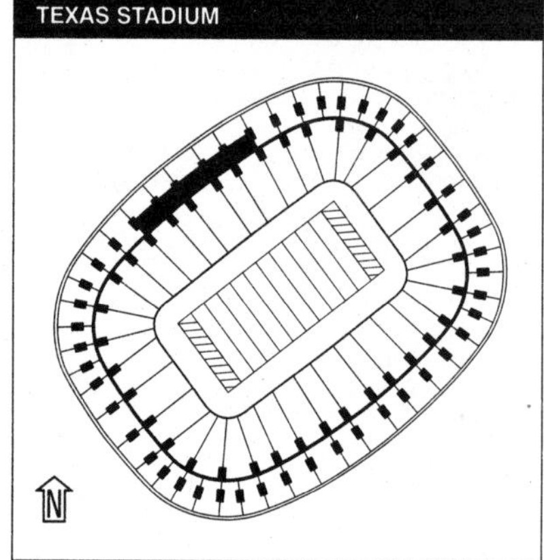

1997 TEAM RECORD

PRESEASON (2-2)

Date	Result		Opponent
8/3	L	27-34	Oakland
8/8	L	10-16	at New England
8/15	W	34-31	St. Louis
8/22	W	34-10	Tennessee

REGULAR SEASON (6-10)

Date	Result		Opponent	Att.
8/31	W	37-7	at Pittsburgh	60,396
9/7	L	22-25	at Arizona (OT)	71,578
9/15	W	21-20	Philadelphia	63,942
9/28	W	27-3	Chicago	64,082
10/5	L	17-20	at New York Giants	77,137
10/13	L	16-21	at Washington	76,159
10/19	W	26-22	Jacksonville	64,464
10/26	L	12-13	at Philadelphia	67,106
11/2	L	10-17	at San Francisco	68,657
11/9	W	24-6	Arizona	64,302
11/16	W	17-14	Washington	64,559
11/23	L	17-45	at Green Bay	60,111
11/27	L	14-27	Tennessee	63,421
12/8	L	13-23	Carolina	63,251
12/14	L	24-31	at Cincinnati	60,043
12/21	L	7-20	New York Giants	63,746

(OT) Overtime

SCORE BY PERIODS

Cowboys	41	95	86	82	0	—	304
Opponents	64	71	86	90	3	—	314

ATTENDANCE

Home 511,767 Away 541,187 Total 1,052,954
Single-game home record, 65,180 (11/12/95)
Single-season home record, 518,167 (1995)

1997 TEAM STATISTICS

	Cowboys	Opp.
Total First Downs	279	281
Rushing	82	104
Passing	170	139
Penalty	27	38
Third Down: Made/Att	83/229	89/233
Third Down Pct.	36.2	38.2
Fourth Down: Made/Att	6/13	5/11
Fourth Down Pct.	46.2	45.5
Total Net Yards	4,778	4,516
Avg. Per Game	298.6	282.3
Total Plays	1,015	1,022
Avg. Per Play	4.7	4.4
Net Yards Rushing	1,637	1,994
Avg. Per Game	102.3	124.6
Total Rushes	423	511
Net Yards Passing	3,141	2,522
Avg. Per Game	196.3	157.6
Sacked/Yards Lost	39/313	38/195
Gross Yards	3,454	2,717
Att./Completions	553/314	473/253
Completion Pct.	56.8	53.5
Had Intercepted	12	7
Punts/Avg.	86/41.8	95/43.6
Net Punting Avg.	86/35.4	95/36.1
Penalties/Yards Lost	116/1,058	99/757
Fumbles/Ball Lost	23/11	27/12
Touchdowns	29	36
Rushing	6	12
Passing	19	20
Returns	4	4
Avg. Time of Possession	29:53	30:07

1997 INDIVIDUAL STATISTICS

Passing	Att.	Comp.	Yds.	Pct.	TD	Int.	Tkld.	Rate
Aikman	518	292	3,283	56.4	19	12	33/269	78.0
Wilson	21	12	115	57.1	0	0	4/26	72.5
Garrett	14	10	56	71.4	0	0	2/18	78.3
Cowboys	553	314	3,454	56.8	19	12	39/313	77.8
Opponents	473	253	2,717	53.5	20	7	38/195	78.5

SCORING	TD R	TD P	TD Rt	PAT	FG	Saf	PTS
Cunningham	0	0	0	24/24	34/37	0	126
Irvin	0	9	0	0/0	0/0	0	54
E. Smith	4	0	0	0/0	0/0	0	26
Miller	0	4	0	0/0	0/0	0	24
LaFleur	0	2	0	0/0	0/0	0	12
Sanders	0	0	2	0/0	0/0	0	12
Walker	0	2	0	0/0	0/0	0	12
Sh. Williams	2	0	0	0/0	0/0	0	12
Coakley	0	0	1	0/0	0/0	0	6
Hennings	0	0	1	0/0	0/0	0	6
Johnston	0	1	0	0/0	0/0	0	6
St. Williams	0	1	0	0/0	0/0	0	6
Bjornson	0	0	0	0/0	0/0	0	2
Gowin	0	0	0	0/0	0/1	0	0
Cowboys	6	19	4	24/24	34/38	0	304
Opponents	12	20	4	34/34	20/27	0	314

2-Point conversions: Bjornson, E. Smith.
Team 2-5, Opponents 2-2.

RUSHING	Att.	Yds.	Avg.	LG	TD
E. Smith	261	1,074	4.1	44	4
Sh. Williams	121	468	3.9	18	2
Aikman	25	79	3.2	13	0
Walker	6	20	3.3	11	0
Miller	1	6	6.0	6	0
Johnston	2	3	1.5	3	0
Wilson	6	-2	-.3	3	0
Sanders	1	-11	-11.0	-11	0
Cowboys	423	1,637	3.9	44	6
Opponents	511	1,994	3.9	31	12

RECEIVING	No.	Yds.	Avg.	LG	TD
Irvin	75	1,180	15.7	55	9
Bjornson	47	442	9.4	32	0
Miller	46	645	14.0	54	4
E. Smith	40	234	5.9	24	0
St. Williams	30	308	10.3	20	1
Sh. Williams	21	159	7.6	18	0
Johnston	18	166	9.2	21	1
LaFleur	18	122	6.8	17	2
Walker	14	149	10.6	64t	2
B. Davis	3	33	11.0	12	0
Galbraith	2	16	8.0	11	0
Sanders	0	0	—	—	0
Cowboys	314	3,454	11.0	64t	19
Opponents	253	2,717	10.7	61	20

INTERCEPTIONS	No.	Yds.	Avg.	LG	TD
Sanders	2	81	40.5	50t	1
Stoutmire	2	8	4.0	8	0
K. Smith	1	21	21.0	21	0
Woodson	1	14	14.0	14	0
Coakley	1	6	6.0	6	0
Cowboys	7	130	18.6	50t	1
Opponents	12	211	17.6	61t	1

PUNTING	No.	Yds.	Avg.	In 20	LG
Gowin	86	3,592	41.8	26	72
Cowboys	86	3,592	41.8	26	72
Opponents	95	4,142	43.6	27	66

PUNT RETURNS	No.	FC	Yds.	Avg.	LG	TD
Sanders	33	12	407	12.3	83t	1
Mathis	11	2	91	8.3	45	0
St. Williams	2	0	14	7.0	14	0
Pittman	1	0	0	0.0	0	0
Cowboys	47	14	512	10.9	83t	1
Opponents	40	19	365	9.1	37	0

KICKOFF RETURNS	No.	Yds.	Avg.	LG	TD
Walker	50	1,167	23.3	49	0
Marion	10	311	31.1	49	0
Galbraith	2	24	12.0	13	0
Sanders	1	18	18.0	18	0
Cowboys	63	1,520	24.1	49	0
Opponents	65	1,172	18.0	34	0

FIELD GOALS	1-19	20-29	30-39	40-49	50+
Cunningham	1/1	16/16	9/9	7/10	1/1
Gowin	0/0	0/0	0/0	0/0	0/1
Cowboys	1/1	16/16	9/9	7/10	1/2
Opponents	2/2	8/8	4/6	6/9	0/2

SACKS	No.
Carver	6.0
Tolbert	5.0
Hennings	4.5
Thomas	3.5
Casillas	3.0
Coakley	2.5
Anderson	2.0
Stoutmire	2.0
C. Williams	2.0
Woodson	2.0
Bates	1.0
Godfrey	1.0
Pittman	1.0
V. Smith	1.0
Lett	0.5
McCormack	0.5
Strickland	0.5
Cowboys	38.0
Opponents	39.0

1998 DRAFT CHOICES

Round	Name	Pos.	College
1	Greg Ellis	DE	North Carolina
2	Flozell Adams	T	Michigan State
4	Michael Myers	DT	Alabama
5	Darren Hambrick	LB	South Carolina
	Oliver Ross	T	Iowa State
6	Izell Reese	DB	Alabama-Birmingham
7	Tarik Smith	RB	California
	Antonio Fleming	G	Georgia
	Rodrick Monroe	TE	Cincinnati

DALLAS COWBOYS

1998 VETERAN ROSTER

No.		Name	Pos.	Ht.	Wt.	Birthdate	NFL Exp.	College	Hometown	How Acq.	'97 Games/ Starts
8		Aikman, Troy	QB	6-4	219	11/21/66	10	UCLA	Henryetta, Okla.	D1-'89	16/16
73		Allen, Larry	G-T	6-3	326	11/27/71	5	Sonoma State	Napa, Calif.	D2-'94	16/16
96		Anderson, Antonio	DT	6-6	318	6/4/73	2	Syracuse	Milford, Conn.	D4a-'97	16/5
40	#	Bates, Bill	S	6-1	213	6/6/61	16	Tennessee	Knoxville, Tenn.	FA-'83	16/0
91		Benson, Darren	DT	6-7	308	8/25/74	4	Trinity Valley C.C.	Memphis, Tenn.	S3-'95	6/0
86	†	Bjornson, Eric	TE	6-4	236	12/15/71	4	Washington	Oakland, Calif.	D4a-'95	14/14
82		Brooks, Macey	WR	6-5	220	2/2/75	2	James Madison	Hampton, Va.	D4b-'97	0*
52		Coakley, Dexter	LB	5-10	215	10/20/72	2	Appalachian State	Mt. Pleasant, S.C.	D3a-'97	16/16
3		Cunningham, Richie	K	5-10	167	8/18/70	2	Southwestern Louisiana	Houma, La.	FA-'97	16/0
87		Davis, Billy	WR	6-1	205	7/6/72	4	Pittsburgh	El Paso, Tex.	FA-'95	16/0
35		Davis, Wendell	CB	5-10	183	6/27/73	3	Oklahoma	Wichita, Kan.	D6-'96	15/0
17		Garrett, Jason	QB	6-2	195	3/28/66	6	Princeton	Chagrin, Ohio	FA-'93	1/0
56		Godfrey, Randall	LB	6-2	237	4/6/73	3	Georgia	Valdosta, Ga.	D2b-'96	16/16
4		Gowin, Toby	P	5-10	167	3/30/75	2	North Texas	Jacksonville, Tex.	FA-'97	16/0
70		Hellestrae, Dale	C-G	6-5	291	7/11/62	14	Southern Methodist	Scottsdale, Ariz.	T(Raid)-'90	16/0
95		Hennings, Chad	DT	6-6	291	10/20/65	7	Air Force	Elberon, Iowa	D11-'88	11/10
66		Hutson, Tony	T	6-3	313	3/13/74	2	Northeastern Oklahoma State	Houston, Tex.	FA-'97	5/1
88		Irvin, Michael	WR	6-2	207	3/5/66	11	Miami, Fla.	Ft. Lauderdale, Fla.	D1-'88	16/16
48		Johnston, Daryl	RB	6-2	242	2/10/66	10	Syracuse	Youngstown, N.Y.	D2-'89	6/6
89		LaFleur, David	TE	6-7	280	1/29/74	2	Louisiana State	Westlake, La.	D1-'97	16/5
78		Lett, Leon	DT	6-6	295	10/12/68	7	Emporia State	Fairhope, Ala.	D7-'91	3/3
23		Mathis, Kevin	CB	5-9	172	4/29/74	2	Texas A&M-Commerce	Gainesville, Tex.	FA-'97	16/3
99		McCormack, Hurvin	DE-DT	6-5	284	4/6/72	5	Indiana	Brooklyn, N.Y.	FA-'94	13/0
67		McIver, Everett	G	6-5	318	8/5/70	5	Elizabeth City State	Fayetteville, N.C.	UFA(Mia)-'98	14/14*
85		Mills, Ernie	WR	5-11	192	10/28/68	8	Florida	Dunnellon, Fla.	FA-'98	10/5*
27		Mobley, Singor	S	5-11	195	10/12/72	2	Washington State	Tacoma, Wash.	FA-'97	12/0
61		Newton, Nate	G	6-3	320	12/20/61	13	Florida A&M	Orlando, Fla.	FA-'86	13/13
83		Oliver, Jimmy	WR	5-10	186	1/30/73	3	Texas Christian	Dallas, Tex.	FA-'98	0*
97		Pittman, Kavika	DE	6-6	267	2/9/74	3	McNeese State	Leesville, La.	D2a-'96	15/0
21		Sanders, Deion	CB-WR	6-1	195	8/9/67	10	Florida State	Fort Myers, Fla.	UFA(SF)-'95	13/12
77		Scifres, Steve	T	6-4	300	1/22/72	2	Wyoming	Colorado Springs, Colo.	D3b-'97	6/0
50		Shiver, Clay	C	6-2	294	12/7/72	3	Florida State	Tifton, Ga.	D3a-'96	16/16
22		Smith, Emmitt	RB	5-9	209	5/15/69	9	Florida	Escambia, Fla.	D1-'90	16/16
93		Smith, Herman	DE	6-5	277	1/25/71	3	Portland State	Ft. Lauderdale, Fla.	FA-'98	0*
26		Smith, Kevin	CB	5-11	190	4/7/70	7	Texas A&M	Orange, Tex.	D1a-'92	16/16
57	#	Smith, Vinson	LB	6-2	247	7/3/65	11	East Carolina	Statesville, N.C.	FA-'97	14/3
24		Stoutmire, Omar	S	5-11	198	7/9/74	2	Fresno State	Long Beach, Calif.	D7-'97	16/2
55		Strickland, Fred	LB	6-2	251	8/15/66	11	Purdue	Wanaque, N.J.	UFA(GB)-'96	15/14
45		Sualua, Nicky	RB	5-11	257	4/16/75	2	Ohio State	Santa Ana, Calif.	D4c-'97	10/1
31		Teague, George	S	6-1	196	2/18/71	6	Alabama	Montgomery, Ala.	FA-'98	15/6*
51		Thomas, Broderick	DE-LB	6-4	254	2/20/67	10	Nebraska	Houston, Tex.	FA-'96	16/0
92		Tolbert, Tony	DE	6-6	263	12/29/67	10	Texas-El Paso	Englewood, N.J.	D4-'89	16/16
37		Vaughn, Lee	CB	5-11	184	11/27/74	2	Wyoming	Cheyenne, Wyo.	D6-'97	0*
34	#	Walker, Herschel	RB	6-1	225	3/3/62	13	Georgia	Wrightsville, Ga.	FA-'96	16/6
42		Warren, Chris	RB	6-2	226	1/24/68	9	Ferrum	Burke, Va.	FA-'98	15/13*
30		Wheaton, Kenny	CB	5-10	190	3/8/75	2	Oregon	Phoenix, Ariz.	D3c-'97	2/0
25		Williams, Charlie	S	6-0	189	2/2/72	4	Bowling Green	Detroit, Mich.	D3-'95	16/0
79		Williams, Erik	T	6-6	328	9/7/68	8	Central State, Ohio	Philadelphia, Pa.	D3c-'91	15/15
20		Williams, Sherman	RB	5-8	202	8/13/73	4	Alabama	Mobile, Ala.	D2a-'95	16/0
80		Williams, Stepfret	WR	6-0	170	6/14/73	3	Northeast Louisiana	Minden, La.	D3b-'96	16/0
28		Woodson, Darren	S	6-1	219	4/25/69	7	Arizona State	Phoenix, Ariz.	D2b-'92	14/14

* Brooks and Vaughn missed '97 season because of injury; McIver played 14 games with Miami; Mills played 10 games with Carolina; Oliver last active with San Diego in '96; H. Smith last active with Tampa Bay in '96; Teague played 15 games with Miami; Warren played 15 games with Seattle.

Unrestricted free agent; subject to developments.

† Restricted free agent; subject to developments.

Retired—Tony Casillas, 12-year defensive tackle, 15 games in '97.

Players lost through free agency (3): C-G John Flannery (StL; 16 games in '97), G-T George Hegamin (Phil; 13), S Brock Marion (Mia; 16).

Also played with Cowboys in '97—DE Shante Carver (16 games), TE Scott Galbraith (16), LB Darryl Hardy (12), LB Nate Hemsley (2), WR Anthony Miller (16), T Mark Tuinei (6), QB Wade Wilson (7).

COACHING STAFF

Head Coach,
Chan Gailey

Pro Career: Chan Gailey became the fourth head coach in Cowboys history on February 12, 1998, after four seasons with the Pittsburgh Steelers, the last two as offensive coordinator. In 10 seasons as an NFL assistant coach with Pittsburgh and Denver, Gailey has appeared in four Super Bowls, six AFC Championship Games, and been a part of seven division winning teams. As an assistant with Pittsburgh, Gailey was instrumental in developing the young offensive talent that helped the Steelers capture four consecutive AFC Central Division titles and appear in three of the last four AFC Championship Games, including an AFC title and Super Bowl XXX appearance following the 1995 season. Gailey was the Pittsburgh offensive coordinator (1996-97) after having served two years (1994-95) as the team's wide receivers coach. Gailey's other NFL experience came during a six-year stint (1985-90) with the Denver Broncos. In his first season with the Broncos, Gailey served as a defensive assistant and special teams coach. The following year he coached special teams-tight ends and in 1987, he was in charge of the tight ends-wide receivers. He took over the quarterback coaching duties in 1988. In 1989, Gailey's first season as the Broncos offensive coordinator, the Broncos earned a berth in Super Bowl XXIV. Sandwiched between his two NFL tours of duty were head coaching stops in the World League with the Birmingham Fire (1991-92) and at Samford University (1993). Gailey is the first former World League head coach to take on NFL head coaching responsibilities.

Background: Gailey was a quarterback at the University of Florida from 1970-73. He received his bachelor's degree in physical education in 1974 and began his coaching career as a graduate assistant at Florida (1974-75). He then served as the secondary coach at Troy State (1976-78). He spent the next four years at the Air Force Academy (1979-82). He returned to Troy State as the head coach (1983-84) and captured the NCAA Division II Championship in 1984. He posted a 36-18-1 (.664) record in his three head coaching stops (five seasons).

Personal: Born in Gainesville, Ga., on January 5, 1952. Was a standout at Americus, Ga., High School. Chan and his wife, Laurie, have two sons, Tate and Andrew.

1998 FRIST-YEAR ROSTER

Name	Pos.	Ht.	Wt.	Birthdate	College	Hometown	How Acq.
Adams, Flozell	T	6-7	335	5/10/75	Michigan State	Maywood, Ill.	D2
Bailey, Ronald	CB	5-11	187	2/14/75	Georgia	Folkston, Ga.	FA
Booth, Kent	G	6-2	290	7/12/75	Northern Illinois	Southfield, Mich.	FA
Bright, Greg	LB	6-1	233	11/16/74	Georgia	Moultrie, Ga.	FA
Cantrell, Barry	K-P	6-1	180	11/2/76	Fordham	Ft. Lauderdale, Fla.	FA
Egbuniwe, Chike	LB	6-1	236	12/25/74	Duke	Dallas, Tex.	FA
Ellis, Greg	DE	6-6	283	8/14/75	North Carolina	Wendell, N.C.	D1
Eubanks, Anthony	WR	6-2	189	12/11/74	Arkansas	Spiro, Okla.	FA
Filikitonga, Junior	DT	6-0	292	4/8/76	Abilene Christian	Hurst, Tex.	FA
Fleming, Antonio	G	6-3	309	2/6/74	Georgia	Edison, Ga.	D7b
Fortney, Denny	DE	6-3	265	12/27/74	Miami	Waynesboro, Pa.	FA
Geason, Cory	TE	6-3	255	8/12/75	Tulane	St. James, La.	FA
Gonzalez, Daniel	QB	6-3	214	9/20/74	East Carolina	Neptune, N.J.	FA
Hambrick, Darren	LB	6-2	216	8/30/75	South Carolina	Pasco, Fla.	D5a
Hemsley, Nate (1)	LB	6-0	219	5/15/74	Syracuse	Delran, N.J.	FA-'97
Hicks, Michael	CB	6-2	210	6/3/76	Texas-El Paso	Houston, Tex.	FA
Johnson, Taj	WR	6-2	203	1/9/75	San Diego State	Ardmore, Okla.	FA
Jones, John (1)	C-G-T	6-1	325	12/8/72	Kansas	Granada Hills, Calif.	FA
Kiselak, Mike (1)	C-G	6-3	300	3/9/67	Maryland	Pine Bush, N.Y.	FA
Knake, Max (1)	QB	6-2	210	4/11/73	Texas Christian	McKinney, Tex.	FA
Lethridge, Zebbie	CB-S	6-0	201	1/31/75	Texas Tech	Lubbock, Tex.	FA
Monroe, Rod	TE	6-4	244	7/30/75	Cincinnati	Hearne, Tex.	D7c
Morgan, Beau (1)	RB	5-10	192	8/4/75	Air Force	Carrollton, Tex.	FA-'97
Myers, Michael	DE-DT	6-2	286	1/20/76	Alabama	Vicksburg, Miss.	D4
Ogden, Jeff	WR	6-0	190	2/22/75	Eastern Washington	Snohomish, Wash.	FA
Perkins, Todd (1)	G	6-4	295	7/10/73	Texas A&M-Kingsville	Mt. Pleasant, Tex.	FA
Reese, Izell	S	6-2	193	5/7/74	Alabama-Birmingham	Dothan, Ala.	D6
Rodriguez, Bobby	RB	5-11	237	11/4/72	Houston	Houston, Tex.	FA
Ross, Oliver	C-G-T	6-4	300	9/27/74	Iowa State	Los Angeles, Calif.	D5b
Simms, Sean (1)	TE	6-2	245	7/5/74	Nevada	Santa Barbara, Calif.	FA
Smith, Tarik	RB	5-10	200	4/16/75	California	Agoura, Calif.	D7a
Thomas, Robert	LB	6-1	255	12/1/74	Henderson State	Jacksonville, Ark.	FA
Williams, Brett (1)	DE	6-4	263	10/15/73	Clemson	Albany, Ga.	FA
Zadel, David	DE-LB	6-5	250	10/12/75	Wake Forest	Cohasset, Mass.	FA

The term NFL Rookie is defined as a player who is in his first season of professional football and has not been on the roster of another professional football team for any regular-season or postseason games. A Rookie is designated by an "R" on NFL rosters. Players who have been active in another professional football league or players who have NFL experience, including either preseason training camp or being on an Active List or Inactive List, or on Reserve/Injured or Reserve/Physically Unable to Perform for fewer than six regular-season games, are termed NFL First-Year Players. An NFL First-Year Player is designated by a "1" on NFL rosters. Thereafter, a player is credited with an additional year of experience for each season in which he accumulates six games on the Active List or Inactive List, or on Reserve/Injured or Reserve/Physically Unable to Perform.

ASSISTANT COACHES

Joe Avezzano, special teams; born November 17, 1943, Yonkers, N.Y., lives in Coppell, Tex. Guard Florida State 1961-65. Pro center Boston Patriots 1966. College coach: Florida State 1968, Iowa State 1969-72, Pittsburgh 1973-76, Tennessee 1977-79, Oregon State 1980-84 (head coach), Texas 1985-88. Pro coach: Joined Cowboys in 1990.

Jim Bates, defensive line; born May 31, 1946, Pontiac, Mich., lives in Irving, Tex. Linebacker Tennessee 1964-67. No pro playing experience. College coach: Tennessee 1968, Southern Mississippi 1972, Villanova 1973-74, Kansas State 1975-76, West Virginia 1977, Texas Tech 1978-83, Tennessee 1989, Florida 1990. Pro coach: San Antonio Gunslingers (USFL) 1984-85 (head coach 1985), Arizona Outlaws (USFL) 1986, Detroit Drive (AFL) 1988, Cleveland Browns 1991-93, 1995, Atlanta Falcons 1994, joined Cowboys in 1996.

Dave Campo, defensive coordinator; born July 18, 1947, New London, Conn., lives in Coppell, Tex. Defensive back Central Connecticut State 1967-70. No pro playing experience. College coach: Central Connecticut State 1971-72, Albany State 1973, Bridgeport 1974, Pittsburgh 1975, Washington State 1976, Boise State 1977-79, Oregon State 1980, Weber State 1981-82, Iowa State 1983, Syracuse 1984-86, Miami 1987-88. Pro coach: Joined Cowboys in 1989.

George Edwards, linebackers; born January 16, 1967, Siler City, N.C., lives in Irving, Tex. Linebacker Duke 1986-89. No pro playing experience. College coach: Florida 1990-91, Appalachian State 1992-95, Duke 1996, Georgia 1997. Pro coach: Joined Cowboys in 1998.

Wayne (Buddy) Geis, quarterbacks; born September 16, 1946, Altoona, Pa., lives in Irving, Tex. Wide receiver Northern Arizona 1965. No pro playing experience. College coach: Arizona 1974-76, Tulane 1977-82, Memphis State 1986-87, Duke 1993, Tulane 1994. Pro coach: Jacksonville Bulls (USFL) 1984-85, Green Bay Packers 1988-91, Memphis Mad Dogs (CFL) 1995, Indianapolis Colts 1996-97, joined Cowboys in 1998.

Steve Hoffman, kickers-research and development; born September 8, 1958, Camden, N.J., lives in Coppell, Tex. Quarterback-running back-wide receiver Dickinson College 1979-82. Pro punter Washington Federals (USFL) 1983. College coach: Miami 1985-87. Pro coach: Joined Cowboys in 1989.

Hudson Houck, offensive line; born January 7, 1943, Los Angeles, Calif., lives in Irving, Tex. Center Southern California 1962-64. No pro playing experience. College coach: Southern California 1970-72, 1976-82, Stanford 1973-75. Pro coach: Los Angeles Rams 1983-91, Seattle Seahawks 1992, joined Cowboys in 1993.

Jim Jeffcoat, defensive line assistant; born April 1, 1961, Cliffwood, N.J., lives in Coppell, Tex. Defensive end Arizona State 1979-82. Pro defensive end Dallas Cowboys 1983-94, Buffalo Bills 1995-97. Pro coach: Joined Cowboys in 1998.

Joe Juraszek, strength and conditioning; born June 8, 1958, Chicago, Ill., lives in Coppell, Tex. Linebacker-defensive end New Mexico 1976-80. No pro playing experience. College coach: Oklahoma 1981-86, 1993-96, Texas Tech 1987-92. Pro coach: Joined Cowboys in 1997.

Les Miles, tight ends; born November 10, 1953, Elyria, Ohio, lives in Irving, Tex. Guard Michigan 1972-75. No pro playing experience. College coach: Colorado 1982-86, Michigan 1987-94, Oklahoma State 1995-97. Pro coach: Joined Cowboys in 1998.

Dwain Painter, wide receivers; born February 13, 1942, Monroeville, Pa., lives in Irving, Tex. Quarterback-defensive back Rutgers 1961-64. No pro playing experience. College coach: San Jose State 1971-72, College of San Mateo 1973, BYU 1974-75, UCLA 1976-78. Northern Arizona 1979-81 (head coach), Georgia Tech 1982-85, Texas 1986, Illinois 1987. Pro coach: Pittsburgh Steelers 1988-91, Indianapolis Colts 1992-93, San Diego Chargers 1994-96, Denver Broncos 1997, joined Cowboys in 1998.

Clancy Pendergast, defensive assistant; born November 29, 1967, Phoenix, Ariz., lives in Irving, Tex. No college or pro playing experience. College coach: Mississippi State 1991, Southern California 1992, Oklahoma 1993-94. Pro coach: Houston Oilers 1995, joined Cowboys in 1996.

Tommie Robinson, offensive assistant; born April 4, 1963, Phenix City, Ala., lives in Fort Worth, Tex. Defensive back Troy State 1981-84. No pro playing experience. College coach: Arkansas 1991, Utah State 1992-93, Texas Christian 1994-97. Pro coach: Joined Cowboys in 1998.

Clarence Shelmon, running backs; born September 17, 1952, Bossier City, La., lives in Irving, Tex. Running back Houston 1971-75. No pro playing experience. College coach: Army 1978-80, Indiana 1981-83, Arizona 1984-86, Southern California 1987-90. Pro coach: Los Angeles Rams 1991, Seattle Seahawks 1992-97, joined Cowboys in 1998.

Mike Zimmer, defensive backs; born June 5, 1956, Peoria, Ill., lives in Grapevine, Tex. Quarterback-linebacker Illinois State 1974-76. No pro playing experience. College coach: Missouri 1979-80, Weber State 1981-88, Washington State 1989-93. Pro coach: Joined Cowboys in 1994.

DETROIT LIONS

National Football Conference
Central Division
Team Colors: Honolulu Blue and Silver
Pontiac Silverdome
1200 Featherstone Road
Pontiac, Michigan 48342
Telephone: (248) 335-4131

CLUB OFFICIALS

Chairman and President: William Clay Ford
Vice Chairman: William Clay Ford, Jr.
Executive Vice President and Chief Operating Officer: Chuck Schmidt
Vice President of Player Personnel: Ron Hughes
Vice President of Communications, Sales and Marketing: Bill Keenist
Vice President of Football Administration: Larry Lee
Vice President of Finance and Chief Financial Officer: Tom Lesnau
Vice President-General Counsel: David Potts
Secretary: David Hempstead
Director of Salary Cap and Stadium Development: Tom Lewand
Director of Pro Personnel: Kevin Colbert
Scouts: Russ Bolinger, Dirk Dierking, Thomas Dimitroff, Scott McEwen, Jim Owens, Charlie Sanders, Sheldon White
Director of Media Relations: Mike Murray
Executive Director of Marketing: Steve Harms
Director of Box Office Operations: Mark Graham
Director of Ticket Sales and Customer Service: Jennifer Manzo
Broadcast Services Coordinator: Bryan Bender
Director of Community Relations and Detroit Lions Charities: Tim Pendell
Head Athletic Trainer: Kent Falb
Equipment Manager: Dan Jaroshewich
Video Director: Steve Hermans
Stadium: Pontiac Silverdome • **Capacity:** 80,311
1200 Featherstone Road
Pontiac, Michigan 48342
Playing Surface: AstroTurf
Training Camp: Saginaw Valley State College
University Center, Michigan 48710

1998 SCHEDULE

PRESEASON

Aug. 7	**Arizona**	7:00
Aug. 14	**Atlanta**	7:00
Aug. 22	at Cincinnati	7:30
Aug. 27	at Indianapolis	7:30

REGULAR SEASON

Sept. 6	at Green Bay	12:01
Sept. 13	**Cincinnati**	1:01
Sept. 20	at Minnesota	12:01
Sept. 28	**Tampa Bay** (Mon.)	8:20
Oct. 4	at Chicago	12:01
Oct. 11	Open Date	
Oct. 15	**Green Bay** (Thurs.)	8:20
Oct. 25	**Minnesota**	1:01
Nov. 1	**Arizona**	1:01
Nov. 8	at Philadelphia	1:01
Nov. 15	**Chicago**	8:20
Nov. 22	at Tampa Bay	1:01
Nov. 26	**Pittsburgh** (Thurs.)	12:35
Dec. 6	at Jacksonville	1:01
Dec. 14	at San Francisco (Mon.)	5:20
Dec. 20	**Atlanta**	1:01
Dec. 27	at Baltimore	1:01

RECORD HOLDERS

INDIVIDUAL RECORDS—CAREER

Category	Name	Performance
Rushing (Yds.)	Barry Sanders, 1989-1997	13,778
Passing (Yds.)	Bobby Layne, 1950-58	15,710
Passing (TDs)	Bobby Layne, 1950-58	118
Receiving (No.)	Herman Moore, 1991-97	528
Receiving (Yds.)	Herman Moore, 1991-97	7,484
Interceptions	Dick LeBeau, 1959-1972	62
Punting (Avg.)	Yale Lary, 1952-53, 1956-1964	44.3
Punt Return (Avg.)	Jack Christiansen, 1951-58	12.8
Kickoff Return (Avg.)	Pat Studstill, 1961-67	25.7
Field Goals	Eddie Murray, 1980-1991	243
Touchdowns (Tot.)	Barry Sanders, 1989-1997	105
Points	Eddie Murray, 1980-1991	1,113

INDIVIDUAL RECORDS—SINGLE SEASON

Category	Name	Performance
Rushing (Yds.)	Barry Sanders, 1997	2,053
Passing (Yds.)	Scott Mitchell, 1995	4,338
Passing (TDs)	Scott Mitchell, 1995	32
Receiving (No.)	Herman Moore, 1995	*123
Receiving (Yds.)	Herman Moore, 1995	1,686
Interceptions	Don Doll, 1950	12
	Jack Christiansen, 1953	12
Punting (Avg.)	Yale Lary, 1963	48.9
Punt Return (Avg.)	Jack Christiansen, 1952	21.5
Kickoff Return (Avg.)	Tom Watkins, 1965	34.4
Field Goals	Jason Hanson, 1993	34
Touchdowns (Tot.)	Barry Sanders, 1991	17
Points	Jason Hanson, 1995	132

INDIVIDUAL RECORDS—SINGLE GAME

Category	Name	Performance
Rushing (Yds.)	Barry Sanders, 11-13-94	237
Passing (Yds.)	Scott Mitchell, 11-23-95	410
Passing (TDs)	Gary Danielson, 12-9-78	5
Receiving (No.)	Herman Moore, 12-4-95	14
Receiving (Yds.)	Cloyce Box, 12-3-50	302
Interceptions	Don Doll, 10-23-49	*4
Field Goals	Garo Yepremian, 11-13-66	6
Touchdowns (Tot.)	Dutch Clark, 10-22-34	4
	Cloyce Box, 12-3-50	4
	Barry Sanders, 11-24-91	4
Points	Dutch Clark, 10-22-34	24
	Cloyce Box, 12-3-50	24
	Barry Sanders, 11-24-91	24

*NFL Record

COACHING HISTORY

Portsmouth Spartans 1930-33
(442-455-32)

1930	Hal (Tubby) Griffen	5-6-3
1931-36	George (Potsy) Clark	49-20-6
1937-38	Earl (Dutch) Clark	14-8-0
1939	Elmer (Gus) Henderson	6-5-0
1940	George (Potsy) Clark	5-5-1
1941-42	Bill Edwards*	4-9-1
1942	John Karcis	0-8-0
1943-47	Charles (Gus) Dorais	20-31-2
1948-50	Alvin (Bo) McMillin	12-24-0
1951-56	Raymond (Buddy) Parker	50-24-2
1957-64	George Wilson	55-45-6
1965-66	Harry Gilmer	10-16-2
1967-72	Joe Schmidt	43-35-7
1973	Don McCafferty	6-7-1
1974-76	Rick Forzano**	15-17-0
1976-77	Tommy Hudspeth	11-13-0
1978-84	Monte Clark	43-63-1
1985-88	Darryl Rogers***	18-40-0
1988-96	Wayne Fontes	67-71-0
1997	Bobby Ross	9-8-0

* Released after three games in 1942
** Resigned after four games in 1976
*** Released after 11 games in 1988

PONTIAC SILVERDOME

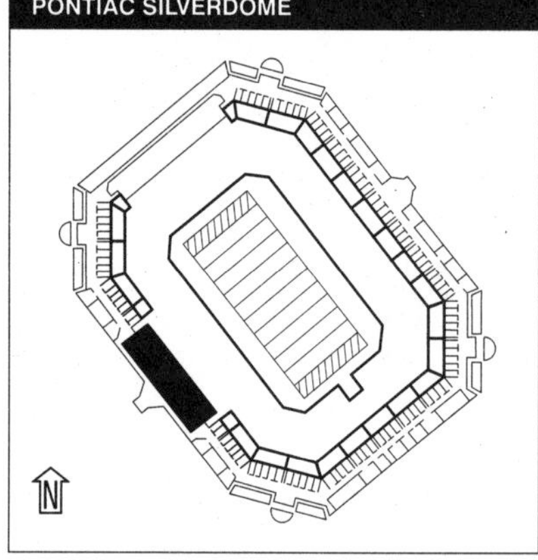

1997 TEAM RECORD

PRESEASON (1-3)

Date	Result		Opponent
8/1	W	20-17	Atlanta
8/8	L	23-27	Cincinnati
8/17	L	20-28	at Pittsburgh
8/21	L	3-16	at Indianapolis

REGULAR SEASON (9-7)

Date	Result		Opponent	Att.
8/31	W	28-17	Atlanta	61,244
9/7	L	17-24	Tampa Bay	58,234
9/14	W	32-7	at Chicago	59,147
9/21	L	17-35	at New Orleans	50,016
9/28	W	26-15	Green Bay	78,110
10/5	L	13-22	at Buffalo	78,025
10/12	W	27-9	at Tampa Bay	72,095
10/19	L	20-26	New York Giants (OT)	70,069
11/2	L	10-20	at Green Bay	60,126
11/9	L	7-30	at Washington	75,261
11/16	W	38-15	Minnesota	68,910
11/23	W	32-10	Indianapolis	62,803
11/27	W	55-20	Chicago	77,904
12/7	L	30-33	at Miami	72,266
12/14	W	14-13	at Minnesota	60,982
12/21	W	13-10	New York Jets	77,624

POSTSEASON (0-1)

Date	Result		Opponent	Att.
12/28	L	10-20	Tampa Bay	73,361

(OT) Overtime

SCORE BY PERIODS

Lions	35	131	87	126	0	— 379
Opponents	100	103	33	64	6	— 306

ATTENDANCE

Home 554,898 Away 527,918 Total 1,082,816
Single-game home record, 80,441 (12/20/81)
Single-season home record, 622,593 (1980)

1997 TEAM STATISTICS

	Lions	Opp.
Total First Downs	304	268
Rushing	120	98
Passing	166	152
Penalty	18	18
Third Down: Made/Att	78/221	85/236
Third Down Pct.	35.3	36.0
Fourth Down: Made/Att	8/18	5/11
Fourth Down Pct.	44.4	45.5
Total Net Yards	5,798	4,947
Avg. Per Game	362.4	309.2
Total Plays	1,028	1,021
Avg. Per Play	5.6	4.8
Net Yards Rushing	2,464	1,833
Avg. Per Game	154.0	114.6
Total Rushes	447	471
Net Yards Passing	3,334	3,114
Avg. Per Game	208.4	194.6
Sacked/Yards Lost	41/271	43/287
Gross Yards	3,605	3,401
Att./Completions	540/304	507/281
Completion Pct.	56.3	55.4
Had Intercepted	17	17
Punts/Avg.	86/41.6	97/44.3
Net Punting Avg.	86/35.6	97/38.4
Penalties/Yards Lost	94/866	112/841
Fumbles/Ball Lost	26/11	24/8
Touchdowns	43	33
Rushing	19	15
Passing	19	15
Returns	5	3
Avg. Time of Possession	28:37	31:23

1997 INDIVIDUAL STATISTICS

Passing	Att.	Comp.	Yds.	Pct.	TD	Int.	Tkld.	Rate
Mitchell	509	293	3,484	57.6	19	14	41/271	79.6
Reich	30	11	121	36.7	0	2	0/0	21.7
Blundin	1	0	0	0.0	0	1	0/0	0.0
Lions	540	304	3,605	56.3	19	17	41/271	75.4
Opponents	507	281	3,401	55.4	15	17	43/287	72.1

SCORING	TD R	TD P	TD Rt	PAT	FG	Saf	PTS
Hanson	0	0	0	39/40	26/29	0	117
Sanders	11	3	0	0/0	0/0	0	84
Moore	0	8	0	0/0	0/0	0	50
Morton	0	6	0	0/0	0/0	0	36
Vardell	6	0	0	0/0	0/0	0	36
Brown	0	0	2	0/0	0/0	0	12
Scroggins	0	0	1	0/0	0/0	1	8
S. Boyd	0	0	1	0/0	0/0	0	6
Chryplewicz	0	1	0	0/0	0/0	0	6
Mitchell	1	0	0	0/0	0/0	0	6
Rivers	1	0	0	0/0	0/0	0	6
Schlesinger	0	1	0	0/0	0/0	0	6
Westbrook	0	0	1	0/0	0/0	0	6
Lions	19	19	5	39/40	26/29	1	379
Opponents	15	15	3	29/30	25/32	1	306

2-Point conversions: Moore. Team 1-3, Opponents 1-2.

RUSHING	Att.	Yds.	Avg.	LG	TD
Sanders	335	2,053	6.1	82t	11
Rivers	29	166	5.7	31	1
Vardell	32	122	3.8	41	6
Mitchell	37	83	2.2	13	1
Morton	3	33	11.0	20	0
Schlesinger	7	11	1.6	4	0
Reich	4	-4	-1.0	-1	0
Lions	447	2,464	5.5	82t	19
Opponents	471	1,833	3.9	74t	15

RECEIVING	No.	Yds.	Avg.	LG	TD
Moore	104	1,293	12.4	79	8
Morton	80	1,057	13.2	73t	6
Sanders	33	305	9.2	66t	3
Sloan	29	264	9.1	25	0
Metzelaars	17	144	8.5	22	0
Vardell	16	218	13.6	37	0
T. Boyd	10	142	14.2	32	0
Milburn	5	77	15.4	43	0
Schlesinger	5	69	13.8	33	1
Chryplewicz	3	27	9.0	12	1
McCorvey	2	9	4.5	6	0
Mitchell	0	0	—	—	0
Lions	304	3,605	11.9	79	19
Opponents	281	3,401	12.1	78t	15

INTERCEPTIONS	No.	Yds.	Avg.	LG	TD
Carrier	5	94	18.8	66	0
Brown	2	83	41.5	45t	2
Westbrook	2	64	32.0	64t	1
Abrams	1	29	29.0	29	0
Rice	1	18	18.0	18	0
Raymond	1	17	17.0	17	0
Porcher	1	5	5.0	5	0
S. Boyd	1	4	4.0	4	0
Bailey	1	0	0.0	0	0
Jeffries	1	0	0.0	0	0
Malone	1	-5	-5.0	-5	0
Lions	17	309	18.2	66	3
Opponents	17	191	11.2	50t	2

PUNTING	No.	Yds.	Avg.	In 20	LG
Jett	84	3,576	35.6	24	60
Lions	84	3,576	35.6	24	60
Opponents	97	4,296	38.4	28	67

PUNT RETURNS	No.	FC	Yds.	Avg.	LG	TD
Milburn	47	26	433	9.2	40	0
Carrier	1	0	0	0.0	0	0
Lions	48	26	433	9.0	40	0
Opponents	51	19	434	8.5	53t	1

KICKOFF RETURNS	No.	Yds.	Avg.	LG	TD
Milburn	55	1,315	23.9	69	0
Rivers	2	34	17.0	23	0
Russell	1	0	0.0	0	0
Vardell	1	15	15.0	15	0
Lions	59	1,364	23.1	69	0
Opponents	61	1,269	20.8	58	0

FIELD GOALS	1-19	20-29	30-39	40-49	50+
Hanson	0/0	10/10	8/9	5/5	3/5
Lions	0/0	10/10	8/9	5/5	3/5
Opponents	2/2	6/6	7/8	6/11	4/5

SACKS	No.
Porcher	12.5
Elliss	8.5
Scroggins	7.5
Brown	2.5
Abrams	2.0
Bailey	2.0
London	2.0
Bonham	1.0
Jamison	1.0
Jeffries	1.0
Rice	1.0
Waldroup	1.0
Wells	1.0
Lions	43.0
Opponents	41.0

1998 DRAFT CHOICES

Round	Name	Pos.	College
1	Terry Fair	DB	Tennessee
2	Germane Crowell	WR	Virginia
	Charlie Batch	QB	Eastern Michigan
6	Jamaal Alexander	DB	Southern Mississippi
7	Chris Liwienski	T	Indiana

DETROIT LIONS

1998 VETERAN ROSTER

No.		Name	Pos.	Ht.	Wt.	Birthdate	NFL Exp.	College	Hometown	How Acq.	'97 Games/ Starts
24		Abrams, Kevin	CB	5-8	175	2/28/74	2	Syracuse	Tampa, Fla.	D2b-'97	15/4
55		Aldridge, Allen	LB	6-1	255	5/30/72	5	Houston	Missouri City, Tex.	UFA(Den)-'98	16/15*
35		Bailey, Robert	CB	5-9	174	9/3/68	8	Miami	Miami, Fla.	FA-'97	15/0
23		Battle, Terry	RB	5-11	197	2/7/76	2	Arizona State	San Diego, Calif.	D7a-'97	0*
57		Boyd, Stephen	LB	6-0	247	8/22/72	4	Boston College	Valley Stream, N.Y.	D5a-'95	16/16
80		Boyd, Tommie	WR	6-0	195	12/21/71	2	Toledo	Lansing, Mich.	FA-'96	16/1
27		Carrier, Mark	S	6-1	192	4/28/68	9	Southern California	Long Beach, Calif.	FA-'97	16/16
81		Chryplewicz, Pete	TE	6-5	253	4/27/74	2	Notre Dame	Sterling Heights, Mich.	D5a-'97	10/0
77		Compton, Mike	G	6-6	297	9/18/70	6	West Virginia	Richland, Va.	D3b-'93	16/16
94		Elliss, Luther	DT	6-5	291	3/22/73	4	Utah	Mancos, Colo.	D1-'95	16/16
53	t-	Fredrickson, Rob	LB	6-4	240	5/13/71	5	Michigan State	St. Joseph, Mich.	T(Oak)-'98	16/14*
50		Hanks, Ben	LB	6-2	222	7/31/72	2	Florida	Miami, Fla.	FA-'97	2/0
4		Hanson, Jason	K	5-11	183	6/17/70	7	Washington State	Spokane, Wash.	D2b-'92	16/0
74		Harrison, Chris	G	6-3	290	2/25/72	3	Virginia	Washington, D.C.	FA-'96	0*
64		Hartings, Jeff	G	6-3	283	9/7/72	3	Penn State	St. Henry, Ohio	D1b-'96	16/16
66		Hempstead, Hessley	C	6-1	295	1/29/72	4	Kansas	Upland, Calif.	D7-'95	16/1
43		Hill, Sean	S	5-10	195	8/14/71	4	Montana State	Colorado Springs, Colo.	FA-'97	0*
58	#	Jamison, George	LB	6-1	235	9/30/62	13	Cincinnati	Bridgeton, N.J.	FA-'97	16/10
25		Jeffries, Greg	CB	5-9	184	10/16/71	6	Virginia	High Point, N.C.	D6-'93	15/2
18		Jett, John	P	6-0	199	11/11/68	6	East Carolina	Reedville, Va.	UFA(Dall)-'97	16/0
70		Johnson, Andre	T	6-5	314	8/25/73	3	Penn State	Southampton, N.Y.	FA-'97	0*
99		Jordan, Richard	LB	6-1	245	12/1/74	2	Missouri Southern	Vian, Okla.	D7c-'97	10/0
67		Kirschke, Travis	DT	6-3	286	9/6/74	2	UCLA	Yorba Linda, Calif.	FA-'97	3/0
52		Kowalkowski, Scott	LB	6-2	228	8/23/68	8	Notre Dame	Orchard Lake, Mich.	FA-'94	16/0
83		McCorvey, Kez	WR	6-0	180	1/23/72	4	Florida State	Pascagoula, Miss.	D5b-'95	7/0
16		Miller, Jim	QB	6-2	210	2/9/71	5	Michigan State	Grosse Pointe, Mich.	UFA(Atl)-'98	0*
19		Mitchell, Scott	QB	6-6	230	1/2/68	9	Utah	Springville, Utah	UFA(Mia)-'94	16/16
84		Moore, Herman	WR	6-3	210	10/20/69	8	Virginia	Danville, Va.	D1-'91	16/16
87		Morton, Johnnie	WR	6-0	190	10/7/71	5	Southern California	Torrance, Calif.	D1-'94	16/16
90		Owens, Dan	DT	6-3	290	3/16/67	9	Southern California	Whittier, Calif.	UFA(Atl)-'98	15/15*
91		Porcher, Robert	DE	6-3	283	7/30/69	7	South Carolina State	Wando, S.C.	D1-'92	16/15
38		Porter, Daryl	CB	5-9	190	1/16/74	2	Boston College	Ft. Lauderdale, Fla.	FA-'97	7/0
61		Pyne, Jim	C	6-2	297	11/23/71	5	Virginia Tech	Milford, Mass.	UFA(TB)-'98	15/14*
75		Ramirez, Tony	T	6-6	296	1/26/73	2	Northern Colorado	Lincoln, Neb.	D6-'97	2/0
89		Rasby, Walter	TE	6-3	247	9/7/72	5	Wake Forest	Washington, N.C.	UFA(Car)-'98	14/2*
14		Reich, Frank	QB	6-4	210	12/4/61	14	Maryland	Lebanon, Pa.	FA-'97	6/0
28	†	Rice, Ron	S	6-1	206	11/9/72	4	Eastern Michigan	Detroit, Mich.	FA-'95	12/8
34		Rivers, Ron	RB	5-8	205	11/13/71	4	Fresno State	Highland, Calif.	FA-'94	16/0
72		Roberts, Ray	T	6-6	308	6/3/69	7	Virginia	Asheville, N.C.	UFA(Sea)-'96	14/14
73		Roque, Juan	T	6-8	333	1/6/74	2	Arizona State	Ontario, Calif.	D2a-'97	13/1
54		Russell, Matt	LB	6-2	245	7/5/73	2	Colorado	Belleville, Ill.	D4-'97	14/0
20		Sanders, Barry	RB	5-8	203	7/16/68	10	Oklahoma State	Wichita, Kan.	D1-'89	16/16
30		Schlesinger, Cory	RB	6-0	230	6/23/72	4	Nebraska	Duncan, Neb.	D6b-'95	16/2
97		Scroggins, Tracy	LB	6-2	255	9/11/69	7	Tulsa	Checotah, Okla.	D2a-'92	15/6
62		Semple, Tony	G	6-4	286	12/20/70	5	Memphis	Lincoln, Ill.	D5-'94	16/1
86	†	Sloan, David	TE	6-6	254	6/8/72	4	New Mexico	Tollhouse, Calif.	D3-'95	14/12
92		Spindler, Marc	DT	6-5	290	11/28/69	9	Pittsburgh	West Scranton, Pa.	FA-'97	10/0
42		Stewart, Ryan	S	6-1	207	9/30/73	3	Georgia Tech	Moncks Corner, S.C.	D3-'96	8/0
81		Stocz, Eric	TE	6-4	278	5/25/74	2	Westminster, Pa.	Trumbull, Ohio	FA-'96	6/0
71	#	Tharpe, Larry	T	6-4	300	11/19/70	7	Tennessee State	Macon, Ga.	FA-'97	16/15
44		Vardell, Tommy	RB	6-2	230	2/20/69	7	Stanford	El Cajon, Calif.	UFA(SF)-'97	16/10
93		Waldroup, Kerwin	DE	6-3	260	8/1/74	3	Central State, Ohio	Country Club Hills, Ill.	D5-'96	11/11
32		Westbrook, Bryant	CB	6-0	199	12/19/74	2	Texas	Oceanside, Calif.	D1-'97	15/14

* Aldridge played 16 games with Denver; Battle inactive for 16 games; Fredrickson played 16 games with Oakland; Harrison missed '97 season because of injury; Hill inactive for 3 games; Johnson inactive for 10 games; Miller inactive for 9 games with Atlanta; Owens played 15 games with Atlanta; Pyne played 15 games with Tampa Bay; Rasby played 14 games with Carolina.

Unrestricted free agent; subject to developments.

† Restricted free agent; subject to developments.

Traded—RB-KR Glyn Milburn (16 games in '97) to Green Bay.

t- Lions traded for Fredrickson (Oakland).

Retired—Pete Metzelaars, 16-year tight end, 16 games in '97.

Players lost to free agency (4): DT Shane Bonham (SF; 16 games in '97), C Kevin Glover (Sea; 16), S Van Malone (Ariz; 8), DT Mike Wells (Chi; 16).

Also played with Lions in '97—QB Matt Blundin (1 game), LB Reggie Brown (16), S Harry Colon (8), TE Kevin Hickman (4), LB Antonio London (16), CB Corey Raymond (13).

COACHING STAFF

Head Coach,
Bobby Ross

Pro Career: Named the Lions' head coach January 13, 1997. In his first season with the Lions, Ross guided the club to victories in five of its final six games to earn a NFC wild-card berth. Joined the Lions following five seasons as the head coach of the San Diego Chargers. Led the Chargers to a 50-36 record, three playoff appearances in five years, including two AFC Western Division titles, and the club's first-ever AFC Championship and an appearance in Super Bowl XXIX. Hired as the ninth coach of the Chargers January 2, 1992. He began his pro coaching career as an assistant with the Kansas City Chiefs in 1978. He coached the Chiefs special teams and defense in 1978-79 and offensive backs in 1980-81. No pro playing experience. Career record: 59-44.
Background: Played quarterback and defensive back for Virginia Military Institute. Began coaching career at VMI in 1965. Moved on as an assistant at William & Mary 1967-70, Rice 1971, and Maryland 1972. Head coach at The Citadel 1973-77. Compiled 39-19-1 record at Maryland (1982-86) as he led the Terrapins to three Atlantic Coast Conference titles and made four bowl game appearances in five seasons. Guided Georgia Tech (1987-91) to first ACC title in school history. Under Ross, the Yellow Jackets won first national championship as country's only undefeated team (11-0-1) in 1990. Named consensus national coach of the year in 1990. Career collegiate record: 94-76-2.
Personal: Born December 23, 1935, Richmond, Va. Bobby and wife, Alice, live in West Bloomfield, Mich. and have five children—Chris, Kevin, Robbie, Mary, and Teresa.

ASSISTANT COACHES

Brian Baker, defensive line; born June 20, 1962, Baltimore, Md., lives in Rochester, Mich. Linebacker Maryland 1980-83. No pro playing experience. College coach: Maryland 1984-85, Army 1986, Georgia Tech 1987-95. Pro coach: San Diego Chargers 1996, joined Lions in 1997.
Don Clemons, defensive asst. & asst. strength coach; born February 15, 1954, Newark, N.J., lives in Rochester, Mich. Defensive end Muhlenberg College 1973-76. No pro playing experience. College coach: Kutztown State 1977-78, New Mexico 1979, Arizona State 1980-84. Pro coach: Joined Lions in 1985.
Sylvester Croom, offensive coordinator; born September 25, 1954, Tuscaloosa, Ala., lives in Rochester, Mich. Center Alabama 1971-74. Pro center New Orleans Saints 1975. College coach: Alabama 1976-86. Pro coach: Tampa Bay Buccaneers 1987-90, Indianapolis Colts 1991, San Diego Chargers 1992-96, joined Lions in 1997.
Frank Falks, running backs; born March 9, 1943, Tampa, Fla., lives in Rochester Hills, Mich. Linebacker Joplin (Mo.) J.C. 1963-64, Parsons College 1965-66. No pro playing experience. College coach: Parsons College 1967-69, Kansas State 1970-72, Arkansas 1973-77, Wyoming 1978-79, San Diego State 1980, Oklahoma State 1981-82, Southern California 1983-86, Arizona State 1987-91, Ohio State 1992-93. Pro coach: San Diego Chargers 1994-96, joined Lions in 1997.
Jack Henry, offensive line; born March 14, 1946, Wilmington, Pa., lives in Rochester Hills, Mich. Linebacker Penn State 1964-65, guard Indiana (Pa.) University 1967-68. No pro playing experience. College coach: West Virginia 1970, 1978-79, Edinboro 1973, Louisville 1974, Millersville 1975-76, Southern Illinois 1977, Appalachian State 1980, Wake Forest 1981-85, Indiana (Pa.) University 1986-89, Pittsburgh 1993-95. Pro coach: Pittsburgh Steelers 1990-91, San Diego Chargers 1996, joined Lions in 1997.
Bert Hill, strength and conditioning; born January 25, 1958, Montgomery, Ala., lives in Rochester Hills, Mich. Linebacker Marion (Ala.) Military Institute 1976-77, Wichita State 1978. No pro playing experience. College coach: Nicholls State 1981-82, Auburn 1983, Texas A&M 1984-88, Ohio State 1989. Pro coach: Joined Lions in 1990.
Stan Kwan, offense and special teams asst.; born November 2, 1967, Phoenix, Ariz., lives in Rochester Hills, Mich. No college or pro playing experience. Pro coach: San Diego Chargers 1991-96, joined Lions in 1997.
John Misciagna, quality control-offense & administrative asst.; born December 11, 1954, Brooklyn, N.Y., lives in Auburn Hills, Mich. Guard Dickinson College 1973-76. No pro playing experience. College coach: Indiana (Pa.) University 1977, Columbia 1978-79, Maryland 1980-88, Georgia Tech 1989-91. Pro coach: San Diego Chargers 1992-96, joined Lions in 1997.
Gary Moeller, linebackers; born January 26, 1941, Lima, Ohio, lives in Ann Arbor, Mich. Center-linebacker Ohio State 1960-62. No pro playing experience. College coach: Miami (Ohio) 1967-68, Michigan 1969-76, 1980-94 (head coach 1990-94), Illinois 1977-79 (head coach). Pro coach: Cincinnati Bengals 1995-96, joined Lions in 1997.
Dennis Murphy, quality control-defense; born October 22, 1940, Endicott, N.Y., lives in Rochester, Mich. Tight end-defensive lineman Notre Dame 1959-61. No pro playing experience. College coach: Notre Dame 1968-74, Colgate 1975, Holy Cross 1976-77, Eastern Michigan 1978-81, Maryland 1982-91, Navy 1992-93. Pro coach: San Diego Chargers 1994-96, joined Lions in 1997.
Bob Palcic, tight ends; born July 2, 1948, Gowanda, N.Y., lives in Rochester, Mich. Linebacker Dayton 1968-70. No pro playing experience. College coach: Dayton 1974-75, Ball State 1976-77, Wisconsin 1978-81, Arizona 1984-85, Ohio State 1986-91, Southern California 1992, UCLA 1993. Pro coach: Atlanta Falcons 1994-96, joined Lions in 1997.
Larry Peccatiello, defensive coordinator; born December 21, 1937, Newark, N.J., lives in Rochester, Mich. Receiver William & Mary 1955-58. No pro playing experience. College coach: William & Mary 1961-68, Navy 1969-70, Rice 1971. Pro coach: Houston Oilers 1972-75, Seattle Seahawks 1976-80, Washington Redskins 1981-93, Cincinnati Bengals 1994-96, joined Lions in 1997.
Chuck Priefer, special teams; born July 26, 1944, Cleveland, Ohio, lives in Rochester Hills, Mich. No college or pro playing experience. College coach: Miami (Ohio) 1977, North Carolina 1978-83, Kent State 1986, Georgia Tech 1987-91. Pro coach: Green Bay Packers 1984-85, San Diego Chargers 1992-96, joined Lions in 1997.
Richard Selcer, defensive backs; born August 22, 1937, Cincinnati, Ohio, lives in Rochester, Mich. Running back Notre Dame 1955-58. No pro playing experience. College coach: Xavier 1962-64, 1970-71 (head coach), Cincinnati 1965-66, Brown 1967-69, Wisconsin 1972-74, Kansas State 1975-77, Southwestern Louisiana 1978-80. Pro coach: Houston Oilers 1981-83, Cincinnati Bengals 1984-91, Los Angeles-St. Louis Rams 1992-96, joined Lions in 1997.
Jerry Sullivan, wide receivers; born July 13, 1944, Miami, Fla., lives in Rochester Hills, Mich. Quarterback Florida State 1963-64. No pro playing experience. College coach: Kansas State 1971-72, Texas Tech 1973-75, South Carolina 1976-82, Indiana 1983, Louisiana State 1984-90, Ohio State 1991. Pro coach: San Diego Chargers 1992-96, joined Lions in 1997.
Jim Zorn, quarterbacks; born May 10, 1953, Whittier, Calif., lives in Bloomfield Hills, Mich. Quarterback Cal Poly Pomona 1973-75. Pro quarterback Seattle Seahawks 1976-84, Green Bay Packers 1985, Winnipeg Blue Bombers (CFL) 1986, Tampa Bay Buccaneers 1987. College coach: Boise State 1989-91, Utah State 1992-94, Minnesota 1995-96. Pro coach: Seattle Seahawks 1997, joined Lions in 1998.

1998 FIRST-YEAR ROSTER

Name	Pos.	Ht.	Wt.	Birthdate	College	Hometown	How Acq.
Alexander, Jamaal	S	5-11	200	9/18/76	Southern Mississippi	New Orleans, La.	D6
Atwell, Tutu	WR	5-8	168	12/11/76	Minnesota	Miami, Fla.	FA
Batch, Charlie	QB	6-2	216	12/5/74	Eastern Michigan	Homestead, Pa.	D2b
Beverly, Eric (1)	G	6-3	279	3/28/74	Miami, Ohio	Bedford Heights, Ohio	FA-'97
Blackman, Jon	TE	6-6	271	10/8/75	Purdue	Yorkville, Ill.	FA
Blaise, Kerlin	G	6-5	306	12/25/74	Miami	Orlando, Fla.	FA
Campbell, Lamar	S	5-11	182	8/29/76	Wisconsin	Chester, Pa.	FA
Coburn, Devon	C	6-3	290	8/19/75	Mississippi	Noxapater, Miss.	FA
Colquitt, Travis (1)	P	6-1	210	7/16/71	Marshall	Knoxville, Tenn.	FA
Crowell, Germane	WR	6-3	213	9/13/76	Virginia	Winston-Salem, N.C.	D2a
Davis, Jerome (1)	DE	6-4	275	3/4/74	Minnesota	Detroit, Mich.	FA-'97
Fair, Terry	CB	5-9	185	7/20/96	Tennessee	Phoenix, Ariz.	D1
Gholston, Kendrick	DE	6-4	269	4/30/75	Louisville	Chicago, Ill.	FA
Green, Clifford (1)	CB	5-8	185	4/15/75	Tennessee State	DeKalb, Ga.	FA
Hogg, Matt	G	6-5	306	12/27/74	Youngstown State	Grove City, Pa.	FA
Liwieniski, Chris	T	6-5	304	8/2/75	Indiana	Sterling Heights, Mich.	D7
Long, Octavis	WR	5-10	178	12/23/74	Michigan State	Lansing, Mich.	FA
Maddox, Deon (1)	WR	5-10	175	2/18/74	Syracuse	Tampa, Fla.	FA-'97
O'Neill, Kevin	LB	6-2	239	4/14/75	Bowling Green	Twinsburg, Ohio	FA
Reece, Travis	RB	6-3	252	4/3/75	Michigan State	Detroit, Mich.	FA
Rush, Clay	K	6-4	218	10/27/73	Missouri Western	Riverview Gardens, Mo.	FA
Settles, Tawambi	S	6-2	191	1/19/76	Duke	Chattanooga, Tenn.	FA
Sheahan, Kevin (1)	DT	6-1	286	6/19/75	Carroll College	Reno, Nev.	FA-'97
Supernaw, Kywin	S	6-1	206	6/2/75	Indiana	Claremore, Okla.	FA
Stuewe, Michael	WR	6-1	187	6/20/74	Virginia Tech	Somerset, N.J.	FA
Thomas, Corey	WR	6-0	164	6/6/75	Duke	Wilson, N.C.	FA
Thomas, Marvin (1)	DE	6-5	264	10/19/73	Memphis	Bay Minette, Ala.	FA-'97
Ward, Phillip (1)	LB	6-2	235	11/11/74	UCLA	Compton, Calif.	FA
Weems, Cyrill (1)	CB	6-2	207	8/1/74	Wisconsin	Detroit, Mich.	FA-'97
Whitehead, Willie (1)	DE	6-3	255	1/16/73	Auburn	Tuskegee, Ala.	FA

The term NFL Rookie is defined as a player who is in his first season of professional football and has not been on the roster of another professional football team for any regular-season or postseason games. A Rookie is designated by an "R" on NFL rosters. Players who have been active in another professional football league or players who have NFL experience, including either preseason training camp or being on an Active List or Inactive List, or on Reserve/Injured or Reserve/Physically Unable to Perform for fewer than six regular-season games, are termed NFL First-Year Players. An NFL First-Year Player is designated by a "1" on NFL rosters. Thereafter, a player is credited with an additional year of experience for each season in which he accumulates six games on the Active List or Inactive List, or on Reserve/Injured or Reserve/Physically Unable to Perform.

NOTES

GREEN BAY PACKERS

National Football Conference
Central Division
Team Colors: Dark Green, Gold, and White
1265 Lombardi Avenue
Green Bay, Wisconsin 54304
Telephone: (920) 496-5700

CLUB OFFICIALS

President, CEO: Bob Harlan
Vice President: John Fabry
Secretary: Peter Platten
Treasurer: John Underwood
Exec. V.P. and General Manager: Ron Wolf
Vice President-Administration/ Chief Financial Officer: Mike Reinfeldt
Exec. Assistant to the President: Phil Pionek
Assistant Vice President-General Counsel: Lance Lopes
Exec. Director of Public Relations: Lee Remmel
Director of Marketing: Jeff Cieply
Assistant Director of Public Relations: Jeff Blumb
Assistant Director of Public Relations/Travel Coordinator: Mark Schiefelbein
Public Relations Assistant: Aaron Popkey
Director of Family Programs/Player Speakers Bureau: Sherry Schuldes
Director of Player Personnel: Ted Thompson
Director of Pro Personnel: Reggie McKenzie
Pro Personnel Assistant: Will Lewis
Director of College Scouting: John Dorsey
College Scouts: Matt Boockmeier, Shaun Herock, Scot McCloughan, Johnny Meads, Sam Seale, Red Cochran
Scouting Coordinator: Danny Mock
Strength and Conditioning Assistant: Barry Rubin
Administrative Assistant-Football: Bill Nayes
Ticket Director: Mark Wagner
Accountants: Duke Copp, Vicki Vannieuwenhoven
Director of Computer Services: Wayne Wichlacz
Video Director: Al Treml
Head Trainer: Pepper Burruss
Equipment Manager: Gordon Batty
Corporate Security Officer: Jerry Parins
Stadium Supervisor: Ted Eisenreich
Fields Supervisor: Todd Edlebeck
Stadium: Lambeau Field •**Capacity:** 60,790
1265 Lombardi Avenue
Green Bay, Wisconsin 54304
Playing Surface: Grass
Training Camp: St. Norbert College
De Pere, Wisconsin 54115

1998 SCHEDULE

PRESEASON

Aug. 1	vs. Kansas City at Tokyo, Japan	9:15
Aug. 8	**New Orleans**	7:00
Aug. 16	**Oakland**	3:00
Aug. 24	at Denver	6:00
Aug. 28	at Miami	7:00

REGULAR SEASON

Sept. 6	**Detroit**	12:01
Sept. 13	**Tampa Bay**	12:01
Sept. 20	at Cincinnati	1:01
Sept. 27	at Carolina	1:01
Oct. 5	**Minnesota** (Mon.)	7:20
Oct. 11	Open Date	
Oct. 15	at Detroit (Thurs.)	8:20
Oct. 25	**Baltimore**	12:01
Nov. 1	**San Francisco**	3:15
Nov. 9	at Pittsburgh (Mon.)	8:20
Nov. 15	at New York Giants	4:15
Nov. 22	at Minnesota	12:01
Nov. 29	**Philadelphia**	3:15
Dec. 7	at Tampa Bay (Mon.)	8:20
Dec. 13	**Chicago**	12:01
Dec. 20	**Tennessee**	12:01
Dec. 27	at Chicago	12:01

RECORD HOLDERS

INDIVIDUAL RECORDS—CAREER

Category	Name	Performance
Rushing (Yds.)	Jim Taylor, 1958-1966	8,207
Passing (Yds.)	Bart Starr, 1956-1971	24,718
Passing (TDs)	Brett Favre, 1992-97	182
Receiving (No.)	Sterling Sharpe, 1988-1994	595
Receiving (Yds.)	James Lofton, 1978-1986	9,656
Interceptions	Bobby Dillon, 1952-59	52
Punting (Avg.)	Craig Hentrich, 1994-97	42.8
Punt Return (Avg.)	Desmond Howard, 1996	15.1
Kickoff Return (Avg.)	Travis Williams, 1967-1970	26.7
Field Goals	Chris Jacke, 1989-1996	173
Touchdowns (Tot.)	Don Hutson, 1935-1945	105
Points	Don Hutson, 1935-1945	823

INDIVIDUAL RECORDS—SINGLE SEASON

Category	Name	Performance
Rushing (Yds.)	Jim Taylor, 1962	1,474
Passing (Yds.)	Lynn Dickey, 1983	4,458
Passing (TDs)	Brett Favre, 1996	39
Receiving (No.)	Sterling Sharpe, 1993	112
Receiving (Yds.)	Robert Brooks, 1995	1,497
Interceptions	Irv Comp, 1943	10
Punting (Avg.)	Craig Hentrich, 1997	45.0
Punt Return (Avg.)	Billy Grimes, 1950	19.1
Kickoff Return (Avg.)	Travis Williams, 1967	*41.1
Field Goals	Chester Marcol, 1972	33
Touchdowns (Tot.)	Jim Taylor, 1962	19
Points	Paul Hornung, 1960	*176

INDIVIDUAL RECORDS—SINGLE GAME

Category	Name	Performance
Rushing (Yds.)	Dorsey Levens, 11-23-97	190
Passing (Yds.)	Lynn Dickey, 10-12-80	418
Passing (TDs)	Many times. Last time by Brett Favre, 9-21-97	5
Receiving (No.)	Don Hutson, 11-22-42	14
Receiving (Yds.)	Bill Howton, 10-21-56	257
Interceptions	Bobby Dillon, 11-26-53	*4
	Willie Buchanon, 9-24-78	*4
Field Goals	Chris Jacke, 11-11-90, 10-14-96	5
Touchdowns (Tot.)	Paul Hornung, 12-12-65	5
Points	Paul Hornung, 10-8-61	33

*NFL Record

COACHING HISTORY

(562-449-36)

1921-49	Earl (Curly) Lambeau	212-106-21
1950-53	Gene Ronzani*	14-31-1
1953	Hugh Devore-Ray (Scooter) McLean**	0-2-0
1954-57	Lisle Blackbourn	17-31-0
1958	Ray (Scooter) McLean	1-10-1
1959-67	Vince Lombardi	98-30-4
1968-70	Phil Bengtson	20-21-1
1971-74	Dan Devine	25-28-4
1975-83	Bart Starr	53-77-3
1984-87	Forrest Gregg	25-37-1
1988-91	Lindy Infante	24-40-0
1992-97	Mike Holmgren	73-36-0

*Resigned after 10 games in 1953
**Co-coaches

LAMBEAU FIELD

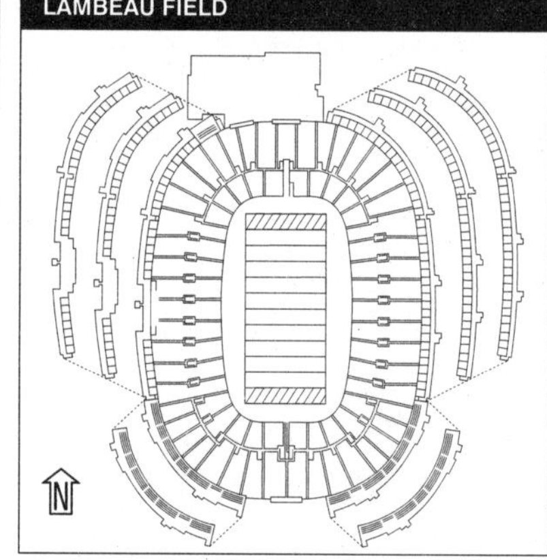

1997 TEAM RECORD

PRESEASON (5-0)

Date	Result		Opponent
7/26	W	20-0	Miami
7/31	W	7-3	New England
8/8	W	37-24	at Oakland
8/16	W	35-3	vs. Buffalo at Toronto, Canada
8/22	W	22-17	vs. N.Y. Giants at Madison, Wis.

REGULAR SEASON (13-3)

Date	Result		Opponent	Att.
9/1	W	38-24	Chicago	60,766
9/7	L	9-10	at Philadelphia	66,803
9/14	W	23-18	Miami	60,075
9/21	W	38-32	Minnesota	60,115
9/28	L	15-26	at Detroit	78,110
10/5	W	21-16	Tampa Bay	60,100
10/12	W	24-23	at Chicago	62,212
10/27	W	28-10	at New England	59,972
11/2	W	20-10	Detroit	60,126
11/9	W	17-7	St. Louis	60,093
11/16	L	38-41	at Indianapolis	60,928
11/23	W	45-17	Dallas	60,111
12/1	W	27-11	at Minnesota	64,001
12/7	W	17-6	at Tampa Bay	73,523
12/14	W	31-10	at Carolina	70,887
12/20	W	31-21	Buffalo	60,108

POSTSEASON (2-1)

Date	Result		Opponent	Att.
1/4	W	21-7	Tampa Bay	60,327
1/11	W	23-10	at San Francisco	68,987
1/25	L	24-31	vs. Denver	68,912

SCORE BY PERIODS

Packers	82	151	87	102	—	422
Opponents	48	78	56	100	—	282

ATTENDANCE

Home 481,494 Away 536,436 Total 1,017,930
Single-game home record, 60,766 (9/1/97)
Single-season home record, 482,988 (1996)

1997 TEAM STATISTICS

	Packers	Opp.
Total First Downs	325	288
Rushing	103	105
Passing	191	156
Penalty	31	27
Third Down: Made/Att	80/202	77/232
Third Down Pct.	39.6	33.2
Fourth Down: Made/Att	5/5	12/24
Fourth Down Pct.	100.0	50.0
Total Net Yards	5,614	4,827
Avg. Per Game	350.9	301.7
Total Plays	1,008	1,047
Avg. Per Play	5.6	4.6
Net Yards Rushing	1,909	1,876
Avg. Per Game	119.3	117.3
Total Rushes	459	443
Net Yards Passing	3,705	2,951
Avg. Per Game	231.6	184.4
Sacked/Yards Lost	26/191	41/274
Gross Yards	3,896	3,225
Att./Completions	523/309	563/288
Completion Pct.	59.1	51.2
Had Intercepted	16	21
Punts/Avg.	75/45.0	90/42.5
Net Punting Avg.	75/36.0	90/36.6
Penalties/Yards Lost.	93/718	114/945
Fumbles/Ball Lost	24/16	25/11
Touchdowns	50	30
Rushing	9	16
Passing	35	10
Returns	6	4
Avg. Time of Possession	30:05	29:55

1997 INDIVIDUAL STATISTICS

Passing	Att.	Comp.	Yds.	Pct.	TD	Int.	Tkld.	Rate
Favre	513	304	3,867	59.3	35	16	25/176	92.6
Bono	10	5	29	50.0	0	0	1/15	56.3
Packers	523	309	3,896	59.1	35	16	26/191	91.9
Opponents	563	288	3,225	51.2	10	21	41/274	59.0

SCORING	TD R	TD P	TD Rt	PAT	FG	Saf	PTS
Longwell	0	0	0	48/48	24/30	0	120
Levens	7	5	0	0/0	0/0	0	74
Freeman	0	12	0	0/0	0/0	0	72
R. Brooks	0	7	0	0/0	0/0	0	42
Chmura	0	6	0	0/0	0/0	0	36
Sharper	0	0	3	0/0	0/0	0	18
T. Davis	0	1	1	0/0	0/0	0	12
Wilkins	0	0	2	0/0	0/0	0	12
Favre	1	0	0	0/0	0/0	0	6
Hayden	1	0	0	0/0	0/0	0	6
Henderson	0	1	0	0/0	0/0	0	6
Mickens	0	1	0	0/0	0/0	0	6
Schroeder	0	1	0	0/0	0/0	0	6
Thomason	0	1	0	0/0	0/0	0	6
Packers	9	35	6	48/48	24/30	0	422
Opponents	16	10	4	18/18	24/30	0	282

2-Point conversions: Levens.
Team 1-2, Opponents 6-12.

RUSHING	Att.	Yds.	Avg.	LG	TD
Levens	329	1,435	4.4	52t	7
Favre	58	187	3.2	16	1
Hayden	32	148	4.6	21	1
Henderson	31	113	3.6	15	0
R. Brooks	2	19	9.5	15	0
Freeman	1	14	14.0	14	0
Bono	3	-3	-1.0	-1	0
Pederson	3	-4	-1.3	-1	0
Packers	459	1,909	4.2	52t	9
Opponents	443	1,876	4.2	68t	16

RECEIVING	No.	Yds.	Avg.	LG	TD
Freeman	81	1,243	15.3	58t	12
R. Brooks	60	1,010	16.8	48	7
Levens	53	370	7.0	56	5
Henderson	41	367	9.0	25	1
Chmura	38	417	11.0	32t	6
Mayes	18	290	16.1	74	0
Thomason	9	115	12.8	27	1
Beebe	2	28	14.0	23	0
T. Davis	2	28	14.0	26	1
Schroeder	2	15	7.5	8	1
Hayden	2	11	5.5	7	0
Mickens	1	2	2.0	2t	1
Packers	309	3,896	12.6	74	35
Opponents	288	3,225	11.2	62	10

INTERCEPTIONS	No.	Yds.	Avg.	LG	TD
Butler	5	4	0.8	2	0
Prior	4	72	18.0	49	0
Evans	3	33	11.0	27	0
Sharper	2	70	35.0	50t	2
B. Williams	2	30	15.0	25	0
Wilkins	1	77	77.0	77t	1
Robinson	1	26	26.0	26	0
Mullen	1	17	17.0	17	0
Harris	1	0	0.0	0	0
T. Williams	1	0	0.0	0	0
Packers	21	329	15.7	77t	3
Opponents	16	305	19.1	52t	3

PUNTING	No.	Yds.	Avg.	In 20	LG
Hentrich	75	3,378	45.0	26	65
Packers	75	3,378	45.0	26	65
Opponents	90	3,828	42.5	29	59

PUNT RETURNS	No.	FC	Yds.	Avg.	LG	TD
Schroeder	33	8	342	10.4	46	0
Mayes	14	3	141	10.1	26	0
Sharper	7	3	32	4.6	23	0
Preston	1	0	0	0.0	0	0
Prior	1	3	0	0.0	0	0
Packers	56	17	515	9.2	46	0
Opponents	32	15	255	8.0	38	0

KICKOFF RETURNS	No.	Yds.	Avg.	LG	TD
Schroeder	24	562	23.4	40	0
Preston	7	211	30.1	43	0
Beebe	6	134	22.3	39	0
Hayden	6	141	23.5	35	0
Darkins	4	68	17.0	20	0
Mickens	1	0	0.0	0	0
Sharper	1	3	3.0	3	0
Packers	49	1,119	22.8	43	0
Opponents	78	1,599	20.5	49	0

FIELD GOALS	1-19	20-29	30-39	40-49	50+
Longwell	4/4	7/8	10/13	2/4	1/1
Packers	4/4	7/8	10/13	2/4	1/1
Opponents	0/0	7/8	8/10	8/11	1/1

SACKS	No.
White	11.0
S. Dotson	5.5
Wilkins	5.5
Brown	3.0
Butler	3.0
Joyner	3.0
Robinson	2.5
McKenzie	1.5
Evans	1.0
Harris	1.0
Smith	1.0
B. Williams	1.0
Packers	41.0
Opponents	26.0

1998 DRAFT CHOICES

Round	Name	Pos.	College
1	Vonnie Holliday	DT	North Carolina
3	Jonathan Brown	DE	Tennessee
4	Roosevelt Blackmon	DB	Morris Brown
5	Corey Bradford	WR	Jackson State
6	Scott McGarrahan	DB	New Mexico
	Matt Hasselbeck	QB	Boston College
7	Edwin Watson	RB	Purdue

GREEN BAY PACKERS

1998 VETERAN ROSTER

No.		Name	Pos.	Ht.	Wt.	Birthdate	NFL Exp.	College	Hometown	How Acq.	'97 Games/ Starts
70		Andruzzi, Joe	G	6-3	313	8/23/75	2	Southern Connecticut State	Staten Island, N.Y.	FA-'97	0*
96	t-	Booker, Vaughn	DE	6-5	295	2/24/68	S	Cincinnati	Cincinnati, Ohio	T(KC)-'98	13/13*
87		Brooks, Robert	WR	6-0	180	6/23/70	7	South Carolina	Greenwood, S.C.	D3-'92	15/15
93		Brown, Gilbert	DT	6-2	345	2/22/71	6	Kansas	Detroit, Mich.	W(Minn)-'93	12/12
68		Bryant, Keif	DT	6-4	285	3/12/73	2	Rutgers	Largo, Fla.	FA-'98	0*
36		Butler, LeRoy	S	6-0	200	7/19/68	9	Florida State	Jacksonville, Fla.	D2-'90	16/16
89		Chmura, Mark	TE	6-5	253	2/22/69	7	Boston College	South Deerfield, Mass.	D6-'92	15/14
10		Conway, Brett	K	6-2	192	3/8/75	2	Penn State	Lilburn, Ga.	D3-'97	0*
75		Curry, Eric	DE	6-6	275	2/3/70	6	Alabama	Thomasville, Ga.	UFA(TB)-'98	6/1*
44		Darkins, Chris	RB	6-0	210	4/30/74	3	Minnesota	Houston, Tex.	D4-'96	14/0
60		Davis, Rob	LS	6-3	288	12/10/68	3	Shippensburg	Greenbelt, Md.	FA-'97	7/0
81		Davis, Tyrone	TE	6-4	245	6/30/72	3	Virginia	Halifax, Va.	FA-'97	13/0
67	#	Dellenbach, Jeff	C-G	6-6	300	2/14/63	13	Wisconsin	Wausau, Wis.	FA-'96	14/5
46		DeRamus, Lee	WR	6-1	205	8/24/72	3	Wisconsin	Tansboro, N.J.	FA-'98	0*
72		Dotson, Earl	T	6-4	315	12/17/70	6	Texas A&I	Beaumont, Tex.	D3-'93	13/13
71		Dotson, Santana	DT	6-5	285	12/19/69	7	Baylor	Houston, Tex.	UFA(TB)-'96	16/16
4		Favre, Brett	QB	6-2	225	10/10/69	8	Southern Mississippi	Kiln, Miss.	T(Atl)-'92	16/16
58		Flanagan, Mike	C	6-5	290	11/10/73	3	UCLA	Sacramento, Calif.	D3a-'96	0*
97		Frase, Paul	DE	6-5	267	5/6/65	10	Syracuse	Rochester, N.H.	T(Jax)-'97	9/0
86	†	Freeman, Antonio	WR	6-1	194	5/27/72	4	Virginia Tech	Baltimore, Md.	D3d-'95	16/16
55		Harris, Bernardo	LB	6-2	247	10/15/71	4	North Carolina	Chapel Hill, N.C.	FA-'95	16/16
24	†	Hayden, Aaron	RB	6-0	216	4/13/73	4	Tennessee	Detroit, Mich.	W(SD)-'97	14/0
33	†	Henderson, William	RB	6-1	249	2/19/71	4	North Carolina	Chester, Va.	D3b-'95	16/14
50		Hicks, Anthony	LB	6-1	242	3/31/74	2	Arkansas	Arkadelphia, Ark.	D5-'97	0*
56		Hollinquest, Lamont	LB	6-3	250	10/24/70	5	Southern California	Downey, Calif.	FA-'96	16/0
32	†	Jervey, Travis	RB	6-0	222	5/5/72	4	Citadel	Mt. Pleasant, S.C.	D5b-'95	16/0
54		Joyner, Seth	LB	6-2	245	11/18/64	13	Texas-El Paso	Spring Valley, N.Y.	FA-'97	11/10
53		Koonce, George	LB	6-1	243	10/15/68	7	East Carolina	Vanceboro, N.C.	FA-'92	4/0
94		Kuberski, Bob	DT	6-4	295	4/5/71	4	Navy	Folsom, Pa.	D7-'93	11/3
7		Landeta, Sean	P	6-0	215	1/6/62	14	Towson State	Towson, Md.	UFA(TB)-'98	10/0*
25		Levens, Dorsey	RB	6-1	230	5/21/70	5	Georgia Tech	Syracuse, N.Y.	D5b-'94	16/16
57		London, Antonio	LB	6-2	240	4/14/71	6	Alabama	Tullahoma, Tenn.	FA-'98	16/6*
8		Longwell, Ryan	K	6-0	185	8/16/74	2	California	Bend, Ore.	W(SF)-'97	16/0
80		Mayes, Derrick	WR	6-0	205	1/28/74	3	Notre Dame	Indianapolis, Ind.	D2-'96	12/3
95		McKenzie, Keith	DE	6-3	265	10/17/73	3	Ball State	Highland Park, Mich.	D7b-'96	16/0
77		Michels, John	T	6-7	304	3/19/73	3	Southern California	La Jolla, Calif.	D1-'96	9/5
30	t-	Milburn, Glyn	RB-KR	5-8	170	2/19/71	6	Stanford	Santa Monica, Calif.	T(Det)-'98	16/1*
28		Mullen, Roderick	CB-S	6-1	204	12/5/72	4	Grambling State	St. Francisville, La.	FA-'95	16/1
21		Newsome, Craig	CB	6-0	190	8/10/71	4	Arizona State	Rialto, Calif.	D1-'95	1/1
73		Nottage, Dexter	DE	6-4	280	11/14/70	4	Florida A&M	Hollywood, Fla.	FA-'98	1/0*
18		Pederson, Doug	QB	6-3	216	1/31/68	6	Northeast Louisiana	Ferndale, Wash.	FA-'95	1/0
49		Preston, Roell	WR-KR	5-10	185	6/23/72	3	Mississippi	Hialeah, Fla.	FA-'97	1/0
39		Prior, Mike	S	6-0	208	11/14/63	13	Illinois State	Chicago Heights, Ill.	FA-'98	16/0
62		Rivera, Marco	G	6-4	295	4/26/72	3	Penn State	Elmont, N.Y.	D6-'96	14/0
84		Schroeder, Bill	WR	6-2	200	1/9/71	3	Wisconsin-La Crosse	Sheboygan, Wis.	FA-'97	15/1
42		Sharper, Darren	S	6-2	205	11/3/75	2	William & Mary	Richmond, Va.	D2-'97	14/0
99		Smith, Jermaine	DT	6-3	289	2/3/72	2	Georgia	Augusta, Ga.	D4-'97	9/0
40		Terrell, Pat	S	6-1	210	3/18/68	9	Notre Dame	Lakewood, Fla.	UFA(Car)-'98	16/5*
83		Thomason, Jeff	TE	6-5	250	12/30/69	6	Oregon	Newport Beach, Calif.	FA-'95	13/1
63		Timmerman, Adam	G	6-4	295	8/14/71	4	South Dakota State	Cherokee, Iowa	D7-'95	16/16
78		Verba, Ross	T	6-4	299	10/31/73	2	Iowa	West Des Moines, Iowa	D1-'97	16/11
92		White, Reggie	DE	6-5	304	12/19/61	14	Tennessee	Chattanooga, Tenn.	UFA(Phil)-'93	16/16
74		Widell, Doug	G	6-4	285	9/23/66	10	Boston College	Hartford, Conn.	FA-'98	16/16*
64		Wilkerson, Bruce	T	6-5	310	7/28/64	12	Tennessee	Loudon, Tenn.	FA-'96	16/3
51		Williams, Brian	LB	6-1	240	12/17/72	4	Southern California	Dallas, Tex.	D3c-'95	16/16
37		Williams, Tyrone	CB	5-11	195	5/31/73	3	Nebraska	Bradenton, Fla.	D3b-'96	16/15
76		Willig, Matt	T	6-7	315	1/21/69	6	Southern California	Santa Fe Springs, Calif.	UFA(Atl)-'98	16/13*
52		Winters, Frank	C	6-3	300	1/23/64	12	Western Illinois	Union City, N.J.	PB(KC)-'92	13/13

* Andruzzi was inactive for 16 games; Booker played 13 games with Kansas City in '97; Bryant last active with Seattle in '96; Conway, Flanagan, and Hicks missed the '97 season because of injury; Curry played 6 games for Tampa Bay in '97; DeRamus last active with New Orleans in '96; Landeta played 10 games with Tampa Bay; London and Milburn played 16 games with Detroit; Nottage played 1 game with Kansas City; Terrell played 16 games with Carolina; Widell played 16 games with Indianapolis; Willig played 12 games with Atlanta.

Unrestricted free agent; subject to developments.

† Restricted free agent; subject to developments.

Traded—QB Steve Bono (2 games in '97) to St. Louis; DT Darius Holland (12 games) to Kansas City.

t- Packers traded for Booker (Kansas City) and Milburn (Detroit).

Players lost through free agency (8): RB Edgar Bennett (Chi; 0 games in '97), CB Mark Collins (Sea; 1), CB Doug Evans (Car; 15), P Craig Hentrich (Tenn; 16), WR Terry Mickens (Oak; 11), S Eugene Robinson (Atl; 16), G Aaron Taylor (SD; 14), DE Gabe Wilkins (SF; 16).

Also played with Packers in '97—WR Don Beebe (10 games), CB Bucky Brooks (3), DE Shannon Clavelle (6), TE Reggie Johnson (4), CB Randy Kinder (6), S Blaine McElmurry (1), LB Wayne Simmons (6), DE Gerald Williams (4).

COACHING STAFF

Head Coach,
Mike Holmgren

Pro Career: Became Packers' eleventh head coach on January 11, 1992. Since that time, he has directed Green Bay to its first NFL championship in 29 years, six consecutive winning seasons, five straight playoff berths for the first time in club history, three consecutive NFC Central titles (the first since 1972), and three straight appearances in the NFC Championship Game. In 1996, he brought the Packers their league-high twelfth NFL championship with a 35-21 victory over the New England Patriots in Super Bowl XXXI. En route, Green Bay won more games (16) than any other team in the organization's history and captured a second consecutive division crown with a 13-3 regular-season record, including a perfect 8-0 mark at home (10-0 counting playoffs). In 1997, Holmgren directed his club to another 13-3 mark, a third straight division title, and a second consecutive appearance in the Super Bowl. In the process, his team went unbeaten at Lambeau Field for the second straight year, stretching its regular-season home winning streak to a club-record 23 games, just four games shy of the Miami Dolphins' all-time league mark of 27 (1971-74). His previous Packer teams went 9-7, 9-7, and 9-7 from 1992-94 and 11-5 in 1995. Holmgren was offensive coordinator for the San Francisco 49ers under George Seifert (1989-91) after spending the three previous seasons (1986-88) as quarterbacks coach under Bill Walsh. During his six-year tenure with San Francisco, the 49ers won five consecutive NFC Western Division championships (1986-1990) and back-to-back Super Bowls (XXIII and XXIV). The 49ers never ranked lower than third overall in his three years as offensive coordinator. Career record: 73-36.

Background: Quarterback at Southern California (1966-69) and was drafted by the St. Louis Cardinals in the eighth round of the 1970 NFL draft. He served as an assistant coach at San Francisco State (1981) and Brigham Young (1982-85) before his tenure with the 49ers. Earned his bachelor of science degree in business finance at Southern California (1970).

Personal: Born June 15, 1948, in San Francisco. He and his wife, Kathy, live in De Pere, Wis. and have four daughters—Calla, Jenny, Emily, and Gretchen.

ASSISTANT COACHES

Larry Brooks, defensive line; born June 10, 1950, Prince George, Va., lives in De Pere, Wis. Defensive lineman Virginia State 1968-71. Pro defensive tackle Los Angeles Rams 1972-82. College coach: Virginia State 1992-93. Pro coach: Los Angeles Rams 1983-90, joined Packers in 1994.

Nolan Cromwell, wide receivers; born January 30, 1955, Smith Center, Kan., lives in Green Bay. Quarterback-safety Kansas 1973-76. Pro defensive back Los Angeles Rams 1977-87. Pro coach: Los Angeles Rams 1991, joined Packers in 1992.

Ken Flajole, defensive assistant-quality control; born October 4, 1954, Seattle, lives in Green Bay. Linebacker Wenatchee (Wash.) Valley C.C. 1973-74, Pacific Lutheran 1975-76. No pro playing experience. College coach: Pacific Lutheran 1977-78, Washington 1979, Montana 1980-85, Texas-El Paso 1986-88, Missouri 1989-93, Richmond 1994, Hawaii 1995, Nevada 1996-97. Pro coach: Joined Packers in 1998.

Johnny Holland, special teams; born March 11, 1965, Belleville, Tex., lives in Green Bay. Linebacker Texas A&M 1983-86. Pro linebacker Green Bay Packers 1987-1993. Pro coach: Joined Packers in 1995.

Kent Johnston, strength and conditioning; born February 21, 1956, Mexia, Tex., lives in Green Bay. Defensive back Stephen F. Austin 1974-77. No pro playing experience. College coach: Northwestern State (Louisiana) 1979, Northeast Louisiana 1980-81, Alabama 1983-86. Pro coach: Tampa Bay Buccaneers 1987-91, joined Packers in 1992.

Sherman Lewis, offensive coordinator; born June 29, 1942, Louisville, Ky., lives in Green Bay. Running back Michigan State 1960-63. Pro running back Toronto Argonauts (CFL) 1964-65, New York Jets 1966. College coach: Michigan State 1969-82. Pro coach: San Francisco 49ers 1983-91, joined Packers in 1992.

Jim Lind, linebackers; born November 11, 1947, Isle, Minn., lives in Green Bay. Linebacker Bethel College 1965-66; defensive back Bemidji State 1971-72. No pro playing experience. College coach: St. Cloud State 1977-78, St. John's (Minn.) 1979-80, Brigham Young 1981-82, Minnesota-Morris 1983-86 (head coach), Wisconsin-Eau Claire 1987-91 (head coach). Pro coach: Joined Packers in 1992.

Tom Lovat, offensive line; born December 28, 1938, Bingham, Utah, lives in Green Bay. Guard-linebacker Utah 1958-60. No pro playing experience. College coach: Utah 1967, 1972-76 (head coach 1974-76), Idaho State 1968-70, Stanford 1977-79, Wyoming 1989. Pro coach: Saskatchewan Roughriders (CFL) 1971, Green Bay Packers 1980, St. Louis-Phoenix Cardinals 1981-84, 1990-91, Indianapolis Colts 1985-88, rejoined Packers in 1992.

Andy Reid, quarterbacks; born March 19, 1958, Los Angeles, lives in Green Bay. Offensive tackle-guard Brigham Young 1978-80. No pro playing experience. College coach: Brigham Young 1982, San Francisco State 1983-85, Northern Arizona 1986, Texas-El Paso 1987, Missouri 1988-91. Pro coach: Joined Packers in 1992.

Gary Reynolds, offensive assistant-quality control; born October 15, 1966, Boston, lives in Green Bay. No college or pro playing experience. College coach Texas A&M 1991, Tennessee 1992. Pro coach: Joined Packers in 1993.

Mike Sherman, tight ends-assistant offensive line; born December 19, 1954, Norwood, Mass., lives in Green Bay. Linebacker-offensive guard-tackle Central Connecticut State 1974, 1976-77. No pro playing experience. College coach: Pittsburgh 1981-82, Tulane 1983-84, Holy Cross 1985-88, Texas A&M 1989-93, 1995-96, UCLA 1994. Pro coach: Joined Packers in 1997.

Fritz Shurmur, defensive coordinator; born July 15, 1932, Riverview, Mich., lives in Suamico, Wis. Center-linebacker Albion 1950-53. No pro playing experience. College coach: Albion 1954-61, Wyoming 1962-74 (head coach 1971-74). Pro coach: Detroit Lions 1975-77, New England Patriots 1978-81, Los Angeles Rams 1982-90, Phoenix Cardinals 1991-93, joined Packers in 1994.

Harry Sydney, running backs; born June 26, 1959, Petersburg, Va., lives in Green Bay. Quarterback-running back Kansas 1978-81. Pro running back Denver Gold (USFL) 1983-84, Memphis Showboats (USFL) 1985, Montreal Alouettes (CFL) 1986, San Francisco 49ers 1987-91, Green Bay Packers 1992. Pro coach: Joined Packers in 1994.

Bob Valesente, defensive backs; born July 19, 1940, Seneca Falls, N.Y., lives in Green Bay. Running back-defensive back Ithaca College 1958-61. No pro playing experience. College coach: Cornell 1964-74, Cincinnati 1975-76, Arizona 1977-79, Mississippi State 1980-81, Kansas 1984-87 (head coach 1986-87), Maryland 1988, Pittsburgh 1989. Pro coach: Baltimore Colts 1982-83, Pittsburgh Steelers 1990-91, joined Packers in 1992.

1998 FIRST-YEAR ROSTER

Name	Pos.	Ht.	Wt.	Birthdate	College	Hometown	How Acq.
Anderson, Ronnie (1)	WR	6-1	195	2/27/74	Allegheny College	Hunting Valley, Ohio	FA-'97
Benton, Magic	WR	6-0	182	1/10/76	Miami	Miami, Fla.	FA
Blackmon, Roosevelt	CB	6-1	180	9/10/74	Morris Brown	Belle Glade, Fla.	D4
Blair, Michael (1)	RB	5-11	245	11/26/74	Ball State	South Holland, Ill.	FA
Bowman, Mike	WR	6-1	198	9/16/74	Valdosta State	Interlachen, Fla.	FA
Bradford, Corey	WR	6-1	200	12/8/75	Jackson State	Clinton, La.	D5
Brown, Jonathan	DE	6-4	270	11/28/75	Tennessee	Tulsa, Okla.	D3
Cromartie, Keaton	LB	6-2	238	4/19/76	Tulane	Bradenton, Fla.	FA
Davis, Jason	P	6-0	219	1/24/75	Oklahoma State	Kerrville, Tex.	FA
Farley, Terrell	CB-S	6-0	195	8/16/75	Nebraska	Columbus, Ga.	FA
Fogle, Anthony (1)	CB	6-0	195	2/23/75	Oklahoma	Houston, Tex.	FA
Hasselbeck, Matt	QB	6-4	219	9/25/75	Boston College	Norfolk, Mass.	D6b
Hoelscher, David	DE	6-6	281	11/27/75	Eastern Kentucky	Versailles, Ohio	FA
Hogue, Chris	P	6-1	204	1/29/75	Tennessee	Memphis, Tenn.	FA
Holliday, Vonnie	DT	6-5	300	12/11/75	North Carolina	Camden, S.C.	D1
Kaczenski, Rick	C	6-4	280	2/15/75	Notre Dame	Erie, Pa.	FA
Lyon, Billy (1)	DE	6-5	295	12/10/73	Marshall	Erlanger, Ky.	FA
McAda, Ronnie (1)	QB	6-3	205	12/6/73	Army	Mesquite, Tex.	D7c-'97
McElmurry, Blaine (1)	S	6-0	188	10/23/73	Montana	Troy, Mont.	FA-'97
McGarrahan, Scott	S	6-1	200	2/12/74	New Mexico	Arlington, Tex.	D6a
McKinney, Anthony (1)	RB	6-2	250	12/8/74	Connecticut	Fairfield, Conn.	FA
Perkins, Delonte	WR	5-11	206	4/5/76	Robert Morris	Cleveland, Ohio	FA
Smith, Emory (1)	RB	6-0	245	5/21/74	Clemson	Pensacola, Fla.	FA
Wachholtz, Kyle (1)	TE	6-4	237	5/17/72	Southern California	Norco, Calif.	FA
Waddy, Jude	LB	6-2	217	9/12/75	William & Mary	Suitland, Md.	FA
Watson, Edwin	RB	6-0	229	9/29/76	Purdue	Pontiac, Mich.	D7
Welsh, Andrew	G	6-6	298	11/17/74	Colorado	Concord, Calif.	FA

The term NFL Rookie is defined as a player who is in his first season of professional football and has not been on the roster of another professional football team for any regular-season or postseason games. A Rookie is designated by an "R" on NFL rosters. Players who have been active in another professional football league or players who have NFL experience, including either preseason training camp or being on an Active List or Inactive List, or on Reserve/Injured or Reserve/Physically Unable to Perform for fewer than six regular-season games, are termed NFL First-Year Players. An NFL First-Year Player is designated by a "1" on NFL rosters. Thereafter, a player is credited with an additional year of experience for each season in which he accumulates six games on the Active List or Inactive List, or on Reserve/Injured or Reserve/Physically Unable to Perform.

NOTES

MINNESOTA VIKINGS

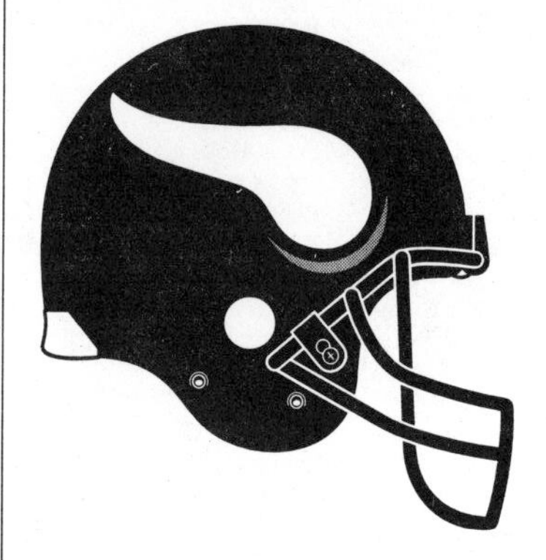

National Football Conference
Central Division
Team Colors: Purple, Gold, and White
9520 Viking Drive
Eden Prairie, Minnesota 55344
Telephone: (612) 828-6500

CLUB OFFICERS

Chairman of the Board: John C. Skoglund
Vice Chairmen: Jaye F. Dyer, Philip S. Maas
Directors: James Binger, N. Bud Grossman, Roger L. Headrick, James R. Jundt, Elizabeth MacMillan, Carol S. Sperry, Wheelock Whitney

CLUB OFFICIALS

President/CEO: Roger L. Headrick
Vice President Administration/Team Operations: Jeff Diamond
Vice President Player Personnel: Frank Gilliam
Vice President of Marketing and Business Development: Stew Widdess
Assistant General Manager/National Scouting: Jerry Reichow
Assistant General Manager/Pro Personnel: Paul Wiggin
Director of Finance: Nick Valentine
Director of Research and Development: Mike Eayrs
Director of Sales: Kernal Buhler
Director of Public Relations: TBA
Director of Team Operations: Breck Spinner
Ticket Manager: Gina Dillon
Director of Security: Steve Rollins
Player Personnel Coordinator: Scott Studwell
Equipment Manager: Dennis Ryan
Trainer: Fred Zamberletti
Video Director: Larry Kohout
Stadium: Hubert H. Humphrey Metrodome
•**Capacity:** 64,182
500 11th Avenue South
Minneapolis, Minnesota 55415
Playing Surface: AstroTurf
Training Camp: Mankato State University
Mankato, Minnesota 56001

1998 SCHEDULE

PRESEASON

Aug. 9	at New England	7:30
Aug. 15	**Kansas City**	7:00
Aug. 22	at Carolina	7:30
Aug. 28	**San Diego**	7:00

REGULAR SEASON

Sept. 6	**Tampa Bay**	12:01
Sept. 13	at St. Louis	12:01
Sept. 20	**Detroit**	12:01
Sept. 27	at Chicago	3:15
Oct. 5	at Green Bay (Mon.)	7:20
Oct. 11	Open Date	
Oct. 18	**Washington**	12:01
Oct. 25	at Detroit	1:01
Nov. 1	at Tampa Bay	1:01
Nov. 8	**New Orleans**	12:01
Nov. 15	**Cincinnati**	12:01
Nov. 22	**Green Bay**	12:01
Nov. 26	at Dallas (Thurs.)	3:05
Dec. 6	**Chicago**	7:20
Dec. 13	at Baltimore	4:15
Dec. 20	**Jacksonville**	7:20
Dec. 26	at Tennessee (Sat.)	11:35 A.M.

RECORD HOLDERS

INDIVIDUAL RECORDS—CAREER

Category	Name	Performance
Rushing (Yds.)	Chuck Foreman, 1973-79	5,879
Passing (Yds.)	Fran Tarkenton, 1961-66, 1972-78	33,098
Passing (TDs)	Fran Tarkenton, 1961-66, 1972-78	239
Receiving (No.)	Cris Carter, 1990-97	667
Receiving (Yds.)	Cris Carter, 1990-97	7,986
Interceptions	Paul Krause, 1968-1979	53
Punting (Avg.)	Harry Newsome, 1990-93	43.8
Punt Return (Avg.)	David Palmer, 1994-97	10.7
Kickoff Return (Avg.)	Charlie West, 1968-1973	25.5
Field Goals	Fred Cox, 1963-1977	282
Touchdowns (Tot.)	Bill Brown, 1962-1974	76
Points	Fred Cox, 1963-1977	1,365

INDIVIDUAL RECORDS—SINGLE SEASON

Category	Name	Performance
Rushing (Yds.)	Robert Smith, 1997	1,266
Passing (Yds.)	Warren Moon, 1994	4,264
Passing (TDs)	Warren Moon, 1995	33
Receiving (No.)	Cris Carter, 1994, 1995	122
Receiving (Yds.)	Cris Carter, 1995	1,371
Interceptions	Paul Krause, 1975	10
Punting (Avg.)	Bobby Walden, 1964	46.4
Punt Return (Avg.)	David Palmer, 1995	13.2
Kickoff Return (Avg.)	John Gilliam, 1972	26.3
Field Goals	Fuad Reveiz, 1994	34
Touchdowns (Tot.)	Chuck Foreman, 1975	22
Points	Chuck Foreman, 1975	132
	Fuad Reveiz, 1994	132

INDIVIDUAL RECORDS—SINGLE GAME

Category	Name	Performance
Rushing (Yds.)	Chuck Foreman, 10-24-76	200
Passing (Yds.)	Tommy Kramer, 11-2-86	490
Passing (TDs)	Joe Kapp, 9-28-69	*7
Receiving (No.)	Rickey Young, 12-16-79	15
Receiving (Yds.)	Sammy White, 11-7-76	210
Interceptions	Many times	3
	Last time by Jack Del Rio, 12-5-93	
Field Goals	Rich Karlis, 11-5-89	*7
Touchdowns (Tot.)	Chuck Foreman, 12-20-75	4
	Ahmad Rashad, 9-2-79	4
Points	Chuck Foreman, 12-20-75	24
	Ahmad Rashad, 9-2-79	24

*NFL Record

VIKINGS COACHING HISTORY

(312-263-9)

1961-66	Norm Van Brocklin	29-51-4
1967-83	Bud Grant	161-99-5
1984	Les Steckel	3-13-0
1985	Bud Grant	7-9-0
1986-91	Jerry Burns	55-46-0
1992-97	Dennis Green	57-45-0

METRODOME

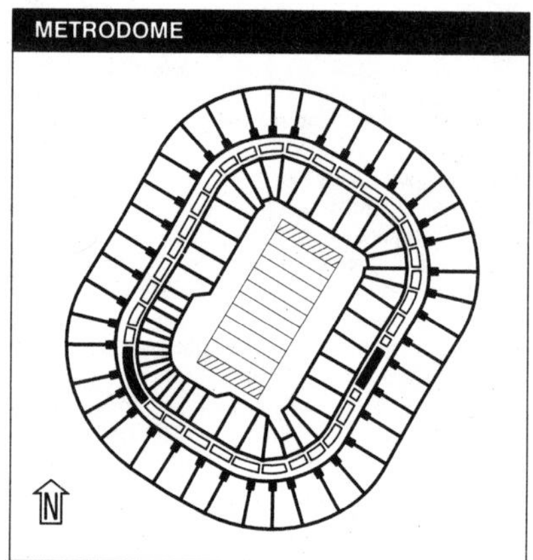

1997 TEAM RECORD

PRESEASON (3-2)

Date	Result		Opponent
7/26	W	28-26	vs. Seattle at Canton, Ohio
8/2	W	24-6	St. Louis
8/8	L	3-19	at Buffalo
8/16	L	13-37	at Cincinnati
8/22	W	28-22	San Diego

REGULAR SEASON (9-7)

Date	Result		Opponent	Att.
8/31	W	34-13	at Buffalo	79,139
9/7	W	27-24	at Chicago	59,263
9/14	L	14-28	Tampa Bay	63,697
9/21	L	32-38	at Green Bay	60,115
9/28	W	28-19	Philadelphia	55,149
10/5	W	20-19	at Arizona	45,550
10/12	W	21-14	Carolina	62,625
10/26	W	10-6	at Tampa Bay	66,815
11/2	W	23-18	New England	62,917
11/9	W	29-22	Chicago	63,443
11/16	L	15-38	at Detroit	68,910
11/23	L	21-23	at New York Jets	70,131
12/1	L	11-27	Green Bay	64,001
12/7	L	17-28	at San Francisco	55,761
12/14	L	13-14	Detroit	60,982
12/21	W	39-28	Indianapolis	54,107

POSTSEASON (1-1)

Date	Result		Opponent	Att.
12/27	W	23-22	at New York Giants	77,497
1/3	L	22-38	at San Francisco	65,018

SCORE BY PERIODS

Vikings	65	96	61	132	—	354
Opponents	54	146	78	81	—	359

ATTENDANCE

Home 486,921 Away 505,684 Total 992,605
Single-game home record, 64,168 (9/22/96)
Single-season home record, 486,921 (1997)

1997 TEAM STATISTICS

	Vikings	Opp.
Total First Downs	293	325
Rushing	96	104
Passing	177	195
Penalty	20	26
Third Down: Made/Att	88/223	88/212
Third Down Pct.	39.5	41.5
Fourth Down: Made/Att	5/11	9/18
Fourth Down Pct.	45.5	50.0
Total Net Yards	5,354	5,687
Avg. Per Game	334.6	355.4
Total Plays	1,022	1,028
Avg. Per Play	5.2	5.5
Net Yards Rushing	2,041	1,983
Avg. Per Game	127.6	123.9
Total Rushes	449	442
Net Yards Passing	3,313	3,704
Avg. Per Game	207.1	231.5
Sacked/Yards Lost	33/224	44/253
Gross Yards	3,537	3,957
Att./Completions	540/319	542/336
Completion Pct.	59.1	62.0
Had Intercepted	16	12
Punts/Avg.	81/42.1	70/41.9
Net Punting Avg.	81/33.8	70/34.4
Penalties/Yards Lost	97/800	81/668
Fumbles/Ball Lost	16/6	31/15
Touchdowns	42	42
Rushing	14	13
Passing	26	28
Returns	2	1
Avg. Time of Possession	29:46	30:14

1997 INDIVIDUAL STATISTICS

Passing	Att.	Comp.	Yds.	Pct.	TD	Int.	Tkld.	Rate
Johnson	452	275	3,036	60.8	20	12	26/164	84.5
Cunningham	88	44	501	50.0	6	4	7/60	71.3
Vikings	540	319	3,537	59.1	26	16	33/224	82.3
Opponents	542	336	3,957	62.0	28	12	44/253	92.2

SCORING	TD R	TD P	TD Rt	PAT	FG	Saf	PTS
Carter	0	13	0	0/0	0/0	0	84
Murray	0	0	0	23/24	12/17	0	59
R. Smith	6	1	0	0/0	0/0	0	42
Reed	0	6	0	0/0	0/0	0	36
Davis	0	0	0	10/10	7/10	0	31
Hoard	4	0	0	0/0	0/0	0	24
Glover	0	3	0	0/0	0/0	0	18
Evans	2	0	0	0/0	0/0	0	14
Palmer	1	1	0	0/0	0/0	0	12
Johnson	0	1	0	0/0	0/0	0	10
Brady	0	0	1	0/0	0/0	0	6
Thomas	0	0	1	0/0	0/0	0	6
Walsh	0	1	0	0/0	0/0	0	6
M. Williams	1	0	0	0/0	0/0	0	6
Vikings	14	26	2	33/34	19/27	0	354
Opponents	13	28	1	36/37	23/30	0	359

2-Point conversions: Carter 3, Johnson 2, Evans. Team 6-8, Opponents 1-5.

RUSHING	Att.	Yds.	Avg.	LG	TD
R. Smith	232	1,266	5.5	78t	6
Hoard	80	235	2.9	20	4
Evans	43	157	3.7	13	2
Johnson	35	139	4.0	28	0
Cunningham	19	127	6.7	28	0
M. Williams	22	59	2.7	8	1
Palmer	11	36	3.3	10	1
Green	6	22	3.7	8	0
Berger	1	0	0.0	0	0
Vikings	449	2,041	4.5	78t	14
Opponents	442	1,983	4.5	60	13

RECEIVING	No.	Yds.	Avg.	LG	TD
Carter	89	1,069	12.0	43	13
Reed	68	1,138	16.7	56	6
R. Smith	37	197	5.3	20	1
Glover	32	378	11.8	43	3
Palmer	26	193	7.4	23	1
Evans	21	152	7.2	17	0
Walsh	11	114	10.4	19	1
Hoard	11	84	7.6	30	0
DeLong	8	75	9.4	23	0
Goodwin	7	61	8.7	14	0
M. Williams	4	14	3.5	7	0
Hatchette	3	54	18.0	38	0
Green	1	5	5.0	5	0
Johnson	1	3	3.0	3t	1
Vikings	319	3,537	11.1	56	26
Opponents	336	3,957	11.8	76	28

INTERCEPTIONS	No.	Yds.	Avg.	LG	TD
Washington	4	71	17.8	27	0
Griffith	2	26	13.0	21	0
Fuller	2	24	12.0	22	0
Thomas	2	1	0.5	1	0
E. McDaniel	1	18	18.0	18	0
Fisk	1	1	1.0	1	0
Vikings	12	141	11.8	27	0
Opponents	16	166	10.4	66	0

PUNTING	No.	Yds.	Avg.	In 20	LG
Berger	73	3,133	42.9	22	65
Cunningham	8	274	34.3	3	65
Vikings	81	3,407	42.1	25	65
Opponents	70	2,932	41.9	25	57

PUNT RETURNS	No.	FC	Yds.	Avg.	LG	TD
Palmer	34	19	444	13.1	57	0
Vikings	34	19	444	13.1	57	0
Opponents	49	10	566	11.6	66t	1

KICKOFF RETURNS	No.	Yds.	Avg.	LG	TD
Palmer	32	711	22.2	62	0
M. Williams	16	388	24.3	74	0
Tate	10	196	19.6	36	0
Morrow	5	99	19.8	42	0
George	1	10	10.0	10	0
Walsh	1	10	10.0	10	0
Vikings	65	1,414	21.8	74	0
Opponents	67	1,398	20.9	61	0

FIELD GOALS	1-19	20-29	30-39	40-49	50+
Murray	0/0	7/7	1/3	4/6	0/1
Davis	0/0	4/5	2/2	1/3	0/0
Vikings	0/0	11/12	3/5	5/9	0/1
Opponents	1/1	14/14	4/8	3/4	1/3

SACKS	No.
Randle	15.5
Clemons	7.0
Rudd	5.0
Alexander	4.5
F. Smith	4.0
Fisk	3.0
Wheeler	2.0
Edwards	1.5
E. McDaniel	1.5
Vikings	44.0
Opponents	33.0

1998 DRAFT CHOICES

Round	Name	Pos.	College
1	Randy Moss	WR	Marshall
2	Kailee Wong	LB	Stanford
3	Ramos McDonald	DB	New Mexico
4	Kivuusama Mays	LB	North Carolina
5	Kerry Cooks	DB	Iowa
6	Matt Birk	T	Harvard
7	Chester Burnett	LB	Arizona
	Tony Darden	DB	Texas Tech

MINNESOTA VIKINGS

1998 VETERAN ROSTER

No.	Name	Pos.	Ht.	Wt.	Birthdate	NFL Exp.	College	Hometown	How Acq.	'97 Games/ Starts
90	Alexander, Derrick	DE	6-4	286	11/13/73	4	Florida State	Jacksonville, Fla.	D1a-'95	14/14
1	Anderson, Gary	K	5-11	178	7/16/59	17	Syracuse	Durban, South Africa	UFA(SF)-'98	16/0*
96	Ball, Jerry	DT	6-1	320	12/15/64	12	Southern Methodist	Beaumont, Tex.	FA-'97	12/6
30	Banks, Antonio	CB	5-10	199	3/12/73	2	Virginia Tech	Newport News, Va.	D4-'97	0*
56	Bercich, Pete	LB	6-1	247	12/23/71	4	Notre Dame	Joliet, Ill.	D7-'94	16/0
17	Berger, Mitch	P	6-2	218	6/24/72	3	Colorado	Vancouver, Canada	FA-'96	14/0
74	Bobo, Orlando	G	6-3	299	2/9/74	2	Northeast Louisiana	Westpoint, Mass.	FA-'96	5/0
43	Briggs, Greg	S	6-3	215	10/1/68	5	Texas Southern	Meadville, Mass.	FA-'97	14/0
31	Butler, Duane	S	6-1	203	11/29/73	2	Illinois State	Trotwood, Ohio	FA-'97	3/0
80	Carter, Cris	WR	6-3	216	11/25/65	12	Ohio State	Missletown, Ohio	W(Phil)-'90	16/16
62	Christy, Jeff	C	6-3	281	2/3/69	6	Pittsburgh	Freeport, Pa.	FA-'93	12/12
92	Clemons, Duane	DE	6-5	277	5/23/74	3	California	Riverside, Calif.	D1-'96	13/3
99	Colinet, Stalin	DE	6-6	274	7/19/74	2	Boston College	New York, N.Y.	D3-'97	10/2
7	Cunningham, Randall	QB	6-4	214	3/27/63	13	Nevada-Las Vegas	Santa Barbara, Calif.	FA-'97	6/3
69	Daniels, LeShun	G	6-1	304	5/30/74	2	Ohio State	Warren, Ohio	FA-'97	1/0
85	DeLong, Greg	TE	6-4	247	4/3/73	4	North Carolina	Orefield, Pa.	FA-'95	16/3
71	Dixon, David	G	6-5	352	1/5/69	5	Arizona	Aukland, New Zealand	FA-'94	13/13
59	Edwards, Dixon	LB	6-1	237	3/25/68	8	Michigan State	Cincinnati, Ohio	UFA(Dall)-'96	16/16
29	Evans, Charles	RB	6-1	243	4/16/67	6	Clark	Augusta, Ga.	D11-'92	16/13
11	Fiedler, Jay	QB	6-2	220	12/29/71	3	Dartmouth	Oceanside, N.Y.	FA-'98	0*
72	Fisk, Jason	DT	6-3	295	9/4/72	4	Stanford	Davis, Calif.	D7b-'95	16/10
27	Fuller, Corey	CB	5-10	206	5/1/71	4	Florida State	Rickards, Fla.	D2b-'95	16/16
82	Glover, Andrew	TE	6-6	253	8/12/67	8	Grambling	Gonzales, La.	UFA(Oak)-'97	13/11
87	Goodwin, Hunter	TE	6-5	273	10/10/72	3	Texas A&M	Bellville, Tex.	D4-'96	16/5
23	Gray, Torrian	S	6-0	198	3/18/74	2	Virginia Tech	Lakeland, Fla.	D2-'97	16/3
24	Griffith, Robert	S	5-11	198	11/30/70	5	San Diego State	San Diego, Calif.	FA-'94	16/16
89	Hatchette, Matthew	WR	6-2	195	5/1/74	2	Langston	Cleveland, Ohio	D7b-'97	16/0
41	t- Hitchcock, Jimmy	CB	5-10	188	11/9/70	4	North Carolina	Concord, N.C.	T(NE)-'98	15/15*
44	Hoard, Leroy	RB	5-11	223	5/15/68	9	Michigan	New Orleans, La.	FA-'96	12/1
55	Houston, Bobby	LB	6-2	245	10/26/67	8	North Carolina	Washington, D.C.	UFA(SD)-'98	2/0*
14	Johnson, Brad	QB	6-5	224	9/13/68	7	Florida State	Black Mountain, N.C.	D9a-'92	13/13
61	Lindsay, Everett	G-C	6-4	302	9/18/70	5	Mississippi State	Raleigh, N.C.	D5-'93	16/3
58	McDaniel, Ed	LB	5-11	230	2/23/69	7	Clemson	Battesburgh, S.C.	D5-'92	16/16
64	McDaniel, Randall	G	6-3	279	12/19/64	11	Arizona	Avondale, Ariz.	D1-'88	16/16
68	Morris, Mike	C	6-5	283	2/22/61	12	Northeast Missouri State	Centerville, Iowa	FA-'91	16/0
33	Morrow, Harold	RB	5-11	215	2/24/73	3	Auburn	Maplesville, Ala.	W(Dall)-'96	16/0
22	Palmer, David	RB	5-8	176	11/19/72	5	Alabama	Birmingham, Ala.	D2a-'94	16/0
28	Phillips, Anthony	CB	6-2	209	10/5/70	4	Texas A&M-Kingsville	Galveston, Tex.	FA-'98	0*
93	Randle, John	DT	6-1	285	12/12/67	9	Texas A&I	Heame, Tex.	FA-'90	16/16
86	Reed, Jake	WR	6-3	219	9/28/67	8	Grambling	Covington, Ga.	D3b-'91	16/16
57	Rudd, Dwayne	LB	6-2	245	2/3/76	2	Alabama	South Panola, Miss.	D1-'97	16/2
78	Sapp, Bob	G	6-4	303	9/22/73	2	Washington	Colorado Springs, Colo.	FA-'97	1/0
95	Smith, Fernando	DE	6-6	283	8/2/71	5	Jackson State	Flint, Mich.	D2b-'94	12/11
26	Smith, Robert	RB	6-2	209	3/4/72	6	Ohio State	Euclid, Ohio	D1-'93	14/14
73	Steussie, Todd	T	6-6	321	12/1/70	5	California	Canoga Park, Calif.	D1b-'94	16/16
77	Stringer, Korey	T	6-4	353	5/8/74	4	Ohio State	Warren, Ohio	D1b-'95	15/15
83	Tate, Robert	WR	5-10	187	10/19/73	2	Cincinnati	Harrisburg, Pa.	D6-'97	4/0
42	Thomas, Orlando	S	6-1	216	10/21/72	4	Southwestern Louisiana	Crowley, La.	D2a-'95	15/13
54	Ulmer, Artie	LB	6-2	243	7/30/73	2	Valdosta State	Rincon, Ga.	D7a-'97	0*
81	Walsh, Chris	WR	6-1	194	12/12/68	6	Stanford	Concord, Calif.	FA-'94	14/0
21	Williams, Moe	RB	6-1	200	7/26/74	3	Kentucky	Columbus, Ga.	D3-'96	14/0
94	Williams, Tony	DT	6-1	291	7/9/75	2	Memphis	Germantown, Tenn.	D5-'97	6/2

* Anderson played 16 games with San Francisco in '97; Banks missed '97 season because of injury; Fiedler last active with Philadelphia in '95; Hitchcock played 15 games with New England; Houston played 2 games with San Diego; Phillips last active with Atlanta in '96; Ulmer was inactive for 11 games.

t- Vikings traded for Hitchcock (New England).

Players lost to free agency (2): CB Dewayne Washington (Pitt; 16 games in '97), CB Leonard Wheeler (Car; 15).

Also played with Vikings in '97—LB Jeff Brady (15 games), K Greg Davis (4), C-G Scott Dill (16), LB Ron George (16), RB Robert Green (3), TE Andrew Jordan (2), K Eddie Murray (12), CB Anthony Prior (12).

COACHING STAFF

Head Coach
Dennis Green

Pro Career: Named the fifth head coach in Vikings history on January 10, 1992, Green is one of only seven people in the history of the league to lead his team to the playoffs in each of his first three seasons as an NFL head coach. He has led Vikings to playoffs five of his six seasons at the helm, including two NFC Central titles. In 1997, Green became the second winningest coach in franchise history. He also led Minnesota to its biggest come-from-behind playoff win, 23-22 over the Giants on December 27, 1997. In 1994, NFL Commissioner Paul Tagliabue appointed Green to the league's Competition Committee. In '92, Green led the Vikings to their best record (11-5) and first division title under a first-year head coach. He earned NFL coach of the year honors from the Washington Touchdown Club and NFC coach of the year honors from *United Press International* and *College & Pro Football Newsweekly*. As receivers coach at San Francisco from 1986-88, Green developed Pro Bowl players Jerry Rice and John Taylor. Green's first pro coaching opportunity came as special teams coach for the 49ers in 1979. Green briefly played defensive back with British Columbia (CFL) in 1971. Career record: 47-37.

Background: A running back at Iowa from 1968-70, Green began his coaching career as a graduate assistant for Iowa in 1972. He coached running backs and receivers at Dayton in 1973, then running backs and receivers at Iowa from 1974-76. Green worked with running backs at Stanford in 1977-78. He returned to Stanford as offensive coordinator in 1980, then was head coach at Northwestern from 1981-85. Green was named Big Ten coach of the year in 1982. As head coach at Stanford from 1989-91, he led the school to the 1991 Aloha Bowl, its first bowl game since 1986.

Personal: Born February 17, 1949 in Harrisburg, Pa., Green earned his degree in recreation from Iowa. He and his wife, Marie, live in Minnetonka, Minn. with their daughter Vanessa. Green also has a daughter, Patti, and a son, Jeremy.

ASSISTANT COACHES

Hubbard Alexander, wide receivers; born February 14, 1939, Winston-Salem, N.C., lives in Eden Prairie, Minn. Center Tennessee State 1958-61. No pro playing experience. College coach: Tennessee State 1962-63, Vanderbilt 1974-78, Miami 1979-88. Pro coach: Dallas Cowboys 1989-97, joined Vikings in 1998.

Dave Atkins, tight ends; born May 18, 1949, Victoria, Tex., lives in Eden Prairie, Minn. Running back Texas-El Paso 1970-72. Pro running back San Francisco 49ers 1973, Honolulu Hawaiians (WFL) 1974, San Diego Chargers 1975. College coach: Texas-El Paso 1979-80, San Diego State 1981-85. Pro coach: Philadelphia Eagles 1986-92, New England Patriots 1993, Arizona Cardinals 1994-95, New Orleans Saints 1996, joined Vikings in 1997.

Brian Billick, offensive coordinator; born February 28, 1954, Redlands, Calif., lives in Eden Prairie, Minn. Tight end Brigham Young 1974-76. Pro tight end Dallas Cowboys 1977. College coach: Brigham Young 1978, Redlands 1979, San Diego State 1981-85, Utah State 1986-88, Stanford 1989-91. Pro coach: Joined Vikings in 1992.

Foge Fazio, defensive coordinator; born February 28, 1939, Dawmont, W. Va., lives in Eden Prairie, Minn. Linebacker-center Pittsburgh 1957-60. No pro playing experience. College coach: Boston University 1967, Harvard 1968, Pittsburgh 1969-72, 1977-85 (head coach 1982-85), Cincinnati 1973-76, Notre Dame 1986-87. Pro coach: Atlanta Falcons 1988-89, New York Jets 1990-94, joined Vikings in 1995.

Jeff Friday, assistant strength and conditioning; born October 11, 1966, Milwaukee, Wis., lives in Eden Prairie, Minn. No college or pro playing experience. College coach: Illinois State 1991-92, Northwestern 1992-95. Pro coach: Joined Vikings in 1996.

Carl Hargrave, running backs; born November 8, 1954, Frankfurt, Germany, lives in Eden Prairie, Minn. Defensive back Upper Iowa 1972-75. No pro playing experience. College coach: Upper Iowa 1977-80, Northwestern 1981-85, Pittsburgh 1986, Houston 1987-91, Iowa 1992-93. Pro coach: Joined Vikings in 1994.

Wade Harman, coaching assistant; born October 1, 1963, Corydon, Iowa, lives in Eden Prairie, Minn. Linebacker Drake 1985, Utah State 1986. College coach: Utah State 1987-91, Pacific 1992-95, Morningside 1996. Pro coach: Joined Vikings in 1997.

Chip Myers, quarterbacks; born July 9, 1945, Panama City, Fla., lives in Eden Prairie, Minn. Receiver Northwestern Oklahoma 1964-66. Pro receiver San Francisco 49ers 1967, Cincinnati Bengals 1969-76. College coach: Illinois 1980-82. Pro coach: Tampa Bay Buccaneers 1983-84, Indianapolis Colts 1985-88, New York Jets 1990-93, New Orleans Saints 1994, joined Vikings in 1995.

Tom Olivadotti, inside linebackers; born September 22, 1945, Long Branch, N.J., lives in Eden Prairie, Minn. Defensive back-wide receiver Upsala 1963-66. No pro playing experience. College coach: Princeton 1975-77, Boston College 1978-79, Miami 1980-83. Pro coach: Cleveland Browns 1985-86, Miami Dolphins 1987-95, joined Vikings in 1996.

Andre Patterson, defensive line; born June 12, 1960, Richmond, Calif., lives in Eden Prairie, Minn. Offensive lineman Contra Costa J.C. 1978-80, Montana 1981. No pro playing experience. College coach: Montana 1982, Weber State 1988, Western Washington 1989, Cornell 1990, Washington State 1992-93, Cal Poly-San Luis Obispo 1994-96 (head coach). Pro coach: New England Patriots 1997, joined Vikings in 1998.

Richard Solomon, defensive backs; born December 8, 1949, New Orleans, La., lives in Eden Prairie, Minn. Running back-defensive back Iowa 1970-73. No pro playing experience. College coach: Dubuque 1973-75, Southern Illinois 1976, Iowa 1977-78, Syracuse 1979, Illinois 1980-86. Pro coach: New York Giants 1987-91 (scout), joined Vikings in 1992.

Mike Tice, offensive line; born February 2, 1959, Bayshore, N.Y., lives in Eden Prairie, Minn. Quarterback Maryland 1977-80. Pro tight end Seattle Seahawks 1981-88, 1990-91, Washington Redskins 1989, Minnesota Vikings 1992-93, 1995. Pro coach: Joined Vikings in 1996.

Trent Walters, outside linebackers; born November 20, 1943, Knoxville, Tenn., lives in Eden Prairie, Minn. Defensive back Indiana 1963-65. Pro defensive back Edmonton Eskimos (CFL) 1966-67. College coach: Indiana 1968-71, Louisville 1972, 1986-90, Indiana 1973-80, Washington 1981-83, Pittsburgh 1985, Texas A&M 1991-93. Pro coach: Cincinnati Bengals 1984, joined Vikings in 1994.

Steve Wetzel, strength and conditioning; born May 11, 1963, Washington D.C., lives in Eden Prairie, Minn. No college or pro playing experience. College coach: Maryland 1985-89, George Mason 1990. Pro coach: Washington Redskins 1990-91, joined Vikings in 1992.

Gary Zauner, special teams; born November 2, 1950, Milwaukee, Wis., lives in Eden Prairie, Minn. Kicker Wisconsin-LaCrosse 1968-72. No pro playing experience. College coach: Brigham Young 1979-80, San Diego State 1981-86, New Mexico 1987-88, Long Beach State 1990-91. Pro coach: Joined Vikings in 1994.

1998 FIRST-YEAR ROSTER

Name	Pos.	Ht.	Wt.	Birthdate	College	Hometown	How Acq.
Ayanbadejo, Obafemi (1)	RB	6-2	230	3/5/75	San Diego State	Santa Cruz, Calif.	FA
Bass, Anthony	CB-S	6-1	192	3/27/75	Bethune-Cookman	St. Alban, W. Va.	FA
Baynham, Grant (1)	TE	6-5	250	10/11/73	Georgia Tech	North Augusta, Sc.	FA-'97
Birk, Matt	T	6-4	308	7/23/76	Harvard	St. Paul, Minn.	D6
Black, Ryan	CB	5-10	194	12/5/74	Colorado	Phoenix, Ariz.	FA
Bland, Tony (1)	WR	6-3	213	12/12/72	Florida A&M	St. Petersburg, Fla.	FA-'96
Bouman, Todd (1)	QB	6-2	195	8/1/72	St. Cloud State	Ruthton, Minn.	FA-'97
Bridges, Corey	WR	5-7	175	6/30/74	South Carolina	Newnan, Ga.	FA
Burnett, Chester	LB	5-10	226	4/15/75	Arizona	Denver, Colo.	D7a
Caflisch, Andy (1)	P	6-3	200	8/7/70	Wisconsin-Stout	River Falls, Wis.	FA
Collins, Ryan	TE	6-7	252	11/1/75	St. Thomas	Robbinsdale, Minn.	FA
Cooks, Kerry	S	5-11	198	3/28/74	Iowa	Irving, Tex.	D5
Darden, Tony	CB	5-11	187	8/11/75	Texas Tech	San Antonio, Tex.	D7b
Kurz, Todd (1)	K	6-3	218	4/20/74	Illinois State	Bloomington, Ill.	FA
Mathis, Claude	RB	5-9	206	11/23/74	Southwest Texas State	Bartletts, Tex.	FA
Mays, Klvuusama	LB	6-3	244	1/7/75	North Carolina	San Antonio, Tex.	D4
McDonald, Ramos	CB	5-11	195	4/30/76	New Mexico	Texarkana, Tex.	D3
Moss, Eric (1)	C-G-T	6-4	325	9/25/74	Ohio State	Belle, W. Va.	FA-'97
Moss, Randy	WR	6-4	194	2/13/77	Marshall	Rand, W. Va.	D1
Murphy, Yo (1)	WR	5-10	178	5/11/71	Idaho	Idaho Falls, Idaho	FA-'97
Stuckey, Shawn	LB	6-0	230	10/22/75	Troy State	Daleville, Ala.	FA
Walker, Anthony (1)	CB-S	6-0	200	12/6/73	Syracuse	Linthicum, Md.	FA-'97
Withrow, Cory	C	6-2	284	4/5/75	Washington State	Spokane, Wash.	FA
Wong, Kailee	LB	6-2	267	5/23/76	Stanford	Eugene, Ore.	D2

The term NFL Rookie is defined as a player who is in his first season of professional football and has not been on the roster of another professional football team for any regular-season or postseason games. A Rookie is designated by an "R" on NFL rosters. Players who have been active in another professional football league or players who have NFL experience, including either preseason training camp or being on an Active List or Inactive List, or on Reserve/Injured or Reserve/Physically Unable to Perform for fewer than six regular-season games, are termed NFL First-Year Players. An NFL First-Year Player is designated by a "1" on NFL rosters. Thereafter, a player is credited with an additional year of experience for each season in which he accumulates six games on the Active List or Inactive List, or on Reserve/Injured or Reserve/Physically Unable to Perform.

NOTES

NEW ORLEANS SAINTS

National Football Conference
Western Division
Team Colors: Old Gold, Black, and White
5800 Airline Drive
Metairie, Louisiana 70003
Telephone: (504) 733-0255

CLUB OFFICIALS

Owner: Tom Benson
President, General Manager, & Chief Operating Officer: Bill Kuharich
Senior Vice President of Marketing & Administration: Greg Suit
Asst. General Manager & Vice President of Football Operations: Chet Franklin
Salary Cap Consultant: Terry O'Neil
Director of College Scouting: Bruce Lemmerman
Treasurer: Bruce Broussard
Comptroller: Charleen Sharpe
Director of Corporate Sales: Greg Seeling
Director of Media and Public Relations: Greg Bensel
Assistant Director of Media and Public Relations: Robert Gunn
Data Processing Manager: Jay Romig
Director of Travel/Entertainment/Special Projects: Barra Birrcher
Club Level Manager/Marketing Assistant: Scott Sidwell
Player Personnel Scouts: Hamp Cook, Hokie Gajan, Cornell Gowdy, Tom Marino
Director of Ticket Sales: Jasen Feyerherm
Trainer: Dean Kleinschmidt
Equipment Manager: Dan Simmons
Video Director: Joe Malota
Facilities Manager: Luke Jenkins
Stadium: Louisiana Superdome
•**Capacity:** 69,028
1500 Poydras Street
New Orleans, Louisiana 70112
Playing Surface: AstroTurf
Training Camp: University of Wisconsin-La Crosse
La Crosse, Wisconsin 54601

1998 SCHEDULE

PRESEASON

Aug. 8	at Green Bay	7:00
Aug. 14	at Denver	7:00
Aug. 22	**Tennessee**	7:00
Aug. 28	**Tampa Bay**	7:30

REGULAR SEASON

Sept. 6	at St. Louis	12:01
Sept. 13	**Carolina**	12:01
Sept. 20	Open Date	
Sept. 27	at Indianapolis	12:01
Oct. 4	**New England**	12:01
Oct. 11	**San Francisco**	12:01
Oct. 18	at Atlanta	1:01
Oct. 25	**Tampa Bay**	12:01
Nov. 1	at Carolina	1:01
Nov. 8	at Minnesota	12:01
Nov. 15	**St. Louis**	12:01
Nov. 22	at San Francisco	5:20
Nov. 29	at Miami	1:01
Dec. 6	**Dallas**	12:01
Dec. 13	**Atlanta**	12:01
Dec. 20	at Arizona	2:15
Dec. 27	**Buffalo**	12:01

RECORD HOLDERS

INDIVIDUAL RECORDS—CAREER

Category	Name	Performance
Rushing (Yds.)	George Rogers, 1981-84	4,267
Passing (Yds.)	Archie Manning, 1971-1982	21,734
Passing (TDs)	Archie Manning, 1971-1982	115
Receiving (No.)	Eric Martin, 1985-1993	532
Receiving (Yds.)	Eric Martin, 1985-1993	7,854
Interceptions	Dave Waymer, 1980-89	37
Punting (Avg.)	Mark Royals, 1997	45.9
Punt Return (Avg.)	Mel Gray, 1986-88	13.4
Kickoff Return (Avg.)	Walter Roberts, 1967	26.3
Field Goals	Morten Andersen, 1982-1994	302
Touchdowns (Tot.)	Dalton Hilliard, 1986-1993	53
Points	Morten Andersen, 1982-1994	1,318

INDIVIDUAL RECORDS—SINGLE SEASON

Category	Name	Performance
Rushing (Yds.)	George Rogers, 1981	1,674
Passing (Yds.)	Jim Everett, 1995	3,970
Passing (TDs)	Jim Everett, 1995	26
Receiving (No.)	Eric Martin, 1988	85
Receiving (Yds.)	Eric Martin, 1989	1,090
Interceptions	Dave Whitsell, 1967	10
Punting (Avg.)	Mark Royals, 1997	45.9
Punt Return (Avg.)	Mel Gray, 1987	14.7
Kickoff Return (Avg.)	Don Shy, 1969	27.9
	Mel Gray, 1986	27.9
Field Goals	Morten Andersen, 1985	31
Touchdowns (Tot.)	Dalton Hilliard, 1989	18
Points	Morten Andersen, 1987	121

INDIVIDUAL RECORDS—SINGLE GAME

Category	Name	Performance
Rushing (Yds.)	George Rogers, 9-4-83	206
Passing (Yds.)	Archie Manning, 12-7-80	377
Passing (TDs)	Billy Kilmer, 11-2-69	6
Receiving (No.)	Tony Galbreath, 9-10-78	14
Receiving (Yds.)	Wes Chandler, 9-2-79	205
Interceptions	Tommy Myers, 9-3-78	3
	Dave Waymer, 10-6-85	3
	Reggie Sutton, 10-18-87	3
	Gene Atkins, 12-22-91	3
Field Goals	Many times	5
	Last time by Morten Andersen, 12-11-94	
Touchdowns (Tot.)	Many times	3
	Last time by Mario Bates, 12-4-94	
Points	Many times	18
	Last time by Mario Bates, 12-4-94	

COACHING HISTORY

(183-282-5)

1967-70	Tom Fears*	13-34-2
1970-72	J.D. Roberts	7-25-3
1973-75	John North**	11-23-0
1975	Ernie Hefferle	1-7-0
1976-77	Hank Stram	7-21-0
1978-80	Dick Nolan***	15-29-0
1980	Dick Stanfel	1-3-0
1981-85	O.A. (Bum) Phillips****	27-42-0
1985	Wade Phillips	1-3-0
1986-96	Jim Mora#	93-78-0
1996	Rick Venturi	1-7-0
1997	Mike Ditka	6-10-0

*Released after seven games in 1970
**Released after six games in 1975
***Released after 12 games in 1980
****Resigned after 12 games in 1985
#Resigned after 8 games in 1996

LOUISIANA SUPREDOME

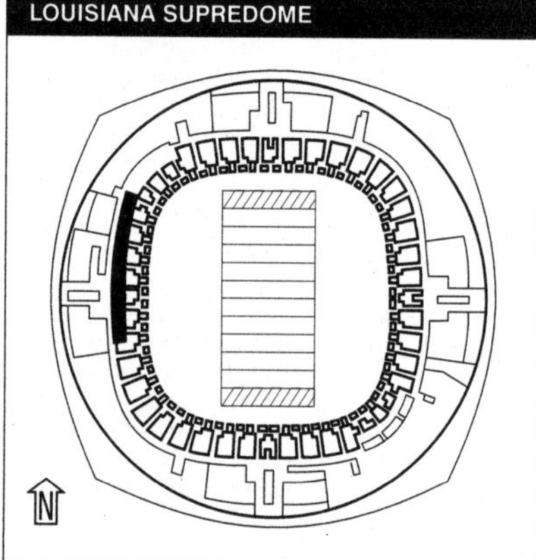

1997 TEAM RECORD

PRESEASON (3-1)

Date	Result		Opponent
8/2	W	21-12	at Tennessee
8/9	W	26-7	Kansas City
8/16	L	16-18	at Oakland
8/22	W	13-7	at Chicago

REGULAR SEASON (6-10)

Date	Result		Opponent	Att.
8/31	L	24-38	at St. Louis	64,575
9/7	L	6-20	San Diego	65,760
9/14	L	7-33	at San Francisco	61,838
9/21	W	35-17	Detroit	50,016
9/28	L	9-14	at New York Giants	68,891
10/5	W	20-17	at Chicago	58,865
10/12	L	17-23	Atlanta	65,619
10/19	L	0-13	Carolina	50,963
10/26	L	0-23	San Francisco	60,443
11/9	W	13-10	at Oakland	40,091
11/16	W	20-17	Seattle (OT)	50,493
11/23	L	3-20	at Atlanta	48,620
11/30	W	16-13	at Carolina	57,957
12/7	L	27-34	St. Louis	54,803
12/14	W	27-10	Arizona	45,517
12/21	L	13-25	at Kansas City	66,772

(OT) Overtime

SCORE BY PERIODS

Saints	22	76	38	98	3	—	237
Opponents	70	107	51	99	0	—	327

ATTENDANCE

Home 444,064 Away 467,609 Total 911,673
Single-game home record, 70,940 (9/2/79)
Single-season home record, 548,728 (1992)

1997 TEAM STATISTICS

	Saints	Opp.
Total First Downs	229	280
Rushing	78	95
Passing	127	168
Penalty	24	17
Third Down: Made/Att	54/207	102/252
Third Down Pct.	26.1	40.5
Fourth Down: Made/Att	14/22	7/12
Fourth Down Pct.	63.6	58.3
Total Net Yards	4,045	4,645
Avg. Per Game	252.8	290.3
Total Plays	925	1,073
Avg. Per Play	4.4	4.3
Net Yards Rushing	1,461	1,764
Avg. Per Game	91.3	110.3
Total Rushes	417	496
Net Yards Passing	2,584	2,881
Avg. Per Game	161.5	180.1
Sacked/Yards Lost	50/317	59/408
Gross Yards	2,901	3,289
Att./Completions	458/228	518/293
Completion Pct.	49.8	56.6
Had Intercepted	33	16
Punts/Avg.	88/45.9	92/39.9
Net Punting Avg.	88/34.9	92/33.0
Penalties/Yards Lost	101/811	110/895
Fumbles/Ball Lost	34/22	31/15
Touchdowns	24	35
Rushing	9	11
Passing	13	21
Returns	2	3
Avg. Time of Possession	27:47	32:13

1997 INDIVIDUAL STATISTICS

Passing	Att.	Comp.	Yds.	Pct.	TD	Int.	Tkld.	Rate
Shuler	203	106	1,288	52.2	2	14	21/132	46.6
Hobert	131	61	891	46.6	6	8	4/29	59.0
Wuerffel	91	42	518	46.2	4	8	18/116	42.3
Nussmeier	32	18	183	56.3	0	3	6/32	33.7
Bates	1	1	21	100.0	1	0	0/0	158.3
Hill	0	0	0	—	0	0	1/8	—
Saints	458	228	2,901	49.8	13	33	50/317	49.4
Opponents	518	293	3,289	56.6	21	16	59/408	76.3

SCORING	TD R	TD P	TD Rt	PAT	FG	Saf	PTS
Brien	0	0	0	22/22	23/27	0	91
Hastings	0	5	0	0/0	0/0	0	32
Bates	4	0	0	0/0	0/0	0	24
Zellars	4	0	0	0/0	0/0	0	24
Guliford	0	1	1	0/0	0/0	0	12
Hill	0	2	0	0/0	0/0	0	12
Poole	0	2	0	0/0	0/0	0	12
Farquhar	0	1	0	0/0	0/0	0	6
Fields	0	0	1	0/0	0/0	0	6
Hobbs	0	1	0	0/0	0/0	0	6
Shuler	1	0	0	0/0	0/0	0	6
I. Smith	0	1	0	0/0	0/0	0	6
Saints	9	13	2	22/22	23/27	0	237
Opponents	11	21	3	33/33	28/36	0	327

2-Point conversions: Hastings.
Team 1-2, Opponents 0-2

RUSHING	Att.	Yds.	Avg.	LG	TD
Zellars	156	552	3.5	27	4
Bates	119	440	3.7	74t	4
T. Davis	75	271	3.6	20	0
Shuler	22	38	1.7	8	1
Hobert	12	36	3.0	15	0
Hastings	4	35	8.8	27	0
Nussmeier	8	30	3.8	15	0
Wuerffel	6	26	4.3	10	0
McCrary	8	15	1.9	8	0
Hill	1	11	11.0	11	0
Bender	5	9	1.8	6	0
Guliford	1	-2	-2.0	-2	0
Saints	417	1,461	3.5	74t	9
Opponents	496	1,764	3.6	50	11

RECEIVING	No.	Yds.	Avg.	LG	TD
Hill	55	761	13.8	89t	2
Hastings	48	722	15.0	39	5
Zellars	31	263	8.5	38	0
Guliford	27	362	13.4	47	1
Farquhar	17	253	14.9	42	1
I. Smith	17	180	10.6	25	1
T. Davis	13	85	6.5	18	0
Bates	5	42	8.4	15	0
Poole	4	98	24.5	49	2
McCrary	4	17	4.3	11	0
Bech	3	50	16.7	22	0
Hobbs	2	41	20.5	21	1
Savoie	1	14	14.0	14	0
T. Johnson	1	13	13.0	13	0
Saints	228	2,901	12.7	89t	13
Opponents	293	3,289	11.2	52	21

INTERCEPTIONS	No.	Yds.	Avg.	LG	TD
Knight	5	75	15.0	39	0
Newman	3	19	6.3	17	0
Washington	2	30	15.0	30	0
Allen	2	27	13.5	27	0
Tubbs	2	21	10.5	15	0
Kelly	1	15	15.0	15	0
Harvey	1	7	7.0	7	0
Saints	16	194	12.1	39	0
Opponents	33	342	10.4	44t	1

PUNTING	No.	Yds.	Avg.	In 20	LG
Royals	88	4,038	45.9	21	66
Saints	88	4,038	45.9	21	66
Opponents	92	3,668	39.9	27	62

PUNT RETURNS	No.	FC	Yds.	Avg.	LG	TD
Guliford	47	26	498	10.6	32	0
Hastings	1	0	-2	-2.0	-2	0
Saints	48	26	496	10.3	32	0
Opponents	50	14	706	14.1	82t	1

KICKOFF RETURNS	No.	Yds.	Avg.	LG	TD
Guliford	43	1,128	26.2	102t	1
T. Davis	9	173	19.2	29	0
Bech	3	47	15.7	30	0
McCrary	2	26	13.0	15	0
Tomich	1	0	0.0	0	0
Saints	58	1,374	23.7	102t	1
Opponents	51	1,139	22.3	59	0

FIELD GOALS	1-19	20-29	30-39	40-49	50+
Brien	1/1	2/2	10/10	6/9	4/5
Saints	1/1	2/2	10/10	6/9	4/5
Opponents	0/0	8/9	12/14	6/11	2/2

SACKS	No.
Martin	10.5
J. Johnson	8.5
Fields	8.0
Glover	6.5
B. Smith	5.0
Mitchell	4.0
Molden	4.0
Mickell	3.5
Harvey	3.0
Tubbs	2.5
Sagapolutele	2.0
Tomich	1.0
Dixon	0.5
Saints	59.0
Opponents	50.0

1998 DRAFT CHOICES

Round	Name	Pos.	College
1	Kyle Turley	T	San Diego State
2	Cameron Cleeland	TE	Washington
4	Fred Weary	DB	Florida
	Julian Pittman	DE	Florida State
5	Wilmont Perry	RB	Livingstone
6	Chris Bordano	LB	Southern Methodist
7	Andy McCullough	WR	Tennessee
	Ron Warner	LB	Kansas

NEW ORLEANS SAINTS

1998 VETERAN ROSTER

No.	Name	Pos.	Ht.	Wt.	Birthdate	NFL Exp.	College	Hometown	How Acq.	'97 Games/ Starts
69	Ackerman, Tom	C-G	6-3	290	9/6/72	3	Eastern Washington	Nooksack, Wash.	D5b-'96	14/0
54	Aleaga, Ink	LB	6-1	225	4/4/73	2	Washington	Honolulu, Hawaii	FA-'97	3/1
89	Bech, Brett	WR	6-1	184	8/20/71	2	Louisiana State	Slidell, La.	FA-'96	10/0
40	Bender, Wes	RB	5-10	249	8/2/70	3	Southern California	Burbank, Calif.	FA-'97	11/0
10	Brien, Doug	K	6-0	180	11/24/70	5	California	Danville, Calif.	FA-'95	16/0
22	# Brown, Derek	RB	5-9	205	4/15/71	6	Nebraska	Anaheim, Calif.	D4b-'93	0*
30	Cherry, Je'Rod	S	6-1	210	5/30/73	3	California	Berkeley, Calif.	D2-'96	16/0
37	Cota, Chad	S	6-1	198	8/13/71	4	Oregon	Ashland, Ore.	RFA(Car)-'98	16/16*
32	Craver, Aaron	RB	6-0	220	12/18/69	8	Fresno State	Compton, Calif.	UFA(SD)-'98	15/5*
53	Davis, Don	LB	6-1	240	12/17/72	3	Kansas	Olathe, Kan.	FA-'96	11/0
73	Davis, Isaac	G	6-3	320	4/8/72	5	Arkansas	Malvern, Ark.	W(SD)-'97	15/14*
28	Davis, Troy	RB	5-7	191	9/14/75	2	Iowa State	Miami, Fla.	D3-'97	16/7
86	Dawkins, Sean	WR	6-4	215	2/3/71	6	California	Homestead, Calif.	UFA(Ind)-'98	14/12*
22	Drakeford, Tyronne	CB	5-11	185	6/21/71	5	Virginia Tech	Camden, S.C.	UFA(SF)-'98	16/2*
87	Farquhar, John	TE	6-6	278	3/22/72	3	Duke	Menlo, Calif.	FA-'97	11/8
55	Fields, Mark	LB	6-2	244	11/9/72	4	Washington State	Cerritos, Calif.	D1-'95	16/15
62	Fontenot, Jerry	C-G	6-3	300	11/21/66	10	Texas A&M	Lafayette, La.	UFA(Chi)-'97	16/16
60	Gammon, Kendall	C	6-4	288	10/23/68	7	Pittsburg State	Rose Hill, Kan.	FA-'96	16/0
97	Glover, La'Roi	DT	6-1	285	7/4/74	3	San Diego State	San Diego, Calif.	W(Oak)-'97	15/2
38	Greer, Donovan	CB	5-9	178	9/11/74	2	Texas A&M	Alief, Tex.	FA-'97	6/1
84	Guliford, Eric	WR	5-8	165	10/25/69	5	Arizona State	Peoria, Ariz.	FA-'97	16/2
80	Harper, Alvin	WR	6-4	218	7/6/68	8	Tennessee	Frostproof, Fla.	W(Wash)-'97	12/0*
52	Harvey, Richard	LB	6-1	242	9/11/66	9	Tulane	Pascagoula, Miss.	UFA(Den)-'95	14/13
88	Hastings, Andre	WR	6-1	190	11/7/71	6	Georgia	Morrow, Ga.	UFA(Pitt)-'97	16/16
23	Hewitt, Chris	S	6-0	210	7/22/74	2	Cincinnati	Englewood, N.J.	FA-'97	11/2
76	Hills, Keno	G-T	6-6	305	6/13/73	3	Southwestern Louisiana	Tampa, Fla.	D6a-'96	9/6
49	Hinton, Marcus	TE	6-4	265	12/27/71	2	Alcorn State	Wiggins, Miss.	FA-'98	0*
12	Hobert, Billy Joe	QB	6-3	230	1/8/71	6	Washington	Puyallup, Wash.	FA-'97	7/4*
82	Ismail, Qadry	WR	6-0	196	11/8/70	6	Syracuse	Wilkes-Barre, Pa.	UFA(Mia)-'98	3/0*
72	Jenkins, Trezelle	T	6-7	317	3/13/73	4	Michigan	Chicago, Ill.	FA-'97	2/1*
94	Johnson, Joe	DT	6-4	270	7/11/72	5	Louisville	St. Louis, Mo.	D1-'94	16/16
61	Johnson, Tony	TE	6-5	255	2/5/72	3	Alabama	Como, Miss.	FA-'96	7/1
58	Jones, Brian	LB	6-1	250	1/22/68	5	Texas	Lubbock, Tex.	FA-'95	0*
74	Jones, Clarence	T	6-6	280	5/6/68	8	Maryland	Central Islip, N.Y.	UFA(StL)-'96	15/15
33	Kelly, Rob	S	6-0	199	6/21/74	2	Ohio State	Newark, Ohio	D2a-'97	16/2
29	Knight, Sammy	S	6-0	205	9/10/75	2	Southern California	Riverside, Calif.	FA-'97	16/12
93	Martin, Wayne	DT	6-5	275	10/26/65	10	Arkansas	Cherry Valley, Ark.	D1-'89	16/16
67	McCollum, Andy	C-G	6-4	295	6/2/70	5	Toledo	Akron, Ohio	FA-'94	16/16
44	McCrary, Fred	RB	6-0	232	9/19/72	3	Mississippi State	Naples, Fla.	FA-'97	7/0
59	Mitchell, Keith	LB	6-2	240	7/24/74	2	Texas A&M	Garland, Tex.	FA-'97	16/2
50	Mitchell, Kevin	LB	6-1	250	1/1/71	5	Syracuse	Harrisburg, Pa.	FA-'98	16/0*
25	Molden, Alex	CB	5-10	190	8/4/73	3	Oregon	Colorado Springs, Colo.	D1-'96	16/15
65	Naeole, Chris	G	6-3	313	12/25/74	2	Colorado	Kaaawa, Hawaii	D1-'97	4/0
83	Poole, Keith	WR	6-0	188	6/18/74	2	Arizona State	Clovis, Calif.	D4b-'97	3/0
77	Roaf, William	T	6-5	300	4/18/70	6	Louisiana Tech	Pine Bluff, Ark.	D1a-'93	16/16
95	Robbins, Austin	DT	6-6	290	3/1/71	5	North Carolina	Washington, D.C.	T(Oak)-'96	12/0
92	Royal, Andre	LB	6-2	238	12/1/72	4	Alabama	Tuscaloosa, Ala.	RFA(Car)-'98	16/13*
3	Royals, Mark	P	6-5	215	6/22/64	9	Appalachian State	Mathews, Va.	UFA(Det)-'97	16/0
99	Sagapolutele, Pio	DT	6-6	297	11/28/69	8	San Diego State	Honolulu, Hawaii	UFA(NE)-'97	14/13
85	Savoie, Nicky	TE	6-5	253	9/21/73	2	Louisiana State	Cut Off, La.	D6-'97	1/0
5	Shuler, Heath	QB	6-2	216	12/31/71	5	Tennessee	Bryson City, N.C.	T(Wash)-'97	10/9
71	Siglar, Ricky	T	6-7	308	6/14/66	7	San Jose State	Albuquerque, N.M.	UFA(KC)-'97	16/1
91	Smith, Brady	DE	6-5	260	6/5/73	3	Colorado State	Barrington, Ill.	D3-'96	16/2
36	Smith, Lamar	RB	5-11	218	11/29/70	5	Houston	Fort Wayne, Ind.	UFA(Sea)-'98	12/2*
16	Stegall, Milt	WR	6-1	185	1/25/70	4	Miami, Ohio	Cincinnati, Ohio	FA-'98	0*
41	Strong, William	CB	5-10	191	11/3/71	2	North Carolina State	Lewisville, S.C.	D5-'95	0*
90	Tomich, Jared	DE	6-2	258	4/24/74	2	Nebraska	St. John, Ind.	D2b-'97	16/1
66	Verstegen, Mike	G-T	6-6	311	10/24/71	4	Wisconsin	Kimberly, Wis.	D3-'95	14/8
26	Washington, Mickey	CB	5-9	195	7/8/68	8	Texas A&M	Beaumont, Tex.	UFA(Jax)-'97	16/2
7	Wuerffel, Danny	QB	6-1	212	5/27/74	2	Florida	Fort Walton, Fla.	D4a-'97	7/2
70	Young, Robert	DE	6-6	273	1/29/69	7	Mississippi State	Carthage, Miss.	FA-'98	0*
34	Zellars, Ray	RB	5-11	233	3/25/73	4	Notre Dame	Pittsburgh, Pa.	D2-'95	16/16

* Brown and B. Jones missed '97 season because of injury; Cota and Royal played 16 games with Carolina; Craver played 15 games with San Diego; I. Davis played 12 games with San Diego; Dawkins played 14 games with Indianapolis; Drakeford and Kevin Mitchell played 16 games with San Francisco; Harper played 12 games with Washington; Hinton last active with Oakland in '96; Hobert played 2 games with Buffalo; Ismail played 3 games with Miami; Jenkins played 2 games with Kansas City; L. Smith played 12 games with Seattle; Stegall last active with Cincinnati in '94; Strong last active with New Orleans in '96; Young last active with Houston in '96.

\# Unrestricted free agent; subject to developments.

Traded—CB Eric Allen (16 games in '97) to Oakland.

Players lost through free agency (6): RB Mario Bates (Ariz; 12 games in '97), LB Ernest Dixon (Car; 15), S Anthony Newman (Oak; 12), QB Doug Nussmeier (Den; 5), TE Irv Smith (SF; 11), LB Winfred Tubbs (SF; 16).

Also played with the Saints in '97—S Vashone Adams (5 games), LB Derrick Barnes (1), WR Mercury Hayes (4), WR Randal Hill (15), WR Daryl Hobbs (4), G Ed King (2), DE Darren Mickell (14).

COACHING STAFF

Head Coach,
Mike Ditka

Pro Career: Named the twelfth head coach in Saints history in January, 1997. Ditka's regular-season and overall career win percentage are second-best among active coaches entering the 1998 NFL season. He is one of just two people (Tom Flores) to have won a Super Bowl ring as a head coach, assistant coach, and player. All three of Ditka's Super Bowl triumphs have taken place in New Orleans. Came to New Orleans after a four-year stint as a broadcaster with NBC. Was head coach of the Chicago Bears for eleven seasons (1982-92). The Bears won the NFC Central Division five consecutive seasons (1984-88) and reached the playoffs seven times during his tenure. The 1985 Bears finished with a 15-1 record and won Super Bowl XX at the Superdome when they defeated the New England Patriots 46-10. Ditka began his pro coaching career as an assistant with the Dallas Cowboys (1973-81). The Cowboys won Super Bowl XII, at the Superdome, when they defeated the Denver Broncos 27-10. As a NFL player, Ditka was chosen in the first round with the fifth overall pick of the 1961 draft by the Chicago Bears. The tight end earned rookie of the year honors by hauling in 56 receptions. Was traded to Philadelphia and played for two seasons (1967-68). From 1969-72 Ditka played for the Cowboys. Dallas defeated Miami 24-3 to capture Super Bowl VI at Tulane Stadium in New Orleans. In that game, Ditka caught a 7-yard touchdown pass from Roger Staubach. Career record: 118-78.

Background: Played tight end at Pittsburgh (1958-60), where he earned all-America honors his senior season. Also played defensive end, linebacker, and ranked among the nation's top punters. Attended Aliquippa High School, where he lettered in football, baseball, and basketball.

Personal: Born October 18, 1939, in Carneige, Pa. Mike and his wife, Diana, live in Metairie, La., and have four children—sons Mike, Mark, and Matthew, and daughter Megan.

ASSISTANT COACHES

Danny Abramowicz, offensive coordinator; born July 13, 1945, Steubenville, Ohio, lives in New Orleans. Wide receiver Xavier 1964-66. Wide receiver New Orleans 1967-72, San Francisco 49ers 1973-74. No college coaching experience. Pro coach: Chicago Bears 1992-96, joined Saints in 1997.

Bobby April, special teams; born April 15, 1953, New Orleans, lives in Mandeville, La. Linebacker-defensive end Nicholls State 1972-75. College coach: Southern Mississippi 1978, Tulane 1979, Arizona 1980-86, Southern California 1987-90. Pro coach: Atlanta Falcons 1991-93, Pittsburgh Steelers 1994-95 , joined Saints in 1996.

Tom Clements, quarterbacks; born June 18, 1953, McKees Rocks, Pa., lives in Harahan, La. Quarterback Notre Dame 1972-74. Pro quarterback Ottawa Rough Riders (CFL) 1975-78, Saskatchewan Roughriders (CFL) 1979, Hamilton Tiger-Cats (CFL) 1979, 1981-83, Kansas City Chiefs 1980, Winnipeg Blue Bombers (CFL) 1983-87. College coach: Notre Dame 1992-95. Pro coach: Joined Saints in 1996.

Walt Corey, defensive line; born May 9, 1938, Latrobe, Pa., lives in River Ridge, La. Defensive end Miami 1956-59. Pro linebacker Dallas Texans/Kansas City Chiefs 1960-66. College coach: Utah State 1967-69, Miami 1970, Coast Guard Academy 1995. Pro coach: Kansas City Chiefs 1971-74, 1978-86, Cleveland Browns 1975-77, Buffalo Bills 1987-94, joined Saints in 1997.

Jack Del Rio, linebackers; born April 4, 1963, Castro Valley, Calif., lives in New Orleans. Linebacker Southern California 1981-84. Pro linebacker New Orleans Saints 1985-86, Kansas City Chiefs 1987-88, Dallas Cowboys 1989-91, Minnesota Vikings 1992-95. No college coaching experience. Pro coach: Joined Saints in 1997.

Judd Garrett, offensive assistant; born June 25, 1967, Abington, Pa., lives in La Place, La. Running back Princeton 1987-89. Pro running back London Monarchs (WLAF) 1991-92, Dallas Cowboys 1993, Las Vegas Posse (CFL) 1994, San Antonio Texans (CFL) 1995. College coach: Princeton 1990. Pro coach: Joined Saints in 1997.

Harold Jackson, wide receivers; born January 6, 1946, Hattiesburg, Miss., lives in River Ridge, La. Wide receiver Jackson State 1964-67. Pro wide receiver Los Angeles Rams 1968, 1973-77, Philadelphia Eagles 1969-72, New England Patriots 1978-81, Seattle Seahawks 1983. College coach: North Carolina Central 1990, Virginia Union 1994 (head coach), Benedict College 1995-96 (head coach). Pro coach: New England Patriots 1985-89, New Orleans Night (Arena League) 1991, Tampa Bay Buccaneers 1992-93, joined Saints in 1997.

Ned James, defensive assistant; born January 18, 1964, Syracuse, N.Y., lives in Metairie, La. Quarterback New Mexico 1985-86. Pro quarterback Montreal Alouettes (CFL) 1987, Dallas Texans (Arena League) 1990. College coach: Arizona State 1987, Long Beach State 1988, Texas Christian 1989-90, Winona State 1992-94. Pro coach: Seattle Seahawks 1995-97, joined Saints in 1998.

Lary Kuharich, running backs; born December 20, 1945, Middletown, N.Y., lives in Metairie, La. Halfback-defensive back Boston College 1964-68. College coach: Boston State 1970-74, Rhode Island 1975, Temple 1977-80, Illinois State 1981, California 1982-83. Pro coach: Hamilton Tiger-Cats (CFL) 1976, San Antonio Gunslingers (USFL) 1984, Oakland Invaders (USFL) 1985, Calgary Stampeders (CFL) 1986-89, British Columbia Lions (CFL) 1990, Tampa Bay Storm (Arena League) 1991-94, Scottish Claymores (WLAF) 1995, Connecticut Coyotes (Arena League) 1996, New York CityHawks (Arena League) 1997, joined Saints in 1998.

Dan Neal, tight ends; born August 30, 1949, Corbin, Ky., lives in Harahan, La. Center Kentucky 1969-72. Pro center Baltimore Colts 1973-74, Chicago Bears 1975-83. College coach: Western Illinois 1996. Pro coach: Philadelphia Eagles 1986-91, Arizona Cardinals 1994-95, joined Saints in 1997.

Markus Paul, asst. strength & conditioning; born April 1, 1966, in Orlando, Fla., lives in Metairie, La. Safety Syracuse 1984-88. Pro safety Chicago Bears 1989-93, Tampa Bay Buccaneers 1993. No college coaching experience. Pro coach: Joined Saints in 1998.

Dick Stanfel, offensive line; born July 20, 1927, San Francisco, Calif., lives in River Ridge, La. Guard San Francisco 1948-50. Pro guard Detroit Lions 1951-55, Washington Redskins 1956-58. College coach: Notre Dame 1959-62, California 1963. Pro coach: Philadelphia Eagles 1964-70, San Francisco 49ers 1971-75, New Orleans Saints 1976-80 (interim head coach for four games, 1980), Chicago Bears 1981-92, rejoined Saints in 1997.

Rick Venturi, asst. head coach-defensive backs; born February 23, 1946, Taylorville, Ill., lives in Destrehan, La. Quarterback-defensive back Northwestern 1965-67. No pro playing experience. College coach: Northwestern 1968-72, 1978-80 (head coach), Purdue 1973-76, Illinois 1977. Pro coach: Hamilton Tiger-Cats (CFL) 1981, Indianapolis Colts 1982-93 (interim head coach for final 11 games of 1991), Cleveland Browns 1994-95, joined Saints in 1996 (interim head coach for final eight games, 1996).

Mike Woicik, strength and conditioning; born September 26, 1956, Baltimore, Md., lives in Kenner, La. Attended Boston College. No college or pro playing experience. College coach: Springfield College 1978-79, Syracuse 1980-89. Pro coach: Dallas Cowboys 1990-96, joined Saints in 1997.

Zaven Yaralian, defensive coordinator; born February 5, 1952, Syria, lives in Metairie, La. Cornerback Nebraska 1972-73. Pro cornerback Green Bay Packers 1974, Philadelphia Bell (WFL) 1975. College coach: Nebraska 1975, Washington State 1976-77, Missouri 1978-82, Florida 1983-87, Colorado 1988-89. Pro coach: Chicago Bears 1990-92, New York Giants 1993-96, joined Saints in 1997.

1998 FIRST-YEAR ROSTER

Name	Pos.	Ht.	Wt.	Birthdate	College	Hometown	How Acq.
Bordano, Chris	LB	6-1	241	12/30/74	Southern Methodist	San Antonio, Tex.	D6
Cleeland, Cam	TE	6-4	272	4/15/75	Washington	Sedro Wooley, Wash.	D2
Cobbs, Anthony (1)	CB	6-0	191	1/9/74	UCLA	Long Beach, Calif.	FA-'97
Danish, Jeff	DE-DT	6-5	282	2/28/75	Syracuse	Staten Island, N.Y.	FA
Delhomme, Jake (1)	QB	6-2	205	1/10/75	Southwestern Louisiana	Lafayette, La.	FA-'97
Fickell, Luke (1)	DT	6-4	284	8/18/73	Ohio State	Columbus, Ohio	FA-'97
Leshinski, Ron (1)	TE	6-2	248	3/6/74	Army	Vermillion, Ohio	FA-'97
Lillibridge, Marc (1)	LB	6-1	245	2/18/72	Iowa State	Marion, Iowa	FA
Little, Earl (1)	CB	6-0	191	3/10/73	Miami	Miami, Fla.	FA-'97
Maranto, Tony	WR	5-11	185	7/28/76	Northwestern St., La.	Port Allen, La.	FA
McCullough, Andy	WR	6-3	210	11/11/75	Tennessee	Dayton, Ohio	D7a
Perry, Wilmont	RB	6-1	230	2/24/75	Livingstone	Franklinton, N.C.	D5
Pittman, Julian	DT	6-4	286	4/22/75	Florida State	Niceville, Fla.	D4b
Ridgley, Troy (1)	DT	6-3	310	10/28/69	Notre Dame	Ambridge, Pa.	FA
Terrell, Daryl	T	6-5	296	1/25/75	Southern Mississippi	Vossburg, Miss.	FA
Townsend, Larry (1)	DT	6-4	315	9/16/74	Nebraska	San Jose, Calif.	FA
Turley, Kyle	T	6-5	307	9/24/75	San Diego State	Moreno Valley, Calif.	D1
Twyner, Gunnard (1)	WR	5-10	165	7/14/73	Western Illinois	Bettendorf, Iowa	FA-'97
Warner, Ron	LB	6-2	246	9/26/75	Kansas	Independence, Kan.	D7b
Weary, Fred	CB	5-10	177	4/12/74	Florida	Jacksonville, Fla.	D4a

The term NFL Rookie is defined as a player who is in his first season of professional football and has not been on the roster of another professional football team for any regular-season or postseason games. A Rookie is designated by an "R" on NFL rosters. Players who have been active in another professional football league or players who have NFL experience, including either preseason training camp or being on an Active List or Inactive List, or on Reserve/Injured or Reserve/Physically Unable to Perform for fewer than six regular-season games, are termed NFL First-Year Players. An NFL First-Year Player is designated by a "1" on NFL rosters. Thereafter, a player is credited with an additional year of experience for each season in which he accumulates six games on the Active List or Inactive List, or on Reserve/Injured or Reserve/Physically Unable to Perform.

NOTES

NEW YORK GIANTS

National Football Conference
Eastern Division
Team Colors: Blue, Red, and White
Giants Stadium
East Rutherford, New Jersey 07073
Telephone: (201) 935-8111

CLUB OFFICIALS

President/Co-CEO: Wellington T. Mara
Chairman/Co-CEO: Preston Robert Tisch
Executive Vice President/General Counsel: John K. Mara, Esq.
Treasurer: Jonathan Tisch
Vice President-General Manager: Ernie Accorsi
Vice President-Player Personnel: Tom Boisture
Vice President-Chief Financial Officer: John Pasquali
Vice President-Marketing: Rusty Hawley
Vice-President-Communications: Pat Hanlon
Assistant General Manager: Rick Donohue
Special Assistant to General Manager: Harry Hulmer
Director of Player Personnel: Marv Sunderland
Director of Pro Personnel: Tim Rooney
Assistant Director of Pro Personnel: David Gettleman
Pro Personnel Assistant: Geoff Mazza
Director of Promotion: Frank Mara
Ticket Manager: John Gormon
Director of Administration: Jim Phelan
Controller: Christine Procops
Director of Community Relations: Allison Stangeby
Director of Media Relations: Aaron Salkin
Director of Sales: Dan Lynch
Assistant Director of Marketing: Bill Smith
Manager of Creative Services: Doug Murphy
Assistant Director of Community and Media Relations: Peter John-Baptiste
Head Trainer: Ronnie Barnes
Assistant Trainers: John Johnson, Steve Kennelly, Michael Colello
Equipment Manager: Ed Wagner, Jr.
Stadium: Giants Stadium • **Capacity:** 79,593
East Rutherford, New Jersey 07073
Playing Surface: AstroTurf
Training Camp: University at Albany
1400 Washington Avenue
Albany, N.Y. 12222

1998 SCHEDULE

PRESEASON

Aug. 8	**Cincinnati**	8:00
Aug. 14	at Jacksonville	8:00
Aug. 20	at New York Jets	8:20
Aug. 28	**Baltimore**	8:00

REGULAR SEASON

Sept. 6	**Washington**	1:01
Sept. 13	at Oakland	1:15
Sept. 21	**Dallas** (Mon.)	8:20
Sept. 27	at San Diego	1:15
Oct. 4	at Tampa Bay	4:15
Oct. 11	**Atlanta**	8:20
Oct. 18	**Arizona**	1:01
Oct. 25	Open Date	
Nov. 1	at Washington	1:01
Nov. 8	at Dallas	12:01
Nov. 15	**Green Bay**	4:15
Nov. 22	**Philadelphia**	1:01
Nov. 30	at San Francisco (Mon.)	5:20
Dec. 6	at Arizona	2:05
Dec. 13	**Denver**	1:01
Dec. 20	**Kansas City**	1:01
Dec. 27	at Philadelphia	4:05

RECORD HOLDERS

INDIVIDUAL RECORDS—CAREER

Category	Name	Performance
Rushing (Yds.)	Rodney Hampton, 1990-97	6,897
Passing (Yds.)	Phil Simms, 1979-1993	33,462
Passing (TDs)	Phil Simms, 1979-1993	199
Receiving (No.)	Joe Morrison, 1959-1972	395
Receiving (Yds.)	Frank Gifford, 1952-1960, 1962-64	5,434
Interceptions	Emlen Tunnell, 1948-1958	74
Punting (Avg.)	Don Chandler, 1956-1964	43.8
Punt Return (Avg.)	David Meggett, 1989-1994	11.0
Kickoff Return (Avg.)	Rocky Thompson, 1971-72	27.2
Field Goals	Pete Gogolak, 1966-1974	126
Touchdowns (Tot.)	Frank Gifford, 1952-1960, 1962-64	78
Points	Pete Gogolak, 1966-1974	646

INDIVIDUAL RECORDS—SINGLE SEASON

Category	Name	Performance
Rushing (Yds.)	Joe Morris, 1986	1,516
Passing (Yds.)	Phil Simms, 1984	4,044
Passing (TDs)	Y.A. Tittle, 1963	36
Receiving (No.)	Earnest Gray, 1983	78
Receiving (Yds.)	Homer Jones, 1967	1,209
Interceptions	Otto Schnellbacher, 1951	11
	Jim Patton, 1958	11
Punting (Avg.)	Don Chandler, 1959	46.6
Punt Return (Avg.)	Merle Hapes, 1942	15.5
Kickoff Return (Avg.)	John Salscheider, 1949	31.6
Field Goals	Ali Haji-Sheikh, 1983	35
Touchdowns (Tot.)	Joe Morris, 1985	21
Points	Ali Haji-Sheikh, 1983	127

INDIVIDUAL RECORDS—SINGLE GAME

Category	Name	Performance
Rushing (Yds.)	Gene Roberts, 11-12-50	218
Passing (Yds.)	Phil Simms, 10-13-85	513
Passing (TDs)	Y.A. Tittle, 10-28-62	*7
Receiving (No.)	Mark Bavaro, 10-13-85	12
Receiving (Yds.)	Del Shofner, 10-28-62	269
Interceptions	Many times	3
	Last time by Terry Kinard, 9-27-87	
Field Goals	Joe Danelo, 10-18-81	6
Touchdowns (Tot.)	Ron Johnson, 10-2-72	4
	Earnest Gray, 9-7-80	4
	Rodney Hampton, 9-24-95	4
Points	Ron Johnson, 10-2-72	24
	Earnest Gray, 9-7-80	24
	Rodney Hampton, 9-24-95	24

*NFL Record

COACHING HISTORY

(537-448-33)

1925	Bob Folwell	8-4-0
1926	Joe Alexander	8-4-1
1927-28	Earl Potteiger	15-8-3
1929-30	LeRoy Andrews*	24-5-1
1930	Benny Friedman	2-0-0
1930-53	Steve Owen	155-108-17
1954-60	Jim Lee Howell	55-29-4
1961-68	Allie Sherman	57-54-4
1969-73	Alex Webster	29-40-1
1974-76	Bill Arnsparger**	7-28-0
1976-78	John McVay	14-23-0
1979-82	Ray Perkins	24-35-0
1983-90	Bill Parcells	85-52-1
1991-92	Ray Handley	14-18-0
1993-96	Dan Reeves	32-34-0
1997	Jim Fassel	10-6-1

*Released after 15 games in 1930

GIANTS STADIUM

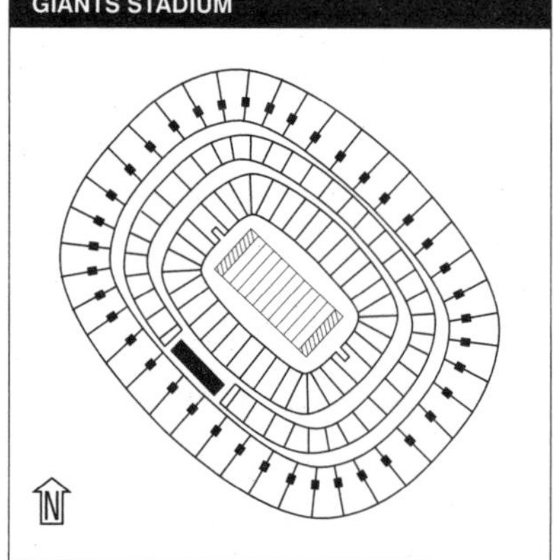

**Released after seven games in 1976

1997 TEAM RECORD

PRESEASON (1-3)

Date	Result		Opponents
8/2	W	21-20	at Baltimore
8/9	L	16-38	Jacksonville
8/16	L	17-27	New York Jets
8/22	L	17-22	vs. Green Bay at Madison, Wis.

REGULAR SEASON (10-5-1)

Date	Result		Opponents	Att.
8/31	W	31-17	Philadelphia	70,296
9/7	L	13-40	at Jacksonville	70,051
9/14	L	23-24	Baltimore	69,768
9/21	L	3-13	at St. Louis	64,642
9/28	W	14-9	New Orleans	68,891
10/5	W	20-17	Dallas	77,137
10/12	W	27-13	at Arizona	38,959
10/19	W	26-20	at Detroit (OT)	70,069
10/26	W	29-27	Cincinnati	72,584
11/9	L	6-10	at Tennessee	26,744
11/16	W	19-10	Arizona	68,316
11/23	T	7-7	at Washington (OT)	75,703
11/30	L	8-20	Tampa Bay	68,678
12/7	W	31-21	at Philadelphia	67,084
12/14	W	30-10	Washington	77,571
12/21	W	20-7	at Dallas	63,746

POSTSEASON (0-1)

Date	Result		Opponents	Att.
12/27	L	22-23	Minnesota	77,710

(OT) Overtime

SCORE BY PERIODS

Giants	68	85	67	81	6	—	307
Opponents	33	93	54	85	0	—	265

ATTENDANCE

Home 573,241 Away 477,528 Total 1,050,769
Single-game home record, 77,454 (9/4/95)
Single-season home record, 599,570 (1990)

1997 TEAM STATISTICS

	Giants	Opp.
Total First Downs	273	310
Rushing	113	82
Passing	124	195
Penalty	36	33
Third Down: Made/Att	74/237	78/227
Third Down Pct.	31.2	34.4
Fourth Down: Made/Att.	5/9	7/20
Fourth Down Pct.	55.6	35.0
Total Net Yards	4513	5067
Avg. Per Game	282.1	316.7
Total Plays	1,027	1,082
Avg. Per Play	4.4	4.7
Net Yards Rushing	1,988	1,451
Avg. Per Game	124.3	90.7
Total Rushes	521	432
Net Yards Passing	2,525	3,616
Avg. Per Game	157.8	226.0
Sacked/Yards Lost	32/238	54/341
Gross Yards	2763	3,957
Att./Completions	474/249	596/325
Completion Pct.	52.5	54.5
Had Intercepted	12	27
Punts/Avg.	112/40.5	89/42.1
Net Punting Avg.	112/34.6	89/35.9
Penalties/Yards Lost	116/1,005	122/1,056
Fumbles/Ball Lost	23/7	33/17
Touchdowns	35	30
Rushing	14	17
Passing	16	10
Returns	5	3
Avg. Time of Possession	29:27	30:33

1997 INDIVIDUAL STATISTICS

Passing	Att.	Comp.	Yds.	Pct.	TD	Int.	Tkld.	Rate
Kanell	294	156	1,740	53.1	11	9	19/171	70.7
Brown	180	93	1,023	51.7	5	3	13/67	71.1
Giants	474	249	2,763	52.5	16	12	32/238	70.9
Opponents	596	325	3,957	54.5	10	27	54/341	61.9

SCORING	TD R	TD P	TD Rt	PAT	FG	Saf	PTS
Daluiso	0	0	0	27/29	22/32	0	93
Calloway	0	8	0	0/0	0/0	0	48
Way	4	1	0	0/0	0/0	0	30
Barber	3	1	0	0/0	0/0	0	26
Wheatley	4	0	0	0/0	0/0	0	24
Cross	0	2	0	0/0	0/0	0	12
Patten	0	2	0	0/0	0/0	0	12
Toomer	0	1	1	0/0	0/0	0	12
Alexander	0	1	0	0/0	0/0	0	6
Armstead	0	0	1	0/0	0/0	0	6
Brown	1	0	0	0/0	0/0	0	6
Garnes	0	0	1	0/0	0/0	0	6
Hampton	1	0	0	0/0	0/0	0	6
Pegram	1	0	0	0/0	0/0	0	6
Sehorn	0	0	1	0/0	0/0	0	6
Wooten	0	0	1	0/0	0/0	0	6
Giants	14	16	5	27/29	22/32	1	307
Opponents	17	10	3	26/27	19/25	0	265

2-Point conversions: Barber.
Team 1-5, Opponents 1-3.

RUSHING	Att.	Yds.	Avg.	LG	TD
Way	151	698	4.6	42	4
Wheatley	152	583	3.8	38	4
Barber	136	511	3.8	42	3
Hampton	23	81	3.5	22	1
Pegram	19	72	3.8	18t	1
Brown	17	29	1.7	7	1
Lane	5	13	2.6	6	0
Kanell	15	2	0.1	8	0
Patten	1	2	2.0	2	0
Calloway	1	-1	-1.0	-1	0
Cherry	1	-2	-2.0	-2	0
Giants	521	1,988	3.8	42	14
Opponents	432	1,451	3.4	37	17

RECEIVING	No.	Yds.	Avg.	LG	TD
Calloway	58	849	14.6	68t	8
Way	37	304	8.2	62	1
Barber	34	299	8.8	29	1
Cross	21	150	7.1	26	2
Pegram	19	83	4.4	14	0
Alexander	18	276	15.3	40	1
Toomer	16	263	16.4	56t	1
Wheatley	16	140	8.8	27	0
Patten	13	226	17.4	40t	2
Pierce	10	47	4.7	14	0
Lewis	5	84	16.8	34	0
Hilliard	2	42	21.0	23	0
Giants	249	2,763	11.1	68t	16
Opponents	325	3,957	12.2	72t	10

INTERCEPTIONS	No.	Yds.	Avg.	LG	TD
Sehorn	6	74	12.3	41	1
Wooten	5	146	29.2	61t	1
Sparks	5	72	14.4	68	0
Ellsworth	4	40	10.0	25	0
Armstead	2	57	28.5	57t	1
Widmer	2	0	0.0	0	0
Garnes	1	95	95.0	95t	1
C. Hamilton	1	18	18.0	18	0
Randolph	1	1	1.0	1	0
Giants	27	503	18.6	95t	4
Opponents	12	230	19.2	64t	2

PUNTING	No.	Yds.	Avg.	In 20	LG
Maynard	111	4,531	40.8	33	57
Giants	112	4,531	40.5	33	57
Opponents	89	3,748	42.1	31	64

PUNT RETURNS	No.	FC	Yds.	Avg.	LG	TD
Toomer	47	19	455	9.7	53t	1
Giants	47	19	455	9.7	53t	1
Opponents	40	27	378	9.5	45	0

KICKOFF RETURNS	No.	Yds.	Avg.	LG	TD
Pegram	22	382	17.4	50	0
Lewis	14	364	26.0	84	0
Patten	8	123	15.4	26	0
Alexander	3	30	10.0	15	0
Way	2	46	23.0	30	0
Pierce	1	10	10.0	10	0
Sparks	1	8	8.0	8	0
Giants	51	963	18.9	84	0
Opponents	49	1,163	23.7	102t	1

FIELD GOALS	1-19	20-29	30-39	40-49	50+
Daluiso	1/1	6/6	6/7	8/14	1/4
Giants	1/1	6/6	6/7	8/14	1/4
Opponents	0/0	6/6	10/10	2/7	1/2

SACKS	No.
Strahan	14.0
Harris	10.0
K. Hamilton	8.0
Armstead	3.5
Bratzke	3.5
Holsey	3.5
Galyon	3.0
Agnew	2.0
Sehorn	1.5
Widmer	1.5
Miller	1.0
Phillips	1.0
Sparks	1.0
Peter	0.5
Giants	54.0
Opponents	32.0

1998 DRAFT CHOICES

Round	Name	Pos.	College
1	Shaun Williams	DB	UCLA
2	Joe Jurevicius	WR	Penn State
3	Brian Alford	WR	Purdue
5	Toby Myles	T	Jackson State
6	Todd Pollack	TE	Boston College
7	Ben Fricke	C	Houston

NEW YORK GIANTS

1998 VETERAN ROSTER

No.		Name	Pos.	Ht.	Wt.	Birthdate	NFL Exp.	College	Hometown	How Acq.	'97 Games/ Starts
98		Armstead, Jessie	LB	6-1	240	10/26/70	6	Miami	Dallas, Tex.	D8-'93	16/16
21		Barber, Tiki	RB	5-10	205	4/7/75	2	Virginia	Montgomery County, Va.	D3-'97	12/6
78		Bishop, Greg	G	6-5	315	5/2/71	6	Pacific	Lodi, Calif.	D4-'93	16/16
77		Bratzke, Chad	DE	6-4	275	9/15/71	5	Eastern Kentucky	Brandon, Fla.	D5-'94	10/10
12		Brice, Will	P	6-4	225	10/24/74	2	Virginia	Lancaster, S.C.	FA-'98	6/0*
33		Brown, Gary	RB	5-11	230	7/1/69	7	Penn State	Williamsport, Pa.	UFA(SD)-'98	15/14*
55		Buckley, Marcus	LB	6-3	240	2/3/71	6	Texas A&M	Fort Worth, Tex.	D3-'93	12/3
80		Calloway, Chris	WR	5-10	191	3/29/68	9	Michigan	Chicago, Ill.	PB-'92	16/16
18		Cherry, Mike	QB	6-3	225	12/15/73	2	Murray State	Texarkana, Ark.	D6-'97	1/0
58		Colman, Doug	LB	6-2	250	6/4/73	3	Nebraska	Somers Point, N.J.	D6a-'96	14/0
87		Cross, Howard	TE	6-5	275	8/8/67	10	Alabama	Huntsville, Ala.	D6-'89	16/16
3		Daluiso, Brad	K	6-2	215	12/31/67	8	UCLA	San Diego, Calif.	FA-'93	16/0
82	#	Douglas, Omar	WR	5-10	180	7/3/72	5	Minnesota	New Orleans, La.	FA-'94	0*
43		Ellsworth, Percy	S	6-2	225	10/19/74	3	Virginia	Drewryville, Va.	FA-'96	16/1
69		Engler, Derek	C	6-5	300	7/11/74	2	Wisconsin	St. Paul, Minn.	FA-'97	5/5
52		Galyon, Scott	LB	6-2	245	3/23/74	3	Tennessee	Seymour, Tenn.	D6b-'96	16/0
20		Garnes, Sam	S	6-3	225	7/12/74	2	Cincinnati	Bronx, N.Y.	D5-'97	16/15
19		Goines, Eddie	WR	6-0	195	8/16/72	2	North Carolina State	Lakeland, Fla.	FA-'98	0*
74	†	Gragg, Scott	T	6-8	325	2/28/72	4	Montana	Silverton, Ore.	D2-'95	16/16
10		Graham, Kent	QB	6-5	240	11/1/68	7	Ohio State	Wheaton, Ill.	UFA(Ariz)-'98	8/6*
41		Hamilton, Conrad	CB	5-10	195	11/5/74	3	Eastern New Mexico	Alamogordo, N.M.	D7-'96	14/0
75		Hamilton, Keith	DT	6-6	300	5/25/71	7	Pittsburgh	Lynchburg, Va.	D4-'92	16/16
97		Harris, Robert	DT	6-4	300	6/13/69	7	Southern	Riviera Beach, Fla.	RFA(Minn)-'95	16/16
88		Hilliard, Ike	WR	5-11	195	4/5/76	2	Florida	Patterson, La.	D1-'97	2/2
79		Holsey, Bernard	DE	6-2	295	12/10/73	3	Duke	Cave Spring, Ga.	FA-'96	16/4
23		Johnson, LeShon	RB	6-0	214	1/15/71	5	Northern Illinois	Haskell, Okla.	UFA(Ariz)-'98	14/0*
94		Jones, Cedric	DE	6-4	275	4/30/74	3	Oklahoma	Houston, Tex.	D1-96	9/2
13		Kanell, Danny	QB	6-3	220	11/21/73	3	Florida State	Ft. Lauderdale, Fla.	D4-'96	16/10
37		Lane, Eric	RB	6-2	240	3/17/74	2	Tennessee	East Orange, N.J.	FA-'97	15/0
44	#	Massey, Robert	CB	5-11	203	2/17/67	10	North Carolina Central	Rock Hill, S.C.	FA-'97	16/0
9		Maynard, Brad	P	6-1	190	2/9/74	2	Ball State	Atlanta, Ind.	D3-'97	16/0
57		Miller, Corey	LB	6-2	252	10/25/68	8	South Carolina	Pageland, S.C.	D6-'91	14/13
51		Monty, Pete	LB	6-2	250	7/13/74	2	Wisconsin	Ft. Collins, Colo.	D4-'97	3/0
72		Oben, Roman	T	6-4	310	10/9/72	3	Louisville	Washington, D.C.	D3-'96	16/16
83		Patten, David	WR	5-9	180	8/19/74	2	Western Carolina	Hopkins, S.C.	FA-'97	16/3
99		Peter, Christian	DT	6-3	300	10/5/72	2	Nebraska	Locust, N.J.	FA-'97	7/0
91		Phillips, Ryan	LB	6-4	252	2/7/74	2	Idaho	Auburn, Wash.	D3-'97	10/0
85		Pupunu, Al	TE	6-2	260	10/17/69	7	Weber State	Salt Lake City, Utah	FA-'97	9/1*
66		Reynolds, Jerry	C-T	6-6	320	4/2/70	5	Nevada-Las Vegas	Fort Thomas, Ky.	FA-'95	5/0
34		Sanders, Brandon	S	5-9	185	6/10/73	2	Arizona	San Diego, Calif.	FA-'97	12/0
53		Scott, Lance	C	6-3	300	2/15/72	4	Utah	Salt Lake City, Utah	FA-'97	16/11
31		Sehorn, Jason	CB	6-2	210	4/15/71	5	Southern California	Mt. Shasta, Calif.	D2-'94	16/16
22		Sparks, Phillippi	CB	5-11	195	4/15/69	7	Arizona State	Glendale, Calif.	D2-'92	13/13
60		Stoltenberg, Bryan	C	6-1	300	8/25/72	3	Colorado	Sugarland, Tex.	FA-'97	3/0
65		Stone, Ron	G	6-5	325	7/20/71	6	Boston College	Roxbury, Mass.	RFA(Dall)-'96	16/16
92		Strahan, Michael	DE	6-4	280	11/21/71	6	Texas Southern	Westbury, Tex.	D2-'93	16/16
81		Toomer, Amani	WR	6-3	202	9/8/74	3	Michigan	Berkeley, Calif.	D2-'96	16/0
30		Way, Charles	RB	6-0	250	12/27/72	4	Virginia	Philadelphia, Pa.	D6-'95	16/16
28		Wheatley, Tyrone	RB	6-0	235	1/19/72	4	Michigan	Inkster, Mich.	D1-'95	14/7
90		Widmer, Corey	LB	6-3	255	12/25/68	7	Montana State	Bozeman, Mont.	D7-'92	16/15
59		Williams, Brian	C	6-5	315	6/8/66	10	Minnesota	Mt. Lebanon, Pa.	D1-'89	0*
29		Wooten, Tito	S	6-0	195	12/12/71	5	Northeast Louisiana	Goldsboro, N.C.	SD4-'94	16/16
47		Young, Rodney	S	6-0	210	1/25/73	4	Louisiana State	Grambling, La.	D3-'95	9/0
73	†	Zatechka, Rob	G	6-4	320	12/1/71	4	Nebraska	Lincoln, Neb.	D4-'95	16/0

* Brice played 6 games with St. Louis in '97; Brown played 15 games with San Diego; Douglas and Williams missed '97 season because of injury; Goines last active with Seattle in '96; Graham played 8 games with Arizona; Johnson played 14 games with Arizona; Pupunu played 8 games with San Diego, 1 with Kansas City.

\# Unrestricted free agent; subject to developments.

† Restricted free agent; subject to developments.

Players lost to free agency (4): DT Ray Agnew (StL; 15 games in '97), WR Kevin Alexander (Mia; 14), WR Thomas Lewis (Chi; 4), CB Thomas Randolph (Cin; 16).

Also played with Giants in '97—QB Dave Brown (7 games), DE Antonio Edwards (3), RB Rodney Hampton (2), RB Erric Pegram (11), TE Aaron Pierce (16).

COACHING STAFF

Head Coach,
Jim Fassel

Pro Career: After being named the fifteenth head coach in Giants history on January 15, 1997, Jim Fassel led his squad to a 10-5-1 record and a berth in the playoffs while capturing the NFC Eastern Division title. Fassel was named Coach of the Year by 11 media outlets, including *The Sporting News*, after helping the Giants improve from a 6-10 record and a last place finish in the NFC East in 1996. Under Fassel's guidance, the Giants became the fifteenth team in NFL history to finish in first place in their division the season after finishing in last place. The worst-to-first turnaround has occurred 13 times, including the 1997 Giants, since the 1970 merger. Fassel's group finished with a 7-0-1 Division record and became the first team ever to go undefeated in NFC Eastern Division play. The 1997 season marked Fassel's return to the Giants organization. He entered the NFL as an assistant coach with the Giants in 1991 as quarterbacks coach, then as offensive coordinator in 1992. Following his service with the Giants, Fassel spent two campaigns as assistant head coach/offensive coordinator for the Denver Broncos in 1993 and 1994. He spent the 1995 season as quarterbacks coach for the Oakland Raiders and was the offensive coordinator and the quarterbacks coach for the Arizona Cardinals in 1996. Under Fassel's guidance, Broncos quarterback John Elway enjoyed his finest season as a pro in 1993, earning honors that included the American Football Conference player of the year and most valuable player. Career record: 10-6-1.

Background: A former collegiate quarterback, Fassel began coaching in 1973 at his alma mater, Fullerton College, then was a player-coach for the Hawaii Hawaiians of the World Football League in 1974. He coached quarterbacks and receivers at Utah in 1976, then served seven seasons as offensive coordinator at both Weber State (1977-78) and Stanford (1979-83). At Stanford, Fassel was credited with recruiting and coaching Elway, who finished second in the balloting for the Heisman Trophy as a senior in 1982. Fassel entered the pro arena in 1984 as offensive coordinator for the New Orleans Breakers of the USFL, then returned to Utah as the school's head coach from 1985-89 where he recruited and coached current Detroit Lions quarterback Scott Mitchell. En route to the NFL under Fassel's tutelage, Mitchell set 10 NCAA and five Western Athletic Conference records in addition to virtually every school passing record.

Personal: A native of Anaheim, California, Fassel was a standout quarterback at Anaheim High School before leading Fullerton College to a 25-1 record over two seasons and winning the junior college national championship in 1967. He also played collegiately at Southern California with Green Bay Packers head coach Mike Holmgren and at Long Beach State. He was drafted by Chicago in the seventh round of the 1972 NFL Draft and played briefly with the Chicago Bears, Houston Oilers, and San Diego Chargers. Born August 31, 1949 in Anaheim, Fassel and his wife, Kitty, have four children, John , Brian, Jana, and Mike. John is a senior quarterback at Weber State.

ASSISTANT COACHES

Dave Brazil, defensive quality control; born March 25, 1936, Detroit, Mich., lives in East Rutherford, N.J. No college or pro playing experience. College coach: Holy Cross 1968, Tulsa 1969-70, Eastern Michigan 1971-73, Boston College 1980, Kent State 1981-82. Pro coach: Detroit Wheels (WFL) 1974, Chicago Wind (WFL) 1975, Kansas City Chiefs 1984-88, Pittsburgh Steelers 1989-91, joined Giants in 1992.

Rod Dowhower, quarterbacks; born April 15, 1943, Ord, Neb. Quarterback San Diego State 1963-65. No pro playing experience. College coach: San Diego State 1966-72, UCLA 1974-75, Boise State 1976, Stanford 1977-79 (head coach 1979), Vanderbilt 1995-96 (head coach). Pro coach: St. Louis Cardinals 1973, 1982-84, Denver Broncos 1980-1981, Indianapolis Colts 1985-86 (head coach), Atlanta Falcons 1987-89, Washington Redskins 1990-93, joined Giants in 1997.

John Dunn, strength and conditioning; born July 22, 1956, Hillsdale, N.Y. Guard Penn State 1974-77. No pro playing experience. College coach: Penn State 1978. Pro coach: Washington Redskins 1984-86, Los Angeles Raiders 1987-89, San Diego Chargers 1990-96, joined Giants in 1997.

John Fox, defensive coordinator; born February 8, 1955, Virginia Beach, Va. Defensive back San Diego State 1975-77. No pro playing experience. College coach: U.S. International 1979, Boise State 1980, Long Beach State 1981, Utah 1982, Kansas 1983, 1985, Iowa State 1984, Pittsburgh 1986-88. Pro coach: Los Angeles Express (USFL) 1985, Pittsburgh Steelers 1989-1991, San Diego Chargers 1992-93, Los Angeles/Oakland Raiders 1994-95, St. Louis Rams 1996, joined Giants in 1997.

Mike Gillhamer, offensive assistant; born February 20, 1954. Defensive back Humbolt State. No pro playing experience. College coach: College of the Sequoias 1979-83, Weber State 1984, Utah 1985-89, San Jose State 1990-93, Nevada 1994-95, Rutgers 1996. Pro coach: Joined Giants in 1997.

Mike Haluchak, linebackers; born November 28, 1949, Concord, Calif. Linebacker Southern California 1967-70. No pro playing experience. College coach: Southern California 1976-77, Cal State-Fullerton 1978, Pacific 1979-80, California 1981, North Carolina State 1982. Pro coach: Oakland Invaders (USFL) 1983-85, San Diego Chargers 1986-91, Cincinnati Bengals 1992-93, Washington Redskins 1994-96, joined Giants in 1997.

Johnnie Lynn, defensive backs; born December 19, 1956, Los Angeles, Calif. Defensive back UCLA 1975-78. Pro defensive back New York Jets 1979-86. College coach: Arizona 1988-93. Pro coach: Tampa Bay Buccaneers 1994-95, San Francisco 49ers 1996, joined Giants in 1997.

Larry MacDuff, special teams; born June 22, 1948, Clinton, Iowa. Defensive end Fullerton Community College 1966-67, Oklahoma 1968-69. No pro playing experience. College coach: Fullerton Community College 1970, 1974-79, Stanford 1980-83, Hawaii 1984-86, Arizona 1987-96. Pro coach: Joined Giants in 1997.

Denny Marcin, defensive line; born April 24, 1942, Cleveland, Ohio. Defensive and offensive line Miami (Ohio) 1961-64. No pro playing experience. College coach: Miami (Ohio) 1974-77, North Carolina 1978-87, Illinois 1988-96. Pro coach: Joined Giants in 1997.

John Matsko, offensive line; born February 2, 1951, Cleveland, Ohio. Fullback Kent State 1970-73. No pro playing experience. College coach: Kent State 1973, Miami (Ohio) 1974-75, 1977, North Carolina 1978-84, Navy 1985, Arizona 1986, Southern California 1987-91. Pro coach: Phoenix Cardinals 1992-93, New Orleans Saints 1994-96, joined Giants in 1997.

Dick Rehbein, tight ends-assistant offensive line; born November 22, 1955, Green Bay, Wis., lives in Wayne, N.J. Center Ripon 1973-77. No pro playing experience. Pro coach: Green Bay Packers 1979-83, Los Angeles Express (USFL) 1984, Minnesota Vikings 1984-91, joined Giants in 1992.

Jimmy Robinson, wide receivers; born January 3, 1953, Atlanta, lives in East Rutherford, N.J. Wide receiver Georgia Tech 1972-74. Pro wide receiver Atlanta Falcons 1975, New York Giants 1976-79, San Francisco 49ers 1980, Denver Broncos 1981. College coach: Georgia Tech 1986-89. Pro coach: Memphis Showboats (USFL) 1984-85, Atlanta Falcons 1990-93, Indianapolis Colts 1994-97, joined Giants in 1998.

Jim Skipper, offensive coordinator-running backs; born January 23, 1949, Breaux Bridge, La. Defensive back Whittier College 1971-72. No pro playing experience. College coach: Cal Poly-Pomona 1974-76, San Jose State 1977-78, Pacific 1979, Oregon 1980-82. Pro coach: Philadelphia/Baltimore Stars (USFL) 1983-85, New Orleans Saints 1986-95, Arizona Cardinals 1996, joined Giants in 1997.

Craig Stoddard, assistant strength and conditioning; born February 8, 1972, North Tarrytown, N.Y. Linebacker Springfield College 1990-93. No pro playing experience. College coach: Penn State 1995-96. Pro coach: San Diego Chargers 1994, joined Giants in 1997.

1998 FIRST-YEAR ROSTER

Name	Pos.	Ht.	Wt.	Birthdate	College	Hometown	How Acq.
Adams, Hunter	DE-DT	6-5	280	2/4/76	Bucknell	Caldwell, N.Y.	FA
Alford, Brian	WR	6-1	190	7/7/75	Purdue	Oak Park, Mich.	D3
Anderson, Ben	QB	6-5	210	5/3/75	Liberty	Chapin, S.C.	FA
Bailey, Corey	C	6-3	300	12/9/75	Fordham	Westwood, Mass.	FA
Ball, Raphaol	CB	5-11	180	12/9/74	Ball State	Cincinnati, Ohio	FA
Bell, Jimmie	DE	6-5	270	11/20/73	Ohio State	Youngstown, Ohio	FA
Blackwell, Kory (1)	CB	5-11	185	8/3/72	Massachusetts	Queens, N.Y.	FA
Comella, Greg	RB	6-1	240	7/29/75	Stanford	Wellesley, Mass.	FA
Estes, Charles (1)	DE	6-3	265	9/30/75	Army	Georgetown, Ky.	FA
Fricke, Ben	C	6-0	295	11/13/75	Houston	Austin, Tex.	D7
Gilliam, Darryl	T	6-6	325	2/17/75	Maryland	Washington, D.C.	FA
Haase, Andy	TE	6-4	260	7/10/74	Northern Colorado	Odessa, Wash.	FA
Hobgood-Chittick, Nate	DT	6-5	295	11/30/74	North Carolina	Allentown, Pa.	FA
Johnson, Rashee	S	5-11	180	3/21/74	Arizona	San Diego, Calif.	FA
Jurevicius, Joe	WR	6-5	230	12/23/74	Penn State	Chardon, Ohio	D2
Lamb, Marc (1)	C	6-5	315	5/4/72	Montana	Yorba Linda, Calif.	FA
Myles, Toby	T	6-5	310	7/23/75	Jackson State	Jackson, Miss.	D5
Nevadomsky, Jason	DE	6-2	240	11/8/75	UCLA	Fullerton, Calif.	FA
Pollack, Todd	TE	6-4	255	12/10/74	Boston College	Rye, N.Y.	D6
Snyder, Chris	DE	6-3	275	12/5/74	Penn State	Chesapeake, Va.	FA
Studdard, Greg	T	6-6	300	9/6/74	Sam Houston	San Antonio, Tex.	FA
Walker, Robert (1)	RB	5-11	210	6/26/72	West Virginia	Huntington, W. Va.	FA
Washington, John (1)	WR	5-9	175	7/8/74	Texas Christian	Longview, Tex.	FA
Whittle, Jason	T	6-6	300	3/7/75	Southwest Missouri State	Springfield, Mo.	FA
Williams, George	DT	6-3	295	12/8/75	North Carolina State	Roseboro, N.C.	FA
Williams, Shaun	S	6-1	215	10/10/76	UCLA	Los Angeles, Calif.	D1
Willis, Marcel	LB	6-4	235	5/12/75	Ohio State	Brook Park, Ohio	FA

The term NFL Rookie is defined as a player who is in his first season of professional football and has not been on the roster of another professional football team for any regular-season or postseason games. A Rookie is designated by an "R" on NFL rosters. Players who have been active in another professional football league or players who have NFL experience, including either preseason training camp or being on an Active List or Inactive List, or on Reserve/Injured or Reserve/Physically Unable to Perform for fewer than six regular-season games, are termed NFL First-Year Players. An NFL First-Year Player is designated by a "1" on NFL rosters. Thereafter, a player is credited with an additional year of experience for each season in which he accumulates six games on the Active List or Inactive List, or on Reserve/Injured or Reserve/Physically Unable to Perform.

PHILADELPHIA EAGLES

National Football Conference
Eastern Division
Team Colors: Midnight Green, Silver, Black, and White
Veterans Stadium
3501 South Broad Street
Philadelphia, Pennsylvania 19148
Telephone: (215) 463-2500

CLUB OFFICIALS

Owner/Chief Executive Officer: Jeffrey Lurie
Executive Vice President: Joe Banner
Director of Football Operations: Tom Modrak
Senior Vice President-Chief Financial Officer: Mimi Box
Senior Vice President, Marketing and Administration: Len Komoroski
Vice President, Sales: Scott O'Neil
Vice President, Corporate Sales: Dave Rowan
Executive Director of Eagles Youth Partnership: Sarah Helfman
Director of College Scouting: John Goeller
College Scouting Coordinator: Bryan Broaddus
Director of Administration: Vicki Chatley
Director of Public Relations: Ron Howard
Assistant Director of Public Relations: Derek Boyko
Director, Broadcasting and Sales: David Perry
Ticket Manager: Leo Carlin
Director of Merchandise: Steve Strawbridge
Director of Advertising and Promotions: Kim Babiak
Office Manager/Travel Coordinator: Tracey Bucher
Director of Security: Anthony (Butch) Buchanico
Director of Penthouse Operations: Christiana Noyalas
Head Athletic Trainer: James Collins
Asst. Athletic Trainers: Scottie Patton and Scott Trulock
Peak Performance Specialist: Baron Baptiste
Video Director: Mike Dougherty
Equipment Manager: Rusty Sweeney
Stadium: Veterans Stadium • **Capacity:** 65,352
3501 South Broad Street
Philadelphia, Pennsylvania 19148
Playing Surface: AstroTurf-8
Training Camp: Lehigh University
Bethlehem, Pennsylvania 18015

1998 SCHEDULE

PRESEASON

Aug. 6	**New York Jets**	8:00
Aug. 14	**Pittsburgh**	8:00
Aug. 24	at Baltimore	7:30
Aug. 29	at New England	8:00

REGULAR SEASON

Sept. 6	**Seattle**	1:01
Sept. 13	at Atlanta	1:01
Sept. 20	at Arizona	5:20
Sept. 27	**Kansas City**	1:01
Oct. 4	at Denver	2:15
Oct. 11	**Washington**	1:01
Oct. 18	at San Diego	1:15
Oct. 25	Open Date	
Nov. 2	**Dallas** (Mon.)	8:20
Nov. 8	**Detroit**	1:01
Nov. 15	at Washington	1:01
Nov. 22	at New York Giants	1:01
Nov. 29	at Green Bay	3:15
Dec. 3	**St. Louis** (Thurs.)	8:20
Dec. 13	**Arizona**	1:01
Dec. 20	at Dallas	3:15
Dec. 27	**New York Giants**	4:05

RECORD HOLDERS

INDIVIDUAL RECORDS—CAREER

Category	Name	Performance
Rushing (Yds.)	Wilbert Montgomery, 1977-1984	6,538
Passing (Yds.)	Ron Jaworski, 1977-1986	26,963
Passing (TDs)	Ron Jaworski, 1977-1986	175
Receiving (No.)	Harold Carmichael, 1971-1983	589
Receiving (Yds.)	Harold Carmichael, 1971-1983	8,978
Interceptions	Bill Bradley, 1969-1976	34
	Eric Allen, 1988-1994	34
Punting (Avg.)	Joe Muha, 1946-1950	42.9
Punt Return (Avg.)	Steve Van Buren, 1944-1951	13.9
Kickoff Return (Avg.)	Steve Van Buren, 1944-1951	26.7
Field Goals	Paul McFadden, 1984-87	91
Touchdowns (Tot.)	Harold Carmichael, 1971-1983	79
Points	Bobby Walston, 1951-1962	881

INDIVIDUAL RECORDS—SINGLE SEASON

Category	Name	Performance
Rushing (Yds.)	Wilbert Montgomery, 1979	1,512
Passing (Yds.)	Randall Cunningham, 1988	3,808
Passing (TDs)	Sonny Jurgensen, 1961	32
Receiving (No.)	Irving Fryar, 1996	88
Receiving (Yds.)	Mike Quick, 1983	1,409
Interceptions	Bill Bradley, 1971	11
Punting (Avg.)	Joe Muha, 1948	47.2
Punt Return (Avg.)	Steve Van Buren, 1944	15.3
Kickoff Return (Avg.)	Al Nelson, 1972	29.1
Field Goals	Paul McFadden, 1984	30
Touchdowns (Tot.)	Steve Van Buren, 1945	18
Points	Paul McFadden, 1984	116

INDIVIDUAL RECORDS—SINGLE GAME

Category	Name	Performance
Rushing (Yds.)	Steve Van Buren, 11-27-49	205
Passing (Yds.)	Randall Cunningham, 9-17-89	447
Passing (TDs)	Adrian Burk, 10-17-54	*7
Receiving (No.)	Don Looney, 12-1-40	14
Receiving (Yds.)	Tommy McDonald, 12-10-60	237
Interceptions	Russ Craft, 9-24-50	*4
Field Goals	Tom Dempsey, 11-12-72	6
Touchdowns (Tot.)	Many times	4
	Last time by Irving Fryar, 10-20-96	
Points	Bobby Walston, 10-17-54	25

*NFL Record

COACHING HISTORY

(397-466-25)

1933-35	Lud Wray	9-21-1
1936-40	Bert Bell	10-44-2
1941-50	Earle (Greasy) Neale*	66-44-5
1951	Alvin (Bo) McMillin**	2-0-0
1951	Wayne Millner	2-8-0
1952-55	Jim Trimble	25-20-3
1956-57	Hugh Devore	7-16-1
1958-60	Lawrence (Buck) Shaw	20-16-1
1961-63	Nick Skorich	15-24-3
1964-68	Joe Kuharich	28-41-1
1969-71	Jerry Williams***	7-22-2
1971-72	Ed Khayat	8-15-2
1973-75	Mike McCormack	16-25-1
1976-82	Dick Vermeil	57-51-0
1983-85	Marion Campbell****	17-29-1
1985	Fred Bruney	1-0-0
1986-90	Buddy Ryan	43-38-1
1991-94	Rich Kotite	37-29-0
1995-97	Ray Rhodes	27-23-1

*Co-coach with Walt Kiesling in Philadelphia-Pittsburgh merger in 1943
**Retired after two games in 1951
***Released after three games in 1971
****Released after 15 games in 1985

VETERANS STADIUM

N

1997 TEAM RECORD

PRESEASON (1-3)

Date	Result		Opponents
8/2	L	17-31	at New York Jets
8/11	L	26-42	at Pittsburgh
8/16	W	24-13	Pittsburgh
8/22	L	14-28	New England

REGULAR SEASON (6-9-1)

Date	Result		Opponents	Att.
8/31	L	17-31	at New York Giants	70,296
9/07	W	10-9	Green Bay	66,803
9/15	L	20-21	at Dallas	63,942
9/28	L	19-28	at Minnesota	55,149
10/5	W	24-10	Washington	67,008
10/12	L	21-38	at Jacksonville	69,150
10/19	W	13-10	Arizona (OT)	66,860
10/26	W	13-12	Dallas	67,106
11/2	L	21-31	at Arizona	39,549
11/10	L	12-24	San Francisco	67,133
11/16	T	10-10	at Baltimore (OT)	63,546
11/23	W	23-20	Pittsburgh	67,166
11/30	W	44-42	Cincinnati	66,623
12/7	L	21-31	New York Giants	67,084
12/14	L	17-20	at Atlanta	42,866
12/21	L	32-35	at Washington	75,939

(OT) Overtime

SCORE BY PERIODS

Eagles	75	71	59	109	3	—	317
Opponents	100	90	68	114	0	—	372

ATTENDANCE

Home 535,783 Away 480,437 Total 1,016,220
Single-game home record, 72,111 (11/1/81)
Single-season home record, 557,325 (1980)

1997 TEAM STATISTICS

	Eagles	Opp.
Total First Downs	326	286
Rushing	105	115
Passing	203	150
Penalty	18	21
Third Down: Made/Att	90/242	80/217
Third Down Pct.	37.2	36.9
Fourth Down: Made/Att	14/22	8/14
Fourth Down Pct.	63.6	57.1
Total Net Yards	5,590	4,932
Avg. Per Game	349.4	308.3
Total Plays	1,116	1,009
Avg. Per Play	5.0	4.9
Net Yards Rushing	1,943	2,009
Avg. Per Game	121.4	125.6
Total Rushes	465	476
Net Yards Passing	3,647	2,923
Avg. Per Game	227.9	182.7
Sacked/Yards Lost	64/362	43/278
Gross Yards	4,009	3,201
Att./Completions	587/330	490/259
Completion Pct.	56.2	52.9
Had Intercepted	16	14
Punts/Avg.	88/41.6	87/41.4
Net Punting Avg.	88/34.6	87/36.0
Penalties/Yards Lost	104/866	86/708
Fumbles/Ball Lost	35/16	25/12
Touchdowns	36	43
Rushing	11	16
Passing	22	20
Returns	3	7
Avg. Time of Possession	31:09	28:51

1997 INDIVIDUAL STATISTICS

Passing	Att.	Comp.	Yds.	Pct.	TD	Int.	Tkld.	Rate
T. Detmer	244	134	1,567	54.9	7	6	19/94	73.9
Hoying	225	128	1,573	56.9	11	6	28/183	83.8
Peete	118	68	869	57.6	4	4	17/85	78.0
Johnson	0	0	0	—	0	0	0/0	—
Eagles	587	330	4,009	56.2	22	16	64/362	78.5
Opponents	490	259	3,201	52.9	20	14	43/278	75.1

SCORING	TD R	TD P	TD Rt	PAT	FG	Saf	PTS
Boniol	0	0	0	33/33	22/31	0	99
Watters	7	0	0	0/0	0/0	0	42
Fryar	0	6	0	0/0	0/0	0	36
Lewis	0	4	0	0/0	0/0	0	24
Solomon	0	3	0	0/0	0/0	0	20
Garner	3	0	0	0/0	0/0	0	18
Turner	0	3	0	0/0	0/0	0	18
Dunn	0	2	0	0/0	0/0	0	12
Timpson	0	2	0	0/0	0/0	0	12
Clark	0	0	1	0/0	0/0	0	6
Dawkins	0	0	1	0/0	0/0	0	6
T. Detmer	1	0	0	0/0	0/0	0	6
Johnson	0	1	0	0/0	0/0	0	6
Seay	0	1	0	0/0	0/0	0	6
W. Thomas	0	0	1	0/0	0/0	0	6
Eagles	11	22	3	33/33	22/31	0	317
Opponents	16	20	7	42/42	24/33	0	372

2-Point conversions: Solomon, Team 1-3, Opponents 0-1

RUSHING	Att.	Yds.	Avg.	LG	TD
Watters	285	1,110	3.9	28	7
Garner	116	547	4.7	26	3
Turner	18	96	5.3	29	0
Hoying	16	78	4.9	30	0
T. Detmer	14	46	3.3	14	1
Peete	8	37	4.6	16	0
Staley	7	29	4.1	12	0
Hutton	1	0	0.0	0	0
Eagles	465	1,943	4.2	30	11
Opponents	476	2,009	4.2	53	16

RECEIVING	No.	Yds.	Avg.	LG	TD
Fryar	86	1,316	15.3	72t	6
Turner	48	443	9.2	36	3
Watters	48	440	9.2	37	0
Timpson	42	484	11.5	26	2
Solomon	29	455	15.7	56	3
Garner	24	225	9.4	27	0
Johnson	14	177	12.6	28	1
Seay	13	187	14.4	38	1
Lewis	12	94	7.8	17	4
Dunn	7	93	13.3	31t	2
C. Jones	5	73	14.6	32	0
Staley	2	22	11.0	22	0
Vincent	0	0	—	—	0
Eagles	330	4,009	12.1	72t	22
Opponents	259	3,201	12.4	62	20

INTERCEPTIONS	No.	Yds.	Avg.	LG	TD
Dawkins	3	76	25.3	64t	1
Vincent	3	14	4.7	14	0
Dimry	2	25	12.5	25	0
W. Thomas	2	11	5.5	11	0
Hall	1	39	39.0	39	0
Zordich	1	21	21.0	21	0
Stevens	1	0	0.0	0	0
Willis	1	0	0.0	0	0
Eagles	14	186	13.3	64t	1
Opponents	16	425	26.6	95t	4

PUNTING	No.	Yds.	Avg.	In 20	LG
Hutton	87	3,660	42.1	19	61
Eagles	88	3,660	41.6	19	61
Opponents	87	3,603	41.4	28	62

PUNT RETURNS	No.	FC	Yds.	Avg.	LG	TD
Seay	16	8	172	10.8	42	0
Solomon	10	7	55	5.5	14	0
Gray	2	5	17	8.5	11	0
Wyatt	2	1	-2	-1.0	0	0
Vincent	1	0	-8	-8.0	-8	0
Eagles	31	21	234	7.5	42	0
Opponents	48	9	515	10.7	73t	1

KICKOFF RETURNS	No.	Yds.	Avg.	LG	TD
Staley	47	1139	24.2	57	0
Witherspoon	9	171	19.0	28	0
Johnson	3	22	7.3	15	0
Turner	3	48	16.0	22	0
Dunn	2	32	16.0	16	0
Wyatt	2	50	25.0	30	0
Clark	1	39	39.0	39t	1
Gray	1	8	8.0	8	0
Lewis	1	11	11.0	11	0
Seay	0	0	—	—	0
Eagles	69	1520	22.0	57	1
Opponents	66	1548	23.5	84	0

FIELD GOALS	1-19	20-29	30-39	40-49	50+
Boniol	0/0	7/7	11/12	4/11	0/1
Eagles	0/0	7/7	11/12	4/11	0/1
Opponents	2/2	10/11	6/6	6/11	0/3

SACKS	No.
Hall	8.0
W. Thomas	5.0
Dent	4.5
Mamula	4.0
Jefferson	3.0
J. Jones	2.5
H. Thomas	2.5
Taylor	2.0
Willis	2.0
Zordich	2.0
Conner	1.5
Farmer	1.0
Harris	1.0
Jasper	1.0
Smith	1.0
Eagles	43.0
Opponents	64.0

1998 DRAFT CHOICES

Round	Name	Pos.	College
1	Tra Thomas	T	Florida State
3	Jeremiah Trotter	LB	Stephen F. Austin
	Allen Rossum	DB	Notre Dame
4	Brandon Whiting	DT	California
	Clarence Love	DB	Toledo
5	Ike Reese	LB	Michigan State
7	Chris Akins	DT	Texas
	Melvin Thomas	G	Colorado

PHILADELPHIA EAGLES

1998 VETERAN ROSTER

No.	Name	Pos.	Ht.	Wt.	Birthdate	NFL Exp.	College	Hometown	How Acq.	'97 Games/ Starts
62	Beckles, Ian	G	6-1	304	7/20/67	9	Indiana	Montreal, Canada	UFA(TB)-'97	9/8
18	Boniol, Chris	K	5-11	167	12/9/71	5	Louisiana Tech	Alexandria, La.	RFA(Dall)-'97	16/0
27	Brice, Alundis	CB	5-10	178	5/1/70	3	Mississippi	Brookhaven, Miss.	FA-'98	0*
76	† Brooks, Barrett	T	6-4	309	5/5/72	4	Kansas State	Florissant, Mo.	D2b-'95	16/14
56	Caldwell, Mike	LB	6-2	237	8/31/71	6	Middle Tennessee State	Oak Ridge, Tenn.	UFA(Ariz)-'98	16/0*
93	# Conner, Darion	DE	6-2	250	9/28/67	9	Jackson State	Prairie Point, Miss.	FA-'96	14/0
77	Cooper, Richard	T	6-5	290	11/1/64	9	Tennessee	Memphis, Tenn.	UFA(NO)-'96	0*
86	Copeland, Russell	WR	6-0	200	11/4/71	6	Memphis State	Tupelo, Miss.	UFA(Buff)-'97	0*
33	Cothran, Jeff	RB	6-1	249	6/28/71	4	Ohio State	Middleton, Ohio	FA-'98	0*
66	Crafts, Jerry	G-T	6-5	334	1/6/68	5	Louisville	Tulsa, Okla.	FA-'97	15/6
57	Darling, James	LB	6-0	250	12/29/74	2	Washington State	Kettle Falls, Wash.	D2-'97	16/6
20	Dawkins, Brian	S	5-11	190	10/13/73	3	Clemson	Jacksonville, Fla.	D2b-'96	15/15
95	# Dent, Richard	DE	6-6	266	12/13/60	15	Tennessee State	Atlanta, Ga.	FA-'97	15/0
10	Detmer, Koy	QB	6-0	180	7/5/73	2	Colorado	San Antonio, Tex.	D7a-'97	0*
38	# Dimry, Charles	CB	6-0	176	1/31/66	11	Nevada-Las Vegas	Oceanside, Calif.	FA-'97	15/9
53	t- Douglas, Hugh	LB-DE	6-2	280	8/23/71	4	Central State, Ohio	Mansfield, Ohio	T(NYJ)-'98	15/15*
75	# Drake, Troy	T	6-6	305	5/15/72	4	Indiana	Byron, Ill.	FA-'95	9/2
87	Dunn, Jason	TE	6-4	257	11/15/73	3	Eastern Kentucky	Harrodsburg, Ky.	D2a-'96	15/4
47	Emanuel, Charles	S	6-0	196	6/3/73	2	West Virginia	Indianatown, Fla.	FA-'97	5/1
61	Everitt, Steve	C	6-5	290	8/21/70	6	Michigan	Miami, Fla.	UFA(Balt)-'97	16/16
55	Farmer, Ray	LB	6-3	225	7/1/74	3	Duke	Kernersville, N.C.	D4-'96	14/5
52	Fogle, DeShawn	LB	6-1	220	4/1/75	2	Kansas State	Manhattan, Kan.	FA-'97	5/0
80	Fryar, Irving	WR	6-0	200	9/28/62	15	Nebraska	Mount Holly, N.J.	UFA(Mia)-'96	16/16
79	Gaines, Wendell	G	6-5	315	1/17/72	3	Oklahoma State	Frederick, Okla.	W(StL)-'98	0*
30	Garner, Charlie	RB	5-9	187	2/13/72	5	Tennessee	Falls Church, Va.	D2b-'94	16/2
81	t- Graham, Jeff	WR	6-2	206	2/14/69	8	Ohio State	Kettering, Ohio	T(NYJ)-'98	16/15*
28	# Gray, Mel	RB-KR	5-9	171	3/16/61	13	Purdue	Williamsburg, Va.	FA-'97	14/0*
97	† Hall, Rhett	DT	6-2	276	12/5/68	8	California	Morgan Hill, Calif.	UFA(SF)-'95	15/15
90	Harris, Jon	DE	6-7	280	6/9/74	2	Virginia	Inwood, N.Y.	D1-'97	8/4
69	Hegamin, George	G-T	6-7	331	2/14/73	5	North Carolina State	Camden, N.J.	UFA(Dall)-'98	13/9*
7	Hoying, Bobby	QB	6-3	221	9/20/72	3	Ohio State	St. Henry, Ohio	D3-'96	7/6
4	Hutton, Tom	P-K	6-1	193	7/8/72	4	Tennessee	Memphis, Tenn.	FA-'95	16/0
74	Jasper, Edward	DT	6-2	295	1/18/73	2	Texas A&M	Troup, Tex.	D6b-'97	10/1
79	† Jefferson, Greg	DE	6-3	257	8/31/71	4	Central Florida	Bartow, Fla.	D3a-'95	12/11
94	Johnson, Bill	DT	6-4	305	12/8/68	7	Michigan State	Chicago, Ill.	UFA(StL)-'98	16/16*
88	Johnson, Jimmie	TE	6-2	257	10/6/66	10	Howard	Augusta, Ga.	FA-'95	16/11
82	† Jones, Chris T.	WR	6-3	209	8/7/71	4	Miami	West Palm Beach, Fla.	D3b-'95	4/1
98	# Jones, Jimmie	DE-DT	6-4	285	1/9/66	9	Miami	Lake Okeechobee, Fla.	FA-'97	14/0
58	Kalu, Ndukwe	LB-DE	6-3	246	8/3/75	2	Rice	San Antonio, Tex.	D5a-'97	3/0
43	Kinder, Randy	CB	6-1	210	4/4/75	2	Notre Dame	East Lansing, Mich.	W(GB)-'97	12/0*
89	Lewis, Chad	TE	6-6	252	10/5/71	2	Brigham Young	Orem, Utah	FA-'97	16/3
64	Love, Sean	G	6-3	305	9/6/68	5	Penn State	Tamaqua, Pa.	FA-'97	0*
59	Mamula, Mike	LB-DE	6-4	252	8/14/73	4	Boston College	Lackawanna, N.Y.	D1-'95	16/16
71	Mayberry, Jermane	T	6-4	325	8/29/73	3	Texas A&M-Kingsville	Floresville, Tex.	D1-'96	16/16
24	McTyer, Tim	CB	5-11	181	12/14/75	2	Brigham Young	Los Angeles, Calif.	FA-'97	10/0
65	Miller, Bubba	C-G	6-1	300	1/24/73	3	Tennessee	Franklin, Tenn.	FA-'96	13/3
9	Peete, Rodney	QB	6-0	225	3/16/66	10	Southern California	Tucson, Ariz.	UFA(Dall)-'95	5/3
67	Sims, Keith	G	6-3	318	6/17/67	9	Iowa State	Warren, N.J.	UFA(Wash)-'98	8/4*
84	Solomon, Freddie	WR	5-10	180	8/15/72	3	South Carolina State	Alachua, Fla.	FA-'97	15/5
22	Staley, Duce	RB	5-11	220	2/27/75	2	South Carolina	Columbia, S.C.	D3-'97	16/0
45	Stevens, Matt	S	6-0	206	6/15/73	3	Appalachian State	Chapel Hill, N.C.	W(Buff)-'97	11/0
21	† Taylor, Bobby	CB	6-3	216	12/28/73	4	Notre Dame	Longview, Tex.	D2a-'95	6/5
78	Thomas, Hollis	DT	6-0	306	1/10/74	3	Northern Illinois	St. Louis, Mo.	FA-'96	16/16
51	Thomas, William	LB	6-2	223	8/13/68	8	Texas A&M	Amarillo, Tex.	D4-'91	14/14
83	# Timpson, Michael	WR	5-10	185	6/6/67	10	Penn State	Hialeah, Fla.	UFA(Chi)-'97	15/10
34	Turner, Kevin	RB	6-1	231	6/12/69	7	Alabama	Prattville, Ala.	RFA(NE)-'95	16/10
68	Unutoa, Morris	C	6-1	284	3/10/71	3	Brigham Young	Carson, Calif.	FA-'96	16/0
23	Vincent, Troy	CB	6-0	194	6/8/70	7	Wisconsin	Trenton, N.J.	RFA(Mia)-'96	16/16
29	Walker, Corey	RB	5-10	188	6/4/73	2	Arkansas State	Memphis, Tenn.	FA-'97	0*
50	Willis, James	LB	6-2	237	9/2/72	6	Auburn	Huntsville, Ala.	FA-'95	15/15
16	Wilson, Sheddrick	WR	6-3	210	11/23/73	2	Louisiana State	Thomasville, Ga.	FA-'98	0*
85	Wyatt, Antwuan	WR	5-10	199	7/18/75	2	Bethune-Cookman	Daytona Beach, Fla.	D6a-'97	1/0
36	Zordich, Michael	S	6-1	212	10/12/63	12	Penn State	Youngstown, Ohio	FA-'94	16/16

* Brice last active with Dallas in '96; Caldwell played 16 games with Arizona in '97; Cooper, K. Detmer, and Walker all missed '97 season because of injury; Copeland inactive for 7 games; Cothran last active with Cincinnati in '96; Douglas played 15 games with the N.Y. Jets; Gaines last active with Arizona in '95; Graham played 16 games with the N.Y. Jets; Gray played 11 games with Tennessee; Hegamin played 13 games with Dallas; B. Johnson played 16 games with St. Louis; Kinder played 6 games with Green Bay; Love inactive for 7 games; Sims played 8 games with Miami; Wilson last active with Houston in '96.

Unrestricted free agent; subject to developments.

† Restricted free agent; subject to developments.

t– Eagles traded for Douglas and Graham (N.Y. Jets).

Players lost through free agency (5): QB Ty Detmer (SF; 8 games in '97), LB Jeff Herrod (Ind; 10), G Joe Panos (Buff; 13), LB Darrin Smith (Sea; 7), RB Ricky Watters (Sea; 16).

Also played with Eagles in '97—WR Justin Armour (1 game), CB Deauntae Brown (1), K Lonny Calicchio (2), CB Willie Clark (16), DT Andy Harmon (5), WR Mark Seay (12), DE Al Wallace (1), S Tim Watson (3), RB Derrick Witherspoon (3), G Mike Zandofsky (5).

COACHING STAFF

Head Coach,
Ray Rhodes

Pro Career: Named the nineteenth head coach in Eagles history on February 2, 1995, after serving as the defensive coordinator for the San Francisco 49ers. After being named the 1995 NFL coach of the year in his inaugural season at the Eagles' helm, Rhodes led the Eagles to another 10-6 season and a wild card playoff berth in 1996. As such, Rhodes became the first coach in team history to lead his team to the playoffs in each of his first two seasons. However, by finishing the 1997 season with a 6-9-1 record, it marked the first season in which Philadelphia has not made the playoffs under Rhodes. In fact, during Rhodes' 17-year coaching career, his teams have been in the postseason in all but four years (1997 Eagles, 1992 Packers, 1991 49ers, and 1982 49ers). Rhodes also suffered just his second losing campaign. (The 1982 49ers finished 3-6 in a strike-shortened season.) In 1995, Rhodes battled through major roster turnover, a slew of injuries to key personnel, an early season quarterback change, and a sluggish 1-3 start to post a 10-6 record, the top wild card berth in the NFC, and a record-setting 58-37 postseason defeat of the Detroit Lions. In 1996, Rhodes' troops again finished second in the NFC East behind the Dallas Cowboys. Philadelphia then closed the '96 season as the fifth of six seeds in the NFC playoffs and fell to the host 49ers in a wild card game. Rhodes came to Philadelphia after assisting George Seifert and the 49ers to that franchise's unprecedented fifth Super Bowl championship. In fact, Rhodes was an assistant on each of the 49ers' championship teams, making him one of only four men in NFL history to have served on the staffs of five Super Bowl winners. Before his most recent stint with San Francisco, Rhodes served two seasons in Green Bay as defensive coordinator under ex-49ers assistant Mike Holmgren, where he elevated the Packers' defense to the second-ranked unit overall in just two seasons. Rhodes ended his seven-year NFL playing career with San Francisco in 1980 and then joined Bill Walsh's coaching staff as an assistant defensive backs coach the following season. In 1982, he was promoted to defensive backs coach and held that position through 1991. Over that period, he developed four Pro Bowl defenders, cornerbacks Ronnie Lott and Eric Wright, and safeties Dwight Hicks and Carlton Williamson. Career record: 27-23-1.

Background: After spending two years at Texas Christian University, Rhodes finished his collegiate career at the University of Tulsa and was selected by the New York Giants in the tenth round of the 1974 NFL draft. He played wide receiver for his first three seasons with the Giants but was switched to defensive back in 1977. In 1979, he was traded to San Francisco in a deal that also saw 49ers defensive back Tony Dungy, presently the head coach of the Tampa Bay Buccaneers, sent to the Giants.

Personal: Born October 20, 1950, in Mexia, Tex. Rhodes and his wife, Carmen, have four daughters: Detra, Candra, Tynesha, and Raven, and reside in Marlton, New Jersey.

ASSISTANT COACHES

Dana Bible, offensive coordinator; born October 30, 1953, Erie, Pa., lives in Philadelphia. Defensive back Cincinnati 1972-76. No pro playing experience. College coach: Cincinnati 1976-80, Miami (Ohio) 1981-82, North Carolina State 1983-85, San Diego State 1986-88, Miami (Ohio) 1989, Cincinnati 1994, Stanford 1995-97. Pro coach: Cincinnati Bengals 1990-92, joined Eagles in 1998.

Jim Bollman, tight ends; born December 1, 1954, Ashtabula, Oh., lives in Philadelphia. Offensive lineman Ohio University 1973-76. No pro playing experience. College coach: Miami (Ohio) 1977-82, North Carolina State 1983-85, Youngstown State 1986-90, Virginia 1991-94, Michigan State 1995-97. Pro coach: Joined Eagles in 1998.

Gerald Carr, wide receivers; born June 28, 1959, Davidson, N.C., lives in Siclerville, N.J. Quarterback Southern Illinois 1977-80. No pro playing experience. College coach: Southern Illinois 1982, Davidson 1983-85, Akron 1986-88, Washington State 1989-90, Arizona 1991, North Carolina 1992-94. Pro coach: Joined Eagles in 1995.

Juan Castillo, offensive line; born October 8, 1959, Port Isabel, Tex., lives in Moorestown, N.J. Linebacker Texas A&M-Kingsville (formerly Texas A&I) 1978-80. Pro linebacker San Antonio Gunslingers (USFL) 1984-85. College coach: Texas A&M-Kingsville 1982-85, 1990-94. Pro coach: Joined Eagles in 1995.

John Harbaugh, special teams; born September 23, 1962, Perrysburg, Oh., lives in Philadelphia. Defensive back Miami (Ohio) 1980-83. No pro playing experience. College coach: Western Michigan 1984-86, Pittsburgh 1987, Morehead State 1998, Cincinnati 1989-96, Indiana 1997. Pro coach: Joined Eagles in 1998.

Chuck Knox, Jr., defensive assistant-quality control; born June 19, 1965, Englewood, N.J., lives in Mt. Laurel, N.J. Running back Arizona 1984-88. No pro playing experience. Pro coach: Los Angeles Rams 1993-94, joined Eagles in 1995.

Sean Payton, quarterbacks; born December 29, 1963, San Mateo, Calif., lives in Marlton, N.J. Quarterback Eastern Illinois 1982-86. Pro quarterback Ottawa Rough Riders (CFL) 1987, Chicago Bears 1987. College coach: San Diego State 1988-89, 1992-93, Indiana State 1990-91, Miami (Ohio) 1994-95, Illinois 1996. Pro coach: Joined Eagles in 1997.

Danny Smith, defensive backs; born November 7, 1953, Pittsburgh, Pa., lives in Mt. Laurel, N.J. Defensive back Edinboro State 1972-75. No pro playing experience. College coach: Edinboro State 1976, Clemson 1979, William & Mary 1980-83, Citadel 1984-86, Georgia Tech 1987-94. Pro coach: Joined Eagles in 1995.

Emmitt Thomas, defensive coordinator; born June 3, 1943, Angleton, Tex., lives in Voorhees, N.J. Quarterback-wide receiver Bishop (Tex.) College 1963-65. Pro defensive back Kansas City Chiefs 1966-78. College coach: Central Missouri State 1979-80. Pro coach: St. Louis Cardinals 1981-85, Washington Redskins 1986-94, joined Eagles in 1995.

Mike Trgovac, defensive line; born February 27, 1959, Youngstown, Ohio, lives in Marlton, N.J. Defensive lineman Michigan 1977-80. No pro playing experience. College coach: Michigan 1984-85, Ball State 1986-88, Navy 1989, Colorado State 1990-91, Notre Dame 1992-94. Pro coach: Joined Eagles in 1995.

Joe Vitt, linebackers; born August 23, 1954, Camden, N.J., lives in Mt. Laurel, N.J. Linebacker Towson State 1973-75. No pro playing experience. Pro coach: Baltimore Colts 1979-81, Seattle Seahawks 1982-91, Los Angeles Rams 1992-94, joined Eagles in 1995.

Ted Williams, running backs; born November 17, 1943, Lyons, Tex., lives in Siclerville, N.J. No college or pro playing experience. College coach: UCLA 1980-89, Washington State 1991-93, Arizona 1994. Pro coach: Joined Eagles in 1995.

Mike Wolf, strength and conditioning; born May 15, 1965, Allentown, Pa., lives in Marlton, N.J. Center Penn State 1983-87. No pro playing experience. College coach: Vanderbilt 1988-89, Lehigh 1990, Penn State 1991. Pro coach: Minnesota Vikings 1992-94, joined Eagles in 1995.

Ken Zampese, offensive assistant; born July 19, 1967, Santa Maria, Calif., lives in Philadelphia. Wide receiver San Diego 1985-88. No pro playing experience. College coach: Southern California 1990-91, Northern Arizona 1992-95, Miami (Ohio) 1996-97. Pro coach: Joined Eagles in 1998.

1998 FIRST-YEAR ROSTER

Name	Pos.	Ht.	Wt.	Birthdate	College	Hometown	How Acq.
Asbell, Troy	LB	6-0	217	9/3/74	Texas A&M-Kingsville	Tyler, Tex.	FA
Akins, Chris	DT	6-1	323	1/7/76	Texas	Paris, Tex.	D7a
Cannon, Rico	WR	6-1	195	11/7/74	Newberry College	Easley, S.C.	FA
Council, Keith	DT	6-6	285	12/3/74	Hampton	Orlando, Fla.	FA
Crawford, Tarren	G	6-6	319	9/23/77	Central State, Ohio	Baltimore, Md.	FA
Dulick, Jason (1)	WR	6-4	200	5/26/74	Illinois	St. Louis, Mo.	FA
Hankton, Karl (1)	WR	6-2	202	7/24/70	Trinity College	Wayne, Pa.	FA
Hoffart, Jake	WR	6-1	200	6/24/75	Pittsburgh	Yuba City, Calif.	FA
Holmes, Jaret	K	6-2	209	3/3/76	Auburn	Clinton, Miss.	FA
Jelks, A.J.	RB	6-2	250	3/25/76	Oregon	Sacramento, Caifl.	FA
Jones, Tevell	CB	6-0	180	11/14/75	Ohio	Detroit, Mich.	FA
Kerrin, Keith	LB	6-0	224	5/3/74	Temple	Gibbsboro, N.J.	FA
Kesi, Pat (1)	G	6-3	319	9/10/73	Washington	Honolulu, Hawaii	FA
Love, Clarence	CB	5-10	181	6/16/76	Toledo	Jackson, Mich.	D4b
McCoy, Mike (1)	QB	6-2	204	4/1/72	Utah	Novato, Calif.	FA
McKenzie, Brian	RB	5-10	200	2/27/75	Brigham Young	Sarasota, Fla.	FA
Middleton, Harvey	WR	5-11	186	4/20/75	Georgia Tech	Jamestown, S.C.	FA
Reed, Mike	RB	6-0	215	1/6/75	Washington	Tacoma, Wash.	FA
Reese, Ike	LB	6-2	222	10/16/73	Michigan State	Cincinnati, Ohio	D5
Rice, Anthony (1)	CB-S	5-9	185	11/29/73	Laverne	Pomona, Calif.	FA-'97
Rossum, Allen	CB-KR	5-8	178	10/22/75	Notre Dame	Dallas, Tex.	D3b
Sinceno, Kaseem	TE	6-4	259	3/26/76	Syracuse	Liberty, N.Y.	FA
Storm, Matt (1)	G	6-3	312	9/2/72	Georgia	Edmonds, Wash.	FA
Thomas, Melvin	G	6-3	322	6/11/75	Colorado	New Orleans, La.	D7b
Thomas, Tra	T	6-7	349	11/20/74	Florida State	Deland, Fla.	D1
Trotter, Jeremiah	LB	6-0	261	1/20/77	Stephen F. Austin	Hooks, Tex.	D3a
Wallace, Al (1)	DE-LB	6-5	258	3/25/74	Maryland	Delray Beach, Fla.	FA
Whiting, Brandon	DT	6-3	278	7/30/76	California	Long Beach, Calif.	D4a

The term NFL Rookie is defined as a player who is in his first season of professional football and has not been on the roster of another professional football team for any regular-season or postseason games. A Rookie is designated by an "R" on NFL rosters. Players who have been active in another professional football league or players who have NFL experience, including either preseason training camp or being on an Active List or Inactive List, or on Reserve/Injured or Reserve/Physically Unable to Perform for fewer than six regular-season games, are termed NFL First-Year Players. An NFL First-Year Player is designated by a "1" on NFL rosters. Thereafter, a player is credited with an additional year of experience for each season in which he accumulates six games on the Active List or Inactive List, or on Reserve/Injured or Reserve/Physically Unable to Perform.

NOTES

ST. LOUIS RAMS

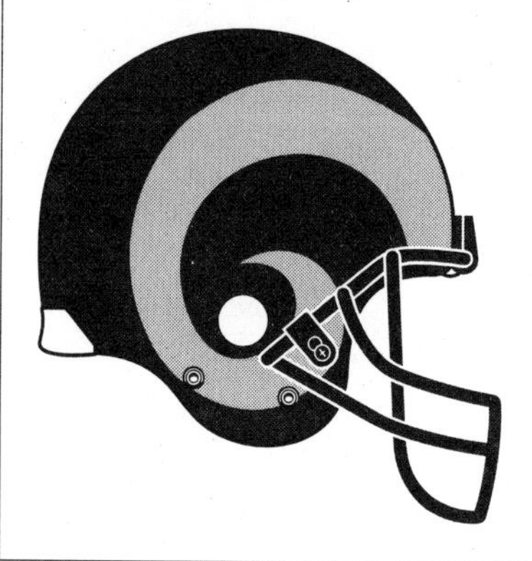

National Football Conference
Western Division
Team Colors: Royal Blue, Gold, and White
One Rams Way
St. Louis County, Missouri 63045
Telephone: (314) 982-7267

CLUB OFFICIALS

Owner/Chairman: Georgia Frontiere
Owner/Vice Chairman: Stan Kroenke
President: John Shaw
President-Football Operations and Head Coach: Dick Vermeil
Executive Vice President: Jay Zygmunt
Senior Vice President-Administration and General Counsel: Bob Wallace
Treasurer: Jeff Brewer
Vice President-Finance: Adrian Barr
Director-College Scouting: John Becker
Vice President-Media and Community Relations: Marshall Klein
Vice President-Football Operations: Lynn Stiles
Vice President-Marketing: Phil Thomas
Vice President-Sales: Brian Ulione
Vice President-Personnel: Charley Armey
Vice President/Player Relations and Football General Counsel: Kevin Warren
Vice President/Player Development: Jackie Slater
Director of Operations: John Oswald
Director of Public Relations: Rick Smith
Assistant Director of Public Relations: Duane Lewis
Head Trainer: Jim Anderson
Assistant Trainers: Dake Walden, Ron DuBuque
Equipment Manager: Todd Hewitt
Scouts: Billy Campfield, Greg Gaines, Kevin McCabe, Lawrence McCutcheon, David Razzano, Paul Russell, Harley Sewell, Howard Tippett
Stadium: Trans World Dome at America's Center
•**Capacity:** 66,000
701 Convention Plaza
St. Louis County, Missouri 63101
Playing Surface: AstroTurf
Training Camp: Western Illinois University
Thompson Hall
Macomb, Illinois 61455

1998 SCHEDULE

PRESEASON

Aug. 8	**Denver**	7:00
Aug. 15	at San Diego	8:00
Aug. 22	**Dallas**	7:00
Aug. 28	at Kansas City	7:00

REGULAR SEASON

Sept. 6	**New Orleans**	12:01
Sept. 13	**Minnesota**	12:01
Sept. 20	at Buffalo	1:01
Sept. 27	**Arizona**	12:01
Oct. 4	Open Date	
Oct. 11	**New York Jets**	3:15
Oct. 18	at Miami	4:15
Oct. 25	**San Francisco**	12:01
Nov. 1	at Atlanta	1:01
Nov. 8	at Chicago	12:01
Nov. 15	at New Orleans	12:01
Nov. 22	**Carolina**	3:05
Nov. 29	**Atlanta**	12:01
Dec. 3	at Philadelphia (Thurs.)	8:20
Dec. 13	**New England**	12:01
Dec. 20	at Carolina	1:01
Dec. 27	at San Francisco	1:05

RECORD HOLDERS

INDIVIDUAL RECORDS—CAREER

Category	Name	Performance
Rushing (Yds.)	Eric Dickerson, 1983-87	7,245
Passing (Yds.)	Jim Everett, 1986-1993	23,758
Passing (TDs)	Roman Gabriel, 1962-1972	154
Receiving (No.)	Henry Ellard, 1983-1993	593
Receiving (Yds.)	Henry Ellard, 1983-1993	9,761
Interceptions	Ed Meador, 1959-1970	46
Punting (Avg.)	Danny Villanueva, 1960-64	44.2
Punt Return (Avg.)	Henry Ellard, 1983-1992	11.3
Kickoff Return (Avg.)	Tom Wilson, 1956-1961	27.1
Field Goals	Mike Lansford, 1982-1990	158
Touchdowns (Tot.)	Eric Dickerson, 1983-87	58
Points	Mike Lansford, 1982-1990	789

INDIVIDUAL RECORDS—SINGLE SEASON

Category	Name	Performance
Rushing (Yds.)	Eric Dickerson, 1984	*2,105
Passing (Yds.)	Jim Everett, 1989	4,310
Passing (TDs)	Jim Everett, 1988	31
Receiving (No.)	Isaac Bruce, 1995	119
Receiving (Yds.)	Isaac Bruce, 1995	1,781
Interceptions	Dick (Night Train) Lane, 1952	*14
Punting (Avg.)	Danny Villanueva, 1962	45.5
Punt Return (Avg.)	Woodley Lewis, 1952	18.5
Kickoff Return (Avg.)	Verda (Vitamin T) Smith, 1950	33.7
Field Goals	David Ray, 1973	30
Touchdowns (Tot.)	Eric Dickerson, 1983	20
Points	David Ray, 1973	130

INDIVIDUAL RECORDS—SINGLE GAME

Category	Name	Performance
Rushing (Yds.)	Eric Dickerson, 1-4-86	248
Passing (Yds.)	Norm Van Brocklin, 9-28-51	*554
Passing (TDs)	Many times	5
	Last time by Jim Everett, 9-25-88	
Receiving (No.)	Tom Fears, 12-3-50	*18
Receiving (Yds.)	Willie Anderson, 11-26-89	*336
Interceptions	Many times	3
	Last time by Keith Lyle, 12-15-96	
Field Goals	Bob Waterfield, 12-9-51	5
Touchdowns (Tot.)	Bob Shaw, 12-11-49	4
	Elroy (Crazylegs) Hirsch, 9-28-51	4
	Harold Jackson, 10-14-73	4
Points	Bob Shaw, 12-11-49	24
	Elroy (Crazylegs) Hirsch, 9-28-51	24
	Harold Jackson, 10-14-73	24

*NFL Record

COACHING HISTORY

Cleveland 1937-1945, Los Angeles 1946-1994
(429-399-20)

1937-38	Hugo Bezdek*	1-13-0
1938	Art Lewis	4-4-0
1939-42	Earl (Dutch) Clark	16-26-2
1944	Aldo (Buff) Donelli	4-6-0
1945-46	Adam Walsh	16-5-1
1947	Bob Snyder	6-6-0
1948-49	Clark Shaughnessy	14-8-3
1950-52	Joe Stydahar**	19-9-0
1952-54	Hamp Pool	23-11-2
1955-59	Sid Gillman	28-32-1
1960-62	Bob Waterfield***	9-24-1
1962-65	Harland Svare	14-31-3
1966-70	George Allen	49-19-4
1971-72	Tommy Prothro	14-12-2
1973-77	Chuck Knox	57-20-1
1978-82	Ray Malavasi	43-36-0
1983-91	John Robinson	79-74-0
1992-94	Chuck Knox	15-33-0
1995-96	Rich Brooks	13-19-0
1997	Dick Vermeil	5-11-0

*Released after three games in 1938
**Resigned after one game in 1952
***Resigned after eight games in 1962

TRANS WORLD DOME

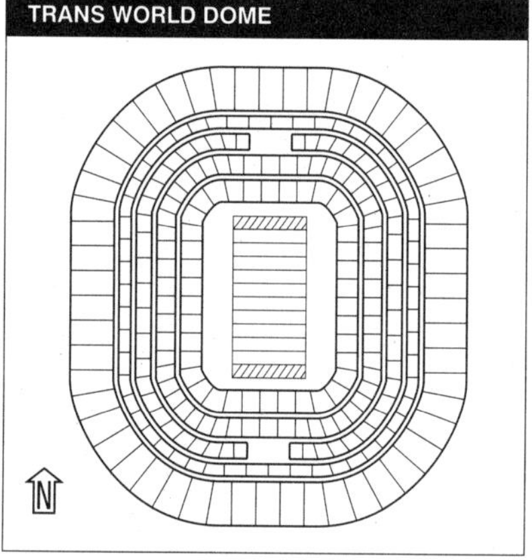

ST. LOUIS RAMS

1997 TEAM RECORD

PRESEASON (2-2)

Date	Result		Opponent
8/2	L	6-24	at Minnesota
8/8	W	12-0	Arizona
8/15	L	31-34	at Dallas
8/22	W	14-13	Kansas City

REGULAR SEASON (5-11)

Date	Result		Opponent	Att.
8/31	W	38-24	New Orleans	64,575
9/7	L	12-15	San Francisco	64,630
9/15	L	14-35	at Denver	74,338
9/21	W	13-3	New York Giants	64,642
9/28	L	17-35	at Oakland	42,506
10/12	L	10-30	at San Francisco	63,825
10/19	L	9-17	Seattle	64,819
10/26	L	20-28	Kansas City	64,864
11/2	L	31-34	at Atlanta	36,583
11/9	L	7-17	at Green Bay	60,093
11/16	L	21-27	Atlanta	64,299
11/23	L	10-16	Carolina	64,609
11/30	W	23-20	at Washington	74,772
12/7	W	34-27	at New Orleans	54,803
12/14	L	10-13	Chicago	66,030
12/20	W	30-18	at Carolina	58,101

SCORE BY PERIODS

Rams	37	121	68	73	—	299
Opponents	57	104	96	102	—	359

ATTENDANCE

Home 518,468 Away 465,021 Total 983,489

Single-game home record, 66,030 (12/14/97)

Single-season home record, 518,468 (1997)

1997 TEAM STATISTICS

	Rams	Opp.
Total First Downs	271	296
Rushing	85	84
Passing	161	177
Penalty	25	35
Third Down: Made/Att	73/223	76/215
Third Down Pct.	32.7	35.3
Fourth Down: Made/Att	4/11	5/11
Fourth Down Pct.	36.4	45.5
Total Net Yards	4,761	5,066
Avg. Per Game	297.6	316.6
Total Plays	1,013	1,021
Avg. Per Play	4.7	5.0
Net Yards Rushing	1,563	1,687
Avg. Per Game	97.7	105.4
Total Rushes	443	440
Net Yards Passing	3,198	3,379
Avg. Per Game	199.9	211.2
Sacked/Yards Lost	44/326	38/296
Gross Yards	3,675	3,379
Att./Completions	526/271	543/288
Completion Pct.	51.5	53.0
Had Intercepted	15	25
Punts/Avg.	95/41.9	82/44.5
Net Punting Avg.	95/33.8	82/39.0
Penalties/Yards Lost	142/1,065	133/1,064
Fumbles/Ball Lost	29/15	27/14
Touchdowns	32	39
Rushing	15	10
Passing	14	26
Returns	3	3
Avg. Time of Possession	29:47	30:13

1997 INDIVIDUAL STATISTICS

Passing	Att.	Comp.	Yds.	Pct.	TD	Int.	Tkld.	Rate
Banks	487	252	3,254	51.7	14	13	43/317	71.5
Rypien	39	19	270	48.7	0	2	1/9	50.2
Rams	526	271	3,524	51.5	14	15	44/326	69.9
Opponents	543	288	3,675	53.0	26	25	38/296	71.3

SCORING	TD R	TD P	TD Rt	PAT	FG	Saf	PTS
Wilkins	0	0	0	32/32	25/37	0	107
Phillips	8	0	0	0/0	0/0	0	48
Bruce	0	5	0	0/0	0/0	0	30
Conwell	0	4	0	0/0	0/0	0	24
Lee	0	3	0	0/0	0/0	0	18
J. Moore	3	0	0	0/0	0/0	0	18
Banks	1	0	0	0/0	0/0	0	6
Heyward	1	0	0	0/0	0/0	0	6
Laing	0	1	0	0/0	0/0	0	6
McNeil	0	0	1	0/0	0/0	0	6
R. Moore	1	0	0	0/0	0/0	0	6
O'Neal	0	0	1	0/0	0/0	0	6
Small	0	1	0	0/0	0/0	0	6
Thompson	1	0	0	0/0	0/0	0	6
Wiegert	0	0	1	0/0	0/0	0	6
Rams	15	14	3	32/32	25/37	0	299
Opponents	10	26	3	31/31	26/31	1	359

2-Point conversions: Team 0-0, Opponents 7-8.

RUSHING	Att.	Yds.	Avg.	LG	TD
Phillips	183	633	3.5	28	8
J. Moore	104	380	3.7	26	3
Banks	47	186	4.0	23	1
Lee	28	104	3.7	14	0
R. Moore	24	103	4.3	27t	1
Heyward	34	84	2.5	8	1
Crawford	2	32	16.0	23	0
Thompson	16	30	1.9	9	1
Kennison	3	13	4.3	6	0
Rypien	1	1	1.0	1	0
Horan	1	-3	-3.0	-3	0
Rams	443	1,563	3.5	28	15
Opponents	440	1,687	3.8	65	10

RECEIVING	No.	Yds.	Avg.	LG	TD
Lee	61	825	13.5	62	3
Bruce	56	815	14.6	59	5
Conwell	38	404	10.6	46t	4
Small	32	488	15.3	46	1
Kennison	25	404	16.2	76	0
Crawford	11	232	21.1	69	0
Phillips	10	33	3.3	17	0
Heyward	8	77	9.6	25	0
J. Moore	8	69	8.6	19	0
Laing	5	31	6.2	11	1
Floyd	4	39	9.8	14	0
R. Moore	4	34	8.5	13	0
Ross	3	37	12.3	14	0
Thomas	2	25	12.5	16	0
Jacoby	2	10	5.0	10	0
Wiegert	1	1	1.0	1	0
Gruttadauria	1	0	0.0	0	0
Rams	271	3,524	13.0	76	14
Opponents	288	3,675	12.8	72t	26

INTERCEPTIONS	No.	Yds.	Avg.	LG	TD
McNeil	9	127	14.1	75t	1
Lyle	8	102	12.8	39	0
Lyght	4	25	6.3	13	0
Farr	1	22	22.0	22	0
O'Neal	1	5	5.0	5	0
M. Jones	1	0	0.0	0	0
McCleon	1	0	0.0	0	0
Rams	25	281	11.2	75t	1
Opponents	15	85	5.7	29	0

PUNTING	No.	Yds.	Avg.	In 20	LG
Horan	53	2,272	42.9	10	60
Brice	41	1,713	41.8	6	61
Rams	95	3,985	41.9	16	61
Opponents	82	3,648	44.5	23	61

PUNT RETURNS	No.	FC	Yds.	Avg.	LG	TD
Kennison	34	20	247	7.3	43	0
Floyd	4	2	15	3.8	8	0
Ross	2	0	12	6.0	6	0
Lee	0	1	0	—	—	0
Rams	40	23	274	6.9	43	0
Opponents	60	14	618	10.3	94t	1

KICKOFF RETURNS	No.	Yds.	Avg.	LG	TD
Thompson	49	1,110	22.7	56	0
Ross	6	130	21.7	42	0
Thomas	5	97	19.4	24	0
Lee	4	71	17.8	19	0
Kennison	1	14	14.0	7	0
R. Moore	1	17	17.0	17	0
J. Williams	1	10	10.0	10	0
Zgonina	1	5	5.0	5	0
Rams	68	1,454	21.4	56	0
Opponents	54	1,262	23.4	102t	1

SACKS	No.
O'Neal	10.0
Carter	7.5
Bill Johnson	4.0
Farr	3.0
M. Jones	2.0
Lyle	2.0
Phifer	2.0
Zgonina	2.0
R. Jones	1.0
Lyght	1.0
McCleon	1.0
B. Robinson	1.0
J. Williams	1.0
J. Robinson	0.5
Rams	38.0
Opponents	44.0

FIELD GOALS	1-19	20-29	30-39	40-49	50+
Wilkins	0/0	8/9	8/12	7/14	2/2
Rams	0/0	8/9	8/12	7/14	2/2
Opponents	1/1	9/10	4/4	8/10	4/6

1998 DRAFT CHOICES

Round	Name	Pos.	College
1	Grant Wistrom	DE	Nebraska
2	Robert Holcombe	RB	Illinois
3	Leonard Little	LB	Tennessee
4	Az-Zahir Hakim	WR	San Diego State
	Roland Williams	TE	Syracuse
5	Raymond Priester	RB	Clemson
6	Glenn Roundtree	G	Clemson
7	Jason Chorak	DE	Washington

ST. LOUIS RAMS

1998 VETERAN ROSTER

No.		Name	Pos.	Ht.	Wt.	Birthdate	NFL Exp.	College	Hometown	How Acq.	'97 Games/ Starts
99		Agnew, Ray	DT	6-3	285	12/9/67	9	North Carolina State	Winston Salem, N.C.	UFA(NYG)-'98	15/0*
20		Allen, Taje	CB	5-10	185	11/6/73	2	Texas	Lubbock, Tex.	D5-'97	14/1
49		Armstrong, Tyji	TE	6-4	250	10/3/70	6	Mississippi	Inkster, Mich.	FA-'98	0*
12		Banks, Tony	QB	6-4	215	4/5/73	3	Michigan State	San Diego, Calif.	D2a-'96	16/16
13	t-	Bono, Steve	QB	6-4	212	5/11/62	14	UCLA	Norristown, Pa.	T(GB)-'98	2/0*
77		Brooks, Ethan	G-T	6-6	299	4/27/72	2	Williams	Simsbury, Conn.	FA-'97	0*
80		Bruce, Isaac	WR	6-0	188	11/10/72	5	Memphis	Ft. Lauderdale, Fla.	D2a-'94	12/12
93		Carter, Kevin	DE	6-5	280	9/21/73	4	Florida	Tallahassee, Fla.	D1-'95	16/16
24		Clark, Willie	CB	5-10	186	1/6/72	5	Notre Dame	Wheatland, Calif.	FA-'98	16/2*
56		Clemons, Charlie	LB	6-2	255	7/4/72	2	Georgia	Griffin, Ga.	FA-'97	5/0
84		Conwell, Ernie	TE	6-1	265	8/17/72	3	Washington	Kent, Wash.	D2b-'96	16/16
55		Dumas, Troy	LB	6-3	242	9/30/72	4	Nebraska	Cheyenne, Wyo.	FA-'97	10/0*
75		Farr, D'Marco	DT	6-1	280	6/9/71	5	Washington	Richmond, Calif.	FA-'94	16/16
63		Flannery, John	C-G	6-3	304	1/13/69	7	Syracuse	Pottsville, Pa.	UFA(Dall)-'98	16/4*
9		Furrer, Will	QB	6-3	215	2/5/68	6	Virginia Tech	Pullman, Wash.	FA-'97	0*
70		Gandy, Wayne	T	6-4	310	2/10/71	5	Auburn	Haines City, Fla.	D1-'94	16/16
66		Gerak, John	G	6-3	300	1/6/70	6	Penn State	Struthers, Ohio	UFA(Minn)-'97	16/16
60		Gruttadauria, Mike	C	6-3	297	12/6/72	3	Central Florida	Tarpon Springs, Fla.	FA-'96	14/14
33		Harris, Derrick	RB	6-0	252	9/18/72	3	Miami	Angleton, Tex.	D6a-'96	0*
34		Heyward, Craig	RB	5-11	265	9/26/66	11	Pittsburgh	Passaic, N.J.	UFA(Atl)-'97	16/12
54		Hill, Eric	LB	6-2	258	11/14/66	10	Louisiana State	Galveston, Tex.	UFA(Ariz)-'98	11/10*
89		Jacoby, Mitch	TE	6-4	260	12/8/73	2	Northern Illinois	Fredonia, Wis.	FA-'97	14/2
22		Jenkins, Jr., Billy	S	5-10	205	7/8/74	2	Howard	Albuquerque, N.M.	FA-'97	16/2
52		Jones, Mike	LB	6-1	240	4/15/69	8	Missouri	Kansas City, Mo.	UFA(Oak)-'97	16/16
59		Kazadi, Muadianvita	LB	6-2	240	12/20/73	2	Tulsa	Newton, Kan.	D6-'97	12/0
88		Kennison, Eddie	WR	6-0	195	1/20/73	3	Louisiana State	Lake Charles, La.	D1b-'96	14/9
86		Laing, Aaron	TE	6-3	260	7/19/71	4	New Mexico State	Houston, Tex.	FA-'96	15/4
31		Lee, Amp	RB	5-11	200	10/1/71	7	Florida State	Chipley, Fla.	FA-'97	16/1
41		Lyght, Todd	CB	6-0	190	2/9/69	8	Notre Dame	Flint, Mich.	D1-'91	16/16
35		Lyle, Keith	S	6-2	210	4/17/72	5	Virginia	Vienna, Va.	D3a-'94	16/16
97		Manley, James	DT	6-3	320	7/11/74	2	Vanderbilt	Birmingham, Ala.	FA-'98	0*
91		Maumalanga, Chris	DT	6-3	300	12/15/71	3	Kansas	Hawthorne, Calif.	FA-'97	0*
23		McBurrows, Gerald	S	5-11	205	10/7/73	4	Kansas	Detroit, Mich.	D7a-'95	8/3
21		McCleon, Dexter	CB	5-10	200	10/9/73	2	Clemson	Meridian, Miss.	D2-'97	16/1
47		McNeil, Ryan	CB	6-2	192	10/4/70	6	Miami	Fort Pierce, Fla.	UFA(Det)-'97	16/16
73		Miller, Fred	T	6-7	315	2/6/73	3	Baylor	Houston, Tex.	D5-'96	15/7
44		Moore, Jerald	RB	5-9	225	11/20/74	3	Oklahoma	Houston, Tex.	D3-'96	9/5
76		Pace, Orlando	T	6-7	340	11/4/75	2	Ohio State	Sandusky, Ohio	D1-'97	13/9
58		Phifer, Roman	LB	6-2	240	3/5/68	8	UCLA	Pineville, N.C.	D2-'91	16/15
79		Phillips, Joe	DT	6-5	305	7/15/63	13	Southern Methodist	Portland, Ore.	FA-'98	15/15*
87		Proehl, Ricky	WR	6-0	190	3/7/68	9	Wake Forest	Hillsborough, N.J.	UFA(Chi)-'98	15/10*
92		Robinson, Bryan	DE	6-4	295	6/22/74	2	Fresno State	Toledo, Ohio	FA-'97	11/0
94		Robinson, Jeff	DE	6-4	275	2/20/70	6	Idaho	Spokane, Wash.	UFA(Den)-'97	16/0
37		Scurlock, Mike	S	5-10	200	2/26/72	4	Arizona	Tucson, Ariz.	FA-'97	5/0
51		Styles, Lorenzo	LB	6-1	245	1/31/74	4	Ohio State	Columbus, Ohio	FA-'97	3/0
83		Thomas, J.T.	WR	5-10	180	7/11/71	4	Arizona State	San Bernardino, Calif.	D7d-'95	4/0
28		Thompson, David	RB	5-8	200	1/13/75	2	Oklahoma State	Okmulgee, Okla.	FA-'97	11/0
50		Tucker, Ryan	C-G	6-5	305	6/12/75	2	Texas Christian	Midland, Tex.	D4-'97	7/0
11		Tuten, Rick	P	6-2	221	1/5/65	9	Florida State	Ocala, Fla.	UFA(Sea)-'98	11/0*
72	†	Wiegert, Zach	G	6-4	310	8/16/72	4	Nebraska	Fremont, Neb.	D2a-'95	15/15
14		Wilkins, Jeff	K	6-2	205	4/19/72	5	Youngstown State	Austintown, Ohio	RFA(SF)-'97	16/0
96		Williams, Jay	DE	6-3	280	10/13/71	3	Wake Forest	Washington, D.C.	FA-'96	16/2
32		Wright, Toby	S	5-11	212	11/19/70	5	Nebraska	Phoenix, Ariz.	D2b-'94	11/11
90		Zgonina, Jeff	DT	6-2	300	5/24/70	6	Purdue	Barrington Hills, Ill.	UFA(Atl)-'97	15/0

* Agnew played 15 games with N.Y. Giants in '97; Armstrong last active with Dallas in '96; Bono played 2 games with Green Bay; Brooks inactive for 5 games; Clark played 16 games with Philadelphia; Dumas played 8 games with Kansas City; Flannery played 16 games with Dallas; Furrer inactive for 16 games; Harris inactive for 15 games; Hill played 11 games with Arizona; Manley inactive for 4 games with Minnesota; Maumalanga inactive for 1 game; Phillips played 15 games with Kansas City; Proehl played 15 games with Chicago; Tuten played 11 games with Seattle.

† Restricted free agent; subject to developments.

t- Rams traded for Bono (Green Bay).

Players lost through free agency (4): WR Keith Crawford (Atl; 15 games in '97), DT Bill Johnson (Phil; 16), QB Mark Rypien (Atl; 5), Torrance Small (Ind; 13).

Also played with Rams in '97—P Will Brice (6 games), C Bern Brostek (1), LB Nate Dingle (9), G Ernest Dye (16), WR Malcolm Floyd (4), LB Britt Hager (13), P Mike Horan (10), LB Robert Jones (16), RB Ronald Moore (7), DE Leslie O'Neal (15), RB Lawrence Phillips (10), WR Jermaine Ross (4), CB Joe Rowe (2), C-G Vernice Smith (10), CB Marquis Walker (11), LB Brett Wallerstedt (2).

COACHING STAFF

Head Coach,
Dick Vermeil

Pro Career: Named twentieth head coach of the Rams on January 22, 1997. Was designated the first special teams coach in NFL history in 1969 for the Los Angeles Rams. After one year of coaching in college, he returned to the Rams as the quarterbacks coach from 1971-73. In 1976, he was named head coach of the Philadelphia Eagles. In 1978, he led the Eagles to their first playoff appearance in eighteen seasons. In 1980, he led the Eagles to Super Bowl XV before losing to the Oakland Raiders. He concluded his stint in Philadelphia in 1982 after piloting the Eagles to four playoff appearances in seven seasons. Career record: 62-62.

Background: Played quarterback at San Jose State from 1956-57 after transferring from Napa Junior College. Began his head coaching career in 1959 at Delmar High School in San Jose, California. He became head coach at Hillsdale High School in San Mateo, California, then moved to College of San Mateo in 1963. The following year he became head coach at Napa College. He was at Stanford for four years beginning in 1965. Returned to college coaching in 1970 when he became the offensive coordinator at UCLA. Vermeil was named head coach at UCLA in 1974. In 1975, the Bruins capped off an improbable season by upsetting No. 1 Ohio State in the Rose Bowl. Has been named Coach of the Year on four levels: high school, junior college, Division I, and NFL. Is the only coach who has guided his team to a Super Bowl and a Rose Bowl.

Personal: Born October 30, 1936, in Calistoga, Calif. Graduated from San Jose State in 1958 with a bachelor of science degree in physical education and in 1959 with a master's degree in physical education. Vermeil and his wife, Carol, reside in St. Charles, Mo., and have three children and ten grandchildren.

1998 FIRST-YEAR ROSTER

Name	Pos.	Ht.	Wt.	Birthdate	College	Hometown	How Acq.
Austin, Billy	S	5-10	195	3/8/75	New Mexico	Houston, Tex.	FA
Baker, Donnell (1)	WR	6-0	200	12/21/73	Southern	Baton Rouge, La.	FA
Bush, Daryl	LB	6-1	248	2/11/75	Florida State	Lake Brantley, Fla.	FA
Chanoine, Roger	T	6-4	270	9/11/76	Temple	Linden, N.J.	FA
Chorak, Jason	LB	6-4	256	9/23/74	Washington	Vashon, Wash.	D7
Fletcher, London	LB	6-0	238	5/19/75	John Carroll	Cleveland, Ohio	FA
Goodson, Tyrone	WR	6-2	191	2/24/74	Auburn	Brooksville, Fla.	FA
Hakim, Az-Zahir	WR	5-10	180	6/3/77	San Diego State	Los Angeles, Calif.	D4a
Henley, June (1)	RB	5-10	226	9/4/75	Kansas	Columbus, Ohio	FA
Holcombe, Robert	RB	5-11	216	12/11/75	Illinois	Mesa, Ariz.	D2
Horne, Tony	WR	5-9	179	3/21/76	Clemson	Rockingham, N.C.	FA
Kempfert, David (1)	C	6-4	290	5/11/74	Montana	Thousands Oaks, Calif.	FA
Little, Leonard	DE	6-3	242	10/19/74	Tennessee	Asheville, N.C.	D3
McKinney, Jeremy	T	6-5	290	1/6/76	Iowa	Brighton, Colo.	FA
Morgan, Omarr	CB	5-9	164	12/4/76	Brigham Young	Los Angeles, Calif.	FA
Nutten, Tom	C	6-4	285	6/8/71	Western Michigan	Magog, Canada	FA
Pollack, Fred	G	6-1	321	2/27/74	Nebraska	Omaha, Neb.	FA
Priester, Raymond	RB	6-1	235	2/3/75	Clemson	Allendale, S.C.	D5
Reem, Matt (1)	T	6-6	270	12/23/72	Minnesota	Minneapolis, Minn.	FA
Rountree, Glenn	G	6-3	308	11/24/73	Clemson	Suffolk, Va.	D6
Rowe, Joe (1)	CB	6-0	195	12/8/73	Virginia	Emporia, Va.	FA
Sellers, Donald (1)	WR	6-0	195	12/30/74	New Mexico	Birmingham, Ala.	FA
Schultis, Mark	P	6-0	188	2/13/75	Texas	Kansas City, Mo.	FA
Sears, Corey	DE-DT	6-2	295	4/15/73	Mississippi State	Universal City, Tex.	FA
Shaw, Russell	WR	5-9	183	2/25/73	Michigan	Los Angeles, Calif.	FA
Warner, Kurt (1)	QB	6-2	220	6/22/71	Northern Iowa	Burlington, Iowa.	FA
Williams, Roland	TE	6-5	266	4/27/75	Syracuse	Rochester, N.Y.	D4b
Wistrom, Grant	DE	6-4	270	7/3/76	Nebraska	Webb City, Mo.	D1
Young, Glenn	DE	6-3	251	9/10/75	Vanderbilt	Detroit, Mich.	FA

The term NFL Rookie is defined as a player who is in his first season of professional football and has not been on the roster of another professional football team for any regular-season or postseason games. A Rookie is designated by an "R" on NFL rosters. Players who have been active in another professional football league or players who have NFL experience, including either preseason training camp or being on an Active List or Inactive List, or on Reserve/Injured or Reserve/Physically Unable to Perform for fewer than six regular-season games, are termed NFL First-Year Players. An NFL First-Year Player is designated by a "1" on NFL rosters. Thereafter, a player is credited with an additional year of experience for each season in which he accumulates six games on the Active List or Inactive List, or on Reserve/Injured or Reserve/Physically Unable to Perform.

ASSISTANT COACHES

Steve Brown, secondary; born March 20, 1960, Sacramento, Calif., lives in Wildhorse, Mo. Defensive back Oregon 1978-82. Pro cornerback Houston Oilers 1983-90. Pro coach: Joined Rams in 1995.

John Bunting, defensive coordinator-linebackers; born July 15, 1950, Portland, Maine, lives in St. Louis. Linebacker North Carolina 1968-71. Pro linebacker Philadelphia Eagles 1972-82, Philadelphia Stars (USFL) 1983-84. College coach: Brown 1986, Rowan College 1987-92 (head coach 1988-92). Pro coach: Baltimore Stars (USFL) 1985, Kansas City Chiefs 1993-96, joined Rams in 1997.

Chris Clausen, strength and conditioning coordinator; born February 21, 1958, Evergreen Park, Ill., lives in St. Louis. Cornerback Indiana 1976-79. No pro playing experience. College coach: San Diego State 1987-88. Pro coach: San Diego Chargers 1989-91, joined Rams in 1992.

Dick Coury, wide receivers; born September 29, 1929, Athens, Ohio, lives in St. Charles, Mo. Quarterback Notre Dame 1950-54. No pro playing experience. College coach: Southern California 1967-69, Cal State-Fullerton 1970-71. Pro coach: Denver Broncos 1972-73, Portland Storm (WFL) 1974 (head coach), San Diego Chargers 1975, Philadelphia Eagles 1976-81, Boston/New Orleans/Portland Breakers (USFL) 1983-85 (head coach), Los Angeles Rams 1986-90, New England Patriots 1991-92, Minnesota Vikings 1993, Houston Oilers 1994-96, rejoined Rams in 1997.

Frank Gansz, special teams-offensive assistant; born November 22, 1938, Altoona, Pa., lives in Chesterfield, Mo. Guard-linebacker Navy 1957-59. No pro playing experience. College coach: Air Force 1964-66, Colgate 1968, Navy 1969-72, Oklahoma State 1973, 1975, Army 1974, UCLA 1976-77. Pro coach: San Francisco 49ers 1978, Cincinnati Bengals 1979-80, Kansas City Chiefs 1981-82, 1986-88 (head coach 1987-88), Philadelphia Eagles 1983-85, Detroit Lions 1989-93, Atlanta Falcons 1994-96, joined Rams in 1997.

Peter Giunta, assistant head coach-defensive coordinator; born August 11, 1956, Salem, Mass., lives in Chesterfield, Mo. Running back-defensive back Northeastern 1974-77. No pro playing experience. College coach: Penn State 1981-83, Brown 1984-87, Lehigh 1988-90. Pro coach: Philadelphia Eagles 1991-94, New York Jets 1995-96, joined Rams in 1997.

Kerry Goode, strength and conditioning coordinator; born July 28, 1965; lives in Wildwood, Mo. Tailback Alabama 1983-1987. Pro running back Tampa Bay Buccaneers 1988, Denver Broncos 1989, Miami Dolphins 1990. No college coaching experience. Pro coach: New York Giants 1993-96, joined Rams in 1997.

Carl Hairston, defensive line; born December 15, 1952, Martinsville, Va., lives in Chesterfield, Mo. Defensive end Maryland-Eastern Shore 1972-75. Pro defensive end Philadelphia Eagles 1976-83, Cleveland Browns 1984-89, Phoenix Cardinals 1990. Pro coach: Kansas City Chiefs 1995-96, joined Rams in 1997.

Jim Hanifan, offensive line; born September 21, 1933, Compton, Calif., lives in St. Charles, Mo. Tight end California 1952-54. Pro tight end Toronto Argonauts (USFL) 1955. College Coach: Yuba City J.C. (Calif.) 1959-61, Glendale J.C. (Calif.) 1964-65, Utah 1966-69, California 1970-71, San Diego State 1972. Pro coach: St. Louis Cardinals 1973-78, 1980-85 (head coach), San Diego Chargers 1979, Atlanta Falcons 1987-89, Washington Redskins 1990-96, joined Rams in 1997.

Todd Howard, defensive assistant; born February 18, 1965, Bryan, Tex., lives in St. Louis. Linebacker Texas A&M 1983-86. Pro linebacker Kansas City Chiefs 1987-88, Barcelona Dragons (WLAF) 1991-92. College coach: Texas A&M 1991-93, Grinnell (Iowa) 1994-97. Pro coach: Joined Rams in 1998.

Wilbert Montgomery, running backs; born September 16, 1954, Greenville, Miss., lives in Chesterfield, Mo. Running back Abilene Christian 1973-76. Pro running back Philadelphia Eagles 1977-84, Detroit Lions 1985-86. Pro coach: joined Rams in 1997.

John Ramsdell, offensive assistant; born August 16, 1954, Lafayette, Ind., lives in Chesterfield, Mo. Running back Springfield (Mass.) College 1972-75. No pro playing experience. College coach: San Francisco State 1976-77, Long Beach State 1978, Pacific 1979-82, Oregon 1983-94. Pro coach: Joined Rams in 1995.

Jerry Rhome, offensive coordinator; born March 6, 1942, in Dallas, Tex., lives in Chesterfield, Mo. Quarterback Southern Methodist 1960-61, Tulsa 1963-64. Pro quarterback Dallas Cowboys 1965-68, Cleveland Browns 1969, Houston Oilers 1970, Los Angeles Rams 1971-72. College coach: Tulsa 1973-75. Pro coach: Seattle Seahawks 1976-82, Washington Redskins 1983-87, San Diego Chargers 1988, Dallas Cowboys 1989, Arizona Cardinals 1990-93, Minnesota Vikings 1994, Houston Oilers 1995-96, rejoined Rams in 1997.

Lynn Stiles, vice president football operations-tight ends; born April 12, 1941, Kermit, Tex., lives in Chesterfield, Mo. Guard Utah 1960-62. No pro playing experience. College coach: Utah 1963-65, Iowa 1966-70, UCLA 1971-75, San Jose State 1976-78 (head coach). Pro coach: Philadelphia Eagles 1979-81, San Francisco 49ers 1987-91, joined Rams in 1997.

Ed White, offensive line; born April 4, 1947, San Diego, lives in Lake St. Louis. Defensive lineman California 1965-68. Pro guard Minnesota Vikings 1969-77, San Diego Chargers 1978-85. College coach: San Diego State 1994-97. Pro coach: San Diego Chargers 1986-87, 1989-93, joined Rams in 1998.

Mike White, assistant head coach-quarterbacks; born January 4, 1936, Berkeley, Calif., lives in Clayton, Mo. Wide receiver California 1955-57. No pro playing experience. College coach: California 1958-63, 1972-1977 (head coach), Stanford 1964-71, Illinois 1980-87 (head coach). Pro coach: San Francisco 49ers 1978-79, Los Angeles-Oakland Raiders 1990-96 (head coach 1995-96), joined Rams in 1997.

SAN FRANCISCO 49ERS

National Football Conference
Western Division
Team Colors: Forty Niners Gold and Cardinal
4949 Centennial Boulevard
Santa Clara, California 95054
Telephone: (408) 562-4949

CLUB OFFICIALS

President: Carmen Policy
Vice President /Director of Football Operations: Dwight Clark
Vice President/Business Operations & C.F.O.: Bill Duffy
Director of Player Personnel: Vinny Cerrato
Pro Personnel: Joe Collins
Director of Public/Community Relations: Rodney Knox
Ticket Manager: Lynn Carrozzi
Director of Stadium Operations: Murlan (Mo) Fowell
Video Director: Robert Yanagi
Trainer: Lindsy McLean
Equipment Manager: Kevin Lartigue
Stadium: 3Com Park •**Capacity:** 70,140
San Francisco, California 94124
Playing Surface: Grass
Training Camp: University of the Pacific
Stockton, California 95211

1998 SCHEDULE

PRESEASON

Aug. 2	**New England**	3:00
Aug. 8	at San Diego	7:00
Aug. 15	vs. Seattle at Vancouver, Canada	5:00
Aug. 23	**Miami**	1:00
Aug. 28	at Seattle	7:00

REGULAR SEASON

Sept. 6	**New York Jets**	1:15
Sept. 14	at Washington (Mon.)	8:20
Sept. 20	Open Date	
Sept. 27	**Atlanta**	1:15
Oct. 4	at Buffalo	1:01
Oct. 11	at New Orleans	12:01
Oct. 18	**Indianapolis**	1:05
Oct. 25	at St. Louis	12:01
Nov. 1	at Green Bay	3:15
Nov. 8	**Carolina**	1:01
Nov. 15	at Atlanta	1:01
Nov. 22	**New Orleans**	5:20
Nov. 30	**N.Y. Giants** (Mon.)	5:20
Dec. 6	at Carolina	1:01
Dec. 14	**Detroit** (Mon.)	5:20
Dec. 20	at New England	1:01
Dec. 27	**St. Louis**	1:05

RECORD HOLDERS

INDIVIDUAL RECORDS—CAREER

Category	Name	Performance
Rushing (Yds.)	Joe Perry, 1950-1960, 1963	7,344
Passing (Yds.)	Joe Montana, 1979-1992	35,124
Passing (TDs)	Joe Montana, 1979-1992	244
Receiving (No.)	Jerry Rice, 1985-1997	*1,057
Receiving (Yds.)	Jerry Rice, 1985-1997	*16,455
Interceptions	Ronnie Lott, 1981-1990	51
Punting (Avg.)	Tommy Davis, 1959-1969	44.7
Punt Return (Avg.)	Dana McLemore, 1982-87	10.8
Kickoff Return (Avg.)	Abe Woodson, 1958-1964	29.4
Field Goals	Ray Wersching, 1977-1987	190
Touchdowns (Tot.)	Jerry Rice, 1985-1997	*166
Points	Jerry Rice, 1985-1997	1,000

INDIVIDUAL RECORDS—SINGLE SEASON

Category	Name	Performance
Rushing (Yds.)	Roger Craig, 1988	1,502
Passing (Yds.)	Steve Young, 1993	4,023
Passing (TDs)	Steve Young, 1994	35
Receiving (No.)	Jerry Rice, 1995	122
Receiving (Yds.)	Jerry Rice, 1995	*1,848
Interceptions	Dave Baker, 1960	10
	Ronnie Lott, 1986	10
Punting (Avg.)	Tommy Davis, 1965	45.8
Punt Return (Avg.)	Dana McLemore, 1982	22.3
Kickoff Return (Avg.)	Joe Arenas, 1953	34.4
Field Goals	Jeff Wilkins, 1996	30
Touchdowns (Tot.)	Jerry Rice, 1987	23
Points	Jerry Rice, 1987	138

INDIVIDUAL RECORDS—SINGLE GAME

Category	Name	Performance
Rushing (Yds.)	Delvin Williams, 10-31-76	194
Passing (Yds.)	Joe Montana, 10-14-90	476
Passing (TDs)	Joe Montana, 10-14-90	6
Receiving (No.)	Jerry Rice, 11-20-94	16
Receiving (Yds.)	Jerry Rice, 12-18-95	289
Interceptions	Dave Baker, 12-4-60	*4
Field Goals	Ray Wersching, 10-16-83	6
	Jeff Wilkins, 9-29-96	6
Touchdowns (Tot.)	Jerry Rice, 10-14-90	5
Points	Jerry Rice, 10-14-90	30

*NFL Record

COACHING HISTORY

(404-302-13)

1950-54	Lawrence (Buck) Shaw	33-25-2
1955	Norman (Red) Strader	4-8-0
1956-58	Frankie Albert	19-17-1
1959-63	Howard (Red) Hickey*	27-27-1
1963-67	Jack Christiansen	26-38-3
1968-75	Dick Nolan	56-56-5
1976	Monte Clark	8-6-0
1977	Ken Meyer	5-9-0
1978	Pete McCulley**	1-8-0
1978	Fred O'Connor	1-6-0
1979-88	Bill Walsh	102-63-1
1989-96	George Seifert	108-35-0
1997	Steve Mariucci	14-4-0

*Resigned after three games in 1963
**Released after nine games in 1978

3COM PARK

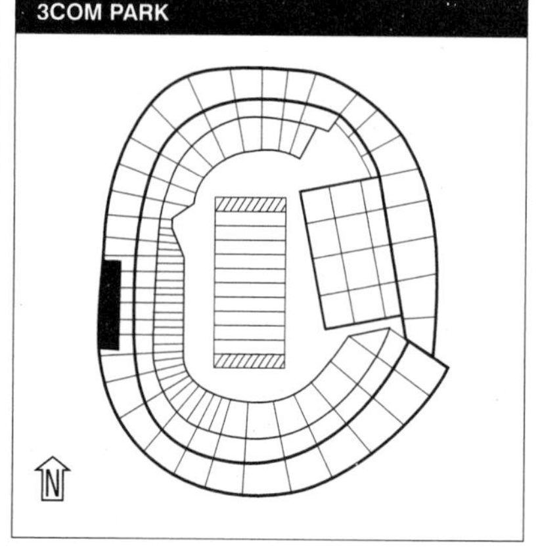

1997 TEAM RECORD

PRESEASON (1-3)

Date	Result		Opponent
8/2	L	13-20	at San Diego
8/9	W	21-17	Seattle
8/18	L	20-28	Jacksonville
8/23	L	17-31	at Denver

REGULAR SEASON (13-3)

Date	Result		Opponent	Att.
8/31	L	6-13	at Tampa Bay	62,554
9/7	W	15-12	at St. Louis	64,630
9/14	W	33-7	New Orleans	61,838
9/21	W	34-7	Atlanta	60,404
9/29	W	34-21	at Carolina	70,972
10/12	W	30-10	St. Louis	63,825
10/19	W	35-28	at Atlanta	53,378
10/26	W	23-0	at New Orleans	60,443
11/2	W	17-10	Dallas	68,657
11/10	W	24-12	at Philadelphia	67,133
11/16	W	27-19	Carolina	61,500
11/23	W	17-10	San Diego	61,195
11/30	L	9-44	at Kansas City	77,535
12/7	W	28-17	Minnesota	55,761
12/15	W	34-17	Denver	68,461
12/21	L	9-38	at Seattle	66,253

POSTSEASON (1-1)

Date	Result		Opponent	Att.
1/3	W	38-22	Minnesota	65,018
1/11	L	10-23	Green Bay	68,987

SCORE BY PERIODS

49ers	90	142	88	55	—	375
Opponents	51	78	66	70	—	265

ATTENDANCE

Home 501,641 Away 522,898 Total 1,024,539
Single-game home record, 69,014 (11/13/94)
Single-season home record, 518,928 (1995)

1997 TEAM STATISTICS

	49ers	Opp.
Total First Downs	294	242
Rushing	106	67
Passing	167	145
Penalty	21	30
Third Down: Made/Att	76/209	76/219
Third Down Pct.	36.4	34.7
Fourth Down: Made/Att	4/8	12/21
Fourth Down Pct.	50.0	57.1
Total Net Yards	5,112	4,013
Avg. Per Game	319.5	250.8
Total Plays	999	949
Avg. Per Play	5.1	4.2
Net Yards Rushing	1,969	1,366
Avg. Per Game	123.1	85.4
Total Rushes	523	386
Net Yards Passing	3,143	2,647
Avg. Per Game	196.4	165.4
Sacked/Yards Lost	44/289	54/364
Gross Yards	3,432	3,011
Att./Completions	432/278	509/258
Completion Pct.	64.4	50.7
Had Intercepted	11	25
Punts/Avg.	79/40.3	83/41.8
Net Punting Avg.	79/34.6	83/33.4
Penalties/Yards Lost	115/979	91/742
Fumbles/Ball Lost	22/9	24/16
Touchdowns	41	31
Rushing	16	5
Passing	20	23
Returns	5	3
Avg. Time of Possession	32:28	27:32

1997 INDIVIDUAL STATISTICS

Passing	Att.	Comp.	Yds.	Pct.	TD	Int.	Tkld.	Rate
S. Young	356	241	3,029	67.7	19	6	35/220	104.7
Druckenmiller	52	21	239	40.4	1	4	4/32	29.2
Brohm	24	16	164	66.7	0	1	5/37	68.8
49ers	432	278	3,432	64.4	20	11	44/289	93.6
Opponents	509	258	3,011	50.7	23	25	54/364	63.6

SCORING	TD R	TD P	TD Rt	PAT	FG	Saf	PTS
Anderson	0	0	0	38/38	29/36	0	125
Kirby	6	1	1	0/0	0/0	0	52
Owens	0	8	0	0/0	0/0	0	48
Hearst	4	2	0	0/0	0/0	0	36
Floyd	3	1	0	0/0	0/0	0	24
Stokes	0	4	0	0/0	0/0	0	24
S. Young	3	0	0	0/0	0/0	0	18
Hanks	0	0	2	0/0	0/0	0	12
Jones	0	2	0	0/0	0/0	0	12
Clark	0	1	0	0/0	0/0	0	6
Greene	0	0	1	0/0	0/0	0	6
Levy	0	0	1	0/0	0/0	0	6
Rice	0	1	0	0/0	0/0	0	6
49ers	16	20	5	38/38	29/36	0	375
Opponents	5	23	3	29/29	16/20	1	265

2-Point conversions: Kirby 2.
Team 2-3, Opponents 0-2.

RUSHING	Att.	Yds.	Avg.	LG	TD
Hearst	234	1,019	4.4	51	4
Kirby	125	418	3.3	38	6
Floyd	78	231	3.0	22	3
S. Young	50	199	4.0	13	3
Levy	16	90	5.6	24	0
Edwards	5	17	3.4	6	0
Brohm	4	11	2.8	10	0
Druckenmiller	10	-6	-0.6	2	0
Rice	1	-10	-10.0	-10	0
49ers	523	1,969	3.8	51	16
Opponents	386	1,366	3.5	46	5

RECEIVING	No.	Yds.	Avg.	LG	TD
Owens	60	936	15.6	56t	8
Stokes	58	733	12.6	36	4
Floyd	37	321	8.7	44t	1
Jones	29	383	13.2	33	2
Kirby	23	279	12.1	82	1
Hearst	21	194	9.2	69	2
Uwaezuoke	14	165	11.8	25	0
Clark	8	96	12.0	23	1
Rice	7	78	11.1	16	1
Edwards	6	48	8.0	19	0
Fann	5	78	15.6	21	0
Levy	5	68	13.6	30	0
Harris	5	53	10.6	16	0
49ers	278	3,432	12.3	82	23
Opponents	258	3,011	11.7	69	23

INTERCEPTIONS	No.	Yds.	Avg.	LG	TD
Hanks	6	103	17.2	55t	1
Drakeford	5	15	3.0	15	0
Woodson	3	81	27.0	41	0
Walker	3	49	16.3	28	0
McDonald	3	34	11.3	17	0
Woodall	2	55	27.5	55	0
Bronson	1	22	22.0	22	0
Pope	1	7	7.0	7	0
Maxie	1	0	0.0	0	0
49ers	25	366	14.6	55t	1
Opponents	11	169	15.4	75t	2

PUNTING	No.	Yds.	Avg.	In 20	LG
Thompson	78	3,182	40.8	22	55
49ers	79	3,182	40.3	22	55
Opponents	83	3,473	41.8	25	59

PUNT RETURNS	No.	FC	Yds.	Avg.	LG	TD
Uwaezuoke	34	14	373	11.0	36	0
Levy	6	2	109	18.2	73t	1
Woodson	1	0	0	0.0	0	0
Mathis	3	1	19	6.3	10	0
Heyward	1	0	0	0.0	0	0
49ers	41	16	482	11.8	73t	1
Opponents	41	9	307	7.5	37	0

KICKOFF RETURNS	No.	Yds.	Avg.	LG	TD
Levy	36	793	22.0	59	0
Uwaezuoke	6	131	21.8	25	0
Kirby	3	124	41.3	101t	1
Owens	2	31	15.5	23	0
Drakeford	1	24	24.0	24	0
Edwards	1	30	30.0	30	0
Fann	1	0	0.0	0	0
49ers	50	1,133	22.7	101t	1
Opponents	82	1,746	21.3	61	0

FIELD GOALS	1-19	20-29	30-39	40-49	50+
Anderson	0/0	11/11	9/12	8/10	1/3
49ers	0/0	11/11	9/12	8/10	1/3
Opponents	0/0	3/4	6/7	6/8	1/1

SACKS	No.
Stubblefield	15.0
Doleman	12.0
Greene	10.5
Barker	5.5
B. Young	4.0
Bryant	2.5
Norton	1.5
Maxie	1.0
Walker	1.0
Washington	1.0
49ers	54.0
Opponents	44.0

1998 DRAFT CHOICES

Round	Name	Pos.	College
1	R.W. McQuarters	DB	Oklahoma State
2	Jeremy Newberry	C	California
3	Chris Ruhman	T	Texas A&M
4	Lance Schulters	DB	Hofstra
5	Phil Ostrowski	G	Penn State
6	Fred Beasley	RB	Auburn
7	Ryan Thelwell	WR	Minnesota

SAN FRANCISCO 49ERS

1998 VETERAN ROSTER

No.		Name	Pos.	Ht.	Wt.	Birthdate	NFL Exp.	College	Hometown	How Acq.	'97 Games/ Starts
92		Barker, Roy	DE	6-5	290	2/14/69	7	North Carolina	Long Island, N.Y.	FA-'96	13/12
79		Barton, Harris	T	6-4	292	4/19/64	12	North Carolina	Atlanta, Ga.	D1a-'87	0*
94		Bonham, Shane	DT	6-2	286	10/18/70	5	Tennessee	Fairbanks, Alaska	UFA(Det)-'98	16/0*
58		Bradford, Vincent	LB	6-2	231	1/22/73	2	Arkansas	Malvern, Ark.	FA-'97	0*
31		Bronson, Zack	S	6-1	191	1/28/74	2	McNeese State	Jasper, Tex.	FA-'97	16/0
72	t-	Brown, Jamie	T	6-8	318	4/24/72	4	Florida A&M	Miami, Fla.	T(Den)-'98	11/2*
65		Brown, Ray	G	6-5	318	12/12/62	13	Arkansas State	Marion, Ark.	FA-'96	15/15
90		Bryant, Junior	DT	6-4	278	1/16/71	4	Notre Dame	Omaha, Neb.	FA-'93	16/3
28		Buckley, Curtis	S	6-0	182	9/25/70	6	East Texas State	Silsbee, Tex.	FA-'96	15/0
85		Clark, Greg	TE	6-4	251	4/7/72	2	Stanford	Bountiful, Utah	D3-'97	15/4
67		Dalman, Chris	C	6-3	297	3/15/70	6	Stanford	Salinas, Calif.	D6-'93	13/13
63		Deese, Derrick	T	6-3	289	5/17/70	7	Southern California	Culver City, Calif.	FA-'92	16/13
11		Detmer, Ty	QB	6-0	194	10/30/67	7	Brigham Young	San Antonio, Tex.	UFA(Phil)-'98	8/7*
56		Doleman, Chris	DE	6-5	289	10/16/61	14	Pittsburgh	York, Pa.	FA-'96	16/16
14		Druckenmiller, Jim	QB	6-4	241	9/19/72	2	Virginia Tech	Northhampton, Pa.	D1-'97	4/1
44		Edwards, Marc	RB	6-0	229	11/17/74	2	Notre Dame	Norwood, Ohio	D2-'97	15/1
86	#	Fann, Chad	TE	6-3	256	6/7/70	5	Florida A&M	Jacksonville, Fla.	FA-'97	11/0
74		Fiore, Dave	T	6-4	288	8/10/74	3	Hofstra	Waldwick, N.J.	FA-'98	0*
66		Gogan, Kevin	G	6-6	330	11/2/64	11	Washington	Pacifica, Calif.	FA-'97	16/16
36		Hanks, Merton	S	6-2	181	3/12/68	8	Iowa	Dallas, Tex.	D5-'91	16/16
77		Hanshaw, Tim	G	6-5	302	4/27/70	3	Brigham Young	Spokane, Wash.	D4-'95	13/3
88		Harris, Mark	WR	6-4	201	4/28/70	2	Stanford	Brigham City, Utah	FA-'97	10/0
20		Hearst, Garrison	RB	5-11	219	1/4/71	6	Georgia	Lincolnton, Ga.	FA-'97	13/13
57		Kirk, Randy	LB-LS	6-2	242	12/27/64	11	San Diego State	San Jose, Calif.	FA-'96	16/0
43		Langham, Antonio	CB	6-0	184	7/31/72	5	Alabama	Town Creek, Ala.	UFA(Balt)-'98	16/15*
32		Levy, Chuck	RB	6-0	206	1/7/72	3	Arizona	Lynwood, Calif.	FA-'96	14/0
46		McDonald, Tim	S	6-2	219	1/6/65	12	Southern California	Fresno, Calif.	FA-'93	15/15
51		Norton Jr., Ken	LB	6-2	254	9/29/66	11	UCLA	Los Angeles, Calif.	FA-'94	16/16
81		Owens, Terrell	WR	6-3	217	12/7/73	3	Tennessee-Chattanooga	Alexander City, Ala.	D3-'96	16/15
50	t-	Peterson, Anthony	LB	6-1	232	1/23/72	5	Notre Dame	Monogahela, Pa.	T(Chi)-'98	16/0*
75		Pollack, Frank	T	6-5	295	11/5/67	8	Northern Arizona	Phoenix, Ariz.	FA-'94	16/0
23		Pope, Marquez	CB	5-11	193	10/2/70	7	Fresno State	Long Beach, Calif.	FA-'95	5/5
91		Price, Daryl	DE	6-3	287	10/23/72	3	Colorado	Galveston, Tex.	D4-'96	5/0
71		Reese, Albert	DT	6-6	294	4/29/73	2	Grambling State	Mobile, Ala.	FA-'97	5/0
80		Rice, Jerry	WR	6-2	196	10/13/62	14	Mississippi Valley State	Crawford, Miss.	D1-'85	2/1
60		Rudolph, Joe	G	6-2	284	7/21/72	3	Wisconsin	Belle Vernon, Pa.	FA-'97	6/1
52		Schwantz, Jim	LB	6-2	240	1/23/70	5	Purdue	Palatine, Ill.	FA-'97	16/0
82		Smith, Irv	TE	6-3	262	10/13/71	6	Notre Dame	Pemberton, N.J.	UFA(NO)-'98	11/8*
83		Stokes, J.J.	WR	6-4	223	10/6/72	4	UCLA	San Diego, Calif.	D1-'95	16/16*
3		Thompson, Tommy	P	5-10	179	4/24/72	4	Oregon	Lompoc, Calif.	FA-'95	16/0
55		Tubbs, Winfred	LB	6-4	260	9/24/70	5	Texas	Fairfield, Tex.	UFA(NO)-'98	16/16*
89		Uwaezuoke, Iheanyi	WR	6-2	198	7/24/73	3	California	Inglewood, Calif.	D5-'96	14/0
38		Walker, Darnell	CB	5-8	167	1/17/70	6	Oklahoma	St. Louis, Mo.	FA-'97	16/11
98		Wilkins, Gabe	DE	6-5	315	9/1/71	5	Gardner-Webb	Cowpens, S.C.	UFA(GB)-'98	16/16
53		Williams, James	LB	6-0	246	10/10/68	8	Mississippi State	Natchez, Miss.	FA-'98	16/0
54		Woodall, Lee	LB	6-1	224	10/31/69	5	West Chester	Carlisle, Pa.	D6b-'94	16/16
97		Young, Bryant	DT	6-3	291	1/27/72	5	Notre Dame	Chicago Heights, Ill.	D1-'94	12/12
8		Young, Steve	QB	6-2	215	10/11/61	14	Brigham Young	Greenwich, Conn.	T(TB)-'87	15/15

* Barton, Bradford, and Fiore missed '97 season because of injury; Bonham played 16 games with Detroit; J. Brown played 11 games with Denver; Detmer played 8 games with Philadelphia; Langham played 16 games with Baltimore; Peterson played 16 games with Chicago; Smith played 11 games with New Orleans; Tubbs played 16 games with New Orleans; Wilkins played 16 games with Green Bay.

\# Unrestricted free agent; subject to developments.

t- Traded for J. Brown (Denver), Peterson (Chicago).

Retired—Brent Jones, 12-year tight end, 13 games in '97; Brett Maxie, 13-year safety, 2 games; Gary Plummer, 12-year linebacker, 16 games.

Players lost through free agency (6): K Gary Anderson (Minn; 16 games in '97), CB Tyronne Drakeford (NO; 16), RB William Floyd (Car; 15), G Rod Milstead (Wash; 4), LB DT Dana Stubblefield (Wash; 16), DE Marvin Washington (Den; 10).

Also played with 49ers in '97—QB Jeff Brohm (5 games), DE Kevin Greene (14), RB Terry Kirby (16), LB Kevin Mitchell (16), S Mike Salmon (1), C Jesse Sapolu (12), T Kirk Scrafford (16), CB-S Frankie Smith (16), CB Rod Woodson (14).

COACHING STAFF

Head Coach,
Steve Mariucci

Pro Career: Became the thirteenth head coach in 49ers' history on January 16, 1997, succeeding George Seifert (1989-96). One of thirteen head coaches since the NFL-AFL merger in 1970 to lead his team to a division title in his first season. He established an NFL record for consecutive wins by a rookie head coach with an 11-game winning streak. In 1996, Mariucci spent one season as head coach at the University of California. He served as the quarterbacks coach of the Green Bay Packers from 1992-95, tutoring the likes of three-time MVP Brett Favre, Mark Brunell, and Ty Detmer. His first pro position was in 1985 when he coached the receivers for the USFL's Orlando Renegades. Later that fall, he had a brief stint with the Los Angeles Rams as quality control coach. No pro playing experience.
Background: Three-time All-America quarterback at Northern Michigan University. Began his coaching career at his alma mater (1978-79), serving as the quarterbacks and running backs coach, then moved to Cal State-Fullerton as the quarterbacks and special teams coordinator (1980-82). In 1983 and 1984, Mariucci was the assistant head coach and offensive coordinator at Louisville. Joined the Southern California staff in 1986, then moved to the University of California as receivers and special teams coach in 1987. In 1990-91, he served as the Bears' offensive coordinator, helping California post a 10-2 record and a number seven national ranking in his final season at Berkeley. Became the head coach at California in 1996 and guided the squad to a 5-0 start and finally a berth in the Aloha Bowl. His offense averaged over 457 yards per game, including a school record 321.5 yards through the air.
Personal: Born November 4, 1955. He and his wife, Gayle, have four children—Tyler, Adam, Stephen, and Brielle—and live in Saratoga, Calif.

ASSISTANT COACHES

Jerry Attaway, physical development; born January 3, 1946, Susanville, Calif., lives in San Jose, Calif. Defensive back Yuba, Calif. J.C. 1964-65, UC Davis 1967. No pro playing experience. College coach: UC Davis 1970-71, Idaho 1972-74, Utah State 1975-77, Southern California 1978-82. Pro coach: Joined 49ers in 1983.
Mike Barnes, strength development; born March 13, 1966, Rochester, N.Y., lives in Dublin, Calif. No college or pro playing experience. College coach: Texas A&M 1990, California 1991-93. Pro coach: Joined 49ers in 1994.
Dwaine Board, defensive line; born November 29, 1956, Rocky Mount, Va., lives in Redwood City, Calif. Defensive lineman North Carolina A&T 1974-77. Pro defensive lineman San Francisco 49ers 1979-87, New Orleans Saints 1988. Pro coach: Joined 49ers in 1991.
Jaime Hill, defensive quality control; born July 6, 1963, Bakersfield, Calif., lives in Fremont, Calif. Wide receiver San Francisco State 1982-85. No pro playing experience. College coach: San Francisco State 1987, UTEP 1988, Northern Arizona 1989, Sonoma State 1990-91, Portland State 1992-96. Pro coach: Joined 49ers in 1997.
Larry Kirksey, wide receivers; born January 6, 1951, Harlan, Ky., lives in Pleasanton, Calif. Wide receiver Eastern Kentucky 1970-72. No pro playing experience. College coach: Miami (Ohio) 1974-76, Kentucky 1977-81, Kansas 1982, Kentucky State 1983 (head coach), Florida 1984-88, Pittsburgh 1989, Alabama 1990-93. Pro coach: Joined 49ers in 1994.
Greg Knapp, offensive assistant-quarterback; born March 5, 1963, Long Beach, Calif., lives in Santa Clara, Calif. Quarterback Cal State-Sacramento 1982-85. No pro playing experience. College coach: Cal State-Sacramento 1986-94. Pro coach: Joined 49ers in 1995.
John Marshall, defensive coordinator; born October 2, 1945, Arroyo Grande, Calif., lives in Pleasanton, Calif. Linebacker Washington State 1964. No pro playing experience. College coach: Oregon 1970-76, Southern California 1977-79. Pro coach: Green Bay Packers 1980-82, Atlanta Falcons 1983-85, Indianapolis Colts 1986-88, joined 49ers in 1989.
Bobb McKittrick, offensive line; born December 29, 1935, Baker, Ore., lives in San Mateo, Calif. Guard Oregon State 1955-57. No pro playing experience. College coach: Oregon State 1961-64, UCLA 1965-70. Pro coach: Los Angeles Rams 1971-72, San Diego Chargers 1974-78, joined 49ers in 1979.
Bill McPherson, defensive assistant; born October 24, 1931, Santa Clara, Calif., lives in San Jose, Calif. Tackle Santa Clara 1950-52. No pro playing experience. College coach: Santa Clara 1963-74, UCLA 1975-77. Pro coach: Philadelphia Eagles 1978, joined 49ers in 1979.
Jim Mora, defensive backs; born November 19, 1961, Los Angeles, Calif., lives in Sunnyvale, Calif. Defensive back Washington 1980-83. No pro playing experience. College coach: Washington 1984. Pro coach: San Diego Chargers 1985-91, New Orleans Saints 1992-96, joined 49ers in 1997.
Marty Mornhinweg, offensive coordinator; born March 29, 1962, Edmond, Okla., lives in Pleasanton, Calif. Quarterback Montana 1980-84. No pro playing experience. College coach: Montana 1985, UTEP 1986-87, Northern Arizona 1988, 1994, Southeast Missouri State 1989-90, Missouri 1991-93. Pro coach: Green Bay Packers 1995-96, joined 49ers in 1997.
Pat Morris, tight ends-asst. offensive line; born April 7, 1954, Cleveland, Ohio, lives in Mountain View, Calif. Offensive lineman Southern California 1972-75. No pro playing experience. College coach: Southern California 1976-77, 1983-86, Northern Arizona 1978, Minnesota 1979-82, Michigan State 1987-94, Stanford 1995-96. Pro coach: Joined 49ers in 1997.
Tom Rathman, running backs; born October 7, 1962, Grand Island, Neb., lives in Redwood City, Calif. Running back Nebraska 1983-85. Pro running back San Francisco 49ers 1986-93, Los Angeles Raiders 1994. College coach: Menlo College 1996. Pro coach: Joined 49ers in 1997.
Richard Smith, linebackers; born October 17, 1955, Los Angeles, Calif., lives in Santa Clara, Calif. Offensive lineman Rio Hondo J.C. 1975-76, Fresno State 1977-78. No pro playing experience. College coach: Rio Hondo J.C. 1979-80, Cal State-Fullerton 1981-83, California 1984-86, Arizona 1987. Pro coach: Houston Oilers 1988-92, Denver Broncos 1993-96, joined 49ers in 1997.
George Stewart, special teams; born December 29, 1958, Little Rock, Ark., lives in Santa Clara, Calif. Guard Arkansas 1977-80. No pro playing experience. College coach: Minnesota 1984-85, Notre Dame 1986-88. Pro coach: Pittsburgh Steelers 1989-91, Tampa Bay Buccaneers 1992-95, joined 49ers in 1996.
Andy Sugarman, offensive quality control; born May 23, 1972, San Francisco, lives in Mountain View, Calif. No college or pro playing experience. College coach: California 1990-97. Pro coach: Joined 49ers in 1998.

1998 FIRST-YEAR ROSTER

Name	Pos.	Ht.	Wt.	Birthdate	College	Hometown	How Acq.
Atkins, Plez	CB	6-0	191	5/22/74	Iowa	Bartlett, Tex	FA
Beasley, Fred	RB	6-0	220	9/18/74	Auburn	Montgomery, Ala.	D6
Becksvoort, John (1)	K	6-1	197	2/26/73	Tennessee	Chattanooga, Tenn.	FA
Blachford, Brock	TE	6-4	242	9/21/73	Northwestern Oklahoma	Tomball, Tex.	FA
Blevins, Tony	CB	6-0	165	1/29/75	Kansas	Kansas City, Mo.	FA
Bradley, Mario (1)	CB-S	6-2	196	4/16/72	Southern California	Long Beach, Calif.	FA
Busby, Thad	QB	6-2	230	11/25/74	Florida State	Pace, Fla.	FA
Charles, Craig	DE	6-5	295	2/26/74	East Tennessee State	Boston, Mass.	FA
Clifton, Andy	LB	6-3	249	10/14/75	Rice	Cleburne, Tex.	FA
Duff, Bill	DT	6-3	284	2/24/74	Tennessee	Delran, N.J.	FA
Eason, Curtis	DT	6-2	292	4/16/76	East Tennessee State	Jacksonville, Fla.	FA
Finn, Dan	G	6-3	307	8/23/76	Northern Arizona	Mesa, Ariz.	FA
Givens, Reggie (1)	LB	6-0	234	10/3/71	Penn State	Sussex, Va.	FA
Henry, Dwight	CB	5-11	179	2/12/74	East Carolina	Fort Lauderdale, Fla.	FA
Lerum, Karl	WR	6-2	200	7/23/74	Pacific Lutheran	Puyallup, Wash.	FA
Lindsey, Steve	K	6-0	166	11/25/74	Mississippi	Hattiesburg, Miss.	FA
Malveaux, Kelly	CB	5-9	175	5/11/76	Arizona	Long Beach, Calif.	FA
McKenzie, Kevin	WR	5-9	187	9/20/75	Washington State	Long Beach, Calif.	FA
McQuarters, R.W.	CB	5-9	198	12/21/76	Oklahoma State	Tulsa, Okla.	D1
Mitchell, Shon (1)	RB	6-1	218	10/8/73	Texas	Austin, Tex.	FA
Nelson, Jim	LB	6-1	235	4/16/75	Penn State	Waldorf, Md.	FA
Newberry, Jeremy	C	6-5	315	3/23/76	California	Antioch, Calif.	D2
Noble, Brandon (1)	DT	6-2	280	4/10/74	Penn State	Virginia Beach, Va.	FA
Olivo, Brock	RB	6-0	226	6/24/76	Missouri	Washington, Mo.	FA
Ostrowski, Phil	G	6-4	291	9/23/75	Penn State	Wilkes-Barre, Pa.	D5
Pearson, Pepe	RB	5-10	208	12/11/75	Ohio State	Euclid, Ohio	FA
Phillips, Tucker (1)	P	6-2	202	2/4/74	Rice	Bellaire, Tex.	FA
Posey, Jeff (1)	DE	6-5	240	8/14/75	Southern Mississippi	Greenville, Miss.	FA
Ruhman, Chris	T	6-5	321	12/19/74	Texas A&M	Houston, Tex.	D3
Rutherford, Reynard (1)	RB	6-0	210	5/15/73	California	Benicia, Calif.	FA
Scales, Shawn	WR	5-10	193	3/5/73	Virginia Tech	Woodbridge, Va.	FA
Schulters, Lance	S	6-2	195	5/27/75	Hofstra	Brooklyn, N.Y.	D4
Scissum, Ed	RB	6-0	229	1/5/76	Alabama	Attalla, Ala.	FA
Shearer, Curtis (1)	WR	5-10	170	6/8/71	San Diego State	San Jose, Calif.	FA
Smith, Tyrone (1)	CB-S	5-11	193	9/29/72	Baylor	Houston, Tex.	FA
Strickland, Vernon (1)	LB	6-4	252	4/9/73	Georgia Tech	Newnan, Ga.	FA
Tarver, Hurley	CB	6-0	176	7/17/75	Central Oklahoma	Fort Worth, Tex.	FA
Thelwell, Ryan	WR	6-2	188	4/6/73	Minnesota	London, Canada	D7
Thornton, Carlos (1)	DT	6-4	308	4/23/74	Alcorn State	Greenville, Miss.	FA-'97

The term NFL Rookie is defined as a player who is in his first season of professional football and has not been on the roster of another professional football team for any regular-season or postseason games. A Rookie is designated by an "R" on NFL rosters. Players who have been active in another professional football league or players who have NFL experience, including either preseason training camp or being on an Active List or Inactive List, or on Reserve/Injured or Reserve/Physically Unable to Perform for fewer than six regular-season games, are termed NFL First-Year Players. An NFL First-Year Player is designated by a "1" on NFL rosters. Thereafter, a player is credited with an additional year of experience for each season in which he accumulates six games on the Active List or Inactive List, or on Reserve/Injured or Reserve/Physically Unable to Perform.

TAMPA BAY BUCCANEERS

National Football Conference
Central Division
Team Colors: Buccaneer Red, Pewter, Black, and Orange
One Buccaneer Place
Tampa, Florida 33607
Telephone: (813) 870-2700

CLUB OFFICIALS

Owner/President: Malcolm Glazer
Executive Vice President: Bryan Glazer
Executive Vice President: Joel Glazer
Executive Vice President: Edward Glazer
General Manager: Rich McKay
Director of Player Personnel: Jerry Angelo
Director of College Scouting: Tim Ruskell
Director of Football Administration: John Idzik
Vice President of Marketing and Communications: Rick McNerney
Vice President of Luxury Services and Guest Relations: Veronica (Roni) Costello
Director of Communications: Reggie Roberts
Director of Marketing: George Woods
Director of Special Events: Meredith Chimerine
Director of Premium Seating: Jim Overton
College Scouts: Mike Ackerley, Joe DiMarzo, Jr., Dennis Hickey, Ruston Webster, Mike Yowarsky
Pro Personnel Assistants: Mark Dominik, Lloyd Richards, Jr.
Ticket and Customer Service Manager: Mike Newquist
Communications Managers: Scott Smith, Nelson Luis
Trainer: Todd Toriscelli
Assistant Trainer: Mark Shermansky
Equipment Manager: Darin Kerns
Video Director: Dave Levy
Assistant Video Director: Pat Brazil
Stadium: New Stadium: Name TBA
•**Capacity:** 65,000
Tampa, Florida 33607
Playing Surface: Grass
Training Camp: University of Tampa
Tampa, Florida 33606

1998 SCHEDULE

PRESEASON

Aug. 1	vs. Pittsburgh at Canton, Ohio	7:00
Aug. 8	vs. Kansas City at Norman, Okla.	7:00
Aug. 13	at Miami	8:20
Aug. 24	at Oakland	6:00
Aug. 28	at New Orleans	7:30

REGULAR SEASON

Sept. 6	at Minnesota	12:01
Sept. 13	at Green Bay	12:01
Sept. 20	**Chicago**	4:05
Sept. 28	at Detroit (Mon.)	8:20
Oct. 4	**New York Giants**	4:15
Oct. 11	Open Date	
Oct. 18	**Carolina**	1:01
Oct. 25	at New Orleans	12:01
Nov. 1	**Minnesota**	1:01
Nov. 8	**Tennessee**	8:20
Nov. 15	at Jacksonville	4:15
Nov. 22	**Detroit**	1:01
Nov. 29	at Chicago	12:01
Dec. 7	**Green Bay** (Mon.)	8:20
Dec. 13	**Pittsburgh**	1:01
Dec. 19	at Washington (Sat.)	4:05
Dec. 27	at Cincinnati	1:01

RECORD HOLDERS

INDIVIDUAL RECORDS—CAREER

Category	Name	Performance
Rushing (Yds.)	James Wilder, 1981-89	5,957
Passing (Yds.)	Vinny Testaverde, 1987-1992	14,820
Passing (TDs)	Vinny Testaverde, 1987-1992	77
Receiving (No.)	James Wilder, 1981-89	430
Receiving (Yds.)	Mark Carrier, 1987-1992	5,018
Interceptions	Cedric Brown, 1977-1984	29
Punting (Avg.)	Frank Garcia, 1983-87	41.1
Punt Return (Avg.)	Karl Williams, 1996-97	14.8
Kickoff Return (Avg.)	Isaac Hagins, 1976-1980	21.9
Field Goals	Michael Husted, 1993-97	96
Touchdowns (Tot.)	James Wilder, 1981-89	46
Points	Donald Igwebuike, 1985-89	416

INDIVIDUAL RECORDS—SINGLE SEASON

Category	Name	Performance
Rushing (Yds.)	James Wilder, 1984	1,544
Passing (Yds.)	Doug Williams, 1981	3,563
Passing (TDs)	Trent Dilfer, 1997	21
Receiving (No.)	Mark Carrier, 1989	86
Receiving (Yds.)	Mark Carrier, 1989	1,422
Interceptions	Cedric Brown, 1981	9
Punting (Avg.)	Tommy Barnhardt, 1996	43.1
Punt Return (Avg.)	Karl Williams, 1996	21.1
Kickoff Return (Avg.)	Karl Williams, 1996	27.4
Field Goals	Michael Husted, 1994, 1996	25
Touchdowns (Tot.)	James Wilder, 1984	13
Points	Donald Igwebuike, 1989	99

INDIVIDUAL RECORDS—SINGLE GAME

Category	Name	Performance
Rushing (Yds.)	James Wilder, 11-6-83	219
Passing (Yds.)	Doug Williams, 11-16-80	486
Passing (TDs)	Steve DeBerg, 9-13-87	5
Receiving (No.)	James Wilder, 9-15-85	13
Receiving (Yds.)	Mark Carrier, 12-6-87	212
Interceptions	Many times Last time by Martin Mayhew, 12-3-95	2
Field Goals	Many times Last time by Michael Husted, 11-17-96	4
Touchdowns (Tot.)	Jimmie Giles, 10-20-85	4
Points	Jimmie Giles, 10-20-85	24

COACHING HISTORY

(112-233-1)

1976-84	John McKay	45-91-1
1985-86	Leeman Bennett	4-28-0
1987-90	Ray Perkins*	19-41-0
1990-91	Richard Williamson	4-15-0
1992-95	Sam Wyche	23-41-0
1996-97	Tony Dungy	17-17-0

*Released after 13 games in 1990

NEW STADIUM: NAME TBA

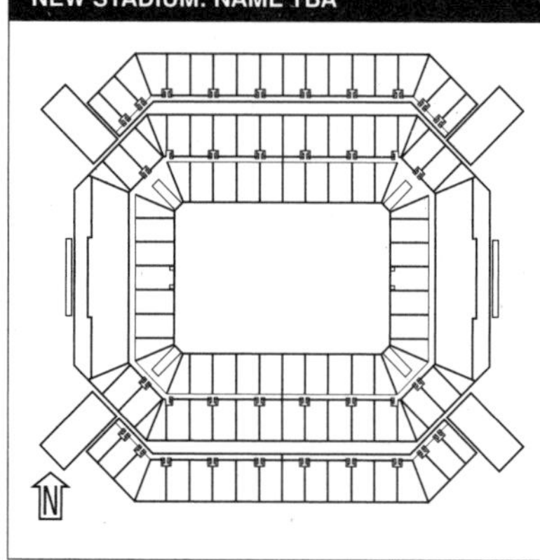

1997 TEAM RECORD

PRESEASON (1-3)

Date	Result		Opponent
8/2	L	8-20	Washington
8/9	L	12-17	at Atlanta
8/16	W	24-10	Miami
8/22	L	9-15	vs. N.Y. Jets at Orlando, Fla. (OT)

REGULAR SEASON (10-6)

Date	Result		Opponent	Att.
8/31	W	13-6	San Francisco	62,554
9/7	W	24-17	at Detroit	58,234
9/14	W	28-14	at Minnesota	63,697
9/21	W	31-21	Miami	73,314
9/28	W	19-18	Arizona	53,804
10/5	L	16-21	at Green Bay	60,100
10/12	L	9-27	Detroit	72,095
10/26	L	6-10	Minnesota	66,815
11/2	W	31-28	at Indianapolis	58,512
11/9	W	31-10	at Atlanta	46,018
11/16	W	27-7	New England	70,479
11/23	L	7-13	at Chicago	43,955
11/30	W	20-8	at New York Giants	68,678
12/7	L	6-17	Green Bay	73,523
12/14	L	0-31	at New York Jets	60,122
12/21	W	31-15	Chicago	70,930

POSTSEASON (1-1)

Date	Result		Opponent	Att.
12/28	W	20-10	Detroit	73,361
1/4	L	7-21	at Green Bay	60,327

SCORE BY PERIODS

Buccaneers	73	78	65	83	—	299
Opponents	36	85	76	66	—	263

ATTENDANCE

Home 543,514 Away 459,316 Total 1,002,830

Single-game home record, 73,523 (12/7/97)

Single-season home record, 545,980 (1979)

1997 TEAM STATISTICS

	Buccaneers	Opp.
Total First Downs	249	265
Rushing	88	96
Passing	134	155
Penalty	27	14
Third Down: Made/Att	79/204	75/220
Third Down Pct.	38.7	34.1
Fourth Down: Made/Att	5/14	11/17
Fourth Down Pct.	35.7	64.7
Total Net Yards	4,376	4,628
Avg. Per Game	273.5	289.3
Total Plays	915	982
Avg. Per Play	4.8	4.7
Net Yards Rushing	1,934	1,617
Avg. Per Game	120.9	101.1
Total Rushes	479	420
Net Yards Passing	2,442	3,011
Avg. Per Game	152.6	188.2
Sacked/Yards Lost	32/196	44/331
Gross Yards	2,638	3,342
Att./Completions	404/224	518/325
Completion Pct.	55.4	62.7
Had Intercepted	12	13
Punts/Avg.	84/42.6	88/41.6
Net Punting Avg.	84/35.8	88/32.5
Penalties/Yards Lost	77/660	93/814
Fumbles/Ball Lost	31/11	21/13
Touchdowns	38	29
Rushing	15	10
Passing	21	13
Returns	2	6
Avg. Time of Possession	29:22	30:38

1997 INDIVIDUAL STATISTICS

Passing	Att.	Comp.	Yds.	Pct.	TD	Int.	Tkld.	Rate
Dilfer	386	217	2,555	56.2	21	11	32/196	82.8
Walsh	17	6	58	35.3	0	1	0/0	21.2
Barnhardt	1	1	25	100.0	0	0	0/0	118.8
Buccaneers	404	224	2,638	55.4	21	12	32/196	80.4
Opponents	518	325	3,342	62.7	13	13	44/331	79.2

SCORING	TD R	TD P	TD Rt	PAT	FG	Saf	PTS
Husted	0	0	0	32/35	13/17	0	71
Alstott	7	3	0	0/0	0/0	0	60
Dunn	4	3	0	0/0	0/0	0	42
Williams	0	4	1	0/0	0/0	0	30
Anthony	0	4	0	0/0	0/0	0	24
Moore	0	4	0	0/0	0/0	0	24
Rhett	3	0	0	0/0	0/0	0	18
Copeland	0	1	0	0/0	0/0	0	6
Dilfer	1	0	0	0/0	0/0	0	6
Hape	0	1	0	0/0	0/0	0	6
Harris	0	1	0	0/0	0/0	0	6
Singleton	0	0	1	0/0	0/0	0	6
Buccaneers	15	21	2	32/35	13/17	0	299
Opponents	10	13	6	25/25	18/29	1	263

2-Point conversions: Team 0-3, Opponents 4-4.

RUSHING	Att.	Yds.	Avg.	LG	TD
Dunn	224	978	4.4	76	4
Alstott	176	665	3.8	47t	7
Dilfer	33	99	3.0	17	1
Rhett	31	96	3.1	21	3
Anthony	5	84	16.8	26	0
Ellison	2	10	5.0	5	0
Williams	1	5	5.0	5	0
Hape	1	1	1.0	1	0
Walsh	6	-4	-0.7	0	0
Buccaneers	479	1,934	4.0	76	15
Opponents	420	1,617	3.9	82t	10

RECEIVING	No.	Yds.	Avg.	LG	TD
Dunn	39	462	11.8	59t	3
Anthony	35	448	12.8	38t	4
Williams	33	486	14.7	55	4
Copeland	33	431	13.1	49	1
Alstott	23	178	7.7	26	3
Moore	19	217	11.4	28	4
Harris	19	197	10.4	39	1
Thomas	13	129	9.9	21	0
Hape	4	22	5.5	13	1
Davis	3	35	11.7	16	0
Bouie	1	25	25.0	25	0
Ellison	1	8	8.0	8	0
Jordan	1	0	0.0	0	0
Buccaneers	224	2,638	11.8	59t	21
Opponents	325	3,342	10.3	79	13

INTERCEPTIONS	No.	Yds.	Avg.	LG	TD
Abraham	5	16	3.2	16	0
Lynch	2	28	14.0	28	0
Brooks	2	13	6.5	13	0
Johnson	1	19	19.0	19	0
Mincy	1	14	14.0	14	0
Parker	1	5	5.0	5	0
Legette	1	0	0.0	0	0
Buccaneers	13	95	7.3	28	0
Opponents	12	370	30.8	77t	4

PUNTING	No.	Yds.	Avg.	In 20	LG
Landeta	54	2,274	42.1	15	74
Barnhardt	29	1,304	45.0	12	61
Buccaneers	84	3,578	42.6	27	74
Opponents	88	3,661	41.6	20	65

PUNT RETURNS	No.	FC	Yds.	Avg.	LG	TD
Williams	46	12	597	13.0	63	1
Dunn	5	0	48	9.6	25	0
Buccaneers	51	12	645	12.6	63	1
Opponents	42	16	388	9.2	57	0

KICKOFF RETURNS	No.	Yds.	Avg.	LG	TD
Anthony	25	592	23.7	51	0
Williams	15	277	18.5	28	0
Dunn	6	129	21.5	30	0
Ellison	2	61	30.5	49	0
Alstott	1	0	0.0	0	0
Rhett	1	16	16.0	16	0
White	1	0	0.0	0	0
Copeland	0	0	—	—	0
Buccaneers	51	1075	21.1	51	0
Opponents	44	957	21.8	101t	1

FIELD GOALS	1-19	20-29	30-39	40-49	50+
Husted	0/0	5/5	2/3	5/6	1/3
Buccaneers	0/0	5/5	2/3	5/6	1/3
Opponents	0/0	5/5	9/13	4/10	0/1

SACKS	No.
Sapp	10.5
Ahanotu	10.0
Culpepper	8.5
Upshaw	7.5
Jackson	2.5
Brooks	1.5
Maniecki	1.0
Nickerson	1.0
Parker	1.0
Porter	0.5
Buccaneers	44.0
Opponents	32.0

1998 DRAFT CHOICES

Round	Name	Pos.	College
2	Jacquez Green	WR	Florida
	Brian Kelly	DB	Southern California
3	Jamie Duncan	LB	Vanderbilt
4	Todd Washington	C	Virginia Tech
6	James Cannida	DT	Nevada
	Shevin Smith	DB	Florida State
7	Chance McCarty	DE	Texas Christian

TAMPA BAY BUCCANEERS

1998 VETERAN ROSTER

No.	Name	Pos.	Ht.	Wt.	Birthdate	NFL Exp.	College	Hometown	How Acq.	'97 Games/ Starts
21	Abraham, Donnie	CB	5-10	190	10/8/73	3	East Tennessee State	Orangeburg, S.C.	D3-'96	16/16
72	Ahanotu, Chidi	DE	6-2	283	10/11/70	6	California	Berkeley, Calif.	D6-'93	16/15
40	Alstott, Mike	RB	6-1	248	12/21/73	3	Purdue	Joliet, Ill.	D2-'96	15/15
85	Anthony, Reidel	WR	5-11	178	10/20/76	2	Florida	South Bay, Fla.	D1b-97	16/13
46	Barber, Kantroy	RB	6-0	243	10/4/73	3	West Virginia	Miami, Fla.	FA-'98	0*
20	Barber, Ronde	CB	5-10	186	4/7/75	2	Virginia	Roanoke, Va.	D3b-'97	1/0
6	Barnhardt, Tommy	P	6-2	228	6/11/63	12	North Carolina	China Grove, N.C.	FA-'96	6/0
52	Bellisari, Greg	LB	6-0	236	6/21/75	2	Ohio State	Boca Raton, Fla.	FA-'97	14/0
23	† Bouie, Tony	S	5-10	190	8/7/72	4	Arizona	New Orleans, La.	FA-'95	16/1
11	Brohm, Jeff	QB	6-1	205	4/24/71	4	Louisville	Louisville, Ky.	FA'-98	5/0*
55	Brooks, Derrick	LB	6-0	235	4/18/73	4	Florida State	Pensacola, Fla.	D1b-'95	16/16
88	Copeland, Horace	WR	6-3	208	1/2/71	6	Miami	Orlando, Fla.	D4b-'93	13/11
77	Culpepper, Brad	DT	6-1	275	5/8/69	7	Florida	Tallahassee, Fla.	W(Minn)-'94	16/16
87	Davis, John	TE	6-4	257	5/14/73	3	Emporia State	Jasper, Tex.	FA-'97	8/2
64	Diaz, Jorge	G	6-4	308	11/15/73	3	Texas A&M-Kingsville	Katy, Tex.	FA-'96	16/16
12	Dilfer, Trent	QB	6-4	234	3/13/72	5	Fresno State	Aptos, Calif.	D1-'94	16/16
65	Dogins, Kevin	C	6-1	295	12/7/72	2	Texas A&M-Kingsville	Eagle Lake, Tex.	FA-'96	0*
28	Dunn, Warrick	RB	5-8	178	1/5/75	2	Florida State	Baton Rouge, La.	D1a-'97	16/10
37	Ellison, Jerry	RB	5-10	207	12/20/71	4	Tennessee-Chattanooga	Augusta, Ga.	FA-'94	16/0
80	Emanuel, Bert	WR	5-10	180	10/26/70	5	Rice	Langham Creek, Tex.	UFA(Atl)-'98	16/16*
50	Gooch, Jeff	LB	5-11	224	10/31/74	3	Austin Peay	Nashville, Tenn.	FA-'96	14/5
74	Gruber, Paul	T	6-5	292	2/24/65	11	Wisconsin	Prairie du Sac, Wis.	D1-'88	16/16
82	Hape, Patrick	TE	6-4	256	6/6/74	2	Alabama	Killen, Ala.	D5-'97	14/3
5	Husted, Michael	K	6-0	190	6/16/70	6	Virginia	Hampton, Va.	FA-'93	16/0
92	Ifeanyi, Israel	DE	6-3	266	11/21/70	2	Southern California	Lagos, Nigeria	FA-'98	0*
67	Ingram, Stephen	G-T	6-4	315	5/8/71	4	Maryland	Seat Pleasant, Md.	D7a-'95	0*
97	† Jackson, Tyoka	DE-DT	6-2	274	11/22/71	4	Penn State	Washington, D.C.	FA-'96	12/0
78	Jones, Marcus	DT	6-6	286	8/15/73	3	North Carolina	Jacksonville, N.C.	D1b-'96	7/1
48	Jordan, Andrew	TE	6-4	254	6/21/72	5	Western Carolina	Charlotte, N.C.	FA-'97	4/0*
45	Legette, Tyrone	CB	5-9	179	2/15/70	7	Nebraska	Columbia, S.C.	UFA(NO)-'96	16/1
47	Lynch, John	S	6-2	214	9/25/71	6	Stanford	Solana Beach, Calif.	D3-'93	16/16
90	Maniecki, Jason	DT	6-4	291	8/15/72	3	Wisconsin	Wisconsin Dells, Wis.	D5-'96	10/0
89	Marshall, Marvin	WR	5-10	170	6/21/72	3	South Carolina State	Augusta, Ga.	FA-'95	0*
68	Mathews, Jason	T	6-5	304	2/9/71	5	Texas A&M	Bridge City, Tex.	UFA(Ind)-'98	16/0*
61	Mayberry, Tony	C	6-4	302	12/8/67	9	Wake Forest	Springfield, Va.	D4b-'90	16/16
73	Middleton, Frank	G	6-3	340	10/25/74	2	Arizona	Beaumont, Tex.	D3a-'97	15/2
13	Milanovich, Scott	QB-P	6-3	220	1/25/73	3	Maryland	Butler, Pa.	FA-'96	0*
22	Mincy, Charles	S	5-11	195	12/16/69	8	Washington	Los Angeles, Calif.	FA-'96	16/9
83	Moore, Dave	TE	6-2	242	11/11/69	6	Pittsburgh	Succasunna, N.J.	FA-'92	16/7
41	t- Neal, Lorenzo	RB	5-11	240	12/27/70	6	Fresno State	Fresno, Calif.	T(NYJ)-'98	16/10*
62	Newnam, Brian	G	6-3	296	2/11/74	2	Tulsa	Stroud, Okla.	FA-'97	0*
56	Nickerson, Hardy	LB	6-2	230	9/1/65	12	California	Compton, Calif.	UFA(Pitt)-'93	16/16
70	Odom, Jason	T	6-5	307	3/31/74	3	Florida	Bartow, Fla.	D4a-'96	16/16
27	Parker, Anthony	CB	5-10	181	2/11/66	8	Arizona State	Tempe, Ariz.	FA-'97	15/14
69	† Pierson, Pete	T	6-5	295	2/4/71	4	Washington	Portland, Ore.	D5-'94	15/0
53	Quarles, Shelton	LB	6-1	236	9/11/71	2	Vanderbilt	Whites Creek, Tenn.	FA-'97	16/0
24	Robinson, Damien	S	6-2	210	12/22/73	2	Iowa	Dallas, Tex.	FA-'97	0*
99	Sapp, Warren	DT	6-2	276	12/19/72	4	Miami	Apopka, Fla.	D1a-'95	15/15
51	Singleton, Alshermond	LB	6-2	227	8/7/75	2	Temple	Irvington, N.J.	D4-97	12/0
84	Thomas, Robb	WR	5-11	178	3/29/66	10	Oregon State	Corvallis, Ore.	FA-'96	16/1
91	Upshaw, Regan	DE	6-4	268	8/12/75	3	California	Pittsburg, Calif.	D1a-'96	15/15
4	Walsh, Steve	QB	6-3	215	12/1/66	10	Miami	St. Paul, Minn.	UFA-'97	12/0
94	White, Steve	DE	6-2	265	10/25/73	3	Tennessee	Memphis, Tenn.	FA-'96	15/1
86	Williams, Karl	WR	5-10	174	4/10/71	3	Texas A&M-Kingsville	Rowlett, Tex.	FA-'96	16/7
58	Willis, Donald	G	6-3	330	7/15/73	3	North Carolina A&T	Lompoc, Calif.	FA-'98	0*
71	Wunsch, Jerry	T	6-6	333	1/21/74	2	Wisconsin	Wausau, Wis.	D2-'97	16/0
31	Young, Floyd	CB	6-0	170	11/23/75	2	Texas A&M-Kingsville	New Orleans, La.	FA-'97	12/1

* K. Barber inactive 6 games with Carolina; Brohm played 5 games with San Francisco; Dogins inactive for 14 games; Emanuel played 16 games with Atlanta; Ifeanyi last active with San Francisco in '96; Ingram, Marshall and Newnam missed '97 season because of injury; Jordan played 2 games with Minnesota; Mathews played 16 games with Indianapolis; Milanovich inactive for 16 games; Neal played 16 games with the N.Y. Jets; Robinson inactive for 13 games; Willis last active with New Orleans in '96.

† Restricted free agents; subject to developments.

t- Buccaneers traded for Neal (N.Y. Jets).

Traded—S Melvin Johnson (16 games in '97) to Kansas City; RB Errict Rhett (11) to Baltimore.

Players lost through free agency (4): DE Eric Curry (GB; 6 games in '97), TE Jackie Harris (Tenn; 12), P Sean Landeta (GB; 10), G Jim Pyne (Det; 15).

Also played with Buccaneers in '97—S Kenny Gant (9 games), WR Brice Hunter (3), LB Rufus Porter (11), CB Reggie Rusk (4).

COACHING STAFF

Head Coach,
Tony Dungy

Pro Career: After 15 years as an NFL assistant coach, was named as the Buccaneers' sixth head coach on January 22, 1996, when he signed a six-year contract. In just his second season as head coach, Dungy's 1997 Buccaneers matched a franchise record with a 10-6 campaign that also included a wild-card playoff victory over the Detroit Lions. Under Dungy's guidance last season, Tampa Bay continued improving on 1996's strong finish in which it won five of its last eight games, completing one of the largest single-season turnarounds in club history. Joined Tampa Bay after serving as Minnesota Vikings' defensive coordinator from 1992-95. Helped Vikings' defense lead NFL with 95 interceptions during his four years in Minnesota. Prior to going to Vikings, spent 1989-1991 as defensive backs coach for Kansas City Chiefs. Also worked eight years as an assistant coach for the Pittsburgh Steelers under Chuck Noll as a defensive assistant (1981), defensive backs coach (1982-83), and as defensive coordinator (1984-88). At 25, was NFL's youngest assistant coach when hired by Steelers in 1981, then became league's youngest coordinator at age of 28. Began coaching career coaching defensive backs at University of Minnesota in 1980. As an NFL player, signed with Pittsburgh as a free agent in 1977 and played safety for Steelers for two seasons (1977-78). Had nine interceptions (second in AFC with 6 in 1978) in 30 games for Pittsburgh and played in Super Bowl XIII victory over Dallas Cowboys. Had unusual distinction of making and throwing an interception in same 1977 game versus Houston Oilers. Traded to San Francisco 49ers during 1979 training camp and played 15 games for 49ers. Was traded again prior to 1980 season to New York Giants in multi-player deal that sent current Philadelphia Eagle head coach Ray Rhodes to 49ers. Career record: 17-17.

Background: Starred as quarterback at University of Minnesota from 1973-76. Finished career as school's all-time leader in attempts, completions, passing yards, and touchdown passes. Left Minnesota in fourth place in Big Ten history in total offense. Two-time team most valuable player, played in Hula Bowl, East-West Shrine Game, and Japan Bowl. Attended Parkside High School in Jackson, Michigan.

Personal: Born October 6, 1955, in Jackson, Michigan. Tony and his wife, Lauren, have three children including daughter Tiara (13), and sons James (11) and Eric (6). The family resides in Tampa.

ASSISTANT COACHES

Mark Asanovich, strength and conditioning; born May 20, 1959, Duluth, Minn., lives in Tampa. No college or pro playing experience. College coach: Ohio State 1985, Citadel 1986. Pro coach: Minnesota Vikings 1995, joined Buccaneers in 1996.

Clyde Christensen, tight ends; born January 28, 1958, Corvine, Calif., lives in Tampa. Quarterback Fresno (Calif.) J.C. 1975, North Carolina 1976-78. No pro playing experience. College coach: East Tennessee State 1980-82, Temple 1983-85, East Carolina 1986-88, Holy Cross 1989-90, South Carolina 1991, Maryland 1992-93, Clemson 1994-95. Pro coach: Joined Buccaneers in 1996.

Herman Edwards, assistant head coach/defensive backs; born April 27, 1954, Monmouth, N.J., lives in Tampa. Defensive back California 1972, 1974, Monterrey Peninsula (Calif.) J.C. 1973, San Diego State 1975-76. Pro defensive back Philadelphia Eagles 1977-85, Los Angeles Rams 1986, Atlanta Falcons 1986. College coach: San Jose State 1987-89. Pro coach: Kansas City Chiefs 1992-94 (scout 1990-91, 1995), joined Buccaneers in 1996.

Chris Foerster, offensive line; born October 12, 1961, Milwaukee, Wis., lives in Tampa. Center Colorado State 1979-82. No pro playing experience. College coach: Colorado State 1983-87, Stanford 1988-91, Minnesota 1992. Pro coach: Minnesota Vikings 1993-95, joined Buccaneers in 1996.

Monte Kiffin, defensive coordinator; born February 29, 1940, Lexington, Neb., lives in Tampa. Offensive/defensive tackle Nebraska 1959-63. Pro defensive end Winnipeg Blue Bombers (CFL) 1965. College coach: Nebraska 1966-76, Arkansas 1977-79, North Carolina State 1980-82 (head coach). Pro coach: Green Bay Packers 1983, Buffalo Bills 1984-85, Minnesota Vikings 1986-89, 1991-94, New York Jets 1990, New Orleans Saints 1995, joined Buccaneers in 1996.

Joe Marciano, special teams; born February 10, 1954, Scranton, Pa., lives in Tampa. Quarterback Temple 1972-75. No pro playing experience. College coach: East Stroudsburg 1977, Rhode Island 1978-79, Villanova 1980, Penn State 1981, Temple 1982. Pro coach: Philadelphia/Baltimore Stars (USFL) 1983-85, New Orleans Saints 1986-95, joined Buccaneers in 1996.

Rod Marinelli, defensive line; born July 13, 1949, Rosemead, Calif., lives in Tampa. Offensive/defensive tackle Utah 1968, offensive tackle California Lutheran 1970-72 (military service 1969-70). No pro playing experience. College coach: Utah State 1976-82, California 1983-91, Arizona State 1992-94, Southern California 1995. Pro coach: Joined Buccaneers in 1996.

Tony Nathan, running backs; born December 14, 1956, Birmingham, Ala., lives in Tampa. Running back Alabama 1975-78. Pro running back Miami Dolphins 1979-87. Pro coach: Miami Dolphins 1988-95, joined Buccaneers in 1996.

Kevin O'Dea, defensive assistant; born June 9, 1960, Williamsport, Va., lives in Tampa. Defensive back/wide receiver Lock Haven 1982-85. No pro playing experience. College coach: Lock Haven 1986, Cornell 1987, Virginia 1988-90, Penn State 1991-93. Pro coach: San Diego Chargers 1994-95, joined Buccaneers in 1996.

Mike Shula, offensive coordinator; born June 3, 1965, Baltimore, Md., lives in Tampa. Quarterback Alabama 1983-86. Pro quarterback Tampa Bay Buccaneers 1987. Pro coach: Tampa Bay Buccaneers 1988-90, Miami Dolphins 1991-92, Chicago Bears 1993-95, rejoined Buccaneers in 1996.

Lovie Smith, linebackers; born May 8, 1958, Gladewater, Tex., lives in Tampa. Linebacker Tulsa 1976-79. No pro playing experience. College coach: Tulsa 1983-86, Wisconsin 1987, Arizona State 1988-91, Kentucky 1992, Tennessee 1993-94, Ohio State 1995. Pro coach: Joined Buccaneers in 1996.

Ricky Thomas, offensive assistant; born March 29, 1965, London, England, lives in Tampa. Safety Alabama 1983-86. Pro safety Seattle Seahawks 1987. College coach: Kentucky 1996, Gardner-Webb 1996. Pro coach: Joined Buccaneers in 1997.

Charlie Williams, wide receivers; born January 31, 1958, Long Beach, Calif., lives in Tampa. Defensive back Long Beach City College 1977-78, Colorado State 1979-80. No pro playing experience. College coach: Colorado State 1981, Long Beach City College 1984-85, New Mexico State 1986-87, Texas Christian 1988-91, Minnesota 1992, Miami 1993-95. Pro coach: Joined Buccaneers in 1996.

1998 FIRST-YEAR ROSTER

Name	Pos.	Ht.	Wt.	Birthdate	College	Hometown	How Acq.
Abdullah, Rabih	RB	6-1	218	4/27/75	Lehigh	Roselle, N.J.	FA
Anderson, Eric	T	6-3	311	7/16/75	Nebraska	Lincoln, Neb.	FA
Brady, Rickey (1)	TE	6-4	264	11/19/70	Oklahoma	Oklahoma City, Okla.	FA-'97
Cannida, James	DT	6-2	275	1/3/75	Nevada	Fremont, Calif.	D6a
Carter, Nigea (1)	WR	6-1	196	9/1/74	Michigan State	Coconut Creek, Fla.	D6b-'97
DeGrate, Anthony (1)	DT	6-1	333	5/24/74	Stephen F. Austin	Waco, Tex.	D7-'97
Duncan, Jamie	LB	6-0	244	7/20/75	Vanderbilt	Wilmington, Del.	D3
Green, Jacquez	WR	5-9	172	1/15/76	Florida	Fort Valley, Ga.	D2a
Hall, Lamont	TE	6-3	251	11/16/74	Clemson	Clover, S.C.	FA
Harris, Al (1)	CB	6-0	185	12/7/74	Texas A&M-Kingsville	Coconut Creek, Fla.	D6a-'97
Hughes, Ralph	DE	6-4	256	10/26/75	Georgia Tech	Montgomery, Ala.	FA
Hunter, Brice (1)	WR	6-0	219	4/21/74	Georgia	Valdosta, Ga.	FA
Kelly, Brian	CB	5-11	196	1/14/76	Southern California	Aurora, Col.	D2b
Kessler, Chad	P	6-1	197	6/24/75	Louisiana State	Lake Mary, Fla.	FA
Lee, Kendrick	WR	5-8	172	9/19/75	Southern Mississippi	Jackson, La.	FA
Lee, Steve (1)	RB	6-0	265	4/16/74	Indiana	Indianapolis, Ind.	FA-'97
McCarty, Chance	DE	6-3	248	8/29/75	Texas Christian	Fort Worth, Tex.	D7
Palmer, Mitch (1)	LB	6-4	245	9/2/73	Colorado State	San Diego, Calif.	FA
Ruhl, Mike	T	6-6	308	4/21/74	Tulsa	Mannheim, Pa.	FA
Simon, Geroy (1)	WR	6-0	183	9/11/75	Maryland	Johnstown, Pa.	FA-'97
Smith, Shevin	S	5-11	196	6/17/75	Florida State	Miami, Fla.	D6b
Vance, Eric (1)	S	6-2	215	7/14/75	Vanderbilt	Hurst, Tex.	FA
Washington, Todd	C-G	6-3	312	7/19/76	Virginia Tech	Melfa, Va.	D4

The term NFL Rookie is defined as a player who is in his first season of professional football and has not been on the roster of another professional football team for any regular-season or postseason games. A Rookie is designated by an "R" on NFL rosters. Players who have been active in another professional football league or players who have NFL experience, including either preseason training camp or being on an Active List or Inactive List, or on Reserve/Injured or Reserve/Physically Unable to Perform for fewer than six regular-season games, are termed NFL First-Year Players. An NFL First-Year Player is designated by a "1" on NFL rosters. Thereafter, a player is credited with an additional year of experience for each season in which he accumulates six games on the Active List or Inactive List, or on Reserve/Injured or Reserve/Physically Unable to Perform.

NOTES

WASHINGTON REDSKINS

National Football Conference
Eastern Division
Team Colors: Burgundy and Gold
Redskin Park
P.O. Box 17247
Washington, D.C. 20041
Telephone: (703) 478-8900

CLUB OFFICIALS

President: John Kent Cooke
House Counsel: Stuart Haney
Controller: Mark Francis
General Manager: Charley Casserly
Assistant General Manager: Bobby Mitchell
Director of Player Development: Joe Mendes
Director of College Scouting: George Saimes
Scouts: Gene Bates, Larry Bryan, Scott Cohen, Mike Maccagnan, Miller McCalmon Joel Patten, Dave Sears
Coordinator of Scouting: Chuck Banker
Scouting Administrator: Ray Wright
Director of Public Relations: Mike McCall
Director of Media Relations: Chris Helein
Publications/Internet Director: Scott McKeen
Community Relations Director: Wendy Brinker
Director of Administration: Barry Asimos
VP Marketing: John Kent Cooke, Jr.
Director of Marketing: John Wagner
Video Director: Donnie Schoenmann
Asst. Video Director: Hugh McPhillips
Ticket Manager: Jeff Ritter
Vice President-Stadium Operations: Jeff Klein
Head Trainer: Bubba Tyer
Assistant Trainers: Al Bellamy, Kevin Bastin
Equipment Manager: Jay Brunetti
Asst. Equipment Manager: Jeff Parsons
Stadium: Jack Kent Cooke Stadium
•**Capacity:** 80,116
Raljon, Maryland 20785-4236
Playing Surface: Grass
Training Camp: Frostburg State University
Frostburg, Maryland 21532-1099

1998 SCHEDULE

PRESEASON

Aug. 8	**Miami**	7:30
Aug. 15	at Tennessee	1:00
Aug. 22	**New England**	7:30
Aug. 28	at Buffalo	7:00

REGULAR SEASON

Sept. 6	at New York Giants	1:01
Sept. 14	**San Francisco** (Mon.)	8:20
Sept. 20	at Seattle	1:05
Sept. 27	**Denver**	1:01
Oct. 4	**Dallas**	1:01
Oct. 11	at Philadelphia	1:01
Oct. 18	at Minnesota	12:01
Oct. 25	Open Date	
Nov. 1	**New York Giants**	1:01
Nov. 8	at Arizona	2:05
Nov. 15	**Philadelphia**	1:01
Nov. 22	**Arizona**	1:01
Nov. 29	at Oakland	1:15
Dec. 6	**San Diego**	1:01
Dec. 13	at Carolina	1:01
Dec. 19	**Tampa Bay** (Sat.)	4:05
Dec. 27	at Dallas	7:20

RECORD HOLDERS

INDIVIDUAL RECORDS—CAREER

Category	Name	Performance
Rushing (Yds.)	John Riggins, 1976-79, 1981-85	7,472
Passing (Yds.)	Joe Theismann, 1974-1985	25,206
Passing (TDs)	Sammy Baugh, 1937-1952	187
Receiving (No.)	Art Monk, 1980-1993	888
Receiving (Yds.)	Art Monk, 1980-1993	12,028
Interceptions	Darrell Green, 1983-1997	44
Punting (Avg.)	Sammy Baugh, 1937-1952	*45.1
Punt Return (Avg.)	Johnny Williams, 1952-53	12.8
Kickoff Return (Avg.)	Bobby Mitchell, 1962-68	28.5
Field Goals	Mark Moseley, 1974-1986	263
Touchdowns (Tot.)	Charley Taylor, 1964-1977	90
Points	Mark Moseley, 1974-1986	1,206

INDIVIDUAL RECORDS—SINGLE SEASON

Category	Name	Performance
Rushing (Yds.)	Terry Allen, 1996	1,353
Passing (Yds.)	Jay Schroeder, 1986	4,109
Passing (TDs)	Sonny Jurgensen, 1967	31
Receiving (No.)	Art Monk, 1984	106
Receiving (Yds.)	Bobby Mitchell, 1963	1,436
Interceptions	Dan Sandifer, 1948	13
Punting (Avg.)	Sammy Baugh, 1940	*51.4
Punt Return (Avg.)	Johnny Williams, 1952	15.3
Kickoff Return (Avg.)	Mike Nelms, 1981	29.7
Field Goals	Mark Moseley, 1983	33
Touchdowns (Tot.)	John Riggins, 1983	24
Points	Mark Moseley, 1983	161

INDIVIDUAL RECORDS—SINGLE GAME

Category	Name	Performance
Rushing (Yds.)	Gerald Riggs, 9-17-89	221
Passing (Yds.)	Sammy Baugh, 10-31-43	446
Passing (TDs)	Sammy Baugh, 10-31-43, 11-23-47	6
	Mark Rypien, 11-10-91	6
Receiving (No.)	Art Monk, 12-15-85	13
	Kelvin Bryant, 12-7-86	13
	Art Monk, 11-4-90	13
Receiving (Yds.)	Anthony Allen, 10-4-87	255
Interceptions	Sammy Baugh, 11-14-43	*4
	Dan Sandifer, 10-31-48	*4
Field Goals	Many times.	5
	Last time by Chip Lohmiller, 10-25-92	
Touchdowns (Tot.)	Dick James, 12-17-61	4
	Larry Brown, 12-16-73	4
Points	Dick James, 12-17-61	24
	Larry Brown, 12-16-73	24

*NFL Record

COACHING HISTORY

Boston 1932-36
(476-414-27)

1932	Lud Wray	4-4-2
1933-34	William (Lone Star) Dietz	11-11-2
1935	Eddie Casey	2-8-1
1936-42	Ray Flaherty	56-23-3
1943	Arthur (Dutch) Bergman	7-4-1
1944-45	Dudley DeGroot	14-6-1
1946-48	Glen (Turk) Edwards	16-18-1
1949	John Whelchel*	3-3-1
1949-51	Herman Ball**	4-16-0
1951	Dick Todd	5-4-0
1952-53	Earl (Curly) Lambeau	10-13-1
1954-58	Joe Kuharich	26-32-2
1959-60	Mike Nixon	4-18-2
1961-65	Bill McPeak	21-46-3
1966-68	Otto Graham	17-22-3
1969	Vince Lombardi	7-5-2
1970	Bill Austin	6-8-0
1971-77	George Allen	69-35-1
1978-80	Jack Pardee	24-24-0
1981-92	Joe Gibbs	140-65-0
1993	Richie Petitbon	4-12-0
1994-97	Norv Turner	26-37-1

*Released after seven games in 1949
**Released after three games in 1951

JACK KENT COOKE STADIUM

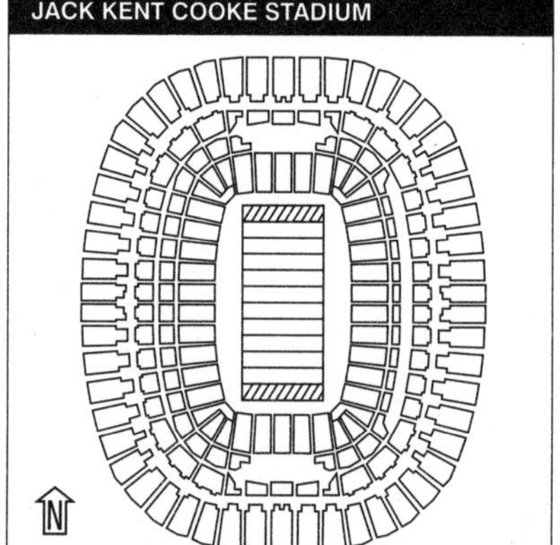

1997 TEAM RECORD

PRESEASON (3-1)

Date	Result		Opponent
8/2	W	20-8	at Tampa Bay
8/9	W	18-12	at Tennessee
8/16	W	35-31	at Atlanta
8/21	L	7-28	at Miami

REGULAR SEASON (8-7-1)

Date	Result		Opponent	Att.
8/31	W	24-10	at Carolina	72,633
9/7	L	13-14	at Pittsburgh	58,059
9/14	W	19-13	Arizona (OT)	78,270
9/28	W	24-12	Jacksonville	74,421
10/5	L	10-24	at Philadelphia	67,008
10/12	W	21-16	Dallas	76,159
10/19	L	14-28	at Tennessee	31,042
10/26	L	17-20	Baltimore	75,067
11/2	W	31-8	at Chicago	53,032
11/9	W	30-7	Detroit	75,261
11/16	L	14-17	at Dallas	64,559
11/23	T	7-7	New York Giants (OT)	75,703
11/30	L	20-23	St. Louis	74,772
12/7	W	38-28	at Arizona	41,537
12/14	L	10-30	at New York Giants	77,571
12/21	W	35-32	Philadelphia	75,939

(OT) Overtime

SCORE BY PERIODS

Redskins	62	101	80	78	—	327
Opponents	64	74	53	98	—	289

ATTENDANCE

Home 605,592 Away 465,441 Total 1,071,033
Single-game home record, 78,270 (9/14/97)
Single-season home record, 605,592 (1997)

1997 TEAM STATISTICS

	Redskins	Opp.
Total First Downs	300	292
Rushing	86	129
Passing	192	149
Penalty	22	14
Third Down: Made/Att	94/222	79/237
Third Down Pct.	42.3	33.3
Fourth Down: Made/Att	5/13	12/21
Fourth Down Pct.	38.5	57.1
Total Net Yards	4,998	5,030
Avg. Per Game	312.4	314.4
Total Plays	1,033	1,058
Avg. Per Play	4.8	4.8
Net Yards Rushing	1,615	2,212
Avg. Per Game	100.9	138.3
Total Rushes	453	508
Net Yards Passing	3,383	2,818
Avg. Per Game	211.4	176.1
Sacked/Yards Lost	33/198	37/280
Gross Yards	3,581	3,098
Att./Completions	547/283	513/267
Completion Pct.	51.7	52.0
Had Intercepted	22	16
Punts/Avg.	85/44.6	95/42.5
Net Punting Avg.	85/39.2	95/35.3
Penalties/Yards Lost	78/639	96/849
Fumbles/Ball Lost	21/7	36/14
Touchdowns	40	32
Rushing	12	15
Passing	22	14
Returns	6	3
Avg. Time of Possession	29:27	30:33

1997 INDIVIDUAL STATISTICS

Passing	Att.	Comp.	Yds.	Pct.	TD	Int.	Tkld.	Rate
Frerotte	402	204	2,682	50.7	17	12	23/146	73.8
Hostetler	144	79	899	54.9	5	10	10/52	56.5
T. Green	1	0	0	0.0	0	0	0/0	39.6
Redskins	547	283	3,581	51.7	22	22	33/198	69.1
Opponents	513	267	3,098	52.0	14	16	37/280	66.7

SCORING	TD R	TD P	TD Rt	PAT	FG	Saf	PTS
Blanton	0	0	0	34/34	16/24	0	82
Allen	4	1	0	0/0	0/0	0	30
Shepherd	0	5	0	0/0	0/0	0	30
Bowie	2	2	0	0/0	0/0	0	24
Ellard	0	4	0	0/0	0/0	0	24
Mitchell	1	1	2	0/0	0/0	0	24
Davis	3	0	0	0/0	0/0	0	18
Jenkins	0	3	0	0/0	0/0	0	18
Westbrook	0	3	0	0/0	0/0	0	18
Connell	0	2	0	0/0	0/0	0	12
Frerotte	2	0	0	0/0	0/0	0	12
Pounds	0	0	2	0/0	0/0	0	12
Asher	0	1	0	0/0	0/0	0	6
Dishman	0	0	1	0/0	0/0	0	6
D. Green	0	0	1	0/0	0/0	0	6
Jacke	0	0	0	5/5	0/0	0	5
Redskins	12	22	6	39/39	16/24	0	327
Opponents	15	14	3	28/28	21/25	0	289

2-Point conversions: Team:0-0, Opponents: 3-4.

RUSHING	Att.	Yds.	Avg.	LG	TD
Allen	210	724	3.4	34	4
Davis	141	567	4.0	18	3
Mitchell	23	107	4.7	26	1
Bowie	28	100	3.6	18	2
Frerotte	24	65	2.7	26	2
Hostetler	14	28	2.0	11	0
Shepherd	4	27	6.8	17	0
Logan	4	5	1.3	4	0
Connell	1	3	3.0	3	0
M. Turk	1	0	0.0	0	0
Westbrook	3	-11	-3.7	7	0
Redskins	453	1615	3.6	34	12
Opponents	508	2212	4.4	51t	15

RECEIVING	No.	Yds.	Avg.	LG	TD
Asher	49	474	9.7	24	1
Mitchell	36	438	12.2	69	1
Westbrook	34	559	16.4	40t	3
Bowie	34	388	11.4	39t	2
Ellard	32	485	15.2	27	4
Shepherd	29	562	19.4	48	5
Allen	20	172	8.6	38	1
Davis	18	134	7.4	19	0
Thomas	11	93	8.5	17	0
Connell	9	138	15.3	41t	2
Jenkins	4	43	10.8	20	3
Logan	3	6	2.0	5	0
Harper	2	65	32.5	52	0
Thrash	2	24	12.0	17	0
Raymer	0	0	—	—	0
Redskins	283	3,581	12.7	69	22
Opponents	267	3,098	11.6	52	14

INTERCEPTIONS	No.	Yds.	Avg.	LG	TD
Dishman	4	47	11.8	29t	1
Richard	4	28	7.0	23	0
Pounds	3	42	14.0	22t	1
M. Patton	2	5	2.5	5	0
D. Green	1	83	83.0	83t	1
Boutte	1	10	10.0	10	0
Campbell	1	7	7.0	7	0
Redskins	16	222	13.9	83t	3
Opponents	22	262	11.9	35t	1

PUNTING	No.	Yds.	Avg.	In 20	LG
M. Turk	84	3,788	45.1	32	62
Redskins	85	3,788	44.6	32	62
Opponents	95	4,038	42.5	33	59

PUNT RETURNS	No.	FC	Yds.	Avg.	LG	TD
Mitchell	38	23	442	11.6	63t	1
Redskins	38	23	442	11.6	63t	1
Opponents	33	18	237	7.2	37	0

KICKOFF RETURNS	No.	Yds.	Avg.	LG	TD
Mitchell	47	1,094	23.3	97t	1
Logan	4	70	17.5	24	0
Davis	3	62	20.7	28	0
Asher	1	17	17.0	17	0
Bowie	1	15	15.0	15	0
D. Green	1	9	9.0	9	0
Jones	1	6	6.0	6	0
M. Patton	1	10	10.0	10	0
Redskins	59	1,283	21.7	97t	1
Opponents	67	1,515	22.6	57	0

FIELD GOALS	1-19	20-29	30-39	40-49	50+
Blanton	2/2	4/4	5/6	4/8	1/4
Redskins	2/2	4/4	5/6	4/8	1/4
Opponents	1/1	6/6	7/8	6/8	1/2

SACKS	No.
Harvey	9.5
M. Patton	4.5
Mims	4.0
Jones	3.5
Owens	2.5
Boutte	2.0
Duff	2.0
Pounds	2.0
Smith	2.0
Dishman	1.5
Lang	1.5
Zorich	1.0
Redskins	*37.0
Opponents	33.0

**Redskins credited with 1 team sack.*

1998 DRAFT CHOICES

Round	Name	Pos.	College
2	Stephen Alexander	TE	Oklahoma
3	Skip Hicks	RB	UCLA
4	Shawn Barber	LB	Richmond
5	Mark Fischer	C	Purdue
6	Patrick Palmer	WR	Northwestern State, La.
7	David Terrell	DB	Texas-El Paso
	Antwaune Ponds	LB	Syracuse

WASHINGTON REDSKINS

1998 VETERAN ROSTER

No.		Name	Pos.	Ht.	Wt.	Birthdate	NFL Exp.	College	Hometown	How Acq.	'97 Games/ Starts
58	†	Alexander, Patrise	LB	6-1	247	10/23/72	3	Southwestern Louisiana	Galveston, Tex.	FA-'96	16/0
21		Allen, Terry	RB	5-10	208	2/21/68	9	Clemson	Commerce, Ga.	FA-'95	10/10
84	†	Asher, Jamie	TE	6-3	241	10/31/72	4	Louisville	Galveston, Tex.	D5a-'95	16/13
74		Badger, Brad	G	6-4	298	1/11/75	2	Stanford	Corvallis, Ore.	D5d-'97	12/1
61		Batiste, Michael	G-T-C	6-3	325	12/24/70	2	Tulane	Beaumont, Tex.	FA-'97	0*
16	†	Blanton, Scott	K	6-2	221	7/1/73	4	Oklahoma	Norman, Okla.	FA-'95	15/0
93		Boutte, Marc	DT	6-4	301	7/26/69	7	Louisiana State	Lake Charles, La.	FA-'94	16/14
47	†	Bowie, Larry	RB	6-0	242	3/21/73	3	Georgia	Anniston, Ala.	FA-'96	15/12
37		Campbell, Jesse	S	6-1	211	4/11/69	8	North Carolina State	Duluth, Ga.	UFA(NYG)-'97	16/16
83		Connell, Albert	WR	6-0	179	5/13/74	2	Texas A&M	Brooklyn, N.Y.	D4-'97	5/1
75		Dahl, Bob	G	6-5	329	1/15/68	7	Notre Dame	Chagrin Falls, Ohio	UFA(Clev)-'96	11/9
48		Davis, Stephen	RB	6-0	230	3/1/74	3	Auburn	Spartanburg, S.C.	D4-'96	14/6
26		Dishman, Cris	CB	6-0	195	8/13/65	11	Purdue	Louisville, Ky.	UFA(Hou)-'97	16/15
92	†	Duff, Jamal	DE	6-7	285	3/11/72	4	San Diego State	Tustin, Calif.	FA-'97	13/5
35		Evans, Leomont	S	6-1	200	7/12/74	3	Clemson	Abbeville, S.C.	D5-'96	16/0
12		Frerotte, Gus	QB	6-2	228	7/3/71	5	Tulsa	Ford Cliff, Pa.	D7-'94	13/13
80		Frisch, David	TE	6-7	260	6/22/70	5	Colorado State	Mouse Springs, Mo.	FA-'97	2/0
28		Green, Darrell	CB	5-8	184	2/15/60	16	Texas A&I	Houston, Tex.	D1-'83	16/16
10		Green, Trent	QB	6-3	215	7/9/70	5	Indiana	St. Louis, Mo.	FA-'95	1/0
57		Harvey, Ken	LB	6-2	236	5/6/65	11	California	Austin, Tex.	UFA(Ariz)-'94	15/14
15		Hostetler, Jeff	QB	6-3	215	4/22/61	15	West Virginia	Davidson, Pa.	UFA(Oak)-'97	6/3
88		Jenkins, James	TE	6-2	249	8/17/67	7	Rutgers	Staten Island, N.Y.	FA-'91	16/5
77		Johnson, Tré	G	6-2	337	8/30/71	5	Temple	Peekskill, N.Y.	D2-'94	11/11
54		Jones, Greg	LB	6-4	238	5/22/74	2	Colorado	Denver, Colo.	D2-'97	16/3
70		Kinney, Kelvin	DE	6-6	252	12/31/72	3	Virginia State	Montgomery, W. Va.	D6-'96	4/1
99	†	Kuehl, Ryan	DT	6-4	276	1/18/72	2	Virginia	Washington, D.C.	FA-'96	12/5
90		Lang, Kenard	DE	6-4	277	1/31/75	2	Miami	Orlando, Fla.	D1-'97	11/11
20		Logan, Marc	RB	6-0	220	5/9/65	11	Kentucky	Lexington, Ky.	UFA(SF)-'95	15/1
32		Lusk, Henry	TE	6-2	250	5/8/72	2	Utah	Carmel, Calif.	FA-'98	0*
36		Maston, LeShai	RB	6-1	242	10/7/70	5	Baylor	Dallas, Tex.	FA-'98	0*
69		Milstead, Rod	G	6-2	290	11/10/69	7	Delaware State	Bryan's Road, Md.	FA-'98	4/0*
30		Mitchell, Brian	RB	5-10	220	8/18/68	9	Southwestern Louisiana	Plaquemine, La.	D5-'90	16/1
96	†	Owens, Rich	DE	6-6	279	5/22/72	4	Lehigh	Philadelphia, Pa.	D5b-'95	16/15
68		Patton, Joe	G	6-5	309	1/5/72	5	Alabama A&M	Birmingham, Ala.	D3b-'94	16/16
53		Patton, Marvcus	LB	6-2	241	5/1/67	9	UCLA	Lawndale, Calif.	UFA(Buff)-'95	16/16
31	†	Pounds, Darryl	CB	5-10	181	7/21/72	4	Nicholls State	Ft. Worth, Tex.	D3-'95	16/0
67		Pourdanesh, Shar	T	6-6	318	7/19/70	3	Nevada-Reno	Tehran, Iran	FA-'96	16/14
52		Raymer, Cory	C	6-2	292	3/3/73	4	Wisconsin	Fond du Lac, Wis.	D2-'95	6/3
24		Richard, Stanley	S	6-2	197	10/21/67	8	Texas	Miniola, Tex.	FA-'95	16/16
98		Russell, Twan	LB	6-1	219	4/25/74	2	Miami	Ft. Lauderdale, Fla.	D5c-'97	15/0
86		Shepherd, Leslie	WR	5-11	180	11/3/69	5	Temple	Forestville, Md.	FA-'94	11/9
50		Smith, Derek	LB	6-2	239	1/18/75	2	Arizona State	American Fork, Utah	D3-'97	16/16
94		Stubblefield, Dana	DT	6-2	315	11/14/70	6	Kansas	Cleves, Ohio	UFA(SF)-'98	16/16*
32		Thibodeaux, Keith	CB	5-11	189	5/16/74	2	Northwestern State, La.	Opelousas, La.	D5b-'97	15/0
89		Thomas, Chris	WR	6-2	190	7/16/71	3	Cal Poly-San Luis Obispo	Burbank, Calif.	FA-'97	13/0
87		Thrash, James	WR	6-0	200	1/28/75	2	Missouri Southern	Wewoka, Okla.	FA-'97	4/0
66		Turk, Dan	C	6-4	290	6/25/62	14	Wisconsin	Greenfield, Wis.	FA-'97	16/0
1		Turk, Matt	P	6-5	234	5/16/68	4	Wisconsin-Whitewater	Greenfield, Wis.	FA-'95	16/0
29	†	Turner, Scott	CB	5-10	180	2/26/72	4	Illinois	Richardson, Tex.	D7-'95	9/0
55		Uhlenhake, Jeff	C	6-3	284	1/28/66	10	Ohio State	Newark, Ohio	FA-'96	14/13
82		Westbrook, Michael	WR	6-3	220	7/7/72	4	Colorado	Detroit, Mich.	D1-'95	13/9
95	t-	Wilkinson, Dan	DT	6-5	313	3/13/73	5	Ohio State	Dayton, Ohio	T(Cin)-'98	15/1*
22		Williams, Jamel	S	5-11	205	12/22/73	2	Nebraska	Gary, Ind.	D5a-'97	16/0

* Batiste last active with Dallas in '95; Lusk last active with New Orleans in '96; Maston last active with Jacksonville in '96; Milstead played 4 games with San Francisco in '97; Stubblefield played 16 games with San Francisco; Wilkinson played 15 games with Cincinnati.

† Restricted free agent; subject to developments.

t- Redskins traded for Wilkinson (Cincinnati).

Players lost to free agency (1): T Darryl Ashmore (Oak; 12 games in '97).

Also played with Redskins in '97—WR Henry Ellard (16 games), DT Steve Emtman (3), DT William Gaines (13), WR Alvin Harper (12), K Chris Jacke (1), DE Chris Mims (11), DT Keith Rucker (2), TE Chris Sanders (1), DE Don Sasa (1), T Ed Simmons (14), S Brian Walker (5), DT Chris Zorich (5).

COACHING STAFF

Head Coach,
Norv Turner

Pro Career: Enters his fifth season as head coach of the Washington Redskins after serving three years as the Dallas Cowboys' offensive coordinator. Turner guided the Cowboys' prolific offense during back-to-back Super Bowl championship seasons. He inherited a Cowboys offense that finished twenty-eighth in total offense in 1990, and a year later improved to ninth. The Cowboys finished fourth in the league offensively in 1992-93. In three seasons under Turner, quarterback Troy Aikman compiled a 91.7 rating, and running back Emmitt Smith won three consecutive NFL rushing titles. Prior to joining the Cowboys, Turner coached six seasons (1985-1990) with the Los Angeles Rams where he oversaw the passing game. Quarterback Jim Everett enjoyed his best seasons under Turner, while Willie Anderson led the NFL in yards per catch in 1989 and 1990, and Henry Ellard was the league's leading receiver in 1988. Career record: 26-37-1.

Background: Turner played quarterback for three seasons at the University of Oregon (1972-74). He began his coaching career as a graduate assistant at Oregon in 1975. A year later, he moved to the University of Southern California, where he coached from 1976-1984.

Personal: Born May 17, 1952, in LeJeune, N.C. Turner and his wife, Nancy, live in Oakton, Va., and have three children—Scott, Stephanie, and Drew.

ASSISTANT COACHES

Jason Arapoff, assistant conditioning; born July 8, 1965, Weymouth, Mass., lives in Centreville, Va. Defensive back Springfield College 1985-88. No pro playing experience. Pro coach: Joined Redskins in 1992.

Jeff Fitzgerald, defensive assistant; born April 18, 1960, Burbank, Calif., lives in Reston, Va. Attended Oregon State. No college or pro playing experience. College coach: Cincinnati 1985-86, Alabama 1986-89, San Diego State 1994-97. Pro coach: Tampa Bay Buccanneers 1990-93, joined Redskins in 1998.

Russ Grimm, offensive line; born May 2, 1959, Scottdale, Pa., lives in Fairfax, Va. Guard-center Pittsburgh 1977-80. Pro guard Washington Redskins 1981-91. Pro coach: Joined Redskins in 1992.

Tom Hayes, defensive backs; born March 26, 1949, Keokuk, Iowa, lives in Ashburn, Va. Defensive back Iowa 1968-71. No pro playing experience. College coach: Coe College 1973, Iowa 1977-78, Cal State-Fullerton 1979, UCLA 1980-88, Texas A&M 1989, Oklahoma 1990-94. Pro coach: Joined Redskins in 1995.

Bobby Jackson, running backs; born February 16, 1940, Forsyth, Ga., lives in Sterling, Va. Linebacker-running back Samford 1959-62. No pro playing experience. College coach: Florida State 1965-69, Kansas State 1970-74, Louisville 1975-76, Tennessee 1977-82. Pro coach: Atlanta Falcons 1983-86, San Diego Chargers 1987-91, Phoenix Cardinals 1992-93, joined Redskins in 1994.

Earl Leggett, defensive line; born March 5, 1935, Jacksonville, Fla., lives in Leesburg, Va. Defensive tackle Hinds J.C. 1953-54, Louisiana State 1955-56. Pro defensive tackle Chicago Bears 1957-65, Los Angeles Rams 1966, New Orleans Saints 1967-68. Pro coach: Seattle Seahawks 1976-77, San Francisco 49ers 1978, Oakland/Los Angeles Raiders 1980-88, 1991-92, Denver Broncos 1989-90, New York Giants 1993-96, joined Redskins in 1997.

Dale Lindsey, linebackers; born January 18, 1943, Bedford, Ind., lives in Ashburn, Va. Linebacker Western Kentucky 1961-64. Pro linebacker Cleveland Browns 1965-73. College coach: Southern Methodist 1988-89. Pro coach: Green Bay Packers 1986-87, New England Patriots 1990, Tampa Bay Buccaneers 1991, San Diego Chargers 1994-96, joined Redskins in 1997.

Mike Martz, quarterbacks; born May 13, 1951, Sioux Falls, S.D., lives in Leesburg, Va. No college or pro playing experience. College coach: San Diego Mesa 1974, 1976-77, San Jose State 1975, Santa Ana College 1978, Fresno State 1979, Pacific 1980-81, Arizona State 1983-91. Pro coach: Los Angeles/St. Louis Rams 1992-96, joined Redskins in 1997.

LeCharls McDaniel, special teams; born October 15, 1958, Fort Bragg, N.C., lives in Ashburn, Va. Cornerback Cal Poly-San Luis Obispo 1976-80. Pro defensive back Washington Redskins 1981-82, New York Giants 1983-84. College coach: Hartnell College (Calif.) 1984-89, Cal Poly-San Luis Obispo 1992, San Diego State 1994-95. Pro coach: San Diego Chargers 1989-91, Phoenix Cardinals 1993, joined Redskins in 1997.

Mike Nolan, defensive coordinator; born March 7, 1959, Baltimore, Md., lives in Oakton, Va. Free safety Oregon 1977-80. No pro playing experience. College coach: Oregon 1981, Stanford 1982-83, Rice 1984-85, Louisiana State 1986. Pro coach: Denver Broncos 1987-92, New York Giants 1993-96, joined Redskins in 1997.

Michael Pope, tight ends; born March 15, 1942, Monroe, N.C., lives in Ashburn, Va. Quarterback Lenoir Rhyne 1962-64. No pro playing experience. College coach: Florida State 1970-74, Texas Tech 1975-77, Mississippi 1978-82. Pro coach: New York Giants 1983-91, Cincinnati Bengals 1992-93, New England Patriots 1994-96, joined Redskins in 1997.

Dan Riley, strength; born October 19, 1949, Syracuse, N.Y., lives in Ashburn, Va. Attended Keene State. No college or pro playing experience. College coach: Army 1973-76, Penn State 1977-81. Pro coach: Joined Redskins in 1982.

Terry Robiskie, receivers; born November 12, 1954, New Orleans, La., lives in Clifton, Va. Running back Louisiana State 1973-76. Pro running back Oakland Raiders 1977-79, Miami Dolphins 1980-81. Pro coach: Los Angeles Raiders 1982-93, joined Redskins in 1994.

Ed Sidwell, offensive assistant; born January 11, 1967, Belleville, Ill., lives in McClean, Va. Attended Ohio State. No college or pro playing experience. College coach: Ohio State 1988-93. Pro coach: San Antonio Texans (CFL) 1995, Houston Oilers 1996, joined Redskins in 1997.

1998 FIRST-YEAR ROSTER

Name	Pos.	Ht.	Wt.	Birthdate	College	Hometown	How Acq.
Alexander, Stephen	TE	6-4	246	11/7/75	Oklahoma	Chickasha, Okla.	D2
Augafa, Patrick (1)	C	6-2	320	11/12/73	Iowa State	Fagaitua, Samoa	FA
Barber, Shawn	LB	6-2	224	1/14/75	Richmond	Richmond, Va.	D4
Brown, Denauld	DT	6-3	298	7/21/75	Kutztown	Westchester, Pa.	FA
Brown, Doug (1)	DT	6-7	290	9/29/74	Simon Fraser	Coquittlam, Canada	FA
Crutchfield, Buddy	CB	6-0	196	3/7/76	North Carolina Central	Raleigh, N.C.	FA
Denton, Tim (1)	CB-S	5-11	182	2/2/73	Sam Houston	Galveston, Tex.	FA
Fischer, Mark	C	6-3	293	7/29/74	Purdue	Cincinnati, Ohio	D5
Hamilton, Malcolm (1)	LB	6-1	235	12/31/72	Baylor	Odessa, Tex.	FA
Hicks, Skip	RB	6-0	230	10/13/74	UCLA	Burkburnett, Tex.	D3
Howard, Eddie (1)	P	6-1	203	10/6/72	Idaho	Covina, Calif.	FA
Kight, Danny (1)	P-K	6-0	200	8/18/71	Auburn	Decatur, Ga.	FA
Lord, Junior	WR	6-1	197	3/11/76	Guilford	Greenwich, Conn.	FA
Malveaux, Felman (1)	WR	6-0	179	8/20/73	Michigan	Beaumont, Tex.	FA
Miller, Norman	RB	5-10	189	8/16/74	Texas A&M-Kingsville	Sacramento, Calif.	FA
Otton, Brad	QB	6-6	235	1/25/72	Southern California	Tumwater, Wash.	FA
Palmer, Pat	WR	6-2	181	7/13/75	Northwestern State	Port Arthur, Tex.	D6
Pesak, Kevin	RB	6-2	222	4/18/75	Sam Houston	Alvin, Tex.	FA
Ponds, Antwaune	LB	6-2	252	6/29/75	Syracuse	Jacksonville, Fla.	D7b
Powell, Ozell (1)	T	6-5	316	11/17/73	Alabama	Greenville, Ala.	FA
Sanders, Chris (1)	TE	6-3	241	4/22/73	Texas A&M	Austin, Tex.	FA
Sellers, Mike	TE	6-3	260	7/21/75	Walla Walla	Lacey, Wash.	FA
Shelton, Chris	RB	5-11	227	7/22/75	New Mexico	Palestine, Tex.	FA
Smith, Neal	DE	6-5	264	11/4/74	Montana State	Polson, Mont.	FA
Stanton, Marcus	S	6-0	187	6/10/75	New Mexico	Killeen, Tex.	FA
Streater, Rahmaan	DE	6-5	263	4/23/75	Richmond	Washington, D.C.	FA
Terrell, David	CB	6-2	172	7/8/75	Texas-El Paso	Sweetwater, Tex.	D7a
Tounkara, Ousmane	WR	6-3	209	12/25/73	Ottawa	Ottawa, Canada	FA

The term NFL Rookie is defined as a player who is in his first season of professional football and has not been on the roster of another professional football team for any regular-season or postseason games. A Rookie is designated by an "R" on NFL rosters. Players who have been active in another professional football league or players who have NFL experience, including either preseason training camp or being on an Active List or Inactive List, or on Reserve/Injured or Reserve/Physically Unable to Perform for fewer than six regular-season games, are termed NFL First-Year Players. An NFL First-Year Player is designated by a "1" on NFL rosters. Thereafter, a player is credited with an additional year of experience for each season in which he accumulates six games on the Active List or Inactive List, or on Reserve/Injured or Reserve/Physically Unable to Perform.

NOTES

1997 Season in Review

TRADES

1997 INTERCONFERENCE TRADES

Defensive back **Chris Hayes** from Green Bay to New York Jets for defensive back **Carl Greenwood** (6/5).

Tight end **Henry Lusk** from New York Jets to Green Bay for past considerations. (6/19)

Guard **Sean Love** from New York Jets to Philadelphia for past considerations. (8/22)

Wide receiver **Qadry Ismail** from Green Bay to Miami for selection choice unannounced. (8/24)

Defensive end **Paul Frase** from Jacksonville to Green Bay for the Packers' sixth-round selection in 1998. Jacksonville selected running back **Kevin McLleod** (Auburn). (8/24)

Tackle **Jimmy Herndon** from Jacksonville to Chicago for the Bears' seventh-round selection in 1998. Jacksonville selected wide receiver **Alvis Whitted** (North Carolina State). (8/24)

Wide receiver **Chris Penn** from Kansas City to Chicago for the Bears' fifth-round selection in 1998. Kansas City selected defensive back **Robert Williams** (North Carolina). (8/24)

Guard **Ben Cavil** from Philadelphia to Baltimore for selection choice unannounced. (8/24)

Defensive end **Israel Raybon** from Pittsburgh to Carolina for the Panthers' seventh-round selection in 1998. Pittsburgh traded the seventh-round selection acquired from Carolina to Atlanta. (8/24)

Tight end **Tyrone Davis** from New York Jets to Green Bay for past considerations. (8/26)

Defensive back **Willie Clark** from Baltimore to Philadelphia for selection choice unannounced. (8/27)

Wide receiver **Daryl Hobbs** from New Orleans to Seattle for the Seahawks' seventh-round selection in 1998. New Orleans selected wide receiver **Andy McCullough** (Tennessee). (9/30)

Linebacker **Wayne Simmons** from Green Bay to Kansas City for the Chiefs' fifth-round selection in 1998. Green Bay selected wide receiver **Corey Bradford** (Jackson State). (10/7)

1998 INTERCONFERENCE TRADES

Running back **Errict Rhett** from Tampa Bay to Baltimore for selection choice unannounced (2/18).

Defensive tackle **Dan Wilkinson** from Cincinnati to Washington for the Redskins' first- and third-round selections in 1998. Cincinnati selected linebacker **Brian Simmons** (North Carolina) and guard **Mike Goff** (Iowa). (2/26)

Cornerback **Eric Allen** from New Orleans to Oakland for the Raiders' fourth-round selection in 1998. New Orleans selected defensive back **Fred Weary** (Florida). (3/5)

Running back **Lorenzo Neal** from New York Jets to Tampa Bay for the Buccaneers' fifth-round selection in 1998. Jets selected tight end **Blake Spence** (Oregon). (3/12)

Defensive end **Hugh Douglas** from New York Jets to Philadelphia for the Eagles' second- and fifth-round selections in 1998. Jets traded the second-round selection acquired from the Eagles to Pittsburgh and selected linebacker **Casey Dailey** (Northwestern). (3/13)

Wide receiver **Eric Metcalf**, linebacker **Patrick Sapp**, and the Chargers' first- and second-round selections in 1998 and first-round selection in 1999 from San Diego to Arizona for the Cardinals' first-round selection in 1998. Arizona selected defensive end **Andre Wadsworth** (Florida State) and defensive back **Corey Chavous** (Vanderbilt). San Diego selected quarterback **Ryan Leaf** (Washington State). (3/16)

Linebacker **Rob Fredrickson** from Oakland to Detroit for the Lions' fourth-round selection in 1998. Oakland traded the selection acquired from the Lions to Washington. (3/24)

Running back **Adrian Murrell** and the New York Jets' seventh-round selection in 1998 to Arizona for the Cardinals' third-round selection in 1998. Arizona selected defensive end **Jomo Cousins** (Florida A&M). The Jets traded the selection acquired from Arizona to St. Louis. (4/7)

Carolina's second-round selection in 1998 to Miami for the selection choice unannounced. (4/16)

Tackle **Jamie Brown** from Denver to San Francisco for the selection choice unannounced. (4/16)

Miami's first-round selection in 1998 to Green Bay for the Packers' first- and second-round selections in 1998. The Packers selected defensive tackle **Vonnie Holiday** (North Carolina). The Dolphins selected running back **John Avery** (Mississippi) and traded the second-round selection acquired from Green Bay to Detroit. (4/18)

Oakland's two second-round selections in 1998 to Tampa Bay for the Buccaneers' first-round selection in 1998. Tampa Bay selected wide receiver **Jacquez Green** (Florida) and traded the second second-round selection acquired from Oakland to San Diego. Oakland selected tackle **Mo Collins** (Florida). (4/18)

Tampa Bay's second-round selection in 1998 to San Diego for the Chargers' first-round selection in 2000. San Diego selected wide receiver **Mikhael Ricks** (Stephen F. Austin). (4/18)

Miami's second-round selection in 1998 to Detroit for the Lions' third-, fifth- and sixth-round selections in 1998. Detroit selected quarterback **Charlie Batch** (Eastern Michigan). Miami selected linebacker **Brad Johnson** (Cincinnati), guard **Scott Shaw** (Michigan State), and quarterback **John Dutton** (Nevada-Reno). (4/18)

New York Jets' third-round selection in 1998 to St. Louis for the Rams' third- and seventh-round selections in 1998. St. Louis selected linebacker **Leonard Little** (Tennessee). The Jets selected defensive back **Scott Frost** (Nebraska) and tight end **Lawrence Hart** (Southern). (4/18)

Atlanta's fifth-round selection in 1998 to Pittsburgh for the Steelers' three seventh-round selections in 1998. Pittsburgh selected defensive back **Jason Simmons** (Arizona State). Atlanta selected tackle **Ephraim Salaam** (San Diego State), defensive tackle **Henry Slay** (West Virginia) and traded the selection acquired from Pittsburgh to San Francisco. (4/19)

Miami's fourth- and fifth-round selections in 1998 to Philadelphia for the Eagles' fourth-round selection in 1998. Philadelphia selected defensive tackle **Brandon Whiting** (California) and linebacker **Ike Reese** (Michigan State). Miami selected defensive end **Lorenzo Bromell** (Clemson). (4/19)

Baltimore's fourth-round selection in 1998 to Tampa Bay for the Buccaneers' third-round selection in 1999. Tampa Bay selected center **Todd Washington** (Virginia Tech). (4/19)

Oakland's fourth- and seventh-round selections in 1998 to Washington for the Redskins' fourth-round selection in 1998. Washington selected linebacker **Shawn Barber** (Richmond) and defensive back **David Terrell** (Texas-El Paso). Oakland selected guard **Gennaro DiNapoli** (Virginia Tech). (4/19)

Dallas' sixth- and seventh-round selections in 1998 to Seattle for the Seahawks' fifth-round selection in 1998. Seattle selected defensive end **Carl Hansen** (Stanford) and center **Jason McEndoo** (Washington State). Dallas selected tackle **Ross Oliver** (Iowa State). (4/19)

Green Bay's fifth-round selection in 1998 to Oakland for the Raiders' sixth-round selections in 1998 and 1999. Oakland selected linebacker **Travian Smith** (Oklahoma). Green Bay selected defensive back **Scott McGarrahan** (New Mexico). (4/19)

Wide receiver **Jeff Graham** from New York Jets to Philadelphia for the Eagles' sixth-round selection in 1998. The Jets selected defensive end **Eric Ogbogu** (Maryland). (4/19)

Denver's sixth-round selection in 1999 to Philadelphia for the Eagles' seventh-round selection in 1998. Denver selected tackle **Trey Teague** (Tennessee). (4/19)

1997 AFC TRADES

Running back **Erric Pegram** from Pittsburgh to San Diego for selection choice unannounced. (7/2)

Tackle **Bernard Dafney** from Pittsburgh to Baltimore for selection choice unannounced. (8/24)

1998 AFC TRADES

Quarterback **Rob Johnson** from Jacksonville to Buffalo for the Bills' first- and fourth-round selections in 1998. Jacksonville selected running back **Fred Taylor** (Florida) and running back **Tavian Banks** (Iowa). (2/13)

Quarterback **Jim Harbaugh** and the Colts' fourth-round selection in 1998 from Indianapolis to Baltimore for the Ravens' third- and fourth-round selections in 1998. Baltimore traded the fourth-round selection acquired from the Colts to Tampa Bay. Indianapolis selected wide receiver **E.G. Green** (Florida State) and traded the fourth-round selection acquired from the Ravens to Baltimore. (2/17)

Quarterback **Paul Justin** from Indianapolis to Cincinnati for the Bengals' fifth-round selection in 1998. Indianapolis selected linebacker **Antony Jordon** (Vanderbilt). (3/26)

New York Jets' second-round selection in 1998 to Pittsburgh for the Steelers' second-, third-, and fifth-round selections in 1998. Pittsburgh selected defensive end **Jeremy Staat** (Arizona State). The New York Jets selected defensive end **Dorian Boose** (Washington State), defensive back **Kevin Williams** (Oklahoma State) and tackle **Eric Bateman** (Brigham Young). (4/18)

Baltimore's fourth-round selection in 1998 to Indianapolis for the Colts' fourth-, fifth- and sixth-round selections in 1998. Indianapolis selected guard **Steve McKinney** (Texas A&M). Baltimore traded the fourth-round selection acquired from Indianapolis to Tampa Bay, selected defensive tackle **Chase Martin** (Oklahoma) and linebacker **Ron Rogers** (Georgia Tech). (4/19)

1998 NFC TRADES

Quarterback **Steve Bono** from Green Bay to St. Louis for selection choice unannounced. (4/6)

Linebacker **Tony Peterson** from Chicago to San Francisco for the 49ers' seventh-round selection in 1998. Chicago selected tackle **Chad Overhauser** (UCLA). (4/16)

Atlanta's second-round selection in 1998 to Tampa Bay for the Buccaneers' second- and fourth-round selections in 1998. Tampa Bay selected defensive back **Brian Kelly** (Southern California). Atlanta selected center **Bob Hallen** (Kent State) and wide receiver **Tim Dwight** (Iowa). (4/18)

Philadelphia's third-round selection in 1998 to the New York Giants for the Giants' third- and fourth-round selections in 1998. The Giants selected wide receiver **Brian Alford** (Purdue). Philadelphia selected defensive back **Allen Rossum** (Notre Dame) and defensive back **Clarence Love** (Toledo). (4/18)

Atlanta's seventh-round selection in 1998 to San Francisco for the 49ers' sixth-round selection in 1999. San Francisco selected wide receiver **Ryan Thelwell** (Minnesota). (4/19)

FINAL STANDINGS

AMERICAN FOOTBALL CONFERENCE

Eastern Division

	W	L	T	Pct.	Pts.	OP
N.Y. Jets	4	0	0	1.000	112	72
New England	3	1	0	.750	78	52
Miami	3	2	0	.600	97	84
Indianapolis	2	2	0	.500	56	87
Buffalo	2	3	0	.400	80	117

Central Division

	W	L	T	Pct.	Pts.	OP
Pittsburgh	5	0	0	1.000	155	96
Jacksonville	4	0	0	1.000	115	62
Cincinnati	2	2	0	.500	108	87
Baltimore	0	4	0	.000	90	115
Tennessee	0	4	0	.000	41	94

Western Division

	W	L	T	Pct.	Pts.	OP
San Diego	3	1	0	.750	86	65
Denver	3	2	0	.600	125	109
Seattle	3	2	0	.600	153	86
Oakland	2	2	0	.500	89	95
Kansas City	1	3	0	.250	64	78

NATIONAL FOOTBALL CONFERENCE

Eastern Division

	W	L	T	Pct.	Pts.	OP
Washington	3	1	0	.750	80	79
Dallas	2	2	0	.500	105	91
Arizona	1	3	0	.250	31	81
N.Y. Giants	1	3	0	.250	71	107
Philadelphia	1	3	0	.250	81	114

Central Division

	W	L	T	Pct.	Pts.	OP
Green Bay	5	0	0	1.000	121	47
Minnesota	3	2	0	.600	96	110
Chicago	2	3	0	.400	80	91
Detroit	1	3	0	.250	66	88
Tampa Bay	1	3	0	.250	53	62

Western Division

	W	L	T	Pct.	Pts.	OP
New Orleans	3	1	0	.750	76	44
St. Louis	2	2	0	.500	63	71
Atlanta	1	3	0	.250	82	93
San Francisco	1	3	0	.250	71	96
Carolina	0	4	0	.000	51	103

AFC PRESEASON RECORDS—TEAM BY TEAM

Eastern Division

BUFFALO (2-3)

10	at Denver	31
17	Chicago (OT)	20
19	Minnesota	3
3	vs. Green Bay+	35
31	at Baltimore	28
80		117

INDIANAPOLIS (2-2)

20	Cincinnati	16
17	at San Diego	23
3	at Seattle	45
16	Detroit	3
56		87

MIAMI (3-2)

0	at Green Bay	20
38	vs. Denver++	19
21	Chicago	14
10	at Tampa Bay	24
28	Washington	7
97		84

NEW ENGLAND (3-1)

3	at Green Bay	7
16	Dallas	10
31	Denver	21
28	at Philadelphia	14
78		52

N.Y. JETS (4-0)

31	Philadelphia	17
39	Baltimore	29
27	at N.Y. Giants	17
15	at Tampa Bay (OT) (ORL)	9
112		72

Central Division

BALTIMORE (0-4)

20	N.Y. Giants	21
29	at N.Y. Jets	39
13	at Philadelphia	24
28	Buffalo	31
90		115

CINCINNATI (2-2)

16	at Indianapolis	20
27	at Detroit	23
37	Minnesota	13
28	Seattle	31
108		87

JACKSONVILLE (4-0)

23	Carolina	9
38	at N.Y. Giants	16
28	at San Francisco	20
26	Atlanta	17
115		62

PITTSBURGH (5-0)

30	vs. Chicago**	17
28	at Kansas City	14
42	Philadelphia	26
28	Detroit	20
27	at Carolina	19
155		96

TENNESSEE (0-4)

12	New Orleans	21
12	Washington	18
7	San Diego	21
10	at Dallas	34
41		94

Western Division

DENVER (3-2)

31	Buffalo	10
19	vs. Miami++	38
23	at Carolina	13
21	at New England	31
31	San Francisco	17
125		109

KANSAS CITY (1-3)

14	Pittsburgh	28
7	at New Orleans	26
30	Carolina	10
13	at St. Louis	14
64		78

OAKLAND (2-2)

34	at Dallas	27
24	Green Bay	37
18	New Orleans	16
13	at Arizona	15
89		95

SAN DIEGO (3-1)

20	San Francisco	13
23	Indianapolis	17
21	at Tennessee	7
22	at Minnesota	28
86		65

SEATTLE (3-2)

26	vs. Minnesota*	28
34	Arizona	6
17	at San Francisco	21
45	Indianapolis	3
31	at Cincinnati	28
153		86

NFC PRESEASON RECORDS—TEAM BY TEAM

Eastern Division

ARIZONA (1-3)

6	at Seattle	34
0	at St. Louis	12
10	at Chicago	22
15	Oakland	13
31		81

DALLAS (2-2)

27	Oakland	34
10	at New England	16
34	St. Louis	31
34	Tennessee	10
105		91

N.Y. GIANTS (1-3)

21	at Baltimore	20
16	Jacksonville	38
17	N.Y. Jets	27
17	at Green Bay (MAD)	22
71		107

PHILADELPHIA (1-3)

17	at N.Y. Jets	31
26	at Pittsburgh	42
24	Baltimore	13
14	New England	28
81		114

WASHINGTON (3-1)

20	at Tampa Bay	8
18	at Tennessee	12
35	at Atlanta	31
7	at Miami	28
80		79

Central Division

CHICAGO (2-3)

17	vs. Pittsburgh**	30
20	at Buffalo (OT)	17
14	at Miami	21
22	Arizona	10
7	New Orleans	13
80		91

DETROIT (1-3)

20	Atlanta	17
23	Cincinnati	27
20	at Pittsburgh	28
3	at Indianapolis	16
66		88

GREEN BAY (5-0)

20	Miami	0
7	New England	3
37	at Oakland	24
35	vs. Buffalo+	3
22	N.Y. Giants (MAD)	17
121		47

MINNESOTA (3-2)

28	vs. Seattle*	26
24	St. Louis	6
3	at Buffalo	19
13	at Cincinnati	37
28	San Diego	22
96		110

TAMPA BAY (1-3)

8	Washington	20
12	at Atlanta	17
24	Miami	10
9	N.Y. Jets (OT) (ORL)	15
53		62

Western Division

ATLANTA (1-3)

17	at Detroit	20
17	Tampa Bay	12
31	Washington	35
17	at Jacksonville	26
82		93

CAROLINA (0-4)

9	at Jacksonville	23
13	Denver	23
10	at Kansas City	30
19	Pittsburgh	27
51		103

NEW ORLEANS (3-1)

21	at Tennessee	12
26	Kansas City	7
16	at Oakland	18
13	at Chicago	7
76		44

ST. LOUIS (2-2)

6	at Minnesota	24
12	Arizona	0
31	at Dallas	34
14	Kansas City	13
63		71

SAN FRANCISCO (1-3)

13	at San Diego	20
21	Seattle	17
20	Jacksonville	28
17	at Denver	31
71		96

(OT) denotes overtime game
* denotes Pro Football Hall of Fame game in Canton, Ohio
** denotes American Bowl in Dublin, Ireland
+ denotes American Bowl in Toronto, Canada
++ denotes American Bowl in Mexico City, Mexico
(MAD) denotes game played in Madison, Wisconsin
(ORL) denotes game played in Orlando, Florida

1997 NFL STANDINGS/RESULTS

FINAL STANDINGS

AMERICAN FOOTBALL CONFERENCE

Eastern Division	W	L	T	Pct.	Pts.	OP
*New England	10	6	0	.625	369	289
#Miami	9	7	0	.563	339	327
New York Jets	9	7	0	.563	.348	287
Buffalo	6	10	0	.375	255	367
Indianapolis	3	13	0	.188	313	401
Central Division						
*Pittsburgh	11	5	0	.688	372	307
#Jacksonville	11	5	0	.688	394	318
Tennessee	8	8	0	.500	333	310
Cincinnati	7	9	0	.438	355	405
Baltimore	6	9	1	.406	326	345
Western Division						
*Kansas City	13	3	0	.813	375	232
#Denver	12	4	0	.750	472	287
Seattle	8	8	0	.500	365	362
Oakland	4	12	0	.250	324	419
San Diego	4	12	0	.250	266	425

NATIONAL FOOTBALL CONFERENCE

Eastern Division	W	L	T	Pct.	Pts.	OP
*N.Y. Giants	10	5	1	.656	307	265
Washington	8	7	1	.531	327	289
Philadelphia	6	9	1	.406	317	372
Dallas	6	10	0	.375	304	314
Arizona	4	12	0	.250	283	379
Central Division						
*Green Bay	13	3	0	.813	422	282
#Tampa Bay	10	6	0	.625	299	263
#Detroit	9	7	0	.563	379	306
#Minnesota	9	7	0	.563	354	359
Chicago	4	12	0	.250	263	421
Western Division						
*San Francisco	13	3	0	.813	375	265
Carolina	7	9	0	.438	265	314
Atlanta	7	9	0	.438	320	361
New Orleans	6	10	0	.375	237	327
St. Louis	5	11	0	.313	299	359

*Division Champion; #Wild Card Team

Miami finished ahead of New York Jets based on head-to-head sweep (2-0). Pittsburgh finished ahead of Jacksonville based on better net division points (78 to Jaguars' 23). Oakland finished ahead of San Diego based on better division record (2-6 to Chargers' 1-7). Detroit finished ahead of Minnesota based on head-to-head sweep (2-0). Carolina finished ahead of Atlanta based on head-to-head sweep (2-0).

WILD CARD PLAYOFFS

AFC

DENVER 42, Jacksonville 17
NEW ENGLAND 17, Miami 3

NFC

Minnesota 23, N.Y. GIANTS 22
TAMPA BAY 20, Detroit 10

DIVISIONAL PLAYOFFS

AFC

PITTSBURGH 7, New England 6
Denver 14, KANSAS CITY 10

NFC

SAN FRANCISCO 38, Minnesota 22
GREEN BAY 21, Tampa Bay 7

CHAMPIONSHIP GAMES

AFC

Denver 24, PITTSBURGH 21

NFC

Green Bay 23, SAN FRANCISCO 10

SUPER BOWL XXXI

Denver (AFC) 31, Green Bay (NFC) 24, at Qualcomm Stadium, San Diego, California

AFC-NFC PRO BOWL

AFC 29, NFC 24, at Aloha Stadium, Honolulu, Hawaii

Home teams in playoff games are indicated in CAPS.

AFC SEASON RECORDS—TEAM BY TEAM

BALTIMORE (6-9-1)

27	JACKSONVILLE	28
23	CINCINNATI	10
24	at N.Y. Giants	23
36	at Tennessee	10
17	at San Diego	21
34	PITTSBURGH	42
	OPEN DATE	
13	MIAMI	24
20	at Washington	17
16	at N.Y. Jets (OT)	19
0	at Pittsburgh	37
10	PHILADELPHIA (OT)	10
13	ARIZONA	16
27	at Jacksonville	29
31	SEATTLE	24
21	TENNESSEE	19
14	at Cincinnati	16
326		345

BUFFALO (6-10)

13	MINNESOTA	34
28	at N.Y. Jets	22
16	at Kansas City	22
37	INDIANAPOLIS	35
	OPEN DATE	
22	DETROIT	13
6	at New England	33
9	at Indianapolis	6
20	DENVER (OT)	23
9	MIAMI	6
10	NEW ENGLAND	31
13	at Miami	30
14	at Tennessee	31
20	N.Y. JETS	10
3	at Chicago	20
14	JACKSONVILLE	20
21	at Green Bay	31
255		367

CINCINNATI (7-9)

24	ARIZONA	21
10	at Baltimore	23
	OPEN DATE	
20	at Denver	38
14	N.Y. JETS	31
13	at Jacksonville	21
7	at Tennessee	30
10	PITTSBURGH	26
27	at N.Y. Giants	29
38	SAN DIEGO	31
28	at Indianapolis	13
3	at Pittsburgh	20
31	JACKSONVILLE	26
42	at Philadelphia	44
41	TENNESSEE	14
31	DALLAS	24
16	BALTIMORE	14
355		405

DENVER (12-4)

19	KANSAS CITY	3
35	at Seattle	14
35	ST. LOUIS	14
38	CINCINNATI	20
29	at Atlanta	21
34	NEW ENGLAND	13
	OPEN DATE	
25	at Oakland	28
23	at Buffalo (OT)	20
30	SEATTLE	27
34	CAROLINA	0
22	at Kansas City	24
31	OAKLAND	3
38	at San Diego	28
24	at Pittsburgh	35
17	at San Francisco	34
38	SAN DIEGO	3
472		287

INDIANAPOLIS (3-13)

10	at Miami	16
6	NEW ENGLAND	31
3	SEATTLE	31
35	at Buffalo	37
	OPEN DATE	
12	N.Y. JETS	16
22	at Pittsburgh	24
6	BUFFALO	9
19	at San Diego	35
28	TAMPA BAY	31
13	CINCINNATI	28
41	GREEN BAY	38
10	at Detroit	32
17	at New England	20
22	at N.Y. Jets	14
41	MIAMI	0
28	at Minnesota	39
313		401

JACKSONVILLE (11-5)

28	at Baltimore	27
40	N.Y. GIANTS	13
	OPEN DATE	
30	PITTSBURGH	21
12	at Washington	24
21	CINCINNATI	13
38	PHILADELPHIA	21
22	at Dallas	26
17	at Pittsburgh (OT)	23
30	at Tennessee	24
24	KANSAS CITY	10
17	TENNESSEE	9
26	at Cincinnati	31
29	BALTIMORE	27
20	NEW ENGLAND	26
20	at Buffalo	14
20	at Oakland	9
394		318

KANSAS CITY (13-3)

3	at Denver	19
28	at Oakland	27
22	BUFFALO	16
35	at Carolina	14
20	SEATTLE (OT)	17
14	at Miami	17
	OPEN DATE	
31	SAN DIEGO	3
28	at St. Louis	20
13	PITTSBURGH	10
10	at Jacksonville	24
24	DENVER	22
19	at Seattle	14
44	SAN FRANCISCO	9
30	OAKLAND	0
29	at San Diego	7
25	NEW ORLEANS	13
375		232

MIAMI (9-7)

16	INDIANAPOLIS	10
16	TENNESSEE (OT)	13
18	at Green Bay	23
21	at Tampa Bay	31
	OPEN DATE	
17	KANSAS CITY	14
31	at N.Y. Jets	20
24	at Baltimore	13
33	CHICAGO (OT)	36
6	at Buffalo	9
24	N.Y. JETS	17
30	BUFFALO	13
24	at New England	27
34	at Oakland	16
33	DETROIT	30
0	at Indianapolis	41
12	NEW ENGLAND	14
339		327

NEW ENGLAND (10-6)

41	SAN DIEGO	7
31	at Indianapolis	6
27	N.Y. JETS (OT)	24
31	CHICAGO	3
	OPEN DATE	
13	at Denver	34
33	BUFFALO	6
19	at N.Y. Jets	24
10	GREEN BAY	28
18	at Minnesota	23
31	at Buffalo	10
7	at Tampa Bay	27
27	MIAMI	24
20	INDIANAPOLIS	17
26	at Jacksonville	20
21	PITTSBURGH (OT)	24
14	at Miami	12
369		289

N.Y. JETS (9-7)

41	at Seattle	3
22	BUFFALO	28
24	at New England	27
23	OAKLAND	22
31	at Cincinnati	14
16	at Indianapolis	12
20	MIAMI	31
24	NEW ENGLAND	19
	OPEN DATE	
19	BALTIMORE (OT)	16
17	at Miami	24
23	at Chicago	15
23	MINNESOTA	21
10	at Buffalo	20
14	INDIANAPOLIS	22
31	TAMPA BAY	0
10	at Detroit	13
348		287

OAKLAND (4-12)

21	at Tennessee	24
27	KANSAS CITY	28
36	at Atlanta	31
22	at N.Y. Jets	23
35	ST. LOUIS	17
10	SAN DIEGO	25
	OPEN DATE	
28	DENVER	25
34	at Seattle	45
14	at Carolina	38
10	NEW ORLEANS	13
38	at San Diego	13
3	at Denver	31
16	MIAMI	34
0	at Kansas City	30
21	SEATTLE	22
9	JACKSONVILLE	20
324		419

PITTSBURGH (11-5)

7	DALLAS	37
14	WASHINGTON	13
	OPEN DATE	
21	at Jacksonville	30
37	TENNESSEE	24
42	at Baltimore	34
24	INDIANAPOLIS	22
26	at Cincinnati	10
23	JACKSONVILLE (OT)	17
10	at Kansas City	13
37	BALTIMORE	0
20	CINCINNATI	3
20	at Philadelphia	23
26	at Arizona (OT)	20
35	DENVER	24
24	at New England (OT)	21
6	at Tennessee	16
372		307

SAN DIEGO (4-12)

7	at New England	41
20	at New Orleans	6
7	CAROLINA	26
22	at Seattle	26
21	BALTIMORE	17
25	at Oakland	10
	OPEN DATE	
3	at Kansas City	31
35	INDIANAPOLIS	19
31	at Cincinnati	38
31	SEATTLE	37
13	OAKLAND	38
10	at San Francisco	17
28	DENVER	38
3	ATLANTA	14
7	KANSAS CITY	29
3	at Denver	38
266		425

SEATTLE (8-8)

3	N.Y. JETS	41
14	DENVER	35
31	at Indianapolis	3
26	SAN DIEGO	22
17	at Kansas City (OT)	20
16	TENNESSEE	13
	OPEN DATE	
17	at St. Louis	9
45	OAKLAND	34
27	at Denver	30
37	at San Diego	31
17	at New Orleans (OT)	20
14	KANSAS CITY	19
17	ATLANTA	24
24	at Baltimore	31
22	at Oakland	21
38	SAN FRANCISCO	9
365		362

TENNESSEE (8-8)

24	OAKLAND (OT)	21
13	at Miami (OT)	16
	OPEN DATE	
10	BALTIMORE	36
24	at Pittsburgh	37
13	at Seattle	16
30	CINCINNATI	7
28	WASHINGTON	14
41	at Arizona	14
24	JACKSONVILLE	30
10	N.Y. GIANTS	6
9	at Jacksonville	17
31	BUFFALO	14
27	at Dallas	14
14	at Cincinnati	41
19	at Baltimore	21
16	PITTSBURGH	6
333		310

(OT) denotes overtime

NFC SEASON RECORDS—TEAM BY TEAM

ARIZONA (4-12)

21	at Cincinnati	24
25	DALLAS (OT)	22
13	at Washington (OT)	19
	OPEN DATE	
18	at Tampa Bay	19
19	MINNESOTA	20
13	N.Y. GIANTS	27
10	at Philadelphia (OT)	13
14	TENNESSEE	41
31	PHILADELPHIA	21
6	at Dallas	24
10	at N.Y. Giants	19
16	at Baltimore	13
20	PITTSBURGH (OT)	26
28	WASHINGTON	38
10	at New Orleans	27
29	ATLANTA	26
283		379

ATLANTA (7-9)

17	at Detroit	28
6	CAROLINA	9
31	OAKLAND	36
7	at San Francisco	34
21	DENVER	29
	OPEN DATE	
23	at New Orleans	17
28	SAN FRANCISCO	35
12	at Carolina	21
34	ST. LOUIS	31
10	TAMPA BAY	31
27	at St. Louis	21
20	NEW ORLEANS	3
24	at Seattle	17
14	at San Diego	3
20	PHILADELPHIA	17
26	at Arizona	29
320		361

CAROLINA (7-9)

10	WASHINGTON	24
9	at Atlanta	6
26	at San Diego	7
14	KANSAS CITY	35
21	SAN FRANCISCO	34
	OPEN DATE	
14	at Minnesota	21
13	at New Orleans	0
21	ATLANTA	12
38	OAKLAND	14
0	at Denver	34
19	at San Francisco	27
16	at St. Louis	10
13	NEW ORLEANS	16
23	at Dallas	13
10	GREEN BAY	31
18	ST. LOUIS	30
265		314

CHICAGO (4-12)

24	at Green Bay	38
24	MINNESOTA	27
7	DETROIT	32
3	at New England	31
3	at Dallas	27
17	NEW ORLEANS	20
23	GREEN BAY	24
	OPEN DATE	
36	at Miami (OT)	33
8	WASHINGTON	31
22	at Minnesota	29
15	N.Y. JETS	23
13	TAMPA BAY	7
20	at Detroit	55
20	BUFFALO	3
13	at St. Louis	10
15	at Tampa Bay	31
263		421

(OT) *denotes overtime*

DALLAS (6-10)

37	at Pittsburgh	7
22	at Arizona (OT)	25
21	PHILADELPHIA	20
	OPEN DATE	
27	CHICAGO	3
17	at N.Y. Giants	20
16	at Washington	21
26	JACKSONVILLE	22
12	at Philadelphia	13
10	at San Francisco	17
24	ARIZONA	6
17	WASHINGTON	14
17	at Green Bay	45
14	TENNESSEE	27
13	CAROLINA	23
24	at Cincinnati	31
7	N.Y. GIANTS	20
304		314

DETROIT (9-7)

28	ATLANTA	17
17	TAMPA BAY	24
32	at Chicago	7
17	at New Orleans	35
26	GREEN BAY	15
13	at Buffalo	22
27	at Tampa Bay	9
20	N.Y. GIANTS (OT)	26
	OPEN DATE	
10	at Green Bay	20
7	at Washington	30
38	MINNESOTA	15
32	INDIANAPOLIS	10
55	CHICAGO	20
30	at Miami	33
14	at Minnesota	13
13	N.Y. JETS	10
379		306

GREEN BAY (13-3)

38	CHICAGO	24
9	at Philadelphia	10
23	MIAMI	18
38	MINNESOTA	32
15	at Detroit	26
21	TAMPA BAY	16
24	at Chicago	23
	OPEN DATE	
28	at New England	10
20	DETROIT	10
17	ST. LOUIS	7
38	at Indianapolis	41
45	DALLAS	17
27	at Minnesota	11
17	at Tampa Bay	6
31	at Carolina	10
31	BUFFALO	21
422		282

MINNESOTA (9-7)

34	at Buffalo	13
27	at Chicago	24
14	TAMPA BAY	28
32	at Green Bay	38
28	PHILADELPHIA	19
20	at Arizona	19
21	CAROLINA	14
	OPEN DATE	
10	at Tampa Bay	6
23	NEW ENGLAND	18
29	CHICAGO	22
15	at Detroit	38
21	at N.Y. Jets	23
11	GREEN BAY	27
17	at San Francisco	28
13	DETROIT	14
39	INDIANAPOLIS	28
354		359

NEW ORLEANS (6-10)

24	at St. Louis	38
6	SAN DIEGO	20
7	at San Francisco	33
35	DETROIT	17
9	at N.Y. Giants	14
20	at Chicago	17
17	ATLANTA	23
0	CAROLINA	13
0	SAN FRANCISCO	23
	OPEN DATE	
13	at Oakland	10
20	SEATTLE (OT)	17
3	at Atlanta	20
16	at Carolina	13
27	ST. LOUIS	34
27	ARIZONA	10
13	at Kansas City	25
237		327

N.Y. GIANTS (10-5-1)

31	PHILADELPHIA	17
13	at Jacksonville	40
23	BALTIMORE	24
3	at St. Louis	13
14	NEW ORLEANS	9
20	DALLAS	17
27	at Arizona	13
26	at Detroit (OT)	20
29	CINCINNATI	27
	OPEN DATE	
6	at Tennessee	10
19	ARIZONA	10
7	at Washington (OT)	7
8	TAMPA BAY	20
31	at Philadelphia	21
30	WASHINGTON	10
20	at Dallas	7
307		265

PHILADELPHIA (6-9-1)

17	at N.Y. Giants	31
10	GREEN BAY	9
20	at Dallas	21
	OPEN DATE	
19	at Minnesota	28
24	WASHINGTON	10
21	at Jacksonville	38
13	ARIZONA (OT)	10
13	DALLAS	12
21	at Arizona	31
12	SAN FRANCISCO	24
10	at Baltimore (OT)	10
23	PITTSBURGH	20
44	CINCINNATI	42
21	N.Y. GIANTS	31
17	at Atlanta	20
32	at Washington	35
317		372

ST. LOUIS (5-11)

38	NEW ORLEANS	24
12	SAN FRANCISCO	15
14	at Denver	35
13	N.Y. GIANTS	3
17	at Oakland	35
	OPEN DATE	
10	at San Francisco	30
9	SEATTLE	17
20	KANSAS CITY	28
31	at Atlanta	34
7	at Green Bay	17
21	ATLANTA	27
10	CAROLINA	16
23	at Washington	20
34	at New Orleans	27
10	CHICAGO	13
30	at Carolina	18
299		359

SAN FRANCISCO (13-3)

6	at Tampa Bay	13
15	at St. Louis	12
33	NEW ORLEANS	7
34	ATLANTA	7
34	at Carolina	21
	OPEN DATE	
30	ST. LOUIS	10
35	at Atlanta	28
23	at New Orleans	0
17	DALLAS	10
24	at Philadelphia	12
27	CAROLINA	19
17	SAN DIEGO	10
9	at Kansas City	44
28	MINNESOTA	17
34	DENVER	17
9	at Seattle	38
375		265

TAMPA BAY (10-6)

13	SAN FRANCISCO	6
24	at Detroit	17
28	at Minnesota	14
31	MIAMI	21
19	ARIZONA	18
16	at Green Bay	21
9	DETROIT	27
	OPEN DATE	
6	MINNESOTA	10
31	at Indianapolis	28
31	at Atlanta	10
27	NEW ENGLAND	7
7	at Chicago	13
20	at N.Y. Giants	8
6	GREEN BAY	17
0	at N.Y. Jets	31
31	CHICAGO	15
299		263

WASHINGTON (8-7-1)

24	at Carolina	10
13	at Pittsburgh	14
19	ARIZONA (OT)	13
	OPEN DATE	
24	JACKSONVILLE	12
10	at Philadelphia	24
21	DALLAS	16
14	at Tennessee	28
17	BALTIMORE	20
31	at Chicago	8
30	DETROIT	7
14	at Dallas	17
7	N.Y. GIANTS (OT)	7
20	ST. LOUIS	23
38	at Arizona	28
10	at N.Y. Giants	30
35	PHILADELPHIA	32
327		289

Attendance figures as they appear in the following, and in the club-by-club sections starting on page 26, are turnstile counts and not paid attendance. Paid attendance totals are on page 242.

FIRST WEEK SUMMARIES

AMERICAN FOOTBALL CONFERENCE

Eastern Division	W	L	T	Pct.	Pts.	OP
Miami	1	0	0	1.000	16	10
New England	1	0	0	1.000	41	7
N.Y. Jets	1	0	0	1.000	41	3
Buffalo	0	1	0	.000	13	34
Indianapolis	0	1	0	.000	10	16
Central Division						
Cincinnati	1	0	0	1.000	24	21
Jacksonville	1	0	0	1.000	28	27
Tennessee	1	0	0	1.000	24	21
Baltimore	0	1	0	.000	27	28
Pittsburgh	0	1	0	.000	7	37
Western Division						
Denver	1	0	0	1.000	19	3
Kansas City	0	1	0	.000	3	19
Oakland	0	1	0	.000	21	24
San Diego	0	1	0	.000	7	41
Seattle	0	1	0	.000	3	41

NATIONAL FOOTBALL CONFERENCE

Eastern Division	W	L	T	Pct.	Pts.	OP
Dallas	1	0	0	1.000	37	7
N.Y. Giants	1	0	0	1.000	31	17
Washington	1	0	0	1.000	24	10
Arizona	0	1	0	.000	21	24
Philadelphia	0	1	0	.000	17	31
Central Division						
Detroit	1	0	0	1.000	28	17
Green Bay	1	0	0	1.000	38	24
Minnesota	1	0	0	1.000	34	13
Tampa Bay	1	0	0	1.000	13	6
Chicago	0	1	0	.000	24	38
Western Division						
St. Louis	1	0	0	1.000	38	24
Atlanta	0	1	0	.000	17	28
Carolina	0	1	0	.000	10	24
New Orleans	0	1	0	.000	24	38
San Francisco	0	1	0	.000	6	13

SUNDAY, AUGUST 31

CINCINNATI 24, ARIZONA 21—at Cinergy Field, attendance 50,298. The Bengals scored 3 fourth-quarter touchdowns, including 2 in the final 2:14, to fend off the upset-minded Cardinals. The Cardinals led 21-3 but Ki-Jana Carter scored from 2 yards to cut the deficit to 21-10 less than a minute into the fourth quarter. The Bengals' defense forced a punt, and Cincinnati got the ball at its own 33-yard line with less than five minutes remaining. Jeff Blake threw 2 completions to Carl Pickens, including a 10-yard pass on fourth-and-4 near midfield, and a 35-yard pass to Carter to set up Carter's second touchdown with 2:14 remaining. The Cardinals were leading 21-17 and attempting to run out the clock when Gerald Dixon stripped Larry Centers of the ball, and John Copeland recovered at the Bengals' 37-yard line with 1:10 left. Blake quickly drove the Bengals downfield and found Pickens for a game-winning 7-yard touchdown pass with 38 seconds left. Kent Graham threw four incompletions from his own 30 to end Arizona's chances. Blake was 24 of 35 for 252 yards, and was 12 of 16 for 123 yards in the fourth quarter. Graham completed 20 of 36 passes for 248 yards. Frank Sanders had 6 receptions for 105 yards.

Arizona	7	7	7	0	—	21
Cincinnati	0	3	0	21	—	24

Ariz — McElrory 17 run (Butler kick)
Cin — FG Pelfrey 38
Ariz — C. Smith 1 run (Butler kick)
Ariz — Centers 1 run (Butler kick)
Cin — Carter 2 run (Pelfrey kick)
Cin — Carter 1 run (pass failed)
Cin — Pickens 7 pass from Blake (McGee pass from Blake)

DETROIT 28, ATLANTA 17—at Pontiac Silverdome, attendance 61,244. The Lions scored 2 defensive touchdowns and 21 of their 28 points off Falcons turnovers to give head coach Bobby Ross a victory in his first game with the Lions. Falcons head coach Dan Reeves lost his first game with the club, despite watching his defense allow just 10 first downs and hold the Lions to a 3 of 15 third-down conversion rate. Ronnie Bradford's blocked punt set up Michael Haynes's touchdown catch and gave the Falcons a 10-7 lead. However, Reggie Brown forced Chris Chandler to fumble, and Stephen Boyd raced 42 yards with the fumble recovery to give the Lions a 14-10 halftime edge. Jamal Anderson's 1-yard run gave the Falcons a 17-14 lead with 9:50 left in the game, and Atlanta got the ball back with six minutes remaining following a punt. However, Boyd intercepted Chandler and returned the ball 4 yards to the Falcons' 25-yard line. Herman Moore caught his second touchdown pass of the day from Scott Mitchell two plays later to give the Lions a 21-17 lead with 5:05 left. Just over one minute later, Brown returned an interception 38 yards to finish the scoring. Mitchell completed just 12 of 30 passes, but he averaged more than 17 yards per completion. Moore had 7 receptions for 115 yards. Chandler was 20 of 36 for 290 yards, with 3 interceptions.

Atlanta	3	7	0	7	—	17
Detroit	0	14	0	14	—	28

Atl — FG Andersen 30
Det — Moore 43 pass from Mitchell (Hanson kick)
Atl — Haynes 24 pass from Chandler (Andersen kick)
Det — Boyd 42 fumble return (Hanson kick)
Atl — Anderson 1 run (Andersen kick)
Det — Moore 25 pass from Mitchell (Hanson kick)
Det — Brown 38 interception return (Hanson kick)

DALLAS 37, PITTSBURGH 7—at Three Rivers Stadium, attendance 60,397. Troy Aikman threw for 295 yards and equaled a career-high with 4 touchdown passes as the Cowboys defeated the Steelers. Two drives of 80 or more yards in the second quarter both ended with Aikman touchdown passes. After forcing a Steelers punt, Aikman completed a 55-yard pass to Michael Irvin on third-and-4 to set up first-year kicker Richie Cunningham's 52-yard field goal just before halftime to give the Cowboys a 17-0 lead. Rookie Dexter Coakley's interception on Pittsburgh's first possession of the second half led to Irvin's second touchdown reception, and after Brock Marion's fumble recovery set up Cunningham's second field goal, the Cowboys led 27-0 with 8:40 left in the third quarter. The Cowboys had twice as many yards (380-174), and converted 8 of 14 third-down opportunities while permitting the Steelers to convert just 1 of 11 chances. Kordell Stewart, in his first game as the Steelers' starting quarterback, was 13 of 28 for 104 yards, with 1 interception, and a touchdown pass to Mark Bruener with 3:04 remaining to avoid the Steelers' first shutout since 1993.

Dallas	0	17	17	3	—	37
Pittsburgh	0	0	0	7	—	7

Dall — Miller 12 pass from Aikman (Cunningham kick)
Dall — Irvin 42 pass from Aikman (Cunningham kick)
Dall — FG Cunningham 52
Dall — Irvin 15 pass from Aikman (Cunningham kick)
Dall — FG Cunningham 24
Dall — Johnston 13 pass from Aikman (Cunningham kick)
Dall — FG Cunningham 28
Pitt — Bruener 4 pass from Stewart (N. Johnson kick)

MIAMI 16, INDIANAPOLIS 10—at Pro Player Stadium, attendance 70,813. Shawn Wooden had 2 interceptions and a fumble recovery and rookie Olindo Mare kicked 3 field goals to enable the Dolphins to defeat the Colts. Miami led 10-7 early in the third quarter when Wooden's fumble recovery set up Mare's second field goal. Wooden intercepted Jim Harbaugh early in the fourth quarter, and Mare's subsequent field goal gave Miami a two-possession lead at 16-7. Paul Justin replaced Harbaugh and drove the Colts to within field-goal range, where Cary Blanchard cut the deficit to 16-10 with 1:00 left. Corey Harris fielded the onside kick for the Dolphins but then fumbled, and Ray McElroy recovered to give the Colts one last chance. Aaron Bailey caught a pass at the 25-yard line, but was tackled in the middle of the field and time ran out before the Colts could get off another play. Blanchard, who established an AFC record with 36 field goals last season, missed 3 out of his 4 attempts for the Colts. The Colts held the Dolphins to 202 total yards, 11 first downs, and they permitted just 3 of 13 third-down opportunities. Mare was also forced to punt 5 times (for an average of 47 yards) when John Kidd sprained his left leg after his first punt. Marshall Faulk caught a pass for a club-record forty-seventh consecutive game for the Colts.

Indianapolis	0	7	0	3	—	10
Miami	3	7	3	3	—	16

Mia — FG Mare 23
Ind — Alexander 43 interception return (Blanchard kick)
Mia — Abdul-Jabbar 9 run (Mare kick)
Mia — FG Mare 34
Mia — FG Mare 18
Ind — FG Blanchard 35

JACKSONVILLE 28, BALTIMORE 27—at Memorial Stadium, attendance 61,018. Rob Johnson, making his first NFL start, threw 2 touchdown passes and ran for another to give the Jaguars a come-from-behind victory. Johnson completed the first drive of the game with a 25-yard scramble to take a 7-0 lead. A 31-yard pass to James Stewart set up Natrone Means's 1-yard run. Vinny Testaverde threw 2 touchdown passes to Jermaine Lewis in the second quarter to tie the score. Chris Hudson's interception resulted in Johnson's 20-yard touchdown pass to Jimmy Smith with 1:08 left in the half to give the Jaguars a 21-14 lead. The Ravens responded with 10 quick points. Matt Stover's field goal ended the half, and the Ravens took their first lead 62 seconds into the third quarter on Testaverde's 54-yard touchdown pass to Michael Jackson. Stover's second field goal put the Ravens ahead 27-21. Johnson, who had left with a sprained ankle, returned and completed a key third-and-6 pass to Pete Mitchell to keep the drive alive. Smith then caught his second touchdown pass, a 28-yard play with 5:47 left, to put the Jaguars ahead. After an exchange of turnovers, Jackson nearly made a diving 18-yard reception at the Jaguars' 32 on fourth-and-18 in the final minute to keep the Ravens' hopes alive, but the catch was ruled a trap and the Jaguars prevailed. Both teams completed at least 50 percent of their third-down opportunities, and tallied 784 yards between them. Johnson, who was playing for injured Mark Brunell, completed 20 of 24 passes for 294 yards. Testaverde was 24 of 41 for 322 yards, but threw 3 interceptions to go along with his 3 touchdown passes. Smith had 106 receiving yards on 6 receptions, while Jackson caught 8 passes for 143 yards.

Jacksonville	14	7	0	7	—	28
Baltimore	0	17	7	3	—	27

Jack — Johnson 25 run (Hollis kick)
Jack — Means 1 run (Hollis kick)
Balt — Lewis 17 pass from Testaverde (Stover kick)
Balt — Lewis 42 pass from Testaverde (Stover kick)
Jack — Smith 20 pass from Johnson (Hollis kick)
Balt — FG Stover 33
Balt — Jackson 54 pass from Testaverde (Stover kick)
Balt — FG Stover 25
Jack — Smith 28 pass from Johnson (Hollis kick)

DENVER 19, KANSAS CITY 3—at Denver Mile High Stadium, attendance 75,600. Terrell Davis rushed for 101 yards and the game's only touchdown, and Jason Elam booted 4 field goals to lead the Broncos to a divisional victory. Chiefs head coach Marty Schottenheimer's career record at Denver Mile High Stadium fell to 2-9 with the defeat. Denver had three times as many yards as the Chiefs (218-72 total yards) in the first half, including a 78-yard pass play from John Elway to Rod Smith, but had to settle for 3 field goals by Elam. Greg Hill's 38-yard run set up Pete Stoyanovich's 20-yard field goal for the Chiefs' lone points. The Broncos scored a touchdown on Davis's 10-yard run early in the fourth quarter to give Denver a 16-3 lead. The Broncos' defense held the Chiefs to just 12 first downs and 108 net passing yards. Elway was 17 of 28 for 246 yards. Smith had 5 receptions for 122 yards. Elvis Grbac, in his first start for the Chiefs, completed 14 of 25 passes for 115 yards. The Chiefs had won seven consecutive opening day games.

Kansas City	0	0	3	0	—	3
Denver	3	6	0	10	—	19

Den — FG Elam 35
Den — FG Elam 36
Den — FG Elam 25
KC — FG Stoyanovich 20

Den — Davis 10 run (Elam kick)
Den — FG Elam 53

MINNESOTA 34, BUFFALO 13—at Rich Stadium, attendance 79,139. Cris Carter had 2 touchdown receptions and Robert Smith had a career-high 169 rushing yards to give the Vikings a victory. Smith's longest career run, a 78-yard touchdown burst, came in the fourth quarter and was less than a minute after Steve Christie's field goal had cut the score to 13-10. Less than three minutes later, Jeff Brady picked up a fumbled snap and lumbered 30 yards to give the Vikings a 27-10 lead with 11:03 to play. Brad Johnson was 17 of 30 for 218 yards, with 1 interception and 2 touchdown passes. Carter had 8 receptions for 121 yards. Todd Collins, the starting quarterback after the retirement of 11-year veteran Jim Kelly following last season, was 25 of 39 for 299 yards, with 2 interceptions. Andre Reed had 7 receptions for 142 yards. Thurman Thomas had 5 receptions, allowing him to join Walter Payton and Marcus Allen as the only players in NFL history with 10,000 rushing yards and 400 career receptions.

Minnesota	0	10	3	21	—	34
Buffalo	0	7	0	6	—	13

Minn — FG Davis 21
Buff — Riemersma 19 pass from Collins (Christie kick)
Minn — Carter 6 pass from Johnson (Davis kick)
Minn — FG Davis 43
Buff — FG Christie 28
Minn — Smith 78 run (Davis kick)
Minn — Brady 30 fumble return (Davis kick)
Buff — FG Christie 46
Minn — Carter 35 pass from Johnson (Davis kick)

ST. LOUIS 38, NEW ORLEANS 24—at Trans World Dome, attendance 64,575. Lawrence Phillips established career highs with 125 rushing yards and 3 touchdowns in a game that featured the return of head coaches Dick Vermeil and Mike Ditka. Vermeil, who had not coached an NFL game since he was with the Philadelphia Eagles in 1982, defeated Ditka, who last coached the 1992 Chicago Bears, to give the Rams four wins in their last five meetings against the Saints. Eric Guliford's kickoff return for a touchdown, and 3 Doug Brien field goals, gave the Saints a 17-14 halftime edge. The Rams then scored 3 touchdowns within four minutes during the third quarter. Tony Banks threw a short pass over the middle to tight end Ernie Conwell, who broke numerous tackles en route to his 48-yard touchdown. After Troy Davis's fumble was recovered by Marquis Walker, Phillips scored on a 25-yard run. Keith Lyle's interception moments later led to Phillips's 5-yard touchdown run and gave the Rams a 35-17 lead with 4:05 left in the third quarter. Banks completed 13 of 21 passes for 226 yards. Heath Shuler, in his first start for the Saints, was just 8 of 21 for 115 yards, with 2 interceptions. Rookie and Heisman Trophy winner Danny Wuerffel guided the Saints to their lone offensive touchdowns. The Rams won despite playing without Pro Bowl wide receiver Isaac Bruce, who was bothered by a pulled right hamstring.

New Orleans	6	11	0	7	—	24
St. Louis	0	14	21	3	—	38

NO — FG Brien 31
NO — FG Brien 53
StL — Phillips 1 run (Wilkins kick)
StL — Small 30 pass from Banks (Wilkins kick)
NO — Guliford 102 kickoff return (Hastings pass from Shuler)
NO — FG Brien 46
StL — Conwell 48 pass from Banks (Wilkins kick)
StL — Phillips 25 run (Wilkins kick)
StL — Phillips 5 run (Wilkins kick)
NO — Hastings 30 pass from Wuerffel (Brien kick)
StL — FG Wilkins 36

N.Y. JETS 41, SEATTLE 3—at Kingdome, attendance 53,893. Neil O'Donnell threw a career-high 5 touchdown passes to make coach Bill Parcells's debut a success. Wayne Chrebet and Jeff Graham each caught 2 touchdowns, and Adrian Murrell rushed for 131 yards. Rookie kicker John Hall made 2 field goals, including a 55-yard boot in the first quarter that equaled the club record. Seattle not only lost the game, but quarterback John Friesz broke his right (throwing) thumb at the end of the first half. His replacement, Warren Moon, completed just 7 of 21 pass attempts in the second half. The Jets led 17-0 after the first quarter, with Hall's field goal set up by Chris Warren's fumble. The Jets wasted little time on offense, as none of their five scoring drives lasted longer than eight plays. O'Donnell completed 18 of 25 passes for 270 yards, while Graham had 100 receiving yards. The Jets outgained the Seahawks (434-247), had more first downs (28-16), and longer time of possession (34:39-25:21).

N.Y. Jets	17	10	14	0	—	41
Seattle	0	3	0	0	—	3

NYJ — Chrebet 35 pass from O'Donnell (Hall kick)
NYJ — FG Hall 55
NYJ — Graham 26 pass from O'Donnell (Hall kick)
NYJ — Brady 1 pass from O'Donnell (Hall kick)
NYJ — FG Hall 28
Sea — FG Peterson 31
NYJ — Chrebet 31 pass from O'Donnell (Hall kick)
NYJ — Graham 47 pass from O'Donnell (Hall kick)

TENNESSEE 24, OAKLAND 21 (OT)—at Liberty Bowl Memorial Stadium, attendance 30,171. Al Del Greco's 33-yard field goal in overtime gave the state of Tennessee its first NFL victory. Eddie George rushed for 216 yards and scored on a 29-yard run, and a subsequent 2-point conversion run, with 2:09 left to put the Oilers ahead 21-14. The Raiders tied the game when Jeff George and Tim Brown connected for their third touchdown with 22 seconds left. After an exchange of possessions in overtime, 2 passes from Steve McNair to Frank Wycheck and an 11-yard scramble by McNair helped set up Del Greco's winning boot. The Oilers held a 10-0 halftime lead and extended it to 13-0 when Del Greco's 37-yard field goal capped a 10:11 second-half opening drive. Jeff George then threw 2 touchdown passes to Brown to give the Raiders a lead with 11:46 remaining in the game. Brown caught 8 passes, all after halftime, for 158 yards. Jeff George was 21 of 37 for 298 yards. The Oilers outgained the Raiders on the ground, 255-45, and the Raiders accumulated just 2 of their 17 first downs via rushing.

Oakland	0	0	7	14	0	—	21
Tennessee	10	0	3	8	3	—	24

Tenn — FG Del Greco 30
Tenn — Sanders 48 pass from McNair (Del Greco kick)
Tenn — FG Del Greco 37
Oak — Brown 59 pass from J. George (Ford kick)
Oak — Brown 27 pass from J. George (Ford kick)
Tenn — E. George 29 run (E. George run)
Oak — Brown 16 pass from J. George (Ford kick)
Tenn — FG Del Greco 33

NEW YORK GIANTS 31, PHILADELPHIA 17—at Giants Stadium, attendance 70,296. Sam Garnes's 95-yard interception return with 4:58 remaining thwarted an Eagles comeback, and the Giants' defense recorded 9 sacks to win their first game under head coach Jim Fassel, who was celebrating his forty-eighth birthday. The Giants led 7-3 when they got the ball after an Eagles punt on their own 40 with 1:32 left before halftime. Tiki Barber's 21-yard run and 28-yard pass reception set up Dave Brown's 9-yard touchdown pass to Chris Calloway with six seconds remaining in the half. Thomas Lewis returned the opening kickoff of the second half 84 yards to allow Barber to score from one yard, giving the Giants 2 touchdowns in the span of 1:04 and a 21-3 lead. After Brad Daluiso's field goal gave the Giants a 24-3 lead, Rodney Peete replaced Ty Detmer at quarterback for the Eagles. Consecutive 10-play scoring drives cut the deficit to 24-17 with 8:15 left in the game. After forcing another punt, the Eagles were driving for the potential game-tying score when Garnes stepped in front of Peete's slant pass, intended for Irving Fryar, and raced 95 yards for the momentum-swinging touchdown. The Eagles recorded twice as many first downs (24-12) and had 157 more total yards of offense, but committed both of the game's turnovers. Dave Brown was 13 of 27 for 193 yards. Peete completed 17 of 23 passes for 268 yards. Michael Timpson had 9 receptions for 125 receiving yards. The Giants started five rookies.

Philadelphia	3	0	7	7	—	17
N.Y. Giants	7	7	10	7	—	31

NYG — Brown 3 run (Daluiso kick)
Phil — FG Boniol 48
NYG — Calloway 9 pass from Brown (Daluiso kick)
NYG — Barber 1 run (Daluiso kick)
NYG — FG Daluiso 39
Phil — Watters 3 run (Boniol kick)
Phil — Turner 14 pass from Peete (Boniol kick)
NYG — Garnes 95 interception return (Daluiso kick)

NEW ENGLAND 41, SAN DIEGO 7—at Foxboro Stadium, attendance 60,190. Drew Bledsoe threw 4 first-half touchdown passes to give head coach Pete Carroll a victory in his debut. Bledsoe was 19 of 24 for 271 yards before halftime, and finished the game completing 26 of 39 passes for 340 yards. The Patriots scored on each of their five first-half possessions. Big plays set up the Patriots' points: Bledsoe's 40-yard pass to Terry Glenn set up the Patriots' first touchdown; a 35-yard pass to Coates led to Adam Vinatieri's first field goal; another 35-yard pass, to Shawn Jefferson, was followed by Sam Gash's touchdown catch; and David Meggett's 35-yard punt return allowed Bledsoe to throw a 2-yard touchdown pass to Keith Byars 37 seconds before halftime to take a 31-0 lead. Meggett had 6 punt returns for the Patriots, setting the NFL record with 305 career punt returns. Chargers head coach Kevin Gilbride lost his coaching debut, and quarterback Stan Humphries separated his left shoulder in the fourth quarter.

San Diego	0	0	7	0	—	7
New England	14	17	0	10	—	41

NE — Coates 4 pass from Bledsoe (Vinatieri kick)
NE — Glenn 25 pass from Bledsoe (Vinatieri kick)
NE — FG Vinatieri 21
NE — Gash 12 pass from Bledsoe (Vinatieri kick)
NE — Byars 2 pass from Bledsoe (Vinatieri kick)
SD — F. Jones 44 pass from Humphries (Carney kick)
NE — FG Vinatieri 26
NE — Clay 53 interception return (Vinatieri kick)

TAMPA BAY 13, SAN FRANCISCO 6—at Houlihan's Stadium, attendance 62,554. The Buccaneers' defense recorded 7 sacks, denied the 49ers a touchdown for the first time since 1991, a span of 86 games, and Jerry Rice was lost for the season with a knee injury to ruin 49ers coach Steve Mariucci's debut. The victory gave the Buccaneers a 2-12 record against the 49ers, with the other victory in 1980. The 49ers led 6-0 at halftime despite Steve Young suffering a concussion on their first possession, and then losing Rice just before halftime. Gary Anderson had an opportunity to give the 49ers a 9-0 lead on the opening possession of the second half, but his 34-yard attempt glanced off the right upright. Tampa Bay drove the length of the field, but Patrick Hape fumbled the ball away at the 4-yard line. On their next possession, Michael Husted missed a 45-yard field goal, but the 49ers were offsides. Husted connected from 40 yards to cut the deficit to 6-3 after three quarters. Mike Alstott caught 2 passes for a total of 41 yards on their next possession to set up Trent Dilfer's 1-yard touchdown pass to Dave Moore. Trailing 10-6, Young returned but was intercepted by Tyrone Legette. Husted's second field goal with 6:49 left ended the scoring. The 49ers were held to 191 total yards, including 20 yards and no first downs on their last five possessions.

San Francisco	3	3	0	0	—	6
Tampa Bay	0	0	3	10	—	13

SF — FG Anderson 30
SF — FG Anderson 40
TB — FG Husted 40
TB — Moore 1 pass from Dilfer (Husted kick)
TB — FG Husted 34

SUNDAY NIGHT, AUGUST 31

WASHINGTON 24, CAROLINA 10—at Ericsson Stadium, attendance 72,633. Terry Allen rushed for 141 yards and 2 touchdowns, and the Redskins forced 4 turnovers to hand the Panthers their first-ever loss at Ericsson Stadium. Carolina was 8-0 at home last season, and defeated the Dallas Cowboys in an NFC Divisional Playoff game. With the score knotted 3-3 in the second quarter, the Panthers drove inside the Redskins' 10-yard line. However, Fred Lane fumbled and Jesse Campbell recovered the ball. The Redskins responded with a 91-yard drive, capped by the first of Allen's 2 touchdown runs. Steve Beuerlein, starting for injured Kerry Collins, threw a 24-yard touchdown pass to Wesley Walls early in the fourth quarter. Washington responded with Allen's second touchdown to finish a 12-play drive. On the ensuing kickoff, rookie linebacker Greg Jones forced kick returner Michael Bates to fumble. Kicker Scott Blanton recovered, and Gus Frerotte tossed a 5-yard touchdown pass to Leslie Shepherd with 6:36 remaining to finish the scoring. The Redskins recorded 7 more first downs (23-16), but also committed zero turnovers while scoring 17 points off the Panthers' 4 turnovers.

Washington	0	10	0	14	—	24
Carolina	3	0	0	7	—	10

Car	— FG Kasay 52
Wash	— FG Blanton 38
Wash	— T. Allen 1 run (Blanton kick)
Car	— Walls 24 pass from Beuerlein (Kasay kick)
Wash	— T. Allen 1 run (Blanton kick)
Wash	— Shepherd 5 pass from Frerotte (Blanton kick)

MONDAY, SEPTEMBER 1

GREEN BAY 38, CHICAGO 24—at Lambeau Field, attendance 60,766. Brett Favre threw for 226 yards and 2 touchdown passes to lead the defending Super Bowl champion Packers to a divisional victory. Chicago led 8-3 and regained possession midway through the second quarter, but Greg Evans intercepted Erik Kramer's pass and returned it 27 yards to the Bears' 1-yard line. Jeff Thomason scored his first NFL touchdown on the next play to give the Packers a 11-8 lead. After Jeff Jaeger's tying field goal with 1:56 left in the half, Favre connected on back-to-back passes to Robert Brooks, the first covering 44 yards and the second an 18-yard touchdown play with 48 seconds remaining before halftime, to give the Packers the lead for good. After an exchange of touchdowns, the Bears, trailing 31-17, forced Green Bay to punt with less than three minutes left. However, Santana Dotson sacked Kramer, forced him to fumble, and Gabe Wilkins recovered the ball for a touchdown with 2:36 left. Rookie Ryan Longwell booted 3 field goals, two of which followed long punt returns by first-year returner Bill Schroeder. The Packers lost cornerback Craig Newsome for the season after he suffered a torn ACL in his knee on the game's first play. Raymont Harris scored 2 touchdowns for Chicago and ran for 122 yards on 13 carries, including a 68-yard touchdown with 2:08 remaining in the game.

Chicago	0	11	0	13	—	24
Green Bay	3	15	6	14	—	38

GB	— FG Longwell 38
Chi	— Harris 1 run (Flanigan pass from Sauerbrun)
GB	— Thomason 1 pass from Favre (Levens pass from Favre)
Chi	— FG Jaeger 42
GB	— Brooks 18 pass from Favre (Longwell kick)
GB	— FG Longwell 36
GB	— FG Longwell 29
GB	— Levens 1 run (Longwell kick)
Chi	— Proehl 22 pass from Kramer (pass failed)
GB	— Wilkins 1 fumble return (Longwell kick)
Chi	— Harris 68 run (Jaeger kick)

SECOND WEEK SUMMARIES

AMERICAN FOOTBALL CONFERENCE						
Eastern Division	**W**	**L**	**T**	**Pct.**	**Pts.**	**OP**
Miami	2	0	0	1.000	32	23
New England	2	0	0	1.000	72	13
Buffalo	1	1	0	.500	41	56
N.Y. Jets	1	1	0	.500	63	31
Indianapolis	0	2	0	.000	16	47
Central Division						
Jacksonville	2	0	0	1.000	68	40
Baltimore	1	1	0	.500	50	38
Cincinnati	1	1	0	.500	34	44
Pittsburgh	1	1	0	.500	21	50
Tennessee	1	1	0	.500	37	37
Western Division						
Denver	2	0	0	1.000	54	17
Kansas City	1	1	0	.500	31	46
San Diego	1	1	0	.500	27	47
Oakland	0	2	0	.000	48	52
Seattle	0	2	0	.000	17	76
NATIONAL FOOTBALL CONFERENCE						
Eastern Division	**W**	**L**	**T**	**Pct.**	**Pts.**	**OP**
Arizona	1	1	0	.500	46	46
Dallas	1	1	0	.500	59	32
N.Y. Giants	1	1	0	.500	44	57
Philadelphia	1	1	0	.500	27	40
Washington	1	1	0	.500	37	24
Central Division						
Minnesota	2	0	0	1.000	61	37
Tampa Bay	2	0	0	1.000	37	23
Detroit	1	1	0	.500	45	41
Green Bay	1	1	0	.500	47	34
Chicago	0	2	0	.000	48	65
Western Division						
Carolina	1	1	0	.500	19	30
San Francisco	1	1	0	.500	21	25
St. Louis	1	1	0	.500	50	39
Atlanta	0	2	0	.000	23	37
New Orleans	0	2	0	.000	30	58

SUNDAY, SEPTEMBER 6

BUFFALO 28, N.Y. JETS 22—at Giants Stadium, attendance 72,988. Todd Collins threw a 10-yard touchdown pass to Jay Riemersma midway through the fourth quarter and the Bills' defense made two big stands in the final moments as Buffalo defeated the Jets. Neil O'Donnell's 19-yard touchdown pass to Dedric Ward less than a minute into the second quarter gave the Jets a 10-0 lead. Todd Collins threw a 45-yard pass to Tim Tindale to set up Thurman Thomas's 2-yard touchdown run, and Andre Reed caught a 10-yard touchdown pass after Chris Spielman's interception to give the Bills the lead at halftime. Steve Tasker's 47-yard punt return early in the third quarter set up Collins's 37-yard touchdown pass to Quinn Early, but Aaron Glenn returned the ensuing kickoff 96 yards for a touchdown. Adrian Murrell was stopped on a 2-point conversion attempt to tie the game, but the Jets retook the lead when James Farrior tackled punter Chris Mohr after a bobbled snap and John Hall drilled a 52-yard field goal with 9:52 to play. The Bills responded with a 7-play, 80-yard drive that featured a 44-yard pass from Collins to Tindale before Riemersma made his winning touchdown catch. Jeff Burris's interception halted one Jets drive, and the Jets reached the Bills' 24 with 2:00 left, but 2 sacks and a fourth-down incompletion ended the comeback attempt. Collins was 15 of 22 for 210 yards and 3 touchdowns, with 2 interceptions. Tindale had 4 receptions for 105 yards. O'Donnell was 16 of 37 for 218 yards and 1 touchdown, with 2 interceptions.

Buffalo	0	14	7	7	—	28
N.Y. Jets	3	10	6	3	—	22

NYJ	— FG Hall 26
NYJ	— Ward 19 pass from O'Donnell (Hall kick)
Buff	— Thomas 2 run (Christie kick)
Buff	— Reed 10 pass from Collins (Christie kick)
NYJ	— FG Hall 19
Buff	— Early 37 pass from Collins (Christie kick)
NYJ	— Glenn 96 kickoff return (run failed)
NYJ	— FG Hall 52
Buff	— Riemersma 10 pass from Collins (Christie kick)

CAROLINA 9, ATLANTA 6—at Georgia Dome, attendance 51,829. John Kasay kicked a 39-yard field goal as time expired to cap a comeback victory for the Panthers. The Falcons capitalized on 2 Panthers' turnovers, a Steve Beuerlein fumble recovered by Lester Archambeau at the Panthers' 15 and a Tyrone Poole fumbled punt return recovered by Craig Sauer at the Panthers' 17, to take a 6-0 lead. Beuerlein connected on a 53-yard pass to Wesley Walls to set up Kasay's first field goal with 12:39 left. Beuerlein threw a 20-yard pass to Raghib Ismail on third-and-10 to the Falcons' 29 to allow Kasay to kick a game-tying 31-yard field goal with 2:39 remaining. The Panthers got the ball back with 1:38 to play at their own 30-yard line. Beuerlein threw a key 10-yard pass to Walls on third-and-9 to the Falcons' 26, setting up Kasay's winning boot as time expired. Beuerlein was 21 of 35 for 268 yards. Chris Chandler was 4 of 6 for 83 yards before leaving the game in the second quarter with an injury. Billy Joe Tolliver was 7 of 17 for 79 yards as Chandler's replacement. The Panthers' defense held the Falcons to 8 first downs and 210 total yards.

Carolina	0	0	0	9	—	9
Atlanta	0	3	3	0	—	6

Atl	— FG Andersen 25
Atl	— FG Andersen 28
Car	— FG Kasay 31
Car	— FG Kasay 31
Car	— FG Kasay 39

BALTIMORE 23, CINCINNATI 10—at Memorial Stadium, attendance 52,968. The Ravens used a balanced attack to outscore the Bengals 20-0 in the second half to claim their first victory. Ashley Ambrose had a fumble recovery at the Bengals' 42 and an interception at the Bengals' 45 that both led directly to Bengals points as Cincinnati took a 10-3 halftime lead. Vinny Testaverde threw a 45-yard pass to Derrick Alexander at the Bengals' 22 to set up Jay Graham's 5-yard touchdown run late in the third quarter to give the Ravens a 13-10 lead. The Ravens then put together a 12-play, 96-yard drive capped by Testaverde's 18-yard touchdown pass to Eric Green. Matt Stover added his third field goal of the game with 3:45 left to finish the scoring. Doug Pelfrey missed field goals of 51, 43, and 46 yards. Testaverde was 25 of 36 for 275 yards and 1 touchdown, with 1 interception. Alexander had 8 receptions for 104 yards. Jeff Blake was 25 of 45 for 317 yards and 1 touchdown, with 2 interceptions. The Ravens' defense permitted just 56 rushing yards, while the offense rolled up 146 yards on the ground.

Cincinnati	0	10	0	0	—	10
Baltimore	0	3	10	10	—	23

Cin	— Pickens 8 pass from Blake (Pelfrey kick)
Balt	— FG Stover 37
Cin	— FG Pelfrey 46
Balt	— FG Stover 32
Balt	— Graham 5 run (Stover kick)
Balt	— Green 18 pass from Testaverde (Stover kick)
Balt	— FG Stover 41

DENVER 35, SEATTLE 14—at Kingdome, attendance 55,859. John Elway threw 2 touchdown passes to Ed McCaffrey and Terrell Davis rushed for 107 yards and 1 touchdown as the Broncos scored the game's final 25 points to defeat the Seahawks. The Broncos put together 32- and 71-yard drives on their first two possessions to take a 10-0 lead, but Warren Moon threw a 12-yard touchdown pass to Carlester Crumpler to finish a 79-yard drive, and Chad Brown returned Elway's fumble, forced by Micheal Sinclair, for a touchdown 16 seconds later to take a 14-10 lead with 55 seconds left in the half. However, Elway threw 10- and 11-yard passes to McCaffrey to set up Jason Elam's 51-yard field goal just before halftime. Elway and McCaffrey hooked up on a 21-yard touchdown pass late in the third quarter, and Shannon Sharpe caught Elway's 2-point conversion pass to take a 21-14 lead. Less than a minute later, Darrien Gordon returned an interception 32 yards for a touchdown to extend the Broncos' lead to 28-14. A 35-yard pass interference penalty to the Seahawks' 1 set up Davis's touchdown for the final points. Elway was 18 of 26 for 197 yards and 2 touchdowns. Moon was 20 of 33 for 222 yards and 1 touchdown, with 1 interception.

Denver	10	3	15	7	—	35
Seattle	0	14	0	0	—	14

Den	— FG Elam 38
Den	— McCaffrey 14 pass from Elway (Elam kick)
Sea	— Crumpler 12 pass from Moon (Peterson kick)
Sea	— Brown 26 fumble return (Peterson kick)
Den	— FG Elam 51
Den	— McCaffrey 32 pass from Elway (Sharpe pass from Elway)
Den	— Gordon 32 interception return (Elam kick)
Den	— Davis 1 run (Elam kick)

PHILADELPHIA 10, GREEN BAY 9—at Veterans Stadium, attendance 66,803. Freddie Solomon caught a touchdown pass with less than two minutes left and Ryan Longwell missed a 28-yard field-goal attempt in the final seconds as the Eagles upset the defending Super Bowl champions. Brett Favre's 30-yard pass to Robert Brooks set up Longwell's first field goal, and a 23-yard pass to Brooks on third-and-5 to the Eagles' 15 allowed Longwell to convert a 18-yard field goal as the half expired for a 6-0 lead. Rhett Hall's 39-yard interception return in the third quarter allowed Chris Boniol to cut the deficit to 6-3, but Longwell extended the lead to six points late in the third quarter with a 27-yard field goal. The Eagles got the ball with 11:18 to play on their own 20 and proceeded to grind out a 19-play, 80-yard drive that featured 11 carries by Ricky Watters and key third-down passes of 13 and 8 yards to Michael Timpson and Irving Fryar to set up Solomon's winning catch on a fourth-and-goal pass to the back of the end zone. Bill Schroeder returned the ensuing kickoff 40 yards and Favre hit Antonio Freeman with a 28-yard pass on fourth-and-16 to put the Packers into field goal position. Dorsey Levens carried five consecutive plays, reaching the Packers' 10 only to watch Longwell's field-goal attempt in the rain sail wide right. Ty Detmer was 19 of 32 for 173 yards and 1 touchdown. Fryar had 8 receptions for 125 yards. Favre was 19 of 41 for 279 yards, with 1 interception.

Green Bay	0	6	3	0	—	9
Philadelphia	0	0	3	7	—	10

GB — FG Longwell 22
GB — FG Longwell 18
Phil — FG Boniol 32
GB — FG Longwell 27
Phil — Solomon 2 pass from Detmer (Boniol kick)

MINNESOTA 27, CHICAGO 24—at Soldier Field, attendance 59,263. Brad Johnson threw a 9-yard touchdown pass to Chris Walsh with 37 seconds left to give the Vikings a comeback victory. Erik Kramer's 25-yard touchdown pass to Ricky Proehl midway through the second quarter snapped a 3-3 tie and gave the Vikings a 10-3 halftime lead. Robert Smith's 39-yard run set up Greg Davis's field goal, and Orlando Thomas's 22-yard fumble return for a touchdown of Rashaan Salaam's turnover gave the Vikings a 13-10 lead. Kramer capped an 11-play drive late in the third quarter with a 10-yard touchdown pass to Bobby Engram. Smith's 22-yard run set up Johnson's 21-yard touchdown pass to Jake Reed less than three minutes later to allow the Vikings to retake the lead. Raymont Harris gave the Bears the lead with a 59-yard burst with 11:52 to play. The Vikings responded with an eight-minute drive, but Johnson's touchdown pass to Walsh was nullified due to a penalty, and Davis missed a 42-yard field goal with 3:30 to play. But the Vikings' defense forced the Bears to punt after three plays, and Johnson completed a 6-yard pass to Paul Palmer on third-and-4 and a 21-yard pass to Carter on fourth-and-2 to the Bears' 12 to set up the winning touchdown pass to Walsh. Johnson was 33 of 44 for 285 yards and 2 touchdowns, with 1 interception. Kramer was 21 of 36 for 174 yards and 2 touchdowns. Reed had 12 catches for 118 yards, while Carter had 9 receptions for 107 yards.

Minnesota	3	0	10	14	—	27
Chicago	0	10	7	7	—	24

Minn — FG Davis 33
Chi — FG Jaeger 39
Chi — Proehl 25 pass from Kramer (Jaeger kick)
Minn — FG Davis 28
Minn — Thomas 22 fumble return (Davis kick)
Chi — Engram 10 pass from Kramer (Jaeger kick)
Minn — Reed 21 pass from Johnson (Davis kick)
Chi — Harris 59 run (Jaeger kick)
Minn — Walsh 9 pass from Johnson (Davis kick)

NEW ENGLAND 31, INDIANAPOLIS 6—at RCA Dome, attendance 53,632. Drew Bledsoe threw 4 touchdown passes to four different receivers for the second consecutive week as the Patriots defeated the Colts. Bledsoe's first touchdown pass was a 34-yard pass to Shawn Jeferson to cap a 10-play, 87-yard drive. Two Cary Blanchard field goals cut the deficit to 7-6, but Bledsoe connected on a 64-yard pass to Jefferson and found Curtis Martin on a 21-yard touchdown pass a few plays later to take a 14-6 lead into the locker room. Bledose threw a 16-yard pass to Ben Coates and a 31-yard pass to Vincent Brisby before tossing a 6-yard touchdown to Brisby in the final minute of the third quarter. Tedy Bruschi recovered a Harbaugh fumble early in the fourth qauarter, and Bledsoe hit Troy Brown with a 21-yard touchdown pass on the next play to take a 28-6 lead with 10:46 left. Bledsoe was 15 of 25 for 267 yards and 4 touchdowns. Martin carried 25 times for 121 yards. Harbaugh was 30 of 38 for 241 yards.

New England	7	7	7	10	—	31
Indianapolis	3	3	0	0	—	6

NE — Jefferson 34 pass from Bledsoe (Vinatieri kick)
Ind — FG Blanchard 45
Ind — FG Blanchard 38
NE — Martin 21 pass from Bledsoe (Vinatieri kick)
NE — Brisby 6 pass from Bledsoe (Vinatieri kick)
NE — Brown 21 pass from Bledsoe (Vinatieri kick)
NE — FG Vinatieri 21

JACKSONVILLE 40, N.Y. GIANTS 13—at ALLTEL Stadium, attendance 70,581. James Stewart and Natrone Means each ran for 2 touchdowns as the Jaguars defeated the Giants. Marcus Buckley's fumble recovery at the Jaguars' 27 set up Tiki Barber's 4-yard touchdown run to give the Giants an early 7-0 lead. Trailing 7-3, Steve Matthews, who started at quarterback in place of injured Mark Brunell and Rob Johnson, was intercepted in the end zone, but a pass interference penalty on the Giants nullified the interception and gave the ball to the Jaguars on the 1-yard line. Stewart scored on the next play to give Jacksonville a 10-0 lead. After Means's first touchdown, Renaldo Wynn recovered Howard Cross's fumble to set up Mike Hollis's 52-yard field goal to end the first half. Leading 23-13 early in the fourth quarter, Matthews completed a 41-yard pass to Jimmy Smith to lead to Hollis's fourth field goal, and Means and Stewart added touchdown runs in the final six minutes to finish the scoring. Matthews, in his first NFL start, completed 23 of 35 passes for 252 yards. Smith had 8 receptions for 117 yards. Dave Brown was 16 of 35 for 182 yards and 1 touchdown, with 1 interception. The Jaguars had more first downs (23-13) and led in time of possession (39:39-20:21).

N.Y. Giants	7	0	6	0	—	13
Jacksonville	0	20	3	17	—	40

NYG — Barber 4 run (Daluiso kick)
Jack — FG Hollis 29
Jack — Stewart 1 run (Hollis kick)
Jack — Means 9 run (Hollis kick)
Jack — FG Hollis 52
Jack — FG Hollis 36
NYG — Calloway 8 pass from Brown (pass failed)
Jack — FG Hollis 42
Jack — Means 5 run (Hollis kick)
Jack — Stewart 12 run (Hollis kick)

SAN DIEGO 20, NEW ORLEANS 6—at Louisiana Superdome, attendance 65,760. The Chargers' defense forced six turnovers and Jim Everett threw a fourth-quarter touchdown pass to help beat his former team. La'Roi Glover's fumble recovery set up Doug Brien's first-quarter field goal, but the Chargers scored when Junior Seau recovered a Heath Shuler fumble, ran to the goal line and fumbled. Rodney Harrison recovered the loose ball in the end zone for a 7-3 lead. After an exchange of field goals in the second quarter, Mike Dumas's recovery of Troy Davis's fumble early in the third quarter set up John Carney's 34-yard field goal to give the Chargers a 13-6 lead. Everett completed a 20-yard pass to Eric Metcalf on third-and-16 to set up his 21-yard touchdown pass to Freddie Jones with 2:10 left to ice the game. Everett was 17 of 29 for 195 yards and 1 touchdown, with 1 interception. Shuler was 20 of 38 for 194 yards, with 3 interceptions.

San Diego	7	3	3	7	—	20
New Orleans	3	3	0	0	—	6

NO — FG Brien 37
SD — Harrison fumble recovery in end zone (Carney kick)
NO — FG Brien 31
SD — FG Carney 37
SD — FG Carney 34
SD — F. Jones 21 pass from Everett (Carney kick)

SAN FRANCISCO 15, ST. LOUIS 12—at Trans World Dome, attendance 64,630. Garrison Hearst's 35-yard touchdown run midway through the fourth quarter lifted the 49ers to their fourteenth consecutive victory against the Rams. Tremaine Ross's 42-yard kickoff return and Todd Lyght's fumble recovery set up 2 Jeff Wilkins field goals to give the Rams a 6-0 lead. Zach Bronson recovered Eddie Kennsion's fumble at the Rams' 21 early in the second quarter, and rookie Jim Druckenmiller threw a 25-yard touchdown pass to J.J. Stokes two plays later to give the 49ers a 7-6 lead. Ryan McNeil's 21-yard interception return set up Wilkins's third field goal of the half. The Rams led 12-7 midway through the fourth quarter when Ken Norton, Jr. forced Lawrence Phillips to fumble and Tim McDonald recovered at the Rams' 47. Hearst scored four plays later, and Druckenmiller threw a 2-point conversion pass to Terry Kirby. The Rams reached the 49ers' 44 on fourth-and-1 with 1:26 left, but Tony Banks was stopped for no gain and the 49ers ran out the clock. The 49ers, who were playing without injured quarterback Steve Young, garnered just 13 first downs but their defense permitted just 11 first downs and 203 total yards. Druckenmiller was 10 of 28 for 102 yards, with 3 interceptions. Banks was 9 of 24 for 123 yards.

San Francisco	0	7	0	8	—	15
St. Louis	3	6	3	0	—	12

StL — FG Wilkins 40
StL — FG Wilkins 49
SF — Stokes 25 pass from Druckenmiller (Anderson kick)
StL — FG Wilkins 52
StL — FG Wilkins 34
SF — Hearst 35 run (Kirby pass from Druckenmiller)

TAMPA BAY 24, DETROIT 17—at Pontiac Silverdome, attendance 58,234. Warrick Dunn rushed for 130 yards as the Buccaneers took a 17-0 lead and held on en route to their first 2-0 start since 1992. Charles Mincy's 14-yard interception return set up Michael Husted's 41-yard field goal five minutes into the game, and Dunn's 49-yard run permitted Trent Dilfer to toss a 1-yard touchdown pass to Patrick Hape. After Jason Hanson missed a 52-yard field goal, the Buccaneers put together a 10-play, 58-yard drive, capped by Dunn's 6-yard run, to take a 17-0 lead. Scott Mitchell's 73-yard touchdown pass to Johnnie Morton midway through the third quarter cut the deficit to 17-10, but the Lions committed a 45-yard pass interference penalty on third-and-19, giving the Buccaneers the ball at the Lions' 1. Mike Alstott scored a few plays later as the Bucs took a 24-10 lead. Barry Sanders dipped and darted his way down field to score on a 66-yard screen pass to give the Lions a chance with 15 seconds left. However, Tampa Bay recovered the onsides kick and ran out the clock. Dilfer was 12 of 24 for 115 yards and 1 touchdown. Mitchell was 29 of 50 for 331 yards and 2 touchdowns, with 1 inteception. Morton had 4 receptions and Sanders had 8 catches as they each garnered 102 receiving yards.

Tampa Bay	10	7	0	7	—	24
Detroit	0	3	7	7	—	17

TB — FG Husted 41
TB — Hape 1 pass from Dilfer (Husted kick)
TB — Dunn 6 run (Husted kick)
Det — FG Hanson 48
Det — Morton 73 pass from Mitchell (Hanson kick)
TB — Alstott 1 run (Husted kick)
Det — Sanders 66 pass from Mitchell (Hanson kick)

MIAMI 16, TENNESSEE 13 (OT)—at Pro Player Stadium, attendance 64,439. Irving Spikes scored the game-tying touchdown in the fourth quarter and his 48-yard kickoff return in overtime set up the winning field goal as the Dolphins fought off the Oilers. Behind the running game of Eddie George, the Oilers led 10-6 late in the third quarter when Rayna Stewart recovered Fred Barnett's fumble at the Dolphins' 25. Al Del Greco kicked his second field goal to give Tennessee a 13-6 lead. Dan Marino threw a 50-yard pass to O.J. McDuffie early in the fourth quarter, and a pass interference penalty on fourth-and-7 gave the Dolphins the ball at the Oilers' 2, setting up Spikes's game-tying score. The Oilers had an opportunity to win in regulation, but Del Greco missed 46-yard field-goal attempt with five seconds left. Spikes's kickoff return gave Mare the chance to avenge a missed 25-yard field goal earlier in the game, which he did to propel the Dolphins to a 2-0 start. Marino was 24 of 43 for 324 yards. McDuffie had 8 receptions for 135 yards. Steve McNair was

7 of 14 for 109 yards, with 1 interception. George had 23 carries for 106 yards.

Tennessee	0	10	3	0	—	13
Miami	0	3	3	7	3 —	16

Mia — FG Mare 23
Tenn — E. George 13 run (Del Greco kick)
Tenn — FG Del Greco 24
Mia — FG Mare 22
Tenn — FG Del Greco 37
Mia — Spikes 2 run (Mare kick)
Mia — FG Mare 29

PITTSBURGH 14, WASHINGTON 13—at Three Rivers Stadium, attendance 58,059. Jerome Bettis rushed for 134 yards and 1 touchdown as the Steelers defeated the Redskins. Will Blackwell's 35-yard kickoff return to start the game propelled the Steelers to a 61-yard drive capped by Kordell Stewart's 1-yard touchdown run. Gus Frerotte completed 29- and 36-yard passes to Michael Westbrook and Leslie Shepherd to set up Scott Blanton's 37-yard second-quarter field goal. Brian Mitchell's 97-yard kickoff return for a touchdown to begin the second half gave the Redskins a 10-7 lead, and they extended it to six points with a 28-yard field goal by Blanton late in the third quarter. However, the Steelers compiled a 9-play, 72-yard drive, which featured 15- and 9-yard runs by Bettis, and took the lead on Bettis's touchdown with 13:23 left. The Redskins outgained the Steelers 354-295 total yards, but the Steelers intercepted Frerotte 3 times, with Chris Oldham's pick in the final minute near midfield clinching the victory. Stewart was 8 of 17 for 82 yards, with 1 interception. Frerotte was 19 of 35 for 270 yards, with 3 interceptions.

Washington	0	3	10	0	—	13
Pittsburgh	7	0	0	7	—	14

Pitt — Stewart 1 run (N. Johnson kick)
Wash — FG Blanton 37
Wash — Mitchell 97 kickoff return (Blanton kick)
Wash — FG Blanton 28
Pitt — Bettis 1 run (N. Johnson kick)

SUNDAY NIGHT, SEPTEMBER 6

ARIZONA 25, DALLAS 22 (OT)—at Sun Devil Stadium, attendance 71,578. Kent Graham threw a touchdown pass to Pat Carter late in regulation and Kevin Butler kicked a field goal in overtime as the Cardinals snapped a 13-game losing streak to the Cowboys. Leeland McElroy's 10-yard touchdown run early in the second quarter gave the Cardinals a 7-6 lead, but the Cowboys scored 13 points in the final five minutes of the half to take a 19-7 halftime lead. Darren Woodson's recovery of Graham's fumble at the Cardinals' 15-yard line 20 seconds into the second half spelled trouble for Arizona. However, the Cardinals' defense forced the Cowboys to settle for Richie Cunningham's fifth field goal, and Arizona put together a 14-play drive late in the third quarter, capped by Graham's 7-yard pass to Frank Sanders, to cut the deficit to 22-14. Michael Bankston blocked Cunningham's 40-yard field-goal attempt, giving Arizona possession at their own 30 with 4:30 to play. Graham completed a 47-yard pass to Rob Moore to the Cowboys' 12 before connecting with Carter for the touchdown with 1:06 left. Graham and Moore hooked up on the 2-point conversion pass to send the game to overtime. In overtime, Sherman Williams, who was in the game for injured Emmitt Smith, fumbled and Terry Irving recovered at the Cardinals' 46. Graham completed a 29-yard pass to Larry Centers to the Cowboys' 3 before Butler converted the winning kick. Graham was 26 of 47 for 249 yards and 2 touchdowns. Moore had 6 receptions for 108 yards. Troy Aikman was 21 of 39 for 171 yards. Smith had 19 carries for 132 yards.

Dallas	6	13	3	0	0	—	22
Arizona	0	7	7	8	3	—	25

Dall — FG Cunningham 24
Dall — FG Cunningham 47
Ariz — McElroy 10 run (Butler kick)
Dall — FG Cunningham 37
Dall — Hennings 4 fumble return (Cunningham kick)
Dall — FG Cunningham 34
Dall — FG Cunningham 28
Ariz — F. Sanders 7 pass from Graham (Butler kick)
Ariz — Carter 1 pass from Graham (Moore pass from Graham)
Ariz — FG Butler 20

MONDAY, SEPTEMBER 7

KANSAS CITY 28, OAKLAND 27—at Oakland-Alameda County Coliseum, attendance 61,523. Elvis Grbac threw a 33-yard touchdown pass to Andre Rison with four seconds left as the Chiefs shocked the Raiders. A 77-yard Raiders' drive culminated in Cole Ford's 32-yard field goal with 1:03 left in the first half to tie the game 10-10. Grbac responded with a 43-yard pass to Rison to set up Pete Stoyanovich's 24-yard field goal in the half's final seconds. The Raiders retook the lead three plays into the second half on Jeff George's 37-yard touchdown pass to Rickey Dudley. Following Napoleon Kaufman's 41-yard run moments later, George and Dudley completed another 3-play drive with a 16-yard touchdown pass to take a 24-13 lead. The Raiders had a chance to pull away when Rob Holmberg recovered Tamarick Vanover's fumble on the ensuing kickoff, but had to settle for Ford's second field goal and a 27-13 lead with 9:50 left in the third quarter. Late in the third quarter, George was pressured and attempted to underhand a pass downfield. Darren Anderson intercepted the errant toss and raced 55 yards for a touchdown, but the Chiefs missed the 2-point conversion attempt and trailed 27-22. Kansas City forced a punt and got the ball back with 58 seconds left on their own 20 with no timeouts. Grbac completed a 21-yard pass to Lake Dawson and a 27-yard pass to Brett Perriman to reach the Raiders' 12. Grbac spiked the ball with 12 seconds left to stop the clock, and then found Rison open in the back of the end zone with four seconds remaining to give the Chiefs the victory. Grbac was 21 of 35 for 312 yards and 2 touchdowns. Rison had 8 catches for 162 yards. George was 19 of 39 for 295 yards and 2 touchdowns, with 2 interceptions. Tim Brown had 11 receptions for 155 yards.

Kansas City	3	10	9	6	—	28
Oakland	7	3	17	0	—	27

Oak — Kaufman 10 run (Ford kick)
KC — FG Stoyanovich 23
KC — Anders 5 pass from Grbac (Stoyanovich kick)
Oak — FG Ford 32
KC — FG Stoyanovich 24
Oak — Dudley 37 pass from George (Ford kick)
Oak — Dudley 16 pass from George (Ford kick)
Oak — FG Ford 34
KC — FG Stoyanovich 23
KC — Anderson 55 interception return (pass failed)
KC — Rison 33 pass from Grbac (pass failed)

THIRD WEEK SUMMARIES

AMERICAN FOOTBALL CONFERENCE

Eastern Division	W	L	T	Pct.	Pts.	OP
New England	3	0	0	1.000	99	37
Miami	2	1	0	.667	50	46
Buffalo	1	2	0	.333	57	78
N.Y. Jets	1	2	0	.333	87	58
Indianapolis	0	3	0	.000	19	78
Central Division						
Jacksonville	2	0	0	1.000	68	40
Baltimore	2	1	0	.667	74	61
Cincinnati	1	1	0	.500	34	44
Pittsburgh	1	1	0	.500	21	50
Tennessee	1	1	0	.500	37	37
Western Division						
Denver	3	0	0	1.000	89	31
Kansas City	2	1	0	.667	53	62
Oakland	1	2	0	.333	84	83
San Diego	1	2	0	.333	34	73
Seattle	1	2	0	.333	48	79

NATIONAL FOOTBALL CONFERENCE

Eastern Division	W	L	T	Pct.	Pts.	OP
Washington	2	1	0	.667	56	37
Dallas	2	1	0	.667	80	52
Philadelphia	1	2	0	.333	47	61
Arizona	1	2	0	.333	59	65
N.Y. Giants	1	2	0	.333	67	81
Central Division						
Tampa Bay	3	0	0	1.000	65	37
Detroit	2	1	0	.667	77	48
Green Bay	2	1	0	.667	70	52
Minnesota	2	1	0	.667	75	65
Chicago	0	3	0	.000	55	97
Western Division						
Carolina	2	1	0	.667	45	37
San Francisco	2	1	0	.667	54	32
St. Louis	1	2	0	.333	64	74
Atlanta	0	3	0	.000	54	73
New Orleans	0	3	0	.000	37	91

SUNDAY, SEPTEMBER 14

WASHINGTON 19, ARIZONA 13 (OT)—at Jack Kent Cooke Stadium, attendance 78,270. Michael Westbrook caught a 40-yard touchdown pass in overtime to give the Redskins a victory in their inaugural game at Jack Kent Cooke Stadium. The Redskins defense permitted the Cardinals just 234 total yards of offense, and kept them out of the end zone. Arizona scored its only touchdown when J.J. McCleskey's blocked punt was recovered in the end zone by Tommy Bennett in the first quarter. The game was tied 10-10 late in the fourth quarter when Ty Howard's pass interference penalty gave the Redskins the ball at the Cardinals' 1-yard line with 1:44 left. The Cardinals, however, stopped the Redskins on three consecutive running plays, and forced Scott Blanton to kick a field goal with 1:13 remaining. Kevin Williams returned the ensuing kickoff 22 yards, and caught Kent Graham's pass on the next play for 16 yards and got out of bounds at the Cardinals' 49 with 1:08 left. Graham completed a third-and-6 pass to Frank Sanders for a first down to set up Kevin Butler's 47-yard field goal with 2 seconds remaining that sent the game to overtime. On the second play of overtime, Marvcus Patton forced Leeland McElroy to fumble, and Derek Smith recovered at the Cardinals' 35-yard line. After Terry Allen lost 5 yards on a running play, Frerotte lofted a pass deep down the left sideline to Westbrook, who leaped and fell on his back while making the winning catch. Frerotte was 19 of 36 for 265 yards. Graham was 17 of 40 for 132 yards. The victory was just the Redskins' second in their last nine games against the Cardinals.

Arizona	7	0	3	3	0	—	13
Washington	3	7	0	3	6	—	19

Wash — FG Blanton 20
Ariz — Bennett recovered blocked punt in end zone (Butler kick)
Wash — Westbrook 5 pass from Frerotte (Blanton kick)
Ariz — FG Butler 32
Wash — FG Blanton 19
Ariz — FG Butler 47
Wash — Westbrook 40 pass from Frerotte (Blanton kick)

BALTIMORE 24, N.Y. GIANTS 23—at Giants Stadium, attendance 69,768. Matt Stover kicked a 37-yard field goal with 34 seconds remaining to give the Ravens their first road victory in franchise history. Each team scored 2 touchdowns in the first half, but the Ravens led 14-12 because of Rob Burnett's blocked extra-point attempt after the Giants' first touchdown and a failed 2-point attempt after the second touchdown. The Giants scored on their first possession of the second half on Tyrone Wheatley's 1-yard touchdown run, and Brad Daluiso's field goal early in the fourth quarter gave the Giants a 23-14 lead. Two possessions later the Ravens drove 83 yards in 10 plays, the key play being Vinny Testaverde's 34-yard pass to Eric Green to set up Michael Jackson's 11-yard touchdown catch with 7:08 left. The Giants drove to the Ravens' 24-yard line, but linebackers Jamie Sharper and Ray Lewis stopped Tiki Barber on third and 1, and Daluiso missed a 41-yard field-goal attempt with 2:59 left. He also had missed a 41-yard attempt earlier in the game. Testaverde completed all 3 of his pass attempts, and Earnest Byner rushed 3 times to set up Stover's winning kick. The Giants were unable to cross midfield before time expired. Testaverde was 22 of 35 for 223 yards and 2 touchdowns, with 1 interception. Dave Brown completed 28 of 46 passes for 269 yards.

Baltimore	7	7	0	10	—	24
N.Y. Giants	0	12	8	3	—	23

Balt — Alexander 22 pass from Testaverde (Stover kick)
NYG — Barber 1 run (kick blocked)
Balt — Graham 1 run (Stover kick)
NYG — Way 1 pass from Brown (pass failed)
NYG — Wheatley 1 run (Barber pass from Brown)
NYG — FG Daluiso 27
Balt — Jackson 11 pass from Testaverde (Stover kick)
Balt — FG Stover 37

KANSAS CITY 22, BUFFALO 16—at Arrowhead Stadium, attendance 78,169. Tamarick Vanover's 94-yard kickoff return for a touchdown and 2 key interceptions by the defense enabled the Chiefs to hold off the Bills. Andre Reed's 77-yard touchdown catch gave the Bills a 10-9 lead early in the third quarter. After Steve Christie's second field goal increased the Bills lead to 13-9, Vanover catapulted the Chiefs back into the lead with his kickoff return. Bills quarterback Todd Collins completed a 45-yard pass to Quinn Early on their next possession, and Christie kicked his third field goal to tie the game with 11:52 remaining. The Bills got the ball back after forcing a punt, but Reggie Tongue intercepted a pass at midfield with 9:50 to play. A pair of 16-yard runs by Greg Hill and Elvis Grbac set up Grbac's 1-yard touchdown pass to Tony Richardson with 6:55 left. However, Phil Hanson blocked the extra point, enabling the Bills to trail by just six points. After an exchange of punts, the Bills began possession at their own 33-yard line with 2:07 remaining. Collins completed a 15-yard pass to Lonnie Johnson to get the Bills down to the Chiefs' 7 with 27 seconds left. Collins threw 3 consecutive incompletions before Mark McMillian intercepted his fourth-down pass in the end zone to preserve the victory for the Chiefs. Grbac was 20 of 37 for 160 yards. Collins completed 22 of 43 passes for 275 yards, with 2 interceptions. Reed had 4 receptions for 113 yards.

Buffalo	0	3	7	6	—	16
Kansas City	6	3	0	13	—	22

KC — FG Stoyanovich 46
KC — FG Stoyanovich 45
Buff — FG Christie 46
KC — FG Stoyanovich 42
Buff — Reed 77 pass from Collins (Chrisite kick)
Buff — FG Christie 33
KC — Vanover 94 kickoff return (Stoyanovich kick)
Buff — FG Chrisite 30
KC — Richardson 1 pass from Grbac (kick blocked)

CAROLINA 26, SAN DIEGO 7—at Qualcomm Stadium, Jack Murphy Field, attendance 70,813. Wesley Walls caught 2 touchdown passes, John Kasay kicked 4 field goals, and the Panthers' defense recovered 4 fumbles to give the Panthers a 3-0 record in the state of California. The Chargers started early, as Stan Humphries's 59-yard pass to Tony Martin set up Erric Pegram's 6-yard touchdown run for their only lead. Big plays led to all six Panthers' scores. Micheal Bates's 56-yard kickoff return set up Walls's first touchdown catch. On the next possession, rookie Rae Carruth blocked Darren Bennett's punt, leading to John Kasay's first field goal and giving the Panthers a 10-7 lead. In the second quarter, Patrick Sapp lined up offsides on a Panthers punt, allowing Carolina to get the ball back for Kasay's second field goal. Fumble recoveries by Micheal Barrow, Barry Minter, and Les Miller in the second half led directly to Carolina's final 13 points. Kerry Collins, who made his first start of the season after suffering a broken jaw in the preseason, was 17 of 36 for 138 yards and 2 touchdowns, with 1 interception. The Panthers gained just 28 more total yards the Chargers, but had nearly twice as many rushing attempts (41-21), and thus maintained possession for more than 36 minutes.

Carolina	10	3	3	10	—	26
San Diego	7	0	0	0	—	7

SD — Pegram 6 run (Carney kick)
Car — Walls 8 pass from Collins (Kasay kick)
Car — FG Kasay 25
Car — FG Kasay 36
Car — FG Kasay 34
Car — FG Kasay 28
Car — Walls 1 pass from Collins (Kasay kick)

DETROIT 32, CHICAGO 7—at Soldier Field, attendance 59,147. Scott Mitchell threw 2 touchdown passes, and Jason Hanson kicked 4 field goals as the Lions won for the sixth time in their last eight meetings with the Bears. Barry Sanders, after having gained only 53 rushing yards the first two games, compiled 161 yards on 19 carries. Raymont Harris scored on the Bears' first possession, but the Lions defense did not allow another point the remainder of the game. After Jason Hanson's first field goal, a 37-yard pass from Mitchell to Tommy Vardell set up Mitchell's 16-yard touchdown pass to Johnnie Morton. Hanson's second field goal in the closing seconds of the first half gave the Lions a 13-7 halftime lead. Detroit's defense set the tone for the third quarter. Reggie Brown sacked Erik Kramer, which forced a fumble recovered by Kerwin Waldroup, leading to Hanson's third field goal. On the Bears next possession, Rick Mirer, who had replaced Kramer, fumbled on fourth-and-1 from their own 49-yard line. Vardell scored nine plays later to give the Lions a 23-7 lead. Mitchell was 16 of 25 for 215 yards. The loss marked the Bears' first 0-3 start since 1969.

Detroit	3	10	10	9	—	32
Chicago	7	0	0	0	—	7

Chi — Harris 7 run (Jaeger kick)
Det — FG Hanson 23
Det — Morton 16 pass from Mitchell (Hanson kick)
Det — FG Hanson 33
Det — FG Hanson 29
Det — Vardell 1 run (Hanson kick)
Det — Moore 27 from Mitchell (Mitchell sacked)
Det — FG Hanson 32

GREEN BAY 23, MIAMI 18—at Lambeau Field, attendance 60,075. Dorsey Levens rushed for a career-high 121 yards, and Brett Favre threw 2 touchdown passes to give the Packers their first-ever win against Miami in nine attempts. The Packers led 13-12 late in the third quarter when Bernie Parmalee's 2-yard run on a fourth-and-11 fake punt gave the Packers the ball at the Dolphins 32-yard line. Ryan Longwell kicked his fourth field goal to give the Packers a 16-12 lead. After a Dolphins punt, the Packers went on a 12-play, 83-yard drive that consumed 6:55, with Favre finding William Henderson for the touchdown to give the Packers a 23-12 lead with 5:33 left. The Dolphins did not score a touchdown until Dan Marino threw a 29-yard pass to Charles Jordan with 1:47 remaining. It was Marino's first touchdown pass of the season. Terry Mickens recovered the ensuing onside kick to clinch the victory for Green Bay. Favre was 24 of 37 for 253 yards. Marino was 21 of 47 for 240 yards, with 1 interception.

Miami	6	3	3	6	—	18
Green Bay	0	10	3	10	—	23

Mia — FG Mare 24
Mia — FG Mare 31
GB — Freeman 2 pass from Favre (Longwell kick)
Mia — FG Mare 22
GB — FG Longwell 26
Mia — FG Mare 34
GB — FG Longwell 24
GB — FG Longwell 39
GB — Henderson 10 pass from Favre (Longwell kick)
Mia — Jordan 29 pass from Marino (pass failed)

SAN FRANCISCO 33, NEW ORLEANS 7—at 3Com Park, attendance 61,838. The 49ers' defense forced 8 turnovers, led by Rod Woodson who had 3 interceptions and a fumble recovery despite leaving the game with an injured calf in the third quarter, that led to 30 points to give coach Steve Mariucci a victory in his first home game. Brent Jones caught 2 touchdown passes in the first half following turnovers to give the 49ers a 23-0 lead. After Heath Shuler threw 3 interceptions in the first half, coach Mike Ditka replaced him with Danny Wuerffel in the second half. Wuerffel threw 3 interceptions himself, of which 2 led to the 49ers' final 10 points. Steve Young returned, after missing the previous game because of a concussion, and completed 18 of 21 passes for 220 yards and 3 touchdowns before sitting out the fourth quarter. Gary Anderson made all 4 of his field-goal attempts. Tyronne Drakeford added 2 interceptions for the 49ers. The Saints committed 19 turnovers in the season's first three games.

New Orleans	0	0	0	7	—	7
San Francisco	13	10	10	0	—	33

SF — FG Anderson 43
SF — Jones 18 pass from Young (Anderson kick)
SF — FG Anderson 22
SF — FG Anderson 40
SF — Jones 1 pass from Young (Anderson kick)
SF — Hearst 1 pass from Young (Anderson kick)
SF — FG Anderson 38
NO — Hastings 8 pass from Wuerffel (Brien kick)

OAKLAND 36, ATLANTA 31—at Georgia Dome, attendance 47,922. On the strength of 58- and 61-yard touchdown runs by Napoleon Kaufman, the Raiders won their first game under head coach Joe Bugel. With the score tied 7-7 in the second quarter, the Falcons took the points from a Morten Andersen field goal off the board after the Raiders John Henry Mills was called for holding. Given the ball on the 1-yard line, Chris Chandler threw a touchdown pass to O.J. Santiago. Cole Ford then booted a field goal to end the half, and the Raiders scored on the opening possession of the second half, with Jeff George's 51-yard touchdown pass to James Jett putting the points on the board. Rookie Byron Hanspard ran 77 yards on the next play from scrimmage, setting up Chandler's 3-yard touchdown pass to Bob Christian. The Falcons forced the Radiers to punt, but James Folston's hit forced Todd Kinchen to fumble. Kenny Shedd recovered the ball and ran 25 yards to give the Raiders a 24-21 lead. After Kaufman's 58-yard touchdown run gave the Raiders a 31-24 lead, Billy Joe Tolliver replaced an injured Chandler and guided the Falcons on a 13-play drive to the tying score midway through the fourth quarter. The Raiders responded when George threw a 76-yard pass to Rickey Dudley on the next play from scrimmage, setting up Ford's go-ahead field goal with 4:24 left. Darrell Russell knocked Billy Joe Tolliver out of the end zone for a safety with 3:19 left to give the Raiders a 36-31 lead. Tolliver's 4th-and-19 pass to Harold Green with 37 seconds left went for 17 yards, and the Raiders prevailed. Atlanta held the ball for 37:06 and permitted just 11 first downs. George was 12 of 22 for 286 yards. Kaufman had 14 carries for 140 yards.

Oakland	7	3	21	5	—	36
Atlanta	7	7	10	7	—	31

Atl — Green 1 run (Andersen kick)
Oak — Kaufman 61 run (Ford kick)
Atl — Santiago 1 pass from Chandler (Andersen kick)
Oak — FG Ford 49
Oak — Jett 51 pass from George (Ford kick)
Atl — Christian 3 pass from Chandler (Andersen kick)
Oak — Shedd 25 fumble return (Ford kick)
Atl — FG Andersen 51
Oak — Kaufman 58 run (Ford kick)
Atl — Mathis 6 pass from Tolliver (Andersen kick)
Oak — FG Ford 31
Oak — Safety, Tolliver sacked by Russell in end zone

DENVER 35, ST. LOUIS 14—at Denver Mile High Stadium, attendance 74,338. John Elway threw 4 touchdown passes, and Darrien Gordon recorded the Broncos first punt return for a touchdown since 1987 as Denver improved to 3-0. Elway threw touchdown passes to Rod Smith and Dwayne Carswell in the first half, but held just a 14-7 halftime lead before Gordon's punt return 1:33 into the third quarter staked the Broncos to a 14-point lead. A 12-yard punt by Will Brice led to Elway's 38-yard touchdown pass to Smith early in the fourth quarter, giving the Broncos a 28-7 lead. Ray Crockett intercepted a pass less than a minute later, returned it to the Rams' 23, and Elway threw a touchdown pass to Ed McCaffrey on the next play. Elway was 16 of 28 for 247 yards, and threw 4 touchdowns for the sixth time in his career. Tony Banks was 18 of 33 for 217 yards. Terrell Davis had 21 carries for 103 yards for his third consecutive 100-yard game. Smith had 126 yards on 4 receptions. The Broncos' defense recorded 5 sacks, 2 by Neil Smith, and had 2 interceptions.

St. Louis	7	0	0	7	—	14
Denver	7	7	7	14	—	35

Den — R. Smith 72 pass from Elway (Elam kick)
StL — Phillips 23 run (Wilkins kick)
Den — Carswell 24 pass from Elway (Elam kick)
Den — Gordon 94 punt return (Elam kick)
Den — R. Smith 38 pass from Elway (Elam kick)
Den — McCaffrey 23 pass from Elway (Elam kick)
StL — R. Moore 27 run (Wilkins kick)

SEATTLE 31, INDIANAPOLIS 3—at RCA Dome, attendance 49,194. In his first start for the Seahawks, Warren Moon threw a touchdown pass and ran for another, and the Seahawks' defense recorded 8 sacks and held the

Colts to 23 net yards passing to win their first game. The Seahawks had more first downs (27-11) and total yards (423-118). Touchdown runs by Lamar Smith and Moon, and Todd Peterson's field goal in the final minute of the half, gave Seattle a 17-3 halftime lead. The 40-year-old Moon set up the Seahawks next score by scrambling 17 yards for a first down before throwing a touchdown pass to Mike Pritchard. Chris Warren's 35-yard run with less than three minutes remaning ended the scoring. The Seahawks limited the Colts in the second half to 30 yards on 24 plays. Moon was 24 of 38 for 270 yards. Jim Harbaugh completed 11 of 17 passes for 77 yards.

Seattle	7	10	0	14	—	31
Indianapolis	3	0	0	0	—	3

Ind — FG Blanchard 46
Sea — Smith 3 run (Peterson kick)
Sea — Moon 1 run (Peterson kick)
Sea — FG Peterson 27
Sea — Pritchard 20 pass from Moon (Peterson kick)
Sea — Warren 35 run (Peterson kick)

TAMPA BAY 28, MINNESOTA 14—at Hubert H. Humphrey Metrodome, attendance 63,697. Trent Dilfer threw 2 touchdown passes as Tampa Bay improved its record to 3-0 for the first time since 1979. Dilfer threw a 49-yard pass to Horace Copeland to set up his first touchdown pass. On their next possession, rookie wide receiver Reidel Anthony went 26 yards on a third-and-1 reverse to ignite a 12-play, 85-yard drive. Mike Alstott's great second-effort rewarded him with a 1-yard touchdown run. On their first possession of the second half, Dilfer and Anthony connected on a 28-yard pass before Copeland caught a 27-yard touchdown pass to give the Buccaneers a 21-3 lead. Dilfer completed 15 of 20 passes for 192 yards. Warrick Dunn had 16 carries for 101 yards, including a 52-yard touchdown scamper in the fourth quarter. Brad Johnson was 29 of 44 for 334 yards, with Jake Reed grabbing 6 passes for 131 receiving yards. Tampa Bay converted 8 of 13 third-down opportunities. The loss broke a streak of 11 consecutive home-opening wins for the Vikings.

Tampa Bay	0	14	7	7	—	28
Minnesota	3	0	3	8	—	14

Minn — FG Davis 25
TB — Harris 5 pass from Dilfer (Husted kick)
TB — Alstott 1 run (Husted kick)
TB — Copeland 27 pass from Dilfer (Husted kick)
Minn — FG Davis 24
TB — Dunn 52 run (Husted kick)
Minn — Carter 30 pass from Johnson (Johnson run)

SUNDAY NIGHT, SEPTEMBER 14

NEW ENGLAND 27, N.Y. JETS 24 (OT)—at Foxboro Stadium, attendance 60,072. Adam Vinatieri's 34-yard field goal 8:03 into overtime averted a near-upset for the Patriots in a game that featured the return of Jets coach Bill Parcells to New England. Amidst a festitve atmosphere, Chris Canty's 63-yard kickoff return began the preceedings. Drew Bledsoe threw a 32-yard touchdown pass to Ben Coates moments later. After 223 career punts, Tom Tupa suffered his first blocked punt, courtesy of ex-Patriots player Corwin Brown, to lead to Neil O'-Donnell's short touchdown run. On the next possession, Curtis Martin had a 33-yard run to set up his own 2-yard jaunt. Trailing 14-10 in the third quarter, Mo Lewis gave the Jets their only lead when he raced 43 yards with an interception. The Patriots responded with a 15-play, 7:58 drive, capped by Vinatieri's tying field goal. Willie McGinest recovered Neil O'Donnell's fumble on the next possession, leading to Lovett Purnell's 10-yard touchdown catch with 12:53 remaining to give the Patriots a 24-17 lead. After two possessions for each club, the Jets got the ball on their own 17-yard line with 2:18 to play. Neil O'Donnell completed 6 of 12 passes on the drive and found Keyshawn Johnson for a 24-yard touchdown with 31 seconds left to tie the game. Derrick Cullors brought the ensuing kickoff out of the end zone, was tackled by Raymond Austin, fumbled, and Chad Cascaden recovered at the 18-yard line. After an 11-yard pass to Jeff Graham, rookie John Hall then made a 24-yard field goal, but the Jets were penalized for delay of game. Hall then attempted a 29-yard field goal, but Mike Jones blocked the game-winning attempt, sending the game to overtime. Otis Smith intercepted Bledsoe near midfield at the beginning of overtime, but the Jets had to punt. The Patriots proceeded to drive 62 yards, with Martin carrying the ball the last six plays, before Vinatieri made the winning kick. Martin finished with 40 carries for 199 yards. Bledsoe was 16 of 34 for 162 yards and 2 touchdowns, with 2 interceptions. O'Donnell was 30 of 50 for 271 yards. Adrian Murrell rushed for 110 yards.

N.Y. Jets	7	3	7	7	0	—	24
New England	14	0	3	7	3	—	27

NE — Coates 32 pass from Bledsoe (Vinatieri kick)
NYJ — O'Donnell 2 run (Hall kick)
NE — Martin 2 run (Vinatieri kick)
NYJ — FG Hall 26
NYJ — Lewis 43 interception return (Hall kick)
NE — FG Vinatieri 33
NE — Purnell 10 pass from Bledsoe (Vinatieri kick)
NYJ — K. Johnson 24 pass from O'Donnell (Hall kick)
NE — FG Vinatieri 34

MONDAY, SEPTEMBER 15

DALLAS 21, PHILADELPHIA 20—at Texas Stadium, attendance 63,942. Holder Tom Hutton fumbled the snap on Chris Boniol's possible game-winning 21-yard field-goal attempt on the final play, as the Cowboys held on to their share of first place in the NFC East. The Eagles led by as many as 14 points, taking a 17-3 lead on Chad Lewis's 12-yard touchdown catch. First-year kicker Richie Cunningham kicked a 48-yard field goal just before halftime, and a 25-yard boot after Herschel Walker opened the second half with a 45-yard kickoff return, to cut the deficit to 17-9. After former Cowboys kicker Boniol made a 44-yard field goal, Cunningham booted 2 more field goals to cut the lead to 20-15 with 5:25 left. After forcing an Eagles punt, the Cowboys faced a fourth-and-5 situation from their own 43, but Charles Dimry was penalized for pass interference. Eric Bjornson's diving catch a few plays later set up Troy Aikman's 14-yard touchdown pass to Anthony Miller with 51 seconds left. Aikman's 2-point conversion pass fell incomplete—but the Cowboys led 21-20. Ty Detmer hit Freddie Solomon for 26 yards and Michael Timpson for 13 to get to midfield with 16 seconds left. Detmer connected with Solomon for 46 yards, with Omar Stoutmire tackling him at the 4-yard line with 4 seconds left. The Eagles lined up for the winning kick, but Hutton had trouble with the snap and attempted to run the ball in, only to get tackled for a loss as time expired. Aikman was 17 of 36 for 205 yards. Detmer was 18 of 30 for 184 yards. Ricky Watters rushed for 106 yards.

Philadelphia	10	7	0	3	—	20
Dallas	3	3	3	12	—	21

Phil — FG Boniol 49
Dall — FG Cunningham 46
Phil — W. Thomas 37 fumble return (Boniol kick)
Phil — Lewis 12 pass from Detmer (Boniol kick)
Dall — FG Cunningham 48
Dall — FG Cunningham 25
Phil — FG Boniol 44
Dall — FG Cunningham 29
Dall — FG Cunningham 22
Dall — Miller 14 pass from Aikman (pass failed)

FOURTH WEEK SUMMARIES

AMERICAN FOOTBALL CONFERENCE

Eastern Division	W	L	T	Pct.	Pts.	OP
New England	4	0	0	1.000	130	40
N.Y. Jets	2	2	0	.500	110	80
Buffalo	2	2	0	.500	94	113
Miami	2	2	0	.500	71	77
Indianapolis	0	4	0	.000	54	115
Central Division						
Jacksonville	3	0	0	1.000	98	61
Baltimore	3	1	0	.750	110	71
Cincinnati	1	2	0	.333	54	82
Pittsburgh	1	2	0	.333	42	80
Tennessee	1	2	0	.333	47	73
Western Division						
Denver	4	0	0	1.000	127	51
Kansas City	3	1	0	.750	88	76
Seattle	2	2	0	.500	74	101
Oakland	1	3	0	.250	106	106
San Diego	1	3	0	.250	56	99

NATIONAL FOOTBALL CONFERENCE

Eastern Division	W	L	T	Pct.	Pts.	OP
Dallas	2	1	0	.667	80	52
Washington	2	1	0	.667	56	37
Arizona	1	2	0	.333	59	65
Philadelphia	1	2	0	.333	47	61
N.Y. Giants	1	3	0	.250	70	94
Central Division						
Tampa Bay	4	0	0	1.000	96	58
Green Bay	3	1	0	.750	108	84
Minnesota	2	2	0	.500	107	103
Detroit	2	2	0	.500	94	83
Chicago	0	4	0	.000	58	128
Western Division						
San Francisco	3	1	0	.750	88	39
Carolina	2	2	0	.500	59	72
St. Louis	2	2	0	.500	77	77
New Orleans	1	3	0	.250	72	108
Atlanta	0	4	0	.000	61	107

SUNDAY, SEPTEMBER 21

SAN FRANCISCO 34, ATLANTA 7—at 3Com Park, attendance 60,404. Steve Young threw 2 touchdown passes and Terry Kirby ran for 2 scores as the 49ers scored 3 touchdowns in an eight-minute span of the second quarter to defeat the Falcons. Young's 69-yard pass to Garrison Hearst set up Gary Anderson's first-quarter field goal. Young directed 7-, 6-, and 5-play touchdown drives in the second quarter, culminating with Young's 56-yard touchdown pass to Terrell Owens with 39 seconds left in the half to give the 49ers a 24-0 halftime edge. Young completed 17 of 24 passes for 336 yards and 2 touchdowns in three quarters of action. Billy Joe Tolliver was 17 of 31 for 162 yards and 1 touchdown, with 1 interception. The 49ers outgained the Falcons 424-211 in total yards.

Atlanta	0	0	7	0	—	7
San Francisco	3	21	7	3	—	34

SF — FG Anderson 22
SF — Stokes 10 pass from Young (Anderson kick)
SF — Kirby 1 run (Anderson kick)
SF — Owens 56 pass from Young (Anderson kick)
SF — Kirby 15 run (Anderson kick)
Atl — Emanuel 16 pass from Tolliver (Andersen kick)
SF — FG Anderson 32

BALTIMORE 36, TENNESSEE 10—at Liberty Bowl Memorial Stadium, attendance 17,737. Vinny Testaverde threw 3 touchdown passes and Matt Stover added 5 field goals as the Ravens' defense forced 5 turnovers in defeating the Oilers. Tony Siragusa's fumble recovery deep in Oilers' territory led to Stover's first field goal. After a masterful 83-yard drive for a touchdown, in which Steve McNair completed all 5 of his pass attempts, the Ravens' defense shut down the Oilers' offense for the remainder of the game. The Ravens had 55- and 87-yard touchdown drives in the second quarter, both capped by Testaverde touchdown passes to Derrick Alexander, to take a 17-7 lead. Earnest Byner recovered Derrick Mason's muffed punt late in the third quarter, setting up Stover's third field goal to give the Ravens a 23-10 lead. Jermaine Lewis's 45-yard punt return set up his 16-yard touchdown reception four minutes into the fourth quarter to take a 30-10 lead and all but ice the game. Testaverde was 23 of 37 for 318 yards and 3 touchdowns. Lewis had 8 receptions for 124 yards. McNair was 20 of 33 for 199 yards and 1 touchdown, with 1 interception.

Baltimore	3	17	3	13	—	36
Tennessee	7	3	0	0	—	10

Balt — FG Stover 38
Tenn — Wycheck 36 pass from McNair (Del Greco kick)
Balt — Alexander 25 pass from Testaverde (Stover kick)
Balt — Alexander 5 pass from Testaverde (Stover kick)
Tenn — FG Del Greco 45
Balt — FG Stover 42
Balt — FG Stover 41
Balt — Lewis 16 pass from Testaverde (Stover kick)
Balt — FG Stover 34
Balt — FG Stover 35

NEW ENGLAND 31, CHICAGO 3—at Foxboro Stadium, attendance 59,873. Drew Bledsoe threw 2 touchdown passes and Curtis Martin had a 70-yard touchdown run as the Patriots' defense permitted just 9 first downs in defeating the Bears. The Patriots led 7-0 with under 3:00 left in the first half when Bledsoe threw a 52-yard touchdown pass to Troy Brown to cap a 79-yard drive. The clubs exchanged field goals before Martin's 70-yard burst to give the Patriots a 24-3 lead midway through the fourth quarter. Scott Zolak added a late touchdown pass to complete the Patriots' scoring. Bledsoe was 24 of 37 for 301 yards and 2 touchdowns, with 1 interception. Brown had 6 receptions for 124 yards. Rick Mirer was 17 of 25 for 154 yards, with 2 interceptions. The Patriots outgained the Bears 402-199 in total yards.

Chicago	0	0	3	0	—	3
New England	7	7	0	17	—	31

NE — Brisby 7 pass from Bledsoe (Vinatieri kick)
NE — T. Brown 52 pass from Bledsoe (Vinatieri kick)
Chi — FG Jaeger 38
NE — FG Vinatieri 27
NE — Martin 70 run (Vinatieri kick)
NE — Purnell 20 pass from Zolak (Vinatieri kick)

DENVER 38, CINCINNATI 20—at Denver Mile High Stadium, attendance 73,871. John Elway threw 3 touchdown passes and Terrell Davis rushed for 215 yards as the Broncos remained undefeated. With the game tied 7-7, Elway completed an 80-yard drive with a 1-yard touchdown pass to Rod Smith with 25 seconds left in the half. The Bengals tied the game when Ki-Jana Carter broke free and raced 79 yards for a touchdown on the first play from scrimmage of the second half. Jeff Blake's 40-yard pass to Carl Pickens on their next possession set up Doug Pelfrey's 38-yard field goal to give the Bengals a 17-14 lead. Elway and Smith culminated a 12-play drive with another touchdown, but Pelfrey responded with his second field goal to cut the deficit to 21-20 with 13:30 to play. On the Broncos' next possession, Davis scampered 50 yards for a touchdown, and his 34-yard run later in the quarter led to Jason Elam's 24-yard field goal to give the Broncos an 11-point lead with 3:26 remaining. The Bengals drove into Broncos' territory, but Neil Smith sacked Blake and forced him to fumble. Alfred Williams scooped up the ball and rumbled 51 yards for the game's final points. Elway was 14 of 26 for 162 yards and 3 touchdowns, with 1 intercepion. Blake was 20 of 30 for 220 yards and 1 touchdown. Carter had 13 carries for 104 yards to become the first Bengals' player to have a 100-yard rushing game since 1992.

Cincinnati	7	0	10	3	—	20
Denver	0	14	7	17	—	38

Cin — McGee 7 pass from Blake (Pelfrey kick)
Den — McCaffrey 32 pass from Elway (Elam kick)
Den — R. Smith 1 pass from Elway (Elam kick)
Cin — Carter 79 run (Pelfrey kick)
Cin — FG Pelfrey 38
Den — R. Smith 18 pass from Elway (Elam kick)
Cin — FG Pelfrey 42
Den — T. Davis 50 run (Elam kick)
Den — FG Elam 24
Den — A. Williams 51 fumble return (Elam kick)

NEW ORLEANS 35, DETROIT 17—at Louisiana Superdome, attendance 50,116. Mario Bates rushed for 162 yards and 2 touchdowns and passed for another as the Saints had their biggest winning margin since 1993. Bates threw a 21-yard touchdown pass to Andre Hastings to cap a drive that began following Anthony Newman's interception. Bates sprinted 74 yards for a touchdown just over two minutes later, and Newman's fumble recovery near midfield set up Heath Shuler's 20-yard touchdown pass to Daryl Hobbs to give the Saints a 21-0 lead. The Lions scored in the final minute of the half, but the Saints took the second half's opening kickoff and marched 64 yards, capped by Shuler's scoring run, to take a 28-7 lead. Bates's 2-yard touchdown run midway through the fourth quarter capped a 15-play, 80-yard drive to give the Saints a 35-10 lead on their way to their first victory. Shuler was 15 of 21 for 202 yards and 1 touchdown. Scott Mitchell was 24 of 43 for 253 yards and 2 touchdowns, with 3 interceptions. Herman Moore had 11 catches for 111 yards.

Detroit	0	7	0	10	—	17
New Orleans	0	21	7	7	—	35

NO — Hastings 21 pass from Bates (Brien kick)
NO — Bates 74 run (Brien kick)
NO — Hobbs 20 pass from Shuler (Brien kick)
Det — Sanders 17 pass from Mitchell (Hanson kick)
NO — Shuler 5 run (Brien kick)
Det — FG Hanson 47
NO — Bates 2 run (Brien kick)
Det — Moore 5 pass from Mitchell (Hanson kick)

BUFFALO 37, INDIANAPOLIS 35—at Rich Stadium, attendance 55,340. Antowain Smith rushed for 3 second-half touchdowns to help overcome a 26-point deficit as the Bills posted the second-best comeback in NFL history. The Colts needed to drive just 16 yards, thanks to Lamont Warren's recovery of Mitchell Galloway's muffed punt, and 57 yards for their first 2 touchdowns to take a 14-0 lead. The Colts had a 17-0 lead when Ellis Johnson intercepted Todd Collins to set up Cary Blanchard's second field goal. Collins fumbled on the first play from scrimmage on successive possessions, with both turnovers concluding with Blanchard field goals, giving the Colts a 26-0 lead with 5:59 left in the first half. The Bills scored on their final 2 possessions of the first half to cut the deficit to 26-10. The Colts drove to the Bills' 34 midway into the third quarter, but Ted Washington stuffed Zack Crockett at the line of scrimmage on fourth-and-1 to enable the Bills to regain possession. Collins guided the Bills on an 11-play, 66-yard drive, capped by Smith's 15-yard touchdown run, but Thurman Thomas was stopped on the 2-point conversion attempt and the score remained 26-16. Henry Jones had the Bills' second muffed punt of the game, and Scott Slutzker recovered early in the fourth quarter. Blanchard's fifth field goal stretched the Colts' lead to 29-16 with 10:19 to play. The Bills responded with a 69-yard drive that took less than four minutes, capped by Collins's 4-yard touchdown pass to Quinn Early with 6:25 remaining to cut the lead to 29-23. The Colts had to punt, and Collins and Early hooked up for a 43-yard pass to the Colts' 1 to set up Smith's second touchdown with 4:43 left to give the Bills their first lead, 30-29. Jim Harbaugh guided the Colts into Bills' territory, but his fourth-and-8 pass was incomplete with 1:24 left. On the first play after regaining possession, Smith raced 54 yards down the left sideline for a touchdown to give the Bllls a 37-29 lead. Harbaugh completed a 22-yard pass to Aaron Bailey on first down, and a 15-yard roughing the passer penalty that knocked Harbaugh out of the game moved the ball to the Bills' 43. Paul Justin entered the game and drove the Colts to the 2-yard line before finding Marvin Harrison for a touchdown with 14 seconds left to cut the score to 37-35. The Colts went to Harrison on the 2-point conversion attempt, but the pass was incomplete and the Bills prevailed. Collins was 23 of 38 for 275 yards and 2 touchdowns, with 1 interception. Smith had 12 carries for 129 yards along with his 3 touchdown runs. Harbaugh was 16 of 31 for 191 yards and 1 touchdown.

Indianapolis	14	12	0	9	—	35
Buffalo	0	10	6	21	—	37

Ind — Bailey 10 pass from Harbaugh (Blanchard kick)
Ind — Faulk 10 run (Blanchard kick)
Ind — FG Blanchard 39
Ind — FG Blanchard 36
Ind — FG Blanchard 49
Ind — FG Blanchard 22
Buff — Johnson 16 pass from Collins (Christie kick)
Buff — FG Christie 27
Buff — Smith 15 run (run failed)
Ind — FG Blanchard 25
Buff — Early 4 pass from Collins (Christie kick)
Buff — Smith 1 run (Christie kick)
Buff — Smith 54 run (Christie kick)
Ind — Harrison 2 pass from Justin (pass failed)

KANSAS CITY 35, CAROLINA 14—at Ericsson Stadium, attendance 67,402. Elvis Grbac threw 3 touchdown passes and the Chiefs' defense forced 3 second-half turnovers to defeat the Panthers. The Chiefs led 14-7 midway through the third quarter when Donnie Edwards intercepted a Kerry Collins pass deep in Panthers territory. Marcus Allen scored four plays later to give the Chiefs a 21-7 lead. Terry Wooden recovered Collins's fumble at the Panthers' 30 late in the third quarter, setting up Grbac's 3-yard touchdown pass to Tony Richardson. Mark McMillian intercepted Collins's pass 37 seconds later and raced 62 yards for a touchdown and a 35-7 Chiefs lead. Grbac was 16 of 29 for 224 yards and 3 touchdowns, with 1 interception. Collins was 24 of 47 for 328 yards and 1 touchdown, with 4 interceptions. Rae Carruth had 8 receptions for 110 yards. The Panthers outgained the Chiefs (364-331 total yards) but committed 5 turnovers while forcing just 1 miscue.

Kansas City	7	7	7	14	—	35
Carolina	0	7	0	7	—	14

KC — Anders 55 pass from Grbac (Stoyanovich kick)
KC — Rison 18 pass from Grbac (Stoyanovich kick)
Car — Lane 8 run (Kasay kick)
KC — Allen 1 run (Stoyanovich kick)
KC — Richardson 3 pass from Grbac (Stoyanovich kick)
KC — McMillian 62 interception return (Stoyanovich kick)
Car — Walls 19 pass from Collins (Kasay kick)

GREEN BAY 38, MINNESOTA 32—at Lambeau Field, attendance 60,115. Brett Favre threw 5 touchdown passes as the Packers held off the Vikings. After the Vikings scored on the game's opening drive, the Packers proceeded to score the next 31 points. Favre threw 4 touchdown passes during a 17-minute stretch, the second touchdown set up by Bill Schroeder's 39-yard punt return and the third by LeRoy Butler's interception. All four drives took just five or fewer plays. Butler's second interception enabled Ryan Longwell to boot a 34-yard field goal to give Green Bay a 31-7 halftime lead. Fortunes turned for the Vikings when Schroeder fumbled the second half's opening kickoff. Brad Johnson capitalized with a 3-yard touchdown pass to Cris Carter. Jason Fisk intercepted Favre 57 seconds later at the Packers' 24, and Johnson threw a 7-yard touchdown pass to Jake Reed two plays later to cut the deficit to 31-22. The Packers responded with an 81-yard touchdown drive, but the Vikings scored on their next two possessions, the final drive consuming 90 yards, to cut the deficit to 38-32 with 6:44 left. The Vikings got the ball back with 2:37 left, but made just one first down before Johnson's fourth down pass fell incomplete. Corey Fuller's pass interference penalty with 1:26 remaining gave the Packers a first down and allowed them to run out the clock. Favre was 18 of 31 for 266 yards and 5 touchdowns, with 2 interceptions. Antonio Freeman had 7 catches for 122 yards. Johnson was 19 of 34 for 217 yards and 3 touchdowns, with 2 interceptions. Robert Smith had 28 carries for 132 yards.

Minnesota	7	0	15	10	—	32
Green Bay	7	24	7	0	—	38

Minn — R. Smith 1 run (Davis kick)
GB — Brooks 19 pass from Favre (Longwell kick)
GB — Freeman 28 pass from Favre (Longwell kick)
GB — Freeman 15 pass from Favre (Longwell kick)
GB — Mickens 2 pass from Favre (Longwell kick)
GB — FG Longwell 34
Minn — Carter 3 pass from Johnson (Davis kick)
Minn — Reed 7 pass from Johnson (Evans run)
GB — Chmura 2 pass from Favre (Longwell kick)
Minn — FG Davis 31
Minn — Reed 27 pass from Johnson (Davis kick)

ST. LOUIS 13, NEW YORK GIANTS 3—at Trans World Dome, attendance 64,642. Craig Heyward scored the game's lone touchdown and the Rams' defense permitted just 11 first downs and 192 total yards as St. Louis evened its record. Brad Daluiso missed 54- and 42-yard field-goal attempts in the first half, but Jeff Wilkins booted a pair of short field goals in the second quarter to give the Rams a 6-0 halftime lead. Neither team threatened to score again until Daluiso connected from 47 yards early in the fourth quarter. An exchange of punts gave the Rams the ball at the Giants' 36 with 5:17 left. The Rams put together a 7-play drive capped by Heyward's 4-yard touchdown run with 2:42 to play in the game. D'Marco Farr sacked Dave Brown on fourth-and-15 near midfield to quell the Giants' final attempt. Tony Banks was 15 of 35 for 176 yards. Brown was 16 of 31 for 163 yards, with 1 interception.

N.Y. Giants	0	0	0	3	—	3
St. Louis	0	6	0	7	—	13

StL — FG Wilkins 23
StL — FG Wilkins 21
NYG — FG Daluiso 47
StL — Heyward 4 run (Wilkins kick)

NEW YORK JETS 23, OAKLAND 22—at Giants Stadium, attendance 72,586. John Hall kicked 3 field goals and Corwin Brown blocked a field-goal attempt that Ray Mickens returned for the game-winning touchdown as the Jets snapped a 13-game home losing streak. Jeff George threw 3 touchdown passes in the game's first 25 minutes, but the Raiders led only 19-10 due to a missed extra-point attempt by Cole Ford and a failed 2-point conversion attempt. James Folston recovered Aaron Glenn's fumbled kickoff on the next play, and Ford booted a 43-yard field goal to give the Raiders a 22-10 lead with 2:14 left in the half. The Raiders had a chance to increase the lead, but Ford's 27-yard field-goal attempt sailed wide left, his second miss of the half, as the second quarter expired. Hall completed the Jets' first two drives of the second half with field goals, the second score set up by Brian Hansen's 26-yard pass on a fake punt to Brown, to cut the deficit to 22-16. Mickens returned Brown's block of Ford's third missed field goal for the go-ahead score with 12:51 remaining to put the Jets ahead 23-22. The Raiders drove to the Jets' 29 with 3:34 remaining, and on fourth-and-2 Ford missed his fourth field goal of the game. The Jets got 2 first downs to run out the clock. Neil O'Donnell was 17 of 32 for 198 yards. George was 26 of 38 for 374 yards and 3 touchdowns. Tim Brown had 10 receptions for 153 yards and James Jett had 5 catches for 148 yards. Napoleon Kaufman had 27 carries for 126 yards.

Oakland	6	16	0	0	—	22
N.Y. Jets	3	7	6	7	—	23

Oak — Jett 56 pass from George (kick failed)
NYJ — FG Hall 34
Oak — Brown 29 pass from George (pass failed)
NYJ — Murrell 4 run (Hall kick)
Oak — Jett 11 pass from George (Ford kick)
Oak — FG Ford 43
NYJ — FG Hall 47
NYJ — FG Hall 26
NYJ — Mickens 72 blocked field goal return (Hall kick)

SEATTLE 26, SAN DIEGO 22—at Kingdome, attendance 51,110. Steve Broussard's touchdown run with 1:22 remaining lifted the Seahawks to a 26-22 victory against AFC Western Division rival San Diego. With the score tied 3-3, Rodney Harrison's 75-yard interception return for a touchdown gave the Chargers their first lead of the game. Eric Metcalf, who set up John Carney's first field goal with an 18-yard punt return, had a 21-yard punt return that led to Carney's second field goal and gave the Chargers a 13-3 lead. The Seahawks scored 10 points in a less than two-minute span late in the half, with Darryl Williams's interception setting up the second score, to tie the game, but Carney added a 26-yard field goal in the closing seconds of the half to give San Diego a 16-13 halftime lead. Terrance Shaw's interception late in the third quarter set up Carney's fourth field goal, but the Seahawks regained the lead 41 seconds later on Warren Moon's 53-yard touchdown pass to Joey Galloway. Harrison recovered Moon's fumble midway through the fourth quarter, and Carney booted his fifth field goal to put the Chargers ahead 22-20 with 5:21 left. The Seahawks put together a 9-play, 80-yard drive, capped by Broussard's touchdown run with 1:22 remaining. The Chargers failed to make a first down in their final attempt. Moon was 17 of 34 for 253 yards and 2 touchdowns, with 2 interceptions. Galloway had 5 receptions for 106 yards. Stan Humphries was 25 of 46 for 239 yards, with 3 interceptions. Williams had all 3 of the Seahawks' interceptions.

San Diego	0	16	0	6	—	22
Seattle	3	10	0	13	—	26

Sea — FG Peterson 41
SD — FG Carney 22
SD — Harrison 75 interception return (Carney kick)
SD — FG Carney 29
Sea — Strong 5 pass from Moon (Peterson kick)
Sea — FG Peterson 37
SD — FG Carney 26
SD — FG Carney 41
Sea — Galloway 53 pass from Moon (Peterson kick)
SD — FG Carney 41
Sea — Broussard 1 run (pass failed)

SUNDAY NIGHT, SEPTEMBER 21

TAMPA BAY 31, MIAMI 21—at Houlihan's Stadium, attendance 73,314. Trent Dilfer threw 4 touchdown passes as the Buccaneers improved their record to 4-0. Karl Williams's 25-yard punt return in the game's opening minutes ignited the Buccaneers and led to Dilfer's 3-yard touchdown pass to Mike Alstott. The Buccaneers put together a 12-play, 76-yard drive in the second quarter, capped by Dilfer's 1-yard touchdown pass to Alstott. The Dolphins responded with a 14-play, 85-yard drive that culminated with O.J. McDuffie's 10-yard touchdown catch 22 seconds before halftime. The Buccaneers scored on their first two possessions of the second half, the second score coming on Dilfer's 38-yard touchdown pass to Reidel Anthony, to take a 24-7 lead. Karim Abdul-Jabbar's touchdown run cut the deficit to 24-14, but the Buccaneers responded with a 71-yard drive, capped by Dilfer's 58-yard touchdown pass to Warrick Dunn with 9:18 to play. Dan Marino threw a touchdown pass to Fred Barnett with 3:25 remaining, but the Buccaneers ran out the clock. Dilfer was 18 of 24 for 248 yards and 4 touchdowns, with 1 interception. Dunn had 6 receptions for 106 yards. Marino was 24 of 37 for 235 yards and 2 touchdowns.

Miami	0	7	0	14	—	21
Tampa Bay	7	7	10	7	—	31

TB — Alstott 3 pass from Dilfer (Husted kick)
TB — Alstott 1 pass from Dilfer (Husted kick)
Mia — McDuffie 10 pass from Marino (Mare kick)
TB — FG Husted 22
TB — Anthony 38 pass from Dilfer (Husted kick)
Mia — Abdul-Jabbar 1 run (Mare kick)
TB — Dunn 58 pass from Dilfer (Husted kick)
Mia — Barnett 1 pass from Marino (Mare kick)

MONDAY, SEPTEMBER 22

JACKSONVILLE 30, PITTSBURGH 21—at ALLTEL Stadium, attendance 73,016. Travis Davis blocked Norm Johnson's field-goal attempt and Chris Hudson returned it 58 yards for a touchdown as time expired as the Jaguars thwarted the Steelers. After each team scored on its first possession, Mark Brunell's 11-yard touchdown pass to Jimmy Smith gave the Jaguars a 14-7 lead early in the second quarter. Aaron Beasley's 5-yard interception return to the Steelers' 35 late in the half led to Mike Hollis's field goal and a 17-7 halftime lead. The Steelers scored on their first two possessions of the second half, with Hollis's second field goal sandwiched in between, to take a 21-20 lead in the opening seconds of the fourth quarter. The Jaguars drove to the Steelers' 19, but Hollis missed a 38-yard field goal. The Jaguars' defense forced a punt, and Jacksonville linked together a 14-play, 72-yard drive, capped by Hollis's 27-yard field goal with 4:14 remaining. Will Blackwell's 30-yard kickoff return gave the Steelers the ball at the Jaguars' 40. Kordell Stewart's 21-yard pass to Yancey Thigpen set up Johnson's game-winning opportunity. However, the snap was low and Davis blocked the kick. Hudson returned it along the Steelers' sideline for a touchdown as time expired. Brunell was 24 of 42 for 306 yards and 1 touchdown. Jimmy Smith had 10 receptions for 164 yards. Stewart was 11 of 16 for 155 yards and 2 touchdowns, with 1 interception. Jerome Bettis had 21 carries for 114 yards.

Pittsburgh	7	0	7	7	—	21
Jacksonville	7	10	3	10	—	30

Jack — Means 1 run (Hollis kick)
Pitt — Stewart 6 run (Johnson kick)
Jack — Smith 11 pass from Brunell (Hollis kick)
Jack — FG Hollis 20
Pitt — Thigpen 4 pass from Stewart (Johnson kick)
Jack — FG Hollis 45
Pitt — Bruener 1 pass from Stewart (Johnson kick)
Jack — FG Hollis 27
Jack — Hudson 58 blocked field goal return (Hollis kick)

FIFTH WEEK SUMMARIES

AMERICAN FOOTBALL CONFERENCE

Eastern Division	W	L	T	Pct.	Pts.	OP
New England	4	0	0	1.000	130	40
N.Y. Jets	3	2	0	.600	141	94
Buffalo	2	2	0	.500	94	113
Miami	2	2	0	.500	71	77
Indianapolis	0	4	0	.000	54	115
Central Division						
Jacksonville	3	1	0	.750	110	85
Baltimore	3	2	0	.600	127	92
Pittsburgh	2	2	0	.500	79	104
Cincinnati	1	3	0	.250	68	113
Tennessee	1	3	0	.250	71	110
Western Division						
Denver	5	0	0	1.000	156	72
Kansas City	4	1	0	.800	108	93
Oakland	2	3	0	.400	141	123
San Diego	2	3	0	.400	77	116
Seattle	2	3	0	.400	91	121

NATIONAL FOOTBALL CONFERENCE

Eastern Division	W	L	T	Pct.	Pts.	OP
Dallas	3	1	0	.750	107	55
Washington	3	1	0	.750	80	49
N.Y. Giants	2	3	0	.400	84	103
Arizona	1	3	0	.250	77	84
Philadelphia	1	3	0	.250	66	89
Central Division						
Tampa Bay	5	0	0	1.000	115	76
Detroit	3	2	0	.600	120	98
Green Bay	3	2	0	.600	123	110
Minnesota	3	2	0	.600	135	122
Chicago	0	5	0	.000	61	155
Western Division						
San Francisco	4	1	0	.800	122	60
Carolina	2	3	0	.400	80	106
St. Louis	2	3	0	.400	94	112
New Orleans	1	4	0	.200	81	122
Atlanta	0	5	0	.000	82	136

SUNDAY, SEPTEMBER 28

TAMPA BAY 19, ARIZONA 18—at Houlihan's Stadium, attendance 53,804. The Buccaneers forced 3 turnovers, blocked a punt and watched Kevin Butler's 47-yard field-goal attempt sail wide as time expired to remain undefeated. Alshermond Singleton returned a blocked punt 28 yards for a touchdown to put the Buccaneers on the board, and punter Tommy Barnhardt threw a 25-yard pass to Tony Bouie on a fake punt to set up Trent Dilfer's 8-yard touchdown pass to Reidel Anthony midway through the second quarter. The Cardinals answered with an 80-yard drive capped by Kent Graham's 21-yard touchdown pass to Rob Moore. Graham and Moore hooked up for a 41-yard pass early in the third quarter to set up Butler's 37-yard field goal that cut the deficit to 12-10. Arizona took the lead on Aeneas Williams's 42-yard interception return late in the third quarter. Trailing 18-12, John Lynch intercepted Graham at the Cardinals' 35 with 7:09 left, and Dilfer threw a 31-yard touchdown pass to Karl Williams to give the Buccaneers a 19-18 lead with 4:48 remaining. After an exchange of punts, the Cardinals got the ball at their own 20-yard line with 46 seconds left. Graham completed a 37-yard pass to Frank Sanders, who was knocked out of bounds at the Buccaneers' 29 with 12 seconds left. After an incompletion, Butler's 47-yard attempt sailed wide right. Dilfer was 11 of 23 for 100 yards and 2 touchdowns, with 1 interception. Graham was 31 of 52 for 339 yards and 1 touchdown, with 2 interceptions. Moore had 8 catches for 147 yards. The Cardinals lost despite more first downs (23-6) and total yards (364-147). The Cardinals' defense permitted the Buccaneers to convert just 2-of-14 third-down conversions.

Arizona	0	7	11	0	—	18
Tampa Bay	6	6	0	7	—	19

TB — Singleton 28 return of blocked punt (kick failed)
TB — Anthony 8 pass from Dilfer (run failed)
Ariz — Moore 21 pass from Graham (Butler kick)
Ariz — FG Butler 37

Ariz — Williams 42 interception return (Sanders pass from Graham)
TB — Williams 31 pass from Dilfer (Husted kick)

SAN DIEGO 21, BALTIMORE 17—at Qualcomm Stadium, Jack Murphy Field, attendance 54,094. Stan Humphries threw 3 long touchdown passes to Tony Martin to lead the Chargers to victory. The duo's first touchdown came midway through the first quarter to complete a 72-yard drive. The Ravens answered with Matt Stover's 47-yard field goal, but Humphries and Martin extended the lead midway through the second quarter on a 72-yard bomb. Stover connected from 35 yards with 29 seconds left in the second quarter and capped the Ravens' opening drive of the third quarter with a 28-yard field goal to cut the lead to 14-9. Baltimore scored on its third consecutive possession as Vinny Testaverde found Jermaine Lewis for a 37-yard touchdown pass. Testaverde's 2-point conversion pass to Michael Jackson increased the lead to 17-14. Late in the third quarter Humphries and Martin hooked up for their third touchdown to take a 21-17 lead. A 34-yard punt return by Derrick Alexander gave the Ravens the ball at the Chargers' 36 with 2:33 remaining, but Testaverde's fourth-and-26 pass was intercepted by Dwayne Harper and the Chargers ran out the clock. Humphries was 17 of 26 for 358 yards and 3 touchdowns, with 2 interceptions. Martin had 4 receptions for 155 yards. Testaverde was 18 of 42 for 228 yards and 1 touchdown, with 2 interceptions.

Baltimore	3	3	11	0	—	17
San Diego	7	7	7	0	—	21

SD — Martin 36 pass from Humphries (Davis kick)
Balt — FG Stover 47
SD — Martin 72 pass from Humphries (Davis kick)
Balt — FG Stover 35
Balt — FG Stover 28
Balt — Lewis 37 pass from Testaverde (Jackson pass from Testaverde)
SD — Martin 38 pass from Humphries (Davis kick)

DALLAS 27, CHICAGO 3—at Texas Stadium, attendance 64,082. Troy Aikman threw 2 touchdown passes and Deion Sanders returned a punt for a touchdown as the Cowboys defeated the Bears. The Bears put together a 16-play, 77-yard drive to begin the game, with Jeff Jaeger's field goal capping the nearly eight-minute drive. The score remained 3-0 Chicago until late in the second quarter when Kevin Smith returned an interception 21 yards to the Bears' 6. Aikman threw a 6-yard touchdown pass to Anthony Miller to give the Cowboys a 7-3 halftime lead. Richie Cunningham's field goal concluded the opening possession of the second half, and Aikman threw a 26-yard touchdown pass to Michael Irvin on their next drive to take a 17-3 lead. The Cowboys' defense forced a punt, and Sanders scampered 83 yards with the return for a touchdown and 24-3 lead. Aikman was 12 of 27 for 144 yards and 2 touchdowns, with 1 interception. Irvin had 6 catches for 105 of the Cowboys' 180 total yards. Rick Mirer was 11 of 21 for 62 yards, with 1 interception. Raymont Harris had 29 carries for 120 yards.

Chicago	3	0	0	0	—	3
Dallas	0	7	17	3	—	27

Chi — FG Jaeger 21
Dall — Miller 6 pass from Aikman (Cunningham kick)
Dall — FG Cunningham 33
Dall — Irvin 26 pass from Aikman (Cunningham kick)
Dall — Sanders 83 punt return (Cunningham kick)
Dall — FG Cunningham 23

DENVER 29, ATLANTA 21—at Georgia Dome, attendance 48,211. John Elway threw 3 touchdown passes as the Broncos held off the Falcons. The Broncos scored on their first two possessions and Terrell Davis's 2-point conversion run due to Jason Elam's hip injury gave the Broncos a 15-0 lead. Trailing 23-0, the Falcons linked together an 8-play, 92-yard drive capped by Chris Chandler's 1-yard touchdown pass to Ed West. Byron Hanspard's 57-yard run in the third quarter set up Chandler's 3-yard touchdown pass to Bert Emanuel to cut the lead to 23-14. The Broncos responded with a 7-play, 60-yard drive that finished with Detron Smith catching Elway's 17-yard touchdown pass. The Broncos missed the 2-point conversion attempt, thus giving the Falcons a chance to tie following Billy Joe Tolliver's 47-yard touchdown pass to Jamal Anderson with 11:18 to play. With Tolliver playing for the injured Chandler, the Falcons got two more possessions but could not penetrate Broncos' territory either time. Elway was 18 of 32 for 243 yards and 3 touchdowns, with 1 interception. Shannon Sharpe had 6 catches for 119 yards. Chandler was 12 of 22 for 137 yards and 2 touchdowns, with 1 interception.

Denver	15	8	6	0	—	29
Atlanta	0	7	7	7	—	21

Den — Sharpe 65 pass from Elway (Elam kick)
Den — Green 10 pass from Elway (Davis run)
Den — Davis 13 run (Davis run)
Atl — West 1 pass from Chandler (Andersen kick)
Atl — Emanuel 3 pass from Chandler (Andersen kick)
Den — D. Smith 17 pass from Elway (pass failed)
Atl — Anderson 47 pass from Tolliver (Andersen kick)

DETROIT 26, GREEN BAY 17—at Pontiac Silverdome, attendance 78,110. Barry Sanders rushed for 139 yards and Jason Hanson kicked 4 field goals as the Lions' defense forced 4 turnovers and defeated the Packers. The Packers kicked field goals to conclude their first two possessions, but Reggie Brown gave the Lions the lead with his 45-yard interception return with 10:00 left in the second quarter. After forcing a punt, the Lions used the impetus of Sanders's 46-yard run to set up Scott Mitchell's 4-yard touchdown pass to Pete Chryplewicz to give the Lions a 14-6 lead. The Packers cut the deficit to 14-9 and were driving late in the half when Robert Porcher intercepted Brett Favre's pass at the Lions' 35, but a facemask penalty on Favre moved the ball to midfield with 30 seconds left. Hanson booted a 53-yard field goal as the half expired to give the Lions a 17-9 lead. The Packers cut the deficit to 17-15 on the opening possession of the second half, but Favre's 2-point conversion pass attempt fell incomplete. The Lions responded with Mitchell's 45-yard pass to Herman Moore to set up Hanson's second field goal. George Jamison's recovery of Dorsey Levens's fumble at the Lions' 19 stopped the Packers' next drive. Hanson added 2 fourth quarter field goals as the Packers never ran a play inside the Lions' 36 in the fourth quarter. Mitchell was 17 of 27 for 215 yards and 1 touchdown. Moore had 6 receptions for 105 yards. Favre was 22 of 43 for 295 yards and 1 touchdown, with 3 interceptions. Levens had 16 carries for 107 yards.

Green Bay	6	3	6	0	—	15
Detroit	0	17	3	6	—	26

GB — FG Longwell 36
GB — FG Longwell 19
Det — R. Brown 45 interception return (Hanson kick)
Det — Chryplewicz 4 pass from Mitchell (Hanson kick)
GB — FG Longwell 50
Det — FG Hanson 53
GB — Schroeder 7 pass from Favre (pass failed)
Det — FG Hanson 44
Det — FG Hanson 22
Det — FG Hanson 39

WASHINGTON 24, JACKSONVILLE 12—at Jack Kent Cooke Stadium, attendance 74,421. Terry Allen had 36 carries for 122 yards and the Redskins' defense forced 3 turnovers to defeat the Jaguars. The Jaguars forced 2 first half turnovers in Redskins' territory, but had to settle for field goals both times. The Redskins took advantage of the short field, driving 28 yards for a touchdown following a 24-yard punt return by Brian Mitchell and then had a 37-yard touchdown drive set up by Stanley Richard's 23-yard interception return, to take a 14-9 halftime lead. The Jaguars trailed 17-12 with 8:52 remaining when Marc Boutte intercepted Mark Brunell deep in Jaguars' territory. Gus Frerotte capped the 17-yard drive with a 13-yard touchdown pass to Leslie Shepherd to finish the scoring. Frerotte was 16 of 24 for 244 yards and 3 touchdowns, with 1 interception. Brunell was 16 of 31 for 153 yards, with 2 interceptions. The Redskins' defense permitted just 11 first downs and allowed the Jaguars to convert just 3 of 13 third-down conversions.

Jacksonville	6	3	3	0	—	12
Washington	0	14	0	10	—	24

Jack — FG Hollis 30
Jack — FG Hollis 42
Jack — FG Hollis 25
Wash — Shephred 10 pass from Frerotte (Blanton kick)
Wash — Asher 8 pass from Frerotte (Blanton kick)
Jack — FG Hollis 47
Wash — FG Blanton 41
Wash — Shepherd 13 pass from Frerotte (Blanton kick)

NEW YORK GIANTS 14, NEW ORLEANS 9—at Giants Stadium, attendance 68,891. Dave Brown threw 2 touchdown passes and the Giants' defense permitted the Saints to convert just 1 of 12 third-down opportunities to defeat New Orleans. One play after Amani Toomer's 44-yard punt return, Brown threw a 32-yard touchdown pass to Kevin Alexander to give the Giants a 7-0 lead. The Saints answered with Doug Brien's field goal, but the Giants took a 14-3 lead on Brown's 14-yard touchdown pass to Chris Calloway to culminate a 12-play, 84-yard drive. The Saints again responded with a field goal to trail 14-6 at halftime. The Saints reached the Giants' 27 at the beginning of the fourth quarter, but Heath Shuler threw 3 consecutive incompletions to turn the ball over on downs. The Saints' defense forced another punt, and Brien kicked his third field goal to cut the deficit to 14-9 with 9:19 to play. The Saints forced a turnover in Giants' territory, but were forced to punt on fourth-and-20 with 3:38 remaining and did not get the ball back. Brown was 16 of 25 for 194 yards and 2 touchdowns, with 1 interception. Shuler was 16 of 31 for 203 yards, with 1 interception.

New Orleans	3	3	0	3	—	9
N.Y. Giants	7	7	0	0	—	14

NYG — Alexander 32 pass from Brown (Daluiso kick)
NO — FG Brien 36
NYG — Calloway 14 pass from Brown (Daluiso kick)
NO — FG Brien 32
NO — FG Brien 39

NEW YORK JETS 31, CINCINNATI 14—at Cinergy Field, attendance 57,209. Neil O'Donnell threw 3 touchdown passes, Adrian Murrell had 40 carries for 156 yards and 1 touchdown, and the Jets' defense permitted just 10 first downs and 215 total yards to defeat the Bengals. The Jets put together two touchdown drives exceeding five minutes, with Jeff Blake's 50-yard touchdown pass to Carl Pickens sandwiched in between, to take a 14-7 lead. Another five-minute-plus drive resulted in John Hall's 44-yard field goal and, following Ray Mickens's interception, O'Donnell threw a 12-yard touchdown pass to Keyshawn Johnson 15 seconds before halftime to take a 24-7 lead. O'Donnell's third touchdown pass, to Richie Anderson less than two minutes into the fourth quarter, extended the Jets' lead to 31-7. Blake found Darnay Scott for a touchdown with 10:06 remaining, but the Bengals turned the ball over on downs on their next possession and the Jets ran the final 6:06 off the clock. O'Donnell was 20 of 34 for 212 yards and 3 touchdowns. Blake was 10 of 21 for 166 yards and 2 touchdowns, with 1 interception.

N.Y. Jets	7	17	0	7	—	31
Cincinnati	0	7	0	7	—	14

NYJ — Baxter 2 pass from O'Donnell (Hall kick)
Cin — Pickens 50 pass from Blake (Pelfrey kick)
NYJ — Murrell 12 run (Hall kick)
NYJ — FG Hall 44
NYJ — Johnson 12 pass from O'Donnell (Hall kick)
NYJ — Anderson 8 pass from O'Donnell (Hall kick)
Cin — Scott 26 pass from Blake (Pelfrey kick)

OAKLAND 35, ST. LOUIS 17—at Oakland-Alameda County Coliseum, attendance 42,506. Jeff George threw 4 touchdown passes, 2 each to James Jett and Rickey Dudley, to lead the Raiders to victory. After a scoreless first quarter, a wild second quarter began with Amp Lee catching Tony Banks's 13-yard touchdown pass. Ryan McNeil's interception less than a minute later set up Banks's 3-yard touchdown pass to Aaron Laing. The Raiders responded with George's 8-yard touchdown pass to Jett and, after Eric Turner's interception, a 34-yard touchdown pass to Dudley on third-and-2. A bobbled snap kept the Raiders from tying the score. However, Turner's second interception led to George's third touchdown pass five minutes into the third quarter. The Raiders scored again less than three minutes later to take a 28-14 lead. After Jeff Wilkins's field goal cut the deficit to 28-17, Napoleon Kaufman broke free for a 65-yard run to set up George's fourth touchdown pass. George was 17 of 30 for 219 yards and 4 touchdowns, with 1 interception. Kaufman had 26 carries for 162 yards. Dudley had 5 receptions for 106 yards. Banks was 24 of 49 for 255 yards and 2 touchdowns, with 3 interceptions. Lee had 10 catches for 109 yards.

St. Louis	0	14	0	3	—	17
Oakland	0	13	15	7	—	35

StL — Lee 13 pass from Banks (Wilkins kick)
StL — Laing 3 pass from Banks (Wilkins kick)
Oak — Jett 8 pass from George (Ford kick)
Oak — Dudley 34 pass from George (bad snap)
Oak — Jett 14 pass from George (Williams pass from George)
Oak — Kaufman 1 run (Ford kick)
StL — FG Wilkins 38
Oak — Dudley 5 pass from George (Ford kick)

KANSAS CITY 20, SEATTLE 17 (OT)—at Arrowhead Stadium, attendance 77,877. Jerome Woods's interception in overtime set up Pete Stoyanovich's game-winning field goal as the Chiefs defeated the Seahawks. Todd Peterson's 44-yard field goal gave the Seahawks a 10-0 second-quarter lead, but Marcus Allen scored on an 8-yard touchdown run on the Chiefs' next drive to cut the deficit to 10-7 at halftime. Allen scored again on their first possession of the second half to take a 14-10 lead, but Warren Moon threw his second long touchdown pass of the game three plays later, a 54-yarder to James McKnight, to retake the lead. The Chiefs answered with a 13-play drive capped by Stoyanovich's 29-yard field goal to tie the game with 13:14 remaining. The Seahawks got the ball on their own 15 with 1:18 left and reached the Chiefs' 40, but Peterson's 58-yard field-goal attempt was not good as time expired. On the Seahawks' second overtime possession, Woods intercepted a long pass and returned it to midfield. Allen got a first down on a third-and-1 2-yard run to allow Stoyanovich the game-winning field goal. Elvis Grbac was 24 of 38 for 274 yards, with 3 interceptions. Moon was 19 of 26 for 252 yards and 2 touchdowns, with 1 interception.

Seattle	7	3	7	0	0	—	17
Kansas City	0	7	7	3	3	—	20

Sea — Galloway 41 pass from Moon (Peterson kick)
Sea — FG Peterson 44
KC — Allen 8 run (Stoyanovich kick)
KC — Allen 1 run (Stoyanovich kick)
Sea — McKnight 54 pass from Moon (Peterson kick)
KC — FG Stoyanovich 29
KC — FG Stoyanovich 41

PITTSBURGH 37, TENNESSEE 24—at Three Rivers Stadium, attendance 57,507. Kordell Stewart threw 1 touchdown pass and ran for 2 other scores as the Steelers defeated the Oilers. After missing a field goal on their first possession, the Steelers scored on their next two drives to take a 10-0 lead. Jason Gildon returned Steve McNair's fumble 12 yards for a touchdown. The Oilers responded with a field goal, but Stewart drove the Steelers 83 yards in 6 plays, capped by his 18-yard touchdown pass to Mark Bruener, to take a 24-3 lead. Levon Kirkland intercepted McNair on the next play from scrimmage, and Stewart's 2-yard run with 22 seconds left in the half gave the Steelers a 31-3 lead. Stewart was 16 of 24 for 244 yards and 1 touchdown. McNair was 22 of 43 for 266 yards and 2 touchdowns, with 2 interceptions.

Tennessee	0	6	3	15	—	24
Pittsburgh	10	21	3	3	—	37

Pitt — Stewart 7 run (Johnson kick)
Pitt — FG Johnson 48
Pitt — Gildon 12 fumble return (Johnson kick)
Tenn — FG Del Greco 37
Pitt — Bruener 18 pass from Stewart (Johnson kick)
Pitt — Stewart 2 run (Johnson kick)
Tenn — FG Del Greco 47
Tenn — FG Del Greco 26
Pitt — FG Johnson 25
Pitt — FG Johnson 44
Tenn — Wycheck 10 pass from McNair (Wycheck pass from McNair)
Tenn — Davis 11 pass from McNair (Del Greco kick)

SUNDAY NIGHT, SEPTEMBER 28

MINNESOTA 28, PHILADELPHIA 19—at Hubert H. Humphrey Metrodome, attendance 55,149. Brad Johnson fired 3 touchdown passes and Robert Smith ran for 125 yards and 1 touchdown and caught 1 touchdown pass as well to lead the Vikings to victory. Dewayne Washington's 27-yard interception return to the Vikings' 48 thwarted the Eagles' initial possession. Three plays later Johnson threw a 48-yard touchdown pass to Jake Reed to give Minnesota a 7-0 lead. The Eagles scored on three of their final four possessions of the half but trailed 14-13. The Eagles' defense forced a punt midway through the third quarter, but Mark Seay muffed the punt and Greg Briggs recovered at the Eagles' 16. Smith scored from 14 yards two plays later to give the Vikings a 21-13 lead. The Eagles scored on their next drive, with Ty Detmer's 20-yard touchdown pass to Kevin Turner cutting the deficit to two points, but Detmer's 2-point conversion pass to Seay was incomplete. The Vikings answered immediately, scoring on Johnson's 18-yard touchdown pass to Cris Carter. The Eagles reached the Vikings' 21 with six minutes left but Washington intercepted his second pass of the game to quell Philadelphia's final threat. Johnson was 17 of 32 for 221 yards and 3 touchdowns, with 1 interception. Reed had 6 receptions for 134 yards. Detmer was 28 of 45 for 298 yards and 2 touchdowns, with 2 interceptions. Irving Fryar had 9 catches for 120 yards.

Philadelphia	3	10	6	0	—	19
Minnesota	7	7	7	7	—	28

Minn — Reed 48 pass from Johnson (Murray kick)
Phil — FG Boniol 47
Phil — Fryar 6 pass from Detmer (Boniol kick)
Minn — Smith 12 pass from Johnson (Murray kick)
Phil — FG Boniol 26
Minn — Smith 14 run (Murray kick)
Phil — Turner 20 pass from Detmer (pass failed)
Minn — Carter 18 pass from Johnson (Murray kick)

MONDAY, SEPTEMBER 29

SAN FRANCISCO 34, CAROLINA 21—at Ericsson Stadium, attendance 70,972. Garrison Hearst ran for 141 yards and 1 touchdown as the 49ers controlled the line of scrimmage and defeated the Panthers. Steve Young orchestrated a 12-play, 79-yard drive to begin the game, capped by his 8-yard touchdown pass to Terrell Owens. After Young's 2-yard touchdown run, Merton Hanks intercepted Kerry Collins's pass to set up Gary Anderson's field goal and a 17-0 49ers lead 2:28 into the second quarter. Micheal Barrow's fumble recovery gave the Panthers momentum, and Collins capitalized with a 17-yard touchdown pass to Rae Carruth. Carolina got the ball back before halftime, but Tyronne Drakeford's interception in the final minute set up Anderson's second field goal and gave the 49ers a 20-7 halftime edge. Hanks's second interception of the game sparked a 31-yard touchdown drive late in the third quarter, capped by Hearst's 3-yard run. The Panthers answered with Steve Beuerlein's 8-yard touchdown pass to Raghib Ismail. The 49ers responded with a pounding 15-play, 81-yard drive that featured 14 running plays and ended with Terry Kirby's 3-yard touchdown run. Young was 16 of 24 for 152 yards and 1 touchdown. Collins was 11 of 24 for 126 yards and 1 touchdown, with 3 interceptions. Beuerlein was 9 of 11 for 94 yards and 2 touchdowns. The 49ers ran the ball 49 times for 219 yards while permitting just 17 carries for 44 yards.

San Francisco	7	13	7	7	—	34
Carolina	0	7	0	14	—	21

SF — Owens 8 pass from Young (Anderson kick)
SF — Young 2 run (Anderson kick)
SF — FG Anderson 25
Car — Carruth 17 pass from Collins (Kasay kick)
SF — FG Anderson 48
SF — Hearst 3 run (Anderson kick)
Car — Ismail 8 pass from Beuerlein (Kasay kick)
SF — Kirby 3 run (Anderson kick)
Car — Carrier 20 pass from Beuerlein (Kasay kick)

SIXTH WEEK SUMMARIES

AMERICAN FOOTBALL CONFERENCE

Eastern Division	**W**	**L**	**T**	**Pct.**	**Pts.**	**OP**
New England	4	1	0	.800	143	74
N.Y. Jets	4	2	0	.667	157	106
Buffalo	3	2	0	.600	116	126
Miami	3	2	0	.600	88	91
Indianapolis	0	5	0	.000	66	131
Central Division						
Jacksonville	4	1	0	.800	131	98
Pittsburgh	3	2	0	.600	121	138
Baltimore	3	3	0	.500	161	134
Cincinnati	1	4	0	.200	81	134
Tennessee	1	4	0	.200	84	126
Western Division						
Denver	6	0	0	1.000	190	85
Kansas City	4	2	0	.667	122	110
San Diego	3	3	0	.500	102	126
Seattle	3	3	0	.500	107	134
Oakland	2	4	0	.333	151	148

NATIONAL FOOTBALL CONFERENCE

Eastern Division	**W**	**L**	**T**	**Pct.**	**Pts.**	**OP**
Dallas	3	2	0	.600	124	75
Washington	3	2	0	.600	90	73
N.Y. Giants	3	3	0	.500	104	120
Philadelphia	2	3	0	.400	90	99
Arizona	1	4	0	.200	96	104
Central Division						
Tampa Bay	5	1	0	.833	131	97
Green Bay	4	2	0	.667	144	126
Minnesota	4	2	0	.667	155	141
Detroit	3	3	0	.500	133	120
Chicago	0	6	0	.000	78	175
Western Division						
San Francisco	4	1	0	.800	122	60
Carolina	2	3	0	.400	80	106
St. Louis	2	3	0	.400	94	112
New Orleans	2	4	0	.333	101	139
Atlanta	0	5	0	.000	82	136

SUNDAY, OCTOBER 5

JACKSONVILLE 21, CINCINNATI 13—at ALLTEL Stadium, attendance 67,728. Mark Brunell threw 3 touchdown passes, and the Jaguars defense stopped the Bengals three times on fourth down, as Jacksonville remained in first place. Eric Bieniemy attempted to run on a fake punt on fourth-and-16 from the Bengals' 14 in the first quarter, but he was stopped at the 20-yard line. Three plays later, Brunell threw a 10-yard touchdown pass to Ty Hallock. It was Hallock's first touchdown since 1993. With the score tied 7-7 at halftime, Jacksonville took the second-half kickoff and marched 69 yards, with James Stewart's touchdown catch putting the Jaguars in front 14-7. The Bengals responded with a 10-play, 72-yard drive, capped by Jeff Blake's 8-yard run, but Tony Brackens blocked the extra-point attempt to allow the Jaguars to maintain the lead. Willie Jackson's 12-yard touchdown catch with 8:49 gave the Jaguars a 21-13 lead. After the Bengals had to punt, the Jaguars went on a drive that exceeded six minutes, only to end with Mike Hollis's missed 27-yard field goal with 1:23 left. The Jaguars defense did not allow the Bengals to get further than their own 39 before stopping them on downs. Brunell was 14 of 27 for 164 yards. Blake completed 16 of 27 passes for 232 yards. Neither team had a turnover, but the Bengals committed 11 penalties.

Cincinnati	0	7	6	0	—	13
Jacksonville	7	0	7	7	—	21

Jack — Hallock 10 pass from Brunell (Hollis kick)
Cin — Carter 1 run (Pelfrey kick)
Jack — Stewart 7 pass from Brunell (Hollis kick)
Cin — Blake 8 run (kick blocked)
Jack — Jackson 12 pass from Brunell (Hollis kick)

NEW YORK GIANTS 20, DALLAS 17—at Giants Stadium, attendance 77,137. Tito Wooten intercepted 2 passes and returned one 61 yards for a touchdown, as the Giants held off a late Cowboys rally to move within one-half game of first place. The Cowboys held a 9-6 lead when Wooten's touchdown, with 40 seconds left in the third quarter, gave the Giants their first lead. Amani Toomer's 37-yard punt return and Kevin Smith's pass interference and unsportsmanlike conduct penalties gave the Giants the ball on the 3-yard line. Charles Way scored on the next play to put the Giants ahead 20-9. The Cowboys responded with a 14-play drive, capped by Troy Aikman's 2-yard touchdown pass to Anthony Miller. The ensuing 2-point conversion pass to Eric Bjornson cut the deficit to 3 points. The Cowboys got the ball back on their own 36 with 48 seconds to play. A third-down pass to Stepfret Williams put the Cowboys into Giants territory. Two plays later, with 18 seconds left, Aikman hit Bjornson with a pass over the middle for 32 yards. Out of the timeouts, the Cowboys scrambled to get to the line of scrimmage to stop the clock. Aikman was able to spike the ball with one second left, but right tackle Erik Williams was not set, and the game ended. The Cowboys dominated the game statistically, in first downs (27-13), total yards (428-166), and time of possession (40:37-19:23). Danny Kanell, who was 10 of 17 for 101 yards, replaced an injured Dave Brown in the first half and directed the Giants' three scoring drives. Aikman was 34 of 52 for 317 yards, with 2 interceptions.

Dallas	3	3	3	8	—	17
N.Y. Giants	0	3	10	7	—	20

Dall — FG Cunningham 38
Dall — FG Cunningham 31
NYG — FG Daluiso 27
NYG — FG Daluiso 22
Dall — FG Cunningham 27
NYG — Wooten 61 interception return (Daluiso kick)
NYG — Way 3 run (Daluiso kick)
Dall — Miller 2 pass from Aikman (Bjornson pass from Aikman)

BUFFALO 22, DETROIT 13—at Rich Stadium, attendance 78,025. Bruce Smith and Phil Hansen tackled Barry Sanders in the end zone for a safety with 2:12 left, and Antowain Smith raced 56 yards for a touchdown 25 seconds later, to propel the Bills to victory. After Jason Hanson's first field goal tied the game 3-3, Eric Moulds ran the ensuing kickoff back 53 yards. Two plays later, Todd Collins threw a 43-yard touchdown pass to Andre Reed. The Bills' special teams made another big play when Ken Irvin blocked John Jett's punt with 11 seconds left in the half, setting up Steve Christie's second field goal. In the fourth quarter, Scott Mitchell and Herman Moore connected for 50 yards on 2 pass plays to set up Mitchell's 8-yard touchdown scramble to tie the score with 5:54 left. The Bills had to punt on their next possession, but Eric Smedley downed Chris Mohr's punt at the 1-yard line with 2:22 left. With left tackle Ray Roberts having left the game with an injury, Bruce Smith and Hansen stopped Sanders for a safety on a running play with 2:12 left. Two plays after the free kick, Antowain Smith broke free for a 56-yard touchdown to ice the game. Collins was 11 of 18 for 122 yards. Mitchell completed 20 of 38 passes for 221 yards. Moore had 8 receptions for 116 yards, while Sanders rushed for 107 yards on 25 carries. The Lions' defense permitted the Bills just 10 first downs and a 2-for-11 third-down conversion rate.

Detroit	0	3	3	7	—	13
Buffalo	3	10	0	9	—	22

Buff — FG Christie 47
Det — FG Hanson 28
Buff — Reed 43 pass from Collins (Christie kick)
Buff — FG Christie 33
Det — FG Hanson 30
Det — Mitchell 8 run (Hanson kick)
Buff — Safety, B. Smith and Hansen tackled Sanders in end zone
Buff — A. Smith 56 run (Christie kick)

MIAMI 17, KANSAS CITY 14—at Pro Player Stadium, attendance 71,794. Olindo Mare kicked a 26-yard field goal, and Anthony Harris's tackle stopped the Chiefs on fourth down with less than two minutes remaining, to give the Dolphins the victory. Dan Marino and O.J. McDuffie had pass plays of 18 and 25 yards to set up Karim Abdul-Jabbar's touchdown run. After Andre Rison nimbly kept his toes inbounds while catching a 16-yard touchdown pass from Elvis Grbac to tie the game, a short punt enabled Grbac to throw a 21-yard touchdown pass to Tony Gonzalez. Miami responded with a 95-yard drive, including 27- and 28-yard passes from Marino to Troy Drayton, capped by Marino's 7-yard touchdown pass to Bernie Parmalee to tie the game at halftime. The game remained tied until the fourth quarter when Mare, who had missed from 41 yards in the third quarter, drilled a 26-yard field goal with 5:40 remaining. The Chiefs drove into Dolphins territory, but on fourth-and-3 from the 39 Grbac threw a swing pass to Marcus Allen, but Anthony Harris tackled him shy of the first down to preserve the victory. Marino was 19 of 31 for 259 yards. Grbac completed 23 of 30 passes for 177 yards. The Dolphins defense held the Chiefs to 96 yards, marking the first time this season Kansas City did not exceed 100 rushing yards. Neither team committed a turnover. The win marked the 300th victory in Dolphins history. The loss snapped a four-game winning streak for the Chiefs.

Kansas City	0	14	0	0	—	14
Miami	7	7	0	3	—	17

Mia — Abdul-Jabbar 10 run (Mare kick)
KC — Rison 16 pass from Grbac (Stoyanovich kick)
KC — Gonzalez 21 pass from Grbac (Stoyanovich kick)
Mia — Parmalee 7 pass from Marino (Mare kick)
Mia — FG Mare 26

MINNESOTA 20, ARIZONA 19—at Sun Devil Stadium, attendance 45,550. Andrew Glover caught a touchdown pass and also had a 43-yard reception to set up Eddie Murray's game-winning field goal with 10 seconds remaining to lift the Vikings to a comeback victory. Trailing 10-3, the Cardinals scored 10 points in the final 1:16 of the first half when Kent Graham threw a 33-yard touchdown pass to Chris Gedney, and J.J. McCleskey's interception set up Kevin Butler's second field goal. After Vikings holder Mitch Berger bobbled the snap on an aborted 39-yard field-goal attempt in the third quarter, Butler made 2 field goals, including a 49-yard kick with 10:22 remaining to give the Cardinals a 19-10 lead. The Vikings responded with a 13-play, 85-yard drive capped by Brad Johnson's 1-yard touchdown pass to Cris Carter with 4:05 left. Kevin Williams returned the ensuing kickoff to the Vikings 45-yard line, and the Cardinals drove downfield. LeShon Johnson ran 9 yards on first down down to the Vikings 6-yard line with 1:49 remaining, but he then lost a yard on second down, and the Vikings defense forced Leeland McElroy to lose 7 yards on third down. Butler, who was 4-for-4 on the day, missed a 31-yard field goal with 52 seconds left. Johnson completed short passes to Robert Smith and Carter before he found Glover open over the middle for 43 yards down to the 20-yard line. Murray, who was playing in just his second game for the team, made the winning 38-yard kick with 10 seconds left. Johnson was 25 of 39 for 292 yards and 2 touchdowns, with 2 interceptions. Graham was 22 of 38 for 293 yards and 1 touchdown. In the fourth quarter Murray tied the NFL record by converting his 234th consecutive extra point. The Cardinals' four losses are by a combined 11 points.

Minnesota	7	3	0	10	—	20
Arizona	3	10	3	3	—	19

Minn — Glover 18 pass from Johnson (Murray kick)
Ariz — FG Butler 23
Minn — FG Murray 49
Ariz — Gedney 33 pass from Graham (Butler kick)
Ariz — FG Butler 23
Ariz — FG Butler 28
Ariz — FG Butler 49
Minn — Carter 1 pass from Johnson (Murray kick)
Minn — FG Murray 38

NEW YORK JETS 16, INDIANAPOLIS 12—at RCA Dome, attendance 48,295. Adrian Murrell rushed for 99 yards and a touchdown as the Jets extended their winning streak to three games. The Jets drove 92 yards on their first possession, capped by Murrell's 24-yard burst up the middle, to take a 7-0 lead. Two field goals by rookie John Hall gave the Jets a 13-0 halftime edge. Marvin Harrison's punt return in the third quarter set up Cary Blanchard's 48-yard field goal to put the Colts on the board. The Jets drove deep into Colts territory late in the third quarter, but Carlton Gray intercepted Neil O'Donnell's pass at the 14-yard line. The turnover sparked a 12-play, 86-yard drive that finished with Marshall Faulk scoring from the 1-yard line to cut the deficit to 13-10 with 10:37 left. The Colts got the ball back with 7:39 left on their own 20 after a punt, but Pepper Johnson intercepted Paul Justin's pass, setting up Hall's third field goal. The Colts reached the Jets 25, but Justin's fourth-and-2 pass fell incomplete. From fourth down on their own 34 with 16 seconds left, O'Donnell consumed some clock before throwing the ball out of the end zone for a safety with 10 seconds left. Aaron Glenn intecepted Justin's Hail Mary pass to end the game. O'Donnell was 15 of 28 for 129 yards, with 1 interception. Harbaugh started and was 8 of 12 for 98 yards, with 1 interception before being replaced by Justin, who was 16 of 33 for 173 yards and 2 interceptions.

N.Y. Jets	7	6	0	3	—	16
Indianapolis	0	0	3	9	—	12

NYJ — Murrell 24 run (Hall kick)
NYJ — FG Hall 53
NYJ — FG Hall 37
Ind — FG Blanchard 48
Ind — Faulk 1 run (Blanchard kick)
NYJ — FG Hall 23
Ind — Safety, O'Donnell threw the ball out of the end zone

PITTSBURGH 42, BALTIMORE 34—at Memorial Stadium, attendance 64,421. Kordell Stewart overcame 3 first-half interceptions to throw 3 touchdown passes and run for 2 others as the Steelers came back to defeat the Ravens before the largest home crowd in franchise history. The Ravens benefitted from Stewart's 3 errant passes to score their final 17 points of the first half to take a 24-7 halftime lead. The Steelers faked a reverse on the second half's opening kickoff, and Will Blackwell raced 97 yards for his first career touchdown. Stewart's 8-yard touchdown pass to Charles Johnson capped a 90-yard drive and pulled the Steelers within 24-21. Mike Vrabel's sack forced Testaverde to fumble, and Kevin Henry recovered the ball to set up Mark Bruener's 4-yard touchdown catch with 9:31 left to give the Steelers their first lead. After forcing a punt, Stewart completed a 63-yard pass to Yancey Thigpen on third-and-8 to set up Charles Johnson's second touchdown catch, giving the Steelers a 35-24 lead with 3:04 left. Jermaine Lewis's 38-yard kickoff return and a 29-yard pass interference penalty on Donnell Woolford allowed Testaverde to throw a 10-yard touchdown pass to Derrick Alexander with 2:27 remaining. The ensuing 2-point conversion pass to Earnest Byner cut the deficit to three points. On third-and-4 from their own 26, Stewart faked a handoff and raced 74 yards for a touchdown with 1:47 to play. Lewis returned the ensuing kickoff 46 yards, and the Ravens were about to score again, but Chris Oldham forced Eric Green to fumble on the 8-yard line, and Myron Bell recovered the ball with 59 seconds left. Punter Josh Miller inadvertently stepped on the back line of the end zone, resulting in a safety with 11 seconds left, but Woolford intercepted Testaverde's Hail Mary pass at the 6-yard line as time expired. Stewart was 18 of 28 for 246 yards and 3 touchdowns, with 3 interceptions. Jerome Bettis had 28 carries for 137 yards, while Thigpen had 162 receiving yards on 7 catches. Testaverde was 28 of 47 for 290 yards and 3 touchdowns, with 2 interceptions. The win broke a streak of five consecutive divisional road losses for the Steelers, while the loss marked the tenth time in their last 17 games that the Ravens had lost after leading in the second half.

Pittsburgh	0	7	14	21	—	42
Baltimore	14	10	0	10	—	34

Balt — Green 22 pass from Testaverde (Stover kick)
Balt — Morris 1 run (Stover kick)
Balt — Kinchen 24 pass from Testaverde (Stover kick)
Pitt — Stewart 1 run (N. Johnson kick)
Balt — FG Stover 34
Pitt — Blackwell 97 kickoff return (N. Johnson kick)
Pitt — C. Johnson 8 pass from Stewart (N. Johnson kick)
Pitt — Bruener 4 pass from Stewart (N. Johnson kick)
Pitt — C. Johnson17 pass from Stewart (N. Johnson kick)
Balt — Alexander 10 pass from Testaverde (Byner pass from Testaverde)
Pitt — Stewart 74 run (N. Johnson kick)
Balt — Safety, Miller ran out of end zone

SAN DIEGO 25, OAKLAND 10—at Oakland-Alameda County Coliseum, attendance 43,648. Gary Brown rushed for 181 yards and Greg Davis kicked 6 field goals to give the Chargers their second consecutive victory. Davis kicked 3 first-half field goals—the first one aided by Raiders punter Leo Araguz dropping the snap and giving the Chargers the ball at the Raiders 10—to give San Diego a 9-0 edge. A 36-yard pass-interference penalty on Terrance Shaw gave the Raiders the ball on the 1-yard line with 19 seconds left in the half. Jeff George threw an apparent touchdown pass to Tim Brown on third down, but an illegal motion penalty nullified the play, and the Raiders had to settle for Cole Ford's field goal. After another Davis field goal, Napoleon Kaufman took a short pass over the middle and burst through the Chargers' secondary for a touchdown to cut the deficit to 12-10. But the Chargers responded with a 80-yard drive, which featured a 32-yard run by Gary Brown to the 1-yard line, setting up Brown's short touchdown run. Davis, who was in his second game with the Chargers John Carney healed a knee injury, tied a club record with 6 field goals. Brown, who was out of football last season, had the second-biggest rushing day of his career. The Chargers' defense held the Raiders to just 11 first downs, none rushing, and sacked Jeff George 6 times, 2 by Raylee Johnson. San Diego outgained Oakland on the ground (180-13) and consumed nearly 39 minutes off the clock. Stan Humphries was 18 of 33 for 226 yards. George was 19 of 42 for 271 yards.

San Diego	6	3	10	6	—	25
Oakland	0	3	7	0	—	10

SD — FG Davis 30
SD — FG Davis 22
SD — FG Davis 38
Oak — FG Ford 24
SD — FG Davis 43
Oak — Kaufman 70 pass from George (Ford kick)
SD — Brown 1 run (Davis kick)
SD — FG Davis 33
SD — FG Davis 33

GREEN BAY 21, TAMPA BAY 16—at Lambeau Field, attendance 60,100. Brett Favre threw 2 touchdown passes to Antonio Freeman, and Gabe Wilkins returned an interception 77 yards for a touchdown, as the Buccaneers suffered their first loss of the season. Tampa Bay scored on its first possession, with Michael Husted booting a 23-yard field goal. The Packers' defense stepped up, as Tyrone Williams forced Warrick Dunn to fumble on the next possession. Brian Williams recovered the ball, and Favre threw a 31-yard touchdown pass to Freeman three plays later. Chidi Ahanotu's fumble recovery at the Packers 18 gave the Buccaneers an opportunity to retake the lead, but on the next play Dilfer threw an interception to Wilkins, who hurdled Dilfer en route to his 77-yard touchdown return. A short punt late in the first half gave the Packers the ball at midfield, and Favre threw his second touchdown pass to Freeman 44 seconds before halftime to take a 21-3 halftime lead. In the third quarter, Hardy Nickerson blocked Ryan Longwell's 47-yard field-goal attempt, and the Buccaneers quickly drove downfield, with Mike Alstott's 1-yard touchdown run cutting the deficit to 21-10. Dunn sparked the Buccaneers next possession with a 44-yard burst, and finished it with a 2-yard touchdown run. Dilfer's pass to Karl Williams on the 2-point conversion fell short, leaving the score at 21-16. The Buccaneers reached the Packers' 42 before being stopped on downs with 1:52 remaining. Tampa Bay got the ball back in the final 38 seconds, but was unable to cross midfield. Favre was 21 of 31 for 191 yards. Dilfer was 16 of 29 for 179 yards, with 1 interception. Dunn had 125 rushing yards. The Buccaneers' defense permitted the Packers just 11 first downs and a 2-for-11 third-down conversion rate.

Tampa Bay	3	0	7	6	—	16
Green Bay	0	21	0	0	—	21

TB — FG Husted 23
GB — Freeman 31 pass from Favre (Longwell kick)
GB — Wilkins 77 interception return (Longwell kick)
GB — Freeman 6 pass from Favre (Longwell kick)
TB — Alstott 1 run (Husted kick)
TB — Dunn 2 run (pass failed)

SEATTLE 16, TENNESSEE 13—at Kingdome, attendance 49,897. Steve Broussard had 2 long touchdown runs to propel the Seahawks to a comeback victory. The Seahawks, who were playing without injured Chris Warren and Joey Galloway, trailed 10-0 in the third quarter when Warren Moon's 25-yard pass to Carlester Crumpler, plus a 15-yard roughing the passer penalty, on third-and-10 set up Todd Peterson's 38-yard field goal. After forcing a punt, Broussard raced 77 yards on the next play to tie the game. Early in the fourth quarter, Moon completed a 8-yard pass to Mike Pritchard on third-and-6 for a first down, and Broussard ran 43 yards for a touchdown to give the Seahawks the lead. Holder Rich Tuten mishandled the extra point, and Al Del Greco's field goal with 3:41 to play cut the advantage to just three points. However, faced with a third-and-9 situation with 1:49 to play, Lamar Smith gained 17 yards to ice the game. Moon was 27 of 40 for 260 yards. Broussard finished with 138 yards on just 6 carries. McNair was 12 of 28 for 101 yards, with 2 interceptions.

Tennessee	3	7	0	3	—	13
Seattle	0	0	10	6	—	16

Tenn — FG Del Greco 37
Tenn — E. George 11 pass from McNair (Del Greco kick)
Sea — FG Peterson 38
Sea — Broussard 77 run (Peterson kick)
Sea — Broussard 43 run (dropped hold)
Tenn — FG Del Greco 43

PHILADELPHIA 24, WASHINGTON 10—at Veterans Stadium, attendance 67,008. Ricky Watters had 104 rushing yards and 2 touchdowns as the Eagles rolled up 449 total yards and defeated the first-place Redskins. The Eagles had touchdown drives of 81 and 75 yards in the first half, and the Redskins only score was set up by Derek Smith's fumble recovery at the Eagles' 23-yard line. Trailing 17-3 in the third quartter, Michael Westbrook's 38-yard catch to the 5-yard line set up Gus Frerotte's 5-yard touchdown pass to Terry Allen. The Eagles responded with Ty Detmer and Irving Fryar hooking up for 26- and 33-yard pass plays to set up Watters's second touchdown run. Washington was stopped on the Eagles 33 with 5:16 to play, and Philadelphia ran out the remainder of the clock. Detmer was 17 of 27 for 246 yards. Frerotte was 16 of 37 for 216 yards and 1 touchdown, with an interception. The Eagles controlled the clock (39:22-20:38), and amassed 203 rushing yards on 50 carries. The Redskins had just 12 carries for 30 yards, all by Allen.

Washington	0	3	7	0	—	10
Philadelphia	7	10	0	7	—	24

Phil — Detmer 3 run (Boniol kick)
Phil — Watters 1 run (Boniol kick)
Wash — FG Blanton 37
Phil — FG Boniol 34
Wash — Allen 5 pass from Frerotte (Blanton kick)
Phil — Watters 1 run (Boniol kick)

SUNDAY NIGHT, OCTOBER 5

NEW ORLEANS 20, CHICAGO 17—at Soldier Field, attendance 58,865. Heath Shuler threw an 89-yard touchdown pass to Randal Hill, the longest in team history, with 5:39 remaining to give the Saints a victory on a night that featured the return of former Bears coach Mike Ditka. Both defenses dominated the first half, as the teams combined for more punts (14) than completed passes (11), and the game was tied 3-3 at intermission. Mario Bates broke through for a 49-yard touchdown run in the opening minutes of the third quarter, and a 15-yard face-masking penalty and 27-yard run by Ray Zellars set up Doug Brien's second field goal. Erik Kramer, who replaced an ineffective Rick Mirer in the third quarter, took advantage of excellent field position, set up by Tyrone Hughes's punt return, and scored on a 1-yard quarterback sneak with 7:44 left. It was the Bears' first touchdown in 15 quarters. Jim Flanigan recovered Shuler's fumble at the 8-yard line moments later, setting up Raymont Harris's 1-yard plunge to give the Bears the lead with 6:02 remaining. After a penalty on the ensuing kickoff pushed the Saints back to the 11-yard line, Shuler connected deep down the left sideline to Hill for the winning touchdown. Kramer's fourth-and-14 pass to Bobby Engram in the final minutes went for 13 yards, thus ending the Bears' chances. Shuler was 9 of 23 for 195 yards. Mirer was 7 of 16 for 58 yards before being replaced by Kramer, who was 12 of 20 for 131 yards. New Orleans had 5 quarterback sacks, while Barry Minter had both of the Bears' sacks. The Saints won despite failing to convert a first down on all 12 third-down attempts.

New Orleans	0	3	10	7	—	20
Chicago	3	0	0	14	—	17

Chi — FG Jaeger 23
NO — FG Brien 38
NO — Bates 49 run (Brien kick)
NO — FG Brien 48
Chi — Kramer 1 run (Jaeger kick)
Chi — Harris 1 run (Jaeger kick)
NO — Hill 89 pass from Shuler (Brien kick)

MONDAY, OCTOBER 6

DENVER 34, NEW ENGLAND 13—at Denver Mile High Stadium, attendance 75,821. Terrell Davis rushed for 171 yards and 2 touchdowns as the Broncos prevailed in the battle of the last two unbeaten teams. The Patriots were driving downfield on the game's first possession when John Mobley forced Terry Glenn to fumble. Steve Atwater recovered the ball at the 25-yard line, and Davis scored from 2 yards out 11 plays later. A punt later in the quarter pinned the Patriots back to the 8-yard line, and Mobley intercepted Drew Bledsoe's pass on the next play and went 13 yards for the touchdown. Willie Clay's 27-yard interception return in the second quarter set up Bledsoe's 44-yard touchdown pass to Keith Byars on the next play. Adam Vinatieri booted 2 field goals, the second of which was set up by another Clay interception, to cut the deficit to 14-13 at halftime. The Broncos took the second-half kickoff and marched 80 yards in 10 plays, the key play being John Elway's 30-yard pass to Rod Smith on third-and-10, to set up Elway's quarterback sneak. On their next possession, a 39-yard pass interference penalty on Jimmy Hitchcock led to Scott Bentley's first NFL field goal. After forcing a punt, Smith caught a 47-yard pass from Elway, allowing Davis to score his second touchdown. Bentley, who was kicking for injured Jason Elam, added a 33-yard field goal in the fourth quarter to finish the scoring. Elway was 13 of 27 for 196 yards, with 2 interceptions. Smith had 5 receptions for 130 receiving yards. Bledsoe was 20 of 41 for 234 yards and 1 touchdown, with 1 interception. Maa Tanuvasa had 3 sacks for the Broncos' defense. Denver had more first downs (25-13) and total yards (380-262).

New England	0	13	0	0	—	13
Denver	14	0	17	3	—	34

Den — Davis 2 run (Bentley kick)
Den — Mobley 13 interception return (Bentley kick)
NE — Byars 44 pass from Bledsoe (Vinatieri kick)
NE — FG Vinatieri 26
NE — FG Vinatieri 49
Den — Elway 1 run (Bentley kick)
Den — FG Bentley 21
Den — Davis 1 run (Bentley kick)
Den — FG Bentley 33

SEVENTH WEEK SUMMARIES

AMERICAN FOOTBALL CONFERENCE

Eastern Division	W	L	T	Pct.	Pts.	OP
New England	5	1	0	.833	176	80
Miami	4	2	0	.667	119	111
N.Y. Jets	4	3	0	.571	177	137
Buffalo	3	3	0	.500	122	159
Indianapolis	0	6	0	.000	88	155
Central Division						
Jacksonville	5	1	0	.833	169	119
Pittsburgh	4	2	0	.667	145	160
Baltimore	3	3	0	.500	161	134
Tennessee	2	4	0	.333	114	133
Cincinnati	1	5	0	.167	88	164
Western Division						
Denver	6	0	0	1.000	190	85
Kansas City	4	2	0	.667	122	110
San Diego	3	3	0	.500	102	126
Seattle	3	3	0	.500	107	134
Oakland	2	4	0	.333	151	148

NATIONAL FOOTBALL CONFERENCE

Eastern Division	W	L	T	Pct.	Pts.	OP
Washington	4	2	0	.667	111	89
N.Y. Giants	4	3	0	.571	131	133
Dallas	3	3	0	.500	140	96
Philadelphia	2	4	0	.333	111	137
Arizona	1	5	0	.167	109	131
Central Division						
Green Bay	5	2	0	.714	168	149
Minnesota	5	2	0	.714	176	155
Tampa Bay	5	2	0	.714	140	124
Detroit	4	3	0	.571	160	129
Chicago	0	7	0	.000	101	199

Western Division

San Francisco	5	1	0	.833	152	70
Carolina	2	4	0	.333	94	127
St. Louis	2	4	0	.333	104	142
New Orleans	2	5	0	.286	118	162
Atlanta	1	5	0	.143	105	153

SUNDAY, OCTOBER 12

ATLANTA 23, NEW ORLEANS 17—at Louisiana Superdome, attendance 65,619. Chuck Smith had 5 of the Falcons club-record 10 sacks, and Michael Booker recorded 2 interceptions as Atlanta won its first game of the season. Todd Kinchen's 10-yard punt return gave the Falcons the ball in Saints territory, leading to the first of Morten Andersen's three field goals against his former team. Heath Shuler fumbled the snap from center on the next play. Rhett Hall recovered it, and Chris Chandler threw a 9-yard touchdown pass to Bert Emanuel to put the Falcons ahead 10-0. A 38-yard pass from Shuler to Andre Hastings set up Doug Brien's 35-yard field goal to cut the deficit to 10-3. Booker's first interception set up Andersen's second field goal, and, after a Saints punt was downed with seven seconds left in the half at the Falcons' 44, Chander threw an 18-yard pass to Terance Mathis to enable Andersen to boot a 55-yard field goal as the half expired. Danny Wuerffel replaced Shuler at halftime, only to be sacked by Smith and fumble on third play of the second half. Dan Owens recovered it and fell forward to the 6-yard line, setting up Jamal Anderson's 2-yard run. Joe Johnson's fumble recovery at the Falcons' 30 led to Wuerffel's 16-yard touchdown pass to Hastings. Byron Hanspard fumbled the ensuing kickoff return, and Brett Bech recovered at the 20-yard line. Mario Bates's touchdown run cut the deficit to six points with 11:30 to play. The Saints got the ball back twice, but Smith sacked Wuerffel on third-and-5 from the Falcons' 36 with six minutes left to force a punt, and Booker grabbed his second interception on fourth down with 1:18 remaining to allow Chandler to run out the clock. Chandler was 10 of 22 for 117 yards and 1 touchdown. Shuler was 5 of 9 for 55 yards, with 1 interception, before Wuerffel was 9 of 13 for 120 yards and 1 touchdown, with 1 interception. Neither offense exceeded 180 total yards, and the defenses permitted just 6 of 26 third-down conversions (2 of 13 by the Saints) to be successful.

Atlanta	10	6	7	0	—	23
New Orleans	0	3	0	14	—	17

Atl — FG Andersen 25
Atl — Emanuel 9 pass from Chandler (Andersen kick)
NO — FG Brien 35
Atl — FG Andersen 32
Atl — FG Andersen 55
Atl — Anderson 2 run (Andersen kick)
NO — Hastings 16 pass from Wuerffel (Brien kick)
NO — Bates 1 run (Brien kick)

NEW ENGLAND 33, BUFFALO 6—at Foxboro Stadium, attendance 59,802. Drew Bledsoe threw 2 touchdown passes and Adam Vinatieri booted 4 field goals as the Patriots posted their ninth consecutive victory against AFC East teams. After forcing a punt on the Bills' initial possession, Bledsoe put the Patriots on the board with a 20-yard touchdown pass to Ben Coates. Tedy Bruschi sacked Todd Collins on the Bills' next possession, knocking him out of the game. Billy Joe Hobert entered and threw interceptions, to Willie Clay and Ty Law, on 2 of his first 3 pass attempts, seting up Vinatieri's first 2 field goals. Derrick Cullors's 33-yard kickoff return to start the second half led to Vinatieri's fourth field goal, and David Meggett's 29-yard punt return moments later led to Curtis Martin's 26-yard touchdown run and a 26-0 lead with 10:42 left in the third quarter. The Patriots scored on their next drive as well, with Bledsoe's 4-yard scoring pass to Keith Byars giving the Patriots a 33-0 lead. Darick Holmes scored on the Bills next possession, but Buffalo could get no closer than the Patriots' 47 the remainder of the game. The Patriots defense permitted the Bills to convert just 1 of 14 third-down opportunities, and intercepted 4 passes. Bledsoe was 14 of 27 for 181 yards and 2 touchdowns, with 1 interception. Hobert was 17 of 30 for 133 yards, with 2 interceptions, before he was replaced in the fourth quarter by Alex Van Pelt, who threw 2 interceptions out of 7 pass attempts. The Patriots improved to 4-0 at home, outscoring their opponents 132-40.

Buffalo	0	0	0	6	—	6
New England	10	6	17	0	—	33

NE — Coates 20 pass from Bledsoe (Vinatieri kick)
NE — FG Viantieri 20
NE — FG Vinatieri 23
NE — FG Vinatieri 41
NE — FG Vinatieri 52
NE — Martin 26 run (Vinatieri kick)
NE — Byars 4 pass from Bledsoe (Vinatieri kick)
Buff — Holmes 1 run (run failed)

MINNESOTA 21, CAROLINA 14—at Hubert H. Humphrey Metrodome, attendance 62,625. Brad Johnson threw 2 touchdown passes, including one to himself, and Robert Smith scored the winning touchdown with 3:47 remaining as the Vikings pulled into a three-way tie for first place in the NFC Central. Lamar Lathon intercepted a pass deep in Panthers territory to halt the Vikings' first drive. But the Vikings struck first, on Johnson's 6-yard touchdown pass to Cris Carter. The Panthers responded with a 10-play, 76-yard drive, capped by Steve Beuerlein's 16-yard touchdown pass to Wesley Walls to tie the game at halftime. The Vikings concluded a 16-play, 91-yard drive, that consumed 9:26, in the opening minute of the fourth quarter when Johnson's pass was batted by Greg Kragen at the line of scrimmage, but Johnson caught the ball and ran into the end zone, the first time in NFC history a quarterback caught his own touchdown pass. The Panthers once again responded immediately, with Rae Carruth catching his first career touchdown pass midway through the fourth quarter to tie the game 14-14. The Panthers forced the Vikings to punt, but Ed McDaniel forced Carruth to fumble on the next play. Fernando Smith recovered the ball and ran 6 yards to the Panthers' 45. Two plays later, Johnson threw a 38-yard pass to Matthew Hatchette on third down, setting up Smith's winning touchdown run. Carolina got as close as the Vikings' 38, but John Randle sacked Beuerlein on first down, and he threw three consecutive incompletions to turn the ball over on downs. Johnson was 17 of 34 for 203 yards and 2 touchdowns, with 1 interception. Smith had 23 carries for 120 rushing yards. Beuerlein was 19 of 35 for 227 yards and 2 touchdowns. Carruth had 6 receptions for 107 yards. The Panthers' defense recorded 5 sacks, while the Vikings' defense forced 3 turnovers.

Carolina	0	7	0	7	—	14
Minnesota	0	7	0	14	—	21

Minn — Carter 6 pass from B. Johnson (Murray kick)
Car — Walls 16 pass from Beuerlein (Kasay kick)
Minn — B. Johnson 3 pass from B. Johnson (Murray kick)
Car — Carruth 5 pass from Beuerlein (Kasay kick)
Minn — R. Smith 4 run (Murray kick)

TENNESSEE 30, CINCINNATI 7—at Liberty Bowl Memorial Stadium, attendance 17,071. Steve McNair threw 3 touchdown passes as the Oilers broke their four-game losing streak. McNair's first touchdown pass, a 9-yard toss to Willie Davis, was started by Joe Bowden's fumble recovery at the Oilers' 40 and set up by his 21-yard pass to Frank Wycheck. Just before halftime, McNair completed a 24-yard pass to Davis on third down before scrambling to his right and finding Wycheck open downfield for a 39-yard touchdown. The Oilers held onto the ball for at least five minutes each of their first three possessions of the second half, and added a 4:21 drive on their fourth possession, to put the game away. Corey Dillon broke free for a 21-yard touchdown run with 2:08 remaining to avert the shutout. The Oilers had more first downs (26-14), total yards (391-191), and time of possession (37:12-22:48). McNair was 16 of 30 for 199 yards and 3 touchdowns. Eddie George gained 106 yards. Jeff Blake was 14 of 27 for 130 yards before Boomer Esiason replaced him and drove the Bengals to their lone touchdown.

Cincinnati	0	0	0	7	—	7
Tennessee	7	7	6	10	—	30

Tenn — W. Davis 9 pass from McNair (Del Greco kick)
Tenn — Wycheck 39 pass from McNair (Del Greco kick)
Tenn — FG Del Greco 47
Tenn — FG Del Greco 45
Tenn — W. Davis 10 pass from McNair (Del Greco kick)
Tenn — FG Del Greco 19
Cin — Dillon 21 run (Pelfrey kick)

DETROIT 27, TAMPA BAY 9—at Houlihan's Stadium, attendance 72,095. Barry Sanders scored 3 touchdowns and became the first player in NFL history with 2 runs of at least 80 yards in the same game as the Lions pulled within one game of first place in the NFC Central. Tampa Bay drove 51 yards on its first possession, concluding with a 25-yard field goal by Michael Husted. Later in the quarter, Sanders raced 80 yards for his first touchdown. On the next drive, Warrick Dunn took a short pass in the flat and raced 59 yards down the left sideline for a touchdown, but a bad hold by Steve Walsh led to a missed extra point. Scott Mitchell completed 4 of 5 passes during the final 1:07 of the first half, allowing Jason Hanson's 34-yard field goal to give the Lions a 10-9 halftime edge. Following a third-quarter punt, Sanders went 82 yards down the right sideline, cutting to the middle of the field behind good downfield blocking by Johnnie Morton. Glyn Milburn's 40-yard punt return set up Hanson's second field goal, and Mitchell's 79-yard pass to Herman Moore set up Sanders's third touchdown on a pass from Mitchell midway through the fourth quarter. Mitchell was 16 of 20 for 222 yards and 1 touchdown. Dilfer was 17 of 31 for 237 yards and 1 touchdown, with 2 interceptions. The Lions averaged 7.8 yards per play.

Detroit	7	3	7	10	—	27
Tampa Bay	9	0	0	0	—	9

TB — FG Husted 25
Det — Sanders 80 run (Hanson kick)
TB — Dunn 59 pass from Dilfer (kick failed)
Det — FG Hanson 34
Det — Sanders 82 run (Hanson kick)
Det — FG Hanson 39
Det — Sanders 7 pass from Mitchell (Hanson kick)

GREEN BAY 24, CHICAGO 23—at Soldier Field, attendance 62,212. Brett Favre threw 3 touchdown passes, and the Packers watched the Bears miss a possible game-winning 2-point conversion attempt, as Green Bay moved into a three-way first-place tie in the NFC Central. Walt Harris's interception on the third play of the game led to Raymont Harris's 1-yard touchdown run three plays later to give the Bears a 7-0 lead. Erik Kramer, who was renamed the Bears' starting quarterback earlier in the week, completed 15-yard passes to Keith Jennings and Ryan Wetnight to set up Jeff Jaeger's 41-yard field goal. The Packers scored twice before halftime, the second touchdown spurred by Tyrone Williams's 25-yard interception return, giving Green Bay a 14-10 halftime lead. The Bears drove 73 yards with the second-half kickoff, keyed by Kramer's quarterback sneak in Bears territory on fourth-and-1 and a 37-yard pass to Curtis Conway, who was playing in his first game of the season after recovering from a broken collarbone, and retook the lead on Kramer's 3-yard run. Later in the quarter, Favre completed 4 of 6 passes for 47 yards on a 55-yard drive, culminating with his second touchdown pass to Mark Chmura. Bernardo Harris's interception led to Ryan Longwell's 37-yard field goal with 2:38 left, giving the Packers a 24-17 lead. Kramer then connected on passes to Conway, Chris Penn, and Mark Engram, setting up a 22-yard touchdown pass to Penn with 1:54 remaining. Trailing by 1 point, the winless Bears went for a 2-point conversion, but Kramer's pass to Harris in the flat fell incomplete. Jeff Thomason recovered the onside kick, allowing the Packers to run out the clock. Favre completed 19 of 35 passes for 177 yards and 3 touchdowns, with 1 interception. Kramer was 22 of 35 for 232 yards and 1 touchdown, with 2 interceptions. Harris tallied 101 rushing yards. The Packers swept the Bears for the fourth consecutive season.

Green Bay	0	14	7	3	—	24
Chicago	10	0	7	6	—	23

Chi — Harris 1 run (Jaeger kick)
Chi — FG Jaeger 41
GB — Chmura 2 pass from Favre (Longwell kick)
GB — Levens 1 pass from Favre (Longwell kick)
Chi — Kramer 3 run (Jaeger kick)
GB — Chmura 12 pass from Favre (Longwell kick)
GB — FG Longwell 37
Chi — Penn 22 pass from Kramer (pass failed)

MIAMI 31, NEW YORK JETS 20—at Giants Stadium, attendance 75,601. Dan Marino threw for 372 yards and 2 touchdowns as the Dolphins rattled off 24 consecutive points en route to moving into second place in the AFC East. Neil O'Donnell completed a 70-yard pass to Wayne Chrebet to set up Leon Johnson's 1-yard touchdown run and give the Jets a 7-0 lead. Karim Abdul-Jabbar recorded a first down on fourth-and-1 from the Jets' 41, and scored moments later when he was left uncovered on a 36-yard touchdown pass from Marino. The Jets responded with a 12-play, 77-yard drive, capped by Keyshawn Johnson's one-handed touchdown catch, to retake the lead. However, Marino completed third-down passes to Lamar Thomas and O.J. McDuffie before finding Thomas from 22 yards out for the tying score. Marino executed the two-minute offense to set up Olindo Mare's field goal as the half expired. After Mare missed a 30-yard field goal in the third quarter, John Hall missed a chance to tie the game from the same spot early in the fourth quarter. After an exchange of punts, the Dolphins drove to the Jets' 26, where Marino completed a 22-yard pass to Charles Jordan on third-and-9. Jordan fumbled, but McDuffie picked up the ball and scored. The Jets were faced with third-and-5 from their own 45 with 3:25 left, but Derrick Rodgers sacked O'Donnell and forced him to fumble. Trace Armstrong recovered, and Marino's 21-yard pass to Bernie Parmalee on third-and-7 set up Irving Spikes's 8-yard touchdown run with 1:56 left to ice the game. Marino was 27 of 38 for 372 yards and 2 touchdowns. O'Donnell was 24 of 37 for 319 yards and 2 touchdowns. Chrebet finished with 5 receptions for 104 yards, including a late touchdown catch. Rodgers had 2 of the Dolphins' 5 sacks.

Miami	0	17	0	14	—	31
N.Y. Jets	7	7	0	6	—	20

NYJ — L. Johnson 1 run (Hall kick)
Mia — Abdul-Jabbar 36 pass from Marino (Mare kick)
NYJ — K. Johnson 7 pass from O'Donnell (Hall kick)
Mia — Thomas 22 pass from Marino (Mare kick)
Mia — FG Mare 23
Mia — McDuffie 4 fumble return (Mare kick)
Mia — Spikes 8 run (Mare kick)
NYJ — Chrebet 8 pass from O'Donnell (pass failed)

NEW YORK GIANTS 27, ARIZONA 13—at Sun Devil Stadium, attendance 38,959. Tyrone Wheatley and Erric Pegram each had touchdown runs in the fourth quarter as the Giants totaled 239 rushing yards and Danny Kanell won his first NFL start. Kanell engineered a 12-play, 58-yard drive to begin the game, capped by Brad Daluiso's 31-yard field goal. Late in the first quarter, Tito Wooten intercepted an errant Kent Graham pass, leading to Daluiso's second field goal. Aeneas Williams intercepted Kanell on the Giants' next possession, returning the ball 30 yards for a touchdown. The play gave Williams a team-record 6 interception returns for touchdowns. Kevin Butler missed the ensuing extra-point attempt, deadlocking the score 6-6 at halftime. Stoney Case, who had replaced an injured Graham in the second quarter, fumbled in the third quarter when Robert Harris sacked him. Harris recovered the ball, and, after Kanell threw a 48-yard pass to Chris Calloway, he threw a 9-yard touchdown pass to David Patten to give the Giants the lead. After an interference penalty on a fair catch gave the Giants the ball in Cardinals territory, Wheatley scored on a 8-yard run. Charles Way's 37-yard run later in the fourth quarter led to Pegram's scoring sprint and gave the Giants a 27-6 lead. Tony McCombs's blocked punt in the closing minutes led to Case's 1-yard quarterback sneak to finish the scoring. The Giants compiled 426 total yards, outgained the Cardinals on the ground 239-27 yards, and maintained possession for nearly 35 minutes. Kanell was 13 of 28 for 198 yards and 1 touchdown, with 1 interception. Wheatley had 103 rushing yards. Graham was just 4 of 14 for 40 yards, with 2 interceptions, before Case entered the game and was 18 of 33 for 222 yards, also with 2 interceptions. Percy Ellsworth had 2 interceptions for the Giants. The win gave former Cardinals offensive coordinator Jim Fassel a victory in his first game against his old club.

N.Y. Giants	3	3	7	14	—	27
Arizona	0	6	0	7	—	13

NYG — FG Daluiso 31
NYG — FG Daluiso 48
Ariz — Williams 30 interception return (kick failed)
NYG — Patten 9 pass from Kanell (Daluiso kick)
NYG — Wheatley 8 run (Daluiso kick)
NYG — Pegram 18 run (Daluiso kick)
Ariz — Case 1 run (Butler kick)

JACKSONVILLE 38, PHILADELPHIA 21—at ALLTEL Stadium, attendance 69,150. James Stewart became the first player in 34 years to rush for 5 touchdowns in a game as the Jaguars won their tenth consecutive home game. After Natrone Means sprained his left ankle on the Jaguars' first drive, Stewart entered the game and scored on the next play to stake the Jaguars to a 7-0 lead. Stewart capped off the next drive with an 8-yard touchdown run, and, after Dave Thomas's blocked punt, Stewart scored his third touchdown of the first quarter. Deion Figures's 32-yard interception return set up Stewart's fourth touchdown, a 1-yard run, and Bryan Schwartz's fumble recovery allowed Stewart to tie Jim Brown and Cookie Gilchrist with 5 rushing touchdowns in a game, falling 1 shy of Ernie Nevers's record. Rodney Peete entered the game and threw 2 fourth-quarter touchdown passes for the Eagles. Mark Brunell was 14 of 19 for 153 yards. Stewart finished with 102 yards on 15 carries. Detmer started for the Eagles and was 15 of 27 for 202 yards and 1 touchdown, with 1 interception. Peete was 12 of 15 for 123 yards and 2 touchdowns. Irving Fryar caught 10 passes for 124 yards and accounted for all 3 Eagles' touchdowns. The loss broke a 10-game winning streak in the month of October for the Eagles under Ray Rhodes.

Philadelphia	0	7	0	14	—	21
Jacksonville	21	0	7	10	—	38

Jack — Stewart 7 run (Hollis kick)
Jack — Stewart 8 run (Hollis kick)
Jack — Stewart 2 run (Hollis kick)
Phil — Fryar 34 pass from Detmer (Boniol kick)
Jack — Stewart 1 run (Hollis kick)
Jack — Stewart 1 run (Hollis kick)
Phil — Fryar 9 pass from Peete (Boniol kick)
Phil — Fryar 15 pass from Peete (Boniol kick)
Jack — FG Hollis 38

SAN FRANCISCO 30, ST. LOUIS 10—at 3Com Park, attendance 63,825. Steve Young threw 3 touchdown passes, 2 to Terrell Owens, and the 49ers' defense did not allow a touchdown, as San Francisco defeated the Rams for the sixteenth consecutive time. The 49ers drove 80 yards with the opening kickoff, with Young's touchdown pass to Owens putting the 49ers ahead 7-0. Kevin Greene recovered Tony Banks's fumble on the next drive, leading to Greg Clark's first career touchdown, a 10-yard reception from Young. The 49ers were driving for another score when Ryan McNeil intercepted an errant Young pass and raced 75 yards for a touchdown. Gary Anderson kicked 2 field goals in the final 1:54 of the half, the second one set up when James Williams recovered Eddie Kennison's fumble, which was forced by Iheanyi Uwaezuoke, on the kickoff return. Junior Bryant blocked Will Brice's punt following the Rams' first possession of the second half, leading to another Anderson field goal. David Thompson fumbled the ensuing kickoff. Uwaezuoke recovered the ball, and Young threw his second touchdown pass to Owens to give the 49ers a 30-7 lead just over five minutes into the third quarter. Young was 19 of 30 for 223 yards and 3 touchdowns, with 1 interception. Banks was 9 of 23 for 119 yards. The 49ers' defense permitted the Rams' offense just 7 first downs and 113 total yards.

St. Louis	0	7	3	0	—	10
San Francisco	14	6	10	0	—	30

SF — Owens 5 pass from Young (Anderson kick)
SF — Clark 10 pass from Young (Anderson kick)
StL — McNeil 75 interception return (Wilkins kick)
SF — FG Anderson 20
SF — FG Anderson 46
SF — FG Anderson 28
SF — Owens 17 pass from Young (Anderson kick)
StL — FG Wilkins 34

SUNDAY NIGHT, OCTOBER 12

PITTSBURGH 24, INDIANAPOLIS 22—at Three Rivers Stadium, attendance 57,925. Jerome Bettis rushed for 164 yards and a touchdown as the Steelers staved off the winless Colts. The Colts scored on their initial possession, keyed by a 16-yard run by Marshall Faulk on fourth-and-1, and Cary Blanchard's field goal a few moments later gave Indianapolis a 10-0 lead less than 10 minutes into the game. The Steelers scored on their next two possessions, and when Carnell Lake sacked Jim Harbaugh, forced him to fumble, scooped up the ball and raced 38 yards for a touchdown, the Steelers had a 17-14 lead. The Steelers responded to Blanchard's second field goal with a 77-yard drive, capped by Mike Tomczak's 28-yard touchdown pass to Courtney Hawkins, to take a 24-13 lead. Pittsburgh was driving for another score with 11 minutes remaining when Dedric Mathis's 31-yard interception return led to Blanchard's third field goal with 7:31 remaining. Ellis Johnson recovered George Jones's fumble at the Colts' 38, and a 42-yard pass interference penalty led to Harbaugh's 5-yard touchdown pass to Brian Stablein with 3:35 to play. Harbaugh's 2-point conversion pass fell incomplete, and the Colts kicked off trailing 24-22. Quentin Coryatt, who knocked quarterback Kordell Stewart out of the game just before halftime, forced Bettis to fumble on the second play after the kickoff. Dan Footman recovered the ball, giving the Colts possession on the Steelers' 23. However, three runs by Marshall Faulk netted a loss of 1 yard, and Blanchard missed a 42-yard field-goal attempt wide left. Stewart was 5 of 11 for 72 yards before Tomczak came in and completed 6 of 11 passes for 70 yards and 1 touchdown, with 2 interceptions. Harbaugh was 19 of 36 for 219 yards and 2 touchdowns, with 1 interception. The Colts forced 6 turnovers, including 4 in the fourth quarter.

Indianapolis	10	0	3	9	—	22
Pittsburgh	7	10	0	7	—	24

Ind — Harrison 18 pass from Harbaugh (Blanchard kick)
Ind — FG Blanchard 37
Pitt — FG N. Johnson 23
Pitt — Bettis 7 run (N. Johnson kick)
Pitt — Lake 38 fumble return (N. Johnson kick)
Ind — FG Blanchard 27
Pitt — Hawkins 28 pass from Tomczak (N. Johnson kick)
Ind — FG Blanchard 35
Ind — Stablein 5 pass from Harbaugh (pass failed)

MONDAY, OCTOBER 13

WASHINGTON 21, DALLAS 16—at Jack Kent Cooke Stadium, attendance 76,159. Stephen Davis, who was playing for injured Terry Allen, rushed for 2 touchdowns as the Redskins defeated the Cowboys at home for the fifth time in six seasons. The Redskins responded to Richie Cunningham's 19-yard field goal with an 80-yard drive, capped by Davis's first touchdown. The Redskins put together another 80-yard drive in the second quarter. Gus Frerotte was 5 for 6 during the drive, and found James Jenkins for a 13-yard touchdown. Early in the third quarter Ken Harvey sacked Troy Aikman and forced him to fumble. Rich Owens recovered the ball at the Cowboys' 25, and Davis carried the ball 6 consecutive times, scoring from 4 yards on the sixth play, to give the Redskins a 21-3 lead. Kevin Smith forced Brian Mitchell to fumble late in the third quarter. Dexter Coakley recovered the fumble and raced 15 yards for his first NFL touchdown to cut the deficit to 21-9. Aikman hooked up with Michael Irvin for 14 yards with 9:40 to play, but the Cowboys could not get closer than the Redskins' 38 the remainder of the game. Frerotte was 12 of 23 for 155 yards and 1 touchdown. Aikman was 17 of 31 for 193 yards and 1 touchdown.

Dallas	3	0	6	7	—	16
Washington	7	7	7	0	—	21

Dall — FG Cunningham 19
Wash — Davis 2 run (Blanton kick)
Wash — Jenkins 13 pass from Frerotte (Blanton kick)
Wash — Davis 4 run (Blanton kick)
Dall — Coakley 15 fumble return (pass failed)
Dall — Irvin 14 pass from Aikman (Cunningham kick)

EIGHTH WEEK SUMMARIES

AMERICAN FOOTBALL CONFERENCE

Eastern Division	W	L	T	Pct.	Pts.	OP
Miami	5	2	0	.714	143	124
New England	5	2	0	.714	195	104
N.Y. Jets	5	3	0	.625	201	156
Buffalo	4	3	0	.571	131	165
Indianapolis	0	7	0	.000	94	164
Central Division						
Jacksonville	5	2	0	.714	191	145
Pittsburgh	5	2	0	.714	171	170
Baltimore	3	4	0	.429	174	158
Tennessee	3	4	0	.429	142	147
Cincinnati	1	6	0	.143	98	190
Western Division						
Denver	6	1	0	.857	215	113
Kansas City	5	2	0	.714	153	113
Seattle	4	3	0	.571	124	143
Oakland	3	4	0	.429	179	173
San Diego	3	4	0	.429	105	157

NATIONAL FOOTBALL CONFERENCE

Eastern Division	W	L	T	Pct.	Pts.	OP
N.Y. Giants	5	3	0	.625	157	153
Dallas	4	3	0	.571	166	118
Washington	4	3	0	.571	125	117
Philadelphia	3	4	0	.429	124	147
Arizona	1	6	0	.143	119	144
Central Division						
Green Bay	5	2	0	.714	168	149
Minnesota	5	2	0	.714	176	155
Tampa Bay	5	2	0	.714	140	124
Detroit	4	4	0	.500	180	155
Chicago	0	7	0	.000	101	199
Western Division						
San Francisco	6	1	0	.857	187	98
Carolina	3	4	0	.429	107	127
St. Louis	2	5	0	.286	113	159
New Orleans	2	6	0	.250	118	175
Atlanta	1	6	0	.143	133	188

THURSDAY, OCTOBER 16

KANSAS CITY 31, SAN DIEGO 3—at Arrowhead Stadium, attendance 77,196. Elvis Grbac threw 2 touchdown passes to Andre Rison, and ran for another, to give the Chiefs their largest margin of victory since 1991. The Chiefs' first touchdown was set up by Grbac's 10-yard scramble on third-and-9 from the 26-yard line. Grbac was dazed on the play, and Rich Gannon entered the game and threw a pass to Rison in the end zone, but Dwayne Harper was called for interference. Grbac re-entered the game and scored on the next play. In the second quarter, the Chiefs' defense gave the offense good field position, and 54- and 36-yard drives culminated with touchdown passes to Rison. Mark McMillian's interception at the Chiefs' 40 with 43 seconds left in the half stifled a Chargers' drive and set up Pete Stoyanovich's 45-yard field goal to give Kansas City a 24-0 halftime lead. Greg Davis booted a short field goal in the third quarter, but Marcus Allen scored his 116th career rushing touchdown with 10:34 left to finish the scoring. Grbac was 20 of 40 for 235 yards. Stan Humphries suffered a concussion late in the first quarter, and Jim Everett was 9 of 25 for 137 yards, with 2 interceptions. The Chiefs' defense allowed 258 total yards, their best game since 1986, permitted the Chargers to complete just 14 of 43 passes, and halted Tony Martin's 53-game streak with at least one reception.

San Diego	0	0	3	0	—	3
Kansas City	7	17	0	7	—	31

KC — Grbac 1 run (Stoyanovich kick)
KC — Rison 10 pass from Grbac (Stoyanovich kick)
KC — Rison 5 pass from Grbac (Stoyanovich kick)
KC — FG Stoyanovich 45
SD — FG Davis 26
KC — Allen 6 run (Stoyanovich kick)

SUNDAY, OCTOBER 19

PHILADELPHIA 13, ARIZONA 10 (OT)—at Veterans Stadium, attendance 66,860. Chris Boniol kicked a 38-yard field goal with 26 seconds left in regulation to tie the game, and a 24-yard field goal in overtime to give the Eagles a comeback victory. Ricky Watters's 2-yard run capped a 10-play, 72-yard drive and gave the Eagles a 7-0 lead. In his first game for the Cardinals, Joe Nedney missed a 40-yard field-goal attempt in the second quarter, but after Eric Swann's fumble recovery he drilled a 23-yarder in the third quarter to cut the deficit to 7-3. Jake Plummer relieved Stoney Case, who was starting his first NFL game, with 10:26 remaining. Plummer guided the Cardinals on a 14-play, 98-yard drive, in which the offense converted 4 third downs, the last one being Plummer's 31-yard touchdown pass to Kevin Williams on third-and-11 with 3:07 remaining. Rodney Peete, who was making his first start of the season, drove the Eagles downfield. Faced with third-and-6 from the Cardinals' 46, Peete completed a 17-yard pass to Freddie Solomon and then scrambled 16 yards on the next play to set up Boniol's game-tying boot. The Cardinals won the overtime coin toss, but were forced to punt. After Peete completed 3 consecutive passes, and Watters ran for 3 yards, Peete hit Charlie Garner for 27 yards down to the 7-yard line to set up Boniol's game-winning field goal. Peete was 23 of 36 for 298 yards, with 2 interceptions, and improved his record as the Eagles' starting quarterback to 13-5. Plummer was 5 of 9 for 98 yards and ran 3 times for 22 yards. Rob Moore had 6 receptions for 101 yards.

Arizona	0	0	3	7	0	—	10
Philadelphia	0	7	0	3	3	—	13

Phil — Watters 2 run (Boniol kick)
Ariz — FG Nedney 23
Ariz — K. Williams 31 pass from Plummer (Nedney kick)
Phil — FG Boniol 38
Phil — FG Boniol 24

CAROLINA 13, NEW ORLEANS 0—at Louisiana Superdome, attendance 50,963. John Kasay kicked 2 field goals and Eric Davis's 2 interceptions led directly to 10 points as the Saints were held scoreless for the first time since 1983. The Panthers drove 13 plays for 47 yards, and converted 3 third-down opportunities, before Kasay kicked his first field goal. Davis intercepted Danny Wuerffel, who was making his first career start, and returned the pickoff 10 yards to the Saints' 32. Kerry Collins's 14-yard touchdown on a screen pass to Anthony Johnson gave the Panthers a 10-0 edge. A long pass intended for Randal Hill was intercepted by Davis in the end zone in the second quarter, leading to a 15-play, 75-yard drive capped by Kasay's second field goal with 11 seconds left in the half. The Saints' best chance in the second half came when they reached the Panthers' 33-yard line with about seven minutes remaining. But Troy Davis was held to no gain, and Wuerffel threw 3 consecutive incompletions. New Orleans got the ball back after a punt deep in their own territory with 3:05 left, but Andre Royal sacked Wuerffel on fourth-and-9 on the Saints' 39 to preserve the Panthers' second shutout in franchise history. Collins, who regained his starting job from Steve Beuerlein, was 23 of 31 for 204 yards. Wuerffel completed 13 of 32 for 132 yards. The Panthers permitted just 200 total yards and recorded 6 sacks, 2 by Micheal Barrow.

Carolina	10	3	0	0	—	13
New Orleans	0	0	0	0	—	0

Car — FG Kasay 25
Car — Johnson 14 pass from Collins (Kasay kick)
Car — FG Kasay 23

OAKLAND 28, DENVER 25—at Oakland-Alameda County Coliseum, attendance 57,006. Napoleon Kaufman rushed for a franchise-record 227 yards, including an 83-yard touchdown run in the fourth quarter, to hand the Broncos, the NFL's last undefeated team, their first loss of the season. Kaufman raced 57 yards on the first play from scrimmage to set up Jeff George's 14-yard touchdown pass to James Jett. After Terrell Davis's 2-yard touchdown run tied the game, George threw a 5-yard touchdown pass to Rickey Dudley. After Jason Elam hit the upright with a 40-yard field-goal attempt, his second missed field goal of the half, Bill Romanowski intercepted George a few plays later to allow Elam to kick a 44-yard field goal as the half ended. The Broncos marched 83 yards in 13 plays and consumed the first 6:23 of the third quarter to take the lead on Davis's second touchdown run. After the Raiders were forced to punt, the Broncos began another drive. On third-and-9 from the Raiders' 33, Lance Johnstone knocked the ball out of a scrambling John Elway's hands. Eric Turner scooped up the bouncing ball and raced 65 yards for the go-ahead touchdown. Midway through the fourth quarter, Kaufman broke through the line on third-and-1 and raced 83 yards for a touchdown. Later in the quarter Elway engineered a 7-play, 67-yard drive that lasted just 1:30, and was capped by his 28-yard touchdown pass to Ed McCaffrey with 2:15 left. Davis's 2-point conversion run pulled the Broncos to within 3 points. However, George fired a 15-yard pass to Tim Brown on third-and-11 to allow the Raiders to run out the clock. George threw just 12 passes, but completed 9 for 96 yards and 2 touchdowns, with 1 interception. Elway was 26 of 46 for 309 yards and a touchdown. The Raiders' defense held Davis, the AFC's leading rusher, to 85 yards on 23 carries.

Denver	7	3	7	8	—	25
Oakland	7	7	7	7	—	28

Oak — Jett 14 pass from George (Ford kick)
Den — Davis 2 run (Elam kick)
Oak — Dudley 5 pass from George (Ford kick)
Den — FG Elam 44
Den — Davis 3 run (Elam kick)
Oak — Turner 65 fumble return (Ford kick)
Oak — Kaufman 83 run (Ford kick)
Den — McCaffrey 28 pass from Elway (Davis run)

DALLAS 26, JACKSONVILLE 22—at Texas Stadium, attendance 64,464. Herschel Walker, making his first start of the season because of an injury to Daryl Johnston, scored the winning touchdown on a 64-yard pass play to propel the Cowboys to victory. After each team scored on its first possession, the Cowboys scored twice in the second quarter. Troy Aikman's 27-yard pass to Michael Irvin set up Emmitt Smith's first touchdown of the season, and a 27-yard pass-interference penalty led to Richie Cunningham's second field goal. A pair of 12-yard runs by Smith set up Stepfret Williams's first career touchdown, staking the Cowboys to 19-7 lead. The Jaguars responded on their next possession as Mark Brunell's 39-yard pass to Keenan McCardell preceeded the duo's 5-yard touchdown. After forcing a punt, the Cowboys were whistled for pass interference in the end zone, setting up Brunell's 2-yard touchdown pass to Derek Brown. The ensuing 2-point conversion pass to Willie Jackson gave the Jaguars a 22-19 lead with 9:06 remaining. However, faced with second-and-22 from their own 36, Walker caught Aikman's short pass, ran through two defenders, and scored the winning touchdown. Brunell threw a 33-yard pass to Pete Mitchell to the Cowboys' 31 with 1:40 left, but Brunell spiked the ball on first down, and, after an incompletion on second down, threw an interception to Omar Stoutmire to finish the Jaguars' chances. Aikman was 21 of 32 for 262 yards and 2 touchdowns. Brunell completed 21 of 31 passes for 242 yards and 3 touchdowns, with 1 interception. McCardell had 7 receptions for 120 yards.

Jacksonville	7	0	7	8	—	22
Dallas	3	10	6	7	—	26

Dall — FG Cunningham 37
Jack — Smith 7 pass from Brunell (Hollis kick)
Dall — E. Smith 1 run (Cunningham kick)
Dall — FG Cunningham 21
Dall — St. Williams 2 pass from Aikman (pass failed)
Jack — McCardell 5 pass from Brunell (Hollis kick)
Jack — Brown 2 pass from Brunell (Jackson pass from Brunell)
Dall — Walker 64 pass from Aikman (Cunningham kick)

MIAMI 24, BALTIMORE 13—at Memorial Stadium, attendance 64,354. Karim Abdul-Jabbar rushed for 108 yards and 3 first-half touchdowns to push the Dolphins into a tie for first place in the AFC East. Jermaine Lewis's 16-yard punt return after the Dolphins' first possession set up Matt Stover's 38-yard field goal. The Dolphins drove 80 yards on their next possession, with Abdul-Jabbar gaining 45 yards on 6 carries and scoring on a 5-yard run. Two plays later, Daryl Gardener forced Byron (Bam) Morris to fumble. Trace Armstrong recovered at the Ravens' 34, leading to Abdul-Jabbar's second touchdown run. In the second quarter, Dan Marino's 18-yard pass to O.J. McDuffie on third-and-17 keyed a 60-yard drive that Abdul-Jabbar capped with his third touchdown run of the half. The Ravens lost opportunities when Vinny Testaverde fumbled on fourth-and-1 from the Dolphins' 25 late in the first half, and had to settle for a 23-yard field goal by Stover in the third quarter. Testaverde's 34-yard touchdown pass to Derrick Alexander with 10:51 remaining cut the deficit to 24-13, but the Ravens could not get any closer. Marino was 19 of 27 for 189 yards. Testaverde completed a career-high 32 passes (out of 47 attempts) for 331 yards. Jermaine Lewis had 6 receptions for 105 yards.

Miami	14	7	0	3	—	24
Baltimore	3	0	3	7	—	13

Balt — FG Stover 38
Mia — Abdul-Jabbar 5 run (Mare kick)
Mia — Abdul-Jabbar 5 run (Mare kick)
Mia — Abdul-Jabbar 6 run (Mare kick)
Balt — FG Stover 23
Mia — FG Mare 23
Balt — Alexander 34 pass from Testaverde (Stover kick)

NEW YORK JETS 24, NEW ENGLAND 19—at Giants Stadium, attendance 77,716. Glenn Foley entered the game in the second half and completed 14 consecutive passes, including a game-winning touchdown pass to Lorenzo Neal, to help the Jets break a six-game losing streak against the Patriots. Both offenses were unproductive in the first half. John Hall's 35-yard field goal was set up by Lawyer Milloy's 39-yard pass interference penalty. New Engalnd scored its points after Larry Whigham downed Tom Tupa's punt at the 3-yard line, enabling Henry Thomas to force Neil O'Donnell into an intentional grounding penalty in the end zone, and, on the next drive following the free kick, Aaron Glenn was offsides on fourth-and-4 from the 40-yard line, allowing Adam Vinatieri to boot a 24-yard field goal in the final minute of the half. Each team scored touchdowns on its first two possessions of the second half. After Drew Bledsoe's 67-yard pass to Troy Brown set up Ben Coates's touchdown catch to give the Patriots a 12-3 lead, Foley replaced O'Donnell. Leon Johnson's 1-yard run capped Foley's first drive, but the Patriots responded with Bledsoe's 23-yard touchdown pass to Brown, only to see Adrian Murrell score from 5 yards to cut the deficit to 19-17. After forcing a Patriots' punt, Foley executed an 8-play, 76-yard drive in which he was 7-for-7 and threw a go-ahead touchdown to Neal with 10:32 remaining. The Patriots reached the Jets' 37, but Bledsoe threw an incomplete pass on fourth down with 5:37 left. Hall, however, missed his third field goal of the game with 2:56 left. The Patriots drove to the Jets' 35, only to have Bledsoe throw an incomplete pass on fourth-and-18. Foley was 17 of 23 for 200 yards. Bledsoe was 24 of 38 for 294 yards and 2 touchdowns, with 1 interception. Brown had 5 receptions for 125 yards. The win marked Jets coach Bill Parcells's first victory against his former club.

New England	0	5	14	0	—	19
N.Y. Jets	3	0	14	7	—	24

NYJ — FG Hall 35
NE — Safety, O'Donnell penalized for intentional grounding in end zone
NE — FG Vinatieri 24
NE — Coates 8 pass from Bledsoe (Vinatieri kick)
NYJ — L. Johnson 1 run (Hall kick)
NE — Brown 23 pass from Bledsoe (Vinatieri kick)
NYJ — Murrell 5 run (Hall kick)
NYJ — Neal 5 pass from Foley (Hall kick)

NEW YORK GIANTS 26, DETROIT 20 (OT)—at Pontiac Silverdome, attendance 70,069. Danny Kanell threw a 68-yard touchdown pass to Chris Calloway in overtime to vault the Giants atop the NFC East standings for the first time since 1993. The Giants were driving deep into Lions territory in the first quarter when Van Malone intercepted Kanell's pass. However, Malone fumbled on the return, and Charles Way recovered at the 16-yard line. Kanell threw a 2-yard touchdown pass to Howard Cross three plays later to give the Giants a 7-0 lead. The score was tied 10-10 in the third quarter when Amani Toomer's 53-yard punt return for a touchdown gave the Giants a 17-10 lead. Glyn Milburn's 36-yard kickoff return set up Jason Hanson's 28-yard field goal to cut the deficit to four points. The Giants extended their lead to seven on the ensuing drive, capped by Brad Daluiso's 47-yard field goal. After two punts by each team, the Lions drove 75 yards in just over four minutes, including converting 3 third-down opportunities, and tied the game on Scott Mitchell's 4-yard touchdown pass to Johnnie Morton with 1:55 remaining. The Giants punted with 24 seconds left, but the Lions had the ball on their own 6 and knelt down to run out the clock. The Giants won the overtime coin toss, and after Way ran 6 yards for a first down, Kanell threw a pass down the right sideline. Corey Raymond fell as Calloway caught the pass, allowing the Giants wide receiver to score the game-winning touchdown. Kanell, in just his second career start, was 17 of 31 for 220 yards and 2 touchdowns, with 1 interception. Calloway finished with 5 receptions for 145 yards. Mitchell was 19 of 32 for 243 yards and 1 touchdown. Barry Sanders had 105 rushing yards.

N.Y. Giants	7	3	7	3	6	—	26
Detroit	0	10	3	7	0	—	20

NYG — Cross 2 pass from Kanell (Daluiso kick)
Det — FG Hanson 22
Det — Sanders 8 run (Hanson kick)
NYG — FG Daluiso 52
NYG — Toomer 53 punt return (Daluiso kick)
Det — FG Hanson 28
NYG — FG Daluiso 47
Det — Morton 4 pass from Mitchell (Hanson kick)
NYG — Calloway 68 pass from Kanell

PITTSBURGH 26, CINCINNATI 10—at Cinergy Field, attendance 60,020. Jerome Bettis rushed for 165 yards and a touchdown, and Kordell Stewart added 2 touchdown passes as the Steelers pulled into a first-place tie in the AFC Central. The Bengals converted two key third-down situations to set up Ki-Jana Carter's 6-yard touchdown run late in the first quarter. Darren Perry's interception near midfield, and Stewart's 35-yard pass to Courtney Hawkins, led to George Jones's 11-yard touchdown catch on a shovel pass from Stewart. Greg Lloyd recovered a Carter fumble at the 22-yard line late in the first half, and the Steelers capitalized when Bettis scored from a yard out moments later. Pittsburgh took the second-half kickoff and marched 12 plays for 68 yards, capped by Stewart's 11-yard touchdown pass to Yancey Thigpen to take a 20-7 lead. Trailing 23-10, Jeff Blake threw a 48-yard pass to Carl Pickens, but Carnell Lake caught him from behind and knocked the ball out of his hands at the 14-yard line. The ball went through the end zone for a touchback, giving the Steelers the ball and dashing the Bengals' hopes. The Steelers controlled the ball for 21:36 of the second half's 30 minutes, and Norm Johnson added 2 field goals to secure the victory. Stewart was 16 of 33 for 246 yards and 2 touchdowns, with 2 interceptions. Thigpen finished with 6 receptions for 120 yards. Blake was 15 of 29 for 178 yards, with 2 interceptions. The Steelers' defense permitted just 236 yards and forced 3 turnovers, while the offense ran nearly 37 minutes off the clock.

Pittsburgh	0	13	7	6	—	26
Cincinnati	7	0	3	0	—	10

Cin — Carter 6 run (Pelfrey kick)
Pitt — Jones 11 pass from Stewart (pass failed)
Pitt — Bettis 1 run (N. Johnson kick)
Pitt — Thigpen 11 pass from Stewart (N. Johnson kick)
Cin — FG Pelfrey 33
Pitt — FG N. Johnson 43
Pitt — FG N. Johnson 32

SAN FRANCISCO 35, ATLANTA 28—at Georgia Dome, attendance 53,378. Terrell Owens caught 2 touchdown passes and Terry Kirby added 2 touchdown runs as the 49ers won their sixth consecutive game. Utilizing the halfback option pass, Jamal Anderson threw a 27-yard touchdown pass to Bert Emanuel to give the Falcons a 7-0 lead. The 49ers scored the next 21 points before Chris Chandler's 7-yard touchdown pass to O.J. Santiago with 48 seconds left cut the deficit to 21-14 at halftime. The 49ers were forced to punt midway through the third quarter, but Atlanta was whistled for roughing-the-punter, and, after a roughing-the-passer call, Steve Young threw a 31-yard touchdown pass to Owens. The Falcons scored three plays later when Chandler hit Todd Kinchen for a 53-yard touchdown. The Falcons then forced the 49ers into a third-and-12 situation, but Young hit Kirby for 82 yards on a screen pass, setting up William Floyd's 1-yard touchdown run and giving the 49ers a 35-21 lead. Billy Joe Tolliver, who replaced an injured Chandler, guided the Falcons on a 13-play, 48-yard drive that lasted 6:04 and consisted of five penalties (three on the 49ers), and the Falcons recovering 2 Tolliver fumbles, before being capped off by Terance Mathis's 4-yard touchdown catch. After each team was whistled once for being offsides on the ensuing onside kick, Juran Bolden recovered Morten Andersen's kick with 1:11 remaining. But Kevin Greene recorded his first sack of the season on fourth down, ending the Falcons' hopes. Young was 16 of 25 for 259 yards. Garrison Hearst had 18 carries for 105 yards, including a 51-yard run in the second quarter to set up Kirby's first touchdown. Chandler was 15 of 29 for 230 yards before his injury. The 49ers converted 8 of 13 third-down conversions and had 438 total yards. Dana Stubblefield and Roy Barker each had 2 of the 49ers' 7 sacks.

San Francisco	7	14	7	7	—	35
Atlanta	7	7	7	7	—	28

Atl — Emanuel 27 pass from Anderson (Andersen kick)
SF — Owens 5 pass from Young (Anderson kick)
SF — Kirby 1 run (pass failed)
SF — Kirby 7 run (Kirby run)
Atl — Santiago 7 pass from Chandler (Andersen kick)
SF — Owens 31 pass from Young (Anderson kick)
Atl — Kinchen 53 pass from Chandler (Andersen kick)
SF — Floyd 1 run (Anderson kick)
Atl — Mathis 4 pass from Tolliver (Andersen kick)

SEATTLE 17, ST. LOUIS 9—at Trans World Dome, attendance 64,819. Warren Moon completed 6 of 9 passes for 68 yards on a 14-play, 76-yard drive leading to Todd Peterson's 24-yard second-quarter field goal. D'Marco Farr intercepted Moon at the 6-yard line and returned the ball 22 yards, setting up Jeff Wilkins's 51-yard field goal just before halftime to tie the game. The Seahawks scored on the opening drive of the second half, keyed by Moon's 34-yard pass to Ronnie Harrris, on Chris Warren's 1-yard run. A 36-yard kickoff retur1-yard run by David Thompson and a defensive holding penalty on third-and-5 set up Wilkins's second field goal to cut the deficit to 10-6, but the Seahawks responded with a 13-play, 78-yard drive that consumed 8:18, and was capped by Steve Broussard's 9-yard touchdown run. Bennie Blades intercepted a pass at the Seahawks' 35 to halt one drive, and, after three punts, Wilkins booted his third field goal with 4:20 remaining to cut the deficit to 17-9. However, the Rams did not get the ball back until there were 24 seconds remaining and were unable to cross midfield. Seattle had more first downs (27-10), total yards (357-192), and time of possession (38:11-21:49). Moon was 24 of 36 for 261 yards, with 2 interceptions. Tony Banks completed 17 of 31 for 164 yards, with 1 interception. The Seahawks improved their record to 8-3 in their last 11 games against the NFC.

Seattle	0	3	7	7	—	17
St. Louis	0	3	3	3	—	9

Sea — FG Peterson 24
StL — FG Wilkins 51
Sea — Warren 1 run (Peterson kick)
StL — FG Wilkins 29
Sea — Broussard 9 run (Peterson kick)
StL — FG Wilkins 46

TENNESSEE 28, WASHINGTON 14—at Liberty Bowl Memorial Stadium, attendance 31,042. Eddie George rushed for 125 yards and 2 touchdowns as the Oilers won their second consecutive game in front of their largest home crowd of the season. It was George's fifth 100-yard rushing game of the season, and his ninth in 23 career games. Steve McNair's 2-yard touchdown run capped a 9-play, 66-yard drive and was keyed by his own 21-yard scramble on third-and-5 from the Redskins' 25. After forcing a punt, the Oilers drove 93 yards, consumed six and a half minutes, and scored on George's 3-yard run. Darryll Lewis's 25-yard interception return stymied the Redskins' opening possession of the second half and resulted in Rodney Thomas's 5-yard touchdown run on third and goal. Gus Frerotte threw 2 touchdown passes to Henry Ellard on consecutive possessions to cut the deficit to 21-14, but Denard Walker's interception at the Oilers' 28 early in the fourth quarter halted a possible game-tying drive. After an exchange of punts, the Oilers drove 80 yards, rushing 8 times for 57 yards, with George's 6-yard run with 2:38 remaining icing the game. Lewis's second interception dashed any comeback hopes for the Redskins. The Oilers rushed for 204 yards and maintained possession for more than 35 minutes. McNair was 13 of 21 for 192 yards and rushed 10 times for 53 yards. Frerotte completed 16 of 31 passes for 228 yards and 2 touchdowns, with 3 interceptions.

Washington	0	0	14	0	—	14
Tennessee	0	14	7	7	—	28

Tenn — McNair 2 run (Del Greco kick)
Tenn — George 3 run (Del Greco kick)
Tenn — Thomas 5 run (Del Greco kick)
Wash — Ellard 13 pass from Frerotte (Blanton kick)
Wash — Ellard 10 pass from Frerotte (Blanton kick)
Tenn — George 6 run (Del Greco kick)

MONDAY, OCTOBER 20

BUFFALO 9, INDIANAPOLIS 6—at RCA Dome, attendance 61,139. Steve Chrisite's 27-yard field goal as time expired gave the Bills a victory in just the second game in NFL history that did not feature a touchdown or a turnover. Todd Collins, who played despite an injured non-throwing shoulder, guided the Bills on a 12-play, 76-yard drive to start the game, concluding with Christie's 22-yard field goal. Jeff Burris's punt return to the Bills' 46 and 17 rushing yards by Thurman Thomas set up Christie's second field goal 4:16 before halftime. The Colts had a chance to score just before intermission, but Jim Harbaugh was sacked on consecutive plays and Cary Blanchard missed a 51-yard field goal. Harbaugh got injured on the first play of the Colts' second possession of the third quarter. Paul Justin entered the game and went 4-for-4 on a 10-play, 52-yard drive that culminated with Blanchard's 39-yard field goal with 34 seconds left in the third quarter. The Bills drove to the Colts' 15, but Christie missed a 32-yard attempt. Justin and the Colts responded with a 11-play, 62-yard drive that stalled when Marvin Harrison dropped Justin's third-and-2 pass at the 15, and had to settle for Blanchard's second field goal with 6:12 remaining. The Bills got out of a third-and-10 situation when Collins completed a 16-yard pass to Quinn Early. Moments later, Collins completed a 14-yard pass to Andre Reed on third-and-3 to get the Bills to the 20-yard line. Buffalo ran three times to set up Christie's winning kick. Collins was 17 of 22 for 184 yards. Harbaugh was 9 of 12 for 109 yards, and Justin was 5 of 6 for 62 yards. The defenses recorded 8 sacks, 5 by the Bills and 2 by Bruce Smith, and held the opposing offense to less than 250 yards. The Colts remained winless, with five of their seven losses totaling a combined 17 points. It was the seventh consecutive game between the teams to be settled by six points or less.

Buffalo	3	3	0	3	—	9
Indianapolis	0	0	3	3	—	6

Buff — FG Christie 22
Buff — FG Christie 47
Ind — FG Blanchard 39
Ind — FG Blanchard 32
Buff — FG Christie 27

NINTH WEEK SUMMARIES

AMERICAN FOOTBALL CONFERENCE

Eastern Division	W	L	T	Pct.	Pts.	OP
Miami	5	3	0	.625	176	160
New England	5	3	0	.625	205	132
N.Y. Jets	5	3	0	.625	201	156
Buffalo	4	4	0	.500	151	188
Indianapolis	0	8	0	.000	113	199
Central Division						
Pittsburgh	6	2	0	.750	194	187
Jacksonville	5	3	0	.625	208	168
Baltimore	4	4	0	.500	194	175
Tennessee	4	4	0	.500	183	161
Cincinnati	1	7	0	.125	125	219
Western Division						
Denver	7	1	0	.875	238	133
Kansas City	6	2	0	.750	181	133
Seattle	5	3	0	.625	169	177
San Diego	4	4	0	.500	140	176
Oakland	3	5	0	.375	213	218

NATIONAL FOOTBALL CONFERENCE

Eastern Division	W	L	T	Pct.	Pts.	OP
N.Y. Giants	6	3	0	.667	186	180
Dallas	4	4	0	.500	178	131
Philadelphia	4	4	0	.500	137	159
Washington	4	4	0	.500	142	137
Arizona	1	7	0	.125	133	185
Central Division						
Green Bay	6	2	0	.750	196	159
Minnesota	6	2	0	.750	186	161
Tampa Bay	5	3	0	.625	146	134
Detroit	4	4	0	.500	180	155
Chicago	1	7	0	.125	137	232
Western Division						
San Francisco	7	1	0	.875	210	98
Carolina	4	4	0	.500	128	139
St. Louis	2	6	0	.250	133	187
New Orleans	2	7	0	.222	118	198
Atlanta	1	7	0	.125	145	209

SUNDAY, OCTOBER 26

BALTIMORE 20, WASHINGTON 17—at Jack Kent Cooke Stadium, attendance 75,067. Byron (Bam) Morris rushed for a career-high 176 yards and scored a touchdown as the Ravens defeated their intrastate rival Washington Redskins in a fierce rainstorm. Vinny Testaverde threw a 39-yard pass to Jermaine Lewis to set up his 13-yard touchdown pass to Derrick Alexander just over five minutes into the game. The Redskins tied the game on their next possession, keyed by Brian Mitchell's 61-yard kickoff return and capped by Gus Frerotte's 15-yard touchdown pass to Leslie Shepherd. The Ravens led 17-7 in the third quarter when Scott Blanton booted a 49-yard field goal for the Redskins. However, the Ravens were penalized for offsides. The Redskins took the points off the board, and were rewarded when Frerotte threw a 6-yard touchdown pass to Mitchell to cut the deficit to 17-14. Matt Stover's second field goal gave the Ravens a six-point lead with 12:16 remaining. Greg Jones forced Testaverde to fumble on the Ravens' next possession. Marvcus Patton recovered the ball at the Ravens' 25, but the Redskins had to settle for Blanton's 26-yard field goal with 6:42 remaining. The Redskins got the ball on their own 11 with 1:52 to play. Frerotte's fourth-and-14 pass to Mitchell was enough for a first down to the Redskins' 42, but his next pass was tipped by Bennie Thompson and intercepted by Ray Lewis to thwart the Redskins' final threat. Testaverde was 10 of 21 for 142 yards and 1 touchdown. Frerotte was 17 of 33 for 199 yards and 2 touchdowns, with 1 interception. The Ravens fumbled 5 times in the wet conditions, but lost the ball just once.

Baltimore	7	7	3	3	—	20
Washington	7	0	7	3	—	17

Balt — Alexander 13 pass from Testaverde (Stover kick)
Wash — Shepherd 15 pass from Frerotte (Blanton kick)
Balt — Morris 4 run (Stover kick)
Balt — FG Stover 34
Wash — Mitchell 6 pass from Frerotte (Blanton kick)
Balt — FG Stover 28
Wash — FG Blanton 26

NEW YORK GIANTS 29, CINCINNATI 27—at Giants Stadium, attendance 72,584. Charles Way and Tyrone Wheatley each rushed for 2 touchdowns, and Jason Sehorn intercepted a possible game-tying 2-point conversion pass in the waning minutes as the Giants won their fifth consecutive game. Each team scored in the first quarter with help of a third-down defensive penalty, as the Bengals took a 7-3 lead. Tito Paul's 24-yard pass interference penalty led to Way's first touchdown. Eric Bieniemy returned the ensuing kickoff a club-record 102 yards to put the Bengals ahead 14-10. The Bengals drove 73 yards in the final minute of the first half, capped by Jeff Blake's 39-yard touchdown pass to David Dunn six seconds before halftime. Trailing 21-10, Percy Ellsworth's 24-yard fumble return and 2 defensive penalties led to Way's second touchdown. Danny Kanell's 23-yard pass to Chris Calloway on third-and-5 to the 1-yard line allowed Wheatley to score less than a minute into the fourth quarter, giving the Giants a 22-21 lead. Kanell's 40-yard pass to Kevin Alexander led to Wheatley's second touchdown and put the Giants ahead by eight points with 3:24 remaining. The Bengals, spurred by 2 defensive penalties, scored when Blake scrambled from four yards to cut the deficit to 29-27 with 1:31 left, but Sehorn intercepted Blake's 2-point conversion pass intended for Carl Pickens. Calloway recovered the onside kick to clinch the victory. Kanell was 18 of 31 for 214 yards. Blake was 17 of 34 for 237 yards and 1 touchdown, with 1 interception. Alexander had 100 receiving yards. Way finished with 75 yards, giving him 256 rushing yards the last three weeks after rushing for 181 yards in his first 38 career games.

Cincinnati	7	14	0	6	—	27
N.Y. Giants	3	7	6	13	—	29

NYG — FG Daluiso 35
Cin — Dillon 1 run (Pelfrey kick)
NYG — Way 1 run (Daluiso kick)
Cin — Bieniemy 102 kickoff return (Pelfrey kick)
Cin — Dunn 39 pass from Blake (Pelfrey kick)
NYG — Way 1 run (run failed)
NYG — Wheatley 1 run (pass failed)
NYG — Wheatley 3 run (Daluiso kick)
Cin — Blake 4 run (pass failed)

PHILADELPHIA 13, DALLAS 12—at Veterans Stadium, attendance 67,106. Rodney Peete's 8-yard touchdown pass to Chad Lewis with 45 seconds remaining propelled the Eagles into a second-place tie in the NFC East. Richie Cunningham booted 3 first-half field goals, one set up by Brock Marion's 47-yard kickoff return and another by an 8-yard punt by Tommy Hutton, to give the Cowboys a 9-0 halftime lead. Special teams led to all three second-half field goals, as Mark Seay's 33-yard punt return and Toby Gowin's 17-yard punt set up Chris Boniol's field goals, and Herschel Walker's 49-yard kickoff return led to Cunningham's fourth field goal with 8:45 remaining. The Eagles regained possession on their own 26 following a punt with 4:20 remaining. Peete, who had been held to 68 passing yards up to this point, threw a 27-yard pass to Kevin Turner and an 11-yard pass to Irving Fryar on fourth-and-11, and Ricky Watters had a 14-yard run to set up the winning pass to Lewis. Emmitt Smith ran out of bounds at his own 43 as time ran out. Peete was 13 of 31 for 126 yards and 1 touchdown. Troy Aikman was 2 of 6 for 21 yards before leaving with a concussion late in the first quarter. Wade Wilson replaced him and was 11 of 16 for 108 yards. Smith had 126 rushing yards. The teams split their season series for the third consecutive year.

Dallas	3	6	0	3	—	12
Philadelphia	0	0	3	10	—	13

Dall — FG Cunningham 26
Dall — FG Cunningham 24
Dall — FG Cunningham 35
Phil — FG Boniol 29
Phil — FG Boniol 37
Dall — FG Cunningham 43
Phil — Lewis 8 pass from Peete (Boniol kick)

DENVER 23, BUFFALO 20 (OT)—at Rich Stadium, attendance 78,458. Terrell Davis rushed for 207 yards and a touchdown and Jason Elam booted a 33-yard field goal in overtime as the Broncos staved off the Bills. Tyrone Braxton's interception and Dwayne Carswell's fumble recovery led to Elam's first 2 field goals, with Davis's 9-yard touchdown run and Keith Traylor's 62-yard interception return accounting for the Broncos' touchdowns and a 20-0 lead entering the fourth quarter. Alex Van Pelt replaced Todd Collins late in the third quarter and two plays after Kurt Schulz's interception Van Pelt threw a 27-yard touchdown pass to Andre Reed. A 40-yard pass interference penalty on the Bills' next possession led to Steve Christie's 30-yard field goal with 9:44 remaining. The Bills reached the Broncos' 25 on their next possession, but Ray Crockett intercepted Van Pelt's pass. However, the Bills' defense forced another punt, and Van Pelt threw a 31-yard touchdown pass to Quinn Early with 2:23 remaining to cut the deficit to 20-17. Denver recovered the ensuing onside kick, but the Bills regained possession on their own 20 following a punt with 56 seconds remaining. A 15-yard pass to Early, a 24-yard pass to Reed, and a 4-yard scramble by Van Pelt enabled Christie to boot a game-tying 55-yard field goal with two seconds left to send the game to overtime. After the Bills had to punt for the second time in overtime, John Elway hit Ed McCaffrey with a 17-yard pass on third-and-10, and then found Rod Smith for 14 yards down to the Bills' 27. Four rushing plays by Davis put Elam in position for his winning kick. Elway was 16 of 30 for 133 yards. Collins was 7 of 18 for 35 yards, with 2 interceptions, before being replaced by Van Pelt, who was 12 of 24 for 177 yards and 2 touchdowns, with 1 interception. The Broncos outgained the Bills 224-25 yards in the first half. Bruce Smith's tenth sack of the season, which came in the first quarter, enabled him to become the first player to record double-digit sacks in 11 seasons. The Broncos, who were trapped in Denver by a blizzard, did not land in Buffalo until 12:57 a.m. Sunday morning.

Denver	0	10	10	0	3	—	23
Buffalo	0	0	0	20	0	—	20

Den — FG Elam 23
Den — Davis 9 run (Elam kick)
Den — FG Elam 22
Den — Traylor 62 interception return (Elam kick)

Buff — Reed 27 pass from Van Pelt (Christie kick)
Buff — FG Christie 30
Buff — Early 31 pass from Van Pelt (Christie kick)
Buff — FG Christie 55
Den — FG Elam 33

SAN DIEGO 35, INDIANAPOLIS 19—at Qualcomm Stadium, Jack Murphy Field, attendance 63,177. Gary Brown rushed for 169 yards and Greg Davis kicked 5 field goals as the Chargers defeated the winless Colts. Davis kicked 4 field goals in the first half, and Brown scored from 1-yard midway through the third quarter to give the Chargers a 19-0 lead. A 36-yard pass-interference penalty set up Paul Justin's 36-yard touchdown pass to Sean Dawkins on the Colts' next possession. The Chargers responded with their fifth scoring drive of the game consisting of at least four minutes, capped by Frank Hartley's 2-yard touchdown catch. Dwayne Harper's 43-yard interception return set up Davis's fifth field goal, giving the Chargers a 29-6 lead. Ellis Johnson blocked Davis's sixth attempt late in the fourth quarter. Ray McElroy recovered the ball and raced 42 yards for a touchdown to cut the deficit to 29-19. The Colts attempted to recover the ensuing onside kick, but Rodney Harrison grabbed the ball and sped 40 yards for the game's final points. Stan Humphries was 21 of 34 for 229 yards and 1 touchdown. Justin was 20 of 39 for 243 yards and 2 touchdowns, with 2 interceptions. The Chargers registered more first downs (24-14) and compiled more total yards (424-250).

Indianapolis	0	0	6	13	—	19
San Diego	3	9	14	9	—	35

SD — FG Davis 45
SD — FG Davis 35
SD — FG Davis 34
SD — FG Davis 31
SD — Brown 1 run (Davis kick)
Ind — Dawkins 36 pass from Justin (pass failed)
SD — Hartley 2 pass from Humphries (Davis kick)
SD — FG Davis 45
Ind — Bailey 10 pass from Justin (Blanchard kick)
Ind — McElroy 42 blocked field goal return (pass failed)
SD — Harrison 40 kickoff return (kick blocked)

PITTSBURGH 23, JACKSONVILLE 17 (OT)—at Three Rivers Stadium, attendance 57,011. Jerome Bettis rumbled 17 yards with a shovel pass in overtime for the game-winning touchdown as the Steelers knocked the Jaguars out of first place in the AFC Central. Jacksonville led 10-0 at halftime on the strength of Willie Jackson's touchdown catch and his 45-yard reception to set up Mike Hollis's field goal. Kordell Stewart directed a 7-play, 80-yard drive in the third quarter, capped by his 28-yard touchdown pass to Courtney Hawkins to cut the deficit to 10-7. The Jaguars drove to the Steelers' 2, but James Stewart was stopped for no gain on third and fourth down, resulting in a change of possession. The Steelers' offense responded with a 15-play, 98-yard drive which lasted 8:48, capped by Stewart's 1-yard run. The Steelers forced a punt, but Tony Brackens stripped Bettis of the ball. Joel Smeenge recovered on the 16-yard line, and Mark Brunell threw a 3-yard touchdown pass to Pete Mitchell moments later to give the Jaguars a 17-14 lead. The Steelers used a 41-yard pass from Stewart to Yancey Thigpen to get deep into Jaguars' territory, but settled for Norm Johnson's 19-yard field goal with 2:21 left, sending the game to overtime. The Steelers won the coin toss, and Stewart and Thigpen hooked up for 9- and 17-yard gains to get Pittsburgh to the Jaguars' 25. On third-and-2, Bettis took a shovel pass from Stewart and rumbled into the end zone. Stewart was 25 of 42 for a career-high 317 yards and 2 touchdowns, with 1 interception. Thigpen established career-highs with 11 catches for 196 yards. Brunell was 15 of 30 for 214 yards and 2 touchdowns. The Steelers outgained the Jaguars (439-267) and dominated time of possession (41:27-24:20).

Jacksonville	0	10	0	7	0	—	17
Pittsburgh	0	0	7	10	6	—	23

Jack — Jackson 8 pass from Brunell (Hollis kick)
Jack — FG Hollis 20
Pitt — Hawkins 28 pass from Stewart (N. Johnson kick)
Pitt — Stewart 1 run (N. Johnson kick)
Jack — Mitchell 3 pass from Brunell (Hollis kick)
Pitt — FG N. Johnson 19
Pitt — Bettis 17 pass from Stewart

KANSAS CITY 28, ST. LOUIS 20—at Trans World Dome, attendance 64,864. Pete Stoyanovich kicked 4 field goals as the Chiefs held off a Rams comeback attempt to defeat their Missouri counterpart. Trailing 3-0 in the first quarter, the Rams scored when Tony Banks threw a 12-yard pass to Isaac Bruce. Elvis Grbac completed 4 passes covering 65 yards, the last pass going 21 yards to Lake Dawson for a touchdown and followed by a 2-point conversion pass, to put the Chiefs ahead 14-7. After Banks had to leave the game for a play, James Hasty intercepted Mark Rypien's pass, which led to Stoyanovich's third field goal. The Rams answered with a 70-yard drive, capped by Lawrence Philllips's 1-yard touchdown run to cut the deficit to 17-14 at halftime. The Chiefs scored twice in just over three minutes, as Marcus Allen's touchdown followed John Browning's fumble recovery at the Rams' 22. Jeff Wilkins added 2 fourth-quarter field goals to cut the lead to 28-20 with 5:07 remaining. However, Donnell Bennett carried five consecutive plays to gain 2 first downs, and Allen got 2 yards on third-and-1 with just under two minutes remaining to ice the game. Grbac was 20 of 37 for 204 yards and 1 touchdown. Banks was 18 of 30 for 268 yards and 1 touchdown. The Rams outgained the Chiefs (360-255), but committed all 4 of the game's turnovers. Leslie O'Neal registered all 4 of the Rams' sacks.

Kansas City	6	11	11	0	—	28
St. Louis	7	7	0	6	—	20

KC — FG Stoyanovich 25
StL — Bruce 12 pass from Banks (Wilkins kick)
KC — FG Stoyanovich 52
KC — Dawson 21 pass from Grbac (Vanover pass from Grbac)
KC — FG Stoyanovich 41
StL — Phillips 1 run (Wilkins kick)
KC — FG Stoyanovich 39
KC — Allen 2 run (Gonzalez pass from Grbac)
StL — FG Wilkins 25
Stl — FG Wilkins 49

MINNESOTA 10, TAMPA BAY 6—at Houlihan's Stadium, attendance 66,815. David Palmer's 57-yard punt return set up the Vikings' only touchdown as Minnesota avoided being swept by the Buccaneers. The Vikings reached the Bucs' 2-yard line early in the second quarter, but Eddie Murray missed a 30-yard field goal, and the game remained scoreless at halftime. The Buccaneers did not run a play inside Vikings' territory until the third quarter, but Tampa Bay was forced to punt. The Vikings drove 75 yards in 7:32, concluding with Murray's 28-yard field goal. After the Vikings' defense stopped the Buccaneers, Palmer returned the ensuing punt to the 8-yard line, setting up Charles Evans's 1-yard touchdown run. The Buccaneers mounted a drive, behind the strength of an 18-yard pass to Dave Moore and a 15-yard run by Warrick Dunn, and scored when Trent Dilfer threw a 2-yard touchdown pass to Reidel Anthony. However, Michael Husted hit the right upright with the extra-point attempt. The Buccaneers reached the 24-yard line in the closing seconds, but Dilfer's pass into the end zone was knocked down. Brad Johnson was 20 of 29 for 230 yards. Dilfer was 15 of 29 for 188 yards and 1 touchdown. The Vikings outgained the Buccaneers (302-229), and controlled the clock (36:59-23:01) on their ability to convert third-down plays (11-of-19) while stopping the Buccaneers (3-of-12). There were no turnovers in the game.

Minnesota	0	0	10	0	—	10
Tampa Bay	0	0	0	6	—	6

Minn — FG Murray 28
Minn — Evans 1 run (Murray kick)
TB — Anthony 2 pass from Dilfer (kick failed)

SEATTLE 45, OAKLAND 34—at Kingdome, attendance 66,264. Warren Moon, 23 days shy of his forty-first birthday, passed for 409 yards and 5 touchdowns to lead the Seahawks to a comeback victory. Moments after Napoleon Kaufman's 55-yard touchdown run gave the Raiders a 7-3 lead, Lorenzo Lynch intercepted a pass to set up James Jett's 13-yard touchdown catch. Trailing 14-6, Joey Galloway's 44-yard reverse set up Moon's first touchdown pass, a 7-yard toss to Brian Blades, to cut the deficit to 14-12. Just over two minutes later, Moon hit James McKnight with a 42-yard touchdown pass. The Raiders responded with Cole Ford's 53-yard field goal 1:09 before halftime, and then caught a break when Moon's pass to Galloway glanced off the receiver's heel. Lionel Washington alertly grabbed the ball out of the air and raced 44 yards for a touchdown just 39 seconds before halftime to give the Raiders a 25-18 lead. The Raiders defense forced the Seahawks to punt the second half's opening possession, and Jeff George threw a 49-yard touchdown pass to Jett on the next play to give the Raiders a 31-18 lead. Moon found McKnight for 41 yards to set up his first of 3 touchdown passes to Galloway. The Raiders maintained possession for nearly six minutes on the next possession, but settled for Ford's 22-yard field goal and a 34-25 lead. The Seahawks answered with a 75-yard drive in less than three minutes, keyed by Moon's 30-yard pass to Carlester Crumpler, and capped by his 28-yard touchdown pass to Galloway. After forcing the Raiders to punt after three plays, Moon found Blades for 27 yards to set up Todd Peterson's go-ahead field goal with 12:55 to play. After yet another punt, Moon hit Galloway for 45 yards to set up Peterson's fourth field goal with 7:24 remaining to put the Seahawks ahead 38-34. On the Raiders next possession, Michael Sinclair sacked George and forced him to fumble near midfield. Dean Wells recovered, and Moon threw a 2-yard touchdown pass to Galloway with 2:26 left as the Seahawks scored 27 of the game's final 30 points. Moon was 28 of 44 for 409 yards and 5 touchdowns, with 2 interceptions. Galloway had 7 receptions for 117 yards and McKnight added 4 catches for 100 yards. George was 18 of 29 for 260 yards and 2 touchdowns. Tim Brown had 7 receptions for 107 yards, and Kaufman added 112 rushing yards. Seattle outgained the Raiders (554-354) and converted 8 of 16 third-down opportunities, while permitting the Raiders to convert just 1 of 10 third-down chances. The Seahawks won for the fifth time in their last six games.

Oakland	14	11	9	0	—	34
Seattle	3	15	14	13	—	45

Sea — FG Peterson 21
Oak — Kaufman 55 run (Ford kick)
Oak — Jett 13 pass from George (Ford kick)
Sea — FG Peterson 40
Sea — Blades 7 pass from Moon (pass failed)
Sea — McKnight 42 pass from Moon (pass failed)
Oak — FG Ford 53
Oak — Washington 44 interception return (Brown pass from George)
Oak — Jett 49 pass from George (bad snap)
Sea — Galloway 17 pass from Moon (Peterson kick)
Oak — FG Ford 32
Sea — Galloway 28 pass from Moon (Peterson kick)
Sea — FG Peterson 38
Sea — FG Peterson 25
Sea — Galloway 2 pass from Moon (Peterson kick)

SAN FRANCISCO 23, NEW ORLEANS 0—at Louisiana Superdome, attendance 60,443. Steve Young threw 2 touchdown passes and the 49ers' defense permitted just 6 first downs as San Francisco won its seventh consecutive game. The 49ers drove 80 yards in just over six minutes in the first quarter, capped by Young's 19-yard touchdown pass to Garrison Hearst. Gary Anderson's 36-yard field goal midway through the second quarter put the 49ers ahead 10-0 and Zach Bronson's interception just before halftime enabled Anderson to kick a 51-yard field goal to increase the lead to 13-0. Anderson added a third field goal in the third quarter, and a 11-play, 77-yard drive in the fourth quarter that ended with Young's 5-yard touchdown pass to J.J. Stokes to ice the game. Young was 20 of 32 for 230 yards and 2 touchdowns. Danny Wuerffel was 7 of 15 for 60 yards, with 1 interception before being replaced by Heath Shuler, who was 1 of 1 for 13 yards. Doug Nussmeier entered the game in the fourth quarter and was 4 of 9 for 36 yards. The 49ers had more yards (347-142) and time of possession (37:41-22:19). The Saints were shut out for the second consecutive week.

San Francisco	7	6	3	7	—	23
New Orleans	0	0	0	0	—	0

SF — Hearst 19 pass from Young (Anderson kick)
SF — FG Anderson 36
SF — FG Anderson 51
SF — FG Anderson 29
SF — Stokes 5 pass from Young (Anderson kick)

TENNESSEE 41, ARIZONA 14—at Sun Devil Stadium, attendance 44,030. Steve McNair threw 2 touchdown passes and ran for 2 more as the Oilers forced 7 turnovers and won their third consecutive game. Denard Walker intercepted Jake Plummer, who was making his first start, and raced 39 yards for a touchdown to give the Oilers a 10-0 lead early in the second quarter. After Al Del Greco's second field goal with 1:46 left in the half, Blaine Bishop recovered Frank Sanders's fumble at the Cardinals' 38. McNair raced 35 yards on a quarterback draw a few plays later to give the Oilers a 20-0 halftime edge. Marcus Robertson, who had 2 interceptions, picked off Plummer's first pass of the second half, returning it 39 yards to the 3-yard line to set up McNair's second scoring run. McNair and Chris Sanders hooked up for 2 scoring passes, as did Plummer and Rob Moore. McNair was 9 of 17 for 146 yards and 2 touchdowns. Plummer was 21 of 40 for 195 yards and 2 touchdowns, with 4 interceptions. Frank Sanders finished with 10 catches for 98 yards.

Tennessee	3	17	14	7	—	41
Arizona	0	0	7	7	—	14

Tenn — FG Del Greco 52
Tenn — Walker 39 interception return (Del Greco kick)
Tenn — FG Del Greco 42
Tenn — McNair 35 run (Del Greco kick)
Tenn — McNair 2 run (Del Greco kick)
Ariz — R. Moore 12 pass from Plummer (Nedney kick)
Tenn — C. Sanders 55 pass from McNair (Del Greco kick)
Tenn — C. Sanders 20 pass from McNair (Del Greco kick)
Ariz — R. Moore 2 pass from Plummer (Nedney kick)

SUNDAY NIGHT, OCTOBER 26

CAROLINA 21, ATLANTA 12—at Ericsson Stadium, attendance 54,675. Tshimanga Biakabutuka rushed for a career-high 104 yards and 2 touchdowns as the Panthers won their first home game in four attempts. Biakabutuka carried 6 times for 39 yards on the game-opening drive, going the final 12 yards for a touchdown. The Panthers had to drive just 40 yards after a 27-yard punt later in the quarter, and Kerry Collins threw a 16-yard touchdown pass to Mark Carrier just before the first quarter expired. Tony Graziani made his first start for the Falcons and was blitzed constantly by the Panthers as Atlanta totaled just 64 total yards of offense in the first half. Billy Joe Tolliver replaced Graziani to start the second half, and guided the Falcons to Morten Andersen's second field goal to cut the deficit to 14-6. Biakabutuka, however, carried 7 times for 50 yards on an 80-yard drive that consumed more than seven minutes, and was capped by his 26-yard touchdown run. Henri Crockett's fumble recovery, forced by Lester Archambeau, at the Panthers' 27 put Tolliver in position to throw a 14-yard touchdown pass to Jamal Anderson with 6:41 left. The Falcons went for 2 points, and Israel Raybon stopped a scrambling Tolliver short of the end zone to keep the score 21-12. Having to score twice, the Falcons reached the 1-yard line with 1:26 left, but Eric Davis recovered Tolliver's fumble and the Panthers ran out the clock. Collins was 12 of 25 for 107 yards and 1 touchdown, with 1 interception. Graziani was 4 of 18 for 24 yards, with 2 interceptions before being replaced by Tolliver, who finished 17 of 28 for 217 yards and 1 touchdown. Atlanta's Terance Mathis had 8 receptions for 107 yards.

Atlanta	0	3	3	6	—	12
Carolina	14	0	0	7	—	21

Car — Biakabutuka 12 run (Kasay kick)
Car — Carrier 16 pass from Collins (Kasay kick)
Atl — FG Andersen 34
Atl — FG Andersen 44
Car — Biakabutuka 26 run (Kasay kick)
Atl — Anderson 14 pass from Tolliver (pass failed)

MONDAY, OCTOBER 27

GREEN BAY 28, NEW ENGLAND 10—at Foxboro Stadium, attendance 59,972. Brett Favre threw 3 touchdown passes as the Packers put together 4 touchdown drives that exceeded 75 yards and won the rematch of Super Bowl XXXI. The Patriots were driving for the game's first score, when Eugene Robinson forced Curtis Martin to fumble. Reggie White recovered at the Packers' 19, and Green Bay drove 81 yards, capped by Favre's 6-yard swing pass to Dorsey Levens. Brian Williams's interception at the Patriots' 30 early in the second quarter gave the Packers great field position, but Favre lost the ball on the next play. Willie McGinest recovered, and Drew Bledsoe threw a 50-yard pass to Terry Glenn before finding Ben Coates with a game-tying touchdown pass. Adam Vinatieri's field goal with 2:12 left in the half gave the Patriots a 10-7 lead, but the Packers responded with a 9-play, 75-yard drive in 1:50, keyed by 2 third-down completions from Favre to Robert Brooks, and capped by Favre's 30-yard bullet pass to Mark Chmura. The Patriots drove to the Packers' 1 early in the third quarter, but Martin was stopped on first down and Bledsoe threw 3 consecutive incomplete passes, the last two batted down by Tyrone Williams. The offense responded with a 17-play, 99-yard drive that lasted 9:31, and was finished by Favre's 20-yard scoring pass to Brooks. After forcing a Patriots' punt, the Packers drove 15 plays for 85 yards. Levens carried 9 times on the 7:24 drive, and his 3-yard run with 2:46 remaining iced the game. Favre was 23 of 34 for 239 yards and 3 touchdowns. Levens had 26 carries for 100 yards. Bledsoe was 20 of 36 for 268 yards and 1 touchdown, with 3 interceptions. Glenn had 7 receptions for 163 yards. The Packers maintained possession for more than 34 minutes, and forced 4 turnovers while committing just 1 themselves.

Green Bay	7	7	7	7	—	28
New England	0	10	0	0	—	10

GB — Levens 6 pass from Favre (Longwell kick)
NE — Coates 11 pass from Bledsoe (Vinatieri kick)
NE — FG Vinatieri 38
GB — Chmura 32 pass from Favre (Longwell kick)
GB — Brooks 20 pass from Favre (Longwell kick)
GB — Levens 3 run (Longwell kick)

CHICAGO 36, MIAMI 33 (OT)—at Pro Player Stadium, attendance 73,156. Jeff Jaeger kicked a 35-yard field goal in overtime as the Bears, in come-from-behind fashion, won their first game of the season. Bryan Cox recovered Dan Marino's fumble at the Dolphins' 20 in the opening minutes, leading to Raymont Harris's 1-yard touchdown run. Jerris McPhail's career-best 71-yard touchdown run tied the game 7-7, but the Bears responded with a field goal capping a five-minute drive, and, just over a minute later, a safety. The Bears put together a 7:58 drive late in the half, concluding with Jaeger's second field goal. The Dolphins drove 75 yards, keyed by a 21-yard pass interference penalty on third down, and scored when Marino found McPhail from 10 yards out to cut the halftime deficit to 15-13. Chicago put together nearly a six-minute drive to start the third quarter, but had to settle for another field goal by Jaeger. After forcing a punt, George Teague stripped Ricky Proehl of the football. Terrell Buckley recovered and went 22 yards for at touchdown to give the Dolphins the lead 19-18. The Dolphins then drove 83 yards for a touchdown, capped by Marino's scoring pass to Troy Drayton. Erik Kramer fumbled moments later, and Trace Armstrong recovered. Karim Abdul-Jabbar scored four plays later, and the Dolphins led 33-18 with 7:26 to play. Kramer responded with a 54-yard pass to Curtis Conway to set up an 8-yard scoring strike to Bobby Engram with 5:48 left. The Bears got the ball with 2:35 remaining, and drove 59 yards in 1:10, capped by Kramer's 25-yard touchdown pass to Chris Penn. Engram made a diving catch for the 2-point conversion to send the game to overtime. After each team had maintained possession for a series in overtime, Barry Minter forced Marino to fumble. Carl Reeves recovered at the Dolphins' 17, and Jaeger kicked the winning field goal to give the Bears their first victory. Kramer was 32 of 50 for 343 yards and 2 touchdowns. Harris rushed for 106 yards, and Conway had 6 receptions for 100 yards. Marino was 18 of 39 for 274 yards and 2 touchdowns, with 1 interception. O.J. McDuffie had 7 receptions for 137 yards. The Bears wore down the Dolphins' defense, controlling the ball 44:53 compared to Miami's 24:32. The game was moved from Sunday because of Game 7 of the World Series.

Chicago	7	8	3	15	3	—	36
Miami	7	6	6	14	0	—	33

Chi — Harris 1 run (Jaeger kick)
Mia — McPhail 71 run (Mare kick)
Chi — FG Jaeger 39
Chi — Safety, Marino sacked by Thierry in end zone
Chi — FG Jaeger 23
Mia — McPhail 10 pass from Marino (pass failed)
Chi — FG Jaeger 47
Mia — Buckley 22 fumble return (pass failed)
Mia — Drayton 22 pass from Marino (Mare kick)
Mia — Abdul-Jabbar 2 run (Mare kick)
Chi — Engram 8 pass from Kramer (Jaeger kick)
Chi — Penn 25 pass from Kramer (Engram pass from Kramer)
Chi — FG Jaeger 35

TENTH WEEK SUMMARIES

AMERICAN FOOTBALL CONFERENCE

Eastern Division	W	L	T	Pct.	Pts.	OP
N.Y. Jets	6	3	0	.667	220	172
Buffalo	5	4	0	.556	160	194
Miami	5	4	0	.556	182	169
New England	5	4	0	.556	223	155
Indianapolis	0	9	0	.000	141	230
Central Division						
Jacksonville	6	3	0	.667	238	192
Pittsburgh	6	3	0	.667	204	200
Baltimore	4	5	0	.444	210	194
Tennessee	4	5	0	.444	207	191
Cincinnati	2	7	0	.222	163	250
Western Division						
Denver	8	1	0	.889	268	160
Kansas City	7	2	0	.778	194	143
Seattle	5	4	0	.556	196	207
San Diego	4	5	0	.444	171	214
Oakland	3	6	0	.333	227	256

NATIONAL FOOTBALL CONFERENCE

Eastern Division	W	L	T	Pct.	Pts.	OP
N.Y. Giants	6	3	0	.667	186	180
Washington	5	4	0	.556	173	145
Dallas	4	5	0	.444	188	148
Philadelphia	4	5	0	.444	158	190
Arizona	2	7	0	.222	164	206
Central Division						
Green Bay	7	2	0	.778	216	169
Minnesota	7	2	0	.778	209	179
Tampa Bay	6	3	0	.667	177	162
Detroit	4	5	0	.444	190	175
Chicago	1	8	0	.111	145	263
Western Division						
San Francisco	8	1	0	.889	227	108
Carolina	5	4	0	.556	166	153
Atlanta	2	7	0	.222	179	240
New Orleans	2	7	0	.222	118	198
St. Louis	2	7	0	.222	164	221

SUNDAY, NOVEMBER 2

NEW YORK JETS 19, BALTIMORE 16 (OT)—at Giants Stadium, attendance 59,524. John Hall kicked 4 field goals, including the game-winner in overtime, as the Jets gained sole possession of first place in the AFC East for the first time since 1986. Leon Johnson's 60-yard punt return was followed by Neil O'Donnell's 13-yard touchdown pass to Fred Baxter on the next play to give the Jets a 7-0 lead just over two minutes into the game. The Jets led 10-9 at halftime, and extended the lead to 13-9 after Otis Smith's 25-yard interception return set up Hall's second field goal. Smith grabbed the interception after Vinny Testaverde attempted to throw from his knee after slipping. Smith then recovered a Byron (Bam) Morris fumble early in the fourth quarter and raced 40 yards to allow Hall to increase the lead to seven points with 11:39 remaining. The Ravens drove to the Jets' 13, but Testaverde, because of pressure by Rick Lyle, threw an incomplete pass on fourth-and-2 to turn the ball over with 6:21 to play. The Ravens forced a punt to get the ball back with 1:57 remaining. Testaverde drove the Ravens down field, with Eric Green being the main contributor with four catches, and they reached the Jets' 16 with 14 seconds left. Testaverde threw a pass to Earnest Byner in the flat. Realizing he would be tackled before he could get out of bounds, and thus the clock would run out, Byner dropped the ball. Faced with fourth-and-1 from the 16 with eight seconds left, Testaverde found Derrick Alexander open in the back of the end zone for the tying touchdown with three seconds left. The Jets won the coin toss to gain possession at the beginning of overtime, and drove 60 yards, with the key play being Glenn Foley's, who had replaced O'Donnell, 9-yard pass to Wayne Chrebet on third-and-7 to reach the Ravens' 22. Hall kicked the winning field goal moments later. O'Donnell was 12 of 20 for 96 yards and 1 touchdown before being replaced by Foley, who was 6 of 13 for 72 yards. Testaverde was 25 of 46 for 288 yards and 1 touchdown, with an interception. Morris had 130 rushing yards. The first half was played in a driving rain.

Baltimore	6	3	0	7	0	—	16
N.Y. Jets	7	3	3	3	3	—	19

NYJ — Baxter 13 pass from O'Donnell (Hall kick)
Balt — FG Stover 41
Balt — FG Stover 22
NYJ — FG Hall 28
Balt — FG Stover 24
NYJ — FG Hall 33
NYJ — FG Hall 31
Balt — Alexander 16 pass from Testaverde (Stover kick)
NYJ — FG Hall 37

SAN FRANCISCO 17, DALLAS 10—at 3Com Park, attendance 68,657. Garrison Hearst and William Floyd each produced a rushing touchdown as the 49ers won their eighth consecutive game. Deion Sanders intercepted Steve Young's first-quarter pass and high-stepped 31 yards, with Young's upending tackle the only act preventing Sanders from scoring. Dallas got a touchdown anyway, as Aikman threw a 5-yard scoring pass to Michael Irvin. The 49ers took the second half's opening kickoff and marched 77 yards, capped by Hearst's 8-yard touchdown run, to tie the game 7-7. Aikman threw a 54-yard pass to Anthony Miller on the next drive, leading to Richie Cunningham's 21-yard field goal. Midway through the fourth quarter, a 23-yard punt gave the 49ers possession at the Cowboys' 39, and J.J. Stokes's diving 29-yard catch to the 1-yard line set up Floyd's go-ahead touchdown run. The 49ers forced another punt when they stopped Sherman Williams on third-and-1, and Iheanyi Uwaezuoke's 34-yard punt return set up Gary Anderson's 28-yard field goal with 2:15 left. The Cowboys reached the 49ers' 39, but after a long pass to Irvin fell incomplete, Tim McDonald intercepted Aikman with 37 seconds left to clinch the victory. The Cowboys lost despite converting 10 of 18 third-down chances, while permitting the 49ers to convert just 2 of 8 third-down opportunities. Young was 15 of 23 for 180 yards, with an interception. Hearst rushed for 104 yards. Dana Stubblefield recorded 2 sacks to earn NFC defensive player-of-the-week honors. Aikman was 22 of 36 for 218 yards and 1 touchdown, with 2 interceptions. Emmitt Smith had 7 carries for 31 yards before leaving with a groin injury just before halftime.

Dallas	7	0	3	0	—	10
San Francisco	0	0	7	10	—	17

Dall — Irvin 5 pass from Aikman (Cunningham kick)
SF — Hearst 8 run (Anderson kick)
Dall — FG Cunningham 21
SF — Floyd 1 run (Anderson kick)
SF — FG Anderson 28

JACKSONVILLE 30, TENNESSEE 24—at Liberty Bowl Memorial Stadium, attendance 27,208. Chris Hudson recovered 2 turnovers that led to 14 points, and Mark Brunell threw and ran for a touchdown as the Jaguars snapped a two-game losing streak and moved back into a first-place tie with Pittsburgh. The Jaguars scored 17 points in a 2-minute, 38-second span late in the first quarter to take a 17-7 lead. Mike Hollis's 30-yard field goal completed a 16-play, 68-yard drive, which lasted 7:25. Hudson gave the Jaguars the lead when Eddie George fumbled on the next play from scrimmage. Hudson recovered the ball and raced 32 yards for the go-ahead score. Hudson then intercepted a pass on the next play from scrimmage, and Brunell threw a 6-yard touchdown pass to Pete Mitchell. Steve McNair answered with a 46-yard pass to Willie Davis to set up Al Del Greco's 36-yard field goal. Brunell's 6-yard touchdown run just before halftime was set up by his 40-yard pass to James Stewart. Reggie Barlow's 52-yard punt return early in the third quarter led to Hollis's second field goal and a 27-10 lead for the Jaguars. Tennessee responded with a 65-yard drive, capped by Rodney Thomas's touchdown run. After Hollis's third field goal, the Oilers took less than a minute to score, as Derrick Mason's 45-yard kickoff return set up George's touchdown run with 12:38 left. The Oilers reached the Jaguars' 2 on their next drive, but on a fourth-and-goal pass Tony Brackens tackled Frank Wycheck for a 2-yard loss. The Oilers were unable to regain possession as Natrone Means gained 4 yards on third-and-3 with 1:34 left to ice the game. Brunell was 17 of 31 for 169 yards and 1 touchdown, with an interception. McNair was 13 of 22 for 211 yards, with an interception. The defeat halted a three-game winning streak for the Oilers.

Jacksonville	17	7	3	3	—	30
Tennessee	7	3	7	7	—	24

Tenn — Lewis 47 interception return (Del Greco kick)
Jack — FG Hollis 30
Jack — Hudson 32 fumble return (Hollis kick)
Jack — Mitchell 6 pass from Brunell (Hollis kick)
Tenn — FG Del Greco 36
Jack — Brunell 6 run (Hollis kick)
Jack — FG Hollis 30
Tenn — Thomas 3 run (Del Greco kick)
Jack — FG Hollis 37
Tenn — George 5 run (Del Greco kick)

BUFFALO 9, MIAMI 6—at Rich Stadium, attendance 78,011. Steve Christie kicked 3 field goals, and Jeff Burris intercepted a pass with just over a minute remaining to propel the Bills into a three-way tie for second place in the AFC East. Alex Van Pelt ran 2 yards on fourth-and-1 to keep alive a first-quarter drive that concluded with Chrisite's first field goal. Van Pelt completed 13- and 15-yard passes to Andre Reed to set up Christie's second field goal. The Dolphins drove to the Bills' 14, only to see Olindo Mare miss a 32-yard field-goal attempt. After Christie missed a 41-yard attempt, Mare converted from 27 yards in the half's final minute to cut the deficit to 6-3. With Craig Erickson in for the injured Dan Marino, the Dolphins used a 25-yard pass to Charles Jordan to set up Mare's tying boot 39 seconds into the final quarter. Van Pelt responded with a 29-yard pass to Eric Moulds that led to Christie's go-ahead field goal with 10:42 remaining. After being forced to punt twice, the Dolphins got the ball back on their own 12-yard line with 2:36 remaining, but upon reaching Bills' territory, Burris picked off Erickson's pass with 1:01 left, and Thurman Thomas rushed for 11 yards on third-and-5 with 51 seconds left to ice the game. Van Pelt was 13 of 22 for 89 yards. Marino was 5 of 15 for 76 yards, with an interception, before leaving with an ankle sprain. Erickson was 8 of 18 for 121 yards, with an interception. The teams combined for less than 500 total yards and each converted just 3 of 14 third-down opportunities. The game was played in rain, and the Bills fumbled 6 times, but lost the ball just once.

Miami	0	3	0	3	—	6
Buffalo	3	3	0	3	—	9

Buff — FG Christie 41
Buff — FG Christie 40
Mia — FG Mare 27
Mia — FG Mare 35
Buff — FG Christie 39

MINNESOTA 23, NEW ENGLAND 18—at Hubert H. Humphrey Metrodome, attendance 62,197. Cris Carter caught 8 passes for 116 yards and a touchdown as the Vikings held off the Patriots to remain tied for first place in the NFC Central. Moe Williams's 74-yard kickoff return to begin the game set up Eddie Murray's first field goal, and Williams scored from 1 yard out on the Vikings' second possession after David Palmer's 19-yard punt return. Drew Bledsoe's 76-yard pass to Shawn Jefferson led to Adam Vinatieri's 22-yard field goal, but the Vikings matched field goals with the Patriots thanks to Brad Johnson's 43-yard pass to Jake Reed. Trailing 16-3 in the fourth quarter, Bledsoe finished a 76-yard drive with a 5-yard touchdown pass to Jefferson with 10:01 left. Holder Tom Tupa dropped the extra-point snap, enabling the Vikings to maintain a seven-point lead. Curtis Martin's 37-yard run on their next possession set up Vinatieri's second field goal, cutting the deficit to 16-12. The Vikings responded with 73-yard drive, capped by Johnson's 28-yard touchdown pass to Carter with 2:39 remaining. The Patriots quickly drove downfield and scored on Terry Glenn's 3-yard touchdown grab, but a 2-point conversion attempt between the same duo fell incomplete. Vinatieri's onside kick went out of bounds, clinching the victory for Minnesota. Johnson was 18 of 31 for 227 yards and a touchdown. Bledsoe was 27 of 42 for 313 yards and 2 touchdowns, with an interception. Curtis Martin had 104 rushing yards, and Jefferson had 4 receptions for 108 yards. The loss marked the Patriots' third consecutive defeat, and their record fell to 0-4 when scoring fewer than 20 points.

New England	0	3	0	15	—	18
Minnesota	10	3	3	7	—	23

Minn — FG Murray 24
Minn — Williams 1 run (Murray kick)
NE — FG Vinatieri 22
Minn — FG Murray 23
Minn — FG Murray 41
NE — Jefferson 5 pass from Bledsoe (bad hold)
NE — FG Vinatieri 25
Minn — Carter 28 pass from Johnson (Murray kick)
NE — Glenn 3 pass from Bledsoe (pass failed)

CAROLINA 38, OAKLAND 14—at Ericsson Stadium, attendance 71,064. Rookie Fred Lane rushed for 147 yards and 3 touchdowns to earn NFC offensive player-of-the-week honors as the Panthers defeated the Raiders. Lane replaced Tshimanga Biakabutuka, who left the game with bruised ribs and did not return, and capped the opening drive with a 14-yard touchdown run. Late in the quarter, Lane finished a 75-yard drive with a 18-yard run in which he spun through numerous tackles on his way to the end zone. Kerry Collins completed a 63-yard drive with a 6-yard scramble to give the Panthers a 21-0 lead. After Napoleon Kaufman caught a 23-yard touchdown pass from Jeff George with 3:24 left in the half, Dwight Stone's 37-yard kickoff return allowed Scott Greene to score from 10 yards and give the Panthers a 28-7 halftime lead. The Raiders scored on the opening drive of the second half, but Sam Mills's interception on the Raiders next possession halted a drive in Panthers' territory. Lane capped the day with a 32-yard touchdown run midway through the fourth quarter to finish the scoring. Collins was 18 of 32 for 198 yards. George was 24 of 38 for 304 yards and 2 touchdowns, with an interception. Oakland's Tim Brown caught 10 passes for 163 yards. Carolina had 216 rushing yards compared to the Raiders' 38 yards on the ground.

Oakland	0	7	7	0	—	14
Carolina	14	14	3	7	—	38

Car — Lane 15 run (Kasay kick)
Car — Lane 18 run (Kasay kick)
Car — Collins 6 run (Kasay kick)
Oak — Kaufman 23 pass from George (Ford kick)
Car — Greene 10 run (Kasay kick)
Oak — Jett 16 pass from George (Ford kick)
Car — FG Kasay 54
Car — Lane 32 run (Kasay kick)

ARIZONA 31, PHILADELPHIA 21—at Sun Devil Stadium, attendance 39,549. Kent Graham scored the first 2 rushing touchdowns of his career in the final 3:10 as the Cardinals snapped a six-game losing streak. The Eagles' first drive ended when Bernard Wilson intercepted a Rodney Peete pass and used a convoy of blockers to rumble 66 yards for his first NFL touchdown. The Cardinals attempted an onside kick on the ensuing kickoff, but Willie Clark alertly grabbed the bouncing ball and sped 39 yards for a touchdown. Kevin Williams's 50-yard punt return in the third quarter was followed on the next play by Jake Plummer's 31-yard scoring pass to Rob Moore to take a 17-7 third-quarter lead. Ty Detmer, who replaced Peete at halftime, guided the Eagles on a 7-play, 82-yard drive, capped by his 19-yard touchdown pass to Mark Seay. Greg Jefferson recovered Plummer's fumble moments later, and Detmer threw a 18-yard touchdown pass to Freddie Solomon to give the Eagles a 21-17 lead. After Joe Nedney missed a 48-yard field-goal attempt early in the fourth quarter, Chris Boniol made a 27-yard field goal. However, the Eagles were whistled for holding, and Boniol's 37-yard attempt hit the left goal post. On the next possession, the Eagles forced the Cardinals to punt with 5:52 remaining in the game, but Seay muffed the fair catch and Cedric Smith recovered at the Eagles' 24. Jimmie Jones jumped offsides on third down to keep the Cardinals' drive alive, and Graham, who had replaced Plummer, scored his first NFL rushing touchdown with 3:10 remaining to give Arizona a 24-21 lead. Mike Caldwell's interception and 5-yard return gave the Cardinals the ball at the Eagles' 20, and Graham scored again, with 24 seconds left, to ice the game. Plummer was 7 of 18 for 132 yards and 1 touchdown, with an interception before being replaced by Graham, who was 5 of 9 for 33 yards. Peete was just 3 of 13 for 54 yards, with an interception before Detmer played the second half and was 15 of 27 for 224 yards and 2 touchdowns, with 2 interceptions. The Eagles committed 15 penalties and 4 turnovers.

Philadelphia	7	0	14	0	—	21
Arizona	7	3	7	14	—	31

Ariz — Wilson 66 interception return (Nedney kick)
Phil — Clark 39 kickoff return (Boniol kick)
Ariz — FG Nedney 45
Ariz — Moore 31 pass from Plummer (Nedney kick)
Phil — Seay 19 pass from Detmer (Boniol kick)
Phil — Solomon 18 pass from Detmer (Boniol kick)
Ariz — Graham 1 run (Nedney kick)
Ariz — Graham 1 run (Nedney kick)

ATLANTA 34, ST. LOUIS 31—at Georgia Dome, attendance 36,583. Morten Andersen's 27-yard field goal with two seconds remaining lifted the Falcons out of last place in the NFC West. After Jeff Wilkins's field goal was the lone score in the first quarter, the teams combined for 38 points in the second quarter. The Falcons drove 84 yards in 5 plays, capped by Chris Chandler's 28-yard touchdown pass to Bert Emanuel. Tony Banks's 59-yard pass to Isaac Bruce set up Lawrence Phillips's 16-yard touchdown run. The Falcons responded with a 6-play, 79-yard drive, with Chandler's 33-yard pass to Emanuel registering points on the scoreboard. The Rams answered with a 6-play, 80-yard drive, with Banks finding Bruce for a touchdown, and, after a punt, Banks found Bruce for another score to complete a 6-play, 58-yard drive that lasted 36 seconds. Brian Kozlowski's 23-yard kickoff return enabled Andersen to kick a 37-yard field goal at the end of the half to cut the deficit to 24-17. The Falcons scored touchdowns on their first two possessions of the second half to take a 31-24 lead, but Tony Banks scrambled and dove into the end zone on fourth-and-goal from the 1 to tie the game with 1:10 remaining. Chandler threw 19- and 22-yard passes to Harold Green to put Andersen in position for his game-winning boot. Chandler was 19 of 32 for 276 yards and 3 touchdowns, with 1 interception. Emanuel had 6 receptions for 108 yards, and Anderson rushed 19 times for 159 yards. Banks was 23 of 34 for a career-high 401 yards and 2 touchdowns, with an interception. Bruce had 10 catches for a career-high 233 yards. The teams combined for 966 yards, including 414 in the second quarter.

St. Louis	3	21	0	7	—	31
Atlanta	0	17	14	3	—	34

StL — FG Wilkins 38
Atl — Emanuel 28 pass from Chandler (Andersen kick)
StL — Phillips 16 run (Wilkins kick)
Atl — Emanuel 33 pass from Chandler (Andersen kick)
StL — Bruce 29 pass from Banks (Wilkins kick)
StL — Bruce 9 pass from Banks (Wilkins kick)
Atl — FG Andersen 37
Atl — Anderson 2 run (Andersen kick)
Atl — Mathis 11 pass from Chandler (Andersen kick)
StL — Banks 1 run (Wilkins kick)
Atl — FG Andersen 27

CINCINNATI 38, SAN DIEGO 31—at Cinergy Field, attendance 53,754. Jeff Blake threw a touchdown pass and ran for another as the Bengals broke a seven-game losing streak despite 2 punt returns for touchdowns by Eric Metcalf. After Doug Pelfrey's field goal cut the Bengals' deficit to 7-3, Bo Orlando recoverd Latario Rachal's fumble on the ensuing kickoff, leading to Blake's 15-yard touchdown pass to Carl Pickens. Metcalf responded less than three minutes later with an 85-yard punt return for a touchdown. Late in the first half, Corey Sawyer's 37-yard interception return down to the 2-yard line set up Brian Milne's touchdown run to give the Bengals a 17-14 edge. Stan Humphries fumbled the snap from center, and five-year veteran John Copeland scooped up the ball and raced 25 yards for his first NFL touchdown. Eric Bieniemy fumbled, however, attempting to run out the clock, and Rodney Harrison recovered with four seconds left to allow Greg Davis to kick a 45-yard field goal to cut the Bengals lead to 24-17. Corey Dillon broke free on a third-and-1 run and scampered 71 yards for a third-quarter touchdown, but Metcalf's 67-yard punt return for a touchdown cut the deficit to 31-24. Blake's 13-yard scramble increased the lead to 14 points with 7:02 remaining, but Craig Whelihan, who replaced an injured Humphries, threw a 44-yard touchdown pass to Charlie Jones. The Chargers got the ball back with 2:05 left, but Whelihan's pass on fourth-and-5 from their own 33 fell incomplete. Blake was 19 of 32 for 172 yards and 1 touchdown. Dillon finished with 123 rushing yards. Humphries was 12 of 25 for 115 yards, with 1 interception. Whelihan was 8 of 16 for 90 yards and 1 touchdown. Metcalf, who finished with 4 punt returns for 168 yards and set an NFL record by becoming the first player with 2 touchdowns in a game two separate times, earned AFC special teams player-of-the-week honors.

San Diego	7	10	0	14	—	31
Cincinnati	0	24	7	7	—	38

SD — Brown 1 run (Davis kick)
Cin — FG Pelfrey 27
Cin — Pickens 15 pass from Blake (Pelfrey kick)
SD — Metcalf 85 punt return (Davis kick)
Cin — Milne 2 run (Pelfrey kick)
Cin — Copeland 25 fumble return (Pelfrey kick)
SD — FG Davis 45
Cin — Dillon 71 run (Pelfrey kick)
SD — Metcalf 67 punt return (Davis kick)
Cin — Blake 13 run (Pelfrey kick)
SD — Jones 44 pass from Whelihan (Davis kick)

DENVER 30, SEATTLE 27—at Denver Mile High Stadium, attendance 74,212. John Elway passed for 252 yards and 2 touchdowns as the Broncos miantained their hold on first place in the AFC West. After an exchange of field goals in the first quarter, John Elway completed a 67-yard drive with a 10-yard touchdown pass to Willie Green. Warren Moon's fumble and Darrien Gordon's recovery led to Jason Elam's second field goal, but the Seahawks responded with a 62-yard drive in less than two minutes, capped by Warren Moon's 20-yard touchdown pass to James McKnight. Glenn Cadrez forced Ronnie Harris to fumble the second half's opening kickoff, and Darrius Johnson picked up the ball and scored to give the Broncos a 20-10 lead. Martin Harrison's fumble recovery set up Todd Peterson's 41-yard field goal, and when Jeremy Lincoln recovered Vaughn Hebron's fumble on the ensuing kickoff, Moon threw a 4-yard pass to Mack Strong to tie the game 20-20. Elway answered with a 59-yard touchdown pass to Rod Smith, but Seattle tied the game with a 10-play, 81-yard drive, capped by Moon's 8-yard scoring pass to Brian Blades with 12:02 remaining. Elway's 49-yard pass to Shannon Sharpe helped drive the Broncos to the Seahawks' 1, but the Seahawks' defense forced Denver to settle for Elam's third field goal. It was enough, as Moon's fourth-and-4 pass from his own 46 with 1:07 left was tipped by Keith Traylor and fell incomplete. Elway, who was the AFC offensive player of the week, was 19 of 30 for 252 yards and 2 touchdowns. Smith had 4 receptions for 100 yards, and Davis finished with 101 rushing yards. Moon was 28 of 46 for 255 yards and 3 touchdowns. Seattle had its three-game winning streak halted.

Seattle	3	7	10	7	—	27
Denver	3	10	14	3	—	30

Sea — FG Peterson 52
Den — FG Elam 23
Den — Green 10 pass from Elway (Elam kick)
Den — FG Elam 48
Sea — McKnight 20 pass from Moon (Peterson kick)
Den — Johnson 6 fumble return (Elam kick)
Sea — FG Peterson 41
Sea — Strong 4 pass from Moon (Peterson kick)
Den — R. Smith 59 pass from Elway (Elam kick)
Sea — Blades 8 pass from Moon (Peterson kick)
Den — FG Elam 22

TAMPA BAY 31, INDIANAPOLIS 28—at RCA Dome, attendance 58,512. Michael Husted's 36-yard field goal with eight seconds left allowed the Buccaneers to break their three-game losing streak and keep the Colts winless. Regan Upshaw's fumble recovery on the Colts' 21 set up Mike Alstott's 1-yard touchdown plunge to give the Buccaneers an early 7-0 lead. Backup quarterback Paul Justin, starting in place of injured Jim Harbaugh, hurt a finger on his throwing hand and had to leave the game. Kelly Holcomb entered his first NFL game and guided the Colts to Marshall Faulk's go-ahead touchdown run early in the second quarter. Karl Williams's 63-yard punt return set up Trent Dilfer's 3-yard touchdown pass to Dave Moore, and Williams caught a 6-yard touchdown pass with 35 seconds left in the half to give Tampa Bay a 21-10 halftime lead. The Colts scored on both of their third-quarter possessions, with Holcomb's 2-point conversion pass to Marcus Pollard tying the game 21-21. Cary Blanchard missed a 30-yard field-goal attempt that would have given the Colts the lead, but Jason Belser forced Alstott to fumble a few plays later. Robert Blackmon recovered the fumble and ran 18 yards to give the Colts the lead. The Buccaneers responded with a 80-yard drive, capped by Williams's second touchdown catch, to tie the game with 6:52 remaining. The Colts drove to the 5-yard line, but Holcomb fumbled a fake handoff, and Chidi Ahanotu recovered with 3:02 left. After an exchange of punts, the Buccaneers got the ball to the Colts' 45, on Williams's 21-yard punt return with 52 seconds left. Dilfer completed passes of 12, 9, and 6 yards to Warrick Dunn, Reidel Anthony, and Moore to set up Husted's heroics. Dilfer was 16 of 25 for 164 yards and 3 touchdowns. Holcomb was 19 of 30 for 181 yards, with 1 interception. Williams earned NFC special teams player-of-the-week honors with his 3 punt returns for 99 yards, and 2 touchdown catches.

Tampa Bay	7	14	0	10	—	31
Indianapolis	3	7	11	7	—	28

TB — Alstott 1 run (Husted kick)
Ind — FG Blanchard 43
Ind — Faulk 4 run (Blanchard kick)
TB — Moore 3 pass from Dilfer (Husted kick)
TB — Williams 6 pass from Dilfer (Husted kick)
Ind — FG Blanchard 36
Ind — Warren 1 run (Pollard pass from Holcomb)
Ind — Blackmon 18 fumble return (Blanchard kick)
TB — Williams 24 pass from Dilfer (Husted kick)
TB — FG Husted 36

WASHINGTON 31, CHICAGO 8—at Soldier Field, attendance 53,032. Terry Allen returned after missing two games and rushed for 125 yards as the Redskins broke a two-game losing streak and defeated the Bears. Allen's 30-yard run on the opening drive keyed a touchdown drive capped by Gus Frerotte's 9-yard touchdown pass to James Jenkins. After forcing a punt, Larry Bowie crashed into the end zone from 5 yards to increase the lead, and Allen's 34-yard run led to Frerotte's 1-yard run on the next drive to give the Redskins a 21-0 lead just 16:26 into the game. The Bears defense stopped the Redskins on their fourth possession, but Tyrone Hughes muffed the punt and Darryl Pounds recovered leading to Scott Blanton's field goal and a 24-0 halftime lead. Frerotte threw a 39-yard touchdown pass to Leslie Shepherd in the third quarter. The Bears drove 98 yards to score their lone points with 5:03 remaining. Frerotte was 14 of 20 for 192 yards and 2 touchdowns. Erik Kramer was 21 of 37 for 237 yards and 1 touchdown, with an interception. The Redskins converted 6 of 11 third-down opportunities, while permitting the Bears just 1 of 9 third-down conversions.

Washington	14	10	7	0	—	31
Chicago	0	0	0	8	—	8

Wash — Jenkins 9 pass from Frerotte (Blanton kick)
Wash — Bowie 5 run (Blanton kick)
Wash — Frerotte 1 run (Blanton kick)
Wash — FG Blanton 38
Wash — Shepherd 39 pass from Frerotte (Blanton kick)
Chi — Proehl 2 pass from Kramer (Proehl pass from Kramer)

SUNDAY NIGHT, NOVEMBER 2

GREEN BAY 20, DETROIT 10—at Lambeau Field, attendance 60,126. Brett Favre threw a touchdown pass, and rookie Darren Sharper scored his first NFL touchdown as the Packers won their twentieth consecutive home game. Scott Mitchell's 33-yard swing pass to Cory Schlesinger on fourth-and-1 to the 1-yard line set up Tommy Vardell's touchdown run. The Packers tied the game in the first minute of the second quarter when Favre threw a 26-yard touchdown pass to Robert Brooks. With just under five minutes left in the half, Sharper intercepted a hurried Mitchell's pass and ran 50 yards for a touchdown. Mark Carrier intercepted Favre just before halftime, enabling Jason Hanson to boot a 34-yard field goal to cut the deficit to 14-10. The Packers tacked on three points with a 68-yard drive to open the second half, and increased the advantage to 10 points with 6:44 remaining on the strength of Favre's 21-yard pass to Brooks on third-and-10. The Lions could not get inside the Packers' 35 during their final two possessions. Favre was 15 of 28 for 181 yards and 1 touchdown, with 1 interception. Mitchell was 21 of 47 for 158 yards, with 4 interceptions. Barry Sanders rushed for 105 yards. The Packers' defense intercepted Mitchell 3 times in the second half, 2 by LeRoy Butler, and permitted the Lions to convert just 2 of 17 third-down chances.

Detroit	7	3	0	0	—	10
Green Bay	0	14	3	3	—	20

Det — Vardell 1 run (Hanson kick)
GB — Brooks 26 pass from Favre (Longwell kick)
GB — Sharper 50 interception return (Longwell kick)
Det — FG Hanson 34
GB — FG Longwell 23
GB — FG Longwell 44

MONDAY, NOVEMBER 3

KANSAS CITY 13, PITTSBURGH 10—at Arrowhead Stadium, attendance 78,301. Marcus Allen threw his first touchdown pass since 1991 as the Chiefs remained a game behind the Denver Broncos. Kordell Stewart threw a 44-yard touchdown pass to Courtney Hawkins to give the Steelers a 7-0 lead. Donnell Woolford's interception and 33-yard return halted a Chiefs drive and led to Norm Johnson's 27-yard field goal. The Chiefs responded with a 12-play, 60-yard drive, which consumed more than six minutes and featured a 30-yard run by Allen, to set up the first of 2 Pete Stoyanovich field goals. Jerome Woods intercepted Stewart on the Steelers' first play after the second field goal, and an 18-yard scramble by Grbac gave the Chiefs a first down at the 14-yard line. On the next play, Allen took a pitch, rolled right, and found Danan Hughes open in the end zone. The Chiefs drove to the Steelers' 3 on the opening drive of the second half, but Darren Perry stopped Allen on fourth down. Neither team ran a play inside the opponents' 30-yard line the remainder of the game. Grbac was 16 of 29 for 172 yards, with 1 interception, before suffering a broken left collarbone in the fourth quarter. Rich Gannon replaced him, and his 13-yard scramble in the final minutes iced the game for Kansas City. Anthony Davis, with 6 tackles, was named AFC defensive player of the week. Stewart was 11 of 21 for 101 yards and 1 touchdown, with an interception. Bettis rushed for 103 yards, giving him five 100-yard rushing games in his last five games on Mondays. The Chiefs had more yards (392-235), first downs (24-12), and time of possession (36:32-23:28).

Pittsburgh	10	0	0	0	—	10
Kansas City	0	13	0	0	—	13

Pitt — Hawkins 44 pass from Stewart (N. Johnson kick)
Pitt — FG N. Johnson 27
KC — FG Stoyanovich 35
KC — FG Stoyanovich 44
KC — Hughes 14 pass from Allen (Stoyanovich kick)

ELEVENTH WEEK SUMMARIES

AMERICAN FOOTBALL CONFERENCE

Eastern Division	W	L	T	Pct.	Pts.	OP
Miami	6	4	0	.600	206	186
New England	6	4	0	.600	254	165
N.Y. Jets	6	4	0	.600	237	196
Buffalo	5	5	0	.500	170	225
Indianapolis	0	10	0	.000	154	258
Central Division						
Jacksonville	7	3	0	.700	262	202
Pittsburgh	7	3	0	.700	241	200
Tennessee	5	5	0	.500	217	197
Baltimore	4	6	0	.400	210	231
Cincinnati	3	7	0	.300	191	263
Western Division						
Denver	9	1	0	.900	302	160
Kansas City	7	3	0	.700	204	167
Seattle	6	4	0	.600	233	238
San Diego	4	6	0	.400	202	251
Oakland	3	7	0	.300	237	269

NATIONAL FOOTBALL CONFERENCE

Eastern Division	W	L	T	Pct.	Pts.	OP
N.Y. Giants	6	4	0	.600	192	190
Washington	6	4	0	.600	203	152
Dallas	5	5	0	.500	212	154
Philadelphia	4	6	0	.400	170	214
Arizona	2	8	0	.200	170	230
Central Division						
Green Bay	8	2	0	.800	233	176
Minnesota	8	2	0	.800	238	201
Tampa Bay	7	3	0	.700	208	172
Detroit	4	6	0	.400	197	205
Chicago	1	9	0	.100	167	292
Western Division						
San Francisco	9	1	0	.900	251	120
Carolina	5	5	0	.500	166	187
New Orleans	3	7	0	.300	131	208
Atlanta	2	8	0	.200	189	271
St. Louis	2	8	0	.200	171	238

SUNDAY, NOVEMBER 9

DALLAS 24, ARIZONA 6—at Texas Stadium, attendance 64,302. Tony Tolbert and Shante Carver each recorded 2 of the Cowboys' 9 sacks as Dallas improved to 4-0 at home. Jake Plummer's 31-yard scramble led to Joe Nedney's 42-yard field goal to stake the Cardinals to a 3-0 lead. In the second quarter, Troy Aikman completed key third-down passes to David LaFleur and Billy Davis to set up Richie Cunningham's tying field goal. Late in the half, the Cowboys drove 81 yards in 3:25, capped by Aikman's 11-yard touchdown pass to Herschel Walker. Ronald McKinnon's interception early in the second half set up Nedney's second field goal, but the Cowboys responded with a touchdown drive, keyed by Aikman's 51-yard pass to Anthony Miller to the 2-yard line, and capped by Sherman Williams's 1-yard run. Later in the third quarter, Fred Strickland recovered Jake Plummer's fumble on the Cardinals' 16, and Emmitt Smith scored from the 5-yard line two plays later to ice the game. Aikman was 15 of 22 for 216 yards and 1 touchdown, with an interception. Plummer was 13 of 22 for 148 yards. Kent Graham replaced Plummer and was 5 of 14 for 74 yards. The Cowboys' defense allowed Arizona to convert just 3 of 15 third-down opportunities.

Arizona	3	0	3	0	—	6
Dallas	0	10	14	0	—	24

Ariz — FG Nedney 42
Dall — FG Cunningham 23
Dall — Walker 11 pass from Aikman (Cunningham kick)
Ariz — FG Nedney 39
Dall — Sh. Williams 1 run (Cunningham kick)
Dall — E. Smith 5 run (Cunningham kick)

DENVER 34, CAROLINA 0—at Denver Mile High Stadium, attendance 71,408. Darrien Gordon returned 2 punts for touchdowns as the Broncos permitted just 7 first downs and recorded their first shutout this season, and just their third this decade. Gordon's punt returns came in a span of just 7:09 in the first quarter. He became the eighth player in NFL history to return 2 punts for touchdowns in the same game. Allen Aldridge forced Fred Lane to fumble at the Broncos' 11-yard line early in the second quarter. John Mobley recovered the fumble to end the Panthers best scoring chance of the game. John Elway threw 36- and 33-yard passes to Shannon Sharpe to set up Jason Elam's field goal in the final minute of the half to increase the lead to 17-0. Elam added a second field goal on the opening drive of the third quarter, and the second of Ray Crockett's 2 interceptions set up Elway's 20-yard touchdown pass to Rod Smith. Tyrone Braxton intercepted an errant pass early in the fourth quarter and raced 27 yards for the final points. Elway was 14 of 23 for 227 yards and 1 touchdown. Sharpe had 8 receptions for 174 yards, and Davis rushed 21 times for 104 yards. Collins was 13 of 29 for 141 yards, with 3 interceptions. The Broncos had more first downs (20-7), total yards (393-147), and time of possession (37:19-22:41). Denver improved to 9-1 for the third time in club history, and won its fourteenth consecutive home game.

Carolina	0	0	0	0	—	0
Denver	14	3	10	7	—	34

Den — Gordon 82 punt return (Elam kick)
Den — Gordon 75 punt return (Elam kick)
Den — FG Elam 25
Den — FG Elam 50
Den — R. Smith 20 pass from Elway (Elam kick)
Den — Braxton 27 interception return (Elam kick)

MINNESOTA 29, CHICAGO 22—at Hubert H. Humphrey Metrodome, attendance 63,443. David Palmer scored 2 touchdowns and set up two more as the Vikings won their sixth consecutive game and maintained a tie for first-place in the NFC Central. Palmer began his exploits with an 8-yard touchdown run midway through the first quarter. Early in the second quarter, Palmer caught 11- and 23-yard passes to set up his own 7-yard touchdown reception. After Jeff Jaeger's field goal cut the deficit to 14-10, Palmer returned the ensuing kickoff 62 yards to lead to Charles Evans's 3-yard touchdown run. After a second Jaeger field goal, Ricky Proehl caught an Erik Kramer pass and scampered 59 yards for a touchdown, but the Bears did not convert the 2-point opportunity and trailed 21-19. Adrian Autry's 19-yard run put the Bears in Vikings' territory, and his 7-yard run on third-and-6 to the Vikings' 25 set up Jaeger's third field goal and gave the Bears the lead with 3:33 remaining. But the Vikings drove 75 yards in 2:39, keyed by Palmer's 7-yard run on third-and-2 to the Bears' 44, and took the lead on Leroy Hoard's 1-yard run with 54 seconds remaining. Cris Carter caught Brad Johnson's 2-point conversion pass to put the Vikings up by 7 points, and the Bears failed to gain a first down, sealing the Viking victory. Johnson was 22 of 33 for 203 yards and 1 touchdown, with 2 interceptions. Kramer was 23 of 35 for 256 yards and 1 touchdown, with an interception. Proehl had 9 receptions for 132 yards.

Chicago	7	3	9	3	—	22
Minnesota	7	14	0	8	—	29

Minn — Palmer 8 run (Murray kick)
Chi — Harris 1 run (Jaeger kick)
Minn — Palmer 7 pass from Johnson (Murray kick)
Chi — FG Jaeger 29
Minn — Evans 3 run (Murray kick)
Chi — FG Jaeger 22
Chi — Proehl 59 pass from Kramer (pass failed)
Chi — FG Jaeger 36
Minn — Hoard 1 run (Carter pass from Johnson)

CINCINNATI 28, INDIANAPOLIS 13—at RCA Dome, attendance 58,473. Boomer Esiason entered the game in the second half for injured Jeff Blake and threw 2 touchdown passes as the Bengals posted consecutive victories for the first time this season. After a scoreless first quarter, James Francis recovered a Marshall Faulk fumble near midfield to set up Blake's 15-yard touchdown pass to Tony McGee. Kelly Holcomb, in his first NFL start, responded with a 66-yard drive, keyed by a 15-yard pass to Marvin Harrison and 14-yard pass to Zack Crockett, that led to his 6-yard touchdown pass to Harrison just before halftime. Cary Blanchard ended the opening drive of the second half with a 42-yard field goal, but the Bengals grabbed the lead for good as Corey Dillon broke free and scooted 46 yards for the go-ahead touchdown. The second of Ashley Ambrose's 2 interceptions, and ensuing 27-yard return, stopped the Colts' next drive. Faced with third-and-1 from his own 48, Esiason hit Marco Battaglia for 29 yards to set up his 5-yard scoring toss to Carl Pickens to give the Bengals a 21-10 lead. James Francis then intercepted Holcomb to halt the Colts' next possession, and Esiason drove the Bengals 65 yards, concluding with a 5-yard touchdown pass to McGee with 7:03 remaining. Blake, who had to leave the game midway through the third quarter with a back strain, was 9 of 15 for 63 yards and a touchdown. Esiason replaced him and was 7 of 10 for 82 yards and 2 touchdown passes. Holcomb, whom it was discovered after the game had played the second half with a broken bone in his nonthrowing hand, was 19 of 32 for 236 yards and 1 touchdown, with 3 interceptions. Faulk rushed 18 times for 110 yards. The Bengals' defense allowed fewer than 21 points for the first time this season, recorded 7 sacks, and forced 4 turnovers.

Cincinnati	0	7	14	7	—	28
Indianapolis	0	7	3	3	—	13

Cin — McGee 15 pass from Blake (Pelfrey kick)
Ind — Harrison 6 pass from Holcomb (Blanchard kick)
Ind — FG Blanchard 42
Cin — Dillon 46 run (Pelfrey kick)
Cin — Pickens 5 pass from Esiason (Pelfrey kick)
Cin — McGee 5 pass from Esiason (Pelfrey kick)
Ind — FG Blanchard 45

WASHINGTON 30, DETROIT 7—at Jack Kent Cooke Stadium, attendance 75,261. Darryl Pounds had 2 interceptions and a touchdown as the Redskins' defense forced 4 turnovers and permitted just 11 first downs to defeat the Lions. Leading 3-0, Jesse Campbell's interception gave the Redskins the ball at the Lions' 30. A 25-yard pass interference penalty set up Gus Frerotte's 1-yard touchdown pass to James Jenkins. Frerotte completed 3 passes in the final 20 seconds of the first half to set up Scott Blanton's 50-yard field goal as the clock expired. Trailing 20-0, Barry Sanders raced 51 yards for a touchdown. In the fourth quarter, Frerotte's 31-yard pass to Michael Westbrook on third-and-1 set up Blanton's third field goal, and Pounds's interception return 28 seconds later finished the scoring. Frerotte was 20 of 41 for 247 yards and a touchdown. Scott Mitchell was 5 of 14 for 53 yards before leaving the game in the second quarter with a hamstring pull. Frank Reich was 10 of 28 for 110 yards, with 2 interceptions, and Matt Blundin threw an interception in his only pass attempt. Sanders finished with 105 rushing yards to move into third place on the NFL's all-time rushing list, and established two NFL records: ninth consecutive 1,000-yard rushing seasons; and eight consecutive 100-yard rushing games on the road. The Redskins held the ball for 40:03 of the game's 60 minutes.

Detroit	0	0	7	0	—	7
Washington	3	10	7	10	—	30

Wash — FG Blanton 22
Wash — Jenkins 1 pass from Frerotte (Blanton kick)
Wash — FG Blanton 50
Wash — Allen 1 run (Blanton kick)
Det — Sanders 51 run (Hanson kick)
Wash — FG Blanton 45
Wash — Pounds 22 interception return (Blanton kick)

JACKSONVILLE 24, KANSAS CITY 10—at ALLTEL Stadium, attendance 70,444. Jeff Lageman had 2 sacks and a fumble recovery as the Jaguars forced 5 turnovers in the Chiefs last 7 possessions and recorded a club-record 6 sacks to extend their home winning-streak to 11 games. Willie Jackson began the game with a 38-yard kickoff return to set up Mark Brunell's 5-yard touchdown pass to Pete Mitchell. Early in the second quarter, the Jaguars drove 93 yards in 5 plays, keyed by Brunell's 75-yard pass to Jimmy Smith, to set up James Stewart's 1-yard touchdown run. The Chiefs answered as Tamarick Vanover's 38-yard kickoff return led to Pete Stoyanovich's 45-yard field goal. But the Jaguars responded with a 7-play, 75-yard drive, capped by Natrone Means's 14-yard touchdown run. Mike Hollis's field goal late in the half gave the Jaguars a 24-3 edge. The only Chiefs touchdown came after Chris Hudson intercepted Rich Gannon, but fumbled on the return, and Danan Hughes scooped up the ball and ran 7 yards for a touchdown. Brunell was 9 of 20 for 199 yards and a touchdown. Smith had 4 receptions for 112 yards. Gannon was 29 of 50 for 314 yards, with 2 interceptions. The Jaguars won despite not converting a third down (0-for-8) and being outgained (424-332 total yards).

Kansas City	0	3	0	7	—	10
Jacksonville	7	17	0	0	—	24

Jack — Mitchell 5 pass from Brunell (Hollis kick)
Jack — Stewart 1 run (Hollis kick)
KC — FG Stoyanovich 45
Jack — Means 14 run (Hollis kick)
Jack — FG Hollis 52
KC — Hughes 7 fumble return (Stoyanovich kick)

NEW ENGLAND 31, BUFFALO 10—at Rich Stadium, attendance 65,783. Derrick Cullors returned a kickoff for a touchdown and Chris Slade scored on an interception return as the Patriots forced 4 turnovers to defeat the Bills. Buffalo scored late in the first quarter, keyed by Brad Van Pelt's 29-yard pass to Tony Cline, and capped by Steve Christie's 23-yard field goal. Cullors, however, returned the ensuing kickoff 86 yards for his first NFL touchdown. Jimmy Hitchcock's interception and 4-yard return to the Patriots' 30 set up Adam Vinatieri's twenty-fifth consecutive field goal. Vinatieri's streak was snapped, however, as he missed a 42-yard field-goal attempt on the Patriots' next possession. On their next drive, Curtis Martin ran 32 yards and Drew Bledsoe connected with Terry Glenn on a 40-yard pass play to set up Bledsoe's 6-yard touchdown pass to Ben Coates to give the Patriots a 17-3 halftime lead. After a punt pinned the Bills back on their own 7-yard line in the third quarter, Slade tipped a pass at the line of scrimmage, caught it, and stepped into the end zone. The Bills responded as they put together an 11-play, 70-yard drive capped by Antowain Smith's 1-yard touchdown run. The Patriots answered with a 71-yard drive, keyed by Bledose's 50-yard pass play to Troy Brown, and capped by Martin's 1-yard run. Bledsoe was 15 of 22 for 200 yards and 1 touchdown. Van Pelt was 3 of 12 for 38 yards, with 3 interceptions. He was replaced at halftime by Todd Collins, who completed 12 of 21 passes for 89 yards, with an interception. The Patriots recorded just 11 first downs and 267 total yards, but did not commit a turnover. Besides their two scoring drives, the Bills did not run a play inside the Patriots' 44-yard line.

New England	7	10	7	7	—	31
Buffalo	3	0	7	0	—	10

Buff — FG Christie 23
NE — Cullors 86 kickoff return (Vinatieri kick)
NE — FG Vinatieri 42
NE — Coates 6 pass from Bledsoe (Vinatieri kick)
NE — Slade 1 interception return (Vinatieri kick)
Buff — Smith 1 run (Christie kick)
NE — Martin 1 run (Vinatieri kick)

NEW ORLEANS 13, OAKLAND 10—at Oakland-Alameda County Coliseum, attendance 40,091. Doug Brien kicked a field goal with 2:57 remaining and Sammy Knight intercepted a pass in the closing minutes as the Saints handed the Raiders their third consecutive defeat. Jeff George hit Rickey Dudley with 26- and 52-yard passes to set up Harvey Williams's first touchdown since 1995 to give the Raiders a 7-0 lead. Dan Land's interception led to Cole Ford's 43-yard field goal to put the Raiders ahead 10-0. The Saints responded, keyed by Heath Shuler's 15-yard pass to Randal Hill on fourth-and-15, and capped by Brien's 48-yard field goal as the half expired. Eric Guliford's 32-yard punt return gave the Saints the ball at the Raiders' 36 and set up Ray Zellars's tying touchdown run on the first play of the fourth quarter. The Saints got the ball back after a punt with 6:19 remaining. Shuler's 14-yard pass to Guliford on third-and-9 allowed the Saints into Raiders territory, and set up Brien's winning boot. Faced with fourth-and-8 from their own 48, George's pass, intended for Tim Brown, was intercepted by Knight with 1:24 to play to seal the victory. Shuler was 21 of 34 for 181 yards, with an interception. George was 17 of 39 for 211 yards, with an interception. Dudley had 5 receptions for 116 yards. In six second-half possessions, the Raiders gained 40 total yards and did not pass the Saints' 49-yard line. New Orleans had been shutout in its previous two games.

New Orleans	0	3	0	10	—	13
Oakland	0	10	0	0	—	10

Oak — Williams 1 run (Ford kick)
Oak — FG Ford 43
NO — FG Brien 48
NO — Zellars 1 run (Brien kick)
NO — FG Brien 44

TENNESSEE 10, NEW YORK GIANTS 6—at Liberty Bowl Memorial Stadium, attendance 26,744. Eddie George rushed for 122 yards and a touchdown as the Oilers won for the fourth time in their last five games and snapped the Giants' five-game winning streak. The Oilers drove for more than 8 minutes before settling for Al Del Greco's 31-yard first-quarter field goal. A 14-play, 84-yard drive, which consumed nearly seven minutes, was capped by George's touchdown run and gave the Oilers a 10-0 lead with 50 seconds left in the half. The Giants responded with Danny Kanell's 27-yard pass to Chris Calloway set up Brad Daluiso's 42-yard field goal as the half expired. Tyrone Wheatley's 34-yard run in the third quarter led to Daluiso's second field goal with 4:54 left in the third quarter. The Giants did not run a play inside Oilers territory the remainder of the game, and Marcus Robertson's interception with just under 2:00 left iced the game. McNair was 13 of 23 for 183 yards, with an interception. Kanell was 15 of 28 for 133 yards, with an interception. The Oilers' defense permitted just 10 first downs, 218 total yards, and allowed just 2 of 12 third-down conversions.

N.Y. Giants	0	3	3	0	—	6
Tennessee	3	7	0	0	—	10

Tenn — FG Del Greco 31
Tenn — George 1 run (Del Greco kick)
NYG — FG Daluiso 42
NYG — FG Daluiso 41

MIAMI 24, NEW YORK JETS 17—at Pro Player Stadium, attendance 73,809. Karim Abdul-Jabbar rushed for 103 yards and 2 touchdowns as the Dolphins staved off the Jets to move into a three-way tie atop the AFC East standings. Abdul-Jabbar capped a game-opening 80-yard drive with a 4-yard scoring jaunt. After John Hall's field goal cut the deficit to 7-3, Glenn Foley completed 20- and 33-yard passes to Dedric Ward to set up his 18-yard scoring toss to Kyle Brady with 1:36 remaining in the half. Dan Marino drove the Dolphins 77 yards in 1:31, capped by his 23-yard touchdown pass to Brett Perriman 5 seconds before halftime to retake the lead. The Dolphins defense forced a punt to begin the third quarter, and Miami drove 66 yards in 5:46, with Abdul-Jabbar scoring his second touchdown to put the Dolphins ahead 21-10. After Olindo Mare added a field goal, Adrian Murrell broke free for a 43-yard touchdown run with 7:37 remaining to cut the deficit to 24-17. The Jets forced a punt, and were driving for the potential tying score when Wayne Chrebet's catch on fourth-and-5 was ruled incomplete with 3:48 left. After forcing another punt, Foley threw a 23-yard pass to Ward to reach the Dolphins' 35 with 1:30 remaining. But on third down, Foley's pass was intercepted by George Teague, thus clinching the game for the Dolphins. Marino was 18 of 29 for 186 yards and a touchdown. Foley, who was making his first start of the season, was 25 of 48 for 322 yards and 1 touchdown, with 1 interception. Ward established career-highs with 6 receptions for 108 yards.

N.Y. Jets	0	10	0	7	—	17
Miami	7	7	7	3	—	24

Mia — Abdul-Jabbar 4 run (Mare kick)
NYJ — FG Hall 29
NYJ — Brady 18 pass from Foley (Hall kick)
Mia — Perriman 23 pass from Marino (Mare kick)
Mia — Abdul-Jabbar 5 run (Mare kick)
Mia — FG Mare 20
NYJ — Murrell 43 run (Hall kick)

GREEN BAY 17, ST. LOUIS 7—at Lambeau Field, attendance 60,093. Brett Favre threw a touchdown pass and ran for another as the Packers won their twenty-first consecutive home game. The game was scoreless until Ryan Longwell's 44-yard field goal, which was set up by Favre's 44-yard pass to Antonio Freeman, with 4:02 left in the half. The Packers marched 80 yards in 7 plays to start the second half, capped by Favre's 25-yard touchdown pass to Freeman. The Rams responded with a 14-play, 75-yard drive that lasted 7:55 and concluded with Lawrence Phillips's 8-yard scoring jaunt. The Packers answered with a 79-yard drive that ended with Favre's 7-yard scramble for the game's final points. The Rams had two more chances, but Jeff Wilkins missed a 36-yard field-goal attempt, his second miss of the day, midway through the fourth quarter, and Mike Prior intercepted Mark Rypien at the Packers' 45 with 3:00 remaining to ice the game. Favre was 18 of 37 for 306 yards and 1 touchdown, with 2 interceptions. Freeman had 7 receptions for 160 yards. Tony Banks started for the Rams and was 9 of 23 for 103 yards, but did not return for the second half because of an upper back strain. In relief, Rypien was 9 of 18 for 132 yards, with an interception. Amp Lee had 5 receptions for 104 yards. The Rams were penalized 15 times for 110 yards.

St. Louis	0	0	7	0	—	7
Green Bay	0	3	7	7	—	17

GB — FG Longwell 44
GB — Freeman 25 pass from Favre (Longwell kick)
StL — Phillips 8 run (Wilkins kick)
GB — Favre 7 run (Longwell kick)

SEATTLE 37, SAN DIEGO 31—at Qualcomm Stadium, Jack Murphy Field, attendance 64,616. Warren Moon threw 2 touchdown passes to Joey Galloway, including the game-winner with 2:20 remaining, as the Seahawks averted a third-place tie with the Chargers. Greg Jackson's 41-yard return of punt-returner Ronnie Harris's fumble gave the Chargers a 7-0 lead 1:30 into the game. Craig Whelihan, who started his first NFL game, threw a 10-yard touchdown pass to Tony Martin to put the Chargers ahead 14-0, and, after the Seahawks kicked a field goal, led the Chargers on a 12-play, 66-yard drive for a field goal of their own. Moon responded with a 60-yard drive in 54 seconds, capped by his 30-yard touchdown pass to Galloway 22 seconds before halftime. The Seahawks tied the game with a 6 minute drive to begin the second half, and took the lead 16 seconds later when Phillip Daniels sacked Whelihan, forced him to fumble, and Michael Sinclair fell on the ball in the end zone. Paul Bradford intercepted Moon and raced 56 yards down the left sideline to register his first NFL touchdown and tie the game 24-24. On their next possession, Whelihan threw a 61-yard bomb to Martin to give the Chargers the lead. The Seahawks responded with a 64-yard drive, but had to settle for Todd Peterson's 28-yard field goal with 6:02 remaining. Whelihan's third-and-1 pass to Terrell Fletcher fell incomplete, which forced the Chargers to punt with 4:25 left. Seattle drove 73 yards, capped by Moon's second touchdown pass to Galloway. Peterson added a third field goal with 1:18 left after the Chargers turned the ball over on downs. San Diego was unable to cross midfield on its final possession. Moon was 24 of 45 for 295 yards and 2 touchdowns, with an interception. Whelihan was 17 of 29 for 206 yards and 2 touchdowns, with an interception. Martin had 5 receptions for 100 yards. Seattle had more first downs (24-13) and total yards (373-260).

Seattle	0	10	14	13	—	37
San Diego	14	3	7	7	—	31

SD — Jackson 41 fumble return (Davis kick)
SD — Martin 10 pass from Whelihan (Davis kick)
Sea — FG Peterson 27
SD — FG Davis 33
Sea — Galloway 30 pass from Moon (Peterson kick)
Sea — Warren 1 run (Peterson kick)
Sea — Sinclair fumble recovery in end zone (Peterson kick)
SD — Bradford 56 interception return (Davis kick)
SD — Martin 61 pass from Whelihan (Davis kick)
Sea — FG Peterson 28
Sea — Galloway 40 pass from Moon (Peterson kick)
Sea — FG Peterson 27

TAMPA BAY 31, ATLANTA 10—at Georgia Dome, attendance 46,018. Warrick Dunn scored 2 touchdowns and Trent Dilfer threw 2 touchdown passes as the Buccaneers defeated the Falcons. Shelton Quarles recovered Todd Kinchen's fumble on a punt return to give the Buccaneers the ball at their own 45. Two plays later, Mike Alstott rumbled 47 yards for a touchdown. The Falcons tied the game when Chris Chandler threw a 30-yard touchdown pass to Bert Emanuel. Tampa Bay answered with a 73-yard drive, capped by Dilfer's 24-yard touchdown pass to Dunn with 45 seconds left in the half. After stopping the Falcons on three plays, Dan Stryzinski's 21-yard punt put Michael Husted in position to drill a 54-yard field goal just before halftime. Morten Andersen kicked a field goal for Atlanta to conclude the opening drive of the second half to cut the deficit to 17-10, but the Buccaneers responded with a 14-play, 81-yard drive that lasted 8:19, which included a third-and-12 pass to Karl Williams for 14 yards and a third-and-8 pass to Dave Moore for 11 yards, and was capped by Dilfer's 14-yard touchdown pass to Moore. Midway through the fourth quarter, Quarles recovered another fumble by Kinchen, and Warrick Dunn raced 30 yards four plays later for the game's final points. Dilfer was 12 of 20 for 150 yards and 2 touchdowns. Chandler was 19 of 27 for 212 yards and 1 touchdown. Brad Culpepper recorded 3 of Tampa Bay's 5 sacks.

Tampa Bay	7	10	7	7	—	31
Atlanta	0	7	3	0	—	10

TB — Alstott 47 run (Husted kick)
Atl — Emanuel 30 pass from Chandler (Andersen kick)
TB — Dunn 24 pass from Dilfer (Husted kick)
TB — FG Husted 54
Atl — FG Andersen 34
TB — Moore 14 pass from Dilfer (Husted kick)
TB — Dunn 30 run (Husted kick)

SUNDAY NIGHT, NOVEMBER 9

PITTSBURGH 37, BALTIMORE 0—at Three Rivers Stadium, attendance 56,669. The Steelers' defense forced 7 turnovers, including 6 in the first half, and allowed just 170 total yards to remain tied for first place in the AFC Central. The Steelers' four scoring drives in the first half consisted of 25, 33, 1 and 0 yards. Steven Conley's interception at the Ravens' 25-yard line 1:25 into the game led to Jerome Bettis's 1-yard touchdown plunge. Chris Oldham's interception and 8-yard return to the Steelers' 33 started a drive that was highlighted by 3 Kordell Stewart-to-Yancey Thigpen passes and concluded with Norm Johnson's 52-yard field goal. Darren Perry's interception and 42-yard return to the Ravens' 1 led to Stewart's 1-yard dive over the top to give the Steelers a 17-0 lead. Greg Lloyd sacked Eric Zeier later in the second quarter and forced him to fumble. Oliver Gibson recovered at the Ravens' 8, but the Steelers did not gain a yard and settled for Johnson's second field goal. The Ravens threw interceptions on each of their first four possessions, the first 3 thrown by starter Vinny Testaverde, and also fumbled twice late in the half. The Steelers did not allow the Ravens inside their own 35-yard line in the second half as they recorded their first shutout since 1993. Stewart was 14 of 27 for 196 yards and a touchdown. Bettis recorded his fourth consecutive 100-yard game as he rushed for 114 yards, and Yancey Thigpen had 6 receptions for 130 yards and a touchdown. Testaverde was 13 of 32 for 120 yards, with 3 interceptions. Zeier played the second quarter and was 2 of 7 for 16 yards, with an interception. The Steelers averaged 4.9 yards per play, and permitted the Ravens just 2.7 yards.

Baltimore	0	0	0	0	—	0
Pittsburgh	10	10	10	7	—	37

Pitt — Bettis 1 run (N. Johnson kick)
Pitt — FG N. Johnson 52
Pitt — Stewart 1 run (N. Johnson kick)
Pitt — FG N. Johnson 22
Pitt — FG N. Johnson 39
Pitt — Thigpen 52 pass from Stewart (N. Johnson kick)
Pitt — Jones 1 run (N. Johnson kick)

MONDAY, NOVEMBER 10

SAN FRANCISCO 24, PHILADELPHIA 12—at Veterans Stadium, attendance 67,133. Merton Hanks returned a fumble for a touchdown, and Chuck Levy scored on a punt return as the 49ers won their ninth consecutive game. Hanks recovered a Ricky Watters fumble, which was forced by Lee Woodall, on the fourth play of the game and raced 38 yards for a touchdown 1:07 into the game. The Eagles converted fourth downs on consecutive possessions later in the first half, with both drives leading to Chris Boniol field goals, to cut the deficit to 7-6. The Eagles' special teams, which had been a concern all season, struggled in the second quarter. First, Freddie Solomon muffed a punt, and Curtis Buckley recovered on the Eagles' 26, which led to Garrison Hearst's touchdown run. Later in the quarter, Chuck Levy fielded a punt and sprinted untouched for a 73-yard touchdown. Moments later, Darnell Walker's interception and 10-yard return to the Eagles' 36 with 39 seconds left in the half led to Gary Anderson's field goal. The Eagles' defense had held the 49ers to scoring drives of 26 and 23 yards, yet trailed 24-6 at halftime. The 49ers maintained possession for more than 21 minutes of the second half, and the defense allowed only a 6-yard touchdown pass from Bobby Hoying to Chad Lewis with 1:14 remaining. Steve Young was 13 of 23 for 103 yards, with an interception. Ty Detmer started for the Eagles and was 13 of 31 for 137 yards, with an interception. Hoying replaced him in the fourth quarter and was 8 of 14 for 94 yards and 1 touchdown. Irving Fryar had 9 receptions for 138 yards. The 49ers' defense registered 8 sacks, spearheaded by Dana Stubblefield's 3.5 sacks, and permitted the Eagles to convert just 4 of 18 third-down opportunities. The 49ers were 7 of 16 on third-down conversions.

San Francisco	7	17	0	0	—	24
Philadelphia	3	3	0	6	—	12

SF — Hanks 38 fumble return (Anderson kick)
Phil — FG Boniol 28
Phil — FG Boniol 34
SF — Hearst 1 run (Anderson kick)
SF — Levy 73 punt return (Anderson kick)
SF — FG Anderson 31
Phil — Lewis 6 pass from Hoying (pass failed)

TWELFTH WEEK SUMMARIES

AMERICAN FOOTBALL CONFERENCE

Eastern Division	W	L	T	Pct.	Pts.	OP
Miami	7	4	0	.636	236	199
N.Y. Jets	7	4	0	.636	260	211
New England	6	5	0	.545	261	192
Buffalo	5	6	0	.455	183	255
Indianapolis	1	10	0	.091	195	296
Central Division						
Jacksonville	8	3	0	.727	279	211
Pittsburgh	8	3	0	.727	261	203
Tennessee	5	6	0	.455	226	214
Baltimore	4	6	1	.409	220	241
Cincinnati	3	8	0	.273	194	283
Western Division						
Denver	9	2	0	.818	324	184
Kansas City	8	3	0	.727	228	189
Seattle	6	5	0	.545	250	258
Oakland	4	7	0	.364	275	282
San Diego	4	7	0	.364	215	289

NATIONAL FOOTBALL CONFERENCE

Eastern Division	W	L	T	Pct.	Pts.	OP
N.Y. Giants	7	4	0	.636	211	200
Dallas	6	5	0	.545	229	168
Washington	6	5	0	.545	217	169
Philadelphia	4	6	1	.409	180	224
Arizona	2	9	0	.182	180	249
Central Division						
Green Bay	8	3	0	.727	271	217
Minnesota	8	3	0	.727	253	239
Tampa Bay	8	3	0	.727	235	179
Detroit	5	6	0	.455	235	220
Chicago	1	10	0	.091	182	315
Western Division						
San Francisco	10	1	0	.909	278	139
Carolina	5	6	0	.455	185	214
New Orleans	4	7	0	.364	151	225
Atlanta	3	8	0	.273	216	292
St. Louis	2	9	0	.182	192	265

SUNDAY, NOVEMBER 16

NEW YORK GIANTS 19, ARIZONA 10—at Giants Stadium, attendance 68,316. Michael Strahan had 3 of the Giants' defenses 8 sacks, and Jason Sehorn had a fumble recovery and interception as the Giants overcame a rookie-record performance by Jake Plummer to defeat the Cardinals. The Cardinals stopped Charles Way and Tiki Barber on back-to-back plays from the 1-yard line early in the second quarter to thwart a scoring threat. But Sehorn forced and recovered Leeland McElroy's fumble on the next possession to set up Brad Daluiso's 33-yard field goal. Two plays after the Giants' defense forced a punt, Danny Kanell threw a 56-yard touchdown pass to Amani Toomer. Three plays into the second half, a scrambling Plummer threw a 70-yard touchdown pass to Frank Sanders. Late in the third quarter, the Cardinals drove 63 yards in 11 plays, with Sanders hauling in 4 receptions on the drive, to set up Joe Nedney's game-tying field goal. The Giants responded with a 17-play, 80-yard drive that lasted 8:55, capped by Kanell's 1-yard touchdown pass to Howard Cross. Daluiso's extra-point attempt sailed wide left, keeping Arizona within six points. Sehorn intercepted Plummer on Arizona's next drive, and Daluiso kicked a 35-yard field goal to increase the advantage to 19-10 with 4:49 left. The Cardinals got the ball back twice but were stopped on downs the first possession, and Tito Wooden intercepted Plummer to ice the game. Kanell was 14 of 21 for 182 yards and 2 touchdowns. Way finished with 114 rushing yards. Plummer established a NFL rookie record with 388 passing yards. He completed 22 of 33 passes for 1 touchdown, with 2 interceptions. Sanders had 9 receptions for 188 yards, and Rob Moore had 8 catches for 139 yards.

Arizona	0	0	10	0	—	10
N.Y. Giants	0	10	0	9	—	19

NYG — FG Daluiso 33

NYG — Toomer 56 pass from Kanell (Daluiso kick)
Ariz — Sanders 70 pass from Plummer (Nedney kick)
Ariz — FG Nedney 34
NYG — Cross 1 pass from Kanell (kick failed)
NYG — FG Daluiso 35

ATLANTA 27, ST. LOUIS 21—at Trans World Dome, attendance 64,299. Jamal Anderson rushed for 2 touchdowns as the Falcons scored the game's final 10 points to sweep the Rams. Anderson carried 7 times on a 12-play, 74-yard drive that consumed 6:47 off the clock and concluded with his 4-yard touchdown run. A 70-yard drive that featured a 19-yard run by Harold Green was capped by Morten Andersen's 27-yard field goal and gave the Falcons a 10-0 lead. The Rams used a 76-yard pass from Tony Banks to Eddie Kennison just before halftime to set up Banks's 1-yard touchdown pass to Ernie Conwell. The Falcons took the second-half kickoff and marched 83 yards, with Anderson's 1-yard touchdown run giving Atlanta a 17-7 lead. The Rams responded with a 74-yard drive that led to Banks's second touchdown pass, this one to Amp Lee, to cut the deficit to 17-14. Two plays later, Kevin Carter's sack of Chris Chandler forced him to fumble. Carter recovered the ball, which enabled Lawrence Phillips to score five plays later to give the Rams a 21-17 lead. However, in the fourth quarter, after Jeff Wilkins missed his second field-goal attempt of the game, Chandler threw a 44-yard pass to Terance Mathis to set up Brian Kozlowski's 2-yard touchdown catch with 6:03 remaining. After the Falcons forced a punt, Andersen booted a 44-yard field goal with 2:43 to play to put the Falcons ahead 27-21. The Rams reached the Falcons' 18, but Banks's fourth-down pass fell incomplete. Chandler was 20 of 30 for 232 yards and 1 touchdown, with 1 interception. Banks was 21 of 38 for 266 yards and 2 touchdowns.

Atlanta	7	3	7	10	—	27
St. Louis	0	7	14	0	—	21

Atl — Anderson 4 run (Andersen kick)
Atl — FG Andersen 27
StL — Conwell 1 pass from Banks (Wilkins kick)
Atl — Anderson 1 run (Andersen kick)
StL — Lee 19 pass from Banks (Wilkins kick)
StL — Phillips 1 run (Wilkins kick)
Atl — Kozlowski 2 pass from Chandler (Andersen kick)
Atl — FG Andersen 44

SAN FRANCISCO 27, CAROLINA 19—at 3Com Park, attendance 61,500. Terry Kirby's 101-yard kickoff return for a touchdown highlighted the 49ers tenth consecutive victory as they clinched the NFC Western Division title. The 49ers controlled the ball for 5:20 on their first possession, and scored on Gary Anderson's 28-yard field goal. Tim McDonald's interception and a 39-yard pass interference penalty on Carolina's Tyrone Poole set up Steve Young's 1-yard touchdown run on the first play of the second quarter. On their next drive, the 49ers drove 89 yards in 7 plays, capped by Young's 44-yard touchdown pass to William Floyd to take a 17-0 lead. John Kasay booted 2 field goals in the final 4:31 of the first half, but Kirby returned the second-half kickoff 101 yards to give the 49ers a 24-6 lead. The Panthers responded with Fred Lane's 4-yard touchdown run to cap a 63-yard drive, and, on their next possession, an 11-play, 53-yard drive concluded with Kerry Collins's 5-yard touchdown pass to Wesley Walls. Lee Woodall's interception early in the fourth quarter set up Anderson's second field goal to put the 49ers ahead 27-19. Anderson attempted another 47-yard field goal with 2:20 remaining, but Tyrone Poole blocked it, and Renaldo Turnbull returned the ball to the 49ers' 40. The Panthers reached the 49ers' 28, but Merton Hanks's interception with 1:41 left sealed the victory. Young was 17 of 22 for 221 yards and 1 touchdown. Collins was 18 of 33 for 190 yards, 1 touchdown, and 3 interceptions. The 49ers became only the second team (1985 Chicago Bears) in a 16-week season to clinch a division title in 11 games.

Carolina	0	6	13	0	—	19
San Francisco	3	14	7	3	—	27

SF — FG Anderson 28
SF — Young 1 run (Anderson kick)
SF — Floyd 44 pass from Young (Anderson kick)
Car — FG Kasay 46
Car — FG Kasay 27
SF — Kirby 101 kickoff return (Anderson kick)
Car — Lane 4 run (Kasay kick)
Car — Walls 5 pass from Collins (run failed)
SF — FG Anderson 43

PITTSBURGH 20, CINCINNATI 3—at Three Rivers Stadium, attendance 55,226. Jerome Bettis reached the 100-yard barrier for the eighth time this season, and Kordell Stewart threw 2 touchdown passes, as the Steelers defeated the Bengals for the twelfth time in their last 14 meetings. Orpheus Roye's sack of Jeff Blake on the Bengals initial possessoin forced him to fumble. Jason Gildon recovered the loose ball and dragged players 20 yards to set up Norm Johnson's first field goal. A 16-play, 85-yard drive, which lasted 6:50 and was keyed by Stewart's 12-yard scramble on third-and-6 and his 25-yard pass to Yancey Thigpen on third-and-5, led to Johnson's 25-yard field goal with five seconds remaining in the half. The Steelers put together a 13-play, 84-yard drive, which consumed 6:55 off the clock and featured a 34-yard pass from Stewart to Thigpen, and concluded with the duo's 20-yard pass play. The Bengals responded with Doug Pelfrey's 25-yard field goal to cut the lead to 13-3, but the Steelers answered with a 69-yard drive, capped by Stewart's 5-yard touchdown pass to Mark Bruener. The Bengals reached the Steelers' 26, but Greg Lloyd sacked Blake and forced him to fumble, and Kevin Henry recovered. The Steelers ran the final 7:39 off the clock. Stewart was 11 of 22 for 128 yards and 2 touchdowns. Thigpen had 5 receptions for 101 yards. Blake was 15 of 21 for 158 yards. The Steelers' defense recorded 4 sacks and forced 3 fumbles.

Cincinnati	0	0	3	0	—	3
Pittsburgh	3	3	7	7	—	20

Pitt — FG N. Johnson 34
Pitt — FG N. Johnson 25
Pitt — Thigpen 20 pass from Stewart (N. Johnson kick)
Cin — FG Pelfrey 25
Pitt — Bruener 5 pass from Stewart (N. Johnson kick)

KANSAS CITY 24, DENVER 22—at Arrowhead Stadium, attendance 77,963. Pete Stoyanovich kicked a 54-yard field goal as time expired to lift the Chiefs to within one-game of the first-place Broncos. The Broncos jumped out to a 13-0 lead on the strength of Shannon Sharpe's 5-yard touchdown catch, keyed by Rod Smith's 43-yard reception, sandwiched between 2 Jason Elam field goals. Tamarick Vanover's 77-yard kickoff return set up Marcus Allen's 6-yard touchdown run. After the Chiefs' defense forced a punt, the Chiefs drove 45 yards in 1:51, capped by Rich Gannon's 5-yard touchdown pass to Danan Hughes. Donnie Edwards recovered John Elway's fumble, setting up Allen's second touchdown run and gave the Chiefs a 21-13 lead. The Broncos reached the Chiefs' 20 on three of their next five possessions, but the Chiefs' defense did not allow them to get inside the 10. Thus, Elam kicked 3 more field goals, the last one with 1:00 remaining, to give Denver a 22-21 advantage. Starting from his own 27 with no timeouts left, Gannon completed 3 consecutive passes to reach the Broncos' 42. After spiking the ball and a delay of game penalty, Gannon completed a 10-yard pass to Andre Rison, who stepped out of bounds at the 37-yard line with four seconds remaining. Stoyanovich's low line-drive kick into the wind just cleared the crossbar, giving the Chiefs a season-series split. Gannon was 11 of 21 for 98 yards and 1 touchdown, with an interception. John Elway was 18 of 31 for 232 yards and 1 touchdown. Smith had 7 receptions for 114 yards, while Terrell Davis rushed for 127 yards, marking his fourth consecutive 100-yard game, and ninth of the season. The Broncos lost despite outgaining the Chiefs (329-202) and maintaing possession for 37:25 of the game's 60 minutes.

Denver	3	10	3	6	—	22
Kansas City	0	14	7	3	—	24

Den — FG Elam 21
Den — Sharpe 5 pass from Elway (Elam kick)
Den — FG Elam 38
KC — Allen 6 run (Stoyanovich kick)
KC — Hughes 5 pass from Gannon (Stoyanovich kick)
KC — Allen 1 run (Stoyanovich kick)
Den — FG Elam 38
Den — FG Elam 28
Den — FG Elam 34
KC — FG Stoyanovich 54

INDIANAPOLIS 41, GREEN BAY 38—at RCA Dome, attendance 60,928. Cary Blanchard kicked a 20-yard field goal as time expired to give the Colts their first victory of the season and mark the third consecutive year Indianapolis had defeated the team that was the defending Super Bowl champion. Dorsey Levens caught a 3-yard touchdown pass from Brett Favre, after the duo's 56-yard pass play two plays earlier, to take a 7-0 lead less than two minutes into the game. After a Blanchard field goal, Levens broke free for a 52-yard touchdown run. The Packers led 14-3 and had run just six plays from scrimmage. The Colts consumed 4:29, driving 80 yards and scoring when Paul Justin's 17-yard pass was caught by Marvin Harrison. On the Packers next possession, Delmonico Montgomery sacked Favre and forced him to fumble. Al Fontenot scooped up the ball and rumbled 33 yards for a touchdown. Midway through the quarter, one play after Blanchard missed a 42-yard field goal, Robert Blackmon intercepted a pass. As he was getting tackled, he lateralled the ball to Jason Belser, who tight-roped 50 yards down the left sideline to score and give the Colts a 24-14 lead. The Packers responded as Favre threw a 74-yard pass to Derrick Mayes down to the Colts' 1, setting up Levens's third touchdown of the half. On the Colts' next drive, Santana Dotson sacked Justin and forced him to fumble. Gabe Wilkins recovered, and Favre threw a 16-yard touchdown pass to Antonio Freeman 44 seconds later to give the Packers a 28-24 lead. Blanchard kicked a pair of field goals, one at the end of the half and the other following an interception by Quentin Coryatt, to take a 30-28 lead into the fourth quarter. The Packers had first-and-goal from the Colts' 5, but Indianapolis' defense held Green Bay to a field goal. The Colts marched 75 yards with the ensuing kickoff, capped by Lamont Warren's 3-yard touchdown run and subsequent 2-point conversion pass from Justin to Harrison. It took the Packers all of three plays to answer, as Favre hit Levens for 30 yards and then found Freeman for 26 yards and a touchdown to tie the game 38-38. But the Colts drained the final 5:19 off the clock, keyed by Justin's 10-yard pass to Sean Dawkins on third-and-10, and a 28-yard pass to Ken Dilger to the Packers' 1 with 1:22 left. Justin took the snap and knelt down three consecutive plays to elapse the remainder of the time off the clock, allowing Blanchard to win the game. Justin was 24 of 30 for 340 yards and 1 touchdown. Marshall Faulk had 116 rushing yards. Favre was 18 of 25 for 363 yards and 3 touchdowns, with 2 interceptions. Levens rushed for 103 yards, and Mayes had 3 receptions for 119 yards. The teams combined for more than 900 total yards, and the Colts maintained possession for nearly 37 of the game's 60 minutes. The Packers lost despite averaging 10 yards per play.

Green Bay	14	14	0	10	—	38
Indianapolis	9	18	3	11	—	41

GB — Levens 3 pass from Favre (Longwell kick)
Ind — FG Blanchard 42
GB — Levens 52 run (Longwell kick)
Ind — Harrison 17 pass from Justin (pass failed)
Ind — Fontenot 33 fumble return (Stablein pass from Justin)
Ind — Belser 50 lateral from Blackmon (Blanchard kick)
GB — Levens 1 run (Longwell kick)
GB — Freeman 16 pass from Favre (Longwell kick)
Ind — FG Blanchard 41
Ind — FG Blanchard 35
GB — FG Longwell 18
Ind — Warren 3 run (Harrison pass from Justin)
GB — Freeman 26 pass from Favre (Longwell kick)
Ind — FG Blanchard 20

DETROIT 38, MINNESOTA 15—at Pontiac Silverdome, attendance 68,910. Barry Sanders rushed for 108 yards, and Tommy Vardell scored 3 touchdowns as the Lions snapped the Vikings' six-game winning streak. Vardell's 41-yard run set up Jason Hanson's first-quarter field goal. Scott Mitchell's 36-yard pass to Herman Moore led to Vardell's first touchdown, and Mitchell's 34-yard pass to Sanders to the Vikings' 2 allowed Vardell to score his second touchdown and give the Lions a 17-0 lead. Robert Smith's 27-yard touchdown run with 2:07 left in the half cut the deficit to 17-7, but Mitchell completed a 32-yard pass to Tommie Boyd, and Sanders's 19-yard run led to Mitchell's 14-yard touchdown pass to Johnnie Morton. Mark Carrier halted the Vikings' opening drive of the second half with a 66-yard interception return to the Vikings' 1, setting up Vardell's third touchdown. The Lions marched 80 yards with their next possession, keyed by a roughing the kicker penalty and capped by Mitchell's 10-yard touchdown pass to Moore and a 38-7 lead. Mitchell was 21 of 29 for 271 yards and 2 touchdowns. Moore had 10 receptions for 130 yards. Brad Johnson was 19 of 37 for 177 yards, with 1 interception. The Lions outgained the Vikings (477-300) in setting their season-high point total.

Minnesota	0	7	0	8	—	15
Detroit	3	21	14	0	—	38

Det — FG Hanson 27
Det — Vardell 1 run (Hanson kick)
Det — Vardell 1 run (Hanson kick)
Min — Smith 27 run (Murray kick)
Det — Morton 14 pass from Mitchell (Hanson kick)
Det — Vardell 1 run (Hanson kick)
Det — Moore 10 pass from Mitchell (Hanson kick)
Min — Hoard 3 run (Carter pass from Johnson)

TAMPA BAY 27, NEW ENGLAND 7—at Houlihan's Stadium, attendance 70,479. The Buccaneers' defense did not allow the Patriots a first down in the first half as they moved into a three-way tie for first place with a 27-7 victory. The Buccaneers engineered a 13-play, 80-yard drive that consumed 8:32, which saw Trent Dilfer complete 5 of 6 passes and ended with Errict Rhett's first touchdown of the season. Late in the first half, Dilfer completed an 18-yard pass to Karl Williams on third-and-9 to set up Michael Husted's 44-yard field goal just before halftime. Tampa Bay outgained New England 248-14 in the first half. Tom Tupa's 20-yard punt and Tedy Bruschi's roughing the passer penalty on third down set up Dilfer's 7-yard touchdown pass to Dave Moore to give the Buccaneers a 17-0 lead four minutes into the third quarter. The Patriots got their initial first down of the game on their next drive, but it was Clifton Abraham's interception early in the fourth quarter that led to the game's next points, a 1-yard run by Mike Alstott. Derrick Brooks's interception on the next drive set up Husted's second field goal. The Patriots drove 75 yards in the final two minutes and scored with eight seconds remaining to avert the Buccaneers' first shutout since 1985. Dilfer was 21 of 29 for 209 yards and 1 touchdown. Drew Bledsoe was 13 of 25 for 117 yards, with 2 interceptions. Scott Zolak guided the Patriots to their lone score, completing 3 of 6 passes for 34 yards and 1 touchdown. The Buccaneers doubled or nearly doubled the Patriots in total yards (343-168), first downs (21-10), and time of possession (39:28-20:32).

New England	0	0	0	7	—	7
Tampa Bay	7	3	7	10	—	27

TB — Rhett 1 run (Husted kick)
TB — FG Husted 44
TB — Moore 7 pass from Dilfer (Husted kick)
TB — Alstott 1 run (Husted kick)
TB — FG Husted 44
NE — Purnell 6 pass from Zolak (Vinatieri kick)

NEW YORK JETS 23, CHICAGO 15—at Soldier Field, attendance 45,642. Otis Smith and Victor Green each had 2 interceptions, and Smith returned one for a touchdown, as the Jets took a 23-0 lead and held on to defeat the Bears and remained tied for first place in the AFC East. Smith's first interception, at the Jets' 49, set up John Hall's first field goal. Green halted a Bears drive with an interception and 24-yard return to the Jets' 44. Glenn Foley completed a 21-yard pass to Kyle Brady and a 35-yard touchdown to Keyshawn Johnson on the following play to give the Jets a 10-0 lead. Leon Johnson's 20-yard punt return led to Hall's second field goal. Marvin Jones recovered Erik Kramer's fumble on the Bears' next possession, and Hall added his third field goal with 6:34 left in the first half. Smith intercepted a pass just over a minute later, and returned it 38 yards for a touchdown. In the third quarter, the Bears took advantage of a 35-yard punt to drive 48 yards and score on Chris Penn's 4-yard touchdown reception. The Bears reached the Jets' 13 with just over 9:00 left, but were stopped on downs. They reached the Jets' 11 with 4:00 left, but Kramer threw 4 consecutive incompletions. Kramer added a 5-yard touchdown pass to Ricky Proehl with 30 seconds left, but Wayne Chrebet recovered the ensuing onside kick to ice the game. Foley was 8 of 13 for 111 yards and 1 touchdown before injuring his left ankle. Neil O'Donnell replaced him and was 4 of 12 for 25 yards. Kramer completed 32 of a team-record 60 attempts for 354 yards and 2 touchdowns, with 3 interceptions. Proehl had 11 receptions for 118 yards. The Bears had more first downs (27-11) and total yards (376-193) but committed 5 turnovers while forcing just 1 turnover, and Jeff Jaeger missed his first 2 field goals of the season. The game was played in a minus-9 degree wind-chill factor.

N.Y. Jets	10	13	0	0	—	23
Chicago	0	0	7	8	—	15

NYJ — FG Hall 34
NYJ — Johnson 35 pass from Foley (Hall kick)
NYJ — FG Hall 36
NYJ — FG Hall 34
NYJ — Smith 38 interception return (Hall kick)
Chi — Penn 4 pass from Kramer (Jaeger kick)
Chi — Proehl 5 pass from Kramer (Autry run)

PHILADELPHIA 10, BALTIMORE 10 (TIE)—at Memorial Stadium, attendance 63,546. Each team missed a field goal in overtime as the Eagles and Ravens battled to the first tie in the NFL since 1989. James Roe's 9-yard punt return to the Eagles' 37 led to Vinny Testaverde's 29-yard touchdown pass to Michael Jackson late in the first quarter. James Willis's interception at the Ravens' 44 in the third quarter, and Bobby Hoying's subsequent 26-yard pass to Irving Fryar, set up Chris Boniol's 33-yard field goal. The Ravens responded with a 14-play, 65-yard drive, with Jay Graham carrying 10 times, that resulted in a 23-yard field goal by Matt Stover. The Eagles gained possession on their own 40, and Charlie Garner scored five plays later to tie the game with 1:25 left. The Eagles threw a Hail Mary pass into the end zone on the final play of regulation, but the ball fell incomplete. In overtime, after the Ravens forced the Eagles to punt, and then reached the Eagles' 36. But William Thomas sacked Testaverde on fourth down. The Eagles reached the Ravens' 33 before Hoying threw 3 consecutive incompletions to turn the ball over on downs. After an exchange of punts, James Darling and Thomas stopped Earnest Byner on third-and-1 from the Eagles' 35, and Stover missed a 53-yard field goal attempt with 2:21 remaining. The Eagles reached the Ravens' 17 with 30 seconds left, but were then whistled for illegal motion. Boniol attempted a 40-yard attempt, but pushed the ball wide right. Hoying, in his first NFL start, was 26 of 38 for 276 yards, despite getting sacked 9 times by the Ravens' defense. Testaverde was 19 of 32 for 140 yards and 1 touchdown, with 2 interceptions. Graham rushed 35 times for 154 yards before leaving with an ankle injury in overtime.

Philadelphia	0	0	3	7	0	—	10
Baltimore	7	0	0	3	0	—	10

Balt — Jackson 29 pass from Testaverde (Stover kick)
Phil — FG Boniol 33
Balt — FG Stover 23
Phil — Garner 2 run (Boniol kick)

NEW ORLEANS 20, SEATTLE 17 (OT)—at Louisiana Superdome, attendance 50,493. Winfred Tubbs's interception on the first play of overtime set up Doug Brien's game-winning field goal as the Saints won their second consecutive game. A 12-play, 49-yard drive strung over the first and second quarters culminated in Todd Peterson's 36-yard field goal. Darryl Williams's 44-yard interception return for a touchdown 1:13 later gave the Seahawks a 10-0 lead. Seahawks' punter Kyle Richardson, playing his first NFL game, bobbled a punt-snap, giving the Saints the ball at the Seahawks' 33. Ten plays later, Ray Zellars crashed into the end zone to pull the Saints to within 3 points at halftime, despite accumulating just 3 first downs. Eric Guliford's 29-yard punt return late in the third quarter allowed the Saints to drive 45 yards to take a 14-10 lead on Ray Zellars's 2-yard run in the opening minutes of the fourth quarter. Chris Hewitt blocked Richardson's punt attempt moments later, setting up Brien's 19-yard field goal to take a 17-10 lead. Williams intercepted Heath Shuler's pass and returned it 24 yards to the Saints' 39 with 2:09 remaining. Four plays later, Warren Moon threw a 34-yard touchdown pass to James McKnight to tie the game with 1:40 left. Doug Nussmeier replaced Shuler and completed his first 3 passes to drive the Saints to the Seahawks' 29 with 54 seconds left, but Nussmeier fumbled and Corwin Brown recovered. The Seahawks reached the 27-yard line with 22 seconds left, but Peterson missed a 45-yard field-goal attempt, his second miss of the game. The Seahawks won the overtime toss, but Tubbs intercepted Moon on the first play, and returned the ball 15 yards to the Seahawks' 20. Brien kicked the game-winning field goal on first down. Shuler was 6 of 14 for 64 yards, with 2 interceptions. Moon was 23 of 46 for 251 yards and 1 touchdown, with 2 interceptions. The Seahawks outgained the Saints 340-173 total yards, but committed 5 of the game's 9 turnovers.

Seattle	0	10	0	7	0	—	17
New Orleans	0	7	0	10	3	—	20

Sea — FG Peterson 36
Sea — Williams 44 interception return (Peterson kick)
NO — Zellars 1 run (Brien kick)
NO — Zellars 2 run (Brien kick)
NO — FG Brien 19
Sea — McKnight 34 pass from Moon (Peterson kick)
NO — FG Brien 38

JACKSONVILLE 17, TENNESSEE 9—at ALLTEL Stadium, attendance 70,070. Mark Brunell completed 22 of 30 passes for 267 yards and 1 touchdown as the Jaguars won their twelfth consecutive home game. After a scoreless first quarter, Mark Brunell completed 20- and 19-yard passes to Jimmy Smith before finding Keenan McCardell for a 17-yard touchdown pass. The Oilers answered with Al Del Greco's 35-yard field goal just before halftime. After an exchange of punts to begin the third quarter, the Jaguars drove 65 yards in 9 plays, keyed by Brunell's 34-yard pass to Smith down to the Oilers' 4, to set up Natrone Means's 1-yard touchdown run. Means fumbled at the end of the third quarter, and Anthony Cook recovered near midfield. It took the Oilers five plays to score, as wide receiver Willie Davis took an end-around and threw a 22-yard touchdown pass to Frank Wycheck. But Renaldo Wynn stopped Rodney Thomas on the ensuing 2-point conversion attempt to allow the Jaguars to maintain a 5-point lead. Mike Hollis concluded the Jaguars' next drive with a 23-yard field goal with 7:17 remaining. The Oilers reached the Jaguars' 40 on each of their final two possessions, but Dave Thomas intercepted Steve McNair on fourth down to stop the first drive, and Eddie Robinson intercepted McNair's Hail Mary attempt as the game ended. Smith had 8 receptions for 158 yards. McNair was 8 of 22 for 162 yards, with 2 interceptions.

Tennessee	0	3	0	6	—	9
Jacksonville	0	7	7	3	—	17

Jack — McCardell 17 pass from Brunell (Hollis kick)
Tenn — FG Del Greco 35
Jack — Means 1 run (Hollis kick)
Tenn — Wycheck 22 pass from Davis (run failed)
Jack — FG Hollis 23

DALLAS 17, WASHINGTON 14—at Texas Stadium, attendance 64,559. Richie Cunningham booted a 42-yard field goal with four seconds remaining as the Cowboys scored 11 points in the final 1:55 to knock the Redskins out of a share of first place in the NFC East. Cunningham kicked a 34-yard field goal to conclude a 7:30 drive, and a 40-yard kick following a 5:05 drive to give Dallas a 6-0 halftime lead. Terry Allen found the end zone to finish a 67-yard drive late in the third quarter to put the Redskins ahead 7-6. After the Redskins' defense forced a punt, Brian Mitchell's 18-yard punt return gave Washington the ball in Cowboys' territory. Four plays later, Gus Frerotte threw a 24-yard touchdown pass to Henry Ellard to give the Redskins a 14-6 lead. An exchange of punts left the Cowboys with the ball at their own 3-yard line with 5:48 remaining. Troy Aikman completed a 21-yard pass to Eric Bjornson, an 18-yard pass to Michael Irvin, and, on fourth-and-2, a 31-yard pass to Irvin to the Redskins' 19. On third-and-goal from the 6-yard line, Aikman found Irvin for a touchdown to finish the 11-play, 97-yard drive. His 2-point conversion pass to Emmitt Smith was successful and tied the game. The Redskins failed to get a first down, and Dallas got the ball on their own 47 with 1:29 left following a 28-yard punt. Aikman completed an 8-yard pass to Anthony Miller on third-and-7 to get the Cowboys close enough for Cunningham's winning kick. Aikman was 25 of 45 for 217 yards and 1 touchdown. Frerotte was 16 of 31 for 157 yards and a touchdown.

Washington	0	0	7	7	—	14
Dallas	0	6	0	11	—	17

Dall — FG Cunningham 34
Dall — FG Cunningham 40
Wash — Allen 4 run (Blanton kick)
Wash — Ellard 24 pass from Frerotte (Blanton kick)
Dall — Irvin 6 pass from Aikman (Smith pass from Aikman)
Dall — FG Cunningham 42

SUNDAY NIGHT, NOVEMBER 16

OAKLAND 38, SAN DIEGO 15—at Qualcomm Stadium, Jack Murphy Field, attendance 65,714. Harvey Williams became just the third Raiders' player to score 4 touchdowns in a game as Oakland defeated the Chargers. Four plays after Greg Jackson's interception return for a touchdown, Williams caught an 8-yard pass from Jeff George. Anthony Smith recovered Craig Whelihan's fumble, and Williams scored from 1-yard out to complete the 17-yard drive and give the Raiders a 14-7 lead. The Raiders led 21-13 at halftime when Jeff George's 33-yard pass to Napoleon Kaufman and 19-yard pass to Williams to the Chargers' 2 set up Williams's third touchdown, a 1-yard run. Late in the third quarter, George and Williams hooked up from 32 yards to give the Raiders a 35-13 lead. Cole Ford added a field goal following James Trapp's fumble recovery to finish the scoring. George was 16 of 34 for 226 yards and 3 touchdowns, with 2 interceptions. Kaufman finished with 109 rushing yards. Whelihan was 14 of 26 for 202 yards. Williams, who had just 4 carries for 7 yards and 3 receptions for 59 yards, joined Art Powell and Marcus Allen as the only Raiders' to score 4 touchdowns in a game. Oakland snapped a three-game losing streak.

Oakland	7	14	14	3	—	38
San Diego	7	6	0	0	—	13

SD — Jackson 36 interception return (Davis kick)
Oak — Williams 8 pass from George (Ford kick)
Oak — Williams 1 run (Ford kick)
SD — FG Davis 45
Oak — Jett 9 pass from George (Ford kick)
SD — FG Davis 22
Oak — Williams 1 run (Ford kick)
Oak — Williams 32 pass from George (Ford kick)
Oak — FG Ford 23

MONDAY, NOVEMBER 17

MIAMI 30, BUFFALO 13—at Pro Player Stadium, attendance 74,155. Dan Marino threw 2 touchdown passes, and Olindo Mare booted 3 field goals as the Dolphins remained tied for first place in the AFC Eastern Division. Mare capped a game-opening 56-yard drive with a 37-yard field goal. The Dolphins drove 90 yards in the second quarter, with Marino completing all 5 of his pass attempts on the drive, and scored on his 3-yard touchdown pass to Ed Perry. George Teague's interception led to Mare's second field goal and a 13-0 halftime lead. Darick Holmes scored from 1-yard out on the Bills' first possession of the second half to cut the deficit to 13-7, but Daryl Gardener recovered Antowain Smith's fumble, and Mare added his third field goal. Steve Christie kicked 2 field goals, the second set up by Steve Tasker's fumble recovery of Irving Spikes's fumbled punt return, to cut the Dolphins lead to 16-13 with 13:56 remaining. Midway through the fourth quarter, Marino hit Brett Perriman with a 26-yard pass on third-and-4 to keep a drive alive, and two plays later found Troy Drayton for a 30-yard touchdown pass wtih 5:11 left. After the Dolphins' defense stopped the Bills on downs, Miami drove 24 yards and scored on Karim Abdul-Jabbar's 1-yard run to ice the game. Marino was 18 of 24 for 234 yards and 2 touchdowns, with an interception. Collins was 19 of 37 for 152 yards, with an interception.

Buffalo	0	0	10	3	—	13
Miami	3	10	3	14	—	30

Mia — FG Mare 37
Mia — Perry 3 pass from Marino (Mare kick)
Mia — FG Mare 30
Buff — Holmes 1 run (Christie kick)
Mia — FG Mare 35
Buff — FG Christie 36
Buff — FG Christie 24
Mia — Drayton 30 pass from Marino (Mare kick)
Mia — Abdul-Jabbar 1 run (Mare kick)

THIRTEENTH WEEK SUMMARIES

AMERICAN FOOTBALL CONFERENCE

Eastern Division	W	L	T	Pct.	Pts.	OP
N.Y. Jets	8	4	0	.667	283	232
Miami	7	5	0	.583	260	226
New England	7	5	0	.583	288	216
Buffalo	5	7	0	.417	197	286
Indianapolis	1	11	0	.083	205	328
Central Division						
Jacksonville	8	4	0	.667	305	242
Pittsburgh	8	4	0	.667	281	226
Tennessee	6	6	0	.500	257	228
Baltimore	4	7	1	.375	233	257
Cincinnati	4	8	0	.333	225	309
Western Division						
Denver	10	2	0	.833	355	187
Kansas City	9	3	0	.750	247	203
Seattle	6	6	0	.500	264	277
Oakland	4	8	0	.333	278	313
San Diego	4	8	0	.333	225	306

NATIONAL FOOTBALL CONFERENCE

Eastern Division	W	L	T	Pct.	Pts.	OP
N.Y. Giants	7	4	1	.625	218	207
Washington	6	5	1	.542	224	176
Dallas	6	6	0	.500	246	213
Philadelphia	5	6	1	.458	203	244
Arizona	3	9	0	.250	196	262
Central Division						
Green Bay	9	3	0	.750	316	234
Minnesota	8	4	0	.667	274	262
Tampa Bay	8	4	0	.667	242	192
Detroit	6	6	0	.500	267	230
Chicago	2	10	0	.167	195	322
Western Division						
San Francisco	11	1	0	.917	295	149
Carolina	6	6	0	.500	201	224
Atlanta	4	8	0	.333	236	295
New Orleans	4	8	0	.333	154	245
St. Louis	2	10	0	.167	202	281

SUNDAY, NOVEMBER 23

ARIZONA 16, BALTIMORE 13—at Memorial Stadium, attendance 53,976. Joe Nedney kicked 3 field goals, including a 43-yard boot as time expired, to give the Cardinals their first road win of the season. Matt Stover's 46-yard field goal, which followed an 8-play, 52-yard drive that lasted 56 seconds, as the first half expired tied the game 3-3. On the opening possession of the second half, Jake Plummer hit Anthony Edwards with a 33-yard pass on third-and-4 to set up Nedney's second field goal. The Ravens responded with a 12-play, 80-yard drive, capped by Byron (Bam) Morris's 1-yard touchdown plunge. Early in the fourth quarter, Kevin Williams's 23-yard punt return gave the Cardinals the ball at the Ravens' 31. Keyed by Plummer's 12-yard run on third-and-10, the Cardinals took a 13-10 lead on Plummer's 4-yard pass to Frank Sanders with 8:34 left. The Ravens appeared to be stopped with three minutes remaining when Testaverde ended up 9 yards shy of a first down on a third-and-18 scramble, but an unnecessary roughness penalty on Mike Caldwell kept the drive alive. Stover's 34-yard field goal with 34 seconds remaining tied the game. Plummer threw 12- and 27-yard passes to Rob Moore to put Nedney in position for the game-winning kick. Plummer was 19 of 34 for 218 yards and 1 touchdown, with 2 interceptions. Moore had 8 receptions for 112 yards. Testaverde was 21 of 37 for 193 yards.

Arizona	3	0	3	10	—	16
Baltimore	0	3	7	3	—	13

Ariz — FG Nedney 22
Balt — FG Stover 46
Ariz — FG Nedney 27
Balt — Morris 1 run (Stover kick)
Ariz — Sanders 4 pass from Plummer (Nedney kick)
Balt — FG Stover 34
Ariz — FG Nedney 43

TENNESSEE 31, BUFFALO 14—at Liberty Bowl Memorial Stadium, attendance 23,571. Steve McNair ran for 2 touchdowns and threw another as the Oilers held the Bills to a team-record-low 4 yards rushing to reach a .500 winning percentage for the first time since week 2. Marcus Robertson recovered Thurman Thomas's fumble on the first play from scrimmage and streaked 27 yards for a touchdown. McNair completed a 69-yard drive later in the quarter and, following Derrick Mason's 27-yard punt return, ran 21 yards on fourth-and-1 to set up his own 3-yard quarterback sneak. The Bills responded with a 63-yard drive, capped by Todd Collins's 9-yard touchdown pass to Quinn Early just before halftime to cut the deficit to 21-7. McNair kept the opening drive of the second half alive with a 15-yard run on third-and-3, allowing Al Del Greco to boot a season-best 51-yard field goal. Early scored his second touchdown early in the fourth quarter, but the Oilers went on a game-breaking 13-play, 60-yard drive that lasted 8:23 and was capped by McNair's 2-yard touchdown pass to Derek Russell. McNair was 15 of 24 for 167 yards and 1 touchdown, with 6 carries for 45 yards. Collins was 25 of 40 for 286 yards and 2 touchdowns, with 1 interception. The Oilers allowed the Bills to convert just 1-of-12 third-down opportunities, while converting 10-of-17 themselves, and maintained possession for 38:35 of the game's 60 minutes. Andre Reed had 5 receptions, including his 820th career catch, which elevated him to third-place on the all-time receiving list.

Buffalo	0	7	0	7	—	14
Tennessee	14	7	3	7	—	31

Tenn — Robertson 27 fumble return (Del Greco kick)
Tenn — McNair 1 run (Del Greco kick)
Tenn — McNair 3 run (Del Greco kick)
Buff — Early 9 pass from Collins (Christie kick)
Tenn — FG Del Greco 51
Buff — Early 6 pass from Collins (Christie kick)
Tenn — Russell 2 pass from McNair (Del Greco kick)

CAROLINA 16, ST. LOUIS 10—at Trans World Dome, attendance 64,609. John Kasay kicked 3 field goals and the Panthers' defense stopped the Rams on four plays from inside the 3-yard line with less than two minutes remaining to defeat the Rams. After a scoreless first quarter, 12-year veteran Leslie O'Neal recovered Kerry Collins's fumble and rumbled 66 yards for his first NFL touchdown. The Panthers tied the game three plays later on Collins's 59-yard touchdown pass to Raghib Ismail. Kasay completed a 53-yard drive late in the half with a 36-yard field goal to give the Panthers a 10-7 halftime edge. On the opening possession of the second half Jeff Wilkins, who missed a 40-yard field goal just before halftime, benefited from a 37-yard pass from Mark Rypien to Eddie Kennison to kick a 26-yard field goal to tie the game. Collins hit Wesley Walls with 13- and 21-yard passes to set up Kasay's second field goal on the ensuing drive. Kasay added a third field goal with 8:04 remaining to give Carolina a 16-10 lead. An exchange of punts gave the Rams the ball at the Panthers' 46 with 4:08 left. A 34-yard pass from Rypien to Ernie Conwell got the Rams to the Panthers' 3 with 2:00 remaining. Rypien threw an incomplete pass on first down, and Jerald Moore gained 1-yard on second and third down, setting up fourth-and-goal from the 1-yard line. Rypien rolled right, but his pass fell incomplete, and the Panthers were able to run out the clock. Collins was 23 of 30 for 286 yards and a touchdown. Walls had 8 receptions for 106 yards. Tony Banks started and was 6 of 13 for 61 yards, with an interception. Rypien replaced Banks, who left the game with an injury, and was 10 of 19 for 138 yards. The Rams lost their eighth consecutive game, while Carolina snapped a two-game losing skid.

Carolina	0	10	3	3	—	16
St. Louis	0	7	3	0	—	10

StL — O'Neal 66 fumble return (Wilkins kick)
Car — Ismail 59 pass from Collins (Kasay kick)
Car — FG Kasay 36
StL — FG Wilkins 26
Car — FG Kasay 53
Car — FG Kasay 27

GREEN BAY 45, DALLAS 17—at Lambeau Field, attendance 60,111. Brett Favre threw 4 touchdown passes and Dorsey Levens rushed for a club-record 190 yards as the Packers broke an eight-game losing streak to the Cowboys. A 36-yard pass from Favre to Robert Brooks set up his first touchdown pass, a 7-yard toss to Levens. Trailing 7-3, Deion Sanders intercepted a Favre pass at midfield and ran 50 yards down the right sideline for a touchdown to give the Cowboys a 10-7 lead with 1:19 remaining in the half. But the Packers drove 57 yards, and Ryan Longwell's 32-yard field goal tied the game at halftime. A 34-yard pass interference penalty on Sanders led to Favre's 4-yard scoring pass to Mark Chmura on the opening drive of the second half. On their next possession, a 16-play, 73-yard drive, keyed by 2 third-down conversions, was capped with a 2-yard scoring pass to Chmura to give the Packers a 24-10 lead. Emmitt Smith cut the deficit to 24-17 with a 21-yard scoring jaunt, but the Packers drove 61 yards, buoyed by Levens's 13-yard run on third-and-4, to score on Favre's 23-yard touchdown pass to Antonio Freeman. Levens had 10 carries for 79 yards on an 11-play, 88-yard drive late in the game that concluded with his 5-yard touchdown run. Darren Sharper finished the scoring when he picked up Sherman Williams's fumble and scored 22 seconds later. Favre was 22 of 35 for 203 yards and 4 touchdowns, with 1 interception. Aikman was 12 of 24 for 130 yards. The Packers had more first downs (29-11), total yards (409-213), time of possession (37:19-22:41), converted 13-of-17 third-down opportunities, and scored on all four of their second-half possessions.

Dallas	3	7	0	7	—	17
Green Bay	7	3	14	21	—	45

GB — Levens 7 pass from Favre (Longwell kick)
Dall — FG Cunningham 29
Dall — Sanders 50 interception return (Cunningham kick)
GB — FG Longwell 32
GB — Chmura 4 pass from Favre (Longwell kick)
GB — Chmura 2 pass from Favre (Longwell kick)
Dall — E. Smith 21 run (Cunningham kick)
GB — Freeman 23 pass from Favre (Longwell kick)
GB — Levens 5 run (Longwell kick)
GB — Sharper 34 fumble return (Longwell kick)

DETROIT 32, INDIANAPOLIS 10—at Pontiac Silverdome, attendance 62,803. Barry Sanders rushed for 216 yards and 2 touchdowns to record his tenth consecutive 100-yard game as the Lions won back-to-back games for the first time this season. Scott Mitchell's quarterback sneak on fourth-and-1 set up Tommy Vardell's first-quarter touchdown plunge. One minute later, Tracy Scroggins sacked Paul Justin in the end zone for a safety to push the Lions lead to 9-0. A 20-yard punt by John Jett later in the quarter set up Justin's 20-yard touchdown pass to Marvin Harrison. Sanders's 51-yard run set up the first of 3 second-quarter field goals by Jason Hanson. The last 2 boots, which came in the final 1:54 of the half and were each longer than 50 yards to give him a club-record 21 consecutive field goals, broke open a 12-10 game and gave Detroit a 18-10 halftime lead. Sanders streaked 80 yards down the right sideline on the opening play of the second half to give the Lions a 25-10 lead. Sanders added a 4-yard scoring run midway through the fourth quarter to conclude the scoring. The Colts only drove into Lions territory once in the second half, getting no closer than the Lions' 38. Mitchell was 16 of 28 for 150 yards. Sanders recorded his fourth career 200-yard game, and second of the season, on just 24 carries. Justin was 6 of 8 for 61 yards and a touchdown before injuring his ankle. Jim Harbaugh was 10 of 16 for 112 yards. The Lions had more first downs (21-12) and total yards (391-173).

Indianapolis	7	3	0	0	—	10
Detroit	9	9	7	7	—	32

Det — Vardell 1 run (Hanson kick)
Det — Safety, Justin sacked in end zone by Scroggins
Ind — Harrison 20 pass from Justin (Blanchard kick)
Det — FG Hanson 38
Ind — FG Blanchard 35
Det — FG Hanson 52
Det — FG Hanson 55
Det — Sanders 80 run (Hanson kick)
Det — Sanders 4 run (Hanson kick)

CINCINNATI 31, JACKSONVILLE 26—at Cinergy Field, attendance 55,158. Boomer Esiason made his first start as the Bengals' quarterback since 1992 a memorable event as he threw 2 touchdown passes en route to an upset victory over the Jaguars. Cincinnati scored touchdowns on 4 of its first 5 possessions. Esiason engineered a 13-play, 63-yard drive to begin the game, capped by Ki-Jana Carter's 1-yard run. Willie Jackson fumbled the ensuing kickoff, and Marco Battaglia recovered. Esiason found Tony McGee in the end zone four plays later to increase the lead to 14-0. After an exchange of punts, Mark Brunell threw a touchdown pass to Pete Mitchell, but David Dunn's 85-yard kickoff return led to Corey Dillon's 3-yard touchdown run. After another punt, the Bengals consumed most of the second quarter with an 18-play, 97-yard drive that lasted 8:14, and concluded with Esiason's 11-yard touchdown pass to Darnay Scott to give the Bengals a 28-7 lead. Mike Hollis kicked a field goal as time expired in the first half, and added another to cap the opening drive of the second half, to cut the deficit to 24-13. Less than two minutes later, a 45-yard pass interference penalty on Jimmy Spencer was followed by Natrone Means's 5-yard touchdown run. Cincinnati responded with its lone points of the second half, a 20-yard field goal by Doug Pelfrey. Brunell's 46-yard pass to Jimmy Smith on the next drive led to Hollis's third field goal and cut the lead to 31-23. Reggie Barlow's 46-yard punt return in the fourth quarter set up Hollis's fourth field goal with 9:12 remaining, but, on the Jaguars' next possession, Tito Paul recovered Means's fumble at the Bengals' 37 with 3:04 remaining to ice the game. Esiason was 26 of 36 for 211 yards and 2 touchdowns. Brunell was 20 of 33 for 286 yards and 1 touchdown, with an interception. Keenan McCardell had 8 receptions for 109 yards, with Smith adding 106 yards on 5 catches.

Jacksonville	7	3	13	3	—	26
Cincinnati	21	7	3	0	—	31

Cin — Carter 1 run (Pelfrey kick)
Cin — McGee 9 pass from Esiason (Pelfrey kick)
Jack — Mitchell 24 pass from Brunell (Hollis kick)
Cin — Dillon 3 run (Pelfrey kick)
Cin — Scott 11 pass from Esiason (Pelfrey kick)
Jack — FG Hollis 21
Jack — FG Hollis 35
Jack — Means 5 run (Hollis kick)
Cin — FG Pelfrey 20
Jack — FG Hollis 29
Jack — FG Hollis 25

KANSAS CITY 19, SEATTLE 14—at Kingdome, attendance 66,264. The Chiefs' defense recorded 5 sacks and forced 3 turnovers, and the special teams made 2 big plays as Kansas City won for the fifth time in its last six games. The Chiefs drove 76 yards with the opening kickoff, keyed by punter Louie Aguiar's 35-yard pass to Kevin Lockett on fourth-and-11 to the Seahawks' 1, and capped by Marcus Allen's 1-yard touchdown run. The touchdown was his club-record forty-first as a Chiefs player. The Seahawks answered with a 77-yard drive that concluded with Warren Moon's 20-yard touchdown pass to Joey Galloway. The Chiefs marched 65 yards on the next drive, with Pete Stoyanovich giving Kansas City a 10-7 lead, but late in the half Kevin Mawae recovered Tamarick Vanover's fumble on a punt return, and Steve Broussard raced 22 yards for the go-ahead touchdown. The Chiefs' defense forced a punt following the second-half kickoff, and Rich Gannon engineered a 54-yard drive, scoring on a 1-yard run to give Kansas City a 17-14 lead. Early in the fourth quarter Joe Horn blocked Kyle Richardson's punt out of the end zone for a safety. The Seahawks reached the Chiefs' 10 with 1:31 remaining, but Moon threw 3 consecutive incomplete passes, and Reggie Tongue sacked him on fourth down. Moon fumbled and Dan Williams recovered, which allowed the Chiefs to kneel-out the clock. Gannon was 15 of 28 for 175 yards. Moon was 20 of 37 for 248 yards and 1 touchdown, with an interception. The game marked the seventh consecutive time the Chiefs' defense had not given up a second-half touchdown.

Kansas City	7	3	7	2	—	19
Seattle	7	7	0	0	—	14

KC — Allen 1 run (Stoyanovich kick)
Sea — Galloway 20 pass from Moon (Peterson kick)
KC — FG Stoyanovich 22
Sea — Broussard 22 run (Peterson kick)
KC — Gannon 1 run (Stoyanovich kick)
KC — Safety, Richardson's punt blocked by Horn and went out of end zone

NEW ENGLAND 27, MIAMI 24—at Foxboro Stadium, attendance 59,002. Larry Whigham and Jimmy Hitchcock each returned interceptions for touchdowns as the Patriots defeated Miami, despite 3 touchdown runs by Karim Abdul-Jabbar, and knocked the Dolphins out of first place in the AFC East. With the game tied 3-3 late in the second quarter, Bledsoe completed a 17-yard pass to Shawn Jefferson on third-and-16 and ran 3 yards on fourth-and-1 to set up David Meggett's 35-yard halfback-option touchdown pass to Troy Brown with 2:37 left in the half. Dan Marino drove the Dolphins to midfield, but Whigham intercepted his pass and raced 60 yards for a touchdown. Undeterred, Marino drove the Dolphins to the Patriots' 7, but Hitchcock intercepted his first-down pass at the goal line and streaked 100 yards for a touchdown to give the Patriots a 24-3 lead with 11 seconds left in the half. Adam Vinatieri added a field goal on the opening drive of the second half to give the Patriots a 27-3 lead. Abdul-Jabbar's first touchdown came on the next drive, and a 14-play, 80-yard drive on their next possession culminated in Abdul-Jabbar's second touchdown and cut the deficit to 27-17 with 11:56 remaining. O.J. Brigance recovered the ensuing onside kick, and the Dolphins drove to the Patriots' 1, but Abdul-Jabbar lost 2- and 3-yards on successive plays, and Marino's third-down pass was intercepted by Whigham in the end zone with 6:45 left. The Patriots drove to the Dolphins' 29, but turned the ball over on downs with 2:39 left. Miami responded with a 16-play, 71-yard drive, capped by Abdul-Jabbar's third touchdown on fourth-and-1 with 10 seconds left. Jerry Wilson recovered the onside kick at the Dolphins' 42, but Marino's last 2 pass attempts fell incomplete. Bledsoe was 15 of 26 for 207 yards. Marino was 38 of 60 for 389 yards, with 3 interceptions. O.J. McDuffie had 9 receptions for 110 yards. The Dolphins had 33 first downs, while allowing just 15 by the Patriots.

Miami	0	3	7	14	—	24
New England	3	21	3	0	—	27

NE — FG Vinatieri 36
Mia — FG Mare 25
NE — Brown 35 pass from Meggett (Vinatieri kick)
NE — Whigham 60 interception return (Vinatieri kick)
NE — Hitchcock 100 interception return (Vinatieri kick)
NE — FG Vinatieri 27
Mia — Abdul-Jabbar 1 run (Mare kick)
Mia — Abdul-Jabbar 1 run (Mare kick)
Mia — Abdul-Jabbar 1 run (Mare kick)

NEW YORK JETS 23, MINNESOTA 21—at Giants Stadium, attendance 70,131. The Jets' defense stopped Robert Smith on a 2-point conversion attempt with no time remaining to propel the Jets into sole possession of first place in the AFC East. Leon Johnson's 66-yard punt return 2:21 into the game gave the Jets a 7-0 lead. John Randle recovered Neil O'Donnell's fumble on the Jets' 20 early in the second quarter, and Brad Johnson threw a 7-yard touchdown pass to an acrobatic Jake Reed three plays later to tie the game. Aaron Glenn's 41-yard kickoff return set up John Hall's 28-yard field goal, and, after a Vikings punt, O'Donnell guided the Jets on a 6-play, 61-yard drive, capped by a 3-yard touchdown pass to Fred Baxter, to give the Jets a 17-7 lead. Hall added field goals just before halftime and early in the third quarter to extend the Jets' lead to 23-7. Jerry Ball's recovery of an O'Donnell fumble at the Jets' 48 set up Johnson's 6-yard touchdown pass to Jake Reed with 11:19 remaining. Johnson ran in the 2-point conversion himself to cut the deficit to 23-15. Hall missed a 42-yard field-goal attempt with 5:30 remaining, but the Vikings were stopped on downs. However, the Vikings forced the Jets to punt, with Brian Hansen's boot travelling just 17 yards. With 1:54 remaining, and the ball on their own 40, the Vikings reached the Jets' 34 with 32 seconds left when Johnson found Cris Carter open downfield. Carter was tackled at the 1-yard line, and fumbled into the end zone. Smith recovered the ball, but per NFL rules the ball was placed on the 1-yard line with 24 seconds left. On first down, Johnson attempted a quarterback sneak, but was stopped. As the clock ran down, Jets cornerback Victor Green ran off with the ball. He was whistled for delay of game, giving the Vikings the ball with three seconds left. Johnson threw a touchdown pass to Andrew Glover as time expired, but the Jets' defense gang-tackled Smith behind the line of scrimmage to thwart his game-tying 2-point conversion effort. O'Donnell was 23 of 34 for 242 yards and 1 touchdown. Keyshawn Johnson had 9 receptions for 104 yards. Brad Johnson was 24 of 35 for 312 yards and 3 touchdowns. Reed had 8 receptions for 150 yards, and Carter added 6 catches for 105 yards.

Minnesota	0	7	0	14	—	21
N.Y. Jets	7	13	3	0	—	23

NYJ — L. Johnson 66 punt return (Hall kick)
Minn — Reed 7 pass from Johnson (Murray kick)
NYJ — FG Hall 28
NYJ — Baxter 3 pass from O'Donnell (Hall kick)
NYJ — FG Hall 27
NYJ — FG Hall 51
Minn — Reed 6 pass from Johnson (Johnson run)
Minn — Glover 1 pass from Johnson (run failed)

ATLANTA 20, NEW ORLEANS 3—at Georgia Dome, attendance 48,620. Chris Chandler threw 2 touchdown passes, and Shane Dronett and Travis Hall each had 2½ of the Falcons' 7 sacks as Atlanta won its second consecutive game. Cornelius Bennett's fumble recovery of Ray Zellars's fumble in the first quarter led to Morten Andersen's first field goal, and Michael Booker's interception midway through the second quarter gave Andersen another field goal and the Falcons a 6-0 lead. The Saints put together their longest drive of the game, but were stopped at the Falcons' 4 and had to settle for Doug Brien's 21-yard field goal just before halftime. In the third quarter, Todd Kinchen's 20-yard punt return into Saints' territory was followed two plays later by Chandler's 36-yard touchdown pass to Bert Emanuel. Chandler and Terance Mathis hooked up for a 4-yard scoring toss on the first play of the fourth quarter to complete the scoring. The Saints ventured into Falcons' territory three times in the second half, but were intercepted twice and had a field-goal attempt blocked by Dronett. Chandler was 17 of 26 for 211 yards. Doug Nussmeier started for the Saints and was 10 of 19 for 101 yards, with 3 interceptions. Billy Joe Hobert, who was just signed earlier in the week, was 4 of 10 for 49 yards, with 1 interception. The Falcons' defense permitted the Saints to convert just 1 of 13 third-down opportunities.

New Orleans	0	3	0	0	—	3
Atlanta	3	3	7	7	—	20

Atl — FG Andersen 43
Atl — FG Andersen 22
NO — FG Brien 21
Atl — Emanuel 36 pass from Chandler (Andersen kick)
Atl — Mathis 4 pass from Chandler (Andersen kick)

PHILADELPHIA 23, PITTSBURGH 20—at Veterans Stadium, attendance 67,166. In his second career start Bobby Hoying threw 2 touchdown passes as the Eagles improved their home record to 5-1 by defeating the Steelers. James Willis's recovery of Jerome Bettis's fumble, and Ricky Watters's 28-yard run, set up Hoying's 31-yard touchdown pass to Jason Dunn less than five minutes into the game. After forcing a punt, Hoying threw 13- and 44-yard passes to Irving Fryar before the duo connected for an 8-yard touchdown. Norm Johnson booted 2 field goals to cut the deficit to 14-6, but Hoying threw a 36-yard pass to Watters, and Charlie Garner had an 18-yard run to the Steelers' 4 before the defense stiffened and held the Eagles to Chris Boniol's 23-yard field goal just before halftime. Charles Dimry halted the Steelers' second-half opening drive with an interception deep in his own territory. The Eagles drove 53 yards, keyed by Hoying's 20-yard pass to Fryar on third-and-18 and 17-yard pass to Fryar on third-and-8, to set up Boniol's second field goal. Kordell Stewart threw a 19-yard touchdown pass to Bettis late in the third quarter, but the Eagles responded with another Boniol field goal to give the Eagles a 23-13 lead. The Steelers' defense stopped the Eagles on downs at their own 10- and 27-yard lines to stay close, but Matt Stevens made a diving, off-balanced interception of Stewart's bomb to Thigpen in the end zone with 1:57 left to halt the drive. After forcing a punt, the Steelers drove 69 yards and scored on Stewart's 30-yard Hail Mary pass to Will Blackwell with 10 seconds remaining. However, William Thomas recovered the ensuing onside kick to seal the victory. Hoying was 15 of 31 for 246 yards and 2 touchdowns. Fryar had 7 catches for 116 yards. Stewart was 20 of 43 for 294 yards and 2 touchdowns, with 3 interceptions. Charles Johnson had 7 receptions for 106 yards.

Pittsburgh	3	3	7	7	—	20
Philadelphia	14	3	3	3	—	23

Phil — Dunn 31 pass from Hoying (Boniol kick)
Phil — Fryar 8 pass from Hoying (Boniol kick)
Pitt — FG N. Johnson 46
Pitt — FG N. Johnson 40
Phil — FG Boniol 23
Phil — FG Boniol 35
Pitt — Bettis 19 pass from Stewart (N. Johnson kick)
Phil — FG Boniol 25
Pitt — Blackwell 30 pass from Stewart (N. Johnson kick)

SAN FRANCISCO 17, SAN DIEGO 10—at 3Com Park, attendance 61,905. Steve Young completed 20 of 30 passes for 245 yards and 2 touchdowns, and Merton Hanks grabbed 2 interceptions as the 49ers' defense permitted just 8 first downs en route to their eleventh consecutive victory. Hanks's first interception, at the Chargers' 34, set up Gary Anderson's 29-yard field goal midway through the first quarter. Iheanyi Uwaezuoke's 30-yard punt return in the final minute of the first half led to Young's 37-yard touchdown pass to Terrell Owens. Michael Swift recovered Uwaezuoke's fumble early in the third quarter to set up Greg Davis's 31-yard field goal. Hanks's second interception, midway through the third quarter, at the Chargers' 34 led to Young's 3-yard touchdown pass to J.J. Stokes and a 17-3 lead. Brett Maxie intercepted Craig Whelihan on the next play from scrimmage, and the 49ers were driving for more points when Marco Coleman forced Garrison Hearst to fumble. Paul Bradford picked up the ball and streaked 78 yards for a touchdown. After the Chargers' defense forced the 49ers to punt, reserve quarterback Todd Philcox threw a 27-yard touchdown pass to Bryan Still, but Isaac Davis's false start penalty negated the play. Davis missed a field goal moments later, and the Chargers failed to reach 49ers' territory the remainder of the game. Whelihan was 4 of 18 for 81 yards, with 3 interceptions. Philcox entered the game in the fourth quarter and was 6 of 10 for 57 yards. The 49ers outgained the Chargers (338-203 total yards) and had more first downs (19-8).

San Diego	0	0	10	0	—	10
San Francisco	3	7	7	0	—	17

SF — FG Anderson 29
SF — Owens 37 pass from Young (Anderson kick)
SD — FG Davis 31
SF — Stokes 3 pass from Young (Anderson kick)
SD — Bradford 78 fumble return (Davis kick)

CHICAGO 13, TAMPA BAY 7—at Soldier Field, attendance 43,955. The Bears turned 2 first-quarter fumbles into 10 points and then held off the Buccaneers to snap Tampa Bay's three-game winning streak. Walt Harris recovered Mike Alstott's fumble on the first play from scrimmage. Erik Kramer scrambled 31 yards on third-and-3, and Raymont Harris scored to give the Bears a 7-0 lead. Moments later, Barry Minter recovered Horace Copeland's fumble, and Jeff Jaeger kicked a 32-yard field goal. Trailing 13-0, the Buccaneers drove 69 yards, to score on Trent Dilfer's 12-yard touchdown pass to Reidel Anthony late in the third quarter. But Michael Husted missed a 40-yard field-goal attempt on Tampa Bay's next possession, and the Bears stopped Alstott a yard short of a first down on fourth-and-2 from their own 40 with 1:43 remaining. The Buccaneers did force the Bears to punt, but Karl Williams muffed the ball, and Fabien Bownes recovered on the Buccaneers' 4 with 38 seconds left to seal the victory. Kramer was 15 of 28 for 110 yards. Harris rushed 33 times for 116 yards. Dilfer was 19 of 33 for 247 yards and 1 touchdown. The game was played in 29-degree weather, which made the Buccaneers 0-17 in games that begin with temperatures colder than 42 degrees.

Tampa Bay	0	0	7	0	—	7
Chicago	10	3	0	0	—	13

Chi — Harris 2 run (Jaeger kick)
Chi — FG Jaeger 32
Chi — FG Jaeger 25
TB — Anthony 12 pass from Dilfer (Husted kick)

SUNDAY NIGHT, NOVEMBER 23

NEW YORK GIANTS 7, WASHINGTON 7 (TIE)—at Jack Kent Cooke Stadium, attendance 75,703. After not having a tie game for eight seasons, the NFL had its second tie in two weeks as the Giants and Redskins struggled to a deadlock. Kenard Lang recovered Danny Kanell's fumble at the Giants' 26, and Gus Frerotte scored five plays later to give the Redskins a 7-0 lead. Frerotte attempted to head-butt the wall at the back of the end zone, and had to leave the game in the third quarter with a jammed neck. The Giants, the fumble notwithstanding, had to punt on their other six first-half possessions, with neither team running a play inside the opponents 37. Phillippi Sparks's interception at the Giants' 46 led to Kanell's 4-yard touchdown pass to Chris Calloway midway through the third quarter to tie the game. The Redskins had an opportunity to score early in the fourth quarter, but Scott Blanton missed a 45-yard field-goal attempt. The Redskins won the overtime toss, but Jason Sehorn intercepted Jeff Hostetler on the third play of overtime. The Giants, however, were forced to punt. The Redskins drove to the Giants' 39, but Michael Strahan forced Hostetler to fumble, and Robert Harris recovered. The Giants once again were forced to punt without gaining a first down. The Redskins drove to the Giants' 41, but Keith Hamilton stopped Terry Allen on fourth-and-1 with 6:04 remaining to give the ball back to the Giants. New York reached the Redskins' 36, but Brad Daluiso, whose first attempt was blocked but the Giants had called time out just before the snap, missed a 54-yard field-goal attempt with 3:18 to play. But Sparks grabbed his second interception, at the Giants' 49, on the next play. However, the Giants decided to forego another 54-yard field-goal attempt, and instead punted into the end zone for a touchback with 2:12 left. Washington reached the Giants' 38, but a penalty on Michael Westbrook pushed the Redskins back, and, after a pass to Henry Ellard got them within field-goal range, Blanton's 54-yard attempt fell short with 11 seconds remaining. Kanell was 20 of 37 for 168 yards and 1 touchdown, with an interception. Hostetler was 19 of 41 for 213 yards, with 3 interceptions. Westbrook had 9 catches for 125 yards.

N.Y. Giants	0	0	7	0	0	—	7
Washington	0	7	0	0	0	—	7

Wash — Frerotte 1 run (Blanton kick)
NYG — Calloway 4 pass from Kanell (Daluiso kick)

MONDAY, NOVEMBER 24

DENVER 31, OAKLAND 3—at Denver Mile High Stadium, attendance 75,307. Terrell Davis scored 3 touchdowns as the Broncos' defense limited the Raiders to 14 first downs and defeated Oakland. In the second quarter James Jett fumbled, and Tyrone Braxton recovered. John Elway hit Ed McCaffrey with a 35-yard pass on the next play, and Davis scored two plays later. After the Broncos' defense forced a punt, Denver drove 71 yards in 9 plays, capped by Davis's 19-yard jaunt around right end. Lance Johnstone recovered an Elway fumble in the final minute of the half to set up Cole Ford's field goal. The Raiders had to punt after the first possession of the second half, and Darrien Gordon's 22-yard punt return and 27- and 10-yard passes from Elway to Shannon Sharpe led to Davis's third touchdown less than four minutes into the third quarter. Mike Lodish recovered Napoleon Kaufman's fumble on the next series, which led to Jason Elam's 36-yard field goal and a 24-3 lead. The Broncos finished the scoring when Elway threw a 15-yard touchdown pass to Rod Smith, one play after a penalty on Anthony Smith on fourth-and-2 extended the drive. Elway was 21 of 32 for 280 yards and 1 touchdown. Sharpe had 10 receptions for 142 yards. Jeff George was 22 of 41 for 185 yards.

Oakland	0	3	0	0	—	3
Denver	0	14	17	0	—	31

Den — Davis 3 run (Elam kick)
Den — Davis 19 run (Elam kick)
Oak — FG Ford 41
Den — Davis 2 run (Elam kick)
Den — FG Elam 36
Den — R. Smith 15 pass from Elway (Elam kick)

FOURTEENTH WEEK SUMMARIES

AMERICAN FOOTBALL CONFERENCE

Eastern Division	**W**	**L**	**T**	**Pct.**	**Pts.**	**OP**
Miami	8	5	0	.615	294	242
New England	8	5	0	.615	308	233
N.Y. Jets	8	5	0	.615	293	252
Buffalo	6	7	0	.462	217	296
Indianapolis	1	12	0	.077	222	348
Central Division						
Jacksonville	9	4	0	.692	334	269
Pittsburgh	9	4	0	.692	307	246
Tennessee	7	6	0	.538	284	242
Baltimore	4	8	1	.346	260	286
Cincinnati	4	9	0	.308	267	353

Western Division						
Denver	11	2	0	.846	393	215
Kansas City	10	3	0	.769	291	212
Seattle	6	7	0	.462	281	301
Oakland	4	9	0	.308	294	347
San Diego	4	9	0	.308	253	344

NATIONAL FOOTBALL CONFERENCE

Eastern Division	W	L	T	Pct.	Pts.	OP
N.Y. Giants	7	5	1	.577	226	227
Philadelphia	6	6	1	.500	247	286
Washington	6	6	1	.500	244	199
Dallas	6	7	0	.462	260	240
Arizona	3	10	0	.231	216	288
Central Division						
Green Bay	10	3	0	.769	343	245
Tampa Bay	9	4	0	.692	262	200
Minnesota	8	5	0	.615	285	289
Detroit	7	6	0	.538	322	250
Chicago	2	11	0	.154	215	377
Western Division						
San Francisco	11	2	0	.846	304	193
Carolina	6	7	0	.462	214	240
Atlanta	5	8	0	.385	260	312
New Orleans	5	8	0	.385	170	258
St. Louis	3	10	0	.231	225	301

THURSDAY, NOVEMBER 27

DETROIT 55, CHICAGO 20—at Pontiac Silverdome, attendance 77,904. Barry Sanders rushed for 167 yards to move into second place on the all-time rushing list, and scored 3 touchdowns as the Lions won their third consecutive game. Erik Kramer threw a 53-yard pass to Ricky Proehl to set up Raymont Harris's 2-yard touchdown run, and the duo connected on the first play of their next drive for a 78-yard touchdown to give the Bears an early 14-0 lead. Glyn Milburn's 69-yard kickoff return sparked the Lions and led to an exchange of field goals. Scott Mitchell's 8-yard pass to Herman Moore completed a 54-yard drive to cut the lead to 17-10 and began a stretch for the Lions of scoring on seven of eight possessions, with six touchdowns. Jeff Jaeger answered Moore's touchdown with a field goal, but the Lions scored the game's next, and final, 45 points. Sanders broke free for a 40-yard touchdown with 47 seconds remaining in the half. Jason Hanson booted a 29-yard field goal to conclude the opening drive of the second half, and, four plays after forcing a punt, Mitchell found a wide-open Johnnie Morton for a 50-yard touchdown to give the Lions a 27-20 lead. Luther Elliss then recovered Erik Kramer's fumble, and Sanders scored on a 25-yard run 1:38 after Morton's touchdown catch to extend the lead. After having a drive thwarted by a Tom Carter interception, Sanders finished a 64-yard drive with a 15-yard scoring run. Ron Rivers added his first touchdown run since 1995, and Tracy Scroggins recovered reserve quarterback Steve Stenstrom's fumble and rumbled 17 yards to cap the scoring. Mitchell was 20 of 31 for 282 yards and 2 touchdowns, with an interception. Sanders needed just 19 carries to gain 167 yards, and tied an NFL record with 11 consecutive 100-yard games. Morton had 7 catches for 120 yards. Kramer was 13 of 26 for 259 yards and 1 touchdown. Detroit rolled up 496 total yards, and its 55 points were a Thanksgiving Day record.

Chicago	14	6	0	0	—	20
Detroit	3	14	17	21	—	55

Chi — Harris 2 run (Jaeger kick)
Chi — Proehl 78 pass from Kramer (Jaeger kick)
Det — FG Hanson 40
Chi — FG Jaeger 52
Det — Moore 8 pass from Mitchell (Hanson kick)
Chi — FG Jaeger 32
Det — Sanders 40 run (Hanson kick)
Det — FG Hanson 29
Det — Morton 50 pass from Mitchell (Hanson kick)
Det — Sanders 25 run (Hanson kick)
Det — Sanders 15 run (Hanson kick)
Det — Rivers 13 run (Hanson kick)
Det — Scroggins 17 fumble return (Hanson kick)

TENNESSEE 27, DALLAS 14—at Texas Stadium, attendance 63,421. Marcus Robertson had a 48-yard interception return and scored on a 42-yard fumble recovery as the Oilers defense forced 5 turnovers, which led to 21 points, and Tennessee handed the Cowboys their first home defeat of the season. Robertson's interception return to the Cowboys' 11 set up Steve McNair's fourth-and- 1 2-yard touchdown pass to tackle-eligible Erik Norgard for his second career touchdown catch. Two posssessions later Troy Aikman, who suffered back spasms a half-hour before game time, threw his second interception of the first quarter. Darryll Lewis returned the pick 34 yards to the Cowboys' 1, and McNair scored on a quarterback sneak. Early in the second quarter, Aikman hit Anthony Miller for 3 passes totalling 59 yards, and then found Michael Irvin for a 19-yard touchdown. The Oilers responded with a 65-yard drive, capped by Al Del Greco's field goal. After an exchange of punts, Aikman hit Eric Bjornson for an 11-yard gain, but Blaine Bishop forced Bjornson to fumble, and Robertson scampered 42 yards down the right sideline to give the Oilers a 24-7 lead with 1:33 left in the first half. A 32-yard pass interference penalty kept a Cowboys' third-quarter drive alive and enabled Aikman and Irvin to hook up for their second touchdown of the game. But Tennessee responded with a grueling 21-play, 90-yard drive that lasted 13:18, and concluded with Del Greco's 19-yard field goal. The Cowboys reached the Oilers' 15 on their next series, but Aikman threw an incompletion on fourth down. Eddie George fumbled two plays later, and the Cowboys were about to score when Sherman Williams caught a screen pass from Aikman and headed for the end zone. However, Rayna Stewart forced him to fumble at the Oilers' 1, and James Roberson recovered with 4:19 left. McNair was 9 of 17 for 81 yards and 1 touchdown. George had 34 carries for 110 yards. Aikman was 27 of 42 for 356 yards and 2 touchdowns, with 3 interceptions. Tennessee maintained possession for 36:02 despite being outgained 386-245 total yards.

Tennessee	14	10	0	3	—	27
Dallas	0	7	7	0	—	14

Tenn — Norgard 2 pass from McNair (Del Greco kick)
Tenn — McNair 1 run (Del Greco kick)
Dall — Irvin 19 pass from Aikman (Cunningham kick)
Tenn — FG Del Greco 29
Tenn — Robertson 42 fumble return (Del Greco kick)
Dall — Irvin 37 pass from Aikman (Cunningham kick)
Tenn — FG Del Greco 19

SUNDAY, NOVEMBER 30

ATLANTA 24, SEATTLE 17—at Kingdome, attendance 52,584. Jamal Anderson scored 2 touchdowns, and Byron Hanspard returned a kickoff 93 yards for a touchdown as the Falcons won their third consecutive game. On the opening drive of the game, a 28-yard pass from Chris Chandler to Brian Kozlowski to the 1-yard line set up Anderson's first touchdown. Todd Kinchen's 28-yard punt return in the second quarter was followed two plays later by Chandler's 13-yard touchdown pass to Anderson. The Falcons settled for an 18-yard Morten Andersen field goal later in the quarter to take a 17-0 lead. The Seahawks responded with a 10-play, 68-yard drive, capped by Warren Moon's 16-yard touchdown pass to Joey Galloway just before halftime. Seattle drove 64 yards to cut the deficit to 17-14 midway through the third quarter on Moon's 20-yard short pass to Steve Broussard, who darted and scampered into the end zone. The Seahawks' momentum lasted all of 17 seconds, as Hanspard returned the ensuing kickoff for a touchdown. Todd Peterson missed a 48-yard field-goal attempt on the Seahawks' next drive, and, after Peterson connected on a 35-yard field goal to cut the lead to 24-17, Lenny McGill thwarted the Seahawks' final drive as he intercepted Moon at the Falcons' 24 with 1:37 remaining to ice the game. Chandler was 15 of 23 for 204 yards and 1 touchdown. Moon was 24 of 38 for 240 yards and 2 touchdowns, with 1 interception. The Falcons held on to win despite gaining just 24 yards and no first downs in five second-half possessions. The Falcons' defense recorded 3 sacks to give them an NFL-high 49 for the season and establish a new club record.

Atlanta	7	10	7	0	—	24
Seattle	0	7	7	3	—	17

Atl — Anderson 1 run (Andersen kick)
Atl — Anderson 13 pass from Chandler (Andersen kick)
Atl — FG Andersen 18
Sea — Galloway 16 pass from Moon (Peterson kick)
Sea — Broussard 20 pass from Moon (Peterson kick)
Atl — Hanspard 93 kickoff return (Andersen kick)
Sea — FG Peterson 35

JACKSONVILLE 29, BALTIMORE 27—at ALLTEL Stadium, attendance 63,712. Mike Hollis kicked 5 field goals, but the Jaguars needed Eric Zeier to trip over Jonathan Ogden on a 2-point conversion attempt with 1:10 remaining to preserve their thirteenth consecutive home victory. The Ravens led 7-3 after the first quarter, thanks to Antonio Langham's interception return. Baltimore extended the lead to 14-3 on the strength of 15- and 29-yard passes to James Roe and Vinny Testaverde's 15-yard touchdown strike to Jermaine Lewis. The Jaguars' defense forced the Ravens to punt following their next 3 possessions, and the offense scored a touchdown, by Natrone Means, and added 2 field goals to give Jacksonville a 16-14 halftime lead. The Jaguars drove 74 yards with the second half's opening kickoff, with the drive being extended by Ray Lewis's 15-yard facemask penalty on third-and-7, and capped by Brunell's 26-yard touchdown pass to Damon Jones. Hollis concluded the ensuing 66- and 60-yard drives with field goals as the Jaguars scored on six consecutive possessions to take a 29-14 lead with 9:04 left in the game. Eric Zeier, who had replaced an injured Testaverde, completed a 29-yard pass to Roe and forced a 32-yard pass interference penalty to set up Kenyon Cotton's first NFL touchdown with 7:13 remaining. The Jaguars failed to record a first down, and the Ravens began their march. Faced with fourth-and-2 from the Jaguars' 27, Zeier hit Michael Jackson with a 9-yard pass. Moments later, Zeier threw a 7-yard touchdown pass to Eric Green with 1:10 left to cut the deficit to 29-27. Attempting the 2-point conversion, Zeier ran a quarterback sneak, but tripped over tackle Ogden's leg and was stopped short of the end zone. Jimmy Smith recovered the ensuing onside kick to ice the game. Brunell was 25 of 40 for 317 yards and 1 touchdown, with 1 interception. Testaverde was 11 of 17 for 101 yards and 1 touchdown, and Zeier completed 7 of 12 attempts for 87 yards and 1 touchdown. The Jaguars had more yards (404-221) and had the ball for 35:11 of the game's 60 minutes.

Baltimore	7	7	0	13	—	27
Jacksonville	3	13	3	10	—	29

Balt — Langham 40 interception return (Stover kick)
Jack — FG Hollis 41
Balt — Lewis 15 pass from Testaverde (Stover kick)
Jack — Means 3 run (Hollis kick)
Jack — FG Hollis 42
Jack — FG Hollis 31
Jack — Jones 26 pass from Brunell (Hollis kick)
Jack — FG Hollis 29
Jack — FG Hollis 22
Balt — Cotton 1 run (Stover kick)
Balt — Green 7 pass from Zeier (run failed)

PHILADELPHIA 44, CINCINNATI 42—at Veterans Stadium, attendance 66,623. Bobby Hoying passed for 313 yards and 4 touchdowns, but the Eagles needed Chris Boniol's 31-yard field goal as time expired to defeat the relentless Bengals. Hoying threw a 23-yard touchdown pass to Michael Timpson to complete the game-opening drive and give the Eagles a 7-0 lead. Boomer Esiason tied the game with a touchdown pass to Darnay Scott, and, just over 2 minutes later and after Ashley Ambrose recovered Ricky Watters's fumble at the Eagles' 44, a scrambling Esiason threw a 36-yard touchdown pass to James Hundon. On their next series, the Bengals were stopped on fourth-and-3 from the Eagles' 34. Philadelphia responded with a 63-yard drive, capped by Hoying's 2-yard scoring pass to Chad Lewis. Michael Zordich recovered Eric Bieniemy's fumble on the ensuing kickoff, and Hoying threw a 16-yard touchdown pass to Jimmie Johnson. The Eagles' defense then forced a punt, and Boniol kicked a 33-yard field goal just before halftime to give Philadelphia a 24-14 lead. William Thomas intercepted Esiason on the third play of the second half, and Boniol's second field goal increased the lead to 27-14. The Bengals drove 90 yards, keyed by a 37-yard run by Corey Dillon, and capped by Ki-Jana Carter's 1-yard scoring run. The Eagles answered with a 71-yard drive that concluded with Kevin Turner's acrobatic 23-yard touchdown catch. After an exchange of punts, Esiason hit David Dunn for 19 yards on third-and-14 and

Hundon for 11 yards on third-and-10 to set up his 9-yard touchdown pass to Tony McGee to cut the deficit to 34-28 with 9:13 remaining. Duce Staley returned the ensuing kickoff 45 yards, and Watters scored from 16 yards with 5:29 remaining. Esiason threw a 41-yard pass to Scott and an 8-yard touchdown pass to Hundon with 3:20 remaining. The Eagles failed to get a first down, and Esiason completed back-to-back passes of 16- and 15-yards to Dunn and Scott to reach the Eagles' 15 with 1:22 remaining. On third-and-10, a pass interference penalty gave the Bengals the ball at the Eagles' 1, and Brian Milne scored on the next play to give Cincinnati a 42-41 lead with 1:00 to play. Hoying hit Fryar for 28 yards to get into Bengals' territory and, from the 31-yard line with 10 seconds left, found Fryar on the left sideline for 18 yards to give Boniol a chip-shot field goal. Hoying was 26 of 42 for 313 yards and 4 touchdowns, with 1 interception. Fryar had 7 catches for 122 yards. Esiason was 27 of 47 for 378 yards and 4 touchdowns, with 1 interception. Dillon had 19 carries for 114 yards. Hundon had 5 receptions for 118 yards. The teams combined for 56 first downs (29 by Cincinnati) and 1,006 total yards (507 by Philadelphia).

Cincinnati	14	0	7	21	—	42
Philadelphia	7	17	10	10	—	44

Phil — Timpson 23 pass from Hoying (Boniol kick)
Cin — Scott 10 pass from Esiason (Pelfrey kick)
Cin — Hundon 36 pass from Esiason (Pelfrey kick)
Phil — Lewis 2 pass from Hoying (Boniol kick)
Phil — Johnson 16 pass from Hoying (Boniol kick)
Phil — FG Boniol 33
Phil — FG Boniol 25
Cin — Carter 1 run (Pelfrey kick)
Phil — Turner 23 pass from Hoying (Boniol kick)
Cin — McGee 9 pass from Esiason (Pelfrey kick)
Phil — Watters 16 run (Boniol kick)
Cin — Hundon 13 pass from Esiason (Pelfrey kick)
Cin — Milne 1 run (Pelfrey kick)
Phil — FG Boniol 31

NEW ENGLAND 20, INDIANAPOLIS 17—at Foxboro Stadium, attendance 58,507. Drew Bledsoe threw 2 touchdown passes as the Patriots pulled into a three-way tie for first place in the AFC East. Willie Clay recovered a Marshall Faulk fumble at the Colts' 44, and Bledsoe completed third-down passes to Vincent Brisby and Ben Coates before finding Sam Gash from 3 yards out to give the Patriots an early 7-0 lead. Cary Blanchard's 24-yard field goal on the next series cut the deficit to 7-3, but Bledsoe responded by hitting Coates and Shawn Jefferson with third-down passes to set up Adam Vinatieri's 32-yard field goal. The Colts reached the Patriots' 19 and faced a fourth-and-1 situation with 1:04 remaining in the half. Indianapolis called time out, and then Jim Harbaugh attempted to draw the Patriots offsides. The attempt failed; the Colts were penalized five yards; and Blanchard missed a 42-yard field-goal attempt. The Patriots drove downfield in 59 seconds, and Vinatieri's 48-yard boot as the half expired extended their lead to 13-3. The Colts scored on their first series of the second half, with Harbaugh's 51-yard pass to Sean Dawkins on third-and-3 setting up his 18-yard scoring toss to Aaron Bailey. David Meggett's 37-yard punt return late in the third quarter led to Bledsoe's 18-yard touchdown pass to Troy Brown on the first play of the fourth quarter to give New England a 20-10 lead. After an exchange of punts, the Colts reached the Patriots' 21 with about 7:00 remaining. Faced with second-and-1, Zack Crockett failed to get a first down on consecutive running plays, and Harbaugh's fourth-down pass was incomplete. The Colts' defense forced another punt, and the offense put together a 15-play (all passing), 75-yard drive, capped by Harbaugh's 11-yard touchdown pass to Sean Dawkins with 1:08 left. Ben Coates recovered the ensuing onside kick to secure the victory. Bledsoe was 20 of 33 for 204 yards and 2 touchdowns. Harbaugh was 22 of 41 for 310 yards and 2 touchdowns. Dawkins had 7 receptions for 120 yards.

Indianapolis	3	0	7	7	—	17
New England	7	6	0	7	—	20

NE — Gash 3 pass from Bledsoe (Vinatieri kick)
Ind — FG Blanchard 24
NE — FG Vinatieri 32
NE — FG Vinatieri 48
Ind — Bailey 18 pass from Harbaugh (Blanchard kick)
NE — Brown 18 pass from Bledsoe (Vinatieri kick)
Ind — Dawkins 11 pass from Harbaugh (Blanchard kick)

MIAMI 34, OAKLAND 16—at Oakland-Alameda County Coliseum, attendance 50,569. Dan Marino threw 2 touchdown passes to Charles Jordan as the Dolphins won for the first time in 10 games in Oakland and moved into a three-way tie for first place in the AFC East. The Raiders struck first, as Jeff George threw a 24-yard touchdown pass to Tim Brown to cap the Raiders' first possession. Marino threw a 12-yard pass to Bernie Parmalee on fourth-and-5 to set up Olindo Mare's 28-yard field goal. On their next series, Marino's 8-yard touchdown pass to Jordan finished a 14-play, 73-yard drive. After another punt, Jordan broke free on a short pass for a 44-yard touchdown. Cole Ford missed a 47-yard field goal just before halftime, as the Dolphins led 17-7. Lorenzo Lynch's interception set up Ford's 44-yard field goal midway through the third quarter, but the Dolphins responded with a 9-play, 79-yard drive, keyed by Marino's 17-yard pass to Jordan on third-and-10, and capped by Karim Abdul-Jabbar's 2-yard touchdown run. Two plays later, Zach Thomas sacked George on his own goal line and forced him to fumble. Tim Bowens recovered the ball for a touchdown and a 31-10 lead. Early in the fourth quarter, on consecutive plays, George hit Jett with a 50-yard pass and a 27-yard scoring strike to cut the deficit to 31-16, but Ford missed the extra point. Eric Turner recovered a Miami fumble at the Dolphins' 30 on the next play from scrimmage, but George threw 3 consecutive incompletions, and Trace Armstrong sacked him on fourth down. Olindo Mare added a field goal, and Sam Madison intercepted George at the Dolphins' 30 with just under five minutes remaining to stifle any comeback attempt. Marino was 19 of 34 for 241 yards and 2 touchdowns, with 1 interception. Jordan had 5 receptions for 106 yards. George was 17 of 34 for 272 yards and 2 touchdowns, with 1 interception. Brown had 8 catches for 125 yards.

Miami	3	14	14	3	—	34
Oakland	7	0	3	6	—	16

Oak — Brown 24 pass from George (Ford kick)
Mia — FG Mare 28
Mia — Jordan 8 pass from Marino (Mare kick)
Mia — Jordan 44 pass from Marino (Mare kick)
Oak — FG Ford 44
Mia — Abdul-Jabbar 2 run (Mare kick)
Mia — Bowens recovered fumble in end zone (Mare kick)
Oak — Jett 27 pass from George (kick failed)
Mia — FG Mare 42

NEW ORLEANS 16, CAROLINA 13—at Ericsson Stadium, attendance 57,957. Doug Brien kicked 3 field goals, including a 45-yard boot with five seconds remaining, to lift the Saints to their third victory in their last four games. Anthony Newman's interception at the Saints' 17 and 17-yard return not only thwarted a Panthers scoring drive, but set up Brien's first field goal, a 50-yard kick, early in the second quarter. Three plays later, Winfred Tubbs recovered Fred Lane's fumble at the Panthers' 41. Billy Joe Hobert, in his first start for the Saints, completed passes of 11 yards to Randal Hill and 20 yards to Irv Smith to set up Ray Zellars's 10-yard scoring run. Lane's 50-yard run on the next series led to John Kasay's 44-yard field goal, and the Panthers reached the Saints' 27 on their next possession, but Sammy Knight's interception stopped the drive. Brien added a 51-yard field goal to give the Saints a 13-3 halftime lead. The Panthers had the best chance to score in the scoreless third quarter, but Darren Mickell blocked Kasay's 26-yard field-goal attempt. Carolina stopped the Saints on fourth-and-1 from the Panthers' 33, and then, faced with fourth-and-9 from the Saints' 37, Steve Beuerlein hit Raghib Ismail with a 35-yard pass to set up Lane's 2-yard touchdown run. Andre Hastings muffed a punt, and Dwight Stone recovered at the Saints' 24 with 9:15 left, but the Panthers had to settle for Kasay's game-tying 31-yard field goal. The Panthers' defense forced a punt, but Carolina had to punt from its own 48. Ken Walter shanked the punt 15 yards, which gave the Saints the ball at their own 37 with 1:10 left. Zellars had 3 carries for 27 yards on the ensuing drive, and Brien booted his game-winning kick with five seconds to spare. Hobert was 14 of 30 for 190 yards, with 1 interception. Kerry Collins started for Carolina and was 7 of 15 for 82 yards, with 2 interceptions. Beuerlein replaced him late in the second quarter, after Collins's left with an injury, and completed 17 of 27 passes for 168 yards, with 1 interception.

New Orleans	0	13	0	3	—	16
Carolina	0	3	0	10	—	13

NO — FG Brien 50
NO — Zellars 10 run (Brien kick)
Car — FG Kasay 44
NO — FG Brien 51
Car — Lane 2 run (Kasay kick)
Car — FG Kasay 31
NO — FG Brien 45

BUFFALO 20, NEW YORK JETS 10—at Rich Stadium, attendance 47,776. Todd Collins threw 2 touchdown passes, and Thurman Thomas recorded his first 100-yard rushing game of the season as the Bills knocked the Jets into a three-way tie atop the AFC East standings. Collins capped the Bills' first possession with a 22-yard touchdown pass to Andre Reed. John Hall missed a 53-yard field-goal attempt late in the first quarter but connected from 22 yards in the second quarter. Phil Hansen sacked Neil O'Donnell and forced him to fumble. Henry Jones recovered at the Jets' 36 with 1:00 left in the half, and Steve Christie kicked a 49-yard field goal to give Buffalo a 10-3 halftime lead. The Jets tied the game one play after Leon Johnson's 28-yard punt return when O'Donnell threw a 29-yard touchdown pass to Keyshawn Johnson. The Bills took the lead early in the fourth quarter when Collins threw a 62-yard touchdown pass to Lonnie Johnson, who ran over two Jets' defenders on his way to the end zone. The Jets were forced to punt on their next drive, and Christie concluded a 56-yard drive with a 34-yard field goal with 5:21 remaining. The Jets failed to cross midfield on their final possession, and the Bills ran out the clock. Collins was 12 of 31 for 164 yards and 2 touchdowns, with an interception. Thomas needed 18 carries for 104 yards to achieve his fifty-second career 100-yard rushing game. O'Donnell was 25 of 47 for 292 yards and 1 touchdown, with 1 interception.

N.Y. Jets	0	3	7	0	—	10
Buffalo	7	3	0	10	—	20

Buff — Reed 22 pass from Collins (Christie kick)
NYJ — FG Hall 22
Buff — FG Christie 49
NYJ — K. Johnson 29 pass from O'Donnell (Hall kick)
Buff — L. Johnson 62 pass from Collins (Chrisite kick)
Buff — FG Christie 34

PITTSBURGH 26, ARIZONA 20 (OT)—at Sun Devil Stadium, attendance 66,341. Jerome Bettis rushed for 142 yards and 3 touchdowns, including the game-winning score in overtime, to allow the Steelers to maintain a share of first place in the AFC Central. Bettis carried 8 times for 39 yards on the Steelers' first series and scored on a 2-yard run. Jake Plummer's 43-yard third-down pass to Rob Moore set up Joe Nedney's 32-yard field goal midway through the second quarter. The Steelers led 10-3 at halftime, but the Cardinals tied the game on their first possession of the second half, with Plummer and Sanders connecting on 11- and 32-yard passes before the duo tied the game from 3 yards out. The Steelers responded with a 12-play, 80-yard drive, keyed by Kordell Stewart's third-down passes to Courtney Hawkins and George Jones, and capped by Bettis's 7-yard run. The Cardinals answered with a 70-yard drive, keyed by Sanders's 26-yard option pass to Moore, to set up Plummer's 11-yard scoring pass to Chris Gedney. Stewart and Bettis each ran for first downs on third-and-short situations, which set up Norm Johnson's 39-yard field goal with 9:12 left to give the Steelers a 20-17 lead. The Cardinals responded with a 44-yard pass from Plummer to Moore on third-and-15 to reach the Steelers' 10.

Pittsburgh	7	3	7	3	6	—	26
Arizona	0	3	14	3	0	—	20

Pitt — Bettis 2 run (N. Johnson kick)
Ariz — FG Nedney 32
Pitt — FG N. Johnson 40
Ariz — Sanders 3 pass from Plummer (Nedney kick)

Pitt — Bettis 7 run (N. Johnson kick)
Ariz — Gedney 11 pass from Plummer (Nedney kick)
Pitt — FG N. Johnson 39
Ariz — FG Nedney 19
Pitt — Bettis 10 run

ST. LOUIS 23, WASHINGTON 20—at Jack Kent Cooke Stadium, attendance 74,772. Amp Lee caught a 36-yard touchdown pass and set up Jeff Wilkins's last-minute game-winning field goal with a 45-yard reception as the Rams snapped an eight-game losing streak. On the opening drive, Gus Frerotte completed third-down passes to Chris Thomas and Jamie Asher before hitting Larry Bowie for a 39-yard touchdown pass. Keith Lyle's 18-yard interception return late in the first quarter led to Wilkins's 30-yard field goal. After Scott Blanton kicked a field goal with 2:09 left in the half to extend the Redskins lead to 10-3, Lee scampered 36 yards after receiving a Tony Banks pass to tie the game at halftime. Banks hit Ernie Conwell with a 25-yard pass and Torrance Small for 15 yards on third-and-3 to set up Jerald Moore's first NFL touchdown. Early in the fourth quarter, Mike Jones stopped Brian Mitchell shy of the goal line on a third-and-goal pass, which forced the Redskins to settle for Blanton's second field goal. After an exchange of punts, Banks threw a 35-yard third-down pass to Eddie Kennison to allow Wilkins to extend the lead to 20-13 with 4:42 left. The Redskins responded with a 15-play, 78-yard drive, keyed by Frerotte's 15-yard pass to Westbrook on third-and-10, the duo's 13-yard pass play on fourth-and-12, and his 19-yard pass to Henry Ellard on fourth-and-10, and capped by Mitchell's game-tying 2-yard run with 1:50 left. David Thompson's 28-yard kickoff return gave the Rams the ball at their own 40, and, on third-and-10 from midfield, Banks hit Lee with a short pass over the middle. Lee raced down to the 5-yard line, and Wilkins booted the game-winning kick two plays later. Banks was 19 of 38 for 298 yards and 1 touchdown. Lee had 6 receptions for 128 yards. Frerotte was 20 of 45 for 258 yards and 1 touchdown, with 2 interceptions, and played the entire fourth quarter with a broken hip.

St. Louis	0	10	7	6	—	23
Washington	7	3	0	10	—	20

StL — Bowie 39 pass from Frerotte (Blanton kick)
StL — FG Wilkins 30
Wash — FG Blanton 43
StL — Lee 36 pass from Banks (Wilkins kick)
StL — Moore 5 run (Wilkins kick)
Wash — FG Blanton 19
StL — FG Wilkins 23
Wash — Mitchell 2 run (Blanton kick)
StL — FG Wilkins 25

KANSAS CITY 44, SAN FRANCISCO 9—at Arrowhead Stadium, attendance 77,535. Rich Gannon threw 3 touchdown passes, including 2 to Andre Rison, and Marcus Allen ran for 1 touchdown and threw for another as the Chiefs snapped the 49ers' 11-game winning streak. The 49ers' defense had entered the game allowing a league-low 12.4 points per game. After an exchange of punts to begin the game, the Chiefs scored on their next four possessions. Gannon hit Rison for an 18-yard completion on third-and-7 to set up the duo's 6-yard scoring connection midway through the first quarter. The 49ers answered with a 72-yard drive, capped by Gary Anderson's 33-yard field goal. The Chiefs came back on the next series with a 12-play, 69-yard drive that ended with Gannon tossing a 2-yard touchdown pass to Tony Gonzalez. Gonzalez blocked Tommy Thompson's punt moments later, and recovered the ball at the 3-yard line, setting up Allen's first touchdown run. The 49ers were once again forced to punt without recording a first down, and the Chiefs drove 57 yards, capped by Allen's 1-yard halfback option touchdown pass to a tip-toeing Ted Popson to give Kansas City a 28-3 lead 26 seconds before halftime. Anderson added field goals as the half expired and at the conclusion of their first series of the second half, but Dale Carter's interception at the Chiefs' 7 ended the 49ers' next drive, and San Francisco did not run a play inside Chiefs' territory in any of its final six possessions. Mark McMillian's 12-yard interception return for a touchdown of reserve Jeff Brohm's pass ended the scoring. Gannon was 12 of 21 for 186 yards and 3 touchdowns, with 1 interception. Rison had 5 catches for 117 yards. Steve Young was 17 of 23 for 184 yards, with 1 interception. The 35-point defeat marked the worst regular-season loss for the 49ers since 1980.

San Francisco	3	3	3	0	—	9
Kansas City	7	21	0	16	—	44

KC — Rison 6 pass from Gannon (Stoyanovich kick)
SF — FG Anderson 33
KC — Gonzalez 2 pass from Gannon (Stoyanovich kick)
KC — Allen 3 run (Stoyanovich kick)
KC — Popson 1 pass from Allen (Stoyanovich kick)
SF — FG Anderson 33
SF — FG Anderson 40
KC — Rison 29 pass from Gannon (Stoyanovich kick)
KC — Safety, Phillips and Edwards tackle Kirby in end zone
KC — McMillian 12 interception return (Stoyanovich kick)

TAMPA BAY 20, NEW YORK GIANTS 8—at Giants Stadium, attendance 77,859. Mike Alstott scored 2 touchdowns, and the Buccaneers' defense did not allow a touchdown as Tampa Bay clinched its first full-schedule winning season since 1981. Brad Daluiso missed a 47-yard field goal at the conclusion of the Giants' opening possession, but Phillippi Sparks's 67-yard interception return to the Buccaneers' 27 gave them another chance to score first. However, Derrick Brooks intercepted Danny Kanell at the 10-yard line to keep the game scoreless. After a second Dilfer interception, Donnie Abraham picked off Kanell's pass at the Buccaneers' 44. Dilfer's 53-yard pass to Warrick Dunn led to his 1-yard touchdown pass to Alstott midway through the second quarter. Dilfer, who had thrown 6 interceptions all season, threw his third of the half, as Tito Wooten raced 53 yards down to the Buccaneers' 28. Daluiso's 45-yard field goal just before halftime cut the deficit to 7-3. Jason Sehorn intercepted Dilfer on the Buccaneers first possession of the second half, but Sehorn was penalized 40 yards for defensive pass interference. Alstott rumbled in from the 9-yard line on the next play to give Tampa Bay a 14-3 lead. John Lynch was flagged for unnecessary roughness and face-mask penalties to extend a Giants' drive late in the third quarter, but New York had to settle for Daluiso's second field goal. Dilfer was blitzed by Conrad Hamilton and was called for intentional grounding in the end zone, which cut the deficit to 14-8 in the first minute of the fourth quarter. But Lynch and Regan Upshaw stopped Tyrone Wheatley for no gain on fourth-and-1 from the Buccaneers' 47, and Tampa Bay, using a 30-yard pass interference penalty and a 17-yard run by Warrick Dunn, scored on Errict Rhett's 1-yard run with 7:22 left to ice the game. Dilfer was 12 of 22 for 152 yards and 1 touchdown, with 3 interceptions. Dunn had 24 carries for 120 yards. Kanell was 14 of 31 for 117 yards, with 2 interceptions. The win was the first in nine attempts for Tampa Bay at Giants Stadium.

Tampa Bay	0	7	7	6	—	20
N.Y. Giants	0	3	3	2	—	8

TB — Alstott 1 pass from Dilfer (Husted kick)
NYG — FG Daluiso 45
TB — Alstott 9 run (Husted kick)
NYG — FG Daluiso 30
NYG — Safety, Dilfer called for intentional grounding in end zone
TB — Rhett 1 run (pass failed)

SUNDAY NIGHT, NOVEMBER 30

DENVER 38, SAN DIEGO 28—at Qualcomm Stadium, Jack Murphy Field, attendance 54,245. John Elway passed for 240 yards and 3 touchdowns, and Terrell Davis added 178 yards and 1 touchdown in his hometown as the Broncos remained a game ahead of the Chiefs. Tyrone Braxton's interception set up Elway's first touchdown pass. Elway's second touchdown pass capped a 74-yard drive early in the second quarter, with Rod Smith's grab giving Denver a 14-0 lead. Kenny Bynum's 57-yard kickoff return led to Craig Whelihan's 4-yard touchdown pass to Tony Martin to cut the deficit to 14-7. However, Davis scored on a 5-yard run with 1:15 left in the half, and 14 seconds later, nine-year veteran safety Steve Atwater scored his first NFL touchdown on an interception return to put the game out of reach. Elway completed 20 of 33 passes. Ed McCaffrey had 7 receptions for 111 yards and 2 touchdowns. Whelihan was 23 of 51 for 222 yards and 2 touchdowns, with 2 interceptions. Eric Metcalf established an NFL record with his ninth career punt return for a touchdown. The Chargers made the game respectable in the fourth quarter, as they ran 40 plays to Denver's five.

Denver	7	21	7	3	—	38
San Diego	0	7	7	14	—	28

Den — McCaffrey 4 pass from Elway (Elam kick)
Den — R. Smith 5 pass from Elway (Elam kick)
SD — Martin 4 pass from Whelihan (Davis kick)
Den — Davis 5 run (Elam kick)
Den — Atwater 22 interception return (Elam kick)
SD — Metcalf 83 punt return (Davis kick)
Den — McCaffrey 21 pass from Elway (Elam kick)
SD — Brown 1 run (Davis kick)
Den — FG Elam 32
SD — Metcalf 11 pass from Whelihan (Davis kick)

MONDAY, DECEMBER 1

GREEN BAY 27, MINNESOTA 11—at Metrodome, attendance 64,001. Dorsey Levens rushed for 108 yards and 2 touchdowns, and the Packers' defense recorded 6 sacks to give Green Bay its first victory in Minnesota since 1991. With the score tied 3-3 in the second quarter, Brett Favre completed 4 passes for 70 yards on an 86-yard drive, capped by Robert Brooks's 18-yard touchdown reception. Doug Evans's interception in the opening moments of the second half led to Levens's first touchdown run and a 17-3 lead. Gabe Wilkins recovered Brad Johnson's fumble on the Vikings' 10, setting up Ryan Longwell's second field goal, from 19 yards, with 8:02 remaining. Randall Cunningham replaced the injured Johnson and engineered a touchdown drive, keyed by his own 24-yard run, to cut the deficit to 20-11 with 3:30 remaining. However, Evans recovered the ensuing onside kick, and Favre completed a 9-yard pass to Mark Chmura on fourth-and-1 with 2:00 remaining to lead to Levens's second touchdown. Favre was 15 of 29 for 196 yards and 1 touchdown. Johnson, who suffered a season-ending nerve injury in his neck, completed 15 of 30 passes for 117 yards, with 1 interception. Cunningham was 6 of 12 for 72 yards. Reggie White had 2½ sacks.

Green Bay	3	7	7	10	—	27
Minnesota	0	3	0	8	—	11

GB — FG Longwell 30
Minn — FG Murray 42
GB — Brooks 18 pass from Favre (Longwell kick)
GB — Levens 3 run (Longwell kick)
GB — FG Longwell 19
Minn — Hoard 4 run (Carter pass from Cunningham)
GB — Levens 5 run (Longwell kick)

FIFTEENTH WEEK SUMMARIES

AMERICAN FOOTBALL CONFERENCE

Eastern Division	W	L	T	Pct.	Pts.	OP
Miami	9	5	0	.643	327	272
New England	9	5	0	.643	334	253
N.Y. Jets	8	6	0	.571	307	274
Buffalo	6	8	0	.429	220	316
Indianapolis	2	12	0	.143	244	362
Central Division						
Pittsburgh	10	4	0	.714	342	270
Jacksonville	9	5	0	.643	354	295
Tennessee	7	7	0	.500	298	283
Baltimore	5	8	1	.393	291	310
Cincinnati	5	9	0	.357	308	367
Western Division						
Denver	11	3	0	.786	417	250
Kansas City	11	3	0	.786	321	212
Seattle	6	8	0	.429	305	332
Oakland	4	10	0	.286	294	377
San Diego	4	10	0	.286	256	358

NATIONAL FOOTBALL CONFERENCE

Eastern Division	W	L	T	Pct.	Pts.	OP
N.Y. Giants	8	5	1	.607	257	248
Washington	7	6	1	.536	282	227
Philadelphia	6	7	1	.464	268	317
Dallas	6	8	0	.429	273	263
Arizona	3	11	0	.214	244	326
Central Division						
Green Bay	11	3	0	.786	360	251
Tampa Bay	9	5	0	.643	268	217
Minnesota	8	6	0	.571	302	317
Detroit	7	7	0	.500	352	283
Chicago	3	11	0	.214	235	380

Western Division

San Francisco	12	2	0	.857	332	210
Carolina	7	7	0	.500	237	253
Atlanta	6	8	0	.429	274	315
New Orleans	5	9	0	.357	197	292
St. Louis	4	10	0	.286	259	328

THURSDAY, DECEMBER 4

CINCINNATI 41, TENNESSEE 14—at Cinergy Field, attendance 49,086. Corey Dillon rushed for an NFL rookie record 246 yards and scored 4 touchdowns, as the Bengals all but knocked the Oilers out of the playoff hunt. The offensive line of Kevin Sargent, Rich Braham, Darrick Brilz, Ken Blackman, and Willie Anderson paved the way for Dillon against the NFL's third-best rushing defense. Boomer Esiason, who had sparked the Bengals offense for 73 points in his previous two starts, completed 4 of 5 passes on the Bengals' first drive, with Dillon scoring on a 2-yard run. After an Oilers punt, Cincinnati drove 66 yards in just over three minutes, capped by Esiason's 1-yard touchdown pass to Tony McGee. After another punt, Esiason once again completed 4 of 5 passes, and Dillon scampered 31 yards up the middle for his second touchdown to give the Bengals a 21-0 lead. Tennessee punted again, and Dillon raced 59 yards on the Bengals' first play to the Oilers' 16. He scored four plays later to give Cincinnati a commanding 28-0 halftime lead. The Bengals did not score on their final drive of the first half, but Esiason completed 3 of 4 passes for 56 yards, and Dillon scored his fourth touchdown on their opening possession of the second half. The Bengals scored on their next drive as well, with Doug Pelfrey's field goal in the final minute of the third quarter giving Cincinnati a 38-0 lead. Steve McNair threw 2 fourth-quarter touchdown passes. Esiason was 20 of 28 for 245 yards and 1 touchdown. Dillon rushed 39 times and doubled his previous career-high in rushing yards (123). McNair was 14 of 25 for 146 yards and 2 touchdowns. Cincinnati had more total yards (515-175), first downs (34-12), and time of possession (40:39-19:21).

Tennessee	0	0	0	14	—	14
Cincinnati	14	14	10	3	—	41

Cin — Dillon 2 run (Pelfrey kick)
Cin — McGee 1 pass from Esiason (Pelfrey kick)
Cin — Dillon 31 run (Pelfrey kick)
Cin — Dillon 1 run (Pelfrey kick)
Cin — Dillon 2 run (Pelfrey kick)
Cin — FG Pelfrey 26
Tenn — Davis 5 pass from McNair (Del Greco kick)
Cin — FG Pelfrey 40
Tenn — Kent 11 pass from McNair (Del Greco kick)

SUNDAY, DECEMBER 7

ATLANTA 14, SAN DIEGO 3—at Qualcomm Stadium, Jack Murphy Field, attendance 46,317. The Falcons used 3 interceptions and Byron Hanspard's 99-yard kickoff return to win for the fifth time in six games. The Chargers reached the Falcons' 15 on their first possession, but Ray Buchanan intercepted Craig Whelihan to halt the drive. Dan Owens's 14-yard interception late in the first quarter gave Atlanta the ball at the Chargers' 36. Chris Chandler threw a 19-yard touchdown pass to Terance Mathis six plays later to give the Falcons a 7-0 lead. Hanspard returned the opening kickoff of the second half for a score, his second touchdown return in two weeks. The Chargers responded with Greg Davis's 37-yard field goal to cut the deficit to 14-3. The Chargers forced a punt and then converted 3 third downs to reach the Falcons' 3, but Buchanan intercepted Whelihan in the end zone with 10:39 left in the game. The Chargers' defense forced another punt, and San Diego reached the Falcons' 24, but Shane Dronett blocked Davis's field-goal attempt, and the Falcons ran the final 5:50 off the clock. The blocked field goal was Dronett's sixth of his career. Chandler was 10 of 23 for 115 yards and 1 touchdown, with 1 interception. Whelihan was 22 of 41 for 259 yards, with 3 interceptions. Eric Metcalf had 8 receptions for 109 yards. The Falcons won three consecutive road games for the first time since 1986.

Atlanta	0	7	7	0	—	14
San Diego	0	0	3	0	—	3

Atl — Mathis 19 pass from Chandler (Andersen kick)
Atl — Hanspard 99 kickoff return (Andersen kick)
SD — FG Davis 37

CHICAGO 20, BUFFALO 3—at Soldier Field, attendance 39,784. Erik Kramer threw 2 touchdown passes during a six-minute stretch of the second quarter, and the Bears' defense permitted just 10 first downs, as Chicago won its third game of the season. Kramer's 42-yard pass to Curtis Conway set up Jeff Jaeger's field goal in the opening minute of the second quarter to give the Bears a 3-0 lead. Kramer threw a 30-yard touchdown pass to Ryan Wetnight midway through the quarter, and connected with Ricky Proehl for a 3-yard touchdown pass with 32 seconds left in the half to take a 17-0 lead. Raymont Harris had a 4-yard run on fourth-and-2 to keep the final scoring drive of the half alive. Steve Tasker's 12-yard return of a squib kick allowed Steve Christie to kick a 43-yard field goal for the Bills' only points. Jaeger added a second field goal early in the fourth quarter to finish the scoring. The Bills did not run a play beyond the Bears' 43-yard line in the second half. Kramer was 23 of 33 for 270 yards and 2 touchdowns, with 2 interceptions. Conway had 7 receptions for 115 yards. Harris gained 59 yards to surpass the 1,000-yard mark for the season, but he fractured his leg in the third quarter and missed the rest of the season. Todd Collins completed 13 of 32 passes for 138 yards. Chicago had more first downs (23-10), total yards (392-160), and time of possession (40:28-19:32).

Buffalo	0	3	0	0	—	3
Chicago	0	17	0	3	—	20

Chi — FG Jaeger 41
Chi — Wetnight 30 pass from Kramer (Jaeger kick)
Chi — Proehl 3 pass from Kramer (Jaeger kick)
Buff — FG Christie 43
Chi — FG Jaeger 38

PITTSBURGH 35, DENVER 24—at Three Rivers Stadium, attendance 59,739. Kordell Stewart threw 3 touchdown passes and ran for 2 scores as the Steelers clinched an AFC playoff spot. The Broncos capitalized on Tyrone Braxton's fumble recovery, as John Elway fired a 37-yard touchdown pass to Rod Smith just over five minutes into the game. The Steelers responded with Stewart's 33-yard touchdown pass to Yancey Thigpen to tie the game. Denver scored on its next drive, with Terrell Davis scoring on a 3-yard touchdown run. Denver took a 21-7 lead on Smith's second touchdown catch, but the Steelers responded three plays later with Thigpen scoring on a 69-yard pass play. Stewart and Thigpen combined for third time, just before halftime, on a 21-yard pass play to tie the score at half. Jason Elam's 35-yard field goal capped the Broncos' opening drive of the second half, but the Steelers answered with Stewart's 4-yard touchdown run to claim their first lead of the game. After forcing a punt, the Steelers drove to the 4-yard line, but Gordon intercepted Stewart's pass in the end zone to halt the drive. Denver drove into Steelers' territory, but Elam missed a 53-yard field-goal attempt with 4:52 to play. Stewart raced 19 yards on fourth-and-2 from the Broncos' 34 before scoring on a 9-yard run with 1:57 remaining to ice the game. Stewart completed 18 of 29 passes for 303 yards and 3 touchdowns, with an interception. Thigpen had 6 receptions for a career-high 175 yards. Jerome Bettis had 24 carries for 125 yards for his tenth 100-yard game of the season. Elway was 17 of 42 for 248 yards and 2 touchdowns, with 1 interception.

Denver	14	7	3	0	—	24
Pittsburgh	7	14	7	7	—	35

Den — R. Smith 37 pass from Elway (Elam kick)
Pitt — Thigpen 33 pass from Stewart (Johnson kick)
Den — Davis 3 run (Elam kick)
Den — R. Smith 25 pass from Elway (Elam kick)
Pitt — Thigpen 69 pass from Stewart (Johnson kick)
Pitt — Thigpen 21 pass from Stewart (Johnson kick)
Den — FG Elam 35
Pitt — Stewart 4 run (Johnson kick)
Pitt — Stewart 9 run (Johnson kick)

GREEN BAY 17, TAMPA BAY 6—at Houlihan's Stadium, attendance 73,523. With first place in the NFC Central on the line, the defending Super Bowl champion Packers' defense allowed just 8 first downs and 161 total yards in defeating the Buccaneers. In the first quarter, Hardy Nickerson recovered Mark Chmura's fumble at the Packers' 13, but Tampa Bay had to settle for Michael Husted's 24-yard field goal. Two plays after Eugene Robinson recovered Mike Alstott's fumble, Brett Favre fired a 43-yard touchdown pass to Robert Brooks. John Lynch's 28-yard interception return late in the second quarter led to Husted's second field goal and cut the Packers lead to 7-6 at halftime. After an exchange of punts to begin the second half, Green Bay drove 73 yards and took a 14-6 lead on Favre's 8-yard scoring pass to Dorsey Levens. A 16-play, 88-yard drive in the fourth quarter culminated with Ryan Longwell's 27-yard field goal to give the Packers an 11-point lead with 6:24 to play. Steve Walsh replaced an injured Trent Dilfer (sprained ankle) and drove the Buccaneers to the Packers' 31, but Mike Prior's interception halted Tampa Bay's deepest penetration of the second half. Favre was 25 of 33 for 280 yards and 2 touchdowns, with 1 interception. Dilfer was 6 of 17 for 67 yards, and Walsh was 4 of 9 for 50 yards, with 1 interception.

Green Bay	7	0	7	3	—	17
Tampa Bay	3	3	0	0	—	6

TB — FG Husted 24
GB — Brooks 43 pass from Favre (Longwell kick)
TB — FG Husted 48
GB — Levens 8 pass from Favre (Longwell kick)
GB — FG Longwell 27

INDIANAPOLIS 22, NEW YORK JETS 14—at Giants Stadium, attendance 61,168. Marshall Faulk rushed for 133 yards and a touchdown as the Colts knocked the Jets out of a first-place tie in the AFC East. Cary Blanchard kicked 2 field goals, and Zack Crockett scored on a 2-yard run to take a 12-0 halftime lead. The Jets were outgained 225-59 in the first half, and John Hall missed a 42-yard field goal for their only scoring opportunity. Faulk had 17- and 20-yard runs to set up the field goals, and caught a 58-yard pass from Jim Harbaugh prior to Crockett's score. Faulk's 22-yard run in the third quarter led to Blanchard's third field goal, and Rico Clark's 14-yard interception return led to Faulk's 2-yard touchdown run on the first play of the fourth quarter. Neil O'Donnell threw 2 touchdown passes to Alex Van Dyke, the second with 1:34 remaining in the game, to cut the deficit to 22-14, but Marcus Pollard recovered the ensuing onside kick to ice the game. Harbaugh was 15 of 24 for 173 yards. O'Donnell was 14 of 32 for 151 yards and 2 touchdowns, with 1 interception. The Colts held a decisive edge in total yards (366-126) and time of possession (40:07-19:53).

Indianapolis	0	12	3	7	—	22
N.Y. Jets	0	0	0	14	—	14

Ind — FG Blanchard 38
Ind — FG Blanchard 20
Ind — Crockett 2 run (pass failed)
Ind — FG Blanchard 42
Ind — Faulk 2 run (Blanchard kick)
NYJ — Van Dyke 17 pass from O'Donnell (Hall kick)
NYJ — Van Dyke 18 pass from O'Donnell (Hall kick)

SAN FRANCISCO 28, MINNESOTA 17—at 3Com Park, attendance 55,761. Steve Young threw 2 touchdown passes and ran for another score as the 49ers defeated the Vikings in the mud and rain of 3Com Park. Precision passing by Young set up his 16-yard touchdown pass to Terry Kirby on the game's initial drive. The 49ers scored on their next possession as well, with William Floyd completing the drive with a 1-yard scoring run. Randall Cunningham responded with a 10-yard touchdown pass to Cris Carter, but the 49ers drove 70 yards on six plays, capped by Young's 21-yard touchdown pass to Terrell Owens. The Vikings stayed in the game with a 15-play, 91-yard drive, which was allowed to continue because of a roughing-the-punter penalty, and cut the deficit to 21-14 on Cunningham's second touchdown pass of the half to Carter. The 49ers drove 91 yards on 10 plays on their first possession of the third quarter, with Young's 31-yard pass to Floyd setting up Young's 4-yard scoring run. Eddie Murray's 42-yard field goal on the next drive cut the deficit to 28-17, but Chris Doleman sacked Cunningham twice and forced him to fumble both times. Doleman recovered the first fumble near midfield, and the second one halted the Vikings' deepest penetration of the fourth quarter. Tyronne Drakeford's interception in Vikings' territory with 54 seconds left iced the game. Young was 20 of 25 for 280 yards and 2 touchdowns. Cunningham, making his first start since 1995 because of Brad Johnson's season-ending injury, was 16 of 31 for 178 yards and 2 touchdowns, with 1 interception.

Minnesota	7	7	3	0	—	17
San Francisco	14	7	7	0	—	28

SF — Kirby 16 pass from Young (Anderson kick)
SF — Floyd 1 run (Anderson kick)
Minn — Carter 10 pass from Cunningham (Murray kick)
SF — Owens 21 pass from Young (Anderson kick)
Minn — Carter 22 pass from Cunningham (Murray kick)
SF — Young 4 run (Anderson kick)
Minn — FG Murray 42

NEW ENGLAND 26, JACKSONVILLE 20—at ALLTEL Stadium, attendance 73,446. Drew Bledsoe threw 2 touchdown passes, and Adam Vinatieri booted 4 field goals as the Patriots snapped the Jaguars' 13-game home winning streak. The Patriots won despite losing the services of two key injured players, Curtis Martin and Terry Glenn. The Patriots scoered on their initial three possessions: Vinatieri's 44-yard field goal capped the Patriots' first drive; Willie McGinest's recovery of Mark Brunell's fumble led to Bledsoe's 9-yard touchdown pass to Troy Brown; and Reggie Barlow's fumble on the ensuing kickoff, and recovery by Tedy Bruschi, set up Vinatieri's second field goal. The Jaguars cut the deficit to 13-7 with a touchdown pass from Brunell to Keenan McCardell with 1:16 left in the half, but the Patriots answered with a 9-play, 78-yard drive, in which Bledsoe completed 7 of 8 passes, capped by Ben Coates's 5-yard touchdown catch. Trailing 23-7, the Jaguars drove 80 yards in 3:09, scoring on Brunell's 12-yard touchdown pass to McCardell. Brown recovered the ensuing onside kick, and Vinatieri's fourth field goal gave the Patriots a 26-13 lead with 2:30 remaining. However, Barlow returned the ensuing kickoff 92 yards for a touchdown, and Vinatieri missed a 32-yard field-goal attempt with 28 seconds left. The Jaguars reached their own 37 before Brunell's final Hail Mary pass was knocked down at the 2-yard line as time expired. Bledsoe was 26 of 35 for 234 yards and 2 touchdowns. Brunell was 25 of 42 for 251 yards and 2 touchdowns. McCardell had 11 receptions for 152 yards.

New England	13	7	3	3	—	26
Jacksonville	0	7	0	13	—	20

NE — FG Vinatieri 44
NE — Brown 9 pass from Bledsoe (Vinatieri kick)
NE — FG Vinatier 41
Jack — McCardell 20 pass from Brunell (Hollis kick)
NE — Coates 5 pass from Bledsoe (Vinatieri kick)
NE — FG Vinatieri 33
Jack — McCardell 12 pass from Brunell (pass failed)
NE — FG Vinatieri 39
Jack — Barlow 92 kickoff return (Hollis kick)

NEW YORK GIANTS 31, PHILADELPHIA 21—at Veterans Stadium, attendance 67,084. Danny Kanell threw 3 touchdown passes, and the Giants rushed for 208 yards and capitalized on 3 first-half turnovers to pull two games ahead of the Eagles. Jessie Armstead's 57-yard interception return 2:41 into the game gave the Giants an early 7-0 lead. Charles Dimry's fumble return to the 3-yard line set up Ricky Watters's game-tying touchdown plunge. Scott Galyon sacked Bobby Hoying and forced him to fumble. Keith Hamilton recovered the fumble at the Eagles' 33, setting up Kanell's 11-yard touchdown pass to Tiki Barber to give the Giants a 14-7 lead. Bernard Holsey sacked Hoying three plays later and also forced him to fumble. Michael Strahan recovered at the Eagles' 40, and Kanell threw a 40-yard bomb to David Patten on the next play to give the Giants 2 touchdowns in 58 seconds. Brian Dawkins's interception return for his first NFL touchdown cut the deficit to 21-14. But the Giants drove 70 yards, keyed by Barber's 42-yard scamper, and culminating with Kanell's 5-yard touchdown pass to Chris Calloway to take a 28-14 lead with 10:51 remaining. After Mel Gray pinned the Eagles deep in their own territory by fair catching a ball at his own 5-yard line, Tommy Hutton proceeded to shank a punt 19 yards, setting up Brad Daluiso's field goal with 3:40 remaining. Hoying threw a 72-yard touchdown pass to Irving Fryar with 2:59 left, but Charles Way recovered the ensuing onside kick, and Barber gained 7 yards on third-and-3 to ice the game. Kanell was 14 of 27 for 153 yards and 3 touchdowns, with 1 interception. Barber rushed for 114 yards. Hoying was 16 of 35 for 209 yards and 1 touchdown, with 3 interceptions and 2 lost fumbles.

N.Y. Giants	7	14	0	10	—	31
Philadelphia	7	0	7	7	—	21

NYG — Armstead 57 interception return (Daluiso kick)
Phil — Watters 1 run (Boniol kick)
NYG — Barber 11 pass from Kanell (Daluiso kick)
NYG — Patten 40 pass from Kanell (Daluiso kick)
Phil — Dawkins 64 interception return (Boniol kick)
NYG — Calloway 5 pass from Kanell (Daluiso kick)
NYG — FG Daluiso 19
Phil — Fryar 72 pass from Hoying (Boniol kick)

KANSAS CITY 30, OAKLAND 0—at Arrowhead Stadium, attendance 76,379. The Chiefs defense allowed just 5 first downs, 93 total yards, and recorded 6 sacks to shutout the Raiders. Rich Gannon's 39-yard pass to Greg Hill on the game's opening drive set up Pete Stoyanovich's 44-yard field goal. The Chiefs converted 3 third-down opportunities on their next scoring drive, as Donnell Bennett's 9-yard run capped the 91-yard drive. Vaughn Booker's fumble recovery on the Raiders' ensuing possession led to another Stoyanovich field goal and a 13-0 Chiefs' lead. The Raiders drove to the Chiefs' 20, but Cole Ford's 38-yard field-goal attempt glanced off the left upright. Kansas City promptly marched 72 yards on 13 plays, with Gannon scoring from 5 yards to give the Chiefs a 20-0 halftime lead. In the first half, Kansas City outgained the Raiders 265-55 and had a 17-2 edge in first downs. Oakland did not run a play inside Chiefs' territory in the second half until they trailed 30-0. Gannon was 15 of 21 for 225 yards and 1 touchdown. The Chiefs recorded 27 first downs and 418 total yards, and had the ball for 41:30. Kansas City is 16-2 against the Raiders in the 1990s.

Oakland	0	0	0	0	—	0
Kansas City	10	10	0	10	—	30

KC — FG Stoyanovich 44
KC — Bennett 9 run (Stoyanovich kick)
KC — FG Stoyanovich 27
KC — Gannon 5 run (Stoyanovich kick)
KC — FG Stoyanovich 40
KC — Richardson 2 pass from Gannon (Stoyanovich kick)

ST. LOUIS 34, NEW ORLEANS 27—at Louisiana Superdome, attendance 54,803. Tony Banks threw 2 fourth-quarter touchdown passes to Isaac Bruce in the final six minutes as the Rams staged a furious fourth-quarter comeback to defeat the Saints for the fourth consecutive time. The Saints capitalized on 2 first-quarter fumble recoveries, one by Richard Harvey to set up a field goal and the other by Mark Fields for a 21-yard touchdown, to take a 10-0 lead. The Rams converted 3 third downs before Banks completed an 84-yard drive with a 3-yard touchdown pass to Ernie Conwell. Fumble recoveries by Toby Wright and Todd Lyght set up 2 Jeff Wilkins field goals, with Doug Brien's boot in between, to send the club's to the locker rooms tied 13-13. The Saints took the lead on Hobert's 34-yard touchdown pass to Andre Hastings late in the third quarter, and used a 36-yard pass play from the same two men early in the fourth quarter to set up Hobert's 1-yard scoring pass to Irv Smith. Trailing 27-13, the Rams used a 59-yard kickoff return by David Thompson and a 38-yard pass interference penalty to set up Jerald Moore's 3-yard touchdown run just 24 seconds after the Saints' tally. The Rams defense forced the Saints to punt, and Eddie Kennison's 43-yard return led to Banks's tying touchdown pass to Bruce with 5:46 remaining. Todd Lyght's interception and return to the Saints' 11 two plays later set up Banks's 5-yard touchdown pass to Bruce with 3:51 left to take a 34-27 lead. The Saints did not reach midfield the remainder of the game. Banks was 22 of 41 for 267 yards and 3 touchdowns, with 1 interception. Bruce had 9 catches for 144 yards. Hobert was 18 of 42 for 259 yards and 2 touchdowns, with 2 interceptions. Hastings had 6 receptions for 120 yards.

St. Louis	0	13	0	21	—	34
New Orleans	10	3	7	7	—	27

NO — FG Brien 49
NO — Fields 21 fumble return (Brien kick)
StL — Conwell 3 pass from Banks (Wilkins kick)
StL — FG Wilkins 37
NO — FG Brien 53
StL — FG Wilkins 34
NO — Hastings 34 pass from Hobert (Brien kick)
NO — Smith 1 pass from Hobert (Brien kick)
StL — Moore 3 run (Wilkins kick)
StL — Bruce 30 pass from Banks (Wilkins kick)

BALTIMORE 31, SEATTLE 24—at Memorial Stadium, attendance 54,395. Jermaine Lewis returned 2 punts for touchdowns and caught a 29-yard scoring pass as the Ravens dealt the Seahawks' playoff hopes a devastating blow. Dan Saleaumua's recovery of Byron (Bam) Morris's fumble on the Ravens' 14 led to Lamar Smith's 4-yard touchdown run. Leading 7-3, Tyree Davis downed Rohn Stark's punt at the 1-yard line, and Saleaumua sacked Eric Zeier for a safety to give Seattle a 9-3 edge. The Seahawks could not score after receiving the free kick, but Lewis returned the ensuing punt 89 yards for a touchdown. Leading 17-10, Lewis returned a punt 66 yards for a touchdown with 35 seconds left in the half to tie the game. He became just the ninth player in NFL history, but the third this year, to return 2 punts for touchdowns in the same quarter. The Seahawks took the lead on their first possession of the third quarter on Warren Moon's 60-yard touchdown pass to James McKnight. Zeier's 29-yard scoring pass to Lewis tied the game late in the third quarter. Stark pinned the Ravens back at their 7-yard line early in the fourth quarter, but Zeier responded with a 92-yard pass to Derrick Alexander to the Seahawks' 1. It was the longest play from scrimmage in Ravens' history. Morris scored on the next play to give Baltimore a 31-24 lead with 10:42 left. John Friesz, who replaced an injured Moon, was intercepted 3 times in the final 5:40 of the game, twice by Ralph Staten and the final time, with 15 seconds left, by Cornell Brown at the Ravens' 14. Zeier, who started for injured Vinny Testaverde, was 17 of 28 for 302 yards and 1 touchdown. Alexander caught 6 passes for 150 yards. Moon was 12 of 19 for 140 yards and 1 touchdown, with an interception. Friesz was 5 of 15 for 59 yards, with 3 interceptions. The Seahawks have lost five of their last six games.

Seattle	7	10	7	0	—	24
Baltimore	3	14	7	7	—	31

Sea — Smith 4 run (Peterson kick)
Balt — FG Stover 24
Sea — Safety, Zeier sacked by Saleaumua in end zone
Balt — Lewis 89 punt return (Stover kick)
Sea — Brown 42 fumble return (Smith run)
Balt — Lewis 66 punt return (Stover kick)
Sea — McKnight 60 pass from Moon (Peterson kick)
Balt — Lewis 29 pass from Zeier (Stover kick)
Balt — Morris 1 run (Stover kick)

WASHINGTON 38, ARIZONA 28—at Sun Devil Stadium, attendance 41,537. Jeff Hostetler threw 3 touchdowns passes in his first start for the Redskins, offsetting Jake Plummer's 4-touchdown performance, as Washington won a wild NFC East game and remained just one game behind the Giants. After Brian Mitchell's 63-yard punt return for a touchdown put the Redskins on the board, Washington scored on its next two possessions as well, with Hostetler's 69-yard pass to Mitchell setting up the first score and Cris Dishman's the second, to take a 17-0 lead. Plummer's 52-yard pass to Frank Sanders led to his first touchdown pass. With 57 seconds left in the first half and on their own 20, Plummer completed 5 of 6 passes for 80 yards, capped by Moore's 29-yard touchdown reception with seven seconds left to cut the halftime deficit to 17-14. Dishman returned his second interception of the game for a touchdown 1:41 into the third quarter, but Plummer completed a 29-yard pass to Sanders on third-and-10, and a 37-yard touchdown pass to Chris Gedney to pull within three points once again. Hostetler's 23-yard touchdown pass to Henry Ellard capped a 13-play, 92-yard drive and gave the Redskins a 31-21 lead early in the fourth quarter. Plummer and Moore connected for a third time, from 47 yards, to cut the lead to 31-28 with 10:03 remaining. The Cardinals forced Washington to punt, but Marvcus Patton sacked Plummer and forced him to fumble. Kenard Lang recovered the ball at the Cardinals' 22 with 5:54 left, and Hostetler threw a 7-yard pass to Albert Connell for his first NFL touchdown three plays later to take a 38-28 lead with 4:17 remaining. The Cardinals got the ball back twice, but could not drive into Redskins' territory. Hostetler, in his first start for injured Gus Frerotte, was 18 of 34 for 226 yards and 3 touchdowns, with 1 interception. Plummer was 19 of 38 for 337 yards and 4 touchdowns, with 2 interceptions. Moore had 5 receptions for 114 yards and a career-high 3 touchdowns.

Washington	7	10	7	14	—	38
Arizona	0	14	7	7	—	28

Wash — Mitchell 63 punt return (Blanton kick)
Wash — Bowie 3 pass from Hostetler (Blanton kick)
Wash — FG Blanton 40
Ariz — Moore 4 pass from Plummer (Nedney kick)
Ariz — Moore 29 pass from Plummer (Nedney kick)
Wash — Dishman 21 interception return (Blanton kick)
Ariz — Gedney 37 pass from Plummer (Nedney kick)
Wash — Ellard 23 pass from Hostetler (Blanton kick)
Ariz — Moore 47 pass from Plummer (Nedney kick)
Wash — Connell 7 pass from Hostetler (Blanton kick)

SUNDAY NIGHT, DECEMBER 7

MIAMI 33, DETROIT 30—at Pro Player Stadium, attendance 72,266. Olindo Mare kicked a 42-yard field goal as time expired as the Dolphins remained tied for first place in the AFC East with a hard-fought victory over the Lions. The Dolphins scored on their first two drives, with a Jason Hanson field goal sandwiched between, to take a 14-3 lead. Detroit drove to the Dolphins' 2, but Scott Mitchell fumbled the snap, and Shane Burton recovered. The Lions forced a punt, but Jason Taylor's recovery of Mitchell's fumble at the Lions' 18 led to Mare's 19-yard field goal and a 17-3 advantage. The Lions responded with an 88-yard drive, keyed by Mitchell's 41-yard pass to Johnnie Morton, and capped by Barry Sanders's 7-yard touchdown run with 56 seconds left in the half. However, Dan Marino completed 4 of 5 passes for 61 yards to allow Mare to kick a 33-yard field goal as the half expired. In the third quarter, O.J. Brigance recovered a punt that deflected off Mark Carrier's leg at the Lions' 18 to set up Mare's second field goal that extended the Dolphins lead to 23-10. On the ensuing possession, Mitchell linked with Morton for a 35-yard scoring toss, but a poor snap kept the Lions behind by seven points. Bryant Westbrook's 64-yard interception return for a touchdown in the first minute of the fourth quarter cut the deficit to 23-22, but Jason Hanson's extra-point attempt hit the right upright. The Lions forced a punt, but Terrell Buckley intercepted Mitchell, and Marino threw a 23-yard touchdown pass to Troy Drayton to give the Dolphins a 30-22 lead with 9:14 remaining. After an exchange of punts, the Lions drove 96 yards in 13 plays, with Mitchell's 16-yard touchdown pass to Herman Moore cutting the deficit to 30-28 with 1:19 left. Following a time out, Mitchell, hooked up with Moore for the 2-point conversion to tie the game. The Dolphins drove to the Lions' 30, and Marino completed a 6-yard pass to Jerris McPhail with four seconds left to set up Mare's winning kick. Marino was 24 of 39 for 310 yards and 2 touchdowns, with 1 interception. Mitchell was 19 of 29 for 288 yards and 2 touchdowns, with 2 interceptions. Sanders had 30 carries for 137 rushing yards, and Morton had 9 catches for 171 yards. Sanders set an NFL record by compiling 12 consecutive 100-yard rushing games.

Detroit	3	7	6	14	—	30
Miami	14	6	3	10	—	33

Mia — Drayton 27 pass from Marino (Mare kick)
Det — FG Hanson 26
Mia — Abdul-Jabbar 1 run (Mare kick)
Mia — FG Mare 19
Det — Sanders 7 run (Hanson kick)
Mia — FG Mare 33
Mia — FG Mare 21
Det — Morton 35 pass from Mitchell (bad snap)
Det — Westbrook 64 interception return (kick failed)
Mia — Drayton 23 pass rom Marino (Mare kick)
Det — Moore 16 pass from Mitchell (Moore pass from Mitchell)
Mia — FG Mare 42

MONDAY, DECEMBER 8

CAROLINA 23, DALLAS 13—at Texas Stadium, attendance 63,251. Kerry Collins threw 2 touchdown passes, and Fred Lane rushed for 138 yards as the Panthers knocked the Cowboys out of the running for their sixth consecutive NFC East title. Lane had 7 carries for all 43 yards of a 9-play first-quarter drive that was capped by John Kasay's 34-yard field goal. Collins threw a 15-yard touchdown pass to Rae Carruth with 4:28 left in the half to take a 10-0 lead. Herschel Walker's 45-yard kickoff return set up Richie Cunningham's 43-yard field goal, and, after Broderick Thomas recovered Collins's fumble at the Panthers' 34, Cunningham added a 32-yard field goal as the half expired. Carolina took the third quarter kickoff and marched 69 yards in 12 plays, with Collins completing all 7 of his pass attempts on the drive, to take a 17-6 lead on Scott Greene's 1-yard touchdown catch. Collins sat a series early in the fourth quarter, and Steve Beuerlein threw a 38-yard pass to Muhsin Muhammad on third-and-16 to set up Kasay's second field goal. The Cowboys responded with a 3-play, 77-yard drive which lasted just 1:28, with Troy Aikman's 52-yard touchdown pass to Michael Irvin cutting the deficit to 20-13 with 6:33 left. The Cowboys forced the Panthers to punt and then faced a fourth-and-1 situation from the Panthers' 45. Aikman attempted to roll out and pass to Irvin or David LaFleur, but both were covered, and Aikman was chased by Chad Cota and Mike Fox and fell 25 yards behind the line of scrimmage. Kasay added his third field goal with 53 seconds left to clinch the victory. Collins was 16 of 28 for 136 yards and 2 touchdowns. Aikman was 14 of 26 for 180 yards and 1 touchdown. The Panthers' defense permitted just 9 first downs.

Carolina	3	7	7	6	—	23
Dallas	0	6	0	7	—	13

Car — FG Kasay 34
Car — Carruth 15 pass from Collins (Kasay kick)
Dall — FG Cunningham 43
Dall — FG Cunningham 32
Car — Greene 1 pass from Collins (Kasay kick)
Car — FG Kasay 40
Dall — Irvin 52 pass from Aikman (Cunningham kick)
Car — FG Kasay 18

SIXTEENTH WEEK SUMMARIES

AMERICAN FOOTBALL CONFERENCE

Eastern Division	W	L	T	Pct.	Pts.	OP
Miami	9	6	0	.600	327	313
New England	9	6	0	.600	355	277
N.Y. Jets	9	6	0	.600	338	274
Buffalo	6	9	0	.400	234	336
Indianapolis	3	12	0	.200	285	362
Central Division						
Pittsburgh	11	4	0	.733	366	291
Jacksonville	10	5	0	.667	374	309
Tennessee	7	8	0	.467	317	304
Baltimore	6	8	1	.433	312	329
Cincinnati	6	9	0	.400	339	391
Western Division						
Kansas City	12	3	0	.800	350	219
Denver	11	4	0	.733	434	284
Seattle	7	8	0	.467	327	353
Oakland	4	11	0	.267	315	399
San Diego	4	11	0	.267	263	387

NATIONAL FOOTBALL CONFERENCE

Eastern Division	W	L	T	Pct.	Pts.	OP
N.Y. Giants	9	5	1	.633	287	258
Washington	7	7	1	.500	292	257
Philadelphia	6	8	1	.433	285	337
Dallas	6	9	0	.400	297	294
Arizona	3	12	0	.200	254	353
Central Division						
Green Bay	12	3	0	.800	391	261
Tampa Bay	9	6	0	.600	268	248
Detroit	8	7	0	.533	366	296
Minnesota	8	7	0	.533	315	331
Chicago	4	11	0	.267	248	390
Western Division						
San Francisco	13	2	0	.867	366	227
Atlanta	7	8	0	.467	294	332
Carolina	7	8	0	.467	247	284
New Orleans	6	9	0	.400	224	302
St. Louis	4	11	0	.267	269	341

SATURDAY, DECEMBER 13

PITTSBURGH 24, NEW ENGLAND 21 (OT)—at Foxboro Stadium, attendance 60,013. Kevin Henry's interception in the final minutes of regulation allowed the Steelers to tie the game, and Norm Johnson's 31-yard field goal in overtime enabled Pittsburgh to maintain a one-game lead in the AFC Central. Interceptions by Lawyer Milloy and Willie Clay set up 27- and 54-yard touchdown drives for the Patriots and allowed them to take a 14-0 lead. The Steelers drove 72 yards and scored on Kordell Stewart's 1-yard run 31 seconds before halftime, and Johnson added a field goal on the first possession of the second half to cut the deficit to 14-10. Darren Perry's 18-yard interception return halted a Patriots' drive and led to Johnson's 34-yard field goal in the opening minutes of the fourth quarter. New England responded with Drew Bledsoe's 49-yard touchdown pass to David Meggett, who weaved his way down the right sideline into the end zone, to take a 21-13 lead with 10:31 remaining. The Patriots had third-and-7 at midfield just before the two-minute warning. The Steelers were out of time outs, and a first down would have iced the game. However, Henry stepped in front of Bledsoe's screen pass and rumbled 36 yards to the Patriots' 13. Henry illegally lateralled the ball to Orpheus Roye placing the ball at the 18-yard line. Yancey Thigpen made a diving catch falling out of bounds at the 4-yard line to keep the Steelers' chances alive, and Stewart threw a 1-yard touchdown pass to Mark Bruener with 38 seconds left. Stewart and Thigpen hooked up for the 2-point conversion to tie the game. The Steelers won the coin toss for overtime, and Stewart's 41-yard pass to Courtney Hawkins on third-and-15 set up Johnson's winning kick. Stewart was 26 of 48 for 266 yards and 1 touchdown, with 2 interceptions. Bledsoe was 21 of 36 for 211 yards and 3 touchdowns, with 2 interceptions. The Steelers outgained New England 404-253 and controlled time of possession (41:04-23:39).

Pittsburgh	0	7	3	11	3	—	24
New England	0	14	0	7	0	—	21

NE — Coates 18 pass from Bledsoe (Vinatieri kick)
NE — Gash 1 pass from Bledsoe (Vinatieri kick)
Pitt — Stewart 1 run (Johnson kick)
Pitt — FG Johnson 36
Pitt — FG Johnson 34
NE — Meggett 49 pass from Bledsoe (Vinatieri kick)
Pitt — Bruener 1 pass from Stewart (Thigpen pass from Stewart)
Pitt — FG Johnson 31

NEW YORK GIANTS 30, WASHINGTON 10—at Giants Stadium, attendance 77,571. The Giants' defense recorded 4 interceptions, including a touchdown by Jason Sehorn, and held the Redskins to 45 rushing yards and 0 rushing first downs to clinch their first NFC East title since 1990. A botched handoff between Jeff Hostetler and Stephen Davis less than two minutes into the game resulted in Jessie Armstead's fumble recovery and Brad Daluiso's 41-yard field goal. Later in the quarter, Matt Turk dropped the ball while attempting to punt. The Giants got the ball on the Redskins' 16, and Charles Way scored two plays later to give the Giants a 10-0 lead. After forcing a punt, Kanell completed 5 of 6 passes on the ensuing 13-play, 76-yard drive, capped by his 7-yard scoring pass to Chris Calloway to take a 17-0 first-quarter lead. The Redskins kicked a field goal on their next possession, but Conrad Hamilton's 18-yard interception return just before halftime added another Daluiso field goal to the board. Hostetler threw a 41-yard touchdown pass to Albert Connell early in the third quarter to cut the deficit to 20-10, and Stanley Richard intercepted 2 passes in the quarter to keep the Giants close. However, Daluiso added a third field goal early in the fourth quarter, and Jason Sehorn's 35-yard interception return 21 seconds later iced the game. Kanell was 13 of 25 for 125 yards and 1 touchdown, with 2 interceptions. Hostetler was 23 of 42 for 288 yards and 1 touchdown, with 4 interceptions.

Washington	0	3	7	0	—	10
N.Y. Giants	17	3	0	10	—	30

NYG — FG Daluiso 41
NYG — Way 15 run (Daluiso kick)
NYG — Calloway 7 pass from Kanell (Daluiso kick)
Wash — FG Blanton 33
NYG — FG Daluiso 28
Wash — Connell 41 pass from Hostetler (Blanton kick)
NYG — FG Daluiso 28
NYG — Sehorn 35 interception return (Daluiso kick)

SUNDAY, DECEMBER 14

NEW ORLEANS 27, ARIZONA 10—at Louisiana Superdome, attendance 45,517. Billy Joe Hobert threw 3 second-half touchdown passes to key a 24-point run by the Saints in handing Arizona its third consecutive loss. Jake Plummer's 10-yard touchdown scramble capped a 15-play, 80-yard drive. The Cardinals led 10-3 and had third-and-goal from the Saints' 5 with 14 seconds left in the half when LaRoi Glover sacked Plummer, forcing him to fumble. Wayne Martin recovered the ball, allowing the Saints to maintain a seven-point deficit. Hobert threw 41- and 17-yard passes to Randal Hill in the third quarter before the pair connected from 9 yards to tie the game. Hobert fired 13- and 44-yard passes to Hill to set up Doug Brien's go-ahead field goal with 13:28 remaining. After forcing a punt, Hobert threw a 49-yard pass to Keith Poole and, three plays later, found Eric Guliford for a 16-yard touchdown. Rob Kelly's 15-yard interception return with 3:16 left led to John Farquhar's 8-yard touchdown catch to ice the game. Hobert was 14 of 24 for 252 yards and 3 touchdowns, with 1 interception. Hill had 5 receptions for 124 yards. Plummer was 17 of 37 for 180 yards, with 2 interceptions.

Arizona	7	3	0	0	—	10
New Orleans	0	3	7	17	—	27

Ariz — Plummer 10 run (Nedney kick)
NO — FG Brien 20
Ariz — FG Nedney 30
NO — Hill 9 pass from Hobert (Brien kick)
NO — FG Brien 33
NO — Guliford 16 pass from Hobert (Brien kick)
NO — Farquhar 8 pass from Hobert (Brien kick)

CINCINNATI 31, DALLAS 24—at Cinergy Field, attendance 60,043. Boomer Esiason threw 2 touchdown passes, and the Bengals scored 4 touchdowns over a 15:38 time period to hand Dallas its fourth consecutive defeat. Richie Cunningham's 23-yard field goal capped the game's opening drive. On their next possession, the Cowboys drove 95 yards in 15 plays, with Sherman Williams's 3-yard run. Trailing 10-3, Eric Bieniemy's 20-yard touchdown run capped an 8-play, 91-yard drive to tie the game. Just before halftime, the Bengals drove 62 yards in 31 seconds, taking the lead on Esiason's 48-yard touchdown pass to Darnay Scott. The Bengals took just 6 plays to drive 64 yards midway through the third quarter, taking a 14-point lead on Corey Dillon's 14-yard run. Corey Sawyer intercepted Troy Aikman on the Cowboys' next possession, and, two plays after Dillon ran 11 yards on fourth-and-1, Esiason threw a 32-yard touchdown pass to David Dunn. Troy Aikman threw 2 touchdown passes to David LaFleur, the second set up by Nate Hemsley's onside kick recovery, to cut the deficit to 31-24 with 6:27 left. The Cowboys defense forced Cincinnati to punt, but Sawyer thwarted the comeback with his second interception, this at the Bengals' 12 with 4:10 remaining. Dallas did not get the ball back until the final minute and were unable to cross midfield. Esiason was 13 of 25 for 269 yards and 2 touchdowns, with 1 interception. Dillon rushed for 127 yards and became the first Bengals' player to break 1,000 yards since 1992. Scott had 4 receptions for 112 yards. Aikman was 28 of 53 for 285 yards and 2 touchdowns, with 2 interceptions. Michael Irvin had 9 receptions for 117 yards. The Bengals have scored at least 30 points in all four of Esiason's starts.

Dallas	10	0	0	14	—	24
Cincinnati	0	17	14	0	—	31

Dall — FG Cunningham 23
Dall — Sh. Williams 3 run (Cunningham kick)
Cin — FG Pelfrey 42
Cin — Bieniemy 20 run (Pelfrey kick)
Cin — Scott 48 pass from Esiason (Pelfrey kick)
Cin — Dillon 14 run (Pelfrey kick)
Cin — Dunn 32 pass from Esiason (Pelfrey kick)
Dall — LaFleur 13 pass from Aikman (Cunningham kick)
Dall — LaFleur 12 pass from Aikman (Cunningham kick)

DETROIT 14, MINNESOTA 13—at Hubert H. Humphrey Metrodome, attendance 60,982. Scott Mitchell threw a 1-yard touchdown pass to Herman Moore with three seconds left to propel the Lions to a comeback victory and give them the tie-breaker edge over the Vikings, who have lost five consecutive games. A 34-yard punt by John Jett allowed the Vikings to travel just 43 yards, capped by Robert Smith's 22-yard touchdown run, to take a 7-0 lead. The Lions used the impetus of Glyn Milburn's 32-yard run to drive 55 yards in 5:00, with Mitchell's touchdown pass to Cory Schlesinger tying the game. A 28-yard scramble by Randall Cunningham set up Eddie Murray's field goal on the next possession. After forcing a punt, the Vikings drove to the Lions' 10 before settling for Murray's second field goal. The Lions missed three scoring opportunities on their next three possessions: Jason Hanson's 50-yard field goal at the end of the half sailed wide right; Dwayne Rudd and Tony Williams stopped Barry Sanders on fourth-and-goal at the Vikings' 1 on Detroit's first possession of the second half; and Hanson's 38-yard field goal also went wide right. However, the Lions' defense forced the Vikings to punt six consecutive possessions until Murray pushed a 37-yard field goal wide right with 1:56 remaining. A pass interference penalty on Dewayne Washington put the ball on the Vikings' 1 with six seconds left. Mitchell then lofted a pass to Moore, who outjumped Washington for the touchdown. Hanson added the extra point to clinch the victory. Mitchell was 23 of 38 for 255 yards and 2 touchdowns, with 1 interception. Sanders recorded his thirteenth consecutive 100-yard game by rushing for 138 yards on 19 carries. Cunningham was 9 of 18 for 77 yards. Smith had 20 carries for 101 yards.

Detroit	0	7	0	7	—	14
Minnesota	7	6	0	0	—	13

Minn — Smith 22 run (Murray kick)
Det — Schlesinger 1 pass from Mitchell (Hanson kick)
Minn — FG Murray 21
Minn — FG Murray 28
Det — Moore 1 pass from Mitchell (Hanson kick)

GREEN BAY 31, CAROLINA 10—at Ericsson Stadium, attendance 70,887. Brett Favre threw 3 touchdown passes as the Packers rolled to their fourth consecutive victory and won the rematch of last season's NFC Championship Game. Favre fired a 58-yard touchdown pass to Antonio Freeman midway through the first quarter, and after the Packers' defense forced their fourth punt of the quarter, Favre orchestrated an 8-play, 61-yard drive capped by his touchdown pass to Robert Brooks to take a 14-0 lead at the end of the first quarter. Chad Cota's interception and 15-yard return into Packers' territory led to John Kasay's 43-yard field goal, but the Packers responded with a 15-play scoring drive, with Ryan Longwell's field goal in the final two minutes of the half giving Green Bay a 17-3 halftime edge. The Packers took the first 7:10 of the second half off the clock before Favre's second touchdown pass to Freeman gave Green Bay a 24-3 lead. Fred Lane's 35-yard touchdown burst in the opening minute of the fourth quarter cut the deficit to 24-10, but the Panthers did not run another play in Packers' territory the remainder of the game. Favre was 18 of 34 for 256 yards and 3 touchdowns, with 1 interception. Freeman had 10 receptions for 166 yards. Kerry Collins completed 7 of 26 passes for 56 yards. The Packers had more first downs (26-9) and total yards (458-172).

Green Bay	14	3	7	7	—	31
Carolina	0	3	0	7	—	10

GB — Freeman 58 pass from Favre (Longwell kick)
GB — Brooks 20 pass from Favre (Longwell kick)
Car — FG Kasay 43
GB — FG Longwell 31
GB — Freeman 6 pass from Favre (Longwell kick)
Car — Lane 35 run (Kasay kick)
GB — Hayden 6 run (Longwell kick)

JACKSONVILLE 20, BUFFALO 14—at Rich Stadium, attendance 41,231. Mark Brunell passed for 317 yards and ran for 1 touchdown as the Jaguars clinched their second playoff berth. Brunell's 60-yard pass to Keenan McCardell on the Jaguars' first play from scrimmage set up Brunell's 13-yard scramble two plays later to take an early 7-0 lead. Brunell completed all 7 of his pass attempts during an 11-play, 90-yard drive, capped by Natrone Means's 2-yard run. A 13-yard sack by Henry Jones on fourth down gave the Bills the ball at the Jaguars' 44 with 43 seconds left in the half. Buffalo moved into field-goal range for Steve Christie just before halftime to cut the deficit to 14-3. On the first drive of the second half, Brunell's 40-yard pass to Jimmy Smith to the Bills' 2 led to Mike Hollis's 19-yard field goal. Buffalo put together a 14-play, 79-yard drive, but had to settle for Christie's second field goal. Alex Van Pelt entered on the Bills' next possession, and promptly drove them 80 yards in less than three minutes to Antowain Smith's 1-yard touchdown. Van Pelt's pass to Eric Moulds for the 2-point conversion cut the deficit to 17-14 with 8:03 left. Mike Logan's 34-yard kickoff return led to Hollis's second field goal with 4:18 remaining. Buffalo had two chances, but Van Pelt lost the ball on a fumble, and, after the Bills forced a punt, he drove Buffalo to the Jaguars' 21 with 1:03 left before throwing across the field and being intercepted by Deon Figures at the Jaguars' 6 to ice the game. Brunell was 24 of 32 for 317 yards, with 1 interception. Collins was 13 of 26 for 107 yards. Van Pelt was 6 of 15 for 103 yards, with 1 interception.

Jacksonville	7	7	3	3	—	20
Buffalo	0	3	0	11	—	14

Jack — Brunell 13 run (Hollis kick)
Jack — Means 2 run (Hollis kick)
Buff — FG Christie 38
Jack — FG Hollis 19
Buff — FG Christie 31
Buff — Smith 1 run (Moulds pass from Van Pelt)
Jack — FG Hollis 47

KANSAS CITY 29, SAN DIEGO 7—at Qualcomm Stadium, Jack Murphy Field, attendance 54,594. The Chiefs moved into first place in the AFC West by handing the Chargers their seventh consecutive defeat. In the first quarter, a pass interference penalty on Terrance Shaw in the end zone on third down enabled Marcus Allen to score his tenth touchdown of the season. The Chargers used the impetus of Kenny Bynum's 35-yard kickoff return to tie the game on Craig Whelihan's 14-yard touchdown pass to Eric Metcalf. Gannon completed 27- and 21-yard passes to Lake Dawson, the second for a touchdown, to give the Chiefs a 14-7 lead. A 37-yard third-down pass interference penalty on Shaw extended the opening drive of the second half, with Pete Stoyanovich capping the possession with a 40-yard field goal. Later in the quarter, the Chiefs downed Louie Aguiar's punt at the Chargers' 2, and Todd Philcox entered the game at quarterback. Derrick Thomas sacked him for a safety three plays later to give the Chiefs a 19-7 lead. After another Stoyanovich field goal, the Chargers drove to the Chiefs' 17 only to watch Mark McMillian intercept a pass and race 87 yards for his third touchdown return of the season. Gannon completed just 8 of 25 passes for 116 yards and 1 touchdown. Whelihan was 13 of 21 for 137 yards and 1 touchdown, while Philcox completed 10 of 17 passes for 116 yards, with 1 interception.

Kansas City	7	7	8	7	—	29
San Diego	0	7	0	0	—	7

KC — Allen 1 run (Stoyanovich kick)
SD — Metcalf 14 pass from Whelihan (Davis kick)
KC — Dawson 21 pass from Gannon (Stoyanovich kick)
KC — FG Stoyanovich 40
KC — Safety, Thomas sacked Philcox in end zone
KC — FG Stoyanovich 48
KC — McMillian 87 interception return (Stoyanovich kick)

INDIANAPOLIS 41, MIAMI 0—at RCA Dome, attendance 61,282. Jim Harbaugh threw 4 touchdown passes, all in the second quarter, as the Colts defeated the playoff-bound Dolphins to record their first shutout since 1987. Harbaugh's 43-yard pass to Ken Dilger on third-and-1 set up his 10-yard touchdown toss to Marshall Faulk to give the Colts a 10-0 lead 35 seconds into the second quarter.

The Dolphins drove to the Colts' 33, but Olindo Mare's field-goal attempt went wide left. Harbaugh's 41-yard pass to Marvin Harrison on third-and-11 led to his 7-yard touchdown pass to Dilger with 8:14 left in the quarter. Two plays later, Dan Footman recovered Dan Marino's fumble and returned it to the Dolphins' 21. The Colts had to settle for Cary Blanchard's 50-yard field goal with 5:39 remaining to take a 20-0 lead. Indianapolis forced another punt, and Harbuagh threw a 31-yard touchdown pass to a wide-open Dilger with 1:55 left. Ellis Johnson recovered another Marino fumble two plays later at the Dolphins' 14, and Harbaugh threw an 8-yard touchdown pass to Dilger with 53 seconds left in the half to take a 34-0 lead. The Dolphins reached the Colts' 4 on their first possession of the second half, but Marino's fourth-down pass was incomplete. Harbaugh was 20 for 26 for 255 yards and 4 touchdowns. Dilger had 5 receptions for 100 yards and 3 touchdowns. Marino was 7 of 15 for 71 yards. Craig Erickson replaced him late in the third quarter and completed 5 of 10 passes for 44 yards. The Colts had more first downs (23-10) and total yards (401-183).

Miami	0	0	0	0	—	0
Indianapolis	3	31	0	7	—	41

Ind — FG Blanchard 21
Ind — Faulk 10 pass from Harbaugh (Blanchard kick)
Ind — Dilger 7 pass from Harbaugh (Blanchard kick)
Ind — FG Blanchard 50
Ind — Dilger 31 pass from Harbaugh (Blanchard kick)
Ind — Dilger 8 pass from Harbaugh (Blanchard kick)
Ind — Faulk 7 run (Blanchard kick)

ATLANTA 20, PHILADELPHIA 17—at Georgia Dome, attendance 42,866. Morten Andersen's 33-yard field goal as time expired lifted the Falcons to their fifth consecutive victory. The Eagles opened the game with an 89-yard touchdown drive to take a 7-0 lead. Byron Hanspard's 53-yard run in the second quarter sparked the Falcons and led to Chris Chandler's 10-yard touchdown pass to Hanspard. Lester Archambeau's interception halted the Eagles' opening drive of the second half, and Jamal Anderson gave Atlanta a 14-7 lead. Andersen's 21-yard field goal capped a 17-play, 65-yard drive to put the Falcons ahead by 10 points with 10:39 left. Bobby Hoying's 56-yard pass to Freddie Solomon set up Ricky Watters's 1-yard touchdown run to cut the deficit to three points with 7:48 remaining. The Eagles forced a punt, but faced fourth-and-5 from the Falcons' 33 with 3:03 left. Hoying completed an 11-yard pass to Irving Fryar for a first down, and Chris Boniol tied the game with a 39-yard field goal with 1:55 left. Chandler dumped a screen pass off to Harold Green, who scampered 47 yards to the Eagles' 18 to set up Andersen's game-winning kick. The field goal moved him into third place on the all-time list. Chandler was 12 of 21 for 210 yards and 1 touchdown. Hoying was 16 of 34 for 180 yards and 1 touchdown, with 1 interception.

Philadelphia	7	0	0	10	—	17
Atlanta	0	7	7	6	—	20

Phil — Timpson 3 pass from Hoying (Boniol kick)
Atl — Hanspard 10 pass from Chandler (Andersen kick)
Atl — Anderson 2 run (Andersen kick)
Atl — FG Andersen 21
Phil — Watters 1 run (Boniol kick)
Phil — FG Boniol 39
Atl — FG Andersen 33

SEATTLE 22, OAKLAND 21—at Oakland-Alameda County Coliseum, attendance 40,124. Todd Peterson's 49-yard field goal with 2:20 left capped a 19-point rally, and Jon Kitna won his first game as a starter as the Seahawks handed the Raiders their fourth consecutive loss. The Raiders scored on their first two possessions, the first a 12-play drive and the second just four plays, but both ending in Jeff George touchdown passes. Oakland would have scored on its third possession as well, but Cole Ford pushed a 24-yard field-goal attempt wide right. A 35-yard pass from Kitna to Joey Galloway set up Todd Peterson's second-quarter field goal, but Grady Jackson blocked Peterson's second attempt of the quarter. Oakland got the ball at midfield, and George threw a 5-yard touchdown pass to Rickey Dudley 1:56 before halftime to take a 21-3 lead. However, Olanda Truitt fumbled the second half kickoff. James Logan recovered at the Raiders' 37, and Kitna hooked up with Galloway four plays later to cut the deficit to 21-9. A 70-yard drive on the Seahawks' next possession netted Peterson's second field goal, and, following a punt, Chris Warren scored from 9 yards to trim the lead to 21-19 with 13:58 remaining in the game. The Raiders drove to the Seahawks' 17, but George threw consecutive incompletions on third- and fourth-and-1 to hand the ball back to Seattle with 9:29 to play. Kitna completed 6 of 7 passes on the ensuing drive, including 2 third-down completions to Galloway, to set up Peterson's winning kick. The Raiders got no closer than midfield before turning the ball over on downs. Kitna was 23 of 37 for 283 yards and 1 touchdown, with 2 interceptions. George was 21 of 31 for 274 yards and 3 touchdowns. Seattle accumulated 15 of its 22 first downs in the second half.

Seattle	0	3	9	10	—	22
Oakland	14	7	0	0	—	21

Oak — Truitt 19 pass from George (Ford kick)
Oak — Jett 37 pass from George (Ford kick)
Sea — FG Peterson 27
Oak — Dudley 5 pass from George (Ford kick)
Sea — Galloway 8 pass from Kitna (pass failed)
Sea — FG Peterson 27
Sea — Warren 9 run (Peterson kick)
Sea — FG Peterson 49

NEW YORK JETS 31, TAMPA BAY 0—at Giants Stadium, attendance 60,122. Otis Smith returned 2 interceptions for touchdowns during a five-minute stretch of the second quarter to allow the Jets to snap a 16-game losing streak during December and January. Their last late-season victory took place in 1993. Ray Lucas's 1-yard run on fourth-and-1 kept alive a late first-quarter drive that led to John Hall's 32-yard field goal. Smith intercepted Trent Dilfer's third-down pass and raced 45 yards for a touchdown. After an exchange of punts, Smith cut in front of Reidel Anthony and scampered 51 yards for his second touchdown to give the Jets a 17-0 lead. Dilfer fumbled at the Jets' 14 just before halftime, and Marvin Jones recovered to keep the shutout intact. Leon Johnson returned the opening kickoff of the second half 101 yards for his second return touchdown of the season. Johnson's 23-yard punt return two minutes later set up Adrian Murrell's 7-yard scoring run. Neither team scored in the final 25:56, and the Buccaneers did not run a play from beyond their own 45-yard line in the second half. Neil O'Donnell was 14 of 22 for 112 yards, with 1 interception. Dilfer was 2 of 15 for 38 yards, with 2 interceptions. The Jets' defense allowed just 6 first downs and 111 total yards in 50 plays.

Tampa Bay	0	0	0	0	—	0
N.Y. Jets	3	14	14	0	—	31

NYJ — FG Hall 32
NYJ — Smith 45 interception return (Hall kick)
NYJ — Smith 51 interception return (Hall kick)
NYJ — Johnson 101 kickoff return (Hall kick)
NYJ — Murrell 7 run (Hall kick)

BALTIMORE 21, TENNESSEE 19—at Memorial Stadium, attendance 60,558. Eric Zeier threw 3 touchdown passes to give the Ravens a victory in the final game at 43-year-old Memorial Stadium. Tyrus McCloud recovered Derrick Mason's muffed punt at the Oilers' 16 less than two minutes into the game to set up Zeier's 8-yard touchdown pass to Michael Jackson. A pair of Al Del Greco field goals, the second set up by Joe Bowden's blocked field goal, cut the deficit to 7-6. However, Zeier completed 4 of 5 passes for 68 yards, including a 37-yard touchdown pass to Eric Green, to give Baltimore a 14-6 halftime lead. Steve McNair scrambled 15 yards for a touchdown in the final minute of the third quarter, but was stopped on a two-point conversion attempt that would have tied the game. The Ravens drove downfield, but Pratt Lyons recorded the Oilers' second blocked field goal of the game. However, Baltimore scored again as James Jones recovered McNair's fumble at the Oilers' 15, and Zeier threw a touchdown pass to Derrick Alexander on the next play to take a 21-12 lead with 9:20 left. McNair scored from 1 yard with 1:03 left, and Terry Killens recovered the ensuing onside kick to give the Oilers a final chance. Tennessee got one first down, but John Williams broke up McNair's fourth-down pass inside the Ravens' 40 with 12 seconds left to clinch the victory. Zeier was 13 of 28 for 204 yards and 3 touchdowns. McNair was 22 of 45 for 219 yards, with 1 interception. Eddie George rushed for 129 yards. Chris Sanders had 7 receptions for 100 yards.

Tennessee	3	3	6	7	—	19
Baltimore	7	7	0	7	—	21

Balt — Jackson 8 pass from Zeier (Stover kick)
Tenn — FG Del Greco 25
Tenn — FG Del Greco 40
Balt — Green 37 pass from Zeier (Stover kick)
Tenn — McNair 15 run (run failed)
Balt — Alexander 19 pass from Zeier (Stover kick)
Tenn — McNair 1 run (Del Greco kick)

SUNDAY NIGHT, DECEMBER 14

CHICAGO 13, ST. LOUIS 10—at Trans World Dome, attendance 66,030. The Bears forced 4 turnovers in the final 16:30 to give Chicago its second consecutive victory and first regular-season road victory in December since 1987. Ryan McNeil's 66-yard return of a blocked field goal to the Bears' 5 led to Jerald Moore's 1-yard touchdown run. The Rams were unable to convert McNeil's 20-yard interception return to the Bears' 19 early in the second quarter into points when Jeff Wilkins hooked his 40-yard field-goal attempt. Chicago responded with Erik Kramer's 55-yard touchdown pass to Curtis Conway to tie the game. The Bears reached the Rams' 21 just before halftime, but a poor snap by Harper LeBel gave Chicago no chance to attempt the go-ahead field goal. A botched fake-punt attempt on fourth-and-1 gave the Rams the ball at midfield on the fourth quarter's first play. Walt Harris intercepted Tony Banks on the next play, but fumbled, and the Rams' Ernie Conwell recovered. The Rams took advantage of their fortune as Wilkins booted a 28-yard field goal with 10:43 left. After an exchange of punts, Rick Mirer, who replaced Kramer, scrambled 20 yards on third-and-4 to set up Jeff Jaeger's tying field goal. Bryan Cox sacked Banks on the next play from scrimmage and forced him to fumble. Jim Flanigan recovered, and Jaeger booted the go-ahead field goal with 2:51 left. The Rams reached the Bears' 21 before Tom Carter's interception in the end zone with 1:38 to play iced the game. Kramer was 14 of 22 for 186 yards and 1 touchdown, with 1 interception. Mirer was 1 of 7 for 8 yards, with 1 interception. Conway had 7 receptions for 109 yards. Banks was 13 of 28 for 147 yards, with 3 interceptions. The Bears' defense recorded 5 sacks, forced 5 turnovers, permitted just 11 first downs, 165 total yards, and allowed the Rams to convert just 1-of-10 third-down opportunities.

Chicago	0	7	0	6	—	13
Miami	7	0	0	3	—	10

StL — Moore 1 run (Wilkins kick)
Chi — Conway 55 pass from Kramer (Jaeger kick)
StL — FG Wilkins 26
Chi — FG Jaeger 27
Chi — FG Jaeger 21

MONDAY, DECEMBER 15

SAN FRANCISCO 34, DENVER 17—at 3Com Park, attendance 68,461. Steve Young passed for 276 yards, including a touchdown pass to Jerry Rice in his first game back from a knee injury, and the 49ers scored 2 defensive touchdowns in the second half to knock the Broncos a game behind Kansas City in the AFC West. Dedrick Dodge's recovery of Iheanyi Uwaezuoke's fumbled punt gave Denver the ball at the 49ers' 6. Terrell Davis scored two plays later to give Denver a 7-0 lead. Trailing 10-0, Young completed all 7 of his pass attempts on a 12-play, 92-yard drive capped by Rice's 14-yard touchdown catch. It was Rice's third catch of the game, but last for the season as he reinjured his knee on the play. Terry Kirby's touchdown with 22 seconds left in the half was offset by Vaughn Hebron's 1-yard touchdown run on the first possession of the second half, which gave Denver a 17-14 lead. Gary Anderson tied the game with a 32-yard field-goal, and Merton Hanks's 55-yard interception return for a touchdown 1:02 later gave the 49ers the lead. Lee Woodall's 55-yard interception return set up Anderson's 20-yard field goal with 9:05 to play, and Kevin Greene's 40-yard fumble return with 4:05 remaining iced the game. Young was 22 of 34 for 276 yards and 1 touchdown. Elway was 16 of 41 for 150 yards, with 2 interceptions. Former 49ers' quarterback Joe Montana had his uniform jersey retired at halftime.

Denver	10	0	7	0	—	17
San Francisco	0	14	10	10	—	34

Den — Davis 4 run (Elam kick)
Den — FG Elam 49
SF — Rice 14 pass from Young (Anderson kick)

SF — Kirby 1 run (Anderson kick)
Den — Hebron 1 run (Elam kick)
SF — FG Anderson 32
SF — Hanks 55 interception return (Anderson kick)
SF — FG Anderson 20
SF — Greene 40 fumble return (Anderson kick)

SEVENTEENTH WEEK SUMMARIES

AMERICAN FOOTBALL CONFERENCE

Eastern Division	W	L	T	Pct.	Pts.	OP
New England	10	6	0	.625	369	289
Miami	9	7	0	.563	339	327
N.Y. Jets	9	7	0	.563	348	287
Buffalo	6	10	0	.375	255	367
Indianapolis	3	13	0	.188	313	401
Central Division						
Pittsburgh	11	5	0	.688	372	307
Jacksonville	11	5	0	.688	394	318
Tennessee	8	8	0	.500	333	310
Cincinnati	7	9	0	.438	355	405
Baltimore	6	9	1	.406	326	345
Western Division						
Kansas City	13	3	0	.813	375	232
Denver	12	4	0	.750	472	287
Seattle	8	8	0	.500	365	362
Oakland	4	12	0	.250	324	419
San Diego	4	12	0	.250	266	425

NATIONAL FOOTBALL CONFERENCE

Eastern Division	W	L	T	Pct.	Pts.	OP
N.Y. Giants	10	5	1	.656	307	265
Washington	8	7	1	.531	327	289
Philadelphia	6	9	1	.406	317	372
Dallas	6	10	0	.375	304	314
Arizona	4	12	0	.250	283	379
Central Division						
Green Bay	13	3	0	.813	422	282
Tampa Bay	10	6	0	.625	299	263
Detroit	9	7	0	.563	379	306
Minnesota	9	7	0	.563	354	359
Chicago	4	12	0	.250	263	421
Western Division						
San Francisco	13	3	0	.813	375	265
Atlanta	7	9	0	.438	320	361
Carolina	7	9	0	.438	265	314
New Orleans	6	10	0	.375	237	327
St. Louis	5	11	0	.313	299	359

SATURDAY, DECEMBER 20

GREEN BAY 31, BUFFALO 21—at Lambeau Field, attendance 60,108. Brett Favre threw 2 first-half touchdown passes as the Packers won 13 games for the second consecutive season. Raymond Jackson muffed Craig Hentrich's punt after the Packers' initial possession at the 6-yard line and Tyrone Davis recovered the ball in the end zone for a touchdown. Seven-time Pro Bowl player Steve Tasker, playing in his last game, was ejected for unsportsmanlike conduct on the play. William Henderson's 3-yard run on fourth-and-1 later in the quarter led to Favre's 4-yard touchdown pass to Antonio Freeman. The Packers' defense stopped Antowain Smith on fourth-and-1 from their own 41 to set up a 6-play, 59-yard drive capped by Favre's 2-yard touchdown pass to Davis in the middle of the second quarter. Mike Prior's 49-yard interception return led to Ryan Longwell's 35-yard field goal to give Green Bay a 24-0 lead. Smith scored 2 touchdowns, the first followed Marcellus Wiley's 40-yard fumble return and the second was set up by Chris Mohr's 29-yard pass to Lonnie Johnson on a fake punt, to cut the deficit to 24-14 with 11:24 remaining. The Bills got the ball with 4:49 left, but Darren Sharper intercepted Alex Van Pelt's pass and returned it 20 yards for a touchdown. Van Pelt scored from 1 yard with 2:05 left, but Sharper recovered the ensuing onside kick to ice the game. Favre, who played just the first half since the Packers' had already clinched the second-best record in the NFC, was 12 of 18 for 156 yards and 2 touchdowns. Steve Bono was 5 of 10 for 29 yards. Van Pelt was 23 of 44 for 255 yards, with 3 interceptions. Quinn Early had 7 receptions for 120 yards.

Buffalo	0	0	8	13	—	21
Green Bay	14	7	3	7	—	31

GB — T. Davis fumble recovery in end zone (Longwell kick)
GB — Freeman 4 pass from Favre (Longwell kick)
GB — T. Davis 2 pass from Favre (Longwell kick)
GB — FG Longwell 35
Buff — Smith 5 run (Riemersma pass from Van Pelt)
Buff — Smith 1 run (pass failed)
GB — Sharper 20 interception return (Longwell kick)
Buff — Van Pelt 1 run (Christie kick)

ST. LOUIS 30, CAROLINA 18—at Ericsson Stadium, attendance 58,101. The Rams scored the first 23 points en route to handing the Panthers their sixth home defeat after having gone 8-0 at home in 1996. Sam Mills forced Jerald Moore to fumble at the 1-yard line and Zach Wiegert recovered in the end zone. Jeff Wilkins added 2 field goals, the second set up by Robert Jones's interception, before the Panthers ran a play in Rams' territory. However, Keith Lyle intercepted Kerry Collins at the Rams' 7, and Wilkins drilled a 47-yard field goal as the half expired to take a 16-0 lead into the locker room. The Rams took the second half's opening kickoff and drove 75 yards and scored on David Thompson's first NFL touchdown to take a 23-0 lead. Collins responded on the next drive with a 35-yard touchdown pass to Rae Carruth, but Lyle's second interception of the game began a 48-yard drive capped by Tony Banks's 1-yard touchdown pass to Ernie Conwell to give the Rams a 30-8 lead with 11:31 remaining in the game. Lyle's third interception of the game was nullified by a Rams' penalty, and the Panthers scored on Steve Beuerlein's touchdown pass to Ernie Mills a few plays later. The Panthers' defense forced a punt, and the offense drove 98 yards, but Taje Allen tackled Muhsin Muhammad at the 1-yard line on fourth down with 1:57 remaining. Punter Mike Horan stepped out of the end zone with 46 seconds remaining to finish the scoring. Banks was 16 of 25 for 163 yards and 1 touchdown. Moore had 27 carries for 112 yards. Collins was 11 of 25 for 132 yards and 1 touchdown, with 3 interceptions. Beuerlein completed 10 of 17 passes for 129 yards and 1 touchdown.

St. Louis	10	6	7	7	—	30
Carolina	0	0	8	10	—	18

StL — Wiegert fumble recovery in end zone (Wilkins kick)
StL — FG Wilkins 49
StL — FG Wilkins 42
StL — FG Wilkins 47
StL — Thompson 7 run (Wilkins kick)
Car — Carruth 35 pass from Collins (Muhammad pass from Collins)
StL — Conwell 1 pass from Banks (Wilkins kick)
Car — Mills 2 pass from Beuerlein (Johnson run)
Car — Safety, Horan stepped out of end zone

SUNDAY, DECEMBER 21

ARIZONA 29, ATLANTA 26—at Sun Devil Stadium, attendance 32,003. Jake Plummer threw 2 fourth-quarter touchdown passes, including one to Larry Centers with five seconds left, to give the Cardinals a comeback victory. William White's interception less than a minute into the game was followed two plays later by Chris Chandler's 38-yard touchdown pass to Bert Emanuel. Kevin Williams's 43-yard kickoff return and Plummer's 44-yard pass to Chris Sanders on third-and-15 set up Plummer's 1-yard touchdown pass to Chris Gedney. The Falcons responded with a 93-yard drive that culminated with Chandler's 17-yard touchdown pass to Terance Mathis. Chuck Smith's 4-yard interception return led to Morten Andersen's 25-yard field goal and a 17-7 Falcons lead, but Plummer completed a fourth-and-4 pass to Williams and scored on a 1-yard run to cut the deficit to 17-14 at halftime. Three Andersen field goals gave the Falcons a 12-point lead with 8:41 to play in the game, but Plummer threw a 21-yard touchdown pass to Rob Moore with 4:55 left and Mike Caldwell stopped Jamal Anderson on third-and-1 with just over two minutes remaining, forcing a punt. Plummer completed a 12-yard pass to Sanders on third-and-11, benefited from a 39-yard pass interference penalty on Ronnie Bradford, and ran for 4 yards on fourth-and-1 from the Falcons' 6 before tossing the winning touchdown to Centers. Plummer was 19 of 40 for 237 yards and 3 touchdowns, with 2 interceptions. Chandler was 13 of 19 for 176 yards and 2 touchdowns. Anderson had 33 carries for 152 yards. By virtue of their victory, the Cardinals gave the Colts the top pick of the 1998 NFL Draft.

Atlanta	14	3	3	6	—	26
Arizona	7	7	0	15	—	29

Atl — Emanuel 38 pass from Chandler (Andersen kick)
Ariz — Gedney 1 pass from Plummer (Nedney kick)
Atl — Mathis 17 pass from Chandler (Andersen kick)
Atl — FG Andersen 25
Ariz — Plummer 1 run (Nedney kick)
Atl — FG Andersen 31
Atl — FG Andersen 20
Atl — FG Andersen 26
Ariz — Moore 21 pass from Plummer (Nedney kick)
Ariz — Centers 1 pass from Plummer (Plummer run)

CINCINNATI 16, BALTIMORE 14—at Cinergy Field, attendance 60,719. Boomer Esiason threw 2 touchdown passes in the final game of his career as the Bengals finished the season winning four of their final five games. The Bengals scored on their opening possession, with Esiason's 8-yard touchdown pass to Marco Battaglia capping a 9-play, 77-yard drive. Neither team drove beyond the opponents' 38-yard line the remainder of the half. Eric Zeier's 83-yard touchdown pass to Derrick Alexander less than five minutes into the second half tied the game. The Bengals responded with a 41-yard drive that allowed Doug Pelfrey to kick a 44-yard field goal. The Bengals' defense then stopped Zeier on fourth-and-1 at their 22-yard line late in the third quarter, and Matt Stover missed a 44-yard field-goal attempt early in the fourth quarter as the score remained 10-7. Faced with second-and-12 and less than four minutes left, Esiason hit Darnay Scott with a 77-yard touchdown pass. However, Pelfrey missed the extra point and Zeier hit Michael Jackson with a 37-yard pass to set up his 12-yard touchdown pass to Eric Green with 1:40 left to cut the deficit to 16-14. But the onside kick was illegally touched before it went ten yards, and the Bengals ran out the clock. Esiason was 21 of 34 for 254 yards and 2 touchdowns. Zeier was 28 of 41 for 349 yards and 2 touchdowns. Gerald Dixon had 3 sacks for the Bengals.

Baltimore	0	0	7	7	—	14
Cincinnati	7	0	3	6	—	16

Cin — Battaglia 8 pass from Esiason (Pelfrey kick)
Balt — Alexander 83 pass from Zeier (Stover kick)
Cin — FG Pelfrey 44
Cin — Scott 77 pass from Esiason (kick failed)
Balt — Green 12 pass from Zeier (Stover kick)

TAMPA BAY 31, CHICAGO 15—at Houlihan's Stadium, attendance 70,930. Karl Williams returned a punt for a touchdown and caught a scoring pass as the Buccaneers clinched their first home playoff game since 1979. Williams caught 2 third-down passes from Trent Dilfer before Dilfer's 7-yard run capped a 68-yard first-quarter drive. Williams's punt return on the last play of the first quarter gave the Buccaneers a 14-0 lead. The Bears responded with a 76-yard drive that culminated with Darnell Autry's first NFL touchdown. Donnie Abraham's interception at the Bears' 36 with 2:25 left in the half set up Dilfer's 7-yard pass to Williams 11 seconds before halftime. Warrick Dunn's 76-yard run in the third quarter led to Michael Husted's field goal, and Errict Rhett scored on the next drive to give Tampa Bay a commanding 31-7 lead. Dilfer was 10 of 18 for 94 yards and 1 touchdown. Erik Kramer was 12 of 19 for 82 yards, with 1 interception and Rick Mirer completed 6 of 10 passes for 39 yards, with 1 interception. The Bears' defense allowed just 12 first downs and 269 total yards, but the offense produced just 203 yards.

Chicago	0	7	0	8	—	15
Tampa Bay	14	7	10	0	—	31

TB — Dilfer 7 run (Husted kick)
TB — Williams 61 punt return (Husted kick)
Chi — Autry 3 run (Jaeger kick)
TB — Williams 7 pass from Dilfer (Husted kick)
TB — FG Husted 20
TB — Rhett 5 run (Husted kick)
Chi — Mirer 1 run (Mirer run)

MINNESOTA 39, INDIANAPOLIS 28—at Hubert H. Humphrey Metrodome, attendance 54,107. Cris Carter caught 3 touchdown passes and the Vikings scored 4 touchdowns in a span of less than 18 minutes to snap their five-game losing streak and earn an NFC Wild Card bid. Steve Morrison's interception set up Marshall Faulk's 1-yard touchdown run in the middle of the first quarter to give the Colts an early lead. David Palmer's 53-yard kickoff return led to Carter's first touchdown off a 16-yard pass from Randall Cunningham. Tied 10-10, Robert Smith broke free for a 76-yard run, and Cunningham found Carter two plays later. Kelly Holcomb, who replaced an injured Jim Harbaugh in the second quarter, threw 2 interceptions and lost a fumble in the final five minutes of the half: Corey Fuller's 22-yard interception return to the Colts' 11 moments later enabled Leroy Hoard to score and; less than three minutes later, Robert Griffith's interception return to the Colts' 36 led to Cunningham's 14-yard touchdown pass to Andrew Glover and a 29-10 halftime lead. Jason Belser's 34-yard interception return to the Vikings' 3 midway through the fourth quarter led to Jim Harbaugh's 2-yard touchdown pass to Marvin Harrison to cut the deficit to 36-28. However, Harbaugh was hurt on the play, and Holcomb fumbled the snap on his first play back in the game with five minutes left. Jerry Ball recovered and Murray's 25-yard field goal with 2:20 remaining proved to be the final margin. By throwing his third interception on the Colts' final possession, Holcomb finished the day with 5 turnovers in six drives. Cunningham was 13 of 27 for 174 yards and 4 touchdowns, with 3 interceptions. Smith had 17 carries for 160 yards. Harbaugh was 15 of 27 for 167 yards and 1 touchdown, while Holcomb completed 5 of 8 passes for 29 yards, with 3 intercepitons. Faulk had 23 carries for 102 yards.

Indianapolis	7	3	8	10	—	28
Minnesota	7	22	7	3	—	39

Ind — Faulk 1 run (Blanchard kick)
Minn — Carter 16 pass from Cunningham (Murray kick)
Minn — FG Murray 29
Ind — FG Blanchard 27
Minn — Carter 3 pass from Cunningham (Murray kick)
Minn — Hoard 6 run (kick blocked)
Minn — Glover 14 pass from Cunningham (pass failed)
Ind — Faulk 3 run (Harrison pass from Harbaugh)
Minn — Carter 13 pass from Cunnigham (Murray kick)
Ind — FG Blanchard 21
Ind — Harrison 2 pass from Harbaugh (Blanchard kick)
Minn — FG Murray 25

JACKSONVILLE 20, OAKLAND 9—at Oakland-Alameda County Coliseum, attendance 40,032. Mark Brunell threw 2 first-quarter touchdown passes as the Jaguars forced the Raiders to finish with their worst record since 1963. Keenan McCardell caught a 35-yard touchdown pass from Brunell to cap the Jaguars' opening drive. Oakland responded by driving downfield, but Tyrone Davis forced James Jett to fumble at the 1-yard line, and Chris Hudson recovered the ball in the end zone for a touchback. James Stewart rattled off a 33-yard run and Brunell culminated the 5-play, 80-yard drive with a 26-yard touchdown pass to Damon Jones. The Raiders drove nearly nine minutes in the second quarter but had to settle for Cole Ford's 33-yard field goal, before reaching the end zone on Rickey Dudley's touchdown catch to culminate a 55-yard drive in the third quarter. However, the 2-point conversion pass attempt failed, and the Jaguars strung together consecutive time-consuming, field-goal ending drives to ice the game. Brunell was 18 of 27 for 243 yards and 2 touchdowns. McCardell had 7 receptions for 116 yards. George was 24 of 37 for 244 yards and 1 touchdown.

Jacksonville	14	0	0	6	—	20
Oakland	0	3	6	0	—	9

Jack — McCardell 35 pass from Brunell (Hollis kick)
Jack — Jones 26 pass from Brunell (Hollis kick)
Oak — FG Ford 33
Oak — Dudley 2 pass from George (pass failed)
Jack — FG Hollis 19
Jack — FG Hollis 23

KANSAS CITY 25, NEW ORLEANS 13—at Arrowhead Stadium, attendance 66,772. Tamarick Vanover used his punt-returning ability to score one touchdown and set up another as the Chiefs finished with the best record in the AFC. Pete Stoyanovich capped the Chiefs' initial drive with a field goal, and, after Dan Williams's fumble recovery, added a second field goal. Tamarick Vanover's 82-yard punt return moments, and Doug Brien missed a 41-yard field-goal attempt just before halftime to allow the Chiefs to maintain a 12-0 lead. Keith Poole caught a 32-yard touchdown on a third-and-11 pass from Billy Joe Hobert to snap the Chiefs NFL-record streak of not allowing a second-half touchdown for 11 consecutive games. Vanover's 48-yard punt return to the Saints' 8 early in the fourth quarter set up Marcus Allen's touchdown run. Mark McMillian's 39-yard interception return to the Saints' 7 23 seconds later led to Rich Gannon's 3-yard touchdown pass with 9:31 left. Danny Wuerffel threw a 14-yard touchdown pass to Poole with 2:23 left. Danan Hughes recovered the ensuing onside kick and the Chiefs ran out the clock. Elvis Grbac was 5 of 14 for 51 yards. Gannon and Billy Joe Tolliver were a combined 4 of 5 for minus-1 yard and 1 touchdown. Hobert was 11 of 25 for 141 yards and 1 touchdown, with 3 interceptions. Wuerffel was 2 of 4 for 18 yards and 1 touchdown. The Saints' defense held the Chiefs to just 20 total passing yards.

New Orleans	0	0	7	6	—	13
Kansas City	3	9	0	13	—	25

KC — FG Stoyanovich 30
KC — FG Stoyanovich 25
KC — Vanover 82 punt return (pass failed)
NO — Poole 32 pass from Hobert (Brien kick)
KC — Allen 3 run (pass failed)
KC — Popson 3 pass from Gannon (Stoyanovich kick)
NO — Poole 14 pass from Wuerffel (run failed)

NEW YORK GIANTS 20, DALLAS 7—at Texas Stadium, attendance 63,746. The Giants' defense limited the Cowboys to 11 first downs and 184 total yards as they became the first team to go undefeated in the NFC East. The Cowboys lost 13 yards on their first possession, and therefore the Giants received the ball at the Cowboys' 48. Danny Kanell's 33-yard pass to David Patten set up Brad Daluiso's field goal. Late in the first quarter Kanell hooked up with Chris Calloway for 41 yards, and, two plays later on third-and-11, hit Calloway for a 21-yard touchdown. After a second Daluiso field goal Jason Sehorn intercepted Troy Aikman's pass to start a 65-yard drive capped by Rodney Hampton's 1-yard touchdown run just before halftime to take a 20-0 lead. Bryan Stoltenberg and Dave Brown fumbled the snap on the first play of the second half. Fred Strickland recovered at the Giants' 20 and Emmitt Smith scored three plays later. Each team missed a field goal, and Ray Agnew halted the Cowboys' best scoring chance by sacking Jason Garrett on fourth down from the Giants' 10. Kanell was 8 of 16 for 129 yards and 1 touchdown. Brown played the second half and was 2 of 9 for 14 yards. Aikman was 6 of 16 for 73 yards, with 1 interception. Garrett completed 10 of 14 passes for 56 yards. The Cowboys finished the season with double-digit losses for the first time since 1989.

N.Y. Giants	10	10	0	0	—	20
Dallas	0	0	7	0	—	7

NYG — FG Daluiso 28
NYG — Calloway 21 pass from Kanell (Daluiso kick)
NYG — FG Daluiso 42
NYG — Hampton 1 run (Daluiso kick)
Dall — Smith 4 run (Cunningham kick)

DETROIT 13, NEW YORK JETS 10—at Pontiac Silverdome, attendance 77,624. In what turned out to be the first true playoff game of 1997, Barry Sanders ran for 184 yards and surpassed the 2,000-yard barrier as the Lions earned a wild-card berth and knocked the Jets out of the playoffs. John Hall's 32-yard field goal capped the Jets opening drive and Neil O'Donnell completed all 4 of his pass attempts on their next possession to set up Adrian Murrell's 14-yard touchdown jaunt to give the Jets a 10-0 lead. The Lions, who scored the most points in the NFL during the final two minutes of the half or game, drove 54 yards in 1:42 to set up Jason Hanson's 44-yard field goal at the halftime gun. Mark Carrier's 11-yard interception return to the Jets' 32 in the third quarter allowed Hanson to cut the deficit to 10-6. The Jets reached the Lions' 19, but a penalty on third-and-4 pushed the Jets back ten yards, and Ron Rice intercepted Ray Lucas's pass on the next play. Late in the third quarter, Sanders broke free for a 47-yard run on third-and-3 to the Jets' 17 and scored moments later on a 15-yard run to put the Lions ahead 13-10 with 13:11 remaining in the game. The Jets responded with a nearly six minute drive to the Lions' 9, but Leon Johnson's halfback-option pass was intercepted by Bryant Westbrook in the end zone. After an exchange of punts, Sanders gained 2 yards on first down to surpass 2,000 rushing yards. On the next play, Sanders scampered 53 yards to the Jets' 3 to seal the victory and move into second place on the single-season rushing list. Scott Mitchell was 15 of 28 for 122 yards. O'Donnell was 21 of 35 for 202 yards, with 1 interception.

N.Y. Jets	10	0	0	0	—	10
Detroit	0	3	3	7	—	13

NYJ — FG Hall 32
NYJ — Murrell 14 run (Hall kick)
Det — FG Hanson 44
Det — FG Hanson 25
Det — Sanders 15 run (Hanson kick)

WASHINGTON 35, PHILADELPHIA 32—at Jack Kent Cooke Stadium, attendance 75,932. The Redskins scored 2 defensive touchdowns as they finished the season above .500 while the Eagles were the only team in the NFL to not win a road game. Darryl Pounds sacked Bobby Hoying and forced him to fumble. Pounds scooped up the ball and ran 18 yards for a touchdown just 1:30 into the game. Later in the quarter, the Eagles drove to the Redskins' 18 before Darrell Green's 83-yard interception return gave the Redskins a 14-0 lead. Duce Staley's 57-yard kickoff return set up Hoying's 31-yard touchdown pass to Jason Dunn 1:39 later. The Redskins responded with a 85-yard drive, capped by Stephen Davis's 1-yard scoring run. It took the Eagles just five plays to answer, with Charlie Garner scoring from 9 yards. But the Redskins drove 88 yards on their next possession and took a 28-14 lead on Larry Bowie's 3-yard scoring run. Troy Vincent's interception inside the Eagles' 20 stopped the Redskins opening drive of the second half, and led to Chris Boniol's 33-yard field goal. Brian Dawkins's interception in Eagles' territory stopped another Redskins drive, and Charlie Garner scord his second touchdwon with 6:41 to play. Hoying's 2-point conversion pass to Freddie Solomon cut the deficit to 28-25. Brian Mitchell returned the ensuing kickoff 74 yards, and Jeff Hostetler threw a 7-yard touchdown pass to Michael Westbrook three plays later. Hoying's 14-yard touchdown pass to Solomon cut the deficit to three points with 1:09 remaining, but Chris Thomas recovered the onside kick to clinch the victory. Hostetler was 16 of 23 for 160 yards and 1 touchdown, with 2 interceptions. Hoying was 21 of 31 for 255 yards and 2 touchdowns, with 1 interception. Garner rushed for 115 yards. The Eagles lost despite outgaining the Redskins 401-221.

Philadelphia	7	7	3	15	—	32
Washington	14	14	0	7	—	35

Wash — Pounds 18 fumble return (Jacke kick)
Wash — Green 83 interception return (Jacke kick)
Phil — Dunn 31 pass from Hoying (Boniol kick)
Wash — Davis 1 run (Jacke kick)
Phil — Garner 9 run (Boniol kick)
Wash — Bowie 3 run (Jacke kick)
Phil — FG Boniol 33
Phil — Garner 1 run (Solomon pass from Hoying)
Wash — Westbrook 7 pass from Hostetler (Jacke kick)
Phil — Solomon 14 pass from Hoying (Boniol kick)

TENNESSEE 16, PITTSBURGH 6—at Liberty Bowl Memorial Stadium, attendance 50,677. Rodney Thomas scored the game's only touchdown as the Oilers finished with an 8-8 record for the second consecutive season and the Steelers won their fourth consecutive AFC Central title. Joe Bowden's 9-yard interception return set up Al Del Greco's first-quarter field goal. The Steelers responded with a 16-play, 70-yard drive that culminated with Norm Johnson's 23-yard field goal. Henry Ford's 13-yard fumble return in the second quarter led to Thomas's 25-yard touchdown run. Steve McNair's 38-yard pass to Derrick Mason enabled Del Greco to kick a 29-yard field goal just before halftime. McNair's 47-yard run in the third quarter set up Del Greco's third field goal. The Steelers responded with scoring drive, capped by Johnson's second field goal. Pittsburgh reached the Oilers' 13 in the final two minutes, but Lenoy Jones forced Fred McAfee to fumble and Darryll Lewis recovered to thwart the Steelers' comeback attempt. McNair was 10 of 26 for 102 yards, with 1 interception. Kordell Stewart played only the first half and was6 of 16 for 87 yards, with 1 interception. Mike Tomczak was 8 of 11 for 89 yards.

Pittsburgh	3	0	0	3	—	6
Tennessee	3	10	3	0	—	16

Tenn — FG Del Greco 34
Pitt — FG N. Johnson 23
Tenn — Thomas 25 run (Del Greco kick)
Tenn — FG Del Greco 29
Tenn — FG Del Greco 26
Pitt — FG N. Johnson 36

DENVER 38, SAN DIEGO 3—at Denver Mile High Stadium, attendance 69,632. The Broncos awoke from their two-game losing streak and outscored the Chargers 38-0 in the final three quarters to prepare for their rematch playoff game against the Jaguars. Greg Davis's 26-yard field goal capped a 14-play drive to give the Chargers a 3-0 lead. Vaughn Hebron's 31-yard kickoff return led to John Elway's 11-yard touchdown pass to Rod Smith. Moments later, Steve Atwater's 20-yard interception return to the Chargers' 29 set up Elway's second touchdown pass to Smith in less than five minutes. Elway completed 12- and 29-yard passes to Shannon Sharpe before connecting with Ed McCaffrey from 1 yard, and drove 75 yards before Jason Elam's 25-yard field goal 13 seconds before halftime finalized the Broncos' 24-point second-quarter explosion. Elway hit Sharpe for a 68-yard touchdown pass on the opening play of the second half, and Derek Loville completed an 18-play, 90-yard drive with a touchdown to finish the scoring. Elway was 17 of 26 for 273 yards and 4 touchdowns, with 1 interception. Craig Whelihan was 15 of 28 for 147 yards, with 1 interception. The Broncos had more first downs (24-9) and total yards (451-203). Terrell Davis sat out the game with a slightly separated shoulder.

San Diego	3	0	0	0	—	3
Denver	0	24	7	7	—	38

SD — FG Davis 26
Den — Smith 11 pass from Elway (Elam kick)
Den — Smith 15 pass from Elway (Elam kick)
Den — McCaffrey 1 pass from Elway (Elam kick)
Den — FG Elam 25
Den — Sharpe 68 pass from Elway (Elam kick)
Den — Loville 6 run (Elam kick)

SUNDAY NIGHT, DECEMBER 21

SEATTLE 38, SAN FRANCISCO 9—at Kingdome, attendance 66,253. Warren Moon threw 4 touchdown passes to enable the Seahawks to finish with a balanced record. Preparing for the playoffs, Steve Young played in just two series, driving the 49ers to Gary Anderson field goals both times. Moon then completed seven-, five-, and four-play drives with touchdown passes to Joey Galloway, James McKnight, and Mike Pritchard in a span of 7:04. Moon responded to Anderson's third field goal with a 35-yard touchdown pass to Galloway to give the Seahawks a commanding 28-9 lead. Jon Kitna led the Seahawks on a 14-play, 92-yard drive in the fourth quarter, running the ball in from 1 yard for his first NFL touchdown, to complete the scoring. Moon was 16 of 26 for 232 yards and 4 touchdowns. Kitna was 8 for 8 for 88 yards. Galloway had 6 receptions for 101 yards. Young, Jeff Brohm, and Jim Druckenmiller combined to complete 18 of 33 passes for 216 yards, with Druckenmiller throwing 1 interception.

San Francisco	6	0	3	0	—	9
Seattle	7	14	7	10	—	38

SF — FG Anderson 33
SF — FG Anderson 40
Sea — Galloway 37 pass from Moon (Peterson kick)
Sea — McKnight 21 pass from Moon (Peterson kick)
Sea — Pritchard 21 pass from Moon (Peterson kick)
SF — FG Anderson 23
Sea — Galloway 35 pass from Moon (Peterson kick)
Sea — FG Peterson 39
Sea — Kitna 1 run (Peterson kick)

MONDAY, DECEMBER 22

NEW ENGLAND 14, MIAMI 12—at Pro Player Stadium, attendance 74,379. A holding penalty on Richmond Webb negated a game-tying 2-point conversion attempt with 3:46 left, and Lawyer Milloy intercepted a pass with 1:10 remaining to give the Patriots the AFC Eastern Division title. By virtue of their victory, the Patriots earned the right to host the Dolphins the following weekend. Olindo Mare kicked 2 first-half field goals to stake the Dolphins to a 6-0 halftime lead. After failing to run a play inside Dolphins' territory in the first half, the Patriots marched 70 yards in nine plays on their first possession of the second half capped by Marrio Grier's 2-yard touchdown run to take a 7-6 lead. David Meggett scored from 5 yards a few drives later to give the Patriots an eight-point edge. The Dolphins responded witha 14-play, 76-yard drive that culminated with Dan Marino's 8-yard touchdown pass to Lamar Thomas with 3:46 left. Karim Abdul-Jabbar ran into the end zone for the 2-point conversion, but Webb's holding penalty nullified the play, and Marino's pass attempt from the 12-yard line fell incomplete. The Dolphins got the ball back with 1:58 left at the Patriots' 47, but Marino's fourth-and-15 pass was intercepted by Milloy. Drew Bledsoe was 18 of 26 for 173 yards, with 1 interception. Marino was 28 for 44 for 275 yards and 1 touchdown, with 1 interception. The teams combined for 89 rushing yards.

New England	0	0	7	7	—	14
Miami	3	3	0	6	—	12

Mia — FG Mare 50
Mia — FG Mare 41
NE — Grier 2 run (Vinatieri kick)
NE — Meggett 5 run (Vinatieri kick)
Mia — Thomas 8 pass from Marino (pass failed)

EIGHTEENTH WEEK SUMMARIES
SATURDAY, DECEMBER 27
NFC WILD CARD PLAYOFF GAME

MINNESOTA 23, NEW YORK GIANTS 22—at Giants Stadium, attendance 77,710. Eddie Murray's 24-yard field goal with 10 seconds remaining capped a 10-point rally in the final 1:30 as the Vikings shocked the Giants. Bernard Holsey and Michael Strahan each recovered first-quarter Randall Cunningham fumbles in Vikings' territory to set up Brad Daluiso field goals. Danny Kanell's 37-yard pass to David Patten led to his 2-yard touchdown pass to Aaron Pierce three plays later to give the Giants a 13-0 lead. Jason Sehorn's interception set up Daluiso's third field goal, and after Duane Butler's fumble recovery of Amani Toomer's punt allowed Murray to put the Vikings on the board, Daluiso added his fourth field goal of the half to give the Giants a 19-3 halftime edge. The Vikings were limited to 68 total yards in the first half. Tony Williams forced Tiki Barber to fumble, and Jerry Ball recovered at the Giants' 4. Leroy Hoard scored on the next play to cut the deficit to 19-10. Murray missed a 48-yard field goal on the their next possession, but a 14-yard punt by Brad Maynard late in the third quarter gave the Vikings good field position and Murray kicked his second field goal fifteen seconds into the fourth quarter. The Giants responded with a 13-play, 74-yard drive capped by Daluiso's fifth field goal, from 22 yards with 7:03 left, to give the NFC East champions a 22-13 lead. When Strahan and Keith Hamilton corralled Robert Smith for a 3-yard loss on third-and-4 from the Vikings' 43, and Minnesota chose to punt, the Giants were in position to run out the clock. But the Vikings forced the Giants to punt, and Maynard's 26-yard boot sailed out of bounds at the Giants' 49 with 2:06 left. Cunningham found Carter for 19 yards between a pair of incompletions before Jake Reed got past Tito Wooten and caught a 30-yard touchdown pass in the back of the end zone with 1:30 left to cut the deficit to 22-20. Chris Calloway bobbled the ensuing onside kick on the wet turf, and Chris Walsh recovered for the Vikings at the 39-yard line. Carter caught a 21-yard pass on third-and-4 to the Giants' 34, and Phillippi Sparks was flagged for pass interference two plays later to put the ball on the 21-yard line with 43 seconds left. Smith broke free for 16 yards to the Giants' 5, and Murray kicked the game-winning field goal with 10 seconds left. Cunningham was 15 of 36 for 203 yards and 1 touchdown, with 1 interception. Kanell was 16 of 32 for 199 yards and 1 touchdown. The victory snapped a six-game postseason losing streak for the Vikings.

Minnesota	0	3	7	13	—	23
N.Y. Giants	6	13	0	3	—	22

NYG — FG Daluiso 43
NYG — FG Daluiso 22
NYG — Pierce 2 pass from Kanell (Daluiso kick)
NYG — FG Daluiso 41
Minn — FG Murray 26
NYG — FG Daluiso 51
Minn — Hoard 4 run (Murray kick)
Minn — FG Murray 26
NYG — FG Daluiso 22
Minn — Reed 30 pass from Cunningham (Murray kick)
Minn — FG Murray 24

AFC WILD CARD PLAYOFF GAME

DENVER 42, JACKSONVILLE 17—at Denver Mile High Stadium, attendance 74,481. Terrell Davis rushed for 184 yards and 2 touchdowns in three quarters as the Broncos avenged last season's playoff loss to the Jaguars. The Broncos marched 73 yards on 15 plays and consumed nearly half the first quarter on their opening possession, capped by Davis's 2-yard touchdown run. John Elway hit Rod Smith with a 43-yard touchdown pass on their next possession, and Davis capped a 92-yard drive on the following possession with a 5-yard run to take a 21-0 lead early in the second quarter. The third possession saw Elway complete passes to Smith, Willie Green, and Smith again on third-and-6, -9, and -13 situations. The Jaguars used a 34-yard pass interference penalty on Darrien Gordon at the Broncos' 4 to set up Natrone Means's 2-yard touchdown run. Reggie Barlow returned the second half's opening kickoff 58 yards to the Broncos' 27, but the Jaguars settled for Mike Hollis's 38-yard field goal to cut the deficit to 21-10. Four minutes later, Travis Davis plucked the ball out of the air, before Mike Horan could punt the ball, and scampered 29 yards for a touchdown. On their next possession the Jaguars drove to the Broncos' 16, but Mark Brunell fumbled the snap and Allen Aldridge recovered. Davis responded with a 59-yard run two plays after the fumble late in the third quarter, but bruised his ribs when he was tackled and did not return. Derek Loville replaced Davis and scored on Denver's next possession on a 25-yard run to give the Broncos a 28-17 cushion. Loville's 44-yard run later in the quarter led to his 8-yard touchdown run with 3:43 left, and Vaughn Hebron added a 6-yard run with 1:11 remaining. Elway was 16 of 24 for 223 yards and 1 touchdown. Loville gained 103 yards on 11 carries and, combined with Davis's 184 yards, became the third duo in playoff history to gain at least 100 yards in a game. Brunell was 18 of 32 for 203 yards with 1 interception. The Broncos more than doubled the Jaguars in first downs (28-14), total yards (511-237), and time of possession (40:31-19:29).

Jacksonville	0	7	10	0	—	17
Denver	14	7	0	21	—	42

Den — Te. Davis 2 run (Elam kick)
Den — R. Smith 43 pass from Elway (Elam kick)
Den — Te. Davis 5 run (Elam kick)
Jack — Means 2 run (Hollis kick)
Jack — FG Hollis 38
Jack — T. Davis 29 return of blocked punt (Hollis kick)
Den — Loville 25 run (Elam kick)
Den — Loville 8 run (Elam kick)
Den — Hebron 6 run (Elam kick)

SUNDAY, DECEMBER 28
AFC WILD CARD PLAYOFF GAME

NEW ENGLAND 17, MIAMI 3—at Foxboro Stadium, attendance 60,041. Todd Collins returned an interception for a touchdown, and Chris Slade's interception set up another as the Patriots' defense permitted just 10 first downs and 162 total yards. Each team punted twice before Collins and Lawyer Milloy stopped Karim Abdul-Jabbar on fourth-and-1 from the Patriots' 39 late in the first quarter. The Patriots reached the Dolphins' 31, but Adam Vinatieri's 48-yard field-goal attempt sailed wide left, keeping the game scoreless. Slade intercepted Marino three plays later, returning the ball to the Dolphins' 29 to set up Drew Bledsoe's 24-yard touchdown pass to Troy Brown. The Patriots had the only other scoring opportunity of the first half, but Vinatieri pushed a 47-yard field goal wide right in the final minute. Collins's interception was on the second play of the second half to give the Patriots a 14-0 lead and, after forcing a punt, Vinatieri capped a 15-play, 66-yard drive with a field goal. Corey Harris returned the kickoff 47 yards to set up Olindo Mare's 38-yard field goal nine seconds into the fourth quarter. Harris recovered the ensuing onside kick, however, Chris Canty forced Marino to fumble on the next play, Chris Slade recovered, and the Dolphins never got inside the Patriots' 43 on their final three possessions. Bledsoe was 16 of 32 for 139 yards and 1 touchdown. Marino was 17 of 43 for 141 yards, with 2 interceptions. Derrick Cullors, who rushed for 101 yards during the season, gained 86 yards on 22 carries in place of injured Curtis Martin. The Dolphins are 0-6 in road playoff games since 1972, and for the first time ever lost to a team three times in one season.

Miami	0	0	0	3	—	3
New England	0	7	10	0	—	17

NE — Brown 24 pass from Bledsoe (Viantieri kick)
NE — Collins 40 interception return (Vinatieri kick)
NE — FG Vinatieri 22
Mia — FG Mare 38

NFC WILD CARD PLAYOFF GAME

TAMPA BAY 20, DETROIT 10—at Houlihan's Stadium, attendance 73,361. The Buccaneers broke out to a 20-0 lead and held on to record their first postseason victory since 1979. Michael Husted's 22-yard field goal with 5:24 left in the first quarter began the Buccaneers' scoring spree. After forcing a punt, Tampa Bay drove 89 yards, with Horace Copeland's 9-yard touchdown catch capping a 17-play drive. On the Lions' next possession, Anthony Parker's 19-yard interception return to the Lions' 20 set up Husted's second field goal. The Buccaneers had a chance to score just before halftime, but Warrick Dunn fumbled at the Lions' 14. However, Mike Alstott capped the Buccaneers' opening drive of the second half with a 31-yard scoring burst. The Lions drove deep into Tampa Bay territory but Scott Mitchell's fourth-and-3 pass from the Buccaneers' 8 fell incomplete. Jason Hanson kicked a 33-yard field goal to cap the Lions' next drive, but Mitchell was injured on the play previous to the field goal. He left the game with a concussion. The Lions forced another punt, and Frank Reich guided the offense to its first touchdown on a 1-yard plunge by Tommy Vardell with 7:48 left. The Lions reached no further than the Buccaneers' 42 on their final drive. Dilfer was 13 of 26 for 181 yards and 1 touchdown, with 1 interception. Mitchell was 10 of 25 for 78 yards, with 1 interception, while Reich was 11 of 15 for 129 yards. Barry Sanders, who gained 2,053 rushing yards during the season, had 18 carries for 65 yards.

Detroit	0	0	3	7	—	10
Tampa Bay	3	10	7	0	—	20

TB — FG Husted 22
TB — Copeland 9 pass from Dilfer (Husted kick)
TB — FG Husted 42
TB — Alstott 31 run (Husted kick)
Det — FG Hanson 33
Det — Vardell 1 run (Hanson kick)

NINETEENTH WEEK SUMMARIES
SATURDAY, JANUARY 3
AFC DIVISIONAL PLAYOFF GAME

PITTSBURGH 7, NEW ENGLAND 6—at Three Rivers Stadium, attendance 61,228. Chad Scott intercepted Drew Bledsoe's long pass intended for Terry Glenn on the game's third play, returning it 27 yards to the Steelers' 38. On second-and-10 from the Patriots' 40, Kordell Stewart ran the option left and tightroped 40 yards down the sideline for a touchdown 5:11 into the game. The Patriots strung together a 10-play, 65-yard drive that culminated with Vinatieri's 31-yard field goal in the middle of the second quarter to cut the deficit to 7-3. After a third quarter that saw neither team drive within the opponents' 40, Vinatieri's second field goal with 12:16 left made it a one-point game. The Steelers reached the Patriots' 1 on fourth down with 3:29 left, but Stewart was stopped at the line of scrimmage by Tedy Bruschi. The Patriots reached their own 42-yard line, but Mark Vrabel sacked Bledsoe with 1:50 left, and Jason Gildon recovered the ensuing fumble. The Steelers were forced to punt, but Bledsoe's desperation pass was intercepted by Levon Kirkland at the Steelers' 20 to end the game. Stewart was 14 of 31 for 134 yards, with 1 interception. Bledsoe was 23 of 44 for 264 yards, with 2 interceptions. Shawn Jefferson had 9 receptions for 104 yards. The Steelers had 1 more first down, and the Patriots gained 1 more yard, but the Steelers had an 11:14 edge in time of possession because of Stewart (68 yards) and Jerome Bettis (67 yards), and forced 4 turnovers.

New England	0	3	0	3	—	6
Pittsburgh	7	0	0	0	—	7

Pitt — Stewart 40 run (Johnson kick)
NE — FG Vinatieri 31
NE — FG Vinatieri 46

NFC DIVISIONAL PLAYOFF GAME

SAN FRANCISCO 38, MINNESOTA 22—at 3Com Park, attendance 65,018. Terry Kirby had 25 carries for 120 yards and 2 touchdowns as the 49ers defeated the Vikings. Mitch Berger's 12-yard punt to the Vikings' 26 enabled William Floyd to score four plays later to give the 49ers a 7-0 lead. Two plays later, Randall Cunningham threw a 66-yard touchdown pass to Cris Carter to tie the game. A 28-yard pass interference penalty on Torrian Gray to the Vikings' 4 set up Terry Kirby's 1-yard run, and Ken Norton's 23-yard interception return 47 seconds later staked the 49ers to 21-7 halftime edge. Gary Anderson's 34-yard field goal capped the 49ers' initial drive of the second half, but the Vikings responded with Cunningham's 53-yard pass to Jake Reed setting up Carter's 3-yard touchdown grab to pull the Vikings within 24-14. However, Steve Young threw a 15-yard touchdown pass to Terrell Owens on their next drive, and Kirby scored two possessions later to give the 49ers a 38-14 lead midway through the fourth quarter. Cunningham threw a 13-yard touchdown pass to Matthew Hatchette, and his 31-yard pass to Andrew Glover got the Vikings to the 49ers' 16 with 2:30 to play, but Cunningham threw 4 consecutive incompletions to end the Vikings' threat. Young was 21 of 30 for 224 yards and 1 touchdown. Cunningham was 18 of 40 for 331 yards and 3 touchdowns, with 1 interception. The 49ers had more first downs (30-16) and led in time of possession (38:04-21:56).

Minnesota	7	0	7	8	—	22
San Francisco	7	14	10	7	—	38

SF — Floyd 1 run (Anderson kick)
Minn — Carter 66 pass from Cunningham (Murray kick)
SF — Kirby 1 run (Anderson kick)
SF — Norton 23 interception return (Anderson kick)
SF — FG Anderson 34
Minn — Carter 3 pass from Cunningham (Murray kick)
SF — Owens 15 pass from Young (Anderson kick)
SF — Kirby 1 run (Anderson kick)
Minn — Hatchette 13 pass from Cunningham (Walsh pass from Cunningham)

SUNDAY, JANUARY 4
NFC DIVISIONAL PLAYOFF GAME

GREEN BAY 21, TAMPA BAY 7—at Lambeau Field, attendance 60,327. Dorsey Levens rushed for 112 yards and 1 touchdown, and the Packers' special teams set up two scores and halted three others as Green Bay advanced to the NFC Championship Game for the third consecutive season. Bob Kuberski blocked Michael Husted's 43-yard field-goal attempt midway through the first quarter to spark a 67-yard drive, capped by Brett Favre's 3-yard touchdown pass to Mark Chmura. Derrick Mayes's 14-yard catch on third-and-9 to the Buccaneers' 3 gave the Packers the impetus to reach the end zone. The Buccaneers reached the Packers' 25 early in the second quarter, but Steve Walsh's fake field-goal attempt pass on fourth-and-2 was incomplete. Warren Sapp forced Levens to fumble and recovered the ball at the Packers' 30 two plays later, but a third field-goal attempt was aborted when Dave Moore's snap sailed past Walsh and was recovered by Husted. LeRoy Butler's 12-yard sack of Trent Dilfer pinned the Buccaneers back to their own 11, and Robert Brooks returned the ensuing punt 28 yards to give the Packers the ball at the Buccaneers' 29 with 4:07 left in the half. The Packers had to settle for Ryan Longwell's 21-yard field goal with 1:52 left in the half, but Tyrone Williams's interception on the next play from scrimmage set up Longwell's second field goal and gave Green Bay a 13-0 lead at halftime. The Packers took the second half's opening kickoff and drove deep into Buccaneers territory before John Lynch hit Favre's arm on a pass attempt and Donnie Abraham intercepted the pass at the 6-yard line. Faced with third-and-11 from their own 5-yard line, Dilfer threw a 53-yard pass to Reidel Anthony. Dilfer then completed a 28-yard pass to Moore on third-and-3, and Mike Alstott scored two plays later to cut the deficit to 13-7. On the last play of the third quarter Favre completed a 23-yard pass to Mayes on third-and-18, and Levens scored three plays later. The Buccaneers drove into Packers territory twice but were stopped on downs, and Mike Prior's interception at the Packers' 34 with 1:49 left iced the game. Favre was 15 of 28 for 190 yards and 1 touchdown, with 2 interceptions. Dilfer was 11 of 36 for 200 yards, with 2 interceptions. With the game-time temperature at 29 degrees, Favre improved his record 23-0 when the temperature is below 35.

Tampa Bay	0	0	7	0	—	7
Green Bay	7	6	0	8	—	21

GB — Chmura 3 pass from Favre (Longwell kick)
GB — FG Longwell 21
GB — FG Longwell 32
TB — Alstott 6 run (Husted kick)
GB — Levens 2 run (Favre run)

AFC DIVISIONAL PLAYOFF GAME

DENVER 14, KANSAS CITY 10—at Arrowhead Stadium, attendance 76,965. Terrell Davis recovered from bruised ribs to rush for 101 yards and 2 touchdowns as the Broncos knocked the number-one seeded Chiefs out of the playoffs. The Chiefs pinned the Broncos deep in their own territory early in the second quarter when Bucky Brooks leaped over the goal line and tipped a punt back onto the field where it was downed at the 2-yard line. Tom Rouen's punt three plays later traveled just 25 yards, giving the Chiefs excellent field position at the Broncos' 30. However, Pete Stoyanovich, who missed just one field goal all season, sailed his 44-yard attempt wide left. The Broncos proceeded to march 65 yards, with Davis's first touchdown with 1:56 left in the half giving Denver a 7-0 lead. Elvis Grbac threw a 34-yard pass to Andre Rison on the first play of the second half to set up Stoyanovich's 20-yard field goal. The Broncos used a 41-yard run by Davis to get deep into Chiefs territory, but John Browning forced Derek Loville to fumble and Reggie Tongue recovered at the Chiefs' 11 to thwart the drive. After an exchange of punts, Grbac connected with Joe Horn on a 50-yard pass and, three plays later, found Tony Gonzalez in the end zone for a touchdown to give the Chiefs a 10-7 lead with 10 seconds left in the third quarter. Loville returned the ensuing kickoff 20 yards, and an unnecessary roughness penalty on Danan Hughes gave the Broncos the ball at the Chiefs' 49. On third-and-5, John Elway threw a short pass to Ed McCaffrey, who tightroped his way 43 yards to the Chiefs' 1. Davis scored three plays later to give Denver a 14-10 advantage with 12:32 left. The Chiefs drove to the Broncos' 37 where they faced fourth-and-6. Kansas City lined up in field-goal formation, but holder Louie Aguiar ran with the ball and was tackled by Gordon three yards shy of the first down. A couple of punts later, the Chiefs began their final drive at their own 17 with 4:04 remaining. Ray Crockett's 29-yard pass interference penalty on the first play moved the ball to the Broncos' 46. Faced with fourth-and-9 from the 47, Grbac hit Lake Dawson with a 12-yard pass and, after getting sacked, connected on a 23-yard pass to Rison to get the Chiefs to the Broncos' 28 with 1:51 left, where they used their final timeout. Grbac netted 1-, 3-, and 4-yard passes to Kimble Anders, Gonzalez, and Ted Popson before Gordon batted down Grbac's final pass attempt in the end zone on fourth-and-2 with 19 seconds left to seal the victory. Elway was 10 of 19 for 170 yards. Elvis Grbac was 24 of 37 for 260 yards and 1 touchdown.

Denver	0	7	0	7	—	14
Kansas City	0	0	10	0	—	10

Den — Davis 1 run (Elam kick)
KC — FG Stoyanovich 20
KC — Gonzalez 12 pass from Grbac (Stoyanovich kick)
Den — Davis 1 run (Elam kick)

TWENTIETH WEEK SUMMARIES
SUNDAY, JANUARY 11
AFC CHAMPIONSHIP PLAYOFF GAME

DENVER 24, PITTSBURGH 21—at Three Rivers Stadium, attendance 61,382. John Elway threw 2 touchdown passes, and the Broncos' defense intercepted 2 passes in the end zone as Denver earned its fifth trip to the Super Bowl. Levon Kirkland intercepted Elway's pass on the second play of the game, but Norm Johnson's 38-yard field-goal attempt sailed wide left. Terrell Davis scampered 43 yards on the next play and scored five plays later to give the Broncos a 7-0 lead. The Steelers responded with a 6-play drive of their own, capped by Kordell Stewart's 33-yard option run down the right side for the game tying touchdown. Darren Perry forced and recovered Davis's fumble at the Steelers' 32 on the next drive, and Pittsburgh marched 68 yards in 11 plays, keyed by 2 third-down passes by Stewart and culminating with Jerome Bettis's

1-yard run. Elway's 17-yard pass to Rod Smith on third-and-10 kept alive the next drive and allowed Jason Elam to cut the deficit to 14-10 with 8:20 left in the half. Ray Crockett intercepted Stewart's bomb in the end zone to halt a Steelers drive with 4:04 left in the half. On the strength of 3 Elway completions, and a 22-yard pass interference penalty by Chad Scott, the Broncos reached the 15-yard line. Elway then threw a swing pass behind Howard Griffith, who reached back and made a one-handed grab before stepping into the end zone with 1:47 remaining. The Broncos forced a punt, and Darrien Gordon's 19-yard return gave them the ball at their own 46 with 43 seconds left in the half. Carnell Lake's 34-yard pass interference penalty put Denver in position, and Elway's 1-yard pass to Ed McCaffrey with 13 seconds left in the half gave Denver a 24-14 lead. The Steelers used nearly the first seven minutes of the second half to drive to the Broncos' 5, only to have Stewart's pass intercepted in the end zone by Allen Aldridge. The next scoring opportunity came when the Steelers got the ball back following a punt with 5:43 left in the game. Stewart threw the ball eight times and ran two times on the 10-play, 79-yard drive, capped by his 15-yard touchdown pass to Charles Johnson with 2:46 left to cut the deficit to 24-21. The Steelers elected to kick deep and had the Broncos pinned at their own 15-yard line on third-and-6 with 2:00 left. But Elway fired an 18-yard pass to Shannon Sharpe. After a Steelers timeout, Elway threw a 10-yard pass to McCaffrey, and Davis broke free for a 19-yard run two plays later to ice the AFC championship. Elway was 18 of 31 for 210 yards and 2 touchdowns, with 1 interception. Davis had 26 carries for 139 yards. Stewart was 18 of 36 for 201 yards and 1 touchdown, with 3 interceptions. Bettis had 23 carries for 105 yards. In what was an evenly matched game, the teams each had 23 first downs, the Steelers had 9 more total yards, while Denver had the ball for two more seconds than Pittsburgh.

Denver	7	17	0	0	—	24
Pittsburgh	7	7	0	7	—	21

Den — Davis 8 run (Elam kick)
Pitt — Stewart 33 run (N. Johnson kick)
Pitt — Bettis 1 run (N. Johnson kick)
Den — FG Elam 43
Den — Griffith 16 pass from Elway (Elam kick)
Den — McCaffrey 1 pass from Elway (Elam kick)
Pitt — C. Johnson 15 pass from Stewart (N. Johnson kick)

NFC CHAMPIONSHIP PLAYOFF GAME

GREEN BAY 23, SAN FRANCISCO 10—at 3Com Park, attendance 68,987. A stifling defensive effort by the Packers limited the 49ers to 33 rushing yards, forced 2 turnovers, and recorded 4 sacks as Green Bay earned their fourth Super Bowl appearance. The Packers forced a punt on the game's initial possession and drove to the 1-yard line, but Gary Plummer batted down Brett Favre's third-and-goal pass, forcing Green Bay to settle for Ryan Longwell's field goal. After an exchange of punts, the 49ers drove to the Packers' 28. However, Eugene Robinson intercepted Steve Young's third-down pass and raced 58 yards. Favre fired a 27-yard touchdown pass to Antonio Freeman two plays later to give the Packers a 10-0 lead. The Packers forced another punt and had a chance to extend their lead, but Longwell's 47-yard field-goal attempt failed. The 49ers resonded with a 10-play drive, capped by Gary Anderson's field goal with 58 seconds left in the half. On their own 35-yard line with time running out in the half, Favre lofted a 40-yard bomb to Freeman with three seconds left in the half. Longwell trotted onto the field and made a 43-yard field goal to give the Packers a 13-3 halftime lead. Each team punted their first three possessions of the second half, but Tommy Thompson's third punt allowed the Packers to begin at the 49ers' 35. Even with great field position, the 49ers' defense held the Packers to Longwell's third field goal with 5:03 left. The 49ers were forced to go for it on fourth-and-10 from their own 20, only to watch Keith McKenzie sack Young for a 9-yard loss. Levens scored two plays later to give Green Bay a 23-3 lead with 3:10 left. Chuck Levy promptly returned the ensuing kickoff 95 yards for a touchdown, but Jeff Thomason recovered the ensuing onside kick and the Packers clinched their second consecutive NFC title. Favre was 16 of 27 for 222 yards and 1 touchdown. Levens rushed 27 times for 114 yards. Freeman had 4 receptions for 107 yards. Young was 23 of 38 for 250 yards, with 1 interception. Terrell Owens had 6 catches for 100 yards.

Green Bay	3	10	0	10	—	23
San Francisco	0	3	0	7	—	10

GB — FG Longwell 19
GB — Freeman 27 pass from Favre (Longwell kick)
SF — FG Anderson 28
GB — FG Longwell 43
GB — FG Longwell 25
GB — Levens 5 run (Longwell kick)
SF — Levy 95 kickoff return (Anderson kick)

TWENTY-FIRST WEEK SUMMARY
SUNDAY, JANUARY 25
SUPER BOWL XXXII

DENVER 31, GREEN BAY 24—at Qualcomm Stadium, attendance 68,912. Terrell Davis rushed for 157 yards and a Super Bowl-record 3 touchdowns to lead the Broncos to their first NFL championship and break the NFC's streak of Super Bowl victories at thirteen. The defending Super Bowl champion Packers took the opening kickoff and marched 76 yards in just over four minutes, scoring the first points on Brett Favre's 22-yard touchdown pass to Antonio Freeman. The Broncos responded with a 10-play, 58-yard drive capped by Davis's 1-yard run to tie the game. Tyrone Braxton intercepted Favre two plays later, and John Elway scored on a third-and-goal play to begin the second quarter. Steve Atwater forced Favre to fumble three plays later, and Neil Smith recovered at the Packers' 33. Jason Elam converted a 51-yard field goal, the second longest in Super Bowl history, to give the Broncos a 17-7 lead with 12:21 left in the half. After an exchange of punts, the Packers produced a 17-play, 95-yard drive that consumed 7:26 and finished with Favre's 6-yard touchdown pass to Mark Chmura on third-and-5 with 12 seconds left in the half. Tyrone Williams forced and recovered Davis's fumble at the Broncos' 26 on the first play from scrimmage in the second half. However, the Broncos' defense kept the Packers out of the end zone as Ryan Longwell's 27-yard field goal tied the game with 11:59 left in the third quarter. After another exchange of punts, Elway's 36-yard pass to Ed McCaffrey keyed a 13-play, 92-yard drive capped by Davis's 1-yard touchdown run with 34 seconds left in the third quarter. Tim McKyer recovered Freeman's fumble at the Packers' 22 on the ensuing kickoff return, giving the Broncos a golden opportunity, but Eugene Robinson intercepted Elway's pass in the end zone on the next play. Sparked by Robinson's play, the Packers took just four plays, three on passes to Freeman, to score the tying touchdown with 13:32 remaining. Each defense stiffened, forcing two punts, but the Broncos got great field position following Craig Hentrich's 39-yard punt to the Packers' 49 with 3:27 left and the score tied 24-24. Davis rushed for 2 yards on the first play, but Darrius Holland's 15-yard face mask penalty moved the ball to the Packers' 32. Elway threw a 23-yard pass to Howard Griffith two plays later, and Davis rushed 7 yards to the Packers' 1 with 1:47 left. After a timeout, Davis waltzed into the end zone to give Denver a 31-24 lead with 1:45 remaining. Freeman returned the kickoff 22 yards to the Broncos' 30, and Favre dumped 22- and 13-yard passes to Dorsey Levens to reach the Broncos' 35 with 1:04 left. But after a 4-yard pass to Levens and incompletions to Freeman and Brooks, John Mobley batted down Favre's fourth-down pass to Chmura with 32 seconds left to give the Broncos the Vince Lombardi trophy. Elway was 12 of 22 for 123 yards, with 1 interception. Favre was 25 of 42 for 256 yards and 1 touchdown, with 1 interception. Freeman had 9 receptions for 126 yards. Davis was named the game's most valuable player.

Green Bay (NFC)	7	7	3	7	—	24
Denver (AFC)	7	10	7	7	—	31

GB — Freeman 22 pass from Favre (Longwell kick) (4:02)
Den — Davis 1 run (Elam kick) (9:21)
Den — Elway 1 run (Elam kick) (:05)
Den — FG Elam 51 (2:29)
GB — Chmura 6 pass from Favre (Longwell kick) (14:48)
GB — FG Longwell 27 (3:01)
Den — Davis 1 run (Elam kick) (14:26)
GB — Freeman 13 pass from Favre (Longwell kick) (1:28)
Den — Davis 1 run (Elam kick) (13:15)

TWENTY-SECOND WEEK SUMMARY
SUNDAY, FEBRUARY 1
AFC-NFC PRO BOWL

AFC 29, NFC 24—at Aloha Stadium, attendance 49,995. Warren Moon guided the AFC to points on all three of his drives, including the winning touchdown from 1 yard with 1:49 left as the AFC scored the game's final 15 points to beat the NFC. Steve Young threw a 22-yard touchdown pass to Herman Moore to cap the game's opening drive and give the NFC a 7-0 lead. Late in the first quarter, Mark Brunell threw a 17-yard touchdown pass to Andre Rison to tie the game. Both touchdown passes came on third-and-8 plays. The NFC responded with a 7-play, 71-yard drive capped by Young's 36-yard touchdown pass to Rob Moore. Trent Difler guided the NFC to its third touchdown, keyed by a 21-yard pass to Irving Fryar and 23-yard pass to Mike Alstott, and capped by Dorsey Levens's 12-yard touchdown run with 1:36 left in the half to give the NFC a 21-7 lead. The NFC had a chance to pad its lead on its first possession of the second half, but Jason Hanson missed a 44-yard field goal. The AFC bounced back with a 10-play, 65-yard drive that culminated with Drew Bledsoe's 14-yard touchdown pass to Jimmy Smith late in the third quarter. After Hanson's 35-yard field goal gave the NFC a 24-14 lead with 13:42 left, Moon entered the game and drove the AFC into field-goal range, where Mike Hollis drilled a 48-yard attempt with 8:51 left. Attempting to grind out the clock, Warrick Dunn fumbled, and Darryl Williams recovered at the AFC's 49 with 3:03 remaining. After a holding penalty moved the AFC back 10 yards, Moon fired a 57-yard pass to Tim Brown to set up Eddie George's 4-yard run with 2:31 left. The AFC went for the lead instead of a tie, but Moon's pass to Rison fell incomplete. However, the AFC got the ball back when Chris Chandler fumbled the snap on the NFC's first play, and Michael Sinclair recovered at the NFC's 16 with 2:19 left. Three runs by George set up Moon's winning sneak with 1:49 remaining. Moon's 2-point conversion pass to Brown was incomplete, keeping the AFC's lead at 29-24. The NFC was unable to move beyond its own 31-yard line in the final moments, and the AFC prevailed. Tim Brown had 5 receptions for 129 yards. Moon, who was 4 of 8 for 89 yards, won player of the game honors.

NFC	7	14	0	3	—	24
AFC	7	0	7	15	—	29

NFC — H. Moore 22 pass from Young (Hanson kick)
AFC — Rison 17 pass from Brunell (Hollis kick)
NFC — R. Moore 36 pass from Young (Hanson kick)
NFC — Levens 12 run (Hanson kick)
AFC — J. Smith 14 pass from Bledsoe (Hollis kick)
NFC — FG Hanson 35
AFC — FG Hollis 48
AFC — George 4 run (pass failed)
AFC — Moon 1 run (pass failed)

1997 PRO FOOTBALL AWARDS

	NFL	AFC	NFC
PRO FOOTBALL WRITERS OF AMERICA			
Most Valuable Player	Barry Sanders		
Rookie of the Year	Warrick Dunn		
Coach of the Year	Jim Fassel		
ASSOCIATED PRESS			
Most Valuable Player	Brett Favre, Barry Sanders		
Offensive Player of the Year	Barry Sanders		
Defensive Player of the Year	Dana Stubblefield		
Offensive Rookie of the Year	Warrick Dunn		
Defensive Rookie of the Year	Peter Boulware		
Coach of the Year	Jim Fassel		
THE SPORTING NEWS			
Player of the Year	Barry Sanders		
Rookie of the Year	Warrick Dunn		
Coach of the Year	Jim Fassel		
FOOTBALL NEWS			
Player of the Year		Terrell Davis	Barry Sanders
Coach of the Year	Jim Fassel		
Rookie of the Year	Warrick Dunn		
PRO FOOTBALL WEEKLY			
Most Valuable Player	Barry Sanders		
Defensive Most Valuable Player	Dana Stubblefield		
Offensive Rookie of the Year	Warrick Dunn		
Defensive Rookie of the Year	Peter Boulware		
Coach of the Year	Jim Fassel		
Assistant Coach of the Year	John Fox		
Golden Toe	Pete Stoyanovich		
Comeback Player of the Year	Robert Brooks		
Executive of the Year	George Young		
FOOTBALL DIGEST			
Player of the Year	Barry Sanders		
Defensive Player of the Year	Dana Stubblefield		
Offensive Rookie of the Year	Warrick Dunn		
Defensive Rookie of the Year	Peter Boulware		
Coach of the Year	Marty Schottenheimer		
SPORTS ILLUSTRATED			
Player of the Year	Barry Sanders		
Coach of the Year	Jim Fassel		
Rookie of the Year	Warrick Dunn		
USA TODAY			
Coach of the Year		Marty Schottenheimer	Jim Fassel
COLLEGE AND PRO FOOTBALL NEWSWEEKLY			
Offensive Player of the Year	Barry Sanders		
Defensive Player of the Year	Dana Stubblefield		
Offensive Rookie of the Year	Warrick Dunn		
Defensive Rookie of the Year	Peter Boulware		
Coach of the Year	Jim Fassel		
Rookie Coach of the Year	Jim Fassel		
NEWSPAPER ENTERPRISE ASSOCIATION			
Tom Landry Award (Offensive Player of the Year)	Barry Sanders		
George Halas Award (Defensive Player of the Year)	Dana Stubblefield		
Bert Bell Trophy (Rookie of the Year)	Warrick Dunn		
MAXWELL CLUB PLAYER OF THE YEAR (Bert Bell Trophy)	Barry Sanders		
MAXWELL CLUB COACH OF THE YEAR (Earle "Greasy" Neale Trophy)	Tony Dungy		
MILLER LITE PLAYER OF THE YEAR	Barry Sanders		
TRUE VALUE NFL MAN OF THE YEAR	Troy Aikman		
SUPER BOWL MOST VALUABLE PLAYER (Pete Rozelle Trophy)	Terrell Davis		
AFC-NFC PRO BOWL PLAYER OF THE GAME (Dan McGuire Award)	Warren Moon		

1997 PLAYERS OF THE WEEK/MONTH

1997 AFC PLAYERS OF THE WEEK

Offense

Week	1	RB	Eddie George, Tennessee
Week	2	QB	Elvis Grbac, Kansas City
Week	3	RB	Curtis Martin, New England
Week	4	RB	Terrell Davis, Denver
Week	5	WR	Tony Martin, San Diego
Week	6	RB	Gary Brown, San Diego
Week	7	RB	James Stewart, Jacksonville
Week	8	RB	Napoleon Kaufman, Oakland
Week	9	QB	Warren Moon, Seattle
Week	10	QB	John Elway, Denver
Week	11	QB	Warren Moon, Seattle
Week	12	QB	Paul Justin, Indianapolis
Week	13	QB	Boomer Esiason, Cincinnati
Week	14	RB	Jerome Bettis, Pittsburgh
Week	15	RB	Corey Dillon, Cincinnati
Week	16	TE	Ken Dilger, Indianapolis
Week	17	WR	Tim Brown, Oakland

Defense

S	Shawn Wooden, Miami
LB	Bryce Paup, Buffalo
LB	Chad Brown, Seattle
S	Darryl Williams, Seattle
S	Jerome Woods, Kansas City
LB	John Mobley, Denver
LB	Derrick Rodgers, Miami
DE	Bruce Smith, Buffalo
LB	Ray Lewis, Baltimore
LB	Anthony Davis, Kansas City
DE	Jeff Lageman, Jacksonville
CB	Otis Smith, New York Jets
S	Larry Whigham, New England
S	Marcus Robertson, Tennessee
CB	Terrell Buckley, Miami
CB	Otis Smith, New York Jets
LB	Gerald Dixon, Cincinnati

Special Teams

K	John Hall, New York Jets
K	Mike Hollis, Jacksonville
KR	Tamarick Vanover, Kansas City
S	Corwin Brown, New York Jets
K	Norm Johnson, Pittsburgh
KR	Will Blackwell, Pittsburgh
K	Adam Vinatieri, New England
P	Reggie Roby, Tennessee
P	Josh Miller, Pittsburgh
KR	Eric Metcalf, San Diego
CB-KR	Darrien Gordon, Denver
KR	Tamarick Vanover, Kansas City
RB-PR	Leon Johnson, New York Jets
K	Mike Hollis, Jacksonville
WR-KR	Jermaine Lewis, Baltimore
K	Pete Stoyanovich, Kansas City
KR	Tamarick Vanover, Kansas City

1997 AFC PLAYERS OF THE MONTH

Offense

September	RB	Terrell Davis, Denver
October	RB	Jerome Bettis, Pittsburgh
November	QB	John Elway, Denver
December	WR	Keenan McCardell, Jacksonville

Defense

LB	Chris Slade, New England
DE	Bruce Smith, Buffalo
S	Jerome Woods, Kansas City
LB	Derrick Thomas, Kansas City

Special Teams

K	Matt Stover, Baltimore
K	Greg Davis, San Diego
WR-PR	Eric Metcalf, San Diego
K	Pete Stoyanovich, Kansas City

1997 NFC PLAYERS OF THE WEEK

Offense

Week	1	QB	Troy Aikman, Dallas
Week	2	RB	Warrick Dunn, Tampa Bay
Week	3	RB	Barry Sanders, Detroit
Week	4	QB	Trent Dilfer, Tampa Bay
Week	5	RB	Garrison Hearst, San Francisco
Week	6	RB	Ricky Watters, Philadelphia
Week	7	RB	Barry Sanders, Detroit
Week	8	WR	Chris Calloway, New York Giants
Week	9	QB	Brett Favre, Green Bay
Week	10	RB	Fred Lane, Carolina
Week	11	WR	Antonio Freeman, Green Bay
Week	12	WR	Herman Moore, Detroit
Week	13	RB	Barry Sanders, Detroit
Week	14	QB	Bobby Hoying, Philadelphia
Week	15	QB	Steve Young, San Francisco
Week	16	WR	Antonio Freeman, Green Bay
Week	17	RB	Barry Sanders, Detroit

Defense

LB	Stephen Boyd, Detroit
CB	Aeneas Williams, Arizona
CB	Rod Woodson, San Francisco
DT	Wayne Martin, New Orleans
CB	Cris Dishman, Washington
DE	Gabe Wilkins, Green Bay
DE	Chuck Smith, Atlanta
CB	Eric Davis, Carolina
DT	Rhett Hall, Philadelphia
DT	Dana Stubblefield, San Francisco
DT	Dana Stubblefield, San Francisco
CB	Jason Sehorn, New York Giants
LB	Ken Harvey, Washington
DT	Travis Hall, Atlanta
LB	Jessie Armstead, New York Giants
CB	Jason Sehorn, New York Giants
CB	Darrell Green, Washington

Special Teams

WR-PR	Bill Schroeder, Green Bay
K	John Kasay, Carolina
P	Ken Walter, Carolina
P	Will Brice, St. Louis
K	Jason Hanson, Detroit
K	Eddie Murray, Minnesota
P	Matt Turk, Washington
WR-PR	Amani Toomer, New York Giants
K	Jeff Jaeger, Chicago
WR-PR	Karl Williams, Tampa Bay
LB	Shelton Quarles, Tampa Bay
S	Chris Hewitt, New Orleans
K	Jason Hanson, Detroit
K	Doug Brien, New Orleans
RB-KR	Byron Hanspard, Atlanta
P	Mark Royals, New Orleans
WR-PR	Karl Williams, Tampa Bay

1997 NFC PLAYERS OF THE MONTH

Offense

September	WR	Jake Reed, Minnesota
October	RB	Barry Sanders, Detroit
November	RB	Barry Sanders, Detroit
December	RB	Barry Sanders, Detroit

Defense

DT	Warren Sapp, Tampa Bay
DT	John Randle, Minnesota
DT	Dana Stubblefield, San Francisco
CB	Jason Sehorn, New York Giants

Special Teams

K	Richie Cunningham, Dallas
P	Matt Turk, Washington
K	Doug Brien, New Orleans
RB-KR	Byron Hanspard, Atlanta

1997 PLAYOFF PLAYERS OF THE WEEK

Offense

Wild Card		Offensive Line, Denver
Divisional	RB	Terry Kirby, San Francisco
Championship	RB	Terrell Davis, Denver

Defense

LB	Chris Slade, New England
LB	Jason Gildon, Pittsburgh
S	Eugene Robinson, Green Bay

Special Teams

K	Eddie Murray, Minnesota
WR-PR	Robert Brooks, Green Bay
P	Craig Hentrich, Green Bay

1997 ROOKIES OF THE MONTH

Offense

September	RB	Warrick Dunn, Tampa Bay (Florida State)
October	T	Walter Jones, Seattle (Florida State)
November	QB	Jake Plummer, Arizona (Arizona State)
December	RB	Corey Dillon, Cincinnati (Washington)

Defense

LB	Peter Boulware, Baltimore (Florida State)
LB	Dexter Coakley, Dallas (Appalachian State)
CB	Paul Bradford, San Diego (Portland State)
LB	Dwayne Rudd, Minnesota (Alabama)

1997 PFW/PFWA ALL-PRO TEAM

Selected by Pro Football Weekly *and the Professional Football Writers of America*

Offense

Herman Moore, Detroit	Wide Receiver
Rob Moore, Arizona	Wide Receiver
Shannon Sharpe, Denver	Tight End
Tony Boselli, Jacksonville	Tackle
Jonathan Ogden, Baltimore	Tackle
Larry Allen, Dallas	Guard
Dave Szott, Kansas City	Guard
Dermontti Dawson, Pittsburgh	Center
Brett Favre, Green Bay	Quarterback
Terrell Davis, Denver	Running Back
Barry Sanders, Detroit	Running Back

Defense

Bruce Smith, Buffalo	End
Michael Strahan, New York Giants	End
John Randle, Minnesota	Tackle
Dana Stubblefield, San Francisco	Tackle
Jessie Armstead, New York Giants	Linebacker
Levon Kirkland, Pittsburgh	Linebacker
John Mobley, Denver	Linebacker
Deion Sanders, Dallas	Cornerback
Aeneas Williams, Arizona	Cornerback
LeRoy Butler, Green Bay	Safety
Carnell Lake, Pittsburgh	Safety

Specialists

Pete Stoyanovich, Kansas City	Kicker
Bryan Barker, Jacksonville	Punter
Michael Bates, Carolina	Kickoff Returner
Darrien Gordon, Denver	Punt Returner
Travis Jervey, Green Bay	Special Teams Player

1997 ASSOCIATED PRESS ALL-PRO TEAM

Selected by the Associated Press

Offense

Herman Moore, Detroit	Wide receiver
Rob Moore, Arizona	Wide receiver
Shannon Sharpe, Denver	Tight end
Tony Boselli, Jacksonville	Tackle
Jonathan Ogden, Baltimore	Tackle
Larry Allen, Dallas	Guard
Dave Szott, Kansas City	Guard
Dermontti Dawson, Pittsburgh	Center
Brett Favre, Green Bay	Quarterback
Terrell Davis, Denver	Running Back
Barry Sanders, Detroit	Running Back
Mike Alstott, Tampa Bay	Fullback

Defense

Bruce Smith, Buffalo	End
Michael Strahan, New York Giants	End
John Randle, Minnesota	Tackle
Dana Stubblefield, San Francisco	Tackle
Jessie Armstead, New York Giants	Linebacker
Levon Kirkland, Pittsburgh	Linebacker
John Mobley, Denver	Linebacker
Hardy Nickerson, Tampa Bay	Linebacker
Deion Sanders, Dallas	Cornerback
Aeneas Williams, Arizona	Cornerback
LeRoy Butler, Green Bay	Safety
Carnell Lake, Pittsburgh	Safety

Specialists

Richie Cunningham, Dallas	Kicker
Bryan Barker, Jacksonville	Punter
Eric Metcalf, San Diego	Kick Returner

1997 ALL-NFL TEAM

Selected by the Associated Press, Pro Football Weekly, *and the Professional Football Writers of America*

Offense

Herman Moore, Detroit (AP, PFW)	Wide Receiver
Rob Moore, Arizona (AP, PFW)	Wide Receiver
Shannon Sharpe, Denver (AP, PFW)	Tight End
Tony Boselli, Jacksonville (AP, PFW)	Tackle
Jonathan Ogden, Baltimore (AP, PFW)	Tackle
Larry Allen, Dallas (AP, PFW)	Guard
Dave Szott, Kansas City (AP, PFW)	Guard
Dermontti Dawson, Pittsburgh (AP, PFW)	Center
Brett Favre, Green Bay (AP, PFW)	Quarterback
Terrell Davis, Denver (AP, PFW)	Running Back
Barry Sanders, Detroit (AP, PFW)	Running Back
Mike Alstott, Tampa Bay (AP)	Fullback

Defense

Bruce Smith, Buffalo (AP, PFW)	End
Michael Strahan, New York Giants (AP, PFW)	End
John Randle, Minnesota (AP, PFW)	Tackle
Dana Stubblefield, San Francisco (AP, PFW)	Tackle
Jessie Armstead, New York Giants (AP, PFW)	Linebacker
Levon Kirkland, Pittsburgh (AP, PFW)	Linebacker
John Mobley, Denver (AP, PFW)	Linebacker
Hardy Nickerson, Tampa Bay (AP)	Linebacker
Deion Sanders, Dallas (AP, PFW)	Cornerback
Aeneas Williams, Arizona (AP, PFW)	Cornerback
LeRoy Butler, Green Bay (AP, PFW)	Safety
Carnell Lake, Pittsburgh (AP, PFW)	Safety

Specialists

Richie Cunningham, Dallas (AP)	Kicker
Pete Stoyanovich, Kansas City (PFW)	Kicker
Bryan Barker, Jacksonville (AP, PFW)	Punter
Michael Bates, Carolina (PFW)	Kickoff Returner
Eric Metcalf, San Diego (AP)	Kick Returner
Darrien Gordon, Denver (PFW)	Punt Returner
Travis Jervey, Green Bay (PFW)	Special Teams Player

1997 ALL-PRO TEAMS

1997 FOOTBALL NEWS ALL-AFC TEAM

Selected by Football News

Offense

Tim Brown, Oakland	Wide Receiver
Yancey Thigpen, Pittsburgh	Wide Receiver
Ben Coates, New England	Tight End
Tony Boselli, Jacksonville	Tackle
Jonathan Ogden, Baltimore	Tackle
Bruce Matthews, Tennessee	Guard
Will Shields, Kansas City	Guard
Dermontti Dawson, Pittsburgh	Center
John Elway, Denver	Quarterback
Jerome Bettis, Pittsburgh	Running Back
Terrell Davis, Denver	Running Back

Defense

Mike Sinclair, Seattle	End
Bruce Smith, Buffalo	End
Joel Steed, Pittsburgh	Tackle
Ted Washington, Buffalo	Tackle
Levon Kirkland, Pittsburgh	Linebacker
Chris Slade, New England	Linebacker
Dale Carter, Kansas City	Cornerback
Aaron Glenn, New York Jets	Cornerback
Carnell Lake, Pittsburgh	Safety
Darryl Williams, Seattle	Safety

Specialists

Adam Vinatieri, New England	Kicker
Leo Araguz, Oakland	Punter
Tamarick Vanover, Kansas City	Kickoff Returner
Darrien Gordon, Denver	Punt Returner

1997 FOOTBALL NEWS ALL-NFC TEAM

Selected by Football News

Offense

Cris Carter, Minnesota	Wide Receiver
Herman Moore, Detroit	Wide Receiver
Wesley Walls, Carolina	Tight End
William Roaf, New Orleans	Tackle
Todd Steussie, Minnesota	Tackle
Larry Allen, Dallas	Guard
Randall McDaniel, Minnesota	Guard
Kevin Glover, Detroit	Center
Brett Favre, Green Bay	Quarterback
Dorsey Levens, Green Bay	Running Back
Barry Sanders, Detroit	Running Back

Defense

Michael Strahan, New York Giants	End
Reggie White, Green Bay	End
John Randle, Minnesota	Tackle
Dana Stubblefield, San Francisco	Tackle
Jessie Armstead, New York Giants	Linebacker
Derrick Brooks, Tampa Bay	Linebacker
Hardy Nickerson, Tampa Bay	Linebacker
Deion Sanders, Dallas	Cornerback
Aeneas Williams, Arizona	Cornerback
LeRoy Butler, Green Bay	Safety
Merton Hanks, San Francisco	Safety

Specialists

Jason Hanson, Detroit	Kicker
Matt Turk, Washington	Punter
Michael Bates, Carolina	Kickoff Returner
Karl Williams, Tampa Bay	Punt Returner

1997 PFW/PFWA ALL-ROOKIE TEAM

Selected by Pro Football Weekly *and the Professional Football Writers of America*

Offense

Reidel Anthony, Tampa Bay	Wide Receiver
Rae Carruth, Carolina	Wide Receiver
Tony Gonzalez, Kansas City	Tight End
Walter Jones, Seattle	Tackle
Ross Verba, Green Bay	Tackle
Tarik Glenn, Indianapolis	Guard
Frank Middleton, Tampa Bay	Guard
Calvin Collins, Atlanta	Center
Jake Plummer, Arizona	Quarterback
Corey Dillon, Cincinnati	Running Back
Warrick Dunn, Tampa Bay	Running Back

Defense

Darrell Russell, Oakland	End
Jason Taylor, Miami	End
Antonio Anderson, Dallas	Tackle
Renaldo Wynn, Jacksonville	Tackle
Peter Boulware, Baltimore	Linebacker
Dexter Coakley, Dallas	Linebacker
Matt Russell, Detroit	Linebacker
Shawn Springs, Seattle	Cornerback
Bryant Westbrook, Detroit	Cornerback
Sam Garnes, New York Giants	Safety
Sammy Knight, New Orleans	Safety

Specialists

John Hall, New York Jets	Kicker
Ken Walter, Carolina	Punter
Byron Hanspard, Atlanta	Kickoff Returner
Leon Johnson, New York Jets	Punt Returner
Randy Kinder, Philadelphia	Special Teams Player

TEN BEST RUSHING PERFORMANCES, 1997

		Att.	Yards	TD
1.	Corey Dillon Cincinnati vs. Tennessee, Dec. 4	39	246	4
2.	Napoleon Kaufman Oakland vs. Denver, Oct. 19	28	227	1
3.	Eddie George Tennessee vs. Oakland, Aug. 31	35	216	1
	Barry Sanders Detroit vs. Indianapolis, Nov. 23	24	216	2
5.	Terrell Davis Denver vs. Cincinnati, Sept. 21	27	215	1
	Barry Sanders Detroit vs. Tampa Bay, Oct. 12	24	215	2
7.	Terrell Davis Denver vs. Buffalo, Oct. 26	42	207	1
8.	Curtis Martin New England vs. N.Y. Jets, Sept. 14	40	199	1
9.	Dorsey Levens Green Bay vs. Dallas, Nov. 23	33	190	1
10.	Barry Sanders Detroit vs. N.Y. Jets, Dec. 21	23	184	1

100-YARD RUSHING PERFORMANCES, 1997

First Week

Eddie George, Tennessee — 216 yards vs. Oakland
Robert Smith, Minnesota — 169 yards vs. Buffalo
Terry Allen, Washington — 141 yards vs. Carolina
Anthony Johnson, Carolina — 134 yards vs. Washington
Adrian Murrell, N.Y. Jets — 131 yards vs. Seattle
Lawrence Phillips, St. Louis — 125 yards vs. New Orleans
Raymont Harris, Chicago — 122 yards vs. Green Bay
Terrell Davis, Denver — 101 yards vs. Kansas City

Second Week

Jerome Bettis, Pittsburgh — 134 yards vs. Washington
Emmitt Smith, Dallas — 132 yards vs. Arizona
Warrick Dunn, Tampa Bay — 130 yards vs. Detroit
Curtis Martin, New England — 121 yards vs. Indianapolis
Terrell Davis, Denver — 107 yards vs. Seattle
Eddie George, Tennessee — 106 yards vs. Miami

Third Week

Curtis Martin, New England — 199 yards vs. N.Y. Jets
Barry Sanders, Detroit — 161 yards vs. Chicago
Napoleon Kaufman, Oakland — 140 yards vs. Atlanta
Dorsey Levens, Green Bay — 121 yards vs. Miami
Adrian Murrell, N.Y. Jets — 110 yards vs. New England
Ricky Watters, Philadelphia — 106 yards vs. Dallas
Terrell Davis, Denver — 103 yards vs. St. Louis
Warrick Dunn, Tampa Bay — 101 yards vs. Minnesota

Fourth Week

Terrell Davis, Denver — 215 yards vs. Cincinnati
Mario Bates, New Orleans — 162 yards vs. Detroit
Robert Smith, Minnesota — 132 yards vs. Green Bay
Antowain Smith, Buffalo — 129 yards vs. Indianapolis
Napoleon Kaufman, Oakland — 126 yards vs. N.Y. Jets
Jerome Bettis, Pittsburgh — 114 yards vs. Jacksonville
Barry Sanders, Detroit — 113 yards vs. New Orleans
Ki-Jana Carter, Cincinnati — 104 yards vs. Denver

Fifth Week

Napoleon Kaufman, Oakland — 162 yards vs. St. Louis
Adrian Murrell, N.Y. Jets — 156 yards vs. Cincinnati
Garrison Hearst, San Francisco — 141 yards vs. Carolina
Barry Sanders, Detroit — 139 yards vs. Green Bay
Robert Smith, Minnesota — 125 yards vs. Philadelphia
Terry Allen, Washington — 122 yards vs. Jacksonville
Raymont Harris, Chicago — 120 yards vs. Dallas
Dorsey Levens, Green Bay — 107 yards vs. Detroit

Sixth Week

Gary Brown, San Diego — 181 yards vs. Oakland
Terrell Davis, Denver — 171 yards vs. New England
Steve Broussard, Seattle — 138 yards vs. Tennessee
Jerome Bettis, Pittsburgh — 137 yards vs. Baltimore
Warrick Dunn, Tampa Bay — 125 yards vs. Green Bay
Eddie George, Tennessee — 116 yards vs. Seattle
Barry Sanders, Detroit — 107 yards vs. Buffalo
Ricky Watters, Philadelphia — 104 yards vs. Washington

Seventh Week

Barry Sanders, Detroit — 215 yards vs. Tampa Bay
Jerome Bettis, Pittsburgh — 164 yards vs. Indianapolis
Robert Smith, Minnesota — 120 yards vs. Carolina
Eddie George, Tennessee — 106 yards vs. Cincinnati
Tyrone Wheatley, N.Y. Giants — 103 yards vs. Arizona
James Stewart, Jacksonville — 102 yards vs. Philadelphia
Raymont Harris, Chicago — 101 yards vs. Green Bay

Eighth Week

Napoleon Kaufman, Oakland — 227 yards vs. Denver
Jerome Bettis, Pittsburgh — 135 yards vs. Cincinnati
Eddie George, Tennessee — 125 yards vs. Washington
Karim Abdul-Jabbar, Miami — 108 yards vs. Baltimore
Garrison Hearst, San Francisco — 105 yards vs. Atlanta
Barry Sanders, Detroit — 105 yards vs. N.Y. Giants

Ninth Week

Terrell Davis, Denver — 207 yards vs. Buffalo
Byron (Bam) Morris, Baltimore — 176 yards vs. Washington
Gary Brown, San Diego — 169 yards vs. Indianapolis
Emmitt Smith, Dallas — 126 yards vs. Philadelphia
Napoleon Kaufman, Oakland — 112 yards vs. Seattle
Raymont Harris, Chicago — 106 yards vs. Miami
Tshimanga Biakabutuka, Carolina — 104 yards vs. Atlanta
Dorsey Levens, Green Bay — 100 yards vs. New England

Tenth Week

Jamal Anderson, Atlanta — 159 yards vs. St. Louis
Fred Lane, Carolina — 147 yards vs. Oakland
Byron (Bam) Morris, Baltimore — 130 yards vs. N.Y. Jets
Terry Allen, Washington — 125 yards vs. Chicago
Corey Dillon, Cincinnati — 123 yards vs. San Diego
Barry Sanders, Detroit — 105 yards vs. Green Bay
Garrison Hearst, San Francisco — 104 yards vs. Dallas
Curtis Martin, New England — 104 yards vs. Minnesota
Jerome Bettis, Pittsburgh — 103 yards vs. Kansas City
Terrell Davis, Denver — 101 yards vs. Seattle

Eleventh Week

Eddie George, Tennessee — 122 yards vs. N.Y. Giants
Jerome Bettis, Pittsburgh — 114 yards vs. Baltimore
Marshall Faulk, Indianapolis — 110 yards vs. Cincinnati
Barry Sanders, Detroit — 105 yards vs. Washington
Terrell Davis, Denver — 104 yards vs. Carolina
Karim Abdul-Jabbar, Miami — 103 yards vs. N.Y. Jets

Twelfth Week

Jay Graham, Baltimore — 154 yards vs. Philadelphia
Terrell Davis, Denver — 127 yards vs. Kansas City
Marshall Faulk, Indianapolis — 116 yards vs. Green Bay
Charles Way, N.Y. Giants — 114 yards vs. Arizona
Napoleon Kaufman, Oakland — 109 yards vs. San Diego
Barry Sanders, Detroit — 108 yards vs. Minnesota
Dorsey Levens, Green Bay — 103 yards vs. Indianapolis
Jerome Bettis, Pittsburgh — 101 yards vs. Cincinnati

Thirteenth Week

Barry Sanders, Detroit — 216 yards vs. Indianapolis
Dorsey Levens, Green Bay — 190 yards vs. Dallas
Raymont Harris, Chicago — 116 yards vs. Tampa Bay

1997 BEST PERFORMANCES

Fourteenth Week

Terrell Davis, Denver	178 yards vs. San Diego
Barry Sanders, Detroit	167 yards vs. Chicago
Jerome Bettis, Pittsburgh	142 yards vs. Arizona
Warrick Dunn, Tampa Bay	120 yards vs. N.Y. Giants
Corey Dillon, Cincinnati	114 yards vs. Philadelphia
Fred Lane, Carolina	112 yards vs. New Orleans
Eddie George, Tennessee	110 yards vs. Dallas
Dorsey Levens, Green Bay	108 yards vs. Minnesota
Thurman Thomas, Buffalo	104 yards vs. N.Y. Jets

Fifteenth Week

Corey Dillon, Cincinnati	246 yards vs. Tennessee
Fred Lane, Carolina	138 yards vs. Dallas
Barry Sanders, Detroit	137 yards vs. Miami
Marshall Faulk, Indianapolis	133 yards vs. N.Y. Jets
Jerome Bettis, Pittsburgh	125 yards vs. Denver
Tiki Barber, N.Y. Giants	114 yards vs. Philadelphia

Sixteenth Week

Barry Sanders, Detroit	138 yards vs. Minnesota
Eddie George, Tennessee	129 yards vs. Baltimore
Corey Dillon, Cincinnati	127 yards vs. Dallas
Fred Lane, Carolina	119 yards vs. Green Bay
Robert Smith, Minnesota	101 yards vs. Detroit

Seventeenth Week

Barry Sanders, Detroit	184 yards vs. N.Y. Jets
Robert Smith, Minnesota	160 yards vs. Indianapolis
Jamal Anderson, Atlanta	152 yards vs. Arizona
Warrick Dunn, Tampa Bay	119 yards vs. Chicago
Charlie Garner, Philadelphia	115 yards vs. Washington
Jerald Moore, St. Louis	113 yards vs. Carolina
Marshall Faulk, Indianapolis	102 yards vs. Minnesota

Times 100 or More (121)
Sanders, 14; Bettis, Davis, 10; George, 8; Kaufman, Levens, R. Smith, 6; Dunn, Harris, 5; Dillon, Faulk, Lane, 4; Allen, Hearst, Martin, Murrell, 3; Abdul-Jabbar, Anderson, Brown, Morris, E. Smith, Watters, 2.

TEN BEST PASSING PERFORMANCES, 1997

		Att.	Comp.	Yards	TD
1.	Warren Moon Seattle vs. Oakland, Oct. 26	44	28	409	5
2.	Tony Banks St. Louis vs. Atlanta, Nov. 2	34	23	401	2
3.	Dan Marino Miami vs. New England, Nov. 23	60	38	389	0
4.	Jake Plummer Arizona vs. N.Y. Giants, Nov. 16	33	22	388	1
5.	Boomer Esiason Cincinnati vs. Philadelphia, Nov. 30	47	27	378	4
6.	Jeff George Oakland vs. N.Y. Jets, Sept. 21	38	26	374	3
7.	Dan Marino Miami vs. N.Y. Jets, Oct. 12	38	27	372	2
8.	Brett Favre Green Bay vs. Indianapolis, Nov. 16	25	18	363	3
9.	Stan Humphries San Diego vs. Baltimore, Sept. 28	26	17	358	3
10.	Troy Aikman Dallas vs. Tennessee, Nov. 27	42	27	356	2

300-YARD PASSING PERFORMANCES, 1997

First Week

Drew Bledsoe, New England	340 yards vs. San Diego
Vinny Testaverde, Baltimore	322 yards vs. Jacksonville

Second Week

Scott Mitchell, Detroit	331 yards vs. Tampa Bay
Dan Marino, Miami	324 yards vs. Tennessee
Jeff Blake, Cincinnati	317 yards vs. Baltimore
Elvis Grbac, Kansas City	312 yards vs. Oakland

Third Week

Brad Johnson, Minnesota	334 yards vs. Tampa Bay

Fourth Week

Jeff George, Oakland	374 yards vs. N.Y. Jets
Steve Young, San Francisco	336 yards vs. Atlanta
Kerry Collins, Carolina	328 yards vs. Kansas City
Vinny Testaverde, Baltimore	318 yards vs. Tennessee
Mark Brunell, Jacksonville	306 yards vs. Pittsburgh
Drew Bledsoe, New England	301 yards vs. Chicago

Fifth Week

Stan Humphries, San Diego	358 yards vs. Baltimore
Kent Graham, Arizona	339 yards vs. Tampa Bay

Sixth Week

Troy Aikman, Dallas	317 yards vs. N.Y. Giants

Seventh Week

Dan Marino, Miami	372 yards vs. N.Y. Jets
Neil O'Donnell, N.Y. Jets	319 yards vs. Miami

Eighth Week

Vinny Testaverde, Baltimore	331 yards vs. Miami
John Elway, Denver	309 yards vs. Oakland

Ninth Week

Warren Moon, Seattle	409 yards vs. Oakland
Erik Kramer, Chicago	343 yards vs. Miami
Kordell Stewart, Pittsburgh	317 yards vs. Jacksonville

Tenth Week

Tony Banks, St. Louis	401 yards vs. Atlanta
Drew Bledsoe, New England	313 yards vs. Minnesota
Jeff George, Oakland	304 yards vs. Carolina

Eleventh Week

Glenn Foley, N.Y. Jets	322 yards vs. Miami
Rich Gannon, Kansas City	314 yards vs. Jacksonville
Brett Favre, Green Bay	306 yards vs. St. Louis

Twelfth Week

Jake Plummer, Arizona	388 yards vs. N.Y. Giants
Brett Favre, Green Bay	363 yards vs. Indianapolis
Erik Kramer, Chicago	354 yards vs. N.Y. Jets
Paul Justin, Indianapolis	340 yards vs. Green Bay
Thirteenth Week	
Dan Marino, Miami	389 yards vs. New England
Brad Johnson, Minnesota	312 yards vs. N.Y. Jets
Fourteenth Week	
Boomer Esiason, Cincinnati	378 yards vs. Philadelphia
Troy Aikman, Dallas	356 yards vs. Tennessee
Mark Brunell, Jacksonville	317 yards vs. Baltimore
Bobby Hoying, Philadelphia	313 yards vs. Cincinnati
Jim Harbaugh, Indianapolis	310 yards vs. New England
Fifteenth Week	
Jake Plummer, Arizona	337 yards vs. Washington
Dan Marino, Miami	310 yards vs. Detroit
Kordell Stewart, Pittsburgh	303 yards vs. Denver
Eric Zeier, Baltimore	302 yards vs. Seattle
Sixteenth Week	
Mark Brunell, Jacksonville	317 yards vs. Buffalo
Seventeenth Week	
Eric Zeier, Baltimore	349 yards vs. Cincinnati

Times 300 or More (46)
Marino, 4; Bledsoe, Brunell, Testaverde, 3; Aikman, Favre, George, Johnson, Kramer, Plummer, Stewart, Zeier, 2.

TEN BEST RECEIVING PERFORMANCES, 1997

		No.	Yards	TD
1.	Isaac Bruce St. Louis vs. Atlanta, Nov. 2	10	233	2
2.	Yancey Thigpen Pittsburgh vs. Jacksonville, Oct. 26	11	196	0
3.	Frank Sanders Arizona vs. N.Y. Giants, Nov. 16	9	188	1
	Rob Moore Arizona vs. Pittsburgh, Nov. 30	8	188	0
5.	Yancey Thigpen Pittsburgh vs. Denver, Dec. 7	6	175	3
6.	Shannon Sharpe Denver vs. Carolina, Nov. 9	8	174	0
7.	Johnnie Morton Detroit vs. Miami, Dec. 7	9	171	1
8.	Antonio Freeman Green Bay vs. Carolina, Dec. 14	10	166	2
9.	Jimmy Smith Jacksonville vs. Pittsburgh, Sept. 22	10	164	1
	Robert Brooks Green Bay vs. Detroit, Sept. 28	9	164	0
	Ricky Proehl Chicago vs. Detroit, Nov. 27	4	164	1
	Tim Brown Oakland vs. Jacksonville, Dec. 21	14	164	0

100-YARD RECEIVING PERFORMANCES, 1997

First Week

Tim Brown, Oakland	158 yards vs. Tennessee
Michael Irvin, Dallas	153 yards vs. Pittsburgh
Michael Jackson, Baltimore	143 yards vs. Jacksonville
Andre Reed, Buffalo	142 yards vs. Minnesota
Michael Timpson, Philadelphia	125 yards vs. N.Y. Giants
Rod Smith, Denver	122 yards vs. Kansas City
Cris Carter, Minnesota	121 yards vs. Buffalo
Herman Moore, Detroit	115 yards vs. Atlanta
Jimmy Smith, Jacksonville	106 yards vs. Baltimore
Frank Sanders, Arizona	105 yards vs. Cincinnati
Jeff Graham, N.Y. Jets	100 yards vs. Seattle
Second Week	
Andre Rison, Kansas City	162 yards vs. Oakland
Tim Brown, Oakland	155 yards vs. Kansas City
Wesley Walls, Carolina	147 yards vs. Atlanta
O.J. McDuffie, Miami	135 yards vs. Tennessee
Irving Fryar, Philadelphia	125 yards vs. Green Bay
Jake Reed, Minnesota	118 yards vs. Chicago
Jimmy Smith, Jacksonville	117 yards vs. N.Y. Giants
Rob Moore, Arizona	108 yards vs. Dallas
Cris Carter, Minnesota	107 yards vs. Chicago
Tim Tindale, Buffalo	105 yards vs. N.Y. Jets
Derrick Alexander, Baltimore	104 yards vs. Cincinnati
Barry Sanders, Detroit	102 yards vs. Tampa Bay
Johnnie Morton, Detroit	102 yards vs. Tampa Bay
Third Week	
Jake Reed, Minnesota	131 yards vs. Tampa Bay
Rod Smith, Denver	126 yards vs. St. Louis
Andre Reed, Buffalo	113 yards vs. Kansas City
Charles Jordan, Miami	100 yards vs. Green Bay
Fourth Week	
Jimmy Smith, Jacksonville	164 yards vs. Pittsburgh
Tim Brown, Oakland	153 yards vs. N.Y. Jets
James Jett, Oakland	148 yards vs. N.Y. Jets
Carl Pickens, Cincinnati	125 yards vs. Denver
Jermaine Lewis, Baltimore	124 yards vs. Tennessee
Troy Brown, New England	124 yards vs. Chicago
Antonio Freeman, Green Bay	122 yards vs. Minnesota

1997 BEST PERFORMANCES

Jake Reed, Minnesota	119 yards vs. Green Bay
Herman Moore, Detroit	111 yards vs. New Orleans
Rae Carruth, Carolina	110 yards vs. Kansas Ctiy
Joey Galloway, Seattle	106 yards vs. San Diego
Warrick Dunn, Tampa Bay	106 yards vs. Miami
Fifth Week	
Robert Brooks, Green Bay	164 yards vs. Detroit
Tony Martin, San Diego	155 yards vs. Baltimore
Rob Moore, Arizona	147 yards vs. Tampa Bay
Jake Reed, Minnesota	134 yards vs. Philadelphia
Irving Fryar, Philadelphia	120 yards vs. Minnesota
Shannon Sharpe, Denver	119 yards vs. Atlanta
Amp Lee, St. Louis	109 yards vs. Oakland
Rickey Dudley, Oakland	106 yards vs. St. Louis
Herman Moore, Detroit	105 yards vs. Green Bay
Michael Irvin, Dallas	105 yards vs. Chicago
Sixth Week	
Yancey Thigpen, Pittsburgh	162 yards vs. Baltimore
Rod Smith, Denver	130 yards vs. New England
Randal Hill, New Orleans	121 yards vs. Chicago
Herman Moore, Detroit	116 yards vs. Buffalo
Rob Moore, Arizona	108 yards vs. Minnesota
Napoleon Kaufman, Oakland	100 yards vs. San Diego
Seventh Week	
Irving Fryar, Philadelphia	124 yards vs. Jacksonville
Herman Moore, Detroit	120 yards vs. Tampa Bay
Rae Carruth, Carolina	107 yards vs. Minnesota
Horace Copeland, Tampa Bay	105 yards vs. Detroit
Wayne Chrebet, N.Y. Jets	104 yards vs. Miami
Eighth Week	
Chris Calloway, N.Y. Giants	145 yards vs. Detroit
Troy Brown, New England	125 yards vs. N.Y. Jets
Keenan McCardell, Jacksonville	120 yards vs. Dallas
Yancey Thigpen, Pittsburgh	120 yards vs. Cincinnati
Jermaine Lewis, Baltimore	105 yards vs. Miami
Rob Moore, Arizona	101 yards vs. Philadelphia
Ninth Week	
Yancey Thigpen, Pittsburgh	196 yards vs. Jacksonville
Terry Glenn, New England	163 yards vs. Green Bay
O.J. McDuffie, Miami	137 yards vs. Chicago
Joey Galloway, Seattle	117 yards vs. Oakland
Tim Brown, Oakland	107 yards vs. Seattle
Terrance Mathis, Atlanta	107 yards vs. Carolina
James McKnight, Seattle	100 yards vs. Oakland
Derrick Alexander, N.Y. Giants	100 yards vs. Cincinnati
Curtis Conway, Chicago	100 yards vs. Miami
Tenth Week	
Isaac Bruce, St. Louis	233 yards vs. Atlanta
Tim Brown, Oakland	163 yards vs. Carolina
Cris Carter, Minnesota	116 yards vs. New England
Robert Smith, Denver	114 yards vs. Seattle
Bert Emanuel, Atlanta	108 yards vs. St. Louis
Shawn Jefferson, New England	108 yards vs. Minnesota
Eleventh Week	
Shannon Sharpe, Denver	174 yards vs. Carolina
Antonio Freeman, Green Bay	160 yards vs. St. Louis
Irving Fryar, Philadelphia	138 yards vs. San Francisco
Ricky Proehl, Chicago	132 yards vs. Minnesota
Yancey Thigpen, Pittsburgh	130 yards vs. Baltimore
Rickey Dudley, Oakland	116 yards vs. New Orleans
Jimmy Smith, Jacksonville	112 yards vs. Kansas City
Dedric Ward, N.Y. Jets	108 yards vs. Miami
Amp Lee, St. Louis	104 yards vs. Green Bay
Tony Martin, San Diego	100 yards vs. Seattle
Twelfth Week	
Frank Sanders, Arizona	188 yards vs. N.Y. Giants
Jimmy Smith, Jacksonville	158 yards vs. Tennessee

Rob Moore, Arizona	139 yards vs. N.Y. Giants
Herman Moore, Detroit	130 yards vs. Minnesota
Derrick Mayes, Green Bay	119 yards vs. Indianapolis
Ricky Proehl, Chicago	118 yards vs. N.Y. Jets
Robert Smith, Denver	114 yards vs. Kansas City
Yancey Thigpen, Pittsburgh	101 yards vs. Cincinnati
Thirteenth Week	
Jake Reed, Minnesota	150 yards vs. N.Y. Jets
Shannon Sharpe, Denver	147 yards vs. Oakland
Michael Westbrook, Washington	125 yards vs. N.Y. Giants
Irving Fryar, Philadelphia	116 yards vs. Pittsburgh
Rob Moore, Arizona	112 yards vs. Baltimore
O.J. McDuffie, Miami	110 yards vs. New England
Keenan McCardell, Jacksonville	109 yards vs. Cincinnati
Wesley Walls, Carolina	106 yards vs. St. Louis
Charles Johnson, Pittsburgh	106 yards vs. Philadelphia
Jimmy Smith, Jacksonville	106 yards vs. Cincinnati
Cris Carter, Minnesota	105 yards vs. N.Y. Jets
Keyshawn Johnson, N.Y. Jets	104 yards vs. Minnesota
Quinn Early, Buffalo	103 yards vs. Tennessee
Fourteenth Week	
Rob Moore, Arizona	188 yards vs. Pittsburgh
Ricky Proehl, Chicago	164 yards vs. Detroit
Amp Lee, St. Louis	128 yards vs. Washington
Tim Brown, Oakland	125 yards vs. Miami
Irving Fryar, Philadelphia	122 yards vs. Cincinnati
Sean Dawkins, Indianapolis	120 yards vs. New England
Johnnie Morton, Detroit	120 yards vs. Chicago
Michael Irvin, Dallas	118 yards vs. Tennessee
James Hundon, Cincinnati	118 yards vs. Philadelphia
Andre Rison, Kansas City	117 yards vs. San Francisco
Ed McCaffrey, Denver	111 yards vs. San Diego
Charles Jordan, Miami	106 yards vs. Oakland
Raghib Ismail, Carolina	102 yards vs. New Orleans
Fifteenth Week	
Yancey Thigpen, Pittsburgh	175 yards vs. Denver
Johnnie Morton, Detroit	171 yards vs. Miami
Keenan McCardell, Jacksonville	152 yards vs. New England
Derrick Alexander, Baltimore	150 yards vs. Seattle
Isaac Bruce, St. Louis	144 yards vs. New Orleans
Andre Hastings, New Orleans	120 yards vs. St. Louis
Robert Smith, Denver	115 yards vs. Pittsburgh
Curtis Conway, Chicago	115 yards vs. Buffalo
Rob Moore, Arizona	114 yards vs. Washington
Eric Metcalf, San Diego	109 yards vs. Atlanta
Sixteenth Week	
Antonio Freeman, Green Bay	166 yards vs. Carolina
Randal Hill, New Orleans	124 yards vs. Arizona
Michael Irvin, Dallas	117 yards vs. Cincinnati
Darnay Scott, Cincinnati	112 yards vs. Dallas
Curtis Conway, Chicago	109 yards vs. St. Louis
Ken Dilger, Indianapolis	100 yards vs. Miami
Chris Sanders, Tennessee	100 yards vs. Baltimore
Seventeenth Week	
Tim Brown, Oakland	164 yards vs. Jacksonville
Shannon Sharpe, Denver	162 yards vs. San Diego
Darnay Scott, Cincinnati	129 yards vs. Baltimore
Quinn Early, Buffalo	120 yards vs. Green Bay
Keenan McCardell, Jacksonville	116 yards vs. Oakland
Derrick Alexander, Baltimore	111 yards vs. Cincinnati
Joey Galloway, Seattle	101 yards vs. San Francisco

Times 100 or More (150)
R. Moore, 8; Tim Brown, 7; Fryar, H. Moore, J. Smith, R. Smith, Thigpen, 6; Reed, 5; Carter, Irvin, McCardell, Sharpe, 4; Alexander, Conway, Freeman, Galloway, Lee, McCardell, McDuffie, Morton, Proehl, 3; Troy Brown, Bruce, Carruth, Dudley, Early, Hill, Jordan, Lewis, Martin, Reed, Rison, F. Sanders, Scott, Walls 2.

TOP QUARTERBACK SACK PERFORMANCES, 1997

(2.5 or More Sacks Per Game Needed to Qualify)

First Week	
Warren Sapp, Tampa Bay	2.5 vs. San Francisco
Michael Strahan, N.Y. Giants	2.5 vs. Philadelphia
Second Week	
Bryce Paup, Buffalo	3.0 vs. N.Y. Jets
Third Week	
Chad Brown, Seattle	3.0 vs. Indianapolis
Andre Royal, Carolina	3.0 vs. San Diego
Chris Slade, New England	3.0 vs. N.Y. Jets
Fourth Week	
Wayne Martin, New Orleans	3.5 vs. Detroit
Tony Bennett, Indianapolis	3.0 vs. Buffalo
Fifth Week	
Brad Culpepper, Tampa Bay	3.0 vs. Arizona
Sixth Week	
Kelvin Pritchett, Jacksonville	3.0 vs. Cincinnati
Maa Tanuvasa, Denver	3.0 vs. New England
Seventh Week	
Chuck Smith, Atlanta	5.0 vs. New Orleans
Travis Hall, Atlanta	3.0 vs. New Orleans
John Randle, Minnesota	3.0 vs. Carolina
Eighth Week	
Bruce Smith, Buffalo	2.5 vs. Indianapolis
Ninth Week	
Leslie O'Neal, St. Louis	4.0 vs. Kansas City
Rhett Hall, Philadelphia	3.5 vs. Dallas
Kenny Holmes, Tennessee	3.0 vs. Arizona
Tenth Week	
None	
Eleventh Week	
Dana Stubblefield, San Francisco	3.5 vs. Philadelphia
Brad Culpepper, Tampa Bay	3.0 vs. Atlanta
Twelfth Week	
Michael McCrary, Baltimore	3.0 vs. Philadelphia
Michael Strahan, N.Y. Giants	3.0 vs. Arizona
Thirteenth Week	
Ken Harvey, Washington	4.0 vs. N.Y. Giants
Robert Porcher, Detroit	3.5 vs. Indianapolis
Tracy Scroggins, Detroit	3.0 vs. Indianapolis
Lester Archambeau, Atlanta	2.5 vs. New Orleans
Shane Dronett, Atlanta	2.5 vs. New Orleans
Fourteenth Week	
Carnell Lake, Pittsburgh	3.0 vs. Arizona
Reggie White, Green Bay	2.5 vs. Minnesota
Fifteenth Week	
Chris Doleman, San Francisco	3.5 vs. Minnesota
Ellis Johnson, Indianapolis	3.0 vs. N.Y. Jets
Sixteenth Week	
John Randle, Minnesota	3.0 vs. Detroit
Derrick Thomas, Kansas City	3.0 vs. San Diego
Seventeenth Week	
Gerald Dixon, Cincinnati	3.0 vs. Baltimore

1997 TEAM STATISTICS

AMERICAN FOOTBALL CONFERENCE OFFENSE

	Balt.	Buff.	Cin.	Den.	Ind.	Jax.	K.C.	Mia.	N.E.	NYJ	Oak.	Pitt.	S.D.	Sea.	Tenn.
First Downs	292	268	310	340	301	308	315	311	267	291	263	326	251	331	288
Rushing	99	98	104	138	109	103	129	87	71	97	74	154	70	98	130
Passing	176	144	171	172	171	187	163	199	173	173	170	157	160	207	136
Penalty	17	26	35	30	21	18	23	25	23	21	19	15	21	26	22
Rushes	420	422	452	520	450	454	529	430	398	431	360	572	409	404	541
Net Yds. Gained	1589	1782	1966	2378	1727	1720	2171	1343	1464	1485	1588	2479	1416	1800	2414
Avg. Gain	3.8	4.2	4.3	4.6	3.8	3.8	4.1	3.1	3.7	3.4	4.4	4.3	3.5	4.5	4.5
Avg. Yds. per Game	99.3	111.4	122.9	148.6	107.9	107.5	135.7	83.9	91.5	92.8	99.3	154.9	88.5	112.5	150.9
Passes Attempted	586	546	504	513	523	504	493	576	532	564	529	466	565	609	420
Completed	338	293	302	287	317	313	281	332	321	319	294	253	291	359	220
% Completed	57.7	53.7	59.9	55.9	60.6	62.1	57.0	57.6	60.3	56.6	55.6	54.3	51.5	58.9	52.4
Total Yds. Gained	3929	3213	3603	3704	3560	3922	3129	3945	3808	3555	3944	3215	3475	4187	2704
Times Sacked	37	46	46	35	62	40	32	22	30	48	58	20	51	36	32
Yds. Lost	227	338	287	210	418	218	236	153	258	313	430	152	386	228	199
Net Yds. Gained	3702	2875	3316	3494	3142	3704	2893	3792	3550	3242	3514	3063	3089	3959	2505
Avg. Yds. per Game	231.4	179.7	207.3	218.4	196.4	231.5	180.8	237.0	221.9	202.6	219.6	191.4	193.1	247.4	156.6
Net Yds. per Pass Play	5.94	4.86	6.03	6.38	5.37	6.81	5.51	6.34	6.32	5.30	5.99	6.30	5.01	6.14	5.54
Yds. Gained per Comp.	11.62	10.97	11.93	12.91	11.23	12.53	11.14	11.88	11.86	11.14	13.41	12.71	11.94	11.66	12.29
Combined Net Yds. Gained	5291	4657	5282	5872	4869	5424	5064	5135	5014	4727	5102	5542	4505	5759	4919
% Total Yds. Rushing	30.0	38.3	37.2	40.5	35.5	31.7	42.9	26.2	29.2	31.4	31.1	44.7	31.4	31.3	49.1
% Total Yds. Passing	70.0	61.7	62.8	59.5	64.5	68.3	57.1	73.8	70.8	68.6	68.9	55.3	68.6	68.7	50.9
Avg. Yds. per Game	330.7	291.1	330.1	367.0	304.3	339.0	316.5	320.9	313.4	295.4	318.9	346.4	281.6	359.9	307.4
Ball Control Plays	1043	1014	1002	1068	1035	998	1054	1028	960	1043	947	1058	1025	1049	993
Avg. Yds. per Play	5.1	4.6	5.3	5.5	4.7	5.4	4.8	5.0	5.2	4.5	5.4	5.2	4.4	5.5	5.0
Avg. Time of Poss.	28:30	27:59	27:56	32:07	32:56	29:40	31:16	30:29	28:08	29:42	26:24	32:05	29:22	30:47	31:27
Third Down Efficiency	36.1	25.0	41.1	42.4	37.9	39.2	41.3	37.8	40.4	38.2	31.9	44.7	32.9	40.6	42.0
Had Intercepted	16	25	9	11	17	9	10	12	15	10	10	19	21	21	13
Yds. Opp Returned	118	359	26	193	285	184	148	307	213	100	192	270	387	372	48
Ret. by Opp. for TD	0	3	0	1	0	2	0	4	2	0	2	0	3	4	0
Punts	83	91	81	60	67	66	83	68	79	75	93	64	90	78	74
Yds. Punted	3540	3764	3471	2598	3034	2964	3489	2962	3569	3212	4189	2729	3972	3144	3081
Avg. Yds. per Punt	42.7	41.4	42.9	43.3	45.3	44.9	42.0	43.6	45.2	42.8	45.0	42.6	44.1	40.3	41.6
Punt Returns	42	39	26	41	31	36	35	32	45	59	27	32	47	37	32
Yds. Returned	564	346	201	555	248	412	383	335	467	674	210	222	489	248	244
Avg. Yds. per Return	13.4	8.9	7.7	13.5	8.0	11.4	10.9	10.5	10.4	11.4	7.8	6.9	10.4	6.7	7.6
Returned for TD	2	0	0	3	0	0	1	0	0	1	0	0	3	0	0
Kickoff Returns	71	78	74	54	68	58	54	63	53	54	81	67	75	76	58
Yds. Returned	1435	1538	1708	1203	1442	1233	1345	1298	1337	1236	1699	1493	1613	1550	1150
Avg. Yds. per Return	20.2	19.7	23.1	22.3	21.2	21.3	24.9	20.6	25.2	22.9	21.0	22.3	21.5	20.4	19.8
Returned for TD	0	0	1	0	0	1	1	0	1	2	0	1	1	0	0
Fumbles	37	39	25	25	23	17	21	23	17	27	25	25	30	26	31
Lost	17	17	13	10	11	11	10	8	7	12	14	14	14	11	13
Out of Bounds	3	1	2	3	3	2	2	2	1	2	1	2	0	3	3
Own Rec. for TD	0	0	0	0	0	0	0	1	0	0	0	1	1	0	0
Opp. Rec. by	11	7	10	13	13	15	13	17	13	7	12	13	11	16	17
Opp. Rec. for TD	0	0	1	2	2	1	1	2	0	0	2	1	2	3	2
Penalties	101	92	98	116	106	110	121	93	99	83	117	95	129	109	103
Yds. Penalized	777	742	877	1006	880	914	1035	783	845	678	976	861	1101	911	814
Total Points Scored	326	255	355	472	313	394	375	339	369	348	324	372	266	365	333
Total TDs	35	26	46	55	31	43	42	37	42	38	41	44	27	43	36
TDs Rushing	7	12	23	18	10	20	15	18	6	10	9	19	5	13	17
TDs Passing	25	14	21	27	16	20	20	16	31	20	29	22	12	26	15
TDs on Ret. and Rec.	3	0	2	10	5	3	7	3	5	8	3	3	10	4	4
Extra Point Kicks	32	21	41	50	21	41	35	33	40	36	33	40	26	37	32
Extra Point Kicks Att.	32	21	43	50	21	41	36	33	40	36	35	40	27	37	32
2Pt Conversions	2	2	1	4	4	1	2	0	0	0	2	1	0	1	2
2Pt Conversions Att.	3	5	3	5	10	2	6	4	2	2	6	2	0	6	4
Safeties	1	1	0	0	1	0	3	0	1	0	1	0	0	1	0
Field Goals Made	26	24	12	28	32	31	26	28	25	28	13	22	26	22	27
Field Goals Attempted	34	30	16	39	41	36	27	36	29	41	22	25	31	28	35
% Successful	76.5	80.0	75.0	71.8	78.0	86.1	96.3	77.8	86.2	68.3	59.1	88.0	83.9	78.6	77.1

AMERICAN FOOTBALL CONFERENCE DEFENSE

	Balt.	Buff.	Cin.	Den.	Ind.	Jax.	K.C.	Mia.	N.E.	NYJ	Oak.	Pitt.	S.D.	Sea.	Tenn.
First Downs	306	265	351	258	280	318	278	299	322	301	345	285	308	286	292
Rushing	101	85	141	83	95	107	94	106	114	103	121	82	92	96	79
Passing	180	160	188	145	163	190	158	176	183	177	199	177	181	166	193
Penalty	25	20	22	30	22	21	26	17	25	21	25	26	35	24	20
Rushes	470	493	514	381	438	455	413	443	436	470	525	403	453	455	414
Net Yds. Gained	1690	1792	2223	1803	2034	1734	1621	1813	1616	1899	2246	1318	1698	1731	1573
Avg. Gain	3.6	3.6	4.3	4.7	4.6	3.8	3.9	4.1	3.7	4.0	4.3	3.3	3.7	3.8	3.8
Avg. Yds. per Game	105.6	112.0	138.9	112.7	127.1	108.4	101.3	113.3	101.0	118.7	140.4	82.4	106.1	108.2	98.3
Passes Attempted	556	502	542	526	453	532	507	530	619	558	552	554	568	462	543
Completed	332	287	309	290	261	320	271	329	368	304	324	295	297	276	321
% Completed	59.7	57.2	57.0	55.1	57.6	60.2	53.5	62.1	59.5	54.5	58.7	53.2	52.3	59.7	59.1
Total Yds. Gained	3966	3405	3668	3166	3067	3835	3618	3782	3772	3663	4109	3681	3632	3356	3898
Times Sacked	42	46	35	44	37	48	54	31	45	29	31	48	27	42	35
Yds. Lost	293	344	209	298	247	331	359	231	303	242	239	294	164	238	240
Net Yds. Gained	3673	3061	3459	2868	2820	3504	3259	3551	3469	3421	3870	3387	3468	3118	3658
Avg. Yds. per Game	229.6	191.3	216.2	179.3	176.3	219.0	203.7	221.9	216.8	213.8	241.9	211.7	216.8	194.9	228.6
Net Yds. per Pass Play	6.14	5.59	5.99	5.03	5.76	6.04	5.81	6.33	5.22	5.83	6.64	5.63	5.83	6.19	6.33
Yds. Gained per Comp.	11.95	11.86	11.87	10.92	11.75	11.98	13.35	11.50	10.25	12.05	12.68	12.48	12.23	12.16	12.14
Combined Net Yds. Gained	5363	4853	5682	4671	4854	5238	4880	5364	5085	5320	6116	4705	5166	4849	5231
% Total Yds. Rushing	31.5	36.9	39.1	38.6	41.9	33.1	33.2	33.8	31.8	35.7	36.7	28.0	32.9	35.7	30.1
% Total Yds. Passing	68.5	63.1	60.9	61.4	58.1	66.9	66.8	66.2	68.2	64.3	63.3	72.0	67.1	64.3	69.9
Avg. Yds. per Game	335.2	303.3	355.1	291.9	303.4	327.4	305.0	335.3	317.8	332.5	382.3	294.1	322.9	303.1	326.9
Ball Control Plays	1068	1041	1091	951	928	1035	974	1004	1100	1057	1108	1005	1048	959	992
Avg. Yds. per Play	5.0	4.7	5.2	4.9	5.2	5.1	5.0	5.3	4.6	5.0	5.5	4.7	4.9	5.1	5.3
Avg. Time of Poss.	31:30	32:01	32:04	27:53	27:04	30:20	28:44	29:31	31:52	30:18	33:36	27:55	30:38	29:13	28:33
Third Down Efficiency	40.3	35.4	44.9	31.4	41.7	45.1	31.6	42.8	38.6	31.6	39.0	44.7	38.5	33.3	39.0
Intercepted By	17	15	13	18	12	14	21	10	19	18	10	20	15	13	14
Yds. Returned By	241	157	183	319	234	145	432	92	366	379	149	253	257	196	328
Returned for TD	1	0	0	5	2	0	4	0	4	4	1	0	3	1	2
Punts	82	86	69	94	64	73	84	63	74	92	77	66	85	74	69
Yds. Punted	3611	3608	3082	4091	2948	3060	3468	2679	3288	3862	3035	2804	3702	3111	3007
Avg. Yds. per Punt	44.0	42.0	44.7	43.5	46.1	41.9	41.3	42.5	44.4	42.0	39.4	42.5	43.6	42.0	43.6
Punt Returns	53	44	35	26	43	29	39	43	38	47	52	23	39	38	36
Yds. Returned	460	366	407	235	491	241	255	323	437	459	431	271	416	463	430
Avg. Yds. per Return	8.7	8.3	11.6	9.0	11.4	8.3	6.5	7.5	11.5	9.8	8.3	11.8	10.7	12.2	11.9
Returned for TD	0	0	2	1	0	0	0	0	0	0	0	0	0	2	0
Kickoff Returns	58	55	67	89	64	77	80	53	75	54	48	74	63	77	71
Yds. Returned	1323	1385	1406	1827	1544	1730	1672	1018	1651	1134	1124	1556	1517	1779	1528
Avg. Yds. per Return	22.8	25.2	21.0	20.5	24.1	22.5	20.9	19.2	22.0	21.0	23.4	21.0	24.1	23.1	21.5
Returned for TD	1	3	0	0	1	0	0	0	1	0	0	1	1	1	0
Fumbles	23	23	23	27	23	26	30	31	30	27	26	26	21	33	32
Lost	11	7	10	13	13	15	13	17	13	7	12	14	11	16	18
Out of Bounds	2	3	2	1	0	3	2	3	2	0	2	5	3	5	4
Own Rec. for TD	0	0	0	0	0	0	0	0	0	1	0	0	0	0	1
Opp. Rec. by	16	17	12	10	11	11	10	8	7	12	14	14	14	11	13
Opp. Rec. for TD	1	3	1	3	1	1	0	0	0	0	1	0	2	2	1
Penalties	106	98	107	130	102	90	113	92	106	99	117	90	101	100	94
Yds. Penalized	828	992	951	1118	861	800	977	892	763	832	977	708	784	820	830
Total Points Scored	345	367	405	287	401	318	232	327	289	287	419	307	425	362	310
Total TDs	39	37	48	35	46	39	23	36	33	33	44	31	50	38	35
TDs Rushing	17	11	15	10	18	12	8	9	16	9	19	5	12	10	12
TDs Passing	20	17	30	20	26	24	15	23	14	23	21	24	31	19	21
TDs on Ret. and Rec.	2	9	3	5	2	3	0	4	3	1	4	2	7	9	2
Extra Point Kicks	33	34	45	35	42	31	22	30	29	27	37	28	46	35	34
Extra Point Kicks Att.	35	35	45	35	44	32	22	32	29	28	37	28	46	35	34
2Pt Conversions	2	0	0	0	0	1	0	2	1	2	2	2	1	2	0
2Pt Conversions Att.	4	2	3	0	2	6	1	4	4	5	7	3	4	3	1
Safeties	1	0	0	0	1	0	0	1	0	2	0	1	1	1	0
Field Goals Made	24	37	24	14	27	17	24	25	20	18	38	29	25	31	22
Field Goals Attempted	34	46	29	19	31	25	33	35	29	27	43	35	26	34	30
% Successful	70.6	80.4	82.8	73.7	87.1	68.0	72.7	71.4	69.0	66.7	88.4	82.9	96.2	91.2	73.3

1997 TEAM STATISTICS

NATIONAL FOOTBALL CONFERENCE OFFENSE

	Ariz.	Atl.	Car.	Chi.	Dall.	Det.	G.B.	Minn.	N.O.	NYG	Phil.	St.L.	S.F.	T.B.	Wash.
First Downs	295	281	284	305	279	304	325	293	229	273	326	271	294	249	300
Rushing	79	88	91	94	82	120	103	96	78	113	105	85	106	88	86
Passing	186	168	170	188	170	166	191	177	127	124	203	161	167	134	192
Penalty	30	25	23	23	27	18	31	20	24	36	18	25	21	27	22
Rushes	395	442	441	490	423	447	459	449	417	521	465	443	523	479	453
Net Yds. Gained	1255	1643	1770	1746	1637	2464	1909	2041	1461	1988	1943	1563	1969	1934	1615
Avg. Gain	3.2	3.7	4.0	3.6	3.9	5.5	4.2	4.5	3.5	3.8	4.2	3.5	3.8	4.0	3.6
Avg. Yds. per Game	78.4	102.7	110.6	109.1	102.3	154.0	119.3	127.6	91.3	124.3	121.4	97.7	123.1	120.9	100.9
Passes Attempted	602	484	534	595	553	540	523	540	458	474	587	526	432	404	547
Completed	317	273	289	336	314	304	309	319	228	249	330	271	278	224	283
% Completed	52.7	56.4	54.1	56.5	56.8	56.3	59.1	59.1	49.8	52.5	56.2	51.5	64.4	55.4	51.7
Total Yds. Gained	3953	3445	3156	3501	3454	3605	3896	3537	2901	2763	4009	3524	3432	2638	3581
Times Sacked	78	54	44	43	39	41	26	33	50	32	64	44	44	32	33
Yds. Lost	495	372	311	257	313	271	191	224	317	238	362	326	289	196	198
Net Yds. Gained	3458	3073	2845	3244	3141	3334	3705	3313	2584	2525	3647	3198	3143	2442	3383
Avg. Yds. per Game	216.1	192.1	177.8	202.8	196.3	208.4	231.6	207.1	161.5	157.8	227.9	199.9	196.4	152.6	211.4
Net Yds. per Pass Play	5.09	5.71	4.92	5.08	5.31	5.74	6.75	5.78	5.09	4.99	5.60	5.61	6.60	5.60	5.83
Yds. Gained per Comp.	12.47	12.62	10.92	10.42	11.00	11.86	12.61	11.09	12.72	11.10	12.15	13.00	12.35	11.78	12.65
Combined Net Yds. Gained	4713	4716	4615	4990	4778	5798	5614	5354	4045	4513	5590	4761	5112	4376	4998
% Total Yds. Rushing	26.6	34.8	38.4	35.0	34.3	42.5	34.0	38.1	36.1	44.1	34.8	32.8	38.5	44.2	32.3
% Total Yds. Passing	73.4	65.2	61.6	65.0	65.7	57.5	66.0	61.9	63.9	55.9	65.2	67.2	61.5	55.8	67.7
Avg. Yds. per Game	294.6	294.8	288.4	311.9	298.6	362.4	350.9	334.6	252.8	282.1	349.4	297.6	319.5	273.5	312.4
Ball Control Plays	1075	980	1019	1128	1015	1028	1008	1022	925	1027	1116	1013	999	915	1033
Avg. Yds. per Play	4.4	4.8	4.5	4.4	4.7	5.6	5.6	5.2	4.4	4.4	5.0	4.7	5.1	4.8	4.8
Avg. Time of Poss.	29:02	31:29	29:43	33:08	29:53	28:37	30:05	29:46	27:47	29:27	31:09	29:47	32:28	29:22	29:27
Third Down Efficiency	35.1	35.2	44.0	36.0	36.2	35.3	39.6	39.5	26.1	31.2	37.2	32.7	36.4	38.7	42.3
Had Intercepted	22	11	24	22	12	17	16	16	33	12	16	15	11	12	22
Yds. Opp Returned	289	124	265	328	211	191	305	166	342	230	425	85	169	370	262
Ret. by Opp. for TD	2	1	2	1	1	2	3	0	1	2	4	0	2	4	1
Punts	92	89	85	96	86	86	75	81	88	112	88	95	79	84	85
Yds. Punted	4028	3498	3604	4077	3592	3576	3378	3407	4038	4531	3660	3985	3182	3578	3788
Avg. Yds. per Punt	43.8	39.3	42.4	42.5	41.8	41.6	45.0	42.1	45.9	40.5	41.6	41.9	40.3	42.6	44.6
Punt Returns	41	52	41	46	47	48	56	34	48	47	31	40	41	51	38
Yds. Returned	461	483	310	321	512	433	515	444	496	455	234	274	482	645	442
Avg. Yds. per Return	11.2	9.3	7.6	7.0	10.9	9.0	9.2	13.1	10.3	9.7	7.5	6.9	11.8	12.6	11.6
Returned for TD	0	0	0	0	1	0	0	0	0	1	0	0	1	1	1
Kickoff Returns	70	51	64	79	63	59	49	65	58	51	69	68	50	51	59
Yds. Returned	1696	1198	1500	1694	1520	1364	1119	1414	1374	963	1520	1454	1133	1075	1283
Avg. Yds. per Return	24.2	23.5	23.4	21.4	24.1	23.1	22.8	21.8	23.7	18.9	22.0	21.4	22.7	21.1	21.7
Returned for TD	0	2	0	0	0	0	0	0	1	0	1	0	1	0	1
Fumbles	27	34	30	33	23	26	24	16	34	23	35	29	22	31	21
Lost	20	13	15	19	11	11	16	6	22	7	16	15	9	11	7
Out of Bounds	0	5	4	2	2	3	1	1	0	4	2	3	0	3	2
Own Rec. for TD	0	0	0	0	0	0	0	0	0	0	0	1	0	0	0
Opp. Rec. by	5	10	11	17	12	8	11	15	15	17	12	14	16	13	14
Opp. Rec. for TD	0	0	0	0	2	2	3	2	1	0	1	1	2	0	1
Penalties	93	101	94	107	116	94	93	97	101	116	104	142	115	77	78
Yds. Penalized	775	773	763	867	1058	866	718	800	811	1005	866	1065	979	660	639
Total Points Scored	283	320	265	263	304	379	422	354	237	307	317	299	375	299	327
Total TDs	32	36	28	28	29	43	50	42	24	35	36	32	41	38	40
TDs Rushing	9	8	11	14	6	19	9	14	9	14	11	15	16	15	12
TDs Passing	19	26	17	14	19	19	35	26	13	16	22	14	20	21	22
TDs on Ret. and Rec.	4	2	0	0	4	5	6	2	2	5	3	3	5	2	6
Extra Point Kicks	28	35	25	20	24	39	48	33	22	27	33	32	38	32	39
Extra Point Kicks Att.	29	35	25	20	24	40	48	34	22	29	33	32	38	35	39
2Pt Conversions	3	0	2	5	2	1	1	6	1	1	1	0	2	0	0
2Pt Conversions Att.	3	1	3	8	5	3	2	8	2	5	3	0	3	3	0
Safeties	0	0	1	1	0	1	0	0	0	1	0	0	0	0	0
Field Goals Made	19	23	22	21	34	26	24	19	23	22	22	25	29	13	16
Field Goals Attempted	29	27	26	26	38	29	30	27	27	32	31	37	36	17	24
% Successful	65.5	85.2	84.6	80.8	89.5	89.7	80.0	70.4	85.2	68.8	71.0	67.6	80.6	76.5	66.7

NATIONAL FOOTBALL CONFERENCE DEFENSE

	Ariz.	Atl.	Car.	Chi.	Dall.	Det.	G.B.	Minn.	N.O.	NYG	Phil.	St.L.	S.F.	T.B.	Wash.
First Downs	298	274	290	281	281	268	288	325	280	310	286	296	242	265	292
Rushing	112	76	112	97	104	98	105	104	95	82	115	84	67	96	129
Passing	167	180	163	156	139	152	156	195	168	195	150	177	145	155	149
Penalty	19	18	15	28	38	18	27	26	17	33	21	35	30	14	14
Rushes	524	409	497	421	511	471	443	442	496	432	476	440	386	420	508
Net Yds. Gained	2180	1666	1973	1858	1994	1833	1876	1983	1764	1451	2009	1687	1366	1617	2212
Avg. Gain	4.2	4.1	4.0	4.4	3.9	3.9	4.2	4.5	3.6	3.4	4.2	3.8	3.5	3.9	4.4
Avg. Yds. per Game	136.3	104.1	123.3	116.1	124.6	114.6	117.3	123.9	110.3	90.7	125.6	105.4	85.4	101.1	138.3
Passes Attempted	491	496	490	476	473	507	563	542	518	596	490	543	509	518	513
Completed	279	275	260	273	253	281	288	336	293	325	259	288	258	325	267
% Completed	56.8	55.4	53.1	57.4	53.5	55.4	51.2	62.0	56.6	54.5	52.9	53.0	50.7	62.7	52.0
Total Yds. Gained	3461	3794	3253	3289	2717	3401	3225	3957	3289	3957	3201	3675	3011	3342	3098
Times Sacked	34	55	36	38	38	43	41	44	59	54	43	38	54	44	37
Yds. Lost	215	354	246	259	195	287	274	253	408	341	278	296	364	331	280
Net Yds. Gained	3246	3440	3007	3030	2522	3114	2951	3704	2881	3616	2923	3379	2647	3011	2818
Avg. Yds. per Game	202.9	215.0	187.9	189.4	157.6	194.6	184.4	231.5	180.1	226.0	182.7	211.2	165.4	188.2	176.1
Net Yds. per Pass Play	6.18	6.24	5.72	5.89	4.94	5.66	4.89	6.32	4.99	5.56	5.48	5.82	4.70	5.36	5.12
Yds. Gained per Comp.	12.41	13.80	12.51	12.05	10.74	12.10	11.20	11.78	11.23	12.18	12.36	12.76	11.67	10.28	11.60
Combined Net Yds. Gained	5426	5106	4980	4888	4516	4947	4827	5687	4645	5067	4932	5066	4013	4628	5030
% Total Yds. Rushing	40.2	32.6	39.6	38.0	44.2	37.1	38.9	34.9	38.0	28.6	40.7	33.3	34.0	34.9	44.0
% Total Yds. Passing	59.8	67.4	60.4	62.0	55.8	62.9	61.1	65.1	62.0	71.4	59.3	66.7	66.0	65.1	56.0
Avg. Yds. per Game	339.1	319.1	311.3	305.5	282.3	309.2	301.7	355.4	290.3	316.7	308.3	316.6	250.8	289.3	314.4
Ball Control Plays	1049	960	1023	935	1022	1021	1047	1028	1073	1082	1009	1021	949	982	1058
Avg. Yds. per Play	5.2	5.3	4.9	5.2	4.4	4.8	4.6	5.5	4.3	4.7	4.9	5.0	4.2	4.7	4.8
Avg. Time of Poss.	30:58	28:31	30:17	26:52	30:07	31:23	29:55	30:14	32:13	30:33	28:51	30:13	27:32	30:38	30:33
Third Down Efficiency	34.2	36.6	36.9	31.7	38.2	36.0	33.2	41.5	40.5	34.4	36.9	35.3	34.7	34.1	33.3
Intercepted By	15	18	11	13	7	17	21	12	16	27	14	25	25	13	16
Yds. Returned By	231	114	72	60	130	309	329	141	194	503	186	281	366	95	222
Returned for TD	3	0	0	0	1	3	3	0	0	4	1	1	1	0	3
Punts	94	90	88	81	95	97	90	70	92	89	87	82	83	88	95
Yds. Punted	4130	3835	3756	3526	4142	4296	3828	2932	3668	3748	3603	3648	3473	3661	4038
Avg. Yds. per Punt	43.9	42.6	42.7	43.5	43.6	44.3	42.5	41.9	39.9	42.1	41.4	44.5	41.8	41.6	42.5
Punt Returns	40	21	38	52	40	51	32	49	50	40	48	60	41	42	33
Yds. Returned	441	55	428	727	365	434	255	566	706	378	515	618	307	388	237
Avg. Yds. per Return	11.0	2.6	11.3	14.0	9.1	8.5	8.0	11.6	14.1	9.5	10.7	10.3	7.5	9.2	7.2
Returned for TD	1	0	2	2	0	1	0	1	1	0	1	1	0	0	0
Kickoff Returns	42	52	55	52	65	61	78	67	51	49	66	54	82	44	67
Yds. Returned	945	1167	1276	1237	1172	1269	1599	1398	1139	1163	1548	1262	1746	957	1515
Avg. Yds. per Return	22.5	22.4	23.2	23.8	18.0	20.8	20.5	20.9	22.3	23.7	23.5	23.4	21.3	21.8	22.6
Returned for TD	1	0	1	0	0	0	0	0	0	1	0	1	0	1	0
Fumbles	16	27	26	25	27	24	25	31	31	33	25	27	24	21	36
Lost	5	10	11	17	12	8	11	15	15	17	12	14	16	13	14
Out of Bounds	1	3	2	1	1	3	2	3	2	2	0	2	1	0	2
Own Rec. for TD	0	0	1	0	0	0	0	0	1	0	0	0	0	0	0
Opp. Rec. by	20	13	15	19	11	11	16	6	22	7	16	15	9	11	7
Opp. Rec. for TD	1	2	1	4	3	0	1	0	0	0	2	1	1	1	1
Penalties	113	115	97	93	99	112	114	81	110	122	86	133	91	93	96
Yds. Penalized	981	872	757	763	757	841	945	668	895	1056	708	1064	742	814	849
Total Points Scored	379	361	314	421	314	306	282	359	327	265	372	359	265	263	289
Total TDs	42	45	36	50	36	33	30	42	35	30	43	39	31	29	32
TDs Rushing	13	18	12	18	12	15	16	13	11	17	16	10	5	10	15
TDs Passing	23	24	17	25	20	15	10	28	21	10	20	26	23	13	14
TDs on Ret. and Rec.	6	3	7	7	4	3	4	1	3	3	7	3	3	6	3
Extra Point Kicks	35	39	35	45	34	29	18	36	33	26	42	31	29	25	28
Extra Point Kicks Att.	37	39	35	45	34	30	18	37	33	27	42	31	29	25	28
2Pt Conversions	1	4	0	2	2	1	6	1	0	1	0	7	0	4	3
2Pt Conversions Att.	3	6	1	5	2	2	12	5	2	3	1	8	2	4	4
Safeties	0	1	0	0	0	1	0	0	0	0	0	1	1	1	0
Field Goals Made	30	14	21	24	20	25	24	23	28	19	24	26	16	18	21
Field Goals Attempted	35	20	25	32	27	32	30	30	36	25	33	31	20	29	25
% Successful	85.7	70.0	84.0	75.0	74.1	78.1	80.0	76.7	77.8	76.0	72.7	83.9	80.0	62.1	84.0

1997 TEAM STATISTICS

AFC, NFC, AND NFL SUMMARY

	AFC Offense Total	AFC Offense Average	AFC Defense Total	AFC Defense Average	NFC Offense Total	NFC Offense Average	NFC Defense Total	NFC Defense Average	NFL Total	NFL Average
First Downs	4462	297.5	4494	299.6	4308	287.2	4276	285.1	8770	292.3
Rushing	1561	104.1	1499	99.9	1414	94.3	1476	98.4	2975	99.2
Passing	2559	170.6	2636	175.7	2524	168.3	2447	163.1	5083	169.4
Penalty	342	22.8	359	23.9	370	24.7	353	23.5	712	23.7
Rushes	6792	452.8	6763	450.9	6847	456.5	6876	458.4	13639	454.6
Net Yds. Gained	27322	1821.5	26791	1786.1	26938	1795.9	27469	1831.3	54260	1808.7
Avg. Gain	—	4.0	—	4.0	—	3.9	—	4.0	—	4.0
Avg. Yds. per Game	—	113.8	—	111.6	—	112.2	—	114.5	—	113.0
Passes Attempted	7930	528.7	8004	533.6	7799	519.9	7725	515.0	15729	524.3
Completed	4520	301.3	4584	305.6	4324	288.3	4260	284.0	8844	294.8
% Completed	—	57.0	—	57.3	—	55.4	—	55.1	—	56.2
Total Yds. Gained	53893	3592.9	54618	3641.2	51395	3426.3	50670	3378.0	105288	3509.6
Times Sacked	595	39.7	594	39.6	657	43.8	658	43.9	1252	41.7
Yds. Lost	4053	270.2	4032	268.8	4360	290.7	4381	292.1	8413	280.4
Net Yds. Gained	49840	3322.7	50586	3372.4	47035	3135.7	46289	3085.9	96875	3229.2
Avg. Yds. per Game	—	207.7	—	210.8	—	196.0	—	192.9	—	201.8
Net Yds. per Pass Play	—	5.85	—	5.88	—	5.56	—	5.52	—	5.70
Yds. Gained per Comp.	—	11.92	—	11.91	—	11.89	—	11.89	—	11.91
Combined Net Yds. Gained	77162	5144.1	77377	5158.5	73973	4931.5	73758	4917.2	151135	5037.8
% Total Yds. Rushing	—	35.4	—	34.6	—	36.4	—	37.2	—	35.9
% Total Yds. Passing	—	64.6	—	65.4	—	63.6	—	62.8	—	64.1
Avg. Yds. per Game	—	321.5	—	322.4	—	308.2	—	307.3	—	314.9
Ball Control Plays	15317	1021.1	15361	1024.1	15303	1020.2	15259	1017.3	30620	1020.7
Avg. Yds. per Play	—	5.0	—	5.0	—	4.8	—	4.8	—	4.9
Third Down Efficiency	—	38.1	—	38.6	—	36.4	—	35.9	—	37.2
Interceptions	218	14.5	229	15.3	261	17.4	250	16.7	479	16.0
Yds. Returned	3202	213.5	3731	248.7	3762	250.8	3233	215.5	6964	232.1
Returned for TD	21	1.4	27	1.8	26	1.7	20	1.3	47	1.6
Punts	1152	76.8	1152	76.8	1321	88.1	1321	88.1	2473	82.4
Yds. Punted	49718	3314.5	49356	3290.4	55922	3728.1	56284	3752.3	105640	3521.3
Avg. Yds. per Punt	—	43.2	—	42.8	—	42.3	—	42.6	—	42.7
Punt Returns	561	37.4	585	39.0	661	44.1	637	42.5	1222	40.7
Yds. Returned	5598	373.2	5685	379.0	6507	433.8	6420	428.0	12105	403.5
Avg. Yds. per Return	—	10.0	—	9.7	—	9.8	—	10.1	—	9.9
Returned for TD	10	0.7	5	0.3	5	0.3	10	0.7	15	0.5
Kickoff Returns	984	65.6	1005	67.0	906	60.4	885	59.0	1890	63.0
Yds. Returned	21280	1418.7	22194	1479.6	20307	1353.8	19393	1292.9	41587	1386.2
Avg. Yds. per Return	—	21.6	—	22.1	—	22.4	—	21.9	—	22.0
Returned for TD	8	0.5	9	0.6	6	0.4	5	0.3	14	0.5
Fumbles	391	26.1	401	26.7	408	27.2	398	26.5	799	26.6
Lost	182	12.1	190	12.7	198	13.2	190	12.7	380	12.7
Out of Bounds	30	2.0	37	2.5	32	2.1	25	1.7	62	2.1
Own Rec. for TD	3	0.2	2	0.1	1	0.1	2	0.1	4	0.1
Opp. Rec.	188	12.5	180	12.0	190	12.7	198	13.2	378	12.6
Opp. Rec. for TD	19	1.3	16	1.1	15	1.0	18	1.2	34	1.1
Penalties	1572	104.8	1545	103.0	1528	101.9	1555	103.7	3100	103.3
Yds. Penalized	13200	880.0	13133	875.5	12645	843.0	12712	847.5	25845	861.5
Total Points Scored	5206	347.1	5081	338.7	4751	316.7	4876	325.1	9957	331.9
Total TDs	586	39.1	567	37.8	534	35.6	553	36.9	1120	37.3
TDs Rushing	202	13.5	183	12.2	182	12.1	201	13.4	384	12.8
TDs Passing	314	20.9	328	21.9	303	20.2	289	19.3	617	20.6
TDs on Ret. and Rec.	70	4.7	56	3.7	49	3.3	63	4.2	119	4.0
Extra Point Kicks	518	34.5	508	33.9	475	31.7	485	32.3	993	33.1
Extra Point Kicks Att.	524	34.9	517	34.5	483	32.2	490	32.7	1007	33.6
2Pt Conversions	22	1.5	15	1.0	25	1.7	32	2.1	47	1.6
2Pt Conversions Att.	60	4.0	49	3.3	49	3.3	60	4.0	109	3.6
Safeties	9	0.6	8	0.5	4	0.3	5	0.3	13	0.4
Field Goals Made	370	24.7	375	25.0	338	22.5	333	22.2	708	23.6
Field Goals Attempted	470	31.3	476	31.7	436	29.1	430	28.7	906	30.2
% Successful	—	78.7	—	78.8	—	77.5	—	77.4	—	78.1

CLUB LEADERS

	Offense	Defense
First Downs	Den. 340	S.F. 242
Rushing	Pitt. 154	S.F. 67
Passing	Sea. 207	Dall. 139
Penalty	N.Y.G. 36	Wash. 14
Rushes	Pitt. 572	Den. 381
Net Yds. Gained	Pitt. 2479	Pitt. 1318
Avg. Gain	Det. 5.5	Pitt. 3.3
Passes Attempted	Sea. 609	Ind. 453
Completed	Sea. 359	Dall. 253
% Completed	S.F. 64.4	S.F. 50.7
Total Yds. Gained	Sea. 4187	Dall. 2717
Times Sacked	Pitt. 20	N.O. 59
Yds. Lost	Pitt. 152	N.O. 408
Net Yds. Gained	Sea. 3959	Dall. 2522
Net Yds. per Pass Play	Jax. 6.81	S.F. 4.70
Yds. Gained per Comp.	Oak. 13.41	N.E. 10.25
Combined Net Yds. Gained	Den. 5872	S.F. 4013
% Total Yds. Rushing	Tenn. 49.1	Pitt. 28.0
% Total Yds. Passing	Mia. 73.8	Dall. 55.8
Ball Control Plays	Chi. 1128	Ind. 928
Avg. Yds. per Play	Det. 5.6	S.F. 4.2
Avg. Time of Poss.	Chi. 33:08	—
Third Down Efficiency	Pitt. 44.7	Den. 31.4
Interceptions	—	N.O. 33
Yds. Returned	—	Phil. 425
Returned for TD	—	Four tied with 4
Punts	N.Y.G. 112	—
Yds. Punted	N.Y.G. 4531	—
Avg. Yds. per Punt	N.O. 45.9	—
Punt Returns	N.Y.J. 59	Atl. 21
Yds. Returned	N.Y.J. 674	Atl. 55
Avg. Yds. per Return	Den. 13.5	Atl. 2.6
Returned for TD	Den. & S.D. 3	—
Kickoff Returns	Oak. 81	Ariz. 42
Yds. Returned	Cin. 1708	Ariz. 945
Avg. Yds. per Return	N.E. 25.2	Dall. 18.0
Returned for TD	Atl. & N.Y.J. 2	—
Total Points Scored	Den. 472	K.C. 232
Total TDs	Den. 55	K.C. 23
TDs Rushing	Cin. 23	Pitt. & S.F. 5
TDs Passing	G.B. 35	G.B. & N.Y.G. 10
TDs on Ret. and Rec.	Den. & S.D. 10	K.C. 0
Extra Points	Den. 50	G.B. 18
2-Point Conversions	Minn. 6	—
Safeties	K.C. 3	—
Field Goals Made	Dall. 34	Atl. & Den. 14
Field Goals Attempted	Ind. & N.Y.J. 41	Den. 19
% Successful	K.C. 96.3	T.B. 62.1

NFL CLUB RANKINGS BY YARDS

	Offense			Defense		
	Total	Rush	Pass	Total	Rush	Pass
Arizona	24	30	10	27	27	15
Atlanta	23	19	22	20	8	20
Baltimore	9	22	5	25	10	28
Buffalo	25	14	25	9	15	12
Carolina	26	15	26	15	22	9
Chicago	17	16	15	12	19	11
Cincinnati	10	9	13	28	29	21
Dallas	20	20	20	2	24	*1
Denver	*1	4	9	5	16	5
Detroit	2	2	12	14	18	13
Green Bay	4	12	3	7	20	8
Indianapolis	19	17	19	10	26	4
Jacksonville	7	18	4	23	13	24
Kansas City	14	5	24	11	7	16
Miami	11	29	2	26	17	25
Minnesota	8	6	14	29	23	29
New England	15	26	7	19	5	23
New Orleans	30	27	27	4	14	6
New York Giants	27	7	28	18	3	26
New York Jets	22	25	16	24	21	19
Oakland	13	23	8	30	30	30
Philadelphia	5	10	6	13	25	7
Pittsburgh	6	*1	23	6	*1	18
St. Louis	21	24	17	17	9	17
San Diego	28	28	21	21	11	22
San Francisco	12	8	18	*1	2	2
Seattle	3	13	*1	8	12	14
Tampa Bay	29	11	30	3	6	10
Tennessee	18	3	29	22	4	27
Washington	16	21	11	16	28	3

* = League Leader

AFC TAKEAWAYS/GIVEAWAYS

	Takeaways			Giveaways			Net
	Int	Fum	Total	Int	Fum	Total	Diff.
Kansas City	21	13	34	10	10	20	+14
Denver	18	13	31	11	10	21	+10
New England	19	13	32	15	7	22	+10
Jacksonville	14	15	29	9	11	20	+9
Miami	10	17	27	12	8	20	+7
Tennessee	14	18	32	13	13	26	+6
New York Jets	18	7	25	10	12	22	+3
Cincinnati	13	10	23	9	13	22	+1
Pittsburgh	20	14	34	19	14	33	+1
Oakland	10	12	22	10	14	24	-2
Indianapolis	12	13	25	17	11	28	-3
Seattle	13	16	29	21	11	32	-3
Baltimore	17	11	28	16	17	33	-5
San Diego	15	11	26	21	14	35	-9
Buffalo	15	7	22	25	17	42	-20

NFC TAKEAWAYS/GIVEAWAYS

	Takeaways			Giveaways			Net
	Int	Fum	Total	Int	Fum	Total	Diff.
New York Giants	27	17	44	12	7	19	+25
San Francisco	25	16	41	11	9	20	+21
St. Louis	25	14	39	15	15	30	+9
Minnesota	12	15	27	16	6	22	+5
Atlanta	18	10	28	11	13	24	+4
Tampa Bay	13	13	26	12	11	23	+3
Washington	16	14	30	22	7	29	+1
Green Bay	21	11	32	16	16	32	0
Detroit	17	8	25	17	11	28	-3
Dallas	7	12	19	12	11	23	-4
Philadelphia	14	12	26	16	16	32	-6
Chicago	13	17	30	22	19	41	-11
Carolina	11	11	22	24	15	39	-17
Arizona	15	5	20	22	20	42	-22
New Orleans	16	15	31	33	22	55	-24

1997 INDIVIDUAL STATISTICS—SCORING

SCORING

Points
- **AFC:** 134—Mike Hollis, Jacksonville
- **NFC:** 126—Richie Cunningham, Dallas

Touchdowns
- **AFC:** 16—Karim Abdul-Jabbar, Miami
- **NFC:** 14—Barry Sanders, Detroit

Extra Points
- **NFC:** 48—Ryan Longwell, Green Bay
- **AFC:** 46—Jason Elam, Denver

Field Goals
- **NFC:** 34—Richie Cunningham, Dallas
- **AFC:** 32—Cary Blanchard, Indianapolis

Field Goal Attempts
- **AFC:** 41—Cary Blanchard, Indianapolis
  John Hall, N.Y. Jets
- **NFC:** 37—Richie Cunningham, Dallas
  Jeff Wilkins, St. Louis

Longest Field Goal
- **AFC:** 55—Steve Christie, Buffalo vs. Denver, October 26
  John Hall, N.Y. Jets at Seattle, August 31
- **NFC:** 55—Morten Andersen, Atlanta at New Orleans, October 12
  Jason Hanson, Detroit vs. Indianapolis, November 23

Most Points, Game
- **AFC:** 30—James Stewart, Jacksonville vs. Philadelphia, October 12 (5 TD)
- **NFC:** 18—by many

Team Leaders, Points

AFC: BALTIMORE: 110, Matt Stover; BUFFALO: 93, Steve Christie; CINCINNATI: 77, Doug Pelfrey; DENVER: 124, Jason Elam; INDIANAPOLIS: 117, Cary Blanchard; JACKSONVILLE: 134, Mike Hollis; KANSAS CITY: 113, Pete Stoyanovich; MIAMI: 117, Olindo Mare; NEW ENGLAND: 115, Adam Vinatieri; N.Y. JETS: 120, John Hall; OAKLAND: 72, Cole Ford, James Jett; PITTSBURGH: 106, Norm Johnson; SAN DIEGO: 78, Greg Davis; SEATTLE: 103, Todd Peterson; TENNESSEE: 113, Al Del Greco

NFC: ARIZONA: 52, Joe Nedney; ATLANTA: 104, Morten Andersen; CAROLINA: 91, John Kasay; CHICAGO: 83, Jeff Jaeger; DALLAS: 126, Richie Cunningham; DETROIT: 117, Jason Hanson; GREEN BAY: 120, Ryan Longwell; MINNESOTA: 84, Cris Carter; NEW ORLEANS: 91, Doug Brien; N.Y. GIANTS: 93, Brad Daluiso; PHILADELPHIA: 99, Chris Boniol; ST. LOUIS: 107, Jeff Wilkins; SAN FRANCISCO: 125, Gary Anderson; TAMPA BAY: 71, Michael Husted; WASHINGTON: 82, Scott Blanton

Team Champion
- **NFC:** 472—Denver
- **AFC:** 422—Green Bay

AFC SCORING—TEAM

					EXTRA PT. KICKS		2-POINT TRIES					
	TD	TDR	TDP	TDM	MADE	ATT.	MADE	ATT.	FG	FGA	SAF	PTS
Denver	55	18	27	10	50	50	4	5	28	39	0	472
Jacksonville	43	20	20	3	41	41	1	2	31	36	0	394
Kansas City	42	15	20	7	35	36	2	6	26	27	3	375
Pittsburgh	44	19	22	3	40	40	1	2	22	25	0	372
New England	42	6	31	5	40	40	0	2	25	29	1	369
Seattle	43	13	26	4	37	37	1	6	22	28	1	365
Cincinnati	46	23	21	2	41	43	1	3	12	16	0	355
N.Y. Jets	38	10	20	8	36	36	0	2	28	41	0	348
Miami	37	18	16	3	33	33	0	4	28	36	0	339
Tennessee	36	17	15	4	32	32	2	4	27	35	0	333
Baltimore	35	7	25	3	32	32	2	3	26	34	1	326
Oakland	41	9	29	3	33	35	2	6	13	22	1	324
Indianapolis	31	10	16	5	21	21	4	10	32	41	1	313
San Diego	27	5	12	10	26	27	0	0	26	31	0	266
Buffalo	26	12	14	0	21	21	2	5	24	30	1	255
AFC Total	586	202	314	70	518	524	22	60	370	470	9	5206
AFC Average	39.1	13.5	20.9	4.7	34.5	34.9	1.5	4	24.7	31.3	0.6	347.1

NFC SCORING—TEAM

					EXTRA PT. KICKS		2-POINT TRIES					
	TD	TDR	TDP	TDM	MADE	ATT.	MADE	ATT.	FG	FGA	SAF	PTS
Green Bay	50	9	35	6	48	48	1	2	24	30	0	422
Detroit	43	19	19	5	39	40	1	3	26	29	1	379
San Francisco	41	16	20	5	38	38	2	3	29	36	0	375
Minnesota	42	14	26	2	33	34	6	8	19	27	0	354
Washington	40	12	22	6	39	39	0	0	16	24	0	327
Atlanta	36	8	26	2	35	35	0	1	23	27	0	320
Philadelphia	36	11	22	3	33	33	1	3	22	31	0	317
N.Y. Giants	35	14	16	5	27	29	1	5	22	32	1	307
Dallas	29	6	19	4	24	24	2	5	34	38	0	304
St. Louis	32	15	14	3	32	32	0	0	25	37	0	299
Tampa Bay	38	15	21	2	32	35	0	3	13	17	0	299
Arizona	32	9	19	4	28	29	3	3	19	29	0	283
Carolina	28	11	17	0	25	25	2	3	22	26	1	265
Chicago	28	14	14	0	20	20	5	8	21	26	1	263
New Orleans	24	9	13	2	22	22	1	2	23	27	0	237
NFC Total	534	182	303	49	475	483	25	49	338	436	4	4751
NFC Average	35.6	12.1	20.2	3.3	31.7	32.2	1.7	3.3	22.5	29.1	0.3	316.7
NFL Total	1120	384	617	119	993	1007	47	109	708	906	13	9957
NFL Average	37.3	12.8	20.6	4	33.1	33.6	1.6	3.6	23.6	30.2	0.4	331.9

1997 INDIVIDUAL STATISTICS—SCORING

NFL TOP TEN SCORERS—NONKICKERS

	TD	TDR	TDP	TDM	2-PT	PTS
Abdul-Jabbar, Karim, Mia.	16	15	1	0	0	96
Davis, Terrell, Den.	15	15	0	0	3	96
Carter, Cris, Min.	13	0	13	0	3	84
Sanders, Barry, Det.	14	11	3	0	0	84
Levens, Dorsey, G.B.	12	7	5	0	1	74
Freeman, Antonio, G.B.	12	0	12	0	0	72
Galloway, Joey, Sea.	12	0	12	0	0	72
Jett, James, Oak.	12	0	12	0	0	72
Smith, Rod, Den.	12	0	12	0	0	72
Allen, Marcus, K.C.	11	11	0	0	0	66
Stewart, Kordell, Pit.	11	11	0	0	0	66

NFL TOP TEN SCORERS—KICKERS

	XP	XPA	FG	FGA	PTS
Hollis, Mike, Jax.	41	41	31	36	134
Cunningham, Richie, Dal.	24	24	34	37	126
Anderson, Gary, S.F.	38	38	29	36	125
Elam, Jason, Den.	46	46	26	36	124
Hall, John, NY-J	36	36	28	41	120
Longwell, Ryan, G.B.	48	48	24	30	120
Blanchard, Cary, Ind.	21	21	32	41	117
Hanson, Jason, Det.	39	40	26	29	117
Mare, Olindo, Mia.	33	33	28	36	117
Vinatieri, Adam, N.E.	40	40	25	29	115

AFC SCORERS—INDIVIDUAL

Kickers

	XP	XPA	FG	FGA	PTS
Hollis, Mike, Jax.	41	41	31	36	134
Elam, Jason, Den.	46	46	26	36	124
Hall, John, NY-J	36	36	28	41	120
Blanchard, Cary, Ind.	21	21	32	41	117
Mare, Olindo, Mia.	33	33	28	36	117
Vinatieri, Adam, N.E.	40	40	25	29	115
Del Greco, Al, Ten.	32	32	27	35	113
Stoyanovich, Pete, K.C.	35	36	26	27	113
Stover, Matt, Bal.	32	32	26	34	110
Davis, Greg, Min.-S.D.	31	32	26	34	109
Johnson, Norm, Pit.	40	40	22	25	106
Peterson, Todd, Sea.	37	37	22	28	103
Christie, Steve, Buf.	21	21	24	30	93
Pelfrey, Doug, Cin.	41	43	12	16	77
Ford, Cole, Oak.	33	35	13	22	72
Carney, John, S.D.	5	5	7	7	26
Bentley, Scott, Den.	4	4	2	3	10

Nonkickers

	TD	TDR	TDP	TDM	2-PT	PTS
Abdul-Jabbar, Karim, Mia.	16	15	1	0	0	96
Davis, Terrell, Den.	15	15	0	0	3	96
Galloway, Joey, Sea.	12	0	12	0	0	72
Jett, James, Oak.	12	0	12	0	0	72
Smith, Rod, Den.	12	0	12	0	0	72
Allen, Marcus, K.C.	11	11	0	0	0	66
Stewart, Kordell, Pit.	11	11	0	0	0	66
Dillon, Corey, Cin.	10	10	0	0	0	60
Alexander, Derrick, Bal.	9	0	9	0	0	54
Bettis, Jerome, Pit.	9	7	2	0	0	54
Means, Natrone, Jax.	9	9	0	0	0	54
Stewart, James, Jax.	9	8	1	0	0	54
Coates, Ben, N.E.	8	0	8	0	0	48
Faulk, Marshall, Ind.	8	7	1	0	0	48
Kaufman, Napoleon, Oak.	8	6	2	0	0	48
Lewis, Jermaine, Bal.	8	0	6	2	0	48
McCaffrey, Ed, Den.	8	0	8	0	0	48
McNair, Steve, Ten.	8	8	0	0	0	48
Phillips, Lawrence, St.L	8	8	0	0	0	48
Smith, Antowain, Buf.	8	8	0	0	0	48
George, Eddie, Ten.	7	6	1	0	1	44
Thigpen, Yancey, Pit.	7	0	7	0	1	44
Carter, Ki-Jana, Cin.	7	7	0	0	0	42
Dudley, Rickey, Oak.	7	0	7	0	0	42
Murrell, Adrian, NY-J	7	7	0	0	0	42
Rison, Andre, K.C.	7	0	7	0	0	42
Harrison, Marvin, Ind.	6	0	6	0	2	40
McGee, Tony, Cin.	6	0	6	0	1	38
Broussard, Steve, Sea.	6	5	1	0	0	36
Brown, Troy, N.E.	6	0	6	0	0	36
Bruener, Mark, Pit.	6	0	6	0	0	36
Martin, Tony, S.D.	6	0	6	0	0	36
McKnight, James, Sea.	6	0	6	0	0	36
Brown, Tim, Oak.	5	0	5	0	1	32
Williams, Harvey, Oak.	5	3	2	0	1	32
Early, Quinn, Buf.	5	0	5	0	0	30
Green, Eric, Bal.	5	0	5	0	0	30
Johnson, Keyshawn, NY-J	5	0	5	0	0	30
Martin, Curtis, N.E.	5	4	1	0	0	30
McCardell, Keenan, Jax.	5	0	5	0	0	30
Metcalf, Eric, S.D.	5	0	2	3	0	30
Pickens, Carl, Cin.	5	0	5	0	0	30
Reed, Andre, Buf.	5	0	5	0	0	30
Scott, Darnay, Cin.	5	0	5	0	0	30
Jackson, Michael, Bal.	4	0	4	0	1	26
Wycheck, Frank, Ten.	4	0	4	0	1	26
Brown, Gary, S.D.	4	4	0	0	0	24
Davis, Willie, Ten.	4	0	4	0	0	24
Drayton, Troy, Mia.	4	0	4	0	0	24
Gordon, Darrien, Den.	4	0	0	4	0	24
Johnson, Leon, NY-J	4	2	0	2	0	24
Mitchell, Pete, Jax.	4	0	4	0	0	24
Morris, Bam, Bal.	4	4	0	0	0	24
Smith, Jimmy, Jax.	4	0	4	0	0	24
Warren, Chris, Sea.	4	4	0	0	0	24
Sharpe, Shannon, Den.	3	0	3	0	1	20
Bailey, Aaron, Ind.	3	0	3	0	0	18
Baxter, Fred, NY-J	3	0	3	0	0	18
Blake, Jeff, Cin.	3	3	0	0	0	18
Byars, Keith, N.E.	3	0	3	0	0	18
Chrebet, Wayne, NY-J	3	0	3	0	0	18
Dilger, Ken, Ind.	3	0	3	0	0	18
Gash, Sam, N.E.	3	0	3	0	0	18
Harrison, Rodney, S.D.	3	0	0	3	0	18
Hawkins, Courtney, Pit.	3	0	3	0	0	18
Hughes, Danan, K.C.	3	0	2	1	0	18
Jordan, Charles, Mia.	3	0	3	0	0	18
McMillian, Mark, K.C.	3	0	0	3	0	18
Purnell, Lovett, N.E.	3	0	3	0	0	18
Richardson, Tony, K.C.	3	0	3	0	0	18
Sanders, Chris, Ten.	3	0	3	0	0	18
Smith, Otis, NY-J	3	0	0	3	0	18
Thomas, Rodney, Ten.	3	3	0	0	0	18
Gonzalez, Tony, K.C.	2	0	2	0	1	14
Jackson, Willie, Jax.	2	0	2	0	1	14
Riemersma, Jay, Buf.	2	0	2	0	1	14
Smith, Lamar, Sea.	2	2	0	0	1	14
Vanover, Tamarick, K.C.	2	0	0	2	1	14
Anders, Kimble, K.C.	2	0	2	0	0	12
Bieniemy, Eric, Cin.	2	1	0	1	0	12
Blackwell, Will, Pit.	2	0	1	1	0	12
Blades, Brian, Sea.	2	0	2	0	0	12
Bradford, Paul, S.D.	2	0	0	2	0	12
Brady, Kyle, NY-J	2	0	2	0	0	12
Brisby, Vincent, N.E.	2	0	2	0	0	12
Brown, Chad, Sea.	2	0	0	2	0	12
Brunell, Mark, Jax.	2	2	0	0	0	12
Dawkins, Sean, Ind.	2	0	2	0	0	12
Dawson, Lake, K.C.	2	0	2	0	0	12
Dunn, David, Cin.	2	0	2	0	0	12
Gannon, Rich, K.C.	2	2	0	0	0	12
Glenn, Terry, N.E.	2	0	2	0	0	12
Graham, Jay, Bal.	2	2	0	0	0	12
Graham, Jeff, NY-J	2	0	2	0	0	12
Green, Willie, Den.	2	0	2	0	0	12
Holmes, Darick, Buf.	2	2	0	0	0	12
Hudson, Chris, Jax.	2	0	0	2	0	12
Hundon, James, Cin.	2	0	2	0	0	12
Jackson, Greg, S.D.	2	0	0	2	0	12
Jefferson, Shawn, N.E.	2	0	2	0	0	12
Johnson, Charles, Pit.	2	0	2	0	0	12
Johnson, Lonnie, Buf.	2	0	2	0	0	12
Jones, Damon, Jax.	2	0	2	0	0	12
Jones, Freddie, S.D.	2	0	2	0	0	12
Jones, George, Pit.	2	1	1	0	0	12
McDuffie, O. J., Mia.	2	0	1	1	0	12
McPhail, Jerris, Mia.	2	1	1	0	0	12
Meggett, David, N.E.	2	1	1	0	0	12
Milne, Brian, Cin.	2	2	0	0	0	12
Popson, Ted, K.C.	2	0	2	0	0	12
Pritchard, Mike, Sea.	2	0	2	0	0	12
Robertson, Marcus, Ten.	2	0	0	2	0	12
Spikes, Irving, Mia.	2	2	0	0	0	12
Strong, Mack, Sea.	2	0	2	0	0	12
Thomas, Lamar, Mia.	2	0	2	0	0	12
Van Dyke, Alex, NY-J	2	0	2	0	0	12

1997 INDIVIDUAL STATISTICS—SCORING

	TD	TDR	TDP	TDM	2-PT	PTS
Warren, Lamont, Ind.	2	2	0	0	0	12
Stablein, Brian, Ind.	1	0	1	0	1	8
Alexander, Elijah, Ind.	1	0	0	1	0	6
Anderson, Darren, K.C.	1	0	0	1	0	6
Anderson, Richie, NY-J	1	0	1	0	0	6
Atwater, Steve, Den.	1	0	0	1	0	6
Barlow, Reggie, Jax.	1	0	0	1	0	6
Barnett, Fred, Mia.	1	0	1	0	0	6
Battaglia, Marco, Cin.	1	0	1	0	0	6
Belser, Jason, Ind.	1	0	0	1	0	6
Bennett, Donnell, K.C.	1	1	0	0	0	6
Blackmon, Robert, Ind.	1	0	0	1	0	6
Bowens, Tim, Mia.	1	0	0	1	0	6
Braxton, Tyrone, Den.	1	0	0	1	0	6
Brown, Derek, Jax.	1	0	1	0	0	6
Buckley, Terrell, Mia.	1	0	0	1	0	6
Carswell, Dwayne, Den.	1	0	1	0	0	6
Clay, Willie, N.E.	1	0	0	1	0	6
Copeland, John, Cin.	1	0	0	1	0	6
Cotton, Kenyon, Bal.	1	1	0	0	0	6
Crockett, Zack, Ind.	1	1	0	0	0	6
Crumpler, Carlester, Sea.	1	0	1	0	0	6
Cullors, Derrick, N.E.	1	0	0	1	0	6
Elway, John, Den.	1	1	0	0	0	6
Fontenot, Al, Ind.	1	0	0	1	0	6
Gildon, Jason, Pit.	1	0	0	1	0	6
Glenn, Aaron, NY-J	1	0	0	1	0	6
Grbac, Elvis, K.C.	1	1	0	0	0	6
Grier, Marrio, N.E.	1	1	0	0	0	6
Hallock, Ty, Jax.	1	0	1	0	0	6
Hartley, Frank, S.D.	1	0	1	0	0	6
Hebron, Vaughn, Den.	1	1	0	0	0	6
Hitchcock, Jimmy, N.E.	1	0	0	1	0	6
Johnson, Darrius, Den.	1	0	0	1	0	6
Johnson, Rob, Jax.	1	1	0	0	0	6
Jones, Charlie, S.D.	1	0	1	0	0	6
Kent, Joey, Ten.	1	0	1	0	0	6
Kinchen, Brian, Bal.	1	0	1	0	0	6
Kitna, Jon, Sea.	1	1	0	0	0	6
Lake, Carnell, Pit.	1	0	0	1	0	6
Langham, Antonio, Bal.	1	0	0	1	0	6
Lewis, Darryll, Ten.	1	0	0	1	0	6
Lewis, Mo, NY-J	1	0	0	1	0	6
Loville, Derek, Den.	1	1	0	0	0	6
McElroy, Ray, Ind.	1	0	0	1	0	6
Mickens, Ray, NY-J	1	0	0	1	0	6
Mobley, John, Den.	1	0	0	1	0	6
Moon, Warren, Sea.	1	1	0	0	0	6
Neal, Lorenzo, NY-J	1	0	1	0	0	6
Norgard, Erik, Ten.	1	0	1	0	0	6
O'Donnell, Neil, NY-J	1	1	0	0	0	6
Parmalee, Bernie, Mia.	1	0	1	0	0	6
Perriman, Brett, Mia.	1	0	1	0	0	6
Perry, Ed, Mia.	1	0	1	0	0	6
Russell, Derek, Ten.	1	0	1	0	0	6
Shedd, Kenny, Oak.	1	0	0	1	0	6
Sinclair, Mike, Sea.	1	0	0	1	0	6
Slade, Chris, N.E.	1	0	0	1	0	6
Smith, Detron, Den.	1	0	1	0	0	6
Thomas, Thurman, Buf.	1	1	0	0	0	6
Traylor, Keith, Den.	1	0	0	1	0	6
Truitt, Olanda, Oak.	1	0	1	0	0	6
Turner, Eric, Oak.	1	0	0	1	0	6
Van Pelt, Alex, Buf.	1	1	0	0	0	6
Walker, Denard, Ten.	1	0	0	1	0	6
Ward, Dedric, NY-J	1	0	1	0	0	6
Washington, Lionel, Oak.	1	0	0	1	0	6
Whigham, Larry, N.E.	1	0	0	1	0	6
Williams, Alfred, Den.	1	0	0	1	0	6
Williams, Darryl, Sea.	1	0	0	1	0	6
Byner, Earnest, Bal.	0	0	0	0	1	2
Hansen, Phil, Buf.	0	0	0	0	0	*2
Moulds, Eric, Buf.	0	0	0	0	1	2
Phillips, Joe, K.C.	0	0	0	0	0	*2
Pollard, Marcus, Ind.	0	0	0	0	1	2
Saleaumua, Dan, Sea.	0	0	0	0	0	*2
Smith, Anthony, Oak.	0	0	0	0	0	*2
Thomas, Derrick, K.C.	0	0	0	0	0	*2

** Safety*

Team safety credited to Tennessee, Oakland, Miami, and New England.

NFC SCORERS—INDIVIDUAL

Kickers

	XP	XPA	FG	FGA	PTS
Cunningham, Richie, Dal.	24	24	34	37	126
Anderson, Gary, S.F.	38	38	29	36	125
Longwell, Ryan, G.B.	48	48	24	30	120
Hanson, Jason, Det.	39	40	26	29	117
Wilkins, Jeff, St.L.	32	32	25	37	107
Andersen, Morten, Atl.	35	35	23	27	104
Boniol, Chris, Phi.	33	33	22	31	99
Daluiso, Brad, NY-G	27	29	22	32	93
Brien, Doug, N.O.	22	22	23	27	91
Kasay, John, Car.	25	25	22	26	91
Jaeger, Jeff, Chi.	20	20	21	26	83
Blanton, Scott, Was.	34	34	16	24	82
Husted, Michael, T.B.	32	35	13	17	71
Murray, Eddie, Min.	23	24	12	17	59
Nedney, Joe, Ariz.	19	19	11	17	52
Butler, Kevin, Ariz.	9	10	8	12	33
Jacke, Chris, Was.	5	5	0	0	5
Gowin, Toby, Dal.	0	0	0	1	0

Nonkickers

	TD	TDR	TDP	TDM	2-PT	PTS
Carter, Cris, Min.	13	0	13	0	3	84
Sanders, Barry, Det.	14	11	3	0	0	84
Levens, Dorsey, G.B.	12	7	5	0	1	74
Freeman, Antonio, G.B.	12	0	12	0	0	72
Alstott, Mike, T.B.	10	7	3	0	0	60
Anderson, Jamal, Atl.	10	7	3	0	0	60
Harris, Raymont, Chi.	10	10	0	0	0	60
Emanuel, Bert, Atl.	9	0	9	0	0	54
Irvin, Michael, Dal.	9	0	9	0	0	54
Kirby, Terry, S.F.	8	6	1	1	2	52
Moore, Herman, Det.	8	0	8	0	1	50
Moore, Rob, Ariz	8	0	8	0	1	50
Calloway, Chris, NY-G	8	0	8	0	0	48
Owens, Terrell, S.F.	8	0	8	0	0	48
Proehl, Ricky, Chi.	7	0	7	0	1	44
Brooks, Robert, G.B.	7	0	7	0	0	42
Dunn, Warrick, T.B.	7	4	3	0	0	42
Lane, Fred, Car.	7	7	0	0	0	42
Smith, Robert, Min.	7	6	1	0	0	42
Watters, Ricky, Phi.	7	7	0	0	0	42
Chmura, Mark, G.B.	6	0	6	0	0	36
Fryar, Irving, Phi.	6	0	6	0	0	36
Hearst, Garrison, S.F.	6	4	2	0	0	36
Mathis, Terance, Atl.	6	0	6	0	0	36
Morton, Johnnie, Det.	6	0	6	0	0	36
Reed, Jake, Min.	6	0	6	0	0	36
Vardell, Tommy, Det.	6	6	0	0	0	36
Walls, Wesley, Car.	6	0	6	0	0	36
Hastings, Andre, N.O.	5	0	5	0	1	32
Allen, Terry, Was.	5	4	1	0	0	30
Bruce, Isaac, St.L.	5	0	5	0	0	30
Shepherd, Leslie, Was.	5	0	5	0	0	30
Way, Charles, NY-G	5	4	1	0	0	30
Williams, Karl, T.B.	5	0	4	1	0	30
Barber, Tiki, NY-G	4	3	1	0	1	26
Sanders, Frank, Ariz.	4	0	4	0	1	26
Smith, Emmitt, Dal.	4	4	0	0	1	26
Anthony, Reidel, T.B.	4	0	4	0	0	24
Bates, Mario, N.O.	4	4	0	0	0	24
Bowie, Larry, Was.	4	2	2	0	0	24
Carruth, Rae, Car.	4	0	4	0	0	24
Conwell, Ernie, St.L.	4	0	4	0	0	24
Ellard, Henry, Was.	4	0	4	0	0	24
Floyd, William, S.F.	4	3	1	0	0	24
Gedney, Chris, Ariz.	4	0	4	0	0	24
Hoard, Leroy, Min.	4	4	0	0	0	24
Lewis, Chad, Phi.	4	0	4	0	0	24
Miller, Anthony, Dal.	4	0	4	0	0	24
Mitchell, Brian, Was.	4	1	1	2	0	24
Moore, Dave, T.B.	4	0	4	0	0	24
Stokes, J.J., S.F.	4	0	4	0	0	24
Wheatley, Tyrone, NY-G	4	4	0	0	0	24
Zellars, Ray, N.O.	4	4	0	0	0	24
Solomon, Freddie, Phi.	3	0	3	0	1	20
Davis, Stephen, Was.	3	3	0	0	0	18
Garner, Charlie, Phi.	3	3	0	0	0	18
Glover, Andrew, Min.	3	0	3	0	0	18
Hanspard, Byron, Atl.	3	0	1	2	0	18
Jenkins, James, Was.	3	0	3	0	0	18
Lee, Amp, St.L.	3	0	3	0	0	18

1997 INDIVIDUAL STATISTICS—SCORING

	TD	TDR	TDP	TDM	2-PT	PTS
Moore, Jerald, St.L.	3	3	0	0	0	18
Penn, Chris, Chi.	3	0	3	0	0	18
Rhett, Errict, T.B.	3	3	0	0	0	18
Sharper, Darren, G.B.	3	0	0	3	0	18
Turner, Kevin, Phi.	3	0	3	0	0	18
Westbrook, Michael, Was.	3	0	3	0	0	18
Young, Steve, S.F.	3	3	0	0	0	18
Engram, Bobby, Chi.	2	0	2	0	1	14
Evans, Chuck, Min.	2	2	0	0	1	14
Plummer, Jake, Ariz.	2	2	0	0	1	14
Biakabutuka, Tim, Car.	2	2	0	0	0	12
Brown, Reggie, Det.	2	0	0	2	0	12
Carrier, Mark, Car.	2	0	2	0	0	12
Centers, Larry, Ariz.	2	1	1	0	0	12
Connell, Albert, Was.	2	0	2	0	0	12
Cross, Howard, NY-G	2	0	2	0	0	12
Davis, Tyrone, G.B.	2	0	1	1	0	12
Dunn, Jason, Phi.	2	0	2	0	0	12
Frerotte, Gus, Was.	2	2	0	0	0	12
Graham, Kent, Ariz.	2	2	0	0	0	12
Greene, Scott, Car.	2	1	1	0	0	12
Guliford, Eric, N.O.	2	0	1	1	0	12
Hanks, Merton, S.F.	2	0	0	2	0	12
Hill, Randal, N.O.	2	0	2	0	0	12
Ismail, Raghib, Car.	2	0	2	0	0	12
Jones, Brent, S.F.	2	0	2	0	0	12
Kramer, Erik, Chi.	2	2	0	0	0	12
LaFleur, David, Dal.	2	0	2	0	0	12
McElroy, Leeland, Ariz.	2	2	0	0	0	12
Palmer, David, Min.	2	1	1	0	0	12
Patten, David, NY-G	2	0	2	0	0	12
Pegram, Erric, S.D.-NY-G	2	2	0	0	0	12
Poole, Keith, N.O.	2	0	2	0	0	12
Pounds, Darryl, Was.	2	0	0	2	0	12
Sanders, Deion, Dal.	2	0	0	2	0	12
Santiago, O.J., Atl.	2	0	2	0	0	12
Timpson, Michael, Phi.	2	0	2	0	0	12
Toomer, Amani, NY-G	2	0	1	1	0	12
Walker, Herschel, Dal.	2	0	2	0	0	12
Wilkins, Gabe, G.B.	2	0	0	2	0	12
Williams, Aeneas, Ariz.	2	0	0	2	0	12
Williams, Sherman, Dal.	2	2	0	0	0	12
Johnson, Brad, Min.	1	0	1	0	2	10
Autry, Darnell, Chi.	1	1	0	0	1	8
Johnson, Anthony, Car.	1	0	1	0	1	8
Mirer, Rick, Chi.	1	1	0	0	1	8
Scroggins, Tracy, Det.	1	0	0	1	0	*8
Alexander, Kevin, NY-G	1	0	1	0	0	6
Armstead, Jessie, NY-G	1	0	0	1	0	6
Asher, Jamie, Was.	1	0	1	0	0	6
Banks, Tony, St.L.	1	1	0	0	0	6
Bennett, Tommy, Ariz.	1	0	0	1	0	6
Boyd, Stephen, Det.	1	0	0	1	0	6
Brady, Jeff, Min.	1	0	0	1	0	6
Brown, Dave, NY-G	1	1	0	0	0	6
Carter, Pat, Ariz.	1	0	1	0	0	6
Case, Stoney, Ariz.	1	1	0	0	0	6
Christian, Bob, Atl.	1	0	1	0	0	6
Chryplewicz, Pete, Det.	1	0	1	0	0	6
Clark, Greg, S.F.	1	0	1	0	0	6
Clark, Willie, Phi.	1	0	0	1	0	6
Coakley, Dexter, Dal.	1	0	0	1	0	6
Collins, Kerry, Car.	1	1	0	0	0	6
Conway, Curtis, Chi.	1	0	1	0	0	6
Copeland, Horace, T.B.	1	0	1	0	0	6
Dawkins, Brian, Phi.	1	0	0	1	0	6
Detmer, Ty, Phi.	1	1	0	0	0	6
Dilfer, Trent, T.B.	1	1	0	0	0	6
Dishman, Cris, Was.	1	0	0	1	0	6
Farquhar, John, N.O.	1	0	1	0	0	6
Favre, Brett, G.B.	1	1	0	0	0	6
Fields, Mark, N.O.	1	0	0	1	0	6
Garnes, Sam, NY-G	1	0	0	1	0	6
Green, Darrell, Was.	1	0	0	1	0	6
Green, Harold, Atl.	1	1	0	0	0	6
Greene, Kevin, S.F.	1	0	0	1	0	6
Hampton, Rodney, NY-G	1	1	0	0	0	6
Hape, Patrick, T.B.	1	0	1	0	0	6
Harris, Jackie, T.B.	1	0	1	0	0	6
Hayden, Aaron, G.B.	1	1	0	0	0	6
Haynes, Michael, Atl.	1	0	1	0	0	6
Henderson, William, G.B.	1	0	1	0	0	6
Hennings, Chad, Dal.	1	0	0	1	0	6
Heyward, Craig, St.L.	1	1	0	0	0	6
Hobbs, Daryl, N.O.	1	0	1	0	0	6
Johnson, Jimmie, Phi.	1	0	1	0	0	6
Johnston, Daryl, Dal.	1	0	1	0	0	6
Kinchen, Todd, Atl.	1	0	1	0	0	6
Kozlowski, Brian, Atl.	1	0	1	0	0	6
Laing, Aaron, St.L.	1	0	1	0	0	6
Levy, Chuck, S.F.	1	0	0	1	0	6
McNeil, Ryan, St.L.	1	0	0	1	0	6
Mickens, Terry, G.B.	1	0	1	0	0	6
Mills, Ernie, Car.	1	0	1	0	0	6
Mitchell, Scott, Det.	1	1	0	0	0	6
Moore, Ronald, St.L.	1	1	0	0	0	6
O'Neal, Leslie, St.L.	1	0	0	1	0	6
Rice, Jerry, S.F.	1	0	1	0	0	6
Rivers, Ron, Det.	1	1	0	0	0	6
Schlesinger, Cory, Det.	1	0	1	0	0	6
Schroeder, Bill, G.B.	1	0	1	0	0	6
Seay, Mark, Phi.	1	0	1	0	0	6
Sehorn, Jason, NY-G	1	0	0	1	0	6
Shuler, Heath, N.O.	1	1	0	0	0	6
Singleton, Alshermond, T.B.	1	0	0	1	0	6
Small, Torrance, St.L.	1	0	1	0	0	6
Smith, Cedric, Ariz.	1	1	0	0	0	6
Smith, Irv, N.O.	1	0	1	0	0	6
Thomas, Orlando, Min.	1	0	0	1	0	6
Thomas, William, Phi.	1	0	0	1	0	6
Thomason, Jeff, G.B.	1	0	1	0	0	6
Thompson, David, St.L.	1	1	0	0	0	6
Walsh, Chris, Min.	1	0	1	0	0	6
West, Ed, Atl.	1	0	1	0	0	6
Westbrook, Bryant, Det.	1	0	0	1	0	6
Wetnight, Ryan, Chi.	1	0	1	0	0	6
Wiegert, Zach, St.L.	1	0	0	1	0	6
Williams, Kevin, Ariz.	1	0	1	0	0	6
Williams, Moe, Min.	1	1	0	0	0	6
Williams, Stepfret, Dal.	1	0	1	0	0	6
Wilson, Bernard, Ariz.	1	0	0	1	0	6
Wooten, Tito, NY-G	1	0	0	1	0	6
Bjornson, Eric, Dal.	0	0	0	0	1	2
Flanigan, Jim, Chi.	0	0	0	0	1	2
Muhammad, Muhsin, Car.	0	0	0	0	1	2
Stone, Dwight, Car.	0	0	0	0	0	*2

** Safety*
Team safety credited to Chicago, N.Y. Giants.

FIELD GOALS

Field Goal Percentage
- **AFC:** .963—Pete Stoyanovich, Kansas City
- **NFC:** .919—Richie Cunningham, Dallas

Field Goals
- **NFC:** 34—Richie Cunningham, Dallas
- **AFC:** 32—Cary Blanchard, Indianapolis

Field Goal Attempts
- **AFC:** 41—Cary Blanchard, Indianapolis
  John Hall, N.Y. Jets
- **NFC:** 37—Richie Cunningham, Dallas
  Jeff Wilkins, St. Louis

Longest Field Goal
- **AFC:** 55—Steve Christie, Buffalo vs. Denver, October 26
  John Hall, N.Y. Jets at Seattle, August 31
- **NFC:** 55—Morten Andersen, Atlanta at New Orleans, October 12
  Jason Hanson, Detroit vs. Indianapolis, November 23

Average Yards Made
- **NFC:** 39.0—Doug Brien, New Orleans
- **AFC:** 36.5—Pete Stoyanovich, Kansas City

1997 INDIVIDUAL STATISTICS—FIELD GOALS

AFC FIELD GOALS—TEAM

	FG	FGA	Pct.	Long
Kansas City	26	27	.963	54
Pittsburgh	22	25	.880	52
New England	25	29	.862	52
Jacksonville	31	36	.861	52
San Diego	26	31	.839	45
Buffalo	24	30	.800	55
Seattle	22	28	.786	52
Indianapolis	32	41	.780	50
Miami	28	36	.778	50
Tennessee	27	35	.771	52
Baltimore	26	34	.765	49
Cincinnati	12	16	.750	46
Denver	28	39	.718	53
N.Y. Jets	28	41	.683	55
Oakland	13	22	.591	53
AFC Total	370	470	—	55
AFC Average	24.7	31.3	.787	—

NFC FIELD GOALS—TEAM

	FG	FGA	Pct.	Long
Detroit	26	29	.897	55
Dallas	34	38	.895	53
Atlanta	23	27	.852	55
New Orleans	23	27	.852	53
Carolina	22	26	.846	54
Chicago	21	26	.808	52
San Francisco	29	36	.806	51
Green Bay	24	30	.800	50
Tampa Bay	13	17	.765	54
Philadelphia	22	31	.710	49
Minnesota	19	27	.704	49
N.Y. Giants	22	32	.688	52
St. Louis	25	37	.676	52
Washington	16	24	.667	50
Arizona	19	29	.655	49
NFC Total	338	436	—	55
NFC Average	22.5	29.1	0.775	—
League Total	708	906	—	55
League Average	23.6	30.2	0.781	

AFC FIELD GOALS—INDIVIDUAL

	1-19 Yards	20-29 Yards	30-39 Yards	40-49 Yards	50 or Longer	Totals	Avg. Yds. Att.	Avg. Yds. Made	Avg. Yds. Miss	Long
Stoyanovich, Pete, K.C.	0-0	9-9	3-3	12-13	2-2	26-27	36.9	36.5	48.0	54
	—	1.000	1.000	.923	1.000	.963				
Johnson, Norm, Pit.	1-1	6-6	8-8	6-8	1-2	22-25	35.9	34.5	46.3	52
	1.000	1.000	1.000	.750	.500	.880				
Vinatieri, Adam, N.E.	0-0	11-11	7-9	6-8	1-1	25-29	33.6	33.0	37.3	52
	—	1.000	.778	.750	1.000	.862				
Hollis, Mike, Jax.	2-2	12-14	8-9	7-9	2-2	31-36	33.0	32.5	36.2	52
	1.000	.857	.889	.778	1.000	.861				
Christie, Steve, Buf.	0-0	6-6	9-12	8-10	1-2	24-30	37.3	36.2	41.5	55
	—	1.000	.750	.800	.500	.800				
Peterson, Todd, Sea.	0-0	9-9	7-10	5-7	1-2	22-28	36.1	34.3	42.7	52
	—	1.000	.700	.714	.500	.786				
Blanchard, Cary, Ind.	0-0	9-9	12-14	10-15	1-3	32-41	37.0	35.5	42.6	50
	—	1.000	.857	.667	.333	.780				
Mare, Olindo, Mia.	2-2	14-15	8-10	3-6	1-3	28-36	31.6	29.3	40.0	50
	1.000	.933	.800	.500	.333	.778				
Del Greco, Al, Ten.	2-2	6-6	10-11	7-14	2-2	27-35	36.6	35.4	40.8	52
	1.000	1.000	.909	.500	1.000	.771				
Davis, Greg, Min.-S.D.	0-0	8-10	12-12	6-12	0-0	26-34	34.2	33.0	38.1	45
	—	.800	1.000	.500	—	.765				
Stover, Matt, Bal.	0-0	8-9	12-12	6-11	0-2	26-34	36.5	34.0	44.4	49
	—	.889	1.000	.545	.000	.765				
Pelfrey, Doug, Cin.	0-0	4-4	3-3	5-7	0-2	12-16	38.6	35.2	49.0	46
	—	1.000	1.000	.714	.000	.750				
Elam, Jason, Den.	0-0	10-11	10-12	3-8	3-5	26-36	36.5	34.2	42.6	53
	—	.909	.833	.375	.600	.722				
Hall, John, NY-J	1-1	10-11	11-17	2-6	4-6	28-41	36.7	34.3	41.8	55
	1.000	.909	.647	.333	.667	.683				
Ford, Cole, Oak.	0-0	3-5	4-6	5-10	1-1	13-22	37.5	36.3	39.2	53
	—	.600	.667	.500	1.000	.591				
Nonqualifiers										
Carney, John, S.D.	0-0	3-3	2-2	2-2	0-0	7-7	32.6	32.6	—	41
	—	1.000	1.000	1.000	—	1.000				
Bentley, Scott, Den.	0-0	1-1	1-1	0-1	0-0	2-3	34.0	27.0	48.0	33
	—	1.000	1.000	.000	—	.667				
AFC Totals	8-8	125-134	125-149	92-144	20-35	370-470	35.8	34.1	41.7	55
	1.000	.933	.839	.639	.571	.787				
League Totals	20-20	243-257	235-280	169-271	41-78	708-906	35.8	34.0	42.3	55
	1.000	.946	.839	.624	.526	.781				

Leader based on percentage, minimum 16 field goal attempts

NFC FIELD GOALS—INDIVIDUAL

	1-19 Yards	20-29 Yards	30-39 Yards	40-49 Yards	50 or Longer	Totals	Avg. Yds. Att.	Avg. Yds. Made	Avg. Yds. Miss	Long
Cunningham, Richie, Dal.	1-1	16-16	9-9	7-10	1-1	34-37	32.6	31.9	41.3	53
	1.000	1.000	1.000	.700	1.000	.919				
Hanson, Jason, Det.	0-0	10-10	8-9	5-5	3-5	26-29	36.6	35.4	46.7	55
	—	1.000	.889	1.000	.600	.897				
Andersen, Morten, Atl.	1-1	10-10	7-7	3-6	2-3	23-27	33.7	31.8	44.8	55
	1.000	1.000	1.000	.500	.667	.852				
Brien, Doug, N.O.	1-1	2-2	10-10	6-9	4-5	23-27	40.0	39.0	45.3	53
	1.000	1.000	1.000	.667	.800	.852				
Kasay, John, Car.	1-1	6-7	8-8	4-4	3-6	22-26	37.1	35.3	47.0	54
	1.000	.857	1.000	1.000	.500	.846				
Jaeger, Jeff, Chi.	0-0	8-9	8-10	4-6	1-1	21-26	33.7	33.4	34.8	52
	—	.889	.800	.667	1.000	.808				
Anderson, Gary, S.F.	0-0	11-11	9-12	8-10	1-3	29-36	35.0	33.2	42.4	51
	—	1.000	.750	.800	.333	.806				
Longwell, Ryan, G.B.	4-4	7-8	10-13	2-4	1-1	24-30	31.9	30.8	36.7	50
	1.000	.875	.769	.500	1.000	.800				
Husted, Michael, T.B.	0-0	5-5	2-3	5-6	1-3	13-17	36.9	35.0	43.3	54
	—	1.000	.667	.833	.333	.765				
Boniol, Chris, Phi.	0-0	7-7	11-12	4-11	0-1	22-31	37.0	34.0	44.4	49
	—	1.000	.917	.364	.000	.710				
Murray, Eddie, Min.	0-0	7-7	1-3	4-6	0-1	12-17	35.5	32.5	42.6	49
	—	1.000	.333	.667	.000	.706				
Daluiso, Brad, NY-G	1-1	6-6	6-7	8-14	1-4	22-32	38.8	35.7	45.7	52
	1.000	1.000	.857	.571	.250	.688				
Wilkins, Jeff, St.L	0-0	8-9	8-12	7-14	2-2	25-37	37.5	36.2	40.3	52
	—	.889	.667	.500	1.000	.676				
Blanton, Scott, Was.	2-2	4-4	5-6	4-8	1-4	16-24	37.5	33.5	45.4	50
	1.000	1.000	.833	.500	.250	.667				
Nedney, Joe, Ariz	1-1	3-3	4-4	3-7	0-2	11-17	37.5	32.4	47.0	45
	1.000	1.000	1.000	.429	.000	.647				
Nonqualifiers										
Butler, Kevin, Ariz	0-0	4-4	2-4	2-4	0-0	8-12	34.5	32.4	38.8	49
	—	1.000	.500	.500	—	.667				
Gowin, Toby, Dal.	0-0	0-0	0-0	0-0	0-1	0-1	63.0	—	63.0	0
	—	—	—	—	.000	.000				
NFC Totals	12-12	118-123	110-131	77-127	21-43	338-436	35.9	33.9	42.8	55
	1.000	.959	.840	.606	.488	.775				
League Totals	20-20	243-257	235-280	169-271	41-78	708-906	35.8	34.0	42.3	55
	1.000	.946	.839	.624	.526	.781				

Leader based on percentage, minimum 16 field-goal attempts

RUSHING

Yards
- **NFC:** 2053—Barry Sanders, Detroit
- **AFC:** 1750—Terrell Davis, Denver

Yards, Game
- **AFC:** 246—Corey Dillon, Cincinnati vs. Tennessee, December 4 (39 attempts, 4 TD)
- **NFC:** 216—Barry Sanders, Detroit vs. Indianapolis, November 23 (24 attempts, 2 TD)

Longest
- **AFC:** 83—Napoleon Kaufman, Oakland vs. Denver, October 19 - TD
- **NFC:** 82—Barry Sanders, Detroit at Tampa Bay, October 12 - TD

Attempts
- **AFC:** 375—Jerome Bettis, Pittsburgh
- **NFC:** 335—Barry Sanders, Detroit

Attempts, Game
- **AFC:** 42—Terrell Davis, Denver at Buffalo, October 26 (207 yards - TD)
- **NFC:** 36—Terry Allen, Washington vs. Jacksonville, September 28 (122 yards)

Yards Per Attempt
- **AFC:** 6.7—Steve McNair, Tennessee
- **NFC:** 6.1—Barry Sanders, Detroit

Touchdowns
- **AFC:** 15—Karim Abdul-Jabbar, Miami
  Terrell Davis, Denver
- **NFC:** 11—Barry Sanders, Detroit

Team Leaders, Yards
- **AFC:** BALTIMORE: 774, Byron (Bam) Morris; BUFFALO: 840, Antowain Smith; CINCINNATI: 1129, Corey Dillon; DENVER: 1750, Terrell Davis; INDIANAPOLIS: 1054, Marshall Faulk; JACKSONVILLE: 823, Natrone Means; KANSAS CITY: 550, Greg Hill; MIAMI: 892, Karim Abdul-Jabbar; NEW ENGLAND: 1160, Curtis Martin; N.Y. JETS: 1086, Adrian Murrell; OAKLAND: 1294, Napoleon Kaufman; PITTSBURGH: 1665, Jerome Bettis; SAN DIEGO: 945, Gary Brown; SEATTLE: 847, Chris Warren; TENNESSEE: 1399, Eddie George
- **NFC:** ARIZONA: 424, Leeland McElroy; ATLANTA: 1002, Jamal Anderson; CAROLINA: 809, Fred Lane; CHICAGO: 1033, Raymont Harris; DALLAS: 1074, Emmitt Smith; DETROIT: 2053, Barry Sanders; GREEN BAY: 1435, Dorsey Levens; MINNESOTA: 1266, Robert Smith; NEW ORLEANS: 552, Ray Zellars; N.Y. GIANTS: 698, Charles Way; PHILADELPHIA: 1110, Ricky Watters; ST. LOUIS: 633, Lawrence Phillips; SAN FRANCISCO: 1019, Garrison Hearst; TAMPA BAY: 978, Warrick Dunn; WASHINGTON: 724, Terry Allen

Team Champion
- **AFC:** 2479—Pittsburgh
- **NFC:** 2464—Detroit

1997 INDIVIDUAL STATISTICS—RUSHING

AFC RUSHING—TEAM

	Att.	Yards	Avg.	Long	TD
Pittsburgh	572	2479	4.3	74t	19
Tennessee	541	2414	4.5	47	17
Denver	520	2378	4.6	50t	18
Kansas City	529	2171	4.1	43	15
Cincinnati	452	1966	4.3	79t	23
Seattle	404	1800	4.5	77t	13
Buffalo	422	1782	4.2	56t	12
Indianapolis	450	1727	3.8	45	10
Jacksonville	454	1720	3.8	33	20
Baltimore	420	1589	3.8	25	7
Oakland	360	1588	4.4	83t	9
N.Y. Jets	431	1485	3.4	43t	10
New England	398	1464	3.7	70t	6
San Diego	409	1416	3.5	32	5
Miami	430	1343	3.1	71t	18
AFC Total	6792	27322	4.0	83t	202
AFC Average	452.8	1821.5	4.0	—	13.5

NFC RUSHING—TEAM

	Att.	Yards	Avg.	Long	TD
Detroit	447	2464	5.5	82t	19
Minnesota	449	2041	4.5	78t	14
N.Y. Giants	521	1988	3.8	42	14
San Francisco	523	1969	3.8	51	16
Philadelphia	465	1943	4.2	30	11
Tampa Bay	479	1934	4.0	76	15
Green Bay	459	1909	4.2	52t	9
Carolina	441	1770	4.0	50	11
Chicago	490	1746	3.6	68t	14
Atlanta	442	1643	3.7	77	8
Dallas	423	1637	3.9	44	6
Washington	453	1615	3.6	34	12
St. Louis	443	1563	3.5	28	15
New Orleans	417	1461	3.5	74t	9
Arizona	395	1255	3.2	31	9
NFC Total	6847	26938	3.9	82t	182
NFC Average	456.5	1795.9	3.9	—	12.1
League Total	13639	54260	—	83t	384
League Average	454.6	1808.7	4.0	—	12.8

NFL TOP TEN RUSHERS

	Att.	Yards	Avg.	Long	TD
Sanders, Barry, Det.	335	2053	6.1	82t	11
Davis, Terrell, Den.	369	1750	4.7	50t	15
Bettis, Jerome, Pit.	375	1665	4.4	34	7
Levens, Dorsey, G.B.	329	1435	4.4	52t	7
George, Eddie, Ten.	357	1399	3.9	30	6
Kaufman, Napoleon, Oak.	272	1294	4.8	83t	6
Smith, Robert, Min.	232	1266	5.5	78t	6
Martin, Curtis, N.E.	274	1160	4.2	70t	4
Dillon, Corey, Cin.	233	1129	4.8	71t	10
Watters, Ricky, Phi.	285	1110	3.9	28	7

AFC RUSHERS—INDIVIDUAL

	Att.	Yards	Avg.	Long	TD
Davis, Terrell, Den.	369	1750	4.7	50t	15
Bettis, Jerome, Pit.	375	1665	4.4	34	7
George, Eddie, Ten.	357	1399	3.9	30	6
Kaufman, Napoleon, Oak.	272	1294	4.8	83t	6
Martin, Curtis, N.E.	274	1160	4.2	70t	4
Dillon, Corey, Cin.	233	1129	4.8	71t	10
Murrell, Adrian, NY-J	300	1086	3.6	43t	7
Faulk, Marshall, Ind.	264	1054	4.0	45	7
Brown, Gary, S.D.	253	945	3.7	32	4
Abdul-Jabbar, Karim, Mia.	283	892	3.2	22	15
Warren, Chris, Sea.	200	847	4.2	36t	4
Smith, Antowain, Buf.	194	840	4.3	56t	8
Means, Natrone, Jax.	244	823	3.4	20	9
Morris, Bam, Bal.	204	774	3.8	25	4
Phillips, Lawrence, St.L-Mia.	201	677	3.4	28	8
McNair, Steve, Ten.	101	674	6.7	47	8
Thomas, Thurman, Buf.	154	643	4.2	24	1
Stewart, James, Jax.	136	555	4.1	33	8
Hill, Greg, K.C.	157	550	3.5	38	0
Allen, Marcus, K.C.	124	505	4.1	30	11
Stewart, Kordell, Pit.	88	476	5.4	74t	11
Carter, Ki-Jana, Cin.	128	464	3.6	79t	7
Broussard, Steve, Sea.	70	418	6.0	77t	5
Anders, Kimble, K.C.	79	397	5.0	43	0
Smith, Lamar, Sea.	91	392	4.3	35	2
Bennett, Donnell, K.C.	94	369	3.9	14	1
Byner, Earnest, Bal.	84	313	3.7	19	0
Thomas, Rodney, Ten.	67	310	4.6	25t	3
Crockett, Zack, Ind.	95	300	3.2	20	1
Graham, Jay, Bal.	81	299	3.7	19	2
Brunell, Mark, Jax.	48	257	5.4	15	2
Jones, George, Pit.	72	235	3.3	32	1
Blake, Jeff, Cin.	45	234	5.2	16	3
Hebron, Vaughn, Den.	49	222	4.5	46	1
Elway, John, Den.	50	218	4.4	23	1
Harbaugh, Jim, Ind.	36	206	5.7	18	0
Spikes, Irving, Mia.	63	180	2.9	14	2
Grbac, Elvis, K.C.	30	168	5.6	20	1
Fletcher, Terrell, S.D.	51	161	3.2	13	0
Johnson, Leon, NY-J	48	158	3.3	20	2
McPhail, Jerris, Mia.	17	146	8.6	71t	1
Testaverde, Vinny, Bal.	34	138	4.1	16	0
Loville, Derek, Den.	25	124	5.0	17	1
Hall, Tim, Oak.	23	120	5.2	15	0
Gannon, Rich, K.C.	33	109	3.3	13	2
Holmes, Darick, Buf.	22	106	4.8	19	2
Cullors, Derrick, N.E.	22	101	4.6	24	0
Bieniemy, Eric, Cin.	21	97	4.6	20t	1
Bynum, Kenny, S.D.	30	97	3.2	19	0
Warren, Lamont, Ind.	28	80	2.9	11	2
Collins, Todd, Buf.	30	77	2.6	11	0
Grier, Marrio, N.E.	33	75	2.3	12	1
Galloway, Joey, Sea.	9	72	8.0	44	0
Craver, Aaron, S.D.	20	71	3.6	22	0
Anderson, Richie, NY-J	21	70	3.3	19	0
Williams, Harvey, Oak.	18	70	3.9	13	3
Groce, Clif, Ind.	10	66	6.6	29	0
Meggett, David, N.E.	20	60	3.0	10	1
Moulds, Eric, Buf.	4	59	14.8	29	0
Parmalee, Bernie, Mia.	18	59	3.3	12	0
Bledsoe, Drew, N.E.	28	55	2.0	8	0
Lucas, Ray, NY-J	6	55	9.2	17	0
Vanover, Tamarick, K.C.	5	50	10.0	17	0
George, Jeff, Oak.	17	44	2.6	12	0
Jones, Charlie, S.D.	4	42	10.5	17	0
McAfee, Fred, Pit.	13	41	3.2	9	0
Moon, Warren, Sea.	17	40	2.4	17	1
O'Donnell, Neil, NY-J	32	36	1.1	19	1
Lewis, Jermaine, Bal.	3	35	11.7	24	0
Sowell, Jerald, NY-J	7	35	5.0	10	0
Griffith, Howard, Den.	9	34	3.8	9	0
Johnson, Rob, Jax.	10	34	3.4	25t	1
Van Pelt, Alex, Buf.	11	33	3.0	9	1
Milne, Brian, Cin.	13	32	2.5	5	2
Whelihan, Craig, S.D.	13	29	2.2	7	0
Neal, Lorenzo, NY-J	10	28	2.8	8	0
Ward, Dedric, NY-J	2	25	12.5	21	0
Byars, Keith, N.E.	11	24	2.2	5	0
Fenner, Derrick, Oak.	7	24	3.4	7	0
Humphries, Stan, S.D.	13	24	1.8	11	0
Hallock, Ty, Jax.	4	21	5.3	11	0
Bailey, Aaron, Ind.	3	20	6.7	18	0
Gardner, Carwell, S.D.	7	20	2.9	5	0
Brown, Tim, Oak.	5	19	3.8	12	0
Hawkins, Courtney, Pit.	5	17	3.4	11	0
Zeier, Eric, Bal.	10	17	1.7	12	0
Smith, Rod, Den.	5	16	3.2	21	0
Blackwell, Will, Pit.	2	14	7.0	11	0
Jackson, Willie, Jax.	3	14	4.7	13	0
Pritchard, Mike, Sea.	1	14	14.0	14	0
Tomczak, Mike, Pit.	7	13	1.9	17	0
Jordan, Charles, Mia.	3	12	4.0	16	0
Roby, Reggie, Ten.	1	12	12.0	12	0
Aguiar, Louie, K.C.	2	11	5.5	6	0
Esiason, Boomer, Cin.	8	11	1.4	8	0
Montgomery, Greg, Bal.	1	11	11.0	11	0
Reed, Andre, Buf.	3	11	3.7	9	0
Richardson, Tony, K.C.	2	11	5.5	6	0
Witman, Jon, Pit.	5	11	2.2	4	0
Aska, Joe, Oak.	12	10	0.8	4	0
Gash, Sam, N.E.	6	10	1.7	4	0
Matthews, Steve, Jax.	1	10	10.0	10	0

1997 INDIVIDUAL STATISTICS—RUSHING

	Att.	Yards	Avg.	Long	TD
Smith, Detron, Den.	4	10	2.5	11	0
Kitna, Jon, Sea.	10	9	0.9	8	1
Lester, Tim, Pit.	2	9	4.5	6	0
Erickson, Craig, Mia.	4	8	2.0	4	0
Strong, Mack, Sea.	4	8	2.0	6	0
Pritchett, Stanley, Mia.	3	7	2.3	4	0
Tolliver, Billy Joe, Atl.-K.C.	9	7	0.8	12	0
Everett, Jim, S.D.	5	6	1.2	6	0
Johnson, Lonnie, Buf.	1	6	6.0	6	0
Ritchey, James, Ten.	1	6	6.0	6	0
Scott, Darnay, Cin.	1	6	6.0	6	0
Holcomb, Kelly, Ind.	5	5	1.0	3	0
Davison, Jerone, Oak.	2	4	2.0	5	0
Kidd, John, Mia.	1	4	4.0	4	0
Potts, Roosevelt, Ind.-Mia.	2	4	2.0	3	0
Shelton, Daimon, Jax.	6	4	0.7	2	0
Levitt, Chad, Oak.	2	3	1.5	2	0
Philcox, Todd, S.D.	1	3	3.0	3	0
Thigpen, Yancey, Pit.	1	3	3.0	3	0
Brister, Bubby, Den.	4	2	0.5	2	0
Cotton, Kenyon, Bal.	2	2	1.0	1t	1
Jordan, Randy, Jax.	1	2	2.0	2	0
Justin, Paul, Ind.	6	2	0.3	3	0
Lewis, Jeff, Den.	5	2	0.4	5	0
Marsh, Curtis, Pit.	1	2	2.0	2	0
Nealy, Ray, Mia.	1	2	2.0	2	0
Rison, Andre, K.C.	1	2	2.0	2	0
Alexander, Derrick, Bal.	1	0	0.0	0	0
Araguz, Leo, Oak.	1	0	0.0	0	0
Barker, Bryan, Jax.	1	0	0.0	0	0
Friesz, John, Sea.	1	0	0.0	0	0
Johnson, Lee, Cin.	1	0	0.0	0	0
Klingler, David, Oak.	1	0	0.0	0	0
Mohr, Chris, Buf.	1	0	0.0	0	0
Richardson, Kyle, Sea.	1	0	0.0	0	0
Graham, Scottie, Cin.	1	-1	-1.0	-1	0
Krieg, Dave, Ten.	4	-2	-0.5	0	0
Clements, Chuck, NY-J	2	-3	-1.5	-1	0
Zolak, Scott, N.E.	3	-3	-1.0	-1	0
Foley, Glenn, NY-J	3	-5	-1.7	-1	0
Metcalf, Eric, S.D.	3	-5	-1.7	2	0
Pickens, Carl, Cin.	1	-6	-6.0	-6	0
Harrison, Marvin, Ind.	2	-7	-3.5	0	0
Mason, Derrick, Ten.	1	-7	-7.0	-7	0
Miller, Josh, Pit.	1	-7	-7.0	-7	0
Sanders, Chris, Ten.	1	-8	-8.0	-8	0
Marino, Dan, Mia.	18	-14	-0.8	1	0
Brown, Troy, N.E.	1	-18	-18.0	-18	0

t = Touchdown

Leader based on most yards gained

NFC RUSHERS—INDIVIDUAL

	Att.	Yards	Avg.	Long	TD
Sanders, Barry, Det.	335	2053	6.1	82t	11
Levens, Dorsey, G.B.	329	1435	4.4	52t	7
Smith, Robert, Min.	232	1266	5.5	78t	6
Watters, Ricky, Phi.	285	1110	3.9	28	7
Smith, Emmitt, Dal.	261	1074	4.1	44	4
Harris, Raymont, Chi.	275	1033	3.8	68t	10
Hearst, Garrison, S.F.	234	1019	4.4	51	4
Anderson, Jamal, Atl.	290	1002	3.5	39	7
Dunn, Warrick, T.B.	224	978	4.4	76	4
Lane, Fred, Car.	182	809	4.4	50	7
Allen, Terry, Was.	210	724	3.4	34	4
Way, Charles, NY-G	151	698	4.6	42	4
Alstott, Mike, T.B.	176	665	3.8	47t	7
Wheatley, Tyrone, NY-G	152	583	3.8	38	4
Davis, Stephen, Was.	141	567	4.0	18	3
Zellars, Ray, N.O.	156	552	3.5	27	4
Garner, Charlie, Phi.	116	547	4.7	26	3
Barber, Tiki, NY-G	136	511	3.8	42	3
Williams, Sherman, Dal.	121	468	3.9	18	2
Bates, Mario, N.O.	119	440	3.7	74t	4
McElroy, Leeland, Ariz	135	424	3.1	18	2
Kirby, Terry, S.F.	125	418	3.3	38	6
Moore, Jerald, St.L	104	380	3.7	26	3
Johnson, Anthony, Car.	97	358	3.7	20	0
Hanspard, Byron, Atl.	53	335	6.3	77	0
Autry, Darnell, Chi.	112	319	2.8	17	1
Biakabutuka, Tim, Car.	75	299	4.0	26t	2
Moore, Ronald, St.L-Ariz	81	278	3.4	27t	1
Centers, Larry, Ariz	101	276	2.7	14	1
Davis, Troy, N.O.	75	271	3.6	20	0
Hoard, Leroy, Min.	80	235	2.9	20	4
Floyd, William, S.F.	78	231	3.0	22	3
Plummer, Jake, Ariz	39	216	5.5	31	2
Young, Steve, S.F.	50	199	4.0	13	3
Favre, Brett, G.B.	58	187	3.2	16	1
Banks, Tony, St.L	47	186	4.0	23	1
Rivers, Ron, Det.	29	166	5.7	31	1
Chandler, Chris, Atl.	43	158	3.7	19	0
Evans, Chuck, Min.	43	157	3.7	13	2
Greene, Scott, Car.	45	157	3.5	10t	1
Hayden, Aaron, G.B.	32	148	4.6	21	1
Johnson, Brad, Min.	35	139	4.0	28	0
Cunningham, Randall, Min.	19	127	6.7	28	0
Vardell, Tommy, Det.	32	122	3.8	41	6
Henderson, William, G.B.	31	113	3.6	15	0
Salaam, Rashaan, Chi.	31	112	3.6	17	0
Mitchell, Brian, Was.	23	107	4.7	26	1
Lee, Amp, St.L	28	104	3.7	14	0
Bowie, Larry, Was.	28	100	3.6	18	2
Dilfer, Trent, T.B.	33	99	3.0	17	1
Rhett, Errict, T.B.	31	96	3.1	21	3
Turner, Kevin, Phi.	18	96	5.3	29	0
Pegram, Erric, S.D.-NY-G	28	95	3.4	18t	2
Levy, Chuck, S.F.	16	90	5.6	24	0
Anthony, Reidel, T.B.	5	84	16.8	26	0
Heyward, Craig, St.L	34	84	2.5	8	1
Kramer, Erik, Chi.	27	83	3.1	31	2
Mitchell, Scott, Det.	37	83	2.2	13	1
Hampton, Rodney, NY-G	23	81	3.5	22	1
Johnson, LeShon, Ariz	23	81	3.5	11	0
Aikman, Troy, Dal.	25	79	3.2	13	0
Green, Harold, Atl.	36	78	2.2	22	1
Hoying, Bobby, Phi.	16	78	4.9	30	0
Mirer, Rick, Chi.	20	78	3.9	20	1
Collins, Kerry, Car.	26	65	2.5	21	1
Frerotte, Gus, Was.	24	65	2.7	26	2
Williams, Moe, Min.	22	59	2.7	8	1
Carter, Tony, Chi.	9	56	6.2	16	0
Detmer, Ty, Phi.	14	46	3.3	14	1
Hobert, Billy Joe, Buf.-N.O.	14	43	3.1	15	0
Shuler, Heath, N.O.	22	38	1.7	8	1
Peete, Rodney, Phi.	8	37	4.6	16	0
Harmon, Ronnie, Ten.-Chi.	10	36	3.6	14	0
Palmer, David, Min.	11	36	3.3	10	1
Hastings, Andre, N.O.	4	35	8.8	27	0
Mathis, Terance, Atl.	3	35	11.7	16	0
Morton, Johnnie, Det.	3	33	11.0	20	0
Beuerlein, Steve, Car.	4	32	8.0	20	0
Crawford, Keith, St.L	2	32	16.0	23	0
Ismail, Raghib, Car.	4	32	8.0	18	0
Nussmeier, Doug, N.O.	8	30	3.8	15	0
Thompson, David, St.L	16	30	1.9	9	1
Brown, Dave, NY-G	17	29	1.7	7	1
Staley, Duce, Phi.	7	29	4.1	12	0
Hostetler, Jeff, Was.	14	28	2.0	11	0
Shepherd, Leslie, Was.	4	27	6.8	17	0
Bouie, Kevin, Ariz	11	26	2.4	6	0
Wuerffel, Danny, N.O.	6	26	4.3	10	0
Carruth, Rae, Car.	6	23	3.8	6	0
Graham, Kent, Ariz	13	23	1.8	10	2
Green, Robert, Min.	6	22	3.7	8	0
Walker, Herschel, Dal.	6	20	3.3	11	0
Brooks, Robert, G.B.	2	19	9.5	15	0
Graziani, Tony, Atl.	3	19	6.3	10	0
Conway, Curtis, Chi.	3	17	5.7	10	0
Edwards, Marc, S.F.	5	17	3.4	6	0
Gedney, Chris, Ariz	1	15	15.0	—	0
McCrary, Fred, N.O.	8	15	1.9	8	0
Freeman, Antonio, G.B.	1	14	14.0	14	0
Hicks, Michael, Chi.	4	14	3.5	8	0
Kennison, Eddie, St.L	3	13	4.3	6	0
Lane, Eric, NY-G	5	13	2.6	6	0
Smith, Eric, Chi.	1	12	12.0	12	0
Brohm, Jeff, S.F.	4	11	2.8	10	0
Hill, Randal, N.O.	1	11	11.0	11	0
Schlesinger, Cory, Det.	7	11	1.6	4	0
Ellison, Jerry, T.B.	2	10	5.0	5	0
Bender, Wes, N.O.	5	9	1.8	6	0
Case, Stoney, Ariz	7	8	1.1	3	1
Christian, Bob, Atl.	7	8	1.1	3	0
Sauerbrun, Todd, Chi.	2	8	4.0	8	0

1997 INDIVIDUAL STATISTICS—PASSING

	Att.	Yards	Avg.	Long	TD
Miller, Anthony, Dal.	1	6	6.0	6	0
Stenstrom, Steve, Chi.	1	6	6.0	6	0
Logan, Marc, Was.	4	5	1.3	4	0
Sanders, Frank, Ariz	1	5	5.0	5	0
Smith, Cedric, Ariz	4	5	1.3	2	1
Williams, Karl, T.B.	1	5	5.0	5	0
Connell, Albert, Was.	1	3	3.0	3	0
Hughes, Tyrone, Chi.	1	3	3.0	3	0
Johnston, Daryl, Dal.	2	3	1.5	3	0
McKinnon, Ronald, Ariz	1	3	3.0	3	0
Kanell, Danny, NY-G	15	2	0.1	8	0
Patten, David, NY-G	1	2	2.0	2	0
Hape, Patrick, T.B.	1	1	1.0	1	0
Rypien, Mark, St.L	1	1	1.0	1	0
Berger, Mitch, Min.	1	0	0.0	0	0
Hutton, Tom, Phi.	1	0	0.0	0	0
LeBel, Harper, Chi.	1	0	0.0	0	0
Oliver, Winslow, Car.	1	0	0.0	0	0
Swann, Eric, Ariz	1	0	0.0	0	0
Turk, Matt, Was.	1	0	0.0	0	0
Calloway, Chris, NY-G	1	-1	-1.0	-1	0
Penn, Chris, Chi.	1	-1	-1.0	-1	0
Cherry, Mike, NY-G	1	-2	-2.0	-2	0
Guliford, Eric, N.O.	1	-2	-2.0	-2	0
Williams, Kevin, Ariz	1	-2	-2.0	-2	0
Wilson, Wade, Dal.	6	-2	-0.3	3	0
Bono, Steve, G.B.	3	-3	-1.0	-1	0
Horan, Mike, St.L	1	-3	-3.0	-3	0
Pederson, Doug, G.B.	3	-4	-1.3	-1	0
Reich, Frank, Det.	4	-4	-1.0	-1	0
Walsh, Steve, T.B.	6	-4	-0.7	0	0
Walter, Ken, Car.	1	-5	-5.0	-5	0
Druckenmiller, Jim, S.F.	10	-6	-0.6	2	0
Rice, Jerry, S.F.	1	-10	-10.0	-10	0
Sanders, Deion, Dal.	1	-11	-11.0	-11	0
Westbrook, Michael, Was.	3	-11	-3.7	7	0

t = Touchdown
Leader based on most yards gained

PASSING

Highest Rating
- **NFC:** 104.7—Steve Young, San Francisco
- **AFC:** 91.2—Mark Brunell, Jacksonville

Completion Percentage
- **NFC:** 67.7—Steve Young, San Francisco
- **AFC:** 61.2—Jim Harbaugh,Indanapolis

Attempts
- **AFC:** 548—Dan Marino, Miami
- **NFC:** 518—Troy Aikman, Dallas

Completions
- **AFC:** 319—Dan Marino, Miami
- **NFC:** 304—Brett Favre, Green Bay

Yards
- **AFC:** 3917—Jeff George, Oakland
- **NFC:** 3867—Brett Favre, Green Bay

Yards, Game
- **AFC:** 409—Warren Moon, Seattle vs. Oakland, October 26 (28-44, 5 TD)
- **NFC:** 401—Tony Banks, St. Louis at Atlanta, November 2 (23-34, 2 TD)

Longest
- **AFC:** 92—Eric Zeier (to Derrick Alexander), Baltimore vs. Seattle, December 7
- **NFC:** 89—Heath Shuler (to Randal Hill), New Orleans at Chicago, October 5 - TD

Yards Per Attempt
- **NFC:** 8.51—Steve Young, San Francisco
- **AFC:** 7.54—Mark Brunell, Jacksonville

Touchdown Passes
- **NFC:** 35—Brett Favre, Green Bay
- **AFC:** 29—Jeff George, Oakland

Touchdown Passes, Game
- **NFC:** 5—Brett Favre, Green Bay vs. Minnesota, September 21 (18-31, 266 yards)
- **AFC:** 5—Neil O'Donnell, N.Y. Jets at Seattle, August 31 (18-25, 270 yards)
  Warren Moon, Seattle vs. Oakland, October 6 (28-44, 409 yards)

Lowest Interception Percentage
- **AFC:** 1.3—Jim Harbaugh, Indianapolis
- **NFC:** 1.7—Steve Young, San Francisco

Team Champion (Most Net Yards)
- **AFC:** 3959—Seattle
- **NFC:** 3705—Green Bay

AFC PASSING—TEAM

	Att.	Comp.	Pct. Comp.	Gross Yards	Sacked	Yds. Lost	Net Yards	Yds./ Att.	Yds./ Comp.	TD	Pct. TD	Long	Int.	Pct. Int.
Seattle	609	359	58.9	4187	36	228	3959	6.88	11.66	26	4.27	61	21	3.4
Miami	576	332	57.6	3945	22	153	3792	6.85	11.88	16	2.78	55	12	2.1
Oakland	529	294	55.6	3944	58	430	3514	7.46	13.41	29	5.48	76	10	1.9
Baltimore	586	338	57.7	3929	37	227	3702	6.70	11.62	25	4.27	92	16	2.7
Jacksonville	504	313	62.1	3922	40	218	3704	7.78	12.53	20	3.97	75	9	1.8
New England	532	321	60.3	3808	30	258	3550	7.16	11.86	31	5.83	76	15	2.8
Denver	513	287	55.9	3704	35	210	3494	7.22	12.91	27	5.26	78	11	2.1
Cincinnati	504	302	59.9	3603	46	287	3316	7.15	11.93	21	4.17	77t	9	1.8
Indianapolis	523	317	60.6	3560	62	418	3142	6.81	11.23	16	3.06	58	17	3.3
N.Y. Jets	564	319	56.6	3555	48	313	3242	6.30	11.14	20	3.55	70	10	1.8
San Diego	565	291	51.5	3475	51	386	3089	6.15	11.94	12	2.12	72t	21	3.7
Pittsburgh	466	253	54.3	3215	20	152	3063	6.90	12.71	22	4.72	69t	19	4.1
Buffalo	546	293	53.7	3213	46	338	2875	5.88	10.97	14	2.56	77t	25	4.6
Kansas City	493	281	57.0	3129	32	236	2893	6.35	11.14	20	4.06	55t	10	2.0
Tennessee	420	220	52.4	2704	32	199	2505	6.44	12.29	15	3.57	55t	13	3.1
AFC Total	7930	4520	—	53893	595	4053	49840	—	—	314	—	92	218	—
AFC Average	528.7	301.3	57.0	3592.9	39.7	270.2	3322.7	6.80	11.92	20.9	4.0	—	14.5	2.7

NFC PASSING—TEAM

	Att.	Comp.	Pct. Comp.	Gross Yards	Sacked	Yds. Lost	Net Yards	Yds./ Att.	Yds./ Comp.	TD	Pct. TD	Long	Int.	Pct. Int.
Philadelphia	587	330	56.2	4009	64	362	3647	6.83	12.15	22	3.75	72t	16	2.7
Arizona	602	317	52.7	3953	78	495	3458	6.57	12.47	19	3.16	70t	22	3.7
Green Bay	523	309	59.1	3896	26	191	3705	7.45	12.61	35	6.69	74	16	3.1
Detroit	540	304	56.3	3605	41	271	3334	6.68	11.86	19	3.52	79	17	3.1
Washington	547	283	51.7	3581	33	198	3383	6.55	12.65	22	4.02	69	22	4.0
Minnesota	540	319	59.1	3537	33	224	3313	6.55	11.09	26	4.81	56	16	3.0
St. Louis	526	271	51.5	3524	44	326	3198	6.70	13.00	14	2.66	76	15	2.9
Chicago	595	336	56.5	3501	43	257	3244	5.88	10.42	14	2.35	78t	22	3.7
Dallas	553	314	56.8	3454	39	313	3141	6.25	11.00	19	3.44	64t	12	2.2
Atlanta	484	273	56.4	3445	54	372	3073	7.12	12.62	26	5.37	56	11	2.3
San Francisco	432	278	64.4	3432	44	289	3143	7.94	12.35	20	4.63	82	11	2.5
Carolina	534	289	54.1	3156	44	311	2845	5.91	10.92	17	3.18	59t	24	4.5
New Orleans	458	228	49.8	2901	50	317	2584	6.33	12.72	13	2.84	89t	33	7.2
N.Y. Giants	474	249	52.5	2763	32	238	2525	5.83	11.10	16	3.38	68t	12	2.5
Tampa Bay	404	224	55.4	2638	32	196	2442	6.53	11.78	21	5.20	59t	12	3.0
NFC Total	7799	4324	—	51395	657	4360	47035	—	—	303	—	89t	261	—
NFC Average	519.9	288.3	55.4	3426.3	43.8	290.7	3135.7	6.59	11.89	20.2	3.9	—	17.4	3.3
League Total	15729	8844	—	105288	1252	8413	96875	—	—	617	—	92	479	—
League Average	524.3	294.8	56.2	3509.6	41.7	280.4	3229.2	6.69	11.91	20.6	3.9	—	16.0	3.0

Leader based on net yards

NFL TOP TEN PASSERS

	Att.	Comp.	Pct. Comp.	Yds.	Avg. Gain	TD	Pct. TD	Long	Int.	Pct. Int.	Sack	Yds. Lost	Rating Points
Young, Steve, S.F.	356	241	67.7	3029	8.51	19	5.3	82	6	1.7	35	220	104.7
Chandler, Chris, Atl.	342	202	59.1	2692	7.87	20	5.8	56	7	2.0	39	261	95.1
Favre, Brett, G.B.	513	304	59.3	3867	7.54	35	6.8	74	16	3.1	25	176	92.6
Brunell, Mark, Jax.	435	264	60.7	3281	7.54	18	4.1	75	7	1.6	33	189	91.2
George, Jeff, Oak.	521	290	55.7	3917	7.52	29	5.6	76	9	1.7	58	430	91.2
Bledsoe, Drew, N.E.	522	314	60.2	3706	7.10	28	5.4	76	15	2.9	30	258	87.7
Elway, John, Den.	502	280	55.8	3635	7.24	27	5.4	78	11	2.2	34	203	87.5
Harbaugh, Jim, Ind.	309	189	61.2	2060	6.67	10	3.2	58	4	1.3	41	256	86.2
Johnson, Brad, Min.	452	275	60.8	3036	6.72	20	4.4	56	12	2.7	26	164	84.5
Hoying, Bobby, Phi.	225	128	56.9	1573	6.99	11	4.9	72t	6	2.7	28	183	83.8

AFC PASSING—INDIVIDUAL

	Att.	Comp.	Pct. Comp.	Yds.	Avg. Gain	TD	Pct. TD	Long	Int.	Pct. Int.	Sack	Yds. Lost	Rating Points
Brunell, Mark, Jax.	435	264	60.7	3281	7.54	18	4.1	75	7	1.6	33	189	91.2
George, Jeff, Oak.	521	290	55.7	3917	7.52	29	5.6	76	9	1.7	58	430	91.2
Bledsoe, Drew, N.E.	522	314	60.2	3706	7.10	28	5.4	76	15	2.9	30	258	87.7
Elway, John, Den.	502	280	55.8	3635	7.24	27	5.4	78	11	2.2	34	203	87.5
Harbaugh, Jim, Ind.	309	189	61.2	2060	6.67	10	3.2	58	4	1.3	41	256	86.2
Moon, Warren, Sea.	528	313	59.3	3678	6.97	25	4.7	60t	16	3.0	30	192	83.7
Marino, Dan, Mia.	548	319	58.2	3780	6.90	16	2.9	55	11	2.0	20	132	80.7
O'Donnell, Neil, NY-J	460	259	56.3	2796	6.08	17	3.7	70	7	1.5	45	289	80.3
Grbac, Elvis, K.C.	314	179	57.0	1943	6.19	11	3.5	55t	6	1.9	19	150	79.1
Blake, Jeff, Cin.	317	184	58.0	2125	6.70	8	2.5	50t	7	2.2	39	244	77.6
Testaverde, Vinny, Bal.	470	271	57.7	2971	6.32	18	3.8	54t	15	3.2	20	129	75.9
Stewart, Kordell, Pit.	440	236	53.6	3020	6.86	21	4.8	69t	17	3.9	20	152	75.2
Humphries, Stan, S.D.	225	121	53.8	1488	6.61	5	2.2	72t	6	2.7	18	144	70.8
McNair, Steve, Ten.	415	216	52.0	2665	6.42	14	3.4	55t	13	3.1	31	190	70.4
Collins, Todd, Buf.	391	215	55.0	2367	6.05	12	3.1	77t	13	3.3	39	278	69.5
Whelihan, Craig, S.D.	237	118	49.8	1357	5.73	6	2.5	61t	10	4.2	21	168	58.3
Nonqualifiers													
Johnson, Rob, Jax.	28	22	78.6	344	12.29	2	7.1	40	2	7.1	6	29	111.9
Esiason, Boomer, Cin.	186	118	63.4	1478	7.95	13	7.0	77t	2	1.1	7	43	106.9
Zeier, Eric, Bal.	116	67	57.8	958	8.26	7	6.0	92	1	0.9	17	98	101.1
Foley, Glenn, NY-J	97	56	57.7	705	7.27	3	3.1	35t	1	1.0	3	24	86.5
Matthews, Steve, Jax.	40	26	65.0	275	6.88	0	0.0	43	0	0.0	1	0	84.9
Tolliver, Billy Joe, Atl.-K.C.	116	64	55.2	677	5.84	5	4.3	47t	1	0.9	14	104	83.2
Kitna, Jon, Sea.	45	31	68.9	371	8.24	1	2.2	61	2	4.4	3	10	82.7
Gannon, Rich, K.C.	175	98	56.0	1144	6.54	7	4.0	47	4	2.3	13	86	79.8
Justin, Paul, Ind.	140	83	59.3	1046	7.47	5	3.6	44	5	3.6	10	86	79.6
Tomczak, Mike, Pit.	24	16	66.7	185	7.71	1	4.2	28t	2	8.3	0	0	68.9
Philcox, Todd, S.D.	28	16	57.1	173	6.18	0	0.0	29	1	3.6	8	44	60.6
Erickson, Craig, Mia.	28	13	46.4	165	5.89	0	0.0	27	1	3.6	2	21	50.4
Everett, Jim, S.D.	75	36	48.0	457	6.09	1	1.3	62	4	5.3	4	30	49.7
Holcomb, Kelly, Ind.	73	45	61.6	454	6.22	1	1.4	41	8	11.0	11	76	44.3
Van Pelt, Alex, Buf.	124	60	48.4	684	5.52	2	1.6	39	10	8.1	4	33	37.2
Friesz, John, Sea.	36	15	41.7	138	3.83	0	0.0	22	3	8.3	2	11	18.1

1997 INDIVIDUAL STATISTICS—PASSING

Fewer than 10 attempts	Att.	Comp.	Pct. Comp.	Yds.	Avg. Gain	TD	Pct. TD	Long	Int.	Pct. Int.	Sack	Yds. Lost	Rating Points
Aguiar, Louie, K.C.	1	1	100.0	35	35.00	0	0.0	35	0	0.0	0	0	118.8
Allen, Marcus, K.C.	2	2	100.0	15	7.50	2	100.0	14t	0	0.0	0	0	137.5
Barker, Bryan, Jax.	1	1	100.0	22	22.00	0	0.0	22	0	0.0	0	0	118.8
Brister, Bubby, Den.	9	6	66.7	48	5.33	0	0.0	15	0	0.0	0	0	79.9
Carter, Ki-Jana, Cin.	1	0	0.0	0	0.00	0	0.0	0	0	0.0	0	0	39.6
Davis, Willie, Ten.	1	1	100.0	22	22.00	1	100.0	22t	0	0.0	0	0	158.3
Galloway, Joey, Sea.	0	0	—	0	—	0	—	—	0	—	1	15	—
Hansen, Brian, NY-J	1	1	100.0	26	26.00	0	0.0	26	0	0.0	0	0	118.8
Johnson, Leon, NY-J	2	0	0.0	0	0.00	0	0.0	0	1	50.0	0	0	0.0
Kaufman, Napoleon, Oak.	1	0	0.0	0	0.00	0	0.0	0	0	0.0	0	0	39.6
Klingler, David, Oak.	7	4	57.1	27	3.86	0	0.0	8	1	14.3	0	0	26.2
Krieg, Dave, Ten.	2	1	50.0	2	1.00	0	0.0	2	0	0.0	0	0	56.3
Lewis, Jeff, Den.	2	1	50.0	21	10.50	0	0.0	21	0	0.0	1	7	87.5
Lucas, Ray, NY-J	4	3	75.0	28	7.00	0	0.0	19	1	25.0	0	0	54.2
Meggett, David, N.E.	1	1	100.0	35	35.00	1	100.0	35t	0	0.0	0	0	158.3
Mohr, Chris, Buf.	1	1	100.0	29	29.00	0	0.0	29	0	0.0	0	0	118.8
Quinn, Mike, Pit.	2	1	50.0	10	5.00	0	0.0	10	0	0.0	0	0	64.6
Reed, Andre, Buf.	0	0	—	0	—	0	—	—	0	—	1	20	—
Ritchey, James, Ten.	2	2	100.0	15	7.50	0	0.0	11	0	0.0	1	9	97.9
Warren, Lamont, Ind.	1	0	0.0	0	0.00	0	0.0	0	0	0.0	0	0	39.6
Zolak, Scott, N.E.	9	6	66.7	67	7.44	2	22.2	20t	0	0.0	0	0	128.2

t = Touchdown
Leader based on rating points, minimum 224 attempts

NFC PASSING—INDIVIDUAL

	Att.	Comp.	Pct. Comp.	Yds.	Avg. Gain	TD	Pct. TD	Long	Int.	Pct. Int.	Sack	Yds. Lost	Rating Points
Young, Steve, S.F.	356	241	67.7	3029	8.51	19	5.3	82	6	1.7	35	220	104.7
Chandler, Chris, Atl.	342	202	59.1	2692	7.87	20	5.8	56	7	2.0	39	261	95.1
Favre, Brett, G.B.	513	304	59.3	3867	7.54	35	6.8	74	16	3.1	25	176	92.6
Johnson, Brad, Min.	452	275	60.8	3036	6.72	20	4.4	56	12	2.7	26	164	84.5
Hoying, Bobby, Phi.	225	128	56.9	1573	6.99	11	4.9	72t	6	2.7	28	183	83.8
Dilfer, Trent, T.B.	386	217	56.2	2555	6.62	21	5.4	59t	11	2.8	32	196	82.8
Mitchell, Scott, Det.	509	293	57.6	3484	6.84	19	3.7	79	14	2.8	41	271	79.6
Aikman, Troy, Dal.	518	292	56.4	3283	6.34	19	3.7	64t	12	2.3	33	269	78.0
Kramer, Erik, Chi.	477	275	57.7	3011	6.31	14	2.9	78t	14	2.9	25	149	74.0
Detmer, Ty, Phi.	244	134	54.9	1567	6.42	7	2.9	57	6	2.5	19	94	73.9
Frerotte, Gus, Was.	402	204	50.7	2682	6.67	17	4.2	52	12	3.0	23	146	73.8
Plummer, Jake, Ariz	296	157	53.0	2203	7.44	15	5.1	70t	15	5.1	52	291	73.1
Banks, Tony, St.L	487	252	51.7	3254	6.68	14	2.9	76	13	2.7	43	317	71.5
Kanell, Danny, NY-G	294	156	53.1	1740	5.92	11	3.7	68t	9	3.1	19	171	70.7
Graham, Kent, Ariz	250	130	52.0	1408	5.63	4	1.6	47	5	2.0	16	115	65.9
Collins, Kerry, Car.	381	200	52.5	2124	5.57	11	2.9	59t	21	5.5	27	200	55.7
Nonqualifiers													
Beuerlein, Steve, Car.	153	89	58.2	1032	6.75	6	3.9	52	3	2.0	17	111	83.6
Garrett, Jason, Dal.	14	10	71.4	56	4.00	0	0.0	12	0	0.0	2	18	78.3
Peete, Rodney, Phi.	118	68	57.6	869	7.36	4	3.4	38	4	3.4	17	85	78.0
Wilson, Wade, Dal.	21	12	57.1	115	5.48	0	0.0	32	0	0.0	4	26	72.5
Cunningham, Randall, Min.	88	44	50.0	501	5.69	6	6.8	34	4	4.5	7	60	71.3
Brown, Dave, NY-G	180	93	51.7	1023	5.68	5	2.8	62	3	1.7	13	67	71.1
Brohm, Jeff, S.F.	24	16	66.7	164	6.83	0	0.0	21	1	4.2	5	37	68.8
Hostetler, Jeff, Was.	144	79	54.9	899	6.24	5	3.5	69	10	6.9	10	52	56.5
Bono, Steve, G.B.	10	5	50.0	29	2.90	0	0.0	14	0	0.0	1	15	56.3
Hobert, Billy Joe, Buf.-N.O.	161	78	48.4	1024	6.36	6	3.7	49	10	6.2	6	36	55.5
Case, Stoney, Ariz	55	29	52.7	316	5.75	0	0.0	30	2	3.6	10	89	54.8
Rypien, Mark, St.L	39	19	48.7	270	6.92	0	0.0	62	2	5.1	1	9	50.2
Shuler, Heath, N.O.	203	106	52.2	1288	6.34	2	1.0	89t	14	6.9	21	132	46.6
Wuerffel, Danny, N.O.	91	42	46.2	518	5.69	4	4.4	47	8	8.8	18	116	42.3
Mirer, Rick, Chi.	103	53	51.5	420	4.08	0	0.0	34	6	5.8	16	89	37.7
Nussmeier, Doug, N.O.	32	18	56.3	183	5.72	0	0.0	24	3	9.4	6	32	33.7
Stenstrom, Steve, Chi.	14	8	57.1	70	5.00	0	0.0	18	2	14.3	2	19	31.0
Druckenmiller, Jim, S.F.	52	21	40.4	239	4.60	1	1.9	33	4	7.7	4	32	29.2
Reich, Frank, Det.	30	11	36.7	121	4.03	0	0.0	27	2	6.7	0	0	21.7
Walsh, Steve, T.B.	17	6	35.3	58	3.41	0	0.0	38	1	5.9	0	0	21.2
Graziani, Tony, Atl.	23	7	30.4	41	1.78	0	0.0	13	2	8.7	1	7	3.7
Fewer than 10 attempts													
Anderson, Jamal, Atl.	4	1	25.0	27	6.75	1	25.0	27t	1	25.0	0	0	55.2
Barnhardt, Tommy, T.B.	1	1	100.0	25	25.00	0	0.0	25	0	0.0	0	0	118.8
Bates, Mario, N.O.	1	1	100.0	21	21.00	1	100.0	21t	0	0.0	0	0	158.3
Blundin, Matt, Det.	1	0	0.0	0	0.00	0	0.0	0	1	100.0	0	0	0.0
Conway, Curtis, Chi.	1	0	0.0	0	0.00	0	0.0	0	0	0.0	0	0	39.6
Green, Trent, Was.	1	0	0.0	0	0.00	0	0.0	0	0	0.0	0	0	39.6
Hill, Randal, N.O.	0	0	—	0	—	0	—	—	0	—	1	8	—
Sanders, Frank, Ariz	1	1	100.0	26	26.00	0	0.0	26	0	0.0	0	0	118.8

t = Touchdown
Leader based on rating points, minimum 224 attempts

PASS RECEIVING

Receptions
- AFC: 104—Tim Brown, Oakland
- NFC: 104—Herman Moore, Detroit

Receptions, Game
- AFC: 14—Tim Brown, Oakland vs. Jacksonville, December 21 (164 yards)
- NFC: 12—Jake Reed, Minnesota at Chicago, September 7 (118 yards - TD)

Yards
- NFC: 1584—Rob Moore, Arizona
- AFC: 1408—Tim Brown, Oakland

Yards, Game
- NFC: 233—Isaac Bruce, St. Louis at Atlanta, November 2 (10 receptions - 2 TD)
- AFC: 196—Yancey Thigpen, Pittsburgh vs. Jacksonville, October 26 (11 receptions)

Longest
- AFC: 92—Derrick Alexander (from Eric Zeier), Baltimore vs. Seattle, December 7
- NFC: 89—Randal Hill (from Heath Shuler), New Orleans at Chicago, October 5 - TD

Yards Per Reception
- AFC: 18.7—James McKnight, Seattle
- NFC: 16.8—Robert Brooks, Green Bay

Touchdowns
- NFC: 13—Cris Carter, Minnesota
- AFC: 12—Joey Galloway, Seattle
  James Jett, Oakland
  Rod Smith, Denver

Team Leaders, Receptions

AFC: BALTIMORE: 69, Michael Jackson; BUFFALO: 60, Quinn Early, Andre Reed; CINCINNATI: 54, Darnay Scott; DENVER: 72, Shannon Sharpe; INDIANAPOLIS: 73, Marvin Harrison; JACKSONVILLE: 85, Keenan McCardell; KANSAS CITY: 72, Andre Rison; MIAMI: 76, O. J. McDuffie; NEW ENGLAND: 66, Ben Coates; N.Y. JETS: 70, Keyshawn Johnson; OAKLAND: 104, Tim Brown; PITTSBURGH: 79, Yancey Thigpen; SAN DIEGO: 63, Tony Martin; SEATTLE: 72, Joey Galloway; TENNESSEE: 63, Frank Wycheck

NFC: ARIZONA: 97, Rob Moore; ATLANTA: 65, Bert Emanuel; CAROLINA: 58, Wesley Walls; CHICAGO: 58, Ricky Proehl; DALLAS: 75, Michael Irvin; DETROIT: 104, Herman Moore; GREEN BAY: 81, Antonio Freeman; MINNESOTA: 89, Cris Carter; NEW ORLEANS: 55, Randal Hill; N.Y. GIANTS: 58, Chris Calloway; PHILADELPHIA: 86, Irving Fryar; ST. LOUIS: 61, Amp Lee; SAN FRANCISCO: 60, Terrell Owens; TAMPA BAY: 39, Warrick Dunn; WASHINGTON: 49, Jamie Asher

NFL TOP TEN PASS RECEIVERS

	No.	Yards	Avg.	Long	TD
Brown, Tim, Oak.	104	1408	13.5	59t	5
Moore, Herman, Det.	104	1293	12.4	79	8
Moore, Rob, Ariz	97	1584	16.3	47t	8
Carter, Cris, Min.	89	1069	12.0	43	13
Fryar, Irving, Phi.	86	1316	15.3	72t	6
McCardell, Keenan, Jax.	85	1164	13.7	60	5
Smith, Jimmy, Jax.	82	1324	16.1	75	4
Freeman, Antonio, G.B.	81	1243	15.3	58t	12
Morton, Johnnie, Det.	80	1057	13.2	73t	6
Thigpen, Yancey, Pit.	79	1398	17.7	69t	7

NFL TOP TEN RECEIVERS BY YARDS

	Yards	No.	Avg.	Long	TD
Moore, Rob, Ariz	1584	97	16.3	47t	8
Brown, Tim, Oak.	1408	104	13.5	59t	5
Thigpen, Yancey, Pit.	1398	79	17.7	69t	7
Smith, Jimmy, Jax.	1324	82	16.1	75	4
Fryar, Irving, Phi.	1316	86	15.3	72t	6
Moore, Herman, Det.	1293	104	12.4	79	8
Freeman, Antonio, G.B.	1243	81	15.3	58t	12
Irvin, Michael, Dal.	1180	75	15.7	55	9
Smith, Rod, Den.	1180	70	16.9	78	12
McCardell, Keenan, Jax.	1164	85	13.7	60	5

AFC RECEIVERS—INDIVIDUAL

	No.	Yards	Avg.	Long	TD
Brown, Tim, Oak.	104	1408	13.5	59t	5
McCardell, Keenan, Jax.	85	1164	13.7	60	5
Smith, Jimmy, Jax.	82	1324	16.1	75	4
Thigpen, Yancey, Pit.	79	1398	17.7	69t	7
McDuffie, O. J., Mia.	76	943	12.4	55	1
Harrison, Marvin, Ind.	73	866	11.9	44	6
Sharpe, Shannon, Den.	72	1107	15.4	68t	3
Rison, Andre, K.C.	72	1092	15.2	45	7
Galloway, Joey, Sea.	72	1049	14.6	53t	12
Smith, Rod, Den.	70	1180	16.9	78	12
Johnson, Keyshawn, NY-J	70	963	13.8	39	5
Jackson, Michael, Bal.	69	918	13.3	54t	4
Dawkins, Sean, Ind.	68	804	11.8	51	2
Coates, Ben, N.E.	66	737	11.2	35	8
Alexander, Derrick, Bal.	65	1009	15.5	92	9
Green, Eric, Bal.	65	601	9.2	37t	5
Pritchard, Mike, Sea.	64	843	13.2	61	2
Martin, Tony, S.D.	63	904	14.3	72t	6
Wycheck, Frank, Ten.	63	748	11.9	42	4
Reed, Andre, Buf.	60	880	14.7	77t	5
Early, Quinn, Buf.	60	853	14.2	45	5
Anders, Kimble, K.C.	59	453	7.7	55t	2
Chrebet, Wayne, NY-J	58	799	13.8	70	3
Jefferson, Shawn, N.E.	54	841	15.6	76	2
Scott, Darnay, Cin.	54	797	14.8	77t	5
Pickens, Carl, Cin.	52	695	13.4	50t	5
Dudley, Rickey, Oak.	48	787	16.4	76	7
Faulk, Marshall, Ind.	47	471	10.0	58	1
Jett, James, Oak.	46	804	17.5	56t	12
Johnson, Charles, Pit.	46	568	12.3	49	2
McCaffrey, Ed, Den.	45	590	13.1	35	8
Hawkins, Courtney, Pit.	45	555	12.3	44t	3
Warren, Chris, Sea.	45	257	5.7	20	0
Davis, Willie, Ten.	43	564	13.1	46	4
Lewis, Jermaine, Bal.	42	648	15.4	42t	6
Graham, Jeff, NY-J	42	542	12.9	47t	2
Davis, Terrell, Den.	42	287	6.8	25	0
Brown, Troy, N.E.	41	607	14.8	67	6
Jones, Freddie, S.D.	41	505	12.3	62	2
Johnson, Lonnie, Buf.	41	340	8.3	62t	2
Stewart, James, Jax.	41	336	8.2	40	1
Martin, Curtis, N.E.	41	296	7.2	22	1
Metcalf, Eric, S.D.	40	576	14.4	62	2
Kaufman, Napoleon, Oak.	40	403	10.1	70t	2
Drayton, Troy, Mia.	39	558	14.3	30t	4
Fletcher, Terrell, S.D.	39	292	7.5	25	0
Mitchell, Pete, Jax.	35	380	10.9	33	4
Popson, Ted, K.C.	35	320	9.1	21	2
McKnight, James, Sea.	34	637	18.7	60t	6
McGee, Tony, Cin.	34	414	12.2	37	6
McPhail, Jerris, Mia.	34	262	7.7	19	1
Gonzalez, Tony, K.C.	33	368	11.2	30	2
Jones, Charlie, S.D.	32	423	13.2	44t	1
Sanders, Chris, Ten.	31	498	16.1	55t	3
Crumpler, Carlester, Sea.	31	361	11.6	30	1
Bieniemy, Eric, Cin.	31	249	8.0	21	0
Blades, Brian, Sea.	30	319	10.6	27	2
Thomas, Thurman, Buf.	30	208	6.9	30	0
Moulds, Eric, Buf.	29	294	10.1	32	0
Abdul-Jabbar, Karim, Mia.	29	261	9.0	36t	1
Morris, Bam, Bal.	29	176	6.1	15	0
Thomas, Lamar, Mia.	28	402	14.4	26	2
Parmalee, Bernie, Mia.	28	301	10.8	29	1
Smith, Antowain, Buf.	28	177	6.3	19	0
Jordan, Charles, Mia.	27	471	17.4	44t	3
Glenn, Terry, N.E.	27	431	16.0	50	2
Dunn, David, Cin.	27	414	15.3	39t	2
Dilger, Ken, Ind.	27	380	14.1	43	3
Baxter, Fred, NY-J	27	276	10.2	37	3
Dillon, Corey, Cin.	27	259	9.6	28	0
Murrell, Adrian, NY-J	27	106	3.9	23	0
Bailey, Aaron, Ind.	26	329	12.7	22	3
Riemersma, Jay, Buf.	26	208	8.0	22	2
Anderson, Richie, NY-J	26	150	5.8	19	1
Perriman, Brett, K.C.-Mia.	25	392	15.7	27	1
Stablein, Brian, Ind.	25	253	10.1	30	1
Still, Bryan, S.D.	24	324	13.5	39	0
Broussard, Steve, Sea.	24	143	6.0	20t	1
Brisby, Vincent, N.E.	23	276	12.0	31	2
Smith, Lamar, Sea.	23	183	8.0	22	0
Milne, Brian, Cin.	23	138	6.0	20	0
Brady, Kyle, NY-J	22	238	10.8	24	2
Gash, Sam, N.E.	22	154	7.0	19	3
Dawson, Lake, K.C.	21	273	13.0	27	2
Carter, Ki-Jana, Cin.	21	157	7.5	35	0
Brown, Gary, S.D.	21	137	6.5	27	0
Byner, Earnest, Bal.	21	128	6.1	17	0
Warren, Lamont, Ind.	20	192	9.6	31	0
Byars, Keith, N.E.	20	189	9.5	51	3

1997 INDIVIDUAL STATISTICS—RECEIVING

	No.	Yards	Avg.	Long	TD
Hartley, Frank, S.D.	19	246	12.9	35	1
Green, Willie, Den.	19	240	12.6	31	2
Meggett, David, N.E.	19	203	10.7	49t	1
Ward, Dedric, NY-J	18	212	11.8	33	1
Hallock, Ty, Jax.	18	131	7.3	23	1
Bruener, Mark, Pit.	18	117	6.5	18t	6
Jackson, Willie, Jax.	17	206	12.1	45	2
Barnett, Fred, Mia.	17	166	9.8	20	1
Hundon, James, Cin.	16	285	17.8	61	2
Yarborough, Ryan, Bal.	16	183	11.4	26	0
Williams, Harvey, Oak.	16	147	9.2	32t	2
Johnson, Leon, NY-J	16	142	8.9	20	0
Jones, George, Pit.	16	96	6.0	25	1
Crockett, Zack, Ind.	15	112	7.5	19	0
Bettis, Jerome, Pit.	15	110	7.3	19t	2
Means, Natrone, Jax.	15	104	6.9	21	0
Mason, Derrick, Ten.	14	186	13.3	38	0
Thomas, Rodney, Ten.	14	111	7.9	22	0
Fenner, Derrick, Oak.	14	92	6.6	13	0
Holmes, Darick, Buf.	13	106	8.2	22	0
Strong, Mack, Sea.	13	91	7.0	20	2
Blackwell, Will, Pit.	12	168	14.0	46	1
Roan, Michael, Ten.	12	159	13.3	26	0
Battaglia, Marco, Cin.	12	149	12.4	34	1
Russell, Derek, Ten.	12	141	11.8	23	1
Hill, Greg, K.C.	12	126	10.5	39	0
Carswell, Dwayne, Den.	12	96	8.0	24t	1
Graham, Jay, Bal.	12	51	4.3	19	0
Kinchen, Brian, Bal.	11	95	8.6	24t	1
Allen, Marcus, K.C.	11	86	7.8	18	0
Griffith, Howard, Den.	11	55	5.0	20	0
Perry, Ed, Mia.	11	45	4.1	10	1
Phillips, Lawrence, St.L-Mia.	11	39	3.5	17	0
Pollard, Marcus, Ind.	10	116	11.6	28	0
Shedd, Kenny, Oak.	10	115	11.5	19	0
Fauria, Christian, Sea.	10	110	11.0	25	0
Lester, Tim, Pit.	10	51	5.1	14	0
Brown, Derek, Jax.	8	84	10.5	21	1
Neal, Lorenzo, NY-J	8	40	5.0	14	1
Roe, James, Bal.	7	124	17.7	29	0
Vanover, Tamarick, K.C.	7	92	13.1	42	0
Truitt, Olanda, Oak.	7	91	13.0	19t	1
Hobbs, Daryl, N.O.-Sea.	7	85	12.1	21	1
Manning, Brian, Mia.	7	85	12.1	21	0
Spikes, Irving, Mia.	7	70	10.0	24	0
Hughes, Danan, K.C.	7	65	9.3	14t	2
George, Eddie, Ten.	7	44	6.3	15	1
Bennett, Donnell, K.C.	7	5	0.7	4	0
Kent, Joey, Ten.	6	55	9.2	19	1
Jones, Damon, Jax.	5	87	17.4	26t	2
Barlow, Reggie, Jax.	5	74	14.8	29	0
Walker, Derrick, K.C.	5	60	12.0	22	0
Purnell, Lovett, N.E.	5	57	11.4	20t	3
Pritchett, Stanley, Mia.	5	35	7.0	17	0
Tindale, Tim, Buf.	4	105	26.3	45	0
Harris, Ronnie, Sea.	4	81	20.3	34	0
Smith, Detron, Den.	4	41	10.3	17t	1
Howard, Desmond, Oak.	4	30	7.5	9	0
Lyons, Mitch, Pit.	4	29	7.3	13	0
Craver, Aaron, S.D.	4	26	6.5	20	0
Van Dyke, Alex, NY-J	3	53	17.7	18t	2
Hebron, Vaughn, Den.	3	36	12.0	21	0
Potts, Roosevelt, Mia.	3	27	9.0	13	0
Jeffers, Patrick, Den.	3	24	8.0	10	0
Slutzker, Scott, Ind.	3	22	7.3	11	0
Richardson, Tony, K.C.	3	6	2.0	3t	3
Horn, Joe, K.C.	2	65	32.5	47	0
Davis, Tyree, Sea.	2	48	24.0	37	0
McAfee, Fred, Pit.	2	44	22.0	30	0
Davison, Jerone, Oak.	2	34	17.0	25	0
Levitt, Chad, Oak.	2	24	12.0	22	0
May, Deems, Sea.	2	21	10.5	11	0
Chamberlain, Byron, Den.	2	18	9.0	9	0
Marsh, Curtis, Pit.	2	14	7.0	8	0
Doering, Chris, Ind.	2	12	6.0	8	0
Gardner, Carwell, S.D.	2	10	5.0	8	0
Loville, Derek, Den.	2	10	5.0	7	0
Cullors, Derrick, N.E.	2	8	4.0	6	0
Bynum, Kenny, S.D.	2	4	2.0	3	0
Adams, Mike, Pit.	1	39	39.0	39	0
Lockett, Kevin, K.C.	1	35	35.0	35	0
Cline, Tony, Buf.	1	29	29.0	29	0
Brown, Corwin, NY-J	1	26	26.0	26	0
Hall, Dana, Jax.	1	22	22.0	22	0
Lynn, Anthony, Den.	1	21	21.0	21	0
Mitchell, Shannon, S.D.	1	14	14.0	14	0
Reese, Jerry, Buf.	1	13	13.0	13	0
Sadowski, Troy, Pit.	1	12	12.0	12	0
Botkin, Kirk, Pit.	1	11	11.0	11	0
Moore, Will, Jax.	1	10	10.0	10	0
Hall, Tim, Oak.	1	9	9.0	9	0
Jells, Dietrich, N.E.	1	9	9.0	9	0
Sowell, Jerald, NY-J	1	8	8.0	8	0
Lewis, Roderick, Ten.	1	7	7.0	7	0
Dotson, DeWayne, Mia.	1	4	4.0	4	0
Glenn, Tarik, Ind.	1	3	3.0	3	0
Witman, Jon, Pit.	1	3	3.0	3	0
Norgard, Erik, Ten.	1	2	2.0	2t	1
Graham, Scottie, Cin.	1	1	1.0	1	0
Nalen, Tom, Den.	1	-1	-1.0	-1	0
Testaverde, Vinny, Bal.	1	-4	-4.0	-4	0

t = Touchdown
Leader based on receptions

NFC RECEIVERS—INDIVIDUAL

	No.	Yards	Avg.	Long	TD
Moore, Herman, Det.	104	1293	12.4	79	8
Moore, Rob, Ariz	97	1584	16.3	47t	8
Carter, Cris, Min.	89	1069	12.0	43	13
Fryar, Irving, Phi.	86	1316	15.3	72t	6
Freeman, Antonio, G.B.	81	1243	15.3	58t	12
Morton, Johnnie, Det.	80	1057	13.2	73t	6
Irvin, Michael, Dal.	75	1180	15.7	55	9
Sanders, Frank, Ariz	75	1017	13.6	70t	4
Reed, Jake, Min.	68	1138	16.7	56	6
Emanuel, Bert, Atl.	65	991	15.2	56	9
Mathis, Terance, Atl.	62	802	12.9	49	6
Lee, Amp, St.L	61	825	13.5	62	3
Brooks, Robert, G.B.	60	1010	16.8	48	7
Owens, Terrell, S.F.	60	936	15.6	56t	8
Calloway, Chris, NY-G	58	849	14.6	68t	8
Proehl, Ricky, Chi.	58	753	13.0	78t	7
Walls, Wesley, Car.	58	746	12.9	52	6
Stokes, J.J., S.F.	58	733	12.6	36	4
Bruce, Isaac, St.L	56	815	14.6	59	5
Hill, Randal, N.O.	55	761	13.8	89t	2
Centers, Larry, Ariz	54	409	7.6	29	1
Levens, Dorsey, G.B.	53	370	7.0	56	5
Asher, Jamie, Was.	49	474	9.7	24	1
Hastings, Andre, N.O.	48	722	15.0	39	5
Turner, Kevin, Phi.	48	443	9.2	36	3
Watters, Ricky, Phi.	48	440	9.2	37	0
Penn, Chris, Chi.	47	576	12.3	33	3
Bjornson, Eric, Dal.	47	442	9.4	32	0
Miller, Anthony, Dal.	46	645	14.0	54	4
Wetnight, Ryan, Chi.	46	464	10.1	34	1
Engram, Bobby, Chi.	45	399	8.9	23	2
Carruth, Rae, Car.	44	545	12.4	52	4
Timpson, Michael, Phi.	42	484	11.5	26	2
Henderson, William, G.B.	41	367	9.0	25	1
Greene, Scott, Car.	40	277	6.9	25	1
Smith, Emmitt, Dal.	40	234	5.9	24	0
Dunn, Warrick, T.B.	39	462	11.8	59t	3
Chmura, Mark, G.B.	38	417	11.0	32t	6
Conwell, Ernie, St.L	38	404	10.6	46t	4
Floyd, William, S.F.	37	321	8.7	44t	1
Way, Charles, NY-G	37	304	8.2	62	1
Smith, Robert, Min.	37	197	5.3	20	1
Mitchell, Brian, Was.	36	438	12.2	69	1
Ismail, Raghib, Car.	36	419	11.6	59t	2
Anthony, Reidel, T.B.	35	448	12.8	38t	4
Westbrook, Michael, Was.	34	559	16.4	40t	3
Bowie, Larry, Was.	34	388	11.4	39t	2
Barber, Tiki, NY-G	34	299	8.8	29	1
Williams, Karl, T.B.	33	486	14.7	55	4
Carrier, Mark, Car.	33	436	13.2	36	2
Copeland, Horace, T.B.	33	431	13.1	49	1
Sanders, Barry, Det.	33	305	9.2	66t	3
Small, Torrance, St.L	32	488	15.3	46	1
Ellard, Henry, Was.	32	485	15.2	27	4
Glover, Andrew, Min.	32	378	11.8	43	3
Zellars, Ray, N.O.	31	263	8.5	38	0
Conway, Curtis, Chi.	30	476	15.9	55t	1

1997 INDIVIDUAL STATISTICS—RECEIVING

	No.	Yards	Avg.	Long	TD
Williams, Stepfret, Dal.	30	308	10.3	20	1
Shepherd, Leslie, Was.	29	562	19.4	48	5
Solomon, Freddie, Phi.	29	455	15.7	56	3
Jones, Brent, S.F.	29	383	13.2	33	2
Green, Harold, Atl.	29	360	12.4	47	0
Anderson, Jamal, Atl.	29	284	9.8	47t	3
Sloan, David, Det.	29	264	9.1	25	0
Harris, Raymont, Chi.	28	115	4.1	16	0
Guliford, Eric, N.O.	27	362	13.4	47	1
Muhammad, Muhsin, Car.	27	317	11.7	38	0
Palmer, David, Min.	26	193	7.4	23	1
Kennison, Eddie, St.L	25	404	16.2	76	0
Garner, Charlie, Phi.	24	225	9.4	27	0
Carter, Tony, Chi.	24	152	6.3	19	0
Kirby, Terry, S.F.	23	279	12.1	82	1
Gedney, Chris, Ariz	23	261	11.3	37t	4
Alstott, Mike, T.B.	23	178	7.7	26	3
Christian, Bob, Atl.	22	154	7.0	19	1
Hearst, Garrison, S.F.	21	194	9.2	69	2
Williams, Sherman, Dal.	21	159	7.6	18	0
Johnson, Anthony, Car.	21	158	7.5	25	1
Evans, Chuck, Min.	21	152	7.2	17	0
Cross, Howard, NY-G	21	150	7.1	26	2
Pegram, Erric, S.D.-NY-G	21	90	4.3	14	0
Williams, Kevin, Ariz	20	273	13.7	31t	1
Edwards, Anthony, Ariz	20	203	10.2	33	0
Allen, Terry, Was.	20	172	8.6	38	1
Moore, Dave, T.B.	19	217	11.4	28	4
Harris, Jackie, T.B.	19	197	10.4	39	1
Mayes, Derrick, G.B.	18	290	16.1	74	0
Alexander, Kevin, NY-G	18	276	15.3	40	1
Harmon, Ronnie, Ten.-Chi.	18	197	10.9	27	0
Johnston, Daryl, Dal.	18	166	9.2	21	1
Davis, Stephen, Was.	18	134	7.4	19	0
LaFleur, David, Dal.	18	122	6.8	17	2
Farquhar, John, N.O.	17	253	14.9	42	1
Santiago, O.J., Atl.	17	217	12.8	30	2
Smith, Irv, N.O.	17	180	10.6	25	1
Metzelaars, Pete, Det.	17	144	8.5	22	0
Kinchen, Todd, Atl.	16	266	16.6	53t	1
Toomer, Amani, NY-G	16	263	16.4	56t	1
Vardell, Tommy, Det.	16	218	13.6	37	0
Wheatley, Tyrone, NY-G	16	140	8.8	27	0
Johnson, Jimmie, Phi.	14	177	12.6	28	1
Uwaezuoke, Iheanyi, S.F.	14	165	11.8	25	0
Jennings, Keith, Chi.	14	164	11.7	23	0
Walker, Herschel, Dal.	14	149	10.6	64t	2
Patten, David, NY-G	13	226	17.4	40t	2
Seay, Mark, Phi.	13	187	14.4	38	1
Thomas, Robb, T.B.	13	129	9.9	21	0
Davis, Troy, N.O.	13	85	6.5	18	0
Haynes, Michael, Atl.	12	154	12.8	24t	1
Bownes, Fabien, Chi.	12	146	12.2	21	0
Lewis, Chad, Phi.	12	94	7.8	17	4
Crawford, Keith, St.L	11	232	21.1	69	0
Mills, Ernie, Car.	11	127	11.5	37	1
Walsh, Chris, Min.	11	114	10.4	19	1
Thomas, Chris, Was.	11	93	8.5	17	0
Hoard, Leroy, Min.	11	84	7.6	30	0
Boyd, Tommie, Det.	10	142	14.2	32	0
Pierce, Aaron, NY-G	10	47	4.7	14	0
Connell, Albert, Was.	9	138	15.3	41t	2
Thomason, Jeff, G.B.	9	115	12.8	27	1
Autry, Darnell, Chi.	9	59	6.6	14	0
Clark, Greg, S.F.	8	96	12.0	23	1
Heyward, Craig, St.L	8	77	9.6	25	0
DeLong, Greg, Min.	8	75	9.4	23	0
Allred, John, Chi.	8	70	8.8	18	0
Moore, Jerald, St.L	8	69	8.6	19	0
Hughes, Tyrone, Chi.	8	68	8.5	16	0
Lane, Fred, Car.	8	27	3.4	7	0
Kozlowski, Brian, Atl.	7	99	14.1	29	1
Dunn, Jason, Phi.	7	93	13.3	31t	2
Rice, Jerry, S.F.	7	78	11.1	16	1
McWilliams, Johnny, Ariz	7	75	10.7	15	0
West, Ed, Atl.	7	63	9.0	23	1
Goodwin, Hunter, Min.	7	61	8.7	14	0
Carter, Pat, Ariz	7	44	6.3	15	1
McElroy, Leeland, Ariz	7	32	4.6	17	0
Hanspard, Byron, Atl.	6	53	8.8	21	1
Edwards, Marc, S.F.	6	48	8.0	19	0
Oliver, Winslow, Car.	6	47	7.8	11	0
Lewis, Thomas, NY-G	5	84	16.8	34	0
Fann, Chad, S.F.	5	78	15.6	21	0
Milburn, Glyn, Det.	5	77	15.4	43	0
Jones, Chris T., Phi.	5	73	14.6	32	0
Schlesinger, Cory, Det.	5	69	13.8	33	1
Levy, Chuck, S.F.	5	68	13.6	30	0
Harris, Mark, S.F.	5	53	10.6	16	0
Bates, Mario, N.O.	5	42	8.4	15	0
Laing, Aaron, St.L	5	31	6.2	11	1
Poole, Keith, N.O.	4	98	24.5	49	2
Mangum, Kris, Car.	4	56	14.0	22	0
Twyner, Gunnard, Cin.	4	45	11.3	16	0
Jenkins, James, Was.	4	43	10.8	20	3
Floyd, Malcolm, St.L	4	39	9.8	14	0
Moore, Ronald, St.L	4	34	8.5	13	0
Hape, Patrick, T.B.	4	22	5.5	13	1
McCrary, Fred, N.O.	4	17	4.3	11	0
Williams, Moe, Min.	4	14	3.5	7	0
Hatchette, Matt, Min.	3	54	18.0	38	0
Bech, Brett, N.O.	3	50	16.7	22	0
Ross, Jermaine, St.L	3	37	12.3	14	0
Davis, John, T.B.	3	35	11.7	16	0
Davis, Billy, Dal.	3	33	11.0	12	0
Chryplewicz, Pete, Det.	3	27	9.0	12	1
Logan, Marc, Was.	3	6	2.0	5	0
Johnson, LeShon, Ariz	3	4	1.3	7	0
Harper, Alvin, Was.	2	65	32.5	52	0
Hilliard, Ike, NY-G	2	42	21.0	23	0
Beebe, Don, G.B.	2	28	14.0	23	0
Davis, Tyrone, G.B.	2	28	14.0	26	1
Thomas, J.T., St.L	2	25	12.5	16	0
Thrash, James, Was.	2	24	12.0	17	0
Smith, Eric, Chi.	2	22	11.0	12	0
Staley, Duce, Phi.	2	22	11.0	22	0
Salaam, Rashaan, Chi.	2	20	10.0	18	0
Smith, Cedric, Ariz	2	20	10.0	18	0
Galbraith, Scott, Dal.	2	16	8.0	11	0
Schroeder, Bill, G.B.	2	15	7.5	8	1
Hayden, Aaron, G.B.	2	11	5.5	7	0
Jacoby, Mitch, St.L	2	10	5.0	10	0
McCorvey, Kez, Det.	2	9	4.5	6	0
Brock, Fred, Ariz	1	29	29.0	29	0
Bouie, Tony, T.B.	1	25	25.0	25	0
Savoie, Nicky, N.O.	1	14	14.0	14	0
Johnson, Tony, N.O.	1	13	13.0	13	0
Allen, Tremayne, Chi.	1	9	9.0	9	0
Ellison, Jerry, T.B.	1	8	8.0	8	0
Pupunu, Alfred, S.D.	1	7	7.0	7	0
Green, Robert, Min.	1	5	5.0	5	0
Johnson, Brad, Min.	1	3	3.0	3t	1
Mickens, Terry, G.B.	1	2	2.0	2t	1
Plummer, Jake, Ariz	1	2	2.0	2	0
Smith, Ed, Atl.	1	2	2.0	2	0
Rasby, Walter, Car.	1	1	1.0	1	0
Wiegert, Zach, St.L	1	1	1.0	1	0
Gruttadauria, Mike, St.L	1	0	0.0	0	0
Jordan, Andrew, T.B.	1	0	0.0	0	0

t = Touchdown
Leader based on receptions

1997 INDIVIDUAL STATISTICS—INTERCEPTIONS

INTERCEPTIONS

Interceptions
- **NFC:** 9—Ryan McNeil, St. Louis
- **AFC:** 8—Mark McMillian, Kansas City
  Darryl Williams, Seattle

Interceptions, Game
- **AFC:** 3—Darryl Williams, Seattle vs. San Diego, September 21
- **NFC:** 3—Rod Woodson, San Francisco vs. New Orleans, September 14

Yards
- **AFC:** 274—Mark McMillian, Kansas City
- **NFC:** 146—Tito Wooten, N.Y. Giants

Longest
- **AFC:** 100—Jimmy Hitchcock, New England vs. Miami, November 23 - TD
- **NFC:** 95—Sam Gârnes, N.Y. Giants vs. Philadelphia, August 31 - TD

Touchdowns
- **AFC:** 3—Mark McMillian, Kansas City
  Otis Smith, N.Y. Jets
- **NFC:** 2—Reggie Brown, Detroit
  Darren Sharper, Green Bay
  Aeneas Williams, Arizona

Team Leaders, Interceptions

AFC: BALTIMORE: 4, Stevon Moore; BUFFALO: 2, Jeff Burris, Ken Irvin, Marlon Kerner, Sean Moran, Kurt Schulz; CINCINNATI: 4, Corey Sawyer; DENVER: 4, Tyrone Braxton, Ray Crockett, Darrien Gordon; INDIANAPOLIS: 2, Jason Belser, Quentin Coryatt, Carlton Gray; JACKSONVILLE: 5, Deon Figures; KANSAS CITY: 8, Mark McMillian; MIAMI: 4, Terrell Buckley; NEW ENGLAND: 6, Willie Clay; N.Y. JETS: 6, Otis Smith; OAKLAND: 2, Lorenzo Lynch, James Trapp, Eric Turner, Lionel Washington; PITTSBURGH: 4, Darren Perry, Donnell Woolford; SAN DIEGO: 2, Paul Bradford, Dwayne Harper, Rodney Harrison, Greg Jackson, Junior Seau; SEATTLE: 8, Darryl Williams; TENNESSEE: 5, Darryll Lewis, Marcus Robertson

NFC: ARIZONA: 6, Aeneas Williams; ATLANTA: 5, Ray Buchanan; CAROLINA: 5, Eric Davis; CHICAGO: 5, Walt Harris; DALLAS: 2, Deion Sanders, Omar Stoutmire; DETROIT: 5, Mark Carrier; GREEN BAY: 5, LeRoy Butler; MINNESOTA: 4, Dewayne Washington; NEW ORLEANS: 5, Sammy Knight; N.Y. GIANTS: 6, Jason Sehorn; PHILADELPHIA: 3, Brian Dawkins, Troy Vincent; ST. LOUIS: 9, Ryan McNeil; SAN FRANCISCO: 6, Merton Hanks; TAMPA BAY: 5, Donnie Abraham; WASHINGTON: 4, Cris Dishman, Stanley Richard

Team Champion
- **AFC:** 27—N.Y. Giants
- **NFC:** 21—Kansas City

AFC INTERCEPTIONS—TEAM

	No.	Yards	Avg.	Long	TD
Kansas City	21	432	20.6	87t	4
Pittsburgh	20	253	12.7	42	0
New England	19	366	19.3	100t	4
Denver	18	319	17.7	62t	5
N.Y. Jets	18	379	21.1	51t	4
Baltimore	17	241	14.2	43	1
Buffalo	15	157	10.5	28	0
San Diego	15	257	17.1	75t	3
Jacksonville	14	145	10.4	32	0
Tennessee	14	328	23.4	48	2
Cincinnati	13	183	14.1	37	0
Seattle	13	196	15.1	44t	1
Indianapolis	12	234	19.5	52t	2
Miami	10	92	9.2	23	0
Oakland	10	149	14.9	44t	1
AFC Total	229	3731	16.3	100t	27
AFC Average	15.3	248.7	16.3	—	1.8

NFC INTERCEPTIONS—TEAM

	No.	Yards	Avg.	Long	TD
N.Y. Giants	27	503	18.6	95t	4
St. Louis	25	281	11.2	75t	1
San Francisco	25	366	14.6	55t	1
Green Bay	21	329	15.7	77t	3
Atlanta	18	114	6.3	31	0
Detroit	17	309	18.2	66	3
New Orleans	16	194	12.1	39	0
Washington	16	222	13.9	83t	3
Arizona	15	231	15.4	66t	3
Philadelphia	14	186	13.3	64t	1
Chicago	13	60	4.6	14	0
Tampa Bay	13	95	7.3	28	0
Minnesota	12	141	11.8	27	0
Carolina	11	72	6.5	18	0
Dallas	7	130	18.6	50t	1
NFC Total	250	3233	12.9	95t	20
NFC Average	16.7	215.5	12.9	—	1.3
League Total	479	6964	—	100t	47
League Average	16.0	232.1	14.5	—	1.6

NFL TOP TEN INTERCEPTORS

	No.	Yards	Avg.	Long	TD
McNeil, Ryan, St.L	9	127	14.1	75t	1
Lyle, Keith, St.L	8	102	12.8	39	0
McMillian, Mark, K.C.	8	274	34.3	87t	3
Williams, Darryl, Sea.	8	172	21.5	44t	1
Clay, Willie, N.E.	6	109	18.2	53t	1
Hanks, Merton, S.F.	6	103	17.2	55t	1
Sehorn, Jason, NY-G	6	74	12.3	41	1
Smith, Otis, NY-J	6	158	26.3	51t	3
Williams, Aeneas, Ariz	6	95	15.8	42t	2
13 tied	5				

AFC INTERCEPTIONS—INDIVIDUAL

	No.	Yards	Avg.	Long	TD
McMillian, Mark, K.C.	8	274	34.3	87t	3
Williams, Darryl, Sea.	8	172	21.5	44t	1
Smith, Otis, NY-J	6	158	26.3	51t	3
Clay, Willie, N.E.	6	109	18.2	53t	1
Robertson, Marcus, Ten.	5	127	25.4	48	0
Lewis, Darryll, Ten.	5	115	23.0	47t	1
Figures, Deon, Jax.	5	48	9.6	32	0
Braxton, Tyrone, Den.	4	113	28.3	43	1
Woolford, Donnell, Pit.	4	91	22.8	34	0
Perry, Darren, Pit.	4	77	19.3	42	0
Gordon, Darrien, Den.	4	64	16.0	32t	1
Woods, Jerome, K.C.	4	57	14.3	27	0
Moore, Stevon, Bal.	4	56	14.0	38	0
Sawyer, Corey, Cin.	4	44	11.0	37	0
Buckley, Terrell, Mia.	4	26	6.5	12	0
Crockett, Ray, Den.	4	18	4.5	10	0
Mickens, Ray, NY-J	4	2	0.5	2	0
Green, Victor, NY-J	3	89	29.7	39	0
Law, Ty, N.E.	3	70	23.3	40	0
Daniel, Eugene, Bal.	3	60	20.0	43	0
Ambrose, Ashley, Cin.	3	56	18.7	29	0
Langham, Antonio, Bal.	3	40	13.3	40t	1
Hudson, Chris, Jax.	3	26	8.7	23	0
Hasty, James, K.C.	3	22	7.3	19	0
Lake, Carnell, Pit.	3	16	5.3	11	0
Milloy, Lawyer, N.E.	3	15	5.0	15	0
Belser, Jason, Ind.	2	121	60.5	50t	1
Hitchcock, Jimmy, N.E.	2	104	52.0	100t	1
Harrison, Rodney, S.D.	2	75	37.5	75t	1
Whigham, Larry, N.E.	2	60	30.0	60t	1
Bradford, Paul, S.D.	2	56	28.0	56t	1
Walker, Denard, Ten.	2	53	26.5	39t	1
Turner, Eric, Oak.	2	45	22.5	29	0
Washington, Lionel, Oak.	2	44	22.0	44t	1
Harper, Dwayne, S.D.	2	43	21.5	43	0
Atwater, Steve, Den.	2	42	21.0	22t	1
Jackson, Greg, S.D.	2	37	18.5	36t	1
Thomas, Dave, Jax.	2	34	17.0	23	0
Seau, Junior, S.D.	2	33	16.5	26	0
Irvin, Ken, Buf.	2	28	14.0	28	0
Teague, George, Mia.	2	25	12.5	23	0
Trapp, James, Oak.	2	24	12.0	25	0

1997 INDIVIDUAL STATISTICS—INTERCEPTIONS

	No.	Yards	Avg.	Long	TD
Schulz, Kurt, Buf.	2	23	11.5	21	0
Kerner, Marlon, Buf.	2	20	10.0	20	0
Burris, Jeff, Buf.	2	19	9.5	10	0
Oldham, Chris, Pit.	2	16	8.0	8	0
Edwards, Donnie, K.C.	2	15	7.5	12	0
Kirkland, Levon, Pit.	2	14	7.0	11	0
Moran, Sean, Buf.	2	12	6.0	12	0
Staten, Ralph, Bal.	2	12	6.0	9	0
Blades, Bennie, Sea.	2	11	5.5	11	0
Wooden, Shawn, Mia.	2	10	5.0	10	0
Carter, Dale, K.C.	2	9	4.5	9	0
Moore, Marty, N.E.	2	7	3.5	7	0
Lynch, Lorenzo, Oak.	2	6	3.0	6	0
Coryatt, Quentin, Ind.	2	3	1.5	3	0
Gray, Carlton, Ind.	2	0	0.0	0	0
Scott, Chad, Pit.	2	-4	-2.0	0	0
Traylor, Keith, Den.	1	62	62.0	62t	1
Anderson, Darren, K.C.	1	55	55.0	55t	1
Henderson, Jerome, NY-J	1	45	45.0	45	0
Alexander, Elijah, Ind.	1	43	43.0	43t	1
Lewis, Mo, NY-J	1	43	43.0	43t	1
Henry, Kevin, Pit.	1	36	36.0	36	0
Mathis, Dedric, Ind.	1	31	31.0	31	0
Mack, Tremain, Cin.	1	29	29.0	29	0
Maddox, Mark, Buf.	1	25	25.0	25	0
Myers, Greg, Cin.	1	25	25.0	25	0
Coleman, Marcus, NY-J	1	24	24.0	24	0
Jones, Roger, Ten.	1	24	24.0	24	0
Davis, Travis, Jax.	1	23	23.0	23	0
Brown, Cornell, Bal.	1	21	21.0	21	0
Madison, Sam, Mia.	1	21	21.0	21	0
Shade, Sam, Cin.	1	21	21.0	21	0
Johnson, Ellis, Ind.	1	18	18.0	18	0
Lewis, Ray, Bal.	1	18	18.0	18	0
McDaniel, Terry, Oak.	1	17	17.0	17	0
Jenkins, DeRon, Bal.	1	15	15.0	15	0
Jones, Rondell, Bal.	1	15	15.0	15	0
Clark, Rico, Ind.	1	14	14.0	14	0
Bellamy, Jay, Sea.	1	13	13.0	13	0
Johnson, Pepper, NY-J	1	13	13.0	13	0
Land, Dan, Oak.	1	13	13.0	13	0
Mobley, John, Den.	1	13	13.0	13t	1
Martin, Emanuel, Buf.	1	12	12.0	12	0
Shaw, Terrance, S.D.	1	11	11.0	11	0
Bell, Myron, Pit.	1	10	10.0	7	0
Thomas, Zach, Mia.	1	10	10.0	10	0
Bowden, Joe, Ten.	1	9	9.0	9	0
Kopp, Jeff, Jax.	1	9	9.0	9	0
Spielman, Chris, Buf.	1	8	8.0	8	0
Francis, James, Cin.	1	7	7.0	7	0
Romanowski, Bill, Den.	1	7	7.0	7	0
Covington, Damien, Buf.	1	6	6.0	6	0
Beasley, Aaron, Jax.	1	5	5.0	5	0
Glenn, Aaron, NY-J	1	5	5.0	5	0
Perry, Marlo, Buf.	1	4	4.0	4	0
Sharper, Jamie, Bal.	1	4	4.0	4	0
Orlando, Bo, Cin.	1	3	3.0	3	0
Blackmon, Robert, Ind.	1	2	2.0	2	0
Coleman, Marco, S.D.	1	2	2.0	2	0
Morrison, Steve, Ind.	1	2	2.0	2	0
Slade, Chris, N.E.	1	1	1.0	1t	1
Dumas, Mike, S.D.	1	0	0.0	0	0
Fuller, William, S.D.	1	0	0.0	0	0
Gouveia, Kurt, S.D.	1	0	0.0	0	0
McKyer, Tim, Den.	1	0	0.0	0	0
Robinson, Eddie, Jax.	1	0	0.0	0	0
Springs, Shawn, Sea.	1	0	0.0	0	0
Tongue, Reggie, K.C.	1	0	0.0	0	0
Williams, Willie, Sea.	1	0	0.0	0	0
Spencer, Jimmy, Cin.	1	-2	-2.0	-2	0
Conley, Steve, Pit.	1	-3	-3.0	-3	0

t = Touchdown
Leader based on interceptions

NFC INTERCEPTIONS—INDIVIDUAL

	No.	Yards	Avg.	Long	TD
McNeil, Ryan, St.L	9	127	14.1	75t	1
Lyle, Keith, St.L	8	102	12.8	39	0
Hanks, Merton, S.F.	6	103	17.2	55t	1
Williams, Aeneas, Ariz	6	95	15.8	42t	2
Sehorn, Jason, NY-G	6	74	12.3	41	1
Wooten, Tito, NY-G	5	146	29.2	61t	1
Carrier, Mark, Det.	5	94	18.8	66	0
Knight, Sammy, N.O.	5	75	15.0	39	0
Sparks, Phillippi, NY-G	5	72	14.4	68	0
Buchanan, Ray, Atl.	5	49	9.8	31	0
Harris, Walt, Chi.	5	30	6.0	12	0
Davis, Eric, Car.	5	25	5.0	17	0
Abraham, Donnie, T.B.	5	16	3.2	16	0
Drakeford, Tyronne, S.F.	5	15	3.0	15	0
Butler, LeRoy, G.B.	5	4	0.8	2	0
Prior, Mike, G.B.	4	72	18.0	49	0
Washington, Dewayne, Min.	4	71	17.8	27	0
Dishman, Cris, Was.	4	47	11.8	29t	1
Ellsworth, Percy, NY-G	4	40	10.0	25	0
Richard, Stanley, Was.	4	28	7.0	23	0
Lyght, Todd, St.L	4	25	6.3	13	0
Bradford, Ronnie, Atl.	4	9	2.3	9	0
Woodson, Rod, S.F.	3	81	27.0	41	0
Dawkins, Brian, Phi.	3	76	25.3	64t	1
Walker, Darnell, S.F.	3	49	16.3	28	0
Pounds, Darryl, Was.	3	42	14.0	22t	1
McKinnon, Ronald, Ariz	3	40	13.3	17	0
McDonald, Tim, S.F.	3	34	11.3	17	0
Evans, Doug, G.B.	3	33	11.0	27	0
Newman, Anthony, N.O.	3	19	6.3	17	0
Booker, Michael, Atl.	3	16	5.3	10	0
Vincent, Troy, Phi.	3	14	4.7	14	0
Carter, Tom, Chi.	3	12	4.0	12	0
Brown, Reggie, Det.	2	83	41.5	45t	2
Sanders, Deion, Dal.	2	81	40.5	50t	1
Sharper, Darren, G.B.	2	70	35.0	50t	2
Westbrook, Bryant, Det.	2	64	32.0	64t	1
Armstead, Jessie, NY-G	2	57	28.5	57t	1
Woodall, Lee, S.F.	2	55	27.5	55	0
Washington, Mickey, N.O.	2	30	15.0	30	0
Williams, Brian, G.B.	2	30	15.0	25	0
Cota, Chad, Car.	2	28	14.0	15	0
Lynch, John, T.B.	2	28	14.0	28	0
Allen, Eric, N.O.	2	27	13.5	27	0
Griffith, Robert, Min.	2	26	13.0	21	0
Dimry, Charles, Phi.	2	25	12.5	25	0
Fuller, Corey, Min.	2	24	12.0	22	0
Tubbs, Winfred, N.O.	2	21	10.5	15	0
Brooks, Derrick, T.B.	2	13	6.5	13	0
Thomas, William, Phi.	2	11	5.5	11	0
Stoutmire, Omar, Dal.	2	8	4.0	8	0
Patton, Marvcus, Was.	2	5	2.5	5	0
Mangum, John, Chi.	2	4	2.0	4	0
Thomas, Orlando, Min.	2	1	0.5	1	0
Marshall, Anthony, Chi.	2	0	0.0	0	0
Poole, Tyrone, Car.	2	0	0.0	0	0
Widmer, Corey, NY-G	2	0	0.0	0	0
Garnes, Sam, NY-G	1	95	95.0	95t	1
Green, Darrell, Was.	1	83	83.0	83t	1
Wilkins, Gabe, G.B.	1	77	77.0	77t	1
Wilson, Bernard, Ariz	1	66	66.0	66t	1
Hall, Rhett, Phi.	1	39	39.0	39	0
Abrams, Kevin, Det.	1	29	29.0	29	0
Robinson, Eugene, G.B.	1	26	26.0	26	0
Bronson, Zack, S.F.	1	22	22.0	22	0
Farr, D'Marco, St.L	1	22	22.0	22	0
Smith, Kevin, Dal.	1	21	21.0	21	0
Zordich, Mike, Phi.	1	21	21.0	21	0
Johnson, Melvin, T.B.	1	19	19.0	19	0
Hamilton, Conrad, NY-G	1	18	18.0	18	0
McDaniel, Ed, Min.	1	18	18.0	18	0
Mills, Sam, Car.	1	18	18.0	18	0
Rice, Ron, Det.	1	18	18.0	18	0
Mullen, Roderick, G.B.	1	17	17.0	17	0
Raymond, Corey, Det.	1	17	17.0	17	0
Kelly, Rob, N.O.	1	15	15.0	15	0
McCleskey, J. J., Ariz	1	15	15.0	15	0
Carter, Marty, Chi.	1	14	14.0	14	0
Mincy, Charles, T.B.	1	14	14.0	14	0
Owens, Dan, Atl.	1	14	14.0	14	0
Woodson, Darren, Dal.	1	14	14.0	14	0
White, William, Atl.	1	11	11.0	11	0
Boutte, Marc, Was.	1	10	10.0	10	0
Lassiter, Kwamie, Ariz	1	10	10.0	10	0
Campbell, Jesse, Was.	1	7	7.0	7	0
Harvey, Richard, N.O.	1	7	7.0	7	0
McGill, Lenny, Atl.	1	7	7.0	7	0

1997 INDIVIDUAL STATISTICS—PUNTING

	No.	Yards	Avg.	Long	TD
Pope, Marquez, S.F.	1	7	7.0	7	0
Coakley, Dexter, Dal.	1	6	6.0	6	0
Caldwell, Mike, Ariz	1	5	5.0	5	0
O'Neal, Leslie, St.L	1	5	5.0	5	0
Parker, Anthony, T.B.	1	5	5.0	5	0
Porcher, Robert, Det.	1	5	5.0	5	0
Boyd, Stephen, Det.	1	4	4.0	4	0
Bush, Devin, Atl.	1	4	4.0	4	0
Smith, Chuck, Atl.	1	4	4.0	4	0
Fisk, Jason, Min.	1	1	1.0	1	0
Lathon, Lamar, Car.	1	1	1.0	1	0
Randolph, Thomas, NY-G	1	1	1.0	1	0
Archambeau, Lester, Atl.	1	0	0.0	0	0
Bailey, Robert, Det.	1	0	0.0	0	0
Bennett, Tommy, Ariz	1	0	0.0	0	0
Harris, Bernardo, G.B.	1	0	0.0	0	0
Jeffries, Greg, Det.	1	0	0.0	0	0
Jones, Mike, St.L	1	0	0.0	0	0
Legette, Tyrone, T.B.	1	0	0.0	0	0
Maxie, Brett, S.F.	1	0	0.0	0	0
McCleon, Dexter, St.L	1	0	0.0	0	0
Rice, Simeon, Ariz	1	0	0.0	0	0
Stevens, Matt, Phi.	1	0	0.0	0	0
Williams, Tyrone, G.B.	1	0	0.0	0	0
Willis, James, Phi.	1	0	0.0	0	0
Malone, Van, Det.	1	-5	-5.0	-5	0

t = Touchdown
Leader based on interceptions

PUNTING

Average Yards Per Punt
NFC: 45.9—Mark Royals, New Orleans
AFC: 45.8—Tom Tupa, New England

Net Average Yards Per Punt
NFC: 39.2—Matt Turk, Washington
AFC: 39.1—Leo Araguz, Oakland

Longest
NFC: 74—Sean Landeta, Tampa Bay at N.Y. Jets, December 14
AFC: 73—Tom Tupa, New England at Denver, October 6

Punts
NFC: 111—Brad Maynard, N.Y. Giants
AFC: 93—Leo Araguz, Oakland

Punts, Game
NFC: 13—Brad Maynard, N.Y. Giants at Washington, November 23 (537 yards)
AFC: 11—Lee Johnson, Cincinnati vs. San Diego, November 2 (474 yards)

Team Champion
NFC: 45.9—New Orleans
AFC: 45.3—Indianapolis

AFC PUNTING—TEAM

	Total Punts	Yards	Long	Avg.	TB	Blk.	Opp. Ret.	Return Yards	Inside the 20	Net. Avg.
Indianapolis	67	3034	72	45.3	6	0	43	491	18	36.2
New England	79	3569	73	45.2	14	1	38	437	24	36.1
Oakland	93	4189	63	45.0	6	0	52	431	28	39.1
Jacksonville	66	2964	64	44.9	8	0	29	241	27	38.8
San Diego	90	3972	66	44.1	8	1	39	416	26	37.7
Miami	68	2962	58	43.6	6	0	43	323	15	37.0
Denver	60	2598	57	43.3	4	0	26	235	22	38.1
Cincinnati	81	3471	66	42.9	8	0	35	407	27	35.9
N.Y. Jets	75	3212	58	42.8	5	1	47	459	20	35.4
Baltimore	83	3540	60	42.7	2	0	53	460	24	36.6
Pittsburgh	64	2729	72	42.6	11	0	23	271	17	35.0
Kansas City	83	3489	65	42.0	4	0	39	255	29	38.0
Tennessee	74	3081	59	41.6	2	0	36	430	25	35.3
Buffalo	91	3764	59	41.4	6	1	44	366	24	36.0
Seattle	78	3144	65	40.3	8	2	38	463	24	32.3
AFC Total	1152	49718	73	—	98	6	585	5685	350	—
AFC Average	76.8	3314.5	—	43.2	6.5	0.4	39.0	379.0	23.3	36.5

NFC PUNTING—TEAM

	Total Punts	Yards	Long	Avg.	TB	Blk.	Opp. Ret.	Return Yards	Inside the 20	Net. Avg.
New Orleans	88	4038	66	45.9	13	0	50	706	21	34.9
Green Bay	75	3378	65	45.0	21	0	32	255	26	36.0
Washington	85	3788	62	44.6	11	1	33	237	32	39.2
Arizona	92	4028	62	43.8	10	1	40	441	24	36.8
Tampa Bay	84	3578	74	42.6	9	1	42	388	27	35.8
Chicago	96	4077	67	42.5	11	0	52	727	26	32.6
Carolina	85	3604	62	42.4	4	0	38	428	29	36.4
Minnesota	81	3407	65	42.1	5	0	49	566	25	33.8
St. Louis	95	3985	61	41.9	8	1	60	618	16	33.8
Dallas	86	3592	72	41.8	9	0	40	365	26	35.4
Philadelphia	88	3660	61	41.6	5	1	48	515	19	34.6
Detroit	86	3576	60	41.6	4	2	51	434	24	35.6
N.Y. Giants	112	4531	57	40.5	14	1	40	378	33	34.6
San Francisco	79	3182	55	40.3	7	1	41	307	22	34.6
Atlanta	89	3498	57	39.3	9	0	21	55	20	36.7
NFC Total	1321	55922	74	—	140	9	637	6420	370	—
NFC Average	88.1	3728.1	—	42.3	9.3	0.6	42.5	428.0	24.7	35.4
NFL Total	2473	105640	74	—	238	15	1222	12,105	720	—
NFL Average	82.4	3521.3	—	42.7	7.9	0.5	40.7	403.5	24.0	35.9

1997 INDIVIDUAL STATISTICS—PUNTING

NFL TOP TEN PUNTERS

	No.	Yards	Long	Avg.	Total Punts	TB	Blk.	Opp. Ret.	Ret. Yds.	In 20	Net. Avg.
Royals, Mark, N.O.	88	4038	66	45.9	88	13	0	50	706	21	34.9
Tupa, Tom, N.E.	78	3569	73	45.8	79	14	1	38	437	24	36.1
Gardocki, Chris, Ind.	67	3034	72	45.3	67	6	0	43	491	18	36.2
Turk, Matt, Was.	84	3788	62	45.1	85	11	1	33	237	32	39.2
Araguz, Leo, Oak.	93	4189	63	45.0	93	6	0	52	431	28	39.1
Hentrich, Craig, G.B.	75	3378	65	45.0	75	21	0	32	255	26	36.0
Barker, Bryan, Jax.	66	2964	64	44.9	66	8	0	29	241	27	38.8
Bennett, Darren, S.D.	89	3972	66	44.6	90	8	1	39	416	26	37.7
Feagles, Jeff, Ariz	91	4028	62	44.3	92	10	1	40	441	24	36.8
Rouen, Tom, Den.	60	2598	57	43.3	60	4	0	26	235	22	38.1

AFC PUNTERS—INDIVIDUAL

	No.	Yards	Long	Avg.	Total Punts	TB	Blk.	Opp. Ret.	Ret. Yds.	In 20	Net. Avg.
Tupa, Tom, N.E.	78	3569	73	45.8	79	14	1	38	437	24	36.1
Gardocki, Chris, Ind.	67	3034	72	45.3	67	6	0	43	491	18	36.2
Araguz, Leo, Oak.	93	4189	63	45.0	93	6	0	52	431	28	39.1
Barker, Bryan, Jax.	66	2964	64	44.9	66	8	0	29	241	27	38.8
Bennett, Darren, S.D.	89	3972	66	44.6	90	8	1	39	416	26	37.7
Rouen, Tom, Den.	60	2598	57	43.3	60	4	0	26	235	22	38.1
Kidd, John, Mia.	52	2247	58	43.2	52	4	0	35	243	13	37.0
Hansen, Brian, NY-J	71	3068	58	43.2	72	5	1	45	429	20	35.3
Johnson, Lee, Cin.	81	3471	66	42.9	81	8	0	35	407	27	35.9
Montgomery, Greg, Bal.	83	3540	60	42.7	83	2	0	53	460	24	36.6
Miller, Josh, Pit.	64	2729	72	42.6	64	11	0	23	271	17	35.0
Aguiar, Louie, K.C.	82	3465	65	42.3	82	4	0	39	255	28	38.2
Mohr, Chris, Buf.	90	3764	59	41.8	91	6	1	44	366	24	36.0
Tuten, Rick, Sea.	48	2007	65	41.8	48	5	0	23	161	15	36.4
Roby, Reggie, Ten.	73	3049	59	41.8	73	1	0	36	430	25	35.6
Nonqualifiers											
Stark, Rohn, Sea.	20	813	52	40.7	20	2	0	10	236	7	26.9
Richardson, Kyle, Mia.-Sea.	19	804	54	42.3	21	3	2	12	142	2	28.7
Mare, Olindo, Mia.	5	235	53	47.0	5	0	0	1	4	2	46.2
Hall, John, NY-J	3	144	57	48.0	3	0	0	2	30	0	38.0
Del Greco, Al, Ten.	1	32	32	32.0	1	1	0	0	0	0	12.0
Stoyanovich, Pete, K.C.	1	24	24	24.0	1	0	0	0	0	1	24.0

Leader based on average, minimum 40 punts

NFC PUNTERS—INDIVIDUAL

	No.	Yards	Long	Avg.	Total Punts	TB	Blk.	Opp. Ret.	Ret. Yds.	In 20	Net. Avg.
Royals, Mark, N.O.	88	4038	66	45.9	88	13	0	50	706	21	34.9
Turk, Matt, Was.	84	3788	62	45.1	85	11	1	33	237	32	39.2
Hentrich, Craig, G.B.	75	3378	65	45.0	75	21	0	32	255	26	36.0
Feagles, Jeff, Ariz	91	4028	62	44.3	92	10	1	40	441	24	36.8
Berger, Mitch, Min.	73	3133	65	42.9	73	5	0	46	545	22	34.1
Horan, Mike, St.L	53	2272	60	42.9	53	4	0	33	266	10	36.3
Sauerbrun, Todd, Chi.	95	4059	67	42.7	95	11	0	52	727	26	32.8
Jett, John, Det.	84	3576	60	42.6	86	4	2	51	434	24	35.6
Walter, Ken, Car.	85	3604	62	42.4	85	4	0	38	428	29	36.4
Landeta, Sean, T.B.	54	2274	74	42.1	55	6	1	28	278	15	34.1
Hutton, Tom, Phi.	87	3660	61	42.1	88	5	1	48	515	19	34.6
Brice, Will, St.L	41	1713	61	41.8	42	4	1	27	352	6	30.5
Gowin, Toby, Dal.	86	3592	72	41.8	86	9	0	40	365	26	35.4
Maynard, Brad, NY-G	111	4531	57	40.8	112	14	1	40	378	33	34.6
Thompson, Tommy, S.F.	78	3182	55	40.8	79	7	1	41	307	22	34.6
Stryzinski, Dan, Atl.	89	3498	57	39.3	89	9	0	21	55	20	36.7
Nonqualifiers											
Barnhardt, Tommy, T.B.	29	1304	61	45.0	29	3	0	14	110	12	39.1
Cunningham, Randall, Min.	8	274	65	34.3	8	0	0	3	21	3	31.6
Jaeger, Jeff, Chi.	1	18	18	18.0	1	0	0	0	0	0	18.0

Leader based on average, minimum 40 punts

1997 INDIVIDUAL STATISTICS—PUNT RETURNS

PUNT RETURNS

Yards Per Return
- **AFC:** 15.6—Jermaine Lewis, Baltimore
- **NFC:** 13.1—David Palmer, Minnesota

Yards
- **AFC:** 619—Leon Johnson, N.Y. Jets
- **NFC:** 597—Karl Williams, Tampa Bay

Yards, Game
- **AFC:** 184—Jermaine Lewis, Baltimore vs. Seattle, December 7 (5 returns - 2 TD)
- **NFC:** 116—Karl Williams, Tampa Bay vs. Chicago, December 21 (6 returns)

Longest
- **AFC:** 94—Darrien Gordon, Denver vs. St. Louis, September 14 - TD
- **NFC:** 83—Deion Sanders, Dallas vs. Chicago, September 28 - TD

Returns
- **NFC:** 52—Todd Kinchen, Atlanta
- **AFC:** 51—Leon Johnson, N.Y. Jets

Returns, Game
- **AFC:** 7—James Roe, Baltimore vs. Philadelphia, Nov. 16 (64 yards)
- **NFC:** 7—Eric Guliford, New Orleans at Oakland, Nov. 9 (90 yards)

Fair Catches
- **NFC:** 26—Eric Guliford, New Orleans; Glyn Milburn, Detroit
- **AFC:** 22—Darrien Gordon, Denver

Touchdowns
- **AFC:** 3—Darrien Gordon, Denver; Eric Metcalf, San Diego
- **NFC:** 1—Chuck Levy, San Francisco; Brian Mitchell, Washington; Deion Sanders, Dallas; Amani Toomer, N.Y. Giants; Karl Williams, Tampa Bay

Team Champion
- **AFC:** 13.5—Denver
- **NFC:** 13.1—Minnesota

AFC PUNT RETURNS—TEAM

	No.	FC	Yards	Avg.	Long	TD
Denver	41	22	555	13.5	94t	3
Baltimore	42	14	564	13.4	89t	2
Jacksonville	36	16	412	11.4	52	0
N.Y. Jets	59	8	674	11.4	66t	1
Kansas City	35	14	383	10.9	82t	1
Miami	32	16	335	10.5	38	0
San Diego	47	8	489	10.4	85t	3
New England	45	8	467	10.4	47	0
Buffalo	39	19	346	8.9	47	0
Indianapolis	31	10	248	8.0	20	0
Oakland	27	20	210	7.8	31	0
Cincinnati	26	19	201	7.7	18	0
Tennessee	32	13	244	7.6	30	0
Pittsburgh	32	10	222	6.9	30	0
Seattle	37	18	248	6.7	28	0
AFC Total	561	215	5598	10.0	94t	10
AFC Average	37.4	14.3	373.2	10.0	—	0.7

NFC PUNT RETURNS—TEAM

	No.	FC	Yards	Avg.	Long	TD
Minnesota	34	19	444	13.1	57	0
Tampa Bay	51	12	645	12.6	63	1
San Francisco	41	16	482	11.8	73t	1
Washington	38	23	442	11.6	63t	1
Arizona	41	16	461	11.2	50	0
Dallas	47	14	512	10.9	83t	1
New Orleans	48	26	496	10.3	32	0
N.Y. Giants	47	19	455	9.7	53t	1
Atlanta	52	14	483	9.3	38	0
Green Bay	56	17	515	9.2	46	0
Detroit	48	26	433	9.0	40	0
Carolina	41	23	310	7.6	40	0
Philadelphia	31	21	234	7.5	42	0
Chicago	46	8	321	7.0	19	0
St. Louis	40	23	274	6.9	43	0
NFC Total	661	277	6507	9.8	83t	5
NFC Average	44.1	18.5	433.8	9.8	—	0.3
League Total	1222	492	12105	—	94t	15
League Average	40.7	16.4	403.5	9.9	—	0.5

NFL TOP TEN PUNT RETURNERS

	No.	FC	Yards	Avg.	Long	TD
Lewis, Jermaine, Bal.	28	13	437	15.6	89t	2
Gordon, Darrien, Den.	40	22	543	13.6	94t	3
Palmer, David, Min.	34	19	444	13.1	57	0
Williams, Karl, T.B.	46	12	597	13.0	63	1
Sanders, Deion, Dal.	33	12	407	12.3	83t	1
Johnson, Leon, NY-J	51	6	619	12.1	66t	1
Mitchell, Brian, Was.	38	23	442	11.6	63t	1
Williams, Kevin, Ariz	40	15	462	11.6	50	0
Barlow, Reggie, Jax.	36	16	412	11.4	52	0
Uwaezuoke, Iheanyi, S.F.	34	14	373	11.0	36	0

AFC—INDIVIDUAL PUNT RETURNERS

	No.	FC	Yards	Avg.	Long	TD
Lewis, Jermaine, Bal.	28	13	437	15.6	89t	2
Gordon, Darrien, Den.	40	22	543	13.6	94t	3
Johnson, Leon, NY-J	51	6	619	12.1	66t	1
Barlow, Reggie, Jax.	36	16	412	11.4	52	0
Vanover, Tamarick, K.C.	35	14	383	10.9	82t	1
Metcalf, Eric, S.D.	45	8	489	10.9	85t	3
Jordan, Charles, Mia.	26	15	273	10.5	38	0
Meggett, David, N.E.	45	8	467	10.4	47	0
Burris, Jeff, Buf.	21	8	198	9.4	32	0
Howard, Desmond, Oak.	27	20	210	7.8	31	0
Myers, Greg, Cin.	26	19	201	7.7	18	0
Harris, Ronnie, Sea.	21	12	144	6.9	19	0
Blackwell, Will, Pit.	23	6	149	6.5	15	0
Nonqualifiers						
Stablein, Brian, Ind.	17	9	133	7.8	20	0
Davis, Tyree, Sea.	16	6	104	6.5	28	0
Jacquet, Nate, Ind.	13	0	96	7.4	17	0
Mason, Derrick, Ten.	13	3	95	7.3	29	0
Tasker, Steve, Buf.	12	9	113	9.4	47	0
Roe, James, Bal.	8	0	72	9.0	14	0
Ward, Dedric, NY-J	8	2	55	6.9	12	0
Ethridge, Ray, Bal.	5	1	21	4.2	16	0
Coleman, Andre, Pit.	5	2	5	1.0	5	0
Hawkins, Courtney, Pit.	4	2	68	17.0	30	0
Buckley, Terrell, Mia.	4	0	58	14.5	26	0
Moulds, Eric, Buf.	2	0	20	10.0	10	0
Galloway, Mitchell, Buf.	2	2	15	7.5	15	0
McDuffie, O. J., Mia.	2	1	4	2.0	3	0
Alexander, Derrick, Bal.	1	0	34	34.0	34	0
Bailey, Aaron, Ind.	1	0	19	19.0	19	0
Smith, Rod, Den.	1	0	12	12.0	12	0
Archie, Mike, Ten.	1	0	5	5.0	5	0
Harrison, Rodney, S.D.	1	0	0	0.0	0	0
Jackson, Greg, S.D.	1	0	0	0.0	0	0
Jackson, Raymond, Buf.	1	0	0	0.0	0	0
Jones, Henry, Buf.	1	0	0	0.0	0	0
Robertson, Marcus, Ten.	1	0	0	0.0	0	0
Harrison, Marvin, Ind.	0	1	0	—	—	0

t = Touchdown
Leader based on average return, minimum 20 returns

NFC—INDIVIDUAL PUNT RETURNERS

	No.	FC	Yards	Avg.	Long	TD
Palmer, David, Min.	34	19	444	13.1	57	0
Williams, Karl, T.B.	46	12	597	13.0	63	1
Sanders, Deion, Dal.	33	12	407	12.3	83t	1
Mitchell, Brian, Was.	38	23	442	11.6	63t	1
Williams, Kevin, Ariz	40	15	462	11.6	50	0
Uwaezuoke, Iheanyi, S.F.	34	14	373	11.0	36	0
Guliford, Eric, N.O.	47	26	498	10.6	32	0
Schroeder, Bill, G.B.	33	8	342	10.4	46	0
Toomer, Amani, NY-G	47	19	455	9.7	53t	1
Milburn, Glyn, Det.	47	26	433	9.2	40	0
Kinchen, Todd, Atl.	52	13	446	8.6	38	0
Poole, Tyrone, Car.	26	18	191	7.3	40	0
Kennison, Eddie, St.L	34	20	247	7.3	43	0
Hughes, Tyrone, Chi.	36	7	258	7.2	19	0
Nonqualifiers						
Gray, Mel, Ten.-Phi.	19	15	161	8.5	30	0
Seay, Mark, Phi.	16	8	172	10.8	42	0
Mayes, Derrick, G.B.	14	3	141	10.1	26	0
Oliver, Winslow, Car.	14	5	111	7.9	26	0
Mathis, Kevin, Dal.	11	2	91	8.3	45	0
Solomon, Freddie, Phi.	10	7	55	5.5	14	0
Proehl, Ricky, Chi.	8	1	59	7.4	14	0
Sharper, Darren, G.B.	7	3	32	4.6	23	0
Levy, Chuck, S.F.	6	2	109	18.2	73t	1

	No.	FC	Yards	Avg.	Long	TD
Dunn, Warrick, T.B.	5	0	48	9.6	25	0
Floyd, Malcolm, St.L	4	2	15	3.8	8	0
Williams, Stepfret, Dal.	2	0	14	7.0	14	0
Ross, Jermaine, St.L	2	0	12	6.0	6	0
Wyatt, Antwuan, Phi.	2	1	-2	-1.0	0	0
Bates, Michael, Car.	1	0	8	8.0	8	0
Engram, Bobby, Chi.	1	0	4	4.0	4	0
Carrier, Mark, Det.	1	0	0	0.0	0	0
Dulaney, Mike, Chi.	1	0	0	0.0	0	0
Pittman, Kavika, Dal.	1	0	0	0.0	0	0
Preston, Roell, G.B.	1	0	0	0.0	0	0
Prior, Mike, G.B.	1	3	0	0.0	0	0
Woodson, Rod, S.F.	1	0	0	0.0	0	0
Edwards, Anthony, Ariz	1	1	-1	-1.0	-1	0
Hastings, Andre, N.O.	1	0	-2	-2.0	-2	0
Vincent, Troy, Phi.	1	0	-8	-8.0	-8	0
Buchanan, Ray, Atl.	0	1	37	—	37	0
Lee, Amp, St.L	0	1	0	—	—	0

t = Touchdown
Leader based on average return, minimum 20 returns

KICKOFF RETURNS

Yards Per Return
- **NFC:** 27.3—Michael Bates, Carolina
- **AFC:** 26.5—Aaron Glenn, N.Y. Jets

Yards
- **NFC:** 1458—Kevin Williams, Arizona
- **AFC:** 1318—Desmond Howard, Oakland

Yards Game
- **AFC:** 223—Desmond Howard, Oakland at Seattle, October 26 (10 returns)
- **NFC:** 211—Roell Preston, Green Bay at Indianapolis, November 16 (7 returns)

Longest
- **AFC:** 102—Eric Bieniemy, Cincinnati at N.Y. Giants, October 26 - TD
- **NFC:** 102—Eric Guliford, New Orleans at St. Louis, August 31 - TD

Returns
- **AFC:** 61—Desmond Howard, Oakland
- **NFC:** 59—Kevin Williams, Arizona

Returns, Game
- **AFC:** 10—Desmond Howard, Oakland at Seattle, October 26 (223 yards)
- **NFC:** 7—by many

Touchdowns
- **NFC:** 2—Byron Hanspard, Atlanta
- **AFC:** 1—by many

Team Champion
- **AFC:** 25.2—New England
- **NFC:** 24.2—Arizona

AFC KICKOFF RETURNS—TEAM

	No.	Yards	Avg.	Long	TD
New England	53	1337	25.2	86t	1
Kansas City	54	1345	24.9	94t	1
Cincinnati	74	1708	23.1	102t	1
N.Y. Jets	54	1236	22.9	101t	2
Pittsburgh	67	1493	22.3	97t	1
Denver	54	1203	22.3	61	0
San Diego	75	1613	21.5	63	1
Jacksonville	58	1233	21.3	92t	1
Indianapolis	68	1442	21.2	61	0
Oakland	81	1699	21.0	45	0
Miami	63	1298	20.6	48	0
Seattle	76	1550	20.4	43	0
Baltimore	71	1435	20.2	51	0
Tennessee	58	1150	19.8	54	0
Buffalo	78	1538	19.7	53	0
AFC Total	984	21280	21.6	102t	8
AFC Average	65.6	1418.7	21.6	—	0.5

NFC KICKOFF RETURNS—TEAM

	No.	Yards	Avg.	Long	TD
Arizona	70	1696	24.2	63	0
Dallas	63	1520	24.1	49	0
New Orleans	58	1374	23.7	102t	1
Atlanta	51	1198	23.5	99t	2
Carolina	64	1500	23.4	56	0
Detroit	59	1364	23.1	69	0
Green Bay	49	1119	22.8	43	0
San Francisco	50	1133	22.7	101t	1
Philadelphia	69	1520	22.0	57	1
Minnesota	65	1414	21.8	74	0
Washington	59	1283	21.7	97t	1
Chicago	79	1694	21.4	58	0
St. Louis	68	1454	21.4	56	0
Tampa Bay	51	1075	21.1	51	0
N.Y. Giants	51	963	18.9	84	0
NFC Total	906	20307	22.4	102t	6
NFC Average	60.4	1353.8	22.4	—	0.4
League Total	1890	41587	—	102t	14
League Average	63.0	1386.2	22.0	—	0.5

NFL TOP TEN KICKOFF RETURNERS

	No.	Yards	Avg.	Long	TD
Bates, Michael, Car.	47	1281	27.3	56	0
Glenn, Aaron, NY-J	28	741	26.5	96t	1
Guliford, Eric, N.O.	43	1128	26.2	102t	1
Vanover, Tamarick, K.C.	51	1308	25.6	94t	1
Meggett, David, N.E.	33	816	24.7	61	0
Blackwell, Will, Pit.	32	791	24.7	97t	1
Williams, Kevin, Ariz	59	1458	24.7	63	0
Hanspard, Byron, Atl.	40	987	24.7	99t	2
Staley, Duce, Phi.	47	1139	24.2	57	0
Milburn, Glyn, Det.	55	1315	23.9	69	0

1997 INDIVIDUAL STATISTICS—KICKOFF RETURNS

AFC KICKOFF RETURNERS—INDIVIDUAL

	No.	Yards	Avg.	Long	TD
Glenn, Aaron, NY-J	28	741	26.5	96t	1
Vanover, Tamarick, K.C.	51	1308	25.6	94t	1
Meggett, Dave, N.E.	33	816	24.7	61	0
Blackwell, Will, Pit.	32	791	24.7	97t	1
Spikes, Irving, Mia.	24	565	23.5	48	0
Hebron, Vaughn, Den.	43	1009	23.5	46	0
Bieniemy, Eric, Cin.	34	789	23.2	102t	1
Lewis, Jermaine, Bal.	41	905	22.1	51	0
Bailey, Aaron, Ind.	55	1206	21.9	61	0
Howard, Desmond, Oak.	61	1318	21.6	45	0
Broussard, Steve, Sea.	50	1076	21.5	43	0
Bynum, Kenny, S.D.	38	814	21.4	57	0
Moulds, Eric, Buf.	43	921	21.4	53	0
Mason, Derrick, Ten.	26	551	21.2	54	0
Coleman, Andre, Sea.-Pit.	27	552	20.4	29	0
Jackson, Willie, Jax.	32	653	20.4	38	0
Holmes, Darick, Buf.	23	430	18.7	36	0
Nonqualifiers					
Dunn, David, Cin.	19	487	25.6	85	0
Thomas, Rodney, Ten.	17	346	20.4	33	0
Metcalf, Eric, S.D.	16	355	22.2	63	0
Cullors, Derrick, N.E.	15	386	25.7	86t	1
Rachal, Latario, S.D.	15	336	22.4	30	0
McPhail, Jerris, Mia.	15	314	20.9	39	0
Harris, Ronnie, Sea.	14	318	22.7	34	0
Johnson, Leon, NY-J	12	319	26.6	101t	1
Harris, Corey, Mia.	11	224	20.4	34	0
Barlow, Reggie, Jax.	10	267	26.7	92t	1
Logan, Mike, Jax.	10	236	23.6	39	0
Adams, Mike, Pit.	10	215	21.5	31	0
Hundon, James, Cin.	10	169	16.9	28	0
Roe, James, Bal.	9	189	21.0	33	0
Hall, Tim, Oak.	9	182	20.2	34	0
Ismail, Qadry, Mia.	8	166	20.8	27	0
Jacquet, Nate, Ind.	8	156	19.5	27	0
Dillon, Corey, Cin.	6	182	30.3	58	0
Van Dyke, Alex, NY-J	6	138	23.0	30	0
Galloway, Mitchell, Buf.	6	130	21.7	30	0
Graham, Jay, Bal.	6	115	19.2	24	0
Loville, Derek, Den.	5	136	27.2	61	0
Brew, Dorian, Bal.	5	88	17.6	24	0
Canty, Chris, N.E.	4	115	28.8	63	0
Twyner, Gunnard, Cin.	4	72	18.0	24	0
Singleton, Nate, Bal.	4	64	16.0	19	0
Burns, Keith, Den.	4	45	11.3	18	0
Craver, Aaron, S.D.	3	68	22.7	27	0
Truitt, Olanda, Oak.	2	51	25.5	30	0
Aska, Joe, Oak.	2	46	23.0	26	0
Shedd, Kenny, Oak.	2	38	19.0	23	0
Ethridge, Ray, Bal.	2	37	18.5	22	0
Davis, Tyree, Sea.	2	25	12.5	23	0
Archie, Mike, Ten.	2	24	12.0	15	0
Hetherington, Chris, Ind.	2	23	11.5	23	0
Neal, Lorenzo, NY-J	2	22	11.0	22	0
Roan, Michael, Ten.	2	20	10.0	12	0
Mitchell, Pete, Jax.	2	17	8.5	12	0
Ward, Dedric, NY-J	2	10	5.0	11	0
Bordelon, Ben, S.D.	2	0	0.0	0	0
Harrison, Rodney, S.D.	1	40	40.0	40t	1
Moore, Will, Jax.	1	36	36.0	36	0
Morris, Bam, Bal.	1	23	23.0	23	0
Neal, Leon, Ind.	1	23	23.0	23	0
Hughes, Danan, K.C.	1	21	21.0	21	0
Coates, Ben, N.E.	1	20	20.0	20	0
Warren, Lamont, Ind.	1	19	19.0	19	0
Biekert, Greg, Oak.	1	16	16.0	16	0
Brown, Reggie, Sea.	1	16	16.0	16	0
Harmon, Ronnie, Ten.	1	16	16.0	16	0
Manusky, Greg, K.C.	1	16	16.0	16	0
Potts, Roosevelt, Mia.	1	16	16.0	16	0
Strong, Mack, Sea.	1	16	16.0	16	0
Groce, Clif, Ind.	1	15	15.0	15	0
Holmberg, Rob, Oak.	1	15	15.0	15	0
Holmes, Priest, Bal.	1	14	14.0	14	0
McKnight, James, Sea.	1	14	14.0	14	0
Morton, Mike, Oak.	1	14	14.0	14	0
Smith, Lamar, Sea.	1	14	14.0	14	0
Chamberlain, Byron, Den.	1	13	13.0	13	0
Coons, Robert, Buf.	1	12	12.0	12	0
Levitt, Chad, Oak.	1	12	12.0	12	0
Tasker, Steve, Buf.	1	12	12.0	12	0
Wiley, Marcellus, Buf.	1	12	12.0	12	0
Pike, Mark, Buf.	1	11	11.0	11	0
Burris, Jeff, Buf.	1	10	10.0	10	0
Carter, Ki-Jana, Cin.	1	9	9.0	9	0
Davis, Travis, Jax.	1	9	9.0	9	0
Parker, Chris, Jax.	1	9	9.0	9	0
May, Deems, Sea.	1	8	8.0	8	0
Brown, Tim, Oak.	1	7	7.0	7	0
Perry, Ed, Mia.	1	7	7.0	7	0
Hallock, Ty, Jax.	1	6	6.0	6	0
Jordan, Charles, Mia.	1	6	6.0	6	0
Chrebet, Wayne, NY-J	1	5	5.0	5	0
Layman, Jason, Ten.	1	5	5.0	5	0
Wycheck, Frank, Ten.	1	3	3.0	3	0
Ferguson, Jason, NY-J	1	1	1.0	1	0
Anders, Kimble, K.C.	1	0	0.0	0	0
Baxter, Fred, NY-J	1	0	0.0	0	0
Beede, Frank, Sea.	1	0	0.0	0	0
Byner, Earnest, Bal.	1	0	0.0	0	0
Cline, Tony, Buf.	1	0	0.0	0	0
Hamilton, Bobby, NY-J	1	0	0.0	0	0
Harris, Anthony, Mia.	1	0	0.0	0	0
Hollier, Dwight, Mia.	1	0	0.0	0	0
McCloud, Tyrus, Bal.	1	0	0.0	0	0
Smith, Detron, Den.	1	0	0.0	0	0
Vrabel, Mike, Pit.	1	0	0.0	0	0
Daniels, Phillip, Sea.	1	-2	-2.0	-2	0

t = Touchdown
Leader based on average return, minimum 20 returns

NFC KICKOFF RETURNERS—INDIVIDUAL

	No.	Yards	Avg.	Long	TD
Bates, Michael, Car.	47	1281	27.3	56	0
Guliford, Eric, N.O.	43	1128	26.2	102t	1
Williams, Kevin, Ariz	59	1458	24.7	63	0
Hanspard, Byron, Atl.	40	987	24.7	99t	2
Staley, Duce, Phi.	47	1139	24.2	57	0
Milburn, Glyn, Det.	55	1315	23.9	69	0
Anthony, Reidel, T.B.	25	592	23.7	51	0
Hughes, Tyrone, Chi.	43	1008	23.4	58	0
Schroeder, Bill, G.B.	24	562	23.4	40	0
Walker, Herschel, Dal.	50	1167	23.3	49	0
Mitchell, Brian, Was.	47	1094	23.3	97t	1
Thompson, David, St.L	49	1110	22.7	56	0
Palmer, David, Min.	32	711	22.2	62	0
Levy, Chuck, S.F.	36	793	22.0	59	0
Pegram, Erric, NY-G	22	382	17.4	50	0
Nonqualifiers					
Bownes, Fabien, Chi.	19	396	20.8	36	0
Williams, Moe, Min.	16	388	24.3	74	0
Williams, Karl, T.B.	15	277	18.5	28	0
Lewis, Thomas, NY-G	14	364	26.0	84	0
Marion, Brock, Dal.	10	311	31.1	49	0
Smith, Eric, Chi.	10	196	19.6	28	0
Tate, Robert, Min.	10	196	19.6	36	0
Gray, Mel, Ten.-Phi.	9	193	21.4	33	0
Davis, Troy, N.O.	9	173	19.2	29	0
Witherspoon, Derrick, Phi.	9	171	19.0	28	0
Patten, David, NY-G	8	123	15.4	26	0
Preston, Roell, G.B.	7	211	30.1	43	0
Hayden, Aaron, G.B.	6	141	23.5	35	0
Bouie, Kevin, Ariz	6	136	22.7	27	0
Beebe, Don, G.B.	6	134	22.3	39	0
Uwaezuoke, Iheanyi, S.F.	6	131	21.8	25	0
Ross, Jermaine, St.L	6	130	21.7	42	0
Dunn, Warrick, T.B.	6	129	21.5	30	0
Bolden, Juran, Atl.	5	106	21.2	34	0
Morrow, Harold, Min.	5	99	19.8	42	0
Thomas, J.T., St.L	5	97	19.4	24	0
Lee, Amp, St.L	4	71	17.8	19	0
Logan, Marc, Was.	4	70	17.5	24	0
Darkins, Chris, G.B.	4	68	17.0	20	0
Mills, Ernie, Car.	4	65	16.3	33	0
Kirby, Terry, S.F.	3	124	41.3	101t	1
Stone, Dwight, Car.	3	76	25.3	37	0
Davis, Stephen, Was.	3	62	20.7	28	0
Smith, Cedric, Ariz	3	50	16.7	21	0
Turner, Kevin, Phi.	3	48	16.0	22	0
Bech, Brett, N.O.	3	47	15.7	30	0
Rasby, Walter, Car.	3	32	10.7	12	0
Alexander, Kevin, NY-G	3	30	10.0	15	0

	No.	Yards	Avg.	Long	TD
Johnson, Jimmie, Phi.	3	22	7.3	15	0
Greene, Scott, Car.	3	18	6.0	8	0
Ellison, Jerry, T.B.	2	61	30.5	49	0
Wyatt, Antwuan, Phi.	2	50	25.0	30	0
Kozlowski, Brian, Atl.	2	49	24.5	26	0
Way, Charles, NY-G	2	46	23.0	30	0
Carter, Tony, Chi.	2	34	17.0	19	0
Rivers, Ron, Det.	2	34	17.0	23	0
Dunn, Jason, Phi.	2	32	16.0	16	0
Owens, Terrell, S.F.	2	31	15.5	23	0
Engram, Bobby, Chi.	2	27	13.5	20	0
Gedney, Chris, Ariz	2	26	13.0	16	0
McCrary, Fred, N.O.	2	26	13.0	15	0
Galbraith, Scott, Dal.	2	24	12.0	13	0
Allred, John, Chi.	2	21	10.5	11	0
Mills, Sam, Car.	2	12	6.0	12	0
Clark, Willie, Phi.	1	39	39.0	39t	1
Edwards, Marc, S.F.	1	30	30.0	30	0
Drakeford, Tyronne, S.F.	1	24	24.0	24	0
Green, Harold, Atl.	1	23	23.0	23	0
Kinchen, Todd, Atl.	1	18	18.0	18	0
Sanders, Deion, Dal.	1	18	18.0	18	0
Asher, Jamie, Was.	1	17	17.0	17	0
Moore, Ronald, St.L	1	17	17.0	17	0
Rhett, Errict, T.B.	1	16	16.0	16	0
Bowie, Larry, Was.	1	15	15.0	15	0
Vardell, Tommy, Det.	1	15	15.0	15	0
Kennison, Eddie, St.L	1	14	14.0	7	0
Garcia, Frank, Car.	1	11	11.0	11	0
Lewis, Chad, Phi.	1	11	11.0	11	0
George, Ron, Min.	1	10	10.0	10	0
Patton, Marvcus, Was.	1	10	10.0	10	0
Pierce, Aaron, NY-G	1	10	10.0	10	0
Walsh, Chris, Min.	1	10	10.0	10	0
Williams, Jay, St.L	1	10	10.0	10	0
Green, Darrell, Was.	1	9	9.0	9	0
Owens, Dan, Atl.	1	9	9.0	9	0
Wetnight, Ryan, Chi.	1	9	9.0	9	0
Sparks, Phillippi, NY-G	1	8	8.0	8	0
Burrough, John, Atl.	1	6	6.0	6	0
Jones, Greg, Was.	1	6	6.0	6	0
Poole, Tyrone, Car.	1	5	5.0	5	0
Zgonina, Jeff, St.L	1	5	5.0	5	0
Sharper, Darren, G.B.	1	3	3.0	3	0
Alstott, Mike, T.B.	1	0	0.0	0	0
Fann, Chad, S.F.	1	0	0.0	0	0
Mickens, Terry, G.B.	1	0	0.0	0	0
Russell, Matt, Det.	1	0	0.0	0	0
Tomich, Jared, N.O.	1	0	0.0	0	0
White, Steve, T.B.	1	0	0.0	0	0
Johnson, LeShon, Ariz	0	26	—	26	0
Marshall, Anthony, Chi.	0	3	—	3	0

t = Touchdown
Leader based on average return, minimum 20 returns

FUMBLES

Most Fumbles
AFC: 16—Steve McNair, Tennessee
NFC: 15—Tony Banks, St. Louis
Scott Mitchell, Detroit

Most Fumbles, Game
AFC: 4—Rich Gannon, Kansas City at Jacksonville, November 9
Steve McNair, Tennessee at Cincinnati, December 4
NFC: 4—Scott Mitchell, Detroit vs. Atlanta, August 31

Own Fumbles Recovered
AFC: 7—Steve McNair, Tennessee
NFC: 4—Warrick Dunn, Tampa Bay
Scott Mitchell, Detroit
Charles Way, N.Y. Giants
Zach Wiegert, St. Louis

Most Own Fumbles Recovered, Game
NFC: 3—Scott Mitchell, Detroit vs. Atlanta, August 31
AFC: 2—by many

Opponents' Fumbles Recovered
AFC: 4—Chad Brown, Seattle
NFC: 3—by many

Most Opponents' Fumbles Recovered, Game
AFC: 2—Blaine Bishop, Tennessee at Seattle, October 5
Chad Brown, Seattle at New Orleans, November 16
NFC: 2—Lester Archambeau, Atlanta at Detroit, August 31
Tim McDonald, San Francisco at St. Louis, September 7
Orlando Thomas, Minnesota at Chicago, September 7
Mike Minter, Carolina at San Diego, September 14
Shelton Quarles, Tampa Bay at Atlanta, November 9
Luther Elliss, Detroit vs. Chicago, November 27

Yards
AFC: 78—Paul Bradford, San Diego
NFC: 66—Leslie O'Neal, St. Louis

Longest
AFC: 78—Paul Bradford, San Diego at San Francisco, November 23 - TD
NFC: 66—Leslie O'Neal, St. Louis vs. Carolina, November 23 - TD

AFC FUMBLES—TEAM

	Fum.	Own. Rec.	Fum. OB	TD	Opp. Rec.	TD	Fum. Yards	Tot. Rec.
Jacksonville	17	4	2	0	15	1	19	19
New England	17	9	1	0	13	0	10	22
Kansas City	21	9	2	0	13	1	23	22
Indianapolis	23	9	3	0	13	2	71	22
Miami	23	13	2	1	17	2	-3	30
Cincinnati	25	11	2	0	10	1	18	21
Denver	25	12	3	0	13	2	74	25
Oakland	25	10	1	0	12	2	52	22
Pittsburgh	25	9	2	1	13	1	136	22
Seattle	26	12	3	0	16	3	57	28
N.Y. Jets	27	13	2	0	7	0	45	20
San Diego	30	16	0	1	11	2	108	27
Tennessee	31	15	3	0	17	2	139	32
Baltimore	37	18	3	0	11	0	-16	29
Buffalo	39	21	1	0	7	0	-23	28
AFC Total	391	181	30	3	188	19	710	369
AFC Average	26.1	12.1	2.0	0.2	12.5	1.3	47.3	24.6

NFC FUMBLES—TEAM

	Fum.	Own. Rec.	Fum. OB	TD	Opp. Rec.	TD	Fum. Yards	Tot. Rec.
Minnesota	16	9	1	0	15	2	58	24
Washington	21	12	2	0	14	1	-10	26
San Francisco	22	13	0	0	16	2	70	29
Dallas	23	10	2	0	12	2	28	22
N.Y. Giants	23	12	4	0	17	0	14	29
Green Bay	24	7	1	0	11	3	19	18
Detroit	26	12	3	0	8	2	48	20
Arizona	27	7	0	0	5	0	-1	12
St. Louis	29	11	3	1	14	1	78	25
Carolina	30	11	4	0	11	0	2	22
Tampa Bay	31	17	3	0	13	0	-2	30
Chicago	33	12	2	0	17	0	-14	29
Atlanta	34	16	5	0	10	0	-16	26
New Orleans	34	12	0	0	15	1	15	27
Philadelphia	35	17	2	0	12	1	70	29
NFC Total	408	178	32	1	190	15	359	368
NFC Average	27.2	11.9	2.1	0.1	12.7	1.0	23.9	24.5
NFL Total	799	359	62	4	378	34	1069	737
NFL Average	26.6	12.0	2.1	0.1	12.6	1.1	35.6	24.6

Fum OB = Fumbled out of bounds, includes fumbled through the end zone.

AFC TOUCHDOWNS ON FUMBLE RECOVERIES

2—Chad Brown, Sea.; 2—Marcus Robertson, Ten.; 1—Robert Blackmon, Ind.; 1—Tim Bowens, Mia.; 1—Paul Bradford, S.D.; 1—Terrell Buckley, Mia.; 1—John Copeland, Cin.; 1—Al Fontenot, Ind.; 1—Jason Gildon, Pit.; 1—Rodney Harrison, S.D.; 1—Chris Hudson, Jax.; 1—Danan Hughes, K.C.; 1—Greg Jackson, S.D.; 1—Darrius Johnson, Den.; 1—Carnell Lake, Pit.; 1—O. J. McDuffie, Mia.; 1—Kenny Shedd, Oak.; 1—Mike Sinclair, Sea.; 1—Eric Turner, Oak.; 1—Alfred Williams, Den.

NFC TOUCHDOWNS ON FUMBLE RECOVERIES

1—Stephen Boyd, Det.; 1—Jeff Brady, Min.; 1—Dexter Coakley, Dal.; 1—Tyrone Davis, G.B.; 1—Mark Fields, N.O.; 1—Kevin Greene, S.F.; 1—Merton Hanks, S.F.; 1—Chad Hennings, Dal.; 1—Leslie O'Neal, St.L; 1—Darryl Pounds, Was.; 1—Tracy Scroggins, Det.; 1—Darren Sharper, G.B.; 1—Orlando Thomas, Min.; 1—William Thomas, Phi.; 1—Zach Wiegert, St.L; 1—Gabe Wilkins, G.B.

1997 INDIVIDUAL STATISTICS—FUMBLES

AFC FUMBLES—INDIVIDUAL

	Fum.	Own Rec.	Opp. Rec.	Yards	Tot. Rec.
Abdul-Jabbar, Karim, Mia.	3	0	0	0	0
Adams, Mike, Pit.	1	0	0	0	0
Alexander, Derrick, Bal.	1	0	0	0	0
Allen, Marcus, K.C.	4	2	0	0	2
Ambrose, Ashley, Cin.	0	0	2	0	2
Anders, Kimble, K.C.	3	1	0	0	1
Anderson, Dunstan, Mia.	0	0	1	0	1
Anderson, Richie, NY-J	2	1	0	0	1
Araguz, Leo, Oak.	1	1	0	-21	1
Archie, Mike, Ten.	0	1	0	0	1
Armstrong, Trace, Mia.	0	0	3	0	3
Atkins, James, Sea.	0	1	0	0	1
Atwater, Steve, Den.	0	0	2	0	2
Bailey, Aaron, Ind.	2	1	0	0	1
Barber, Mike, Sea.	0	0	1	0	1
Barker, Bryan, Jax.	1	0	0	-19	0
Barlow, Reggie, Jax.	2	1	0	0	1
Barnett, Fred, Mia.	1	0	0	0	0
Battaglia, Marco, Cin.	2	1	1	0	2
Baxter, Fred, NY-J	1	0	0	0	0
Beede, Frank, Sea.	1	0	0	0	0
Bell, Myron, Pit.	0	0	1	0	1
Berti, Tony, S.D.	0	1	0	0	1
Bettis, Jerome, Pit.	6	1	0	0	1
Bieniemy, Eric, Cin.	2	0	0	0	0
Bishop, Blaine, Ten.	0	0	2	0	2
Blackmon, Robert, Ind.	0	0	1	18	1
Blackwell, Will, Pit.	3	2	0	0	2
Blades, Brian, Sea.	1	0	0	0	0
Blake, Jeff, Cin.	7	0	0	0	0
Bledsoe, Drew, N.E.	4	3	0	-4	3
Booker, Vaughn, K.C.	0	0	1	0	1
Bowden, Joe, Ten.	0	0	1	0	1
Bowens, Tim, Mia.	0	0	1	0	1
Brackens, Tony, Jax.	0	0	1	0	1
Bradford, Paul, S.D.	0	0	1	78	1
Brady, Donny, Bal.	0	0	1	0	1
Brady, Kyle, NY-J	1	0	0	0	0
Brandenburg, Dan, Buf.	0	1	0	0	1
Braxton, Tyrone, Den.	0	0	3	45	3
Brigance, O.J., Mia.	0	0	1	0	1
Brilz, Darrick, Cin.	0	1	0	0	1
Brown, Chad, Sea.	0	0	4	68	4
Brown, Gary, S.D.	2	0	0	0	0
Brown, Ruben, Buf.	0	1	0	0	1
Brown, Tim, Oak.	1	0	0	0	0
Browning, John, K.C.	0	0	1	0	1
Bruener, Mark, Pit.	1	0	0	0	0
Brunell, Mark, Jax.	4	0	0	-5	0
Bruschi, Tedy, N.E.	0	0	2	0	2
Buckley, Terrell, Mia.	0	0	2	23	2
Burnett, Rob, Bal.	0	0	1	0	1
Burris, Jeff, Buf.	3	1	0	0	1
Burton, Shane, Mia.	0	0	1	0	1
Byars, Keith, N.E.	1	0	0	0	0
Byner, Earnest, Bal.	2	2	1	0	3
Cain, Joe, Sea.	0	0	1	0	1
Canty, Chris, N.E.	0	2	0	9	2
Carswell, Dwayne, Den.	0	0	1	0	1
Carter, Ki-Jana, Cin.	3	2	0	0	2
Cascadden, Chad, NY-J	0	0	1	0	1
Chamberlain, Byron, Den.	1	0	0	0	0
Clay, Willie, N.E.	0	0	2	0	2
Coleman, Andre, Sea.-Pit.	2	0	0	0	0
Coleman, Marcus, NY-J	0	0	1	0	1
Collins, Andre, Cin.	0	0	1	0	1
Collins, Todd, Buf.	10	0	0	-30	0
Collons, Ferric, N.E.	0	0	1	5	1
Cook, Anthony, Ten.	0	0	2	0	2
Copeland, John, Cin.	0	0	2	25	2
Craver, Aaron, S.D.	0	1	0	0	1
Crawford, Vernon, N.E.	0	1	0	0	1
Crockett, Zack, Ind.	3	0	0	0	0
Cullors, Derrick, N.E.	3	0	0	0	0
Daniels, Phillip, Sea.	1	0	0	0	0
Davis, Anthony, K.C.	0	0	1	2	1
Davis, Terrell, Den.	4	2	0	-7	2
Davis, Travis, Jax.	0	0	3	10	3
Davis, Tyree, Sea.	1	1	0	0	1
Dillon, Corey, Cin.	1	1	0	4	1
Dodge, Dedrick, Den.	0	0	1	0	1
Duffy, Roger, NY-J	2	1	0	-22	1
Dumas, Mike, S.D.	0	0	1	0	1
Dunn, David, Cin.	1	1	0	0	1
Edwards, Donnie, K.C.	0	0	1	0	1
Elway, John, Den.	11	1	0	-21	1
Erickson, Craig, Mia.	2	2	0	-13	2
Esiason, Boomer, Cin.	1	0	0	0	0
Ethridge, Ray, Bal.	2	0	0	0	0
Evans, Josh, Ten.	0	0	1	0	1
Everett, Jim, S.D.	2	1	0	-8	1
Faulk, Marshall, Ind.	5	1	0	0	1
Fenner, Derrick, Oak.	1	0	0	0	0
Fina, John, Buf.	0	1	0	0	1
Fletcher, Terrell, S.D.	4	0	0	0	0
Flowers, Lethon, Pit.	0	1	0	0	1
Foley, Glenn, NY-J	1	0	0	0	0
Folston, James, Oak.	0	0	1	0	1
Fontenot, Al, Ind.	0	0	3	35	3
Footman, Dan, Ind.	0	0	2	14	2
Ford, Henry, Ten.	0	0	2	13	2
Francis, James, Cin.	0	0	1	0	1
Frederick, Mike, Bal.	0	0	1	0	1
Friesz, John, Sea.	1	1	0	-2	1
Galloway, Joey, Sea.	1	1	0	0	1
Galloway, Mitchell, Buf.	1	0	0	0	0
Gannon, Rich, K.C.	5	0	0	0	0
Gardener, Daryl, Mia.	0	0	1	0	1
George, Eddie, Ten.	4	0	0	0	0
George, Jeff, Oak.	7	3	0	-14	3
Gibson, Oliver, Pit.	0	0	1	0	1
Gildon, Jason, Pit.	0	1	1	32	2
Glenn, Aaron, NY-J	1	0	0	0	0
Glenn, Tarik, Ind.	0	1	0	0	1
Glenn, Terry, N.E.	1	0	0	0	0
Gordon, Darrien, Den.	3	3	1	0	4
Graham, Jay, Bal.	2	1	0	0	1
Graham, Jeff, NY-J	0	1	0	0	1
Grant, Steve, Ind.	0	0	1	0	1
Gray, Mel, Ten.	1	0	0	0	0
Grbac, Elvis, K.C.	1	0	0	0	0
Green, Eric, Bal.	1	0	0	0	0
Griffith, Howard, Den.	0	1	0	0	1
Grunhard, Tim, K.C.	0	1	0	0	1
Harbaugh, Jim, Ind.	4	1	0	0	1
Harper, Dwayne, S.D.	0	0	1	0	1
Harris, Ronnie, Sea.	4	2	0	0	2
Harrison, Martin, Sea.	0	0	1	0	1
Harrison, Marvin, Ind.	2	1	0	5	1
Harrison, Rodney, S.D.	0	1	2	0	3
Hasty, James, K.C.	0	0	1	0	1
Hauck, Tim, Sea.	0	0	1	8	1
Hawkins, Courtney, Pit.	1	0	0	0	0
Hebron, Vaughn, Den.	1	1	0	0	1
Henry, Kevin, Pit.	0	0	2	0	2
Herring, Kim, Bal.	0	0	1	0	1
Hill, Greg, K.C.	1	0	0	0	0
Hobbs, Daryl, Sea.	1	0	0	0	0
Holcomb, Kelly, Ind.	4	1	0	-8	1
Holmberg, Rob, Oak.	0	0	1	0	1
Holmes, Darick, Buf.	1	1	0	0	1
Holmes, Earl, Pit.	0	0	1	0	1
Holmes, Kenny, Ten.	0	0	1	0	1
Hopkins, Brad, Ten.	0	1	0	0	1
Howard, Desmond, Oak.	2	2	0	0	2
Hudson, Chris, Jax.	1	0	2	32	2
Hughes, Danan, K.C.	0	1	1	7	2
Humphries, Stan, S.D.	7	1	0	-10	1
Hundon, James, Cin.	1	0	0	0	0
Jackson, Calvin, Mia.	0	1	0	0	1
Jackson, Greg, S.D.	0	0	1	41	1
Jackson, Michael, Bal.	2	0	0	0	0
Jackson, Raymond, Buf.	1	0	0	0	0
Jackson, Willie, Jax.	1	0	0	0	0
Jacquet, Nate, Ind.	1	1	0	0	1
Jefferson, Shawn, N.E.	2	0	0	0	0
Jenkins, DeRon, Bal.	0	0	1	0	1
Jett, James, Oak.	2	1	0	0	1
Johnson, Darrius, Den.	0	0	1	6	1
Johnson, Ellis, Ind.	0	0	2	0	2
Johnson, Lee, Cin.	0	2	0	0	2

	Fum.	Own Rec.	Opp. Rec.	Yards	Tot. Rec.
Johnson, Leon, NY-J	5	5	0	0	5
Johnson, Lonnie, Buf.	2	1	0	0	1
Johnstone, Lance, Oak.	0	0	1	2	1
Jones, Donta, Pit.	0	1	0	6	1
Jones, George, Pit.	3	1	0	0	1
Jones, Henry, Buf.	1	0	1	0	1
Jones, James, Bal.	0	0	1	0	1
Jones, Marvin, NY-J	0	0	1	0	1
Jones, Mike, N.E.	0	0	1	0	1
Jordan, Charles, Mia.	2	1	0	0	1
Justin, Paul, Ind.	1	0	0	0	0
Kaufman, Napoleon, Oak.	7	1	0	0	1
Kerner, Marlon, Buf.	0	1	0	0	1
Kirkland, Levon, Pit.	0	0	1	0	1
Kitna, Jon, Sea.	1	1	0	-2	1
Klingler, David, Oak.	1	1	0	-5	1
Lacina, Corbin, Buf.	0	1	0	0	1
Lageman, Jeff, Jax.	0	0	1	0	1
Lake, Carnell, Pit.	0	0	1	38	1
Lane, Max, N.E.	0	1	0	0	1
Law, Ty, N.E.	1	0	1	0	1
Leeuwenburg, Jay, Ind.	1	0	0	-20	0
Lewis, Darryll, Ten.	1	1	2	68	3
Lewis, Jermaine, Bal.	3	2	0	0	2
Lewis, Mo, NY-J	0	0	1	26	1
Lewis, Ray, Bal.	0	1	0	0	1
Lincoln, Jeremy, Sea.	0	0	1	0	1
Lloyd, Greg, Pit.	1	0	3	61	3
Lodish, Mike, Den.	0	0	1	0	1
Logan, James, Sea.	0	0	1	0	1
Lott, Anthone, Cin.	0	1	0	0	1
Loville, Derek, Den.	1	0	0	0	0
Lyle, Rick, NY-J	0	0	1	2	1
Mandarich, Tony, Ind.	0	1	0	0	1
Manning, Brian, Mia.	0	1	0	-1	1
Manusky, Greg, K.C.	0	1	0	0	1
Marino, Dan, Mia.	8	3	0	-17	3
Martin, Curtis, N.E.	3	0	0	0	0
Marts, Lonnie, Ten.	0	0	1	0	1
Mason, Derrick, Ten.	5	0	0	0	0
Matthews, Bruce, Ten.	0	2	0	0	2
Matthews, Steve, Jax.	1	0	0	0	0
Mawae, Kevin, Sea.	0	1	1	0	2
McAfee, Fred, Pit.	1	0	0	0	0
McCaffrey, Ed, Den.	0	1	1	0	2
McCloud, Tyrus, Bal.	1	0	1	0	1
McCrary, Michael, Bal.	0	0	2	0	2
McDaniel, Terry, Oak.	1	0	0	0	0
McDaniels, Pellom, K.C.	0	0	1	0	1
McDuffie, O. J., Mia.	0	2	0	3	2
McGinest, Willie, N.E.	0	0	3	0	3
McGlockton, Chester, Oak.	0	0	1	0	1
McKenzie, Raleigh, S.D.	0	1	0	0	1
McKnight, James, Sea.	1	0	0	0	0
McNair, Steve, Ten.	16	7	0	-2	7
McPhail, Jerris, Mia.	1	0	0	4	0
Means, Natrone, Jax.	5	0	0	0	0
Meggett, David, N.E.	2	1	0	0	1
Metcalf, Eric, S.D.	4	2	0	0	2
Milloy, Lawyer, N.E.	0	0	2	0	2
Mitchell, Pete, Jax.	0	1	0	0	1
Mobley, John, Den.	0	0	1	0	1
Mohr, Chris, Buf.	1	1	0	-10	1
Moon, Warren, Sea.	7	1	0	-2	1
Moran, Sean, Buf.	0	0	1	0	1
Morris, Bam, Bal.	4	4	0	0	4
Morrison, Steve, Ind.	0	0	2	27	2
Morton, Mike, Oak.	0	0	1	0	1
Moss, Winston, Sea.	0	0	1	0	1
Moulds, Eric, Buf.	3	1	0	0	1
Murrell, Adrian, NY-J	4	2	0	0	2
Myers, Greg, Cin.	3	2	0	0	2
Norgard, Erik, Ten.	0	1	0	0	1
O'Donnell, Neil, NY-J	9	2	0	-1	2
Orlando, Bo, Cin.	0	0	1	0	1
Ostroski, Jerry, Buf.	0	3	0	0	3
Palelei, Lonnie, NY-J	0	1	0	0	1
Parker, Vaughn, S.D.	0	2	0	0	2
Parmalee, Bernie, Mia.	1	0	0	-2	0
Parrella, John, S.D.	0	0	1	0	1
Paul, Tito, Cin.	0	0	1	0	1

	Fum.	Own Rec.	Opp. Rec.	Yards	Tot. Rec.
Paup, Bryce, Buf.	0	0	1	0	1
Perry, Ed, Mia.	0	1	0	0	1
Perry, Marlo, Buf.	0	1	0	0	1
Philcox, Todd, S.D.	2	0	0	0	0
Phillips, Joe, K.C.	0	0	1	0	1
Pickens, Carl, Cin.	1	0	0	0	0
Pritchard, Mike, Sea.	2	0	0	0	0
Pritchett, Kelvin, Jax.	0	0	1	0	1
Pupunu, Alfred, S.D.	0	1	0	0	1
Purnell, Lovett, N.E.	0	1	0	0	1
Rachal, Latario, S.D.	1	0	1	0	1
Reed, Andre, Buf.	1	0	0	0	0
Richardson, Kyle, Sea.	1	0	0	-13	0
Riemersma, Jay, Buf.	1	0	0	0	0
Roberson, James, Ten.	0	0	1	0	1
Robertson, Marcus, Ten.	0	0	3	67	3
Robinson, Eddie, Jax.	0	0	2	0	2
Rodgers, Derrick, Mia.	0	0	1	0	1
Roe, James, Bal.	1	1	0	0	1
Saleaumua, Dan, Sea.	0	0	1	0	1
Sanders, Chris, Ten.	1	0	0	0	0
Schlereth, Mark, Den.	0	1	0	0	1
Schwartz, Bryan, Jax.	0	0	1	0	1
Seau, Junior, S.D.	1	0	2	5	2
Shade, Sam, Cin.	1	0	1	0	1
Sharpe, Shannon, Den.	1	0	0	0	0
Sharper, Jamie, Bal.	1	0	0	0	0
Shaw, Terrance, S.D.	0	1	0	0	1
Shedd, Kenny, Oak.	0	0	2	25	2
Shelton, Daimon, Jax.	1	0	0	0	0
Sienkiewicz, Troy, S.D.	0	2	0	7	2
Sinclair, Mike, Sea.	0	0	1	0	1
Siragusa, Tony, Bal.	0	0	1	7	1
Slutzker, Scott, Ind.	0	1	1	0	2
Smeenge, Joel, Jax.	0	0	2	1	2
Smith, Anthony, Oak.	0	0	1	0	1
Smith, Antowain, Buf.	4	0	0	0	0
Smith, Jimmy, Jax.	1	1	0	0	1
Smith, Otis, NY-J	0	0	2	40	2
Smith, Rod, Den.	3	1	0	0	1
Smith, Thomas, Buf.	1	0	1	1	1
Spikes, Irving, Mia.	3	2	0	0	2
Steed, Joel, Pit.	0	0	1	0	1
Stepnoski, Mark, Ten.	2	1	0	-7	1
Stewart, Kordell, Pit.	6	1	0	-1	1
Stewart, Rayna, Ten.	0	0	1	0	1
Strong, Mack, Sea.	0	1	0	0	1
Swift, Michael, S.D.	0	0	1	6	1
Szott, David, K.C.	0	1	0	0	1
Tasker, Steve, Buf.	1	1	1	0	2
Taylor, Jason, Mia.	0	0	2	0	2
Testaverde, Vinny, Bal.	11	5	0	-9	5
Thigpen, Yancey, Pit.	1	1	0	0	1
Thomas, Dave, Jax.	0	0	1	0	1
Thomas, Henry, N.E.	0	0	1	0	1
Thomas, Lamar, Mia.	1	0	0	0	0
Thomas, Rodney, Ten.	1	0	0	0	0
Thomas, Thurman, Buf.	2	0	0	0	0
Thompson, Bennie, Bal.	0	2	0	0	2
Tolliver, Billy Joe, Atl.-K.C.	7	2	0	-1	2
Trapp, James, Oak.	0	1	1	0	2
Truitt, Greg, Cin.	2	0	0	-11	0
Truitt, Olanda, Oak.	1	0	0	0	0
Turner, Eric, Oak.	1	0	3	65	3
Vanover, Tamarick, K.C.	6	1	0	0	1
Van Pelt, Alex, Buf.	3	3	0	-7	3
Veland, Tony, Den.	0	1	0	0	1
Vrabel, Mike, Pit.	0	0	1	0	1
Walker, Bracey, Mia.	0	0	1	0	1
Ward, Dedric, NY-J	1	0	0	0	0
Warren, Chris, Sea.	2	0	0	0	0
Warren, Lamont, Ind.	0	0	1	0	1
Washington, Ted, Buf.	0	0	1	0	1
Wells, Dean, Sea.	0	0	1	0	1
Whelihan, Craig, S.D.	7	2	0	-11	2
Widell, Dave, Jax.	0	1	0	0	1
Wiley, Marcellus, Buf.	1	1	1	40	2
Williams, Alfred, Den.	0	0	1	51	1
Williams, Dan, K.C.	0	0	2	2	2
Williams, Darryl, Sea.	0	0	1	0	1
Williams, Grant, Sea.	0	2	0	0	2

1997 INDIVIDUAL STATISTICS—FUMBLES

	Fum.	Own Rec.	Opp. Rec.	Yards	Tot. Rec.
Wilson, Jerry, Mia.	0	0	1	0	1
Wooden, Shawn, Mia.	1	0	2	0	2
Wooden, Terry, K.C.	0	0	1	0	1
Woods, Jerome, K.C.	0	0	2	13	2
Wycheck, Frank, Ten.	0	1	0	0	1
Wynn, Renaldo, Jax.	0	0	1	0	1
Yarborough, Ryan, Bal.	3	0	0	0	0
Zeier, Eric, Bal.	3	0	0	-14	0
Zeigler, Dusty, Buf.	1	1	0	-12	1

Yards includes aborted plays, own recoveries and opponents' recoveries.

NFC FUMBLES—INDIVIDUAL

	Fum.	Own Rec.	Opp. Rec.	Yards	Tot. Rec.
Abraham, Donnie, T.B.	0	0	1	2	1
Agnew, Ray, NY-G	0	0	1	0	1
Ahanotu, Chidi, T.B.	0	0	2	0	2
Aikman, Troy, Dal.	6	0	0	-5	0
Alexander, Derrick, Min.	0	1	0	0	1
Allen, Terry, Was.	2	1	0	0	1
Alstott, Mike, T.B.	5	0	0	0	0
Anderson, Jamal, Atl.	4	1	0	0	1
Archambeau, Lester, Atl.	0	0	3	0	3
Armstead, Jessie, NY-G	0	0	1	0	1
Asher, Jamie, Was.	0	2	0	0	2
Autry, Darnell, Chi.	2	0	0	0	0
Ball, Jerry, Min.	0	0	2	0	2
Banks, Tony, St.L	15	3	0	-27	3
Barber, Tiki, NY-G	3	0	0	0	0
Barrow, Micheal, Car.	0	0	2	0	2
Bates, Mario, N.O.	2	0	0	0	0
Bates, Michael, Car.	4	2	0	0	2
Bech, Brett, N.O.	0	0	1	0	1
Beckles, Ian, Phi.	0	2	0	0	2
Bender, Wes, N.O.	1	0	0	0	0
Bennett, Cornelius, Atl.	0	0	1	0	1
Berger, Mitch, Min.	1	0	0	-9	0
Beuerlein, Steve, Car.	1	0	0	0	0
Biakabutuka, Tim, Car.	1	0	0	0	0
Bishop, Greg, NY-G	0	1	0	0	1
Bjornson, Eric, Dal.	2	0	0	0	0
Blanton, Scott, Was.	0	0	1	0	1
Bono, Steve, G.B.	1	0	0	0	0
Bouie, Tony, T.B.	0	1	0	0	1
Bowie, Larry, Was.	2	1	0	0	1
Bownes, Fabien, Chi.	0	0	1	0	1
Boyd, Stephen, Det.	0	0	1	42	1
Brady, Jeff, Min.	0	0	3	30	3
Bratzke, Chad, NY-G	0	0	2	0	2
Briggs, Greg, Min.	0	0	1	0	1
Brohm, Jeff, S.F.	3	0	0	0	0
Bronson, Zack, S.F.	0	0	1	3	1
Brooks, Barrett, Phi.	0	2	0	0	2
Brooks, Derrick, T.B.	1	0	1	0	1
Brown, Dave, NY-G	1	0	0	0	0
Bruce, Isaac, St.L	1	0	0	0	0
Buckley, Curtis, S.F.	0	0	1	0	1
Buckley, Marcus, NY-G	0	0	1	0	1
Burger, Todd, Chi.	0	1	0	0	1
Bush, Devin, Atl.	0	0	1	0	1
Butler, LeRoy, G.B.	0	1	0	0	1
Campbell, Jesse, Was.	0	1	1	-1	2
Carrier, Mark, Car.	1	0	0	0	0
Carrier, Mark, Det.	1	0	0	0	0
Carruth, Rae, Car.	2	0	0	0	0
Carter, Tony, Chi.	0	1	0	0	1
Carter, Cris, Min.	3	0	0	0	0
Carter, Kevin, St.L	0	0	2	5	2
Case, Stoney, Ariz	3	0	0	0	0
Centers, Larry, Ariz	1	0	0	0	0
Chandler, Chris, Atl.	9	3	0	-18	3
Chmura, Mark, G.B.	1	0	0	0	0
Christian, Bob, Atl.	3	1	0	0	1
Clemons, Duane, Min.	0	0	1	0	1
Coakley, Dexter, Dal.	0	0	1	16	1
Collins, Kerry, Car.	8	2	0	-14	2
Conwell, Ernie, St.L	0	0	1	0	1
Copeland, Horace, T.B.	3	0	0	0	0
Cota, Chad, Car.	0	0	1	0	1
Cox, Bryan, Chi.	0	0	1	0	1
Crawford, Keith, St.L	0	1	0	0	1
Crockett, Henri, Atl.	0	0	1	0	1
Cross, Howard, NY-G	1	1	0	0	1
Cunningham, Randall, Min.	4	2	0	0	2
Dahl, Bob, Was.	0	1	0	0	1
Dalman, Chris, S.F.	0	1	0	0	1
Darby, Matt, Ariz	0	0	2	0	2
Davis, Antone, Atl.	0	1	0	0	1
Davis, Eric, Car.	0	0	1	2	1
Davis, Stephen, Was.	1	1	0	0	1
Davis, Troy, N.O.	3	0	0	0	0
Davis, Tyrone, G.B.	0	0	1	0	1
Davis, Wendell, Dal.	0	1	1	0	2
Deese, Derrick, S.F.	0	1	0	0	1
DeLong, Greg, Min.	1	0	0	0	0
Detmer, Ty, Phi.	6	1	0	-2	1
Devlin, Mike, Ariz	0	1	0	0	1
Diaz, Jorge, T.B.	0	1	0	0	1
Dilfer, Trent, T.B.	9	3	0	-22	3
Dimry, Charles, Phi.	1	1	1	34	2
Dishman, Cris, Was.	0	0	1	0	1
Doleman, Chris, S.F.	0	0	1	0	1
Dotson, Earl, G.B.	0	1	0	0	1
Dulaney, Mike, Chi.	1	0	0	0	0
Dunn, Warrick, T.B.	4	4	0	0	4
Edwards, Anthony, Ariz	0	1	0	0	1
Edwards, Dixon, Min.	0	0	1	0	1
Ellison, Jerry, T.B.	0	1	0	0	1
Elliss, Luther, Det.	0	0	2	0	2
Ellsworth, Percy, NY-G	0	0	2	24	2
Emanuel, Bert, Atl.	2	1	1	0	2
Engler, Derek, NY-G	1	0	0	-2	0
Engram, Bobby, Chi.	1	1	0	0	1
Evans, Chuck, Min.	0	1	0	0	1
Evans, Leomont, Was.	0	0	1	0	1
Everitt, Steve, Phi.	0	1	0	0	1
Farmer, Ray, Phi.	0	0	1	0	1
Farr, D'Marco, St.L	0	0	2	0	2
Favre, Brett, G.B.	7	1	0	-10	1
Feagles, Jeff, Ariz	1	1	0	0	1
Fields, Mark, N.O.	0	0	2	28	2
Fisk, Jason, Min.	0	0	1	0	1
Flanigan, Jim, Chi.	0	0	3	3	3
Floyd, William, S.F.	2	0	0	0	0
Fontenot, Jerry, N.O.	3	0	0	0	0
Freeman, Antonio, G.B.	1	0	0	0	0
Frerotte, Gus, Was.	8	2	0	-16	2
Fryar, Irving, Phi.	1	0	0	0	0
Garner, Charlie, Phi.	1	0	0	0	0
Gedney, Chris, Ariz	1	0	0	0	0
Glover, Kevin, Det.	0	1	0	0	1
Glover, La'Roi, N.O.	0	0	1	0	1
Godfrey, Randall, Dal.	0	0	1	0	1
Gragg, Scott, NY-G	0	1	0	0	1
Graham, Aaron, Ariz	0	1	0	0	1
Graham, Kent, Ariz	5	0	0	0	0
Grasmanis, Paul, Chi.	0	0	1	0	1
Green, Harold, Atl.	0	1	0	0	1
Green, Robert, Min.	0	1	0	0	1
Greene, Kevin, S.F.	0	0	2	40	2
Greene, Scott, Car.	1	0	0	0	0
Gruber, Paul, T.B.	0	1	0	0	1
Guliford, Eric, N.O.	2	1	0	0	1
Hall, Travis, Atl.	0	0	1	0	1
Hamilton, Keith, NY-G	0	0	3	0	3
Hanks, Merton, S.F.	0	0	2	38	2
Hanspard, Byron, Atl.	3	2	0	0	2
Hape, Patrick, T.B.	1	0	0	0	0
Harris, Raymont, Chi.	1	0	0	0	0
Harris, Robert, NY-G	0	0	2	0	2
Harris, Walt, Chi.	1	0	1	0	1
Harvey, Richard, N.O.	0	0	1	0	1
Hastings, Andre, N.O.	1	0	0	0	0
Hearst, Garrison, S.F.	2	2	0	0	2
Hegamin, George, Dal.	0	1	0	0	1
Henderson, William, G.B.	1	2	0	0	2
Hennings, Chad, Dal.	0	0	1	4	1
Hewitt, Chris, N.O.	0	0	1	0	1
Heyward, Craig, St.L	1	0	0	0	0
Hill, Randal, N.O.	0	1	0	0	1
Hobert, Billy Joe, Buf.-N.O.	3	1	0	-5	1

1997 INDIVIDUAL STATISTICS—FUMBLES

	Fum.	Own Rec.	Opp. Rec.	Yards	Tot. Rec.
Hostetler, Jeff, Was.	3	1	0	0	1
Hoying, Bobby, Phi.	7	1	0	0	1
Hughes, Tyrone, Chi.	2	2	0	0	2
Hutton, Tom, Phi.	1	1	0	-1	1
Irving, Terry, Ariz	0	0	1	0	1
Jamison, George, Det.	0	0	1	0	1
Jefferson, Greg, Phi.	0	0	1	0	1
Johnson, Anthony, Car.	2	2	0	0	2
Johnson, Bill, St.L	0	0	1	0	1
Johnson, Brad, Min.	4	3	0	0	3
Johnson, Jimmie, Phi.	1	0	0	0	0
Johnson, Joe, N.O.	0	0	1	0	1
Johnson, Tony, N.O.	1	0	0	0	0
Johnston, Daryl, Dal.	1	0	0	0	0
Jones, Brent, S.F.	1	0	0	0	0
Jones, Clarence, N.O.	0	2	0	0	2
Jones, Marcus, T.B.	0	0	1	0	1
Kanell, Danny, NY-G	6	0	0	-10	0
Kennison, Eddie, St.L	2	0	0	0	0
Kinchen, Todd, Atl.	5	2	0	0	2
Kirby, Terry, S.F.	3	2	0	0	2
Knight, Sammy, N.O.	0	0	1	0	1
Kramer, Erik, Chi.	11	3	0	-14	3
LaFleur, David, Dal.	1	0	0	0	0
Lane, Fred, Car.	4	2	0	0	2
Lang, Kenard, Was.	0	0	2	0	2
LeBel, Harper, Chi.	1	0	1	0	1
Levens, Dorsey, G.B.	5	1	0	-7	1
Levy, Chuck, S.F.	1	0	0	0	0
Logan, Marc, Was.	1	1	0	0	1
Lyght, Todd, St.L	0	0	2	0	2
Lynch, John, T.B.	0	0	2	0	2
Malone, Van, Det.	1	0	0	0	0
Mangum, John, Chi.	0	0	3	0	3
Maniecki, Jason, T.B.	0	0	1	0	1
Marion, Brock, Dal.	0	0	1	13	1
Marshall, Anthony, Chi.	1	1	1	10	2
Martin, Wayne, N.O.	0	0	1	0	1
Mathis, Kevin, Dal.	2	1	1	0	2
Mayberry, Jermane, Phi.	0	0	1	0	1
McDonald, Tim, S.F.	0	0	3	0	3
McElroy, Leeland, Ariz	3	0	0	0	0
McNeil, Ryan, St.L	1	0	1	0	1
Mickell, Darren, N.O.	0	0	1	11	1
Milburn, Glyn, Det.	3	2	0	0	2
Miller, Anthony, Dal.	1	1	0	0	1
Miller, Les, Car.	0	0	1	3	1
Mills, Sam, Car.	1	0	0	0	0
Mincy, Charles, T.B.	0	1	0	0	1
Minter, Barry, Chi.	0	0	3	0	3
Minter, Mike, Car.	0	0	2	0	2
Mirer, Rick, Chi.	4	1	0	-4	1
Mitchell, Brian, Was.	3	0	0	0	0
Mitchell, Scott, Det.	15	4	0	-15	4
Molden, Alex, N.O.	0	0	2	0	2
Moore, Jerald, St.L	4	2	0	0	2
Morabito, Tim, Car.	0	0	1	0	1
Morton, Johnnie, Det.	2	0	0	0	0
Mullen, Roderick, G.B.	0	0	1	1	1
Newman, Anthony, N.O.	0	0	1	0	1
Newton, Nate, Dal.	0	1	0	0	1
Nickerson, Hardy, T.B.	0	1	1	0	2
Norton, Ken, S.F.	0	0	2	0	2
Nussmeier, Doug, N.O.	1	0	0	-4	0
Oliver, Winslow, Car.	2	0	0	0	0
O'Neal, Leslie, St.L	0	0	2	66	2
Owens, Dan, Atl.	1	0	1	2	1
Owens, Rich, Was.	0	0	1	0	1
Owens, Terrell, S.F.	1	1	0	0	1
Pace, Orlando, St.L	0	1	0	0	1
Palmer, David, Min.	2	0	0	0	0
Panos, Joe, Phi.	0	1	0	0	1
Parker, Anthony, T.B.	1	0	0	0	0
Patten, David, NY-G	2	0	1	0	1
Patton, Joe, Was.	0	1	0	0	1
Patton, Marvcus, Was.	0	0	1	0	1
Peete, Rodney, Phi.	5	2	0	-2	2
Pegram, Erric, NY-G	1	1	0	0	1
Penn, Chris, Chi.	1	0	0	0	0
Peterson, Tony, Chi.	0	1	0	0	1
Phillips, Lawrence, St.L	3	0	0	0	0

	Fum.	Own Rec.	Opp. Rec.	Yards	Tot. Rec.
Pilgrim, Evan, Chi.	0	1	0	0	1
Plummer, Jake, Ariz	6	1	0	-1	1
Poole, Tyrone, Car.	3	2	1	11	3
Pounds, Darryl, Was.	0	0	3	18	3
Prior, Mike, G.B.	1	0	0	0	0
Proehl, Ricky, Chi.	2	0	0	0	0
Pyne, Jim, T.B.	1	0	0	-5	0
Quarles, Shelton, T.B.	0	0	2	0	2
Randle, John, Min.	0	0	2	5	2
Reeves, Carl, Chi.	0	0	1	0	1
Richard, Stanley, Was.	0	0	1	0	1
Rivers, Ron, Det.	0	1	0	0	1
Roberts, Ray, Det.	0	2	0	4	2
Robinson, Eugene, G.B.	1	0	2	0	2
Royal, Andre, Car.	0	0	1	0	1
Russell, Matt, Det.	0	0	1	0	1
Salaam, Rashaan, Chi.	2	0	0	0	0
Sanders, Barry, Det.	3	1	0	0	1
Sanders, Deion, Dal.	1	0	0	0	0
Sanders, Frank, Ariz	3	0	0	0	0
Santiago, O.J., Atl.	1	0	0	0	0
Sapp, Warren, T.B.	0	0	1	23	1
Sauer, Craig, Atl.	0	0	1	0	1
Sauerbrun, Todd, Chi.	1	0	0	-9	0
Schroeder, Bill, G.B.	4	1	0	0	1
Scroggins, Tracy, Det.	0	0	1	17	1
Seay, Mark, Phi.	3	1	0	0	1
Sehorn, Jason, NY-G	0	0	1	2	1
Sharper, Darren, G.B.	1	0	1	34	1
Shiver, Clay, Dal.	2	1	0	0	1
Shuler, Heath, N.O.	8	3	0	-20	3
Smith, Cedric, Ariz	0	0	1	0	1
Smith, Darrin, Phi.	0	0	1	0	1
Smith, Derek, Was.	0	0	2	5	2
Smith, Emmitt, Dal.	1	1	0	0	1
Smith, Fernando, Min.	0	0	1	6	1
Smith, Frankie, S.F.	0	1	0	0	1
Smith, Irv, N.O.	1	0	0	0	0
Smith, Robert, Min.	0	1	0	0	1
Solomon, Freddie, Phi.	3	1	0	0	1
Staley, Duce, Phi.	0	1	0	0	1
Stenstrom, Steve, Chi.	1	0	0	0	0
Stevens, Matt, Phi.	0	0	1	0	1
Stokes, J.J., S.F.	1	2	0	0	2
Stoltenberg, Bryan, NY-G	1	0	0	0	0
Stone, Dwight, Car.	0	0	1	0	1
Stone, Ron, NY-G	0	1	0	0	1
Stoutmire, Omar, Dal.	0	1	0	0	1
Strahan, Mike, NY-G	0	0	1	0	1
Strickland, Fred, Dal.	0	0	2	0	2
Swann, Eric, Ariz	1	0	1	0	1
Terrell, Pat, Car.	0	1	0	0	1
Thomas, Broderick, Dal.	0	0	1	0	1
Thomas, Hollis, Phi.	0	0	1	0	1
Thomas, Mark, Chi.	0	0	1	0	1
Thomas, Orlando, Min.	1	0	2	26	2
Thomas, William, Phi.	0	0	1	37	1
Thomason, Jeff, G.B.	1	0	0	0	0
Thompson, David, St.L	2	0	1	0	1
Timpson, Michael, Phi.	1	0	0	0	0
Tobeck, Robbie, Atl.	0	1	0	0	1
Tomich, Jared, N.O.	1	1	0	0	1
Tubbs, Winfred, N.O.	0	0	2	0	2
Turk, Matt, Was.	1	0	0	-16	0
Turner, Kevin, Phi.	1	0	0	0	0
Upshaw, Regan, T.B.	0	0	1	0	1
Uwaezuoke, Iheanyi, S.F.	4	1	1	0	2
Vardell, Tommy, Det.	1	1	0	0	1
Vincent, Troy, Phi.	1	1	1	5	2
Waldroup, Kerwin, Det.	0	0	1	0	1
Walker, Herschel, Dal.	0	1	1	0	2
Walker, Marquis, St.L	0	0	1	0	1
Walsh, Steve, T.B.	1	2	0	0	2
Washington, Marvin, S.F.	0	0	1	0	1
Watters, Ricky, Phi.	3	1	0	0	1
Way, Charles, NY-G	3	4	1	0	5
Wells, Mike, Det.	0	0	1	0	1
Wetnight, Ryan, Chi.	1	0	0	0	0
Wheatley, Tyrone, NY-G	3	3	0	0	3
Wheeler, Leonard, Min.	0	0	1	0	1
White, Reggie, G.B.	0	0	2	0	2

1997 INDIVIDUAL STATISTICS—SACKS

	Fum.	Own Rec.	Opp. Rec.	Yards	Tot. Rec.
Wiegert, Zach, St.L	0	4	0	0	4
Wilkins, Gabe, G.B.	0	0	3	1	3
Williams, Brian, G.B.	0	0	1	0	1
Williams, Gene, Atl.	0	2	0	0	2
Williams, James, S.F.	0	0	1	0	1
Williams, Karl, T.B.	5	1	0	0	1
Williams, Kevin, Ariz	3	1	0	0	1
Williams, Sherman, Dal.	5	1	0	0	1
Willis, James, Phi.	0	0	2	0	2
Wolf, Joe, Ariz	0	1	0	0	1
Woodson, Darren, Dal.	1	0	2	0	2
Woodson, Rod, S.F.	0	0	1	0	1
Wooten, Tito, NY-G	1	0	1	0	1
Wright, Toby, St.L	0	0	1	34	1
Wuerffel, Danny, N.O.	2	2	0	0	2
Wunsch, Jerry, T.B.	0	1	0	0	1
Young, Steve, S.F.	4	2	0	-11	2
Zellars, Ray, N.O.	6	2	0	0	2
Zordich, Mike, Phi.	0	0	1	-1	1

Yards includes aborted plays, own recoveries, and opponents' recoveries.

SACKS

Most Sacks

NFC: 15.5—John Randle, Minnesota

AFC: 14.0—Bruce Smith, Buffalo

Most Sacks, Game

NFC: 5.0—Chuck Smith, Atlanta at New Orleans, October 12

AFC: 3.5—Gerald Dixon, Cincinnati vs. Baltimore, December 21

Team Champion

NFC: 59—New Orleans

AFC: 54—Kansas City

Team Leaders, Sacks

AFC: BALTIMORE: 11.5, Peter Boulware; BUFFALO: 14, Bruce Smith; CINCINNATI: 8.5, Gerald Dixon; DENVER: 8.5, Neil Smith, Maa Tanuvasa, Alfred Williams; INDIANAPOLIS: 10.5, Dan Footman; JACKSONVILLE: 8.5, Clyde Simmons; KANSAS CITY: 10.5, Dan Williams; MIAMI: 5.5, Trace Armstrong; NEW ENGLAND: 9, Chris Slade; N.Y. JETS: 8, Mo Lewis; OAKLAND: 6.5, Anthony Smith; PITTSBURGH: 6, Carnell Lake; SAN DIEGO: 7, Junior Seau; SEATTLE: 12, Mike Sinclair; TENNESSEE: 7, Kenny Holmes, Gary Walker

NFC: ARIZONA: 7.5, Eric Swann; ATLANTA: 12, Chuck Smith; CAROLINA: 8.5, Micheal Barrow; CHICAGO: 6, Jim Flanigan, Barry Minter; DALLAS: 6, Shante Carver; DETROIT: 12.5, Robert Porcher; GREEN BAY: 11, Reggie White; MINNESOTA: 15.5, John Randle; NEW ORLEANS: 10.5, Wayne Martin; N.Y. GIANTS: 14, Mike Strahan; PHILADELPHIA: 8, Rhett Hall; ST. LOUIS: 10, Leslie O'Neal; SAN FRANCISCO: 15, Dana Stubblefield; TAMPA BAY: 10.5, Warren Sapp; WASHINGTON: 9.5, Ken Harvey

AFC SACKS—TEAM

	Sacks	Yards
Kansas City	54	359
Jacksonville	48	331
Pittsburgh	48	294
Buffalo	46	344
New England	45	303
Denver	44	298
Baltimore	42	293
Seattle	42	238
Indianapolis	37	247
Cincinnati	35	209
Tennessee	35	240
Miami	31	231
Oakland	31	239
N.Y. Jets	29	242
San Diego	27	164
AFC Total	594	4032
AFC Average	39.6	268.8

NFC SACKS—TEAM

	Sacks	Yards
New Orleans	59	408
Atlanta	55	354
N.Y. Giants	54	341
San Francisco	54	364
Minnesota	44	253
Tampa Bay	44	331
Detroit	43	287
Philadelphia	43	278
Green Bay	41	274
Chicago	38	259
Dallas	38	195
St. Louis	38	296
Washington	37	280
Carolina	36	246
Arizona	34	215
NFC Total	658	4381
NFC Average	43.9	292.1
League Total	1252	8413
League Average	41.7	280.4

SACKS—TOP TEN LEADERS

Randle, John, Min.	15.5
Stubblefield, Dana, S.F.	15.0
Smith, Bruce, Buf.	14.0
Strahan, Mike, NYG	14.0
Porcher, Robert, Det.	12.5
Doleman, Chris, S.F.	12.0
Sinclair, Mike, Sea.	12.0
Smith, Chuck, Atl.	12.0
Boulware, Peter, Bal.	11.5
White, Reggie, G.B.	11.0

AFC SACKS—INDIVIDUAL

Smith, Bruce, Buf.	14.0
Sinclair, Mike, Sea.	12.0
Boulware, Peter, Bal.	11.5
Footman, Dan, Ind.	10.5
Williams, Dan, K.C.	10.5
Paup, Bryce, Buf.	9.5
Thomas, Derrick, K.C.	9.5
McCrary, Michael, Bal.	9.0
Slade, Chris, N.E.	9.0
Dixon, Gerald, Cin.	8.5
Simmons, Clyde, Jax.	8.5
Smith, Neil, Den.	8.5
Tanuvasa, Maa, Den.	8.5
Williams, Alfred, Den.	8.5
Lewis, Mo, NY-J	8.0
Adams, Sam, Sea.	7.0
Brackens, Tony, Jax.	7.0
Holmes, Kenny, Ten.	7.0
Seau, Junior, S.D.	7.0
Thomas, Henry, N.E.	7.0
Walker, Gary, Ten.	7.0
Brown, Chad, Sea.	6.5
Smeenge, Joel, Jax.	6.5
Smith, Anthony, Oak.	6.5
Hansen, Phil, Buf.	6.0
Jones, James, Bal.	6.0
Lake, Carnell, Pit.	6.0
Armstrong, Trace, Mia.	5.5
Bowens, Tim, Mia.	5.0
Ford, Henry, Ten.	5.0
Gildon, Jason, Pit.	5.0
Kirkland, Levon, Pit.	5.0
Lageman, Jeff, Jax.	5.0
Rodgers, Derrick, Mia.	5.0
Taylor, Jason, Mia.	5.0
Wilkinson, Dan, Cin.	5.0
Fontenot, Al, Ind.	4.5
Henry, Kevin, Pit.	4.5
Johnson, Ellis, Ind.	4.5
Maryland, Russell, Oak.	4.5
McGlockton, Chester, Oak.	4.5
Moran, Sean, Buf.	4.5
Booker, Vaughn, K.C.	4.0
Browning, John, K.C.	4.0
Bruschi, Tedy, N.E.	4.0
Burnett, Rob, Bal.	4.0
Burton, Shane, Mia.	4.0
Conley, Steve, Pit.	4.0
Daniels, Phillip, Sea.	4.0
Douglas, Hugh, NY-J	4.0
Harrison, Nolan, Pit.	4.0
Harrison, Rodney, S.D.	4.0
Holmes, Earl, Pit.	4.0
Johnson, Ted, N.E.	4.0
Jones, Mike, N.E.	4.0
Lewis, Ray, Bal.	4.0
Mobley, John, Den.	4.0
Oldham, Chris, Pit.	4.0
Shade, Sam, Cin.	4.0
Washington, Ted, Buf.	4.0
Wheeler, Mark, N.E.	4.0
Davis, Anthony, K.C.	3.5
Ferguson, Jason, NY-J	3.5
Francis, James, Cin.	3.5
Johnstone, Lance, Oak.	3.5
Lloyd, Greg, Pit.	3.5
McDaniels, Pellom, K.C.	3.5
Parrella, John, S.D.	3.5
Rogers, Sam, Buf.	3.5
Russell, Darrell, Oak.	3.5
Saleaumua, Dan, Sea.	3.5
Simmons, Wayne, K.C.	3.5
Bennett, Tony, Ind.	3.0
Blackmon, Robert, Ind.	3.0
Collins, Andre, Cin.	3.0
Copeland, John, Cin.	3.0
Davey, Don, Jax.	3.0
Fuller, William, S.D.	3.0
Jones, Marvin, NY-J	3.0
LaBounty, Matt, Sea.	3.0
Lee, Shawn, S.D.	3.0
Lyle, Rick, NY-J	3.0
Pritchett, Kelvin, Jax.	3.0
Sharper, Jamie, Bal.	3.0
Wilson, Reinard, Cin.	3.0
Biekert, Greg, Oak.	2.5
Bowden, Joe, Ten.	2.5
Edwards, Donnie, K.C.	2.5
Hardy, Kevin, Jax.	2.5

Johnson, Raylee, S.D.	2.5
Lyons, Pratt, Ten.	2.5
McCoy, Tony, Ind.	2.5
Tongue, Reggie, K.C.	2.5
Wynn, Renaldo, Jax.	2.5
Anderson, Darren, K.C.	2.0
Barndt, Tom, K.C.	2.0
Bellamy, Jay, Sea.	2.0
Canty, Chris, N.E.	2.0
Coleman, Marco, S.D.	2.0
Coryatt, Quentin, Ind.	2.0
Davis, Travis, Jax.	2.0
Evans, Josh, Ten.	2.0
Fredrickson, Rob, Oak.	2.0
Gordon, Darrien, Den.	2.0
Hall, Lemanski, Ten.	2.0
Hasty, James, K.C.	2.0
Jones, Henry, Buf.	2.0
Kennedy, Cortez, Sea.	2.0
Lewis, Albert, Oak.	2.0
McGinest, Willie, N.E.	2.0
Pryce, Trevor, Den.	2.0
Roberson, James, Ten.	2.0
Robinson, Eddie, Jax.	2.0
Romanowski, Bill, Den.	2.0
Terry, Rick, NY-J	2.0
Traylor, Keith, Den.	2.0
Washington, Keith, Bal.	2.0
Whigham, Larry, N.E.	2.0
Wilson, Jerry, Mia.	2.0
Wooden, Terry, K.C.	2.0
Bell, Myron, Pit.	1.5
Bishop, Blaine, Ten.	1.5
Boyer, Brant, Jax.	1.5
Collins, Todd, N.E.	1.5
Farrior, James, NY-J	1.5
Gardener, Daryl, Mia.	1.5
Hasselbach, Harald, Den.	1.5
Holecek, John, Buf.	1.5
Vrabel, Mike, Pit.	1.5
Alexander, Elijah, Ind.	1.0
Ambrose, Ashley, Cin.	1.0
Atwater, Steve, Den.	1.0
Belser, Jason, Ind.	1.0
Blades, Bennie, Sea.	1.0
Bruce, Aundray, Oak.	1.0
Burroughs, Sammie, Ind.	1.0
Collons, Ferric, N.E.	1.0
Dumas, Mike, S.D.	1.0
Dumas, Troy, K.C.	1.0
Eaton, Chad, N.E.	1.0
Fuller, Randy, Pit.	1.0
Gibson, Oliver, Pit.	1.0
Gordon, Dwayne, NY-J	1.0
Green, Victor, NY-J	1.0
Hamilton, Bobby, NY-J	1.0
Hamilton, James, Jax.	1.0
Hand, Norman, S.D.	1.0
Harris, Anthony, Mia.	1.0
Herring, Kim, Bal.	1.0
Israel, Steve, N.E.	1.0
Jackson, Steve, Ten.	1.0
Jones, Lenoy, Ten.	1.0
Kopp, Jeff, Jax.	1.0
Langford, Jevon, Cin.	1.0
Langham, Antonio, Bal.	1.0
Lodish, Mike, Den.	1.0
Lynch, Lorenzo, Oak.	1.0
Marts, Lonnie, Ten.	1.0
McDonald, Ricardo, Cin.	1.0
McGruder, Mike, N.E.	1.0
McKyer, Tim, Den.	1.0
Mickens, Ray, NY-J	1.0
Montgomery, Delmonico, Ind.	1.0
Morrison, Steve, Ind.	1.0
Orlando, Bo, Cin.	1.0
Perry, Darren, Pit.	1.0
Roye, Orpheus, Pit.	1.0
Shello, Kendel, Ind.	1.0
Steed, Joel, Pit.	1.0
Stubbs, Danny, Mia.	1.0
Tuaolo, Esera, Jax.	1.0
Tumulty, Tom, Cin.	1.0
Wells, Dean, Sea.	1.0
Woods, Jerome, K.C.	1.0
Braxton, Tyrone, Den.	0.5
Brown, Cornell, Bal.	0.5
Covington, Damien, Buf.	0.5
Jackson, Calvin, Mia.	0.5
Jeffcoat, Jim, Buf.	0.5
Law, Ty, N.E.	0.5
Phillips, Joe, K.C.	0.5
Richie, David, Den.	0.5
Schwartz, Bryan, Jax.	0.5
Stewart, Rayna, Ten.	0.5
Thomas, Zach, Mia.	0.5

NFC SACKS—INDIVIDUAL

Randle, John, Min.	15.5
Stubblefield, Dana, S.F.	15.0
Strahan, Mike, NY-G	14.0
Porcher, Robert, Det.	12.5
Doleman, Chris, S.F.	12.0
Smith, Chuck, Atl.	12.0
White, Reggie, G.B.	11.0
Greene, Kevin, S.F.	10.5
Hall, Travis, Atl.	10.5
Martin, Wayne, N.O.	10.5
Sapp, Warren, T.B.	10.5
Ahanotu, Chidi, T.B.	10.0
Harris, Robert, NY-G	10.0
O'Neal, Leslie, St.L	10.0
Harvey, Ken, Was.	9.5
Archambeau, Lester, Atl.	8.5
Barrow, Micheal, Car.	8.5
Culpepper, Brad, T.B.	8.5
Elliss, Luther, Det.	8.5
Johnson, Joe, N.O.	8.5
Fields, Mark, N.O.	8.0
Hall, Rhett, Phi.	8.0
Hamilton, Keith, NY-G	8.0
Owens, Dan, Atl.	8.0
Carter, Kevin, St.L	7.5
Scroggins, Tracy, Det.	7.5
Swann, Eric, Ariz	7.5
Upshaw, Regan, T.B.	7.5
Bennett, Cornelius, Atl.	7.0
Clemons, Duane, Min.	7.0
Glover, La'Roi, N.O.	6.5
Carver, Shante, Dal.	6.0
Flanigan, Jim, Chi.	6.0
Minter, Barry, Chi.	6.0
Smith, Mark, Ariz	6.0
Barker, Roy, S.F.	5.5
Dotson, Santana, G.B.	5.5
Miller, Jamir, Ariz	5.5
Miller, Les, Car.	5.5
Wilkins, Gabe, G.B.	5.5
Cox, Bryan, Chi.	5.0
Rice, Simeon, Ariz	5.0
Royal, Andre, Car.	5.0
Rudd, Dwayne, Min.	5.0
Smith, Brady, N.O.	5.0
Thomas, William, Phi.	5.0
Tolbert, Tony, Dal.	5.0
Alexander, Derrick, Min.	4.5
Dent, Richard, Phi.	4.5
Hennings, Chad, Dal.	4.5
Patton, Marvcus, Was.	4.5
Simpson, Carl, Chi.	4.5
Thomas, Mark, Chi.	4.5
Johnson, Bill, St.L	4.0
Mamula, Mike, Phi.	4.0
Mims, Chris, Was.	4.0
Mitchell, Keith, N.O.	4.0
Molden, Alex, N.O.	4.0
Smith, Fernando, Min.	4.0
Young, Bryant, S.F.	4.0
Armstead, Jessie, NY-G	3.5
Bratzke, Chad, NY-G	3.5
Holsey, Bernard, NY-G	3.5
Jones, Greg, Was.	3.5
Mickell, Darren, N.O.	3.5
Minter, Mike, Car.	3.5
Thomas, Broderick, Dal.	3.5
Brown, Gilbert, G.B.	3.0
Butler, LeRoy, G.B.	3.0
Casillas, Tony, Dal.	3.0
Dronett, Shane, Atl.	3.0
Farr, D'Marco, St.L	3.0
Fisk, Jason, Min.	3.0
Galyon, Scott, NY-G	3.0
Harvey, Richard, N.O.	3.0
Jefferson, Greg, Phi.	3.0
Joyner, Seth, G.B.	3.0
Lassiter, Kwamie, Ariz	3.0
Marshall, Anthony, Chi.	3.0
Thierry, John, Chi.	3.0
Brown, Reggie, Det.	2.5
Bryant, Junior, S.F.	2.5
Coakley, Dexter, Dal.	2.5
Jackson, Tyoka, T.B.	2.5
Jones, Jimmie, Phi.	2.5
Owens, Rich, Was.	2.5
Robinson, Eugene, G.B.	2.5
Thomas, Hollis, Phi.	2.5
Tubbs, Winfred, N.O.	2.5
Abrams, Kevin, Det.	2.0
Agnew, Ray, NY-G	2.0
Anderson, Antonio, Dal.	2.0
Bailey, Robert, Det.	2.0
Bankston, Michael, Ariz	2.0
Boutte, Marc, Was.	2.0
Caldwell, Mike, Ariz	2.0
Crockett, Henri, Atl.	2.0
Duff, Jamal, Was.	2.0
Jones, Mike, St.L	2.0
King, Shawn, Car.	2.0
Kragen, Greg, Car.	2.0
Lathon, Lamar, Car.	2.0
London, Antonio, Det.	2.0
Lyle, Keith, St.L	2.0
Phifer, Roman, St.L	2.0
Pounds, Darryl, Was.	2.0
Sagapolutele, Pio, N.O.	2.0
Smith, Derek, Was.	2.0
Spellman, Alonzo, Chi.	2.0
Stoutmire, Omar, Dal.	2.0
Taylor, Bobby, Phi.	2.0
Wheeler, Leonard, Min.	2.0
Williams, Charlie, Dal.	2.0
Willis, James, Phi.	2.0
Woodson, Darren, Dal.	2.0
Zgonina, Jeff, St.L	2.0
Zordich, Mike, Phi.	2.0
Brooks, Derrick, T.B.	1.5
Conner, Darion, Phi.	1.5
Dishman, Cris, Was.	1.5
Edwards, Dixon, Min.	1.5
Lang, Kenard, Was.	1.5
McDaniel, Ed, Min.	1.5
McKenzie, Keith, G.B.	1.5
Norton, Ken, S.F.	1.5
Sehorn, Jason, NY-G	1.5
Tuggle, Jessie, Atl.	1.5
Widmer, Corey, NY-G	1.5
Bates, Bill, Dal.	1.0
Bonham, Shane, Det.	1.0
Brandon, David, Atl.	1.0
Burrough, John, Atl.	1.0
Carter, Marty, Chi.	1.0
Cook, Toi, Car.	1.0
Cota, Chad, Car.	1.0
Cox, Ron, Chi.	1.0
Evans, Doug, G.B.	1.0
Farmer, Ray, Phi.	1.0
Godfrey, Randall, Dal.	1.0
Harris, Bernardo, G.B.	1.0
Harris, Jon, Phi.	1.0
Howard, Ty, Ariz	1.0
Jamison, George, Det.	1.0
Jasper, Edward, Phi.	1.0
Jeffries, Greg, Det.	1.0
Jones, Robert, St.L	1.0
Lyght, Todd, St.L	1.0
Mangum, John, Chi.	1.0
Maniecki, Jason, T.B.	1.0
Maxie, Brett, S.F.	1.0
McCleon, Dexter, St.L	1.0
McCleskey, J. J., Ariz	1.0
McKinnon, Ronald, Ariz	1.0
Miller, Corey, NY-G	1.0
Nickerson, Hardy, T.B.	1.0
Parker, Anthony, T.B.	1.0
Phillips, Ryan, NY-G	1.0
Pittman, Kavika, Dal.	1.0
Poole, Tyrone, Car.	1.0
Rice, Ron, Det.	1.0
Robinson, Bryan, St.L	1.0
Saleh, Tarek, Car.	1.0
Seals, Ray, Car.	1.0
Smith, Darrin, Phi.	1.0
Smith, Jermaine, G.B.	1.0
Smith, Vinson, Dal.	1.0
Sparks, Phillippi, NY-G	1.0
Tomich, Jared, N.O.	1.0
Turnbull, Renaldo, Car.	1.0
Waldroup, Kerwin, Det.	1.0
Walker, Darnell, S.F.	1.0
Washington, Marvin, S.F.	1.0
Wells, Mike, Det.	1.0
Williams, Brian, G.B.	1.0
Williams, Jay, St.L	1.0
Zorich, Chris, Was.	1.0
Dixon, Ernest, N.O.	0.5
Grasmanis, Paul, Chi.	0.5
Lett, Leon, Dal.	0.5
McCormack, Hurvin, Dal.	0.5
Peter, Christian, NY-G	0.5
Pleasant, Anthony, Atl.	0.5
Porter, Rufus, T.B.	0.5
Raybon, Israel, Car.	0.5
Reeves, Carl, Chi.	0.5
Robinson, Jeff, St.L	0.5
Strickland, Fred, Dal.	0.5

1997 ATTENDANCE

1997 NFL PAID ATTENDANCE BREAKDOWN

	Games	Attendance	Average
AFC Preseason	11	564,507	51,319
NFC Preseason	10	520,791	52,079
AFC-NFC Interconference	43	2,195,395	51,056
NFL Preseason Total	**64**	**3,280,693**	**51,261**
AFC Regular Season	90	5,476,598	60,851
NFC Regular Season	90	5,694,595	63,273
AFC-NFC Regular Season, Interconference	60	3,796,121	63,269
NFL Regular Season Total	**240**	**14,967,314**	**62,364**
AFC Wild Card Playoffs	2		
Jacksonville at Denver		74,512	
Miami at New England		60,452	
AFC Divisional Playoffs	2		
New England at Pittsburgh		60,517	
Denver at Kansas City		79,254	
AFC Championship Game	1		
Denver at Pittsburgh		61,068	
NFC Wild Card Playoffs	2		
Minnesota at N.Y. Giants		77,210	
Detroit at Tampa Bay		72,720	
NFC Divisional Playoffs	2		
Minnesota at San Francisco		67,252	
Tampa Bay at Green Bay		60,323	
NFC Championship Game	1		
Green Bay at San Francisco		69,664	
Super Bowl XXXII at San Diego, California	1		
Denver vs. Green Bay		68,912	
AFC-NFC Pro Bowl at Honolulu, Hawaii	1	49,995	
NFL Postseason Total	**12**	**801,879**	**66,823**
NFL All Games	**316**	**19,049,886**	**60,284**

ONE MILLION PLUS CLUB

During the 1997 season, 18 clubs drew a combined home and away paid attendance of more than 1 million. The Kansas City Chiefs drew an NFL-leading 1,177,972 fans in 1997.

Team	Total Paid Home Attendance	Total Paid Visiting Attendance	Total Paid Attendance
Kansas City	629,763	548,209	1,177,972
Denver	595,217	511,852	1,107,069
New York Jets	613,513	479,619	1,093,132
Miami	573,728	518,267	1,091,995
New York Giants	613,109	471,510	1,084,619
Detroit	555,421	529,150	1,084,571
Washington	592,761	474,245	1,067,006
Carolina	573,361	493,427	1,066,788
San Francisco	545,540	518,720	1,064,260
Chicago	526,484	532,413	1,058,897
Tampa Bay	538,616	500,072	1,038,688
Dallas	499,675	537,086	1,036,761
New England	479,763	546,243	1,026,006
Buffalo	528,055	494,701	1,022,756
Green Bay	480,850	535,317	1,016,167
San Diego	519,342	492,139	1,011,481
Philadelphia	527,033	484,260	1,011,293
Minnesota	478,805	529,946	1,008,751

Note: *For complete year-by-year paid attendance and attendance records,* *see page 377.*

Inside the Numbers

INSIDE THE NUMBERS

RECORDS FOR NFL TEAMS FOR MOST POINTS IN A GAME (REGULAR SEASON ONLY)

***Note:** When the record has been achieved more than once, only the most recent game is shown; summaries are listed in alphabetical order by conference. Bold face indicates team holding record.*

BALTIMORE RAVENS
October 6, 1996, at Baltimore

New England 3 17 15 11 — 46
Baltimore 0 14 0 24 — 38

TDs: Balt—Earnest Byner 2, Michael Jackson 2, Derrick Alexander; NE—Shawn Jefferson 2, Ben Coates, Mike Bartrum, Ted Bruschi. TD Passes: Balt—Vinny Testaverde 3; NE—Drew Bledsoe 4. FGs: NE—Adam Vinatieri 3.

BUFFALO BILLS
September 18, 1966, at Buffalo

Miami 3 7 0 14 — 24
Buffalo 21 27 3 7 — 58

TDs: Buff—Bobby Burnett 2, Butch Byrd 2, Jack Spikes 2, Bobby Crockett, Jack Kemp; Mia—Dave Kocourek, Bo Roberson, John Roderick. TD Passes: Buff—Jack Kemp, Daryle Lamonica; Mia—George Wilson 3. FGs: Buff—Booth Lusteg; Mia—Gene Mingo.

CINCINNATI BENGALS
December 17, 1989, at Cincinnati

Houston 0 0 0 7 — 7
Cincinnati 21 10 21 9 — 61

TDs: Cin—Eddie Brown 2, Eric Ball, James Brooks, Ira Hillary, Rodney Holman, Tim McGee, Craig Taylor; Hou—Lorenzo White. TD Passes: Cin—Boomer Esiason 4, Erik Wilhelm. FGs: Cin—Jim Breech 2.

CLEVELAND BROWNS
November 7, 1954, at Cleveland

Washington 0 3 0 0 — 3
Cleveland 13 14 21 14 — 62

TDs: Clev—Darrell Brewster 2, Mo Bassett, Ken Gorgal, Otto Graham, Dub Jones, Dante Lavelli, Curley Morrison. TD Passes: Clev—George Ratterman 3, Otto Graham. FGs: Clev—Lou Groza 2; Wash—Vic Janowicz.

DENVER BRONCOS
October 6, 1963, at Denver

San Diego 13 7 0 14 — 34
Denver 3 14 9 24 — 50

TDs: Den—Lionel Taylor 2, Goose Gonsoulin, Gene Prebola, Donnie Stone; SD—Keith Lincoln 2, Lance Alworth, Paul Lowe, Jacque MacKinnon. TD Passes: Den—John McCormick 3; SD—Tobin Rote 3, John Hadl 2. FGs: Den—Gene Mingo 5.

INDIANAPOLIS COLTS
December 12, 1976, at Baltimore

Buffalo 3 3 7 7 — 20
Baltimore Colts 7 13 28 10 — 58

TDs: Balt—Roger Carr, Raymond Chester, Glenn Doughty, Roosevelt Leaks, Derrel Luce, Lydell Mitchell, Howard Stevens; Buff—Bob Chandler, O.J. Simpson. TD Passes: Balt—Bert Jones 3; Buff—Gary Marangi. FGs: Balt—Toni Linhart 3; Buff—George Jakowenko 2.

JACKSONVILLE JAGUARS
September, 7 1997, at Jacksonville

N.Y. Giants 7 0 6 0 — 13
Jacksonville 0 20 3 17 — 40

TDs: Jax—Natrone Means 2, James Stewart 2; NYG—Tiki Barber, Chris Calloway. TD Passes: NYG—Dave Brown. FGs: Jax—Mike Hollis 4.

KANSAS CITY CHIEFS
September 7, 1963, at Denver

Kansas City 14 14 21 10 — 59
Denver 0 7 0 0 — 7

TDs: KC—Chris Burford 2, Frank Jackson 2, Dave Grayson, Abner Haynes, Sherrill Headrick, Curtis McClinton; Den—Lionel Taylor. TD Passes: KC—Len Dawson 4, Curtis McClinton; Den—Mickey Slaughter. FG: KC—Tommy Brooker.

MIAMI DOLPHINS
November 24, 1977, at St. Louis

Miami 14 14 20 7 — 55
St. Louis Cardinals 7 0 0 7 — 14

TDs: Mia—Nat Moore 3, Gary Davis, Duriel Harris, Leroy Harris, Benny Malone, Andre Tillman; StL—Ike Harris, Terry Metcalf. TD Passes: Mia—Bob Griese 6; StL—Jim Hart.

NEW ENGLAND PATRIOTS
September 9, 1979, at New England

New York Jets 3 0 0 0 — 3
New England 14 21 7 14 — 56

TDs: NE—Harold Jackson 3, Stanley Morgan 2, Allan Clark, Andy Johnson, Don Westbrook. TD Passes: NE—Steve Grogan 5, Tom Owen. FG: NYJ—Pat Leahy.

NEW YORK JETS
November 17, 1985, at New York

Tampa Bay 14 7 7 0 — 28
New York Jets 17 24 14 7 — 62

TDs: NYJ—Mickey Shuler 3, Johnny Hector 2, Tony Paige, Al Toon, Wesley Walker; TB—James Wilder 2, Kevin House, Calvin Magee. TD Passes: NYJ—Ken O'Brien 5; TB—Steve DeBerg 2. FGs: NYJ—Pat Leahy 2.

OAKLAND RAIDERS
December 22, 1963, at Oakland

Houston 14 21 14 0 — 49
Oakland 7 28 7 10 — 52

TDs: Oak—Art Powell 4, Clem Daniels, Claude Gibson, Ken Herock; Hou—Willard Dewveall 2, Dave Smith 2, Charley Hennigan, Bob McLeod, Charley Tolar. TD Passes: Oak—Tom Flores 6; Hou—George Blanda 5. FG: Oak—Mike Mercer.

PITTSBURGH STEELERS
November 30, 1952, at Pittsburgh

New York Giants 0 0 7 0 — 7
Pittsburgh 14 14 7 28 — 63

TDs: Pitt—Lynn Chandnois 2, Dick Hensley 2, Jack Butler, George Hays, Ray Mathews, Ed Modzelewski, Elbie Nickel; NYG—Bill Stribling. TD Passes: Pitt—Jim Finks 4, Gary Kerkorian; NYG—Tom Landry.

SAN DIEGO CHARGERS
December 22, 1963, at San Diego

Denver 7 10 3 0 — 20
San Diego 10 16 10 22 — 58

TDs: SD—Paul Lowe 2, Chuck Allen, Bobby Jackson, Dave Kocourek, Keith Lincoln, Jacque MacKinnon; Den—Billy Joe, Donnie Stone. TD Passes: SD—John Hadl, Tobin Rote; Den—Don Breaux. FGs: SD—George Blair 3; Den—Gene Mingo 2.

SEATTLE SEAHAWKS
October 30, 1977, at Seattle

Buffalo 3 0 7 7 — 17
Seattle 14 28 7 7 — 56

TDs: Sea—Steve Largent 2, Duke Fergerson, Al Hunter, David Sims, Sherman Smith, Don Testerman, Jim Zorn; Buff—Joe Ferguson, John Kimbrough. TD Passes: Sea—Jim Zorn 4; Buff—Joe Ferguson. FG: Buff—Carson Long.

TENNESSEE OILERS
December 9, 1990, at Houston

Cleveland 0 7 7 0 — 14
Houston Oilers 14 31 7 6 — 58

TDs: Hou—Lorenzo White 4, Ernest Givins, Leonard Harris, Tony Jones, Terry Kinard; Clev—Eric Metcalf 2. TD Passes: Hou—Warren Moon 2, Cody Carlson; Clev—Bernie Kosar. FG: Hou—Teddy Garcia.

ARIZONA CARDINALS
November 13, 1949, at New York

Chicago Cardinals 7 31 14 13 — 65
New York Bulldogs 7 0 6 7 — 20

TDs: Chi—Red Cochran 2, Pat Harder 2, Bill Dewell, Mel Kutner, Bob Ravensburg, Vic Schwall, Charlie Trippi; NY—Joe Golding, Frank Muehlheuser, Johnny Rauch. TD Passes: Chi—Paul Christman 3, Jim Hardy 3; NY—Bobby Layne. FG: Chi—Pat Harder.

ATLANTA FALCONS
September 16, 1973, at New Orleans

Atlanta 0 24 21 17 — 62
New Orleans 0 0 7 0 — 7

TDs: Atl—Ken Burrow 2, Eddie Ray 2, Wes Chesson, Tom Hayes, Art Malone, Joe Profit; NO—Bill Butler. TD Passes: Atl—Dick Shiner 3, Bob Lee; NO—Archie Manning. FGs: Atl—Nick Mike-Mayer 2.

CAROLINA PANTHERS
October 13, 1996, at Carolina

St. Louis 0 13 0 0 — 13
Carolina 14 14 10 7 — 45

TDs: Car—Wesley Walls 2, Kevin Greene, Muhsin Muhammad, Michael Bates, Dino Philyaw; StL—Anthony Parker, Eddie Kennison. TD Passes: Car—Kerry Collins 3; StL—Tony Banks. FG: Car—John Kasay.

CHICAGO BEARS
December 7, 1980, at Chicago

Green Bay 0 7 0 0 — 7
Chicago 0 28 13 20 — 61

TDs: Chi—Walter Payton 3, Brian Baschnagel, Robin Earl, Roland Harper, Willie McClendon, Len Walterscheid, Rickey Watts; GB—James Lofton. TD Passes: Chi—Vince Evans 3; GB—Lynn Dickey.

DALLAS COWBOYS
October 12, 1980, at Dallas

San Francisco 0 7 0 7 — 14
Dallas 14 24 14 7 — 59

TDs: Dall—Drew Pearson 3, Ron Springs 2, Tony Dorsett, Billy Joe DuPree, Robert Newhouse; SF—Dwight Clark 2. TD Passes: Dall—Danny White 4; SF—Steve DeBerg 2. FG: Dall—Rafael Septien.

DETROIT LIONS
November 27, 1997, at Detroit

Chicago 14 6 0 0 — 20
Detroit 3 14 17 21 — 55

TDs: Det—Herman Moore, Johnnie Morton, Ron Rivers, Barry Sanders 3, Tracy Scroggins; Chi—Raymont Harris, Ricky Proehl. TD Passes: Det—Scott Mitchell 2; Chi—Erik Kramer. FGs: Det—Jason Hanson 2; Chi—Jeff Jaeger 2.

GREEN BAY PACKERS
October 7, 1945, at Milwaukee

Detroit 0 7 7 7 — 21
Green Bay 0 41 9 7 — 57

TDs: GB—Don Hutson 4, Charley Brock, Irv Comp, Ted Fritsch, Clyde Goodnight; Det—Chuck Fenenbock, John Greene, Bob Westfall. TD Passes: GB—Tex McKay 4, Lou Brock, Irv Comp; Det—Dave Ryan.

MINNESOTA VIKINGS
October 18, 1970, at Minnesota

Dallas 3 3 0 7 — 13
Minnesota 14 20 17 3 — 54

TDs: Minn—Clint Jones 2, Ed Sharockman 2, John Beasley, Dave Osborn; Dall—Calvin Hill. TD Pass: Minn—Gary Cuozzo. FGs: Minn—Fred Cox 4; Dall—Mike Clark 2.

NEW ORLEANS SAINTS
November 21, 1976, at Seattle

New Orleans 3 17 28 3 — 51
Seattle 6 0 7 14 — 27

TDs: NO—Bobby Douglass 2, Tony Galbreath, Chuck Muncie, Tom Myers, Elex Price; Sea—Sherman Smith 2, Steve Largent, Jim Zorn. TD Pass: Sea—Bill Munson. FGs: NO—Rich Szaro 3.

NEW YORK GIANTS
November 26, 1972, at New York

Philadelphia 3 7 0 0 — 10
New York Giants 14 24 10 14 — 62

TDs: NYG—Don Herrmann 2, Ron Johnson 2, Bob Tucker 2, Randy Johnson; Phil—Harold Jackson. TD Passes: NYG—Norm Snead 3, Randy Johnson 2; Phil—John Reaves. FGs: NYG—Pete Gogolak 2; Phil—Tom Dempsey.

PHILADELPHIA EAGLES
November 6, 1934, at Philadelphia

Cincinnati Reds 0 0 0 0 — 0
Philadelphia 26 6 12 20 — 64

TDs: Phil—Joe Carter 3, Swede Hanson 3, Marvin Ellstrom, Roger Kirkman, Ed Matesic, Ed Storm. TD Passes: Phil—Ed Matesic 2, Albert Weiner 2, Marvin Elstrom.

ST. LOUIS RAMS
October 22, 1950, at Los Angeles

Baltimore 13 0 7 7 — 27
Los Angeles Rams 21 14 14 21 — 70

TDs: LA—Bob Boyd 2, Vitamin T. Smith 2, Tom Fears, Elroy (Crazylegs) Hirsch, Dick Hoerner, Ralph

Pasquariello, Dan Towler, Bob Waterfield; Balt—Chet Mutryn 2, Adrian Burk, Billy Stone. TD Passes: LA—Norm Van Brocklin 2, Bob Waterfield 2, Glenn Davis; Balt—Adrian Burk 3.

SAN FRANCISCO 49ERS
October 18, 1992, at San Francisco

Atlanta	7	3	0	7	— 17
San Francisco	21	21	14	0	— 56

TDs: SF—Jerry Rice 3, Ricky Watters 3, Brent Jones, Tom Rathman; Atl—Michael Haynes, Jason Phillips. TD Passes: SF—Steve Young 3; Atl—Chris Miller, Wade Wilson. FG: Atl—Norm Johnson.

TAMPA BAY BUCCANEERS
September 13, 1987, at Tampa Bay

Atlanta	0	3	0	7	— 10
Tampa Bay	14	13	7	14	— 48

TDs: TB—Gerald Carter 2, Cliff Austin, Steve Bartalo, Mark Carrier, Phil Freeman, Calvin Magee; Atl—Stacey Bailey. TD Passes: TB—Steve DeBerg 5; Atl—Scott Campbell. FG: Atl—Mick Luckhurst.

WASHINGTON REDSKINS
November 27, 1966, at Washington

New York Giants	0	14	14	13	— 41
Washington	13	21	14	24	— 72

TDs: Wash—A.D. Whitfield 3, Brig Owens 2, Charley Taylor 2, Rickie Harris, Joe Don Looney, Bobby Mitchell; NYG—Allen Jacobs, Homer Jones, Dan Lewis, Joe Morrison, Aaron Thomas, Gary Wood. TD Passes: Wash—Sonny Jurgensen 3; NYG—Gary Wood 2, Tom Kennedy. FG: Wash—Charlie Gogolak.

TEAMS THAT FINISHED IN FIRST PLACE IN THEIR DIVISION THE SEASON AFTER FINISHING IN LAST PLACE

Season	Team	Record	Previous Season
1967	Houston	9-4-1	*3-11
1968	Minnesota	8-6	3-8-3
1970	Cincinnati	8-6	4-9-1
1970	San Francisco	10-3-1	4-8-2
1972	Green Bay	10-4	4-8-2
1975	Baltimore	10-4	2-12
1979	Tampa Bay	10-6	5-11
1981	Cincinnati	12-4	6-10
1987	Indianapolis	9-6	3-13
1988	Cincinnati	12-4	4-11
1990	Cincinnati	9-7	8-8
1991	Denver	12-4	5-11
1992	San Diego	11-5	4-12
1993	Detroit	10-6	5-11
1997	N.Y. Giants	10-5-1	6-10

**tied for last place*

RECORDS OF NFL TEAMS, 1988-1997

AFC	W	L	T	Pct.	Division Titles	Playoff Berths	Postseason Record	Super Bowl Record
Buffalo	103	57	0	.644	6	8	11-8	0-4
Kansas City	98	60	2	.619	3	7	3-7	0-0
Pittsburgh	94	66	0	.588	5	7	6-7	0-1
Denver	93	67	0	.581	3	5	7-4	1-1
Miami	90	70	0	.563	2	5	3-5	0-0
Tennessee	86	74	0	.538	2	6	2-6	0-0
Oakland	81	79	0	.506	1	3	2-3	0-0
Jacksonville	24	24	0	.500	0	2	2-2	0-0
Cleveland	58	69	1	.457	1	3	2-3	0-0
San Diego	73	87	0	.456	2	3	3-3	0-1
Seattle	69	91	0	.431	1	1	0-1	0-0
Indianapolis	67	93	0	.419	0	2	2-2	0-0
Cincinnati	65	95	0	.406	2	2	3-2	0-1
New England	65	95	0	.406	2	3	3-3	0-1
N.Y. Jets	57	102	1	.359	0	1	0-1	0-0
Baltimore	10	21	1	.328	0	0	0-0	0-0

Oakland totals include L.A. Raiders, 1988-94
Tennessee totals include Houston, 1988-96

NFC	W	L	T	Pct.	Division Titles	Playoff Berths	Postseason Record	Super Bowl Record
San Francisco	121	39	0	.756	8	9	14-6	3-0
Philadelphia	93	66	1	.584	1	6	2-6	0-0
Minnesota	91	69	0	.569	3	7	2-7	0-0
N.Y. Giants	90	69	1	.566	3	4	4-3	1-0
Green Bay	88	72	0	.550	3	5	9-4	1-1
Dallas	87	73	0	.544	5	6	12-3	3-0
Carolina	26	22	0	.542	1	1	1-1	0-0
Chicago	81	79	0	.506	2	4	3-4	0-0
New Orleans	81	79	0	.506	1	3	0-3	0-0
Washington	80	79	1	.503	1	3	5-2	1-0
Detroit	77	83	0	.481	2	5	1-5	0-0
St. Louis	62	98	0	.388	0	2	2-2	0-0
Atlanta	61	99	0	.381	0	2	1-2	0-0
Tampa Bay	58	102	0	.363	0	1	1-1	0-0
Arizona	55	105	0	.344	0	0	0-0	0-0

Arizona totals include Phoenix, 1988-93
St. Louis totals include L.A. Rams, 1988-94

HOME RECORDS, 1988-1997

AFC	W-L-T	Pct.	NFC	W-L-T	Pct.
Buffalo	62-18-0	.775	San Francisco	63-17-0	.788
Denver	61-19-0	.763	Green Bay	55-25-0	.688
Kansas City	61-19-0	.763	Minnesota	54-26-0	.675
Pittsburgh	59-21-0	.738	Philadelphia	54-26-0	.675
Jacksonville	16- 8-0	.667	Carolina	15- 9-0	.625
Miami	51-29-0	.638	N.Y. Giants	50-30-0	.625
Tennessee	51-29-0	.638	Chicago	49-31-0	.613
Oakland	45-35-0	.563	Dallas	48-32-0	.600
Cincinnati	44-36-0	.550	Detroit	48-32-0	.600
Cleveland	33-30-1	.523	Washington	45-34-1	.569
San Diego	40-40-0	.500	New Orleans	43-37-0	.538
Indianapolis	39-41-0	.488	Atlanta	42-38-0	.525
Seattle	39-41-0	.488	Tampa Bay	37-43-0	.463
New Engand	38-42-0	.475	Arizona	34-46-0	.425
Baltimore	7- 8-1	.469	St. Louis	34-46-0	.425
N.Y. Jets	30-49-1	.381			

Arizona totals include Phoenix, 1988-93
Oakland totals include L.A. Raiders, 1988-94
St. Louis totals include L.A. Rams, 1988-94
Tennessee totals include Houston, 1988-96

ROAD RECORDS, 1988-1997

AFC	W-L-T	Pct.	NFC	W-L-T	Pct.
Buffalo	41-39-0	.513	San Francisco	58-22-0	.725
Miami	39-41-0	.488	N.Y. Giants	40-39-1	.506
Kansas City	37-41-2	.475	Philadelphia	39-40-1	.494
Oakland	36-44-0	.450	Dallas	39-41-0	.488
Pittsburgh	35-45-0	.438	New Orleans	38-42-0	.475
Tennessee	35-45-0	.438	Minnesota	37-43-0	.463
San Diego	33-47-0	.413	Carolina	11-13-0	.458
Denver	32-48-0	.400	Washington	35-45-0	.438
Cleveland	25-39-0	.391	Green Bay	33-47-0	.413
Seattle	30-50-0	.375	Chicago	32-48-0	.400
Indianapolis	28-52-0	.350	Detroit	29-51-0	.363
New England	27-53-0	.338	St. Louis	28-52-0	.350
N.Y. Jets	27-53-0	.338	Arizona	21-59-0	.263
Jacksonville	8-16-0	.333	Tampa Bay	21-59-0	.263
Cincinnati	21-59-0	.263	Atlanta	19-61-0	.238
Baltimore	3-13-0	.188			

Arizona totals include Phoenix, 1988-93
Oakland totals include L.A. Raiders, 1988-94
St. Louis totals include L.A. Rams, 1988-94
Tennessee totals include Houston, 1988-96

RECORDS BY MONTHS, 1988-1997

AFC	Sept. W-L-T	Oct. W-L-T	Nov. W-L-T	Dec. W-L-T	Total W-L-T	Pct.
Buffalo	30- 8	26-13	28-15	19-21	103- 57-0	.644
Kansas City	27-14	19-19-1	28-12-1	24-15	98- 60-2	.619
Pittsburgh	19-20	24-16	27-15	24-15	94- 66-0	.588
Denver	26-15	23-15	27-14	17-23	93- 67-0	.581
Miami	23-14	27-14	22-20	18-22	90- 70-0	.563
Tennessee	19-20	23-17	22-19	22-18	86- 74-0	.538
Oakland	19-22	24-15	18-22	20-20	81- 79-0	.506
Jacksonville	5- 8	6- 7	6- 5	7- 4	24- 24-0	.500
Cleveland	17-14	19-13	10-21-1	12-21	58- 69-1	.457
San Diego	19-22	14-25	20-21	20-19	73- 87-0	.456
Seattle	15-25	20-21	15-24	19-21	69- 91-0	.431
Indianapolis	12-25	19-23	15-26	21-19	67- 93-0	.419
Cincinnati	15-23	10-31	19-22	21-19	65- 95-0	.406
New England	14-24	13-28	19-22	19-21	65- 95-0	.406
N.Y. Jets	16-25	13-26-1	19-21	9-30	57-102-1	.359
Baltimore	5- 4	2- 5	0- 8-1	3- 4	10- 21-1	.328

Oakland totals include L.A. Raiders, 1988-94
Tennessee totals include Houston, 1988-96
September totals include August
December totals include January

NFC	Sept. W-L-T	Oct. W-L-T	Nov. W-L-T	Dec. W-L-T	Total W-L-T	Pct.
San Francisco	29-11	30- 9	31-10	31- 9	121- 39-0	.756
Philadelphia	20-18	26-14	24-17-1	23-17	93- 66-1	.584
Minnesota	24-17	20-18	24-17	23-17	91- 69-0	.569
N.Y. Giants	23-16	24-16	21-20-1	22-17	90- 69-1	.566

INSIDE THE NUMBERS

	Sept. W-L-T	Oct. W-L-T	Nov. W-L-T	Dec. W-L-T	Total W-L-T	Pct.
Green Bay	19-22	20-17	24-17	25-16	88- 72-0	.550
Dallas	21-17	23-18	23-21	20-17	87- 73-0	.544
Carolina	5- 7	7- 5	7- 6	7- 4	26- 22-0	.542
Chicago	22-19	23-14	22-21	14-25	81- 79-0	.506
New Orleans	18-23	22-17	21-19	20-20	81- 79-0	.506
Washington	23-16	20-20	14-27-1	23-16	80- 79-1	.503
Detroit	19-23	16-21	18-25	24-14	77- 83-0	.481
St. Louis	23-17	11-28	11-30	17-23	62- 98-0	.388
Atlanta	11-29	14-25	23-18	13-27	61- 99-0	.381
Tampa Bay	17-24	11-28	15-26	15-24	58-102-0	.363
Arizona	13-26	15-26	15-27	12-26	55-105-0	.344

Arizona totals include Phoenix, 1988
St. Louis totals include L.A. Rams, 1988-94
September totals include August
December totals include January

TAKEAWAYS/GIVEAWAYS IN 1988-1997

AFC	Takeaways Int.	Fum.	Total	Giveaways Int.	Fum.	Total	Net.Diff.
Kansas City	179	172	351	133	122	255	96
Pittsburgh	212	156	368	158	150	308	60
San Diego	197	116	313	183	117	300	13
N.Y. Jets	178	151	329	176	146	322	7
Jacksonville	40	40	80	44	34	78	2
Cincinnati	172	131	303	162	141	303	0
Denver	164	138	302	166	143	309	- 7
Buffalo	187	141	328	190	152	342	-14
Tennessee	191	155	346	181	179	360	- 14
Indianapolis	146	135	281	170	126	296	- 15
Baltimore	32	18	50	36	30	66	- 16
Miami	160	126	286	170	138	308	- 22
Cleveland	136	98	234	141	116	257	- 23
Seattle	165	151	316	200	143	343	- 27
Oakland	142	129	271	173	131	304	- 33
New England	168	144	312	213	144	357	- 45

Oakland totals include L.A. Raiders, 1988-94
Tennessee totals include Houston, 1988-96

NFC	Takeaways Int.	Fum.	Total	Giveaways Int.	Fum.	Total	Net.Diff.
N.Y. Giants	185	136	321	126	114	240	81
San Francisco	202	135	337	133	127	260	77
Minnesota	222	140	362	177	122	299	63
Philadelphia	224	156	380	166	151	317	63
Washington	199	122	321	193	113	306	15
Chicago	190	127	317	175	144	319	-2
Green Bay	190	137	327	181	150	331	-4
Carolina	54	43	97	60	45	105	-8
Detroit	169	139	308	183	135	318	- 10
New Orleans	165	162	327	192	152	344	- 17
Atlanta	168	133	301	189	139	328	- 27
Dallas	138	118	256	161	123	284	- 28
St. Louis	182	128	310	191	154	345	- 35
Tampa Bay	160	142	302	230	128	358	- 56
Arizona	158	140	298	222	150	372	- 74

Arizona totals include Phoenix, 1988-93
St. Louis totals include L.A. Rams, 1988-94

BEST TAKEAWAY/GIVEAWAY DIFFERENTIAL, SEASON

+43 Washington, 1983
+26 Kansas City, 1990
+25 N.Y. Giants, 1997

HIGH AND LOW SINGLE-GAME YARDAGE TOTALS, 1988-1997

Most Total Yards, Game
676 Washington vs. Detroit, Nov. 4, 1990 (OT)
615 Arizona vs. Washington, Nov. 10, 1996 (OT)
598 San Francisco vs. Buffalo, Sept. 13, 1992
597 N.Y. Jets vs. Miami, Nov. 27, 1988
590 San Francisco vs. Atlanta, Oct. 18, 1992

Fewest Total Yards, Game
53 Pittsburgh vs. Cleveland, Sept. 10, 1989
60 Detroit vs. Minnesota, Nov. 24, 1988
62 Seattle vs. Dallas, Oct. 11, 1992
65 Seattle vs. New England, Dec. 4, 1988
82 Denver vs. Philadelphia, Sept. 20, 1992

Most Yards Rushing, Game
315 Buffalo vs. Atlanta, Nov. 22, 1992
310 Kansas City vs. Detroit, Oct. 14, 1990
305 Pittsburgh vs. Miami, Dec. 18, 1988
304 Philadelphia vs. New England, Nov. 4, 1990
296 Minnesota vs. Tampa Bay, Dec. 8, 1991

Fewest Yards Rushing, Game
0 Buffalo vs. Chicago, Oct. 2, 1988
1 Tampa Bay vs. Washington, Oct. 22, 1989
4 Indianapolis vs. Detroit, Sept. 22, 1991
Buffalo vs. Tennessee, Nov. 23, 1997
6 N.Y. Giants vs. L.A. Rams, Nov. 12, 1989

Most Yards Passing, Game
521 Miami vs. N.Y. Jets, Oct. 23, 1988
507 Arizona vs. Washington, Nov. 10, 1996 (OT)
505 Houston vs. Kansas City, Dec. 16, 1990
483 Cincinnati vs. L.A. Rams, Oct. 7, 1990 (OT)
482 Washington vs. Detroit, Nov. 4, 1990 (OT)

Fewest Yards Passing, Game
12 Carolina vs. Buffalo, Sept. 10, 1995
13 Seattle vs. Oakland, Dec. 22, 1996
15 New England vs. Atlanta, Nov. 29, 1992
17 Pittsburgh vs. Cleveland, Sept. 10, 1989
19 L.A. Raiders vs Cincinnati, Nov. 24, 1991

NFL INDIVIDUAL LEADERS, 1988-1997

Points	Touchdowns	Field Goals
1,095 Morten Andersen	123 Jerry Rice	253 Morten Andersen
1,072 Gary Anderson	119 Emmitt Smith	248 Gary Anderson
1,027 Norm Johnson	105 Barry Sanders	223 Norm Johnson
972 Pete Stoyanovich	88 Cris Carter	219 Pete Stoyanovich
942 Al Del Greco	83 Thurman Thomas	209 Al Del Greco
		209 Nick Lowery

Rushes	Rushing Yards	Rushing TDs
2,720 Thurman Thomas	13,778 Barry Sanders	112 Emmitt Smith
2,719 Barry Sanders	11,405 Thurman Thomas	95 Barry Sanders
2,595 Emmitt Smith	11,234 Emmitt Smith	69 Marcus Allen
1,824 Rodney Hampton	6,897 Rodney Hampton	63 Thurman Thomas
1,628 Ricky Watters	6,706 Chris Warren	58 Terry Allen

Attempts	Completions	Passing Yards
4,958 Dan Marino	2,941 Dan Marino	35,994 Dan Marino
4,845 Warren Moon	2,928 Warren Moon	35,123 Warren Moon
4,736 John Elway	2,745 John Elway	33,834 John Elway
4,474 Jim Everett	2,606 Jim Everett	31,755 Jim Everett
4,012 Vinny Testaverde	2,339 Jim Kelly	29,076 Jim Kelly

TD Passes	Receptions	Reception Yards
218 Warren Moon	857 Jerry Rice	12,880 Jerry Rice
217 Dan Marino	751 Cris Carter	10,715 Henry Ellard
196 Jim Kelly	668 Andre Reed	10,680 Michael Irvin
193 John Elway	666 Michael Irvin	9,636 Andre Reed
185 Jim Everett	641 Andre Rison	9,389 Irving Fryar

Receiving TDs	Interceptions	Sacks
115 Jerry Rice	41 Eugene Robinson	124.5 Reggie White
87 Cris Carter	40 Rod Woodson	120.5 Bruce Smith
73 Andre Rison	39 Eric Allen	119.5 Kevin Greene
65 Sterling Sharpe	38 Aeneas Williams	113.0 Chris Doleman
64 Andre Reed	36 Deion Sanders	110.0 Leslie O'Neal
	36 Donnell Woolford	

NFL GAMES IN WHICH A TEAM HAS SCORED 60 OR MORE POINTS

(Home team in capitals)

Regular Season
WASHINGTON 72, New York Giants 41....November 27, 1966
LOS ANGELES RAMS 70, Baltimore 27....October 22, 1950
Chicago Cardinals 65, NEW YORK BULLDOGS 20....November 13, 1949
LOS ANGELES RAMS 65, Detroit 24....October 29, 1950
PHILADELPHIA 64, Cincinnati 0....November 6, 1934
CHICAGO CARDINALS 63, New York Giants 35....October 17, 1948
AKRON 62, Oorang 0....October 29, 1922
PITTSBURGH 62, New York Giants 7....November 30, 1952
CLEVELAND 62, New York Giants 14....December 6, 1953
CLEVELAND 62, Washington 3....November 7, 1954
NEW YORK GIANTS 62, Philadelphia 10....November 26, 1972
Atlanta 62, NEW ORLEANS 7....September 16, 1973
NEW YORK JETS 62, Tampa Bay 28....November 17, 1985
CHICAGO 61, San Francisco 20....December 12, 1965
Cincinnati 61, HOUSTON 17....December 17, 1972
CHICAGO 61, Green Bay 7....December 7, 1980
CINCINNATI 61, Houston 7....December 17, 1989
ROCK ISLAND 60, Evansville 0....October 15, 1922
CHICAGO CARDINALS 60, Rochester 0....October 7, 1923

Postseason
Chicago Bears 73, WASHINGTON 0....December 8, 1940

YOUNGEST AND OLDEST PLAYERS IN NFL IN 1997

10 Youngest Players	Birthdate	Games	Starts	Position
Reidel Anthony, Tampa Bay	10/20/76	16	13	WR
Darnell Autry, Chicago	6/19/76	13	3	RB
Darrell Russell, Oakland	5/27/76	16	10	DE
Tarik Glenn, Indianapolis	5/25/76	16	16	G
Ike Hilliard, N.Y. Giants	4/5/76	2	2	WR
Chris Canty, New England	3/30/76	16	1	CB
Tony Gonzalez, Kansas City	2/27/76	16	0	TE
Dwayne Rudd, Minnesota	2/3/76	16	2	LB
Byron Hanspard, Atlanta	1/23/76	16	0	RB
Tim McTyer, Philadelphia	12/14/75	10	0	CB

10 Oldest Players	Birthdate	Games	Starts	Position
Eddie Murray, Minnesota	8/29/56	12	0	K
Warren Moon, Seattle	11/18/56	15	14	QB
Dave Krieg, Tennessee	10/20/58	8	0	QB
Wade Wilson, Dallas	2/1/59	7	0	QB
Mike Horan, St. Louis	2/1/59	10	0	P
Rohn Stark, Seattle	5/4/59	4	0	P
Sam Mills, Carolina	6/3/59	16	16	LB
Gary Anderson, San Francisco	7/16/59	16	0	K
Gary Plummer, San Francisco	1/26/60	16	16	LB
Darrell Green, Washington	2/15/60	16	16	CB

YOUNGEST AND OLDEST REGULAR STARTERS BY POSITION IN 1997

Minimum: 8 Games Started

	Youngest		Oldest	
QB	12/19/74	Jake Plummer, Ariz	11/18/56	Warren Moon, Sea.
RB	5/12/75	Lawrence Phillips, St. L.-Mia.	10/14/63	Keith Byars, N.E.
WR	10/20/76	Reidel Anthony, T.B.	7/21/61	Henry Ellard, Wash.
TE	9/16/74	Freddie Jones, S.D.	2/12/63	Brent Jones, S.F.
C	1/5/74	Calvin Collins, Atl.	2/8/63	Raleigh McKenzie, S.D.
G	5/25/76	Tarik Glenn, Ind.	8/8/61	Bruce Matthews, Tenn.
T	11/4/75	Orlando Pace, St. L.	12/13/61	Gary Zimmerman, Den.
DE	5/27/76	Darrell Russell, Oak.	10/16/61	Chris Doleman, S.F.
DT	9/3/74	Renaldo Wynn, Jack.	3/4/62	Greg Kragen, Car.
LB	5/15/75	Ray Lewis, Balt.	6/3/59	Sam Mills, Car.
CB	3/11/75	Shawn Springs, Sea.	2/15/60	Darrell Green, Wash.
S	9/10/75	Sammy Knight, N.O.	5/28/63	Eugene Robinson, G.B.

EMMITT SMITH'S CAREER RUSHING VS. EACH OPPONENT

Opponent	Games	Rushes	Yards	Yards Per Rush	Yards Per Game	TD
Arizona	16	319	1,376	4.3	86.3	20
Atlanta	6	114	586	5.1	97.7	7
Buffalo	1	15	25	1.7	25.0	1
Carolina	1	2	3	1.5	3.0	0
Chicago	3	51	244	4.8	81.3	1
Cincinnati	3	56	222	4.0	74.0	1
Cleveland	2	58	224	3.9	112.0	1
Denver	2	52	176	3.4	88.0	2
Detroit	3	64	276	4.3	92.0	4
Green Bay	6	139	567	4.1	94.5	6
Indianapolis	2	51	205	4.0	102.5	2
Jacksonville	1	24	75	3.1	75.0	1
Kansas City	2	42	151	3.6	75.5	2
Miami	2	38	125	3.3	62.5	0
Minnesota	2	39	254	6.5	127.0	3
New England	1	27	85	3.1	85.0	0
New Orleans	3	66	271	4.1	90.3	2
N.Y. Giants	15	296	1,357	4.6	90.5	14
N.Y. Jets	2	35	146	4.2	73.0	0
Oakland	2	58	262	4.5	131.0	6
Philadelphia	16	371	1,756	4.7	109.8	11
Pittsburgh	3	89	349	3.9	116.3	2
St. Louis	2	40	134	3.4	67.0	1
San Diego	2	24	70	2.9	35.0	2
San Francisco	6	110	422	3.8	70.3	4
Seattle	1	22	78	3.5	78.0	2
Tampa Bay	2	39	169	4.3	84.5	1
Tennessee	3	49	161	3.3	53.7	1
Washington	14	305	1,465	4.8	104.6	15
Totals	124	2,595	11,234	4.3	90.6	112

Arizona totals include eight games vs. Phoenix
Oakland totals include one game vs. L.A. Raiders
St. Louis totals include two games vs. L.A. Rams
Tennessee totals include two games vs. Houston

BARRY SANDERS'S CAREER RUSHING VS. EACH OPPONENT

Opponent	Games	Rushes	Yards	Yards Per Rush	Yards Per Game	TD
Arizona	3	56	308	5.5	102.7	2
Atlanta	7	144	586	4.1	83.7	5
Buffalo	3	70	260	3.7	86.7	2
Chicago	17	330	1,704	5.2	100.2	12
Cincinnati	2	47	265	5.6	132.5	2
Cleveland	3	76	389	5.1	129.7	4
Dallas	3	79	357	4.5	119.0	0
Denver	1	23	147	6.4	147.0	1
Green Bay	17	342	1,843	5.4	107.9	6
Indianapolis	2	54	395	7.3	197.5	4
Jacksonville	1	22	76	3.5	76.0	2
Kansas City	2	36	167	4.6	83.5	2
Miami	3	74	332	4.5	110.7	1
Minnesota	17	317	1,662	5.2	97.8	11
New England	2	50	279	5.6	139.5	2
New Orleans	5	75	307	4.1	61.4	2
N.Y. Giants	5	89	424	4.8	84.8	2
N.Y. Jets	3	66	425	6.4	141.7	3
Oakland	2	34	212	6.2	106.0	2
Philadelphia	1	16	49	3.1	49.0	2
Pittsburgh	3	47	203	4.3	67.7	1
St. Louis	2	52	148	2.8	74.0	1
San Diego	1	16	51	3.2	51.0	2
San Francisco	5	93	424	4.6	84.8	2
Seattle	3	47	258	5.5	86.0	2
Tampa Bay	17	344	1,998	5.8	117.5	14
Tennessee	3	60	199	3.3	66.3	4
Washington	4	60	319	5.3	79.8	2
Totals	137	2,719	13,778	5.1	100.6	95

Arizona totals include two games vs. Phoenix
Oakland totals include one game vs. L.A. Raiders
St. Louis totals include two games vs. L.A. Rams
Tennessee totals include three games vs. Houston

THURMAN THOMAS'S CAREER RUSHING VS. EACH OPPONENT

Opponent	Games	Rushes	Yards	Yards Per Rush	Yards Per Game	TD
Arizona	1	26	112	4.3	112.0	0
Atlanta	3	51	264	5.2	88.0	1
Carolina	1	22	91	4.1	91.0	1
Chicago	3	37	151	4.1	50.3	1
Cincinnati	4	69	312	4.5	78.0	1
Cleveland	2	40	144	3.6	72.0	2
Dallas	2	47	126	2.7	63.0	1
Denver	6	93	390	4.2	65.0	3
Detroit	2	30	131	4.4	65.5	0
Green Bay	4	85	330	3.9	82.5	2
Indianapolis	18	293	1,181	4.0	65.6	7
Jacksonville	1	8	30	3.8	30.0	0
Kansas City	5	76	213	2.8	42.6	1
Miami	18	349	1,563	4.5	86.8	8
Minnesota	3	48	199	4.1	66.3	1
New England	20	386	1,723	4.5	86.2	10
New Orleans	2	40	155	3.9	77.5	2
N.Y. Giants	3	79	279	3.5	93.0	2
N.Y. Jets	20	335	1,561	4.7	78.1	7
Oakland	5	79	356	4.5	71.2	3
Philadelphia	3	53	174	3.3	58.0	1
Pittsburgh	6	118	510	4.3	85.0	1
St. Louis	3	70	337	4.8	112.3	3
San Francisco	3	35	132	3.8	44.0	1
Seattle	4	68	216	3.2	54.0	0
Tampa Bay	2	24	55	2.3	27.5	0
Tennessee	7	103	434	4.2	62.0	2
Washington	3	56	236	4.2	78.7	2
Totals	154	2,720	11,405	4.2	74.1	63

Arizona totals include one game vs. Phoenix
Oakland totals include five games vs. L.A. Raiders
St. Louis totals include two games vs. L.A. Rams
Tennessee totals include six games vs. Houston

INSIDE THE NUMBERS

DAN MARINO'S CAREER PASSING VS. EACH OPPONENT

Opponent	Games	Att.	Cmp.	Pct.	Yards	Avg. Gain	TD	Int.	Sacked
Arizona	3	84	56	66.7	812	9.67	7	0	3/21
Atlanta	3	130	75	57.7	896	6.89	4	6	1/2
Baltimore	1	27	19	70.4	189	7.00	0	0	0/0
Buffalo	27	904	563	62.3	6,947	7.68	47	33	35/289
Chicago	5	156	81	51.9	1,129	7.24	8	5	12/78
Cincinnati	6	219	143	65.3	1,680	7.67	11	2	6/47
Cleveland	6	205	126	61.5	1,661	8.10	11	5	4/33
Dallas	4	142	78	54.9	1,033	7.27	7	4	4/36
Denver	1	43	25	58.1	390	9.07	3	0	3/25
Detroit	4	152	89	58.6	1,016	6.68	4	3	4/28
Green Bay	6	218	133	61.0	1,568	7.19	12	7	6/37
Indianapolis	29	903	544	60.2	6,489	7.19	46	15	27/172
Kansas City	7	243	142	58.4	1,687	6.94	12	4	4/35
Minnesota	2	91	49	53.8	695	7.64	5	6	1/5
New England	27	944	560	59.3	6,806	7.21	40	41	25/191
New Orleans	3	105	65	61.9	650	6.19	5	2	6/42
N.Y. Giants	2	60	30	50.0	324	5.40	1	4	4/25
N.Y. Jets	26	945	565	59.8	7,699	8.15	67	28	32/179
Oakland	9	314	174	55.4	2,186	6.96	17	11	11/90
Philadelphia	3	127	72	56.7	987	7.77	6	2	5/45
Pittsburgh	9	284	179	63.0	2,082	7.33	12	10	9/64
St. Louis	4	156	98	62.8	1,195	7.66	11	5	3/14
San Diego	5	202	128	63.4	1,534	7.59	11	3	6/42
San Francisco	4	144	84	58.3	942	6.54	5	5	8/56
Seattle	2	68	40	58.8	504	7.41	3	4	3/25
Tampa Bay	4	154	98	63.6	1,110	7.21	9	1	1/10
Tennessee	9	291	161	55.3	2,025	6.96	11	11	13/88
Washington	4	141	76	53.9	1,180	8.37	10	3	2/7
Totals	215	7,452	4,453	59.8	55,416	7.44	385	220	238/1,686

Arizona totals include one game vs. St. Louis, one game vs. Phoenix
Indianapolis totals include two games vs. Baltimore Colts
Oakland totals include seven games vs. L.A. Raiders
St. Louis totals include three games vs. L.A. Rams
Tennessee totals include eight games vs. Houston

JOHN ELWAY'S CAREER PASSING VS. EACH OPPONENT

Opponent	Games	Att.	Cmp.	Pct.	Yards	Avg. Gain	TD	Int.	Sacked
Arizona	3	83	55	66.3	748	9.01	6	5	4/26
Atlanta	4	139	80	57.6	1,151	8.28	9	4	12/87
Baltimore	1	39	25	64.1	326	8.36	3	1	0/0
Buffalo	7	226	119	52.7	1,469	6.50	6	8	19/125
Carolina	1	23	14	60.9	227	9.87	1	0	3/15
Chicago	6	150	84	56.0	961	6.41	4	4	13/79
Cincinnati	6	176	106	60.2	1,353	7.69	12	3	13/105
Cleveland	9	251	147	58.6	2,005	7.99	14	7	16/126
Dallas	2	48	23	47.9	352	7.33	5	1	3/24
Detroit	3	88	56	63.6	699	7.94	2	2	7/72
Green Bay	4	153	88	57.5	913	5.97	2	5	5/38
Indianapolis	7	213	118	55.4	1,545	7.25	8	2	17/129
Jacksonville	1	34	22	64.7	286	8.41	4	1	0/0
Kansas City	28	873	487	55.8	6,206	7.11	26	34	78/560
Miami	1	37	18	48.6	250	6.76	0	1	3/24
Minnesota	6	166	111	66.9	1,257	7.57	12	3	16/125
New England	9	276	156	56.5	1,944	7.04	10	8	11/73
New Orleans	2	79	46	58.2	519	6.57	4	2	4/35
N.Y. Giants	3	103	58	56.3	724	7.03	2	3	3/19
N.Y. Jets	5	165	96	58.2	1,177	7.13	6	6	10/61
Oakland	26	822	449	54.6	5,583	6.79	31	27	67/541
Philadelphia	5	105	54	51.4	680	6.48	5	6	16/119
Pittsburgh	8	234	122	52.1	1,614	6.90	8	6	16/126
St. Louis	4	147	79	53.7	989	6.73	11	3	5/43
San Diego	29	902	528	58.5	6,297	6.98	34	33	60/406
San Francisco	4	140	67	47.9	681	4.86	3	6	12/89
Seattle	28	894	508	56.8	6,490	7.26	38	25	64/426
Tampa Bay	2	75	51	68.0	405	5.40	1	2	1/0
Tennessee	4	139	81	58.3	1,081	7.78	8	6	11/109
Washington	3	114	65	57.0	737	6.46	3	2	9/68
Totals	221	6,894	3,913	56.8	48,669	7.06	278	216	498/3,650

Arizona totals include two games vs. Phoenix
Oakland totals include 20 games vs. L.A. Raiders
St. Louis totals include three games vs. L.A. Rams
Tennessee totals include four games vs. Houston

BRETT FAVRE'S CAREER PASSING VS. EACH OPPONENT

Opponent	Games	Att.	Cmp.	Pct.	Yards	Avg. Gain	TD	Int.	Sacked
Atlanta	2	87	62	71.3	597	6.86	3	2	4/26
Buffalo	2	58	34	58.6	370	6.38	5	1	1/9
Carolina	1	34	18	52.9	256	7.53	3	1	3/16
Chicago	12	366	229	62.6	2,821	7.71	27	10	21/133
Cincinnati	2	82	53	64.6	628	7.66	5	1	6/36
Cleveland	2	61	43	70.5	433	7.10	3	0	4/22
Dallas	5	190	112	58.9	1,123	5.91	10	2	9/75
Denver	2	70	40	57.1	515	7.36	5	5	1/4
Detroit	12	413	263	63.7	3,121	7.56	22	18	22/143
Indianapolis	1	25	18	72.0	363	14.52	3	2	3/29
Jacksonville	1	30	20	66.7	202	6.73	2	1	2/9
Kansas City	2	83	47	56.6	527	6.35	3	4	8/50
Miami	2	88	55	62.5	615	6.99	4	1	5/20
Minnesota	11	328	192	58.5	2,144	6.54	18	12	25/149
New England	2	81	48	59.3	533	6.58	4	2	5/42
New Orleans	2	62	39	62.9	458	7.39	5	0	8/39
N.Y. Giants	2	69	41	59.4	420	6.09	2	3	5/34
N.Y. Jets	1	28	20	71.4	183	6.54	2	0	1/11
Oakland	1	28	14	50.0	190	6.79	1	0	2/9
Philadelphia	5	174	95	54.6	1,206	6.93	8	7	11/61
Pittsburgh	2	51	37	72.5	511	10.02	4	0	4/27
St. Louis	7	219	130	59.4	1,471	6.72	10	10	15/124
San Diego	2	56	35	62.5	377	6.73	3	2	4/49
San Francisco	1	61	28	45.9	395	6.48	1	2	2/17
Seattle	1	34	20	58.8	209	6.15	4	0	2/7
Tampa Bay	12	393	259	65.9	2,768	7.04	24	6	17/87
Tennessee	1	30	19	63.3	155	5.17	1	1	3/1
Washington	1	5	0	0.0	0	0.00	0	2	1/11
Totals	97	3,206	1,971	61.5	22,591	7.05	182	95	194/1,240

Oakland totals include one game vs. L.A. Raiders
St. Louis totals include four games vs. L.A. Rams
Tennessee totals include one game vs. Houston

WARREN MOON'S CAREER PASSING VS. EACH OPPONENT

Opponent	Games	Att.	Cmp.	Pct.	Yards	Avg. Gain	TD	Int.	Sacked
Arizona	4	151	84	55.6	1,150	7.62	9	4	9/76
Atlanta	5	194	111	57.2	1,429	7.37	11	6	12/55
Baltimore	1	19	12	63.2	140	7.37	1	1	3/23
Buffalo	8	206	117	56.8	1,528	7.42	7	9	12/94
Carolina	1	34	19	55.9	209	6.15	2	1	4/17
Chicago	8	281	168	59.8	2,019	7.19	9	8	19/141
Cincinnati	20	649	383	59.0	4,902	7.55	37	22	37/310
Cleveland	19	590	336	56.9	4,315	7.31	25	22	42/314
Dallas	4	149	89	59.7	1,058	7.10	4	4	19/130
Denver	5	166	98	59.0	1,255	7.56	9	3	12/79
Detroit	7	223	142	63.7	1,824	8.18	9	8	12/95
Green Bay	6	222	126	56.8	1,291	5.82	8	10	14/133
Indianapolis	8	293	184	62.8	2,426	8.28	14	8	15/97
Kansas City	10	330	205	62.1	2,506	7.59	13	9	34/237
Miami	6	148	102	68.9	1,236	8.35	8	6	11/112
Minnesota	3	95	58	61.1	592	6.23	2	2	14/106
New England	4	136	76	55.9	946	6.96	6	4	5/41
New Orleans	7	248	144	58.1	1,746	7.04	11	6	16/107
N.Y. Giants	4	142	84	59.2	1,008	7.10	4	4	8/56
N.Y. Jets	5	192	125	65.1	1,500	7.81	8	7	10/86
Oakland	5	182	96	52.7	1,413	7.76	11	7	13/115
Philadelphia	1	46	24	52.2	262	5.70	0	0	4/36
Pittsburgh	20	621	350	56.4	4,421	7.12	24	29	42/320
St. Louis	5	193	109	56.5	1,424	7.38	4	9	11/81
San Diego	8	280	149	53.2	1,910	6.82	11	9	13/87
San Francisco	6	192	109	56.8	1,359	7.08	14	8	16/98
Seattle	4	145	87	60.0	970	6.69	5	6	6/44
Tampa Bay	6	216	132	61.1	1,498	6.94	7	7	9/63
Tennessee	2	83	55	66.3	549	6.61	2	2	3/30
Washington	3	102	53	52.0	579	5.68	4	3	6/46
Totals	195	6,528	3,827	58.6	47,465	7.27	279	224	431/3,229

Arizona totals include one game vs. St. Louis, one game vs. Phoenix
Oakland totals include four games vs. L.A. Raiders
St. Louis totals include four games vs. L.A. Rams
Tennessee totals include one game vs. Houston

TROY AIKMAN'S CAREER PASSING VS. EACH OPPONENT

Opponent	Games	Att.	Cmp.	Pct.	Yards	Avg. Gain	TD	Int.	Sacked
Arizona	16	422	264	62.6	3,450	8.18	16	11	20/131
Atlanta	4	93	67	72.0	943	10.14	8	3	3/19
Buffalo	2	78	44	56.4	461	5.91	0	5	2/11
Carolina	1	26	14	53.8	180	6.92	1	0	4/42
Chicago	3	84	43	51.2	414	4.93	2	2	6/41
Cincinnati	3	108	62	57.4	833	7.71	5	5	2/23
Cleveland	2	73	45	61.6	462	6.33	3	2	4/20
Denver	2	66	43	65.2	427	6.47	5	1	2/9
Detroit	3	106	70	66.0	765	7.22	3	3	4/30
Green Bay	6	182	127	69.8	1,381	7.59	4	4	7/44
Indianapolis	2	55	38	69.1	429	7.80	2	0	2/14
Jacksonville	1	32	21	65.6	262	8.19	2	0	2/24
Kansas City	2	58	42	72.4	384	6.62	3	2	3/26
Miami	3	117	86	73.5	805	6.88	5	2	1/4
Minnesota	2	67	43	64.2	454	6.78	2	0	2/13
New England	1	28	16	57.1	169	6.04	0	2	3/25
New Orleans	3	84	53	63.1	532	6.33	1	4	4/46
N.Y. Giants	18	454	301	66.3	3,238	7.13	15	11	21/129
N.Y. Jets	2	67	46	68.7	501	7.48	2	5	6/40
Oakland	2	49	35	71.4	461	9.41	1	0	6/31
Philadelphia	16	404	214	53.0	2,317	5.74	11	15	42/263
Pittsburgh	2	62	40	64.5	540	8.71	5	1	0/0
St. Louis	3	103	58	56.3	754	7.32	7	2	4/25
San Diego	2	59	34	57.6	415	7.03	1	1	6/39
San Francisco	6	179	103	57.5	1,155	6.45	3	8	14/97
Seattle	1	23	15	65.2	173	7.52	0	2	1/3
Tampa Bay	2	53	30	56.6	332	6.26	2	2	5/38
Tennessee	3	106	65	61.3	844	7.96	4	4	8/38
Washington	16	458	273	59.6	2,935	6.41	16	13	34//244
Totals	129	3,696	2,292	62.0	26,016	7.04	129	110	218/1,469

Arizona totals include eight games vs. Phoenix
Oakland totals include one game vs. L.A. Raiders
St. Louis totals include three games vs. L.A. Rams
Tennessee totals include two games vs. Houston

STEVE YOUNG'S CAREER PASSING VS. EACH OPPONENT

Opponent	Games	Att.	Cmp.	Pct.	Yards	Avg. Gain	TD	Int.	Sacked
Arizona	5	131	69	52.7	885	6.76	5	2	10/71
Atlanta	17	440	293	66.6	4,055	9.22	32	13	24/139
Buffalo	4	124	77	62.1	1,051	8.48	4	4	12/88
Carolina	5	172	115	66.9	1,369	7.96	8	4	14/50
Chicago	6	136	75	55.1	993	7.30	8	3	9/52
Cincinnati	2	55	32	58.2	453	8.24	2	5	5/29
Cleveland	3	34	19	55.9	274	8.06	0	3	1/8
Dallas	6	108	71	65.7	887	8.21	6	2	11/53
Denver	3	66	42	63.6	626	9.48	4	3	3/19
Detroit	9	218	149	68.3	1,764	8.09	13	3	15/115
Green Bay	5	109	59	54.1	668	6.13	2	6	24/177
Indianapolis	2	65	42	64.6	480	7.38	2	3	8/43
Kansas City	4	81	54	66.7	617	7.62	2	4	13/78
Miami	1	27	19	70.4	220	8.15	2	1	0/0
Minnesota	10	268	174	64.9	2,218	8.28	14	9	30/139
New England	3	81	59	72.8	706	8.72	8	2	7/30
New Orleans	17	376	254	67.6	2,812	7.48	20	4	50/304
N.Y. Giants	5	87	53	60.9	506	5.82	3	1	5/26
N.Y. Jets	2	43	28	65.1	345	8.02	3	0	1/4
Oakland	2	67	37	55.2	525	7.84	4	3	4/20
Philadelphia	5	115	73	63.5	805	7.00	5	3	9/59
Pittsburgh	3	72	48	66.7	493	6.85	6	3	4/21
St. Louis	15	361	244	67.6	3,053	8.46	23	5	22/118
San Diego	4	101	73	72.3	911	9.02	7	1	9/50
Seattle	2	18	11	61.1	136	7.56	1	0	0/0
Tampa Bay	5	95	66	69.5	883	9.29	8	0	5/28
Tennessee	3	30	16	53.3	187	6.23	0	2	2/10
Washington	3	68	48	70.6	586	8.62	1	2	6/28
Totals	151	3,548	2,300	64.8	28,508	8.03	193	91	302/1,758

Arizona totals include two games vs. St. Louis, three games vs. Phoenix
Oakland totals include two games vs. L.A. Raiders
St. Louis totals include 12 games vs. L.A. Rams
Tennessee totals include three games vs. Houston

JERRY RICE'S CAREER RECEIVING VS. EACH OPPONENT

Opponent	Games	Rec.	Yards	Yds./Rec.	Yds./Game	TD
Arizona	5	25	465	18.6	93.0	5
Atlanta	23	140	2,150	15.4	93.5	22
Baltimore	1	6	58	9.7	58.0	1
Buffalo	3	11	104	9.5	34.7	1
Carolina	4	34	488	14.4	122.0	1
Chicago	5	24	424	17.7	84.8	7
Cincinnati	4	23	351	15.3	87.8	2
Cleveland	3	19	275	14.5	91.7	4
Dallas	7	43	671	15.6	95.9	4
Denver	4	19	306	16.1	76.5	2
Detroit	8	38	533	14.0	66.6	2
Green Bay	5	30	516	17.2	103.2	6
Indianapolis	3	18	378	21.0	126.0	5
Kansas City	3	13	178	13.7	59.3	2
Miami	3	18	304	16.9	101.3	5
Minnesota	9	50	874	17.5	97.1	10
New England	4	19	294	15.5	73.5	5
New Orleans	24	120	1,751	14.6	73.0	13
N.Y. Giants	7	34	525	15.4	75.0	5
N.Y. Jets	3	15	265	17.7	88.3	2
Oakland	4	18	362	20.1	90.5	2
Philadelphia	6	31	490	15.8	81.7	5
Pittsburgh	4	27	278	10.3	69.5	4
St. Louis	24	134	2,134	15.9	88.9	18
San Diego	3	27	465	17.2	155.0	4
Seattle	3	14	272	19.4	90.7	4
Tampa Bay	8	47	710	15.1	88.8	10
Tennessee	4	28	274	9.8	68.5	2
Washington	6	32	560	17.5	93.3	2
Totals	190	1,057	16,455	15.6	86.6	155

Arizona totals include one game vs. St. Louis, four games vs. Phoenix
Oakland totals include four games vs. L.A. Raiders
St. Louis totals include 20 games vs. L.A. Rams
Tennessee totals include four games vs. Houston

ANDRE REED'S CAREER RECEIVING VS. EACH OPPONENT

Opponent	Games	Rec.	Yards	Yds./Rec.	Yds./Game	TD
Arizona	2	0	0	—	0.0	0
Atlanta	2	9	170	18.9	85.0	1
Carolina	1	0	0	—	0.0	0
Chicago	4	16	185	11.6	46.3	0
Cincinnati	6	17	276	16.2	46.0	2
Cleveland	5	25	347	13.9	69.4	2
Dallas	2	6	46	7.7	23.0	0
Denver	7	34	478	14.1	68.3	3
Detroit	3	15	184	12.3	61.3	2
Green Bay	3	21	249	11.9	83.0	3
Indianapolis	24	108	1,472	13.6	61.3	14
Jacksonville	1	1	8	8.0	8.0	0
Kansas City	7	36	557	15.5	79.6	5
Miami	24	113	1,621	14.3	67.5	10
Minnesota	4	18	247	13.7	61.8	0
New England	22	91	1,479	16.3	67.2	7
New Orleans	2	6	54	9.0	27.0	0
N.Y. Giants	3	12	233	19.4	77.7	2
N.Y. Jets	25	98	1,289	13.2	51.6	12
Oakland	5	28	406	14.5	81.2	1
Philadelphia	4	17	183	10.8	45.8	3
Pittsburgh	8	33	389	11.8	48.6	3
St. Louis	2	10	135	13.5	67.5	1
San Diego	2	9	138	15.3	69.0	0
San Francisco	2	20	259	13.0	129.5	0
Seattle	3	6	123	20.5	41.0	1
Tampa Bay	3	8	119	14.9	39.7	0
Tennessee	10	49	756	15.4	75.6	6
Washington	4	20	361	18.1	90.3	2
Totals	190	826	11,764	14.2	61.9	80

Arizona totals include one game vs. St. Louis, one game vs. Phoenix
Oakland totals include five games vs. L.A. Raiders
St. Louis totals include two games vs. L.A. Rams
Tennessee totals include nine games vs. Houston

MICHAEL IRVIN'S CAREER RECEIVING VS. EACH OPPONENT

Opponent	Games	Rec.	Yards	Yds./Rec.	Yds./Game	TD
Arizona	18	72	1,364	18.9	75.8	8
Atlanta	8	41	660	16.1	82.5	3
Buffalo	1	8	115	14.4	115.0	0
Carolina	1	2	67	33.5	67.0	1
Chicago	2	11	151	13.7	75.5	1
Cincinnati	4	24	431	18.0	107.8	1
Cleveland	3	18	248	13.8	82.7	1
Denver	2	12	156	13.0	78.0	2
Detroit	3	16	304	19.0	101.3	1
Green Bay	7	38	633	16.7	90.4	4
Indianapolis	1	7	112	16.0	112.0	0
Jacksonville	1	3	57	19.0	57.0	0
Kansas City	2	17	205	12.1	102.5	1
Miami	2	15	217	14.5	108.5	1
Minnesota	3	18	274	15.2	91.3	2
New England	1	6	76	12.7	76.0	0
New Orleans	5	17	268	15.8	53.6	0
N.Y. Giants	16	67	1,017	15.2	63.6	4
N.Y. Jets	2	10	184	18.4	92.0	2
Oakland	2	10	163	16.3	81.5	1
Philadelphia	17	56	951	17.0	55.9	4
Pittsburgh	4	26	522	20.1	130.5	4
St. Louis	2	10	239	23.9	119.5	2
San Diego	1	7	103	14.7	103.0	0
San Francisco	7	43	508	11.8	72.6	3
Seattle	1	6	113	18.8	113.0	0
Tampa Bay	2	2	42	21.0	21.0	1
Tennessee	4	16	259	16.2	64.8	3
Washington	17	88	1,241	14.1	73.0	11
Totals	139	666	10,680	16.0	76.8	61

Arizona totals include 10 games vs. Phoenix
Oakland totals include one game vs. L.A. Raiders
St. Louis totals include two games vs. L.A. Rams
Tennessee totals include three games vs. Houston

HERMAN MOORE'S CAREER RECEIVING VS. EACH OPPONENT

Opponent	Games	Rec.	Yards	Yds./Rec.	Yds./Game	TD
Arizona	3	14	212	15.1	70.7	1
Atlanta	5	29	595	20.5	119.0	6
Buffalo	3	17	310	18.2	103.3	1
Chicago	14	72	969	13.5	69.2	5
Cincinnati	1	5	86	17.2	86.0	0
Cleveland	2	11	177	16.1	88.5	0
Dallas	3	12	156	13.0	52.0	1
Green Bay	14	60	845	14.1	60.4	9
Indianapolis	2	2	16	8.0	8.0	0
Jacksonville	1	5	59	11.8	59.0	0
Kansas City	1	7	84	12.0	84.0	0
Miami	3	11	133	12.1	44.3	1
Minnesota	13	64	1,038	16.2	79.8	7
New England	2	10	141	14.1	70.5	0
New Orleans	2	15	153	10.2	76.5	1
N.Y. Giants	3	20	243	12.2	81.0	2
N.Y. Jets	2	10	109	10.9	54.5	0
Oakland	1	10	109	10.9	109.0	2
Philadelphia	1	6	88	14.7	88.0	0
Pittsburgh	2	15	202	13.5	101.0	1
St. Louis	1	6	120	20.0	120.0	0
San Diego	1	3	39	13.0	39.0	0
San Francisco	6	29	360	12.4	60.0	4
Seattle	2	14	153	10.9	76.5	3
Tampa Bay	11	57	756	13.3	68.7	4
Tennessee	2	9	193	21.4	96.5	3
Washington	3	15	138	9.2	46.0	1
Totals	104	528	7,484	14.2	72.0	52

Arizona totals include two games vs. Phoenix
St. Louis totals include one game vs. L.A. Rams
Tennessee totals include two games vs. Houston

CRIS CARTER'S CAREER RECEIVING VS. EACH OPPONENT

Opponent	Games	Rec.	Yards	Yds./Rec.	Yds./Game	TD
Arizona	12	53	774	14.6	64.5	11
Atlanta	3	13	254	19.5	84.7	5
Buffalo	3	18	242	13.4	80.7	2
Carolina	2	9	108	12.0	54.0	3
Chicago	17	103	1,096	10.6	64.5	4
Cincinnati	3	20	223	11.2	74.3	3
Cleveland	3	12	166	13.8	55.3	0
Dallas	6	22	252	11.5	42.0	5
Denver	5	20	259	13.0	51.8	3
Detroit	16	74	798	10.8	49.9	6
Green Bay	15	74	830	11.2	55.3	7
Indianapolis	1	5	89	17.8	89.0	3
Kansas City	3	14	177	12.6	59.0	3
Miami	2	7	81	11.6	40.5	3
Minnesota	2	5	30	6.0	15.0	1
New England	4	24	276	11.5	69.0	1
New Orleans	6	31	362	11.7	60.3	3
N.Y. Giants	9	19	329	17.3	36.6	2
N.Y. Jets	3	18	219	12.2	73.0	2
Oakland	4	21	257	12.2	64.3	1
Philadelphia	2	11	209	19.0	104.5	3
Pittsburgh	2	9	140	15.6	70.0	2
St. Louis	3	8	105	13.1	35.0	0
San Diego	2	9	122	13.6	61.0	0
San Francisco	7	31	283	9.1	40.4	5
Seattle	3	12	217	18.1	72.3	1
Tampa Bay	17	76	1,014	13.3	59.6	6
Tennessee	3	17	211	12.4	70.3	3
Washington	7	21	313	14.9	44.7	1
Totals	165	756	9,436	12.5	57.2	89

Arizona totals include two games vs. St. Louis, six games vs. Phoenix
Oakland totals include three games vs. L.A. Raiders
St. Louis totals include three games vs. L.A. Rams
Tennessee totals include three games vs. Houston

MORTEN ANDERSEN'S CAREER KICKING VS. EACH OPPONENT

Opponent	Games	FG	FGA	FG%	Long FG	XP	XPA	Pts.
Arizona	11	18	18	100.0	52	28	29	82
Atlanta	25	40	51	78.4	49	56	58	176
Buffalo	4	7	11	63.6	50	7	7	28
Carolina	6	12	14	85.7	51	6	6	42
Chicago	5	3	6	50.0	60	12	12	21
Cincinnati	5	5	8	62.5	49	17	17	32
Cleveland	4	7	8	87.5	53	7	7	28
Dallas	10	18	24	75.0	54	17	17	71
Denver	4	4	8	50.0	55	14	15	26
Detroit	8	9	15	60.0	50	15	15	42
Green Bay	6	10	11	90.9	52	15	15	45
Indianapolis	2	3	4	75.0	46	7	7	16
Jacksonville	1	1	2	50.0	46	2	2	5
Kansas City	4	4	5	80.0	50	7	7	19
Miami	4	4	5	80.0	32	10	10	22
Minnesota	9	15	17	88.2	47	15	15	60
New England	5	8	9	88.9	54	11	11	35
New Orleans	6	15	19	78.9	55	12	12	57
N.Y. Giants	7	13	15	86.7	45	11	11	50
N.Y. Jets	5	9	10	90.0	53	12	12	39
Oakland	5	7	9	77.8	51	11	11	32
Philadelphia	9	17	21	81.0	56	17	17	68
Pittsburgh	5	7	9	77.8	50	9	9	30
St. Louis	29	44	51	86.3	51	73	75	205
San Diego	4	3	7	42.9	35	9	9	18
San Francisco	31	50	61	82.0	59	45	46	195
Seattle	4	6	7	85.7	47	8	8	26
Tampa Bay	14	23	31	74.2	50	32	32	101
Tennessee	5	8	12	66.7	47	11	11	35
Washington	7	8	14	57.1	45	11	11	35
Totals	244	378	482	78.4	60	507	514	1,641

Arizona totals include five games vs. St. Louis, four games vs. Phoenix
Oakland totals include four games vs. L.A. Raiders
St. Louis totals include 23 games vs. L.A. Rams
Tennessee totals include five games vs. Houston

STARTING RECORDS OF ACTIVE NFL QUARTERBACKS

Minimum: 10 starts

Player	W - L - T	Pct.
Danny Kanell	7 - 2 - 1	.750
Elvis Grbac	14 - 5	.737
Steve Bono	28 - 12	.700
Kordell Stewart	11 - 5	.688
Brett Favre	63 - 30	.677
Steve Young	81 - 44	.648
John Elway	138 - 80 - 1	.632
Dan Marino	132 - 81	.620
Brad Johnson	13 - 8	.619
Jeff Hostetler	51 - 32	.614
Mike Tomczak	41 - 27	.603
Mark Rypien	47 - 31	.603
Troy Aikman	76 - 53	.589
Randall Cunningham	64 - 45 - 1	.586
Neil O'Donnell	47 - 34	.580
Kerry Collins	22 - 16	.579
Drew Bledsoe	42 - 33	.560
Dave Krieg	98 - 77	.560
Steve McNair	12 - 10	.545
Rich Gannon	26 - 22	.542
Wade Wilson	35 - 31	.530
Rodney Peete	36 - 32	.529
Steve Walsh	20 - 18	.526
Mark Brunell	21 - 19	.525
Warren Moon	98 - 94	.510
Ty Detmer	9 - 9	.500
Jim Harbaugh	55 - 56	.495
Steve Beuerlein	26 - 27	.491
Scott Mitchell	30 -32	.484
Erik Kramer	26 - 29	.473
Bubby Brister	33 - 38	.465
Trent Dilfer	23 - 27	.460
Gus Frerotte	19 - 24 - 1	.443
Dave Brown	23 - 30	.434
Jim Everett	64 - 89	.418
Chris Chandler	35 - 49	.417
Todd Collins	7 - 10	.412
Jeff Blake	21 - 31	.404
Craig Erickson	14 - 21	.400
Rick Mirer	20 - 34	.370
Vinny Testaverde	48 - 83 - 1	.367
Heath Shuler	8 - 14	.364
Billy Joe Tolliver	13 - 23	.361
Tony Banks	10 - 19	.345
Jeff George	34 - 66	.340
John Friesz	12 - 25	.324
Tom Tupa	4 - 9	.308
Kent Graham	5 - 13	.278
David Klingler	4 - 20	.167

ALL-TIME RANKINGS OF PLAYERS IN FOUR CATEGORIES THAT DETERMINE NFL PASSER RATING

Minimum: 1,500 Attempts

COMPLETION PERCENTAGE	Pct.	Att.	Comp.
Steve Young	64.83	3,548	2,300
Joe Montana	63.24	5,391	3,409
Troy Aikman	62.01	3,696	2,292
Brett Favre	61.48	3,206	1,971
Jim Kelly	60.14	4,779	2,874
Ken Stabler	59.85	3,793	2,270
Dan Marino	59.76	7,452	4,453
Danny White	59.69	2,950	1,761
Ken Anderson	59.31	4,475	2,654
Bernie Kosar	59.26	3,365	1,994

AVERAGE YARDS PER PASS	Avg.	Att.	Yards
Otto Graham	8.63	1,565	13,499
Sid Luckman	8.42	1,744	14,686
Norm Van Brocklin	8.16	2,895	23,611
Steve Young	8.03	3,548	28,508
Ed Brown	7.85	1,987	15,600
Bart Starr	7.85	3,149	24,718
Johnny Unitas	7.76	5,186	40,239
Earl Morrall	7.74	2,689	20,809
Dan Fouts	7.68	5,604	43,040
Len Dawson	7.67	3,741	28,711

TOUCHDOWN PERCENTAGE	Pct.	Att.	TD
Sid Luckman	7.86	1,744	137
Frank Ryan	6.99	2,133	149
Len Dawson	6.39	3,741	239
Daryle Lamonica	6.31	2,601	164
Sammy Baugh	6.24	2,995	187
Charley Conerly	6.11	2,833	173
Bob Waterfield	6.00	1,617	97
Earl Morrall	5.99	2,689	161
Sonny Jurgensen	5.98	4,262	255
Norm Van Brocklin	5.98	2,895	173

INTERCEPTION PERCENTAGE	Pct.	Att.	Int.
Neil O'Donnell	2.10	2,519	53
Steve Bono	2.43	1,564	38
Steve Young	2.56	3,548	91
Joe Montana	2.58	5,391	139
Bernie Kosar	2.59	3,365	87
Jeff George	2.69	3,233	87
Ken O'Brien	2.72	3,602	98
Jim Harbaugh	2.74	2,989	82
Jeff Blake	2.75	1,748	48
Neil Lomax	2.85	3,153	90

HIGHEST NFL POSTSEASON PASSER RATINGS (MINIMUM: 150 ATTEMPTS)

	Games	Att.	Comp.	Pct.	Yds.	Avg. Gain	TD	Int.	Rating
Bart Starr	10	213	130	61.0	1,753	8.23	15	3	104.8
Troy Aikman	14	415	276	66.5	3,372	8.13	22	13	96.0
Joe Montana	23	734	460	62.7	5,772	7.86	45	21	95.6
Ken Anderson	6	166	110	66.3	1,321	7.96	9	6	93.5
Brett Favre	13	414	250	60.4	3,098	7.48	23	10	92.0
Joe Theismann	10	211	128	60.7	1,782	8.45	11	7	91.4
Steve Young	20	402	251	62.4	2,855	7.10	16	8	88.7
Warren Moon	10	403	259	64.3	2,870	7.12	17	14	84.9
Ken Stabler	13	351	203	57.8	2,641	7.52	19	13	84.2
Bernie Kosar	10	270	152	56.3	1,953	7.23	16	10	83.5

HIGHEST NFL POSTSEASON PASSER RATINGS, ACTIVE PLAYERS (MINIMUM: 150 ATTEMPTS)

	Games	Att.	Comp.	Pct.	Yds.	Avg. Gain	TD	Int.	Rating
Troy Aikman	14	415	276	66.5	3,372	8.13	22	13	96.0
Brett Favre	13	414	250	60.4	3,098	7.48	23	10	92.0
Steve Young	20	402	251	62.4	2,855	7.10	16	8	88.7
Warren Moon	10	403	259	64.3	2,870	7.12	17	14	84.9
Dan Marino	14	561	308	54.9	3,741	6.67	29	19	78.7
John Elway	19	565	310	54.9	4,273	7.56	24	20	78.7
Wade Wilson	7	185	99	53.5	1,322	7.15	7	6	75.6
Neil O'Donnell	7	273	158	57.9	1,690	6.19	9	8	74.9
Dave Krieg	12	282	144	51.1	1,895	6.72	11	9	72.3
Mark Rypien	8	234	126	53.8	1,776	7.54	8	10	72.2

NFL INDIVIDUAL LEADERS OVER RECENT SEASONS

Points

Last 2 Seasons		Last 3 Seasons		Last 4 Seasons	
252	Cary Blanchard	365	Jason Elam	484	Jason Elam
251	Mike Hollis	358	Al Del Greco	460	Chris Boniol
244	Al Del Greco	353	Norm Johnson	448	Norm Johnson
240	Gary Anderson	346	Chris Boniol	442	Gary Anderson
237	Jeff Wilkins	341	John Kasay	439	Morten Andersen

Touchdowns

Last 2 Seasons		Last 3 Seasons		Last 4 Seasons	
30	Terrell Davis	44	Emmitt Smith	66	Emmitt Smith
27	Karim Abdul-Jabbar	40	Cris Carter	47	Cris Carter
26	Terry Allen	38	Terrell Davis	45	Terry Allen
25	Barry Sanders	37	Terry Allen	45	Carl Pickens
23	Cris Carter	37	Curtis Martin	45	Barry Sanders
		37	Barry Sanders		

Field Goals

Last 2 Seasons		Last 3 Seasons		Last 4 Seasons	
68	Cary Blanchard	87	Cary Blanchard	108	Jason Elam
61	Mike Hollis	86	Al Del Greco	105	John Kasay
59	Al Del Greco	85	John Kasay	104	Morten Andersen
59	John Kasay	81	Mike Hollis	103	Chris Boniol
55	Jeff Wilkins	81	Chris Boniol	103	Steve Christie

Rushes

Last 2 Seasons		Last 3 Seasons		Last 4 Seasons	
714	Terrell Davis	975	Ricky Watters	1,333	Emmitt Smith
695	Jerome Bettis	965	Emmitt Smith	1,287	Barry Sanders
692	Eddie George	958	Curtis Martin	1,214	Ricky Watters
642	Barry Sanders	956	Barry Sanders	1,197	Jerome Bettis
638	Ricky Watters	951	Terrell Davis	1,150	Terry Allen

Rushing Yards

Last 2 Seasons		Last 3 Seasons		Last 4 Seasons	
3,606	Barry Sanders	5,106	Barry Sanders	6,989	Barry Sanders
3,288	Terrell Davis	4,405	Terrell Davis	5,535	Emmitt Smith
3,096	Jerome Bettis	4,051	Emmitt Smith	4,758	Jerome Bettis
2,767	Eddie George	3,799	Curtis Martin	4,671	Ricky Watters
2,521	Ricky Watters	3,794	Ricky Watters	4,593	Chris Warren

Rushing TDs

Last 2 Seasons		Last 3 Seasons		Last 4 Seasons	
28	Terrell Davis	41	Emmitt Smith	62	Emmitt Smith
26	Karim Abdul-Jabbar	35	Terry Allen	43	Terry Allen
25	Terry Allen	35	Terrell Davis	40	Barry Sanders
22	Barry Sanders	33	Barry Sanders	37	Ricky Watters
20	Marcus Allen	32	Curtis Martin	36	Marshall Faulk
20	Ricky Watters				

Passes

Last 2 Seasons		Last 3 Seasons		Last 4 Seasons	
1,145	Drew Bledsoe	1,781	Drew Bledsoe	2,472	Drew Bledsoe
1,056	Brett Favre	1,626	Brett Favre	2,208	Brett Favre
1,019	Vinny Testaverde	1,529	Scott Mitchell	2,018	Dan Marino
992	Mark Brunell	1,510	John Elway	2,004	John Elway
983	Troy Aikman	1,433	Jeff Blake	1,982	Warren Moon

Completions

Last 2 Seasons		Last 3 Seasons		Last 4 Seasons	
687	Drew Bledsoe	1,010	Drew Bledsoe	1,410	Drew Bledsoe
629	Brett Favre	988	Brett Favre	1,351	Brett Favre
617	Mark Brunell	892	Scott Mitchell	1,234	Dan Marino
596	Vinny Testaverde	883	John Elway	1,195	Warren Moon
588	Troy Aikman	868	Troy Aikman	1,190	John Elway

Passing Yards

Last 2 Seasons		Last 3 Seasons		Last 4 Seasons	
7,792	Drew Bledsoe	12,179	Brett Favre	16,061	Brett Favre
7,766	Brett Favre	11,299	Drew Bledsoe	15,854	Drew Bledsoe
7,648	Mark Brunell	10,933	John Elway	14,696	Dan Marino
7,148	Vinny Testaverde	10,739	Scott Mitchell	14,423	John Elway
6,963	John Elway	10,243	Dan Marino	13,780	Warren Moon

Touchdown Passes

Last 2 Seasons		Last 3 Seasons		Last 4 Seasons	
74	Brett Favre	112	Brett Favre	145	Brett Favre
55	Drew Bledsoe	79	John Elway	95	John Elway
53	John Elway	68	Drew Bledsoe	93	Drew Bledsoe
51	Vinny Testaverde	68	Scott Mitchell	88	Steve Young
37	Mark Brunell	68	Vinny Testaverde	87	Dan Marino
37	Brad Johnson				

Receptions

Last 2 Seasons		Last 3 Seasons		Last 4 Seasons	
210	Herman Moore	333	Herman Moore	429	Cris Carter
194	Tim Brown	307	Cris Carter	405	Herman Moore
185	Cris Carter	283	Tim Brown	372	Tim Brown
174	Irving Fryar	259	Isaac Bruce	349	Jerry Rice
170	Keenan McCardell	254	Larry Centers	331	Larry Centers

Reception Yards

Last 2 Seasons		Last 3 Seasons		Last 4 Seasons	
2,600	Rob Moore	4,275	Herman Moore	5,448	Herman Moore
2,589	Herman Moore	3,934	Isaac Bruce	5,163	Tim Brown
2,568	Jimmy Smith	3,854	Tim Brown	4,986	Michael Irvin
2,512	Tim Brown	3,745	Michael Irvin	4,859	Cris Carter
2,511	Irving Fryar	3,625	Jake Reed	4,800	Jake Reed

Receiving Touchdowns

Last 2 Seasons		Last 3 Seasons		Last 4 Seasons	
23	Cris Carter	40	Cris Carter	47	Cris Carter
21	Antonio Freeman	34	Carl Pickens	45	Carl Pickens
20	Tony Martin	31	Herman Moore	42	Herman Moore
19	Joey Galloway	27	Michael Jackson	37	Jerry Rice
18	Derrick Alexander	26	Joey Galloway	33	Tim Brown
18	Michael Jackson	26	Tony Martin	33	Tony Martin
				33	Terance Mathis

Interceptions

Last 2 Seasons		Last 3 Seasons		Last 4 Seasons	
17	Keith Lyle	20	Keith Lyle	27	Aeneas Williams
14	Ryan McNeil	18	Willie Clay	22	Merton Hanks
13	Tyrone Braxton	18	Aeneas Williams	22	Keith Lyle
13	Darryl Williams	16	Darryll Lewis	21	Willie Clay
12	Aeneas Williams	16	Ryan McNeil	21	Darryll Lewis
		16	Orlando Thomas		

Sacks

Last 2 Seasons		Last 3 Seasons		Last 4 Seasons	
27.5	Bruce Smith	38.0	Bruce Smith	51.0	John Randle
27.0	John Randle	37.5	John Randle	48.0	Kevin Greene
25.0	Kevin Greene	34.5	Wayne Martin	48.0	Bruce Smith
25.0	Mike Sinclair	34.0	Kevin Greene	44.5	Wayne Martin
23.0	Chris Doleman	33.0	Bryce Paup	42.0	Leslie O'Neal

NFL TEAM LEADERS OVER RECENT SEASONS

Highest Won-Lost Percentage

Last 2 Seasons		Last 3 Seasons		Last 4 Seasons	
.813	Green Bay	.771	Green Bay	.766	San Francisco
.781	Denver	.750	San Francisco	.719	Green Bay
.781	San Francisco	.729	Kansas City	.688	Kansas City
.688	Kansas City	.688	Denver	.688	Pittsburgh
.656	New England	.667	Pittsburgh	.625	Dallas
.656	Pittsburgh			.625	Denver

Most Points

Last 2 Seasons		Last 3 Seasons		Last 4 Seasons	
878	Green Bay	1,282	Green Bay	1,735	San Francisco
863	Denver	1,251	Denver	1,664	Green Bay
787	New England	1,230	San Francisco	1,598	Denver
773	San Francisco	1,123	Pittsburgh	1,474	Detroit
727	Cincinnati	1,117	Detroit	1,465	Miami

Most Total Yards

Last 2 Seasons		Last 3 Seasons		Last 4 Seasons	
11,663	Denver	17,703	Denver	23,190	Denver
11,217	Philadelphia	16,924	Detroit	22,765	San Francisco
11,184	Jacksonville	16,899	Green Bay	22,344	Minnesota
11,149	Green Bay	16,705	San Francisco	22,215	Green Bay
11,014	Baltimore	16,496	Minnesota	22,094	Miami

Most Rushing Yards

Last 2 Seasons		Last 3 Seasons		Last 4 Seasons	
4,778	Pittsburgh	6,735	Denver	8,810	Pittsburgh
4,740	Denver	6,630	Pittsburgh	8,205	Denver
4,364	Tennessee	6,402	Kansas City	8,134	Kansas City
4,274	Detroit	6,028	Tennessee	8,107	Detroit
4,180	Kansas City	6,027	Detroit	8,059	Seattle

Most Passing Yards

Last 2 Seasons		Last 3 Seasons		Last 4 Seasons	
7,814	Jacksonville	11,724	Green Bay	15,965	Miami
7,680	Baltimore	11,545	Miami	15,573	San Francisco
7,451	New England	11,410	San Francisco	15,500	Minnesota
7,402	Green Bay	11,176	Minnesota	15,497	Green Bay
7,392	Philadelphia	11,042	New England	15,486	New England

*Fewest Turnovers

Last 2 Seasons		Last 3 Seasons		Last 4 Seasons	
44	Kansas City	65	Kansas City	91	Kansas City
44	Miami	72	San Francisco	96	San Francisco
44	San Francisco	74	Indianapolis	99	Dallas
47	Cincinnati	75	Dallas	99	Green Bay
47	Washington	76	Miami	103	Detroit

*Fewest Points Allowed

Last 2 Seasons		Last 3 Seasons		Last 4 Seasons	
492	Green Bay	773	Kansas City	1,071	Kansas City
522	San Francisco	780	San Francisco	1,076	San Francisco
532	Carolina	806	Green Bay	1,093	Green Bay
532	Kansas City	855	Dallas	1,103	Dallas
556	Tampa Bay	857	Carolina	1,125	Pittsburgh

Last 2 Seasons		Last 3 Seasons		Last 4 Seasons	
***Fewest Total Yards Allowed**					
8,674	San Francisco	13,072	San Francisco	17,911	San Francisco
8,898	Dallas	13,628	Pittsburgh	17,954	Pittsburgh
8,983	Green Bay	13,942	Dallas	18,255	Dallas
9,067	Pittsburgh	14,132	Philadelphia	18,842	Philadelphia
9,141	Denver	14,138	Green Bay	18,902	Green Bay
***Fewest Rushing Yards Allowed**					
2,733	Pittsburgh	3,924	San Francisco	5,262	San Francisco
2,863	San Francisco	4,054	Pittsburgh	5,506	Pittsburgh
2,958	Tennessee	4,484	Tennessee	6,170	Green Bay
3,118	New England	4,614	Kansas City	6,348	Kansas City
3,134	Denver	4,807	Green Bay	6,368	Minnesota
***Fewest Passing Yards Allowed**					
5,328	Dallas	8,600	Dallas	11,352	Dallas
5,691	Green Bay	8,718	Philadelphia	11,812	Philadelphia
5,715	New Orleans	9,148	San Francisco	12,448	Pittsburgh
5,811	San Francisco	9,305	Denver	12,649	San Francisco
5,902	Philadelphia	9,331	Green Bay	12,732	Green Bay
Most Opponents' Turnovers					
79	N.Y. Giants	114	St. Louis	144	San Francisco
78	St. Louis	110	N.Y. Giants	142	N.Y. Giants
75	San Francisco	109	San Francisco	139	Pittsburgh
74	Pittsburgh	108	Pittsburgh	136	Minnesota
71	Green Bay	102	Minnesota	135	New England

**Carolina and Jacksonville excluded from last four seasons lists; Baltimore excluded from last three and four seasons lists; Cleveland excluded from all lists.*

RECORDS OF TEAMS ON OPENING DAY, 1933-1997

AFC	W	L	T	Pct.	Longest W Strk.	Longest L Strk.	Current Streak
Jacksonville	2	1	0	.667	2	1	W-2
Denver	24	13	1	.649	3	4	W-3
Kansas City	22	16	0	.579	7	4	L-1
Cleveland	26	20	0	.565	5	5	L-1
Oakland	21	17	0	.553	5	5	L-2
San Diego	21	17	0	.553	6	6	L-1
Miami	17	14	1	.548	6	5	W-6
Indianapolis	23	22	1	.511	8	8	L-1
Pittsburgh	30	29	4	.508	4	3	L-2
Baltimore	1	1	0	.500	1	1	L-1
Cincinnati	15	15	0	.500	4	4	W-1
Tennessee	19	19	0	.500	4	3	W-1
New England	18	20	0	.474	6	3	W-1
Buffalo	16	22	0	.421	6	5	L-1
N.Y. Jets	16	22	0	.421	3	5	W-1
Seattle	5	17	0	.227	3	8	L-3

NFC	W	L	T	Pct.	Longest W Strk.	Longest L Strk.	Current Streak
Dallas	28	9	1	.757	17	3	W-1
Chicago	38	26	1	.594	9	6	L-1
N.Y. Giants	36	25	4	.590	4	3	W-1
Minnesota	20	16	1	.556	4	3	W-2
St. Louis	33	27	0	.550	5	6	W-4
Green Bay	33	29	3	.532	5	6	W-2
Detroit	33	30	2	.524	7	4	W-1
San Francisco	24	23	1	.511	5	3	L-1
Washington	31	30	4	.508	6	5	W-1
Atlanta	16	16	0	.500	5	3	L-2
Arizona	26	37	1	.413	6	6	L-6
Philadelphia	26	37	1	.413	5	9	L-1
Tampa Bay	9	13	0	.409	3	5	W-1
Carolina	1	2	0	.333	1	1	L-1
New Orleans	7	24	0	.226	1	6	L-4

Kansas City totals include Dallas Texans, 1960-62.
Oakland totals include L.A. Raiders, 1982-94.
San Diego totals include L.A. Chargers, 1960.
Indianapolis totals include Baltimore, 1953-83.
Tennessee totals include Houston, 1960-96.
New England totals include Boston, 1960-70.
St. Louis totals include Cleveland, 1937-42 and 1944-45, and L.A. Rams, 1946-94.
Detroit totals include Portsmouth, 1933.
Arizona totals include Chi. Cardinals, 1933-59, St. Louis, 1960-87, and Phoenix, 1988-93.
NOTE: All tied games occurred prior to 1972, when calculation of ties in percentages as half-win, half-loss was begun.

OLDEST INDIVIDUAL SINGLE-SEASON OR SINGLE-GAME RECORDS IN NFL RECORD & FACT BOOK

Regular-Season Records That Have Not Been Surpassed or Tied

Most Points, Game—40, Ernie Nevers, Chi. Cardinals vs. Chi. Bears, Nov. 28, 1929 (6-td, 4-pat)

Most Touchdowns Rushing, Game—6, Ernie Nevers, Chi. Cardinals vs. Chi. Bears, Nov. 28, 1929

Highest Punting Average, Season (Qualifiers)—51.40, Sammy Baugh, Washington, 1940 (35-1,799)

Highest Punting Average, Game (minimum: 4 punts)—61.75, Bob Cifers, Detroit vs. Chi. Bears, Nov. 24, 1946 (4-247)

Highest Average Gain, Pass Receptions, Season (minimum: 24 receptions)—32.58, Don Currivan, Boston, 1947 (24-782)

Highest Average Gain, Passing, Game (minimum: 20 passes)—18.58, Sammy Baugh, Washington vs. Boston, Oct. 31, 1948 (24-446)

Most Touchdowns, Fumble Recoveries, Game—2, Fred (Dippy) Evans, Chi. Bears vs. Washington, Nov. 28, 1948

Most Yards Gained, Intercepted Passes, Rookie, Season—301, Don Doll, Detroit, 1949

Most Passes Had Intercepted, Game—8, Jim Hardy, Chi. Cardinals vs. Philadelphia, Sept. 24, 1950

Highest Average Gain, Rushing, Game (minimum: 10 attempts)—17.09, Marion Motley, Cleveland vs. Pittsburgh, Oct. 29, 1950 (11-188)

Highest Kickoff Return Average, Game (minimum: 3 returns)—73.50, Wally Triplett, Detroit vs. Los Angeles, Oct. 29, 1950 (4-294)

Most Pass Receptions, Game—18, Tom Fears, Los Angeles vs. Green Bay, Dec. 3, 1950

Highest Punt Return Average, Season (Qualifiers)—23.00, Herb Rich, Baltimore, 1950 (12-276)

Highest Punt Return Average, Rookie, Season (Qualifiers)—23.00, Herb Rich, Baltimore, 1950 (12-276)

Most Yards Passing, Game—554, Norm Van Brocklin, Los Angeles vs. N.Y. Yanks, Sept. 28, 1951

Most Touchdowns, Punt Returns, Rookie, Season—4, Jack Christiansen, Detroit, 1951

Most Interceptions By, Season—14, Dick (Night Train) Lane, Los Angeles, 1952

Most Interceptions By, Rookie, Season—14, Dick (Night Train) Lane, Los Angeles, 1952

Highest Average Gain, Passing, Season (Qualifiers)—11.17, Tommy O'Connell, Cleveland, 1957 (110-1,229)

Most Points, Season—176, Paul Hornung, Green Bay, 1960 (15-td, 41-pat,15-fg)

Most Yards Gained, Pass Receptions, Rookie, Season—1,473, Bill Groman, Houston, 1960

LARGEST TRADES IN NFL HISTORY

(Based on number of players or draft choices involved)

18—October 13, 1989—RB Herschel Walker from the Dallas Cowboys to Minnesota. Dallas also traded its third-round choice in 1990, its tenth-round choice in 1990, and its third-round choice in 1991 to Minnesota. Minnesota traded LB Jesse Solomon, LB David Howard, CB Issiac Holt, and DE Alex Stewart along with its first-round choice in 1990, its second-round choice in 1990, its sixth-round choice in 1990, its first-round choice in 1991, its second-round choice in 1991, its first-round choice in 1992, its second-round choice in 1992, and its third-round choice in 1992 to Dallas. Minnesota traded RB Darrin Nelson to Dallas, which traded Nelson to San Diego for the Chargers' fifth-round choice in 1990, which Dallas then sent to Minnesota.

15—March 26, 1953—T Mike McCormack, DT Don Colo, LB Tom Catlin, DB John Petitbon, and G Herschell Forester from Baltimore to Cleveland for DB Don Shula, DB Bert Rechichar, DB Carl Taseff, LB Ed Sharkey, E Gern Nagler, QB Harry Agganis, T Dick Batten, T Stu Sheets, G Art Spinney, and G Elmer Willhoite.

15—January 28, 1971—LB Marlin McKeever, first- and third-round choices in 1971, and third-, fourth-, fifth-, sixth-, and seventh-round choices in 1972 from Washington to the Los Angeles Rams for LB Maxie Baughan, LB Jack Pardee, LB Myron Pottios, RB Jeff Jordan, G John Wilbur, DT Diron Talbert, and a fifth-round choice in 1971.

12—June 13, 1952—Selection rights to Les Richter from the Dallas Texans to the Los Angeles Rams for RB Dick Hoerner, DB Tom Keane, DB George Sims, C Joe Reid, HB Billy Baggett, T Jack Halliday, FB Dick McKissack, LB Vic Vasicek, E Richard Wilkins, C Aubrey Phillips, and RB Dave Anderson.

10—March 23, 1959—HB Ollie Matson from the Chicago Cardinals to the Los Angeles Rams for T Frank Fuller, DE Glenn Holtzman, T Ken Panfil, DT Art Hauser, E John Tracey, FB Larry Hickman, HB Don Brown, the Rams second-round choice in 1960, and a player to be delivered during the 1959 training camp.

10—October 31, 1987—RB Eric Dickerson from the Los Angeles Rams to Indianapolis. The rights to LB Cornelius Bennett from Indianapolis to Buffalo. Indianapolis running back Owen Gill and the Colts' first- and second-round choices in 1988 and second-round choice in 1989, plus Bills running back Greg Bell and Buffalo's first-round choice in 1988 and first- and second-round choices in 1989 to the Rams.

INSIDE THE NUMBERS

RETIRED UNIFORM NUMBERS IN NFL

AFC

Buffalo:	None	
Cincinnati:	Bob Johnson	54
Cleveland:	Otto Graham	14
	Jim Brown	32
	Ernie Davis	45
	Don Fleming	46
	Lou Groza	76
Denver:	Frank Tripucka	18
	Floyd Little	44
Indianapolis:	Johnny Unitas	19
	Buddy Young	22
	Lenny Moore	24
	Art Donovan	70
	Jim Parker	77
	Raymond Berry	82
	Gino Marchetti	89
Jacksonville	None	
Kansas City:	Jan Stenerud	3
	Len Dawson	16
	Abner Haynes	28
	Stone Johnson	33
	Mack Lee Hill	36
	Willie Lanier	63
	Bobby Bell	78
	Buck Buchanan	86
Miami:	Bob Griese	12
New England:	Gino Cappelletti	20
	Mike Haynes	40
	Steve Nelson	57
	John Hannah	73
	Jim Hunt	79
	Bob Dee	89
New York Jets:	Joe Namath	12
	Don Maynard	13
Oakland:	None	
Pittsburgh:	None	
San Diego:	Dan Fouts	14
Seattle:	"Fans/the twelfth man"	12
	Steve Largent	80
Tennessee:	Earl Campbell	34
	Jim Norton	43
	Mike Munchak	63
	Elvin Bethea	65

NFC

Arizona:	Larry Wilson	8
	Stan Mauldin	77
	J.V. Cain	88
	Marshall Goldberg	99
Atlanta:	Steve Bartowski	10
	William Andrews	31
	Jeff Van Note	57
	Tommy Nobis	60
Carolina	None	
Chicago:	Bronko Nagurski	3
	George McAfee	5
	George Halas	7
	Willie Galimore	28
	Walter Payton	34
	Gale Sayers	40
	Brian Piccolo	41
	Sid Luckman	42
	Dick Butkus	51
	Bill Hewitt	56
	Bill George	61
	Bulldog Turner	66
	Red Grange	77
Dallas:	None	
Detroit:	Dutch Clark	7
	Bobby Layne	22
	Doak Walker	37
	Joe Schmidt	56
	Chuck Hughes	85
	Charlie Sanders	88
Green Bay:	Tony Canadeo	3
	Don Hutson	14
	Bart Starr	15
	Ray Nitschke	66
Minnesota:	Fran Tarkenton	10
	Alan Page	88
New Orleans:	Jim Taylor	31
	Doug Atkins	81
New York Giants:	Ray Flaherty	1
	Tuffy Leemans	4
	Mel Hein	7
	Phil Simms	11
	Y.A. Tittle	14
	Al Blozis	32
	Joe Morrison	40
	Charlie Conerly	42
	Ken Strong	50
	Lawrence Taylor	56
Philadelphia:	Steve Van Buren	15
	Tom Brookshier	40
	Pete Retzlaff	44
	Chuck Bednarik	60
	Al Wistert	70
	Jerome Brown	99
St. Louis:	Bob Waterfield	7
	Merlin Olsen	74
	Jackie Slater	78
San Francisco:	John Brodie	12
	Joe Montana	16
	Joe Perry	34
	Jimmy Johnson	37
	Hugh McElhenny	39
	Charlie Krueger	70
	Leo Nomellini	73
	Dwight Clark	87
Tampa Bay:	Lee Roy Selmon	63
Washington:	Sammy Baugh	33

1997 NFL SCORE BY QUARTERS

AFC Offense	1	2	3	4	OT	PTS
Denver	107	140	137	85	3	472
Jacksonville	117	111	66	100	0	394
Kansas City	63	149	59	101	3	375
Pittsburgh	67	98	86	106	15	372
New England	82	126	61	97	3	369
Seattle	44	126	92	103	0	365
Cincinnati	77	110	80	88	0	355
N.Y. Jets	91	116	74	64	3	348
Miami	67	103	49	117	3	339
Tennessee	74	107	55	94	3	333
Baltimore	67	98	58	103	0	326
Oakland	69	100	113	42	0	324
Indianapolis	62	103	50	98	0	313
San Diego	61	71	71	63	0	266
Buffalo	19	66	45	125	0	255

NFC Offense	1	2	3	4	OT	PTS
Green Bay	82	151	87	102	0	422
Detroit	35	131	87	126	0	379
San Francisco	90	142	88	55	0	375
Minnesota	65	96	61	132	0	354
Washington	62	101	80	78	6	327
Atlanta	58	97	99	66	0	320
Philadelphia	75	71	59	109	3	317
N.Y. Giants	68	85	67	81	6	307
Dallas	41	95	86	82	0	304
St. Louis	37	121	68	73	0	299
Tampa Bay	73	78	65	83	0	299
Arizona	44	67	85	84	3	283
Carolina	54	70	37	104	0	265
Chicago	61	72	36	91	3	263
New Orleans	22	76	38	98	3	237

AFC Defense	1	2	3	4	OT	PTS
Kansas City	61	80	47	44	0	232
Denver	34	100	68	85	0	287
N.Y. Jets	40	97	47	100	3	287
New England	60	39	89	98	3	289
Pittsburgh	69	106	65	67	0	307
Tennessee	54	93	77	83	3	310
Jacksonville	65	91	58	98	6	318
Miami	43	135	51	95	3	327
Baltimore	89	92	81	80	3	345
Seattle	101	111	93	51	6	362
Buffalo	78	118	68	100	3	367
Indianapolis	74	141	65	121	0	401
Cincinnati	65	108	90	142	0	405
Oakland	87	123	102	104	3	419
San Diego	64	170	98	93	0	425

NFC Defense	1	2	3	4	OT	PTS
Tampa Bay	36	85	76	66	0	263
N.Y. Giants	33	93	54	85	0	265
San Francisco	51	78	66	70	0	265
Green Bay	48	78	56	100	0	282
Washington	64	74	53	98	0	289
Detroit	100	103	33	64	6	306
Carolina	62	102	61	89	0	314
Dallas	64	71	86	90	3	314
New Orleans	70	107	51	99	0	327
Minnesota	54	146	78	81	0	359
St. Louis	57	104	96	102	0	359
Atlanta	70	118	72	101	0	361
Philadelphia	100	90	68	114	0	372
Arizona	63	101	83	117	15	379
Chicago	78	123	107	113	0	421
NFL Totals	1,934	3,077	2,139	2,750	57	9,957

TEAM LEADERS

Offense	Most Scored	Fewest Scored
1st Quarter	117 Jacksonville	19 Buffalo
2nd Quarter	151 Green Bay	66 Buffalo
3rd Quarter	137 Denver	36 Chicago
4th Quarter	132 Minnesota	42 Oakland

Defense	Most Allowed	Fewest Allowed
1st Quarter	101 Seattle	33 N.Y. Giants
2nd Quarter	170 San Diego	39 New England
3rd Quarter	107 Chicago	33 Detroit
4th Quarter	142 Cincinnati	44 Kansas City

INSIDE THE NUMBERS

GREATEST COMEBACKS IN NFL HISTORY
(Most Points Overcome To Win Game)

REGULAR SEASON GAMES

FROM 28 POINTS BEHIND TO WIN:
December 7, 1980, at San Francisco

New Orleans	14	21	0	0	0	— 35
San Francisco	0	7	14	14	3	— 38

NO — Harris 33 pass from Manning (Ricardo kick)
NO — Childs 21 pass from Manning (Ricardo kick)
NO — Holmes 1 run (Ricardo kick)
SF — Solomon 57 punt return (Wersching kick)
NO — Holmes 1 run (Ricardo kick)
NO — Harris 41 pass from Manning (Ricardo kick)
SF — Montana 1 run (Wersching kick)
SF — Clark 71 pass from Montana (Wersching kick)
SF — Solomon 14 pass from Montana (Wersching kick)
SF — Elliott 7 run (Wersching kick)
SF — FG Wersching 36

	N.O.	S.F.
First Downs	27	24
Total Yards	519	430
Yards Rushing	143	176
Yards Passing	376	254
Turnovers	3	0

FROM 26 POINTS BEHIND TO WIN:
September 21, 1997, at Buffalo

Indianapolis	14	12	0	9	— 35
Buffalo	0	10	6	21	— 37

Ind — Bailey 10 pass from Harbaugh (Blanchard kick)
Ind — Faulk 10 run (Blanchard kick)
Ind — FG Blanchard 39
Ind — FG Blanchard 36
Ind — FG Blanchard 49
Ind — FG Blanchard 22
Buff — Johnson 16 pass from Collins (Christie kick)
Buff — FG Christie 27
Buff — A. Smith 15 run (2-pt attempt failed)
Ind — FG Blanchard 25
Buff — Early 4 pass from Collins (Christie kick)
Buff — A. Smith 1 run (Christie kick)
Buff — A. Smith 54 run (Christie kick)
Ind — Harrison 2 pass from Justin (2-pt attempt failed)

	Ind.	Buff.
First Downs	17	25
Total Yards	322	393
Yards Rushing	124	163
Yards Passing	198	230
Turnovers	1	5

FROM 25 POINTS BEHIND TO WIN:
November 8, 1987, at St. Louis

Tampa Bay	7	7	14	0	— 28
St. Louis	0	3	0	28	— 31

TB — Carrier 5 pass from DeBerg (Igwebuike kick)
TB — Carter 3 pass from DeBerg (Igwebuike kick)
StL — FG Gallery 31
TB — Smith 34 pass from DeBerg (Igwebuike kick)
TB — Smith 3 run (Igwebuike kick)
StL — Awalt 4 pass from Lomax (Gallery kick)
StL — Noga 23 fumble recovery (Gallery kick)
StL — J. Smith 11 pass from Lomax (Gallery kick)
StL — J. Smith 17 pass from Lomax (Gallery kick)

	T.B.	St.L.
First Downs	26	26
Total Yards	377	415
Yards Rushing	83	137
Yards Passing	294	278
Turnovers	1	2

FROM 24 POINTS BEHIND TO WIN:
October 27, 1946, at Washington

Philadelphia	0	0	14	14	— 28
Washington	10	14	0	0	— 24

Wash — Rosato 2 run (Poillon kick)
Wash — FG Poillon 28
Wash — Rosato 4 run (Poillon kick)
Wash — Lapka recovered fumble in end zone (Poillon kick)
Phil — Steele 1 run (Lio kick)
Phil — Pritchard 45 pass from Thompson (Lio kick)
Phil — Steinke 7 pass from Thompson (Lio kick)
Phil — Ferrante 30 pass from Thompson (Lio kick)

	Phil.	Wash.
First Downs	14	8
Total Yards	262	127
Yards Rushing	34	66
Yards Passing	228	61
Turnovers	6	3

FROM 24 POINTS BEHIND TO WIN:
October 20, 1957, at Detroit

Baltimore	7	14	6	0	— 27
Detroit	0	3	7	21	— 31

Balt — Mutscheller 15 pass from Unitas (Rechichar kick)
Det — FG Martin 47
Balt — Moore 72 pass from Unitas (Rechichar kick)
Balt — Mutscheller 52 pass from Unitas (Rechichar kick)
Balt — Moore 4 pass from Unitas (kick failed)
Det — Junker 14 pass from Rote (Layne kick)
Det — Cassady 26 pass from Layne (Layne kick)
Det — Johnson 1 run (Layne kick)
Det — Cassady 29 pass from Layne (Layne kick)

	Balt.	Det.
First Downs	15	20
Total Yards	322	369
Yards Rushing	117	178
Yards Passing	205	191
Turnovers	6	4

FROM 24 POINTS BEHIND TO WIN:
October 25, 1959, at Minneapolis

Philadelphia	0	0	21	7	— 28
Chicago Cardinals	7	10	7	0	— 24

Cardinals — Crow 10 pass from Roach (Conrad kick)
Cardinals — J. Hill 77 blocked field goal return (Conrad kick)
Cardinals — FG Conrad 15
Cardinals — Lane 37 interception return (Conrad kick)
Phil — Barnes 1 run (Walston kick)
Phil — McDonald 29 pass from Van Brocklin (Walston kick)
Phil — Barnes 2 run (Walston kick)
Phil — McDonald 22 pass from Van Brocklin (Walston kick)

	Phil.	Cardinals
First Downs	22	14
Total Yards	399	313
Yards Rushing	168	163
Yards Passing	231	150
Turnovers	2	6

FROM 24 POINTS BEHIND TO WIN:
October 23, 1960, at Denver

Boston	10	7	7	0	— 24
Denver	0	0	14	17	— 31

Bos — FG Cappelletti 12
Bos — Colclough 10 pass from Songin (Cappelletti kick)
Bos — Wells 6 pass from Songin (Cappelletti kick)
Bos — Miller 47 pass from Songin (Cappelletti kick)
Den — Carmichael 21 pass from Tripucka (Mingo kick)
Den — Jessup 19 pass from Tripucka (Mingo kick)
Den — Carmichael 35 lateral from Taylor, pass from Tripucka (Mingo kick)
Den — Taylor 8 pass from Tripucka (Mingo kick)
Den — FG Mingo 9

	Bos.	Den.
First Downs	19	16
Total Yards	434	326
Yards Rushing	211	65
Yards Passing	223	261
Turnovers	7	4

FROM 24 POINTS BEHIND TO WIN:
December 15, 1974, at Miami

New England	21	3	0	3	— 27
Miami	0	17	7	10	— 34

NE — Hannah recovered fumble in end zone (J. Smith kick)
NE — Sanders 23 interception return (J. Smith kick)
NE — Herron 4 pass from Plunkett (J. Smith kick)
NE — FG J. Smith 46
Mia — Nottingham 1 run (Yepremian kick)
Mia — Baker 37 pass from Morrall (Yepremian kick)
Mia — FG Yepremian 28
Mia — Baker 46 pass from Morrall (Yepremian kick)
NE — FG J. Smith 34
Mia — Nottingham 2 run (Yepremian kick)
Mia — FG Yepremian 40

	N.E.	Mia.
First Downs	18	18
Total Yards	333	333
Yards Rushing	114	61
Yards Passing	219	272
Turnovers	3	4

FROM 24 POINTS BEHIND TO WIN:
December 4, 1977, at Minnesota

San Francisco	0	10	14	3	— 27
Minnesota	0	0	7	21	— 28

SF — Delvin Williams 2 run (Wersching kick)
SF — FG Wersching 31
SF — Dave Williams 80 kickoff return (Wersching kick)
SF — Delvin Williams 5 run (Wersching kick)
Minn— McClanahan 15 pass from Lee (Cox kick)
Minn— Rashad 8 pass from Kramer (Cox kick)
Minn— Tucker 9 pass from Kramer (Cox kick)
SF — FG Wersching 31
Minn— S. White 69 pass from Kramer (Cox kick)

	S.F.	Minn.
First Downs	19	18
Total Yards	243	309
Yards Rushing	196	52
Yards Passing	47	257
Turnovers	2	5

FROM 24 POINTS BEHIND TO WIN:
September 23, 1979, at Denver

Seattle	10	10	14	0	— 34
Denver	0	10	21	6	— 37

Sea — FG Herrera 28
Sea — Doornink 5 run (Herrera kick)
Den — FG Turner 27
Sea — Doornink 5 run (Herrera kick)
Den — Armstrong 2 run (Turner kick)
Sea — FG Herrera 22
Sea — McCullum 13 pass from Zorn (Herrera kick)
Sea — Smith 1 run (Herrera kick)
Den — Studdard 2 pass from Morton (Turner kick)
Den — Moses 11 pass from Morton (Turner kick)
Den — Upchurch 35 pass from Morton (Turner kick)
Den — Lytle 1 run (kick failed)

	Sea.	Den.
First Downs	22	23
Total Yards	350	344
Yards Rushing	153	90
Yards Passing	197	254
Turnovers	4	3

FROM 24 POINTS BEHIND TO WIN:
September 23, 1979, at Cincinnati

Houston	0	10	17	0	3	—30
Cincinnati	14	10	0	3	0	—27

Cin — Johnson 1 run (Bahr kick)
Cin — Alexander 2 run (Bahr kick)
Cin — Johnson 1 run (Bahr kick)
Cin — FG Bahr 52
Hou — Burrough 35 pass from Pastorini (Fritsch kick)
Hou — FG Fritsch 33
Hou — Campbell 8 run (Fritsch kick)
Hou — Caster 22 pass from Pastorini (Fritsch kick)
Hou — FG Fritsch 47
Cin — FG Bahr 55
Hou — FG Fritsch 29

	Hou.	Cin.
First Downs	19	21
Total Yards	361	265
Yards Rushing	177	165
Yards Passing	184	100
Turnovers	3	2

FROM 24 POINTS BEHIND TO WIN:
November 22, 1982, at Los Angeles

San Diego	10	14	0	0	— 24
L.A. Raiders	0	7	14	7	— 28

SD — FG Benirschke 19
SD — Scales 29 pass from Fouts (Benirschke kick)
SD — Muncie 2 run (Benirschke kick)
SD — Muncie 1 run (Benirschke kick)
Raiders — Christensen 1 pass from Plunkett (Bahr kick)
Raiders — Allen 3 run (Bahr kick)
Raiders — Allen 6 run (Bahr kick)
Raiders — Hawkins 1 run (Bahr kick)

	S.D.	Raiders
First Downs	26	23
Total Yards	411	326
Yards Rushing	72	181
Yards Passing	339	145
Turnovers	4	2

FROM 24 POINTS BEHIND TO WIN:
September 26, 1988, at Denver

L.A. Raiders	0	0	14	13	3 — 30
Denver	7	17	0	3	0 — 27

Den — Dorsett 1 run (Karlis kick)
Den — Dorsett 1 run (Karlis kick)
Den — Sewell 7 pass from Elway (Karlis kick)
Den — FG Karlis 39
Raiders — Smith 40 pass from Schroeder (Bahr kick)
Raiders — Smith 42 pass from Schroeder (Bahr kick)
Raiders — FG Bahr 28
Raiders — Allen 4 run (Bahr kick)
Den — FG Karlis 25
Raiders — FG Bahr 44
Raiders — FG Bahr 35

	Raiders	Den.
First Downs	20	23
Total Yards	363	398
Yards Rushing	128	189
Yards Passing	235	209
Turnovers	1	5

FROM 24 POINTS BEHIND TO WIN:
December 6, 1992, at Tampa

L.A. Rams	0	3	21	7	— 31
Tampa Bay	6	21	0	0	— 27

TB — FG Murray 34
TB — FG Murray 47
TB — Armstrong 81 pass from Testaverde (Murray kick)
TB — Jones 26 fumble recovery (Murray kick)
Rams — FG Zendejas 18
TB — Carrier 10 pass from Testaverde (Murray kick)
Rams — Anderson 40 pass from Everett (Zendejas kick)
Rams — Chadwick 27 pass from Everett (Zendejas kick)
Rams — Lang 1 run (Zendejas kick)
Rams — Carter 8 pass from Everett (Zendejas kick)

	Rams	T.B.
First Downs	21	16
Total Yards	405	313
Yards Rushing	63	150
Yards Passing	342	163
Turnovers	3	3

POSTSEASON GAMES

FROM 32 POINTS BEHIND TO WIN:
AFC First-Round Playoff Game
January 3, 1993, at Buffalo

Houston	7	21	7	3	0 — 38
Buffalo	3	0	28	7	3 — 41

Hou — Jeffires 3 pass from Moon (Del Greco kick)
Buff — FG Christie 36
Hou — Slaughter 7 pass from Moon (Del Greco kick)
Hou — Duncan 26 pass from Moon (Del Greco kick)
Hou — Jeffires 27 pass from Moon (Del Greco kick)
Hou — McDowell 58 interception return (Del Greco kick)
Buff — Davis 1 run (Christie kick)
Buff — Beebe 38 pass from Reich (Christie kick)
Buff — Reed 26 pass from Reich (Christie kick)
Buff — Reed 18 pass from Reich (Christie kick)
Buff — Reed 17 pass from Reich (Christie kick)
Hou — FG Del Greco 26
Buff — FG Christie 32

	Hou.	Buff.
First Downs	27	19
Total Yards	429	366
Yards Rushing	82	98
Yards Passing	347	268
Turnovers	2	1

FROM 20 POINTS BEHIND TO WIN:
Western Conference Playoff Game
December 22, 1957, at San Francisco

Detroit	0	7	14	10	— 31
San Francisco	14	10	3	0	— 27

SF — Owens 34 pass from Tittle (Soltau kick)
SF — McElhenny 47 pass from Tittle (Soltau kick)
Det — Junker 4 pass from Rote (Martin kick)
SF — Wilson 12 pass from Tittle (Soltau kick)
SF — FG Soltau 25
SF — FG Soltau 10
Det — Tracy 2 run (Martin kick)
Det — Tracy 58 run (Martin kick)
Det — Gedman 3 run (Martin kick)
Det — FG Martin 14

	Det.	S.F.
First Downs	22	20
Total Yards	324	351
Yards Rushing	129	127
Yards Passing	195	224
Turnovers	5	4

FROM 18 POINTS BEHIND TO WIN:
NFC Divisional Playoff Game
December 23, 1972, at San Francisco

Dallas	3	10	0	17	— 30
San Francisco	7	14	7	0	— 28

SF — Washington 97 kickoff return (Gossett kick)
Dall — FG Fritsch 37
SF — Schreiber 1 run (Gossett kick)
SF — Schreiber 1 run (Gossett kick)
Dall — FG Fritsch 45
Dall — Alworth 28 pass from Morton (Fritsch kick)
SF — Schreiber 1 run (Gossett kick)
Dall — FG Fritsch 27
Dall — Parks 20 pass from Staubach (Fritsch kick)
Dall — Sellers 10 pass from Staubach (Fritsch kick)

	Dall.	S.F.
First Downs	22	13
Total Yards	402	255
Yards Rushing	165	105
Yards Passing	237	150
Turnovers	5	3

FROM 18 POINTS BEHIND TO WIN:
AFC Divisional Playoff Game
January 4, 1986, at Miami

Cleveland	7	7	7	0	— 21
Miami	3	0	14	7	— 24

Mia — FG Reveiz 51
Clev — Newsome 16 pass from Kosar (Bahr kick)
Clev — Byner 21 run (Bahr kick)
Clev — Byner 66 run (Bahr kick)
Mia — Moore 6 pass from Marino (Reveiz kick)
Mia — Davenport 31 run (Reveiz kick)
Mia — Davenport 1 run (Reveiz kick)

	Clev.	Mia.
First Downs	17	20
Total Yards	313	330
Yards Rushing	251	92
Yards Passing	62	238
Turnovers	1	1

RECORDS OF NFL TEAMS SINCE 1970 AFL-NFL MERGER

AFC	W-L-T	Pct.	Division Titles	Playoff Berths	Post-season Record	Super Bowl Record
Miami	274-148-2	.649	11	17	17-15	2-3
Oakland	255-163-6	.610	9	15	18-12	3-0
Pittsburgh	256-167-1	.605	14	18	21-14	4-1
Denver	242-176-6	.578	8	12	13-11	1-4
Kansas City	212-205-7	.508	4	9	3-9	0-0
Jacksonville**	24- 24-0	.500	0	2	2-2	0-0
Cleveland+	194-195-3	.499	6	10	4-10	0-0
Buffalo	202-220-2	.479	7	11	12-11	0-4
Cincinnati	200-224-0	.472	5	7	5-7	0-2
New England	195-229-0	.460	4	8	6-8	0-2
Seattle*	156-184-0	.459	1	4	3-4	0-0
San Diego	191-228-5	.456	5	7	6-7	0-1
Tennessee	189-233-2	.448	2	10	7-10	0-0
Indianapolis	177-245-2	.420	5	8	6-7	1-0
N.Y. Jets	171-251-2	.406	0	5	3-5	0-0
Baltimore***	10- 21-1	.328	0	0	0-0	0-0

NFC	W-L-T	Pct.	Division Titles	Playoff Berths	Post-season Record	Super Bowl Record
Dallas	267-157-0	.630	14	20	31-15	5-3
San Francisco	261-160-3	.619	16	18	23-13	5-0
Washington	251-171-2	.595	5	13	18-10	3-2
Minnesota	246-176-2	.583	12	18	12-18	0-3
Carolina**	26- 22-0	.542	1	1	1-1	0-0
St. Louis	225-195-4	.536	8	14	10-14	0-1
Chicago	215-208-1	.508	6	10	7-9	1-0
Philadelphia	204-213-7	.489	2	10	5-10	0-1
N.Y. Giants	199-222-3	.473	4	8	10-6	2-0
Green Bay	196-220-8	.472	4	7	10-6	1-1
Detroit	193-227-4	.460	3	8	1-8	0-0
Arizona	174-244-6	.417	2	3	0-3	0-0
New Orleans	171-249-4	.407	1	4	0-4	0-0
Atlanta	170-250-4	.405	1	5	2-5	0-0
Tampa Bay*	110-229-1	.325	2	4	2-4	0-0

*entered NFL in 1976.
**entered NFL in 1995.
***entered NFL in 1996.
+ Suspended play in 1996. Will return for 1999 season.
Oakland totals include L.A. Raiders, 1982-94.
Tennessee totals include Houston, 1960-96.
Indianapolis totals include Baltimore, 1970-83.
St. Louis totals include L.A. Rams, 1970-94.
Arizona totals include St. Louis, 1970-87, and Phoenix, 1988-93.
Tie games before 1972 are not calculated in won-lost percentage.
In 1982, because of players' strike, the divisional format was abandoned; L.A. Raiders and Washington won regular-season conference titles, not included in "Division Titles" totals listed above. Sixteen teams were awarded playoff berths, included in totals listed above.

INSIDE THE NUMBERS

LONGEST WINNING STREAKS SINCE 1970

Regular-Season Games

16	Miami, 1971-73	(1 in 1971, 14 in 1972, 1 in 1973)
16	Miami, 1983-84	(5 in 1983, 11 in 1984)
15	San Francisco, 1989-90	(5 in 1989, 10 in 1990)
14	Oakland, 1976-77	(10 in 1976, 4 in 1977)
13	Minnesota, 1974-75	(3 in 1974, 10 in 1975)
13	Chicago, 1984-85	(1 in 1984, 12 in 1985)
13	N.Y. Giants, 1989-90	(3 in 1989, 10 in 1990)
12	Washington, 1990-91	(1 in 1990, 11 in 1991)
11	Pittsburgh, 1975	
11	Baltimore, 1975-76	(9 in 1975, 2 in 1976)
11	Chicago, 1986-87	(7 in 1986, 4 in 1987)
11	Houston, 1993	
11	San Francisco, 1997	
10	Miami, 1973	
10	Pittsburgh, 1976-77	(9 in 1976, 1 in 1977)
10	Denver, 1984	
10	San Francisco, 1994	

NFL PLAYOFF APPEARANCES BY SEASONS

Team	Number of Seasons in Playoffs
Dallas	24
N.Y. Giants	24
Cleveland	23
St. Louis	22
Chicago	21
Minnesota	20
Washington	19
Pittsburgh	19
San Francisco	19
Green Bay	18
Oakland	18
Miami	17
Buffalo	15
Tennessee	15
Philadelphia	14
Detroit	13
Indianapolis	13
Kansas City	13
Denver	12
San Diego	12
New England	9
Cincinnati	7
N.Y. Jets	7
Arizona	5
Atlanta	5
New Orleans	4
Seattle	4
Tampa Bay	4
Jacksonville	2
Carolina	1

TEAMS IN SUPER BOWL CONTENTION, 1978-1997

	With 3 Weeks to Play	With 2 Weeks to Play	With 1 Week to Play
1997	22	18	14
1996	23	21	13
1995	*27	21	*18
1994	25	*22	15
1993	20	18	16
1992	20	16	14
1991	20	18	13
1990	23	20	15
1989	21	18	17
1988	21	18	15
1987	19	19	15
1986	19	17	14
1985	21	18	13
1984	18	14	13
1983	24	19	15
1982	20	17	16
1981	21	20	16
1980	20	14	12
1979	19	15	13
1978	20	17	12

*NFL Record

GAMES DECIDED BY 7 POINTS OR LESS AND 3 POINTS OR LESS (1970-1997)

	Games Decided by 7 Points or Less	Games Decided by 3 Points or Less
1970	59 of 182 (32.4%)	34 of 182 (18.7%)
1971	76 of 182 (41.8%)	35 of 182 (19.2%)
1972	71 of 182 (39.0%)	38 of 182 (20.9%)
1973	60 of 182 (32.9%)	28 of 182 (15.4%)
1974	91 of 182 (50.0%)	37 of 182 (20.3%)
1975	62 of 182 (34.1%)	35 of 182 (19.2%)
1976	73 of 196 (37.2%)	38 of 196 (19.4%)
1977	85 of 196 (43.4%)	36 of 196 (18.4%)
1978	108 of 224 (48.2%)	49 of 224 (21.9%)
1979	104 of 224 (46.4%)	51 of 224 (22.8%)
1980	108 of 224 (48.2%)	58 of 224 (25.9%)
1981	91 of 224 (40.6%)	**60 of 224 (26.8%)
1982	61 of 126 (48.4%)	33 of 126 (26.2%)
1983	106 of 224 (47.3%)	54 of 224 (24.1%)
1984	95 of 224 (42.4%)	58 of 224 (25.9%)
1985	87 of 224 (38.8%)	38 of 224 (17.0%)
1986	106 of 224 (47.3%)	48 of 224 (21.4%)
1987	99 of 210 (47.1%)	40 of 210 (19.0%)
1988	113 of 224 (50.4%)	62 of 224 (27.7%)
1989	107 of 224 (47.8%)	55 of 224 (24.6%)
1990	97 of 224 (43.3%)	54 of 224 (24.1%)
1991	112 of 224 (50.0%)	57 of 224 (25.4%)
1992	88 of 224 (39.3%)	**48 of 224 (21.4%)
1993	*105 of 224 (46.9%)	53 of 224 (23.7%)
1994	115 of 224 (51.3%)	60 of 224 (26.8%)
1995	115 of 240 (47.9%)	61 of 240 (25.4%)
1996	109 of 240 (45.4%)	47 of 240 (19.6%)
1997	111 of 240 (46.3%)	67 of 240 (27.9%)

*Week record: Dec. 11-13, 1993 (Week 15), 12 of 14 games (86%) decided by 7 points or less.
**Week record: Nov. 8-9, 1981 (Week 10), 8 of 14 games (57%), and Nov. 15-16, 1992 (Week 11), 8 of 14 games (57%) decided by 3 points or less.

1997 RECORDS OF TEAMS IN CLOSE GAMES

AFC	Overall Record	Decided by 8 Pts. or Less	Decided By 3 Pts. or Less
Baltimore	6-9-1	4-7-1	3-5-1
Buffalo	6-10	4-3	3-1
Cincinnati	7-9	5-3	2-2
Denver	12-4	3-2	2-2
Indianapolis	3-13	2-7	1-5
Jacksonville	11-5	6-4	2-0
Kansas City	13-3	7-1	4-1
Miami	9-7	5-5	3-4
New England	10-6	5-3	4-1
N.Y. Jets	9-7	6-5	3-2
Oakland	4-12	2-5	1-5
Pittsburgh	11-5	6-2	3-2
San Diego	4-12	1-4	0-0
Seattle	8-8	5-6	2-3
Tennessee	8-8	2-5	1-3

NFC	Overall Record	Decided by 8 Pts. or Less	Decided By 3 Pts. or Less
Arizona	4-12	3-6	3-4
Atlanta	7-9	5-5	2-2
Carolina	7-9	2-3	1-1
Chicago	4-12	3-5	2-3
Dallas	6-10	3-6	2-3
Detroit	9-7	2-3	2-1
Green Bay	13-3	4-2	1-2
Minnesota	9-7	6-3	2-2
New Orleans	6-10	4-3	4-0
N.Y. Giants	10-5-1	4-2-1	2-1-1
Philadelphia	6-9-1	5-3-1	5-3-1
St. Louis	5-11	2-7	1-3
San Francisco	13-3	5-1	1-0
Tampa Bay	10-6	4-3	2-0
Washington	8-7-1	3-4-1	1-4-1

SUPER BOWL CHAMPIONS WHO DID NOT MAKE PLAYOFFS THE FOLLOWING YEAR

N.Y. Giants—Super Bowl XXV champions did not make playoffs in the 1991 season.
Washington—Super Bowl XXII champions did not make playoffs in the 1988 season.
N.Y. Giants—Super Bowl XXI champions did not make playoffs in the 1987 season.
San Francisco—Super Bowl XVI champions did not make playoffs in the 1982 season.
Oakland—Super Bowl XV champions did not make playoffs in the 1981 season.
Pittsburgh—Super Bowl XIV champions did not make playoffs in the 1980 season.
Kansas City—Super Bowl IV champions did not make playoffs in the 1970 season.
Green Bay—Super Bowl II champions did not make playoffs in the 1968 season.

NON-DIVISION WINNERS THAT PLAYED IN SUPER BOWL

1997	Denver Broncos (Defeated Green Bay, 31-24)	Super Bowl XXXII
1992	Buffalo Bills (Lost to Dallas, 52-17)	Super Bowl XXVII
1985	New England Patriots (Lost to Chicago, 46-10)	Super Bowl XX
1980	Oakland Raiders (Defeated Philadelphia, 27-10)	Super Bowl XV
1975	Dallas Cowboys (Lost to Pittsburgh, 21-17)	Super Bowl X
1969	Kansas City Chiefs (Defeated Minnesota, 23-7)	Super Bowl IV

TEAMS AT OR UNDER .500 IN POSTSEASON PLAY

1991	New York Jets	8-8
1990	New Orleans Saints	8-8
1985	Cleveland Browns	8-8
1982	Cleveland Browns	4-5
1982	Detroit Lions	4-5
1969	Houston Oilers	6-6-2

COLDEST NFL GAMES ON RECORD

-13 degrees (-48 degree wind chill)—December 31, 1967, Lambeau Field, Green Bay, Wisconsin, NFL Championship (Green Bay 21, Dallas 17)
-9 degrees (-59 degree wind chill)—January 10, 1982, Riverfront Stadium, Cincinnati, Ohio, AFC Championship (Cincinnati 27, San Diego 7)
0 degrees (-32 degree wind chill)—January 15, 1994, Rich Stadium, Orchard Park, New York, AFC Divisional Playoff (Buffalo 29, Los Angeles Raiders 23)
1 degree (wind chill not recorded)—January 4, 1981, Cleveland Stadium, Cleveland, Ohio, AFC Divisional Playoff (Oakland 14, Cleveland 12)

ALL-TIME REGULAR-SEASON RECORDS OF CURRENT NFL TEAMS

AFC

BALTIMORE RAVENS

	All Games			Home Games			Road Games		
Season	W	L	T	W	L	T	W	L	T
1996	4	12		4	4		0	8	
1997	6	9	1	3	4	1	3	5	
Total	10	21	1	7	8	1	3	13	

BUFFALO BILLS

	All Games			Home Games			Road Games		
Season	W	L	T	W	L	T	W	L	T
1960	5	8	1	3	4		2	4	1
1961	6	8		2	5		4	3	
1962	7	6	1	3	3	1	4	3	
1963	7	6	1	4	2	1	3	4	
1964	12	2		6	1		6	1	
1965	10	3	1	5	2		5	1	1
1966	9	4	1	4	2	1	5	2	
1967	4	10		2	5		2	5	
1968	1	12	1	1	6		0	6	1
1969	4	10		4	3		0	7	
1970	3	10	1	1	6		2	4	1
1971	1	13		1	6		0	7	
1972	4	9	1	2	4	1	2	5	
1973	9	5		5	2		4	3	
1974	9	5		5	2		4	3	
1975	8	6		3	4		5	2	
1976	2	12		1	6		1	6	
1977	3	11		1	6		2	5	
1978	5	11		4	4		1	7	
1979	7	9		3	5		4	4	

	All Games			Home Games			Road Games		
Season	W	L	T	W	L	T	W	L	T
1980	11	5		6	2		5	3	
1981	10	6		7	1		3	5	
1982	4	5		4	1		0	4	
1983	8	8		3	5		5	3	
1984	2	14		2	6		0	8	
1985	2	14		2	6		0	8	
1986	4	12		3	5		1	7	
1987	7	8		4	4		3	4	
1988	12	4		8	0		4	4	
1989	9	7		6	2		3	5	
1990	13	3		8	0		5	3	
1991	13	3		7	1		6	2	
1992	11	5		6	2		5	3	
1993	12	4		6	2		6	2	
1994	7	9		4	4		3	5	
1995	10	6		6	2		4	4	
1996	10	6		7	1		3	5	
1997	6	10		4	4		2	6	
Total	267	289	8	153	126	4	114	163	4

CINCINNATI BENGALS

	All Games			Home Games			Road Games		
Season	W	L	T	W	L	T	W	L	T
1968	3	11		2	5		1	6	
1969	4	9	1	4	3		0	6	1
1970	8	6		5	2		3	4	
1971	4	10		3	4		1	6	
1972	8	6		4	3		4	3	
1973	10	4		7	0		3	4	
1974	7	7		4	3		3	4	
1975	11	3		6	1		5	2	
1976	10	4		6	1		4	3	
1977	8	6		5	2		3	4	
1978	4	12		3	5		1	7	
1979	4	12		4	4		0	8	
1980	6	10		3	5		3	5	
1981	12	4		6	2		6	2	
1982	7	2		4	0		3	2	
1983	7	9		4	4		3	5	
1984	8	8		5	3		3	5	
1985	7	9		5	3		2	6	
1986	10	6		6	2		4	4	
1987	4	11		1	7		3	4	
1988	12	4		8	0		4	4	
1989	8	8		5	3		3	5	
1990	9	7		5	3		4	4	
1991	3	13		3	5		0	8	
1992	5	11		3	5		2	6	
1993	3	13		3	5		0	8	
1994	3	13		2	6		1	7	
1995	7	9		3	5		4	4	
1996	8	8		6	2		2	6	
1997	7	9		6	2		1	7	
Total	207	244	1	131	95		76	149	1

CLEVELAND BROWNS

	All Games			Home Games			Road Games		
Season	W	L	T	W	L	T	W	L	T
1950	10	2		5	1		5	1	
1951	11	1		6	0		5	1	
1952	8	4		4	2		4	2	
1953	11	1		6	0		5	1	
1954	9	3		5	1		4	2	
1955	9	2	1	5	1		4	1	1
1956	5	7		1	5		4	2	
1957	9	2	1	6	0		3	2	1
1958	9	3		4	2		5	1	
1959	7	5		3	3		4	2	
1960	8	3	1	4	2		4	1	1
1961	8	5	1	4	3		4	2	1
1962	7	6	1	4	2	1	3	4	
1963	10	4		5	2		5	2	
1964	10	3	1	5	1	1	5	2	
1965	11	3		5	2		6	1	
1966	9	5		5	2		4	3	
1967	9	5		6	1		3	4	
1968	10	4		5	2		5	2	
1969	10	3	1	5	1	1	5	2	
1970	7	7		4	3		3	4	
1971	9	5		4	3		5	2	
1972	10	4		4	3		6	1	

	All Games			Home Games			Road Games		
Season	W	L	T	W	L	T	W	L	T
1973	7	5	2	5	1	1	2	4	1
1974	4	10		3	4		1	6	
1975	3	11		3	4		0	7	
1976	9	5		6	1		3	4	
1977	6	8		2	5		4	3	
1978	8	8		5	3		3	5	
1979	9	7		5	3		4	4	
1980	11	5		6	2		5	3	
1981	5	11		3	5		2	6	
1982	4	5		2	2		2	3	
1983	9	7		6	2		3	5	
1984	5	11		2	6		3	5	
1985	8	8		5	3		3	5	
1986	12	4		6	2		6	2	
1987	10	5		5	2		5	3	
1988	10	6		6	2		4	4	
1989	9	6	1	5	2	1	4	4	
1990	3	13		2	6		1	7	
1991	6	10		3	5		3	5	
1992	7	9		4	4		3	5	
1993	7	9		4	4		3	5	
1994	11	5		6	2		5	3	
1995	5	11		3	5		2	6	
Total	374	266	10	202	117	5	172	149	5

DENVER BRONCOS

	All Games			Home Games			Road Games		
Season	W	L	T	W	L	T	W	L	T
1960	4	9	1	2	4	1	2	5	
1961	3	11		2	5		1	6	
1962	7	7		3	4		4	3	
1963	2	11	1	2	5		0	6	1
1964	2	11	1	2	4	1	0	7	
1965	4	10		2	5		2	5	
1966	4	10		3	4		1	6	
1967	3	11		1	6		2	5	
1968	5	9		3	4		2	5	
1969	5	8	1	4	2	1	1	6	
1970	5	8	1	3	3	1	2	5	
1971	4	9	1	2	4	1	2	5	
1972	5	9		3	4		2	5	
1973	7	5	2	3	3	1	4	2	1
1974	7	6	1	3	3	1	4	3	
1975	6	8		5	2		1	6	
1976	9	5		6	1		3	4	
1977	12	2		6	1		6	1	
1978	10	6		6	2		4	4	
1979	10	6		6	2		4	4	
1980	8	8		4	4		4	4	
1981	10	6		8	0		2	6	
1982	2	7		1	4		1	3	
1983	9	7		6	2		3	5	
1984	13	3		7	1		6	2	
1985	11	5		6	2		5	3	
1986	11	5		7	1		4	4	
1987	10	4	1	7	1		3	3	1
1988	8	8		6	2		2	6	
1989	11	5		6	2		5	3	
1990	5	11		4	4		1	7	
1991	12	4		7	1		5	3	
1992	8	8		7	1		1	7	
1993	9	7		5	3		4	4	
1994	7	9		4	4		3	5	
1995	8	8		6	2		2	6	
1996	13	3		8	0		5	3	
1997	12	4		8	0		4	4	
Total	281	273	10	174	102	7	107	171	3

INDIANAPOLIS COLTS*

	All Games			Home Games			Road Games		
Season	W	L	T	W	L	T	W	L	T
1953	3	9		2	4		1	5	
1954	3	9		2	4		1	5	
1955	5	6	1	4	1	1	1	5	
1956	5	7		4	2		1	5	
1957	7	5		4	2		3	3	
1958	9	3		6	0		3	3	
1959	9	3		4	2		5	1	
1960	6	6		4	2		2	4	
1961	8	6		5	2		3	4	
1962	7	7		3	4		4	3	
1963	8	6		4	3		4	3	
1964	12	2		7	1		5	1	
1965	10	3	1	5	2		5	1	1
1966	9	5		5	2		4	3	
1967	11	1	2	6	0	1	5	1	1
1968	13	1		6	1		7	0	
1969	8	5	1	4	2	1	4	3	
1970	11	2	1	5	1	1	6	1	
1971	10	4		5	2		5	2	
1972	5	9		2	5		3	4	
1973	4	10		3	4		1	6	
1974	2	12		0	7		2	5	
1975	10	4		5	2		5	2	
1976	11	3		6	1		5	2	
1977	10	4		6	1		4	3	
1978	5	11		2	6		3	5	
1979	5	11		3	5		2	6	
1980	7	9		2	6		5	3	
1981	2	14		1	7		1	7	
1982	0	8	1	0	3	1	0	5	
1983	7	9		3	5		4	4	
1984	4	12		2	6		2	6	
1985	5	11		4	4		1	7	
1986	3	13		1	7		2	6	
1987	9	6		4	4		5	2	
1988	9	7		6	2		3	5	
1989	8	8		6	2		2	6	
1990	7	9		3	5		4	4	
1991	1	15		0	8		1	7	
1992	9	7		4	4		5	3	
1993	4	12		2	6		2	6	
1994	8	8		5	3		3	5	
1995	9	7		5	3		4	4	
1996	9	7		6	2		3	5	
1997	3	13		2	6		1	7	
Total	310	329	7	168	151	5	142	178	2

includes Baltimore Colts (1953-83).

JACKSONVILLE JAGUARS

	All Games			Home Games			Road Games		
Season	W	L	T	W	L	T	W	L	T
1995	4	12		2	6		2	6	
1996	9	7		7	1		2	6	
1997	11	5		7	1		4	4	
Total	24	24		16	8		8	16	

KANSAS CITY CHIEFS*

	All Games			Home Games			Road Games		
Season	W	L	T	W	L	T	W	L	T
1960	8	6		5	2		3	4	
1961	6	8		4	3		2	5	
1962	11	3		6	1		5	2	
1963	5	7	2	4	3		1	4	2
1964	7	7		4	3		3	4	
1965	7	5	2	5	2		2	3	2
1966	11	2	1	4	2	1	7	0	
1967	9	5		4	3		5	2	
1968	12	2		6	1		6	1	
1969	11	3		6	1		5	2	
1970	7	5	2	4	1	2	3	4	
1971	10	3	1	7	0		3	3	1
1972	8	6		3	4		5	2	
1973	7	5	2	5	1	1	2	4	1
1974	5	9		1	6		4	3	
1975	5	9		3	4		2	5	
1976	5	9		1	6		4	3	
1977	2	12		1	6		1	6	
1978	4	12		3	5		1	7	
1979	7	9		3	5		4	4	
1980	8	8		3	5		5	3	
1981	9	7		5	3		4	4	
1982	3	6		2	2		1	4	
1983	6	10		5	3		1	7	
1984	8	8		5	3		3	5	
1985	6	10		5	3		1	7	
1986	10	6		6	2		4	4	
1987	4	11		3	4		1	7	
1988	4	11	1	4	4		0	7	1
1989	8	7	1	5	3		3	4	1
1990	11	5		6	2		5	3	
1991	10	6		6	2		4	4	

Season	All Games W	L	T	Home Games W	L	T	Road Games W	L	T
1992	10	6		7	1		3	5	
1993	11	5		7	1		4	4	
1994	9	7		5	3		4	4	
1995	13	3		8	0		5	3	
1996	9	7		5	3		4	4	
1997	13	3		8	0		5	3	
Total	299	253	12	174	103	4	125	150	8

**includes Dallas Texans (1960-62).*

MIAMI DOLPHINS

Season	All Games W	L	T	Home Games W	L	T	Road Games W	L	T
1966	3	11		2	5		1	6	
1967	4	10		4	3		0	7	
1968	5	8	1	1	5	1	4	3	
1969	3	10	1	2	4	1	1	6	
1970	10	4		6	1		4	3	
1971	10	3	1	6	1		4	2	1
1972	14	0		7	0		7	0	
1973	12	2		7	0		5	2	
1974	11	3		7	0		4	3	
1975	10	4		5	2		5	2	
1976	6	8		3	4		3	4	
1977	10	4		6	1		4	3	
1978	11	5		7	1		4	4	
1979	10	6		6	2		4	4	
1980	8	8		5	3		3	5	
1981	11	4	1	6	1	1	5	3	
1982	7	2		4	0		3	2	
1983	12	4		7	1		5	3	
1984	14	2		7	1		7	1	
1985	12	4		8	0		4	4	
1986	8	8		4	4		4	4	
1987	8	7		4	3		4	4	
1988	6	10		4	4		2	6	
1989	8	8		4	4		4	4	
1990	12	4		7	1		5	3	
1991	8	8		5	3		3	5	
1992	11	5		6	2		5	3	
1993	9	7		4	4		5	3	
1994	10	6		6	2		4	4	
1995	9	7		5	3		4	4	
1996	8	8		4	4		4	4	
1997	9	7		6	2		3	5	
Total	289	187	4	165	71	3	124	116	1

NEW ENGLAND PATRIOTS*

Season	All Games W	L	T	Home Games W	L	T	Road Games W	L	T
1960	5	9		3	4		2	5	
1961	9	4	1	4	2	1	5	2	
1962	9	4	1	6	1		3	3	1
1963	7	6	1	5	1	1	2	5	
1964	10	3	1	4	2	1	6	1	
1965	4	8	2	1	4	2	3	4	
1966	8	4	2	4	2	1	4	2	1
1967	3	10	1	2	4		1	6	1
1968	4	10		2	5		2	5	
1969	4	10		2	5		2	5	
1970	2	12		1	6		1	6	
1971	6	8		5	2		1	6	
1972	3	11		2	5		1	6	
1973	5	9		3	4		2	5	
1974	7	7		3	4		4	3	
1975	3	11		2	5		1	6	
1976	11	3		6	1		5	2	
1977	9	5		6	1		3	4	
1978	11	5		5	3		6	2	
1979	9	7		6	2		3	5	
1980	10	6		6	2		4	4	
1981	2	14		2	6		0	8	
1982	5	4		3	1		2	3	
1983	8	8		5	3		3	5	
1984	9	7		5	3		4	4	
1985	11	5		7	1		4	4	
1986	11	5		4	4		7	1	
1987	8	7		5	3		3	4	
1988	9	7		7	1		2	6	
1989	5	11		3	5		2	6	
1990	1	15		0	8		1	7	
1991	6	10		4	4		2	6	
1992	2	14		1	7		1	7	
1993	5	11		3	5		2	6	
1994	10	6		5	3		5	3	
1995	6	10		3	5		3	5	
1996	11	5		6	2		5	3	
1997	10	6		6	2		4	4	
Total	258	297	9	147	128	6	111	169	3

**includes Boston Patriots (1960-70).*

NEW YORK JETS*

Season	All Games W	L	T	Home Games W	L	T	Road Games W	L	T
1960	7	7		3	4		4	3	
1961	7	7		5	2		2	5	
1962	5	9		2	5		3	4	
1963	5	8	1	4	2	1	1	6	
1964	5	8	1	5	1	1	0	7	
1965	5	8	1	3	3	1	2	5	
1966	6	6	2	4	3		2	3	2
1967	8	5	1	4	2	1	4	3	
1968	11	3		6	1		5	2	
1969	10	4		5	2		5	2	
1970	4	10		2	5		2	5	
1971	6	8		4	3		2	5	
1972	7	7		4	3		3	4	
1973	4	10		2	4		2	6	
1974	7	7		3	4		4	3	
1975	3	11		1	6		2	5	
1976	3	11		2	5		1	6	
1977	3	11		1	6		2	5	
1978	8	8		4	4		4	4	
1979	8	8		6	2		2	6	
1980	4	12		2	6		2	6	
1981	10	5	1	6	2		4	3	1
1982	6	3		3	1		3	2	
1983	7	9		2	6		5	3	
1984	7	9		3	5		4	4	
1985	11	5		7	1		4	4	
1986	10	6		5	3		5	3	
1987	6	9		4	4		2	5	
1988	8	7	1	5	2	1	3	5	
1989	4	12		1	7		3	5	
1990	6	10		3	5		3	5	
1991	8	8		4	4		4	4	
1992	4	12		3	5		1	7	
1993	8	8		3	5		5	3	
1994	6	10		4	4		2	6	
1995	3	13		2	6		1	7	
1996	1	15		0	8		1	7	
1997	9	7		5	3		4	4	
Total	240	316	8	132	144	5	108	172	3

**includes New York Titans (1960-62).*

OAKLAND RAIDERS*

Season	All Games W	L	T	Home Games W	L	T	Road Games W	L	T
1960	6	8		3	4		3	4	
1961	2	12		1	6		1	6	
1962	1	13		1	6		0	7	
1963	10	4		6	1		4	3	
1964	5	7	2	5	2		0	5	2
1965	8	5	1	5	2		3	3	1
1966	8	5	1	3	3	1	5	2	
1967	13	1		7	0		6	1	
1968	12	2		6	1		6	1	
1969	12	1	1	7	0		5	1	1
1970	8	4	2	6	1		2	3	2
1971	8	4	2	5	1	1	3	3	1
1972	10	3	1	5	1	1	5	2	
1973	9	4	1	5	2		4	2	1
1974	12	2		6	1		6	1	
1975	11	3		6	1		5	2	
1976	13	1		7	0		6	1	
1977	11	3		6	1		5	2	
1978	9	7		4	4		5	3	
1979	9	7		6	2		3	5	
1980	11	5		6	2		5	3	
1981	7	9		4	4		3	5	
1982	8	1		4	0		4	1	
1983	12	4		6	2		6	2	
1984	11	5		6	2		5	3	
1985	12	4		7	1		5	3	
1986	8	8		3	5		5	3	
1987	5	10		3	5		2	5	
1988	7	9		3	5		4	4	
1989	8	8		7	1		1	7	
1990	12	4		6	2		6	2	
1991	9	7		5	3		4	4	
1992	7	9		5	3		2	6	
1993	10	6		5	3		5	3	
1994	9	7		4	4		5	3	
1995	8	8		4	4		4	4	
1996	7	9		4	4		3	5	
1997	4	12		2	6		2	6	
Total	332	221	11	184	95	3	148	126	8

**includes Los Angeles Raiders (1982-94).*

PITTSBURGH STEELERS*

Season	All Games W	L	T	Home Games W	L	T	Road Games W	L	T
1933	3	6	2	2	3		1	3	2
1934	2	10		1	5		1	5	
1935	4	8		2	5		2	3	
1936	6	6		4	1		2	5	
1937	4	7		2	4		2	3	
1938	2	9		0	5		2	4	
1939	1	9	1	1	4		0	5	1
1940	2	7	2	1	2	2	1	5	
1941	1	9	1	1	4		0	5	1
1942	7	4		3	2		4	2	
1945	2	8		1	4		1	4	
1946	5	5	1	4	1		1	4	1
1947	8	4		5	1		3	3	
1948	4	8		4	2		0	6	
1949	6	5	1	3	2	1	3	3	
1950	6	6		2	4		4	2	
1951	4	7	1	1	4	1	3	3	
1952	5	7		2	4		3	3	
1953	6	6		3	3		3	3	
1954	5	7		4	2		1	5	
1955	4	8		3	2		1	6	
1956	5	7		3	3		2	4	
1957	6	6		4	2		2	4	
1958	7	4	1	5	1		2	3	1
1959	6	5	1	3	2	1	3	3	
1960	5	6	1	4	2		1	4	1
1961	6	8		4	3		2	5	
1962	9	5		4	3		5	2	
1963	7	4	3	5	0	2	2	4	1
1964	5	9		2	5		3	4	
1965	2	12		1	6		1	6	
1966	5	8	1	3	3	1	2	5	
1967	4	9	1	1	6		3	3	1
1968	2	11	1	1	6		1	5	1
1969	1	13		1	6		0	7	
1970	5	9		4	3		1	6	
1971	6	8		5	2		1	6	
1972	11	3		7	0		4	3	
1973	10	4		7	1		3	3	
1974	10	3	1	5	2		5	1	1
1975	12	2		6	1		6	1	
1976	10	4		6	1		4	3	
1977	9	5		6	1		3	4	
1978	14	2		7	1		7	1	
1979	12	4		8	0		4	4	
1980	9	7		6	2		3	5	
1981	8	8		5	3		3	5	
1982	6	3		4	0		2	3	
1983	10	6		4	4		6	2	
1984	9	7		6	2		3	5	
1985	7	9		5	3		2	6	
1986	6	10		4	4		2	6	
1987	8	7		4	3		4	4	
1988	5	11		4	4		1	7	
1989	9	7		4	4		5	3	
1990	9	7		6	2		3	5	
1991	7	9		5	3		2	6	
1992	11	5		7	1		4	4	
1993	9	7		6	2		3	5	
1994	12	4		7	1		5	3	
1995	11	5		6	2		5	3	
1996	10	6		7	1		3	5	

	All Games			Home Games			Road Games		
Season	W	L	T	W	L	T	W	L	T
1997	11	5		7	1		4	4	
Total	413	420	19	248	166	8	165	254	11

*includes Pittsburgh Pirates (1933-40).

SAN DIEGO CHARGERS*

	All Games			Home Games			Road Games		
Season	W	L	T	W	L	T	W	L	T
1960	10	4		5	2		5	2	
1961	12	2		6	1		6	1	
1962	4	10		3	4		1	6	
1963	11	3		6	1		5	2	
1964	8	5	1	4	3		4	2	1
1965	9	2	3	4	1	2	5	1	1
1966	7	6	1	5	2		2	4	1
1967	8	5	1	5	2	1	3	3	
1968	9	5		4	3		5	2	
1969	8	6		5	2		3	4	
1970	5	6	3	2	3	2	3	3	1
1971	6	8		6	1		0	7	
1972	4	9	1	2	5		2	4	1
1973	2	11	1	2	5		0	6	1
1974	5	9		3	4		2	5	
1975	2	12		1	6		1	6	
1976	6	8		3	4		3	4	
1977	7	7		3	4		4	3	
1978	9	7		5	3		4	4	
1979	12	4		7	1		5	3	
1980	11	5		6	2		5	3	
1981	10	6		5	3		5	3	
1982	6	3		3	1		3	2	
1983	6	10		4	4		2	6	
1984	7	9		4	4		3	5	
1985	8	8		6	2		2	6	
1986	4	12		2	6		2	6	
1987	8	7		4	3		4	4	
1988	6	10		3	5		3	5	
1989	6	10		4	4		2	6	
1990	6	10		3	5		3	5	
1991	4	12		3	5		1	7	
1992	11	5		6	2		5	3	
1993	8	8		4	4		4	4	
1994	11	5		5	3		6	2	
1995	9	7		5	3		4	4	
1996	8	8		5	3		3	5	
1997	4	12		2	6		2	6	
Total	277	276	11	155	122	5	122	154	6

*includes Los Angeles Chargers (1960).

SEATTLE SEAHAWKS

	All Games			Home Games			Road Games		
Season	W	L	T	W	L	T	W	L	T
1976	2	12		1	6		1	6	
1977	5	9		3	4		2	5	
1978	9	7		5	3		4	4	
1979	9	7		5	3		4	4	
1980	4	12		0	8		4	4	
1981	6	10		5	3		1	7	
1982	4	5		3	2		1	3	
1983	9	7		5	3		4	4	
1984	12	4		7	1		5	3	
1985	8	8		5	3		3	5	
1986	10	6		7	1		3	5	
1987	9	6		6	2		3	4	
1988	9	7		5	3		4	4	
1989	7	9		3	5		4	4	
1990	9	7		5	3		4	4	
1991	7	9		5	3		2	6	
1992	2	14		1	7		1	7	
1993	6	10		4	4		2	6	
1994	6	10		3	5		3	5	
1995	8	8		5	3		3	5	
1996	7	9		4	4		3	5	
1997	8	8		4	4		4	4	
Total	156	184		91	80		65	104	

TENNESSEE OILERS*

	All Games			Home Games			Road Games		
Season	W	L	T	W	L	T	W	L	T
1960	10	4		6	1		4	3	
1961	10	3	1	6	1		4	2	1
1962	11	3		6	1		5	2	
1963	6	8		4	3		2	5	
1964	4	10		3	4		1	6	
1965	4	10		3	4		1	6	
1966	3	11		3	4		0	7	
1967	9	4	1	5	2		4	2	1
1968	7	7		3	4		4	3	
1969	6	6	2	4	2	1	2	4	1
1970	3	10	1	1	6		2	4	1
1971	4	9	1	3	3	1	1	6	
1972	1	13		1	6		0	7	
1973	1	13		0	7		1	6	
1974	7	7		3	4		4	3	
1975	10	4		5	2		5	2	
1976	5	9		3	4		2	5	
1977	8	6		5	2		3	4	
1978	10	6		5	3		5	3	
1979	11	5		6	2		5	3	
1980	11	5		6	2		5	3	
1981	7	9		5	3		2	6	
1982	1	8		1	4		0	4	
1983	2	14		2	6		0	8	
1984	3	13		2	6		1	7	
1985	5	11		4	4		1	7	
1986	5	11		4	4		1	7	
1987	9	6		5	2		4	4	
1988	10	6		7	1		3	5	
1989	9	7		6	2		3	5	
1990	9	7		6	2		3	5	
1991	11	5		7	1		4	4	
1992	10	6		5	3		5	3	
1993	12	4		7	1		5	3	
1994	2	14		2	6		0	8	
1995	7	9		3	5		4	4	
1996	8	8		2	6		6	2	
1997	8	8		6	2		2	6	
Total	259	299	6	155	125	2	104	174	4

*includes Houston Oilers (1960-96).

NFC

ARIZONA CARDINALS*

	All Games			Home Games			Road Games		
Season	W	L	T	W	L	T	W	L	T
1920	6	2	2	5	1	1	1	1	1
1921	3	3	2	3	3	1	0	0	1
1922	8	3		8	3		0	0	
1923	8	4		8	3		0	1	
1924	5	4	1	5	3	1	0	1	
1925	11	2	1	11	2		0	0	1
1926	5	6	1	3	3		2	3	1
1927	3	7	1	2	3	1	1	4	
1928	1	5		1	1		0	4	
1929	6	6	1	3	2		3	4	1
1930	5	6	2	3	2		2	4	2
1931	5	4		3	0		2	4	
1932	2	6	2	1	2	1	1	4	1
1933	1	9	1	0	4	1	1	5	
1934	5	6		2	2		3	4	
1935	6	4	2	2	2		4	2	2
1936	3	8	1	3	1	1	0	7	
1937	5	5	1	1	3		4	2	1
1938	2	9		1	4		1	5	
1939	1	10		0	4		1	6	
1940	2	7	2	2	1	1	0	6	1
1941	3	7	1	0	3	1	3	4	
1942	3	8		2	2		1	6	
1943	0	10		0	3		0	7	
1945	1	9		0	3		1	6	
1946	6	5		2	2		4	3	
1947	9	3		5	0		4	3	
1948	11	1		5	1		6	0	
1949	6	5	1	2	3	1	4	2	
1950	5	7		3	3		2	4	
1951	3	9		1	5		2	4	
1952	4	8		2	4		2	4	
1953	1	10	1	0	5	1	1	5	
1954	2	10		2	4		0	6	
1955	4	7	1	3	2	1	1	5	
1956	7	5		4	2		3	3	
1957	3	9		0	6		3	3	
1958	2	9	1	1	4	1	1	5	
1959	2	10		2	4		0	6	
1960	6	5	1	3	2	1	3	3	
1961	7	7		3	4		4	3	
1962	4	9	1	2	4	1	2	5	
1963	9	5		3	4		6	1	
1964	9	3	2	4	1	1	5	2	1
1965	5	9		2	5		3	4	
1966	8	5	1	5	1	1	3	4	
1967	6	7	1	3	3	1	3	4	
1968	9	4	1	4	2	1	5	2	
1969	4	9	1	3	4		1	5	1
1970	8	5	1	6	1		2	4	1
1971	4	9	1	1	5	1	3	4	
1972	4	9	1	2	5		2	4	1
1973	4	9	1	2	4	1	2	5	
1974	10	4		5	2		5	2	
1975	11	3		6	1		5	2	
1976	10	4		6	1		4	3	
1977	7	7		4	3		3	4	
1978	6	10		3	5		3	5	
1979	5	11		3	5		2	6	
1980	5	11		2	6		3	5	
1981	7	9		5	3		2	6	
1982	5	4		1	3		4	1	
1983	8	7	1	4	3	1	4	4	
1984	9	7		5	3		4	4	
1985	5	11		4	4		1	7	
1986	4	11	1	3	5		1	6	1
1987	7	8		4	3		3	5	
1988	7	9		4	4		3	5	
1989	5	11		2	6		3	5	
1990	5	11		3	5		2	6	
1991	4	12		2	6		2	6	
1992	4	12		3	5		1	7	
1993	7	9		4	4		3	5	
1994	8	8		5	3		3	5	
1995	4	12		3	5		1	7	
1996	7	9		5	3		2	6	
1997	4	12		3	5		1	7	
Total	406	555	39	233	243	22	173	312	17

*includes Chicago Cardinals (1920-59), St. Louis Cardinals (1960-87), and Phoenix Cardinals (1988-93).

ATLANTA FALCONS

	All Games			Home Games			Road Games		
Season	W	L	T	W	L	T	W	L	T
1966	3	11		1	6		2	5	
1967	1	12	1	1	5	1	0	7	
1968	2	12		1	6		1	6	
1969	6	8		4	3		2	5	
1970	4	8	2	3	4		1	4	2
1971	7	6	1	4	3		3	3	1
1972	7	7		4	3		3	4	
1973	9	5		4	3		5	2	
1974	3	11		2	5		1	6	
1975	4	10		3	4		1	6	
1976	4	10		3	4		1	6	
1977	7	7		4	3		3	4	
1978	9	7		7	1		2	6	
1979	6	10		3	5		3	5	
1980	12	4		6	2		6	2	
1981	7	9		4	4		3	5	
1982	5	4		2	3		3	1	
1983	7	9		4	4		3	5	
1984	4	12		2	6		2	6	
1985	4	12		3	5		1	7	
1986	7	8	1	2	5	1	5	3	
1987	3	12		2	6		1	6	
1988	5	11		2	6		3	5	
1989	3	13		3	5		0	8	
1990	5	11		5	3		0	8	
1991	10	6		6	2		4	4	
1992	6	10		5	3		1	7	
1993	6	10		4	4		2	6	
1994	7	9		5	3		2	6	
1995	9	7		7	1		2	6	
1996	3	13		2	6		1	7	
1997	7	9		3	5		4	4	
Total	182	293	5	111	128	2	71	165	3

CAROLINA PANTHERS

	All Games			Home Games			Road Games		
Season	W	L	T	W	L	T	W	L	T
1995	7	9		5	3		2	6	
1996	12	4		8	0		4	4	
1997	7	9		2	6		5	3	
Total	26	22		15	9		11	13	

CHICAGO BEARS*

	All Games			Home Games			Road Games		
Season	W	L	T	W	L	T	W	L	T
1920	10	1	2	6	0	1	4	1	1
1921	9	1	1	9	1	1	0	0	
1922	9	3		7	1		2	2	
1923	9	2	1	7	1	1	2	1	
1924	6	1	4	5	0	3	1	1	1
1925	9	5	3	7	1	1	2	4	2
1926	12	1	3	10	0	2	2	1	1
1927	9	3	2	7	1	1	2	2	1
1928	7	5	1	6	3		1	2	1
1929	4	9	2	1	5	2	3	4	
1930	9	4	1	5	2	1	4	2	
1931	8	5		6	3		2	2	
1932	7	1	6	6	1	1	1	0	5
1933	10	2	1	6	0		4	2	1
1934	13	0		5	0		8	0	
1935	6	4	2	1	2	2	5	2	
1936	9	3		3	1		6	2	
1937	9	1	1	4	1		5	0	1
1938	6	5		2	3		4	2	
1939	8	3		4	1		4	2	
1940	8	3		5	0		3	3	
1941	10	1		5	1		5	0	
1942	11	0		6	0		5	0	
1943	8	1	1	5	0		3	1	1
1944	6	3	1	4	0	1	2	3	
1945	3	7		2	3		1	4	
1946	8	2	1	4	1	1	4	1	
1947	8	4		4	2		4	2	
1948	10	2		5	1		5	1	
1949	9	3		5	1		4	2	
1950	9	3		6	0		3	3	
1951	7	5		3	3		4	2	
1952	5	7		3	3		2	4	
1953	3	8	1	1	4	1	2	4	
1954	8	4		4	2		4	2	
1955	8	4		5	1		3	3	
1956	9	2	1	6	0		3	2	1
1957	5	7		2	4		3	3	
1958	8	4		5	1		3	3	
1959	8	4		4	2		4	2	
1960	5	6	1	4	2		1	4	1
1961	8	6		5	2		3	4	
1962	9	5		4	3		5	2	
1963	11	1	2	6	0	1	5	1	1
1964	5	9		2	5		3	4	
1965	9	5		5	2		4	3	
1966	5	7	2	4	1	2	1	6	
1967	7	6	1	3	3	1	4	3	
1968	7	7		2	5		5	2	
1969	1	13		1	6		0	7	
1970	6	8		3	4		3	4	
1971	6	8		4	3		2	5	
1972	4	9	1	1	5	1	3	4	
1973	3	11		1	6		2	5	
1974	4	10		4	3		0	7	
1975	4	10		3	4		1	6	
1976	7	7		4	3		3	4	
1977	9	5		5	2		4	3	
1978	7	9		4	4		3	5	
1979	10	6		6	2		4	4	
1980	7	9		5	3		2	6	
1981	6	10		4	4		2	6	
1982	3	6		2	2		1	4	
1983	8	8		5	3		3	5	
1984	10	6		6	2		4	4	
1985	15	1		8	0		7	1	
1986	14	2		7	1		7	1	
1987	11	4		6	2		5	2	
1988	12	4		7	1		5	3	
1989	6	10		4	4		2	6	
1990	11	5		7	1		4	4	
1991	11	5		6	2		5	3	
1992	5	11		4	4		1	7	
1993	7	9		3	5		4	4	
1994	9	7		5	3		4	4	
1995	9	7		5	3		4	4	
1996	7	9		6	2		1	7	
1997	4	12		2	6		2	6	
Total	602	406	42	354	169	24	248	237	18

**includes Decatur Staleys (1920) and Chicago Staleys (1921).*

DALLAS COWBOYS

	All Games			Home Games			Road Games		
Season	W	L	T	W	L	T	W	L	T
1960	0	11	1	0	6		0	5	1
1961	4	9	1	2	4	1	2	5	
1962	5	8	1	2	4	1	3	4	
1963	4	10		3	4		1	6	
1964	5	8	1	2	4	1	3	4	
1965	7	7		5	2		2	5	
1966	10	3	1	6	1		4	2	1
1967	9	5		5	2		4	3	
1968	12	2		5	2		7	0	
1969	11	2	1	6	0	1	5	2	
1970	10	4		6	1		4	3	
1971	11	3		6	1		5	2	
1972	10	4		5	2		5	2	
1973	10	4		6	1		4	3	
1974	8	6		5	2		3	4	
1975	10	4		5	2		5	2	
1976	11	3		6	1		5	2	
1977	12	2		6	1		6	1	
1978	12	4		7	1		5	3	
1979	11	5		6	2		5	3	
1980	12	4		8	0		4	4	
1981	12	4		8	0		4	4	
1982	6	3		3	2		3	1	
1983	12	4		6	2		6	2	
1984	9	7		5	3		4	4	
1985	10	6		7	1		3	5	
1986	7	9		3	5		4	4	
1987	7	8		3	4		4	4	
1988	3	13		1	7		2	6	
1989	1	15		0	8		1	7	
1990	7	9		5	3		2	6	
1991	11	5		6	2		5	3	
1992	13	3		7	1		6	2	
1993	12	4		6	2		6	2	
1994	12	4		6	2		6	2	
1995	12	4		6	2		6	2	
1996	10	6		6	2		4	4	
1997	6	10		5	3		1	7	
Total	334	222	6	185	92	4	149	130	2

DETROIT LIONS*

	All Games			Home Games			Road Games		
Season	W	L	T	W	L	T	W	L	T
1930	5	6	3	5	1	2	0	5	1
1931	11	3		8	0		3	3	
1932	6	2	4	3	0	2	3	2	2
1933	6	5		4	1		2	4	
1934	10	3		6	2		4	1	
1935	7	3	2	5	0	1	2	3	1
1936	8	4		5	1		3	3	
1937	7	4		4	2		3	2	
1938	7	4		4	3		3	1	
1939	6	5		4	2		2	3	
1940	5	5	1	3	3		2	2	1
1941	4	6	1	3	2		1	4	1
1942	0	11		0	7		0	4	
1943	3	6	1	2	2	1	1	4	
1944	6	3	1	4	2		2	1	1
1945	7	3		4	1		3	2	
1946	1	10		1	5		0	5	
1947	3	9		2	4		1	5	
1948	2	10		2	4		0	6	
1949	4	8		2	4		2	4	
1950	6	6		4	2		2	4	
1951	7	4	1	3	3	1	4	1	
1952	9	3		6	1		3	2	
1953	10	2		5	1		5	1	
1954	9	2	1	5	0	1	4	2	
1955	3	9		3	4		0	5	
1956	9	3		5	1		4	2	
1957	8	4		5	1		3	3	
1958	4	7	1	2	4		2	3	1
1959	3	8	1	2	4		1	4	1
1960	7	5		5	1		2	4	
1961	8	5	1	2	5		6	0	1
1962	11	3		7	0		4	3	
1963	5	8	1	3	3	1	2	5	
1964	7	5	2	3	3	1	4	2	1
1965	6	7	1	2	4	1	4	3	
1966	4	9	1	3	4		1	5	1
1967	5	7	2	3	4		2	3	2
1968	4	8	2	1	4	2	3	4	
1969	9	4	1	5	2		4	2	1
1970	10	4		6	1		4	3	
1971	7	6	1	3	4		4	2	1
1972	8	5	1	5	2		3	3	1
1973	6	7	1	4	3		2	4	1
1974	7	7		5	2		2	5	
1975	7	7		4	3		3	4	
1976	6	8		5	2		1	6	
1977	6	8		5	2		1	6	
1978	7	9		5	3		2	6	
1979	2	14		2	6		0	8	
1980	9	7		6	2		3	5	
1981	8	8		7	1		1	7	
1982	4	5		2	3		2	2	
1983	9	7		6	2		3	5	
1984	4	11	1	2	5	1	2	6	
1985	7	9		6	2		1	7	
1986	5	11		1	7		4	4	
1987	4	11		1	6		3	5	
1988	4	12		2	6		2	6	
1989	7	9		4	4		3	5	
1990	6	10		3	5		3	5	
1991	12	4		8	0		4	4	
1992	5	11		3	5		2	6	
1993	10	6		5	3		5	3	
1994	9	7		6	2		3	5	
1995	10	6		7	1		3	5	
1996	5	11		4	4		1	7	
1997	9	7		6	2		3	5	
Total	435	446	32	268	185	14	167	261	18

**includes Portsmouth Spartans (1930-33).*

GREEN BAY PACKERS

	All Games			Home Games			Road Games		
Season	W	L	T	W	L	T	W	L	T
1921	3	2	1	2	1		1	1	1
1922	4	3	3	4	1	1	0	2	2
1923	7	2	1	4	2	1	3	0	
1924	7	4		5	0		2	4	
1925	8	5		6	0		2	5	
1926	7	3	3	4	1	2	3	2	1
1927	7	2	1	6	1		1	1	1
1928	6	4	3	2	2	2	4	2	1
1929	12	0	1	5	0		7	0	1
1930	10	3	1	6	0		4	3	1
1931	12	2		8	0		4	2	
1932	10	3	1	5	0	1	5	3	
1933	5	7	1	3	2	1	2	5	
1934	7	6		4	2		3	4	
1935	8	4		5	2		3	2	
1936	10	1	1	5	1		5	0	1
1937	7	4		3	2		4	2	
1938	8	3		4	2		4	1	
1939	9	2		4	1		5	1	
1940	6	4	1	4	2		2	2	1
1941	10	1		4	1		6	0	
1942	8	2	1	4	1		4	1	1
1943	7	2	1	2	1	1	5	1	
1944	8	2		5	0		3	2	
1945	6	4		4	1		2	3	
1946	6	5		2	3		4	2	
1947	6	5	1	4	2		2	3	1
1948	3	9		2	4		1	5	
1949	2	10		1	5		1	5	
1950	3	9		3	3		0	6	
1951	3	9		2	4		1	5	
1952	6	6		3	3		3	3	
1953	2	9	1	1	5		1	4	1

Season	All Games W	L	T	Home Games W	L	T	Road Games W	L	T
1954	4	8		2	4		2	4	
1955	6	6		5	1		1	5	
1956	4	8		2	4		2	4	
1957	3	9		1	5		2	4	
1958	1	10	1	1	4	1	0	6	
1959	7	5		4	2		3	3	
1960	8	4		4	2		4	2	
1961	11	3		6	1		5	2	
1962	13	1		7	0		6	1	
1963	11	2	1	6	1		5	1	1
1964	8	5	1	4	3		4	2	1
1965	10	3	1	6	1		4	2	1
1966	12	2		6	1		6	1	
1967	9	4	1	4	2	1	5	2	
1968	6	7	1	2	5		4	2	1
1969	8	6		5	2		3	4	
1970	6	8		4	3		2	5	
1971	4	8	2	3	3	1	1	5	1
1972	10	4		4	3		6	1	
1973	5	7	2	3	2	2	2	5	
1974	6	8		4	3		2	5	
1975	4	10		3	4		1	6	
1976	5	9		4	3		1	6	
1977	4	10		2	5		2	5	
1978	8	7	1	5	2	1	3	5	
1979	5	11		4	4		1	7	
1980	5	10	1	4	4		1	6	1
1981	8	8		4	4		4	4	
1982	5	3	1	3	1		2	2	1
1983	8	8		5	3		3	5	
1984	8	8		5	3		3	5	
1985	8	8		5	3		3	5	
1986	4	12		1	7		3	5	
1987	5	9	1	2	5	1	3	4	
1988	4	12		2	6		2	6	
1989	10	6		6	2		4	4	
1990	6	10		3	5		3	5	
1991	4	12		2	6		2	6	
1992	9	7		6	2		3	5	
1993	9	7		6	2		3	5	
1994	9	7		7	1		2	6	
1995	11	5		7	1		4	4	
1996	13	3		8	0		5	3	
1997	13	3		8	0		5	3	
Total	540	440	36	311	180	16	229	260	20

MINNESOTA VIKINGS

Season	All Games W	L	T	Home Games W	L	T	Road Games W	L	T
1961	3	11		3	4		0	7	
1962	2	11	1	1	5	1	1	6	
1963	5	8	1	3	4		2	4	1
1964	8	5	1	4	3		4	2	1
1965	7	7		2	5		5	2	
1966	4	9	1	2	5		2	4	1
1967	3	8	3	1	4	2	2	4	1
1968	8	6		4	3		4	3	
1969	12	2		7	0		5	2	
1970	12	2		7	0		5	2	
1971	11	3		5	2		6	1	
1972	7	7		3	4		4	3	
1973	12	2		7	0		5	2	
1974	10	4		4	3		6	1	
1975	12	2		7	0		5	2	
1976	11	2	1	6	0	1	5	2	
1977	9	5		5	2		4	3	
1978	8	7	1	5	3		3	4	1
1979	7	9		5	3		2	6	
1980	9	7		5	3		4	4	
1981	7	9		5	3		2	6	
1982	5	4		4	1		1	3	
1983	8	8		3	5		5	3	
1984	3	13		2	6		1	7	
1985	7	9		4	4		3	5	
1986	9	7		5	3		4	4	
1987	8	7		5	3		3	4	
1988	11	5		7	1		4	4	
1989	10	6		8	0		2	6	
1990	6	10		4	4		2	6	
1991	8	8		4	4		4	4	
1992	11	5		5	3		6	2	
1993	9	7		4	4		5	3	
1994	10	6		6	2		4	4	
1995	8	8		6	2		2	6	
1996	9	7		5	3		4	4	
1997	9	7		5	3		4	4	
Total	298	243	9	168	104	4	130	139	5

NEW ORLEANS SAINTS

Season	All Games W	L	T	Home Games W	L	T	Road Games W	L	T
1967	3	11		2	5		1	6	
1968	4	9	1	3	4		1	5	1
1969	5	9		3	4		2	5	
1970	2	11	1	2	5		0	6	1
1971	4	8	2	2	4	1	2	4	1
1972	2	11	1	2	5		0	6	1
1973	5	9		5	2		0	7	
1974	5	9		4	3		1	6	
1975	2	12		2	5		0	7	
1976	4	10		2	5		2	5	
1977	3	11		2	5		1	6	
1978	7	9		3	5		4	4	
1979	8	8		3	5		5	3	
1980	1	15		0	8		1	7	
1981	4	12		2	6		2	6	
1982	4	5		2	3		2	2	
1983	8	8		5	3		3	5	
1984	7	9		3	5		4	4	
1985	5	11		3	5		2	6	
1986	7	9		4	4		3	5	
1987	12	3		6	1		6	2	
1988	10	6		5	3		5	3	
1989	9	7		5	3		4	4	
1990	8	8		5	3		3	5	
1991	11	5		6	2		5	3	
1992	12	4		6	2		6	2	
1993	8	8		4	4		4	4	
1994	7	9		3	5		4	4	
1995	7	9		4	4		3	5	
1996	3	13		2	6		1	7	
1997	6	10		3	5		3	5	
Total	183	278	5	103	129	1	80	149	4

NEW YORK GIANTS

Season	All Games W	L	T	Home Games W	L	T	Road Games W	L	T
1925	8	4		7	2		1	2	
1926	8	4	1	5	2	1	3	2	
1927	11	1	1	7	1		4	0	1
1928	4	7	2	1	2	2	3	5	
1929	13	1	1	7	1		6	0	1
1930	13	4		6	2		7	2	
1931	7	6	1	4	2	1	3	4	
1932	4	6	2	3	2	1	1	4	1
1933	11	3		7	0		4	3	
1934	8	5		5	1		3	4	
1935	9	3		4	2		5	1	
1936	5	6	1	3	3	1	2	3	
1937	6	3	2	4	2	1	2	1	1
1938	8	2	1	6	1		2	1	1
1939	9	1	1	6	0		3	1	1
1940	6	4	1	4	3		2	1	1
1941	8	3		5	2		3	1	
1942	5	5	1	3	2	1	2	3	
1943	6	3	1	4	2		2	1	1
1944	8	1	1	5	1		3	0	1
1945	3	6	1	2	4		1	2	1
1946	7	3	1	5	1	1	2	2	
1947	2	8	2	2	3	1	0	5	1
1948	4	8		2	4		2	4	
1949	6	6		2	4		4	2	
1950	10	2		5	1		5	1	
1951	9	2	1	5	1		4	1	1
1952	7	5		2	4		5	1	
1953	3	9		2	4		1	5	
1954	7	5		4	2		3	3	
1955	6	5	1	4	1	1	2	4	
1956	8	3	1	4	1	1	4	2	
1957	7	5		3	3		4	2	
1958	9	3		5	1		4	2	
1959	10	2		5	1		5	1	
1960	6	4	2	1	3	2	5	1	
1961	10	3	1	4	2	1	6	1	
1962	12	2		6	1		6	1	
1963	11	3		5	2		6	1	
1964	2	10	2	2	5		0	5	2
1965	7	7		3	4		4	3	
1966	1	12	1	1	6		0	6	1
1967	7	7		5	2		2	5	
1968	7	7		3	4		4	3	
1969	6	8		5	2		1	6	
1970	9	5		5	2		4	3	
1971	4	10		1	6		3	4	
1972	8	6		4	3		4	3	
1973	2	11	1	2	4	1	0	7	
1974	2	12		0	7		2	5	
1975	5	9		2	5		3	4	
1976	3	11		3	4		0	7	
1977	5	9		3	4		2	5	
1978	6	10		5	3		1	7	
1979	6	10		4	4		2	6	
1980	4	12		2	6		2	6	
1981	9	7		4	4		5	3	
1982	4	5		2	3		2	2	
1983	3	12	1	1	7		2	5	1
1984	9	7		6	2		3	5	
1985	10	6		6	2		4	4	
1986	14	2		8	0		6	2	
1987	6	9		5	3		1	6	
1988	10	6		5	3		5	3	
1989	12	4		7	1		5	3	
1990	13	3		7	1		6	2	
1991	8	8		5	3		3	5	
1992	6	10		4	4		2	6	
1993	11	5		6	2		5	3	
1994	9	7		4	4		5	3	
1995	5	11		3	5		2	6	
1996	6	10		3	5		3	5	
1997	10	5	1	6	2		4	3	1
Total	523	429	33	296	198	16	227	231	17

PHILADELPHIA EAGLES

Season	All Games W	L	T	Home Games W	L	T	Road Games W	L	T
1933	3	5	1	2	3	1	1	2	
1934	4	7		2	4		2	3	
1935	2	9		0	5		2	4	
1936	1	11		1	6		0	5	
1937	2	8	1	0	5	1	2	3	
1938	5	6		2	3		3	3	
1939	1	9	1	1	3	1	0	6	
1940	1	10		1	4		0	6	
1941	2	8	1	1	4	1	1	4	
1942	2	9		0	5		2	4	
1944	7	1	2	3	1	2	4	0	
1945	7	3		6	0		1	3	
1946	6	5		3	2		3	3	
1947	8	4		6	1		2	3	
1948	9	2	1	6	0		3	2	1
1949	11	1		6	0		5	1	
1950	6	6		2	4		4	2	
1951	4	8		1	5		3	3	
1952	7	5		4	2		3	3	
1953	7	4	1	5	0	1	2	4	
1954	7	4	1	5	1		2	3	1
1955	4	7	1	4	2		0	5	1
1956	3	8	1	2	3	1	1	5	
1957	4	8		3	3		1	5	
1958	2	9	1	2	4		0	5	1
1959	7	5		5	1		2	4	
1960	10	2		5	1		5	1	
1961	10	4		5	2		5	2	
1962	3	10	1	2	5		1	5	1
1963	2	10	2	1	5	1	1	5	1
1964	6	8		3	4		3	4	
1965	5	9		2	5		3	4	
1966	9	5		5	2		4	3	
1967	6	7	1	5	2		1	5	1
1968	2	12		1	6		1	6	
1969	4	9	1	2	5		2	4	1
1970	3	10	1	3	3	1	0	7	
1971	6	7	1	3	4		3	3	1

INSIDE THE NUMBERS

Season	All Games W	L	T	Home Games W	L	T	Road Games W	L	T
1972	2	11	1	0	6	1	2	5	
1973	5	8	1	4	3		1	5	1
1974	7	7		5	2		2	5	
1975	4	10		2	5		2	5	
1976	4	10		2	5		2	5	
1977	5	9		4	3		1	6	
1978	9	7		5	3		4	4	
1979	11	5		5	3		6	2	
1980	12	4		7	1		5	3	
1981	10	6		6	2		4	4	
1982	3	6		1	4		2	2	
1983	5	11		1	7		4	4	
1984	6	9	1	5	3		1	6	1
1985	7	9		4	4		3	5	
1986	5	10	1	2	5	1	3	5	
1987	7	8		4	4		3	4	
1988	10	6		5	3		5	3	
1989	11	5		6	2		5	3	
1990	10	6		6	2		4	4	
1991	10	6		4	4		6	2	
1992	11	5		8	0		3	5	
1993	8	8		3	5		5	3	
1994	7	9		5	3		2	6	
1995	10	6		6	2		4	4	
1996	10	6		5	3		5	3	
1997	6	9	1	6	2		0	7	1
Total	383	451	24	221	201	12	162	250	12

ST. LOUIS RAMS*

Season	All Games W	L	T	Home Games W	L	T	Road Games W	L	T
1937	1	10		0	5		1	5	
1938	4	7		2	2		2	5	
1939	5	5	1	3	2	1	2	3	
1940	4	6	1	3	1	1	1	5	
1941	2	9		1	4		1	5	
1942	5	6		3	2		2	4	
1944	4	6		1	2		3	4	
1945	9	1		4	0		5	1	
1946	6	4	1	3	2		3	2	1
1947	6	6		3	3		3	3	
1948	6	5	1	3	2	1	3	3	
1949	8	2	2	5	1		3	1	2
1950	9	3		5	1		4	2	
1951	8	4		5	2		3	2	
1952	9	3		5	1		4	2	
1953	8	3	1	5	1		3	2	1
1954	6	5	1	3	2	1	3	3	
1955	8	3	1	5	1		3	2	1
1956	4	8		4	2		0	6	
1957	6	6		5	1		1	5	
1958	8	4		4	2		4	2	
1959	2	10		0	6		2	4	
1960	4	7	1	2	3	1	2	4	
1961	4	10		4	3		0	7	
1962	1	12	1	0	7		1	5	1
1963	5	9		3	4		2	5	
1964	5	7	2	3	2	2	2	5	
1965	4	10		3	4		1	6	
1966	8	6		5	2		3	4	
1967	11	1	2	5	1	1	6	0	1
1968	10	3	1	5	2		5	1	1
1969	11	3		5	2		6	1	
1970	9	4	1	3	3	1	6	1	
1971	8	5	1	4	2	1	4	3	
1972	6	7	1	4	3		2	4	1
1973	12	2		7	0		5	2	
1974	10	4		6	1		4	3	
1975	12	2		6	1		6	1	
1976	10	3	1	5	2		5	1	1
1977	10	4		7	0		3	4	
1978	12	4		6	2		6	2	
1979	9	7		4	4		5	3	
1980	11	5		6	2		5	3	
1981	6	10		4	4		2	6	
1982	2	7		1	4		1	3	
1983	9	7		5	3		4	4	
1984	10	6		5	3		5	3	
1985	11	5		6	2		5	3	
1986	10	6		6	2		4	4	
1987	6	9		3	4		3	5	
1988	10	6		4	4		6	2	
1989	11	5		6	2		5	3	
1990	5	11		2	6		3	5	
1991	3	13		2	6		1	7	
1992	6	10		4	4		2	6	
1993	5	11		3	5		2	6	
1994	4	12		3	5		1	7	
1995	7	9		4	4		3	5	
1996	6	10		4	4		2	6	
1997	5	11		2	6		3	5	
Total	416	379	20	229	163	10	187	216	10

**includes Cleveland Rams (1937-42, 1944-45) and Los Angeles Rams (1946-94).*

SAN FRANCISCO 49ERS

Season	All Games W	L	T	Home Games W	L	T	Road Games W	L	T
1950	3	9		3	3		0	6	
1951	7	4	1	5	1		2	3	1
1952	7	5		3	3		4	2	
1953	9	3		5	1		4	2	
1954	7	4	1	4	2		3	2	1
1955	4	8		2	4		2	4	
1956	5	6	1	3	3		2	3	1
1957	8	4		5	1		3	3	
1958	6	6		4	2		2	4	
1959	7	5		4	2		3	3	
1960	7	5		3	3		4	2	
1961	7	6	1	5	1	1	2	5	
1962	6	8		1	6		5	2	
1963	2	12		2	5		0	7	
1964	4	10		3	4		1	6	
1965	7	6	1	4	2	1	3	4	
1966	6	6	2	4	2	1	2	4	1
1967	7	7		3	4		4	3	
1968	7	6	1	3	3	1	4	3	
1969	4	8	2	3	3	1	1	5	1
1970	10	3	1	5	1	1	5	2	
1971	9	5		4	3		5	2	
1972	8	5	1	4	2	1	4	3	
1973	5	9		3	4		2	5	
1974	6	8		3	4		3	4	
1975	5	9		2	5		3	4	
1976	8	6		4	3		4	3	
1977	5	9		3	4		2	5	
1978	2	14		2	6		0	8	
1979	2	14		2	6		0	8	
1980	6	10		4	4		2	6	
1981	13	3		7	1		6	2	
1982	3	6		0	5		3	1	
1983	10	6		4	4		6	2	
1984	15	1		7	1		8	0	
1985	10	6		5	3		5	3	
1986	10	5	1	6	2		4	3	1
1987	13	2		6	1		7	1	
1988	10	6		4	4		6	2	
1989	14	2		6	2		8	0	
1990	14	2		6	2		8	0	
1991	10	6		7	1		3	5	
1992	14	2		7	1		7	1	
1993	10	6		6	2		4	4	
1994	13	3		7	1		6	2	
1995	11	5		6	2		5	3	
1996	12	4		6	2		6	2	
1997	13	3		8	0		5	3	
Total	381	288	13	203	131	7	178	157	6

TAMPA BAY BUCCANEERS

Season	All Games W	L	T	Home Games W	L	T	Road Games W	L	T
1976	0	14		0	7		0	7	
1977	2	12		1	6		1	6	
1978	5	11		3	5		2	6	
1979	10	6		5	3		5	3	
1980	5	10	1	2	5	1	3	5	
1981	9	7		6	2		3	5	
1982	5	4		4	1		1	3	
1983	2	14		1	7		1	7	
1984	6	10		6	2		0	8	
1985	2	14		2	6		0	8	
1986	2	14		1	7		1	7	
1987	4	11		2	5		2	6	
1988	5	11		3	5		2	6	
1989	5	11		2	6		3	5	
1990	6	10		4	4		2	6	
1991	3	13		3	5		0	8	
1992	5	11		3	5		2	6	
1993	5	11		3	5		2	6	
1994	6	10		4	4		2	6	
1995	7	9		5	3		2	6	
1996	6	10		5	3		1	7	
1997	10	6		5	3		5	3	
Total	110	229	1	70	99	1	40	130	

WASHINGTON REDSKINS*

Season	All Games W	L	T	Home Games W	L	T	Road Games W	L	T
1932	4	4	2	2	3	1	2	1	1
1933	5	5	2	4	2		1	3	2
1934	6	6		4	3		2	3	
1935	2	8	1	2	5		0	3	1
1936	7	5		4	3		3	2	
1937	8	3		4	2		4	1	
1938	6	3	2	3	1	1	3	2	1
1939	8	2	1	5	0	1	3	2	
1940	9	2		6	0		3	2	
1941	6	5		4	2		2	3	
1942	10	1		5	1		5	0	
1943	6	3	1	4	2		2	1	1
1944	6	3	1	4	2		2	1	1
1945	8	2		6	0		2	2	
1946	5	5	1	3	2	1	2	3	
1947	4	8		4	2		0	6	
1948	7	5		4	2		3	3	
1949	4	7	1	3	3		1	4	1
1950	3	9		1	5		2	4	
1951	5	7		2	4		3	3	
1952	4	8		1	5		3	3	
1953	6	5	1	3	3		3	2	1
1954	3	9		3	3		0	6	
1955	8	4		3	3		5	1	
1956	6	6		4	2		2	4	
1957	5	6	1	2	3	1	3	3	
1958	4	7	1	3	2	1	1	5	
1959	3	9		2	4		1	5	
1960	1	9	2	1	4	1	0	5	1
1961	1	12	1	1	6		0	6	1
1962	5	7	2	3	4		2	3	2
1963	3	11		1	6		2	5	
1964	6	8		4	3		2	5	
1965	6	8		3	4		3	4	
1966	7	7		4	3		3	4	
1967	5	6	3	2	4	1	3	2	2
1968	5	9		3	4		2	5	
1969	7	5	2	4	2	1	3	3	1
1970	6	8		4	3		2	5	
1971	9	4	1	4	2	1	5	2	
1972	11	3		6	1		5	2	
1973	10	4		7	0		3	4	
1974	10	4		6	1		4	3	
1975	8	6		5	2		3	4	
1976	10	4		5	2		5	2	
1977	9	5		5	2		4	3	
1978	8	8		5	3		3	5	
1979	10	6		6	2		4	4	
1980	6	10		4	4		2	6	
1981	8	8		5	3		3	5	
1982	8	1		3	1		5	0	
1983	14	2		7	1		7	1	
1984	11	5		7	1		4	4	
1985	10	6		5	3		5	3	
1986	12	4		7	1		5	3	
1987	11	4		6	1		5	3	
1988	7	9		4	4		3	5	
1989	10	6		4	4		6	2	
1990	10	6		7	1		3	5	
1991	14	2		7	1		7	1	
1992	9	7		6	2		3	5	
1993	4	12		3	5		1	7	
1994	3	13		0	8		3	5	
1995	6	10		4	4		2	6	
1996	9	7		5	3		4	4	
1997	8	7	1	5	2	1	3	5	
Total	455	400	27	263	176	11	192	224	16

**includes Boston Braves (1932) and Boston Redskins (1933-36).*

History

PRO FOOTBALL HALL OF FAME

The Professional Football Hall of Fame is located in Canton, Ohio, site of the organizational meeting on September 17, 1920, from which the National Football League evolved. The NFL recognized Canton as the Hall of Fame site on April 27, 1961. Canton area individuals, foundations, and companies donated almost $400,000 in cash and services to provide funds for the construction of the original two-building complex, which was dedicated on September 7, 1963. Since that time, the Hall added three buildings with major expansion projects in 1971, 1978, and 1995. The Hall's largest-ever expansion, a $9.2 million project, was completed in early fall 1995. With the new fifth building, the Hall's size is now 82,307-square feet, more than four times its original size.

The expanded Hall represents the sport of pro football in many ways—through (1) GameDay Stadium, a dynamic two-part turntable theater featuring NFL action in Cinemascope for the first time, (2) a standard theater showing NFL films hourly, (3) six large exhibition areas where the history of pro football is detailed in memento, picture, and story form, (4) an extensive library and research center, and (5) a new and enlarged museum store.

In recent years, the Pro Football Hall of Fame has become an extremely popular tourist attraction. At the end of 1997, a total of 6,316,549 fans had visited the Hall of Fame.

New members of the Pro Football Hall of Fame are elected annually by a 36-member National Board of Selectors, made up of media representatives from every league city, five at-large representatives, and a representative of the Pro Football Writers of America. Between four and seven new members are elected each year. An affirmative vote of approximately 80 percent is needed for election.

Any fan may nominate any eligible player or contributor simply by writing to the Pro Football Hall of Fame. Players must be retired five years to be eligible, while a coach need only to be retired with no time limit specified. Contributors (administrators, owners, *et al.*) may be elected while they are still active.

The charter class of 17 enshrinees was elected in 1963 and the honor roll now stands at 194 with the election of a five-man class in 1998. That class consists of Paul Krause, Tommy McDonald, Anthony Muñoz, Mike Singletary, and Dwight Stephenson.

ROSTER OF MEMBERS

HERB ADDERLEY
Defensive back. 6-1, 200. Born in Philadelphia, Pennsylvania, June 8, 1939. Michigan State. Inducted in 1980. 1961-69 Green Bay Packers, 1970-72 Dallas Cowboys. **Highlights:** 48 interceptions, 7 touchdowns. Played in four Super Bowls, five Pro Bowls.

LANCE ALWORTH
Wide receiver. 6-0, 184. Born in Houston, Texas, August 3, 1940. Arkansas. Inducted in 1978. 1962-70 San Diego Chargers, 1971-72 Dallas Cowboys. **Highlights:** 542 receptions for 10,266 yards, 85 touchdowns. All-AFL seven times, seven All-Star games.

DOUG ATKINS
Defensive end. 6-8, 275. Born in Humboldt, Tennessee, May 8, 1930. Tennessee. Inducted in 1982. 1953-54 Cleveland Browns, 1955-66 Chicago Bears, 1967-69 New Orleans Saints. **Highlights:** Eight Pro Bowls, All-NFL three times. Played for 17 years, 205 games.

MORRIS (RED) BADGRO
End. 6-0, 190. Born in Orilla, Washington, December 1, 1902. Southern California. Inducted in 1981. 1927 New York Yankees, 1930-35 New York Giants, 1936 Brooklyn Dodgers. **Highlights:** All-NFL four times. Scored first touchdown in NFL championship game series.

LEM BARNEY
Cornerback. 6-0, 190. Born in Gulfport, Mississippi, September 8, 1945. Jackson State. Inducted in 1992. 1967-77 Detroit Lions. **Highlights:** 56 interceptions for 1,077 yards, 11 touchdowns (7 defensive, 4 special teams). Seven Pro Bowls, All-NFL/NFC three times.

CLIFF BATTLES
Halfback. 6-1, 201. Born in Akron, Ohio, May 1, 1910. Died April 28, 1981. West Virginia Wesleyan. Inducted in 1968. 1932 Boston Braves, 1933-36 Boston Redskins, 1937 Washington Redskins. **Highlights:** NFL rushing champion 1932, 1937. First to gain more than 200 yards in a game, 1933.

SAMMY BAUGH
Quarterback. 6-2, 180. Born in Temple, Texas, March 17, 1914. Texas Christian. Inducted in 1963. 1937-52 Washington Redskins. **Highlights:** Charter enshrinee. Six-time NFL passing leader. NFL passing, punting, interception champ, 1943.

CHUCK BEDNARIK
Center-linebacker. 6-3, 230. Born in Bethlehem, Pennsylvania, May 1, 1925. Pennsylvania. Inducted in 1967. 1949-62 Philadelphia Eagles. **Highlights:** Eight Pro Bowls. Missed three games in 14 years. Named NFL all-time center, 1969.

BERT BELL
Team owner. Commissioner. Born in Philadelphia, Pennsylvania, February 25, 1895. Died October 11, 1959. Pennsylvania. Inducted in 1963. 1933-40 Philadelphia Eagles, 1941-42 Pittsburgh Steelers, 1943 Phil-Pitt, 1944 Card-Pitt, 1945-46 Pittsburgh Steelers. Commissioner, 1946-59. **Highlights:** Charter enshrinee. Built NFL image as commissioner, 1946-1959. Set up long-term television policies.

BOBBY BELL
Linebacker. 6-4, 225. Born in Shelby, North Carolina, June 17, 1940. Minnesota. Inducted in 1983. 1963-74 Kansas City Chiefs. **Highlights:** 25 interceptions. All-AFL/AFC nine times. Eight career touchdowns, 1 on onside kick return.

RAYMOND BERRY
End. 6-2, 187. Born in Corpus Christi, Texas, February 27, 1933. Southern Methodist. Inducted in 1973. 1955-67 Baltimore Colts. **Highlights:** 631 receptions for 9,275 yards, 68 touchdowns. Set NFL title game mark with 12 catches for 178 yards, 1958.

CHARLES W. BIDWILL, SR.
Team owner. Born in Chicago, Illinois, September 16, 1895. Died April 19, 1947. Loyola of Chicago. Inducted in 1967. 1933-43 Chicago Cardinals, 1944 Card-Pitt, 1945-47 Chicago Cardinals. **Highlights:** Guiding light for NFL during depression years. Built famous "Dream Backfield."

FRED BILETNIKOFF
Wide receiver. 6-1, 190. Born in Erie, Pennsylvania, February 23, 1943. Florida State. Inducted in 1988. 1965-78 Oakland Raiders. **Highlights:** 589 receptions for 8,974 yards, 76 touchdowns. 40 catches 10 straight years. MVP, Super Bowl XI.

GEORGE BLANDA
Quarterback-kicker. 6-2, 215. Born in Youngwood, Pennsylvania, September 17, 1927. Kentucky. Inducted in 1981. 1949-58 Chicago Bears, 1950 Baltimore Colts, 1960-66 Houston Oilers, 1967-75 Oakland Raiders. **Highlights:** Record 2,002 career points. 26-season, 340-game career longest in NFL history.

MEL BLOUNT
Cornerback. 6-3, 205. Born in Vidalia, Georgia, April 10, 1948. Southern University. Inducted in 1989. 1970-83 Pittsburgh Steelers. **Highlights:** 57 interceptions for 736 yards. NFL defensive MVP, 1975. Played in five Pro Bowls.

TERRY BRADSHAW
Quarterback. 6-3, 210. Born in Shreveport, Louisiana, September 2, 1948. Louisiana Tech. Inducted in 1989. 1970-83 Pittsburgh Steelers. **Highlights:** 27,989 yards passing, 212 touchdowns. MVP in Super Bowls XIII, XIV.

JIM BROWN
Fullback. 6-2, 228. Born in St. Simons, Georgia, February 17, 1936. Syracuse. Inducted in 1971. 1957-65 Cleveland Browns. **Highlights:** 12,312 yards rushing, 756 points. Led NFL rushers eight years. Nine consecutive Pro Bowls.

PAUL BROWN
Coach. Born in Norwalk, Ohio, September 7, 1908. Died August 5, 1991. Miami (Ohio). Inducted in 1967. 1946-49 Cleveland Browns (AAFC), 1950-62 Cleveland Browns. **Highlights:** Built Cleveland dynasty with 167-53-8 record, four AAFC titles, three NFL crowns. Returned to coaching with Cincinnati Bengals after induction, 1968-1975.

ROOSEVELT BROWN
Tackle. 6-3, 255. Born in Charlottesville, Virginia, October 20, 1932. Morgan State. Inducted in 1975. 1953-65 New York Giants. **Highlights:** All-NFL eight consecutive years, nine Pro Bowls. NFL's Lineman of Year, 1956.

WILLIE BROWN
Cornerback. 6-1, 210. Born in Yazoo City, Mississippi, December 2, 1940. Grambling. Inducted in 1984. 1963-66 Denver Broncos, 1967-78 Oakland Raiders. **Highlights:** 54 interceptions for 472 yards. Scored on 75-yard interception in Super Bowl XI.

BUCK BUCHANAN
Defensive tackle. 6-7, 274. Born in Gainesville, Alabama, September 10, 1940. Died July 16, 1992. Grambling. Inducted in 1990. 1963-75 Kansas City Chiefs. **Highlights:** Led Chiefs defensive efforts in Super Bowl I, IV. Missed one game in 13 years.

DICK BUTKUS
Linebacker. 6-3, 245. Born in Chicago, Illinois, December 9, 1942. Illinois. Inducted in 1979. 1965-73 Chicago Bears. **Highlights:** All-NFL seven years, eight consecutive Pro Bowls. 25 fumble recoveries.

EARL CAMPBELL
Running back. 5-11, 233. Born in Tyler, Texas, March 29, 1955. Texas. Inducted in 1991. 1978-84 Houston Oilers, 1984-85 New Orleans Saints. **Highlights:** 9,407 yards rushing, 74 touchdowns. 1,934 yards rushing in 1980, including four games with at least 200 yards.

TONY CANADEO
Halfback. 5-11, 195. Born in Chicago, Illinois, May 5, 1919. Gonzaga. Inducted in 1974. 1941-44, 1946-52 Green Bay Packers. **Highlights:** Two-way player. Third player to rush for 1,000 yards in single season, 1949.

JOE CARR
NFL president. Born in Columbus, Ohio, October 22, 1880. Died May 20, 1939. Did not attend college. Inducted in 1963. President, 1921-39 National Football League. **Highlights:** Charter enshrinee. NFL co-organizer, 1920. Introduced standard player's contract.

GUY CHAMBERLIN
End. Coach. 6-2, 210. Born in Blue Springs, Nebraska, January 16, 1894. Died April 4, 1967. Nebraska. Inducted in 1965. 1919 Canton Bulldogs, 1920 Decatur Staleys, 1921 Chicago Staleys, player-coach 1922-23 Canton Bulldogs, 1924 Cleveland Bulldogs, 1925-26 Frankford Yellow Jackets, 1927-28 Chicago Cardinals. **Highlights:** Player-coach of four NFL championship teams. Six-year coaching record 56-14-5.

JACK CHRISTIANSEN
Safety. 6-1, 185. Born in Sublette, Kansas, December 20, 1928. Died June 29, 1986. Colorado State. Inducted in 1970. 1951-58 Detroit Lions. **Highlights:** 46 interceptions. NFL interception leader, 1953, 1957. NFL record 8 punt returns for touchdowns.

EARL (DUTCH) CLARK
Quarterback. 6-0, 185. Born in Fowler, Colorado, October 11, 1906. Died August 5, 1978. Colorado College.

Inducted in 1963. 1931-32 Portsmouth Spartans, 1934-38 Detroit Lions. **Highlights:** Charter enshrinee. NFL scoring champion three years. Led Lions to 1935 NFL title.

GEORGE CONNOR
Tackle-linebacker. 6-3, 240. Born in Chicago, Illinois, January 21, 1925. Holy Cross, Notre Dame. Inducted in 1975. 1948-55 Chicago Bears. **Highlights:** All-NFL at three positions—T, DT, LB. All-NFL five years. Played in first four Pro Bowls.

JIMMY CONZELMAN
Quarterback. Coach. Team owner. 6-0, 180. Born in St. Louis, Missouri, March 6, 1898. Died July 31, 1970. Washington of St. Louis. Inducted in 1964. 1920 Decatur Staleys, 1921-22 Rock Island Independents, 1923-24 Milwaukee Badgers; owner-coach 1925-26 Detroit Panthers; player-coach 1927-29, coach 1930 Providence Steam Roller; coach 1940-42, 1946-48 Chicago Cardinals. **Highlights:** Player-coach of four NFL teams in 1920's. Coached Cardinals to 1947 NFL crown.

LOU CREEKMUR
Tackle-guard. 6-4, 255. Born in Hopelawn, New Jersey. January 22, 1927. William & Mary. Inducted in 1996. 1950-59 Detroit Lions. **Highlights:** All-NFL six times, twice at guard and four times at tackle. Selected to eight Pro Bowls and played on three NFL Championship teams.

LARRY CSONKA
Running back. 6-3, 235. Born in Stow, Ohio, December 25, 1946. Syracuse. Inducted in 1987. 1968-74, 1979 Miami Dolphins, 1976-78 New York Giants. **Highlights:** 8,081 yards rushing, 68 touchdowns. MVP Super Bowl VIII. Only 21 fumbles in 1,997 carries.

AL DAVIS
Team, League Administrator. Born in Brockton, Massachusetts, July 4, 1929. Wittenberg, Syracuse. Inducted in 1992. 1963-81, 1995-present Oakland Raiders, 1982-94 Los Angeles Raiders, 1966 American Football League. **Highlights:** Only person to serve in pros as personnel assistant, scout, assistant coach, head coach, general manager, commissioner, team owner/CEO.

WILLIE DAVIS
Defensive end. 6-3, 245. Born in Lisbon, Louisiana, July 24, 1934. Grambling. Inducted in 1981. 1958-59 Cleveland Browns, 1960-69 Green Bay Packers. **Highlights:** All-NFL five seasons, five Pro Bowls. Did not miss game in 12-year career.

LEN DAWSON
Quarterback. 6-0, 190. Born in Alliance, Ohio, June 20, 1935. Purdue. Inducted in 1987. 1957-59 Pittsburgh Steelers, 1960-61 Cleveland Browns, 1962 Dallas Texans, 1963-75 Kansas City Chiefs. **Highlights:** 28,711 yards passing, 239 touchdowns. Four AFL passing crowns. MVP, Super Bowl IV.

DAN DIERDORF
Tackle. 6-3, 290. Born in Canton, Ohio, June 29, 1949. Michigan. Inducted in 1996. 1971-83 St. Louis Cardinals. **Highlights:** All-Pro five times, played in six Pro Bowls, named NFL's best blocker three times.

MIKE DITKA
Tight end. 6-3, 225. Born in Carnegie, Pennsylvania, October 18, 1939. Pittsburgh. Inducted in 1988. 1961-66 Chicago Bears, 1967-68 Philadelphia Eagles, 1969-72 Dallas Cowboys. **Highlights:** 427 receptions for 5,812 yards, 43 touchdowns. First tight end selected to Hall of Fame. Five consecutive Pro Bowls.

ART DONOVAN
Defensive tackle. 6-3, 265. Born in Bronx, New York, June 5, 1925. Boston College. Inducted in 1968. 1950 Baltimore Colts, 1951 New York Yanks, 1952 Dallas Texans, 1953-61 Baltimore Colts. **Highlights:** Five Pro Bowls. Vital part of Baltimore's climb to powerhouse status in 1950s.

TONY DORSETT
Running back. 5-11, 184. Born in Rochester, Pennsylvania, April 7, 1954. Pittsburgh. Inducted in 1994. 1977-87 Dallas Cowboys, 1988 Denver Broncos. **Highlights:** 12,739 yards rushing, 398 receptions, 90 touchdowns. Ran record 99 yards for touchdown vs. Minnesota, January, 1983.

JOHN (PADDY) DRISCOLL
Quarterback. 5-11, 160. Born in Evanston, Illinois, January 11, 1896. Died June 29, 1968. Northwestern. Inducted in 1965. 1919 Hammond Pros, 1920 Decatur Staleys, 1920-25 Chicago Cardinals, 1926-29 Chicago Bears. **Highlights:** All-NFL six times. Dropkicked record 4 field goals in one game, 1925.

BILL DUDLEY
Halfback. 5-10, 176. Born in Bluefield, Virginia, December 24, 1921. Virginia. Inducted in 1966. 1942, 1945-46 Pittsburgh Steelers, 1947-49 Detroit Lions, 1950-51, 1953 Washington Redskins. **Highlights:** Won NFL rushing, interception, punt return titles, 1946. All-NFL 1942, 1946.

ALBERT GLEN (TURK) EDWARDS
Tackle. 6-2, 260. Born in Mold, Washington, September 28, 1907. Died January 12, 1973. Washington State. Inducted in 1969. 1932 Boston Braves, 1933-36 Boston Redskins, 1937-40 Washington Redskins. **Highlights:** All-NFL 1932-33, 1936, 1937. Steamrolling blocker, smothering tackler.

WEEB EWBANK
Coach. Born in Richmond, Indiana, May 6, 1907. Miami (Ohio). Inducted in 1978. 1954-62 Baltimore Colts, 1963-73 New York Jets. **Highlights:** Only coach to win championships in both NFL, AFL. Led both Colts (1958) and Jets (1968) to championships.

TOM FEARS
End. 6-2, 215. Born in Los Angeles, California, December 3, 1923. Santa Clara, UCLA. Inducted in 1970. 1948-56 Los Angeles Rams. **Highlights:** 400 receptions for 5,397 yards, 38 touchdowns. Led NFL receivers first three seasons. Record 18 receptions in single game.

JIM FINKS
Administrator. Born in St. Louis, Missouri, August 31, 1927. Died May 8, 1994. Tulsa. Inducted 1995. 1964-73 Minnesota Vikings, 1974-82 Chicago Bears, 1986-93 New Orleans Saints. **Highlights:** Developed Vikings, Bears, Saints—all teams with losing records—into winners.

RAY FLAHERTY
Coach. Born in Spokane, Washington, September 1, 1903. Died July 19, 1994. Gonzaga. Inducted in 1976. 1936 Boston Redskins, 1937-42 Washington Redskins, 1946-48 New York Yankees (AAFC), 1949 Chicago Hornets (AAFC). **Highlights:** 80-37-5 coaching record. Introduced screen pass in 1937 title game and platoon system.

LEN FORD
Defensive end. 6-5, 260. Born in Washington, D.C., February 18, 1926. Died March 14, 1972. Morgan State, Michigan. Inducted in 1976. 1948-49 Los Angeles Dons (AAFC), 1950-57 Cleveland Browns, 1958 Green Bay Packers. **Highlights:** All-NFL five times, four Pro Bowls. Recovered 20 opponent's fumbles.

DAN FORTMANN
Guard. 6-0, 210. Born in Pearl River, New York, April 11, 1916. Died May 24, 1995. Colgate. Inducted in 1965. 1936-43 Chicago Bears. **Highlights:** At 20, became youngest starter in NFL. All-NFL six consecutive years.

DAN FOUTS
Quarterback. 6-3, 210. Born in San Francisco, California, June 10, 1951. Oregon. Inducted in 1993. 1973-1987 San Diego Chargers. **Highlights:** 43,040 passing yards, 254 touchdowns. Six Pro Bowls, NFL MVP, 1982.

FRANK GATSKI
Center. 6-3, 240. Born in Farmington, West Virginia, March 18, 1922. Marshall, Auburn. Inducted in 1985. 1946-49 Cleveland Browns (AAFC), 1950-56 Cleveland Browns, 1957 Detroit Lions. **Highlights:** Never missed game in high school, college, or pro football. Played 11 championship games, winning eight.

BILL GEORGE
Linebacker. 6-2, 230. Born in Waynesburg, Pennsylvania, October 27, 1930. Died September 30, 1982. Wake Forest. Inducted in 1974. 1952-65 Chicago Bears, 1966 Los Angeles Rams. **Highlights:** All-NFL eight years, eight consecutive Pro Bowls. 14 years of service, longest of any Bears player.

JOE GIBBS
Coach. Born in Mocksville, North Carolina, November 25, 1940. Cerritos (Calif.) J.C., San Diego State. Inducted in 1996. 1981-92 Washington Redskins. **Highlights:** 124-60-0 record in regular season, 16-5 in postseason, including four Super Bowl appearances—winning three. Won 10 or more games eight times.

FRANK GIFFORD
Halfback. 6-1, 195. Born in Santa Monica, California, August 16, 1930. Southern California. Inducted in 1977. 1952-60, 1962-64 New York Giants. **Highlights:** Starred on both offense and defense. Seven Pro Bowls, 1956 NFL Player of the Year.

SID GILLMAN
Coach. Born in Minneapolis, Minnesota, October 26, 1911. Ohio State. Inducted in 1983. 1955-59 Los Angeles Rams, 1960 Los Angeles Chargers, 1961-69, 1971 San Diego Chargers, 1973-74 Houston Oilers. **Highlights:** 123-104-7 coaching record. First to win division titles in both NFL, AFL.

OTTO GRAHAM
Quarterback. 6-1, 195. Born in Waukegan, Illinois, December 6, 1921. Northwestern. Inducted in 1965. 1946-49 Cleveland Browns (AAFC), 1950-55 Cleveland Browns. **Highlights:** 23,584 passing yards, 174 touchdowns. Guided Browns to 10 division or league crowns in 10 years.

HAROLD (RED) GRANGE
Halfback. 6-0, 185. Born in Forksville, Pennsylvania, June 13, 1903. Died January 28, 1991. Illinois. Inducted in 1963. 1925 Chicago Bears, 1926 New York Yankees (AFL), 1927 New York Yankees, 1929-34 Chicago Bears. **Highlights:** Nicknamed "Galloping Ghost." Name produced first huge pro football crowds.

BUD GRANT
Coach. Born in Superior, Wisconsin, May 20, 1927. Minnesota. Inducted in 1994. 1967-83, 1985 Minnesota Vikings. **Highlights:** 168-108-5 coaching record. Led Vikings to 11 division championships, four Super Bowls.

JOE GREENE
Defensive tackle. 6-4, 260. Born in Temple, Texas, September 24, 1946. North Texas State. Inducted in 1987. 1969-81 Pittsburgh Steelers. **Highlights:** NFL Defensive Player of the Year, 1972, 1974. Four-time Super Bowl champion, 10 Pro Bowls.

FORREST GREGG
Tackle. 6-4, 250. Born in Birthright, Texas, October 18, 1933. Southern Methodist. Inducted in 1977. 1956, 1958-70 Green Bay Packers, 1971 Dallas Cowboys. **Highlights:** Played 188 consecutive games. Nine Pro Bowls. Played on seven NFL championship teams, three Super Bowl winners.

BOB GRIESE
Quarterback. 6-1, 190. Born in Evansville, Indiana, February 3, 1945. Purdue. Inducted in 1990. 1967-80 Miami Dolphins. **Highlights:** 25,092 passing yards, 192 touchdowns. Led Miami to three AFC titles, Super Bowl VII, VIII wins.

LOU GROZA
Tackle-kicker. 6-3, 250. Born in Martins Ferry, Ohio, January 25, 1924.

Ohio State. Inducted in 1974. 1946-49 Cleveland Browns (AAFC), 1950-59, 1961-67 Cleveland Browns. **Highlights:** 1,608 points in 21 years. Nine Pro Bowls, All-NFL six years. NFL Player of the Year, 1954.

JOE GUYON
Halfback. 6-1, 180. Born on White Earth Indian Reservation, Minnesota, November 26, 1892. Died November 27, 1971. Carlisle, Georgia Tech. Inducted in 1966. 1919-20 Canton Bulldogs, 1921 Cleveland Indians, 1922-23 Oorang Indians, 1924 Rock Island Independents, 1924-25 Kansas City Cowboys, 1927 New York Giants. **Highlights:** Touchdown pass gave Giants victory over Bears to win 1927 Championship.

GEORGE HALAS
End. Coach. Team owner. Born in Chicago, Illinois, February 2, 1895. Died October 31, 1983. Illinois. Inducted in 1963. Player-coach 1920 Decatur Staleys, 1921 Chicago Staleys, 1922-29 Chicago Bears; coach 1933-42, 1946-55, 1958-67 Chicago Bears. **Highlights:** Charter enshrinee. 324 coaching wins. Only person associated with NFL throughout first 50 years. Coached Bears 40 seasons, won seven NFL titles.

JACK HAM
Linebacker. 6-1, 225. Born in Johnstown, Pennsylvania, December 23, 1948. Penn State. Inducted in 1988. 1971-82 Pittsburgh Steelers. **Highlights:** Won four Super Bowls, 21 opponent's fumbles recovered, 32 interceptions. Eight consecutive Pro Bowls.

JOHN HANNAH
Guard. 6-3, 265. Born in Canton, Georgia, April 4, 1951. Alabama. Inducted in 1991. 1973-85 New England Patriots. **Highlights:** Renowned as premier guard of era. All-Pro 10 years, eight Pro Bowls.

FRANCO HARRIS
Running back. 6-2, 225. Born in Fort Dix, New Jersey, March 7, 1950. Penn State. Inducted in 1990. 1972-83 Pittsburgh Steelers, 1984 Seattle Seahawks. **Highlights:** 12,120 rushing yards, 100 total touchdowns. 1,556 rushing yards in 19 postseason games. MVP in Super Bowl IX.

MIKE HAYNES
Cornerback. 6-2, 195. Born in Denison, Texas, July 1, 1953. Arizona State. Inducted in 1997. 1976-82 New England Patriots, 1983-89 Los Angeles Raiders. **Highlights:** Defensive Rookie of the Year. Selected to nine Pro Bowls and intercepted 46 passes, plus one pick in Super Bowl XVIII.

ED HEALEY
Tackle. 6-3, 220. Born in Indian Orchard, Massachusetts, December 28, 1894. Died December 9, 1978. Dartmouth. Inducted in 1964. 1920-22 Rock Island Independents, 1922-27 Chicago Bears. **Highlights:** Two-way star. Perennial all-pro with Bears.

MEL HEIN
Center. 6-2, 225. Born in Redding, California, August 22, 1909. Died January 31, 1992. Washington State. Inducted in 1963. 1931-45 New York Giants. **Highlights:** Charter enshrinee. 60-minute regular for 15 years. All-NFL eight consecutive years.

TED HENDRICKS
Linebacker. 6-7, 235. Born in Guatemala City, Guatemala, November 1, 1947. Miami. Inducted in 1990. 1969-73 Baltimore Colts, 1974 Green Bay Packers, 1975-81 Oakland Raiders, 1982-83 Los Angeles Raiders. **Highlights:** 25 blocked field goals or extra points, 26 interceptions. Played in 215 consecutive games.

WILBUR (PETE) HENRY
Tackle. 6-0, 250. Born in Mansfield, Ohio, October 31, 1897. Died February 7, 1952. Washington & Jefferson. Inducted in 1963. 1920-23, 1925-26 Canton Bulldogs, 1927 New York Giants, 1927-28 Pottsville Maroons. **Highlights:** Largest player of his time at 250 pounds. Bulwark of Canton's championship lines.

ARNIE HERBER
Quarterback. 6-0, 200. Born in Green Bay, Wisconsin, April 2, 1910. Died October 14, 1969. Wisconsin, Regis College. Inducted in 1966. 1930-40 Green Bay Packers, 1944-45 New York Giants. **Highlights:** NFL passing leader 1932, 1934, 1936. Came out of retirement to lead 1944 Giants to NFL Eastern crown.

BILL HEWITT
End. 5-11, 191. Born in Bay City, Michigan, October 8, 1909. Died January 14, 1947. Michigan. Inducted in 1971. 1932-36 Chicago Bears, 1937-39 Philadelphia Eagles, 1943 Phil-Pitt. **Highlights:** First to be named all-NFL with two teams—1933, 1934, 1936 Bears; 1937 Eagles.

CLARKE HINKLE
Fullback. 5-11, 201. Born in Toronto, Ohio, April 10, 1909. Died November 9, 1988. Bucknell. Inducted in 1964. 1932-41 Green Bay Packers. **Highlights:** 3,860 yards rushing, 373 points, 43.4 punting average. Fullback on offense, linebacker on defense.

ELROY (CRAZYLEGS) HIRSCH
Halfback-end. 6-2, 190. Born in Wausau, Wisconsin, June 17, 1923. Wisconsin, Michigan. Inducted in 1968. 1946-48 Chicago Rockets (AAFC), 1949-57 Los Angeles Rams. **Highlights:** 387 receptions for 7,029 yards, 60 touchdowns. Key part of Rams' revolutionary "three end" offense, 1949.

PAUL HORNUNG
Halfback. 6-2, 220. Born in Louisville, Kentucky, December 23, 1935. Notre Dame. Inducted in 1986. 1957-62, 1964-66 Green Bay Packers. **Highlights:** 760 points. Led NFL scorers three years, including record 176 points, 1960. Record 19 points scored in 1961 NFL title game.

KEN HOUSTON
Safety. 6-3, 198. Born in Lufkin, Texas, November 12, 1944. Prairie View A&M. Inducted in 1986. 1967-72 Houston Oilers, 1973-80 Washington Redskins. **Highlights:** 49 interceptions, 898 yards, 9 touchdowns. NFL's premier strong safety of 1970s. 10 Pro Bowls.

ROBERT (CAL) HUBBARD
Tackle. 6-5, 250. Born in Keytesville, Missouri, October 31, 1900. Died October 17, 1977. Centenary, Geneva. Inducted in 1963. 1927-28 New York Giants, 1929-33, 1935 Green Bay Packers, 1936 New York Giants, 1936 Pittsburgh Pirates. **Highlights:** Charter enshrinee. Most feared lineman of his time. All-NFL six years, 1928-33.

SAM HUFF
Linebacker. 6-1, 230. Born in Morgantown, West Virginia, October 4, 1934. West Virginia. Inducted in 1982. 1956-63 New York Giants, 1964-67, 1969 Washington Redskins. **Highlights:** 30 interceptions. Played in six NFL title games, five Pro Bowls. Redskins player-coach, 1969.

LAMAR HUNT
Team owner. Born in El Dorado, Arkansas, August 2, 1932. Southern Methodist. Inducted in 1972. 1960-62 Dallas Texans, 1963-present Kansas City Chiefs. **Highlights:** Driving force behind organization of AFL. Spearheaded merger negotiations with NFL, 1966.

DON HUTSON
End. 6-1, 180. Born in Pine Bluff, Arkansas, January 31, 1913. Died June 26, 1997. Alabama. Inducted in 1963. 1935-45 Green Bay Packers. **Highlights:** 488 receptions for 7,991 yards, 99 touchdowns. NFL receiving champion eight years. NFL MVP, 1941, 1942.

JIMMY JOHNSON
Cornerback. 6-2, 187. Born in Dallas, Texas, March 31, 1938. UCLA. Inducted in 1994. 1961-76 San Francisco 49ers. **Highlights:** 47 interceptions for 615 yards. Five Pro Bowls. Opposing passers avoided throwing in his area.

JOHN HENRY JOHNSON
Fullback. 6-2, 225. Born in Waterproof, Louisiana, November 24, 1929. St. Mary's, Arizona State. Inducted in 1987. 1954-56 San Francisco 49ers, 1957-59 Detroit Lions, 1960-65 Pittsburgh Steelers, 1966 Houston Oilers. **Highlights:** 6,803 yards rushing, 48 touchdowns. Member of San Francisco's "Fabulous Foursome" backfield.

CHARLIE JOINER
Wide receiver. 5-11, 180. Born in Many, Louisiana, October 14, 1947. Grambling. Inducted in 1996. 1969-72 Houston Oilers, 1972-75 Cincinnati Bengals, 1976-86 San Diego Chargers. **Highlights:** 750 receptions for 12,146 yards and 65 touchdowns. Played 18 seasons, 239 games, most ever for wide receiver.

DAVID (DEACON) JONES
Defensive end. 6-5, 260. Born in Eatonville, Florida, December 9, 1938. South Carolina State, Mississippi Vocational. Inducted in 1980. 1961-71 Los Angeles Rams, 1972-73 San Diego Chargers, 1974 Washington Redskins. **Highlights:** Specialized in quarterback 'sacks,' a name he invented. Unanimous all-league six consecutive years.

STAN JONES
Guard-defensive tackle. 6-1, 250. Born in Altoona, Pennsylvania, November 24, 1931. Maryland. Inducted in 1991. 1954-65 Chicago Bears, 1966 Washington Redskins. **Highlights:** Seven consecutive Pro Bowls. First to rely on weightlifting for football preparation.

HENRY JORDAN
Defensive tackle, 6-3, 240. Born in Emporia, Virginia, January 26, 1935. Died February 21, 1977. Virginia. Inducted in 1995. 1957-58 Cleveland Browns, 1959-69 Green Bay Packers. **Highlights:** 11-year fixture at DT. Played in four Pro Bowls, seven NFL title games, Super Bowls I, II.

SONNY JURGENSEN
Quarterback. 6-0, 203. Born in Wilmington, North Carolina, August 23, 1934. Duke. Inducted in 1983. 1957-63 Philadelphia Eagles, 1964-74 Washington Redskins. **Highlights:** 32,224 yards passing, 255 touchdowns, 82.63 passer rating. Surpassed 3,000 yards passing in five seasons.

LEROY KELLY
Running back. 6-0, 205. Born in Philadelphia, Pennsylvania, May 20, 1942. Morgan State. Inducted in 1994. 1964-73 Cleveland Browns. **Highlights:** 7,274 yards rushing, 90 total touchdowns, 1,000-yard rusher first three years as regular starter. Two-time punt return champion.

WALT KIESLING
Guard. Coach. 6-2, 245. Born in St. Paul, Minnesota, March 27, 1903. Died March 2, 1962. St. Thomas (Minnesota). Inducted in 1966. 1926-27 Duluth Eskimos, 1928 Pottsville Maroons, 1929-33 Chicago Cardinals, 1934 Chicago Bears, 1935-36 Green Bay Packers, 1937-38 Pittsburgh Pirates; coach, 1939 Pittsburgh Pirates, 1940-42 Pittsburgh Steelers; co-coach, 1943 Phil-Pitt, 1944 Card-Pitt; coach, 1954-56 Pittsburgh Steelers. **Highlights:** 34-year career as pro player, assistant coach, head coach. Led Steelers to first winning season, 1942.

FRANK (BRUISER) KINARD
Tackle. 6-1, 210. Born in Pelahatchie, Mississippi, October 23, 1914. Died September 7, 1985. Mississippi. Inducted in 1971. 1938-43 Brooklyn Dodgers, 1944 Brooklyn Tigers, 1946-47 New York Yankees (AAFC). **Highlights:** First man to earn both All-NFL, All-AAFC honors. Out because of injury only once.

PAUL KRAUSE
Saftey. 6-3, 200. Born in Flint, Michigan, February 19, 1942. Iowa. Inducted in 1998. 1964-67 Washington Redskins, 1968-79 Minnesota Vikings. **Highlights:** NFL all-time leader with

81 interceptions. Played in eight Pro Bowls. Starting safety in four Super Bowls.

EARL (CURLY) LAMBEAU
Coach. Born in Green Bay, Wisconsin, April 9, 1898. Died June 1, 1965. Notre Dame. Inducted in 1963. 1919-49 Green Bay Packers, 1950-51 Chicago Cardinals, 1952-53 Washington Redskins. **Highlights:** 229-134-22 coaching record with six NFL championships. Founded pre-NFL Packers, 1919.

JACK LAMBERT
Linebacker. 6-4, 220. Born in Mantua, Ohio, July 8, 1952. Kent State. Inducted in 1990. 1974-84 Pittsburgh Steelers. **Highlights:** Prototype middle linebacker. Two-time NFL Defensive Player of Year, nine Pro Bowls.

TOM LANDRY
Coach. Born in Mission, Texas, September 11, 1924. Texas. Inducted in 1990. 1960-88 Dallas Cowboys. **Highlights:** 270-178-6 coaching record. 20 consecutive winning seasons. Perfected flex defense, shotgun offense.

DICK (NIGHT TRAIN) LANE
Cornerback. 6-2, 210. Born in Austin, Texas, April 16, 1928. Scottsbluff Junior College. Inducted in 1974. 1952-53 Los Angeles Rams, 1954-59 Chicago Cardinals, 1960-65 Detroit Lions. **Highlights:** 68 interceptions for 1,207 yards, 5 touchdowns. Record 14 interceptions as rookie. Six Pro Bowls.

JIM LANGER
Center. 6-2, 255. Born in Little Falls, Minnesota, May 16, 1948. South Dakota State. Inducted in 1987. 1970-79 Miami Dolphins, 1980-81 Minnesota Vikings. **Highlights:** Played every offensive down in Dolphins' perfect 1972 season. Six Pro Bowls.

WILLIE LANIER
Linebacker. 6-1, 245. Born in Clover, Virginia, August 21, 1945. Morgan State. Inducted in 1986. 1967-77 Kansas City Chiefs. **Highlights:** 27 interceptions. Defensive star in Super Bowl IV upset. Nicknamed 'Contact' for ferocious tackling.

STEVE LARGENT
Wide receiver. 5-11, 191. Born in Tulsa, Oklahoma, September 28, 1954, Tulsa. Inducted in 1995. 1976-89 Seattle Seahawks. **Highlights:** 819 receptions for 13,089 yards, 100 touchdowns. Receptions in 177 consecutive games.

YALE LARY
Defensive back-punter. 5-11, 189. Born in Fort Worth, Texas, November 24, 1930. Texas A&M. Inducted in 1979. 1952-53, 1956-64 Detroit Lions. **Highlights:** 50 interceptions. Three NFL punting crowns, three touchdowns on punt returns. Nine Pro Bowls.

DANTE LAVELLI
End. 6-0, 199. Born in Hudson, Ohio, February 23, 1923. Ohio State. Inducted in 1975. 1946-49 Cleveland Browns (AAFC), 1950-56 Cleveland Browns. **Highlights:** 386 receptions for 6,488 yards, 62 touchdowns. 24 catches in six NFL title games.

BOBBY LAYNE
Quarterback. 6-2, 190. Born in Santa Ana, Texas, December 19, 1926. Died December 1, 1986. Texas. Inducted in 1967. 1948 Chicago Bears, 1949 New York Bulldogs, 1950-58 Detroit Lions, 1958-62 Pittsburgh Steelers. **Highlights:** 26,768 yards passing, 196 touchdowns, 2,451 yards rushing. Last-second touchdown pass won 1953 NFL title game.

ALPHONSE (TUFFY) LEEMANS
Fullback. 6-0, 200. Born in Superior, Wisconsin, November 12, 1912. Died January 19, 1979. Oregon, George Washington. Inducted in 1978. 1936-43 New York Giants. **Highlights:** 3,142 yards rushing, 2,324 yards passing, 442 yards receiving. Led NFL rushers as rookie, 1936.

BOB LILLY
Defensive tackle. 6-5, 260. Born in Olney, Texas, July 26, 1939. Texas Christian. Inducted in 1980. 1961-74 Dallas Cowboys. **Highlights:** 11 Pro Bowls. Missed one game in 14 years. Foundation of great Dallas defensive units.

LARRY LITTLE
Guard. 6-1, 265. Born in Groveland, Georgia, November 2, 1945. Bethune-Cookman. Inducted in 1993. 1967-68 San Diego Chargers, 1969-80 Miami Dolphins. **Highlights:** Five Pro Bowls, started in three Super Bowls. Epitome of powerful Dolphins rushing game of 1970s.

VINCE LOMBARDI
Coach. Born in Brooklyn, New York, June 11, 1913. Died September 3, 1970. Fordham. Inducted in 1971. 1959-67 Green Bay Packers, 1969 Washington Redskins. **Highlights:** 105-35-6 coaching record in 10 years, including five NFL titles and victories in Super Bowl I and II.

SID LUCKMAN
Quarterback. 6-0, 195. Born in Brooklyn, New York, November 21, 1916. Columbia. Inducted in 1965. 1939-50 Chicago Bears. **Highlights:** 139 touchdown passes. All-NFL team five times. League MVP in 1943.

WILLIAM ROY (LINK) LYMAN
Tackle. 6-2, 252. Born in Table Rock, Nebraska, November 30, 1898. Died December 16, 1972. Nebraska. Inducted in 1964. 1922-23, 1925 Canton Bulldogs, 1924 Cleveland Bulldogs, 1925 Frankford Yellow Jackets, 1926-28, 1930-31, 1933-34 Chicago Bears. **Highlights:** Played for four NFL champions. In 16 seasons of college and pro football, played on one losing team.

JOHN MACKEY
Tight end. 6-2, 224. Born in New York, New York, September 24, 1941. Syracuse. Inducted in 1992. 1963-71 Baltimore Colts, 1972 San Diego Chargers. **Highlights:** 331 receptions for 5,236 yards, 38 touchdowns. Second tight end to enter Hall of Fame.

TIM MARA
Team owner. Born in New York, New York, July 29, 1887. Died February 17, 1959. Did not attend college. Inducted in 1963. 1925-59 New York Giants. **Highlights:** Charter enshrinee. Founder of New York Giants. Built team into powerhouse winning three NFL titles, eight division titles.

WELLINGTON MARA
Team owner. Born in New York, New York, August 14, 1916. Fordham. Inducted in 1997. 1937-present New York Giants. **Highlights:** Lifetime contributor to NFL and New York Giants. Worked as Giants' ballboy, secretary, vice-president, president and co-CEO. NFC president 1984-present.

GINO MARCHETTI
Defensive end. 6-4, 245. Born in Smithers, West Virginia, January 2, 1927. San Francisco. Inducted in 1972. 1952 Dallas Texans, 1953-64, 1966 Baltimore Colts. **Highlights:** Named top defensive end of NFL's first 50 years. 11 consecutive Pro Bowls. All-NFL seven times.

GEORGE PRESTON MARSHALL
Team owner. Born in Grafton, West Virginia, October 11, 1897. Died August 9, 1969. Randolph-Macon. Inducted in 1963. 1932 Boston Braves, 1933-36 Boston Redskins, 1937-69 Washington Redskins. **Highlights:** Charter enshrinee. Sponsored progressive rules changes. Organized first team band, pioneered halftime shows.

OLLIE MATSON
Halfback. 6-2, 220. Born in Trinity, Texas, May 1, 1930. San Francisco. Inducted in 1972. 1952, 1954-58 Chicago Cardinals, 1959-62 Los Angeles Rams, 1963 Detroit Lions, 1964-66 Philadelphia Eagles. **Highlights:** NFL-record 9 touchdowns on kickoff, punt returns. Traded for nine players in 1959.

DON MAYNARD
Wide receiver. 6-1, 185. Born in Crosbyton, Texas, January 25, 1935. Texas Western. Inducted in 1987. 1958 New York Giants, 1960-62 New York Titans, 1963-72 New York Jets, 1973 St. Louis Cardinals. **Highlights:** 633 receptions for 11,834 yards, 88 touchdowns. At least 50 catches and 1,000 yards in five different seasons.

GEORGE McAFEE
Halfback. 6-0, 177. Born in Corbin, Kentucky, March 13, 1918. Duke. Inducted in 1966. 1940-41, 1945-50 Chicago Bears. **Highlights:** Two-way star. 21 interceptions, 234 points. Career punt return record of 12.78 yards per return.

MIKE McCORMACK
Tackle. 6-4, 250. Born in Chicago, Illinois, June 21, 1930. Kansas. Inducted in 1984. 1951 New York Yanks, 1954-62 Cleveland Browns. **Highlights:** Excelled as offensive right tackle for eight years. Six Pro Bowls.

TOMMY McDONALD
Wide receiver. 5-9, 175. Born in Roy, New Mexico, July 26, 1934. Oklahoma. Inducted in 1998. 1957-63 Philadelphia Eagles, 1964 Dallas Cowboys, 1965-66 Los Angeles Rams, 1967 Atlanta Falcons, 1968 Cleveland Browns. **Highlights:** Recorded 495 receptions for 8,410 yards, 84 touchdowns.

HUGH McELHENNY
Halfback. 6-1, 198. Born in Los Angeles, California, December 31, 1928. Washington. Inducted in 1970. 1952-60 San Francisco 49ers, 1961-62 Minnesota Vikings, 1963 New York Giants, 1964 Detroit Lions. **Highlights:** 5,281 rushing yards, 360 points. Scored 40-yard touchdown run on first pro play.

JOHNNY (BLOOD) McNALLY
Halfback. 6-0, 185. Born in New Richmond, Wisconsin, November 27, 1903. Died November 28, 1985. Notre Dame, St. John's (Minnesota). Inducted in 1963. 1925-26 Milwaukee Badgers, 1926-27 Duluth Eskimos, 1928 Pottsville Maroons, 1929-33, 1935-36 Green Bay Packers, 1934 Pittsburgh Pirates; player-coach, 1937-39 Pittsburgh Pirates. **Highlights:** 37 touchdowns, 224 points in 15 seasons with five teams.

MIKE MICHALSKE
Guard. 6-0, 209. Born in Cleveland, Ohio, April 24, 1903. Died October 26, 1983. Penn State. Inducted in 1964. 1926 New York Yankees (AFL), 1927-28 New York Yankees, 1929-35, 1937 Green Bay Packers. **Highlights:** Anchored Packers' championship lines, 1929-1931. First-ever guard enshrined in Canton.

WAYNE MILLNER
End. 6-0, 191. Born in Roxbury, Massachusetts, January 31, 1913. Died November 19, 1976. Notre Dame. Inducted in 1968. 1936 Boston Redskins, 1937-41, 1945 Washington Redskins. **Highlights:** Redskins' all-time leader with 124 catches when retired. 55- and 78-yard touchdown receptions in 1937 NFL championship.

BOBBY MITCHELL
Running back-wide receiver. 6-0, 195. Born in Hot Springs, Arkansas, June 6, 1935. Illinois. Inducted in 1983. 1958-61 Cleveland Browns, 1962-68 Washington Redskins. **Highlights:** 91 touchdowns, including 8 on kickoff and punt returns. 14,078 combined yards.

RON MIX
Tackle. 6-4, 255. Born in Los Angeles, California, March 10, 1938. Southern California. Inducted in 1979. 1960 Los Angeles Chargers, 1961-69 San Diego Chargers, 1971 Oakland Raiders. **Highlights:** All-AFL tackle eight times. Only two holding penalties in 10 years with the Chargers.

LENNY MOORE
Flanker-running back. 6-1, 198. Born

in Reading, Pennsylvania, November 25, 1933. Penn State. Inducted in 1975. 1956-67 Baltimore Colts. **Highlights:** From 1963-65, scored touchdowns in record 18 consecutive games. 113 career touchdowns, 12,451 combined net yards.

MARION MOTLEY
Fullback. 6-1, 238. Born in Leesburg, Georgia, June 5, 1920. South Carolina State, Nevada. Inducted in 1968. 1946-49 Cleveland Browns (AAFC), 1950-53 Cleveland Browns, 1955 Pittsburgh Steelers. **Highlights:** AAFC's all-time rushing champion. Led league in rushing in first NFL season.

ANTHONY MUÑOZ
Tackle. 6-6, 278. Born in Ontario, California, August 19, 1958. Southern California. Inducted in 1998. 1980-92 Cincinnati Bengals. **Highlights:** All-Pro choice 11 consecutive years, 1981-91. Selected to 11 straight Pro Bowls.

GEORGE MUSSO
Guard-tackle. 6-2, 270. Born in Collinsville, Illinois. April 8, 1910. Millikin. Inducted in 1982. 1933-44 Chicago Bears. **Highlights:** First player to achieve All-NFL status at two positions—tackle in 1935 and guard in 1937.

BRONKO NAGURSKI
Fullback. 6-2, 225. Born in Rainy River, Ontario, Canada, November 3, 1908. Died January 7, 1990. Minnesota. Inducted in 1963. 1930-37, 1943 Chicago Bears. **Highlights:** Charter enshrinee. 4,031 rushing yards in nine seasons. All-NFL three times.

JOE NAMATH
Quarterback. 6-2, 200. Born in Beaver Falls, Pennsylvania, May 31, 1943. Alabama. Inducted in 1985. 1965-76 New York Jets, 1977 Los Angeles Rams. **Highlights:** First quarterback to pass for more than 4,000 yards in season, 1967. Guaranteed, delivered victory over Colts in Super Bowl III.

EARLE (GREASY) NEALE
Coach. Born in Parkersburg, West Virginia, November 5, 1891. Died November 2, 1973. West Virginia Wesleyan. Inducted in 1969. 1941-42, 1944-50 Philadelphia Eagles; co-coach, 1943 Phil-Pitt. **Highlights:** Turned Eagles into winners with three consecutive division crowns, NFL championships in 1948 and 1949.

ERNIE NEVERS
Fullback. 6-1, 205. Born in Willow River, Minnesota, June 11, 1903. Died May 3, 1976. Stanford. Inducted in 1963. 1926-27 Duluth Eskimos, 1929-31 Chicago Cardinals. **Highlights:** Charter enshrinee. Holds NFL's longest-standing record, 40 points in one game in 1929.

RAY NITSCHKE
Linebacker. 6-3, 235. Born in Elmwood Park, Illinois, December 29, 1936. Died March 8, 1998. Illinois. Inducted in 1978. 1958-72 Green Bay Packers. **Highlights:** MVP of 1962 title game. Named NFL's all-time linebacker in 1969.

CHUCK NOLL
Coach. Born in Cleveland, Ohio, January 5, 1932. Dayton. Inducted in 1993. 1969-91 Pittsburgh Steelers. **Highlights:** Coached for 23 years. Only coach to win four Super Bowl titles (IX, X, XIII, XIV).

LEO NOMELLINI
Defensive tackle. 6-3, 264. Born in Lucca, Italy, June 19, 1924. Minnesota. Inducted in 1969. 1950-63 San Francisco 49ers. **Highlights:** Played every 49ers game for 14 seasons. 10 Pro Bowls.

MERLIN OLSEN
Defensive tackle. 6-5, 270. Born in Logan, Utah, September 15, 1940. Utah State. Inducted in 1982. 1962-76 Los Angeles Rams. **Highlights:** Member of the Fearsome Foursome. Named to 14 consecutive Pro Bowls, Rams' all-time team.

JIM OTTO
Center. 6-2, 255. Born in Wausau, Wisconsin, January 5, 1938. Miami. Inducted in 1980. 1960-74 Oakland Raiders. **Highlights:** Named AFL's all-time center. Played in 308 games, 12 all-star games, six AFL/AFC title games.

STEVE OWEN
Tackle. Coach. 6-2, 235. Born in Cleo Springs, Oklahoma, April 21, 1898. Died May 17, 1964. Phillips. Inducted in 1966. 1924-25 Kansas City Cowboys, 1925 Cleveland Bulldogs, 1926-31, 1933 New York Giants; coach, 1931-53 New York Giants. **Highlights:** Both player and coach. Coached Giants to record of 153-108-17, eight divisional titles, two NFL championships.

ALAN PAGE
Defensive tackle. 6-4, 225. Born in Canton, Ohio, August 7, 1945. Notre Dame. Inducted in 1988. 1967-78 Minnesota Vikings, 1978-81 Chicago Bears. **Highlights:** NFL iron man. Played in 236 consecutive games, four Super Bowls. League MVP in 1971.

CLARENCE (ACE) PARKER
Quarterback. 5-11, 168. Born in Portsmouth, Virginia, May 17, 1912. Duke. Inducted in 1972. 1937-41 Brooklyn Dodgers, 1945 Boston Yanks, 1946 New York Yankees (AAFC). **Highlights:** Two-way threat. Two-time All-NFL performer, league MVP in 1940.

JIM PARKER
Guard-tackle. 6-3, 273. Born in Macon, Georgia, April 3, 1934. Ohio State. Inducted in 1973. 1957-67 Baltimore Colts. **Highlights:** First full-time offensive lineman elected to Hall of Fame. All-NFL eight consecutive years, eight Pro Bowls.

WALTER PAYTON
Running back. 5-10, 202. Born in Columbia, Mississippi, July 25, 1954. Jackson State. Inducted in 1993. 1975-87 Chicago Bears. **Highlights:** NFL's all-time leading rusher with 16,726 yards. Holds single-game rushing record of 275 yards.

JOE PERRY
Fullback. 6-0, 200. Born in Stevens, Arkansas, January 22, 1927. Compton Junior College. Inducted in 1969. 1948-49 San Francisco 49ers (AAFC), 1950-60, 1963 San Francisco 49ers, 1961-62 Baltimore Colts. **Highlights:** First player in NFL history to gain 1,000 yards two consecutive seasons. 12,505 combined yards.

PETE PIHOS
End. 6-1, 210. Born in Orlando, Florida, October 22, 1923. Indiana. Inducted in 1970. 1947-55 Philadelphia Eagles. **Highlights:** Three-time NFL receiving champion. Caught winning touchdown in 1949 NFL Championship Game.

HUGH (SHORTY) RAY
Supervisor of officials 1938-52. Born in Highland Park, Illinois, September 21, 1884. Died September 16, 1956. Illinois. Inducted in 1966. **Highlights:** Supervisor of Officials, 1938-1952. Streamlined rules to improve game tempo, player safety.

DAN REEVES
Team owner. Born in New York, New York, June 30, 1912. Died April 15, 1971. Georgetown. Inducted in 1967. 1941-45 Cleveland Rams, 1946-71 Los Angeles Rams. **Highlights:** Moved Rams to Los Angeles in 1946 and opened up west coast to pro football. First post-war owner to sign African-American player.

MEL RENFRO
Cornerback-safety. 6-0, 192. Born in Houston, Texas, December 30, 1941. Oregon. Inducted in 1996. 1964-77 Dallas Cowboys. **Highlights:** 52 interceptions for 626 yards and 3 touchdowns. Also added 849 yards on punt returns, 2,246 yards on kickoff returns. Elected to Pro Bowl first 10 seasons.

JOHN RIGGINS
Running back. 6-2, 240. Born in Seneca, Kansas, August 4, 1949. Kansas. Inducted in 1992. 1971-75 New York Jets, 1976-79, 1981-85 Washington Redskins. **Highlights:** 11,352 rushing yards, 104 touchdowns. MVP of Super Bowl XVII with 166 rushing yards including game-winning 43-yard touchdown.

JIM RINGO
Center. 6-2, 230. Born in Orange, New Jersey, November 21, 1931. Syracuse. Inducted in 1981. 1953-63 Green Bay Packers, 1964-67 Philadelphia Eagles. **Highlights:** Ten-time Pro Bowl selection, six-time All-NFL selection. Started in then-record 182 consecutive games.

ANDY ROBUSTELLI
Defensive end. 6-0, 230. Born in Stamford, Connecticut, December 6, 1925. Arnold College. Inducted in 1971. 1951-55 Los Angeles Rams, 1956-64 New York Giants. **Highlights:** Anchored defense in eight championship games. Named NFL's top player in 1962.

ART ROONEY
Team owner. Born in Coulterville, Pennsylvania, January 27, 1901. Died August 25, 1988. Georgetown, Duquesne. Inducted in 1964. 1933-39 Pittsburgh Pirates, 1940-42, 1945-88 Pittsburgh Steelers, 1943 Phil-Pitt, 1944 Card-Pitt. **Highlights:** Founded Pittsburgh Pirates in 1933 and renamed them Steelers in 1940. Team won four Super Bowls in 1970s.

PETE ROZELLE
Commissioner. Born in South Gate, California, March 1, 1926. Died December 6, 1996. Compton Junior College, San Francisco. Inducted in 1985. Commissioner, 1960-89. **Highlights:** Negotiated first league-wide television contract in 1962. Generally recognized as premiere commissioner in all of sports. Credited with making NFL the nation's most popular sport.

BOB ST. CLAIR
Tackle. 6-9, 265. Born in San Francisco, California, February 18, 1931. San Francisco, Tulsa. Inducted in 1990. 1953-63 San Francisco 49ers. **Highlights:** Exceptional offensive lineman. Also played goal-line defense and had 10 blocked field goals, 1956.

GALE SAYERS
Running back. 6-0, 200. Born in Wichita, Kansas, May 30, 1943. Kansas. Inducted in 1977. 1965-71 Chicago Bears. **Highlights:** Broke into league by scoring rookie-record 22 touchdowns. Led league in rushing in 1966, 1969. MVP of three Pro Bowls.

JOE SCHMIDT
Linebacker. 6-0, 222. Born in Pittsburgh, Pennsylvania, January 18, 1932. Pittsburgh. Inducted in 1973. 1953-65 Detroit Lions. **Highlights:** 24 interceptions. Lions team captain for nine years. Mastered middle linebacker position which evolved in 1950s.

TEX SCHRAMM
Team president-general manager. Born in San Gabriel, California, June 2, 1920. Texas. Inducted in 1991. 1947-56 Los Angeles Rams. 1960-89 Dallas Cowboys. **Highlights:** Played prominent role in AFL-NFL merger. Chairman of Competition Committee from 1966-1988.

LEE ROY SELMON
Defensive end. 6-3, 250. Born in Eufaula, Oklahoma, October 20, 1954. Oklahoma. Inducted in 1995. 1976-84 Tampa Bay Buccaneers. **Highlights:** 78½ sacks, 380 quarterback pressures, forced 28 fumbles. Five consecutive Pro Bowls.

ART SHELL
Tackle. 6-5, 285. Born in Charleston, South Carolina, November 26, 1946. Maryland State-Eastern Shore. Inducted in 1989. 1968-81 Oakland Raiders, 1982 Los Angeles Raiders. **Highlights:** Cornerstone of Raiders' offensive line in 1970s. 207 regular-season games, 24 postseason games, eight Pro Bowls.

DON SHULA
Coach. Born in Painesville, Ohio, January 4, 1930. John Carroll. Inducted in 1997. 1963-69 Baltimore Colts, 1970-1995 Miami Dolphins. **Highlights:** Won more games (347) than any coach in NFL history. Won two Super Bowl titles, including Super Bowl VII when Dolphins recorded NFL's only perfect season (17-0).

O.J. SIMPSON
Running back. 6-1, 212. Born in San Francisco, California, July 9, 1947. City College (San Francisco), Southern California. Inducted in 1985. 1969-77 Buffalo Bills, 1978-79 San Francisco 49ers. **Highlights:** In 1973, became first player to rush for 2,000 yards in season. Finished career with four rushing titles, 11,236 yards.

MIKE SINGLETARY
Linebacker. 6-0, 230. Born in Houston, Texas, October 9, 1958. Baylor. Inducted in 1998. 1981-92 Chicago Bears. **Highlights:** All-Pro choice eight times and All-NFC nine consecutive seasons. Selected to 10 Pro Bowls.

JACKIE SMITH
Tight end. 6-4, 232. Born in Columbia, Mississippi, February 23, 1940. Northwestern State (Louisiana). Inducted in 1994. 1963-77 St. Louis Cardinals, 1978 Dallas Cowboys. **Highlights:** 480 receptions for 7,918 yards, 40 touchdowns. Third tight end to be elected to Hall of Fame.

BART STARR
Quarterback. 6-1, 200. Born in Montgomery, Alabama, January 9, 1934. Alabama. Inducted in 1977. 1956-71 Green Bay Packers. **Highlights:** Quarterbacked Packers to six division titles, five NFL titles including first two Super Bowls in which he was MVP.

ROGER STAUBACH
Quarterback. 6-3, 202. Born in Cincinnati, Ohio, February 5, 1942. New Mexico Military Institute, Navy. Inducted in 1985. 1969-79 Dallas Cowboys. **Highlights:** Led Cowboys to four NFC titles and victories in Super Bowls VI, XII. When retired, 83.4 career passer rating was best of all time.

ERNIE STAUTNER
Defensive tackle. 6-2, 235. Born in Prinzing-by-Cham, Bavaria, April 20, 1925. Boston College. Inducted in 1969. 1950-63 Pittsburgh Steelers. **Highlights:** Played in nine Pro Bowls and won the best lineman award in 1957. Recorded 3 safeties.

JAN STENERUD
Kicker. 6-2, 190. Born in Fetsund, Norway, November 26, 1942. Montana State. Inducted in 1991. 1967-79 Kansas City Chiefs, 1980-83 Green Bay Packers, 1984-85 Minnesota Vikings. **Highlights:** 1,699 points on 580 extra points, 373 field goals. First pure placekicker to enter Hall of Fame.

DWIGHT STEPHENSON
Center. 6-2, 255. Born in Murfreesboro, North Carolina, November 20, 1957. Alabama. Inducted in 1998. 1980-87 Miami Dolphins. **Highlights:** Recognized as premier center of his time. All-Pro, All-AFC five straight years. Selected to five Pro Bowls.

KEN STRONG
Halfback. 5-11, 210. Born in West Haven, Connecticut, August 6, 1906. Died October 5, 1979. New York University. Inducted in 1967. 1929-32 Staten Island Stapletons, 1933-35, 1939, 1944-47 New York Giants, 1936-37 New York Yanks (AFL). **Highlights:** Scored 17 points to lead Giants to victory in 1934 'Sneakers' game, led NFL with 64 points, 1933.

JOE STYDAHAR
Tackle. 6-4, 230. Born in Kaylor, Pennsylvania, March 17, 1912. Died March 23, 1977. West Virginia. Inducted in 1967. 1936-42, 1945-46 Chicago Bears. **Highlights:** One of stalwarts of Bears' 'Monsters of the Midway.' Played on five divisional, three NFL championship teams.

FRAN TARKENTON
Quarterback. 6-0, 185. Born in Richmond, Virginia, February 3, 1940. Georgia. Inducted in 1986. 1961-66, 1972-78 Minnesota Vikings, 1967-71 New York Giants. **Highlights:** At retirement, held NFL records for attempts (6,467), completions (3,686), yards (47,003), and touchdowns (342). Four touchdowns passes in first NFL game.

CHARLEY TAYLOR
Running back-wide receiver. 6-3, 210. Born in Grand Prairie, Texas, September 28, 1941. Arizona State. Inducted in 1984. 1964-75, 1977 Washington Redskins. **Highlights:** Won Rookie of Year honors as running back. Switched to wide receiver and won receiving titles in 1966, 1967.

JIM TAYLOR
Fullback. 6-0, 216. Born in Baton Rouge, Louisiana, September 20, 1935. Louisiana State. Inducted in 1976. 1958-66 Green Bay Packers, 1967 New Orleans Saints. **Highlights:** 8,597 rushing yards, 558 points. In 1962, led league in rushing and scoring with 19 touchdowns.

JIM THORPE
Halfback. 6-1, 190. Born in Prague, Oklahoma, May 28, 1888. Died March 28, 1953. Carlisle. Inducted in 1963. 1915-17, 1919-20, 1926 Canton Bulldogs, 1921 Cleveland Indians, 1922-23 Oorang Indians, 1924 Rock Island Independents, 1925 New York Giants, 1928 Chicago Cardinals. **Highlights:** Charter enshrinee. First president of American Professional Football Association, 1920. Played for 12 seasons.

Y.A. TITTLE
Quarterback. 6-0, 200. Born in Marshall, Texas, October 24, 1926. Louisiana State. Inducted in 1971. 1948-49 Baltimore Colts (AAFC), 1950 Baltimore Colts, 1951-60 San Francisco 49ers, 1961-64 New York Giants. **Highlights:** 33,070 yards, 242 touchdowns. 33 touchdown passes in 1962 and 36 in 1963. Two-time league MVP.

GEORGE TRAFTON
Center. 6-2, 235. Born in Chicago, Illinois, December 6, 1896. Died September 5, 1971. Notre Dame. Inducted in 1964. 1920 Decatur Staleys, 1921 Chicago Staleys, 1922-32 Chicago Bears. **Highlights:** First center to snap with one hand. Named top NFL center of 1920s.

CHARLEY TRIPPI
Halfback-quarterback. 6-0, 185. Born in Pittston, Pennsylvania, December 14, 1922. Georgia. Inducted in 1968. 1947-55 Chicago Cardinals. **Highlights:** One of football's most versatile performers. Played halfback five years, quarterback for two, defense for two.

EMLEN TUNNELL
Safety. 6-1, 200. Born in Bryn Mawr, Pennsylvania, March 29, 1925. Died July 22, 1975. Toledo, Iowa. Inducted in 1967. 1948-58 New York Giants, 1959-61 Green Bay Packers. **Highlights:** 79 interceptions. Gained more yards on kickoffs and interceptions (923) in 1952 than that season's NFL rushing leader.

CLYDE (BULLDOG) TURNER
Center. 6-2, 235. Born in Sweetwater, Texas, November 10, 1919. Hardin-Simmons. Inducted in 1966. 1940-52 Chicago Bears. **Highlights:** Anchored defense for four NFL championship teams, including 4 interceptions in five title games.

JOHNNY UNITAS
Quarterback. 6-1, 195. Born in Pittsburgh, Pennsylvania, May 7, 1933. Louisville. Inducted in 1979. 1956-72 Baltimore Colts, 1973 San Diego Chargers. **Highlights:** 40,239 passing yards, 290 touchdowns. Led Colts to two NFL championships. Passed for at least one touchdown in 47 consecutive games.

GENE UPSHAW
Guard. 6-5, 255. Born in Robstown, Texas, August 15, 1945. Texas A & I. Inducted in 1987. 1967-81 Oakland Raiders. **Highlights:** Played in 10 AFL/AFC Championship Games, three Super Bowls, seven Pro Bowls—307 total games.

NORM VAN BROCKLIN
Quarterback. 6-1, 190. Born in Eagle Butte, South Dakota, March 15, 1926. Died May 2, 1983. Oregon. Inducted in 1971. 1949-57 Los Angeles Rams, 1958-60 Philadelphia Eagles. **Highlights:** NFL-record 554 yards passing in 1951 season opener. Guided Eagles to NFL crown as league MVP in 1960.

STEVE VAN BUREN
Halfback. 6-1, 200. Born in La Ceiba, Honduras, December 28, 1920. Louisiana State. Inducted in 1965. 1944-51 Philadelphia Eagles. **Highlights:** Four-time rushing champion. Won 1944 punt return title and was 1945 kick return champion.

DOAK WALKER
Halfback. 5-11, 173. Born in Dallas, Texas, January 1, 1927. Southern Methodist. Inducted in 1986. 1950-55 Detroit Lions. **Highlights:** 534 points. Won two NFL scoring titles. Had winning 67-yard scoring run in 1952 title game.

BILL WALSH
Coach. Born in Los Angeles, California, November 30, 1931. San Jose State. Inducted in 1993. 1979-88 San Francisco 49ers. **Highlights:** 102-63-1 coaching record. Guided 49ers to three Super Bowl titles (XVI, XIX, XXIII) in 10 years.

PAUL WARFIELD
Wide receiver. 6-0, 188. Born in Warren, Ohio, November 28, 1942. Ohio State. Inducted in 1983. 1964-69, 1976-77 Cleveland Browns, 1970-74 Miami Dolphins. **Highlights:** 8,565 yards receiving, 85 touchdowns. Eight-time Pro Bowl player. Key to both Cleveland and Miami offenses.

BOB WATERFIELD
Quarterback. 6-2, 200. Born in Elmira, New York, July 26, 1920. Died March 25, 1983. UCLA. Inducted in 1965. 1945 Cleveland Rams, 1946-52 Los Angeles Rams. **Highlights:** NFL MVP as rookie in 1945 and led Rams to NFL title. Grabbed 20 interceptions in limited defensive duties.

MIKE WEBSTER
Center. 6-2, 260. Born in Tomahawk, Wisconsin, March 18, 1952. Wisconsin. Inducted in 1997. 1974-88 Pittsburgh Steelers, 1989-90 Kansas City Chiefs. **Highlights:** Played in 245 games, nine Pro Bowls, and won four Super Bowls during 17-year career.

ARNIE WEINMEISTER
Defensive tackle. 6-4, 235. Born in Rhein, Saskatchewan, Canada, March 23, 1923. Washington. Inducted in 1984. 1948-49 New York Yankees (AAFC), 1950-53 New York Giants. **Highlights:** Dominant defensive tackle of his time. Four-time All-NFL selection, four Pro Bowls.

RANDY WHITE
Defensive tackle. 6-4, 265. Born in Pittsburgh, Pennsylvania, January 15, 1953. Maryland. Inducted in 1994. 1975-88 Dallas Cowboys. **Highlights:** Missed only one game in 14 seasons. Co-MVP of Super Bowl XII. Nine-time Pro Bowl selection.

BILL WILLIS
Guard. 6-2, 215. Born in Columbus, Ohio, October 5, 1921. Ohio State. Inducted in 1977. 1946-49 Cleveland Browns (AAFC), 1950-53 Cleveland Browns. **Highlights:** Two-way player who excelled on defense. Four-time All-NFL player, played in three Pro Bowls.

LARRY WILSON
Safety. 6-0, 190. Born in Rigby, Idaho, March 24, 1938. Utah. Inducted in 1978. 1960-72 St. Louis Cardinals. **Highlights:** 52 interceptions. Had interception in seven consecutive games in 1966. Made "safety blitz" famous.

KELLEN WINSLOW
Tight end. 6-5, 250. Born in St. Louis,

Missouri, November 5, 1957. Missouri. Inducted in 1995. 1979-87 San Diego Chargers **Highlights:** 541 receptions for 6,741 yards, 45 touchdowns. 13 catches, blocked field goal in 1981 playoff win over Miami.

ALEX WOJCIECHOWICZ
Center. 6-0, 235. Born in South River, New Jersey, August 12, 1915. Died July 13, 1992. Fordham. Inducted in 1968. 1938-46 Detroit Lions, 1946-50 Philadelphia Eagles. **Highlights:** One of league's first iron men. Played both ways for eight years with Lions.

WILLIE WOOD
Safety. 5-10, 190. Born in Washington, D.C., December 23, 1936. Southern California. Inducted in 1989. 1960-71 Green Bay Packers. **Highlights:** 48 interceptions. Competed in six NFL championship games including Super Bowls I and II.

ENSHRINEES BY YEAR OF INDUCTION

**Deceased*
(Date of enshrinement in parentheses)

1963 CHARTER CLASS
(September 7, 1963)
Sammy Baugh
Bert Bell*
Joe Carr*
Earl (Dutch) Clark*
Harold (Red) Grange*
George Halas*
Mel Hein*
Wilbur (Pete) Henry*
Robert (Cal) Hubbard*
Don Hutson*
Earl (Curly) Lambeau*
Tim Mara*
George Preston Marshall*
John (Blood) McNally*
Bronko Nagurski*
Ernie Nevers*
Jim Thorpe*

CLASS OF 1964
(September 6, 1964)
Jimmy Conzelman*
Ed Healey*
Clarke Hinkle*
William Roy (Link) Lyman*
Mike Michalske*
Art Rooney*
George Trafton*

CLASS OF 1965
(September 12, 1965)
Guy Chamberlin*
John (Paddy) Driscoll*
Dan Fortmann*
Otto Graham
Sid Luckman
Steve Van Buren
Bob Waterfield*

CLASS OF 1966
(September 17, 1966)
Bill Dudley
Joe Guyon*
Arnie Herber*
Walt Kiesling*
George McAfee
Steve Owen*
Hugh (Shorty) Ray*
Clyde (Bulldog) Turner

CLASS OF 1967
(August 5, 1967)
Chuck Bednarik
Charles W. Bidwill, Sr.*
Paul Brown*
Bobby Layne*
Dan Reeves*
Ken Strong*
Joe Stydahar*
Emlen Tunnell*

CLASS OF 1968
(August 3, 1968)
Cliff Battles*
Art Donovan
Elroy (Crazylegs) Hirsch
Wayne Millner*
Marion Motley
Charley Trippi
Alex Wojciechowicz*

CLASS OF 1969
(September 13, 1969)
Albert Glen (Turk) Edwards*
Earle (Greasy) Neale*
Leo Nomellini
Joe Perry
Ernie Stautner

CLASS OF 1970
(August 8, 1970)
Jack Christiansen*
Tom Fears
Hugh McElhenny
Pete Pihos

CLASS OF 1971
(July 31, 1971)
Jim Brown
Bill Hewitt*
Frank (Bruiser) Kinard*
Vince Lombardi*
Andy Robustelli
Y. A. Tittle
Norm Van Brocklin*

CLASS OF 1972
(July 29, 1972)
Lamar Hunt
Gino Marchetti
Ollie Matson
Clarence (Ace) Parker

CLASS OF 1973
(July 28, 1973)
Raymond Berry
Jim Parker
Joe Schmidt

CLASS OF 1974
(July 27, 1974)
Tony Canadeo
Bill George*
Lou Groza
Dick (Night Train) Lane

CLASS OF 1975
(August 2, 1975)
Roosevelt Brown
George Connor
Dante Lavelli
Lenny Moore

CLASS OF 1976
(July 24, 1976)
Ray Flaherty*
Len Ford*
Jim Taylor

CLASS OF 1977
(July 30, 1977)
Frank Gifford
Forrest Gregg
Gale Sayers
Bart Starr
Bill Willis

CLASS OF 1978
(July 29, 1978)
Lance Alworth
Weeb Ewbank
Alphonse (Tuffy) Leemans*
Ray Nitschke*
Larry Wilson

CLASS OF 1979
(July 28, 1979)
Dick Butkus
Yale Lary
Ron Mix
Johnny Unitas

CLASS OF 1980
(August 2, 1980)
Herb Adderley
David (Deacon) Jones
Bob Lilly
Jim Otto

CLASS OF 1981
(August 1, 1981)
Morris (Red) Badgro
George Blanda
Willie Davis
Jim Ringo

CLASS OF 1982
(August 7, 1982)
Doug Atkins
Sam Huff
George Musso
Merlin Olsen

CLASS OF 1983
(July 30, 1983)
Bobby Bell
Sid Gillman
Sonny Jurgensen
Bobby Mitchell
Paul Warfield

CLASS OF 1984
(July 28, 1984)
Willie Brown
Mike McCormack
Charley Taylor
Arnie Weinmeister

CLASS OF 1985
(August 3, 1985)
Frank Gatski
Joe Namath
Pete Rozelle*
O. J. Simpson
Roger Staubach

CLASS OF 1986
(August 2, 1986)
Paul Hornung
Ken Houston
Willie Lanier
Fran Tarkenton
Doak Walker

CLASS OF 1987
(August 8, 1987)
Larry Csonka
Len Dawson
Joe Greene
John Henry Johnson
Jim Langer
Don Maynard
Gene Upshaw

CLASS OF 1988
(July 30, 1988)
Fred Biletnikoff
Mike Ditka
Jack Ham
Alan Page

CLASS OF 1989
(August 5, 1989)
Mel Blount
Terry Bradshaw
Art Shell
Willie Wood

CLASS OF 1990
(August 4, 1989)
Buck Buchanan*
Bob Griese
Franco Harris
Ted Hendricks
Jack Lambert
Tom Landry
Bob St. Clair

CLASS OF 1991
(July 27, 1991)
Earl Campbell
John Hannah
Stan Jones
Tex Schramm
Jan Stenerud

CLASS OF 1992
(August 1, 1992)
Lem Barney
Al Davis
John Mackey
John Riggins

CLASS OF 1993
(July 31, 1993)
Dan Fouts
Larry Little
Chuck Noll
Walter Payton
Bill Walsh

CLASS OF 1994
(July 30, 1994)
Tony Dorsett
Bud Grant
Jimmy Johnson
Leroy Kelly
Jackie Smith
Randy White

CLASS OF 1995
(July 29, 1995)
Jim Finks*
Henry Jordan*
Steve Largent
Lee Roy Selmon
Kellen Winslow

CLASS OF 1996
(July 27, 1996)
Lou Creekmur
Dan Dierdorf
Joe Gibbs
Charlie Joiner
Mel Renfro

CLASS OF 1997
(July 26, 1997)
Mike Haynes
Wellington Mara
Don Shula
Mike Webster

CLASS OF 1998
(August 1, 1998)
Paul Krause
Tommy McDonald
Anthony Muñoz
Mike Singletary
Dwight Stephenson

1869
Rutgers and Princeton played a college soccer football game, the first ever, November 6. The game used modified London Football Association rules. During the next seven years, rugby gained favor with the major eastern schools over soccer, and modern football began to develop from rugby.

1876
At the Massasoit convention, the first rules for American football were written. Walter Camp, who would become known as the father of American football, first became involved with the game.

1892
In an era in which football was a major attraction of local athletic clubs, an intense competition between two Pittsburgh-area clubs, the Allegheny Athletic Association (AAA) and the Pittsburgh Athletic Club (PAC), led to the making of the first professional football player. Former Yale All-America guard William (Pudge) Heffelfinger was paid $500 by the AAA to play in a game against the PAC, becoming the first person to be paid to play football, November 12. The AAA won the game 4-0 when Heffelfinger picked up a PAC fumble and ran 25 yards for a touchdown.

1893
The Pittsburgh Athletic Club signed one of its players, probably halfback Grant Dibert, to the first known pro football contract, which covered all of the PAC's games for the year.

1895
John Brallier became the first football player to openly turn pro, accepting $10 and expenses to play for the Latrobe YMCA against the Jeannette Athletic Club.

1896
The Allegheny Athletic Association team fielded the first completely professional team for its abbreviated two-game season.

1897
The Latrobe Athletic Association football team went entirely professional, becoming the first team to play a full season with only professionals.

1898
A touchdown was changed from four points to five.

1899
Chris O'Brien formed a neighborhood team, which played under the name the Morgan Athletic Club, on the south side of Chicago. The team later became known as the Normals, then the Racine (for a street in Chicago) Cardinals, the Chicago Cardinals, the St. Louis Cardinals, the Phoenix Cardinals, and, in 1994, the Arizona Cardinals. The team remains the oldest continuing operation in pro football.

1900
William C. Temple took over the team payments for the Duquesne Country and Athletic Club, becoming the first known individual club owner.

1902
Baseball's Philadelphia Athletics, managed by Connie Mack, and the Philadelphia Phillies formed professional football teams, joining the Pittsburgh Stars in the first attempt at a pro football league, named the National Football League. The Athletics won the first night football game ever played, 39-0 over Kanaweola AC at Elmira, New York, November 21.

All three teams claimed the pro championship for the year, but the league president, Dave Berry, named the Stars the champions. Pitcher Rube Waddell was with the Athletics, and pitcher Christy Mathewson a fullback for Pittsburgh.

The first World Series of pro football, actually a five-team tournament, was played among a team made up of players from both the Athletics and the Phillies, but simply named New York; the New York Knickerbockers; the Syracuse AC; the Warlow AC; and the Orange (New Jersey) AC at New York's original Madison Square Garden. New York and Syracuse played the first indoor football game before 3,000, December 28. Syracuse, with Glen (Pop) Warner at guard, won 6-0 and went on to win the tournament.

1903
The Franklin (Pa.) Athletic Club won the second and last World Series of pro football over the Oreos AC of Asbury Park, New Jersey; the Watertown Red and Blacks; and the Orange AC.

Pro football was popularized in Ohio when the Massillon Tigers, a strong amateur team, hired four Pittsburgh pros to play in the season-ending game against Akron. At the same time, pro football declined in the Pittsburgh area, and the emphasis on the pro game moved west from Pennsylvania to Ohio.

1904
A field goal was changed from five points to four.

Ohio had at least seven pro teams, with Massillon winning the Ohio Independent Championship, that is, the pro title. Talk surfaced about forming a state-wide league to end spiraling salaries brought about by constant bidding for players and to write universal rules for the game. The feeble attempt to start the league failed.

Halfback Charles Follis signed a contract with the Shelby (Ohio) AC, making him the first known black pro football player.

1905
The Canton AC, later to become known as the Bulldogs, became a professional team. Massillon again won the Ohio League championship.

1906
The forward pass was legalized. The first authenticated pass completion in a pro game came on October 27, when George (Peggy) Parratt of Massillon threw a completion to Dan (Bullet) Riley in a victory over a combined Benwood-Moundsville team.

Arch-rivals Canton and Massillon, the two best pro teams in America, played twice, with Canton winning the first game but Massillon winning the second and the Ohio League championship. A betting scandal and the financial disaster wrought upon the two clubs by paying huge salaries caused a temporary decline in interest in pro football in the two cities and, somewhat, throughout Ohio.

1909
A field goal dropped from four points to three.

1912
A touchdown was increased from five points to six.

Jack Cusack revived a strong pro team in Canton.

1913
Jim Thorpe, a former football and track star at the Carlisle Indian School (Pa.) and a double gold medal winner at the 1912 Olympics in Stockholm, played for the Pine Village Pros in Indiana.

1915
Massillon again fielded a major team, reviving the old rivalry with Canton. Cusack signed Thorpe to play for Canton for $250 a game.

1916
With Thorpe and former Carlisle teammate Pete Calac starring, Canton went 9-0-1, won the Ohio League championship, and was acclaimed the pro football champion.

1917
Despite an upset by Massillon, Canton again won the Ohio League championship.

1919
Canton again won the Ohio League championship, despite the team having been turned over from Cusack to Ralph Hay. Thorpe and Calac were joined in the backfield by Joe Guyon.

Earl (Curly) Lambeau and George Calhoun organized the Green Bay Packers. Lambeau's employer at the Indian Packing Company provided $500 for equipment and allowed the team to use the company field for practices. The Packers went 10-1.

1920
Pro football was in a state of confusion due to three major problems: dramatically rising salaries; players continually jumping from one team to another following the highest offer; and the use of college players still enrolled in school. A league in which all the members would follow the same rules seemed the answer. An organizational meeting, at which the Akron Pros, Canton Bulldogs, Cleveland Indians, and Dayton Triangles were represented, was held at the Jordan and Hupmobile auto showroom in Canton, Ohio, August 20. This meeting resulted in the formation of the American Professional Football Conference.

A second organizational meeting was held in Canton, September 17. The teams were from four states—Akron, Canton, Cleveland, and Dayton from Ohio; the Hammond Pros and Muncie Flyers from Indiana; the Rochester Jeffersons from New York; and the Rock Island Independents, Decatur Staleys, and Racine Cardinals from Illinois. The name of the league was changed to the American Professional Football Association. Hoping to capitalize on his fame, the members elected Thorpe president; Stanley Cofall of Cleveland was elected vice president. A membership fee of $100 per team was charged to give an appearance of respectability, but no team ever paid it. Scheduling was left up to the teams, and there were wide variations, both in the overall number of games played and in the number played against APFA member teams.

Four other teams—the Buffalo All-Americans, Chicago Tigers, Columbus Panhandles, and Detroit Heralds—joined the league sometime during the year. On September 26, the first game featuring an APFA team was played at Rock Island's Douglas Park. A crowd of 800 watched the Independents defeat the St. Paul Ideals 48-0. A week later, October 3, the first game matching two APFA teams was held. At Triangle Park, Dayton defeated Columbus 14-0, with Lou Partlow of Dayton scoring the first touchdown in a game between Association teams. The same day, Rock Island defeated Muncie 45-0.

By the beginning of December, most of the teams in the APFA had abandoned their hopes for a championship, and some of them, including the Chicago Tigers and the Detroit Heralds, had finished their seasons, disbanded, and had their franchises canceled by the Association. Four teams—Akron, Buffalo, Canton, and Decatur—still had championship aspirations, but a series of late-season games among them left Akron as the only undefeated team in the Association. At one of these games, Akron sold tackle Bob Nash to Buffalo for $300 and five percent of the gate receipts—the first APFA player deal.

1921
At the league meeting in Akron, April 30, the championship of the 1920 season was awarded to the Akron Pros. The APFA was reorganized, with Joe Carr of the Columbus Panhandles named president and Carl Storck of Dayton secretary-treasurer. Carr moved the Association's headquarters to Columbus, drafted a league constitution and by-laws, gave teams territorial rights, restricted player movements, developed membership criteria for the franchises, and issued standings for the first time, so that the APFA would have a clear champion.

The Association's membership increased to 22 teams, including the Green Bay Packers, who were awarded to John Clair of the Acme Packing Company.

Thorpe moved from Canton to the Cleveland Indians, but he was hurt early in the season and played very little.

A.E. Staley turned the Decatur Staleys over to player-coach George Halas, who moved the team to Cubs Park in Chicago. Staley paid Halas

$5,000 to keep the name Staleys for one more year. Halas made halfback Ed (Dutch) Sternaman his partner.

Player-coach Fritz Pollard of the Akron Pros became the first black head coach.

The Staleys claimed the APFA championship with a 9-1-1 record, as did Buffalo at 9-1-2. Carr ruled in favor of the Staleys, giving Halas his first championship.

1922
After admitting the use of players who had college eligibility remaining during the 1921 season, Clair and the Green Bay management withdrew from the APFA, January 28. Curly Lambeau promised to obey league rules and then used $50 of his own money to buy back the franchise. Bad weather and low attendance plagued the Packers, and Lambeau went broke, but local merchants arranged a $2,500 loan for the club. A public nonprofit corporation was set up to operate the team, with Lambeau as head coach and manager.

The American Professional Football Association changed its name to the National Football League, June 24. The Chicago Staleys became the Chicago Bears.

The NFL fielded 18 teams, including the new Oorang Indians of Marion, Ohio, an all-Indian team featuring Thorpe, Joe Guyon, and Pete Calac, and sponsored by the Oorang dog kennels.

Canton, led by player-coach Guy Chamberlin and tackles Link Lyman and Wilbur (Pete) Henry, emerged as the league's first true powerhouse, going 10-0-2.

1923
For the first time, all of the franchises considered to be part of the NFL fielded teams. Thorpe played first for Oorang, then for the Toledo Maroons. Against the Bears, Thorpe fumbled, and Halas picked up the ball and returned it 98 yards for a touchdown, a record that would last until 1972.

Canton had its second consecutive undefeated season, going 11-0-1 for the NFL title.

1924
The league had 18 franchises, including new ones in Kansas City, Kenosha, and Frankford, a section of Philadelphia. League champion Canton, successful on the field but not at the box office, was purchased by the owner of the Cleveland franchise, who kept the Canton franchise inactive, while using the best players for his Cleveland team, which he renamed the Bulldogs. Cleveland won the title with a 7-1-1 record.

1925
Five new franchises were admitted to the NFL—the New York Giants, who were awarded to Tim Mara and Billy Gibson for $500; the Detroit Panthers, featuring Jimmy Conzelman as owner, coach, and tailback; the Providence Steam Roller; a new Canton Bulldogs team; and the Pottsville Maroons, who had been perhaps the most successful independent pro team. The NFL established its first player limit, at 16 players.

Late in the season, the NFL made its greatest coup in gaining national recognition. Shortly after the University of Illinois season ended in November, All-America halfback Harold (Red) Grange signed a contract to play with the Chicago Bears. On Thanksgiving Day, a crowd of 36,000—the largest in pro football history—watched Grange and the Bears play the Chicago Cardinals to a scoreless tie at Wrigley Field. At the beginning of December, the Bears left on a barnstorming tour that saw them play eight games in 12 days, in St. Louis, Philadelphia, New York City, Washington, Boston, Pittsburgh, Detroit, and Chicago. A crowd of 73,000 watched the game against the Giants at the Polo Grounds, helping assure the future of the troubled NFL franchise in New York. The Bears then played nine more games in the South and West, including a game in Los Angeles, in which 75,000 fans watched them defeat the Los Angeles Tigers in the Los Angeles Memorial Coliseum.

Pottsville and the Chicago Cardinals were the top contenders for the league title, with Pottsville winning a late-season meeting 21-7. Pottsville scheduled a game against a team of former Notre Dame players for Shibe Park in Philadelphia. Frankford lodged a protest not only because the game was in Frankford's protected territory, but because it was being played the same day as a Yellow Jackets home game. Carr gave three different notices forbidding Pottsville to play the game, but Pottsville played anyway, December 12. That day, Carr fined the club, suspended it from all rights and privileges (including the right to play for the NFL championship), and returned its franchise to the league. The Cardinals, who ended the season with the best record in the league, were named the 1925 champions.

1926
Grange's manager, C.C. Pyle, told the Bears that Grange wouldn't play for them unless he was paid a five-figure salary and given one-third ownership of the team. The Bears refused. Pyle leased Yankee Stadium in New York City, then petitioned for an NFL franchise. After he was refused, he started the first American Football League. It lasted one season and included Grange's New York Yankees and eight other teams. The AFL champion Philadelphia Quakers played a December game against the New York Giants, seventh in the NFL, and the Giants won 31-0. At the end of the season, the AFL folded.

Halas pushed through a rule that prohibited any team from signing a player whose college class had not graduated.

The NFL grew to 22 teams, including the Duluth Eskimos, who signed All-America fullback Ernie Nevers of Stanford, giving the league a gate attraction to rival Grange. The 15-member Eskimos, dubbed the Iron Men of the North, played 29 exhibition and league games, 28 on the road, and Nevers played in all but 29 minutes of them.

Frankford edged the Bears for the championship, despite Halas having obtained John (Paddy) Driscoll from the Cardinals. On December 4, the Yellow Jackets scored in the final two minutes to defeat the Bears 7-6 and move ahead of them in the standings.

1927
At a special meeting in Cleveland, April 23, Carr decided to secure the NFL's future by eliminating the financially weaker teams and consolidating the quality players onto a limited number of more successful teams. The new-look NFL dropped to 12 teams, and the center of gravity of the league left the Midwest, where the NFL had started, and began to emerge in the large cities of the East. One of the new teams was Grange's New York Yankees, but Grange suffered a knee injury and the Yankees finished in the middle of the pack. The NFL championship was won by the cross-town rival New York Giants, who posted 10 shutouts in 13 games.

1928
Grange and Nevers both retired from pro football, and Duluth disbanded, as the NFL was reduced to only 10 teams. The Providence Steam Roller of Jimmy Conzelman and Pearce Johnson won the championship, playing in the Cycledrome, a 10,000-seat oval that had been built for bicycle races.

1929
Chris O'Brien sold the Chicago Cardinals to David Jones, July 27.

The NFL added a fourth official, the field judge, July 28.

Grange and Nevers returned to the NFL. Nevers scored six rushing touchdowns and four extra points as the Cardinals beat Grange's Bears 40-6, November 28. The 40 points set a record that remains the NFL's oldest.

Providence became the first NFL team to host a game at night under floodlights, against the Cardinals, November 3.

The Packers added back Johnny Blood (McNally), tackle Cal Hubbard, and guard Mike Michalske, and won their first NFL championship, edging the Giants, who featured quarterback Benny Friedman.

1930
Dayton, the last of the NFL's original franchises, was purchased by William B. Dwyer and John C. Depler, moved to Brooklyn, and renamed the Dodgers. The Portsmouth, Ohio, Spartans entered the league.

The Packers edged the Giants for the title, but the most improved team was the Bears. Halas retired as a player and replaced himself as coach of the Bears with Ralph Jones, who refined the T-formation by introducing wide ends and a halfback in motion. Jones also introduced rookie All-America fullback-tackle Bronko Nagurski.

The Giants defeated a team of former Notre Dame players coached by Knute Rockne 22-0 before 55,000 at the Polo Grounds, December 14. The proceeds went to the New York Unemployment Fund to help those suffering because of the Great Depression, and the easy victory helped give the NFL credibility with the press and the public.

1931
The NFL decreased to 10 teams, and halfway through the season the Frankford franchise folded. Carr fined the Bears, Packers, and Portsmouth $1,000 each for using players whose college classes had not graduated.

The Packers won an unprecedented third consecutive title, beating out the Spartans, who were led by rookie backs Earl (Dutch) Clark and Glenn Presnell.

1932
George Preston Marshall, Vincent Bendix, Jay O'Brien, and M. Dorland Doyle were awarded a franchise for Boston, July 9. Despite the presence of two rookies—halfback Cliff Battles and tackle Glen (Turk) Edwards—the new team, named the Braves, lost money and Marshall was left as the sole owner at the end of the year.

NFL membership dropped to eight teams, the lowest in history. Official statistics were kept for the first time. The Bears and the Spartans finished the season in the first-ever tie for first place. After the season finale, the league office arranged for the first playoff game in NFL history. The game was moved indoors to Chicago Stadium because of bitter cold and heavy snow. The arena allowed only an 80-yard field that came right to the walls. The goal posts were moved from the end lines to the goal lines and, for safety, inbounds lines or hashmarks where the ball would be put in play were drawn 10 yards from the walls that butted against the sidelines. The Bears won 9-0, December 18, scoring the winning touchdown on a two-yard pass from Nagurski to Grange. The Spartans claimed Nagurski's pass was thrown from less than five yards behind the line of scrimmage, violating the existing passing rule, but the play stood.

1933
The NFL, which long had followed the rules of college football, made a number of significant changes from the college game for the first time and began to develop rules serving its needs and the style of play it preferred. The innovations from the 1932 championship game—inbounds line or hashmarks and goal posts on the goal lines—were adopted. Also the forward pass was legalized from anywhere behind the line of scrimmage, February 25.

Marshall and Halas pushed through a proposal that divided the NFL into two divisions, with the winners to meet in an annual championship game, July 8.

Three new franchises joined the league—the Pittsburgh Pirates of Art Rooney, the Philadelphia Eagles of Bert Bell and Lud Wray, and the Cincinnati Reds. The Staten Island Stapletons suspended operations for a year, but never returned to the league.

Halas bought out Sternaman, became sole owner of the Bears, and reinstated himself as head coach. Marshall changed the name of the Boston Braves to the Redskins. David Jones sold the Chicago Cardinals to Charles W. Bidwill.

In the first NFL Championship Game scheduled before the season, the Western Division champion Bears defeated the Eastern Division champion Giants 23-21 at Wrigley Field, December 17.

1934
G.A. (Dick) Richards purchased the Portsmouth Spartans, moved them to Detroit, and renamed them the Lions.

Professional football gained new prestige when the Bears were matched against the best college football players in the first Chicago College All-Star Game, August 31. The game ended in a scoreless tie before 79,432 at Soldier Field.

The Cincinnati Reds lost their first eight games, then were suspended from the league for defaulting on payments. The St. Louis Gunners, an independent team, joined the NFL by buying the Cincinnati franchise and went 1-2 the last three weeks.

Rookie Beattie Feathers of the Bears became the NFL's first 1,000-yard rusher, gaining 1,004 on 101 carries. The Thanksgiving Day game between the Bears and the Lions became the first NFL game broadcast nationally, with Graham McNamee the announcer for NBC radio.

In the championship game, on an extremely cold and icy day at the Polo Grounds, the Giants trailed the Bears 13-3 in the third quarter before changing to basketball shoes for better footing. The Giants won 30-13 in what has come to be known as the Sneakers Game, December 9.

The player waiver rule was adopted, December 10.

1935
The NFL adopted Bert Bell's proposal to hold an annual draft of college players, to begin in 1936, with teams selecting in an inverse order of finish, May 19. The inbounds line or hashmarks were moved nearer the center of the field, 15 yards from the sidelines.

All-America end Don Hutson of Alabama joined Green Bay. The Lions defeated the Giants 26-7 in the NFL Championship Game, December 15.

1936
There were no franchise transactions for the first year since the formation of the NFL. It also was the first year in which all member teams played the same number of games.

The Eagles made University of Chicago halfback and Heisman Trophy winner Jay Berwanger the first player ever selected in the NFL draft, February 8. The Eagles traded his rights to the Bears, but Berwanger never played pro football. The first player selected to actually sign was the number-two pick, Riley Smith of Alabama, who was selected by Boston.

A rival league was formed, and it became the second to call itself the American Football League. The Boston Shamrocks were its champions.

Because of poor attendance, Marshall, the owner of the host team, moved the Championship Game from Boston to the Polo Grounds in New York. Green Bay defeated the Redskins 21-6, December 13.

1937
Homer Marshman was granted a Cleveland franchise, named the Rams, February 12. Marshall moved the Redskins to Washington, D.C., February 13. The Redskins signed TCU All-America tailback Sammy Baugh, who led them to a 28-21 victory over the Bears in the NFL Championship Game, December 12.

The Los Angeles Bulldogs had an 8-0 record to win the AFL title, but then the 2-year-old league folded.

1938
At the suggestion of Halas, Hugh (Shorty) Ray became a technical advisor on rules and officiating to the NFL. A new rule called for a 15-yard penalty for roughing the passer.

Rookie Byron (Whizzer) White of the Pittsburgh Pirates led the NFL in rushing. The Giants defeated the Packers 23-17 for the NFL title, December 11.

Marshall, *Los Angeles Times* sports editor Bill Henry, and promoter Tom Gallery established the Pro Bowl game between the NFL champion and a team of pro all-stars.

1939
The New York Giants defeated the Pro All-Stars 13-10 in the first Pro Bowl, at Wrigley Field, Los Angeles, January 15.

Carr, NFL president since 1921, died in Columbus, May 20. Carl Storck was named acting president, May 25.

An NFL game was televised for the first time when NBC broadcast the Brooklyn Dodgers-Philadelphia Eagles game from Ebbets Field to the approximately 1,000 sets then in New York.

Green Bay defeated New York 27-0 in the NFL Championship Game, December 10 at Milwaukee. NFL attendance exceeded 1 million in a season for the first time, reaching 1,071,200.

1940
A six-team rival league, the third to call itself the American Football League, was formed, and the Columbus Bullies won its championship.

Halas's Bears, with additional coaching by Clark Shaughnessy of Stanford, defeated the Redskins 73-0 in the NFL Championship Game, December 8. The game, which was the most decisive victory in NFL history, popularized the Bears' T-formation with a man-in-motion. It was the first championship carried on network radio, broadcast by Red Barber to 120 stations of the Mutual Broadcasting System, which paid $2,500 for the rights.

Art Rooney sold the Pittsburgh franchise to Alexis Thompson, December 9, then bought part interest in the Philadelphia Eagles.

1941
Elmer Layden was named the first Commissioner of the NFL, March 1; Storck, the acting president, resigned, April 5. NFL headquarters were moved to Chicago.

Bell and Rooney traded the Eagles to Thompson for the Pirates, then re-named their new team the Steelers. Homer Marshman sold the Rams to Daniel F. Reeves and Fred Levy, Jr.

The league by-laws were revised to provide for playoffs in case there were ties in division races, and sudden-death overtimes in case a playoff game was tied after four quarters. An official *NFL Record Manual* was published for the first time.

Columbus again won the championship of the AFL, but the two-year-old league then folded.

The Bears and the Packers finished in a tie for the Western Division championship, setting up the first divisional playoff game in league history. The Bears won 33-14, then defeated the Giants 37-9 for the NFL championship, December 21.

1942
Players departing for service in World War II depleted the rosters of NFL teams. Halas left the Bears in midseason to join the Navy, and Luke Johnsos and Heartley (Hunk) Anderson served as co-coaches as the Bears went 11-0 in the regular season. The Redskins defeated the Bears 14-6 in the NFL Championship Game, December 13.

1943
The Cleveland Rams, with co-owners Reeves and Levy in the service, were granted permission to suspend operations for one season, April 6. Levy transferred his stock in the team to Reeves, April 16.

The NFL adopted free substitution, April 7. The league also made the wearing of helmets mandatory and approved a 10-game schedule for all teams.

Philadelphia and Pittsburgh were granted permission to merge for one season, June 19. The team, known as Phil-Pitt (and called the Steagles by fans), divided home games between the two cities, and Earle (Greasy) Neale of Philadelphia and Walt Kiesling of Pittsburgh served as co-coaches. The merger automatically dissolved the last day of the season, December 5.

Ted Collins was granted a franchise for Boston, to become active in 1944.

Sammy Baugh led the league in passing, punting, and interceptions. He led the Redskins to a tie with the Giants for the Eastern Division title, and then to a 28-0 victory in a divisional playoff game. The Bears beat the Redskins 41-21 in the NFL Championship Game, December 26.

1944
Collins, who had wanted a franchise in Yankee Stadium in New York, named his new team in Boston the Yanks. Cleveland resumed operations. The Brooklyn Dodgers changed their name to the Tigers.

Coaching from the bench was legalized, April 20.

The Cardinals and the Steelers were granted permission to merge for one year under the name Card-Pitt, April 21. Phil Handler of the Cardinals and Walt Kiesling of the Steelers served as co-coaches. The merger automatically dissolved the last day of the season, December 3.

In the NFL Championship Game, Green Bay defeated the New York Giants 14-7, December 17.

1945
The inbounds lines or hashmarks were moved from 15 yards away from the sidelines to nearer the center of the field—20 yards from the sidelines.

Brooklyn and Boston merged into a team that played home games in both cities and was known simply as The Yanks. The team was coached by former Boston head coach Herb Kopf. In December, the Brooklyn franchise withdrew from the NFL to join the new All-America Football Conference; all the players on its active and reserve lists were assigned to The Yanks, who once again became the Boston Yanks.

Halas rejoined the Bears late in the season after service with the U.S. Navy. Although Halas took over much of the coaching duties, Anderson and Johnsos remained the coaches of record throughout the season.

Steve Van Buren of Philadelphia led the NFL in rushing, kickoff returns, and scoring.

After the Japanese surrendered ending World War II, a count showed that the NFL service roster, limited to men who had played in league games, totaled 638, 21 of whom had died in action.

Rookie quarterback Bob Waterfield led Cleveland to a 15-14 victory over Washington in the NFL Championship Game, December 16.

1946
The contract of Commissioner Layden was not renewed, and Bert Bell, the co-owner of the Steelers, replaced him, January 11. Bell moved the league headquarters from Chicago to the Philadelphia suburb of Bala-Cynwyd.

Free substitution was withdrawn and substitutions were limited to no more than three men at a time. Forward passes were made automatically incomplete upon striking the goal posts, January 11.

The NFL took on a truly national appearance for the first time when Reeves was granted permission by the league to move his NFL champion Rams to Los Angeles.

Halfback Kenny Washington (March 21) and end Woody Strode (May 7) signed with the Los Angeles Rams to become the first African-Americans to play in the NFL in the modern era. Guard Bill Willis (August 6) and running back Marion Motley (August 9) joined the AAFC with the Cleveland Browns.

The rival All-America Football Conference began play with eight teams. The Cleveland Browns, coached by Paul Brown, won the AAFC's first championship, defeating the New York Yankees 14-9.

CHRONOLOGY OF PROFESSIONAL FOOTBALL

Bill Dudley of the Steelers led the NFL in rushing, interceptions, and punt returns, and won the league's most valuable player award.

Backs Frank Filchock and Merle Hapes of the Giants were questioned about an attempt by a New York man to fix the championship game with the Bears. Bell suspended Hapes but allowed Filchock to play; he played well, but Chicago won 24-14, December 15.

1947
The NFL added a fifth official, the back judge.

A bonus choice was made for the first time in the NFL draft. One team each year would select the special choice before the first round began. The Chicago Bears won a lottery and the rights to the first choice and drafted back Bob Fenimore of Oklahoma A&M.

The Cleveland Browns again won the AAFC title, defeating the New York Yankees 14-3.

Charles Bidwill, Sr., owner of the Cardinals, died April 19, but his wife and sons retained ownership of the team. On December 28, the Cardinals won the NFL Championship Game 28-21 over the Philadelphia Eagles, who had beaten Pittsburgh 21-0 in a playoff.

1948
Plastic helmets were prohibited. A flexible artificial tee was permitted at the kickoff. Officials other than the referee were equipped with whistles, not horns, January 14.

Fred Mandel sold the Detroit Lions to a syndicate headed by D. Lyle Fife, January 15.

Halfback Fred Gehrke of the Los Angeles Rams painted horns on the Rams' helmets, the first modern helmet emblems in pro football.

The Cleveland Browns won their third straight championship in the AAFC, going 14-0 and then defeating the Buffalo Bills 49-7.

In a blizzard, the Eagles defeated the Cardinals 7-0 in the NFL Championship Game, December 19.

1949
Alexis Thompson sold the champion Eagles to a syndicate headed by James P. Clark, January 15. The Boston Yanks became the New York Bulldogs, sharing the Polo Grounds with the Giants.

Free substitution was adopted for one year, January 20.

The NFL had two 1,000-yard rushers in the same season for the first time—Steve Van Buren of Philadelphia and Tony Canadeo of Green Bay.

The AAFC played its season with a one-division, seven-team format. On December 9, Bell announced a merger agreement in which three AAFC franchises—Cleveland, San Francisco, and Baltimore—would join the NFL in 1950. The Browns won their fourth consecutive AAFC title, defeating the 49ers 21-7, December 11.

In a heavy rain, the Eagles defeated the Rams 14-0 in the NFL Championship Game, December 18.

1950
Unlimited free substitution was restored, opening the way for the era of two platoons and specialization in pro football, January 20.

Curly Lambeau, founder of the franchise and Green Bay's head coach since 1921, resigned under fire, February 1.

The name National Football League was restored after about three months as the National-American Football League. The American and National conferences were created to replace the Eastern and Western divisions, March 3.

The New York Bulldogs became the Yanks and divided the players of the former AAFC Yankees with the Giants. A special allocation draft was held in which the 13 teams drafted the remaining AAFC players, with special consideration for Baltimore, which received 15 choices compared to 10 for other teams.

The Los Angeles Rams became the first NFL team to have all of its games—both home and away—televised. The Washington Redskins followed the Rams in arranging to televise their games; other teams made deals to put selected games on television.

In the first game of the season, former AAFC champion Cleveland defeated NFL champion Philadelphia 35-10. For the first time, deadlocks occurred in both conferences and playoffs were necessary. The Browns defeated the Giants in the American and the Rams defeated the Bears in the National. Cleveland defeated Los Angeles 30-28 in the NFL Championship Game, December 24.

1951
The Pro Bowl game, dormant since 1942, was revived under a new format matching the all-stars of each conference at the Los Angeles Memorial Coliseum. The American Conference defeated the National Conference 28-27, January 14.

Abraham Watner returned the Baltimore franchise and its player contracts back to the NFL for $50,000. Baltimore's former players were made available for drafting at the same time as college players, January 18.

A rule was passed that no tackle, guard, or center would be eligible to catch a forward pass, January 18.

The Rams reversed their television policy and televised only road games.

The NFL Championship Game was televised coast-to-coast for the first time, December 23. The DuMont Network paid $75,000 for the rights to the game, in which the Rams defeated the Browns 24-17.

1952
Ted Collins sold the New York Yanks' franchise back to the NFL, January 19. A new franchise was awarded to a group in Dallas after it purchased the assets of the Yanks, January 24. The new Texans went 1-11, with the owners turning the franchise back to the league in midseason. For the last five games of the season, the commissioner's office operated the Texans as a road team, using Hershey, Pennsylvania, as a home base. At the end of the season the franchise was canceled, the last time an NFL team failed.

The Pittsburgh Steelers abandoned the Single-Wing for the T-formation, the last pro team to do so.

The Detroit Lions won their first NFL championship in 17 years, defeating the Browns 17-7 in the title game, December 28.

1953
A Baltimore group headed by Carroll Rosenbloom was granted a franchise and was awarded the holdings of the defunct Dallas organization, January 23. The team, named the Colts, put together the largest trade in league history, acquiring 10 players from Cleveland in exchange for five.

The names of the American and National conferences were changed to the Eastern and Western conferences, January 24.

Jim Thorpe died, March 28.

Mickey McBride, founder of the Cleveland Browns, sold the franchise to a syndicate headed by Dave R. Jones, June 10.

The NFL policy of blacking out home games was upheld by Judge Allan K. Grim of the U.S. District Court in Philadelphia, November 12.

The Lions again defeated the Browns in the NFL Championship Game, winning 17-16, December 27.

1954
The Canadian Football League began a series of raids on NFL teams, signing quarterback Eddie LeBaron and defensive end Gene Brito of Washington and defensive tackle Arnie Weinmeister of the Giants, among others.

Fullback Joe Perry of the 49ers became the first player in league history to gain 1,000 yards rushing in consecutive seasons.

Cleveland defeated Detroit 56-10 in the NFL Championship Game, December 26.

1955
The sudden-death overtime rule was used for the first time in a preseason game between the Rams and Giants at Portland, Oregon, August 28. The Rams won 23-17 three minutes into overtime.

A rule change declared the ball dead immediately if the ball carrier touched the ground with any part of his body except his hands or feet while in the grasp of an opponent.

The Baltimore Colts made an 80-cent phone call to Johnny Unitas and signed him as a free agent. Another quarterback, Otto Graham, played his last game as the Browns defeated the Rams 38-14 in the NFL Championship Game, December 26. Graham had quarterbacked the Browns to 10 championship-game appearances in 10 years.

NBC replaced DuMont as the network for the title game, paying a rights fee of $100,000.

1956
The NFL Players Association was founded.

Grabbing an opponent's facemask (other than the ball carrier) was made illegal. Using radio receivers to communicate with players on the field was prohibited. A natural leather ball with white end stripes replaced the white ball with black stripes for night games.

The Giants moved from the Polo Grounds to Yankee Stadium.

Halas retired as coach of the Bears, and was replaced by Paddy Driscoll.

CBS became the first network to broadcast some NFL regular-season games to selected television markets across the nation.

The Giants routed the Bears 47-7 in the NFL Championship Game, December 30.

1957
Pete Rozelle was named general manager of the Rams. Anthony J. Morabito, founder and co-owner of the 49ers, died of a heart attack during a game against the Bears at Kezar Stadium, October 28. An NFL-record crowd of 102,368 saw the 49ers-Rams game at the Los Angeles Memorial Coliseum, November 10.

The Lions came from 20 points down to post a 31-27 playoff victory over the 49ers, December 22. Detroit defeated Cleveland 59-14 in the NFL Championship Game, December 29.

1958
The bonus selection in the draft was eliminated, January 29. The last selection was quarterback King Hill of Rice by the Chicago Cardinals.

Halas reinstated himself as coach of the Bears.

Jim Brown of Cleveland gained an NFL-record 1,527 yards rushing. In a divisional playoff game, the Giants held Brown to eight yards and defeated Cleveland 10-0.

Baltimore, coached by Weeb Ewbank, defeated the Giants 23-17 in the first sudden-death overtime in an NFL Championship Game, December 28. The game ended when Colts fullback Alan Ameche scored on a one-yard touchdown run after 8:15 of overtime.

1959
Vince Lombardi was named head coach of the Green Bay Packers, January 28. Tim Mara, the co-founder of the Giants, died, February 17.

Lamar Hunt of Dallas announced his intentions to form a second pro football league. The first meeting was held in Chicago, August 14, and consisted of Hunt representing Dallas; Bob Howsam, Denver; K.S. (Bud) Adams, Houston; Barron Hilton, Los Angeles; Max Winter and Bill Boyer, Minneapolis; and Harry Wismer, New York City. They made plans to begin play in 1960.

The new league was named the American Football League, August 22. Buffalo, owned by Ralph Wilson, became the seventh franchise, October 28. Boston, owned by William H. Sullivan, became the eighth team, November 22. The first AFL draft, lasting 33 rounds, was held, November 22. Joe Foss was named AFL Commissioner, November 30. An additional draft of 20 rounds was held by the AFL, December 2.

NFL Commissioner Bert Bell died of a heart attack suffered at Franklin

Field, Philadelphia, during the last two minutes of a game between the Eagles and the Steelers, October 11. Treasurer Austin Gunsel was named president in the office of the commissioner, October 14.

The Colts again defeated the Giants in the NFL Championship Game, 31-16, December 27.

1960

Pete Rozelle was elected NFL Commissioner as a compromise choice on the twenty-third ballot, January 26. Rozelle moved the league offices to New York City.

Hunt was elected AFL president for 1960, January 26. Minneapolis withdrew from the AFL, January 27, and the same ownership was given an NFL franchise for Minnesota (to start in 1961), January 28. Dallas received an NFL franchise for 1960, January 28. Oakland received an AFL franchise, January 30.

The AFL adopted the two-point option on points after touchdown, January 28. A no-tampering verbal pact, relative to players' contracts, was agreed to between the NFL and AFL, February 9.

The NFL owners voted to allow the transfer of the Chicago Cardinals to St. Louis, March 13.

The AFL signed a five-year television contract with ABC, June 9.

The Boston Patriots defeated the Buffalo Bills 28-7 before 16,000 at Buffalo in the first AFL preseason game, July 30. The Denver Broncos defeated the Patriots 13-10 before 21,597 at Boston in the first AFL regular-season game, September 9.

Philadelphia defeated Green Bay 17-13 in the NFL Championship Game, December 26.

1961

The Houston Oilers defeated the Los Angeles Chargers 24-16 before 32,183 in the first AFL Championship Game, January 1.

Detroit defeated Cleveland 17-16 in the first Playoff Bowl, or Bert Bell Benefit Bowl, between second-place teams in each conference in Miami, January 7.

End Willard Dewveall of the Bears played out his option and joined the Oilers, becoming the first player to move deliberately from one league to the other, January 14.

Ed McGah, Wayne Valley, and Robert Osborne bought out their partners in the ownership of the Raiders, January 17. The Chargers were transferred to San Diego, February 10. Dave R. Jones sold the Browns to a group headed by Arthur B. Modell, March 22. The Howsam brothers sold the Broncos to a group headed by Calvin Kunz and Gerry Phipps, May 26.

NBC was awarded a two-year contract for radio and television rights to the NFL Championship Game for $615,000 annually, $300,000 of which was to go directly into the NFL Player Benefit Plan, April 5.

Canton, Ohio, where the league that became the NFL was formed in 1920, was chosen as the site of the Pro Football Hall of Fame, April 27. Dick McCann, a former Redskins executive, was named executive director.

A bill legalizing single-network television contracts by professional sports leagues was introduced in Congress by Representative Emanuel Celler. It passed the House and Senate and was signed into law by President John F. Kennedy, September 30.

Houston defeated San Diego 10-3 for the AFL championship, December 24. Green Bay won its first NFL championship since 1944, defeating the New York Giants 37-0, December 31.

1962

The Western Division defeated the Eastern Division 47-27 in the first AFL All-Star Game, played before 20,973 in San Diego, January 7.

Both leagues prohibited grabbing any player's facemask. The AFL voted to make the scoreboard clock the official timer of the game.

The NFL entered into a single-network agreement with CBS for telecasting all regular-season games for $4.65 million annually, January 10.

Judge Roszel Thompson of the U.S. District Court in Baltimore ruled against the AFL in its antitrust suit against the NFL, May 21. The AFL had charged the NFL with monopoly and conspiracy in areas of expansion, television, and player signings. The case lasted two and a half years, the trial two months.

McGah and Valley acquired controlling interest in the Raiders, May 24. The AFL assumed financial responsibility for the New York Titans, November 8. With Commissioner Rozelle as referee, Daniel F. Reeves regained the ownership of the Rams, outbidding his partners in sealed-envelope bidding for the team, November 27.

The Dallas Texans defeated the Oilers 20-17 for the AFL championship at Houston after 17 minutes, 54 seconds of overtime on a 25-yard field goal by Tommy Brooker, December 23. The game lasted a record 77 minutes, 54 seconds.

Judge Edward Weinfeld of the U.S. District Court in New York City upheld the legality of the NFL's television blackout within a 75-mile radius of home games and denied an injunction that would have forced the championship game between the Giants and the Packers to be televised in the New York City area, December 28. The Packers beat the Giants 16-7 for the NFL title, December 30.

1963

The Dallas Texans transferred to Kansas City, becoming the Chiefs, February 8. The New York Titans were sold to a five-man syndicate headed by David (Sonny) Werblin, March 28. Weeb Ewbank became the Titans' new head coach and the team's name was changed to the Jets, April 15. They began play in Shea Stadium.

NFL Properties, Inc., was founded to serve as the licensing arm of the NFL.

Rozelle indefinitely suspended Green Bay halfback Paul Hornung and Detroit defensive tackle Alex Karras for placing bets on their own teams and on other NFL games; he also fined five other Detroit players $2,000 each for betting on one game in which they did not participate, and the Detroit Lions Football Company $2,000 on each of two counts for failure to report information promptly and for lack of sideline supervision.

Paul Brown, head coach of the Browns since their inception, was fired and replaced by Blanton Collier. Don Shula replaced Weeb Ewbank as head coach of the Colts.

The AFL allowed the Jets and Raiders to select players from other franchises in hopes of giving the league more competitive balance, May 11.

NBC was awarded exclusive network broadcasting rights for the 1963 AFL Championship Game for $926,000, May 23.

The Pro Football Hall of Fame was dedicated at Canton, Ohio, September 7.

The U.S. Fourth Circuit Court of Appeals reaffirmed the lower court's finding for the NFL in the $10-million suit brought by the AFL, ending three and a half years of litigation, November 21.

Jim Brown of Cleveland rushed for an NFL single-season record 1,863 yards.

Boston defeated Buffalo 26-8 in the first divisional playoff game in AFL history, December 28.

The Bears defeated the Giants 14-10 in the NFL Championship Game, a record sixth and last title for Halas in his thirty-sixth season as the Bears' coach, December 29.

1964

The Chargers defeated the Patriots 51-10 in the AFL Championship Game, January 5.

William Clay Ford, the Lions' president since 1961, purchased the team, January 10. A group representing the late James P. Clark sold the Eagles to a group headed by Jerry Wolman, January 21. Carroll Rosenbloom, the majority owner of the Colts since 1953, acquired complete ownership of the team, January 23.

The AFL signed a five-year, $36-million television contract with NBC to begin with the 1965 season, January 29.

Commissioner Rozelle negotiated an agreement on behalf of the NFL clubs to purchase Ed Sabol's Blair Motion Pictures, which was renamed NFL Films, March 5.

Hornung and Karras were reinstated by Rozelle, March 16.

CBS submitted the winning bid of $14.1 million per year for the NFL regular-season television rights for 1964 and 1965, January 24. CBS acquired the rights to the championship games for 1964 and 1965 for $1.8 million per game, April 17.

Pete Gogolak of Cornell signed a contract with Buffalo, becoming the first soccer-style kicker in pro football.

Buffalo defeated San Diego 20-7 in the AFL Championship Game, December 26. Cleveland defeated Baltimore 27-0 in the NFL Championship Game, December 27.

1965

The NFL teams pledged not to sign college seniors until completion of all their games, including bowl games, and empowered the Commissioner to discipline the clubs up to as much as the loss of an entire draft list for a violation of the pledge, February 15.

The NFL added a sixth official, the line judge, February 19. The color of the officials' penalty flags was changed from white to bright gold, April 5.

Atlanta was awarded an NFL franchise for 1966, with Rankin Smith, Sr., as owner, June 30. Miami was awarded an AFL franchise for 1966, with Joe Robbie and Danny Thomas as owners, August 16.

Field Judge Burl Toler became the first black official in NFL history, September 19.

According to a Harris survey, sports fans chose professional football (41 percent) as their favorite sport, overtaking baseball (38 percent) for the first time, October.

Green Bay defeated Baltimore 13-10 in sudden-death overtime in a Western Conference playoff game. Don Chandler kicked a 25-yard field goal for the Packers after 13 minutes, 39 seconds of overtime, December 26. The Packers then defeated the Browns 23-12 in the NFL Championship Game, January 2.

In the AFL Championship Game, the Bills again defeated the Chargers, 23-0, December 26.

CBS acquired the rights to the NFL regular-season games in 1966 and 1967, with an option for 1968, for $18.8 million per year, December 29.

1966

The AFL-NFL war reached its peak, as the leagues spent a combined $7 million to sign their 1966 draft choices. The NFL signed 75 percent of its 232 draftees, the AFL 46 percent of its 181. Of the 111 common draft choices, 79 signed with the NFL, 28 with the AFL, and 4 went unsigned.

Buddy Young became the first African-American to work in the league office when Commissioner Rozelle named him director of player relations, February 1.

The rights to the 1966 and 1967 NFL Championship Games were sold to CBS for $2 million per game, February 14.

Foss resigned as AFL Commissioner, April 7. Al Davis, the head coach and general manager of the Raiders, was named to replace him, April 8.

Goal posts offset from the goal line, painted bright yellow, and with uprights 20 feet above the cross-bar were made standard in the NFL, May 16.

A series of secret meetings regarding a possible AFL-NFL merger were held in the spring between Hunt of Kansas City and Tex Schramm of Dallas. Rozelle announced the merger, June 8. Under the agreement, the two leagues would combine to form an expanded league with 24 teams, to be increased to 26 in 1968 and to 28 by 1970 or soon thereafter. All existing franchises would be retained, and no franchises would be transferred outside their metropolitan areas. While maintaining separate schedules through 1969, the leagues agreed to play an annual AFL-NFL World Championship Game beginning in January, 1967, and to hold a combined draft, also beginning in 1967. Preseason games would be held between teams of each league starting in 1967. Official regular-season play would start in 1970 when the two leagues would officially merge to form one league with two conferences. Rozelle was named Commissioner of the expanded league setup.

Davis rejoined the Raiders, and Milt Woodard was named president of the AFL, July 25.

The St. Louis Cardinals moved into newly constructed Busch Memorial Stadium.

Barron Hilton sold the Chargers to a group headed by Eugene Klein and Sam Schulman, August 25.

Congress approved the AFL-NFL merger, passing legislation exempting the agreement itself from antitrust action, October 21.

New Orleans was awarded an NFL franchise to begin play in 1967, November 1. John Mecom, Jr., of Houston was designated majority stockholder and president of the franchise, December 15.

The NFL was realigned for the 1967-69 seasons into the Capitol and Century Divisions in the Eastern Conference and the Central and Coastal Divisions in the Western Conference, December 2. New Orleans and the New York Giants agreed to switch divisions in 1968 and return to the 1967 alignment in 1969.

The rights to the Super Bowl for four years were sold to CBS and NBC for $9.5 million, December 13.

1967

Green Bay earned the right to represent the NFL in the first AFL-NFL World Championship Game by defeating Dallas 34-27, January 1. The same day, Kansas City defeated Buffalo 31-7 to represent the AFL. The Packers defeated the Chiefs 35-10 before 61,946 fans at the Los Angeles Memorial Coliseum in the first game between AFL and NFL teams, January 15. The winning players' share for the Packers was $15,000 each, and the losing players' share for the Chiefs was $7,500 each. The game was televised by both CBS and NBC.

The "sling-shot" goal post and a six-foot-wide border around the field were made standard in the NFL, February 22.

Baltimore made Bubba Smith, a Michigan State defensive lineman, the first choice in the first combined AFL-NFL draft, March 14.

The AFL awarded a franchise to begin play in 1968 to Cincinnati, May 24. A group with Paul Brown as part owner, general manager, and head coach, was awarded the Cincinnati franchise, September 27.

Arthur B. Modell, the president of the Cleveland Browns, was elected president of the NFL, May 28.

Defensive back Emlen Tunnell of the New York Giants became the first black player to enter the Pro Football Hall of Fame, August 5.

An AFL team defeated an NFL team for the first time, when Denver beat Detroit 13-7 in a preseason game, August 5.

Green Bay defeated Dallas 21-17 for the NFL championship on a last-minute 1-yard quarterback sneak by Bart Starr in 13-below-zero temperature at Green Bay, December 31. The same day, Oakland defeated Houston 40-7 for the AFL championship.

1968

Green Bay defeated Oakland 33-14 in Super Bowl II at Miami, January 14. The game had the first $3-million gate in pro football history.

Vince Lombardi resigned as head coach of the Packers, but remained as general manager, January 28.

Werblin sold his shares in the Jets to his partners Don Lillis, Leon Hess, Townsend Martin, and Phil Iselin, May 21. Lillis assumed the presidency of the club, but then died July 23. Iselin was appointed president, August 6.

Halas retired for the fourth and last time as head coach of the Bears, May 27.

The Oilers left Rice Stadium for the Astrodome and became the first NFL team to play its home games in a domed stadium.

The movie *Heidi* became a footnote in sports history when NBC didn't show the last 1:05 of the Jets-Raiders game in order to permit the children's special to begin on time. The Raiders scored two touchdowns in the last 42 seconds to win 43-32, November 17.

Ewbank became the first coach to win titles in both the NFL and AFL when his Jets defeated the Raiders 27-23 for the AFL championship, December 29. The same day, Baltimore defeated Cleveland 34-0.

1969

The AFL established a playoff format for the 1969 season, with the winner in one division playing the runner-up in the other, January 11.

An AFL team won the Super Bowl for the first time, as the Jets defeated the Colts 16-7 at Miami, January 12 in Super Bowl III. The title Super Bowl was recognized by the NFL for the first time.

Vince Lombardi became part owner, executive vice-president, and head coach of the Washington Redskins, February 7.

Wolman sold the Eagles to Leonard Tose, May 1.

Baltimore, Cleveland, and Pittsburgh agreed to join the AFL teams to form the 13-team American Football Conference of the NFL in 1970, May 17. The NFL also agreed on a playoff format that would include one "wild-card" team per conference—the second-place team with the best record.

Monday Night Football was signed for 1970. ABC acquired the rights to televise 13 NFL regular-season Monday night games in 1970, 1971, and 1972.

George Preston Marshall, president emeritus of the Redskins, died at 72, August 9.

The NFL marked its fiftieth year by the wearing of a special patch by each of the 16 teams.

1970

Kansas City defeated Minnesota 23-7 in Super Bowl IV at New Orleans, January 11. The gross receipts of approximately $3.8 million were the largest ever for a one-day sports event.

Four-year television contracts, under which CBS would televise all NFC games and NBC all AFC games (except Monday night games) and the two would divide televising the Super Bowl and AFC-NFC Pro Bowl games, were announced, January 26.

Art Modell resigned as president of the NFL, March 12. Milt Woodard resigned as president of the AFL, March 13. Lamar Hunt was elected president of the AFC and George Halas was elected president of the NFC, March 19.

The merged 26-team league adopted rules changes putting names on the backs of players' jerseys, making a point after touchdown worth only one point, and making the scoreboard clock the official timing device of the game, March 18.

The Players Negotiating Committee and the NFL Players Association announced a four-year agreement guaranteeing approximately $4,535,000 annually to player pension and insurance benefits, August 3. The owners also agreed to contribute $250,000 annually to improve or implement items such as disability payments, widows' benefits, maternity benefits, and dental benefits. The agreement also provided for increased preseason game and per diem payments, averaging approximately $2.6 million annually.

The Pittsburgh Steelers moved into Three Rivers Stadium. The Cincinnati Bengals moved to Riverfront Stadium.

Lombardi died of cancer at 57, September 3.

Tom Dempsey of New Orleans kicked a game-winning NFL-record 63-yard field goal against Detroit, November 8.

1971

Baltimore defeated Dallas 16-13 on Jim O'Brien's 32-yard field goal with five seconds to go in Super Bowl V at Miami, January 17. The NBC telecast was viewed in an estimated 23,980,000 homes, the largest audience ever for a one-day sports event.

The NFC defeated the AFC 27-6 in the first AFC-NFC Pro Bowl at Los Angeles, January 24.

The Boston Patriots changed their name to the New England Patriots, March 25. Their new stadium, Schaefer Stadium, was dedicated in a 20-14 preseason victory over the Giants.

The Philadelphia Eagles left Franklin Field and played their games at the new Veterans Stadium.

The San Francisco 49ers left Kezar Stadium and moved their games to Candlestick Park.

Daniel F. Reeves, the president and general manager of the Rams, died at 58, April 15.

The Dallas Cowboys moved from the Cotton Bowl into their new home, Texas Stadium, October 24.

Miami defeated Kansas City 27-24 in sudden-death overtime in an AFC Divisional Playoff Game, December 25. Garo Yepremian kicked a 37-yard field goal for the Dolphins after 22 minutes, 40 seconds of overtime, as the game lasted 82 minutes, 40 seconds overall, making it the longest game in history.

1972

Dallas defeated Miami 24-3 in Super Bowl VI at New Orleans, January 16. The CBS telecast was viewed in an estimated 27,450,000 homes, the top-rated one-day telecast ever.

The inbounds lines or hashmarks were moved nearer the center of the field, 23 yards, 1 foot, 9 inches from the sidelines, March 23. The method of determining won-lost percentage in standings changed. Tie games, previously not counted in the standings, were made equal to a half-game won and a half-game lost, May 24.

Robert Irsay purchased the Los Angeles Rams and transferred ownership of the club to Carroll Rosenbloom in exchange for the Baltimore Colts, July 13.

William V. Bidwill purchased the stock of his brother Charles (Stormy) Bidwill to become the sole owner of the St. Louis Cardinals, September 2.

The National District Attorneys Association endorsed the position of professional leagues in opposing proposed legalization of gambling on professional team sports, September 28.

Franco Harris's "Immaculate Reception" gave the Steelers their first postseason win ever, 13-7 over the Raiders, December 23.

1973

Rozelle announced that all Super Bowl VII tickets were sold and that the game would be telecast in Los Angeles, the site of the game, on an experimental basis, January 3.

Miami defeated Washington 14-7 in Super Bowl VII at Los Angeles, completing a 17-0 season, the first perfect-record regular-season and post-season mark in NFL history, January 14. The NBC telecast was viewed by approximately 75 million people.

The AFC defeated the NFC 33-28 in the Pro Bowl in Dallas, the first time since 1942 that the game was played outside Los Angeles, January 21.

A jersey numbering system was adopted, April 5: 1-19 for quarterbacks and specialists, 20-49 for running backs and defensive backs, 50-59 for centers and linebackers, 60-79 for defensive linemen and interior offensive linemen other than centers, and 80-89 for wide receivers and tight ends. Players who had been in the NFL in 1972 could continue to use old numbers.

NFL Charities, a nonprofit organization, was created to derive an income from monies generated from NFL Properties' licensing of NFL trademarks and team names, June 26. NFL Charities was set up to support education and charitable activities and to supply economic support to persons formerly associated with professional football who are no longer able to support themselves.

Congress adopted experimental legislation (for three years) requiring any NFL game that had been declared a sellout 72 hours prior to kickoff to be made available for local televising, September 14. The legislation provided for an annual review to be made by the Federal Communications Commission.

The Buffalo Bills moved their home games from War Memorial Stadium to Rich Stadium in nearby Orchard Park. The Giants tied the Eagles 23-23 in the final game in Yankee Stadium, September 23. The Giants played the rest of their home games at the Yale Bowl in New Haven, Connecticut.

A rival league, the World Football League, was formed and was reported in operation, October 2. It had plans to start play in 1974.

O.J. Simpson of Buffalo became the first player to rush for more than 2,000 yards in a season, gaining 2,003.

1974

Miami defeated Minnesota 24-7 in Super Bowl VIII at Houston, the second consecutive Super Bowl championship for the Dolphins, January 13. The CBS telecast was viewed by approximately 75 million people.

Rozelle was given a 10-year contract effective January 1, 1973, February 27.

Tampa Bay was awarded a franchise to begin operation in 1976, April 24.

Sweeping rules changes were adopted to add action and tempo to games: one sudden-death overtime period was added for preseason and regular-season games; the goal posts were moved from the goal line to the end lines; kickoffs were moved from the 40- to the 35-yard line; after missed field goals from beyond the 20, the ball was to be returned to the line of scrimmage; restrictions were placed on members of the punting team to open up return possibilities; roll-blocking and cutting of wide receivers was eliminated; the extent of downfield contact a defender could have with an eligible receiver was restricted; the penalties for offensive holding, illegal use of the hands, and tripping were reduced from 15 to 10 yards; wide receivers blocking back toward the ball within three yards of the line of scrimmage were prevented from blocking below the waist, April 25.

The Toronto Northmen of the WFL signed Larry Csonka, Jim Kiick, and Paul Warfield of Miami, March 31.

Seattle was awarded an NFL franchise to begin play in 1976, June 4. Lloyd W. Nordstrom, president of the Seattle Seahawks, and Hugh Culverhouse, president of the Tampa Bay Buccaneers, signed franchise agreements, December 5.

The Birmingham Americans defeated the Florida Blazers 22-21 in the WFL World Bowl, winning the league championship, December 5.

1975

Pittsburgh defeated Minnesota 16-6 in Super Bowl IX at New Orleans, the Steelers' first championship since entering the NFL in 1933. The NBC telecast was viewed by approximately 78 million people.

The divisional winners with the highest won-loss percentage were made the home team for the divisional playoffs, and the surviving winners with the highest percentage made home teams for the championship games, June 26.

Referees were equipped with wireless microphones for all preseason, regular-season, and playoff games.

The Lions moved to the new Pontiac Silverdome. The Giants played their home games in Shea Stadium. The Saints moved into the Louisiana Superdome.

The World Football League folded, October 22.

1976

Pittsburgh defeated Dallas 21-17 in Super Bowl X in Miami. The Steelers joined Green Bay and Miami as the only teams to win two Super Bowls; the Cowboys became the first wild-card team to play in the Super Bowl. The CBS telecast was viewed by an estimated 80 million people, the largest television audience in history.

Lloyd Nordstrom, the president of the Seahawks, died at 66, January 20. His brother Elmer succeeded him as majority representative of the team.

The owners awarded Super Bowl XII, to be played on January 15, 1978, to New Orleans. They also adopted the use of two 30-second clocks for all games, visible to both players and fans to note the official time between the ready-for-play signal and snap of the ball, March 16.

A veteran player allocation was held to stock the Seattle and Tampa Bay franchises with 39 players each, March 30-31. In the college draft, Seattle and Tampa Bay each received eight extra choices, April 8-9.

The Giants moved into new Giants Stadium in East Rutherford, New Jersey.

The Steelers defeated the College All-Stars in a storm-shortened Chicago College All-Star Game, the last of the series, July 23. St. Louis defeated San Diego 20-10 in a preseason game before 38,000 in Korakuen Stadium, Tokyo, in the first NFL game outside of North America, August 16.

1977

Oakland defeated Minnesota 32-14 in Super Bowl XI at Pasadena, January 9. The paid attendance was a pro record 103,438. The NBC telecast was viewed by 81.9 million people, the largest ever to view a sports event. The victory was the fifth consecutive for the AFC in the Super Bowl.

The NFL Players Association and the NFL Management Council ratified a collective bargaining agreement extending until 1982, covering five football seasons while continuing the pension plan—including years 1974, 1975, and 1976—with contributions totaling more than $55 million. The total cost of the agreement was estimated at $107 million. The agreement called for a college draft at least through 1986; contained a no-strike, no-suit clause; established a 43-man active player limit; reduced pension vesting to four years; provided for increases in minimum salaries and preseason and postseason pay; improved insurance, medical, and dental benefits; modified previous practices in player movement and control; and reaffirmed the NFL Commissioner's disciplinary authority. Additionally, the agreement called for the NFL member clubs to make payments totaling $16 million the next 10 years to settle various legal disputes, February 25.

The San Francisco 49ers were sold to Edward J. DeBartolo, Jr., March 28.

A 16-game regular season, 4-game preseason was adopted to begin in 1978, March 29. A second wild-card team was adopted for the playoffs beginning in 1978, with the wild-card teams to play each other and the winners advancing to a round of eight postseason series.

The Seahawks were permanently aligned in the AFC Western Division and the Buccaneers in the NFC Central Division, March 31.

The owners awarded Super Bowl XIII, to be played on January 21, 1979, to Miami, to be played in the Orange Bowl; Super Bowl XIV, to be played January 20, 1980, was awarded to Pasadena, to be played in the Rose Bowl, June 14.

Rules changes were adopted to open up the passing game and to cut down on injuries. Defenders were permitted to make contact with eligible receivers only once; the head slap was outlawed; offensive linemen were prohibited from thrusting their hands to an opponent's neck, face, or head; and wide receivers were prohibited from clipping, even in the legal clipping zone.

Rozelle negotiated contracts with the three television networks to televise all NFL regular-season and postseason games, plus selected preseason games, for four years beginning with the 1978 season. ABC was awarded yearly rights to 16 Monday night games, four prime-time games, the AFC-NFC Pro Bowl, and the Hall of Fame games. CBS received the rights to all NFC regular-season and postseason games (except those in the ABC package) and to Super Bowls XIV and XVI. NBC received the rights to all AFC regular-season and postseason games (except those in the ABC package) and to Super Bowls XIII and XV. Industry sources considered it the largest single television package ever negotiated, October 12.

Chicago's Walter Payton set a single-game rushing record with 275 yards (40 carries) against Minnesota, November 20.

1978

Dallas defeated Denver 27-10 in Super Bowl XII, held indoors for the first time, at the Louisiana Superdome in New Orleans, January 15. The CBS telecast was viewed by more than 102 million people, meaning the game was watched by more viewers than any other show of any kind in the history of television. Dallas's victory was the first for the NFC in six years.

According to a Louis Harris Sports Survey, 70 percent of the nation's sports fans said they followed football, compared to 54 percent who followed baseball. Football increased its lead as the country's favorite, 26 percent to 16 percent for baseball, January 19.

A seventh official, the side judge, was added to the officiating crew, March 14.

The NFL continued a trend toward opening up the game. Rules changes permitted a defender to maintain contact with a receiver within five yards of the line of scrimmage, but restricted contact beyond that point. The pass-blocking rule was interpreted to permit the extending of arms and open hands, March 17.

A study on the use of instant replay as an officiating aid was made during seven nationally televised preseason games.

The NFL played for the first time in Mexico City, with the Saints defeating the Eagles 14-7 in a preseason game, August 5.

Bolstered by the expansion of the regular-season schedule from 14 to 16 weeks, NFL paid attendance exceeded 12 million (12,771,800) for the first time. The per-game average of 57,017 was the third-highest in league history and the most since 1973.

1979

Pittsburgh defeated Dallas 35-31 in Super Bowl XIII at Miami to become the first team ever to win three Super Bowls, January 21. The NBC telecast was viewed in 35,090,000 homes, by an estimated 96.6 million fans.

The owners awarded three future Super Bowl sites: Super Bowl XV to the Louisiana Superdome in New Orleans, to be played on January 25, 1981; Super Bowl XVI to the Pontiac Silverdome in Pontiac, Michigan, to be played on January 24, 1982; and Super Bowl XVII to Pasadena's Rose Bowl, to be played on January 30, 1983, March 13.

NFL rules changes emphasized additional player safety. The changes prohibited players on the receiving team from blocking below the waist during kickoffs, punts, and field-goal attempts; prohibited the wearing of torn or altered equipment and exposed pads that could be hazardous; extended the zone in which there could be no crackback blocks; and instructed officials to quickly whistle a play dead when a quarterback was clearly in the grasp of a tackler, March 16.

Rosenbloom, the president of the Rams, drowned at 72, April 2. His widow, Georgia, assumed control of the club.

1980

Pittsburgh defeated the Los Angeles Rams 31-19 in Super Bowl XIV at Pasadena to become the first team to win four Super Bowls, January 20. The game was viewed in a record 35,330,000 homes.

The AFC-NFC Pro Bowl, won 37-27 by the NFC, was played before 48,060 fans at Aloha Stadium in Honolulu, Hawaii. It was the first time in the 30-year history of the Pro Bowl that the game was played in a non-NFL city.

Rules changes placed greater restrictions on contact in the area of the head, neck, and face. Under the heading of "personal foul," players were prohibited from directly striking, swinging, or clubbing on the head, neck, or face. Starting in 1980, a penalty could be called for such contact whether or not the initial contact was made below the neck area.

CBS, with a record bid of $12 million, won the national radio rights to 26 NFL regular-season games, including Monday Night Football, and all 10 postseason games for the 1980-83 seasons.

The Los Angeles Rams moved their home games to Anaheim Stadium in nearby Orange County, California.

The Oakland Raiders joined the Los Angeles Coliseum Commission's antitrust suit against the NFL. The suit contended the league violated antitrust laws in declining to approve a proposed move by the Raiders from Oakland to Los Angeles.

NFL regular-season attendance of nearly 13.4 million set a record for the third year in a row. The average paid attendance for the 224-game 1980 regular season was 59,787, the highest in the league's 61-year history. NFL games in 1980 were played before 92.4 percent of total stadium capacity.

Television ratings in 1980 were the second-best in NFL history, trailing only the combined ratings of the 1976 season. All three networks posted gains, and NBC's 15.0 rating was its best ever. CBS and ABC had their best ratings since 1977, with 15.3 and 20.8 ratings, respectively. CBS Radio reported a record audience of 7 million for Monday night and special games.

1981

Oakland defeated Philadelphia 27-10 in Super Bowl XV at the Louisiana Superdome in New Orleans, to become the first wild-card team to win a Super Bowl, January 25.

Edgar F. Kaiser, Jr., purchased the Denver Broncos from Gerald and Allan Phipps, February 26.

The owners adopted a disaster plan for re-stocking a team should the club be involved in a fatal accident, March 20.

The owners awarded Super Bowl XVIII to Tampa, to be played in Tampa Stadium on January 22, 1984, June 3.

A CBS-New York Times poll showed that 48 percent of sports fans preferred football to 31 percent for baseball.

The NFL teams hosted 167 representatives from 44 predominantly black colleges during training camps for a total of 289 days. The program was adopted for renewal during each training camp period.

NFL regular-season attendance—13.6 million for an average of 60,745—set a record for the fourth year in a row. It also was the first time the per-game average exceeded 60,000. NFL games in 1981 were played before 93.8 percent of total stadium capacity.

ABC and CBS set all-time rating highs. ABC finished with a 21.7 rating and CBS with a 17.5 rating. NBC was down slightly to 13.9.

1982

San Francisco defeated Cincinnati 26-21 in Super Bowl XVI at the Pontiac Silverdome, in the first Super Bowl held in the North, January 24. The CBS telecast achieved the highest rating of any televised sports event ever, 49.1 with a 73.0 share. The game was viewed by a record 110.2 million fans. CBS Radio reported a record 14 million listeners for the game.

The NFL signed a five-year contract with the three television networks (ABC, CBS, and NBC) to televise all NFL regular-season and postseason games starting with the 1982 season.

The owners awarded the 1983, 1984, and 1985 AFC-NFC Pro Bowls to Honolulu's Aloha Stadium.

A jury ruled against the NFL in the antitrust trial brought by the Los Angeles Coliseum Commission and the Oakland Raiders, May 7. The verdict cleared the way for the Raiders to move to Los Angeles, where they defeated Green Bay 24-3 in their first preseason game, August 29.

The 1982 season was reduced from a 16-game schedule to nine as the result of a 57-day players' strike. The strike was called by the NFLPA at midnight on Monday, September 20, following the Green Bay at New York Giants game. Play resumed November 21-22 following ratification of the Collective Bargaining Agreement by NFL owners, November 17 in New York.

Under the Collective Bargaining Agreement, which was to run through the 1986 season, the NFL draft was extended through 1992 and the veteran free-agent system was left basically unchanged. A minimum salary schedule for years of experience was established; training camp and postseason pay were increased; players' medical, insurance, and retirement benefits were increased; and a severance-pay system was introduced to aid in career transition, a first in professional sports.

Despite the players' strike, the average paid attendance in 1982 was 58,472, the fifth-highest in league history.

The owners awarded the sites of two Super Bowls, December 14: Super Bowl XIX, to be played on January 20, 1985, to Stanford University Stadium in Stanford, California, with San Francisco as host team; and Super Bowl XX, to be played on January 26, 1986, to the Louisiana Superdome in New Orleans.

1983

Because of the shortened season, the NFL adopted a format of 16 teams competing in a Super Bowl Tournament for the 1982 playoffs. The NFC's number-one seed, Washington, defeated the AFC's number-two seed, Miami, 27-17 in Super Bowl XVII at the Rose Bowl in Pasadena, January 30.

Super Bowl XVII was the second-highest rated live television program of all time, giving the NFL a sweep of the top 10 live programs in television history. The game was viewed in more than 40 million homes, the largest ever for a live telecast.

Halas, the owner of the Bears and the last surviving member of the NFL's second organizational meeting, died at 88, October 31.

1984

The Los Angeles Raiders defeated Washington 38-9 in Super Bowl XVIII at Tampa Stadium, January 22. The game achieved a 46.4 rating and 71.0 share.

An 11-man group headed by H.R. (Bum) Bright purchased the Dallas Cowboys from Clint Murchison, Jr., March 20. Club president Tex Schramm was designated as managing general partner.

Patrick Bowlen purchased a majority interest in the Denver Broncos from Edgar Kaiser, Jr., March 21.

The Colts relocated to Indianapolis, March 28. Their new home became the Hoosier Dome.

The owners awarded two Super Bowl sites at their May 23-25 meetings: Super Bowl XXI, to be played on January 25, 1987, to the Rose Bowl in Pasadena; and Super Bowl XXII, to be played on January 31, 1988, to San Diego Jack Murphy Stadium.

The New York Jets moved their home games to Giants Stadium in East Rutherford, New Jersey.

Alex G. Spanos purchased a majority interest in the San Diego Chargers from Eugene V. Klein, August 28.

Houston defeated Pittsburgh 23-20 to mark the one-hundredth overtime game in regular-season play since overtime was adopted in 1974, December 2.

On the field, many all-time records were set: Dan Marino of Miami passed for 5,084 yards and 48 touchdowns; Eric Dickerson of the Los Angeles Rams rushed for 2,105 yards; Art Monk of Washington caught 106 passes; and Walter Payton of Chicago broke Jim Brown's career rushing mark, finishing the season with 13,309 yards.

According to a CBS Sports/*New York Times* survey, 53 percent of the nation's sports fans said they most enjoyed watching football, compared to 18 percent for baseball, December 2-4.

NFL paid attendance exceeded 13 million for the fifth consecutive complete regular season when 13,398,112, an average of 59,813, attended games. The figure was the second-highest in league history. Teams averaged 42.4 points per game, the second-highest total since the 1970 merger.

1985

San Francisco defeated Miami 38-16 in Super Bowl XIX at Stanford Stadium in Stanford, California, January 20. The game was viewed on television by more people than any other live event in history. President Ronald Reagan, who took his second oath of office before tossing the coin for the game, was one of 115,936,000 viewers. The game drew a 46.4 rating and a 63.0 share. In addition, 6 million people watched the Super Bowl in the United Kingdom and a similar number in Italy. Super Bowl XIX had a direct economic impact of $113.5 million on the San Francisco Bay area.

NBC Radio and the NFL entered into a two-year agreement granting NBC the radio rights to a 37-game package in each of the 1985-86 seasons, March 6. The package included 27 regular-season games and 10 postseason games.

The owners awarded two Super Bowl sites at their annual meeting, March 10-15: Super Bowl XXIII, to be played on January 22, 1989, to the proposed Dolphins Stadium in Miami; and Super Bowl XXIV, to be played on January 28, 1990, to the Louisiana Superdome in New Orleans.

Norman Braman, in partnership with Edward Leibowitz, bought the Philadelphia Eagles from Leonard Tose, April 29.

Bruce Smith, a Virginia Tech defensive lineman selected by Buffalo, was the first player chosen in the fiftieth NFL draft, April 30.

A group headed by Tom Benson, Jr., was approved to purchase the New Orleans Saints from John W. Mecom, Jr., June 3.

The NFL owners adopted a resolution calling for a series of overseas preseason games, beginning in 1986, with one game to be played in England/Europe and/or one game in Japan each year. The game would be a fifth preseason game for the clubs involved and all arrangements and selection of the clubs would be under the control of the Commissioner, May 23.

The league-wide conversion to videotape from movie film for coaching study was approved.

Commissioner Rozelle was authorized to extend the commitment to Honolulu's Aloha Stadium for the AFC-NFC Pro Bowl for 1988, 1989, and 1990, October 15.

The NFL set a single-weekend paid attendance record when 902,657 tickets were sold for the weekend of October 27-28.

A Louis Harris poll in December revealed that pro football remained the sport most followed by Americans. Fifty-nine percent of those surveyed followed pro football, compared with 54 percent who followed baseball.

The Chicago-Miami Monday game had the highest rating, 29.6, and share, 46.0, of any prime-time game in NFL history, December 2. The game was viewed in more than 25 million homes.

The NFL showed a ratings increase on all three networks for the season, gaining 4 percent on NBC, 10 on CBS, and 16 on ABC.

1986

Chicago defeated New England 46-10 in Super Bowl XX at the Louisiana Superdome, January 26. The Patriots had earned the right to play the Bears by becoming the first wild-card team to win three consecutive games on the road. The NBC telecast replaced the final episode of *M*A*S*H* as the most-viewed television program in history, with an audience of 127 million viewers, according to A.C. Nielsen figures. In addition to drawing a 48.3 rating and a 70 percent share in the United States, Super Bowl XX was televised to 59 foreign countries and beamed via satellite to the QE II. An estimated 300 million Chinese viewed a tape delay of the game in March. NBC Radio figures indicated an audience of 10 million for the game.

Super Bowl XX injected more than $100 million into the New Orleans-area economy, and fans spent $250 per day and a record $17.69 per person on game day.

The owners adopted limited use of instant replay as an officiating aid, prohibited players from wearing or otherwise displaying equipment, apparel, or other items that carry commercial names, names of organizations, or personal messages of any type, March 11.

After an 11-week trial, a jury in U.S. District Court in New York awarded the United States Football League one dollar in its $1.7 billion antitrust suit against the NFL. The jury rejected all of the USFL's television-related claims, which were the self-proclaimed heart of the USFL's case, July 29.

Chicago defeated Dallas 17-6 at Wembley Stadium in London in the first American Bowl. The game drew a sellout crowd of 82,699 and the NBC national telecast in this country produced a 12.4 rating and 36 percent share, making it the second-highest-rated daytime preseason game and highest daytime preseason television audience ever with 10.65-million viewers, August 3.

Monday Night Football became the longest-running prime-time series in the history of the ABC network.

Instant replay was used to reverse two plays in 31 preseason games. During the regular season, 374 plays were closely reviewed by replay officials, leading to 38 reversals in 224 games. Eighteen plays were closely reviewed by instant replay in 10 postseason games with three reversals.

1987
The New York Giants defeated Denver 39-20 in Super Bowl XXI and captured their first NFL title since 1956. The game, played in Pasadena's Rose Bowl, drew a sellout crowd of 101,063. According to A.C. Nielsen figures, the CBS broadcast of the game was viewed in the U.S. on television by 122.64-million people, making the telecast the second most-watched television show of all-time behind Super Bowl XX. The game was watched live or on tape in 55 foreign countries and NBC Radio's broadcast of the game was heard by a record 10.1 million people.

The NFL set an all-time paid attendance mark of 17,304,463 for all games, including preseason, regular-season, and postseason. Average regular-season game attendance (60,663) exceeded the 60,000 figure for only the second time in league history.

New three-year TV contracts with ABC, CBS, and NBC were announced for 1987-89 at the NFL annual meeting in Maui, Hawaii, March 15. Commissioner Rozelle and Broadcast Committee Chairman Art Modell also announced a three-year contract with ESPN to televise 13 prime-time games each season. The ESPN contract was the first with a cable network. However, NFL games on ESPN also were scheduled for regular television in the city of the visiting team and in the home city if the game was sold out 72 hours in advance.

Owners also voted to continue in effect for one year the instant replay system used during the 1986 season.

A special payment program was adopted to benefit nearly 1,000 former NFL players who participated in the League before the current Bert Bell NFL Pension Plan was created and made retroactive to the 1959 season. Players covered by the new program spent at least five years in the League and played all or part of their career prior to 1959. Each vested player would receive $60 per month for each year of service in the League for life.

Possible sites for Super Bowl XXV were reduced to five locations by the NFL Super Bowl XXV Site Selection Committee: Anaheim Stadium, Los Angeles Memorial Coliseum, Joe Robbie Stadium, San Diego Jack Murphy Stadium, and Tampa Stadium.

NFL and CBS Radio jointly announced agreement granting CBS the radio rights to a 40-game package in each of the next three NFL seasons, 1987-89, April 7.

NFL owners awarded Super Bowl XXV, to be played on January 27, 1991, to Tampa Stadium, May 20.

Over 400 former NFL players from the pre-1959 era received first payments from NFL owners, July 1.

The NFL's debut on ESPN produced the two highest-rated and most-watched sports programs in basic cable history. The Chicago at Miami game on August 16 drew an 8.9 rating in 3.81 million homes. Those records fell two weeks later when the Los Angeles Raiders at Dallas game achieved a 10.2 cable rating in 4.36 million homes.

Fifty-eight preseason games drew a record paid attendance of 3,116,870.

The 1987 season was reduced from a 16-game season to 15 as the result of a 24-day players' strike. The strike was called by the NFLPA on Tuesday, September 22, following the New England at New York Jets game. Games scheduled for the third weekend were canceled but the games of weeks four, five, and six were played with replacement teams. Striking players returned for the seventh week of the season, October 25.

In a three-team deal involving 10 players and/or draft choices, the Los Angeles Rams traded running back Eric Dickerson to the Indianapolis Colts for six draft choices and two players. Buffalo obtained the rights to linebacker Cornelius Bennett from Indianapolis, sending Greg Bell and three draft choices to the Rams. The Colts added Owen Gill and three draft choices of their own to complete the deal with the Rams, October 31.

The Chicago at Minnesota game became the highest-rated and most-watched sports program in basic cable history when it drew a 14.4 cable rating in 6.5 million homes, December 6.

Instant replay was used to reverse eight plays in 52 preseason games. During the strike-shortened 210-game regular season, 490 plays were closely reviewed by replay officials, leading to 57 reversals. Eighteen plays were closely reviewed by instant replay in 10 postseason games, with three reversals.

1988
Washington defeated Denver 42-10 in Super Bowl XXII to earn its second victory this decade in the NFL Championship Game. The game, played for the first time in San Diego Jack Murphy Stadium, drew a sellout crowd of 73,302. According to A.C. Nielsen figures, the ABC broadcast of the game was viewed in the U.S. on television by 115,000,000 people. The game was seen live or on tape in 60 foreign countries, including the People's Republic of China, and CBS's radio broadcast of the game was heard by 13.7 million people.

A total of 811 players shared in the postseason pool of $16.9 million, the most ever distributed in a single season.

In a unanimous 3-0 decision, the 2nd Circuit Court of Appeals in New York upheld the verdict of the jury that in July, 1986, had awarded the United States Football League one dollar in its $1.7 billion antitrust suit against the NFL. In a 91-page opinion, Judge Ralph K. Winter said the USFL sought through court decree the success it failed to gain among football fans, March 10.

By a 23-5 margin, owners voted to continue the instant replay system for the third consecutive season with the Instant Replay Official to be assigned to a regular seven-man, on-the-field crew. At the NFL annual meeting in Phoenix, Arizona, a 45-second clock was also approved to replace the 30-second clock. For a normal sequence of plays, the interval between plays was changed to 45 seconds from the time the ball is signaled dead until it is snapped on the succeeding play.

NFL owners approved the transfer of the Cardinals' franchise from St. Louis to Phoenix; approved two supplemental drafts each year—one prior to training camp and one prior to the regular season; and voted to initiate an annual series of games in Japan/Asia as early as the 1989 preseason, March 14-18.

The NFL Annual Selection Meeting returned to a separate two-day format and for the first time originated on a Sunday. ESPN drew a 3.6 rating during their seven-hour coverage of the draft, which was viewed in 1.6 million homes, April 24-25.

Art Rooney, founder and owner of the Steelers, died at 87, August 25.

Johnny Grier became the first African-American referee in NFL history, September 4.

Paid and average attendance of 934,271 and 66,734 at 14 games on October 16-17 set single weekend records.

Commissioner Rozelle announced that two teams would play a preseason game as part of the American Bowl series on August 6, 1989, in the Korakuen Tokyo Dome in Japan, December 16.

NFL regular-season paid attendance of 13,535,335 and the average of 60,427 was the third highest all-time. Buffalo set an NFL team single-season, in-house attendance mark of 622,793.

1989
San Francisco defeated Cincinnati 20-16 in Super Bowl XXIII. The game, played for the first time at Joe Robbie Stadium in Miami, was attended by a sellout crowd of 75,129. NBC's telecast of the game was watched by an estimated 110,780,000 viewers, according to A.C. Nielsen, making it the sixth most-watched program in television history. The game was seen live or on tape in 60 foreign countries, including an estimated 300 million in China. The CBS Radio broadcast of the game was heard by 11.2 million people.

Commissioner Rozelle announced his retirement, pending the naming of a successor, March 22 at the NFL annual meeting in Palm Desert, California.

Following the announcement, AFC president Lamar Hunt and NFC president Wellington Mara announced the formation of a six-man search committee composed of Art Modell, Robert Parins, Dan Rooney, and Ralph Wilson. Hunt and Mara served as co-chairmen.

By a 24-4 margin, owners voted to continue the instant replay system for the fourth straight season. A strengthened policy regarding anabolic steroids and masking agents was announced by Commissioner Rozelle. NFL clubs called for strong disciplinary measures in cases of feigned injuries and adopted a joint proposal by the Long-Range Planning and Finance committees regarding player personnel rules, March 19-23.

Two hundred twenty-nine unconditional free agents signed with new teams under management's Plan B system, April 1.

Jerry Jones purchased a majority interest in the Dallas Cowboys from H.R. (Bum) Bright, April 18.

Tex Schramm was named president of the new World League of American Football to work with a six-man committee of Dan Rooney, chairman; Norman Braman, Lamar Hunt, Victor Kiam, Mike Lynn, and Bill Walsh, April 18.

NFL and CBS Radio jointly announced agreement extending CBS's radio rights to an annual 40-game package through the 1994 season, April 18.

NFL owners awarded Super Bowl XXVI, to be played on January 26, 1992, to Minneapolis, May 24.

As of opening day, September 10, of the 229 Plan B free agents, 111 were active and 23 others were on teams' reserve lists. Ninety-two others were waived and three retired.

Art Shell was named head coach of the Los Angeles Raiders making him the NFL's first black head coach since Fritz Pollard coached the Akron Pros in 1921, October 3.

The site of the New England Patriots at San Francisco 49ers game scheduled for Candlestick Park on October 22 was switched to Stanford Stadium in the aftermath of the Bay Area Earthquake of October 17. The change was announced on October 19.

Paul Tagliabue became the seventh

chief executive of the NFL on October 26 when he was chosen to succeed Commissioner Pete Rozelle on the sixth ballot of a three-day meeting in Cleveland, Ohio.

In all, 12 ballots were required to select Tagliabue. Two were conducted at a meeting in Chicago on July 6, and four at a meeting in Dallas on October 10-11. On the twelfth ballot, with Seattle absent, Tagliabue received more than the 19 affirmative votes required for election from among the 27 clubs present.

The transfer from Commissioner Rozelle to Commissioner Tagliabue took place at 12:01 A.M. on Sunday, November 5.

NFL Charities donated $1 million through United Way to benefit Bay Area earthquake victims, November 6.

NFL paid attendance of 17,399,538 was the highest total in league history. This included a total of 13,625,662 for an average of 60,829—both NFL records—for the 224-game regular season.

1990

San Francisco defeated Denver 55-10 in Super Bowl XXIV at the Louisiana Superdome, January 28. San Francisco joined Pittsburgh as the NFL's only teams to win four Super Bowls.

The NFL announced revisions in its 1990 draft eligibility rules. College juniors became eligible but must renounce their collegiate football eligibility before applying for the NFL Draft, February 16.

Commissioner Tagliabue announced NFL teams will play their 16-game schedule over 17 weeks in 1990 and 1991 and 16 games over 18 weeks in 1992 and 1993, February 27.

The NFL revised its playoff format to include two additional wild-card teams (one per conference).

Commissioner Tagliabue and Broadcast Committee Chairman Art Modell announced a four-year contract with Turner Broadcasting to televise nine Sunday-night games.

New four-year TV agreements were ratified for 1990-93 for ABC, CBS, NBC, ESPN, and TNT at the NFL annual meeting in Orlando, Florida, March 12. The contracts totaled $3.6 billion, the largest in TV history.

The NFL announced plans to expand its American Bowl series of preseason games. In addition to games in London and Tokyo, American Bowl games were scheduled for Berlin, Germany, and Montreal, Canada, in 1990.

For the fifth straight year, NFL owners voted to continue a limited system of Instant Replay. Beginning in 1990, the replay official will have a two-minute time limit to make a decision. The vote was 21-7, March 12.

Commissioner Tagliabue announced the formation of a Committee on Expansion and Realignment, March 13. He also named a Player Advisory Council, comprised of 12 former NFL players, March 14.

One-hundred eighty-four Plan B unconditional free agents signed with new teams, April 2.

Commissioner Tagliabue appointed Dr. John Lombardo as the League's Drug Advisor for Anabolic Steroids, April 25 and named Dr. Lawrence Brown as the League's Advisor for Drugs of Abuse, May 17.

NFL owners awarded Super Bowl XXVIII, to be played in 1994, to the proposed Georgia Dome, May 23.

Commissioner Tagliabue named NFL referee Jerry Seeman as NFL Director of Officiating, replacing Art McNally, who announced his retirement after 31 years on the field and at the league office, July 12.

NFL International Week was celebrated with four preseason games in seven days in Tokyo, London, Berlin, and Montreal. More than 200,000 fans on three continents attended the four games, August 4-11.

Commissioner Tagliabue announced the NFL Teacher of the Month program in which the League furnishes grants and scholarships in recognition of teachers who provided a positive influence upon NFL players in elementary and secondary schools, September 20.

For the first time since 1957, every NFL club won at least one of its first four games, October 1.

NFL total paid attendance of 17,665,671 was the highest total in League history. The regular-season total paid attendance of 13,959,896 and average of 62,321 for 224 games were the highest ever, surpassing the previous records set in the 1989 season.

1991

The New York Giants defeated Buffalo 20-19 in Super Bowl XXV to capture their second title in five years. The game was played before a sellout crowd of 73,813 at Tampa Stadium and became the first Super Bowl decided by one point, January 26. The ABC broadcast of the game was seen by more than 112-million people in the United States and was seen live or taped in 60 other countries.

NFL playoff games earned the top television rating spot of the week for each week of the month-long playoffs, January 29.

A total of 693 players shared in the postseason pool of $14.9 million.

New York businessman Robert Tisch purchased a 50 percent interest in the New York Giants from Mrs. Helen Mara Nugent and her children, Tim Mara and Maura Mara Concannon, February 2.

Commissioner Tagliabue named Neil Austrian to the newly created position of President of the NFL to be chief operating officer for League-wide business and financial operations, February 27.

NFL clubs voted to continue a limited system of Instant Replay for the sixth consecutive year. The vote was 21-7, March 19.

The NFL launched the World League of American Football, the first sports league to operate on a weekly basis on two separate continents, March 23.

NFL Charities presented a $250,000 donation to the United Service Organization. The donation was the second largest single grant ever by NFL Charities, April 5.

Commissioner Tagliabue named Harold Henderson as Executive Vice President for Labor Relations and Chairman of the NFL Management Council Executive Committee, April 8.

Russell Maryland, a University of Miami defensive lineman, was selected by Dallas, becoming the first player chosen in the 1991 NFL draft, April 21.

NFL clubs approved a recommendation by the Expansion and Realignment Committee to add two teams for the 1994 season, resulting in six divisions of five teams each, May 22.

NFL clubs awarded Super Bowl XXIX, to be played on January 29, 1995, to Miami, May 23.

"NFL International Week" featured six 1990 playoff teams playing nationally televised games in London, Berlin, and Tokyo on July 28 and August 3-4. The games drew more than 150,000 fans.

Paul Brown, founder of the Cleveland Browns and Cincinnati Bengals, died at age 82, August 5.

NFL clubs approved a resolution establishing an international division, reporting to the President of the NFL. A three-year financial plan for the World League was approved by NFL clubs at a meeting in Dallas, October 23.

1992

The NFL agreed to provide a minimum of $2.5 million in financial support to the NFL Alumni Association and assistance to NFL Alumni-related programs. The agreement included contributions from NFL Charities to the Pre-59ers and Dire Need Programs for former players, January 25.

The Washington Redskins defeated the Buffalo Bills 37-24 in Super Bowl XXVI to capture their third world championship in 10 years, January 26. The game was played before a sellout crowd of 63,130 at the Hubert H. Humphrey Metrodome in Minneapolis and attracted the second largest television audience in Super Bowl history. The CBS broadcast was seen by more than 123 million people nationally, second only to the 127 million who viewed Super Bowl XX.

For the third consecutive season, NFL total paid attendance reached a record level. Total paid attendance was 17,752,139 for the 296 preseason, regular-season, and postseason games, February 3.

The use in officiating of a limited system of Instant Replay for a seventh consecutive year was not approved. The vote was 17-11 in favor of approval (21 votes were required), March 18.

Steve Emtman, a University of Washington defensive lineman, was selected by Indianapolis, becoming the first player chosen in the 1992 NFL draft, April 26.

St. Louis businessman James Orthwein purchased controlling interest in the New England Patriots from Victor Kiam, May 11.

In a Harris Poll taken during the NFL offseason, professional football again was declared the nation's most popular sport. Professional football finished atop similar surveys conducted by Harris in 1985 and 1989, May 23.

NFL clubs accepted the report of the Expansion Committee at a league meeting in Pasadena. The report names five cities as finalists for the two expansion teams—Baltimore, Charlotte, Jacksonville, Memphis, and St. Louis, May 19.

At a league meeting in Dallas, NFL clubs approved a proposal by the World League Board of Directors to restructure the World League and place future emphasis on its international success, September 17.

1993

The NFL and lawyers for the players announced a settlement of various lawsuits and an agreement on the terms of a seven-year deal that included a new player system to be in place through the 1999 season, January 6.

Commissioner Tagliabue announced the establishment of the "NFL World Partnership Program" to develop amateur football internationally through a series of clinics conducted by former NFL players and coaches, January 14.

As part of Super Bowl XXVII, the NFL announced the creation of the first NFL Youth Education Town, a facility located in south central Los Angeles for inner city youth. January 25.

The Dallas Cowboys defeated the Buffalo Bills 52-17 in Super Bowl XXVII to capture their first NFL title since 1978. The game was played before a crowd of 98,374 at the Rose Bowl in Pasadena, California. The NBC broadcast of the game was the most watched program in television history and was seen by 133,400,000 people in the United States. The game also was seen live or taped in 101 other countries. The rating for the game was 45.1, the tenth highest for any televised sports event, January 31.

A total of 695 players shared in the postseason pool of $14.9 million, February 15.

For the fourth consecutive season, the NFL total paid attendance reached a record level. Total paid attendance was 17,784,354 for the 296 preseason, regular-season, and postseason games, March 4.

NFL clubs awarded Super Bowl XXX to the city of Phoenix, to be played on January 28, 1996, at Sun Devil Stadium, March 23.

Drew Bledsoe, a quarterback from Washington State, was selected by New England, becoming the first player chosen in the 1993 NFL draft, April 25.

The NFL and the NFL Players Association officially signed a 7-year Collective Bargaining Agreement in Washington, D.C., which guarantees more than $1 billion in pension, health, and post-career benefits for current and retired players—the most extensive benefits plan in pro sports. It was the NFL's first CBA since the 1982 agreement expired in 1987, June 29.

Ron Bernard was named president of NFL Enterprises, a newly formed division of the NFL responsible for NFL Films, home video, and special domestic and international television programming, August 19.

NFL announced plans to allow fans, for the first time ever, to join players and coaches in selecting the annual AFC and NFC Pro Bowl teams, October 12.

NFL clubs unanimously awarded

the league's twenty-ninth franchise to the Carolina Panthers at a meeting in Chicago. NFL clubs also awarded Super Bowl XXXI to New Orleans and Super Bowl XXXII to San Diego, October 26.

At the same meeting in Chicago, NFL clubs approved a plan to form a European league with joint venture partners, October 27.

Don Shula became the winningest coach in NFL history when Miami beat Philadelphia to give Shula his 325th victory, one more than George Halas, November 14.

NFL clubs awarded the league's thirtieth franchise to the Jacksonville Jaguars at a meeting in Chicago, November 30.

The NFL announced new 4-year television agreements with ABC, ESPN, TNT, and NFL newcomer FOX, which took over the NFC package from CBS, December 18.

The NFL completed its new TV agreements by announcing that NBC would retain the rights to the AFC package, December 20.

1994

The NFL announced that a regular-season paid attendance record was set in 1993. Attendance averaged 62,354, topping the previous record of 62,321 set in 1990, January 6.

The Dallas Cowboys defeated the Buffalo Bills 30-13 in Super Bowl XXVIII to become the fifth team to win back-to-back Super Bowl titles. The game was viewed by the largest U.S. audience in television history—134.8 million people. The game's 45.5 rating was the highest for a Super Bowl since 1987 and the tenth highest-rated Super Bowl ever, January 30.

NFL clubs unanimously approved the transfer of the New England Patriots from James Orthwein to Robert Kraft at a meeting in Orlando, February 22.

In an effort to increase offensive production, NFL clubs at the league's annual meeting in Orlando adopted a package of changes, including modifications in line play, chucking rules, and the roughing-the-passer rule, plus the adoption of the two-point conversion and moving the spot of the kickoff back to the 30-yard line, March 22.

NFL clubs approved the transfer of the majority interest in the Miami Dolphins from the Robbie family to H. Wayne Huizenga, March 23.

The NFL and FOX announced the formation of a joint venture to create a six-team World League to begin play in Europe in April, 1995, March 23.

The NFL announced a total paid attendance record for the fifth consecutive year, with 17,951,831 in paid attendance for all 1993 games, March 23.

Dan Wilkinson, a defensive tackle from Ohio State, was selected by Cincinnati as the first overall selection in the draft, April 24.

The Carolina Panthers earned the right to select first in the 1995 NFL draft by winning a coin toss with the Jacksonville Jaguars. The Jaguars received the second selection in the 1995 draft, April 24.

NFL clubs approved the transfer of the Philadelphia Eagles from Norman Braman to Jeffrey Lurie, May 6.

The NFL launched "NFL Sunday Ticket," a new season subscription service for satellite television dish owners, June 1.

Sara Levinson, president/business director of MTV, was named president of NFL Properties, July 12.

An all-time NFL record crowd of 112,376 attended the American Bowl game between Dallas and Houston in Mexico City. It concluded the biggest American Bowl series in NFL history with four games attracting a record 256,666 fans, August 15.

The NFL 75th Anniversary All-Time Team was announced at a press conference at Radio City Music Hall, August 30.

The NFL reached agreement on a new seven-year contract with its game officials, September 22.

The NFL Management Council and the NFL Players Association announced an agreement on the formulation and implementation of the most comprehensive drug and alcohol policy in sports, October 28.

At an NFL meeting in Chicago, Commissioner Tagliabue slotted the two new expansion teams into the AFC Central (Jacksonville Jaguars) and NFC West (Carolina Panthers) for the 1995 season only. He also appointed a special committee on realignment to make recommendations on the 1996 season and beyond, November 2.

The NFL set a regular-season paid attendance record for the second consecutive year, topping 14 million for the first time (14,034,977), December 27.

1995

The San Francisco 49ers became the first team to win five Super Bowls when they defeated the San Diego Chargers 49-26 in Super Bowl XXIX at Joe Robbie Stadium in Miami, January 29.

Carolina and Jacksonville stocked their expansion rosters with a total of 66 players from other NFL teams in a veteran player allocation draft in New York, February 16.

CBS Radio and the NFL agreed to a new four-year contract for an annual 53-game package of games, continuing a relationship that spanned 15 of the past 17 years, February 22.

NFL total paid attendance for all 1994 season games reached a record level for the sixth consecutive year, exceeding 18 million for the first time (18,010,264), March 9.

NFL clubs approved the transfer of the Tampa Bay Buccaneers from the estate of the late Hugh Culverhouse to South Florida businessman Malcolm Glazer, March 13.

A total of $20.3 million, the largest NFL postseason pool ever, was divided among 729 players who participated in the 1994 playoffs, March 13.

A series of safety-related rules changes were adopted at a league meeting in Phoenix, primarily related to the use of the helmet against defenseless players, March 14.

After a two-year hiatus, the World League of American Football returned to action with six teams in Europe, April 8.

The NFL became the first major sports league to establish a site on the Internet system of on-line computer communication, April 10.

The transfer of the Rams from Los Angeles to St. Louis was approved by a vote of the NFL clubs at a meeting in Dallas, April 12.

ABC's *NFL Monday Night Football* finished the 1994-95 television season as the fifth highest-rated show out of 146 with a 17.8 average rating, the highest finish in the 25-year history of the series, April 18.

Ki-Jana Carter, a running back from Penn State, was selected by the Cincinnati Bengals as the first overall selection in the draft, April 22.

In an ABC News Poll taken during the NFL offseason, America's sports fans chose football as their favorite spectator sport by more than a 2-to-1 margin over basketball and baseball (35%-16%-12%), April 26.

The Frankfurt Galaxy defeated the Amsterdam Admirals 26-22 to win the 1995 World Bowl before a crowd of 23,847 in Amsterdam's Olympic Stadium, June 23.

Former NFL quarterback and Rhein Fire general manager Oliver Luck was named President of the World League, July 13.

The transfer of the Raiders from Los Angeles to Oakland was approved by a vote of the NFL clubs at a meeting in Chicago, July 22.

Jacksonville Municipal Stadium opened before a sold-out crowd of more than 70,000 for the first preseason game in Jaguars history, August 18.

NFL Charities and 50 NFL players donated $1 million to the United Negro College Fund in honor of the fiftieth anniversity of the UNCF and the integration of the modern NFL, September 15.

The Pro Football Hall Of Fame in Canton, Ohio, completed an $8.9 million expansion including a $4 million contribution by the NFL clubs, October 14.

The Trans World Dome opened in St. Louis before a sold-out crowd of 65,598 as the Rams defeated the Carolina Panthers 28-17, November 12.

NFL paid attendance totaled 963,521 for 15 games in Week 12, the highest weekend total in the league's 76-year history, November 19-20.

On the field, many significant records and milestones were achieved: Miami's Dan Marino surpassed Pro Football Hall of Famer Fran Tarkenton in four major passing categories—attempts, completions, yards, and touchdowns—to become the NFL's all-time career leader. San Francisco's Jerry Rice became the all-time reception and receiving-yardage leader with career totals of 942 catches and 15,123 yards. Dallas' Emmitt Smith scored 25 touchdowns, breaking the season record of 24 set by Washington's John Riggins in 1983.

1996

The Dallas Cowboys won their third Super Bowl title in four years when they defeated the Pittsburgh Steelers 27-17 in Super Bowl XXX at Sun Devil Stadium in Tempe, Arizona. The game was viewed by the largest audience in U.S. television history—138.5 million people, January 28.

An agreement between the NFL and the city of Cleveland regarding the Cleveland Browns' relocation was approved by a vote of the NFL clubs, February 9. According to the agreement, the city of Cleveland retained the Browns' heritage and records, including the name, logo, colors, history, playing records, trophies, and memorabilia, and committed to building a new 72,000-seat stadium for a reactivated Browns' franchise to begin play there no later than 1999. Art Modell received approval to move his franchise to Baltimore and rename it.

NFL total paid attendance for all 1995 games reached a record level for the seventh consecutive year, exceeding 19 million for the first time (19,202,757), March 7.

A total of $21.5 million, the largest NFL postseason pool ever, was divided among 717 players who participated in the 1995 playoffs, March 11.

Keyshawn Johnson, a wide receiver from Southern California, was selected by the New York Jets as the first overall selection in the draft, April 20.

The transfer of the Oilers from Houston to Nashville for the 1998 season was approved by a vote of the NFL clubs at a meeting in Atlanta, April 30.

The Scottish Claymores defeated the Frankfurt Galaxy 32-27 to win the 1996 World Bowl in front of 38,982 at Murrayfield Stadium in Edinburgh, Scotland, June 23.

The NFL returned to Baltimore when the new Baltimore Ravens defeated the Philadelphia Eagles 17-9 in a preseason game before a crowd of 63,804 at Memorial Stadium, August 3.

Ericsson Stadium opened in Charlotte, North Carolina before a crowd of 65,350 as the Carolina Panthers defeated the Chicago Bears 30-12 in a preseason game, August 3.

Points scored totaled 762 and NFL paid attendance totaled 964,079 for 15 games in Week 11, the highest weekend totals in either category in the league's 77-year history, November 10-11.

Former NFL Commissioner Pete Rozelle died at his home in Rancho Santa Fe, California. Rozelle, regarded as the premiere commissioner in sports history, led the NFL for 29 years, from 1960-1989, December 6.

1997

Indianapolis Colts owner Robert Irsay died from complications related to a stroke he suffered in 1995. Irsay acquired the club in 1972 when he traded his Los Angeles Rams to Carrol Rosenbloom for the Colts. He later moved the Colts from Baltimore to Indianapolis in 1984, January 14.

The Green Bay Packers won their first NFL title in 29 years by defeating the New England Patriots 35-21 in Super Bowl XXXI at the Louisiana Superdome in New Orleans. The game was viewed by the fourth-largest audience in U.S. television history—128 million people, January 26.

A total of $24.3 million, the largest NFL postseason pool ever, was divided among 730 players who participated in the 1996 playoffs, March 11.

The rules governing cross-ownership were modified, permitting NFL club owners to also own teams in other sports in their home market or markets without NFL teams. The vote was 24-5 (one abstention) in favor of approval, March 11.

Washington Redskins owner Jack Kent Cooke died at his home in Washington, D.C. Cooke became majority owner in 1974 and the Redskins won three Super Bowls under his leadership, April 6.

Orlando Pace, an offensive tackle from Ohio State, was selected by the St. Louis Rams as the first overall selection in the draft, April 19.

The Barcelona Dragons defeated the Rhein Fire 38-24 to win the 1997 World Bowl in front of 31,100 fans at Estadi Olimpic de Montjuic in Barcelona, Spain, June 22.

Jack Kent Cooke Stadium opened in Raljon, Maryland before a crowd of 78,270 as the Washington Redskins defeated the Arizona Cardinals 19-13, September 14.

The 10,000th regular-season game in NFL history was played when the Seattle Seahawks defeated the Tennessee Oilers 16-13 at the Kingdome in Seattle, October 5.

Atlanta Falcons owner Rankin Smith died of heart failure three days prior to his seventy-third birthday. Smith was the founder of the Falcons and was instrumental in bringing Super Bowls XXVIII and XXXIV to Atlanta, October 26.

NFL paid attendance totaled 999,778 for 15 games in Week 12, the highest weekend total in league history, November 16-17.

Regular-season paid attendance in 1997 rose to 14,967,314 for an average of 62,364 per game. That total was the second-highest all-time, behind the 15,043,562 of 1995, December 23.

1998

The NFL reached agreement on record eight-year television contracts with four networks. ABC (*Monday Night Football*) and FOX (NFC) retained their previous rights, CBS took over the AFC package from NBC, and ESPN won the right to broadcast the entire Sunday night cable package, January 13.

The World League was renamed the NFL Europe League, January 22.

The Denver Broncos won their first Super Bowl by defeating the defending champion Green Bay Packers 31-24 in Super Bowl XXXII at Qualcomm Stadium in San Diego. The game tied Super Bowl XXVII for the third-largest audience in U.S. television history with 133.4 million viewers, January 25.

The NFL clubs approved a six-year extension of the Collective Bargaining Agreement through 2003. The extended CBA also created a $100 million fund for youth football, March 22.

The NFL clubs unanimously approved an expansion team for Cleveland to fulfill the commitment to return the Browns to the field in 1999, March 23.

NFL paid attendance of 19,049,886 for all games played during the 1997 season was the second highest in league history. In 1995, 19,202,757 fans paid to attend games, March 23.

A total of $25.1 million, the largest NFL postseason pool ever, was divided among 737 players who participated in the 1997 playoffs, March 24.

Peyton Manning, a quarterback from Tennessee, was selected by the Indianapolis Colts as the first overall selection in the draft, April 18.

NFL COMMISSIONERS AND PRESIDENTS*

1920................Jim Thorpe, President
1921-39................Joe Carr, President
1939-41............Carl Storck, President
1941-46........................Elmer Layden, Commissioner
1946-59........Bert Bell, Commissioner
1960-89..........................Pete Rozelle, Commissioner
1989-present..............Paul Tagliabue, Commissioner

**NFL treasurer Austin Gunsel served as president in the office of the commissioner following the death of Bert Bell (Oct. 11, 1959) until the election of Pete Rozelle (Jan. 26, 1960).*

1997

AMERICAN CONFERENCE

Eastern Division

	W	L	T	Pct.	Pts.	OP
New England	10	6	0	.625	369	289
Miami*	9	7	0	.563	339	327
New York Jets	9	7	0	.563	348	287
Buffalo	6	10	0	.375	255	367
Indianapolis	3	13	0	.188	313	401

Central Division

	W	L	T	Pct.	Pts.	OP
Pittsburgh	11	5	0	.688	372	307
Jacksonville*	11	5	0	.688	394	318
Tennessee	8	8	0	.500	333	310
Cincinnati	7	9	0	.438	355	405
Baltimore	6	9	1	.406	326	345

Western Division

	W	L	T	Pct.	Pts.	OP
Kansas City	13	3	0	.813	375	232
Denver*	12	4	0	.750	472	287
Seattle	8	8	0	.500	365	362
Oakland	4	12	0	.250	324	419
San Diego	4	12	0	.250	266	425

NATIONAL CONFERENCE

Eastern Division

	W	L	T	Pct.	Pts.	OP
N.Y. Giants	10	5	1	.656	307	265
Washington	8	7	1	.531	327	289
Philadelphia	6	9	1	.406	317	372
Dallas	6	10	0	.375	304	314
Arizona	4	12	0	.250	283	379

Central Division

	W	L	T	Pct.	Pts.	OP
Green Bay	13	3	0	.813	422	282
Tampa Bay*	10	6	0	.625	299	263
Detroit*	9	7	0	.563	379	306
Minnesota*	9	7	0	.563	354	359
Chicago	4	12	0	.250	263	421

Western Division

	W	L	T	Pct.	Pts.	OP
San Francisco	13	3	0	.813	375	265
Carolina	7	9	0	.438	265	314
Atlanta	7	9	0	.438	320	361
New Orleans	6	10	0	.375	237	327
St. Louis	5	11	0	.313	299	359

**Wild-Card qualifier for playoffs*

Miami finished ahead of New York Jets based on head-to-head sweep (2-0). Pittsburgh finished ahead of Jacksonville based on better net division points (78 to Jaguars' 23). Oakland finished ahead of San Diego based on better division record (2-6 to Chargers' 1-7). Detroit finished ahead of Minnesota based on head-to-head sweep (2-0). Carolina finished ahead of Atlanta based on head-to-head sweep (2-0).

Wild-Card playoffs: DENVER 42, Jacksonville 17; NEW ENGLAND 17, Miami 3
Divisional playoffs: PITTSBURGH 7, New England 6; Denver 14, KANSAS CITY 10
AFC championship: Denver 24, PITTSBURGH 21
Wild-Card playoffs: Minnesota 23, N.Y. GIANTS 22; TAMPA BAY 20, Detroit 10
Divisional playoffs: SAN FRANCISCO 38, Minnesota 22; GREEN BAY 21, Tampa Bay 7
NFC championship: Green Bay 23, SAN FRANCISCO 10
Super Bowl XXXII: Denver (AFC) 31, Green Bay (NFC) 24, at Qualcomm Stadium, San Diego, California

In Past Standings section, home teams in playoff games are indicated by capital letters.

1996

AMERICAN CONFERENCE

Eastern Division

	W	L	T	Pct.	Pts.	OP
New England	11	5	0	.688	418	313
Buffalo*	10	6	0	.625	319	266
Indianapolis*	9	7	0	.563	317	334
Miami	8	8	0	.500	339	325
N.Y. Jets	1	15	0	.063	279	454

Central Division

	W	L	T	Pct.	Pts.	OP
Pittsburgh	10	6	0	.625	344	257
Jacksonville*	9	7	0	.563	325	335
Cincinnati	8	8	0	.500	372	369
Houston	8	8	0	.500	345	319
Baltimore	4	12	0	.250	371	441

Western Division

	W	L	T	Pct.	Pts.	OP
Denver	13	3	0	.813	391	275
Kansas City	9	7	0	.563	297	300
San Diego	8	8	0	.500	310	376
Oakland	7	9	0	.438	340	293
Seattle	7	9	0	.438	317	376

NATIONAL CONFERENCE

Eastern Division

	W	L	T	Pct.	Pts.	OP
Dallas	10	6	0	.625	286	250
Philadelphia*	10	6	0	.625	363	341
Washington	9	7	0	.563	364	312
Arizona	7	9	0	.438	300	397
N.Y. Giants	6	10	0	.375	242	297

Central Division

	W	L	T	Pct.	Pts.	OP
Green Bay	13	3	0	.813	456	210
Minnesota*	9	7	0	.563	298	315
Chicago	7	9	0	.438	283	305
Tampa Bay	6	10	0	.375	221	293
Detroit	5	11	0	.313	302	368

Western Division

	W	L	T	Pct.	Pts.	OP
Carolina	12	4	0	.750	367	218
San Francisco*	12	4	0	.750	398	257
St. Louis	6	10	0	.375	303	409
Atlanta	3	13	0	.188	309	461
New Orleans	3	13	0	.188	229	339

**Wild-Card qualifier for playoffs*

Jacksonville finished ahead of Indianapolis and Kansas City based on better conference record (7-5 to Colts' 6-6 and Chiefs' 5-7). Indianapolis was third Wild Card based on head-to-head victory over Kansas City (1-0). Cincinnati finished ahead of Houston based on better net division points (19 to Oilers' 11). Oakland finished ahead of Seattle based on better division record (3-5 to Seahawks' 2-6). Dallas finished ahead of Philadelphia based on better record against common opponents (8-5 to Eagles' 7-6). Minnesota was third Wild Card based on better conference record than Washington (8-4 to Redskins' 6-6). Carolina finished ahead of San Francisco based on head-to-head sweep (2-0). Atlanta finished ahead of New Orleans based on head-to-head sweep (2-0).

Wild-Card playoffs: Jacksonville 30, BUFFALO 27; PITTSBURGH 42, Indianapolis 14
Divisional playoffs: Jacksonville 30, DENVER 27; NEW ENGLAND 28, Pittsburgh 3
AFC championship: NEW ENGLAND 20, Jacksonville 6
Wild-Card playoffs: DALLAS 40, Minnesota 15; SAN FRANCISCO 14, Philadelphia 0
Divisional playoffs: GREEN BAY 35, San Francisco 14; CAROLINA 26, Dallas 17
NFC championship: GREEN BAY 30, Carolina 13
Super Bowl XXXI: Green Bay (NFC) 35, New England (AFC) 21, at Louisiana Superdome, New Orleans, Louisiana

1995

AMERICAN CONFERENCE

Eastern Division

	W	L	T	Pct.	Pts.	OP
Buffalo	10	6	0	.625	350	335
Indianapolis*	9	7	0	.563	331	316
Miami*	9	7	0	.563	398	332
New England	6	10	0	.375	294	377
N.Y. Jets	3	13	0	.188	233	384

Central Division

	W	L	T	Pct.	Pts.	OP
Pittsburgh	11	5	0	.688	407	327
Cincinnati	7	9	0	.438	349	374
Houston	7	9	0	.438	348	324
Cleveland	5	11	0	.313	289	356
Jacksonville	4	12	0	.250	275	404

Western Division

	W	L	T	Pct.	Pts.	OP
Kansas City	13	3	0	.813	358	241
San Diego*	9	7	0	.563	321	323
Seattle	8	8	0	.500	363	366
Denver	8	8	0	.500	388	345
Oakland	8	8	0	.500	348	332

NATIONAL CONFERENCE

Eastern Division

	W	L	T	Pct.	Pts.	OP
Dallas	12	4	0	.750	435	291
Philadelphia*	10	6	0	.625	318	338
Washington	6	10	0	.375	326	359
N.Y. Giants	5	11	0	.313	290	340
Arizona	4	12	0	.250	275	422

Central Division

	W	L	T	Pct.	Pts.	OP
Green Bay	11	5	0	.688	404	314
Detroit*	10	6	0	.625	436	336
Chicago	9	7	0	.563	392	360
Minnesota	8	8	0	.500	412	385
Tampa Bay	7	9	0	.438	238	335

Western Division

	W	L	T	Pct.	Pts.	OP
San Francisco	11	5	0	.688	457	258
Atlanta*	9	7	0	.563	362	349
St. Louis	7	9	0	.438	309	418
Carolina	7	9	0	.438	289	325
New Orleans	7	9	0	.438	319	348

**Wild-Card qualifier for playoffs*

Indianapolis finished ahead of Miami based on head-to-head sweep (2-0). San Diego was first Wild Card based on head-to-head victory over Indianapolis (1-0). Cincinnati finished ahead of Houston based on better division record (4-4 to Oilers' 3-5). Seattle finished ahead of Denver and Oakland based on best head-to-head record (3-1 to Broncos' 2-2 and Raiders' 1-3). Denver finished ahead of Oakland based on head-to-head sweep (2-0). Philadelphia was first Wild Card ahead of Detroit based on better conference record (9-3 to Lions' 7-5). Atlanta was third Wild Card ahead of Chicago based on better record against common opponents (4-2 to Bears' 3-3). St. Louis finished ahead of Carolina and New Orleans based on best head-to-head record (3-1 to Panthers' 1-3 and Saints' 2-2). Carolina finished ahead of New Orleans based on better conference record (4-8 to 3-9).

Wild-Card playoffs: BUFFALO 37, Miami 22; Indianapolis 35, SAN DIEGO 20
Divisional playoffs: PITTSBURGH 40, Buffalo 21; Indianapolis 10, KANSAS CITY 7
AFC championship: PITTSBURGH 20, Indianapolis 16
Wild-Card playoffs: PHILADELPHIA 58, Detroit 37; GREEN BAY 37, Atlanta 20
Divisional playoffs: Green Bay 27, SAN FRANCISCO 17; DALLAS 30, Philadelphia 11
NFC championship: DALLAS 38, Green Bay 27
Super Bowl XXX: Dallas (NFC) 27, Pittsburgh (AFC)17, at Sun Devil Stadium, Tempe, Arizona

1994

AMERICAN CONFERENCE

Eastern Division

	W	L	T	Pct.	Pts.	OP
Miami	10	6	0	.625	389	327
New England*	10	6	0	.625	351	312
Indianapolis	8	8	0	.500	307	320
Buffalo	7	9	0	.438	340	356
N.Y. Jets	6	10	0	.375	264	320

Central Division

	W	L	T	Pct.	Pts.	OP
Pittsburgh	12	4	0	.750	316	234
Cleveland*	11	5	0	.688	340	204
Cincinnati	3	13	0	.188	276	406
Houston	2	14	0	.125	226	352

Western Division

	W	L	T	Pct.	Pts.	OP
San Diego	11	5	0	.688	381	306
Kansas City*	9	7	0	.563	319	298
L.A. Raiders	9	7	0	.563	303	327
Denver	7	9	0	.438	347	396
Seattle	6	10	0	.375	287	323

NATIONAL CONFERENCE

Eastern Division

	W	L	T	Pct.	Pts.	OP
Dallas	12	4	0	.750	414	248
N.Y. Giants	9	7	0	.563	279	305
Arizona	8	8	0	.500	235	267
Philadelphia	7	9	0	.438	308	308
Washington	3	13	0	.188	320	412

Central Division

	W	L	T	Pct.	Pts.	OP
Minnesota	10	6	0	.625	356	314
Green Bay*	9	7	0	.563	382	287
Detroit*	9	7	0	.563	357	342
Chicago*	9	7	0	.563	271	307
Tampa Bay	6	10	0	.375	251	351

Western Division

	W	L	T	Pct.	Pts.	OP
San Francisco	13	3	0	.813	505	296
New Orleans	7	9	0	.438	348	407
Atlanta	7	9	0	.438	317	385
L.A. Rams	4	12	0	.250	286	365

**Wild-Card qualifier for playoffs*

Miami finished ahead of New England based on a head-to-head sweep (2-0). Kansas City finished ahead of L.A. Raiders based on a head-to-head sweep (2-0). Green Bay was first Wild Card based on best head-to-head record (3-1) vs. Detroit (2-2) and Chicago (1-3) and better conference record (8-4) than N.Y. Giants (6-6). Detroit was second Wild Card based on better division record (4-4) than Chicago (3-5) and head-to-head sweep of N.Y. Giants (1-0). Chicago was third Wild Card based on better record vs. common opponents (4-4) than N.Y. Giants (3-5). New Orleans finished ahead of Atlanta based on a head-to-head sweep (2-0).

Wild-Card playoffs: MIAMI 27, Kansas City 17; CLEVELAND 20, New England 13
Divisional playoffs: PITTSBURGH 29, Cleveland 9; SAN DIEGO 22, Miami 21
AFC championship: San Diego 17, PITTSBURGH 13
Wild-Card playoffs: GREEN BAY 16, Detroit 12; Chicago 35, MINNESOTA 18
Divisional playoffs: SAN FRANCISCO 44, Chicago 15; DALLAS 35, Green Bay 9
NFC championship: SAN FRANCISCO 38, Dallas 28
Super Bowl XXIX: San Francisco (NFC) 49, San Diego (AFC) 26, at Joe Robbie Stadium, Miami, Florida

PAST STANDINGS

1993

AMERICAN CONFERENCE

Eastern Division

	W	L	T	Pct.	Pts.	OP
Buffalo	12	4	0	.750	329	242
Miami	9	7	0	.563	349	351
N.Y. Jets	8	8	0	.500	270	247
New England	5	11	0	.313	238	286
Indianapolis	4	12	0	.250	189	378

Central Division

	W	L	T	Pct.	Pts.	OP
Houston	12	4	0	.750	368	238
Pittsburgh*	9	7	0	.563	308	281
Cleveland	7	9	0	.438	304	307
Cincinnati	3	13	0	.188	187	319

Western Division

	W	L	T	Pct.	Pts.	OP
Kansas City	11	5	0	.688	328	291
L.A. Raiders*	10	6	0	.625	306	326
Denver*	9	7	0	.563	373	284
San Diego	8	8	0	.500	322	290
Seattle	6	10	0	.375	280	314

NATIONAL CONFERENCE

Eastern Division

	W	L	T	Pct.	Pts.	OP
Dallas	12	4	0	.750	376	229
N.Y. Giants*	11	5	0	.688	288	205
Philadelphia	8	8	0	.500	293	315
Phoenix	7	9	0	.438	326	269
Washington	4	12	0	.250	230	345

Central Division

	W	L	T	Pct.	Pts.	OP
Detroit	10	6	0	.625	298	292
Minnesota*	9	7	0	.563	277	290
Green Bay*	9	7	0	.563	340	282
Chicago	7	9	0	.438	234	230
Tampa Bay	5	11	0	.313	237	376

Western Division

	W	L	T	Pct.	Pts.	OP
San Francisco	10	6	0	.625	473	295
New Orleans	8	8	0	.500	317	343
Atlanta	6	10	0	.375	316	385
L.A. Rams	5	11	0	.313	221	367

**Wild-Card qualifier for playoffs*

Minnesota finished ahead of Green Bay based on a head-to-head sweep (2-0).

Wild-Card playoffs: KANSAS CITY 27, Pittsburgh 24 (OT); L.A. RAIDERS 42, Denver 24

Divisional playoffs: BUFFALO 29, L.A. Raiders 23; Kansas City 28, HOUSTON 20

AFC championship: BUFFALO 30, Kansas City 13

Wild-Card playoffs: Green Bay 28, DETROIT 24; N.Y. GIANTS 17, Minnesota 10

Divisional playoffs: SAN FRANCISCO 44, N.Y. Giants 3; DALLAS 27, Green Bay 17

NFC championship: DALLAS 38, San Francisco 21

Super Bowl XXVIII: Dallas (NFC) 30, Buffalo (AFC) 13, at Georgia Dome, Atlanta, Georgia

1992

AMERICAN CONFERENCE

Eastern Division

	W	L	T	Pct.	Pts.	OP
Miami	11	5	0	.688	340	281
Buffalo*	11	5	0	.688	381	283
Indianapolis	9	7	0	.563	216	302
N.Y. Jets	4	12	0	.250	220	315
New England	2	14	0	.125	205	363

Central Division

	W	L	T	Pct.	Pts.	OP
Pittsburgh	11	5	0	.688	299	225
Houston*	10	6	0	.625	352	258
Cleveland	7	9	0	.438	272	275
Cincinnati	5	11	0	.313	274	364

Western Division

	W	L	T	Pct.	Pts.	OP
San Diego	11	5	0	.688	335	241
Kansas City*	10	6	0	.625	348	282
Denver	8	8	0	.500	262	329
L.A. Raiders	7	9	0	.438	249	281
Seattle	2	14	0	.125	140	312

NATIONAL CONFERENCE

Eastern Division

	W	L	T	Pct.	Pts.	OP
Dallas	13	3	0	.813	409	243
Philadelphia*	11	5	0	.688	354	245
Washington*	9	7	0	.563	300	255
N.Y. Giants	6	10	0	.375	306	367
Phoenix	4	12	0	.250	243	332

Central Division

	W	L	T	Pct.	Pts.	OP
Minnesota	11	5	0	.688	374	249
Green Bay	9	7	0	.563	276	296
Tampa Bay	5	11	0	.313	267	365
Chicago	5	11	0	.313	295	361
Detroit	5	11	0	.313	273	332

Western Division

	W	L	T	Pct.	Pts.	OP
San Francisco	14	2	0	.875	431	236
New Orleans*	12	4	0	.750	330	202
Atlanta	6	10	0	.375	327	414
L.A. Rams	6	10	0	.375	313	383

**Wild-Card qualifier for playoffs*

Miami finished ahead of Buffalo based on better conference record (9-3 to 7-5). Tampa Bay finished ahead of Chicago and Detroit based on better conference record (5-9 to Bears' 4-8 and Lions' 3-9). Atlanta finished ahead of L.A. Rams based on better record versus common opponents (5-7 to 4-8).

Wild-Card playoffs: SAN DIEGO 17, Kansas City 0; BUFFALO 41, Houston 38 (OT)

Divisional playoffs: Buffalo 24, PITTSBURGH 3; MIAMI 31, San Diego 0

AFC championship: Buffalo 29, MIAMI 10

Wild-Card playoffs: Washington 24, MINNESOTA 7; Philadelphia 36, NEW ORLEANS 20

Divisional playoffs: SAN FRANCISCO 20, Washington 13; DALLAS 34, Philadelphia 10

NFC championship: Dallas 30, SAN FRANCISCO 20

Super Bowl XXVII: Dallas (NFC) 52, Buffalo (AFC) 17, at Rose Bowl, Pasadena, California

1991

AMERICAN CONFERENCE

Eastern Division

	W	L	T	Pct.	Pts.	OP
Buffalo	13	3	0	.813	458	318
N.Y. Jets*	8	8	0	.500	314	293
Miami	8	8	0	.500	343	349
New England	6	10	0	.375	211	305
Indianapolis	1	15	0	.063	143	381

Central Division

	W	L	T	Pct.	Pts.	OP
Houston	11	5	0	.688	386	251
Pittsburgh	7	9	0	.438	292	344
Cleveland	6	10	0	.375	293	298
Cincinnati	3	13	0	.188	263	435

Western Division

	W	L	T	Pct.	Pts.	OP
Denver	12	4	0	.750	304	235
Kansas City*	10	6	0	.625	322	252
L.A. Raiders*	9	7	0	.563	298	297
Seattle	7	9	0	.438	276	261
San Diego	4	12	0	.250	274	342

NATIONAL CONFERENCE

Eastern Division

	W	L	T	Pct.	Pts.	OP
Washington	14	2	0	.875	485	224
Dallas*	11	5	0	.688	342	310
Philadelphia	10	6	0	.625	285	244
N.Y. Giants	8	8	0	.500	281	297
Phoenix	4	12	0	.250	196	344

Central Division

	W	L	T	Pct.	Pts.	OP
Detroit	12	4	0	.750	339	295
Chicago*	11	5	0	.688	299	269
Minnesota	8	8	0	.500	301	306
Green Bay	4	12	0	.250	273	313
Tampa Bay	3	13	0	.188	199	365

Western Division

	W	L	T	Pct.	Pts.	OP
New Orleans	11	5	0	.688	341	211
Atlanta*	10	6	0	.625	361	338
San Francisco	10	6	0	.625	393	239
L.A. Rams	3	13	0	.188	234	390

**Wild-Card qualifiers for playoffs*

New York Jets finished ahead of Miami based on head-to-head sweep (2-0). Atlanta finished ahead of San Francisco based on head-to-head sweep (2-0).

Wild-Card playoffs: KANSAS CITY 10, L.A. Raiders 6; HOUSTON 17, N.Y. Jets 10

Divisional playoffs: DENVER 26, Houston 24; BUFFALO 37, Kansas City 14

AFC championship: BUFFALO 10, Denver 7

Wild-Card playoffs: Atlanta 27, NEW ORLEANS 20; Dallas 17, CHICAGO 13

Divisional playoffs: WASHINGTON 24, Atlanta 7; DETROIT 38, Dallas 6

NFC championship: WASHINGTON 41, Detroit 10

Super Bowl XXVI: Washington (NFC) 37, Buffalo (AFC) 24, at Hubert H. Humphrey Metrodome, Minneapolis, Minnesota

1990

AMERICAN CONFERENCE

Eastern Division

	W	L	T	Pct.	Pts.	OP
Buffalo	13	3	0	.813	428	263
Miami*	12	4	0	.750	336	242
Indianapolis	7	9	0	.438	281	353
N.Y. Jets	6	10	0	.375	295	345
New England	1	15	0	.063	181	446

Central Division

	W	L	T	Pct.	Pts.	OP
Cincinnati	9	7	0	.563	360	352
Houston*	9	7	0	.563	405	307
Pittsburgh	9	7	0	.563	292	240
Cleveland	3	13	0	.188	228	462

Western Division

	W	L	T	Pct.	Pts.	OP
L.A. Raiders	12	4	0	.750	337	268
Kansas City*	11	5	0	.688	369	257
Seattle	9	7	0	.563	306	286
San Diego	6	10	0	.375	315	281
Denver	5	11	0	.313	331	374

NATIONAL CONFERENCE

Eastern Division

	W	L	T	Pct.	Pts.	OP
N.Y. Giants	13	3	0	.813	335	211
Philadelphia*	10	6	0	.625	396	299
Washington*	10	6	0	.625	381	301
Dallas	7	9	0	.438	244	308
Phoenix	5	11	0	.313	268	396

Central Division

	W	L	T	Pct.	Pts.	OP
Chicago	11	5	0	.688	348	280
Tampa Bay	6	10	0	.375	264	367
Detroit	6	10	0	.375	373	413
Green Bay	6	10	0	.375	271	347
Minnesota	6	10	0	.375	351	326

Western Division

	W	L	T	Pct.	Pts.	OP
San Francisco	14	2	0	.875	353	239
New Orleans*	8	8	0	.500	274	275
L.A. Rams	5	11	0	.313	345	412
Atlanta	5	11	0	.313	348	365

**Wild-Card qualifiers for playoffs*

Cincinnati won AFC Central title based on best head-to-head record (3-1) vs. Houston (2-2) and Pittsburgh (1-3). Houston was Wild Card based on better conference record (8-4) than Seattle (7-5) and Pittsburgh (6-6). Philadelphia finished second in the NFC East based on better division record (5-3) than Washington (4-4). Tampa Bay was second in NFC Central based on 5-1 record vs. Detroit, Green Bay, and Minnesota. Detroit finished third based on best net division points (minus 8) vs. Green Bay (minus 40) in fourth. Minnesota was fifth based on 4-8 conference record. The Los Angeles Rams finished third in NFC West based on net points in division (plus 1) vs. Atlanta (minus 31).

Wild-Card playoffs: MIAMI 17, Kansas City 16; CINCINNATI 41, Houston 14

Divisional playoffs: BUFFALO 44, Miami 34; L.A. RAIDERS 20, Cincinnati 10

AFC championship: BUFFALO 51, L.A. Raiders 3

Wild-Card playoffs: Washington 20, PHILADELPHIA 6; CHICAGO 16, New Orleans 6

Divisional playoffs: SAN FRANCISCO 28, Washington 10; N.Y. GIANTS 31, Chicago 3

NFC championship: N.Y. Giants 15, SAN FRANCISCO 13

Super Bowl XXV: N.Y. Giants (NFC) 20, Buffalo (AFC) 19, at Tampa Stadium, Tampa, Florida

1989

AMERICAN CONFERENCE

Eastern Division

	W	L	T	Pct.	Pts.	OP
Buffalo	9	7	0	.563	409	317
Indianapolis	8	8	0	.500	298	301
Miami	8	8	0	.500	331	379
New England	5	11	0	.313	297	391
N.Y. Jets	4	12	0	.250	253	411

Central Division

	W	L	T	Pct.	Pts.	OP
Cleveland	9	6	1	.594	334	254
Houston*	9	7	0	.563	365	412
Pittsburgh*	9	7	0	.563	265	326
Cincinnati	8	8	0	.500	404	285

Western Division

	W	L	T	Pct.	Pts.	OP
Denver	11	5	0	.688	362	226
Kansas City	8	7	1	.531	318	286
L.A. Raiders	8	8	0	.500	315	297
Seattle	7	9	0	.438	241	327
San Diego	6	10	0	.375	266	290

NATIONAL CONFERENCE

Eastern Division

	W	L	T	Pct.	Pts.	OP
N.Y. Giants	12	4	0	.750	348	252
Philadelphia*	11	5	0	.688	342	274
Washington	10	6	0	.625	386	308
Phoenix	5	11	0	.313	258	377
Dallas	1	15	0	.063	204	393

Central Division

	W	L	T	Pct.	Pts.	OP
Minnesota	10	6	0	.625	351	275
Green Bay	10	6	0	.625	362	356
Detroit	7	9	0	.438	312	364
Chicago	6	10	0	.375	358	377
Tampa Bay	5	11	0	.313	320	419

Western Division

	W	L	T	Pct.	Pts.	OP
San Francisco	14	2	0	.875	442	253
L.A. Rams*	11	5	0	.688	426	344
New Orleans	9	7	0	.563	386	301
Atlanta	3	13	0	.188	279	437

**Wild-Card qualifiers for playoffs*

Indianapolis finished ahead of Miami in AFC East because of better conference record (7-5 vs. 6-8). Houston finished ahead of Pittsburgh in AFC Central because of head-to-head sweep (2-0). Minnesota finished ahead of Green Bay in NFC Central because of better division record (6-2 vs. 5-3).

Wild-Card playoff: Pittsburgh 26, HOUSTON 23 (OT)
Divisional playoffs: CLEVELAND 34, Buffalo 30; DENVER 24, Pittsburgh 23
AFC championship: DENVER 37, Cleveland 21
Wild-Card playoff: L.A. Rams 21, PHILADELPHIA 7
Divisional playoffs: L.A. Rams 19, N.Y. GIANTS 13 (OT); SAN FRANCISCO 41, Minnesota 13
NFC championship: SAN FRANCISCO 30, L.A. Rams 3
Super Bowl XXIV: San Francisco (NFC) 55, Denver (AFC) 10, at Louisiana Superdome, New Orleans, Louisiana

1988

AMERICAN CONFERENCE

Eastern Division

	W	L	T	Pct.	Pts.	OP
Buffalo	12	4	0	.750	329	237
Indianapolis	9	7	0	.563	354	315
New England	9	7	0	.563	250	284
N.Y. Jets	8	7	1	.531	372	354
Miami	6	10	0	.375	319	380

Central Division

	W	L	T	Pct.	Pts.	OP
Cincinnati	12	4	0	.750	448	329
Cleveland*	10	6	0	.625	304	288
Houston*	10	6	0	.625	424	365
Pittsburgh	5	11	0	.313	336	421

Western Division

	W	L	T	Pct.	Pts.	OP
Seattle	9	7	0	.563	339	329
Denver	8	8	0	.500	327	352
L.A. Raiders	7	9	0	.438	325	369
San Diego	6	10	0	.375	231	332
Kansas City	4	11	1	.281	254	320

NATIONAL CONFERENCE

Eastern Division

	W	L	T	Pct.	Pts.	OP
Philadelphia	10	6	0	.625	379	319
N.Y. Giants	10	6	0	.625	359	304
Washington	7	9	0	.438	345	387
Phoenix	7	9	0	.438	344	398
Dallas	3	13	0	.188	265	381

Central Division

	W	L	T	Pct.	Pts.	OP
Chicago	12	4	0	.750	312	215
Minnesota*	11	5	0	.688	406	233
Tampa Bay	5	11	0	.313	261	350
Detroit	4	12	0	.250	220	313
Green Bay	4	12	0	.250	240	315

Western Division

	W	L	T	Pct.	Pts.	OP
San Francisco	10	6	0	.625	369	294
L.A. Rams*	10	6	0	.625	407	293
New Orleans	10	6	0	.625	312	283
Atlanta	5	11	0	.313	244	315

**Wild-Card qualifiers for playoffs*

Indianapolis finished second in AFC East on basis of better record versus common opponents (7-5) over New England (6-6). Cleveland gained first AFC Wild-Card position based on better division record (4-2) over Houston (3-3). Philadelphia finished first in NFC East on basis of head-to-head sweep over New York Giants. Washington finished third in NFC East on basis of better division record (4-4) over Phoenix (3-5). Detroit finished fourth in NFC Central on basis of head-to-head sweep over Green Bay. San Francisco finished first in NFC West based on better head-to-head record (3-1) over Los Angeles Rams (2-2) and New Orleans (1-3). Los Angeles Rams finished second in NFC West on basis of better division record (4-2) over New Orleans (3-3) and earned Wild-Card position based on better conference record (8-4) over New York Giants (9-5) and New Orleans (6-6).

Wild-Card playoff: Houston 24, CLEVELAND 23
Divisional playoffs: CINCINNATI 21, Seattle 13; BUFFALO 17, Houston 10
AFC championship: CINCINNATI 21, Buffalo 10
Wild-Card playoff: MINNESOTA 28, Los Angeles Rams 17
Divisional playoffs: CHICAGO 20, Philadelphia 12; SAN FRANCISCO 34, Minnesota 9
NFC championship: San Francisco 28, CHICAGO 3
Super Bowl XXIII: San Francisco (NFC) 20, Cincinnati (AFC) 16, at Joe Robbie Stadium, Miami, Florida

1987

AMERICAN CONFERENCE

Eastern Division

	W	L	T	Pct.	Pts.	OP
Indianapolis	9	6	0	.600	300	238
New England	8	7	0	.533	320	293
Miami	8	7	0	.533	362	335
Buffalo	7	8	0	.467	270	305
N.Y. Jets	6	9	0	.400	334	360

Central Division

	W	L	T	Pct.	Pts.	OP
Cleveland	10	5	0	.667	390	239
Houston*	9	6	0	.600	345	349
Pittsburgh	8	7	0	.533	285	299
Cincinnati	4	11	0	.267	285	370

Western Division

	W	L	T	Pct.	Pts.	OP
Denver	10	4	1	.700	379	288
Seattle*	9	6	0	.600	371	314
San Diego	8	7	0	.533	253	317
L.A. Raiders	5	10	0	.333	301	289
Kansas City	4	11	0	.267	273	388

NATIONAL CONFERENCE

Eastern Division

	W	L	T	Pct.	Pts.	OP
Washington	11	4	0	.733	379	285
Dallas	7	8	0	.467	340	348
St. Louis	7	8	0	.467	362	368
Philadelphia	7	8	0	.467	337	380
N.Y. Giants	6	9	0	.400	280	312

Central Division

	W	L	T	Pct.	Pts.	OP
Chicago	11	4	0	.733	356	282
Minnesota*	8	7	0	.533	336	335
Green Bay	5	9	1	.367	255	300
Tampa Bay	4	11	0	.267	286	360
Detroit	4	11	0	.267	269	384

Western Division

	W	L	T	Pct.	Pts.	OP
San Francisco	13	2	0	.867	459	253
New Orleans*	12	3	0	.800	422	283
L.A. Rams	6	9	0	.400	317	361
Atlanta	3	12	0	.200	205	436

**Wild-Card qualifiers for playoffs*

Houston gained first AFC Wild-Card position on better conference record (7-4) over Seattle (5-6).

Wild-Card playoff: HOUSTON 23, Seattle 20 (OT)
Divisional playoffs: CLEVELAND 38, Indianapolis 21; DENVER 34, Houston 10
AFC championship: DENVER 38, Cleveland 33
Wild-Card playoff: Minnesota 44, NEW ORLEANS 10
Divisional playoffs: Minnesota 36, SAN FRANCISCO 24; Washington 21, CHICAGO 17
NFC championship: WASHINGTON 17, Minnesota 10
Super Bowl XXII: Washington (NFC) 42, Denver (AFC) 10, at San Diego Jack Murphy Stadium, San Diego, California

Note: 1987 regular season was reduced from 16 to 15 games for each team due to players' strike.

1986

AMERICAN CONFERENCE

Eastern Division

	W	L	T	Pct.	Pts.	OP
New England	11	5	0	.688	412	307
N.Y. Jets*	10	6	0	.625	364	386
Miami	8	8	0	.500	430	405
Buffalo	4	12	0	.250	287	348
Indianapolis	3	13	0	.188	229	400

Central Division

	W	L	T	Pct.	Pts.	OP
Cleveland	12	4	0	.750	391	310
Cincinnati	10	6	0	.625	409	394
Pittsburgh	6	10	0	.375	307	336
Houston	5	11	0	.313	274	329

Western Division

	W	L	T	Pct.	Pts.	OP
Denver	11	5	0	.688	378	327
Kansas City*	10	6	0	.625	358	326
Seattle	10	6	0	.625	366	293
L.A. Raiders	8	8	0	.500	323	346
San Diego	4	12	0	.250	335	396

NATIONAL CONFERENCE

Eastern Division

	W	L	T	Pct.	Pts.	OP
N.Y. Giants	14	2	0	.875	371	236
Washington*	12	4	0	.750	368	296
Dallas	7	9	0	.438	346	337
Philadelphia	5	10	1	.344	256	312
St. Louis	4	11	1	.281	218	351

Central Division

	W	L	T	Pct.	Pts.	OP
Chicago	14	2	0	.875	352	187
Minnesota	9	7	0	.563	398	273
Detroit	5	11	0	.313	277	326
Green Bay	4	12	0	.250	254	418
Tampa Bay	2	14	0	.125	239	473

Western Division

	W	L	T	Pct.	Pts.	OP
San Francisco	10	5	1	.656	374	247
L.A. Rams*	10	6	0	.625	309	267
Atlanta	7	8	1	.469	280	280
New Orleans	7	9	0	.438	288	287

**Wild-Card qualifiers for playoffs*

New York Jets gained first AFC Wild-Card position on better conference record (8-4) over Kansas City (9-5), Seattle (7-5), and Cincinnati (7-5). Kansas City gained second Wild Card based on better conference record (9-5) over Seattle (7-5) and Cincinnati (7-5).

Wild-Card playoff: NEW YORK JETS 35, Kansas City 15
Divisional playoffs: CLEVELAND 23, New York Jets 20 (OT); DENVER 22, New England 17
AFC championship: Denver 23, CLEVELAND 20 (OT)
Wild-Card playoff: WASHINGTON 19, Los Angeles Rams 7
Divisional playoffs: Washington 27, CHICAGO 13 NEW YORK GIANTS 49, San Francisco 3
NFC championship: NEW YORK GIANTS 17, Washington 0
Super Bowl XXI: New York Giants (NFC) 39, Denver (AFC) 20, at Rose Bowl, Pasadena, California

PAST STANDINGS

1985

AMERICAN CONFERENCE

Eastern Division

	W	L	T	Pct.	Pts.	OP
Miami	12	4	0	.750	428	320
N.Y. Jets*	11	5	0	.688	393	264
New England*	11	5	0	.688	362	290
Indianapolis	5	11	0	.313	320	386
Buffalo	2	14	0	.125	200	381

Central Division

	W	L	T	Pct.	Pts.	OP
Cleveland	8	8	0	.500	287	294
Cincinnati	7	9	0	.438	441	437
Pittsburgh	7	9	0	.438	379	355
Houston	5	11	0	.313	284	412

Western Division

	W	L	T	Pct.	Pts.	OP
L.A. Raiders	12	4	0	.750	354	308
Denver	11	5	0	.688	380	329
Seattle	8	8	0	.500	349	303
San Diego	8	8	0	.500	467	435
Kansas City	6	10	0	.375	317	360

NATIONAL CONFERENCE

Eastern Division

	W	L	T	Pct.	Pts.	OP
Dallas	10	6	0	.625	357	333
N.Y. Giants*	10	6	0	.625	399	283
Washington	10	6	0	.625	297	312
Philadelphia	7	9	0	.438	286	310
St. Louis	5	11	0	.313	278	414

Central Division

	W	L	T	Pct.	Pts.	OP
Chicago	15	1	0	.938	456	198
Green Bay	8	8	0	.500	337	355
Minnesota	7	9	0	.438	346	359
Detroit	7	9	0	.438	307	366
Tampa Bay	2	14	0	.125	294	448

Western Division

	W	L	T	Pct.	Pts.	OP
L.A. Rams	11	5	0	.688	340	277
San Francisco*	10	6	0	.625	411	263
New Orleans	5	11	0	.313	294	401
Atlanta	4	12	0	.250	282	452

**Wild-Card qualifiers for playoffs*

New York Jets gained first AFC Wild-Card position on better conference record (9-3) over New England (8-4) and Denver (8-4). New England gained second AFC Wild-Card position based on better record vs. common opponents (4-2) than Denver (3-3). Dallas won NFC Eastern Division title based on better record (4-0) vs. New York Giants (1-3) and Washington (1-3). New York Giants gained first NFC Wild Card position based on better conference record (8-4) over San Francisco (7-5) and Washington (6-6). San Francisco gained second NFC Wild-Card position based on head-to-head victory over Washington.

Wild-Card playoff: New England 26, NEW YORK JETS 14
Divisional playoffs: MIAMI 24, Cleveland 21;
New England 27, LOS ANGELES RAIDERS 20
AFC championship: New England 31, MIAMI 14
Wild-Card playoff: NEW YORK GIANTS 17, San Francisco 3
Divisional playoffs: LOS ANGELES RAMS 20, Dallas 0;
CHICAGO 21, New York Giants 0
NFC championship: CHICAGO 24, Los Angeles Rams 0
Super Bowl XX: Chicago (NFC) 46, New England (AFC) 10, at Louisiana Superdome, New Orleans, Louisiana

1984

AMERICAN CONFERENCE

Eastern Division

	W	L	T	Pct.	Pts.	OP
Miami	14	2	0	.875	513	298
New England	9	7	0	.563	362	352
N.Y. Jets	7	9	0	.438	332	364
Indianapolis	4	12	0	.250	239	414
Buffalo	2	14	0	.125	250	454

Central Division

	W	L	T	Pct.	Pts.	OP
Pittsburgh	9	7	0	.563	387	310
Cincinnati	8	8	0	.500	339	339
Cleveland	5	11	0	.313	250	297
Houston	3	13	0	.188	240	437

Western Division

	W	L	T	Pct.	Pts.	OP
Denver	13	3	0	.813	353	241
Seattle*	12	4	0	.750	418	282
L.A. Raiders*	11	5	0	.688	368	278
Kansas City	8	8	0	.500	314	324
San Diego	7	9	0	.438	394	413

NATIONAL CONFERENCE

Eastern Division

	W	L	T	Pct.	Pts.	OP
Washington	11	5	0	.688	426	310
N.Y. Giants*	9	7	0	.563	299	301
St. Louis	9	7	0	.563	423	345
Dallas	9	7	0	.563	308	308
Philadelphia	6	9	1	.406	278	320

Central Division

	W	L	T	Pct.	Pts.	OP
Chicago	10	6	0	.625	325	248
Green Bay	8	8	0	.500	390	309
Tampa Bay	6	10	0	.375	335	380
Detroit	4	11	1	.281	283	408
Minnesota	3	13	0	.188	276	484

Western Division

	W	L	T	Pct.	Pts.	OP
San Francisco	15	1	0	.938	475	227
L.A. Rams*	10	6	0	.625	346	316
New Orleans	7	9	0	.438	298	361
Atlanta	4	12	0	.250	281	382

**Wild-Card qualifiers for playoffs*

New York Giants clinched Wild-Card berth based on 3-1 record vs. St. Louis's 2-2 and Dallas's 1-3. St. Louis finished ahead of Dallas based on better division record (5-3 to 3-5).

Wild-Card playoff: SEATTLE 13, Los Angeles Raiders 7
Divisional playoffs: MIAMI 31, Seattle 10; Pittsburgh 24, DENVER 17
AFC championship: MIAMI 45, Pittsburgh 28
Wild-Card playoff: New York Giants 16, LOS ANGELES RAMS 13
Divisional playoffs: SAN FRANCISCO 21, New York Giants 10;
Chicago 23, WASHINGTON 19
NFC championship: SAN FRANCISCO 23, Chicago 0
Super Bowl XIX: San Francisco (NFC) 38, Miami (AFC) 16, at Stanford Stadium, Stanford, California

1983

AMERICAN CONFERENCE

Eastern Division

	W	L	T	Pct.	Pts.	OP
Miami	12	4	0	.750	389	250
New England	8	8	0	.500	274	289
Buffalo	8	8	0	.500	283	351
Baltimore	7	9	0	.438	264	354
N.Y. Jets	7	9	0	.438	313	331

Central Division

	W	L	T	Pct.	Pts.	OP
Pittsburgh	10	6	0	.625	355	303
Cleveland	9	7	0	.563	356	342
Cincinnati	7	9	0	.438	346	302
Houston	2	14	0	.125	288	460

Western Division

	W	L	T	Pct.	Pts.	OP
L.A. Raiders	12	4	0	.750	442	338
Seattle*	9	7	0	.563	403	397
Denver*	9	7	0	.563	302	327
San Diego	6	10	0	.375	358	462
Kansas City	6	10	0	.375	386	367

NATIONAL CONFERENCE

Eastern Division

	W	L	T	Pct.	Pts.	OP
Washington	14	2	0	.875	541	332
Dallas*	12	4	0	.750	479	360
St. Louis	8	7	1	.531	374	428
Philadelphia	5	11	0	.313	233	322
N.Y. Giants	3	12	1	.219	267	347

Central Division

	W	L	T	Pct.	Pts.	OP
Detroit	9	7	0	.563	347	286
Green Bay	8	8	0	.500	429	439
Chicago	8	8	0	.500	311	301
Minnesota	8	8	0	.500	316	348
Tampa Bay	2	14	0	.125	241	380

Western Division

	W	L	T	Pct.	Pts.	OP
San Francisco	10	6	0	.625	432	293
L.A. Rams*	9	7	0	.563	361	344
New Orleans	8	8	0	.500	319	337
Atlanta	7	9	0	.438	370	389

**Wild-Card qualifiers for playoffs*

Seattle and Denver gained Wild-Card berths over Cleveland because of their victories over the Browns.

Wild-Card playoff: SEATTLE 31, Denver 7
Divisional playoffs: Seattle 27, MIAMI 20; LOS ANGELES RAIDERS 38, Pittsburgh 10
AFC championship: LOS ANGELES RAIDERS 30, Seattle 14
Wild-Card playoff: Los Angeles Rams 24, DALLAS 17
Divisional playoffs: SAN FRANCISCO 24, Detroit 23; WASHINGTON 51, L.A. Rams 7
NFC championship: WASHINGTON 24, San Francisco 21
Super Bowl XVIII: Los Angeles Raiders (AFC) 38, Washington (NFC) 9, at Tampa Stadium, Tampa, Florida

1982

AMERICAN CONFERENCE

	W	L	T	Pct.	Pts.	OP
L.A. Raiders	8	1	0	.889	260	200
Miami	7	2	0	.778	198	131
Cincinnati	7	2	0	.778	232	177
Pittsburgh	6	3	0	.667	204	146
San Diego	6	3	0	.667	288	221
N.Y. Jets	6	3	0	.667	245	166
New England	5	4	0	.556	143	157
Cleveland	4	5	0	.444	140	182
Buffalo	4	5	0	.444	150	154
Seattle	4	5	0	.444	127	147
Kansas City	3	6	0	.333	176	184
Denver	2	7	0	.222	148	226
Houston	1	8	0	.111	136	245
Baltimore	0	8	1	.056	113	236

NATIONAL CONFERENCE

	W	L	T	Pct.	Pts.	OP
Washington	8	1	0	.889	190	128
Dallas	6	3	0	.667	226	145
Green Bay	5	3	1	.611	226	169
Minnesota	5	4	0	.556	187	198
Atlanta	5	4	0	.556	183	199
St. Louis	5	4	0	.556	135	170
Tampa Bay	5	4	0	.556	158	178
Detroit	4	5	0	.444	181	176
New Orleans	4	5	0	.444	129	160
N.Y. Giants	4	5	0	.444	164	160
San Francisco	3	6	0	.333	209	206
Chicago	3	6	0	.333	141	174
Philadelphia	3	6	0	.333	191	195
L.A. Rams	2	7	0	.222	200	250

As the result of a 57-day players' strike, the 1982 NFL regular season schedule was reduced from 16 weeks to 9. At the conclusion of the regular season, the NFL conducted a 16-team postseason Super Bowl Tournament. Eight teams from each conference were seeded 1-8 based on their records during the season.

Miami finished ahead of Cincinnati based on better conference record (6-1 to 6-2). Pittsburgh won common games tie-breaker with San Diego (3-1 to 2-1) after New York Jets were eliminated from three-way tie based on conference record (Pittsburgh and San Diego 5-3 vs. Jets 2-3). Cleveland finished ahead of Buffalo and Seattle based on better conference record (4-3 to 3-3 to 3-5). Minnesota (4-1), Atlanta (4-3), St. Louis (5-4), Tampa Bay (3-3) seeds were determined by best won-lost record in conference games. Detroit finished ahead of New Orleans and the New York Giants based on better conference record (4-4 to 3-5 to 3-5).

First round playoff: MIAMI 28, New England 13
LOS ANGELES RAIDERS 27, Cleveland 10
New York Jets 44, CINCINNATI 17
San Diego 31, PITTSBURGH 28
Second round playoff: New York Jets 17, LOS ANGELES RAIDERS 14
MIAMI 34, San Diego 13
AFC championship: MIAMI 14, New York Jets 0
First round playoff: WASHINGTON 31, Detroit 7
GREEN BAY 41, St. Louis 16
MINNESOTA 30, Atlanta 24
DALLAS 30, Tampa Bay 17
Second round playoff: WASHINGTON 21, Minnesota 7
DALLAS 37, Green Bay 26
NFC championship: WASHINGTON 31, Dallas 17
Super Bowl XVII: Washington (NFC) 27, Miami (AFC) 17, at Rose Bowl, Pasadena, California

1981

AMERICAN CONFERENCE

Eastern Division

	W	L	T	Pct.	Pts.	OP
Miami	11	4	1	.719	345	275
N.Y. Jets*	10	5	1	.656	355	287
Buffalo*	10	6	0	.625	311	276
Baltimore	2	14	0	.125	259	533
New England	2	14	0	.125	322	370

Central Division

	W	L	T	Pct.	Pts.	OP
Cincinnati	12	4	0	.750	421	304
Pittsburgh	8	8	0	.500	356	297
Houston	7	9	0	.438	281	355
Cleveland	5	11	0	.313	276	375

Western Division

	W	L	T	Pct.	Pts.	OP
San Diego	10	6	0	.625	478	390
Denver	10	6	0	.625	321	289
Kansas City	9	7	0	.563	343	290
Oakland	7	9	0	.438	273	343
Seattle	6	10	0	.375	322	388

NATIONAL CONFERENCE

Eastern Division

	W	L	T	Pct.	Pts.	OP
Dallas	12	4	0	.750	367	277
Philadelphia*	10	6	0	.625	368	221
N.Y. Giants*	9	7	0	.563	295	257
Washington	8	8	0	.500	347	349
St. Louis	7	9	0	.438	315	408

Central Division

	W	L	T	Pct.	Pts.	OP
Tampa Bay	9	7	0	.563	315	268
Detroit	8	8	0	.500	397	322
Green Bay	8	8	0	.500	324	361
Minnesota	7	9	0	.438	325	369
Chicago	6	10	0	.375	253	324

Western Division

	W	L	T	Pct.	Pts.	OP
San Francisco	13	3	0	.813	357	250
Atlanta	7	9	0	.438	426	355
Los Angeles	6	10	0	.375	303	351
New Orleans	4	12	0	.250	207	378

**Wild-Card qualifiers for playoffs*

San Diego won AFC Western title over Denver on the basis of a better division record (6-2 to 5-3). Buffalo won a Wild-Card playoff berth over Denver as the result of a 9-7 victory in head-to-head competition.

Wild-Card playoff: Buffalo 31, NEW YORK JETS 27

Divisional playoffs: San Diego 41, MIAMI 38 (OT); CINCINNATI 28, Buffalo 21

AFC championship: CINCINNATI 27, San Diego 7

Wild-Card playoff: New York Giants 27, PHILADELPHIA 21

Divisional playoffs: DALLAS 38, Tampa Bay 0; SAN FRANCISCO 38, New York Giants 24

NFC championship: SAN FRANCISCO 28, Dallas 27

Super Bowl XVI: San Francisco (NFC) 26, Cincinnati (AFC) 21, at Silverdome, Pontiac, Michigan

1980

AMERICAN CONFERENCE

Eastern Division

	W	L	T	Pct.	Pts.	OP
Buffalo	11	5	0	.688	320	260
New England	10	6	0	.625	441	325
Miami	8	8	0	.500	266	305
Baltimore	7	9	0	.438	355	387
N.Y. Jets	4	12	0	.250	302	395

Central Division

	W	L	T	Pct.	Pts.	OP
Cleveland	11	5	0	.688	357	310
Houston*	11	5	0	.688	295	251
Pittsburgh	9	7	0	.563	352	313
Cincinnati	6	10	0	.375	244	312

Western Division

	W	L	T	Pct.	Pts.	OP
San Diego	11	5	0	.688	418	327
Oakland*	11	5	0	.688	364	306
Kansas City	8	8	0	.500	319	336
Denver	8	8	0	.500	310	323
Seattle	4	12	0	.250	291	408

NATIONAL CONFERENCE

Eastern Division

	W	L	T	Pct.	Pts.	OP
Philadelphia	12	4	0	.750	384	222
Dallas*	12	4	0	.750	454	311
Washington	6	10	0	.375	261	293
St. Louis	5	11	0	.313	299	350
N.Y. Giants	4	12	0	.250	249	425

Central Division

	W	L	T	Pct.	Pts.	OP
Minnesota	9	7	0	.563	317	308
Detroit	9	7	0	.563	334	272
Chicago	7	9	0	.438	304	264
Tampa Bay	5	10	1	.344	271	341
Green Bay	5	10	1	.344	231	371

Western Division

	W	L	T	Pct.	Pts.	OP
Atlanta	12	4	0	.750	405	272
Los Angeles*	11	5	0	.688	424	289
San Francisco	6	10	0	.375	320	415
New Orleans	1	15	0	.063	291	487

**Wild-Card qualifiers for playoffs*

Philadelphia won division title over Dallas on the basis of best net points in division games (plus 84 net points to plus 50). Minnesota won division title because of a better conference record than Detroit (8-4 to 9-5). Cleveland won division title because of a better conference record than Houston (8-4 to 7-5). San Diego won division title over Oakland on the basis of best net points in division games (plus 60 net points to plus 37).

Wild-Card playoff: OAKLAND 27, Houston 7

Divisional playoffs: SAN DIEGO 20, Buffalo 14; Oakland 14, CLEVELAND 12

AFC championship: Oakland 34, SAN DIEGO 27

Wild-Card playoff: DALLAS 34, Los Angeles 13

Divisional playoffs: PHILADELPHIA 31, Minnesota 16; Dallas 30, ATLANTA 27

NFC championship: PHILADELPHIA 20, Dallas 7

Super Bowl XV: Oakland (AFC) 27, Philadelphia (NFC) 10, at Louisiana Superdome, New Orleans, Louisiana

1979

AMERICAN CONFERENCE

Eastern Division

	W	L	T	Pct.	Pts.	OP
Miami	10	6	0	.625	341	257
New England	9	7	0	.563	411	326
N.Y. Jets	8	8	0	.500	337	383
Buffalo	7	9	0	.438	268	279
Baltimore	5	11	0	.313	271	351

Central Division

	W	L	T	Pct.	Pts.	OP
Pittsburgh	12	4	0	.750	416	262
Houston*	11	5	0	.688	362	331
Cleveland	9	7	0	.563	359	352
Cincinnati	4	12	0	.250	337	421

Western Division

	W	L	T	Pct.	Pts.	OP
San Diego	12	4	0	.750	411	246
Denver*	10	6	0	.625	289	262
Seattle	9	7	0	.563	378	372
Oakland	9	7	0	.563	365	337
Kansas City	7	9	0	.438	238	262

NATIONAL CONFERENCE

Eastern Division

	W	L	T	Pct.	Pts.	OP
Dallas	11	5	0	.688	371	313
Philadelphia*	11	5	0	.688	339	282
Washington	10	6	0	.625	348	295
N.Y. Giants	6	10	0	.375	237	323
St. Louis	5	11	0	.313	307	358

Central Division

	W	L	T	Pct.	Pts.	OP
Tampa Bay	10	6	0	.625	273	237
Chicago*	10	6	0	.625	306	249
Minnesota	7	9	0	.438	259	337
Green Bay	5	11	0	.313	246	316
Detroit	2	14	0	.125	219	365

Western Division

	W	L	T	Pct.	Pts.	OP
Los Angeles	9	7	0	.563	323	309
New Orleans	8	8	0	.500	370	360
Atlanta	6	10	0	.375	300	388
San Francisco	2	14	0	.125	308	416

**Wild-Card qualifiers for playoffs*

Dallas won division title because of a better conference record than Philadelphia (10-2 to 9-3). Tampa Bay won division title because of a better division record than Chicago (6-2 to 5-3). Chicago won a Wild-Card berth over Washington on the basis of best net points in all games (plus 57 net points to plus 53).

Wild-Card playoff: HOUSTON 13, Denver 7

Divisional playoffs: Houston 17, SAN DIEGO 14; PITTSBURGH 34, Miami 14

AFC championship: PITTSBURGH 27, Houston 13

Wild-Card playoff: PHILADELPHIA 27, Chicago 17

Divisional playoffs: TAMPA BAY 24, Philadelphia 17; Los Angeles 21, DALLAS 19

NFC championship: Los Angeles 9, TAMPA BAY 0

Super Bowl XIV: Pittsburgh (AFC) 31, Los Angeles (NFC) 19, at Rose Bowl, Pasadena, California

1978

AMERICAN CONFERENCE

Eastern Division

	W	L	T	Pct.	Pts.	OP
New England	11	5	0	.688	358	286
Miami*	11	5	0	.688	372	254
N.Y. Jets	8	8	0	.500	359	364
Buffalo	5	11	0	.313	302	354
Baltimore	5	11	0	.313	239	421

Central Division

	W	L	T	Pct.	Pts.	OP
Pittsburgh	14	2	0	.875	356	195
Houston*	10	6	0	.625	283	298
Cleveland	8	8	0	.500	334	356
Cincinnati	4	12	0	.250	252	284

Western Division

	W	L	T	Pct.	Pts.	OP
Denver	10	6	0	.625	282	198
Oakland	9	7	0	.563	311	283
Seattle	9	7	0	.563	345	358
San Diego	9	7	0	.563	355	309
Kansas City	4	12	0	.250	243	327

NATIONAL CONFERENCE

Eastern Division

	W	L	T	Pct.	Pts.	OP
Dallas	12	4	0	.750	384	208
Philadelphia*	9	7	0	.563	270	250
Washington	8	8	0	.500	273	283
St. Louis	6	10	0	.375	248	296
N.Y. Giants	6	10	0	.375	264	298

Central Division

	W	L	T	Pct.	Pts.	OP
Minnesota	8	7	1	.531	294	306
Green Bay	8	7	1	.531	249	269
Detroit	7	9	0	.438	290	300
Chicago	7	9	0	.438	253	274
Tampa Bay	5	11	0	.313	241	259

Western Division

	W	L	T	Pct.	Pts.	OP
Los Angeles	12	4	0	.750	316	245
Atlanta*	9	7	0	.563	240	290
New Orleans	7	9	0	.438	281	298
San Francisco	2	14	0	.125	219	350

**Wild-Card qualifiers for playoffs*

New England won division title on the basis of a better division record than Miami (6-2 to 5-3). Minnesota won division title because of a better head-to-head record against Green Bay (1-0-1).

Wild-Card playoff: Houston 17, MIAMI 9

Divisional playoffs: Houston 31, NEW ENGLAND 14; PITTSBURGH 33, Denver 10

AFC championship: PITTSBURGH 34, Houston 5

Wild-Card playoff: ATLANTA 14, Philadelphia 13

Divisional playoffs: DALLAS 27, Atlanta 20; LOS ANGELES 34, Minnesota 10

NFC championship: Dallas 28, LOS ANGELES 0

Super Bowl XIII: Pittsburgh (AFC) 35, Dallas (NFC) 31, at Orange Bowl, Miami, Florida

PAST STANDINGS

1977

AMERICAN CONFERENCE

Eastern Division

	W	L	T	Pct.	Pts.	OP
Baltimore	10	4	0	.714	295	221
Miami	10	4	0	.714	313	197
New England	9	5	0	.643	278	217
N.Y. Jets	3	11	0	.214	191	300
Buffalo	3	11	0	.214	160	313

Central Division

	W	L	T	Pct.	Pts.	OP
Pittsburgh	9	5	0	.643	283	243
Houston	8	6	0	.571	299	230
Cincinnati	8	6	0	.571	238	235
Cleveland	6	8	0	.429	269	267

Western Division

	W	L	T	Pct.	Pts.	OP
Denver	12	2	0	.857	274	148
Oakland*	11	3	0	.786	351	230
San Diego	7	7	0	.500	222	205
Seattle	5	9	0	.357	282	373
Kansas City	2	12	0	.143	225	349

NATIONAL CONFERENCE

Eastern Division

	W	L	T	Pct.	Pts.	OP
Dallas	12	2	0	.857	345	212
Washington	9	5	0	.643	196	189
St. Louis	7	7	0	.500	272	287
Philadelphia	5	9	0	.357	220	207
N.Y. Giants	5	9	0	.357	181	265

Central Division

	W	L	T	Pct.	Pts.	OP
Minnesota	9	5	0	.643	231	227
Chicago*	9	5	0	.643	255	253
Detroit	6	8	0	.429	183	252
Green Bay	4	10	0	.286	134	219
Tampa Bay	2	12	0	.143	103	223

Western Division

	W	L	T	Pct.	Pts.	OP
Los Angeles	10	4	0	.714	302	146
Atlanta	7	7	0	.500	179	129
San Francisco	5	9	0	.357	220	260
New Orleans	3	11	0	.214	232	336

**Wild-Card qualifier for playoffs*

Baltimore won division title on the basis of a better conference record than Miami (9-3 to 8-4). Chicago won a Wild-Card berth over Washington on the basis of best net points in conference games (plus 48 net points to plus 4).

Divisional playoffs: DENVER 34, Pittsburgh 21; Oakland 37, BALTIMORE 31 (OT)
AFC championship: DENVER 20, Oakland 17
Divisional playoffs: DALLAS 37, Chicago 7; Minnesota 14, LOS ANGELES 7
NFC championship: DALLAS 23, Minnesota 6
Super Bowl XII: Dallas (NFC) 27, Denver (AFC) 10, at Louisiana Superdome, New Orleans, Louisiana

1976

AMERICAN CONFERENCE

Eastern Division

	W	L	T	Pct.	Pts.	OP
Baltimore	11	3	0	.786	417	246
New England*	11	3	0	.786	376	236
Miami	6	8	0	.429	263	264
N.Y. Jets	3	11	0	.214	169	383
Buffalo	2	12	0	.143	245	363

Central Division

	W	L	T	Pct.	Pts.	OP
Pittsburgh	10	4	0	.714	342	138
Cincinnati	10	4	0	.714	335	210
Cleveland	9	5	0	.643	267	287
Houston	5	9	0	.357	222	273

Western Division

	W	L	T	Pct.	Pts.	OP
Oakland	13	1	0	.929	350	237
Denver	9	5	0	.643	315	206
San Diego	6	8	0	.429	248	285
Kansas City	5	9	0	.357	290	376
Tampa Bay	0	14	0	.000	125	412

NATIONAL CONFERENCE

Eastern Division

	W	L	T	Pct.	Pts.	OP
Dallas	11	3	0	.786	296	194
Washington*	10	4	0	.714	291	217
St. Louis	10	4	0	.714	309	267
Philadelphia	4	10	0	.286	165	286
N.Y. Giants	3	11	0	.214	170	250

Central Division

	W	L	T	Pct.	Pts.	OP
Minnesota	11	2	1	.821	305	176
Chicago	7	7	0	.500	253	216
Detroit	6	8	0	.429	262	220
Green Bay	5	9	0	.357	218	299

Western Division

	W	L	T	Pct.	Pts.	OP
Los Angeles	10	3	1	.750	351	190
San Francisco	8	6	0	.571	270	190
Atlanta	4	10	0	.286	172	312
New Orleans	4	10	0	.286	253	346
Seattle	2	12	0	.143	229	429

**Wild-Card qualifier for playoffs*

Baltimore won division title on the basis of a better division record than New England (7-1 to 6-2). Pittsburgh won division title because of a two-game sweep over Cincinnati. Washington won Wild-Card berth over St. Louis because of a two-game sweep over Cardinals.

Divisional playoffs: OAKLAND 24, New England 21; Pittsburgh 40, BALTIMORE 14
AFC championship: OAKLAND 24, Pittsburgh 7
Divisional playoffs: MINNESOTA 35, Washington 20; Los Angeles 14, DALLAS 12
NFC championship: MINNESOTA 24, Los Angeles 13
Super Bowl XI: Oakland (AFC) 32, Minnesota (NFC) 14, at Rose Bowl, Pasadena, California

1975

AMERICAN CONFERENCE

Eastern Division

	W	L	T	Pct.	Pts.	OP
Baltimore	10	4	0	.714	395	269
Miami	10	4	0	.714	357	222
Buffalo	8	6	0	.571	420	355
New England	3	11	0	.214	258	358
N.Y. Jets	3	11	0	.214	258	433

Central Division

	W	L	T	Pct.	Pts.	OP
Pittsburgh	12	2	0	.857	373	162
Cincinnati*	11	3	0	.786	340	246
Houston	10	4	0	.714	293	226
Cleveland	3	11	0	.214	218	372

Western Division

	W	L	T	Pct.	Pts.	OP
Oakland	11	3	0	.786	375	255
Denver	6	8	0	.429	254	307
Kansas City	5	9	0	.357	282	341
San Diego	2	12	0	.143	189	345

NATIONAL CONFERENCE

Eastern Division

	W	L	T	Pct.	Pts.	OP
St. Louis	11	3	0	.786	356	276
Dallas*	10	4	0	.714	350	268
Washington	8	6	0	.571	325	276
N.Y. Giants	5	9	0	.357	216	306
Philadelphia	4	10	0	.286	225	302

Central Division

	W	L	T	Pct.	Pts.	OP
Minnesota	12	2	0	.857	377	180
Detroit	7	7	0	.500	245	262
Chicago	4	10	0	.286	191	379
Green Bay	4	10	0	.286	226	285

Western Division

	W	L	T	Pct.	Pts.	OP
Los Angeles	12	2	0	.857	312	135
San Francisco	5	9	0	.357	255	286
Atlanta	4	10	0	.286	240	289
New Orleans	2	12	0	.143	165	360

**Wild-Card qualifier for playoffs*

Baltimore won division title on the basis of a two-game sweep over Miami.

Divisional playoffs: PITTSBURGH 28, Baltimore 10; OAKLAND 31, Cincinnati 28
AFC championship: PITTSBURGH 16, Oakland 10
Divisional playoffs: LOS ANGELES 35, St. Louis 23; Dallas 17, MINNESOTA 14
NFC championship: Dallas 37, LOS ANGELES 7
Super Bowl X: Pittsburgh (AFC) 21, Dallas (NFC) 17, at Orange Bowl, Miami, Florida

1974

AMERICAN CONFERENCE

Eastern Division

	W	L	T	Pct.	Pts.	OP
Miami	11	3	0	.786	327	216
Buffalo*	9	5	0	.643	264	244
New England	7	7	0	.500	348	289
N.Y. Jets	7	7	0	.500	279	300
Baltimore	2	12	0	.143	190	329

Central Division

	W	L	T	Pct.	Pts.	OP
Pittsburgh	10	3	1	.750	305	189
Cincinnati	7	7	0	.500	283	259
Houston	7	7	0	.500	236	282
Cleveland	4	10	0	.286	251	344

Western Division

	W	L	T	Pct.	Pts.	OP
Oakland	12	2	0	.857	355	228
Denver	7	6	1	.536	302	294
Kansas City	5	9	0	.357	233	293
San Diego	5	9	0	.357	212	285

NATIONAL CONFERENCE

Eastern Division

	W	L	T	Pct.	Pts.	OP
St. Louis	10	4	0	.714	285	218
Washington*	10	4	0	.714	320	196
Dallas	8	6	0	.571	297	235
Philadelphia	7	7	0	.500	242	217
N.Y. Giants	2	12	0	.143	195	299

Central Division

	W	L	T	Pct.	Pts.	OP
Minnesota	10	4	0	.714	310	195
Detroit	7	7	0	.500	256	270
Green Bay	6	8	0	.429	210	206
Chicago	4	10	0	.286	152	279

Western Division

	W	L	T	Pct.	Pts.	OP
Los Angeles	10	4	0	.714	263	181
San Francisco	6	8	0	.429	226	236
New Orleans	5	9	0	.357	166	263
Atlanta	3	11	0	.214	111	271

**Wild-Card qualifier for playoffs*

St. Louis won division title because of a two-game sweep over Washington.

Divisional playoffs: OAKLAND 28, Miami 26; PITTSBURGH 32, Buffalo 14
AFC championship: Pittsburgh 24, OAKLAND 13
Divisional playoffs: MINNESOTA 30, St. Louis 14; LOS ANGELES 19, Washington 10
NFC championship: MINNESOTA 14, Los Angeles 10
Super Bowl IX: Pittsburgh (AFC) 16, Minnesota (NFC) 6, at Tulane Stadium, New Orleans, Louisiana

1973

AMERICAN CONFERENCE

Eastern Division

	W	L	T	Pct.	Pts.	OP
Miami	12	2	0	.857	343	150
Buffalo	9	5	0	.643	259	230
New England	5	9	0	.357	258	300
Baltimore	4	10	0	.286	226	341
N.Y. Jets	4	10	0	.286	240	306

Central Division

	W	L	T	Pct.	Pts.	OP
Cincinnati	10	4	0	.714	286	231
Pittsburgh*	10	4	0	.714	347	210
Cleveland	7	5	2	.571	234	255
Houston	1	13	0	.071	199	447

Western Division

	W	L	T	Pct.	Pts.	OP
Oakland	9	4	1	.679	292	175
Denver	7	5	2	.571	354	296
Kansas City	7	5	2	.571	231	192
San Diego	2	11	1	.179	188	386

NATIONAL CONFERENCE

Eastern Division

	W	L	T	Pct.	Pts.	OP
Dallas	10	4	0	.714	382	203
Washington*	10	4	0	.714	325	198
Philadelphia	5	8	1	.393	310	393
St. Louis	4	9	1	.321	286	365
N.Y. Giants	2	11	1	.179	226	362

Central Division

	W	L	T	Pct.	Pts.	OP
Minnesota	12	2	0	.857	296	168
Detroit	6	7	1	.464	271	247
Green Bay	5	7	2	.429	202	259
Chicago	3	11	0	.214	195	334

Western Division

	W	L	T	Pct.	Pts.	OP
Los Angeles	12	2	0	.857	388	178
Atlanta	9	5	0	.643	318	224
New Orleans	5	9	0	.357	163	312
San Francisco	5	9	0	.357	262	319

**Wild-Card qualifier for playoffs*

Cincinnati won division title on the basis of a better conference record than Pittsburgh (8-3 to 7-4). Dallas won division title on the basis of a better point differential vs. Washington (net 13 points).

Divisional playoffs: OAKLAND 33, Pittsburgh 14; MIAMI 34, Cincinnati 16
AFC championship: MIAMI 27, Oakland 10
Divisional playoffs: MINNESOTA 27, Washington 20; DALLAS 27, Los Angeles 16
NFC championship: Minnesota 27, DALLAS 10
Super Bowl VIII: Miami (AFC) 24, Minnesota (NFC) 7, at Rice Stadium, Houston, Texas

1972

AMERICAN CONFERENCE

Eastern Division

	W	L	T	Pct.	Pts.	OP
Miami	14	0	0	1.000	385	171
N.Y. Jets	7	7	0	.500	367	324
Baltimore	5	9	0	.357	235	252
Buffalo	4	9	1	.321	257	377
New England	3	11	0	.214	192	446

Central Division

	W	L	T	Pct.	Pts.	OP
Pittsburgh	11	3	0	.786	343	175
Cleveland*	10	4	0	.714	268	249
Cincinnati	8	6	0	.571	299	229
Houston	1	13	0	.071	164	380

Western Division

	W	L	T	Pct.	Pts.	OP
Oakland	10	3	1	.750	365	248
Kansas City	8	6	0	.571	287	254
Denver	5	9	0	.357	325	350
San Diego	4	9	1	.321	264	344

NATIONAL CONFERENCE

Eastern Division

	W	L	T	Pct.	Pts.	OP
Washington	11	3	0	.786	336	218
Dallas*	10	4	0	.714	319	240
N.Y. Giants	8	6	0	.571	331	247
St. Louis	4	9	1	.321	193	303
Philadelphia	2	11	1	.179	145	352

Central Division

	W	L	T	Pct.	Pts.	OP
Green Bay	10	4	0	.714	304	226
Detroit	8	5	1	.607	339	290
Minnesota	7	7	0	.500	301	252
Chicago	4	9	1	.321	225	275

Western Division

	W	L	T	Pct.	Pts.	OP
San Francisco	8	5	1	.607	353	249
Atlanta	7	7	0	.500	269	274
Los Angeles	6	7	1	.464	291	286
New Orleans	2	11	1	.179	215	361

**Wild-Card qualifier for playoffs*

Divisional playoffs: PITTSBURGH 13, Oakland 7; MIAMI 20, Cleveland 14
AFC championship: Miami 21, PITTSBURGH 17
Divisional playoffs: Dallas 30, SAN FRANCISCO 28; WASHINGTON 16, Green Bay 3
NFC championship: WASHINGTON 26, Dallas 3
Super Bowl VII: Miami (AFC) 14, Washington (NFC) 7, at Memorial Coliseum, Los Angeles, California

1971

AMERICAN CONFERENCE

Eastern Division

	W	L	T	Pct.	Pts.	OP
Miami	10	3	1	.769	315	174
Baltimore*	10	4	0	.714	313	140
New England	6	8	0	.429	238	325
N.Y. Jets	6	8	0	.429	212	299
Buffalo	1	13	0	.071	184	394

Central Division

	W	L	T	Pct.	Pts.	OP
Cleveland	9	5	0	.643	285	273
Pittsburgh	6	8	0	.429	246	292
Houston	4	9	1	.308	251	330
Cincinnati	4	10	0	.286	284	265

Western Division

	W	L	T	Pct.	Pts.	OP
Kansas City	10	3	1	.769	302	208
Oakland	8	4	2	.667	344	278
San Diego	6	8	0	.429	311	341
Denver	4	9	1	.308	203	275

NATIONAL CONFERENCE

Eastern Division

	W	L	T	Pct.	Pts.	OP
Dallas	11	3	0	.786	406	222
Washington*	9	4	1	.692	276	190
Philadelphia	6	7	1	.462	221	302
St. Louis	4	9	1	.308	231	279
N.Y. Giants	4	10	0	.286	228	362

Central Division

	W	L	T	Pct.	Pts.	OP
Minnesota	11	3	0	.786	245	139
Detroit	7	6	1	.538	341	286
Chicago	6	8	0	.429	185	276
Green Bay	4	8	2	.333	274	298

Western Division

	W	L	T	Pct.	Pts.	OP
San Francisco	9	5	0	.643	300	216
Los Angeles	8	5	1	.615	313	260
Atlanta	7	6	1	.538	274	277
New Orleans	4	8	2	.333	266	347

**Wild-Card qualifier for playoffs*

Divisional playoffs: Miami 27, KANSAS CITY 24 (OT); Baltimore 20, CLEVELAND 3
AFC championship: MIAMI 21, Baltimore 0
Divisional playoffs: Dallas 20, MINNESOTA 12; SAN FRANCISCO 24, Washington 20
NFC championship: DALLAS 14, San Francisco 3
Super Bowl VI: Dallas (NFC) 24, Miami (AFC) 3, at Tulane Stadium, New Orleans, Louisiana

1970

AMERICAN CONFERENCE

Eastern Division

	W	L	T	Pct.	Pts.	OP
Baltimore	11	2	1	.846	321	234
Miami*	10	4	0	.714	297	228
N.Y. Jets	4	10	0	.286	255	286
Buffalo	3	10	1	.231	204	337
Boston Patriots	2	12	0	.143	149	361

Central Division

	W	L	T	Pct.	Pts.	OP
Cincinnati	8	6	0	.571	312	255
Cleveland	7	7	0	.500	286	265
Pittsburgh	5	9	0	.357	210	272
Houston	3	10	1	.231	217	352

Western Division

	W	L	T	Pct.	Pts.	OP
Oakland	8	4	2	.667	300	293
Kansas City	7	5	2	.583	272	244
San Diego	5	6	3	.455	282	278
Denver	5	8	1	.385	253	264

NATIONAL CONFERENCE

Eastern Division

	W	L	T	Pct.	Pts.	OP
Dallas	10	4	0	.714	299	221
N.Y. Giants	9	5	0	.643	301	270
St. Louis	8	5	1	.615	325	228
Washington	6	8	0	.429	297	314
Philadelphia	3	10	1	.231	241	332

Central Division

	W	L	T	Pct.	Pts.	OP
Minnesota	12	2	0	.857	335	143
Detroit*	10	4	0	.714	347	202
Chicago	6	8	0	.429	256	261
Green Bay	6	8	0	.429	196	293

Western Division

	W	L	T	Pct.	Pts.	OP
San Francisco	10	3	1	.769	352	267
Los Angeles	9	4	1	.692	325	202
Atlanta	4	8	2	.333	206	261
New Orleans	2	11	1	.154	172	347

**Wild-Card qualifier for playoffs*

Divisional playoffs: BALTIMORE 17, Cincinnati 0; OAKLAND 21, Miami 14
AFC championship: BALTIMORE 27, Oakland 17
Divisional playoffs: DALLAS 5, Detroit 0; San Francisco 17, MINNESOTA 14
NFC championship: Dallas 17, SAN FRANCISCO 10
Super Bowl V: Baltimore (AFC) 16, Dallas (NFC) 13, at Orange Bowl, Miami, Florida

PAST STANDINGS

1969 NFL

EASTERN CONFERENCE

Capitol Division

	W	L	T	Pct.	Pts.	OP
Dallas	11	2	1	.846	369	223
Washington	7	5	2	.583	307	319
New Orleans	5	9	0	.357	311	393
Philadelphia	4	9	1	.308	279	377

Century Division

	W	L	T	Pct.	Pts.	OP
Cleveland	10	3	1	.769	351	300
N.Y. Giants	6	8	0	.429	264	298
St. Louis	4	9	1	.308	314	389
Pittsburgh	1	13	0	.071	218	404

WESTERN CONFERENCE

Coastal Division

	W	L	T	Pct.	Pts.	OP
Los Angeles	11	3	0	.786	320	243
Baltimore	8	5	1	.615	279	268
Atlanta	6	8	0	.429	276	268
San Francisco	4	8	2	.333	277	319

Central Division

	W	L	T	Pct.	Pts.	OP
Minnesota	12	2	0	.857	379	133
Detroit	9	4	1	.692	259	188
Green Bay	8	6	0	.571	269	221
Chicago	1	13	0	.071	210	339

Conference championships: Cleveland 38, DALLAS 14; MINNESOTA 23, Los Angeles 20
NFL championship: MINNESOTA 27, Cleveland 7
Super Bowl IV: Kansas City (AFL) 23, Minnesota (NFL) 7, at Tulane Stadium, New Orleans, Louisiana

1969 AFL

EASTERN DIVISION

	W	L	T	Pct.	Pts.	OP
N.Y. Jets	10	4	0	.714	353	269
Houston	6	6	2	.500	278	279
Boston Patriots	4	10	0	.286	266	316
Buffalo	4	10	0	.286	230	359
Miami	3	10	1	.231	233	332

WESTERN DIVISION

	W	L	T	Pct.	Pts.	OP
Oakland	12	1	1	.923	377	242
Kansas City	11	3	0	.786	359	177
San Diego	8	6	0	.571	288	276
Denver	5	8	1	.385	297	344
Cincinnati	4	9	1	.308	280	367

Divisional playoffs: Kansas City 13, N.Y. JETS 6; OAKLAND 56, Houston 7
AFL championship: Kansas City 17, OAKLAND 7

1968 NFL

EASTERN CONFERENCE

Capitol Division

	W	L	T	Pct.	Pts.	OP
Dallas	12	2	0	.857	431	186
N.Y. Giants	7	7	0	.500	294	325
Washington	5	9	0	.357	249	358
Philadelphia	2	12	0	.143	202	351

Century Division

	W	L	T	Pct.	Pts.	OP
Cleveland	10	4	0	.714	394	273
St. Louis	9	4	1	.692	325	289
New Orleans	4	9	1	.308	246	327
Pittsburgh	2	11	1	.154	244	397

WESTERN CONFERENCE

Coastal Division

	W	L	T	Pct.	Pts.	OP
Baltimore	13	1	0	.929	402	144
Los Angeles	10	3	1	.769	312	200
San Francisco	7	6	1	.538	303	310
Atlanta	2	12	0	.143	170	389

Central Division

	W	L	T	Pct.	Pts.	OP
Minnesota	8	6	0	.571	282	242
Chicago	7	7	0	.500	250	333
Green Bay	6	7	1	.462	281	227
Detroit	4	8	2	.333	207	241

Conference championships: CLEVELAND 31, Dallas 20; BALTIMORE 24, Minnesota 14
NFL championship: Baltimore 34, CLEVELAND 0
Super Bowl III: N.Y. Jets (AFL) 16, Baltimore (NFL) 7, at Orange Bowl, Miami, Florida

1968 AFL

EASTERN DIVISION

	W	L	T	Pct.	Pts.	OP
N.Y. Jets	11	3	0	.786	419	280
Houston	7	7	0	.500	303	248
Miami	5	8	1	.385	276	355
Boston Patriots	4	10	0	.286	229	406
Buffalo	1	12	1	.077	199	367

WESTERN DIVISION

	W	L	T	Pct.	Pts.	OP
Oakland	12	2	0	.857	453	233
Kansas City	12	2	0	.857	371	170
San Diego	9	5	0	.643	382	310
Denver	5	9	0	.357	255	404
Cincinnati	3	11	0	.214	215	329

Western Division playoff: OAKLAND 41, Kansas City 6
AFL championship: N.Y. JETS 27, Oakland 23

1967 NFL

EASTERN CONFERENCE

Capitol Division

	W	L	T	Pct.	Pts.	OP
Dallas	9	5	0	.643	342	268
Philadelphia	6	7	1	.462	351	409
Washington	5	6	3	.455	347	353
New Orleans	3	11	0	.214	233	379

Century Division

	W	L	T	Pct.	Pts.	OP
Cleveland	9	5	0	.643	334	297
N.Y. Giants	7	7	0	.500	369	379
St. Louis	6	7	1	.462	333	356
Pittsburgh	4	9	1	.308	281	320

WESTERN CONFERENCE

Coastal Division

	W	L	T	Pct.	Pts.	OP
Los Angeles	11	1	2	.917	398	196
Baltimore	11	1	2	.917	394	198
San Francisco	7	7	0	.500	273	337
Atlanta	1	12	1	.077	175	422

Central Division

	W	L	T	Pct.	Pts.	OP
Green Bay	9	4	1	.692	332	209
Chicago	7	6	1	.538	239	218
Detroit	5	7	2	.417	260	259
Minnesota	3	8	3	.273	233	294

Los Angeles won division title on the basis of advantage in points (58-34) in two games vs. Baltimore.
Conference championships: DALLAS 52, Cleveland 14; GREEN BAY 28, Los Angeles 7
NFL championship: GREEN BAY 21, Dallas 17
Super Bowl II: Green Bay (NFL) 33, Oakland (AFL) 14, at Orange Bowl, Miami, Florida

1967 AFL

EASTERN DIVISION

	W	L	T	Pct.	Pts.	OP
Houston	9	4	1	.692	258	199
N.Y. Jets	8	5	1	.615	371	329
Buffalo	4	10	0	.286	237	285
Miami	4	10	0	.286	219	407
Boston Patriots	3	10	1	.231	280	389

WESTERN DIVISION

	W	L	T	Pct.	Pts.	OP
Oakland	13	1	0	.929	468	233
Kansas City	9	5	0	.643	408	254
San Diego	8	5	1	.615	360	352
Denver	3	11	0	.214	256	409

AFL championship: OAKLAND 40, Houston 7

1966 NFL

EASTERN CONFERENCE

	W	L	T	Pct.	Pts.	OP
Dallas	10	3	1	.769	445	239
Cleveland	9	5	0	.643	403	259
Philadelphia	9	5	0	.643	326	340
St. Louis	8	5	1	.615	264	265
Washington	7	7	0	.500	351	355
Pittsburgh	5	8	1	.385	316	347
Atlanta	3	11	0	.214	204	437
N.Y. Giants	1	12	1	.077	263	501

WESTERN CONFERENCE

	W	L	T	Pct.	Pts.	OP
Green Bay	12	2	0	.857	335	163
Baltimore	9	5	0	.643	314	226
Los Angeles	8	6	0	.571	289	212
San Francisco	6	6	2	.500	320	325
Chicago	5	7	2	.417	234	272
Detroit	4	9	1	.308	206	317
Minnesota	4	9	1	.308	292	304

NFL championship: Green Bay 34, DALLAS 27
Super Bowl I: Green Bay (NFL) 35, Kansas City (AFL) 10, at Memorial Coliseum, Los Angeles, California

1966 AFL

EASTERN DIVISION

	W	L	T	Pct.	Pts.	OP
Buffalo	9	4	1	.692	358	255
Boston Patriots	8	4	2	.677	315	283
N.Y. Jets	6	6	2	.500	322	312
Houston	3	11	0	.214	335	396
Miami	3	11	0	.214	213	362

WESTERN DIVISION

	W	L	T	Pct.	Pts.	OP
Kansas City	11	2	1	.846	448	276
Oakland	8	5	1	.615	315	288
San Diego	7	6	1	.538	335	284
Denver	4	10	0	.286	196	381

AFL championship: Kansas City 31, BUFFALO 7

1965 NFL

EASTERN CONFERENCE

	W	L	T	Pct.	Pts.	OP
Cleveland	11	3	0	.786	363	325
Dallas	7	7	0	.500	325	280
N.Y. Giants	7	7	0	.500	270	338
Washington	6	8	0	.429	257	301
Philadelphia	5	9	0	.357	363	359
St. Louis	5	9	0	.357	296	309
Pittsburgh	2	12	0	.143	202	397

WESTERN CONFERENCE

	W	L	T	Pct.	Pts.	OP
Green Bay	10	3	1	.769	316	224
Baltimore	10	3	1	.769	389	284
Chicago	9	5	0	.643	409	275
San Francisco	7	6	1	.538	421	402
Minnesota	7	7	0	.500	383	403
Detroit	6	7	1	.462	257	295
Los Angeles	4	10	0	.286	269	328

Western Conference playoff: GREEN BAY 13, Baltimore 10 (OT)
NFL championship: GREEN BAY 23, Cleveland 12

1965 AFL

EASTERN DIVISION

	W	L	T	Pct.	Pts.	OP
Buffalo	10	3	1	.769	313	226
N.Y. Jets	5	8	1	.385	285	303
Boston Patriots	4	8	2	.333	244	302
Houston	4	10	0	.286	298	429

WESTERN DIVISION

	W	L	T	Pct.	Pts.	OP
San Diego	9	2	3	.818	340	227
Oakland	8	5	1	.615	298	239
Kansas City	7	5	2	.583	322	285
Denver	4	10	0	.286	303	392

AFL championship: Buffalo 23, SAN DIEGO 0

1964 NFL

EASTERN CONFERENCE

	W	L	T	Pct.	Pts.	OP
Cleveland	10	3	1	.769	415	293
St. Louis	9	3	2	.750	357	331
Philadelphia	6	8	0	.429	312	313
Washington	6	8	0	.429	307	305
Dallas	5	8	1	.385	250	289
Pittsburgh	5	9	0	.357	253	315
N.Y. Giants	2	10	2	.167	241	399

WESTERN CONFERENCE

	W	L	T	Pct.	Pts.	OP
Baltimore	12	2	0	.857	428	225
Green Bay	8	5	1	.615	342	245
Minnesota	8	5	1	.615	355	296
Detroit	7	5	2	.583	280	260
Los Angeles	5	7	2	.417	283	339
Chicago	5	9	0	.357	260	379
San Francisco	4	10	0	.286	236	330

NFL championship: CLEVELAND 27, Baltimore 0

1964 AFL

EASTERN DIVISION

	W	L	T	Pct.	Pts.	OP
Buffalo	12	2	0	.857	400	242
Boston Patriots	10	3	1	.769	365	297
N.Y. Jets	5	8	1	.385	278	315
Houston	4	10	0	.286	310	355

WESTERN DIVISION

	W	L	T	Pct.	Pts.	OP
San Diego	8	5	1	.615	341	300
Kansas City	7	7	0	.500	366	306
Oakland	5	7	2	.417	303	350
Denver	2	11	1	.154	240	438

AFL championship: BUFFALO 20, San Diego 7

1963 NFL

EASTERN CONFERENCE	W	L	T	Pct.	Pts.	OP
N.Y. Giants	11	3	0	.786	448	280
Cleveland	10	4	0	.714	343	262
St. Louis	9	5	0	.643	341	283
Pittsburgh	7	4	3	.636	321	295
Dallas	4	10	0	.286	305	378
Washington	3	11	0	.214	279	398
Philadelphia	2	10	2	.167	242	381

WESTERN CONFERENCE	W	L	T	Pct.	Pts.	OP
Chicago	11	1	2	.917	301	144
Green Bay	11	2	1	.846	369	206
Baltimore	8	6	0	.571	316	285
Detroit	5	8	1	.385	326	265
Minnesota	5	8	1	.385	309	390
Los Angeles	5	9	0	.357	210	350
San Francisco	2	12	0	.143	198	391

NFL championship: CHICAGO 14, N.Y. Giants 10

1963 AFL

EASTERN DIVISION	W	L	T	Pct.	Pts.	OP
Boston Patriots	7	6	1	.538	327	257
Buffalo	7	6	1	.538	304	291
Houston	6	8	0	.429	302	372
N.Y. Jets	5	8	1	.385	249	399

WESTERN DIVISION	W	L	T	Pct.	Pts.	OP
San Diego	11	3	0	.786	399	255
Oakland	10	4	0	.714	363	282
Kansas City	5	7	2	.417	347	263
Denver	2	11	1	.154	301	473

Eastern Division playoff: Boston 26, BUFFALO 8
AFL championship: SAN DIEGO 51, Boston 10

1962 NFL

EASTERN CONFERENCE	W	L	T	Pct.	Pts.	OP
N.Y. Giants	12	2	0	.857	398	283
Pittsburgh	9	5	0	.643	312	363
Cleveland	7	6	1	.538	291	257
Washington	5	7	2	.417	305	376
Dallas Cowboys	5	8	1	.385	398	402
St. Louis	4	9	1	.308	287	361
Philadelphia	3	10	1	.231	282	356

WESTERN CONFERENCE	W	L	T	Pct.	Pts.	OP
Green Bay	13	1	0	.929	415	148
Detroit	11	3	0	.786	315	177
Chicago	9	5	0	.643	321	287
Baltimore	7	7	0	.500	293	288
San Francisco	6	8	0	.429	282	331
Minnesota	2	11	1	.154	254	410
Los Angeles	1	12	1	.077	220	334

NFL championship: Green Bay 16, N.Y. GIANTS 7

1962 AFL

EASTERN DIVISION	W	L	T	Pct.	Pts.	OP
Houston	11	3	0	.786	387	270
Boston Patriots	9	4	1	.692	346	295
Buffalo	7	6	1	.538	309	272
N.Y. Titans	5	9	0	.357	278	423

WESTERN DIVISION	W	L	T	Pct.	Pts.	OP
Dallas Texans	11	3	0	.786	389	233
Denver	7	7	0	.500	353	334
San Diego	4	10	0	.286	314	392
Oakland	1	13	0	.071	213	370

AFL championship: Dallas Texans 20, HOUSTON 17 (OT)

1961 NFL

EASTERN CONFERENCE	W	L	T	Pct.	Pts.	OP
N.Y. Giants	10	3	1	.769	368	220
Philadelphia	10	4	0	.714	361	297
Cleveland	8	5	1	.615	319	270
St. Louis	7	7	0	.500	279	267
Pittsburgh	6	8	0	.429	295	287
Dallas Cowboys	4	9	1	.308	236	380
Washington	1	12	1	.077	174	392

WESTERN CONFERENCE	W	L	T	Pct.	Pts.	OP
Green Bay	11	3	0	.786	391	223
Detroit	8	5	1	.615	270	258
Baltimore	8	6	0	.571	302	307
Chicago	8	6	0	.571	326	302
San Francisco	7	6	1	.538	346	272
Los Angeles	4	10	0	.286	263	333
Minnesota	3	11	0	.214	285	407

NFL championship: GREEN BAY 37, N.Y. Giants 0

1961 AFL

EASTERN DIVISION	W	L	T	Pct.	Pts.	OP
Houston	10	3	1	.769	513	242
Boston Patriots	9	4	1	.692	413	313
N.Y. Titans	7	7	0	.500	301	390
Buffalo	6	8	0	.429	294	342

WESTERN DIVISION	W	L	T	Pct.	Pts.	OP
San Diego	12	2	0	.857	396	219
Dallas Texans	6	8	0	.429	334	343
Denver	3	11	0	.214	251	432
Oakland	2	12	0	.143	237	458

AFL championship: Houston 10, SAN DIEGO 3

1960 NFL

EASTERN CONFERENCE	W	L	T	Pct.	Pts.	OP
Philadelphia	10	2	0	.833	321	246
Cleveland	8	3	1	.727	362	217
N.Y. Giants	6	4	2	.600	271	261
St. Louis	6	5	1	.545	288	230
Pittsburgh	5	6	1	.455	240	275
Washington	1	9	2	.100	178	309

WESTERN CONFERENCE	W	L	T	Pct.	Pts.	OP
Green Bay	8	4	0	.667	332	209
Detroit	7	5	0	.583	239	212
San Francisco	7	5	0	.583	208	205
Baltimore	6	6	0	.500	288	234
Chicago	5	6	1	.455	194	299
L.A. Rams	4	7	1	.364	265	297
Dallas Cowboys	0	11	1	.000	177	369

NFL championship: PHILADELPHIA 17, Green Bay 13

1960 AFL

EASTERN CONFERENCE	W	L	T	Pct.	Pts.	OP
Houston	10	4	0	.714	379	285
N.Y. Titans	7	7	0	.500	382	399
Buffalo	5	8	1	.385	296	303
Boston	5	9	0	.357	286	349

WESTERN CONFERENCE	W	L	T	Pct.	Pts.	OP
L.A. Chargers	10	4	0	.714	373	336
Dallas Texans	8	6	0	.571	362	253
Oakland	6	8	0	.429	319	388
Denver	4	9	1	.308	309	393

AFL championship: HOUSTON 24, L.A. Chargers 16

1959

EASTERN CONFERENCE	W	L	T	Pct.	Pts.	OP
N.Y. Giants	10	2	0	.833	284	170
Cleveland	7	5	0	.583	270	214
Philadelphia	7	5	0	.583	268	278
Pittsburgh	6	5	1	.545	257	216
Washington	3	9	0	.250	185	350
Chi. Cardinals	2	10	0	.167	234	324

WESTERN CONFERENCE	W	L	T	Pct.	Pts.	OP
Baltimore	9	3	0	.750	374	251
Chi. Bears	8	4	0	.667	252	196
Green Bay	7	5	0	.583	248	246
San Francisco	7	5	0	.583	255	237
Detroit	3	8	1	.273	203	275
Los Angeles	2	10	0	.167	242	315

NFL championship: BALTIMORE 31, N.Y. Giants 16

1958

EASTERN CONFERENCE	W	L	T	Pct.	Pts.	OP
N.Y. Giants	9	3	0	.750	246	183
Cleveland	9	3	0	.750	302	217
Pittsburgh	7	4	1	.636	261	230
Washington	4	7	1	.364	214	268
Chi. Cardinals	2	9	1	.182	261	356
Philadelphia	2	9	1	.182	235	306

WESTERN CONFERENCE	W	L	T	Pct.	Pts.	OP
Baltimore	9	3	0	.750	381	203
Chi. Bears	8	4	0	.667	298	230
Los Angeles	8	4	0	.667	344	278
San Francisco	6	6	0	.500	257	324
Detroit	4	7	1	.364	261	276
Green Bay	1	10	1	.091	193	382

Eastern Conference playoff: N.Y. GIANTS 10, Cleveland 0
NFL championship: Baltimore 23, N.Y. GIANTS 17 (OT)

1957

EASTERN CONFERENCE	W	L	T	Pct.	Pts.	OP
Cleveland	9	2	1	.818	269	172
N.Y. Giants	7	5	0	.583	254	211
Pittsburgh	6	6	0	.500	161	178
Washington	5	6	1	.455	251	230
Philadelphia	4	8	0	.333	173	230
Chi. Cardinals	3	9	0	.250	200	299

WESTERN CONFERENCE	W	L	T	Pct.	Pts.	OP
Detroit	8	4	0	.667	251	231
San Francisco	8	4	0	.667	260	264
Baltimore	7	5	0	.583	303	235
Los Angeles	6	6	0	.500	307	278
Chi. Bears	5	7	0	.417	203	211
Green Bay	3	9	0	.250	218	311

Western Conference playoff: Detroit 31, SAN FRANCISCO 27
NFL championship: DETROIT 59, Cleveland 14

1956

EASTERN CONFERENCE	W	L	T	Pct.	Pts.	OP
N.Y. Giants	8	3	1	.727	264	197
Chi. Cardinals	7	5	0	.583	240	182
Washington	6	6	0	.500	183	225
Cleveland	5	7	0	.417	167	177
Pittsburgh	5	7	0	.417	217	250
Philadelphia	3	8	1	.273	143	215

WESTERN CONFERENCE	W	L	T	Pct.	Pts.	OP
Chi. Bears	9	2	1	.818	363	246
Detroit	9	3	0	.750	300	188
San Francisco	5	6	1	.455	233	284
Baltimore	5	7	0	.417	270	322
Green Bay	4	8	0	.333	264	342
Los Angeles	4	8	0	.333	291	307

NFL championship: N.Y. GIANTS 47, Chi. Bears 7

1955

EASTERN CONFERENCE	W	L	T	Pct.	Pts.	OP
Cleveland	9	2	1	.818	349	218
Washington	8	4	0	.667	246	222
N.Y. Giants	6	5	1	.545	267	223
Chi. Cardinals	4	7	1	.364	224	252
Philadelphia	4	7	1	.364	248	231
Pittsburgh	4	8	0	.333	195	285

WESTERN CONFERENCE	W	L	T	Pct.	Pts.	OP
Los Angeles	8	3	1	.727	260	231
Chi. Bears	8	4	0	.667	294	251
Green Bay	6	6	0	.500	258	276
Baltimore	5	6	1	.455	214	239
San Francisco	4	8	0	.333	216	298
Detroit	3	9	0	.250	230	275

NFL championship: Cleveland 38, LOS ANGELES 14

1954

EASTERN CONFERENCE	W	L	T	Pct.	Pts.	OP
Cleveland	9	3	0	.750	336	162
Philadelphia	7	4	1	.636	284	230
N.Y. Giants	7	5	0	.583	293	184
Pittsburgh	5	7	0	.417	219	263
Washington	3	9	0	.250	207	432
Chi. Cardinals	2	10	0	.167	183	347

WESTERN CONFERENCE	W	L	T	Pct.	Pts.	OP
Detroit	9	2	1	.818	337	189
Chi. Bears	8	4	0	.667	301	279
San Francisco	7	4	1	.636	313	251
Los Angeles	6	5	1	.545	314	285
Green Bay	4	8	0	.333	234	251
Baltimore	3	9	0	.250	131	279

NFL championship: CLEVELAND 56, Detroit 10

PAST STANDINGS

1953

EASTERN CONFERENCE

	W	L	T	Pct.	Pts.	OP
Cleveland	11	1	0	.917	348	162
Philadelphia	7	4	1	.636	352	215
Washington	6	5	1	.545	208	215
Pittsburgh	6	6	0	.500	211	263
N.Y. Giants	3	9	0	.250	179	277
Chi. Cardinals	1	10	1	.091	190	337

WESTERN CONFERENCE

	W	L	T	Pct.	Pts.	OP
Detroit	10	2	0	.833	271	205
San Francisco	9	3	0	.750	372	237
Los Angeles	8	3	1	.727	366	236
Chi. Bears	3	8	1	.273	218	262
Baltimore	3	9	0	.250	182	350
Green Bay	2	9	1	.182	200	338

NFL championship: DETROIT 17, Cleveland 16

1952

AMERICAN CONFERENCE

	W	L	T	Pct.	Pts.	OP
Cleveland	8	4	0	.667	310	213
N.Y. Giants	7	5	0	.583	234	231
Philadelphia	7	5	0	.583	252	271
Pittsburgh	5	7	0	.417	300	273
Chi. Cardinals	4	8	0	.333	172	221
Washington	4	8	0	.333	240	287

NATIONAL CONFERENCE

	W	L	T	Pct.	Pts.	OP
Detroit	9	3	0	.750	344	192
Los Angeles	9	3	0	.750	349	234
San Francisco	7	5	0	.583	285	221
Green Bay	6	6	0	.500	295	312
Chi. Bears	5	7	0	.417	245	326
Dallas Texans	1	11	0	.083	182	427

National Conference playoff: DETROIT 31, Los Angeles 21
NFL championship: Detroit 17, CLEVELAND 7

1951

AMERICAN CONFERENCE

	W	L	T	Pct.	Pts.	OP
Cleveland	11	1	0	.917	331	152
N.Y. Giants	9	2	1	.818	254	161
Washington	5	7	0	.417	183	296
Pittsburgh	4	7	1	.364	183	235
Philadelphia	4	8	0	.333	234	264
Chi. Cardinals	3	9	0	.250	210	287

NATIONAL CONFERENCE

	W	L	T	Pct.	Pts.	OP
Los Angeles	8	4	0	.667	392	261
Detroit	7	4	1	.636	336	259
San Francisco	7	4	1	.636	255	205
Chi. Bears	7	5	0	.583	286	282
Green Bay	3	9	0	.250	254	375
N.Y. Yanks	1	9	2	.100	241	382

NFL championship: LOS ANGELES 24, Cleveland 17

1950

AMERICAN CONFERENCE

	W	L	T	Pct.	Pts.	OP
Cleveland	10	2	0	.833	310	144
N.Y. Giants	10	2	0	.833	268	150
Philadelphia	6	6	0	.500	254	141
Pittsburgh	6	6	0	.500	180	195
Chi. Cardinals	5	7	0	.417	233	287
Washington	3	9	0	.250	232	326

NATIONAL CONFERENCE

	W	L	T	Pct.	Pts.	OP
Los Angeles	9	3	0	.750	466	309
Chi. Bears	9	3	0	.750	279	207
N.Y. Yanks	7	5	0	.583	366	367
Detroit	6	6	0	.500	321	285
Green Bay	3	9	0	.250	244	406
San Francisco	3	9	0	.250	213	300
Baltimore	1	11	0	.083	213	462

American Conference playoff: CLEVELAND 8, N.Y. Giants 3
National Conference playoff: LOS ANGELES 24, Chi. Bears 14
NFL championship: CLEVELAND 30, Los Angeles 28

1949

EASTERN DIVISION

	W	L	T	Pct.	Pts.	OP
Philadelphia	11	1	0	.917	364	134
Pittsburgh	6	5	1	.545	224	214
N.Y. Giants	6	6	0	.500	287	298
Washington	4	7	1	.364	268	339
N.Y. Bulldogs	1	10	1	.091	153	368

WESTERN DIVISION

	W	L	T	Pct.	Pts.	OP
Los Angeles	8	2	2	.800	360	239
Chi. Bears	9	3	0	.750	332	218
Chi. Cardinals	6	5	1	.545	360	301
Detroit	4	8	0	.333	237	259
Green Bay	2	10	0	.167	114	329

NFL championship: Philadelphia 14, LOS ANGELES 0

1948

EASTERN DIVISION

	W	L	T	Pct.	Pts.	OP
Philadelphia	9	2	1	.818	376	156
Washington	7	5	0	.583	291	287
N.Y. Giants	4	8	0	.333	297	388
Pittsburgh	4	8	0	.333	200	243
Boston	3	9	0	.250	174	372

WESTERN DIVISION

	W	L	T	Pct.	Pts.	OP
Chi. Cardinals	11	1	0	.917	395	226
Chi. Bears	10	2	0	.833	375	151
Los Angeles	6	5	1	.545	327	269
Green Bay	3	9	0	.250	154	290
Detroit	2	10	0	.167	200	407

NFL championship: PHILADELPHIA 7, Chi. Cardinals 0

1947

EASTERN DIVISION

	W	L	T	Pct.	Pts.	OP
Philadelphia	8	4	0	.667	308	242
Pittsburgh	8	4	0	.667	240	259
Boston	4	7	1	.364	168	256
Washington	4	8	0	.333	295	367
N.Y. Giants	2	8	2	.200	190	309

WESTERN DIVISION

	W	L	T	Pct.	Pts.	OP
Chi. Cardinals	9	3	0	.750	306	231
Chi. Bears	8	4	0	.667	363	241
Green Bay	6	5	1	.545	274	210
Los Angeles	6	6	0	.500	259	214
Detroit	3	9	0	.250	231	305

Eastern Division playoff: Philadelphia 21, PITTSBURGH 0
NFL championship: CHI. CARDINALS 28, Philadelphia 21

1946

EASTERN DIVISION

	W	L	T	Pct.	Pts.	OP
N.Y. Giants	7	3	1	.700	236	162
Philadelphia	6	5	0	.545	231	220
Washington	5	5	1	.500	171	191
Pittsburgh	5	5	1	.500	136	117
Boston	2	8	1	.200	189	273

WESTERN DIVISION

	W	L	T	Pct.	Pts.	OP
Chi. Bears	8	2	1	.800	289	193
Los Angeles	6	4	1	.600	277	257
Green Bay	6	5	0	.545	148	158
Chi. Cardinals	6	5	0	.545	260	198
Detroit	1	10	0	.091	142	310

NFL championship: Chi. Bears 24, N.Y. GIANTS 14

1945

EASTERN DIVISION

	W	L	T	Pct.	Pts.	OP
Washington	8	2	0	.800	209	121
Philadelphia	7	3	0	.700	272	133
N.Y. Giants	3	6	1	.333	179	198
Boston	3	6	1	.333	123	211
Pittsburgh	2	8	0	.200	79	220

WESTERN DIVISION

	W	L	T	Pct.	Pts.	OP
Cleveland	9	1	0	.900	244	136
Detroit	7	3	0	.700	195	194
Green Bay	6	4	0	.600	258	173
Chi. Bears	3	7	0	.300	192	235
Chi. Cardinals	1	9	0	.100	98	228

NFL championship: CLEVELAND 15, Washington 14

1944

EASTERN DIVISION

	W	L	T	Pct.	Pts.	OP
N.Y. Giants	8	1	1	.889	206	75
Philadelphia	7	1	2	.875	267	131
Washington	6	3	1	.667	169	180
Boston	2	8	0	.200	82	233
Brooklyn	0	10	0	.000	69	166

WESTERN DIVISION

	W	L	T	Pct.	Pts.	OP
Green Bay	8	2	0	.800	238	141
Chi. Bears	6	3	1	.667	258	172
Detroit	6	3	1	.667	216	151
Cleveland	4	6	0	.400	188	224
Card-Pitt	0	10	0	.000	108	328

NFL championship: Green Bay 14, N.Y. GIANTS 7

1943

EASTERN DIVISION

	W	L	T	Pct.	Pts.	OP
Washington	6	3	1	.667	229	137
N.Y. Giants	6	3	1	.667	197	170
Phil-Pitt	5	4	1	.556	225	230
Brooklyn	2	8	0	.200	65	234

WESTERN DIVISION

	W	L	T	Pct.	Pts.	OP
Chi. Bears	8	1	1	.889	303	157
Green Bay	7	2	1	.778	264	172
Detroit	3	6	1	.333	178	218
Chi. Cardinals	0	10	0	.000	95	238

Eastern Division playoff: Washington 28, N.Y. GIANTS 0
NFL championship: CHI. BEARS 41, Washington 21

1942

EASTERN DIVISION

	W	L	T	Pct.	Pts.	OP
Washington	10	1	0	.909	227	102
Pittsburgh	7	4	0	.636	167	119
N.Y. Giants	5	5	1	.500	155	139
Brooklyn	3	8	0	.273	100	168
Philadelphia	2	9	0	.182	134	239

WESTERN DIVISION

	W	L	T	Pct.	Pts.	OP
Chi. Bears	11	0	0	1.000	376	84
Green Bay	8	2	1	.800	300	215
Cleveland	5	6	0	.455	150	207
Chi. Cardinals	3	8	0	.273	98	209
Detroit	0	11	0	.000	38	263

NFL championship: WASHINGTON 14, Chi. Bears 6

1941

EASTERN DIVISION

	W	L	T	Pct.	Pts.	OP
N.Y. Giants	8	3	0	.727	238	114
Brooklyn	7	4	0	.636	158	127
Washington	6	5	0	.545	176	174
Philadelphia	2	8	1	.200	119	218
Pittsburgh	1	9	1	.100	103	276

WESTERN DIVISION

	W	L	T	Pct.	Pts.	OP
Chi. Bears	10	1	0	.909	396	147
Green Bay	10	1	0	.909	258	120
Detroit	4	6	1	.400	121	195
Chi. Cardinals	3	7	1	.300	127	197
Cleveland	2	9	0	.182	116	244

Western Division playoff: CHI. BEARS 33, Green Bay 14
NFL championship: CHI. BEARS 37, N.Y. Giants 9

1940

EASTERN DIVISION

	W	L	T	Pct.	Pts.	OP
Washington	9	2	0	.818	245	142
Brooklyn	8	3	0	.727	186	120
N.Y. Giants	6	4	1	.600	131	133
Pittsburgh	2	7	2	.222	60	178
Philadelphia	1	10	0	.091	111	211

WESTERN DIVISION

	W	L	T	Pct.	Pts.	OP
Chi. Bears	8	3	0	.727	238	152
Green Bay	6	4	1	.600	238	155
Detroit	5	5	1	.500	138	153
Cleveland	4	6	1	.400	171	191
Chi. Cardinals	2	7	2	.222	139	222

NFL championship: Chi. Bears 73, WASHINGTON 0

1939

EASTERN DIVISION

	W	L	T	Pct.	Pts.	OP
N.Y. Giants	9	1	1	.900	168	85
Washington	8	2	1	.800	242	94
Brooklyn	4	6	1	.400	108	219
Philadelphia	1	9	1	.100	105	200
Pittsburgh	1	9	1	.100	114	216

WESTERN DIVISION

	W	L	T	Pct.	Pts.	OP
Green Bay	9	2	0	.818	233	153
Chi. Bears	8	3	0	.727	298	157
Detroit	6	5	0	.545	145	150
Cleveland	5	5	1	.500	195	164
Chi. Cardinals	1	10	0	.091	84	254

NFL championship: GREEN BAY 27, N.Y. Giants 0

1938

EASTERN DIVISION

	W	L	T	Pct.	Pts.	OP
N.Y. Giants	8	2	1	.800	194	79
Washington	6	3	2	.667	148	154
Brooklyn	4	4	3	.500	131	161
Philadelphia	5	6	0	.455	154	164
Pittsburgh	2	9	0	.182	79	169

WESTERN DIVISION

	W	L	T	Pct.	Pts.	OP
Green Bay	8	3	0	.727	223	118
Detroit	7	4	0	.636	119	108
Chi. Bears	6	5	0	.545	194	148
Cleveland	4	7	0	.364	131	215
Chi. Cardinals	2	9	0	.182	111	168

NFL championship: N.Y. GIANTS 23, Green Bay 17

1937

EASTERN DIVISION

	W	L	T	Pct.	Pts.	OP
Washington	8	3	0	.727	195	120
N.Y. Giants	6	3	2	.667	128	109
Pittsburgh	4	7	0	.364	122	145
Brooklyn	3	7	1	.300	82	174
Philadelphia	2	8	1	.200	86	177

WESTERN DIVISION

	W	L	T	Pct.	Pts.	OP
Chi. Bears	9	1	1	.900	201	100
Green Bay	7	4	0	.636	220	122
Detroit	7	4	0	.636	180	105
Chi. Cardinals	5	5	1	.500	135	165
Cleveland	1	10	0	.091	75	207

NFL championship: Washington 28, CHI. BEARS 21

1936

EASTERN DIVISION

	W	L	T	Pct.	Pts.	OP
Boston	7	5	0	.583	149	110
Pittsburgh	6	6	0	.500	98	187
N.Y. Giants	5	6	1	.455	115	163
Brooklyn	3	8	1	.273	92	161
Philadelphia	1	11	0	.083	51	206

WESTERN DIVISION

	W	L	T	Pct.	Pts.	OP
Green Bay	10	1	1	.909	248	118
Chi. Bears	9	3	0	.750	222	94
Detroit	8	4	0	.667	235	102
Chi. Cardinals	3	8	1	.273	74	143

NFL championship: Green Bay 21, Boston 6, at Polo Grounds, N.Y.

1935

EASTERN DIVISION

	W	L	T	Pct.	Pts.	OP
N.Y. Giants	9	3	0	.750	180	96
Brooklyn	5	6	1	.455	90	141
Pittsburgh	4	8	0	.333	100	209
Boston	2	8	1	.200	65	123
Philadelphia	2	9	0	.182	60	179

WESTERN DIVISION

	W	L	T	Pct.	Pts.	OP
Detroit	7	3	2	.700	191	111
Green Bay	8	4	0	.667	181	96
Chi. Bears	6	4	2	.600	192	106
Chi. Cardinals	6	4	2	.600	99	97

NFL championship: DETROIT 26, N.Y. Giants 7
One game between Boston and Philadelphia was canceled.

1934

EASTERN DIVISION

	W	L	T	Pct.	Pts.	OP
N.Y. Giants	8	5	0	.615	147	107
Boston	6	6	0	.500	107	94
Brooklyn	4	7	0	.364	61	153
Philadelphia	4	7	0	.364	127	85
Pittsburgh	2	10	0	.167	51	206

WESTERN DIVISION

	W	L	T	Pct.	Pts.	OP
Chi. Bears	13	0	0	1.000	286	86
Detroit	10	3	0	.769	238	59
Green Bay	7	6	0	.538	156	112
Chi. Cardinals	5	6	0	.455	80	84
St. Louis	1	2	0	.333	27	61
Cincinnati	0	8	0	.000	10	243

NFL championship: N.Y. GIANTS 30, Chi. Bears 13

1933

EASTERN DIVISION

	W	L	T	Pct.	Pts.	OP
N.Y. Giants	11	3	0	.786	244	101
Brooklyn	5	4	1	.556	93	54
Boston	5	5	2	.500	103	97
Philadelphia	3	5	1	.375	77	158
Pittsburgh	3	6	2	.333	67	208

WESTERN DIVISION

	W	L	T	Pct.	Pts.	OP
Chi. Bears	10	2	1	.833	133	82
Portsmouth	6	5	0	.545	128	87
Green Bay	5	7	1	.417	170	107
Cincinnati	3	6	1	.333	38	110
Chi. Cardinals	1	9	1	.100	52	101

NFL championship: CHI. BEARS 23, N.Y. Giants 21

1932

	W	L	T	Pct.
Chicago Bears	7	1	6	.875
Green Bay Packers	10	3	1	.769
Portsmouth Spartans	6	2	4	.750
Boston Braves	4	4	2	.500
New York Giants	4	6	2	.400
Brooklyn Dodgers	3	9	0	.250
Chicago Cardinals	2	6	2	.250
Staten Island Stapletons	2	7	3	.222

Chicago Bears and Portsmouth finished regularly scheduled games tied for first place. Bears won playoff game, which counted in standings, 9-0.

1931

	W	L	T	Pct.
Green Bay Packers	12	2	0	.857
Portsmouth Spartans	11	3	0	.786
Chicago Bears	8	5	0	.615
Chicago Cardinals	5	4	0	.556
New York Giants	7	6	1	.538
Providence Steam Roller	4	4	3	.500
Staten Island Stapletons	4	6	1	.400
Cleveland Indians	2	8	0	.200
Brooklyn Dodgers	2	12	0	.143
Frankford Yellow Jackets	1	6	1	.143

1930

	W	L	T	Pct.
Green Bay Packers	10	3	1	.769
New York Giants	13	4	0	.765
Chicago Bears	9	4	1	.692
Brooklyn Dodgers	7	4	1	.636
Providence Steam Roller	6	4	1	.600
Staten Island Stapletons	5	5	2	.500
Chicago Cardinals	5	6	2	.455
Portsmouth Spartans	5	6	3	.455
Frankford Yellow Jackets	4	13	1	.222
Minneapolis Red Jackets	1	7	1	.125
Newark Tornadoes	1	10	1	.091

1929

	W	L	T	Pct.
Green Bay Packers	12	0	1	1.000
New York Giants	13	1	1	.929
Frankford Yellow Jackets	10	4	5	.714
Chicago Cardinals	6	6	1	.500
Boston Bulldogs	4	4	0	.500
Staten Island Stapletons	3	4	3	.429
Providence Steam Roller	4	6	2	.400
Orange Tornadoes	3	5	4	.375
Chicago Bears	4	9	2	.308
Buffalo Bisons	1	7	1	.125
Minneapolis Red Jackets	1	9	0	.100
Dayton Triangles	0	6	0	.000

1928

	W	L	T	Pct.
Providence Steam Roller	8	1	2	.889
Frankford Yellow Jackets	11	3	2	.786
Detroit Wolverines	7	2	1	.778
Green Bay Packers	6	4	3	.600
Chicago Bears	7	5	1	.583
New York Giants	4	7	2	.364
New York Yankees	4	8	1	.333
Pottsville Maroons	2	8	0	.200
Chicago Cardinals	1	5	0	.167
Dayton Triangles	0	7	0	.000

1927

	W	L	T	Pct.
New York Giants	11	1	1	.917
Green Bay Packers	7	2	1	.778
Chicago Bears	9	3	2	.750
Cleveland Bulldogs	8	4	1	.667
Providence Steam Roller	8	5	1	.615
New York Yankees	7	8	1	.467
Frankford Yellow Jackets	6	9	3	.400
Pottsville Maroons	5	8	0	.385
Chicago Cardinals	3	7	1	.300
Dayton Triangles	1	6	1	.143
Duluth Eskimos	1	8	0	.111
Buffalo Bisons	0	5	0	.000

1926

	W	L	T	Pct.
Frankford Yellow Jackets	14	1	2	.933
Chicago Bears	12	1	3	.923
Pottsville Maroons	10	2	2	.833
Kansas City Cowboys	8	3	0	.727
Green Bay Packers	7	3	3	.700
Los Angeles Buccaneers	6	3	1	.667
New York Giants	8	4	1	.667
Duluth Eskimos	6	5	3	.545
Buffalo Rangers	4	4	2	.500
Chicago Cardinals	5	6	1	.455
Providence Steam Roller	5	7	1	.417
Detroit Panthers	4	6	2	.400
Hartford Blues	3	7	0	.300
Brooklyn Lions	3	8	0	.273
Milwaukee Badgers	2	7	0	.222
Akron Pros	1	4	3	.200
Dayton Triangles	1	4	1	.200
Racine Tornadoes	1	4	0	.200
Columbus Tigers	1	6	0	.143
Canton Bulldogs	1	9	3	.100
Hammond Pros	0	4	0	.000
Louisville Colonels	0	4	0	.000

1925

	W	L	T	Pct.
Chicago Cardinals	11	2	1	.846
Pottsville Maroons	10	2	0	.833
Detroit Panthers	8	2	2	.800
New York Giants	8	4	0	.667
Akron Indians	4	2	2	.667
Frankford Yellow Jackets	13	7	0	.650
Chicago Bears	9	5	3	.643
Rock Island Independents	5	3	3	.625
Green Bay Packers	8	5	0	.615
Providence Steam Roller	6	5	1	.545
Canton Bulldogs	4	4	0	.500
Cleveland Bulldogs	5	8	1	.385
Kansas City Cowboys	2	5	1	.286
Hammond Pros	1	4	0	.200
Buffalo Bisons	1	6	2	.143
Duluth Kelleys	0	3	0	.000
Rochester Jeffersons	0	6	1	.000
Milwaukee Badgers	0	6	0	.000
Dayton Triangles	0	7	1	.000
Columbus Tigers	0	9	0	.000

1924

	W	L	T	Pct.
Cleveland Bulldogs	7	1	1	.875
Chicago Bears	6	1	4	.857
Frankford Yellow Jackets	11	2	1	.846
Duluth Kelleys	5	1	0	.833
Rock Island Independents	5	2	2	.714
Green Bay Packers	7	4	0	.636
Racine Legion	4	3	3	.571
Chicago Cardinals	5	4	1	.556
Buffalo Bisons	6	5	0	.545
Columbus Tigers	4	4	0	.500
Hammond Pros	2	2	1	.500
Milwaukee Badgers	5	8	0	.385
Akron Indians	2	6	0	.250
Dayton Triangles	2	6	0	.250
Kansas City Blues	2	7	0	.222
Kenosha Maroons	0	4	1	.000
Minneapolis Marines	0	6	0	.000
Rochester Jeffersons	0	7	0	.000

1923

	W	L	T	Pct.
Canton Bulldogs	11	0	1	1.000
Chicago Bears	9	2	1	.818
Green Bay Packers	7	2	1	.778
Milwaukee Badgers	7	2	3	.778
Cleveland Indians	3	1	3	.750
Chicago Cardinals	8	4	0	.667
Duluth Kelleys	4	3	0	.571
Buffalo All-Americans	5	4	3	.556
Columbus Tigers	5	4	1	.556
Racine Legion	4	4	2	.500
Toledo Maroons	3	3	2	.500
Rock Island Independents	2	3	3	.400
Minneapolis Marines	2	5	2	.286
St. Louis All-Stars	1	4	2	.200
Hammond Pros	1	5	1	.167
Dayton Triangles	1	6	1	.143
Akron Indians	1	6	0	.143
Oorang Indians	1	10	0	.091
Louisville Brecks	0	3	0	.000
Rochester Jeffersons	0	4	0	.000

PAST STANDINGS

1922

	W	L	T	Pct.
Canton Bulldogs	10	0	2	1.000
Chicago Bears	9	3	0	.750
Chicago Cardinals	8	3	0	.727
Toledo Maroons	5	2	2	.714
Rock Island Independents	4	2	1	.667
Racine Legion	6	4	1	.600
Dayton Triangles	4	3	1	.571
Green Bay Packers	4	3	3	.571
Buffalo All-Americans	5	4	1	.556
Akron Pros	3	5	2	.375
Milwaukee Badgers	2	4	3	.333
Oorang Indians	3	6	0	.333
Minneapolis Marines	1	3	0	.250
Louisville Brecks	1	3	0	.250
Evansville Crimson Giants	0	3	0	.000
Rochester Jeffersons	0	4	1	.000
Hammond Pros	0	5	1	.000
Columbus Panhandles	0	8	0	.000

1921

	W	L	T	Pct.
Chicago Staleys	9	1	1	.900
Buffalo All-Americans	9	1	2	.900
Akron Pros	8	3	1	.727
Canton Bulldogs	5	2	3	.714
Rock Island Independents	4	2	1	.667
Evansville Crimson Giants	3	2	0	.600
Green Bay Packers	3	2	1	.600
Dayton Triangles	4	4	1	.500
Chicago Cardinals	3	3	2	.500
Rochester Jeffersons	2	3	0	.400
Cleveland Indians	3	5	0	.375
Washington Senators	1	2	0	.333
Cincinnati Celts	1	3	0	.250
Hammond Pros	1	3	1	.250
Minneapolis Marines	1	3	0	.250
Detroit Heralds	1	5	1	.167
Columbus Panhandles	1	8	0	.111
Tonawanda Kardex	0	1	0	.000
Muncie Flyers	0	2	0	.000
Louisville Brecks	0	2	0	.000
New York Giants	0	2	0	.000

1920*

	W	L	T	Pct.
Akron Pros	8	0	3	1.000
Decatur Staleys	10	1	2	.909
Buffalo All-Americans	9	1	1	.900
Chicago Cardinals	6	2	2	.750
Rock Island Independents	6	2	2	.750
Dayton Triangles	5	2	2	.714
Rochester Jeffersons	6	3	2	.667
Canton Bulldogs	7	4	2	.636
Detroit Heralds	2	3	3	.400
Cleveland Tigers	2	4	2	.333
Chicago Tigers	2	5	1	.286
Hammond Pros	2	5	0	.286
Columbus Panhandles	2	6	2	.250
Muncie Flyers	0	1	0	.000

**No official standing was maintained for the 1920 season, and the championship was awarded to the Akron Pros in a League meeting on April 30, 1921. Clubs played schedules which included games against non-league opponents.*

RS=REGULAR SEASON
PS=POSTSEASON

***ARIZONA vs. ATLANTA**
RS: Cardinals lead series, 13-6
1966—Falcons, 16-10 (A)
1968—Cardinals, 17-12 (StL)
1971—Cardinals, 26-9 (A)
1973—Cardinals, 32-10 (A)
1975—Cardinals, 23-20 (StL)
1978—Cardinals, 42-21 (StL)
1980—Falcons, 33-27 (StL) OT
1981—Falcons, 41-20 (A)
1982—Cardinals, 23-20 (A)
1986—Falcons, 33-13 (A)
1987—Cardinals, 34-21 (A)
1989—Cardinals, 34-20 (P)
1990—Cardinals, 24-13 (A)
1991—Cardinals, 16-10 (P)
1992—Falcons, 20-17 (A)
1993—Cardinals, 27-10 (A)
1994—Falcons, 10-6 (Atl)
1995—Cardinals, 40-37 (Ariz) OT
1997—Cardinals, 29-26 (Ariz)
(RS Pts.—Cardinals 460, Falcons 382)
**Franchise known as Phoenix prior to 1994 and in St. Louis prior to 1988*

***ARIZONA vs. BALTIMORE**
RS: Cardinals lead series, 1-0
1997—Cardinals, 16-13 (B)
(RS Pts.—Cardinals 16, Ravens 13)

***ARIZONA vs. BUFFALO**
RS: Series tied, 3-3
1971—Cardinals, 28-23 (B)
1975—Bills, 32-14 (StL)
1981—Cardinals, 24-0 (StL)
1984—Cardinals, 37-7 (StL)
1986—Bills, 17-10 (B)
1990—Bills, 45-14 (B)
(RS Pts.—Cardinals 127, Bills 124)
**Franchise known as Phoenix prior to 1994 and in St. Louis prior to 1988*

ARIZONA vs. CAROLINA
RS: Panthers lead series, 1-0
1995—Panthers, 27-7 (C)
(RS Pts.—Panthers 27, Cardinals 7)

***ARIZONA vs. **CHICAGO**
RS: Bears lead series, 52-25-6
(NP denotes Normal Park;
Wr denotes Wrigley Field;
Co denotes Comiskey Park;
So denotes Soldier Field;
all Chicago)
1920—Cardinals, 7-6 (NP)
Staleys, 10-0 (Wr)
1921—Tie, 0-0 (Wr)
1922—Cardinals, 6-0 (Co)
Cardinals, 9-0 (Co)
1923—Bears, 3-0 (Wr)
1924—Bears, 6-0 (Wr)
Bears, 21-0 (Co)
1925—Cardinals, 9-0 (Co)
Tie, 0-0 (Wr)
1926—Bears, 16-0 (Wr)
Bears, 10-0 (So)
Tie, 0-0 (Wr)
1927—Bears, 9-0 (NP)
Cardinals, 3-0 (Wr)
1928—Bears, 15-0 (NP)
Bears, 34-0 (Wr)
1929—Tie, 0-0 (Wr)
Cardinals, 40-6 (Co)
1930—Bears, 32-6 (Co)
Bears, 6-0 (Wr)
1931—Bears, 26-13 (Wr)
Bears, 18-7 (Wr)
1932—Tie, 0-0 (Wr)
Bears, 34-0 (Wr)
1933—Bears, 12-9 (Wr)
Bears, 22-6 (Wr)
1934—Bears, 20-0 (Wr)
Bears, 17-6 (Wr)
1935—Tie, 7-7 (Wr)
Bears, 13-0 (Wr)
1936—Bears, 7-3 (Wr)
Cardinals, 14-7 (Wr)
1937—Bears, 16-7 (Wr)
Bears, 42-28 (Wr)
1938—Bears, 16-13 (So)
Bears, 34-28 (Wr)
1939—Bears, 44-7 (Wr)
Bears, 48-7 (Co)
1940—Cardinals, 21-7 (Co)
Bears, 31-23 (Wr)
1941—Bears, 53-7 (Wr)
Bears, 34-24 (Co)
1942—Bears, 41-14 (Wr)
Bears, 21-7 (Co)
1943—Bears, 20-0 (Wr)
Bears, 35-24 (Co)
1945—Cardinals, 16-7 (Wr)
Bears, 28-20 (Co)
1946—Bears, 34-17 (Co)
Cardinals, 35-28 (Wr)
1947—Cardinals, 31-7 (Co)
Cardinals, 30-21 (Wr)
1948—Bears, 28-17 (Co)
Cardinals, 24-21 (Wr)
1949—Bears, 17-7 (Co)
Bears, 52-21 (Wr)
1950—Bears, 27-6 (Wr)
Cardinals, 20-10 (Co)
1951—Cardinals, 28-14 (Co)
Cardinals, 24-14 (Wr)
1952—Cardinals, 21-10 (Co)
Bears, 10-7 (Wr)
1953—Cardinals, 24-17 (Wr)
1954—Bears, 29-7 (Co)
1955—Cardinals, 53-14 (Co)
1956—Bears, 10-3 (Wr)
1957—Bears, 14-6 (Co)
1958—Bears, 30-14 (Wr)
1959—Bears, 31-7 (So)
1965—Bears, 34-13 (Wr)
1966—Cardinals, 24-17 (StL)
1967—Bears, 30-3 (Wr)
1969—Cardinals, 20-17 (StL)
1972—Bears, 27-10 (StL)
1975—Cardinals, 34-20 (So)
1977—Cardinals, 16-13 (StL)
1978—Bears, 17-10 (So)
1979—Bears, 42-6 (So)
1982—Cardinals, 10-7 (So)
1984—Cardinals, 38-21 (StL)
1990—Bears, 31-21 (P)
1994—Bears, 19-16 (A) OT
(RS Pts.—Bears 1,567, Cardinals 1,014)
**Franchise known as Phoenix prior to 1994, in St. Louis prior to 1988, and in Chicago prior to 1960*
***Franchise in Decatur prior to 1921 and known as Staleys prior to 1922*

***ARIZONA vs. CINCINNATI**
RS: Bengals lead series, 4-2
1973—Bengals, 42-24 (C)
1979—Bengals, 34-28 (C)
1985—Cardinals, 41-27 (StL)
1988—Bengals, 21-14 (C)
1994—Cardinals, 28-7 (A)
1997—Bengals, 24-21 (C)
(RS Pts.—Cardinals 156, Bengals 155)
**Franchise known as Phoenix prior to 1994 and in St. Louis prior to 1988*

***ARIZONA vs. CLEVELAND**
RS: Browns lead series, 32-10-3
1950—Browns, 34-24 (Cle)
Browns, 10-7 (Chi)
1951—Browns, 34-17 (Chi)
Browns, 49-28 (Cle)
1952—Browns, 28-13 (Cle)
Browns, 10-0 (Chi)
1953—Browns, 27-7 (Chi)
Browns, 27-16 (Cle)
1954—Browns, 31-7 (Cle)
Browns, 35-3 (Chi)
1955—Browns, 26-20 (Chi)
Browns, 35-24 (Cle)
1956—Cardinals, 9-7 (Chi)
Cardinals, 24-7 (Cle)
1957—Browns, 17-7 (Chi)
Browns, 31-0 (Cle)
1958—Browns, 35-28 (Cle)
Browns, 38-24 (Chi)
1959—Browns, 34-7 (Chi)
Browns, 17-7 (Cle)
1960—Browns, 28-27 (Cle)
Tie, 17-17 (StL)
1961—Browns, 20-17 (Cle)
Browns, 21-10 (StL)
1962—Browns, 34-7 (StL)
Browns, 38-14 (Cle)
1963—Cardinals, 20-14 (Cle)
Browns, 24-10 (StL)
1964—Tie, 33-33 (Cle)
Cardinals, 28-19 (StL)
1965—Cardinals, 49-13 (Cle)
Browns, 27-24 (StL)
1966—Cardinals, 34-28 (Cle)
Browns, 38-10 (StL)
1967—Browns, 20-16 (Cle)
Browns, 20-16 (StL)
1968—Cardinals, 27-21 (Cle)
Cardinals, 27-16 (StL)
1969—Tie, 21-21 (Cle)
Browns, 27-21 (StL)
1974—Cardinals, 29-7 (StL)
1979—Browns, 38-20 (StL)
1985—Cardinals, 27-24 (Cle) OT
1988—Browns, 29-21 (P)
1994—Browns, 32-0 (Cle)
(RS Pts.—Browns 1,141, Cardinals 797)
**Franchise known as Phoenix prior to 1994, in St. Louis prior to 1988, and in Chicago prior to 1960*

***ARIZONA vs. DALLAS**
RS: Cowboys lead series, 47-23-1
1960—Cardinals, 12-10 (StL)
1961—Cardinals, 31-17 (D)
Cardinals, 31-13 (StL)
1962—Cardinals, 28-24 (D)
Cardinals, 52-20 (StL)
1963—Cardinals, 34-7 (D)
Cowboys, 28-24 (StL)
1964—Cardinals, 16-6 (D)
Cowboys, 31-13 (StL)
1965—Cardinals, 20-13 (StL)
Cowboys, 27-13 (D)
1966—Tie, 10-10 (StL)
Cowboys, 31-17 (D)
1967—Cowboys, 46-21 (D)
1968—Cowboys, 27-10 (StL)
1969—Cowboys, 24-3 (D)
1970—Cardinals, 20-7 (StL)
Cardinals, 38-0 (D)
1971—Cowboys, 16-13 (StL)
Cowboys, 31-12 (D)
1972—Cowboys, 33-24 (D)
Cowboys, 27-6 (StL)
1973—Cowboys, 45-10 (D)
Cowboys, 30-3 (StL)
1974—Cardinals, 31-28 (StL)
Cowboys, 17-14 (D)
1975—Cowboys, 37-31 (D) OT
Cardinals, 31-17 (StL)
1976—Cardinals, 21-17 (StL)
Cowboys, 19-14 (D)
1977—Cowboys, 30-24 (StL)
Cardinals, 24-17 (D)
1978—Cowboys, 21-12 (D)
Cowboys, 24-21 (StL) OT
1979—Cowboys, 22-21 (StL)
Cowboys, 22-13 (D)
1980—Cowboys, 27-24 (StL)
Cowboys, 31-21 (D)
1981—Cowboys, 30-17 (D)
Cardinals, 20-17 (StL)
1982—Cowboys, 24-7 (StL)
1983—Cowboys, 34-17 (StL)
Cowboys, 35-17 (D)
1984—Cardinals, 31-20 (D)
Cowboys, 24-17 (StL)
1985—Cardinals, 21-10 (StL)
Cowboys, 35-17 (D)
1986—Cowboys, 31-7 (StL)
Cowboys, 37-6 (D)
1987—Cardinals, 24-13 (StL)
Cowboys, 21-16 (D)
1988—Cowboys, 17-14 (P)
Cardinals, 16-10 (D)
1989—Cardinals, 19-10 (D)
Cardinals, 24-20 (P)
1990—Cardinals, 20-3 (P)
Cowboys, 41-10 (D)
1991—Cowboys, 17-9 (P)
Cowboys, 27-7 (D)
1992—Cowboys, 31-20 (D)
Cowboys, 16-10 (P)
1993—Cowboys, 17-10 (P)
Cowboys, 20-15 (D)
1994—Cowboys, 38-3 (D)
Cowboys, 28-21 (A)
1995—Cowboys, 34-20 (D)
Cowboys, 37-13 (A)
1996—Cowboys, 17-3 (D)
Cowboys, 10-6 (A)
1997—Cardinals, 25-22 (A) OT
Cowboys, 24-6 (D)
(RS Pts.—Cowboys 1,622, Cardinals 1,251)
**Franchise known as Phoenix prior to 1994 and in St. Louis prior to 1988*

***ARIZONA vs. DENVER**
RS: Broncos lead series, 4-0-1
1973—Tie, 17-17 (StL)
1977—Broncos, 7-0 (D)
1989—Broncos, 37-0 (P)
1991—Broncos, 24-19 (D)
1995—Broncos, 38-6 (D)
(RS Pts.—Broncos 123, Cardinals 42)
**Franchise known as Phoenix prior to 1994 and in St. Louis prior to 1988*

***ARIZONA vs. **DETROIT**
RS: Lions lead series, 27-17-5
1930—Tie, 0-0 (Port)
Cardinals, 23-0 (C)
1931—Cardinals, 20-19 (C)
1932—Tie, 7-7 (Port)
1933—Spartans, 7-6 (Port)
1934—Lions, 6-0 (D)
Lions, 17-13 (C)
1935—Tie, 10-10 (D)
Lions, 7-6 (C)
1936—Lions, 39-0 (D)
Lions, 14-7 (C)
1937—Lions, 16-7 (C)
Lions, 16-7 (D)
1938—Lions, 10-0 (D)
Lions, 7-3 (C)
1939—Lions, 21-3 (D)
Lions, 17-3 (C)
1940—Tie, 0-0 (Buffalo)
Lions, 43-14 (C)
1941—Tie, 14-14 (C)
Lions, 21-3 (D)
1942—Cardinals, 13-0 (C)
Cardinals, 7-0 (D)
1943—Lions, 35-17 (D)
Lions, 7-0 (Buffalo)
1945—Lions, 10-0 (Milwaukee)
Lions, 26-0 (D)
1946—Cardinals, 34-14 (C)
Cardinals, 36-14 (D)
1947—Cardinals, 45-21 (C)
Cardinals, 17-7 (D)
1948—Cardinals, 56-20 (C)
Cardinals, 28-14 (D)
1949—Lions, 24-7 (C)
Cardinals, 42-19 (D)
1959—Lions, 45-21 (D)
1961—Lions, 45-14 (StL)
1967—Cardinals, 38-28 (StL)
1969—Lions, 20-0 (D)
1970—Lions, 16-3 (D)
1973—Lions, 20-16 (StL)

1975—Cardinals, 24-13 (D)
1978—Cardinals, 21-14 (StL)
1980—Lions, 20-7 (D)
Cardinals, 24-23 (StL)
1989—Cardinals, 16-13 (D)
1993—Lions, 26-20 (D)
Lions, 21-14 (Phx)
1995—Cardinals, 20-17 (D)
(RS Pts.—Lions 823, Cardinals 696)
Franchise known as Phoenix prior to 1994, in St. Louis prior to 1988, and in Chicago prior to 1960
***Franchise in Portsmouth prior to 1934 and known as the Spartans*

***ARIZONA vs. GREEN BAY**
RS: Packers lead series, 39-21-4
PS: Packers lead series, 1-0
1921—Tie, 3-3 (C)
1922—Cardinals, 16-3 (C)
1924—Cardinals, 3-0 (C)
1925—Cardinals, 9-6 (C)
1926—Cardinals, 13-7 (GB)
Packers, 3-0 (C)
1927—Packers, 13-0 (GB)
Tie, 6-6 (C)
1928—Packers, 20-0 (GB)
1929—Packers, 9-2 (GB)
Packers, 7-6 (C)
Packers, 12-0 (C)
1930—Packers, 14-0 (GB)
Cardinals, 13-6 (C)
1931—Packers, 26-7 (GB)
Cardinals, 21-13 (C)
1932—Packers, 15-7 (GB)
Packers, 19-9 (C)
1933—Packers, 14-6 (C)
1934—Packers, 15-0 (GB)
Cardinals, 9-0 (Mil)
Cardinals, 6-0 (C)
1935—Cardinals, 7-6 (GB)
Cardinals, 3-0 (Mil)
Cardinals, 9-7 (C)
1936—Packers, 10-7 (GB)
Packers, 24-0 (Mil)
Tie, 0-0 (C)
1937—Cardinals, 14-7 (GB)
Packers, 34-13 (Mil)
1938—Packers, 28-7 (Mil)
Packers, 24-22 (Buffalo)
1939—Packers, 14-10 (GB)
Packers, 27-20 (Mil)
1940—Packers, 31-6 (Mil)
Packers, 28-7 (C)
1941—Packers, 14-13 (Mil)
Packers, 17-9 (GB)
1942—Packers, 17-13 (C)
Packers, 55-24 (GB)
1943—Packers, 28-7 (C)
Packers, 35-14 (Mil)
1945—Packers, 33-14 (GB)
1946—Packers, 19-7 (C)
Cardinals, 24-6 (GB)
1947—Cardinals, 14-10 (GB)
Cardinals, 21-20 (C)
1948—Cardinals, 17-7 (Mil)
Cardinals, 42-7 (C)
1949—Cardinals, 39-17 (Mil)
Cardinals, 41-21 (C)
1955—Packers, 31-14 (GB)
1956—Packers, 24-21 (C)
1962—Packers, 17-0 (Mil)
1963—Packers, 30-7 (StL)
1967—Packers, 31-23 (StL)
1969—Packers, 45-28 (GB)
1971—Tie, 16-16 (StL)
1973—Packers, 25-21 (GB)
1976—Cardinals, 29-0 (StL)
1982—**Packers, 41-16 (GB)
1984—Packers, 24-23 (GB)
1985—Cardinals, 43-28 (StL)
1988—Packers, 26-17 (P)
1990—Packers, 24-21 (P)
(RS Pts.—Packers 1,078, Cardinals 823)
(PS Pts.—Packers 41, Cardinals 16)
**Franchise known as Phoenix prior to 1994, in St. Louis prior to 1988, and in Chicago prior to 1960*
***NFC First-Round Playoff*

***ARIZONA vs. **INDIANAPOLIS**
RS: Series tied, 6-6
1961—Colts, 16-0 (B)
1964—Colts, 47-27 (B)
1968—Colts, 27-0 (B)
1972—Cardinals, 10-3 (B)
1976—Cardinals, 24-17 (StL)
1978—Colts, 30-17 (StL)
1980—Cardinals, 17-10 (B)
1981—Cardinals, 35-24 (B)
1984—Cardinals, 34-33 (I)
1990—Cardinals, 20-17 (P)
1992—Colts, 16-13 (I)
1996—Colts, 20-13 (I)
(RS Pts.—Colts 260, Cardinals 210)
**Franchise known as Phoenix prior to 1994 and in St. Louis prior to 1988*
***Franchise in Baltimore prior to 1984*

***ARIZONA vs. KANSAS CITY**
RS: Chiefs lead series, 4-1-1
1970—Tie, 6-6 (KC)
1974—Chiefs, 17-13 (StL)
1980—Chiefs, 21-13 (StL)
1983—Chiefs, 38-14 (KC)
1986—Cardinals, 23-14 (StL)
1995—Chiefs, 24-3 (A)
(RS Pts.—Chiefs 120, Cardinals 72)
**Franchise known as Phoenix prior to 1994 and in St. Louis prior to 1988*

***ARIZONA vs. MIAMI**
RS: Dolphins lead series, 7-0
1972—Dolphins, 31-10 (M)
1977—Dolphins, 55-14 (StL)
1978—Dolphins, 24-10 (M)
1981—Dolphins, 20-7 (StL)
1984—Dolphins, 36-28 (StL)
1990—Dolphins, 23-3 (M)
1996—Dolphins, 38-10 (A)
(RS Pts.—Dolphins 227, Cardinals 82)
**Franchise known as Phoenix prior to 1994 and in St. Louis prior to 1988*

***ARIZONA vs. MINNESOTA**
RS: Cardinals lead series, 8-7
PS: Vikings lead series, 1-0
1963—Cardinals, 56-14 (M)
1967—Cardinals, 34-24 (M)
1969—Vikings, 27-10 (StL)
1972—Cardinals, 19-17 (M)
1974—Vikings, 28-24 (StL)
**Vikings, 30-14 (M)
1977—Cardinals, 27-7 (M)
1979—Cardinals, 37-7 (StL)
1981—Cardinals, 30-17 (StL)
1983—Cardinals, 41-31 (StL)
1991—Vikings, 34-7 (M)
Vikings, 28-0 (P)
1994—Cardinals, 17-7 (A)
1995—Vikings, 30-24 (A) OT
1996—Vikings, 41-17 (M)
1997—Vikings, 20-19 (A)
(RS Pts.—Cardinals 362, Vikings 332)
(PS Pts.—Vikings 30, Cardinals 14)
**Franchise known as Phoenix prior to 1994 and in St. Louis prior to 1988*
***NFC Divisional Playoff*

***ARIZONA vs. **NEW ENGLAND**
RS: Cardinals lead series, 6-3
1970—Cardinals, 31-0 (StL)
1975—Cardinals, 24-17 (StL)
1978—Patriots, 16-6 (StL)
1981—Cardinals, 27-20 (NE)
1984—Cardinals, 33-10 (NE)
1990—Cardinals, 34-14 (P)
1991—Cardinals, 24-10 (P)
1993—Patriots, 23-21 (P)
1996—Patriots, 31-0 (NE)
(RS Pts.—Cardinals 200, Patriots 141)
**Franchise known as Phoenix prior to 1994 and in St. Louis prior to 1988*
***Franchise in Boston prior to 1971*

***ARIZONA vs. NEW ORLEANS**
RS: Cardinals lead series, 11-10
1967—Cardinals, 31-20 (StL)
1968—Cardinals, 21-20 (NO)
Cardinals, 31-17 (StL)
1969—Saints, 51-42 (StL)
1970—Cardinals, 24-17 (StL)
1974—Saints, 14-0 (NO)
1977—Cardinals, 49-31 (StL)
1980—Cardinals, 40-7 (NO)
1981—Cardinals, 30-3 (StL)
1982—Cardinals, 21-7 (NO)
1983—Saints, 28-17 (NO)
1984—Saints, 34-24 (NO)
1985—Cardinals, 28-16 (StL)
1986—Saints, 16-7 (StL)
1987—Cardinals, 24-19 (StL)
1990—Saints, 28-7 (NO)
1991—Saints, 27-3 (P)
1992—Saints, 30-21 (P)
1993—Saints, 20-17 (P)
1996—Cardinals, 28-14 (NO)
1997—Saints, 27-10 (NO)
(RS Pts.—Cardinals 475, Saints 446)
**Franchise known as Phoenix prior to 1994 and in St. Louis prior to 1988*

***ARIZONA vs. N.Y. GIANTS**
RS: Giants lead series, 71-37-2
1926—Giants, 20-0 (NY)
1927—Giants, 28-7 (NY)
1929—Giants, 24-21 (NY)
1930—Giants, 25-12 (NY)
Giants, 13-7 (C)
1935—Cardinals, 14-13 (NY)
1936—Giants, 14-6 (NY)
1938—Giants, 6-0 (NY)
1939—Giants, 17-7 (NY)
1941—Cardinals, 10-7 (NY)
1942—Giants, 21-7 (NY)
1943—Giants, 24-13 (NY)
1946—Giants, 28-24 (NY)
1947—Giants, 35-31 (NY)
1948—Cardinals, 63-35 (NY)
1949—Giants, 41-38 (C)
1950—Cardinals, 17-3 (C)
Giants, 51-21 (NY)
1951—Giants, 28-17 (NY)
Giants, 10-0 (C)
1952—Cardinals, 24-23 (NY)
Giants, 28-6 (C)
1953—Giants, 21-7 (NY)
Giants, 23-20 (C)
1954—Giants, 41-10 (C)
Giants, 31-17 (NY)
1955—Cardinals, 28-17 (C)
Giants, 10-0 (NY)
1956—Cardinals, 35-27 (C)
Giants, 23-10 (NY)
1957—Giants, 27-14 (NY)
Giants, 28-21 (C)
1958—Giants, 37-7 (Buffalo)
Cardinals, 23-6 (NY)
1959—Giants, 9-3 (NY)
Giants, 30-20 (Minn)
1960—Giants, 35-14 (StL)
Cardinals, 20-13 (NY)
1961—Cardinals, 21-10 (NY)
Giants, 24-9 (StL)
1962—Giants, 31-14 (StL)
Giants, 31-28 (NY)
1963—Giants, 38-21 (StL)
Cardinals, 24-17 (NY)
1964—Giants, 34-17 (NY)
Tie, 10-10 (StL)
1965—Giants, 14-10 (NY)
Giants, 28-15 (StL)
1966—Cardinals, 24-19 (StL)
Cardinals, 20-17 (NY)
1967—Giants, 37-20 (StL)
Giants, 37-14 (NY)
1968—Cardinals, 28-21 (NY)
1969—Cardinals, 42-17 (StL)
Giants, 49-6 (NY)
1970—Giants, 35-17 (NY)
Giants, 34-17 (StL)
1971—Giants, 21-20 (StL)
Cardinals, 24-7 (NY)
1972—Giants, 27-21 (NY)
Giants, 13-7 (StL)
1973—Cardinals, 35-27 (StL)
Giants, 24-13 (New Haven)
1974—Cardinals, 23-21 (New Haven)
Cardinals, 26-14 (StL)
1975—Cardinals, 26-14 (StL)
Cardinals, 20-13 (NY)
1976—Cardinals, 27-21 (StL)
Cardinals, 17-14 (NY)
1977—Cardinals, 28-0 (StL)
Giants, 27-7 (NY)
1978—Cardinals, 20-10 (StL)
Giants, 17-0 (NY)
1979—Cardinals, 27-14 (NY)
Cardinals, 29-20 (StL)
1980—Giants, 41-35 (StL)
Cardinals, 23-7 (NY)
1981—Giants, 34-14 (NY)
Giants, 20-10 (StL)
1982—Cardinals, 24-21 (StL)
1983—Tie, 20-20 (StL) OT
Cardinals, 10-6 (NY)
1984—Giants, 16-10 (NY)
Cardinals, 31-21 (StL)
1985—Giants, 27-17 (NY)
Giants, 34-3 (StL)
1986—Giants, 13-6 (StL)
Giants, 27-7 (NY)
1987—Giants, 30-7 (NY)
Cardinals, 27-24 (StL)
1988—Cardinals, 24-17 (P)
Giants, 44-7 (NY)
1989—Giants, 35-7 (NY)
Giants, 20-13 (P)
1990—Giants, 20-19 (NY)
Giants, 24-21 (P)
1991—Giants, 20-9 (NY)
Giants, 21-14 (P)
1992—Giants, 31-21 (NY)
Cardinals, 19-0 (P)
1993—Giants, 19-17 (NY)
Cardinals, 17-6 (P)
1994—Giants, 20-17 (A)
Cardinals, 10-9 (NY)
1995—Giants, 27-21 (NY) OT
Giants, 10-6 (A)
1996—Giants, 16-8 (NY)
Cardinals, 31-23 (A)
1997—Giants, 27-13 (A)
Giants, 19-10 (NY)
(RS Pts.—Giants 2,428, Cardinals 1,869)
**Franchise known as Phoenix prior to 1994, in St. Louis prior to 1988, and in Chicago prior to 1960*

***ARIZONA vs. N.Y. JETS**
RS: Series tied, 2-2
1971—Cardinals, 17-10 (StL)
1975—Cardinals, 37-6 (NY)
1978—Jets, 23-10 (NY)
1996—Jets, 31-21 (A)
(RS Pts.—Cardinals 85, Jets 70)
**Franchise known as Phoenix prior to 1994 and in St. Louis prior to 1988*

***ARIZONA vs. **OAKLAND**
RS: Raiders lead series, 2-1
1973—Raiders, 17-10 (StL)
1983—Cardinals, 34-24 (LA)
1989—Raiders, 16-14 (LA)
(RS Pts.—Cardinals 58, Raiders 57)
**Franchise known as Phoenix prior to 1994 and in St. Louis prior to 1988*
***Franchise in Los Angeles from 1982-1994*

***ARIZONA vs. PHILADELPHIA**
RS: Eagles lead series, 48-47-5
PS: Series tied, 1-1

1935—Cardinals, 12-3 (C)
1936—Cardinals, 13-0 (C)
1937—Tie, 6-6 (P)
1938—Eagles, 7-0 (Erie, Pa.)
1941—Eagles, 21-14 (P)
1945—Eagles, 21-6 (P)
1947—Cardinals, 45-21 (P)
**Cardinals, 28-21 (C)
1948—Cardinals, 21-14 (C)
**Eagles, 7-0 (P)
1949—Eagles, 28-3 (P)
1950—Eagles, 45-7 (C)
Cardinals, 14-10 (P)
1951—Eagles, 17-14 (C)
1952—Eagles, 10-7 (P)
Cardinals, 28-22 (C)
1953—Eagles, 56-17 (C)
Eagles, 38-0 (P)
1954—Eagles, 35-16 (C)
Eagles, 30-14 (P)
1955—Tie, 24-24 (C)
Eagles, 27-3 (P)
1956—Cardinals, 20-6 (P)
Cardinals, 28-17 (C)
1957—Eagles, 38-21 (C)
Cardinals, 31-27 (P)
1958—Tie, 21-21 (C)
Eagles, 49-21 (P)
1959—Eagles, 28-24 (Minn)
Eagles, 27-17 (P)
1960—Eagles, 31-27 (P)
Eagles, 20-6 (StL)
1961—Cardinals, 30-27 (P)
Eagles, 20-7 (StL)
1962—Cardinals, 27-21 (P)
Cardinals, 45-35 (StL)
1963—Cardinals, 28-24 (P)
Cardinals, 38-14 (StL)
1964—Cardinals, 38-13 (P)
Cardinals, 36-34 (StL)
1965—Eagles, 34-27 (P)
Eagles, 28-24 (StL)
1966—Cardinals, 16-13 (StL)
Cardinals, 41-10 (P)
1967—Cardinals, 48-14 (StL)
1968—Cardinals, 45-17 (P)
1969—Eagles, 34-30 (StL)
1970—Cardinals, 35-20 (P)
Cardinals, 23-14 (StL)
1971—Eagles, 37-20 (StL)
Eagles, 19-7 (P)
1972—Tie, 6-6 (P)
Cardinals, 24-23 (StL)
1973—Cardinals, 34-23 (P)
Eagles, 27-24 (StL)
1974—Cardinals, 7-3 (StL)
Cardinals, 13-3 (P)
1975—Cardinals, 31-20 (StL)
Cardinals, 24-23 (P)
1976—Cardinals, 33-14 (StL)
Cardinals, 17-14 (P)
1977—Cardinals, 21-17 (P)
Cardinals, 21-16 (StL)
1978—Cardinals, 16-10 (P)
Eagles, 14-10 (StL)
1979—Eagles, 24-20 (StL)
Eagles, 16-13 (P)
1980—Cardinals, 24-14 (StL)
Eagles, 17-3 (P)
1981—Eagles, 52-10 (StL)
Eagles, 38-0 (P)
1982—Cardinals, 23-20 (P)
1983—Cardinals, 14-11 (P)
Cardinals, 31-7 (StL)
1984—Cardinals, 34-14 (P)
Cardinals, 17-16 (StL)
1985—Eagles, 30-7 (P)
Eagles, 24-14 (StL)
1986—Cardinals, 13-10 (StL)
Tie, 10-10 (P) OT
1987—Eagles, 28-23 (StL)
Cardinals, 31-19 (P)
1988—Eagles, 31-21 (P)
Eagles, 23-17 (Phx)
1989—Eagles, 17-5 (Phx)
Eagles, 31-14 (P)
1990—Cardinals, 23-21 (P)
Eagles, 23-21 (Phx)
1991—Cardinals, 26-10 (P)
Eagles, 34-14 (Phx)
1992—Eagles, 31-14 (Phx)
Eagles, 7-3 (P)
1993—Eagles, 23-17 (P)
Cardinals, 16-3 (Phx)
1994—Eagles, 17-7 (P)
Cardinals, 12-6 (A)
1995—Eagles, 31-19 (A)
Eagles, 21-20 (P)
1996—Cardinals, 36-30 (A)
Eagles, 29-19 (P)
1997—Eagles, 13-10 (P) OT
Cardinals, 31-21 (A)
(RS Pts.—Eagles 2,140, Cardinals 1,986)
(PS Pts.—Eagles 28, Cardinals 28)
Franchise known as Phoenix prior to 1994, in St. Louis prior to 1988, and in Chicago prior to 1960
***NFL Championship*

***ARIZONA vs. **PITTSBURGH**
RS: Steelers lead series, 30-22-3
1933—Pirates, 14-13 (C)
1935—Pirates, 17-13 (P)
1936—Cardinals, 14-6 (C)
1937—Cardinals, 13-7 (P)
1939—Cardinals, 10-0 (P)
1940—Tie, 7-7 (P)
1942—Steelers, 19-3 (P)
1945—Steelers, 23-0 (P)
1946—Steelers, 14-7 (P)
1948—Cardinals, 24-7 (P)
1950—Steelers, 28-17 (C)
Steelers, 28-7 (P)
1951—Steelers, 28-14 (C)
1952—Steelers, 34-28 (C)
Steelers, 17-14 (P)
1953—Steelers, 31-28 (P)
Steelers, 21-17 (C)
1954—Cardinals, 17-14 (C)
Steelers, 20-17 (P)
1955—Steelers, 14-7 (P)
Cardinals, 27-13 (C)
1956—Steelers, 14-7 (P)
Cardinals, 38-27 (C)
1957—Steelers, 29-20 (P)
Steelers, 27-2 (C)
1958—Steelers, 27-20 (C)
Steelers, 38-21 (P)
1959—Cardinals, 45-24 (C)
Steelers, 35-20 (P)
1960—Steelers, 27-14 (P)
Cardinals, 38-7 (StL)
1961—Steelers, 30-27 (P)
Cardinals, 20-0 (StL)
1962—Steelers, 26-17 (StL)
Steelers, 19-7 (P)
1963—Steelers, 23-10 (P)
Cardinals, 24-23 (StL)
1964—Cardinals, 34-30 (StL)
Cardinals, 21-20 (P)
1965—Cardinals, 20-7 (P)
Cardinals, 21-17 (StL)
1966—Steelers, 30-9 (P)
Cardinals, 6-3 (StL)
1967—Cardinals, 28-14 (P)
Tie, 14-14 (StL)
1968—Tie, 28-28 (StL)
Cardinals, 20-10 (P)
1969—Cardinals, 27-14 (P)
Cardinals, 47-10 (StL)
1972—Steelers, 25-19 (StL)
1979—Steelers, 24-21 (StL)
1985—Steelers, 23-10 (P)
1988—Cardinals, 31-14 (Phx)
1994—Cardinals, 20-17 (A) OT
1997—Steelers, 26-20 (A) OT
(RS Pts.—Steelers 1,064, Cardinals 1,023)
Franchise known as Phoenix prior to 1994, in St. Louis prior to 1988, and in Chicago prior to 1960
***Steelers known as Pirates prior to 1941*

***ARIZONA vs. **ST. LOUIS**
RS: Rams lead series, 23-20-2
PS: Rams lead series, 1-0
1937—Cardinals, 6-0 (Clev)
Cardinals, 13-7 (Chi)
1938—Cardinals, 7-6 (Clev)
Cardinals, 31-17 (Chi)
1939—Rams, 24-0 (Chi)
Rams, 14-0 (Clev)
1940—Rams, 26-14 (Clev)
Cardinals, 17-7 (Chi)
1941—Rams, 10-6 (Clev)
Cardinals, 7-0 (Chi)
1942—Cardinals, 7-0 (Buffalo)
Rams, 7-3 (Clev)
1945—Rams, 21-0 (Clev)
Rams, 35-21 (Chi)
1946—Cardinals, 34-10 (Chi)
Rams, 17-14 (LA)
1947—Rams, 27-7 (LA)
Cardinals, 17-10 (Chi)
1948—Cardinals, 27-22 (LA)
Cardinals, 27-24 (Chi)
1949—Tie, 28-28 (Chi)
Cardinals, 31-27 (LA)
1951—Rams, 45-21 (LA)
1953—Tie, 24-24 (Chi)
1954—Rams, 28-17 (LA)
1958—Rams, 20-14 (Chi)
1960—Cardinals, 43-21 (LA)
1965—Rams, 27-3 (StL)
1968—Rams, 24-13 (StL)
1970—Rams, 34-13 (LA)
1972—Cardinals, 24-14 (StL)
1975—***Rams, 35-23 (LA)
1976—Cardinals, 30-28 (LA)
1979—Rams, 21-0 (LA)
1980—Rams, 21-13 (StL)
1984—Rams, 16-13 (StL)
1985—Rams, 46-14 (LA)
1986—Rams, 16-10 (StL)
1987—Rams, 27-24 (StL)
1988—Cardinals, 41-27 (LA)
1989—Rams, 37-14 (LA)
1991—Cardinals, 24-14 (LA)
1992—Cardinals, 20-14 (LA)
1993—Cardinals, 38-10 (P)
1994—Rams, 14-12 (LA)
1996—Cardinals, 31-28 (A) OT
(RS Pts.—Rams 895, Cardinals 773)
(PS Pts.—Rams 35, Cardinals 23)
Franchise known as Phoenix prior to 1994, in St. Louis prior to 1988, and in Chicago prior to 1960
***Franchise in Los Angeles prior to 1995 and in Cleveland prior to 1946*
****NFC Divisional Playoff*

***ARIZONA vs. SAN DIEGO**
RS: Chargers lead series, 6-1
1971—Chargers, 20-17 (SD)
1976—Chargers, 43-24 (SD)
1983—Cardinals, 44-14 (StL)
1987—Chargers, 28-24 (SD)
1989—Chargers, 24-13 (P)
1992—Chargers, 27-21 (P)
1995—Chargers, 28-25 (SD)
(RS Pts.—Chargers 184, Cardinals 168)
Franchise known as Phoenix prior to 1994, in St. Louis prior to 1988,

***ARIZONA vs. SAN FRANCISCO**
RS: 49ers lead series, 10-9
1951—Cardinals, 27-21 (SF)
1957—Cardinals, 20-10 (SF)
1962—49ers, 24-17 (StL)
1964—Cardinals, 23-13 (SF)
1968—49ers, 35-17 (SF)
1971—49ers, 26-14 (StL)
1974—Cardinals, 34-9 (SF)
1976—Cardinals, 23-20 (StL) OT
1978—Cardinals, 16-10 (SF)
1979—Cardinals, 13-10 (StL)
1980—49ers, 24-21 (SF) OT
1982—49ers, 31-20 (StL)
1983—49ers, 42-27 (StL)
1986—49ers, 43-17 (SF)
1987—49ers, 34-28 (SF)
1988—Cardinals, 24-23 (P)
1991—49ers, 14-10 (SF)
1992—Cardinals, 24-14 (P)
1993—49ers, 28-14 (SF)
(RS Pts.—49ers 431, Cardinals 389)
Franchise known as Phoenix prior to 1994, in St. Louis prior to 1988, and in Chicago prior to 1960

***ARIZONA vs. SEATTLE**
RS: Cardinals lead series, 5-0
1976—Cardinals, 30-24 (S)
1983—Cardinals, 33-28 (StL)
1989—Cardinals, 34-24 (S)
1993—Cardinals, 30-27 (S) OT
1995—Cardinals, 20-14 (A) OT
(RS Pts.—Cardinals 147, Seahawks 117)
Franchise known as Phoenix prior to 1994 and in St. Louis prior to 1988

***ARIZONA vs. TAMPA BAY**
RS: Series tied, 7-7
1977—Buccaneers, 17-7 (TB)
1981—Buccaneers, 20-10 (TB)
1983—Cardinals, 34-27 (TB)
1985—Buccaneers, 16-0 (TB)
1986—Cardinals, 30-19 (TB)
Cardinals, 21-17 (StL)
1987—Cardinals, 31-28 (StL)
Cardinals, 31-14 (TB)
1988—Cardinals, 30-24 (TB)
1989—Buccaneers, 14-13 (P)
1992—Buccaneers, 23-7 (TB)
Buccaneers, 7-3 (P)
1996—Cardinals, 13-9 (A)
1997—Buccaneers, 19-18 (TB)
(RS Pts.—Buccaneers 254, Cardinals 248)
Franchise known as Phoenix prior to 1994 and in St. Louis prior to 1988

***ARIZONA vs. **TENNESSEE**
RS: Cardinals lead series, 4-3
1970—Cardinals, 44-0 (StL)
1974—Cardinals, 31-27 (H)
1979—Cardinals, 24-17 (H)
1985—Oilers, 20-10 (StL)
1988—Oilers, 38-20 (H)
1994—Cardinals, 30-12 (H)
1997—Oilers, 41-14 (T)
(RS Pts.—Cardinals 173, Oilers 155)
Franchise known as Phoenix prior to 1994 and in St. Louis prior to 1988
***Franchise in Houston prior to 1997*

***ARIZONA vs. **WASHINGTON**
RS: Redskins lead series, 64-41-2
1932—Cardinals, 9-0 (B)
Braves, 8-6 (C)
1933—Redskins, 10-0 (C)
Tie, 0-0 (B)
1934—Redskins, 9-0 (B)
1935—Cardinals, 6-0 (B)
1936—Redskins, 13-10 (B)
1937—Cardinals, 21-14 (W)
1939—Redskins, 28-7 (W)
1940—Redskins, 28-21 (W)
1942—Redskins, 28-0 (W)
1943—Redskins, 13-7 (W)
1945—Redskins, 24-21 (W)
1947—Redskins, 45-21 (W)
1949—Cardinals, 38-7 (C)
1950—Cardinals, 38-28 (W)
1951—Redskins, 7-3 (C)
Redskins, 20-17 (W)
1952—Redskins, 23-7 (C)
Cardinals, 17-6 (W)
1953—Redskins, 24-13 (C)
Redskins, 28-17 (W)
1954—Cardinals, 38-16 (C)
Redskins, 37-20 (W)

ALL-TIME TEAM VS. TEAM RESULTS

1955—Cardinals, 24-10 (W)
Redskins, 31-0 (C)
1956—Cardinals, 31-3 (W)
Redskins, 17-14 (C)
1957—Redskins, 37-14 (C)
Cardinals, 44-14 (W)
1958—Cardinals, 37-10 (C)
Redskins, 45-31 (W)
1959—Cardinals, 49-21 (C)
Redskins, 23-14 (W)
1960—Cardinals, 44-7 (StL)
Cardinals, 26-14 (W)
1961—Cardinals, 24-0 (W)
Cardinals, 38-24 (StL)
1962—Redskins, 24-14 (W)
Tie, 17-17 (StL)
1963—Cardinals, 21-7 (W)
Cardinals, 24-20 (StL)
1964—Cardinals, 23-17 (W)
Cardinals, 38-24 (StL)
1965—Cardinals, 37-16 (W)
Redskins, 24-20 (StL)
1966—Cardinals, 23-7 (StL)
Redskins, 26-20 (W)
1967—Cardinals, 27-21 (W)
1968—Cardinals, 41-14 (StL)
1969—Redskins, 33-17 (W)
1970—Cardinals, 27-17 (StL)
Redskins, 28-27 (W)
1971—Redskins, 24-17 (StL)
Redskins, 20-0 (W)
1972—Redskins, 24-10 (W)
Redskins, 33-3 (StL)
1973—Cardinals, 34-27 (StL)
Redskins, 31-13 (W)
1974—Cardinals, 17-10 (W)
Cardinals, 23-20 (StL)
1975—Redskins, 27-17 (W)
Cardinals, 20-17 (StL) OT
1976—Redskins, 20-10 (W)
Redskins, 16-10 (StL)
1977—Redskins, 24-14 (W)
Redskins, 26-20 (StL)
1978—Redskins, 28-10 (StL)
Cardinals, 27-17 (W)
1979—Redskins, 17-7 (StL)
Redskins, 30-28 (W)
1980—Redskins, 23-0 (W)
Redskins, 31-7 (StL)
1981—Cardinals, 40-30 (StL)
Redskins, 42-21 (W)
1982—Redskins, 12-7 (StL)
Redskins, 28-0 (W)
1983—Redskins, 38-14 (StL)
Redskins, 45-7 (W)
1984—Cardinals, 26-24 (StL)
Redskins, 29-27 (W)
1985—Redskins, 27-10 (W)
Redskins, 27-16 (StL)
1986—Redskins, 28-21 (W)
Redskins, 20-17 (StL)
1987—Redskins, 28-21 (W)
Redskins, 34-17 (StL)
1988—Cardinals, 30-21 (P)
Redskins, 33-17 (W)
1989—Redskins, 30-28 (W)
Redskins, 29-10 (P)
1990—Redskins, 31-0 (W)
Redskins, 38-10 (P)
1991—Redskins, 34-0 (W)
Redskins, 20-14 (P)
1992—Cardinals, 27-24 (P)
Redskins, 41-3 (W)
1993—Cardinals, 17-10 (W)
Cardinals, 36-6 (P)
1994—Cardinals, 19-16 (W) OT
Cardinals, 17-15 (A)
1995—Redskins, 27-7 (W)
Cardinals, 24-20 (A)
1996—Cardinals, 37-34 (W) OT
Cardinals, 27-26 (A)
1997—Redskins, 19-13 (W) OT
Redskins, 38-28 (A)
(RS Pts.—Redskins 2,356, Cardinals 1,998)
**Franchise known as Phoenix prior to 1994, in St. Louis prior to 1988, and in Chicago prior to 1960*
***Franchise in Boston prior to 1937 and known as Braves prior to 1933*

ATLANTA vs. ARIZONA
RS: Cardinals lead series, 13-6;
See Arizona vs. Atlanta

ATLANTA vs. BUFFALO
RS: Bills lead series, 4-3
1973—Bills, 17-6 (A)
1977—Bills, 3-0 (B)
1980—Falcons, 30-14 (B)
1983—Falcons, 31-14 (A)
1989—Falcons, 30-28 (A)
1992—Bills, 41-14 (B)
1995—Bills, 23-17 (B)
(RS Pts.—Bills 140, Falcons 128)

ATLANTA vs. CAROLINA
RS: Panthers lead series, 4-2
1995—Falcons, 23-20 (A) OT
Panthers, 21-17 (C)
1996—Panthers, 29-6 (C)
Falcons, 20-17 (A)
1997—Panthers, 9-6 (A)
Panthers, 21-12 (C)
(RS Pts.—Panthers 117, Falcons 84)

ATLANTA vs. CHICAGO
RS: Series tied, 9-9
1966—Bears, 23-6 (C)
1967—Bears, 23-14 (A)
1968—Falcons, 16-13 (C)
1969—Falcons, 48-31 (A)
1970—Bears, 23-14 (A)
1972—Falcons, 37-21 (C)
1973—Falcons, 46-6 (A)
1974—Falcons, 13-10 (A)
1976—Falcons, 10-0 (C)
1977—Falcons, 16-10 (C)
1978—Bears, 13-7 (C)
1980—Falcons, 28-17 (A)
1983—Falcons, 20-17 (C)
1985—Bears, 36-0 (C)
1986—Bears, 13-10 (A)
1990—Bears, 30-24 (C)
1992—Bears, 41-31 (C)
1993—Bears, 6-0 (C)
(RS Pts.—Falcons 340, Bears 333)

ATLANTA vs. CINCINNATI
RS: Bengals lead series, 7-2
1971—Falcons, 9-6 (C)
1975—Bengals, 21-14 (A)
1978—Bengals, 37-7 (C)
1981—Bengals, 30-28 (A)
1984—Bengals, 35-14 (C)
1987—Bengals, 16-10 (A)
1990—Falcons, 38-17 (A)
1993—Bengals, 21-17 (C)
1996—Bengals, 41-31 (C)
(RS Pts.—Bengals 224, Falcons 168)

ATLANTA vs. CLEVELAND
RS: Browns lead series, 8-2
1966—Browns, 49-17 (A)
1968—Browns, 30-7 (C)
1971—Falcons, 31-14 (C)
1976—Browns, 20-17 (A)
1978—Browns, 24-16 (A)
1981—Browns, 28-17 (C)
1984—Browns, 23-7 (A)
1987—Browns, 38-3 (C)
1990—Browns, 13-10 (C)
1993—Falcons, 17-14 (A)
(RS Pts.—Browns 253, Falcons 142)

ATLANTA vs. DALLAS
RS: Cowboys lead series, 11-6
PS: Cowboys lead series, 2-0
1966—Cowboys, 47-14 (A)
1967—Cowboys, 37-7 (D)
1969—Cowboys, 24-17 (A)
1970—Cowboys, 13-0 (D)
1974—Cowboys, 24-0 (A)
1976—Falcons, 17-10 (A)
1978—*Cowboys, 27-20 (D)
1980—*Cowboys, 30-27 (A)
1985—Cowboys, 24-10 (D)
1986—Falcons, 37-35 (D)
1987—Falcons, 21-10 (D)
1988—Cowboys, 26-20 (D)
1989—Falcons 27-21 (A)
1990—Falcons, 26-7 (A)
1991—Cowboys, 31-27 (D)
1992—Cowboys, 41-17 (A)
1993—Falcons, 27-14 (A)
1995—Cowboys, 28-13 (A)
1996—Cowboys, 32-28 (D)
(RS Pts.—Cowboys 424, Falcons 308)
(PS Pts.—Cowboys 57, Falcons 47)
**NFC Divisional Playoff*

ATLANTA vs. DENVER
RS: Broncos lead series, 6-3
1970—Broncos, 24-10 (D)
1972—Falcons, 23-20 (A)
1975—Falcons, 35-21 (A)
1979—Broncos, 20-17 (A) OT
1982—Falcons, 34-27 (D)
1985—Broncos, 44-28 (A)
1988—Broncos, 30-14 (D)
1994—Broncos, 32-28 (D)
1997—Broncos, 29-21 (A)
(RS Pts.—Broncos 247, Falcons 210)

ATLANTA vs. DETROIT
RS: Lions lead series, 20-6
1966—Lions, 28-10 (D)
1967—Lions, 24-3 (D)
1968—Lions, 24-7 (A)
1969—Lions, 27-21 (D)
1971—Lions, 41-38 (D)
1972—Lions, 26-23 (A)
1973—Lions, 31-6 (D)
1975—Lions, 17-14 (A)
1976—Lions, 24-10 (D)
1977—Falcons, 17-6 (A)
1978—Falcons, 14-0 (A)
1979—Lions, 24-23 (D)
1980—Falcons, 43-28 (A)
1983—Falcons, 30-14 (D)
1984—Lions, 27-24 (A) OT
1985—Lions, 28-27 (A)
1986—Falcons, 20-6 (D)
1987—Lions, 30-13 (A)
1988—Lions, 31-17 (D)
1989—Lions, 31-24 (A)
1990—Lions, 21-14 (D)
1993—Lions, 30-13 (D)
1994—Lions, 31-28 (D) OT
1995—Falcons, 34-22 (A)
1996—Lions, 28-24 (D)
1997—Lions, 28-17 (D)
(RS Pts.—Lions 627, Falcons 514)

ATLANTA vs. GREEN BAY
RS: Packers lead series, 10-9
PS: Packers lead series, 1-0
1966—Packers, 56-3 (Mil)
1967—Packers, 23-0 (Mil)
1968—Packers, 38-7 (A)
1969—Packers, 28-10 (GB)
1970—Packers, 27-24 (GB)
1971—Falcons, 28-21 (A)
1972—Falcons, 10-9 (Mil)
1974—Falcons, 10-3 (A)
1975—Packers, 22-13 (GB)
1976—Packers, 24-20 (A)
1979—Falcons, 25-7 (A)
1981—Falcons, 31-17 (GB)
1982—Packers, 38-7 (A)
1983—Falcons, 47-41 (A) OT
1988—Falcons, 20-0 (A)
1989—Packers, 23-21 (Mil)
1991—Falcons, 35-31 (A)
1992—Falcons, 24-10 (A)
1994—Packers, 21-17 (Mil)
1995—*Packers, 37-20 (GB)
(RS Pts.—Packers 439, Falcons 352)
(PS Pts.—Packers 37, Falcons 20)
**NFC First-Round Playoff*

ATLANTA vs. *INDIANAPOLIS
RS: Colts lead series, 10-0
1966—Colts, 19-7 (A)
1967—Colts, 38-31 (B)
Colts, 49-7 (A)
1968—Colts, 28-20 (A)
Colts, 44-0 (B)
1969—Colts, 21-14 (A)
Colts, 13-6 (B)
1974—Colts, 17-7 (A)
1986—Colts, 28-23 (A)
1989—Colts, 13-9 (I)
(RS Pts.—Colts 270, Falcons 124)
**Franchise in Baltimore prior to 1984*

ATLANTA vs. JACKSONVILLE
RS: Jaguars lead series, 1-0
1996—Jaguars, 19-17 (J)
(RS Pts.—Jaguars, 19, Falcons 17)

ATLANTA vs. KANSAS CITY
RS: Chiefs lead series, 4-0
1972—Chiefs, 17-14 (A)
1985—Chiefs, 38-10 (KC)
1991—Chiefs, 14-3 (KC)
1994—Chiefs, 30-10 (A)
(RS Pts.—Chiefs 99, Falcons 37)

ATLANTA vs. MIAMI
RS: Dolphins lead series, 6-1
1970—Dolphins, 20-7 (A)
1974—Dolphins, 42-7 (M)
1980—Dolphins, 20-17 (A)
1983—Dolphins, 31-24 (M)
1986—Falcons, 20-14 (M)
1992—Dolphins, 21-17 (M)
1995—Dolphins, 21-20 (M)
(RS Pts.—Dolphins 169, Falcons 112)

ATLANTA vs. MINNESOTA
RS: Vikings lead series, 12-6
PS: Vikings lead series, 1-0
1966—Falcons, 20-13 (M)
1967—Falcons, 21-20 (A)
1968—Vikings, 47-7 (M)
1969—Falcons, 10-3 (A)
1970—Vikings, 37-7 (A)
1971—Vikings, 24-7 (M)
1973—Falcons, 20-14 (A)
1974—Vikings, 23-10 (M)
1975—Vikings, 38-0 (M)
1977—Vikings, 14-7 (A)
1980—Vikings, 24-23 (M)
1981—Falcons, 31-30 (A)
1982—*Vikings, 30-24 (M)
1984—Vikings, 27-20 (M)
1985—Falcons, 14-13 (A)
1987—Vikings, 24-13 (M)
1989—Vikings, 43-17 (M)
1991—Vikings, 20-19 (A)
1996—Vikings, 23-17 (A)
(RS Pts.—Vikings 437, Falcons 263)
(PS Pts.—Vikings 30, Falcons 24)
**NFC First-Round Playoff*

ATLANTA vs. NEW ENGLAND
RS: Falcons lead series, 5-3
1972—Patriots, 21-20 (NE)
1977—Patriots, 16-10 (A)
1980—Falcons, 37-21 (NE)
1983—Falcons, 24-13 (A)
1986—Patriots, 25-17 (NE)
1989—Falcons, 16-15 (A)
1992—Falcons, 34-0 (A)
1995—Falcons, 30-17 (A)
(RS Pts.—Falcons 188, Patriots 128)

ATLANTA vs. NEW ORLEANS
RS: Falcons lead series, 33-24
PS: Falcons lead series, 1-0
1967—Saints, 27-24 (NO)
1969—Falcons, 45-17 (A)
1970—Falcons, 14-3 (NO)
Falcons, 32-14 (A)
1971—Falcons, 28-6 (A)
Falcons, 24-20 (NO)
1972—Falcons, 21-14 (NO)
Falcons, 36-20 (A)

1973—Falcons, 62-7 (NO)
Falcons, 14-10 (A)
1974—Saints, 14-13 (NO)
Saints, 13-3 (A)
1975—Falcons, 14-7 (A)
Saints, 23-7 (NO)
1976—Saints, 30-0 (NO)
Falcons, 23-20 (A)
1977—Saints, 21-20 (NO)
Falcons, 35-7 (A)
1978—Falcons, 20-17 (NO)
Falcons, 20-17 (A)
1979—Falcons, 40-34 (NO) OT
Saints, 37-6 (A)
1980—Falcons, 41-14 (NO)
Falcons, 31-13 (A)
1981—Falcons, 27-0 (A)
Falcons, 41-10 (NO)
1982—Falcons, 35-0 (A)
Saints, 35-6 (NO)
1983—Saints, 19-17 (A)
Saints, 27-10 (NO)
1984—Falcons, 36-28 (NO)
Saints, 17-13 (A)
1985—Falcons, 31-24 (A)
Falcons, 16-10 (NO)
1986—Falcons, 31-10 (NO)
Saints, 14-9 (A)
1987—Saints, 38-0 (A)
1988—Saints, 29-21 (A)
Saints, 10-9 (NO)
1989—Saints, 20-13 (NO)
Saints, 26-17 (A)
1990—Falcons, 28-27 (A)
Saints, 10-7 (NO)
1991—Saints, 27-6 (A)
Falcons, 23-20 (NO) OT
*Falcons, 27-20 (NO)
1992—Saints, 10-7 (A)
Saints, 22-14 (NO)
1993—Saints, 34-31 (A)
Falcons, 26-15 (NO)
1994—Saints, 33-32 (NO)
Saints, 29-20 (A)
1995—Falcons, 27-24 (NO) OT
Falcons, 19-14 (A)
1996—Falcons, 17-15 (A)
Falcons, 31-15 (NO)
1997—Falcons, 23-17 (NO)
Falcons, 20-3 (A)
(RS Pts.—Falcons 1,236, Saints 1,037)
(PS Pts.—Falcons 27, Saints 20)
NFC First-Round Playoff

ATLANTA vs. N.Y. GIANTS
RS: Series tied, 6-6
1966—Falcons, 27-16 (NY)
1968—Falcons, 24-21 (A)
1971—Giants, 21-17 (A)
1974—Falcons, 14-7 (New Haven)
1977—Falcons, 17-3 (A)
1978—Falcons, 23-20 (A)
1979—Giants, 24-3 (NY)
1981—Giants, 27-24 (A) OT
1982—Falcons, 16-14 (NY)
1983—Giants, 16-13 (A) OT
1984—Giants, 19-7 (A)
1988—Giants, 23-16 (A)
(RS Pts.—Giants 211, Falcons 201)

ATLANTA vs. N.Y. JETS
RS: Falcons lead series, 4-3
1973—Falcons, 28-20 (NY)
1980—Jets, 14-7 (A)
1983—Falcons, 27-21 (NY)
1986—Jets, 28-14 (A)
1989—Jets, 27-7 (NY)
1992—Falcons, 20-17 (A)
1995—Falcons, 13-3 (A)
(RS Pts.—Jets 130, Falcons 116)

ATLANTA vs. *OAKLAND
RS: Raiders lead series, 6-3
1971—Falcons, 24-13 (A)
1975—Raiders, 37-34 (O) OT
1979—Raiders, 50-19 (O)
1982—Raiders, 38-14 (A)
1985—Raiders, 34-24 (A)
1988—Falcons, 12-6 (LA)
1991—Falcons, 21-17 (A)
1994—Raiders, 30-17 (LA)
1997—Raiders, 36-31 (A)
(RS Pts.—Raiders 261, Falcons 196)
Franchise in Los Angeles from 1982-1994

ATLANTA vs. PHILADELPHIA
RS: Eagles lead series, 9-8-1
PS: Falcons lead series, 1-0
1966—Eagles, 23-10 (P)
1967—Eagles, 38-7 (A)
1969—Falcons, 27-3 (P)
1970—Tie, 13-13 (P)
1973—Falcons, 44-27 (P)
1976—Eagles, 14-13 (A)
1978—*Falcons, 14-13 (A)
1979—Falcons, 14-10 (P)
1980—Falcons, 20-17 (P)
1981—Eagles, 16-13 (P)
1983—Eagles, 28-24 (A)
1984—Falcons, 26-10 (A)
1985—Eagles, 23-17 (P) OT
1986—Eagles, 16-0 (A)
1988—Falcons, 27-24 (P)
1990—Eagles, 24-23 (A)
1994—Falcons, 28-21 (A)
1996—Eagles, 33-18 (A)
1997—Falcons, 20-17 (A)
(RS Pts.—Eagles 357, Falcons 344)
(PS Pts.—Falcons 14, Eagles 13)
NFC First-Round Playoff

ATLANTA vs. PITTSBURGH
RS: Steelers lead series, 10-1
1966—Steelers, 57-33 (A)
1968—Steelers, 41-21 (A)
1970—Falcons, 27-16 (A)
1974—Steelers, 24-17 (P)
1978—Steelers, 31-7 (P)
1981—Steelers, 34-20 (A)
1984—Steelers, 35-10 (P)
1987—Steelers, 28-12 (A)
1990—Steelers, 21-9 (P)
1993—Steelers, 45-17 (A)
1996—Steelers, 20-17 (A)
(RS Pts.—Steelers 352, Falcons 190)

ATLANTA vs. *ST. LOUIS
RS: Rams lead series, 39-21-2
1966—Rams, 19-14 (A)
1967—Rams, 31-3 (A)
Rams, 20-3 (LA)
1968—Rams, 27-14 (LA)
Rams, 17-10 (A)
1969—Rams, 17-7 (LA)
Rams, 38-6 (A)
1970—Tie, 10-10 (LA)
Rams, 17-7 (A)
1971—Tie, 20-20 (LA)
Rams, 24-16 (A)
1972—Falcons, 31-3 (A)
Rams, 20-7 (LA)
1973—Rams, 31-0 (LA)
Falcons, 15-13 (A)
1974—Rams, 21-0 (LA)
Rams, 30-7 (A)
1975—Rams, 22-7 (LA)
Rams, 16-7 (A)
1976—Rams, 30-14 (A)
Rams, 59-0 (LA)
1977—Falcons, 17-6 (A)
Rams, 23-7 (LA)
1978—Rams, 10-0 (LA)
Falcons, 15-7 (A)
1979—Rams, 20-14 (LA)
Rams, 34-13 (A)
1980—Falcons, 13-10 (A)
Rams, 20-17 (LA) OT
1981—Rams, 37-35 (A)
Rams, 21-16 (LA)
1982—Falcons, 34-17 (A)
1983—Rams, 27-21 (LA)
Rams, 36-13 (A)
1984—Falcons, 30-28 (LA)
Rams, 24-10 (A)
1985—Rams, 17-6 (LA)
Falcons, 30-14 (A)
1986—Falcons, 26-14 (A)
Rams, 14-7 (LA)
1987—Falcons, 24-20 (A)
Rams, 33-0 (LA)
1988—Rams, 33-0 (A)
Rams, 22-7 (LA)
1989—Rams, 31-21 (A)
Rams, 26-14 (LA)
1990—Rams, 44-24 (LA)
Falcons, 20-13 (A)
1991—Falcons, 31-14 (A)
Falcons, 31-14 (LA)
1992—Falcons, 30-28 (A)
Rams, 38-27 (LA)
1993—Falcons, 30-24 (A)
Falcons, 13-0 (LA)
1994—Falcons, 31-13 (A)
Falcons, 8-5 (LA)
1995—Rams, 21-19 (StL)
Falcons, 31-6 (A)
1996—Rams, 59-16 (StL)
Rams, 34-27 (A)
1997—Falcons, 34-31 (A)
Falcons, 27-21 (StL)
(RS Pts.—Rams 1,394, Falcons 987)
Franchise in Los Angeles prior to 1995

ATLANTA vs. SAN DIEGO
RS: Falcons lead series, 5-1
1973—Falcons, 41-0 (SD)
1979—Falcons, 28-26 (SD)
1988—Chargers, 10-7 (A)
1991—Falcons, 13-10 (SD)
1994—Falcons, 10-9 (A)
1997—Falcons, 14-3 (SD)
(RS Pts.—Falcons 113, Chargers 58)

ATLANTA vs. SAN FRANCISCO
RS: 49ers lead series, 39-22-1
1966—49ers, 44-7 (A)
1967—49ers, 38-7 (SF)
49ers, 34-28 (A)
1968—49ers, 28-13 (SF)
49ers, 14-12 (A)
1969—Falcons, 24-12 (A)
Falcons, 21-7 (SF)
1970—Falcons, 21-20 (A)
49ers, 24-20 (SF)
1971—Falcons, 20-17 (A)
49ers, 24-3 (SF)
1972—49ers, 49-14 (A)
49ers, 20-0 (SF)
1973—49ers, 13-9 (A)
Falcons, 17-3 (SF)
1974—49ers, 16-10 (A)
49ers, 27-0 (SF)
1975—Falcons, 17-3 (SF)
Falcons, 31-9 (A)
1976—49ers, 15-0 (SF)
Falcons, 21-16 (A)
1977—Falcons, 7-0 (SF)
49ers, 10-3 (A)
1978—Falcons, 20-17 (SF)
Falcons, 21-10 (A)
1979—49ers, 20-15 (SF)
Falcons, 31-21 (A)
1980—Falcons, 20-17 (SF)
Falcons, 35-10 (A)
1981—Falcons, 34-17 (A)
49ers, 17-14 (SF)
1982—Falcons, 17-7 (SF)
1983—49ers, 24-20 (SF)
Falcons, 28-24 (A)
1984—49ers, 14-5 (SF)
49ers, 35-17 (A)
1985—49ers, 35-16 (SF)
49ers, 38-17 (A)
1986—Tie, 10-10 (A) OT
49ers, 20-0 (SF)
1987—49ers, 25-17 (A)
49ers, 35-7 (SF)
1988—Falcons, 34-17 (SF)
49ers, 13-3 (A)
1989—49ers, 45-3 (SF)
49ers, 23-10 (A)
1990—49ers, 19-13 (SF)
49ers, 45-35 (A)
1991—Falcons, 39-34 (SF)
Falcons, 17-14 (A)
1992—49ers, 56-17 (SF)
49ers, 41-3 (A)
1993—49ers, 37-30 (SF)
Falcons, 27-24 (A)
1994—49ers, 42-3 (A)
49ers, 50-14 (SF)
1995—49ers, 41-10 (SF)
Falcons, 28-27 (A)
1996—49ers, 39-17 (SF)
49ers, 34-10 (A)
1997—49ers, 34-7 (SF)
49ers, 35-28 (A)
(RS Pts.—49ers 1,509, Falcons 997)

ATLANTA vs. SEATTLE
RS: Seahawks lead series, 4-2
1976—Seahawks, 30-13 (S)
1979—Seahawks, 31-28 (A)
1985—Seahawks, 30-26 (S)
1988—Seahawks, 31-20 (A)
1991—Falcons, 26-13 (A)
1997—Falcons, 24-17 (S)
(RS Pts.—Seahawks 152, Falcons 137)

ATLANTA vs. TAMPA BAY
RS: Falcons lead series, 8-7
1977—Falcons, 17-0 (TB)
1978—Buccaneers, 14-9 (TB)
1979—Falcons, 17-14 (A)
1981—Buccaneers, 24-23 (TB)
1984—Buccaneers, 23-6 (TB)
1986—Falcons, 23-20 (TB) OT
1987—Buccaneers, 48-10 (TB)
1988—Falcons, 17-10 (A)
1990—Buccaneers, 23-17 (TB)
1991—Falcons, 43-7 (A)
1992—Falcons, 35-7 (TB)
1993—Buccaneers, 31-24 (A)
1994—Falcons, 34-13 (A)
1995—Falcons, 24-21 (TB)
1997—Buccaneers, 31-10 (A)
(RS Pts.—Falcons 309, Buccaneers 286)

ATLANTA vs. *TENNESSEE
RS: Falcons lead series, 5-4
1972—Falcons, 20-10 (A)
1976—Oilers, 20-14 (H)
1978—Falcons, 20-14 (A)
1981—Falcons, 31-27 (H)
1984—Falcons, 42-10 (A)
1987—Oilers, 37-33 (H)
1990—Falcons, 47-27 (A)
1993—Oilers, 33-17 (H)
1996—Oilers, 23-13 (A)
(RS Pts.—Falcons 237, Oilers 201)
Franchise in Houston prior to 1997

ATLANTA vs. WASHINGTON
RS: Redskins lead series, 13-4-1
PS: Redskins lead series, 1-0
1966—Redskins, 33-20 (W)
1967—Tie, 20-20 (A)
1969—Redskins, 27-20 (W)
1972—Redskins, 24-13 (W)
1975—Redskins, 30-27 (A)
1977—Redskins, 10-6 (W)
1978—Falcons, 20-17 (A)
1979—Redskins, 16-7 (A)
1980—Falcons, 10-6 (A)
1983—Redskins, 37-21 (W)
1984—Redskins, 27-14 (W)
1985—Redskins, 44-10 (A)
1987—Falcons, 21-20 (A)
1989—Redskins, 31-30 (A)
1991—Redskins, 56-17 (W)
*Redskins, 24-7 (W)
1992—Redskins, 24-17 (W)
1993—Redskins, 30-17 (W)

ALL-TIME TEAM VS. TEAM RESULTS

1994—Falcons, 27-20 (W)
(RS Pts.—Redskins 472, Falcons 317)
(PS Pts.—Redskins 24, Falcons 7)
NFC Divisional Playoff

BALTIMORE vs. ARIZONA
RS: Cardinals lead series, 1-0;
See Arizona vs. Baltimore
BALTIMORE vs. CAROLINA
RS: Panthers lead series, 1-0
1996—Panthers, 27-16 (C)
(RS Pts.—Panthers 27, Ravens 16)
BALTIMORE vs. CINCINNATI
RS: Bengals lead series, 3-1
1996—Bengals, 24-21 (B)
Bengals, 21-14 (C)
1997—Ravens, 23-10 (B)
Bengals, 16-14 (C)
(RS Pts.—Ravens 72, Bengals 71)
BALTIMORE vs. DENVER
RS: Broncos lead series, 1-0
1996—Broncos, 45-34 (D)
(RS Pts.—Broncos 45, Ravens 34)
BALTIMORE vs. INDIANAPOLIS
RS: Colts lead series, 1-0
1996—Colts, 26-21 (I)
(RS Pts.—Colts 26, Ravens 21)
BALTIMORE vs. JACKSONVILLE
RS: Jaguars lead series, 4-0
1996—Jaguars, 30-27 (J)
Jaguars, 28-25 (B) OT
1997—Jaguars, 28-27 (B)
Jaguars, 29-27 (J)
(RS Pts.—Jaguars 115, Ravens 106)
BALTIMORE vs. MIAMI
RS: Dolphins lead series, 1-0
1997—Dolphins, 24-13 (B)
(RS Pts.—Dolphins 24, Ravens 13)
BALTIMORE vs. NEW ENGLAND
RS: Patriots lead series, 1-0
1996—Patriots, 46-38 (B)
(RS Pts.—Patriots 46, Ravens 38)
BALTIMORE vs. NEW ORLEANS
RS: Ravens lead series, 1-0
1996—Ravens, 17-10 (B)
(RS Pts.—Ravens 17, Saints 10)
BALTIMORE vs. N.Y. GIANTS
RS: Ravens lead series, 1-0
1997—Ravens, 24-23 (NY)
(RS Pts.—Ravens 24, Giants 23)
BALTIMORE vs. N.Y. JETS
RS: Jets lead series, 1-0
1997—Jets, 19-16 (NY) OT
(RS Pts.—Jets 19, Ravens 16)
BALTIMORE vs. OAKLAND
RS: Ravens lead series, 1-0
1996—Ravens, 19-14 (B)
(RS Pts.—Ravens 19, Raiders 14)
BALTIMORE vs. PHILADELPHIA
RS: Series tied, 0-0-1
1997—Tie, 10-10 (B) OT
(RS Pts.—Ravens 10, Eagles 10)
BALTIMORE vs. PITTSBURGH
RS: Steelers lead series, 3-1
1996—Steelers, 31-17 (P)
Ravens, 31-17 (B)
1997—Steelers, 42-34 (B)
Steelers, 37-0 (P)
(RS Pts.—Steelers 127, Ravens 82)
BALTIMORE vs. ST. LOUIS
RS: Ravens lead series, 1-0
1996—Ravens, 37-31 (B) OT
(RS Pts.—Ravens 37, Rams 31)
BALTIMORE vs. SAN DIEGO
RS: Chargers lead series, 1-0
1997—Chargers, 21-17 (SD)
(RS Pts.—Chargers 21, Ravens 17)
BALTIMORE vs. SAN FRANCISCO
RS: 49ers lead series, 1-0
1996—49ers, 38-20 (SF)
(RS Pts.—49ers 38, Ravens 20)
BALTIMORE vs. SEATTLE
RS: Ravens lead series, 1-0
1997—Ravens, 31-24 (B)
(RS Pts.—Ravens 31, Seahawks 24)
BALTIMORE vs. *TENNESSEE
RS: Series tied, 2-2
1996—Oilers, 29-13 (H)
Oilers, 24-21 (B)
1997—Ravens, 36-10 (T)
Ravens, 21-19 (B)
(RS Pts.—Ravens 91, Oilers 82)
Franchise in Houston prior to 1997
BALTIMORE vs. WASHINGTON
RS: Ravens lead series, 1-0
1997—Ravens, 20-17 (W)
(RS Pts.—Ravens 20, Redskins 17)

BUFFALO vs. ARIZONA
RS: Series tied, 3-3;
See Arizona vs. Buffalo
BUFFALO vs. ATLANTA
RS: Bills lead series, 4-3;
See Atlanta vs. Buffalo
BUFFALO vs. CAROLINA
RS: Bills lead series, 1-0
1995—Bills, 31-9 (B)
(RS Pts.—Bills 31, Panthers 9)
BUFFALO vs. CHICAGO
RS: Bears lead series, 5-2
1970—Bears, 31-13 (C)
1974—Bills, 16-6 (B)
1979—Bears, 7-0 (B)
1988—Bears, 24-3 (C)
1991—Bills, 35-20 (B)
1994—Bears, 20-13 (C)
1997—Bears, 20-3 (C)
(RS Pts.—Bears 128, Bills 83)
BUFFALO vs. CINCINNATI
RS: Bengals lead series, 9-8
PS: Bengals lead series, 2-0
1968—Bengals, 34-23 (C)
1969—Bills, 16-13 (B)
1970—Bengals, 43-14 (B)
1973—Bengals, 16-13 (B)
1975—Bengals, 33-24 (C)
1978—Bills, 5-0 (B)
1979—Bills, 51-24 (B)
1980—Bills, 14-0 (C)
1981—Bengals, 27-24 (C) OT
*Bengals, 28-21 (C)
1983—Bills, 10-6 (C)
1984—Bengals, 52-21 (C)
1985—Bengals, 23-17 (B)
1986—Bengals, 36-33 (C) OT
1988—Bengals, 35-21 (C)
**Bengals, 21-10 (C)
1989—Bills, 24-7 (B)
1991—Bills, 35-16 (B)
1996—Bills, 31-17 (B)
(RS Pts.—Bengals 382, Bills 376)
(PS Pts.—Bengals 49, Bills 31)
AFC Divisional Playoff
***AFC Championship*
BUFFALO vs. CLEVELAND
RS: Browns lead series, 7-4
PS: Browns lead series, 1-0
1972—Browns, 27-10 (C)
1974—Bills, 15-10 (C)
1977—Browns, 27-16 (B)
1978—Browns, 41-20 (C)
1981—Bills, 22-13 (B)
1984—Browns, 13-10 (B)
1985—Browns, 17-7 (C)
1986—Browns, 21-17 (B)
1987—Browns, 27-21 (C)
1989—*Browns, 34-30 (C)
1990—Bills, 42-0 (C)
1995—Bills, 22-19 (C)
(RS Pts.—Browns 215, Bills 202)
(PS Pts.—Browns 34, Bills 30)
AFC Divisional Playoff
BUFFALO vs. DALLAS
RS: Series tied, 3-3
PS: Cowboys lead series, 2-0
1971—Cowboys, 49-37 (B)
1976—Cowboys, 17-10 (D)
1981—Cowboys, 27-14 (D)
1984—Bills, 14-3 (B)
1992—*Cowboys, 52-17 (Pasadena)
1993—Bills, 13-10 (D)
**Cowboys, 30-13 (Atlanta)
1996—Bills, 10-7 (B)
(RS Pts.—Cowboys 113, Bills 98)
(PS Pts.—Cowboys 82, Bills 30)
Super Bowl XXVII
***Super Bowl XXVIII*
BUFFALO vs. DENVER
RS: Bills lead series, 17-12-1
PS: Bills lead series, 1-0
1960—Broncos, 27-21 (B)
Tie, 38-38 (D)
1961—Broncos, 22-10 (B)
Bills, 23-10 (D)
1962—Broncos, 23-20 (B)
Bills, 45-38 (D)
1963—Bills, 30-28 (D)
Bills, 27-17 (B)
1964—Bills, 30-13 (B)
Bills, 30-19 (D)
1965—Bills, 30-15 (D)
Bills, 31-13 (B)
1966—Bills, 38-21 (B)
1967—Bills, 17-16 (D)
Broncos, 21-20 (B)
1968—Broncos, 34-32 (D)
1969—Bills, 41-28 (B)
1970—Broncos, 25-10 (B)
1975—Bills, 38-14 (B)
1977—Broncos, 26-6 (D)
1979—Broncos, 19-16 (B)
1981—Bills, 9-7 (B)
1984—Broncos, 37-7 (B)
1987—Bills, 21-14 (B)
1989—Broncos, 28-14 (B)
1990—Bills, 29-28 (B)
1991—*Bills, 10-7 (B)
1992—Bills, 27-17 (B)
1994—Bills, 27-20 (B)
1995—Broncos, 22-7 (D)
1997—Broncos, 23-20 (B) OT
(RS Pts.—Bills 714, Broncos 663)
(PS Pts.—Bills 10, Broncos 7)
*AFC Championship
BUFFALO vs. DETROIT
RS: Lions lead series, 3-2-1
1972—Tie, 21-21 (B)
1976—Lions, 27-14 (D)
1979—Bills, 20-17 (D)
1991—Lions, 17-14 (B) OT
1994—Lions, 35-21 (D)
1997—Bills, 22-13 (B)
(RS Pts.—Lions 130, Bills 112)
BUFFALO vs. GREEN BAY
RS: Bills lead series, 5-2
1974—Bills, 27-7 (GB)
1979—Bills, 19-12 (B)
1982—Packers, 33-21 (Mil)
1988—Bills, 28-0 (B)
1991—Bills, 34-24 (Mil)
1994—Bills 29-20 (B)
1997—Packers, 31-21 (GB)
(RS Pts.—Bills 179, Packers 127)
BUFFALO vs. *INDIANAPOLIS
RS: Bills lead series, 31-23-1
1970—Tie, 17-17 (Balt)
Colts, 20-14 (Buff)
1971—Colts, 43-0 (Buff)
Colts, 24-0 (Balt)
1972—Colts, 17-0 (Buff)
Colts, 35-7 (Balt)
1973—Bills, 31-13 (Buff)
Bills, 24-17 (Balt)
1974—Bills, 27-14 (Balt)
Bills, 6-0 (Buff)
1975—Bills, 38-31 (Balt)
Colts, 42-35 (Buff)
1976—Colts, 31-13 (Buff)
Colts, 58-20 (Balt)
1977—Colts, 17-14 (Balt)
Colts, 31-13 (Buff)
1978—Bills, 24-17 (Buff)
Bills, 21-14 (Balt)
1979—Bills, 31-13 (Balt)
Colts, 14-13 (Buff)
1980—Colts, 17-12 (Buff)
Colts, 28-24 (Balt)
1981—Bills, 35-3 (Balt)
Bills, 23-17 (Buff)
1982—Bills, 20-0 (Buff)
1983—Bills, 28-23 (Buff)
Bills, 30-7 (Balt)
1984—Colts, 31-17 (I)
Bills, 21-15 (Buff)
1985—Colts, 49-17 (I)
Bills, 21-9 (Buff)
1986—Bills, 24-13 (Buff)
Colts, 24-14 (I)
1987—Colts, 47-6 (Buff)
Bills, 27-3 (I)
1988—Bills, 34-23 (Buff)
Colts, 17-14 (I)
1989—Colts, 37-14 (I)
Bills, 30-7 (Buff)
1990—Bills, 26-10 (Buff)
Bills, 31-7 (I)
1991—Bills, 42-6 (Buff)
Bills, 35-7 (I)
1992—Bills, 38-0 (Buff)
Colts, 16-13 (I) OT
1993—Bills, 23-9 (Buff)
Bills, 30-10 (I)
1994—Colts, 27-17 (Buff)
Colts, 10-9 (I)
1995—Bills, 20-14 (Buff)
Bills, 16-10 (I)
1996—Bills, 16-13 (Buff) OT
Colts, 13-10 (I) OT
1997—Bills, 37-35 (B)
Bills, 9-6 (I)
(RS Pts.—Bills 1,131, Colts 1,031)
Franchise in Baltimore prior to 1984
BUFFALO vs. JACKSONVILLE
RS: Jaguars lead series, 1-0
PS: Jaguars lead series, 1-0
1996—*Jaguars 30-27 (B)
1997—Jaguars , 20-14 (B)
(RS Pts.—Jaguars 20, Bills 14)
(PS Pts.—Jaguars 30, Bills 27)
AFC First-Round Playoff
BUFFALO vs. *KANSAS CITY
RS: Bills lead series, 17-14-1
PS: Bills lead series, 2-1
1960—Texans, 45-28 (B)
Texans, 24-7 (D)
1961—Bills, 27-24 (B)
Bills, 30-20 (D)
1962—Texans, 41-21 (D)
Bills, 23-14 (B)
1963—Tie, 27-27 (B)
Bills, 35-26 (KC)
1964—Bills, 34-17 (B)
Bills, 35-22 (KC)
1965—Bills, 23-7 (KC)
Bills, 34-25 (B)
1966—Chiefs, 42-20 (B)
Bills, 29-14 (KC)
**Chiefs, 31-7 (B)
1967—Chiefs, 23-13 (KC)
1968—Chiefs, 18-7 (B)
1969—Chiefs, 29-7 (B)
Chiefs, 22-19 (KC)
1971—Chiefs, 22-9 (KC)
1973—Bills, 23-14 (B)
1976—Bills, 50-17 (B)
1978—Bills, 28-13 (B)
Chiefs, 14-10 (KC)
1982—Bills, 14-9 (B)
1983—Bills, 14-9 (KC)
1986—Chiefs, 20-17 (B)
Bills, 17-14 (KC)
1991—Chiefs, 33-6 (KC)

***Bills, 37-14 (B)
1993—Chiefs, 23-7 (KC)
****Bills, 30-13 (B)
1994—Bills, 44-10 (B)
1996—Bills, 20-9 (B)
1997—Chiefs, 22-16 (KC)
(RS Pts.—Bills 694, Chiefs 669)
(PS Pts.—Bills 74, Chiefs 58)
Franchise in Dallas prior to 1963 and known as Texans
***AFL Championship*
****AFC Divisional Playoff*
*****AFC Championship*

BUFFALO vs. MIAMI
RS: Dolphins lead series, 41-22-1
PS: Bills lead series, 3-0
1966—Bills, 58-24 (B)
Bills, 29-0 (M)
1967—Bills, 35-13 (B)
Dolphins, 17-14 (M)
1968—Tie, 14-14 (M)
Dolphins, 21-17 (B)
1969—Dolphins, 24-6 (M)
Bills, 28-3 (B)
1970—Dolphins, 33-14 (B)
Dolphins, 45-7 (M)
1971—Dolphins, 29-14 (B)
Dolphins, 34-0 (M)
1972—Dolphins, 24-23 (M)
Dolphins, 30-16 (B)
1973—Dolphins, 27-6 (M)
Dolphins, 17-0 (B)
1974—Dolphins, 24-16 (B)
Dolphins, 35-28 (M)
1975—Dolphins, 35-30 (B)
Dolphins, 31-21 (M)
1976—Dolphins, 30-21 (B)
Dolphins, 45-27 (M)
1977—Dolphins, 13-0 (B)
Dolphins, 31-14 (M)
1978—Dolphins, 31-24 (M)
Dolphins, 25-24 (B)
1979—Dolphins, 9-7 (B)
Dolphins, 17-7 (M)
1980—Bills, 17-7 (B)
Dolphins, 17-14 (M)
1981—Bills, 31-21 (B)
Dolphins, 16-6 (M)
1982—Dolphins, 9-7 (B)
Dolphins, 27-10 (M)
1983—Dolphins, 12-0 (B)
Bills, 38-35 (M) OT
1984—Dolphins, 21-17 (B)
Dolphins, 38-7 (M)
1985—Dolphins, 23-14 (B)
Dolphins, 28-0 (M)
1986—Dolphins, 27-14 (M)
Dolphins, 34-24 (B)
1987—Bills, 34-31 (M) OT
Bills, 27-0 (B)
1988—Bills, 9-6 (B)
Bills, 31-6 (M)
1989—Bills, 27-24 (M)
Bills, 31-17 (B)
1990—Dolphins, 30-7 (M)
Bills, 24-14 (B)
*Bills, 44-34 (B)
1991—Bills, 35-31 (B)
Bills, 41-27 (M)
1992—Dolphins, 37-10 (B)
Bills, 26-20 (M)
**Bills, 29-10 (M)
1993—Dolphins, 22-13 (B)
Bills, 47-34 (M)
1994—Bills, 21-11 (B)
Bills, 42-31 (M)
1995—Dolphins, 23-6 (M)
Bills, 23-20 (B)
***Bills, 37-22 (B)
1996—Dolphins, 21-7 (B)
Dolphins, 16-14 (M)
1997—Bills, 9-6 (B)
Dolphins, 30-13 (M)
(RS Pts.—Dolphins 1,453, Bills 1,196)
(PS Pts.—Bills 110, Dolphins 66)
**AFC Divisional Playoff*
***AFC Championship*
****AFC First-Round Playoff*

BUFFALO vs. MINNESOTA
RS: Vikings lead series, 6-2
1971—Vikings, 19-0 (M)
1975—Vikings, 35-13 (B)
1979—Vikings, 10-3 (M)
1982—Bills, 23-22 (B)
1985—Vikings, 27-20 (B)
1988—Bills, 13-10 (B)
1994—Vikings, 21-17 (B)
1997—Vikings, 34-13 (B)
(RS Pts.—Vikings 178, Bills 102)

BUFFALO vs. *NEW ENGLAND
RS: Patriots lead series, 39-35-1
PS: Patriots lead series, 1-0
1960—Bills, 13-0 (Bos)
Bills, 38-14 (Buff)
1961—Patriots, 23-21 (Buff)
Patriots, 52-21 (Bos)
1962—Tie, 28-28 (Buff)
Patriots, 21-10 (Bos)
1963—Bills, 28-21 (Buff)
Patriots, 17-7 (Bos)
**Patriots, 26-8 (Buff)
1964—Patriots, 36-28 (Buff)
Bills, 24-14 (Bos)
1965—Bills, 24-7 (Buff)
Bills, 23-7 (Bos)
1966—Patriots, 20-10 (Buff)
Patriots, 14-3 (Bos)
1967—Patriots, 23-0 (Buff)
Bills, 44-16 (Bos)
1968—Patriots, 16-7 (Buff)
Patriots, 23-6 (Bos)
1969—Bills, 23-16 (Buff)
Patriots, 35-21 (Bos)
1970—Bills, 45-10 (Bos)
Patriots, 14-10 (Buff)
1971—Patriots, 38-33 (NE)
Bills, 27-20 (Buff)
1972—Bills, 38-14 (Buff)
Bills, 27-24 (NE)
1973—Bills, 31-13 (NE)
Bills, 37-13 (Buff)
1974—Bills, 30-28 (Buff)
Bills, 29-28 (NE)
1975—Bills, 45-31 (Buff)
Bills, 34-14 (NE)
1976—Patriots, 26-22 (Buff)
Patriots, 20-10 (NE)
1977—Bills, 24-14 (NE)
Patriots, 20-7 (Buff)
1978—Patriots, 14-10 (Buff)
Patriots, 26-24 (NE)
1979—Patriots, 26-6 (Buff)
Bills, 16-13 (NE) OT
1980—Bills, 31-13 (Buff)
Patriots, 24-2 (NE)
1981—Bills, 20-17 (Buff)
Bills, 19-10 (NE)
1982—Patriots, 30-19 (NE)
1983—Patriots, 31-0 (Buff)
Patriots, 21-7 (NE)
1984—Patriots, 21-17 (Buff)
Patriots, 38-10 (NE)
1985—Patriots, 17-14 (Buff)
Patriots, 14-3 (NE)
1986—Patriots, 23-3 (Buff)
Patriots, 22-19 (NE)
1987—Patriots, 14-7 (NE)
Patriots, 13-7 (Buff)
1988—Bills, 16-14 (NE)
Bills, 23-20 (Buff)
1989—Bills, 31-10 (Buff)
Patriots, 33-24 (NE)
1990—Bills, 27-10 (NE)
Bills, 14-0 (Buff)
1991—Bills, 22-17 (Buff)
Patriots, 16-13 (NE)
1992—Bills, 41-7 (NE)
Bills, 16-7 (Buff)
1993—Bills, 38-14 (Buff)
Bills, 13-10 (NE) OT
1994—Bills, 38-35 (NE)
Patriots, 41-17 (Buff)
1995—Patriots, 27-14 (NE)
Patriots, 35-25 (Buff)
1996—Bills, 17-10 (Buff)
Patriots, 28-25 (NE)
1997—Patriots, 33-6 (NE)
Patriots, 31-10 (B)
(RS Pts.—Bills 1,515, Patriots 1,492)
(PS Pts.—Patriots 26, Bills 8)
**Franchise in Boston prior to 1971*
***Division Playoff*

BUFFALO vs. NEW ORLEANS
RS: Bills lead series, 3-2
1973—Saints, 13-0 (NO)
1980—Bills, 35-26 (NO)
1983—Bills, 27-21 (B)
1989—Saints, 22-19 (B)
1992—Bills, 20-16 (NO)
(RS Pts.—Bills 101, Saints 98)

BUFFALO vs. N.Y. GIANTS
RS: Bills lead series, 5-2
PS: Giants lead series, 1-0
1970—Giants, 20-6 (NY)
1975—Giants, 17-14 (B)
1978—Bills, 41-17 (B)
1987—Bills, 6-3 (B) OT
1990—Bills, 17-13 (NY)
*Giants, 20-19 (Tampa)
1993—Bills, 17-14 (B)
1996—Bills, 23-20 (NY) OT
(RS Pts.—Bills 124, Giants 104)
(PS Pts.—Giants 20, Bills 19)
**Super Bowl XXV*

BUFFALO vs. *N.Y. JETS
RS: Bills lead series, 43-31
PS: Bills lead series, 1-0
1960—Titans, 27-3 (NY)
Titans, 17-13 (B)
1961—Bills, 41-31 (B)
Titans, 21-14 (NY)
1962—Titans, 17-6 (B)
Bills, 20-3 (NY)
1963—Bills, 45-14 (B)
Bills, 19-10 (NY)
1964—Bills, 34-24 (B)
Bills, 20-7 (NY)
1965—Bills, 33-21 (B)
Jets, 14-12 (NY)
1966—Bills, 33-23 (NY)
Bills, 14-3 (B)
1967—Bills, 20-17 (B)
Jets, 20-10 (NY)
1968—Bills, 37-35 (B)
Jets, 25-21 (NY)
1969—Jets, 33-19 (B)
Jets, 16-6 (NY)
1970—Bills, 34-31 (B)
Bills, 10-6 (NY)
1971—Jets, 28-17 (NY)
Jets, 20-7 (B)
1972—Jets, 41-24 (B)
Jets, 41-3 (NY)
1973—Bills, 9-7 (B)
Bills, 34-14 (NY)
1974—Bills, 16-12 (B)
Jets, 20-10 (NY)
1975—Bills, 42-14 (B)
Bills, 24-23 (NY)
1976—Jets, 17-14 (NY)
Jets, 19-14 (B)
1977—Jets, 24-19 (B)
Bills, 14-10 (NY)
1978—Jets, 21-20 (B)
Jets, 45-14 (NY)
1979—Bills, 46-31 (B)
Bills, 14-12 (NY)
1980—Bills, 20-10 (B)
Bills, 31-24 (NY)
1981—Bills, 31-0 (B)
Jets, 33-14 (NY)
**Bills, 31-27 (NY)
1983—Jets, 34-10 (B)
Bills, 24-17 (NY)
1984—Jets, 28-26 (B)
Jets, 21-17 (NY)
1985—Jets, 42-3 (NY)
Jets, 27-7 (B)
1986—Jets, 28-24 (B)
Jets, 14-13 (NY)
1987—Jets, 31-28 (B)
Bills, 17-14 (NY)
1988—Bills, 37-14 (NY)
Bills, 9-6 (B) OT
1989—Bills, 34-3 (B)
Bills, 37-0 (NY)
1990—Bills, 30-7 (NY)
Bills, 30-27 (B)
1991—Bills, 23-20 (NY)
Bills, 24-13 (B)
1992—Bills, 24-20 (NY)
Jets, 24-17 (B)
1993—Bills, 19-10 (NY)
Bills, 16-14 (B)
1994—Jets, 23-3 (B)
Jets, 22-17 (NY)
1995—Bills, 29-10 (B)
Bills, 28-26 (NY)
1996—Bills, 25-22 (NY)
Bills, 35-10 (B)
1997—Bills, 28-22 (NY)
Bills, 20-10 (B)
(RS Pts.—Bills 1,555, Jets 1,440)
(PS Pts.—Bills 31, Jets 27)
**Jets known as Titans prior to 1963*
***AFC First-Round Playoff*

BUFFALO vs. *OAKLAND
RS: Raiders lead series, 15-14
PS: Bills lead series, 2-0
1960—Bills, 38-9 (B)
Raiders, 20-7 (O)
1961—Raiders, 31-22 (B)
Bills, 26-21 (O)
1962—Bills, 14-6 (B)
Bills, 10-6 (O)
1963—Raiders, 35-17 (O)
Bills, 12-0 (B)
1964—Bills, 23-20 (B)
Raiders, 16-13 (O)
1965—Bills, 17-12 (B)
Bills, 17-14 (O)
1966—Bills, 31-10 (O)
1967—Raiders, 24-20 (B)
Raiders, 28-21 (O)
1968—Raiders, 48-6 (B)
Raiders, 13-10 (O)
1969—Raiders, 50-21 (O)
1972—Raiders, 28-16 (O)
1974—Bills, 21-20 (B)
1977—Raiders, 34-13 (O)
1980—Bills, 24-7 (B)
1983—Raiders, 27-24 (B)
1987—Raiders, 34-21 (LA)
1988—Bills, 37-21 (B)
1990—Bills, 38-24 (B)
**Bills, 51-3 (B)
1991—Bills, 30-27 (LA) OT
1992—Raiders, 20-3 (LA)
1993—Raiders, 25-24 (B)
***Bills, 29-23 (B)
(RS Pts.—Raiders 630, Bills 576)
(PS Pts.—Bills 80, Raiders 26)
**Franchise in Los Angeles from 1982-1994*
***AFC Championship*
****AFC Divisional Playoff*

BUFFALO vs. PHILADELPHIA
RS: Series tied, 4-4
1973—Bills, 27-26 (B)
1981—Eagles, 20-14 (B)
1984—Eagles, 27-17 (B)
1985—Eagles, 21-17 (P)

1987—Eagles, 17-7 (P)
1990—Bills, 30-23 (B)
1993—Bills, 10-7 (P)
1996—Bills, 24-17 (P)
(RS Pts.—Eagles 158, Bills 146)

BUFFALO vs. PITTSBURGH
RS: Steelers lead series, 8-7
PS: Steelers lead series, 2-1
1970—Steelers, 23-10 (P)
1972—Steelers, 38-21 (B)
1974—*Steelers, 32-14 (P)
1975—Bills, 30-21 (P)
1978—Steelers, 28-17 (B)
1979—Steelers, 28-0 (P)
1980—Bills, 28-13 (B)
1982—Bills, 13-0 (B)
1985—Steelers, 30-24 (P)
1986—Bills, 16-12 (B)
1988—Bills, 36-28 (B)
1991—Bills, 52-34 (B)
1992—Bills, 28-20 (B)
*Bills, 24-3 (P)
1993—Steelers, 23-0 (P)
1994—Steelers, 23-10 (P)
1995—*Steelers, 40-21 (P)
1996—Steelers, 24-6 (P)
(RS Pts.—Steelers 345, Bills 291)
(PS Pts.—Steelers 75, Bills 59)
AFC Divisional Playoff

BUFFALO vs. *ST. LOUIS
RS: Bills lead series, 4-3
1970—Rams, 19-0 (B)
1974—Rams, 19-14 (LA)
1980—Bills, 10-7 (B) OT
1983—Rams, 41-17 (LA)
1989—Bills, 23-20 (B)
1992—Bills, 40-7 (B)
1995—Bills, 45-27 (StL)
(RS Pts.—Bills 149, Rams 140)
Franchise in Los Angeles prior to 1995

BUFFALO vs. *SAN DIEGO
RS: Chargers lead series, 16-7-2
PS: Bills lead series, 2-1
1960—Chargers, 24-10 (B)
Bills, 32-3 (LA)
1961—Chargers, 19-11 (B)
Chargers, 28-10 (SD)
1962—Bills, 35-10 (B)
Bills, 40-20 (SD)
1963—Chargers, 14-10 (SD)
Chargers, 23-13 (B)
1964—Bills, 30-3 (B)
Bills, 27-24 (SD)
**Bills, 20-7 (B)
1965—Chargers, 34-3 (B)
Tie, 20-20 (SD)
**Bills, 23-0 (SD)
1966—Chargers, 27-7 (SD)
Tie, 17-17 (B)
1967—Chargers, 37-17 (B)
1968—Chargers, 21-6 (B)
1969—Chargers, 45-6 (SD)
1971—Chargers, 20-3 (SD)
1973—Chargers, 34-7 (SD)
1976—Chargers, 34-13 (B)
1979—Chargers, 27-19 (SD)
1980—Bills, 26-24 (SD)
***Chargers, 20-14 (SD)
1981—Bills, 28-27 (SD)
1985—Chargers, 14-9 (B)
Chargers, 40-7 (SD)
(RS Pts.—Chargers 589, Bills 406)
(PS Pts.—Bills 57, Chargers 27)
Franchise in Los Angeles prior to 1961
**AFL Championship*
***AFC Divisional Playoff*

BUFFALO vs. SAN FRANCISCO
RS: Series tied, 3-3
1972—Bills, 27-20 (B)
1980—Bills, 18-13 (SF)
1983—49ers, 23-10 (B)
1989—49ers, 21-10 (SF)
1992—Bills, 34-31 (SF)
1995—49ers, 27-17 (SF)
(RS Pts.—49ers 135, Bills 116)

BUFFALO vs. SEATTLE
RS: Seahawks lead series, 4-2
1977—Seahawks, 56-17 (S)
1984—Seahawks, 31-28 (S)
1988—Bills, 13-3 (S)
1989—Seahawks, 17-16 (S)
1995—Bills, 27-21 (B)
1996—Seahawks, 26-18 (S)
(RS Pts.—Seahawks 154, Bills 119)

BUFFALO vs. TAMPA BAY
RS: Buccaneers lead series, 4-2
1976—Bills, 14-9 (TB)
1978—Buccaneers, 31-10 (TB)
1982—Buccaneers, 24-23 (TB)
1986—Buccaneers, 34-28 (TB)
1988—Buccaneers, 10-5 (TB)
1991—Bills, 17-10 (TB)
(RS Pts.—Buccaneers 118, Bills 97)

BUFFALO vs. *TENNESSEE
RS: Oilers lead series, 22-13
PS: Bills lead series, 2-0
1960—Bills, 25-24 (B)
Oilers, 31-23 (H)
1961—Bills, 22-12 (H)
Oilers, 28-16 (B)
1962—Oilers, 28-23 (B)
Oilers, 17-14 (H)
1963—Oilers, 31-20 (B)
Oilers, 28-14 (H)
1964—Bills, 48-17 (H)
Bills, 24-10 (B)
1965—Oilers, 19-17 (B)
Bills, 29-18 (H)
1966—Bills, 27-20 (B)
Bills, 42-20 (H)
1967—Oilers, 20-3 (B)
Oilers, 10-3 (H)
1968—Oilers, 30-7 (B)
Oilers, 35-6 (H)
1969—Oilers, 17-3 (B)
Oilers, 28-14 (H)
1971—Oilers, 20-14 (B)
1974—Oilers, 21-9 (B)
1976—Oilers, 13-3 (B)
1978—Oilers, 17-10 (H)
1983—Bills, 30-13 (B)
1985—Bills, 20-0 (B)
1986—Oilers, 16-7 (H)
1987—Bills, 34-30 (B)
1988—**Bills, 17-10 (B)
1989—Bills, 47-41 (H) OT
1990—Oilers, 27-24 (H)
1992—Oilers, 27-3 (H)
***Bills, 41-38 (B) OT
1993—Bills, 35-7 (B)
1994—Bills, 15-7 (H)
1995—Oilers, 28-17 (B)
1997—Oilers, 31-14 (T)
(RS Pts.—Oilers 741, Bills 662)
(PS Pts.—Bills 58, Oilers 48)
Franchise in Houston prior to 1997
**AFC Divisional Playoff*
***AFC First-Round Playoff*

BUFFALO vs. WASHINGTON
RS: Series tied, 4-4
PS: Redskins lead series, 1-0
1972—Bills, 24-17 (W)
1977—Redskins, 10-0 (B)
1981—Bills, 21-14 (B)
1984—Redskins, 41-14 (W)
1987—Redskins, 27-7 (B)
1990—Redskins, 29-14 (W)
1991—*Redskins, 37-24 (Minneapolis)
1993—Bills, 24-10 (B)
1996—Bills, 38-13 (B)
(RS Pts.—Redskins 161, Bills 142)
(PS Pts.—Redskins 37, Bills 24)
Super Bowl XXVI

CAROLINA vs. ARIZONA
RS: Panthers lead series, 1-0;
See Arizona vs. Carolina

CAROLINA vs. ATLANTA
RS: Panthers lead series, 4-2;
See Atlanta vs. Carolina

CAROLINA vs. BALTIMORE
RS: Panthers lead series, 1-0
See Baltimore vs. Carolina

CAROLINA vs. BUFFALO
RS: Bills lead series, 1-0;
See Buffalo vs. Carolina

CAROLINA vs. CHICAGO
RS: Bears lead series, 1-0
1995—Bears, 31-27 (Chi)
(RS Pts.—Bears 31, Panthers 27)

CAROLINA vs. DALLAS
RS: Panthers lead seies, 1-0
PS: Panthers lead series, 1-0
1996—*Panthers, 26-17 (C)
1997—Panthers, 23-13 (D)
(RS Pts.—Panthers 23, Cowboys 13)
(PS Pts.—Panthers 26, Cowboys 17)
NFC Divisional Playoff

CAROLINA vs. DENVER
RS: Broncos lead series, 1-0
1997—Broncos, 34-0 (D)
(RS Pts.—Broncos 34, Panthers 0)

CAROLINA vs. GREEN BAY
RS: Packers lead series, 1-0
PS: Packers lead series, 1-0
1996—*Packers, 30-13 (GB)
1997—Packers, 31-10 (C)
(RS Pts.—Packers 31, Panthers 10)
(PS Pts.—Packers 30, Panthers 13)
NFC Championship

CAROLINA vs. INDIANAPOLIS
RS: Panthers lead series, 1-0
1995—Panthers, 13-10 (C)
(RS Pts.—Panthers 13, Colts 10)

CAROLINA vs. JACKSONVILLE
RS: Jaguars lead series, 1-0
1996—Jaguars, 24-14 (J)
(RS Pts.—Jaguars 24, Panthers 14)

CAROLINA vs. KANSAS CITY
RS: Chiefs lead series, 1-0
1997—Chiefs, 35-14 (C)
(RS Pts.—Chiefs 35, Panthers 14)

CAROLINA vs. MINNESOTA
RS: Vikings lead series, 2-0
1996—Vikings, 14-12 (M)
1997—Vikings, 21-14 (M)
(RS Pts.—Vikings 35, Panthers 26)

CAROLINA vs. NEW ENGLAND
RS: Panthers lead series, 1-0
1995—Panthers, 20-17 (NE) OT
(RS Pts.—Panthers 20, Patriots 17)

CAROLINA vs. NEW ORLEANS
RS: Panthers lead series, 4-2
1995—Panthers, 20-3 (C)
Saints, 34-26 (NO)
1996—Panthers, 22-20 (NO)
Panthers, 19-7 (C)
1997—Panthers, 13-0 (NO)
Saints, 16-13 (C)
(RS Pts.—Panthers 113, Saints 80)

CAROLINA vs. N.Y. GIANTS
RS: Panthers lead series, 1-0
1995—Panthers, 27-17 (C)
(RS Pts.—Panthers 27, Giants 17)

CAROLINA vs. N.Y. JETS
RS: Panthers lead series, 1-0
1995—Panthers, 26-15 (C)
(RS Pts.—Panthers 26, Jets 15)

CAROLINA vs. OAKLAND
RS: Panthers lead series, 1-0
1997—Panthers, 38-14 (C)
(RS Pts.—Panthers 38, Raiders 14)

CAROLINA vs. PHILADELPHIA
RS: Eagles lead series, 1-0
1996—Eagles, 20-9 (P)
(RS Pts.—Eagles 20, Panthers 9)

CAROLINA vs. PITTSBURGH
RS: Panthers lead series, 1-0
1996—Panthers, 18-14 (C)
(RS Pts.—Panthers 18, Steelers 14)

CAROLINA vs. ST. LOUIS
RS: Series tied, 3-3
1995—Rams, 31-10 (C)
Rams, 28-17 (StL)
1996—Panthers, 45-13 (C)
Panthers, 20-10 (StL)
1997—Panthers, 16-10 (StL)
Rams, 30-18 (C)
(RS Pts.—Panthers 126, Rams 122)

CAROLINA vs. SAN DIEGO
RS: Panthers lead series, 1-0
1997—Panthers, 26-7 (SD)
(RS Pts.—Panthers 26, Chargers 7)

CAROLINA vs. SAN FRANCISCO
RS: Series tied, 3-3
1995—Panthers, 13-7 (SF)
49ers, 31-10 (C)
1996—Panthers, 23-7 (C)
Panthers, 30-24 (SF)
1997—49ers, 34-21 (C)
49ers, 27-19 (SF)
(RS Pts.—49ers 130, Panthers 116)

CAROLINA vs. TAMPA BAY
RS: Series tied, 1-1
1995—Buccaneers, 20-13 (C)
1996—Panthers, 24-0 (C)
(RS Pts.—Panthers 37, Buccaneers 20)

CAROLINA vs. *TENNESSEE
RS: Panthers lead series, 1-0
1996—Panthers, 31-6 (H)
(RS Pts.—Panthers 31, Oilers 6)
Franchise in Houston prior to 1997

CAROLINA vs. WASHINGTON
RS: Redskins lead series, 2-0
1995—Redskins, 20-17 (W)
1997—Redskins, 24-10 (C)
(RS Pts.—Redskins 44, Panthers 27)

CHICAGO vs. ARIZONA
RS: Bears lead series, 52-25-6;
See Arizona vs. Chicago

CHICAGO vs. ATLANTA
RS: Series tied, 9-9;
See Atlanta vs. Chicago

CHICAGO vs. BUFFALO
RS: Bears lead series, 5-2;
See Buffalo vs. Chicago

CHICAGO vs. CAROLINA
RS: Bears lead series, 1-0;
See Carolina vs. Chicago

CHICAGO vs. CINCINNATI
RS: Bengals lead series, 4-2
1972—Bengals, 13-3 (Chi)
1980—Bengals, 17-14 (Chi) OT
1986—Bears, 44-7 (Cin)
1989—Bears, 17-14 (Chi)
1992—Bengals, 31-28 (Chi) OT
1995—Bengals, 16-10 (Cin)
(RS Pts.—Bears 116, Bengals 98)

CHICAGO vs. CLEVELAND
RS: Browns lead series, 8-3
1951—Browns, 42-21 (Cle)
1954—Browns, 39-10 (Chi)
1960—Browns, 42-0 (Cle)
1961—Bears, 17-14 (Chi)
1967—Browns, 24-0 (Cle)
1969—Browns, 28-24 (Chi)
1972—Bears, 17-0 (Cle)
1980—Browns, 27-21 (Cle)
1986—Bears, 41-31 (Chi)
1989—Browns, 27-7 (Cle)
1992—Browns, 27-14 (Cle)
(RS Pts.—Browns 301, Bears 172)

CHICAGO vs. DALLAS
RS: Cowboys lead series, 9-7
PS: Cowboys lead series, 2-0
1960—Bears, 17-7 (C)
1962—Bears, 34-33 (D)
1964—Cowboys, 24-10 (C)
1968—Cowboys, 34-3 (C)
1971—Bears, 23-19 (C)
1973—Cowboys, 20-17 (C)

1976—Cowboys, 31-21 (D)
1977—*Cowboys, 37-7 (D)
1979—Cowboys, 24-20 (D)
1981—Cowboys, 10-9 (D)
1984—Cowboys, 23-14 (C)
1985—Bears, 44-0 (D)
1986—Bears, 24-10 (D)
1988—Bears, 17-7 (C)
1991—**Cowboys, 17-13 (C)
1992—Cowboys, 27-14 (D)
1996—Bears, 22-6 (C)
1997—Cowboys, 27-3 (D)
(RS Pts.—Cowboys 302, Bears 292)
(PS Pts.—Cowboys 54, Bears 20)
NFC Divisional Playoff
**NFC First-Round Playoff*

CHICAGO vs. DENVER
RS: Broncos lead series, 6-5
1971—Broncos, 6-3 (D)
1973—Bears, 33-14 (D)
1976—Broncos, 28-14 (C)
1978—Broncos, 16-7 (D)
1981—Bears, 35-24 (C)
1983—Bears, 31-14 (C)
1984—Bears, 27-0 (C)
1987—Broncos, 31-29 (D)
1990—Bears, 16-13 (D) OT
1993—Broncos, 13-3 (C)
1996—Broncos, 17-12 (D)
(RS Pts.—Bears 210, Broncos 176)

CHICAGO vs. *DETROIT
RS: Bears lead series, 76-55-5
1930—Spartans, 7-6 (P)
Bears, 14-6 (C)
1931—Bears, 9-6 (C)
Spartans, 3-0 (P)
1932—Tie, 13-13 (C)
Tie, 7-7 (P)
Bears, 9-0 (C)
1933—Bears, 17-14 (C)
Bears, 17-7 (P)
1934—Bears, 19-16 (D)
Bears, 10-7 (C)
1935—Tie, 20-20 (C)
Lions, 14-2 (D)
1936—Bears, 12-10 (C)
Lions, 13-7 (D)
1937—Bears, 28-20 (C)
Bears, 13-0 (D)
1938—Lions, 13-7 (C)
Lions, 14-7 (D)
1939—Lions, 10-0 (C)
Bears, 23-13 (D)
1940—Bears, 7-0 (C)
Lions, 17-14 (D)
1941—Bears, 49-0 (C)
Bears, 24-7 (D)
1942—Bears, 16-0 (C)
Bears, 42-0 (D)
1943—Bears, 27-21 (D)
Bears, 35-14 (C)
1944—Tie, 21-21 (C)
Lions, 41-21 (D)
1945—Lions, 16-10 (D)
Lions, 35-28 (C)
1946—Bears, 42-6 (C)
Bears, 45-24 (D)
1947—Bears, 33-24 (C)
Bears, 34-14 (D)
1948—Bears, 28-0 (C)
Bears, 42-14 (D)
1949—Bears, 27-24 (C)
Bears, 28-7 (D)
1950—Bears, 35-21 (D)
Bears, 6-3 (C)
1951—Bears, 28-23 (D)
Lions, 41-28 (C)
1952—Bears, 24-23 (C)
Lions, 45-21 (D)
1953—Lions, 20-16 (C)
Lions, 13-7 (D)
1954—Lions, 48-23 (D)
Bears, 28-24 (C)
1955—Bears, 24-14 (D)
Bears, 21-20 (C)
1956—Lions, 42-10 (D)
Bears, 38-21 (C)
1957—Bears, 27-7 (D)
Lions, 21-13 (C)
1958—Bears, 20-7 (D)
Bears, 21-16 (C)
1959—Bears, 24-14 (D)
Bears, 25-14 (C)
1960—Bears, 28-7 (C)
Lions, 36-0 (D)
1961—Bears, 31-17 (D)
Lions, 16-15 (C)
1962—Lions, 11-3 (D)
Bears, 3-0 (C)
1963—Bears, 37-21 (D)
Bears, 24-14 (C)
1964—Lions, 10-0 (C)
Bears, 27-24 (D)
1965—Bears, 38-10 (C)
Bears, 17-10 (D)
1966—Lions, 14-3 (D)
Tie, 10-10 (C)
1967—Bears, 14-3 (C)
Bears, 27-13 (D)
1968—Lions, 42-0 (D)
Lions, 28-10 (C)
1969—Lions, 13-7 (D)
Lions, 20-3 (C)
1970—Lions, 28-14 (D)
Lions, 16-10 (C)
1971—Bears, 28-23 (D)
Lions, 28-3 (C)
1972—Lions, 38-24 (C)
Lions, 14-0 (D)
1973—Lions, 30-7 (C)
Lions, 40-7 (D)
1974—Bears, 17-9 (C)
Lions, 34-17 (D)
1975—Lions, 27-7 (D)
Bears, 25-21 (C)
1976—Bears, 10-3 (C)
Lions, 14-10 (D)
1977—Bears, 30-20 (C)
Bears, 31-14 (D)
1978—Bears, 19-0 (D)
Lions, 21-17 (C)
1979—Bears, 35-7 (C)
Lions, 20-0 (D)
1980—Bears, 24-7 (C)
Bears, 23-17 (D) OT
1981—Lions, 48-17 (D)
Lions, 23-7 (C)
1982—Lions, 17-10 (D)
Bears, 20-17 (C)
1983—Lions, 31-17 (D)
Lions, 38-17 (C)
1984—Bears, 16-14 (C)
Bears, 30-13 (D)
1985—Bears, 24-3 (C)
Bears, 37-17 (D)
1986—Bears, 13-7 (C)
Bears, 16-13 (D)
1987—Bears, 30-10 (C)
1988—Bears, 24-7 (D)
Bears, 13-12 (C)
1989—Bears, 47-27 (D)
Lions, 27-17 (C)
1990—Bears, 23-17 (C) OT
Lions, 38-21 (D)
1991—Bears, 20-10 (C)
Lions, 16-6 (D)
1992—Bears, 27-24 (C)
Lions, 16-3 (D)
1993—Bears, 10-6 (D)
Lions, 20-14 (C)
1994—Lions, 21-16 (D)
Bears, 20-10 (C)
1995—Lions, 24-17 (C)
Lions, 27-7 (D)
1996—Lions, 35-16 (D)
Bears, 31-14 (C)
1997—Lions, 32-7 (C)
Lions, 55-20 (D)
(RS Pts.—Bears 2,520, Lions 2,374)
Franchise in Portsmouth prior to 1934 and known as the Spartans

***CHICAGO vs. GREEN BAY**
RS: Bears lead series, 81-67-6
PS: Bears lead series, 1-0
1921—Staleys, 20-0 (C)
1923—Bears, 3-0 (GB)
1924—Bears, 3-0 (C)
1925—Packers, 14-10 (GB)
Bears, 21-0 (C)
1926—Tie, 6-6 (GB)
Bears, 19-13 (C)
Tie, 3-3 (C)
1927—Bears, 7-6 (GB)
Bears, 14-6 (C)
1928—Tie, 12-12 (GB)
Packers, 16-6 (C)
Packers, 6-0 (C)
1929—Packers, 23-0 (GB)
Packers, 14-0 (C)
Packers, 25-0 (C)
1930—Packers, 7-0 (GB)
Packers, 13-12 (C)
Bears, 21-0 (C)
1931—Packers, 7-0 (GB)
Packers, 6-2 (C)
Bears, 7-6 (C)
1932—Tie, 0-0 (GB)
Packers, 2-0 (C)
Bears, 9-0 (C)
1933—Bears, 14-7 (GB)
Bears, 10-7 (C)
Bears, 7-6 (C)
1934—Bears, 24-10 (GB)
Bears, 27-14 (C)
1935—Packers, 7-0 (GB)
Packers, 17-14 (C)
1936—Bears, 30-3 (GB)
Packers, 21-10 (C)
1937—Bears, 14-2 (GB)
Packers, 24-14 (C)
1938—Bears, 2-0 (GB)
Packers, 24-17 (C)
1939—Packers, 21-16 (GB)
Bears, 30-27 (C)
1940—Bears, 41-10 (GB)
Bears, 14-7 (C)
1941—Bears, 25-17 (GB)
Packers, 16-14 (C)
**Bears, 33-14 (C)
1942—Bears, 44-28 (GB)
Bears, 38-7 (C)
1943—Tie, 21-21 (GB)
Bears, 21-7 (C)
1944—Packers, 42-28 (GB)
Bears, 21-0 (C)
1945—Packers, 31-21 (GB)
Bears, 28-24 (C)
1946—Bears, 30-7 (GB)
Bears, 10-7 (C)
1947—Packers, 29-20 (GB)
Bears, 20-17 (C)
1948—Bears, 45-7 (GB)
Bears, 7-6 (C)
1949—Bears, 17-0 (GB)
Bears, 24-3 (C)
1950—Packers, 31-21 (GB)
Bears, 28-14 (C)
1951—Bears, 31-20 (GB)
Bears, 24-13 (C)
1952—Bears, 24-14 (GB)
Packers, 41-28 (C)
1953—Bears, 17-13 (GB)
Tie, 21-21 (C)
1954—Bears, 10-3 (GB)
Bears, 28-23 (C)
1955—Packers, 24-3 (GB)
Bears, 52-31 (C)
1956—Bears, 37-21 (GB)
Bears, 38-14 (C)
1957—Packers, 21-17 (GB)
Bears, 21-14 (C)
1958—Bears, 34-20 (GB)
Bears, 24-10 (C)
1959—Packers, 9-6 (GB)
Bears, 28-17 (C)
1960—Bears, 17-14 (GB)
Packers, 41-13 (C)
1961—Packers, 24-0 (GB)
Packers, 31-28 (C)
1962—Packers, 49-0 (GB)
Packers, 38-7 (C)
1963—Bears, 10-3 (GB)
Bears, 26-7 (C)
1964—Packers, 23-12 (GB)
Packers, 17-3 (C)
1965—Packers, 23-14 (GB)
Bears, 31-10 (C)
1966—Packers, 17-0 (C)
Packers, 13-6 (GB)
1967—Packers, 13-10 (GB)
Packers, 17-13 (C)
1968—Bears, 13-10 (GB)
Packers, 28-27 (C)
1969—Packers, 17-0 (GB)
Packers, 21-3 (C)
1970—Packers, 20-19 (GB)
Bears, 35-17 (C)
1971—Packers, 17-14 (C)
Packers, 31-10 (GB)
1972—Packers, 20-17 (GB)
Packers, 23-17 (C)
1973—Bears, 31-17 (GB)
Packers, 21-0 (C)
1974—Bears, 10-9 (C)
Packers, 20-3 (Mil)
1975—Bears, 27-14 (C)
Packers, 28-7 (GB)
1976—Bears, 24-13 (C)
Bears, 16-10 (GB)
1977—Bears, 26-0 (GB)
Bears, 21-10 (C)
1978—Packers, 24-14 (GB)
Bears, 14-0 (C)
1979—Bears, 6-3 (C)
Bears, 15-14 (GB)
1980—Packers, 12-6 (GB) OT
Bears, 61-7 (C)
1981—Packers, 16-9 (C)
Packers, 21-17 (GB)
1983—Packers, 31-28 (GB)
Bears, 23-21 (C)
1984—Bears, 9-7 (GB)
Packers, 20-14 (C)
1985—Bears, 23-7 (C)
Bears, 16-10 (GB)
1986—Bears, 25-12 (GB)
Bears, 12-10 (C)
1987—Bears, 26-24 (GB)
Bears, 23-10 (C)
1988—Bears, 24-6 (GB)
Bears, 16-0 (C)
1989—Packers, 14-13 (GB)
Packers, 40-28 (C)
1990—Bears, 31-13 (GB)
Bears, 27-13 (C)
1991—Bears, 10-0 (GB)
Bears, 27-13 (C)
1992—Bears, 30-10 (GB)
Packers, 17-3 (C)
1993—Packers, 17-3 (GB)
Bears, 30-17 (C)
1994—Packers, 33-6 (C)
Packers, 40-3 (GB)
1995—Packers, 27-24 (C)
Packers, 35-28 (GB)
1996—Packers, 37-6 (C)
Packers, 28-17 (GB)
1997—Packers, 38-24 (GB)
Packers, 24-23 (C)
(RS Pts.—Bears 2,609, Packers 2,392)
(PS Pts.—Bears 33, Packers 14)
Bears known as Staleys prior to 1922

***Division Playoff*

CHICAGO vs. *INDIANAPOLIS

RS: Colts lead series, 21-16

1953—Colts, 13-9 (B)
Colts, 16-14 (C)
1954—Bears, 28-9 (C)
Bears, 28-13 (B)
1955—Colts, 23-17 (B)
Bears, 38-10 (C)
1956—Colts, 28-21 (B)
Bears, 58-27 (C)
1957—Colts, 21-10 (B)
Colts, 29-14 (C)
1958—Colts, 51-38 (B)
Colts, 17-0 (C)
1959—Bears, 26-21 (B)
Colts, 21-7 (C)
1960—Colts, 42-7 (B)
Colts, 24-20 (C)
1961—Bears, 24-10 (C)
Bears, 21-20 (B)
1962—Bears, 35-15 (C)
Bears, 57-0 (B)
1963—Bears, 10-3 (C)
Bears, 17-7 (B)
1964—Colts, 52-0 (B)
Colts, 40-24 (C)
1965—Colts, 26-21 (C)
Bears, 13-0 (B)
1966—Bears, 27-17 (C)
Colts, 21-16 (B)
1967—Colts, 24-3 (C)
1968—Colts, 28-7 (B)
1969—Colts, 24-21 (C)
1970—Colts, 21-20 (B)
1975—Colts, 35-7 (C)
1983—Colts, 22-19 (B) OT
1985—Bears, 17-10 (C)
1988—Bears, 17-13 (I)
1991—Bears, 31-17 (I)
(RS Pts.—Colts 770, Bears 742)

**Franchise in Baltimore prior to 1984*

CHICAGO vs. JACKSONVILLE

RS: Bears lead series, 1-0

1995—Bears, 30-27 (J)
(RS Pts.—Bears 30, Jaguars 27)

CHICAGO vs. KANSAS CITY

RS: Bears lead series, 4-3

1973—Chiefs, 19-7 (KC)
1977—Bears, 28-27 (C)
1981—Bears, 16-13 (KC) OT
1987—Bears, 31-28 (C)
1990—Chiefs, 21-10 (C)
1993—Bears, 19-17 (KC)
1996—Chiefs, 14-10 (KC)
(RS Pts.—Chiefs 139, Bears 121)

CHICAGO vs. MIAMI

RS: Dolphins lead series, 5-3

1971—Dolphins, 34-3 (M)
1975—Dolphins, 46-13 (C)
1979—Dolphins, 31-16 (M)
1985—Dolphins, 38-24 (M)
1988—Bears, 34-7 (C)
1991—Dolphins, 16-13 (C) OT
1994—Bears, 17-14 (M)
1997—Bears, 36-33 (M) OT
(RS Pts.—Dolphins 219, Bears 156)

CHICAGO vs. MINNESOTA

RS: Vikings lead series, 39-32-2
PS: Bears lead series, 1-0

1961—Vikings, 37-13 (M)
Bears, 52-35 (C)
1962—Bears, 13-0 (M)
Bears, 31-30 (C)
1963—Bears, 28-7 (M)
Tie, 17-17 (C)
1964—Bears, 34-28 (M)
Vikings, 41-14 (C)
1965—Bears, 45-37 (M)
Vikings, 24-17 (C)
1966—Bears, 13-10 (M)
Bears, 41-28 (C)
1967—Bears, 17-7 (M)
Tie, 10-10 (C)
1968—Bears, 27-17 (M)
Bears, 26-24 (C)
1969—Vikings, 31-0 (C)
Vikings, 31-14 (M)
1970—Vikings, 24-0 (C)
Vikings, 16-13 (M)
1971—Bears, 20-17 (M)
Vikings, 27-10 (C)
1972—Bears, 13-10 (C)
Vikings, 23-10 (M)
1973—Vikings, 22-13 (C)
Vikings, 31-13 (M)
1974—Vikings, 11-7 (M)
Vikings, 17-0 (C)
1975—Vikings, 28-3 (M)
Vikings, 13-9 (C)
1976—Vikings, 20-19 (M)
Bears, 14-13 (C)
1977—Vikings, 22-16 (M) OT
Bears, 10-7 (C)
1978—Vikings, 24-20 (C)
Vikings, 17-14 (M)
1979—Bears, 26-7 (C)
Vikings, 30-27 (M)
1980—Vikings, 34-14 (C)
Vikings, 13-7 (M)
1981—Vikings, 24-21 (M)
Bears, 10-9 (C)
1982—Vikings, 35-7 (M)
1983—Vikings, 23-14 (C)
Bears, 19-13 (M)
1984—Bears, 16-7 (C)
Bears, 34-3 (M)
1985—Bears, 33-24 (M)
Bears, 27-9 (C)
1986—Bears, 23-0 (C)
Vikings, 23-7 (M)
1987—Bears, 27-7 (C)
Bears, 30-24 (M)
1988—Vikings, 31-7 (C)
Vikings, 28-27 (M)
1989—Bears, 38-7 (C)
Vikings, 27-16 (M)
1990—Bears, 19-16 (C)
Vikings, 41-13 (M)
1991—Bears, 10-6 (C)
Bears, 34-17 (M)
1992—Vikings, 21-20 (M)
Vikings, 38-10 (C)
1993—Vikings, 10-7 (M)
Vikings, 19-12 (C)
1994—Vikings, 42-14 (C)
Vikings, 33-27 (M) OT
*Bears, 35-18 (M)
1995—Bears, 31-14 (C)
Bears, 14-6 (M)
1996—Vikings, 20-14 (C)
Bears, 15-13 (M)
1997—Vikings, 27-24 (C)
Vikings, 29-22 (M)
(RS Pts.—Vikings 1,486, Bears 1,332)
(PS Pts.—Bears 35, Vikings 18)

**NFC First-Round Playoff*

CHICAGO vs. NEW ENGLAND

RS: Patriots lead series, 5-2
PS: Bears lead series, 1-0

1973—Patriots, 13-10 (C)
1979—Patriots, 27-7 (C)
1982—Bears, 26-13 (C)
1985—Bears, 20-7 (C)
*Bears, 46-10 (New Orleans)
1988—Patriots, 30-7 (NE)
1994—Patriots, 13-3 (C)
1997—Patriots, 31-3 (NE)
(RS Pts.—Patriots 134, Bears 76)
(PS Pts.—Bears 46, Patriots 10)

**Super Bowl XX*

CHICAGO vs. NEW ORLEANS

RS: Bears lead series, 9-8
PS: Bears lead series, 1-0

1968—Bears, 23-17 (NO)
1970—Bears, 24-3 (NO)
1971—Bears, 35-14 (C)
1973—Saints, 21-16 (NO)
1974—Bears, 24-10 (C)
1975—Bears, 42-17 (NO)
1977—Saints, 42-24 (C)
1980—Bears, 22-3 (C)
1982—Saints, 10-0 (C)
1983—Saints, 34-31 (NO) OT
1984—Bears, 20-7 (C)
1987—Saints, 19-17 (C)
1990—*Bears, 16-6 (C)
1991—Bears, 20-17 (NO)
1992—Saints, 28-6 (NO)
1994—Bears, 17-7 (C)
1996—Saints, 27-24 (NO)
1997—Saints, 20-17 (C)
(RS Pts.—Bears 362, Saints 296)
(PS Pts.—Bears 16, Saints 6)

**NFC First-Round Playoff*

CHICAGO vs. N.Y. GIANTS

RS: Bears lead series, 25-16-2
PS: Bears lead series, 5-3

1925—Bears, 19-7 (NY)
Giants, 9-0 (C)
1926—Bears, 7-0 (C)
1927—Giants, 13-7 (NY)
1928—Bears, 13-0 (C)
1929—Giants, 26-14 (C)
Giants, 34-0 (NY)
Giants, 14-9 (C)
1930—Giants, 12-0 (C)
Bears, 12-0 (NY)
1931—Bears, 6-0 (C)
Bears, 12-6 (NY)
Giants, 25-6 (C)
1932—Bears, 28-8 (NY)
Bears, 6-0 (C)
1933—Bears, 14-10 (C)
Giants, 3-0 (NY)
*Bears, 23-21 (C)
1934—Bears, 27-7 (C)
Bears, 10-9 (NY)
*Giants, 30-13 (NY)
1935—Bears, 20-3 (NY)
Giants, 3-0 (C)
1936—Bears, 25-7 (NY)
1937—Tie, 3-3 (NY)
1939—Giants, 16-13 (NY)
1940—Bears, 37-21 (NY)
1941—*Bears, 37-9 (C)
1942—Bears, 26-7 (NY)
1943—Bears, 56-7 (NY)
1946—Giants, 14-0 (NY)
*Bears, 24-14 (NY)
1948—Bears, 35-14 (C)
1949—Giants, 35-28 (NY)
1956—Tie, 17-17 (NY)
*Giants, 47-7 (NY)
1962—Giants, 26-24 (C)
1963—*Bears, 14-10 (C)
1965—Bears, 35-14 (NY)
1967—Bears, 34-7 (C)
1969—Giants, 28-24 (NY)
1970—Bears, 24-16 (NY)
1974—Bears, 16-13 (C)
1977—Bears, 12-9 (NY) OT
1985—**Bears, 21-0 (C)
1987—Bears, 34-19 (C)
1990—**Giants, 31-3 (NY)
1991—Bears, 20-17 (C)
1992—Giants, 27-14 (C)
1993—Giants, 26-20 (C)
1995—Bears, 27-24 (NY)
(RS Pts.—Bears 734, Giants 556)
(PS Pts.—Giants 162, Bears 142)

**NFL Championship*
***NFC Divisional Playoff*

CHICAGO vs. N.Y. JETS

RS: Bears lead series, 4-2

1974—Jets, 23-21 (C)
1979—Bears, 23-13 (C)
1985—Bears, 19-6 (NY)
1991—Bears, 19-13 (C) OT
1994—Bears, 19-7 (NY)
1997—Jets, 23-15 (C)
(RS Pts.—Bears 116, Jets 85)

CHICAGO vs. *OAKLAND

RS: Raiders lead series, 5-4

1972—Raiders, 28-21 (O)
1976—Raiders, 28-27 (C)
1978—Raiders, 25-19 (C) OT
1981—Bears, 23-6 (O)
1984—Bears, 17-6 (C)
1987—Bears, 6-3 (LA)
1990—Raiders, 24-10 (LA)
1993—Raiders, 16-14 (C)
1996—Bears, 19-17 (C)
(RS Pts.—Bears 156, Raiders 153)

**Franchise in Los Angeles from 1982-1994*

CHICAGO vs. PHILADELPHIA

RS: Bears lead series, 24-4-1
PS: Series tied, 1-1

1933—Tie, 3-3 (P)
1935—Bears, 39-0 (P)
1936—Bears, 17-0 (P)
Bears, 28-7 (P)
1938—Bears, 28-6 (P)
1939—Bears, 27-14 (C)
1941—Bears, 49-14 (P)
1942—Bears, 45-14 (C)
1944—Bears, 28-7 (P)
1946—Bears, 21-14 (C)
1947—Bears, 40-7 (C)
1948—Eagles, 12-7 (P)
1949—Bears, 38-21 (C)
1955—Bears, 17-10 (C)
1961—Eagles, 16-14 (P)
1963—Bears, 16-7 (C)
1968—Bears, 29-16 (P)
1970—Bears, 20-16 (C)
1972—Bears, 21-12 (P)
1975—Bears, 15-13 (C)
1979—*Eagles, 27-17 (P)
1980—Eagles, 17-14 (P)
1983—Bears, 7-6 (P)
Bears, 17-14 (C)
1986—Bears, 13-10 (C) OT
1987—Bears, 35-3 (P)
1988—**Bears, 20-12 (C)
1989—Bears, 27-13 (C)
1993—Bears, 17-6 (P)
1994—Eagles, 30-22 (P)
1995—Bears, 20-14 (C)
(RS Pts.—Bears 674, Eagles 322)
(PS Pts.—Eagles 39, Bears 37)

**NFC First-Round Playoff*
***NFC Divisional Playoff*

CHICAGO vs. *PITTSBURGH

RS: Bears lead series, 16-5-1

1934—Bears, 28-0 (P)
1935—Bears, 23-7 (P)
1936—Bears, 27-9 (P)
Bears, 26-6 (C)
1937—Bears, 7-0 (P)
1939—Bears, 32-0 (P)
1941—Bears, 34-7 (C)
1945—Bears, 28-7 (C)
1947—Bears, 49-7 (C)
1949—Bears, 30-21 (C)
1958—Steelers, 24-10 (P)
1959—Bears, 27-21 (C)
1963—Tie, 17-17 (P)
1967—Steelers, 41-13 (P)
1969—Bears, 38-7 (C)
1971—Bears, 17-15 (C)
1975—Steelers, 34-3 (P)
1980—Steelers, 38-3 (P)
1986—Bears, 13-10 (C) OT
1989—Bears, 20-0 (P)
1992—Bears, 30-6 (C)
1995—Steelers, 37-34 (C) OT
(RS Pts.—Bears 509, Steelers 314)

**Steelers known as Pirates prior to 1941*

CHICAGO vs. *ST. LOUIS

RS: Bears lead series, 47-30-3

PS: Series tied, 1-1
1937—Bears, 20-2 (Clev)
Bears, 15-7 (C)
1938—Rams, 14-7 (C)
Rams, 23-21 (Clev)
1939—Bears, 30-21 (Clev)
Bears, 35-21 (C)
1940—Bears, 21-14 (Clev)
Bears, 47-25 (C)
1941—Bears, 48-21 (Clev)
Bears, 31-13 (C)
1942—Bears, 21-7 (Clev)
Bears, 47-0 (C)
1944—Rams, 19-7 (Clev)
Bears, 28-21 (C)
1945—Rams, 17-0 (Clev)
Rams, 41-21 (C)
1946—Tie, 28-28 (C)
Bears, 27-21 (LA)
1947—Bears, 41-21 (LA)
Rams, 17-14 (C)
1948—Bears, 42-21 (C)
Bears, 21-6 (LA)
1949—Rams, 31-16 (C)
Rams, 27-24 (LA)
1950—Bears, 24-20 (LA)
Bears, 24-14 (C)
**Rams, 24-14 (LA)
1951—Rams, 42-17 (C)
1952—Rams, 31-7 (LA)
Rams, 40-24 (C)
1953—Rams, 38-24 (LA)
Bears, 24-21 (C)
1954—Rams, 42-38 (LA)
Bears, 24-13 (C)
1955—Bears, 31-20 (LA)
Bears, 24-3 (C)
1956—Bears, 35-24 (LA)
Bears, 30-21 (C)
1957—Bears, 34-26 (C)
Bears, 16-10 (LA)
1958—Bears, 31-10 (C)
Rams, 41-35 (LA)
1959—Rams, 28-21 (C)
Bears, 26-21 (LA)
1960—Bears, 34-27 (C)
Tie, 24-24 (LA)
1961—Bears, 21-17 (LA)
Bears, 28-24 (C)
1962—Bears, 27-23 (LA)
Bears, 30-14 (C)
1963—Bears, 52-14 (LA)
Bears, 6-0 (C)
1964—Bears, 38-17 (C)
Bears, 34-24 (LA)
1965—Rams, 30-28 (LA)
Bears, 31-6 (C)
1966—Rams, 31-17 (LA)
Bears, 17-10 (C)
1967—Rams, 28-17 (C)
1968—Bears, 17-16 (LA)
1969—Rams, 9-7 (C)
1971—Rams, 17-3 (LA)
1972—Tie, 13-13 (C)
1973—Rams, 26-0 (C)
1975—Rams, 38-10 (LA)
1976—Rams, 20-12 (LA)
1977—Bears, 24-23 (C)
1979—Bears, 27-23 (C)
1981—Rams, 24-7 (C)
1982—Bears, 34-26 (LA)
1983—Rams, 21-14 (LA)
1984—Rams, 29-13 (LA)
1985—***Bears, 24-0 (C)
1986—Rams, 20-17 (C)
1988—Rams, 23-3 (LA)
1989—Bears, 20-10 (C)
1990—Bears, 38-9 (C)
1993—Rams, 20-6 (LA)
1994—Bears, 27-13 (C)
1995—Rams, 34-28 (StL)
1996—Bears, 35-9 (C)
1997—Bears, 13-10 (StL)
(RS Pts.—Bears 1,873, Rams 1,625)
(PS Pts.—Bears 38, Rams 24)
Franchise in Los Angeles prior to 1995 and in Cleveland prior to 1946
***Conference Playoff*
****NFC Championship*

CHICAGO vs. SAN DIEGO
RS: Chargers lead series, 4-3
1970—Chargers, 20-7 (C)
1974—Chargers, 28-21 (SD)
1978—Chargers, 40-7 (SD)
1981—Bears, 20-17 (C) OT
1984—Chargers, 20-7 (SD)
1993—Bears, 16-13 (SD)
1996—Bears, 27-14 (C)
(RS Pts.—Chargers 152, Bears 105)

CHICAGO vs. SAN FRANCISCO
RS: Series tied, 25-25-1
PS: 49ers lead series, 3-0
1950—Bears, 32-20 (SF)
Bears, 17-0 (C)
1951—Bears, 13-7 (C)
1952—49ers, 40-16 (C)
Bears, 20-17 (SF)
1953—49ers, 35-28 (C)
49ers, 24-14 (SF)
1954—49ers, 31-24 (C)
Bears, 31-27 (SF)
1955—49ers, 20-19 (C)
Bears, 34-23 (SF)
1956—Bears, 31-7 (C)
Bears, 38-21 (SF)
1957—49ers, 21-17 (C)
49ers, 21-17 (SF)
1958—Bears, 28-6 (C)
Bears, 27-14 (SF)
1959—49ers, 20-17 (SF)
Bears, 14-3 (C)
1960—Bears, 27-10 (C)
49ers, 25-7 (SF)
1961—Bears, 31-0 (C)
49ers, 41-31 (SF)
1962—Bears, 30-14 (SF)
49ers, 34-27 (C)
1963—49ers, 20-14 (SF)
Bears, 27-7 (C)
1964—49ers, 31-21 (SF)
Bears, 23-21 (C)
1965—49ers, 52-24 (SF)
Bears, 61-20 (C)
1966—Tie, 30-30 (C)
49ers, 41-14 (SF)
1967—Bears, 28-14 (SF)
1968—Bears, 27-19 (C)
1969—49ers, 42-21 (SF)
1970—49ers, 37-16 (C)
1971—49ers, 13-0 (SF)
1972—49ers, 34-21 (C)
1974—49ers, 34-0 (C)
1975—49ers, 31-3 (SF)
1976—Bears, 19-12 (SF)
1978—Bears, 16-13 (SF)
1979—Bears, 28-27 (SF)
1981—49ers, 28-17 (SF)
1983—Bears, 13-3 (C)
1984—*49ers, 23-0 (SF)
1985—Bears, 26-10 (SF)
1987—49ers, 41-0 (SF)
1988—Bears, 10-9 (C)
*49ers, 28-3 (C)
1989—49ers, 26-0 (SF)
1991—49ers, 52-14 (SF)
1994—**49ers, 44-15 (SF)
(RS Pts.—49ers 1,148, Bears 1,063)
(PS Pts.—49ers 95, Bears 18)
**NFC Championship*
***NFC Divisional Playoff*

CHICAGO vs. SEATTLE
RS: Seahawks lead series, 4-2
1976—Bears, 34-7 (S)
1978—Seahawks, 31-29 (C)
1982—Seahawks, 20-14 (S)
1984—Seahawks, 38-9 (S)
1987—Seahawks, 34-21 (C)
1990—Bears, 17-0 (C)
(RS Pts.—Seahawks 130, Bears 124)

CHICAGO vs. TAMPA BAY
RS: Bears lead series, 30-10
1977—Bears, 10-0 (TB)
1978—Buccaneers, 33-19 (TB)
Bears, 14-3 (C)
1979—Buccaneers, 17-13 (C)
Bears, 14-0 (TB)
1980—Bears, 23-0 (C)
Bears, 14-13 (TB)
1981—Bears, 28-17 (C)
Buccaneers, 20-10 (TB)
1982—Buccaneers, 26-23 (TB) OT
1983—Bears, 17-10 (C)
Bears, 27-0 (TB)
1984—Bears, 34-14 (C)
Bears, 44-9 (TB)
1985—Bears, 38-28 (C)
Bears, 27-19 (TB)
1986—Bears, 23-3 (TB)
Bears, 48-14 (C)
1987—Bears, 20-3 (C)
Bears, 27-26 (TB)
1988—Bears, 28-10 (C)
Bears, 27-15 (TB)
1989—Buccaneers, 42-35 (TB)
Buccaneers, 32-31 (C)
1990—Bears, 26-6 (TB)
Bears, 27-14 (C)
1991—Bears, 21-20 (TB)
Bears, 27-0 (C)
1992—Bears, 31-14 (C)
Buccaneers, 20-17 (TB)
1993—Bears, 47-17 (C)
Buccaneers, 13-10 (TB)
1994—Bears, 21-9 (C)
Bears, 20-6 (TB)
1995—Bears, 25-6 (TB)
Bears, 31-10 (C)
1996—Bears, 13-10 (C)
Buccaneers, 34-19 (TB)
1997—Bears, 13-7 (C)
Buccaneers, 31-15 (TB)
(RS Pts.—Bears 957, Buccaneers 571)

CHICAGO vs. *TENNESSEE
RS: Oilers lead series, 4-3
1973—Bears, 35-14 (C)
1977—Oilers, 47-0 (H)
1980—Oilers, 10-6 (C)
1986—Bears, 20-7 (H)
1989—Oilers, 33-28 (C)
1992—Oilers, 24-7 (H)
1995—Bears, 35-32 (C)
(RS Pts.—Oilers 167, Bears 131)
**Franchise in Houston prior to 1997*

CHICAGO vs. *WASHINGTON
RS: Bears lead series, 18-14-1
PS: Redskins lead series, 4-3
1932—Tie, 7-7 (B)
1933—Bears, 7-0 (C)
Redskins, 10-0 (B)
1934—Bears, 21-0 (B)
1935—Bears, 30-14 (B)
1936—Bears, 26-0 (B)
1937—**Redskins, 28-21 (C)
1938—Bears, 31-7 (C)
1940—Redskins, 7-3 (W)
**Bears, 73-0 (W)
1941—Bears, 35-21 (C)
1942—**Redskins, 14-6 (W)
1943—Redskins, 21-7 (W)
**Bears, 41-21 (C)
1945—Redskins, 28-21 (W)
1946—Bears, 24-20 (C)
1947—Bears, 56-20 (W)
1948—Bears, 48-13 (C)
1949—Bears, 31-21 (W)
1951—Bears, 27-0 (W)
1953—Bears, 27-24 (W)
1957—Redskins, 14-3 (C)
1964—Redskins, 27-20 (W)
1968—Redskins, 38-28 (C)
1971—Bears, 16-15 (C)
1974—Redskins, 42-0 (W)
1976—Bears, 33-7 (C)
1978—Bears, 14-10 (W)
1980—Bears, 35-21 (C)
1981—Redskins, 24-7 (C)
1984—***Bears, 23-19 (W)
1985—Bears, 45-10 (C)
1986—***Redskins, 27-13 (C)
1987—***Redskins, 21-17 (C)
1988—Bears, 34-14 (W)
1989—Redskins, 38-14 (W)
1990—Redskins, 10-9 (W)
1991—Redskins, 20-7 (C)
1996—Redskins, 10-3 (W)
1997—Redskins, 31-8 (C)
(RS Pts.—Bears 677, Redskins 544)
(PS Pts.—Bears 194, Redskins 130)
**Franchise in Boston prior to 1937 and known as Braves prior to 1933*
***NFL Championship*
****NFC Divisional Playoff*

CINCINNATI vs. ARIZONA
RS: Bengals lead series, 4-2;
See Arizona vs. Cincinnati

CINCINNATI vs. ATLANTA
RS: Bengals lead series, 7-2;
See Atlanta vs. Cincinnati

CINCINNATI vs. BALTIMORE
RS: Bengals lead series, 3-1;
See Baltimore vs. Cincinnati

CINCINNATI vs. BUFFALO
RS: Bengals lead series, 9-8
PS: Bengals lead series, 2-0;
See Buffalo vs. Cincinnati

CINCINNATI vs. CHICAGO
RS: Bengals lead series, 4-2;
See Chicago vs. Cincinnati

CINCINNATI vs. CLEVELAND
RS: Browns lead series, 27-24
1970—Browns, 30-27 (Cle)
Bengals, 14-10 (Cin)
1971—Browns, 27-24 (Cin)
Browns, 31-27 (Cle)
1972—Browns, 27-6 (Cle)
Browns, 27-24 (Cin)
1973—Browns, 17-10 (Cle)
Bengals, 34-17 (Cin)
1974—Bengals, 33-7 (Cin)
Bengals, 34-24 (Cle)
1975—Bengals, 24-17 (Cin)
Browns, 35-23 (Cle)
1976—Bengals, 45-24 (Cle)
Bengals, 21-6 (Cin)
1977—Browns, 13-3 (Cin)
Bengals, 10-7 (Cle)
1978—Browns, 13-10 (Cle) OT
Bengals, 48-16 (Cin)
1979—Browns, 28-27 (Cle)
Bengals, 16-12 (Cin)
1980—Browns, 31-7 (Cle)
Browns, 27-24 (Cin)
1981—Browns, 20-17 (Cin)
Bengals, 41-21 (Cle)
1982—Bengals, 23-10 (Cin)
1983—Browns, 17-7 (Cle)
Bengals, 28-21 (Cin)
1984—Bengals, 12-9 (Cin)
Bengals, 20-17 (Cle) OT
1985—Bengals, 27-10 (Cin)
Browns, 24-6 (Cle)
1986—Bengals, 30-13 (Cle)
Browns, 34-3 (Cin)
1987—Browns, 34-0 (Cin)
Browns, 38-24 (Cle)
1988—Bengals, 24-17 (Cin)
Browns, 23-16 (Cle)
1989—Bengals, 21-14 (Cin)
Bengals, 21-0 (Cle)
1990—Bengals, 34-13 (Cle)
Bengals, 21-14 (Cin)

ALL-TIME TEAM VS. TEAM RESULTS

1991—Browns, 14-13 (Cle)
Bengals, 23-21 (Cin)
1992—Bengals, 30-10 (Cin)
Browns, 37-21 (Cle)
1993—Browns, 27-14 (Cle)
Browns, 28-17 (Cin)
1994—Browns, 28-20 (Cin)
Browns, 37-13 (Cle)
1995—Browns, 29-26 (Cin) OT
Browns, 26-10 (Cle)
(RS Pts.—Bengals 1,053, Browns 1,052)

CINCINNATI vs. DALLAS

RS: Cowboys lead series, 4-3
1973—Cowboys, 38-10 (D)
1979—Cowboys, 38-13 (D)
1985—Bengals, 50-24 (C)
1988—Bengals, 38-24 (D)
1991—Cowboys, 35-23 (D)
1994—Cowboys, 23-20 (C)
1997—Bengals, 31-24 (C)
(RS Pts.—Cowboys 206, Bengals 185)

CINCINNATI vs. DENVER

RS: Broncos lead series, 13-6
1968—Bengals, 24-10 (C)
Broncos, 10-7 (D)
1969—Broncos, 30-23 (C)
Broncos, 27-16 (D)
1971—Bengals, 24-10 (D)
1972—Bengals, 21-10 (C)
1973—Broncos, 28-10 (D)
1975—Bengals, 17-16 (D)
1976—Bengals, 17-7 (C)
1977—Broncos, 24-13 (C)
1979—Broncos, 10-0 (D)
1981—Bengals, 38-21 (C)
1983—Broncos, 24-17 (D)
1984—Broncos, 20-17 (D)
1986—Broncos, 34-28 (D)
1991—Broncos, 45-14 (D)
1994—Broncos, 15-13 (D)
1996—Broncos, 14-10 (C)
1997—Broncos, 38-20 (D)
(RS Pts.—Broncos 393, Bengals 329)

CINCINNATI vs. DETROIT

RS: Series tied, 3-3
1970—Lions, 38-3 (D)
1974—Lions, 23-19 (C)
1983—Bengals, 17-9 (C)
1986—Bengals, 24-17 (D)
1989—Bengals, 42-7 (C)
1992—Lions, 19-13 (C)
(RS Pts.—Bengals 118, Lions 113)

CINCINNATI vs. GREEN BAY

RS: Series tied, 4-4
1971—Packers, 20-17 (GB)
1976—Bengals, 28-7 (C)
1977—Bengals, 17-7 (Mil)
1980—Packers, 14-9 (GB)
1983—Bengals, 34-14 (C)
1986—Bengals, 34-28 (Mil)
1992—Packers, 24-23 (GB)
1995—Packers, 24-10 (GB)
(RS Pts.—Bengals 172, Packers 138)

CINCINNATI vs. *INDIANAPOLIS

RS: Colts lead series, 9-8
PS: Colts lead series, 1-0
1970—**Colts, 17-0 (B)
1972—Colts, 20-19 (C)
1974—Bengals, 24-14 (B)
1976—Colts, 28-27 (B)
1979—Colts, 38-28 (B)
1980—Bengals, 34-33 (C)
1981—Bengals, 41-19 (B)
1982—Bengals, 20-17 (B)
1983—Colts, 34-31 (C)
1987—Bengals, 23-21 (I)
1989—Colts, 23-12 (C)
1990—Colts, 34-20 (C)
1992—Colts, 21-17 (C)
1993—Colts, 9-6 (C)
1994—Colts, 17-13 (C)
1995—Bengals, 24-21 (I) OT
1996—Bengals, 31-24 (C)
1997—Bengals, 28-13 (I)
(RS Pts.—Colts 398, Bengals 386)
(PS Pts.—Colts 17, Bengals 0)
**Franchise in Baltimore prior to 1984*
***AFC Divisional Playoff*

CINCINNATI vs. JACKSONVILLE

RS: Bengals lead series, 4-2
1995—Bengals, 24-17 (C)
Bengals, 17-13 (J)
1996—Bengals, 28-21 (C)
Jaguars, 30-27 (J)
1997—Jaguars, 21-13 (J)
Bengals, 31-26 (C)
(RS Pts.—Bengals 140, Jaguars 128)

CINCINNATI vs. KANSAS CITY

RS: Chiefs lead series, 11-9
1968—Chiefs, 13-3 (KC)
Chiefs, 16-9 (C)
1969—Bengals, 24-19 (C)
Chiefs, 42-22 (KC)
1970—Chiefs, 27-19 (C)
1972—Bengals, 23-16 (KC)
1973—Bengals, 14-6 (C)
1974—Bengals, 33-6 (C)
1976—Bengals, 27-24 (KC)
1977—Bengals, 27-7 (KC)
1978—Chiefs, 24-23 (C)
1979—Chiefs, 10-7 (C)
1980—Bengals, 20-6 (KC)
1983—Chiefs, 20-15 (KC)
1984—Chiefs, 27-22 (C)
1986—Chiefs, 24-14 (KC)
1987—Bengals, 30-27 (C) OT
1988—Chiefs, 31-28 (KC)
1989—Bengals, 21-17 (KC)
1993—Chiefs, 17-15 (KC)
(RS Pts.—Bengals 396, Chiefs 379)

CINCINNATI vs. MIAMI

RS: Dolphins lead series, 11-3
PS: Dolphins lead series, 1-0
1968—Dolphins, 24-22 (C)
Bengals, 38-21 (M)
1969—Bengals, 27-21 (C)
1971—Dolphins, 23-13 (C)
1973—*Dolphins, 34-16 (M)
1974—Dolphins, 24-3 (M)
1977—Bengals, 23-17 (C)
1978—Dolphins, 21-0 (M)
1980—Dolphins, 17-16 (M)
1983—Dolphins, 38-14 (M)
1987—Dolphins, 20-14 (C)
1989—Dolphins, 20-13 (C)
1991—Dolphins, 37-13 (M)
1994—Dolphins, 23-7 (C)
1995—Dolphins, 26-23 (C)
(RS Pts.—Dolphins 366, Bengals 242)
(PS Pts.—Dolphins 34, Bengals 16)
**AFC Divisional Playoff*

CINCINNATI vs. MINNESOTA

RS: Series tied, 4-4
1973—Bengals, 27-0 (C)
1977—Vikings, 42-10 (M)
1980—Bengals, 14-0 (C)
1983—Vikings, 20-14 (M)
1986—Bengals, 24-20 (C)
1989—Vikings, 29-21 (M)
1992—Vikings, 42-7 (C)
1995—Bengals, 27-24 (C)
(RS Pts.—Vikings 177, Bengals 144)

CINCINNATI vs. *NEW ENGLAND

RS: Patriots lead series, 9-7
1968—Patriots, 33-14 (B)
1969—Patriots, 25-14 (C)
1970—Bengals, 45-7 (C)
1972—Bengals, 31-7 (NE)
1975—Bengals, 27-10 (C)
1978—Patriots, 10-3 (C)
1979—Patriots, 20-14 (C)
1984—Patriots, 20-14 (NE)
1985—Patriots, 34-23 (NE)
1986—Bengals, 31-7 (NE)
1988—Patriots, 27-21 (NE)
1990—Bengals, 41-7 (C)
1991—Bengals, 29-7 (C)
1992—Bengals, 20-10 (C)
1993—Patriots, 7-2 (NE)
1994—Patriots, 31-28 (C)
(RS Pts.—Bengals 357, Patriots 262)
**Franchise in Boston prior to 1971*

CINCINNATI vs. NEW ORLEANS

RS: Saints lead series, 5-4
1970—Bengals, 26-6 (C)
1975—Bengals, 21-0 (NO)
1978—Saints, 20-18 (C)
1981—Saints, 17-7 (NO)
1984—Bengals, 24-21 (NO)
1987—Saints, 41-24 (C)
1990—Saints, 21-7 (C)
1993—Saints, 20-13 (NO)
1996—Bengals, 30-15 (C))
(RS Pts.—Bengals 170, Saints 161)

CINCINNATI vs. N.Y. GIANTS

RS: Bengals lead series, 4-2
1972—Bengals, 13-10 (C)
1977—Bengals, 30-13 (C)
1985—Bengals, 35-30 (C)
1991—Bengals, 27-24 (C)
1994—Giants, 27-20 (NY)
1997—Giants, 29-27 (NY)
(RS Pts.—Bengals 152, Giants 133)

CINCINNATI vs. N.Y. JETS

RS: Jets lead series, 10-6
PS: Jets lead series, 1-0
1968—Jets, 27-14 (NY)
1969—Jets, 21-7 (C)
Jets, 40-7 (NY)
1971—Jets, 35-21 (NY)
1973—Bengals, 20-14 (C)
1976—Bengals, 42-3 (NY)
1981—Bengals, 31-30 (NY)
1982—*Jets, 44-17 (C)
1984—Jets, 43-23 (NY)
1985—Jets, 29-20 (C)
1986—Bengals, 52-21 (C)
1987—Jets, 27-20 (NY)
1988—Bengals, 36-19 (C)
1990—Bengals, 25-20 (C)
1992—Jets, 17-14 (NY)
1993—Jets, 17-12 (NY)
1997—Jets, 31-14 (C)
(RS Pts.—Jets 394, Bengals 358)
(PS Pts.—Jets 44, Bengals 17)
**AFC First-Round Playoff*

CINCINNATI vs. *OAKLAND

RS: Raiders lead series, 15-7
PS: Raiders lead series, 2-0
1968—Raiders, 31-10 (O)
Raiders, 34-0 (C)
1969—Bengals, 31-17 (C)
Raiders, 37-17 (O)
1970—Bengals, 31-21 (C)
1971—Raiders, 31-27 (O)
1972—Raiders, 20-14 (C)
1974—Raiders, 30-27 (O)
1975—Bengals, 14-10 (C)
**Raiders, 31-28 (O)
1976—Raiders, 35-20 (O)
1978—Raiders, 34-21 (C)
1980—Raiders, 28-17 (O)
1982—Bengals, 31-17 (C)
1983—Raiders, 20-10 (C)
1985—Raiders, 13-6 (LA)
1988—Bengals, 45-21 (LA)
1989—Raiders, 28-7 (LA)
1990—Raiders, 24-7 (LA)
**Raiders, 20-10 (LA)
1991—Raiders, 38-14 (C)
1992—Bengals, 24-21 (C) OT
1993—Bengals, 16-10 (C)
1995—Raiders, 20-17 (C)
(RS Pts.—Raiders 540, Bengals 406)
(PS Pts.—Raiders 51, Bengals 38)
**Franchise in Los Angeles from 1982-1994*
***AFC Divisional Playoff*

CINCINNATI vs. PHILADELPHIA

RS: Bengals lead series, 6-2
1971—Bengals, 37-14 (C)
1975—Bengals, 31-0 (P)
1979—Bengals, 37-13 (C)
1982—Bengals, 18-14 (P)
1988—Bengals, 28-24 (P)
1991—Eagles, 17-10 (P)
1994—Bengals, 33-30 (C)
1997—Eagles, 44-42 (P)
(RS Pts.—Bengals 236, Eagles 156)

CINCINNATI vs. PITTSBURGH

RS: Steelers lead series, 32-23
1970—Steelers, 21-10 (P)
Bengals, 34-7 (C)
1971—Steelers, 21-10 (P)
Steelers, 21-13 (C)
1972—Bengals, 15-10 (C)
Steelers, 40-17 (P)
1973—Bengals, 19-7 (C)
Steelers, 20-13 (P)
1974—Bengals, 17-10 (C)
Steelers, 27-3 (P)
1975—Steelers, 30-24 (C)
Steelers, 35-14 (P)
1976—Steelers, 23-6 (P)
Steelers, 7-3 (C)
1977—Steelers, 20-14 (P)
Bengals, 17-10 (C)
1978—Steelers, 28-3 (C)
Steelers, 7-6 (P)
1979—Bengals, 34-10 (C)
Steelers, 37-17 (P)
1980—Bengals, 30-28 (C)
Bengals, 17-16 (P)
1981—Bengals, 34-7 (C)
Bengals, 17-10 (P)
1982—Steelers, 26-20 (P) OT
1983—Steelers, 24-14 (C)
Bengals, 23-10 (P)
1984—Steelers, 38-17 (P)
Bengals, 22-20 (C)
1985—Bengals, 37-24 (P)
Bengals, 26-21 (C)
1986—Bengals, 24-22 (C)
Steelers, 30-9 (P)
1987—Steelers, 23-20 (P)
Steelers, 30-16 (C)
1988—Bengals, 17-12 (P)
Bengals, 42-7 (C)
1989—Bengals, 41-10 (C)
Bengals, 26-16 (P)
1990—Bengals, 27-3 (C)
Bengals, 16-12 (P)
1991—Steelers, 33-27 (C) OT
Steelers, 17-10 (P)
1992—Steelers, 20-0 (P)
Steelers, 21-9 (C)
1993—Steelers, 34-7 (P)
Steelers, 24-16 (C)
1994—Steelers, 14-10 (P)
Steelers, 38-15 (C)
1995—Bengals, 27-9 (P)
Steelers, 49-31 (C)
1996—Steelers, 20-10 (P)
Bengals, 34-24 (C)
1997—Steelers, 26-10 (C)
Steelers, 20-3 (P)
(RS Pts.—Steelers 1,129, Bengals 993)

CINCINNATI vs. *ST. LOUIS

RS: Bengals lead series, 5-3
1972—Rams, 15-12 (LA)
1976—Bengals, 20-12 (C)
1978—Bengals, 20-19 (LA)
1981—Bengals, 24-10 (C)
1984—Rams, 24-14 (C)
1990—Bengals, 34-31 (LA) OT
1993—Bengals, 15-3 (C)
1996—Rams, 26-16 (StL)
(RS Pts.—Bengals 155, Rams 140)
**Franchise in Los Angeles prior to 1995*

CINCINNATI vs. SAN DIEGO

RS: Chargers lead series, 14-9
PS: Bengals lead series, 1-0

1968—Chargers, 29-13 (SD)
Chargers, 31-10 (C)
1969—Bengals, 34-20 (C)
Chargers, 21-14 (SD)
1970—Bengals, 17-14 (SD)
1971—Bengals, 31-0 (C)
1973—Bengals, 20-13 (SD)
1974—Chargers, 20-17 (C)
1975—Bengals, 47-17 (C)
1977—Chargers, 24-3 (SD)
1978—Chargers, 22-13 (SD)
1979—Chargers, 26-24 (C)
1980—Chargers, 31-14 (C)
1981—Bengals, 40-17 (SD)
*Bengals, 27-7 (C)
1982—Chargers, 50-34 (SD)
1985—Chargers, 44-41 (C)
1987—Chargers, 10-9 (C)
1988—Bengals, 27-10 (C)
1990—Bengals, 21-16 (SD)
1992—Chargers, 27-10 (SD)
1994—Chargers, 27-10 (SD)
1996—Chargers, 27-14 (SD)
1997—Bengals, 38-31 (C)
(RS Pts.—Chargers 527, Bengals 501)
(PS Pts.—Bengals 27, Chargers 7)
*AFC Championship

CINCINNATI vs. SAN FRANCISCO
RS: 49ers lead series, 7-1
PS: 49ers lead series, 2-0
1974—Bengals, 21-3 (SF)
1978—49ers, 28-12 (SF)
1981—49ers, 21-3 (C)
*49ers, 26-21 (Detroit)
1984—49ers, 23-17 (SF)
1987—49ers, 27-26 (C)
1988—**49ers, 20-16 (Miami)
1990—49ers, 20-17 (C) OT
1993—49ers, 21-8 (SF)
1996—49ers, 28-21 (SF)
(RS Pts.—49ers 171, Bengals 125)
(PS Pts.—49ers 46, Bengals 37)
*Super Bowl XVI
**Super Bowl XXIII

CINCINNATI vs. SEATTLE
RS: Series tied, 7-7
PS: Bengals lead series, 1-0
1977—Bengals, 42-20 (C)
1981—Bengals, 27-21 (C)
1982—Bengals, 24-10 (C)
1984—Seahawks, 26-6 (C)
1985—Seahawks, 28-24 (C)
1986—Bengals, 34-7 (C)
1987—Bengals, 17-10 (S)
1988—*Bengals, 21-13 (C)
1989—Seahawks, 24-17 (C)
1990—Seahawks, 31-16 (S)
1991—Seahawks, 13-7 (C)
1992—Bengals, 21-3 (S)
1993—Seahawks, 19-10 (C)
1994—Bengals, 20-17 (S) OT
1995—Seahawks, 24-21 (S)
(RS Pts.—Bengals 286, Seahawks 253)
(PS Pts.—Bengals 21, Seahawks 13)
*AFC Divisional Playoff

CINCINNATI vs. TAMPA BAY
RS: Bengals lead series, 3-2
1976—Bengals, 21-0 (C)
1980—Buccaneers, 17-12 (C)
1983—Bengals, 23-17 (TB)
1989—Bengals, 56-23 (C)
1995—Buccaneers, 19-16 (TB)
(RS Pts.—Bengals 128, Buccaneers 76)

CINCINNATI vs. *TENNESSEE
RS: Oilers lead series, 29-28-1
PS: Bengals lead series, 1-0
1968—Oilers, 27-17 (C)
1969—Tie, 31-31 (H)
1970—Oilers, 20-13 (C)
Bengals, 30-20 (H)
1971—Oilers, 10-6 (H)
Bengals, 28-13 (C)
1972—Bengals, 30-7 (C)
Bengals, 61-17 (H)
1973—Bengals, 24-10 (C)
Bengals, 27-24 (H)
1974—Oilers, 34-21 (C)
Oilers, 20-3 (H)
1975—Bengals, 21-19 (H)
Bengals, 23-19 (C)
1976—Bengals, 27-7 (H)
Bengals, 31-27 (C)
1977—Bengals, 13-10 (C) OT
Oilers, 21-16 (H)
1978—Bengals, 28-13 (C)
Oilers, 17-10 (H)
1979—Oilers, 30-27 (C) OT
Oilers, 42-21 (H)
1980—Oilers, 13-10 (C)
Oilers, 23-3 (H)
1981—Oilers, 17-10 (H)
Bengals, 34-21 (C)
1982—Bengals, 27-6 (C)
Bengals, 35-27 (H)
1983—Bengals, 55-14 (H)
Bengals, 38-10 (C)
1984—Bengals, 13-3 (C)
Bengals, 31-13 (H)
1985—Oilers, 44-27 (H)
Bengals, 45-27 (C)
1986—Bengals, 31-28 (C)
Oilers, 32-28 (H)
1987—Oilers, 31-29 (C)
Oilers, 21-17 (H)
1988—Bengals, 44-21 (C)
Oilers, 41-6 (H)
1989—Oilers, 26-24 (H)
Bengals, 61-7 (C)
1990—Oilers, 48-17 (H)
Bengals, 40-20 (C)
**Bengals, 41-14 (C)
1991—Oilers, 30-7 (C)
Oilers, 35-3 (H)
1992—Oilers, 38-24 (C)
Oilers, 26-10 (H)
1993—Oilers, 28-12 (H)
Oilers, 38-3 (C)
1994—Oilers, 20-13 (H)
Bengals, 34-31 (C)
1995—Oilers, 38-28 (C)
Bengals, 32-25 (H)
1996—Oilers, 30-27 (C) OT
Bengals, 21-13 (H)
1997—Oilers, 30-7 (T)
Bengals, 41-14 (C)
(RS Pts.—Bengals 1,395, Oilers 1,327)
(PS Pts.—Bengals 41, Oilers 14)
*Franchise in Houston prior to 1997
**AFC First-Round Playoff

CINCINNATI vs. WASHINGTON
RS: Redskins lead series, 4-2
1970—Redskins, 20-0 (W)
1974—Bengals, 28-17 (C)
1979—Redskins, 28-14 (W)
1985—Redskins, 27-24 (W)
1988—Bengals, 20-17 (C) OT
1991—Redskins, 34-27 (C)
(RS Pts.—Redskins 143, Bengals 113)

CLEVELAND vs. ARIZONA
RS: Browns lead series, 32-10-3;
See Arizona vs. Cleveland

CLEVELAND vs. ATLANTA
RS: Browns lead series, 8-2;
See Atlanta vs. Cleveland

CLEVELAND vs. BUFFALO
RS: Browns lead series, 7-4
PS: Browns lead series, 1-0;
See Buffalo vs. Cleveland

CLEVELAND vs. CHICAGO
RS: Browns lead series, 8-3;
See Chicago vs. Cleveland

CLEVELAND vs. CINCINNATI
RS: Browns lead series, 27-24;
See Cincinnati vs. Cleveland

CLEVELAND vs. DALLAS
RS: Browns lead series, 15-9
PS: Browns lead series, 2-1
1960—Browns, 48-7 (D)
1961—Browns, 25-7 (C)
Browns, 38-17 (D)
1962—Browns, 19-10 (C)
Cowboys, 45-21 (D)
1963—Browns, 41-24 (D)
Browns, 27-17 (C)
1964—Browns, 27-6 (C)
Browns, 20-16 (D)
1965—Browns, 23-17 (C)
Browns, 24-17 (D)
1966—Browns, 30-21 (C)
Cowboys, 26-14 (D)
1967—Cowboys, 21-14 (C)
*Cowboys, 52-14 (D)
1968—Cowboys, 28-7 (C)
*Browns, 31-20 (C)
1969—Browns, 42-10 (C)
*Browns, 38-14 (D)
1970—Cowboys, 6-2 (C)
1974—Cowboys, 41-17 (D)
1979—Browns, 26-7 (C)
1982—Cowboys, 31-14 (D)
1985—Cowboys, 20-7 (D)
1988—Browns, 24-21 (C)
1991—Cowboys, 26-14 (C)
1994—Browns, 19-14 (D)
(RS Pts.—Browns 543, Cowboys 455)
(PS Pts.—Cowboys 86, Browns 83)
*Conference Championship

CLEVELAND vs. DENVER
RS: Broncos lead series, 13-5
PS: Broncos lead series, 3-0
1970—Browns, 27-13 (D)
1971—Broncos, 27-0 (C)
1972—Browns, 27-20 (D)
1974—Browns, 23-21 (C)
1975—Broncos, 16-15 (D)
1976—Broncos, 44-13 (D)
1978—Broncos, 19-7 (C)
1980—Broncos, 19-16 (C)
1981—Broncos, 23-20 (D) OT
1983—Broncos, 27-6 (D)
1984—Broncos, 24-14 (C)
1986—*Broncos, 23-20 (C) OT
1987—*Broncos, 38-33 (D)
1988—Broncos, 30-7 (D)
1989—Browns, 16-13 (C)
*Broncos, 37-21 (D)
1990—Browns, 30-29 (D)
1991—Broncos, 17-7 (C)
1992—Broncos, 12-0 (C)
1993—Broncos, 29-14 (C)
1994—Broncos, 26-14 (D)
(RS Pts.—Broncos 409, Browns 256)
(PS Pts.—Broncos 98, Browns 74)
*AFC Championship

CLEVELAND vs. DETROIT
RS: Lions lead series, 12-3
PS: Lions lead series, 3-1
1952—Lions, 17-6 (D)
*Lions, 17-7 (C)
1953—*Lions, 17-16 (D)
1954—Lions, 14-10 (C)
*Browns, 56-10 (C)
1957—Lions, 20-7 (D)
*Lions, 59-14 (D)
1958—Lions, 30-10 (C)
1963—Lions, 38-10 (D)
1964—Browns, 37-21 (C)
1967—Lions, 31-14 (D)
1969—Lions, 28-21 (C)
1970—Lions, 41-24 (C)
1975—Lions, 21-10 (D)
1983—Browns, 31-26 (D)
1986—Browns, 24-21 (C)
1989—Lions, 13-10 (D)
1992—Lions, 24-14 (D)
1995—Lions, 38-20 (D)
(RS Pts.—Lions 383, Browns 248)
(PS Pts.—Lions 103, Browns 93)
*NFL Championship

CLEVELAND vs. GREEN BAY
RS: Packers lead series, 8-6
PS: Packers lead series, 1-0
1953—Browns, 27-0 (Mil)
1955—Browns, 41-10 (C)
1956—Browns, 24-7 (Mil)
1961—Packers, 49-17 (C)
1964—Packers, 28-21 (Mil)
1965—*Packers, 23-12 (GB)
1966—Packers, 21-20 (C)
1967—Packers, 55-7 (Mil)
1969—Browns, 20-7 (C)
1972—Packers, 26-10 (C)
1980—Browns, 26-21 (C)
1983—Packers, 35-21 (Mil)
1986—Packers, 17-14 (C)
1992—Browns, 17-6 (C)
1995—Packers, 31-20 (C)
(RS Pts.—Packers 313, Browns 285)
(PS Pts.—Packers 23, Browns 12)
*NFL Championship

CLEVELAND vs. *INDIANAPOLIS
RS: Browns lead series, 13-7
PS: Series tied, 2-2
1956—Colts, 21-7 (C)
1959—Browns, 38-31 (B)
1962—Colts, 36-14 (C)
1964—**Browns, 27-0 (C)
1968—Browns, 30-20 (B)
**Colts, 34-0 (C)
1971—Browns, 14-13 (B)
***Colts, 20-3 (C)
1973—Browns, 24-14 (C)
1975—Colts, 21-7 (B)
1978—Browns, 45-24 (B)
1979—Browns, 13-10 (C)
1980—Browns, 28-27 (B)
1981—Browns, 42-28 (C)
1983—Browns, 41-23 (C)
1986—Browns, 24-9 (I)
1987—Colts, 9-7 (C)
***Browns, 38-21 (C)
1988—Browns, 23-17 (C)
1989—Colts, 23-17 (I) OT
1991—Browns, 31-0 (I)
1992—Colts, 14-3 (I)
1993—Colts, 23-10 (I)
1994—Browns, 21-14 (I)
(RS Pts.—Browns 439, Colts 377)
(PS Pts.—Colts 75, Browns 68)
*Franchise in Baltimore prior to 1984
**NFL Championship
***AFC Divisional Playoff

CLEVELAND vs. JACKSONVILLE
RS: Jaguars lead series, 2-0
1995—Jaguars, 23-15 (C)
Jaguars, 24-21 (J)
(RS Pts.—Jaguars 47, Browns 36)

CLEVELAND vs. KANSAS CITY
RS: Browns lead series, 8-7-2
1971—Chiefs, 13-7 (KC)
1972—Chiefs, 31-7 (C)
1973—Tie, 20-20 (KC)
1975—Browns, 40-14 (C)
1976—Chiefs, 39-14 (KC)
1977—Browns, 44-7 (C)
1978—Chiefs, 17-3 (KC)
1979—Browns, 27-24 (KC)
1980—Browns, 20-13 (C)
1984—Chiefs, 10-6 (KC)
1986—Browns, 20-7 (C)
1988—Browns, 6-3 (KC)
1989—Tie, 10-10 (C) OT
1990—Chiefs, 34-0 (KC)
1991—Browns, 20-15 (C)
1994—Chiefs, 20-13 (KC)
1995—Browns, 35-17 (C)
(RS Pts.—Chiefs 294, Browns 292)

CLEVELAND vs. MIAMI
RS: Dolphins lead series, 6-4
PS: Dolphins lead series, 2-0
1970—Browns, 28-0 (M)

ALL-TIME TEAM VS. TEAM RESULTS

1972—*Dolphins, 20-14 (M)
1973—Dolphins, 17-9 (C)
1976—Browns, 17-13 (C)
1979—Browns, 30-24 (C) OT
1985—*Dolphins, 24-21 (M)
1986—Browns, 26-16 (C)
1988—Dolphins, 38-31 (M)
1989—Dolphins, 13-10 (M) OT
1990—Dolphins, 30-13 (C)
1992—Dolphins, 27-23 (C)
1993—Dolphins, 24-14 (C)
(RS Pts.—Dolphins 202, Browns 201)
(PS Pts.—Dolphins 44, Browns 35)
AFC Divisional Playoff

CLEVELAND vs. MINNESOTA
RS: Vikings lead series, 8-3
PS: Vikings lead series, 1-0
1965—Vikings, 27-17 (C)
1967—Browns, 14-10 (C)
1969—Vikings, 51-3 (M)
*Vikings, 27-7 (M)
1973—Vikings, 26-3 (M)
1975—Vikings, 42-10 (C)
1980—Vikings, 28-23 (M)
1983—Vikings, 27-21 (C)
1986—Browns, 23-20 (M)
1989—Browns, 23-17 (C) OT
1992—Vikings, 17-13 (M)
1995—Vikings, 27-11 (M)
(RS Pts.—Vikings 292, Browns 161)
(PS Pts.—Vikings 27, Browns 7)
NFL Championship

CLEVELAND vs. NEW ENGLAND
RS: Browns lead series, 10-4
PS: Browns lead series, 1-0
1971—Browns, 27-7 (C)
1974—Browns, 21-14 (NE)
1977—Browns, 30-27 (C) OT
1980—Patriots, 34-17 (NE)
1982—Browns, 10-7 (C)
1983—Browns, 30-0 (NE)
1984—Patriots, 17-16 (C)
1985—Browns, 24-20 (C)
1987—Browns, 20-10 (NE)
1991—Browns, 20-0 (NE)
1992—Browns, 19-17 (NE)
1993—Patriots, 20-17 (C)
1994—Browns, 13-6 (C)
*Browns, 20-13 (C)
1995—Patriots, 17-14 (NE)
(RS Pts.—Browns 278, Patriots 196)
(PS Pts.—Browns 20, Patriots 13)
AFC First-Round Playoff

CLEVELAND vs. NEW ORLEANS
RS: Browns lead series, 9-3
1967—Browns, 42-7 (NO)
1968—Browns, 24-10 (NO)
Browns, 35-17 (C)
1969—Browns, 27-17 (NO)
1971—Browns, 21-17 (NO)
1975—Browns, 17-16 (C)
1978—Browns, 24-16 (NO)
1981—Browns, 20-17 (C)
1984—Saints, 16-14 (C)
1987—Saints, 28-21 (NO)
1990—Saints, 25-20 (NO)
1993—Browns, 17-13 (C)
(RS Pts.—Browns 282, Saints 199)

CLEVELAND vs. N.Y. GIANTS
RS: Browns lead series, 25-17-2
PS: Series tied, 1-1
1950—Giants, 6-0 (C)
Giants, 17-13 (NY)
*Browns, 8-3 (C)
1951—Browns, 14-13 (C)
Browns, 10-0 (NY)
1952—Giants, 17-9 (C)
Giants, 37-34 (NY)
1953—Browns, 7-0 (NY)
Browns, 62-14 (C)
1954—Browns, 24-14 (C)
Browns, 16-7 (NY)
1955—Browns, 24-14 (C)
Tie, 35-35 (NY)
1956—Giants, 21-9 (C)
Browns, 24-7 (NY)
1957—Browns, 6-3 (C)
Browns, 34-28 (NY)
1958—Giants, 21-17 (C)
Giants, 13-10 (NY)
*Giants, 10-0 (NY)
1959—Giants, 10-6 (C)
Giants, 48-7 (NY)
1960—Giants, 17-13 (C)
Browns, 48-34 (NY)
1961—Giants, 37-21 (C)
Tie, 7-7 (NY)
1962—Browns, 17-7 (C)
Giants, 17-13 (NY)
1963—Browns, 35-24 (NY)
Giants, 33-6 (C)
1964—Browns, 42-20 (C)
Browns, 52-20 (NY)
1965—Browns, 38-14 (NY)
Browns, 34-21 (C)
1966—Browns, 28-7 (NY)
Browns, 49-40 (C)
1967—Giants, 38-34 (NY)
Browns, 24-14 (C)
1968—Browns, 45-10 (C)
1969—Browns, 28-17 (C)
Giants, 27-14 (NY)
1973—Browns, 12-10 (C)
1977—Browns, 21-7 (NY)
1985—Browns, 35-33 (NY)
1991—Giants, 13-10 (NY)
1994—Giants, 16-13 (C)
(RS Pts.—Browns 1,000, Giants 808)
(PS Pts.—Giants 13, Browns 8)
Conference Playoff

CLEVELAND vs. N.Y. JETS
RS: Browns lead series, 9-6
PS: Browns lead series, 1-0
1970—Browns, 31-21 (C)
1972—Browns, 26-10 (NY)
1976—Browns, 38-17 (C)
1978—Browns, 37-34 (C) OT
1979—Browns, 25-22 (NY) OT
1980—Browns, 17-14 (C)
1981—Jets, 14-13 (C)
1983—Browns, 10-7 (C)
1984—Jets, 24-20 (C)
1985—Jets, 37-10 (NY)
1986—*Browns, 23-20 (C) OT
1988—Jets, 23-3 (C)
1989—Browns, 38-24 (C)
1990—Jets, 24-21 (NY)
1991—Jets, 17-14 (C)
1994—Browns, 27-7 (C)
(RS Pts.—Browns 330, Jets 295)
(PS Pts.—Browns 23, Jets 20)
AFC Divisional Playoff

CLEVELAND vs. *OAKLAND
RS: Raiders lead series, 8-4
PS: Raiders lead series, 2-0
1970—Raiders, 23-20 (O)
1971—Raiders, 34-20 (C)
1973—Browns, 7-3 (O)
1974—Raiders, 40-24 (C)
1975—Raiders, 38-17 (O)
1977—Raiders, 26-10 (C)
1979—Raiders, 19-14 (O)
1980—**Raiders, 14-12 (C)
1982—***Raiders, 27-10 (LA)
1985—Raiders, 21-20 (C)
1986—Raiders, 27-14 (LA)
1987—Browns, 24-17 (LA)
1992—Browns, 28-16 (LA)
1993—Browns, 19-16 (LA)
(RS Pts.—Raiders 280, Browns 217)
(PS Pts.—Raiders 41, Browns 22)
*Franchise in Los Angeles from 1982-1994
**AFC Divisional Playoff
***AFC First-Round Playoff

CLEVELAND vs. PHILADELPHIA
RS: Browns lead series, 31-12-1
1950—Browns, 35-10 (P)
Browns, 13-7 (C)
1951—Browns, 20-17 (C)
Browns, 24-9 (P)
1952—Browns, 49-7 (P)
Eagles, 28-20 (C)
1953—Browns, 37-13 (C)
Eagles, 42-27 (P)
1954—Eagles, 28-10 (P)
Browns, 6-0 (C)
1955—Browns, 21-17 (C)
Eagles, 33-17 (P)
1956—Browns, 16-0 (P)
Browns, 17-14 (C)
1957—Browns, 24-7 (C)
Eagles, 17-7 (P)
1958—Browns, 28-14 (C)
Browns, 21-14 (P)
1959—Browns, 28-7 (C)
Browns, 28-21 (P)
1960—Browns, 41-24 (P)
Eagles, 31-29 (C)
1961—Eagles, 27-20 (P)
Browns, 45-24 (C)
1962—Eagles, 35-7 (P)
Tie, 14-14 (C)
1963—Browns, 37-7 (C)
Browns, 23-17 (P)
1964—Browns, 28-20 (P)
Browns, 38-24 (C)
1965—Browns, 35-17 (P)
Browns, 38-34 (C)
1966—Browns, 27-7 (C)
Eagles, 33-21 (P)
1967—Eagles, 28-24 (P)
1968—Browns, 47-13 (C)
1969—Browns, 27-20 (P)
1972—Browns, 27-17 (P)
1976—Browns, 24-3 (C)
1979—Browns, 24-19 (P)
1982—Eagles, 24-21 (C)
1988—Browns, 19-3 (C)
1991—Eagles, 32-30 (C)
1994—Browns, 26-7 (P)
(RS Pts.—Browns 1,120, Eagles 785)

CLEVELAND vs. PITTSBURGH
RS: Browns lead series, 52-40
PS: Steelers lead series, 1-0
1950—Browns, 30-17 (P)
Browns, 45-7 (C)
1951—Browns, 17-0 (C)
Browns, 28-0 (P)
1952—Browns, 21-20 (P)
Browns, 29-28 (C)
1953—Browns, 34-16 (C)
Browns, 20-16 (P)
1954—Steelers, 55-27 (P)
Browns, 42-7 (C)
1955—Browns, 41-14 (C)
Browns, 30-7 (P)
1956—Browns, 14-10 (P)
Steelers, 24-16 (C)
1957—Browns, 23-12 (P)
Browns, 24-0 (C)
1958—Browns, 45-12 (P)
Browns, 27-10 (C)
1959—Steelers, 17-7 (P)
Steelers, 21-20 (C)
1960—Browns, 28-20 (C)
Steelers, 14-10 (P)
1961—Browns, 30-28 (P)
Steelers, 17-13 (C)
1962—Browns, 41-14 (P)
Browns, 35-14 (C)
1963—Browns, 35-23 (C)
Steelers, 9-7 (P)
1964—Steelers, 23-7 (C)
Browns, 30-17 (P)
1965—Browns, 24-19 (C)
Browns, 42-21 (P)
1966—Browns, 41-10 (C)
Steelers, 16-6 (P)
1967—Browns, 21-10 (C)
Browns, 34-14 (P)
1968—Browns, 31-24 (C)
Browns, 45-24 (P)
1969—Browns, 42-31 (C)
Browns, 24-3 (P)
1970—Browns, 15-7 (C)
Steelers, 28-9 (P)
1971—Browns, 27-17 (C)
Steelers, 26-9 (P)
1972—Browns, 26-24 (C)
Steelers, 30-0 (P)
1973—Steelers, 33-6 (P)
Browns, 21-16 (C)
1974—Steelers, 20-16 (P)
Steelers, 26-16 (C)
1975—Steelers, 42-6 (C)
Steelers, 31-17 (P)
1976—Steelers, 31-14 (P)
Browns, 18-16 (C)
1977—Steelers, 28-14 (C)
Steelers, 35-31 (P)
1978—Steelers, 15-9 (P) OT
Steelers, 34-14 (C)
1979—Steelers, 51-35 (C)
Steelers, 33-30 (P) OT
1980—Browns, 27-26 (C)
Steelers, 16-13 (P)
1981—Steelers, 13-7 (P)
Steelers, 32-10 (C)
1982—Browns, 10-9 (C)
Steelers, 37-21 (P)
1983—Steelers, 44-17 (P)
Browns, 30-17 (C)
1984—Browns, 20-10 (C)
Steelers, 23-20 (P)
1985—Browns, 17-7 (C)
Steelers, 10-9 (P)
1986—Browns, 27-24 (P)
Browns, 37-31 (C) OT
1987—Browns, 34-10 (C)
Browns, 19-13 (P)
1988—Browns, 23-9 (P)
Browns, 27-7 (C)
1989—Browns, 51-0 (P)
Steelers, 17-7 (C)
1990—Browns, 13-3 (C)
Steelers, 35-0 (P)
1991—Browns, 17-14 (C)
Steelers, 17-10 (P)
1992—Browns, 17-9 (C)
Steelers, 23-13 (P)
1993—Browns, 28-23 (C)
Steelers, 16-9 (P)
1994—Steelers, 17-10 (C)
Steelers, 17-7 (P)
*Steelers, 29-9 (P)
1995—Steelers, 20-3 (P)
Steelers, 20-17 (C)
(RS Pts.—Browns 1,989, Steelers 1,756)
(PS Pts.—Steelers 29, Browns 9)
AFC Divisional Playoff

CLEVELAND vs. *ST. LOUIS
RS: Browns lead series, 8-7
PS: Browns lead series, 2-1
1950—**Browns, 30-28 (C)
1951—Browns, 38-23 (LA)
**Rams, 24-17 (LA)
1952—Browns, 37-7 (C)
1955—**Browns, 38-14 (LA)
1957—Browns, 45-31 (C)
1958—Browns, 30-27 (LA)
1963—Browns, 20-6 (C)
1965—Rams, 42-7 (LA)
1968—Rams, 24-6 (C)
1973—Rams, 30-17 (LA)
1977—Rams, 9-0 (C)
1978—Browns, 30-19 (C)
1981—Rams, 27-16 (LA)
1984—Rams, 20-17 (LA)
1987—Browns, 30-17 (C)
1990—Rams, 38-23 (C)
1993—Browns, 42-14 (LA)

(RS Pts.—Browns 358, Rams 334)
(PS Pts.—Browns 85, Rams 66)
Franchise in Los Angeles prior to 1995
***NFL Championship*

CLEVELAND vs. SAN DIEGO
RS: Chargers lead series, 9-6-1
1970—Chargers, 27-10 (C)
1972—Browns, 21-17 (SD)
1973—Tie, 16-16 (C)
1974—Chargers, 36-35 (SD)
1976—Browns, 21-17 (C)
1977—Chargers, 37-14 (SD)
1981—Chargers, 44-14 (C)
1982—Chargers, 30-13 (C)
1983—Browns, 30-24 (SD) OT
1985—Browns, 21-7 (SD)
1986—Browns, 47-17 (C)
1987—Chargers, 27-24 (SD) OT
1990—Chargers, 24-14 (C)
1991—Browns, 30-24 (SD) OT
1992—Chargers, 14-13 (C)
1995—Chargers, 31-13 (SD)
(RS Pts.—Chargers 392, Browns 336)

CLEVELAND vs. SAN FRANCISCO
RS: Browns lead series, 9-6
1950—Browns, 34-14 (C)
1951—49ers, 24-10 (SF)
1953—Browns, 23-21 (C)
1955—Browns, 38-3 (SF)
1959—49ers, 21-20 (C)
1962—Browns, 13-10 (SF)
1968—Browns, 33-21 (SF)
1970—49ers, 34-31 (SF)
1974—Browns, 7-0 (C)
1978—Browns, 24-7 (C)
1981—Browns, 15-12 (SF)
1984—49ers, 41-7 (C)
1987—49ers, 38-24 (SF)
1990—49ers, 20-17 (SF)
1993—Browns, 23-13 (C)
(RS Pts.—Browns 319, 49ers 279)

CLEVELAND vs. SEATTLE
RS: Seahawks lead series, 9-4
1977—Seahawks, 20-19 (S)
1978—Seahawks, 47-24 (S)
1979—Seahawks, 29-24 (C)
1980—Browns, 27-3 (S)
1981—Seahawks, 42-21 (S)
1982—Browns, 21-7 (S)
1983—Seahawks, 24-9 (C)
1984—Seahawks, 33-0 (S)
1985—Seahawks, 31-13 (S)
1988—Seahawks, 16-10 (C)
1989—Browns, 17-7 (S)
1993—Seahawks, 22-5 (S)
1994—Browns, 35-9 (C)
(RS Pts.—Seahawks 290, Browns 225)

CLEVELAND vs. TAMPA BAY
RS: Browns lead series, 5-0
1976—Browns, 24-7 (TB)
1980—Browns, 34-27 (TB)
1983—Browns, 20-0 (C)
1989—Browns, 42-31 (TB)
1995—Browns, 22-6 (C)
(RS Pts.—Browns 142, Buccaneers 71)

CLEVELAND vs. *TENNESSEE
RS: Browns lead series, 30-21
PS: Oilers lead series, 1-0
1970—Browns, 28-14 (C)
Browns, 21-10 (H)
1971—Browns, 31-0 (C)
Browns, 37-24 (H)
1972—Browns, 23-17 (H)
Browns, 20-0 (C)
1973—Browns, 42-13 (C)
Browns, 23-13 (H)
1974—Browns, 20-7 (C)
Oilers, 28-24 (H)
1975—Oilers, 40-10 (C)
Oilers, 21-10 (H)
1976—Browns, 21-7 (H)
Browns, 13-10 (C)
1977—Browns, 24-23 (H)
Oilers, 19-15 (C)
1978—Oilers, 16-13 (C)
Oilers, 14-10 (H)
1979—Oilers, 31-10 (H)
Browns, 14-7 (C)
1980—Oilers, 16-7 (C)
Browns, 17-14 (H)
1981—Oilers, 9-3 (C)
Oilers, 17-13 (H)
1982—Browns, 20-14 (H)
1983—Browns, 25-19 (C) OT
Oilers, 34-27 (H)
1984—Browns, 27-10 (C)
Browns, 27-20 (H)
1985—Browns, 21-6 (H)
Browns, 28-21 (C)
1986—Browns, 23-20 (H)
Browns, 13-10 (C) OT
1987—Oilers, 15-10 (C)
Browns, 40-7 (H)
1988—Oilers, 24-17 (H)
Browns, 28-23 (C)
**Oilers, 24-23 (C)
1989—Browns, 28-17 (C)
Browns, 24-20 (H)
1990—Oilers, 35-23 (C)
Oilers, 58-14 (H)
1991—Oilers, 28-24 (H)
Oilers, 17-14 (C)
1992—Browns, 24-14 (H)
Oilers, 17-14 (C)
1993—Oilers, 27-20 (C)
Oilers, 19-17 (H)
1994—Browns, 11-8 (H)
Browns, 34-10 (C)
1995—Browns, 14-7 (H)
Oilers, 37-10 (C)
(RS Pts.—Browns 1,026, Oilers 907)
(PS Pts.—Oilers 24, Browns 23)
Franchise in Houston prior to 1997
***AFC First-Round Playoff*

CLEVELAND vs. WASHINGTON
RS: Browns lead series, 32-9-1
1950—Browns, 20-14 (C)
Browns, 45-21 (W)
1951—Browns, 45-0 (C)
1952—Browns, 19-15 (C)
Browns, 48-24 (W)
1953—Browns, 30-14 (W)
Browns, 27-3 (C)
1954—Browns, 62-3 (C)
Browns, 34-14 (W)
1955—Redskins, 27-17 (C)
Browns, 24-14 (W)
1956—Redskins, 20-9 (W)
Redskins, 20-17 (C)
1957—Browns, 21-17 (C)
Tie, 30-30 (W)
1958—Browns, 20-10 (W)
Browns, 21-14 (C)
1959—Browns, 34-7 (C)
Browns, 31-17 (W)
1960—Browns, 31-10 (W)
Browns, 27-16 (C)
1961—Browns, 31-7 (C)
Browns, 17-6 (W)
1962—Redskins, 17-16 (C)
Redskins, 17-9 (W)
1963—Browns, 37-14 (C)
Browns, 27-20 (W)
1964—Browns, 27-13 (W)
Browns, 34-24 (C)
1965—Browns, 17-7 (W)
Browns, 24-16 (C)
1966—Browns, 38-14 (W)
Browns, 14-3 (C)
1967—Browns, 42-37 (C)
1968—Browns, 24-21 (W)
1969—Browns, 27-23 (C)
1971—Browns, 20-13 (W)
1975—Redskins, 23-7 (C)
1979—Redskins, 13-9 (C)
1985—Redskins, 14-7 (C)
1988—Browns, 17-13 (W)
1991—Redskins, 42-17 (W)
(RS Pts.—Browns 1,073, Redskins 667)

DALLAS vs. ARIZONA
RS: Cowboys lead series, 47-23-1;
See Arizona vs. Dallas

DALLAS vs. ATLANTA
RS: Cowboys lead series, 11-6
PS: Cowboys lead series, 2-0;
See Atlanta vs. Dallas

DALLAS vs. BUFFALO
RS: Series tied, 3-3
PS: Cowboys lead series, 2-0;
See Buffalo vs. Dallas

DALLAS vs. CAROLINA
RS: Panthers lead series, 1-0
PS: Panthers lead series, 1-0;
See Carolina vs. Dallas

DALLAS vs. CHICAGO
RS: Cowboys lead series, 9-7
PS: Cowboys lead series, 2-0;
See Chicago vs. Dallas

DALLAS vs. CINCINNATI
RS: Cowboys lead series, 4-3;
See Cincinnati vs. Dallas

DALLAS vs. CLEVELAND
RS: Browns lead series, 15-9
PS: Browns lead series, 2-1;
See Cleveland vs. Dallas

DALLAS vs. DENVER
RS: Cowboys lead series, 4-2
PS: Cowboys lead series, 1-0
1973—Cowboys, 22-10 (Den)
1977—Cowboys, 14-6 (Dal)
*Cowboys, 27-10 (New Orleans)
1980—Broncos, 41-20 (Den)
1986—Broncos, 29-14 (Den)
1992—Cowboys, 31-27 (Den)
1995—Cowboys, 31-21 (Dal)
(RS Pts.—Broncos 134, Cowboys 132)
(PS Pts.—Cowboys 27, Broncos 10)
**Super Bowl XII*

DALLAS vs. DETROIT
RS: Cowboys lead series, 7-6
PS: Series tied, 1-1
1960—Lions, 23-14 (Det)
1963—Cowboys, 17-14 (Dal)
1968—Cowboys, 59-13 (Dal)
1970—*Cowboys, 5-0 (Dal)
1972—Cowboys, 28-24 (Dal)
1975—Cowboys, 36-10 (Det)
1977—Cowboys, 37-0 (Dal)
1981—Lions, 27-24 (Det)
1985—Lions, 26-21 (Det)
1986—Cowboys, 31-7 (Det)
1987—Lions, 27-17 (Det)
1991—Lions, 34-10 (Det)
*Lions, 38-6 (Det)
1992—Cowboys, 37-3 (Det)
1994—Lions, 20-17 (Dal) OT
(RS Pts.—Cowboys 348, Lions 228)
(PS Pts.—Lions 38, Cowboys 11)
**NFC Divisional Playoff*

DALLAS vs. GREEN BAY
RS: Series tied, 9-9
PS: Cowboys lead series, 4-2
1960—Packers, 41-7 (GB)
1964—Packers, 45-21 (D)
1965—Packers, 13-3 (Mil)
1966—*Packers, 34-27 (D)
1967—*Packers, 21-17 (GB)
1968—Packers, 28-17 (D)
1970—Cowboys, 16-3 (D)
1972—Packers, 16-13 (Mil)
1975—Packers, 19-17 (D)
1978—Cowboys, 42-14 (Mil)
1980—Cowboys, 28-7 (Mil)
1982—**Cowboys, 37-26 (D)
1984—Cowboys, 20-6 (D)
1989—Packers, 31-13 (GB)
Packers, 20-10 (D)
1991—Cowboys, 20-17 (Mil)
1993—Cowboys, 36-14 (D)
***Cowboys, 27-17 (D)
1994—Cowboys, 42-31 (D)
***Cowboys, 35-9 (D)
1995—Cowboys, 34-24 (D)
****Cowboys, 38-27 (D)
1996—Cowboys, 21-6 (D)
1997—Packers, 45-17 (GB)
(RS Pts.—Packers 380, Cowboys 377)
(PS Pts.—Cowboys 181, Packers 134)
**NFL Championship*
***NFC Second-Round Playoff*
****NFC Divisional Playoff*
*****NFC Championship*

DALLAS vs. *INDIANAPOLIS
RS: Cowboys lead series, 7-3
PS: Colts lead series, 1-0
1960—Colts, 45-7 (D)
1967—Colts, 23-17 (B)
1969—Cowboys, 27-10 (D)
1970—**Colts, 16-13 (Miami)
1972—Cowboys, 21-0 (B)
1976—Cowboys, 30-27 (D)
1978—Cowboys, 38-0 (D)
1981—Cowboys, 37-13 (B)
1984—Cowboys, 22-3 (D)
1993—Cowboys, 27-3 (I)
1996—Colts, 25-24 (D)
(RS Pts.—Cowboys 250, Colts 149)
(PS Pts.—Colts 16, Cowboys 13)
**Franchise in Baltimore prior to 1984*
***Super Bowl V*

DALLAS VS. JACKSONVILLE
RS: Cowboys lead series, 1-0
1997—Cowboys, 26-22 (D)
(RS Pts.—Cowboys 26, Jaguars 22)

DALLAS vs. KANSAS CITY
RS: Cowboys lead series, 4-2
1970—Cowboys, 27-16 (KC)
1975—Chiefs, 34-31 (D)
1983—Cowboys, 41-21 (D)
1989—Chiefs, 36-28 (KC)
1992—Cowboys, 17-10 (D)
1995—Cowboys, 24-12 (D)
(RS Pts.—Cowboys 168, Chiefs 129)

DALLAS vs. MIAMI
RS: Dolphins lead series, 6-2
PS: Cowboys lead series, 1-0
1971—*Cowboys, 24-3 (New Orleans)
1973—Dolphins, 14-7 (D)
1978—Dolphins, 23-16 (M)
1981—Cowboys, 28-27 (D)
1984—Dolphins, 28-21 (M)
1987—Dolphins, 20-14 (D)
1989—Dolphins, 17-14 (D)
1993—Dolphins, 16-14 (D)
1996—Cowboys, 29-10 (M)
(RS Pts.—Dolphins 155, Cowboys 143)
(PS Pts.—Cowboys 24, Dolphins 3)
**Super Bowl VI*

DALLAS vs. MINNESOTA
RS: Cowboys lead series, 9-6
PS: Cowboys lead series, 4-1
1961—Cowboys, 21-7 (D)
Cowboys, 28-0 (M)
1966—Cowboys, 28-17 (D)
1968—Cowboys, 20-7 (M)
1970—Vikings, 54-13 (M)
1971—*Cowboys, 20-12 (M)
1973—**Vikings, 27-10 (D)
1974—Vikings, 23-21 (D)
1975—*Cowboys, 17-14 (M)
1977—Cowboys, 16-10 (M) OT
**Cowboys, 23-6 (D)
1978—Vikings, 21-10 (D)
1979—Cowboys, 36-20 (M)
1982—Vikings, 31-27 (M)
1983—Cowboys, 37-24 (M)
1987—Vikings, 44-38 (D) OT
1988—Vikings, 43-3 (D)
1993—Cowboys, 37-20 (M)
1995—Cowboys, 23-17 (M) OT
1996—***Cowboys, 40-15 (D)

ALL-TIME TEAM VS. TEAM RESULTS

(RS Pts.—Cowboys 358, Vikings 338)
(PS Pts.—Cowboys 110, Vikings 74)
**NFC Divisional Playoff*
***NFC Championship*
****NFC First-Round Playoff*

DALLAS vs. NEW ENGLAND
RS: Cowboys lead series, 7-0
1971—Cowboys, 44-21 (D)
1975—Cowboys, 34-31 (NE)
1978—Cowboys, 17-10 (D)
1981—Cowboys, 35-21 (NE)
1984—Cowboys, 20-17 (D)
1987—Cowboys, 23-17 (NE) OT
1996—Cowboys, 12-6 (D)
(RS Pts.—Cowboys 185, Patriots 123)

DALLAS vs. NEW ORLEANS
RS: Cowboys lead series, 14-3
1967—Cowboys, 14-10 (D)
Cowboys, 27-10 (NO)
1968—Cowboys, 17-3 (NO)
1969—Cowboys, 21-17 (NO)
Cowboys, 33-17 (D)
1971—Saints, 24-14 (NO)
1973—Cowboys, 40-3 (D)
1976—Cowboys, 24-6 (NO)
1978—Cowboys, 27-7 (D)
1982—Cowboys, 21-7 (D)
1983—Cowboys, 21-20 (D)
1984—Cowboys, 30-27 (D) OT
1988—Saints, 20-17 (NO)
1989—Saints, 28-0 (NO)
1990—Cowboys, 17-13 (D)
1991—Cowboys, 23-14 (D)
1994—Cowboys, 24-16 (NO)
(RS Pts.—Cowboys 370, Saints 242)

DALLAS vs. N.Y. GIANTS
RS: Cowboys lead series, 44-25-2
1960—Tie, 31-31 (NY)
1961—Giants, 31-10 (D)
Cowboys, 17-16 (NY)
1962—Giants, 41-10 (D)
Giants, 41-31 (NY)
1963—Giants, 37-21 (NY)
Giants, 34-27 (D)
1964—Tie, 13-13 (D)
Cowboys, 31-21 (NY)
1965—Cowboys, 31-2 (D)
Cowboys, 38-20 (NY)
1966—Cowboys, 52-7 (D)
Cowboys, 17-7 (NY)
1967—Cowboys, 38-24 (D)
1968—Giants, 27-21 (D)
Cowboys, 28-10 (NY)
1969—Cowboys, 25-3 (D)
1970—Cowboys, 28-10 (D)
Giants, 23-20 (NY)
1971—Cowboys, 20-13 (D)
Cowboys, 42-14 (NY)
1972—Cowboys, 23-14 (NY)
Giants, 23-3 (D)
1973—Cowboys, 45-28 (D)
Cowboys, 23-10 (New Haven)
1974—Giants, 14-6 (D)
Cowboys, 21-7 (New Haven)
1975—Cowboys, 13-7 (NY)
Cowboys, 14-3 (D)
1976—Cowboys, 24-14 (NY)
Cowboys, 9-3 (D)
1977—Cowboys, 41-21 (D)
Cowboys, 24-10 (NY)
1978—Cowboys, 34-24 (NY)
Cowboys, 24-3 (D)
1979—Cowboys, 16-14 (NY)
Cowboys, 28-7 (D)
1980—Cowboys, 24-3 (D)
Giants, 38-35 (NY)
1981—Cowboys, 18-10 (D)
Giants, 13-10 (NY) OT
1983—Cowboys, 28-13 (D)
Cowboys, 38-20 (NY)
1984—Giants, 28-7 (NY)
Giants, 19-7 (D)
1985—Cowboys, 30-29 (NY)
Cowboys, 28-21 (D)
1986—Cowboys, 31-28 (D)
Giants, 17-14 (NY)
1987—Cowboys, 16-14 (NY)
Cowboys, 33-24 (D)
1988—Giants, 12-10 (D)
Giants, 29-21 (NY)
1989—Giants, 30-13 (D)
Giants, 15-0 (NY)
1990—Giants, 28-7 (D)
Giants, 31-17 (NY)
1991—Cowboys, 21-16 (D)
Giants, 22-9 (NY)
1992—Cowboys, 34-28 (NY)
Cowboys, 30-3 (D)
1993—Cowboys, 31-9 (D)
Cowboys, 16-13 (NY) OT
1994—Cowboys, 38-10 (D)
Giants, 15-10 (NY)
1995—Cowboys, 35-0 (NY)
Cowboys, 21-20 (D)
1996—Cowboys, 27-0 (D)
Giants, 20-6 (NY)
1997—Giants, 20-17 (NY)
Giants, 20-7 (D)
(RS Pts.—Cowboys 1,588, Giants 1,245)

DALLAS vs. N.Y. JETS
RS: Cowboys lead series, 5-1
1971—Cowboys, 52-10 (D)
1975—Cowboys, 31-21 (NY)
1978—Cowboys, 30-7 (NY)
1987—Cowboys, 38-24 (NY)
1990—Jets, 24-9 (NY)
1993—Cowboys, 28-7 (NY)
(RS Pts.—Cowboys 188, Jets 93)

DALLAS vs. *OAKLAND
RS: Series tied, 3-3
1974—Raiders, 27-23 (O)
1980—Cowboys, 19-13 (O)
1983—Raiders, 40-38 (D)
1986—Raiders, 17-13 (D)
1992—Cowboys, 28-13 (LA)
1995—Cowboys, 34-21 (O)
(RS Pts.—Cowboys 155, Raiders 131)
**Franchise in Los Angeles from 1982-1994*

DALLAS vs. PHILADELPHIA
RS: Cowboys lead series, 45-29
PS: Cowboys lead series, 2-1
1960—Eagles, 27-25 (D)
1961—Eagles, 43-7 (D)
Eagles, 35-13 (P)
1962—Cowboys, 41-19 (D)
Eagles, 28-14 (P)
1963—Eagles, 24-21 (P)
Cowboys, 27-20 (D)
1964—Eagles, 17-14 (D)
Eagles, 24-14 (P)
1965—Eagles, 35-24 (D)
Cowboys, 21-19 (P)
1966—Cowboys, 56-7 (D)
Eagles, 24-23 (P)
1967—Eagles, 21-14 (P)
Cowboys, 38-17 (D)
1968—Cowboys, 45-13 (P)
Cowboys, 34-14 (D)
1969—Cowboys, 38-7 (P)
Cowboys, 49-14 (D)
1970—Cowboys, 17-7 (P)
Cowboys, 21-17 (D)
1971—Cowboys, 42-7 (P)
Cowboys, 20-7 (D)
1972—Cowboys, 28-6 (D)
Cowboys, 28-7 (P)
1973—Eagles, 30-16 (P)
Cowboys, 31-10 (D)
1974—Eagles, 13-10 (P)
Cowboys, 31-24 (D)
1975—Cowboys, 20-17 (P)
Cowboys, 27-17 (D)
1976—Cowboys, 27-7 (D)
Cowboys, 26-7 (P)
1977—Cowboys, 16-10 (P)
Cowboys, 24-14 (D)
1978—Cowboys, 14-7 (D)
Cowboys, 31-13 (P)
1979—Eagles, 31-21 (D)
Cowboys, 24-17 (P)
1980—Eagles, 17-10 (P)
Cowboys, 35-27 (D)
*Eagles, 20-7 (P)
1981—Cowboys, 17-14 (P)
Cowboys, 21-10 (D)
1982—Eagles, 24-20 (D)
1983—Cowboys, 37-7 (D)
Cowboys, 27-20 (P)
1984—Cowboys, 23-17 (D)
Cowboys, 26-10 (P)
1985—Eagles, 16-14 (P)
Cowboys, 34-17 (D)
1986—Cowboys, 17-14 (P)
Eagles, 23-21 (D)
1987—Cowboys, 41-22 (D)
Eagles, 37-20 (P)
1988—Eagles, 24-23 (P)
Eagles, 23-7 (D)
1989—Eagles, 27-0 (D)
Eagles, 20-10 (P)
1990—Eagles, 21-20 (D)
Eagles, 17-3 (P)
1991—Eagles, 24-0 (D)
Cowboys, 25-13 (P)
1992—Eagles, 31-7 (P)
Cowboys, 20-10 (D)
**Cowboys, 34-10 (D)
1993—Cowboys, 23-10 (P)
Cowboys, 23-17 (D)
1994—Cowboys, 24-13 (D)
Cowboys, 31-19 (P)
1995—Cowboys, 34-12 (D)
Eagles, 20-17 (P)
**Cowboys, 30-11 (D)
1996—Cowboys, 23-19 (P)
Eagles, 31-21 (D)
1997—Cowboys, 21-20 (D)
Eagles, 13-12 (P)
(RS Pts.—Cowboys 1,699, Eagles 1,335)
(PS Pts.—Cowboys 71, Eagles 41)
**NFC Championship*
***NFC Divisional Playoff*

DALLAS vs. PITTSBURGH
RS: Cowboys lead series, 14-11
PS: Steelers lead series, 2-1
1960—Steelers, 35-28 (D)
1961—Cowboys, 27-24 (D)
Steelers, 37-7 (P)
1962—Steelers, 30-28 (D)
Cowboys, 42-27 (P)
1963—Steelers, 27-21 (P)
Steelers, 24-19 (D)
1964—Steelers, 23-17 (P)
Cowboys, 17-14 (D)
1965—Steelers, 22-13 (P)
Cowboys, 24-17 (D)
1966—Cowboys, 52-21 (D)
Cowboys, 20-7 (P)
1967—Cowboys, 24-21 (P)
1968—Cowboys, 28-7 (D)
1969—Cowboys, 10-7 (P)
1972—Cowboys, 17-13 (D)
1975—*Steelers, 21-17 (Miami)
1977—Steelers, 28-13 (P)
1978—**Steelers, 35-31 (Miami)
1979—Steelers, 14-3 (P)
1982—Steelers, 36-28 (D)
1985—Cowboys, 27-13 (D)
1988—Steelers, 24-21 (P)
1991—Cowboys, 20-10 (D)
1994—Cowboys, 26-9 (P)
1995—***Cowboys, 27-17 (Tempe)
1997—Cowboys, 37-7 (P)
(RS Pts.—Cowboys 569, Steelers 497)
(PS Pts.—Cowboys 75, Steelers 73)
**Super Bowl X*
***Super Bowl XIII*
****Super Bowl XXX*

DALLAS vs. *ST. LOUIS
RS: Rams lead series, 9-8
PS: Series tied, 4-4
1960—Rams, 38-13 (D)
1962—Cowboys, 27-17 (LA)
1967—Rams, 35-13 (D)
1969—Rams, 24-23 (LA)
1971—Cowboys, 28-21 (D)
1973—Rams, 37-31 (LA)
**Cowboys, 27-16 (D)
1975—Cowboys, 18-7 (D)
***Cowboys, 37-7 (LA)
1976—**Rams, 14-12 (D)
1978—Rams, 27-14 (LA)
***Cowboys, 28-0 (LA)
1979—Cowboys, 30-6 (D)
**Rams, 21-19 (D)
1980—Rams, 38-14 (LA)
****Cowboys, 34-13 (D)
1981—Cowboys, 29-17 (D)
1983—****Rams, 24-17 (D)
1984—Cowboys, 20-13 (LA)
1985—**Rams, 20-0 (LA)
1986—Rams, 29-10 (LA)
1987—Cowboys, 29-21 (LA)
1989—Rams, 35-31 (D)
1990—Cowboys, 24-21 (LA)
1992—Rams, 27-23 (D)
(RS Pts.—Rams 413, Cowboys 377)
(PS Pts.—Cowboys 174, Rams 115)
**Franchise in Los Angeles prior to 1995*
***NFC Divisional Playoff*
****NFC Championship*
*****NFC First-Round Playoff*

DALLAS vs. SAN DIEGO
RS: Cowboys lead series, 5-1
1972—Cowboys, 34-28 (SD)
1980—Cowboys, 42-31 (D)
1983—Chargers, 24-23 (SD)
1986—Cowboys, 24-21 (SD)
1990—Cowboys, 17-14 (D)
1995—Cowboys, 23-9 (SD)
(RS Pts.—Cowboys 163, Chargers 127)

DALLAS vs. SAN FRANCISCO
RS: 49ers lead series, 12-7-1
PS: Cowboys lead series, 5-2
1960—49ers, 26-14 (D)
1963—49ers, 31-24 (SF)
1965—Cowboys, 39-31 (D)
1967—49ers, 24-16 (SF)
1969—Tie, 24-24 (D)
1970—*Cowboys, 17-10 (SF)
1971—*Cowboys, 14-3 (D)
1972—49ers, 31-10 (D)
**Cowboys, 30-28 (SF)
1974—Cowboys, 20-14 (D)
1977—Cowboys, 42-35 (SF)
1979—Cowboys, 21-13 (SF)
1980—Cowboys, 59-14 (D)
1981—49ers, 45-14 (SF)
*49ers, 28-27 (SF)
1983—49ers, 42-17 (SF)
1985—49ers, 31-16 (SF)
1989—49ers, 31-14 (D)
1990—49ers, 24-6 (D)
1992—*Cowboys, 30-20 (SF)
1993—Cowboys, 26-17 (D)
*Cowboys, 38-21 (D)
1994—49ers, 21-14 (SF)
*49ers, 38-28 (SF)
1995—49ers, 38-20 (D)
1996—Cowboys, 20-17 (SF) OT
1997—49ers, 17-10 (SF)
(RS Pts.—49ers 526, Cowboys 426)
(PS Pts.—Cowboys 184, 49ers 148)
**NFC Championship*
***NFC Divisional Playoff*

DALLAS vs. SEATTLE
RS: Cowboys lead series, 4-1
1976—Cowboys, 28-13 (S)
1980—Cowboys, 51-7 (D)
1983—Cowboys, 35-10 (S)
1986—Seahawks, 31-14 (D)

1992—Cowboys, 27-0 (D)
(RS Pts.—Cowboys 155, Seahawks 61)

DALLAS vs. TAMPA BAY
RS: Cowboys lead series, 6-0
PS: Cowboys lead series, 2-0
1977—Cowboys, 23-7 (D)
1980—Cowboys, 28-17 (D)
1981—*Cowboys, 38-0 (D)
1982—Cowboys, 14-9 (D)
**Cowboys, 30-17 (D)
1983—Cowboys, 27-24 (D) OT
1990—Cowboys, 14-10 (D)
Cowboys, 17-13 (TB)
(RS Pts.—Cowboys 123, Buccaneers 80)
(PS Pts.—Cowboys 68, Buccaneers 17)
NFC Divisional Playoff
***NFC First-Round Playoff*

DALLAS vs. *TENNESSEE
RS: Cowboys lead series, 5-4
1970—Cowboys, 52-10 (D)
1974—Cowboys, 10-0 (H)
1979—Oilers, 30-24 (D)
1982—Cowboys, 37-7 (H)
1985—Cowboys, 17-10 (H)
1988—Oilers, 25-17 (D)
1991—Oilers, 26-23 (H) OT
1994—Cowboys, 20-17 (D)
1997—Oilers, 27-14 (D)
(RS Pts.—Cowboys 214, Oilers 152)
Franchise in Houston prior to 1997

DALLAS vs. WASHINGTON
RS: Cowboys lead series, 41-31-2
PS: Redskins lead series, 2-0
1960—Redskins, 26-14 (W)
1961—Tie, 28-28 (D)
Redskins, 34-24 (W)
1962—Tie, 35-35 (D)
Cowboys, 38-10 (W)
1963—Redskins, 21-17 (W)
Cowboys, 35-20 (D)
1964—Cowboys, 24-18 (D)
Redskins, 28-16 (W)
1965—Cowboys, 27-7 (D)
Redskins, 34-31 (W)
1966—Cowboys, 31-30 (W)
Redskins, 34-31 (D)
1967—Cowboys, 17-14 (W)
Redskins, 27-20 (D)
1968—Cowboys, 44-24 (W)
Cowboys, 29-20 (D)
1969—Cowboys, 41-28 (W)
Cowboys, 20-10 (D)
1970—Cowboys, 45-21 (W)
Cowboys, 34-0 (D)
1971—Redskins, 20-16 (D)
Cowboys, 13-0 (W)
1972—Redskins, 24-20 (W)
Cowboys, 34-24 (D)
*Redskins, 26-3 (W)
1973—Redskins, 14-7 (W)
Cowboys, 27-7 (D)
1974—Redskins, 28-21 (W)
Cowboys, 24-23 (D)
1975—Redskins, 30-24 (W) OT
Cowboys, 31-10 (D)
1976—Cowboys, 20-7 (W)
Redskins, 27-14 (D)
1977—Cowboys, 34-16 (D)
Cowboys, 14-7 (W)
1978—Redskins, 9-5 (W)
Cowboys, 37-10 (D)
1979—Redskins, 34-20 (W)
Cowboys, 35-34 (D)
1980—Cowboys, 17-3 (W)
Cowboys, 14-10 (D)
1981—Cowboys, 26-10 (W)
Cowboys, 24-10 (D)
1982—Cowboys, 24-10 (W)
*Redskins, 31-17 (W)
1983—Cowboys, 31-30 (W)
Redskins, 31-10 (D)
1984—Redskins, 34-14 (W)
Redskins, 30-28 (D)
1985—Cowboys, 44-14 (D)
Cowboys, 13-7 (W)
1986—Cowboys, 30-6 (D)
Redskins, 41-14 (W)
1987—Redskins, 13-7 (D)
Redskins, 24-20 (W)
1988—Redskins, 35-17 (D)
Cowboys, 24-17 (W)
1989—Redskins, 30-7 (D)
Cowboys, 13-3 (W)
1990—Redskins, 19-15 (W)
Cowboys, 27-17 (D)
1991—Redskins, 33-31 (D)
Cowboys, 24-21 (W)
1992—Cowboys, 23-10 (D)
Redskins, 20-17 (W)
1993—Redskins, 35-16 (W)
Cowboys, 38-3 (D)
1994—Cowboys, 34-7 (W)
Cowboys, 31-7 (D)
1995—Redskins, 27-23 (W)
Redskins, 24-17 (D)
1996—Cowboys, 21-10 (D)
Redskins, 37-10 (W)
1997—Redskins, 21-16 (W)
Cowboys, 17-14 (D)
(RS Pts.—Cowboys 1,734, Redskins 1,456)
(PS Pts.—Redskins 57, Cowboys 20)
NFC Championship

DENVER vs. ARIZONA
RS: Broncos lead series, 4-0-1;
See Arizona vs. Denver

DENVER vs. ATLANTA
RS: Broncos lead series, 6-3;
See Atlanta vs. Denver

DENVER vs. BALTIMORE
RS: Broncos lead series, 1-0;
See Baltimore vs. Denver

DENVER vs. BUFFALO
RS: Bills lead series, 17-12-1
PS: Bills lead series, 1-0;
See Buffalo vs. Denver

DENVER vs. CAROLINA
RS: Broncos lead series, 1-0;
See Carolina vs. Denver

DENVER vs. CHICAGO
RS: Broncos lead series, 6-5;
See Chicago vs. Denver

DENVER vs. CINCINNATI
Broncos lead series, 13-6;
See Cincinnati vs. Denver

DENVER vs. CLEVELAND
RS: Broncos lead series, 13-5
PS: Broncos lead series, 3-0;
See Cleveland vs. Denver

DENVER vs. DALLAS
RS: Cowboys lead series, 4-2
PS: Cowboys lead series, 1-0;
See Dallas vs. Denver

DENVER vs. DETROIT
RS: Broncos lead series, 4-3
1971—Lions, 24-20 (Den)
1974—Broncos, 31-27 (Det)
1978—Lions, 17-14 (Det)
1981—Broncos, 27-21 (Den)
1984—Broncos, 28-7 (Det)
1987—Broncos, 34-0 (Den)
1990—Lions, 40-27 (Det)
(RS Pts.—Broncos 181, Lions 136)

DENVER vs. GREEN BAY
RS: Broncos lead series, 4-3-1
PS: Broncos lead series, 1-0
1971—Packers, 34-13 (Mil)
1975—Broncos, 23-13 (D)
1978—Broncos, 16-3 (D)
1984—Broncos, 17-14 (D)
1987—Tie, 17-17 (Mil) OT
1990—Broncos, 22-13 (D)
1993—Packers, 30-27 (GB)
1996—Packers, 41-6 (GB)
1997—*Broncos, 31-24 (San Diego)
(RS Pts.—Packers 165, Broncos 141)
(PS Pts.—Broncos 31, Packers 24)
Super Bowl XXXII

DENVER vs. *INDIANAPOLIS
RS: Broncos lead series, 9-2
1974—Broncos, 17-6 (B)
1977—Broncos, 27-13 (D)
1978—Colts, 7-6 (B)
1981—Broncos, 28-10 (D)
1983—Broncos, 17-10 (B)
Broncos, 21-19 (D)
1985—Broncos, 15-10 (I)
1988—Colts, 55-23 (I)
1989—Broncos, 14-3 (D)
1990—Broncos, 27-17 (I)
1993—Broncos, 35-13 (D)
(RS Pts.—Broncos 230, Colts 163)
Franchise in Baltimore prior to 1984

DENVER vs. JACKSONVILLE
RS: Broncos lead series, 1-0
PS: Series tied, 1-1
1995—Broncos, 31-23 (D)
1996—*Jaguars, 30-27 (D)
1997—**Broncos, 42-17 (D)
(RS Pts.—Broncos 31, Jaguars 23)
(PS Pts.—Broncos 69, Jaguars 47)
AFC Divisional Playoff
***AFC First-Round Playoff*

DENVER vs. *KANSAS CITY
RS: Chiefs lead series, 43-32
PS: Broncos lead series, 1-0
1960—Texans, 17-14 (D)
Texans, 34-7 (Dal)
1961—Texans, 19-12 (D)
Texans, 49-21 (Dal)
1962—Texans, 24-3 (D)
Texans, 17-10 (Dal)
1963—Chiefs, 59-7 (D)
Chiefs, 52-21 (KC)
1964—Broncos, 33-27 (D)
Chiefs, 49-39 (KC)
1965—Chiefs, 31-23 (D)
Chiefs, 45-35 (KC)
1966—Chiefs, 37-10 (KC)
Chiefs, 56-10 (D)
1967—Chiefs, 52-9 (KC)
Chiefs, 38-24 (D)
1968—Chiefs, 34-2 (KC)
Chiefs, 30-7 (D)
1969—Chiefs, 26-13 (D)
Chiefs, 31-17 (KC)
1970—Broncos, 26-13 (D)
Chiefs, 16-0 (KC)
1971—Chiefs, 16-3 (D)
Chiefs, 28-10 (KC)
1972—Chiefs, 45-24 (D)
Chiefs, 24-21 (KC)
1973—Chiefs, 16-14 (KC)
Broncos, 14-10 (D)
1974—Broncos, 17-14 (KC)
Chiefs, 42-34 (D)
1975—Broncos, 37-33 (D)
Chiefs, 26-13 (KC)
1976—Broncos, 35-26 (KC)
Broncos, 17-16 (D)
1977—Broncos, 23-7 (D)
Broncos, 14-7 (KC)
1978—Broncos, 23-17 (KC) OT
Broncos, 24-3 (D)
1979—Broncos, 24-10 (KC)
Broncos, 20-3 (D)
1980—Chiefs, 23-17 (D)
Chiefs, 31-14 (KC)
1981—Chiefs, 28-14 (KC)
Broncos, 16-13 (D)
1982—Chiefs, 37-16 (D)
1983—Broncos, 27-24 (D)
Chiefs, 48-17 (KC)
1984—Broncos, 21-0 (D)
Chiefs, 16-13 (KC)
1985—Broncos, 30-10 (KC)
Broncos, 14-13 (D)
1986—Broncos, 38-17 (D)
Chiefs, 37-10 (KC)
1987—Broncos, 26-17 (KC)
Broncos, 20-17 (D)
1988—Chiefs, 20-13 (KC)
Broncos, 17-11 (D)
1989—Broncos, 34-20 (D)
Broncos, 16-13 (KC)
1990—Broncos, 24-23 (D)
Chiefs, 31-20 (KC)
1991—Broncos, 19-16 (D)
Broncos, 24-20 (KC)
1992—Broncos, 20-19 (D)
Chiefs, 42-20 (KC)
1993—Chiefs, 15-7 (KC)
Broncos, 27-21 (D)
1994—Chiefs, 31-28 (D)
Broncos, 20-17 (KC) OT
1995—Chiefs, 21-7 (D)
Chiefs, 20-17 (KC)
1996—Chiefs, 17-14 (KC)
Broncos, 34-7 (D)
1997—Broncos, 19-3 (D)
Chiefs, 24-22 (KC)
**Broncos, 14-10 (KC)
(RS Pts.—Chiefs 1,821, Broncos 1,405)
(PS Pts.—Broncos 14, Chiefs 10)
Franchise in Dallas prior to 1963 and known as Texans
***AFC Divisional Playoff*

DENVER vs. MIAMI
RS: Dolphins lead series, 5-2-1
1966—Dolphins, 24-7 (M)
Broncos, 17-7 (D)
1967—Dolphins, 35-21 (M)
1968—Broncos, 21-14 (D)
1969—Dolphins, 27-24 (M)
1971—Tie, 10-10 (D)
1975—Dolphins, 14-13 (M)
1985—Dolphins, 30-26 (D)
(RS Pts.—Dolphins 161, Broncos 139)

DENVER vs. MINNESOTA
RS: Vikings lead series, 5-4
1972—Vikings, 23-20 (D)
1978—Vikings, 12-9 (M) OT
1981—Broncos, 19-17 (D)
1984—Broncos, 42-21 (D)
1987—Vikings, 34-27 (M)
1990—Vikings, 27-22 (M)
1991—Broncos, 13-6 (M)
1993—Vikings, 26-23 (D)
1996—Broncos, 21-17 (M)
1997—Broncos, 34-13 (D)
(RS Pts.—Broncos 196, Vikings 183)

DENVER vs. *NEW ENGLAND
RS: Broncos lead series, 19-12
PS: Broncos lead series, 1-0
1960—Broncos, 13-10 (B)
Broncos, 31-24 (D)
1961—Patriots, 45-17 (B)
Patriots, 28-24 (D)
1962—Patriots, 41-16 (B)
Patriots, 33-29 (D)
1963—Broncos, 14-10 (D)
Patriots, 40-21 (B)
1964—Patriots, 39-10 (D)
Patriots, 12-7 (B)
1965—Broncos, 27-10 (B)
Patriots, 28-20 (D)
1966—Patriots, 24-10 (D)
Broncos, 17-10 (B)
1967—Broncos, 26-21 (D)
1968—Patriots, 20-17 (D)
Broncos, 35-14 (B)
1969—Broncos, 35-7 (D)
1972—Broncos, 45-21 (D)
1976—Patriots, 38-14 (NE)
1979—Broncos, 45-10 (D)
1980—Patriots, 23-14 (NE)
1984—Broncos, 26-19 (D)
1986—Broncos, 27-20 (D)
**Broncos, 22-17 (D)
1987—Broncos, 31-20 (D)
1988—Broncos, 21-10 (D)
1991—Broncos, 9-6 (NE)

ALL-TIME TEAM VS. TEAM RESULTS

Broncos, 20-3 (D)
1995—Broncos, 37-3 (NE)
1996—Broncos, 34-8 (NE)
1997—Broncos, 34-13 (D)
(RS Pts.—Broncos 726, Patriots 610)
(PS Pts.—Broncos 22, Patriots 17)
Franchise in Boston prior to 1971
**AFC Divisional Playoff*

DENVER vs. NEW ORLEANS
RS: Broncos lead series, 4-2
1970—Broncos, 31-6 (NO)
1974—Broncos, 33-17 (D)
1979—Broncos, 10-3 (D)
1985—Broncos, 34-23 (D)
1988—Saints, 42-0 (NO)
1994—Saints, 30-28 (D)
(RS Pts.—Broncos 136, Saints 121)

DENVER vs. N.Y. GIANTS
RS: Series tied, 3-3
PS: Giants lead series, 1-0
1972—Giants, 29-17 (NY)
1976—Broncos, 14-13 (D)
1980—Broncos, 14-9 (NY)
1986—Giants, 19-16 (NY)
*Giants, 39-20 (Pasadena)
1989—Giants, 14-7 (D)
1992—Broncos, 27-13 (D)
(RS Pts.—Giants 97, Broncos 95)
(PS Pts.—Giants 39, Broncos 20)
Super Bowl XXI

DENVER vs. *N.Y. JETS
RS: Broncos lead series, 13-12-1
1960—Titans, 28-24 (NY)
Titans, 30-27 (D)
1961—Titans, 35-28 (NY)
Broncos, 27-10 (D)
1962—Broncos, 32-10 (NY)
Titans, 46-45 (D)
1963—Tie, 35-35 (NY)
Jets, 14-9 (D)
1964—Jets, 30-6 (NY)
Broncos, 20-16 (D)
1965—Broncos, 16-13 (D)
Jets, 45-10 (NY)
1966—Jets, 16-7 (D)
1967—Jets, 38-24 (D)
Broncos, 33-24 (NY)
1968—Broncos, 21-13 (NY)
1969—Broncos, 21-19 (D)
1973—Broncos, 40-28 (NY)
1976—Broncos, 46-3 (D)
1978—Jets, 31-28 (D)
1980—Broncos, 31-24 (D)
1986—Jets, 22-10 (NY)
1992—Broncos, 27-16 (D)
1993—Broncos, 26-20 (NY)
1994—Jets, 25-22 (NY) OT
1996—Broncos, 31-6 (D)
(RS Pts.—Broncos 646, Jets 597)
Jets known as Titans prior to 1963

DENVER vs. *OAKLAND
RS: Raiders lead series, 49-24-2
PS: Series tied, 1-1
1960—Broncos, 31-14 (D)
Raiders, 48-10 (O)
1961—Raiders, 33-19 (O)
Broncos, 27-24 (D)
1962—Broncos, 44-7 (D)
Broncos, 23-6 (O)
1963—Raiders, 26-10 (D)
Raiders, 35-31 (O)
1964—Raiders, 40-7 (O)
Tie, 20-20 (D)
1965—Raiders, 28-20 (D)
Raiders, 24-13 (O)
1966—Raiders, 17-3 (D)
Raiders, 28-10 (O)
1967—Raiders, 51-0 (O)
Raiders, 21-17 (D)
1968—Raiders, 43-7 (D)
Raiders, 33-27 (O)
1969—Raiders, 24-14 (D)
Raiders, 41-10 (O)
1970—Raiders, 35-23 (O)
Raiders, 24-19 (D)
1971—Raiders, 27-16 (D)
Raiders, 21-13 (O)
1972—Broncos, 30-23 (O)
Raiders, 37-20 (D)
1973—Tie, 23-23 (D)
Raiders, 21-17 (O)
1974—Raiders, 28-17 (D)
Broncos, 20-17 (O)
1975—Raiders, 42-17 (D)
Raiders, 17-10 (O)
1976—Raiders, 17-10 (D)
Raiders, 19-6 (O)
1977—Broncos, 30-7 (O)
Raiders, 24-14 (D)
**Broncos, 20-17 (D)
1978—Broncos, 14-6 (D)
Broncos, 21-6 (O)
1979—Raiders, 27-3 (O)
Raiders, 14-10 (D)
1980—Raiders, 9-3 (O)
Raiders, 24-21 (D)
1981—Broncos, 9-7 (D)
Broncos, 17-0 (O)
1982—Raiders, 27-10 (LA)
1983—Raiders, 22-7 (D)
Raiders, 22-20 (LA)
1984—Broncos, 16-13 (D)
Broncos, 22-19 (LA) OT
1985—Raiders, 31-28 (LA) OT
Raiders, 17-14 (D) OT
1986—Broncos, 38-36 (D)
Broncos, 21-10 (LA)
1987—Broncos, 30-14 (D)
Broncos, 23-17 (LA)
1988—Raiders, 30-27 (D) OT
Raiders, 21-20 (LA)
1989—Broncos, 31-21 (D)
Raiders, 16-13 (LA) OT
1990—Raiders, 14-9 (LA)
Raiders, 23-20 (D)
1991—Raiders, 16-13 (LA)
Raiders, 17-16 (D)
1992—Broncos, 17-13 (D)
Raiders, 24-0 (LA)
1993—Raiders, 23-20 (D)
Raiders, 33-30 (LA) OT
***Raiders, 42-24 (LA)
1994—Raiders, 48-16 (D)
Raiders, 23-13 (LA)
1995—Broncos, 27-0 (D)
Broncos, 31-28 (O)
1996—Broncos, 22-21 (O)
Broncos, 24-19 (D)
1997—Raiders, 28-25 (O)
Broncos, 31-3 (D)
(RS Pts.—Raiders 1,687, Broncos 1,360)
(PS Pts.—Raiders 59, Broncos 44)
Franchise in Los Angeles from 1982-1994
**AFC Championship*
***AFC First-Round Playoff*

DENVER vs. PHILADELPHIA
RS: Eagles lead series, 6-2
1971—Eagles, 17-16 (P)
1975—Broncos, 25-10 (D)
1980—Eagles, 27-6 (P)
1983—Eagles, 13-10 (D)
1986—Broncos, 33-7 (P)
1989—Eagles, 28-24 (D)
1992—Eagles, 30-0 (P)
1995—Eagles, 31-13 (P)
(RS Pts.—Eagles 163, Broncos 127)

DENVER vs. PITTSBURGH
RS: Broncos lead series, 10-6-1
PS: Broncos lead series, 3-2
1970—Broncos, 16-13 (D)
1971—Broncos, 22-10 (P)
1973—Broncos, 23-13 (P)
1974—Tie, 35-35 (D) OT
1975—Steelers, 20-9 (P)
1977—Broncos, 21-7 (D)
*Broncos, 34-21 (D)
1978—Steelers, 21-17 (D)
*Steelers, 33-10 (P)
1979—Steelers, 42-7 (P)
1983—Broncos, 14-10 (P)
1984—*Steelers, 24-17 (D)
1985—Broncos, 31-23 (P)
1986—Broncos, 21-10 (P)
1988—Steelers, 39-21 (P)
1989—Broncos, 34-7 (D)
*Broncos, 24-23 (D)
1990—Steelers, 34-17 (D)
1991—Broncos, 20-13 (D)
1993—Broncos, 37-13 (D)
1997—Steelers, 35-24 (P)
**Broncos, 24-21 (P)
(RS Pts.—Broncos 369, Steelers 345)
(PS Pts.—Steelers 122, Broncos 109)
AFC Divisional Playoff
**AFC Championship*

DENVER vs. *ST. LOUIS
RS: Series tied, 4-4
1972—Broncos, 16-10 (LA)
1974—Rams, 17-10 (D)
1979—Rams, 13-9 (D)
1982—Broncos, 27-24 (LA)
1985—Rams, 20-16 (LA)
1988—Broncos, 35-24 (D)
1994—Rams, 27-21 (LA)
1997—Broncos, 35-14 (D)
(RS Pts.—Rams 169, Broncos 149)
Franchise in Los Angeles prior to 1995

DENVER vs. *SAN DIEGO
RS: Broncos lead series, 40-35-1
1960—Chargers, 23-19 (D)
Chargers, 41-33 (LA)
1961—Chargers, 37-0 (SD)
Chargers, 19-16 (D)
1962—Broncos, 30-21 (D)
Broncos, 23-20 (SD)
1963—Broncos, 50-34 (D)
Chargers, 58-20 (SD)
1964—Chargers, 42-14 (SD)
Chargers, 31-20 (D)
1965—Chargers, 34-31 (SD)
Chargers, 33-21 (D)
1966—Chargers, 24-17 (SD)
Broncos, 20-17 (D)
1967—Chargers, 38-21 (D)
Chargers, 24-20 (SD)
1968—Chargers, 55-24 (SD)
Chargers, 47-23 (D)
1969—Broncos, 13-0 (D)
Chargers, 45-24 (SD)
1970—Chargers, 24-21 (SD)
Tie, 17-17 (D)
1971—Broncos, 20-16 (D)
Chargers, 45-17 (SD)
1972—Chargers, 37-14 (SD)
Broncos, 38-13 (D)
1973—Broncos, 30-19 (D)
Broncos, 42-28 (SD)
1974—Broncos, 27-7 (D)
Chargers, 17-0 (SD)
1975—Broncos, 27-17 (SD)
Broncos, 13-10 (D) OT
1976—Broncos, 26-0 (D)
Broncos, 17-0 (SD)
1977—Broncos, 17-14 (SD)
Broncos, 17-9 (D)
1978—Broncos, 27-14 (D)
Chargers, 23-0 (SD)
1979—Broncos, 7-0 (D)
Chargers, 17-7 (SD)
1980—Chargers, 30-13 (D)
Broncos, 20-13 (SD)
1981—Broncos, 42-24 (D)
Chargers, 34-17 (SD)
1982—Chargers, 23-3 (D)
Chargers, 30-20 (SD)
1983—Broncos, 14-6 (D)
Chargers, 31-7 (SD)
1984—Broncos, 16-13 (SD)
Broncos, 16-13 (D)
1985—Chargers, 30-10 (SD)
Broncos, 30-24 (D) OT
1986—Broncos, 31-14 (SD)
Chargers, 9-3 (D)
1987—Broncos, 31-17 (SD)
Broncos, 24-0 (D)
1988—Broncos, 34-3 (D)
Broncos, 12-0 (SD)
1989—Broncos, 16-10 (D)
Chargers, 19-16 (SD)
1990—Chargers, 19-7 (SD)
Broncos, 20-10 (D)
1991—Broncos, 27-19 (D)
Broncos, 17-14 (SD)
1992—Broncos, 21-13 (D)
Chargers, 24-21 (SD)
1993—Broncos, 34-17 (D)
Chargers, 13-10 (SD)
1994—Chargers, 37-34 (D)
Broncos, 20-15 (SD)
1995—Chargers, 17-6 (SD)
Broncos, 30-27 (D)
1996—Broncos, 28-17 (D)
Chargers, 16-10 (SD)
1997—Broncos, 38-28 (SD)
Broncos, 38-3 (D)
(RS Pts.—Chargers 1,602, Broncos 1,559)
Franchise in Los Angeles prior to 1961

DENVER vs. SAN FRANCISCO
RS: Series tied, 4-4
PS: 49ers lead series, 1-0
1970—49ers, 19-14 (SF)
1973—49ers, 36-34 (D)
1979—Broncos, 38-28 (SF)
1982—Broncos, 24-21 (D)
1985—Broncos, 17-16 (D)
1988—Broncos, 16-13 (SF) OT
1989—*49ers, 55-10 (New Orleans)
1994—49ers, 42-19 (SF)
1997—49ers, 34-17 (SF)
(RS Pts.—49ers 209, Broncos 179)
(PS Pts.—49ers 55, Broncos 10)
Super Bowl XXIV

DENVER vs. SEATTLE
RS: Borncos lead series, 26-15
PS: Seahawks lead series, 1-0
1977—Broncos, 24-13 (S)
1978—Broncos, 28-7 (D)
Broncos, 20-17 (S) OT
1979—Broncos, 37-34 (D)
Seahawks, 28-23 (S)
1980—Broncos, 36-20 (D)
Broncos, 25-17 (S)
1981—Seahawks, 13-10 (S)
Broncos, 23-13 (D)
1982—Seahawks, 17-10 (D)
Seahawks, 13-11 (S)
1983—Seahawks, 27-19 (S)
Broncos, 38-27 (D)
*Seahawks, 31-7 (S)
1984—Seahawks, 27-24 (D)
Broncos, 31-14 (S)
1985—Broncos, 13-10 (D) OT
Broncos, 27-24 (S)
1986—Broncos, 20-13 (D)
Seahawks, 41-16 (S)
1987—Broncos, 40-17 (D)
Seahawks, 28-21 (S)
1988—Seahawks, 21-14 (D)
Seahawks, 42-14 (S)
1989—Broncos, 24-21 (S) OT
Broncos, 41-14 (D)
1990—Broncos, 34-31 (D) OT
Seahawks, 17-12 (S)
1991—Broncos, 16-10 (D)
Seahawks, 13-10 (S)
1992—Seahawks, 16-13 (S) OT
Broncos, 10-6 (D)
1993—Broncos, 28-17 (D)
Broncos, 17-9 (S)
1994—Broncos, 16-9 (S)
Broncos, 17-10 (D)

1995—Seahawks, 27-10 (S)
Seahawks, 31-27 (D)
1996—Broncos, 30-20 (S)
Broncos, 34-7 (D)
1997—Broncos, 35-14 (S)
Broncos, 30-27 (D)
(RS Pts.—Broncos 928, Seahawks 782)
(PS Pts.—Seahawks 31, Broncos 7)
AFC First-Round Playoff

DENVER vs. TAMPA BAY
RS: Broncos lead series, 3-1
1976—Broncos, 48-13 (D)
1981—Broncos, 24-7 (TB)
1993—Buccaneers, 17-10 (D)
1996—Broncos, 27-23 (D)
(RS Pts.—Broncos 109, Buccaneers 60)

DENVER vs. *TENNESSEE
RS: Oilers lead series, 20-11-1
PS: Broncos lead series, 2-1
1960—Oilers, 45-25 (D)
Oilers, 20-10 (H)
1961—Oilers, 55-14 (D)
Oilers, 45-14 (H)
1962—Broncos, 20-10 (D)
Oilers, 34-17 (H)
1963—Oilers, 20-14 (H)
Oilers, 33-24 (D)
1964—Oilers, 38-17 (D)
Oilers, 34-15 (H)
1965—Broncos, 28-17 (D)
Broncos, 31-21 (H)
1966—Oilers, 45-7 (H)
Broncos, 40-38 (D)
1967—Oilers, 10-6 (H)
Oilers, 20-18 (D)
1968—Oilers, 38-17 (H)
1969—Oilers, 24-21 (H)
Tie, 20-20 (D)
1970—Oilers, 31-21 (H)
1972—Broncos, 30-17 (D)
1973—Broncos, 48-20 (H)
1974—Broncos, 37-14 (D)
1976—Oilers, 17-3 (H)
1977—Broncos, 24-14 (H)
1979—**Oilers, 13-7 (H)
1980—Oilers, 20-16 (D)
1983—Broncos, 26-14 (H)
1985—Broncos, 31-20 (D)
1987—Oilers, 40-10 (D)
***Broncos, 34-10 (D)
1991—Oilers, 42-14 (H)
***Broncos, 26-24 (D)
1992—Broncos, 27-21 (D)
1995—Oilers, 42-33 (H)
(RS Pts.—Oilers 879, Broncos 678)
(PS Pts.—Broncos 67, Oilers 47)
Franchise in Houston prior to 1997
**AFC First-Round Playoff*
***AFC Divisional Playoff*

DENVER vs. WASHINGTON
RS: Broncos lead series, 4-3
PS: Redskins lead series, 1-0
1970—Redskins, 19-3 (D)
1974—Redskins, 30-3 (W)
1980—Broncos, 20-17 (D)
1986—Broncos, 31-30 (D)
1987—*Redskins, 42-10 (San Diego)
1989—Broncos, 14-10 (W)
1992—Redskins, 34-3 (W)
1995—Broncos, 38-31 (D)
(RS Pts.—Redskins 171, Broncos 112)
(PS Pts.—Redskins 42, Broncos 10)
Super Bowl XXII

DETROIT vs. ARIZONA
RS: Lions lead series, 27-17-5;
See Arizona vs. Detroit

DETROIT vs. ATLANTA
RS: Lions lead series, 20-6;
See Atlanta vs. Detroit

DETROIT vs. BUFFALO
RS: Lions lead series, 3-2-1;
See Buffalo vs. Detroit

DETROIT vs. CHICAGO
RS: Bears lead series, 76-55-5;
See Chicago vs. Detroit

DETROIT vs. CINCINNATI
RS: Series tied, 3-3;
See Cincinnati vs. Detroit

DETROIT vs. CLEVELAND
RS: Lions lead series, 12-3
PS: Lions lead series, 3-1;
See Cleveland vs. Detroit

DETROIT vs. DALLAS
RS: Cowboys lead series, 7-6
PS: Series tied, 1-1;
See Dallas vs. Detroit

DETROIT vs. DENVER
RS: Broncos lead series, 4-3;
See Denver vs. Detroit

***DETROIT vs. GREEN BAY**
RS: Packers lead series, 69-59-7
PS: Packers lead series, 2-0
1930—Packers, 47-13 (GB)
Tie, 6-6 (P)
1932—Packers, 15-10 (GB)
Spartans, 19-0 (P)
1933—Packers, 17-0 (GB)
Spartans, 7-0 (P)
1934—Lions, 3-0 (GB)
Packers, 3-0 (D)
1935—Packers, 13-9 (Mil)
Packers, 31-7 (GB)
Lions, 20-10 (D)
1936—Packers, 20-18 (GB)
Packers, 26-17 (D)
1937—Packers, 26-6 (GB)
Packers, 14-13 (D)
1938—Lions, 17-7 (GB)
Packers, 28-7 (D)
1939—Packers, 26-7 (GB)
Packers, 12-7 (D)
1940—Lions, 23-14 (GB)
Packers, 50-7 (D)
1941—Packers, 23-0 (GB)
Packers, 24-7 (D)
1942—Packers, 38-7 (Mil)
Packers, 28-7 (D)
1943—Packers, 35-14 (GB)
Packers, 27-6 (D)
1944—Packers, 27-6 (Mil)
Packers, 14-0 (D)
1945—Packers, 57-21 (Mil)
Lions, 14-3 (D)
1946—Packers, 10-7 (Mil)
Packers, 9-0 (D)
1947—Packers, 34-17 (GB)
Packers, 35-14 (D)
1948—Packers, 33-21 (GB)
Lions, 24-20 (D)
1949—Packers, 16-14 (Mil)
Lions, 21-7 (D)
1950—Lions, 45-7 (GB)
Lions, 24-21 (D)
1951—Lions, 24-17 (GB)
Lions, 52-35 (D)
1952—Lions, 52-17 (GB)
Lions, 48-24 (D)
1953—Lions, 14-7 (GB)
Lions, 34-15 (D)
1954—Lions, 21-17 (GB)
Lions, 28-24 (D)
1955—Packers, 20-17 (GB)
Lions, 24-10 (D)
1956—Lions, 20-16 (GB)
Packers, 24-20 (D)
1957—Lions, 24-14 (GB)
Lions, 18-6 (D)
1958—Tie, 13-13 (GB)
Lions, 24-14 (D)
1959—Packers, 28-10 (GB)
Packers, 24-17 (D)
1960—Packers, 28-9 (GB)
Lions, 23-10 (D)
1961—Lions, 17-13 (Mil)
Packers, 17-9 (D)
1962—Packers, 9-7 (GB)
Lions, 26-14 (D)
1963—Packers, 31-10 (Mil)
Tie, 13-13 (D)
1964—Packers, 14-10 (D)
Packers, 30-7 (GB)
1965—Packers, 31-21 (D)
Lions, 12-7 (GB)
1966—Packers, 23-14 (GB)
Packers, 31-7 (D)
1967—Tie, 17-17 (GB)
Packers, 27-17 (D)
1968—Lions, 23-17 (GB)
Tie, 14-14 (D)
1969—Packers, 28-17 (D)
Lions, 16-10 (GB)
1970—Lions, 40-0 (GB)
Lions, 20-0 (D)
1971—Lions, 31-28 (D)
Tie, 14-14 (Mil)
1972—Packers, 24-23 (D)
Packers, 33-7 (GB)
1973—Tie, 13-13 (GB)
Lions, 34-0 (D)
1974—Packers, 21-19 (Mil)
Lions, 19-17 (D)
1975—Lions, 30-16 (Mil)
Lions, 13-10 (D)
1976—Packers, 24-14 (GB)
Lions, 27-6 (D)
1977—Lions, 10-6 (D)
Packers, 10-9 (GB)
1978—Packers, 13-7 (D)
Packers, 35-14 (Mil)
1979—Packers, 24-16 (Mil)
Packers, 18-13 (D)
1980—Lions, 29-7 (Mil)
Lions, 24-3 (D)
1981—Lions, 31-27 (D)
Packers, 31-17 (GB)
1982—Lions, 30-10 (GB)
Lions, 27-24 (D)
1983—Lions, 38-14 (D)
Lions, 23-20 (Mil) OT
1984—Packers, 41-9 (GB)
Lions, 31-28 (D)
1985—Packers, 43-10 (GB)
Packers, 26-23 (D)
1986—Lions, 21-14 (GB)
Packers, 44-40 (D)
1987—Lions, 19-16 (GB) OT
Packers, 34-33 (D)
1988—Lions, 19-9 (Mil)
Lions, 30-14 (D)
1989—Packers, 23-20 (Mil) OT
Lions, 31-22 (D)
1990—Packers, 24-21 (D)
Lions, 24-17 (GB)
1991—Lions, 23-14 (D)
Lions, 21-17 (GB)
1992—Packers, 27-13 (D)
Packers, 38-10 (Mil)
1993—Packers, 26-17 (Mil)
Lions, 30-20 (D)
**Packers, 28-24 (D)
1994—Packers, 38-30 (Mil)
Lions, 34-31 (D)
**Packers, 16-12 (GB)
1995—Packers, 30-21 (GB)
Lions, 24-16 (D)
1996—Packers, 28-18 (GB)
Packers, 31-3 (D)
1997—Lions, 26-15 (D)
Packers, 20-10 (GB)
(RS: Pts.—Packers 2,696, Lions 2,437)
(PS Pts.—Packers 44, Lions 36)
Franchise in Portsmouth prior to 1934 and known as the Spartans
**NFC First-Round Playoff*

DETROIT vs. *INDIANAPOLIS
RS: Lions lead series, 18-17-2
1953—Lions, 27-17 (B)
Lions, 17-7 (D)
1954—Lions, 35-0 (D)
Lions, 27-3 (B)
1955—Colts, 28-13 (B)
Lions, 24-14 (D)
1956—Lions, 31-14 (B)
Lions, 27-3 (D)
1957—Colts, 34-14 (B)
Lions, 31-27 (D)
1958—Colts, 28-15 (B)
Colts, 40-14 (D)
1959—Colts, 21-9 (B)
Colts, 31-24 (D)
1960—Lions, 30-17 (D)
Lions, 20-15 (B)
1961—Lions, 16-15 (B)
Colts, 17-14 (D)
1962—Lions, 29-20 (B)
Lions, 21-14 (D)
1963—Colts, 25-21 (D)
Colts, 24-21 (B)
1964—Colts, 34-0 (D)
Lions, 31-14 (B)
1965—Colts, 31-7 (B)
Tie, 24-24 (D)
1966—Colts, 45-14 (B)
Lions, 20-14 (D)
1967—Colts, 41-7 (B)
1968—Colts, 27-10 (D)
1969—Tie, 17-17 (B)
1973—Colts, 29-27 (D)
1977—Lions, 13-10 (B)
1980—Colts, 10-9 (D)
1985—Colts, 14-6 (I)
1991—Lions, 33-24 (I)
1997—Lions, 32-10 (D)
(RS Pts.—Colts 758, Lions 730)
Franchise in Baltimore prior to 1984

DETROIT vs. JACKSONVILLE
RS: Lions lead series, 1-0
1995—Lions, 44-0 (D)
(RS Pts.—Lions 44, Jaguars 0)

DETROIT vs. KANSAS CITY
RS: Chiefs lead series, 5-3
1971—Lions, 32-21 (D)
1975—Chiefs, 24-21 (KC) OT
1980—Chiefs, 20-17 (KC)
1981—Lions, 27-10 (D)
1987—Chiefs, 27-20 (D)
1988—Lions, 7-6 (KC)
1990—Chiefs, 43-24 (KC)
1996—Chiefs, 28-24 (D)
(RS Pts.—Chiefs 179, Lions 172)

DETROIT vs. MIAMI
RS: Dolphins lead series, 4-2
1973—Dolphins, 34-7 (M)
1979—Dolphins, 28-10 (D)
1985—Lions, 31-21 (D)
1991—Lions, 17-13 (D)
1994—Dolphins, 27-20 (M)
1997—Dolphins, 33-30 (M)
(RS Pts.—Dolphins 156, Lions 115)

DETROIT vs. MINNESOTA
RS: Vikings lead series, 44-27-2
1961—Lions, 37-10 (M)
Lions, 13-7 (D)
1962—Lions, 17-6 (M)
Lions, 37-23 (D)
1963—Lions, 28-10 (D)
Vikings, 34-31 (M)
1964—Lions, 24-20 (M)
Tie, 23-23 (D)
1965—Lions, 31-29 (M)
Vikings, 29-7 (D)
1966—Lions, 32-31 (M)
Vikings, 28-16 (D)
1967—Tie, 10-10 (M)
Lions, 14-3 (D)
1968—Vikings, 24-10 (M)
Vikings, 13-6 (D)
1969—Vikings, 24-10 (M)
Vikings, 27-0 (D)
1970—Vikings, 30-17 (D)
Vikings, 24-20 (M)

1971—Vikings, 16-13 (D)
Vikings, 29-10 (M)
1972—Vikings, 34-10 (D)
Vikings, 16-14 (M)
1973—Vikings, 23-9 (D)
Vikings, 28-7 (M)
1974—Vikings, 7-6 (D)
Lions, 20-16 (M)
1975—Vikings, 25-19 (M)
Lions, 17-10 (D)
1976—Vikings, 10-9 (D)
Vikings, 31-23 (M)
1977—Vikings, 14-7 (M)
Vikings, 30-21 (D)
1978—Vikings, 17-7 (M)
Lions, 45-14 (D)
1979—Vikings, 13-10 (D)
Vikings, 14-7 (M)
1980—Lions, 27-7 (D)
Vikings, 34-0 (M)
1981—Vikings, 26-24 (M)
Lions, 45-7 (D)
1982—Vikings, 34-31 (D)
1983—Vikings, 20-17 (M)
Lions, 13-2 (D)
1984—Vikings, 29-28 (D)
Lions, 16-14 (M)
1985—Vikings, 16-13 (M)
Lions, 41-21 (D)
1986—Lions, 13-10 (M)
Vikings, 24-10 (D)
1987—Vikings, 34-19 (M)
Vikings, 17-14 (D)
1988—Vikings, 44-17 (M)
Vikings, 23-0 (D)
1989—Vikings, 24-17 (M)
Vikings, 20-7 (D)
1990—Lions, 34-27 (M)
Vikings, 17-7 (D)
1991—Lions, 24-20 (D)
Lions, 34-14 (M)
1992—Lions, 31-17 (D)
Vikings, 31-14 (M)
1993—Lions, 30-27 (M)
Vikings, 13-0 (D)
1994—Vikings, 10-3 (M)
Lions, 41-19 (D)
1995—Vikings, 20-10 (M)
Lions, 44-38 (D)
1996—Vikings, 17-13 (M)
Vikings, 24-22 (D)
1997—Lions, 38-15 (D)
Lions, 14-13 (M)
(RS Pts.—Vikings 1,483, Lions 1,348)

DETROIT vs. NEW ENGLAND
RS: Series tied, 3-3
1971—Lions, 34-7 (NE)
1976—Lions, 30-10 (D)
1979—Patriots, 24-17 (NE)
1985—Patriots, 23-6 (NE)
1993—Lions, 19-16 (NE) OT
1994—Patriots, 23-17 (D)
(RS Pts.—Lions 123, Patriots 103)

DETROIT vs. NEW ORLEANS
RS: Saints lead series, 8-6-1
1968—Tie, 20-20 (D)
1970—Saints, 19-17 (NO)
1972—Lions, 27-14 (D)
1973—Saints, 20-13 (NO)
1974—Lions, 19-14 (D)
1976—Saints, 17-16 (NO)
1977—Lions, 23-19 (D)
1979—Saints, 17-7 (NO)
1980—Lions, 24-13 (D)
1988—Saints, 22-14 (D)
1989—Lions, 21-14 (D)
1990—Lions, 27-10 (NO)
1992—Saints, 13-7 (D)
1993—Saints, 14-3 (NO)
1997—Saints, 35-17 (NO)
(RS Pts.—Saints 261, Lions 255)

***DETROIT vs. N.Y. GIANTS**
RS: Lions lead series, 18-17-1
PS: Lions lead series, 1-0
1930—Giants, 19-6 (P)
1931—Spartans, 14-6 (P)
Giants, 14-0 (NY)
1932—Spartans, 7-0 (P)
Spartans, 6-0 (NY)
1933—Spartans, 17-7 (P)
Giants, 13-10 (NY)
1934—Lions, 9-0 (D)
1935—**Lions, 26-7 (D)
1936—Giants, 14-7 (NY)
Lions, 38-0 (D)
1937—Lions, 17-0 (NY)
1939—Lions, 18-14 (D)
1941—Giants, 20-13 (NY)
1943—Tie, 0-0 (D)
1945—Giants, 35-14 (NY)
1947—Lions, 35-7 (D)
1949—Lions, 45-21 (NY)
1953—Lions, 27-16 (NY)
1955—Giants, 24-19 (D)
1958—Giants, 19-17 (D)
1962—Giants, 17-14 (NY)
1964—Lions, 26-3 (D)
1967—Lions, 30-7 (NY)
1969—Lions, 24-0 (D)
1972—Lions, 30-16 (D)
1974—Lions, 20-19 (D)
1976—Giants, 24-10 (NY)
1982—Giants, 13-6 (D)
1983—Lions, 15-9 (D)
1988—Giants, 30-10 (NY)
Giants, 13-10 (D) OT
1989—Giants, 24-14 (NY)
1990—Giants, 20-0 (NY)
1994—Lions, 28-25 (NY) OT
1996—Giants, 35-7 (D)
1997—Giants, 26-20 (D) OT
(RS Pts.—Lions 583, Giants 510)
(PS Pts.—Lions 26, Giants 7)
**Franchise in Portsmouth prior to 1934 and known as the Spartans*
***NFL Championship*

DETROIT vs. N.Y. JETS
RS: Lions lead series, 5-3
1972—Lions, 37-20 (D)
1979—Jets, 31-10 (NY)
1982—Jets, 28-13 (D)
1985—Lions, 31-20 (D)
1988—Jets, 17-10 (D)
1991—Lions, 34-20 (D)
1994—Lions, 18-7 (NY)
1997—Lions, 13-10 (D)
(RS Pts.—Lions 166, Jets 153)

DETROIT vs. *OAKLAND
RS: Raiders lead series, 6-2
1970—Lions, 28-14 (D)
1974—Raiders, 35-13 (O)
1978—Raiders, 29-17 (O)
1981—Lions, 16-0 (D)
1984—Raiders, 24-3 (D)
1987—Raiders, 27-7 (LA)
1990—Raiders, 38-31 (D)
1996—Raiders, 37-21 (O)
(RS Pts.—Raiders 204, Lions 136)
**Franchise in Los Angeles from 1982-1994*

***DETROIT vs. PHILADELPHIA**
RS: Lions lead series, 12-10-2
PS: Eagles lead series, 1-0
1933—Spartans, 25-0 (P)
1934—Lions, 10-0 (P)
1935—Lions, 35-0 (D)
1936—Lions, 23-0 (P)
1938—Eagles, 21-7 (D)
1940—Lions, 21-0 (P)
1941—Lions, 21-17 (D)
1945—Lions, 28-24 (D)
1948—Eagles, 45-21 (P)
1949—Eagles, 22-14 (D)
1951—Lions, 28-10 (P)
1954—Tie, 13-13 (D)
1957—Lions, 27-16 (P)
1960—Eagles, 28-10 (P)
1961—Eagles, 27-24 (D)
1965—Lions, 35-28 (P)
1968—Eagles, 12-0 (D)
1971—Eagles, 23-20 (D)
1974—Eagles, 28-17 (P)
1977—Lions, 17-13 (D)
1979—Eagles, 44-7 (P)
1984—Tie, 23-23 (D) OT
1986—Lions, 13-11 (P)
1995—**Eagles, 58-37 (P)
1996—Eagles, 24-17 (P)
(RS Pts.—Lions 456, Eagles 429)
(PS Pts.—Eagles 58, Lions 37)
**Franchise in Portsmouth prior to 1934 and known as the Spartans*
***NFC First-Round Playoff*

DETROIT vs. *PITTSBURGH
RS: Lions lead series, 13-12-1
1934—Lions, 40-7 (D)
1936—Lions, 28-3 (D)
1937—Lions, 7-3 (D)
1938—Lions, 16-7 (D)
1940—Pirates, 10-7 (D)
1942—Steelers, 35-7 (D)
1946—Lions, 17-7 (D)
1947—Steelers, 17-10 (P)
1948—Lions, 17-14 (D)
1949—Steelers, 14-7 (P)
1950—Lions, 10-7 (D)
1952—Lions, 31-6 (P)
1953—Lions, 38-21 (D)
1955—Lions, 31-28 (P)
1956—Lions, 45-7 (D)
1959—Tie, 10-10 (P)
1962—Lions, 45-7 (D)
1966—Steelers, 17-3 (P)
1967—Steelers, 24-14 (D)
1969—Steelers, 16-13 (P)
1973—Steelers, 24-10 (P)
1983—Lions, 45-3 (D)
1986—Steelers, 27-17 (P)
1989—Steelers, 23-3 (D)
1992—Steelers, 17-14 (P)
1995—Steelers, 23-20 (P)
(RS Pts.—Lions 505, Steelers 377)
**Steelers known as Pirates prior to 1941*

DETROIT vs. *ST. LOUIS
RS: Rams lead series, 39-35-1
PS: Lions lead series, 1-0
1937—Lions, 28-0 (C)
Lions, 27-7 (D)
1938—Rams, 21-17 (C)
Lions, 6-0 (D)
1939—Lions, 15-7 (D)
Rams, 14-3 (C)
1940—Lions, 6-0 (D)
Rams, 24-0 (C)
1941—Lions, 17-7 (D)
Lions, 14-0 (C)
1942—Rams, 14-0 (D)
Rams, 27-7 (C)
1944—Rams, 20-17 (D)
Lions, 26-14 (C)
1945—Rams, 28-21 (D)
1946—Rams, 35-14 (LA)
Rams, 41-20 (D)
1947—Rams, 27-13 (D)
Rams, 28-17 (LA)
1948—Rams, 44-7 (LA)
Rams, 34-27 (D)
1949—Rams, 27-24 (LA)
Rams, 21-10 (D)
1950—Rams, 30-28 (D)
Rams, 65-24 (LA)
1951—Rams, 27-21 (D)
Lions, 24-22 (LA)
1952—Lions, 17-14 (LA)
Lions, 24-16 (D)
**Lions, 31-21 (D)
1953—Rams, 31-19 (D)
Rams, 37-24 (LA)
1954—Lions, 21-3 (D)
Lions, 27-24 (LA)
1955—Rams, 17-10 (D)
Rams, 24-13 (LA)
1956—Lions, 24-21 (D)
Lions, 16-7 (LA)
1957—Lions, 10-7 (D)
Rams, 35-17 (LA)
1958—Rams, 42-28 (D)
Lions, 41-24 (LA)
1959—Lions, 17-7 (LA)
Lions, 23-17 (D)
1960—Rams, 48-35 (LA)
Lions, 12-10 (D)
1961—Lions, 14-13 (D)
Lions, 28-10 (LA)
1962—Lions, 13-10 (D)
Lions, 12-3 (LA)
1963—Lions, 23-2 (LA)
Rams, 28-21 (D)
1964—Tie, 17-17 (LA)
Lions, 37-17 (D)
1965—Lions, 20-0 (D)
Lions, 31-7 (LA)
1966—Rams, 14-7 (D)
Rams, 23-3 (LA)
1967—Rams, 31-7 (D)
1968—Rams, 10-7 (LA)
1969—Lions, 28-0 (D)
1970—Lions, 28-23 (LA)
1971—Rams, 21-13 (D)
1972—Lions, 34-17 (LA)
1974—Rams, 16-13 (LA)
1975—Rams, 20-0 (D)
1976—Rams, 20-17 (D)
1980—Lions, 41-20 (LA)
1981—Rams, 20-13 (LA)
1982—Lions, 19-14 (LA)
1983—Rams, 21-10 (LA)
1986—Rams, 14-10 (LA)
1987—Rams, 37-16 (D)
1988—Rams, 17-10 (LA)
1991—Lions, 21-10 (D)
1993—Lions, 16-13 (LA)
(RS Pts.—Rams 1,436, Lions 1,340)
(PS Pts.—Lions 31, Rams 21)
**Franchise in Los Angeles prior to 1995 and in Cleveland prior to 1946*
***Conference Playoff*

DETROIT vs. SAN DIEGO
RS: Series tied, 3-3
1972—Lions, 34-20 (D)
1977—Lions, 20-0 (D)
1978—Lions, 31-14 (D)
1981—Chargers, 28-23 (SD)
1984—Chargers, 27-24 (SD)
1996—Chargers, 27-21 (SD)
(RS Pts.—Lions 153, Chargers 116)

DETROIT vs. SAN FRANCISCO
RS: 49ers lead series, 28-26-1
PS: Series tied, 1-1
1950—Lions, 24-7 (D)
49ers, 28-27 (SF)
1951—49ers, 20-10 (D)
49ers, 21-17 (SF)
1952—49ers, 17-3 (SF)
49ers, 28-0 (D)
1953—Lions, 24-21 (D)
Lions, 14-10 (SF)
1954—49ers, 37-31 (SF)
Lions, 48-7 (D)
1955—49ers, 27-24 (D)
49ers, 38-21 (SF)
1956—Lions, 20-17 (D)
Lions, 17-13 (SF)
1957—49ers, 35-31 (SF)
Lions, 31-10 (D)
*Lions, 31-27 (SF)
1958—49ers, 24-21 (SF)
Lions, 35-21 (D)
1959—49ers, 34-13 (D)
49ers, 33-7 (SF)
1960—49ers, 14-10 (D)
Lions, 24-0 (SF)

1961—49ers, 49-0 (D)
Tie, 20-20 (SF)
1962—Lions, 45-24 (D)
Lions, 38-24 (SF)
1963—Lions, 26-3 (D)
Lions, 45-7 (SF)
1964—Lions, 26-17 (SF)
Lions, 24-7 (D)
1965—49ers, 27-21 (D)
49ers, 17-14 (SF)
1966—49ers, 27-24 (SF)
49ers, 41-14 (D)
1967—Lions, 45-3 (SF)
1968—49ers, 14-7 (D)
1969—Lions, 26-14 (SF)
1970—Lions, 28-7 (D)
1971—49ers, 31-27 (SF)
1973—Lions, 30-20 (D)
1974—Lions, 17-13 (D)
1975—Lions, 28-17 (SF)
1977—49ers, 28-7 (SF)
1978—Lions, 33-14 (D)
1980—Lions, 17-13 (D)
1981—Lions, 24-17 (D)
1983—**49ers, 24-23 (SF)
1984—49ers, 30-27 (D)
1985—Lions, 23-21 (D)
1988—49ers, 20-13 (SF)
1991—49ers, 35-3 (SF)
1992—49ers, 24-6 (SF)
1993—49ers, 55-17 (D)
1994—49ers, 27-21 (D)
1995—Lions, 27-24 (D)
1996—49ers, 24-14 (SF)
(RS Pts.—Lions 1,189, 49ers 1,176)
(PS Pts.—Lions 54, 49ers 51)
Conference Playoff
***NFC Divisional Playoff*

DETROIT vs. SEATTLE
RS: Seahawks lead series, 4-3
1976—Lions, 41-14 (S)
1978—Seahawks, 28-16 (S)
1984—Seahawks, 38-17 (S)
1987—Seahawks, 37-14 (D)
1990—Seahawks, 30-10 (S)
1993—Lions, 30-10 (D)
1996—Lions, 17-16 (D)
(RS Pts.—Seahawks 173, Lions 145)

DETROIT vs. TAMPA BAY
RS: Lions lead series, 22-18
PS: Buccaneers lead series, 1-0
1977—Lions, 16-7 (D)
1978—Lions, 15-7 (TB)
Lions, 34-23 (D)
1979—Buccaneers, 31-16 (TB)
Buccaneers, 16-14 (D)
1980—Lions, 24-10 (TB)
Lions, 27-14 (D)
1981—Buccaneers, 28-10 (TB)
Buccaneers, 20-17 (D)
1982—Buccaneers, 23-21 (TB)
1983—Lions, 11-0 (TB)
Lions, 23-20 (D)
1984—Buccaneers, 21-17 (TB)
Lions, 13-7 (D) OT
1985—Lions, 30-9 (D)
Buccaneers, 19-16 (TB) OT
1986—Buccaneers, 24-20 (D)
Lions, 38-17 (TB)
1987—Buccaneers, 31-27 (D)
Lions, 20-10 (TB)
1988—Buccaneers, 23-20 (D)
Buccaneers, 21-10 (TB)
1989—Lions, 17-16 (TB)
Lions, 33-7 (D)
1990—Buccaneers, 38-21 (D)
Buccaneers, 23-20 (TB)
1991—Lions, 31-3 (D)
Buccaneers, 30-21 (TB)
1992—Buccaneers, 27-23 (D)
Lions, 38-7 (TB)
1993—Buccaneers, 27-10 (TB)
Lions, 23-0 (D)
1994—Buccaneers, 24-14 (TB)
Lions, 14-9 (D)
1995—Lions, 27-24 (D)
Lions, 37-10 (TB)
1996—Lions, 21-6 (D)
Lions, 27-0 (TB)
1997—Buccaneers, 24-17 (D)
Lions, 27-9 (TB)
*Buccaneers, 20-10 (TB)
(RS Pts.—Lions 860, Buccaneers 665)
(PS Pts.—Buccaneers 20, Lions 10)
**NFC First-Round Playoff*

DETROIT vs. *TENNESSEE
RS: Oilers lead series, 4-3
1971—Lions, 31-7 (H)
1975—Oilers, 24-8 (H)
1983—Oilers, 27-17 (H)
1986—Lions, 24-13 (D)
1989—Oilers, 35-31 (H)
1992—Oilers, 24-21 (D)
1995—Lions, 24-17 (H)
(RS Pts.—Lions 156, Oilers 147)
**Franchise in Houston prior to 1997*

***DETROIT vs. **WASHINGTON**
RS: Redskins lead series, 24-8
PS: Redskins lead series, 2-0
1932—Spartans, 10-0 (P)
1933—Spartans, 13-0 (B)
1934—Lions, 24-0 (D)
1935—Lions, 17-7 (B)
Lions, 14-0 (D)
1938—Redskins, 7-5 (D)
1939—Redskins, 31-7 (W)
1940—Redskins, 20-14 (D)
1942—Redskins, 15-3 (D)
1943—Redskins, 42-20 (W)
1946—Redskins, 17-16 (W)
1947—Lions, 38-21 (D)
1948—Redskins, 46-21 (W)
1951—Lions, 35-17 (D)
1956—Redskins, 18-17 (W)
1965—Lions, 14-10 (D)
1968—Redskins, 14-3 (W)
1970—Redskins, 31-10 (W)
1973—Redskins, 20-0 (D)
1976—Redskins, 20-7 (W)
1978—Redskins, 21-19 (D)
1979—Redskins, 27-24 (D)
1981—Redskins, 33-31 (W)
1982—***Redskins, 31-7 (W)
1983—Redskins, 38-17 (W)
1984—Redskins, 28-14 (W)
1985—Redskins, 24-3 (W)
1987—Redskins, 20-13 (W)
1990—Redskins, 41-38 (D)
1991—Redskins, 45-0 (W)
****Redskins, 41-10 (W)
1992—Redskins, 13-10 (W)
1995—Redskins, 36-30 (W) OT
1997—Redskins, 30-7 (W)
(RS Pts.—Redskins 692, Lions 494)
(PS Pts.—Redskins 72, Lions 17)
**Franchise in Portsmouth prior to 1934 and known as the Spartans.*
***Franchise in Boston prior to 1937*
****NFC First-Round Playoff*
*****NFC Championship*

GREEN BAY vs. ARIZONA
RS: Packers lead series, 39-21-4
PS: Packers lead series, 1-0;
See Arizona vs. Green Bay

GREEN BAY vs. ATLANTA
RS: Packers lead series, 10-9
PS: Packers lead series, 1-0;
See Atlanta vs. Green Bay

GREEN BAY vs. BUFFALO
RS: Bills lead series, 5-2
See Buffalo vs. Green Bay

GREEN BAY vs. CAROLINA
RS: Packers lead series, 1-0
PS: Packers lead series, 1-0;
See Carolina vs. Green Bay

GREEN BAY vs. CHICAGO
RS: Bears lead series, 81-67-6
PS: Bears lead series, 1-0;
See Chicago vs. Green Bay

GREEN BAY vs. CINCINNATI
RS: Series tied, 4-4;
See Cincinnati vs. Green Bay

GREEN BAY vs. CLEVELAND
RS: Packers lead series, 8-6
PS: Packers lead series, 1-0;
See Cleveland vs. Green Bay

GREEN BAY vs. DALLAS
RS: Series tied, 9-9
PS: Cowboys lead series, 4-2;
See Dallas vs. Green Bay

GREEN BAY vs. DENVER
RS: Broncos lead series, 4-3-1
PS: Broncos lead series, 1-0;
See Denver vs. Green Bay

GREEN BAY vs. DETROIT
RS: Packers lead series, 69-59-7
PS: Packers lead series, 2-0;
See Detroit vs. Green Bay

GREEN BAY vs. *INDIANAPOLIS
RS: Colts lead series, 19-18-1
PS: Packers lead series, 1-0
1953—Packers, 37-14 (GB)
Packers, 35-24 (B)
1954—Packers, 7-6 (B)
Packers, 24-13 (Mil)
1955—Colts, 24-20 (Mil)
Colts, 14-10 (B)
1956—Packers, 38-33 (Mil)
Colts, 28-21 (B)
1957—Colts, 45-17 (Mil)
Packers, 24-21 (B)
1958—Colts, 24-17 (Mil)
Colts, 56-0 (B)
1959—Colts, 38-21 (B)
Colts, 28-24 (Mil)
1960—Packers, 35-21 (GB)
Colts, 38-24 (B)
1961—Packers, 45-7 (GB)
Colts, 45-21 (B)
1962—Packers, 17-6 (B)
Packers, 17-13 (GB)
1963—Packers, 31-20 (GB)
Packers, 34-20 (B)
1964—Colts, 21-20 (GB)
Colts, 24-21 (B)
1965—Packers, 20-17 (Mil)
Packers, 42-27 (B)
**Packers, 13-10 (GB) OT
1966—Packers, 24-3 (Mil)
Packers, 14-10 (B)
1967—Colts, 13-10 (B)
1968—Colts, 16-3 (GB)
1969—Colts, 14-6 (B)
1970—Colts, 13-10 (Mil)
1974—Packers, 20-13 (B)
1982—Tie, 20-20 (B) OT
1985—Colts, 37-10 (I)
1988—Colts, 20-13 (GB)
1991—Packers, 14-10 (Mil)
1997—Colts, 41-38 (I)
(RS Pts.—Colts 837, Packers 804)
(PS Pts.—Packers 13, Colts 10)
**Franchise in Baltimore prior to 1984*
***Conference Playoff*

GREEN BAY vs. JACKSONVILLE
RS: Packers lead series, 1-0
1995—Packers, 24-14 (J)
(RS Pts.—Packers 24, Jaguars 14)

GREEN BAY vs. KANSAS CITY
RS: Chiefs lead series, 5-1-1
PS: Packers lead series, 1-0
1966—*Packers, 35-10 (Los Angeles)
1973—Tie, 10-10 (Mil)
1977—Chiefs, 20-10 (KC)
1987—Packers, 23-3 (KC)
1989—Chiefs, 21-3 (GB)
1990—Chiefs, 17-3 (GB)
1993—Chiefs, 23-16 (KC)
1996—Chiefs, 27-20 (KC)
(RS Pts.—Chiefs 121, Packers 85)
(PS Pts.—Packers 35, Chiefs 10)
**Super Bowl I*

GREEN BAY vs. MIAMI
RS: Dolphins lead series, 8-1
1971—Dolphins, 27-6 (Mia)
1975—Dolphins, 31-7 (GB)
1979—Dolphins, 27-7 (Mia)
1985—Dolphins, 34-24 (GB)
1988—Dolphins, 24-17 (Mia)
1989—Dolphins, 23-20 (Mia)
1991—Dolphins, 16-13 (Mia)
1994—Dolphins, 24-14 (Mil)
1997—Packers, 23-18 (GB)
(RS Pts.—Dolphins 224, Packers 131)

GREEN BAY vs. MINNESOTA
RS: Series tied, 36-36-1
1961—Packers, 33-7 (Minn)
Packers, 28-10 (Mil)
1962—Packers, 34-7 (GB)
Packers, 48-21 (Minn)
1963—Packers, 37-28 (Minn)
Packers, 28-7 (GB)
1964—Vikings, 24-23 (GB)
Packers, 42-13 (Minn)
1965—Packers, 38-13 (Minn)
Packers, 24-19 (GB)
1966—Vikings, 20-17 (GB)
Packers, 28-16 (Minn)
1967—Vikings, 10-7 (Mil)
Packers, 30-27 (Minn)
1968—Vikings, 26-13 (Mil)
Vikings, 14-10 (Minn)
1969—Vikings, 19-7 (Minn)
Vikings, 9-7 (Mil)
1970—Packers, 13-10 (Mil)
Vikings, 10-3 (Minn)
1971—Vikings, 24-13 (GB)
Vikings, 3-0 (Minn)
1972—Vikings, 27-13 (GB)
Packers, 23-7 (Minn)
1973—Vikings, 11-3 (Minn)
Vikings, 31-7 (GB)
1974—Vikings, 32-17 (GB)
Packers, 19-7 (Minn)
1975—Vikings, 28-17 (GB)
Vikings, 24-3 (Minn)
1976—Vikings, 17-10 (Mil)
Vikings, 20-9 (Minn)
1977—Vikings, 19-7 (Minn)
Vikings, 13-6 (GB)
1978—Vikings, 21-7 (Minn)
Tie, 10-10 (GB) OT
1979—Vikings, 27-21 (Minn) OT
Packers, 19-7 (Mil)
1980—Packers, 16-3 (GB)
Packers, 25-13 (Minn)
1981—Vikings, 30-13 (Mil)
Packers, 35-23 (Minn)
1982—Packers, 26-7 (Mil)
1983—Vikings, 20-17 (GB) OT
Packers, 29-21 (Minn)
1984—Packers, 45-17 (Mil)
Packers, 38-14 (Minn)
1985—Packers, 20-17 (Mil)
Packers, 27-17 (Minn)
1986—Vikings, 42-7 (Minn)
Vikings, 32-6 (GB)
1987—Packers, 23-16 (Minn)
Packers, 16-10 (Mil)
1988—Packers, 34-14 (Minn)
Packers, 18-6 (GB)
1989—Vikings, 26-14 (Minn)
Packers, 20-19 (Mil)
1990—Packers, 24-10 (Mil)
Vikings, 23-7 (Minn)
1991—Vikings, 35-21 (GB)
Packers, 27-7 (Minn)
1992—Vikings, 23-20 (GB) OT
Vikings, 27-7 (Minn)
1993—Vikings, 15-13 (Minn)
Vikings, 21-17 (Mil)

ALL-TIME TEAM VS. TEAM RESULTS

1994—Packers, 16-10 (GB)
Vikings, 13-10 (M) OT
1995—Packers, 38-21 (GB)
Vikings, 27-24 (M)
1996—Vikings, 30-21 (M)
Packers, 38-10 (GB)
1997—Packers, 38-32 (GB)
Packers, 27-11 (M)
(RS Pts.—Packers 1,451, Vikings 1,300)

GREEN BAY vs. NEW ENGLAND
RS: Series tied, 3-3
PS: Packers lead series, 1-0
1973—Patriots, 33-24 (NE)
1979—Packers, 27-14 (GB)
1985—Patriots, 26-20 (NE)
1988—Packers, 45-3 (Mil)
1994—Patriots, 17-16 (NE)
1996—*Packers, 35-21 (New Orleans)
1997—Packers, 28-10 (NE)
(RS Pts.—Packers 160, Patriots 103)
(PS Pts.—Packers 35, Patriots 21)
Super Bowl XXXI

GREEN BAY vs. NEW ORLEANS
RS: Packers lead series, 13-4
1968—Packers, 29-7 (Mil)
1971—Saints, 29-21 (Mil)
1972—Packers, 30-20 (NO)
1973—Packers, 30-10 (Mil)
1975—Saints, 20-19 (NO)
1976—Packers, 32-27 (Mil)
1977—Packers, 24-20 (NO)
1978—Packers, 28-17 (Mil)
1979—Packers, 28-19 (Mil)
1981—Packers, 35-7 (NO)
1984—Packers, 23-13 (NO)
1985—Packers, 38-14 (Mil)
1986—Saints, 24-10 (NO)
1987—Saints, 33-24 (NO)
1989—Packers, 35-34 (GB)
1993—Packers, 19-17 (NO)
1995—Packers, 34-23 (NO)
(RS Pts.—Packers 459, Saints 334)

GREEN BAY vs. N.Y. GIANTS
RS: Packers lead series, 22-20-2
PS: Packers lead series, 4-1
1928—Giants, 6-0 (GB)
Packers, 7-0 (NY)
1929—Packers, 20-6 (NY)
1930—Packers, 14-7 (GB)
Giants, 13-6 (NY)
1931—Packers, 27-7 (GB)
Packers, 14-10 (NY)
1932—Packers, 13-0 (GB)
Giants, 6-0 (NY)
1933—Giants, 10-7 (Mil)
Giants, 17-6 (NY)
1934—Packers, 20-6 (Mil)
Giants, 17-3 (NY)
1935—Packers, 16-7 (GB)
1936—Packers, 26-14 (NY)
1937—Giants, 10-0 (NY)
1938—Giants, 15-3 (NY)
*Giants, 23-17 (NY)
1939—*Packers, 27-0 (Mil)
1940—Giants, 7-3 (NY)
1942—Tie, 21-21 (NY)
1943—Packers, 35-21 (NY)
1944—Giants, 24-0 (NY)
*Packers, 14-7 (NY)
1945—Packers, 23-14 (NY)
1947—Tie, 24-24 (NY)
1948—Giants, 49-3 (Mil)
1949—Giants, 30-10 (GB)
1952—Packers, 17-3 (NY)
1957—Giants, 31-17 (GB)
1959—Giants, 20-3 (NY)
1961—Packers, 20-17 (Mil)
*Packers, 37-0 (GB)
1962—*Packers, 16-7 (NY)
1967—Packers, 48-21 (NY)
1969—Packers, 20-10 (Mil)
1971—Giants, 42-40 (GB)
1973—Packers, 16-14 (New Haven)
1975—Packers, 40-14 (Mil)
1980—Giants, 27-21 (NY)
1981—Packers, 27-14 (NY)
Packers, 26-24 (Mil)
1982—Packers, 27-19 (NY)
1983—Giants, 27-3 (NY)
1985—Packers, 23-20 (GB)
1986—Giants, 55-24 (NY)
1987—Giants, 20-10 (NY)
1992—Giants, 27-7 (NY)
1995—Packers, 14-6 (GB)
(RS Pts.—Giants 752, Packers 704)
(PS Pts.—Packers 111, Giants 37)
NFL Championship

GREEN BAY vs. N.Y. JETS
RS: Jets lead series, 5-2
1973—Packers, 23-7 (Mil)
1979—Jets, 27-22 (GB)
1981—Jets, 28-3 (NY)
1982—Jets, 15-13 (NY)
1985—Jets, 24-3 (Mil)
1991—Jets, 19-16 (NY) OT
1994—Packers, 17-10 (GB)
(RS Pts.—Jets 130, Packers 97)

GREEN BAY vs. *OAKLAND
RS: Raiders lead series, 5-2
PS: Packers lead series, 1-0
1967—**Packers, 33-14 (Miami)
1972—Raiders, 20-14 (GB)
1976—Raiders, 18-14 (O)
1978—Raiders, 28-3 (GB)
1984—Raiders, 28-7 (LA)
1987—Raiders, 20-0 (GB)
1990—Packers, 29-16 (LA)
1993—Packers, 28-0 (GB)
(RS Pts.—Raiders 130, Packers 95)
(PS Pts.—Packers 33, Raiders 14)
Franchise in Los Angeles from 1982-1994
**Super Bowl II*

GREEN BAY vs. PHILADELPHIA
RS: Packers lead series, 20-9
PS: Eagles lead series, 1-0
1933—Packers, 35-9 (GB)
Packers, 10-0 (P)
1934—Packers, 19-6 (GB)
1935—Packers, 13-6 (P)
1937—Packers, 37-7 (Mil)
1939—Packers, 23-16 (P)
1940—Packers, 27-20 (GB)
1942—Packers, 7-0 (P)
1946—Packers, 19-7 (P)
1947—Eagles, 28-14 (P)
1951—Packers, 37-24 (GB)
1952—Packers, 12-10 (Mil)
1954—Packers, 37-14 (P)
1958—Packers, 38-35 (GB)
1960—*Eagles, 17-13 (P)
1962—Packers, 49-0 (P)
1968—Packers, 30-13 (GB)
1970—Packers, 30-17 (Mil)
1974—Eagles, 36-14 (P)
1976—Packers, 28-13 (GB)
1978—Eagles, 10-3 (P)
1979—Eagles, 21-10 (GB)
1987—Packers, 16-10 (GB) OT
1990—Eagles, 31-0 (P)
1991—Eagles, 20-3 (GB)
1992—Packers, 27-24 (Mil)
1993—Eagles, 20-17 (GB)
1994—Eagles, 13-7 (P)
1996—Packers, 39-13 (GB)
1997—Eagles, 10-9 (P)
(RS Pts.—Packers 610, Eagles 433)
(PS Pts.—Eagles 17, Packers 13)
NFL Championship

GREEN BAY vs. *PITTSBURGH
RS: Packers lead series, 18-11
1933—Packers, 47-0 (GB)
1935—Packers, 27-0 (GB)
Packers, 34-14 (P)
1936—Packers, 42-10 (Mil)
1938—Packers, 20-0 (GB)
1940—Packers, 24-3 (Mil)
1941—Packers, 54-7 (P)
1942—Packers, 24-21 (Mil)
1946—Packers, 17-7 (GB)
1947—Steelers, 18-17 (Mil)
1948—Steelers, 38-7 (P)
1949—Steelers, 30-7 (Mil)
1951—Packers, 35-33 (Mil)
Steelers, 28-7 (P)
1953—Steelers, 31-14 (P)
1954—Steelers, 21-20 (GB)
1957—Packers, 27-10 (P)
1960—Packers, 19-13 (P)
1963—Packers, 33-14 (Mil)
1965—Packers, 41-9 (P)
1967—Steelers, 24-17 (GB)
1969—Packers, 38-34 (P)
1970—Packers, 20-12 (P)
1975—Steelers, 16-13 (Mil)
1980—Steelers, 22-20 (P)
1983—Steelers, 25-21 (GB)
1986—Steelers, 27-3 (P)
1992—Packers, 17-3 (GB)
1995—Packers, 24-19 (GB)
(RS Pts.—Packers 689, Steelers 489)
Steelers known as Pirates prior to 1941

GREEN BAY vs. *ST. LOUIS
RS: Rams lead series, 43-39-2
PS: Packers lead series, 1-0
1937—Packers, 35-10 (C)
Packers, 35-7 (GB)
1938—Packers, 26-17 (GB)
Packers, 28-7 (C)
1939—Rams, 27-24 (GB)
Packers, 7-6 (C)
1940—Packers, 31-14 (GB)
Tie, 13-13 (C)
1941—Packers, 24-7 (Mil)
Packers, 17-14 (C)
1942—Packers, 45-28 (GB)
Packers, 30-12 (C)
1944—Packers, 30-21 (GB)
Packers, 42-7 (C)
1945—Rams, 27-14 (GB)
Rams, 20-7 (C)
1946—Rams, 21-17 (Mil)
Rams, 38-17 (LA)
1947—Packers, 17-14 (Mil)
Packers, 30-10 (LA)
1948—Packers, 16-0 (GB)
Rams, 24-10 (LA)
1949—Rams, 48-7 (GB)
Rams, 35-7 (LA)
1950—Rams, 45-14 (Mil)
Rams, 51-14 (LA)
1951—Rams, 28-0 (Mil)
Rams, 42-14 (LA)
1952—Rams, 30-28 (Mil)
Rams, 45-27 (LA)
1953—Rams, 38-20 (Mil)
Rams, 33-17 (LA)
1954—Packers, 35-17 (Mil)
Rams, 35-27 (LA)
1955—Packers, 30-28 (Mil)
Rams, 31-17 (LA)
1956—Packers, 42-17 (Mil)
Rams, 49-21 (LA)
1957—Rams, 31-27 (Mil)
Rams, 42-17 (LA)
1958—Rams, 20-7 (GB)
Rams, 34-20 (LA)
1959—Rams, 45-6 (Mil)
Packers, 38-20 (LA)
1960—Rams, 33-31 (Mil)
Packers, 35-21 (LA)
1961—Packers, 35-17 (GB)
Packers, 24-17 (LA)
1962—Packers, 41-10 (Mil)
Packers, 20-17 (LA)
1963—Packers, 42-10 (GB)
Packers, 31-14 (LA)
1964—Rams, 27-17 (Mil)
Tie, 24-24 (LA)
1965—Packers, 6-3 (Mil)
Rams, 21-10 (LA)
1966—Packers, 24-13 (GB)
Packers, 27-23 (LA)
1967—Rams, 27-24 (LA)
**Packers, 28-7 (Mil)
1968—Rams, 16-14 (Mil)
1969—Rams, 34-21 (LA)
1970—Rams, 31-21 (GB)
1971—Rams, 30-13 (LA)
1973—Rams, 24-7 (LA)
1974—Packers, 17-6 (Mil)
1975—Rams, 22-5 (LA)
1977—Rams, 24-6 (Mil)
1978—Rams, 31-14 (LA)
1980—Rams, 51-21 (LA)
1981—Rams, 35-23 (LA)
1982—Packers, 35-23 (Mil)
1983—Packers, 27-24 (Mil)
1984—Packers, 31-6 (Mil)
1985—Rams, 34-17 (LA)
1988—Rams, 34-7 (GB)
1989—Rams, 41-38 (LA)
1990—Packers, 36-24 (GB)
1991—Rams, 23-21 (LA)
1992—Packers, 28-13 (GB)
1993—Packers, 36-6 (Mil)
1994—Packers, 24-17 (GB)
1995—Rams, 17-14 (GB)
1996—Packers, 24-9 (StL)
1997—Packers, 17-7 (GB)
(RS Pts.—Rams 1,967, Packers 1,858)
(PS Pts.—Packers 28, Rams 7)
Franchise in Los Angeles prior to 1995 and in Cleveland prior to 1946
**Conference Championship*

GREEN BAY vs. SAN DIEGO
RS: Packers lead series, 5-1
1970—Packers, 22-20 (SD)
1974—Packers, 34-0 (GB)
1978—Packers, 24-3 (SD)
1984—Chargers, 34-28 (GB)
1993—Packers, 20-13 (SD)
1996—Packers, 42-10 (GB)
(RS Pts.—Packers 170, Chargers 80)

GREEN BAY vs. SAN FRANCISCO
RS: 49ers lead series, 25-22-1
PS: Packers lead series, 3-0
1950—Packers, 25-21 (GB)
49ers, 30-14 (SF)
1951—49ers, 31-19 (SF)
1952—49ers, 24-14 (SF)
1953—49ers, 37-7 (Mil)
49ers, 48-14 (SF)
1954—49ers, 23-17 (Mil)
49ers, 35-0 (SF)
1955—Packers, 27-21 (Mil)
Packers, 28-7 (SF)
1956—49ers, 17-16 (GB)
49ers, 38-20 (SF)
1957—49ers, 24-14 (Mil)
49ers, 27-20 (SF)
1958—49ers, 33-12 (Mil)
49ers, 48-21 (SF)
1959—Packers, 21-20 (GB)
Packers, 36-14 (SF)
1960—Packers, 41-14 (Mil)
Packers, 13-0 (SF)
1961—Packers, 30-10 (GB)
49ers, 22-21 (SF)
1962—Packers, 31-13 (Mil)
Packers, 31-21 (SF)
1963—Packers, 28-10 (Mil)
Packers, 21-17 (SF)
1964—Packers, 24-14 (Mil)
49ers, 24-14 (SF)
1965—Packers, 27-10 (GB)
Tie, 24-24 (SF)
1966—49ers, 21-20 (SF)
Packers, 20-7 (Mil)
1967—Packers, 13-0 (GB)
1968—49ers, 27-20 (SF)
1969—Packers, 14-7 (Mil)

1970—49ers, 26-10 (SF)
1972—Packers, 34-24 (Mil)
1973—49ers, 20-6 (SF)
1974—49ers, 7-6 (SF)
1976—49ers, 26-14 (GB)
1977—Packers, 16-14 (Mil)
1980—Packers, 23-16 (Mil)
1981—49ers, 13-3 (Mil)
1986—49ers, 31-17 (Mil)
1987—49ers, 23-12 (GB)
1989—Packers, 21-17 (SF)
1990—49ers, 24-20 (GB)
1995—*Packers, 27-17 (SF)
1996—Packers, 23-20 (GB) OT
*Packers, 35-14 (GB)
1997—**Packers, 23-10 (GB)
(RS Pts.—49ers 1,000, Packers 922)
(PS Pts.—Packers 85, 49ers 41)
NFC Divisional Playoff
**NFC Championship*

GREEN BAY vs. SEATTLE
RS: Packers lead series, 4-3
1976—Packers, 27-20 (Mil)
1978—Packers, 45-28 (Mil)
1981—Packers, 34-24 (GB)
1984—Seahawks, 30-24 (Mil)
1987—Seahawks, 24-13 (S)
1990—Seahawks, 20-14 (Mil)
1996—Packers, 31-10 (S)
(RS Pts.—Packers 188, Seahawks 156)

GREEN BAY vs. TAMPA BAY
RS: Packers lead series, 24-13-1
PS: Packers lead series, 1-0
1977—Packers, 13-0 (TB)
1978—Packers, 9-7 (GB)
Packers, 17-7 (TB)
1979—Buccaneers, 21-10 (GB)
Buccaneers, 21-3 (TB)
1980—Tie, 14-14 (TB) OT
Buccaneers, 20-17 (Mil)
1981—Buccaneers, 21-10 (GB)
Buccaneers, 37-3 (TB)
1983—Packers, 55-14 (GB)
Packers, 12-9 (TB) OT
1984—Buccaneers, 30-27 (TB) OT
Packers, 27-14 (GB)
1985—Packers, 21-0 (GB)
Packers, 20-17 (TB)
1986—Packers, 31-7 (Mil)
Packers, 21-7 (TB)
1987—Buccaneers, 23-17 (Mil)
1988—Buccaneers, 13-10 (GB)
Buccaneers, 27-24 (TB)
1989—Buccaneers, 23-21 (GB)
Packers, 17-16 (TB)
1990—Buccaneers, 26-14 (TB)
Packers, 20-10 (Mil)
1991—Packers, 15-13 (GB)
Packers, 27-0 (TB)
1992—Buccaneers, 31-3 (TB)
Packers, 19-14 (Mil)
1993—Packers, 37-14 (TB)
Packers, 13-10 (GB)
1994—Packers, 30-3 (GB)
Packers, 34-19 (TB)
1995—Packers, 35-13 (GB)
Buccaneers, 13-10 (TB) OT
1996—Packers, 34-3 (TB)
Packers, 13-7 (GB)
1997—Packers, 21-16 (GB)
Packers, 17-6 (TB)
*Packers, 21-7 (GB)
(RS Pts.—Packers 741, Buccaneers 546)
(PS Pts.—Packers 21, Buccaneers 7)
NFC Divisional Playoff

GREEN BAY vs. *TENNESSEE
RS: Series tied, 3-3
1972—Packers, 23-10 (H)
1977—Oilers, 16-10 (GB)
1980—Oilers, 22-3 (GB)
1983—Packers, 41-38 (H) OT
1986—Oilers, 31-3 (GB)
1992—Packers, 16-14 (H)
(RS Pts.—Oilers 131, Packers 96)
Franchise in Houston prior to 1997

GREEN BAY vs. *WASHINGTON
RS: Packers lead series, 13-12-1
PS: Series tied, 1-1
1932—Packers, 21-0 (B)
1933—Tie, 7-7 (GB)
Redskins, 20-7 (B)
1934—Packers, 10-0 (B)
1936—Packers, 31-2 (GB)
Packers, 7-3 (B)
**Packers, 21-6 (New York)
1937—Redskins, 14-6 (W)
1939—Packers, 24-14 (Mil)
1941—Packers, 22-17 (W)
1943—Redskins, 33-7 (Mil)
1946—Packers, 20-7 (W)
1947—Packers, 27-10 (Mil)
1948—Redskins, 23-7 (Mil)
1949—Redskins, 30-0 (W)
1950—Packers, 35-21 (Mil)
1952—Packers, 35-20 (Mil)
1958—Redskins, 37-21 (W)
1959—Packers, 21-0 (GB)
1968—Packers, 27-7 (W)
1972—Redskins, 21-16 (W)
***Redskins, 16-3 (W)
1974—Redskins, 17-6 (GB)
1977—Redskins, 10-9 (W)
1979—Redskins, 38-21 (W)
1983—Packers, 48-47 (GB)
1986—Redskins, 16-7 (GB)
1988—Redskins, 20-17 (Mil)
(RS Pts.—Packers 459, Redskins 434)
(PS Pts.—Packers 24, Redskins 22)
Franchise in Boston prior to 1937 and known as Braves prior to 1933
**NFL Championship*
***NFC Divisional Playoff*

INDIANAPOLIS vs. ARIZONA
RS: Series tied, 6-6;
See Arizona vs. Indianapolis

INDIANAPOLIS vs. ATLANTA
RS: Colts lead series, 10-0;
See Atlanta vs. Indianapolis

INDIANAPOLIS vs. BALTIMORE
RS: Colts lead series, 1-0;
See Baltimore vs. Indianapolis

INDIANAPOLIS vs. BUFFALO
RS: Bills lead series, 31-23-1;
See Buffalo vs. Indianapolis

INDIANAPOLIS vs. CAROLINA
RS: Panthers lead series, 1-0;
See Carolina vs. Indianapolis

INDIANAPOLIS vs. CHICAGO
RS: Colts lead series, 21-16;
See Chicago vs. Indianapolis

INDIANAPOLIS vs. CINCINNATI
RS: Colts lead series, 9-8
PS: Colts lead series, 1-0;
See Cincinnati vs. Indianapolis

INDIANAPOLIS vs. CLEVELAND
RS: Browns lead series, 13-7
PS: Series tied, 2-2;
See Cleveland vs. Indianapolis

INDIANAPOLIS vs. DALLAS
RS: Cowboys lead series, 7-3
PS: Colts lead series, 1-0;
See Dallas vs. Indianapolis

INDIANAPOLIS vs. DENVER
RS: Broncos lead series, 9-2;
See Denver vs. Indianapolis

INDIANAPOLIS vs. DETROIT
RS: Lions lead series, 18-17-2;
See Detroit vs. Indianapolis

INDIANAPOLIS vs. GREEN BAY
RS: Colts lead series, 19-18-1
PS: Packers lead series, 1-0;
See Green Bay vs. Indianapolis

INDIANAPOLIS vs. JACKSONVILLE
RS: Colts lead series, 1-0
1995—Colts, 41-31 (J)
(RS Pts.—Colts 41, Jaguars 31)

***INDIANAPOLIS vs. KANSAS CITY**
RS: Chiefs lead series, 6-5
PS: Colts lead series, 1-0
1970—Chiefs, 44-24 (B)
1972—Chiefs, 24-10 (KC)
1975—Colts, 28-14 (B)
1977—Colts, 17-6 (KC)
1979—Chiefs, 14-0 (KC)
Chiefs, 10-7 (B)
1980—Colts, 31-24 (KC)
Chiefs, 38-28 (B)
1985—Chiefs, 20-7 (KC)
1990—Colts, 23-19 (I)
1995—**Colts, 10-7 (KC)
1996—Colts, 24-19 (KC)
(RS Pts.—Chiefs 232, Colts 199)
(PS Pts.—Colts 10, Chiefs 7)
Franchise in Baltimore prior to 1984
**AFC Divisional Playoff*

***INDIANAPOLIS vs. MIAMI**
RS: Dolphins lead series, 37-19
PS: Dolphins lead series, 1-0
1970—Colts, 35-0 (B)
Dolphins, 34-17 (M)
1971—Dolphins, 17-14 (M)
Colts, 14-3 (B)
**Dolphins, 21-0 (M)
1972—Dolphins, 23-0 (B)
Dolphins, 16-0 (M)
1973—Dolphins, 44-0 (M)
Colts, 16-3 (B)
1974—Dolphins, 17-7 (M)
Dolphins, 17-16 (B)
1975—Colts, 33-17 (M)
Colts, 10-7 (B) OT
1976—Colts, 28-14 (B)
Colts, 17-16 (M)
1977—Colts, 45-28 (B)
Dolphins, 17-6 (M)
1978—Dolphins, 42-0 (B)
Dolphins, 26-8 (M)
1979—Dolphins, 19-0 (M)
Dolphins, 28-24 (B)
1980—Colts, 30-17 (M)
Dolphins, 24-14 (B)
1981—Dolphins, 31-28 (B)
Dolphins, 27-10 (M)
1982—Dolphins, 24-20 (M)
Dolphins, 34-7 (B)
1983—Dolphins, 21-7 (B)
Dolphins, 37-0 (M)
1984—Dolphins, 44-7 (M)
Dolphins, 35-17 (I)
1985—Dolphins, 30-13 (M)
Dolphins, 34-20 (I)
1986—Dolphins, 30-10 (M)
Dolphins, 17-13 (I)
1987—Dolphins, 23-10 (I)
Colts, 40-21 (M)
1988—Colts, 15-13 (I)
Colts, 31-28 (M)
1989—Dolphins, 19-13 (M)
Colts, 42-13 (I)
1990—Dolphins, 27-7 (I)
Dolphins, 23-17 (M)
1991—Dolphins, 17-6 (M)
Dolphins, 10-6 (I)
1992—Colts, 31-20 (M)
Dolphins, 28-0 (I)
1993—Dolphins, 24-20 (I)
Dolphins, 41-27 (M)
1994—Dolphins, 22-21 (M)
Colts, 10-6 (I)
1995—Colts, 27-24 (M) OT
Colts, 36-28 (I)
1996—Colts, 10-6 (I)
Dolphins, 37-13 (M)
1997—Dolphins, 16-10 (M)
Colts, 41-0 (I)
(RS Pts.—Dolphins 1,239, Colts 919)
(PS Pts.—Dolphins 21, Colts 0)
Franchise in Baltimore prior to 1984
**AFC Championship*

***INDIANAPOLIS vs. MINNESOTA**
RS: Colts lead series, 11-7-1
PS: Colts lead series, 1-0
1961—Colts, 34-33 (B)
Vikings, 28-20 (M)
1962—Colts, 34-7 (M)
Colts, 42-17 (B)
1963—Colts, 37-34 (M)
Colts, 41-10 (B)
1964—Vikings, 34-24 (M)
Colts, 17-14 (B)
1965—Colts, 35-16 (B)
Colts, 41-21 (M)
1966—Colts, 38-23 (M)
Colts, 20-17 (B)
1967—Tie, 20-20 (M)
1968—Colts, 21-9 (B)
**Colts, 24-14 (B)
1969—Vikings, 52-14 (M)
1971—Vikings, 10-3 (M)
1982—Vikings, 13-10 (M)
1988—Vikings, 12-3 (M)
1997—Vikings, 39-28 (M)
(RS Pts.—Colts 482, Vikings 409)
(PS Pts.—Colts 24, Vikings 14)
Franchise in Baltimore prior to 1984
**Conference Championship*

***INDIANAPOLIS vs. **NEW ENGLAND**
RS: Colts lead series, 33-32
1970—Colts, 14-6 (Bos)
Colts, 27-3 (Balt)
1971—Colts, 23-3 (NE)
Patriots, 21-17 (Balt)
1972—Colts, 24-17 (NE)
Colts, 31-0 (Balt)
1973—Patriots, 24-16 (NE)
Colts, 18-13 (Balt)
1974—Patriots, 42-3 (NE)
Patriots, 27-17 (Balt)
1975—Patriots, 21-10 (NE)
Colts, 34-21 (Balt)
1976—Colts, 27-13 (NE)
Patriots, 21-14 (Balt)
1977—Patriots, 17-3 (NE)
Colts, 30-24 (Balt)
1978—Colts, 34-27 (NE)
Patriots, 35-14 (Balt)
1979—Colts, 31-26 (Balt)
Patriots, 50-21 (NE)
1980—Patriots, 37-21 (Balt)
Patriots, 47-21 (NE)
1981—Colts, 29-28 (NE)
Colts, 23-21 (Balt)
1982—Patriots, 24-13 (Balt)
1983—Colts, 29-23 (NE) OT
Colts, 12-7 (Balt)
1984—Patriots, 50-17 (I)
Patriots, 16-10 (NE)
1985—Patriots, 34-15 (NE)
Patriots, 38-31 (I)
1986—Patriots, 33-3 (NE)
Patriots, 30-21 (I)
1987—Colts, 30-16 (I)
Patriots, 24-0 (NE)
1988—Patriots, 21-17 (NE)
Colts, 24-21 (I)
1989—Patriots, 23-20 (I) OT
Patriots, 22-16 (NE)
1990—Patriots, 16-14 (I)
Colts, 13-10 (NE)
1991—Patriots, 16-7 (I)
Patriots, 23-17 (NE) OT
1992—Patriots, 37-34 (I) OT
Colts, 6-0 (NE)
1993—Colts, 9-6 (I)
Patriots, 38-0 (NE)
1994—Patriots, 12-10 (I)
Patriots, 28-13 (NE)
1995—Colts, 24-10 (NE)
Colts, 10-7 (I)
1996—Patriots, 27-9 (I)
Patriots, 27-13 (NE)

ALL-TIME TEAM VS. TEAM RESULTS

1997—Patriots, 31-6 (I)
Patriots, 20-17 (NE)
(RS Pts.—Patriots 1,234, Colts 962)
Franchise in Baltimore prior to 1984
***Franchise in Boston prior to 1971*

***INDIANAPOLIS vs. NEW ORLEANS**
RS: Series tied, 3-3
1967—Colts, 30-10 (B)
1969—Colts, 30-10 (NO)
1973—Colts, 14-10 (B)
1986—Saints, 17-14 (I)
1989—Saints, 41-6 (NO)
1995—Saints, 17-14 (NO)
(RS Pts.—Colts 108, Saints 105)
Franchise in Baltimore prior to 1984

***INDIANAPOLIS vs. N.Y. GIANTS**
RS: Series tied, 5-5
PS: Colts lead series, 2-0
1954—Colts, 20-14 (B)
1955—Giants, 17-7 (NY)
1958—Giants, 24-21 (NY)
**Colts, 23-17 (NY) OT
1959—**Colts, 31-16 (B)
1963—Giants, 37-28 (B)
1968—Colts, 26-0 (NY)
1971—Colts, 31-7 (NY)
1975—Colts, 21-0 (NY)
1979—Colts, 31-7 (NY)
1990—Giants, 24-7 (I)
1993—Giants, 20-6 (NY)
(RS Pts.—Colts 198, Giants 150)
(PS Pts.—Colts 54, Giants 33)
Franchise in Baltimore prior to 1984
***NFL Championship*

***INDIANAPOLIS vs. N.Y. JETS**
RS: Colts lead series, 33-22
PS: Jets lead series, 1-0
1968—**Jets 16-7 (Miami)
1970—Colts, 29-22 (NY)
Colts, 35-20 (B)
1971—Colts, 22-0 (B)
Colts, 14-13 (NY)
1972—Jets, 44-34 (B)
Jets, 24-20 (NY)
1973—Jets, 34-10 (B)
Jets, 20-17 (NY)
1974—Colts, 35-20 (NY)
Jets, 45-38 (B)
1975—Colts, 45-28 (NY)
Colts, 52-19 (B)
1976—Colts, 20-0 (NY)
Colts, 33-16 (B)
1977—Colts, 20-12 (NY)
Colts, 33-12 (B)
1978—Jets, 33-10 (B)
Jets, 24-16 (NY)
1979—Colts, 10-8 (B)
Jets, 30-17 (NY)
1980—Colts, 17-14 (NY)
Colts, 35-21 (B)
1981—Jets, 41-14 (B)
Jets, 25-0 (NY)
1982—Jets, 37-0 (NY)
1983—Colts, 17-14 (NY)
Jets, 10-6 (B)
1984—Jets, 23-14 (I)
Colts, 9-5 (NY)
1985—Jets, 25-20 (NY)
Jets, 35-17 (I)
1986—Jets, 26-7 (I)
Jets, 31-16 (NY)
1987—Colts, 6-0 (I)
Colts, 19-14 (NY)
1988—Colts, 38-14 (I)
Jets, 34-16 (NY)
1989—Colts, 17-10 (NY)
Colts, 27-10 (I)
1990—Colts, 17-14 (I)
Colts, 29-21 (NY)
1991—Jets, 17-6 (I)
Colts, 28-27 (NY)
1992—Colts, 6-3 (I) OT
Colts, 10-6 (NY)
1993—Jets, 31-17 (I)
Colts, 9-6 (NY)
1994—Jets, 16-6 (NY)
Colts, 28-25 (I)
1995—Colts, 27-24 (NY) OT
Colts, 17-10 (I)
1996—Colts, 21-7 (NY)
Colts, 34-29 (I)
1997—Jets, 16-12 (I)
Colts, 22-14 (NY)
(RS Pts.—Colts 1,094, Jets 1,079)
(PS Pts.—Jets 16, Colts 7)
Franchise in Baltimore prior to 1984
***Super Bowl III*

***INDIANAPOLIS vs **OAKLAND**
RS: Raiders lead series, 5-2
PS: Series tied, 1-1
1970—***Colts, 27-17 (B)
1971—Colts, 37-14 (O)
1973—Raiders, 34-21 (B)
1975—Raiders, 31-20 (B)
1977—****Raiders, 37-31 (B) OT
1984—Raiders, 21-7 (LA)
1986—Colts, 30-24 (LA)
1991—Raiders, 16-0 (LA)
1995—Raiders, 30-17 (O)
(RS Pts.—Raiders 170, Colts 132)
(PS Pts.—Colts 58, Raiders 54)
Franchise in Baltimore prior to 1984
***Franchise in Los Angeles from 1982-1994*
****AFC Championship*
*****AFC Divisional Playoff*

***INDIANAPOLIS vs. PHILADELPHIA**
RS: Colts lead series, 7-6
1953—Eagles, 45-14 (P)
1965—Colts, 34-24 (B)
1967—Colts, 38-6 (P)
1969—Colts, 24-20 (B)
1970—Colts, 29-10 (B)
1974—Eagles, 30-10 (P)
1978—Eagles, 17-14 (B)
1981—Eagles, 38-13 (P)
1983—Colts, 22-21 (P)
1984—Eagles, 16-7 (P)
1990—Colts, 24-23 (P)
1993—Eagles, 20-10 (I)
1996—Colts, 37-10 (I)
(RS Pts.—Eagles 280, Colts 276)
Franchise in Baltimore prior to 1984

***INDIANAPOLIS vs. PITTSBURGH**
RS: Steelers lead series, 12-4
PS: Steelers lead series, 4-0
1957—Steelers, 19-13 (B)
1968—Colts, 41-7 (P)
1971—Colts, 34-21 (P)
1974—Steelers, 30-0 (B)
1975—**Steelers, 28-10 (P)
1976—**Steelers, 40-14 (B)
1977—Colts, 31-21 (B)
1978—Steelers, 35-13 (P)
1979—Steelers, 17-13 (P)
1980—Steelers, 20-17 (B)
1983—Steelers, 24-13 (B)
1984—Colts, 17-16 (I)
1985—Steelers, 45-3 (P)
1987—Steelers, 21-7 (P)
1991—Steelers, 21-3 (I)
1992—Steelers, 30-14 (P)
1994—Steelers, 31-21 (P)
1995—***Steelers, 20-16 (P)
1996—****Steelers, 42-14 (P)
1997—Steelers, 24-22 (P)
(RS Pts.—Steelers 382, Colts 262)
(PS Pts.—Steelers 130, Colts 54)
Franchise in Baltimore prior to 1984
***AFC Divisional Playoff*
****AFC Championship*
*****AFC First-Round Playoff*

***INDIANAPOLIS vs. **ST. LOUIS**
RS: Colts lead series, 21-16-2
1953—Rams, 21-13 (B)
Rams, 45-2 (LA)
1954—Rams, 48-0 (B)
Colts, 22-21 (LA)
1955—Tie, 17-17 (B)
Rams, 20-14 (LA)
1956—Colts, 56-21 (B)
Rams, 31-7 (LA)
1957—Colts, 31-14 (B)
Rams, 37-21 (LA)
1958—Colts, 34-7 (B)
Rams, 30-28 (LA)
1959—Colts, 35-21 (B)
Colts, 45-26 (LA)
1960—Colts, 31-17 (B)
Rams, 10-3 (LA)
1961—Colts, 27-24 (B)
Rams, 34-17 (LA)
1962—Colts, 30-27 (B)
Colts, 14-2 (LA)
1963—Rams, 17-16 (LA)
Colts, 19-16 (B)
1964—Colts, 35-20 (B)
Colts, 24-7 (LA)
1965—Colts, 35-20 (B)
Colts, 20-17 (LA)
1966—Colts, 17-3 (LA)
Rams, 23-7 (B)
1967—Tie, 24-24 (B)
Rams, 34-10 (LA)
1968—Colts, 27-10 (B)
Colts, 28-24 (LA)
1969—Rams, 27-20 (B)
Colts, 13-7 (LA)
1971—Colts, 24-17 (B)
1975—Rams, 24-13 (LA)
1986—Rams, 24-7 (I)
1989—Rams, 31-17 (LA)
1995—Colts, 21-18 (I)
(RS Pts.—Rams 836, Colts 824)
Franchise in Baltimore prior to 1984
***Franchise in Los Angeles prior to 1995*

***INDIANAPOLIS vs. SAN DIEGO**
RS: Chargers lead series, 12-5
PS: Colts lead series, 1-0
1970—Colts, 16-14 (SD)
1972—Chargers, 23-20 (B)
1976—Colts, 37-21 (SD)
1981—Chargers, 43-14 (B)
1982—Chargers, 44-26 (SD)
1984—Chargers, 38-10 (I)
1986—Chargers, 17-3 (I)
1987—Chargers, 16-13 (I)
Colts, 20-7 (SD)
1988—Colts, 16-0 (SD)
1989—Colts, 10-6 (I)
1992—Chargers, 34-14 (I)
Chargers, 26-0 (SD)
1993—Chargers, 31-0 (I)
1995—Chargers, 27-24 (I)
**Colts, 35-20 (SD)
1996—Chargers, 26-19 (I)
1997—Chargers, 35-19 (SD)
(RS Pts.—Chargers 408, Colts 261)
(PS Pts.—Colts 35, Chargers 20)
Franchise in Baltimore prior to 1984
***AFC First-Round Playoff*

***INDIANAPOLIS vs. SAN FRANCISCO**
RS: Colts lead series, 22-16
1953—49ers, 38-21 (B)
49ers, 45-14 (SF)
1954—Colts, 17-13 (B)
49ers, 10-7 (SF)
1955—Colts, 26-14 (B)
49ers, 35-24 (SF)
1956—49ers, 20-17 (B)
49ers, 30-17 (SF)
1957—Colts, 27-21 (B)
49ers, 17-13 (SF)
1958—Colts, 35-27 (B)
49ers, 21-12 (SF)
1959—Colts, 45-14 (B)
Colts, 34-14 (SF)
1960—49ers, 30-22 (B)
49ers, 34-10 (SF)
1961—Colts, 20-17 (B)
Colts, 27-24 (SF)
1962—49ers, 21-13 (B)
Colts, 22-3 (SF)
1963—Colts, 20-14 (SF)
Colts, 20-3 (B)
1964—Colts, 37-7 (B)
Colts, 14-3 (SF)
1965—Colts, 27-24 (B)
Colts, 34-28 (SF)
1966—Colts, 36-14 (B)
Colts, 30-14 (SF)
1967—Colts, 41-7 (B)
Colts, 26-9 (SF)
1968—Colts, 27-10 (B)
Colts, 42-14 (SF)
1969—49ers, 24-21 (B)
49ers, 20-17 (SF)
1972—49ers, 24-21 (SF)
1986—49ers, 35-14 (SF)
1989—49ers, 30-24 (I)
1995—Colts, 18-17 (I)
(RS Pts.—Colts 892, 49ers 745)
Franchise in Baltimore prior to 1984

***INDIANAPOLIS vs. SEATTLE**
RS: Colts lead series, 4-2
1977—Colts, 29-14 (S)
1978—Colts, 17-14 (S)
1991—Seahawks, 31-3 (S)
1994—Colts, 17-15 (I)
Colts, 31-19 (S)
1997—Seahawks, 31-3 (I)
(RS Pts.—Seahawks 124, Colts 100)
Franchise in Baltimore prior to 1984

***INDIANAPOLIS vs. TAMPA BAY**
RS: Colts lead series, 5-4
1976—Colts, 42-17 (B)
1979—Buccaneers, 29-26 (B) OT
1985—Colts, 31-23 (TB)
1987—Colts, 24-6 (I)
1988—Colts, 35-31 (I)
1991—Buccaneers, 17-3 (TB)
1992—Colts, 24-14 (TB)
1994—Buccaneers, 24-10 (TB)
1997—Buccaneers, 31-28 (I)
(RS Pts.—Colts 223, Buccaneers 192)
Franchise in Baltimore prior to 1984

***INDIANAPOLIS vs. **TENNESSEE**
RS: Series tied, 7-7
1970—Colts, 24-20 (H)
1973—Oilers, 31-27 (B)
1976—Colts, 38-14 (B)
1979—Oilers, 28-16 (B)
1980—Oilers, 21-16 (H)
1983—Colts, 20-10 (B)
1984—Colts, 35-21 (H)
1985—Colts, 34-16 (I)
1986—Oilers, 31-17 (H)
1987—Colts, 51-27 (I)
1988—Oilers, 17-14 (I) OT
1990—Oilers, 24-10 (H)
1992—Oilers, 20-10 (I)
1994—Colts, 45-21 (I)
(RS Pts.—Colts 357, Oilers 301)
Franchise in Baltimore prior to 1984
***Franchise in Houston prior to 1997*

***INDIANAPOLIS vs. WASHINGTON**
RS: Colts lead series, 16-9
1953—Colts, 27-17 (B)
1954—Redskins, 24-21 (W)
1955—Redskins, 14-13 (B)
1956—Colts, 19-17 (B)
1957—Colts, 21-17 (W)
1958—Colts, 35-10 (B)
1959—Redskins, 27-24 (W)
1960—Colts, 20-0 (B)
1961—Colts, 27-6 (W)
1962—Colts, 34-21 (B)
1963—Colts, 36-20 (W)
1964—Colts, 45-17 (B)
1965—Colts, 38-7 (W)
1966—Colts, 37-10 (B)
1967—Colts, 17-13 (W)

1969—Colts, 41-17 (B)
1973—Redskins, 22-14 (W)
1977—Colts, 10-3 (B)
1978—Colts, 21-17 (B)
1981—Redskins, 38-14 (W)
1984—Redskins, 35-7 (I)
1990—Colts, 35-28 (I)
1993—Redskins, 30-24 (W)
1994—Redskins, 41-27 (I)
1996—Redskins, 31-16 (W)
(RS Pts.—Colts 623, Redskins 482)
Franchise in Baltimore prior to 1984

JACKSONVILLE vs. ATLANTA
RS: Jaguars lead series, 1-0;
See Atlanta vs. Jacksonville
JACKSONVILLE vs. BALTIMORE
RS: Jaguars lead series, 4-0;
See Baltimore vs. Jacksonville
JACKSONVILLE vs. BUFFALO
RS: Jaguars lead series, 1-0
PS: Jaguars lead series, 1-0;
See Buffalo vs. Jacksonville
JACKSONVILLE vs. CAROLINA
RS: Jaguars lead series, 1-0;
See Carolina vs. Jacksonville
JACKSONVILLE vs. CHICAGO
RS: Bears lead series, 1-0;
See Chicago vs. Jacksonville
JACKSONVILLE vs. CINCINNATI
RS: Bengals lead series, 4-2;
See Cincinnati vs. Jacksonville
JACKSONVILLE vs. CLEVELAND
RS: Jaguars lead series, 2-0;
See Cleveland vs. Jacksonville
JACKSONVILLE vs. DALLAS
RS: Cowboys lead series, 1-0;
See Dallas vs. Jacksonville
JACKSONVILLE vs. DENVER
RS: Broncos lead series, 1-0
PS: Series tied, 1-1;
See Denver vs. Jacksonville
JACKSONVILLE vs. DETROIT
RS: Lions lead series, 1-0;
See Detroit vs. Jacksonville
JACKSONVILLE vs. GREEN BAY
RS: Packers lead series, 1-0;
See Green Bay vs. Jacksonville
JACKSONVILLE vs. INDIANAPOLIS
RS: Colts lead series, 1-0;
See Indianapolis vs. Jacksonville
JACKSONVILLE vs. KANSAS CITY
RS: Jaguars lead series, 1-0
1997—Jaguars, 24-10 (J)
(RS Pts.—Jaguars 24, Chiefs 10)
JACKSONVILLE vs. NEW ENGLAND
RS: Patriots lead series, 2-0
PS: Patriots lead series, 1-0
1996—Patriots, 28-25 (NE) OT
*Patriots, 20-6 (NE)
1997—Patriots, 26-20 (J)
(RS Pts.—Patriots 54, Jaguars 45)
(PS Pts.—Patriots 20, Jaguars 6)
AFC Championship
JACKSONVILLE vs. NEW ORLEANS
RS: Saints lead series, 1-0
1996—Saints, 17-13 (NO)
(RS Pts.—Saints 17, Jaguars 13)
JACKSONVILLE vs. N.Y. GIANTS
RS: Jaguars lead series, 1-0
1997—Jaguars, 40-13 (J)
(RS Pts.—Jaguars 40, Giants 13)
JACKSONVILLE vs. N.Y. JETS
RS: Series tied, 1-1
1995—Jets, 27-10 (NY)
1996—Jaguars, 21-17 (J)
(RS Pts.—Jets 44, Jaguars 31)
JACKSONVILLE vs. OAKLAND
RS: Series tied, 1-1
1996—Raiders, 17-3 (O)
1997—Jaguars, 20-9 (O)
(RS Pts.—Raiders 26, Jaguars 23)
JACKSONVILLE vs. PHILADELPHIA
RS: Jaguars lead series, 1-0
1997—Jaguars, 38-21 (J)
(RS Pts.—Jaguars 38, Eagles 21)
JACKSONVILLE vs. PITTSBURGH
RS: Series tied, 3-3
1995—Jaguars, 20-16 (J)
Steelers, 24-7 (P)
1996—Jaguars, 24-9 (J)
Steelers, 28-3 (P)
1997—Jaguars, 30-21 (J)
Steelers, 23-17 (P) OT
(RS Pts.—Steelers 121, Jaguars 101)
JACKSONVILLE vs. ST. LOUIS
RS: Rams lead series, 1-0
1996—Rams, 17-14 (StL)
(RS Pts.—Rams 17, Jaguars 14)
JACKSONVILLE vs. SEATTLE
RS: Series tied, 1-1
1995—Seahawks, 47-30 (J)
1996—Jaguars, 20-13 (J)
(RS Pts.—Seahawks 60, Jaguars 50)
JACKSONVILLE vs. TAMPA BAY
RS: Buccaneers lead series, 1-0
1995—Buccaneers, 17-16 (TB)
(RS Pts.—Buccaneers 17, Jaguars 16)
JACKSONVILLE vs. *TENNESSEE
RS: Jaguars lead series 4-2
1995—Oilers, 10-3 (J)
Jaguars, 17-16 (H)
1996—Oilers, 34-27 (J)
Jaguars, 23-17 (H)
1997—Jaguars, 30-24 (T)
Jaguars, 17-9 (J)
(RS Pts.—Jaguars 117, Oilers 110)
Franchise in Houston prior to 1997
JACKSONVILLE vs. WASHINGTON
RS: Redskins lead series, 1-0
1997—Redskins, 24-12 (W)
(RS Pts.—Redskins 24, Jaguars 12)

KANSAS CITY vs. ARIZONA
RS: Chiefs lead series, 4-1-1;
See Arizona vs. Kansas City
KANSAS CITY vs. ATLANTA
RS: Chiefs lead series, 4-0;
See Atlanta vs. Kansas City
KANSAS CITY vs. BUFFALO
RS: Bills lead series, 17-14-1
PS: Bills lead series, 2-1;
See Buffalo vs. Kansas City
KANSAS CITY vs. CARLOINA
RS: Chiefs lead series, 1-0;
See Carolina vs. Kansas City
KANSAS CITY vs. CHICAGO
RS: Bears lead series, 4-3;
See Chicago vs. Kansas City
KANSAS CITY vs. CINCINNATI
RS: Chiefs lead series, 11-9;
See Cincinnati vs. Kansas City
KANSAS CITY vs. CLEVELAND
RS: Browns lead series, 8-7-2;
See Cleveland vs. Kansas City
KANSAS CITY vs. DALLAS
RS: Cowboys lead series, 4-2;
See Dallas vs. Kansas City
KANSAS CITY vs. DENVER
RS: Chiefs lead series, 43-32
PS: Broncos lead series, 1-0;
See Denver vs. Kansas City
KANSAS CITY vs. DETROIT
RS: Chiefs lead series, 5-3;
See Detroit vs. Kansas City
KANSAS CITY vs. GREEN BAY
RS: Chiefs lead series, 5-1-1
PS: Packers lead series, 1-0;
See Green Bay vs. Kansas City
KANSAS CITY vs. INDIANAPOLIS
RS: Chiefs lead series, 6-5
PS: Colts lead series, 1-0;
See Indianapolis vs. Kansas City
KANSAS CITY vs. JACKSONVILLE
RS: Jaguars lead series, 1-0;
See Jacksonville vs. Kansas City

KANSAS CITY vs. MIAMI
RS: Series tied, 10-10
PS: Dolphins lead series, 3-0
1966—Chiefs, 34-16 (KC)
Chiefs, 19-18 (M)
1967—Chiefs, 24-0 (M)
Chiefs, 41-0 (KC)
1968—Chiefs, 48-3 (M)
1969—Chiefs, 17-10 (KC)
1971—*Dolphins, 27-24 (KC) OT
1972—Dolphins, 20-10 (KC)
1974—Dolphins, 9-3 (M)
1976—Chiefs, 20-17 (M) OT
1981—Dolphins, 17-7 (KC)
1983—Dolphins, 14-6 (M)
1985—Dolphins, 31-0 (M)
1987—Dolphins, 42-0 (M)
1989—Chiefs, 26-21 (KC)
Chiefs, 27-24 (M)
1990—**Dolphins, 17-16 (M)
1991—Chiefs, 42-7 (KC)
1993—Dolphins, 30-10 (M)
1994—Dolphins, 45-28 (M)
**Dolphins, 27-17 (M)
1995—Dolphins, 13-6 (M)
1997—Dolphins, 17-14 (M)
(RS Pts.—Chiefs 382, Dolphins 354)
(PS Pts.—Dolphins 71, Chiefs 57)
*AFC Divisional Playoff
**AFC First-Round Playoff
KANSAS CITY vs. MINNESOTA
RS: Series tied, 3-3
PS: Chiefs lead series, 1-0
1969—*Chiefs, 23-7 (New Orleans)
1970—Vikings, 27-10 (M)
1974—Vikings, 35-15 (KC)
1981—Chiefs, 10-6 (M)
1990—Chiefs, 24-21 (KC)
1993—Vikings, 30-10 (M)
1996—Chiefs, 21-6 (M)
(RS Pts.—Vikings 125, Chiefs 90)
(PS Pts.—Chiefs 23, Vikings 7)
Super Bowl IV
***KANSAS CITY vs. **NEW ENGLAND**
RS: Chiefs lead series, 14-7-3
1960—Patriots, 42-14 (B)
Texans, 34-0 (D)
1961—Patriots, 18-17 (D)
Patriots, 28-21 (B)
1962—Texans, 42-28 (D)
Texans, 27-7 (B)
1963—Tie, 24-24 (B)
Chiefs, 35-3 (KC)
1964—Patriots, 24-7 (B)
Patriots, 31-24 (KC)
1965—Chiefs, 27-17 (KC)
Tie, 10-10 (B)
1966—Chiefs, 43-24 (B)
Tie, 27-27 (KC)
1967—Chiefs, 33-10 (B)
1968—Chiefs, 31-17 (KC)
1969—Chiefs, 31-0 (B)
1970—Chiefs, 23-10 (KC)
1973—Chiefs, 10-7 (NE)
1977—Patriots, 21-17 (NE)
1981—Patriots, 33-17 (NE)
1990—Chiefs, 37-7 (NE)
1992—Chiefs, 27-20 (KC)
1995—Chiefs, 31-26 (KC)
(RS Pts.—Chiefs 609, Patriots 434)
*Franchise located in Dallas prior to 1963 and known as Texans
**Franchise in Boston prior to 1971
KANSAS CITY vs. NEW ORLEANS
RS: Chiefs lead series, 4-3
1972—Chiefs, 20-17 (NO)
1976—Saints, 27-17 (KC)
1982—Saints, 27-17 (NO)
1985—Chiefs, 47-27 (NO)
1991—Saints, 17-10 (KC)
1994—Chiefs, 30-17 (NO)
1997—Chiefs, 25-13 (KC)
(RS Pts.—Chiefs 166, Saints 145)

KANSAS CITY vs. N.Y. GIANTS
RS: Giants lead series, 6-2
1974—Giants, 33-27 (KC)
1978—Giants, 26-10 (NY)
1979—Giants, 21-17 (KC)
1983—Chiefs, 38-17 (KC)
1984—Giants, 28-27 (NY)
1988—Giants, 28-12 (NY)
1992—Giants, 35-21 (NY)
1995—Chiefs, 20-17 (KC) OT
(RS Pts.—Giants 205, Chiefs 172)
***KANSAS CITY vs. **N.Y. JETS**
RS: Chiefs lead series, 14-12-1
PS: Series tied, 1-1
1960—Titans, 37-35 (D)
Titans, 41-35 (NY)
1961—Titans, 28-7 (NY)
Texans, 35-24 (D)
1962—Texans, 20-17 (D)
Texans, 52-31 (NY)
1963—Jets, 17-0 (NY)
Chiefs, 48-0 (KC)
1964—Jets, 27-14 (NY)
Chiefs, 24-7 (KC)
1965—Chiefs, 14-10 (NY)
Jets, 13-10 (KC)
1966—Chiefs, 32-24 (NY)
1967—Chiefs, 42-18 (KC)
Chiefs, 21-7 (NY)
1968—Jets, 20-19 (KC)
1969—Chiefs, 34-16 (NY)
***Chiefs, 13-6 (NY)
1971—Jets, 13-10 (NY)
1974—Chiefs, 24-16 (KC)
1975—Jets, 30-24 (KC)
1982—Chiefs, 37-13 (KC)
1984—Jets, 17-16 (KC)
Jets, 28-7 (NY)
1986—****Jets, 35-15 (NY)
1987—Jets, 16-9 (KC)
1988—Tie, 17-17 (NY)
Chiefs, 38-34 (KC)
1992—Chiefs, 23-7 (NY)
(RS Pts.—Chiefs 647, Jets 528)
(PS Pts.—Jets 41, Chiefs 28)
*Franchise in Dallas prior to 1963 and known as Texans
**Jets known as Titans prior to 1963
***Inter-Divisional Playoff
****AFC First-Round Playoff
***KANSAS CITY vs. **OAKLAND**
RS: Chiefs lead series, 37-36-2
PS: Chiefs lead series, 2-1
1960—Texans, 34-16 (O)
Raiders, 20-19 (D)
1961—Texans, 42-35 (O)
Texans, 43-11 (D)
1962—Texans, 26-16 (O)
Texans, 35-7 (D)
1963—Raiders, 10-7 (O)
Raiders, 22-7 (KC)
1964—Chiefs, 21-9 (O)
Chiefs, 42-7 (KC)
1965—Raiders, 37-10 (O)
Chiefs, 14-7 (KC)
1966—Chiefs, 32-10 (O)
Raiders, 34-13 (KC)
1967—Raiders, 23-21 (O)
Raiders, 44-22 (KC)
1968—Chiefs, 24-10 (KC)
Raiders, 38-21 (O)
***Raiders, 41-6 (O)
1969—Raiders, 27-24 (KC)
Raiders, 10-6 (O)
****Chiefs, 17-7 (O)
1970—Tie, 17-17 (KC)
Raiders, 20-6 (O)
1971—Tie, 20-20 (O)
Chiefs, 16-14 (KC)
1972—Chiefs, 27-14 (KC)
Raiders, 26-3 (O)
1973—Chiefs, 16-3 (KC)
Raiders, 37-7 (O)

ALL-TIME TEAM VS. TEAM RESULTS

1974—Raiders, 27-7 (O)
Raiders, 7-6 (KC)
1975—Chiefs, 42-10 (KC)
Raiders, 28-20 (O)
1976—Raiders, 24-21 (KC)
Raiders, 21-10 (O)
1977—Raiders, 37-28 (KC)
Raiders, 21-20 (O)
1978—Raiders, 28-6 (O)
Raiders, 20-10 (KC)
1979—Chiefs, 35-7 (KC)
Chiefs, 24-21 (O)
1980—Raiders, 27-14 (KC)
Chiefs, 31-17 (O)
1981—Chiefs, 27-0 (KC)
Chiefs, 28-17 (O)
1982—Raiders, 21-16 (KC)
1983—Raiders, 21-20 (LA)
Raiders, 28-20 (KC)
1984—Raiders, 22-20 (KC)
Raiders, 17-7 (LA)
1985—Chiefs, 36-20 (KC)
Raiders, 19-10 (LA)
1986—Raiders, 24-17 (KC)
Chiefs, 20-17 (LA)
1987—Raiders, 35-17 (LA)
Chiefs, 16-10 (KC)
1988—Raiders, 27-17 (KC)
Raiders, 17-10 (LA)
1989—Chiefs, 24-19 (KC)
Raiders, 20-14 (LA)
1990—Chiefs, 9-7 (KC)
Chiefs, 27-24 (LA)
1991—Chiefs, 24-21 (KC)
Chiefs, 27-21 (LA)
*****Chiefs, 10-6 (KC)
1992—Chiefs, 27-7 (KC)
Raiders, 28-7 (LA)
1993—Chiefs, 24-9 (KC)
Chiefs, 31-20 (LA)
1994—Chiefs, 13-3 (KC)
Chiefs, 19-9 (LA)
1995—Chiefs, 23-17 (KC) OT
Chiefs, 29-23 (O)
1996—Chiefs, 19-3 (KC)
Raiders, 26-7 (O)
1997—Chiefs, 28-27 (O)
Chiefs, 30-0 (KC)
(RS Pts.—Chiefs 1,512, Raiders 1,418)
(PS Pts.—Raiders 54, Chiefs 33)
Franchise in Dallas prior to 1963 and known as Texans
***Franchise in Los Angeles from 1982-1994*
****Division Playoff*
*****AFL Championship*
******AFC First-Round Playoff*

KANSAS CITY vs. PHILADELPHIA
RS: Series tied, 1-1
1972—Eagles, 21-20 (KC)
1992—Chiefs, 24-17 (KC)
(RS Pts.—Chiefs 44, Eagles 38)

KANSAS CITY vs. PITTSBURGH
RS: Steelers lead series, 14-6
PS: Chiefs lead series, 1-0
1970—Chiefs, 31-14 (P)
1971—Chiefs, 38-16 (KC)
1972—Steelers, 16-7 (P)
1974—Steelers, 34-24 (KC)
1975—Steelers, 28-3 (P)
1976—Steelers, 45-0 (KC)
1978—Steelers, 27-24 (P)
1979—Steelers, 30-3 (KC)
1980—Steelers, 21-16 (P)
1981—Chiefs, 37-33 (P)
1982—Steelers, 35-14 (P)
1984—Chiefs, 37-27 (P)
1985—Steelers, 36-28 (KC)
1986—Chiefs, 24-19 (P)
1987—Steelers, 17-16 (KC)
1988—Steelers, 16-10 (P)
1989—Steelers, 23-17 (P)
1992—Steelers, 27-3 (KC)
1993—*Chiefs, 27-24 (KC) OT
1996—Steelers, 17-7 (KC)
1997—Chiefs, 13-10 (KC)
(RS Pts.—Steelers 491, Chiefs 352)
(PS Pts.—Chiefs 27, Steelers 24)
**AFC First-Round Playoff*

KANSAS CITY vs. *ST. LOUIS
RS: Rams lead series, 4-2
1973—Rams, 23-13 (KC)
1982—Rams, 20-14 (LA)
1985—Rams, 16-0 (KC)
1991—Chiefs, 27-20 (LA)
1994—Rams, 16-0 (KC)
1997—Chiefs, 28-20 (StL)
(RS Pts.—Rams 115, Chiefs 82)
**Franchise in Los Angeles prior to 1995*

***KANSAS CITY vs. **SAN DIEGO**
RS: Chiefs lead series, 39-35-1
PS: Chargers lead series, 1-0
1960—Chargers, 21-20 (LA)
Texans, 17-0 (D)
1961—Chargers, 26-10 (D)
Chargers, 24-14 (SD)
1962—Chargers, 32-28 (SD)
Texans, 26-17 (D)
1963—Chargers, 24-10 (SD)
Chargers, 38-17 (KC)
1964—Chargers, 28-14 (KC)
Chiefs, 49-6 (SD)
1965—Tie, 10-10 (SD)
Chiefs, 31-7 (KC)
1966—Chiefs, 24-14 (KC)
Chiefs, 27-17 (SD)
1967—Chargers, 45-31 (SD)
Chargers, 17-16 (KC)
1968—Chiefs, 27-20 (KC)
Chiefs, 40-3 (SD)
1969—Chiefs, 27-9 (SD)
Chiefs, 27-3 (KC)
1970—Chiefs, 26-14 (KC)
Chargers, 31-13 (SD)
1971—Chargers, 21-14 (SD)
Chiefs, 31-10 (KC)
1972—Chiefs, 26-14 (SD)
Chargers, 27-17 (KC)
1973—Chiefs, 19-0 (SD)
Chiefs, 33-6 (KC)
1974—Chiefs, 24-14 (SD)
Chargers, 14-7 (KC)
1975—Chiefs, 12-10 (SD)
Chargers, 28-20 (KC)
1976—Chargers, 30-16 (KC)
Chiefs, 23-20 (SD)
1977—Chargers, 23-7 (KC)
Chiefs, 21-16 (SD)
1978—Chargers, 29-23 (SD) OT
Chiefs, 23-0 (KC)
1979—Chargers, 20-14 (KC)
Chargers, 28-7 (SD)
1980—Chargers, 24-7 (KC)
Chargers, 20-7 (SD)
1981—Chargers, 42-31 (KC)
Chargers, 22-20 (SD)
1982—Chiefs, 19-12 (KC)
1983—Chargers, 17-14 (KC)
Chargers, 41-38 (SD)
1984—Chiefs, 31-13 (KC)
Chiefs, 42-21 (SD)
1985—Chargers, 31-20 (SD)
Chiefs, 38-34 (KC)
1986—Chiefs, 42-41 (KC)
Chiefs, 24-23 (SD)
1987—Chiefs, 20-13 (KC)
Chargers, 42-21 (SD)
1988—Chargers, 24-23 (KC)
Chargers, 24-13 (SD)
1989—Chargers, 21-6 (SD)
Chargers, 20-13 (KC)
1990—Chiefs, 27-10 (KC)
Chiefs, 24-21 (SD)
1991—Chiefs, 14-13 (SD)
Chiefs, 20-17 (KC) OT
1992—Chiefs, 24-10 (SD)
Chiefs, 16-14 (KC)
***Chargers, 17-0 (SD)
1993—Chiefs, 17-14 (SD)
Chiefs, 28-24 (KC)
1994—Chargers, 20-6 (SD)
Chargers, 14-13 (KC)
1995—Chiefs, 29-23 (KC) OT
Chiefs, 22-7 (SD)
1996—Chargers, 22-19 (SD)
Chargers, 28-14 (KC)
1997—Chiefs, 31-3 (KC)
Chiefs, 29-7 (SD)
(RS Pts.—Chiefs 1,603, Chargers 1,448)
(PS Pts.—Chargers 17, Chiefs 0)
**Franchise in Dallas prior to 1963 and known as Texans*
***Franchise in Los Angeles prior to 1961*
****AFC First-Round Playoff*

KANSAS CITY vs. SAN FRANCISCO
RS: 49ers lead series, 4-3
1971—Chiefs, 26-17 (SF)
1975—49ers, 20-3 (KC)
1982—49ers, 26-13 (KC)
1985—49ers, 31-3 (SF)
1991—49ers, 28-14 (SF)
1994—Chiefs, 24-17 (KC)
1997—Chiefs, 44-9 (KC)
(PS Pts.—49ers 148, Chiefs 127)

KANSAS CITY vs. SEATTLE
RS: Chiefs lead series, 26-13
1977—Seahawks, 34-31 (KC)
1978—Seahawks, 13-10 (KC)
Seahawks, 23-19 (S)
1979—Chiefs, 24-6 (S)
Chiefs, 37-21 (KC)
1980—Seahawks, 17-16 (KC)
Chiefs, 31-30 (S)
1981—Chiefs, 20-14 (S)
Chiefs, 40-13 (KC)
1983—Chiefs, 17-13 (KC)
Seahawks, 51-48 (S) OT
1984—Seahawks, 45-0 (S)
Chiefs, 34-7 (KC)
1985—Chiefs, 28-7 (KC)
Seahawks, 24-6 (S)
1986—Seahawks, 23-17 (S)
Chiefs, 27-7 (KC)
1987—Seahawks, 43-14 (S)
Chiefs, 41-20 (KC)
1988—Seahawks, 31-10 (S)
Chiefs, 27-24 (KC)
1989—Chiefs, 20-16 (S)
Chiefs, 20-10 (KC)
1990—Seahawks, 19-7 (S)
Seahawks, 17-16 (KC)
1991—Chiefs, 20-13 (KC)
Chiefs, 19-6 (S)
1992—Chiefs, 26-7 (KC)
Chiefs, 24-14 (S)
1993—Chiefs, 31-16 (S)
Chiefs, 34-24 (KC)
1994—Chiefs, 38-23 (KC)
Seahawks, 10-9 (S)
1995—Chiefs, 34-10 (S)
Chiefs, 26-3 (KC)
1996—Chiefs, 35-17 (S)
Chiefs, 34-16 (KC)
1997—Chiefs, 20-17 (KC) OT
Chiefs, 19-14 (S)
(RS Pts.—Chiefs 929, Seahawks 718)

KANSAS CITY vs. TAMPA BAY
RS: Chiefs lead series, 5-2
1976—Chiefs, 28-19 (TB)
1978—Buccaneers, 30-13 (KC)
1979—Buccaneers, 3-0 (TB)
1981—Chiefs, 19-10 (KC)
1984—Chiefs, 24-20 (KC)
1986—Chiefs, 27-20 (KC)
1993—Chiefs, 27-3 (TB)
1995—Chiefs, 24-3 (KC)
(RS Pts.—Chiefs 138, Buccaneers 105)

***KANSAS CITY vs. **TENNESSEE**
RS: Chiefs lead series, 24-17
PS: Chiefs lead series, 2-0
1960—Oilers, 20-10 (H)
Texans, 24-0 (D)
1961—Texans, 26-21 (D)
Oilers, 38-7 (H)
1962—Texans, 31-7 (H)
Oilers, 14-6 (D)
***Texans, 20-17 (H) OT
1963—Chiefs, 28-7 (KC)
Oilers, 28-7 (H)
1964—Chiefs, 28-7 (KC)
Chiefs, 28-19 (H)
1965—Chiefs, 52-21 (KC)
Oilers, 38-36 (H)
1966—Chiefs, 48-23 (KC)
1967—Chiefs, 25-20 (H)
Oilers, 24-19 (KC)
1968—Chiefs, 26-21 (H)
Chiefs, 24-10 (KC)
1969—Chiefs, 24-0 (KC)
1970—Chiefs, 24-9 (KC)
1971—Chiefs, 20-16 (H)
1973—Chiefs, 38-14 (KC)
1974—Chiefs, 17-7 (H)
1975—Oilers, 17-13 (KC)
1977—Oilers, 34-20 (H)
1978—Oilers, 20-17 (KC)
1979—Oilers, 20-6 (H)
1980—Chiefs, 21-20 (KC)
1981—Chiefs, 23-10 (KC)
1983—Chiefs, 13-10 (H) OT
1984—Oilers, 17-16 (KC)
1985—Oilers, 23-20 (H)
1986—Chiefs, 27-13 (KC)
1988—Oilers, 7-6 (H)
1989—Chiefs, 34-0 (KC)
1990—Oilers, 27-10 (KC)
1991—Oilers, 17-7 (H)
1992—Oilers, 23-20 (H) OT
1993—Oilers, 30-0 (H)
****Chiefs, 28-20 (H)
1994—Chiefs, 31-9 (KC)
1995—Chiefs, 20-13 (KC)
1996—Chiefs, 20-19 (H)
(RS Pts.—Chiefs 872, Oilers 693)
(PS Pts.—Chiefs 48, Oilers 37)
**Franchise in Dallas prior to 1963 and known as Texans*
***Franchise in Houston prior to 1997*
****AFL Championship*
*****AFC Divisional Playoff*

KANSAS CITY vs. WASHINGTON
RS: Chiefs lead series, 4-1
1971—Chiefs, 27-20 (KC)
1976—Chiefs, 33-30 (W)
1983—Redskins, 27-12 (W)
1992—Chiefs, 35-16 (KC)
1995—Chiefs, 24-3 (KC)
(RS Pts.—Chiefs 131, Redskins 96)

MIAMI vs. ARIZONA
RS: Dolphins lead series, 7-0;
See Arizona vs. Miami

MIAMI vs. ATLANTA
RS: Dolphins lead series, 6-1;
See Atlanta vs. Miami

MIAMI vs. BALTIMORE
RS: Dolphins lead series, 1-0;
See Baltimore vs. Miami

MIAMI vs. BUFFALO
RS: Dolphins lead series, 41-22-1
PS: Bills lead series, 3-0;
See Buffalo vs. Miami

MIAMI vs. CHICAGO
RS: Dolphins lead series, 5-3;
See Chicago vs. Miami

MIAMI vs. CINCINNATI
RS: Dolphins lead series, 11-3
PS: Dolphins lead series, 1-0;
See Cincinnati vs. Miami

MIAMI vs. CLEVELAND
RS: Dolphins lead series, 6-4
PS: Dolphins lead series, 2-0;

See Cleveland vs. Miami

MIAMI vs. DALLAS
RS: Dolphins lead series, 6-2
PS: Cowboys lead series, 1-0;
See Dallas vs. Miami

MIAMI vs. DENVER
RS: Dolphins lead series, 5-2-1;
See Denver vs. Miami

MIAMI vs. DETROIT
RS: Dolphins lead series, 4-2;
See Detroit vs. Miami

MIAMI vs. GREEN BAY
RS: Dolphins lead series, 8-1;
See Green Bay vs. Miami

MIAMI vs. INDIANAPOLIS
RS: Dolphins lead series, 37-19
PS: Dolphins lead series, 1-0;
See Indianapolis vs. Miami

MIAMI vs. KANSAS CITY
RS: Series tied, 10-10
PS: Dolphins lead series, 3-0;
See Kansas City vs. Miami

MIAMI vs. MINNESOTA
RS: Dolphins lead series, 4-2
PS: Dolphins lead series, 1-0
1972—Dolphins, 16-14 (Minn)
1973—*Dolphins, 24-7 (Houston)
1976—Vikings, 29-7 (Mia)
1979—Dolphins, 27-12 (Minn)
1982—Dolphins, 22-14 (Mia)
1988—Dolphins, 24-7 (Mia)
1994—Vikings, 38-35 (M)
(RS Pts.—Dolphins 131, Vikings 114)
(PS Pts.—Dolphins 24, Vikings 7)
Super Bowl VIII

MIAMI vs. *NEW ENGLAND
RS: Dolphins lead series, 37-25
PS: Patriots lead series, 2-1
1966—Patriots, 20-14 (M)
1967—Patriots, 41-10 (B)
Dolphins, 41-32 (M)
1968—Dolphins, 34-10 (B)
Dolphins, 38-7 (M)
1969—Dolphins, 17-16 (B)
Patriots, 38-23 (Tampa)
1970—Patriots, 27-14 (B)
Dolphins, 37-20 (M)
1971—Dolphins, 41-3 (M)
Patriots, 34-13 (NE)
1972—Dolphins, 52-0 (M)
Dolphins, 37-21 (NE)
1973—Dolphins, 44-23 (M)
Dolphins, 30-14 (NE)
1974—Patriots, 34-24 (NE)
Dolphins, 34-27 (M)
1975—Dolphins, 22-14 (NE)
Dolphins, 20-7 (M)
1976—Patriots, 30-14 (NE)
Dolphins, 10-3 (M)
1977—Dolphins, 17-5 (M)
Patriots, 14-10 (NE)
1978—Patriots, 33-24 (NE)
Dolphins, 23-3 (M)
1979—Patriots, 28-13 (NE)
Dolphins, 39-24 (M)
1980—Patriots, 34-0 (NE)
Dolphins, 16-13 (M) OT
1981—Dolphins, 30-27 (NE) OT
Dolphins, 24-14 (M)
1982—Patriots, 3-0 (NE)
**Dolphins, 28-13 (M)
1983—Dolphins, 34-24 (M)
Patriots, 17-6 (NE)
1984—Dolphins, 28-7 (M)
Dolphins, 44-24 (NE)
1985—Patriots, 17-13 (NE)
Dolphins, 30-27 (M)
***Patriots, 31-14 (M)
1986—Patriots, 34-7 (NE)
Patriots, 34-27 (M)
1987—Patriots, 28-21 (NE)
Patriots, 24-10 (M)
1988—Patriots, 21-10 (NE)
Patriots, 6-3 (M)
1989—Dolphins, 24-10 (NE)
Dolphins, 31-10 (M)
1990—Dolphins, 27-24 (NE)
Dolphins, 17-10 (M)
1991—Dolphins, 20-10 (NE)
Dolphins, 30-20 (M)
1992—Dolphins, 38-17 (M)
Dolphins, 16-13 (NE) OT
1993—Dolphins, 17-13 (M)
Patriots, 33-27 (NE) OT
1994—Dolphins, 39-35 (M)
Dolphins, 23-3 (NE)
1995—Dolphins, 20-3 (NE)
Patriots, 34-17 (M)
1996—Dolphins, 24-10 (M)
Patriots, 42-23 (NE)
1997—Patriots, 27-24 (NE)
Patriots, 14-12 (M)
**Patriots, 17-3 (NE)
(RS Pts.—Dolphins 1,427, Patriots 1,210)
(PS Pts.—Patriots 61, Dolphins 45)
Franchise in Boston prior to 1971
***AFC First-Round Playoff*
****AFC Championship*

MIAMI vs. NEW ORLEANS
RS: Dolphins lead series, 4-3
1970—Dolphins, 21-10 (M)
1974—Dolphins, 21-0 (NO)
1980—Dolphins, 21-16 (M)
1983—Saints, 17-7 (NO)
1986—Dolphins, 31-27 (NO)
1992—Saints, 24-13 (NO)
1995—Saints, 33-30 (NO)
(RS Pts.—Dolphins 144, Saints 127)

MIAMI vs. N.Y. GIANTS
RS: Giants lead series, 3-1
1972—Dolphins, 23-13 (NY)
1990—Giants, 20-3 (NY)
1993—Giants, 19-14 (M)
1996—Giants, 17-7 (M)
(RS Pts.—Giants 69, Dolphins 47)

MIAMI vs. N.Y. JETS
RS: Dolphins lead series, 34-29-1
PS: Dolphins lead series, 1-0
1966—Jets, 19-14 (M)
Jets, 30-13 (NY)
1967—Jets, 29-7 (NY)
Jets, 33-14 (M)
1968—Jets, 35-17 (NY)
Jets, 31-7 (M)
1969—Jets, 34-31 (NY)
Jets, 27-9 (M)
1970—Dolphins, 20-6 (NY)
Dolphins, 16-10 (M)
1971—Jets, 14-10 (M)
Dolphins, 30-14 (NY)
1972—Dolphins, 27-17 (NY)
Dolphins, 28-24 (M)
1973—Dolphins, 31-3 (M)
Dolphins, 24-14 (NY)
1974—Dolphins, 21-17 (M)
Jets, 17-14 (NY)
1975—Dolphins, 43-0 (NY)
Dolphins, 27-7 (M)
1976—Dolphins, 16-0 (M)
Dolphins, 27-7 (NY)
1977—Dolphins, 21-17 (M)
Dolphins, 14-10 (NY)
1978—Jets, 33-20 (NY)
Jets, 24-13 (M)
1979—Jets, 33-27 (NY)
Jets, 27-24 (M)
1980—Jets, 17-14 (NY)
Jets, 24-17 (M)
1981—Tie, 28-28 (M) OT
Jets, 16-15 (NY)
1982—Dolphins, 45-28 (NY)
Dolphins, 20-19 (M)
*Dolphins, 14-0 (M)
1983—Dolphins, 32-14 (NY)
Dolphins, 34-14 (M)
1984—Dolphins, 31-17 (NY)
Dolphins, 28-17 (M)
1985—Jets, 23-7 (NY)
Dolphins, 21-17 (M)
1986—Jets, 51-45 (NY) OT
Dolphins, 45-3 (M)
1987—Jets, 37-31 (NY) OT
Dolphins, 37-28 (M)
1988—Jets, 44-30 (M)
Jets, 38-34 (NY)
1989—Jets, 40-33 (M)
Dolphins, 31-23 (NY)
1990—Dolphins, 20-16 (M)
Dolphins, 17-3 (NY)
1991—Jets, 41-23 (NY)
Jets, 23-20 (M) OT
1992—Jets, 26-14 (NY)
Dolphins, 19-17 (M)
1993—Jets, 24-14 (M)
Jets, 27-10 (NY)
1994—Dolphins, 28-14 (M)
Dolphins, 28-24 (NY)
1995—Dolphins, 52-14 (M)
Jets, 17-16 (NY)
1996—Dolphins, 36-27 (M)
Dolphins, 31-28 (NY)
1997—Dolphins, 31-20 (NY)
Dolphins, 24-17 (M)
(RS Pts.—Dolphins 1,526, Jets 1,368)
(PS Pts.—Dolphins 14, Jets 0)
AFC Championship

MIAMI vs. *OAKLAND
RS: Raiders lead series, 15-6-1
PS: Raiders lead series, 2-1
1966—Raiders, 23-14 (M)
Raiders, 21-10 (O)
1967—Raiders, 31-17 (O)
1968—Raiders, 47-21 (M)
1969—Raiders, 20-17 (O)
Tie, 20-20 (M)
1970—Dolphins, 20-13 (M)
**Raiders, 21-14 (O)
1973—Raiders, 12-7 (O)
***Dolphins, 27-10 (M)
1974—**Raiders, 28-26 (O)
1975—Raiders, 31-21 (M)
1978—Dolphins, 23-6 (M)
1979—Raiders, 13-3 (O)
1980—Raiders, 16-10 (O)
1981—Raiders, 33-17 (M)
1983—Raiders, 27-14 (LA)
1984—Raiders, 45-34 (M)
1986—Raiders, 30-28 (M)
1988—Dolphins, 24-14 (LA)
1990—Raiders, 13-10 (M)
1992—Dolphins, 20-7 (M)
1994—Dolphins, 20-17 (M) OT
1996—Raiders, 17-7 (O)
1997—Dolphins, 34-16 (O)
(RS Pts.—Raiders 472, Dolphins 391)
(PS Pts.—Dolphins 67, Raiders 59)
Franchise in Los Angeles from 1982-1994
***AFC Divisional Playoff*
****AFC Championship*

MIAMI vs. PHILADELPHIA
RS: Dolphins lead series, 6-3
1970—Eagles, 24-17 (P)
1975—Dolphins, 24-16 (M)
1978—Eagles, 17-3 (P)
1981—Dolphins, 13-10 (M)
1984—Dolphins, 24-23 (M)
1987—Dolphins, 28-10 (P)
1990—Dolphins, 23-20 (M) OT
1993—Dolphins, 19-14 (P)
1996—Eagles, 35-28 (P)
(RS Pts.—Dolphins 179, Eagles 169)

MIAMI vs. PITTSBURGH
RS: Dolphins lead series, 8-7
PS: Dolphins lead series, 2-1
1971—Dolphins, 24-21 (M)
1972—*Dolphins, 21-17 (P)
1973—Dolphins, 30-26 (M)
1976—Steelers, 14-3 (P)
1979—**Steelers, 34-14 (P)
1980—Steelers, 23-10 (P)
1981—Dolphins, 30-10 (M)
1984—Dolphins, 31-7 (P)
*Dolphins, 45-28 (M)
1985—Dolphins, 24-20 (M)
1987—Dolphins, 35-24 (M)
1988—Steelers, 40-24 (P)
1989—Steelers, 34-14 (M)
1990—Dolphins, 28-6 (P)
1993—Steelers, 21-20 (M)
1994—Steelers, 16-13 (P) OT
1995—Dolphins, 23-10 (M)
1996—Steelers, 24-17 (M)
(RS Pts.—Dolphins 326, Steelers 296)
(PS Pts.—Dolphins 80, Steelers 79)
AFC Championship
***AFC Divisional Playoff*

MIAMI vs. *ST. LOUIS
RS: Dolphins lead series, 6-1
1971—Dolphins, 20-14 (LA)
1976—Rams, 31-28 (M)
1980—Dolphins, 35-14 (LA)
1983—Dolphins, 30-14 (M)
1986—Dolphins, 37-31 (LA) OT
1992—Dolphins, 26-10 (M)
1995—Dolphins, 41-22 (StL)
(RS Pts.—Dolphins 217, Rams 136)
Franchise in Los Angeles prior to 1995

MIAMI vs. SAN DIEGO
RS: Chargers lead series, 10-6
PS: Series tied, 2-2
1966—Chargers, 44-10 (SD)
1967—Chargers, 24-0 (SD)
Dolphins, 41-24 (M)
1968—Chargers, 34-28 (SD)
1969—Chargers, 21-14 (M)
1972—Dolphins, 24-10 (M)
1974—Dolphins, 28-21 (SD)
1977—Chargers, 14-13 (M)
1978—Dolphins, 28-21 (SD)
1980—Chargers, 27-24 (M) OT
1981—*Chargers, 41-38 (M) OT
1982—**Dolphins, 34-13 (M)
1984—Chargers, 34-28 (SD) OT
1986—Chargers, 50-28 (SD)
1988—Dolphins, 31-28 (M)
1991—Chargers, 38-30 (SD)
1992—*Dolphins, 31-0 (M)
1993—Chargers, 45-20 (SD)
1994—*Chargers, 22-21 (SD)
1995—Dolphins, 24-14 (SD)
(RS Pts.—Chargers 449, Dolphins 371)
(PS Pts.—Dolphins 124, Chargers 76)
AFC Divisional Playoff
***AFC Second-Round Playoff*

MIAMI vs. SAN FRANCISCO
RS: Dolphins lead series, 4-3
PS: 49ers lead series, 1-0
1973—Dolphins, 21-13 (M)
1977—Dolphins, 19-15 (SF)
1980—Dolphins, 17-13 (M)
1983—Dolphins, 20-17 (SF)
1984—*49ers, 38-16 (Stanford)
1986—49ers, 31-16 (M)
1992—49ers, 27-3 (SF)
1995—49ers, 44-20 (M)
(RS Pts.—49ers 160, Dolphins 116)
(PS Pts.—49ers 38, Dolphins 16)
Super Bowl XIX

MIAMI vs. SEATTLE
RS: Dolphins lead series, 4-2
PS: Series tied, 1-1
1977—Dolphins, 31-13 (M)
1979—Dolphins, 19-10 (M)
1983—*Seahawks, 27-20 (M)
1984—*Dolphins, 31-10 (M)
1987—Seahawks, 24-20 (S)
1990—Dolphins, 24-17 (M)
1992—Dolphins, 19-17 (S)
1996—Seahawks, 22-15 (M)
(RS Pts.—Dolphins 128, Seahawks 103)
(PS Pts.—Dolphins 51, Seahawks 37)

**AFC Divisional Playoff*

MIAMI vs. TAMPA BAY
RS: Dolphins lead series, 4-2
1976—Dolphins, 23-20 (TB)
1982—Buccaneers, 23-17 (TB)
1985—Dolphins, 41-38 (M)
1988—Dolphins, 17-14 (TB)
1991—Dolphins, 33-14 (M)
1997—Buccaneers, 31-21 (TB)
(RS Pts.—Dolphins 152, Buccaneers 140)

MIAMI vs. *TENNESSEE
RS: Dolphins lead series, 13-11
PS: Oilers lead series, 1-0
1966—Dolphins, 20-13 (H)
Dolphins, 29-28 (M)
1967—Oilers, 17-14 (H)
Oilers, 41-10 (M)
1968—Oilers, 24-10 (M)
Dolphins, 24-7 (H)
1969—Oilers, 22-10 (H)
Oilers, 32-7 (M)
1970—Dolphins, 20-10 (H)
1972—Dolphins, 34-13 (M)
1975—Oilers, 20-19 (H)
1977—Dolphins, 27-7 (M)
1978—Oilers, 35-30 (H)
**Oilers, 17-9 (M)
1979—Oilers, 9-6 (M)
1981—Dolphins, 16-10 (H)
1983—Dolphins, 24-17 (H)
1984—Dolphins, 28-10 (M)
1985—Oilers, 26-23 (H)
1986—Dolphins, 28-7 (M)
1989—Oilers, 39-7 (H)
1991—Oilers, 17-13 (M)
1992—Dolphins, 19-16 (M)
1996—Dolphins, 23-20 (H)
1997—Dolphins, 16-13 (M) OT
(RS Pts.—Dolphins 457, Oilers 453)
(PS Pts.—Oilers 17, Dolphins 9)
**Franchise in Houston prior to 1997*
***AFC First-Round Playoff*

MIAMI vs. WASHINGTON
RS: Dolphins lead series, 5-2
PS: Series tied, 1-1
1972—*Dolphins, 14-7 (Los Angeles)
1974—Redskins, 20-17 (W)
1978—Dolphins, 16-0 (W)
1981—Dolphins, 13-10 (M)
1982—**Redskins, 27-17 (Pasadena)
1984—Dolphins, 35-17 (W)
1987—Dolphins, 23-21 (M)
1990—Redskins, 42-20 (W)
1993—Dolphins, 17-10 (M)
(RS Pts.—Dolphins 141, Redskins 120)
(PS Pts.—Redskins 34, Dolphins 31)
**Super Bowl VII*
***Super Bowl XVII*

MINNESOTA vs. ARIZONA
RS: Cardinals lead series, 8-7
PS: Vikings lead series, 1-0;
See Arizona vs. Minnesota

MINNESOTA vs. ATLANTA
RS: Vikings lead series, 12-6
PS: Vikings lead series, 1-0;
See Atlanta vs. Minnesota

MINNESOTA vs. BUFFALO
RS: Vikings lead series, 6-2;
See Buffalo vs. Minnesota

MINNESOTA vs. CAROLINA
RS: Vikings lead series, 2-0;
See Carolina vs. Minnesota

MINNESOTA vs. CHICAGO
RS: Vikings lead series, 39-32-2
PS: Bears lead series, 1-0;
See Chicago vs. Minnesota

MINNESOTA vs. CINCINNATI
RS: Series tied, 4-4;
See Cincinnati vs. Minnesota

MINNESOTA vs. CLEVELAND
RS: Vikings lead series, 8-3
PS: Vikings lead series, 1-0;
See Cleveland vs. Minnesota

MINNESOTA vs. DALLAS
RS: Cowboys lead series, 9-6
PS: Cowboys lead series, 4-1;
See Dallas vs. Minnesota

MINNESOTA vs. DENVER
RS: Vikings lead series, 5-4;
See Denver vs. Minnesota

MINNESOTA vs. DETROIT
RS: Vikings lead series, 44-27-2;
See Detroit vs. Minnesota

MINNESOTA vs. GREEN BAY
RS: Series tied, 36-36-1;
See Green Bay vs. Minnesota

MINNESOTA vs. INDIANAPOLIS
RS: Colts lead series, 11-7-1
PS: Colts lead series, 1-0;
See Indianapolis vs. Minnesota

MINNESOTA vs. KANSAS CITY
RS: Series tied, 3-3
PS: Chiefs lead series, 1-0;
See Kansas City vs. Minnesota

MINNESOTA vs. MIAMI
RS: Dolphins lead series, 4-2
PS: Dolphins lead series, 1-0;
See Miami vs. Minnesota

MINNESOTA vs. *NEW ENGLAND
RS: Patriots lead series, 4-3
1970—Vikings, 35-14 (B)
1974—Patriots, 17-14 (M)
1979—Patriots, 27-23 (NE)
1988—Vikings, 36-6 (M)
1991—Patriots, 26-23 (NE) OT
1994—Patriots, 26-20 (NE) OT
1997—Vikings, 23-18 (M)
(RS Pts.—Vikings 174, Patriots 134)
**Franchise in Boston prior to 1971*

MINNESOTA vs. NEW ORLEANS
RS: Vikings lead series, 13-6
PS: Vikings lead series, 1-0
1968—Saints, 20-17 (NO)
1970—Vikings, 26-0 (M)
1971—Vikings, 23-10 (NO)
1972—Vikings, 37-6 (M)
1974—Vikings, 29-9 (M)
1975—Vikings, 20-7 (NO)
1976—Vikings, 40-9 (NO)
1978—Saints, 31-24 (NO)
1980—Vikings, 23-20 (NO)
1981—Vikings, 20-10 (M)
1983—Saints, 17-16 (NO)
1985—Saints, 30-23 (M)
1986—Vikings, 33-17 (M)
1987—*Vikings, 44-10 (NO)
1988—Vikings, 45-3 (M)
1990—Vikings, 32-3 (M)
1991—Saints, 26-0 (NO)
1993—Saints, 17-14 (M)
1994—Vikings, 21-20 (M)
1995—Vikings, 43-24 (M)
(RS Pts.—Vikings 486, Saints 279)
(PS Pts.—Vikings 44, Saints 10)
**NFC First-Round Playoff*

MINNESOTA vs. N.Y. GIANTS
RS: Vikings lead series, 7-5
PS: Series tied, 1-1
1964—Vikings, 30-21 (NY)
1965—Vikings, 40-14 (M)
1967—Vikings, 27-24 (M)
1969—Giants, 24-23 (NY)
1971—Vikings, 17-10 (NY)
1973—Vikings, 31-7 (New Haven)
1976—Vikings, 24-7 (M)
1986—Giants, 22-20 (M)
1989—Giants, 24-14 (NY)
1990—Giants, 23-15 (NY)
1993—*Giants, 17-10 (NY)
1994—Vikings, 27-10 (NY)
1996—Giants, 15-10 (NY)
1997—*Vikings, 23-22 (NY)
(RS Pts.—Vikings 278, Giants 201)
(PS Pts.—Giants 39, Vikings 33)
**NFC First-Round Playoff*

MINNESOTA vs. N.Y. JETS
RS: Jets lead series, 5-1
1970—Jets, 20-10 (NY)
1975—Vikings, 29-21 (M)
1979—Jets, 14-7 (NY)
1982—Jets, 42-14 (M)
1994—Jets, 31-21 (M)
1997—Jets, 23-21 (NY)
(RS Pts.—Jets 151, Vikings 102)

MINNESOTA vs. *OAKLAND
RS: Raiders lead series, 6-3
PS: Raiders lead series, 1-0
1973—Vikings, 24-16 (M)
1976—**Raiders, 32-14 (Pasadena)
1977—Raiders, 35-13 (O)
1978—Raiders, 27-20 (O)
1981—Raiders, 36-10 (M)
1984—Raiders, 23-20 (LA)
1987—Vikings, 31-20 (M)
1990—Raiders, 28-24 (M)
1993—Raiders, 24-7 (LA)
1996—Vikings, 16-13 (O) OT
(RS Pts.—Raiders 222, Vikings 165)
(PS Pts.—Raiders 32, Vikings 14)
**Franchise in Los Angeles from 1982-1994*
***Super Bowl XI*

MINNESOTA vs. PHILADELPHIA
RS: Vikings lead series, 11-6
PS: Eagles lead series, 1-0
1962—Vikings, 31-21 (M)
1963—Vikings, 34-13 (P)
1968—Vikings, 24-17 (P)
1971—Vikings, 13-0 (P)
1973—Vikings, 28-21 (M)
1976—Vikings, 31-12 (P)
1978—Vikings, 28-27 (M)
1980—Eagles, 42-7 (M)
*Eagles, 31-16 (P)
1981—Vikings, 35-23 (M)
1984—Eagles, 19-17 (P)
1985—Vikings, 28-23 (P)
Eagles, 37-35 (M)
1988—Vikings, 23-21 (M)
1989—Eagles, 10-9 (P)
1990—Eagles, 32-24 (P)
1992—Eagles, 28-17 (P)
1997—Vikings, 28-19 (M)
(RS Pts.—Vikings 412, Eagles 365)
(PS Pts.—Eagles 31, Vikings 16)
**NFC Divisional Playoff*

MINNESOTA vs. PITTSBURGH
RS: Vikings lead series, 8-4
PS: Steelers lead series, 1-0
1962—Steelers, 39-31 (P)
1964—Vikings, 30-10 (M)
1967—Vikings, 41-27 (P)
1969—Vikings, 52-14 (M)
1972—Steelers, 23-10 (P)
1974—*Steelers, 16-6 (New Orleans)
1976—Vikings, 17-6 (M)
1980—Steelers, 23-17 (M)
1983—Vikings, 17-14 (P)
1986—Vikings, 31-7 (M)
1989—Steelers, 27-14 (P)
1992—Vikings, 6-3 (P)
1995—Vikings, 44-24 (P)
(RS Pts.—Vikings 310, Steelers 217)
(PS Pts.—Steelers 16, Vikings 6)
**Super Bowl IX*

MINNESOTA vs. *ST. LOUIS
RS: Vikings lead series, 15-11-2
PS: Vikings lead series, 5-1
1961—Rams, 31-17 (LA)
Vikings, 42-21 (M)
1962—Vikings, 38-14 (LA)
Tie, 24-24 (M)
1963—Rams, 27-24 (LA)
Vikings, 21-13 (M)
1964—Rams, 22-13 (LA)
Vikings, 34-13 (M)
1965—Vikings, 38-35 (LA)
Vikings, 24-13 (M)
1966—Vikings, 35-7 (M)
Rams, 21-6 (LA)
1967—Rams, 39-3 (LA)
1968—Rams, 31-3 (M)
1969—Vikings, 20-13 (LA)
**Vikings, 23-20 (M)
1970—Vikings, 13-3 (M)
1972—Vikings, 45-41 (LA)
1973—Vikings, 10-9 (M)
1974—Rams, 20-17 (LA)
***Vikings, 14-10 (M)
1976—Tie, 10-10 (M) OT
***Vikings, 24-13 (M)
1977—Rams, 35-3 (LA)
****Vikings, 14-7 (LA)
1978—Rams, 34-17 (M)
****Rams, 34-10 (LA)
1979—Rams, 27-21 (LA) OT
1985—Rams, 13-10 (LA)
1987—Vikings, 21-16 (LA)
1988—*****Vikings, 28-17 (M)
1989—Vikings, 23-21 (M) OT
1991—Vikings, 20-14 (M)
1992—Vikings, 31-17 (LA)
(RS Pts.—Rams 584, Vikings 583)
(PS Pts.—Vikings 113, Rams 101)
**Franchise in Los Angeles prior to 1995*
***Conference Championship*
****NFC Championship*
*****NFC Divisional Playoff*
******NFC First-Round Playoff*

MINNESOTA vs. SAN DIEGO
RS: Chargers lead series, 4-3
1971—Chargers, 30-14 (SD)
1975—Vikings, 28-13 (M)
1978—Chargers, 13-7 (M)
1981—Vikings, 33-31 (SD)
1984—Chargers, 42-13 (M)
1985—Vikings, 21-17 (M)
1993—Chargers, 30-17 (M)
(RS Pts.—Chargers 176, Vikings 133)

MINNESOTA vs. SAN FRANCISCO
RS: 49ers lead series, 17-16-1
PS: 49ers lead series, 4-1
1961—49ers, 38-24 (M)
49ers, 38-28 (SF)
1962—49ers, 21-7 (SF)
49ers, 35-12 (M)
1963—Vikings, 24-20 (SF)
Vikings, 45-14 (M)
1964—Vikings, 27-22 (SF)
Vikings, 24-7 (M)
1965—Vikings, 42-41 (SF)
49ers, 45-24 (M)
1966—Tie, 20-20 (SF)
Vikings, 28-3 (SF)
1967—49ers, 27-21 (M)
1968—Vikings, 30-20 (SF)
1969—Vikings, 10-7 (M)
1970—*49ers, 17-14 (M)
1971—49ers, 13-9 (M)
1972—49ers, 20-17 (SF)
1973—Vikings, 17-13 (SF)
1975—Vikings, 27-17 (M)
1976—49ers, 20-16 (SF)
1977—Vikings, 28-27 (M)
1979—Vikings, 28-22 (M)
1983—49ers, 48-17 (M)
1984—49ers, 51-7 (SF)
1985—Vikings, 28-21 (M)
1986—Vikings, 27-24 (SF) OT
1987—*Vikings, 36-24 (SF)
1988—49ers, 24-21 (SF)
*49ers, 34-9 (SF)
1989—*49ers, 41-13 (SF)
1990—49ers, 20-17 (M)
1991—Vikings, 17-14 (M)
1992—49ers, 20-17 (M)
1993—49ers, 38-19 (SF)
1994—Vikings, 21-14 (M)
1995—49ers, 37-30 (SF)
1997—49ers, 28-17 (SF)
*49ers, 38-22 (SF)

(RS Pts.—49ers 829, Vikings 746)
(PS Pts.—49ers 154, Vikings 94)
*NFC Divisional Playoff

MINNESOTA vs. SEATTLE
RS: Seahawks lead series, 4-2
1976—Vikings, 27-21 (M)
1978—Seahawks, 29-28 (S)
1984—Seahawks, 20-12 (M)
1987—Seahawks, 28-17 (S)
1990—Vikings, 24-21 (S)
1996—Seahawks, 42-23 (S)
(RS Pts.—Seahawks 161, Vikings 131)

MINNESOTA vs. TAMPA BAY
RS: Vikings lead series, 27-13
1977—Vikings, 9-3 (TB)
1978—Buccaneers, 16-10 (M)
Vikings, 24-7 (TB)
1979—Buccaneers, 12-10 (M)
Vikings, 23-22 (TB)
1980—Vikings, 38-30 (M)
Vikings, 21-10 (TB)
1981—Buccaneers, 21-13 (TB)
Vikings, 25-10 (M)
1982—Vikings, 17-10 (M)
1983—Vikings, 19-16 (TB) OT
Buccaneers, 17-12 (M)
1984—Buccaneers, 35-31 (TB)
Vikings, 27-24 (M)
1985—Vikings, 31-16 (TB)
Vikings, 26-7 (M)
1986—Vikings, 23-10 (TB)
Vikings, 45-13 (M)
1987—Buccaneers, 20-10 (TB)
Vikings, 23-17 (M)
1988—Vikings, 14-13 (M)
Vikings, 49-20 (TB)
1989—Vikings, 17-3 (M)
Vikings, 24-10 (TB)
1990—Buccaneers, 23-20 (M) OT
Buccaneers, 26-13 (TB)
1991—Vikings, 28-13 (M)
Vikings, 26-24 (TB)
1992—Vikings, 26-20 (M)
Vikings, 35-7 (TB)
1993—Vikings, 15-0 (M)
Buccaneers, 23-10 (TB)
1994—Vikings, 36-13 (TB)
Buccaneers, 20-17 (M) OT
1995—Buccaneers, 20-17 (TB) OT
Vikings, 31-17 (M)
1996—Buccaneers, 24-13 (TB)
Vikings, 21-10 (M)
1997—Buccaneers, 28-14 (M)
Vikings, 10-6 (TB)
(RS Pts.—Vikings 873, Buccaneers 636)

MINNESOTA vs. *TENNESSEE
RS: Vikings lead series, 4-3
1974—Vikings, 51-10 (M)
1980—Oilers, 20-16 (H)
1983—Vikings, 34-14 (M)
1986—Oilers, 23-10 (H)
1989—Vikings, 38-7 (M)
1992—Oilers, 17-13 (M)
1995—Vikings, 23-17 (M) OT
(RS Pts.—Vikings 185, Oilers 108)
*Franchise in Houston prior to 1997

MINNESOTA vs. WASHINGTON
RS: Redskins lead series, 6-4
PS: Redskins lead series, 3-2
1968—Vikings, 27-14 (M)
1970—Vikings, 19-10 (W)
1972—Redskins, 24-21 (M)
1973—*Vikings, 27-20 (M)
1975—Redskins, 31-30 (W)
1976—*Vikings, 35-20 (M)
1980—Vikings, 39-14 (W)
1982—**Redskins, 21-7 (W)
1984—Redskins, 31-17 (M)
1986—Redskins, 44-38 (W) OT
1987—Redskins, 27-24 (M) OT
***Redskins, 17-10 (W)
1992—Redskins, 15-13 (M)
****Redskins, 24-7 (M)
1993—Vikings, 14-9 (W)
(RS Pts.—Vikings 242, Redskins 219)
(PS Pts.—Redskins 102, Vikings 86)
*NFC Divisional Playoff
**NFC Second-Round Playoff
***NFC Championship
****NFC First-Round Playoff

NEW ENGLAND vs. ARIZONA
RS: Cardinals lead series, 6-3;
See Arizona vs. New England

NEW ENGLAND vs. ATLANTA
RS: Falcons lead series, 5-3;
See Atlanta vs. New England

NEW ENGLAND vs. BALTIMORE
RS: Patriots lead series, 1-0;
See Baltimore vs. New England

NEW ENGLAND vs. BUFFALO
RS: Patriots lead series, 39-35-1
PS: Patriots lead series, 1-0;
See Buffalo vs. New England

NEW ENGLAND vs. CAROLINA
RS: Panthers lead series, 1-0;
See Carolina vs. New England

NEW ENGLAND vs. CHICAGO
RS: Patriots lead series, 5-2
PS: Bears lead series, 1-0;
See Chicago vs. New England

NEW ENGLAND vs. CINCINNATI
RS: Patriots lead series, 9-7;
See Cincinnati vs. New England

NEW ENGLAND vs. CLEVELAND
RS: Browns lead series, 10-4
PS: Browns lead series, 1-0;
See Cleveland vs. New England

NEW ENGLAND vs. DALLAS
RS: Cowboys lead series, 7-0;
See Dallas vs. New England

NEW ENGLAND vs. DENVER
RS: Broncos lead series, 19-12
PS: Broncos lead series, 1-0;
See Denver vs. New England

NEW ENGLAND vs. DETROIT
RS: Series tied, 3-3;
See Detroit vs. New England

NEW ENGLAND vs. GREEN BAY
RS: Series tied, 3-3
PS: Packers lead series, 1-0;
See Green Bay vs. New England

NEW ENGLAND vs. INDIANAPOLIS
RS: Patriots lead series, 33-22;
See Indianapolis vs. New England

NEW ENGLAND vs. JACKSONVILLE
RS: Patriots lead series, 2-0
PS: Patriots lead series, 1-0;
See Jacksonville vs. New England

NEW ENGLAND vs. KANSAS CITY
RS: Chiefs lead series, 14-7-3;
See Kansas City vs. New England

NEW ENGLAND vs. MIAMI
RS: Dolphins lead series, 37-25
PS: Patriots lead series, 2-1;
See Miami vs. New England

NEW ENGLAND vs. MINNESOTA
RS: Patriots lead series, 4-3;
See Minnesota vs. New England

NEW ENGLAND vs. NEW ORLEANS
RS: Patriots lead series, 5-3
1972—Patriots, 17-10 (NO)
1976—Patriots, 27-6 (NE)
1980—Patriots, 38-27 (NO)
1983—Patriots, 7-0 (NE)
1986—Patriots, 21-20 (NO)
1989—Saints, 28-24 (NE)
1992—Saints, 31-14 (NE)
1995—Saints, 31-17 (NE)
(RS Pts.—Patriots 165, Saints 153)

***NEW ENGLAND vs. N.Y. GIANTS**
RS: Giants lead series, 3-2
1970—Giants, 16-0 (B)
1974—Patriots, 28-20 (New Haven)
1987—Giants, 17-10 (NY)
1990—Giants, 13-10 (NE)
1996—Patriots, 23-22 (NY)
(RS Pts.—Giants 88, Patriots 71)
*Franchise in Boston prior to 1971

***NEW ENGLAND vs. **N.Y. JETS**
RS: Jets lead series, 40-34-1
PS: Patriots lead series, 1-0
1960—Patriots, 28-24 (NY)
Patriots, 38-21 (B)
1961—Titans, 21-20 (B)
Titans, 37-30 (NY)
1962—Patriots, 43-14 (NY)
Patriots, 24-17 (B)
1963—Patriots, 38-14 (B)
Jets, 31-24 (NY)
1964—Patriots, 26-10 (B)
Jets, 35-14 (NY)
1965—Jets, 30-20 (B)
Patriots, 27-23 (NY)
1966—Tie, 24-24 (B)
Jets, 38-28 (NY)
1967—Jets, 30-23 (NY)
Jets, 29-24 (B)
1968—Jets, 47-31 (Birmingham)
Jets, 48-14 (NY)
1969—Jets, 23-14 (B)
Jets, 23-17 (NY)
1970—Jets, 31-21 (B)
Jets, 17-3 (NY)
1971—Patriots, 20-0 (NE)
Jets, 13-6 (NY)
1972—Jets, 41-13 (NE)
Jets, 34-10 (NY)
1973—Jets, 9-7 (NE)
Jets, 33-13 (NY)
1974—Patriots, 24-0 (NY)
Jets, 21-16 (NE)
1975—Jets, 36-7 (NY)
Jets, 30-28 (NE)
1976—Patriots, 41-7 (NE)
Patriots, 38-24 (NY)
1977—Jets, 30-27 (NY)
Patriots, 24-13 (NE)
1978—Patriots, 55-21 (NE)
Patriots, 19-17 (NY)
1979—Patriots, 56-3 (NE)
Jets, 27-26 (NY)
1980—Patriots, 21-11 (NY)
Patriots, 34-21 (NE)
1981—Jets, 28-24 (NY)
Jets, 17-6 (NE)
1982—Jets, 31-7 (NE)
1983—Patriots, 23-13 (NE)
Jets, 26-3 (NY)
1984—Patriots, 28-21 (NY)
Patriots, 30-20 (NE)
1985—Patriots, 20-13 (NE)
Jets, 16-13 (NY) OT
***Patriots, 26-14 (NY)
1986—Patriots, 20-6 (NY)
Jets, 31-24 (NE)
1987—Jets, 43-24 (NY)
Patriots, 42-20 (NE)
1988—Patriots, 28-3 (NE)
Patriots, 14-13 (NY)
1989—Patriots, 27-24 (NY)
Jets, 27-26 (NE)
1990—Jets, 37-13 (NE)
Jets, 42-7 (NY)
1991—Jets, 28-21 (NE)
Patriots, 6-3 (NY)
1992—Jets, 30-21 (NY)
Patriots, 24-3 (NE)
1993—Jets, 45-7 (NY)
Jets, 6-0 (NE)
1994—Jets, 24-17 (NY)
Patriots, 24-13 (NE)
1995—Patriots, 20-7 (NY)
Patriots, 31-28 (NE)
1996—Patriots, 31-27 (NY)
Patriots, 34-10 (NE)
1997—Patriots, 27-24 (NE) OT
Jets, 24-19 (NY)
(RS Pts.—Jets 1,681, Patriots 1,677)
(PS Pts.—Patriots 26, Jets 14)
*Franchise in Boston prior to 1971
**Jets known as Titans prior to 1963
***AFC First-Round Playoff

***NEW ENGLAND vs. **OAKLAND**
RS: Raiders lead series, 13-12-1
PS: Series tied, 1-1
1960—Raiders, 27-14 (O)
Patriots, 34-28 (B)
1961—Patriots, 20-17 (B)
Patriots, 35-21 (O)
1962—Patriots, 26-16 (B)
Raiders, 20-0 (O)
1963—Patriots, 20-14 (O)
Patriots, 20-14 (B)
1964—Patriots, 17-14 (O)
Tie, 43-43 (B)
1965—Raiders, 24-10 (B)
Raiders, 30-21 (O)
1966—Patriots, 24-21 (B)
1967—Raiders, 35-7 (O)
Raiders, 48-14 (B)
1968—Raiders, 41-10 (O)
1969—Raiders, 38-23 (B)
1971—Patriots, 20-6 (NE)
1974—Raiders, 41-26 (O)
1976—Patriots, 48-17 (NE)
***Raiders, 24-21 (O)
1978—Patriots, 21-14 (O)
1981—Raiders, 27-17 (O)
1985—Raiders, 35-20 (NE)
***Patriots, 27-20 (LA)
1987—Patriots, 26-23 (NE)
1989—Raiders, 24-21 (LA)
1994—Raiders, 21-17 (NE)
(RS Pts.—Raiders 659, Patriots 554)
(PS Pts.—Patriots 48, Raiders 44)
*Franchise in Boston prior to 1971
**Franchise in Los Angeles from 1982-1994
***AFC Divisional Playoff

NEW ENGLAND vs. PHILADELPHIA
RS: Eagles lead series, 5-2
1973—Eagles, 24-23 (P)
1977—Patriots, 14-6 (NE)
1978—Patriots, 24-14 (NE)
1981—Eagles, 13-3 (P)
1984—Eagles, 27-17 (P)
1987—Eagles, 34-31 (NE) OT
1990—Eagles, 48-20 (P)
(RS Pts.—Eagles 166, Patriots 132)

NEW ENGLAND vs. PITTSBURGH
RS: Steelers lead series, 11-3
PS: Series tied, 1-1
1972—Steelers, 33-3 (P)
1974—Steelers, 21-17 (NE)
1976—Patriots, 30-27 (P)
1979—Steelers, 16-13 (NE) OT
1981—Steelers, 27-21 (P) OT
1982—Steelers, 37-14 (P)
1983—Patriots, 28-23 (P)
1986—Patriots, 34-0 (P)
1989—Steelers, 28-10 (P)
1990—Steelers, 24-3 (P)
1991—Steelers, 20-6 (P)
1993—Steelers, 17-14 (P)
1995—Steelers, 41-27 (P)
1996—*Patriots, 28-3 (NE)
1997—Steelers, 24-21 (NE) OT
*Steelers, 7-6 (P)
(RS Pts.—Steelers 338, Patriots 241)
(PS Pts.—Patriots 34, Steelers 10)
*AFC Divisional Playoff

NEW ENGLAND vs. *ST. LOUIS
RS: Series tied, 3-3
1974—Patriots, 20-14 (NE)
1980—Rams, 17-14 (NE)
1983—Patriots, 21-7 (LA)
1986—Patriots, 30-28 (LA)
1989—Rams, 24-20 (NE)
1992—Rams, 14-0 (LA)
(RS Pts.—Patriots 105, Rams 104)
*Franchise in Los Angeles prior to 1995

ALL-TIME TEAM VS. TEAM RESULTS

***NEW ENGLAND vs. **SAN DIEGO**
RS: Patriots lead series, 16-11-2
PS: Chargers lead series, 1-0
1960—Patriots, 35-0 (LA)
Chargers, 45-16 (B)
1961—Chargers, 38-27 (B)
Patriots, 41-0 (SD)
1962—Patriots, 24-20 (B)
Patriots, 20-14 (SD)
1963—Chargers, 17-13 (SD)
Chargers, 7-6 (B)
***Chargers, 51-10 (SD)
1964—Patriots, 33-28 (SD)
Chargers, 26-17 (B)
1965—Tie, 10-10 (B)
Patriots, 22-6 (SD)
1966—Chargers, 24-0 (SD)
Patriots, 35-17 (B)
1967—Chargers, 28-14 (SD)
Tie, 31-31 (SD)
1968—Chargers, 27-17 (B)
1969—Chargers, 13-10 (B)
Chargers, 28-18 (SD)
1970—Chargers, 16-14 (B)
1973—Patriots, 30-14 (NE)
1975—Patriots, 33-19 (SD)
1977—Patriots, 24-20 (SD)
1978—Patriots, 28-23 (NE)
1979—Patriots, 27-21 (NE)
1983—Patriots, 37-21 (NE)
1994—Patriots, 23-17 (NE)
1996—Patriots, 45-7 (SD)
1997—Patriots, 41-7 (NE)
(RS Pts.—Patriots 691, Chargers 544)
(PS Pts.—Chargers 51, Patriots 10)
**Franchise in Boston prior to 1971*
***Franchise in Los Angeles prior to 1961*
****AFL Championship*

NEW ENGLAND vs. SAN FRANCISCO
RS: 49ers lead series, 7-1
1971—49ers, 27-10 (SF)
1975—Patriots, 24-16 (NE)
1980—49ers, 21-17 (SF)
1983—49ers, 33-13 (NE)
1986—49ers, 29-24 (NE)
1989—49ers, 37-20 (SF)
1992—49ers, 24-12 (NE)
1995—49ers, 28-3 (SF)
(RS Pts.—49ers 215, Patriots 123)

NEW ENGLAND vs. SEATTLE
RS: Seahawks lead series, 7-6
1977—Patriots, 31-0 (NE)
1980—Patriots, 37-31 (S)
1982—Patriots, 16-0 (S)
1983—Seahawks, 24-6 (S)
1984—Patriots, 38-23 (NE)
1985—Patriots, 20-13 (S)
1986—Seahawks, 38-31 (NE)
1988—Patriots, 13-7 (NE)
1989—Seahawks, 24-3 (NE)
1990—Seahawks, 33-20 (NE)
1992—Seahawks, 10-6 (NE)
1993—Seahawks, 17-14 (NE)
Seahawks, 10-9 (S)
(RS Pts.—Patriots 244, Seahawks 230)

NEW ENGLAND vs. TAMPA BAY
RS: Patriots lead series, 3-1
1976—Patriots, 31-14 (TB)
1985—Patriots, 32-14 (TB)
1988—Patriots, 10-7 (NE) OT
1997—Buccaneers, 27-7 (TB)
(RS Pts.—Patriots 80, Buccaneers 62)

***NEW ENGLAND vs. **TENNESSEE**
RS: Patriots lead series, 17-14-1
PS: Oilers lead series, 1-0
1960—Oilers, 24-10 (B)
Oilers, 37-21 (H)
1961—Tie, 31-31 (B)
Oilers, 27-15 (H)
1962—Patriots, 34-21 (B)
Oilers, 21-17 (H)
1963—Patriots, 45-3 (B)
Patriots, 46-28 (H)
1964—Patriots, 25-24 (B)
Patriots, 34-17 (H)
1965—Oilers, 31-10 (H)
Patriots, 42-14 (B)
1966—Patriots, 27-21 (B)
Patriots, 38-14 (H)
1967—Patriots, 18-7 (B)
Oilers, 27-6 (H)
1968—Oilers, 16-0 (B)
Oilers, 45-17 (H)
1969—Patriots, 24-0 (B)
Oilers, 27-23 (H)
1971—Patriots, 28-20 (NE)
1973—Patriots, 32-0 (H)
1975—Oilers, 7-0 (NE)
1978—Oilers, 26-23 (NE)
***Oilers, 31-14 (NE)
1980—Oilers, 38-34 (H)
1981—Patriots, 38-10 (NE)
1982—Patriots, 29-21 (NE)
1987—Patriots, 21-7 (H)
1988—Oilers, 31-6 (H)
1989—Patriots, 23-13 (NE)
1991—Patriots, 24-20 (NE)
1993—Oilers, 28-14 (NE)
(RS Pts.—Patriots 755, Oilers 656)
(PS Pts.—Oilers 31, Patriots 14)
**Franchise in Boston prior to 1971*
***Franchise in Houston prior to 1997*
****AFC Divisional Playoff*

NEW ENGLAND vs. WASHINGTON
RS: Redskins lead series, 5-1
1972—Patriots, 24-23 (NE)
1978—Redskins, 16-14 (NE)
1981—Redskins, 24-22 (W)
1984—Redskins, 26-10 (NE)
1990—Redskins, 25-10 (NE)
1996—Redskins, 27-22 (NE)
(RS Pts.—Redskins 141, Patriots 102)

NEW ORLEANS vs. ARIZONA
RS: Cardinals lead series, 11-10;
See Arizona vs. New Orleans

NEW ORLEANS vs. ATLANTA
RS: Falcons lead series, 33-24
PS: Falcons lead series, 1-0;
See Atlanta vs. New Orleans

NEW ORLEANS vs. BALTIMORE
RS: Ravens lead series, 1-0;
See Baltimore vs. New Orleans

NEW ORLEANS vs. BUFFALO
RS: Bills lead series, 3-2;
See Buffalo vs. New Orleans

NEW ORLEANS vs. CAROLINA
RS: Panthers lead series, 4-2;
See Carolina vs. New Orleans

NEW ORLEANS vs. CHICAGO
RS: Bears lead series, 9-8
PS: Bears lead series, 1-0;
See Chicago vs. New Orleans

NEW ORLEANS vs. CINCINNATI
RS: Saints lead series, 5-4;
See Cincinnati vs. New Orleans

NEW ORLEANS vs. CLEVELAND
RS: Browns lead series, 9-3;
See Cleveland vs. New Orleans

NEW ORLEANS vs. DALLAS
RS: Cowboys lead series, 14-3;
See Dallas vs. New Orleans

NEW ORLEANS vs. DENVER
RS: Broncos lead series, 4-2;
See Denver vs. New Orleans

NEW ORLEANS vs. DETROIT
RS: Saints lead series, 8-6-1;
See Detroit vs. New Orleans

NEW ORLEANS vs. GREEN BAY
RS: Packers lead series, 13-4;
See Green Bay vs. New Orleans

NEW ORLEANS vs. INDIANAPOLIS
RS: Series tied, 3-3;
See Indianapolis vs. New Orleans

NEW ORLEANS vs. JACKSONVILLE
RS: Saints lead series, 1-0;
See Jacksonville vs. New Orleans

NEW ORLEANS vs. KANSAS CITY
RS: Chiefs lead series, 4-3;
See Kansas City vs. New Orleans

NEW ORLEANS vs. MIAMI
RS: Dolphins lead series, 4-3;
See Miami vs. New Orleans

NEW ORLEANS vs. MINNESOTA
RS: Vikings lead series, 13-6
PS: Vikings lead series, 1-0;
See Minnesota vs. New Orleans

NEW ORLEANS vs. NEW ENGLAND
RS: Patriots lead series, 5-3;
See New England vs. New Orleans

NEW ORLEANS vs. N.Y. GIANTS
RS: Giants lead series, 11-8
1967—Giants, 27-21 (NY)
1968—Giants, 38-21 (NY)
1969—Saints, 25-24 (NY)
1970—Saints, 14-10 (NO)
1972—Giants, 45-21 (NY)
1975—Giants, 28-14 (NY)
1978—Saints, 28-17 (NO)
1979—Saints, 24-14 (NO)
1981—Giants, 20-7 (NY)
1984—Saints, 10-3 (NY)
1985—Giants, 21-13 (NO)
1986—Giants, 20-17 (NY)
1987—Saints, 23-14 (NO)
1988—Giants, 13-12 (NO)
1993—Giants, 24-14 (NO)
1994—Saints, 27-22 (NO)
1995—Giants, 45-29 (NY)
1996—Saints 17-3 (NY)
1997—Giants, 14-9 (NY)
(RS Pts.—Giants 402, Saints 346)

NEW ORLEANS vs. N.Y. JETS
RS: Series tied, 4-4
1972—Jets, 18-17 (NY)
1977—Jets, 16-13 (NO)
1980—Saints, 21-20 (NY)
1983—Jets, 31-28 (NO)
1986—Jets, 28-23 (NY)
1989—Saints, 29-14 (NO)
1992—Saints, 20-0 (NY)
1995—Saints, 12-0 (NY)
(RS Pts.—Saints 163, Jets 127)

NEW ORLEANS vs. *OAKLAND
RS: Raiders lead series, 4-3-1
1971—Tie, 21-21 (NO)
1975—Raiders, 48-10 (O)
1979—Raiders, 42-35 (NO)
1985—Raiders, 23-13 (LA)
1988—Saints, 20-6 (NO)
1991—Saints, 27-0 (NO)
1994—Raiders, 24-19 (LA)
1997—Saints, 13-10 (O)
(RS Pts.—Raiders 174, Saints 158)
**Franchise in Los Angeles from 1982-1994*

NEW ORLEANS vs. PHILADELPHIA
RS: Eagles lead series, 12-8
PS: Eagles lead series, 1-0
1967—Saints, 31-24 (NO)
Eagles, 48-21 (P)
1968—Eagles, 29-17 (P)
1969—Eagles, 13-10 (P)
Saints, 26-17 (NO)
1972—Saints, 21-3 (NO)
1974—Saints, 14-10 (NO)
1977—Eagles, 28-7 (P)
1978—Eagles, 24-17 (NO)
1979—Eagles, 26-14 (NO)
1980—Eagles, 34-21 (NO)
1981—Eagles, 31-14 (NO)
1983—Saints, 20-17 (P) OT
1985—Saints, 23-21 (NO)
1987—Eagles, 27-17 (P)
1989—Saints, 30-20 (NO)
1991—Saints, 13-6 (P)
1992—Eagles, 15-13 (P)
*Eagles, 36-20 (NO)
1993—Eagles, 37-26 (P)
1995—Eagles, 15-10 (NO)
(RS Pts.—Eagles 445, Saints 365)
(PS Pts.—Eagles 36, Saints 20)
**NFC First-Round Playoff*

NEW ORLEANS vs. PITTSBURGH
RS: Steelers lead series, 6-5
1967—Steelers, 14-10 (NO)
1968—Saints, 16-12 (P)
Saints, 24-14 (NO)
1969—Saints, 27-24 (NO)
1974—Steelers, 28-7 (NO)
1978—Steelers, 20-14 (P)
1981—Steelers, 20-6 (NO)
1984—Saints, 27-24 (NO)
1987—Saints, 20-16 (P)
1990—Steelers, 9-6 (NO)
1993—Steelers, 37-14 (P)
(RS Pts.—Steelers 218, Saints 171)

NEW ORLEANS vs. *ST. LOUIS
RS: Rams lead series, 32-24
1967—Rams, 27-13 (NO)
1969—Rams, 36-17 (LA)
1970—Rams, 30-17 (NO)
Rams, 34-16 (LA)
1971—Saints, 24-20 (NO)
Rams, 45-28 (LA)
1972—Rams, 34-14 (LA)
Saints, 19-16 (NO)
1973—Rams, 29-7 (LA)
Rams, 24-13 (NO)
1974—Rams, 24-0 (LA)
Saints, 20-7 (NO)
1975—Rams, 38-14 (LA)
Rams, 14-7 (NO)
1976—Rams, 16-10 (NO)
Rams, 33-14 (LA)
1977—Rams, 14-7 (LA)
Saints, 27-26 (NO)
1978—Rams, 26-20 (NO)
Saints, 10-3 (LA)
1979—Rams, 35-17 (NO)
Saints, 29-14 (LA)
1980—Rams, 45-31 (LA)
Rams, 27-7 (NO)
1981—Saints, 23-17 (NO)
Saints, 21-13 (LA)
1983—Rams, 30-27 (LA)
Rams, 26-24 (NO)
1984—Rams, 28-10 (NO)
Rams, 34-21 (LA)
1985—Rams, 28-10 (LA)
Saints, 29-3 (NO)
1986—Saints, 6-0 (NO)
Rams, 26-13 (LA)
1987—Saints, 37-10 (NO)
Saints, 31-14 (LA)
1988—Rams, 12-10 (NO)
Saints, 14-10 (LA)
1989—Saints, 40-21 (LA)
Rams, 20-17 (NO) OT
1990—Saints, 24-20 (LA)
Saints, 20-17 (NO)
1991—Saints, 24-7 (NO)
Saints, 24-17 (LA)
1992—Saints, 13-10 (NO)
Saints, 37-14 (LA)
1993—Saints, 37-6 (LA)
Rams, 23-20 (NO)
1994—Saints, 37-34 (NO)
Saints, 31-15 (LA)
1995—Rams, 17-13 (StL)
Saints, 19-10 (NO)
1996—Rams, 26-10 (NO)
Rams, 14-13 (StL)
1997—Rams, 38-24 (StL)
Rams, 34-27 (NO)
(RS Pts.—Rams 1,211, Saints 1,087)
**Franchise in Los Angeles prior to 1995*

NEW ORLEANS vs. SAN DIEGO
RS: Chargers lead series, 6-1
1973—Chargers, 17-14 (SD)
1977—Chargers, 14-0 (NO)
1979—Chargers, 35-0 (NO)

1988—Saints, 23-17 (SD)
1991—Chargers, 24-21 (SD)
1994—Chargers, 36-22 (NO)
1997—Chargers, 20-6 (NO)
(RS Pts.—Chargers 163, Saints 86)

NEW ORLEANS vs. SAN FRANCISCO
RS: 49ers lead series, 40-15-2
1967—49ers, 27-13 (SF)
1969—Saints, 43-38 (NO)
1970—Tie, 20-20 (SF)
49ers, 38-27 (NO)
1971—49ers, 38-20 (NO)
Saints, 26-20 (SF)
1972—49ers, 37-2 (NO)
Tie, 20-20 (SF)
1973—49ers, 40-0 (SF)
Saints, 16-10 (NO)
1974—49ers, 17-13 (NO)
49ers, 35-21 (SF)
1975—49ers, 35-21 (SF)
49ers, 16-6 (NO)
1976—49ers, 33-3 (SF)
49ers, 27-7 (NO)
1977—49ers, 10-7 (NO) OT
49ers, 20-17 (SF)
1978—Saints, 14-7 (SF)
Saints, 24-13 (NO)
1979—Saints, 30-21 (SF)
Saints, 31-20 (NO)
1980—49ers, 26-23 (NO)
49ers, 38-35 (SF) OT
1981—49ers, 21-14 (SF)
49ers, 21-17 (NO)
1982—Saints, 23-20 (SF)
1983—49ers, 32-13 (NO)
49ers, 27-0 (SF)
1984—49ers, 30-20 (SF)
49ers, 35-3 (NO)
1985—Saints, 20-17 (SF)
49ers, 31-19 (NO)
1986—49ers, 26-17 (SF)
Saints, 23-10 (NO)
1987—49ers, 24-22 (NO)
Saints, 26-24 (SF)
1988—49ers, 34-33 (NO)
49ers, 30-17 (SF)
1989—49ers, 24-20 (NO)
49ers, 31-13 (SF)
1990—49ers, 13-12 (NO)
Saints, 13-10 (SF)
1991—Saints, 10-3 (NO)
49ers, 38-24 (SF)
1992—49ers, 16-10 (NO)
49ers, 21-20 (SF)
1993—Saints, 16-13 (NO)
49ers, 42-7 (SF)
1994—49ers, 24-13 (SF)
49ers, 35-14 (NO)
1995—49ers, 24-22 (NO)
Saints, 11-7 (SF)
1996—49ers, 27-11 (SF)
49ers, 24-17 (NO)
1997—49ers, 33-7 (SF)
49ers, 23-0 (NO)
(RS Pts.—49ers 1,396, Saints 946)

NEW ORLEANS vs. SEATTLE
RS: Saints lead series, 4-2
1976—Saints, 51-27 (S)
1979—Seahawks, 38-24 (S)
1985—Seahawks, 27-3 (NO)
1988—Saints, 20-19 (S)
1991—Saints, 27-24 (NO)
1997—Saints, 20-17 (NO) OT
(RS Pts.—Seahawks 152, Saints 145)

NEW ORLEANS vs. TAMPA BAY
RS: Saints lead series, 12-5
1977—Buccaneers, 33-14 (NO)
1978—Saints, 17-10 (TB)
1979—Saints, 42-14 (TB)
1981—Buccaneers, 31-14 (NO)
1982—Buccaneers, 13-10 (NO)
1983—Saints, 24-21 (TB)
1984—Saints, 17-13 (NO)
1985—Saints, 20-13 (NO)
1986—Saints, 38-7 (NO)
1987—Saints, 44-34 (NO)
1988—Saints, 13-9 (NO)
1989—Buccaneers, 20-10 (TB)
1990—Saints, 35-7 (NO)
1991—Saints, 23-7 (NO)
1992—Saints, 23-21 (NO)
1994—Saints, 9-7 (TB)
1996—Buccaneers, 13-7 (TB)
(RS Pts.—Saints 360, Buccaneers 273)

NEW ORLEANS vs. *TENNESSEE
RS: Series tied, 4-4-1
1971—Tie, 13-13 (H)
1976—Oilers, 31-26 (NO)
1978—Oilers, 17-12 (NO)
1981—Saints, 27-24 (H)
1984—Saints, 27-10 (H)
1987—Saints, 24-10 (NO)
1990—Oilers, 23-10 (H)
1993—Saints, 33-21 (NO)
1996—Oilers, 31-14 (NO)
(RS Pts.—Saints 186, Oilers 180)
Franchise in Houston prior to 1997

NEW ORLEANS vs. WASHINGTON
RS: Redskins lead series, 12-5
1967—Redskins, 30-10 (NO)
Saints, 30-14 (W)
1968—Saints, 37-17 (NO)
1969—Redskins, 26-20 (NO)
Redskins, 17-14 (W)
1971—Redskins, 24-14 (W)
1973—Saints, 19-3 (NO)
1975—Redskins, 41-3 (W)
1979—Saints, 14-10 (W)
1980—Redskins, 22-14 (W)
1982—Redskins, 27-10 (NO)
1986—Redskins, 14-6 (NO)
1988—Redskins, 27-24 (W)
1989—Redskins, 16-14 (NO)
1990—Redskins, 31-17 (W)
1992—Saints, 20-3 (NO)
1994—Redskins, 38-24 (NO)
(RS Pts.—Redskins 360, Saints 290)

N.Y. GIANTS vs. ARIZONA
RS: Giants lead series, 71-37-2;
See Arizona vs. N.Y. Giants

N.Y. GIANTS vs. ATLANTA
RS: Series tied, 6-6;
See Atlanta vs. N.Y. Giants

N.Y. GIANTS vs. BALTIMORE
RS: Ravens lead series, 1-0;
See Baltimore vs. N.Y. Giants

N.Y. GIANTS vs. BUFFALO
RS: Bills lead series, 5-2
PS: Giants lead series, 1-0;
See Buffalo vs. N.Y. Giants

N.Y. GIANTS vs. CAROLINA
RS: Panthers lead series, 1-0;
See Carolina vs. N.Y. Giants

N.Y. GIANTS vs. CHICAGO
RS: Bears lead series, 25-16-2
PS: Bears lead series, 5-3;
See Chicago vs. N.Y. Giants

N.Y. GIANTS vs. CINCINNATI
RS: Bengals lead series, 4-2;
See Cincinnati vs. N.Y. Giants

N.Y. GIANTS vs. CLEVELAND
RS: Browns lead series, 25-17-2
PS: Series tied, 1-1;
See Cleveland vs. N.Y. Giants

N.Y. GIANTS vs. DALLAS
RS: Cowboys lead series, 44-25-2;
See Dallas vs. N.Y. Giants

N.Y. GIANTS vs. DENVER
RS: Series tied, 3-3
PS: Giants lead series, 1-0;
See Denver vs. N.Y. Giants

N.Y. GIANTS vs. DETROIT
RS: Lions lead series, 18-17-1
PS: Lions lead series, 1-0;
See Detroit vs. N.Y. Giants

N.Y. GIANTS vs. GREEN BAY
RS: Packers lead series, 22-20-2
PS: Packers lead series, 4-1;
See Green Bay vs. N.Y. Giants

N.Y. GIANTS vs. INDIANAPOLIS
RS: Series tied, 5-5
PS: Colts lead series, 2-0;
See Indianapolis vs. N.Y. Giants

N.Y. GIANTS vs. JACKSONVILLE
RS: Jaguars lead series, 1-0;
See Jacksonville vs. N.Y. Giants

N.Y. GIANTS vs. KANSAS CITY
RS: Giants lead series, 6-2;
See Kansas City vs. N.Y. Giants

N.Y. GIANTS vs. MIAMI
RS: Giants lead series, 3-1;
See Miami vs. N.Y. Giants

N.Y. GIANTS vs. MINNESOTA
RS: Vikings lead series, 7-5
PS: Series tied, 1-1;
See Minnesota vs. N.Y. Giants

N.Y. GIANTS vs. NEW ENGLAND
RS: Giants lead series, 3-2;
See New England vs. N.Y. Giants

N.Y. GIANTS vs. NEW ORLEANS
RS: Giants lead series, 11-8;
See New Orleans vs. N.Y. Giants

N.Y. GIANTS vs. N.Y. JETS
RS: Series tied, 4-4
1970—Giants, 22-10 (NYJ)
1974—Jets, 26-20 (New Haven) OT
1981—Jets, 26-7 (NYG)
1984—Giants, 20-10 (NYJ)
1987—Giants, 20-7 (NYG)
1988—Jets, 27-21 (NYJ)
1993—Jets, 10-6 (NYG)
1996—Giants, 13-6 (NYJ)
(RS Pts.—Giants 129, Jets 122)

N.Y. GIANTS vs. *OAKLAND
RS: Raiders lead series, 5-2
1973—Raiders, 42-0 (O)
1980—Raiders, 33-17 (NY)
1983—Raiders, 27-12 (LA)
1986—Giants, 14-9 (LA)
1989—Giants, 34-17 (NY)
1992—Raiders, 13-10 (LA)
1995—Raiders, 17-13 (NY)
(RS Pts.—Raiders 158, Giants 100)
Franchise in Los Angeles from 1982-1994

N.Y. GIANTS vs. PHILADELPHIA
RS: Giants lead series, 66-58-2
PS: Giants lead series, 1-0
1933—Giants, 56-0 (NY)
Giants, 20-14 (P)
1934—Giants, 17-0 (NY)
Eagles, 6-0 (P)
1935—Giants, 10-0 (NY)
Giants, 21-14 (P)
1936—Eagles, 10-7 (P)
Giants, 21-17 (NY)
1937—Giants, 16-7 (P)
Giants, 21-0 (NY)
1938—Eagles, 14-10 (P)
Giants, 17-7 (NY)
1939—Giants, 13-3 (P)
Giants, 27-10 (NY)
1940—Giants, 20-14 (P)
Giants, 17-7 (NY)
1941—Giants, 24-0 (P)
Giants, 16-0 (NY)
1942—Giants, 35-17 (NY)
Giants, 14-0 (P)
1944—Eagles, 24-17 (NY)
Tie, 21-21 (P)
1945—Eagles, 38-17 (P)
Giants, 28-21 (NY)
1946—Eagles, 24-14 (P)
Giants, 45-17 (NY)
1947—Eagles, 23-0 (P)
Eagles, 41-24 (NY)
1948—Eagles, 45-0 (P)
Eagles, 35-14 (NY)
1949—Eagles, 24-3 (NY)
Eagles, 17-3 (P)
1950—Giants, 7-3 (NY)
Giants, 9-7 (P)
1951—Giants, 26-24 (NY)
Giants, 23-7 (P)
1952—Giants, 31-7 (P)
Eagles, 14-10 (NY)
1953—Eagles, 30-7 (P)
Giants, 37-28 (NY)
1954—Giants, 27-14 (NY)
Eagles, 29-14 (P)
1955—Eagles, 27-17 (P)
Giants, 31-7 (NY)
1956—Giants, 20-3 (NY)
Giants, 21-7 (P)
1957—Giants, 24-20 (P)
Giants, 13-0 (NY)
1958—Eagles, 27-24 (P)
Giants, 24-10 (NY)
1959—Eagles, 49-21 (P)
Giants, 24-7 (NY)
1960—Eagles, 17-10 (NY)
Eagles, 31-23 (P)
1961—Giants, 38-21 (NY)
Giants, 28-24 (P)
1962—Giants, 29-13 (P)
Giants, 19-14 (NY)
1963—Giants, 37-14 (P)
Giants, 42-14 (NY)
1964—Eagles, 38-7 (P)
Eagles, 23-17 (NY)
1965—Giants, 16-14 (P)
Giants, 35-27 (NY)
1966—Eagles, 35-17 (P)
Eagles, 31-3 (NY)
1967—Giants, 44-7 (NY)
1968—Giants, 34-25 (P)
Giants, 7-6 (NY)
1969—Eagles, 23-20 (NY)
1970—Giants, 30-23 (NY)
Eagles, 23-20 (P)
1971—Eagles, 23-7 (P)
Eagles, 41-28 (NY)
1972—Giants, 27-12 (P)
Giants, 62-10 (NY)
1973—Tie, 23-23 (NY)
Eagles, 20-16 (P)
1974—Eagles, 35-7 (P)
Eagles, 20-7 (New Haven)
1975—Giants, 23-14 (P)
Eagles, 13-10 (NY)
1976—Eagles, 20-7 (P)
Eagles, 10-0 (NY)
1977—Eagles, 28-10 (NY)
Eagles, 17-14 (P)
1978—Eagles, 19-17 (NY)
Eagles, 20-3 (P)
1979—Eagles, 23-17 (P)
Eagles, 17-13 (NY)
1980—Eagles, 35-3 (P)
Eagles, 31-16 (NY)
1981—Eagles, 24-10 (NY)
Giants, 20-10 (P)
*Giants, 27-21 (P)
1982—Giants, 23-7 (NY)
Giants, 26-24 (P)
1983—Eagles, 17-13 (NY)
Giants, 23-0 (P)
1984—Giants, 28-27 (NY)
Eagles, 24-10 (P)
1985—Giants, 21-0 (NY)
Giants, 16-10 (P) OT
1986—Giants, 35-3 (NY)
Giants, 17-14 (P)
1987—Giants, 20-17 (P)
Giants, 23-20 (NY) OT
1988—Eagles, 24-13 (P)
Eagles, 23-17 (NY) OT
1989—Eagles, 21-19 (P)
Eagles, 24-17 (NY)
1990—Giants, 27-20 (NY)
Eagles, 31-13 (P)

ALL-TIME TEAM VS. TEAM RESULTS

1991—Eagles, 30-7 (P)
Eagles, 19-14 (NY)
1992—Eagles, 47-34 (NY)
Eagles, 20-10 (P)
1993—Giants, 21-10 (NY)
Giants, 7-3 (P)
1994—Giants, 28-23 (NY)
Giants, 16-13 (P)
1995—Eagles, 17-14 (NY)
Eagles, 28-19 (P)
1996—Eagles, 19-10 (NY)
Eagles, 24-0 (P)
1997—Giants, 31-17 (NY)
Giants, 31-21 (P)
(RS Pts.—Giants 2,397, Eagles 2,275)
(PS Pts.—Giants 27, Eagles 21)
NFC First-Round Playoff

N.Y. GIANTS vs. *PITTSBURGH
RS: Giants lead series, 42-27-3
1933—Giants, 23-2 (P)
Giants, 27-3 (NY)
1934—Giants, 14-12 (P)
Giants, 17-7 (NY)
1935—Giants, 42-7 (P)
Giants, 13-0 (NY)
1936—Pirates, 10-7 (P)
1937—Giants, 10-7 (P)
Giants, 17-0 (NY)
1938—Giants, 27-14 (P)
Pirates, 13-10 (NY)
1939—Giants, 14-7 (P)
Giants, 23-7 (NY)
1940—Tie, 10-10 (P)
Giants, 12-0 (NY)
1941—Giants, 37-10 (P)
Giants, 28-7 (NY)
1942—Steelers, 13-10 (P)
Steelers, 17-9 (NY)
1945—Giants, 34-6 (P)
Steelers, 21-7 (NY)
1946—Giants, 17-14 (P)
Giants, 7-0 (NY)
1947—Steelers, 38-21 (NY)
Steelers, 24-7 (P)
1948—Giants, 34-27 (NY)
Steelers, 38-28 (P)
1949—Steelers, 28-7 (P)
Steelers, 21-17 (NY)
1950—Giants, 18-7 (P)
Steelers, 17-6 (NY)
1951—Tie, 13-13 (P)
Giants, 14-0 (NY)
1952—Steelers, 63-7 (P)
1953—Steelers, 24-14 (P)
Steelers, 14-10 (NY)
1954—Giants, 30-6 (P)
Giants, 24-3 (NY)
1955—Steelers, 30-23 (P)
Steelers, 19-17 (NY)
1956—Giants, 38-10 (NY)
Giants, 17-14 (P)
1957—Giants, 35-0 (NY)
Steelers, 21-10 (P)
1958—Giants, 17-6 (NY)
Steelers, 31-10 (P)
1959—Giants, 21-16 (P)
Steelers, 14-9 (NY)
1960—Giants, 19-17 (P)
Giants, 27-24 (NY)
1961—Giants, 17-14 (P)
Giants, 42-21 (NY)
1962—Giants, 31-27 (P)
Steelers, 20-17 (NY)
1963—Steelers, 31-0 (P)
Giants, 33-17 (NY)
1964—Steelers, 27-24 (P)
Steelers, 44-17 (NY)
1965—Giants, 23-13 (P)
Giants, 35-10 (NY)
1966—Tie, 34-34 (P)
Steelers, 47-28 (NY)
1967—Giants, 27-24 (P)
Giants, 28-20 (NY)
1968—Giants, 34-20 (P)
1969—Giants, 10-7 (NY)
Giants, 21-17 (P)
1971—Steelers, 17-13 (P)
1976—Steelers, 27-0 (NY)
1985—Giants, 28-10 (NY)
1991—Giants, 23-20 (P)
1994—Steelers, 10-6 (NY)
(RS Pts.—Giants 1,399, Steelers 1,189)
Steelers known as Pirates prior to 1941

N.Y. GIANTS vs. *ST. LOUIS
RS: Rams lead series, 22-9
PS: Series tied, 1-1
1938—Giants, 28-0 (NY)
1940—Rams, 13-0 (NY)
1941—Giants, 49-14 (NY)
1945—Rams, 21-17 (NY)
1946—Rams, 31-21 (NY)
1947—Rams, 34-10 (LA)
1948—Rams, 52-37 (NY)
1953—Rams, 21-7 (LA)
1954—Rams, 17-16 (NY)
1959—Giants, 23-21 (LA)
1961—Giants, 24-14 (NY)
1966—Rams, 55-14 (LA)
1968—Rams, 24-21 (LA)
1970—Rams, 31-3 (NY)
1973—Rams, 40-6 (LA)
1976—Rams, 24-10 (LA)
1978—Rams, 20-17 (NY)
1979—Giants, 20-14 (LA)
1980—Rams, 28-7 (NY)
1981—Giants, 10-7 (NY)
1983—Rams, 16-6 (NY)
1984—Rams, 33-12 (LA)
**Giants, 16-13 (LA)
1985—Giants, 24-19 (NY)
1988—Rams, 45-31 (NY)
1989—Rams, 31-10 (LA)
***Rams, 19-13 (NY) OT
1990—Giants, 31-7 (LA)
1991—Rams, 19-13 (NY)
1992—Rams, 38-17 (LA)
1993—Giants, 20-10 (NY)
1994—Rams, 17-10 (LA)
1997—Rams, 13-3 (StL)
(RS Pts.—Rams 729, Giants 517)
(PS Pts.—Rams 32, Giants 29)
Franchise in Los Angeles prior to 1995 and in Cleveland prior to 1946
***NFC First-Round Playoff*
****NFC Divisional Playoff*

N.Y. GIANTS vs. SAN DIEGO
RS: Giants lead series, 4-3
1971—Giants, 35-17 (NY)
1975—Giants, 35-24 (NY)
1980—Chargers, 44-7 (SD)
1983—Chargers, 41-34 (NY)
1986—Giants, 20-7 (NY)
1989—Giants, 20-13 (SD)
1995—Chargers, 27-17 (NY)
(RS Pts.—Chargers 173, Giants 168)

N.Y. GIANTS vs. SAN FRANCISCO
RS: Series tied, 11-11
PS: Series tied, 3-3
1952—Giants, 23-14 (NY)
1956—Giants, 38-21 (SF)
1957—49ers, 27-17 (NY)
1960—Giants, 21-19 (SF)
1963—Giants, 48-14 (NY)
1968—49ers, 26-10 (NY)
1972—Giants, 23-17 (SF)
1975—Giants, 26-23 (SF)
1977—Giants, 20-17 (NY)
1978—Giants, 27-10 (NY)
1979—Giants, 32-16 (NY)
1980—49ers, 12-0 (SF)
1981—49ers, 17-10 (SF)
*49ers, 38-24 (SF)
1984—49ers, 31-10 (NY)
*49ers, 21-10 (SF)
1985—**Giants, 17-3 (NY)
1986—Giants, 21-17 (SF)
*Giants, 49-3 (NY)
1987—49ers, 41-21 (NY)
1988—49ers, 20-17 (NY)
1989—49ers, 34-24 (SF)
1990—49ers, 7-3 (SF)
***Giants, 15-13 (SF)
1991—Giants, 16-14 (NY)
1992—49ers, 31-14 (NY)
1993—*49ers, 44-3 (SF)
1995—49ers, 20-6 (SF)
(RS Pts.—49ers 451, Giants 427)
(PS Pts.—49ers 119, Giants 118)
**NFC Divisional Playoff*
***NFC First-Round Playoff*
****NFC Championship*

N.Y. GIANTS vs. SEATTLE
RS: Giants lead series, 5-3
1976—Giants, 28-16 (NY)
1980—Giants, 27-21 (S)
1981—Giants, 32-0 (S)
1983—Seahawks, 17-12 (NY)
1986—Seahawks, 17-12 (S)
1989—Giants, 15-3 (NY)
1992—Giants, 23-10 (NY)
1995—Seahawks, 30-28 (S)
(RS Pts.—Giants 177, Seahawks 114)

N.Y. GIANTS vs. TAMPA BAY
RS: Giants lead series, 8-4
1977—Giants, 10-0 (TB)
1978—Giants, 19-13 (TB)
Giants, 17-14 (NY)
1979—Giants, 17-14 (NY)
Buccaneers, 31-3 (TB)
1980—Buccaneers, 30-13 (TB)
1984—Giants, 17-14 (NY)
Buccaneers, 20-17 (TB)
1985—Giants, 22-20 (NY)
1991—Giants, 21-14 (TB)
1993—Giants, 23-7 (NY)
1997—Buccaneers, 20-8 (NY)
(RS Pts.—Buccaneers 197, Giants 187)

N.Y. GIANTS vs. *TENNESSEE
RS: Giants lead series, 5-1
1973—Giants, 34-14 (NY)
1982—Giants, 17-14 (NY)
1985—Giants, 35-14 (H)
1991—Giants, 24-20 (NY)
1994—Giants, 13-10 (H)
1997—Oilers, 10-6 (T)
(RS Pts.—Giants 129, Oilers 82)
Franchise in Houston prior to 1997

N.Y. GIANTS vs. *WASHINGTON
RS: Giants lead series, 74-52-4
PS: Series tied, 1-1
1932—Braves, 14-6 (B)
Tie, 0-0 (NY)
1933—Redskins, 21-20 (B)
Giants, 7-0 (NY)
1934—Giants, 16-13 (B)
Giants, 3-0 (NY)
1935—Giants, 20-12 (B)
Giants, 17-6 (NY)
1936—Giants, 7-0 (B)
Redskins, 14-0 (NY)
1937—Redskins, 13-3 (W)
Redskins, 49-14 (NY)
1938—Giants, 10-7 (W)
Giants, 36-0 (NY)
1939—Tie, 0-0 (W)
Giants, 9-7 (NY)
1940—Redskins, 21-7 (W)
Giants, 21-7 (NY)
1941—Giants, 17-10 (W)
Giants, 20-13 (NY)
1942—Giants, 14-7 (W)
Redskins, 14-7 (NY)
1943—Giants, 14-10 (NY)
Giants, 31-7 (W)
**Redskins, 28-0 (NY)
1944—Giants, 16-13 (NY)
Giants, 31-0 (W)
1945—Redskins, 24-14 (NY)
Redskins, 17-0 (W)
1946—Redskins, 24-14 (W)
Giants, 31-0 (NY)
1947—Redskins, 28-20 (W)
Giants, 35-10 (NY)
1948—Redskins, 41-10 (W)
Redskins, 28-21 (NY)
1949—Giants, 45-35 (W)
Giants, 23-7 (NY)
1950—Giants, 21-17 (W)
Giants, 24-21 (NY)
1951—Giants, 35-14 (W)
Giants, 28-14 (NY)
1952—Giants, 14-10 (W)
Redskins, 27-17 (NY)
1953—Redskins, 13-9 (W)
Redskins, 24-21 (NY)
1954—Giants, 51-21 (W)
Giants, 24-7 (NY)
1955—Giants, 35-7 (NY)
Giants, 27-20 (W)
1956—Redskins, 33-7 (W)
Giants, 28-14 (NY)
1957—Giants, 24-20 (W)
Redskins, 31-14 (NY)
1958—Giants, 21-14 (W)
Giants, 30-0 (NY)
1959—Giants, 45-14 (NY)
Giants, 24-10 (W)
1960—Tie, 24-24 (NY)
Giants, 17-3 (W)
1961—Giants, 24-21 (W)
Giants, 53-0 (NY)
1962—Giants, 49-34 (NY)
Giants, 42-24 (W)
1963—Giants, 24-14 (W)
Giants, 44-14 (NY)
1964—Giants, 13-10 (NY)
Redskins, 36-21 (W)
1965—Redskins, 23-7 (NY)
Giants, 27-10 (W)
1966—Giants, 13-10 (NY)
Redskins, 72-41 (W)
1967—Redskins, 38-34 (W)
1968—Giants, 48-21 (NY)
Giants, 13-10 (W)
1969—Redskins, 20-14 (W)
1970—Giants, 35-33 (NY)
Giants, 27-24 (W)
1971—Redskins, 30-3 (NY)
Redskins, 23-7 (W)
1972—Redskins, 23-16 (NY)
Redskins, 27-13 (W)
1973—Redskins, 21-3 (New Haven)
Redskins, 27-24 (W)
1974—Redskins, 13-10 (New Haven)
Redskins, 24-3 (W)
1975—Redskins, 49-13 (W)
Redskins, 21-13 (NY)
1976—Redskins, 19-17 (W)
Giants, 12-9 (NY)
1977—Giants, 20-17 (NY)
Giants, 17-6 (W)
1978—Giants, 17-6 (NY)
Redskins, 16-13 (W) OT
1979—Redskins, 27-0 (W)
Giants, 14-6 (NY)
1980—Redskins, 23-21 (NY)
Redskins, 16-13 (W)
1981—Giants, 17-7 (W)
Redskins, 30-27 (NY) OT
1982—Redskins, 27-17 (NY)
Redskins, 15-14 (W)
1983—Redskins, 33-17 (NY)
Redskins, 31-22 (W)
1984—Redskins, 30-14 (W)
Giants, 37-13 (NY)
1985—Giants, 17-3 (NY)
Redskins, 23-21 (W)
1986—Giants, 27-20 (NY)
Giants, 24-14 (W)
***Giants, 17-0 (NY)
1987—Redskins, 38-12 (NY)
Redskins, 23-19 (W)

1988—Giants, 27-20 (NY)
Giants, 24-23 (W)
1989—Giants, 27-24 (W)
Giants, 20-17 (NY)
1990—Giants, 24-20 (W)
Giants, 21-10 (NY)
1991—Redskins, 17-13 (NY)
Redskins, 34-17 (W)
1992—Giants, 24-7 (W)
Redskins, 28-10 (NY)
1993—Giants, 41-7 (W)
Giants, 20-6 (NY)
1994—Giants, 31-23 (NY)
Giants, 21-19 (W)
1995—Giants, 24-15 (W)
Giants, 20-13 (NY)
1996—Redskins, 31-10 (NY)
Redskins, 31-21 (W)
1997—Tie, 7-7 (W) OT
Giants, 30-10 (NY)
(RS Pts.—Giants 2,594, Redskins 2,316)
(PS Pts.—Redskins 28, Giants 17)
Franchise in Boston prior to 1937 and known as Braves prior to 1933
***Division Playoff*
****NFC Championship*

N.Y. JETS vs. ARIZONA
RS: Series tied, 2-2;
See Arizona vs. N.Y. Jets
N.Y. JETS vs. ATLANTA
RS: Falcons lead series, 4-3;
See Atlanta vs. N.Y. Jets
N.Y. JETS vs BALTIMORE
RS: Ravens lead series, 1-0;
See Baltimore vs. N.Y. Jets
N.Y. JETS vs. BUFFALO
RS: Bills lead series, 43-31
PS: Bills lead series, 1-0;
See Buffalo vs. N.Y. Jets
N.Y. JETS vs. CAROLINA
RS: Panthers lead series, 1-0;
See Carolina vs. N.Y. Jets
N.Y. JETS vs. CHICAGO
RS: Bears lead series, 4-2;
See Chicago vs. N.Y. Jets
N.Y. JETS vs. CINCINNATI
RS: Jets lead series, 10-6
PS: Jets lead series, 1-0;
See Cincinnati vs. N.Y. Jets
N.Y. JETS vs. CLEVELAND
RS: Browns lead series, 9-6
PS: Browns lead series, 1-0;
See Cleveland vs. N.Y. Jets
N.Y. JETS vs. DALLAS
RS: Cowboys lead series, 5-1;
See Dallas vs. N.Y. Jets
N.Y. JETS vs. DENVER
RS: Broncos lead series, 13-12-1;
See Denver vs. N.Y. Jets
N.Y. JETS vs. DETROIT
RS: Lions lead series, 5-3;
See Detroit vs. N.Y. Jets
N.Y. JETS vs. GREEN BAY
RS: Jets lead series, 5-2;
See Green Bay vs. N.Y. Jets
N.Y. JETS vs. INDIANAPOLIS
RS: Colts lead series, 33-22
PS: Jets lead series, 1-0;
See Indianapolis vs. N.Y. Jets
N.Y. JETS vs. JACKSONVILLE
RS: Series tied, 1-1;
See Jacksonville vs. N.Y. Jets
N.Y. JETS vs. KANSAS CITY
RS: Chiefs lead series, 14-12-1
PS: Series tied, 1-1;
See Kansas City vs. N.Y. Jets
N.Y. JETS vs. MIAMI
RS: Dolphins lead series, 34-29-1
PS: Dolphins lead series, 1-0;
See Miami vs. N.Y. Jets
N.Y. JETS vs. MINNESOTA
RS: Jets lead series, 5-1;
See Minnesota vs. N.Y. Jets
N.Y. JETS vs. NEW ENGLAND
RS: Jets lead series, 40-34-1
PS: Patriots lead series, 1-0;
See New England vs. N.Y. Jets
N.Y. JETS vs. NEW ORLEANS
RS: Series tied, 4-4;
See New Orleans vs. N.Y. Jets
N.Y. JETS vs. N.Y. GIANTS
RS: Series tied, 4-4;
See N.Y. Giants vs. N.Y. Jets
***N.Y. JETS vs. **OAKLAND**
RS: Raiders lead series, 16-10-2
PS: Jets lead series, 2-0
1960—Raiders, 28-27 (NY)
Titans, 31-28 (O)
1961—Titans, 14-6 (O)
Titans, 23-12 (NY)
1962—Titans, 28-17 (O)
Titans, 31-21 (NY)
1963—Jets, 10-7 (NY)
Raiders, 49-26 (O)
1964—Jets, 35-13 (NY)
Raiders, 35-26 (O)
1965—Tie, 24-24 (NY)
Raiders, 24-14 (O)
1966—Raiders, 24-21 (NY)
Tie, 28-28 (O)
1967—Jets, 27-14 (NY)
Raiders, 38-29 (O)
1968—Raiders, 43-32 (O)
***Jets, 27-23 (NY)
1969—Raiders, 27-14 (NY)
1970—Raiders, 14-13 (NY)
1972—Raiders, 24-16 (O)
1977—Raiders, 28-27 (NY)
1979—Jets, 28-19 (NY)
1982—****Jets, 17-14 (LA)
1985—Raiders, 31-0 (LA)
1989—Raiders, 14-7 (NY)
1993—Raiders, 24-20 (LA)
1995—Raiders, 47-10 (NY)
1996—Raiders, 34-13 (NY)
1997—Jets 23-22 (NY)
(RS Pts.—Raiders 695, Jets 597)
(PS Pts.—Jets 44, Raiders 37)
**Jets known as Titans prior to 1963*
***Franchise in Los Angeles from 1982-1994*
****AFL Championship*
*****AFC Second-Round Playoff*
N.Y. JETS vs. PHILADELPHIA
RS: Eagles lead series, 6-0
1973—Eagles, 24-23 (P)
1977—Eagles, 27-0 (P)
1978—Eagles, 17-9 (P)
1987—Eagles, 38-27 (NY)
1993—Eagles, 35-30 (NY)
1996—Eagles, 21-20 (NY)
(RS Pts.—Eagles 162, Jets 109)
N.Y. JETS vs. PITTSBURGH
RS: Steelers lead series, 12-1
1970—Steelers, 21-17 (P)
1973—Steelers, 26-14 (P)
1975—Steelers, 20-7 (NY)
1977—Steelers, 23-20 (NY)
1978—Steelers, 28-17 (NY)
1981—Steelers, 38-10 (P)
1983—Steelers, 34-7 (NY)
1984—Steelers, 23-17 (NY)
1986—Steelers, 45-24 (NY)
1988—Jets, 24-20 (NY)
1989—Steelers, 13-0 (NY)
1990—Steelers, 24-7 (NY)
1992—Steelers, 27-10 (P)
(RS Pts.—Steelers 342, Jets 174)
N.Y. JETS vs. *ST. LOUIS
RS: Rams lead series, 6-2
1970—Jets, 31-20 (LA)
1974—Rams, 20-13 (NY)
1980—Rams, 38-13 (LA)
1983—Jets, 27-24 (NY) OT
1986—Rams, 17-3 (NY)
1989—Rams, 38-14 (LA)
1992—Rams, 18-10 (LA)
1995—Rams, 23-20 (NY)
(RS Pts.—Rams 198, Jets 131)
**Franchise in Los Angeles prior to 1995*
***N.Y. JETS vs. **SAN DIEGO**
RS: Chargers lead series, 17-9-1
1960—Chargers, 21-7 (NY)
Chargers, 50-43 (LA)
1961—Chargers, 25-10 (NY)
Chargers, 48-13 (SD)
1962—Chargers, 40-14 (SD)
Titans, 23-3 (NY)
1963—Chargers, 24-20 (SD)
Chargers, 53-7 (NY)
1964—Tie, 17-17 (NY)
Chargers, 38-3 (SD)
1965—Chargers, 34-9 (NY)
Chargers, 38-7 (SD)
1966—Jets, 17-16 (NY)
Chargers, 42-27 (SD)
1967—Jets, 42-31 (SD)
1968—Jets, 23-20 (NY)
Jets, 37-15 (SD)
1969—Chargers, 34-27 (SD)
1971—Chargers, 49-21 (SD)
1974—Jets, 27-14 (NY)
1975—Chargers, 24-16 (SD)
1983—Jets, 41-29 (SD)
1989—Jets, 20-17 (SD)
1990—Chargers, 39-3 (NY)
Chargers, 38-17 (SD)
1991—Jets, 24-3 (NY)
1994—Chargers, 21-6 (NY)
(RS Pts.—Chargers 783, Jets 521)
**Jets known as Titans prior to 1963*
***Franchise in Los Angeles prior to 1961*
N.Y. JETS vs. SAN FRANCISCO
RS: 49ers lead series, 6-1
1971—49ers, 24-21 (NY)
1976—49ers, 17-6 (SF)
1980—49ers, 37-27 (NY)
1983—Jets, 27-13 (SF)
1986—49ers, 24-10 (SF)
1989—49ers, 23-10 (NY)
1992—49ers, 31-14 (NY)
(RS Pts.—49ers 169, Jets 115)
N.Y. JETS vs. SEATTLE
RS: Seahawks lead series, 8-5
1977—Seahawks, 17-0 (NY)
1978—Seahawks, 24-17 (NY)
1979—Seahawks, 30-7 (S)
1980—Seahawks, 27-17 (NY)
1981—Seahawks, 19-3 (NY)
Seahawks, 27-23 (S)
1983—Seahawks, 17-10 (NY)
1985—Jets, 17-14 (NY)
1986—Jets, 38-7 (S)
1987—Jets, 30-14 (NY)
1991—Seahawks, 20-13 (S)
1995—Jets, 16-10 (S)
1997—Jets, 41-3 (S)
(RS Pts.—Jets 232, Seahawks 229)
N.Y. JETS vs. TAMPA BAY
RS: Jets lead series, 6-1
1976—Jets, 34-0 (NY)
1982—Jets, 32-17 (NY)
1984—Buccaneers, 41-21 (TB)
1985—Jets, 62-28 (NY)
1990—Jets, 16-14 (TB)
1991—Jets, 16-13 (NY)
1997—Jets, 31-0 (NY)
(RS Pts.—Jets 212, Buccaneers 113)
***N.Y. JETS vs. **TENNESSEE**
RS: Oilers lead series, 20-12-1
PS: Oilers lead series, 1-0
1960—Oilers, 27-21 (H)
Oilers, 42-28 (NY)
1961—Oilers, 49-13 (H)
Oilers, 48-21 (NY)
1962—Oilers, 56-17 (H)
Oilers, 44-10 (NY)
1963—Jets, 24-17 (NY)
Oilers, 31-27 (H)
1964—Jets, 24-21 (NY)
Oilers, 33-17 (H)
1965—Oilers, 27-21 (H)
Jets, 41-14 (NY)
1966—Jets, 52-13 (NY)
Oilers, 24-0 (H)
1967—Tie, 28-28 (NY)
1968—Jets, 20-14 (H)
Jets, 26-7 (NY)
1969—Jets, 26-17 (NY)
Jets, 34-26 (H)
1972—Oilers, 26-20 (H)
1974—Oilers, 27-22 (NY)
1977—Oilers, 20-0 (H)
1979—Oilers, 27-24 (H) OT
1980—Jets, 31-28 (NY) OT
1981—Jets, 33-17 (NY)
1984—Oilers, 31-20 (H)
1988—Jets, 45-3 (NY)
1990—Jets, 17-12 (H)
1991—Oilers, 23-20 (NY)
***Oilers, 17-10 (H)
1993—Oilers, 24-0 (H)
1994—Oilers, 24-10 (H)
1995—Oilers, 23-6 (H)
1996—Oilers, 35-10 (NY)
(RS Pts.—Oilers 858, Jets 708)
(PS Pts.—Oilers 17, Jets 10)
**Jets known as Titans prior to 1963*
***Franchise in Houston prior to 1997*
****AFC First-Round Playoff*
N.Y. JETS vs. WASHINGTON
RS: Redskins lead series, 5-1
1972—Redskins, 35-17 (NY)
1976—Redskins, 37-16 (NY)
1978—Redskins, 23-3 (W)
1987—Redskins, 17-16 (W)
1993—Jets, 3-0 (W)
1996—Redskins, 31-16 (W)
(RS Pts.—Redskins 143, Jets 71)

OAKLAND vs. ARIZONA
RS: Raiders lead series, 2-1;
See Arizona vs. Oakland
OAKLAND vs. ATLANTA
RS: Raiders lead series, 6-3;
See Atlanta vs. Oakland
OAKLAND vs. BALTIMORE
RS: Ravens lead series, 1-0;
See Baltimore vs. Oakland
OAKLAND vs. BUFFALO
RS: Raiders lead series, 15-14
PS: Bills lead series, 2-0;
See Buffalo vs. Oakland
OAKLAND vs CAROLINA
RS: Panthers lead series, 1-0;
See Carolina vs Oakland
OAKLAND vs. CHICAGO
RS: Raiders lead series, 5-4;
See Chicago vs. Oakland
OAKLAND vs. CINCINNATI
RS: Raiders lead series, 15-7
PS: Raiders lead series, 2-0;
See Cincinnati vs. Oakland
OAKLAND vs. CLEVELAND
RS: Raiders lead series, 8-4
PS: Raiders lead series, 2-0;
See Cleveland vs. Oakland
OAKLAND vs. DALLAS
RS: Series tied, 3-3;
See Dallas vs. Oakland
OAKLAND vs. DENVER
RS: Raiders lead series, 49-24-2
PS: Series tied, 1-1;
See Denver vs. Oakland
OAKLAND vs. DETROIT
RS: Raiders lead series, 6-2;
See Detroit vs. Oakland
OAKLAND vs. GREEN BAY
RS: Raiders lead series, 5-2
PS: Packers lead series, 1-0;
See Green Bay vs. Oakland

ALL-TIME TEAM VS. TEAM RESULTS

OAKLAND vs. INDIANAPOLIS
RS: Raiders lead series, 5-2
PS: Series tied, 1-1;
See Indianapolis vs. Oakland
OAKLAND vs. JACKSONVILLE
RS: Series tied, 1-1;
See Jacksonville vs. Oakland
OAKLAND vs. KANSAS CITY
RS: Chiefs lead series, 37-36-2
PS: Chiefs lead series, 2-1;
See Kansas City vs. Oakland
OAKLAND vs. MIAMI
RS: Raiders lead series, 15-6-1
PS: Raiders lead series, 2-1;
See Miami vs. Oakland
OAKLAND vs. MINNESOTA
RS: Raiders lead series, 6-3
PS: Raiders lead series, 1-0;
See Minnesota vs. Oakland
OAKLAND vs. NEW ENGLAND
RS: Raiders lead series, 13-12-1
PS: Series tied, 1-1;
See New England vs. Oakland
OAKLAND vs. NEW ORLEANS
RS: Raiders lead series, 4-3-1;
See New Orleans vs. Oakland
OAKLAND vs. N.Y. GIANTS
RS: Raiders lead series, 5-2
See N.Y. Giants vs. Oakland
OAKLAND vs. N.Y. JETS
RS: Raiders lead series, 16-10-2
PS: Jets lead series, 2-0;
See N.Y. Jets vs. Oakland
***OAKLAND vs. PHILADELPHIA**
RS: Eagles lead series, 4-3
PS: Raiders lead series, 1-0
1971—Raiders, 34-10 (O)
1976—Raiders, 26-7 (P)
1980—Eagles, 10-7 (P)
**Raiders, 27-10 (New Orleans)
1986—Eagles, 33-27 (LA) OT
1989—Eagles, 10-7 (P)
1992—Eagles, 31-10 (P)
1995—Raiders, 48-17 (O)
(RS Pts.—Raiders 159, Eagles 118)
(PS Pts.—Raiders 27, Eagles 10)
**Franchise in Los Angeles from 1982-1994*
***Super Bowl XV*
***OAKLAND vs. PITTSBURGH**
RS: Raiders lead series, 7-5
PS: Series tied, 3-3
1970—Raiders, 31-14 (O)
1972—Steelers, 34-28 (P)
**Steelers, 13-7 (P)
1973—Steelers, 17-9 (O)
**Raiders, 33-14 (O)
1974—Raiders, 17-0 (P)
***Steelers, 24-13 (O)
1975—***Steelers, 16-10 (P)
1976—Raiders, 31-28 (O)
***Raiders, 24-7 (O)
1977—Raiders, 16-7 (P)
1980—Raiders, 45-34 (P)
1981—Raiders, 30-27 (O)
1983—**Raiders, 38-10 (LA)
1984—Steelers, 13-7 (LA)
1990—Raiders, 20-3 (LA)
1994—Steelers, 21-3 (LA)
1995—Steelers, 29-10 (O)
(RS Pts.—Raiders 247, Steelers 227)
(PS Pts.—Raiders 125, Steelers 84)
**Franchise in Los Angeles from 1982-1994*
***AFC Divisional Playoff*
****AFC Championship*
***OAKLAND vs. **ST. LOUIS**
RS: Raiders lead series, 7-2
1972—Raiders, 45-17 (O)
1977—Rams, 20-14 (LA)
1979—Raiders, 24-17 (LA)
1982—Raiders, 37-31 (LA Raiders)
1985—Raiders, 16-6 (LA Rams)
1988—Rams, 22-17 (LA Raiders)
1991—Raiders, 20-17 (LA Raiders)
1994—Raiders, 20-17 (LA Rams)
1997—Raiders, 35-17 (O)
(RS Pts.—Raiders 228, Rams 164)
**Franchise in Los Angeles from 1982-1994*
***Franchise in Los Angeles prior to 1995*
***OAKLAND vs. **SAN DIEGO**
RS: Raiders lead series, 45-29-2
PS: Raiders lead series, 1-0
1960—Chargers, 52-28 (LA)
Chargers, 41-17 (O)
1961—Chargers, 44-0 (SD)
Chargers, 41-10 (O)
1962—Chargers, 42-33 (O)
Chargers, 31-21 (SD)
1963—Raiders, 34-33 (SD)
Raiders, 41-27 (O)
1964—Chargers, 31-17 (SD)
Raiders, 21-20 (O)
1965—Chargers, 17-6 (O)
Chargers, 24-14 (SD)
1966—Chargers, 29-20 (O)
Raiders, 41-19 (SD)
1967—Raiders, 51-10 (O)
Raiders, 41-21 (SD)
1968—Chargers, 23-14 (O)
Raiders, 34-27 (SD)
1969—Raiders, 24-12 (SD)
Raiders, 21-16 (O)
1970—Tie, 27-27 (SD)
Raiders, 20-17 (O)
1971—Raiders, 34-0 (SD)
Raiders, 34-33 (O)
1972—Tie, 17-17 (O)
Raiders, 21-19 (SD)
1973—Raiders, 27-17 (SD)
Raiders, 31-3 (O)
1974—Raiders, 14-10 (SD)
Raiders, 17-10 (O)
1975—Raiders, 6-0 (SD)
Raiders, 25-0 (O)
1976—Raiders, 27-17 (SD)
Raiders, 24-0 (O)
1977—Raiders, 24-0 (O)
Chargers, 12-7 (SD)
1978—Raiders, 21-20 (SD)
Chargers, 27-23 (O)
1979—Chargers, 30-10 (SD)
Raiders, 45-22 (O)
1980—Chargers, 30-24 (SD) OT
Raiders, 38-24 (O)
***Raiders, 34-27 (SD)
1981—Chargers, 55-21 (O)
Chargers, 23-10 (SD)
1982—Raiders, 28-24 (LA)
Raiders, 41-34 (SD)
1983—Raiders, 42-10 (SD)
Raiders, 30-14 (LA)
1984—Raiders, 33-30 (LA)
Raiders, 44-37 (SD)
1985—Raiders, 34-21 (LA)
Chargers, 40-34 (SD) OT
1986—Raiders, 17-13 (LA)
Raiders, 37-31 (SD) OT
1987—Chargers, 23-17 (LA)
Chargers, 16-14 (SD)
1988—Raiders, 24-13 (LA)
Raiders, 13-3 (SD)
1989—Raiders, 40-14 (LA)
Chargers, 14-12 (SD)
1990—Raiders, 24-9 (SD)
Raiders, 17-12 (LA)
1991—Chargers, 21-13 (LA)
Raiders, 9-7 (SD)
1992—Chargers, 27-3 (SD)
Chargers, 36-14 (LA)
1993—Chargers, 30-23 (LA)
Raiders, 12-7 (SD)
1994—Chargers, 26-24 (LA)
Raiders, 24-17 (SD)
1995—Raiders, 17-7 (O)
Chargers, 12-6 (SD)
1996—Chargers, 40-34 (O)
Raiders, 23-14 (SD)
1997—Chargers, 25-10 (O)
Raiders, 38-13 (SD)
(RS Pts.—Raiders 1,786, Chargers 1,613)
(PS Pts.—Raiders 34, Chargers 27)
**Franchise in Los Angeles from 1982-1994*
***Franchise in Los Angeles prior to 1961*
****AFC Championship*
***OAKLAND vs. SAN FRANCISCO**
RS: Raiders lead series, 5-3
1970—49ers, 38-7 (O)
1974—Raiders, 35-24 (SF)
1979—Raiders, 23-10 (O)
1982—Raiders, 23-17 (SF)
1985—49ers, 34-10 (LA)
1988—Raiders, 9-3 (SF)
1991—Raiders, 12-6 (LA)
1994—49ers, 44-14 (SF)
(RS Pts.—49ers 176, Raiders 133)
**Franchise in Los Angeles from 1982-1994*
***OAKLAND vs. SEATTLE**
RS: Raiders lead series, 21-19
PS: Series tied, 1-1
1977—Raiders, 44-7 (O)
1978—Seahawks, 27-7 (S)
Seahawks, 17-16 (O)
1979—Seahawks, 27-10 (S)
Seahawks, 29-24 (O)
1980—Raiders, 33-14 (O)
Raiders, 19-17 (S)
1981—Raiders, 20-10 (O)
Raiders, 32-31 (S)
1982—Raiders, 28-23 (LA)
1983—Seahawks, 38-36 (S)
Seahawks, 34-21 (LA)
**Raiders, 30-14 (LA)
1984—Raiders, 28-14 (LA)
Seahawks, 17-14 (S)
***Seahawks, 13-7 (S)
1985—Seahawks, 33-3 (S)
Raiders, 13-3 (LA)
1986—Raiders, 14-10 (LA)
Seahawks, 37-0 (S)
1987—Seahawks, 35-13 (LA)
Raiders, 37-14 (S)
1988—Seahawks, 35-27 (S)
Seahawks, 43-37 (LA)
1989—Seahawks, 24-20 (LA)
Seahawks, 23-17 (S)
1990—Raiders, 17-13 (S)
Raiders, 24-17 (LA)
1991—Raiders, 23-20 (S) OT
Raiders, 31-7 (LA)
1992—Raiders, 19-0 (S)
Raiders, 20-3 (LA)
1993—Raiders, 17-13 (S)
Raiders, 27-23 (LA)
1994—Seahawks, 38-9 (LA)
Raiders, 17-16 (S)
1995—Raiders, 34-14 (O)
Seahawks, 44-10 (S)
1996—Raiders, 27-21 (S)
Seahawks, 28-21 (O)
1997—Seahawks, 45-34 (S)
Seahawks, 22-21 (O)
(RS Pts.—Seahawks 886, Raiders 864)
(PS Pts.—Raiders 37, Seahawks 27)
**Franchise in Los Angeles from 1982-1994*
***AFC Championship*
****AFC First-Round Playoff*
***OAKLAND vs. TAMPA BAY**
RS: Raiders lead series, 3-1
1976—Raiders, 49-16 (O)
1981—Raiders, 18-16 (O)
1993—Raiders, 27-20 (LA)
1996—Buccaneers, 20-17 (TB) OT
(RS Pts.—Raiders 111, Buccaneers 72)
**Franchise in Los Angeles from 1982-1994*
***OAKLAND vs. **TENNESSEE**
RS: Raiders lead series, 20-14
PS: Raiders lead series, 3-0
1960—Oilers, 37-22 (O)
Raiders, 14-13 (H)
1961—Oilers, 55-0 (H)
Oilers, 47-16 (O)
1962—Oilers, 28-20 (O)
Oilers, 32-17 (H)
1963—Raiders, 24-13 (H)
Raiders, 52-49 (O)
1964—Oilers, 42-28 (H)
Raiders, 20-10 (O)
1965—Raiders, 21-17 (O)
Raiders, 33-21 (H)
1966—Oilers, 31-0 (H)
Raiders, 38-23 (O)
1967—Raiders, 19-7 (H)
***Raiders, 40-7 (O)
1968—Raiders, 24-15 (H)
1969—Raiders, 21-17 (O)
****Raiders, 56-7 (O)
1971—Raiders, 41-21 (O)
1972—Raiders, 34-0 (H)
1973—Raiders, 17-6 (H)
1975—Oilers, 27-26 (O)
1976—Raiders, 14-13 (H)
1977—Raiders, 34-29 (O)
1978—Raiders, 21-17 (O)
1979—Oilers, 31-17 (H)
1980—*****Raiders, 27-7 (O)
1981—Oilers, 17-16 (H)
1983—Raiders, 20-6 (LA)
1984—Raiders, 24-14 (H)
1986—Raiders, 28-17 (H)
1988—Oilers, 38-35 (H)
1989—Oilers, 23-7 (H)
1991—Oilers, 47-17 (H)
1994—Raiders, 17-14 (LA)
1997—Oilers, 24-21 (T) OT
(RS Pts.—Oilers 801, Raiders 758)
(PS Pts.—Raiders 123, Oilers 21)
**Franchise in Los Angeles from 1982-1994*
***Franchise in Houston prior to 1997*
****AFL Championship*
*****Inter-Divisional Playoff*
******AFC First-Round Playoff*
***OAKLAND vs. WASHINGTON**
RS: Raiders lead series, 6-2
PS: Raiders lead series, 1-0
1970—Raiders, 34-20 (O)
1975—Raiders, 26-23 (W) OT
1980—Raiders, 24-21 (O)
1983—Redskins, 37-35 (W)
**Raiders, 38-9 (Tampa)
1986—Redskins, 10-6 (W)
1989—Raiders, 37-24 (LA)
1992—Raiders, 21-20 (W)
1995—Raiders, 20-8 (W)
(RS Pts.—Raiders 203, Redskins 163)
(PS Pts.—Raiders 38, Redskins 9)
**Franchise in Los Angeles from 1982-1994*
***Super Bowl XVIII*

PHILADELPHIA vs. ARIZONA
RS: Eagles lead series, 48-47-5
PS: Series tied, 1-1;
See Arizona vs. Philadelphia
PHILADELPHIA vs. ATLANTA
RS: Eagles lead series, 9-8-1
PS: Falcons lead series, 1-0;
See Atlanta vs. Philadelphia
PHILADELPHIA vs. BALTIMORE
RS: Series tied, 0-0-1;
See Baltimore vs. Philadelphia
PHILADELPHIA vs. BUFFALO
RS: Series tied, 4-4;
See Buffalo vs. Philadelphia
PHILADELPHIA vs. CAROLINA
RS: Eagles lead series, 1-0;

See Carolina vs. Philadelphia
PHILADELPHIA vs. CHICAGO
RS: Bears lead series, 24-4-1
PS: Series tied, 1-1;
See Chicago vs. Philadelphia
PHILADELPHIA vs. CINCINNATI
RS: Bengals lead series, 6-2;
See Cincinnati vs. Philadelphia
PHILADELPHIA vs. CLEVELAND
RS: Browns lead series, 31-12-1;
See Cleveland vs. Philadelphia
PHILADELPHIA vs. DALLAS
RS: Cowboys lead series, 45-29
PS: Cowboys lead series, 2-1;
See Dallas vs. Philadelphia
PHILADELPHIA vs. DENVER
RS: Eagles lead series, 6-2;
See Denver vs. Philadelphia
PHILADELPHIA vs. DETROIT
RS: Lions lead series, 12-10-2
PS: Eagles lead series, 1-0;
See Detroit vs. Philadelphia
PHILADELPHIA vs. GREEN BAY
RS: Packers lead series, 20-9
PS: Eagles lead series, 1-0;
See Green Bay vs. Philadelphia
PHILADELPHIA vs. INDIANAPOLIS
RS: Colts lead series, 7-6;
See Indianapolis vs. Philadelphia
PHILADELPHIA vs. JACKSONVILLE
RS: Jaguars lead series, 1-0;
See Jacksonville vs. Philadelphia
PHILADELPHIA vs. KANSAS CITY
RS: Series tied, 1-1;
See Kansas City vs. Philadelphia
PHILADELPHIA vs. MIAMI
RS: Dolphins lead series, 6-3;
See Miami vs. Philadelphia
PHILADELPHIA vs. MINNESOTA
RS: Vikings lead series, 11-6
PS: Eagles lead series, 1-0;
See Minnesota vs. Philadelphia
PHILADELPHIA vs. NEW ENGLAND
RS: Eagles lead series, 5-2;
See New England vs. Philadelphia
PHILADELPHIA vs. NEW ORLEANS
RS: Eagles lead series, 12-8
PS; Eagles lead series, 1-0;
See New Orleans vs. Philadelphia
PHILADELPHIA vs. N.Y. GIANTS
RS: Giants lead series, 66-58-2
PS: Giants lead series, 1-0;
See N.Y. Giants vs. Philadelphia
PHILADELPHIA vs. N.Y. JETS
RS: Eagles lead series, 6-0;
See N.Y. Jets vs. Philadelphia
PHILADELPHIA vs. OAKLAND
RS: Eagles lead series, 4-3
PS: Raiders lead series, 1-0;
See Oakland vs. Philadelphia
PHILADELPHIA vs. *PITTSBURGH
RS: Eagles lead series, 44-26-3
PS: Eagles lead series, 1-0
1933—Eagles, 25-6 (Phila)
1934—Eagles, 17-0 (Pitt)
Pirates, 9-7 (Phila)
1935—Pirates, 17-7 (Phila)
Eagles, 17-6 (Pitt)
1936—Pirates, 17-0 (Pitt)
Pirates, 6-0 (Johnstown, Pa.)
1937—Pirates, 27-14 (Pitt)
Pirates, 16-7 (Pitt)
1938—Eagles, 27-7 (Buffalo)
Eagles, 14-7 (Charleston, W. Va.)
1939—Eagles, 17-14 (Phila)
Pirates, 24-12 (Pitt)
1940—Pirates, 7-3 (Pitt)
Eagles, 7-0 (Phila)
1941—Eagles, 10-7 (Pitt)
Tie, 7-7 (Phila)
1942—Eagles, 24-14 (Pitt)
Steelers, 14-0 (Phila)
1945—Eagles, 45-3 (Pitt)
Eagles, 30-6 (Phila)
1946—Steelers, 10-7 (Pitt)
Eagles, 10-7 (Phila)
1947—Steelers, 35-24 (Pitt)
Eagles, 21-0 (Phila)
**Eagles, 21-0 (Pitt)
1948—Eagles, 34-7 (Pitt)
Eagles, 17-0 (Phila)
1949—Eagles, 38-7 (Pitt)
Eagles, 34-17 (Phila)
1950—Eagles, 17-10 (Pitt)
Steelers, 9-7 (Phila)
1951—Eagles, 34-13 (Pitt)
Steelers, 17-13 (Phila)
1952—Eagles, 31-25 (Pitt)
Eagles, 26-21 (Phila)
1953—Eagles, 23-17 (Phila)
Eagles, 35-7 (Pitt)
1954—Eagles, 24-22 (Phila)
Steelers, 17-7 (Pitt)
1955—Steelers, 13-7 (Pitt)
Eagles, 24-0 (Phila)
1956—Eagles, 35-21 (Pitt)
Eagles, 14-7 (Phila)
1957—Steelers, 6-0 (Pitt)
Eagles, 7-6 (Phila)
1958—Steelers, 24-3 (Pitt)
Steelers, 31-24 (Phila)
1959—Eagles, 28-24 (Phila)
Steelers, 31-0 (Pitt)
1960—Eagles, 34-7 (Phila)
Steelers, 27-21 (Pitt)
1961—Eagles, 21-16 (Phila)
Eagles, 35-24 (Pitt)
1962—Steelers, 13-7 (Pitt)
Steelers, 26-17 (Phila)
1963—Tie, 21-21 (Phila)
Tie, 20-20 (Pitt)
1964—Eagles, 21-7 (Phila)
Eagles, 34-10 (Pitt)
1965—Steelers, 20-14 (Phila)
Eagles, 47-13 (Pitt)
1966—Eagles, 31-14 (Pitt)
Eagles, 27-23 (Phila)
1967—Eagles, 34-24 (Phila)
1968—Steelers, 6-3 (Pitt)
1969—Eagles, 41-27 (Phila)
1970—Eagles, 30-20 (Phila)
1974—Steelers, 27-0 (Pitt)
1979—Eagles, 17-14 (Phila)
1988—Eagles, 27-26 (Pitt)
1991—Eagles, 23-14 (Phila)
1994—Steelers, 14-3 (Pitt)
1997—Eagles, 23-20 (Phila)
(RS Pts.—Eagles 1,385, Steelers 1,041)
(PS Pts.—Eagles 21, Steelers 0)
Steelers known as Pirates prior to 1941
***Division Playoff*
PHILADELPHIA vs. *ST. LOUIS
RS: Rams lead series, 15-12-1
PS: Series tied, 1-1
1937—Rams, 21-3 (P)
1939—Rams, 35-13 (Colorado Springs)
1940—Rams, 21-13 (C)
1942—Rams, 24-14 (Akron)
1944—Eagles, 26-13 (P)
1945—Eagles, 28-14 (P)
1946—Eagles, 25-14 (LA)
1947—Eagles, 14-7 (P)
1948—Tie, 28-28 (LA)
1949—Eagles, 38-14 (P)
**Eagles, 14-0 (LA)
1950—Eagles, 56-20 (P)
1955—Rams, 23-21 (P)
1956—Rams, 27-7 (LA)
1957—Rams, 17-13 (LA)
1959—Eagles, 23-20 (P)
1964—Rams, 20-10 (LA)
1967—Rams, 33-17 (LA)
1969—Rams, 23-17 (P)
1972—Rams, 34-3 (P)
1975—Rams, 42-3 (P)
1977—Rams, 20-0 (LA)
1978—Rams, 16-14 (P)
1983—Eagles, 13-9 (P)
1985—Rams, 17-6 (P)
1986—Eagles, 34-20 (P)
1988—Eagles, 30-24 (P)
1989—***Rams, 21-7 (P)
1990—Eagles, 27-21 (LA)
1995—Eagles, 20-9 (P)
(RS Pts.—Rams 586, Eagles 516)
(PS Pts.—Rams 21, Eagles 21)
Franchise in Los Angeles prior to 1995 and in Cleveland prior to 1946
***NFL Championship*
****NFC First-Round Playoff*
PHILADELPHIA vs. SAN DIEGO
RS: Chargers lead series, 4-2
1974—Eagles, 13-7 (SD)
1980—Chargers, 22-21 (SD)
1985—Chargers, 20-14 (SD)
1986—Eagles, 23-7 (P)
1989—Chargers, 20-17 (SD)
1995—Chargers, 27-21 (P)
(RS Pts.—Eagles 109, Chargers 103)
PHILADELPHIA vs. SAN FRANCISCO
RS: 49ers lead series, 14-6-1
PS: 49ers lead series, 1-0
1951—Eagles, 21-14 (P)
1953—49ers, 31-21 (SF)
1956—Tie, 10-10 (P)
1958—49ers, 30-24 (P)
1959—49ers, 24-14 (SF)
1964—49ers, 28-24 (P)
1966—Eagles, 35-34 (SF)
1967—49ers, 28-27 (P)
1969—49ers, 14-13 (SF)
1971—49ers, 31-3 (P)
1973—49ers, 38-28 (SF)
1975—Eagles, 27-17 (P)
1983—Eagles, 22-17 (SF)
1984—49ers, 21-9 (P)
1985—49ers, 24-13 (SF)
1989—49ers, 38-28 (P)
1991—49ers, 23-7 (P)
1992—49ers, 20-14 (SF)
1993—Eagles, 37-34 (SF) OT
1994—Eagles, 40-8 (SF)
1996—*49ers, 14-0 (SF)
1997—49ers, 24-12 (P)
(RS Pts.—49ers 508, Eagles 429)
(PS Pts.—49ers 14, Eagles 0)
NFC First-Round Playoff
PHILADELPHIA vs. SEATTLE
RS: Eagles lead series, 4-2
1976—Eagles, 27-10 (P)
1980—Eagles, 27-20 (S)
1986—Seahawks, 24-20 (S)
1989—Eagles, 31-7 (P)
1992—Eagles, 20-17 (S) OT
1995—Seahawks, 26-10 (S)
(RS Pts.—Eagles 135, Seahawks 104)
PHILADELPHIA vs. TAMPA BAY
RS: Eagles lead series, 3-2
PS: Buccaneers lead series, 1-0
1977—Eagles, 13-3 (P)
1979—*Buccaneers, 24-17 (TB)
1981—Eagles, 20-10 (P)
1988—Eagles, 41-14 (TB)
1991—Buccaneers, 14-13 (TB)
1995—Buccaneers, 21-6 (P)
(RS Pts.—Eagles 93, Buccaneers 62)
(PS Pts.—Buccaneers 24, Eagles 17)
NFC Divisional Playoff
PHILADELPHIA vs. *TENNESSEE
RS: Eagles lead series, 6-0
1972—Eagles, 18-17 (H)
1979—Eagles, 26-20 (H)
1982—Eagles, 35-14 (P)
1988—Eagles, 32-23 (P)
1991—Eagles, 13-6 (H)
1994—Eagles, 21-6 (P)
(RS Pts.—Eagles 145, Oilers 86)
Franchise in Houston prior to 1997
PHILADELPHIA vs. *WASHINGTON
RS: Redskins lead series, 68-52-5
PS: Redskins lead series, 1-0
1934—Redskins, 6-0 (B)
Redskins, 14-7 (P)
1935—Eagles, 7-6 (B)
1936—Redskins, 26-3 (P)
Redskins, 17-7 (B)
1937—Eagles, 14-0 (W)
Redskins, 10-7 (P)
1938—Redskins, 26-23 (P)
Redskins, 20-14 (W)
1939—Redskins, 7-0 (P)
Redskins, 7-6 (W)
1940—Redskins, 34-17 (P)
Redskins, 13-6 (W)
1941—Redskins, 21-17 (P)
Redskins, 20-14 (W)
1942—Redskins, 14-10 (P)
Redskins, 30-27 (W)
1944—Tie, 31-31 (P)
Eagles, 37-7 (W)
1945—Redskins, 24-14 (W)
Eagles, 16-0 (P)
1946—Eagles, 28-24 (W)
Redskins, 27-10 (P)
1947—Eagles, 45-42 (P)
Eagles, 38-14 (W)
1948—Eagles, 45-0 (W)
Eagles, 42-21 (P)
1949—Eagles, 49-14 (P)
Eagles, 44-21 (W)
1950—Eagles, 35-3 (P)
Eagles, 33-0 (W)
1951—Redskins, 27-23 (P)
Eagles, 35-21 (W)
1952—Eagles, 38-20 (P)
Redskins, 27-21 (W)
1953—Tie, 21-21 (P)
Redskins, 10-0 (W)
1954—Eagles, 49-21 (W)
Eagles, 41-33 (P)
1955—Redskins, 31-30 (P)
Redskins, 34-21 (W)
1956—Eagles, 13-9 (P)
Redskins, 19-17 (W)
1957—Eagles, 21-12 (P)
Redskins, 42-7 (W)
1958—Redskins, 24-14 (P)
Redskins, 20-0 (W)
1959—Eagles, 30-23 (P)
Eagles, 34-14 (W)
1960—Eagles, 19-13 (P)
Eagles, 38-28 (W)
1961—Eagles, 14-7 (P)
Eagles, 27-24 (W)
1962—Redskins, 27-21 (P)
Eagles, 37-14 (W)
1963—Eagles, 37-24 (W)
Redskins, 13-10 (P)
1964—Redskins, 35-20 (W)
Redskins, 21-10 (P)
1965—Redskins, 23-21 (W)
Eagles, 21-14 (P)
1966—Redskins, 27-13 (P)
Eagles, 37-28 (W)
1967—Eagles, 35-24 (P)
Tie, 35-35 (W)
1968—Redskins, 17-14 (W)
Redskins, 16-10 (P)
1969—Tie, 28-28 (W)
Redskins, 34-29 (P)
1970—Redskins, 33-21 (P)
Redskins, 24-6 (W)
1971—Tie, 7-7 (W)
Redskins, 20-13 (P)
1972—Redskins, 14-0 (W)
Redskins, 23-7 (P)
1973—Redskins, 28-7 (P)
Redskins, 38-20 (W)
1974—Redskins, 27-20 (P)
Redskins, 26-7 (W)
1975—Eagles, 26-10 (P)
Eagles, 26-3 (W)

ALL-TIME TEAM VS. TEAM RESULTS

1976—Redskins, 20-17 (P) OT
Redskins, 24-0 (W)
1977—Redskins, 23-17 (W)
Redskins, 17-14 (P)
1978—Redskins, 35-30 (W)
Eagles, 17-10 (P)
1979—Eagles, 28-17 (P)
Redskins, 17-7 (W)
1980—Eagles, 24-14 (P)
Eagles, 24-0 (W)
1981—Eagles, 36-13 (P)
Redskins, 15-13 (W)
1982—Redskins, 37-34 (P) OT
Redskins, 13-9 (W)
1983—Redskins, 23-13 (P)
Redskins, 28-24 (W)
1984—Redskins, 20-0 (W)
Eagles, 16-10 (P)
1985—Eagles, 19-6 (W)
Redskins, 17-12 (P)
1986—Redskins, 41-14 (W)
Redskins, 21-14 (P)
1987—Redskins, 34-24 (W)
Eagles, 31-27 (P)
1988—Redskins, 17-10 (W)
Redskins, 20-19 (P)
1989—Eagles, 42-37 (W)
Redskins, 10-3 (P)
1990—Redskins, 13-7 (W)
Eagles, 28-14 (P)
**Redskins, 20-6 (P)
1991—Redskins, 23-0 (W)
Eagles, 24-22 (P)
1992—Redskins, 16-12 (W)
Eagles, 17-13 (P)
1993—Eagles, 34-31 (P)
Eagles, 17-14 (W)
1994—Eagles, 21-17 (P)
Eagles, 31-29 (W)
1995—Eagles, 37-34 (P) (OT)
Eagles, 14-7 (W)
1996—Eagles, 17-14 (W)
Redskins, 26-21 (P)
1997—Eagles, 24-10 (P)
Redskins, 35-32 (W)
(RS Pts.—Eagles 2,544, Redskins 2,496)
(PS Pts.—Redskins 20, Eagles 6)
Franchise in Boston prior to 1937
**NFC First-Round Playoff*

PITTSBURGH vs. ARIZONA
RS: Steelers lead series, 30-22-3;
See Arizona vs. Pittsburgh
PITTSBURGH vs. ATLANTA
RS: Steelers lead series, 10-1;
See Atlanta vs. Pittsburgh
PITTSBURGH vs. BALTIMORE
RS: Steelers lead series, 3-1;
See Baltimore vs. Pittsburgh
PITTSBURGH vs. BUFFALO
RS: Steelers lead series, 8-7
PS: Steelers lead series, 2-1;
See Buffalo vs. Pittsburgh
PITTSBURGH vs. CAROLINA
RS: Panthers lead series, 1-0;
See Carolina vs. Pittsburgh
PITTSBURGH vs. CHICAGO
RS: Bears lead series, 16-5-1;
See Chicago vs. Pittsburgh
PITTSBURGH vs. CINCINNATI
RS: Steelers lead series, 32-23;
See Cincinnati vs. Pittsburgh
PITTSBURGH vs. CLEVELAND
RS: Browns lead series, 52-40
PS: Steelers lead series, 1-0;
See Cleveland vs. Pittsburgh
PITTSBURGH vs. DALLAS
RS: Cowboys lead series, 14-11
PS: Steelers lead series, 2-1;
See Dallas vs. Pittsburgh
PITTSBURGH vs. DENVER
RS: Broncos lead series, 10-6-1
PS: Broncos lead series, 3-2;
See Denver vs. Pittsburgh
PITTSBURGH vs. DETROIT
RS: Lions lead series, 13-12-1;
See Detroit vs. Pittsburgh
PITTSBURGH vs. GREEN BAY
RS: Packers lead series, 18-11;
See Green Bay vs. Pittsburgh
PITTSBURGH vs. INDIANAPOLIS
RS: Steelers lead series, 12-4
PS: Steelers lead series, 4-0;
See Indianapolis vs. Pittsburgh
PITTSBURGH vs. JACKSONVILLE
RS: Series tied, 3-3;
See Jacksonville vs. Pittsburgh
PITTSBURGH vs. KANSAS CITY
RS: Steelers lead series, 14-6
PS: Chiefs lead series, 1-0;
See Kansas City vs. Pittsburgh
PITTSBURGH vs. MIAMI
RS: Dolphins lead series, 8-7
PS: Dolphins lead series, 2-1;
See Miami vs. Pittsburgh
PITTSBURGH vs. MINNESOTA
RS: Vikings lead series, 8-4
PS: Steelers lead series, 1-0;
See Minnesota vs. Pittsburgh
PITTSBURGH vs. NEW ENGLAND
RS: Steelers lead series, 11-3
PS: Series tied, 1-1;
See New England vs. Pittsburgh
PITTSBURGH vs. NEW ORLEANS
RS: Steelers lead series, 6-5;
See New Orleans vs. Pittsburgh
PITTSBURGH vs. N.Y. GIANTS
RS: Giants lead series, 42-27-3;
See N.Y. Giants vs. Pittsburgh
PITTSBURGH vs. N.Y. JETS
RS: Steelers lead series, 12-1;
See N.Y. Jets vs. Pittsburgh
PITTSBURGH vs. OAKLAND
RS: Raiders lead series, 7-5
PS: Series tied, 3-3;
See Oakland vs. Pittsburgh
PITTSBURGH vs. PHILADELPHIA
RS: Eagles lead series, 44-26-3
PS: Eagles lead series, 1-0;
See Philadelphia vs. Pittsburgh
***PITTSBURGH vs. **ST. LOUIS**
RS: Rams lead series, 14-5-2
PS: Steelers lead series, 1-0
1938—Rams, 13-7 (New Orleans)
1939—Tie, 14-14 (C)
1941—Rams, 17-14 (Akron)
1947—Rams, 48-7 (P)
1948—Rams, 31-14 (LA)
1949—Tie, 7-7 (P)
1952—Rams, 28-14 (LA)
1955—Rams, 27-26 (LA)
1956—Steelers, 30-13 (P)
1961—Rams, 24-14 (LA)
1964—Rams, 26-14 (P)
1968—Rams, 45-10 (LA)
1971—Rams, 23-14 (P)
1975—Rams, 10-3 (LA)
1978—Rams, 10-7 (LA)
1979—***Steelers, 31-19 (Pasadena)
1981—Steelers, 24-0 (P)
1984—Steelers, 24-14 (P)
1987—Rams, 31-21 (LA)
1990—Steelers, 41-10 (P)
1993—Rams, 27-0 (LA)
1996—Steelers, 42-6 (P)
(RS Pts.—Rams 424, Steelers 347)
(PS Pts.—Steelers 31, Rams 19)
Steelers known as Pirates prior to 1941
**Franchise in Los Angeles prior to 1995 and in Cleveland prior to 1946*
***Super Bowl XIV*
PITTSBURGH vs. SAN DIEGO
RS: Steelers lead series, 16-5
PS: Chargers lead series, 2-0
1971—Steelers, 21-17 (P)
1972—Steelers, 24-2 (SD)
1973—Steelers, 38-21 (P)
1975—Steelers, 37-0 (SD)
1976—Steelers, 23-0 (P)
1977—Steelers, 10-9 (SD)
1979—Chargers, 35-7 (SD)
1980—Chargers, 26-17 (SD)
1982—*Chargers, 31-28 (P)
1983—Steelers, 26-3 (P)
1984—Steelers, 52-24 (P)
1985—Chargers, 54-44 (SD)
1987—Steelers, 20-16 (SD)
1988—Chargers, 20-14 (SD)
1989—Steelers, 20-17 (P)
1990—Steelers, 36-14 (P)
1991—Steelers, 26-20 (P)
1992—Steelers, 23-6 (SD)
1993—Steelers,.16-3 (P)
1994—Chargers, 37-34 (SD)
**Chargers, 17-13 (P)
1995—Steelers, 31-16 (P)
1996—Steelers, 16-3 (P)
(RS Pts.—Steelers 535, Chargers 343)
(PS Pts.—Chargers 48, Steelers 41)
AFC First-Round Playoff
**AFC Championship*
PITTSBURGH vs. SAN FRANCISCO
RS: 49ers lead series, 9-7
1951—49ers, 28-24 (P)
1952—Steelers, 24-7 (SF)
1954—49ers, 31-3 (SF)
1958—49ers, 23-20 (SF)
1961—Steelers, 20-10 (P)
1965—49ers, 27-17 (SF)
1968—49ers, 45-28 (P)
1973—Steelers, 37-14 (SF)
1977—Steelers, 27-0 (P)
1978—Steelers, 24-7 (SF)
1981—49ers, 17-14 (P)
1984—Steelers, 20-17 (SF)
1987—Steelers, 30-17 (P)
1990—49ers, 27-7 (SF)
1993—49ers, 24-13 (P)
1996—49ers, 25-15 (P)
(RS Pts.—Steelers 323, 49ers 319)
PITTSBURGH vs. SEATTLE
RS: Seahawks lead series, 6-5
1977—Steelers, 30-20 (P)
1978—Steelers, 21-10 (P)
1981—Seahawks, 24-21 (S)
1982—Seahawks, 16-0 (S)
1983—Steelers, 27-21 (S)
1986—Seahawks, 30-0 (S)
1987—Steelers, 13-9 (P)
1991—Seahawks, 27-7 (P)
1992—Steelers, 20-14 (P)
1993—Seahawks, 16-6 (S)
1994—Seahawks, 30-13 (S)
(RS Pts.—Seahawks 217, Steelers 158)
PITTSBURGH vs. TAMPA BAY
RS: Steelers lead series, 4-0
1976—Steelers, 42-0 (P)
1980—Steelers, 24-21 (TB)
1983—Steelers, 17-12 (P)
1989—Steelers, 31-22 (TB)
(RS Pts.—Steelers 114, Buccaneers 55)
PITTSBURGH vs. *TENNESSEE
RS: Steelers lead series, 35-20
PS: Steelers lead series, 3-0
1970—Oilers, 19-7 (P)
Steelers, 7-3 (H)
1971—Steelers, 23-16 (P)
Oilers, 29-3 (H)
1972—Steelers, 24-7 (P)
Steelers, 9-3 (H)
1973—Steelers, 36-7 (H)
Steelers, 33-7 (P)
1974—Steelers, 13-7 (H)
Oilers, 13-10 (P)
1975—Steelers, 24-17 (P)
Steelers, 32-9 (H)
1976—Steelers, 32-16 (P)
Steelers, 21-0 (H)
1977—Oilers, 27-10 (H)
Steelers, 27-10 (P)
1978—Oilers, 24-17 (P)
Steelers, 13-3 (H)
**Steelers, 34-5 (P)
1979—Steelers, 38-7 (P)
Oilers, 20-17 (H)
**Steelers, 27-13 (P)
1980—Steelers, 31-17 (P)
Oilers, 6-0 (H)
1981—Steelers, 26-13 (P)
Oilers, 21-20 (H)
1982—Steelers, 24-10 (H)
1983—Steelers, 40-28 (H)
Steelers, 17-10 (P)
1984—Steelers, 35-7 (P)
Oilers, 23-20 (H) OT
1985—Steelers, 20-0 (P)
Steelers, 30-7 (H)
1986—Steelers, 22-16 (H) OT
Steelers, 21-10 (P)
1987—Oilers, 23-3 (P)
Oilers, 24-16 (H)
1988—Oilers, 34-14 (P)
Steelers, 37-34 (H)
1989—Oilers, 27-0 (H)
Oilers, 23-16 (P)
***Steelers, 26-23 (H) OT
1990—Steelers, 20-9 (P)
Oilers, 34-14 (H)
1991—Steelers, 26-14 (P)
Oilers, 31-6 (H)
1992—Steelers, 29-24 (H)
Steelers, 21-20 (P)
1993—Oilers, 23-3 (H)
Oilers, 26-17 (P)
1994—Steelers, 30-14 (P)
Steelers, 12-9 (H) OT
1995—Steelers, 34-17 (H)
Steelers, 21-7 (P)
1996—Steelers, 30-16 (P)
Oilers, 23-13 (H)
1997—Steelers, 37-24 (P)
Oilers, 16-6 (T)
(RS Pts.—Steelers 1,107, Oilers 884)
(PS Pts.—Steelers 87, Oilers 41)
Franchise in Houston prior to 1997
**AFC Championship*
***AFC First-Round Playoff*
***PITTSBURGH vs. **WASHINGTON**
RS: Redskins lead series, 42-28-3
1933—Redskins, 21-6 (P)
Pirates, 16-14 (B)
1934—Redskins, 7-0 (P)
Redskins, 39-0 (B)
1935—Pirates, 6-0 (P)
Redskins, 13-3 (B)
1936—Pirates, 10-0 (P)
Redskins, 30-0 (B)
1937—Redskins, 34-20 (W)
Pirates, 21-13 (P)
1938—Redskins, 7-0 (P)
Redskins, 15-0 (W)
1939—Redskins, 44-14 (W)
Redskins, 21-14 (P)
1940—Redskins, 40-10 (P)
Redskins, 37-10 (W)
1941—Redskins, 24-20 (P)
Redskins, 23-3 (W)
1942—Redskins, 28-14 (W)
Redskins, 14-0 (P)
1945—Redskins, 14-0 (P)
Redskins, 24-0 (W)
1946—Tie, 14-14 (W)
Steelers, 14-7 (P)
1947—Redskins, 27-26 (W)
Steelers, 21-14 (P)
1948—Redskins, 17-14 (W)
Steelers, 10-7 (P)
1949—Redskins, 27-14 (P)
Redskins, 27-14 (W)
1950—Steelers, 26-7 (W)
Redskins, 24-7 (P)
1951—Redskins, 22-7 (P)

Steelers, 20-10 (W)
1952—Redskins, 28-24 (P)
Steelers, 24-23 (W)
1953—Redskins, 17-9 (P)
Steelers, 14-13 (W)
1954—Steelers, 37-7 (P)
Redskins, 17-14 (W)
1955—Redskins, 23-14 (P)
Redskins, 28-17 (W)
1956—Steelers, 30-13 (P)
Steelers, 23-0 (W)
1957—Steelers, 28-7 (P)
Redskins, 10-3 (W)
1958—Steelers, 24-16 (P)
Tie, 14-14 (W)
1959—Redskins, 23-17 (P)
Steelers, 27-6 (W)
1960—Tie, 27-27 (W)
Steelers, 22-10 (P)
1961—Steelers, 20-0 (P)
Steelers, 30-14 (W)
1962—Steelers, 23-21 (P)
Steelers, 27-24 (W)
1963—Steelers, 38-27 (P)
Steelers, 34-28 (W)
1964—Redskins, 30-0 (P)
Steelers, 14-7 (W)
1965—Redskins, 31-3 (P)
Redskins, 35-14 (W)
1966—Redskins, 33-27 (P)
Redskins, 24-10 (W)
1967—Redskins, 15-10 (P)
1968—Redskins, 16-13 (W)
1969—Redskins, 14-7 (P)
1973—Steelers, 21-16 (P)
1979—Steelers, 38-7 (P)
1985—Redskins, 30-23 (P)
1988—Redskins, 30-29 (W)
1991—Redskins, 41-14 (P)
1997—Steelers, 14-13 (P)
(RS Pts.—Redskins 1,403, Steelers 1,131)
Steelers known as Pirates prior to 1941
***Franchise in Boston prior to 1937*

ST. LOUIS vs. ARIZONA
RS: Rams lead series, 23-20-2
PS: Rams lead series, 1-0;
See Arizona vs. St. Louis
ST. LOUIS vs. ATLANTA
RS: Rams lead series, 39-21-2;
See Atlanta vs. St. Louis
ST. LOUIS vs. BALTIMORE
RS: Ravens lead series, 1-0;
See Baltimore vs. St. Louis
ST. LOUIS vs. BUFFALO
RS: Bills lead series, 4-3;
See Buffalo vs. St. Louis
ST. LOUIS vs. CAROLINA
RS: Series tied, 3-3;
See Carolina vs. St. Louis
ST. LOUIS vs. CHICAGO
RS: Bears lead series, 47-30-3
PS: Series tied, 1-1;
See Chicago vs. St. Louis
ST. LOUIS vs. CINCINNATI
RS: Bengals lead series, 5-3;
See Cincinnati vs. St. Louis
ST. LOUIS vs. CLEVELAND
RS: Browns lead series, 8-7
PS: Browns lead series, 2-1;
See Cleveland vs. St. Louis
ST. LOUIS vs. DALLAS
RS: Rams lead series, 9-8
PS: Series tied, 4-4;
See Dallas vs. St. Louis
ST. LOUIS vs. DENVER
RS: Series tied, 4-4;
See Denver vs. St. Louis
ST. LOUIS vs. DETROIT
RS: Rams lead series, 39-35-1
PS: Lions lead series, 1-0;
See Detroit vs. St. Louis
ST. LOUIS vs. GREEN BAY
RS: Rams lead series, 43-39-2
PS: Packers lead series, 1-0;
See Green Bay vs. St. Louis
ST. LOUIS vs. INDIANAPOLIS
RS: Colts lead series, 21-16-2;
See Indianapolis vs. St. Louis
ST. LOUIS vs. JACKSONVILLE
RS: Rams lead series, 1-0;
See Jacksonville vs. St. Louis
ST. LOUIS vs. KANSAS CITY
RS: Rams lead series, 4-2;
See Kansas City vs. St. Louis
ST. LOUIS vs. MIAMI
RS: Dolphins lead series, 6-1;
See Miami vs. St. Louis
ST. LOUIS vs. MINNESOTA
RS: Vikings lead series, 15-11-2
PS: Vikings lead series, 5-1;
See Minnesota vs. St. Louis
ST. LOUIS vs. NEW ENGLAND
RS: Series tied, 3-3;
See New England vs. St. Louis
ST. LOUIS vs. NEW ORLEANS
RS: Rams lead series, 32-24;
See New Orleans vs. St. Louis
ST. LOUIS vs. N.Y. GIANTS
RS: Rams lead series, 22-9
PS: Series tied, 1-1;
See N.Y. Giants vs. St. Louis
ST. LOUIS vs. N.Y. JETS
RS: Rams lead series, 6-2;
See N.Y. Jets vs. St. Louis
ST. LOUIS vs. OAKLAND
RS: Raiders lead series, 7-2;
See Oakland vs. St. Louis
ST. LOUIS vs. PHILADELPHIA
RS: Rams lead series, 15-12-1
PS: Series tied, 1-1;
See Philadelphia vs. St. Louis
ST. LOUIS vs. PITTSBURGH
RS: Rams lead series, 14-5-2
PS: Steelers lead series, 1-0;
See Pittsburgh vs. St. Louis
***ST. LOUIS vs. SAN DIEGO**
RS: Series tied, 3-3
1970—Rams, 37-10 (LA)
1975—Rams, 13-10 (SD) OT
1979—Chargers, 40-16 (LA)
1988—Chargers, 38-24 (LA)
1991—Rams, 30-24 (LA)
1994—Chargers, 31-17 (SD)
(RS Pts.—Chargers 153, Rams 137)
**Franchise in Los Angeles prior to 1995*
***ST. LOUIS vs. SAN FRANCISCO**
RS: Rams lead series, 48-46-2
PS: 49ers lead series, 1-0
1950—Rams, 35-14 (SF)
Rams, 28-21 (LA)
1951—49ers, 44-17 (SF)
Rams, 23-16 (LA)
1952—Rams, 35-9 (LA)
Rams, 34-21 (SF)
1953—49ers, 31-30 (SF)
49ers, 31-27 (LA)
1954—Tie, 24-24 (LA)
Rams, 42-34 (SF)
1955—Rams, 23-14 (SF)
Rams, 27-14 (LA)
1956—49ers, 33-30 (SF)
Rams, 30-6 (LA)
1957—49ers, 23-20 (SF)
Rams, 37-24 (LA)
1958—Rams, 33-3 (SF)
Rams, 56-7 (LA)
1959—49ers, 34-0 (SF)
49ers, 24-16 (LA)
1960—49ers, 13-9 (SF)
49ers, 23-7 (LA)
1961—49ers, 35-0 (SF)
Rams, 17-7 (LA)
1962—Rams, 28-14 (SF)
49ers, 24-17 (LA)
1963—Rams, 28-21 (LA)
Rams, 21-17 (SF)
1964—Rams, 42-14 (LA)
49ers, 28-7 (SF)
1965—49ers, 45-21 (LA)
49ers, 30-27 (SF)
1966—Rams, 34-3 (LA)
49ers, 21-13 (SF)
1967—49ers, 27-24 (LA)
Rams, 17-7 (SF)
1968—Rams, 24-10 (LA)
Tie, 20-20 (SF)
1969—Rams, 27-21 (SF)
Rams, 41-30 (LA)
1970—49ers, 20-6 (LA)
Rams, 30-13 (SF)
1971—Rams, 20-13 (SF)
Rams, 17-6 (LA)
1972—Rams, 31-7 (LA)
Rams, 26-16 (SF)
1973—Rams, 40-20 (SF)
Rams, 31-13 (LA)
1974—Rams, 37-14 (LA)
Rams, 15-13 (SF)
1975—Rams, 23-14 (SF)
49ers, 24-23 (LA)
1976—49ers, 16-0 (LA)
Rams, 23-3 (SF)
1977—Rams, 34-14 (LA)
Rams, 23-10 (SF)
1978—Rams, 27-10 (LA)
Rams, 31-28 (SF)
1979—Rams, 27-24 (LA)
Rams, 26-20 (SF)
1980—Rams, 48-26 (LA)
Rams, 31-17 (SF)
1981—49ers, 20-17 (SF)
49ers, 33-31 (LA)
1982—49ers, 30-24 (LA)
Rams, 21-20 (SF)
1983—Rams, 10-7 (SF)
49ers, 45-35 (LA)
1984—49ers, 33-0 (LA)
49ers, 19-16 (SF)
1985—49ers, 28-14 (LA)
Rams, 27-20 (SF)
1986—Rams, 16-13 (LA)
49ers, 24-14 (SF)
1987—49ers, 31-10 (LA)
49ers, 48-0 (SF)
1988—49ers, 24-21 (LA)
Rams, 38-16 (SF)
1989—Rams, 13-12 (SF)
49ers, 30-27 (LA)
**49ers, 30-3 (SF)
1990—Rams, 28-17 (SF)
49ers, 26-10 (LA)
1991—49ers, 27-10 (SF)
49ers, 33-10 (LA)
1992—49ers, 27-24 (SF)
49ers, 27-10 (LA)
1993—49ers, 40-17 (SF)
49ers, 35-10 (LA)
1994—49ers, 34-19 (LA)
49ers, 31-27 (SF)
1995—49ers, 44-10 (StL)
49ers, 41-13 (SF)
1996—49ers, 34-0 (SF)
49ers, 28-11 (StL)
1997—49ers, 15-12 (StL)
49ers, 30-10 (SF)
(RS Pts.—49ers 2,120, Rams 2,115)
(PS Pts.—49ers 30, Rams 3)
**Franchise in Los Angeles prior to 1995*
***NFC Championship*
***ST. LOUIS vs. SEATTLE**
RS: Rams lead series, 4-2
1976—Rams, 45-6 (LA)
1979—Rams, 24-0 (S)
1985—Rams, 35-24 (S)
1988—Rams, 31-10 (LA)
1991—Seahawks, 23-9 (S)
1997—Seahawks, 17-9 (StL)
(RS Pts.—Rams 153, Seahawks 80)
**Franchise in Los Angeles prior to 1995*
***ST. LOUIS vs. TAMPA BAY**
RS: Rams lead series, 8-3
PS: Rams lead series, 1-0
1977—Rams, 31-0 (LA)
1978—Rams, 26-23 (LA)
1979—Buccaneers, 21-6 (TB)
**Rams, 9-0 (TB)
1980—Buccaneers, 10-9 (TB)
1984—Rams, 34-33 (TB)
1985—Rams, 31-27 (TB)
1986—Rams, 26-20 (LA) OT
1987—Rams, 35-3 (LA)
1990—Rams, 35-14 (TB)
1992—Rams, 31-27 (TB)
1994—Buccaneers, 24-14 (TB)
(RS Pts.—Rams 278, Buccaneers 202)
(PS Pts.—Rams 9, Buccaneers 0)
**Franchise in Los Angeles prior to 1995*
***NFC Championship*
***ST. LOUIS vs. **TENNESSEE**
RS: Rams lead series, 5-2
1973—Rams, 31-26 (H)
1978—Rams, 10-6 (H)
1981—Oilers, 27-20 (LA)
1984—Rams, 27-16 (LA)
1987—Oilers, 20-16 (H)
1990—Rams, 17-13 (LA)
1993—Rams, 28-13 (H)
(RS Pts.—Rams 149, Oilers 121)
**Franchise in Los Angeles prior to 1995*
***Franchise in Houston prior to 1997*
***ST. LOUIS vs. WASHINGTON**
RS: Redskins lead series, 17-6-1
PS: Series tied, 2-2
1937—Redskins, 16-7 (C)
1938—Redskins, 37-13 (W)
1941—Redskins, 17-13 (W)
1942—Redskins, 33-14 (W)
1944—Redskins, 14-10 (W)
1945—**Rams, 15-14 (C)
1948—Rams, 41-13 (W)
1949—Rams, 53-27 (LA)
1951—Redskins, 31-21 (W)
1962—Redskins, 20-14 (W)
1963—Redskins, 37-14 (LA)
1967—Tie, 28-28 (LA)
1969—Rams, 24-13 (W)
1971—Redskins, 38-24 (LA)
1974—Redskins, 23-17 (LA)
***Rams, 19-10 (LA)
1977—Redskins, 17-14 (W)
1981—Redskins, 30-7 (LA)
1983—Redskins, 42-20 (LA)
***Redskins, 51-7 (W)
1986—****Redskins, 19-7 (W)
1987—Rams, 30-26 (W)
1991—Redskins, 27-6 (LA)
1993—Rams, 10-6 (LA)
1994—Redskins, 24-21 (LA)
1995—Redskins, 35-23 (StL)
1996—Redskins, 17-10 (StL)
1997—Rams, 23-20 (W)
(RS Pts.—Redskins 591, Rams 457)
(PS Pts.—Redskins 94, Rams 48)
**Franchise in Los Angeles prior to 1995 and in Cleveland prior to 1946*
***NFL Championship*
****NFC Divisional Playoff*
*****NFC First-Round Playoff*

SAN DIEGO vs. ARIZONA
RS: Chargers lead series, 6-1;
See Arizona vs. San Diego
SAN DIEGO vs. ATLANTA
RS: Falcons lead series, 5-1;
See Atlanta vs. San Diego
SAN DIEGO vs BALTIMORE
RS: Chargers lead series, 1-0;
See Baltimore vs. San Diego
SAN DIEGO vs. BUFFALO
RS: Chargers lead series, 16-7-2
PS: Bills lead series, 2-1;

ALL-TIME TEAM VS. TEAM RESULTS

See Buffalo vs. San Diego
SAN DIEGO vs. CAROLINA
RS: Panthers lead series, 1-0;
See Carolina vs. San Diego
SAN DIEGO vs. CHICAGO
RS: Chargers lead series, 4-3;
See Chicago vs. San Diego
SAN DIEGO vs. CINCINNATI
RS: Chargers lead series, 14-9
PS: Bengals lead series, 1-0;
See Cincinnati vs. San Diego
SAN DIEGO vs. CLEVELAND
RS: Chargers lead series, 9-6-1;
See Cleveland vs. San Diego
SAN DIEGO vs. DALLAS
RS: Cowboys lead series, 5-1;
See Dallas vs. San Diego
SAN DIEGO vs. DENVER
RS: Broncos lead series, 40-35-1;
See Denver vs. San Diego
SAN DIEGO vs. DETROIT
RS: Series tied, 3-3;
See Detroit vs. San Diego
SAN DIEGO vs. GREEN BAY
RS: Packers lead series, 5-1;
See Green Bay vs. San Diego
SAN DIEGO vs. INDIANAPOLIS
RS: Chargers lead series, 12-5
PS: Colts lead series, 1-0;
See Indianapolis vs. San Diego
SAN DIEGO vs. KANSAS CITY
RS: Chiefs lead series, 39-35-1
PS: Chargers lead series, 1-0;
See Kansas City vs. San Diego
SAN DIEGO vs. MIAMI
RS: Chargers lead series, 10-6
PS: Series tied, 2-2;
See Miami vs. San Diego
SAN DIEGO vs. MINNESOTA
RS: Chargers lead series, 4-3;
See Minnesota vs. San Diego
SAN DIEGO vs. NEW ENGLAND
RS: Patriots lead series, 16-11-2
PS: Chargers lead series, 1-0;
See New England vs. San Diego
SAN DIEGO vs. NEW ORLEANS
RS: Chargers lead series, 6-1;
See New Orleans vs. San Diego
SAN DIEGO vs. N.Y. GIANTS
RS: Giants lead series, 4-3;
See N.Y. Giants vs. San Diego
SAN DIEGO vs. N.Y. JETS
RS: Chargers lead series, 17-9-1;
See N.Y. Jets vs. San Diego
SAN DIEGO vs. OAKLAND
RS: Raiders lead series, 45-29-2
PS: Raiders lead series, 1-0;
See Oakland vs. San Diego
SAN DIEGO vs. PHILADELPHIA
RS: Chargers lead series, 4-2;
See Philadelphia vs. San Diego
SAN DIEGO vs. PITTSBURGH
RS: Steelers lead series, 16-5
PS: Chargers lead series, 2-0;
See Pittsburgh vs. San Diego
SAN DIEGO vs. ST. LOUIS
RS: Series tied, 3-3
See St. Louis vs. San Diego
SAN DIEGO vs. SAN FRANCISCO
RS: 49ers lead series, 5-3
PS: 49ers lead series, 1-0
1972—49ers, 34-3 (SF)
1976—Chargers, 13-7 (SD) OT
1979—Chargers, 31-9 (SD)
1982—Chargers, 41-37 (SF)
1988—49ers, 48-10 (SD)
1991—49ers, 34-14 (SF)
1994—49ers, 38-15 (SD)
*49ers, 49-26 (Miami)
1997—49ers, 17-10 (SF)
(RS Pts.—49ers 224, Chargers 137)
(PS Pts.—49ers 49, Chargers 26)
**Super Bowl XXIX*

SAN DIEGO vs. SEATTLE
RS: Chargers lead series, 20-18
1977—Chargers, 30-28 (S)
1978—Chargers, 24-20 (S)
Chargers, 37-10 (SD)
1979—Chargers, 33-16 (S)
Chargers, 20-10 (SD)
1980—Chargers, 34-13 (S)
Chargers, 21-14 (SD)
1981—Chargers, 24-10 (SD)
Seahawks, 44-23 (S)
1983—Seahawks, 34-31 (S)
Chargers, 28-21 (SD)
1984—Seahawks, 31-17 (S)
Seahawks, 24-0 (SD)
1985—Seahawks, 49-35 (SD)
Seahawks, 26-21 (S)
1986—Seahawks, 33-7 (S)
Seahawks, 34-24 (SD)
1987—Seahawks, 34-3 (S)
1988—Chargers, 17-6 (SD)
Seahawks, 17-14 (S)
1989—Seahawks, 17-16 (SD)
Seahawks, 10-7 (S)
1990—Chargers, 31-14 (S)
Seahawks, 13-10 (SD) OT
1991—Seahawks, 20-9 (S)
Chargers, 17-14 (SD)
1992—Chargers, 17-6 (SD)
Chargers, 31-14 (S)
1993—Chargers, 18-12 (SD)
Seahawks, 31-14 (S)
1994—Chargers, 24-10 (S)
Chargers, 35-15 (SD)
1995—Chargers, 14-10 (SD)
Chargers, 35-25 (S)
1996—Chargers, 29-7 (SD)
Seahawks, 32-13 (S)
1997—Seahawks, 26-22 (S)
Seahawks, 37-31 (SD)
(RS Pts.—Chargers 816, Seahawks 787)
SAN DIEGO vs. TAMPA BAY
RS: Chargers lead series, 6-1
1976—Chargers, 23-0 (TB)
1981—Chargers, 24-23 (TB)
1987—Chargers, 17-13 (TB)
1990—Chargers, 41-10 (SD)
1992—Chargers, 29-14 (SD)
1993—Chargers, 32-17 (TB)
1996—Buccaneers, 25-17 (SD)
(RS Pts.—Chargers 183, Buccaneers 102)
***SAN DIEGO vs. **TENNESSEE**
RS: Chargers lead series, 18-13-1
PS: Oilers lead series, 3-0
1960—Oilers, 38-28 (H)
Chargers, 24-21 (LA)
***Oilers, 24-16 (H)
1961—Chargers, 34-24 (SD)
Oilers, 33-13 (H)
***Oilers, 10-3 (SD)
1962—Oilers, 42-17 (SD)
Oilers, 33-27 (H)
1963—Chargers, 27-0 (SD)
Chargers 20-14 (H)
1964—Chargers, 27-21 (SD)
Chargers, 20-17 (H)
1965—Chargers, 31-14 (SD)
Chargers, 37-26 (H)
1966—Chargers, 28-22 (H)
1967—Chargers, 13-3 (SD)
Oilers, 24-17 (H)
1968—Chargers, 30-14 (SD)
1969—Chargers, 21-17 (H)
1970—Tie, 31-31 (SD)
1971—Oilers, 49-33 (H)
1972—Chargers, 34-20 (SD)
1974—Oilers, 21-14 (H)
1975—Oilers, 33-17 (H)
1976—Chargers, 30-27 (SD)
1978—Chargers, 45-24 (H)
1979—****Oilers, 17-14 (SD)
1984—Chargers, 31-14 (SD)
1985—Oilers, 37-35 (H)
1986—Chargers, 27-0 (SD)
1987—Oilers, 33-18 (H)
1989—Oilers, 34-27 (SD)
1990—Oilers, 17-7 (SD)
1992—Oilers, 27-0 (H)
1993—Chargers, 18-17 (SD)
(RS Pts.—Chargers 781, Oilers 747)
(PS Pts.—Oilers 51, Chargers 33)
**Franchise in Los Angeles prior to 1961*
***Franchise in Houston prior to 1997*
****AFL Championship*
*****AFC Divisional Playoff*
SAN DIEGO vs. WASHINGTON
RS: Redskins lead series, 5-0
1973—Redskins, 38-0 (W)
1980—Redskins, 40-17 (W)
1983—Redskins, 27-24 (SD)
1986—Redskins, 30-27 (SD)
1989—Redskins, 26-21 (W)
(RS Pts.—Redskins 161, Chargers 89)

SAN FRANCISCO vs. ARIZONA
RS: 49ers lead series, 10-9;
See Arizona vs. San Francisco
SAN FRANCISCO vs. ATLANTA
RS: 49ers lead series, 39-22-1;
See Atlanta vs. San Francisco
SAN FRANCISCO vs. BALTIMORE
RS: 49ers lead series, 1-0;
See Baltimore vs. San Francisco
SAN FRANCISCO vs. BUFFALO
RS: Series tied, 3-3;
See Buffalo vs. San Francisco
SAN FRANCISCO vs. CAROLINA
RS: Series tied, 3-3;
See Carolina vs. San Francisco
SAN FRANCISCO vs. CHICAGO
RS: Series tied, 25-25-1
PS: 49ers lead series, 3-0;
See Chicago vs. San Francisco
SAN FRANCISCO vs. CINCINNATI
RS: 49ers lead series, 7-1
PS: 49ers lead series, 2-0;
See Cincinnati vs. San Francisco
SAN FRANCISCO vs. CLEVELAND
RS: Browns lead series, 9-6;
See Cleveland vs. San Francisco
SAN FRANCISCO vs. DALLAS
RS: 49ers lead series, 12-7-1
PS: Cowboys lead series, 5-2;
See Dallas vs. San Francisco
SAN FRANCISCO vs. DENVER
RS: Series tied, 4-4
PS: 49ers lead series, 1-0;
See Denver vs. San Francisco
SAN FRANCISCO vs. DETROIT
RS: 49ers lead series, 28-26-1
PS: Series tied, 1-1;
See Detroit vs. San Francisco
SAN FRANCISCO vs. GREEN BAY
RS: 49ers lead series, 25-22-1
PS: Packers lead series, 3-0;
See Green Bay vs. San Francisco
SAN FRANCISCO vs. INDIANAPOLIS
RS: Colts lead series, 22-16;
See Indianapolis vs. San Francisco
SAN FRANCISCO vs. KANSAS CITY
RS: 49ers lead series, 4-3;
See Kansas City vs. San Francisco
SAN FRANCISCO vs. MIAMI
RS: Dolphins lead series, 4-3
PS: 49ers lead series, 1-0;
See Miami vs. San Francisco
SAN FRANCISCO vs. MINNESOTA
RS: 49ers lead series, 17-16-1
PS: 49ers lead series, 4-1;
See Minnesota vs. San Francisco
SAN FRANCISCO vs. NEW ENGLAND
RS: 49ers lead series, 7-1;
See New England vs. San Francisco
SAN FRANCISCO vs. NEW ORLEANS
RS: 49ers lead series, 40-15-2;
See New Orleans vs. San Francisco

SAN FRANCISCO vs. N.Y. GIANTS
RS: Series tied, 11-11
PS: Series tied, 3-3;
See N.Y. Giants vs. San Francisco
SAN FRANCISCO vs. N.Y. JETS
RS: 49ers lead series, 6-1;
See N.Y. Jets vs. San Francisco
SAN FRANCISCO vs. OAKLAND
RS: Raiders lead series, 5-3;
See Oakland vs. San Francisco
SAN FRANCISCO vs. PHILADELPHIA
RS: 49ers lead series, 14-6-1
PS: 49ers lead series, 1-0;
See Philadelphia vs. San Francisco
SAN FRANCISCO vs. PITTSBURGH
RS: 49ers lead series, 9-7;
See Pittsburgh vs. San Francisco
SAN FRANCISCO vs. ST. LOUIS
RS: Rams lead series, 48-46-2
PS: 49ers lead series, 1-0;
See St. Louis vs. San Francisco
SAN FRANCISCO vs. SAN DIEGO
RS: 49ers lead series, 5-3
PS: 49ers lead series, 1-0;
See San Diego vs. San Francisco
SAN FRANCISCO vs. SEATTLE
RS: 49ers lead series, 4-2
1976—49ers, 37-21 (S)
1979—Seahawks, 35-24 (SF)
1985—49ers, 19-6 (SF)
1988—49ers, 38-7 (S)
1991—49ers, 24-22 (S)
1997—Seahawks, 38-9 (S)
(RS Pts.—49ers 151, Seahawks 129)
SAN FRANCISCO vs. TAMPA BAY
RS: 49ers lead series, 12-2
1977—49ers, 20-10 (SF)
1978—49ers, 6-3 (SF)
1979—49ers, 23-7 (SF)
1980—Buccaneers, 24-23 (SF)
1983—49ers, 35-21 (SF)
1984—49ers, 24-17 (SF)
1986—49ers, 31-7 (TB)
1987—49ers, 24-10 (TB)
1989—49ers, 20-16 (TB)
1990—49ers, 31-7 (SF)
1992—49ers, 21-14 (SF)
1993—49ers, 45-21 (TB)
1994—49ers, 41-16 (SF)
1997—Buccaneers, 13-6 (TB)
(RS Pts.—49ers 350, Buccaneers 186)
SAN FRANCISCO vs. *TENNESSEE
RS: 49ers lead series, 6-3
1970—49ers, 30-20 (H)
1975—Oilers, 27-13 (SF)
1978—Oilers, 20-19 (H)
1981—49ers, 28-6 (SF)
1984—49ers, 34-21 (H)
1987—49ers, 27-20 (SF)
1990—49ers, 24-21 (H)
1993—Oilers, 10-7 (SF)
1996—49ers, 10-9 (H)
(RS Pts.—49ers 192, Oilers 154)
**Franchise in Houston prior to 1997*
SAN FRANCISCO vs. WASHINGTON
RS: 49ers lead series, 11-6-1
PS: 49ers lead series, 3-1
1952—49ers, 23-17 (W)
1954—49ers, 41-7 (SF)
1955—Redskins, 7-0 (W)
1961—49ers, 35-3 (SF)
1967—Redskins, 31-28 (W)
1969—Tie, 17-17 (SF)
1970—49ers, 26-17 (SF)
1971—*49ers, 24-20 (SF)
1973—Redskins, 33-9 (W)
1976—Redskins, 24-21 (SF)
1978—Redskins, 38-20 (W)
1981—49ers, 30-17 (W)
1983—**Redskins, 24-21 (W)
1984—49ers, 37-31 (SF)
1985—49ers, 35-8 (W)
1986—Redskins, 14-6 (W)

1988—49ers, 37-21 (SF)
1990—49ers, 26-13 (SF)
*49ers, 28-10 (SF)
1992—*49ers, 20-13 (SF)
1994—49ers, 37-22 (W)
1996—49ers, 19-16 (W) OT
(RS Pts.—49ers 447, Redskins 336)
(PS Pts.—49ers 93, Redskins 67)
NFC Divisional Playoff
**NFC Championship*

SEATTLE vs. ARIZONA
RS: Cardinals lead series, 5-0;
See Arizona vs. Seattle
SEATTLE vs. ATLANTA
RS: Seahawks lead series, 4-2;
See Atlanta vs. Seattle
SEATTLE vs. BALTIMORE
RS: Ravens lead series, 1-0;
See Baltimore vs. Seattle
SEATTLE vs. BUFFALO
RS: Seahawks lead series, 4-2;
See Buffalo vs. Seattle
SEATTLE vs. CHICAGO
RS: Seahawks lead series, 4-2;
See Chicago vs. Seattle
SEATTLE vs. CINCINNATI
RS: Series tied, 7-7
PS: Bengals lead series, 1-0;
See Cincinnati vs. Seattle
SEATTLE vs. CLEVELAND
RS: Seahawks lead series, 9-4;
See Cleveland vs. Seattle
SEATTLE vs. DALLAS
RS: Cowboys lead series, 4-1;
See Dallas vs. Seattle
SEATTLE vs. DENVER
RS: Broncos lead series, 26-15
PS: Seahawks lead series, 1-0;
See Denver vs. Seattle
SEATTLE vs. DETROIT
RS: Seahawks lead series, 4-3;
See Detroit vs. Seattle
SEATTLE vs. GREEN BAY
RS: Packers lead series, 4-3;
See Green Bay vs. Seattle
SEATTLE vs. INDIANAPOLIS
RS: Colts lead series, 4-2;
See Indianapolis vs. Seattle
SEATTLE vs. JACKSONVILLE
RS: Series tied, 1-1;
See Jacksonville vs. Seattle
SEATTLE vs. KANSAS CITY
RS: Chiefs lead series, 26-13;
See Kansas City vs. Seattle
SEATTLE vs. MIAMI
RS: Dolphins lead series, 4-2
PS: Series tied, 1-1;
See Miami vs. Seattle
SEATTLE vs. MINNESOTA
RS: Seahawks lead series, 4-2;
See Minnesota vs. Seattle
SEATTLE vs. NEW ENGLAND
RS: Seahawks lead series, 7-6;
See New England vs. Seattle
SEATTLE vs. NEW ORLEANS
RS: Saints lead series, 4-2;
See New Orleans vs. Seattle
SEATTLE vs. N.Y. GIANTS
RS: Seahawks lead series, 8-5;
See N.Y. Giants vs. Seattle
SEATTLE vs. N.Y. JETS
RS: Seahawks lead series, 8-5;
See N.Y. Jets vs. Seattle
SEATTLE vs. OAKLAND
RS: Raiders lead series, 21-19
PS: Series tied, 1-1;
See Oakland vs. Seattle
SEATTLE vs. PHILADELPHIA
RS: Eagles lead series, 4-2;
See Philadelphia vs. Seattle
SEATTLE vs. PITTSBURGH
RS: Seahawks lead series, 6-5;
See Pittsburgh vs. Seattle
SEATTLE vs. ST. LOUIS
RS: Rams lead series, 4-2;
See St. Louis vs. Seattle
SEATTLE vs. SAN DIEGO
RS: Chargers lead series, 20-18;
See San Diego vs. Seattle
SEATTLE vs. SAN FRANCISCO
RS: 49ers lead series, 4-2;
See San Francisco vs. Seattle
SEATTLE vs. TAMPA BAY
RS: Seahawks lead series, 4-0
1976—Seahawks, 13-10 (TB)
1977—Seahawks, 30-23 (S)
1994—Seahawks, 22-21 (S)
1996—Seahawks, 17-13 (TB)
(RS Pts.—Seahawks 82, Buccaneers 67)
SEATTLE vs. *TENNESSEE
RS: Seahawks lead series, 7-4
PS: Oilers lead series, 1-0
1977—Oilers, 22-10 (S)
1979—Seahawks, 34-14 (S)
1980—Seahawks, 26-7 (H)
1981—Oilers, 35-17 (H)
1982—Oilers, 23-21 (H)
1987—**Oilers, 23-20 (H) OT
1988—Seahawks, 27-24 (S)
1990—Seahawks, 13-10 (S) OT
1993—Oilers, 24-14 (H)
1994—Seahawks, 16-14 (H)
1996—Seahawks, 23-16 (S)
1997—Seahawks, 16-13 (S)
(RS Pts.—Seahawks 217, Oilers 202)
(PS Pts.—Oilers 23, Seahawks 20)
Franchise in Houston prior to 1997
**AFC First-Round Playoff*
SEATTLE vs. WASHINGTON
RS: Redskins lead series, 5-3
1976—Redskins, 31-7 (W)
1980—Seahawks, 14-0 (W)
1983—Redskins, 27-17 (S)
1986—Redskins, 19-14 (W)
1989—Redskins, 29-0 (S)
1992—Redskins, 16-3 (S)
1994—Seahawks, 28-7 (W)
1995—Seahawks, 27-20 (W)
(RS Pts.—Redskins 149, Seahawks 110)

TAMPA BAY vs. ARIZONA
RS: Series tied, 7-7;
See Arizona vs. Tampa Bay
TAMPA BAY vs. ATLANTA
RS: Falcons lead series, 8-7;
See Atlanta vs. Tampa Bay
TAMPA BAY vs. BUFFALO
RS: Buccaneers lead series, 4-2;
See Buffalo vs. Tampa Bay
TAMPA BAY vs. CAROLINA
RS: Series tied, 1-1;
See Carolina vs. Tampa Bay
TAMPA BAY vs. CHICAGO
RS: Bears lead series, 30-10;
See Chicago vs. Tampa Bay
TAMPA BAY vs. CINCINNATI
RS: Bengals lead series, 3-2;
See Cincinnati vs. Tampa Bay
TAMPA BAY vs. CLEVELAND
RS: Browns lead series, 5-0;
See Cleveland vs. Tampa Bay
TAMPA BAY vs. DALLAS
RS: Cowboys lead series, 6-0
PS: Cowboys lead series, 2-0;
See Dallas vs. Tampa Bay
TAMPA BAY vs. DENVER
RS: Broncos lead series, 3-1;
See Denver vs. Tampa Bay
TAMPA BAY vs. DETROIT
RS: Lions lead series, 22-18
PS: Buccaneers lead series, 1-0;
See Detroit vs. Tampa Bay
TAMPA BAY vs. GREEN BAY
RS: Packers lead series, 24-13-1
PS: Packers lead series, 1-0;
See Green Bay vs. Tampa Bay
TAMPA BAY vs. INDIANAPOLIS
RS: Colts lead series, 5-4;
See Indianapolis vs. Tampa Bay
TAMPA BAY vs. JACKSONVILLE
RS: Buccaneers lead series, 1-0;
See Jacksonville vs. Tampa Bay
TAMPA BAY vs. KANSAS CITY
RS: Chiefs lead series, 5-2;
See Kansas City vs. Tampa Bay
TAMPA BAY vs. MIAMI
RS: Dolphins lead series, 4-2;
See Miami vs. Tampa Bay
TAMPA BAY vs. MINNESOTA
RS: Vikings lead series, 27-13;
See Minnesota vs. Tampa Bay
TAMPA BAY vs. NEW ENGLAND
RS: Patriots lead series, 3-1;
See New England vs. Tampa Bay
TAMPA BAY vs. NEW ORLEANS
RS: Saints lead series, 12-5;
See New Orleans vs. Tampa Bay
TAMPA BAY vs. N.Y. GIANTS
RS: Giants lead series, 8-4;
See N.Y. Giants vs. Tampa Bay
TAMPA BAY vs. N.Y. JETS
RS: Jets lead series, 6-1;
See N.Y. Jets vs. Tampa Bay
TAMPA BAY vs. OAKLAND
RS: Raiders lead series, 3-1;
See Oakland vs. Tampa Bay
TAMPA BAY vs. PHILADELPHIA
RS: Eagles lead series, 3-2
PS: Buccaneers lead series, 1-0;
See Philadelphia vs. Tampa Bay
TAMPA BAY vs. PITTSBURGH
RS: Steelers lead series, 4-0;
See Pittsburgh vs. Tampa Bay
TAMPA BAY vs. ST. LOUIS
RS: Rams lead series, 8-3
PS: Rams lead series, 1-0;
See St. Louis vs. Tampa Bay
TAMPA BAY vs. SAN DIEGO
RS: Chargers lead series, 6-1;
See San Diego vs. Tampa Bay
TAMPA BAY vs. SAN FRANCISCO
RS: 49ers lead series, 12-2;
See San Francisco vs. Tampa Bay
TAMPA BAY vs. SEATTLE
RS: Seahawks lead series, 4-0;
See Seattle vs. Tampa Bay
TAMPA BAY vs. *TENNESSEE
RS: Oilers lead series, 4-1
1976—Oilers, 20-0 (H)
1980—Oilers, 20-14 (H)
1983—Buccaneers, 33-24 (TB)
1989—Oilers, 20-17 (H)
1995—Oilers, 19-7 (H)
(RS Pts.—Oilers 103, Buccaneers 71)
Franchise in Houston prior to 1997
TAMPA BAY vs. WASHINGTON
RS: Series tied, 4-4
1977—Redskins, 10-0 (TB)
1982—Redskins, 21-13 (TB)
1989—Redskins, 32-28 (W)
1993—Redskins, 23-17 (TB)
1994—Buccaneers, 26-21 (TB)
Buccaneers, 17-14 (W)
1995—Buccaneers, 14-6 (TB)
1996—Buccaneers, 24-10 (TB)
(RS Pts.—Buccaneers 139, Redskins 137)

TENNESSEE VS. ARIZONA
RS: Cardinals lead series, 4-3;
See Arizona vs. Tennessee
TENNESSEE vs. ATLANTA
RS: Falcons lead series, 5-4;
See Atlanta vs. Tennessee
TENNESSEE vs. BALTIMORE
RS: Series tied, 2-2;
See Baltimore vs. Tennessee
TENNESSEE vs. BUFFALO
RS: Oilers lead series, 22-13
PS: Bills lead series, 2-0;
See Buffalo vs. Tennessee
TENNESSEE vs. CAROLINA
RS: Panthers lead series, 1-0;
See Carolina vs. Tennessee
TENNESSEE vs. CHICAGO
RS: Oilers lead series, 4-3;
See Chicago vs. Tennessee
TENNESSEE vs. CINCINNATI
RS: Oilers lead series, 29-28-1
PS: Bengals lead series, 1-0;
See Cincinnati vs. Tennessee
TENNESSEE vs. CLEVELAND
RS: Browns lead series, 30-21
PS: Oilers lead series, 1-0;
See Cleveland vs. Tennessee
TENNESSEE vs. DALLAS
RS: Cowboys lead series, 5-4
See Dallas vs. Tennessee
TENNESSEE vs. DENVER
RS: Oilers lead series, 20-11-1
PS: Broncos lead series, 2-1;
See Denver vs. Tennessee
TENNESSEE vs. DETROIT
RS: Oilers lead series, 4-3;
See Detroit vs. Tennessee
TENNESSEE vs. GREEN BAY
RS: Series tied, 3-3;
See Green Bay vs. Tennessee
TENNESSEE vs. INDIANAPOLIS
RS: Series tied, 7-7;
See Indianapolis vs. Tennessee
TENNESSEE vs. JACKSONVILLE
RS: Jaguars lead series, 4-2;
See Jacksonville vs. Tennessee
TENNESSEE vs. KANSAS CITY
RS: Chiefs lead series, 24-17
PS: Chiefs lead series, 2-0;
See Kansas City vs. Tennessee
TENNESSEE vs. MIAMI
RS: Dolphins lead series, 13-11
PS: Oilers lead series, 1-0;
See Miami vs. Tennessee
TENNESSEE vs. MINNESOTA
RS: Vikings lead series, 4-3;
See Minnesota vs. Tennessee
TENNESSEE vs. NEW ENGLAND
RS: Patriots lead series, 17-14-1
PS: Oilers lead series, 1-0;
See New England vs. Tennessee
TENNESSEE vs. NEW ORLEANS
RS: Series tied, 4-4-1;
See New Orleans vs. Tennessee
TENNESSEE vs. N.Y. GIANTS
RS: Giants lead series, 5-1;
See N.Y. Giants vs. Tennessee
TENNESSEE vs. N.Y. JETS
RS: Oilers lead series, 20-12-1
PS: Oilers lead series, 1-0;
See N.Y. Jets vs. Tennessee
TENNESSEE vs. OAKLAND
RS: Raiders lead series, 20-14
PS: Raiders lead series, 3-0;
See Oakland vs. Tennessee
TENNESSEE vs. PHILADELPHIA
RS: Eagles lead series, 6-0;
See Philadelphia vs. Tennessee
TENNESSEE vs. PITTSBURGH
RS: Steelers lead series, 35-20
PS: Steelers lead series, 3-0;
See Pittsburgh vs. Tennessee
TENNESSEE vs. ST. LOUIS
RS: Rams lead series, 5-2;
See St. Louis vs. Tennessee
TENNESSEE vs. SAN DIEGO
RS: Chargers lead series, 18-13-1
PS: Oilers lead series, 3-0;
See San Diego vs. Tennessee
TENNESSEE vs. SAN FRANCISCO
RS: 49ers lead series, 6-3;
See San Francisco vs. Tennessee
TENNESSEE vs. SEATTLE
RS: Seahawks lead series, 7-4

ALL-TIME TEAM VS. TEAM RESULTS

PS: Oilers lead series, 1-0;
See Seattle vs. Tennessee
TENNESSEE vs. TAMPA BAY
RS: Oilers lead series, 4-3
See Tampa Bay vs. Tennessee
***TENNESSEE vs. WASHINGTON**
RS: Oilers lead series, 4-3
1971—Redskins, 22-13 (W)
1975—Oilers, 13-10 (H)
1979—Oilers, 29-27 (W)
1985—Redskins, 16-13 (W)
1988—Oilers, 41-17 (H)
1991—Redskins, 16-13 (W) OT
1997—Oilers, 28-14 (T)
(RS Pts.—Oilers 150, Redskins 122)
**Franchise in Houston prior to 1997*

WASHINGTON vs. ARIZONA
RS: Redskins lead series, 64-41-2;
See Arizona vs. Washington
WASHINGTON vs. ATLANTA
RS: Redskins lead series, 13-4-1
PS: Redskins lead series, 1-0;
See Atlanta vs. Washington
WASHINGTON vs BALTIMORE
RS: Ravens lead series, 1-0;
See Baltimore vs. Washington
WASHINGTON vs. BUFFALO
RS: Series tied, 4-4
PS: Redskins lead series, 1-0;
See Buffalo vs. Washington
WASHINGTON vs. CAROLINA
RS: Redskins lead series, 2-0;
See Carolina vs. Washington
WASHINGTON vs. CHICAGO
RS: Bears lead series, 18-14-1
PS: Redskins lead series, 4-3;
See Chicago vs. Washington
WASHINGTON vs. CINCINNATI
RS: Redskins lead series, 4-2;
See Cincinnati vs. Washington
WASHINGTON vs. CLEVELAND
RS: Browns lead series, 32-9-1;
See Cleveland vs. Washington
WASHINGTON vs. DALLAS
RS: Cowboys lead series, 41-31-2
PS: Redskins lead series, 2-0;
See Dallas vs. Washington
WASHINGTON vs. DENVER
RS: Broncos lead series, 4-3
PS: Redskins lead series, 1-0;
See Denver vs. Washington
WASHINGTON vs. DETROIT
RS: Redskins lead series, 24-8
PS: Redskins lead series, 2-0;
See Detroit vs. Washington
WASHINGTON vs. GREEN BAY
RS: Packers lead series, 13-12-1
PS: Series tied, 1-1;
See Green Bay vs. Washington
WASHINGTON vs. INDIANAPOLIS
RS: Colts lead series, 16-9;
See Indianapolis vs. Washington
WASHINGTON vs. JACKSONVILLE
RS: Redskins lead series, 1-0;
See Jacksonville vs. Washington
WASHINGTON vs. KANSAS CITY
RS: Chiefs lead series, 4-1;
See Kansas City vs. Washington
WASHINGTON vs. MIAMI
RS: Dolphins lead series, 5-2
PS: Series tied, 1-1;
See Miami vs. Washington
WASHINGTON vs. MINNESOTA
RS: Redskins lead series, 6-4
PS: Redskins lead series, 3-2;
See Minnesota vs. Washington
WASHINGTON vs. NEW ENGLAND
RS: Redskins lead series, 5-1;
See New England vs. Washington
WASHINGTON vs. NEW ORLEANS
RS: Redskins lead series, 12-5;
See New Orleans vs. Washington
WASHINGTON vs. N.Y. GIANTS
RS: Giants lead series, 74-52-4
PS: Series tied, 1-1;
See N.Y. Giants vs. Washington
WASHINGTON vs. N.Y. JETS
RS: Redskins lead series, 5-1;
See N.Y. Jets vs. Washington
WASHINGTON vs. OAKLAND
RS: Raiders lead series, 6-2
PS: Raiders lead series, 1-0;
See Oakland vs. Washington
WASHINGTON vs. PHILADELPHIA
RS: Redskins lead series, 68-52-5
PS: Redskins lead series, 1-0;
See Philadelphia vs. Washington
WASHINGTON vs. PITTSBURGH
RS: Redskins lead series, 42-28-3;
See Pittsburgh vs. Washington
WASHINGTON vs. ST. LOUIS
RS: Redskins lead series, 17-6-1
PS: Series tied, 2-2;
See St. Louis vs. Washington
WASHINGTON vs. SAN DIEGO
RS: Redskins lead series, 5-0;
See San Diego vs. Washington
WASHINGTON vs. SAN FRANCISCO
RS: 49ers lead series, 11-6-1
PS: 49ers lead series, 3-1;
See San Francisco vs. Washington
WASHINGTON vs. SEATTLE
RS: Redskins lead series, 5-3;
See Seattle vs. Washington
WASHINGTON vs. TAMPA BAY
RS: Series tied, 4-4;
See Tampa Bay vs. Washington
WASHINGTON vs. TENNESSEE
RS: Oilers lead series, 4-3;
See Tennessee vs. Washington

RESULTS

Super Bowl	Date	Winner (Share)	Loser (Share)	Score	Site	Attendance
XXXII	1-25-98	Denver ($48,000)	Green Bay ($29,000)	31-24	San Diego	68,912
XXXI	1-26-97	Green Bay ($48,000)	New England ($29,000)	35-21	New Orleans	72,301
XXX	1-28-96	Dallas ($42,000)	Pittsburgh ($27,000)	27-17	Tempe	76,347
XXIX	1-29-95	San Francisco ($42,000)	San Diego ($26,000)	49-26	Miami	74,107
XXVIII	1-30-94	Dallas ($38,000)	Buffalo ($23,500)	30-13	Atlanta	72,817
XXVII	1-31-93	Dallas ($36,000)	Buffalo ($18,000)	52-17	Pasadena	98,374
XXVI	1-26-92	Washington ($36,000)	Buffalo ($18,000)	37-24	Minneapolis	63,130
XXV	1-27-91	N.Y. Giants ($36,000)	Buffalo ($18,000)	20-19	Tampa	73,813
XXIV	1-28-90	San Francisco ($36,000)	Denver ($18,000)	55-10	New Orleans	72,919
XXIII	1-22-89	San Francisco ($36,000)	Cincinnati ($18,000)	20-16	Miami	75,129
XXII	1-31-88	Washington ($36,000)	Denver ($18,000)	42-10	San Diego	73,302
XXI	1-25-87	N.Y. Giants ($36,000)	Denver ($18,000)	39-20	Pasadena	101,063
XX	1-26-86	Chicago ($36,000)	New England ($18,000)	46-10	New Orleans	73,818
XIX	1-20-85	San Francisco ($36,000)	Miami ($18,000)	38-16	Stanford	84,059
XVIII	1-22-84	L.A. Raiders ($36,000)	Washington ($18,000)	38-9	Tampa	72,920
XVII	1-30-83	Washington ($36,000)	Miami ($18,000)	27-17	Pasadena	103,667
XVI	1-24-82	San Francisco ($18,000)	Cincinnati ($9,000)	26-21	Pontiac	81,270
XV	1-25-81	Oakland ($18,000)	Philadelphia ($9,000)	27-10	New Orleans	76,135
XIV	1-20-80	Pittsburgh ($18,000)	Los Angeles ($9,000)	31-19	Pasadena	103,985
XIII	1-21-79	Pittsburgh ($18,000)	Dallas ($9,000)	35-31	Miami	79,484
XII	1-15-78	Dallas ($18,000)	Denver ($9,000)	27-10	New Orleans	75,583
XI	1-9-77	Oakland ($15,000)	Minnesota ($7,500)	32-14	Pasadena	103,438
X	1-18-76	Pittsburgh ($15,000)	Dallas ($7,500)	21-17	Miami	80,187
IX	1-12-75	Pittsburgh ($15,000)	Minnesota ($7,500)	16-6	New Orleans	80,997
VIII	1-13-74	Miami ($15,000)	Minnesota ($7,500)	24-7	Houston	71,882
VII	1-14-73	Miami ($15,000)	Washington ($7,500)	14-7	Los Angeles	90,182
VI	1-16-72	Dallas ($15,000)	Miami ($7,500)	24-3	New Orleans	81,023
V	1-17-71	Baltimore ($15,000)	Dallas ($7,500)	16-13	Miami	79,204
IV	1-11-70	Kansas City ($15,000)	Minnesota ($7,500)	23-7	New Orleans	80,562
III	1-12-69	N.Y. Jets ($15,000)	Baltimore ($7,500)	16-7	Miami	75,389
II	1-14-68	Green Bay ($15,000)	Oakland ($7,500)	33-14	Miami	75,546
I	1-15-67	Green Bay ($15,000)	Kansas City ($7,500)	35-10	Los Angeles	61,946

SUPER BOWL COMPOSITE STANDINGS

	W	L	Pct.	Pts.	OP
San Francisco 49ers	5	0	1.000	188	89
New York Giants	2	0	1.000	59	39
Chicago Bears	1	0	1.000	46	10
New York Jets	1	0	1.000	16	7
Pittsburgh Steelers	4	1	.800	120	100
Green Bay Packers	3	1	.750	127	76
Oakland/L.A. Raiders	3	1	.750	111	66
Dallas Cowboys	5	3	.625	221	132
Washington Redskins	3	2	.600	122	103
Baltimore Colts	1	1	.500	23	29
Kansas City Chiefs	1	1	.500	33	42
Miami Dolphins	2	3	.400	74	103
Denver Broncos	1	4	.200	81	187
Los Angeles Rams	0	1	.000	19	31
Philadelphia Eagles	0	1	.000	10	27
San Diego Chargers	0	1	.000	26	49
Cincinnati Bengals	0	2	.000	37	46
New England Patriots	0	2	.000	31	81
Buffalo Bills	0	4	.000	73	139
Minnesota Vikings	0	4	.000	34	95

SUPER BOWL MOST VALUABLE PLAYERS*

Super Bowl I — QB Bart Starr, Green Bay
Super Bowl II — QB Bart Starr, Green Bay
Super Bowl III — QB Joe Namath, N.Y. Jets
Super Bowl IV — QB Len Dawson, Kansas City
Super Bowl V — LB Chuck Howley, Dallas
Super Bowl VI — QB Roger Staubach, Dallas
Super Bowl VII — S Jake Scott, Miami
Super Bowl VIII — RB Larry Csonka, Miami
Super Bowl IX — RB Franco Harris, Pittsburgh
Super Bowl X — WR Lynn Swann, Pittsburgh
Super Bowl XI — WR Fred Biletnikoff, Oakland
Super Bowl XII — DT Randy White and DE Harvey Martin, Dallas
Super Bowl XIII — QB Terry Bradshaw, Pittsburgh
Super Bowl XIV — QB Terry Bradshaw, Pittsburgh
Super Bowl XV — QB Jim Plunkett, Oakland
Super Bowl XVI — QB Joe Montana, San Francisco
Super Bowl XVII — RB John Riggins, Washington
Super Bowl XVIII — RB Marcus Allen, L.A. Raiders
Super Bowl XIX — QB Joe Montana, San Francisco
Super Bowl XX — DE Richard Dent, Chicago
Super Bowl XXI — QB Phil Simms, N.Y. Giants
Super Bowl XXII — QB Doug Williams, Washington
Super Bowl XXIII — WR Jerry Rice, San Francisco
Super Bowl XXIV — QB Joe Montana, San Francisco
Super Bowl XXV — RB Ottis Anderson, N.Y. Giants
Super Bowl XXVI — QB Mark Rypien, Washington
Super Bowl XXVII — QB Troy Aikman, Dallas
Super Bowl XXVIII — RB Emmitt Smith, Dallas
Super Bowl XXIX — QB Steve Young, San Francisco
Super Bowl XXX — CB Larry Brown, Dallas
Super Bowl XXXI — KR-PR Desmond Howard, Green Bay
Super Bowl XXXII — RB Terrell Davis, Denver

** Award named Pete Rozelle Trophy since Super Bowl XXV.*

SUPER BOWL XXXII

Qualcomm Stadium, San Diego, California
January 25, 1998; Attendance: 68,912

DENVER 31, GREEN BAY 24—Terrell Davis rushed for 157 yards and a Super Bowl-record 3 touchdowns to lead the Broncos to their first NFL championship and break the NFC's streak of Super Bowl victories at thirteen. The defending Super Bowl champion Packers took the opening kickoff and marched 76 yards in just over four minutes, scoring the first points on Brett Favre's 22-yard touchdown pass to Antonio Freeman. The Broncos responded with a 10-play, 58-yard drive capped by Davis's 1-yard run to tie the game. Tyrone Braxton intercepted Favre two plays later, and John Elway scored on a third-and-goal play to begin the second quarter. Steve Atwater forced Favre to fumble three plays later, and Neil Smith recovered at the Packers' 33. Jason Elam converted a 51-yard field goal, the second longest in Super Bowl history, to give the Broncos a 17-7 lead with 12:21 left in the half. After an exchange of punts, the Packers produced a 17-play, 95-yard drive that consumed 7:26 and finished with Favre's 6-yard touchdown pass to Mark Chmura on third-and-5 with 12 seconds left in the half. Tyrone Williams forced and recovered Davis's fumble at the Broncos' 26 on the first play from scrimmage in the second half. However, the Broncos' defense kept the Packers out of the end zone as Ryan Longwell's 27-yard field goal tied the game with 11:59 left in the third quarter. After another exchange of punts, Elway's 36-yard pass to Ed McCaffrey keyed a 13-play, 92-yard drive capped by Davis's 1-yard touchdown run with 34 seconds left in the third quarter. Tim McKyer recovered Freeman's fumble at the Packers' 22 on the ensuing kickoff return, giving the Broncos a golden opportunity, but Eugene Robinson intercepted Elway's pass in the end zone on the next play. Sparked by Robinson's play, the Packers took just four plays, three on passes to Freeman, to score the tying touchdown with 13:32 remaining. Each defense stiffened, forcing two punts, but the Broncos got great field position following Craig Hentrich's 39-yard punt to the Packers' 49 with 3:27 left and the score tied 24-24. Davis rushed for 2 yards on the first play, but Darrius Holland's 15-yard face mask penalty moved the ball to the Packers' 32. Elway threw a 23-yard pass to Howard Griffith two plays later, and Davis rushed 7 yards to the Packers' 1 with 1:47 left. After a timeout, Davis waltzed into the end zone to give Denver a 31-24 lead with 1:45 remaining. Freeman returned the kickoff 22 yards to the Broncos' 30, and Favre dumped 22- and 13-yard passes to Dorsey Levens to reach the Broncos' 35 with 1:04 left. But after a 4-yard pass to Levens and incompletions to Freeman and Brooks, John Mobley batted down Favre's pass to Chmura with 32 seconds left to give the Broncos the Vince Lombardi trophy. Elway was 12 of 22 for 123 yards, with 1 interception. Favre was 25 of 42 for 256 yards and 1 touchdown, with 1 interception. Freeman had 9 receptions for 126 yards. Davis was named the game's most valuable player.

Green Bay (24)	Offense	Denver (31)
Antonio Freeman	WR	Rod Smith
Ross Verba	LT	Gary Zimmerman
Aaron Taylor	LG	Mark Schlereth
Frank Winters	C	Tom Nalen
Adam Timmerman	RG	Brian Habib
Earl Dotson	RT	Tony Jones
Mark Chmura	TE	Shannon Sharpe
Robert Brooks	WR	Ed McCaffrey
Brett Favre	QB	John Elway
Dorsey Levens	RB	Terrell Davis
William Henderson	RB	Howard Griffith
	Defense	
Reggie White	LE	Neil Smith
Santana Dotson	DT-LT	Keith Traylor
Gilbert Brown	NT-RT	Maa Tanuvasa
Gabe Wilkins	RE	Alfred Williams
Seth Joyner	LLB-WLB	John Mobley
Bernardo Harris	MLB	Allen Aldridge
Brian Williams	RLB-SLB	Bill Romanowski
Tyrone Williams	LCB	Ray Crockett
Doug Evans	RCB	Darrien Gordon

LeRoy Butler	SS	Tyrone Braxton
Eugene Robinson	FS	Steve Atwater

SUBSTITUTIONS

GREEN BAY—Offense: G—Rob Davis, Marco Rivera. T—Bruce Wilkerson. TE—Tyrone Davis, Jeff Thomason. WR—Derrick Mayes, Terry Mickens. RB—Chris Darkins, Aaron Hayden, Travis Jervey. P—Craig Hentrich. K—Ryan Longwell. Defense: DT—Darius Holland, Bob Kuberski. DE—Keith McKenzie. LB—Lamont Hollinquest, George Koonce. DB—Mark Collins, Roderick Mullen, Mike Prior, Darren Sharper. DNP—Steve Bono, Jeff Dellenbach

DENVER—Offense: G—David Diaz-Infante. T—Harry Swayne. TE—Dwayne Carswell. WR—Willie Green, Patrick Jeffers. RB—Vaughn Hebron, Derek Loville, Anthony Lynn, Detron Smith. P—Tom Rouen. K—Jason Elam. Defense: NT—Mike Lodish. DT—Trevor Pryce. DE—Harald Hasselbach. LB—Keith Burns, Glenn Cadrez. DB—Dedrick Dodge, Randy Hilliard, Darrius Johnson, Tim McKyer, Tony Veland. DNP—Bubby Brister, Byron Chamberlain.

OFFICIALS

Referee—Ed Hochuli. Umpire—Jim Quirk. Head Linesman—John Schleyer. Line Judge—Ben Montgomery. Back Judge—Paul Baetz. Field Judge—Don Dorkowski. Side Judge—Doug Toole.

SCORING

Green Bay (NFC)	7	7	3	7	—	24
Denver (AFC)	7	10	7	7	—	31

GB — Freeman 22 pass from Favre (Longwell kick) (4:02)
Den — Davis 1 run (Elam kick) (9:21)
Den — Elway 1 run (Elam kick) (:05)
Den — FG Elam 51 (2:39)
GB — Chmura 6 pass from Favre (Longwell kick) (14:48)
GB — FG Longwell 27 (3:01)
Den — Davis 1 run (Elam kick) (14:26)
GB — Freeman 13 pass from Favre (Longwell kick) (1:28)
Den — Davis 1 run (Elam kick) (13:15)

TEAM STATISTICS	G.B.	DEN.
Total First Downs	21	21
Rushing	4	14
Passing	14	5
Penalty	3	2
Total Net Yardage	350	302
Total Offensive Plays	63	61
Average Gain Per Offensive Play	5.6	5.0
Rushes	20	39
Yards Gained Rushing (Net)	95	179
Average Yards per Rush	4.8	4.6
Passes Attempted	42	22
Passes Completed	25	12
Had Intercepted	1	1
Tackled Attempting to Pass	1	0
Yards Lost Attempting to Pass	1	0
Yards Gained Passing (Net)	255	123
Punts	4	4
Average Distance	35.5	36.5
Punt Returns	0	0
Punt Return Yardage	0	0
Kickoff Returns	6	5
Kickoff Return Yardage	104	95
Interception Return Yardage	17	0
Total Return Yardage	121	95
Fumbles	2	1
Fumbles Lost	2	1
Own Fumbles Recovered	0	0
Opponent Fumbles Recovered	1	2
Penalties	9	7
Yards Penalized	59	65
Field Goals	1	1
Field Goals Attempted	1	1
Third-Down Efficiency	5/14	5/10
Fourth-Down Efficiency	0/1	0/0
Time of Possession	27:35	32:25

INDIVIDUAL STATISTICS

RUSHING: GB: Levens 19-90, R. Brooks 1-5. DEN: Davis 30-157, Elway 5-17, Hebron 3-3, Griffith 1-2.
PASSING: GB: Favre 25-42-256-3. DEN: Elway 12-22-123-0.
RECEIVING: GB: Freeman 9-126, Levens 6-56, Chmura 4-43, R. Brooks 3-16, Henderson 2-9, Mickens 1-6. DEN: Sharpe 5-38, McCaffrey 2-45, Davis 2-8, Griffith 1-23, Hebron 1-5, Carswell 1-4.
KICKOFF RETURNS: GB: Freeman 6-104. DEN: Hebron 4-79, Burns 1-16.
PUNTING: GB: Hentrich 4-142-35.5. DEN: Rouen 4-146-36.5.
INTERCEPTIONS: GB: Robinson 1-17. DEN: Braxton 1-0.
SACKS: DEN: Atwater 1.

SUPER BOWL XXXI

Louisiana Superdome, New Orleans, Louisiana
January 26, 1997, Attendance: 72,301

GREEN BAY 35, NEW ENGLAND 21— Desmond Howard returned a kickoff 99 yards for a touchdown and Brett Favre threw 2 touchdown passes and ran for a score as the Packers won their first Super Bowl in twenty-nine years. Howard, en route to garnering the MVP trophy, established a Super Bowl record with 244 total return yards. It was Favre's arm that struck first, as he hit Andre Rison for a 54-yard touchdown pass on the Packers' second play from scrimmage to take a 7-0 lead. Two plays later Doug Evans made a diving interception of Drew Bledsoe's pass at the 28-yard line, setting up Chris Jacke's field goal and giving the Packers a 10-0 lead just 6:18 into the Super Bowl. The Patriots answered with touchdowns on their next two possessions. Craig Newsome's pass interference penalty set up the first touchdown and a 44-yard completion from Bledsoe to Terry Glenn preceeding Ben Coates's touchdown gave New England its first and only lead. The 24 combined first quarter points were the most in Super Bowl history. Green Bay struck again 56 seconds into the second quarter as Favre hit Antonio Freeman with a Super Bowl-record 81-yard touchdown bomb. Jacke booted his second field goal on Green Bay's next possession. After a Mike Prior interception, Favre orchestrated a 74-yard, nearly 6-minute drive which concluded with a diving Favre touching the ball against the pylon to give Green Bay a 27-14 halftime lead. Curtis Martin brought the Patriots to within a score by running in from 18 yards out with 3:27 left in the third quarter. But Howard broke the Patriots' spirit by returning the ensuing kickoff a Super Bowl-record 99 yards. Favre found Mark Chmura for the 2-point conversion to finish the scoring. Bledsoe was intercepted twice in the fourth quarter as the Patriots never crossed midfield in 4 fourth-quarter possessions. Reggie White set a Super Bowl record with 3 sacks. Favre completed 14 of 27 passes for 246 yards, 2 touchdowns, 0 interceptions, and 1 rushing TD. Bledsoe completed 11 more passes than Favre, but for just 7 more yards, and threw 4 interceptions.

New England (AFC)	14	0	7	0	—	21
Green Bay (NFC)	10	17	8	0	—	35

GB — Rison 54 pass from Favre (Jacke kick) (3:32)
GB — FG Jacke 37 (6:18)
NE — Byars 1 pass from Bledsoe (Vinatieri kick) (8:25)
NE — Coates 4 pass from Bledsoe (Vinatieri kick) (12:27)
GB — Freeman 81 pass from Favre (Jacke kick) (0:56)
GB — FG Jacke 31 (6:45)
GB — Favre 2 run (Jacke kick) (13:49)
NE — Martin 18 run (Vinatieri kick) (11:33)
GB — Howard 99 kick return (Chmura pass from Favre) (11:50)

SUPER BOWL XXX

Sun Devil Stadium, Tempe, Arizona
January 28, 1996, Attendance: 76,347

DALLAS 27, PITTSBURGH 17—Cornerback Larry Brown's 2 interceptions led to 14 second-half points and helped lift the Cowboys to their third Super Bowl victory in the last four seasons and their record-tying fifth title overall. Brown's interceptions foiled the comeback efforts of the Steelers, and earned him the Pete Rozelle Trophy as the game's most valuable player. Dallas scored on each of its first three possessions, taking a 13-0 lead on Troy Aikman's 3-yard touchdown pass to Jay Novacek and a pair of field goals by Chris Boniol. Neil O'Donnell's 6-yard touchdown pass to Yancey Thigpen 13 seconds before halftime pulled Pittsburgh within 6 points, and the Steelers had the ball near midfield midway through the third quarter. But O'Donnell's third-down pass was intercepted by Brown at the Cowboys' 38-yard line, and his 44-yard return carried to Pittsburgh's 18. After Aikman's 17-yard completion to Michael Irvin, Emmitt Smith ran 1 yard for the touchdown that put Dallas ahead again by 13 points. The Steelers rallied, though, behind Norm Johnson's 46-yard field goal, a successful surprise onside kick, and Byron (Bam) Morris's 1-yard touchdown run with 6:36 to play in the game. And when they forced a punt and took possession at their own 32-yard line trailing only 20-17 with 4:15 remaining, it appeared they might have a chance to break the NFC's recent domination in the Super Bowl. But on second down, Brown struck again, intercepting O'Donnell's pass at the 39 and returning it 33 yards to the 6. Two plays later, Smith barreled over from 4 yards out for the clinching touchdown with 3:43 to go. Pittsburgh limited the Cowboys' powerful running game to only 56 yards and enjoyed a whopping 201-61 advantage in total yards in the second half, but could not overcome the 3 interceptions (another came on the game's final play) thrown by O'Donnell, the NFL's career leader for fewest interceptions per pass attempt. In all, O'Donnell completed 28 of 49 passes for 239 yards. Morris rushed for a game-high 73 yards on 19 carries. For Dallas, Aikman completed 15 of 23 pass attempts for 209 yards. The Cowboys' victory was the twelfth in a row for NFC teams over AFC teams in the Super Bowl.

Dallas (NFC)	10	3	7	7	—	27
Pittsburgh (AFC)	0	7	0	10	—	17

Dall — FG Boniol 42 (2:55)
Dall — Novacek 3 pass from Aikman (Boniol kick) (9:37)
Dall — FG Boniol 35 (8:57)
Pitt — Thigpen 6 pass from O'Donnell (N. Johnson kick) (14:47)
Dall — E. Smith 1 run (Boniol kick) (8:18)
Pitt — FG N. Johnson 46 (3:40)
Pitt — Morris 1 run (N. Johnson kick) (8:24)
Dall — E. Smith 4 run (Boniol kick) (11:17)

SUPER BOWL XXIX

Joe Robbie Stadium, Miami, Florida
January 29, 1995, Attendance: 74,107

SAN FRANCISCO 49, SAN DIEGO 26—Steve Young threw a record 6 touchdown passes, and the 49ers became the first team to win five Super Bowls when they routed the Chargers. Young, the game's most valuable player, directed an explosive offense that generated 7 touchdowns, 28 first downs, and 455 total yards. He completed 24 of 36 passes for 325 yards, and broke former 49ers quarterback Joe Montana's previous record of 5 touchdown passes in Super Bowl XXIV. San Francisco wasted little time scoring, taking the lead for good on Young's 44-yard touchdown pass to Jerry Rice only three plays and 1:24 into the game. The next time they had the ball, the 49ers marched 79 yards in four plays, taking a 14-0 lead when Young teamed with running back Ricky Watters on a 51-yard touchdown pass with 10:05 still to play in the opening period. San Diego then put together its most impressive possession of the game, a 13-play, 78-yard drive that consumed more than 7 minutes and was capped by Natrone Means's 1-yard touchdown run, to cut its deficit to 14-7 late in the quarter. But San Francisco countered with a 70-yard drive of its own, and Young's 5-yard touchdown pass to fullback William Floyd made it 21-7. Young's fourth touchdown pass of the half, 8 yards to Watters 4:44 before halftime, increased the advantage to 28-7, and the Chargers could get no closer than 18 points after that. Watters, who ran 9 yards for a touchdown in the third quarter, equaled the Super Bowl record with 3 touchdowns. Rice also scored 3 touchdowns (the second time in his career he'd done that in a Super Bowl) while catching 10 passes for 149 yards. He established career records for receptions, yards, and touchdowns in a Super Bowl. Young, who scrambled 21 yards and 15 yards to set up touchdowns in the first half, was the game's leading rusher with 49 yards on 5 carries. San Diego's Means, who rushed for 1,350 yards during the regular season, was limited to 33 yards on 13 attempts. Chargers quarterback Stan Humphries completed 24 of 49 passes for 275 yards. Rookie Andre Coleman became only the third player in Super Bowl history to return a kickoff for a touchdown, going 98 yards in the third quarter. The 75 points scored by the two teams established another record, breaking the previous mark of 69 set in Dallas's 52-17 victory over Buffalo in XXVII. The 49ers' victory was the eleventh straight for NFC teams over AFC teams in the Super Bowl.

San Diego (AFC)	7	3	8	8	— 26
San Francisco (NFC)	14	14	14	7	— 49

SF — Rice 44 pass from S. Young (Brien kick) (1:24)
SF — Watters 51 pass from S. Young (Brien kick) (4:55)
SD — Means 1 run (Carney kick) (12:16)
SF — Floyd 5 pass from S. Young (Brien kick) (1:58)
SF — Watters 8 pass from S. Young (Brien kick) (10:16)
SD — FG Carney 31 (13:16)
SF — Watters 9 run (Brien kick) (5:25)
SF — Rice 15 pass from S. Young (Brien kick) (11:42)
SD — Coleman 98 kickoff return (Seay pass from Humphries) (11:59)
SF — Rice 7 pass from S. Young (Brien kick) (1:11)
SD — Martin 30 pass from Humphries (Pupunu pass from Humphries) (12:35)

SUPER BOWL XXVIII

Georgia Dome, Atlanta, Georgia
January 30, 1994, Attendance: 72,817

DALLAS 30, BUFFALO 13—Emmitt Smith rushed for 132 yards and 2 second-half touchdowns to power the Cowboys to their second consecutive NFL title. By winning, Dallas joined San Francisco and Pittsburgh as the only franchises with four Super Bowl victories. The Bills, meanwhile, extended a dubious string by losing in the Super Bowl for the fourth consecutive year. To win, the Cowboys had to rally from a 13-6 halftime deficit. Buffalo had forged its lead on Thurman Thomas's 4-yard touchdown run and a pair of field goals by Steve Christie, including a 54-yard kick, the longest in Super Bowl history. But just 55 seconds into the second half, Thomas was stripped of the ball by Dallas defensive tackle Leon Lett. Safety James Washington recovered and weaved his way 46 yards for a touchdown to tie the game at 13-13. After forcing the Bills to punt, the Cowboys began their next possession on their 36-yard line and Smith, the game's most valuable player, took over. He carried 7 times for 61 yards on the ensuing 8-play, 64-yard drive, capping the march with a 15-yard touchdown run to give Dallas the lead for good with 8:42 remaining in the third quarter. Early in the fourth quarter, Washington intercepted Jim Kelly's pass and returned it 12 yards to Buffalo's 34. A penalty moved the ball back to the 39, but Smith carried twice for 10 yards and caught a screen pass for 9, and quarterback Troy Aikman completed a 16-yard pass to Alvin Harper to give the Cowboys a first-and-goal at the 6. Smith took it from there, cracking the end zone on fourth-and-goal from the 1 to put Dallas ahead 27-13 with 9:50 remaining. Eddie Murray's third field goal, from 20 yards with 2:50 left, ended any doubt about the game's outcome. Smith had 30 carries in all, with 19 of his attempts and 92 yards coming after intermission. Washington, normally a reserve who played most of the game because the Cowboys used five defensive backs to combat the Bills' No-Huddle offense, had 11 tackles and forced another fumble by Thomas in the first quarter. Aikman completed 19 of 27 passes for 207 yards. Buffalo's Kelly completed a Super Bowl-record 31 passes in 50 attempts for 260 yards. Dallas, the first team in NFL history to begin the regular season 0-2 and go on to win the Super Bowl, also became the fifth to win back-to-back titles, following Green Bay, Miami, Pittsburgh (the Steelers did it twice), and San Francisco. Buffalo became the third team, along with Minnesota and Denver, to lose four Super Bowls. The Cowboys' victory was the tenth in succession for the NFC over the AFC.

Dallas (NFC)	6	0	14	10	— 30
Buffalo (AFC)	3	10	0	0	— 13

Dall — FG Murray 41 (2:19)
Buff — FG Christie 54 (4:41)
Dall — FG Murray 24 (11:05)
Buff — Thomas 4 run (Christie kick) (2:34)
Buff — FG Christie 28 (15:00)
Dall — Washington 46 fumble return (Murray kick) (0:55)
Dall — E. Smith 15 run (Murray kick) (6:18)
Dall — E. Smith 1 run (Murray kick) (5:10)
Dall — FG Murray 20 (12:10)

SUPER BOWL XXVII

Rose Bowl, Pasadena, California
January 31, 1993, Attendance: 98,374

DALLAS 52, BUFFALO 17—Troy Aikman threw 4 touchdown passes, Emmitt Smith rushed for 108 yards, and the Cowboys converted 9 turnovers into 35 points while coasting to the victory. Dallas's win was its third in its record sixth Super Bowl appearance; the Bills became the first team to drop three in succession. Buffalo led 7-0 until the first 2 of its record number of turnovers helped the Cowboys take the lead for good late in the opening quarter. First, Dallas safety James Washington intercepted a Jim Kelly pass and returned it 13 yards to the Bills' 47, setting up Aikman's 23-yard touchdown pass to tight end Jay Novacek with 1:36 rèmaining in the period. On the next play from scrimmage, Kelly was sacked by Charles Haley and fumbled at the Bills' 2-yard line where the Cowboys' Jimmie Jones picked up the loose ball and ran 2 yards for a touchdown. Dallas, which recovered 5 fumbles and intercepted 4 passes, struck just as quickly late in the first half, when Aikman tossed 19- and 18-yard touchdown passes to Michael Irvin 15 seconds apart to give the Cowboys a 28-10 lead at intermission. The second score was set up when Bills running back Thurman Thomas lost a fumble at his 19-yard line. Buffalo scored for the last time when backup quarterback Frank Reich, playing because Kelly was injured while attempting to pass midway through the second quarter, threw a 40-yard touchdown pass to Don Beebe on the final play of the third period to trim the deficit to 31-17. But Dallas put the game out of reach by scoring three times in a span of 2:33 of the fourth quarter. Aikman, the game's most valuable player, completed 22 of 30 passes for 273 yards. The victory was the ninth in succession for the NFC over the AFC.

Buffalo (AFC)	7	3	7	0	— 17
Dallas (NFC)	14	14	3	21	— 52

Buff — Thomas 2 run (Christie kick) (5:00)
Dall — Novacek 23 pass from Aikman (Elliott kick) (13:24)
Dall — J. Jones 2 fumble recovery return (Elliott kick) (13:39)
Buff — FG Christie 21 (11:36)
Dall — Irvin 19 pass from Aikman (Elliott kick) (13:06)
Dall — Irvin 18 pass from Aikman (Elliott kick) (13:24)
Dall — FG Elliott 20 (6:39)
Buff — Beebe 40 pass from Reich (Christie kick) (15:00)
Dall — Harper 45 pass from Aikman (Elliott kick) (4:56)
Dall — E. Smith 10 run (Elliott kick) (6:48)
Dall — Norton 9 fumble recovery return (Elliott kick) (7:29)

SUPER BOWL XXVI

Metrodome, Minneapolis, Minnesota
January 26, 1992, Attendance: 63,130

WASHINGTON 37, BUFFALO 24—Mark Rypien passed for 292 yards and 2 touchdowns as the Redskins overwhelmed the Bills to win their third Super Bowl in the past 10 years. Rypien, the game's most valuable player, completed 18 of 33 passes, including a 10-yard scoring strike to Earnest Byner and a 30-yard touchdown to Gary Clark. The latter came late in the third quarter after Buffalo had trimmed a 24-0 deficit to 24-10, and effectively put the game out of reach. Washington went on to lead by as much as 37-10 before the Bills made it close wih a pair of touchdowns in the final six minutes. Though the Redskins struggled early, converting their first three drives inside the Bills' 20-yard line into only 3 points, they built a 17-0 halftime lead. And they made it 24-0 just 16 seconds into the second half, after Kurt Gouveia intercepted Buffalo quarterback Jim Kelly's pass on the first play of the third quarter and returned it 23 yards to the Bills' 2. One play later, Gerald Riggs scored his second touchdown of the game to make it 24-0. Kelly, forced to bring Buffalo from behind, completed 28 of a Super Bowl-record 58 passes for 275 yards and 2 touchdowns, but was intercepted 4 times. Bills running back Thurman Thomas, who had an AFC-high 1,407 yards rushing and an NFL-best 2,038 total yards from scrimmage during the regular season, ran for only 13 yards on 10 carries and was limited to 27 yards on 4 receptions. Clark had 7 catches for 114 yards and Art Monk added 7 for 113 for the Redskins, who amassed 417 yards of total offense while limiting the explosive Bills to 283. Washington's Joe Gibbs became only the third head coach to win three Super Bowls.

Washington (NFC)	0	17	14	6	— 37
Buffalo (AFC)	0	0	10	14	— 24

Wash — FG Lohmiller 34 (1:58)
Wash — Byner 10 pass from Rypien (Lohmiller kick) (5:06)
Wash — Riggs 1 run (Lohmiller kick) (7:43)
Wash — Riggs 2 run (Lohmiller kick) (0:16)
Buff — FG Norwood 21 (3:01)
Buff — Thomas 1 run (Norwood kick) (9:02)
Wash — Clark 30 pass from Rypien(Lohmiller kick) (13:36)
Wash — FG Lohmiller 25 (0:06)
Wash — FG Lohmiller 39 (3:24)
Buff — Metzelaars 2 pass from Kelly (Norwood kick) (9:01)
Buff — Beebe 4 pass from Kelly (Norwood kick) (11:05)

SUPER BOWL XXV

Tampa Stadium, Tampa, Florida
January 27, 1991, Attendance: 73,813

NEW YORK GIANTS 20, BUFFALO 19—The NFC champion New York Giants won their second Super Bowl in five years with a 20-19 victory over AFC titlist Buffalo. New York, employing its ball-control offense, had possession for 40 minutes, 33 seconds, a Super Bowl record. The Bills, who scored 95 points in their previous two playoff games leading to Super Bowl XXV, had the ball for less than eight minutes in the second half and just 19:27 for the game. Fourteen of New York's 73 plays came on its initial drive of the third quarter, which covered 75 yards and consumed a Super Bowl-record 9:29 before running back Ottis Anderson ran 1 yard for a touchdown. Giants quarterback Jeff Hostetler kept the long drive going by converting three third-down plays—an 11-yard pass to running back David Meggett on third-and-eight, a 14-yard toss to wide receiver Mark Ingram on third-and-13, and a 9-yard pass to Howard Cross on third-and-four—to give New York a 17-12 lead in the third quarter. Buffalo jumped to a 12-3 lead midway through the second quarter before Hostetler completed a 14-yard scoring strike to wide receiver Stephen Baker to close the score to 12-10 at halftime. Buffalo's Thurman Thomas ran 31 yards for a touchdown on the opening play of the fourth quarter to help Buffalo recapture the lead 19-17. Matt Bahr's

21-yard field goal gave the Giants a 20-19 lead, but Buffalo's Scott Norwood had a chance to win the game with seconds remaining before his 47-yard field-goal attempt sailed wide right. Hostetler completed 20 of 32 passes for 222 yards and 1 touchdown. Anderson rushed 21 times for 102 yards and 1 touchdown to capture the most-valuable-player honors. Thomas totaled 190 scrimmage yards, rushing 15 times for 135 yards and catching 5 passes for 55 yards.

Buffalo (AFC)	3	9	0	7	— 19
N.Y. Giants (NFC)	3	7	7	3	— 20

NYG — FG Bahr 28 (7:46)
Buff — FG Norwood 23 (9:09)
Buff — D. Smith 1 run (Norwood kick) (2:30)
Buff — Safety, B. Smith tackled Hostetler in end zone (6:33)
NYG — Baker 14 pass from Hostetler (Bahr kick) (14:35)
NYG — Anderson 1 run (Bahr kick) (9:29)
Buff — Thomas 31 run (Norwood kick) (0:08)
NYG — FG Bahr 21 (7:40)

SUPER BOWL XXIV

Louisiana Superdome, New Orleans, Louisiana
January 28, 1990, Attendance: 72,919

SAN FRANCISCO 55, DENVER 10—NFC titlist San Francisco won its fourth Super Bowl championship with a 55-10 victory over AFC champion Denver. The 49ers, who also won Super Bowls XVI, XIX, and XXIII, tied the Pittsburgh Steelers for most Super Bowl victories. The Steelers captured Super Bowls IX, X, XIII, and XIV. San Francisco's 55 points broke the previous Super Bowl scoring mark of 46 points by Chicago in Super Bowl XX. San Francisco scored touchdowns on four of its six first-half possessions to hold a 27-3 lead at halftime. Interceptions by Michael Walter and Chet Brooks ended the Broncos' first two possessions of the second half. San Francisco quarterback Joe Montana was named the Super Bowl most valuable player for a record third time. Montana completed 22 of 29 passes for 297 yards and a Super Bowl-record 5 touchdowns. Jerry Rice, Super Bowl XXIII most valuable player, caught 7 passes for 148 yards and three touchdowns. The 49ers' domination included first downs (28 to 12), net yards (461 to 167), and time of possession (39:31 to 20:29).

San Francisco (NFC)	13	14	14	14	— 55
Denver (AFC)	3	0	7	0	— 10

SF — Rice 20 pass from Montana (Cofer kick) (4:54)
Den — FG Treadwell 42 (8:13)
SF — Jones 7 pass from Montana (kick failed) (14:57)
SF — Rathman 1 run (Cofer kick) (7:45)
SF — Rice 38 pass from Montana (Cofer kick) (14:26)
SF — Rice 28 pass from Montana (Cofer kick) (2:12)
SF — Taylor 35 pass from Montana (Cofer kick) (5:16)
Den — Elway 3 run (Treadwell kick) (8:07)
SF — Rathman 3 run (Cofer kick) (0:03)
SF — Craig 1 run (Cofer kick) (1:13)

SUPER BOWL XXIII

Joe Robbie Stadium, Miami, Florida
January 22, 1989, Attendance: 75,129

SAN FRANCISCO 20, CINCINNATI 16—NFC champion San Francisco captured its third Super Bowl of the 1980s by defeating AFC champion Cincinnati 20-16. The 49ers, who also won Super Bowls XVI and XIX, are the first NFC team to win three Super Bowls. Pittsburgh, with four Super Bowl titles (IX, X, XIII, and XIV), and the Oakland/Los Angeles Raiders, with three (XI, XV, and XVIII), lead AFC franchises. Even though San Francisco held an advantage in total net yards (453 to 229), the 49ers found themselves trailing the Bengals late in the game. With the score 13-13, Cincinnati took a 16-13 lead on Jim Breech's 40-yard field goal with 3:20 remaining. It was Breech's third field goal of the day, following earlier successes from 34 and 43 yards. The 49ers started their winning drive at their 8-yard line. Over the next 11 plays, San Francisco covered 92 yards with the decisive score coming on a 10-yard pass from quarterback Joe Montana to wide receiver John Taylor with 34 seconds remaining. At halftime, the score was 3-3, the first time in Super Bowl history the game was tied at intermission. After the teams traded third-period field goals, the Bengals jumped ahead 13-6 on Stanford Jennings's 93-yard kickoff return for a touchdown with 34 seconds remaining in the quarter. The 49ers didn't waste any time coming back as they covered 85 yards in four plays, concluding with Montana's 14-yard scoring pass to Jerry Rice 57 seconds into the final stanza. Rice was named the game's most valuable player after compiling 11 catches for a Super Bowl-record 215 yards. Montana completed 23 of 36 passes for a Super Bowl-record 357 yards and 2 touchdowns.

Cincinnati (AFC)	0	3	10	3	— 16
San Francisco (NFC)	3	0	3	14	— 20

SF — FG Cofer 41 (11:46)
Cin — FG Breech 34 (13:45)
Cin — FG Breech 43 (9:21)
SF — FG Cofer 32 (14:10)
Cin — Jennings 93 kickoff return (Breech kick) (14:26)
SF — Rice 14 pass from Montana (Cofer kick) (0:57)
Cin — FG Breech 40 (11:40)
SF — Taylor 10 pass from Montana (Cofer kick) (14:26)

SUPER BOWL XXII

San Diego Jack Murphy Stadium, San Diego, California
January 31, 1988, Attendance: 73,302

WASHINGTON 42, DENVER 10—NFC champion Washington won Super Bowl XXII and its second NFL championship of the 1980s with a 42-10 decision over AFC champion Denver. The Redskins, who also won Super Bowl XVII, enjoyed a record-setting second quarter en route to the victory. The Broncos broke in front 10-0 when quarterback John Elway threw a 56-yard touchdown pass to wide receiver Ricky Nattiel on the Broncos' first play from scrimmage. Following a Washington punt, Denver's Rich Karlis kicked a 24-yard field goal to cap a seven-play, 61-yard scoring drive. The Redskins then erupted for 35 points on five straight possessions in the second period and coasted thereafter. The 35 points established an NFL postseason mark for most points in a period, bettering the previous total of 21 by San Francisco in Super Bowl XIX and Chicago in Super Bowl XX. Redskins quarterback Doug Williams led the second-period explosion by throwing a Super Bowl record-tying 4 touchdown passes, including 80- and 50-yard passes to wide receiver Ricky Sanders, a 27-yard toss to wide receiver Gary Clark, and an 8-yard pass to tight end Clint Didier. Washington scored 5 touchdowns in 18 plays with total time of possession of only 5:47. Overall, Williams completed 18 of 29 passes for 340 yards and was named the game's most valuable player. His passyardage total eclipsed the Super Bowl record of 331 yards by Joe Montana of San Francisco in Super Bowl XIX. Sanders ended with 193 yards on 8 catches, breaking the previous Super Bowl yardage record of 161 yards by Lynn Swann of Pittsburgh in Game X. Rookie running back Timmy Smith was the game's leading rusher with 22 carries for a Super Bowl-record 204 yards, breaking the previous mark of 191 yards by Marcus Allen of the Raiders in Game XVIII. Smith also scored twice on runs of 58 and 4 yards. Washington's 6 touchdowns and 602 total yards gained also set Super Bowl records. Redskins cornerback Barry Wilburn had 2 of the team's 3 interceptions, and strong safety Alvin Walton had 2 of Washington's 5 sacks.

Washington (NFC)	0	35	0	7	— 42
Denver (AFC)	10	0	0	0	— 10

Den — Nattiel 56 pass from Elway (Karlis kick) (1:57)
Den — FG Karlis 24 (5:51)
Wash — Sanders 80 pass from Williams (Haji-Sheikh kick) (0:53)
Wash — Clark 27 pass from Williams (Haji-Sheikh kick) (4:45)
Wash — Smith 58 run (Haji-Sheikh kick) (8:33)
Wash — Sanders 50 pass from Williams (Haji-Sheikh kick) (11:18)
Wash — Didier 8 pass from Williams (Haji-Sheikh kick) (13:56)
Wash — Smith 4 run (Haji-Sheikh kick) (1:51)

SUPER BOWL XXI

Rose Bowl, Pasadena, California
January 25, 1987, Attendance: 101,063

NEW YORK GIANTS 39, DENVER 20—The NFC champion New York Giants captured their first NFL title since 1956 when they downed the AFC champion Denver Broncos 39-20 in Super Bowl XXI. The victory marked the NFC's fifth NFL title in the past six seasons. The Broncos, behind the passing of quarterback John Elway, who was 13 of 20 for 187 yards in the first half, held a 10-9 lead at intermission, the narrowest halftime margin in Super Bowl history. Denver's Rich Karlis opened the scoring with a Super Bowl record-tying 48-yard field goal. New York drove 78 yards in nine plays on the next series to take a 7-3 lead on quarterback Phil Simms's 6-yard touchdown pass to tight end Zeke Mowatt. The Broncos came right back with a 58-yard scoring drive on six plays capped by Elway's 4-yard touchdown run. The only scoring in the second period was the sack of Elway in the end zone by defensive end George Martin for a New York safety. The Giants produced a key defensive stand early in the second quarter when the Broncos had a first down at the New York 1-yard line, but failed to score on three running plays and Karlis's 23-yard missed field-goal attempt. The Giants took command of the game in the third period en route to a 30-point second half, the most ever scored in one half of Super Bowl play. New York took the lead for good on tight end Mark Bavaro's 13-yard touchdown catch 4:52 into the third period. The nine-play, 63-yard scoring drive included the successful conversion of a fourth-and-1 play on the New York 46-yard line. Denver was limited to only 2 net yards on 10 offensive plays in the third period. Simms set Super Bowl records for most consecutive completions (10) and highest completion percentage (88 percent on 22 completions in 25 attempts). He also passed for 268 yards and 3 touchdowns and was named the game's most valuable player. New York running back Joe Morris was the game's leading rusher with 20 carries for 67 yards. Denver wide receiver Vance Johnson led all receivers with 5 catches for 121 yards. The Giants defeated their three playoff opponents by a cumulative total of 82 points (New York 105, opponents 23), the largest such margin by a Super Bowl winner.

Denver (AFC)	10	0	0	10	— 20
N.Y. Giants (NFC)	7	2	17	13	— 39

Den — FG Karlis 48 (4:09)
NYG — Mowatt 6 pass from Simms (Allegre kick) (9:33)
Den — Elway 4 run (Karlis kick) (12:54)
NYG — Safety, Martin tackled Elway in end zone (12:14)
NYG — Bavaro 13 pass from Simms (Allegre kick) (4:52)
NYG — FG Allegre 21 (11:06)
NYG — Morris 1 run (Allegre kick) (14:36)
NYG — McConkey 6 pass from Simms (Allegre kick) (4:04)
Den — FG Karlis 28 (8:59)
NYG — Anderson 2 run (kick failed) (10:42)
Den — V. Johnson 47 pass from Elway (Karlis kick) (12:54)

SUPER BOWL XX

Louisiana Superdome, New Orleans, Louisiana
January 26, 1986, Attendance: 73,818

CHICAGO 46, NEW ENGLAND 10—The NFC champion Chicago Bears, seeking their first NFL title since 1963, scored a Super Bowl-record 46 points in downing AFC champion New England 46-10 in Super Bowl XX. The previous record for most points in a Super Bowl was 38, shared by San Francisco in XIX and the Los Angeles Raiders in XVIII. The Bears' league-leading defense tied the Super Bowl record for sacks (7) and limited the Patriots to a record-low 7 rushing yards. New England took the quickest lead in Super Bowl history when Tony Franklin kicked a 36-yard field goal with 1:19 elapsed in the first period. The score came about because of Larry McGrew's fumble recovery at the Chicago 19-yard line. However, the Bears rebounded for a 23-3 first-half lead, while building a yardage advantage of 236 total yards to New England's minus 19. Running back Matt Suhey rushed 8 times for 37 yards, including an 11-yard touchdown run, and caught 1 pass for 24 yards in the first half. After the Patriots first drive of the second half ended with a punt to the Bears' 4-yard line, Chicago marched 96 yards in nine plays with quarterback Jim McMahon's 1-yard scoring run capping the drive. McMahon became the first quarterback in Super Bowl history to rush for a pair of touchdowns. The Bears completed their scoring via a 28-yard interception return by reserve cornerback Reggie Phillips, a 1-yard run by defensive tackle/fullback William Perry, and a safety when defensive end Henry Waechter tackled Patriots quarterback Steve Grogan in the end zone. Bears defensive end Richard Dent became the fourth defender to be named the game's most valuable player after contributing 1½ sacks. The Bears' victory margin of 36 points was the largest in Super Bowl history, bettering the previous mark of 29 by the Los Angeles Raiders when they topped Washington 38-9 in Game XVIII. McMahon completed 12 of 20 passes for 256 yards before leaving the game in the fourth period with a wrist injury. The NFL's all-time leading rusher, Bears running back Walter Payton, carried 22 times for 61 yards. Wide receiver Willie Gault caught 4 passes for 129 yards, the fourth-most receiving yards in a Super Bowl. Chicago coach Mike Ditka became the second man (Tom Flores of Raiders was the other) who played in a Super Bowl and coached a team to a victory in the game.

Chicago (NFC)	13	10	21	2	— 46
New England (AFC)	3	0	0	7	— 10

NE — FG Franklin 36 (1:19)
Chi — FG Butler 28 (5:40)
Chi — FG Butler 24 (13:34)
Chi — Suhey 11 run (Butler kick) (14:37)
Chi — McMahon 2 run (Butler kick) (7:36)
Chi — FG Butler 24 (15:00)
Chi — McMahon 1 run (Butler kick) (7:38)
Chi — Phillips 28 interception return (Butler kick) (8:44)
Chi — Perry 1 run (Butler kick) (11:38)
NE — Fryar 8 pass from Grogan (Franklin kick) (1:46)
Chi — Safety, Waechter tackled Grogan in end zone (9:24)

SUPER BOWL XIX

Stanford Stadium, Stanford, California
January 20, 1985, Attendance: 84,059

SAN FRANCISCO 38, MIAMI 16—The San Francisco 49ers captured their second Super Bowl title with a dominating offense and a defense that tamed Miami's explosive passing attack. The Dolphins held a 10-7 lead at the end of the first period, which represented the most points scored by two teams in an opening quarter of a Super Bowl. However, the 49ers used excellent field position in the second period to build a 28-16 halftime lead. Running back Roger Craig set a Super Bowl record by scoring 3 touchdowns on pass receptions of 8 and 16 yards and a run of 2 yards. San Francisco's Joe Montana was voted the game's most valuable player. He joined Green Bay's Bart Starr and Pittsburgh's Terry Bradshaw as the only two-time Super Bowl most valuable players. Montana completed 24 of 35 passes for a Super Bowl-record 331 yards and 3 touchdowns, and rushed 5 times for 59 yards, including a 6-yard touchdown. Craig had 58 yards on 15 carries and caught 7 passes for 77 yards. Wendell Tyler rushed 13 times for 65 yards and had 4 catches for 70 yards. Dwight Clark had 6 receptions for 77 yards, while Russ Francis had 5 for 60. San Francisco's 537 total net yards bettered the previous Super Bowl record of 429 yards by Oakland in Super Bowl XI. The 49ers also held a time of possession advantage over the Dolphins of 37:11 to 22:49.

Miami (AFC)	10	6	0	0	— 16
San Francisco (NFC)	7	21	10	0	— 38

Mia — FG von Schamann 37 (7:36)
SF — Monroe 33 pass from Montana (Wersching kick) (11:48)
Mia — D. Johnson 2 pass from Marino (von Schamann kick) (14:15)
SF — Craig 8 pass from Montana (Wersching kick) (3:26)
SF — Montana 6 run (Wersching kick) (8:02)
SF — Craig 2 run (Wersching kick) (12:55)
Mia — FG von Schamann 31 (14:48)
Mia — FG von Schamann 30 (15:00)
SF — FG Wersching 27 (4:48)
SF — Craig 16 pass from Montana (Wersching kick) (8:42)

SUPER BOWL XVIII

Tampa Stadium, Tampa, Florida
January 22, 1984, Attendance: 72,920

LOS ANGELES RAIDERS 38, WASHINGTON 9—The Los Angeles Raiders dominated the Washington Redskins from the beginning in Super Bowl XVIII and achieved the most lopsided victory in Super Bowl history, surpassing Green Bay's 35-10 win over Kansas City in Super Bowl I. The Raiders took a 7-0 lead 4:52 into the game when Derrick Jensen blocked a Jeff Hayes punt and recovered it in the end zone for a touchdown. With 9:14 remaining in the first half, Raiders quarterback Jim Plunkett threw a 12-yard touchdown pass to wide receiver Cliff Branch to complete a three-play, 65-yard drive. Washington cut the Raiders' lead to 14-3 on a 24-yard field goal by Mark Moseley. With seven seconds left in the first half, Raiders linebacker Jack Squirek intercepted a Joe Theismann pass at the Redskins' 5-yard line and ran it in for a touchdown to give Los Angeles a 21-3 halftime lead. In the third period, running back Marcus Allen, who rushed for a Super Bowl-record 191 yards on 20 carries, increased the Raiders' lead to 35-9 on touchdown runs of 5 and 74 yards, the latter erasing the Super Bowl record of 58 yards set by Baltimore's Tom Matte in Game III. Allen was named the game's most valuable player. The victory over Washington raised Raiders coach Tom Flores' playoff record to 8-1, including a 27-10 win against Philadelphia in Super Bowl XV. The 38 points scored by the Raiders were the highest total by a Super Bowl team. The previous high was 35 points by Green Bay in Game I.

Washington (NFC)	0	3	6	0	— 9
L.A. Raiders (AFC)	7	14	14	3	— 38

Raiders — Jensen recovered blocked punt in end zone (Bahr kick) (4:52)
Raiders — Branch 12 pass from Plunkett (Bahr kick) (5:46)
Wash — FG Moseley 24 (11:55)
Raiders — Squirek 5 interception return (Bahr kick) (14:53)
Wash — Riggins 1 run (kick blocked) (4:08)
Raiders — Allen 5 run (Bahr kick) (7:54)
Raiders — Allen 74 run (Bahr kick) (15:00)
Raiders — FG Bahr 21 (12:36)

SUPER BOWL XVII

Rose Bowl, Pasadena, California
January 30, 1983, Attendance: 103,667

WASHINGTON 27, MIAMI 17—Fullback John Riggins ran for a Super Bowl-record 166 yards on 38 carries to spark Washington to a 27-17 victory over AFC champion Miami. It was Riggins's fourth straight 100-yard rushing game during the playoffs, also a record. The win marked Washington's first NFL title since 1942, and was only the second time in Super Bowl history NFL/NFC teams scored consecutive victories (Green Bay did it in Super Bowls I and II and San Francisco won Super Bowl XVI). The Redskins, under second-year head coach Joe Gibbs, used a balanced offense that accounted for 400 total yards (a Super Bowl-record 276 yards rushing and 124 passing), second in Super Bowl history to 429 yards by Oakland in Super Bowl XI. The Dolphins built a 17-10 halftime lead on a 76-yard touchdown pass from quarterback David Woodley to wide receiver Jimmy Cefalo 6:49 into the first period, a 20-yard field goal by Uwe von Schamann with 6:00 left in the half, and a Super Bowl-record 98-yard kickoff return by Fulton Walker with 1:38 remaining. Washington had tied the score at 10-10 with 1:51 left on a four-yard touchdown pass from Joe Theismann to wide receiver Alvin Garrett. Mark Moseley started the Redskins' scoring with a 31-yard field goal late in the first period, and added a 20-yarder midway through the third period to cut the Dolphins' lead to 17-13. Riggins, who was voted the game's most valuable player, gave Washington its first lead of the game with 10:01 left when he ran 43 yards off left tackle for a touchdown in a fourth-and-1 situation. Wide receiver Charlie Brown caught a six-yard scoring pass from Theismann with 1:55 left to complete the scoring. The Dolphins managed only 176 yards (142 in first half). Theismann completed 15 of 23 passes for 143 yards, with 2 touchdowns and 2 interceptions. For Miami, Woodley was 4 of 14 for 97 yards, with 1 touchdown, and 1 interception. Don Strock was 0 for 3 in relief.

Miami (AFC)	7	10	0	0	— 17
Washington (NFC)	0	10	3	14	— 27

Mia — Cefalo 76 pass from Woodley (von Schamann kick) (6:49)
Wash — FG Moseley 31 (0:21)
Mia — FG von Schamann 20 (9:00)
Wash — Garrett 4 pass from Theismann (Moseley kick) (13:09)
Mia — Walker 98 kickoff return (von Schamann kick) (13:22)
Wash — FG Moseley 20 (6:51)
Wash — Riggins 43 run (Moseley kick) (4:59)
Wash — Brown 6 pass from Theismann (Moseley kick) (13:05)

SUPER BOWL XVI

Pontiac Silverdome, Pontiac, Michigan
January 24, 1982, Attendance: 81,270

SAN FRANCISCO 26, CINCINNATI 21—Ray Wersching's Super Bowl record-tying 4 field goals and Joe Montana's controlled passing helped lift the San Francisco 49ers to their first NFL championship with a 26-21 victory over Cincinnati. The 49ers built a game-record 20-0 halftime lead via Montana's 1-yard touchdown run, which capped an 11-play, 68-yard drive; fullback Earl Cooper's 11-yard scoring-pass from Montana, which climaxed a Super Bowl record 92-yard drive on 12 plays; and Wersching's 22- and 26-yard field goals. The Bengals rebounded in the second half, closing the gap to 20-14 on quarterback Ken Anderson's 5-yard run and Dan Ross's 4-yard reception from Anderson, who established Super Bowl passing records for completions (25) and completion percentage (73.5 percent on 25 of 34). Wersching added early fourth-period field goals of 40 and 23 yards to increase the 49ers' lead to 26-14. The Bengals managed to score on an Anderson-to-Ross 3-yard pass with only 16 seconds remaining. Ross set a Super Bowl record with 11 receptions for 104 yards. Montana, the game's most valuable player, completed 14 of 22 passes for 157 yards. Cincinnati compiled 356 yards to San Francisco's 275, which marked the first time in Super Bowl history that the team that gained the most yards from scrimmage lost the game.

San Francisco (NFC)	7	13	0	6	— 26
Cincinnati (AFC)	0	0	7	14	— 21

SF — Montana 1 run (Wersching kick) (9:08)
SF — Cooper 11 pass from Montana (Wersching kick) (8:07)
SF — FG Wersching 22 (14:45)
SF — FG Wersching 26 (14:58)
Cin — Anderson 5 run (Breech kick) (3:35)

Cin — Ross 4 pass from Anderson (Breech kick) (4:54)
SF — FG Wersching 40 (9:35)
SF — FG Wersching 23 (13:03)
Cin — Ross 3 pass from Anderson (Breech kick) (14:44)

SUPER BOWL XV

Louisiana Superdome, New Orleans, Louisiana
January 25, 1981, Attendance: 76,135

OAKLAND 27, PHILADELPHIA 10—Jim Plunkett threw 3 touchdown passes, including an 80-yard strike to Kenny King, as the Raiders became the first wild-card team to win the Super Bowl. Plunkett's touchdown bomb to King—the longest play in Super Bowl history—gave Oakland a decisive 14-0 lead with nine seconds left in the first period. Linebacker Rod Martin had set up Oakland's first touchdown, a 2-yard reception by Cliff Branch, with a 17-yard interception return to the Eagles' 30-yard line. The Eagles never recovered from that early deficit, managing only a Tony Franklin field goal (30 yards) and an 8-yard touchdown pass from Ron Jaworski to Keith Krepfle. Plunkett, who became a starter in the sixth game of the season, completed 13 of 21 for 261 yards and was named the game's most valuable player. Oakland won 9 of 11 games with Plunkett starting, but that was good enough only for second place in the AFC West, although they tied division winner San Diego with an 11-5 record. The Raiders, who had previously won Super Bowl XI over Minnesota, had to win three playoff games to get to the championship game. Oakland defeated Houston 27-7 at home followed by road victories over Cleveland (14-12) and San Diego (34-27). Oakland's Mark van Eeghen was the game's leading rusher with 75 yards on 18 carries. Philadelphia's Wilbert Montgomery led all receivers with 6 receptions for 91 yards. Branch had 5 for 67 and Harold Carmichael of Philadelphia 5 for 83. Martin finished the game with 3 interceptions, a Super Bowl record.

Oakland (AFC)	14	0	10	3	—	27
Philadelphia (NFC)	0	3	0	7	—	10

Oak — Branch 2 pass from Plunkett (Bahr kick) (6:04)
Oak — King 80 pass from Plunkett (Bahr kick) (14:51)
Phil — FG Franklin 30 (4:32)
Oak — Branch 29 pass from Plunkett (Bahr kick) (2:36)
Oak — FG Bahr 46 (10:25)
Phil — Krepfle 8 pass from Jaworski (Franklin kick) (1:01)
Oak — FG Bahr 35 (6:31)

SUPER BOWL XIV

Rose Bowl, Pasadena, California
January 20, 1980, Attendance: 103,985

PITTSBURGH 31, LOS ANGELES 19—Terry Bradshaw completed 14 of 21 passes for 309 yards and set two passing records as the Steelers became the first team to win four Super Bowls. Despite 3 interceptions by the Rams, Bradshaw kept his poise and brought the Steelers from behind twice in the second half. Trailing 13-10 at halftime, Pittsburgh went ahead 17-13 when Bradshaw hit Lynn Swann with a 47-yard touchdown pass after 2:48 of the third quarter. On the Rams' next possession Vince Ferragamo, who completed 15 of 25 passes for 212 yards, responded with a 50-yard pass to Billy Waddy that moved Los Angeles from its 26 to the Steelers' 24. On the following play, Lawrence McCutcheon connected with Ron Smith on a halfback option pass that gave the Rams a 19-17 lead. On Pittsburgh's initial possession of the final period, Bradshaw lofted a 73-yard scoring pass to John Stallworth to put the Steelers in front to stay 24-19. Franco Harris scored on a 1-yard run later in the quarter to seal the verdict. A 45-yard pass from Bradshaw to Stallworth was the key play in the drive to Harris's score. Bradshaw, the game's most valuable player for the second straight year, set career Super Bowl records for most touchdown passes (9) and most passing yards (932). Larry Anderson gave the Steelers excellent field position throughout the game with 5 kickoff returns for a record 162 yards.

Los Angeles (NFC)	7	6	6	0	—	19
Pittsburgh (AFC)	3	7	7	14	—	31

Pitt — FG Bahr 41 (7:29)
LA — Bryant 1 run (Corral kick) (12:16)
Pitt — Harris 1 run (Bahr kick) (2:08)
LA — FG Corral 31 (7:39)
LA — FG Corral 45 (14:46)
Pitt — Swann 47 pass from Bradshaw (Bahr kick) (2:48)
LA — Smith 24 pass from McCutcheon (kick failed) (4:45)
Pitt — Stallworth 73 pass from Bradshaw (Bahr kick) (2:56)
Pitt — Harris 1 run (Bahr kick) (13:11)

SUPER BOWL XIII

Orange Bowl, Miami, Florida
January 21, 1979, Attendance: 79,484

PITTSBURGH 35, DALLAS 31—Terry Bradshaw threw a record 4 touchdown passes to lead the Steelers to victory. The Steelers became the first team to win three Super Bowls, mostly because of Bradshaw's accurate arm. Bradshaw, voted the game's most valuable player, completed 17 of 30 passes for 318 yards, a personal high. Four of those passes went for touchdowns—2 to John Stallworth and the third, with 26 seconds remaining in the second period, to Rocky Bleier for a 21-14 halftime lead. The Cowboys scored twice before intermission on Roger Staubach's 39-yard pass to Tony Hill and a 37-yard fumble return by linebacker Mike Hegman, who stole the ball from Bradshaw. The Steelers broke open the contest with 2 touchdowns in a span of 19 seconds midway through the final period. Franco Harris rambled 22 yards up the middle to give the Steelers a 28-17 lead with 7:10 left. Pittsburgh got the ball right back when Randy White fumbled the kickoff and Dennis Winston recovered for the Steelers. On first down, Bradshaw fired his fourth touchdown pass, an 18-yard pass to Lynn Swann to boost the Steelers' lead to 35-17 with 6:51 to play. The Cowboys refused to let the Steelers run away with the contest. Staubach connected with Billy Joe DuPree on a 7-yard scoring pass with 2:23 left. Then the Cowboys recovered an onside kick and Staubach took them in for another score, passing 4 yards to Butch Johnson with 22 seconds remaining. Bleier recovered another onside kick with 17 seconds left to seal the victory for the Steelers.

Pittsburgh (AFC)	7	14	0	14	—	35
Dallas (NFC)	7	7	3	14	—	31

Pitt — Stallworth 28 pass from Bradshaw (Gerela kick) (5:13)
Dall — Hill 39 pass from Staubach (Septien kick) (15:00)
Dall — Hegman 37 fumble recovery return (Septien kick) (2:52)
Pitt — Stallworth 75 pass from Bradshaw (Gerela kick) (4:35)
Pitt — Bleier 7 pass from Bradshaw (Gerela kick) (14:34)
Dall — FG Septien 27 (12:24)
Pitt — Harris 22 run (Gerela kick) (7:50)
Pitt — Swann 18 pass from Bradshaw (Gerela kick) (8:09)
Dall — DuPree 7 pass from Staubach (Septien kick) (12:37)
Dall — B. Johnson 4 pass from Staubach (Septien kick) (14:38)

SUPER BOWL XII

Louisiana Superdome, New Orleans, Louisiana
January 15, 1978, Attendance: 75,583

DALLAS 27, DENVER 10—The Cowboys evened their Super Bowl record at 2-2 by defeating Denver before a sellout crowd of 75,583, plus 102,010,000 television viewers, the largest audience ever to watch a sporting event. Dallas converted 2 interceptions into 10 points and Efren Herrera added a 35-yard field goal for a 13-0 halftime advantage. In the third period Craig Morton engineered a drive to the Cowboys' 30 and Jim Turner's 47-yard field goal made the score 13-3. After an exchange of punts, Butch Johnson made a spectacular diving catch in the end zone to complete a 45-yard pass from Roger Staubach and put the Cowboys ahead 20-3. Following Rick Upchurch's 67-yard kickoff return, Norris Weese guided the Broncos to a touchdown to cut the Dallas lead to 20-10. Dallas clinched the victory when running back Robert Newhouse threw a 29-yard touchdown pass to Golden Richards with 7:04 remaining in the game. It was the first pass thrown by Newhouse since 1975. Harvey Martin and Randy White, who were named co-most valuable players, led the Cowboys' defense, which recovered 4 fumbles and intercepted 4 passes.

Dallas (NFC)	10	3	7	7	—	27
Denver (AFC)	0	0	10	0	—	10

Dall — Dorsett 3 run (Herrera kick) (10:31)
Dall — FG Herrera 35 (13:29)
Dall — FG Herrera 43 (3:44)
Den — FG Turner 47 (2:28)
Dall — Johnson 45 pass from Staubach (Herrera kick) (8:01)
Den — Lytle 1 run (Turner kick) (9:21)
Dall — Richards 29 pass from Newhouse (Herrera kick) (7:56)

SUPER BOWL XI

Rose Bowl, Pasadena, California
January 9, 1977, Attendance: 103,438

OAKLAND 32, MINNESOTA 14—The Raiders won their first NFL championship before a record Super Bowl crowd plus 81 million television viewers, the largest audience ever to watch a sporting event. The Raiders gained a record-breaking 429 yards, including running back Clarence Davis's 137 rushing yards. Wide receiver Fred Biletnikoff made 4 key receptions, which earned him the game's most valuable player trophy. Oakland scored on three successive possessions in the second quarter to build a 16-0 halftime lead. Errol Mann's 24-yard field goal opened the scoring, then the AFC champions put together drives of 64 and 35 yards, scoring on a 1-yard pass from Ken Stabler to Dave Casper and a 1-yard run by Pete Banaszak. The Raiders increased their lead to 19-0 on a 40-yard field goal in the third quarter, but Minnesota responded with a 12-play, 58-yard drive late in the period, with Fran Tarkenton passing 8 yards to wide receiver Sammy White to cut the deficit to 19-7. Two fourth-quarter interceptions clinched the title for the Raiders. One set up Banaszak's second touchdown run, the other resulted in cornerback Willie Brown's Super Bowl-record 75-yard interception return.

Oakland (AFC)	0	16	3	13	—	32
Minnesota (NFC)	0	0	7	7	—	14

Oak — FG Mann 24 (0:48)
Oak — Casper 1 pass from Stabler (Mann kick) (7:50)
Oak — Banaszak 1 run (kick failed) (11:27)
Oak — FG Mann 40 (9:44)
Minn — S. White 8 pass from Tarkenton (Cox kick) (14:13)
Oak — Banaszak 2 run (Mann kick) (7:21)
Oak — Brown 75 interception return (kick failed) (9:17)
Minn — Voigt 13 pass from Lee (Cox kick) (14:35)

SUPER BOWL X

Orange Bowl, Miami, Florida
January 18, 1976, Attendance: 80,187

PITTSBURGH 21, DALLAS 17—The Steelers won the Super Bowl for the second year in a row on Terry Bradshaw's 64-yard touchdown pass to Lynn Swann and an aggressive defense that snuffed out a late rally by the Cowboys with an end-zone interception on the final play of the game. In the fourth quarter, Pittsburgh ran on fourth down and gave up the ball on the Cowboys' 39 with 1:22 to play. Roger Staubach ran and passed for 2 first downs but his last desperation pass was picked off by Glen

Edwards. Dallas's scoring was the result of 2 touchdown passes by Staubach, one to Drew Pearson for 29 yards and the other to Percy Howard for 34 yards. Toni Fritsch had a 36-yard field goal. The Steelers scored on 2 touchdown passes by Bradshaw, 1 to Randy Grossman for 7 yards and the long bomb to Swann. Roy Gerela had 36- and 18-yard field goals. Reggie Harrison blocked a punt through the end zone for a safety. Swann set a Super Bowl record by gaining 161 yards on his 4 receptions.

Dallas (NFC)	7	3	0	7	— 17
Pittsburgh (AFC)	7	0	0	14	— 21

Dall — D. Pearson 29 pass from Staubach (Fritsch kick) (4:36)
Pitt — Grossman 7 pass from Bradshaw (Gerela kick) (9:03)
Dall — FG Fritsch 36 (0:15)
Pitt — Safety, Harrison blocked Hoopes's punt through end zone (3:32)
Pitt — FG Gerela 36 (6:19)
Pitt — FG Gerela 18 (8:23)
Pitt — Swann 64 pass from Bradshaw (kick failed) (11:58)
Dall — P. Howard 34 pass from Staubach (Fritsch kick) (13:12)

SUPER BOWL IX

Tulane Stadium, New Orleans, Louisiana
January 12, 1975, Attendance: 80,997

PITTSBURGH 16, MINNESOTA 6—AFC champion Pittsburgh, in its initial Super Bowl appearance, and NFC champion Minnesota, making a third bid for its first Super Bowl title, struggled through a first half in which the only score was produced by the Steelers' defense when Dwight White downed Vikings' quarterback Fran Tarkenton in the end zone for a safety 7:49 into the second period. The Steelers forced another break and took advantage on the second-half kickoff when Minnesota's Bill Brown fumbled and Marv Kellum recovered for Pittsburgh on the Vikings' 30. After Rocky Bleier failed to gain on first down, Franco Harris carried 3 consecutive times for 24 yards, a loss of 3, and a 9-yard touchdown and a 9-0 lead. Though its offense was completely stymied by Pittsburgh's defense, Minnesota managed to move into a threatening position after 4:27 of the final period when Matt Blair blocked Bobby Walden's punt and Terry Brown recovered the ball in the end zone for a touchdown. Fred Cox's kick failed and the Steelers led 9-6. Pittsburgh wasted no time putting the victory away. The Steelers took the ensuing kickoff and marched 66 yards in 11 plays, climaxed by Terry Bradshaw's 4-yard scoring pass to Larry Brown with 3:31 left. Pittsburgh's defense permitted Minnesota only 119 yards total offense, including a Super Bowl low of 17 rushing yards. The Steelers, meanwhile, gained 333 yards, including Harris's record 158 yards on 34 carries.

Pittsburgh (AFC)	0	2	7	7	— 16
Minnesota (NFC)	0	0	0	6	— 6

Pitt — Safety, White downed Tarkenton in end zone (7:49)
Pitt — Harris 9 run (Gerela kick) (1:35)
Minn — T. Brown recovered blocked punt in end zone (kick failed) (4:27)
Pitt — L. Brown 4 pass from Bradshaw (Gerela kick) (11:29)

SUPER BOWL VIII

Rice Stadium, Houston, Texas
January 13, 1974, Attendance: 71,882

MIAMI 24, MINNESOTA 7—The defending NFL champion Dolphins, representing the AFC for the third straight year, scored the first two times they had possession on marches of 62 and 56 yards while the Miami defense limited the Vikings to only seven plays in the first period. Larry Csonka climaxed the initial 10-play drive with a 5-yard touchdown bolt through right guard after 5:27 had elapsed. Four plays later, Miami began another 10-play scoring drive, which ended with Jim Kiick bursting 1 yard through the middle for another touchdown after 13:38 of the period. Garo Yepremian added a 28-yard field goal midway in the second period for a 17-0 Miami lead. Minnesota then drove from its 20 to a second-and-2 situation on the Miami 7 yard line with 1:18 left in the half. But on two plays, Miami limited Oscar Reed to 1 yard. On fourth-and-1 from the 6, Reed went over right tackle, but Dolphins middle linebacker Nick Buoniconti jarred the ball loose and Jake Scott recovered for Miami to halt the Minnesota threat. The Vikings were unable to muster enough offense in the second half to threaten the Dolphins. Csonka rushed 33 times for a Super Bowl-record 145 yards. Bob Griese of Miami completed 6 of 7 passes for 73 yards.

Minnesota (NFC)	0	0	0	7	— 7
Miami (AFC)	14	3	7	0	— 24

Mia — Csonka 5 run (Yepremian kick) (9:33)
Mia — Kiick 1 run (Yepremian kick) (13:38)
Mia — FG Yepremian 28 (8:58)
Mia — Csonka 2 run (Yepremian kick) (6:16)
Minn — Tarkenton 4 run (Cox kick) (1:35)

SUPER BOWL VII

Memorial Coliseum, Los Angeles, California
January 14, 1973, Attendance: 90,182

MIAMI 14, WASHINGTON 7—The Dolphins played virtually perfect football in the first half as their defense permitted the Redskins to cross midfield only once and their offense turned good field position into 2 touchdowns. On its third possession, Miami opened its first scoring drive from the Dolphins' 37 yard line. An 18-yard pass from Bob Griese to Paul Warfield preceded by three plays Griese's 28-yard touchdown pass to Howard Twilley. After Washington moved from its 17 to the Miami 48 with two minutes remaining in the first half, Dolphins linebacker Nick Buoniconti intercepted a Billy Kilmer pass at the Miami 41 and returned it to the Washington 27. Jim Kiick ran for 3 yards, Larry Csonka for 3, Griese passed to Jim Mandich for 19, and Kiick gained 1 to the 1-yard line. With 18 seconds left until intermission, Kiick scored from the 1. Washington's only touchdown came with 2:07 left in the game and resulted from a misplayed field-goal attempt and fumble by Garo Yepremian, with the Redskins' Mike Bass picking the ball out of the air and running 49 yards for the score. Dolphins safety Jake Scott, who had 2 interceptions, including 1 in the end zone to kill a Redskins' drive, was voted the game's most valuable player.

Miami (AFC)	7	7	0	0	— 14
Washington (NFC)	0	0	0	7	— 7

Mia — Twilley 28 pass from Griese (Yepremian kick) (14:59)
Mia — Kiick 1 run (Yepremian kick) (14:42)
Wash — Bass 49 fumble recovery return (Knight kick) (12:53)

SUPER BOWL VI

Tulane Stadium, New Orleans, Louisiana
January 16, 1972, Attendance: 81,023

DALLAS 24, MIAMI 3—The Cowboys rushed for a record 252 yards and their defense limited the Dolphins to a low of 185 yards while not permitting a touchdown for the first time in Super Bowl history. Dallas converted Chuck Howley's recovery of Larry Csonka's first fumble of the season into a 3-0 advantage and led at halftime 10-3. After Dallas received the second-half kickoff, Duane Thomas led a 71-yard march in eight plays for a 17-3 margin. Howley intercepted Bob Griese's pass at the 50 and returned it to the Miami 9 early in the fourth period, and three plays later Roger Staubach passed 7 yards to Mike Ditka for the final touchdown. Thomas rushed for 95 yards and Walt Garrison gained 74. Staubach, voted the game's most valuable player, completed 12 of 19 passes for 119 yards and 2 touchdowns.

Dallas (NFC)	3	7	7	7	— 24
Miami (AFC)	0	3	0	0	— 3

Dall — FG Clark 9 (13:37)
Dall — Alworth 7 pass from Staubach (Clark kick) (13:45)
Mia — FG Yepremian 31 (14:56)
Dall — D. Thomas 3 run (Clark kick) (5:17)
Dall — Ditka 7 pass from Staubach (Clark kick) (3:18)

SUPER BOWL V

Orange Bowl, Miami, Florida
January 17, 1971, Attendance: 79,204

BALTIMORE 16, DALLAS 13—A 32-yard field goal by rookie kicker Jim O'Brien brought the Baltimore Colts a victory over the Dallas Cowboys in the final five seconds of Super Bowl V. The game between the champions of the AFC and NFC was played on artificial turf for the first time. Dallas led13-6 at the half but interceptions by Rick Volk and Mike Curtis set up a Baltimore touchdown and O'Brien's decisive kick in the fourth period. Earl Morrall relieved an injured Johnny Unitas late in the firsthalf, although Unitas completed the Colts' only scoring pass. It caromed off receiver Eddie Hinton's fingertips, off Dallas defensive back Mel Renfro, and finally settled into the grasp of John Mackey, who went 45 yards to score on a 75-yard play.

Baltimore (AFC)	0	6	0	10	— 16
Dallas (NFC)	3	10	0	0	— 13

Dall — FG Clark 14 (9:28)
Dall — FG Clark 30 (0:08)
Balt — Mackey 75 pass from Unitas (kick blocked) (0:05)
Dall — Thomas 7 pass from Morton (Clark kick) (7:07)
Balt — Nowatzke 2 run (O'Brien kick) (7:25)
Balt — FG O'Brien 32 (14:55)

SUPER BOWL IV

Tulane Stadium, New Orleans, Louisiana
January 11, 1970, Attendance: 80,562

KANSAS CITY 23, MINNESOTA 7—The AFL squared the Super Bowl at two games apiece with the NFL, building a 16-0 halftime lead behind Len Dawson's superb quarterbacking and a powerful defense. Dawson, the fourth consecutive quarterback to be chosen the Super Bowl's top player, called an almost flawless game, completing 12 of 17 passes and hitting Otis Taylor on a 46-yard play for the final Chiefs touchdown. The Kansas City defense limited Minnesota's strong rushing game to 67 yards and had 3 interceptions and 2 fumble recoveries. The crowd of 80,562 set a Super Bowl record, as did the gross receipts of $3,817,872.69.

Minnesota (NFL)	0	0	7	0	— 7
Kansas City (AFL)	3	13	7	0	— 23

KC — FG Stenerud 48 (8:08)
KC — FG Stenerud 32 (1:40)
KC — FG Stenerud 25 (7:08)
KC — Garrett 5 run (Stenerud kick) (9:26)
Minn — Osborn 4 run (Cox kick) (10:28)
KC — Taylor 46 pass from Dawson (Stenerud kick) (13:38)

SUPER BOWL III

Orange Bowl, Miami, Florida
January 12, 1969, Attendance: 75,389

NEW YORK JETS 16, BALTIMORE 7—Jets quarterback Joe Namath "guaranteed" victory on the Thursday before the game, then went out and led the AFL to its first Super Bowl victory over a Baltimore team that had lost only once in 16 games all season. Namath, chosen the outstanding player, completed 17 of 28 passes for 206 yards and directed a steady attack that dominated the NFL champions after the Jets' defense had intercepted Colts quarterback Earl Morrall 3 times in the first half. The Jets had 337 total yards, including 121 rushing yards by Matt Snell. Johnny Unitas, who had missed most of the season with a sore elbow, came off the bench and led Baltimore to its only touchdown late in the fourth quarter after New York led 16-0.

New York Jets (AFL)	0	7	6	3	— 16
Baltimore (NFL)	0	0	0	7	— 7

NYJ — Snell 4 run (Turner kick) (5:57)
NYJ — FG Turner 32 (4:52)
NYJ — FG Turner 30 (11:02)
NYJ — FG Turner 9 (1:34)
Balt — Hill 1 run (Michaels kick) (11:41)

SUPER BOWL II

Orange Bowl, Miami, Florida
January 14, 1968, Attendance: 75,546

GREEN BAY 33, OAKLAND 14—Green Bay, after winning its third consecutive NFL championship, won the Super Bowl title for the second straight year, defeating the AFL champion Raiders in a game that drew the first $3-million gate in football history. Bart Starr again was chosen the game's most valuable player as he completed 13 of 24 passes for 202 yards and 1 touchdown and directed a Packers attack that was in control all the way after building a 16-7 halftime lead. Don Chandler kicked 4 field goals and all-pro cornerback Herb Adderley capped the Green Bay scoring with a 60-yard interception return. The game marked the last for Vince Lombardi as Packers coach, ending nine years at Green Bay in which he won six Western Conference championships, five NFL championships, and two Super Bowls.

Green Bay (NFL)	3	13	10	7	— 33
Oakland (AFL)	0	7	0	7	— 14

GB — FG Chandler 39 (5:07)
GB — FG Chandler 20 (3:08)
GB — Dowler 62 pass from Starr (Chandler kick) (4:10)
Oak — Miller 23 pass from Lamonica (Blanda kick) (8:45)
GB — FG Chandler 43 (14:59)
GB — Anderson 2 run (Chandler kick) (9:06)
GB — FG Chandler 31 (14:58)
GB — Adderley 60 interception return (Chandler kick) (3:57)
Oak — Miller 23 pass from Lamonica (Blanda kick) (5:47)

SUPER BOWL I

Memorial Coliseum, Los Angeles, California
January 15, 1967, Attendance: 61,946

GREEN BAY 35, KANSAS CITY 10—The Green Bay Packers opened the Super Bowl series by defeating the AFL champion Chiefs behind the passing of Bart Starr, the receiving of Max McGee, and a key interception by all-pro safety Willie Wood. Green Bay broke open the game with 3 second-half touchdowns, the first of which was set up by Wood's 50-yard return of an interception. McGee, filling in for ailing Boyd Dowler after having caught only 4 passes all season, caught 7 from Starr for 138 yards and 2 touchdowns. Elijah Pitts ran for two other scores. The Chiefs' 10 points came in the second quarter, the only touchdown on a 7-yard pass from Len Dawson to Curtis McClinton. Starr completed 16 of 23 passes for 250 yards and 2 touchdowns and was chosen the most valuable player. The Packers collected $15,000 per man and the Chiefs $7,500—the largest single-game shares in the history of team sports.

Kansas City (AFL)	0	10	0	0	— 10
Green Bay (NFL)	7	7	14	7	— 35

GB — McGee 37 pass from Starr (Chandler kick) (8:56)
KC — McClinton 7 pass from Dawson (Mercer kick) (4:20)
GB — Taylor 14 run (Chandler kick) (10:23)
KC — FG Mercer 31 (14:06)
GB — Pitts 5 run (Chandler kick) (2:27)
GB — McGee 13 pass from Starr (Chandler kick) (14:09)
GB — Pitts 1 run (Chandler kick) (8:25)

AFC CHAMPIONSHIP GAME RESULTS

Includes AFL Championship Games (1960-69)

Season	Date	Winner (Share)	Loser (Share)	Score	Site	Attendance
1997	Jan. 11	Denver ($30,000)	Pittsburgh ($30,000)	24-21	Pittsburgh	61,382
1996	Jan. 12	New England ($29,000)	Jacksonville ($29,000)	20-6	New England	60,190
1995	Jan. 14	Pittsburgh ($27,000)	Indianapolis ($27,000)	20-16	Pittsburgh	61,062
1994	Jan. 15	San Diego ($26,000)	Pittsburgh ($26,000)	17-13	Pittsburgh	61,545
1993	Jan. 23	Buffalo ($23,500)	Kansas City ($23,500)	30-13	Buffalo	76,642
1992	Jan. 17	Buffalo ($18,000)	Miami ($18,000)	29-10	Miami	72,703
1991	Jan. 12	Buffalo ($18,000)	Denver ($18,000)	10-7	Buffalo	80,272
1990	Jan. 20	Buffalo ($18,000)	L.A. Raiders ($18,000)	51-3	Buffalo	80,325
1989	Jan. 14	Denver ($18,000)	Cleveland ($18,000)	37-21	Denver	76,046
1988	Jan. 8	Cincinnati ($18,000)	Buffalo ($18,000)	21-10	Cincinnati	59,747
1987	Jan. 17	Denver ($18,000)	Cleveland ($18,000)	38-33	Denver	76,197
1986	Jan. 11	Denver ($18,000)	Cleveland ($18,000)	23-20*	Cleveland	79,973
1985	Jan. 12	New England ($18,000)	Miami ($18,000)	31-14	Miami	75,662
1984	Jan. 6	Miami ($18,000)	Pittsburgh ($18,000)	45-28	Miami	76,029
1983	Jan. 8	L.A. Raiders ($18,000)	Seattle ($18,000)	30-14	Los Angeles	91,445
1982	Jan. 23	Miami ($18,000)	N.Y. Jets ($18,000)	14-0	Miami	67,396
1981	Jan. 10	Cincinnati ($9,000)	San Diego ($9,000)	27-7	Cincinnati	46,302
1980	Jan. 11	Oakland ($9,000)	San Diego ($9,000)	34-27	San Diego	52,675
1979	Jan. 6	Pittsburgh ($9,000)	Houston ($9,000)	27-13	Pittsburgh	50,475
1978	Jan. 7	Pittsburgh ($9,000)	Houston ($9,000)	34-5	Pittsburgh	50,725
1977	Jan. 1	Denver ($9,000)	Oakland ($9,000)	20-17	Denver	75,044
1976	Dec. 26	Oakland ($8,500)	Pittsburgh ($5,500)	24-7	Oakland	53,821
1975	Jan. 4	Pittsburgh ($8,500)	Oakland ($5,500)	16-10	Pittsburgh	50,609
1974	Dec. 29	Pittsburgh ($8,500)	Oakland ($5,500)	24-13	Oakland	53,800
1973	Dec. 30	Miami ($8,500)	Oakland ($5,500)	27-10	Miami	79,325
1972	Dec. 31	Miami ($8,500)	Pittsburgh ($5,500)	21-17	Pittsburgh	50,845
1971	Jan. 2	Miami ($8,500)	Baltimore ($5,500)	21-0	Miami	76,622
1970	Jan. 3	Baltimore ($8,500)	Oakland ($5,500)	27-17	Baltimore	54,799
1969	Jan. 4	Kansas City ($7,755)	Oakland ($6,252)	17-7	Oakland	53,564
1968	Dec. 29	N.Y. Jets ($7,007)	Oakland ($5,349)	27-23	New York	62,627
1967	Dec. 31	Oakland ($6,321)	Houston ($4,996)	40-7	Oakland	53,330
1966	Jan. 1	Kansas City ($5,309)	Buffalo ($3,799)	31-7	Buffalo	42,080
1965	Dec. 26	Buffalo ($5,189)	San Diego ($3,447)	23-0	San Diego	30,361
1964	Dec. 26	Buffalo ($2,668)	San Diego ($1,738)	20-7	Buffalo	40,242
1963	Jan. 5	San Diego ($2,498)	Boston ($1,596)	51-10	San Diego	30,127
1962	Dec. 23	Dallas ($2,206)	Houston ($1,471)	20-17*	Houston	37,981
1961	Dec. 24	Houston ($1,792)	San Diego ($1,111)	10-3	San Diego	29,556
1960	Jan. 1	Houston ($1,025)	L.A. Chargers ($718)	24-16	Houston	32,183

*Sudden death overtime.

AFC CHAMPIONSHIP GAME COMPOSITE STANDINGS

	W	L	Pct.	Pts.	OP
Cincinnati Bengals	2	0	1.000	48	17
Denver Broncos	5	1	.833	149	122
Buffalo Bills	6	2	.750	180	92
Kansas City Chiefs*	3	1	.750	81	61
Miami Dolphins	5	2	.714	152	115
New England Patriots**	2	1	.667	61	71
Pittsburgh Steelers	5	5	.500	207	188
New York Jets	1	1	.500	27	37
Tennessee Oilers##	2	4	.333	76	140
Indianapolis Colts#	1	2	.333	43	58
Oakland/L.A. Raiders	4	8	.333	228	264
San Diego Chargers***	2	6	.250	128	161
Jacksonville Jaguars	0	1	.000	6	20
Seattle Seahawks	0	1	.000	14	30
Cleveland Browns	0	3	.000	74	98

*One game played when franchise was in Dallas (Texans). (Won 20-17)

**One game played when franchise was in Boston. (Lost 51-10)

***One game played when franchise was in Los Angeles. (Lost 24-16)

#Two games played when franchise was in Baltimore. (Won 27-17, lost 21-0)

##Six games played when franchise was in Houston. (Won 2, lost 4)

1997 AFC CHAMPIONSHIP GAME

Three Rivers Stadium, Pittsburgh, Pennsylvania
January 11, 1998, Attendance: 61,382

DENVER 24, PITTSBURGH 21—John Elway threw 2 touchdown passes, and the Broncos' defense intercepted 2 passes in the end zone as Denver earned its fifth trip to the Super Bowl. Levon Kirkland intercepted Elway's pass on the second play of the game, but Norm Johnson's 38-yard field-goal attempt sailed wide left. Terrell Davis scampered 43 yards on the next play and scored five plays later to give the Broncos a 7-0 lead. The Steelers responded with a 6-play drive of their own, capped by Kordell Stewart's 33-yard option run down the right side for the game tying touchdown. Darren Perry forced and recovered Davis's fumble at the Steelers' 32 on the next drive, and Pittsburgh marched 68 yards in 11 plays, keyed by 2 third-down passes by Stewart and culminating with Jerome Bettis's 1-yard run. Elway's 17-yard pass to Rod Smith on third-and-10 kept alive the next drive and allowed Jason Elam to cut the deficit to 14-10 with 8:20 left in the half. Ray Crockett intercepted Stewart's bomb in the end zone to halt a Steelers drive with 4:04 left in the half. On the strength of 3 Elway completions, and a 22-yard pass interference penalty by Chad Scott, the Broncos reached the 15-yard line. Elway then threw a swing pass behind Howard Griffith, who reached back and made a one-handed grab before stepping into the end zone with 1:47 remaining. The Broncos forced a punt, and Darrien Gordon's 19-yard return gave them the ball at their own 46 with 43 seconds left in the half. Carnell Lake's 34-yard pass interference penalty put Denver in position, and Elway's 1-yard pass to Ed McCaffrey with 13 seconds left in the half gave Denver a 24-14 lead. The Steelers used nearly the first seven minutes of the second half to drive to the Broncos' 5, only to have Stewart's pass intercepted in the end zone by Allen Aldridge. The next scoring opportunity came when the Steelers got the ball back following a punt with 5:43 left in the game. Stewart threw the ball eight times and ran two times on the 10-play, 79-yard drive, capped by his 15-yard touchdown pass to Charles Johnson with 2:46 left to cut the deficit to 24-21. The Steelers elected to kick deep and had the Broncos pinned at their own 15-yard line on third-and-6 with 2:00 left. But Elway fired an 18-yard pass to Shannon Sharpe. After a Steelers timeout, Elway threw a 10-yard pass to McCaffrey, and Davis broke free for a 19-yard run two plays later to ice the AFC championship. Elway was 18 of 31 for 210 yards and 2 touchdowns, with 1 interception. Davis had 26 carries for 139 yards. Stewart was 18 of 36 for 201 yards and 1 touchdown, with 3 interceptions. Bettis had 23 carries for 105 yards. In what was an evenly matched game, the teams each had 23 first downs, the Steelers had 9 more total yards, while Denver had the ball for two more seconds than Pittsburgh.

Denver (24)	Offense	Pittsburgh (21)
Rod Smith	WR	Yancey Thigpen
Gary Zimmerman	LT	John Jackson
Mark Schlereth	LG	Will Wolford
Tom Nalen	C	Dermontti Dawson
Brian Habib	RG	Brenden Stai
Tony Jones	RT	Justin Strzelczyk
Shannon Sharpe	TE	Mark Bruener
Ed McCaffrey	WR	Charles Johnson
John Elway	QB	Kordell Stewart
Howard Griffith	RB	Tim Lester
Terrell Davis	RB	Jerome Bettis
	Defense	
Neil Smith	LE	Nolan Harrison
Keith Traylor	LT-NT	Joel Steed
Maa Tanuvasa	RT-RE	Kevin Henry
Alfred Williams	RE-LOLB	Jason Gildon
John Mobley	WLB-LILB	Levon Kirkland
Allen Aldridge	MLB-RILB	Earl Holmes
Bill Romanowski	SLB-ROLB	Donta Jones
Ray Crockett	LCB-LCB	Chad Scott
Darrien Gordon	RCB-RCB	Carnell Lake
Tyrone Braxton	SS	Myron Bell
Steve Atwater	FS	Darren Perry

SUBSTITUTIONS

Denver—Offense: T—Harry Swayne. TE—Dwayne Carswell. WR—Willie Green, Patrick Jeffers. RB—Vaughn Hebron, Derek Loville, Anthony Lynn, Detron Smith. P—Tom Rouen. K—Jason Elam. Defense: NT—Mike Lodish. DT—Trevor Pryce. DE—Harald Hasselbach. LB—Keith Burns, Glenn Cadrez. DB—Dedrick Dodge, Randy Hilliard, Darrius Johnson, Tim McKyer, Tony Veland. DNP—Bubby Brister,

Byron Chamberlain.
Pittsburgh—Offense: C—Jim Sweeney. G—Tom Myslinski. TE—Kirk Botkin, Troy Sadowski. WR—Will Blackwell, Andre Coleman, Courtney Hawkins. RB—Fred McAfee, Jon Witman. QB—Mike Tomczak. P—Josh Miller. K—Norm Johnson. Defense: DT—Oliver Gibson. DE—Orpheus Roye, Mike Vrabel. LB—Steven Conley, Carlos Emmons, Jerry Olsavsky. DB—J.B. Brown, Lethon Flowers, Randy Fuller, Chris Oldham. DNP—Donnell Woolford.

OFFICIALS
Referee—Ron Blum. Umpire—Bob Boylston. Head Linesman—Mark Baltz. Line Judge—Ron Winter. Back Judge—Bill Lovett. Field Judge—Don Hakes. Side Judge—Dave Wyant.

SCORING

Denver	7	17	0	0	— 24
Pittsburgh	7	7	0	7	— 21

Den — Davis 8 run (Elam kick)
Pitt — Stewart 33 run (N. Johnson kick)
Pitt — Bettis 1 run (N. Johnson kick)
Den — FG Elam 43
Den — Griffith 16 pass from Elway (Elam kick)
Den — McCaffrey 1 pass from Elway (Elam kick)
Pitt — C. Johnson 15 pass from Stewart (N. Johnson kick)

TEAM STATISTICS	Den	Pit
Total First Downs	23	23
Rushing	6	8
Passing	15	13
Penalty	2	2
Total Net Yardage	345	351
Total Offensive Plays	63	66
Average Gain Per Offensive Play	5.5	5.3
Rushes	30	27
Yards Gained Rushing (Net)	150	161
Average Yards per Rush	5.0	6.0
Passes Attempted	31	36
Passes Completed	18	18
Had Intercepted	1	3
Tackled Attempting to Pass	2	3
Yards Lost Attempting to Pass	15	11
Yards Gained Passing (Net)	195	190
Punts	5	4
Average Distance	31.4	42.0
Punt Returns	2	1
Punt Return Yardage	19	19
Kickoff Returns	4	4
Kickoff Return Yardage	69	62
Interception Return Yardage	6	0
Total Return Yardage	95	81
Fumbles	2	1
Fumbles Lost	1	1
Own Fumbles Recovered	1	0
Opponent Fumbles Recovered	1	1
Penalties	4	4
Yards Penalized	21	71
Field Goals	1	0
Field Goals Attempted	1	1
Third-Down Efficiency	8/14	6/11
Fourth-Down Efficiency	0/0	0/0
Time of Possession	30:01	29:59

INDIVIDUAL STATISTICS
RUSHING: DEN: Davis 26-139, Elway 2-9, Hebron 2-2. PIT: Bettis 23-105, Stewart 3-44, McAfee 1-12.
PASSING: DEN: Elway 18-31-210-2. PIT: Stewart 18-36-201-1.
RECEIVING: DEN: R. Smith 6-87, McCaffrey 5-37, Sharpe 3-49, Griffith 2-26, Hebron 1-9, Davis 1-2. PIT: Thigpen 6-92, Hawkins 4-30, C. Johnson 3-34, Blackwell 2-19, Bruener 1-16, Lester 1-7, Bettis 1-3.
KICKOFF RETURNS: DEN: Hebron 4-69. PIT: Blackwell 3-52, Witman 1-10.
PUNT RETURNS: DEN: Gordon 2-19. PIT: Blackwell 1-19.
PUNTING: DEN: Rouen 5-157-31.4. PIT: Miller 4-168-42.0.
INTERCEPTIONS: DEN: Braxton 1-6, Aldridge 1-0, Crockett 1-0. PIT: Kirkland 1-0.
SACKS: DEN: Crockett 1, N. Smith 1, Traylor 1. PIT: Bell 1, Kirkland 1.

NFC CHAMPIONSHIP GAME RESULTS

Includes NFL Championship Games (1933-69)

Season	Date	Winner (Share)	Loser (Share)	Score	Site	Attendance
1997	Jan. 11	Green Bay ($30,000)	San Francisco ($30,000)	23-10	San Francisco	68,987
1996	Jan. 12	Green Bay ($29,000)	Carolina ($29,000)	30-13	Green Bay	60,216
1995	Jan. 14	Dallas ($27,000)	Green Bay ($27,000)	38-27	Dallas	65,135
1994	Jan. 15	San Francisco ($26,000)	Dallas ($26,000)	38-28	San Francisco	69,125
1993	Jan. 23	Dallas ($23,500)	San Francisco ($23,500)	38-21	Dallas	64,902
1992	Jan. 17	Dallas ($18,000)	San Francisco ($18,000)	30-20	San Francisco	64,920
1991	Jan. 12	Washington ($18,000)	Detroit ($18,000)	41-10	Washington	55,585
1990	Jan. 20	N.Y. Giants ($18,000)	San Francisco ($18,000)	15-13	San Francisco	65,750
1989	Jan. 14	San Francisco ($18,000)	L.A. Rams ($18,000)	30-3	San Francisco	65,634
1988	Jan. 8	San Francisco ($18,000)	Chicago ($18,000)	28-3	Chicago	66,946
1987	Jan. 17	Washington ($18,000)	Minnesota ($18,000)	17-10	Washington	55,212
1986	Jan. 11	New York Giants ($18,000)	Washington ($18,000)	17-0	East Rutherford	76,891
1985	Jan. 12	Chicago ($18,000)	L.A. Rams ($18,000)	24-0	Chicago	66,030
1984	Jan. 6	San Francisco ($18,000)	Chicago ($18,000)	23-0	San Francisco	61,336
1983	Jan. 8	Washington ($18,000)	San Francisco ($18,000)	24-21	Washington	55,363
1982	Jan. 22	Washington ($18,000)	Dallas ($18,000)	31-17	Washington	55,045
1981	Jan. 10	San Francisco ($9,000)	Dallas ($9,000)	28-27	San Francisco	60,525
1980	Jan. 11	Philadelphia ($9,000)	Dallas ($9,000)	20-7	Philadelphia	71,522
1979	Jan. 6	Los Angeles ($9,000)	Tampa Bay ($9,000)	9-0	Tampa Bay	72,033
1978	Jan. 7	Dallas ($9,000)	Los Angeles ($9,000)	28-0	Los Angeles	71,086
1977	Jan. 1	Dallas ($9,000)	Minnesota ($9,000)	23-6	Dallas	64,293
1976	Dec. 26	Minnesota ($8,500)	Los Angeles ($5,500)	24-13	Minnesota	48,379
1975	Jan. 4	Dallas ($8,500)	Los Angeles ($5,500)	37-7	Los Angeles	88,919
1974	Dec. 29	Minnesota ($8,500)	Los Angeles ($5,500)	14-10	Minnesota	48,444
1973	Dec. 30	Minnesota ($8,500)	Dallas ($5,500)	27-10	Dallas	64,422
1972	Dec. 31	Washington ($8,500)	Dallas ($5,500)	26-3	Washington	53,129
1971	Jan. 2	Dallas ($8,500)	San Francisco ($5,500)	14-3	Dallas	63,409
1970	Jan. 3	Dallas ($8,500)	San Francisco ($5,500)	17-10	San Francisco	59,364
1969	Jan. 4	Minnesota ($7,930)	Cleveland ($5,118)	27-7	Minnesota	46,503
1968	Dec. 29	Baltimore ($9,306)	Cleveland ($5,963)	34-0	Cleveland	78,410
1967	Dec. 31	Green Bay ($7,950)	Dallas ($5,299)	21-17	Green Bay	50,861
1966	Jan. 1	Green Bay ($9,813)	Dallas ($6,527)	34-27	Dallas	74,152
1965	Jan. 2	Green Bay ($7,819)	Cleveland ($5,288)	23-12	Green Bay	50,777
1964	Dec. 27	Cleveland ($8,052)	Baltimore ($5,571)	27-0	Cleveland	79,544
1963	Dec. 29	Chicago ($5,899)	New York ($4,218)	14-10	Chicago	45,801
1962	Dec. 30	Green Bay ($5,888)	New York ($4,166)	16-7	New York	64,892
1961	Dec. 31	Green Bay ($5,195)	New York ($3,339)	37-0	Green Bay	39,029
1960	Dec. 26	Philadelphia ($5,116)	Green Bay ($3,105)	17-13	Philadelphia	67,325
1959	Dec. 27	Baltimore ($4,674)	New York ($3,083)	31-16	Baltimore	57,545
1958	Dec. 28	Baltimore ($4,718)	New York ($3,111)	23-17*	New York	64,185
1957	Dec. 29	Detroit ($4,295)	Cleveland ($2,750)	59-14	Detroit	55,263
1956	Dec. 30	New York ($3,779)	Chi. Bears ($2,485)	47-7	New York	56,836
1955	Dec. 26	Cleveland ($3,508)	Los Angeles ($2,316)	38-14	Los Angeles	85,693
1954	Dec. 26	Cleveland ($2,478)	Detroit ($1,585)	56-10	Cleveland	43,827
1953	Dec. 27	Detroit ($2,424)	Cleveland ($1,654)	17-16	Detroit	54,577
1952	Dec. 28	Detroit ($2,274)	Cleveland ($1,712)	17-7	Cleveland	50,934
1951	Dec. 23	Los Angeles ($2,108)	Cleveland ($1,483)	24-17	Los Angeles	57,522
1950	Dec. 24	Cleveland ($1,113)	Los Angeles ($686)	30-28	Cleveland	29,751
1949	Dec. 18	Philadelphia ($1,094)	Los Angeles ($739)	14-0	Los Angeles	27,980
1948	Dec. 19	Philadelphia ($1,540)	Chi. Cardinals ($874)	7-0	Philadelphia	36,309
1947	Dec. 28	Chi. Cardinals ($1,132)	Philadelphia ($754)	28-21	Chicago	30,759

Season	Date	Winner (Share)	Loser (Share)	Score	Site	Attendance
1946	Dec. 15	Chi. Bears ($1,975)	New York ($1,295)	24-14	New York	58,346
1945	Dec. 16	Cleveland ($1,469)	Washington ($902)	15-14	Cleveland	32,178
1944	Dec. 17	Green Bay ($1,449)	New York ($814)	14-7	New York	46,016
1943	Dec. 26	Chi. Bears ($1,146)	Washington ($765)	41-21	Chicago	34,320
1942	Dec. 13	Washington ($965)	Chi. Bears ($637)	14-6	Washington	36,006
1941	Dec. 21	Chi. Bears ($430)	New York ($288)	37-9	Chicago	13,341
1940	Dec. 8	Chi. Bears ($873)	Washington ($606)	73-0	Washington	36,034
1939	Dec. 10	Green Bay ($703.97)	New York ($455.57)	27-0	Milwaukee	32,279
1938	Dec. 11	New York ($504.45)	Green Bay ($368.81)	23-17	New York	48,120
1937	Dec. 12	Washington ($225.90)	Chi. Bears ($127.78)	28-21	Chicago	15,870
1936	Dec. 13	Green Bay ($250)	Boston ($180)	21-6	New York	29,545
1935	Dec. 15	Detroit ($313.35)	New York ($200.20)	26-7	Detroit	15,000
1934	Dec. 9	New York ($621)	Chi. Bears ($414.02)	30-13	New York	35,059
1933	Dec. 17	Chi. Bears ($210.34)	New York ($140.22)	23-21	Chicago	26,000

*Sudden death overtime.

NFC CHAMPIONSHIP GAME COMPOSITE STANDINGS

	W	L	Pct.	Pts.	OP
Philadelphia Eagles	4	1	.800	79	48
Green Bay Packers	10	3	.769	303	177
Baltimore Colts	3	1	.750	88	60
Detroit Lions	4	2	.667	139	141
Minnesota Vikings	4	2	.667	108	80
Washington Redskins*	7	5	.583	222	255
Chicago Bears	7	6	.538	286	245
Dallas Cowboys	8	8	.500	361	319
Arizona Cardinals**	1	1	.500	28	28
San Francisco 49ers	5	7	.417	245	222
Cleveland Browns	4	7	.364	224	253
New York Giants	5	11	.313	240	322
St. Louis Rams***	3	9	.250	123	270
Carolina Panthers	0	1	.000	13	30
Tampa Bay Buccaneers	0	1	.000	0	9

*One game played when franchise was in Boston. (Lost 21-6)

**Both games played when franchise was in Chicago. (Won 28-21, lost 7-0)

***One game played when franchise was in Cleveland (Won 15-14), and 11 games when franchise was in Los Angeles (Won 2, lost 9, scored 108 points, allowed 256 points).

1997 NFC CHAMPIONSHIP GAME

3Com Park, San Francisco, California
January 11, 1998, Attendance: 68,987

GREEN BAY 23, SAN FRANCISCO 10—A stifling defensive effort by the Packers limited the 49ers to 33 rushing yards, forced 2 turnovers, and recorded 4 sacks as Green Bay earned their fourth Super Bowl appearance. The Packers forced a punt on the game's initial possession and drove to the 1-yard line, but Gary Plummer batted down Brett Favre's third-and-goal pass, forcing Green Bay to settle for Ryan Longwell's field goal. After an exchange of punts, the 49ers drove to the Packers' 28. However, Eugene Robinson intercepted Steve Young's third-down pass and raced 58 yards. Favre fired a 27-yard touchdown pass to Antonio Freeman two plays later to give the Packers a 10-0 lead. The Packers forced another punt and had a chance to extend their lead, but Longwell's 47-yard field-goal attempt failed. The 49ers responded with a 10-play drive, capped by Gary Anderson's field goal with 58 seconds left in the half. On their own 35-yard line with time running out in the half, Favre lofted a 40-yard bomb to Freeman with three seconds left in the half. Longwell trotted onto the field and made a 43-yard field goal to give the Packers a 13-3 halftime lead. Each team punted their first three possessions of the second half, but Tommy Thompson's third punt allowed the Packers to begin at the 49ers' 35. Even with great field position, the 49ers' defense held the Packers to Longwell's third field goal with 5:03 left. The 49ers were forced to go for it on fourth-and-10 from their own 20, only to watch Keith McKenzie sack Young for a 9-yard loss. Levens scored two plays later to give Green Bay a 23-3 lead with 3:10 left. Chuck Levy promptly returned the ensuing kickoff 95 yards for a touchdown, but Jeff Thomason recovered the ensuing onside kick and the Packers clinched their second consecutive NFC title. Favre was 16 of 27 for 222 yards and 1 touchdown. Levens rushed 27 times for 114 yards. Freeman had 4 receptions for 107 yards. Young was 23 of 38 for 250 yards, with 1 interception. Terrell Owens had 6 catches for 100 yards.

Green Bay (23)	Offense	San Francisco (10)
Antonio Freeman	WR	J.J. Stokes
Ross Verba	LT	Derrick Deese
Aaron Taylor	LG	Roy Brown
Frank Winters	C	Chris Dalman
Adam Timmerman	RG	Kevin Gogan
Earl Dotson	RT	Kirk Scrafford
Mark Chmura	TE	Greg Clark
Robert Brooks	WR	Terrell Owens
Brett Favre	QB	Steve Young
Dorsey Levens	RB	Terry Kirby
William Henderson	RB	William Floyd
	Defense	
Reggie White	DE	Roy Barker
Santana Dotson	NT-DT	Bryant Young
Gilbert Brown	DE-DT	Dana Stubblefield
Gabe Wilkins	LOLB-DE	Chris Doleman
Seth Joyner	LILB-LLB	Lee Woodall
Bernardo Harris	RILB-MLB	Gary Plummer
Brian Williams	ROLB-RLB	Ken Norton, Jr.
Tyrone Williams	LCB	Rod Woodson
Doug Evans	RCB	Marquez Pope
LeRoy Butler	SS	Tim McDonald
Eugene Robinson	FS	Merton Hanks

SUBSTITUTIONS

Green Bay—Offense: G—Rob Davis, Marco Rivera. T—Bruce Wilkerson. TE—Tyrone Davis, Jeff Thomason. WR—Derrick Mayes, Terry Mickens. RB—Chris Darkins, Aaron Hayden, Travis Jervey. P—Craig Hentrich. K—Ryan Longwell. Defense: DT—Darius Holland, Bob Kuberski. DE—Paul Frase. LB—Lamont Hollinquest, George Koonce. DB—Mike Prior, Darren Sharper. DNP—Steve Bonom, Jeff Dellenbach.

San Francisco—C—Jesse Sapolu. G—Tim Hanshaw. T—Frank Pollack. TE—Chad Fann, Brent Jones. WR—Iheanyi Uwaezuoke. RB—Marc Edwards, Garrison Hearst, Chuck Levy. P—Tommy Thompson. K—Gary Anderson. Defense: DE—Junior Bryant, Kevin Greene. LB—Randy Kirk, Kevin Mitchell, Jim Schwantz, James Williams. DB—Zack Bronson, Curtis Buckley, Tyronne Drakeford, Frankie Smith, Darnell Walker. DNP—Jeff Brohm.

OFFICIALS

Referee—Dick Hantak. Umpire—Ron Botchan. Head Linesman—Sanford Rivers. Line Judge—Byron Boston. Back Judge—Tony Corrente. Field Judge—Don Dorkowski. Side Judge—Dean Look.

SCORING

Green Bay	3	10	0	10	— 23
San Francisco	0	3	0	7	— 10

GB — FG Longwell 19
GB — Freeman 27 pass from Favre (Longwell kick)
SF — FG Anderson 28
GB — FG Longwell 43
GB — FG Longwell 25
GB — Levens 5 run (Longwell kick)
SF — Levy 95 kickoff return (Anderson kick)

TEAM STATISTICS	GB	SF
Total First Downs	19	15
Rushing	8	1
Passing	10	11
Penalty	1	3
Total Net Yardage	325	257
Total Offensive Plays	60	60
Average Gain Per Offensive Play	5.4	4.3
Rushes	32	18
Yards Gained Rushing (Net)	106	33
Average Yards per Rush	3.3	1.8
Passes Attempted	27	38
Passes Completed	16	23
Had Intercepted	0	1
Tackled Attempting to Pass	1	4
Yards Lost Attempting to Pass	3	26
Yards Gained Passing (Net)	219	224
Punts	5	6
Average Distance	36.6	33.8
Punt Returns	2	2
Punt Return Yardage	27	2
Kickoff Returns	2	4
Kickoff Return Yardage	37	134
Interception Return Yardage	58	0
Total Return Yardage	122	136
Fumbles	1	4
Fumbles Lost	0	1
Own Fumbles Recovered	0	2
Opponent Fumbles Recovered	1	0
Penalties	9	6
Yards Penalized	62	64
Field Goals	3	1
Field Goals Attempted	4	1
Third-Down Efficiency	4/12	3/14
Fourth-Down Efficiency	0/0	2/3
Time of Possession	31:48	28:12

INDIVIDUAL STATISTICS

RUSHING: GB: Levens 27-114, Henderson 3-2, Favre 2-(-10). SF: Kirby 6-21, Hearst 8-12, S. Young 2-1, Floyd 2-(-1).

PASSING: GB: Favre 16-27-222-1. SF: S. Young 23-38-250-0.

RECEIVING: GB: Freeman 4-107, Levens 4-27, R. Brooks 3-36, Chmura 2-18, T. Davis 1-17, Mayes 1-10, Henderson 1-7. SF: Owens 6-100, Stokes 6-87, Kirby 4-7, Hearst 3-14, Uwaezuoke 2-14, Clark 1-16, Jones 1-12.

KICKOFF RETURNS: GB: Hayden 1-19, Freeman 1-18. SF: Levy 3-127, Pollack 1-7.

PUNT RETURNS: GB: R. Brooks 2-27. SF: Levy 2-2.

PUNTING: GB: Hentrich 5-183-36.6. SF: Thompson 6-203-33.8.

INTERCEPTIONS: GB: Robinson 1-58.

SACKS: GB: McKenzie 2, Harris 1, White 1. SF: McDonald 1.

AFC DIVISIONAL PLAYOFFS RESULTS

Includes Second-Round Playoff Games (1982), AFC Inter-Divisional Games (1969), and special playoff games to break ties for AFL Division Championships (1963, 1968)

Season	Date	Winner (Share)	Loser (Share)	Score	Site	Attendance
1997	Jan. 4	Denver ($15,000)	Kansas City ($15,000)	14-10	Kansas City	76,965
	Jan. 3	Pittsburgh ($15,000)	New England ($15,000)	7-6	Pittsburgh	61,228
1996	Jan. 5	New England ($14,000)	Pittsburgh ($14,000)	28-3	New England	60,188
	Jan. 4	Jacksonville ($14,000)	Denver ($14,000)	30-27	Denver	75,678
1995	Jan. 7	Indianapolis ($13,000)	Kansas City ($13,000)	10-7	Kansas City	77,594
	Jan. 6	Pittsburgh ($13,000)	Buffalo ($13,000)	40-21	Pittsburgh	59,072
1994	Jan. 8	San Diego ($12,000)	Miami ($12,000)	22-21	San Diego	63,381
	Jan. 7	Pittsburgh ($12,000)	Cleveland ($12,000)	29-9	Pittsburgh	58,185
1993	Jan. 16	Kansas City ($12,000)	Houston ($12,000)	28-20	Houston	64,011
	Jan. 15	Buffalo ($12,000)	L.A. Raiders ($12,000)	29-23	Buffalo	61,923
1992	Jan. 10	Miami ($10,000)	San Diego ($10,000)	31-0	Miami	71,224
	Jan. 9	Buffalo ($10,000)	Pittsburgh ($10,000)	24-3	Pittsburgh	60,407
1991	Jan. 5	Buffalo ($10,000)	Kansas City ($10,000)	37-14	Buffalo	80,182
	Jan. 4	Denver ($10,000)	Houston ($10,000)	26-24	Denver	75,301
1990	Jan. 13	L.A. Raiders ($10,000)	Cincinnati ($10,000)	20-10	Los Angeles	92,045
	Jan. 12	Buffalo ($10,000)	Miami ($10,000)	44-34	Buffalo	77,087
1989	Jan. 7	Denver ($10,000)	Pittsburgh ($10,000)	24-23	Denver	75,477
	Jan. 6	Cleveland ($10,000)	Buffalo ($10,000)	34-30	Cleveland	78,921
1988	Jan. 1	Buffalo ($10,000)	Houston ($10,000)	17-10	Buffalo	79,532
	Dec. 31	Cincinnati ($10,000)	Seattle ($10,000)	21-13	Cincinnati	58,560
1987	Jan. 10	Denver ($10,000)	Houston ($10,000)	34-10	Denver	75,440
	Jan. 9	Cleveland ($10,000)	Indianapolis ($10,000)	38-21	Cleveland	79,372
1986	Jan. 4	Denver ($10,000)	New England ($10,000)	22-17	Denver	75,262
	Jan. 3	Cleveland ($10,000)	N.Y. Jets ($10,000)	23-20*	Cleveland	79,720
1985	Jan. 5	New England ($10,000)	L.A. Raiders ($10,000)	27-20	Los Angeles	87,163
	Jan. 4	Miami ($10,000)	Cleveland ($10,000)	24-21	Miami	74,667
1984	Dec. 30	Pittsburgh ($10,000)	Denver ($10,000)	24-17	Denver	74,981
	Dec. 29	Miami ($10,000)	Seattle ($10,000)	31-10	Miami	73,469
1983	Jan. 1	L.A. Raiders ($10,000)	Pittsburgh ($10,000)	38-10	Los Angeles	90,380
	Dec. 31	Seattle ($10,000)	Miami ($10,000)	27-20	Miami	74,136
1982	Jan. 16	Miami ($10,000)	San Diego ($10,000)	34-13	Miami	71,383
	Jan. 15	N.Y. Jets ($10,000)	L.A. Raiders ($10,000)	17-14	Los Angeles	90,038
1981	Jan. 3	Cincinnati ($5,000)	Buffalo ($5,000)	28-21	Cincinnati	55,420
	Jan. 2	San Diego ($5,000)	Miami ($5,000)	41-38*	Miami	73,735
1980	Jan. 4	Oakland ($5,000)	Cleveland ($5,000)	14-12	Cleveland	78,245
	Jan. 3	San Diego ($5,000)	Buffalo ($5,000)	20-14	San Diego	52,253
1979	Dec. 30	Pittsburgh ($5,000)	Miami ($5,000)	34-14	Pittsburgh	50,214
	Dec. 29	Houston ($5,000)	San Diego ($5,000)	17-14	San Diego	51,192
1978	Dec. 31	Houston ($5,000)	New England ($5,000)	31-14	New England	60,735
	Dec. 30	Pittsburgh ($5,000)	Denver ($5,000)	33-10	Pittsburgh	50,230
1977	Dec. 24	Oakland ($5,000)	Baltimore ($5,000)	37-31*	Baltimore	59,925
	Dec. 24	Denver ($5,000)	Pittsburgh ($5,000)	34-21	Denver	75,059
1976	Dec. 19	Pittsburgh [$]	Baltimore [$]	40-14	Baltimore	59,296
	Dec. 18	Oakland [$]	New England [$]	24-21	Oakland	53,050
1975	Dec. 28	Oakland [$]	Cincinnati [$]	31-28	Oakland	53,030
	Dec. 27	Pittsburgh [$]	Baltimore [$]	28-10	Pittsburgh	49,557
1974	Dec. 22	Pittsburgh [$]	Buffalo [$]	32-14	Pittsburgh	49,841
	Dec. 21	Oakland [$]	Miami [$]	28-26	Oakland	53,023
1973	Dec. 23	Miami [$]	Cincinnati [$]	34-16	Miami	78,928
	Dec. 22	Oakland [$]	Pittsburgh [$]	33-14	Oakland	52,646
1972	Dec. 24	Miami [$]	Cleveland [$]	20-14	Miami	78,916
	Dec. 23	Pittsburgh [$]	Oakland [$]	13-7	Pittsburgh	50,327
1971	Dec. 26	Baltimore [$]	Cleveland [$]	20-3	Cleveland	70,734
	Dec. 25	Miami [$]	Kansas City [$]	27-24*	Kansas City	45,822
1970	Dec. 27	Oakland [$]	Miami [$]	21-14	Oakland	52,594
	Dec. 26	Baltimore [$]	Cincinnati [$]	17-0	Baltimore	49,694
1969	Dec. 21	Oakland [$]	Houston [$]	56-7	Oakland	53,539
	Dec. 20	Kansas City [$]	N.Y. Jets [$]	13-6	New York	62,977
1968	Dec. 22	Oakland [$]	Kansas City [$]	41-6	Oakland	53,605
1963	Dec. 28	Boston [$]	Buffalo [$]	26-8	Buffalo	33,044

**Sudden Death Overtime.*

$ Players received 1/14 of annual salary for playoff appearances.

1997 AFC DIVISIONAL PLAYOFF GAMES

Arrowhead Stadium, Kansas City, Missouri
January 4, 1998, Attendance: 76,965

DENVER 14, KANSAS CITY 10—Terrell Davis recovered from bruised ribs to rush for 101 yards and 2 touchdowns as the Broncos knocked the number-one seeded Chiefs out of the playoffs. The Chiefs pinned the Broncos deep in their own territory early in the second quarter when Bucky Brooks leaped over the goal line and tipped a punt back onto the field where it was downed at the 2-yard line. Tom Rouen's punt three plays later traveled just 25 yards, giving the Chiefs excellent field position at the Broncos' 30. However, Pete Stoyanovich, who missed just one field goal all season, sailed his 44-yard attempt wide left. The Broncos proceeded to march 65 yards, with Davis's first touchdown with 1:56 left in the half giving Denver a 7-0 lead. Elvis Grbac threw a 34-yard pass to Andre Rison on the first play of the second half to set up Stoyanovich's 20-yard field goal. The Broncos used a 41-yard run by Davis to get deep into Chiefs territory, but John Browning forced Derek Loville to fumble and Reggie Tongue recovered at the Chiefs' 11 to thwart the drive. After an exchange of punts, Grbac connected with Joe Horn on a 50-yard pass and, three plays later, found Tony Gonzalez in the end zone for a touchdown to give the Chiefs a 10-7 lead with 10 seconds left in the third quarter. Loville returned the ensuing kickoff 20 yards, and an unnecessary roughness penalty on Danan Hughes gave the Broncos the ball at the Chiefs' 49. On third-and-5, John Elway threw a short pass to Ed McCaffrey, who tightroped his way 43 yards to the Chiefs' 1. Davis scored three plays later to give Denver a 14-10 advantage with 12:32 left. The Chiefs drove to the Broncos' 37 where they faced fourth-and-6. Kansas City lined up in field-goal formation, but holder Louie Aguiar ran with the ball and was tackled by Gordon three yards shy of the first down. A couple of punts later, the Chiefs began their final drive at their own 17 with 4:04 remaining. Faced with fourth-and-9 from the 47, Grbac hit Lake Dawson with a 12-yard pass and, after getting sacked, connected on a 23-yard pass to Rison to get the Chiefs to the Broncos' 28 with 1:51 left, where they used their final timeout. Grbac netted 1-, 3-, and 4-yard passes to Kimble Anders, Gonzalez, and Ted Popson before Gordon batted down Grbac's final pass attempt in the end zone on fourth-and-2 with 19 seconds left to seal the victory. Elway was 10 of 19 for 170 yards. Grbac was 24 of 37 for 260 yards and 1 touchdown.

Denver	0	7	0	7	—	14
Kansas City	0	0	10	0	—	10

Den — Davis 1 run (Elam kick)
KC — FG Stoyanovich 20
KC — Gonzalez 12 pass from Grbac (Stoyanovich kick)
Den — Davis 1 run (Elam kick)

Three Rivers Stadium, Pittsburgh Pennsylvania
January 3, 1998, Attendance: 61,228
PITTSBURGH 7, NEW ENGLAND 6—Chad Scott intercepted Drew Bledsoe's long pass intended for Terry Glenn on the game's third play, returning it 27 yards to the Steelers' 38. On second-and-10 from the Patriots' 40, Kordell Stewart ran the option left and tightroped 40 yards down the sideline for a touchdown. The Patriots strung together a 10-play, 65-yard drive that culminated with Vinatieri's 31-yard field goal in the middle of the second quarter to cut the deficit to 7-3. After a third quarter that saw neither team drive within the opponents' 40, Vinatieri's second field goal with 12:16 left made it a one-point game. The Steelers reached the Patriots' 1 on fourth down with 3:29 left, but Stewart was stopped at the line of scrimmage. The Patriots reached their own 42-yard line, but Mark Vrabel sacked Bledsoe with 1:50 left, and Jason Gildon recovered the ensuing fumble. The Steelers were forced to punt, but Bledsoe's desperation pass was intercepted by Levon Kirkland at the Steelers' 20 to end the game. Stewart was 14 of 31 for 134 yards, with 1 interception. Bledsoe was 23 of 44 for 264 yards, with 2 interceptions. Shawn Jefferson had 9 receptions for 104 yards. The Steelers had 1 more first down, and the Patriots gained 1 more yard, but the Steelers had an 11:14 edge in time of possession because of Stewart (68 yards) and Jerome Bettis (67 yards), and forced 4 turnovers.

New England	0	3	0	3	—	6
Pittsburgh	7	0	0	0	—	7

Pitt — Stewart 40 run (Johnson kick)
NE — FG Vinatieri 31
NE — FG Vinatieri 46

NFC DIVISIONAL PLAYOFFS RESULTS

Includes Second-Round Playoff Games (1982), NFL Conference Championship Games (1967-69), and special playoff games to break ties for NFL Division or Conference Championships (1941, 1943, 1947, 1950, 1952, 1957, 1958, 1965)

Season	Date	Winner (Share)	Loser (Share)	Score	Site	Attendance
1997	Jan. 4	Green Bay ($15,000)	Tampa Bay ($15,000)	21-7	Green Bay	60,327
	Jan. 3	San Francisco ($15,000)	Minnesota ($15,000)	38-22	San Francisco	65,018
1996	Jan. 5	Carolina ($14,000)	Dallas ($14,000)	26-17	Carolina	72,808
	Jan. 4	Green Bay ($14,000)	San Francisco ($14,000)	35-14	Green Bay	60,787
1995	Jan. 7	Dallas ($13,000)	Philadelphia ($13,000)	30-11	Dallas	64,371
	Jan. 6	Green Bay ($13,000)	San Francisco ($13,000)	27-17	San Francisco	69,311
1994	Jan. 8	Dallas ($12,000)	Green Bay ($12,000)	35-9	Dallas	64,745
	Jan. 7	San Francisco ($12,000)	Chicago ($12,000)	44-15	San Francisco	64,644
1993	Jan. 16	Dallas ($12,000)	Green Bay ($12,000)	27-17	Dallas	64,790
	Jan. 15	San Francisco ($12,000)	N.Y. Giants ($12,000)	44-3	San Francisco	67,143
1992	Jan. 10	Dallas ($10,000)	Philadelphia ($10,000)	34-10	Dallas	63,721
	Jan. 9	San Francisco ($10,000)	Washington ($10,000)	20-13	San Francisco	64,991
1991	Jan. 5	Detroit ($10,000)	Dallas ($10,000)	38-6	Detroit	78,290
	Jan. 4	Washington ($10,000)	Atlanta ($10,000)	24-7	Washington	55,181
1990	Jan. 13	N.Y. Giants ($10,000)	Chicago ($10,000)	31-3	East Rutherford	77,025
	Jan. 12	San Francisco ($10,000)	Washington ($10,000)	28-10	San Francisco	65,292
1989	Jan. 7	L.A. Rams ($10,000)	N.Y. Giants ($10,000)	19-13*	East Rutherford	76,526
	Jan. 6	San Francisco ($10,000)	Minnesota ($10,000)	41-13	San Francisco	64,918
1988	Jan. 1	San Francisco ($10,000)	Minnesota ($10,000)	34-9	San Francisco	61,848
	Dec. 31	Chicago ($10,000)	Philadelphia ($10,000)	20-12	Chicago	65,534
1987	Jan. 10	Washington ($10,000)	Chicago ($10,000)	21-17	Chicago	65,268
	Jan. 9	Minnesota ($10,000)	San Francisco ($10,000)	36-24	San Francisco	63,008
1986	Jan. 4	N.Y. Giants ($10,000)	San Francisco ($10,000)	49-3	East Rutherford	75,691
	Jan. 3	Washington ($10,000)	Chicago ($10,000)	27-13	Chicago	65,524
1985	Jan. 5	Chicago ($10,000)	N.Y. Giants ($10,000)	21-0	Chicago	65,670
	Jan. 4	L.A. Rams ($10,000)	Dallas ($10,000)	20-0	Anaheim	66,581
1984	Dec. 30	Chicago ($10,000)	Washington ($10,000)	23-19	Washington	55,431
	Dec. 29	San Francisco ($10,000)	N.Y. Giants ($10,000)	21-10	San Francisco	60,303
1983	Jan. 1	Washington ($10,000)	L.A. Rams ($10,000)	51-7	Washington	54,440
	Dec. 31	San Francisco ($10,000)	Detroit ($10,000)	24-23	San Francisco	59,979
1982	Jan. 16	Dallas ($10,000)	Green Bay ($10,000)	37-26	Dallas	63,972
	Jan. 15	Washington ($10,000)	Minnesota ($10,000)	21-7	Washington	54,593
1981	Jan. 3	San Francisco ($5,000)	N.Y. Giants ($5,000)	38-24	San Francisco	58,360
	Jan. 2	Dallas ($5,000)	Tampa Bay ($5,000)	38-0	Dallas	64,848
1980	Jan. 4	Dallas ($5,000)	Atlanta ($5,000)	30-27	Atlanta	59,793
	Jan. 3	Philadelphia ($5,000)	Minnesota ($5,000)	31-16	Philadelphia	70,178
1979	Dec. 30	Los Angeles ($5,000)	Dallas ($5,000)	21-19	Dallas	64,792
	Dec. 29	Tampa Bay ($5,000)	Philadelphia ($5,000)	24-17	Tampa Bay	71,402
1978	Dec. 31	Los Angeles ($5,000)	Minnesota ($5,000)	34-10	Los Angeles	70,436
	Dec. 30	Dallas ($5,000)	Atlanta ($5,000)	27-20	Dallas	63,406
1977	Dec. 26	Dallas ($5,000)	Chicago ($5,000)	37-7	Dallas	63,260
	Dec. 26	Minnesota ($5,000)	Los Angeles ($5,000)	14-7	Los Angeles	70,203
1976	Dec. 19	Los Angeles [$]	Dallas [$]	14-12	Dallas	63,283
	Dec. 18	Minnesota [$]	Washington [$]	35-20	Minnesota	47,466
1975	Dec. 28	Dallas [$]	Minnesota [$]	17-14	Minnesota	48,050
	Dec. 27	Los Angeles [$]	St. Louis [$]	35-23	Los Angeles	73,459
1974	Dec. 22	Los Angeles [$]	Washington [$]	19-10	Los Angeles	77,925
	Dec. 21	Minnesota [$]	St. Louis [$]	30-14	Minnesota	48,150
1973	Dec. 23	Dallas [$]	Los Angeles [$]	27-16	Dallas	63,272
	Dec. 22	Minnesota [$]	Washington [$]	27-20	Minnesota	48,040
1972	Dec. 24	Washington [$]	Green Bay [$]	16-3	Washington	52,321
	Dec. 23	Dallas [$]	San Francisco [$]	30-28	San Francisco	59,746
1971	Dec. 26	San Francisco [$]	Washington [$]	24-20	San Francisco	45,327
	Dec. 25	Dallas [$]	Minnesota [$]	20-12	Minnesota	47,307
1970	Dec. 27	San Francisco [$]	Minnesota [$]	17-14	Minnesota	45,103
	Dec. 26	Dallas [$]	Detroit [$]	5-0	Dallas	69,613
1969	Dec. 28	Cleveland [$]	Dallas [$]	38-14	Dallas	69,321
	Dec. 27	Minnesota [$]	Los Angeles [$]	23-20	Minnesota	47,900
1968	Dec. 22	Baltimore [$]	Minnesota [$]	24-14	Baltimore	60,238
	Dec. 21	Cleveland [$]	Dallas [$]	31-20	Cleveland	81,497
1967	Dec. 24	Dallas [$]	Cleveland [$]	52-14	Dallas	70,786
	Dec. 23	Green Bay [$]	Los Angeles [$]	28-7	Milwaukee	49,861

1965	Dec. 26	Green Bay [$]	Baltimore [$]	13-10*	Green Bay	50,484
1958	Dec. 21	N.Y. Giants (#)	Cleveland (#)	10-0	New York	61,274
1957	Dec. 22	Detroit (#)	San Francisco (#)	31-27	San Francisco	60,118
1952	Dec. 21	Detroit (#)	Los Angeles (#)	31-21	Detroit	47,645
1950	Dec. 17	Los Angeles (#)	Chicago Bears (#)	24-14	Los Angeles	83,501
	Dec. 17	Cleveland (#)	N.Y. Giants (#)	8-3	Cleveland	33,054
1947	Dec. 21	Philadelphia (#)	Pittsburgh (#)	21-0	Pittsburgh	35,729
1943	Dec. 19	Washington (¢)	N.Y. Giants (¢)	28-0	New York	42,800
1941	Dec. 14	Chicago Bears (¢)	Green Bay (¢)	33-14	Chicago	43,425

** Sudden Death Overtime.*
[$] Players received 1/14 of annual salary for playoff appearances.
 # Players received 1/12 of annual salary for playoff appearances.
¢ Players received 1/10 of annual salary for playoff appearances.

1997 NFC DIVISIONAL PLAYOFF GAMES

Lambeau Field, Green Bay, Wisconsin
January 4, 1998, Attendance: 60,327

GREEN BAY 21, TAMPA BAY 7—Dorsey Levens rushed for 112 yards and 1 touchdown, and the Packers' special teams set up two scores and halted three others as Green Bay advanced to the NFC Championship Game for the third consecutive season. Bob Kuberski blocked Michael Husted's 43-yard field-goal attempt midway through the first quarter to spark a 67-yard drive, capped by Brett Favre's 3-yard touchdown pass to Mark Chmura. Derrick Mayes's 14-yard catch on third-and-9 to the Buccaneers' 3 gave the Packers the impetus to reach the end zone. The Buccaneers reached the Packers' 25 early in the second quarter, but Steve Walsh's fake field-goal attempt pass on fourth-and-2 was incomplete. Warren Sapp forced Levens to fumble and recovered the ball at the Packers' 30 two plays later, but a third field-goal attempt was aborted when Dave Moore's snap sailed past Walsh and was recovered by Husted. LeRoy Butler's 12-yard sack of Trent Dilfer pinned the Buccaneers back to their own 11, and Robert Brooks returned the ensuing punt 28 yards to give the Packers the ball at the Buccaneers' 29 with 4:07 left in the half. The Packers had to settle for Ryan Longwell's 21-yard field goal with 1:52 left in the half, but Tyrone Williams's interception on the next play from scrimmage set up Longwell's second field goal and gave Green Bay a 13-0 lead at halftime. The Packers took the second half's opening kickoff and drove deep into Buccaneers territory before John Lynch hit Favre's arm on a pass attempt and Donnie Abraham intercepted the pass at the 6-yard line. Faced with third-and-11 from their own 5-yard line, Dilfer threw a 53-yard pass to Reidel Anthony. Dilfer then completed a 28-yard pass to Moore on third-and-3, and Mike Alstott scored two plays later to cut the deficit to 13-7. On the last play of the third quarter Favre completed a 23-yard pass to Mayes on third-and-18, and Levens scored three plays later. The Buccaneers drove into Packers territory twice but were stopped on downs, and Mike Prior's interception at the Packers' 34 with 1:49 left iced the game. Favre was 15 of 28 for 190 yards and 1 touchdown, with 2 interceptions. Dilfer was 11 of 36 for 200 yards, with 2 interceptions. With the game-time temperature at 29 degrees, Favre improved his record 23-0 when the temperature is below 35.

Tampa Bay	0	0	7	0	—	7
Green Bay	7	6	0	8	—	21

GB —Chmura 3 pass from Favre (Longwell kick)
GB —FG Longwell 21
GB —FG Longwell 32
TB —Alstott 6 run (Husted kick)
GB —Levens 2 run (Favre run)

3Com Park, San Francisco, California
January 3, 1998, Attendance: 65,018

SAN FRANCISCO 38, MINNESOTA 22—Terry Kirby had 25 carries for 120 yards and 2 touchdowns as the 49ers defeated the Vikings. Mitch Berger's 12-yard punt to the Vikings' 26 enabled William Floyd to score four plays later to give the 49ers a 7-0 lead. Two plays later, Randall Cunningham threw a 66-yard touchdown pass to Cris Carter to tie the game. A 28-yard pass interference penalty on Torrian Gray to the Vikings' 4 set up Terry Kirby's 1-yard run, and Ken Norton's 23-yard interception return 47 seconds later staked the 49ers to a 21-7 halftime edge. Gary Anderson's 34-yard field goal capped the 49ers' initial drive of the second half, but the Vikings responded with Cunningham's 53-yard pass to Jake Reed setting up Carter's 3-yard touchdown grab to pull the Vikings within 24-14. However, Steve Young threw a 15-yard touchdown pass to Terrell Owens on their next drive, and Kirby scored two possessions later to give the 49ers a 38-14 lead midway through the fourth quarter. Cunningham threw a 13-yard touchdown pass to Matthew Hatchette, and the Vikings drove to the 49ers' 16 with 2:30 to play, but Cunningham threw 4 consecutive incompletions to end the Vikings' threat. Young was 21 of 30 for 224 yards and 1 touchdown. Cunningham was 18 of 40 for 331 yards and 3 touchdowns, with 1 interception. The 49ers had more first downs (30-16) and led in time of possession (38:04-21:56).

Minnesota	7	0	7	8	—	22
San Francisco	7	14	10	7	—	38

SF — Floyd 1 run (Anderson kick)
Minn — Carter 66 pass from Cunningham (Murray kick)
SF — Kirby 1 run (Anderson kick)
SF — Norton 23 interception return (Anderson kick)
SF — FG Anderson 34
Minn — Carter 3 pass from Cunningham (Murray kick)
SF — Owens 15 pass from Young (Anderson kick)
SF — Kirby 1 run (Anderson kick)
Minn — Hatchette 13 pass from Cunningham (Walsh pass from Cunningham)

AFC WILD CARD PLAYOFF GAMES RESULTS

Season	Date	Winner (Share)	Loser (Share)	Score	Site	Attendance
1997	Dec. 28	New England ($15,000)	Miami ($10,000)	17-3	New England	60,041
	Dec. 27	Denver ($10,000)	Jacksonville ($10,000)	42-17	Denver	74,481
1996	Dec. 29	Pittsburgh ($14,000)	Indianapolis ($10,000)	42-14	Pittsburgh	58,078
	Dec. 28	Jacksonville ($10,000)	Buffalo ($10,000)	30-27	Buffalo	70,213
1995	Dec. 31	Indianapolis ($7,500)	San Diego ($7,500)	35-20	San Diego	61,182
	Dec. 30	Buffalo ($13,000)	Miami ($7,500)	37-22	Buffalo	73,103
1994	Jan. 1	Cleveland ($7,500)	New England ($7,500)	20-13	Cleveland	77,452
	Dec. 31	Miami ($12,000)	Kansas City ($7,500)	27-17	Miami	67,487
1993	Jan. 9	L.A. Raiders ($7,500)	Denver ($7,500)	42-24	Los Angeles	65,314
	Jan. 8	Kansas City ($12,000)	Pittsburgh ($7,500)	27-24*	Kansas City	74,515
1992	Jan. 3	Buffalo ($6,000)	Houston ($6,000)	41-38*	Buffalo	75,141
	Jan. 2	San Diego ($10,000)	Kansas City ($6,000)	17-0	San Diego	58,278
1991	Dec. 29	Houston ($10,000)	N.Y. Jets ($6,000)	17-10	Houston	61,485
	Dec. 28	Kansas City ($6,000)	L.A. Raiders ($6,000)	10-6	Kansas City	75,827
1990	Jan. 6	Cincinnati ($10,000)	Houston ($6,000)	41-14	Cincinnati	60,012
	Jan. 5	Miami ($6,000)	Kansas City ($6,000)	17-16	Miami	67,276
1989	Dec. 31	Pittsburgh ($6,000)	Houston ($6,000)	26-23*	Houston	59,406
1988	Dec. 26	Houston ($6,000)	Cleveland ($6,000)	24-23	Cleveland	75,896
1987	Jan. 3	Houston ($6,000)	Seattle ($6,000)	23-20*	Houston	50,519
1986	Dec. 28	N.Y. Jets ($6,000)	Kansas City ($6,000)	35-15	East Rutherford	75,210
1985	Dec. 28	New England ($6,000)	N.Y. Jets ($6,000)	26-14	East Rutherford	75,945
1984	Dec. 22	Seattle ($6,000)	L.A. Raiders ($6,000)	13-7	Seattle	62,049
1983	Dec. 24	Seattle ($6,000)	Denver ($6,000)	31-7	Seattle	64,275
1982	Jan. 9	N.Y. Jets ($6,000)	Cincinnati ($6,000)	44-17	Cincinnati	57,560
	Jan. 9	San Diego ($6,000)	Pittsburgh ($6,000)	31-28	Pittsburgh	53,546
	Jan. 8	L.A. Raiders ($6,000)	Cleveland ($6,000)	27-10	Los Angeles	56,555
	Jan. 8	Miami ($6,000)	New England ($6,000)	28-13	Miami	68,842
1981	Dec. 27	Buffalo ($3,000)	N.Y. Jets ($3,000)	31-27	New York	57,050
1980	Dec. 28	Oakland ($3,000)	Houston ($3,000)	27-7	Oakland	53,333
1979	Dec. 23	Houston ($3,000)	Denver ($3,000)	13-7	Houston	48,776
1978	Dec. 24	Houston ($3,000)	Miami ($3,000)	17-9	Miami	72,445

1997 AFC WILD CARD PLAYOFF GAMES

Foxboro Stadium, Foxboro, Massachusetts
December 28, 1997, Attendance: 60,041

NEW ENGLAND 17, MIAMI 3—at Foxboro Stadium, attendance 60,041. Todd Collins returned an interception for a touchdown, and Chris Slade's interception set up another as the Patriots' defense permitted just 10 first downs and 162 total yards. Each team punted twice before Collins and Lawyer Milloy stopped Karim Abdul-Jabbar on fourth-and-1 from the Patriots' 39 late in the first quarter. The Patriots reached the Dolphins' 31, but Adam Vinatieri's 48-yard field-goal attempt sailed wide left, keeping the game scoreless. Slade intercepted Dan Marino three plays later, returning the ball to the Dolphins' 29 to set up Drew Bledsoe's 24-yard touchdown pass to Troy Brown. The Patriots had the only other scoring opportunity of the first half, but Vinatieri pushed a 47-yard field goal attempt wide right in the final minute. Collins's interception was on the second play of the second half to give the Patriots a 14-0 lead, and, after forcing a punt, Vinatieri capped a 15-play, 66-yard drive with a field goal. Corey Harris returned the kickoff 47 yards to set up Olindo Mare's 38-yard field goal nine seconds into the fourth quarter. Harris recovered the ensuing onside kick, however, Chris Canty forced Marino to fumble on the next play, Slade recovered, and the Dolphins never got inside the Patriots' 43 on their final three possessions. Bledsoe was 16 of 32 for 139 yards and 1 touchdown. Marino was 17 of 43 for 141 yards, with 2 interceptions. Derrick Cullors, who rushed for 101 yards during the season, gained 86 yards on 22 carries in place of injured Curtis Martin. The Dolphins are 0-6 in road playoff games since 1972, and, for the first time ever, lost to a team three times in one season.

Miami	0	0	0	3	—	3
New England	0	7	10	0	—	17

NE — Brown 24 pass from Bledsoe (Viantieri kick)
NE — Collins 40 interception return (Vinatieri kick)
NE — FG Vinatieri 22
Mia — FG Mare 38

Denver Mile High Stadium, Denver, Colorado
December 27, 1997, Attendance: 74,481

DENVER 42, JACKSONVILLE 17—Terrell Davis rushed for 184 yards and 2 touchdowns in three quarters as the Broncos avenged last season's playoff loss to the Jaguars. The Broncos marched 73 yards on 15 plays and consumed nearly half the first quarter on their opening possession, capped by Davis's 2-yard touchdown run. John Elway hit Rod Smith with a 43-yard touchdown pass on their next possession, and Davis capped a 92-yard drive on the following possession with a 5-yard run to take a 21-0 lead early in the second quarter. The third possession saw Elway complete passes to Smith, Willie Green, and Smith again on third-and-6, -9, and -13 situations. The Jaguars used a 34-yard pass interference penalty on Darrien Gordon at the Broncos' 4 to set up Natrone Means's 2-yard touchdown run. Reggie Barlow returned the second half's opening kickoff 58 yards to the Broncos' 27, but the Jaguars settled for Mike Hollis's 38-yard field goal to cut the deficit to 21-10. Four minutes later, Travis Davis plucked the ball out of the air, before Mike Horan could punt the ball, and scampered 29 yards for a touchdown. On their next possession the Jaguars drove to the Broncos' 16, but Mark Brunell fumbled the snap and Allen Aldridge recovered. Davis responded with a 59-yard run two plays after the fumble late in the third quarter, but bruised his ribs when he was tackled and did not return. Derek Loville replaced Davis and scored on Denver's next possession on a 25-yard run to give the Broncos a 28-17 cushion. Loville's 44-yard run later in the quarter led to his 8-yard touchdown run with 3:43 left, and Vaughn Hebron added a 6-yard run with 1:11 remaining. Elway was 16 of 24 for 223 yards and 1 touchdown. Loville gained 103 yards on 11 carries and, combined with Davis's 184 yards, became the third duo in playoff history to gain at least 100 yards in a game. Brunell was 18 of 32 for 203 yards with 1 interception. The Broncos more than doubled the Jaguars in first downs (28-14), total yards (511-237), and time of possession (40:31-19:29).

Jacksonville	0	7	10	0	—	17
Denver	14	7	0	21	—	42

Den — Te. Davis 2 run (Elam kick)
Den — R. Smith 43 pass from Elway (Elam kick)
Den — Te. Davis 5 run (Elam kick)
Jack — Means 2 run (Hollis kick)
Jack — FG Hollis 38
Jack — T. Davis 29 return of blocked punt (Hollis kick)
Den — Loville 25 run (Elam kick)
Den — Loville 8 run (Elam kick)
Den — Hebron 6 run (Elam kick)

NFC WILD CARD PLAYOFF GAMES RESULTS

Season	Date	Winner (Share)	Loser (Share)	Score	Site	Attendance
1997	Dec. 28	Tampa Bay ($10,000)	Detroit ($10,000)	20-10	Tampa Bay	73,361
	Dec. 27	Minnesota ($10,000)	N.Y. Giants ($15,000)	23-22	East Rutherford	77,497
1996	Dec. 29	San Francisco ($10,000)	Philadelphia ($10,000)	14-0	San Francisco	56,460
	Dec. 28	Dallas ($14,000)	Minnesota ($10,000)	40-15	Dallas	64,682
1995	Dec. 31	Green Bay ($13,000)	Atlanta ($7,500)	37-20	Green Bay	60,453
	Dec. 30	Philadelphia ($7,500)	Detroit ($7,500)	58-37	Philadelphia	66,099
1994	Jan. 1	Chicago ($7,500)	Minnesota ($12,000)	35-18	Minneapolis	60,347
	Dec. 31	Green Bay ($7,500)	Detroit ($7,500)	16-12	Green Bay	58,125
1993	Jan. 9	N.Y. Giants ($7,500)	Minnesota ($7,500)	17-10	East Rutherford	75,089
	Jan. 8	Green Bay ($7,500)	Detroit ($12,000)	28-24	Detroit	68,479
1992	Jan. 3	Philadelphia ($6,000)	New Orleans ($6,000)	36-20	New Orleans	68,893
	Jan. 2	Washington ($6,000)	Minnesota ($10,000)	24-7	Minneapolis	57,353
1991	Dec. 29	Dallas ($6,000)	Chicago ($6,000)	17-13	Chicago	62,594
	Dec. 28	Atlanta ($6,000)	New Orleans ($10,000)	27-20	New Orleans	68,794
1990	Jan. 6	Chicago ($10,000)	New Orleans ($6,000)	16-6	Chicago	60,767
	Jan. 5	Washington ($6,000)	Philadelphia ($6,000)	20-6	Philadelphia	65,287
1989	Dec. 31	L.A. Rams ($6,000)	Philadelphia ($6,000)	21-7	Philadelphia	65,479
1988	Dec. 26	Minnesota ($6,000)	L.A. Rams ($6,000)	28-17	Minnesota	61,204
1987	Jan. 3	Minnesota ($6,000)	New Orleans ($6,000)	44-10	New Orleans	68,546
1986	Dec. 28	Washington ($6,000)	L.A. Rams ($6,000)	19-7	Washington	54,567
1985	Dec. 29	N.Y. Giants ($6,000)	San Francisco ($6,000)	17-3	East Rutherford	75,131
1984	Dec. 23	N.Y. Giants ($6,000)	L.A. Rams ($6,000)	16-3	Anaheim	67,037
1983	Dec. 26	L.A. Rams ($6,000)	Dallas ($6,000)	24-17	Dallas	62,118
1982	Jan. 9	Dallas ($6,000)	Tampa Bay ($6,000)	30-17	Dallas	65,042
	Jan. 9	Minnesota ($6,000)	Atlanta ($6,000)	30-24	Minnesota	60,560
	Jan. 8	Green Bay ($6,000)	St. Louis ($6,000)	41-16	Green Bay	54,282
	Jan. 8	Washington ($6,000)	Detroit ($6,000)	31-7	Washington	55,045
1981	Dec. 27	N.Y. Giants ($3,000)	Philadelphia ($3,000)	27-21	Philadelphia	71,611
1980	Dec. 28	Dallas ($3,000)	Los Angeles ($3,000)	34-13	Dallas	63,052
1979	Dec. 23	Philadelphia ($3,000)	Chicago ($3,000)	27-17	Philadelphia	69,397
1978	Dec. 24	Atlanta ($3,000)	Philadelphia ($3,000)	14-13	Atlanta	59,403

1997 NFC WILD CARD PLAYOFF GAMES

Houlihan's Stadium, Tampa, Florida
December 28, 1997, Attendance: 73,361

TAMPA BAY 20, DETROIT 10—The Buccaneers broke out to a 20-0 lead and held on to record their first postseason victory since 1979. Michael Husted's 22-yard field goal with 5:24 left in the first quarter began the Buccaneers' scoring spree. After forcing a punt, Tampa Bay drove 89 yards, with Horace Copeland's 9-yard touchdown catch capping a 17-play drive. On the Lions' next possession, Anthony Parker's 19-yard interception return to the Lions' 20 set up Husted's second field goal. The Buccaneers had a chance to score just before halftime, but Warrick Dunn fumbled at the Lions' 14. However, Mike Alstott capped the Buccaneers' opening drive of the second half with a 31-yard scoring burst. The Lions drove deep into Tampa Bay territory but Scott Mitchell's fourth-and-3 pass from the Buccaneers' 8 fell incomplete. Jason Hanson kicked a 33-yard field goal to cap the Lions' next drive, but Mitchell was injured on the play previous to the field goal. He left the game with a concussion. The Lions forced another punt, and Frank Reich guided the offense to its first touchdown on a 1-yard plunge by Tommy Vardell with 7:48 left. The Lions reached no farther than the Buccaneers' 42 on their final drive. Trent Dilfer was 13 of 26 for 181 yards and 1 touchdown, with 1 interception. Mitchell was 10 of 25 for 78 yards, with 1 interception, while Reich was 11 of 15 for 129 yards. Barry Sanders, who gained 2,053 rushing yards during the season, had 18 carries for 65 yards.

Detroit	0	0	3	7	—	10
Tampa Bay	3	10	7	0	—	20

TB —FG Husted 22
TB — Copeland 9 pass from Dilfer (Husted kick)
TB — FG Husted 42
TB — Alstott 31 run (Husted kick)
Det — FG Hanson 33
Det — Vardell 1 run (Hanson kick)

Giants Stadium, East Rutherford, New Jersey
December 27,1997, Attendance: 77,497

MINNESOTA 23, NEW YORK GIANTS 22—Eddie Murray's 24-yard field goal with 10 seconds remaining capped a 10-point rally in the final 1:30 as the Vikings shocked the Giants. Bernard Holsey and Michael Strahan each recovered first-quarter Randall Cunningham fumbles in Vikings' territory to set up Brad Daluiso field goals. Danny Kanell's 37-yard pass to David Patten led to his 2-yard touchdown pass to Aaron Pierce three plays later to give the Giants a 13-0 lead. Jason Sehorn's interception set up Daluiso's third field goal, and after Duane Butler's fumble recovery of Amani Toomer's punt allowed Murray to put the Vikings on the board, Daluiso added his fourth field goal of the half to give the Giants a 19-3 halftime edge. The Vikings were limited to 68 total yards in the first half. Tony Williams forced Tiki Barber to fumble, and Jerry Ball recovered at the Giants' 4. Leroy Hoard scored on the next play to cut the deficit to 19-10. Murray missed a 48-yard field-goal attempt on the their next possession, but a 14-yard punt by Brad Maynard late in the third quarter gave the Vikings good field position and Murray kicked his second field goal fifteen seconds into the fourth quarter. The Giants responded with a 13-play, 74-yard drive capped by Daluiso's fifth field goal, from 22 yards with 7:03 left, to give the NFC East champions a 22-13 lead. When Strahan and Keith Hamilton corralled Robert Smith for a 3-yard loss on third-and-4 from the Vikings' 43, and Minnesota chose to punt, the Giants were in position to run out the clock. But the Vikings forced the Giants to punt, and Maynard's 26-yard boot sailed out of bounds at the Giants' 49 with 2:06 left. Cunningham found Carter for 19 yards between a pair of incompletions before Jake Reed got past Tito Wooten and caught a 30-yard touchdown pass in the back of the end zone with 1:30 left to cut the deficit to 22-20. Chris Calloway bobbled the ensuing onside kick on the wet turf, and Chris Walsh recovered for the Vikings at the 39-yard line. Carter caught a 21-yard pass on third-and-4 to the Giants' 34, and Phillippi Sparks was flagged for pass interference two plays later to put the ball on the 21-yard line with 43 seconds left. Smith broke free for 16 yards to the Giants' 5, and Murray kicked the game-winning field goal with 10 seconds left. Cunningham was 15 of 36 for 203 yards and 1 touchdown, with 1 interception. Kanell was 16 of 32 for 199 yards and 1 touchdown. The victory snapped a six-game postseason losing streak for the Vikings.

Minnesota	0	3	7	13	—	23
N.Y. Giants	6	13	0	3	—	22

NYG — FG Daluiso 43
NYG — FG Daluiso 22
NYG — Pierce 2 pass from Kanell (Daluiso kick)
NYG — FG Daluiso 41
Minn — FG Murray 26
NYG — FG Daluiso 51
Minn — Hoard 4 run (Murray kick)
Minn — FG Murray 26
NYG — FG Daluiso 22
Minn — Reed 30 pass from Cunningham (Murray kick)
Minn — FG Murray 24

AFC-NFC PRO BOWL AT A GLANCE RESULTS (1971-1998)

NFC leads series, 15-12

Year	Date	Winner (Share)	Loser (Share)	Score	Site	Attendance
1998	Feb. 1	AFC ($25,000)	NFC ($12,500)	29-24	Honolulu	49,995
1997	Feb. 2	AFC ($20,000)	NFC ($10,000)	26-23 (OT)	Honolulu	50,031
1996	Feb. 4	NFC ($20,000)	AFC ($10,000)	20-13	Honolulu	50,034
1995	Feb. 5	AFC ($20,000)	NFC ($10,000)	41-13	Honolulu	49,121
1994	Feb. 6	NFC ($20,000)	AFC ($10,000)	17-3	Honolulu	50,026
1993	Feb. 7	AFC ($10,000)	NFC ($5,000)	23-20 (OT)	Honolulu	50,007
1992	Feb. 2	NFC ($10,000)	AFC ($5,000)	21-15	Honolulu	50,209
1991	Feb. 3	AFC ($10,000)	NFC ($5,000)	23-21	Honolulu	50,345
1990	Feb. 4	NFC ($10,000)	AFC ($5,000)	27-21	Honolulu	50,445
1989	Jan. 29	NFC ($10,000)	AFC ($5,000)	34-3	Honolulu	50,113
1988	Feb. 7	AFC ($10,000)	NFC ($5,000)	15-6	Honolulu	50,113
1987	Feb. 1	AFC ($10,000)	NFC ($5,000)	10-6	Honolulu	50,101
1986	Feb. 2	NFC ($10,000)	AFC ($5,000)	28-24	Honolulu	50,101
1985	Jan. 27	AFC ($10,000)	NFC ($5,000)	22-14	Honolulu	50,385
1984	Jan. 29	NFC ($10,000)	AFC ($5,000)	45-3	Honolulu	50,445
1983	Feb. 6	NFC ($10,000)	AFC ($5,000)	20-19	Honolulu	49,883
1982	Jan. 31	AFC ($5,000)	NFC ($2,500)	16-13	Honolulu	50,402
1981	Feb. 1	NFC ($5,000)	AFC ($2,500)	21-7	Honolulu	50,360
1980	Jan. 27	NFC ($5,000)	AFC ($2,500)	37-27	Honolulu	49,800
1979	Jan. 29	NFC ($5,000)	AFC ($2,500)	13-7	Los Angeles	46,281
1978	Jan. 23	NFC ($5,000)	AFC ($2,500)	14-13	Tampa	51,337
1977	Jan. 17	AFC ($2,000)	NFC ($1,500)	24-14	Seattle	64,752
1976	Jan. 26	NFC ($2,000)	AFC ($1,500)	23-20	New Orleans	30,546
1975	Jan. 20	NFC ($2,000)	AFC ($1,500)	17-10	Miami	26,484
1974	Jan. 20	AFC ($2,000)	NFC ($1,500)	15-13	Kansas City	66,918
1973	Jan. 21	AFC ($2,000)	NFC ($1,500)	33-28	Dallas	37,091
1972	Jan. 23	AFC ($2,000)	NFC ($1,500)	26-13	Los Angeles	53,647
1971	Jan. 24	NFC ($2,000)	AFC ($1,500)	27-6	Los Angeles	48,222

1998 AFC-NFC PRO BOWL

Aloha Stadium, Honolulu, Hawaii
February 1, 1998, Attendance: 49,995

AFC 29, NFC 24—Warren Moon guided the AFC to points on all three of his drives, including the winning touchdown from 1 yard with 1:49 left as the AFC scored the game's final 15 points to beat the NFC. Steve Young threw a 22-yard touchdown pass to Herman Moore to cap the game's opening drive and give the NFC a 7-0 lead. Late in the first quarter, Mark Brunell threw a 17-yard touchdown pass to Andre Rison to tie the game. Both touchdown passes came on third-and-8 plays. The NFC responded with a 7-play, 71-yard drive capped by Young's 36-yard touchdown pass to Rob Moore. Trent Dilfer guided the NFC to its third touchdown, keyed by a 21-yard pass to Irving Fryar and 23-yard pass to Mike Alstott, and capped by Dorsey Levens's 12-yard touchdown run with 1:36 left in the half to give the NFC a 21-7 lead. The NFC had a chance to pad its lead on its first possession of the second half, but Jason Hanson missed a 44-yard field goal. The AFC bounced back with a 10-play, 65-yard drive that culminated with Drew Bledsoe's 14-yard touchdown pass to Jimmy Smith late in the third quarter. After Hanson's 35-yard field goal gave the NFC a 24-14 lead with 13:42 left, Moon entered the game and drove the AFC into field-goal range, where Mike Hollis drilled a 48-yard attempt with 8:51 left. Attempting to grind out the clock, Warrick Dunn fumbled, and Darryl Williams recovered at the AFC's 49 with 3:03 remaining. After a holding penalty moved the AFC back 10 yards, Moon fired a 57-yard pass to Tim Brown to set up Eddie George's 4-yard run with 2:31 left. The AFC went for the lead instead of a tie, but Moon's pass to Rison fell incomplete. However, the AFC got the ball back when Chris Chandler fumbled the snap on the NFC's first play, and Michael Sinclair recovered at the NFC's 16 with 2:19 left. Three runs by George set up Moon's winning sneak with 1:49 remaining. Moon's 2-point conversion pass to Brown was incomplete, keeping the AFC's lead at 29-24. The NFC was unable to move beyond its own 31-yard line in the final moments, and the AFC prevailed. Tim Brown had 5 receptions for 129 yards. Moon, who was 4 of 8 for 89 yards, earned player of the game honors.

AFC (29)	Offense	NFC (24)
Tim Brown (Oakland)	WR	Cris Carter (Minnesota)
Tony Boselli (Jacksonville)	LT	William Roaf (New Orleans)
Ruben Brown (Buffalo)	LG	Larry Allen (Dallas)
Dermontti Dawson (Pittsburgh)	C	Kevin Glover (Detroit)
Will Shields (Kansas City)	RG	Randall McDaniel (Minnesota)
Jonathan Ogden (Baltimore)	RT	Todd Steussie (Minnesota)
Shannon Sharpe (Denver)	TE	Wesley Walls (Carolina)
Yancey Thigpen (Pittsburgh)	WR	Herman Moore (Detroit)
Mark Brunell (Jacksonville)	QB	Steve Young (San Francisco)
Terrell Davis (Denver)	RB	Barry Sanders (Detroit)
Jerome Bettis (Pittsburgh)	RB	Mike Alstott (Tampa Bay)
	Defense	
Bruce Smith (Buffalo)	LE	Michael Strahan (N.Y. Giants)
Joel Steed (Pittsburgh)	IL	Dana Stubblefield (San Francisco)
Ted Washington (Buffalo)	IL	John Randle (Minnesota)
Neil Smith (Denver)	RE	Chris Doleman (San Francisco)
Bryce Paup (Buffalo)	LOLB	Jessie Armstead (N.Y. Giants)
Levon Kirkland (Pittsburgh)	ILB	Hardy Nickerson (Tampa Bay)
Chris Slade (New England)	ROLB	Derrick Brooks (Tampa Bay)
Dale Carter (Kansas City)	LCB	Darrell Green (Washington)
Aaron Glenn (N.Y. Jets)	RCB	Aeneas Williams (Arizona)
Carnell Lake (Pittsburgh)	SS	LeRoy Butler (Green Bay)
Darryl Williams (Seattle)	FS	Merton Hanks (San Francisco)

SUBSTITUTIONS

AFC—Offense: C—Tom Nalen (Denver). G—Steve Wisniewski (Oakland). T—Bruce Armstrong (New England). TE—Ben Coates (New England). WR—Eric Metcalf (San Diego), Andre Rison (Kansas City), Jimmy Smith (Jacksonville). RB—Eddie George (Tennessee), Kimble Anders (Kansas City). QB—Drew Bledsoe (New England), Warren Moon (Seattle). P—Bryan Barker (Jacksonville). K—Mike Hollis (Jacksonville). Defense: IL—Chester McGlockton (Oakland). DE—Mike Sinclair (Seattle). LB—Derrick Thomas (Kansas City), Junior Seau (San Diego), Ray Lewis (Baltimore). DB—Larry Whigham (New England), James Hasty (Kansas City), Blaine Bishop (Tennessee).

NFC—Offense: C—Tony Mayberry (Tampa Bay). G—Kevin Gogan (San Francisco). T—Erik Williams (Dallas). TE—Mark Chmura (Green Bay). WR—Michael Bates (Carolina), Irving Fryar (Philadelphia), Rob Moore (Arizona). RB—Warrick Dunn (Tampa Bay), Travis Jervey (Green Bay), Dorsey Levens (Green Bay). QB—Chris Chandler (Atlanta), Trent Dilfer (Tampa Bay). P—Matt Turk (Washington). K—Jason Hanson (Detroit). Defense: IL—Warren Sapp (Tampa Bay). DE—Robert Porcher (Detroit). LB—Ken Norton (San Francisco), Lee Woodall (San Francisco), Jessie Tuggle (Atlanta). DB—Cris Dishman (Washington), John Lynch (Tampa Bay).

HEAD COACHES

AFC—Bill Cowher (Pittsburgh)
NFC—Steve Mariucci (San Francisco)

OFFICIALS

Referee—Gary Lane. Umpire—Hendi Ancich. Head Linesman—Dale Williams. Line Judge—Bill Spyksma. Back Judge—Boris Cheek. Field Judge— Ron Spitler. Side Judge—Howard Slavin.

SCORING

AFC	7	0	7	15	—	29
NFC	7	14	0	3	—	24

NFC —H. Moore 22 pass from Young (Hanson kick)
AFC —Rison 17 pass from Brunell (Hollis kick)
NFC —R. Moore 36 pass from Young (Hanson kick)
NFC —Levens 12 run (Hanson kick)
AFC —J. Smith 14 pass from Bledsoe (Hollis kick)
NFC —FG Hanson 35
AFC —FG Hollis 48
AFC —George 4 run (pass failed)
AFC —Moon 1 run (pass failed)

TEAM STATISTICS	AFC	NFC
Total First Downs	19	20
Rushing	7	8
Passing	11	11
Penalty	1	1
Total Net Yardage	304	364
Total Offensive Plays	73	67
Average Gain Per Offensive Play	4.2	5.4
Rushes	33	34

Yards Gained Rushing (Net)	107	110
Average Yards per Rush	3.2	3.2
Passes Attempted	36	33
Passes Completed	14	15
Had Intercepted	0	0
Tackled Attempting to Pass	4	0
Yards Lost Attempting to Pass	15	0
Yards Gained Passing (Net)	197	254
Punts	5	4
Average Distance	36.0	39.8
Punt Returns	3	2
Punt Return Yardage	28	10
Kickoff Returns	6	5
Kickoff Return Yardage	122	109
Interception Return Yardage	0	0
Total Return Yardage	150	116
Fumbles	3	3
Fumbles Lost	3	3
Own Fumbles Recovered	0	0
Opponent Fumbles Recovered	3	3
Penalties	3	7
Yards Penalized	20	37
Field Goals	1	1
Field Goals Attempted	2	1
Third-Down Efficiency	9/18	5/13
Fourth-Down Efficiency	0/1	1/2
Time of Possession	32:22	27:38

INDIVIDUAL STATISTICS

RUSHING: NFC: Dunn (T.B.) 11-26, Levens (G.B.) 6-24, Sanders (Det.) 7-22, S. Young (S.F.) 2-20, Alstott (T.B.) 4-14, Chandler (Atl.) 3-1. AFC: E. George (Tenn.) 12-43, Bettis (Pitt.) 11-34, Davis (Den.) 6-27, Metcalf (S.D.) 1-6, Brunell (Jax.) 1-2, Moon (Sea.) 2-0, T. Brown (Oak.) 1-(-2).

PASSING: NFC: S. Young (S.F.) 5-11-103-0, Dilfer (T.B.) 8-18-98-0, Chandler (Atl.) 1-7-11-0. AFC: Brunell (Jax.) 6-11-98-0, Moon (Sea.) 4-8-89-0, Bledsoe (N.E.) 5-14-67-0.

RECEIVING: NFC: Fryar (Phil.) 3-46, Walls (Car.) 3-36, Rob Moore (Ariz.) 2-47, Carter (Minn.) 2-12, Alstott (T.B.) 1-23, Moore (Det.) 1-22, Chmura (G.B.) 1-16, Dunn (T.B.) 1-10. AFC: T. Brown (Oak.) 5-129, Smith (Jax.) 2-31, Anders (K.C.) 2-29, Bettis (Pitt.) 2-9, E. George (Tenn.) 1-23, Rison (K.C.) 1-17, Coates (N.E.) 1-8, Metcalf (S.D.) 1-8.

KICKOFF RETURNS: NFC: Bates (Car.) 6-122. AFC: Metcalf (S.D.) 5-109.

PUNT RETURNS: NFC: Dunn (T.B.) 3-28. AFC: Metcalf (S.D.) 2-10.

PUNTING: NFC: M. Turk (Wash.) 5-180-36.0. AFC: Barker (Jax.) 4-159-39.8.

SACKS: AFC: B. Smith (Buff.) 2.5, McGlockton (Oak.) 1, Sinclair (Sea.) 0.5.

1997 AFC-NFC PRO BOWL

Aloha Stadium, Honolulu, Hawaii
February 2, 1997, Attendance: 50,031

AFC 26, NFC 23 (OT)—Cary Blanchard's 37-yard field goal 8:16 into overtime gave the AFC a 26-23 victory. The field goal was an ironic ending to a game that saw Blanchard and NFC kicker John Kasay, who each broke the previous single-season record of 35 field goals, combine to miss 5 of 8 field-goal attempts. The NFC scored on its first two possessions, with Vikings guard Randall McDaniel, who lined up as a fullback, scoring his first professional touchdown to give the NFC a 9-0 lead. However, the follies of the kicking unit began as holder Matt Turk muffed the snap on the extra point attempt. Blanchard booted a 28-yard field goal with 27 seconds left in the half to cut the NFC's lead to 9-3. In the third quarter, Barry Sanders scored from 6 yards out, but Kerry Collins was sacked on the 2-point attempt. A 41-yard pass from Drew Bledsoe to Tony Martin led to Curtis Martin's 3-yard run, and after Ashley Ambrose ran an interception back 54 yards for a touchdown 11 seconds into the fourth quarter, the AFC found itself with a 16-15 lead. The NFC drove for more than six minutes, only to have Kasay miss a 40-yard field goal attempt. After an AFC punt, Cris Carter caught a 47-yard touchdown bomb from Gus Frerotte to put the NFC ahead 23-16. After each team punted, the AFC got the ball on its own 20-yard line with 55 seconds left. Mark Brunell hit Tim Brown with an 80-yard bomb down the right sideline to tie the game with 44 seconds left. Wesley Walls caught a 33-yard pass to give the NFC a chance to win in regulation, but Kasay missed a 39-yard attempt and the game went to overtime. The AFC won the overtime toss, but Blanchard missed a 41-yard field goal attempt. The NFC had to punt after three plays, and Brunell hit Ben Coates with a 43-yard pass on the AFC's first play. After three running plays failed to gain a first down, Blanchard trotted onto the field and made the game-winning kick. The teams combined for a Pro Bowl record 962 total yards. Brunell, who completed 12 of 22 pass attempts for 236 yards, was selected as the player of the game.

AFC	0	3	7	13	3 — 26
NFC	9	0	6	8	0 — 23

NFC — FG Kasay 20
NFC — R. McDaniel 5 pass from Favre (muffed snap)
AFC — FG Blanchard 28
NFC — Sanders 6 run (pass failed)
AFC — Martin 3 run (Blanchard kick)
AFC — Ambrose 54 interception return (pass failed)
NFC — Carter 53 pass from Frerotte (Walls pass from Frerotte)
AFC — T. Brown 80 pass from Brunell (Blanchard kick)
AFC — FG Blanchard 37

1996 AFC-NFC PRO BOWL

Aloha Stadium, Honolulu, Hawaii
February 4, 1996, Attendance: 50,034

NFC 20, AFC 13—Jerry Rice had 6 receptions for 82 yards and 1 touchdown to earn player of the game honors in the NFC's victory. The 49ers' wide receiver, who was named to the Pro Bowl for the tenth consecutive year, caught a 1-yard touchdown pass from Packers quarterback Brett Favre 1:41 into the second quarter to cap an 80-yard drive and give the NFC the lead for good at 10-7. The AFC had taken a 7-0 lead 2:26 into the game when Bengals quarterback Jeff Blake connected with Steelers wide receiver Yancey Thigpen on a Pro Bowl-record 93-yard touchdown pass. The NFC increased its advantage to 20-7 at halftime on Redskins linebacker Ken Harvey's 36-yard interception return for a touchdown and Falcons kicker Morten Andersen's 24-yard field goal. The AFC trimmed its deficit to 20-13 when Colts quarterback Jim Harbaugh teamed with Patriots running back Curtis Martin on a 17-yard touchdown pass in the final minute of the third quarter, but its bid to win or tie was rebuffed twice in the final minutes of the fourth quarter. First, 49ers safety Tim McDonald intercepted Harbaugh's pass in the end zone with 1:50 remaining. Then, after the AFC forced a punt and got the ball back near midfield, Harbaugh drove his team to the NFC's 9-yard line in the closing seconds. But he spiked the ball once to stop the clock and threw 3 consecutive incompletions as time ran out. The AFC outgained the NFC 390 total yards to 287, but its quarterbacks suffered 4 interceptions, including 3 off Harbaugh, the NFL's leading passer during the regular season. The NFC raised its edge to 15-11 in Pro Bowl games since the AFL-NFL merger in 1970.

NFC	3	17	0	0	—	20
AFC	7	0	6	0	—	13

AFC — Thigpen 93 pass from Blake (Elam kick)
NFC — FG Andersen 36
NFC — Rice 1 pass from Favre (Andersen kick)
NFC — Harvey 36 interception return (Andersen kick)
NFC — FG Andersen 24
AFC — Martin 17 pass from Harbaugh (kick failed)

1995 AFC-NFC PRO BOWL

Aloha Stadium, Honolulu, Hawaii
February 5, 1995, Attendance: 49,121

AFC 41, NFC 13—Colts rookie Marshall Faulk rushed for a Pro Bowl-record 180 yards to key the AFC's rout of the NFC. Faulk, who earned the Dan McGuire Trophy as the player of the game, averaged nearly 14 yards on his 13 carries and shattered the previous rushing mark of 112 yards set by O.J. Simpson in the 1973 game. Faulk's 49-yard touchdown run from punt formation in the fourth quarter was the longest in Pro Bowl history. The Seahawks' Chris Warren added 127 yards on 14 carries as the AFC amassed records for rushing yards (400) and total yards (552). Steelers tight end Eric Green caught 2 touchdown passes for the victors. The NFC managed only 196 total yards, a large chunk coming when 49ers quarterback Steve Young and Vikings wide receiver Cris Carter teamed on a 51-yard touchdown pass in the first quarter. That gave the NFC a 10-0 advantage, but the AFC rallied in the second quarter and took the lead for good when the Browns' Leroy Hoard scored on a 4-yard touchdown run 2:07 before halftime.

AFC	0	17	3	21	—	41
NFC	10	0	3	0	—	13

NFC — FG Reveiz 28
NFC — Carter 51 pass from Young (Reveiz kick)
AFC — Green 22 pass from Elway (Carney kick)
AFC — FG Carney 22
AFC — Hoard 4 run (Carney kick)
NFC — FG Reveiz 49
AFC — FG Carney 23
AFC — Warren 11 run (Carney kick)
AFC — Green 16 pass from Hostetler (Carney kick)
AFC — Faulk 49 run (Carney kick)

1994 AFC-NFC PRO BOWL

Aloha Stadium, Honolulu, Hawaii
February 6, 1994, Attendance: 50,026

NFC 17, AFC 3—The NFC converted a blocked punt and a fumble recovery into touchdowns just 2:20 apart in the second half of its victory over the AFC. With the score tied 3-3 late in the third quarter, Saints linebacker Renaldo Turnbull deflected a punt by the Oilers' Greg Montgomery, and the NFC took possession at the AFC's 48-yard line. A 32-yard pass from Bobby Hebert to Falcons teammate Andre Rison positioned Rams running back Jerome Bettis for a 4-yard touchdown run with 1:27 left in the third quarter. Moments later, Rams defensive tackle Sean Gilbert recovered a fumble by Oilers quarterback Warren Moon at the AFC's 19. Hebert then teamed with the Vikings' Cris Carter on a 15-yard touchdown pass 53 seconds into the fourth period. The NFC kept the AFC out of the end zone by maintaining possession for more than 38 minutes and forcing 6 turnovers. Rison earned the Dan McGuire Trophy as the player of the game by catching 6 passes for 86 yards. The victory was the fourth in the last six years for the NFC, which leads the series 14-10.

NFC	3	0	7	7	—	17
AFC	0	3	0	0	—	3

NFC — FG Johnson 35
AFC — FG Anderson 25
NFC — Bettis 4 run (Johnson kick)
NFC — Carter 15 pass from Hebert (Johnson kick)

1993 AFC-NFC PRO BOWL

Aloha Stadium, Honolulu, Hawaii
February 7, 1993, Attendance: 50,007

AFC 23, NFC 20—Nick Lowery's 33-yard field goal 4:09 into overtime gave the American Conference allstars an unlikely 23-20 victory over the National Conference. Despite being overwhelmed by the NFC in first downs (30-9), and total yards (471-114), the AFC won because it forced 6 turnovers, blocked a pair of field goals (1 of which was returned for a touchdown), and returned an interception for a score. Special-teams star Steve Tasker of the Bills earned the Dan McGuire Trophy as the player of the game for making 4 tackles, forcing a fumble, and blocking a field goal. The block came with eight minutes left in regulation and the game tied at 13-13. The Raiders' Terry McDaniel picked up the loose ball and ran 28 yards for a touchdown and a 20-13 AFC lead. The NFC rallied behind 49ers quarterback Steve Young, whose fourth-down, 23-yard touchdown pass to Giants running back Rodney Hampton tied the game at 20-20 with 10 seconds left in regulation. Young completed 18 of 32 passes for 196 yards but was intercepted 3 times and lost a fumble when sacked in overtime. Raiders defensive end Howie Long fell on that fumble at the NFC 28-yard line, and five plays later, Lowery converted the winning field goal.

AFC	0	10	3	7	3 — 23
NFC	3	10	0	7	0 — 20

NFC — FG Andersen 27
AFC — Seau 31 interception return (Lowery kick)
NFC — FG Andersen 37
NFC — Irvin 9 pass from Aikman (Andersen kick)
AFC — FG Lowery 42
AFC — FG Lowery 29
AFC — McDaniel 28 blocked field goal return (Lowery kick)
NFC — Hampton 23 pass from Young (Andersen kick)
AFC — FG Lowery 33

1992 AFC-NFC PRO BOWL

Aloha Stadium, Honolulu, Hawaii
February 2, 1992, Attendance: 50,209

NFC 21, AFC 15—Atlanta's Chris Miller threw an 11-yard touchdown pass to San Francisco's Jerry Rice with 4:04 remaining in the game to lift the NFC over the AFC. It was the NFC's thirteenth win in the 22-game series. The AFC had taken a 15-14 lead when the Raiders' Jeff Jaeger kicked a 27-yard field goal 1:49 into the fourth quarter. But the NFC, aided by a key roughing-the-passer penalty on a third-down incompletion from the AFC 24-yard line, drove 85 yards to the winning score. The Cowboys' Michael Irvin, playing in his first Pro Bowl, caught 8 passes for 125 yards, including a 13-yard touchdown in the first quarter, and was named the player of the game. Rice had 7 catches for 77 yards. Mark Rypien of Washington, the Super Bowl most valuable player one week earlier, completed 11 of 18 passes for 165 yards and 2 touchdowns for the NFC, including a 35-yard pass to Redskins teammate Gary Clark just 26 seconds before halftime. Miller completed 7 of his 10 attempts for 85 yards.

NFC	7	7	0	7	—	21
AFC	7	5	0	3	—	15

AFC — Clayton 4 pass from Kelly (Jaeger kick)
NFC — Irvin 13 pass from Rypien (Lohmiller kick)
AFC — Safety, Townsend tackled Byner in end zone
AFC — FG Jaeger 48
NFC — Clark 35 pass from Rypien (Lohmiller kick)
AFC — FG Jaeger 27
NFC — Rice 11 pass from Miller (Lohmiller kick)

1991 AFC-NFC PRO BOWL

Aloha Stadium, Honolulu, Hawaii
February 3, 1991, Attendance: 50,345

AFC 23, NFC 21—Buffalo's Jim Kelly and Houston's Ernest Givins combined for a 13-yard scoring pass late in the fourth quarter to rally the AFC over the NFC. Phoenix rookie Johnny Johnson scored on runs of 1 and 9 yards to put the NFC ahead 14-3 in the third quarter. Buffalo's Andre Reed, who led all receivers with 4 catches for 80 yards, caught a 20-yard scoring reception from Kelly early in the fourth quarter to move the AFC to within 1 point. Barry Sanders ran 22 yards for a touchdown to increase the NFC's lead to 21-13. Miami's Jeff Cross blocked a 46-yard field-goal attempt by New Orleans's Morten Andersen with seven seconds remaining to preserve the win. Buffalo's Bruce Smith recorded 3 sacks and also had a blocked field goal. Kelly, who completed 13 of 19 passes for 210 yards and 2 touchdowns, was presented the Dan McGuire Award as player of the game. The AFC's victory narrowed the NFC's Pro Bowl series lead to 12-9.

AFC	3	0	3	17	—	23
NFC	0	7	7	7	—	21

AFC — FG Lowery 26
NFC — J. Johnson 1 run (Andersen kick)
AFC — FG Lowery 43
NFC — J. Johnson 9 run (Andersen kick)
AFC — Reed 20 pass from Kelly (Lowery kick)
NFC — Sanders 22 run (Andersen kick)
AFC — FG Lowery 34
AFC — Givins 13 pass from Kelly (Lowery kick)

1990 AFC-NFC PRO BOWL

Aloha Stadium, Honolulu, Hawaii
February 4, 1990, Attendance: 50,445

NFC 27, AFC 21—The NFC captured its second straight Pro Bowl as the defense accounted for a pair of touchdowns and forced 5 turnovers before the eleventh consecutive sellout crowd at Aloha Stadium. The AFC held a 7-6 halftime edge on a 1-yard scoring run by Christian Okoye of the Chiefs. The NFC then rallied with 21 unanswered points in the third quarter. David Meggett of the Giants began the comeback with an 11-yard touchdown reception from Philadelphia's Randall Cunningham. The Rams' Jerry Gray followed with a 51-yard interception return for a score and the Vikings' Keith Millard added an 8-yard fumble return for a touchdown four minutes later to give the NFC a commanding 27-7 lead. Seattle's Dave Krieg rallied the AFC with a 5-yard touchdown pass to Miami's Ferrell Edmunds. Cleveland's Mike Johnson then returned an interception 22 yards for a score to pull the AFC to within 27-21. Gray, who was credited with 7 tackles, was given the Dan McGuire Award as player of the game. Krieg led all quarterbacks by completing 15 of 23 for 148 yards and 1 touchdown. Buffalo's Thurman Thomas topped all receivers with 5 catches for 47 yards, while Indianapolis's Eric Dickerson led all rushers with 46 yards on 15 carries. The win gave the NFC a 12-8 advantage in Pro Bowl games since 1971.

NFC	3	3	21	0	—	27
AFC	0	7	0	14	—	21

NFC — FG Murray 23
NFC — FG Murray 41
AFC — Okoye 1 run (Treadwell kick)
NFC — Meggett 11 pass from Cunningham (Murray kick)
NFC — Gray 51 interception return (Murray kick)
NFC — Millard 8 fumble recovery return (Murray kick)
AFC — Edmunds 5 pass from Krieg (Treadwell kick)
AFC — M. Johnson 22 interception return (Treadwell kick)

1989 AFC-NFC PRO BOWL

Aloha Stadium, Honolulu, Hawaii
January 29, 1989, Attendance: 50,113

NFC 34, AFC 3—The NFC scored 34 unanswered points to snap a two-game losing streak to the AFC before the tenth straight sellout crowd in Honolulu's Aloha Stadium. Bills kicker Scott Norwood provided the AFC's only points on a 38-yard field goal 6:23 into the game. Touchdown runs by Dallas's Herschel Walker (4 yards) and Atlanta's John Settle (1) brought the NFC a 14-3 halftime lead. Walker added a 7-yard scoring run, the Saints' Morten Andersen kicked field goals of 27 and 51 yards, and Los Angeles Rams' wide receiver Henry Ellard caught an 8-yard scoring pass from Minnesota quarterback Wade Wilson in the second half to complete the scoring. Chicago running back Neal Anderson and Philadelphia quarterback Randall Cunningham, who were both appearing in their first Pro Bowl, also played major roles in the NFC's victory. Anderson rushed 13 times for 85 yards and had 2 receptions for 17. Cunningham, who was voted the game's outstanding player, completed 10 of 14 passes for 63 yards and rushed for 49 yards. The NFC, which had 5 takeaways, outgained the AFC 355 yards to 167 and held a time-of-possession advantage of 35:18 to 24:42. Houston quarterback Warren Moon completed 13 of 20 passes for 134 yards for the AFC. The win gave the NFC an 11-8 advantage in Pro Bowl games.

AFC	3	0	0	0	—	3
NFC	7	7	10	10	—	34

AFC — FG Norwood 38
NFC — Walker 4 run (Andersen kick)
NFC — Settle 1 run (Andersen kick)
NFC — FG Andersen 27
NFC — Walker 7 run (Andersen kick)
NFC — FG Andersen 51
NFC — Ellard 8 pass from Wilson (Andersen kick)

1988 AFC-NFC PRO BOWL

Aloha Stadium, Honolulu, Hawaii
February 7, 1988, Attendance: 50,113

AFC 15, NFC 6—Led by a tenacious pass rush, the AFC defeated the NFC for the second consecutive year before the ninth straight sellout crowd in Honolulu's Aloha Stadium. Buffalo quarterback Jim Kelly scored the game's lone touchdown on a 1-yard run for a 7-6 halftime lead. Colts kicker Dean Biasucci added field goals from 37 and 30 yards to complete the AFC's scoring. Saints kicker Morten Andersen had 25- and 36-yard field goals to account for the NFC's points. AFC defenders held the NFC to 213 yards and recorded 8 sacks. Bills defensive end Bruce Smith, who had 2 sacks among his 5 tackles, was voted the game's outstanding player. Oilers running back Mike Rozier led all rushers with 49 yards on 9 carries. Jets wide receiver Al Toon had 5 receptions for 75 yards. The AFC generated 341 yards total offense and held a time-of-possession advantage of 34:14 to 25:46. By winning, the AFC cut the NFC's lead in the Pro Bowl series to 10-8.

NFC	0	6	0	0	—	6
AFC	0	7	6	2	—	15

NFC — FG Andersen 25
AFC — Kelly 1 run (Biasucci kick)
NFC — FG Andersen 36
AFC — FG Biasucci 37
AFC — FG Biasucci 30
AFC — Safety, Montana forced out of end zone

1987 AFC-NFC PRO BOWL

Aloha Stadium, Honolulu, Hawaii
February 1, 1987, Attendance: 50,101

AFC 10, NFC 6—The AFC defeated the NFC in the lowest-scoring game in AFC-NFC Pro Bowl history. The AFC took a 10-0 halftime lead on Broncos quarterback John Elway's 10-yard touchdown pass to Raiders tight end Todd Christensen and Patriots kicker Tony Franklin's 26-yard field goal. The AFC defense made the lead stand by forcing the NFC to settle for a pair of field goals from 38 and 19 yards by Saints kicker Morten Andersen after the NFC had first downs at the AFC 31-, 7-, 16-, 15-, 5-, and 7-yard lines. Both AFC scores were set up by fumble recoveries by Seahawks linebacker Fredd Young and Dolphins linebacker John Offerdahl, respectively. Eagles defensive end Reggie White, who tied a Pro Bowl record with 4 sacks among his 7 solo tackles, was voted the game's outstanding player. The AFC victory cut the NFC's lead in the Pro Bowl series to 10-7.

AFC	7	3	0	0	—	10
NFC	0	0	3	3	—	6

AFC — Christensen 10 pass from Elway (Franklin kick)
AFC — FG Franklin 26
NFC — FG Andersen 38
NFC — FG Andersen 19

1986 AFC-NFC PRO BOWL

Aloha Stadium, Honolulu, Hawaii
February 2, 1986, Attendance: 50,101

NFC 28, AFC 24—New York Giants quarterback Phil Simms brought the NFC back from a 24-7 halftime deficit to defeat the AFC. Simms, who completed 15 of 27 passes for 212 yards and 3 touchdowns, was named the most valuable player of the game. The AFC had taken its first-half lead behind a 2-yard run by Los Angeles Raiders running back Marcus Allen, who also threw a 51-yard scoring pass to San Diego wide receiver Wes Chandler, an 11-yard touchdown catch by Pittsburgh wide receiver Louis Lipps, and a 34-yard field goal by Steelers kicker Gary Anderson. Minnesota's Joey Browner accounted for the NFC's only score before halftime with a 48-yard interception return. After intermission, the NFC blanked the AFC while scoring 3 touchdowns via a 15-yard catch by Washington wide receiver Art Monk, a 2-yard reception by Dallas tight end Doug Cosbie, and a 15-yard catch by Tampa Bay tight end Jimmie Giles with 2:47 remaining in the game. The victory gave the NFC a 10-6 Pro Bowl record against the AFC.

NFC	0	7	7	14	—	28
AFC	7	17	0	0	—	24

AFC — Allen 2 run (Anderson kick)
NFC — Browner 48 interception return (Andersen kick)
AFC — Chandler 51 pass from Allen (Anderson kick)
AFC — FG Anderson 34
AFC — Lipps 11 pass from O'Brien (Anderson kick)
NFC — Monk 15 pass from Simms (Andersen kick)
NFC — Cosbie 2 pass from Simms (Andersen kick)
NFC — Giles 15 pass from Simms (Andersen kick)

1985 AFC-NFC PRO BOWL

Aloha Stadium, Honolulu, Hawaii
January 27, 1985, Attendance: 50,385

AFC 22, NFC 14—Defensive end Art Still of the Kansas City Chiefs recovered a fumble and returned it 83 yards for a touchdown to clinch the AFC's victory over the NFC. Still's touchdown came in the fourth period with the AFC trailing 14-12 and was one of several outstanding defensive plays in a Pro Bowl dominated by two record-breaking defenses. The teams combined for a Pro Bowl-record 17 sacks, including 4 by New York Jets defensive end Mark Gastineau, who was named the game's outstanding player. The AFC's first score came on a safety when Gastineau tackled running back Eric Dickerson of the Los Angeles Rams in the end zone. The AFC's second score, a 6-yard pass from Miami's Dan Marino to Los Angeles Raiders running back Marcus Allen, was set up by a partial block of a punt by Seahawks linebacker Fredd Young. The NFC leads the series 9-6.

AFC	0	9	0	13	—	22
NFC	0	0	7	7	—	14

AFC — Safety, Gastineau tackled Dickerson in end zone
AFC — Allen 6 pass from Marino (Johnson kick)
NFC — Lofton 13 pass from Montana (Stenerud kick)
NFC — Payton 1 run (Stenerud kick)
AFC — FG Johnson 33
AFC — Still 83 fumble recovery return (Johnson kick)
AFC — FG Johnson 22

1984 AFC-NFC PRO BOWL

Aloha Stadium, Honolulu, Hawaii
January 29, 1984, Attendance: 50,445

NFC 45, AFC 3—The NFC won its sixth Pro Bowl in the last seven seasons by routing the AFC. The NFC was led by the passing of most valuable player Joe Theismann of Washington, who completed 21 of 27 passes for 242 yards and 3 touchdowns. Theismann set Pro Bowl records for completions and touchdown passes. The NFC established Pro Bowl marks for most points scored and fewest points allowed. Running back William Andrews of Atlanta had 6 carries for 43 yards and caught 4 passes for 49 yards, including scoring receptions of 16 and 2 yards. Los Angeles Rams rookie Eric Dickerson gained 46 yards on 11 carries, including a 14-yard touchdown run, and had 45 yards on 5 catches. Rams safety Nolan Cromwell had a 44-yard interception return for a touchdown early in the third period to give the NFC a commanding 24-3 lead. Green Bay wide receiver James Lofton caught an 8-yard touchdown pass, while tight end teammate Paul Coffman had a 6-yard scoring catch.

NFC	3	14	14	14	—	45
AFC	0	3	0	0	—	3

NFC — FG Haji-Sheikh 23
NFC — Andrews 16 pass from Theismann (Haji-Sheikh kick)
NFC — Andrews 2 pass from Montana (Haji-Sheikh kick)
AFC — FG Anderson 43
NFC — Cromwell 44 interception return (Haji-Sheikh kick)
NFC — Lofton 8 pass from Theismann (Haji-Sheikh kick)
NFC — Coffman 6 pass from Theismann (Haji-Sheikh kick)
NFC — Dickerson 14 run (Haji-Sheikh kick)

1983 AFC-NFC PRO BOWL

Aloha Stadium, Honolulu, Hawaii
February 6, 1983, Attendance: 49,883

NFC 20, AFC 19—Dallas's Danny White threw an 11-yard touchdown pass to the Packers' John Jefferson with 35 seconds remaining to rally the NFC over the AFC. White, who completed 14 of 26 passes for 162 yards, kept the winning 65-yard drive alive with a 14-yard completion to Jefferson on a fourth-and-7 play at the AFC 25. The AFC was ahead 12-10 at halftime and increased the lead to 19-10 in the third period, when Marcus Allen scored on a 1-yard run. San Diego's Dan Fouts, who attempted 30 passes, set Pro Bowl records for most completions (17) and yards (274). Pittsburgh's John Stallworth was the AFC's leading receiver with 7 catches for 67 yards. William Andrews topped the NFC with 5 receptions for 48 yards. Fouts and Jefferson were co-winners of the player of the game award.

AFC	9	3	7	0	—	19
NFC	0	10	0	10	—	20

AFC — Walker 34 pass from Fouts (Benirschke kick)
AFC — Safety, Still tackled Theismann in end zone
NFC — Andrews 3 run (Moseley kick)
NFC — FG Moseley 35
AFC — FG Benirschke 29
AFC — Allen 1 run (Benirschke kick)
NFC — FG Moseley 41
NFC — Jefferson 11 pass from D. White (Moseley kick)

1982 AFC-NFC PRO BOWL

Aloha Stadium, Honolulu, Hawaii
January 31, 1982, Attendance: 50,402

AFC 16, NFC 13—Nick Lowery of Kansas City kicked a 23-yard field goal with three seconds remaining to give the AFC a last-second victory over the NFC. Lowery's kick climaxed a 69-yard drive directed by quarterback Dan Fouts. The NFC gained a 13-13 tie with 2:43 to go when Dallas's Tony Dorsett ran 4 yards for a touchdown. In the drive to the winning field goal, Fouts completed 3 passes, including a 23-yard toss to San Diego teammate Kellen Winslow that put the ball on the NFC's 5-yard line. Two plays later, Lowery kicked the field goal. Winslow, who caught 6 passes for 86 yards, was named co-player of the game along with Tampa Bay defensive end Lee Roy Selmon.

NFC	0	6	0	7	—	13
AFC	0	0	13	3	—	16

NFC — Giles 4 pass from Montana (kick blocked)
AFC — Muncie 2 run (kick failed)
AFC — Campbell 1 run (Lowery kick)
NFC — Dorsett 4 run (Septien kick)
AFC — FG Lowery 23

1981 AFC-NFC PRO BOWL

Aloha Stadium, Honolulu, Hawaii
February 1, 1981, Attendance: 50,360

NFC 21, AFC 7—Eddie Murray kicked 4 field goals and Steve Bartkowski fired a 55-yard scoring pass to Alfred Jenkins to lead the NFC to its fourth straight victory over the AFC and a 7-4 edge in the series. Murray was named the game's most valuable player and missed tying Garo Yepremian's Pro Bowl record of 5 field goals when a 37-yard attempt hit the crossbar with 22 seconds remaining. The AFC's only score came on a 9-yard pass from Brian Sipe to Stanley Morgan in the second period. Bartkowski completed 9 of 21 passes for 173 yards, while Sipe connected on 10 of 15 for 142 yards. Ottis Anderson led all rushers with 70 yards on 10 carries. Earl Campbell, the NFL's leading rusher in 1980, was limited to 24 yards on 8 attempts.

AFC	0	7	0	0	—	7
NFC	3	6	0	12	—	21

NFC — FG Murray 31
AFC — Morgan 9 pass from Sipe (J. Smith kick)
NFC — FG Murray 31
NFC — FG Murray 34
NFC — Jenkins 55 pass from Bartkowski (Murray kick)
NFC — FG Murray 36
NFC — Safety, Shell called for holding in end zone

1980 AFC-NFC PRO BOWL

Aloha Stadium, Honolulu, Hawaii
January 27, 1980, Attendance: 49,800

NFC 37, AFC 27—Running back Chuck Muncie of New Orleans ran for 2 touchdowns and threw a 25-yard option pass for another score to give the NFC its third consecutive victory over the AFC. Muncie, who was selected the game's most valuable player, snapped a 3-3 tie on a 1-yard touchdown run at 1:41 of the second quarter, then scored on an 11-yard run in the fourth quarter for the NFC's final touchdown. Two scoring records were set in the game— 37 points by the NFC, eclipsing the 33 by the AFC in 1973, and the 64 points by both teams, surpassing the 61 scored in 1973.

NFC	3	20	7	7	—	37
AFC	3	7	10	7	—	27

NFC — FG Moseley 37
AFC — FG Fritsch 19
NFC — Muncie 1 run (Moseley kick)
AFC — Pruitt 1 pass from Bradshaw (Fritsch kick)
NFC — D. Hill 13 pass from Manning (kick failed)
NFC — T. Hill 25 pass from Muncie (Moseley kick)
NFC — Henry 86 punt return (Moseley kick)
AFC — Campbell 2 run (Fritsch kick)
AFC — FG Fritsch 29
NFC — Muncie 11 run (Moseley kick)
AFC — Campbell 1 run (Fritsch kick)

1979 AFC-NFC PRO BOWL

Memorial Coliseum, Los Angeles, California
January 29, 1979, Attendance: 46,281

NFC 13, AFC 7—Roger Staubach completed 9 of 15 passes for 125 yards, including the winning touchdown on a 19-yard strike to Dallas Cowboys teammate Tony Hill in the third period. The winning drive began at the AFC's 45-yard line after a shanked punt. Staubach hit Ahmad Rashad with passes of 15 and 17 yards to set up Hill's decisive catch. The victory gave the NFC a 5-4 advantage in Pro Bowl games. Rashad, who accounted for 89 yards on 5 receptions, was named the player of the game. The AFC led 7-6 at halftime on Bob Griese's 8-yard scoring toss to Steve Largent late in the second quarter. Largent finished the game with 5 receptions for 75 yards. The NFC scored first as Archie Manning marched his team 70 yards in 11 plays, capped by Wilbert Montgomery's 2-yard touchdown run. The AFC's Earl Campbell was the game's leading rusher with 66 yards on 12 carries.

AFC	0	7	0	0	—	7
NFC	0	6	7	0	—	13

NFC — Montgomery 2 run (kick failed)
AFC — Largent 8 pass from Griese (Yepremian kick)
NFC — T. Hill 19 pass from Staubach (Corral kick)

1978 AFC-NFC PRO BOWL

Tampa Stadium, Tampa, Florida
January 23, 1978, Attendance: 51,337

NFC 14, AFC 13—Walter Payton, the NFL's leading rusher in 1977, sparked a second-half comeback to give the NFC the win and tie the series between the two conferences at four victories each. Payton, who was the game's most valuable player, gained 77 yards on 13 carries and scored the tying touchdown on a 1-yard burst with 7:37 left in the game. Efren Herrera kicked the winning extra point. The AFC dominated the first half of the game, taking a 13-0 lead on field goals of 21 and 39 yards by Toni Linhart and a 10-yard touchdown pass from Ken Stabler to Oakland teammate Cliff Branch. On the NFC's first possession of the second half, Pat Haden put together the first touchdown drive after Eddie Brown returned Ray Guy's punt to the AFC 46-yard line. Haden connected on all 4 of his passes on that drive, finally hitting Terry Metcalf with a 4-yard scoring toss. The NFC continued to rally and, with Jim Hart at quarterback, moved 63 yards in 12 plays for the go-ahead score. During the winning drive, Hart completed 5 of 6 passes for 38 yards and Payton picked up 20 more on the ground.

AFC	3	10	0	0	—	13
NFC	0	0	7	7	—	14

AFC — FG Linhart 21
AFC — Branch 10 pass from Stabler (Linhart kick)
AFC — FG Linhart 39
NFC — Metcalf 4 pass from Haden (Herrera kick)
NFC — Payton 1 run (Herrera kick)

1977 AFC-NFC PRO BOWL

Kingdome, Seattle, Washington
January 17, 1977, Attendance: 64,752

AFC 24, NFC 14—O.J. Simpson's 3-yard touchdown burst at 7:03 of the first quarter gave the AFC a lead it would not surrender, breaking a two-game NFC win streak and giving the American Conference stars a 4-3 series lead. The AFC took a 17-7 lead midway through the second period on the first of 2 Ken Anderson touchdown passes, a 12-yard toss to Charlie Joiner. But the NFC mounted a 73-yard drive capped by Lawrence McCutcheon's 1-yard touchdown plunge to pull within 17-14 at the half. Following a scoreless third quarter, player of the game Mel Blount thwarted a possible NFC score when he intercepted Jim Hart's pass in the end zone. Less than three minutes later, Blount again picked off a Hart pass, returning it 16 yards to the NFC 27. That set up Anderson's 27-yard touchdown strike to the Raiders' Cliff Branch for the final score.

NFC	0	14	0	0	—	14
AFC	10	7	0	7	—	24

AFC — Simpson 3 run (Linhart kick)
AFC — FG Linhart 31
NFC — Thomas 15 run (Bakken kick)
AFC — Joiner 12 pass from Anderson (Linhart kick)
NFC — McCutcheon 1 run (Bakken kick)
AFC — Branch 27 pass from Anderson (Linhart kick)

1976 AFC-NFC PRO BOWL

Superdome, New Orleans, Louisiana
January 26, 1976, Attendance: 30,546

NFC 23, AFC 20—Mike Boryla, a late substitute who did not enter the game until 5:39 remained, lifted the National Football Conference to the victory over the American Football Conference with 2 touchdown passes in the final minutes. It was the second straight NFC win, squaring the series at 3-3. Until Boryla started firing the ball the AFC was in control, leading 13-0 at the half. Boryla entered the game after Billy Johnson had raced 90 yards with a punt to make the score 20-9 in favor of the AFC. He floated a 14-yard touchdown pass to Terry Metcalf and later fired an 8-yard scoring pass to Mel Gray for the winner.

AFC	0	13	0	7	—	20
NFC	0	0	9	14	—	23

AFC — FG Stenerud 20
AFC — FG Stenerud 35
AFC — Burrough 64 pass from Pastorini (Stenerud kick)
NFC — FG Bakken 42
NFC — Foreman 4 pass from Hart (kick blocked)
AFC — Johnson 90 punt return (Stenerud kick)
NFC — Metcalf 14 pass from Boryla (Bakken kick)
NFC — Gray 8 pass from Boryla (Bakken kick)

1975 AFC-NFC PRO BOWL

Orange Bowl, Miami, Florida
January 20, 1975, Attendance: 26,484

NFC 17, AFC 10—Los Angeles quarterback James Harris, who took over the NFC offense after Jim Hart of St. Louis suffered a laceration above his right eye in the second period, threw 2 touchdown passes early in the fourth period to pace the NFC to its second victory in the five-game Pro Bowl series. The NFC win snapped a three-game AFC victory string. Harris, who was named the player of the game, connected with St. Louis's Mel Gray for an 8-yard touchdown 2:03 into the final period. One minute and 24 seconds later, following a fumble recovery by Washington's Ken Houston, Harris tossed another 8-yard scoring pass to Washington's Charley Taylor for the decisive points.

NFC	0	3	0	14	—	17
AFC	0	0	10	0	—	10

NFC — FG Marcol 33
AFC — Warfield 32 pass from Griese (Gerela kick)
AFC — FG Gerela 33
NFC — Gray 8 pass from J. Harris (Marcol kick)
NFC — Taylor 8 pass from J. Harris (Marcol kick)

1974 AFC-NFC PRO BOWL

Arrowhead Stadium, Kansas City, Missouri
January 20, 1974, Attendance: 66,918

AFC 15, NFC 13—Miami's Garo Yepremian's fifth field goal—a 42-yard kick with 21 seconds remaining—gave the AFC its third straight victory since the NFC won the inaugural game following the 1970 season. The field goal by Yepremian, who was voted the game's outstanding player, offset a 21-yard field goal by Atlanta's Nick Mike-Mayer that had given the NFC a 13-12 advantage with 1:41 remaining. The only touchdown in the game was scored by the NFC on a 14-yard pass from Philadelphia's Roman Gabriel to Lawrence McCutcheon of the Los Angeles Rams.

NFC	0	10	0	3	—	13
AFC	3	3	3	6	—	15

AFC — FG Yepremian 16
NFC — FG Mike-Mayer 27
NFC — McCutcheon 14 pass from Gabriel (Mike-Mayer kick)
AFC — FG Yepremian 37
AFC — FG Yepremian 27
AFC — FG Yepremian 41
NFC — FG Mike-Mayer 21
AFC — FG Yepremian 42

1973 AFC-NFC PRO BOWL

Texas Stadium, Irving, Texas
January 21, 1973, Attendance: 37,091

AFC 33, NFC 28—Paced by the rushing and receiving of player of the game O.J. Simpson, the AFC erased a 14-0 first period deficit and built a commanding 33-14 lead midway through the fourth period before the NFC managed 2 touchdowns in the final minute of play. Simpson rushed for 112 yards and caught 3 passes for 58 more to gain unanimous recognition in the balloting for player of the game. John Brockington scored 3 touchdowns for the NFC.

AFC	0	10	10	13	—	33
NFC	14	0	0	14	—	28

NFC — Brockington 1 run (Marcol kick)
NFC — Brockington 3 pass from Kilmer (Marcol kick)
AFC — Simpson 7 run (Gerela kick)
AFC — FG Gerela 18
AFC — FG Gerela 22
AFC — Hubbard 11 run (Gerela kick)
AFC — O. Taylor 5 pass from Lamonica (kick failed)
AFC — Bell 12 interception return (Gerela kick)
NFC — Brockington 1 run (Marcol kick)
NFC — Kwalick 12 pass from Snead (Marcol kick)

1972 AFC-NFC PRO BOWL

Memorial Coliseum, Los Angeles, California
January 23, 1972, Attendance: 53,647

AFC 26, NFC 13—Kansas City's Jan Stenerud kicked 4 field goals to lead the AFC from a 6-0 deficit to victory. The AFC defense picked off 3 passes. Stenerud was selected as the outstanding offensive player and his Kansas City teammate, linebacker Willie Lanier, was the game's outstanding defensive player.

AFC	0	3	13	10	—	26
NFC	0	6	0	7	—	13

NFC — Grim 50 pass from Landry (kick failed)
AFC — FG Stenerud 25
AFC — FG Stenerud 23
AFC — FG Stenerud 48
AFC — Morin 5 pass from Dawson (Stenerud kick)
AFC — FG Stenerud 42
NFC — V. Washington 2 run (Knight kick)
AFC — F. Little 6 run (Stenerud kick)

1971 AFC-NFC PRO BOWL

Memorial Coliseum, Los Angeles, California
January 24, 1971, Attendance: 48,222

NFC 27, AFC 6—Mel Renfro of Dallas broke open the first meeting between the American Football Conference and National Football Conference all-star teams as he returned a pair of punts 82 and 56 yards for touchdowns in the final period to clinch the NFC victory over the AFC. Renfro was voted the game's outstanding back and linebacker Fred Carr of Green Bay the outstanding lineman.

AFC	0	3	3	0	—	6
NFC	0	3	10	14	—	27

AFC — FG Stenerud 37
NFC — FG Cox 13
NFC — Osborn 23 pass from Brodie (Cox kick)
NFC — FG Cox 35
AFC — FG Stenerud 16
NFC — Renfro 82 punt return (Cox kick)
NFC — Renfro 56 punt return (Cox kick)

PRO BOWL ALL-TIME RESULTS

PRO BOWL ALL-TIME RESULTS

Date	Result	Site (attendance)	Honored players
Jan. 15, 1939	New York Giants 13, Pro All-Stars 10	Wrigley Field, Los Angeles (20,000)	
Jan. 14, 1940	Green Bay 16, NFL All-Stars 7	Gilmore Stadium, Los Angeles (18,000)	
Dec. 29, 1940	Chicago Bears 28, NFL All-Stars 14	Gilmore Stadium, Los Angeles (21,624)	
Jan. 4, 1942	Chicago Bears 35, NFL All-Stars 24	Polo Grounds, New York (17,725)	
Dec. 27, 1942	NFL All-Stars 17, Washington 14	Shibe Park, Philadelphia (18,671)	
Jan. 14, 1951	American Conf. 28, National Conf. 27	Los Angeles Memorial Coliseum (53,676)	Otto Graham, Cleveland, player of the game
Jan. 12, 1952	National Conf. 30, American Conf. 13	Los Angeles Memorial Coliseum (19,400)	Dan Towler, Los Angeles, player of the game
Jan. 10, 1953	National Conf. 27, American Conf. 7	Los Angeles Memorial Coliseum (34,208)	Don Doll, Detroit, player of the game
Jan. 17, 1954	East 20, West 9	Los Angeles Memorial Coliseum (44,214)	Chuck Bednarik, Philadelphia, player of the game
Jan. 16, 1955	West 26, East 19	Los Angeles Memorial Coliseum (43,972)	Billy Wilson, San Francisco, player of the game
Jan. 15, 1956	East 31, West 30	Los Angeles Memorial Coliseum (37,867)	Ollie Matson, Chi. Cardinals, player of the game
Jan. 13, 1957	West 19, East 10	Los Angeles Memorial Coliseum (44,177)	Bert Rechichar, Baltimore, outstanding back Ernie Stautner, Pittsburgh, outstanding lineman
Jan. 12, 1958	West 26, East 7	Los Angeles Memorial Coliseum (66,634)	Hugh McElhenny, San Francisco, outstanding back Gene Brito, Washington, outstanding lineman
Jan. 11, 1959	East 28, West 21	Los Angeles Memorial Coliseum (72,250)	Frank Gifford, N.Y. Giants, outstanding back Doug Atkins, Chi. Bears, outstanding lineman
Jan. 17, 1960	West 38, East 21	Los Angeles Memorial Coliseum (56,876)	Johnny Unitas, Baltimore, outstanding back Gene (Big Daddy) Lipscomb, Baltimore, outstanding lineman
Jan. 15, 1961	West 35, East 31	Los Angeles Memorial Coliseum (62,971)	Johnny Unitas, Baltimore, outstanding back Sam Huff, N.Y. Giants, outstanding lineman
Jan. 7, 1962	AFL West 47, East 27	Balboa Stadium, San Diego (20,973)	Cotton Davidson, Dallas Texans, player of the game
Jan. 14, 1962	NFL West 31, East 30	Los Angeles Memorial Coliseum (57,409)	Jim Brown, Cleveland, outstanding back Henry Jordan, Green Bay, outstanding lineman
Jan. 13, 1963	AFL West 21, East 14	Balboa Stadium, San Diego (27,641)	Curtis McClinton, Dallas Texans, outstanding offensive player Earl Faison, San Diego, outstanding defensive player
Jan. 13, 1963	NFL East 30, West 20	Los Angeles Memorial Coliseum (61,374)	Jim Brown, Cleveland, outstanding back Gene (Big Daddy) Lipscomb, Pittsburgh, outstanding lineman
Jan. 12, 1964	NFL West 31, East 17	Los Angeles Memorial Coliseum (67,242)	Johnny Unitas, Baltimore, player of the game Gino Marchetti, Baltimore, outstanding lineman
Jan. 19, 1964	AFL West 27, East 24	Balboa Stadium, San Diego (20,016)	Keith Lincoln, San Diego, outstanding offensive player Archie Matsos, Oakland, outstanding defensive player
Jan. 10, 1965	NFL West 34, East 14	Los Angeles Memorial Coliseum (60,598)	Fran Tarkenton, Minnesota, outstanding back Terry Barr, Detroit, outstanding lineman
Jan. 16, 1965	AFL West 38, East 14	Jeppesen Stadium, Houston (15,446)	Keith Lincoln, San Diego, outstanding offensive player Willie Brown, Denver, outstanding defensive player
Jan. 15, 1966	AFL All-Stars 30, Buffalo 19	Rice Stadium, Houston (35,572)	Joe Namath, N.Y. Jets, most valuable player, offense Frank Buncom, San Diego, most valuable player, defense
Jan. 15, 1966	NFL East 36, West 7	Los Angeles Memorial Coliseum (60,124)	Jim Brown, Cleveland, outstanding back Dale Meinert, St. Louis, outstanding lineman
Jan. 21, 1967	AFL East 30, West 23	Oakland-Alameda County Coliseum (18,876)	Babe Parilli, Boston, outstanding offensive player Verlon Biggs, N.Y. Jets, outstanding defensive player
Jan. 22, 1967	NFL East 20, West 10	Los Angeles Memorial Coliseum (15,062)	Gale Sayers, Chicago, outstanding back Floyd Peters, Philadelphia, outstanding lineman
Jan. 21, 1968	AFL East 25, West 24	Gator Bowl, Jacksonville, Fla. (40,103)	Joe Namath and Don Maynard, N.Y. Jets, out. off. players Leslie (Speedy) Duncan, San Diego, out. def. player
Jan. 21, 1968	NFL West 38, East 20	Los Angeles Memorial Coliseum (53,289)	Gale Sayers, Chicago, outstanding back Dave Robinson, Green Bay, outstanding lineman
Jan. 19, 1969	AFL West 38, East 25	Gator Bowl, Jacksonville, Fla. (41,058)	Len Dawson, Kansas City, outstanding offensive player George Webster, Houston, outstanding defensive player
Jan. 19, 1969	NFL West 10, East 7	Los Angeles Memorial Coliseum (32,050)	Roman Gabriel, Los Angeles, outstanding back Merlin Olsen, Los Angeles, outstanding lineman
Jan. 17, 1970	AFL West 26, East 3	Astrodome, Houston (30,170)	John Hadl, San Diego, player of the game
Jan. 18, 1970	NFL West 16, East 13	Los Angeles Memorial Coliseum (57,786)	Gale Sayers, Chicago, outstanding back George Andrie, Dallas, outstanding lineman
Jan. 24, 1971	NFC 27, AFC 6	Los Angeles Memorial Coliseum (48,222)	Mel Renfro, Dallas, outstanding back Fred Carr, Green Bay, outstanding lineman
Jan. 23, 1972	AFC 26, NFC 13	Los Angeles Memorial Coliseum (53,647)	Jan Stenerud, Kansas City, outstanding offensive player Willie Lanier, Kansas City, outstanding defensive player
Jan. 21, 1973	AFC 33, NFC 28	Texas Stadium, Irving (37,091)	O.J. Simpson, Buffalo, player of the game
Jan. 20, 1974	AFC 15, NFC 13	Arrowhead Stadium, Kansas City (66,918)	Garo Yepremian, Miami, player of the game
Jan. 20, 1975	NFC 17, AFC 10	Orange Bowl, Miami (26,484)	James Harris, Los Angeles, player of the game
Jan. 26, 1976	NFC 23, AFC 20	Louisiana Superdome, New Orleans (30,546)	Billy Johnson, Houston, player of the game
Jan. 17, 1977	AFC 24, NFC 14	Kingdome, Seattle (64,752)	Mel Blount, Pittsburgh, player of the game
Jan. 23, 1978	NFC 14, AFC 13	Tampa Stadium (51,337)	Walter Payton, Chicago, player of the game
Jan. 29, 1979	NFC 13, AFC 7	Los Angeles Memorial Coliseum (46,281)	Ahmad Rashad, Minnesota, player of the game
Jan. 27, 1980	NFC 37, AFC 27	Aloha Stadium, Honolulu (49,800)	Chuck Muncie, New Orleans, player of the game
Feb. 1, 1981	NFC 21, AFC 7	Aloha Stadium, Honolulu (50,360)	Eddie Murray, Detroit, player of the game
Jan. 31, 1982	AFC 16, NFC 13	Aloha Stadium, Honolulu (50,402)	Kellen Winslow, San Diego, and Lee Roy Selmon, Tampa Bay, players of the game
Feb. 6, 1983	NFC 20, AFC 19	Aloha Stadium, Honolulu (49,883)	Dan Fouts, San Diego, and John Jefferson, Green Bay, players of the game
Jan. 29, 1984	NFC 45, AFC 3	Aloha Stadium, Honolulu (50,445)	Joe Theismann, Washington, player of the game
Jan. 27, 1985	AFC 22, NFC 14	Aloha Stadium, Honolulu (50,385)	Mark Gastineau, N.Y. Jets, player of the game
Feb. 2, 1986	NFC 28, AFC 24	Aloha Stadium, Honolulu (50,101)	Phil Simms, N.Y. Giants, player of the game
Feb. 1, 1987	AFC 10, NFC 6	Aloha Stadium, Honolulu (50,101)	Reggie White, Philadelphia, player of the game
Feb. 7, 1988	AFC 15, NFC 6	Aloha Stadium, Honolulu (50,113)	Bruce Smith, Buffalo, player of the game
Jan. 29, 1989	NFC 34, AFC 3	Aloha Stadium, Honolulu (50,113)	Randall Cunningham, Philadelphia, player of the game
Feb. 4, 1990	NFC 27, AFC 21	Aloha Stadium, Honolulu (50,445)	Jerry Gray, L.A. Rams, player of the game
Feb. 3, 1991	AFC 23, NFC 21	Aloha Stadium, Honolulu (50,345)	Jim Kelly, Buffalo, player of the game
Feb. 2, 1992	NFC 21, AFC 15	Aloha Stadium, Honolulu (50,209)	Michael Irvin, Dallas, player of the game
Feb. 7, 1993	AFC 23, NFC 20 (OT)	Aloha Stadium, Honolulu (50,007)	Steve Tasker, Buffalo, player of the game
Feb. 6, 1994	NFC 17, AFC 3	Aloha Stadium, Honolulu (50,026)	Andre Rison, Atlanta, player of the game
Feb. 5, 1995	AFC 41, NFC 13	Aloha Stadium, Honolulu (49,121)	Marshall Faulk, Indianapolis, player of the game
Feb. 4, 1996	NFC 20, AFC 13	Aloha Stadium, Honolulu (50,034)	Jerry Rice, San Francisco, player of the game
Feb. 2, 1997	AFC 26, NFC 23 (OT)	Aloha Stadium, Honolulu (50,031)	Mark Brunell, Jacksonville, player of the game
Feb. 1, 1998	AFC 29, NFC 24	Aloha Stadium, Honolulu (49,995)	Warren Moon, Seattle, player of the game

PRO FOOTBALL HALL OF FAME GAME

1962	New York Giants 21, St. Louis Cardinals 21
1963	Pittsburgh Steelers 16, Cleveland Browns 7
1964	Baltimore Colts 48, Pittsburgh Steelers 17
1965	Washington Redskins 20, Detroit Lions 3
1966	No game
1967	Philadelphia Eagles 28, Cleveland Browns 13
1968	Chicago Bears 30, Dallas Cowboys 24
1969	Green Bay Packers 38, Atlanta Falcons 24
1970	New Orleans Saints 14, Minnesota Vikings 13
1971	Los Angeles Rams (NFC) 17, Houston Oilers (AFC) 6
1972	Kansas City Chiefs (AFC) 23, New York Giants (NFC) 17
1973	San Francisco 49ers (NFC) 20, New England Patriots (AFC) 7
1974	St. Louis Cardinals (NFC) 21, Buffalo Bills (AFC) 13
1975	Washington Redskins (NFC) 17, Cincinnati Bengals (AFC) 9
1976	Denver Broncos (AFC) 10, Detroit Lions (NFC) 7
1977	Chicago Bears (NFC) 20, New York Jets (AFC) 6
1978	Philadelphia Eagles (NFC) 17, Miami Dolphins (AFC) 3
1979	Oakland Raiders (AFC) 20, Dallas Cowboys (NFC) 13
1980*	San Diego Chargers (AFC) 0, Green Bay Packers (NFC) 0
1981	Cleveland Browns (AFC) 24, Atlanta Falcons (NFC) 10
1982	Minnesota Vikings (NFC) 30, Baltimore Colts (AFC) 14
1983	Pittsburgh Steelers (AFC) 27, New Orleans Saints (NFC) 14
1984	Seattle Seahawks (AFC) 38, Tampa Bay Buccaneers (NFC) 0
1985	New York Giants (NFC) 21, Houston Oilers (AFC) 20
1986	New England Patriots (AFC) 21, St. Louis Cardinals (NFC) 16
1987	San Francisco 49ers (NFC) 20, Kansas City Chiefs (AFC) 7
1988	Cincinnati Bengals (AFC) 14, Los Angeles Rams (NFC) 7
1989	Washington Redskins (NFC) 31, Buffalo Bills (AFC) 6
1990	Chicago Bears (NFC) 13, Cleveland Browns (AFC) 0
1991	Detroit Lions (NFC) 14, Denver Broncos (AFC) 3
1992	New York Jets (AFC) 41, Philadelphia Eagles (NFC) 14
1993	Los Angeles Raiders (AFC) 19, Green Bay Packers (NFC) 3
1994	Atlanta Falcons (NFC) 21, San Diego Chargers (AFC) 17
1995	Carolina Panthers (NFC) 20, Jacksonville Jaguars (AFC) 14
1996	Indianapolis Colts (AFC) 10, New Orleans Saints (NFC) 3
1997	Minnesota Vikings (NFC) 28, Seattle Seahawks (AFC) 26

Game called with 5:29 remaining due to severe thunder and lightning.

NFL INTERNATIONAL GAMES

Date	Site	Teams
Aug. 12, 1950	Ottawa, Canada	N.Y. Giants 27, Ottawa Rough Riders 6
Aug. 11, 1951	Ottawa, Canada	N.Y. Giants 41, Ottawa Rough Riders 18
Aug. 5, 1959	Toronto, Canada	Chi. Cardinals 55, Tor. Argonauts 26
Aug. 3, 1960	Toronto, Canada	Pittsburgh 43, Toronto Argonauts 16
Aug. 15, 1960	Toronto, Canada	Chicago 16, N.Y. Giants 7
Aug. 2, 1961	Toronto, Canada	St. Louis 36, Toronto Argonauts 7
Aug. 5, 1961	Montreal, Canada	Chicago 34, Montreal Allouettes 16
Aug. 8, 1961	Hamilton, Canada	Hamilton Tiger-Cats 38, Buffalo 21
Sept. 11, 1969	Montreal, Canada	Pittsburgh 17, N.Y. Giants 13
Aug. 25, 1969	Montreal, Canada	Detroit 22, Boston 9
Aug. 16, 1976	Tokyo, Japan	St. Louis 20, San Diego 10
Aug. 5, 1978	Mexico City, Mexico	New Orleans 14, Philadelphia 7
Aug. 6, 1983	London, England	Minnesota 28, St. Louis 10
*Aug. 3, 1986	London, England	Chicago 17, Dallas 6
*Aug. 9, 1987	London, England	L.A. Rams 28, Denver 27
*July 31, 1988	London, England	Miami 27, San Francisco 21
Aug. 14, 1988	Goteborg, Sweden	Minnesota 28, Chicago 21
Aug. 18, 1988	Montreal, Canada	N.Y. Jets 11, Cleveland 7
*Aug. 5, 1989	Tokyo, Japan	L.A. Rams 16, San Francisco 13 (OT)
*Aug. 6, 1989	London, England	Philadelphia 17, Cleveland 13
*Aug. 4, 1990	Tokyo, Japan	Denver 10, Seattle 7
*Aug. 5, 1990	London, England	New Orleans 17, L.A. Raiders 10
*Aug. 9, 1990	Montreal, Canada	Pittsburgh 30, New England 14
*Aug. 11, 1990	Berlin, Germany	L.A. Rams 19, Kansas City 3
*July 28, 1991	London, England	Buffalo 17, Philadelphia 13
*Aug. 3, 1991	Berlin, Germany	San Francisco 21, Chicago 7
*Aug. 3, 1991	Tokyo, Japan	Miami 19, L.A. Raiders 17
*Aug. 1, 1992	Tokyo, Japan	Houston 34, Dallas 23
*Aug. 15, 1992	Berlin, Germany	Miami 31, Denver 27
*Aug. 16, 1992	London, England	San Francisco 17, Washington 15
*July 31, 1993	Tokyo, Japan	New Orleans 28, Philadelphia 16
*Aug. 1, 1993	Barcelona, Spain	San Francisco 21, Pittsburgh 14
*Aug. 7, 1993	Berlin, Germany	Minnesota 20, Buffalo 6
*Aug. 8, 1993	London, England	Dallas 13, Detroit 13 (OT)
Aug. 14, 1993	Toronto, Canada	Cleveland 12, New England 9
*July 31, 1994	Barcelona, Spain	L.A. Raiders 25, Denver 22
*Aug. 6, 1994	Tokyo, Japan	Minnesota 17, Kansas City 9
*Aug. 13, 1994	Berlin, Germany	N.Y. Giants 28, San Diego 20
*Aug. 15, 1994	Mexico City, Mexico	Houston 6, Dallas 0
*Aug. 5, 1995	Tokyo, Japan	Denver 24, San Francisco 10
*Aug. 12, 1995	Toronto, Canada	Buffalo 9, Dallas 7
*July 27, 1996	Tokyo, Japan	San Diego 20, Pittsburgh 10
*Aug. 5, 1996	Monterrey, Mexico	Kansas City 32, Dallas 6
*July 27, 1997	Dublin, Ireland	Pittsburgh 30, Chicago 17
*Aug. 4, 1997	Mexico City, Mexico	Miami 38, Denver 19
*Aug. 16, 1997	Toronto, Canada	Green Bay 35, Buffalo 3

**American Bowl Game*

CHICAGO ALL-STAR GAME

Pro teams won 31, lost 9, and tied 2. The game was discontinued after 1976.

Year	Date	Winner	Loser	Attendance
1976*	July 23	Pittsburgh 24	All-Stars 0	52,895
1975	Aug. 1	Pittsburgh 21	All-Stars 14	54,103
1974		No game was played		
1973	July 27	Miami 14	All-Stars 3	54,103
1972	July 28	Dallas 20	All-Stars 7	54,162
1971	July 30	Baltimore 24	All-Stars 17	52,289
1970	July 31	Kansas City 24	All-Stars 3	69,940
1969	Aug. 1	N.Y. Jets 26	All-Stars 24	74,208
1968	Aug. 2	Green Bay 34	All-Stars 17	69,917
1967	Aug. 4	Green Bay 27	All-Stars 0	70,934
1966	Aug. 5	Green Bay 38	All-Stars 0	72,000
1965	Aug. 6	Cleveland 24	All-Stars 16	68,000
1964	Aug. 7	Chicago 28	All-Stars 17	65,000
1963	Aug. 2	All-Stars 20	Green Bay 17	65,000
1962	Aug. 3	Green Bay 42	All-Stars 20	65,000
1961	Aug. 4	Philadelphia 28	All-Stars 14	66,000
1960	Aug. 12	Baltimore 32	All-Stars 7	70,000
1959	Aug. 14	Baltimore 29	All-Stars 0	70,000
1958	Aug. 15	All-Stars 35	Detroit 19	70,000
1957	Aug. 9	N.Y. Giants 22	All-Stars 12	75,000
1956	Aug. 10	Cleveland 26	All-Stars 0	75,000
1955	Aug. 12	All-Stars 30	Cleveland 27	75,000
1954	Aug. 13	Detroit 31	All-Stars 6	93,470
1953	Aug. 14	Detroit 24	All-Stars 10	93,818
1952	Aug. 15	Los Angeles 10	All-Stars 7	88,316
1951	Aug. 17	Cleveland 33	All-Stars 0	92,180
1950	Aug. 11	All-Stars 17	Philadelphia 7	88,885
1949	Aug. 12	Philadelphia 38	All-Stars 0	93,780
1948	Aug. 20	Chi. Cardinals 28	All-Stars 0	101,220
1947	Aug. 22	All-Stars 16	Chi. Bears 0	105,840
1946	Aug. 23	All-Stars 16	Los Angeles 0	97,380
1945	Aug. 30	Green Bay 19	All-Stars 7	92,753
1944	Aug. 30	Chi. Bears 24	All-Stars 21	48,769
1943	Aug. 25	All-Stars 27	Washington 7	48,471
1942	Aug. 28	Chi. Bears 21	All-Stars 0	101,100
1941	Aug. 28	Chi. Bears 37	All-Stars 13	98,203
1940	Aug. 29	Green Bay 45	All-Stars 28	84,567
1939	Aug. 30	N.Y. Giants 9	All-Stars 0	81,456
1938	Aug. 31	All-Stars 28	Washington 16	74,250
1937	Sept. 1	All-Stars 6	Green Bay 0	84,560
1936	Sept. 3	Detroit 7	All-Stars 7 (tie)	76,000
1935	Aug. 29	Chi. Bears 5	All-Stars 0	77,450
1934	Aug. 31	Chi. Bears 0	All-Stars 0 (tie)	79,432

**Game shortened due to thunderstorms.*

NFL PLAYOFF BOWL

Western Conference won 8, Eastern Conference won 2.
All games played at Miami's Orange Bowl.

1970	Los Angeles Rams 31, Dallas Cowboys 0
1969	Dallas Cowboys 17, Minnesota Vikings 13
1968	Los Angeles Rams 30, Cleveland Browns 6
1967	Baltimore Colts 20, Philadelphia Eagles 14
1966	Baltimore Colts 35, Dallas Cowboys 3
1965	St. Louis Cardinals 24, Green Bay Packers 17
1964	Green Bay Packers 40, Cleveland Browns 23
1963	Detroit Lions 17, Pittsburgh Steelers 10
1962	Detroit Lions 28, Philadelphia Eagles 10
1961	Detroit Lions 17, Cleveland Browns 16

INTERCONFERENCE GAMES

AFC VS. NFC (REGULAR SEASON), 1970-1997

	1970	1971	1972	1973	1974	1975	1976	1977	1978	1979	1980	1981	1982	1983	1984	1985	1986	1987	1988	1989	1990	1991	1992	1993	1994	1995	1996	1997	Totals
Miami	2-1	3-0	3-0	3-0	2-1	3-0	0-2	2-0	3-1	4-0	4-0	3-1	1-1	3-1	4-0	3-1	2-2	3-0	3-1	2-0	2-2	3-1	2-2	3-1	2-2	2-2	1-3	1-3	69-28
Oakland	1-2	1-1-1	3-0	2-1	3-0	3-0	3-0	1-1	4-0	4-0	2-2	2-2	3-0	2-2	3-1	3-1	1-3	2-2	1-3	2-2	3-1	2-2	2-2	3-1	3-1	3-1	1-3	2-2	65-36-1
Pittsburgh	0-3	1-2	2-1	3-0	3-0	2-1	1-1	2-0	3-1	3-1	4-0	3-1	1-0	2-2	3-1	1-3	2-2	2-2	1-3	3-1	3-1	0-4	1-3	2-2	2-2	2-2	2-2	2-2	56-43
Baltimore																											2-2	2-1-1	4-3-1
Kansas City	0-2-1	2-1	2-1	1-1-1	1-2	2-1	1-1	1-1	0-2	0-2	2-0	2-2	0-3	2-2	1-1	2-2	1-1	1-2	0-2	2-0	4-0	2-2	2-2	2-2	3-1	3-1	4-0	4-0	47-37-2
Denver	2-2	1-3	1-3	0-3-1	2-2	2-1	2-0	1-1	2-2	3-1	3-1	3-1	2-1	0-2	3-1	3-1	3-1	2-1-1	3-1	2-2	1-3	2-0	1-3	1-3	1-3	2-2	3-1	3-1	54-46-2
Cincinnati	1-2	1-2	2-1	2-1	2-1	3-0	2-0	2-1	2-2	2-2	2-2	2-2	1-0	3-1	2-2	2-2	3-1	1-2	4-0	2-2	1-3	1-3	1-3	2-2	1-3	2-2	2-2	2-2	53-46
Cleveland	0-3	2-1	1-2	1-2	1-2	1-3	2-0	1-1	4-0	3-1	3-1	3-1	0-2	2-2	1-3	1-3	2-2	2-2	4-0	3-1	1-3	0-4	2-2	3-1	3-1	1-3			47-46
Seattle								1-0	3-1	3-1	1-3	0-2	1-0	1-3	4-0	2-2	3-1	4-0	1-3	0-4	2-2	1-3	0-4	0-2	2-0	3-1	2-2	2-2	36-36
Buffalo	0-3	0-3	2-0-1	2-1	2-1	1-2	0-2	1-1	1-1	2-2	3-1	1-3	1-2	1-3	1-3	0-2	1-1	1-2	2-2	1-3	3-1	3-1	4-0	4-0	1-3	3-1	4-0	1-3	46-47-1
San Diego	1-2	2-1	0-3	1-2	1-2	0-3	2-0	1-1	2-2	3-1	2-2	2-2	1-0	2-2	4-0	1-1	0-4	2-0	2-2	2-2	1-1	1-3	2-0	2-2	2-2	3-1	1-3	1-3	44-47
Tennessee	0-3	0-2-1	0-3	0-3	0-3	3-0	2-0	2-0	2-2	2-2	4-0	1-3	0-3	1-3	0-4	1-3	2-2	2-2	3-1	3-1	1-3	1-3	3-1	2-2	0-4	1-3	2-2	4-0	42-58-1
Indianapolis	3-0	2-1	0-3	2-1	1-2	2-1	0-2	1-1	2-2	1-1	1-1	0-4	0-1-1	2-0	0-4	3-1	1-3	1-0	2-2	1-3	2-2	0-4	2-0	0-4	0-2	2-2	3-1	1-3	35-51-1
N.Y. Jets	2-1	0-3	1-2	0-3	2-1	0-3	0-2	1-1	1-3	3-1	1-3	2-0	4-0	3-1	0-2	2-2	2-2	0-4	2-0	1-3	2-0	2-2	0-4	2-2	1-3	0-4	1-3	3-1	38-56
New England	0-3	0-3	3-0	2-1	3-0	1-2	1-1	2-0	2-2	3-1	1-3	0-4	0-1	2-2	0-4	3-1	3-1	0-3	2-2	0-4	0-4	1-1	0-4	1-1	4-0	0-4	2-2	1-3	37-57
Jacksonville																										0-4	2-2	2-2	4-8
Tampa Bay							0-1																						0-1
TOTALS	12-27-1	15-23-2	20-19-1	19-19-2	23-17	23-17	16-12	19-9	31-21	36-16	33-19	24-28	15-14-1	26-26	26-26	27-25	26-26	23-22-1	30-22	24-28	26-26	19-33	22-30	27-25	25-27	27-33	32-28	31-28-1	677-646-9

NFC VS. AFC (REGULAR SEASON), 1970-1997

	1970	1971	1972	1973	1974	1975	1976	1977	1978	1979	1980	1981	1982	1983	1984	1985	1986	1987	1988	1989	1990	1991	1992	1993	1994	1995	1996	1997	Totals
Carolina																										3-1	3-1	2-2	8-4
Dallas	3-0	3-0	3-0	2-1	2-1	2-1	2-0	1-1	3-1	1-3	3-1	4-0	2-1	2-2	2-2	3-1	1-3	2-1	0-4	0-2	1-1	3-1	4-0	2-2	3-1	4-0	2-2	2-2	62-34
San Francisco	4-0	2-1	2-1	1-2	0-3	1-2	1-1	0-2	1-3	0-4	2-2	3-1	1-3	2-2	3-1	3-1	4-0	3-1	2-2	4-0	4-0	3-1	3-1	2-2	3-1	3-1	4-0	2-2	63-40
Philadelphia	2-1	1-2	2-1	2-1	2-1	0-3	0-2	1-1	3-1	2-2	3-1	3-1	2-1	1-1	3-1	1-1	2-2	3-1	2-2	3-1	1-3	4-0	3-1	2-2	1-3	1-3	2-2	2-1-1	54-42-1
Washington	2-1	1-2	1-2	2-1	2-1	1-2	1-1	1-1	2-2	2-2	1-3	2-2		4-0	3-1	4-0	3-1	2-1	1-3	2-2	3-1	4-0	2-2	1-3	1-1	0-4	3-1	1-3	52-43
Minnesota	2-1	2-1	1-2	2-1	2-1	4-0	2-0	1-1	1-3	1-3	1-3	1-3	1-3	4-0	0-4	2-0	1-3	2-1	2-2	2-2	2-2	0-2	3-1	2-2	2-2	3-1	1-3	3-1	50-48
St. Louis	2-1	1-2	1-2	3-0	3-1	3-0	1-1	2-0	2-2	2-2	2-2	1-3	1-2	1-3	3-1	3-1	2-2	1-2	2-2	3-1	2-2	1-3	2-2	2-2	2-2	1-3	2-2	0-4	51-50
N.Y. Giants	3-0	1-2	1-2	1-2	1-2	2-1	0-2	0-2	1-1	1-1	1-3	1-1	1-0	0-4	2-0	2-2	3-1	2-1	1-1	4-0	3-1	3-1	2-2	2-2	3-1	0-4	2-2	1-3	44-44
Chicago	1-2	1-2	1-2	2-2	0-3	0-3	0-2	1-1	0-4	2-2	0-4	4-0	1-1	1-1	2-2	3-1	4-0	2-2	3-1	2-2	2-2	2-2	1-3	2-2	3-1	2-2	2-2	2-2	46-53
Detroit	3-0	4-0	2-0-1	0-3	1-2	1-2	2-0	2-0	2-2	0-4	0-2	2-2	0-1	1-3	0-4	2-2	1-3	0-4	1-1	1-3	1-3	4-0	2-2	2-0	2-2	3-1	1-3	2-2	42-51-1
New Orleans	0-3	0-1-2	0-3	1-2	0-3	0-3	1-2	0-2	1-3	0-4	1-3	2-2	1-0	1-3	3-1	0-4	1-3	4-0	4-0	4-0	2-2	3-1	3-1	2-2	1-3	4-0	1-3	2-2	42-56-2
Arizona	2-0-1	2-1	1-2	0-2-1	2-1	2-1	1-1	0-2	0-4	1-3	1-1	3-1		3-1	3-1	2-2	1-1	0-1	1-3	1-3	2-2	1-1	0-2	1-1	3-1	1-3	0-4	1-3	35-48-2
Green Bay	2-1	2-1	2-1	1-1-1	2-1	0-3	0-2	0-3	2-2	1-3	1-3	1-1	1-1-1	2-2	0-4	0-4	1-3	1-2-1	1-3	0-2	1-3	1-3	3-1	3-1	1-3	4-0	3-1	3-1	39-56-3
Atlanta	1-2	3-0	2-2	2-1	0-3	1-2	0-2	0-2	1-3	1-3	2-2	1-3	1-1	3-1	1-3	0-4	1-3	0-4	1-3	2-2	2-2	3-1	2-2	1-3	1-3	2-2	0-4	2-2	36-65
Tampa Bay								0-1	2-0	2-0	1-3	0-4	2-1	1-3	1-1	0-4	1-1	0-2	1-3	0-4	0-2	1-3	0-2	1-3	1-1	2-2	2-2	3-1	21-43
Seattle							1-0																						1-0
TOTALS	27-12-1	23-15-2	19-20-1	19-19-2	17-23	17-23	12-16	9-19	21-31	16-36	19-33	28-24	14-15-1	26-26	26-26	25-27	26-26	22-23-1	22-30	28-24	26-26	33-19	30-22	25-27	27-25	33-27	28-32	28-31-1	646-677-9

1997 INTERCONFERENCE GAMES

(Home Team in capital letters)

AFC 31, NFC 28, Ties 1

AFC Victories

CINCINNATI 24, Arizona 21
JACKSONVILLE 40, New York Giants 13
San Diego 20, NEW ORLEANS 6
PITTSBURGH 14, Washington 13
Baltimore 24, NEW YORK GIANTS 23
Oakland 36, ATLANTA 31
DENVER 35, St. Louis 14
NEW ENGLAND 31, Chicago 3
Kansas City 35, CAROLINA 14
Denver 29, ATLANTA 21
OAKLAND 35, St. Louis 17
BUFFALO 22, Detroit 13
JACKSONVILLE 38, Philadelphia 21
Seattle 17, ST. LOUIS 9
TENNESSEE 28, Washington 14
Baltimore 20, WASHINGTON 17
Kansas City 28, ST. LOUIS 20
Tennessee 41, ARIZONA 14
DENVER 34, Carolina 0
TENNESSEE 10, New York Giants 6
INDIANAPOLIS 41, Green Bay 38
New York Jets 23, CHICAGO 15
NEW YORK JETS 23, Minnesota 21
Tennessee 27, DALLAS 14
Pittsburgh 26, ARIZONA 20 (OT)
KANSAS CITY 44, San Francisco 9
MIAMI 33, Detroit 30
CINCINNATI 31, Dallas 24
NEW YORK JETS 31, Tampa Bay 0
KANSAS CITY 25, New Orleans 13
SEATTLE 38, San Francisco 9

NFC Victories

Dallas 37, PITTSBURGH 7
Minnesota 34, BUFFALO 13
Carolina 26, SAN DIEGO 7
GREEN BAY 23, Miami 18
TAMPA BAY 31, Miami 21
WASHINGTON 24, Jacksonville 12
DALLAS 26, Jacksonville 22
Chicago 36, MIAMI 33 (OT)
NEW YORK GIANTS 29, Cincinnati 27
Green Bay 28, NEW ENGLAND 10
MINNESOTA 23, New England 18
CAROLINA 38, Oakland 14
Tampa Bay 31, INDIANAPOLIS 28
New Orleans 13, OAKLAND 10
TAMPA BAY 27, New England 7
NEW ORLEANS 20, Seattle 17 (OT)
Arizona 16, BALTIMORE 13
DETROIT 32, Indianapolis 10
PHILADELPHIA 23, Pittsburgh 20
SAN FRANCISCO 17, San Diego 10
Atlanta 24, SEATTLE 17
PHILADELPHIA 44, Cincinnati 42
Atlanta 14, SAN DIEGO 3
CHICAGO 20, Buffalo 3
SAN FRANCISCO 34, Denver 17
GREEN BAY 31, Buffalo 21
MINNESOTA 39, Indianapolis 28
DETROIT 13, New York Jets 10

TIE

BALTIMORE 10, Philadelphia 10 (OT)

REGULAR SEASON INTERCONFERENCE RECORDS, 1970-1997

AMERICAN FOOTBALL CONFERENCE

Eastern Division	W	L	T	Pct.
Miami	69	28	0	.711
Buffalo	46	47	1	.495
Indianapolis	35	51	1	.408
New York Jets	38	56	0	.404
New England	37	57	0	.394
Central Division				
Pittsburgh	56	43	0	.566
Baltimore	4	3	1	.563
Cincinnati	53	46	0	.535
Cleveland	47	46	0	.505
Tennessee	42	58	1	.421
Jacksonville	4	8	0	.333
Western Division				
Oakland	65	36	1	.642
Kansas City	47	37	2	.558
Denver	54	46	2	.539
Seattle*	36	36	0	.500
San Diego	44	47	0	.484

NATIONAL FOOTBALL CONFERENCE

Eastern Division	W	L	T	Pct.
Dallas	62	34	0	.646
Philadelphia	54	42	1	.562
Washington	52	43	0	.547
New York Giants	44	44	0	.500
Arizona	35	48	2	.424
Central Division				
Minnesota	50	48	0	.510
Chicago	46	53	0	.465
Detroit	42	51	1	.452
Green Bay	39	56	3	.413
Tampa Bay*	21	44	0	.328
Western Division				
Carolina	8	4	0	.667
San Francisco	63	40	0	.612
St. Louis	51	50	0	.505
New Orleans	42	56	2	.430
Atlanta	36	65	0	.356

**Records include one game played between Seattle and Tampa Bay, won by the Seahwaks 13-10, in their inaugural season (1976) when Seattle competed in the NFC and Tampa Bay in the AFC.*

INTERCONFERENCE VICTORIES, 1970-1997

REGULAR SEASON

	AFC	NFC	Tie
1970	12	27	1
1971	15	23	2
1972	20	19	1
1973	19	19	2
1974	23	17	0
1975	23	17	0
1976	16	12	0
1977	19	9	0
1978	31	21	0
1979	36	16	0
1980	33	19	0
1981	24	28	0
1982	15	14	1
1983	26	26	0
1984	26	26	0
1985	27	25	0
1986	26	26	0
1987	23	22	1
1988	30	22	0
1989	24	28	0
1990	26	26	0
1991	19	33	0
1992	22	30	0
1993	27	25	0
1994	25	27	0
1995	27	33	0
1996	32	28	0
1997	31	28	1
Total	677	646	9

PRESEASON

	AFC	NFC	Tie
1970	21	28	1
1971	28	28	3
1972	27	25	4
1973	23	35	2
1974	35	25	0
1975	30	26	1
1976	30	31	0
1977	38	25	0
1978	20	19	0
1979	25	18	0
1980	22	20	1
1981	18	19	0
1982	25	16	0
1983	15	24	0
1984	16	19	0
1985	10	22	1
1986	22	17	0
1987	22	22	0
1988	23	16	1
1989	16	27	0
1990	15	29	0
1991	19	27	0
1992	30	22	0
1993	17	22	0
1994	22	16	0
1995	19	26	0
1996	27	19	0
1997	26	17	0
Total	641	640	14

RECORDS AFTER BYE WEEKS, 1990-97

AFC

Team	Record	Team	Record
Baltimore	1-1	Miami	8-1
Buffalo	8-1	New England	3-6
Cincinnati	2-7	N.Y. Jets	3-6
Cleveland	2-5	Oakland	4-5
Denver	7-2	Pittsburgh	5-4
Indianapolis	4-5	San Diego	4-5
Jacksonville	2-1	Seattle	2-7
Kansas City	7-2	Tennessee	4-5

RECORDS AFTER BYE WEEKS, 1990-97

NFC

Team	Record	Team	Record
Arizona	4-5	New Orleans	4-5
Atlanta	7-2	N.Y. Giants	2-7
Carolina	1-2	Philadelphia	6-3
Chicago	7-2	St. Louis	3-6
Dallas	7-2	San Francisco	4-5
Detroit	4-5	Tampa Bay	2-7
Green Bay	4-5	Washington	3-6
Minnesota	7-2		

MONDAY NIGHT FOOTBALL, 1970-1997

(Home Team in capitals, games listed in chronological order.)

1997
GREEN BAY 38, Chicago 24
Kansas City 28, OAKLAND 27
DALLAS 21, Philadelphia 20
JACKSONVILLE 30, Pittsburgh 21
San Francisco 34, CAROLINA 21
DENVER 34, New England 13
WASHINGTON 21, Dallas 16
Buffalo 9, INDIANAPOLIS 6
Green Bay 28, NEW ENGLAND 10
KANSAS CITY 13, Pittsburgh 10
San Francisco 24, PHILADELPHIA 12
MIAMI 30, Buffalo 13
DENVER 31, Oakland 3
Green Bay 27, MINNESOTA 11
Carolina 23, DALLAS 13
SAN FRANCISCO 34, Denver 17
New England 14, MIAMI 12

1996
CHICAGO 22, Dallas 6
GREEN BAY 39, Philadelphia 13
PITTSBURGH 24, Buffalo 6
INDIANAPOLIS 10, Miami 6
Dallas 23, PHILADELPHIA 19
Pittsburgh 17, KANSAS CITY 7
GREEN BAY 23, San Francisco 20 (OT)
Oakland 23, SAN DIEGO 14
Chicago 15, MINNESOTA 13
Denver 22, OAKLAND 21
SAN DIEGO 27, Detroit 21
DALLAS 21, Green Bay 6
Pittsburgh 24, MIAMI 17
San Francisco 34, ATLANTA 10
OAKLAND 26, Kansas City 7
MIAMI 16, Buffalo 14
SAN FRANCISCO 24, Detroit 14

1995
Dallas 35, NEW YORK GIANTS 0
Green Bay 27, CHICAGO 24
MIAMI 23, Pittsburgh 10
DETROIT 27, San Francisco 24
Buffalo 22, CLEVELAND 19
KANSAS CITY 29, San Diego 23 (OT)
DENVER 27, Oakland 0
NEW ENGLAND 27, Buffalo 14
Chicago 14, MINNESOTA 6
DALLAS 34, Philadelphia 12
PITTSBURGH 20, Cleveland 3
San Francisco 44, MIAMI 20
SAN DIEGO 12, Oakland 6
DETROIT 27, Chicago 7
MIAMI 13, Kansas City 6
SAN FRANCISCO 37, Minnesota 30
Dallas 37, ARIZONA 13

1994
SAN FRANCISCO 44, Los Angeles Raiders 14
PHILADELPHIA 30, Chicago 22
Detroit 20, DALLAS 17 (OT)
BUFFALO 27, Denver 20
PITTSBURGH 30, Houston 14
Minnesota 27, NEW YORK GIANTS 10
Kansas City 31, DENVER 28
PHILADELPHIA 21, Houston 6
Green Bay 33, CHICAGO 6
DALLAS 38, New York Giants 10
PITTSBURGH 23, Buffalo 10
New York Giants 13, HOUSTON 10
San Francisco 35, NEW ORLEANS 14
Los Angeles Raiders 24, SAN DIEGO 17
MIAMI 45, Kansas City 28
Dallas 24, NEW ORLEANS 16
MINNESOTA 21, San Francisco 14

1993
WASHINGTON 35, Dallas 16
CLEVELAND 23, San Francisco 13
KANSAS CITY 15, Denver 7
Pittsburgh 45, ATLANTA 17
MIAMI 17, Washington 10
BUFFALO 35, Houston 7
Los Angeles Raiders 23, DENVER 20
Minnesota 19, CHICAGO 12
BUFFALO 24, Washington 10
KANSAS CITY 23, Green Bay 16
PITTSBURGH 23, Buffalo 0
SAN FRANCISCO 42, New Orleans 7
San Diego 31, INDIANAPOLIS 0
DALLAS 23, Philadelphia 17
Pittsburgh 21, MIAMI 20
New York Giants 24, NEW ORLEANS 14
SAN DIEGO 45, Miami 20
Philadelphia 37, SAN FRANCISCO 34 (OT)

1992
DALLAS 23, Washington 10
Miami 27, CLEVELAND 23
New York Giants 27, CHICAGO 14
KANSAS CITY 27, Los Angeles Raiders 7
PHILADELPHIA 31, Dallas 7
WASHINGTON 34, Denver 3
PITTSBURGH 20, Cincinnati 0
Buffalo 24, NEW YORK JETS 20
Minnesota 38, CHICAGO 10
San Francisco 41, ATLANTA 3
Buffalo 26, MIAMI 20
NEW ORLEANS 20, Washington 3
SEATTLE 16, Denver 13 (OT)
HOUSTON 24, Chicago 7
MIAMI 20, Los Angeles Raiders 7
Dallas 41, ATLANTA 17
SAN FRANCISCO 24, Detroit 6

1991
NEW YORK GIANTS 16, San Francisco 14
Washington 33, DALLAS 31
HOUSTON 17, Kansas City 7
CHICAGO 19, New York Jets 13 (OT)
WASHINGTON 23, Philadelphia 0
KANSAS CITY 33, Buffalo 6
New York Giants 23, PITTSBURGH 20
BUFFALO 35, Cincinnati 16
KANSAS CITY 24, Los Angeles Raiders 21
PHILADELPHIA 30, New York Giants 7
Chicago 34, MINNESOTA 17
Buffalo 41, MIAMI 27
San Francisco 33, LOS ANGELES RAMS 10
Philadelphia 13, HOUSTON 6
MIAMI 37, Cincinnati 13
NEW ORLEANS 27, Los Angeles Raiders 0
SAN FRANCISCO 52, Chicago 14

1990
San Francisco 13, NEW ORLEANS 12
DENVER 24, Kansas City 23
Buffalo 30, NEW YORK JETS 7
SEATTLE 31, Cincinnati 16
Cleveland 30, DENVER 29
PHILADELPHIA 32, Minnesota 24
Cincinnati 34, CLEVELAND 13
PITTSBURGH 41, Los Angeles Rams 10
New York Giants 24, INDIANAPOLIS 7
PHILADELPHIA 28, Washington 14
Los Angeles Raiders 13, MIAMI 10
HOUSTON 27, Buffalo 24
SAN FRANCISCO 7, New York Giants 3
Los Angeles Raiders 38, DETROIT 31
San Francisco 26, LOS ANGELES RAMS 10
NEW ORLEANS 20, Los Angeles Rams 17

1989
New York Giants 27, WASHINGTON 24
Denver 28, BUFFALO 14
CINCINNATI 21, Cleveland 14
CHICAGO 27, Philadelphia 13
Los Angeles Raiders 14, NEW YORK JETS 7
BUFFALO 23, Los Angeles Rams 20
CLEVELAND 27, Chicago 7
NEW YORK GIANTS 24, Minnesota 14
SAN FRANCISCO 31, New Orleans 13
HOUSTON 26, Cincinnati 24
Denver 14, WASHINGTON 10
SAN FRANCISCO 34, New York Giants 24
SEATTLE 17, Buffalo 16
San Francisco 30, LOS ANGELES RAMS 27
NEW ORLEANS 30, Philadelphia 20
MINNESOTA 29, Cincinnati 21

1988
NEW YORK GIANTS 27, Washington 20
Dallas 17, PHOENIX 14
CLEVELAND 23, Indianapolis 17
Los Angeles Raiders 30, DENVER 27 (OT)
NEW ORLEANS 20, Dallas 17
PHILADELPHIA 24, New York Giants 13
Buffalo 37, NEW YORK JETS 14
CHICAGO 10, San Francisco 9
INDIANAPOLIS 55, Denver 23
HOUSTON 24, Cleveland 17
Buffalo 31, MIAMI 6
SAN FRANCISCO 37, Washington 21
SEATTLE 35, Los Angeles Raiders 27
LOS ANGELES RAMS 23, Chicago 3
MIAMI 38, Cleveland 31
MINNESOTA 28, Chicago 27

1987
CHICAGO 34, New York Giants 19
NEW YORK JETS 43, New England 24
San Francisco 41, NEW YORK GIANTS 21
DENVER 30, Los Angeles Raiders 14
Washington 13, DALLAS 7
CLEVELAND 30, Los Angeles Rams 17
MINNESOTA 34, Denver 27
DALLAS 33, New York Giants 24
NEW YORK JETS 30, Seattle 14
DENVER 31, Chicago 29
Los Angeles Rams 30, WASHINGTON 26
Los Angeles Raiders 37, SEATTLE 14
MIAMI 37, New York Jets 28
SAN FRANCISCO 41, Chicago 0
Dallas 29, LOS ANGELES RAMS 21
New England 24, MIAMI 10

1986
DALLAS 31, New York Giants 28
Denver 21, PITTSBURGH 10
Chicago 25, GREEN BAY 12
Dallas 31, ST. LOUIS 7
SEATTLE 33, San Diego 7
CINCINNATI 24, Pittsburgh 22
NEW YORK JETS 22, Denver 10
NEW YORK GIANTS 27, Washington 20
Los Angeles Rams 20, CHICAGO 17
CLEVELAND 26, Miami 16
WASHINGTON 14, San Francisco 6
MIAMI 45, New York Jets 3
New York Giants 21, SAN FRANCISCO 17
SEATTLE 37, Los Angeles Raiders 0
Chicago 16, DETROIT 13
New England 34, MIAMI 27

1985
DALLAS 44, Washington 14
CLEVELAND 17, Pittsburgh 7
Los Angeles Rams 35, SEATTLE 24
Cincinnati 37, PITTSBURGH 24
WASHINGTON 27, St. Louis 10
NEW YORK JETS 23, Miami 7
CHICAGO 23, Green Bay 7
LOS ANGELES RAIDERS 34, San Diego 21
ST. LOUIS 21, Dallas 10
DENVER 17, San Francisco 16
WASHINGTON 23, New York Giants 21
SAN FRANCISCO 19, Seattle 6
MIAMI 38, Chicago 24
Los Angeles Rams 27, SAN FRANCISCO 20
MIAMI 30, New England 27
L.A. Raiders 16, L.A. RAMS 6

1984
Dallas 20, LOS ANGELES RAMS 13
SAN FRANCISCO 37, Washington 31
Miami 21, BUFFALO 17
LOS ANGELES RAIDERS 33, San Diego 30
PITTSBURGH 38, Cincinnati 17
San Francisco 31, NEW YORK GIANTS 10
DENVER 17, Green Bay 14
Los Angeles Rams 24, ATLANTA 10
Seattle 24, SAN DIEGO 0
WASHINGTON 27, Atlanta 14
SEATTLE 17, Los Angeles Raiders 14
NEW ORLEANS 27, Pittsburgh 24
MIAMI 28, New York Jets 17
SAN DIEGO 20, Chicago 7
Los Angeles Raiders 24, DETROIT 3
MIAMI 28, Dallas 21

1983
Dallas 31, WASHINGTON 30
San Diego 17, KANSAS CITY 14
LOS ANGELES RAIDERS 27, Miami 14
NEW YORK GIANTS 27, Green Bay 3
New York Jets 34, BUFFALO 10
Pittsburgh 24, CINCINNATI 14
GREEN BAY 48, Washington 47
ST. LOUIS 20, New York Giants 20 (OT)
Washington 27, SAN DIEGO 24
DETROIT 15, New York Giants 9
Los Angeles Rams 36, ATLANTA 13
New York Jets 31, NEW ORLEANS 28
MIAMI 38, Cincinnati 14
DETROIT 13, Minnesota 2
Green Bay 12, TAMPA BAY 9 (OT)
SAN FRANCISCO 42, Dallas 17

1982
Pittsburgh 36, DALLAS 28
Green Bay 27, NEW YORK GIANTS 19
LOS ANGELES RAIDERS 28, San Diego 24
TAMPA BAY 23, Miami 17
New York Jets 28, DETROIT 13
Dallas 37, HOUSTON 7
SAN DIEGO 50, Cincinnati 34
MIAMI 27, Buffalo 10
MINNESOTA 31, Dallas 27

1981
San Diego 44, CLEVELAND 14
Oakland 36, MINNESOTA 10
Dallas 35, NEW ENGLAND 21
Los Angeles 24, CHICAGO 7
PHILADELPHIA 16, Atlanta 13
BUFFALO 31, Miami 21
DETROIT 48, Chicago 17
PITTSBURGH 26, Houston 13
DENVER 19, Minnesota 17
DALLAS 27, Buffalo 14
SEATTLE 44, San Diego 23
ATLANTA 31, Minnesota 30
MIAMI 13, Philadelphia 10
OAKLAND 30, Pittsburgh 27
LOS ANGELES 21, Atlanta 16
SAN DIEGO 23, Oakland 10

1980
Dallas 17, WASHINGTON 3
Houston 16, CLEVELAND 7
PHILADELPHIA 35, New York Giants 3
NEW ENGLAND 23, Denver 14
CHICAGO 23, Tampa Bay 0
DENVER 20, Washington 17
Oakland 45, PITTSBURGH 34
NEW YORK JETS 17, Miami 14
CLEVELAND 27, Chicago 21
HOUSTON 38, New England 34
Oakland 19, SEATTLE 17
Los Angeles 27, NEW ORLEANS 7
OAKLAND 9, Denver 3
MIAMI 16, New England 13 (OT)
LOS ANGELES 38, Dallas 14
SAN DIEGO 26, Pittsburgh 17

1979
Pittsburgh 16, NEW ENGLAND 13 (OT)
Atlanta 14, PHILADELPHIA 10
WASHINGTON 27, New York Giants 0
CLEVELAND 26, Dallas 7
GREEN BAY 27, New England 14
OAKLAND 13, Miami 3
NEW YORK JETS 14, Minnesota 7
PITTSBURGH 42, Denver 7
Seattle 31, ATLANTA 28
Houston 9, MIAMI 6
Philadelphia 31, DALLAS 21
LOS ANGELES 20, Atlanta 14
SEATTLE 30, New York Jets 7
Oakland 42, NEW ORLEANS 35
HOUSTON 20, Pittsburgh 17
SAN DIEGO 17, Denver 7

1978
DALLAS 38, Baltimore 0
MINNESOTA 12, Denver 9 (OT)
Baltimore 34, NEW ENGLAND 27
Minnesota 24, CHICAGO 20
WASHINGTON 9, Dallas 5
MIAMI 21, Cincinnati 0
DENVER 16, Chicago 7
Houston 24, PITTSBURGH 17
ATLANTA 15, Los Angeles 7
BALTIMORE 21, Washington 17
Oakland 34, CINCINNATI 21
HOUSTON 35, Miami 30
Pittsburgh 24, SAN FRANCISCO 7
SAN DIEGO 40, Chicago 7
Cincinnati 20, LOS ANGELES 19
MIAMI 23, New England 3

1977
PITTSBURGH 27, San Francisco 0
CLEVELAND 30, New England 27 (OT)
Oakland 37, KANSAS CITY 28
CHICAGO 24, Los Angeles 23
PITTSBURGH 20, Cincinnati 14
LOS ANGELES 35, Minnesota 3
ST. LOUIS 28, New York Giants 0
BALTIMORE 10, Washington 3
St. Louis 24, DALLAS 17
WASHINGTON 10, Green Bay 9
OAKLAND 34, Buffalo 13
MIAMI 17, Baltimore 6
Dallas 42, SAN FRANCISCO 35

1976
Miami 30, BUFFALO 21
Oakland 24, KANSAS CITY 21
Washington 20, PHILADELPHIA 17 (OT)
MINNESOTA 17, Pittsburgh 6
San Francisco 16, LOS ANGELES 0
NEW ENGLAND 41, New York Jets 7
WASHINGTON 20, St. Louis 10
BALTIMORE 38, Houston 14
CINCINNATI 20, Los Angeles 12
DALLAS 17, Buffalo 10
Baltimore 17, MIAMI 16
SAN FRANCISCO 20, Minnesota 16
OAKLAND 35, Cincinnati 20

1975
Oakland 31, MIAMI 21
DENVER 23, Green Bay 13
Dallas 36, DETROIT 10
WASHINGTON 27, St. Louis 17
New York Giants 17, BUFFALO 14
Minnesota 13, CHICAGO 9
Los Angeles 42, PHILADELPHIA 3
Kansas City 34, DALLAS 31
CINCINNATI 33, Buffalo 24
Pittsburgh 32, HOUSTON 9
MIAMI 20, New England 7
OAKLAND 17, Denver 10
SAN DIEGO 24, New York Jets 16

1974
BUFFALO 21, Oakland 20
PHILADELPHIA 13, Dallas 10
WASHINGTON 30, Denver 3
MIAMI 21, New York Jets 17
DETROIT 17, San Francisco 13
CHICAGO 10, Green Bay 9
PITTSBURGH 24, Atlanta 17
Los Angeles 15, SAN FRANCISCO 13
Minnesota 28, ST. LOUIS 24
Kansas City 42, DENVER 34
Pittsburgh 28, NEW ORLEANS 7
MIAMI 24, Cincinnati 3
Washington 23, LOS ANGELES 17

1973
GREEN BAY 23, New York Jets 7
DALLAS 40, New Orleans 3
DETROIT 31, Atlanta 6
WASHINGTON 14, Dallas 7
Miami 17, CLEVELAND 9
DENVER 23, Oakland 23
BUFFALO 23, Kansas City 14
PITTSBURGH 21, Washington 16
KANSAS CITY 19, Chicago 7
ATLANTA 20, Minnesota 14
SAN FRANCISCO 20, Green Bay 6
MIAMI 30, Pittsburgh 26
LOS ANGELES 40, New York Giants 6

1972
Washington 24, MINNESOTA 21
Kansas City 20, NEW ORLEANS 17
New York Giants 27, PHILADELPHIA 12
Oakland 34, HOUSTON 0
Green Bay 24, DETROIT 23
CHICAGO 13, Minnesota 10
DALLAS 28, Detroit 24
Baltimore 24, NEW ENGLAND 17
Cleveland 21, SAN DIEGO 17
WASHINGTON 24, Atlanta 13
MIAMI 31, St. Louis 10
Los Angeles 26, SAN FRANCISCO 16
OAKLAND 24, New York Jets 16

1971
Minnesota 16, DETROIT 13
ST. LOUIS 17, New York Jets 10
Oakland 34, CLEVELAND 20
DALLAS 20, New York Giants 13
KANSAS CITY 38, Pittsburgh 16
MINNESOTA 10, Baltimore 3
GREEN BAY 14, Detroit 14
BALTIMORE 24, Los Angeles 17
SAN DIEGO 20, St. Louis 17
ATLANTA 28, Green Bay 21
MIAMI 34, Chicago 3
Kansas City 26, SAN FRANCISCO 17
Washington 38, LOS ANGELES 24

1970
CLEVELAND 31, New York Jets 21
Kansas City 44, BALTIMORE 24
DETROIT 28, Chicago 14
Green Bay 22, SAN DIEGO 20
OAKLAND 34, Washington 20
MINNESOTA 13, Los Angeles 3
PITTSBURGH 21, Cincinnati 10
Baltimore 13, GREEN BAY 10
St. Louis 38, DALLAS 0
PHILADELPHIA 23, New York Giants 20
Miami 20, ATLANTA 7
Cleveland 21, HOUSTON 10
Detroit 28, LOS ANGELES 23

MONDAY NIGHT WON-LOST RECORDS, 1970-1997

AMERICAN FOOTBALL CONFERENCE

	Balt.	Buff.	Cin.	Clev.	Den.	Ind.	Jax.	K.C.	Mia.	N.E.	N.Y.J.	Oak.	Pitt.	S.D.	Sea.	Tenn.
Total	0-0	16-19	7-16	13-11	16-20-1	10-8	1-0	16-10	33-23	6-14	9-16	33-16-1	28-15	14-12	11-5	11-11
1997		1-1			2-1	0-1	1-0	2-0	1-1	1-2		0-2	3-0			
1996		0-2			1-0	1-0		0-2	1-2			2-1	3-0	1-1		
1995		1-1		0-2	1-0			1-1	2-1	1-0		0-2	1-1	1-1		
1994		1-1			0-2			1-1	1-0			1-1	2-0	0-1		0-3
1993		2-1		1-0	0-2	0-1		2-0	1-2			1-0	3-0	2-0		0-1
1992		2-0	0-1	0-1	0-2			1-0	2-1		0-1	0-2	1-0		1-0	1-0
1991		2-1	0-2					2-1	1-1		0-1	0-2	0-1			1-1
1990		1-1	1-1	1-1	1-1	0-1		0-1	0-1		0-1	2-0	1-0		1-0	1-0
1989		1-2	1-2	1-1	2-0						0-1	1-0			1-0	1-0
1988		2-0		1-2	0-2	1-1			1-1		0-1	1-1			1-0	1-0
1987				1-0	2-1				1-1	1-1	2-1	1-1			0-2	
1986			1-0	1-0	1-1				1-2	1-0	1-1	0-1	0-2	0-1	2-0	
1985			1-0	1-0	1-0				2-1	0-1	1-0	2-0	0-2	0-1	0-2	
1984		0-1	0-1		1-0				3-0		0-1	2-1	1-1	1-2	2-0	
1983		0-1	0-2					0-1	1-1		2-0	1-0	1-0	1-1		
1982		0-1	0-1		0-1				1-1		1-0	1-0	1-0	1-1		0-1
1981		1-1		0-1	1-0				1-1	0-1		2-1	1-1	2-1	1-0	0-1
1980				1-1	1-2				1-1	1-2	1-0	3-0	0-2	1-0	0-1	2-0
1979				1-0	0-2				0-2	0-2	1-1	2-0	2-1	1-0	2-0	2-0
1978			1-2		1-1	2-1			2-1	0-2		1-0	1-1	1-0		2-0
1977		0-1	0-1	1-0		1-1		0-1	1-0	0-1		2-0	2-0			
1976		0-2	1-1			2-0		0-1	1-1	1-0	0-1	2-0	0-1			0-1
1975		0-2	1-0		1-1			1-0	1-1	0-1	0-1	2-0	1-0	1-0		0-1
1974		1-0	0-1		0-2			1-0	2-0		0-1	0-1	2-0			
1973		1-0		0-1	0-0-1			1-1	2-0		0-1	0-0-1	1-1			
1972				1-0		1-0		1-0	1-0	0-1	0-1	2-0		0-1		0-1
1971				0-1		1-1		2-0	1-0		0-1	1-0	0-1	1-0		
1970			0-1	2-0		1-1		1-0	1-0		0-1	1-0	1-0	0-1		0-1

NATIONAL FOOTBALL CONFERENCE

	Ariz.	Atl.	Car.	Chi.	Dall.	Det.	G.B.	Minn.	N.O.	N.Y.G.	Phil.	St. L.	S.F.	T.B.	Wash.
Total	5-9-1	5-15	1-1	15-28	30-23	10-11-1	14-12-1	16-17	6-12	14-21-1	14-14	17-20	30-18	1-2	23-21
1997			1-1	0-1	1-2		3-0	0-1			0-2		3-0		1-0
1995	0-1			1-2	3-0	2-0	1-0	0-2		0-1	0-1		2-1		
1994				0-2	2-1	1-0	1-0	2-0	0-2	1-2	2-0		2-1		
1993		0-1		0-1	1-1		0-1	1-0	0-2	1-0	1-1		1-2		1-2
1992		0-2		0-3	2-1	0-1		1-0	1-0	1-0	1-0		2-0		1-2
1991				2-1	0-1			0-1	1-0	2-1	2-1	0-1	2-1		2-0
1990						0-1		0-1	1-1	1-1	2-0	0-3	3-0		0-1
1989				1-1				1-1	1-1	2-1	0-2	0-2	3-0		0-2
1988	0-1			1-2	1-1			1-0	1-0	1-0	1-1	1-0	1-1		0-2
1987				1-2	2-1			1-0		0-3		1-2	2-0		1-1
1986	0-1			2-1	2-0	0-1	0-1			2-1		1-0	0-2		1-1
1985	1-1			1-1	1-1		0-1			0-1		2-1	1-2		2-1
1984		0-2		0-1	1-1	0-1	0-1		1-0	0-1		1-1	2-0		1-1
1983	0-0-1	0-1			1-1	2-0	2-1	0-1	0-1	1-1-1		1-0	1-0	0-1	1-2
1982					1-2	0-1	1-0	1-0		0-1				1-0	
1981		1-2		0-2	2-0	1-0		0-3			1-1	2-0			
1980				1-1	1-1				0-1	0-1	1-0	2-0		0-1	0-2
1979		1-2			0-2		1-0	0-1	0-1	0-1	1-1	1-0			1-0
1978	2-0	1-0		0-3	1-1			2-0				0-2	0-1		1-1
1977	0-1			1-0	1-1		0-1	0-1		0-1		1-1	0-2		1-1
1976	0-1				1-0			1-1			0-1	0-2	2-0		2-0
1975	0-1			0-1	1-1	0-1	0-1	1-0		1-0	0-1	1-0			1-0
1974		0-1		1-0	0-1	1-0	0-1	1-0	0-1		1-0	1-1	0-2		2-0
1973	0-1	1-1		0-1	1-1	1-0	1-1	0-1	0-1	0-1		1-0	1-0		1-1
1972	1-1	0-1		1-0	1-0	0-2	1-0	0-2	0-1	1-0	0-1	1-0	0-1		2-0
1971	1-0	1-0		0-1	1-0	0-1-1	0-1-1	2-0		0-1		0-2	0-1		1-0
1970		0-1		0-1	0-1	2-0	1-1	1-0		0-1	1-0	0-2			0-1

Compiled by Elias Sports Bureau
*Set or tied NFL all-time record.

MONDAY NIGHT RECORDS

SCORING
TOUCHDOWNS
Most Touchdowns, Game
4 Ron Johnson, N.Y. Giants at Philadelphia, Oct. 2, 1972
4 Earl Campbell, Houston vs. Miami, Nov. 20, 1978
4 Marcus Allen, L.A. Raiders vs. San Diego, Sept. 24, 1984
4 Eric Dickerson, Indianapolis vs. Denver, Oct. 31, 1988
4 Emmitt Smith, Dallas at N.Y. Giants, Sept. 4. 1995

FIELD GOALS
Most Field Goals, Game
7 Chris Boniol, Dallas vs. Green Bay, Nov. 18, 1996*
5 Tim Mazzetti, Atlanta vs. Los Angeles, Oct. 30, 1978
5 Roger Ruzek, Dallas at L.A. Rams, Dec. 21, 1987
5 Rich Karlis, Minnesota vs. Cincinnati, Dec. 25, 1989
5 Nick Lowery, Kansas City vs. Denver, Sept. 20, 1993
5 Chris Jacke, Green Bay vs. San Francisco, Oct. 14, 1996 (OT)
5 Richie Cunningham, Dallas vs. Philadelphia, Sept. 15, 1997

RUSHING
YARDS GAINED
Most Yards Rushing, Game
221 Bo Jackson, L.A. Raiders at Seattle, Nov. 30, 1987
214 Thurman Thomas, Buffalo at N.Y. Jets, Sept. 24, 1990
199 Earl Campbell, Houston vs. Miami, Nov. 20, 1978

Longest Run From Scrimage, Game
99 Tony Dorsett, Dallas at Minnesota, Jan. 3, 1983 (TD)*
91 Bo Jackson, L.A. Raiders at Seattle, Nov. 30, 1987 (TD)
83 James Lofton, Green Bay at N.Y. Giants, Sept. 20, 1982 (TD)

TOUCHDOWNS
Most Rushing Touchdowns, Game
4 Earl Campbell, Houston vs. Miami, Nov. 20, 1978
4 Eric Dickerson, Indianapolis vs. Denver, Oct. 31, 1988
4 Emmitt Smith, Dallas at N.Y. Giants, Sept. 4, 1995

PASSING
YARDS GAINED
Most Yards Passing, Game
458 Joe Montana, San Francisco at L.A. Rams, Dec. 11, 1989
447 Ken Anderson, Cincinnati vs. Buffalo, Nov. 17, 1975
445 Charley Johnson, Denver vs. Kansas City, Nov. 18, 1974

Longest Pass Play
99 Brett Favre to Robert Brooks, Green Bay at Chicago, Sept. 11, 1995 (TD)*
97 Bernie Kosar to Webster Slaughter, Cleveland vs. Chicago, Oct. 23, 1989 (TD)
95 Joe Montana to John Taylor, San Francisco at L.A. Rams, Dec. 11, 1989 (TD)

TOUCHDOWNS
Most Touchdown Passes, Game
5 Dave Krieg, Seattle vs. L.A. Raiders, Nov. 28, 1988
5 Jim Kelly, Buffalo vs. Cincinnati, Oct. 21, 1991

PASS RECEIVING
RECEPTIONS
Most Pass Receptions, Game
14 Herman Moore, Detroit vs. Chicago, Dec. 4, 1995
14 Jerry Rice, San Francisco vs. Minnesota, Dec. 18, 1995
13 Andre Reed, Buffalo vs. Denver, Sept. 18, 1989

YARDS GAINED
Most Yards on Pass Receptions, Game
289 Jerry Rice, San Francisco vs. Minnesota, Dec. 18, 1995
286 John Taylor, San Francisco at L.A. Rams, Dec. 11, 1989
260 Wes Chandler, San Diego vs. Cincinnati, Dec. 20, 1982

TOUCHDOWNS
Most Touchdown Pass Receptions, Game
3 Ron Johnson, N.Y. Giants at Philadelphia, Oct. 2, 1972
3 Wesley Walker, N.Y. Jets at Detroit, Dec. 6, 1982
3 Steve Largent, Seattle at San Diego, Oct. 29, 1984
3 Mark Clayton, Miami vs. Dallas, Dec. 17, 1984
3 Jerry Rice, San Francisco vs. Chicago, Dec. 14, 1987
3 Jerry Rice, San Francisco vs. Minnesota, Dec. 18, 1995

INTERCEPTIONS BY
Most Interceptions, Game
4 Dick Anderson, Miami vs. Pittsburgh, Dec. 3, 1973*
3 Johnny Robinson, Kansas City at Baltimore, Sept. 28, 1970
3 Charlie Babb, Miami vs. Oakland, Sept. 22, 1975
3 Charles Phillips, Oakland vs. Denver, Dec. 8, 1975
3 Mark Murphy, Washington at San Diego, Oct. 31, 1983
3 Ken Easley, Seattle at San Diego, Oct. 29, 1984
3 Dwayne Harper, San Diego vs. Oakland, Nov. 27, 1995

Longest Interception Return
102 Eddie Anderson, L.A. Raiders at Miami, Dec. 14, 1992 (TD)
94 Nolan Cromwell, L.A. Rams vs. Atlanta, Dec. 14, 1981
94 Walker Lee Ashley, Minnesota vs. Chicago, Dec. 19, 1988 (TD)

PUNTING
Longest Punt
74 Craig Colquitt, Pittsburgh vs. Oakland, Dec. 7, 1981
73 Tom Tupa, New England at Denver, Oct. 6, 1997
72 Bill Van Heusen, Denver at Oakland, Oct. 22, 1973

PUNT RETURNS
Longest Punt Return
95 John Taylor, San Francisco vs. Washington, Nov. 21, 1988 (TD)
94 Dennis McKinnon, Chicago vs. N.Y. Giants, Sept. 14, 1987 (TD)
91 JoJo Townsell, N.Y. Jets vs. Seattle, Nov. 9, 1987 (TD)

KICKOFF RETURNS
Longest Kickoff Return
102 Harold Hart, Oakland at Miami, Sept. 22, 1975 (TD)
99 Eddie Payton, Minnesota vs. Oakland, Sept. 14, 1981 (TD)
99 Gaston Green, L.A. Rams at Pittsburgh, Oct. 29, 1990 (TD)

FUMBLES
Longest Fumble Return
99 Don Griffin, San Francisco vs. Chicago, Dec. 23, 1991 (TD)
96 Joe Lavender, Philadelphia vs. Dallas, Sept. 23, 1974 (TD)
86 Michael Downs, Dallas at Houston, Dec. 13, 1982 (TD)
86 Tyrone Hughes, New Orleans vs. San Francisco, Nov. 28, 1994 (TD)

THANKSGIVING DAY RECORDS

SCORING
Most Touchdowns, Game
6 Ernie Nevers, Chi. Cardinals vs. Chi. Bears, Nov. 28, 1929*
4 Sterling Sharpe, Green Bay at Dallas, Nov. 24, 1994
3 By many players

RUSHING
Most Yards Rushing, Game
273 O.J. Simpson, Buffalo at Detroit, Nov. 25, 1976
198 Bob Hoernschemeyer, Detroit vs. N.Y. Yankees, Nov. 23, 1950
195 Earl Campbell, Houston at Dallas, Nov. 22, 1979

PASSING
Most Yards Passing, Game
410 Scott Mitchell, Detroit vs. Minnesota, Nov. 23, 1995
384 Warren Moon, Minnesota at Detroit, Nov. 23, 1995
356 Troy Aikman, Dallas vs. Tennessee, Nov. 27, 1997

PASS RECEIVING
RECEPTIONS
Most Pass Receptions, Game
12 Brett Perriman, Detroit vs. Minnesota, Nov. 23, 1995
11 Daryl Johnston, Dallas vs. Miami, Nov. 25, 1993
Michael Irvin, Dallas vs Kansas City, Nov. 23 1995

YARDS GAINED
Most Yards on Pass Receptions, Game
303 Jim Benton, Cleveland at Detroit, Nov. 22, 1945
185 Lance Alworth, San Diego vs. Buffalo, Nov. 26, 1964
184 Anthony Carter, Minnesota at Dallas, Nov. 26, 1987 (OT)

THURSDAY-SUNDAY NIGHT FOOTBALL

THURSDAY-SUNDAY NIGHT FOOTBALL, 1974-1997

(Home Team in capitals, games listed in chronological order.)

1997
Washington 24, CAROLINA 10 (Sun.)
ARIZONA 25, Dallas 22 (OT) (Sun.)
NEW ENGLAND 27, New York Jets 24 (OT) (Sun.)
TAMPA BAY 31, Miami 21 (Sun.)
MINNESOTA 28, Philadelphia 19 (Sun.)
New Orleans 20, CHICAGO 17 (Sun.)
PITTSBURGH 24, Indianapolis 22 (Sun.)
KANSAS CITY 31, San Diego 3 (Thurs.)
CAROLINA 21, Atlanta 12 (Sun.)
GREEN BAY 20, Detroit 10 (Sun.)
PITTSBURGH 37, Baltimore 0 (Sun.)
Oakland 38, SAN DIEGO 13 (Sun.)
WASHINGTON 7, New York Giants 7 (OT) (Sun.)
Denver 38, SAN DIEGO 28 (Sun.)
CINCINNATI 41, Tennessee 14 (Thurs.)
MIAMI 33, Detroit 30 (Sun.)
Chicago 13, ST. LOUIS 10 (Sun.)
SEATTLE 38, San Francisco 9 (Sun.)

1996
Buffalo 23, NEW YORK GIANTS 20 (OT) (Sun.)
Miami 38, ARIZONA 10 (Sun.)
DENVER 27, Tampa Bay 23 (Sun.)
Philadelphia 33, ATLANTA 18 (Sun.)
WASHINGTON 31, New York Jets 16 (Sun.)
Houston 30, CINCINNATI 27 (OT) (Sun.)
INDIANAPOLIS 26, Baltimore 21 (Sun.)
KANSAS CITY 34, Seattle 16 (Thurs.)
NEW ENGLAND 28, Buffalo 25 (Sun.)
San Francisco 24, NEW ORLEANS 17 (Sun.)
CAROLINA 27, New York Giants 17 (Sun.)
Minnesota 16, OAKLAND 13 (OT) (Sun.)
Green Bay 24, ST. LOUIS 9 (Sun.)
New England 45, SAN DIEGO 7 (Sun.)
INDIANAPOLIS 37, Philadelphia 10 (Thurs.)
Minnesota 24, DETROIT 22 (Sun.)
JACKSONVILLE 20, Seattle 13 (Sun.)
SAN DIEGO 16, Denver 10 (Sun.)

1995
DENVER 22, Buffalo 7 (Sun.)
Philadelphia 31, ARIZONA 19 (Sun.)
Dallas 23, MINNESOTA 17 (OT) (Sun.)
Green Bay 24, JACKSONVILLE 14 (Sun.)
Oakland 47, NEW YORK JETS 10 (Sun.)
Denver 37, NEW ENGLAND 3 (Sun.)
ST. LOUIS 21, Atlanta 19 (Thurs.)
Cincinnati 27, PITTSBURGH 9 (Thurs.)
New York Giants 24, WASHINGTON 15 (Sun.)
Miami 24, SAN DIEGO 14 (Sun.)
PHILADELPHIA 31, Denver 13 (Sun.)
KANSAS CITY 20, Houston 13 (Sun.)
NEW ORLEANS 34, Carolina 26 (Sun.)
New York Giants 10, ARIZONA 6 (Thurs.)
SAN FRANCISCO 27, Buffalo 17 (Sun.)
TAMPA BAY 13, Green Bay 10 (OT) (Sun.)
SEATTLE 44, Oakland 10 (Sun.)
INDIANAPOLIS 10, New England 7 (Sat.)

1994
San Diego 17, DENVER 34 (Sun.)
New York Giants 20, ARIZONA 17 (Sun.)
Kansas City 30, ATLANTA 10 (Sun.)
Chicago 19, NEW YORK JETS 7 (Sun.)
Miami 23, CINCINNATI 7 (Sun.)
PHILADELPHIA 21, Washington 17 (Sun.)
Cleveland 11, HOUSTON 8 (Thurs.)
MINNESOTA 13, Green Bay 10 (OT) (Thurs.)
ARIZONA 20, Pittsburgh 17 (OT) (Sun.)
KANSAS CITY 13, Los Angeles Raiders 3 (Sun.)
DETROIT 14, Tampa Bay 9 (Sun.)
SAN FRANCISCO 31, Los Angeles Rams 27 (Sun.)
New England 12, INDIANAPOLIS 10 (Sun.)
MINNESOTA 33, Chicago 27 (OT) (Thurs.)
Buffalo 42, MIAMI 31 (Sun.)
New Orleans 29, ATLANTA 20 (Sun.)
Los Angeles Raiders 17, SEATTLE 16 (Sun.)
MIAMI 27, Detroit 20 (Sun.)

1993
NEW ORLEANS 33, Houston 21 (Sun.)
Los Angeles Raiders 17, SEATTLE 13 (Sun.)
Dallas 17, PHOENIX 10 (Sun.)
NEW YORK JETS 45, New England 7 (Sun.)
BUFFALO 17, New York Giants 14 (Sun.)
GREEN BAY 30, Denver 27 (Sun.)
ATLANTA 30, Los Angeles Rams 24 (Thurs.)
MIAMI 41, Indianapolis 27 (Sun.)
Detroit 30, MINNESOTA 27 (Sun.)
WASHINGTON 30, Indianapolis 24 (Sun.)
Chicago 16, SAN DIEGO 13 (Sun.)
TAMPA BAY 23, Minnesota 10 (Sun.)
HOUSTON 23, Pittsburgh 3 (Sun.)
SAN FRANCISCO 21, Cincinnati 8 (Sun.)
Green Bay 20, SAN DIEGO 13 (Sun.)
Philadelphia 20, INDIANAPOLIS 10 (Sun.)
MINNESOTA 30, Kansas City 10 (Sun.)
HOUSTON 24, New York Jets 0 (Sun.)

1992
DENVER 17, Los Angeles Raiders 13 (Sun.)
Philadelphia 31, PHOENIX 14 (Sun.)
BUFFALO 38, Indianapolis 0 (Sun.)
San Francisco 16, NEW ORLEANS 10 (Sun.)
NEW YORK JETS 30, New England 21 (Sun.)
NEW ORLEANS 13, Los Angeles Rams 10 (Sun.)
MINNESOTA 31, Detroit 14 (Thurs.)
Pittsburgh 27, KANSAS CITY 3 (Sun.)
New York Giants 24, WASHINGTON 7 (Sun.)
Cincinnati 31, CHICAGO 28 (OT) (Sun.)
DENVER 27, New York Giants 13 (Sun.)
Kansas City 24, SEATTLE 14 (Sun.)
SAN DIEGO 27, Los Angeles Raiders 3 (Sun.)
NEW ORLEANS 22, Atlanta 14 (Thurs.)
Los Angeles Rams 31, TAMPA BAY 27 (Sun.)
Green Bay 16, HOUSTON 14 (Sun.)
MIAMI 19, New York Jets 17 (Sun.)
HOUSTON 27, Buffalo 3 (Sun.)

1991
WASHINGTON 45, Detroit 0 (Sun.)
Houston 30, CINCINNATI 7 (Sun.)
NEW ORLEANS 24, Los Angeles Rams 7 (Sun.)
Dallas 17, PHOENIX 9 (Sun.)
Denver 13, MINNESOTA 6 (Sun.)
Pittsburgh 21, INDIANAPOLIS 3 (Sun.)
Los Angeles Raiders 23, SEATTLE 20 (Sun.)
Chicago 10, GREEN BAY 0 (Thurs.)
Washington 17, NEW YORK GIANTS 13 (Sun.)
DENVER 20, Pittsburgh 13 (Sun.)
MIAMI 30, New England 20 (Sun.)
HOUSTON 28, Cleveland 24 (Sun.)
Atlanta 23, NEW ORLEANS 20 (OT) (Sun.)
Los Angeles Raiders 9, SAN DIEGO 7 (Sun.)
Minnesota 26, TAMPA BAY 24 (Sun.)
Buffalo 35, INDIANAPOLIS 7 (Sun.)
SEATTLE 23, Los Angeles Rams 9 (Sun.)

1990
NEW YORK GIANTS 27, Philadelphia 20 (Sun.)
PITTSBURGH 20, Houston 9 (Sun.)
TAMPA BAY 23, Detroit 20 (Sun.)
Washington 38, PHOENIX 10 (Sun.)
BUFFALO 38, Los Angeles Raiders 24 (Sun.)
CHICAGO 38, Los Angeles Rams 9 (Sun.)
MIAMI 17, New England 10 (Thurs.)
ATLANTA 38, Cincinnati 17 (Sun.)
MINNESOTA 27, Denver 22 (Sun.)
San Francisco 24, DALLAS 6 (Sun.)
CINCINNATI 27, Pittsburgh 3 (Sun.)
Seattle 13, SAN DIEGO 10 (Sun.)
MINNESOTA 23, Green Bay 7 (Sun.)
MIAMI 23, Philadelphia 20 (Sun.)
DETROIT 38, Chicago 21 (Sun.)
INDIANAPOLIS 35, Washington 28 (Sat.)
SEATTLE 17, Denver 12 (Sun.)
HOUSTON 34, Pittsburgh 14 (Sun.)

1989
Dallas 13, WASHINGTON 3 (Sun.)
SAN DIEGO 14, Los Angeles Raiders 12 (Sun.)
INDIANAPOLIS 27, New York Jets 10 (Sun.)
Los Angeles Rams 20, NEW ORLEANS 17 (Sun.)
MINNESOTA 27, Chicago 16 (Sun.)
MIAMI 31, New England 10 (Sun.)
SEATTLE 23, Los Angeles Raiders 17 (Sun.)
Cleveland 24, HOUSTON 20 (Sat.)

1988
HOUSTON 41, Washington 17 (Sun.)
Los Angeles Raiders 13, SAN DIEGO 3 (Sun.)
Minnesota 43, DALLAS 3 (Sun.)
New England 6, MIAMI 3 (Sun.)
New York Giants 13, NEW ORLEANS 12 (Sun.)
Pittsburgh 37, HOUSTON 34 (Sun.)
SEATTLE 42, Denver 14 (Sun.)
Los Angeles Rams 38, SAN FRANCISCO 16 (Sun.)

1987
NEW YORK GIANTS 17, New England 10 (Sun.)
SAN DIEGO 16, Los Angeles Raiders 14 (Sun.)
Miami 20, DALLAS 14 (Sun.)
SAN FRANCISCO 38, Cleveland 24 (Sun.)
Chicago 30, MINNESOTA 24 (Sun.)
SEATTLE 28, Denver 21 (Sun.)
MIAMI 23, Washington 21 (Sun.)
SAN FRANCISCO 48, Los Angeles Rams 0 (Sun.)

1986
New England 20, NEW YORK JETS 6 (Thurs.)
Cincinnati 30, CLEVELAND 13 (Thurs.)
Los Angeles Raiders 37, SAN DIEGO 31 (OT) (Thurs.)
LOS ANGELES RAMS 29, Dallas 10 (Sun.)
SAN FRANCISCO 24, Los Angeles Rams 14 (Fri.)

1985
KANSAS CITY 36, Los Angeles Raiders 20 (Thurs.)
Chicago 33, MINNESOTA 24 (Thurs.)
Dallas 30, NEW YORK GIANTS 29 (Sun.)
SAN DIEGO 54, Pittsburgh 44 (Sun.)
Denver 27, SEATTLE 24 (Fri.)

1984
Pittsburgh 23, NEW YORK JETS 17 (Thurs.)
Denver 24, CLEVELAND 14 (Sun.)
DALLAS 30, New Orleans 27 (Sun.)
Washington 31, MINNESOTA 17 (Thurs.)
SAN FRANCISCO 19, Los Angeles Rams 16 (Fri.)

1983
San Francisco 48, MINNESOTA 17 (Thurs.)
CLEVELAND 17, Cincinnati 7 (Thurs.)
Los Angeles Raiders 40, DALLAS 38 (Sun.)
Los Angeles Raiders 42, SAN DIEGO 10 (Thurs.)
MIAMI 34, New York Jets 14 (Fri.)

1982
BUFFALO 23, Minnesota 22 (Thurs.)
SAN FRANCISCO 30, Los Angeles Rams 24 (Thurs.)
ATLANTA 17, San Francisco 7 (Sun.)

1981
MIAMI 30, Pittsburgh 10 (Thurs.)
Philadelphia 20, BUFFALO 14 (Thurs.)
DALLAS 29, Los Angeles 17 (Sun.)
HOUSTON 17, Cleveland 13 (Thurs.)

1980
TAMPA BAY 10, Los Angeles 9 (Thurs.)
DALLAS 42, San Diego 31 (Sun.)
San Diego 27, MIAMI 24 (OT) (Thurs.)
HOUSTON 6, Pittsburgh 0 (Thurs.)

1979
Los Angeles 13, DENVER 9 (Thurs.)
DALLAS 30, Los Angeles 6 (Sun.)
OAKLAND 45, San Diego 22 (Thurs.)
MIAMI 39, New England 24 (Thurs.)

1978
New England 21, OAKLAND 14 (Sun.)
Minnesota 21, DALLAS 10 (Thurs.)
LOS ANGELES 10, Pittsburgh 7 (Sun.)
Denver 21, OAKLAND 6 (Sun.)

1977
Minnesota 30, DETROIT 21 (Sat.)

1976
Los Angeles 20, DETROIT 17 (Sat.)

1975
LOS ANGELES 10, Pittsburgh 3 (Sat.)

1974
OAKLAND 27, Dallas 23 (Sat.)

OVERTIME GAMES

HISTORY OF OVERTIME GAMES

PRESEASON

Aug. 28, 1955	Los Angeles 23, New York Giants 17, at Portland, Oregon
Aug. 24, 1962	Denver 27, Dallas Texans 24, at Fort Worth, Texas
Aug. 10, 1974	San Diego 20, New York Jets 14, at San Diego
Aug. 17, 1974	Pittsburgh 33, Philadelphia 30, at Philadelphia
Aug. 17, 1974	Dallas 19, Houston 13, at Dallas
Aug. 17, 1974	Cincinnati 13, Atlanta 7, at Atlanta
Sept. 6, 1974	Buffalo 23, New York Giants 17, at Buffalo
Aug. 9, 1975	Baltimore 23, Denver 20, at Denver
Aug. 30, 1975	New England 20, Green Bay 17, at Milwaukee
Sept. 13, 1975	Minnesota 14, San Diego 14, at San Diego
Aug. 1, 1976	New England 13, New York Giants 7, at New England
Aug. 2, 1976	Kansas City 9, Houston 3, at Kansas City
Aug. 20, 1976	New Orleans 26, Baltimore 20, at Baltimore
Sept. 4, 1976	Dallas 26, Houston 20, at Dallas
Aug. 13, 1977	Seattle 23, Dallas 17, at Seattle
Aug. 28, 1977	New England 13, Pittsburgh 10, at New England
Aug. 28, 1977	New York Giants 24, Buffalo 21, at East Rutherford, N.J.
Aug. 2, 1979	Seattle 12, Minnesota 9, at Minnesota
Aug. 4, 1979	Los Angeles 20, Oakland 14, at Los Angeles
Aug. 24, 1979	Denver 20, New England 17, at Denver
Aug. 23, 1980	Tampa Bay 20, Cincinnati 14, at Tampa Bay
Aug. 5, 1981	San Francisco 27, Seattle 24, at Seattle
Aug. 29, 1981	New Orleans 20, Detroit 17, at New Orleans
Aug. 28, 1982	Miami 17, Kansas City 17, at Kansas City
Sept. 3, 1982	Miami 16, New York Giants 13, at Miami
Aug. 6, 1983	L.A. Raiders 26, San Francisco 23, at Los Angeles
Aug. 6, 1983	Atlanta 13, Washington 10, at Atlanta
Aug. 13, 1983	St. Louis 27, Chicago 24, at St. Louis
Aug. 18, 1983	New York Jets 20, Cincinnati 17, at Cincinnati
Aug. 27, 1983	Chicago 20, Kansas City 17, at Chicago
Aug. 11, 1984	Pittsburgh 20, Philadelphia 17, at Pittsburgh
Aug. 9, 1985	Buffalo 10, Detroit 10, at Pontiac, Mich.
Aug. 10, 1985	Minnesota 16, Miami 13, at Miami
Aug. 17, 1985	Dallas 27, San Diego 24, at San Diego
Aug. 24, 1985	N.Y. Giants 34, N.Y. Jets 31, at East Rutherford, N.J.
Aug. 15, 1986	Washington 27, Pittsburgh 24, at Washington
Aug. 15, 1986	Detroit 30, Seattle 27, at Detroit
Aug. 23, 1986	Los Angeles Rams 20, San Diego 17, at Anaheim
Aug. 30, 1986	Minnesota 23, Indianapolis 20, at Indianapolis
Aug. 23, 1987	Philadelphia 19, New England 13, at New England
Sept. 5, 1987	Cleveland 30, Green Bay 24, at Milwaukee
Sept. 6, 1987	Kansas City 13, St. Louis 10, at Memphis, Tenn.
Aug. 11, 1988	Seattle 16, Detroit 13, at Detroit
Aug. 19, 1988	Miami 16, Denver 13, at Miami
Aug. 19, 1988	Green Bay 21, Kansas City 21, at Milwaukee
Aug. 20, 1988	Houston 20, Los Angeles Rams 17, at Anaheim
Aug. 21, 1988	Minnesota 19, Phoenix 16, at Phoenix
Aug. 5, 1989	Los Angeles Rams 16, San Francisco 13, at Tokyo, Japan
Aug. 26, 1989	Denver 24, Dallas 21, at Denver
Sept. 1, 1989	N.Y. Jets 15, Kansas City 13, at Kansas City
Aug. 24, 1990	Cincinnati 13, New England 10, at New England
Aug. 16, 1991	Cleveland 24, Washington 21, at Washington
Aug. 17, 1991	Cincinnati 27, Minnesota 24, at Cincinnati
Aug. 23, 1991	Dallas 20, Atlanta 17, at Dallas
Aug. 24, 1991	Cincinnati 19, Green Bay 16, at Green Bay
Aug. 22, 1992	Los Angeles Rams 16, Green Bay 13, at Anaheim
Aug. 8, 1993	Dallas 13, Detroit 13, at London, England
Aug. 12, 1995	Washington 16, Houston 13, at Knoxville, Tenn.
Aug. 19, 1995	Indianapolis 20, Green Bay 17, at Green Bay
Aug. 3, 1996	Minnesota 23, San Diego 20, at Minnesota
Aug. 10, 1996	San Francisco 16, San Diego 13, at San Francisco

REGULAR SEASON

Sept. 22, 1974—Pittsburgh 35, Denver 35, at Denver; Steelers win toss. Gilliam's pass intercepted and returned by Rowser to Denver's 42. Turner misses 41-yard field goal. Walden punts and Greer returns to Broncos' 39. Van Heusen punts and Edwards returns to Steelers' 16. Game ends with Steelers on own 26.

Nov. 10, 1974—New York Jets 26, New York Giants 20, at New Haven, Conn.; Giants win toss. Gogolak misses 42-yard field goal. Namath passes to Boozer for five yards and touchdown at 6:53.

Sept. 28, 1975—Dallas 37, St. Louis 31, at Dallas; Cardinals win toss. Hart's pass intercepted and returned by Jordan to Cardinals' 37. Staubach passes to DuPree for three yards and touchdown at 7:53.

Oct. 12, 1975—Los Angeles 13, San Diego 10, at San Diego; Chargers win toss. Partee punts to Rams' 14. Dempsey kicks 22-yard field goal at 9:27.

Nov. 2, 1975—Washington 30, Dallas 24, at Washington; Cowboys win toss. Staubach's pass intercepted and returned by Houston to Cowboys' 35. Kilmer runs one yard for touchdown at 6:34.

Nov. 16, 1975—St. Louis 20, Washington 17, at St. Louis; Cardinals win toss. Bakken kicks 37-yard field goal at 7:00.

Nov. 23, 1975—Kansas City 24, Detroit 21, at Kansas City; Lions win toss. Chiefs take over on downs at own 38. Stenerud kicks 26-yard field goal at 6:44.

Nov. 23, 1975—Oakland 26, Washington 23, at Washington; Redskins win toss. Bragg punts to Raiders' 42. Blanda kicks 27-yard field goal at 7:13.

Nov. 30, 1975—Denver 13, San Diego 10, at Denver; Broncos win toss. Turner kicks 25-yard field goal at 4:13.

Nov. 30, 1975—Oakland 37, Atlanta 34, at Oakland; Falcons win toss. James punts to Raiders' 16. Guy punts and Herron returns to Falcons' 41. Nick Mike-Mayer misses 45-yard field goal. Guy punts into Falcons' end zone. James punts to Raiders' 39. Blanda kicks 36-yard field goal at 15:00.

Dec. 14, 1975—Baltimore 10, Miami 7, at Baltimore; Dolphins win toss. Seiple punts to Colts' 4. Linhart kicks 31-yard field goal at 12:44.

Sept. 19, 1976—Minnesota 10, Los Angeles 10, at Minnesota; Vikings win toss. Tarkenton's pass intercepted by Monte Jackson and returned to Minnesota 16. Allen blocks Dempsey's 30-yard field goal attempt, ball rolls into end zone for touchback. Clabo punts and Scribner returns to Rams' 20. Rusty Jackson punts to Vikings' 35. Tarkenton's pass intercepted by Kay at Rams' 1, no return. Game ends with Rams on own 3.

***Sept. 27, 1976—Washington 20, Philadelphia 17,** at Philadelphia; Eagles win toss. Jones punts and E. Brown loses one yard on return to Redskins' 40. Bragg punts 51 yards into end zone for touchback. Jones punts and E. Brown returns to Redskins' 42. Bragg punts and Marshall returns to Eagles' 41. Boryla's pass intercepted by Dusek at Redskins' 37, no return. Bragg punts and Bradley returns. Philadelphia holding penalty moves ball back to Eagles' 8. Boryla pass intercepted by E. Brown and returned to Eagles' 22. Moseley kicks 29-yard field goal at 12:49.

Oct. 17, 1976—Kansas City 20, Miami 17, at Miami; Chiefs win toss. Wilson punts into end zone for touchback. Bulaich fumbles into Kansas City end zone, Collier recovers for touchback. Stenerud kicks 34-yard field goal at 14:48.

Oct. 31, 1976—St. Louis 23, San Francisco 20, at St. Louis; Cardinals win toss. Joyce punts and Leonard fumbles on return, Jones recovers at 49ers' 43. Bakken kicks 21-yard field goal at 6:42.

Dec. 5, 1976—San Diego 13, San Francisco 7, at San Diego; Chargers win toss. Morris runs 13 yards for touchdown at 5:12.

Sept. 18, 1977—Dallas 16, Minnesota 10, at Minnesota; Vikings win toss. Dallas starts on Vikings' 47 after a punt early in the overtime period. Staubach scores seven plays later on a four-yard run at 6:14.

***Sept. 26, 1977—Cleveland 30, New England 27,** at Cleveland; Browns win toss. Sipe throws a 22-yard pass to Logan at Patriots' 19. Cockroft kicks 35-yard field goal at 4:45.

Oct. 16, 1977—Minnesota 22, Chicago 16, at Minnesota; Bears win toss. Parsons punts 53 yards to Vikings' 18. Minnesota drives to Bears' 11. On a first-and-10, Vikings fake a field goal and holder Krause hits Voigt with a touchdown pass at 6:45.

Oct. 30, 1977—Cincinnati 13, Houston 10, at Cincinnati; Bengals win toss. Bahr kicks a 22-yard field goal at 5:51.

Nov. 13, 1977—San Francisco 10, New Orleans 7, at New Orleans; Saints win toss. Saints fail to move ball and Blanchard punts to 49ers' 41. Wersching kicks a 33-yard field goal at 6:33.

Dec. 18, 1977—Chicago 12, New York Giants 9, at East Rutherford, N.J.; Giants win toss. The ball changes hands eight times before Thomas kicks a 28-yard field goal at 14:51.

Sept. 10, 1978—Cleveland 13, Cincinnati 10, at Cleveland; Browns win toss. Collins returns kickoff 41 yards to Browns' 47. Cockroft kicks 27-yard field goal at 4:30.

***Sept. 11, 1978—Minnesota 12, Denver 9,** at Minnesota; Vikings win toss. Danmeier kicks 44-yard field goal at 2:56.

Sept. 24, 1978—Pittsburgh 15, Cleveland 9, at Pittsburgh; Steelers win toss. Cunningham scores on a 37-yard "gadget" pass from Bradshaw at 3:43. Steelers start winning drive on their 21.

Sept. 24, 1978—Denver 23, Kansas City 17, at Kansas City; Broncos win toss. Dilts punts to Kansas City. Chiefs advance to Broncos' 40 where Reed fails to make first down on fourth-and-one situation. Broncos march downfield. Preston scores two-yard touchdown at 10:28.

Oct. 1, 1978—Oakland 25, Chicago 19, at Chicago; Bears win toss. Both teams punt on first possession. On Chicago's second offensive series, Colzie intercepts Avellini's pass and returns it to Bears' 3. Three plays later, Whittington runs two yards for a touchdown at 5:19.

Oct. 15, 1978—Dallas 24, St. Louis 21, at St. Louis; Cowboys win toss. Dallas drives from its 23 into field goal range. Septien kicks 27-yard field goal at 3:28.

Oct. 29, 1978—Denver 20, Seattle 17, at Seattle; Broncos win toss. Ball changes hands four times before Turner kicks 18-yard field goal at 12:59.

Nov. 12, 1978—San Diego 29, Kansas City 23, at San Diego; Chiefs win toss. Fouts hits Jefferson for decisive 14-yard touchdown pass on the last play (15:00) of overtime period.

Nov. 12, 1978—Washington 16, New York Giants 13, at Washington; Redskins win toss. Moseley kicks winning 45-yard field goal at 8:32 after missing first down field goal attempt of 35 yards at 4:50.

Nov. 26, 1978—Green Bay 10, Minnesota 10, at Green Bay; Packers win toss. Both teams have possession of the ball four times.

Dec. 9, 1978—Cleveland 37, New York Jets 34, at Cleveland; Browns win toss. Cockroft kicks 22-yard field goal at 3:07.

Sept. 2, 1979—Atlanta 40, New Orleans 34, at New Orleans; Falcons win toss.

Bartkowski's pass intercepted by Myers and returned to Falcons' 46. Erxleben punts to Falcons' 4. James punts to Chandler on Saints' 43. Erxleben punts and Ryckman returns to Falcons' 28. James punts and Chandler returns to Saints' 36. Erxleben retrieves punt snap on Saints' 1 and attempts pass. Mayberry intercepts and returns six yards for touchdown at 8:22.

Sept. 2, 1979—Cleveland 25, New York Jets 22, at New York; Jets win toss. Leahy's 43-yard field goal attempt goes wide right at 4:41. Evans's punt blocked by Dykes is recovered by Newton. Ramsey punts into end zone for touchback. Evans punts and Harper returns to Jets' 24. Robinson's pass intercepted by Davis and returned 33 yards to Jets' 31. Cockroft kicks 27-yard field goal at 14:45.

***Sept. 3, 1979—Pittsburgh 16, New England 13,** at Foxboro; Patriots win toss. Hare punts to Swann at Steelers' 31. Bahr kicks 41-yard field goal at 5:10.

Sept. 9, 1979—Tampa Bay 29, Baltimore 26, at Baltimore; Colts win toss. Landry fumbles, recovered by Kollar at Colts' 14. O'Donoghue kicks 31-yard, first-down field goal at 1:41.

Sept. 16, 1979—Denver 20, Atlanta 17, at Atlanta; Broncos win toss. Broncos march 65 yards to Falcons' 7. Turner kicks 24-yard field goal at 6:15.

Sept. 23, 1979—Houston 30, Cincinnati 27, at Cincinnati; Oilers win toss. Parsley punts and Lusby returns to Bengals' 33. Bahr's 32-yard field goal attempt is wide right at 8:05. Parsley's punt downed on Bengals' 5. McInally punts and Ellender returns to Bengals' 42. Fritsch's third down, 29-yard field goal attempt hits left upright and bounces through at 14:28.

Sept. 23, 1979—Minnesota 27, Green Bay 21, at Minnesota; Vikings win toss. Kramer throws 50-yard touchdown pass to Rashad at 3:18.

Oct. 28, 1979—Houston 27, New York Jets 24, at Houston; Oilers win toss. Oilers march 58 yards to Jets' 18. Fritsch kicks 35-yard field goal at 5:10.

Nov. 18, 1979—Cleveland 30, Miami 24, at Cleveland; Browns win toss. Sipe passes 39 yards to Rucker for touchdown at 1:59.

Nov. 25, 1979—Pittsburgh 33, Cleveland 30, at Pittsburgh; Browns win toss. Sipe's pass intercepted by Blount on Steelers' 4. Bradshaw pass intercepted by Bolton on Browns' 12. Evans punts and Bell returns to Steelers' 17. Bahr kicks 37-yard field goal at 14:51.

Nov. 25, 1979—Buffalo 16, New England 13, at Foxboro; Patriots win toss. Hare's punt downed on Bills' 38. Jackson punts and Morgan returns to Patriots' 20. Grogan's pass intercepted by Haslett and returned to Bills' 42. Ferguson's 51-yard pass to Butler sets up N. Mike-Mayer's 29-yard field goal at 9:15.

Dec. 2, 1979—Los Angeles 27, Minnesota 21, at Los Angeles; Rams win toss. Clark punts and Miller returns to Vikings' 25. Kramer's pass intercepted by Brown and returned to Rams' 40. Cromwell, holding for 22-yard field goal attempt, runs around left end untouched for winning score at 6:53.

Sept. 7, 1980—Green Bay 12, Chicago 6, at Green Bay; Bears win toss. Parsons punts and Nixon returns 16 yards. Five plays later, Marcol returns own blocked field goal attempt 24 yards for touchdown at 6:00.

Sept. 14, 1980—San Diego 30, Oakland 24, at San Diego; Raiders win toss. Pastorini's first-down pass intercepted by Edwards. Millen intercepts Fouts' first-down pass and returns to San Diego 46. Bahr's 50-yard field goal attempt partially blocked by Williams and recovered on Chargers' 32. Eight plays later, Fouts throws 24-yard touchdown pass to Jefferson at 8:09.

Sept. 14, 1980—San Francisco 24, St. Louis 21, at San Francisco; Cardinals win toss. Swider punts and Robinson returns to 49ers' 32. San Francisco drives 52 yards to St. Louis 16, where Wersching kicks 33-yard field goal at 4:12.

Oct. 12, 1980—Green Bay 14, Tampa Bay 14, at Tampa Bay; Packers win toss. Teams trade punts twice. Lee returns second Tampa Bay punt to Green Bay 42. Dickey completes three passes to Buccaneers' 18, where Birney's 36-yard field goal attempt is wide right as time expires.

Nov. 9, 1980—Atlanta 33, St. Louis 27, at St. Louis; Falcons win toss. Strong runs 21 yards for touchdown at 4:20.

#Nov. 20, 1980—San Diego 27, Miami 24, at Miami; Chargers win toss. Partridge punts into end zone, Dolphins take over on their own 20. Woodley's pass for Nathan intercepted by Lowe and returned 28 yards to Dolphins' 12. Benirschke kicks 28-yard field goal at 7:14.

Nov. 23, 1980—New York Jets 31, Houston 28, at New York; Jets win toss. Leahy kicks 38-yard field goal at 3:58.

Nov. 27, 1980—Chicago 23, Detroit 17, at Detroit; Bears win toss. Williams returns kickoff 95 yards for touchdown at 0:21.

Dec. 7, 1980—Buffalo 10, Los Angeles 7, at Buffalo; Rams win toss. Corral punts and Hooks returns to Bills' 34. Ferguson's 30-yard pass to Lewis sets up N. Mike-Mayer's 30-yard field goal at 5:14.

Dec. 7, 1980—San Francisco 38, New Orleans 35, at San Francisco; Saints win toss. Erxleben's punt downed by Hardy on 49ers' 27. Wersching kicks 36-yard field goal at 7:40.

***Dec. 8, 1980—Miami 16, New England 13,** at Miami; Dolphins win toss. Von Schamann kicks 23-yard field goal at 3:20.

Dec. 14, 1980—Cincinnati 17, Chicago 14, at Chicago; Bengals win toss. Breech kicks 28-yard field goal at 4:23.

Dec. 21, 1980—Los Angeles 20, Atlanta 17, at Los Angeles; Rams win toss. Corral's punt downed at Rams' 37. James punts into end zone for touchback. Corral's punt downed on Falcons' 17. Bartkowski fumbles when hit by Harris, recovered by Delaney. Corral kicks 23-yard field goal on first play of possession at 7:00.

Sept. 27, 1981—Cincinnati 27, Buffalo 24, at Cincinnati; Bills win toss. Cater punts into end zone for touchback. Bengals drive to the Bills' 10 where Breech kicks 28-yard field goal at 9:33.

Sept. 27, 1981—Pittsburgh 27, New England 21, at Pittsburgh; Patriots win toss. Hubach punts and Smith returns five yards to midfield. Four plays later Bradshaw throws 24-yard touchdown pass to Swann at 3:19.

Oct. 4, 1981—Miami 28, New York Jets 28, at Miami; Jets win toss. Teams trade punts twice. Leahy's 48-yard field goal attempt is wide right as time expires.

Oct. 25, 1981—New York Giants 27, Atlanta 24, at Atlanta; Giants win toss. Jennings' punt goes out of bounds at New York 47. Bright returns Atlanta punt to Giants' 14. Woerner fair catches punt at own 28. Andrews fumbles on first play, recovered by Van Pelt. Danelo kicks 40-yard field goal four plays later at 9:20.

Oct. 25, 1981—Chicago 20, San Diego 17, at Chicago; Bears win toss. Teams trade punts. Bears' second punt returned by Brooks to Chargers' 33. Fouts pass intercepted by Fencik and returned 32 yards to San Diego 27. Roveto kicks 27-yard field goal seven plays later at 9:30.

Nov. 8, 1981—Chicago 16, Kansas City 13, at Kansas City; Bears win toss. Teams trade punts. Kansas City takes over on downs on its own 38. Fuller's fumble recovered by Harris on Chicago 36. Roveto's 37-yard field goal wide, but Chiefs penalized for leverage. Roveto's 22-yard field goal attempt three plays later is good at 13:07.

Nov. 8, 1981—Denver 23, Cleveland 20, at Denver; Browns win toss. D. Smith recovers Hill's fumble at Denver 48. Morton's 33-yard pass to Upchurch and 6-yard run by Preston set up Steinfort's 30-yard field goal at 4:10.

Nov. 8, 1981—Miami 30, New England 27, at New England; Dolphins win toss. Orosz punts and Morgan returns six yards to New England 26. Grogan's pass intercepted by Brudzinski who returns 19 yards to Patriots' 26. Von Schamann kicks 30-yard field goal on first down at 7:09.

Nov. 15, 1981—Washington 30, New York Giants 27, at New York; Giants win toss. Nelms returns Giants' punt 26 yards to New York 47. Five plays later Moseley kicks 48-yard field goal at 3:44.

Dec. 20, 1981—New York Giants 13, Dallas 10, at New York; Cowboys win toss and kick off. Jennings punts to Dallas 40. Taylor recovers Dorsett's fumble on second down. Danelo's 33-yard field goal attempt hits right upright and bounces back. White's pass for Pearson intercepted by Hunt and returned seven yards to Dallas 24. Four plays later Danelo kicks 35-yard field goal at 6:19.

Sept. 12, 1982—Washington 37, Philadelphia 34, at Philadelphia; Redskins win toss. Theismann completes five passes for 63 yards to set up Moseley's 26-yard field goal at 4:47.

Sept. 19, 1982—Pittsburgh 26, Cincinnati 20, at Pittsburgh; Bengals win toss. Anderson's pass intended for Kreider intercepted by Woodruff and returned 30 yards to Cincinnati 2. Bradshaw completes two-yard touchdown pass to Stallworth on first down at 1:08.

Dec. 19, 1982—Baltimore 20, Green Bay 20, at Baltimore; Packers win toss. K. Anderson intercepts Dickey's first-down pass and returns to Packers' 42. Miller's 44-yard field goal attempt blocked by G. Lewis. Teams trade punts before Stenerud's 47-yard field goal attempt is wide right. Teams trade punts again before time expires in Colts possession.

Jan. 2, 1983—Tampa Bay 26, Chicago 23, at Tampa; Bears win toss. Parsons punts to T. Bell at Buccaneers' 40. Capece kicks 33-yard field goal at 3:14.

Sept. 4, 1983—Baltimore 29, New England 23, at New England; Patriots win toss. Cooks runs 52 yards with fumble recovery three plays into overtime at 0:30.

Sept. 4, 1983—Green Bay 41, Houston 38, at Houston; Packers win toss. Stenerud kicks 42-yard field goal at 5:55.

Sept. 11, 1983—New York Giants 16, Atlanta 13, at Atlanta; Giants win toss. Dennis returns kickoff 54 yards to Atlanta 41. Haji-Sheikh kicks 30-yard field goal at 3:38.

Sept. 18, 1983—New Orleans 34, Chicago 31, at New Orleans; Bears win toss. Parsons punts and Groth returns five yards to New Orleans 34. Stabler pass intercepted by Schmidt at Chicago 47. Parsons punt downed by Gentry at New Orleans 2. Stabler gains 36 yards in four passes; Wilson 38 on six carries. Andersen kicks 41-yard field goal at 10:57.

Sept. 18, 1983—Minnesota 19, Tampa Bay 16, at Tampa; Vikings win toss. Coleman punts and Bell returns eight yards to Tampa Bay 47. Capece's 33-yard field goal attempt sails wide at 7:26. Dils and Young combine for 48-yard gain to Tampa Bay 27. Ricardo kicks 42-yard field goal at 9:27.

Sept. 25, 1983—Baltimore 22, Chicago 19, at Baltimore; Colts win toss. Allegre kicks 33-yard field goal nine plays later at 4:51.

Sept. 25, 1983—Cleveland 30, San Diego 24, at San Diego; Browns win toss. Walker returns kickoff 33 yards to Cleveland 37. Sipe completes 48-yard touchdown pass to Holt four plays later at 1:53.

Sept. 25, 1983—New York Jets 27, Los Angeles Rams 24, at New York; Jets win toss. Ramsey punts to Irvin who returns to 25 but penalty puts Rams on own 13. Holmes 30-yard interception return sets up Leahy's 26-yard field goal at 3:22.

Oct. 9, 1983—Buffalo 38, Miami 35, at Miami; Dolphins win toss. Von Schamann's 52-yard field goal attempt goes wide at 12:36. Cater punts to Clayton who loses 11 to own 13. Von Schamann's 43-yard field goal attempt sails wide at 5:15. Danelo kicks 36-yard field goal nine plays later at 13:58.

Oct. 9, 1983—Dallas 27, Tampa Bay 24, at Dallas; Cowboys win toss. Septien's 51-yard field goal attempt goes wide but Buccaneers penalized for roughing kicker. Septien kicks 42-yard field goal at 4:38.

Oct. 23, 1983—Kansas City 13, Houston 10, at Houston; Chiefs win toss. Lowery kicks 41-yard field goal 13 plays later at 7:41.

Oct. 23, 1983—Minnesota 20, Green Bay 17, at Green Bay; Packers win toss.

OVERTIME GAMES

Scribner's punt downed on Vikings' 42. Ricardo kicks 32-yard field goal eight plays later at 5:05.

***Oct. 24, 1983—New York Giants 20, St. Louis 20,** at St. Louis; Cardinals win toss. Teams trade punts before O'Donoghue's 44-yard field goal attempt is wide left. Jennings' punt returned by Bird to St. Louis 21. Lomax pass intercepted by Haynes who loses six yards to New York 33. Jennings' punt downed on St. Louis 17. O'Donoghue's 19-yard field goal attempt is wide right. Rutledge's pass intercepted by L. Washington who returns 25 yards to New York 25. O'Donoghue's 42-yard field goal attempt is wide right. Rutledge's pass intercepted by W. Smith at St. Louis 33 to end game.

Oct. 30, 1983—Cleveland 25, Houston 19, at Cleveland; Oilers win toss. Teams trade punts. Nielsen's pass intercepted by Whitwell who returns to Houston 20. Green runs 20 yards for touchdown on first down at 6:34.

Nov. 20, 1983—Detroit 23, Green Bay 20, at Milwaukee; Packers win toss. Scribner punts and Jenkins returns 14 yards to Green Bay 45. Murray's 33-yard field goal attempt is wide left at 9:32. Whitehurst's pass intercepted by Watkins and returned to Green Bay 27. Murray kicks 37-yard field goal four plays later at 8:30.

Nov. 27, 1983—Atlanta 47, Green Bay 41, at Atlanta; Packers win toss. K. Johnson returns interception 31 yards for touchdown at 2:13.

Nov. 27, 1983—Seattle 51, Kansas City 48, at Seattle; Seahawks win toss. Dixon's 47-yard kickoff return sets up N. Johnson's 42-yard field goal at 1:36.

Dec. 11, 1983—New Orleans 20, Philadelphia 17, at Philadelphia; Eagles win toss. Runager punts to Groth who fair catches on New Orleans 32. Stabler completes two passes for 36 yards to Goodlow to set up Andersen's 50-yard field goal at 5:30.

***Dec. 12, 1983—Green Bay 12, Tampa Bay 9,** at Tampa; Packers win toss. Stenerud kicks 23-yard field goal 11 plays later at 4:07.

Sept. 9, 1984—Detroit 27, Atlanta 24, at Atlanta; Lions win toss. Murray kicks 48-yard field goal nine plays later at 5:06.

Sept. 30, 1984—Tampa Bay 30, Green Bay 27, at Tampa; Packers win toss. Scribner punts 44 yards to Tampa Bay 2. Epps returns Garcia's punt three yards to Green Bay 27. Scribner's punt downed on Buccaneers' 33. Ariri kicks 46-yard field goal 11 plays later at 10:32.

Oct. 14, 1984—Detroit 13, Tampa Bay 7, at Detroit; Buccaneers win toss. Tampa Bay drives to Lions' 39 before Wilder fumbles. Five plays later Danielson hits Thompson with 37-yard touchdown pass at 4:34.

Oct. 21, 1984—Dallas 30, New Orleans 27, at Dallas; Cowboys win toss. Septien kicks 41-yard field goal eight plays later at 3:42.

Oct. 28, 1984—Denver 22, Los Angeles Raiders 19, at Los Angeles; Raiders win toss. Hawkins fumble recovered by Foley at Denver 7. Teams trade punts. Karlis's 42-yard field goal attempt is wide left. Teams trade punts. Wilson pass intercepted by R. Jackson at Los Angeles 45, returned 23 yards to Los Angeles 22. Karlis kicks 35-yard field goal two plays later at 15:00.

Nov. 4, 1984—Philadelphia 23, Detroit 23, at Detroit; Lions win toss. Lions drive to Eagles' 3 in eight plays. Murray's 21-yard field goal attempt hits right upright and bounces back. Jaworski's pass intercepted by Watkins at Detroit 5. Teams trade punts. Cooper returns Black's punt five yards to Eagles' 14. Time expires four plays later with Eagles on own 21.

Nov. 18, 1984—San Diego 34, Miami 28, at San Diego; Chargers win toss. McGee scores eight plays later on a 25-yard run at 3:17.

Dec. 2, 1984—Cincinnati 20, Cleveland 17, at Cleveland; Browns win toss. Simmons returns Cox's punt 30 yards to Cleveland 35. Breech kicks 35-yard field goal seven plays later at 4:34.

Dec. 2, 1984—Houston 23, Pittsburgh 20, at Houston; Oilers win toss. Cooper kicks 30-yard field goal 16 plays later at 5:53.

Sept. 8, 1985—St. Louis 27, Cleveland 24, at Cleveland; Cardinals win toss. O'Donoghue kicks 35-yard field goal nine plays later at 5:27.

Sept. 29, 1985—New York Giants 16, Philadelphia 10, at Philadelphia; Eagles win toss. Jaworski's pass tipped by Quick and intercepted by Patterson who returns 29 yards for touchdown at 0:55.

Oct. 20, 1985—Denver 13, Seattle 10, at Denver; Seahawks win toss. Teams trade punts twice. Krieg's pass intercepted by Hunter and returned to Seahawks' 15. Karlis kicks 24-yard field goal four plays later at 9:19.

Nov. 10, 1985—Philadelphia 23, Atlanta 17, at Philadelphia; Falcons win toss. Donnelly's 62-yard punt goes out of bounds at Eagles' 1. Jaworski completes 99-yard touchdown pass to Quick two plays later at 1:49.

Nov. 10, 1985—San Diego 40, Los Angeles Raiders 34, at San Diego; Chargers win toss. James scores on 17-yard run seven plays later at 3:44.

Nov. 17, 1985—Denver 30, San Diego 24, at Denver; Chargers win toss. Thomas' 40-yard field goal attempt blocked by Smith and returned 60 yards by Wright for touchdown at 4:45.

Nov. 24, 1985—New York Jets 16, New England 13, at New York; Jets win toss. Teams trade punts twice. Patriots' second punt returned 46 yards by Sohn to Patriots' 15. Leahy kicks 32-yard field goal one play later at 10:05.

Nov. 24, 1985—Tampa Bay 19, Detroit 16, at Tampa; Lions win toss. Teams trade punts. Lions' punt downed on Buccaneers' 38. Igwebuike kicks 24-yard field goal 11 plays later at 12:31.

Nov. 24, 1985—Los Angeles Raiders 31, Denver 28, at Los Angeles; Raiders win toss. Bahr kicks 32-yard field goal six plays later at 2:42.

Dec. 8, 1985—Los Angeles Raiders 17, Denver 14, at Denver; Broncos win toss. Teams trade punts twice. Elway's fumble recovered by Townsend at Broncos' 8. Bahr kicks 26-yard field goal one play later at 4:55.

Sept. 14, 1986—Chicago 13, Philadelphia 10, at Chicago; Eagles win toss. Crawford's fumble of kickoff recovered by Jackson at Eagles' 35. Butler kicks 23-yard field goal 10 plays later at 5:56.

Sept. 14, 1986—Cincinnati 36, Buffalo 33, at Cincinnati; Bills win toss. Zander intercepts Kelly's first-down pass and returns it to Bills' 17. Breech kicks 20-yard field goal two plays later at 0:56.

Sept. 21, 1986—New York Jets 51, Miami 45, at New York; Jets win toss. O'Brien completes 43-yard touchdown pass to Walker five plays later at 2:35.

Sept. 28, 1986—Pittsburgh 22, Houston 16, at Houston; Oilers win toss. Johnson's punt returned 41 yards by Woods to Oilers' 15. Abercrombie scores on three-yard run three plays later at 2:35.

Sept. 28, 1986—Atlanta 23, Tampa Bay 20, at Tampa; Falcons win toss. Teams trade punts. Luckhurst kicks 34-yard field goal 10 plays later at 12:35.

Oct. 5, 1986—Los Angeles Rams 26, Tampa Bay 20, at Anaheim; Rams win toss. Dickerson scores four plays later on 42-yard run at 2:16.

Oct. 12, 1986—Minnesota 27, San Francisco 24, at San Francisco; Vikings win toss. C. Nelson kicks 28-yard field goal nine plays later at 4:27.

Oct. 19, 1986—San Francisco 10, Atlanta 10, at Atlanta; Falcons win toss. Teams trade punts twice. Donnelly punts to 49ers' 27. The following play Wilson recovers Rice's fumble at 49ers' 46 as time expires.

Nov. 2, 1986—Washington 44, Minnesota 38, at Washington; Redskins win toss. Schroeder completes 38-yard touchdown pass to Clark four plays later at 1:46.

Nov. 20, 1986—Los Angeles Raiders 37, San Diego 31, at San Diego; Raiders win toss. Teams trade punts. Allen scores five plays later on 28-yard run at 8:33.

Nov. 23, 1986—Cleveland 37, Pittsburgh 31, at Cleveland; Browns win toss. Teams trade punts. Six plays later Kosar hits Slaughter with 36-yard touchdown pass at 6:37.

Nov. 30, 1986—Chicago 13, Pittsburgh 10, at Chicago; Bears win toss and kick off. Newsome's punt returned by Barnes to Chicago 49. Butler kicks 42-yard field goal five plays later at 3:55.

Nov. 30, 1986—Philadelphia 33, Los Angeles Raiders 27, at Los Angeles; Eagles win toss. Teams trade punts. Long recovers Cunningham's fumble at Philadelphia 42. Waters returns Allen's fumble 81 yards to Los Angeles 4. Cunningham scores on one-yard run two plays later at 6:53.

Nov. 30, 1986—Cleveland 13, Houston 10, at Cleveland; Oilers win toss and kick off. Gossett punts to Houston 39. Luck's pass intercepted by Minnifield at Cleveland 21. Gossett punts to Houston 34. Luck's pass intercepted by Minnifield at Cleveland 43 who returns 20 yards to Houston 37. Moseley kicks 29-yard field goal nine plays later at 14:44.

Dec. 7, 1986—St. Louis 10, Philadelphia 10, at Philadelphia; Cardinals win toss. White blocks Schubert's 40-yard field goal attempt. Teams trade punts. McFadden's 43-yard field goal attempt is wide left. Schubert's 37-yard field goal attempt is wide right. Cavanaugh's pass intercepted by Carter and returned to Eagles' 48 to end game.

Dec. 14, 1986—Miami 37, Los Angeles Rams 31, at Anaheim; Dolphins win toss. Marino completes 20-yard touchdown pass to Duper six plays later at 3:04.

Sept. 20, 1987—Denver 17, Green Bay 17, at Milwaukee; Packers win toss. Del Greco's 47-yard field goal attempt is short. Teams trade punts. Elway intercepted by Noble who returns 10 yards to Green Bay 34. Davis fumbles on next play and Smith recovers. Two plays later, Karlis's 40-yard field goal attempt is wide left. Time expires two plays later with Packers on own 23.

Oct. 11, 1987—Detroit 19, Green Bay 16, at Green Bay; Lions win toss. Prindle's 42-yard field goal attempt is wide left. Packers punt downed on Detroit 17. Prindle kicks 31-yard field goal 16 plays later at 12:26.

Oct. 18, 1987—New York Jets 37, Miami 31, at New York; Jets win toss. Teams trade punts. Ryan intercepted by Hooper at Jets' 47 who returns 11 yards. Mackey intercepted by Haslett at Jets' 37 who returns 9 yards. Jets punt. Mackey intercepted by Radachowsky who returns 45 yards to Miami 24. Ryan completes eight-yard touchdown pass to Hunter five plays later at 14:26.

Oct. 18, 1987—Green Bay 16, Philadelphia 10, at Green Bay; Packers win toss. Hargrove scores on seven-yard run 10 plays later at 5:04.

Oct. 18, 1987—Buffalo 6, New York Giants 3, at Buffalo; Bills win toss. Schlopy's 28-yard field goal attempt is wide left. Teams trade punts. Rutledge intercepted by Clark who returns 23 yards to Buffalo 40. Schlopy kicks 27-yard field goal nine plays later at 14:41.

Oct. 25, 1987—Buffalo 34, Miami 31, at Miami; Bills win toss. Norwood kicks 27-yard field goal seven plays later at 4:12.

Nov. 1, 1987—San Diego 27, Cleveland 24, at San Diego; Browns win toss. Kosar intercepted by Glenn who returns 20 yards to Browns' 25. Abbott kicks 33-yard field goal three plays later at 2:16.

Nov. 15, 1987—Dallas 23, New England 17, at New England; Cowboys win toss. Walker scores on 60-yard run four plays later at 1:50.

Nov. 26, 1987—Minnesota 44, Dallas 38, at Dallas; Vikings win toss. Coleman's punt downed by Hilton at Cowboys' 37. White intercepted by Studwell who returns 12 yards to Vikings' 37. D. Nelson scores on 24-yard run seven plays later at 7:51.

Nov. 29, 1987—Philadelphia 34, New England 31, at New England; Patriots win toss. Ramsey intercepted by Joyner who returns 29 yards to Eagles' 32. Fryar fair catches Teltschik's punt at Patriots' 13. Franklin's 46-yard field goal attempt is short. McFadden's 39-yard field goal attempt is wide left. Tatupu fumbles on next play and Cobb recovers. McFadden kicks 38-yard field goal four plays later at 12:16.

Dec. 6, 1987—New York Giants 23, Philadelphia 20, at New York; Giants win toss and kick off. Teams trade punts twice. Teltschik's punt is returned 16 yards by McConkey to Eagles' 33. Three plays later, Allegre's 50-yard field goal attempt is blocked by Joyner and returned 25 yards by Hoage to Eagles' 30. McConkey returns Teltschik's punt four yards to Giants' 44. Allegre kicks 28-yard field goal four plays later at 10:42.

Dec. 6, 1987—Cincinnati 30, Kansas City 27, at Cincinnati; Bengals win toss. Teams trade punts. Breech kicks 32-yard field goal 16 plays later at 9:44.

Dec. 26, 1987—Washington 27, Minnesota 24, at Minnesota; Redskins win toss. Haji-Sheikh kicks 26-yard field goal six plays later at 2:09.

Sept. 4, 1988—Houston 17, Indianapolis 14, at Indianapolis; Colts win toss. Dickerson fumble recovered by Lyles who returns six yards to Colts' 42. Zendejas kicks 35-yard field goal six plays later at 3:51.

***Sept. 26, 1988—Los Angeles Raiders 30, Denver 27,** at Denver; Broncos win toss. Teams trade punts twice. Elway intercepted by Lee who returns 20 yards to Broncos' 31. Bahr kicks 35-yard field goal four plays later at 12:35.

Oct. 2, 1988—New York Jets 17, Kansas City 17, at New York; Chiefs win toss. Chiefs punt goes into end zone for touchback. Leahy's 44-yard field goal attempt is wide right. Chiefs punt is returned by Townsell to Jets' 26. Burruss recovers McNeil's fumble at Chiefs' 11. DeBerg intercepted by Humphery at Jets' 49. Three plays later, time expires.

Oct. 9, 1988—Denver 16, San Francisco 13, at San Francisco; Broncos win toss and kick off. Young intercepted by Haynes at Broncos' 32. Denver punt downed at 49ers' 5. Young intercepted by Wilson who returns seven yards to 49ers' 5. Karlis kicks 22-yard field goal two plays later at 8:11.

Oct. 30, 1988—New York Giants 13, Detroit 10, at Detroit; Lions win toss. James's fumble recovered by Taylor at Lions' 22. Three plays later, McFadden kicks 33-yard field goal at 1:13.

Nov. 20, 1988—Buffalo 9, New York Jets 6, at Buffalo; Jets win toss. Vick's fumble recovered by Bennett at Bills' 32. Norwood kicks 30-yard field goal five plays later at 3:47.

Nov. 20, 1988—Philadelphia 23, New York Giants 17, at New York; Eagles win toss. Philadelphia's punt goes into end zone for touchback. Hostetler intercepted by Hoage who returns 11 yards to Giants' 41. Six plays later, Zendejas's 30-yard field-goal attempt is blocked and ball is recovered behind line of scrimmage by Eagles' Simmons, who runs 15 yards for touchdown at 3:09.

Dec. 11, 1988—New England 10, Tampa Bay 7, at New England; Buccaneers win toss and kick off. Staurovsky kicks 27-yard field goal six plays later at 3:08.

Dec. 17, 1988—Cincinnati 20, Washington 17, at Cincinnati; Bengals win toss. Cincinnati's punt returned by Oliphant to Redskins' 16. Grant recovers Williams's fumble at Redskins' 17. Breech kicks 20-yard field goal three plays later at 7:01.

Sept. 24, 1989—Buffalo 47, Houston 41, at Houston; Oilers win toss. Johnson returns Brady's kickoff 17 yards to Oilers' 19. Oilers drive to Buffalo 25, Zendejas's 37-yard field goal blocked, but Bills offsides and Zendejas's second attempt is wide left. Bills' ball and Kelly completes series of passes, including 28-yard game-winner to Andre Reed, at 8:42.

Oct. 8, 1989—Miami 13, Cleveland 10, at Miami; Browns win toss. Metcalf returns Stoyanovich's kickoff 20 yards to Browns' 28. Browns drive ball 46 yards in eight plays; Bahr wide left on 44-yard field goal attempt. Dolphins ball. Browns called for pass interference on Marino pass to Banks at Cleveland 47. Two plays later, Banks's 20-yard reception at Browns' 23 sets up winning 35-yard field goal by Stoyanovich at 6:23.

Oct. 22, 1989—Denver 24, Seattle 21, at Seattle; Seahawks win toss. Treadwell's 56-yard kickoff returned 18 yards by Jefferson to Seahawks' 27. Seahawks drive to Broncos' 22 in 10 plays, but Johnson's 40-yard field goal attempt wide left. Smith intercepts a Krieg pass and returns it 28 yards to Seahawks' 10. Treadwell kicks winning 27-yard field goal at 7:46.

Oct. 29, 1989—New England 23, Indianapolis 20, at Indianapolis; Patriots win toss. Biasucci kickoff returned 13 yards to Patriots' 23 by Martin. Holding penalty brings ball back to Patriots' 13. After six plays, Feagles punt returned 11 yards by Verdin to Colts' 28. Six plays later, Colts punt to Martin at Patriots' 12. Grogan completes three straight passes to Patriots' 44. Five consecutive runs put New England on Colts' 33. Davis kicks a 51-yard winning field goal for Patriots at 9:46.

Oct. 29, 1989—Green Bay 23, Detroit 20, at Milwaukee; Lions win toss. Sanders touchback on Jacke kickoff. On first play, Murphy intercepts Lions' Peete and returns it three yards to Lions' 26. Fullwood gains five yards on three plays to set up Jacke's 38-yard field goal at 2:14.

Nov. 5, 1989—Minnesota 23, Los Angeles Rams 21, at Minneapolis; Rams win toss. Karlis's kick returned 18 yards by Delpino to Rams' 19. Drive stops at Rams' 28. Merriweather blocks Hatcher's punt at 12. Ball rolls out of end zone for safety.

Nov. 19, 1989—Cleveland 10, Kansas City 10, at Cleveland; Browns win toss. Browns punt three times; Chiefs twice; before Kansas City's Lowery misses 47-yard field goal with 17 seconds remaining in overtime. Kosar's pass intercepted as time expired.

Nov. 26, 1989—Los Angeles Rams 20, New Orleans 17, at New Orleans; Saints win toss. Lansford's kickoff returned 27 yards to Saints' 30. After four plays, Barnhardt punts to Rams' 15. Saints penalized 35 yards for interference to Rams' 43. Three plays later, Everett hits Anderson with 14-yard pass to Saints' 40, then 26-yarder to put Rams in field goal position. Lansford kicks 31-yard field goal at 6:38.

Dec. 3, 1989—Los Angeles Raiders 16, Denver 13, at Los Angeles; Broncos win toss. Bell returns Jaeger kickoff 14 yards to Broncos' 18. Broncos' penalized for illegal block to Broncos' 9. Elway completes three passes for two first downs. On third and eight Elway sacked for 10-yard loss. Horan punts, Adams calls for fair catch at Raiders' 29. Dyal's 26-yard reception moves Raiders to Denver 43. Raiders move ball 34 yards in three plays to set up Jaeger's 26-yard field goal at 7:02.

Dec. 10, 1989—Indianapolis 23, Cleveland 17, at Indianapolis; Browns win toss. Teams trade punts. McNeil returns Colts' punt 42 yards to 42. Seven plays later, Bahr misses 35-yard field goal attempt. Three plays later, Stark punts and McNeil returns ball to 50-yard line. Two plays later, Prior intercepts Kosar's pass at Colts' 42 and returns it 58 yards for touchdown at 10:54.

Dec. 17, 1989—Cleveland 23, Minnesota 17, at Cleveland; Browns win toss. Browns punt to Vikings' 18. Six plays later, Vikings punt to Browns' 22. Nine plays later, Bahr lines up to attempt 31-yard field goal. Holder Pagel takes snap and passes 14 yards to Waiters for touchdown at 9:30.

Sept. 23, 1990—Denver 34, Seattle 31, at Denver; Seahawks win toss. Loville returns kickoff 19 yards to Seahawks' 27. Seahawks drive to Broncos' 26, where Johnson misses 44-yard field goal wide right. Broncos take over and Elway completes series of passes to set up Treadwell's 25-yard field goal at 9:14.

Sept. 30, 1990—Tampa Bay 23, Minnesota 20, at Minnesota; Vikings win toss. Vikings drive to Buccaneers' 31; Igwebuike's 48-yard field goal attempt wide left. Buccaneers drive to Vikings' 43 and punt. Gannon's pass is intercepted at Vikings' 26 by Wayne Haddix. Buccaneers drive to Vikings' 19 to set up Christie's 36-yard field goal at 9:11.

Oct. 7, 1990—Cincinnati 34, Los Angeles Rams 31, at Anaheim; Rams win toss. Berry returns kickoff to Rams' 21. After 3 plays, English punts and Green downs ball at Bengals' 25. After 3 plays, Johnson punts and Sutton downs ball at Rams' 29-yard line. After 3 plays, English punts and Price signals fair catch at Bengals' 47. Esiason completes series of passes to 26-yard line to set up Breech's 44-yard field goal at 11:56.

Nov. 4, 1990—Washington 41, Detroit 38, at Detroit; Redskins win toss. Howard downs kickoff on Redskins' 15. After 3 plays, Mojsiejenko punts to Redskins' 45. After 3 plays, Arnold punts to Redskins' 10. Rutledge completes series of passes to set up Lohmiller's 34-yard field goal at 9:10.

Nov. 18, 1990—Chicago 16, Denver 13, at Denver; Broncos win toss. Ezor returns kickoff to Broncos' 12. Both teams have ball twice and have to punt after each possession. Broncos punt after third possession of overtime and Bailey returns 20 yards to Broncos' 34. Harbaugh completes 10-yard pass to Thornton to set up Butler's 44-yard field goal at 13:14.

Nov. 25, 1990—Seattle 13, San Diego 10, at San Diego; Chargers win toss. Lewis returns kickoff to Chargers' 22. After 2 plays, Cox fumbles and ball is recovered by Porter at Chargers' 23. After two plays, Johnson kicks 40-yard field goal at 3:01.

Dec. 2, 1990—Chicago 23, Detroit 17, at Chicago; Lions win toss. Gray returns kickoff to Lions' 35. After 10 plays, Murray misses 35-yard field goal. Bears take possession at Chicago 20. Harbaugh completes 50-yard game-winning pass to Anderson at 10:57.

Dec. 2, 1990—Seattle 13, Houston 10, at Seattle; Seahawks win toss. Warren returns kickoff to Seahawks' 13. After 5 plays, Donnelly punts to Oilers' 23-yard line. Ford's fumble recovered by Wyman. Seahawks take possession at Oilers' 27. After 2 plays, Johnson kicks 42-yard field goal at 4:25.

Dec. 9, 1990—Miami 23, Philadelphia 20, at Miami; Eagles win toss. After 11 plays, Feagles punts to Dolphins' 26. After 6 plays, Roby punts to Eagles' 14 and Harris returns to 25. After 3 plays, Feagles punts to Dolphins' 43. Marino completes series of passes to Eagles' 22. Stoyanovich kicks 39-yard field goal at 12:32.

Dec. 9, 1990—San Francisco 20, Cincinnati 17, at Cincinnati; 49ers win toss. Carter returns kickoff to 49ers' 19. After 10 plays, Cofer kicks 23-yard field goal at 6:12.

Sept. 23, 1991—Chicago 19, New York Jets 13, at Chicago; Jets win toss. Mathis returns kickoff seven yards to New York's 12. Jets drive to New York 26; Bailey returns punt to Chicago 39. Bears drive to Jets' 44-yard line and punt into the end zone. Jets drive to Bears' 11 where Leahy's 28-yard field goal attempt is wide left. Bears drive from 20 to Jets' 1 where Harbaugh runs for touchdown at 14:42.

Oct. 13, 1991—Los Angeles Raiders 23, Seattle 20, at Seattle. Seahawks win toss. Seahawks begin on 20. After 5 plays, Tuten punts and Brown signals fair catch at Raiders' 24. After 3 plays, Gossett punts and Land downs ball at Seattle 9. After 1 play, Lott intercepts at Seahawks' 19 to set up Jaeger's game-winning 37-yard field goal at 6:37.

Oct. 20, 1991—Cleveland 30, San Diego 24, at San Diego; Chargers win toss. After kickoff, Chargers drive to Browns' 45 and punt to Browns' 6 where Hendrickson downs ball. Browns drive to 38 and punt; Taylor fair catches on Chargers' 14. After 3 plays, Brandon intercepts at Chargers' 30 and scores at 5:58.

Oct. 20, 1991—New England 26, Minnesota 23, at New England; Patriots win toss. Martin returns kickoff 18 yards to New England 22. Patriots drive to Minnesota 19. Staurovsky's 36-yard field goal attempt is wide left. Minnesota drives to the 50 where Newsome punts into end zone. On first play, McMillian intercepts at the 40 for Minnesota. After 2 plays, Marion causes Jordan fumble and Pool recovers at New England 20. New England drives to Minnesota 24 where Staurovsky kicks 42-yard field goal as time expires.

Nov. 3, 1991—New York Jets 19, Green Bay 16, at New York; Packers win toss. Thompson returns kickoff 30 yards to Packers' 39. Green Bay drives to New York 24 where Jacke's 42-yard field goal attempt is wide right. Jets drive to 50. Aguiar's punt is fumbled by Sikahema and recovered by New York at Packers' 23. After 2 plays, Leahy kicks 37-yard field goal at 9:40.

Nov. 3, 1991—Washington 16, Houston 13, at Washington; Redskins win toss. Mitchell returns kickoff 9 yards to Washington 14. After 4 plays, Goodburn punts and Givins returns to Houston 31. After 1 play, Moon's pass is intercepted by

Green at Oilers' 35. After 3 plays, Lohmiller kicks 41-yard field goal at 4:01.
Nov. 10, 1991—Houston 26, Dallas 23, at Houston; Oilers win toss. Pinkett returns kickoff 20 yards to Houston 24. After 6 plays, Montgomery punts and Martin returns to Dallas 24. Cowboys drive to Oilers' 24 where Smith fumbles and McDowell recovers at Oilers' 15. Houston drives to Dallas 5 where Del Greco kicks 23-yard field goal at 14:31.
Nov. 10, 1991—Pittsburgh 33, Cincinnati 27, at Cincinnati; Pittsburgh wins toss. Woodson downs kickoff for touchback. After 3 plays, Stryzinski punts and Barber returns 7 yards to Cincinnati 38. Bengals drive to Pittsburgh 37 where Woods fumbles and Lloyd returns recovery to Cincinnati 44. After 2 plays, O'Donnell passes to Green for 26-yard touchdown at 6:32.
Nov. 24, 1991—Atlanta 23, New Orleans 20, at New Orleans; Atlanta wins toss. Falcons begin at 20. After 3 plays, Fulhage punts and Fenerty signals fair catch at New Orleans 43. After 3 plays, Barnhardt punts and Thompson downs ball at Atlanta 23. After 3 plays, Fulhage punts and Fenerty fair catches at New Orleans 25. Saints drive to Atlanta 38 where Andersen misses 55-yard field-goal attempt. After 1 play, Rozier fumbles and Martin recovers on 50. Saints drive to Atlanta 38 where Barnhardt punts to Falcons' 2. Atlanta drives to New Orleans 33 where Johnson kicks 50-yard field goal at 13:03.
Nov. 24, 1991—Miami 16, Chicago 13, at Chicago; Miami wins toss. Butler kicks to Miami 20 where Paige returns kickoff 15 yards to 35. Miami drives to Chicago 9 where Stoyanovich kicks 27-yard field goal at 4:11.
Dec. 8, 1991—Buffalo 30, Los Angeles Raiders 27, at Los Angeles; Raiders win toss. Daluiso kicks into end zone for touchback. On third play, Kelso intercepts for Buffalo and returns ball to Bills' 36. Bills drive to Los Angeles 24 where Norwood kicks 42-yard field goal at 2:34.
Dec. 8, 1991—Kansas City 20, San Diego 17, at Kansas City; Chiefs win toss. Carney kicks to Kansas City 10 where Stradford returns 23 yards to 33. After 3 plays, Barker punts to San Diego 4. Chargers drive to 40 where Kidd punts 60 yards into end zone for touchback. Kansas City drives to San Diego 39 where Barker punts 38 yards to 1. After 3 plays, Kidd punts 41 yards to San Diego 42 where Stradford returns 12 yards to 30. Chiefs drive to San Diego 1 where Lowery kicks 18-yard field goal at 11:26.
Dec. 8, 1991—New England 23, Indianapolis 17, at New England; Indianapolis wins toss. Baumann kicks off to Indianapolis 2 where Martin returns 23 yards to 25. After 3 downs, Stark punts to New England 17 where Henderson returns 8 yards to 25. New England drives to 50 where McCarthy punts and Prior signals fair catch at Indianapolis 15. After 3 plays, Stark punts to New England 40 where Henderson returns 7 yards to 47. After 2 plays, Millen passes to Timpson for 45-yard touchdown at 8:55.
Dec. 22, 1991—Detroit 17, Buffalo 14, at Buffalo; Detroit wins toss. Daluiso kicks off to Detroit 20 where Dozier returns 15 yards to Lions 35. Lions drive to Bills' 3 where Murray kicks 21-yard field goal at 4:23.
Dec. 22, 1991—New York Jets 23, Miami 20, at Miami; Jets win toss. Aguiar kicks to Miami's 30 where Logan returns 3 yards to the 33. After 4 downs, Stoyanovich punts to Jets' 15 where Baty returns 8 yards to 23. Jets drive to Miami 12 where Allegre kicks 30-yard field goal at 6:33.
Sept. 6, 1992—Minnesota 23, Green Bay 20, at Green Bay. Vikings win toss. Nelson returns kickoff 14 yards to the Minnesota 23. After 5 plays, Newsome punts 49 yards to Green Bay 21 where Brooks returns 12 yards to the 33. After 2 plays, Glenn intercepts pass at the Vikings' 48. On first play, Allen fumbles and Billups recovers at Green Bay 35. After 3 plays, McJulien punts 33 yards to Vikings' 35. Vikings drive to Minnesota 48; Newsome punts 52 yards for touchback. After 3 plays, McJulien punts and Parker returns 10 yards to Green Bay 48. Vikings drive to Packers' 9 where Reveiz kicks 26-yard field goal at 10:20.
Sept. 13, 1992—Cincinnati 24, Los Angeles Raiders 21, at Cincinnati. Raiders win toss. Land returns kickoff 13 yards but fumbles at Los Angeles's 20; ball recovered by Bengals' Bennett at Raiders' 21. After 1 play, Breech kicks 34-yard field goal at 1:01.
Sept. 20, 1992—Houston 23, Kansas City 20, at Houston. Chiefs win toss. Carter returns kickoff 25 yards to Kansas City 28. On third play of drive, Birden fumbles at Kansas City 34; ball recovered by Houston's D. Smith at Chiefs' 23. After one play, Del Greco kicks 39-yard field goal at 1:55.
Oct. 11, 1992—Indianapolis 6, New York Jets 3, at Indianapolis. Colts win toss. Verdin returns kickoff 33 yards to Colts' 36. Colts drive to Jets' 30 where Biasucci kicks 47-yard field goal at 3:01.
Nov. 8, 1992—Cincinnati 31, Chicago 28, at Chicago. Bears win toss. Lewis returns kickoff 22 yards to Chicago's 29. Bears drive to Chicago's 46 where Gardocki punts; fair catch by Wright at the Cincinnati 17. Bengals drive to Bears' 18 where Breech kicks 36-yard field goal at 8:39.
Nov. 15, 1992—New England 37, Indianapolis 34, at Indianapolis. Colts win toss. Verdin returns kickoff 10 yards to Colts' 20; holding penalty brings ball back to Colts' 10. After two plays, Henderson intercepts pass at Colts' 38 and returns it 9 yards to the 29. In three plays, Patriots drive to 1 where Baumann kicks 18-yard field goal at 3:25.
Nov. 29, 1992—Indianapolis 16, Buffalo 13, at Indianapolis. Colts win toss. Verdin returns kickoff 24 yards to Colts' 22. Colts drive to Buffalo 22 where Biasucci kicks 40-yard field goal at 3:51.
***Nov. 30, 1992—Seattle 16, Denver 13,** at Seattle. Seahawks win toss. Daluiso kicks through end zone for touchback. After three plays, Tuten punts 53 yards to Denver 18 where Marshall returns for no gain. After three plays, Rodriguez punts 29 yards to Seattle 45 where Warren signals fair catch. Seahawks drive to Denver 15 where Kasay's 33-yard field goal attempt misses. Broncos take over at Denver 20. After three plays, Rodriguez punts 43 yards to Seattle 38 where Warren signals for fair catch. After four plays, Tuten punts 39 yards to Denver 4 where Daniels downs punt. After three plays, Rodriguez punts 46 yards to Denver 48 where Warren returns 10 yards to the 38. Seahawks drive to Denver 14 where Kasay kicks 32-yard field goal at 11:10.
Dec. 13, 1992—Philadelphia 20, Seattle 17, at Seattle. Eagles win toss. Sydner returns kick 12 yards to Eagles' 16; illegal block penalty brings ball back to 8. Eagles drive to Philadelphia 45 where Feagles punts for a touchback. After 6 plays, Tuten punts 45 yards to Philadelphia 22 where Sydner returns 7 yards to 29. After 6 plays, Feagles punts 44 yards to Seattle 26 where Warren returns 5 yards to 31. After 5 plays, Tuten punts 32 yards to Philadelphia 20 where Sydner signals for fair catch. Eagles drive to Seattle 27 where Ruzek kicks 44-yard field goal with no time remaining.
Dec. 27, 1992—Miami 16, New England 13, at New England. Patriots win toss. Lockwood returns kickoff 15 yards to Patriots' 21. After three plays, McCarthy punts 39 yards to Miami 33 where Miller returns 2 yards to the 35. Miami drives to New England 18 where Stoyanovich kicks 35-yard field goal at 8:17.
Sept. 12, 1993—Detroit 19, New England 16, at New England. Patriots win toss. Patriots begin at 20. After 3 plays, Saxon punts 42 yards to Detroit 29 where Gray returns 12 yards to the 41. After 3 plays, Arnold punts 41 yards to New England 12 where Brown returns 16 yards to the 28. Patriots drive to Detroit 44 where Saxon punts into the end zone for a touchback. Detroit drives to New England 20 where Hanson kicks 38-yard field goal at 11:04.
Nov. 7, 1993—Buffalo 13, New England 10, at New England. Patriots win toss. T. Brown returns kickoff 27 yards to Patriots 30. Patriots drive to Buffalo 48 where Bills take over on downs. Bills drive to New England 25 where Metzelaars fumbles, and C. Brown recovers. After 3 plays, Saxon punts 46 yards to Buffalo 24 where Copeland returns 11 yards to the 35. Bills drive to New England 14 where Christie kicks 32-yard field goal at 9:22.
Dec. 19, 1993—Phoenix 30, Seattle 27, at Seattle. Cardinals win toss. Bailey returns kickoff 14 yards to Cardinals 20. Cardinals drive to Seattle 23 where Davis kicks 41-yard field goal at 6:45.
Jan. 2, 1994—Dallas 16, New York Giants 13, at New York. Giants win toss. Meggett returns kickoff 19 yards to Giants 19. After 6 plays, Horan punts 45 yards to Cowboys 25 where Widmer downs punt. Cowboys drive to Giants' 23 where Murray kicks 41-yard field goal at 10:44.
Jan. 2, 1994—New England 33, Miami 27, at New England. Dolphins win toss. McDuffie returns kickoff 21 yards to Miami 27. After 3 plays, Hatcher punts 43 yards to New England 29 where Harris returns 6 yards to the 35. After 2 plays, Brown intercepts pass from Bledsoe and returns 3 yards to Miami 49. After 3 plays, Hatcher punts 37 yards to New England 14 where Harris returns 18 yards to the 32. After 2 plays, Bledsoe passes 36 yards to Timpson for touchdown at 4:44.
Jan. 2, 1994—Los Angeles Raiders 33, Denver 30, at Los Angeles. Broncos win toss. Delpino returns kickoff 12 yards to Denver 25. Broncos drive to Los Angeles 22 where Elam's 40-yard field goal attempt is wide left. Raiders drive to Denver 29 where Jaeger kicks 47-yard field goal at 7:10.
***Jan. 3, 1994—Philadelphia 37, San Francisco 34,** at San Francisco. 49ers win toss. Walker returns kickoff, 19 yards to San Francisco 27. 49ers drive to Philadelphia 14 where Cofer misses 32-yard field goal. Eagles start at their 20-yard line, and, after 3 plays, Feagles punts 48 yards to San Francisco 36 where Carter fumbles and 49ers recover. After 7 plays, Wilmsmeyer punts 57 yards to Philadelphia 6 where Sikahema returns 16 yards to the 22. Eagles drive to San Francisco 10 where Ruzek kicks 28-yard field goal with no time remaining.
Sept. 4, 1994—Detroit 31, Atlanta 28, at Detroit. Falcons win toss. Falcons start at their own 16 after holding penalty on kickoff. After 3 plays, Alexander punts 41 yards to Detroit 39 where Clay returns 12 yards to Atlanta 49. Detroit drives to Atlanta 20 where Hanson kicks 37-yard field goal with 9:46 remaining.
Sept. 11, 1994—New York Jets 25, Denver 22, at New York. Jets win toss. Murrell returns kickoff 24 yards to New York 33. Jets drive to Denver 22 where Lowery kicks 39-yard field goal with 11:03 remaining.
***Sept. 19, 1994—Detroit 20, Dallas 17,** at Dallas. Lions win toss. Gray returns kickoff 24 yards to Detroit 32. Lions drive to Dallas 34 where Hanson's 51-yard field-goal attempt is blocked by Lett. Cowboys take possession at Dallas 42. Cowboys drive to Detroit 37 where Kennard fumbles and Swilling recovers. Lions take possession at Detroit 45. After 6 plays, Montgomery punts 31 yards to Dallas 16. Cowboys drive to Dallas 49 where Aikman fumbles and Thomas recovers at Dallas 43. Lions drive to Dallas 26 where Hanson kicks 44-yard field goal with 27 seconds remaining.
Oct. 16, 1994—Arizona 19, Washington 16, at Washington. Redskins win toss. Mitchell returns kickoff 27 yards to Washington 41. Redskins drive to Arizona 34 where Lohmiller's 51-yard field-goal attempt is blocked by Joyner and recovered by Williams who returns it to the Washington 37. After 5 plays, Peterson's 45-yard field-goal attempt is wide right. Redskins take possession at the Washington 36. After 3 plays, Roby punts 36 yards to the Arizona 37 where Robinson returns 3 yards to the 40. After 3 plays, Feagles punts 51 yards for a touchback. After 1 play, Shuler's pass is intercepted by Hoage who returns it to the Washington 12. Peterson kicks 29-yard field goal with 5:00 remaining.
Oct. 16, 1994—Miami 20, Los Angeles Raiders 17, at Miami. Dolphins win toss. McDuffie returns kickoff 19 yards to Miami 23. Dolphins drive to Los Angeles 12 where Stoyanovich kicks 29-yard field goal with 9:14 remaining.
#Oct. 20, 1994—Minnesota 13, Green Bay 10, at Minnesota. Vikings win toss. Ismail returns kickoff 22 yards to Minnesota 29. Vikings drive to Green Bay 9 where Fuad Reveiz kicks 27-yard field goal with 10:34 remaining.

Oct. 30, 1994—Detroit 28, New York Giants 25, at New York. Giants win toss. Lewis returns kickoff 16 yards to New York 27. After 3 plays, Horan punts 42 yards to Detroit 24 where Gray calls for fair catch. Detroit drives to New York 6 where Hanson kicks 24-yard field goal with 8:17 remaining.

Oct. 30, 1994—Arizona 20, Pittsburgh 17, at Arizona. Steelers win toss. Johnson returns kickoff 24 yards to Pittsburgh 30 where he fumbles and Arizona's Merritt recovers at Pittsburgh 32. After 3 plays, Davis kicks 51-yard field goal with 13:20 remaining.

Nov. 6, 1994—Cincinnati 20, Seattle 17, at Seattle. Seahawks win toss. Warren returns kickoff 32 yards to Seattle 33. After 3 plays, Tuten punts 37 yards to Cincinnati 28 where Sawyer calls for fair catch. After 3 plays, Johnson punts 64 yards to Seattle 2 where Truitt downs ball. Seahawks drive to Seattle 38 where Tuten punts 50 yards to Cincinnati 12 and Sawyer returns 5 yards to 17. Blake passes to Scott for 76 yards to Seattle 7. Pelfrey kicks 26-yard field goal with 6:46 remaining.

Nov. 6, 1994—Pittsburgh 12, Houston 9, at Houston. Steelers win toss. Stone returns kickoff 15 yards to Pittsburgh 28. After 3 plays, Royals punts 53 yards to Houston 13 where Givins downs ball. After 3 plays, Camarillo punts 57 yards to Pittsburgh 31 where Woodson returns 20 yards to Houston 49. After 3 plays, Royals punts 43 yards to Houston 15 where Coleman returns 3 yards to 18. After 5 plays, Camarillo punts 57 yards to Pittsburgh 12 where Hastings returns 12 yards to 24. Steelers drive to Houston 41 where Royals punts 29 yards to Houston 12, and Coleman calls for fair catch. Brown fumbles on first play and Jones recovers at Houston 22. After 1 play, Anderson kicks 40-yard field goal with 3:36 remaining.

Nov. 13, 1994—New England 26, Minnesota 20, at New England. Patriots win toss. Thompson returns kickoff 27 yards to New England 33. Patriots drive to Minnesota 14 where Bledsoe passes 14 yards to Turner for touchdown with 10:50 remaining.

Nov. 20, 1994—Pittsburgh 16, Miami 13, at Pittsburgh. Steelers win toss. Stone returns kickoff 15 yards to Pittsburgh 16. Steelers drive to Miami 39 where they lose possession on downs. Dolphins drive to Pittsburgh 47 where Arnold punts 35 yards to Pittsburgh 12 and Oliver downs ball. Steelers drive to Miami 21 where Anderson kicks 39-yard field goal with 4:41 remaining.

Nov. 27, 1994—Chicago 19, Arizona 16, at Arizona. Cardinals win toss. Levy returns kickoff 31 yards to Arizona 45. After 5 plays, Feagles punts 38 yards to the end zone for a touchback. Bears drive to Arizona 10 where Butler kicks 27-yard field goal with 6:49 remaining.

Nov. 27, 1994—Tampa Bay 20, Minnesota 17, at Minnesota. Buccaneers win toss. Harris returns kickoff 12 yards to Tampa Bay 38. After 6 plays, Stryzinski punts 40 yards to Minnesota 4 where Guliford muffs punt and Buccaneers' Brady recovers. Husted kicks 22-yard field goal with 12:52 remaining.

#Dec. 1, 1994—Minnesota 33, Chicago 27, at Minnesota. Bears win toss. Lewis returns kickoff 23 yards to Chicago 33. Bears drive to Minnesota 22 where Butler's 40-yard field goal attempt is wide left. After 1 play, Moon passes 65 yards to Carter for touchdown with 9:14 remaining.

Dec. 4, 1994—Denver 20, Kansas City 17, at Kansas City. Broncos win toss. Milburn returns kickoff 24 yards to Denver 29. After 3 plays, Millen fumbles and Phillips recovers at Denver 35. After 4 plays, Allen fumbles and Smith recovers at Denver 27. After 6 plays, Rouen punts 45 yards to Kansas City 25 where Hughes calls for fair catch. After 3 plays, Aguiar punts 33 yards to Denver 42 where Chiefs down ball. Broncos drive to Kansas City 17 where Elam kicks 34-yard field goal with 2:48 remaining.

Sept. 3, 1995—Cincinnati 24, Indianapolis 21, at Indianapolis. Bengals win toss. Dunn returns kickoff 15 yards to Bengals' 17. Cincinnati drives to Indianapolis 29 where Pelfrey kicks 47-yard field goal with 12:24 remaining.

Sept. 3, 1995—Atlanta 23, Carolina 20, at Atlanta. Panthers win toss. Baldwin downs kickoff for touchback. Panthers drive to Carolina 42 where Reich fumbles and ball is recovered by Archambeau at Carolina 31. Falcons drive to Panthers' 16 where Andersen kicks 35-yard field goal with 8:43 remaining.

Sept. 10, 1995—Indianapolis 27, New York Jets 24, at New York. Jets win toss. Carter downs kickoff for touchback. Jets punt downed at Colts' 37. Colts drive to Jets' 35 where Cofer kicks 52-yard field goal with 10:33 remaining.

Sept. 10, 1995—Kansas City 20, New York Giants 17, at Kansas City. Chiefs win toss. Vanover returns kickoff 30 yards to Chiefs' 28. Aguiar punts to Giants' 3. Horan punts to Chiefs' 49. Chiefs drive to Giants' 6 where Elliott kicks 23-yard field goal with 7:11 left.

Sept. 17, 1995—Dallas 23, Minnesota 17, at Minnesota. Cowboys win toss. K. Williams returns kickoff 23 yards to Cowboys' 27. E. Smith scores on 31-yard run with 12:34 left.

Sept. 17, 1995—Kansas City 23, Oakland 17, at Kansas City. Chiefs win toss. Vanover returns kickoff 28 yards to Chiefs' 41. M. Allen fumbles, ball recovered by Robbins at Raiders' 38. Hasty intercepts pass at Chiefs' 36 and returns it 64 yards for touchdown with 10:33 left.

Sept. 17, 1995—Atlanta 27, New Orleans 24, at Atlanta. Saints win toss. Hughes returns kickoff 21 yards to Saints' 17. Metcalf returns Wilmsmeyer's punt 18 yards to Saints' 39. Stryzinski punts, fair catch by Hughes at Saints' 14. Wilmsmeyer punt downed at Falcons' 6. Falcons drive to Saints' 3 where Andersen kicks 21-yard field goal with 7:02 left.

Oct. 8, 1995—Indianapolis 27, Miami 24, at Miami. Colts win toss. Warren returns kickoff 25 yards to Colts' 33. Colts drive to Dolphins' 10 where Blanchard kicks 27-yard field goal with 10:02 left.

Oct. 8, 1995—New York Giants 27, Arizona 21, at New York. Cardinals win toss. Terry returns kickoff 20 yards to Cardinals' 23. Hamilton recovers Krieg's fumble at Cardinals' 36. Lynch recovers Brown's fumble at Cardinals' 38. Armstead intercepts pass at Giants' 42 and returns it 58 yards for touchdown with 10:55 left.

Oct. 8, 1995—Minnesota 23, Houston 17, at Minnesota. Vikings win toss. Palmer returns kickoff 10 yards to Vikings' 15. Saxon's punt downed at Oilers' 8. Washington intercepts pass at Vikings' 47 and returns it 25 yards to Oilers' 28. R. Smith scores on 20-yard run with 7:50 left.

Oct. 8, 1995—Philadelphia 37, Washington 34, at Philadelphia. Redskins win toss. Redskins take possession at their 20 after touchback. Turk punt out of bounds at Eagles' 9. Eagles drive to Redskins' 18 where Anderson kicks 35-yard field goal with 4:54 left.

*** Oct. 9, 1995—Kansas City 29, San Diego 23,** at Kansas City. Chargers win toss. Coleman returns kickoff 24 yards to Chargers' 28. Vanover makes fair catch of Bennett's punt at Chiefs' 15. Coleman makes fair catch of Aguiar's punt at Chargers' 43. Vanover returns Bennett's punt 86 yards for a touchdown with 7:33 left.

Oct. 15, 1995—Tampa Bay 20, Minnesota 17, at Tampa Bay. Buccaneers win toss. Edmonds returns kickoff 19 yards to Buccaneers' 22. A. Lee returns Roby's punt to Vikings' 48. Vikings drive to Tampa Bays' 35 where Reveiz's 53-yard field-goal attempt is wide right. Buccaneers take over at own 43 and drive to Vikings' 33 where Husted kicks 51-yard field goal with 8:37 left.

Oct. 22, 1995—Washington 36, Detroit 30, at Washington. Redskins win toss. B. Mitchell returns kickoff 16 yards to Redskins' 27. Turk's punt downed at Lions' 4. D. Green intercepts S. Mitchell's pass and returns it 7 yards for touchdown with 11:19 left.

Oct. 29, 1995—Carolina 20, New England 17, at New England. Panthers win toss. Baldwin returns kickoff 22 yards to Panthers' 25. Meggett makes fair catch of Barnhardt's punt at Patriots' 9. Guliford returns O'Neill's punt 9 yards to Patriots' 32. Panthers drive to Patriots' 12 where Kasay kicks 29-yard field goal with 7:52 left.

Oct. 29, 1995—Cleveland 29, Cincinnati 26, at Cincinnati. Browns win toss. Hunter returns kickoff 31 yards to Browns' 31. Bieniemy returns Tupa's punt 9 yards to Bengals' 37. McCardell makes fair catch of Johnson's punt at Browns' 12. Bieniemy returns Tupa's punt 0 yards to Bengals' 38. Hall intercepts Blake's pass and returns it 5 yards to Bengals' 45. Browns drive to Bengals' 11 where Stover kicks 28-yard field goal with 8:30 left.

Oct. 29, 1995—Arizona 20, Seattle 14, at Arizona. Cardinals win toss. Dowdell returns kickoff 16 yards to Cardinals' 25. Cardinals drive to Seahawks' 10 where G. Davis' 27-yard field goal attempt is blocked. L. Lynch intercepts Friesz's pass at Cardinals' 28 and returns it 72 yards for a touchdown with 3:44 left.

Nov. 5, 1995—Pittsburgh 37, Chicago 34, at Chicago. Bears win toss. Timpson returns kickoff 23 yards to Bears' 33. Hastings returns Sauerbrun's punt 2 yards to Steelers' 31. Steelers drive to Bears' 6 where N. Johnson kicks 24-yard field goal with 6:41 left.

Nov. 12, 1995—Minnesota 30, Arizona 24, at Arizona. Vikings win toss. A. Lee returns kickoff 20 yards to Vikings' 25. Moon throws 50-yard touchdown pass to Ismail with 12:44 left.

Nov. 26, 1995—Arizona 40, Atlanta 37, at Arizona. Falcons win toss. J. Anderson returns kickoff 20 yards to Falcons' 20. Stryzinski fumbles punt snap. Recovered by England at Falcons' 10 where G. Davis kicks 28-yard field goal with 13:17 left.

Dec. 10, 1995—Tampa Bay 13, Green Bay 10, at Tampa Bay. Buccaneers win toss. Edmonds returns kickoff 24 yards to Buccaneers' 23. Tampa Bay drives to Packers' 29 where Husted kicks 47-yard field goal with 11:14 remaining.

Sept. 1, 1996—Buffalo 23, New York Giants 20, at New York. Bills win toss. Daluiso kick is a touchback. Bills drive to Buffalo 46. Toomer returns Mohr's punt to Giants' 16. Dave Brown's fumble recovered by Spielman at Giants' 33. Bills drive to Giants' 16 where Christie kicks 34-yard field goal with 5:52 remaining.

Sept. 22, 1996—New England 28, Jacksonville 25, at New England. Patriots win toss. T. Brown returns kickoff 18 yards to Patriots' 29. Patriots drive to Jaguars' 22 where Vinatieri kicks 40-yard field goal with 12:24 remaining.

Sept. 29, 1996—Arizona 31, St. Louis 28, at Arizona. Cardinals win toss. Lohmiller kick is a touchback. Cardinals drive to Rams' 7 where G. Davis kicks 24-yard field goal with 13:06 remaining.

Oct. 6, 1996—Buffalo 16, Indianapolis 13, at Buffalo. Colts win toss. Christie kick is a touchback. Colts drive to Indianapolis 32. Burris returns Gardocki's punt to Bills' 35. Bills drive to Colts' 48. Mohr punts out of bounds at Colts' 14. Colts drive to Indianapolis 9. Burris returns Gardocki's punt to Colts' 48. Bills drive to Colts' 22 where Christie kicks 39-yard field goal with 5:38 remaining.

Oct. 6, 1996—Houston 30, Cincinnati 27, at Cincinnati. Bengals win toss. Dunn returns kickoff 23 yards to Bengals' 34. Bengals drive to Cincinnati 36. Floyd returns L. Johnson's punt to Oilers' 18. Oilers drive to Bengals' 31 where Del Greco kicks 49-yard field goal with 7:53 remaining.

*** Oct. 14, 1996—Green Bay 23, San Francisco 20,** at Green Bay. 49ers win toss. D. Carter returns kickoff 23 yards to 49ers' 22. 49ers' drive to San Francisco 25. Howard makes fair catch of Thompson's punt at Packers' 44. Packers drive to 49ers' 35 where Jacke kicks 53-yard field goal with 11:19 remaining.

Oct. 27, 1996—Baltimore 37, St. Louis 31, at Baltimore. Rams win toss. J. Thomas returns kickoff 17 yard to Rams' 17. Rams drive to Ravens' 15. F. Miller fumble in field goal formation recovered by S. Moore at Ravens' 17. Ravens drive to Baltimore 49 and turn ball over on downs. Rams drive to Ravens' 40 and turn ball over on downs. Testaverde throws 22-yard scoring pass to M. Jackson with 10 seconds remaining.

Nov. 10, 1996—Dallas 20, San Francisco 17, at San Francisco. Cowboys win

OVERTIME GAMES

toss. H. Walker returns kickoff 10 yards to Cowboys' 23. Cowboys drive to 49ers' 11 where Boniol kicks 29-yard field goal with 8:43 remaining.
Nov. 10, 1996—Arizona 37, Washington 34, at Washington. Arizona wins toss. Blanton's kickoff is a touchback. Cardinals drive to Redskins' 15 where Butler misses 32-yard field goal. Redskins drive to Cardinals' 43 where Turk punts for touchback. L. Johnson fumble returned by Morrison to Cardinals' 27. Redskins drive to Cardinals' 31 where Blanton misses 48-yard field goal. Cardinals drive to Redskins' 15 where Butler kicks 32-yard field goal with 33 seconds remaining.
Nov. 10, 1996—Tampa Bay 20, Oakland 17, at Tampa Bay. Tampa Bay wins toss. M. Marshall returns kickoff 15 yards to Bucs' 17. Bucs drive to Tampa Bay 36. T. Brown returns Barnhardt's punt four yards to Raiders' 22. Raiders drive to Oakland 25. M. Marshall returns Gossett's punt nine yards to Bucs' 39. Bucs drive to Raiders' 4 where Husted kicks 23-yard field goal with 3:04 remaining.
Nov. 17, 1996—Minnesota 16, Oakland 13, at Oakland. Oakland wins toss. Kaufman returns kickoff 32 yards to Raiders' 27. Raiders drive to Oakland 46 where Gossett punts to Vikings' 17. Vikings drive to Raiders' 12 where Sisson kicks 31-yard field goal with 3:07 remaining.
Nov. 24, 1996—Jacksonville 28, Baltimore 25, at Baltimore. Jacksonville wins toss. Jordon returns kickoff 16 yards to Jaguars' 30. Jaguars drive to Jacksonville 37. Barker's punt is downed at Ravens' 6. Ravens drive to Jaguars' 37 where Pritchett recovers Byner's fumble. Jaguars drive to Ravens' 15 where Hollis kicks 34-yard field goal with 5:54 remaining.
Nov. 24, 1996—San Francisco 19, Washington 16, at Washington. San Francisco wins toss. D. Carter returns kickoff 20 yards to 49ers' 32. 49ers drive to Redskins' 20 where WIlkins kicks 38-yard field goal with 11:36 remaining.
Dec. 1, 1996—Indianapolis 13, Buffalo 10, at Indianapolis. Buffalo wins toss. Moulds returns kickoff 26 yards to Bills' 25. Bills drive to Buffalo 49. Stock returns Mohr's punt one yard to Colts' 16. Colts drive to Bills' 32 where Blanchard kicks 49-yard field goal with 4:14 remaining.
Aug. 31, 1997—Tennessee 24, Oakland 21, at Tennessee. Oilers win toss. Gray returns kickoff 32 yards to Tennessee 33. Oilers drive to Tennessee 38. Roby's punt is downed at the Oakland 33. Raiders drive to Oakland 32. Gray returns Araguz punt to Tennessee 35. Oilers drive to Oakland 15 where Del Greco kicks 33-yard field goal with 8:03 remaining.
Sept. 7, 1997—Miami 16, Tennessee 13, at Miami. Dolphins win toss. Spikes returns kickoff 48 yards to Tennessee 45. Dolphins drive to Tennessee 11 where Mare kicks 29-yard field goal with 12:45 remaining.
Sept. 7, 1997— Arizona 25, Dallas 22, at Arizona. Cowboys win toss. Walker returns kickoff 21 yards to Dallas 25. Cowboys drive to Arizona 43. Gowin punts 43 yards for a touchback. Cardinals drive to Dallas 44. Graham fumbles. Cowboys drive to Arizona 42. Williams fumbles. Cardinals drive to Dallas 3 where Butler kicks 20-yard field goal with 6:30 remaining.
Sept. 14, 1997—Washington 19, Arizona 13, at Washington. Cardinals win toss. K. Williams returns kickoff 27 yards to Arizona 34. Cardinals drive to Arizona 40. McElroy fumbles. Redskins drive to Arizona 40. Westbrook catches 40-yard touchdown pass from Frerotte with 13:24 remaining.
Sept. 14, 1997—New England 27, New York Jets 24, at New England. Patriots win toss. Hall's kickoff is a touchback. Patriots drive to New England 15. Bledsoe pass intercepted by O. Smith. Jets drive to New York 46. Hansen punts 47 yards. Meggett returns to New England 21. Patriots drive to New York 17 where Vinatieri kicks 34-yard field goal with 6:57 remaining.
Sept. 28, 1997—Kansas City 20, Seattle 17, at Kansas City. Seahawks win toss. Broussard returns kickoff 12 yards to Seattle 14. Seahawks drive to Seattle 17. Vanover returns Tuten punt 8 yards to Kansas City 26. Chiefs drive to Seattle 44. Aguiar punt downed at Seattle 11. Seahawks drive to Seattle 26. Moon pass intercepted by Woods and returned 13 yards to 50. Chiefs drive to Seattle 23 where Stoyanovich kicks 41-yard field goal with 1:56 remaining.
Oct. 20, 1997—Philadelphia 13, Arizona 10, at Philadelphia. Cardinals win toss. K. Williams returns kickoff 28 yards to Arizona 42. Cardinals drive to Philadelphia 48. Feagles punts 48 yards for touchback. Eagles drive to Arizona 7 where Boniol kicks 24-yard field goal with 10:58 remaining.
Oct. 20, 1997—New York Giants 26, Detroit 20, at Detroit. Giants win toss. Pegram returns kickoff 16 yards to New York 18. Giants drive to New York 32. Calloway catches 68-yard touchdown pass from Kanell with 13:20 remaining.
Oct. 26, 1997—Denver 23, Buffalo 20, at Buffalo. Denver wins toss and elects to kickoff. Holmes returns kickoff 20 yards to Buffalo 25. Bills drive to Buffalo 23. Mohr punt downed at Denver 40. Broncos drive to Buffalo 48. Rouen punt downed at Buffalo 1. Bills drive to Buffalo 20. Gordon returns Mohr punt to Denver 42. Broncos drive to Buffalo 15 where Elam kicks 33-yard field goal with 1:56 remaining.
Oct. 26, 1997—Pittsburgh 23, Jacksonville 17, at Pittsburgh. Pittsburgh wins toss. Coleman returns kickoff 23 yards to Pittsburgh 23. Steelers drive to Jacksonville 17. Bettis catches 17-yard touchdown pass from Stewart with 11:13 remaining.
Oct. 27, 1997—Chicago 36, Miami 33, at Miami. Miami wins toss. McPhail returns kickoff 23 yards to Miami 27. Dolphins drive to Miami 36. Kidd punts out of bounds at Chicago 10. Bears drive to the Chicago 39. Sauerbrun punt out of bounds at Miami 27. Reeves recovers Marino fumble at Miami 17. Bears drive to Miami 17 where Jaeger kicks 35-yard field goal with 5:35 remaining.
Nov. 2, 1997—New York Jets 19, Baltimore 16, at New York. New York wins toss. Stover's kickoff is a touchback. Jets drive to Baltimore 20 where Hall kicks 37-yard field goal with 10:02 remaining.
Nov. 16, 1997—Philadelphia 10, Baltimore 10, at Baltimore. Philadelphia wins toss. Stover's kickoff is a touchback. Eagles drive to Philadelphia 19. Hutton punts 36 yards to Baltimore 45. Ravens drive to Baltimore 36 where Eagles take over on downs. Eagles drive to Baltimore 33 where Ravens take over on downs. Ravens drive to Baltimore 37. Montgomery punts 55 yards, and Solomon returns to Philadelphia 22. Eagles drive to Philadelphia 16. Hutton punts 41 yards, and Roe returns to Baltimore 46. Ravens drive to Philadelphia 35 where Stover's 53-yard field-goal attempt is no good. Eagles drive to Baltimore 22 where Boniol's 40-yard field-goal is no good as time expires.
Nov. 16, 1997—New Orleans 20, Seattle 17, at New Orleans. Seattle wins toss. Brien's kickoff is a touchback. Seahawks start at Seattle 20 where Moon's pass intercepted by Tubbs who returns 15 yards to Seattle 20. Saints Brien kicks 38-yard field goal with 14:43 remaining.
Nov. 23, 1997—New York Giants 7, Washington 7, at Washington. Washington wins toss. Davis returns kickoff 28 yards to Washington 39. Redskins drive to Washington 36 where Hostetler's pass intercepted by Sehorn who returns minus-2 yards before lateralling to Wooten who returns 5 yards to New York 41. Giants drive to New York 26 where Maynard punts 37 yards to Washington 37. Redskins drive to New York 39 where Hostetler fumble is recovered by Harris at New York 40. Giants drive to New York 43 where Maynard punts 57 yards for a touchback. Washington drives to New York 41. Giants take over on downs at New York 40. Giants drive to Washington 36 where Daluiso's 54-yard field-goal attempt is no good. Redskins drive to Washington 45 where Hostetler's pass intercepted by Sparks at New York 49. Giants drive to Washington 36 where Maynard punts 36 yards for a touchback. Redskins drive to New York 36 where Blanton's 54-yard field-goal attempt is no good. Giants drive to New York 45 where Kanell's pass intercepted by Patton who laterals to Pounds who returns 11 yards to Washington 24 as time expires.
Nov. 30, 1997—Pittsburgh 26, Arizona 20, at Arizona. Arizona wins toss. K. Williams returns kickoff 11 yards to Arizona 23. Cardinals drive to Arizona 18 where Feagles punts 43 yards. Hawkins returns punt 9 yards to Pittsburgh 48. Steelers drive to Arizona 10 where Bettis scores on a 10-yard touchdown run with 9:26 remaining.
Dec. 13, 1997—Pittsburgh 24, New England 21, at New England. Pittsburgh wins toss. Coleman returns kickoff 19 yards to Pittsburgh 26. Steelers drive to New England 13 where Johnson kicks a 31-yard field goal with 10:17 remaining.
**indicates Monday night game*
#indicates Thursday night game

POSTSEASON
Dec. 28, 1958—Baltimore 23, New York Giants 17, at New York in NFL Championship Game. Giants win toss. Maynard returns kickoff to Giants' 20. Chandler punts and Taseff returns one yard to Colts' 20. Colts win at 8:15 on a 1-yard run by Ameche.
Dec. 23, 1962—Dallas Texans 20, Houston Oilers 17, at Houston in AFL Championship Game. Texans win toss and kick off. Jancik returns kickoff to Oilers' 33. Norton punts and Jackson makes fair catch on Texans' 22. Wilson punts and Jancik makes fair catch on Oilers' 45. Robinson intercepts Blanda's pass and returns 13 yards to Oilers' 47. Wilson's punt rolls dead at Oilers' 12. Hull intercepts Blanda's pass and returns 23 yards to midfield. Texans win at 17:54 on a 25-yard field goal by Brooker.
Dec. 26, 1965—Green Bay 13, Baltimore 10, at Green Bay in NFL Divisional Playoff Game. Packers win toss. Moore returns kickoff to Packers' 22. Chandler punts and Haymond returns nine yards to Colts' 41. Gilburg punts and Wood makes fair catch at Packers' 21. Chandler punts and Haymond returns one yard to Colts' 41. Michaels misses 47-yard field goal. Packers win at 13:39 on 25-yard field goal by Chandler.
Dec. 25, 1971—Miami 27, Kansas City 24, at Kansas City in AFC Divisional Playoff Game. Chiefs win toss. Podolak, after a lateral from Buchanan, returns kickoff to Chiefs' 46. Stenerud's 42-yard field goal is blocked. Seiple punts and Podolak makes fair catch at Chiefs' 17. Wilson punts and Scott returns 18 yards to Dolphins' 39. Yepremian misses 62-yard field goal. Scott intercepts Dawson's pass and returns 13 yards to Dolphins' 46. Seiple punts and Podolak loses one yard to Chiefs' 15. Wilson punts and Scott makes fair catch on Dolphins' 30. Dolphins win at 22:40 on a 37-yard field goal by Yepremian.
Dec. 24, 1977—Oakland 37, Baltimore 31, at Baltimore in AFC Divisional Playoff Game. Colts win toss. Raiders start on own 42 following a punt late in the first overtime. Oakland works way into field-goal range on Stabler's 19-yard pass to Branch at Colts' 26. Four plays later, on the second play of the second overtime, Stabler hits Casper with a 10-yard touchdown pass at 15:43.
Jan. 2, 1982—San Diego 41, Miami 38, at Miami in AFC Divisional Playoff Game. Chargers win toss. San Diego drives from its 13 to Miami 8. On second-and-goal, Benirschke misses 27-yard field goal attempt wide left at 9:15. Miami has the ball twice and San Diego twice more before the Dolphins get their third possession. Miami drives from the San Diego 46 to Chargers' 17 and on fourth-and-two, von Schamann's 34-yard field goal attempt is blocked by San Diego's Winslow after 11:27. Fouts then completes four of five passes, including a 39-yarder to Joiner that puts the ball on Dolphins' 10. On first down, Benirschke kicks a 29-yard field goal at 13:52. San Diego's winning drive covered 74 yards in six plays.
Jan. 3, 1987—Cleveland 23, New York Jets 20, at Cleveland in AFC Divisional Playoff Game. Jets win toss. Jets' punt downed at Browns' 26. Moseley's 23-yard field goal attempt is wide right. Teams trade punts. Jets' second punt

downed at Browns' 31. First overtime period expires eight plays later with Browns in possession at Jets' 42. Moseley kicks 27-yard field goal four plays into second overtime at 17:02.

Jan. 11, 1987—Denver 23, Cleveland 20, at Cleveland in AFC Championship Game. Browns win toss. Broncos hold Browns on four downs. Browns' punt returned four yards to Denver's 25. Elway completes 22- and 28-yard passes to set up Karlis's 33-yard field goal nine plays into drive at 5:38.

Jan. 3, 1988—Houston 23, Seattle 20, at Houston in AFC Wild Card Game. Seahawks win toss. Rodriguez punts to K. Johnson who returns one yard to Houston 15. Zendejas kicks 32-yard field goal 12 plays later at 8:05.

Dec. 31, 1989—Pittsburgh 26, Houston 23, at Houston in AFC Wild Card Playoff Game. Steelers win toss. Steelers punt to Oilers. Oilers' fumble recovered by Woodson and returned three yards. Four plays and 13 yards later, Anderson kicks a 50-yard field goal at 3:26.

Jan. 7, 1990—Los Angeles Rams 19, New York Giants 13, at New York in NFC Divisional Game. Rams win toss. Everett completes two passes to move ball to Giants' 48. White called for pass interference; ball spotted on Giants' 25. Everett hits Anderson with a 30-yard touchdown pass at 1:06.

Jan. 3, 1993—Buffalo 41, Houston 38, at Buffalo in AFC Wild Card Game. Houston wins toss. Oilers begin at 20. After 2 plays, Moon's pass is intercepted by Odomes who returns ball 2 yards to Houston 35. After 2 plays, Christie kicks 32-yard field goal at 3:06.

Jan. 8, 1994—Kansas City 27, Pittsburgh 24, at Kansas City in AFC Wild Card Game. Kansas City wins toss. Hughes returns kickoff 20 yards to Kansas City 25. After 3 plays, Barker punts 48 yards to Pittsburgh 18 where Woodson returns 8 yards to the 26. After 6 plays, Royals punts 30 yards to Kansas City 20. Kansas City drives to Pittsburgh 14 where Lowery kicks 32-yard field goal at 11:03.

NFL POSTSEASON OVERTIME GAMES

(BY LENGTH OF GAME)

Date	Game	Length
Dec. 25, 1971	Miami 27, KANSAS CITY 24	82:40
Dec. 23, 1962	Dallas Texans 20, HOUSTON 17	77:54
Jan. 3, 1987	CLEVELAND 23, New York Jets 20	77:02
Dec. 24, 1977	Oakland 37, BALTIMORE 31	75:43
Jan. 2, 1982	San Diego 41, MIAMI 38	73:52
Dec. 26, 1965	GREEN BAY 13, Baltimore 10	73:39
Jan. 8, 1994	KANSAS CITY 27, Pittsburgh 24	71:03
Dec. 28, 1958	Baltimore 23, N.Y. GIANTS 17	68:15
Jan. 3, 1988	HOUSTON 23, Seattle 20	68:05
Jan. 11, 1987	Denver 23, CLEVELAND 20	65:38
Dec. 31, 1989	Pittsburgh 26, HOUSTON 23	63:26
Jan. 3, 1993	BUFFALO 41, Houston 38	63:06
Jan. 7, 1990	Los Angeles Rams 19, N.Y. GIANTS 13	61:06

Home team in CAPS

There have been 13 overtime postseason games dating back to 1958. In 12 cases, both teams had at least one possession. Last time: 1/8/94, Kansas City 27, Pittsburgh 24.

OVERTIME WON-LOST RECORDS, 1974-1997

(REGULAR SEASON)

AFC	W	L	T	Pct.
Baltimore	1	2	1	.375
Buffalo	11	6	0	.647
Cincinnati	12	7	0	.632
Cleveland	12	8	1	.595
Denver	13	9	2	.583
Indianapolis	9	7	1	.559
Jacksonville	1	2	0	.333
Kansas City	8	7	2	.529
Miami	9	14	1	.396
New England	9	15	0	.375
New York Jets	10	8	2	.555
Oakland	10	11	0	.476
Pittsburgh	13	4	1	.750
San Diego	7	10	0	.412
Seattle	4	11	0	.267
Tennessee	8	13	0	.380

NFC	W	L	T	Pct.
Arizona	11	10	2	.571
Atlanta	7	9	1	.441
Carolina	1	1	0	.500
Chicago	11	11	0	.500
Dallas	9	6	0	.600
Detroit	9	9	1	.500
Green Bay	6	10	4	.400
Minnesota	13	12	2	.519
New Orleans	3	7	0	.300
New York Giants	8	10	2	.450
Philadelphia	8	8	3	.500
St. Louis	6	7	1	.464
San Francisco	5	7	1	.423
Tampa Bay	9	7	1	.559
Washington	11	7	1	.605

OVERTIME GAMES BY YEAR

(REGULAR SEASON)

1997-17	1991-15	1985-10	1979-12
1996-14	1990-10	1984- 9	1978-11
1995-21	1989-11	1983-19	1977- 6
1994-16	1988- 9	1982- 4	1976- 5
1993-7	1987-13	1981-10	1975- 9
1992-10	1986-16	1980-13	1974- 2

OVERTIME GAME SUMMARY—1974-1997

There have been 269 overtime games in regular-season play since the rule was adopted in 1974 (17 in 1997 season). Breakdown follows:

200 (12) times both teams had at least one possession (74%)
132 (8) times the team which won the toss won the game (49%)
122 (7) times the team which lost the toss won the game (45%)
15 (2) games ended tied (6%). Last time: Nov. 23, 1997, New York Giants 7, at Washington 7
69 (5) times the team which won the toss drove for winning score (49 FG, 20 TD) (26%)
186 (11) games were decided by a field goal (69%)
67 (4) games were decided by a touchdown (25%)
1 (0) game was decided by a safety (0.4%)

Note: The number in parentheses represents the 1997 season total in each category.

MOST OVERTIME GAMES, SEASON

5 Green Bay Packers, 1983
4 Denver Broncos, 1985
Cleveland Browns, 1989
Minnesota Vikings, 1994
Arizona Cardinals, 1995
Minnesota Vikings, 1995
Arizona Cardinals, 1997
3 By many teams, last time: Pittsburgh Steelers, 1997

LONGEST CONSECUTIVE GAME STREAKS WITHOUT OVERTIME (Current)

35 Denver Broncos (last OT game, 12/4/94 at Kansas City)
30 New York Jets (last OT game, 9/10/95 vs. Indianapolis)
29 New Orleans Saints (last OT game, 9/17/95 vs. Atlanta)
(Record: 110, Phoenix Cardinals, 12/7/86-12/19/93)

OVERTIME GAMES

SHORTEST OVERTIME GAMES

0:17 New Orleans 20, Seattle 17; 11/16/97
0:21 Chicago 23, Detroit 17; 11/27/80—only kickoff return for TD
0:30 Baltimore 29, New England 23; 9/4/83

LONGEST OVERTIME GAMES
(ALL POSTSEASON GAMES)

22:40 Miami 27, Kansas City 24; 12/25/71
17:54 Dallas Texans 20, Houston 17; 12/23/62
17:02 Cleveland 23, New York Jets 20; 1/3/87

OVERTIME SCORING SUMMARY

186 were decided by a field goal
29 were decided by a touchdown pass
20 were decided by a touchdown run
9 were decided by interceptions (Atlanta 40, New Orleans 34, 9/2/79; Atlanta 47, Green Bay 41, 11/27/83; New York Giants 16, Philadelphia 10, 9/29/85; Indianapolis 23, Cleveland 17, 12/10/89; Cleveland 30, San Diego 24, 10/20/91; Kansas City 23, Oakland 17, 9/17/95; New York Giants 27, Arizona 21, 10/8/95; Washington 36, Detroit 30, 10/22/95; Arizona 20, Seattle 14, 10/29/95)
2 were decided on a fake field goal/touchdown pass (Minnesota 22, Chicago 16, 10/16/77; Cleveland 23, Minnesota 17, 12/17/89)
1 was decided by a kickoff return (Chicago 23, Detroit 17, 11/27/80)
1 was decided by a punt return (Kansas City 29, San Diego 23, 10/9/95)
1 was decided by a fumble recovery (Baltimore 29, New England 23, 9/4/83)
1 was decided on a fake field goal/touchdown run (Los Angeles Rams 27, Minnesota 21, 12/2/79)
1 was decided on a blocked field goal (Denver 30, San Diego 24, 11/17/85)
1 was decided on a blocked field goal/recovery by kicker (Green Bay 12, Chicago 6, 9/7/80)
1 was decided on a blocked field goal/recovery by kicking team (Philadelphia 23, New York Giants 17, 11/20/88)
1 was decided by a safety (Minnesota 23, Los Angeles Rams 21, 11/5/89)
15 ended tied

OVERTIME RECORDS

Longest Touchdown Pass
99 Yards — Ron Jaworski to Mike Quick, Philadelphia 23, Atlanta 17 (11/10/85)
68 Yards — Danny Kanell to Chris Calloway, New York Giants 26, Detroit 20 (10/20/97)
65 Yards — Warren Moon to Cris Carter, Minnesota 33, Chicago 27 (12/1/94)

Longest Touchdown Run
60 Yards — Herschel Walker, Dallas 23, New England 17 (11/15/87)
42 Yards — Eric Dickerson, Los Angeles Rams 26, Tampa Bay 20 (10/5/86)
31 Yards — Emmitt Smith, Dallas 23, Minnesota 17 (9/17/95)

Longest Field Goal
53 Yards — Chris Jacke, Green Bay 23, San Francisco 20 (10/4/96)
52 Yards — Mike Cofer, Indianapolis 27, N.Y. Jets 24 (9/10/95)
51 Yards — Greg Davis, New England 23, Indianapolis 20 (10/29/89)
Greg Davis, Arizona 20, Pittsburgh 17 (10/30/94)
Michael Husted, Tampa Bay 20, Minnesota 17 (10/15/95)

Longest Touchdown Plays
99 Yards — (Pass) Ron Jaworski to Mike Quick, Philadelphia 23, Atlanta 17 (11/10/85)
95 Yards — (Kickoff return) Dave Williams, Chicago 23, Detroit 17 (11/27/80)
86 Yards — (Punt return) Tamarick Vanover, Kansas City 29, San Diego 23 (10/9/95)
72 Yards — (Interception return) Lorenzo Lynch, Arizona 20, Seattle 14 (10/29/95)

NFL PAID ATTENDANCE

For detailed 1997 attendance, see page 242.

Year	Regular Season	Average	Postseason	Total
1997	14,967,314 (240 games)	62,364	801,879 (12)	15,769,193
1996	14,612,417 (240 games)	60,885	769,310 (12)	15,381,727
1995	#15,043,562 (240 games)	#62,682	790,906 (12)	#15,834,468
1994	14,030,435 (224 games)	62,636	779,738 (12)	14,810,173
1993	13,966,843 (224 games)	62,352	814,607 (12)	14,781,450
1992	13,828,887 (224 games)	61,736	815,910 (12)	14,644,797
1991	13,841,459 (224 games)	61,792	813,247 (12)	14,654,706
1990	13,959,896 (224 games)	62,321	847,543 (12)	14,807,439
1989	13,625,662 (224 games)	60,829	685,771 (10)	14,311,433
1988	13,539,848 (224 games)	60,446	658,317 (10)	14,198,165
1987	*11,406,166 (210 games)	54,315	656,977 (10)	12,063,143
1986	13,588,551 (224 games)	60,663	734,002 (10)	14,322,553
1985	13,345,047 (224 games)	59,567	710,768 (10)	14,055,815
1984	13,398,112 (224 games)	59,813	665,194 (10)	14,063,306
1983	13,277,222 (224 games)	59,273	675,513 (10)	13,952,735
1982	**7,367,438 (126 games)	58,472	1,033,153 (16)	8,400,591
1981	13,606,990 (224 games)	60,745	637,763 (10)	14,244,753
1980	13,392,230 (224 games)	59,787	624,430 (10)	14,016,660
1979	13,182,039 (224 games)	58,848	630,326 (10)	13,812,365
1978	12,771,800 (224 games)	57,017	624,388 (10)	13,396,188
1977	11,018,632 (196 games)	56,218	534,925 (8)	11,553,557
1976	11,070,543 (196 games)	56,482	492,884 (8)	11,563,427
1975	10,213,193 (182 games)	56,116	475,919 (8)	10,689,112
1974	10,236,322 (182 games)	56,244	438,664 (8)	10,674,986
1973	10,730,933 (182 games)	58,961	525,433 (8)	11,256,366
1972	10,445,827 (182 games)	57,395	483,345 (8)	10,929,172
1971	10,076,035 (182 games)	55,363	483,891 (8)	10,559,926
1970	9,533,333 (182 games)	52,381	458,493 (8)	9,991,826
1969	6,096,127 (112 games) NFL	54,430	162,279 (3)	6,258,406
	2,843,373 (70 games) AFL	40,620	167,088 (3)	3,010,461
1968	5,882,313 (112 games) NFL	52,521	215,902 (3)	6,098,215
	2,635,004 (70 games) AFL	37,643	114,438 (2)	2,749,442
1967	5,938,924 (112 games) NFL	53,026	166,208 (3)	6,105,132
	2,295,697 (63 games) AFL	36,439	53,330 (1)	2,349,027
1966	5,337,044 (105 games) NFL	50,829	74,152 (1)	5,411,196
	2,160,369 (63 games) AFL	34,291	42,080 (1)	2,202,449
1965	4,634,021 (98 games) NFL	47,286	100,304 (2)	4,734,325
	1,782,384 (56 games) AFL	31,828	30,361 (1)	1,812,745
1964	4,563,049 (98 games) NFL	46,562	79,544 (1)	4,642,593
	1,447,875 (56 games) AFL	25,855	40,242 (1)	1,488,117
1963	4,163,643 (98 games) NFL	42,486	45,801 (1)	4,209,444
	1,208,697 (56 games) AFL	21,584	63,171 (2)	1,271,868
1962	4,003,421 (98 games) NFL	40,851	64,892 (1)	4,068,313
	1,147,302 (56 games) AFL	20,487	37,981 (1)	1,185,283
1961	3,986,159 (98 games) NFL	40,675	39,029 (1)	4,025,188
	1,002,657 (56 games) AFL	17,904	29,556 (1)	1,032,213
1960	3,128,296 (78 games) NFL	40,106	67,325 (1)	3,195,621
	926,156 (56 games) AFL	16,538	32,183 (1)	958,339
1959	3,140,000 (72 games)	43,617	57,545 (1)	3,197,545
1958	3,006,124 (72 games)	41,752	123,659 (2)	3,129,783
1957	2,836,318 (72 games)	39,393	119,579 (2)	2,955,897
1956	2,551,263 (72 games)	35,434	56,836 (1)	2,608,099
1955	2,521,836 (72 games)	35,026	85,693 (1)	2,607,529
1954	2,190,571 (72 games)	30,425	43,827 (1)	2,234,398
1953	2,164,585 (72 games)	30,064	54,577 (1)	2,219,162
1952	2,052,126 (72 games)	28,502	97,507 (2)	2,149,633
1951	1,913,019 (72 games)	26,570	57,522 (1)	1,970,541
1950	1,977,753 (78 games)	25,356	136,647 (3)	2,114,400
1949	1,391,735 (60 games)	23,196	27,980 (1)	1,419,715
1948	1,525,243 (60 games)	25,421	36,309 (1)	1,561,552
1947	1,837,437 (60 games)	30,624	66,268 (2)	1,903,705
1946	1,732,135 (55 games)	31,493	58,346 (1)	1,790,481
1945	1,270,401 (50 games)	25,408	32,178 (1)	1,302,579
1944	1,019,649 (50 games)	20,393	46,016 (1)	1,065,665
1943	969,128 (40 games)	24,228	71,315 (2)	1,040,443
1942	887,920 (55 games)	16,144	36,006 (1)	923,926
1941	1,108,615 (55 games)	20,157	55,870 (2)	1,164,485
1940	1,063,025 (55 games)	19,328	36,034 (1)	1,099,059
1939	1,071,200 (55 games)	19,476	32,279 (1)	1,103,479
1938	937,197 (55 games)	17,040	48,120 (1)	985,317
1937	963,039 (55 games)	17,510	15,878 (1)	978,917
1936	816,007 (54 games)	15,111	29,545 (1)	845,552
1935	638,178 (53 games)	12,041	15,000 (1)	653,178
1934	492,684 (60 games)	8,211	35,059 (1)	527,743

 # Record

**Players' 24-day strike reduced 224-game schedule to 210 games.*

***Players' 57-day strike reduced 224-game schedule to 126 games.*

ATTENDANCE/TV RATINGS

NFL'S TOP 10 PAID ATTENDANCE WEEKENDS

Weekend	Games	Attendance
November 23-24, 1997	15	999,778
December 4, 7-8, 1997	15	983,684
November 10-11, 1996	15	964,079
December 9-11, 1995	15	963,521
November 19-20, 1995	15	962,523
September 17-18, 1995	15	958,105
December 16-18, 1995	15	956,675
December 13-15, 1997	15	955,388
December 21-23, 1996	15	952,460
November 30, December 3-4, 1995	15	940,032

NFL'S 10 HIGHEST SCORING WEEKENDS

Point Total	Date	Weekend
762	November 10-11, 1996	11th
761	October 16-17, 1983	7th
739	November 23, 26-27, 1995	13th
736	October 25-26, 1987	7th
734	November 19-20, 1995	12th
732	November 9-10, 1980	10th
725	November 24, 27-28, 1983	13th
719	November 27, 30-December 1, 1997	14th
714	September 17-18, 1989	2nd
711	November 26, 29-30, 1987	12th

TOP 10 TELEVISED SPORTS EVENTS OF ALL-TIME

(Based on A.C. Nielsen Figures)

Program	Date	Network	Share	Rating
Super Bowl XVI	1/24/82	CBS	73.0	49.1
Super Bowl XVII	1/30/83	NBC	69.0	48.6
Winter Olympics	2/23/94	CBS	64.0	48.5
Super Bowl XX	1/26/86	NBC	70.0	48.3
Super Bowl XII	1/15/78	CBS	67.0	47.2
Super Bowl XIII	1/21/79	NBC	74.0	47.1
Super Bowl XVIII	1/22/84	CBS	71.0	46.4
Super Bowl XIX	1/20/85	ABC	63.0	46.4
Super Bowl XIV	1/20/80	CBS	67.0	46.3
Super Bowl XXX	1/28/96	NBC	68.0	46.0

TEN MOST WATCHED TV PROGRAMS & ESTIMATED TOTAL NUMBER OF VIEWERS

(Based on A.C. Nielsen Figures)

Program	Date	Network	*Total Viewers
Super Bowl XXX	Jan. 28, 1996	NBC	138,488,000
Super Bowl XXVIII	Jan. 30, 1994	NBC	134,800,000
Super Bowl XXXII	Jan. 25, 1998	NBC	133,400,000
Super Bowl XXVII	Jan. 31, 1993	NBC	133,400,000
Super Bowl XXXI	Jan. 26, 1997	FOX	128,900,000
Super Bowl XX	Jan. 26, 1986	NBC	127,000,000
Winter Olympics	Feb. 23, 1994	CBS	126,686,000
Super Bowl XXIX	Jan. 29, 1995	ABC	125,216,000
Super Bowl XXI	Jan. 25, 1987	CBS	122,640,000
M*A*S*H (Special)	Feb. 28, 1983	CBS	121,624,000

**Watched some portion of the broadcast*

NFL'S TOP 10 TEAM SINGLE-SEASON HOME PAID ATTENDANCE TOTALS

Year	Club	Games	Attendance
1980	Detroit Lions	8	634,204
1988	Buffalo Bills	8	631,818
1991	Buffalo Bills	8	631,786
1992	Buffalo Bills	8	630,978
1997	Kansas City Chiefs	8	629,763
1996	Kansas City Chiefs	8	628,460
1994	Kansas City Chiefs	8	626,612
1989	Buffalo Bills	8	626,399
1995	Kansas City Chiefs	8	625,936
1989	Cleveland Browns	8	625,240

NFL'S TOP FIVE PAID ATTENDANCE TOTALS FOR ALL GAMES

Year	Preseason	Regular Season	Postseason	All Games
1995	3,368,289	15,043,562	790,906	19,202,757
1997	3,280,693	14,967,314	801,879	19,049,886
1996	3,267,254	14,612,417	769,310	18,648,981
1994	3,200,091	14,030,435	779,738	18,010,264
1993	3,170,381	13,966,843	814,607	17,951,831

TEN HIGHEST-RATED ABC NFL MONDAY NIGHT FOOTBALL GAMES OF ALL-TIME

(Based on A.C. Nielsen Figures)

Game	Date	Share	Rating
Chicago at Miami	12/2/85	46.0	29.6
N.Y. Giants at San Francisco	12/3/90	42.0	26.9
Dallas at Washington	10/2/78	43.0	26.8
Pittsburgh at San Diego	12/22/80	40.0	25.3
Philadelphia at Miami	11/30/81	40.0	25.3
Pittsburgh at Houston	12/10/79	40.0	25.1
Dallas at Miami	12/17/84	40.0	25.1
Pittsburgh at Dallas	9/13/82	42.0	24.9
Cincinnati at Oakland	12/6/76	40.0	24.7
Dallas at Washington	10/8/73	40.0	24.6
Minnesota at Atlanta	11/19/73	40.0	24.6

NFL'S 10 BIGGEST SINGLE-GAME ATTENDANCE TOTALS

Date	Site	Game	Teams	Attendance
August 15, 1994	Azteca Stadium	American Bowl (Mexico City)	Cowboys vs. Oilers	112,376
August 22, 1947	Soldier Field	College All-Star	Bears vs. All-Stars	105,840
August 4, 1997	Estadio Guillermo Canedo	American Bowl (Mexico City)	Broncos vs. Dolphins	104,629
January 20, 1980	Rose Bowl	Super Bowl XIV	Steelers vs. Rams	103,985
January 30, 1983	Rose Bowl	Super Bowl XVII	Redskins vs. Dolphins	103,667
January 9, 1977	Rose Bowl	Super Bowl XI	Raiders vs. Vikings	103,438
November 10, 1957	L.A. Coliseum	Regular Season	49ers at Rams	102,368
January 25, 1987	Rose Bowl	Super Bowl XXI	Giants vs. Broncos	101,643
August 20, 1948	Soldier Field	College All-Star	Cardinals vs. All-Stars	101,220
August 28, 1942	Soldier Field	College All-Star	Bears vs. All-Stars	101,100

NUMBER-ONE DRAFT CHOICES

Season	Date	Team	Player	Position	College
1998	April 18-19	Indianapolis	Peyton Manning	QB	Tennessee
1997	April 19-20	St. Louis	Orlando Pace	T	Ohio State
1996	April 20-21	New York Jets	Keyshawn Johnson	WR	Southern California
1995	April 22-23	Cincinnati	Ki-Jana Carter	RB	Penn State
1994	April 24-25	Cincinnati	Dan Wilkinson	DT	Ohio State
1993	April 25-26	New England	Drew Bledsoe	QB	Washington State
1992	April 26-27	Indianapolis	Steve Emtman	DT	Washington
1991	April 21-22	Dallas	Russell Maryland	DT	Miami
1990	April 22-23	Indianapolis	Jeff George	QB	Illinois
1989	April 23-24	Dallas	Troy Aikman	QB	UCLA
1988	April 24-25	Atlanta	Aundray Bruce	LB	Auburn
1987	April 28-29	Tampa Bay	Vinny Testaverde	QB	Miami
1986	April 29-30	Tampa Bay	Bo Jackson	RB	Auburn
1985	April 30-May 1	Buffalo	Bruce Smith	DE	Virginia Tech
1984	May 1-2	New England	Irving Fryar	WR	Nebraska
1983	April 26-27	Baltimore	John Elway	QB	Stanford
1982	April 27-28	New England	Kenneth Sims	DT	Texas
1981	April 28-29	New Orleans	George Rogers	RB	South Carolina
1980	April 29-30	Detroit	Billy Sims	RB	Oklahoma
1979	May 3-4	Buffalo	Tom Cousineau	LB	Ohio State
1978	May 2-3	Houston	Earl Campbell	RB	Texas
1977	May 3-4	Tampa Bay	Ricky Bell	RB	Southern California
1976	April 8-9	Tampa Bay	Lee Roy Selmon	DE	Oklahoma
1975	January 28-29	Atlanta	Steve Bartkowski	QB	California
1974	January 29-30	Dallas	Ed Jones	DE	Tennessee State
1973	January 30-31	Houston	John Matuszak	DE	Tampa
1972	February 1-2	Buffalo	Walt Patulski	DE	Notre Dame
1971	January 28-29	New England	Jim Plunkett	QB	Stanford
1970	January 27-28	Pittsburgh	Terry Bradshaw	QB	Louisiana Tech
1969	January 28-29	Buffalo (AFL)	O.J. Simpson	RB	Southern California
1968	January 30-31	Minnesota	Ron Yary	T	Southern California
1967	March 14	Baltimore	Bubba Smith	DT	Michigan State
1966	November 27, 1965	Atlanta	Tommy Nobis	LB	Texas
	November 28, 1965	Miami (AFL)	Jim Grabowski	RB	Illinois
1965	November 28, 1964	New York Giants	Tucker Frederickson	RB	Auburn
	November 28, 1964	Houston (AFL)	Lawrence Elkins	E	Baylor
1964	December 2, 1963	San Francisco	Dave Parks	E	Texas Tech
	November 30, 1963	Boston (AFL)	Jack Concannon	QB	Boston College
1963	December 3, 1962	Los Angeles	Terry Baker	QB	Oregon State
	December 1, 1962	Kansas City (AFL)	Buck Buchanan	DT	Grambling
1962	December 4, 1961	Washington	Ernie Davis	RB	Syracuse
	December 2, 1961	Oakland (AFL)	Roman Gabriel	QB	North Carolina State
1961	December 27-28, 1960	Minnesota	Tommy Mason	RB	Tulane
	November 23, 1960	Buffalo (AFL)	Ken Rice	G	Auburn
1960	Secret Draft	Los Angeles	Billy Cannon	RB	Louisiana State
	November 22, December 2, 1959	(AFL had no formal first pick)			
1959	December 2, 1958	Green Bay	Randy Duncan	QB	Iowa
1958	December 2, 1957	Chicago Cardinals	King Hill	QB	Rice
1957	November 27, 1956	Green Bay	Paul Hornung	HB	Notre Dame
1956	November 29, 1955	Pittsburgh	Gary Glick	DB	Colorado A&M
1955	January 27-28	Baltimore	George Shaw	QB	Oregon
1954	January 28	Cleveland	Bobby Garrett	QB	Stanford
1953	January 22	San Francisco	Harry Babcock	E	Georgia
1952	January 17	Los Angeles	Bill Wade	QB	Vanderbilt
1951	January 18-19	New York Giants	Kyle Rote	HB	Southern Methodist
1950	January 21-22	Detroit	Leon Hart	E	Notre Dame
1949	December 21, 1948	Philadelphia	Chuck Bednarik	C	Pennsylvania
1948	December 19, 1947	Washington	Harry Gilmer	QB	Alabama
1947	December 16, 1946	Chicago Bears	Bob Fenimore	HB	Oklahoma A&M
1946	January 14	Boston	Frank Dancewicz	QB	Notre Dame
1945	April 6	Chicago Cardinals	Charley Trippi	HB	Georgia
1944	April 19	Boston	Angelo Bertelli	QB	Notre Dame
1943	April 8	Detroit	Frank Sinkwich	HB	Georgia
1942	December 22, 1941	Pittsburgh	Bill Dudley	HB	Virginia
1941	December 10, 1940	Chicago Bears	Tom Harmon	HB	Michigan
1940	December 9, 1939	Chicago Cardinals	George Cafego	HB	Tennessee
1939	December 8, 1938	Chicago Cardinals	Ki Aldrich	C	Texas Christian
1938	December 12, 1937	Cleveland	Corbett Davis	FB	Indiana
1937	December 12, 1936	Philadelphia	Sam Francis	FB	Nebraska
1936	February 8	Philadelphia	Jay Berwanger	HB	Chicago

Note: From 1947 through 1958, the first selection in the draft was a Bonus pick, awarded to the winner of a random draw. That club, in turn, forfeited its last-round draft choice. The winner of the Bonus choice was eliminated from future draws. The system was abolished after 1958, by which time all clubs had received a Bonus choice.

FIRST-ROUND SELECTIONS

FIRST-ROUND SELECTIONS
If club had no first-round selection, first player drafted is listed with round in parentheses.

ARIZONA CARDINALS

Year	Player, College, Position
1936	Jim Lawrence, Texas Christian, B
1937	Ray Buivid, Marquette, B
1938	Jack Robbins, Arkansas, B
1939	Charles (Ki) Aldrich, Texas Christian, C
1940	George Cafego, Tennessee, B
1941	John Kimbrough, Texas A&M, B
1942	Steve Lach, Duke, B
1943	Glenn Dobbs, Tulsa, B
1944	Pat Harder, Wisconsin, B
1945	Charley Trippi, Georgia, B
1946	Dub Jones, Louisiana State, B
1947	DeWitt (Tex) Coulter, Army, T
1948	Jim Spavital, Oklahoma A&M, B
1949	Bill Fischer, Notre Dame, G
1950	Jack Jennings, Ohio State, T (2)
1951	Jerry Groom, Notre Dame, C
1952	Ollie Matson, San Francisco, B
1953	Johnny Olszewski, California, B
1954	Lamar McHan, Arkansas, B
1955	Max Boydston, Oklahoma, E
1956	Joe Childress, Auburn, B
1957	Jerry Tubbs, Oklahoma, C
1958	King Hill, Rice, B
	John David Crow, Texas A&M, B
1959	Bill Stacy, Mississippi State, B
1960	George Izo, Notre Dame, QB
1961	Ken Rice, Auburn, T
1962	Fate Echols, Northwestern, DT
	Irv Goode, Kentucky, C
1963	Jerry Stovall, Louisiana State, S
	Don Brumm, Purdue, DE
1964	Ken Kortas, Louisville, DT
1965	Joe Namath, Alabama, QB
1966	Carl McAdams, Oklahoma, LB
1967	Dave Williams, Washington, WR
1968	MacArthur Lane, Utah State, RB
1969	Roger Wehrli, Missouri, DB
1970	Larry Stegent, Texas A&M, RB
1971	Norm Thompson, Utah, CB
1972	Bobby Moore, Oregon, RB-WR
1973	Dave Butz, Purdue, DT
1974	J.V. Cain, Colorado, TE
1975	Tim Gray, Texas A&M, DB
1976	Mike Dawson, Arizona, DT
1977	Steve Pisarkiewicz, Missouri, QB
1978	Steve Little, Arkansas, K
	Ken Greene, Washington State, DB
1979	Ottis Anderson, Miami, RB
1980	Curtis Greer, Michigan, DE
1981	E.J. Junior, Alabama, LB
1982	Luis Sharpe, UCLA, T
1983	Leonard Smith, McNeese State, DB
1984	Clyde Duncan, Tennessee, WR
1985	Freddie Joe Nunn, Mississippi, LB
1986	Anthony Bell, Michigan State, LB
1987	Kelly Stouffer, Colorado State, QB
1988	Ken Harvey, California, LB
1989	Eric Hill, Louisiana State, LB
	Joe Wolf, Boston College, G
1990	Anthony Thompson, Indiana, RB (2)
1991	Eric Swann, No College, DE
1992	Tony Sacca, Penn State, QB (2)
1993	Garrison Hearst, Georgia, RB
	Ernest Dye, South Carolina, T
1994	Jamir Miller, UCLA, LB
1995	Frank Sanders, Auburn, WR (2)
1996	Simeon Rice, Illinois, DE
1997	Tom Knight, Iowa, DB
1998	Andre Wadsworth, Florida State, DE

ATLANTA FALCONS

Year	Player, College, Position
1966	Tommy Nobis, Texas, LB
	Randy Johnson, Texas A&I, QB
1967	Leo Carroll, San Diego State, DE (2)
1968	Claude Humphrey, Tennessee State, DE
1969	George Kunz, Notre Dame, T
1970	John Small, Citadel, LB
1971	Joe Profit, Northeast Louisiana, RB
1972	Clarence Ellis, Notre Dame, DB
1973	Greg Marx, Notre Dame, DT (2)
1974	Gerald Tinker, Kent State, WR (2)
1975	Steve Bartkowski, California, QB
1976	Bubba Bean, Texas A&M, RB
1977	Warren Bryant, Kentucky, T
	Wilson Faumuina, San Jose State, DT
1978	Mike Kenn, Michigan, T
1979	Don Smith, Miami, DE
1980	Junior Miller, Nebraska, TE
1981	Bobby Butler, Florida State, DB
1982	Gerald Riggs, Arizona State, RB
1983	Mike Pitts, Alabama, DE
1984	Rick Bryan, Oklahoma, DT
1985	Bill Fralic, Pittsburgh, T
1986	Tony Casillas, Oklahoma, NT
	Tim Green, Syracuse, LB
1987	Chris Miller, Oregon, QB
1988	Aundray Bruce, Auburn, LB
1989	Deion Sanders, Florida State, DB
	Shawn Collins, Northern Arizona, WR
1990	Steve Broussard, Washington State, RB
1991	Bruce Pickens, Nebraska, DB
	Mike Pritchard, Colorado, WR
1992	Bob Whitfield, Stanford, T
	Tony Smith, Southern Mississippi, RB
1993	Lincoln Kennedy, Washington, T
1994	Bert Emanuel, Rice, WR (2)
1995	Devin Bush, Florida State, DB
1996	Shannon Brown, Alabama, DT (3)
1997	Michael Booker, Nebraska, DB
1998	Keith Brooking, Georgia Tech, LB

BALTIMORE RAVENS

Year	Player, College, Position
1996	Jonathan Ogden, UCLA, T
	Ray Lewis, Miami, LB
1997	Peter Boulware, Florida State, DE
1998	Duane Starks, Miami, DB

BUFFALO BILLS

Year	Player, College, Position
1960	Richie Lucas, Penn State, QB
1961	Ken Rice, Auburn, T
1962	Ernie Davis, Syracuse, RB
1963	Dave Behrman, Michigan State, C
1964	Carl Eller, Minnesota, DE
1965	Jim Davidson, Ohio State, T
1966	Mike Dennis, Mississippi, RB
1967	John Pitts, Arizona State, S
1968	Haven Moses, San Diego State, WR
1969	O.J. Simpson, Southern California, RB
1970	Al Cowlings, Southern California, DE
1971	J.D. Hill, Arizona State, WR
1972	Walt Patulski, Notre Dame, DE
1973	Paul Seymour, Michigan, TE
	Joe DeLamielleure, Michigan State, G
1974	Reuben Gant, Oklahoma State, TE
1975	Tom Ruud, Nebraska, LB
1976	Mario Clark, Oregon, DB
1977	Phil Dokes, Oklahoma State, DT
1978	Terry Miller, Oklahoma State, RB
1979	Tom Cousineau, Ohio State, LB
	Jerry Butler, Clemson, WR
1980	Jim Ritcher, North Carolina State, C
1981	Booker Moore, Penn State, RB
1982	Perry Tuttle, Clemson, WR
1983	Tony Hunter, Notre Dame, TE
	Jim Kelly, Miami, QB
1984	Greg Bell, Notre Dame, RB
1985	Bruce Smith, Virginia Tech, DE
	Derrick Burroughs, Memphis State, DB
1986	Ronnie Harmon, Iowa, RB
	Will Wolford, Vanderbilt, T
1987	Shane Conlan, Penn State, LB
1988	Thurman Thomas, Oklahoma State, RB (2)
1989	Don Beebe, Chadron, Neb., WR (3)
1990	James Williams, Fresno State, DB
1991	Henry Jones, Illinois, DB
1992	John Fina, Arizona, T
1993	Thomas Smith, North Carolina, DB
1994	Jeff Burris, Notre Dame, DB
1995	Ruben Brown, Pittsburgh, G
1996	Eric Moulds, Mississippi State, WR
1997	Antowain Smith, Houston, RB
1998	Sam Cowart, Florida State, LB (2)

CAROLINA PANTHERS

Year	Player, College, Position
1995	Kerry Collins, Penn State, QB
	Tyrone Poole, Ft. Valley State, DB
	Blake Brockermeyer, Texas, T
1996	Tim Biakabutuka, Michigan, RB
1997	Rae Carruth, Colorado, WR
1998	Jason Peter, Nebraska, DT

CHICAGO BEARS

Year	Player, College, Position
1936	Joe Stydahar, West Virginia, T
1937	Les McDonald, Nebraska, E
1938	Joe Gray, Oregon State, B
1939	Sid Luckman, Columbia, QB
	Bill Osmanski, Holy Cross, B
1940	Clyde (Bulldog) Turner, Hardin-Simmons, C
1941	Tom Harmon, Michigan, B
	Norm Standlee, Stanford, B
	Don Scott, Ohio State, B
1942	Frankie Albert, Stanford, B
1943	Bob Steber, Missouri, B
1944	Ray Evans, Kansas, B
1945	Don Lund, Michigan, B
1946	Johnny Lujack, Notre Dame, QB
1947	Bob Fenimore, Oklahoma State, B
	Don Kindt, Wisconsin, B
1948	Bobby Layne, Texas, QB
	Max Bumgardner, Texas, E
1949	Dick Harris, Texas, C
1950	Chuck Hunsinger, Florida, B
	Fred Morrison, Ohio State, B
1951	Bob Williams, Notre Dame, B
	Billy Stone, Bradley, B
	Gene Schroeder, Virginia, E
1952	Jim Dooley, Miami, B
1953	Billy Anderson, Compton (Calif.) J.C., B
1954	Stan Wallace, Illinois, B
1955	Ron Drzewiecki, Marquette, B
1956	Menan (Tex) Schriewer, Texas, E
1957	Earl Leggett, Louisiana State, T
1958	Chuck Howley, West Virginia, G
1959	Don Clark, Ohio State, B
1960	Roger Davis, Syracuse, G
1961	Mike Ditka, Pittsburgh, E
1962	Ronnie Bull, Baylor, RB
1963	Dave Behrman, Michigan State, C
1964	Dick Evey, Tennessee, DT
1965	Dick Butkus, Illinois, LB
	Gale Sayers, Kansas, RB
	Steve DeLong, Tennessee, T
1966	George Rice, Louisiana State, DT
1967	Loyd Phillips, Arkansas, DE
1968	Mike Hull, Southern California, RB
1969	Rufus Mayes, Ohio State, T
1970	George Farmer, UCLA, WR (3)
1971	Joe Moore, Missouri, RB
1972	Lionel Antoine, Southern Illinois, T
	Craig Clemons, Iowa, DB
1973	Wally Chambers, Eastern Kentucky, DE
1974	Waymond Bryant, Tennessee State, LB
	Dave Gallagher, Michigan, DT
1975	Walter Payton, Jackson State, RB
1976	Dennis Lick, Wisconsin, T
1977	Ted Albrecht, California, T
1978	Brad Shearer, Texas, DT (3)
1979	Dan Hampton, Arkansas, DT
	Al Harris, Arizona State, DE
1980	Otis Wilson, Louisville, LB
1981	Keith Van Horne, Southern California, T
1982	Jim McMahon, Brigham Young, QB
1983	Jim Covert, Pittsburgh, T
	Willie Gault, Tennessee, WR
1984	Wilber Marshall, Florida, LB
1985	William Perry, Clemson, DT
1986	Neal Anderson, Florida, RB
1987	Jim Harbaugh, Michigan, QB

1988 Brad Muster, Stanford, RB
Wendell Davis, Louisiana State, WR
1989 Donnell Woolford, Clemson, DB
Trace Armstrong, Florida, DE
1990 Mark Carrier, Southern California, DB
1991 Stan Thomas, Texas, T
1992 Alonzo Spellman, Ohio State, DE
1993 Curtis Conway, Southern California, WR
1994 John Thierry, Alcorn State, DE
1995 Rashaan Salaam, Colorado, RB
1996 Walt Harris, Mississippi State, DB
1997 John Allred, Southern California, TE (2)
1998 Curtis Enis, Penn State, RB

CINCINNATI BENGALS

Year	Player, College, Position
1968	Bob Johnson, Tennessee, C
1969	Greg Cook, Cincinnati, QB
1970	Mike Reid, Penn State, DT
1971	Vernon Holland, Tennessee State, T
1972	Sherman White, California, DE
1973	Isaac Curtis, San Diego State, WR
1974	Bill Kollar, Montana State, DT
1975	Glenn Cameron, Florida, LB
1976	Billy Brooks, Oklahoma, WR
	Archie Griffin, Ohio State, RB
1977	Eddie Edwards, Miami, DT
	Wilson Whitley, Houston, DT
	Mike Cobb, Michigan State, TE
1978	Ross Browner, Notre Dame, DT
	Blair Bush, Washington, C
1979	Jack Thompson, Washington State, QB
	Charles Alexander, Louisiana State, RB
1980	Anthony Muñoz, Southern California, T
1981	David Verser, Kansas, WR
1982	Glen Collins, Mississippi State, DE
1983	Dave Rimington, Nebraska, C
1984	Ricky Hunley, Arizona, LB
	Pete Koch, Maryland, DE
	Brian Blados, North Carolina, T
1985	Eddie Brown, Miami, WR
	Emanuel King, Alabama, LB
1986	Joe Kelly, Washington, LB
	Tim McGee, Tennessee, WR
1987	Jason Buck, Brigham Young, DE
1988	Rickey Dixon, Oklahoma, DB
1989	Eric Ball, UCLA, RB (2)
1990	James Francis, Baylor, LB
1991	Alfred Williams, Colorado, LB
1992	David Klingler, Houston, QB
	Darryl Williams, Miami, DB
1993	John Copeland, Alabama, DE
1994	Dan Wilkinson, Ohio State, DT
1995	Ki-Jana Carter, Penn State, RB
1996	Willie Anderson, Auburn, T
1997	Reinard Wilson, Florida State, LB
1998	Takeo Spikes, Cincinnati, LB
	Brian Simmons, North Carolina, LB

CLEVELAND BROWNS

Year	Player, College, Position
1950	Ken Carpenter, Oregon State, B
1951	Ken Konz, Louisiana State, B
1952	Bert Rechichar, Tennessee, DB
	Harry Agganis, Boston U., QB
1953	Doug Atkins, Tennessee, DE
1954	Bobby Garrett, Stanford, QB
	John Bauer, Illinois, G
1955	Kurt Burris, Oklahoma, C
1956	Preston Carpenter, Arkansas, B
1957	Jim Brown, Syracuse, RB
1958	Jim Shofner, Texas Christian, DB
1959	Rich Kreitling, Illinois, DE
1960	Jim Houston, Ohio State, DE
1961	Bobby Crespino, Mississippi, TE
1962	Gary Collins, Maryland, WR
	Leroy Jackson, Western Illinois, RB
1963	Tom Hutchinson, Kentucky, WR
1964	Paul Warfield, Ohio State, WR
1965	James Garcia, Purdue, T (2)
1966	Milt Morin, Massachusetts, TE
1967	Bob Matheson, Duke, LB
1968	Marvin Upshaw, Trinity, Tex., DT-DE
1969	Ron Johnson, Michigan, RB
1970	Mike Phipps, Purdue, QB
	Bob McKay, Texas, T
1971	Clarence Scott, Kansas State, CB
1972	Thom Darden, Michigan, DB
1973	Steve Holden, Arizona State, WR
	Pete Adams, Southern California, T
1974	Billy Corbett, Johnson C. Smith, T (2)
1975	Mack Mitchell, Houston, DE
1976	Mike Pruitt, Purdue, RB
1977	Robert Jackson, Texas A&M, LB
1978	Clay Matthews, Southern California, LB
	Ozzie Newsome, Alabama, TE
1979	Willis Adams, Houston, WR
1980	Charles White, Southern California, RB
1981	Hanford Dixon, Southern Mississippi, DB
1982	Chip Banks, Southern California, LB
1983	Ron Brown, Arizona State, WR (2)
1984	Don Rogers, UCLA, DB
1985	Greg Allen, Florida State, RB (2)
1986	Webster Slaughter, San Diego State, WR (2)
1987	Mike Junkin, Duke, LB
1988	Clifford Charlton, Florida, LB
1989	Eric Metcalf, Texas, RB
1990	Leroy Hoard, Michigan, RB (2)
1991	Eric Turner, UCLA, DB
1992	Tommy Vardell, Stanford, RB
1993	Steve Everitt, Michigan, C
1994	Antonio Langham, Alabama, DB
	Derrick Alexander, Michigan, WR
1995	Craig Powell, Ohio State, LB

DALLAS COWBOYS

Year	Player, College, Position
1960	None
1961	Bob Lilly, Texas Christian, DT
1962	Sonny Gibbs, Texas Christian, QB (2)
1963	Lee Roy Jordan, Alabama, LB
1964	Scott Appleton, Texas, DT
1965	Craig Morton, California, QB
1966	John Niland, Iowa, G
1967	Phil Clark, Northwestern, DB (3)
1968	Dennis Homan, Alabama, WR
1969	Calvin Hill, Yale, RB
1970	Duane Thomas, West Texas State, RB
1971	Tody Smith, Southern California, DE
1972	Bill Thomas, Boston College, RB
1973	Billy Joe DuPree, Michigan State, TE
1974	Ed (Too Tall) Jones, Tennessee State, DE
	Charley Young, North Carolina State, RB
1975	Randy White, Maryland, LB
	Thomas Henderson, Langston, LB
1976	Aaron Kyle, Wyoming, DB
1977	Tony Dorsett, Pittsburgh, RB
1978	Larry Bethea, Michigan State, DE
1979	Robert Shaw, Tennessee, C
1980	Bill Roe, Colorado, LB (3)
1981	Howard Richards, Missouri, T
1982	Rod Hill, Kentucky State, DB
1983	Jim Jeffcoat, Arizona State, DE
1984	Billy Cannon, Jr., Texas A&M, LB
1985	Kevin Brooks, Michigan, DE
1986	Mike Sherrard, UCLA, WR
1987	Danny Noonan, Nebraska, DT
1988	Michael Irvin, Miami, WR
1989	Troy Aikman, UCLA, QB
1990	Emmitt Smith, Florida, RB
1991	Russell Maryland, Miami, DT
	Alvin Harper, Tennessee, WR
	Kelvin Pritchett, Mississippi, DT
1992	Kevin Smith, Texas A&M, DB
	Robert Jones, East Carolina, LB
1993	Kevin Williams, Miami, WR (2)
1994	Shante Carver, Arizona State, DE
1995	Sherman Williams, Alabama, RB (2)
1996	Kavika Pittman, McNeese State, DE (2)
1997	David LaFleur, Louisiana State, TE
1998	Greg Ellis, North Carolina, DE

DENVER BRONCOS

Year	Player, College, Position
1960	Roger LeClerc, Trinity, Conn., C
1961	Bob Gaiters, New Mexico State, RB
1962	Merlin Olsen, Utah State, DT
1963	Kermit Alexander, UCLA, CB
1964	Bob Brown, Nebraska, T
1965	Dick Butkus, Illinois, LB (2)
1966	Jerry Shay, Purdue, DT
1967	Floyd Little, Syracuse, RB
1968	Curley Culp, Arizona State, DE (2)
1969	Grady Cavness, Texas-El Paso, DB (2)
1970	Bob Anderson, Colorado, RB
1971	Marv Montgomery, Southern California, T
1972	Riley Odoms, Houston, TE
1973	Otis Armstrong, Purdue, RB
1974	Randy Gradishar, Ohio State, LB
1975	Louis Wright, San Jose State, DB
1976	Tom Glassic, Virginia, G
1977	Steve Schindler, Boston College, G
1978	Don Latimer, Miami, DT
1979	Kelvin Clark, Nebraska, T
1980	Rulon Jones, Utah State, DE (2)
1981	Dennis Smith, Southern California, DB
1982	Gerald Willhite, San Jose State, RB
1983	Chris Hinton, Northwestern, G
1984	Andre Townsend, Mississippi, DE (2)
1985	Steve Sewell, Oklahoma, RB
1986	Jim Juriga, Illinois, T (4)
1987	Ricky Nattiel, Florida, WR
1988	Ted Gregory, Syracuse, NT
1989	Steve Atwater, Arkansas, DB
1990	Alton Montgomery, Houston, DB (2)
1991	Mike Croel, Nebraska, LB
1992	Tommy Maddox, UCLA, QB
1993	Dan Williams, Toledo, DE
1994	Allen Aldridge, Houston, LB (2)
1995	Jamie Brown, Florida A&M, T (4)
1996	John Mobley, Kutztown, LB
1997	Trevor Pryce, Clemson, DT
1998	Marcus Nash, Tennessee, WR

DETROIT LIONS

Year	Player, College, Position
1936	Sid Wagner, Michigan State, G
1937	Lloyd Cardwell, Nebraska, B
1938	Alex Wojciechowicz, Fordham, C
1939	John Pingel, Michigan State, B
1940	Doyle Nave, Southern California, B
1941	Jim Thomason, Texas A&M, B
1942	Bob Westfall, Michigan, B
1943	Frank Sinkwich, Georgia, B
1944	Otto Graham, Northwestern, B
1945	Frank Szymanski, Notre Dame, C
1946	Bill Dellastatious, Missouri, B
1947	Glenn Davis, Army, B
1948	Y.A. Tittle, Louisiana State, B
1949	John Rauch, Georgia, B
1950	Leon Hart, Notre Dame, E
	Joe Watson, Rice, C
1951	Dick Stanfel, San Francisco, G (2)
1952	Yale Lary, Texas A&M, B (3)
1953	Harley Sewell, Texas, G
1954	Dick Chapman, Rice, T
1955	Dave Middleton, Auburn, B
1956	Hopalong Cassady, Ohio State, B
1957	Bill Glass, Baylor, G
1958	Alex Karras, Iowa, T
1959	Nick Pietrosante, Notre Dame, B
1960	John Robinson, Louisiana State, S
1961	Danny LaRose, Missouri, T (2)
1962	John Hadl, Kansas, QB
1963	Daryl Sanders, Ohio State, T
1964	Pete Beathard, Southern California, QB
1965	Tom Nowatzke, Indiana, RB
1966	Nick Eddy, Notre Dame, RB (2)
1967	Mel Farr, UCLA, RB
1968	Greg Landry, Massachusetts, QB
	Earl McCullouch, Southern California, WR
1969	Altie Taylor, Utah State, RB (2)
1970	Steve Owens, Oklahoma, RB
1971	Bob Bell, Cincinnati, DT
1972	Herb Orvis, Colorado, DE
1973	Ernie Price, Texas A&I, DE
1974	Ed O'Neil, Penn State, LB
1975	Lynn Boden, South Dakota State, G
1976	James Hunter, Grambling, DB

Year	Player, College, Position
	Lawrence Gaines, Wyoming, RB
1977	Walt Williams, New Mexico State, DB (2)
1978	Luther Bradley, Notre Dame, DB
1979	Keith Dorney, Penn State, T
1980	Billy Sims, Oklahoma, RB
1981	Mark Nichols, San Jose State, WR
1982	Jimmy Williams, Nebraska, LB
1983	James Jones, Florida, RB
1984	David Lewis, California, TE
1985	Lomas Brown, Florida, T
1986	Chuck Long, Iowa, QB
1987	Reggie Rogers, Washington, DE
1988	Bennie Blades, Miami, DB
1989	Barry Sanders, Oklahoma State, RB
1990	Andre Ware, Houston, QB
1991	Herman Moore, Virginia, WR
1992	Robert Porcher, South Carolina State, DE
1993	Ryan McNeil, Miami, DB (2)
1994	Johnnie Morton, Southern California, WR
1995	Luther Elliss, Utah, DT
1996	Reggie Brown, Texas A&M, LB
	Jeff Hartings, Penn State, G
1997	Bryant Westbrook, Texas, DB
1998	Terry Fair, Tennessee, DB

GREEN BAY PACKERS

Year	Player, College, Position
1936	Russ Letlow, San Francisco, G
1937	Eddie Jankowski, Wisconsin, B
1938	Cecil Isbell, Purdue, B
1939	Larry Buhler, Minnesota, B
1940	Harold Van Every, Minnesota, B
1941	George Paskvan, Wisconsin, B
1942	Urban Odson, Minnesota, T
1943	Dick Wildung, Minnesota, T
1944	Merv Pregulman, Michigan, G
1945	Walt Schlinkman, Texas Tech, B
1946	Johnny (Strike) Strzykalski, Marquette, B
1947	Ernie Case, UCLA, B
1948	Earl (Jug) Girard, Wisconsin, B
1949	Stan Heath, Nevada, B
1950	Clayton Tonnemaker, Minnesota, C
1951	Bob Gain, Kentucky, T
1952	Babe Parilli, Kentucky, QB
1953	Al Carmichael, Southern California, B
1954	Art Hunter, Notre Dame, T
	Veryl Switzer, Kansas State, B
1955	Tom Bettis, Purdue, G
1956	Jack Losch, Miami, B
1957	Paul Hornung, Notre Dame, B
	Ron Kramer, Michigan, E
1958	Dan Currie, Michigan State, C
1959	Randy Duncan, Iowa, B
1960	Tom Moore, Vanderbilt, RB
1961	Herb Adderley, Michigan State, CB
1962	Earl Gros, Louisiana State, RB
1963	Dave Robinson, Penn State, LB
1964	Lloyd Voss, Nebraska, DT
1965	Donny Anderson, Texas Tech, RB
	Lawrence Elkins, Baylor, E
1966	Jim Grabowski, Illinois, RB
	Gale Gillingham, Minnesota, T
1967	Bob Hyland, Boston College, C
	Don Horn, San Diego State, QB
1968	Fred Carr, Texas-El Paso, LB
	Bill Lueck, Arizona, G
1969	Rich Moore, Villanova, DT
1970	Mike McCoy, Notre Dame, DT
	Rich McGeorge, Elon, TE
1971	John Brockington, Ohio State, RB
1972	Willie Buchanon, San Diego State, DB
	Jerry Tagge, Nebraska, QB
1973	Barry Smith, Florida State, WR
1974	Barty Smith, Richmond, RB
1975	Bill Bain, Southern California, G (2)
1976	Mark Koncar, Colorado, T
1977	Mike Butler, Kansas, DE
	Ezra Johnson, Morris Brown, DE
1978	James Lofton, Stanford, WR
	John Anderson, Michigan, LB
1979	Eddie Lee Ivery, Georgia Tech, RB
1980	Bruce Clark, Penn State, DE
	George Cumby, Oklahoma, LB
1981	Rich Campbell, California, QB
1982	Ron Hallstrom, Iowa, G
1983	Tim Lewis, Pittsburgh, DB
1984	Alphonso Carreker, Florida State, DE
1985	Ken Ruettgers, Southern California, T
1986	Kenneth Davis, Texas Christian, RB (2)
1987	Brent Fullwood, Auburn, RB
1988	Sterling Sharpe, South Carolina, WR
1989	Tony Mandarich, Michigan State, T
1990	Tony Bennett, Mississippi, LB
	Darrell Thompson, Minnesota, RB
1991	Vinnie Clark, Ohio State, DB
1992	Terrell Buckley, Florida State, DB
1993	Wayne Simmons, Clemson, LB
	George Teague, Alabama, DB
1994	Aaron Taylor, Notre Dame, T
1995	Craig Newsome, Arizona State, DB
1996	John Michels, Southern California, T
1997	Ross Verba, Iowa, T
1998	Vonnie Holliday, North Carolina, DT

INDIANAPOLIS COLTS

Year	Player, College, Position
1953	Billy Vessels, Oklahoma, B
1954	Cotton Davidson, Baylor, B
1955	George Shaw, Oregon, B
	Alan Ameche, Wisconsin, FB
1956	Lenny Moore, Penn State, B
1957	Jim Parker, Ohio State, G
1958	Lenny Lyles, Louisville, B
1959	Jackie Burkett, Auburn, C
1960	Ron Mix, Southern California, T
1961	Tom Matte, Ohio State, RB
1962	Wendell Harris, Louisiana State, S
1963	Bob Vogel, Ohio State, T
1964	Marv Woodson, Indiana, CB
1965	Mike Curtis, Duke, LB
1966	Sam Ball, Kentucky, T
1967	Bubba Smith, Michigan State, DT
	Jim Detwiler, Michigan, RB
1968	John Williams, Minnesota, G
1969	Eddie Hinton, Oklahoma, WR
1970	Norman Bulaich, Texas Christian, RB
1971	Don McCauley, North Carolina, RB
	Leonard Dunlap, North Texas State, DB
1972	Tom Drougas, Oregon, T
1973	Bert Jones, Louisiana State, QB
	Joe Ehrmann, Syracuse, DT
1974	John Dutton, Nebraska, DE
	Roger Carr, Louisiana Tech, WR
1975	Ken Huff, North Carolina, G
1976	Ken Novak, Purdue, DT
1977	Randy Burke, Kentucky, WR
1978	Reese McCall, Auburn, TE
1979	Barry Krauss, Alabama, LB
1980	Curtis Dickey, Texas A&M, RB
	Derrick Hatchett, Texas, DB
1981	Randy McMillan, Pittsburgh, RB
	Donnell Thompson, North Carolina, DT
1982	Johnie Cooks, Mississippi State, LB
	Art Schlichter, Ohio State, QB
1983	John Elway, Stanford, QB
1984	Leonard Coleman, Vanderbilt, DB
	Ron Solt, Maryland, G
1985	Duane Bickett, Southern California, LB
1986	Jon Hand, Alabama, DE
1987	Cornelius Bennett, Alabama, LB
1988	Chris Chandler, Washington, QB (3)
1989	Andre Rison, Michigan State, WR
1990	Jeff George, Illinois, QB
1991	Shane Curry, Miami, DE (2)
1992	Steve Emtman, Washington, DT
	Quentin Coryatt, Texas A&M, LB
1993	Sean Dawkins, California, WR
1994	Marshall Faulk, San Diego State, RB
	Trev Alberts, Nebraska, LB
1995	Ellis Johnson, Florida, DT
1996	Marvin Harrison, Syracuse, WR
1997	Tarik Glenn, California, T
1998	Peyton Manning, Tennessee, QB

JACKSONVILLE JAGUARS

Year	Player, College, Position
1995	Tony Boselli, Southern California, T
	James Stewart, Tennessee, RB
1996	Kevin Hardy, Illinois, LB
1997	Renaldo Wynn, Notre Dame, DT
1998	Fred Taylor, Florida, RB
	Donovin Darius, Syracuse, DB

KANSAS CITY CHIEFS

Year	Player, College, Position
1960	Don Meredith, Southern Methodist, QB
1961	E.J. Holub, Texas Tech, C
1962	Ronnie Bull, Baylor, RB
1963	Buck Buchanan, Grambling, DT
	Ed Budde, Michigan State, G
1964	Pete Beathard, Southern California, QB
1965	Gale Sayers, Kansas, RB
1966	Aaron Brown, Minnesota, DE
1967	Gene Trosch, Miami, DE-DT
1968	Mo Moorman, Texas A&M, G
	George Daney, Texas-El Paso, G
1969	Jim Marsalis, Tennessee State, CB
1970	Sid Smith, Southern California, T
1971	Elmo Wright, Houston, WR
1972	Jeff Kinney, Nebraska, RB
1973	Gary Butler, Rice, TE (2)
1974	Woody Green, Arizona State, RB
1975	Elmore Stephens, Kentucky, TE (2)
1976	Rod Walters, Iowa, G
1977	Gary Green, Baylor, DB
1978	Art Still, Kentucky, DE
1979	Mike Bell, Colorado State, DE
	Steve Fuller, Clemson, QB
1980	Brad Budde, Southern California, G
1981	Willie Scott, South Carolina, TE
1982	Anthony Hancock, Tennessee, WR
1983	Todd Blackledge, Penn State, QB
1984	Bill Maas, Pittsburgh, DT
	John Alt, Iowa, T
1985	Ethan Horton, North Carolina, RB
1986	Brian Jozwiak, West Virginia, T
1987	Paul Palmer, Temple, RB
1988	Neil Smith, Nebraska, DE
1989	Derrick Thomas, Alabama, LB
1990	Percy Snow, Michigan State, LB
1991	Harvey Williams, Louisiana State, RB
1992	Dale Carter, Tennessee, DB
1993	Will Shields, Nebraska, G (3)
1994	Greg Hill, Texas A&M, RB
1995	Trezelle Jenkins, Michigan, T
1996	Jerome Woods, Memphis, DB
1997	Tony Gonzalez, California, TE
1998	Victor Riley, Auburn, T

MIAMI DOLPHINS

Year	Player, College, Position
1966	Jim Grabowski, Illinois, RB
	Rick Norton, Kentucky, QB
1967	Bob Griese, Purdue, QB
1968	Larry Csonka, Syracuse, RB
	Doug Crusan, Indiana, T
1969	Bill Stanfill, Georgia, DE
1970	Jim Mandich, Michigan, TE (2)
1971	Otto Stowe, Iowa State, WR (2)
1972	Mike Kadish, Notre Dame, DT
1973	Chuck Bradley, Oregon, C (2)
1974	Donald Reese, Jackson State, DE
1975	Darryl Carlton, Tampa, T
1976	Larry Gordon, Arizona State, LB
	Kim Bokamper, San Jose State, LB
1977	A.J. Duhe, Louisiana State, DT
1978	Guy Benjamin, Stanford, QB (2)
1979	Jon Giesler, Michigan, T
1980	Don McNeal, Alabama, DB
1981	David Overstreet, Oklahoma, RB
1982	Roy Foster, Southern California, G
1983	Dan Marino, Pittsburgh, QB
1984	Jackie Shipp, Oklahoma, LB
1985	Lorenzo Hampton, Florida, RB
1986	John Offerdahl, Western Michigan, LB (2)
1987	John Bosa, Boston College, DE
1988	Eric Kumerow, Ohio State, DE

1989 Sammie Smith, Florida State, RB
Louis Oliver, Florida, DB
1990 Richmond Webb, Texas A&M, T
1991 Randal Hill, Miami, WR
1992 Troy Vincent, Wisconsin, DB
Marco Coleman, Georgia Tech, LB
1993 O.J. McDuffie, Penn State, WR
1994 Tim Bowens, Mississippi, DT
1995 Billy Milner, Houston, T
1996 Daryl Gardener, Baylor, DT
1997 Yatil Green, Miami, WR
1998 John Avery, Mississippi, RB

MINNESOTA VIKINGS

Year	Player, College, Position
1961	Tommy Mason, Tulane, RB
1962	Bill Miller, Miami, WR (3)
1963	Jim Dunaway, Mississippi, T
1964	Carl Eller, Minnesota, DE
1965	Jack Snow, Notre Dame, WR
1966	Jerry Shay, Purdue, DT
1967	Clint Jones, Michigan State, RB
	Gene Washington, Michigan State, WR
	Alan Page, Notre Dame, DT
1968	Ron Yary, Southern California, T
1969	Ed White, California, G (2)
1970	John Ward, Oklahoma State, DT
1971	Leo Hayden, Ohio State, RB
1972	Jeff Siemon, Stanford, LB
1973	Chuck Foreman, Miami, RB
1974	Fred McNeill, UCLA, LB
	Steve Riley, Southern California, T
1975	Mark Mullaney, Colorado State, DE
1976	James White, Oklahoma State, DT
1977	Tommy Kramer, Rice, QB
1978	Randy Holloway, Pittsburgh, DE
1979	Ted Brown, North Carolina State, RB
1980	Doug Martin, Washington, DT
1981	Mardye McDole, Mississippi State, WR (2)
1982	Darrin Nelson, Stanford, RB
1983	Joey Browner, Southern California, DB
1984	Keith Millard, Washington State, DE
1985	Chris Doleman, Pittsburgh, LB
1986	Gerald Robinson, Auburn, DE
1987	D.J. Dozier, Penn State, RB
1988	Randall McDaniel, Arizona State, G
1989	David Braxton, Wake Forest, LB (2)
1990	Mike Jones, Texas A&M, TE (3)
1991	Carlos Jenkins, Michigan State, LB (3)
1992	Robert Harris, Southern University, DE (2)
1993	Robert Smith, Ohio State, RB
1994	DeWayne Washington, N. Carolina St., DB
	Todd Steussie, California, T
1995	Derrick Alexander, Florida State, DE
	Korey Stringer, Ohio State, T
1996	Duane Clemons, California, DE
1997	Dwayne Rudd, Alabama, LB
1998	Randy Moss, Marshall, WR

NEW ENGLAND PATRIOTS

Year	Player, College, Position
1960	Ron Burton, Northwestern, RB
1961	Tommy Mason, Tulane, RB
1962	Gary Collins, Maryland, WR
1963	Art Graham, Boston College, WR
1964	Jack Concannon, Boston College, QB
1965	Jerry Rush, Michigan State, DE
1966	Karl Singer, Purdue, T
1967	John Charles, Purdue, S
1968	Dennis Byrd, North Carolina State, DE
1969	Ron Sellers, Florida State, WR
1970	Phil Olsen, Utah State, DE
1971	Jim Plunkett, Stanford, QB
1972	Tom Reynolds, San Diego State, WR (2)
1973	John Hannah, Alabama, G
	Sam Cunningham, So. California, RB
	Darryl Stingley, Purdue, WR
1974	Steve Corbett, Boston College, G (2)
1975	Russ Francis, Oregon, TE
1976	Mike Haynes, Arizona State, DB
	Pete Brock, Colorado, C
	Tim Fox, Ohio State, DB
1977	Raymond Clayborn, Texas, DB
	Stanley Morgan, Tennessee, WR
1978	Bob Cryder, Alabama, G
1979	Rick Sanford, South Carolina, DB
1980	Roland James, Tennessee, DB
	Vagas Ferguson, Notre Dame, RB
1981	Brian Holloway, Stanford, T
1982	Kenneth Sims, Texas, DT
	Lester Williams, Miami, DT
1983	Tony Eason, Illinois, QB
1984	Irving Fryar, Nebraska, WR
1985	Trevor Matich, Brigham Young, C
1986	Reggie Dupard, Southern Methodist, RB
1987	Bruce Armstrong, Louisville, T
1988	John Stephens, Northwestern St., La., RB
1989	Hart Lee Dykes, Oklahoma State, WR
1990	Chris Singleton, Arizona, LB
	Ray Agnew, North Carolina State, DE
1991	Pat Harlow, Southern California, T
	Leonard Russell, Arizona State, RB
1992	Eugene Chung, Virginia Tech, T
1993	Drew Bledsoe, Washington State, QB
1994	Willie McGinest, Southern California, DE
1995	Ty Law, Michigan, DB
1996	Terry Glenn, Ohio State, WR
1997	Chris Canty, Kansas State, DB
1998	Robert Edwards, Georgia, RB
	Tebucky Jones, Syracuse, DB

NEW ORLEANS SAINTS

Year	Player, College, Position
1967	Les Kelley, Alabama, RB
1968	Kevin Hardy, Notre Dame, DE
1969	John Shinners, Xavier, G
1970	Ken Burrough, Texas Southern, WR
1971	Archie Manning, Mississippi, QB
1972	Royce Smith, Georgia, G
1973	Derland Moore, Oklahoma, DE (2)
1974	Rick Middleton, Ohio State, LB
1975	Larry Burton, Purdue, WR
	Kurt Schumacher, Ohio State, T
1976	Chuck Muncie, California, RB
1977	Joe Campbell, Maryland, DE
1978	Wes Chandler, Florida, WR
1979	Russell Erxleben, Texas, P-K
1980	Stan Brock, Colorado, T
1981	George Rogers, South Carolina, RB
1982	Lindsay Scott, Georgia, WR
1983	Steve Korte, Arkansas, G (2)
1984	James Geathers, Wichita State, DE
1985	Alvin Toles, Tennessee, LB
1986	Jim Dombrowski, Virginia, T
1987	Shawn Knight, Brigham Young, DT
1988	Craig Heyward, Pittsburgh, RB
1989	Wayne Martin, Arkansas, DE
1990	Renaldo Turnbull, West Virginia, DE
1991	Wesley Carroll, Miami, WR (2)
1992	Vaughn Dunbar, Indiana, RB
1993	Willie Roaf, Louisiana Tech, T
	Irv Smith, Notre Dame, TE
1994	Joe Johnson, Louisville, DE
1995	Mark Fields, Washington State, LB
1996	Alex Molden, Oregon, DB
1997	Chris Naeole, Colorado, G
1998	Kyle Turley, San Diego State, T

NEW YORK GIANTS

Year	Player, College, Position
1936	Art Lewis, Ohio U., T
1937	Ed Widseth, Minnesota, T
1938	George Karamatic, Gonzaga, B
1939	Walt Neilson, Arizona, B
1940	Grenville Lansdell, Southern California, B
1941	George Franck, Minnesota, B
1942	Merle Hapes, Mississippi, B
1943	Steve Filipowicz, Fordham, B
1944	Billy Hillenbrand, Indiana, B
1945	Elmer Barbour, Wake Forest, B
1946	George Connor, Notre Dame, T
1947	Vic Schwall, Northwestern, B
1948	Tony Minisi, Pennsylvania, B
1949	Paul Page, Southern Methodist, B
1950	Travis Tidwell, Auburn, B
1951	Kyle Rote, Southern Methodist, B
	Jim Spavital, Oklahoma A&M, B
1952	Frank Gifford, Southern California, B
1953	Bobby Marlow, Alabama, B
1954	Ken Buck, Pacific, C (2)
1955	Joe Heap, Notre Dame, B
1956	Henry Moore, Arkansas, B (2)
1957	Sam DeLuca, South Carolina, T (2)
1958	Phil King, Vanderbilt, B
1959	Lee Grosscup, Utah, B
1960	Lou Cordileone, Clemson, G
1961	Bruce Tarbox, Syracuse, G (2)
1962	Jerry Hillebrand, Colorado, LB
1963	Frank Lasky, Florida, T (2)
1964	Joe Don Looney, Oklahoma, RB
1965	Tucker Frederickson, Auburn, RB
1966	Francis Peay, Missouri, T
1967	Louis Thompson, Alabama, DT (4)
1968	Dick Buzin, Penn State, T (2)
1969	Fred Dryer, San Diego State, DE
1970	Jim Files, Oklahoma, LB
1971	Rocky Thompson, West Texas State, WR
1972	Eldridge Small, Texas A&I, DB
	Larry Jacobson, Nebraska, DE
1973	Brad Van Pelt, Michigan State, LB (2)
1974	John Hicks, Ohio State, G
1975	Al Simpson, Colorado State, T (2)
1976	Troy Archer, Colorado, DE
1977	Gary Jeter, Southern California, DT
1978	Gordon King, Stanford, T
1979	Phil Simms, Morehead State, QB
1980	Mark Haynes, Colorado, DB
1981	Lawrence Taylor, North Carolina, LB
1982	Butch Woolfolk, Michigan, RB
1983	Terry Kinard, Clemson, DB
1984	Carl Banks, Michigan State, LB
	William Roberts, Ohio State, T
1985	George Adams, Kentucky, RB
1986	Eric Dorsey, Notre Dame, DE
1987	Mark Ingram, Michigan State, WR
1988	Eric Moore, Indiana, T
1989	Brian Williams, Minnesota, C-G
1990	Rodney Hampton, Georgia, RB
1991	Jarrod Bunch, Michigan, RB
1992	Derek Brown, Notre Dame, TE
1993	Michael Strahan, Texas Southern, DE (2)
1994	Thomas Lewis, Indiana, WR
1995	Tyrone Wheatley, Michigan, RB
1996	Cedric Jones, Oklahoma, DE
1997	Ike Hilliard, Florida, WR
1998	Shaun Williams, UCLA, DB

NEW YORK JETS

Year	Player, College, Position
1960	George Izo, Notre Dame, QB
1961	Tom Brown, Minnesota, G
1962	Sandy Stephens, Minnesota, QB
1963	Jerry Stovall, Louisiana State, S
1964	Matt Snell, Ohio State, RB
1965	Joe Namath, Alabama, QB
	Tom Nowatzke, Indiana, RB
1966	Bill Yearby, Michigan, DT
1967	Paul Seiler, Notre Dame, T
1968	Lee White, Weber State, RB
1969	Dave Foley, Ohio State, T
1970	Steve Tannen, Florida, CB
1971	John Riggins, Kansas, RB
1972	Jerome Barkum, Jackson State, WR
	Mike Taylor, Michigan, LB
1973	Burgess Owens, Miami, DB
1974	Carl Barzilauskas, Indiana, DT
1975	Anthony Davis, Southern California, RB (2)
1976	Richard Todd, Alabama, QB
1977	Marvin Powell, Southern California, T
1978	Chris Ward, Ohio State, T
1979	Marty Lyons, Alabama, DE
1980	Johnny (Lam) Jones, Texas, WR
1981	Freeman McNeil, UCLA, RB
1982	Bob Crable, Notre Dame, LB
1983	Ken O'Brien, Cal-Davis, QB
1984	Russell Carter, Southern Methodist, DB
	Ron Faurot, Arkansas, DE
1985	Al Toon, Wisconsin, WR

FIRST-ROUND SELECTIONS

1986 Mike Haight, Iowa, T
1987 Roger Vick, Texas A&M, RB
1988 Dave Cadigan, Southern California, T
1989 Jeff Lageman, Virginia, LB
1990 Blair Thomas, Penn State, RB
1991 Browning Nagle, Louisville, QB (2)
1992 Johnny Mitchell, Nebraska, TE
1993 Marvin Jones, Florida State, LB
1994 Aaron Glenn, Texas A&M, DB
1995 Kyle Brady, Penn State, TE
Hugh Douglas, Central State, Ohio, DE
1996 Keyshawn Johnson, Southern California, WR
1997 James Farrior, Virginia, LB
1998 Dorian Boose, Washington State, DE (2)

OAKLAND RAIDERS

Year Player, College, Position

1960 Dale Hackbart, Wisconsin, CB
1961 Joe Rutgens, Illinois, DT
1962 Roman Gabriel, North Carolina State, QB
1963 George Wilson, Alabama, RB (6)
1964 Tony Lorick, Arizona State, RB
1965 Harry Schuh, Memphis State, T
1966 Rodger Bird, Kentucky, S
1967 Gene Upshaw, Texas A&I, G
1968 Eldridge Dickey, Tennessee State, QB
1969 Art Thoms, Syracuse, DT
1970 Raymond Chester, Morgan State, TE
1971 Jack Tatum, Ohio State, S
1972 Mike Siani, Villanova, WR
1973 Ray Guy, Southern Mississippi, P
1974 Henry Lawrence, Florida A&M, T
1975 Neal Colzie, Ohio State, DB
1976 Charles Philyaw, Texas Southern, DT (2)
1977 Mike Davis, Colorado, DB (2)
1978 Dave Browning, Washington, DE (2)
1979 Willie Jones, Florida State, DE (2)
1980 Marc Wilson, Brigham Young, QB
1981 Ted Watts, Texas Tech, DB
Curt Marsh, Washington, T
1982 Marcus Allen, Southern California, RB
1983 Don Mosebar, Southern California, T
1984 Sean Jones, Northeastern, DE (2)
1985 Jessie Hester, Florida State, WR
1986 Bob Buczkowski, Pittsburgh, DE
1987 John Clay, Missouri, T
1988 Tim Brown, Notre Dame, WR
Terry McDaniel, Tennessee, DB
Scott Davis, Illinois, DE
1989 Jeff Francis, Tennessee, QB (6)
1990 Anthony Smith, Arizona, DE
1991 Todd Marinovich, Southern California, QB
1992 Chester McGlockton, Clemson, DE
1993 Patrick Bates, Texas A&M, DB
1994 Rob Fredrickson, Michigan State, LB
1995 Napoleon Kaufman, Washington, RB
1996 Rickey Dudley, Ohio State, TE
1997 Darrell Russell, Southern California, DT
1998 Charles Woodson, Michigan, DB
Mo Collins, Florida, T

PHILADELPHIA EAGLES

Year Player, College, Position

1936 Jay Berwanger, Chicago, B
1937 Sam Francis, Nebraska, B
1938 Jim McDonald, Ohio State, B
1939 Davey O'Brien, Texas Christian, B
1940 George McAfee, Duke, B
1941 Art Jones, Richmond, B (2)
1942 Pete Kmetovic, Stanford, B
1943 Joe Muha, Virginia Military, B
1944 Steve Van Buren, Louisiana State, B
1945 John Yonaker, Notre Dame, E
1946 Leo Riggs, Southern California, B
1947 Neill Armstrong, Oklahoma A&M, E
1948 Clyde (Smackover) Scott, Arkansas, B
1949 Chuck Bednarik, Pennsylvania, C
Frank Tripucka, Notre Dame, B
1950 Harry (Bud) Grant, Minnesota, E
1951 Ebert Van Buren, Louisiana State, B
Chet Mutryn, Xavier, B
1952 Johnny Bright, Drake, B
1953 Al Conway, Army, B (2)
1954 Neil Worden, Notre Dame, B
1955 Dick Bielski, Maryland, B
1956 Bob Pellegrini, Maryland, C
1957 Clarence Peaks, Michigan State, B
1958 Walt Kowalczyk, Michigan State, B
1959 J.D. Smith, Rice, T (2)
1960 Ron Burton, Northwestern, RB
1961 Art Baker, Syracuse, RB
1962 Pete Case, Georgia, G (2)
1963 Ed Budde, Michigan State, G
1964 Bob Brown, Nebraska, T
1965 Ray Rissmiller, Georgia, T (2)
1966 Randy Beisler, Indiana, DE
1967 Harry Jones, Arkansas, RB
1968 Tim Rossovich, Southern California, DE
1969 Leroy Keyes, Purdue, RB
1970 Steve Zabel, Oklahoma, TE
1971 Richard Harris, Grambling, DE
1972 John Reaves, Florida, QB
1973 Jerry Sisemore, Texas, T
Charle Young, Southern California, TE
1974 Mitch Sutton, Kansas, DT (3)
1975 Bill Capraun, Miami, T (7)
1976 Mike Smith, Florida, DE (4)
1977 Skip Sharp, Kansas, DB (5)
1978 Reggie Wilkes, Georgia Tech, LB (3)
1979 Jerry Robinson, UCLA, LB
1980 Roynell Young, Alcorn State, DB
1981 Leonard Mitchell, Houston, DE
1982 Mike Quick, North Carolina State, WR
1983 Michael Haddix, Mississippi State, RB
1984 Kenny Jackson, Penn State, WR
1985 Kevin Allen, Indiana, T
1986 Keith Byars, Ohio State, RB
1987 Jerome Brown, Miami, DT
1988 Keith Jackson, Oklahoma, TE
1989 Jessie Small, Eastern Kentucky, LB (2)
1990 Ben Smith, Georgia, DB
1991 Antone Davis, Tennessee, T
1992 Siran Stacy, Alabama, RB (2)
1993 Lester Holmes, Jackson State, T
Leonard Renfro, Colorado, DT
1994 Bernard Williams, Georgia, T
1995 Mike Mamula, Boston College, DE
1996 Jermane Mayberry, Texas A&M-Kingsville, T
1997 Jon Harris, Virginia, DE
1998 Tra Thomas, Florida State, T

PITTSBURGH STEELERS

Year Player, College, Position

1936 Bill Shakespeare, Notre Dame, B
1937 Mike Basrak, Duquesne, C
1938 Byron (Whizzer) White, Colorado, B
1939 Bill Patterson, Baylor, B (3)
1940 Kay Eakin, Arkansas, B
1941 Chet Gladchuk, Boston College, C (2)
1942 Bill Dudley, Virginia, B
1943 Bill Daley, Minnesota, B
1944 Johnny Podesto, St. Mary's, Calif., B
1945 Paul Duhart, Florida, B
1946 Felix (Doc) Blanchard, Army, B
1947 Hub Bechtol, Texas, E
1948 Dan Edwards, Georgia, E
1949 Bobby Gage, Clemson, B
1950 Lynn Chandnois, Michigan State, B
1951 Butch Avinger, Alabama, B
1952 Ed Modzelewski, Maryland, B
1953 Ted Marchibroda, St. Bonaventure, B
1954 Johnny Lattner, Notre Dame, B
1955 Frank Varrichione, Notre Dame, T
1956 Gary Glick, Colorado A&M, B
Art Davis, Mississippi State, B
1957 Len Dawson, Purdue, B
1958 Larry Krutko, West Virginia, B (2)
1959 Tom Barnett, Purdue, B (8)
1960 Jack Spikes, Texas Christian, RB
1961 Myron Pottios, Notre Dame, LB (2)
1962 Bob Ferguson, Ohio State, RB
1963 Frank Atkinson, Stanford, T (8)
1964 Paul Martha, Pittsburgh, S
1965 Roy Jefferson, Utah, WR (2)
1966 Dick Leftridge, West Virginia, RB
1967 Don Shy, San Diego State, RB (2)
1968 Mike Taylor, Southern California, T
1969 Joe Greene, North Texas State, DT
1970 Terry Bradshaw, Louisiana Tech, QB
1971 Frank Lewis, Grambling, WR
1972 Franco Harris, Penn State, RB
1973 J.T. Thomas, Florida State, DB
1974 Lynn Swann, Southern California, WR
1975 Dave Brown, Michigan, DB
1976 Bennie Cunningham, Clemson, TE
1977 Robin Cole, New Mexico, LB
1978 Ron Johnson, Eastern Michigan, DB
1979 Greg Hawthorne, Baylor, RB
1980 Mark Malone, Arizona State, QB
1981 Keith Gary, Oklahoma, DE
1982 Walter Abercrombie, Baylor, RB
1983 Gabriel Rivera, Texas Tech, DT
1984 Louis Lipps, Southern Mississippi, WR
1985 Darryl Sims, Wisconsin, DE
1986 John Rienstra, Temple, G
1987 Rod Woodson, Purdue, DB
1988 Aaron Jones, Eastern Kentucky, DE
1989 Tim Worley, Georgia, RB
Tom Ricketts, Pittsburgh, T
1990 Eric Green, Liberty, TE
1991 Huey Richardson, Florida, DE
1992 Leon Searcy, Miami, T
1993 Deon Figures, Colorado, DB
1994 Charles Johnson, Colorado, WR
1995 Mark Bruener, Washington, TE
1996 Jamain Stephens, North Carolina A&T, T
1997 Chad Scott, Maryland, DB
1998 Alan Faneca, Louisiana State, G

ST. LOUIS RAMS

Year Player, College, Position

1937 Johnny Drake, Purdue, B
1938 Corbett Davis, Indiana, B
1939 Parker Hall, Mississippi, B
1940 Ollie Cordill, Rice, B
1941 Rudy Mucha, Washington, C
1942 Jack Wilson, Baylor, B
1943 Mike Holovak, Boston College, B
1944 Tony Butkovich, Illinois, B
1945 Elroy (Crazylegs) Hirsch, Wisconsin, B
1946 Emil Sitko, Notre Dame, B
1947 Herman Wedemeyer, St. Mary's, Calif., B
1948 Tom Keane, West Virginia, B (2)
1949 Bobby Thomason, Virginia Military, B
1950 Ralph Pasquariello, Villanova, B
Stan West, Oklahoma, G
1951 Bud McFadin, Texas, G
1952 Bill Wade, Vanderbilt, QB
Bob Carey, Michigan State, E
1953 Donn Moomaw, UCLA, C
Ed Barker, Washington State, E
1954 Ed Beatty, Cincinnati, C
1955 Larry Morris, Georgia Tech, C
1956 Joe Marconi, West Virginia, B
Charles Horton, Vanderbilt, B
1957 Jon Arnett, Southern California, B
Del Shofner, Baylor, E
1958 Lou Michaels, Kentucky, T
Jim Phillips, Auburn, E
1959 Dick Bass, Pacific, B
Paul Dickson, Baylor, T
1960 Billy Cannon, Louisiana State, RB
1961 Marlin McKeever, Southern California, E-LB
1962 Roman Gabriel, North Carolina State, QB
Merlin Olsen, Utah State, DT
1963 Terry Baker, Oregon State, QB
Rufus Guthrie, Georgia Tech, G
1964 Bill Munson, Utah State, QB
1965 Clancy Williams, Washington State, CB
1966 Tom Mack, Michigan, G
1967 Willie Ellison, Texas Southern, RB (2)
1968 Gary Beban, UCLA, QB (2)
1969 Larry Smith, Florida, RB
Jim Seymour, Notre Dame, WR
Bob Klein, Southern California, TE
1970 Jack Reynolds, Tennessee, LB
1971 Isiah Robertson, Southern, LB
Jack Youngblood, Florida, DE
1972 Jim Bertelsen, Texas, RB (2)

1973 Cullen Bryant, Colorado, DB (2)
1974 John Cappelletti, Penn State, RB
1975 Mike Fanning, Notre Dame, DT
Dennis Harrah, Miami, T
Doug France, Ohio State, T
1976 Kevin McLain, Colorado State, LB
1977 Bob Brudzinski, Ohio State, LB
1978 Elvis Peacock, Oklahoma, RB
1979 George Andrews, Nebraska, LB
Kent Hill, Georgia Tech, T
1980 Johnnie Johnson, Texas, DB
1981 Mel Owens, Michigan, LB
1982 Barry Redden, Richmond, RB
1983 Eric Dickerson, Southern Methodist, RB
1984 Hal Stephens, East Carolina, DE (5)
1985 Jerry Gray, Texas, DB
1986 Mike Schad, Queen's University, Canada, T
1987 Donald Evans, Winston-Salem, DE (2)
1988 Gaston Green, UCLA, RB
Aaron Cox, Arizona State, WR
1989 Bill Hawkins, Miami, DE
Cleveland Gary, Miami, RB
1990 Bern Brostek, Washington, C
1991 Todd Lyght, Notre Dame, DB
1992 Sean Gilbert, Pittsburgh, DE
1993 Jerome Bettis, Notre Dame, RB
1994 Wayne Gandy, Auburn, T
1995 Kevin Carter, Florida, DE
1996 Lawrence Phillips, Nebraska, RB
Eddie Kennison, Louisiana State, WR
1997 Orlando Pace, Ohio State, T
1998 Grant Wistrom, Nebraska, DE

SAN DIEGO CHARGERS

Year	Player, College, Position
1960	Monty Stickles, Notre Dame, E
1961	Earl Faison, Indiana, DE
1962	Bob Ferguson, Ohio State, RB
1963	Walt Sweeney, Syracuse, G
1964	Ted Davis, Georgia Tech, LB
1965	Steve DeLong, Tennessee, DE
1966	Don Davis, Cal State-Los Angeles, DT
1967	Ron Billingsley, Wyoming, DE
1968	Russ Washington, Missouri, DT
	Jimmy Hill, Texas A&I, DB
1969	Marty Domres, Columbia, QB
	Bob Babich, Miami, Ohio, LB
1970	Walker Gillette, Richmond, WR
1971	Leon Burns, Long Beach State, RB
1972	Pete Lazetich, Stanford, DE (2)
1973	Johnny Rodgers, Nebraska, WR
1974	Bo Matthews, Colorado, RB
	Don Goode, Kansas, LB
1975	Gary Johnson, Grambling, DT
	Mike Williams, Louisiana State, DB
1976	Joe Washington, Oklahoma, RB
1977	Bob Rush, Memphis State, C
1978	John Jefferson, Arizona State, WR
1979	Kellen Winslow, Missouri, TE
1980	Ed Luther, San Jose State, QB (4)
1981	James Brooks, Auburn, RB
1982	Hollis Hall, Clemson, DB (7)
1983	Billy Ray Smith, Arkansas, LB
	Gary Anderson, Arkansas, WR
	Gill Byrd, San Jose State, DB
1984	Mossy Cade, Texas, DB
1985	Jim Lachey, Ohio State, G
1986	Leslie O'Neal, Oklahoma State, DE
	James FitzPatrick, Southern California, T
1987	Rod Bernstine, Texas A&M, TE
1988	Anthony Miller, Tennessee, WR
1989	Burt Grossman, Pittsburgh, DE
1990	Junior Seau, Southern California, LB
1991	Stanley Richard, Texas, DB
1992	Chris Mims, Tennessee, DE
1993	Darrien Gordon, Stanford, DB
1994	Isaac Davis, Arkansas, G (2)
1995	Terrance Shaw, Stephen F. Austin, DB (2)
1996	Bryan Still, Virginia Tech, WR (2)
1997	Freddie Jones, North Carolina, TE (2)
1998	Ryan Leaf, Washington State, QB

SAN FRANCISCO 49ERS

Year	Player, College, Position
1950	Leo Nomellini, Minnesota, T
1951	Y.A. Tittle, Louisiana State, B
1952	Hugh McElhenny, Washington, B
1953	Harry Babcock, Georgia, E
	Tom Stolhandske, Texas, E
1954	Bernie Faloney, Maryland, B
1955	Dickie Moegle, Rice, B
1956	Earl Morrall, Michigan State, B
1957	John Brodie, Stanford, B
1958	Jim Pace, Michigan, B
	Charlie Krueger, Texas A&M, T
1959	Dave Baker, Oklahoma, B
	Dan James, Ohio State, C
1960	Monty Stickles, Notre Dame, E
1961	Jimmy Johnson, UCLA, CB
	Bernie Casey, Bowling Green, WR
	Bill Kilmer, UCLA, QB
1962	Lance Alworth, Arkansas, WR
1963	Kermit Alexander, UCLA, CB
1964	Dave Parks, Texas Tech, WR
1965	Ken Willard, North Carolina, RB
	George Donnelly, Illinois, DB
1966	Stan Hindman, Mississippi, DE
1967	Steve Spurrier, Florida, QB
	Cas Banaszek, Northwestern, T
1968	Forrest Blue, Auburn, C
1969	Ted Kwalick, Penn State, TE
	Gene Washington, Stanford, WR
1970	Cedrick Hardman, North Texas State, DE
	Bruce Taylor, Boston U., DB
1971	Tim Anderson, Ohio State, DB
1972	Terry Beasley, Auburn, WR
1973	Mike Holmes, Texas Southern, DB
1974	Wilbur Jackson, Alabama, RB
	Bill Sandifer, UCLA, DT
1975	Jimmy Webb, Mississippi State, DT
1976	Randy Cross, UCLA, C (2)
1977	Elmo Boyd, Eastern Kentucky, WR (3)
1978	Ken MacAfee, Notre Dame, TE
	Dan Bunz, Cal State-Long Beach, LB
1979	James Owens, UCLA, WR (2)
1980	Earl Cooper, Rice, RB
	Jim Stuckey, Clemson, DT
1981	Ronnie Lott, Southern California, DB
1982	Bubba Paris, Michigan, T (2)
1983	Roger Craig, Nebraska, RB (2)
1984	Todd Shell, Brigham Young, LB
1985	Jerry Rice, Mississippi Valley State, WR
1986	Larry Roberts, Alabama, DE (2)
1987	Harris Barton, North Carolina, T
	Terrence Flagler, Clemson, RB
1988	Danny Stubbs, Miami, DE (2)
1989	Keith DeLong, Tennessee, LB
1990	Dexter Carter, Florida State, RB
1991	Ted Washington, Louisville, DT
1992	Dana Hall, Washington, DB
1993	Dana Stubblefield, Kansas, DT
	Todd Kelly, Tennessee, DE
1994	Bryant Young, Notre Dame, DT
	William Floyd, Florida State, RB
1995	J.J. Stokes, UCLA, WR
1996	Israel Ifeanyi, Southern California, DE (2)
1997	Jim Druckenmiller, Virginia Tech, QB
1998	R.W. McQuarters, Oklahoma State, DB

SEATTLE SEAHAWKS

Year	Player, College, Position
1976	Steve Niehaus, Notre Dame, DT
1977	Steve August, Tulsa, G
1978	Keith Simpson, Memphis State, DB
1979	Manu Tuiasosopo, UCLA, DT
1980	Jacob Green, Texas A&M, DE
1981	Ken Easley, UCLA, DB
1982	Jeff Bryant, Clemson, DE
1983	Curt Warner, Penn State, RB
1984	Terry Taylor, Southern Illinois, DB
1985	Owen Gill, Iowa, RB (2)
1986	John L. Williams, Florida, RB
1987	Tony Woods, Pittsburgh, LB
1988	Brian Blades, Miami, WR (2)
1989	Andy Heck, Notre Dame, T
1990	Cortez Kennedy, Miami, DT
1991	Dan McGwire, San Diego State, QB
1992	Ray Roberts, Virginia, T
1993	Rick Mirer, Notre Dame, QB
1994	Sam Adams, Texas A&M, DT
1995	Joey Galloway, Ohio State, WR
1996	Pete Kendall, Boston College, T
1997	Shawn Springs, Ohio State, DB
	Walter Jones, Florida State, T
1998	Anthony Simmons, Clemson, LB

TAMPA BAY BUCCANEERS

Year	Player, College, Position
1976	Lee Roy Selmon, Oklahoma, DT
1977	Ricky Bell, Southern California, RB
1978	Doug Williams, Grambling, QB
1979	Greg Roberts, Oklahoma, G (2)
1980	Ray Snell, Wisconsin, G
1981	Hugh Green, Pittsburgh, LB
1982	Sean Farrell, Penn State, G
1983	Randy Grimes, Baylor, C (2)
1984	Keith Browner, Southern California, LB (2)
1985	Ron Holmes, Washington, DE
1986	Bo Jackson, Auburn, RB
	Roderick Jones, Southern Methodist, DB
1987	Vinny Testaverde, Miami, QB
1988	Paul Gruber, Wisconsin, T
1989	Broderick Thomas, Nebraska, LB
1990	Keith McCants, Alabama, LB
1991	Charles McRae, Tennessee, T
1992	Courtney Hawkins, Michigan State, WR (2)
1993	Eric Curry, Alabama, DE
1994	Trent Dilfer, Fresno State, QB
1995	Warren Sapp, Miami, DT
	Derrick Brooks, Florida State, LB
1996	Regan Upshaw, California, DE
	Marcus Jones, North Carolina, DT
1997	Warrick Dunn, Florida State, RB
	Reidel Anthony, Florida, WR
1998	Jacquez Green, Florida, WR (2)

TENNESSEE OILERS

Year	Player, College, Position
1960	Billy Cannon, Louisiana State, RB
1961	Mike Ditka, Pittsburgh, E
1962	Ray Jacobs, Howard Payne, DT
1963	Danny Brabham, Arkansas, LB
1964	Scott Appleton, Texas, DT
1965	Lawrence Elkins, Baylor, WR
1966	Tommy Nobis, Texas, LB
1967	George Webster, Michigan State, LB
	Tom Regner, Notre Dame, G
1968	Mac Haik, Mississippi, WR (2)
1969	Ron Pritchard, Arizona State, LB
1970	Doug Wilkerson, N. Carolina Central, G
1971	Dan Pastorini, Santa Clara, QB
1972	Greg Sampson, Stanford, DE
1973	John Matuszak, Tampa, DE
	George Amundson, Iowa State, RB
1974	Steve Manstedt, Nebraska, LB (4)
1975	Robert Brazile, Jackson State, LB
	Don Hardeman, Texas A&I, RB
1976	Mike Barber, Louisiana Tech, TE (2)
1977	Morris Towns, Missouri, T
1978	Earl Campbell, Texas, RB
1979	Mike Stensrud, Iowa State, DE (2)
1980	Angelo Fields, Michigan State, T (2)
1981	Michael Holston, Morgan State, WR (3)
1982	Mike Munchak, Penn State, G
1983	Bruce Matthews, Southern California, T
1984	Dean Steinkuhler, Nebraska, T
1985	Ray Childress, Texas A&M, DE
	Richard Johnson, Wisconsin, DB
1986	Jim Everett, Purdue, QB
1987	Alonzo Highsmith, Miami, RB
	Haywood Jeffires, North Carolina St., WR
1988	Lorenzo White, Michigan State, RB
1989	David Williams, Florida, T
1990	Lamar Lathon, Houston, LB
1991	Mike Dumas, Indiana, DB (2)
1992	Eddie Robinson, Alabama State, LB (2)
1993	Brad Hopkins, Illinois, T
1994	Henry Ford, Arkansas, DE

FIRST-ROUND SELECTIONS

1995 Steve McNair, Alcorn State, QB
1996 Eddie George, Ohio State, RB
1997 Kenny Holmes, Miami, DE
1998 Kevin Dyson, Utah, WR

WASHINGTON REDSKINS

Year	Player, College, Position
1936	Riley Smith, Alabama, B
1937	Sammy Baugh, Texas Christian, B
1938	Andy Farkas, Detroit, B
1939	I.B. Hale, Texas Christian, T
1940	Ed Boell, New York U., B
1941	Forest Evashevski, Michigan, B
1942	Orban (Spec) Sanders, Texas, B
1943	Jack Jenkins, Missouri, B
1944	Mike Micka, Colgate, B
1945	Jim Hardy, Southern California, B
1946	Casl Rossi, UCLA, B*
1947	Casl Rossi, UCLA, B
1948	Harry Gilmer, Alabama, B
	Lowell Tew, Alabama, B
1949	Rob Goode, Texas A&M, B
1950	George Thomas, Oklahoma, B
1951	Leon Heath, Oklahoma, B
1952	Larry Isbell, Baylor, B
1953	Jack Scarbath, Maryland, B
1954	Steve Meilinger, Kentucky, E
1955	Ralph Guglielmi, Notre Dame, B
1956	Ed Vereb, Maryland, B
1957	Don Bosseler, Miami, B
1958	Mike Sommer, George Washington, B (2)
1959	Don Allard, Boston College, B
1960	Richie Lucas, Penn State, QB
1961	Norman Snead, Wake Forest, QB
	Joe Rutgens, Illinois, DT
1962	Ernie Davis, Syracuse, RB
1963	Pat Richter, Wisconsin, TE
1964	Charley Taylor, Arizona State, RB-WR
1965	Bob Breitenstein, Tulsa, T (2)
1966	Charlie Gogolak, Princeton, K
1967	Ray McDonald, Idaho, RB
1968	Jim Smith, Oregon, DB
1969	Eugene Epps, Texas-El Paso, DB (2)
1970	Bill Bundige, Colorado, DT (2)
1971	Cotton Speyrer, Texas, WR (2)
1972	Moses Denson, Maryland State, RB (8)
1973	Charles Cantrell, Lamar, G (5)
1974	Jon Keyworth, Colorado, TE (6)
1975	Mike Thomas, Nevada-Las Vegas, RB (6)
1976	Mike Hughes, Baylor, G (5)
1977	Duncan McColl, Stanford, DE (4)
1978	Tony Green, Florida, RB (6)
1979	Don Warren, San Diego State, TE (4)
1980	Art Monk, Syracuse, WR
1981	Mark May, Pittsburgh, T
1982	Vernon Dean, San Diego State, DB (2)
1983	Darrell Green, Texas A&I, DB
1984	Bob Slater, Oklahoma, DT (2)
1985	Tory Nixon, San Diego State, DB (2)
1986	Markus Koch, Boise State, DE (2)
1987	Brian Davis, Nebraska, DB (2)
1988	Chip Lohmiller, Minnesota, K (2)
1989	Tracy Rocker, Auburn, DT (3)
1990	Andre Collins, Penn State, LB (2)
1991	Bobby Wilson, Michigan State, DT
1992	Desmond Howard, Michigan, WR
1993	Tom Carter, Notre Dame, DB
1994	Heath Shuler, Tennessee, QB
1995	Michael Westbrook, Colorado, WR
1996	Andre Johnson, Penn State, T
1997	Kenard Lang, Miami, DE
1998	Stephen Alexander, Oklahoma, TE (2)

**Choice lost due to ineligibility*

ASSOCIATED PRESS NFL MOST VALUABLE PLAYERS

NFL MOST VALUABLE PLAYERS NAMED BY *ASSOCIATED PRESS* IN BALLOTING BY A NATIONWIDE PANEL OF MEDIA:

YEAR	PLAYER	POS.	TEAM	ACCOMPLISHMENTS
1957	Jim Brown	RB	Cleveland Browns	Rushed for league-leading 942 yards and added 9 TDs as a rookie.
1958	Gino Marchetti	DE	Baltimore Colts	Leader of defense that permitted league-low 1,291 rushing yards and division-low 203 points.
1959	Charley Conerly	QB	New York Giants	Passed for 14 TDs vs. 4 interceptions. Led offense to division-leading 284 points.
1960	Norm Van Brocklin	QB	Philadelphia Eagles	Guided Eagles to first division title since 1949. Passed for 2,471 yards and 24 TDs.
	Joe Schmidt	LB	Detroit Lions	Team went 7-2 after 0-3 start when he returned from injury. Scored 2 defensive TDs.
1961	Paul Hornung	RB	Green Bay Packers	Led league in scoring for second straight season with 146 points (10 TD, 15 FG, 41 PAT).
1962	Jim Taylor	RB	Green Bay Packers	League rushing champion with 1,474 yards. Scored then all-time record 19 touchdowns.
1963	Y.A. Tittle	QB	New York Giants	Set then all-time season record with 36 TD passes. Guided league's top offense (5,024 yards).
1964	Johnny Unitas	QB	Baltimore Colts	Guided Colts to NFL's best record (12-2) and league's top offensive attack (4,779 yards).
1965	Jim Brown	RB	Cleveland Browns	Leader of NFL's top rushing attack. Led league with 1,544 yards, added 21 total TDs.
1966	Bart Starr	QB	Green Bay Packers	Passed for 14 touchdowns vs. 3 interceptions. Led Packers to league-best 12-2 record.
1967	Johnny Unitas	QB	Baltimore Colts	Passed for 3,428 yards and 20 touchdowns. Led Colts to 11-1-2 record.
1968	Earl Morrall	QB	Baltimore Colts	Guided Colts to NFL-best 13-1 record. Led league with 26 touchdown passes.
1969	Roman Gabriel	QB	Los Angeles Rams	Led NFL with 24 touchdown passes. Guided Rams to 11-3 record.
1970	John Brodie	QB	San Francisco 49ers	Took 49ers to first-ever division title. Threw NFL-best 24 TD passes.
1971	Alan Page	DT	Minnesota Vikings	Led defense that allowed NFL-low 139 points. Vikings won fourth straight NFC Central title.
1972	Larry Brown	RB	Washington Redskins	Led conference with 1,216 rushing yards. Redskins had NFC-best 11-3 record.
1973	O.J. Simpson	RB	Buffalo Bills	Rushed for then all-time record 2,003 yards, including three 200-yard performances.
1974	Ken Stabler	QB	Oakland Raiders	Led league with 26 touchdown passes vs. 12 interceptions. Raiders had NFL-best 12-2 record.
1975	Fran Tarkenton	QB	Minnesota Vikings	Tied for league-best 12-2 record. Led NFC with 91.7 passer rating.
1976	Bert Jones	QB	Baltimore Colts	Threw 24 touchdowns vs. 9 interceptions for 102.5 passer rating.
1977	Walter Payton	RB	Chicago Bears	Rushed for league-leading 1,852 yards and 16 total touchdowns.
1978	Terry Bradshaw	QB	Pittsburgh Steelers	Led Steelers to league-leading 14-2 mark. Set team record with 28 TD passes.
1979	Earl Campbell	RB	Houston Oilers	Led league with 1,697 rushing yards and 19 touchdowns.
1980	Brian Sipe	QB	Cleveland Browns	NFL-best 91.4 passer rating. Set Browns' records with 30 TD passes and 4,132 yards.
1981	Ken Anderson	QB	Cincinnati Bengals	Led Bengals to first division title since 1973. NFL-high 98.5 passer rating.
1982	Mark Moseley	K	Washington Redskins	Converted 20 of 21 FGs. Set then consecutive field-goal record at 23 (including last three in '81).
1983	Joe Theismann	QB	Washington Redskins	Leader of offense that scored NFL record 541 points. Redskins had NFL-best 14-2 record.
1984	Dan Marino	QB	Miami Dolphins	Set NFL records with 5,084 yards and 48 TD passes. Led Dolphins to AFC-best 14-2 mark.
1985	Marcus Allen	RB	Los Angeles Raiders	Rushed for league-leading 1,759 yards. Tied for AFC lead with 11 rushing touchdowns.
1986	Lawrence Taylor	LB	New York Giants	Recorded league-high 20.5 sacks, and led Giants' second-ranked defense (297.3).
1987	John Elway	QB	Denver Broncos	In 12 games, passed for 19 TDs and 3,198 yards, including four 300-yard games.
1988	Boomer Esiason	QB	Cincinnati Bengals	Led NFL with 97.4 passer rating. Tied for AFC lead with 28 TD passes.
1989	Joe Montana	QB	San Francisco 49ers	Set then NFL record with 112.4 passer rating, including 70.2 completion percentage.
1990	Joe Montana	QB	San Francisco 49ers	Led 49ers to league-best 14-2 record. Completed NFC-high 61.7 percent of passes.
1991	Thurman Thomas	RB	Buffalo Bills	Recorded league-high 2,038 yards from scrimmage (1,407 rushing, 631 receiving).
1992	Steve Young	QB	San Francisco 49ers	NFL's top passer with 107.0 rating. Led 49ers to league-best 14-2 record.
1993	Emmitt Smith	RB	Dallas Cowboys	Led league in rushing (1,486 yards) for third straight year despite missing first two games.
1994	Steve Young	QB	San Francisco 49ers	Compiled NFL all-time best 112.8 passer rating. Completed more than 70 percent of his passes.
1995	Brett Favre	QB	Green Bay Packers	Led league with 38 touchdown passes and NFC with 99.5 passer rating.
1996	Brett Favre	QB	Green Bay Packers	Led Packers to top conference record (13-3). Threw NFL-best 39 TD passes.
1997	Brett Favre	QB	Green Bay Packers	Led league with 35 touchdown passes. Led NFC with 3,867 passing yards
	Barry Sanders	RB	Detroit Lions	Rushed for all-time second-best 2,053 yards, including record 14 straight 100-yard games.

Total *Associated Press* NFL MVPs: 43
Two-time Winners: Jim Brown, Brett Favre (3), Joe Montana, Johnny Unitas, Steve Young

ASSOCIATED PRESS NFL MVP BY POSITION

Quarterback:	26	**Defensive End:**	1
Running Back:	12	**Defensive Tackle:**	1
Linebacker:	2	**Kicker:**	1

ASSOCIATED PRESS MVPs WHO WON SUPER BOWL/NFL CHAMPIONSHIP IN SAME SEASON: 12

1958	Gino Marchetti	Baltimore Colts
1960	Norm Van Brocklin	Philadelphia Eagles
1961	Paul Hornung	Green Bay Packers
1962	Jim Taylor	Green Bay Packers
1966	Bart Starr	Green Bay Packers
1978	Terry Bradshaw	Pittsburgh Steelers
1982	Mark Moseley	Washington Redskins
1986	Lawrence Taylor	New York Giants
1989	Joe Montana	San Francisco 49ers
1993	Emmitt Smith	Dallas Cowboys
1994	Steve Young	San Francisco 49ers
1996	Brett Favre	Green Bay Packers

ASSOCIATED PRESS MVPs BY TEAM

6	Green Bay Packers
5	Baltimore Colts San Francisco 49ers
3	Cleveland Browns New York Giants Washington Redskins
2	Buffalo Bills Cincinnati Bengals Detroit Lions Minnesota Vikings Oakland/Los Angeles Raiders
1	Chicago Bears Dallas Cowboys Denver Broncos Houston Oilers Los Angeles Rams Miami Dolphins Philadelphia Eagles Pittsburgh Steelers

MILLER LITE PLAYERS OF THE YEAR

YEAR	PLAYER	POS.	TEAM
1989	Joe Montana	QB	San Francisco 49ers
1990	Joe Montana	QB	San Francisco 49ers
1991	Thurman Thomas	RB	Buffalo Bills
1992	Steve Young	QB	San Francisco 49ers
1993	Emmitt Smith	RB	Dallas Cowboys
1994	Steve Young	QB	San Francisco 49ers
1995	Brett Favre	QB	Green Bay Packers
1996	Brett Favre	QB	Green Bay Packers
1997	Barry Sanders	RB	Detroit Lions

ALL-TIME NFL TEAMS

75TH ANNIVERSARY ALL-TIME TEAM

Chosen by a selection committee of media and league personnel in 1994.

Position	Name	Team(s)	Ht.	Wt.	College
OFFENSE					
QB	Sammy Baugh	Washington Redskins (1937-52)	6-2	180	Texas Christian
QB	Otto Graham	Cleveland Browns (1946-55)	6-1	195	Northwestern
QB	Joe Montana	San Francisco 49ers (1979-92), Kansas City Chiefs (1993-94)	6-2	195	Notre Dame
QB	Johnny Unitas	Baltimore Colts (1956-72), San Diego Chargers (1973)	6-1	195	Louisville
RB	Jim Brown	Cleveland Browns (1957-65)	6-2	232	Syracuse
RB	Marion Motley	Cleveland Browns (1946-53), Pittsburgh Steelers (1955)	6-1	238	Nevada-Reno
RB	Bronko Nagurski	Chicago Bears (1930-37, 1943)	6-2	225	Minnesota
RB	Walter Payton	Chicago Bears (1975-87)	5-10	202	Jackson State
RB	Gale Sayers	Chicago Bears (1965-71)	6-0	200	Kansas
RB	O.J. Simpson	Buffalo Bills (1969-77), San Francisco 49ers (1978-79)	6-1	212	Southern California
RB	Steve Van Buren	Philadelphia Eagles (1944-51)	6-1	200	Louisiana State
WR	Lance Alworth	San Diego Chargers (1962-70), Dallas Cowboys (1971-72)	6-0	184	Arkansas
WR	Raymond Berry	Baltimore Colts (1955-67)	6-2	187	Southern Methodist
WR	Don Hutson	Green Bay Packers (1935-45)	6-1	180	Alabama
WR	Jerry Rice	San Francisco 49ers (1985-present)	6-2	200	Miss. Valley State
TE	Mike Ditka	Chicago Bears (1961-66), Philadelphia Eagles (1967-68), Dallas Cowboys (1969-72)	6-3	225	Pittsburgh
TE	Kellen Winslow	San Diego Chargers (1979-87)	6-5	250	Missouri
T	Roosevelt Brown	New York Giants (1953-65)	6-3	255	Morgan State
T	Forrest Gregg	Green Bay Packers (1956, 1958-70)	6-4	250	Southern Methodist
T	Anthony Muñoz	Cincinnati Bengals (1980-92)	6-6	285	Southern California
G	John Hannah	New England Patriots (1973-85)	6-3	265	Alabama
G	Jim Parker	Baltimore Colts (1957-67)	6-3	273	Ohio State
G	Gene Upshaw	Oakland Raiders (1967-81)	6-5	255	Texas A&I
C	Mel Hein	New York Giants (1931-45)	6-2	225	Washington State
C	Mike Webster	Pittsburgh Steelers (1974-88), Kansas City Chiefs (1989-90)	6-2	250	Wisconsin
DEFENSE					
DE	David (Deacon) Jones	Los Angeles Rams (1961-71), San Diego Chargers (1972-73), Washington Redskins (1974)	6-5	250	Miss. Vocational
DE	Gino Marchetti	Dallas Texans (1952), Baltimore Colts (1953-64,1966)	6-4	245	San Francisco
DE	Reggie White	Philadelphia Eagles (1985-95), Green Bay Packers (1993-present)	6-5	290	Tennessee
DT	Joe Greene	Pittsburgh Steelers (1969-81)	6-4	260	North Texas State
DT	Bob Lilly	Dallas Cowboys (1961-74)	6-5	260	Texas Christian
DT	Merlin Olsen	Los Angeles Rams (1962-76)	6-5	270	Utah State
LB	Dick Butkus	Chicago Bears (1965-73)	6-3	245	Illinois
LB	Jack Ham	Pittsburgh Steelers (1971-82)	6-1	225	Penn State
LB	Ted Hendricks	Baltimore Colts (1969-73), Green Bay Packers (1974), Oakland/L.A. Raiders (1975-83)	6-7	235	Miami
LB	Jack Lambert	Pittsburgh Steelers (1974-84)	6-4	220	Kent State
LB	Willie Lanier	Kansas City Chiefs (1967-77)	6-1	245	Morgan State
LB	Ray Nitschke	Green Bay Packers (1958-72)	6-3	235	Illinois
LB	Lawrence Taylor	New York Giants (1981-93)	6-3	243	North Carolina
CB	Mel Blount	Pittsburgh Steelers (1970-83)	6-3	205	Southern
CB	Mike Haynes	New England Patriots (1976-82), Los Angeles Raiders (1983-89)	6-2	190	Arizona State
CB	Dick (Night Train) Lane	Los Angeles Rams (1952-53), Chicago Cardinals (1954-59), Detroit Lions (1960-65)	6-2	210	Scottsbluff JC
CB	Rod Woodson	Pittsburgh Steelers (1987-96), San Francisco 49ers (1997)	6-0	200	Purdue
S	Ken Houston	Houston Oilers (1967-72), Washington Redskins (1973-80)	6-3	198	Prairie View A&M
S	Ronnie Lott	San Francisco 49ers (1981-90), Los Angeles Raiders (1991-92), New York Jets (1993-94)	6-0	200	Southern California
S	Larry Wilson	St. Louis Cardinals (1960-72)	6-0	190	Utah
SPECIAL TEAMS					
P	Ray Guy	Oakland/L.A. Raiders (1973-86)	6-3	190	Southern Miss.
K	Jan Stenerud	Kansas City Chiefs (1967-79), Green Bay Packers (1980-83), Minnesota Vikings (1984-85)	6-2	190	Montana State
PR	Billy (White Shoes) Johnson	Houston Oilers (1974-80), Atlanta Falcons (1982-87), Washington Redskins (1988)	5-9	170	Widener
KR	Gale Sayers	Chicago Bears (1965-71)	6-0	200	Kansas

75TH ANNIVERSARY ALL-TWO-WAY TEAM

Positions	
Quarterback, Defensive Halfback, Punter	Sammy Baugh
Center, Linebacker	Chuck Bednarik
Quarterback, Defensive Halfback, Punter	Earl (Dutch) Clark
Tackle, Defensive Tackle	George Connor
Guard, Defensive Tackle	Danny Fortmann
Center, Defensive Tackle	Mel Hein
Tackle, Defensive Tackle, Punter	Wilbur (Pete) Henry
Back, Defensive Halfback	Bill Hewitt
Fullback, Linebacker, Kicker	Clarke Hinkle
Tackle, Defensive Tackle	Cal Hubbard
End, Defensive Halfback	Don Hutson
Back, Defensive Back	George McAfee
Fullback, Linebacker	Marion Motley
Guard-Tackle, Defensive Tackle	George Musso
Fullback, Linebacker	Bronko Nagurski
Halfback, Defensive Halfback	Ernie Nevers
End, Defensive Back	Pete Pihos
Tackle, Defensive Tackle	Joe Stydahar
Running Back, Defensive Back	Steve Van Buren

50TH ANNIVERSARY TEAM

Chosen by the Hall of Fame Selection Committee in 1969.

Offense

Split End	Don Hutson
Tight End	John Mackey
Tackle	Cal Hubbard
Guard	Jerry Kramer
Center	Chuck Bednarik
Flanker	Elroy Hirsch
Quarterback	Johnny Unitas
Halfback	Jim Thorpe
Halfback	Gale Sayers
Fullback	Jim Brown
Kicker	Lou Groza

Defense

End	Gino Marchetti
Tackle	Leo Nomellini
Linebacker	Ray Nitschke
Cornerback	Dick (Night Train) Lane
Safety	Emlen Tunnell

ALL-TIME AFL TEAM

Chosen by 1969 AFL Hall of Fame Selection Committee members.

Offense

Flanker	Lance Alworth
End	Don Maynard
Tight End	Fred Arbanas
Tackle	Ron Mix
Tackle	Jim Tyrer
Guard	Ed Budde
Guard	Billy Shaw
Center	Jim Otto
Quarterback	Joe Namath
Running Back	Clemon Daniels
Running Back	Paul Lowe

Defense

End	Jerry Mays
End	Gerry Philbin
Tackle	Houston Antwine
Tackle	Tom Sestak
Linebacker	Bobby Bell
Linebacker	George Webster
Linebacker	Nick Buoniconti
Cornerback	Willie Brown
Cornerback	Dave Grayson
Safety	Johnny Robinson
Safety	George Saimes

Special Teams

Kicker	George Blanda
Punter	Jerrel Wilson

SUPER BOWL SILVER ANNIVERSARY TEAM

Chosen by the fans prior to Super Bowl XXV in 1990.

Head Coach Vince Lombardi

Offense

Quarterback	Joe Montana
Running Back	Franco Harris
Running Back	Larry Csonka
Wide Receiver	Lynn Swann
Wide Receiver	Jerry Rice
Tight End	Dave Casper
Tackle	Art Shell
Tackle	Forrest Gregg
Guard	Gene Upshaw
Guard	Jerry Kramer
Center	Mike Webster

Defense

Defensive End	L.C. Greenwood
Defensive End	Ed (Too Tall) Jones
Defensive Tackle	Joe Greene
Defensive Tackle	Randy White
Inside Linebacker	Jack Lambert
Inside Linebacker	Mike Singletary
Outside Linebacker	Jack Ham
Outside Linebacker	Ted Hendricks
Cornerback	Ronnie Lott
Cornerback	Mel Blount
Safety	Donnie Shell
Safety	Willie Wood

Special Teams

Punter	Ray Guy
Kicker	Jan Stenerud
Kick Returner	John Taylor

ALL-TIME NFL TEAMS

All-Decade teams chosen by the Pro Football Hall of Fame Board of Selectors.

1920's ALL-DECADE TEAM

Back	Paddy Driscoll
Halfback	Red Grange
Halfback	Jim Thorpe
Fullback	Ernie Nevers
End	Guy Chamberlin
End	Lavern Dilweg
Tackle	Wilbur (Pete) Henry
Tackle	Cal Hubbard
Guard	Walt Kiesling
Guard	Mike Michalske
Center	George Trafton

1930's ALL-DECADE TEAM

Back	Earl (Dutch) Clark
Halfback	Cliff Battles
Halfback	Clarke Hinkle
Fullback	Bronko Nagurski
End	Bill Hewitt
End	Don Hutson
Tackle	Glen (Turk) Edwards
Tackle	Joe Stydahar
Guard	Grover (Ox) Emerson
Guard	Dan Fortmann
Center	Mel Hein

1940's ALL-DECADE TEAM

Quarterback	Sammy Baugh
Halfback	George McAfee
Halfback	Steve Van Buren
Fullback	Marion Motley
End	Dante Lavelli
End	Pete Pihos
Tackle	George Conner
Tackle	Al Wistert
Guard	Bruno Banducci
Guard	Bill Willis
Center	Clyde (Bulldog) Turner

1950's ALL-DECADE TEAM

Offense

Quarterback	Otto Graham
Halfback	Ollie Matson
Halfback	Hugh McElhenny
Fullback	Joe Perry
End	Raymond Berry
End	Tom Fears
Flanker	Elroy (Crazylegs) Hirsch
Tackle	Roosevelt Brown
Tackle	Bob St. Clair
Guard	Jim Parker
Guard	Dick Stanfel
Center	Chuck Bednarik

Defense

Defensive End	Len Ford
Defensive End	Gino Marchetti
Defensive Tackle	Leo Nomellini
Defensive Tackle	Ernie Stautner
Linebacker	Bill George
Linebacker	Sam Huff
Linebacker	Joe Schmidt
Defensive Halfback	Jack Butler
Defensive Halfback	Dick (Night Train) Lane
Safety	Jack Christiansen
Safety	Emlen Tunnell

Special Teams

Kicker	Lou Groza

1960's ALL-DECADE TEAM

Offense

Quarterback	Johnny Unitas
Halfback	Paul Hornung
Halfback	Gale Sayers
Fullback	Jim Brown
Wide Receiver	Lance Alworth
Wide Receiver	Charley Taylor
Tight End	John Mackey
Tackle	Forrest Gregg
Tackle	Ron Mix
Guard	Jerry Kramer
Guard	Billy Shaw
Center	Jim Otto

Defense

Defensive End	Willie Davis
Defensive End	David (Deacon) Jones
Defensive Tackle	Bob Lilly
Defensive Tackle	Merlin Olsen
Linebacker	Bobby Bell
Linebacker	Dick Butkus
Linebacker	Ray Nitschke
Cornerback	Herb Adderley
Cornerback	Willie Brown
Safety	Johnny Robinson
Safety	Larry Wilson

Special Teams

Punter	Don Chandler
Kicker	Jim Bakken

1970's ALL-DECADE TEAM

Offense

Quarterback	Terry Bradshaw
Running Back	Walter Payton
Running Back	O.J. Simpson
Wide Receiver	Drew Pearson
Wide Receiver	Lynn Swann
Tight End	Dave Casper
Tackle	Art Shell
Tackle	Ron Yary
Guard	Joe DeLamielleure
Guard	Larry Little
Center	Jim Langer

Defense

Defensive End	Carl Eller
Defensive End	Jack Youngblood
Defensive Tackle	Joe Greene
Defensive Tackle	Bob Lilly
Outside Linebacker	Jack Ham
Middle Linebacker	Dick Butkus
Outside Linebacker	Ted Hendricks
Cornerback	Willie Brown
Cornerback	Jimmy Johnson
Safety	Cliff Harris
Safety	Ken Houston

Special Teams

Punter	Ray Guy
Kicker	Garo Yepremian
Kick Returner	Rick Upchurch

1980's ALL-DECADE TEAM

Offense

Quarterback	Joe Montana
Running Back	Eric Dickerson
Running Back	Walter Payton
Wide Receiver	Steve Largent
Wide Receiver	Jerry Rice
Tight End	Kellen Winslow
Tackle	Jim Covert
Tackle	Anthony Muñoz
Guard	Russ Grimm
Guard	John Hannah
Center	Dwight Stephenson

Defense

Defensive End	Howie Long
Defensive End	Reggie White
Defensive Tackle	Dan Hampton
Defensive Tackle	Randy White
Linebacker	Ted Hendricks
Inside Linebacker	Mike Singletary
Outside Linebacker	Lawrence Taylor
Cornerback	Mel Blount
Cornerback	Mike Haynes
Safety	Kenny Easley
Safety	Ronnie Lott

Special Teams

Punter	Sean Landeta
Kicker	Morten Andersen
Punt Returner	Billy (White Shoes) Johnson
Kick Returner	Mike Nelms

Records

ALL-TIME RECORDS

Compiled by Elias Sports Bureau

The following records reflect all available official information on the National Football League from its formation in 1920 to date. Also included are all applicable records from the American Football League, 1960-69.

Individuals eligible for Rookie records are players who were in their first season of professional football and had not been on the roster of another professional football team, including teams in other leagues, for any regular-season or postseason games in a previous season. Eligible players, therefore, include those who were under contract to a National Football League club for a previous season but were terminated prior to their club's first regular-season game and not re-signed, or who were placed on Reserve/Injured (or another category of the Reserve List) prior to their club's first regular-season game and were not activated during the rest of the regular season or postseason.

INDIVIDUAL RECORDS

SERVICE

Most Seasons

26 George Blanda, Chi. Bears, 1949, 1950-58; Baltimore, 1950; Houston, 1960-66; Oakland, 1967-75
21 Earl Morrall, San Francisco, 1956; Pittsburgh, 1957-58; Detroit, 1958-64; N.Y. Giants, 1965-67; Baltimore, 1968-71; Miami, 1972-76
20 Jim Marshall, Cleveland, 1960; Minnesota, 1961-79
Jackie Slater, L.A. Rams, 1976-94; St. Louis, 1995

Most Seasons, One Club

20 Jackie Slater, L.A. Rams, 1976-94; St. Louis, 1995
19 Jim Marshall, Minnesota, 1961-79
18 Jim Hart, St. Louis, 1966-83
Jeff Van Note, Atlanta, 1969-86
Pat Leahy, N.Y. Jets, 1974-91

Most Games Played, Career

340 George Blanda, Chi. Bears, 1949, 1950-58; Baltimore, 1950; Houston, 1960-66; Oakland, 1967-75
282 Jim Marshall, Cleveland, 1960; Minnesota, 1961-79
278 Clay Matthews, Cleveland, 1978-93; Atlanta, 1994-96

Most Consecutive Games Played, Career

282 Jim Marshall, Cleveland, 1960; Minnesota, 1961-79
240 Mick Tingelhoff, Minnesota, 1962-78
234 Jim Bakken, St. Louis, 1962-78

SCORING

Most Seasons Leading League

5 Don Hutson, Green Bay, 1940-44
Gino Cappelletti, Boston, 1961, 1963-66
3 Earl (Dutch) Clark, Portsmouth, 1932; Detroit, 1935-36
Pat Harder, Chi. Cardinals, 1947-49
Paul Hornung, Green Bay, 1959-61
2 Jack Manders, Chi. Bears, 1934, 1937
Gordy Soltau, San Francisco, 1952-53
Doak Walker, Detroit, 1950, 1955
Gene Mingo, Denver, 1960, 1962
Jim Turner, N.Y. Jets, 1968-69
Fred Cox, Minnesota, 1969-70
Chester Marcol, Green Bay, 1972, 1974
John Smith, New England, 1979-80

Most Consecutive Seasons Leading League

5 Don Hutson, Green Bay, 1940-44
4 Gino Cappelletti, Boston, 1963-66
3 Pat Harder, Chi. Cardinals, 1947-49
Paul Hornung, Green Bay, 1959-61

POINTS

Most Points, Career

2,002 George Blanda, Chi. Bears, 1949, 1950-58; Baltimore, 1950; Houston, 1960-66; Oakland, 1967-75 (9-td, 943-pat, 335-fg)
1,711 Nick Lowery, New England, 1978; Kansas City, 1980-93; N.Y. Jets, 1994-96 (562-pat, 383-fg)
1,699 Jan Stenerud, Kansas City, 1967-79; Green Bay, 1980-83; Minnesota, 1984-85 (580-pat, 373-fg)

Most Points, Season

176 Paul Hornung, Green Bay, 1960 (15-td, 41-pat, 15-fg)
161 Mark Moseley, Washington, 1983 (62-pat, 33-fg)
155 Gino Cappelletti, Boston, 1964 (7-td, 38-pat, 25-fg)

Most Points, No Touchdowns, Season

161 Mark Moseley, Washington, 1983 (62-pat, 33-fg)
149 Chip Lohmiller, Washington, 1991 (56-pat, 31-fg)
145 Jim Turner, N.Y. Jets, 1968 (43-pat, 34-fg)
John Kasay, Carolina, 1996 (34-pat, 37-fg)

Most Seasons, 100 or More Points

11 Nick Lowery, Kansas City, 1981, 1983-86, 1988-93
Morten Andersen, New Orleans, 1985-89, 1991-94; Atlanta, 1995, 1997
10 Gary Anderson, Pittsburgh, 1983-85, 1988, 1991-94; Philadelphia, 1996; San Francisco, 1997
9 Norm Johnson, Seattle, 1983-84, 1986, 1988, 1990; Atlanta, 1993; Pittsburgh, 1995-97

Most Points, Rookie, Season

144 Kevin Butler, Chicago, 1985 (51-pat, 31-fg)
132 Gale Sayers, Chicago, 1965 (22-td)
128 Doak Walker, Detroit, 1950 (11-td, 38-pat, 8-fg)
Chester Marcol, Green Bay, 1972 (29-pat, 33-fg)

Most Points, Game

40 Ernie Nevers, Chi. Cardinals vs. Chi. Bears, Nov. 28, 1929 (6-td, 4-pat)
36 Dub Jones, Cleveland vs. Chi. Bears, Nov. 25, 1951 (6-td)
Gale Sayers, Chicago vs. San Francisco, Dec. 12, 1965 (6-td)
33 Paul Hornung, Green Bay vs. Baltimore, Oct. 8, 1961 (4-td, 6-pat, 1-fg)

Most Consecutive Games Scoring

222 Morten Andersen, New Orleans, 1982-94; Atlanta, 1995-97 (current)
186 Jim Breech, Oakland, 1979; Cincinnati, 1980-92
155 Ray Wersching, San Francisco, 1977-87

TOUCHDOWNS

Most Seasons Leading League

8 Don Hutson, Green Bay, 1935-38, 1941-44
3 Jim Brown, Cleveland, 1958-59, 1963
Lance Alworth, San Diego, 1964-66
Emmitt Smith, Dallas, 1992, 1994-95
2 By many players

Most Consecutive Seasons Leading League

4 Don Hutson, Green Bay, 1935-38, 1941-44
3 Lance Alworth, San Diego, 1964-66
2 By many players

Most Touchdowns, Career

166 Jerry Rice, San Francisco, 1985-97 (10-r, 155-p, 1-ret)
145 Marcus Allen, L.A. Raiders, 1982-92; Kansas City, 1993-97 (123-r, 21-p, 1-ret)
126 Jim Brown, Cleveland, 1957-65 (106-r, 20-p)

Most Touchdowns, Season

25 Emmitt Smith, Dallas, 1995 (25-r)
24 John Riggins, Washington, 1983 (24-r)
23 O.J. Simpson, Buffalo, 1975 (16-r, 7-p)
Jerry Rice, San Francisco, 1987 (1-r, 22-p)

Most Touchdowns, Rookie, Season

22 Gale Sayers, Chicago, 1965 (14-r, 6-p, 2-ret)
20 Eric Dickerson, L.A. Rams, 1983 (18-r, 2-p)
16 Billy Sims, Detroit, 1980 (13-r, 3-p)

Most Touchdowns, Game

6 Ernie Nevers, Chi. Cardinals vs. Chi. Bears, Nov. 28, 1929 (6-r)
Dub Jones, Cleveland vs. Chi. Bears, Nov. 25, 1951 (4-r, 2-p)
Gale Sayers, Chicago vs. San Francisco, Dec. 12, 1965 (4-r, 1-p, 1-ret)
5 Bob Shaw, Chi. Cardinals vs. Baltimore, Oct. 2, 1950 (5-p)
Jim Brown, Cleveland vs. Baltimore, Nov. 1, 1959 (5-r)
Abner Haynes, Dall. Texans vs. Oakland, Nov. 26, 1961 (4-r, 1-p)
Billy Cannon, Houston vs. N.Y. Titans, Dec. 10, 1961 (3-r, 2-p)
Cookie Gilchrist, Buffalo vs. N.Y. Jets, Dec. 8, 1963 (5-r)
Paul Hornung, Green Bay vs. Baltimore, Dec. 12, 1965 (3-r, 2-p)
Kellen Winslow, San Diego vs. Oakland, Nov. 22, 1981 (5-p)
Jerry Rice, San Francisco vs. Atlanta, Oct. 14, 1990 (5-p)
James Stewart, Jacksonville vs. Pittsburgh, Oct. 12, 1997 (5-r)
4 By many players. Last time: Corey Dillon, Cincinnati vs. Tennessee, Dec. 4, 1997 (4-r)

Most Consecutive Games Scoring Touchdowns

18 Lenny Moore, Baltimore, 1963-65
14 O.J. Simpson, Buffalo, 1975
13 John Riggins, Washington, 1982-83
George Rogers, Washington, 1985-86
Jerry Rice, San Francisco, 1986-87

POINTS AFTER TOUCHDOWN

Most Seasons Leading League

8 George Blanda, Chi. Bears, 1956; Houston, 1961-62; Oakland, 1967-69, 1972, 1974
4 Bob Waterfield, Cleveland, 1945; Los Angeles, 1946, 1950, 1952
3 Earl (Dutch) Clark, Portsmouth, 1932; Detroit, 1935-36
Jack Manders, Chi. Bears, 1933-35
Don Hutson, Green Bay, 1941-42, 1945

Most (Kicking) Points After Touchdown Attempted, Career

959 George Blanda, Chi. Bears, 1949, 1950-58; Baltimore, 1950; Houston, 1960-66; Oakland, 1967-75
657 Lou Groza, Cleveland, 1950-59, 1961-67
601 Jan Stenerud, Kansas City, 1967-79; Green Bay, 1980-83; Minnesota, 1984-85

Most (Kicking) Points After Touchdown Attempted, Season

70 Uwe von Schamann, Miami, 1984
65 George Blanda, Houston, 1961

63 Mark Moseley, Washington, 1983

Most (Kicking) Points After Touchdown Attempted, Game
10 Charlie Gogolak, Washington vs. N.Y. Giants, Nov. 27, 1966
9 Pat Harder, Chi. Cardinals vs. N.Y. Giants, Oct. 17, 1948; vs. N.Y. Bulldogs, Nov. 13, 1949
Bob Waterfield, Los Angeles vs. Baltimore, Oct. 22, 1950
Bob Thomas, Chicago vs. Green Bay, Dec. 7, 1980
8 By many players

Most (One-Point) Points After Touchdown, Career
943 George Blanda, Chi. Bears, 1949, 1950-58; Baltimore, 1950; Houston, 1960-66; Oakland, 1967-75
641 Lou Groza, Cleveland, 1950-59, 1961-67
592 Norm Johnson, Seattle, 1982-90; Atlanta, 1991-94; Pittsburgh, 1995-97

Most (One-Point) Points After Touchdown, Season
66 Uwe von Schamann, Miami, 1984
64 George Blanda, Houston, 1961
62 Mark Moseley, Washington, 1983

Most (One-Point) Points After Touchdown, Game
9 Pat Harder, Chi. Cardinals vs. N.Y. Giants, Oct. 17, 1948
Bob Waterfield, Los Angeles vs. Baltimore, Oct. 22, 1950
Charlie Gogolak, Washington vs. N.Y. Giants, Nov. 27, 1966
8 By many players

Most Consecutive (Kicking) Points After Touchdown
255 Norm Johnson, Atlanta, 1991-94; Pittsburgh, 1995-97 (current)
250 Eddie Murray, Detroit, 1988-91; Kansas City, 1992; Tampa Bay, 1992; Dallas, 1993; Philadelphia, 1994; Washington, 1995; Minnesota, 1997
234 Tommy Davis, San Francisco, 1959-65

Highest (Kicking) Points After Touchdown Percentage, Career (200 points after touchdown)
99.50 Jason Elam, Denver, 1993-97 (202-201)
99.43 Tommy Davis, San Francisco, 1959-69 (350-348)
99.10 Jason Hanson, Detroit, 1992-97 (222-220)

Most (Kicking) Points After Touchdown, No Misses, Season
56 Danny Villanueva, Dallas, 1966
Ray Wersching, San Francisco, 1984
Chip Lohmiller, Washington, 1991
54 Mike Clark, Dallas, 1968
George Blanda, Oakland, 1968
53 Pat Harder, Chi. Cardinals, 1948

Most (Kicking) Points After Touchdown, No Misses, Game
9 Pat Harder, Chi. Cardinals vs. N.Y. Giants, Oct. 17, 1948
Bob Waterfield, Los Angeles vs. Baltimore, Oct. 22, 1950
8 By many players

Most Two-Point Conversions, Career
6 Terance Mathis, Atlanta, 1994-97
5 Cris Carter, Minnesota, 1994-97
Rob Moore, N.Y. Jets, 1994; Arizona, 1995-97
4 Gino Cappelletti, Boston, 1960-69
Lamar Smith, Seattle, 1994-97

Most Two-Point Conversions, Season
3 Gino Cappelletti, Boston, 1960
Richie Lucas, Buffalo, 1961
Ronnie Harmon, San Diego, 1994
Haywood Jeffires, Houston, 1994
Tom Tupa, Cleveland, 1994
Terance Mathis, Atlanta, 1995
Lamar Smith, Seattle, 1996
Cris Carter, Minnesota, 1997
Terrell Davis, Denver, 1997
2 By many players

Most Two-Point Conversions, Game
2 Brett Perriman, Detroit vs. Green Bay, Nov. 6, 1994
Michael Jackson, Baltimore vs. New England, Oct. 6, 1996
Terrell Davis, Denver vs. Atlanta, Sept. 28, 1997

FIELD GOALS

Most Seasons Leading League
5 Lou Groza, Cleveland, 1950, 1952-54, 1957
4 Jack Manders, Chi. Bears, 1933-34, 1936-37
Ward Cuff, N.Y. Giants, 1938-39, 1943; Green Bay, 1947
Mark Moseley, Washington, 1976-77, 1979, 1982
3 Bob Waterfield, Los Angeles, 1947, 1949, 1951
Gino Cappelletti, Boston, 1961, 1963-64
Fred Cox, Minnesota, 1965, 1969-70
Jan Stenerud, Kansas City, 1967, 1970, 1975

Most Consecutive Seasons Leading League
3 Lou Groza, Cleveland, 1952-54
2 Jack Manders, Chi. Bears, 1933-34
Armand Niccolai, Pittsburgh, 1935-36
Jack Manders, Chi. Bears, 1936-37
Ward Cuff, N.Y. Giants, 1938-39
Clark Hinkle, Green Bay, 1940-41
Cliff Patton, Philadelphia, 1948-49
Gino Cappelletti, Boston, 1963-64
Jim Turner, N.Y. Jets, 1968-69
Fred Cox, Minnesota, 1969-70
Mark Moseley, Washington, 1976-77
Chip Lohmiller, Washington, 1991-92
Pete Stoyanovich, Miami, 1991-92

Most Field Goals Attempted, Career
637 George Blanda, Chi. Bears, 1949, 1950-58; Baltimore, 1950; Houston, 1960-66; Oakland, 1967-75
558 Jan Stenerud, Kansas City, 1967-79; Green Bay, 1980-83; Minnesota, 1984-85
490 Gary Anderson, Pittsburgh, 1982-94; Philadelphia, 1995-96; San Francisco, 1997

Most Field Goals Attempted, Season
49 Bruce Gossett, Los Angeles, 1966
Curt Knight, Washington, 1971
48 Chester Marcol, Green Bay, 1972
47 Jim Turner, N.Y. Jets, 1969
David Ray, Los Angeles, 1973
Mark Moseley, Washington, 1983

Most Field Goals Attempted, Game
9 Jim Bakken, St. Louis vs. Pittsburgh, Sept. 24, 1967
8 Lou Michaels, Pittsburgh vs. St. Louis, Dec. 2, 1962
Garo Yepremian, Detroit vs. Minnesota, Nov. 13, 1966
Jim Turner, N.Y. Jets vs. Buffalo, Nov. 3, 1968
7 By many players

Most Field Goals, Career
385 Gary Anderson, Pittsburgh, 1982-94; Philadelphia, 1995-96; San Francisco, 1997
383 Nick Lowery, New England, 1978; Kansas City, 1980-93; N.Y. Jets, 1994-96
378 Morten Andersen, New Orleans, 1982-94; Atlanta, 1995-97

Most Field Goals, Season
37 John Kasay, Carolina, 1996
36 Cary Blanchard, Indianapolis, 1996
35 Ali Haji-Sheikh, N.Y. Giants, 1983
Jeff Jaeger, L.A. Raiders, 1993

Most Field Goals, Rookie, Season
35 Ali Haji-Sheikh, N.Y. Giants, 1983
34 Richie Cunningham, Dallas, 1997
33 Chester Marcol, Green Bay, 1972

Most Field Goals, Game
7 Jim Bakken, St. Louis vs. Pittsburgh, Sept. 24, 1967
Rich Karlis, Minnesota vs. L.A. Rams, Nov. 5, 1989 (OT)
Chris Boniol, Dallas vs. Green Bay, Nov. 18, 1996
6 Gino Cappelletti, Boston vs. Denver, Oct. 4, 1964
Garo Yepremian, Detroit vs. Minnesota, Nov. 13, 1966
Jim Turner, N.Y. Jets vs. Buffalo, Nov. 3, 1968
Tom Dempsey, Philadelphia vs. Houston, Nov. 12, 1972
Bobby Howfield, N.Y. Jets vs. New Orleans, Dec. 3, 1972
Jim Bakken, St. Louis vs. Atlanta, Dec. 9, 1973
Joe Danelo, N.Y. Giants vs. Seattle, Oct. 18, 1981
Ray Wersching, San Francisco vs. New Orleans, Oct. 16, 1983
Gary Anderson, Pittsburgh vs. Denver, Oct. 23, 1988
John Carney, San Diego vs. Seattle, Sept. 5, 1993
John Carney, San Diego vs. Houston, Sept. 19, 1993
Doug Pelfrey, Cincinnati vs. Seattle, Nov. 6, 1994 (OT)
Norm Johnson, Atlanta vs. New Orleans, Nov. 13, 1994
Jeff Wilkins, San Francisco vs. Atlanta, Sept. 29, 1996
Steve Christie, Buffalo vs. N.Y. Jets, Oct. 20, 1996
Greg Davis, San Diego vs. Oakland, Oct. 5, 1997
5 By many players

Most Field Goals, One Quarter
4 Garo Yepremian, Detroit vs. Minnesota, Nov. 13, 1966 (second quarter)
Curt Knight, Washington vs. N.Y. Giants, Nov. 15, 1970 (second quarter)
Roger Ruzek, Dallas vs. N.Y. Giants, Nov. 2, 1987 (fourth quarter)
3 By many players

Most Consecutive Games Scoring Field Goals
31 Fred Cox, Minnesota, 1968-70
28 Jim Turner, N.Y. Jets, 1970; Denver, 1971-72
Chip Lohmiller, Washington, 1988-90
23 Morten Andersen, New Orleans, 1986-88

Most Consecutive Field Goals
31 Fuad Reveiz, Minnesota, 1994-95
29 John Carney, San Diego, 1992-93
28 Chris Boniol, Dallas, 1996; Philadelphia, 1997

Longest Field Goal
63 Tom Dempsey, New Orleans vs. Detroit, Nov. 8, 1970
60 Steve Cox, Cleveland vs. Cincinnati, Oct. 21, 1984
Morten Andersen, New Orleans vs. Chicago, Oct. 27, 1991
59 Tony Franklin, Philadelphia vs. Dallas, Nov. 12, 1979
Pete Stoyanovich, Miami vs. N.Y. Jets, Nov. 12, 1989

Steve Christie, Buffalo vs. Miami, Sept. 26, 1993
Morten Andersen, Atlanta vs. San Francisco, Dec. 24, 1995

Highest Field Goal Percentage, Career (100 field goals)
83.06 Chris Boniol, Dallas, 1994-1996; Philadelphia, 1997 (124-103)
80.56 Doug Pelfrey, Cincinnati, 1993-97 (144-116)
80.34 John Carney, Tampa Bay, 1988-89; L.A. Rams, 1990; San Diego, 1990-97 (234-188)

Highest Field Goal Percentage, Season (Qualifiers)
100.00 Tony Zendejas, L.A. Rams, 1991 (17-17)
96.43 Chris Boniol, Dallas, 1995 (28-27)
96.30 Norm Johnson, Atlanta, 1993 (27-26)
Pete Stoyanovich, Kansas City, 1997 (27-26)

Most Field Goals, No Misses, Game
7 Rich Karlis, Minnesota vs. L.A. Rams, Nov. 5, 1989 (OT)
Chris Boniol, Dallas vs. Green Bay, Nov. 18, 1996
6 Gino Cappelletti, Boston vs. Denver, Oct. 4, 1964
Joe Danelo, N.Y. Giants vs. Seattle, Oct. 18, 1981
Ray Wersching, San Francisco vs. New Orleans, Oct. 16, 1983
Gary Anderson, Pittsburgh vs. Denver, Oct. 23, 1988
John Carney, San Diego vs. Seattle, Sept. 5, 1993
John Carney, San Diego vs. Houston, Sept. 19, 1993
Doug Pelfrey, Cincinnati vs. Seattle, Nov. 6, 1994 (OT)
Norm Johnson, Atlanta vs. New Orleans, Nov. 13, 1994
Jeff Wilkins, San Francisco vs. Atlanta, Sept. 29, 1996
Greg Davis, San Diego vs. Oakland, Oct. 5, 1997
5 By many players

Most Field Goals, 50 or More Yards, Career
33 Morten Andersen, New Orleans, 1982-94; Atlanta, 1995-97
22 Nick Lowery, New England, 1978; Kansas City, 1980-93; N.Y. Jets, 1994-96
21 Eddie Murray, Detroit, 1980-91; Kansas City, 1992; Tampa Bay, 1992; Dallas, 1993; Philadelphia, 1994; Washington, 1995; Minnesota, 1997

Most Field Goals, 50 or More Yards, Season
8 Morten Andersen, Atlanta, 1995
6 Dean Biasucci, Indianapolis, 1988
Chris Jacke, Green Bay, 1993
Tony Zendejas, L.A. Rams, 1993
5 Fred Steinfort, Denver, 1980
Norm Johnson, Seattle, 1986
Kevin Butler, Chicago, 1993
Jason Elam, Denver, 1995
Cary Blanchard, Indianapolis, 1996

Most Field Goals, 50 or More Yards, Game
3 Morten Andersen, Atlanta vs. New Orleans, Dec. 10, 1995
2 By many players. Last time:
Doug Brien, New Orleans vs. Carolina, Nov. 30, 1997

SAFETIES

Most Safeties, Career
4 Ted Hendricks, Baltimore, 1969-73; Green Bay, 1974; Oakland, 1975-81; L.A. Raiders, 1982-83
Doug English, Detroit, 1975-79, 1981-85
3 Bill McPeak, Pittsburgh, 1949-57
Charlie Krueger, San Francisco, 1959-73
Ernie Stautner, Pittsburgh, 1950-63
Jim Katcavage, N.Y. Giants, 1956-68
Roger Brown, Detroit, 1960-66; Los Angeles, 1967-69
Bruce Maher, Detroit, 1960-67; N.Y. Giants, 1968-69
Ron McDole, St. Louis, 1961; Houston, 1962; Buffalo, 1963-70; Washington, 1971-78
Alan Page, Minnesota, 1967-78; Chicago, 1979-81
Lyle Alzado, Denver, 1971-78; Cleveland, 1979-81; L.A. Raiders, 1982-85
Rulon Jones, Denver, 1980-88
Steve McMichael, New England, 1980; Chicago, 1981-93; Green Bay, 1994
Kevin Greene, L.A. Rams, 1985-92; Pittsburgh, 1993-95; Carolina 1996
Burt Grossman, San Diego, 1989-93; Philadelphia, 1994
Eric Swann, Phoenix, 1991-93; Arizona, 1994-96
Dan Saleaumua, Detroit, 1987-88; Kansas City, 1989-96; Seattle, 1997
2 By many players

Most Safeties, Season
2 Tom Nash, Green Bay, 1932
Roger Brown, Detroit, 1962
Ron McDole, Buffalo, 1964
Alan Page, Minnesota, 1971
Fred Dryer, Los Angeles, 1973
Benny Barnes, Dallas, 1973
James Young, Houston, 1977
Tom Hannon, Minnesota, 1981
Doug English, Detroit, 1983
Don Blackmon, New England, 1985
Tim Harris, Green Bay, 1988
Brian Jordan, Atlanta, 1991
Burt Grossman, San Diego, 1992
Rod Stephens, Seattle, 1993
Bryant Young, San Francisco, 1996

Most Safeties, Game
2 Fred Dryer, Los Angeles vs. Green Bay, Oct. 21, 1973

RUSHING

Most Seasons Leading League
8 Jim Brown, Cleveland, 1957-61, 1963-65
4 Steve Van Buren, Philadelphia, 1945, 1947-49
O.J. Simpson, Buffalo, 1972-73, 1975-76
Eric Dickerson, L.A. Rams, 1983-84, 1986; Indianapolis, 1988
Emmitt Smith, Dallas, 1991-93, 1995
Barry Sanders, Detroit, 1990, 1994, 1996-97
3 Earl Campbell, Houston, 1978-80

Most Consecutive Seasons Leading League
5 Jim Brown, Cleveland, 1957-61
3 Steve Van Buren, Philadelphia, 1947-49
Jim Brown, Cleveland, 1963-65
Earl Campbell, Houston, 1978-80
Emmitt Smith, Dallas, 1991-93
2 Bill Paschal, N.Y. Giants, 1943-44
Joe Perry, San Francisco, 1953-54
Jim Nance, Boston, 1966-67
Leroy Kelly, Cleveland, 1967-68
O.J. Simpson, Buffalo, 1972-73; 1975-76
Eric Dickerson, L.A. Rams, 1983-84
Barry Sanders, Detroit, 1996-97

ATTEMPTS

Most Seasons Leading League
6 Jim Brown, Cleveland, 1958-59, 1961, 1963-65
4 Steve Van Buren, Philadelphia, 1947-50
Walter Payton, Chicago, 1976-79
3 Cookie Gilchrist, Buffalo, 1963-64; Denver, 1965
Jim Nance, Boston, 1966-67, 1969
O.J. Simpson, Buffalo, 1973-75
Eric Dickerson, L.A. Rams, 1983, 1986; Indianapolis, 1988
Emmitt Smith, Dallas, 1991, 1994-95

Most Consecutive Seasons Leading League
4 Steve Van Buren, Philadelphia, 1947-50
Walter Payton, Chicago, 1976-79
3 Jim Brown, Cleveland, 1963-65
Cookie Gilchrist, Buffalo, 1963-64; Denver, 1965
O.J. Simpson, Buffalo, 1973-75
2 By many players

Most Attempts, Career
3,838 Walter Payton, Chicago, 1975-87
3,022 Marcus Allen, L.A. Raiders, 1982-92; Kansas City, 1993-97
2,996 Eric Dickerson, L.A. Rams, 1983-87; Indianapolis, 1987-91; L.A. Raiders, 1992; Atlanta, 1993

Most Attempts, Season
407 James Wilder, Tampa Bay, 1984
404 Eric Dickerson, L.A. Rams, 1986
397 Gerald Riggs, Atlanta, 1985

Most Attempts, Rookie, Season
390 Eric Dickerson, L.A. Rams, 1983
378 George Rogers, New Orleans, 1981
368 Curtis Martin, New England, 1995

Most Attempts, Game
45 Jamie Morris, Washington vs. Cincinnati, Dec. 17, 1988 (OT)
43 Butch Woolfolk, N.Y. Giants vs. Philadelphia, Nov. 20, 1983
James Wilder, Tampa Bay vs. Green Bay, Sept. 30, 1984 (OT)
42 James Wilder, Tampa Bay vs. Pittsburgh, Oct. 30, 1983
Terrell Davis, Denver vs. Buffalo, Oct. 26, 1997 (OT)

YARDS GAINED

Most Yards Gained, Career
16,726 Walter Payton, Chicago, 1975-87
13,778 Barry Sanders, Detroit, 1989-97
13,259 Eric Dickerson, L.A. Rams, 1983-87; Indianapolis, 1987-91; L.A. Raiders, 1992; Atlanta, 1993

Most Seasons, 1,000 or More Yards Rushing
10 Walter Payton, Chicago, 1976-81, 1983-86
9 Barry Sanders, Detroit, 1989-97
8 Franco Harris, Pittsburgh, 1972, 1974-79, 1983
Tony Dorsett, Dallas, 1977-81, 1983-85
Thurman Thomas, Buffalo, 1989-96

Most Consecutive Seasons, 1,000 or More Yards Rushing
9 Barry Sanders, Detroit, 1989-97 (current)
8 Thurman Thomas, Buffalo, 1989-96
7 Eric Dickerson, L.A. Rams, 1983-86; L.A. Rams-Indianapolis, 1987; Indianapolis, 1988-89
Emmitt Smith, Dallas, 1991-97 (current)

Most Yards Gained, Season
2,105 Eric Dickerson, L.A. Rams, 1984
2,053 Barry Sanders, Detroit, 1997
2,003 O.J. Simpson, Buffalo, 1973

Most Yards Gained, Rookie, Season
1,808 Eric Dickerson, L.A. Rams, 1983
1,674 George Rogers, New Orleans, 1981
1,605 Ottis Anderson, St. Louis, 1979

Most Yards Gained, Game
275 Walter Payton, Chicago vs. Minnesota, Nov. 20, 1977
273 O.J. Simpson, Buffalo vs. Detroit, Nov. 25, 1976
250 O.J. Simpson, Buffalo vs. New England, Sept. 16, 1973

Most Games, 200 or More Yards Rushing, Career
6 O.J. Simpson, Buffalo, 1969-77; San Francisco, 1978-79
4 Jim Brown, Cleveland, 1957-65
Earl Campbell, Houston, 1978-84; New Orleans, 1984-85
Barry Sanders, Detroit, 1989-97
3 Eric Dickerson, L.A. Rams, 1983-87; Indianapolis, 1987-91; L.A. Raiders, 1992; Atlanta, 1993
Greg Bell, Buffalo, 1984-87; L.A. Rams, 1987-89; L.A. Raiders, 1990

Most Games, 200 or More Yards Rushing, Season
4 Earl Campbell, Houston, 1980
3 O.J. Simpson, Buffalo, 1973
2 Jim Brown, Cleveland, 1963
O.J. Simpson, Buffalo, 1976
Walter Payton, Chicago, 1977
Eric Dickerson, L.A. Rams, 1984
Greg Bell, L.A. Rams, 1989
Terrell Davis, Denver, 1997
Barry Sanders, Detroit, 1997

Most Consecutive Games, 200 or More Yards Rushing
2 O.J. Simpson, Buffalo, 1973, 1976
Earl Campbell, Houston, 1980

Most Games, 100 or More Yards Rushing, Career
77 Walter Payton, Chicago, 1975-87
68 Barry Sanders, Detroit, 1989-97
64 Eric Dickerson, L.A. Rams, 1983-87; Indianapolis, 1987-91; L.A. Raiders, 1992; Atlanta, 1993

Most Games, 100 or More Yards Rushing, Season
14 Barry Sanders, Detroit, 1997
12 Eric Dickerson, L.A. Rams, 1984
Barry Foster, Pittsburgh, 1992
11 O.J. Simpson, Buffalo, 1973
Earl Campbell, Houston, 1979
Marcus Allen, L.A. Raiders, 1985
Eric Dickerson, L.A. Rams, 1986
Emmitt Smith, Dallas, 1995

Most Consecutive Games, 100 or More Yards Rushing
14 Barry Sanders, Detroit, 1997 (current)
11 Marcus Allen, L.A. Raiders, 1985-86
9 Walter Payton, Chicago, 1985

Longest Run From Scrimmage
99 Tony Dorsett, Dallas vs. Minnesota, Jan. 3, 1983 (TD)
97 Andy Uram, Green Bay vs. Chi. Cardinals, Oct. 8, 1939 (TD)
Bob Gage, Pittsburgh vs. Chi. Bears, Dec. 4, 1949 (TD)
96 Jim Spavital, Baltimore vs. Green Bay, Nov. 5, 1950 (TD)
Bob Hoernschemeyer, Detroit vs. N.Y. Yanks, Nov. 23, 1950 (TD)

AVERAGE GAIN

Highest Average Gain, Career (750 attempts)
5.22 Jim Brown, Cleveland, 1957-65 (2,359-12,312)
5.14 Eugene (Mercury) Morris, Miami, 1969-75; San Diego, 1976 (804-4,133)
5.07 Barry Sanders, Detroit, 1989-97 (2,719-13,778)

Highest Average Gain, Season (Qualifiers)
8.44 Beattie Feathers, Chi. Bears, 1934 (119-1,004)
7.98 Randall Cunningham, Philadelphia 1990 (118-942)
6.87 Bobby Douglass, Chicago, 1972 (141-968)

Highest Average Gain, Game (10 attempts)
17.09 Marion Motley, Cleveland vs. Pittsburgh, Oct. 29, 1950 (11-188)
16.70 Bill Grimes, Green Bay vs. N.Y. Yanks, Oct. 8, 1950 (10-167)
16.57 Bobby Mitchell, Cleveland vs. Washington, Nov. 15, 1959 (14-232)

TOUCHDOWNS

Most Seasons Leading League
5 Jim Brown, Cleveland, 1957-59, 1963, 1965
4 Steve Van Buren, Philadelphia, 1945, 1947-49
3 Abner Haynes, Dall. Texans, 1960-62
Cookie Gilchrist, Buffalo, 1962-64
Paul Lowe, L.A. Chargers, 1960; San Diego, 1961, 1965
Leroy Kelly, Cleveland, 1966-68
Emmitt Smith, Dallas, 1992, 1994-95

Most Consecutive Seasons Leading League
3 Steve Van Buren, Philadelphia, 1947-49
Jim Brown, Cleveland, 1957-59
Abner Haynes, Dall. Texans, 1960-62
Cookie Gilchrist, Buffalo, 1962-64
Leroy Kelly, Cleveland, 1966-68

Most Touchdowns, Career
123 Marcus Allen, L.A. Raiders, 1982-92; Kansas City, 1993-97
112 Emmitt Smith, Dallas, 1990-97
110 Walter Payton, Chicago, 1975-87

Most Touchdowns, Season
25 Emmitt Smith, Dallas, 1995
24 John Riggins, Washington, 1983
21 Joe Morris, N.Y. Giants, 1985
Emmitt Smith, Dallas, 1994
Terry Allen, Washington, 1996

Most Touchdowns, Rookie, Season
18 Eric Dickerson, L.A. Rams, 1983
15 Ickey Woods, Cincinnati, 1988
14 Gale Sayers, Chicago, 1965
Barry Sanders, Detroit, 1989
Curtis Martin, New England, 1995

Most Touchdowns, Game
6 Ernie Nevers, Chi. Cardinals vs. Chi. Bears, Nov. 28, 1929
5 Jim Brown, Cleveland vs. Baltimore, Nov. 1, 1959
Cookie Gilchrist, Buffalo vs. N.Y. Jets, Dec. 8, 1963
James Stewart, Jacksonville vs. Philadelphia, Oct. 12, 1997
4 By many players

Most Consecutive Games Rushing for Touchdowns
13 John Riggins, Washington, 1982-83
George Rogers, Washington, 1985-86
11 Lenny Moore, Baltimore, 1963-64
Emmitt Smith, Dallas, 1994-95
Emmitt Smith, Dallas, 1995
10 Greg Bell, L.A. Rams, 1988-89
Terry Allen, Washington, 1995-96

PASSING

Most Seasons Leading League
6 Sammy Baugh, Washington, 1937, 1940, 1943, 1945, 1947, 1949
Steve Young San Francisco, 1991-94, 1996-97
4 Len Dawson, Dall. Texans; 1962; Kansas City, 1964, 1966, 1968
Roger Staubach, Dallas, 1971, 1973, 1978-79
Ken Anderson, Cincinnati, 1974-75, 1981-82
3 Arnie Herber, Green Bay, 1932, 1934, 1936
Norm Van Brocklin, Los Angeles, 1950, 1952, 1954
Bart Starr, Green Bay, 1962, 1964, 1966

Most Consecutive Seasons Leading League
4 Steve Young, San Francisco, 1991-94
2 Cecil Isbell, Green Bay, 1941-42
Milt Plum, Cleveland, 1960-61
Ken Anderson, Cincinnati, 1974-75, 1981-82
Roger Staubach, Dallas, 1978-79
Steve Young, San Francisco, 1996-97

PASS RATING

Highest Pass Rating, Career (1,500 attempts)
97.0 Steve Young, Tampa Bay, 1985-86; San Francisco, 1987-97
92.3 Joe Montana, San Francisco, 1979-90, 1992; Kansas City, 1993-94
89.3 Brett Favre, Atlanta, 1991; Green Bay, 1992-97

Highest Pass Rating, Season (Qualifiers)
112.8 Steve Young, San Francisco, 1994
112.4 Joe Montana, San Francisco, 1989
110.4 Milt Plum, Cleveland, 1960

Highest Pass Rating, Rookie, Season (Qualifiers)
96.0 Dan Marino, Miami, 1983
88.2 Greg Cook, Cincinnati, 1969
84.0 Charlie Conerly, N.Y. Giants, 1948

ATTEMPTS

Most Seasons Leading League
5 Dan Marino, Miami, 1984, 1986, 1988, 1992, 1997
4 Sammy Baugh, Washington, 1937, 1943, 1947-48
Johnny Unitas, Baltimore, 1957, 1959-61
George Blanda, Chi. Bears, 1953; Houston, 1963-65
3 Arnie Herber, Green Bay, 1932, 1934, 1936
Sonny Jurgensen, Washington, 1966-67, 1969
Drew Bledsoe, New England, 1994-96

ALL-TIME RECORDS

Most Consecutive Seasons Leading League
3 Johnny Unitas, Baltimore, 1959-61
George Blanda, Houston, 1963-65
Drew Bledsoe, New England, 1994-96
2 By many players

Most Passes Attempted, Career
7,452 Dan Marino, Miami, 1983-97
6,894 John Elway, Denver, 1983-97
6,528 Warren Moon, Houston, 1984-93; Minnesota, 1994-96; Seattle, 1997

Most Passes Attempted, Season
691 Drew Bledsoe, New England, 1994
655 Warren Moon, Houston, 1991
636 Drew Bledsoe, New England, 1995

Most Passes Attempted, Rookie, Season
486 Rick Mirer, Seattle, 1993
439 Jim Zorn, Seattle, 1976
433 Kerry Collins, Carolina, 1995

Most Passes Attempted, Game
70 Drew Bledsoe, New England vs. Minnesota, Nov. 13, 1994 (OT)
68 George Blanda, Houston vs. Buffalo, Nov. 1, 1964
66 Chris Miller, Atlanta vs. Detroit, Dec. 24, 1989

COMPLETIONS

Most Seasons Leading League
6 Dan Marino, Miami, 1984-86, 1988, 1992, 1997
5 Sammy Baugh, Washington, 1937, 1943, 1945, 1947-48
4 George Blanda, Chi. Bears, 1953; Houston, 1963-65
Sonny Jurgensen, Philadelphia, 1961; Washington, 1966-67, 1969

Most Consecutive Seasons Leading League
3 George Blanda, Houston, 1963-65
Dan Marino, Miami, 1984-86
2 By many players

Most Passes Completed, Career
4,453 Dan Marino, Miami, 1983-97
3,913 John Elway, Denver, 1983-97
3,827 Warren Moon, Houston, 1984-93; Minnesota, 1994-96; Seattle, 1997

Most Passes Completed, Season
404 Warren Moon, Houston, 1991
400 Drew Bledsoe, New England, 1994
385 Dan Marino, Miami, 1994

Most Passes Completed, Rookie, Season
274 Rick Mirer, Seattle, 1993
214 Drew Bledsoe, New England, 1993
Kerry Collins, Carolina, 1995
208 Jim Zorn, Seattle, 1976

Most Passes Completed, Game
45 Drew Bledsoe, New England vs. Minnesota, Nov. 13, 1994 (OT)
42 Richard Todd, N.Y. Jets vs. San Francisco, Sept. 21, 1980
41 Warren Moon, Houston vs. Dallas, Nov. 10, 1991 (OT)

Most Consecutive Passes Completed
22 Joe Montana, San Francisco vs. Cleveland (5), Nov. 29, 1987; vs. Green Bay (17), Dec. 6, 1987
20 Ken Anderson, Cincinnati vs. Houston, Jan. 2, 1983
Hugh Millen, Denver vs. L.A. Raiders (7), Dec. 11, 1994; vs. San Francisco (13), Dec. 17, 1994
Steve Young, San Francisco vs. Washington, Nov. 24, 1996
18 Steve DeBerg, Denver vs. L.A. Rams (17), Dec. 12, 1982; vs. Kansas City (1), Dec. 19, 1982
Lynn Dickey, Green Bay vs. Houston, Sept. 4, 1983
Joe Montana, San Francisco vs. L.A. Rams (13), Oct. 28, 1984; vs. Cincinnati (5), Nov. 4, 1984
Don Majkowski, Green Bay vs. New Orleans, Sept. 18, 1989
Boomer Esiason, N.Y. Jets vs. Miami (5), Sept. 12, 1993; vs. New England (13), Sept. 26, 1993

COMPLETION PERCENTAGE

Most Seasons Leading League
8 Len Dawson, Dall. Texans, 1962; Kansas City, 1964-69, 1975
7 Sammy Baugh, Washington, 1940, 1942-43, 1945, 1947-49
5 Joe Montana, San Francisco, 1980-81, 1985, 1987, 1989
Steve Young, San Francisco, 1992, 1994-97

Most Consecutive Seasons Leading League
6 Len Dawson, Kansas City, 1964-69
4 Steve Young, San Francisco, 1994-97
3 Sammy Baugh, Washington, 1947-49
Otto Graham, Cleveland, 1953-55
Milt Plum, Cleveland, 1959-61

Highest Completion Percentage, Career (1,500 attempts)
64.83 Steve Young, Tampa Bay, 1985-86; San Francisco, 1987-97 (3,548-2,300)
63.24 Joe Montana, San Francisco, 1979-90, 1992; Kansas City, 1993-94 (5,391-3,409)
62.01 Troy Aikman, Dallas, 1989-97 (3,696-2,292)

Highest Completion Percentage, Season (Qualifiers)
70.55 Ken Anderson, Cincinnati, 1982 (309-218)
70.33 Sammy Baugh, Washington, 1945 (182-128)
70.28 Steve Young, San Francisco, 1994 (461-324)

Highest Completion Percentage, Rookie, Season (Qualifiers)
58.45 Dan Marino, Miami, 1983 (296-173)
57.14 Jim McMahon, Chicago, 1982 (210-120)
56.38 Rick Mirer, Seattle, 1993 (486-274)

Highest Completion Percentage, Game (20 attempts)
91.30 Vinny Testaverde, Cleveland vs. L.A. Rams, Dec. 26, 1993 (23-21)
90.91 Ken Anderson, Cincinnati vs. Pittsburgh, Nov. 10, 1974 (22-20)
90.48 Lynn Dickey, Green Bay vs. New Orleans, Dec. 13, 1981 (21-19)

YARDS GAINED

Most Seasons Leading League
5 Sonny Jurgensen, Philadelphia, 1961-62; Washington, 1966-67, 1969
Dan Marino, Miami, 1984-86, 1988, 1992
4 Sammy Baugh, Washington, 1937, 1940, 1947-48
Johnny Unitas, Baltimore, 1957, 1959-60, 1963
Dan Fouts, San Diego, 1979-82
3 Arnie Herber, Green Bay, 1932, 1934, 1936
Sid Luckman, Chi. Bears, 1943, 1945-46
John Brodie, San Francisco, 1965, 1968, 1970
John Hadl, San Diego, 1965, 1968, 1971
Joe Namath, N.Y. Jets, 1966-67, 1972

Most Consecutive Seasons Leading League
4 Dan Fouts, San Diego, 1979-82
3 Dan Marino, Miami, 1984-86
2 By many players

Most Yards Gained, Career
55,416 Dan Marino, Miami, 1983-97
48,669 John Elway, Denver, 1983-97
47,465 Warren Moon, Houston, 1984-93; Minnesota, 1994-96; Seattle, 1997

Most Seasons, 3,000 or More Yards Passing
12 Dan Marino, Miami, 1984-92, 1994-95, 1997
John Elway, Denver, 1985-91, 1993-97
9 Warren Moon, Houston, 1984, 1986, 1989-91, 1993; Minnesota, 1994-95; Seattle, 1997
8 Joe Montana, San Francisco, 1981, 1983-85, 1987, 1989-90; Kansas City, 1994
Jim Kelly, Buffalo, 1986, 1988-89, 1991-95

Most Yards Gained, Season
5,084 Dan Marino, Miami, 1984
4,802 Dan Fouts, San Diego, 1981
4,746 Dan Marino, Miami, 1986

Most Yards Gained, Rookie, Season
2,833 Rick Mirer, Seattle, 1993
2,717 Kerry Collins, Carolina, 1995
2,571 Jim Zorn, Seattle, 1976

Most Yards Gained, Game
554 Norm Van Brocklin, Los Angeles vs. N.Y. Yanks, Sept. 28, 1951
527 Warren Moon, Houston vs. Kansas City, Dec. 16, 1990
522 Boomer Esiason, Arizona vs. Washington, Nov. 10, 1996

Most Games, 400 or More Yards Passing, Career
13 Dan Marino, Miami, 1983-97
7 Joe Montana, San Francisco, 1979-90, 1992; Kansas City, 1993-94
Warren Moon, Houston, 1984-93; Minnesota, 1994-96; Seattle, 1997
6 Dan Fouts, San Diego, 1973-87

Most Games, 400 or More Yards Passing, Season
4 Dan Marino, Miami, 1984
3 Dan Marino, Miami, 1986
2 By many players

Most Consecutive Games, 400 or More Yards Passing
2 Dan Fouts, San Diego, 1982
Dan Marino, Miami, 1984
Phil Simms, N.Y. Giants, 1985

Most Games, 300 or More Yards Passing, Career
56 Dan Marino, Miami, 1983-97
51 Dan Fouts, San Diego, 1973-87
49 Warren Moon, Houston, 1984-93; Minnesota, 1994-96; Seattle, 1997

Most Games, 300 or More Yards Passing, Season
9 Dan Marino, Miami, 1984
Warren Moon, Houston, 1990
8 Dan Fouts, San Diego, 1980
7 Dan Fouts, San Diego, 1981
Bill Kenney, Kansas City, 1983
Neil Lomax, St. Louis, 1984
Dan Fouts, San Diego, 1985
Brett Favre, Green Bay, 1995

Most Consecutive Games, 300 or More Yards Passing
5 Joe Montana, San Francisco, 1982
4 Dan Fouts, San Diego, 1979
Dan Fouts, San Diego, 1980-81

Bill Kenney, Kansas City, 1983
Joe Montana, San Francisco, 1985-86
Joe Montana, San Francisco, 1990
Warren Moon, Houston, 1990
Drew Bledsoe, New England, 1993-94
3 By many players

Longest Pass Completion (All TDs except as noted)
99 Frank Filchock (to Farkas), Washington vs. Pittsburgh, Oct. 15, 1939
George Izo (to Mitchell), Washington vs. Cleveland, Sept. 15, 1963
Karl Sweetan (to Studstill), Detroit vs. Baltimore, Oct. 16, 1966
Sonny Jurgensen (to Allen), Washington vs. Chicago, Sept. 15, 1968
Jim Plunkett (to Branch), L.A. Raiders vs. Washington, Oct. 2, 1983
Ron Jaworski (to Quick), Philadelphia vs. Atlanta, Nov. 10, 1985
Stan Humphries (to Martin), San Diego vs. Seattle, Sept. 18, 1994
Brett Favre (to Brooks), Green Bay vs. Chicago, Sept. 11, 1995
98 Doug Russell (to Tinsley), Chi. Cardinals vs. Cleveland, Nov. 27, 1938
Ogden Compton (to Lane), Chi. Cardinals vs. Green Bay, Nov. 13, 1955
Bill Wade (to Farrington), Chicago Bears vs. Detroit, Oct. 8, 1961
Jacky Lee (to Dewveall), Houston vs. San Diego, Nov. 25, 1962
Earl Morrall (to Jones), N.Y. Giants vs. Pittsburgh, Sept. 11, 1966
Jim Hart (to Moore), St. Louis vs. Los Angeles, Dec. 10, 1972 (no TD)
Bobby Hebert (to Haynes), Atlanta vs. New Orleans, Sept. 12, 1993
97 Pat Coffee (to Tinsley), Chi. Cardinals vs. Chi. Bears, Dec. 5, 1937
Bobby Layne (to Box), Detroit vs. Green Bay, Nov. 26, 1953
George Shaw (to Tarr), Denver vs. Boston, Sept. 21, 1962
Bernie Kosar (to Slaughter), Cleveland vs. Chicago, Oct. 23, 1989
Steve Young (to Taylor), San Francisco vs. Atlanta, Nov. 3, 1991

AVERAGE GAIN

Most Seasons Leading League
7 Sid Luckman, Chi. Bears, 1939-43, 1946-47
5 Steve Young, San Francisco, 1991-94, 1997
3 Arnie Herber, Green Bay, 1932, 1934, 1936
Norm Van Brocklin, Los Angeles, 1950, 1952, 1954
Len Dawson, Dall. Texans, 1962; Kansas City, 1966, 1968
Bart Starr, Green Bay, 1966-68

Most Consecutive Seasons Leading League
5 Sid Luckman, Chi. Bears, 1939-43
4 Steve Young, San Francisco, 1991-94
3 Bart Starr, Green Bay, 1966-68

Highest Average Gain, Career (1,500 attempts)
8.63 Otto Graham, Cleveland, 1950-55 (1,565-13,499)
8.42 Sid Luckman, Chi. Bears, 1939-50 (1,744-14,686)
8.16 Norm Van Brocklin, Los Angeles, 1949-57; Philadelphia, 1958-60 (2,895-23,611)

Highest Average Gain, Season (Qualifiers)
11.17 Tommy O'Connell, Cleveland, 1957 (110-1,229)
10.86 Sid Luckman, Chi. Bears, 1943 (202-2,194)
10.55 Otto Graham, Cleveland, 1953 (258-2,722)

Highest Average Gain, Rookie, Season (Qualifiers)
9.411 Greg Cook, Cincinnati, 1969 (197-1,854)
9.409 Bob Waterfield, Cleveland, 1945 (171-1,609)
8.36 Zeke Bratkowski, Chi. Bears, 1954 (130-1,087)

Highest Average Gain, Game (20 attempts)
18.58 Sammy Baugh, Washington vs. Boston, Oct. 31, 1948 (24-446)
18.50 Johnny Unitas, Baltimore vs. Atlanta, Nov. 12, 1967 (20-370)
17.71 Joe Namath, N.Y. Jets vs. Baltimore, Sept. 24, 1972 (28-496)

TOUCHDOWNS

Most Seasons Leading League
4 Johnny Unitas, Baltimore, 1957-60
Len Dawson, Dall. Texans, 1962; Kansas City, 1963, 1965-66
3 Arnie Herber, Green Bay, 1932, 1934, 1936
Sid Luckman, Chi. Bears, 1943, 1945-46
Y.A. Tittle, San Francisco, 1955; N.Y. Giants, 1962-63
Dan Marino, Miami, 1984-86
Steve Young, San Francisco, 1992-94
Brett Favre, Green Bay, 1995-97
2 By many players

Most Consecutive Seasons Leading League
4 Johnny Unitas, Baltimore, 1957-60
3 Dan Marino, Miami, 1984-86
Steve Young, San Francisco, 1992-94
Brett Favre, Green Bay, 1995-97
2 By many players

Most Touchdown Passes, Career
385 Dan Marino, Miami, 1983-97
342 Fran Tarkenton, Minnesota, 1961-66, 1972-78; N.Y. Giants, 1967-71
290 Johnny Unitas, Baltimore, 1956-72: San Diego, 1973

Most Touchdown Passes, Season
48 Dan Marino, Miami, 1984
44 Dan Marino, Miami, 1986
39 Brett Favre, Green Bay, 1996

Most Touchdown Passes, Rookie, Season
22 Charlie Conerly, N.Y. Giants, 1948
20 Dan Marino, Miami, 1983
19 Jim Plunkett, New England, 1971

Most Touchdown Passes, Game
7 Sid Luckman, Chi. Bears vs. N.Y. Giants, Nov. 14, 1943
Adrian Burk, Philadelphia vs. Washington, Oct. 17, 1954
George Blanda, Houston vs. N.Y. Titans, Nov. 19, 1961
Y.A. Tittle, N.Y. Giants vs. Washington, Oct. 28, 1962
Joe Kapp, Minnesota vs. Baltimore, Sept. 28, 1969
6 By many players. Last time:
Mark Rypien, Washington vs. Atlanta, Nov. 10, 1991

Most Games, Four or More Touchdown Passes, Career
20 Dan Marino, Miami, 1983-97
17 Johnny Unitas, Baltimore, 1956-72; San Diego, 1973
13 George Blanda, Chi. Bears, 1949, 1950-58; Baltimore, 1950; Houston, 1960-66; Oakland, 1967-75

Most Games, Four or More Touchdown Passes, Season
6 Dan Marino, Miami, 1984
5 Dan Marino, Miami, 1986
Brett Favre, Green Bay, 1996
4 George Blanda, Houston, 1961
Vince Ferragamo, Los Angeles, 1980

Most Consecutive Games, Four or More Touchdown Passes
4 Dan Marino, Miami, 1984
2 By many players

Most Consecutive Games, Touchdown Passes
47 Johnny Unitas, Baltimore, 1956-60
30 Dan Marino, Miami, 1985-87
28 Dave Krieg, Seattle, 1983-85

HAD INTERCEPTED

Most Consecutive Passes Attempted, None Intercepted
308 Bernie Kosar, Cleveland, 1990-91
294 Bart Starr, Green Bay, 1964-65
279 Jeff George, Indianapolis, 1993; Atlanta, 1994

Most Passes Had Intercepted, Career
277 George Blanda, Chi. Bears, 1949, 1950-58; Baltimore, 1950; Houston, 1960-66; Oakland, 1967-75
268 John Hadl, San Diego, 1962-72; Los Angeles, 1973-74; Green Bay, 1974-75; Houston, 1976-77
266 Fran Tarkenton, Minnesota, 1961-66, 1972-78; N.Y. Giants, 1967-71

Most Passes Had Intercepted, Season
42 George Blanda, Houston, 1962
35 Vinny Testaverde, Tampa Bay, 1988
34 Frank Tripucka, Denver, 1960

Most Passes Had Intercepted, Game
8 Jim Hardy, Chi. Cardinals vs. Philadelphia, Sept. 24, 1950
7 Parker Hall, Cleveland vs. Green Bay, Nov. 8, 1942
Frank Sinkwich, Detroit vs. Green Bay, Oct. 24, 1943
Bob Waterfield, Los Angeles vs. Green Bay, Oct. 17, 1948
Zeke Bratkowski, Chicago vs. Baltimore, Oct. 2, 1960
Tommy Wade, Pittsburgh vs. Philadelphia, Dec. 12, 1965
Ken Stabler, Oakland vs. Denver, Oct. 16, 1977
Steve DeBerg, Tampa Bay vs. San Francisco, Sept. 7, 1986
6 By many players

Most Attempts, No Interceptions, Game
70 Drew Bledsoe, New England vs. Minnesota, Nov. 13, 1994 (OT)
63 Rich Gannon, Minnesota vs. New England, Oct. 20, 1991 (OT)
60 Davey O'Brien, Philadelphia vs. Washington, Dec. 1, 1940

LOWEST PERCENTAGE, PASSES HAD INTERCEPTED

Most Seasons Leading League, Lowest Percentage, Passes Had Intercepted
5 Sammy Baugh, Washington, 1940, 1942, 1944-45, 1947
3 Charlie Conerly, N.Y. Giants, 1950, 1956, 1959
Bart Starr, Green Bay, 1962, 1964, 1966
Roger Staubach, Dallas, 1971, 1977, 1979
Ken Anderson, Cincinnati, 1972, 1981-82
Ken O'Brien, N.Y. Jets, 1985, 1987-88
2 By many players

Lowest Percentage, Passes Had Intercepted, Career (1,500 attempts)
2.10 Neil O'Donnell, Pittsburgh, 1991-95; N.Y. Jets, 1997 (2,519-53)
2.43 Steve Bono, Minnesota, 1985-86; Pittsburgh, 1987-88; San Francisco, 1989, 1991-93; Kansas City, 1994-96; Green Bay, 1997 (1,564-38)
2.56 Steve Young, Tampa Bay, 1985-86; San Francisco, 1987-97, (3,548-91)

Lowest Percentage, Passes Had Intercepted, Season (Qualifiers)
0.66 Joe Ferguson, Buffalo, 1976 (151-1)
0.90 Steve DeBerg, Kansas City, 1990 (444-4)
1.16 Steve Bartkowski, Atlanta, 1983 (432-5)

Lowest Percentage, Passes Had Intercepted, Rookie, Season (Qualifiers)
2.03 Dan Marino, Miami, 1983 (296-6)
2.10 Gary Wood, N.Y. Giants, 1964 (143-3)
2.82 Bernie Kosar, Cleveland, 1985 (248-7)

TIMES SACKED
Times Sacked has been compiled since 1963.

Most Times Sacked, Career
498 John Elway, Denver, 1983-97
492 Dave Krieg, Seattle, 1980-91; Kansas City, 1992-93; Detroit, 1994; Arizona, 1995; Chicago, 1996; Tennessee, 1997
483 Fran Tarkenton, Minnesota, 1963-66, 1972-78; N.Y. Giants, 1967-71

Most Times Sacked, Season
72 Randall Cunningham, Philadelphia, 1986
62 Ken O'Brien, N.Y. Jets, 1985
61 Neil Lomax, St. Louis, 1985

Most Times Sacked, Game
12 Bert Jones, Baltimore vs. St. Louis, Oct. 26, 1980
Warren Moon, Houston vs. Dallas, Sept. 29, 1985
11 Charley Johnson, St. Louis vs. N.Y. Giants, Nov. 1, 1964
Bart Starr, Green Bay vs. Detroit, Nov. 7, 1965
Jack Kemp, Buffalo vs. Oakland, Oct. 15, 1967
Bob Berry, Atlanta vs. St. Louis, Nov. 24, 1968
Greg Landry, Detroit vs. Dallas, Oct. 6, 1975
Ron Jaworski, Philadelphia vs. St. Louis, Dec. 18, 1983
Paul McDonald, Cleveland vs. Kansas City, Sept. 30, 1984
Archie Manning, Minnesota vs. Chicago, Oct. 28, 1984
Steve Pelluer, Dallas vs. San Diego, Nov. 16, 1986
Randall Cunningham, Philadelphia vs. L.A. Raiders, Nov. 30, 1986 (OT)
David Norrie, N.Y. Jets vs. Dallas, Oct. 4, 1987
Troy Aikman, Dallas vs. Philadelphia, Sept. 15, 1991
Bernie Kosar, Cleveland vs. Indianapolis, Sept. 6, 1992
10 By many players

PASS RECEIVING
Most Seasons Leading League
8 Don Hutson, Green Bay, 1936-37, 1939, 1941-45
5 Lionel Taylor, Denver, 1960-63, 1965
3 Tom Fears, Los Angeles, 1948-50
Pete Pihos, Philadelphia, 1953-55
Billy Wilson, San Francisco, 1954, 1956-57
Raymond Berry, Baltimore, 1958-60
Lance Alworth, San Diego, 1966, 1968-69
Sterling Sharpe, Green Bay, 1989, 1992-93

Most Consecutive Seasons Leading League
5 Don Hutson, Green Bay, 1941-45
4 Lionel Taylor, Denver, 1960-63
3 Tom Fears, Los Angeles, 1948-50
Pete Pihos, Philadelphia, 1953-55
Raymond Berry, Baltimore, 1958-60

Most Pass Receptions, Career
1,057 Jerry Rice, San Francisco, 1985-97
940 Art Monk, Washington, 1980-93; N.Y. Jets, 1994; Philadelphia, 1995
826 Andre Reed, Buffalo, 1985-97

Most Seasons, 50 or More Pass Receptions
11 Jerry Rice, San Francisco, 1986-96
Andre Reed, Buffalo, 1986-94, 1996-97
10 Steve Largent, Seattle, 1976, 1978-81, 1983-87
Gary Clark, Washington, 1985-92; Phoenix, 1993; Arizona, 1994
Henry Ellard, L.A. Rams, 1985, 1987-91, 1993; Washington, 1994-96
9 Art Monk, Washington, 1980-81, 1984-86, 1988-91
James Lofton, Green Bay, 1979-81, 1983-86; Buffalo, 1991-92

Most Pass Receptions, Season
123 Herman Moore, Detroit, 1995
122 Cris Carter, Minnesota, 1994
Cris Carter, Minnesota, 1995
Jerry Rice, San Francisco, 1995
119 Isaac Bruce, St. Louis, 1995

Most Pass Receptions, Rookie, Season
90 Terry Glenn, New England, 1996
83 Earl Cooper, San Francisco, 1980
81 Keith Jackson, Philadelphia, 1988

Most Pass Receptions, Game
18 Tom Fears, Los Angeles vs. Green Bay, Dec. 3, 1950
17 Clark Gaines, N.Y. Jets vs. San Francisco, Sept. 21, 1980
16 Sonny Randle, St. Louis vs. N.Y. Giants, Nov. 4, 1962
Jerry Rice, San Francisco vs. L.A. Rams, Nov. 20, 1994
Keenan McCardell, Jacksonville vs. St. Louis, Oct. 20, 1996

Most Consecutive Games, Pass Receptions
183 Art Monk, Washington, 1980-93; N.Y. Jets, 1994; Philadelphia, 1995
177 Steve Largent, Seattle, 1977-89
Jerry Rice, San Francisco, 1985-97 (current)
150 Ozzie Newsome, Cleveland, 1979-89

YARDS GAINED
Most Seasons Leading League
7 Don Hutson, Green Bay, 1936, 1938-39, 1941-44
6 Jerry Rice, San Francisco, 1986, 1989-90, 1993-95
3 Raymond Berry, Baltimore, 1957, 1959-60
Lance Alworth, San Diego, 1965-66, 1968

Most Consecutive Seasons Leading League
4 Don Hutson, Green Bay, 1941-44
3 Jerry Rice, San Francisco, 1993-95
2 By many players

Most Yards Gained, Career
16,455 Jerry Rice, San Francisco, 1985-97
14,004 James Lofton, Green Bay, 1978-86; L.A. Raiders, 1987-88; Buffalo, 1989-92; L.A. Rams, 1993; Philadelphia, 1993
13,662 Henry Ellard, L.A. Rams, 1983-1993; Washington, 1994-97

Most Seasons, 1,000 or More Yards, Pass Receiving
11 Jerry Rice, San Francisco, 1986-96
8 Steve Largent, Seattle, 1978-81, 1983-86
7 Lance Alworth, San Diego, 1963-69
Henry Ellard, L.A. Rams, 1988-91; Washington 1994-96

Most Yards Gained, Season
1,848 Jerry Rice, San Francisco, 1995
1,781 Isaac Bruce, St. Louis, 1995
1,746 Charley Hennigan, Houston, 1961

Most Yards Gained, Rookie, Season
1,473 Bill Groman, Houston, 1960
1,231 Bill Howton, Green Bay, 1952
1,132 Terry Glenn, New England, 1996

Most Yards Gained, Game
336 Willie Anderson, L.A. Rams vs. New Orleans, Nov. 26, 1989 (OT)
309 Stephone Paige, Kansas City vs. San Diego, Dec. 22, 1985
303 Jim Benton, Cleveland vs. Detroit, Nov. 22, 1945

Most Games, 200 or More Yards Pass Receiving, Career
5 Lance Alworth, San Diego, 1962-70; Dallas, 1971-72
4 Don Hutson, Green Bay, 1935-45
Charley Hennigan, Houston, 1960-66
Jerry Rice, San Francisco, 1985-97
3 Don Maynard, N.Y. Giants, 1958; N.Y. Jets, 1960-72; St. Louis, 1973
Wes Chandler, New Orleans, 1978-81; San Diego, 1981-87; San Francisco, 1988
Isaac Bruce, L.A. Rams, 1994; St. Louis, 1995-97

Most Games, 200 or More Yards Pass Receiving, Season
3 Charley Hennigan, Houston, 1961
2 Don Hutson, Green Bay, 1942
Gene Roberts, N.Y. Giants, 1949
Lance Alworth, San Diego, 1963
Don Maynard, N.Y. Jets, 1968

Most Games, 100 or More Yards Pass Receiving, Career
61 Jerry Rice, San Francisco, 1985-97
50 Don Maynard, N.Y. Giants, 1958; N.Y. Jets, 1960-72; St. Louis, 1973
43 James Lofton, Green Bay, 1978-86; L.A. Raiders, 1987-88; Buffalo, 1989-92; L.A. Rams, 1993; Philadelphia, 1993
Michael Irvin, Dallas, 1988-97

Most Games, 100 or More Yards Pass Receiving, Season
11 Michael Irvin, Dallas, 1995
10 Charley Hennigan, Houston, 1961
Herman Moore, Detroit, 1995
9 Elroy (Crazylegs) Hirsch, Los Angeles, 1951
Bill Groman, Houston, 1960
Lance Alworth, San Diego, 1965
Don Maynard, N.Y. Jets, 1967
Stanley Morgan, New England, 1986
Mark Carrier, Tampa Bay, 1989
Robert Brooks, Green Bay, 1995
Isaac Bruce, St. Louis, 1995
Jerry Rice, San Francisco, 1995

Most Consecutive Games, 100 or More Yards Pass Receiving
7 Charley Hennigan, Houston, 1961
Bill Groman, Houston, 1961
Michael Irvin, Dallas, 1995
6 Raymond Berry, Baltimore, 1960
Pat Studstill, Detroit, 1966
Isaac Bruce, St. Louis, 1995
5 Elroy (Crazylegs) Hirsch, Los Angeles, 1951
Bob Boyd, Los Angeles, 1954
Terry Barr, Detroit, 1963
Lance Alworth, San Diego, 1966
Don Maynard, N.Y. Jets, 1968-69
Harold Jackson, Philadelphia, 1971-72

Longest Pass Reception (All TDs except as noted)
99 Andy Farkas (from Filchock), Washington vs. Pittsburgh, Oct. 15, 1939
Bobby Mitchell (from Izo), Washington vs. Cleveland, Sept. 15, 1963
Pat Studstill (from Sweetan), Detroit vs. Baltimore, Oct. 16, 1966

Gerry Allen (from Jurgensen), Washington vs. Chicago, Sept. 15, 1968
Cliff Branch (from Plunkett), L.A. Raiders vs. Washington, Oct. 2, 1983
Mike Quick (from Jaworski), Philadelphia vs. Atlanta, Nov. 10, 1985
Tony Martin (from Humphries), San Diego vs. Seattle, Sept. 18, 1994
Robert Brooks (from Favre), Green Bay vs. Chicago, Sept. 11, 1995
98 Gaynell Tinsley (from Russell), Chi. Cardinals vs. Cleveland, Nov. 17, 1938
Dick (Night Train) Lane (from Compton), Chi. Cardinals vs. Green Bay, Nov. 13, 1955
John Farrington (from Wade), Chicago vs. Detroit, Oct. 8, 1961
Willard Dewveall (from Lee), Houston vs. San Diego, Nov. 25, 1962
Homer Jones (from Morrall), N.Y. Giants vs. Pittsburgh, Sept. 11, 1966
Bobby Moore (from Hart), St. Louis vs. Los Angeles, Dec. 10, 1972 (no TD)
Michael Haynes (from Hebert), Atlanta vs. New Orleans, Sept. 12, 1993
97 Gaynell Tinsley (from Coffee), Chi. Cardinals vs. Chi. Bears, Dec. 5, 1937
Cloyce Box (from Layne), Detroit vs. Green Bay, Nov. 26, 1953
Jerry Tarr (from Shaw), Denver vs. Boston, Sept. 21, 1962
Webster Slaughter (from Kosar), Cleveland vs. Chicago, Oct. 23, 1989
John Taylor (from Young), San Francisco vs. Atlanta, Nov. 3, 1991

AVERAGE GAIN

Highest Average Gain, Career (200 receptions)
22.26 Homer Jones, N.Y. Giants, 1964-69; Cleveland, 1970 (224-4,986)
20.83 Buddy Dial, Pittsburgh, 1959-63; Dallas, 1964-66 (261-5,436)
20.24 Harlon Hill, Chi. Bears, 1954-61; Pittsburgh, 1962; Detroit, 1962 (233-4,717)

Highest Average Gain, Season (24 receptions)
32.58 Don Currivan, Boston, 1947 (24-782)
31.44 Bucky Pope, Los Angeles, 1964 (25-786)
28.60 Bobby Duckworth, San Diego, 1984 (25-715)

Highest Average Gain, Game (3 receptions)
60.67 Bill Groman, Houston vs. Denver, Nov. 20, 1960 (3-182)
Homer Jones, N.Y. Giants vs. Washington, Dec. 12, 1965 (3-182)
60.33 Don Currivan, Boston vs. Washington, Nov. 30, 1947 (3-181)
59.67 Bobby Duckworth, San Diego vs. Chicago, Dec. 3, 1984 (3-179)

TOUCHDOWNS

Most Seasons Leading League
9 Don Hutson, Green Bay, 1935-38, 1940-44
6 Jerry Rice, San Francisco, 1986-87, 1989-91, 1993
3 Lance Alworth, San Diego, 1964-66

Most Consecutive Seasons Leading League
5 Don Hutson, Green Bay, 1940-44
4 Don Hutson, Green Bay, 1935-38
3 Lance Alworth, San Diego, 1964-66
Jerry Rice, San Francisco, 1989-91

Most Touchdowns, Career
155 Jerry Rice, San Francisco, 1985-97
100 Steve Largent, Seattle, 1976-89
99 Don Hutson, Green Bay, 1935-45

Most Touchdowns, Season
22 Jerry Rice, San Francisco, 1987
18 Mark Clayton, Miami, 1984
Sterling Sharpe, Green Bay, 1994
17 Don Hutson, Green Bay, 1942
Elroy (Crazylegs) Hirsch, Los Angeles, 1951
Bill Groman, Houston, 1961
Jerry Rice, San Francisco, 1989
Cris Carter, Minnesota, 1995
Carl Pickens, Cincinnati, 1995

Most Touchdowns, Rookie, Season
13 Bill Howton, Green Bay, 1952
John Jefferson, San Diego, 1979
12 Harlon Hill, Chi. Bears, 1954
Bill Groman, Houston, 1960
Mike Ditka, Chicago, 1961
Bob Hayes, Dallas, 1965
10 Bill Swiacki, N.Y. Giants, 1948
Bucky Pope, Los Angeles, 1964
Sammy White, Minnesota, 1976
Daryl Turner, Seattle, 1984

Most Touchdowns, Game
5 Bob Shaw, Chi. Cardinals vs. Baltimore, Oct. 2, 1950
Kellen Winslow, San Diego vs. Oakland, Nov. 22, 1981
Jerry Rice, San Francisco vs. Atlanta, Oct. 14, 1990
4 By many players. Last time:
Irving Fryar, Philadelphia vs. Miami,Oct. 20, 1996

Most Consecutive Games, Touchdowns
13 Jerry Rice, San Francisco, 1986-87

11 Elroy (Crazylegs) Hirsch, Los Angeles, 1950-51
Buddy Dial, Pittsburgh, 1959-60
10 Carl Pickens, Cincinnati, 1994-95

INTERCEPTIONS BY

Most Seasons Leading League
3 Everson Walls, Dallas, 1981-82, 1985
2 Dick (Night Train) Lane, Los Angeles, 1952; Chi. Cardinals, 1954
Jack Christiansen, Detroit, 1953, 1957
Milt Davis, Baltimore, 1957, 1959
Dick Lynch, N.Y. Giants, 1961, 1963
Johnny Robinson, Kansas City, 1966, 1970
Bill Bradley, Philadelphia, 1971-72
Emmitt Thomas, Kansas City, 1969, 1974
Ronnie Lott, San Francisco, 1986; L.A. Raiders, 1991

Most Interceptions By, Career
81 Paul Krause, Washington, 1964-67; Minnesota, 1968-79
79 Emlen Tunnell, N.Y. Giants, 1948-58; Green Bay, 1959-61
68 Dick (Night Train) Lane, Los Angeles, 1952-53; Chi. Cardinals, 1954-59; Detroit, 1960-65

Most Interceptions By, Season
14 Dick (Night Train) Lane, Los Angeles, 1952
13 Dan Sandifer, Washington, 1948
Orban (Spec) Sanders, N.Y. Yanks, 1950
Lester Hayes, Oakland, 1980
12 By nine players

Most Interceptions By, Rookie, Season
14 Dick (Night Train) Lane, Los Angeles, 1952
13 Dan Sandifer, Washington, 1948
12 Woodley Lewis, Los Angeles, 1950
Paul Krause, Washington, 1964

Most Interceptions By, Game
4 Sammy Baugh, Washington vs. Detroit, Nov. 14, 1943
Dan Sandifer, Washington vs. Boston, Oct. 31, 1948
Don Doll, Detroit vs. Chi. Cardinals, Oct. 23, 1949
Bob Nussbaumer, Chi. Cardinals vs. N.Y. Bulldogs, Nov. 13, 1949
Russ Craft, Philadelphia vs. Chi. Cardinals, Sept. 24, 1950
Bobby Dillon, Green Bay vs. Detroit, Nov. 26, 1953
Jack Butler, Pittsburgh vs. Washington, Dec. 13, 1953
Austin (Goose) Gonsoulin, Denver vs. Buffalo, Sept. 18, 1960
Jerry Norton, St. Louis vs. Washington, Nov. 20, 1960; vs. Pittsburgh, Nov. 26, 1961
Dave Baker, San Francisco vs. L.A. Rams, Dec. 4, 1960
Bobby Ply, Dall. Texans vs. San Diego, Dec. 16, 1962
Bobby Hunt, Kansas City vs. Houston, Oct. 4, 1964
Willie Brown, Denver vs. N.Y. Jets, Nov. 15, 1964
Dick Anderson, Miami vs. Pittsburgh, Dec. 3, 1973
Willie Buchanon, Green Bay vs. San Diego, Sept. 24, 1978
Deron Cherry, Kansas City vs. Seattle, Sept. 29, 1985

Most Consecutive Games, Passes Intercepted By
8 Tom Morrow, Oakland, 1962-63
7 Paul Krause, Washington, 1964
Larry Wilson, St. Louis, 1966
Ben Davis, Cleveland, 1968
6 Dick (Night Train) Lane, Chi. Cardinals, 1954-55
Will Sherman, Los Angeles, 1954-55
Jim Shofner, Cleveland, 1960
Paul Krause, Minnesota, 1968
Willie Williams, N.Y. Giants, 1968
Kermit Alexander, San Francisco, 1968-69
Mel Blount, Pittsburgh, 1975
Lemar Parrish, Washington, 1978-79
Eric Harris, Kansas City, 1980
Lester Hayes, Oakland, 1980
Barry Wilburn, Washington, 1987

YARDS GAINED

Most Seasons Leading League
2 Dick (Night Train) Lane, Los Angeles, 1952; Chi. Cardinals, 1954
Herb Adderley, Green Bay, 1965, 1969
Dick Anderson, Miami, 1968, 1970

Most Yards Gained, Career
1,282 Emlen Tunnell, N.Y. Giants, 1948-58; Green Bay, 1959-61
1,207 Dick (Night Train) Lane, Los Angeles, 1952-53; Chi. Cardinals, 1954-59; Detroit, 1960-65
1,185 Paul Krause, Washington, 1964-67; Minnesota, 1968-79

Most Yards Gained, Season
349 Charlie McNeil, San Diego, 1961
303 Deion Sanders, San Francisco, 1994
301 Don Doll, Detroit, 1949

Most Yards Gained, Rookie, Season
301 Don Doll, Detroit, 1949
298 Dick (Night Train) Lane, Los Angeles, 1952

275 Woodley Lewis, Los Angeles, 1950

Most Yards Gained, Game

177 Charlie McNeil, San Diego vs. Houston, Sept. 24, 1961
170 Louis Oliver, Miami vs. Buffalo, Oct. 4, 1992
167 Dick Jauron, Detroit vs. Chicago, Nov. 18, 1973

Longest Return (All TDs)

103 Vencie Glenn, San Diego vs. Denver, Nov. 29, 1987
Louis Oliver, Miami vs. Buffalo, Oct. 4, 1992
102 Bob Smith, Detroit vs. Chi. Bears, Nov. 24, 1949
Erich Barnes, N.Y. Giants vs. Dall. Cowboys, Oct. 15, 1961
Gary Barbaro, Kansas City vs. Seattle, Dec. 11, 1977
Louis Breeden, Cincinnati vs. San Diego, Nov. 8, 1981
Eddie Anderson, L.A. Raiders vs. Miami, Dec. 14, 1992
Donald Frank, San Diego vs. L.A. Raiders, Oct. 31, 1993
101 Richie Petitbon, Chicago vs Los Angeles, Dec. 9, 1962
Henry Carr, N.Y. Giants vs. Los Angeles, Nov. 13, 1966
Tony Greene, Buffalo vs. Kansas City, Oct. 3, 1976
Tom Pridemore, Atlanta vs. San Francisco, Sept. 20, 1981

TOUCHDOWNS

Most Touchdowns, Career

9 Ken Houston, Houston, 1967-72; Washington, 1973-80
7 Herb Adderley, Green Bay, 1961-69; Dallas, 1970-72
Erich Barnes, Chi. Bears, 1958-60; N.Y. Giants, 1961-64; Cleveland, 1965-70
Lem Barney, Detroit, 1967-77
Deion Sanders, Atlanta, 1989-93; San Francisco, 1994; Dallas, 1995-97
6 Tom Janik, Denver, 1963-64; Buffalo, 1965-68; Boston, 1969-70; New England, 1971
Miller Farr, Denver, 1965; San Diego, 1965-66; Houston, 1967-69; St. Louis, 1970-72; Detroit, 1973
Bobby Bell, Kansas City, 1963-74
Darrell Green, Washington, 1983-97
Aeneas Williams, Phoenix, 1991-93; Arizona, 1994-97

Most Touchdowns, Season

4 Ken Houston, Houston, 1971
Jim Kearney, Kansas City, 1972
Eric Allen, Philadelphia, 1993
3 Dick Harris, San Diego, 1961
Dick Lynch, N.Y. Giants, 1963
Herb Adderley, Green Bay, 1965
Lem Barney, Detroit, 1967
Miller Farr, Houston, 1967
Monte Jackson, Los Angeles, 1976
Rod Perry, Los Angeles, 1978
Ronnie Lott, San Francisco, 1981
Lloyd Burruss, Kansas City, 1986
Wayne Haddix, Tampa Bay, 1990
Robert Massey, Phoenix, 1992
Ray Buchanan, Indianapolis, 1994
Deion Sanders, San Francisco, 1994
Mark McMillian, Kansas City, 1997
Otis Smith, N.Y. Jets, 1997
2 By many players

Most Touchdowns, Rookie, Season

3 Lem Barney, Detroit, 1967
Ronnie Lott, San Francisco, 1981
2 By many players

Most Touchdowns, Game

2 Bill Blackburn, Chi. Cardinals vs. Boston, Oct. 24, 1948
Dan Sandifer, Washington vs. Boston, Oct. 31, 1948
Bob Franklin, Cleveland vs. Chicago, Dec. 11, 1960
Bill Stacy, St. Louis vs. Dall. Cowboys, Nov. 5, 1961
Jerry Norton, St. Louis vs. Pittsburgh, Nov. 26, 1961
Miller Farr, Houston vs. Buffalo, Dec. 7, 1968
Ken Houston, Houston vs. San Diego, Dec. 19, 1971
Jim Kearney, Kansas City vs. Denver, Oct. 1, 1972
Lemar Parrish, Cincinnati vs. Houston, Dec. 17, 1972
Dick Anderson, Miami vs. Pittsburgh, Dec. 3, 1973
Prentice McCray, New England vs. N.Y. Jets, Nov. 21, 1976
Kenny Johnson, Atlanta vs. Green Bay, Nov. 27, 1983 (OT)
Mike Kozlowski, Miami vs. N.Y. Jets, Dec. 16, 1983
Dave Brown, Seattle vs. Kansas City, Nov. 4, 1984
Lloyd Burruss, Kansas City vs. San Diego, Oct. 19, 1986
Henry Jones, Buffalo vs. Indianapolis, Sept. 20, 1992
Robert Massey, Phoenix vs. Washington, Oct. 4, 1992
Eric Allen, Philadelphia vs. New Orleans, Dec. 26, 1993
Ken Norton, San Francisco vs. St. Louis, Oct. 22, 1995
Otis Smith, N.Y. Jets vs. Tampa Bay, Dec. 14, 1997

PUNTING

Most Seasons Leading League

4 Sammy Baugh, Washington, 1940-43
Jerrel Wilson, Kansas City, 1965, 1968, 1972-73
3 Yale Lary, Detroit, 1959, 1961, 1963
Jim Fraser, Denver, 1962-64
Ray Guy, Oakland, 1974-75, 1977
Rohn Stark, Baltimore, 1983; Indianapolis, 1985-86
2 By many players

Most Consecutive Seasons Leading League

4 Sammy Baugh, Washington, 1940-43
3 Jim Fraser, Denver, 1962-64
2 By many players

PUNTS

Most Punts, Career

1,154 Dave Jennings, N.Y. Giants, 1974-84; N.Y. Jets, 1985-87
1,141 Rohn Stark, Baltimore, 1982-83; Indianapolis, 1984-94; Pittsburgh, 1995; Carolina, 1996; Seattle, 1997
1,083 John James, Atlanta, 1972-81; Detroit, 1982, Houston, 1982-84

Most Punts, Season

114 Bob Parsons, Chicago, 1981
111 Brad Maynard, N.Y. Giants, 1997
109 John James, Atlanta, 1978

Most Punts, Rookie, Season

111 Brad Maynard, N.Y. Giants, 1997
108 John Teltschik, Philadelphia, 1986
99 Lewis Colbert, Kansas City, 1986

Most Punts, Game

15 John Teltschik, Philadelphia vs. N.Y. Giants, Dec. 6, 1987 (OT)
14 Dick Nesbitt, Chi. Cardinals vs. Chi. Bears, Nov. 30, 1933
Keith Molesworth, Chi. Bears vs. Green Bay, Dec. 10, 1933
Sammy Baugh, Washington vs. Philadelphia, Nov. 5, 1939
Carl Kinscherf, N.Y. Giants vs. Detroit, Nov. 7, 1943
George Taliaferro, N.Y. Yanks vs. Los Angeles, Sept. 28, 1951
13 Brad Maynard, N.Y. Giants vs. Washington, Nov. 23, 1997 (OT)

Longest Punt

98 Steve O'Neal, N.Y. Jets vs. Denver, Sept. 21, 1969
94 Joe Lintzenich, Chi. Bears vs. N.Y. Giants, Nov. 16, 1931
93 Shawn McCarthy, New England vs. Buffalo, Nov. 3, 1991

AVERAGE YARDAGE

Highest Average, Punting, Career (250 punts)

45.10 Sammy Baugh, Washington, 1937-52 (338-15,245)
44.68 Tommy Davis, San Francisco, 1959-69 (511-22,833)
44.29 Yale Lary, Detroit, 1952-53, 1956-64 (503-22,279)

Highest Average, Punting, Season (Qualifiers)

51.40 Sammy Baugh, Washington, 1940 (35-1,799)
48.94 Yale Lary, Detroit, 1963 (35-1,713)
48.73 Sammy Baugh, Washington, 1941 (30-1,462)

Highest Average, Punting, Rookie, Season (Qualifiers)

45.92 Frank Sinkwich, Detroit, 1943 (12-551)
45.66 Tommy Davis, San Francisco, 1959 (59-2,694)
45.57 David Lee, Baltimore, 1966 (49-2,233)

Highest Average, Punting, Game (4 punts)

61.75 Bob Cifers, Detroit vs. Chi. Bears, Nov. 24, 1946 (4-247)
61.60 Roy McKay, Green Bay vs. Chi. Cardinals, Oct. 28, 1945 (5-308)
59.50 Darren Bennett, San Diego vs. Pittsburgh, Oct. 1, 1995 (4-238)

PUNTS HAD BLOCKED

Most Consecutive Punts, None Blocked

623 Dave Jennings, N.Y. Giants, 1976-83
619 Ray Guy, Oakland, 1979-81; L.A. Raiders, 1982-86
578 Bobby Walden, Minnesota, 1964-67; Pittsburgh, 1968-72

Most Punts Had Blocked, Career

14 Herman Weaver, Detroit, 1970-76; Seattle, 1977-80
Harry Newsome, Pittsburgh, 1985-89; Minnesota, 1990-93
12 Jerrel Wilson, Kansas City, 1963-77; New England, 1978
Tom Blanchard, N.Y. Giants, 1971-73; New Orleans, 1974-78; Tampa Bay, 1979-81
11 David Lee, Baltimore, 1966-78

Most Punts Had Blocked, Season

6 Harry Newsome, Pittsburgh, 1988
4 Bryan Wagner, Cleveland, 1990
3 By many players

PUNT RETURNS

Most Seasons Leading League

3 Les (Speedy) Duncan, San Diego, 1965-66; Washington, 1971
Rick Upchurch, Denver, 1976, 1978, 1982

2 Dick Christy, N.Y. Titans, 1961-62
Claude Gibson, Oakland, 1963-64
Billy (White Shoes) Johnson, Houston, 1975, 1977
Mel Gray, New Orleans, 1987; Detroit, 1991

PUNT RETURNS

Most Punt Returns, Career
344 David Meggett, N.Y. Giants, 1989-94; New England, 1995-97
301 Tim Brown, L.A. Raiders, 1989-94; Oakland, 1995-97
292 Vai Sikahema, St. Louis, 1986-87; Phoenix, 1988-90; Green Bay, 1991; Philadelphia, 1992-93

Most Punt Returns, Season
70 Danny Reece, Tampa Bay, 1979
62 Fulton Walker, Miami-L.A. Raiders, 1985
58 J.T. Smith, Kansas City, 1979
Greg Pruitt, L.A. Raiders, 1983
Leo Lewis, Minnesota, 1988
Desmond Howard, Green Bay, 1996

Most Punt Returns, Rookie, Season
57 Lew Barnes, Chicago, 1986
54 James Jones, Dallas, 1980
53 Louis Lipps, Pittsburgh, 1984

Most Punt Returns, Game
11 Eddie Brown, Washington vs. Tampa Bay, Oct. 9, 1977
10 Theo Bell, Pittsburgh vs. Buffalo, Dec. 16, 1979
Mike Nelms, Washington vs. New Orleans, Dec. 26, 1982
Ronnie Harris, New England vs. Pittsburgh, Dec. 5, 1993
9 Rodger Bird, Oakland vs. Denver, Sept. 10, 1967
Ralph McGill, San Francisco vs. Atlanta, Oct. 29, 1972
Ed Podolak, Kansas City vs. San Diego, Nov. 10, 1974
Anthony Leonard, San Francisco vs. New Orleans, Oct. 17, 1976
Butch Johnson, Dallas vs. Buffalo, Nov. 15, 1976
Larry Marshall, Philadelphia vs. Tampa Bay, Sept. 18, 1977
Nesby Glasgow, Baltimore vs. Kansas City, Sept. 2, 1979
Mike Nelms, Washington vs. St. Louis, Dec. 21, 1980
Leon Bright, N.Y. Giants vs. Philadelphia, Dec. 11, 1982
Pete Shaw, N.Y. Giants vs. Philadelphia, Nov. 20, 1983
Cleotha Montgomery, L.A. Raiders vs. Detroit, Dec. 10, 1984
Phil McConkey, N.Y. Giants vs. Philadelphia, Dec. 6, 1987 (OT)
Andre Hastings, Pittsburgh vs. Cleveland, Nov. 13, 1995

FAIR CATCHES

Most Fair Catches, Career
121 Mel Gray, New Orleans, 1986-88; Detroit, 1989-94; Houston, 1995-96; Tennessee, 1997; Philadelphia, 1997
119 Brian Mitchell, Washington, 1990-97
114 David Meggett, N.Y. Giants, 1989-94; New England, 1995-97

Most Fair Catches, Season
27 Leo Lewis, Minnesota, 1989
26 Eric Guliford, New Orleans, 1997
Glyn Milburn, Detroit, 1997
25 Mark Konecny, Philadelphia, 1988
Phil McConkey, N.Y. Giants, 1988
Chris Warren, Seattle, 1992

Most Fair Catches, Game
7 Lem Barney, Detroit vs. Chicago, Nov. 21, 1976
Bobby Morse, Philadelphia vs. Buffalo, Dec. 27, 1987
6 Jake Scott, Miami vs. Buffalo, Dec. 20, 1970
Greg Pruitt, L.A. Raiders vs. Seattle, Oct. 7, 1984
Phil McConkey, San Diego vs. Kansas City, Dec. 17, 1989
Gerald McNeil, Houston vs. Pittsburgh, Sept. 16, 1990
Bobby Engram, Chicago vs. Minnesota, Sept. 15, 1996
5 By many players

YARDS GAINED

Most Seasons Leading League
3 Alvin Haymond, Baltimore, 1965-66; Los Angeles, 1969
2 Bill Dudley, Pittsburgh, 1942, 1946
Emlen Tunnell, N.Y. Giants, 1951-52
Dick Christy, N.Y. Titans, 1961-62
Claude Gibson, Oakland, 1963-64
Rodger Bird, Oakland, 1966-67
J.T. Smith, Kansas City, 1979-80
Vai Sikahema, St. Louis, 1986-87
David Meggett, N.Y. Giants, 1989-90

Most Yards Gained, Career
3,668 David Meggett, N.Y. Giants, 1989-94; New England, 1995-97
3,317 Billy (White Shoes) Johnson, Houston, 1974-80; Atlanta, 1982-87; Washington, 1988
3,169 Vai Sikahema, St. Louis, 1986-87; Phoenix, 1988-90; Green Bay, 1991; Philadelphia, 1992-93

Most Yards Gained, Season
875 Desmond Howard, Green Bay, 1996
692 Fulton Walker, Miami-L.A. Raiders, 1985
666 Greg Pruitt, L.A. Raiders, 1983

Most Yards Gained, Rookie, Season
656 Louis Lipps, Pittsburgh, 1984
655 Neal Colzie, Oakland, 1975
619 Leon Johnson, N.Y. Jets, 1997

Most Yards Gained, Game
207 LeRoy Irvin, Los Angeles vs. Atlanta, Oct. 11, 1981
205 George Atkinson, Oakland vs. Buffalo, Sept. 15, 1968
184 Tom Watkins, Detroit vs. San Francisco, Oct. 6, 1963
Jermaine Lewis, Baltimore vs. Seattle, Dec. 7, 1997

Longest Punt Return (All TDs)
103 Robert Bailey, L.A. Rams vs. New Orleans, Oct. 23, 1994
98 Gil LeFebvre, Cincinnati vs. Brooklyn, Dec. 3, 1933
Charlie West, Minnesota vs. Washington, Nov. 3, 1968
Dennis Morgan, Dallas vs. St. Louis, Oct. 13, 1974
Terance Mathis, N.Y. Jets vs. Dallas, Nov. 4, 1990
97 Greg Pruitt, L.A. Raiders vs. Washington, Oct. 2, 1983

AVERAGE YARDAGE

Highest Average, Career (75 returns)
13.64 Darrien Gordon, San Diego, 1993-94, 1996; Denver, 1997 (143-1,950)
12.78 George McAfee, Chi. Bears, 1940-41, 1945-50 (112-1,431)
12.75 Jack Christiansen, Detroit, 1951-58 (85-1,084)

Highest Average, Season (Qualifiers)
23.00 Herb Rich, Baltimore, 1950 (12-276)
21.47 Jack Christiansen, Detroit, 1952 (15-322)
21.28 Dick Christy, N.Y. Titans, 1961 (18-383)

Highest Average, Rookie, Season (Qualifiers)
23.00 Herb Rich, Baltimore, 1950 (12-276)
20.88 Jerry Davis, Chi. Cardinals, 1948 (16-334)
20.73 Frank Sinkwich, Detroit, 1943 (11-228)

Highest Average, Game (3 returns)
47.67 Chuck Latourette, St. Louis vs. New Orleans, Sept. 29, 1968 (3-143)
47.33 Johnny Roland, St. Louis vs. Philadelphia, Oct. 2, 1966 (3-142)
45.67 Dick Christy, N.Y. Titans vs. Denver, Sept. 24, 1961 (3-137)

TOUCHDOWNS

Most Touchdowns, Career
9 Eric Metcalf, Cleveland, 1989-94; Atlanta, 1995-96; San Diego, 1997
8 Jack Christiansen, Detroit, 1951-58
Rick Upchurch, Denver, 1975-83
7 David Meggett, N.Y. Giants, 1989-94; New England, 1995-97
Brian Mitchell, Washington, 1990-97

Most Touchdowns, Season
4 Jack Christiansen, Detroit, 1951
Rick Upchurch, Denver, 1976
3 Emlen Tunnell, N.Y. Giants, 1951
Billy (White Shoes) Johnson, Houston, 1975
LeRoy Irvin, Los Angeles, 1981
Desmond Howard, Green Bay, 1996
Darrien Gordon, Denver, 1997
Eric Metcalf, San Diego, 1997
2 By many players

Most Touchdowns, Rookie, Season
4 Jack Christiansen, Detroit, 1951
2 By many players

Most Touchdowns, Game
2 Jack Christiansen, Detroit vs. Los Angeles, Oct. 14, 1951; vs. Green Bay, Nov. 22, 1951
Dick Christy, N.Y. Titans vs. Denver, Sept. 24, 1961
Rick Upchurch, Denver vs. Cleveland, Sept. 26, 1976
LeRoy Irvin, Los Angeles vs. Atlanta, Oct. 11, 1981
Vai Sikahema, St. Louis vs. Tampa Bay, Dec. 21, 1986
Todd Kinchen, L.A. Rams vs. Atlanta, Dec. 27, 1992
Eric Metcalf, Cleveland vs. Pittsburgh, Oct. 24, 1993; San Diego vs. Cincinnati, Nov. 2, 1997
Darrien Gordon, Denver vs. Carolina, Nov. 9, 1997
Jermaine Lewis, Baltimore vs. Seattle, Dec. 7, 1997

KICKOFF RETURNS

Most Seasons Leading League
3 Abe Woodson, San Francisco, 1959, 1962-63
2 Lynn Chandnois, Pittsburgh, 1951-52
Bobby Jancik, Houston, 1962-63
Travis Williams, Green Bay, 1967; Los Angeles, 1971
Mel Gray, Detroit, 1991, 1994
Michael Bates, Carolina, 1996-97

KICKOFF RETURNS

Most Kickoff Returns, Career
421 Mel Gray, New Orleans, 1986-88; Detroit, 1989-94; Houston, 1995-96; Tennessee, 1997; Philadelphia, 1997

319 Brian Mitchell, Washington, 1990-97
275 Ron Smith, Chicago, 1965, 1970-72; Atlanta, 1966-67; Los Angeles, 1968-69; San Diego, 1973; Oakland, 1974

Most Kickoff Returns, Season
70 Tyrone Hughes, New Orleans, 1996
66 Tyrone Hughes, New Orleans, 1995
64 Glyn Milburn, Detroit, 1996

Most Kickoff Returns, Rookie, Season
55 Stump Mitchell, St. Louis, 1981
54 Leeland McElroy, Arizona, 1996
53 Buster Rhymes, Minnesota, 1985

Most Kickoff Returns, Game
10 Desmond Howard, Oakland vs. Seattle, Oct. 26, 1997
9 Noland Smith, Kansas City vs. Oakland, Nov. 23, 1967
Dino Hall, Cleveland vs. Pittsburgh, Oct. 7, 1979
Paul Palmer, Kansas City vs. Seattle, Sept. 20, 1987
Eric Metcalf, Atlanta vs. San Francisco, Sept. 29, 1996; vs. St. Louis, Nov. 10, 1996
8 By many players

YARDS GAINED

Most Seasons Leading League
3 Bruce Harper, N.Y. Jets, 1977-79
Tyrone Hughes, New Orleans, 1994-96
2 Marshall Goldberg, Chi. Cardinals, 1941-42
Woodley Lewis, Los Angeles, 1953-54
Al Carmichael, Green Bay, 1956-57
Timmy Brown, Philadelphia, 1961, 1963
Bobby Jancik, Houston, 1963, 1966
Ron Smith, Atlanta, 1966-67
Tyrone Hughes, New Orleans, 1994-95

Most Yards Gained, Career
10,250 Mel Gray, New Orleans, 1986-88; Detroit, 1989-94; Houston, 1995-96; Tennessee, 1997; Philadelphia, 1997
7,356 Brian Mitchell, Washington, 1990-97
6,922 Ron Smith, Chicago, 1965, 1970-72; Atlanta, 1966-67; Los Angeles, 1968-69; San Diego, 1973; Oakland, 1974

Most Yards Gained, Season
1,791 Tyrone Hughes, New Orleans, 1996
1,627 Glyn Milburn, Detroit, 1996
1,617 Tyrone Hughes, New Orleans, 1995

Most Yards Gained, Rookie, Season
1,345 Buster Rhymes, Minnesota, 1985
1,293 Andre Coleman, San Diego, 1994
1,292 Stump Mitchell, St. Louis, 1981

Most Yards Gained, Game
304 Tyrone Hughes, New Orleans vs. L.A. Rams, Oct. 23, 1994
294 Wally Triplett, Detroit vs. Los Angeles, Oct. 29, 1950
253 Derrick Witherspoon, Philadelphia vs. Arizona, Nov. 24, 1996

Longest Kickoff Return (All TDs)
106 Al Carmichael, Green Bay vs. Chi. Bears, Oct. 7, 1956
Noland Smith, Kansas City vs. Denver, Dec. 17, 1967
Roy Green, St. Louis vs. Dallas, Oct. 21, 1979
105 Frank Seno, Chi. Cardinals vs. N.Y. Giants, Oct. 20, 1946
Ollie Matson, Chi. Cardinals vs. Washington, Oct. 14, 1956
Abe Woodson, San Francisco vs. Los Angeles, Nov. 8, 1959
Timmy Brown, Philadelphia vs. Cleveland, Sept. 17, 1961
Jon Arnett, Los Angeles vs. Detroit, Oct. 29, 1961
Eugene (Mercury) Morris, Miami vs. Cincinnati, Sept. 14, 1969
Travis Williams, Los Angeles vs. New Orleans, Dec. 5, 1971
104 By many players

AVERAGE YARDAGE

Highest Average, Career (75 returns)
30.56 Gale Sayers, Chicago, 1965-71 (91-2,781)
29.57 Lynn Chandnois, Pittsburgh, 1950-56 (92-2,720)
28.69 Abe Woodson, San Francisco, 1958-64; St. Louis, 1965-66 (193-5,538)

Highest Average, Season (Qualifiers)
41.06 Travis Williams, Green Bay, 1967 (18-739)
37.69 Gale Sayers, Chicago, 1967 (16-603)
35.50 Ollie Matson, Chi. Cardinals, 1958 (14-497)

Highest Average, Rookie, Season (Qualifiers)
41.06 Travis Williams, Green Bay, 1967 (18-739)
33.08 Tom Moore, Green Bay, 1960 (12-397)
32.88 Duriel Harris, Miami, 1976 (17-559)

Highest Average, Game (3 returns)
73.50 Wally Triplett, Detroit vs. Los Angeles, Oct. 29, 1950 (4-294)
67.33 Lenny Lyles, San Francisco vs. Baltimore, Dec. 18, 1960 (3-202)
65.33 Ken Hall, Houston vs. N.Y. Titans, Oct. 23, 1960 (3-196)

TOUCHDOWNS

Most Touchdowns, Career
6 Ollie Matson, Chi. Cardinals, 1952, 1954-58; L.A. Rams, 1959-62; Detroit, 1963; Philadelphia, 1964
Gale Sayers, Chicago, 1965-71
Travis Williams, Green Bay, 1967-70; Los Angeles, 1971
Mel Gray, New Orleans, 1986-88; Detroit, 1989-94; Houston, 1995-96; Tennessee, 1997; Philadelphia, 1997
5 Bobby Mitchell, Cleveland, 1958-61; Washington, 1962-68
Abe Woodson, San Francisco, 1958-64; St. Louis, 1965-66
Timmy Brown, Green Bay, 1959; Philadelphia, 1960-67; Baltimore, 1968
4 Cecil Turner, Chicago, 1968-73
Ron Brown, L.A. Rams, 1984-89, 1991; L.A. Raiders, 1990
Jon Vaughn, New England, 1991-92; Seattle, 1993-94; Kansas City, 1994
Andre Coleman, San Diego, 1994-96; Seattle, 1997; Pittsburgh, 1997
Tamarick Vanover, Kansas City, 1995-97

Most Touchdowns, Season
4 Travis Williams, Green Bay, 1967
Cecil Turner, Chicago, 1970
3 Verda (Vitamin T) Smith, Los Angeles, 1950
Abe Woodson, San Francisco, 1963
Gale Sayers, Chicago, 1967
Raymond Clayborn, New England, 1977
Ron Brown, L.A. Rams, 1985
Mel Gray, Detroit, 1994
2 By many players

Most Touchdowns, Rookie, Season
4 Travis Williams, Green Bay, 1967
3 Raymond Clayborn, New England, 1977
2 By ten players

Most Touchdowns, Game
2 Timmy Brown, Philadelphia vs. Dallas, Nov. 6, 1966
Travis Williams, Green Bay vs. Cleveland, Nov. 12, 1967
Ron Brown, L.A. Rams vs. Green Bay, Nov. 24, 1985
Tyrone Hughes, New Orleans vs. L.A. Rams, Oct. 23, 1994

COMBINED KICK RETURNS

Most Combined Kick Returns, Career
673 Mel Gray, New Orleans, 1986-88; Detroit, 1989-94; Houston, 1995-96; Tennessee, 1997; Philadelphia, 1997 (p-252, k-421)
595 David Meggett, N.Y. Giants, 1989-94; New England, 1995-97 (p-344, k-251)
552 Brian Mitchell, Washington, 1990-97 (p-233, k-319)

Most Combined Kick Returns, Season
102 Glyn Milburn, Detroit, 1997 (p-47, k-55)
100 Larry Jones, Washington, 1975 (p-53, k-47)
Tyrone Hughes, New Orleans, 1996 (p-30, k-70)
99 Kevin Williams, Arizona, 1997 (p-40, k-59)

Most Combined Kick Returns, Game
13 Stump Mitchell, St. Louis vs. Atlanta, Oct. 18, 1981 (p-6, k-7)
Ronnie Harris, New England vs. Pittsburgh, Dec. 5, 1993 (p-10, k-3)
12 Mel Renfro, Dallas vs. Green Bay, Nov. 29, 1964 (p-4, k-8)
Larry Jones, Washington vs. Dallas, Dec. 13, 1975 (p-6, k-6)
Eddie Brown, Washington vs. Tampa Bay, Oct. 9, 1977 (p-11, k-1)
Nesby Glasgow, Baltimore vs. Denver, Sept. 2, 1979 (p-9, k-3)
11 By many players

YARDS GAINED

Most Yards Returned, Career
13,003 Mel Gray, New Orleans, 1986-88; Detroit, 1989-94; Houston, 1995-96; Tennessee, 1997; Philadelphia, 1997 (p-2,753, k-10,250)
9,994 Brian Mitchell, Washington, 1990-97 (p-2,638, k-7,356)
9,218 David Meggett, N.Y. Giants, 1989-94; New England, 1995-97 (p-3,668, k-5,550)

Most Yards Returned, Season
1,943 Tyrone Hughes, New Orleans, 1996 (p-152, k-1,791)
1,930 Brian Mitchell, Washington, 1994 (p-452, k-1,478)
1,920 Kevin Williams, Arizona, 1997 (p-462, k-1,458)

Most Yards Returned, Game
347 Tyrone Hughes, New Orleans vs. L.A. Rams, Oct. 23, 1994 (p-43, k-304)
294 Wally Triplett, Detroit vs. Los Angeles, Oct. 29, 1950 (k-294)
Woodley Lewis, Los Angeles vs. Detroit, Oct. 18, 1953 (p-120, k-174)
289 Eddie Payton, Detroit vs. Minnesota, Dec. 17, 1977 (p-105, k-184)

TOUCHDOWNS

Most Touchdowns, Career
11 Eric Metcalf, Cleveland, 1989-94; Atlanta, 1995-96; San Diego, 1997 (p-9, k-2)
9 Ollie Matson, Chi. Cardinals, 1952, 1954-58; Los Angeles, 1959-62; Detroit, 1963; Philadelphia, 1964-66 (p-3, k-6)

Mel Gray, New Orleans, 1986-88; Detroit, 1989-94; Houston, 1995-96; Tennessee, 1997; Philadelphia, 1997 (p-3, k-6)
8 Jack Christiansen, Detroit, 1951-58 (p-8)
Bobby Mitchell, Cleveland, 1958-61; Washington, 1962-68 (p-3, k-5)
Gale Sayers, Chicago, 1965-71 (p-2, k-6)
Rick Upchurch, Denver, 1975-83 (p-8)
Billy (White Shoes) Johnson, Houston, 1974-80; Atlanta, 1982-87; Washington, 1988 (p-6, k-2)
David Meggett, N.Y. Giants, 1989-94; New England, 1995-97 (p-7, k-1)
Brian Mitchell, Washington, 1990-97 (p-3, k-5)

Most Touchdowns, Season
4 Jack Christiansen, Detroit, 1951 (p-4)
Emlen Tunnell, N.Y. Giants, 1951 (p-3, k-1)
Gale Sayers, Chicago, 1967 (p-1, k-3)
Travis Williams, Green Bay, 1967 (k-4)
Cecil Turner, Chicago, 1970 (k-4)
Billy Johnson, Houston, 1975 (p-3, k-1)
Rick Upchurch, Denver, 1976 (p-4)
3 Verda (Vitamin T) Smith, Los Angeles, 1950 (k-3)
Abe Woodson, San Francisco, 1963 (k-3)
Raymond Clayborn, New England, 1977 (k-3)
Billy Johnson, Houston, 1977 (p-2, k-1)
LeRoy Irvin, Los Angeles, 1981 (p-3)
Ron Brown, L.A. Rams, 1985 (k-3)
Tyrone Hughes, New Orleans, 1993 (p-2, k-1)
Mel Gray, Detroit, 1994 (k-3)
Tamarick Vanover, Kansas City, 1995 (p-1, k-2)
Desmond Howard, Green Bay, 1996 (p-3)
Darrien Gordon, Denver, 1997 (p-3)
Eric Metcalf, San Diego, 1997 (p-3)
2 By many players

Most Touchdowns, Game
2 Jack Christiansen, Detroit vs. Los Angeles, Oct. 14, 1951 (p-2); vs. Green Bay, Nov. 22, 1951 (p-2)
Jim Patton, N.Y. Giants vs. Washington, Oct. 30, 1955 (p-1, k-1)
Bobby Mitchell, Cleveland vs. Philadelphia, Nov. 23, 1958 (p-1, k-1)
Dick Christy, N.Y. Titans vs. Denver, Sept. 24, 1961 (p-2)
Al Frazier, Denver vs. Boston, Dec. 3, 1961 (p-1, k-1)
Timmy Brown, Philadelphia vs. Dallas, Nov. 6, 1966 (k-2)
Travis Williams, Green Bay vs. Cleveland, Nov. 12, 1967 (k-2); vs. Pittsburgh, Nov. 2, 1969 (p-1, k-1)
Gale Sayers, Chicago vs. San Francisco, Dec. 3, 1967 (p-1, k-1)
Rick Upchurch, Denver vs. Cleveland, Sept. 26, 1976 (p-2)
Eddie Payton, Detroit vs. Minnesota, Dec. 17, 1977 (p-1, k-1)
LeRoy Irvin, Los Angeles vs. Atlanta, Oct. 11, 1981 (p-2)
Ron Brown, L.A. Rams vs. Green Bay, Nov. 24, 1985 (k-2)
Vai Sikahema, St. Louis vs. Tampa Bay, Dec. 21, 1986 (p-2)
Eric Metcalf, Cleveland vs. Pittsburgh, Oct. 24, 1993 (p-2); San Diego vs. Cincinnati, Nov. 2, 1997 (p-2)
Tyrone Hughes, New Orleans vs. L.A. Rams, Oct. 23, 1994 (k-2)
Darrien Gordon, Denver vs. Carolina, Nov. 9, 1997 (p-2)
Jermaine Lewis, Baltimore vs. Seattle, Dec. 7, 1997 (p-2)

FUMBLES

Most Fumbles, Career
152 Warren Moon, Houston, 1984-93; Minnesota, 1994-96; Seattle, 1997
150 Dave Krieg, Seattle, 1980-91; Kansas City, 1992-93; Detroit, 1994; Arizona, 1995; Chicago, 1996; Tennessee, 1997
130 John Elway, Denver, 1983-97

Most Fumbles, Season
21 Tony Banks, St. Louis, 1996
18 Dave Krieg, Seattle, 1989
Warren Moon, Houston, 1990
17 Dan Pastorini, Houston, 1973
Warren Moon, Houston, 1984
Randall Cunningham, Philadelphia, 1989

Most Fumbles, Game
7 Len Dawson, Kansas City vs. San Diego, Nov. 15, 1964
6 Sam Etcheverry, St. Louis vs. N.Y. Giants, Sept, 17, 1961
Dave Krieg, Seattle vs. Kansas City, Nov. 5, 1989
5 Paul Christman, Chi. Cardinals vs. Green Bay, Nov. 10, 1946
Charlie Conerly, N.Y. Giants vs. San Francisco, Dec. 1, 1957
Jack Kemp, Buffalo vs. Houston, Oct. 29, 1967
Roman Gabriel, Philadelphia vs. Oakland, Nov. 21, 1976
Randall Cunningham, Philadelphia vs. L.A. Raiders, Nov. 30, 1986 (OT)
Willie Totten, Buffalo vs. Indianapolis, Oct. 4, 1987
Dave Walter, Cincinnati vs. Seattle, Oct. 11, 1987
Dave Krieg, Seattle vs. San Diego, Nov. 25, 1990 (OT)
Andre Ware, Detroit vs. Green Bay, Dec. 6, 1992

FUMBLES RECOVERED

Most Fumbles Recovered, Career, Own and Opponents'
54 Warren Moon, Houston, 1984-93, Minnesota, 1994-96; Seattle, 1997 (54 own)
46 Dave Krieg, Seattle, 1980-91; Kansas City, 1992-93; Detroit, 1994; Arizona, 1995; Chicago, 1996; Tennessee, 1997 (46 own)
45 Boomer Esiason, Cincinnati, 1984-92, 1997; N.Y. Jets, 1993-95; Arizona, 1996 (45 own)

Most Fumbles Recovered, Season, Own and Opponents'
9 Don Hultz, Minnesota, 1963 (9 opp)
Dave Krieg, Seattle, 1989 (9 own)
8 Paul Christman, Chi. Cardinals, 1945 (8 own)
Joe Schmidt, Detroit, 1955 (8 opp)
Bill Butler, Minnesota, 1963 (8 own)
Kermit Alexander, San Francisco, 1965 (4 own, 4 opp)
Jack Lambert, Pittsburgh, 1976 (1 own, 7 opp)
Danny White, Dallas, 1981 (8 own)
Dan Marino, Miami, 1988 (7 own, 1 opp)
7 By many players

Most Fumbles Recovered, Game, Own and Opponents'
4 Otto Graham, Cleveland vs. N.Y. Giants, Oct. 25, 1953 (4 own)
Sam Etcheverry, St. Louis vs. N.Y. Giants, Sept. 17, 1961 (4 own)
Roman Gabriel, Los Angeles vs. San Francisco, Oct. 12, 1969 (4 own)
Joe Ferguson, Buffalo vs. Miami, Sept. 18, 1977 (4 own)
Randall Cunningham, Philadelphia vs. L.A. Raiders, Nov. 30, 1986 (OT) (4 own)
3 By many players

OWN FUMBLES RECOVERED

Most Own Fumbles Recovered, Career
54 Warren Moon, Houston, 1984-93, Minnesota, 1994-96 ; Seattle, 1997 (54 own)
46 Dave Krieg, Seattle, 1980-91; Kansas City, 1992-93; Detroit, 1994; Arizona, 1995; Chicago, 1996; Tennessee, 1997 (46 own)
45 Boomer Esiason, Cincinnati, 1984-92, 1997; N.Y. Jets, 1993-95; Arizona, 1996 (45 own)

Most Own Fumbles Recovered, Season
9 Dave Krieg, Seattle, 1989
8 Paul Christman, Chi. Cardinals, 1945
Bill Butler, Minnesota, 1963
Danny White, Dallas, 1981
7 By many players

Most Own Fumbles Recovered, Game
4 Otto Graham, Cleveland vs. N.Y. Giants, Oct. 25, 1953
Sam Etcheverry, St. Louis vs. N.Y. Giants, Sept. 17, 1961
Roman Gabriel, Los Angeles vs. San Francisco, Oct. 12, 1969
Joe Ferguson, Buffalo vs. Miami, Sept. 18, 1977
Randall Cunningham, Philadelphia vs. L.A. Raiders, Nov. 30, 1986 (OT)
3 By many players

OPPONENTS' FUMBLES RECOVERED

Most Opponents' Fumbles Recovered, Career
29 Jim Marshall, Cleveland, 1960; Minnesota, 1961-79
28 Rickey Jackson, New Orleans, 1981-93; San Francisco, 1994-95
25 Dick Butkus, Chicago, 1965-73

Most Opponents' Fumbles Recovered, Season
9 Don Hultz, Minnesota, 1963
8 Joe Schmidt, Detroit, 1955
7 Alan Page, Minnesota, 1970
Jack Lambert, Pittsburgh, 1976
Ray Childress, Houston, 1988
Rickey Jackson, New Orleans, 1990

Most Opponents' Fumbles Recovered, Game
3 Corwin Clatt, Chi. Cardinals vs. Detroit, Nov. 6, 1949
Vic Sears, Philadelphia vs. Green Bay, Nov. 2, 1952
Ed Beatty, San Francisco vs. Los Angeles, Oct. 7, 1956
Ron Carroll, Houston vs. Cincinnati, Oct. 27, 1974
Maurice Spencer, New Orleans vs. Atlanta, Oct. 10, 1976
Steve Nelson, New England vs. Philadelphia, Oct. 8, 1978
Charles Jackson, Kansas City vs. Pittsburgh, Sept. 6, 1981
Willie Buchanon, San Diego vs. Denver, Sept. 27, 1981
Joey Browner, Minnesota vs. San Francisco, Sept. 8, 1985
Ray Childress, Houston vs. Washington, Oct. 30, 1988
John Thierry, Chicago vs. Houston, Oct. 22, 1995
2 By many players

YARDS RETURNING FUMBLES

Longest Fumble Run (All TDs)
104 Jack Tatum, Oakland vs. Green Bay, Sept. 24, 1972
100 Chris Martin, Kansas City vs. Miami, Oct. 13, 1991
99 Don Griffin, San Francisco vs. Chicago, Dec. 23, 1991

ALL-TIME RECORDS

TOUCHDOWNS

Most Touchdowns, Career (Total)

4 Bill Thompson, Denver, 1969-81
Jessie Tuggle, Atlanta, 1987-97
3 Ralph Heywood, Detroit, 1947-48; Boston, 1948; N.Y. Bulldogs, 1949
Leo Sugar, Chi. Cardinals, 1954-59; St. Louis, 1960; Philadelphia, 1961; Detroit, 1962
Bud McFadin, Los Angeles, 1952-56; Denver, 1960-63; Houston, 1964-65
Doug Cline, Houston, 1960-66; San Diego, 1966
Bob Lilly, Dall. Cowboys, 1961-74
Chris Hanburger, Washington, 1965-78
Lemar Parrish, Cincinnati, 1970-77; Washington, 1978-81; Buffalo, 1982
Paul Krause, Washington, 1964-67; Minnesota, 1968-79
Brad Dusek, Washington, 1974-81
David Logan, Tampa Bay, 1979-86; Green Bay, 1987
Thomas Howard, Kansas City, 1977-83; St. Louis, 1984-85
Greg Townsend, L.A. Raiders, 1983-93; Philadelphia, 1994; Oakland, 1997
Les Miller, San Diego, 1987-90, 1994; New Orleans, 1991-94; Carolina, 1996-97
Chris Martin, New Orleans, 1983; Minnesota, 1984-88; Kansas City, 1989-92; L.A. Rams, 1993-94
Seth Joyner, Philadelphia, 1986-93; Arizona, 1994-96; Green Bay, 1997
Derrick Thomas, Kansas City, 1989-97
Tony Bennett, Green Bay, 1990-93; Indianapolis, 1994-97
Sam Mills, New Orleans, 1986-94; Carolina, 1995-97
Anthony Parker, Indianapolis, 1989; Kansas City, 1991; Minnesota, 1992-94; St. Louis, 1995-96, Tampa Bay, 1997
Marcus Robertson, Houston, 1991-96; Tennessee, 1997
2 By many players

Most Touchdowns, Season (Total)

2 Harold McPhail, Boston, 1934
Harry Ebding, Detroit, 1937
John Morelli, Boston, 1944
Frank Maznicki, Boston, 1947
Fred (Dippy) Evans, Chi. Bears, 1948
Ralph Heywood, Boston, 1948
Art Tait, N.Y. Yanks, 1951
John Dwyer, Los Angeles, 1952
Leo Sugar, Chi. Cardinals, 1957
Doug Cline, Houston, 1961
Jim Bradshaw, Pittsburgh, 1964
Royce Berry, Cincinnati, 1970
Ahmad Rashad, Buffalo, 1974
Tim Gray, Kansas City, 1977
Charles Phillips, Oakland, 1978
Kenny Johnson, Atlanta, 1981
George Martin, N.Y. Giants, 1981
Del Rodgers, Green Bay, 1982
Mike Douglass, Green Bay, 1983
Shelton Robinson, Seattle, 1983
Erik McMillan, N.Y. Jets, 1989
Les Miller, San Diego, 1990
Seth Joyner, Philadelphia, 1991
Robert Goff, New Orleans, 1992
Willie Clay, Detroit, 1993
Tyrone Hughes, New Orleans, 1994
Chad Brown, Seattle, 1997
Marcus Robertson, Tennessee, 1997

Most Touchdowns, Career (Own recovered)

2 Ken Kavanaugh, Chi. Bears, 1940-41, 1945-50
Mike Ditka, Chicago, 1961-66; Philadelphia, 1967-68; Dallas, 1969-72
Gail Cogdill, Detroit, 1960-68; Baltimore, 1968; Atlanta, 1969-70
Ahmad Rashad, St. Louis, 1972-73; Buffalo, 1974; Minnesota, 1976-82
Jim Mitchell, Atlanta, 1969-79
Drew Pearson, Dallas, 1973-83
Del Rodgers, Green Bay, 1982, 1984; San Francisco, 1987-88

Most Touchdowns, Season (Own recovered)

2 Ahmad Rashad, Buffalo, 1974
Del Rodgers, Green Bay, 1982
1 By many players

Most Touchdowns, Career (Opponents' recovered)

4 Jessie Tuggle, Atlanta, 1987-97
3 Leo Sugar, Chi. Cardinals, 1954-59; St. Louis, 1960; Philadelphia, 1961; Detroit, 1962
Doug Cline, Houston, 1960-66; San Diego, 1966
Bud McFadin, Los Angeles, 1952-56; Denver, 1960-63; Houston, 1964-65
Bob Lilly, Dall. Cowboys, 1961-74
Chris Hanburger, Washington, 1965-78
Paul Krause, Washington, 1964-67; Minnesota, 1968-79
Lemar Parrish, Cincinnati, 1970-77; Washington, 1978-81; Buffalo, 1982
Bill Thompson, Denver, 1969-81
Brad Dusek, Washington, 1974-81
David Logan, Tampa Bay, 1979-86; Green Bay, 1987
Thomas Howard, Kansas City, 1977-83; St. Louis, 1984-85
Greg Townsend, L.A. Raiders, 1983-93; Philadelphia, 1994; Oakland, 1997
Les Miller, San Diego, 1987-90, 1994; New Orleans, 1991-94, Carolina, 1996-97
Chris Martin, New Orleans, 1983; Minnesota, 1984-88; Kansas City, 1989-92; L.A. Rams, 1993-94
Seth Joyner, Philadelphia, 1986-93; Arizona, 1994-96; Green Bay, 1997
Derrick Thomas, Kansas City, 1989-97
Tony Bennett, Green Bay, 1990-93; Indianapolis, 1994-97
Sam Mills, New Orleans, 1986-94; Carolina, 1995-97
Marcus Robertson, Houston, 1991-96; Tennessee, 1997
2 By many players

Most Touchdowns, Season (Opponents' recovered)

2 Harold McPhail, Boston, 1934
Harry Ebding, Detroit, 1937
John Morelli, Boston, 1944
Frank Maznicki, Boston, 1947
Fred (Dippy) Evans, Chi. Bears, 1948
Ralph Heywood, Boston, 1948
Art Tait, N.Y. Yanks, 1951
John Dwyer, Los Angeles, 1952
Leo Sugar, Chi. Cardinals, 1957
Doug Cline, Houston, 1961
Jim Bradshaw, Pittsburgh, 1964
Royce Berry, Cincinnati, 1970
Tim Gray, Kansas City, 1977
Charles Phillips, Oakland, 1978
Kenny Johnson, Atlanta, 1981
George Martin, N.Y. Giants, 1981
Mike Douglass, Green Bay, 1983
Shelton Robinson, Seattle, 1983
Erik McMillan, N.Y. Jets, 1989
Les Miller, San Diego, 1990
Seth Joyner, Philadelphia, 1991
Robert Goff, New Orleans, 1992
Willie Clay, Detroit, 1993
Tyrone Hughes, New Orleans, 1994
Chad Brown, Seattle, 1997
Marcus Robertson, Tennessee, 1997

Most Touchdowns, Game (Opponents' recovered)

2 Fred (Dippy) Evans, Chi. Bears vs. Washington, Nov. 28, 1948

COMBINED NET YARDS GAINED

Rushing, receiving, interception returns, punt returns, kickoff returns, and fumble returns

Most Seasons Leading League

5 Jim Brown, Cleveland, 1958-61, 1964
3 Cliff Battles, Boston, 1932-33; Washington, 1937
Gale Sayers, Chicago, 1965-67
Eric Dickerson, L.A. Rams, 1983-84, 1986
Thurman Thomas, Buffalo, 1989, 1991-92
Brian Mitchell, Washington, 1994-96
2 By many players

Most Consecutive Seasons Leading League

4 Jim Brown, Cleveland, 1958-61
3 Gale Sayers, Chicago, 1965-67
Brian Mitchell, Washington, 1994-96
2 Cliff Battles, Boston, 1932-33
Charley Trippi, Chi. Cardinals, 1948-49
Timmy Brown, Philadelphia, 1962-63
Floyd Little, Denver, 1967-68
James Brooks, San Diego, 1981-82
Eric Dickerson, L.A. Rams, 1983-84
Thurman Thomas, Buffalo, 1991-92

ATTEMPTS

Most Attempts, Career

4,368 Walter Payton, Chicago, 1975-87
3,624 Marcus Allen, L.A. Raiders, 1982-92; Kansas City, 1993-97
3,351 Tony Dorsett, Dallas, 1977-87; Denver, 1988

Most Attempts, Season

496 James Wilder, Tampa Bay, 1984
449 Marcus Allen, L.A. Raiders, 1985
442 Eric Dickerson, L.A. Rams, 1983

Most Attempts, Rookie, Season

442 Eric Dickerson, L.A. Rams, 1983
395 George Rogers, New Orleans, 1981

390 Joe Cribbs, Buffalo, 1980

Most Attempts, Game

48 James Wilder, Tampa Bay vs. Pittsburgh, Oct. 30, 1983
47 James Wilder, Tampa Bay vs. Green Bay, Sept. 30, 1984 (OT)
Terrell Davis, Denver vs. Buffalo, Oct. 26, 1997 (OT)
46 Gerald Riggs, Atlanta vs. L.A. Rams, Nov. 17, 1985

YARDS GAINED

Most Yards Gained, Career

21,803 Walter Payton, Chicago, 1975-87
18,168 Herschel Walker, Dallas, 1986-89, 1996-97; Minnesota, 1989-91; Philadelphia, 1992-94; N.Y. Giants, 1995
17,648 Marcus Allen, L.A. Raiders, 1982-92; Kansas City, 1993-97

Most Yards Gained, Season

2,535 Lionel James, San Diego, 1985
2,477 Brian Mitchell, Washington, 1994
2,462 Terry Metcalf, St. Louis, 1975

Most Yards Gained, Rookie, Season

2,317 Tim Brown, L.A. Raiders, 1988
2,272 Gale Sayers, Chicago, 1965
2,212 Eric Dickerson, L.A. Rams, 1983

Most Yards Gained, Game

404 Glyn Milburn, Denver vs. Seattle, Dec. 10, 1995
373 Billy Cannon, Houston vs. N.Y. Titans, Dec. 10, 1961
347 Tyrone Hughes, New Orleans vs. L.A. Rams, Oct. 23, 1994

SACKS

Sacks have been compiled since 1982.

Most Seasons Leading League

2 Mark Gastineau, N.Y. Jets, 1983-84
Reggie White, Philadelphia, 1987-88
Kevin Greene, Pittsburgh, 1994; Carolina, 1996

Most Sacks, Career

176.5 Reggie White, Philadelphia, 1985-92; Green Bay, 1993-97
154.0 Bruce Smith, Buffalo, 1985-97
137.5 Richard Dent, Chicago, 1983-93, 1995; San Francisco, 1994; Indianapolis, 1996; Philadelphia, 1997

Most Sacks, Season

22 Mark Gastineau, N.Y. Jets, 1984
21 Reggie White, Philadelphia, 1987
Chris Doleman, Minnesota, 1989
20.5 Lawrence Taylor, N.Y. Giants, 1986

Most Sacks, Rookie, Season

12.5 Leslie O'Neal, San Diego, 1986
Simeon Rice, Arizona, 1996
12 Charles Haley, San Francisco, 1986
11.5 Peter Boulware, Baltimore, 1997

Most Sacks, Game

7 Derrick Thomas, Kansas City vs. Seattle, Nov. 11, 1990
6 Fred Dean, San Francisco vs. New Orleans, Nov. 13, 1983
5.5 William Gay, Detroit vs. Tampa Bay, Sept. 4, 1983

Most Seasons, 10 or More Sacks

11 Reggie White, Philadelphia, 1985-92; Green Bay, 1993, 1995, 1997
Bruce Smith, Buffalo, 1986-1990, 1992-97
8 Richard Dent, Chicago, 1984-88, 1990-91, 1993
Leslie O'Neal, San Diego, 1986, 1989-90, 1992-95; St. Louis, 1997
Kevin Greene, L.A. Rams, 1988-90, 1992; Pittsburgh, 1993-94; Carolina, 1996; San Francisco, 1997
7 Lawrence Taylor, N.Y. Giants, 1984-1990
Greg Townsend, L.A. Raiders, 1983, 1985-86, 1988-91
Chris Doleman, Minnesota, 1987, 1989-90, 1992-93; San Francisco, 1996-97

Most Consecutive Seasons, 10 or More Sacks

9 Reggie White, Philadelphia, 1985-92; Green Bay, 1993
7 Lawrence Taylor, N.Y. Giants, 1984-1990
6 John Randle, Minnesota, 1992-97
Bruce Smith, Buffalo, 1992-97

MISCELLANEOUS

Longest Return of Missed Field Goal (All TDs)

101 Al Nelson, Philadelphia vs. Dallas, Sept. 26, 1971
100 Al Nelson, Philadelphia vs. Cleveland, Dec. 11, 1966
Ken Ellis, Green Bay vs. N.Y. Giants, Sept. 19, 1971
99 Jerry Williams, Los Angeles vs. Green Bay, Dec. 16, 1951
Carl Taseff, Baltimore vs. Los Angeles, Dec. 12, 1959
Timmy Brown, Philadelphia vs. St. Louis, Sept. 16, 1962

TEAM RECORDS

CHAMPIONSHIPS

Most Seasons League Champion

12 Green Bay, 1929-31, 1936, 1939, 1944, 1961-62, 1965-67, 1996
9 Chi. Bears, 1921, 1932-33, 1940-41, 1943, 1946, 1963, 1985
6 N.Y. Giants, 1927, 1934, 1938, 1956, 1986, 1990

Most Consecutive Seasons League Champion

3 Green Bay, 1929-31
Green Bay, 1965-67
2 Canton, 1922-23
Chi. Bears, 1932-33
Chi. Bears, 1940-41
Philadelphia, 1948-49
Detroit, 1952-53
Cleveland, 1954-55
Baltimore, 1958-59
Houston, 1960-61
Green Bay, 1961-62
Buffalo, 1964-65
Miami, 1972-73
Pittsburgh, 1974-75
Pittsburgh, 1978-79
San Francisco, 1988-89
Dallas, 1992-93

Most Times Finishing First, Regular Season

19 N.Y. Giants, 1927, 1933-35, 1938-39, 1941, 1944, 1946, 1956, 1958-59, 1961-63, 1986, 1989-90, 1997
18 Clev. Browns, 1950-55, 1957, 1964-65, 1967-69, 1971, 1980, 1985-87, 1989
Chi. Bears, 1921, 1932-34, 1937, 1940-43, 1946, 1956, 1963, 1984-88, 1990
Dallas, 1966-71, 1973, 1976-79, 1981, 1985, 1992-96
17 Green Bay, 1929-31, 1936, 1938-39, 1944, 1960-62, 1965-67, 1972, 1995-97

Most Consecutive Times Finishing First, Regular Season

7 Los Angeles, 1973-79
6 Cleveland, 1950-55
Dallas, 1966-71
Minnesota, 1973-78
Pittsburgh, 1974-79
5 Oakland, 1972-76
Chicago, 1984-88
San Francisco, 1986-90
Dallas, 1992-96

GAMES WON

Most Consecutive Games Won

17 Chi. Bears, 1933-34
16 Chi. Bears, 1941-42
Miami, 1971-73
Miami, 1983-84
15 L.A. Chargers/San Diego, 1960-61
San Francisco, 1989-90

Most Consecutive Games Without Defeat

25 Canton, 1921-23 (won 22, tied 3)
24 Chi. Bears, 1941-43 (won 23, tied 1)
23 Green Bay, 1928-30 (won 21, tied 2)

Most Games Won, Season

15 San Francisco, 1984
Chicago, 1985
14 Frankford, 1926
Miami, 1972
Pittsburgh, 1978
Washington, 1983
Miami, 1984
Chicago, 1986
N.Y. Giants, 1986
San Francisco, 1989
San Francisco, 1990
Washington, 1991
San Francisco, 1992
13 By many teams

Most Consecutive Games Won, Season

14 Miami, 1972
13 Chi. Bears, 1934
12 Minnesota, 1969
Chicago, 1985

Most Consecutive Games Won, Start of Season

14 Miami, 1972, entire season
13 Chi. Bears, 1934, entire season
12 Chicago, 1985

Most Consecutive Games Won, End of Season

14 Miami, 1972, entire season
13 Chi. Bears, 1934, entire season
11 Chi. Bears, 1942, entire season
Cleveland, 1951
Houston, 1993

Most Consecutive Games Without Defeat, Season
14 Miami, 1972 (won 14)
13 Chi. Bears, 1926 (won 11, tied 2)
Green Bay, 1929 (won 12, tied 1)
Chi. Bears, 1934 (won 13)
Baltimore, 1967 (won 11, tied 2)
12 Canton, 1922 (won 10, tied 2)
Canton, 1923 (won 11, tied 1)
Minnesota, 1969 (won 12)
Chicago, 1985 (won 12)

Most Consecutive Games Without Defeat, Start of Season
14 Miami, 1972 (won 14), entire season
13 Chi. Bears, 1926 (won 11, tied 2)
Green Bay, 1929 (won 12, tied 1), entire season
Chi. Bears, 1934 (won 13), entire season
Baltimore, 1967 (won 11, tied 2)
12 Canton, 1922 (won 10, tied 2), entire season
Canton, 1923 (won 11, tied 1), entire season
Chicago, 1985 (won 12)

Most Consecutive Games Without Defeat, End of Season
14 Miami, 1972 (won 14), entire season
13 Green Bay, 1929 (won 12, tied 1), entire season
Chi. Bears, 1934 (won 13), entire season
12 Canton, 1922 (won 10, tied 2), entire season
Canton, 1923 (won 11, tied 1), entire season

Most Consecutive Home Games Won
27 Miami, 1971-74
23 Green Bay, 1995-97 (current)
20 Green Bay, 1929-32

Most Consecutive Home Games Without Defeat
30 Green Bay, 1928-33 (won 27, tied 3)
27 Miami, 1971-74 (won 27)
25 Chi. Bears, 1923-25 (won 19, tied 6)

Most Consecutive Road Games Won
18 San Francisco, 1988-90
11 L.A. Chargers/San Diego, 1960-61
San Francisco, 1987-88
10 Chi. Bears, 1941-42
Dallas, 1968-69
New Orleans, 1987-88

Most Consecutive Road Games Without Defeat
18 San Francisco, 1988-90 (won 18)
13 Chi. Bears, 1941-43 (won 12, tied 1)
12 Green Bay, 1928-30 (won 10, tied 2)

Most Shutout Games Won or Tied, Season
10 Pottsville, 1926 (won 9, tied 1)
N.Y. Giants, 1927 (won 9, tied 1)
9 Akron, 1921 (won 8, tied 1)
Canton, 1922 (won 7, tied 2)
Frankford, 1926 (won 9)
Frankford, 1929 (won 6, tied 3)
8 By many teams

Most Consecutive Shutout Games Won or Tied
13 Akron, 1920-21 (won 10, tied 3)
7 Pottsville, 1926 (won 6, tied 1)
Detroit, 1934 (won 7)
6 Buffalo, 1920-21 (won 5, tied 1)
Frankford, 1926 (won 6)
Detroit, 1926 (won 4, tied 2)
N.Y. Giants, 1926-27 (won 5, tied 1)

GAMES LOST

Most Consecutive Games Lost
26 Tampa Bay, 1976-77
19 Chi. Cardinals, 1942-43, 1945
Oakland, 1961-62
18 Houston, 1972-73

Most Consecutive Games Without Victory
26 Tampa Bay, 1976-77 (lost 26)
23 Rochester, 1922-25 (lost 21, tied 2)
Washington, 1960-61 (lost 20, tied 3)
19 Dayton, 1927-29 (lost 18, tied 1)
Chi. Cardinals, 1942-43, 1945 (lost 19)
Oakland, 1961-62 (lost 19)

Most Games Lost, Season
15 New Orleans, 1980
Dallas, 1989
New England, 1990
Indianapolis, 1991
N.Y. Jets, 1996
14 By many teams

Most Consecutive Games Lost, Season
14 Tampa Bay, 1976
New Orleans, 1980
Baltimore, 1981
New England, 1990
13 Oakland, 1962
Pittsburgh, 1969
Indianapolis, 1986
12 Tampa Bay, 1977

Most Consecutive Games Lost, Start of Season
14 Tampa Bay, 1976, entire season
New Orleans, 1980
13 Oakland, 1962
Indianapolis, 1986
12 Tampa Bay, 1977

Most Consecutive Games Lost, End of Season
14 Tampa Bay, 1976, entire season
New England, 1990
13 Pittsburgh, 1969
11 Philadelphia, 1936
Detroit, 1942, entire season
Houston, 1972

Most Consecutive Games Without Victory, Season
14 Tampa Bay, 1976 (lost 14), entire season
New Orleans, 1980 (lost 14)
Baltimore, 1981 (lost 14)
New England, 1990 (lost 14)
13 Washington, 1961 (lost 12, tied 1)
Oakland, 1962 (lost 13)
Pittsburgh, 1969 (lost 13)
Indianapolis, 1986 (lost 13)
12 Dall. Cowboys, 1960 (lost 11, tied 1), entire season
Tampa Bay, 1977 (lost 12)

Most Consecutive Games Without Victory, Start of Season
14 Tampa Bay, 1976 (lost 14), entire season
New Orleans, 1980 (lost 14)
13 Washington, 1961 (lost 12, tied 1)
Oakland, 1962 (lost 13)
Indianapolis, 1986 (lost 13)
12 Dall. Cowboys, 1960 (lost 11, tied 1), entire season
Tampa Bay, 1977 (lost 12)

Most Consecutive Games Without Victory, End of Season
14 Tampa Bay, 1976, (lost 14), entire season
New England, 1990 (lost 14)
13 Pittsburgh, 1969 (lost 13)
12 Dall. Cowboys, 1960 (lost 11, tied 1), entire season

Most Consecutive Home Games Lost
14 Dallas, 1988-89
13 Houston, 1972-73
Tampa Bay, 1976-77
N.Y. Jets, 1995-97
11 Oakland, 1961-62
Los Angeles, 1961-63

Most Consecutive Home Games Without Victory
14 Dallas, 1988-89 (lost 14)
13 Houston, 1972-73 (lost 13)
Tampa Bay, 1976-77 (lost 13)
N.Y. Jets, 1995-97 (lost 13)
12 Philadelphia, 1936-38 (lost 11, tied 1)

Most Consecutive Road Games Lost
23 Houston, 1981-84
22 Buffalo, 1983-86
19 Tampa Bay, 1983-85
Atlanta, 1988-91

Most Consecutive Road Games Without Victory
23 Houston, 1981-84 (lost 23)
22 Buffalo, 1983-86 (lost 22)
19 Tampa Bay, 1983-85 (lost 19)
Atlanta, 1988-91 (lost 19)

Most Shutout Games Lost or Tied, Season
8 Frankford, 1927 (lost 6, tied 2)
Brooklyn, 1931 (lost 8)
7 Dayton, 1925 (lost 6, tied 1)
Orange, 1929 (lost 4, tied 3)
Frankford, 1931 (lost 6, tied 1)
6 By many teams

Most Consecutive Shutout Games Lost or Tied
8 Rochester, 1922-24 (lost 8)
7 Hammond, 1922-23 (lost 6, tied 1)
6 Providence, 1926-27 (lost 5, tied 1)
Brooklyn, 1942-43 (lost 6)

TIE GAMES

Most Tie Games, Season
6 Chi. Bears, 1932
5 Frankford, 1929
4 Chi. Bears, 1924
Orange, 1929
Portsmouth, 1932

Most Consecutive Tie Games
3 Chi. Bears, 1932
2 By many teams

SCORING

Most Seasons Leading League
10 Chi. Bears, 1932, 1934-35, 1939, 1941-43, 1946-47, 1956
9 San Francisco, 1953, 1965, 1970, 1987, 1989, 1992-95
7 Green Bay, 1931, 1936-38, 1961-62, 1996

Most Consecutive Seasons Leading League
4 San Francisco, 1992-1996
3 Green Bay, 1936-38
Chi. Bears, 1941-43
Los Angeles, 1950-52
Oakland, 1967-69
2 By many teams

POINTS

Most Points, Season
541 Washington, 1983
513 Houston, 1961
Miami, 1984
505 San Francisco, 1994

Fewest Points, Season (Since 1932)
37 Cincinnati/St. Louis, 1934
38 Cincinnati, 1933
Detroit, 1942
51 Pittsburgh, 1934
Philadelphia, 1936

Most Points, Game
72 Washington vs. N.Y. Giants, Nov. 27, 1966
70 Los Angeles vs. Baltimore, Oct. 22, 1950
65 Chi. Cardinals vs. N.Y. Bulldogs, Nov. 13, 1949
Los Angeles vs. Detroit, Oct. 29, 1950

Most Points, Both Teams, Game
113 Washington (72) vs. N.Y. Giants (41), Nov. 27, 1966
101 Oakland (52) vs. Houston (49), Dec. 22, 1963
99 Seattle (51) vs. Kansas City (48), Nov. 27, 1983 (OT)

Fewest Points, Both Teams, Game
0 In many games. Last time: N.Y. Giants vs. Detroit, Nov. 7, 1943

Most Points, Shutout Victory, Game
64 Philadelphia vs. Cincinnati, Nov. 6, 1934
62 Akron vs. Oorang, Oct. 29, 1922
60 Rock Island vs. Evansville, Oct. 15, 1922
Chi. Cardinals vs. Rochester, Oct. 7, 1923

Fewest Points, Shutout Victory, Game
2 Green Bay vs. Chi. Bears, Oct. 16, 1932
Chi. Bears vs. Green Bay, Sept. 18, 1938

Most Points Overcome to Win Game
28 San Francisco vs. New Orleans, Dec. 7, 1980 (OT) (trailed 7-35, won 38-35)
26 Buffalo vs. Indianapolis, Sept., 21, 1997 (trailed 26-0, won 37-35)
25 St. Louis vs. Tampa Bay, Nov. 8, 1987 (trailed 3-28, won 31-28)

Most Points Overcome to Tie Game
31 Denver vs. Buffalo, Nov. 27, 1960 (trailed 7-38, tied 38-38)
28 Los Angeles vs. Philadelphia, Oct. 3, 1948 (trailed 0-28, tied 28-28)

Most Points, Each Half
1st: 49 Green Bay vs. Tampa Bay, Oct. 2, 1983
48 Buffalo vs. Miami, Sept. 18, 1966
45 Green Bay vs. Cleveland, Nov. 12, 1967
Indianapolis vs. Denver, Oct. 31, 1988
Houston vs. Cleveland, Dec. 9, 1990
2nd: 49 Chi. Bears vs. Philadelphia, Nov. 30, 1941
48 Chi. Cardinals vs. Baltimore, Oct. 2, 1950
N.Y. Giants vs. Baltimore, Nov. 19, 1950
45 Cincinnati vs. Houston, Dec. 17, 1972

Most Points, Both Teams, Each Half
1st: 70 Houston (35) vs. Oakland (35), Dec. 22, 1963
62 N.Y. Jets (41) vs. Tampa Bay (21), Nov. 17, 1985
59 St. Louis (31) vs. Philadelphia (28), Dec. 16, 1962
2nd: 65 Washington (38) vs. N.Y. Giants (27), Nov. 27, 1966
62 L.A. Raiders (31) vs. San Diego (31), Jan. 2, 1983
58 New England (37) vs. Baltimore (21), Nov. 23, 1980
N.Y. Jets (37) vs. New England (21), Sept. 21, 1987

Most Points, One Quarter
41 Green Bay vs. Detroit, Oct. 7, 1945 (second quarter)
Los Angeles vs. Detroit, Oct. 29, 1950 (third quarter)
37 Los Angeles vs. Green Bay, Sept. 21, 1980 (second quarter)
35 Chi. Cardinals vs. Boston, Oct. 24, 1948 (third quarter)
Green Bay vs. Cleveland, Nov. 12, 1967 (first quarter)
Green Bay vs. Tampa Bay, Oct. 2, 1983 (second quarter)

Most Points, Both Teams, One Quarter
49 Oakland (28) vs. Houston (21), Dec. 22, 1963 (second quarter)
48 Green Bay (41) vs. Detroit (7), Oct. 7, 1945 (second quarter)
Los Angeles (41) vs. Detroit (7), Oct. 29, 1950 (third quarter)
47 St. Louis (27) vs. Philadelphia (20), Dec. 13, 1964 (second quarter)

Most Points, Each Quarter
1st: 35 Green Bay vs. Cleveland, Nov. 12, 1967
31 Buffalo vs. Kansas City, Sept. 13, 1964
28 By seven teams
2nd: 41 Green Bay vs. Detroit, Oct. 7, 1945
37 Los Angeles vs. Green Bay, Sept. 21, 1980
35 Green Bay vs. Tampa Bay, Oct. 2, 1983
3rd: 41 Los Angeles vs. Detroit, Oct. 29, 1950
35 Chi. Cardinals vs. Boston, Oct. 24, 1948
28 By 10 teams
4th: 31 Oakland vs. Denver, Dec. 17, 1960
Oakland vs. San Diego, Dec. 8, 1963
Atlanta vs. Green Bay, Sept. 13, 1981
28 By many teams

Most Points, Both Teams, Each Quarter
1st: 42 Green Bay (35) vs. Cleveland (7), Nov. 12, 1967
35 Dall. Texans (21) vs. N.Y. Titans (14), Nov. 11, 1962
Dallas (28) vs. Philadelphia (7), Oct. 19, 1969
Kansas City (21) vs. Seattle (14), Dec. 11, 1977
Detroit (21) vs. L.A. Raiders (14), Dec. 10, 1990
Dallas (21) vs. Atlanta (14), Dec. 22, 1991
34 Los Angeles (21) vs. Baltimore (13), Oct. 22, 1950
Oakland (21) vs. Atlanta (13), Nov. 30, 1975
2nd: 49 Oakland (28) vs. Houston (21), Dec. 22, 1963
48 Green Bay (41) vs. Detroit (7), Oct. 7, 1945
47 St. Louis (27) vs. Philadelphia (20), Dec. 13, 1964
3rd: 48 Los Angeles (41) vs. Detroit (7), Oct. 29, 1950
42 Washington (28) vs. Philadelphia (14), Oct. 1, 1955
41 Green Bay (21) vs. N.Y. Yanks (20), Oct. 8, 1950
4th: 42 Chi. Cardinals (28) vs. Philadelphia (14), Dec. 7, 1947
Green Bay (28) vs. Chi. Bears (14), Nov. 6, 1955
N.Y. Jets (28) vs. Boston (14), Oct. 27, 1968
Pittsburgh (21) vs. Cleveland (21), Oct. 18, 1969
41 Baltimore (27) vs. New England (14), Sept. 18, 1978
New England (27) vs. Baltimore (14), Nov. 23, 1980
40 Chicago (21) vs. Tampa Bay (19), Nov. 19, 1989

Most Consecutive Games Scoring
322 San Francisco, 1977-97 (current)
274 Cleveland, 1950-71
218 Dallas, 1970-85

TOUCHDOWNS

Most Seasons Leading League, Touchdowns
13 Chi. Bears, 1932, 1934-35, 1939, 1941-44, 1946-48, 1956, 1965
7 Dallas, 1966, 1968, 1971, 1973, 1977-78, 1980
San Francisco, 1953, 1970, 1987, 1992-95
6 Oakland, 1967-69, 1972, 1974, 1977
San Diego, 1963, 1965, 1979, 1981-82, 1985
Green Bay, 1932, 1937-38, 1961-62, 1996

Most Consecutive Seasons Leading League, Touchdowns
4 Chi. Bears, 1941-44
Los Angeles, 1949-52
San Francisco, 1992-95
3 Chi. Bears, 1946-48
Baltimore, 1957-59
Oakland, 1967-69
2 By many teams

Most Touchdowns, Season
70 Miami, 1984
66 Houston, 1961
San Francisco, 1994
64 Los Angeles, 1950

Fewest Touchdowns, Season (Since 1932)
3 Cincinnati, 1933
4 Cincinnati/St. Louis, 1934
5 Detroit, 1942

Most Touchdowns, Game
10 Philadelphia vs. Cincinnati, Nov. 6, 1934
Los Angeles vs. Baltimore, Oct. 22, 1950
Washington vs. N.Y. Giants, Nov. 27, 1966

9 Chi. Cardinals vs. Rochester, Oct. 7, 1923
Chi. Cardinals vs. N.Y. Giants, Oct. 17, 1948
Chi. Cardinals vs. N.Y. Bulldogs, Nov. 13, 1949
Los Angeles vs. Detroit, Oct. 29, 1950
Pittsburgh vs. N.Y. Giants, Nov. 30, 1952
Chicago vs. San Francisco, Dec. 12, 1965
Chicago vs. Green Bay, Dec. 7, 1980
8 By many teams.

Most Touchdowns, Both Teams, Game
16 Washington (10) vs. N.Y. Giants (6), Nov. 27, 1966
14 Chi. Cardinals (9) vs. N.Y. Giants (5), Oct. 17, 1948
Los Angeles (10) vs. Baltimore (4), Oct. 22, 1950
Houston (7) vs. Oakland (7), Dec. 22, 1963
13 New Orleans (7) vs. St. Louis (6), Nov. 2, 1969
Kansas City (7) vs. Seattle (6), Nov. 27, 1983 (OT)
San Diego (8) vs. Pittsburgh (5), Dec. 8, 1985
N.Y. Jets (7) vs. Miami (6), Sept. 21, 1986 (OT)

Most Consecutive Games Scoring Touchdowns
166 Cleveland, 1957-69
97 Oakland, 1966-73
96 Kansas City, 1963-70

POINTS AFTER TOUCHDOWN

Most (One-Point) Points After Touchdown, Season
66 Miami, 1984
65 Houston, 1961
62 Washington, 1983

Fewest (One-Point) Points After Touchdown, Season
2 Chi. Cardinals, 1933
3 Cincinnati, 1933
Pittsburgh, 1934
4 Cincinnati/St. Louis, 1934

Most (One-Point) Points After Touchdown, Game
10 Los Angeles vs. Baltimore, Oct. 22, 1950
9 Chi. Cardinals vs. N.Y. Giants, Oct. 17, 1948
Pittsburgh vs. N.Y. Giants, Nov. 30, 1952
Washington vs. N.Y. Giants, Nov. 27, 1966
8 By many teams

Most (One-Point) Points After Touchdown, Both Teams, Game
14 Chi. Cardinals (9) vs. N.Y. Giants (5), Oct. 17, 1948
Houston (7) vs. Oakland (7), Dec. 22, 1963
Washington (9) vs. N.Y. Giants (5), Nov. 27, 1966
13 Los Angeles (10) vs. Baltimore (3), Oct. 22, 1950
12 In many games

Most Two-Point Conversions, Season
6 Miami, 1994
Minnesota, 1997
5 Arizona, 1995
Baltimore, 1996
Jacksonville, 1996
Chicago, 1997
4 By many teams

Most Two-Point Conversions, Game
3 Baltimore vs. New England, Oct. 6, 1996
2 Denver vs. Oakland, Oct. 1, 1961
Oakland vs. San Diego, Sept. 30, 1962
Kansas City vs. Houston, Oct. 24, 1965
Houston vs. N.Y. Jets, Dec. 6, 1969
Seattle vs. Kansas City, Oct. 23, 1994
Tampa Bay vs. San Francisco, Oct. 23, 1994
Detroit vs. Green Bay, Nov. 6, 1994
Washington vs. San Francisco, Nov. 6, 1994
Carolina vs. New Orleans, Nov. 26, 1995
Miami vs. Indianapolis, Nov. 26, 1995
New England vs. Baltimore, Oct. 6, 1996
Minnesota vs. Seattle, Nov. 10, 1996
Denver vs. Atlanta, Sept. 28, 1997
Kansas City vs. St. Louis, Oct. 26, 1997
Indianapolis vs. Green Bay, Nov. 16, 1997
Carolina vs. St. Louis, Dec. 20, 1997

Most Two-Point Conversions, Both Teams, Game
5 Baltimore (3) vs. New England (2), Oct. 6, 1996
3 Seattle (2) vs. Kansas City (1), Oct. 23, 1994
Minnesota (2) vs. Seattle (1), Nov. 10, 1996
2 In many games

FIELD GOALS

Most Seasons Leading League, Field Goals
11 Green Bay, 1935-36, 1940-43, 1946-47, 1955, 1972, 1974
8 Washington, 1945, 1956, 1971, 1976-77, 1979, 1982, 1992
7 N.Y. Giants, 1933, 1937, 1939, 1941, 1944, 1959, 1983

Most Consecutive Seasons Leading League, Field Goals
4 Green Bay, 1940-43
3 Cleveland, 1952-54
2 By many teams

Most Field Goals Attempted, Season
49 Los Angeles, 1966
Washington, 1971
48 Green Bay, 1972
47 N.Y. Jets, 1969
Los Angeles, 1973
Washington, 1983

Fewest Field Goals Attempted, Season (Since 1938)
0 Chi. Bears, 1944
2 Cleveland, 1939
Card-Pitt, 1944
Boston, 1946
Chi. Bears, 1947
3 Chi. Bears, 1945
Cleveland, 1945

Most Field Goals Attempted, Game
9 St. Louis vs. Pittsburgh, Sept. 24, 1967
8 Pittsburgh vs. St. Louis, Dec. 2, 1962
Detroit vs. Minnesota, Nov. 13, 1966
N.Y. Jets vs. Buffalo, Nov. 3, 1968
7 By many teams

Most Field Goals Attempted, Both Teams, Game
11 St. Louis (6) vs. Pittsburgh (5), Nov. 13, 1966
Washington (6) vs. Chicago (5), Nov. 14, 1971
Green Bay (6) vs. Detroit (5), Sept. 29, 1974
Washington (6) vs. N.Y. Giants (5), Nov. 14, 1976
10 In many games

Most Field Goals, Season
37 Carolina, 1996
36 Indianapolis, 1996
35 N.Y. Giants, 1983
L.A. Raiders, 1993

Fewest Field Goals, Season (Since 1932)
0 Boston, 1932, 1935
Chi. Cardinals, 1932, 1945
Green Bay, 1932, 1944
N.Y. Giants, 1932
Brooklyn, 1944
Card-Pitt, 1944
Chi. Bears, 1944, 1947
Boston, 1946
Baltimore, 1950
Dallas, 1952

Most Field Goals, Game
7 St. Louis vs. Pittsburgh, Sept. 24, 1967
Minnesota vs. L.A. Rams, Nov. 5, 1989 (OT)
Dallas vs. Green Bay, Nov. 18, 1996
6 Boston vs. Denver, Oct. 4, 1964
Detroit vs. Minnesota, Nov. 13, 1966
N.Y. Jets vs. Buffalo, Nov. 3, 1968
Philadelphia vs. Houston, Nov. 12, 1972
N.Y. Jets vs. New Orleans, Dec. 3, 1972
St. Louis vs. Atlanta, Dec. 9, 1973
N.Y. Giants vs. Seattle, Oct. 18, 1981
San Francisco vs. New Orleans, Oct. 16, 1983
Pittsburgh vs. Denver, Oct. 23, 1988
San Diego vs. Seattle, Sept. 5, 1993
San Diego vs. Houston, Sept. 19, 1993
Cincinnati vs. Seattle, Nov. 6, 1994
Atlanta vs. New Orleans, Nov. 13, 1994
San Francisco vs. Atlanta, Sept. 29, 1996
Buffalo vs. N.Y. Jets, Oct. 20, 1996
San Diego vs. Oakland, Oct. 5, 1997
5 By many teams

Most Field Goals, Both Teams, Game
9 San Diego (5) vs. Kansas City (4), Sept. 29, 1996
8 Cleveland (4) vs. St. Louis (4), Sept. 20, 1964
Chicago (5) vs. Philadelphia (3), Oct. 20, 1968
Washington (5) vs. Chicago (3), Nov. 14, 1971
Kansas City (5) vs. Buffalo (3), Dec. 19, 1971
Detroit (4) vs. Green Bay (4), Sept. 29, 1974
Cleveland (5) vs. Denver (3), Oct. 19, 1975
New England (4) vs. San Diego (4), Nov. 9, 1975
San Francisco (6) vs. New Orleans (2), Oct. 16, 1983
Seattle (5) vs. L.A. Raiders (3), Dec. 18, 1988
Atlanta (6) vs. New Orleans (2), Nov. 13, 1994
Indianapolis (4) vs. San Diego (4), Nov. 3, 1996
7 In many games

Most Consecutive Games Scoring Field Goals
31 Minnesota, 1968-70
28 Washington, 1988-90

22 San Francisco, 1988-89

SAFETIES

Most Safeties, Season
4 Cleveland, 1927
Detroit, 1962
Seattle, 1993
San Francisco, 1996
3 By many teams

Most Safeties, Game
3 L.A. Rams vs. N.Y. Giants, Sept. 30, 1984
2 N.Y. Giants vs. Pottsville, Oct. 30, 1927
Chi. Bears vs. Pottsville, Nov. 13, 1927
Detroit vs. Brooklyn, Dec. 1, 1935
N.Y. Giants vs. Pittsburgh, Sept. 17, 1950
N.Y. Giants vs. Washington, Nov. 5, 1961
Chicago vs. Pittsburgh, Nov. 9, 1969
Dallas vs. Philadelphia, Nov. 19, 1972
Los Angeles vs. Green Bay, Oct. 21, 1973
Oakland vs. San Diego, Oct. 26, 1975
Denver vs. Seattle, Jan. 2, 1983
New Orleans vs. Cleveland, Sept. 13, 1987
Buffalo vs. Denver, Nov. 8, 1987
San Francisco vs. St. Louis, Sept. 8, 1996

Most Safeties, Both Teams, Game
3 L.A. Rams (3) vs. N.Y. Giants (0), Sept. 30, 1984
2 Chi. Cardinals (1) vs. Frankford (1), Nov. 19, 1927
Chi. Cardinals (1) vs. Cincinnati (1), Nov. 12, 1933
Chi. Bears (1) vs. San Francisco (1), Oct. 19, 1952
Cincinnati (1) vs. Los Angeles (1), Oct. 22, 1972
Chi. Bears (1) vs. San Francisco (1), Sept. 19, 1976
Baltimore (1) vs. Miami (1), Oct. 29, 1978
Atlanta (1) vs. Detroit (1), Oct. 5, 1980
Houston (1) vs. Philadelphia (1), Oct. 2, 1988
Cleveland (1) vs. Seattle (1), Nov. 14, 1993
Arizona (1) vs. Houston (1), Dec. 4, 1994
(Also see previous record)

FIRST DOWNS

Most Seasons Leading League
9 Chi. Bears, 1935, 1939, 1941, 1943, 1945, 1947-49, 1955
7 San Diego, 1965, 1969, 1980-83, 1985
6 L.A. Rams, 1946, 1950-51, 1954, 1957, 1973

Most Consecutive Seasons Leading League
4 San Diego, 1980-83
3 Chi. Bears, 1947-49
2 By many teams

Most First Downs, Season
387 Miami, 1984
380 San Diego, 1985
379 San Diego, 1981

Fewest First Downs, Season
51 Cincinnati, 1933
64 Pittsburgh, 1935
67 Philadelphia, 1937

Most First Downs, Game
39 N.Y. Jets vs. Miami, Nov. 27, 1988
Washington vs. Detroit, Nov. 4, 1990 (OT)
38 Los Angeles vs. N.Y. Giants, Nov. 13, 1966
37 Green Bay vs. Philadelphia, Nov. 11, 1962

Fewest First Downs, Game
0 N.Y. Giants vs. Green Bay, Oct. 1, 1933
Pittsburgh vs. Boston, Oct. 29, 1933
Philadelphia vs. Detroit, Sept. 20, 1935
N.Y. Giants vs. Washington, Sept. 27, 1942
Denver vs. Houston, Sept. 3, 1966

Most First Downs, Both Teams, Game
62 San Diego (32) vs. Seattle (30), Sept. 15, 1985
59 Miami (31) vs. Buffalo (28), Oct. 9, 1983 (OT)
Seattle (33) vs. Kansas City (26), Nov. 27, 1983 (OT)
N.Y. Jets (32) vs. Miami (27), Sept. 21, 1986 (OT)
N.Y. Jets (39) vs. Miami (20), Nov. 27, 1988
58 Los Angeles (30) vs. Chi. Bears (28), Oct. 24, 1954
Denver (34) vs. Kansas City (24), Nov. 18, 1974
Atlanta (35) vs. New Orleans (23), Sept. 2, 1979 (OT)
Pittsburgh (36) vs. Cleveland (22), Nov. 25, 1979 (OT)
San Diego (34) vs. Miami (24), Nov. 18, 1984 (OT)
Cincinnati (32) vs. San Diego (26), Sept. 22, 1985

Fewest First Downs, Both Teams, Game
7 Chi. Cardinals (2) vs. Detroit (5), Sept. 15, 1940
9 Pittsburgh (1) vs. Boston (8), Oct. 27, 1935
Boston (4) vs. Brooklyn (5), Nov. 24, 1935
N.Y. Giants (3) vs. Detroit (6), Nov. 7, 1943
Pittsburgh (4) vs. Chi. Cardinals (5), Nov. 11, 1945
N.Y. Bulldogs (1) vs. Philadelphia (8), Sept. 22, 1949
10 N.Y. Giants (4) vs. Washington (6), Dec. 11, 1960

Most First Downs, Rushing, Season
181 New England, 1978
177 Los Angeles, 1973
176 Chicago, 1985

Fewest First Downs, Rushing, Season
36 Cleveland, 1942
Boston, 1944
39 Brooklyn, 1943
40 Philadelphia, 1940
Detroit, 1945

Most First Downs, Rushing, Game
25 Philadelphia vs. Washington, Dec. 2, 1951
23 St. Louis vs. New Orleans, Oct. 5, 1980
21 Cleveland vs. Philadelphia, Dec. 13, 1959
Green Bay vs. Philadelphia, Nov. 11, 1962
Los Angeles vs. New Orleans, Nov. 25, 1973
Pittsburgh vs. Kansas City, Nov. 7, 1976
New England vs. Denver, Nov. 28, 1976
Oakland vs. Green Bay, Sept. 17, 1978
Buffalo vs. Washington, Nov. 3, 1996

Fewest First Downs, Rushing, Game
0 By many teams. Last time: Washington vs. N.Y. Giants, Dec. 13, 1997

Most First Downs, Rushing, Both Teams, Game
36 Philadelphia (25) vs. Washington (11), Dec. 2, 1951
31 Detroit (18) vs. Washington (13), Sept. 30, 1951
30 Los Angeles (17) vs. Minnesota (13), Nov. 5, 1961
New Orleans (17) vs. Green Bay (13), Sept. 9, 1979
New Orleans (16) vs. San Francisco (14), Nov. 11, 1979
New England (16) vs. Kansas City (14), Oct. 4, 1981

Fewest First Downs, Rushing, Both Teams, Game
2 Houston (0) vs. Denver (2), Dec. 2, 1962
N.Y. Jets, (1) vs. St. Louis (1), Dec. 3, 1995
3 Philadelphia (1) vs. Pittsburgh (2), Oct. 27, 1957
Boston (1) vs. Buffalo (2), Nov. 15, 1964
Los Angeles (0) vs. San Francisco (3), Dec. 6, 1964
Pittsburgh (1) vs. St. Louis (2), Nov. 13, 1966
Seattle (1) vs. New Orleans (2), Sept. 1, 1991
New Orleans (0) vs. N.Y. Jets (3), Dec. 24, 1995
Philadelphia (1) vs. Carolina (2), Oct. 27, 1996
San Diego (1) vs. New Orleans (2), Sept. 7, 1997
4 In many games

Most First Downs, Passing, Season
259 San Diego, 1985
251 Houston, 1990
250 Miami, 1986

Fewest First Downs, Passing, Season
18 Pittsburgh, 1941
23 Brooklyn, 1942
N.Y. Giants, 1944
24 N.Y. Giants, 1943

Most First Downs, Passing, Game
29 N.Y. Giants vs. Cincinnati, Oct. 13, 1985
27 San Diego vs. Seattle, Sept. 15, 1985
26 Miami vs. Cleveland, Dec. 12, 1988

Fewest First Downs, Passing, Game
0 By many teams. Last time:
Houston vs. Kansas City, Oct. 9, 1988

Most First Downs, Passing, Both Teams, Game
43 San Diego (23) vs. Cincinnati (20), Dec. 20, 1982
Miami (24) vs. N.Y. Jets (19), Sept. 21, 1986 (OT)
42 San Francisco (22) vs. San Diego (20), Dec. 11, 1982
41 San Diego (27) vs. Seattle (14), Sept. 15, 1985
Miami (26) vs. Cleveland (15), Dec. 12, 1988

Fewest First Downs, Passing, Both Teams, Game
0 Brooklyn vs. Pittsburgh, Nov. 29, 1942
1 Green Bay (0) vs. Cleveland (1), Sept. 21, 1941
Pittsburgh (0) vs. Brooklyn (1), Oct. 11, 1942
N.Y. Giants (0) vs. Detroit (1), Nov. 7, 1943
Pittsburgh (0) vs. Chi. Cardinals (1), Nov. 11, 1945
N.Y. Bulldogs (0) vs. Philadelphia (1), Sept. 22, 1949
Chicago (0) vs. Buffalo (1), Oct. 7, 1979
2 In many games

Most First Downs, Penalty, Season
43 Denver, 1994
42 Chicago, 1987
41 Denver, 1986

Fewest First Downs, Penalty, Season
2 Brooklyn, 1940
4 Chi. Cardinals, 1940
N.Y. Giants, 1942, 1944

Washington, 1944
Cleveland, 1952
Kansas City, 1969
5 Brooklyn, 1939
Chi. Bears, 1939
Detroit, 1953
Los Angeles, 1953
Houston, 1982

Most First Downs, Penalty, Game
11 Denver vs. Houston, Oct. 6, 1985
9 Chi. Bears vs. Cleveland, Nov. 25, 1951
Baltimore vs. Pittsburgh, Oct. 30, 1977
N.Y. Jets vs. Houston, Sept. 18, 1988
8 Philadelphia vs. Detroit, Dec. 2, 1979
Cincinnati vs. N.Y. Jets, Oct. 6, 1985
Buffalo vs. Houston, Sept. 20, 1987
Houston vs. Atlanta, Sept. 9, 1990
Kansas City vs. L.A. Raiders, Oct. 3, 1993

Most First Downs, Penalty, Both Teams, Game
11 Chi. Bears (9) vs. Cleveland (2), Nov. 25, 1951
Cincinnati (8) vs. N.Y. Jets (3), Oct. 6, 1985
Denver (11) vs. Houston (0), Oct. 6, 1985
Detroit (6) vs. Dallas (5), Nov. 8, 1987
N.Y. Jets (9) vs. Houston (2), Sept. 18, 1988
Kansas City (8) vs. L.A. Raiders (3), Oct. 3, 1993
Detroit (6) vs. San Diego (5), Nov. 11, 1996
10 In many games

NET YARDS GAINED RUSHING AND PASSING

Most Seasons Leading League
12 Chi. Bears, 1932, 1934-35, 1939, 1941-44, 1947, 1949, 1955-56
7 San Diego, 1963, 1965, 1980-83, 1985
6 L.A. Rams, 1946, 1950-51, 1954, 1957, 1973
Baltimore, 1958-60, 1964, 1967, 1976
Dall. Cowboys, 1966, 1968-69, 1971, 1974, 1977

Most Consecutive Seasons Leading League
4 Chi. Bears, 1941-44
San Diego, 1980-83
3 Baltimore, 1958-60
Houston, 1960-62
Oakland, 1968-70
2 By many teams

Most Yards Gained, Season
6,936 Miami, 1984
6,744 San Diego, 1981
6,535 San Diego, 1985

Fewest Yards Gained, Season
1,150 Cincinnati, 1933
1,443 Chi. Cardinals, 1934
1,486 Chi. Cardinals, 1933

Most Yards Gained, Game
735 Los Angeles vs. N.Y. Yanks, Sept. 28, 1951
683 Pittsburgh vs. Chi. Cardinals, Dec. 13, 1958
682 Chi. Bears vs. N.Y. Giants, Nov. 14, 1943

Fewest Yards Gained, Game
–7 Seattle vs. Los Angeles, Nov. 4, 1979
–5 Denver vs. Oakland, Sept. 10, 1967
14 Chi. Cardinals vs. Detroit, Sept. 15, 1940

Most Yards Gained, Both Teams, Game
1,133 Los Angeles (636) vs. N.Y. Yanks (497), Nov. 19, 1950
1,102 San Diego (661) vs. Cincinnati (441), Dec. 20, 1982
1,087 St. Louis (589) vs. Philadelphia (498), Dec. 16, 1962

Fewest Yards Gained, Both Teams, Game
30 Chi. Cardinals (14) vs. Detroit (16), Sept. 15, 1940
136 Chi. Cardinals (50) vs. Green Bay (86), Nov. 18, 1934
154 N.Y. Giants (51) vs. Washington (103), Dec. 11, 1960

Most Consecutive Games, 400 or More Yards Gained
11 San Diego, 1982-83
6 Houston, 1961-62
San Diego, 1981
San Francisco, 1987
5 Chi. Bears, 1947
Philadelphia, 1953
Chi. Bears, 1955
Oakland, 1968
New England, 1981
Cincinnati, 1986
San Francisco, 1994

Most Consecutive Games, 300 or More Yards Gained
29 Los Angeles, 1949-51
26 Miami, 1983-85
25 Miami, 1993-95

RUSHING

Most Seasons Leading League
16 Chi. Bears, 1932, 1934-35, 1939-42, 1951, 1955-56, 1968, 1977, 1983-86
7 Buffalo, 1962, 1964, 1973, 1975, 1982, 1991-92
6 Cleveland, 1958-59, 1963, 1965-67

Most Consecutive Seasons Leading League
4 Chi. Bears, 1939-42
Chi. Bears, 1983-86
3 Detroit, 1936-38
San Francisco, 1952-54
Cleveland, 1965-67
2 By many teams

ATTEMPTS

Most Rushing Attempts, Season
681 Oakland, 1977
674 Chicago, 1984
671 New England, 1978

Fewest Rushing Attempts, Season
211 Philadelphia, 1982
219 San Francisco, 1982
225 Houston, 1982

Most Rushing Attempts, Game
72 Chi. Bears vs. Brooklyn, Oct. 20, 1935
70 Chi. Cardinals vs. Green Bay, Dec. 5, 1948
69 Chi. Cardinals vs. Green Bay, Dec. 6, 1936
Kansas City vs. Cincinnati, Sept. 3, 1978

Fewest Rushing Attempts, Game
6 Chi. Cardinals vs. Boston, Oct. 29, 1933
7 Oakland vs. Buffalo, Oct. 15, 1963
Houston vs. N.Y. Giants, Dec. 8, 1985
Seattle vs. L.A. Raiders, Nov. 17, 1991
Green Bay vs. Miami, Sept. 11, 1994
8 Denver vs. Oakland, Dec. 17, 1960
Buffalo vs. St. Louis, Sept. 9, 1984
Detroit vs. San Francisco, Oct. 20, 1991
Atlanta vs. Detroit, Sept. 5, 1993

Most Rushing Attempts, Both Teams, Game
108 Chi. Cardinals (70) vs. Green Bay (38), Dec. 5, 1948
105 Oakland (62) vs. Atlanta (43), Nov. 30, 1975 (OT)
104 Chi. Bears (64) vs. Pittsburgh (40), Oct. 18, 1936

Fewest Rushing Attempts, Both Teams, Game
34 Atlanta (12) vs. Houston (22), Dec. 5, 1993
Atlanta (15) vs. San Francisco (19), Dec. 24, 1995
35 Seattle (15) vs. New Orleans (20), Sept. 1, 1991
36 Houston (15) vs. N.Y. Jets (21), Oct. 13, 1991

YARDS GAINED

Most Yards Gained Rushing, Season
3,165 New England, 1978
3,088 Buffalo, 1973
2,986 Kansas City, 1978

Fewest Yards Gained Rushing, Season
298 Philadelphia, 1940
467 Detroit, 1946
471 Boston, 1944

Most Yards Gained Rushing, Game
426 Detroit vs. Pittsburgh, Nov. 4, 1934
423 N.Y. Giants vs. Baltimore, Nov. 19, 1950
420 Boston vs. N.Y. Giants, Oct. 8, 1933

Fewest Yards Gained Rushing, Game
–53 Detroit vs. Chi. Cardinals, Oct. 17, 1943
–36 Philadelphia vs. Chi. Bears, Nov. 19, 1939
–33 Phil-Pitt vs. Brooklyn, Oct. 2, 1943

Most Yards Gained Rushing, Both Teams, Game
595 Los Angeles (371) vs. N.Y. Yanks (224), Nov. 18, 1951
574 Chi. Bears (396) vs. Pittsburgh (178), Oct. 10, 1934
558 Boston (420) vs. N.Y. Giants (138), Oct. 8, 1933

Fewest Yards Gained Rushing, Both Teams, Game
–15 Detroit (–53) vs. Chi. Cardinals (38), Oct. 17, 1943
4 Detroit (–10) vs. Chi. Cardinals (14), Sept. 15, 1940
62 L.A. Rams (15) vs. San Francisco (47), Dec. 6, 1964

AVERAGE GAIN

Highest Average Gain, Rushing, Season
5.74 Cleveland, 1963
5.65 San Francisco, 1954
5.56 San Diego, 1963

Lowest Average Gain, Rushing, Season
0.94 Philadelphia, 1940
1.45 Boston, 1944
1.55 Pittsburgh, 1935

TOUCHDOWNS
Most Touchdowns, Rushing, Season
36 Green Bay, 1962
33 Pittsburgh, 1976
30 Chi. Bears, 1941
New England, 1978
Washington, 1983

Fewest Touchdowns, Rushing, Season
1 Brooklyn, 1934
2 Chi. Cardinals, 1933
Cincinnati, 1933
Pittsburgh, 1934
Philadelphia, 1935
Philadelphia, 1936
Philadelphia, 1937
Philadelphia, 1938
Pittsburgh, 1940
Philadelphia, 1972
N.Y. Jets, 1995
3 By many teams

Most Touchdowns, Rushing, Game
7 Los Angeles vs. Atlanta, Dec. 4, 1976
6 By many teams

Most Touchdowns, Rushing, Both Teams, Game
8 Los Angeles (6) vs. N.Y. Yanks (2), Nov. 18, 1951
Chi. Bears (5) vs. Green Bay (3), Nov. 6, 1955
Cleveland (6) vs. Los Angeles (2), Nov. 24, 1957
7 In many games

PASSING
ATTEMPTS
Most Passes Attempted, Season
709 Minnesota, 1981
699 New England, 1994
686 New England, 1995

Fewest Passes Attempted, Season
102 Cincinnati, 1933
106 Boston, 1933
120 Detroit, 1937

Most Passes Attempted, Game
70 New England vs. Minnesota, Nov. 13, 1994
68 Houston vs. Buffalo, Nov 1, 1964
66 Atlanta vs. Detroit, Dec. 24, 1989

Fewest Passes Attempted, Game
0 Green Bay vs. Portsmouth, Oct. 8, 1933
Detroit vs. Cleveland, Sept. 10, 1937
Pittsburgh vs. Brooklyn, Nov. 16, 1941
Pittsburgh vs. Los Angeles, Nov. 13, 1949
Cleveland vs. Philadelphia, Dec. 3, 1950

Most Passes Attempted, Both Teams, Game
112 New England (70) vs. Minnesota (42), Nov. 13, 1994
104 Miami (55) vs. N.Y. Jets (49), Oct. 18, 1987 (OT)
102 San Francisco (57) vs. Atlanta (45), Oct. 6, 1985

Fewest Passes Attempted, Both Teams, Game
4 Chi. Cardinals (1) vs. Detroit (3), Nov. 3, 1935
Detroit (0) vs. Cleveland (4), Sept. 10, 1937
6 Chi. Cardinals (2) vs. Detroit (4), Sept. 15, 1940
8 Brooklyn (2) vs. Philadelphia (6), Oct. 1, 1939

COMPLETIONS
Most Passes Completed, Season
432 San Francisco, 1995
411 Houston, 1991
409 Minnesota, 1994

Fewest Passes Completed, Season
25 Cincinnati, 1933
33 Boston, 1933
34 Chi. Cardinals, 1934
Detroit, 1934

Most Passes Completed, Game
45 New England vs. Minnesota, Nov. 13, 1994 (OT)
42 N.Y. Jets vs. San Francisco, Sept. 21, 1980
41 Houston vs. Dallas, Nov. 10, 1991 (OT)

Fewest Passes Completed, Game
0 By many teams. Last time: Buffalo vs. N.Y. Jets, Sept. 29, 1974

Most Passes Completed, Both Teams, Game
71 New England (45) vs. Minnesota (26), Nov. 13, 1994
68 San Francisco (37) vs. Atlanta (31), Oct. 6, 1985
66 Cincinnati (40) vs. San Diego (26), Dec. 20, 1982

Fewest Passes Completed, Both Teams, Game
1 Chi. Cardinals (0) vs. Philadelphia (1), Nov. 8, 1936
Detroit (0) vs. Cleveland (1), Sept. 10, 1937
Chi. Cardinals (0) vs. Detroit (1), Sept. 15, 1940
Brooklyn (0) vs. Pittsburgh (1), Nov. 29, 1942
2 Chi. Cardinals (0) vs. Detroit (2), Nov. 3, 1935
Buffalo (0) vs. N.Y. Jets (2), Sept. 29, 1974
Chi. Cardinals (0) vs. Green Bay (2), Nov. 18, 1934
3 In seven games

YARDS GAINED
Most Seasons Leading League, Passing Yardage
10 San Diego, 1965, 1968, 1971, 1978-83, 1985
8 Chi. Bears, 1932, 1939, 1941, 1943, 1945, 1949, 1954, 1964
Washington, 1938, 1940, 1944, 1947-48, 1967, 1974, 1989
7 Houston, 1960-61, 1963-64, 1990-92

Most Consecutive Seasons Leading League, Passing Yardage
6 San Diego, 1978-83
4 Green Bay, 1934-37
3 Miami, 1986-88
Houston, 1990-92

Most Yards Gained, Passing, Season
5,018 Miami, 1984
4,870 San Diego, 1985
4,805 Houston, 1990

Fewest Yards Gained, Passing, Season
302 Chi. Cardinals, 1934
357 Cincinnati, 1933
459 Boston, 1934

Most Yards Gained, Passing, Game
554 Los Angeles vs. N.Y. Yanks, Sept. 28, 1951
530 Minnesota vs. Baltimore, Sept. 28, 1969
521 Miami vs. N.Y. Jets, Oct. 23, 1988

Fewest Yards Gained, Passing, Game
–53 Denver vs. Oakland, Sept. 10, 1967
–52 Cincinnati vs. Houston, Oct. 31, 1971
–39 Atlanta vs. San Francisco, Oct. 23, 1976

Most Yards Gained, Passing, Both Teams, Game
884 N.Y. Jets (449) vs. Miami (435), Sept. 21, 1986 (OT)
883 San Diego (486) vs. Cincinnati (397), Dec. 20, 1982
874 Miami (456) vs. New England (418), Sept. 4, 1994

Fewest Yards Gained, Passing, Both Teams, Game
–11 Green Bay (–10) vs. Dallas (–1), Oct. 24, 1965
1 Chi. Cardinals (0) vs. Philadelphia (1), Nov. 8, 1936
7 Brooklyn (0) vs. Pittsburgh (7), Nov. 29, 1942

TIMES SACKED
Most Seasons Leading League, Fewest Times Sacked
10 Miami, 1973, 1982-90
4 San Diego, 1963-64, 1967-68
San Francisco, 1964-65, 1970-71
N.Y. Jets, 1965-66, 1968, 1993
3 Houston, 1961-62, 1978
St. Louis, 1974-76
Washington, 1966-67, 1991

Most Consecutive Seasons Leading League, Fewest Times Sacked
9 Miami, 1982-90
3 St. Louis, 1974-76
2 By many teams

Most Times Sacked, Season
104 Philadelphia, 1986
78 Arizona, 1997
72 Philadelphia, 1987

Fewest Times Sacked, Season
7 Miami, 1988
8 San Francisco, 1970
St. Louis, 1975
9 N.Y. Jets, 1966
Washington, 1991

Most Times Sacked, Game
12 Pittsburgh vs. Dallas, Nov. 20, 1966
Baltimore vs. St. Louis, Oct. 26, 1980
Detroit vs. Chicago, Dec. 16, 1984
Houston vs. Dallas, Sept. 29, 1985
11 St. Louis vs. N.Y. Giants, Nov. 1, 1964
Los Angeles vs. Baltimore, Nov. 22, 1964
Denver vs. Buffalo, Dec. 13, 1964
Green Bay vs. Detroit, Nov. 7, 1965
Buffalo vs. Oakland, Oct. 15, 1967
Denver vs. Oakland, Nov. 5, 1967
Atlanta vs. St. Louis, Nov. 24, 1968
Detroit vs. Dallas, Oct. 6, 1975

Philadelphia vs. St. Louis, Dec. 18, 1983
Cleveland vs. Kansas City, Sept. 30, 1984
Minnesota vs. Chicago, Oct. 28, 1984
Atlanta vs. Cleveland, Nov. 18, 1984
Dallas vs. San Diego, Nov. 16, 1986
Philadelphia vs. Detroit, Nov. 16, 1986
Philadelphia vs. L.A. Raiders, Nov. 30, 1986 (OT)
L.A. Raiders vs. Seattle, Dec. 8, 1986
N.Y. Jets vs. Dallas, Oct. 4, 1987
Philadelphia vs. Chicago, Oct. 4, 1987
Dallas vs. Philadelphia, Sept. 15, 1991
Cleveland vs. Indianapolis, Sept. 6, 1992
10 By many teams

Most Times Sacked, Both Teams, Game
18 Green Bay (10) vs. San Diego (8), Sept. 24, 1978
17 Buffalo (10) vs. N.Y. Titans (7), Nov. 23, 1961
Pittsburgh (12) vs. Dallas (5), Nov. 20, 1966
Atlanta (9) vs. Philadelphia (8), Dec. 16, 1984
Philadelphia (11) vs. L.A. Raiders (6), Nov. 30, 1986 (OT)
16 Los Angeles (11) vs. Baltimore (5), Nov. 22, 1964
Buffalo (11) vs. Oakland (5), Oct. 15, 1967

COMPLETION PERCENTAGE

Most Seasons Leading League, Completion Percentage
14 San Francisco, 1952, 1957-58, 1965, 1981, 1983, 1987, 1989, 1992-97
11 Washington, 1937, 1939-40, 1942-45, 1947-48, 1969-70
7 Green Bay, 1936, 1941, 1961-62, 1964, 1966, 1968

Most Consecutive Seasons Leading League, Completion Percentage
6 San Francisco, 1992-97
4 Washington, 1942-45
Kansas City, 1966-69
San Francisco, 1992-95
3 Cleveland, 1953-55

Highest Completion Percentage, Season
70.65 Cincinnati, 1982 (310-219)
70.25 San Francisco, 1994 (511-359)
70.19 San Francisco, 1989 (483-339)

Lowest Completion Percentage, Season
22.9 Philadelphia, 1936 (170-39)
24.5 Cincinnati, 1933 (102-25)
25.0 Pittsburgh, 1941 (168-42)

TOUCHDOWNS

Most Touchdowns, Passing, Season
49 Miami, 1984
48 Houston, 1961
46 Miami, 1986

Fewest Touchdowns, Passing, Season
0 Cincinnati, 1933
Pittsburgh, 1945
1 Boston, 1932
Boston, 1933
Chi. Cardinals, 1934
Cincinnati/St. Louis, 1934
Detroit, 1942
2 Chi. Cardinals, 1932
Stapleton, 1932
Chi. Cardinals, 1935
Brooklyn, 1936
Pittsburgh, 1942

Most Touchdowns, Passing, Game
7 Chi. Bears vs. N.Y. Giants, Nov. 14, 1943
Philadelphia vs. Washington, Oct. 17, 1954
Houston vs. N.Y. Titans, Nov. 19, 1961
Houston vs. N.Y. Titans, Oct. 14, 1962
N.Y. Giants vs. Washington, Oct. 28, 1962
Minnesota vs. Baltimore, Sept. 28, 1969
San Diego vs. Oakland, Nov. 22, 1981
6 By many teams.

Most Touchdowns, Passing, Both Teams, Game
12 New Orleans (6) vs. St. Louis (6), Nov. 2, 1969
11 N.Y. Giants (7) vs. Washington (4), Oct. 28, 1962
Oakland (6) vs. Houston (5), Dec. 22, 1963
10 San Diego (5) vs. Seattle (5), Sept. 15, 1985
Miami (6) vs. N.Y. Jets (4), Sept. 21, 1986 (OT)

PASSES HAD INTERCEPTED

Most Passes Had Intercepted, Season
48 Houston, 1962
45 Denver, 1961
41 Card-Pitt, 1944

Fewest Passes Had Intercepted, Season
5 Cleveland, 1960
Green Bay, 1966
Kansas City, 1990
N.Y. Giants, 1990
6 Green Bay, 1964
St. Louis, 1982
Dallas, 1993
7 Los Angeles, 1969

Most Passes Had Intercepted, Game
9 Detroit vs. Green Bay, Oct. 24, 1943
Pittsburgh vs. Philadelphia, Dec. 12, 1965
8 Green Bay vs. N.Y. Giants, Nov. 21, 1948
Chi. Cardinals vs. Philadelphia, Sept. 24, 1950
N.Y. Yanks vs. N.Y. Giants, Dec. 16, 1951
Denver vs. Houston, Dec. 2, 1962
Chi. Bears vs. Detroit, Sept. 22, 1968
Baltimore vs. N.Y. Jets, Sept. 23, 1973
7 By many teams. Last time:
Green Bay vs. New Orleans, Sept. 14, 1986

Most Passes Had Intercepted, Both Teams, Game
13 Denver (8) vs. Houston (5), Dec. 2, 1962
11 Philadelphia (7) vs. Boston (4), Nov. 3, 1935
Boston (6) vs. Pittsburgh (5), Dec. 1, 1935
Cleveland (7) vs. Green Bay (4), Oct. 30, 1938
Green Bay (7) vs. Detroit (4), Oct. 20, 1940
Detroit (7) vs. Chi. Bears (4), Nov. 22, 1942
Detroit (7) vs. Cleveland (4), Nov. 26, 1944
Chi. Cardinals (8) vs. Philadelphia (3), Sept. 24, 1950
Washington (7) vs. N.Y. Giants (4), Dec. 8, 1963
Pittsburgh (9) vs. Philadelphia (2), Dec 12, 1965
10 In many games

PUNTING

Most Seasons Leading League (Average Distance)
6 Washington, 1940-43, 1945, 1958
Denver, 1962-64, 1966-67, 1982
Kansas City, 1968, 1971-73, 1979, 1984
5 L.A. Rams, 1946, 1949, 1955-56, 1994

Most Consecutive Seasons Leading League (Average Distance)
4 Washington, 1940-43
3 Cleveland, 1950-52
Denver, 1962-64
Kansas City, 1971-73

Most Punts, Season
114 Chicago, 1981
113 Boston, 1934
Brooklyn, 1934
112 Boston, 1935
N.Y. Giants, 1997

Fewest Punts, Season
23 San Diego, 1982
31 Cincinnati, 1982
32 Chi. Bears, 1941

Most Punts, Game
17 Chi. Bears vs. Green Bay, Oct. 22, 1933
Cincinnati vs. Pittsburgh, Oct. 22, 1933
16 Cincinnati vs. Portsmouth, Sept. 17, 1933
Chi. Cardinals vs. Chi. Bears, Nov. 30, 1933
Chi. Cardinals vs. Detroit, Sept. 15, 1940
15 N.Y. Giants vs. Chi. Bears, Nov. 17, 1935
Philadelphia vs. N.Y. Giants, Dec. 6, 1987 (OT)

Fewest Punts, Game
0 By many teams. Last time: Tampa Bay vs. Miami, Sept. 21, 1997

Most Punts, Both Teams, Game
31 Chi. Bears (17) vs. Green Bay (14), Oct. 22, 1933
Cincinnati (17), vs. Pittsburgh (14), Oct. 22, 1933
29 Chi. Cardinals (15) vs. Cincinnati (14), Nov. 12, 1933
Chi. Cardinals (16) vs. Chi. Bears (13), Nov. 30, 1933
Chi. Cardinals (16) vs. Detroit (13), Sept. 15, 1940
28 Philadelphia (14) vs. Washington (14), Nov. 5, 1939

Fewest Punts, Both Teams, Game
0 Buffalo vs. San Francisco, Sept. 13, 1992
1 Baltimore (0) vs. Cleveland (1), Nov. 1, 1959
Dall. Cowboys (0) vs. Cleveland (1), Dec. 3, 1961
Chicago (0) vs. Detroit (1), Oct. 1, 1972
San Francisco (0) vs. N.Y. Giants (1), Oct. 15, 1972
Green Bay (0) vs. Buffalo (1), Dec. 5, 1982
Miami (0) vs. Buffalo (1), Oct. 12, 1986
Green Bay (0) vs. Chicago (1), Dec. 17, 1989
2 In many games

AVERAGE YARDAGE

Highest Average Distance, Punting, Season
47.6 Detroit, 1961 (56-2,664)
47.0 Pittsburgh, 1961 (73-3,431)
46.9 Pittsburgh, 1953 (80-3,752)

Lowest Average Distance, Punting, Season
32.7 Card-Pitt, 1944 (60-1,964)
33.8 Cincinnati, 1986 (59-1,996)
33.9 Detroit, 1969 (74-2,510)

PUNT RETURNS

Most Seasons Leading League (Average Return)
9 Detroit, 1943-45, 1951-52, 1962, 1966, 1969, 1991
7 Chi. Cardinals/St. Louis, 1948-49, 1955-56, 1959, 1986-87
6 Green Bay, 1950, 1953-54, 1961, 1972, 1996

Most Consecutive Seasons Leading League (Average Return)
3 Detroit, 1943-45
2 By many teams

Most Punt Returns, Season
71 Pittsburgh, 1976
Tampa Bay, 1979
L.A. Raiders, 1985
67 Pittsburgh, 1974
Los Angeles, 1978
L.A. Raiders, 1984
65 San Francisco, 1976

Fewest Punt Returns, Season
12 Baltimore, 1981
San Diego, 1982
14 Los Angeles, 1961
Philadelphia, 1962
Baltimore, 1982
15 Houston, 1960
Washington, 1960
Oakland, 1961
N.Y. Giants, 1969
Philadelphia, 1973
Kansas City, 1982

Most Punt Returns, Game
12 Philadelphia vs. Cleveland, Dec. 3, 1950
11 Chi. Bears vs. Chi. Cardinals, Oct. 8, 1950
Washington vs. Tampa Bay, Oct. 9, 1977
10 Philadelphia vs. N.Y. Giants, Nov. 26, 1950
Philadelphia vs. Tampa Bay, Sept. 18, 1977
Pittsburgh vs. Buffalo, Dec. 16, 1979
Washington vs. New Orleans, Dec. 26, 1982
Philadelphia vs. Seattle, Dec. 13, 1992 (OT)
New England vs. Pittsburgh, Dec. 5, 1993

Most Punt Returns, Both Teams, Game
17 Philadelphia (12) vs. Cleveland (5), Dec. 3, 1950
16 N.Y. Giants (9) vs. Philadelphia (7), Dec. 12, 1954
Washington (11) vs. Tampa Bay (5), Oct. 9, 1977
15 Detroit (8) vs. Cleveland (7), Sept. 27, 1942
Los Angeles (8) vs. Baltimore (7), Nov. 27, 1966
Pittsburgh (8) vs. Houston (7), Dec. 1, 1974
Philadelphia (10) vs. Tampa Bay (5), Sept. 18, 1977
Baltimore (9) vs. Kansas City (6), Sept. 2, 1979
Washington (10) vs. New Orleans (5), Dec. 26, 1982
L.A. Raiders (8) vs. Cleveland (7), Nov. 16, 1986

FAIR CATCHES

Most Fair Catches, Season
34 Baltimore, 1971
32 San Diego, 1969
31 Minnesota, 1996

Fewest Fair Catches, Season
0 San Diego, 1975
New England, 1976
Tampa Bay, 1976
Pittsburgh, 1977
Dallas, 1982
1 Cleveland, 1974
San Francisco, 1975
Kansas City, 1976
St. Louis, 1976
San Diego, 1976
L.A. Rams, 1982
St. Louis, 1982
Tampa Bay, 1982
2 By many teams

Most Fair Catches, Game
7 Minnesota vs. Dallas, Sept. 25, 1966
Detroit vs. Chicago, Nov. 21, 1976
Philadelphia vs. Buffalo, Dec. 27, 1987
6 By many teams

YARDS GAINED

Most Yards, Punt Returns, Season
875 Green Bay, 1996
785 L.A. Raiders, 1985
781 Chi. Bears, 1948

Fewest Yards, Punt Returns, Season
27 St. Louis, 1965
35 N.Y. Giants, 1965
37 New England, 1972

Most Yards, Punt Returns, Game
231 Detroit vs. San Francisco, Oct. 6, 1963
225 Oakland vs. Buffalo, Sept. 15, 1968
219 Los Angeles vs. Atlanta, Oct. 11, 1981

Fewest Yards, Punt Returns, Game
-28 Washington vs. Dallas, Dec. 11, 1966
-23 N.Y. Giants vs. Buffalo, Oct. 20, 1975
Pittsburgh vs. Houston, Sept. 20, 1970
-20 New Orleans vs. Pittsburgh, Oct. 20, 1968

Most Yards, Punt Returns, Both Teams, Game
282 Los Angeles (219) vs. Atlanta (63), Oct. 11, 1981
245 Detroit (231) vs. San Francisco (14), Oct. 6, 1963
244 Oakland (225) vs. Buffalo (19), Sept. 15, 1968

Fewest Yards, Punt Returns, Both Teams, Game
-18 Buffalo (-18) vs. Pittsburgh (0), Oct. 29, 1972
-14 Miami (-14) vs. Boston (0), Nov. 30, 1969
-13 N.Y. Giants (-13) vs. Cleveland (0), Nov. 14, 1965

AVERAGE YARDS RETURNING PUNTS

Highest Average, Punt Returns, Season
20.2 Chi. Bears, 1941 (27-546)
19.1 Chi. Cardinals, 1948 (35-669)
18.2 Chi. Cardinals, 1949 (30-546)

Lowest Average, Punt Returns, Season
1.2 St. Louis, 1965 (23-27)
1.5 N.Y. Giants, 1965 (24-35)
1.7 Washington, 1970 (27-45)

TOUCHDOWNS RETURNING PUNTS

Most Touchdowns, Punt Returns, Season
5 Chi. Cardinals, 1959
4 Chi. Cardinals, 1948
Detroit, 1951
N.Y. Giants, 1951
Denver, 1976
3 Washington, 1941
Detroit, 1952
Pittsburgh, 1952
Houston, 1975
Los Angeles, 1981
Cleveland, 1993
Green Bay, 1996
Denver, 1997
San Diego, 1997

Most Touchdowns, Punt Returns, Game
2 Detroit vs. Los Angeles, Oct. 14, 1951
Detroit vs. Green Bay, Nov. 22, 1951
Chi. Cardinals vs. Pittsburgh, Nov. 1, 1959
Chi. Cardinals vs. N.Y. Giants, Nov. 22, 1959
N.Y. Titans vs. Denver, Sept. 24, 1961
Denver vs. Cleveland, Sept. 26, 1976
Los Angeles vs. Atlanta, Oct. 11, 1981
St. Louis vs. Tampa Bay, Dec. 21, 1986
L.A. Rams vs. Atlanta, Dec. 27, 1992
Cleveland vs. Pittsburgh, Oct. 24, 1993
San Diego vs. Cincinnati, Nov. 2, 1997
Denver vs. Carolina, Nov. 9, 1997
Baltimore vs. Seattle, Dec. 7, 1997

Most Touchdowns, Punt Returns, Both Teams, Game
2 Philadelphia (1) vs. Washington (1), Nov. 9, 1952
Kansas City (1) vs. Buffalo (1), Sept. 11, 1966
Baltimore (1) vs. New England (1), Nov. 18, 1979
L.A. Raiders (1) vs. Philadelphia (1), Nov. 30, 1986 (OT)
Cincinnati (1) vs. Green Bay (1), Sept. 20, 1992
(Also see previous record)

KICKOFF RETURNS

Most Seasons Leading League (Average Return)
8 Washington, 1942, 1947, 1962-63, 1973-74, 1981, 1995
6 Chicago Bears, 1943, 1948, 1958, 1966, 1972, 1985
5 N.Y. Giants, 1944, 1946, 1949, 1951, 1953

Most Consecutive Seasons Leading League (Average Return)
3 Denver, 1965-67
2 By many teams

Most Kickoff Returns, Season
88 New Orleans, 1980
87 Atlanta, 1996
86 Minnesota, 1984
Cincinnati, 1994
Baltimore, 1996

Fewest Kickoff Returns, Season
17 N.Y. Giants, 1944
20 N.Y. Giants, 1941, 1943
Chi. Bears, 1942
23 Washington, 1942

Most Kickoff Returns, Game
12 N.Y. Giants vs. Washington, Nov. 27, 1966
10 By many teams

Most Kickoff Returns, Both Teams, Game
19 N.Y. Giants (12) vs. Washington (7), Nov. 27, 1966
18 Houston (10) vs. Oakland (8), Dec. 22, 1963
17 Washington (9) vs. Green Bay (8), Oct. 17, 1983
San Diego (9) vs. Pittsburgh (8), Dec. 8, 1985
Detroit (9) vs. Green Bay (8), Nov. 27, 1986
L.A. Raiders (9) vs. Seattle (8), Dec. 18, 1988
Oakland (10) vs. Seattle (7), Oct. 26, 1997

YARDS GAINED

Most Yards, Kickoff Returns, Season
1,973 New Orleans, 1980
1,899 New Orleans, 1996
1,840 New Orleans, 1994

Fewest Yards, Kickoff Returns, Season
282 N.Y. Giants, 1940
381 Green Bay, 1940
424 Chicago, 1963

Most Yards, Kickoff Returns, Game
362 Detroit vs. Los Angeles, Oct. 29, 1950
304 Chi. Bears vs. Green Bay, Nov. 9, 1952
New Orleans vs. L.A. Rams, Oct. 23, 1994
295 Denver vs. Boston, Oct. 4, 1964

Most Yards, Kickoff Returns, Both Teams, Game
560 Detroit (362) vs. Los Angeles (198), Oct. 29, 1950
501 New Orleans (304) vs. L.A. Rams (197), Oct. 23, 1994
453 Washington (236) vs. Philadelphia (217), Sept. 28, 1947

AVERAGE YARDAGE

Highest Average, Kickoff Returns, Season
29.4 Chicago, 1972 (52-1,528)
28.9 Pittsburgh, 1952 (39-1,128)
28.2 Washington, 1962 (61-1,720)

Lowest Average, Kickoff Returns, Season
14.7 N.Y. Jets, 1993 (46-675)
15.8 N.Y. Giants, 1993 (32-507)
15.9 Tampa Bay, 1993 (58-922)

TOUCHDOWNS

Most Touchdowns, Kickoff Returns, Season
4 Green Bay, 1967
Chicago, 1970
Detroit, 1994
3 Los Angeles, 1950
Chi. Cardinals, 1954
San Francisco, 1963
Denver, 1966
Chicago, 1967
New England, 1977
L.A. Rams, 1985
2 By many teams

Most Touchdowns, Kickoff Returns, Game
2 Chi. Bears vs. Green Bay, Sept. 22, 1940
Chi. Bears vs. Green Bay, Nov. 9, 1952
Philadelphia vs. Dallas, Nov. 6, 1966
Green Bay vs. Cleveland, Nov. 12, 1967
L.A. Rams vs. Green Bay, Nov. 24, 1985
New Orleans vs. L.A. Rams, Oct. 23, 1994

Most Touchdowns, Kickoff Returns, Both Teams, Game
2 Washington (1) vs. Philadelphia (1), Nov. 1, 1942
Washington (1) vs. Philadelphia (1), Sept. 28, 1947
Los Angeles (1) vs. Detroit (1), Oct. 29, 1950
N.Y. Yanks (1) vs. N.Y. Giants (1), Nov. 4, 1951 (consecutive)
Baltimore (1) vs. Chi. Bears (1), Oct. 4, 1958
Buffalo (1) vs. Boston (1), Nov. 3, 1962
Pittsburgh (1) vs. Dallas (1), Oct. 30, 1966
St. Louis (1) vs. Washington (1), Sept. 23, 1973 (consecutive)
Atlanta (1) vs. San Francisco (1), Dec. 20, 1987 (consecutive)
Houston (1) vs. Pittsburgh (1), Dec. 4, 1988
(Also see previous record)

FUMBLES

Most Fumbles, Season
56 Chi. Bears, 1938
San Francisco, 1978
54 Philadelphia, 1946
51 New England, 1973

Fewest Fumbles, Season
8 Cleveland, 1959
11 Green Bay, 1944
12 Brooklyn, 1934
Detroit, 1943
Cincinnati, 1982
Minnesota, 1982

Most Fumbles, Game
10 Phil-Pitt vs. N.Y. Giants, Oct. 9, 1943
Detroit vs. Minnesota, Nov. 12, 1967
Kansas City vs. Houston, Oct. 12, 1969
San Francisco vs. Detroit, Dec. 17, 1978
9 Philadelphia vs. Green Bay, Oct. 13, 1946
Kansas City vs. San Diego, Nov. 15, 1964
N.Y. Giants vs. Buffalo, Oct. 20, 1975
St. Louis vs. Washington, Oct. 25, 1976
San Diego vs. Green Bay, Sept. 24, 1978
Pittsburgh vs. Cincinnati, Oct. 14, 1979
Cleveland vs. Seattle, Dec. 20, 1981
Cleveland vs. Pittsburgh, Dec. 23, 1990
Oakland vs. Seattle, Dec. 22, 1996
8 By many teams

Most Fumbles, Both Teams, Game
14 Washington (8) vs. Pittsburgh (6), Nov. 14, 1937
Chi. Bears (7) vs. Cleveland (7), Nov. 24, 1940
St. Louis (8) vs. N.Y. Giants (6), Sept. 17, 1961
Kansas City (10) vs. Houston (4), Oct. 12, 1969
13 Washington (8) vs. Pittsburgh (5), Nov. 14, 1937
Philadelphia (7) vs. Boston (6), Dec. 8, 1946
N.Y. Giants (7) vs. Washington (6), Nov. 5, 1950
Kansas City (9) vs. San Diego (4), Nov. 15, 1964
Buffalo (7) vs. Denver (6), Dec. 13, 1964
N.Y. Jets (7) vs. Houston (6), Sept. 12, 1965
Houston (8) vs. Pittsburgh (5), Dec. 9, 1973
St. Louis (9) vs. Washington (4), Oct. 25, 1976
Cleveland (9) vs. Seattle (4), Dec. 20, 1981
Green Bay (7) vs. Detroit (6), Oct. 6, 1985
12 In many games

FUMBLES LOST

Most Fumbles Lost, Season
36 Chi. Cardinals, 1959
31 Green Bay, 1952
29 Chi. Cardinals, 1946
Pittsburgh, 1950

Fewest Fumbles Lost, Season
3 Philadelphia, 1938
Minnesota, 1980
4 San Francisco, 1960
Kansas City, 1982
5 Chi. Cardinals, 1943
Detroit, 1943
N.Y. Giants, 1943
Cleveland, 1959
Minnesota, 1982
San Diego, 1993
Detroit, 1996

Most Fumbles Lost, Game
8 St. Louis vs. Washington, Oct. 25, 1976
Cleveland vs. Pittsburgh, Dec. 23, 1990
7 Cincinnati vs. Buffalo, Nov. 30, 1969
Pittsburgh vs. Cincinnati, Oct. 14, 1979
Cleveland vs. Seattle, Dec. 20, 1981
6 By many teams

FUMBLES RECOVERED

Most Fumbles Recovered, Season, Own and Opponents'
58 Minnesota, 1963 (27 own, 31 opp)
51 Chi. Bears, 1938 (37 own, 14 opp)
San Francisco, 1978 (24 own, 27 opp)
50 Philadelphia, 1987 (23 own, 27 opp)

Fewest Fumbles Recovered, Season, Own and Opponents'
9 San Francisco, 1982 (5 own, 4 opp)
11 Cincinnati, 1982 (5 own, 6 opp)
12 Washington, 1994 (6 own, 6 opp)
Arizona, 1997 (7 own, 5 opp)

Most Fumbles Recovered, Game, Own and Opponents'
10 Denver vs. Buffalo, Dec. 13, 1964 (5 own, 5 opp)
Pittsburgh vs. Houston, Dec. 9, 1973 (5 own, 5 opp)
Washington vs. St. Louis, Oct. 25, 1976 (2 own, 8 opp)
9 St. Louis vs. N.Y. Giants, Sept. 17, 1961 (6 own, 3 opp)
Houston vs. Cincinnati, Oct. 27, 1974 (4 own, 5 opp)
Kansas City vs. Dallas, Nov. 10, 1975 (4 own, 5 opp)
Green Bay vs. Detroit, Oct. 6, 1985 (5 own, 4 opp)
8 By many teams

Most Own Fumbles Recovered, Season
37 Chi. Bears, 1938
28 Pittsburgh, 1987
27 Philadelphia, 1946
Minnesota, 1963

Fewest Own Fumbles Recovered, Season
2 Washington, 1958
3 Detroit, 1956
Cleveland, 1959
Houston, 1982
4 By many teams

Most Opponents' Fumbles Recovered, Season
31 Minnesota, 1963
29 Cleveland, 1951
28 Green Bay, 1946
Houston, 1977
Seattle, 1983

Fewest Opponents' Fumbles Recovered, Season
3 Los Angeles, 1974
Green Bay, 1995
4 Philadelphia, 1944
San Francisco, 1982
5 Baltimore, 1982
Arizona, 1997

Most Opponents' Fumbles Recovered, Game
8 Washington vs. St. Louis, Oct. 25, 1976
Pittsburgh vs. Cleveland, Dec. 23, 1990
7 Buffalo vs. Cincinnati, Nov. 30, 1969
Cincinnati vs. Pittsburgh, Oct. 14, 1979
Seattle vs. Cleveland, Dec. 20, 1981
6 By many teams

TOUCHDOWNS

Most Touchdowns, Fumbles Recovered, Season, Own and Opponents'
5 Chi. Bears, 1942 (1 own, 4 opp)
Los Angeles, 1952 (1 own, 4 opp)
San Francisco, 1965 (1 own, 4 opp)
Oakland, 1978 (2 own, 3 opp)
4 Chi. Bears, 1948 (1 own, 3 opp)
Boston, 1948 (4 opp)
Denver, 1979 (1 own, 3 opp)
Atlanta, 1981 (1 own, 3 opp)
Denver, 1984 (4 opp)
St. Louis, 1987 (4 opp)
Minnesota, 1989 (4 opp)
Atlanta, 1991 (4 opp)
Philadelphia, 1995 (4 opp)
3 By many teams

Most Touchdowns, Own Fumbles Recovered, Season
2 Chi. Bears, 1953
New England, 1973
Buffalo, 1974
Denver, 1975
Oakland, 1978
Green Bay, 1982
New Orleans, 1983
Cleveland, 1986
Green Bay, 1989
Miami, 1996

Most Touchdowns, Opponents' Fumbles Recovered, Season
4 Detroit, 1937
Chi. Bears, 1942
Boston, 1948
Los Angeles, 1952
San Francisco, 1965
Denver, 1984
St. Louis, 1987
Minnesota, 1989
Atlanta, 1991
Philadelphia, 1995
3 By many teams

Most Touchdowns, Fumbles Recovered, Game, Own and Opponents'
2 By many teams

Most Touchdowns, Fumbled Recovered, Game, Both Teams, Own and Opponents'
3 Detroit (2) vs. Minnesota (1), Dec. 9, 1962 (2 own, 1 opp)
Green Bay (2) vs. Dallas (1), Nov. 29, 1964 (3 opp)
Oakland (2) vs. Buffalo (1), Dec. 24, 1967 (3 opp)
Oakland (2) vs. Philadelphia (1), Sept. 24, 1995 (3 opp)

Most Touchdowns, Own Fumbles Recovered, Game
2 Miami vs. New England, Sept.1, 1996

Most Touchdowns, Opponents' Fumbles Recovered, Game
2 Detroit vs. Cleveland, Nov. 7, 1937
Philadelphia vs. N.Y. Giants, Sept. 25, 1938
Chi. Bears vs. Washington, Nov. 28, 1948
N.Y. Giants vs. Pittsburgh, Sept. 17, 1950
Cleveland vs. Dall. Cowboys, Dec. 3, 1961
Cleveland vs. N.Y. Giants, Oct. 25, 1964
Green Bay vs. Dallas, Nov. 29, 1964
San Francisco vs. Detroit, Nov. 14, 1965
Oakland vs. Buffalo, Dec. 24, 1967
N.Y. Giants vs. Green Bay, Sept. 19, 1971
Washington vs. San Diego, Sept. 16, 1973
New Orleans vs. San Francisco, Oct. 19, 1975
Cincinnati vs. Pittsburgh, Oct. 14, 1979
Atlanta vs. Detroit, Oct. 5, 1980
Kansas City vs. Oakland, Oct. 5, 1980
New England vs. Baltimore, Nov. 23, 1980
Denver vs. Green Bay, Oct. 15, 1984
Miami vs. Kansas City, Oct. 11, 1987
St. Louis vs. New Orleans, Oct. 11, 1987
Minnesota vs. Atlanta, Dec. 10, 1989
Philadelphia vs. Phoenix, Nov. 24, 1991
Cincinnati vs. Seattle, Sept. 6, 1992
Oakland vs. Philadelphia, Sept. 24, 1995
Pittsburgh vs. New England, Dec. 16, 1995
New England vs. San Diego, Dec.1, 1996

Most Touchdowns, Opponents' Fumbled Recovered, Game, Both Teams
3 Green Bay (2) vs. Dallas (1), Nov. 29, 1964
Oakland (2) vs. Buffalo (1), Dec. 24, 1967
Oakland (2) vs. Philadelphia (1), Sept. 24, 1995

TURNOVERS

(Number of times losing the ball on interceptions and fumbles.)

Most Turnovers, Season
63 San Francisco, 1978
58 Chi. Bears, 1947
Pittsburgh, 1950
N.Y. Giants, 1983
57 Green Bay, 1950
Houston, 1962, 1963
Pittsburgh, 1965

Fewest Turnovers, Season
12 Kansas City, 1982
14 N.Y. Giants, 1943
Cleveland, 1959
N.Y. Giants, 1990
16 San Francisco, 1960
Cincinnati, 1982
St. Louis, 1982
Washington, 1982

Most Turnovers, Game
12 Detroit vs. Chi. Bears, Nov. 22, 1942
Chi. Cardinals vs. Philadelphia, Sept. 24, 1950
Pittsburgh vs. Philadelphia, Dec. 12, 1965
11 San Diego vs. Green Bay, Sept. 24, 1978
10 Washington vs. N.Y. Giants, Dec. 4, 1938
Pittsburgh vs. Green Bay, Nov. 23, 1941
Detroit vs. Green Bay, Oct. 24, 1943
Chi. Cardinals vs. Green Bay, Nov. 10, 1946
Chi. Cardinals vs. N.Y. Giants, Nov. 2, 1952
Minnesota vs. Detroit, Dec. 9, 1962
Houston vs. Oakland, Sept. 7, 1963
Washington vs. N.Y. Giants, Dec. 8, 1963
Chicago vs. Detroit, Sept. 22, 1968
St. Louis vs. Washington, Oct. 25, 1976

N.Y. Jets vs. New England, Nov. 21, 1976
San Francisco vs. Dallas, Oct. 12, 1980
Cleveland vs. Seattle, Dec. 20, 1981
Detroit vs. Denver, Oct. 7, 1984

Most Turnovers, Both Teams, Game
17 Detroit (12) vs. Chi. Bears (5), Nov. 22, 1942
Boston (9) vs. Philadelphia (8), Dec. 8, 1946
16 Chi. Cardinals (12) vs. Philadelphia (4), Sept. 24, 1950
Chi. Cardinals (8) vs. Chi. Bears (8), Dec. 7, 1958
Minnesota (10) vs. Detroit (6), Dec. 9, 1962
Houston (9) vs. Kansas City (7), Oct. 12, 1969
15 Philadelphia (8) vs. Chi. Cardinals (7), Oct. 3, 1954
Denver (9) vs. Houston (6), Dec. 2, 1962
Washington (10) vs. N.Y. Giants (5), Dec. 8, 1963
St. Louis (9) vs. Kansas City (6), Oct. 2, 1983

PENALTIES

Most Seasons Leading League, Fewest Penalties
13 Miami, 1968, 1976-84, 1986, 1990-91
9 Pittsburgh, 1946-47, 1950-52, 1954, 1963, 1965, 1968
7 Boston/New England, 1962, 1964-65, 1973, 1987, 1989, 1993

Most Consecutive Seasons Leading League, Fewest Penalties
9 Miami, 1976-84
3 Pittsburgh, 1950-52
2 By many teams

Most Seasons Leading League, Most Penalties
16 Chi. Bears, 1941-44, 1946-49, 1951, 1959-61, 1963, 1965, 1968, 1976
12 Oakland/L.A. Raiders, 1963, 1966, 1968-69, 1975, 1982, 1984, 1991, 1993-96
7 L.A./St. Louis Rams, 1950, 1952, 1962, 1969, 1978, 1980, 1997

Most Consecutive Seasons Leading League, Most Penalties
4 Chi. Bears, 1941-44, 1946-49
L.A./Oakland Raiders, 1993-96
3 Chi. Cardinals, 1954-56
Chi. Bears, 1959-61
Houston, 1988-90

Fewest Penalties, Season
19 Detroit, 1937
21 Boston, 1935
24 Philadelphia, 1936

Most Penalties, Season
156 L.A. Raiders, 1994
Oakland, 1996
149 Houston, 1989
148 L.A. Raiders, 1993

Fewest Penalties, Game
0 By many teams. Last time:
Buffalo vs. Jacksonville, Dec. 14, 1997
Carolina vs. Green Bay, Dec. 14, 1997

Most Penalties, Game
22 Brooklyn vs. Green Bay, Sept. 17, 1944
Chi. Bears vs. Philadelphia, Nov. 26, 1944
21 Cleveland vs. Chi. Bears, Nov. 25, 1951
20 Tampa Bay vs. Seattle, Oct. 17, 1976
Oakland vs. Denver, Dec. 15, 1996

Fewest Penalties, Both Teams, Game
0 Brooklyn vs. Pittsburgh, Oct. 28, 1934
Brooklyn vs. Boston, Sept. 28, 1936
Cleveland vs. Chi. Bears, Oct. 9, 1938
Pittsburgh vs. Philadelphia, Nov. 10, 1940

Most Penalties, Both Teams, Game
37 Cleveland (21) vs. Chi. Bears (16), Nov. 25, 1951
35 Tampa Bay (20) vs. Seattle (15), Oct. 17, 1976
33 Brooklyn (22) vs. Green Bay (11), Sept. 17, 1944

YARDS PENALIZED

Most Seasons Leading League, Fewest Yards Penalized
13 Miami, 1967-68, 1973, 1977-84, 1990-91
10 Boston/Washington, 1935, 1953-54, 1956-58, 1970, 1985, 1995, 1997
7 Pittsburgh, 1946-47, 1950, 1952, 1962, 1965, 1968
Boston/New England, 1962, 1964-66, 1987, 1989, 1993

Most Consecutive Seasons Leading League, Fewest Yards Penalized
8 Miami, 1977-84
3 Washington, 1956-58
Boston, 1964-66
2 By many teams

Most Seasons Leading League, Most Yards Penalized
15 Chi. Bears, 1935, 1937, 1939-44, 1946-47, 1949, 1951, 1961-62, 1968
12 Oakland/L.A. Raiders, 1963-64, 1968-69, 1975, 1982, 1984, 1991, 1993-94, 1996
6 Buffalo, 1962, 1967, 1970, 1972, 1981, 1983
Houston, 1961, 1985-86, 1988-90

Most Consecutive Seasons Leading League, Most Yards Penalized
6 Chi. Bears, 1939-44
3 Cleveland, 1976-78
Houston, 1988-90
2 By many teams

Fewest Yards Penalized, Season
139 Detroit, 1937
146 Philadelphia, 1937
159 Philadelphia, 1936

Most Yards Penalized, Season
1,274 Oakland, 1969
1,266 Oakland, 1996
1,239 Baltimore, 1979

Fewest Yards Penalized, Game
0 By many teams. Last time:
Buffalo vs. Jacksonville, Dec. 14, 1997
Carolina vs. Green Bay, Dec. 14, 1997

Most Yards Penalized, Game
209 Cleveland vs. Chi. Bears, Nov. 25, 1951
191 Philadelphia vs. Seattle, Dec. 13, 1992 (OT)
190 Tampa Bay vs. Seattle, Oct. 17, 1976

Fewest Yards Penalized, Both Teams, Game
0 Brooklyn vs. Pittsburgh, Oct. 28, 1934
Brooklyn vs. Boston, Sept. 28, 1936
Cleveland vs. Chi. Bears, Oct. 9, 1938
Pittsburgh vs. Philadelphia, Nov. 10, 1940

Most Yards Penalized, Both Teams, Game
374 Cleveland (209) vs. Chi. Bears (165), Nov. 25, 1951
310 Tampa Bay (190) vs. Seattle (120), Oct. 17, 1976
309 Green Bay (184) vs. Boston (125), Oct. 21, 1945

DEFENSE

SCORING

Most Seasons Leading League, Fewest Points Allowed
11 N.Y. Giants, 1927, 1935, 1938-39, 1941, 1944, 1958-59, 1961, 1990, 1993
9 Chi. Bears, 1932, 1936-37, 1942, 1948, 1963, 1985-86, 1988
7 Cleveland, 1951, 1953-57, 1994
Green Bay, 1929, 1935, 1947, 1962, 1965-66, 1996

Most Consecutive Seasons Leading League, Fewest Points Allowed
5 Cleveland, 1953-57
3 Buffalo, 1964-66
Minnesota, 1969-71
2 By many teams

Fewest Points Allowed, Season (Since 1932)
44 Chi. Bears, 1932
54 Brooklyn, 1933
59 Detroit, 1934

Most Points Allowed, Season
533 Baltimore, 1981
501 N.Y. Giants, 1966
487 New Orleans, 1980

Fewest Touchdowns Allowed, Season (Since 1932)
6 Chi. Bears, 1932
Brooklyn, 1933
7 Detroit, 1934
8 Green Bay, 1932

Most Touchdowns Allowed, Season
68 Baltimore, 1981
66 N.Y. Giants, 1966
63 Baltimore, 1950

FIRST DOWNS

Fewest First Downs Allowed Season
77 Detroit, 1935
79 Boston, 1935
82 Washington, 1937

Most First Downs Allowed, Season
406 Baltimore, 1981
371 Seattle, 1981
366 Green Bay, 1983

Fewest First Downs Allowed, Rushing, Season
35 Chi. Bears, 1942
40 Green Bay, 1939
41 Brooklyn, 1944

Most First Downs Allowed, Rushing, Season
179 Detroit, 1985
178 New Orleans, 1980
175 Seattle, 1981

Fewest First Downs Allowed, Passing, Season
33 Chi. Bears, 1943
34 Pittsburgh, 1941
Washington, 1943
35 Detroit, 1940
Philadelphia, 1940, 1944

Most First Downs Allowed, Passing, Season
230 Atlanta, 1995
218 San Diego, 1985
216 San Diego, 1981
N.Y. Jets, 1986

Fewest First Downs Allowed, Penalty, Season
1 Boston, 1944
3 Philadelphia, 1940
Pittsburgh, 1945
Washington, 1957
4 Cleveland, 1940
Green Bay, 1943
N.Y. Giants, 1943

Most First Downs Allowed, Penalty, Season
48 Houston, 1985
46 Houston, 1986
43 L.A. Raiders, 1984

NET YARDS ALLOWED RUSHING AND PASSING

Most Seasons Leading League, Fewest Yards Allowed
8 Chi. Bears, 1942-43, 1948, 1958, 1963, 1984-86
6 N.Y. Giants, 1938, 1940-41, 1951, 1956, 1959
Philadelphia, 1944-45, 1949, 1953, 1981, 1991
Minnesota, 1969-70, 1975, 1988-89, 1993
5 Boston/Washington, 1935-37, 1939, 1946

Most Consecutive Seasons Leading League, Fewest Yards Allowed
3 Boston/Washington, 1935-37
Chicago, 1984-86
2 By many teams

Fewest Yards Allowed, Season
1,539 Chi. Cardinals, 1934
1,703 Chi. Bears, 1942
1,789 Brooklyn, 1933

Most Yards Allowed, Season
6,793 Baltimore, 1981
6,403 Green Bay, 1983
6,352 Minnesota, 1984

RUSHING

Most Seasons Leading League, Fewest Yards Allowed
10 Chi. Bears, 1937, 1939, 1942, 1946, 1949, 1963, 1984-85, 1987-88
7 Detroit, 1938, 1950, 1952, 1962, 1970, 1980-81
Philadelphia, 1944-45, 1947-48, 1953, 1990-91
Dallas, 1966-69, 1972, 1978, 1992
5 N.Y. Giants, 1940, 1951, 1956, 1959, 1986

Most Consecutive Seasons Leading League, Fewest Yards Allowed
4 Dallas, 1966-69
2 By many teams

Fewest Yards Allowed, Rushing, Season
519 Chi. Bears, 1942
558 Philadelphia, 1944
762 Pittsburgh, 1982

Most Yards Allowed, Rushing, Season
3,228 Buffalo, 1978
3,106 New Orleans, 1980
3,010 Baltimore, 1978

Fewest Touchdowns Allowed, Rushing, Season
2 Detroit, 1934
Dallas, 1968
Minnesota, 1971
3 By many teams

Most Touchdowns Allowed, Rushing, Season
36 Oakland, 1961
31 N.Y. Giants, 1980
Tampa Bay, 1986
30 Baltimore, 1981

PASSING

Most Seasons Leading League, Fewest Yards Allowed
9 Green Bay, 1947-48, 1962, 1964-68, 1996
7 Washington, 1939, 1942, 1945, 1952-53, 1980, 1985
6 Chi. Bears, 1938, 1943-44, 1958, 1960, 1963
Minnesota, 1969-70, 1972, 1975-76, 1989
Pittsburgh, 1941, 1946, 1951, 1955, 1974, 1990
Philadelphia, 1934, 1936, 1940, 1949, 1981, 1991

Most Consecutive Seasons Leading League, Fewest Yards Allowed
5 Green Bay, 1964-68
2 By many teams

Fewest Yards Allowed, Passing, Season
545 Philadelphia, 1934
558 Portsmouth, 1933
585 Chi. Cardinals, 1934

Most Yards Allowed, Passing, Season
4,541 Atlanta, 1995
4,389 N.Y. Jets, 1986
4,311 San Diego, 1981

Fewest Touchdowns Allowed, Passing, Season
1 Portsmouth, 1932
Philadelphia, 1934
2 Brooklyn, 1933
Chi. Bears, 1934
3 Chi. Bears, 1932
Green Bay, 1932
Green Bay, 1934
Chi. Bears, 1936
New York, 1939
New York, 1944

Most Touchdowns Allowed, Passing, Season
40 Denver, 1963
38 St. Louis, 1969
37 Washington, 1961
Baltimore, 1981

SACKS

Most Seasons Leading League
5 Oakland/L.A. Raiders, 1966-68, 1982, 1986
4 Boston/New England, 1961, 1963, 1977, 1979
Dallas, 1966, 1968-69, 1978
Dallas/Kansas City, 1960, 1965, 1969, 1990
3 San Francisco, 1967, 1972, 1976
L.A. Rams, 1968, 1970, 1988

Most Consecutive Seasons Leading League
3 Oakland, 1966-68
2 Dallas, 1968-69

Most Sacks, Season
72 Chicago, 1984
71 Minnesota, 1989
70 Chicago, 1987

Fewest Sacks, Season
11 Baltimore, 1982
12 Buffalo, 1982
13 Baltimore, 1981

Most Sacks, Game
12 Dallas vs. Pittsburgh, Nov. 20, 1966
St. Louis vs. Baltimore, Oct. 26, 1980
Chicago vs. Detroit, Dec. 16, 1984
Dallas vs. Houston, Sept. 29, 1985
11 N.Y. Giants vs. St. Louis, Nov. 1, 1964
Baltimore vs. Los Angeles, Nov. 22, 1964
Buffalo vs. Denver, Dec. 13, 1964
Detroit vs. Green Bay, Nov. 7, 1965
Oakland vs. Buffalo, Oct. 15, 1967
Oakland vs. Denver, Nov. 5, 1967
St. Louis vs. Atlanta, Nov. 24, 1968
Dallas vs. Detroit, Oct. 6, 1975
St. Louis vs. Philadelphia, Dec. 18, 1983
Kansas City vs. Cleveland, Sept. 30, 1984
Chicago vs. Minnesota, Oct. 28, 1984
Cleveland vs. Atlanta, Nov. 18, 1984
Detroit vs. Philadelphia, Nov. 16, 1986
San Diego vs. Dallas, Nov. 16, 1986
L.A. Raiders vs. Philadelphia, Nov. 30, 1986 (OT)
Seattle vs. L.A. Raiders, Dec. 8, 1986
Chicago vs. Philadelphia, Oct. 4, 1987
Dallas vs. N.Y. Jets, Oct. 4, 1987
Indianapolis vs. Cleveland, Sept. 6, 1992
10 By many teams

Most Opponents Yards Lost Attempting to Pass, Season
666 Oakland, 1967
583 Chicago, 1984
573 San Francisco, 1976

Fewest Opponents Yards Lost Attempting to Pass, Season
72 Jacksonville, 1995
75 Green Bay, 1956
77 N.Y. Bulldogs, 1949

ALL-TIME RECORDS

INTERCEPTIONS BY

Most Seasons Leading League
10 N.Y. Giants, 1933, 1937-39, 1944, 1948, 1951, 1954, 1961, 1997
8 Green Bay, 1940, 1942-43, 1947, 1955, 1957, 1962, 1965
Chi. Bears, 1935-36, 1941-42, 1946, 1963, 1985, 1990
6 Kansas City, 1966-70, 1974

Most Consecutive Seasons Leading League
5 Kansas City, 1966-70
3 N.Y. Giants, 1937-39
2 By many teams

Most Passes Intercepted By, Season
49 San Diego, 1961
42 Green Bay, 1943
41 N.Y. Giants, 1951

Fewest Passes Intercepted By, Season
3 Houston, 1982
5 Baltimore, 1982
6 Houston, 1972
St. Louis, 1982
Atlanta, 1996

Most Passes Intercepted By, Game
9 Green Bay vs. Detroit, Oct. 24, 1943
Philadelphia vs. Pittsburgh, Dec. 12, 1965
8 N.Y. Giants vs. Green Bay, Nov. 21, 1948
Philadelphia vs. Chi. Cardinals, Sept. 24, 1950
N.Y. Giants vs. N.Y. Yanks, Dec. 16, 1951
Houston vs. Denver, Dec. 2, 1962
Detroit vs. Chicago, Sept. 22, 1968
N.Y. Jets vs. Baltimore, Sept. 23, 1973
7 By many teams. Last time:
New Orleans vs. Green Bay, Sept. 14, 1986

Most Consecutive Games, One or More Interceptions By
46 L.A. Chargers/San Diego, 1960-63
37 Detroit, 1960-63
36 Boston, 1944-47

Most Yards Returning Interceptions, Season
929 San Diego, 1961
712 Los Angeles, 1952
697 Seattle, 1984

Fewest Yards Returning Interceptions, Season
5 Los Angeles, 1959
37 Dallas, 1989
41 Atlanta, 1996

Most Yards Returning Interceptions, Game
325 Seattle vs. Kansas City, Nov. 4, 1984
314 Los Angeles vs. San Francisco, Oct. 18, 1964
245 Houston vs. N.Y. Jets, Oct. 15, 1967

Most Yards Returning Interceptions, Both Teams, Game
356 Seattle (325) vs. Kansas City (31), Nov. 4, 1984
338 Los Angeles (314) vs. San Francisco (24), Oct. 18, 1964
308 Dallas (182) vs. Los Angeles (126), Nov. 2, 1952

Most Touchdowns, Returning Interceptions, Season
9 San Diego, 1961
7 Seattle, 1984
6 Cleveland, 1960
Green Bay, 1966
Detroit, 1967
Houston, 1967

Most Touchdowns Returning Interceptions, Game
4 Seattle vs. Kansas City, Nov. 4, 1984
3 Baltimore vs. Green Bay, Nov. 5, 1950
Cleveland vs. Chicago, Dec. 11, 1960
Philadelphia vs. Pittsburgh, Dec. 12, 1965
Baltimore vs. Pittsburgh, Sept. 29, 1968
Buffalo vs. N.Y. Jets, Sept. 29, 1968
Houston vs. San Diego, Dec. 19, 1971
Cincinnati vs. Houston, Dec. 17, 1972
Tampa Bay vs. New Orleans, Dec. 11, 1977
2 By many teams

Most Touchdown Returning Interceptions, Both Teams, Game
4 Philadelphia (3) vs. Pittsburgh (1), Dec. 12, 1965
Seattle (4) vs. Kansas City (0), Nov. 4, 1984
3 Los Angeles (2) vs. Detroit (1), Nov. 1, 1953
Cleveland (2) vs. N.Y. Giants (1), Dec. 18, 1960
Pittsburgh (2) vs. Cincinnati (1), Oct. 10, 1983
Kansas City (2) vs. San Diego (1), Oct. 19, 1986
(Also see previous record)

PUNT RETURNS

Fewest Opponents Punt Returns, Season
7 Washington, 1962
San Diego, 1982
10 Buffalo, 1982
11 Boston, 1962

Most Opponents Punt Returns, Season
71 Tampa Bay, 1976, 1977
69 N.Y. Giants, 1953
68 Cleveland, 1974

Fewest Yards Allowed, Punt Returns, Season
22 Green Bay, 1967
34 Washington, 1962
39 Cleveland, 1959
Washington, 1972

Most Yards Allowed, Punt Returns, Season
932 Green Bay, 1949
913 Boston, 1947
906 New Orleans, 1974

Lowest Average Allowed, Punt Returns, Season
1.20 Chi. Cardinals, 1954 (46-55)
1.22 Cleveland, 1959 (32-39)
1.55 Chi. Cardinals, 1953 (44-68)

Highest Average Allowed, Punt Returns, Season
18.6 Green Bay, 1949 (50-932)
18.0 Cleveland, 1977 (31-558)
17.9 Boston, 1960 (20-357)

Most Touchdowns Allowed, Punt Returns, Season
4 New York, 1959
Atlanta, 1992
3 Green Bay, 1949
Chi. Cardinals, 1951
L.A. Rams, 1951, 1994
Washington, 1952
Dallas, 1952
Pittsburgh, 1959, 1993
N.Y. Jets, 1968
Cleveland, 1977
Atlanta, 1986
Tampa Bay, 1986
2 By many teams

KICKOFF RETURNS

Fewest Opponents Kickoff Returns, Season
10 Brooklyn, 1943
13 Denver, 1992
15 Detroit, 1942
Brooklyn, 1944

Most Opponents Kickoff Returns, Season
91 Washington, 1983
89 New England, 1980
San Francisco, 1994
Denver, 1997
88 San Diego, 1981
Pittsburgh, 1995

Fewest Yards Allowed, Kickoff Returns, Season
225 Brooklyn, 1943
254 Denver, 1992
293 Brooklyn, 1944

Most Yards Allowed, Kickoff Returns, Season
2,045 Kansas City, 1966
1,912 San Francisco, 1994
1,857 San Francisco, 1995

Lowest Average Allowed, Kickoff Returns, Season
14.3 Cleveland, 1980 (71-1,018)
14.9 Indianapolis, 1993 (37-551)
15.0 Seattle, 1982 (24-361)

Highest Average Allowed, Kickoff Returns, Season
29.5 N.Y. Jets, 1972 (47-1,386)
29.4 Los Angeles, 1950 (48-1,411)
29.1 New England, 1971 (49-1,427)

Most Touchdowns Allowed, Kickoff Returns, Season
3 Minnesota, 1963, 1970
Dallas, 1966
Detroit, 1980
Pittsburgh, 1986
Buffalo, 1997
2 By many teams

FUMBLES

Fewest Opponents Fumbles, Season
11 Cleveland, 1956
Baltimore, 1982

12 Green Bay, 1995
13 Los Angeles, 1956
Chicago, 1960
Cleveland, 1963
Cleveland, 1965
Detroit, 1967
San Diego, 1969

Most Opponents Fumbles, Season

50 Minnesota, 1963
San Francisco, 1978
48 N.Y. Giants, 1980
N.Y. Jets, 1986
47 N.Y. Giants, 1977
Seattle, 1984

TURNOVERS

(Number of times losing the ball on interceptions and fumbles.)

Fewest Opponents Turnovers, Season

11 Baltimore, 1982
13 San Francisco, 1982
15 St. Louis, 1982

Most Opponents Turnovers, Season

66 San Diego, 1961
63 Seattle, 1984
61 Washington, 1983

Most Opponents Turnovers, Game

12 Chi. Bears vs. Detroit, Nov. 22, 1942
Philadelphia vs. Chi. Cardinals, Sept. 24, 1950
Philadelphia vs. Pittsburgh, Dec. 12, 1965
11 Green Bay vs. San Diego, Sept. 24, 1978
10 By 14 teams

OUTSTANDING PERFORMERS

1,000 YARDS RUSHING IN A SEASON

Year	Player, Team	Att.	Yards	Avg.	Long	TD
1997	Barry Sanders, Detroit[9]	335	2,053	6.1	82	11
	Terrell Davis, Denver[3]	369	1,750	4.7	50	15
	Jerome Bettis, Pittsburgh[4]	375	1,665	4.4	34	7
	Dorsey Levens, Green Bay	329	1,435	4.4	52	7
	Eddie George, Tennessee[2]	357	1,399	3.9	30	6
	Napoleon Kaufman, Oakland	272	1,294	4.8	83	6
	Robert Smith, Minnesota	232	1,266	5.5	78	6
	Curtis Martin, New England[3]	274	1,160	4.2	70	4
	*Corey Dillon, Cincinnati	233	1,129	4.8	71	10
	Ricky Watters, Philadelphia[4]	285	1,110	3.9	28	7
	Adrian Murrell, N.Y. Jets[2]	300	1,086	3.6	43	7
	Emmitt Smith, Dallas[7]	261	1,074	4.1	44	4
	Marshall Faulk, Indianapolis[3]	264	1,054	4.0	45	7
	Raymont Harris, Chicago	275	1,033	3.8	68	10
	Garrison Hearst, San Francisco[2]	234	1,019	4.4	51	4
	Jamal Anderson, Atlanta[2]	290	1,002	3.5	39	7
1996	Barry Sanders, Detroit[8]	307	1,553	5.1	54	11
	Terrell Davis, Denver[2]	345	1,538	4.5	71	13
	Jerome Bettis, Pittsburgh[3]	320	1,431	4.5	50	11
	Ricky Watters, Philadelphia[3]	353	1,411	4.0	56	13
	*Eddie George, Houston	335	1,368	4.1	76	8
	Terry Allen, Washington[4]	347	1,353	3.9	49	21
	Adrian Murrell, N.Y. Jets	301	1,249	4.1	78	6
	Emmitt Smith, Dallas[6]	327	1,204	3.7	42	12
	Curtis Martin, New England[2]	316	1,152	3.6	57	14
	Anthony Johnson, Carolina	300	1,120	3.7	29	6
	*Karim Abdul-Jabbar, Miami	307	1,116	3.6	29	11
	Jamal Anderson, Atlanta	232	1,055	4.5	32	5
	Thurman Thomas, Buffalo[8]	281	1,033	3.7	36	8
1995	Emmitt Smith, Dallas[5]	377	1,773	4.7	60	25
	Barry Sanders, Detroit[7]	314	1,500	4.8	75	11
	*Curtis Martin, New England	368	1,487	4.0	49	14
	Chris Warren, Seattle[4]	310	1,346	4.3	52	15
	Terry Allen, Washington[3]	338	1,309	3.9	28	10
	Ricky Watters, Philadelphia[2]	337	1,273	3.8	57	11
	Errict Rhett, Tampa Bay[2]	332	1,207	3.6	21	11
	Rodney Hampton, N.Y. Giants[5]	306	1,182	3.9	32	10
	*Terrell Davis, Denver	237	1,117	4.7	60	7
	Harvey Williams, Oakland	255	1,114	4.4	60	9
	Craig Heyward, Atlanta	236	1,083	4.6	31	6
	Marshall Faulk, Indianapolis[2]	289	1,078	3.7	40	11
	*Rashaan Salaam, Chicago	296	1,074	3.6	42	10
	Garrison Hearst, Arizona	284	1,070	3.8	38	1
	Edgar Bennett, Green Bay	316	1,067	3.4	23	3
	Thurman Thomas, Buffalo[7]	267	1,005	3.8	49	6
1994	Barry Sanders, Detroit[6]	331	1,883	5.7	85	7
	Chris Warren, Seattle[3]	333	1,545	4.6	41	9
	Emmitt Smith, Dallas[4]	368	1,484	4.0	46	21
	Natrone Means, San Diego	343	1,350	3.9	25	12
	*Marshall Faulk, Indianapolis	314	1,282	4.1	52	11
	Thurman Thomas, Buffalo[6]	287	1,093	3.8	29	7
	Rodney Hampton, N.Y. Giants[4]	327	1,075	3.3	27	6
	Terry Allen, Minnesota[2]	255	1,031	4.0	45	8
	Jerome Bettis, L.A. Rams[2]	319	1,025	3.2	19	3
	*Errict Rhett, Tampa Bay	284	1,011	3.6	27	7
1993	Emmitt Smith, Dallas[3]	283	1,486	5.3	62	9
	*Jerome Bettis, L.A. Rams	294	1,429	4.9	71	7
	Thurman Thomas, Buffalo[5]	355	1,315	3.7	27	6
	Erric Pegram, Atlanta	292	1,185	4.1	29	3
	Barry Sanders, Detroit[5]	243	1,115	4.6	42	3
	Leonard Russell, New England	300	1,088	3.6	21	7
	Rodney Hampton, N.Y. Giants[3]	292	1,077	3.7	20	5
	Chris Warren, Seattle[2]	273	1,072	3.9	45	7
	*Reggie Brooks, Washington	223	1,063	4.8	85	3
	*Ron Moore, Phoenix	263	1,018	3.9	20	9
	Gary Brown, Houston	195	1,002	5.1	26	6
1992	Emmitt Smith, Dallas[2]	373	1,713	4.6	68	18
	Barry Foster, Pittsburgh	390	1,690	4.3	69	11
	Thurman Thomas, Buffalo[4]	312	1,487	4.8	44	9
	Barry Sanders, Detroit[4]	312	1,352	4.3	55	9
	Lorenzo White, Houston	265	1,226	4.6	44	7
	Terry Allen, Minnesota	266	1,201	4.5	51	13
	Reggie Cobb, Tampa Bay	310	1,171	3.8	25	9
	Harold Green, Cincinnati	265	1,170	4.4	53	2
	Rodney Hampton, N.Y. Giants[2]	257	1,141	4.4	63	14
	Cleveland Gary, L.A. Rams	279	1,125	4.0	63	7
	Herschel Walker, Philadelphia[2]	267	1,070	4.0	38	8
	Chris Warren, Seattle	223	1,017	4.6	52	3
	Ricky Watters, San Francisco	206	1,013	4.9	43	9
1991	Emmitt Smith, Dallas	365	1,563	4.3	75	12
	Barry Sanders, Detroit[3]	342	1,548	4.5	69	16
	Thurman Thomas, Buffalo[3]	288	1,407	4.9	33	7
	Rodney Hampton, N.Y. Giants	256	1,059	4.1	44	10
	Earnest Byner, Washington[3]	274	1,048	3.8	32	5
	Gaston Green, Denver	261	1,037	4.0	63	4
	Christian Okoye, Kansas City[2]	225	1,031	4.6	48	9
1990	Barry Sanders, Detroit[2]	255	1,304	5.1	45	13
	Thurman Thomas, Buffalo[2]	271	1,297	4.8	80	11
	Marion Butts, San Diego	265	1,225	4.6	52	8
	Earnest Byner, Washington[2]	297	1,219	4.1	22	6
	Bobby Humphrey, Denver[2]	288	1,202	4.2	37	7
	Neal Anderson, Chicago[3]	260	1,078	4.1	52	10
	Barry Word, Kansas City	204	1,015	5.0	53	4
	James Brooks, Cincinnati[3]	195	1,004	5.1	56	5
1989	Christian Okoye, Kansas City	370	1,480	4.0	59	12
	*Barry Sanders, Detroit	280	1,470	5.3	34	14
	Eric Dickerson, Indianapolis[7]	314	1,311	4.2	21	7
	Neal Anderson, Chicago[2]	274	1,275	4.7	73	11
	Dalton Hilliard, New Orleans	344	1,262	3.7	40	13
	Thurman Thomas, Buffalo	298	1,244	4.2	38	6
	James Brooks, Cincinnati[2]	221	1,239	5.6	65	7
	*Bobby Humphrey, Denver	294	1,151	3.9	40	7
	Greg Bell, L.A. Rams[3]	272	1,137	4.2	47	15
	Roger Craig, San Francisco[3]	271	1,054	3.9	27	6
	Ottis Anderson, N.Y. Giants[6]	325	1,023	3.1	36	14
1988	Eric Dickerson, Indianapolis[6]	388	1,659	4.3	41	14
	Herschel Walker, Dallas	361	1,514	4.2	38	5
	Roger Craig, San Francisco[2]	310	1,502	4.8	46	9
	Greg Bell, L.A. Rams[2]	288	1,212	4.2	44	16
	*John Stephens, New England	297	1,168	3.9	52	4
	Gary Anderson, San Diego	225	1,119	5.0	36	3
	Neal Anderson, Chicago	249	1,106	4.4	80	12
	Joe Morris, N.Y. Giants[3]	307	1,083	3.5	27	5
	*Ickey Woods, Cincinnati	203	1,066	5.3	56	15
	Curt Warner, Seattle[4]	266	1,025	3.9	29	10
	John Settle, Atlanta	232	1,024	4.4	62	7
	Mike Rozier, Houston	251	1,002	4.0	28	10
1987	Charles White, L.A. Rams	324	1,374	4.2	58	11
	Eric Dickerson, L.A. Rams-Indianapolis[5]	283	1,288	4.6	57	6
1986	Eric Dickerson, L.A. Rams[4]	404	1,821	4.5	42	11
	Joe Morris, N.Y. Giants[2]	341	1,516	4.4	54	14
	Curt Warner, Seattle[3]	319	1,481	4.6	60	13
	*Rueben Mayes, New Orleans	286	1,353	4.7	50	8
	Walter Payton, Chicago[10]	321	1,333	4.2	41	8
	Gerald Riggs, Atlanta[3]	343	1,327	3.9	31	9
	George Rogers, Washington[4]	303	1,203	4.0	42	18
	James Brooks, Cincinnati	205	1,087	5.3	56	5
1985	Marcus Allen, L.A. Raiders[3]	390	1,759	4.6	61	11
	Gerald Riggs, Atlanta[2]	397	1,719	4.3	50	10
	Walter Payton, Chicago[9]	324	1,551	4.8	40	9
	Joe Morris, N.Y. Giants	294	1,336	4.5	65	21
	Freeman McNeil, N.Y. Jets[2]	294	1,331	4.5	69	3
	Tony Dorsett, Dallas[8]	305	1,307	4.3	60	7
	James Wilder, Tampa Bay[2]	365	1,300	3.6	28	10
	Eric Dickerson, L.A. Rams[3]	292	1,234	4.2	43	12
	Craig James, New England	263	1,227	4.7	65	5
	Kevin Mack, Cleveland	222	1,104	5.0	61	7
	Curt Warner, Seattle[2]	291	1,094	3.8	38	8
	George Rogers, Washington[3]	231	1,093	4.7	35	7
	Roger Craig, San Francisco	214	1,050	4.9	62	9
	Earnest Jackson, Philadelphia[2]	282	1,028	3.6	59	5
	Stump Mitchell, St. Louis	183	1,006	5.5	64	7
	Earnest Byner, Cleveland	244	1,002	4.1	36	8
1984	Eric Dickerson, L.A. Rams[2]	379	2,105	5.6	66	14
	Walter Payton, Chicago[8]	381	1,684	4.4	72	11
	James Wilder, Tampa Bay	407	1,544	3.8	37	13
	Gerald Riggs, Atlanta	353	1,486	4.2	57	13
	Wendell Tyler, San Francisco[3]	246	1,262	5.1	40	7
	John Riggins, Washington[5]	327	1,239	3.8	24	14
	Tony Dorsett, Dallas[7]	302	1,189	3.9	31	6
	Earnest Jackson, San Diego	296	1,179	4.0	32	8
	Ottis Anderson, St. Louis[5]	289	1,174	4.1	24	6
	Marcus Allen, L.A. Raiders[2]	275	1,168	4.2	52	13
	Sammy Winder, Denver	296	1,153	3.9	24	4
	*Greg Bell, Buffalo	262	1,100	4.2	85	7
	Freeman McNeil, N.Y. Jets	229	1,070	4.7	53	5
1983	*Eric Dickerson, L.A. Rams	390	1,808	4.6	85	18
	William Andrews, Atlanta[4]	331	1,567	4.7	27	7
	*Curt Warner, Seattle	335	1,449	4.3	60	13
	Walter Payton, Chicago[7]	314	1,421	4.5	49	6
	John Riggins, Washington[4]	375	1,347	3.6	44	24
	Tony Dorsett, Dallas[6]	289	1,321	4.6	77	8
	Earl Campbell, Houston[5]	322	1,301	4.0	42	12
	Ottis Anderson, St. Louis[4]	296	1,270	4.3	43	5

	Mike Pruitt, Cleveland[4]	293	1,184	4.0	27	10
	George Rogers, New Orleans[2]	256	1,144	4.5	76	5
	Joe Cribbs, Buffalo[3]	263	1,131	4.3	45	3
	Curtis Dickey, Baltimore	254	1,122	4.4	56	4
	Tony Collins, New England	219	1,049	4.8	50	10
	Billy Sims, Detroit[3]	220	1,040	4.7	41	7
	Marcus Allen, L.A. Raiders	266	1,014	3.8	19	9
	Franco Harris, Pittsburgh[8]	279	1,007	3.6	19	5
1981	*George Rogers, New Orleans	378	1,674	4.4	79	13
	Tony Dorsett, Dallas[5]	342	1,646	4.8	75	4
	Billy Sims, Detroit[2]	296	1,437	4.9	51	13
	Wilbert Montgomery, Philadelphia[3]	286	1,402	4.9	41	8
	Ottis Anderson, St. Louis[3]	328	1,376	4.2	28	9
	Earl Campbell, Houston[4]	361	1,376	3.8	43	10
	William Andrews, Atlanta[3]	289	1,301	4.5	29	10
	Walter Payton, Chicago[6]	339	1,222	3.6	39	6
	Chuck Muncie, San Diego[2]	251	1,144	4.6	73	19
	*Joe Delaney, Kansas City	234	1,121	4.8	82	3
	Mike Pruitt, Cleveland[3]	247	1,103	4.5	21	7
	Joe Cribbs, Buffalo[2]	257	1,097	4.3	35	3
	Pete Johnson, Cincinnati	274	1,077	3.9	39	12
	Wendell Tyler, Los Angeles[2]	260	1,074	4.1	69	12
	Ted Brown, Minnesota	274	1,063	3.9	34	6
1980	Earl Campbell, Houston[3]	373	1,934	5.2	55	13
	Walter Payton, Chicago[5]	317	1,460	4.6	69	6
	Ottis Anderson, St. Louis[2]	301	1,352	4.5	52	9
	William Andrews, Atlanta[2]	265	1,308	4.9	33	4
	*Billy Sims, Detroit	313	1,303	4.2	52	13
	Tony Dorsett, Dallas[4]	278	1,185	4.3	56	11
	*Joe Cribbs, Buffalo	306	1,185	3.9	48	11
	Mike Pruitt, Cleveland[2]	249	1,034	4.2	56	6
1979	Earl Campbell, Houston[2]	368	1,697	4.6	61	19
	Walter Payton, Chicago[4]	369	1,610	4.4	43	14
	*Ottis Anderson, St. Louis	331	1,605	4.8	76	8
	Wilbert Montgomery, Philadelphia[2]	338	1,512	4.5	62	9
	Mike Pruitt, Cleveland	264	1,294	4.9	77	9
	Ricky Bell, Tampa Bay	283	1,263	4.5	49	7
	Chuck Muncie, New Orleans	238	1,198	5.0	69	11
	Franco Harris, Pittsburgh[7]	267	1,186	4.4	71	11
	John Riggins, Washington[3]	260	1,153	4.4	66	9
	Wendell Tyler, Los Angeles	218	1,109	5.1	63	9
	Tony Dorsett, Dallas[3]	250	1,107	4.4	41	6
	*William Andrews, Atlanta	239	1,023	4.3	23	3
1978	*Earl Campbell, Houston	302	1,450	4.8	81	13
	Walter Payton, Chicago[3]	333	1,395	4.2	76	11
	Tony Dorsett, Dallas[2]	290	1,325	4.6	63	7
	Delvin Williams, Miami[2]	272	1,258	4.6	58	8
	Wilbert Montgomery, Philadelphia	259	1,220	4.7	47	9
	Terdell Middleton, Green Bay	284	1,116	3.9	76	11
	Franco Harris, Pittsburgh[6]	310	1,082	3.5	37	8
	Mark van Eeghen, Oakland[3]	270	1,080	4.0	34	9
	*Terry Miller, Buffalo	238	1,060	4.5	60	7
	Tony Reed, Kansas City	206	1,053	5.1	62	5
	John Riggins, Washington[2]	248	1,014	4.1	31	5
1977	Walter Payton, Chicago[2]	339	1,852	5.5	73	14
	Mark van Eeghen, Oakland[2]	324	1,273	3.9	27	7
	Lawrence McCutcheon, Los Angeles[4]	294	1,238	4.2	48	7
	Franco Harris, Pittsburgh[5]	300	1,162	3.9	61	11
	Lydell Mitchell, Baltimore[3]	301	1,159	3.9	64	3
	Chuck Foreman, Minnesota[3]	270	1,112	4.1	51	6
	Greg Pruitt, Cleveland[3]	236	1,086	4.6	78	3
	Sam Cunningham, New England	270	1,015	3.8	31	4
	*Tony Dorsett, Dallas	208	1,007	4.8	84	12
1976	O.J. Simpson, Buffalo[5]	290	1,503	5.2	75	8
	Walter Payton, Chicago	311	1,390	4.5	60	13
	Delvin Williams, San Francisco	248	1,203	4.9	80	7
	Lydell Mitchell, Baltimore[2]	289	1,200	4.2	43	5
	Lawrence McCutcheon, Los Angeles[3]	291	1,168	4.0	40	9
	Chuck Foreman, Minnesota[2]	278	1,155	4.2	46	13
	Franco Harris, Pittsburgh[4]	289	1,128	3.9	30	14
	Mike Thomas, Washington	254	1,101	4.3	28	5
	Rocky Bleier, Pittsburgh	220	1,036	4.7	28	5
	Mark van Eeghen, Oakland	233	1,012	4.3	21	3
	Otis Armstrong, Denver[2]	247	1,008	4.1	31	5
	Greg Pruitt, Cleveland[2]	209	1,000	4.8	64	4
1975	O.J. Simpson, Buffalo[4]	329	1,817	5.5	88	16
	Franco Harris, Pittsburgh[3]	262	1,246	4.8	36	10
	Lydell Mitchell, Baltimore	289	1,193	4.1	70	11
	Jim Otis, St. Louis	269	1,076	4.0	30	5
	Chuck Foreman, Minnesota	280	1,070	3.8	31	13
	Greg Pruitt, Cleveland	217	1,067	4.9	50	8
	John Riggins, N.Y. Jets	238	1,005	4.2	42	8
	Dave Hampton, Atlanta	250	1,002	4.0	22	5
1974	Otis Armstrong, Denver	263	1,407	5.3	43	9
	*Don Woods, San Diego	227	1,162	5.1	56	7
	O.J. Simpson, Buffalo[3]	270	1,125	4.2	41	3
	Lawrence McCutcheon, Los Angeles[2]	236	1,109	4.7	23	3
	Franco Harris, Pittsburgh[2]	208	1,006	4.8	54	5
1973	O.J. Simpson, Buffalo[2]	332	2,003	6.0	80	12
	John Brockington, Green Bay[3]	265	1,144	4.3	53	3
	Calvin Hill, Dallas[2]	273	1,142	4.2	21	6
	Lawrence McCutcheon, Los Angeles	210	1,097	5.2	37	2
	Larry Csonka, Miami[3]	219	1,003	4.6	25	5
1972	O.J. Simpson, Buffalo	292	1,251	4.3	94	6
	Larry Brown, Washington[2]	285	1,216	4.3	38	8
	Ron Johnson, N.Y. Giants[2]	298	1,182	4.0	35	9
	Larry Csonka, Miami[2]	213	1,117	5.2	45	6
	Marv Hubbard, Oakland	219	1,100	5.0	39	4
	*Franco Harris, Pittsburgh	188	1,055	5.6	75	10
	Calvin Hill, Dallas	245	1,036	4.2	26	6
	Mike Garrett, San Diego[2]	272	1,031	3.8	41	6
	John Brockington, Green Bay[2]	274	1,027	3.7	30	8
	Eugene (Mercury) Morris, Miami	190	1,000	5.3	33	12
1971	Floyd Little, Denver	284	1,133	4.0	40	6
	*John Brockington, Green Bay	216	1,105	5.1	52	4
	Larry Csonka, Miami	195	1,051	5.4	28	7
	Steve Owens, Detroit	246	1,035	4.2	23	8
	Willie Ellison, Los Angeles	211	1,000	4.7	80	4
1970	Larry Brown, Washington	237	1,125	4.7	75	5
	Ron Johnson, N.Y. Giants	263	1,027	3.9	68	8
1969	Gale Sayers, Chicago[2]	236	1,032	4.4	28	8
1968	Leroy Kelly, Cleveland[3]	248	1,239	5.0	65	16
	*Paul Robinson, Cincinnati	238	1,023	4.3	87	8
1967	Jim Nance, Boston[2]	269	1,216	4.5	53	7
	Leroy Kelly, Cleveland[2]	235	1,205	5.1	42	11
	Hoyle Granger, Houston	236	1,194	5.1	67	6
	Mike Garrett, Kansas City	236	1,087	4.6	58	9
1966	Jim Nance, Boston	299	1,458	4.9	65	11
	Gale Sayers, Chicago	229	1,231	5.4	58	8
	Leroy Kelly, Cleveland	209	1,141	5.5	70	15
	Dick Bass, Los Angeles[2]	248	1,090	4.4	50	8
1965	Jim Brown, Cleveland[7]	289	1,544	5.3	67	17
	Paul Lowe, San Diego[2]	222	1,121	5.0	59	7
1964	Jim Brown, Cleveland[6]	280	1,446	5.2	71	7
	Jim Taylor, Green Bay[5]	235	1,169	5.0	84	12
	John Henry Johnson, Pittsburgh[2]	235	1,048	4.5	45	7
1963	Jim Brown, Cleveland[5]	291	1,863	6.4	80	12
	Clem Daniels, Oakland	215	1,099	5.1	74	3
	Jim Taylor, Green Bay[4]	248	1,018	4.1	40	9
	Paul Lowe, San Diego	177	1,010	5.7	66	8
1962	Jim Taylor, Green Bay[3]	272	1,474	5.4	51	19
	John Henry Johnson, Pittsburgh	251	1,141	4.5	40	7
	Cookie Gilchrist, Buffalo	214	1,096	5.1	44	13
	Abner Haynes, Dall. Texans	221	1,049	4.7	71	13
	Dick Bass, Los Angeles	196	1,033	5.3	57	6
	Charlie Tolar, Houston	244	1,012	4.1	25	7
1961	Jim Brown, Cleveland[4]	305	1,408	4.6	38	8
	Jim Taylor, Green Bay[2]	243	1,307	5.4	53	15
1960	Jim Brown, Cleveland[3]	215	1,257	5.8	71	9
	Jim Taylor, Green Bay	230	1,101	4.8	32	11
	John David Crow, St. Louis	183	1,071	5.9	57	6
1959	Jim Brown, Cleveland[2]	290	1,329	4.6	70	14
	J.D. Smith, San Francisco	207	1,036	5.0	73	10
1958	Jim Brown, Cleveland	257	1,527	5.9	65	17
1956	Rick Casares, Chi. Bears	234	1,126	4.8	68	12
1954	Joe Perry, San Francisco[2]	173	1,049	6.1	58	8
1953	Joe Perry, San Francisco	192	1,018	5.3	51	10
1949	Steve Van Buren, Philadelphia[2]	263	1,146	4.4	41	11
	Tony Canadeo, Green Bay	208	1,052	5.1	54	4
1947	Steve Van Buren, Philadelphia	217	1,008	4.6	45	13
1934	*Beattie Feathers, Chi. Bears	119	1,004	8.4	82	8

**First season of professional football.*

200 YARDS RUSHING IN A GAME

Date	Player, Team, Opponent	Att.	Yards	TD
Dec. 4, 1997	*Corey Dillon, Cincinnati vs. Tennessee	39	246	4
Nov. 23, 1997	Barry Sanders, Detroit vs. Indianapolis	24	216	2
Oct. 26, 1997	Terrell Davis, Denver vs. Buffalo (OT)	42	207	1
Oct. 19, 1997	Napoleon Kaufman, Oakland vs. Denver	28	227	1
Oct. 12, 1997	Barry Sanders, Detroit vs. Tampa Bay	24	215	2
Sept. 21, 1997	Terrell Davis, Denver vs. Cincinnati	27	215	1
Aug. 31, 1997	Eddie George, Tennessee vs. Oakland (OT)	35	216	1
Sept. 22, 1996	LeShon Johnson, Arizona vs. New Orleans	21	214	2
Nov. 13, 1994	Barry Sanders, Detroit vs. Tampa Bay	26	237	0
Dec. 12, 1993	*Jerome Bettis, L.A. Rams vs. New Orleans	28	212	1
Oct. 31, 1993	Emmitt Smith, Dallas vs. Philadelphia	30	237	1

OUTSTANDING PERFORMERS

Nov. 24, 1991	Barry Sanders, Detroit vs. Minnesota	23	220	4
Dec. 23, 1990	James Brooks, Cincinnati vs. Houston	20	201	1
Oct. 14, 1990	Barry Word, Kansas City vs. Detroit	18	200	2
Sept. 24, 1990	Thurman Thomas, Buffalo vs. N.Y. Jets	18	214	0
Dec. 24, 1989	Greg Bell, L.A. Rams vs. New England	26	210	1
Sept. 24, 1989	Greg Bell, L.A. Rams vs. Green Bay	28	221	2
Sept. 17, 1989	Gerald Riggs, Washington vs. Philadelphia	29	221	1
Dec. 18, 1988	Gary Anderson, San Diego vs. Kansas City	34	217	1
Nov. 30, 1987	*Bo Jackson, L.A. Raiders vs. Seattle	18	221	2
Nov. 15, 1987	Charles White, L.A. Rams vs. St. Louis	34	213	1
Dec. 7, 1986	Rueben Mayes, New Orleans vs. Miami	28	203	2
Oct. 5, 1986	Eric Dickerson, L.A. Rams vs. Tampa Bay (OT)	30	207	2
Dec. 21, 1985	George Rogers, Washington vs. St. Louis	34	206	1
Dec. 21, 1985	Joe Morris, N.Y. Giants vs. Pittsburgh	36	202	3
Dec. 9, 1984	Eric Dickerson, L.A. Rams vs. Houston	27	215	2
Nov. 18, 1984	*Greg Bell, Buffalo vs. Dallas	27	206	1
Nov. 4, 1984	Eric Dickerson, L.A. Rams vs. St. Louis	21	208	0
Sept. 2, 1984	Gerald Riggs, Atlanta vs. New Orleans	35	202	2
Nov. 27, 1983	*Curt Warner, Seattle vs. Kansas City (OT)	32	207	3
Nov. 6, 1983	James Wilder, Tampa Bay vs. Minnesota	31	219	1
Sept. 18, 1983	Tony Collins, New England vs. N.Y. Jets	23	212	3
Sept. 4, 1983	George Rogers, New Orleans vs. St. Louis	24	206	2
Dec. 21, 1980	Earl Campbell, Houston vs. Minnesota	29	203	1
Nov. 16, 1980	Earl Campbell, Houston vs. Chicago	31	206	0
Oct. 26, 1980	Earl Campbell, Houston vs. Cincinnati	27	202	2
Oct. 19, 1980	Earl Campbell, Houston vs. Tampa Bay	33	203	0
Nov. 26, 1978	*Terry Miller, Buffalo vs. N.Y. Giants	21	208	2
Dec. 4, 1977	*Tony Dorsett, Dallas vs. Philadelphia	23	206	2
Nov. 20, 1977	Walter Payton, Chicago vs. Minnesota	40	275	1
Oct. 30, 1977	Walter Payton, Chicago vs. Green Bay	23	205	2
Dec. 5, 1976	O.J. Simpson, Buffalo vs. Miami	24	203	1
Nov. 25, 1976	O.J. Simpson, Buffalo vs. Detroit	29	273	2
Oct. 24, 1976	Chuck Foreman, Minnesota vs. Philadelphia	28	200	2
Dec. 14, 1975	Greg Pruitt, Cleveland vs. Kansas City	26	214	3
Sept. 28, 1975	O.J. Simpson, Buffalo vs. Pittsburgh	28	227	1
Dec. 16, 1973	O.J. Simpson, Buffalo vs. N.Y. Jets	34	200	1
Dec. 9, 1973	O.J. Simpson, Buffalo vs. New England	22	219	1
Sept. 16, 1973	O.J. Simpson, Buffalo vs. New England	29	250	2
Dec. 5, 1971	Willie Ellison, Los Angeles vs. New Orleans	26	247	1
Dec. 20, 1970	John (Frenchy) Fuqua, Pittsburgh vs. Philadelphia	20	218	2
Nov. 3, 1968	Gale Sayers, Chicago vs. Green Bay	24	205	0
Oct. 30, 1966	Jim Nance, Boston vs. Oakland	38	208	2
Oct. 10, 1964	John Henry Johnson, Pittsburgh vs. Cleveland	30	200	3
Dec. 8, 1963	Cookie Gilchrist, Buffalo vs. N.Y. Jets	36	243	5
Nov. 3, 1963	Jim Brown, Cleveland vs. Philadelphia	28	223	1
Oct. 20, 1963	Clem Daniels, Oakland vs. N.Y. Jets	27	200	2
Sept. 22, 1963	Jim Brown, Cleveland vs. Dallas	20	232	2
Dec. 10, 1961	Billy Cannon, Houston vs. N.Y. Titans	25	216	3
Nov. 19, 1961	Jim Brown, Cleveland vs. Philadelphia	34	237	4
Dec. 18, 1960	John David Crow, St. Louis vs. Pittsburgh	24	203	0
Nov. 15, 1959	Bobby Mitchell, Cleveland vs. Washington	14	232	3
Nov. 24, 1957	*Jim Brown, Cleveland vs. Los Angeles	31	237	4
Dec. 16, 1956	*Tom Wilson, Los Angeles vs. Green Bay	23	223	0
Nov. 22, 1953	Dan Towler, Los Angeles vs. Baltimore	14	205	1
Nov. 12, 1950	Gene Roberts, N.Y. Giants vs. Chi. Cardinals	26	218	2
Nov. 27, 1949	Steve Van Buren, Philadelphia vs. Pittsburgh	27	205	0
Oct. 8, 1933	Cliff Battles, Boston vs. N.Y. Giants	16	215	1

**First season of professional football.*

TIMES 200 OR MORE

68 times by 46 players...Simpson 6; Brown, Campbell, Sanders 4; Bell, Dickerson 3; Davis, Payton, Riggs, Rogers 2.

4,000 YARDS PASSING IN A SEASON

Year	Player, Team	Att.	Comp.	Pct.	Yards	TD	Int.
1996	Mark Brunell, Jacksonville	557	353	63.4	4,367	19	20
	Vinny Testaverde, Baltimore	549	325	59.2	4,177	33	19
	Drew Bledsoe, New England[2]	623	373	59.9	4,086	27	15
1995	Brett Favre, Green Bay	570	359	63.0	4,413	38	13
	Scott Mitchell, Detroit	583	346	59.3	4,338	32	12
	Warren Moon, Minnesota[4]	606	377	62.2	4,228	33	14
	Jeff George, Atlanta	557	336	60.3	4,143	24	11
1994	Drew Bledsoe, New England	691	400	57.9	4,555	25	27
	Dan Marino, Miami[6]	615	385	62.6	4,453	30	17
	Warren Moon, Minnesota[3]	601	371	61.7	4,264	18	19
1993	John Elway, Denver	551	348	63.2	4,030	25	10
	Steve Young, San Francisco	462	314	68.0	4,023	29	16
1992	Dan Marino, Miami[5]	554	330	59.6	4,116	24	16
1991	Warren Moon, Houston[2]	655	404	61.7	4,690	23	21
1990	Warren Moon, Houston	584	362	62.0	4,689	33	13
1989	Don Majkowski, Green Bay	599	353	58.9	4,318	27	20
	Jim Everett, L.A. Rams	518	304	58.7	4,310	29	17
1988	Dan Marino, Miami[4]	606	354	58.4	4,434	28	23
1986	Dan Marino, Miami[3]	623	378	60.7	4,746	44	23
	Jay Schroeder, Washington	541	276	51.0	4,109	22	22
1985	Dan Marino, Miami[2]	567	336	59.3	4,137	30	21
1984	Dan Marino, Miami	564	362	64.2	5,084	48	17
	Neil Lomax, St. Louis	560	345	61.6	4,614	28	16
	Phil Simms, N.Y. Giants	533	286	53.7	4,044	22	18
1983	Lynn Dickey, Green Bay	484	289	59.7	4,458	32	29
	Bill Kenney, Kansas City	603	346	57.4	4,348	24	18
1981	Dan Fouts, San Diego[3]	609	360	59.1	4,802	33	17
1980	Dan Fouts, San Diego[2]	589	348	59.1	4,715	30	24
	Brian Sipe, Cleveland	554	337	60.8	4,132	30	14
1979	Dan Fouts, San Diego	530	332	62.6	4,082	24	24
1967	Joe Namath, N.Y. Jets	491	258	52.5	4,007	26	28

400 YARDS PASSING IN A GAME

Date	Player, Team, Opponent	Att.	Comp.	Yards	TD
Nov. 2, 1997	Tony Banks, St. Louis vs. Atlanta	34	23	401	2
Oct. 26, 1997	Warren Moon, Seattle vs. Oakland	44	28	409	5
Nov. 10, 1996	Boomer Esiason, Arizona vs. Washington (OT)	59	35	522	3
Nov. 3, 1996	Drew Bledsoe, New England vs. Miami	41	30	419	3
Oct. 27, 1996	Vinny Testaverde, Baltimore vs. St. Louis (OT)	51	31	429	3
Oct. 20, 1996	Mark Brunell, Jacksonville vs. St. Louis	52	37	421	0
Sept. 22, 1996	Mark Brunell, Jacksonville vs. New England (OT)	39	23	432	3
Dec. 18, 1995	Steve Young, San Francisco vs. Minnesota	49	30	425	3
Nov. 26, 1995	Dave Krieg, Arizona vs. Atlanta (OT)	43	27	413	4
Nov. 23, 1995	Scott Mitchell, Detroit vs. Minnesota	45	30	410	4
Oct. 1, 1995	Dan Marino, Miami vs. Cincinnati	48	33	450	2
Nov. 20, 1994	Warren Moon, Minnesota vs. N.Y. Jets	50	33	400	2
Nov. 13, 1994	Drew Bledsoe, New England vs. Minnesota (OT)	70	45	426	3
Nov. 6, 1994	Warren Moon, Minnesota vs. New Orleans	57	33	420	3
Sept. 25, 1994	Dan Marino, Miami vs. Minnesota	54	29	431	3
Sept. 4, 1994	Dan Marino, Miami vs. New England (OT)	42	23	473	5
Sept. 4, 1994	Drew Bledsoe, New England vs. Miami (OT)	51	32	421	4
Dec. 19, 1993	Steve Beuerlein, Phoenix vs. Seattle	53	34	431	3
Dec. 5, 1993	Brett Favre, Green Bay vs. Chicago	54	36	402	2
Nov. 28, 1993	Steve Young, San Francisco vs. L.A. Rams	32	26	462	4
Oct. 31, 1993	Jeff Hostetler, L.A. Raiders vs. San Diego	32	20	424	2
Sept. 13, 1992	Steve Young, San Francisco vs. Buffalo	37	26	449	3
Sept. 13, 1992	Jim Kelly, Buffalo vs. San Francisco	33	22	403	3
Nov. 10, 1991	Warren Moon, Houston vs. Dallas (OT)	56	41	432	0
Nov. 10, 1991	Mark Rypien, Washington vs. Atlanta	31	16	442	6
Oct. 13, 1991	Warren Moon, Houston vs. N.Y. Jets	50	35	423	2
Dec. 16, 1990	Warren Moon, Houston vs. Kansas City	45	27	527	3
Nov. 4, 1990	Joe Montana, San Francisco vs. Green Bay	40	25	411	3
Oct. 14, 1990	Joe Montana, San Francisco vs. Atlanta	49	32	476	6
Oct. 7, 1990	Boomer Esiason, Cincinnati vs. L.A. Rams (OT)	45	31	490	3
Dec. 23, 1989	Warren Moon, Houston vs. Cleveland	51	32	414	2
Dec. 11, 1989	Joe Montana, San Francisco vs. L.A. Rams	42	30	458	3
Nov. 26, 1989	Jim Everett, L.A. Rams vs. New Orleans (OT)	51	29	454	1
Nov. 26, 1989	Mark Rypien, Washington vs. Chicago	47	30	401	4
Oct. 2, 1989	Randall Cunningham, Philadelphia vs. Chicago	62	32	401	1
Sept. 24, 1989	Joe Montana, San Francisco vs. Philadelphia	34	25	428	5
Sept. 24, 1989	Dan Marino, Miami vs. N.Y. Jets	55	33	427	3
Sept. 17, 1989	Randall Cunningham, Phil. vs. Washington	46	34	447	5
Dec. 18, 1988	Dave Krieg, Seattle vs. L.A. Raiders	32	19	410	4
Dec. 12, 1988	Dan Marino, Miami vs. Cleveland	50	30	404	4
Oct. 23, 1988	Dan Marino, Miami vs. N.Y. Jets	60	35	521	3
Oct. 16, 1988	Vinny Testaverde, Tampa Bay vs. Indianapolis	42	25	469	2
Sept. 11, 1988	Doug Williams, Washington vs. Pittsburgh	52	30	430	2
Nov. 29, 1987	Tom Ramsey, New England vs. Philadelphia	53	34	402	3
Nov. 22, 1987	Boomer Esiason, Cincinnati vs. Pittsburgh	53	30	409	0
Sept. 20, 1987	Neil Lomax, St. Louis vs. San Diego	61	32	457	3
Dec. 21, 1986	Boomer Esiason, Cincinnati vs. N.Y. Jets	30	23	425	5
Dec. 14, 1986	Dan Marino, Miami vs. L.A. Rams (OT)	46	29	403	5
Nov. 23, 1986	Bernie Kosar, Cleveland vs. Pittsburgh (OT)	46	28	414	2
Nov. 17, 1986	Joe Montana, San Francisco vs. Washington	60	33	441	0
Nov. 16, 1986	Dan Marino, Miami vs. Buffalo	54	39	404	4
Nov. 10, 1986	Bernie Kosar, Cleveland vs. Miami	50	32	401	0
Nov. 2, 1986	Tommy Kramer, Minnesota vs. Washington (OT)	35	20	490	4
Nov. 2, 1986	Ken O'Brien, N.Y. Jets vs. Seattle	32	26	431	4
Oct. 27, 1986	Jay Schroeder, Washington vs. N.Y. Giants	40	22	420	1
Oct. 12, 1986	Steve Grogan, New England vs. N.Y. Jets	42	23	401	3
Sept. 21, 1986	Ken O'Brien, N.Y. Jets vs. Miami (OT)	43	29	479	4
Sept. 21, 1986	Dan Marino, Miami vs. N.Y. Jets (OT)	50	30	448	6
Sept. 21, 1986	Tony Eason, New England vs. Seattle	45	26	414	3
Dec. 20, 1985	John Elway, Denver vs. Seattle	42	24	432	1
Nov. 10, 1985	Dan Fouts, San Diego vs. L.A. Raiders (OT)	41	26	436	4
Oct. 13, 1985	Phil Simms, N.Y. Giants vs. Cincinnati	62	40	513	1
Oct. 13, 1985	Dave Krieg, Seattle vs. Atlanta	51	33	405	4
Oct. 6, 1985	Phil Simms, N.Y. Giants vs. Dallas	36	18	432	3
Oct. 6, 1985	Joe Montana, San Francisco vs. Atlanta	57	37	429	5

Sept. 19, 1985	Tommy Kramer, Minnesota vs. Chicago	55	28	436	3
Sept. 15, 1985	Dan Fouts, San Diego vs. Seattle	43	29	440	4
Dec. 16, 1984	Neil Lomax, St. Louis vs. Washington	46	37	468	2
Dec. 9, 1984	Dan Marino, Miami vs. Indianapolis	41	29	404	4
Dec. 2, 1984	Dan Marino, Miami vs. L.A. Raiders	57	35	470	4
Nov. 25, 1984	Dave Krieg, Seattle vs. Denver	44	30	406	3
Nov. 4, 1984	Dan Marino, Miami vs. N.Y. Jets	42	23	422	2
Oct. 21, 1984	Dan Fouts, San Diego vs. L.A. Raiders	45	24	410	3
Sept. 30, 1984	Dan Marino, Miami vs. St. Louis	36	24	429	3
Sept. 2, 1984	Phil Simms, N.Y. Giants vs. Philadelphia	30	23	409	4
Dec. 11, 1983	Bill Kenney, Kansas City vs. San Diego	41	31	411	4
Nov. 20, 1983	Dave Krieg, Seattle vs. Denver	42	31	418	3
Oct. 9, 1983	Joe Ferguson, Buffalo vs. Miami (OT)	55	38	419	5
Oct. 2, 1983	Joe Theismann, Washington vs. L.A. Raiders	39	23	417	3
Sept. 25, 1983	Richard Todd, N.Y. Jets vs. L.A. Rams (OT)	50	37	446	2
Dec. 26, 1982	Vince Ferragamo, L.A. Rams vs. Chicago	46	30	509	3
Dec. 20, 1982	Dan Fouts, San Diego vs. Cincinnati	40	25	435	1
Dec. 20, 1982	Ken Anderson, Cincinnati vs. San Diego	56	40	416	2
Dec. 11, 1982	Dan Fouts, San Diego vs. San Francisco	48	33	444	5
Nov. 21, 1982	Joe Montana, San Francisco vs. St. Louis	39	26	408	3
Nov. 15, 1981	Steve Bartkowski, Atlanta vs. Pittsburgh	50	33	416	2
Oct. 25, 1981	Brian Sipe, Cleveland vs. Baltimore	41	30	444	4
Oct. 25, 1981	David Woodley, Miami vs. Dallas	37	21	408	3
Oct. 11, 1981	Tommy Kramer, Minnesota vs. San Diego	43	27	444	4
Dec. 14, 1980	Tommy Kramer, Minnesota vs. Cleveland	49	38	456	4
Nov. 16, 1980	Doug Williams, Tampa Bay vs. Minnesota	55	30	486	4
Oct. 19, 1980	Dan Fouts, San Diego vs. N.Y. Giants	41	26	444	3
Oct. 12, 1980	Lynn Dickey, Green Bay vs. Tampa Bay (OT)	51	35	418	1
Sept. 21, 1980	Richard Todd, N.Y. Jets vs. San Francisco	60	42	447	3
Oct. 3, 1976	James Harris, Los Angeles vs. Miami	29	17	436	2
Nov. 17, 1975	Ken Anderson, Cincinnati vs. Buffalo	46	30	447	2
Nov. 18, 1974	Charley Johnson, Denver vs. Kansas City	42	28	445	2
Dec. 11, 1972	Joe Namath, N.Y. Jets vs. Oakland	46	25	403	1
Sept. 24, 1972	Joe Namath, N.Y. Jets vs. Baltimore	28	15	496	6
Dec. 21, 1969	Don Horn, Green Bay vs. St. Louis	31	22	410	5
Sept. 28, 1969	Joe Kapp, Minnesota vs. Baltimore	43	28	449	7
Sept. 9, 1968	Pete Beathard, Houston vs. Kansas City	48	23	413	2
Nov. 26, 1967	Sonny Jurgensen, Washington vs. Cleveland	50	32	418	3
Oct. 1, 1967	Joe Namath, N.Y. Jets vs. Miami	39	23	415	3
Sept. 17, 1967	Johnny Unitas, Baltimore vs. Atlanta	32	22	401	2
Nov. 13, 1966	Don Meredith, Dallas vs. Washington	29	21	406	2
Nov. 28, 1965	Sonny Jurgensen, Washington vs. Dallas	43	26	411	3
Oct. 24, 1965	Fran Tarkenton, Minnesota vs. San Francisco	35	21	407	3
Nov. 1, 1964	Len Dawson, Kansas City vs. Denver	38	23	435	6
Oct. 25, 1964	Cotton Davidson, Oakland vs. Denver	36	23	427	5
Oct. 16, 1964	Babe Parilli, Boston vs. Oakland	47	25	422	4
Dec. 22, 1963	Tom Flores, Oakland vs. Houston	29	17	407	6
Nov. 17, 1963	Norm Snead, Washington vs. Pittsburgh	40	23	424	2
Nov. 10, 1963	Don Meredith, Dallas vs. San Francisco	48	30	460	3
Oct. 13, 1963	Charley Johnson, St. Louis vs. Pittsburgh	41	20	428	2
Dec. 16, 1962	Sonny Jurgensen, Philadelphia vs. St. Louis	34	15	419	5
Nov. 18, 1962	Bill Wade, Chicago vs. Dall. Cowboys	46	28	466	2
Oct. 28, 1962	Y.A. Tittle, N.Y. Giants vs. Washington	39	27	505	7
Sept. 15, 1962	Frank Tripucka, Denver vs. Buffalo	56	29	447	2
Dec. 17, 1961	Sonny Jurgensen, Philadelphia vs. Detroit	42	27	403	3
Nov. 19, 1961	George Blanda, Houston vs. N.Y. Titans	32	20	418	7
Oct. 29, 1961	George Blanda, Houston vs. Buffalo	32	18	464	4
Oct. 29, 1961	Sonny Jurgensen, Philadelphia vs. Washington	41	27	436	3
Oct. 13, 1961	Jacky Lee, Houston vs. Boston	41	27	457	2
Dec. 13, 1958	Bobby Layne, Pittsburgh vs. Chi. Cardinals	49	23	409	2
Nov. 8, 1953	Bobby Thomason, Philadelphia vs. N.Y. Giants	44	22	437	4
Oct. 4, 1952	Otto Graham, Cleveland vs. Pittsburgh	49	21	401	3
Sept. 28, 1951	Norm Van Brocklin, Los Angeles vs. N.Y. Yanks	41	27	554	5
Dec. 11, 1949	Johnny Lujack, Chi. Bears vs. Chi. Cardinals	39	24	468	6
Oct. 31, 1948	Sammy Baugh, Washington vs. Boston	24	17	446	4
Oct. 31, 1948	Jim Hardy, Los Angeles vs. Chi. Cardinals	53	28	406	3
Nov. 14, 1943	Sid Luckman, Chi. Bears vs. N.Y. Giants	32	21	433	7

TIMES 400 OR MORE

130 times by 66 players…Marino 13; Montana, Moon 7; Fouts 6; Jurgensen, Krieg 5; Esiason, Kramer 4; Bledsoe, Namath, Simms, Young 3; Anderson, Blanda, Brunell, Cunningham, Johnson, Kosar, Lomax, Meredith, O'Brien, Rypien, Testaverde, Todd, Williams 2.

100 PASS RECEPTIONS IN A SEASON

Year	Player, Team	No.	Yards	Avg.	Long	TD
1997	Tim Brown, Oakland	104	1,408	13.5	59	5
	Herman Moore, Detroit[3]	104	1,293	12.4	79	8
1996	Jerry Rice, San Francisco[4]	108	1,254	11.6	39	8
	Herman Moore, Detroit[2]	106	1,296	12.2	50	9
	Carl Pickens, Cincinnati	100	1,180	11.8	61	12
1995	Herman Moore, Detroit	123	1,686	13.7	69	14
	Jerry Rice, San Francisco[3]	122	1,848	15.1	81	15
	Cris Carter, Minnesota[2]	122	1,371	11.2	60	17
	Isaac Bruce, St. Louis	119	1,781	15.0	72	13
	Michael Irvin, Dallas	111	1,603	14.4	50	10
	Brett Perriman, Detroit	108	1,488	13.8	91	9
	Eric Metcalf, Atlanta	104	1,189	11.4	62	8
	Robert Brooks, Green Bay	102	1,497	14.7	99	13
	Larry Centers, Arizona	101	962	9.5	32	2
1994	Cris Carter, Minnesota	122	1,256	10.3	65	7
	Jerry Rice, San Francisco[2]	112	1,499	13.4	69	13
	Terance Mathis, Atlanta	111	1,342	12.1	81	11
1993	Sterling Sharpe, Green Bay[2]	112	1,274	11.4	54	11
1992	Sterling Sharpe, Green Bay	108	1,461	13.5	76	13
1991	Haywood Jeffires, Houston	100	1,181	11.8	44	7
1990	Jerry Rice, San Francisco	100	1,502	15.0	64	13
1984	Art Monk, Washington	106	1,372	12.9	72	7
1964	Charley Hennigan, Houston	101	1,546	15.3	53	8
1961	Lionel Taylor, Denver	100	1,176	11.8	52	4

1,000 YARDS PASS RECEIVING IN A SEASON

Year	Player, Team	No.	Yards	Avg.	Long	TD
1997	Rob Moore, Arizona[3]	97	1,584	16.3	47	8
	Tim Brown, Oakland[5]	104	1,408	13.5	59	5
	Yancey Thigpen, Pittsburgh[2]	79	1,398	17.7	69	7
	Jimmy Smith, Jacksonville[2]	82	1,324	16.1	75	4
	Irving Fryar, Philadelphia[5]	86	1,316	15.3	72	6
	Herman Moore, Detroit[4]	104	1,293	12.4	79	8
	Antonio Freeman, Green Bay	81	1,243	15.3	58	12
	Michael Irvin, Dallas[6]	75	1,180	15.7	55	9
	Rod Smith, Denver	70	1,180	16.9	78	12
	Keenan McCardell, Jacksonville[2]	85	1,164	13.7	60	5
	Jake Reed, Minnesota[4]	68	1,138	16.7	56	6
	Shannon Sharpe, Denver[3]	72	1,107	15.4	68	3
	Andre Rison, Kansas City[5]	72	1,092	15.2	45	7
	Cris Carter, Minnesota[5]	89	1,069	12.0	43	13
	Johnnie Morton, Detroit	80	1,057	13.2	73	6
	Joey Galloway, Seattle[2]	72	1,049	14.6	53	12
	Frank Sanders, Arizona	75	1,017	13.6	70	4
	Robert Brooks, Green Bay[2]	60	1,010	16.8	48	7
	Derrick Alexander, Baltimore[2]	65	1,009	15.5	92	9
1996	Isaac Bruce, St. Louis[2]	84	1,338	15.9	70	7
	Jake Reed, Minnesota[3]	72	1,320	18.3	82	7
	Herman Moore, Detroit[3]	106	1,296	12.2	50	9
	Jerry Rice, San Francisco[11]	108	1,254	11.6	39	8
	Jimmy Smith, Jacksonville	83	1,244	15.0	62	7
	Michael Jackson, Baltimore	76	1,201	15.8	86	14
	Irving Fryar, Philadelphia[4]	88	1,195	13.6	42	11
	Carl Pickens, Cincinnati[3]	100	1,180	11.8	61	12
	Tony Martin, San Diego[2]	85	1,171	13.8	55	14
	Cris Carter, Minnesota[4]	96	1,163	12.1	43	10
	*Terry Glenn, New England	90	1,132	12.6	37	6
	Keenan McCardell, Jacksonville	85	1,129	13.3	52	3
	Tim Brown, Oakland[4]	90	1,104	12.3	42	9
	Derrick Alexander, Baltimore	62	1,099	17.7	64	9
	Shannon Sharpe, Denver[2]	80	1,062	13.3	51	10
	Curtis Conway, Chicago[2]	81	1,049	13.0	58	7
	Andre Reed, Buffalo[4]	66	1,036	15.7	67	6
	Brett Perriman, Detroit[2]	94	1,021	10.9	44	5
	Rob Moore, Arizona[2]	58	1,016	17.5	69	4
	Henry Ellard, Washington[7]	52	1,014	19.5	51	2
	Charles Johnson, Pittsburgh	60	1,008	16.8	70	3
1995	Jerry Rice, San Francisco[10]	122	1,848	15.1	81	15
	Isaac Bruce, St. Louis	119	1,781	15.0	72	13
	Herman Moore, Detroit[2]	123	1,686	13.7	69	14
	Michael Irvin, Dallas[5]	111	1,603	14.4	50	10
	Robert Brooks, Green Bay	102	1,497	14.7	99	13
	Brett Perriman, Detroit	108	1,488	13.8	91	9
	Cris Carter, Minnesota[3]	122	1,371	11.2	60	17
	Tim Brown, Oakland[3]	89	1,342	15.1	80	10
	Yancey Thigpen, Pittsburgh	85	1,307	15.4	43	5
	Jeff Graham, Chicago	82	1,301	15.9	51	4
	Carl Pickens, Cincinnati[2]	99	1,234	12.5	68	17
	Tony Martin, San Diego	90	1,224	13.6	51	6
	Eric Metcalf, Atlanta	104	1,189	11.4	62	8
	Jake Reed, Minnesota[2]	72	1,167	16.2	55	9
	Quinn Early, New Orleans	81	1,087	13.4	70	8
	Anthony Miller, Denver[5]	59	1,079	18.3	62	14
	Bert Emanuel, Atlanta	74	1,039	14.0	52	5
	*Joey Galloway, Seattle	67	1,039	15.5	59	7
	Terance Mathis, Atlanta[2]	78	1,039	13.3	54	9
	Curtis Conway, Chicago	62	1,037	16.7	76	12
	Henry Ellard, Washington[6]	56	1,005	17.9	59	5

OUTSTANDING PERFORMERS

	Mark Carrier, Carolina[2]	66	1,002	15.2	66	3
	Brian Blades, Seattle[4]	77	1,001	13.0	49	4
1994	Jerry Rice, San Francisco[9]	112	1,499	13.4	69	13
	Henry Ellard, Washington[5]	74	1,397	18.9	73	6
	Terance Mathis, Atlanta	111	1,342	12.1	81	11
	Tim Brown, L.A. Raiders[2]	89	1,309	14.7	77	9
	Andre Reed, Buffalo[2]	90	1,303	14.5	83	8
	Irving Fryar, Miami[3]	73	1,270	17.4	54	7
	Cris Carter, Minnesota[2]	122	1,256	10.3	65	7
	Michael Irvin, Dallas[4]	79	1,241	15.7	65	6
	Jake Reed, Minnesota	85	1,175	13.8	59	4
	Ben Coates, New England	96	1,174	12.2	62	7
	Herman Moore, Detroit	72	1,173	16.3	51	11
	Fred Barnett, Philadelphia[2]	78	1,127	14.4	54	5
	Carl Pickens, Cincinnati	71	1,127	15.9	70	11
	Sterling Sharpe, Green Bay[4]	94	1,119	11.9	49	18
	Anthony Miller, Denver[4]	60	1,107	18.5	76	5
	Andre Rison, Atlanta[3]	81	1,088	13.4	69	8
	Brian Blades, Seattle[3]	81	1,088	13.4	45	4
	Rob Moore, N.Y. Jets	78	1,010	12.9	41	6
	Shannon Sharpe, Denver	87	1,010	11.6	44	4
1993	Jerry Rice, San Francisco[8]	98	1,503	15.3	80	15
	Michael Irvin, Dallas[3]	88	1,330	15.1	61	7
	Sterling Sharpe, Green Bay[4]	112	1,274	11.4	54	11
	Andre Rison, Atlanta[3]	86	1,242	14.4	53	15
	Tim Brown, L.A. Raiders	80	1,180	14.8	71	7
	Anthony Miller, San Diego[3]	84	1,162	13.8	66	7
	Cris Carter, Minnesota	86	1,071	12.5	58	9
	Reggie Langhorne, Indianapolis	85	1,038	12.2	72	3
	Irving Fryar, Miami[2]	64	1,010	15.8	65	5
1992	Sterling Sharpe, Green Bay[3]	108	1,461	13.5	76	13
	Michael Irvin, Dallas[2]	78	1,396	17.9	87	7
	Jerry Rice, San Francisco[7]	84	1,201	14.3	80	10
	Andre Rison, Atlanta[2]	93	1,119	12.0	71	11
	Fred Barnett, Philadelphia	67	1,083	16.2	71	6
	Anthony Miller, San Diego[2]	72	1,060	14.7	67	7
	Eric Martin, New Orleans[3]	68	1,041	15.3	52	5
1991	Michael Irvin, Dallas	93	1,523	16.4	66	8
	Gary Clark, Washington[5]	70	1,340	19.1	82	10
	Jerry Rice, San Francisco[6]	80	1,206	15.1	73	14
	Haywood Jeffires, Houston[2]	100	1,181	11.8	44	7
	Michael Haynes, Atlanta	50	1,122	22.4	80	11
	Andre Reed, Buffalo[2]	81	1,113	13.7	55	10
	Drew Hill, Houston[5]	90	1,109	12.3	61	4
	Mark Duper, Miami[4]	70	1,085	15.5	43	5
	James Lofton, Buffalo[6]	57	1,072	18.8	77	8
	Mark Clayton, Miami[5]	70	1,053	15.0	43	12
	Henry Ellard, L.A. Rams[4]	64	1,052	16.4	38	3
	Art Monk, Washington[5]	71	1,049	14.8	64	8
	Irving Fryar, New England	68	1,014	14.9	56	3
	John Taylor, San Francisco[2]	64	1,011	15.8	97	9
	Brian Blades, Seattle[2]	70	1,003	14.3	52	2
1990	Jerry Rice, San Francisco[5]	100	1,502	15.0	64	13
	Henry Ellard, L.A. Rams[3]	76	1,294	17.0	50	4
	Andre Rison, Atlanta	82	1,208	14.7	75	10
	Gary Clark, Washington[4]	75	1,112	14.8	53	8
	Sterling Sharpe, Green Bay[2]	67	1,105	16.5	76	6
	Willie Anderson, L.A. Rams[2]	51	1,097	21.5	55	4
	Haywood Jeffires, Houston	74	1,048	14.2	87	8
	Stephone Paige, Kansas City	65	1,021	15.7	86	5
	Drew Hill, Houston[4]	74	1,019	13.8	57	5
	Anthony Carter, Minnesota[3]	70	1,008	14.4	56	8
1989	Jerry Rice, San Francisco[4]	82	1,483	18.1	68	17
	Sterling Sharpe, Green Bay	90	1,423	15.8	79	12
	Mark Carrier, Tampa Bay	86	1,422	16.5	78	9
	Henry Ellard, L.A. Rams[2]	70	1,382	19.7	53	8
	Andre Reed, Buffalo	88	1,312	14.9	78	9
	Anthony Miller, San Diego	75	1,252	16.7	69	10
	Webster Slaughter, Cleveland	65	1,236	19.0	97	6
	Gary Clark, Washington[3]	79	1,229	15.6	80	9
	Tim McGee, Cincinnati	65	1,211	18.6	74	8
	Art Monk, Washington[4]	86	1,186	13.8	60	8
	Willie Anderson, L.A. Rams	44	1,146	26.0	78	5
	Ricky Sanders, Washington[2]	80	1,138	14.2	68	4
	Vance Johnson, Denver	76	1,095	14.4	69	7
	Richard Johnson, Detroit	70	1,091	15.6	75	8
	Eric Martin, New Orleans[2]	68	1,090	16.0	53	8
	John Taylor, San Francisco	60	1,077	18.0	95	10
	Mervyn Fernandez, L.A. Raiders	57	1,069	18.8	75	9
	Anthony Carter, Minnesota[2]	65	1,066	16.4	50	4
	Brian Blades, Seattle	77	1,063	13.8	60	5
	Mark Clayton, Miami[4]	64	1,011	15.8	78	9
1988	Henry Ellard, L.A. Rams	86	1,414	16.4	68	10
	Jerry Rice, San Francisco[3]	64	1,306	20.4	96	9
	Eddie Brown, Cincinnati	53	1,273	24.0	86	9
	Anthony Carter, Minnesota	72	1,225	17.0	67	6
	Ricky Sanders, Washington	73	1,148	15.7	55	12
	Drew Hill, Houston[3]	72	1,141	15.8	57	10
	Mark Clayton, Miami[3]	86	1,129	13.1	45	14
	Roy Green, Phoenix[3]	68	1,097	16.1	52	7
	Eric Martin, New Orleans	85	1,083	12.7	40	7
	Al Toon, N.Y. Jets[2]	93	1,067	11.5	42	5
	Bruce Hill, Tampa Bay	58	1,040	17.9	42	9
	Lionel Manuel, N.Y. Giants	65	1,029	15.8	46	4
1987	J.T. Smith, St. Louis[2]	91	1,117	12.3	38	8
	Jerry Rice, San Francisco[2]	65	1,078	16.6	57	22
	Gary Clark, Washington[2]	56	1,066	19.0	84	7
	Carlos Carson, Kansas City[3]	55	1,044	19.0	81	7
1986	Jerry Rice, San Francisco	86	1,570	18.3	66	15
	Stanley Morgan, New England[3]	84	1,491	17.8	44	10
	Mark Duper, Miami[3]	67	1,313	19.6	85	11
	Gary Clark, Washington	74	1,265	17.1	55	7
	Al Toon, N.Y. Jets	85	1,176	13.8	62	8
	Todd Christensen, L.A. Raiders[3]	95	1,153	12.1	35	8
	Mark Clayton, Miami[2]	60	1,150	19.2	68	10
	*Bill Brooks, Indianapolis	65	1,131	17.4	84	8
	Drew Hill, Houston[2]	65	1,112	17.1	81	5
	Steve Largent, Seattle[8]	70	1,070	15.3	38	9
	Art Monk, Washington[3]	73	1,068	14.6	69	4
	*Ernest Givins, Houston	61	1,062	17.4	60	3
	Cris Collinsworth, Cincinnati[4]	62	1,024	16.5	46	10
	Wesley Walker, N.Y. Jets[2]	49	1,016	20.7	83	12
	J.T. Smith, St. Louis	80	1,014	12.7	45	6
	Mark Bavaro, N.Y. Giants	66	1,001	15.2	41	4
1985	Steve Largent, Seattle[7]	79	1,287	16.3	43	6
	Mike Quick, Philadelphia[3]	73	1,247	17.1	99	11
	Art Monk, Washington[2]	91	1,226	13.5	53	2
	Wes Chandler, San Diego[4]	67	1,199	17.9	75	10
	Drew Hill, Houston	64	1,169	18.3	57	9
	James Lofton, Green Bay[5]	69	1,153	16.7	56	4
	Louis Lipps, Pittsburgh	59	1,134	19.2	51	12
	Cris Collinsworth, Cincinnati[3]	65	1,125	17.3	71	5
	Tony Hill, Dallas[3]	74	1,113	15.0	53	7
	Lionel James, San Diego	86	1,027	11.9	67	6
	Roger Craig, San Francisco	92	1,016	11.0	73	6
1984	Roy Green, St. Louis[2]	78	1,555	19.9	83	12
	John Stallworth, Pittsburgh[3]	80	1,395	17.4	51	11
	Mark Clayton, Miami	73	1,389	19.0	65	18
	Art Monk, Washington	106	1,372	12.9	72	7
	James Lofton, Green Bay[4]	62	1,361	22.0	79	7
	Mark Duper, Miami[2]	71	1,306	18.4	80	8
	Steve Watson, Denver[3]	69	1,170	17.0	73	7
	Steve Largent, Seattle[6]	74	1,164	15.7	65	12
	Tim Smith, Houston[2]	69	1,141	16.5	75	4
	Stacey Bailey, Atlanta	67	1,138	17.0	61	6
	Carlos Carson, Kansas City[2]	57	1,078	18.9	57	4
	Mike Quick, Philadelphia[2]	61	1,052	17.2	90	9
	Todd Christensen, L.A. Raiders[2]	80	1,007	12.6	38	7
	Kevin House, Tampa Bay[2]	76	1,005	13.2	55	5
	Ozzie Newsome, Cleveland[2]	89	1,001	11.2	52	5
1983	Mike Quick, Philadelphia	69	1,409	20.4	83	13
	Carlos Carson, Kansas City	80	1,351	16.9	50	7
	James Lofton, Green Bay[3]	58	1,300	22.4	74	8
	Todd Christensen, L.A. Raiders	92	1,247	13.6	45	12
	Roy Green, St. Louis	78	1,227	15.7	71	14
	Charlie Brown, Washington	78	1,225	15.7	75	8
	Tim Smith, Houston	83	1,176	14.2	47	6
	Kellen Winslow, San Diego[3]	88	1,172	13.3	46	8
	Earnest Gray, N.Y. Giants	78	1,139	14.6	62	5
	Steve Watson, Denver[2]	59	1,133	19.2	78	5
	Cris Collinsworth, Cincinnati[2]	66	1,130	17.1	63	5
	Steve Largent, Seattle[5]	72	1,074	14.9	46	11
	Mark Duper, Miami	51	1,003	19.7	85	10
1982	Wes Chandler, San Diego[3]	49	1,032	21.1	66	9
1981	Alfred Jenkins, Atlanta[2]	70	1,358	19.4	67	13
	James Lofton, Green Bay[2]	71	1,294	18.2	75	8
	Steve Watson, Denver	60	1,244	20.7	95	13
	Frank Lewis, Buffalo[2]	70	1,244	17.8	33	4
	Steve Largent, Seattle[4]	75	1,224	16.3	57	9
	Charlie Joiner, San Diego[4]	70	1,188	17.0	57	7
	Kevin House, Tampa Bay	56	1,176	21.0	84	9
	Wes Chandler, N.O.-San Diego[2]	69	1,142	16.6	51	6
	Dwight Clark, San Francisco	85	1,105	13.0	78	4
	John Stallworth, Pittsburgh[2]	63	1,098	17.4	55	5
	Kellen Winslow, San Diego[2]	88	1,075	12.2	67	10
	Pat Tilley, St. Louis	66	1,040	15.8	75	3

Year	Player, Team	No.	Yards	Avg.	Long	TD
	Stanley Morgan, New England[2]	44	1,029	23.4	76	6
	Harold Carmichael, Philadelphia[3]	61	1,028	16.9	85	6
	Freddie Scott, Detroit	53	1,022	19.3	48	5
	*Cris Collinsworth, Cincinnati	67	1,009	15.1	74	8
	Joe Senser, Minnesota	79	1,004	12.7	53	8
	Ozzie Newsome, Cleveland	69	1,002	14.5	62	6
	Sammy White, Minnesota	66	1,001	15.2	53	3
1980	John Jefferson, San Diego[3]	82	1,340	16.3	58	13
	Kellen Winslow, San Diego	89	1,290	14.5	65	9
	James Lofton, Green Bay	71	1,226	17.3	47	4
	Charlie Joiner, San Diego[3]	71	1,132	15.9	51	4
	Ahmad Rashad, Minnesota[2]	69	1,095	15.9	76	5
	Steve Largent, Seattle[3]	66	1,064	16.1	67	6
	Tony Hill, Dallas[2]	60	1,055	17.6	58	8
	Alfred Jenkins, Atlanta	57	1,026	18.0	57	6
1979	Steve Largent, Seattle[2]	66	1,237	18.7	55	9
	John Stallworth, Pittsburgh	70	1,183	16.9	65	8
	Ahmad Rashad, Minnesota	80	1,156	14.5	52	9
	John Jefferson, San Diego[2]	61	1,090	17.9	65	10
	Frank Lewis, Buffalo	54	1,082	20.0	55	2
	Wes Chandler, New Orleans	65	1,069	16.4	85	6
	Tony Hill, Dallas	60	1,062	17.7	75	10
	Drew Pearson, Dallas[2]	55	1,026	18.7	56	8
	Wallace Francis, Atlanta	74	1,013	13.7	42	8
	Harold Jackson, New England[3]	45	1,013	22.5	59	7
	Charlie Joiner, San Diego[2]	72	1,008	14.0	39	4
	Stanley Morgan, New England	44	1,002	22.8	63	12
1978	Wesley Walker, N.Y. Jets	48	1,169	24.4	77	8
	Steve Largent, Seattle	71	1,168	16.5	57	8
	Harold Carmichael, Philadelphia[2]	55	1,072	19.5	56	8
	*John Jefferson, San Diego	56	1,001	17.9	46	13
1976	Roger Carr, Baltimore	43	1,112	25.9	79	11
	Cliff Branch, Oakland[2]	46	1,111	24.2	88	12
	Charlie Joiner, San Diego	50	1,056	21.1	81	7
1975	Ken Burrough, Houston	53	1,063	20.1	77	8
1974	Cliff Branch, Oakland	60	1,092	18.2	67	13
	Drew Pearson, Dallas	62	1,087	17.5	50	2
1973	Harold Carmichael, Philadelphia	67	1,116	16.7	73	9
1972	Harold Jackson, Philadelphia[2]	62	1,048	16.9	77	4
	John Gilliam, Minnesota	47	1,035	22.0	66	7
1971	Otis Taylor, Kansas City[2]	57	1,110	19.5	82	7
1970	Gene Washington, San Francisco	53	1,100	20.8	79	12
	Marlin Briscoe, Buffalo	57	1,036	18.2	48	8
	Dick Gordon, Chicago	71	1,026	14.5	69	13
	Gary Garrison, San Diego[2]	44	1,006	22.9	67	12
1969	Warren Wells, Oakland[2]	47	1,260	26.8	80	14
	Harold Jackson, Philadelphia	65	1,116	17.2	65	9
	Roy Jefferson, Pittsburgh[2]	67	1,079	16.1	63	9
	Dan Abramowicz, New Orleans	73	1,015	13.9	49	7
	Lance Alworth, San Diego[7]	64	1,003	15.7	76	4
1968	Lance Alworth, San Diego[6]	68	1,312	19.3	80	10
	Don Maynard, N.Y. Jets[5]	57	1,297	22.8	87	10
	George Sauer, N.Y. Jets[3]	66	1,141	17.3	43	3
	Warren Wells, Oakland	53	1,137	21.5	94	11
	Gary Garrison, San Diego	52	1,103	21.2	84	10
	Roy Jefferson, Pittsburgh	58	1,074	18.5	62	11
	Paul Warfield, Cleveland	50	1,067	21.3	65	12
	Homer Jones, N.Y. Giants[3]	45	1,057	23.5	84	7
	Fred Biletnikoff, Oakland	61	1,037	17.0	82	6
	Lance Rentzel, Dallas	54	1,009	18.7	65	6
1967	Don Maynard, N.Y. Jets[4]	71	1,434	20.2	75	10
	Ben Hawkins, Philadelphia	59	1,265	21.4	87	10
	Homer Jones, N.Y. Giants[2]	49	1,209	24.7	70	13
	Jackie Smith, St. Louis	56	1,205	21.5	76	9
	George Sauer, N.Y. Jets[2]	75	1,189	15.9	61	6
	Lance Alworth, San Diego[5]	52	1,010	19.4	71	9
1966	Lance Alworth, San Diego[4]	73	1,383	18.9	78	13
	Otis Taylor, Kansas City	58	1,297	22.4	89	8
	Pat Studstill, Detroit	67	1,266	18.9	99	5
	Bob Hayes, Dallas[2]	64	1,232	19.3	95	13
	Charlie Frazier, Houston	57	1,129	19.8	79	12
	Charley Taylor, Washington	72	1,119	15.5	86	12
	George Sauer, N.Y. Jets	63	1,081	17.2	77	5
	Homer Jones, N.Y. Giants	48	1,044	21.8	98	8
	Art Powell, Oakland[5]	53	1,026	19.4	46	11
1965	Lance Alworth, San Diego[3]	69	1,602	23.2	85	14
	Dave Parks, San Francisco	80	1,344	16.8	53	12
	Don Maynard, N.Y. Jets[3]	68	1,218	17.9	56	14
	Pete Retzlaff, Philadelphia	66	1,190	18.0	78	10
	Lionel Taylor, Denver[4]	85	1,131	13.3	63	6
	Tommy McDonald, Los Angeles[3]	67	1,036	15.5	51	9
	*Bob Hayes, Dallas	46	1,003	21.8	82	12
1964	Charley Hennigan, Houston[3]	101	1,546	15.3	53	8
	Art Powell, Oakland[4]	76	1,361	17.9	77	11
	Lance Alworth, San Diego[2]	61	1,235	20.2	82	13
	Johnny Morris, Chicago	93	1,200	12.9	63	10
	Elbert Dubenion, Buffalo	42	1,139	27.1	72	10
	Terry Barr, Detroit[2]	57	1,030	18.1	58	9
1963	Bobby Mitchell, Washington[2]	69	1,436	20.8	99	7
	Art Powell, Oakland[3]	73	1,304	17.9	85	16
	Buddy Dial, Pittsburgh[2]	60	1,295	21.6	83	9
	Lance Alworth, San Diego	61	1,205	19.8	85	11
	Del Shofner, N.Y. Giants[4]	64	1,181	18.5	70	9
	Lionel Taylor, Denver[3]	78	1,101	14.1	72	10
	Terry Barr, Detroit	66	1,086	16.5	75	13
	Charley Hennigan, Houston[2]	61	1,051	17.2	83	10
	Sonny Randle, St. Louis[2]	51	1,014	19.9	68	12
	Bake Turner, N.Y. Jets	71	1,009	14.2	53	6
1962	Bobby Mitchell, Washington	72	1,384	19.2	81	11
	Sonny Randle, St. Louis	63	1,158	18.4	86	7
	Tommy McDonald, Philadelphia[2]	58	1,146	19.8	60	10
	Del Shofner, N.Y. Giants[3]	53	1,133	21.4	69	12
	Art Powell, N.Y. Titans[2]	64	1,130	17.7	80	8
	Frank Clarke, Dall. Cowboys	47	1,043	22.2	66	14
	Don Maynard, N.Y. Titans[2]	56	1,041	18.6	86	8
1961	Charley Hennigan, Houston	82	1,746	21.3	80	12
	Lionel Taylor, Denver[2]	100	1,176	11.8	52	4
	Bill Groman, Houston[2]	50	1,175	23.5	80	17
	Tommy McDonald, Philadelphia	64	1,144	17.9	66	13
	Del Shofner, N.Y. Giants[2]	68	1,125	16.5	46	11
	Jim Phillips, Los Angeles	78	1,092	14.0	69	5
	*Mike Ditka, Chicago	56	1,076	19.2	76	12
	Dave Kocourek, San Diego	55	1,055	19.2	76	4
	Buddy Dial, Pittsburgh	53	1,047	19.8	88	12
	R.C. Owens, San Francisco	55	1,032	18.8	54	5
1960	*Bill Groman, Houston	72	1,473	20.5	92	12
	Raymond Berry, Baltimore	74	1,298	17.5	70	10
	Don Maynard, N.Y. Titans	72	1,265	17.6	65	6
	Lionel Taylor, Denver	92	1,235	13.4	80	12
	Art Powell, N.Y. Titans	69	1,167	16.9	76	14
1958	Del Shofner, Los Angeles	51	1,097	21.5	92	8
1956	Bill Howton, Green Bay[2]	55	1,188	21.6	66	12
	Harlon Hill, Chi. Bears[2]	47	1,128	24.0	79	11
1954	Bob Boyd, Los Angeles	53	1,212	22.9	80	6
	*Harlon Hill, Chi. Bears	45	1,124	25.0	76	12
1953	Pete Pihos, Philadelphia	63	1,049	16.7	59	10
1952	*Bill Howton, Green Bay	53	1,231	23.2	90	13
1951	Elroy (Crazylegs) Hirsch, Los Angeles	66	1,495	22.7	91	17
1950	Tom Fears, Los Angeles[2]	84	1,116	13.3	53	7
	Cloyce Box, Detroit	50	1,009	20.2	82	11
1949	Bob Mann, Detroit	66	1,014	15.4	64	4
	Tom Fears, Los Angeles	77	1,013	13.2	51	9
1945	Jim Benton, Cleveland	45	1,067	23.7	84	8
1942	Don Hutson, Green Bay	74	1,211	16.4	73	17

First season of professional football.

250 YARDS PASS RECEIVING IN A GAME

Date	Player, Team, Opponent	No.	Yards	TD
Dec. 18, 1995	Jerry Rice, San Francisco vs. Minnesota	14	289	3
Dec. 11, 1989	John Taylor, San Francisco vs. L.A. Rams	11	286	2
Nov. 26, 1989	Willie Anderson, L.A. Rams vs. New Orleans (OT)	15	336	1
Oct. 18, 1987	Steve Largent, Seattle vs. Detroit	15	261	3
Oct. 4, 1987	Anthony Allen, Washington vs. St. Louis	7	255	3
Dec. 22, 1985	Stephone Paige, Kansas City vs. San Diego	8	309	2
Dec. 20, 1982	Wes Chandler, San Diego vs. Cincinnati	10	260	2
Sept. 23, 1979	*Jerry Butler, Buffalo vs. N.Y. Jets	10	255	4
Nov. 4, 1962	Sonny Randle, St. Louis vs. N.Y. Giants	16	256	1
Oct. 28, 1962	Del Shofner, N.Y. Giants vs. Washington	11	269	1
Oct. 13, 1961	Charley Hennigan, Houston vs. Boston	13	272	1
Oct. 21, 1956	Billy Howton, Green Bay vs. Los Angeles	7	257	2
Dec. 3, 1950	Cloyce Box, Detroit vs. Baltimore	12	302	4
Nov. 22, 1945	Jim Benton, Cleveland vs. Detroit	10	303	1

First season of professional football.

2,000 COMBINED NET YARDS GAINED IN A SEASON

Year	Player, Team	Rushing Att.-Yds.	Pass Rec.	Punt Ret.	Kickoff Ret.	Fum. Runs	Total Yds.
1997	Barry Sanders, Detroit	335-2,053	33-305	0-0	0-0	1-0	369-2,358
	Kevin Williams, Arizona	1-(-2)	20-273	40-462	59-1,458	1-0	121-2,191
	Brian Mitchell, Wash.	23-107	36-438	38-442	47-1,094	0-0	144-2,081
	Terrell Davis, Denver	369-1,750	42-287	0-0	0-0	2-(-7)	413-2,030
	Jermaine Lewis, Balt.	3-35	42-648	28-437	41-905	2-0	116-2,025
1995	Brian Mitchell, Wash.	46-301	38-324	25-315	55-1,408	0-0	164-2,348
	Emmitt Smith, Dallas	377-1,773	62-375	0-0	0-0	0-0	439-2,148
	Glyn Milburn, Denver	49-266	22-191	31-354	47-1,269	0-0	149-2,080
	Ernie Mills, Pittsburgh	5-39	39-679	0-0	54-1,306	0-0	98-2,024

1994	Brian Mitchell, Wash.	78-311	26-236	32-452	58-1,478	0-0	194-2,477
	Barry Sanders, Detroit	331-1,883	44-283	0-0	0-0	0-0	375-2,166
1992	Thurman Thomas, Buffalo	312-1,487	58-626	0-0	0-0	1-0	371-2,113
	Emmitt Smith, Dallas	373-1,713	59-335	0-0	0-0	1-0	433-2,048
	Barry Foster, Pittsburgh	390-1,690	36-344	0-0	0-0	2-(–20)	428-2,014
1991	Thurman Thomas, Buffalo	288-1,407	62-631	0-0	0-0	0-0	350-2,038
1990	Herschel Walker, Minnesota	184-770	35-315	0-0	44-966	4-0	267-2,051
1988	*Tim Brown, L.A. Raiders	14-50	43-725	49-444	41-1,098	7-0	154-2,317
	Roger Craig, San Fran.	310-1,502	76-534	0-0	2-32	2-0	390-2,068
	Eric Dickerson, Indianapolis	388-1,659	36-377	0-0	0-0	1-0	425-2,036
	Herschel Walker, Dallas	361-1,514	53-505	0-0	0-0	3-0	417-2,019
1986	Eric Dickerson, L.A. Rams	404-1,821	26-205	0-0	0-0	2-0	432-2,026
	Gary Anderson, San Diego	127-442	80-871	25-227	24-482	2-0	258-2,022
1985	Lionel James, San Diego	105-516	86-1,027	25-213	36-779	1-0	253-2,535
	Marcus Allen, L.A. Raiders	380-1,759	67-555	0-0	0-0	2-(–6)	449-2,308
	Roger Craig, San Fran.	214-1,050	92-1,016	0-0	0-0	0-0	306-2,066
	Walter Payton, Chicago	324-1,551	49-483	0-0	0-0	1-0	374-2,034
1984	Eric Dickerson, L.A. Rams	379-2,105	21-139	0-0	0-0	4-15	404-2,259
	James Wilder, Tampa Bay	407-1,544	85-685	0-0	0-0	4-0	496-2,229
	Walter Payton, Chicago	381-1,684	45-368	0-0	0-0	1-0	427-2,052
1983	*Eric Dickerson, L.A. Rams	390-1,808	51-404	0-0	0-0	1-0	442-2,212
	William Andrews, Atlanta	331-1,567	59-609	0-0	0-0	2-0	392-2,176
	Walter Payton, Chicago	314-1,421	53-607	0-0	0-0	2-0	369-2,028
1981	*James Brooks, San Diego	109-525	46-329	22-290	40-949	2-0	219-2,093
	William Andrews, Atlanta	289-1,301	81-735	0-0	0-0	0-0	370-2,036
1980	Bruce Harper, N.Y. Jets	45-126	50-634	28-242	49-1,070	3-0	175-2,072
1979	Wilbert Montgomery, Phil.	338-1,512	41-494	0-0	1-6	2-0	382-2,012
1978	Bruce Harper, N.Y. Jets	58-303	13-196	30-378	55-1,280	1-0	157-2,157
1977	Walter Payton, Chicago	339-1,852	27-269	0-0	2-95	5-0	373-2,216
	Terry Metcalf, St. Louis	149-739	34-403	14-108	32-772	1-0	230-2,022
1975	Terry Metcalf, St. Louis	165-816	43-378	23-285	35-960	2-23	268-2,462
	O.J. Simpson, Buffalo	329-1,817	28-426	0-0	0-0	1-0	358-2,243
1974	Mack Herron, New England	231-824	38-474	35-517	28-629	3-0	335-2,444
	Otis Armstrong, Denver	263-1,407	38-405	0-0	16-386	1-0	318-2,198
	Terry Metcalf, St. Louis	152-718	50-377	26-340	20-623	7-0	255-2,058
1973	O.J. Simpson, Buffalo	332-2,003	6-70	0-0	0-0	0-0	338-2,073
1966	Gale Sayers, Chicago	229-1,231	34-447	6-44	23-718	3-0	295-2,440
	Leroy Kelly, Cleveland	209-1,141	32-366	13-104	19-403	0-0	273-2,014
1965	*Gale Sayers, Chicago	166-867	29-507	16-238	21-660	4-0	236-2,272
1963	Timmy Brown, Philadelphia	192-841	36-487	16-152	33-945	2-3	279-2,428
	Jim Brown, Cleveland	291-1,863	24-268	0-0	0-0	0-0	315-2,131
1962	Timmy Brown, Philadelphia	137-545	52-849	6-81	30-831	4-0	229-2,306
	Dick Christy, N.Y. Titans	114-535	62-538	15-250	38-824	2-0	231-2,147
1961	Billy Cannon, Houston	200-948	43-586	9-70	18-439	2-0	272-2,043
1960	*Abner Haynes, Dall. Texans	156-875	55-576	14-215	19-434	4-0	248-2,100

**First season of professional football.*

300 COMBINED NET YARDS GAINED IN A GAME

Date	Player, Team, Opponent	No.	Yards	TD
Dec. 7, 1997	Jermaine Lewis, Baltimore vs. Seattle	10	308	3
Dec. 25, 1995	Kevin Williams, Dallas vs. Arizona	16	307	2
Dec. 10, 1995	Glyn Milburn, Denver vs. Seattle	33	404	0
Oct. 23, 1994	Tyrone Hughes, New Orleans vs. L.A. Rams	11	347	2
Dec. 11, 1989	John Taylor, San Francisco vs. L.A. Rams	14	321	2
Nov. 26, 1989	Willie Anderson, L.A. Rams vs. New Orleans (OT)	15	336	1
Nov. 28, 1988	*Tim Brown, L.A. Raiders vs. Seattle	12	308	1
Dec. 22, 1985	Stephone Paige, Kansas City vs. San Diego	8	309	2
Nov. 10, 1985	Lionel James, San Diego vs. L.A. Raiders (OT)	23	345	0
Sept. 22, 1985	Lionel James, San Diego vs. Cincinnati	20	316	2
Dec. 21, 1975	*Walter Payton, Chicago vs. New Orleans	32	300	1
Nov. 23, 1975	Greg Pruitt, Cleveland vs. Cincinnati	28	304	2
Nov. 1, 1970	Eugene (Mercury) Morris, Miami vs. Baltimore	17	302	0
Oct. 4, 1970	O.J. Simpson, Buffalo vs. N.Y. Jets	26	303	2
Dec. 6, 1969	Jerry LeVias, Houston vs. N.Y. Jets	18	329	1
Nov. 2, 1969	Travis Williams, Green Bay vs. Pittsburgh	11	314	3
Dec. 18, 1966	Gale Sayers, Chicago vs. Minnesota	20	339	2
Dec. 12, 1965	*Gale Sayers, Chicago vs. San Francisco	17	336	6
Nov. 17, 1963	Gary Ballman, Pittsburgh vs. Washington	12	320	2
Dec. 16, 1962	Timmy Brown, Philadelphia vs. St. Louis	19	341	2
Dec. 10, 1961	Billy Cannon, Houston vs. N.Y. Titans	32	373	5
Nov. 19, 1961	Jim Brown, Cleveland vs. Philadelphia	38	313	4
Dec. 3, 1950	Cloyce Box, Detroit vs. Baltimore	13	302	4
Oct. 29, 1950	Wally Triplett, Detroit vs. Los Angeles	11	331	1
Nov. 22, 1945	Jim Benton, Cleveland vs. Detroit	10	303	1

**First season of professional football.*

TOP 20 SCORERS

Player	Years	TD	FG	PAT	TP
George Blanda	26	9	335	943	2,002
Nick Lowery	18	0	383	562	1,711
Jan Stenerud	19	0	373	580	1,699
Gary Anderson	16	0	385	526	1,681
Morten Andersen	16	0	378	507	1,641
Norm Johnson	16	0	322	592	1,558
Eddie Murray	19	0	337	521	1,532
Pat Leahy	18	0	304	558	1,470
Jim Turner	16	1	304	521	1,439
Matt Bahr	17	0	300	522	1,422
Mark Moseley	16	0	300	482	1,382
Jim Bakken	17	0	282	534	1,380
Fred Cox	15	0	282	519	1,365
Lou Groza	17	1	234	641	1,349
Jim Breech	14	0	243	517	1,246
Al Del Greco	14	0	263	435	1,224
Chris Bahr	14	0	241	490	1,213
Kevin Butler	13	0	265	413	1,208
Gino Cappelletti	11	42	176	342	1,130
Ray Wersching	15	0	222	456	1,122

Cappelletti's total includes 4 two-point conversions.

TOP 20 TOUCHDOWN SCORERS

Player	Years	Rush	Rec.	Total Returns	TD
Jerry Rice	13	10	155	1	166
Marcus Allen	16	123	21	1	145
Jim Brown	9	106	20	0	126
Walter Payton	13	110	15	0	125
Emmitt Smith	8	112	7	0	119
John Riggins	14	104	12	0	116
Lenny Moore	12	63	48	2	113
Don Hutson	11	3	99	3	105
Barry Sanders	9	95	10	0	105
Steve Largent	14	1	100	0	101
Franco Harris	13	91	9	0	100
Eric Dickerson	11	90	6	0	96
Jim Taylor	10	83	10	0	93
Tony Dorsett	12	77	13	1	91
Bobby Mitchell	11	18	65	8	91
Cris Carter	11	0	89	1	90
Leroy Kelly	10	74	13	3	90
Charley Taylor	13	11	79	0	90
Don Maynard	15	0	88	0	88
Lance Alworth	1	2	85	0	87

TOP 20 RUSHERS

Player	Years	Att.	Yards	Avg.	Long	TD
Walter Payton	13	3,838	16,726	4.4	76	110
Barry Sanders	9	2,719	13,778	5.1	85	95
Eric Dickerson	11	2,996	13,259	4.4	85	90
Tony Dorsett	12	2,936	12,739	4.3	99	77
Jim Brown	9	2,359	12,312	5.2	80	106
Marcus Allen	16	3,022	12,243	4.1	61	123
Franco Harris	13	2,949	12,120	4.1	75	91
Thurman Thomas	10	2,720	11,405	4.2	80	63
John Riggins	14	2,916	11,352	3.9	66	104
O.J. Simpson	11	2,404	11,236	4.7	94	61
Emmitt Smith	8	2,595	11,234	4.3	75	112
Ottis Anderson	14	2,562	10,273	4.0	76	81
Earl Campbell	8	2,187	9,407	4.3	81	74
Jim Taylor	10	1,941	8,597	4.4	84	83
Joe Perry	14	1,737	8,378	4.8	78	53
Earnest Byner	14	2,095	8,261	3.9	54	56
Herschel Walker	12	1,954	8,225	4.2	91	61
Roger Craig	11	1,991	8,189	4.1	71	56
Gerald Riggs	10	1,989	8,188	4.1	58	69
Larry Csonka	11	1,891	8,081	4.3	54	64
Freeman McNeil	12	1,798	8,074	4.5	69	38

TOP 20 COMBINED YARDS GAINED

	Years	Tot.	Rush.	Rec.	Int. Ret.	Punt Ret.	Kickoff Ret.	Fumble Ret.
Walter Payton	13	21,803	16,726	4,538	0	0	539	0
Herschel Walker	12	18,168	8,225	4,859	0	0	5,084	0
Marcus Allen	16	17,648	12,243	5,411	0	0	0	-6
Jerry Rice	13	17,075	614	16,455	0	0	6	0
Barry Sanders	9	16,528	13,778	2,632	0	0	118	0
Tony Dorsett	12	16,326	12,739	3,554	0	0	0	33
Henry Ellard	15	15,603	50	13,662	0	1,527	364	0
Thruman Thomas	10	15,489	11,405	4,084	0	0	0	0
Jim Brown	9	15,459	12,312	2,499	0	0	648	0
Eric Dickerson	11	15,411	13,259	2,137	0	0	0	15
James Brooks	12	14,910	7,962	3,621	0	565	2,762	0
Franco Harris	13	14,622	12,120	2,287	0	0	233	–18
Eric Metcalf	9	14,443	2,365	5,096	0	2,509	4,473	0
O.J. Simpson	11	14,368	11,236	2,142	0	0	990	0
James Lofton	16	14,277	246	14,004	0	0	0	27

Irving Fryar 14	14,174	180	11,427	0	2,055	505	7
Bobby Mitchell 11	14,078	2,735	7,954	0	699	2,690	0
David Meggett.........9	13,901	1,660	3,023	0	3,668	5,550	0
Emmitt Smith...........8	13,668	11,234	2,434	0	0	0	0
Earnest Byner........14	13,497	8,261	4,605	0	0	576	55

TOP 20 PASSERS

Player	Years	Att.	Comp.	Pct. Comp.	Yards	Avg. Gain	TD	Pct. TD	Int.	Pct. Int.	Rating
Steve Young	13	3,548	2,300	64.8	28,508	8.03	193	5.4	91	2.6	97.0
Joe Montana	15	5,391	3,409	63.2	40,551	7.52	273	5.1	139	2.6	92.3
Brett Favre	7	3,206	1,971	61.5	22,591	7.05	182	5.7	95	3.0	89.3
Dan Marino	15	7,452	4,453	59.8	55,416	7.44	385	5.2	220	3.0	87.8
Jim Kelly	11	4,779	2,874	60.1	35,467	7.42	237	5.0	175	3.7	84.4
R. Staubach	11	2,958	1,685	57.0	22,700	7.67	153	5.2	109	3.7	83.4
Neil Lomax	8	3,153	1,817	57.6	22,771	7.22	136	4.3	90	2.9	82.7
S. Jurgensen	18	4,262	2,433	57.1	32,224	7.56	255	6.0	189	4.4	82.6
Len Dawson	19	3,741	2,136	57.1	28,711	7.67	239	6.4	183	4.9	82.6
Troy Aikman	9	3,696	2,292	62.0	26,016	7.04	129	3.5	110	3.0	82.3
Ken Anderson	16	4,475	2,654	59.3	32,838	7.34	197	4.4	160	3.6	81.9
Bernie Kosar	12	3,365	1,994	59.3	23,301	6.92	124	3.7	87	2.6	81.8
Danny White	13	2,950	1,761	59.7	21,959	7.44	155	5.3	132	4.5	81.7
Dave Krieg	18	5,290	3,093	58.5	37,948	7.17	261	4.9	199	3.8	81.5
Warren Moon	14	6,528	3,827	58.6	47,465	7.27	279	4.3	224	3.4	81.2
Boomer Esiason	14	5,205	2,969	57.0	37,920	7.29	247	4.7	184	3.5	81.1
Jeff Hostetler	14	2,338	1,357	58.0	16,430	7.03	94	4.0	71	3.0	80.5
Neil O'Donnell	8	2,519	1,438	57.1	16,810	6.67	89	3.5	53	2.1	80.5
Bart Starr	16	3,149	1,808	57.4	24,718	7.85	152	4.8	138	4.4	80.5
Ken O'Brien	10	3,602	2,110	58.6	25,094	6.97	128	3.6	98	2.7	80.4

1,500 or more attempts. The passing ratings are based on performance standards established for completion percentage, interception percentage, touchdown percentage, and average gain. Please consult page 16 for more information.

TOP 20 LEADERS IN PASSES COMPLETED

Dan Marino 4,453
John Elway 3,913
Warren Moon 3,827
Fran Tarkenton 3,686
Joe Montana 3,409
Dan Fouts 3,297
Dave Krieg 3,093
Boomer Esiason 2,969
Jim Kelly 2,874
Steve DeBerg 2,844
Jim Everett 2,841
Johnny Unitas 2,830
Ken Anderson 2,654
Jim Hart 2,593
Phil Simms 2,576
John Brodie 2,469
Sonny Jurgensen 2,433
Joe Ferguson 2,369
Roman Gabriel 2,366
John Hadl 2,363

TOP 20 LEADERS IN PASSING YARDS

Dan Marino 55,416
John Elway 48,669
Warren Moon 47,465
Fran Tarkenton 47,003
Dan Fouts 43,040
Joe Montana 40,551
Johnny Unitas 40,239
Dave Krieg 37,948
Boomer Esiason 37,920
Jim Kelly 35,467
Jim Everett 34,837
Jim Hart 34,665
Steve DeBerg 33,872
John Hadl 33,503
Phil Simms 33,462
Ken Anderson 32,838
Sonny Jurgensen 32,224
John Brodie 31,548
Norm Snead 30,797
Joe Ferguson 29,817

TOP 20 LEADERS IN TOUCHDOWN PASSES

Dan Marino 385
Fran Tarkenton 342
Johnny Unitas 290
Warren Moon 279
John Elway 278
Joe Montana 273
Dave Krieg 261
Sonny Jurgensen 255
Dan Fouts 254
Boomer Esiason 247
John Hadl 244
Len Dawson 239
Jim Kelly 237
George Blanda 236
John Brodie 214
Terry Bradshaw 212
Y.A. Tittle 212
Jim Hart 209
Jim Everett 203
Roman Gabriel 201

TOP 20 PASS RECEIVERS

Player	Years	No.	Yards	Avg.	Long	TD
Jerry Rice	13	1,057	16,455	15.6	96	155
Art Monk	16	940	12,721	13.5	79	68
Andre Reed	13	826	11,764	14.2	83	80
Steve Largent	14	819	13,089	16.0	74	100
Henry Ellard	15	807	13,662	16.9	81	65
James Lofton	16	764	14,004	18.3	80	75
Cris Carter	11	756	9,436	12.5	80	89
Charlie Joiner	18	750	12,146	16.2	87	65
Irving Fryar	14	736	11,427	15.5	80	75
Gary Clark	11	699	10,856	15.5	84	65
Michael Irvin	10	666	10,680	16.0	87	61
Ozzie Newsome	13	662	7,980	12.1	74	47
Charley Taylor	13	649	9,110	14.0	88	79
Andre Rison	9	641	8,839	13.8	75	73
Drew Hill	14	634	9,831	15.5	81	60
Don Maynard	15	633	11,834	18.7	87	88
Raymond Berry	13	631	9,275	14.7	70	68
Tim Brown	10	599	8,588	14.3	80	60
Anthony Miller	10	595	9,148	15.4	76	63
Sterling Sharpe	7	595	8,134	13.7	79	65

TOP 20 LEADERS IN RECEPTION YARDS

Jerry Rice 16,455
James Lofton 14,004
Henry Ellard 13,662
Steve Largent 13,089
Art Monk 12,721
Charlie Joiner 12,146
Don Maynard 11,834
Andre Reed 11,764
Irving Fryar 11,427
Gary Clark 10,856
Stanley Morgan 10,716
Michael Irvin 10,680
Harold Jackson 10,372
Lance Alworth 10,266
Drew Hill 9,831
Cris Carter 9,436
Raymond Berry 9,275
Anthony Miller 9,148
Charley Taylor 9,110
Harold Carmichael 8,985

TOP 20 INTERCEPTORS

Player	Years	No.	Yards	Avg.	Long	TD
Paul Krause	16	81	1,185	14.6	81	3
Emlen Tunnell	14	79	1,282	16.2	55	4
Dick (Night Train) Lane	14	68	1,207	17.8	80	5
Ken Riley	15	65	596	9.2	66	5
Ronnie Lott	14	63	730	11.6	83	5
Dick LeBeau	13	62	762	12.3	70	3
Dave Brown	15	62	698	11.3	90	5
Emmitt Thomas	13	58	937	16.2	73	5
Bobby Boyd	9	57	994	17.4	74	4
Johnny Robinson	12	57	741	13.0	57	1
Mel Blount	14	57	736	12.9	52	2
Everson Walls	13	57	504	8.8	40	1
Lem Barney	11	56	1,077	19.2	71	7
Pat Fischer	17	56	941	16.8	69	4
Willie Brown	16	54	472	8.7	45	2
Bobby Dillon	8	52	976	18.8	61	5
Jack Butler	9	52	826	15.9	52	4
Larry Wilson	13	52	800	15.4	96	5
Jim Patton	12	52	712	13.7	51	2
Mel Renfro	14	52	626	12.0	90	3

OUTSTANDING PERFORMERS

TOP 20 PUNTERS

Player	Years	No.	Yards	Avg.	Long	Blk.
Sammy Baugh	16	338	15,245	45.1	85	9
Tommy Davis	11	511	22,833	44.7	82	2
Yale Lary	11	503	22,279	44.3	74	4
Bob Scarpitto	8	283	12,408	43.8	87	4
Horace Gillom	7	385	16,872	43.8	80	5
Jerry Norton	11	358	15,671	43.8	78	2
David Lewis	4	285	12,447	43.7	63	0
Sean Landeta	13	861	37,569	43.6	74	5
Greg Montgomery	9	524	22,831	43.6	77	8
Don Chandler	12	660	28,678	43.5	90	4
Reggie Roby	15	932	40,440	43.4	77	5
Rick Tuten	9	614	26,629	43.4	73	2
Rohn Stark	16	1,141	49,471	43.4	72	7
Tom Tupa	9	292	12,630	43.3	73	1
Tom Rouen	5	320	13,779	43.1	62	2
Jerrel Wilson	16	1,072	46,139	43.0	72	12
Norm Van Brocklin	12	523	22,413	42.9	72	3
Tommy Barnhardt	11	648	27,707	42.8	65	3
Craig Hentrich	4	289	12,355	42.8	70	2
Danny Villanueva	8	488	20,862	42.8	68	2

250 or more punts.

TOP 20 PUNT RETURNERS

Player	Years	No.	Yards	Avg.	Long	TD
Darrien Gordon	5	143	1,950	13.6	94	6
George McAfee	8	112	1,431	12.8	74	2
Jack Christiansen	8	85	1,084	12.8	89	8
Claude Gibson	5	110	1,381	12.6	85	3
Bill Dudley	9	124	1,515	12.2	96	3
Rick Upchurch	9	248	3,008	12.1	92	8
Desmond Howard	6	119	1,440	12.1	92	4
Billy Johnson	14	282	3,317	11.8	87	6
Mack Herron	3	84	982	11.7	66	0
Billy Thompson	13	157	1,814	11.6	60	0
Brian Mitchell	8	233	2,638	11.3	84	7
Henry Ellard	15	135	1,527	11.3	83	4
Rodger Bird	3	94	1,063	11.3	78	0
Bosh Pritchard	6	95	1,072	11.3	81	2
Terry Metcalf	6	84	936	11.1	69	1
Bob Hayes	11	104	1,158	11.1	90	3
Floyd Little	9	81	893	11.0	72	2
Louis Lipps	9	112	1,234	11.0	76	3
Bobby Joe Edmonds	5	134	1,471	11.0	75	1
Mel Gray	12	252	2,753	10.9	80	3

75 or more returns.

TOP 20 KICKOFF RETURNERS

Player	Years	No.	Yards	Avg.	Long	TD
Gale Sayers	7	91	2,781	30.6	103	6
Lynn Chandnois	7	92	2,720	29.6	93	3
Abe Woodson	9	193	5,538	28.7	105	5
Claude (Buddy) Young	6	90	2,514	27.9	104	2
Travis Williams	5	102	2,801	27.5	105	6
Joe Arenas	7	139	3,798	27.3	96	1
Clarence Davis	8	79	2,140	27.1	76	0
Steve Van Buren	8	76	2,030	26.7	98	3
Lenny Lyles	12	81	2,161	26.7	103	3
Eugene (Mercury) Morris	8	111	2,947	26.5	105	3
Bobby Jancik	6	158	4,185	26.5	61	0
Mel Renfro	14	85	2,246	26.4	100	2
Bobby Mitchell	11	102	2,690	26.4	98	5
Ollie Matson	14	143	3,746	26.2	105	6
Alvin Haymond	10	170	4,438	26.1	98	2
Noland Smith	3	82	2,137	26.1	106	1
Al Nelson	9	101	2,625	26.0	78	0
Tim Brown	11	184	4,781	26.0	105	5
Vic Washington	6	129	3,341	25.9	98	1
Dave Hampton	8	113	2,923	25.9	101	3

75 or more returns.

TOP 20 LEADERS IN SACKS

Player	*Years	No.
Reggie White	13	176.5
Bruce Smith	13	154.0
Richard Dent	15	137.5
Kevin Greene	13	133.0
Lawrence Taylor	12	132.5
Rickey Jackson	14	128.0
Chris Doleman	13	127.5
Leslie O'Neal	11	122.5
Sean Jones	13	113.0
Greg Townsend	13	109.5
Clyde Simmons	12	109.0
Derrick Thomas	9	107.5
Pat Swilling	11	105.5
Jim Jeffcoat	15	102.5
Andre Tippett	11	100.0
Simon Fletcher	11	97.5
William Fuller	12	97.5
Jacob Green	11	97.5
Charles Haley	11	97.5
Dexter Manley	10	97.5

**Since NFL began compiling statistics in 1982.*

POSTSEASON LEADERS

TOP 10 RUSHERS

Player	Att.	Yards	Avg.	Long	TD
Franco Harris	400	1,556	3.9	50	16
Emmitt Smith	318	1,413	4.4	38	18
Thurman Thomas	327	1,399	4.3	40	15
Tony Dorsett	302	1,383	4.6	53	9
Marcus Allen	267	1,347	5.0	74	11
John Riggins	251	996	4.0	43	12
Larry Csonka	225	891	4.0	49	9
Chuck Foreman	229	860	3.8	62	7
Roger Craig	208	841	4.0	80	7
Earnest Byner	186	839	4.5	66	5

TOP 10 POSTSEASON PASSERS

Player	Att.	Comp.	Pct. Comp.	Yards	Avg. Gain	TD	Pct. TD	Int.	Pct. Int.	Rating
Bart Starr	213	130	61.0	1,753	8.23	15	7.0	3	1.4	104.8
Troy Aikman	415	276	66.5	3,372	8.13	22	5.3	13	3.1	96.0
Joe Montana	734	460	62.7	5,772	7.86	45	6.1	21	2.9	95.6
Ken Anderson	166	110	66.3	1,321	7.96	9	5.4	6	3.6	93.5
Brett Favre	414	250	60.4	3,098	7.48	23	5.6	10	2.4	92.0
Joe Theismann	211	128	60.7	1,782	8.45	11	5.2	7	3.3	91.4
Steve Young	402	251	62.4	2,855	7.10	16	4.0	8	2.0	88.7
Warren Moon	403	259	64.3	2,870	7.12	17	4.2	14	3.5	84.9
Ken Stabler	351	203	57.8	2,641	7.52	19	5.4	13	3.7	84.2
Bernie Kosar	270	152	56.3	1,953	7.23	16	5.9	10	3.7	83.5

150 or more attempts. The passing ratings are based on performance standards established for completion percentage, interception percentage, touchdown percentage, and average gain. Please consult page 16 for more information.

TOP 10 POSTSEASON PASS RECEIVERS

Player	No.	Yards	Avg.	Long	TD
Jerry Rice	120	1,742	14.5	72	18
Michael Irvin	83	1,283	15.5	53	8
Andre Reed	80	1,169	14.6	72	9
Thurman Thomas	75	669	8.9	27	5
Cliff Branch	73	1,289	17.7	72	5
Fred Biletnikoff	70	1,167	16.7	57	10
Art Monk	69	1,062	15.4	48	7
Drew Pearson	67	1,105	16.5	83	8
Tony Nathan	65	649	10.0	39	2
Roger Craig	63	606	9.6	40	2

TOP 10 POSTSEASON INTERCEPTION LEADERS

Player	Interceptions
Ronnie Lott	9
Bill Simpson	9
Charlie Waters	9
Lester Hayes	8
Willie Brown	7
Dennis Thurman	7
Bobby Bryant	6
Eric Davis	6
Glen Edwards	6
Cliff Harris	6
Vernon Perry	6

TOP 10 POSTSEASON SACK LEADERS

Player	Sacks
Bruce Smith	12.0
Reggie White	12.0
Charles Haley	11.0
Richard Dent	10.5
Charles Mann	10.0
Tony Tolbert	10.0
Jeff Wright	9.0
Kevin Greene	8.5
Dexter Manley	8.0
Mark Gastineau	7.5
Greg Townsend	7.5

ANNUAL SCORING LEADERS

Year	Player, Team	TD	FG	PAT	TP
1997	Mike Hollis, Jacksonville, AFC	0	31	41	134
	Richie Cunningham, Dallas, NFC	0	34	24	126
1996	John Kasay, Carolina, NFC	0	37	34	145
	Cary Blanchard, Indianapolis, AFC	0	36	27	135
1995	Emmitt Smith, Dallas, NFC	25	0	0	150
	Norm Johnson, Pittsburgh, AFC	0	34	39	141
1994	John Carney, San Diego, AFC	0	34	33	135
	Fuad Reveiz, Minnesota, NFC	0	34	30	132
1993	Jeff Jaeger, L.A. Raiders, AFC	0	35	27	132
	Jason Hanson, Detroit, NFC	0	34	28	130
1992	Pete Stoyanovich, Miami, AFC	0	30	34	124
	Morten Andersen, New Orleans, NFC	0	29	33	120
	Chip Lohmiller, Washington, NFC	0	30	30	120
1991	Chip Lohmiller, Washington, NFC	0	31	56	149
	Pete Stoyanovich, Miami, AFC	0	31	28	121
1990	Nick Lowery, Kansas City, AFC	0	34	37	139
	Chip Lohmiller, Washington, NFC	0	30	41	131
1989	Mike Cofer, San Francisco, NFC	0	29	49	136
	*David Treadwell, Denver, AFC	0	27	39	120
1988	Scott Norwood, Buffalo, AFC	0	32	33	129
	Mike Cofer, San Francisco, NFC	0	27	40	121
1987	Jerry Rice, San Francisco, NFC	23	0	0	138
	Jim Breech, Cincinnati, AFC	0	24	25	97
1986	Tony Franklin, New England, AFC	0	32	44	140
	Kevin Butler, Chicago, NFC	0	28	36	120
1985	*Kevin Butler, Chicago, NFC	0	31	51	144
	Gary Anderson, Pittsburgh, AFC	0	33	40	139
1984	Ray Wersching, San Francisco, NFC	0	25	56	131
	Gary Anderson, Pittsburgh, AFC	0	24	45	117
1983	Mark Moseley, Washington, NFC	0	33	62	161
	Gary Anderson, Pittsburgh, AFC	0	27	38	119
1982	*Marcus Allen, L.A. Raiders, AFC	14	0	0	84
	Wendell Tyler, L.A. Rams, NFC	13	0	0	78
1981	Ed Murray, Detroit, NFC	0	25	46	121
	Rafael Septien, Dallas, NFC	0	27	40	121
	Jim Breech, Cincinnati, AFC	0	22	49	115
	Nick Lowery, Kansas City, AFC	0	26	37	115
1980	John Smith, New England, AFC	0	26	51	129
	*Ed Murray, Detroit, NFC	0	27	35	116
1979	John Smith, New England, AFC	0	23	46	115
	Mark Moseley, Washington, NFC	0	25	39	114
1978	*Frank Corral, Los Angeles, NFC	0	29	31	118
	Pat Leahy, N.Y. Jets, AFC	0	22	41	107
1977	Errol Mann, Oakland, AFC	0	20	39	99
	Walter Payton, Chicago, NFC	16	0	0	96
1976	Toni Linhart, Baltimore, AFC	0	20	49	109
	Mark Moseley, Washington, NFC	0	22	31	97
1975	O.J. Simpson, Buffalo, AFC	23	0	0	138
	Chuck Foreman, Minnesota, NFC	22	0	0	132
1974	Chester Marcol, Green Bay, NFC	0	25	19	94
	Roy Gerela, Pittsburgh, AFC	0	20	33	93
1973	David Ray, Los Angeles, NFC	0	30	40	130
	Roy Gerela, Pittsburgh, AFC	0	29	36	123
1972	*Chester Marcol, Green Bay, NFC	0	33	29	128
	Bobby Howfield, N.Y. Jets, AFC	0	27	40	121
1971	Garo Yepremian, Miami, AFC	0	28	33	117
	Curt Knight, Washington, NFC	0	29	27	114
1970	Fred Cox, Minnesota, NFC	0	30	35	125
	Jan Stenerud, Kansas City, AFC	0	30	26	116
1969	Jim Turner, N.Y. Jets, AFL	0	32	33	129
	Fred Cox, Minnesota, NFL	0	26	43	121
1968	Jim Turner, N.Y. Jets, AFL	0	34	43	145
	Leroy Kelly, Cleveland, NFL	20	0	0	120
1967	Jim Bakken, St. Louis, NFL	0	27	36	117
	George Blanda, Oakland, AFL	0	20	56	116
1966	Gino Cappelletti, Boston, AFL	6	16	35	119
	Bruce Gossett, Los Angeles, NFL	0	28	29	113
1965	*Gale Sayers, Chicago, NFL	22	0	0	132
	Gino Cappelletti, Boston, AFL	9	17	27	132
1964	Gino Cappelletti, Boston, AFL	7	25	36	#155
	Lenny Moore, Baltimore, NFL	20	0	0	120
1963	Gino Cappelletti, Boston, AFL	2	22	35	113
	Don Chandler, N.Y. Giants, NFL	0	18	52	106
1962	Gene Mingo, Denver, AFL	4	27	32	137
	Jim Taylor, Green Bay, NFL	19	0	0	114
1961	Gino Cappelletti, Boston, AFL	8	17	48	147
	Paul Hornung, Green Bay, NFL	10	15	41	146
1960	Paul Hornung, Green Bay, NFL	15	15	41	176
	*Gene Mingo, Denver, AFL	6	18	33	123
1959	Paul Hornung, Green Bay	7	7	31	94
1958	Jim Brown, Cleveland	18	0	0	108
1957	Sam Baker, Washington	1	14	29	77
	Lou Groza, Cleveland	0	15	32	77
1956	Bobby Layne, Detroit	5	12	33	99
1955	Doak Walker, Detroit	7	9	27	96
1954	Bobby Walston, Philadelphia	11	4	36	114
1953	Gordy Soltau, San Francisco	6	10	48	114
1952	Gordy Soltau, San Francisco	7	6	34	94
1951	Elroy (Crazylegs) Hirsch, Los Angeles	17	0	0	102
1950	*Doak Walker, Detroit	11	8	38	128
1949	Pat Harder, Chi. Cardinals	8	3	45	102
	Gene Roberts, N.Y. Giants	17	0	0	102
1948	Pat Harder, Chi. Cardinals	6	7	53	110
1947	Pat Harder, Chi. Cardinals	7	7	39	102
1946	Ted Fritsch, Green Bay	10	9	13	100
1945	Steve Van Buren, Philadelphia	18	0	2	110
1944	Don Hutson, Green Bay	9	0	31	85
1943	Don Hutson, Green Bay	12	3	36	117
1942	Don Hutson, Green Bay	17	1	33	138
1941	Don Hutson, Green Bay	12	1	20	95
1940	Don Hutson, Green Bay	7	0	15	57
1939	Andy Farkas, Washington	11	0	2	68
1938	Clarke Hinkle, Green Bay	7	3	7	58
1937	Jack Manders, Chi. Bears	5	8	15	69
1936	Earl (Dutch) Clark, Detroit	7	4	19	73
1935	Earl (Dutch) Clark, Detroit	6	1	16	55
1934	Jack Manders, Chi. Bears	3	10	31	79
1933	Ken Strong, N.Y. Giants	6	5	13	64
	Glenn Presnell, Portsmouth	6	6	10	64
1932	Earl (Dutch) Clark, Portsmouth	6	3	10	55

**First season of professional football.*
#Cappelletti's total includes a two-point conversion.

ANNUAL TOUCHDOWN LEADERS

Year	Player, Team	TD	Rush	Pass	Ret.
1997	Karim Abdul-Jabbar, Miami, AFC	16	15	1	0
	Barry Sanders, Detroit, NFC	14	11	3	0
1996	Terry Allen, Washington, NFC	21	21	0	0
	Curtis Martin, New England, AFC	17	14	3	0
1995	Emmitt Smith, Dallas, NFC	25	25	0	0
	Carl Pickens, Cincinnati, AFC	17	0	17	0
1994	Emmitt Smith, Dallas, NFC	22	21	1	0
	*Marshall Faulk, Indianapolis, AFC	12	11	1	0
	Natrone Means, San Diego, AFC	12	12	0	0
1993	Jerry Rice, San Francisco, NFC	16	1	15	0
	Marcus Allen, Kansas City, AFC	15	12	3	0
1992	Emmitt Smith, Dallas, NFC	19	18	1	0
	Thurman Thomas, Buffalo, AFC	12	9	3	0
1991	Barry Sanders, Detroit, NFC	17	16	1	0
	Mark Clayton, Miami, AFC	12	0	12	0
	Thurman Thomas, Buffalo, AFC	12	7	5	0
1990	Barry Sanders, Detroit, NFC	16	13	3	0
	Derrick Fenner, Seattle, AFC	15	14	1	0
1989	Dalton Hilliard, New Orleans, NFC	18	13	5	0
	Christian Okoye, Kansas City, AFC	12	12	0	0
	Thurman Thomas, Buffalo, AFC	12	6	6	0
1988	Greg Bell, L.A. Rams, NFC	18	16	2	0
	Eric Dickerson, Indianapolis, AFC	15	14	1	0
	*Ickey Woods, Cincinnati, AFC	15	15	0	0
1987	Jerry Rice, San Francisco, NFC	23	1	22	0
	Johnny Hector, N.Y. Jets, AFC	11	11	0	0
1986	George Rogers, Washington, NFC	18	18	0	0
	Sammy Winder, Denver, AFC	14	9	5	0
1985	Joe Morris, N.Y. Giants, NFC	21	21	0	0
	Louis Lipps, Pittsburgh, AFC	15	1	12	2
1984	Marcus Allen, L.A. Raiders, AFC	18	13	5	0
	Mark Clayton, Miami, AFC	18	0	18	0
	Eric Dickerson, L.A. Rams, NFC	14	14	0	0
	John Riggins, Washington, NFC	14	14	0	0
1983	John Riggins, Washington, NFC	24	24	0	0
	Pete Johnson, Cincinnati, AFC	14	14	0	0
	*Curt Warner, Seattle, AFC	14	13	1	0
1982	*Marcus Allen, L.A. Raiders, AFC	14	11	3	0
	Wendell Tyler, L.A. Rams, NFC	13	9	4	0
1981	Chuck Muncie, San Diego, AFC	19	19	0	0
	Wendell Tyler, Los Angeles, NFC	17	12	5	0
1980	*Billy Sims, Detroit, NFC	16	13	3	0
	Earl Campbell, Houston, AFC	13	13	0	0
	*Curtis Dickey, Baltimore, AFC	13	11	2	0
	John Jefferson, San Diego, AFC	13	0	13	0
1979	Earl Campbell, Houston, AFC	19	19	0	0
	Walter Payton, Chicago, NFC	16	14	2	0
1978	David Sims, Seattle, AFC	15	14	1	0
	Terdell Middleton, Green Bay, NFC	12	11	1	0

YEARLY STATISTICAL LEADERS

Year	Player, Team				
1977	Walter Payton, Chicago, NFC	16	14	2	0
	Nat Moore, Miami, AFC	13	1	12	0
1976	Chuck Foreman, Minnesota, NFC	14	13	1	0
	Franco Harris, Pittsburgh, AFC	14	14	0	0
1975	O.J. Simpson, Buffalo, AFC	23	16	7	0
	Chuck Foreman, Minnesota, NFC	22	13	9	0
1974	Chuck Foreman, Minnesota, NFC	15	9	6	0
	Cliff Branch, Oakland, AFC	13	0	13	0
1973	Larry Brown, Washington, NFC	14	8	6	0
	Floyd Little, Denver, AFC	13	12	1	0
1972	Emerson Boozer, N.Y. Jets, AFC	14	11	3	0
	Ron Johnson, N.Y. Giants, NFC	14	9	5	0
1971	Duane Thomas, Dallas, NFC	13	11	2	0
	Leroy Kelly, Cleveland, AFC	12	10	2	0
1970	Dick Gordon, Chicago, NFC	13	0	13	0
	MacArthur Lane, St. Louis, NFC	13	11	2	0
	Gary Garrison, San Diego, AFC	12	0	12	0
1969	Warren Wells, Oakland, AFL	14	0	14	0
	Tom Matte, Baltimore, NFL	13	11	2	0
	Lance Rentzel, Dallas, NFL	13	0	12	1
1968	Leroy Kelly, Cleveland, NFL	20	16	4	0
	Warren Wells, Oakland, AFL	12	1	11	0
1967	Homer Jones, N.Y. Giants, NFL	14	1	13	0
	Emerson Boozer, N.Y. Jets, AFL	13	10	3	0
1966	Leroy Kelly, Cleveland, NFL	16	15	1	0
	Dan Reeves, Dallas, NFL	16	8	8	0
	Lance Alworth, San Diego, AFL	13	0	13	0
1965	*Gale Sayers, Chicago, NFL	22	14	6	2
	Lance Alworth, San Diego, AFL	14	0	14	0
	Don Maynard, N.Y. Jets, AFL	14	0	14	0
1964	Lenny Moore, Baltimore, NFL	20	16	3	1
	Lance Alworth, San Diego, AFL	15	2	13	0
1963	Art Powell, Oakland, AFL	16	0	16	0
	Jim Brown, Cleveland, NFL	15	12	3	0
1962	Abner Haynes, Dallas, AFL	19	13	6	0
	Jim Taylor, Green Bay, NFL	19	19	0	0
1961	Bill Groman, Houston, AFL	18	1	17	0
	Jim Taylor, Green Bay, NFL	16	15	1	0
1960	Paul Hornung, Green Bay, NFL	15	13	2	0
	Sonny Randle, St. Louis, NFL	15	0	15	0
	Art Powell, N.Y. Titans, AFL	14	0	14	0
1959	Raymond Berry, Baltimore	14	0	14	0
	Jim Brown, Cleveland	14	14	0	0
1958	Jim Brown, Cleveland	18	17	1	0
1957	Lenny Moore, Baltimore	11	3	7	1
1956	Rick Casares, Chi. Bears	14	12	2	0
1955	*Alan Ameche, Baltimore	9	9	0	0
	Harlon Hill, Chi. Bears	9	0	9	0
1954	*Harlon Hill, Chi. Bears	12	0	12	0
1953	Joseph Perry, San Francisco	13	10	3	0
1952	Cloyce Box, Detroit	15	0	15	0
1951	Elroy (Crazylegs) Hirsch, Los Angeles	17	0	17	0
1950	Bob Shaw, Chi. Cardinals	12	0	12	0
1949	Gene Roberts, N.Y. Giants	17	9	8	0
1948	Mal Kutner, Chi. Cardinals	15	1	14	0
1947	Steve Van Buren, Philadelphia	14	13	0	1
1946	Ted Fritsch, Green Bay	10	9	1	0
1945	Steve Van Buren, Philadelphia	18	15	2	1
1944	Don Hutson, Green Bay	9	0	9	0
	Bill Paschal, N.Y. Giants	9	9	0	0
1943	Don Hutson, Green Bay	12	0	11	1
	*Bill Paschal, N.Y. Giants	12	10	2	0
1942	Don Hutson, Green Bay	17	0	17	0
1941	Don Hutson, Green Bay	12	2	10	0
	George McAfee, Chi. Bears	12	6	3	3
1940	John Drake, Cleveland	9	9	0	0
	Richard Todd, Washington	9	4	4	1
1939	Andrew Farkas, Washington	11	5	5	1
1938	Don Hutson, Green Bay	9	0	9	0
1937	Cliff Battles, Washington	7	5	1	1
	Clarke Hinkle, Green Bay	7	5	2	0
	Don Hutson, Green Bay	7	0	7	0
1936	Don Hutson, Green Bay	9	0	8	1
1935	*Don Hutson, Green Bay	7	0	6	1
1934	*Beattie Feathers, Chi. Bears	9	8	1	0
1933	*Charlie (Buckets) Goldenberg, Green Bay	7	4	1	2
	John (Shipwreck) Kelly, Brooklyn	7	2	3	2
	*Elvin (Kink) Richards, N.Y. Giants	7	4	3	0
1932	Earl (Dutch) Clark, Portsmouth	6	3	3	0
	Red Grange, Chi. Bears	6	3	3	0

**First season of professional football.*

ANNUAL LEADERS—MOST FIELD GOALS MADE

Year	Player, Team	Att.	Made	Pct.
1997	Richie Cunningham, Dallas, NFC	37	34	91.9
	Cary Blanchard, Indianapolis, AFC	41	32	78.1
1996	John Kasay, Carolina, NFC	45	37	82.2
	Cary Blanchard, Indianapolis, AFC	40	36	90.0
1995	Norm Johnson, Pittsburgh, AFC	41	34	82.9
	Morten Andersen, Atlanta, NFC	37	31	83.8
1994	John Carney, San Diego, AFC	38	34	89.5
	Fuad Reveiz, Minnesota, NFC	39	34	87.2
1993	Jeff Jaeger, L.A. Raiders, AFC	44	35	79.5
	Jason Hanson, Detroit, NFC	43	34	79.1
1992	Pete Stoyanovich, Miami, AFC	37	30	81.1
	Chip Lohmiller, Washington, NFC	40	30	75.0
1991	Pete Stoyanovich, Miami, AFC	37	31	83.8
	Chip Lohmiller, Washington, NFC	43	31	72.1
1990	Nick Lowery, Kansas City, AFC	37	34	91.9
	Chip Lohmiller, Washington, NFC	40	30	75.0
1989	Rich Karlis, Minnesota, NFC	39	31	79.5
	*David Treadwell, Denver, AFC	33	27	81.8
1988	Scott Norwood, Buffalo, AFC	37	32	86.5
	Mike Cofer, San Francisco, NFC	38	27	71.1
1987	Morten Andersen, New Orleans, NFC	36	28	77.8
	Dean Biasucci, Indianpolis, AFC	27	24	88.9
	Jim Breech, Cincinnati, AFC	30	24	80.0
1986	Tony Franklin, New England, AFC	41	32	78.0
	Kevin Butler, Chicago, NFC	41	28	68.3
1985	Gary Anderson, Pittsburgh, AFC	42	33	78.6
	Morten Andersen, New Orleans, NFC	35	31	88.6
	*Kevin Butler, Chicago, NFC	37	31	83.8
1984	*Paul McFadden, Philadelphia, NFC	37	30	81.1
	Gary Anderson, Pittsburgh, AFC	32	24	75.0
	Matt Bahr, Cleveland, AFC	32	24	75.0
1983	*Ali-Haji-Sheikh, N.Y. Giants, NFC	42	35	83.3
	*Raul Allegre, Baltimore, AFC	35	30	85.7
1982	Mark Moseley, Washington, NFC	21	20	95.2
	Nick Lowery, Kansas City, AFC	24	19	79.2
1981	Rafael Septien, Dallas, NFC	35	27	77.1
	Nick Lowery, Kansas City, AFC	36	26	72.2
1980	*Ed Murray, Detroit, NFC	42	27	64.3
	John Smith, New England, AFC	34	26	76.5
	Fred Steinfort, Denver, AFC	34	26	76.5
1979	Mark Moseley, Washington, NFC	33	25	75.8
	John Smith, New England, AFC	33	23	69.7
1978	*Frank Corral, Los Angeles, NFC	43	29	67.4
	Pat Leahy, N.Y. Jets, AFC	30	22	73.3
1977	Mark Moseley, Washington, NFC	37	21	56.8
	Errol Mann, Oakland, AFC	28	20	71.4
1976	Mark Moseley, Washington, NFC	34	22	64.7
	Jan Stenerud, Kansas City, AFC	38	21	55.3
1975	Jan Stenerud, Kansas City, AFC	32	22	68.8
	Toni Fritsch, Dallas, NFC	35	22	62.9
1974	Chester Marcol, Green Bay, NFC	39	25	64.1
	Roy Gerela, Pittsburgh, AFC	29	20	69.0
1973	David Ray, Los Angeles, NFC	47	30	63.8
	Roy Gerela, Pittsburgh, AFC	43	29	67.4
1972	*Chester Marcol, Green Bay, NFC	48	33	68.8
	Roy Gerela, Pittsburgh, AFC	41	28	68.3
1971	Curt Knight, Washington, NFC	49	29	59.2
	Garo Yepremian, Miami, AFC	40	28	70.0
1970	Jan Stenerud, Kansas City, AFC	42	30	71.4
	Fred Cox, Minnesota, NFC	46	30	65.2
1969	Jim Turner, N.Y. Jets, AFL	47	32	68.1
	Fred Cox, Minnesota, NFL	37	26	70.3
1968	Jim Turner, N.Y. Jets, AFL	46	34	73.9
	Mac Percival, Chicago, NFL	36	25	69.4
1967	Jim Bakken, St. Louis, NFL	39	27	69.2
	Jan Stenerud, Kansas City, AFL	36	21	58.3
1966	Bruce Gossett, Los Angeles, NFL	49	28	57.1
	Mike Mercer, Oakland-Kansas City, AFL	30	21	70.0
1965	Pete Gogolak, Buffalo, AFL	46	28	60.9
	Fred Cox, Minnesota, NFL	35	23	65.7
1964	Jim Bakken, St. Louis, NFL	38	25	65.8
	Gino Cappelletti, Boston, AFL	39	25	64.1
1963	Jim Martin, Baltimore, NFL	39	24	61.5
	Gino Cappelletti, Boston, AFL	38	22	57.9
1962	Gene Mingo, Denver, AFL	39	27	69.2
	Lou Michaels, Pittsburgh, NFL	42	26	61.9
1961	Steve Myhra, Baltimore, NFL	39	21	53.8
	Gino Cappelletti, Boston, AFL	32	17	53.1
1960	Tommy Davis, San Francisco, NFL	32	19	59.4
	*Gene Mingo, Denver, AFL	28	18	64.3

1959	Pat Summerall, N.Y. Giants	29	20	69.0
1958	Paige Cothren, Los Angeles	25	14	56.0
	*Tom Miner, Pittsburgh	28	14	50.0
1957	Lou Groza, Cleveland	22	15	68.2
1956	Sam Baker, Washington	25	17	68.0
1955	Fred Cone, Green Bay	24	16	66.7
1954	Lou Groza, Cleveland	24	16	66.7
1953	Lou Groza, Cleveland	26	23	88.5
1952	Lou Groza, Cleveland	33	19	57.6
1951	Bob Waterfield, Los Angeles	23	13	56.5
1950	Lou Groza, Cleveland	19	13	68.4
1949	Cliff Patton, Philadelphia	18	9	50.0
	Bob Waterfield, Los Angeles	16	9	56.3
1948	Cliff Patton, Philadelphia	12	8	66.7
1947	Ward Cuff, Green Bay	16	7	43.8
	Pat Harder, Chi. Cardinals	10	7	70.0
	Bob Waterfield, Los Angeles	16	7	43.8
1946	Ted Fritsch, Green Bay	17	9	52.9
1945	Joe Aguirre, Washington	13	7	53.8
1944	Ken Strong, N.Y. Giants	12	6	50.0
1943	Ward Cuff, N.Y. Giants	9	3	33.3
	Don Hutson, Green Bay	5	3	60.0
1942	Bill Daddio, Chi. Cardinals	10	5	50.0
1941	Clarke Hinkle, Green Bay	14	6	42.9
1940	Clarke Hinkle, Green Bay	14	9	64.3
1939	Ward Cuff, N.Y. Giants	16	7	43.8
1938	Ward Cuff, N.Y. Giants	9	5	55.6
	Ralph Kercheval, Brooklyn	13	5	38.5
1937	Jack Manders, Chi. Bears		8	
1936	Jack Manders, Chi. Bears		7	
	Armand Niccolai, Pittsburgh		7	
1935	Armand Niccolai, Pittsburgh		6	
	Bill Smith, Chi. Cardinals		6	
1934	Jack Manders, Chi. Bears		10	
1933	*Jack Manders, Chi. Bears		6	
	Glenn Presnell, Portsmouth		6	
1932	Earl (Dutch) Clark, Portsmouth		3	

**First season of professional football.*

ANNUAL RUSHING LEADERS

Year	Player, Team	Att.	Yards	Avg.	TD
1997	Barry Sanders, Detroit, NFC	335	2,053	6.1	11
	Terrell Davis, Denver, AFC	369	1,750	4.7	15
1996	Barry Sanders, Detroit, NFC	307	1,553	5.1	11
	Terrell Davis, Denver, AFC	345	1,538	4.5	13
1995	Emmitt Smith, Dallas, NFC	377	1,773	4.7	25
	*Curtis Martin, New England, AFC	368	1,487	4.0	14
1994	Barry Sanders, Detroit, NFC	331	1,883	5.7	7
	Chris Warren, Seattle, AFC	333	1,545	4.6	9
1993	Emmitt Smith, Dallas, NFC	283	1,486	5.3	9
	Thurman Thomas, Buffalo, AFC	355	1,315	3.7	6
1992	Emmitt Smith, Dallas, NFC	373	1,713	4.6	18
	Barry Foster, Pittsburgh, AFC	390	1,690	4.3	11
1991	Emmitt Smith, Dallas, NFC	365	1,563	4.3	12
	Thurman Thomas, Buffalo, AFC	288	1,407	4.9	7
1990	Barry Sanders, Detroit, NFC	255	1,304	5.1	13
	Thurman Thomas, Buffalo, AFC	271	1,297	4.8	11
1989	Christian Okoye, Kansas City, AFC	370	1,480	4.0	12
	*Barry Sanders, Detroit, NFC	280	1,470	5.3	14
1988	Eric Dickerson, Indianapolis, AFC	388	1,659	4.3	14
	Herschel Walker, Dallas, NFC	361	1,514	4.2	5
1987	Charles White, L.A. Rams, NFC	324	1,374	4.2	11
	Eric Dickerson, Indianapolis, AFC	223	1,011	4.5	5
1986	Eric Dickerson, L.A. Rams, NFC	404	1,821	4.5	11
	Curt Warner, Seattle, AFC	319	1,481	4.6	13
1985	Marcus Allen, L.A. Raiders, AFC	380	1,759	4.6	11
	Gerald Riggs, Atlanta, NFC	397	1,719	4.3	10
1984	Eric Dickerson, L.A. Rams, NFC	379	2,105	5.6	14
	Earnest Jackson, San Diego, AFC	296	1,179	4.0	8
1983	*Eric Dickerson, L.A. Rams, NFC	390	1,808	4.6	18
	*Curt Warner, Seattle, AFC	335	1,449	4.3	13
1982	Freeman McNeil, N.Y. Jets, AFC	151	786	5.2	6
	Tony Dorsett, Dallas, NFC	177	745	4.2	5
1981	*George Rogers, New Orleans, NFC	378	1,674	4.4	13
	Earl Campbell, Houston, AFC	361	1,376	3.8	10
1980	Earl Campbell, Houston, AFC	373	1,934	5.2	13
	Walter Payton, Chicago, NFC	317	1,460	4.6	6
1979	Earl Campbell, Houston, AFC	368	1,697	4.6	19
	Walter Payton, Chicago, NFC	369	1,610	4.4	14
1978	*Earl Campbell, Houston, AFC	302	1,450	4.8	13
	Walter Payton, Chicago, NFC	333	1,395	4.2	11
1977	Walter Payton, Chicago, NFC	339	1,852	5.5	14
	Mark van Eeghen, Oakland, AFC	324	1,273	3.9	7
1976	O.J. Simpson, Buffalo, AFC	290	1,503	5.2	8
	Walter Payton, Chicago, NFC	311	1,390	4.5	13
1975	O.J. Simpson, Buffalo, AFC	329	1,817	5.5	16
	Jim Otis, St. Louis, NFC	269	1,076	4.0	5
1974	Otis Armstrong, Denver, AFC	263	1,407	5.3	9
	Lawrence McCutcheon, Los Angeles, NFC	236	1,109	4.7	3
1973	O.J. Simpson, Buffalo, AFC	332	2,003	6.0	12
	John Brockington, Green Bay, NFC	265	1,144	4.3	3
1972	O.J. Simpson, Buffalo, AFC	292	1,251	4.3	6
	Larry Brown, Washington, NFC	285	1,216	4.3	8
1971	Floyd Little, Denver, AFC	284	1,133	4.0	6
	*John Brockington, Green Bay, NFC	216	1,105	5.1	4
1970	Larry Brown, Washington, NFC	237	1,125	4.7	5
	Floyd Little, Denver, AFC	209	901	4.3	3
1969	Gale Sayers, Chicago, NFL	236	1,032	4.4	8
	Dickie Post, San Diego, AFL	182	873	4.8	6
1968	Leroy Kelly, Cleveland, NFL	248	1,239	5.0	16
	*Paul Robinson, Cincinnati, AFL	238	1,023	4.3	8
1967	Jim Nance, Boston, AFL	269	1,216	4.5	7
	Leroy Kelly, Cleveland, NFL	235	1,205	5.1	11
1966	Jim Nance, Boston, AFL	299	1,458	4.9	11
	Gale Sayers, Chicago, NFL	229	1,231	5.4	8
1965	Jim Brown, Cleveland, NFL	289	1,544	5.3	17
	Paul Lowe, San Diego, AFL	222	1,121	5.0	7
1964	Jim Brown, Cleveland, NFL	280	1,446	5.2	7
	Cookie Gilchrist, Buffalo, AFL	230	981	4.3	6
1963	Jim Brown, Cleveland, NFL	291	1,863	6.4	12
	Clem Daniels, Oakland, AFL	215	1,099	5.1	3
1962	Jim Taylor, Green Bay, NFL	272	1,474	5.4	19
	Cookie Gilchrist, Buffalo, AFL	214	1,096	5.1	13
1961	Jim Brown, Cleveland, NFL	305	1,408	4.6	8
	Billy Cannon, Houston, AFL	200	948	4.7	6
1960	Jim Brown, Cleveland, NFL	215	1,257	5.8	9
	*Abner Haynes, Dall. Texans, AFL	156	875	5.6	9
1959	Jim Brown, Cleveland	290	1,329	4.6	14
1958	Jim Brown, Cleveland	257	1,527	5.9	17
1957	*Jim Brown, Cleveland	202	942	4.7	9
1956	Rick Casares, Chi. Bears	234	1,126	4.8	12
1955	*Alan Ameche, Baltimore	213	961	4.5	9
1954	Joe Perry, San Francisco	173	1,049	6.1	8
1953	Joe Perry, San Francisco	192	1,018	5.3	10
1952	Dan Towler, Los Angeles	156	894	5.7	10
1951	Eddie Price, N.Y. Giants	271	971	3.6	7
1950	Marion Motley, Cleveland	140	810	5.8	3
1949	Steve Van Buren, Philadelphia	263	1,146	4.4	11
1948	Steve Van Buren, Philadelphia	201	945	4.7	10
1947	Steve Van Buren, Philadelphia	217	1,008	4.6	13
1946	Bill Dudley, Pittsburgh	146	604	4.1	3
1945	Steve Van Buren, Philadelphia	143	832	5.8	15
1944	Bill Paschal, N.Y. Giants	196	737	3.8	9
1943	*Bill Paschal, N.Y. Giants	147	572	3.9	10
1942	*Bill Dudley, Pittsburgh	162	696	4.3	5
1941	Clarence (Pug) Manders, Brooklyn	111	486	4.4	5
1940	Byron (Whizzer) White, Detroit	146	514	3.5	5
1939	*Bill Osmanski, Chicago	121	699	5.8	7
1938	*Byron (Whizzer) White, Pittsburgh	152	567	3.7	4
1937	Cliff Battles, Washington	216	874	4.0	5
1936	*Alphonse (Tuffy) Leemans, N.Y. Giants	206	830	4.0	2
1935	Doug Russell, Chi. Cardinals	140	499	3.6	0
1934	*Beattie Feathers, Chi. Bears	119	1,004	8.4	8
1933	Jim Musick, Boston	173	809	4.7	5
1932	*Cliff Battles, Boston	148	576	3.9	3

**First season of professional football.*

ANNUAL PASSING LEADERS

(Current rating system implemented in 1973)

Year	Player, Team	Att.	Comp.	Yards	TD	Int.	Rating
1997	Steve Young, San Francisco, NFC	356	241	3,029	19	6	104.7
	Mark Brunell, Jacksonville, AFC	435	264	3,281	18	7	91.2
1996	Steve Young, San Francisco, NFC	316	214	2,410	14	6	97.2
	John Elway, Denver, AFC	466	287	3,328	26	14	89.2
1995	Jim Harbaugh, Indianapolis, AFC	314	200	2,575	17	5	100.7
	Brett Favre, Green Bay, NFC	570	359	4,413	38	13	99.5
1994	Steve Young, San Francisco, NFC	461	324	3,969	35	10	112.8
	Dan Marino, Miami, AFC	615	385	4,453	30	17	89.2
1993	Steve Young, San Francisco, NFC	462	314	4,023	29	16	101.5
	John Elway, Denver, AFC	551	348	4,030	25	10	92.8
1992	Steve Young, San Francisco, NFC	402	268	3,465	25	7	107.0
	Warren Moon, Houston, AFC	346	224	2,521	18	12	89.3
1991	Steve Young, San Francisco, NFC	279	180	2,517	17	8	101.8
	Jim Kelly, Buffalo, AFC	474	304	3,844	33	17	97.6
1990	Jim Kelly, Buffalo, AFC	346	219	2,829	24	9	101.2
	Phil Simms, N.Y. Giants, NFC	311	184	2,284	15	4	92.7

1989	Joe Montana, San Francisco, NFC	386	271	3,521	26	8	112.4
	Boomer Esiason, Cincinnati, AFC	455	258	3,525	28	11	92.1
1988	Boomer Esiason, Cincinnati, AFC	388	223	3,572	28	14	97.4
	Wade Wilson, Minnesota, NFC	332	204	2,746	15	9	91.5
1987	Joe Montana, San Francisco, NFC	398	266	3,054	31	13	102.1
	Bernie Kosar, Cleveland, AFC	389	241	3,033	22	9	95.4
1986	Tommy Kramer, Minnesota, NFC	372	208	3,000	24	10	92.6
	Dan Marino, Miami, AFC	623	378	4,746	44	23	92.5
1985	Ken O'Brien, N.Y. Jets, AFC	488	297	3,888	25	8	96.2
	Joe Montana, San Francisco, NFC	494	303	3,653	27	13	91.3
1984	Dan Marino, Miami, AFC	564	362	5,084	48	17	108.9
	Joe Montana, San Francisco, NFC	432	279	3,630	28	10	102.9
1983	Steve Bartkowski, Atlanta, NFC	432	274	3,167	22	5	97.6
	*Dan Marino, Miami, AFC	296	173	2,210	20	6	96.0
1982	Ken Anderson, Cincinnati, AFC	309	218	2,495	12	9	95.3
	Joe Theismann, Washington, NFC	252	161	2,033	13	9	91.3
1981	Ken Anderson, Cincinnati, AFC	479	300	3,754	29	10	98.4
	Joe Montana, San Francisco, NFC	488	311	3,565	19	12	88.4
1980	Brian Sipe, Cleveland, AFC	554	337	4,132	30	14	91.4
	Ron Jaworski, Philadelphia, NFC	451	257	3,529	27	12	91.0
1979	Roger Staubach, Dallas, NFC	461	267	3,586	27	11	92.3
	Dan Fouts, San Diego, AFC	530	332	4,082	24	24	82.6
1978	Roger Staubach, Dallas, NFC	413	231	3,190	25	16	84.9
	Terry Bradshaw, Pittsburgh, AFC	368	207	2,915	28	20	84.7
1977	Bob Griese, Miami, AFC	307	180	2,252	22	13	87.8
	Roger Staubach, Dallas, NFC	361	210	2,620	18	9	87.0
1976	Ken Stabler, Oakland, AFC	291	194	2,737	27	17	103.4
	James Harris, Los Angeles, NFC	158	91	1,460	8	6	89.6
1975	Ken Anderson, Cincinnati, AFC	377	228	3,169	21	11	93.9
	Fran Tarkenton, Minnesota, NFC	425	273	2,994	25	13	91.8
1974	Ken Anderson, Cincinnati, AFC	328	213	2,667	18	10	95.7
	Sonny Jurgensen, Washington, NFC	167	107	1,185	11	5	94.5
1973	Roger Staubach, Dallas, NFC	286	179	2,428	23	15	94.6
	Ken Stabler, Oakland, AFC	260	163	1,997	14	10	88.3
1972	Norm Snead, N.Y. Giants, NFC	325	196	2,307	17	12	
	Earl Morrall, Miami, AFC	150	83	1,360	11	7	
1971	Roger Staubach, Dallas, NFC	211	126	1,882	15	4	
	Bob Griese, Miami, AFC	263	145	2,089	19	9	
1970	John Brodie, San Francisco, NFC	378	223	2,941	24	10	
	Daryle Lamonica, Oakland, AFC	356	179	2,516	22	15	
1969	Sonny Jurgensen, Washington, NFL	442	274	3,102	22	15	
	*Greg Cook, Cincinnati, AFL	197	106	1,854	15	11	
1968	Len Dawson, Kansas City, AFL	224	131	2,109	17	9	
	Earl Morrall, Baltimore, NFL	317	182	2,909	26	17	
1967	Sonny Jurgensen, Washington, NFL	508	288	3,747	31	16	
	Daryle Lamonica, Oakland, AFL	425	220	3,228	30	20	
1966	Bart Starr, Green Bay, NFL	251	156	2,257	14	3	
	Len Dawson, Kansas City, AFL	284	159	2,527	26	10	
1965	Rudy Bukich, Chicago, NFL	312	176	2,641	20	9	
	John Hadl, San Diego, AFL	348	174	2,798	20	21	
1964	Len Dawson, Kansas City, AFL	354	199	2,879	30	18	
	Bart Starr, Green Bay, NFL	272	163	2,144	15	4	
1963	Y.A. Tittle, N.Y. Giants, NFL	367	221	3,145	36	14	
	Tobin Rote, San Diego, AFL	286	170	2,510	20	17	
1962	Len Dawson, Dall. Texans, AFL	310	189	2,759	29	17	
	Bart Starr, Green Bay, NFL	285	178	2,438	12	9	
1961	George Blanda, Houston, AFL	362	187	3,330	36	22	
	Milt Plum, Cleveland, NFL	302	177	2,416	18	10	
1960	Milt Plum, Cleveland, NFL	250	151	2,297	21	5	
	Jack Kemp, L.A. Chargers, AFL	406	211	3,018	20	25	
1959	Charlie Conerly, N.Y. Giants	194	113	1,706	14	4	
1958	Eddie LeBaron, Washington	145	79	1,365	11	10	
1957	Tommy O'Connell, Cleveland	110	63	1,229	9	8	
1956	Ed Brown, Chi. Bears	168	96	1,667	11	12	
1955	Otto Graham, Cleveland	185	98	1,721	15	8	
1954	Norm Van Brocklin, Los Angeles	260	139	2,637	13	21	
1953	Otto Graham, Cleveland	258	167	2,722	11	9	
1952	Norm Van Brocklin, Los Angeles	205	113	1,736	14	17	
1951	Bob Waterfield, Los Angeles	176	88	1,566	13	10	
1950	Norm Van Brocklin, Los Angeles	233	127	2,061	18	14	
1949	Sammy Baugh, Washington	255	145	1,903	18	14	
1948	Tommy Thompson, Philadelphia	246	141	1,965	25	11	
1947	Sammy Baugh, Washington	354	210	2,938	25	15	
1946	Bob Waterfield, Los Angeles	251	127	1,747	18	17	
1945	Sammy Baugh, Washington	182	128	1,669	11	4	
	Sid Luckman, Chi. Bears	217	117	1,725	14	10	
1944	Frank Filchock, Washington	147	84	1,139	13	9	
1943	Sammy Baugh, Washington	239	133	1,754	23	19	
1942	Cecil Isbell, Green Bay	268	146	2,021	24	14	
1941	Cecil Isbell, Green Bay	206	117	1,479	15	11	
1940	Sammy Baugh, Washington	177	111	1,367	12	10	
1939	*Parker Hall, Cleveland	208	106	1,227	9	13	
1938	Ed Danowski, N.Y. Giants	129	70	848	7	8	
1937	*Sammy Baugh, Washington	171	81	1,127	8	14	
1936	Arnie Herber, Green Bay	173	77	1,239	11	13	
1935	Ed Danowski, N.Y. Giants	113	57	794	10	9	
1934	Arnie Herber, Green Bay	115	42	799	8	12	
1933	*Harry Newman, N.Y. Giants	136	53	973	11	17	
1932	Arnie Herber, Green Bay	101	37	639	9	9	

First season of professional football.

ANNUAL PASSING TOUCHDOWN LEADERS

Year	Player, Team	TD
1997	Brett Favre, Green Bay, NFC	35
	Jeff George, Oakland, AFC	29
1996	Brett Favre, Green Bay, NFC	39
	Vinny Testaverde, Baltimore, AFC	33
1995	Brett Favre, Green Bay, NFC	38
	Jeff Blake, Cincinnati, AFC	28
1994	Steve Young, San Francisco, NFC	35
	Dan Marino, Miami, AFC	30
1993	Steve Young, San Francisco, NFC	29
	John Elway, Denver, AFC	25
1992	Steve Young, San Francisco, NFC	25
	Dan Marino, Miami, AFC	24
1991	Jim Kelly, Buffalo, AFC	33
	Mark Rypien, Washington, NFC	28
1990	Warren Moon, Houston, AFC	33
	Randall Cunningham, Philadelphia, NFC	30
1989	Jim Everett, L.A. Rams, NFC	29
	Boomer Esiason, Cincinnati, AFC	28
1988	Jim Everett, L.A. Rams, NFC	31
	Boomer Esiason, Cincinnati, AFC	28
	Dan Marino, Miami, AFC	28
1987	Joe Montana, San Francisco, NFC	31
	Dan Marino, Miami, AFC	26
1986	Dan Marino, Miami, AFC	44
	Tommy Kramer, Minnesota, NFC	24
1985	Dan Marino, Miami, AFC	30
	Joe Montana, San Francisco, NFC	27
1984	Dan Marino, Miami, AFC	48
	Neil Lomax, St. Louis, NFC	28
	Joe Montana, San Francisco, NFC	28
1983	Lynn Dickey, Green Bay, NFC	32
	Joe Ferguson, Buffalo, AFC	26
	Brian Sipe, Cleveland, AFC	26
1982	Terry Bradshaw, Pittsburgh, AFC	17
	Dan Fouts, San Diego, AFC	17
	Joe Montana, San Francisco, NFC	17
1981	Dan Fouts, San Diego, AFC	33
	Steve Bartkowski, Atlanta, NFC	30
1980	Steve Bartkowski, Atlanta, NFC	31
	Dan Fouts, San Diego, AFC	30
	Brian Sipe, Cleveland, AFC	30
1979	Steve Grogan, New England, AFC	28
	Brian Sipe, Cleveland, AFC	28
	Roger Staubach, Dallas, NFC	27
1978	Terry Bradshaw, Pittsburgh, AFC	28
	Roger Staubach, Dallas, NFC	25
	Fran Tarkenton, Minnesota, NFC	25
1977	Bob Griese, Miami, AFC	22
	Ron Jaworski, Philadelphia, NFC	18
	Roger Staubach, Dallas, NFC	18
1976	Ken Stabler, Oakland, AFC	27
	Jim Hart, St. Louis, NFC	18
1975	Joe Ferguson, Buffalo, AFC	25
	Fran Tarkenton, Minnesota, NFC	25
1974	Ken Stabler, Oakland, AFC	26
	Jim Hart, St. Louis, NFC	20
1973	Roman Gabriel, Philadelphia, NFC	23
	Roger Staubach, Dallas, NFC	23
	Charley Johnson, Denver, AFC	20
1972	Billy Kilmer, Washington, NFC	19
	Joe Namath, N.Y. Jets, AFC	19
1971	John Hadl, San Diego, AFC	21
	John Brodie, San Francisco, NFC	18
1970	John Brodie, San Francisco, NFC	24
	John Hadl, San Diego, AFC	22
	Daryle Lamonica, Oakland, AFC	22
1969	Daryle Lamonica, Oakland, AFL	34
	Roman Gabriel, Los Angeles, NFL	24
1968	John Hadl, San Diego, AFL	27
	Earl Morrall, Baltimore, NFL	26
1967	Sonny Jurgensen, Washington, NFL	31
	Daryle Lamonica, Oakland, AFL	30

1966	Frank Ryan, Cleveland, NFL	29
	Len Dawson, Kansas City, AFL	26
1965	John Brodie, San Francisco, NFL	30
	Len Dawson, Kansas City, AFL	21
1964	Babe Parilli, Boston, AFL	31
	Frank Ryan, Cleveland, NFL	25
1963	Y.A. Tittle, N.Y. Giants, NFL	36
	Len Dawson, Kansas City, AFL	26
1962	Y.A. Tittle, N.Y. Giants, NFL	33
	Len Dawson, Dallas, AFL	29
1961	George Blanda, Houston, AFL	36
	Sonny Jurgensen, Philadelphia, NFL	32
1960	Al Dorow, N.Y. Titans, AFL	26
	Johnny Unitas, Baltimore, NFL	25
1959	Johnny Unitas, Baltimore	32
1958	Johnny Unitas, Baltimore	19
1957	Johnny Unitas, Baltimore	24
1956	Tobin Rote, Green Bay	18
1955	Tobin Rote, Green Bay	17
	Y.A. Tittle, San Francisco	17
1954	Adrian Burk, Philadelphia	23
1953	Robert Thomason, Philadelphia	21
1952	Jim Finks, Pittsburgh	20
	Otto Graham, Cleveland	20
1951	Bobby Layne, Detroit	26
1950	George Ratterman, N.Y. Yanks	22
1949	Johnny Lujack, Chi. Bears	23
1948	Tommy Thompson, Philadelphia	25
1947	Sammy Baugh, Washington	25
1946	Sid Luckman, Chi. Bears	17
	Bob Waterfield, Los Angeles	17
1945	Sid Luckman, Chi. Bears	14
	*Bob Waterfield, Cleveland	14
1944	Frank Filchock, Washington	13
1943	Sid Luckman, Chi. Bears	28
1942	Cecil Isbell, Green Bay	24
1941	Cecil Isbell, Green Bay	15
1940	Sammy Baugh, Washington	12
1939	Frank Filchock, Washington	11
1938	Bob Monnett, Green Bay	9
1937	Bernie Masterson, Chi. Bears	9
1936	Arnie Herber, Green Bay	11
1935	Ed Danowski, N.Y. Giants	10
1934	Arnie Herber, Green Bay	8
1933	*Harry Newman, N.Y. Giants	11
1932	Arnie Herber, Green Bay	9

**First season of professional football.*

ANNUAL PASS RECEIVING LEADERS

Year	Player, Team	No.	Yards	Avg.	TD
1997	Tim Brown, Oakland, AFC	104	1,408	13.5	5
	Herman Moore, Detroit, NFC	104	1,293	12.4	8
1996	Jerry Rice, San Francisco, NFC	108	1,254	11.6	8
	Carl Pickens, Cincinnati, AFC	100	1,180	11.8	12
1995	Herman Moore, Detroit, NFC	123	1,686	13.7	14
	Carl Pickens, Cincinnati, AFC	99	1,234	12.5	17
1994	Cris Carter, Minnesota, NFC	122	1,256	10.3	7
	Ben Coates, New England, AFC	96	1,174	12.2	7
1993	Sterling Sharpe, Green Bay, NFC	112	1,274	11.4	11
	Reggie Langhorne, Indianapolis, AFC	85	1,038	12.2	3
1992	Sterling Sharpe, Green Bay, NFC	108	1,461	13.5	13
	Haywood Jeffires, Houston, AFC	90	913	10.1	9
1991	Haywood Jeffires, Houston, AFC	100	1,181	11.8	7
	Michael Irvin, Dallas, NFC	93	1,523	16.4	8
1990	Jerry Rice, San Francisco, NFC	100	1,502	15.0	13
	Haywood Jeffires, Houston, AFC	74	1,048	14.2	8
	Drew Hill, Houston, AFC	74	1,019	13.8	5
1989	Sterling Sharpe, Green Bay, NFC	90	1,423	15.8	12
	Andre Reed, Buffalo, AFC	88	1,312	14.9	9
1988	Al Toon, N.Y. Jets, AFC	93	1,067	11.5	5
	Henry Ellard, L.A. Rams, NFC	86	1,414	16.4	10
1987	J.T. Smith, St. Louis, NFC	91	1,117	12.3	8
	Al Toon, N.Y. Jets, AFC	68	976	14.4	5
1986	Todd Christensen, L.A. Raiders, AFC	95	1,153	12.1	8
	Jerry Rice, San Francisco, NFC	86	1,570	18.3	15
1985	Roger Craig, San Francisco, NFC	92	1,016	11.0	6
	Lionel James, San Diego, AFC	86	1,027	11.9	6
1984	Art Monk, Washington, NFC	106	1,372	12.9	7
	Ozzie Newsome, Cleveland, AFC	89	1,001	11.2	5
1983	Todd Christensen, L.A. Raiders, AFC	92	1,247	13.6	12
	Roy Green, St. Louis, NFC	78	1,227	15.7	14
	Charlie Brown, Washington, NFC	78	1,225	15.7	8
	Earnest Gray, N.Y. Giants, NFC	78	1,139	14.6	5
1982	Dwight Clark, San Francisco, NFC	60	913	15.2	5
	Kellen Winslow, San Diego, AFC	54	721	13.4	6
1981	Kellen Winslow, San Diego, AFC	88	1,075	12.2	10
	Dwight Clark, San Francisco, NFC	85	1,105	13.0	4
1980	Kellen Winslow, San Diego, AFC	89	1,290	14.5	9
	*Earl Cooper, San Francisco, NFC	83	567	6.8	4
1979	Joe Washington, Baltimore, AFC	82	750	9.1	3
	Ahmad Rashad, Minnesota, NFC	80	1,156	14.5	9
1978	Rickey Young, Minnesota, NFC	88	704	8.0	5
	Steve Largent, Seattle, AFC	71	1,168	16.5	8
1977	Lydell Mitchell, Baltimore, AFC	71	620	8.7	4
	Ahmad Rashad, Minnesota, NFC	51	681	13.4	2
1976	MacArthur Lane, Kansas City, AFC	66	686	10.4	1
	Drew Pearson, Dallas, NFC	58	806	13.9	6
1975	Chuck Foreman, Minnesota, NFC	73	691	9.5	9
	Reggie Rucker, Cleveland, AFC	60	770	12.8	3
	Lydell Mitchell, Baltimore, AFC	60	544	9.1	4
1974	Lydell Mitchell, Baltimore, AFC	72	544	7.6	2
	Charles Young, Philadelphia, NFC	63	696	11.0	3
1973	Harold Carmichael, Philadelphia, NFC	67	1,116	16.7	9
	Fred Willis, Houston, AFC	57	371	6.5	1
1972	Harold Jackson, Philadelphia, NFC	62	1,048	16.9	4
	Fred Biletnikoff, Oakland, AFC	58	802	13.8	7
1971	Fred Biletnikoff, Oakland, AFC	61	929	15.2	9
	Bob Tucker, N.Y. Giants, NFC	59	791	13.4	4
1970	Dick Gordon, Chicago, NFC	71	1,026	14.5	13
	Marlin Briscoe, Buffalo, AFC	57	1,036	18.2	8
1969	Dan Abramowicz, New Orleans, NFL	73	1,015	13.9	7
	Lance Alworth, San Diego, AFL	64	1,003	15.7	4
1968	Clifton McNeil, San Francisco, NFL	71	994	14.0	7
	Lance Alworth, San Diego, AFL	68	1,312	19.3	10
1967	George Sauer, N.Y. Jets, AFL	75	1,189	15.9	6
	Charley Taylor, Washington, NFL	70	990	14.1	9
1966	Lance Alworth, San Diego, AFL	73	1,383	18.9	13
	Charley Taylor, Washington, NFL	72	1,119	15.5	12
1965	Lionel Taylor, Denver, AFL	85	1,131	13.3	6
	Dave Parks, San Francisco, NFL	80	1,344	16.8	12
1964	Charley Hennigan, Houston, AFL	101	1,546	15.3	8
	Johnny Morris, Chicago, NFL	93	1,200	12.9	10
1963	Lionel Taylor, Denver, AFL	78	1,101	14.1	10
	Bobby Joe Conrad, St. Louis, NFL	73	967	13.2	10
1962	Lionel Taylor, Denver, AFL	77	908	11.8	4
	Bobby Mitchell, Washington, NFL	72	1,384	19.2	11
1961	Lionel Taylor, Denver, AFL	100	1,176	11.8	4
	Jim (Red) Phillips, Los Angeles, NFL	78	1,092	14.0	5
1960	Lionel Taylor, Denver, AFL	92	1,235	13.4	12
	Raymond Berry, Baltimore, NFL	74	1,298	17.5	10
1959	Raymond Berry, Baltimore	66	959	14.5	14
1958	Raymond Berry, Baltimore	56	794	14.2	9
	Pete Retzlaff, Philadelphia	56	766	13.7	2
1957	Billy Wilson, San Francisco	52	757	14.6	6
1956	Billy Wilson, San Francisco	60	889	14.8	5
1955	Pete Pihos, Philadelphia	62	864	13.9	7
1954	Pete Pihos, Philadelphia	60	872	14.5	10
	Billy Wilson, San Francisco	60	830	13.8	5
1953	Pete Pihos, Philadelphia	63	1,049	16.7	10
1952	Mac Speedie, Cleveland	62	911	14.7	5
1951	Elroy (Crazylegs) Hirsch, Los Angeles	66	1,495	22.7	17
1950	Tom Fears, Los Angeles	84	1,116	13.3	7
1949	Tom Fears, Los Angeles	77	1,013	13.2	9
1948	*Tom Fears, Los Angeles	51	698	13.7	4
1947	Jim Keane, Chi. Bears	64	910	14.2	10
1946	Jim Benton, Los Angeles	63	981	15.6	6
1945	Don Hutson, Green Bay	47	834	17.7	9
1944	Don Hutson, Green Bay	58	866	14.9	9
1943	Don Hutson, Green Bay	47	776	16.5	11
1942	Don Hutson, Green Bay	74	1,211	16.4	17
1941	Don Hutson, Green Bay	58	738	12.7	10
1940	*Don Looney, Philadelphia	58	707	12.2	4
1939	Don Hutson, Green Bay	34	846	24.9	6
1938	Gaynell Tinsley, Chi. Cardinals	41	516	12.6	1
1937	Don Hutson, Green Bay	41	552	13.5	7
1936	Don Hutson, Green Bay	34	536	15.8	8
1935	*Tod Goodwin, N.Y. Giants	26	432	16.6	4
1934	Joe Carter, Philadelphia	16	238	14.9	4
	Morris (Red) Badgro, N.Y. Giants	16	206	12.9	1
1933	John (Shipwreck) Kelly, Brooklyn	22	246	11.2	3
1932	Ray Flaherty, N.Y. Giants	21	350	16.7	3

**First season of professional football.*

YEARLY STATISTICAL LEADERS

ANNUAL PASS RECEIVING LEADERS (YARDS)

Year	Player, Team	No.	Yards	Avg.	TD
1997	Rob Moore, Arizona, NFC	97	1,584	16.3	8
	Tim Brown, Oakland, AFC	104	1,408	13.5	5
1996	Isaac Bruce, St. Louis, NFC	84	1,338	15.9	7
	Jimmy Smith, Jacksonville, AFC	83	1,244	15.0	7
1995	Jerry Rice, San Francisco, NFC	122	1,848	15.1	15
	Tim Brown, Oakland, AFC	89	1,342	15.1	10
1994	Jerry Rice, San Francisco, NFC	112	1,499	13.4	13
	Tim Brown, L.A. Raiders, AFC	89	1,309	14.7	9
1993	Jerry Rice, San Francisco, NFC	98	1,503	15.3	15
	Tim Brown, L.A. Raiders, AFC	80	1,180	14.8	7
1992	Sterling Sharpe, Green Bay, NFC	108	1,461	13.5	13
	Anthony Miller, San Diego, AFC	72	1,060	14.7	7
1991	Michael Irvin, Dallas, NFC	93	1,523	16.4	8
	Haywood Jeffires, Houston, AFC	100	1,181	11.8	7
1990	Jerry Rice, San Francisco, NFC	100	1,502	15.0	13
	Haywood Jeffires, Houston, AFC	74	1,048	14.2	8
1989	Jerry Rice, San Francisco, NFC	82	1,483	18.1	17
	Andre Reed, Buffalo, AFC	88	1,312	14.9	9
1988	Henry Ellard, L.A. Rams, NFC	86	1,414	16.4	10
	Eddie Brown, Cincinnati, AFC	53	1,273	24.0	9
1987	J.T. Smith, St. Louis, NFC	91	1,117	12.3	8
	Carlos Carson, Kansas City, AFC	55	1,044	19.0	7
1986	Jerry Rice, San Francisco, NFC	86	1,570	18.3	15
	Stanley Morgan, New England, AFC	84	1,491	17.8	10
1985	Steve Largent, Seattle, AFC	79	1,287	16.3	6
	Mike Quick, Philadelphia, NFC	73	1,247	17.1	11
1984	Roy Green, St. Louis, NFC	78	1,555	19.9	12
	John Stallworth, Pittsburgh, AFC	80	1,395	17.4	11
1983	Mike Quick, Philadelphia, NFC	69	1,409	20.4	13
	Carlos Carson, Kansas City, AFC	80	1,351	16.9	7
1982	Wes Chandler, San Diego, AFC	49	1,032	21.1	9
	Dwight Clark, San Francisco, NFC	60	913	15.2	5
1981	Alfred Jenkins, Atlanta, NFC	70	1,358	19.4	13
	Frank Lewis, Buffalo, AFC	70	1,244	17.8	4
	Steve Watson, Denver, AFC	60	1,244	20.7	13
1980	John Jefferson, San Diego, AFC	82	1,340	16.3	13
	James Lofton, Green Bay, NFC	71	1,226	17.3	4
1979	Steve Largent, Seattle, AFC	66	1,237	18.7	9
	Ahmad Rashad, Minnesota, NFC	80	1,156	14.5	9
1978	Wesley Walker, N.Y. Jets, AFC	48	1,169	24.4	8
	Harold Carmichael, Philadelphia, NFC	55	1,072	19.5	8
1977	Drew Pearson, Dallas, NFC	48	870	18.1	2
	Ken Burrough, Houston, AFC	43	816	19.0	8
1976	Roger Carr, Baltimore, AFC	43	1,112	25.9	11
	*Sammy White, Minnesota, NFC	51	906	17.8	10
1975	Ken Burrough, Houston, AFC	53	1,063	20.1	8
	Mel Gray, St. Louis, NFC	48	926	19.3	11
1974	Cliff Branch, Oakland, AFC	60	1,092	18.2	13
	Drew Pearson, Dallas, NFC	62	1,087	17.5	2
1973	Harold Carmichael, Philadelphia, NFC	67	1,116	16.7	9
	*Isaac Curtis, Cincinnati, AFC	45	843	18.7	9
1972	Harold Jackson, Philadelphia, NFC	62	1,048	16.9	4
	Rich Caster, N.Y. Jets, AFC	39	833	21.4	10
1971	Otis Taylor, Kansas City, AFC	57	1,110	19.5	7
	Gene Washington, San Francisco, NFC	46	884	19.2	4
1970	Gene Washington, San Francisco, NFC	53	1,100	20.8	12
	Marlin Briscoe, Buffalo, AFC	57	1,036	18.2	8
1969	Warren Wells, Oakland, AFL	47	1,260	26.8	14
	Harold Jackson, Philadelphia, NFL	65	1,116	17.2	9
1968	Lance Alworth, San Diego, AFL	68	1,312	19.3	10
	Roy Jefferson, Pittsburgh, NFL	58	1,074	18.5	11
1967	Don Maynard, N.Y. Jets, AFL	71	1,434	20.3	10
	Ben Hawkins, Philadelphia, NFL	59	1,265	21.4	10
1966	Lance Alworth, San Diego, AFL	73	1,383	18.9	13
	Pat Studstill, Detroit, NFL	67	1,266	18.9	5
1965	Lance Alworth, San Diego, AFL	69	1,602	23.2	14
	Dave Parks, San Francisco, NFL	80	1,344	16.8	12
1964	Charley Hennigan, Houston, AFL	101	1,546	15.3	8
	Johnny Morris, Chicago, NFL	93	1,200	12.9	10
1963	Bobby Mitchell, Washington, NFL	69	1,436	20.8	7
	Art Powell, Oakland, AFL	73	1,304	17.8	16
1962	Bobby Mitchel, Washington, NFL	72	1,384	19.2	11
	Art Powell, N.Y. Titans, AFL	64	1,130	17.6	8
1961	Charley Hennigan, Houston, AFL	82	1,746	21.3	12
	Tommy McDonald, Philadelphia, NFL	64	1,144	17.9	13
1960	*Bill Groman, Houston, AFL	72	1,473	20.5	12
	Raymond Berry, Baltimore, NFL	74	1,298	17.5	10
1959	Raymond Berry, Baltimore	66	959	14.5	14
1958	Del Shofner, Los Angeles	51	1,097	21.5	8
1957	Raymond Berry, Baltimore	47	800	17.0	6
1956	Billy Howton, Green Bay	55	1,188	21.6	12
1955	Pete Pihos, Philadelphia	62	864	13.9	7
1954	Bob Boyd, Los Angeles	53	1,212	22.9	6
1953	Pete Pihos, Philadelphia	63	1,049	16.7	10
1952	*Bill Howton, Green Bay	53	1,231	23.2	13
1951	Elroy (Crazylegs) Hirsch, Los Angeles	66	1,495	22.7	17
1950	Tom Fears, Los Angeles	84	1,116	13.3	7
1949	Bob Mann, Detroit	66	1,014	15.4	4
1948	Mal Kutner, Chi. Cardinals	41	943	23.0	14
1947	Mal Kutner, Chi. Cardinals	43	944	21.9	7
1946	Jim Benton, Los Angeles	63	981	15.5	6
1945	Jim Benton, Cleveland	45	1,067	23.7	8
1944	Don Hutson, Green Bay	58	866	14.6	9
1943	Don Hutson, Green Bay	47	776	16.5	11
1942	Don Hutson, Green Bay	74	1,211	16.4	17
1941	Don Hutson, Green Bay	58	738	12.7	10
1940	*Don Looney, Philadelphia	58	707	12.2	4
1939	Don Hutson, Green Bay	34	846	24.9	6
1938	Don Hutson, Green Bay	32	548	17.1	9
1937	*Gaynell Tinsley, Chi. Cardinals	36	675	18.8	5
1936	Don Hutson, Green Bay	34	526	15.5	8
1935	Charley Malone, Boston	22	433	19.7	2
1934	Harry Ebding, Detroit	9	257	28.6	2
1933	*Paul Moss, Pittsburgh	18	383	21.3	2
1932	Johnny Blood (McNally), Green Bay	19	326	17.2	3

**First season of professional football.*

ANNUAL INTERCEPTION LEADERS

Year	Player, Team	No.	Yards	TD
1997	Ryan McNeil, St. Louis, NFC	9	127	1
	Mark McMillian, Kansas City, AFC	8	274	3
	Darryl Williams, Seattle, AFC	8	172	1
1996	Tyrone Braxton, Denver, AFC	9	128	1
	Keith Lyle, St. Louis, NFC	9	152	0
1995	*Orlando Thomas, Minnesota, NFC	9	108	1
	Willie Williams, Pittsburgh, AFC	7	122	1
1994	Eric Turner, Cleveland, AFC	9	199	1
	Aeneas Williams, Arizona, NFC	9	89	0
1993	Eugene Robinson, Seattle, AFC	9	80	0
	Nate Odomes, Buffalo, AFC	9	65	0
	Deion Sanders, Atlanta, NFC	7	91	0
1992	Henry Jones, Buffalo, AFC	8	263	2
	Audray McMillian, Minnesota, NFC	8	157	2
1991	Ronnie Lott, L.A. Raiders, AFC	8	52	0
	Ray Crockett, Detroit, NFC	6	141	1
	Deion Sanders, Atlanta, NFC	6	119	1
	*Aeneas Williams, Phoenix, NFC	6	60	0
	Tim McKyer, Atlanta, NFC	6	24	0
1990	*Mark Carrier, Chicago, NFC	10	39	0
	Richard Johnson, Houston, AFC	8	100	1
1989	Felix Wright, Cleveland, AFC	9	91	1
	Eric Allen, Philadelphia, NFC	8	38	0
1988	Scott Case, Atlanta, NFC	10	47	0
	Erik McMillan, N.Y. Jets, AFC	8	168	2
1987	Barry Wilburn, Washington, NFC	9	135	1
	Mike Prior, Indianapolis, AFC	6	57	0
	Mark Kelso, Buffalo, AFC	6	25	0
	Keith Bostic, Houston, AFC	6	-14	0
1986	Ronnie Lott, San Francisco, NFC	10	134	1
	Deron Cherry, Kansas City, AFC	9	150	0
1985	Everson Walls, Dallas, NFC	9	31	0
	Albert Lewis, Kansas City, AFC	8	59	0
	Eugene Daniel, Indianapolis, AFC	8	53	0
1984	Ken Easley, Seattle, AFC	10	126	2
	*Tom Flynn, Green Bay, NFC	9	106	0
1983	Mark Murphy, Washington, NFC	9	127	0
	Ken Riley, Cincinnati, AFC	8	89	2
	Vann McElroy, L.A. Raiders, AFC	8	68	0
1982	Everson Walls, Dallas, NFC	7	61	0
	Ken Riley, Cincinnati, AFC	5	88	1
	Bobby Jackson, N.Y Jets, AFC	5	84	1
	Dwayne Woodruff, Pittsburgh, AFC	5	53	0
	Donnie Shell, Pittsburgh, AFC	5	27	0
1981	*Everson Walls, Dallas, NFC	11	133	0
	John Harris, Seattle, AFC	10	155	2
1980	Lester Hayes, Oakland, AFC	13	273	1
	Nolan Cromwell, Los Angeles, NFC	8	140	1
1979	Mike Reinfeldt, Houston, AFC	12	205	0
	Lemar Parrish, Washiongton, NFC	9	65	0
1978	Thom Darden, Cleveland, AFC	10	200	0
	Ken Stone, St. Louis, NFC	9	139	0
	Willie Buchanon, Green Bay, NFC	9	93	1
1977	Lyle Blackwood, Baltimore, AFC	10	163	0
	Rolland Lawrence, Atlanta, NFC	7	138	0

1976	Monte Jackson, Los Angeles, NFC	10	173	3
	Ken Riley, Cincinnati, AFC	9	141	1
1975	Mel Blount, Pittsburgh, AFC	11	121	0
	Paul Krause, Minnesota, NFC	10	201	0
1974	Emmitt Thomas, Kansas City, AFC	12	214	2
	Ray Brown, Atlanta, NFC	8	164	1
1973	Dick Anderson, Miami, AFC	8	163	2
	Mike Wagner, Pittsburgh, AFC	8	134	0
	Bobby Bryant, Minnesota, NFC	7	105	1
1972	Bill Bradley, Philadelphia, NFC	9	73	0
	Mike Sensibaugh, Kansas City, AFC	8	65	0
1971	Bill Bradley, Philadelphia, NFC	11	248	0
	Ken Houston, Houston, AFC	9	220	4
1970	Johnny Robinson, Kansas City, AFC	10	155	0
	Dick LeBeau, Detroit, NFC	9	96	0
1969	Mel Renfro, Dallas, NFL	10	118	0
	Emmitt Thomas, Kansas City, AFL	9	146	1
1968	Dave Grayson, Oakland, AFL	10	195	1
	Willie Williams, N.Y. Giants, NFL	10	103	0
1967	Miller Farr, Houston, AFL	10	264	3
	*Lem Barney, Detroit, NFL	10	232	3
	Tom Janik, Buffalo, AFL	10	222	2
	Dave Whitsell, New Orleans, NFL	10	178	2
	Dick Westmoreland, Miami, AFL	10	127	1
1966	Larry Wilson, St. Louis, NFL	10	180	2
	Johnny Robinson, Kansas City, AFL	10	136	1
	Bobby Hunt, Kansas City, AFL	10	113	0
1965	W.K. Hicks, Houston, AFL	9	156	0
	Bobby Boyd, Baltimore, NFL	9	78	1
1964	Dainard Paulson, N.Y. Jets, AFL	12	157	1
	*Paul Krause, Washington, NFL	12	140	1
1963	Fred Glick, Houston, AFL	12	180	1
	Dick Lynch, N.Y. Giants, NFL	9	251	3
	Roosevelt Taylor, Chicago, NFL	9	172	1
1962	Lee Riley, N.Y. Titans, AFL	11	122	0
	Willie Wood, Green Bay, NFL	9	132	0
1961	Billy Atkins, Buffalo, AFL	10	158	0
	Dick Lynch, N.Y. Giants, NFL	9	60	0
1960	*Austin (Goose) Gonsoulin, Denver, AFL	11	98	0
	Dave Baker, San Francisco, NFL	10	96	0
	Jerry Norton, St. Louis, NFL	10	96	0
1959	Dean Derby, Pittsburgh	7	127	0
	Milt Davis, Baltimore	7	119	1
	Don Shinnick, Baltimore	7	70	0
1958	Jim Patton, N.Y. Giants	11	183	0
1957	Milt Davis, Baltimore	10	219	2
	Jack Christiansen, Detroit	10	137	1
	Jack Butler, Pittsburgh	10	85	0
1956	Linden Crow, Chi. Cardinals	11	170	0
1955	Will Sherman, Los Angeles	11	101	0
1954	Dick (Night Train) Lane, Chi. Cardinals	10	181	0
1953	Jack Christiansen, Detroit	12	238	1
1952	*Dick (Night Train) Lane, Los Angeles	14	298	2
1951	Otto Schnellbacher, N.Y. Giants	11	194	2
1950	Orban (Spec) Sanders, N.Y. Yanks	13	199	0
1949	Bob Nussbaumer, Chi. Cardinals	12	157	0
1948	*Dan Sandifer, Washington	13	258	2
1947	Frank Reagan, N.Y. Giants	10	203	0
	Frank Seno, Boston	10	100	0
1946	Bill Dudley, Pittsburgh	10	242	1
1945	Roy Zimmerman, Philadelphia	7	90	0
1944	*Howard Livingston, N.Y. Giants	9	172	1
1943	Sammy Baugh, Washington	11	112	0
1942	Clyde (Bulldog) Turner, Chi. Bears	8	96	1
1941	Marshall Goldberg, Chi. Cardinals	7	54	0
	*Art Jones, Pittsburgh	7	35	0
1940	Clarence (Ace) Parker, Brooklyn	6	146	1
	Kent Ryan, Detroit	6	65	0
	Don Hutson, Green Bay	6	24	0

**First season of professional football.*

ANNUAL PUNTING LEADERS

Year	Player, Team	No.	Avg.	Long
1997	Mark Royals, New Orleans, NFC	88	45.9	66
	Tom Tupa, New England, AFC	78	45.8	73
1996	John Kidd, Miami, AFC	78	46.3	63
	Matt Turk, Washington, NFC	75	45.1	63
1995	Rick Tuten, Seattle, AFC	83	45.0	73
	Sean Landeta, St. Louis, NFC	83	44.3	63
1994	Sean Landeta, L.A. Rams, NFC	78	44.8	62
	Jeff Gossett, L.A. Raiders, AFC	77	43.9	65
1993	Greg Montgomery, Houston, AFC	54	45.6	77
	Jim Arnold, Detroit, NFC	72	44.5	68
1992	Greg Montgomery, Houston, AFC	53	46.9	66
	Harry Newsome, Minnesota, NFC	72	45.0	84
1991	Reggie Roby, Miami, AFC	54	45.7	64
	Harry Newsome, Minnesota, AFC	68	45.5	65
1990	Mike Horan, Denver, AFC	58	44.4	67
	Sean Landeta, N.Y. Giants, NFC	75	44.1	67
1989	Rich Camarillo, Phoenix, NFC	76	43.4	58
	Greg Montgomery, Hounton, AFC	56	43.3	63
1988	Harry Newsome, Pittsburgh, AFC	65	45.4	62
	Jim Arnold, Detroit, NFC	97	42.4	69
1987	Rick Donnelly, Atlanta, NFC	61	44.0	62
	Ralf Mojsiejenko, San Diego, AFC	67	42.9	57
1986	Rohn Stark, Indianapolis, AFC	76	45.2	63
	Sean Landeta, N.Y. Giants, NFC	79	44.8	61
1985	Rohn Stark, Indianapolis, AFC	78	45.9	68
	*Rick Donnelly, Atlanta, NFC	59	43.6	68
1984	Jim Arnold, Kansas City, AFC	98	44.9	63
	*Brian Hansen, New Orleans, NFC	69	43.8	66
1983	Rohn Stark, Baltimore, AFC	91	45.3	68
	Frank Garcia, Tampa Bay, NFC	95	42.2	64
1982	Luke Prestridge, Denver, AFC	45	45.0	65
	Carl Birdsong, St. Louis, NFC	54	43.8	65
1981	Pat McInally, Cincinnati, AFC	72	45.4	62
	Tom Skladany, Detroit, NFC	64	43.5	74
1980	Dave Jennings, N.Y. Giants, NFC	94	44.8	63
	Luke Prestridge, Denver, AFC	70	43.9	57
1979	*Bob Grupp, Kansas City, AFC	89	43.6	74
	Dave Jennings, N.Y. Giants, NFC	104	42.7	72
1978	Pat McInally, Cincinnati, AFC	91	43.1	65
	*Tom Skladany, Detroit, NFC	86	42.5	63
1977	Ray Guy, Oakland, AFC	59	43.3	74
	Tom Blanchard, New Orleans, NFC	82	42.4	66
1976	Marv Bateman, Buffalo, AFC	86	42.8	78
	John James, Atlanta, NFC	101	42.1	67
1975	Ray Guy, Oakland, AFC	68	43.8	64
	Herman Weaver, Detroit, NFC	80	42.0	61
1974	Ray Guy, Oakland, AFC	74	42.2	66
	Tom Blanchard, New Orleans, NFC	88	42.1	71
1973	Jerrel Wilson, Kansas City, AFC	80	45.5	68
	*Tom Wittum, San Francisco, NFC	79	43.7	62
1972	Jerrel Wilson, Kansas City, AFC	66	44.8	69
	Dave Chapple, Los Angeles, NFC	53	44.2	70
1971	Dave Lewis, Cincinnati, AFC	72	44.8	56
	Tom McNeill, Philadelphia, NFC	73	42.0	64
1970	Dave Lewis, Cincinnati, AFC	79	46.2	63
	*Julian Fagan, New Orleans, NFC	77	42.5	64
1969	David Lee, Baltimore, NFL	57	45.3	66
	Dennis Partee, San Diego, AFL	71	44.6	62
1968	Jerrel Wilson, Kansas City, AFL	63	45.1	70
	Billy Lothridge, Atlanta, NFL	75	44.3	70
1967	Bob Scarpitto, Denver, AFL	105	44.9	73
	Billy Lothridge, Atlanta, NFL	87	43.7	62
1966	Bob Scarpitto, Denver, AFL	76	45.8	70
	*David Lee, Baltimore, NFL	49	45.6	64
1965	Gary Collins, Cleveland, NFL	65	46.7	71
	Jerrel Wilson, Kansas City, AFL	69	45.4	64
1964	Bobby Walden, Minnesota, NFL	72	46.4	73
	Jim Fraser, Denver, AFL	73	44.2	67
1963	Yale Lary, Detroit, NFL	35	48.9	73
	Jim Fraser, Denver, AFL	81	44.4	66
1962	Tommy Davis, San Francisco, NFL	48	45.6	82
	Jim Fraser, Denver, AFL	55	43.6	75
1961	Yale Lary, Detroit, NFL	52	48.4	71
	Billy Atkins, Buffalo, AFL	85	44.5	70
1960	Jerry Norton, St. Louis, NFL	39	45.6	62
	*Paul Maguire, L.A. Chargers, AFL	43	40.5	61
1959	Yale Lary, Detroit	45	47.1	67
1958	Sam Baker, Washington	48	45.4	64
1957	Don Chandler, N.Y. Giants	60	44.6	61
1956	Norm Van Brocklin, Los Angeles	48	43.1	72
1955	Norm Van Brocklin, Los Angeles	60	44.6	61
1954	Pat Brady, Pittsburgh	66	43.2	72
1953	Pat Brady, Pittsburgh	80	46.9	64
1952	Horace Gillom, Cleveland	61	45.7	73
1951	Horace Gillom, Cleveland	73	45.5	66
1950	*Fred (Curly) Morrison, Chi. Bears	57	43.3	65
1949	*Mike Boyda, N.Y. Bulldogs	56	44.2	61
1948	Joe Muha, Philadelphia	57	47.3	82
1947	Jack Jacobs, Green Bay	57	43.5	74
1946	Roy McKay, Green Bay	64	42.7	64
1945	Roy McKay, Green Bay	44	41.2	73
1944	Frank Sinkwich, Detroit	45	41.0	73
1943	Sammy Baugh, Washington	50	45.9	81

Year	Player, Team	No.	Avg.	Long
1942	Sammy Baugh, Washington	37	48.2	74
1941	Sammy Baugh, Washington	30	48.7	75
1940	Sammy Baugh, Washington	35	51.4	85
1939	*Parker Hall, Cleveland	58	40.8	80

First season of professional football.

ANNUAL PUNT RETURN LEADERS

Year	Player, Team	No.	Yards	Avg.	Long	TD
1997	Jermaine Lewis, Baltimore, AFC	28	437	15.6	89	2
	David Palmer, Minnesota, NFC	34	444	13.1	57	0
1996	Desmond Howard, Green Bay, NFC	58	875	15.1	92	3
	Darrien Gordon, San Diego, AFC	36	537	14.9	81	1
1995	David Palmer, Minnesota, NFC	26	342	13.2	74	1
	Andre Coleman, San Diego, AFC	28	326	11.6	88	1
1994	Brian Mitchell, Washington, NFC	32	452	14.1	78	2
	Darrien Gordon, San Diego, AFC	36	475	13.2	90	2
1993	*Tyrone Hughes, New Orleans, NFC	37	503	13.6	83	2
	Eric Metcalf, Cleveland, AFC	36	464	12.9	91	2
1992	Johnny Bailey, Phoenix, NFC	20	263	13.2	65	0
	Rod Woodson, Pittsburgh, AFC	32	364	11.4	80	1
1991	Mel Gray, Detroit, NFC	25	385	15.4	78	1
	Rod Woodson, Pittsburgh, AFC	28	320	11.4	40	0
1990	Clarence Verdin, Indianapolis, AFC	31	396	12.8	36	0
	*Johnny Bailey, Chicago, NFC	36	399	11.1	95	1
1989	Walter Stanley, Detroit, NFC	36	496	13.8	74	0
	Clarence Verdin, Indianapolis, AFC	23	296	12.9	49	1
1988	John Taylor, San Francisco, NFC	44	556	12.6	95	2
	JoJo Townsell, N.Y. Jets, AFC	35	409	11.7	59	1
1987	Mel Gray, New Orleans, NFC	24	352	14.7	80	0
	Bobby Joe Edmonds, Seattle, AFC	20	251	12.6	40	0
1986	*Bobby Joe Edmonds, Seattle, AFC	34	419	12.3	75	1
	*Vai Sikahema, St. Louis, NFC	43	522	12.1	71	2
1985	Irving Fryar, New England, AFC	37	520	14.1	85	2
	Henry Ellard, L.A. Rams, NFC	37	501	13.5	80	1
1984	Mike Martin, Cincinnati, AFC	24	376	15.7	55	0
	Henry Ellard, L.A. Rams, NFC	30	403	13.4	83	2
1983	*Henry Ellard, L.A. Rams, NFC	16	217	13.6	72	1
	Kirk Springs, N.Y. Jets, AFC	23	287	12.5	76	1
1982	Rick Upchurch, Denver, AFC	15	242	16.1	78	2
	Billy Johnson, Atlanta, NFC	24	273	11.4	71	0
1981	LeRoy Irvin, Los Angeles, NFC	46	615	13.4	84	3
	*James Brooks, San Diego, AFC	22	290	13.2	42	0
1980	J.T. Smith, Kansas City, AFC	40	581	14.5	75	2
	*Kenny Johnson, Atlanta, NFC	23	281	12.2	56	0
1979	John Sciarra, Philadelphia, NFC	16	182	11.4	38	0
	*Tony Nathan, Miami, AFC	28	306	10.9	86	1
1978	Rick Upchurch, Denver, AFC	36	493	13.7	75	1
	Jackie Wallace, Los Angeles, NFC	52	618	11.9	58	0
1977	Billy Johnson, Houston, AFC	35	539	15.4	87	2
	Larry Marshall, Philadelphia, NFC	46	489	10.6	48	0
1976	Rick Upchurch, Denver, AFC	39	536	13.7	92	4
	Eddie Brown, Washington, NFC	48	646	13.5	71	1
1975	Billy Johnson, Houston, AFC	40	612	15.3	83	3
	Terry Metcalf, St. Louis, NFC	23	285	12.4	69	1
1974	Lemar Parrish, Cincinnati, AFC	18	338	18.8	90	2
	Dick Jauron, Detroit, NFC	17	286	16.8	58	0
1973	Bruce Taylor, San Francisco, NFC	15	207	13.8	61	0
	Ron Smith, San Diego, AFC	27	352	13.0	84	2
1972	Ken Ellis, Green Bay, NFC	14	215	15.4	80	1
	Chris Farasopoulos, N.Y. Jets, AFC	17	179	10.5	65	1
1971	Les (Speedy) Duncan, Washington, NFC	22	233	10.6	33	0
	Leroy Kelly, Cleveland, AFC	30	292	9.7	74	0
1970	Ed Podolak, Kansas City, AFC	23	311	13.5	60	0
	*Bruce Taylor, San Francisco, NFC	43	516	12.0	76	0
1969	Alvin Haymond, Los Angeles, NFL	33	435	13.2	52	0
	*Bill Thompson, Denver, AFL	25	288	11.5	40	0
1968	Bob Hayes, Dallas, NFL	15	312	20.8	90	2
	Noland Smith, Kansas City, AFL	18	270	15.0	80	1
1967	Floyd Little, Denver, AFL	16	270	16.9	72	1
	Ben Davis, Cleveland, NFL	18	229	12.7	52	1
1966	Les (Speedy) Duncan, San Diego, AFL	18	238	13.2	81	1
	Johnny Roland, St. Louis, NFL	20	221	11.1	86	1
1965	Leroy Kelly, Cleveland, NFL	17	265	15.6	67	2
	Les (Speedy) Duncan, San Diego, AFL	30	464	15.5	66	2
1964	Bobby Jancik, Houston, AFL	12	220	18.3	82	1
	Tommy Watkins, Detroit, NFL	16	238	14.9	68	2
1963	Dick James, Washington, NFL	16	214	13.4	39	0
	Claude (Hoot) Gibson, Oakland, AFL	26	307	11.8	85	2
1962	Dick Christy, N.Y. Titans, AFL	15	250	16.7	73	2
	Pat Studstill, Detroit, NFL	29	457	15.8	44	0
1961	Dick Christy, N.Y. Titans, AFL	18	383	21.3	70	2
	Willie Wood, Green Bay, NFL	14	225	16.1	72	2
1960	*Abner Haynes, Dall. Texans, AFL	14	215	15.4	46	0
	Abe Woodson, San Francisco, NFL	13	174	13.4	48	0
1959	Johnny Morris, Chi. Bears	14	171	12.2	78	1
1958	Jon Arnett, Los Angeles	18	223	12.4	58	0
1957	Bert Zagers, Washington	14	217	15.5	76	2
1956	Ken Konz, Cleveland	13	187	14.4	65	1
1955	Ollie Matson, Chi. Cardinals	13	245	18.8	78	2
1954	*Veryl Switzer, Green Bay	24	306	12.8	93	1
1953	Charley Trippi, Chi. Cardinals	21	239	11.4	38	0
1952	Jack Christiansen, Detroit	15	322	21.5	79	2
1951	Claude (Buddy) Young, N.Y. Yanks	12	231	19.3	79	1
1950	*Herb Rich, Baltimore	12	276	23.0	86	1
1949	Verda (Vitamin T) Smith, Los Angeles	27	427	15.8	85	1
1948	George McAfee, Chi. Bears	30	417	13.9	60	1
1947	*Walt Slater, Pittsburgh	28	435	15.5	33	0
1946	Bill Dudley, Pittsburgh	27	385	14.3	52	0
1945	*Dave Ryan, Detroit	15	220	14.7	56	0
1944	*Steve Van Buren, Philadelphia	15	230	15.3	55	1
1943	Andy Farkas, Washington	15	168	11.2	33	0
1942	Merlyn Condit, Brooklyn	21	210	10.0	23	0
1941	Byron (Whizzer) White, Detroit	19	262	13.8	64	0

First season of professional football.

ANNUAL KICKOFF RETURN LEADERS

Year	Player, Team	No.	Yards	Avg.	Long	TD
1997	Michael Bates, Carolina, NFC	47	1,281	27.3	56	0
	Aaron Glenn, N.Y. Jets, AFC	28	741	26.5	96	1
1996	Michael Bates, Carolina, NFC	33	998	30.2	93	1
	Tamarick Vanover, Kansas City, AFC	33	854	25.9	97	1
1995	Ron Carpenter, N.Y. Jets, AFC	20	553	27.7	58	0
	Brian Mitchell, Washington, NFC	55	1,408	25.6	59	0
1994	Mel Gray, Detroit, NFC	45	1,276	28.4	102	3
	Randy Baldwin, Cleveland, AFC	28	753	26.9	85	1
1993	Robert Brooks, Green Bay, NFC	23	611	26.6	95	1
	*Raghib Ismail, L.A. Raiders, AFC	25	605	24.2	66	0
1992	Jon Vaughn, New England, AFC	20	564	28.2	100	1
	Deion Sanders, Atlanta, NFC	40	1,067	26.7	99	2
1991	Mel Gray, Detroit, NFC	36	929	25.8	71	0
	Nate Lewis, San Diego, AFC	23	578	25.1	95	1
1990	Kevin Clark, Denver, AFC	20	505	25.3	75	0
	David Meggett, N.Y. Giants, NFC	21	492	23.4	58	0
1989	Rod Woodson, Pittsburgh, AFC	36	982	27.3	84	1
	Mel Gray, Detroit, NFC	24	640	26.7	57	0
1988	*Tim Brown, L.A. Raiders, AFC	41	1,098	26.8	97	1
	Donnie Elder, Tampa Bay, NFC	34	772	22.7	51	0
1987	Sylvester Stamps, Atlanta, NFC	24	660	27.5	97	1
	Paul Palmer, Kansas City, AFC	38	923	24.3	95	2
1986	Dennis Gentry, Chicago, NFC	20	576	28.8	91	1
	Lupe Sanchez, Pittsburgh, AFC	25	591	23.6	64	0
1985	Ron Brown, L.A. Rams, NFC	28	918	32.8	98	3
	Glen Young, Cleveland, AFC	35	898	25.7	63	0
1984	*Bobby Humphery, N.Y. Jets, AFC	22	675	30.7	97	1
	Barry Redden, L.A. Rams, NFC	23	530	23.0	40	0
1983	Fulton Walker, Miami, AFC	36	962	26.7	78	0
	Darrin Nelson, Minnesota, NFC	18	445	24.7	50	0
1982	*Mike Mosley, Buffalo, AFC	18	487	27.1	66	0
	Alvin Hall, Detroit, NFC	16	426	26.6	96	1
1981	Mike Nelms, Washington, NFC	37	1,099	29.7	84	0
	Carl Roaches, Houston, AFC	28	769	27.5	96	1
1980	Horace Ivory, New England, AFC	36	992	27.6	98	1
	Rich Mauti, New Orleans, NFC	31	798	25.7	52	0
1979	Larry Brunson, Oakland, AFC	17	441	25.9	89	0
	Jimmy Edwards, Minnesota, NFC	44	1,103	25.1	83	0
1978	Steve Odom, Green Bay, NFC	25	677	27.1	95	1
	*Keith Wright, Cleveland, AFC	30	789	26.3	86	0
1977	*Raymond Clayborn, New England, AFC	28	869	31.0	101	3
	*Wilbert Montgomery, Philadelphia, NFC	23	619	26.9	99	1
1976	*Duriel Harris, Miami, AFC	17	559	32.9	69	0
	Cullen Bryant, Los Angeles, NFC	16	459	28.7	90	1
1975	*Walter Payton, Chicago, NFC	14	444	31.7	70	0
	Harold Hart, Oakland, AFC	17	518	30.5	102	1
1974	Terry Metcalf, St. Louis, NFC	20	623	31.2	94	1
	Greg Pruitt, Cleveland, AFC	22	606	27.5	88	1
1973	Carl Garrett, Chicago, NFC	16	486	30.4	67	0
	*Wallace Francis, Buffalo, AFC	23	687	29.9	101	2
1972	Ron Smith, Chicago, NFC	30	924	30.8	94	1
	*Bruce Laird, Baltimore, AFC	29	843	29.1	73	0
1971	Travis Williams, Los Angeles, NFC	25	743	29.7	105	1
	Eugene (Mercury) Morris, Miami, AFC	15	423	28.2	94	1
1970	Jim Duncan, Baltimore, AFC	20	707	35.4	99	1
	Cecil Turner, Chicago, NFC	23	752	32.7	96	4
1969	Bobby Williams, Detroit, NFL	17	563	33.1	96	1
	*Bill Thompson, Denver, AFL	18	513	28.5	63	0

Year	Player, Team					
1968	Preston Pearson, Baltimore, NFL	15	527	35.1	102	2
	*George Atkinson, Oakland, AFL	32	802	25.1	60	0
1967	*Travis Williams, Green Bay, NFL	18	739	41.1	104	4
	*Zeke Moore, Houston, AFL	14	405	28.9	92	1
1966	Gale Sayers, Chicago, NFL	23	718	31.2	93	2
	*Goldie Sellers, Denver, AFL	19	541	28.5	100	2
1965	Tommy Watkins, Detroit, NFL	17	584	34.4	94	0
	Abner Haynes, Denver, AFL	34	901	26.5	60	0
1964	*Clarence Childs, N.Y. Giants, NFL	34	987	29.0	100	1
	Bo Roberson, Oakland, AFL	36	975	27.1	59	0
1963	Abe Woodson, San Francisco, NFL	29	935	32.2	103	3
	Bobby Jancik, Houston, AFL	45	1,317	29.3	53	0
1962	Abe Woodson, San Francisco, NFL	37	1,157	31.3	79	0
	*Bobby Jancik, Houston, AFL	24	826	30.3	61	0
1961	Dick Bass, Los Angeles, NFL	23	698	30.3	64	0
	*Dave Grayson, Dall. Texans, AFL	16	453	28.3	73	0
1960	*Tom Moore, Green Bay, NFL	12	397	33.1	84	0
	Ken Hall, Houston, AFL	19	594	31.3	104	1
1959	Abe Woodson, San Francisco	13	382	29.4	105	1
1958	Ollie Matson, Chi. Cardinals	14	497	35.5	101	2
1957	*Jon Arnett, Los Angeles	18	504	28.0	98	1
1956	*Tom Wilson, Los Angeles	15	477	31.8	103	1
1955	Al Carmichael, Green Bay	14	418	29.9	100	1
1954	Billy Reynolds, Cleveland	14	413	29.5	51	0
1953	Joe Arenas, San Francisco	16	551	34.4	82	0
1952	Lynn Chandnois, Pittsburgh	17	599	35.2	93	2
1951	Lynn Chandnois, Pittsburgh	12	390	32.5	55	0
1950	Verda (Vitamin T) Smith, Los Angeles	22	742	33.7	97	3
1949	*Don Doll, Detroit	21	536	25.5	56	0
1948	*Joe Scott, N.Y. Giants	20	569	28.5	99	1
1947	Eddie Saenz, Washington	29	797	27.5	94	2
1946	Abe Karnofsky, Boston	21	599	28.5	97	1
1945	Steve Van Buren, Philadelphia	13	373	28.7	98	1
1944	Bob Thurbon, Card.-Pitt.	12	291	24.3	55	0
1943	Ken Heineman, Brooklyn	16	444	27.8	69	0
1942	Marshall Goldberg, Chi. Cardinals	15	393	26.2	95	1
1941	Marshall Goldberg, Chi. Cardinals	12	290	24.2	41	0

First season of professional football.

ANNUAL LEADERS IN SACKS (SINCE 1982)

Year	Player, Team	Sacks
1997	John Randle, Minnesota, NFC	15.5
	Bruce Smith, Buffalo, AFC	14
1996	Kevin Greene, Carolina, NFC	14.5
	Michael McCrary, Seattle, AFC	13.5
	Bruce Smith, Buffalo, AFC	13.5
1995	Bryce Paup, Buffalo, AFC	17.5
	William Fuller, Philadelphia, NFC	13
	Wayne Martin, New Orleans, NFC	13
1994	Kevin Greene, Pittsburgh, AFC	14
	Ken Harvey, Washington, NFC	13.5
	John Randle, Minnesota, NFC	13.5
1993	Neil Smith, Kansas City, AFC	15
	Renaldo Turnbull, New Orleans, NFC	13
	Reggie White, Green Bay, NFC	13
1992	Clyde Simmons, Philadelphia, NFC	19
	Leslie O'Neal, San Diego, AFC	17
1991	Pat Swilling, New Orleans, NFC	17
	William Fuller, Houston, AFC	15
1990	Derrick Thomas, Kansas City, AFC	20
	Charles Haley, San Francisco, NFC	16
1989	Chris Doleman, Minnesota, NFC	21
	Lee Williams, San Diego, AFC	14
1988	Reggie White, Philadelphia, NFC	18
	G. Townsend, L.A. Raiders, AFC	11.5
1987	Reggie White, Philadelphia, NFC	21
	Andre Tippett, New England, AFC	12.5
1986	Lawrence Taylor, N.Y. Giants, NFC	20.5
	Sean Jones, L.A. Raiders, AFC	15.5
1985	Richard Dent, Chicago, NFC	17
	Andre Tippett, New England, AFC	16.5
1984	Mark Gastineau, N.Y. Jets, AFC	22
	Richard Dent, Chicago, NFC	17.5
1983	Mark Gastineau, N.Y. Jets, AFC	19
	Fred Dean, San Francisco, NFC	17.5
1982	Doug Martin, Minnesota, NFC	11.5
	Jesse Baker, Houston, AFC	7.5

POINTS SCORED

Year	Team	Points
1997	Denver, AFC	472
	Green Bay, NFC	422
1996	Green Bay, NFC	456
	New England, AFC	418
1995	San Francisco, NFC	457
	Pittsburgh, AFC	407
1994	San Francisco, NFC	505
	Miami, AFC	389
1993	San Francisco, NFC	473
	Denver, AFC	373
1992	San Francisco, NFC	431
	Buffalo, AFC	381
1991	Washington, NFC	485
	Buffalo, AFC	458
1990	Buffalo, AFC	428
	Philadelphia, NFC	396
1989	San Francisco, NFC	442
	Buffalo, AFC	409
1988	Cincinnati, AFC	448
	L.A. Rams, NFC	407
1987	San Francisco, NFC	459
	Cleveland, AFC	390
1986	Miami, AFC	430
	Minnesota, NFC	398
1985	San Diego, AFC	467
	Chicago, NFC	456
1984	Miami, AFC	513
	San Francisco, NFC	475
1983	Washington, NFC	541
	L.A. Raiders, AFC	442
1982	San Diego, AFC	288
	Dallas, NFC	226
	Green Bay, NFC	226
1981	San Diego, AFC	478
	Atlanta, NFC	426
1980	Dallas, NFC	454
	New England, AFC	441
1979	Pittsburgh, AFC	416
	Dallas, NFC	371
1978	Dallas, NFC	384
	Miami, AFC	372
1977	Oakland, AFC	351
	Dallas, NFC	345
1976	Baltimore, AFC	417
	Los Angeles, NFC	351
1975	Buffalo, AFC	420
	Minnesota, NFC	377
1974	Oakland, AFC	355
	Washington, NFC	320
1973	Los Angeles, NFC	388
	Denver, AFC	354
1972	Miami, AFC	385
	San Francisco, NFC	353
1971	Dallas, NFC	406
	Oakland, AFC	344
1970	San Francisco, NFC	352
	Baltimore, AFC	321
1969	Minnesota, NFL	379
	Oakland, AFL	377
1968	Oakland, AFL	453
	Dallas, NFL	431
1967	Oakland, AFL	468
	Los Angeles, NFL	398
1966	Kansas City, AFL	448
	Dallas, NFL	445
1965	San Francisco, NFL	421
	San Diego, AFL	340
1964	Baltimore, NFL	428
	Buffalo, AFL	400
1963	N.Y. Giants, NFL	448
	San Diego, AFL	399
1962	Green Bay, NFL	415
	Dall. Texans, AFL	389
1961	Houston, AFL	513
	Green Bay, NFL	391
1960	N.Y. Titans, AFL	382
	Cleveland, NFL	362
1959	Baltimore	374
1958	Baltimore	381
1957	Los Angeles	307
1956	Chi. Bears	363
1955	Cleveland	349
1954	Detroit	337
1953	San Francisco	372
1952	Los Angeles	349
1951	Los Angeles	392
1950	Los Angeles	466
1949	Philadelphia	364
1948	Chi. Cardinals	395
1947	Chi. Bears	363
1946	Chi. Bears	289
1945	Philadelphia	272
1944	Philadelphia	267
1943	Chi. Bears	303
1942	Chi. Bears	376
1941	Chi. Bears	396
1940	Washington	245
1939	Chi. Bears	298
1938	Green Bay	223
1937	Green Bay	220
1936	Green Bay	248
1935	Chi. Bears	192
1934	Chi. Bears	286
1933	N.Y. Giants	244
1932	Chicago Bears	160

TOTAL YARDS GAINED

Year	Team	Yards
1997	Denver, AFC	5,872
	Detroit, NFC	5,798
1996	Denver, AFC	5,791
	Philadelphia, NFC	5,627
1995	Detroit, NFC	6,113
	Denver, AFC	6,040
1994	Miami, AFC	6,078
	San Francisco, NFC	6,060
1993	San Francisco, NFC	6,435
	Miami, AFC	5,812
1992	San Francisco, NFC	6,195
	Buffalo, AFC	5,893
1991	Buffalo, AFC	6,252
	San Francisco, NFC	5,858
1990	Houston, AFC	6,222
	San Francisco, NFC	5,895
1989	San Francisco, NFC	6,268
	Cincinnati, AFC	6,101
1988	Cincinnati, AFC	6,057
	San Francisco, NFC	5,900
1987	San Francisco, NFC	5,987
	Denver, AFC	5,624
1986	Cincinnati, AFC	6,490
	San Francisco, NFC	6,082
1985	San Diego, AFC	6,535
	San Francisco, NFC	5,920
1984	Miami, AFC	6,936
	San Francisco, NFC	6,366
1983	San Diego, AFC	6,197
	Green Bay, NFC	6,172
1982	San Diego, AFC	4,048
	San Francisco, NFC	3,242
1981	San Diego, AFC	6,744
	Detroit, NFC	5,933
1980	San Diego, AFC	6,410
	Los Angeles, NFC	6,006
1979	Pittsburgh, AFC	6,258
	Dallas, NFC	5,968
1978	New England, AFC	5,965
	Dallas, NFC	5,959
1977	Dallas, NFC	4,812
	Oakland, AFC	4,736
1976	Baltimore, AFC	5,236
	St. Louis, NFC	5,136
1975	Buffalo, AFC	5,467
	Dallas, NFC	5,025
1974	Dallas, NFC	4,983
	Oakland, AFC	4,718
1973	Los Angeles, NFC	4,906
	Oakland, AFC	4,773
1972	Miami, AFC	5,036
	N.Y. Giants, NFC	4,483
1971	Dallas, NFC	5,035
	San Diego, AFC	4,738
1970	Oakland, AFC	4,829
	San Francisco, NFC	4,503

1969	Dallas, NFL	5,122
	Oakland, AFL	5,036
1968	Oakland, AFL	5,696
	Dallas, NFL	5,117
1967	N.Y. Jets, AFL	5,152
	Baltimore, NFL	5,008
1966	Dallas, NFL	5,145
	Kansas City, AFL	5,114
1965	San Francisco, NFL	5,270
	San Diego, AFL	5,188
1964	Buffalo, AFL	5,206
	Baltimore, NFL	4,779
1963	San Diego, AFL	5,153
	N.Y. Giants, NFL	5,024
1962	N.Y. Giants, NFL	5,005
	Houston, AFL	4,971
1961	Houston, AFL	6,288
	Philadelphia, NFL	5,112
1960	Houston, AFL	4,936
	Baltimore, NFL	4,245
1959	Baltimore	4,458
1958	Baltimore	4,539
1957	Los Angeles	4,143
1956	Chi. Bears	4,537
1955	Chi. Bears	4,316
1954	Los Angeles	5,187
1953	Philadelphia	4,811
1952	Cleveland	4,352
1951	Los Angeles	5,506
1950	Los Angeles	5,420
1949	Chi. Bears	4,873
1948	Chi. Cardinals	4,705
1947	Chi. Bears	5,053
1946	Los Angeles	3,793
1945	Washington	3,549
1944	Chi. Bears	3,239
1943	Chi. Bears	4,045
1942	Chi. Bears	3,900
1941	Chi. Bears	4,265
1940	Green Bay	3,400
1939	Chi. Bears	3,988
1938	Green Bay	3,037
1937	Green Bay	3,201
1936	Detroit	3,703
1935	Chi. Bears	3,454
1934	Chi. Bears	3,900
1933	N.Y. Giants	2,973
1932	Chi. Bears	2,755

YARDS RUSHING

Year	Team	Yards
1997	Pittsburgh, AFC	2,479
	Detroit, NFC	2,464
1996	Denver, AFC	2,362
	Washington, NFC	1,910
1995	Kansas City, AFC	2,222
	Dallas, NFC	2,201
1994	Pittsburgh, AFC	2,180
	Detroit, NFC	2,080
1993	N.Y. Giants, NFC	2,210
	Seattle, AFC	2,015
1992	Buffalo, AFC	2,436
	Philadelphia, NFC	2,388
1991	Buffalo, AFC	2,381
	Minnesota, NFC	2,201
1990	Philadelphia, NFC	2,556
	San Diego, AFC	2,257
1989	Cincinnati, AFC	2,483
	Chicago, NFC	2,287
1988	Cincinnati, AFC	2,710
	San Francisco, NFC	2,523
1987	San Francisco, NFC	2,237
	L.A. Raiders, AFC	2,197
1986	Chicago, NFC	2,700
	Cincinnati, AFC	2,533
1985	Chicago, NFC	2,761
	Indianapolis, AFC	2,439
1984	Chicago, NFC	2,974
	N.Y. Jets, AFC	2,189
1983	Chicago, NFC	2,727
	Baltimore, AFC	2,695
1982	Buffalo, AFC	1,371
	Dallas, NFC	1,313
1981	Detroit, NFC	2,795
	Kansas City, AFC	2,633
1980	Los Angeles, NFC	2,799
	Houston, AFC	2,635
1979	N.Y. Jets, AFC	2,646
	St. Louis, NFC	2,582
1978	New England, AFC	3,165
	Dallas, NFC	2,783
1977	Chicago, NFC	2,811
	Oakland, AFC	2,627
1976	Pittsburgh, AFC	2,971
	Los Angeles, NFC	2,528
1975	Buffalo, AFC	2,974
	Dallas, NFC	2,432
1974	Dallas, NFC	2,454
	Pittsburgh, AFC	2,417
1973	Buffalo, AFC	3,088
	Los Angeles, NFC	2,925
1972	Miami, AFC	2,960
	Chicago, NFC	2,360
1971	Miami, AFC	2,429
	Detroit, NFC	2,376
1970	Dallas, NFC	2,300
	Miami, AFC	2,082
1969	Dallas, NFL	2,276
	Kansas City, AFL	2,220
1968	Chicago, NFL	2,377
	Kansas City, AFL	2,227
1967	Cleveland, NFL	2,139
	Houston, AFL	2,122
1966	Kansas City, AFL	2,274
	Cleveland, NFL	2,166
1965	Cleveland, NFL	2,331
	San Diego, AFL	2,085
1964	Green Bay, NFL	2,276
	Buffalo, AFL	2,040
1963	Cleveland, NFL	2,639
	San Diego, AFL	2,203
1962	Buffalo, AFL	2,480
	Green Bay, NFL	2,460
1961	Green Bay, NFL	2,350
	Dall. Texans, AFL	2,189
1960	St. Louis, NFL	2,356
	Oakland, AFL	2,056
1959	Cleveland	2,149
1958	Cleveland	2,526
1957	Los Angeles	2,142
1956	Chi. Bears	2,468
1955	Chi. Bears	2,388
1954	San Francisco	2,498
1953	San Francisco	2,230
1952	San Francisco	1,905
1951	Chi. Bears	2,408
1950	N.Y. Giants	2,336
1949	Philadelphia	2,607
1948	Chi. Cardinals	2,560
1947	Los Angeles	2,171
1946	Green Bay	1,765
1945	Cleveland	1,714
1944	Philadelphia	1,661
1943	Phil-Pitt	1,730
1942	Chi. Bears	1,881
1941	Chi. Bears	2,263
1940	Chi. Bears	1,818
1939	Chi. Bears	2,043
1938	Detroit	1,893
1937	Detroit	2,074
1936	Detroit	2,885
1935	Chi. Bears	2,096
1934	Chi. Bears	2,847
1933	Boston	2,260
1932	Chi. Bears	1,770

YARDS PASSING

Leadership in this category has been based on net yards since 1952.

Year	Team	Yards
1997	Seattle, AFC	3,959
	Green Bay, NFC	3,705
1996	Jacksonville, AFC	4,110
	Philadelphia, NFC	3,745
1995	San Francisco, NFC	4,608
	Miami, AFC	4,210
1994	New England, AFC	4,444
	Minnesota, NFC	4,324
1993	Miami, AFC	4,353
	San Francisco, NFC	4,302
1992	Houston, AFC	4,029
	San Francisco, NFC	3,880
1991	Houston, AFC	4,621
	San Francisco, NFC	3,997
1990	Houston, AFC	4,805
	San Francisco, NFC	4,177
1989	Washington, NFC	4,349
	Miami, AFC	4,216
1988	Miami, AFC	4,516
	Washington, NFC	4,136
1987	Miami, AFC	3,876
	San Francisco, NFC	3,750
1986	Miami, AFC	4,779
	San Francisco, NFC	4,096
1985	San Diego, AFC	4,870
	Dallas, NFC	3,861
1984	Miami, AFC	5,018
	St. Louis, NFC	4,257
1983	San Diego, AFC	4,661
	Green Bay, NFC	4,365
1982	San Diego, AFC	2,927
	San Francisco, NFC	2,502
1981	San Diego, AFC	4,739
	Minnesota, NFC	4,333
1980	San Diego, AFC	4,531
	Minnesota, NFC	3,688
1979	San Diego, AFC	3,915
	San Francisco, NFC	3,641
1978	San Diego, AFC	3,375
	Minnesota, NFC	3,243
1977	Buffalo, AFC	2,530
	St. Louis, NFC	2,499
1976	Baltimore, AFC	2,933
	Minnesota, NFC	2,855
1975	Cincinnati, AFC	3,241
	Washington, NFC	2,917
1974	Washington, NFC	2,978
	Cincinnati, AFC	2,804
1973	Philadelphia, NFC	2,998
	Denver, AFC	2,519
1972	N.Y. Jets, AFC	2,777
	San Francisco, NFC	2,735
1971	San Diego, AFC	3,134
	Dallas, NFC	2,786
1970	San Francisco, NFC	2,923
	Oakland, AFC	2,865
1969	Oakland, AFL	3,271
	San Francisco, NFL	3,158
1968	San Diego, AFL	3,623
	Dallas, NFL	3,026
1967	N.Y. Jets, AFL	3,845
	Washington, NFL	3,730
1966	N.Y. Jets, AFL	3,464
	Dallas, NFL	3,023
1965	San Francisco, NFL	3,487
	San Diego, AFL	3,103
1964	Houston, AFL	3,527
	Chicago, NFL	2,841
1963	Baltimore, NFL	3,296
	Houston, AFL	3,222
1962	Denver, AFL	3,404
	Philadelphia, NFL	3,385
1961	Houston, AFL	4,392
	Philadelphia, NFL	3,605
1960	Houston, AFL	3,203
	Baltimore, NFL	2,956
1959	Baltimore	2,753
1958	Pittsburgh	2,752
1957	Baltimore	2,388
1956	Los Angeles	2,419
1955	Philadelphia	2,472
1954	Chi. Bears	3,104
1953	Philadelphia	3,089
1952	Cleveland	2,566
1951	Los Angeles	3,296
1950	Los Angeles	3,709
1949	Chi. Bears	3,055
1948	Washington	2,861
1947	Washington	3,336
1946	Los Angeles	2,080
1945	Chi. Bears	1,857
1944	Washington	2,021
1943	Chi. Bears	2,310
1942	Green Bay	2,407
1941	Chi. Bears	2,002
1940	Washington	1,887
1939	Chi. Bears	1,965
1938	Washington	1,536
1937	Green Bay	1,398
1936	Green Bay	1,629
1935	Green Bay	1,449
1934	Green Bay	1,165
1933	N.Y. Giants	1,348
1932	Chi. Bears	1,013

FEWEST POINTS ALLOWED

Year	Team	Points
1997	Kansas City, AFC	232
	Tampa Bay, NFC	263
1996	Green Bay, NFC	210
	Pittsburgh, AFC	257
1995	Kansas City, AFC	241
	San Francisco, NFC	258
1994	Cleveland, AFC	204
	Dallas, NFC	248
1993	N.Y. Giants, NFC	205
	Houston, AFC	238
1992	New Orleans, NFC	202
	Pittsburgh, AFC	225
1991	New Orleans, NFC	211
	Denver, AFC	235
1990	N.Y. Giants, NFC	211
	Pittsburgh, AFC	240
1989	Denver, AFC	226
	N.Y. Giants, NFC	252
1988	Chicago, NFC	215
	Buffalo, AFC	237
1987	Indianapolis, AFC	238
	San Francisco, NFC	253
1986	Chicago, NFC	187
	Seattle, AFC	293
1985	Chicago, NFC	198
	N.Y. Jets, AFC	264
1984	San Francisco, NFC	227
	Denver, AFC	241
1983	Miami, AFC	250
	Detroit, NFC	286
1982	Washington, NFC	128
	Miami, AFC	131
1981	Philadelphia, NFC	221
	Miami, AFC	275
1980	Philadelphia, NFC	222
	Houston, AFC	251
1979	Tampa Bay, NFC	237
	San Diego, AFC	246
1978	Pittsburgh, AFC	195
	Dallas, NFC	208
1977	Atlanta, NFC	129
	Denver, AFC	148
1976	Pittsburgh, AFC	138
	Minnesota, NFC	176
1975	Los Angeles, NFC	135
	Pittsburgh, AFC	162
1974	Los Angeles, NFC	181
	Pittsburgh, AFC	189
1973	Miami, AFC	150
	Minnesota, NFC	168
1972	Miami, AFC	171
	Washington, NFC	218
1971	Minnesota, NFC	139
	Baltimore, AFC	140
1970	Minnesota, NFC	143
	Miami, AFC	228
1969	Minnesota, NFL	133
	Kansas City, AFL	177
1968	Baltimore, NFL	144
	Kansas City, AFL	170
1967	Los Angeles, NFL	196
	Houston, AFL	199
1966	Green Bay, NFL	163
	Buffalo, AFL	255

1965 Green Bay, NFL 224
Buffalo, AFL 226
1964 Baltimore, NFL 225
Buffalo, AFL 242
1963 Chicago, NFL 144
San Diego, AFL 255
1962 Green Bay, NFL 148
Dall. Texans, AFL 233
1961 San Diego, AFL 219
N.Y. Giants, NFL 220
1960 San Francisco, NFL 205
Dall. Texans, AFL 253
1959 N.Y. Giants 170
1958 N.Y. Giants 183
1957 Cleveland 172
1956 Cleveland 177
1955 Cleveland 218
1954 Cleveland 162
1953 Cleveland 162
1952 Detroit 192
1951 Cleveland 152
1950 Philadelphia 141
1949 Philadelphia 134
1948 Chi. Bears 151
1947 Green Bay 210
1946 Pittsburgh 117
1945 Washington 121
1944 N.Y. Giants 75
1943 Washington 137
1942 Chi. Bears 84
1941 N.Y. Giants 114
1940 Brooklyn 120
1939 N.Y. Giants 85
1938 N.Y. Giants 79
1937 Chi. Bears 100
1936 Chi. Bears 94
1935 Green Bay 96
N.Y. Giants 96
1934 Detroit 59
1933 Brooklyn 54
1932 Chi. Bears 44

FEWEST TOTAL YARDS ALLOWED

Year Team Yards
1997 San Francisco, NFC 4,013
Denver, AFC 4,671
1996 Greem Bay, NFC 4,156
Pittsburgh, AFC 4,362
1995 San Francisco, NFC 4,398
Kansas City, AFC 4,549
1994 Dallas, NFC 4,313
Pittsburgh, AFC 4,326
1993 Minnesota, NFC 4,406
Pittsburgh, AFC 4,531
1992 Dallas, NFC 3,931
Houston, AFC 4,211
1991 Philadelphia, NFC 3,549
Denver, AFC 4,549
1990 Pittsburgh, AFC 4,115
N.Y. Giants, NFC 4,206
1989 Minnesota, NFC 4,184
Kansas City, AFC 4,293
1988 Minnesota, NFC 4,091
Buffalo, AFC 4,578
1987 San Francisco, NFC 4,095
Cleveland, AFC 4,264
1986 Chicago, NFC 4,130
L.A. Raiders, AFC 4,804
1985 Chicago, NFC 4,135
L.A. Raiders, AFC 4,603
1984 Chicago, NFC 3,863
Cleveland, AFC 4,641
1983 Cincinnati, AFC 4,327
New Orleans, NFC 4,691
1982 Miami, AFC 2,312
Tampa Bay, NFC 2,442
1981 Philadelphia, NFC 4,447
N.Y. Jets, AFC 4,871
1980 Buffalo, AFC 4,101
Philadelphia, NFC 4,443
1979 Tampa Bay, NFC 3,949
Pittsburgh, AFC 4,270
1978 Los Angeles, NFC 3,893
Pittsburgh, AFC 4,168
1977 Dallas, NFC 3,213
New England, AFC 3,638
1976 Pittsburgh, AFC 3,323
San Francisco, NFC 3,562
1975 Minnesota, NFC 3,153
Oakland, AFC 3,629
1974 Pittsburgh, AFC 3,074
Washington, NFC 3,285
1973 Los Angeles, NFC 2,951
Oakland, AFC 3,160
1972 Miami, AFC 3,297
Green Bay, NFC 3,474
1971 Baltimore, AFC 2,852
Minnesota, NFC 3,406
1970 Minnesota, NFC 2,803
N.Y. Jets, AFC 3,655
1969 Minnesota, NFL 2,720
Kansas City, AFL 3,163
1968 Los Angeles, NFL 3,118
N.Y. Jets, AFL 3,363
1967 Oakland, AFL 3,294
Green Bay, NFL 3,300
1966 St. Louis, NFL 3,492
Oakland, AFL 3,910
1965 San Diego, AFL 3,262
Detroit, NFL 3,557
1964 Green Bay, NFL 3,179
Buffalo, AFL 3,878
1963 Chicago, NFL 3,176
Boston, AFL 3,834
1962 Detroit, NFL 3,217
Dall. Texans, AFL 3,951
1961 San Diego, AFL 3,726
Baltimore, NFL 3,782
1960 St. Louis, NFL 3,029
Buffalo, AFL 3,866
1959 N.Y. Giants 2,843
1958 Chi. Bears 3,066
1957 Pittsburgh 2,791
1956 N.Y. Giants 3,081
1955 Cleveland 2,841
1954 Cleveland 2,658
1953 Philadelphia 2,998
1952 Cleveland 3,075
1951 N.Y. Giants 3,250
1950 Cleveland 3,154
1949 Philadelphia 2,831
1948 Chi. Bears 2,931
1947 Green Bay 3,396
1946 Washington 2,451
1945 Philadelphia 2,073
1944 Philadelphia 1,943
1943 Chi. Bears 2,262
1942 Chi. Bears 1,703
1941 N.Y. Giants 2,368
1940 N.Y. Giants 2,219
1939 Washington 2,116
1938 N.Y. Giants 2,029
1937 Washington 2,123
1936 Boston 2,181
1935 Boston 1,996
1934 Chi. Cardinals 1,539
1933 Brooklyn 1,789

FEWEST RUSHING YARDS ALLOWED

Year Team Yards
1997 Pittsburgh, AFC 1,318
San Francisco, NFC 1,366
1996 Denver, AFC 1,331
Green Bay, NFC 1,416
1995 San Francisco, NFC 1,061
Pittsburgh, AFC 1,321
1994 Minnesota, NFC 1,090
San Diego, AFC 1,404
1993 Houston, AFC 1,273
Minnesota, NFC 1,536
1992 Dallas, NFC 1,244
Buffalo, AFC 1,395
San Diego, AFC 1,395
1991 Philadelphia, NFC 1,136
N.Y. Jets, AFC 1,442
1990 Philadelphia, NFC 1,169
San Diego, AFC 1,515
1989 New Orleans, NFC 1,326
Denver, AFC 1,580
1988 Chicago, NFC 1,326
Houston, AFC 1,592
1987 Chicago, NFC 1,413
Cleveland, AFC 1,433
1986 N.Y. Giants, NFC 1,284
Denver, AFC 1,651
1985 Chicago, NFC 1,319
N.Y. Jets, AFC 1,516
1984 Chicago, NFC 1,377
Pittsburgh, AFC 1,617
1983 Washington, NFC 1,289
Cincinnati, AFC 1,499
1982 Pittsburgh, AFC 762
Detroit, NFC 854
1981 Detroit, NFC 1,623
Kansas City, AFC 1,747
1980 Detroit, NFC 1,599
Cincinnati, AFC 1,680
1979 Denver, AFC 1,693
Tampa Bay, NFC 1,873
1978 Dallas, NFC 1,721
Pittsburgh, AFC 1,774
1977 Denver, AFC 1,531
Dallas, NFC 1,651
1976 Pittsburgh, AFC 1,457
Los Angeles, NFC 1,564
1975 Minnesota, NFC 1,532
Houston, AFC 1,680
1974 Los Angeles, NFC 1,302
New England, AFC 1,587
1973 Los Angeles, NFC 1,270
Oakland, AFC 1,470
1972 Dallas, NFC 1,515
Miami, AFC 1,548
1971 Baltimore, AFC 1,113
Dallas, NFC 1,144
1970 Detroit, NFC 1,152
N.Y. Jets, AFC 1,283
1969 Dallas, NFL 1,050
Kansas City, AFL 1,091
1968 Dallas, NFL 1,195
N.Y. Jets, AFL 1,195
1967 Dallas, NFL 1,081
Oakland, AFL 1,129
1966 Buffalo, AFL 1,051
Dallas, NFL 1,176
1965 San Diego, AFL 1,094
Los Angeles, NFL 1,409
1964 Buffalo, AFL 913
Los Angeles, NFL 1,501
1963 Boston, AFL 1,107
Chicago, NFL 1,442
1962 Detroit, NFL 1,231
Dall. Texans, AFL 1,250
1961 Boston, AFL 1,041
Pittsburgh, NFL 1,463
1960 St. Louis, NFL 1,212
Dall. Texans, AFL 1,338
1959 N.Y. Giants 1,261
1958 Baltimore 1,291
1957 Baltimore 1,174
1956 N.Y. Giants 1,443
1955 Cleveland 1,189
1954 Cleveland 1,050
1953 Philadelphia 1,117
1952 Detroit 1,145
1951 N.Y. Giants 913
1950 Detroit 1,367
1949 Chi. Bears 1,196
1948 Philadelphia 1,209
1947 Philadelphia 1,329
1946 Chi. Bears 1,060
1945 Philadelphia 817
1944 Philadelphia 558
1943 Phil-Pitt 793
1942 Chi. Bears 519
1941 Washington 1,042
1940 N.Y. Giants 977
1939 Chi. Bears 812
1938 Detroit 1,081
1937 Chi. Bears 933
1936 Boston 1,148
1935 Boston 998
1934 Chi. Cardinals 954
1933 Brooklyn 964

FEWEST PASSING YARDS ALLOWED

Leadership in this category has been based on net yards since 1952.

Year Team Yards
1997 Dallas, NFC 2,522
Indianapolis, AFC 2,820
1996 Green Bay, NFC 2,740
Pittsburgh, AFC 2,947
1995 N.Y. Jets, AFC 2,740
Philadelphia, NFC 2,816
1994 Dallas, NFC 2,752
Houston, AFC 2,795
1993 New Orleans, NFC 2,606
Cincinnati, AFC 2,798
1992 New Orleans, NFC 2,470
Kansas City, AFC 2,537
1991 Philadelphia, NFC 2,413
Denver, AFC 2,755
1990 Pittsburgh, AFC 2,500
Dallas, NFC 2,639
1989 Minnesota, NFC 2,501
Kansas City, AFC 2,527
1988 Kansas City, AFC 2,434
Minnesota, NFC 2,489
1987 San Francisco, NFC 2,484
L.A. Raiders, AFC 2,727
1986 St. Louis, NFC 2,637
New England, AFC 2,978
1985 Washington, NFC 2,746
Pittsburgh, AFC 2,783
1984 New Orleans, NFC 2,453
Cleveland, AFC 2,696
1983 New Orleans, NFC 2,691
Cincinnati, AFC 2,828
1982 Miami, AFC 1,027
Tampa Bay, NFC 1,384
1981 Philadelphia, NFC 2,696
Buffalo, AFC 2,870
1980 Washington, NFC 2,171
Buffalo, AFC 2,282
1979 Tampa Bay, NFC 2,076
Buffalo, AFC 2,530
1978 Buffalo, AFC 1,960
Los Angeles, NFC 2,048
1977 Atlanta, NFC 1,384
San Diego, AFC 1,725
1976 Minnesota, NFC 1,575
Cincinnati, AFC 1,758
1975 Minnesota, NFC 1,621
Cincinnati, AFC 1,729
1974 Pittsburgh, AFC 1,466
Atlanta, NFC 1,572
1973 Miami, AFC 1,290
Atlanta, NFC 1,430
1972 Minnesota, NFC 1,699
Cleveland, AFC 1,736
1971 Atlanta, NFC 1,638
Baltimore, AFC 1,739
1970 Minnesota, NFC 1,438
Kansas City, AFC 2,010
1969 Minnesota, NFL 1,631
Kansas City, AFL 2,072
1968 Houston, AFL 1,671
Green Bay, NFL 1,796
1967 Green Bay, NFL 1,377
Buffalo, AFL 1,825
1966 Green Bay, NFL 1,959
Oakland, AFL 2,118
1965 Green Bay, NFL 1,981
San Diego, AFL 2,168
1964 Green Bay, NFL 1,647
San Diego, AFL 2,518
1963 Chicago, NFL 1,734
Oakland, AFL 2,589

1962 Green Bay, NFL 1,746
Oakland, AFL..................2,306
1961 Baltimore, NFL................1,913
San Diego, AFL...............2,363
1960 Chicago, NFL..................1,388
Buffalo, AFL 2,124
1959 N.Y. Giants 1,582
1958 Chi. Bears 1,769
1957 Cleveland.........................1,300
1956 Cleveland.........................1,103
1955 Pittsburgh 1,295
1954 Cleveland.........................1,608
1953 Washington......................1,751
1952 Washington......................1,580
1951 Pittsburgh 1,687
1950 Cleveland.........................1,581
1949 Philadelphia.....................1,607
1948 Green Bay........................1,626
1947 Green Bay........................1,790
1946 Pittsburgh 939
1945 Washington......................1,121
1944 Chi. Bears 1,052
1943 Chi. Bears 980
1942 Washington......................1,093
1941 Pittsburgh 1,168
1940 Philadelphia.....................1,012
1939 Washington......................1,116
1938 Chi. Bears 897
1937 Detroit 804
1936 Philadelphia........................853
1935 Chi. Cardinals 793
1934 Philadelphia........................545
1933 Portsmouth 558

Compiled by Elias Sports Bureau

1967: Super Bowl I	1978: Super Bowl XII	1989: Super Bowl XXIII
1968: Super Bowl II	1979: Super Bowl XIII	1990: Super Bowl XXIV
1969: Super Bowl III	1980: Super Bowl XIV	1991: Super Bowl XXV
1970: Super Bowl IV	1981: Super Bowl XV	1992: Super Bowl XXVI
1971: Super Bowl V	1982: Super Bowl XVI	1993: Super Bowl XXVII
1972: Super Bowl VI	1983: Super Bowl XVII	1994: Super Bowl XXVIII
1973: Super Bowl VII	1984: Super Bowl XVIII	1995: Super Bowl XXIX
1974: Super Bowl VIII	1985: Super Bowl XIX	1996: Super Bowl XXX
1975: Super Bowl IX	1986: Super Bowl XX	1997: Super Bowl XXXI
1976: Super Bowl X	1987: Super Bowl XXI	1998: Super Bowl XXXII
1977: Super Bowl XI	1988: Super Bowl XXII	

INDIVIDUAL RECORDS

SERVICE

Most Games

5 Marv Fleming, Green Bay, 1967-68; Miami, 1972-74
Larry Cole, Dallas, 1971-72, 1976, 1978-79
Cliff Harris, Dallas, 1971-72, 1976, 1978-79
Charles Haley, San Francisco, 1989-90; Dallas, 1993-94, 1996
D.D. Lewis, Dallas, 1971-72, 1976, 1978-79
Mike Lodish, Buffalo, 1991-94; Denver, 1998
Preston Pearson, Baltimore, 1969; Pittsburgh, 1975; Dallas, 1976, 1978-79
Charlie Waters, Dallas, 1971-72, 1976, 1978-79
Rayfield Wright, Dallas, 1971-72, 1976, 1978-79
4 By many players

Most Games, Winning Team

5 Charles Haley, San Francisco, 1989-90; Dallas, 1993-94, 1996
4 By many players

Most Games, Coach

6 Don Shula, Baltimore, 1969; Miami, 1972-74, 1983, 1985
5 Tom Landry, Dallas, 1971-72, 1976, 1978-79
4 Bud Grant, Minnesota, 1970, 1974-75, 1977
Chuck Noll, Pittsburgh, 1975-76, 1979-80
Joe Gibbs, Washington, 1983-84, 1988, 1992
Marv Levy, Buffalo, 1991-94

Most Games, Winning Team, Coach

4 Chuck Noll, Pittsburgh, 1975-76, 1979-80
3 Bill Walsh, San Francisco, 1982, 1985, 1989
Joe Gibbs, Washington, 1983, 1988, 1992
2 Vince Lombardi, Green Bay, 1967-68
Tom Landry, Dallas, 1972, 1978
Don Shula, Miami, 1973-74
Tom Flores, Oakland, 1981; L.A. Raiders, 1984
Bill Parcells, N.Y. Giants, 1987, 1991
Jimmy Johnson, Dallas, 1993-94
George Seifert, San Francisco, 1990, 1995

Most Games, Losing Team, Coach

4 Bud Grant, Minnesota, 1970, 1974-75, 1977
Don Shula, Baltimore, 1969; Miami, 1972, 1983, 1985
Marv Levy, Buffalo, 1991-94
3 Tom Landry, Dallas, 1971, 1976, 1979
Dan Reeves, Denver, 1987-88, 1990

SCORING

POINTS

Most Points, Career

42 Jerry Rice, San Francisco, 3 games (7-td)
30 Emmitt Smith, Dallas, 3 games (5-td)
24 Franco Harris, Pittsburgh, 4 games (4-td)
Roger Craig, San Francisco, 3 games (4-td)
Thurman Thomas, Buffalo, 4 games (4-td)

Most Points, Game

18 Roger Craig, San Francisco vs. Miami, 1985 (3-td)
Jerry Rice, San Francisco vs. Denver, 1990 (3-td); vs. San Diego, 1995 (3-td)
Ricky Watters, San Francisco vs. San Diego, 1995 (3-td)
Terrell Davis, Denver vs. Green Bay, 1998 (3-td)
15 Don Chandler, Green Bay vs. Oakland, 1968 (3-pat, 4-fg)
14 Ray Wersching, San Francisco vs. Cincinnati, 1982 (2-pat, 4-fg)
Kevin Butler, Chicago vs. New England, 1986 (5-pat, 3-fg)

TOUCHDOWNS

Most Touchdowns, Career

7 Jerry Rice, San Francisco, 3 games (7-p)
5 Emmitt Smith, Dallas, 3 games (5-r)
4 Franco Harris, Pittsburgh, 4 games (4-r)
Roger Craig, San Francisco, 3 games (2-r, 2-p)
Thurman Thomas, Buffalo, 4 games (4-r)

Most Touchdowns, Game

3 Roger Craig, San Francisco vs. Miami, 1985 (1-r, 2-p)
Jerry Rice, San Francisco. vs. Denver, 1990 (3-p); vs. San Diego, 1995 (3-p)
Ricky Watters, San Francisco vs. San Diego, 1995 (1-r, 2-p)
Terrell Davis, Denver vs. Green Bay, 1998 (3-r)
2 Max McGee, Green Bay vs. Kansas City, 1967 (2-p)
Elijah Pitts, Green Bay vs. Kansas City, 1967 (2-r)
Bill Miller, Oakland vs. Green Bay, 1968 (2-p)
Larry Csonka, Miami vs. Minnesota, 1974 (2-r)
Pete Banaszak, Oakland vs. Minnesota, 1977 (2-r)
John Stallworth, Pittsburgh vs. Dallas, 1979 (2-p)
Franco Harris, Pittsburgh vs. Los Angeles, 1980 (2-r)
Cliff Branch, Oakland vs. Philadelphia, 1981 (2-p)
Dan Ross, Cincinnati vs. San Francisco, 1982 (2-p)
Marcus Allen, L.A. Raiders vs. Washington, 1984 (2-r)
Jim McMahon, Chicago vs. New England, 1986 (2-r)
Ricky Sanders, Washington vs. Denver, 1988 (2-p)
Timmy Smith, Washington vs. Denver, 1988 (2-r)
Tom Rathman, San Francisco vs. Denver, 1990 (2-r)
Gerald Riggs, Washington vs. Buffalo, 1992 (2-r)
Michael Irvin, Dallas vs. Buffalo, 1993 (2-p)
Emmitt Smith, Dallas vs. Buffalo, 1994 (2-r)
Emmitt Smith, Dallas vs. Pittsburgh, 1996 (2-r)
Antonio Freeman, Green Bay vs. Denver, 1998 (2-p)

POINTS AFTER TOUCHDOWN

Most (One-Point) Points After Touchdown, Career

9 Mike Cofer, San Francisco, 2 games (10 att)
8 Don Chandler, Green Bay, 2 games (8 att)
Roy Gerela, Pittsburgh, 3 games (9 att)
Chris Bahr, Oakland-L.A. Raiders, 2 games (8 att)
7 Ray Wersching, San Francisco, 2 games (7 att)
Lin Elliott, Dallas, 1 game (7 att)
Doug Brien, San Francisco, 1 game (7 att)

Most (One-Point) Points After Touchdown, Game

7 Mike Cofer, San Francisco vs. Denver, 1990 (8 att)
Lin Elliott, Dallas vs. Buffalo, 1993 (7 att)
Doug Brien, San Francisco vs. San Diego, 1995 (7 att)
6 Ali Haji-Sheikh, Washington vs. Denver, 1988 (6 att)
5 Don Chandler, Green Bay vs. Kansas City, 1967 (5 att)
Roy Gerela, Pittsburgh vs. Dallas, 1979 (5 att)
Chris Bahr, L.A. Raiders vs. Washington, 1984 (5 att)
Ray Wersching, San Francisco vs. Miami, 1985 (5 att)
Kevin Butler, Chicago vs. New England, 1986 (5 att)

Most Two-Point Conversions, Game

1 Mark Seay, San Diego vs. San Francisco, 1995
Alfred Pupunu, San Diego vs. San Francisco, 1995
Mark Chmura, Green Bay vs. New England, 1997

FIELD GOALS

Field Goals Attempted, Career

6 Jim Turner, N.Y. Jets-Denver, 2 games
Roy Gerela, Pittsburgh, 3 games
Rich Karlis, Denver, 2 games
5 Efren Herrera, Dallas, 1 game
Ray Wersching, San Francisco, 2 games

Most Field Goals Attempted, Game

5 Jim Turner, N.Y. Jets vs. Baltimore, 1969
Efren Herrera, Dallas vs. Denver, 1978
4 Don Chandler, Green Bay vs. Oakland, 1968
Roy Gerela, Pittsburgh vs. Dallas, 1976
Ray Wersching, San Francisco vs. Cincinnati, 1982
Rich Karlis, Denver vs. N.Y. Giants, 1987
Mike Cofer, San Francisco vs. Cincinnati, 1989

Most Field Goals, Career

5 Ray Wersching, San Francisco, 2 games (5 att)
4 Don Chandler, Green Bay, 2 games (4 att)
Jim Turner, N.Y. Jets-Denver, 2 games (6 att)
Uwe von Schamann, Miami, 2 games (4 att)
3 Mike Clark, Dallas, 2 games (3 att)
Jan Stenerud, Kansas City, 1 game (3 att)
Chris Bahr, Oakland-L.A. Raiders, 2 games (4 att)
Mark Moseley, Washington, 2 games (4 att)
Kevin Butler, Chicago, 1 game (3 att)
Rich Karlis, Denver, 2 games (6 att)
Jim Breech, Cincinnati, 2 games (3 att)
Matt Bahr, Pittsburgh-N.Y. Giants, 2 games (3 att)
Chip Lohmiller, Washington, 1 game (3 att)
Steve Christie, Buffalo, 2 games (3 att)
Eddie Murray, Dallas, 1 game (3 att)

Most Field Goals, Game

4 Don Chandler, Green Bay vs. Oakland, 1968
Ray Wersching, San Francisco vs. Cincinnati, 1982
3 Jim Turner, N.Y. Jets vs. Baltimore, 1969

Jan Stenerud, Kansas City vs. Minnesota, 1970
Uwe von Schamann, Miami vs. San Francisco, 1985
Kevin Butler, Chicago vs. New England, 1986
Jim Breech, Cincinnati vs. San Francisco, 1989
Chip Lohmiller, Washington vs. Buffalo, 1992
Eddie Murray, Dallas vs. Buffalo, 1994

Longest Field Goal
54 Steve Christie, Buffalo vs. Dallas, 1994
51 Jason Elam, Denver vs. Green Bay, 1998
48 Jan Stenerud, Kansas City vs. Minnesota, 1970
Rich Karlis, Denver vs. N.Y. Giants, 1987

SAFETIES

Most Safeties, Game
1 Dwight White, Pittsburgh vs. Minnesota, 1975
Reggie Harrison, Pittsburgh vs. Dallas, 1976
Henry Waechter, Chicago vs. New England, 1986
George Martin, N.Y. Giants vs. Denver, 1987
Bruce Smith, Buffalo vs. N.Y. Giants, 1991

RUSHING

ATTEMPTS

Most Attempts, Career
101 Franco Harris, Pittsburgh, 4 games
70 Emmitt Smith, Dallas, 3 games
64 John Riggins, Washington, 2 games

Most Attempts, Game
38 John Riggins, Washington vs. Miami, 1983
34 Franco Harris, Pittsburgh vs. Minnesota, 1975
33 Larry Csonka, Miami vs. Minnesota, 1974

YARDS GAINED

Most Yards Gained, Career
354 Franco Harris, Pittsburgh, 4 games
297 Larry Csonka, Miami, 3 games
289 Emmitt Smith, Dallas, 3 games

Most Yards Gained, Game
204 Timmy Smith, Washington vs. Denver, 1988
191 Marcus Allen, L.A. Raiders vs. Washington, 1984
166 John Riggins, Washington vs. Miami, 1983

Longest Run From Scrimmage
74 Marcus Allen, L.A. Raiders vs. Washington, 1984 (TD)
58 Tom Matte, Baltimore vs. N.Y. Jets, 1969
Timmy Smith, Washington vs. Denver, 1988 (TD)
49 Larry Csonka, Miami vs. Washington, 1973

AVERAGE GAIN

Highest Average Gain, Career (20 attempts)
9.6 Marcus Allen, L.A. Raiders, 1 game (20-191)
9.3 Timmy Smith, Washington, 1 game (22-204)
5.3 Walt Garrison, Dallas, 2 games (26-139)

Highest Average Gain, Game (10 attempts)
10.5 Tom Matte, Baltimore vs. N.Y. Jets, 1969 (11-116)
9.6 Marcus Allen, L.A. Raiders vs. Washington, 1984 (20-191)
9.3 Timmy Smith, Washington vs. Denver, 1988 (22-204)

TOUCHDOWNS

Most Touchdowns, Career
5 Emmitt Smith, Dallas, 3 games
4 Franco Harris, Pittsburgh, 4 games
Thurman Thomas, Buffalo, 4 games
3 Terrell Davis, Denver, 1 game
John Elway, Denver, 4 games

Most Touchdowns, Game
3 Terrell Davis, Denver vs. Green Bay, 1998
2 Elijah Pitts, Green Bay vs. Kansas City, 1967
Larry Csonka, Miami vs. Minnesota, 1974
Pete Banaszak, Oakland vs. Minnesota, 1977
Franco Harris, Pittsburgh vs. Los Angeles, 1980
Marcus Allen, L.A. Raiders vs. Washington, 1984
Jim McMahon, Chicago vs. New England, 1986
Timmy Smith, Washington vs. Denver, 1988
Tom Rathman, San Francisco vs. Denver, 1990
Gerald Riggs, Washington vs. Buffalo, 1992
Emmitt Smith, Dallas vs. Buffalo, 1994
Emmitt Smith, Dallas vs. Pittsburgh, 1996

PASSING

PASSER RATING

Highest Passer Rating, Career (40 attempts)
127.8 Joe Montana, San Francisco, 4 games
122.8 Jim Plunkett, Oakland-L.A. Raiders, 2 games
112.8 Terry Bradshaw, Pittsburgh, 4 games

ATTEMPTS

Most Passes Attempted, Career
145 Jim Kelly, Buffalo, 4 games
123 John Elway, Denver, 4 games
122 Joe Montana, San Francisco, 4 games

Most Passes Attempted, Game
58 Jim Kelly, Buffalo vs. Washington, 1992
50 Dan Marino, Miami vs. San Francisco, 1985
Jim Kelly, Buffalo vs. Dallas, 1994
49 Stan Humphries, San Diego vs. San Francisco, 1995
Neil O'Donnell, Pittsburgh vs. Dallas, 1996

COMPLETIONS

Most Passes Completed, Career
83 Joe Montana, San Francisco, 4 games
81 Jim Kelly, Buffalo, 4 games
61 Roger Staubach, Dallas, 4 games

Most Passes Completed, Game
31 Jim Kelly, Buffalo vs. Dallas, 1994
29 Dan Marino, Miami vs. San Francisco, 1985
28 Jim Kelly, Buffalo vs. Washington, 1992
Neil O'Donnell, Pittsburgh vs. Dallas, 1996

Most Consecutive Completions, Game
13 Joe Montana, San Francisco vs. Denver, 1990
10 Phil Simms, N.Y. Giants vs. Denver, 1987
Troy Aikman, Dallas vs. Pittsburgh, 1996
9 Jim Kelly, Buffalo vs. Dallas, 1994
Neil O'Donnell, Pittsburgh vs. Dallas, 1996

COMPLETION PERCENTAGE

Highest Completion Percentage, Career (40 attempts)
70.0 Troy Aikman, Dallas, 3 games, (80-56)
68.0 Joe Montana, San Francisco, 4 games (122-83)
63.6 Len Dawson, Kansas City, 2 games (44-28)

Highest Completion Percentage, Game (20 attempts)
88.0 Phil Simms, N.Y. Giants vs. Denver, 1987 (25-22)
75.9 Joe Montana, San Francisco vs. Denver, 1990 (29-22)
73.5 Ken Anderson, Cincinnati vs. San Francisco, 1982 (34-25)

YARDS GAINED

Most Yards Gained, Career
1,142 Joe Montana, San Francisco, 4 games
932 Terry Bradshaw, Pittsburgh, 4 games
829 Jim Kelly, Buffalo, 4 games

Most Yards Gained, Game
357 Joe Montana, San Francisco vs. Cincinnati, 1989
340 Doug Williams, Washington vs. Denver, 1988
331 Joe Montana, San Francisco vs. Miami, 1985

Longest Pass Completion
81 Brett Favre (to Freeman), Green Bay vs. New England, 1997 (TD)
80 Jim Plunkett (to King), Oakland vs. Philadelphia, 1981 (TD)
Doug Williams (to Sanders), Washington vs. Denver, 1988 (TD)
76 David Woodley (to Cefalo), Miami vs. Washington, 1983 (TD)

AVERAGE GAIN

Highest Average Gain, Career (40 attempts)
11.10 Terry Bradshaw, Pittsburgh, 4 games (84-932)
9.62 Bart Starr, Green Bay, 2 games (47-452)
9.41 Jim Plunkett, Oakland-L.A. Raiders, 2 games (46-433)

Highest Average Gain, Game (20 attempts)
14.71 Terry Bradshaw, Pittsburgh vs. Los Angeles, 1980 (21-309)
12.80 Jim McMahon, Chicago vs. New England, 1986 (20-256)
12.43 Jim Plunkett, Oakland vs. Philadelphia, 1981 (21-261)

TOUCHDOWNS

Most Touchdown Passes, Career
11 Joe Montana, San Francisco, 4 games
9 Terry Bradshaw, Pittsburgh, 4 games
8 Roger Staubach, Dallas, 4 games

Most Touchdown Passes, Game
6 Steve Young, San Francisco vs. San Diego, 1995
5 Joe Montana, San Francisco vs. Denver, 1990
4 Terry Bradshaw, Pittsburgh vs. Dallas, 1979
Doug Williams, Washington vs. Denver, 1988
Troy Aikman, Dallas vs. Buffalo, 1993

HAD INTERCEPTED

Lowest Percentage, Passes Had Intercepted, Career (40 attempts)

0.00 Jim Plunkett, Oakland-L.A. Raiders, 2 games (46-0)
Joe Montana, San Francisco, 4 games (122-0)
1.25 Troy Aikman, Dallas, 3 games (80-1)
1.45 Brett Favre, Green Bay, 2 games (69-1)

Most Attempts, Without Interception, Game

36 Joe Montana, San Francisco vs. Cincinnati, 1989
Steve Young, San Francisco vs. San Diego, 1995
35 Joe Montana, San Francisco vs. Miami, 1985
32 Jeff Hostetler, N.Y. Giants vs. Buffalo, 1991

Most Passes Had Intercepted, Career

7 Craig Morton, Dallas-Denver, 2 games
Jim Kelly, Buffalo, 4 games
John Elway, Denver, 4 games
6 Fran Tarkenton, Minnesota, 3 games
4 Earl Morrall, Baltimore-Miami, 4 games
Roger Staubach, Dallas, 4 games
Terry Bradshaw, Pittsburgh, 4 games
Joe Theismann, Washington, 2 games
Drew Bledsoe, New England, 1 game

Most Passes Had Intercepted, Game

4 Craig Morton, Denver vs. Dallas, 1978
Jim Kelly, Buffalo vs. Washington, 1992
Drew Bledsoe, New England vs. Green Bay, 1997
3 By nine players

PASS RECEIVING

RECEPTIONS

Most Receptions, Career

28 Jerry Rice, San Francisco, 3 games
27 Andre Reed, Buffalo, 4 games
20 Roger Craig, San Francisco, 3 games
Thurman Thomas, Buffalo, 4 games

Most Receptions, Game

11 Dan Ross, Cincinnati vs. San Francisco, 1982
Jerry Rice, San Francisco vs. Cincinnati, 1989
10 Tony Nathan, Miami vs. San Francisco, 1985
Jerry Rice, San Francisco vs. San Diego, 1995
Andre Hastings, Pittsburgh vs. Dallas, 1996
9 Ricky Sanders, Washington vs. Denver, 1988
Antonio Freeman, Green Bay vs. Denver, 1998

YARDS GAINED

Most Yards Gained, Career

512 Jerry Rice, San Francisco, 3 games
364 Lynn Swann, Pittsburgh, 4 games
323 Andre Reed, Buffalo, 4 games

Most Yards Gained, Game

215 Jerry Rice, San Francisco vs. Cincinnati, 1989
193 Ricky Sanders, Washington vs. Denver, 1988
161 Lynn Swann, Pittsburgh vs. Dallas, 1976

Longest Reception

81 Antonio Freeman (from Favre), Green Bay vs. New England, 1997 (TD)
80 Kenny King (from Plunkett), Oakland vs. Philadelphia, 1981 (TD)
Ricky Sanders (from Williams), Washington vs. Denver, 1988 (TD)
76 Jimmy Cefalo (from Woodley), Miami vs. Washington, 1983 (TD)

AVERAGE GAIN

Highest Average Gain, Career (8 receptions)

24.4 John Stallworth, Pittsburgh, 4 games (11-268)
23.4 Ricky Sanders, Washington, 2 games (10-234)
22.8 Lynn Swann, Pittsburgh, 4 games (16-364)

Highest Average Gain, Game (3 receptions)

40.33 John Stallworth, Pittsburgh vs. Los Angeles, 1980 (3-121)
40.25 Lynn Swann, Pittsburgh vs. Dallas, 1979 (4-161)
38.33 John Stallworth, Pittsburgh vs. Dallas, 1979 (3-115)

TOUCHDOWNS

Most Touchdowns, Career

7 Jerry Rice, San Francisco, 3 games
3 John Stallworth, Pittsburgh, 4 games
Lynn Swann, Pittsburgh, 4 games
Cliff Branch, Oakland-L.A. Raiders, 3 games
Antonio Freeman, Green Bay, 2 games
2 Max McGee, Green Bay, 2 games
Bill Miller, Oakland, 1 game
Butch Johnson, Dallas, 2 games
Dan Ross, Cincinnati, 1 game
Roger Craig, San Francisco, 3 games
Ricky Sanders, Washington, 2 games
John Taylor, San Francisco, 3 games
Gary Clark, Washington, 2 games
Don Beebe, Buffalo-Green Bay, 4 games
Michael Irvin, Dallas, 2 games
Ricky Watters, San Francisco, 1 game
Jay Novacek, Dallas, 3 games

Most Touchdowns, Game

3 Jerry Rice, San Francisco vs. San Diego, 1995; vs. Denver, 1990
2 Max McGee, Green Bay vs. Kansas City, 1967
Bill Miller, Oakland vs. Green Bay, 1968
John Stallworth, Pittsburgh vs. Dallas, 1979
Cliff Branch, Oakland vs. Philadelphia, 1981
Dan Ross, Cincinnati vs. San Francisco, 1982
Roger Craig, San Francisco vs. Miami, 1985
Ricky Sanders, Washington vs. Denver, 1988
Michael Irvin, Dallas vs. Buffalo, 1993
Ricky Watters, San Francisco vs. San Diego, 1995
Antonio Freeman, Green Bay vs. Denver, 1998

INTERCEPTIONS BY

Most Interceptions By, Career

3 Chuck Howley, Dallas, 2 games
Rod Martin, Oakland-L.A. Raiders, 2 games
Larry Brown, Dallas, 3 games
2 Randy Beverly, N.Y. Jets, 1 game
Jake Scott, Miami, 3 games
Mike Wagner, Pittsburgh, 3 games
Mel Blount, Pittsburgh, 4 games
Eric Wright, San Francisco, 4 games
Barry Wilburn, Washington, 1 game
Brad Edwards, Washington, 1 game
Thomas Everett, Dallas, 2 games
James Washington, Dallas, 2 games

Most Interceptions By, Game

3 Rod Martin, Oakland vs. Philadelphia, 1981
2 Randy Beverly, N.Y. Jets vs. Baltimore, 1969
Chuck Howley, Dallas vs. Baltimore, 1971
Jake Scott, Miami vs. Washington, 1973
Barry Wilburn, Washington vs. Denver, 1988
Brad Edwards, Washington vs. Buffalo, 1992
Thomas Everett, Dallas vs. Buffalo, 1993
Larry Brown, Dallas vs. Pittsburgh, 1996

YARDS GAINED

Most Yards Gained, Career

77 Larry Brown, Dallas, 3 games
75 Willie Brown, Oakland, 2 games
63 Chuck Howley, Dallas, 2 games
Jake Scott, Miami, 3 games

Most Yards Gained, Game

77 Larry Brown, Dallas vs. Pittsburgh, 1996
75 Willie Brown, Oakland vs. Minnesota, 1977
63 Jake Scott, Miami vs. Washington, 1973

Longest Return

75 Willie Brown, Oakland vs. Minnesota, 1977 (TD)
60 Herb Adderley, Green Bay vs. Oakland, 1968 (TD)
55 Jake Scott, Miami vs. Washington, 1973

TOUCHDOWNS

Most Touchdowns, Game

1 Herb Adderley, Green Bay vs. Oakland, 1968
Willie Brown, Oakland vs. Minnesota, 1977
Jack Squirek, L.A. Raiders vs. Washington, 1984
Reggie Phillips, Chicago vs. New England, 1986

PUNTING

Most Punts, Career

17 Mike Eischeid, Oakland-Minnesota, 3 games
15 Larry Seiple, Miami, 3 games
Mike Horan, Denver, 3 games
14 Ron Widby, Dallas, 2 games
Ray Guy, Oakland-L.A. Raiders, 3 games
Chris Mohr, Buffalo, 3 games

Most Punts, Game

9 Ron Widby, Dallas vs. Baltimore, 1971
8 Tom Tupa, New England vs. Green Bay, 1997
7 By nine players

Longest Punt

63 Lee Johnson, Cincinnati vs. San Francisco, 1989
62 Rich Camarillo, New England vs. Chicago, 1986
61 Jerrel Wilson, Kansas City vs. Green Bay, 1967

AVERAGE YARDAGE

Highest Average, Punting, Career (10 punts)

46.5 Jerrel Wilson, Kansas City, 2 games (11-511)

41.9 Ray Guy, Oakland-L.A. Raiders, 3 games (14-587)
41.3 Larry Seiple, Miami, 3 games (15-620)

Highest Average, Punting, Game (4 punts)
48.8 Bryan Wagner, San Diego vs. San Francisco, 1995 (4-195)
48.5 Jerrel Wilson, Kansas City vs. Minnesota, 1970 (4-194)
46.3 Jim Miller, San Francisco vs. Cincinnati, 1982 (4-185)

PUNT RETURNS

Most Punt Returns, Career
6 Willie Wood, Green Bay, 2 games
Jake Scott, Miami, 3 games
Theo Bell, Pittsburgh, 2 games
Mike Nelms, Washington, 1 game
John Taylor, San Francisco, 3 games
Desmond Howard, Green Bay, 1 game
David Meggett, N.Y. Giants-New England, 2 games
5 Dana McLemore, San Francisco, 1 game
4 By eight players

Most Punt Returns, Game
6 Mike Nelms, Washington vs. Miami, 1983
Desmond Howard, Green Bay vs. New England, 1997
5 Willie Wood, Green Bay vs. Oakland, 1968
Dana McLemore, San Francisco vs. Miami, 1985
4 By seven players

Most Fair Catches, Game
3 Ron Gardin, Baltimore vs. Dallas, 1971
Golden Richards, Dallas vs. Pittsburgh, 1976
Greg Pruitt, L.A. Raiders vs. Washington, 1984
Al Edwards, Buffalo vs. N.Y. Giants, 1991
David Meggett, N.Y. Giants vs. Buffalo, 1991

YARDS GAINED

Most Yards Gained, Career
94 John Taylor, San Francisco, 3 games
90 Desmond Howard, Green Bay, 1 game
67 David Meggett, N.Y. Giants-New England, 2 games

Most Yards Gained, Game
90 Desmond Howard, Green Bay vs. New England, 1997
56 John Taylor, San Francisco vs. Cincinnati, 1989
52 Mike Nelms, Washington vs. Miami, 1983

Longest Return
45 John Taylor, San Francisco vs. Cincinnati, 1989
34 Darrell Green, Washington vs. L.A. Raiders, 1984
Desmond Howard, Green Bay vs. New England, 1997
32 Desmond Howard, Green Bay vs. New England, 1997

AVERAGE YARDAGE

Highest Average, Career (4 returns)
15.7 John Taylor, San Francisco, 3 games (6-94)
15.0 Desmond Howard, Green Bay, 1 game (6-90)
11.2 David Meggett, N.Y. Giants-New England, 2 games (6-67)

Highest Average, Game (3 returns)
18.7 John Taylor, San Francisco vs. Cincinnati, 1989 (3-56)
15.0 Desmond Howard, Green Bay vs. New England, 1997 (6-90)
12.7 John Taylor, San Francisco vs. Denver, 1990 (3-38)

TOUCHDOWNS

Most Touchdowns, Game
None

KICKOFF RETURNS

Most Kickoff Returns, Career
10 Ken Bell, Denver, 3 games
8 Larry Anderson, Pittsburgh, 2 games
Fulton Walker, Miami, 2 games
Andre Coleman, San Diego, 1 game
7 Preston Pearson, Baltimore-Pittsburgh-Dallas, 5 games
Stephen Starring, New England, 1 game
David Meggett, N.Y. Giants-New England, 2 games

Most Kickoff Returns, Game
8 Andre Coleman, San Diego vs. San Francisco, 1995
7 Stephen Starring, New England vs. Chicago, 1986
6 Darren Carrington, Denver vs. San Francisco, 1990
Antonio Freeman, Green Bay vs. Denver, 1998

YARDS GAINED

Most Yards Gained, Career
283 Fulton Walker, Miami, 2 games
244 Andre Coleman, San Diego, 1 game
207 Larry Anderson, Pittsburgh, 2 games

Most Yards Gained, Game
244 Andre Coleman, San Diego vs. San Francisco, 1995
190 Fulton Walker, Miami vs. Washington, 1983
162 Larry Anderson, Pittsburgh vs. Los Angeles, 1980

Longest Return
99 Desmond Howard, Green Bay vs. New England, 1997 (TD)
98 Fulton Walker, Miami vs. Washington, 1983 (TD)
Andre Coleman, San Diego vs. San Francisco, 1995 (TD)
93 Stanford Jennings, Cincinnati vs. San Francisco, 1989 (TD)

AVERAGE YARDAGE

Highest Average, Career (4 returns)
38.5 Desmond Howard, Green Bay, 1 game (4-154)
35.4 Fulton Walker, Miami, 2 games (8-283)
30.5 Andre Coleman, San Diego, 1 game (8-244)

Highest Average, Game (3 returns)
47.5 Fulton Walker, Miami vs. Washington, 1983 (4-190)
38.5 Desmond Howard, Green Bay vs. New England, 1997 (4-154)
32.4 Larry Anderson, Pittsburgh vs. Los Angeles, 1980 (5-162)

TOUCHDOWNS

Most Touchdowns, Game
1 Fulton Walker, Miami vs. Washington, 1983
Stanford Jennings, Cincinnati vs. San Francisco, 1989
Andre Coleman, San Diego vs. San Francisco, 1995
Desmond Howard, Green Bay vs. New England, 1997

FUMBLES

Most Fumbles, Career
5 Roger Staubach, Dallas, 4 games
4 Jim Kelly, Buffalo, 4 games
3 Franco Harris, Pittsburgh, 4 games
Terry Bradshaw, Pittsburgh, 4 games
John Elway, Denver, 4 games
Frank Reich, Buffalo, 4 games
Thurman Thomas, Buffalo, 4 games

Most Fumbles, Game
3 Roger Staubach, Dallas vs. Pittsburgh, 1976
Jim Kelly, Buffalo vs. Washington, 1992
Frank Reich, Buffalo vs. Dallas, 1993
2 Franco Harris, Pittsburgh vs. Minnesota, 1975
Butch Johnson, Dallas vs. Denver, 1978
Terry Bradshaw, Pittsburgh vs. Dallas, 1979
Joe Montana, San Francisco vs. Cincinnati, 1989
John Elway, Denver vs. San Francisco, 1990
Thurman Thomas, Buffalo vs. Dallas, 1994

RECOVERIES

Most Fumbles Recovered, Career
2 Jake Scott, Miami, 3 games (1 own, 1 opp)
Fran Tarkenton, Minnesota, 3 games (2 own)
Franco Harris, Pittsburgh, 4 games (2 own)
Roger Staubach, Dallas, 4 games (2 own)
Bobby Walden, Pittsburgh, 2 games (2 own)
John Fitzgerald, Dallas, 4 games (2 own)
Randy Hughes, Dallas, 3 games (2 opp)
Butch Johnson, Dallas, 2 games (2 own)
Mike Singletary, Chicago, 1 game (2 opp)
John Elway, Denver, 4 games (2 own)
Jimmie Jones, Dallas, 2 games (2 opp)
Kenneth Davis, Buffalo, 4 games (2 own)

Most Fumbles Recovered, Game
2 Jake Scott, Miami vs. Minnesota, 1974 (1 own, 1 opp)
Roger Staubach, Dallas vs. Pittsburgh, 1976 (2 own)
Randy Hughes, Dallas vs. Denver, 1978 (2 opp)
Butch Johnson, Dallas vs. Denver, 1978 (2 own)
Mike Singletary, Chicago vs. New England, 1986 (2 opp)
Jimmie Jones, Dallas vs. Buffalo, 1993 (2 opp)

YARDS GAINED

Most Yards Gained, Game
64 Leon Lett, Dallas vs. Buffalo, 1993 (opp)
49 Mike Bass, Washington vs. Miami, 1973 (opp)
46 James Washington, Dallas vs. Buffalo, 1994 (opp)

Longest Return
64 Leon Lett, Dallas vs. Buffalo, 1993
49 Mike Bass, Washington vs. Miami, 1973 (TD)
46 James Washington, Dallas vs. Buffalo, 1994 (TD)

TOUCHDOWNS

Most Touchdowns, Game
1 Mike Bass, Washington vs. Miami, 1973 (opp 49 yds)
Mike Hegman, Dallas vs. Pittsburgh, 1979 (opp 37 yds)
Jimmie Jones, Dallas vs. Buffalo, 1993 (opp 2 yds)
Ken Norton, Dallas vs. Buffalo, 1993 (opp 9 yds)
James Washington, Dallas vs. Buffalo, 1994 (opp 46 yds)

COMBINED NET YARDS GAINED

(Rushing, receiving, interception returns, punt returns, kickoff returns, and fumble returns)

ATTEMPTS

Most Attempts, Career
108 Franco Harris, Pittsburgh, 4 games
81 Emmitt Smith, Dallas, 3 games
72 Roger Craig, San Francisco, 3 games
Thurman Thomas, Buffalo, 4 games

Most Attempts, Game
39 John Riggins, Washington vs. Miami, 1983
35 Franco Harris, Pittsburgh vs. Minnesota, 1975
34 Matt Snell, N.Y. Jets vs. Baltimore, 1969
Emmitt Smith, Dallas vs. Buffalo, 1994

YARDS GAINED

Most Yards Gained, Career
527 Jerry Rice, San Francisco, 3 games
468 Franco Harris, Pittsburgh, 4 games
410 Roger Craig, San Francisco, 3 games

Most Yards Gained, Game
244 Desmond Howard, Green Bay vs. New England, 1997
Andre Coleman, San Diego vs. San Francisco, 1995
235 Ricky Sanders, Washington vs. Denver, 1988
230 Antonio Freeman, Green Bay vs. Denver, 1998

SACKS

Sacks have been compiled since 1983.

Most Sacks, Career
4.5 Charles Haley, San Francisco-Dallas, 5 games
3 Danny Stubbs, San Francisco, 2 games
Leonard Marshall, N.Y. Giants, 2 games
Jeff Wright, Buffalo, 4 games
Reggie White, Green Bay, 1 game
2.5 Dexter Manley, Washington, 3 games

Most Sacks, Game
3 Reggie White, Green Bay vs. New England, 1997
2 Dwaine Board, San Francisco vs. Miami, 1985
Dennis Owens, New England vs. Chicago, 1986
Otis Wilson, Chicago vs. New England, 1986
Leonard Marshall, N.Y. Giants vs. Denver, 1987
Alvin Walton, Washington vs. Denver, 1988
Charles Haley, San Francisco vs. Cincinnati, 1989
Danny Stubbs, San Francisco vs. Denver, 1990
Jeff Wright, Buffalo vs. Dallas, 1994
Raylee Johnson, San Diego vs. San Francisco, 1995
Chad Hennings, Dallas vs. Pittsburgh, 1996
Tedy Bruschi, New England vs. Green Bay, 1997

TEAM RECORDS

GAMES, VICTORIES, DEFEATS

Most Games
8 Dallas, 1971-72, 1976, 1978-79, 1993-94, 1996
5 Miami, 1972-74, 1983, 1985
Washington, 1973, 1983-84, 1988, 1992
San Francisco, 1982, 1985, 1989-90, 1995
Pittsburgh, 1975-76, 1979-80, 1996
Denver, 1978, 1987-88, 1990, 1998
4 Minnesota, 1970, 1974-75, 1977
Oakland/L.A. Raiders, 1968, 1977, 1981, 1984
Buffalo, 1991-94
Green Bay, 1967-68, 1997-98

Most Consecutive Games
4 Buffalo, 1991-94
3 Miami, 1972-74
2 Green Bay, 1967-68
Dallas, 1971-72; 1978-79; 1993-94
Minnesota, 1974-75
Pittsburgh, 1975-76, 1979-80
Washington, 1983-84
Denver, 1987-88
San Francisco 1989-90
Green Bay, 1997-98

Most Games Won
5 San Francisco, 1982, 1985, 1989-90, 1995
Dallas, 1972, 1978, 1993-94, 1996
4 Pittsburgh, 1975-76, 1979-80
3 Oakland/L.A. Raiders, 1977, 1981, 1984
Washington, 1983, 1988, 1992
Green Bay, 1967-68, 1997

Most Consecutive Games Won
2 Green Bay, 1967-68
Miami, 1973-74
Pittsburgh, 1975-76, 1979-80
San Francisco, 1989-90
Dallas, 1993-94

Most Games Lost
4 Minnesota, 1970, 1974-75, 1977
Denver, 1978, 1987-88, 1990
Buffalo, 1991-94
3 Dallas, 1971, 1976, 1979
Miami, 1972, 1983, 1985
2 Washington, 1973, 1984
Cincinnati, 1982, 1989
New England, 1986, 1997

Most Consecutive Games Lost
4 Buffalo, 1991-94
2 Minnesota, 1974-75
Denver, 1987-88

SCORING

Most Points, Game
55 San Francisco vs. Denver, 1990
52 Dallas vs. Buffalo, 1993
49 San Francisco vs. San Diego, 1995

Fewest Points, Game
3 Miami vs. Dallas, 1972
6 Minnesota vs. Pittsburgh, 1975
7 By four teams

Most Points, Both Teams, Game
75 San Francisco (49) vs. San Diego (26), 1995
69 Dallas (52) vs. Buffalo (17), 1993
66 Pittsburgh (35) vs. Dallas (31), 1979

Fewest Points, Both Teams, Game
21 Washington (7) vs. Miami (14), 1973
22 Minnesota (6) vs. Pittsburgh (16), 1975
23 Baltimore (7) vs. N.Y. Jets (16), 1969

Largest Margin of Victory, Game
45 San Francisco vs. Denver, 1990 (55-10)
36 Chicago vs. New England, 1986 (46-10)
35 Dallas vs. Buffalo, 1993 (52-17)

Most Points, Each Half
1st: 35 Washington vs. Denver, 1988
2nd: 30 N.Y. Giants vs. Denver, 1987

Most Points, Each Quarter
1st: 14 Miami vs. Minnesota, 1974
Oakland vs. Philadelphia, 1981
Dallas vs. Buffalo, 1993
San Francisco vs. San Diego, 1995
New England vs. Green Bay, 1997
2nd: 35 Washington vs. Denver, 1988
3rd: 21 Chicago vs. New England, 1986
4th: 21 Dallas vs. Buffalo, 1993

Most Points, Both Teams, Each Half
1st: 45 Washington (35) vs. Denver (10), 1988
2nd: 44 Buffalo (24) vs. Washington (20), 1992

Fewest Points, Both Teams, Each Half
1st: 2 Minnesota (0) vs. Pittsburgh (2), 1975
2nd: 7 Miami (0) vs. Washington (7), 1973
Denver (0) vs. Washington (7), 1988

Most Points, Both Teams, Each Quarter
1st: 24 New England (14) vs. Green Bay (10), 1997
2nd: 35 Washington (35) vs. Denver (0), 1988
3rd: 24 Washington (14) vs. Buffalo (10), 1992
4th: 28 Dallas (14) vs. Pittsburgh (14), 1979

TOUCHDOWNS

Most Touchdowns, Game
8 San Francisco vs. Denver, 1990
7 Dallas vs. Buffalo, 1993
San Francisco vs. San Diego, 1995
6 Washington vs. Denver, 1988

Fewest Touchdowns, Game
0 Miami vs. Dallas, 1972
1 By 17 teams

Most Touchdowns, Both Teams, Game
10 San Francisco (7) vs. San Diego (3), 1995
9 Pittsburgh (5) vs. Dallas (4), 1979
San Francisco (8) vs. Denver (1), 1990
Dallas (7) vs. Buffalo (2), 1993
7 N.Y. Giants (5) vs. Denver (2), 1987
Washington (6) vs. Denver (1), 1988
Washington (4) vs. Buffalo (3), 1992

Green Bay (4) vs. New England (3), 1997
Denver (4) vs. Green Bay (3), 1998

Fewest Touchdowns, Both Teams, Game
2 Baltimore (1) vs. N.Y. Jets (1), 1969
3 In six games

POINTS AFTER TOUCHDOWN

Most (One-Point) Points After Touchdown, Game
7 San Francisco vs. Denver, 1990
Dallas vs. Buffalo, 1993
San Francisco vs. San Diego, 1995
6 Washington vs. Denver, 1988
5 Green Bay vs. Kansas City, 1967
Pittsburgh vs. Dallas, 1979
L.A. Raiders vs. Washington, 1984
San Francisco vs. Miami, 1985
Chicago vs. New England, 1986

Most (One-Point) Points After Touchdown, Both Teams, Game
9 Pittsburgh (5) vs. Dallas (4), 1979
Dallas (7) vs. Buffalo (2), 1993
8 San Francisco (7) vs. Denver (1), 1990
San Francisco (7) vs. San Diego (1), 1995
7 Washington (6) vs. Denver (1), 1988
Washington (4) vs. Buffalo (3), 1992
Denver (4) vs. Green Bay (3), 1998

Fewest (One-Point) Points After Touchdown, Both Teams, Game
2 Baltimore (1) vs. N.Y. Jets (1), 1969
Baltimore (1) vs. Dallas (1), 1971
Minnesota (0) vs. Pittsburgh (2), 1975

Most Two-Point Conversions, Game
2 San Diego vs. San Francisco, 1995

Most Two-Point Conversions, Both Teams, Game
2 San Diego (2) vs. San Francisco (0), 1995

FIELD GOALS

Most Field Goals Attempted, Game
5 N.Y. Jets vs. Baltimore, 1969
Dallas vs. Denver, 1978
4 Green Bay vs. Oakland, 1968
Pittsburgh vs. Dallas, 1976
San Francisco vs. Cincinnati, 1982; 1989
Denver vs. N.Y. Giants, 1987

Most Field Goals Attempted, Both Teams, Game
7 N.Y. Jets (5) vs. Baltimore (2), 1969
San Francisco (4) vs. Cincinnati (3), 1989
6 Dallas (5) vs. Denver (1), 1978
5 Green Bay (4) vs. Oakland (1), 1968
Pittsburgh (4) vs. Dallas (1), 1976
Oakland (3) vs. Philadelphia (2), 1981
Denver (4) vs. N.Y. Giants (1), 1987
Dallas (3) vs. Buffalo (2), 1994

Fewest Field Goals Attempted, Both Teams, Game
1 Minnesota (0) vs. Miami (1), 1974
San Francisco (0) vs. Denver (1), 1990
2 Green Bay (0) vs. Kansas City (2), 1967
Miami (1) vs. Washington (1), 1973
Dallas (1) vs. Pittsburgh (1), 1979
Dallas (1) vs. Buffalo (1), 1993
San Diego (1) vs. San Francisco (1), 1995
Denver (1) vs. Green Bay (1), 1998

Most Field Goals, Game
4 Green Bay vs. Oakland, 1968
San Francisco vs. Cincinnati, 1982
3 N.Y. Jets vs. Baltimore, 1969
Kansas City vs. Minnesota, 1970
Miami vs. San Francisco, 1985
Chicago vs. New England, 1986
Cincinnati vs. San Francisco, 1989
Washington vs. Buffalo, 1992
Dallas vs. Buffalo, 1994

Most Field Goals, Both Teams, Game
5 Cincinnati (3) vs. San Francisco (2), 1989
Dallas (3) vs. Buffalo (2), 1994
4 Green Bay (4) vs. Oakland (0), 1968
San Francisco (4) vs. Cincinnati (0), 1982
Miami (3) vs. San Francisco (1), 1985
Chicago (3) vs. New England (1), 1986
Washington (3) vs. Buffalo (1), 1992
3 In eleven games

Fewest Field Goals, Both Teams, Game
0 Miami vs. Washington, 1973
Pittsburgh vs. Minnesota, 1975
1 Green Bay (0) vs. Kansas City (1), 1967
Minnesota (0) vs. Miami (1), 1974
Pittsburgh (0) vs. Dallas (1), 1979
Washington (0) vs. Denver (1), 1988
San Francisco (0) vs. Denver (1), 1990
San Francisco (0) vs. San Diego (1), 1995

SAFETIES

Most Safeties, Game
1 Pittsburgh vs. Minnesota, 1975; vs. Dallas, 1976
Chicago vs. New England, 1986
N.Y. Giants vs. Denver, 1987
Buffalo vs. N.Y. Giants, 1991

FIRST DOWNS

Most First Downs, Game
31 San Francisco vs. Miami, 1985
28 San Francisco vs. Denver, 1990
San Francisco vs. San Diego, 1995
25 Washington vs. Denver, 1988
Buffalo vs. Washington, 1992
Pittsburgh vs. Dallas, 1996

Fewest First Downs, Game
9 Minnesota vs. Pittsburgh, 1975
Miami vs. Washington, 1983
10 Dallas vs. Baltimore, 1971
Miami vs. Dallas, 1972
11 Denver vs. Dallas, 1978

Most First Downs, Both Teams, Game
50 San Francisco (31) vs. Miami (19), 1985
49 Buffalo (25) vs. Washington (24), 1992
48 San Francisco (28) vs. San Diego (20), 1995

Fewest First Downs, Both Teams, Game
24 Dallas (10) vs. Baltimore (14), 1971
26 Minnesota (9) vs. Pittsburgh (17), 1975
27 Pittsburgh (13) vs. Dallas (14), 1976

RUSHING

Most First Downs, Rushing, Game
16 San Francisco vs. Miami, 1985
15 Dallas vs. Miami, 1972
14 Washington vs. Miami, 1983
San Francisco vs. Denver, 1990
Denver vs. Green Bay, 1998

Fewest First Downs, Rushing, Game
1 New England vs. Chicago, 1986
2 Minnesota vs. Kansas City, 1970; vs. Pittsburgh, 1975; vs. Oakland, 1977
Pittsburgh vs. Dallas, 1979
Miami vs. San Francisco, 1985
3 Miami vs. Dallas, 1972
Philadelphia vs. Oakland, 1981
New England vs. Green Bay, 1997

Most First Downs, Rushing, Both Teams, Game
21 Washington (14) vs. Miami (7), 1983
19 Washington (13) vs. Denver (6), 1988
San Francisco (14) vs. Denver (5), 1990
18 Dallas (15) vs. Miami (3), 1972
Miami (13) vs. Minnesota (5), 1974
San Francisco (16) vs. Miami (2), 1985
N.Y. Giants (10) vs. Buffalo (8), 1991
Denver (14) vs. Green Bay (4), 1998

Fewest First Downs, Rushing, Both Teams, Game
8 Baltimore (4) vs. Dallas (4), 1971
Pittsburgh (2) vs. Dallas (6), 1979
9 Philadelphia (3) vs. Oakland (6), 1981
10 Minnesota (2) vs. Kansas City (8), 1970

PASSING

Most First Downs, Passing, Game
18 Buffalo vs. Washington, 1992
17 Miami vs. San Francisco, 1985
San Francisco vs. San Diego, 1995
16 Denver vs. N.Y. Giants, 1987
San Francisco vs. Cincinnati, 1989

Fewest First Downs, Passing, Game
1 Denver vs. Dallas, 1978
2 Miami vs. Washington, 1983
4 Miami vs. Minnesota, 1974

Most First Downs, Passing, Both Teams, Game
32 Miami (17) vs. San Francisco (15), 1985
31 San Francisco (17) vs. San Diego (14), 1995
30 Buffalo (18) vs. Washington (12), 1992

Fewest First Downs, Passing, Both Teams, Game
9 Denver (1) vs. Dallas (8), 1978
10 Minnesota (5) vs. Pittsburgh (5), 1975
11 Dallas (5) vs. Baltimore (6), 1971
Miami (2) vs. Washington (9), 1983

PENALTY
Most First Downs, Penalty, Game
4 Baltimore vs. Dallas, 1971
Miami vs. Minnesota, 1974
Cincinnati vs. San Francisco, 1982
Buffalo vs. Dallas, 1993
3 Kansas City vs. Minnesota, 1970
Minnesota vs. Oakland, 1977
Buffalo vs. Washington, 1992
Green Bay vs. Denver, 1998
Most First Downs, Penalty, Both Teams, Game
6 Cincinnati (4) vs. San Francisco (2), 1982
5 Baltimore (4) vs. Dallas (1), 1971
Miami (4) vs. Minnesota (1), 1974
Buffalo (3) vs. Washington (2), 1992
Green Bay (3) vs. Denver (2), 1998
4 Kansas City (3) vs. Minnesota (1), 1970
Buffalo (4) vs. Dallas (0), 1993
Fewest First Downs, Penalty, Both Teams, Game
0 Dallas vs. Miami, 1972
Miami vs. Washington, 1973
Dallas vs. Pittsburgh, 1976
Miami vs. San Francisco, 1985
1 Green Bay (0) vs. Kansas City (1), 1967
Miami (0) vs. Washington (1), 1983
Cincinnati (0) vs. San Francisco (1), 1989
San Francisco (0) vs. Denver (1), 1990
Dallas (0) vs. Buffalo (1), 1994
Dallas (0) vs. Pittsburgh (1), 1996

NET YARDS GAINED RUSHING AND PASSING
Most Yards Gained, Game
602 Washington vs. Denver, 1988
537 San Francisco vs. Miami, 1985
461 San Francisco vs. Denver, 1990
Fewest Yards Gained, Game
119 Minnesota vs. Pittsburgh, 1975
123 New England vs. Chicago, 1986
156 Denver vs. Dallas, 1978
Most Yards Gained, Both Teams, Game
929 Washington (602) vs. Denver (327), 1988
851 San Francisco (537) vs. Miami (314), 1985
809 San Francisco (455) vs. San Diego (354), 1995
Fewest Yards Gained, Both Teams, Game
452 Minnesota (119) vs. Pittsburgh (333), 1975
481 Washington (228) vs. Miami (253), 1973
Denver (156) vs. Dallas (325), 1978
497 Minnesota (238) vs. Miami (259), 1974

RUSHING
ATTEMPTS
Most Attempts, Game
57 Pittsburgh vs. Minnesota, 1975
53 Miami vs. Minnesota, 1974
52 Oakland vs. Minnesota, 1977
Washington vs. Miami, 1983
Fewest Attempts, Game
9 Miami vs. San Francisco, 1985
11 New England vs. Chicago, 1986
13 New England vs. Green Bay, 1997
Most Attempts, Both Teams, Game
81 Washington (52) vs. Miami (29), 1983
78 Pittsburgh (57) vs. Minnesota (21), 1975
Oakland (52) vs. Minnesota (26), 1977
77 Miami (53) vs. Minnesota (24), 1974
Pittsburgh (46) vs. Dallas (31), 1976
Fewest Attempts, Both Teams, Game
49 Miami (9) vs. San Francisco (40), 1985
New England (13) vs. Green Bay (36), 1997
51 San Diego (19) vs. San Francisco (32), 1995
53 Kansas City (19) vs. Green Bay (34), 1967

YARDS GAINED
Most Yards Gained, Game
280 Washington vs. Denver, 1988
276 Washington vs. Miami, 1983
266 Oakland vs. Minnesota, 1977
Fewest Yards Gained, Game
7 New England vs. Chicago, 1986
17 Minnesota vs. Pittsburgh, 1975
25 Miami vs. San Francisco, 1985
Most Yards Gained, Both Teams, Game
377 Washington (280) vs. Denver (97), 1988
372 Washington (276) vs. Miami (96), 1983
338 N.Y. Giants (172) vs. Buffalo (166), 1991
Fewest Yards Gained, Both Teams, Game
158 New England (43) vs. Green Bay (115), 1997
159 Dallas (56) vs. Pittsburgh (103), 1996
168 Buffalo (43) vs. Washington (125), 1992

AVERAGE GAIN
Highest Average Gain, Game
7.00 L.A. Raiders vs. Washington, 1984 (33-231)
Washington vs. Denver, 1988 (40-280)
6.64 Buffalo vs. N.Y. Giants, 1991 (25-166)
6.22 Baltimore vs. N.Y. Jets, 1969 (23-143)
Lowest Average Gain, Game
0.64 New England vs. Chicago, 1986 (11-7)
0.81 Minnesota vs. Pittsburgh, 1975 (21-17)
2.23 Baltimore vs. Dallas, 1971 (31-69)

TOUCHDOWNS
Most Touchdowns, Game
4 Chicago vs. New England, 1986
Denver vs. Green Bay, 1998
3 Green Bay vs. Kansas City, 1967
Miami vs. Minnesota, 1974
San Francisco vs. Denver, 1990
2 Oakland vs. Minnesota, 1977
Pittsburgh vs. Los Angeles, 1980
L.A. Raiders vs. Washington, 1984
San Francisco vs. Miami, 1985
N.Y. Giants vs. Denver, 1987
Washington vs. Denver, 1988; vs. Buffalo, 1992
Buffalo vs. N.Y. Giants, 1991
Dallas vs. Buffalo, 1994; vs. Pittsburgh, 1996
Fewest Touchdowns, Game
0 By 19 teams
Most Touchdowns, Both Teams, Game
4 Miami (3) vs. Minnesota (1), 1974
Chicago (4) vs. New England (0), 1986
San Francisco (3) vs. Denver (1), 1990
Denver (4) vs. Green Bay (0), 1998
3 Green Bay (3) vs. Kansas City (0), 1967
Pittsburgh (2) vs. Los Angeles (1), 1980
L.A. Raiders (2) vs. Washington (1), 1984
N.Y. Giants (2) vs. Denver (1), 1987
Buffalo (2) vs. N.Y. Giants (1), 1991
Washington (2) vs. Buffalo (1), 1992
Dallas (2) vs. Buffalo (1), 1994
Dallas (2) vs. Pittsburgh (1), 1996
Fewest Touchdowns, Both Teams, Game
0 Pittsburgh vs. Dallas, 1976
Oakland vs. Philadelphia, 1981
Cincinnati vs. San Francisco, 1989
1 In seven games

PASSING
ATTEMPTS
Most Passes Attempted, Game
59 Buffalo vs. Washington, 1992
55 San Diego vs. San Francisco, 1995
50 Miami vs. San Francisco, 1985
Buffalo vs. Dallas, 1994
Fewest Passes Attempted, Game
7 Miami vs. Minnesota, 1974
11 Miami vs. Washington, 1973
14 Pittsburgh vs. Minnesota, 1975
Most Passes Attempted, Both Teams, Game
93 San Diego (55) vs. San Francisco (38), 1995
92 Buffalo (59) vs. Washington (33), 1992
85 Miami (50) vs. San Francisco (35), 1985
Fewest Passes Attempted, Both Teams, Game
35 Miami (7) vs. Minnesota (28), 1974
39 Miami (11) vs. Washington (28), 1973
40 Pittsburgh (14) vs. Minnesota (26), 1975
Miami (17) vs. Washington (23), 1983

SUPER BOWL RECORDS

COMPLETIONS

Most Passes Completed, Game

31 Buffalo vs. Dallas, 1994
29 Miami vs. San Francisco, 1985
Buffalo vs. Washington, 1992
28 Pittsburgh vs. Dallas, 1996

Fewest Passes Completed, Game

4 Miami vs. Washington, 1983
6 Miami vs. Minnesota, 1974
8 Miami vs. Washington, 1973
Denver vs. Dallas, 1978

Most Passes Completed, Both Teams, Game

53 Miami (29) vs. San Francisco (24), 1985
52 San Diego (27) vs. San Francisco (25), 1995
50 Buffalo (31) vs. Dallas (19), 1994

Fewest Passes Completed, Both Teams, Game

19 Miami (4) vs. Washington (15), 1983
20 Pittsburgh (9) vs. Minnesota (11), 1975
22 Miami (8) vs. Washington (14), 1973

COMPLETION PERCENTAGE

Highest Completion Percentage, Game (20 attempts)

88.0 N.Y. Giants vs. Denver, 1987 (25-22)
75.0 San Francisco vs. Denver, 1990 (32-24)
73.5 Cincinnati vs. San Francisco, 1982 (34-25)

Lowest Completion Percentage, Game (20 attempts)

32.0 Denver vs. Dallas, 1978 (25-8)
37.9 Denver vs. San Francisco, 1990 (29-11)
38.5 Denver vs. Washington, 1988 (39-15)

YARDS GAINED

Most Yards Gained, Game

341 San Francisco vs. Cincinnati, 1989
326 San Francisco vs. Miami, 1985
322 Washington vs. Denver, 1988

Fewest Yards Gained, Game

35 Denver vs. Dallas, 1978
63 Miami vs. Minnesota, 1974
69 Miami vs. Washington, 1973

Most Yards Gained, Both Teams, Game

615 San Francisco (326) vs. Miami (289), 1985
603 San Francisco (316) vs. San Diego (287), 1995
583 Denver (320) vs. N.Y. Giants (263), 1987

Fewest Yards Gained, Both Teams, Game

156 Miami (69) vs. Washington (87), 1973
186 Pittsburgh (84) vs. Minnesota (102), 1975
204 Miami (80) vs. Washington (124), 1983

TIMES SACKED

Most Times Sacked, Game

7 Dallas vs. Pittsburgh, 1976
New England vs. Chicago, 1986
6 Kansas City vs. Green Bay, 1967
Washington vs. L.A. Raiders, 1984
Denver vs. San Francisco, 1990
5 Dallas vs. Denver, 1978; vs. Pittsburgh, 1979
Cincinnati vs. San Francisco, 1982; 1989
Denver vs. Washington, 1988
Buffalo vs. Washington, 1992
Green Bay vs. New England, 1997
New England vs. Green Bay, 1997

Fewest Times Sacked, Game

0 Baltimore vs. N.Y. Jets, 1969; vs. Dallas, 1971
Minnesota vs. Pittsburgh, 1975
Pittsburgh vs. Los Angeles, 1980
Philadelphia vs. Oakland, 1981
Washington vs. Buffalo, 1992
Denver vs. Green Bay, 1998
1 By 12 teams

Most Times Sacked, Both Teams, Game

10 New England (7) vs. Chicago (3), 1986
Green Bay (5) vs. New England (5), 1997
9 Kansas City (6) vs. Green Bay (3), 1967
Dallas (7) vs. Pittsburgh (2), 1976
Dallas (5) vs. Denver (4), 1978
Dallas (5) vs. Pittsburgh (4), 1979
Cincinnati (5) vs. San Francisco (4), 1989
8 Washington (6) vs. L.A. Raiders (2), 1984

Fewest Times Sacked, Both Teams, Game

1 Philadelphia (0) vs. Oakland (1), 1981
Denver (0) vs. Green Bay (1), 1998

2 Baltimore (0) vs. N.Y. Jets (2), 1969
Baltimore (0) vs. Dallas (2), 1971
Minnesota (0) vs. Pittsburgh (2), 1975
3 In four games

TOUCHDOWNS

Most Touchdowns, Game

6 San Francisco vs. San Diego, 1995
5 San Francisco vs. Denver, 1990
4 Pittsburgh vs. Dallas, 1979
Washington vs. Denver, 1988
Dallas vs. Buffalo, 1993

Fewest Touchdowns, Game

0 By 17 teams

Most Touchdowns, Both Teams, Game

7 Pittsburgh (4) vs. Dallas (3), 1979
San Francisco (6) vs. San Diego (1), 1995
5 Washington (4) vs. Denver (1), 1988
San Francisco (5) vs. Denver (0), 1990
Dallas (4) vs. Buffalo (1), 1993
4 Dallas (2) vs. Pittsburgh (2), 1976
Oakland (3) vs. Philadelphia (1), 1981
San Francisco (3) vs. Miami (1), 1985
N.Y. Giants (3) vs. Denver (1), 1987
Washington (2) vs. Buffalo (2), 1992
Green Bay (2) vs. New England (2), 1997

Fewest Touchdowns, Both Teams, Game

0 N.Y. Jets vs. Baltimore, 1969
Miami vs. Minnesota, 1974
Buffalo vs. Dallas, 1994
1 In six games

INTERCEPTIONS BY

Most Interceptions By, Game

4 N.Y. Jets vs. Baltimore, 1969
Dallas vs. Denver, 1978
Washington vs. Buffalo, 1992
Dallas vs. Buffalo, 1993
Green Bay vs. New England, 1997
3 By 11 teams

Most Interceptions By, Both Teams, Game

6 Baltimore (3) vs. Dallas (3), 1971
5 Washington (4) vs. Buffalo (1), 1992
4 In eight games

Fewest Interceptions By, Both Teams, Game

0 Buffalo vs. N.Y. Giants, 1991
1 Oakland (0) vs. Green Bay (1), 1968
Miami (0) vs. Dallas (1), 1972
Minnesota (0) vs. Miami (1), 1974
N.Y. Giants (0) vs. Denver (1), 1987
Cincinnati (0) vs. San Francisco (1), 1989

YARDS GAINED

Most Yards Gained, Game

95 Miami vs. Washington, 1973
91 Oakland vs. Minnesota, 1977
89 Pittsburgh vs. Dallas, 1976

Most Yards Gained, Both Teams, Game

95 Miami (95) vs. Washington (0), 1973
91 Oakland (91) vs. Minnesota (0), 1977
89 Pittsburgh (89) vs. Dallas (0), 1976

TOUCHDOWNS

Most Touchdowns, Game

1 Green Bay vs. Oakland, 1968
Oakland vs. Minnesota, 1977
L.A. Raiders vs. Washington, 1984
Chicago vs. New England, 1986

PUNTING

Most Punts, Game

9 Dallas vs. Baltimore, 1971
8 Washington vs. L.A. Raiders, 1984
New England vs. Green Bay, 1997
7 By eight teams

Fewest Punts, Game

2 Pittsburgh vs. Los Angeles, 1980
Denver vs. N.Y. Giants, 1987
3 By 10 teams

Most Punts, Both Teams, Game

15 Washington (8) vs. L.A. Raiders (7), 1984
New England (8) vs. Green Bay (7), 1997

13 Dallas (9) vs. Baltimore (4), 1971
Pittsburgh (7) vs. Minnesota (6), 1975
12 In three games

Fewest Punts, Both Teams, Game
5 Denver (2) vs. N.Y. Giants (3), 1987
6 Oakland (3) vs. Philadelphia (3), 1981
7 In five games

AVERAGE YARDAGE

Highest Average, Game (4 punts)
48.75 San Diego vs. San Francisco, 1995 (4-195)
48.50 Kansas City vs. Minnesota, 1970 (4-194)
46.25 San Francisco vs. Cincinnati, 1982 (4-185)

Lowest Average, Game (4 punts)
31.20 Washington vs. Miami, 1973 (5-156)
32.38 Washington vs. L.A. Raiders, 1984 (8-259)
32.40 Oakland vs. Minnesota, 1977 (5-162)

PUNT RETURNS

Most Punt Returns, Game
6 Washington vs. Miami, 1983
Green Bay vs. New England, 1997
5 By five teams

Fewest Punt Returns, Game
0 Minnesota vs. Miami, 1974
Buffalo vs. N.Y. Giants, 1991
Washington vs. Buffalo, 1992
Denver vs. Green Bay, 1998
Green Bay vs. Denver, 1998
1 By 15 teams

Most Punt Returns, Both Teams, Game
10 Green Bay (6) vs. New England (4), 1997
9 Pittsburgh (5) vs. Minnesota (4), 1975
8 Green Bay (5) vs. Oakland (3), 1968
Baltimore (5) vs. Dallas (3), 1971
Washington (6) vs. Miami (2), 1983

Fewest Punt Returns, Both Teams, Game
0 Denver vs. Green Bay, 1998
2 Dallas (1) vs. Miami (1), 1972
Denver (1) vs. N.Y. Giants (1), 1987
Buffalo (0) vs. N.Y. Giants (2), 1991
Buffalo (1) vs. Dallas (1), 1994
3 Kansas City (1) vs. Minnesota (2), 1970
Minnesota (0) vs. Miami (3), 1974
Washington (1) vs. Denver (2), 1988
Washington (0) vs. Buffalo (3), 1992
Dallas (1) vs. Pittsburgh (2), 1996
4 L.A. Raiders (2) vs. Washington (2), 1984
Chicago (2) vs. New England (2), 1986
Buffalo (1) vs. Dallas (3), 1993

YARDS GAINED

Most Yards Gained, Game
90 Green Bay vs. New England, 1997
56 San Francisco vs. Cincinnati, 1989
52 Washington vs. Miami, 1983

Fewest Yards Gained, Game
–1 Dallas vs. Miami, 1972
0 By ten teams

Most Yards Gained, Both Teams, Game
120 Green Bay (90) vs. New England (30), 1997
74 Washington (52) vs. Miami (22), 1983
66 San Francisco (51) vs. Miami (15), 1985

Fewest Yards Gained, Both Teams, Game
0 Denver vs. Green Bay, 1998
9 Washington (0) vs. Bufffalo (9), 1992
10 Buffalo (5) vs. Dallas (5), 1994

AVERAGE RETURN

Highest Average, Game (3 returns)
18.7 San Francisco vs. Cincinnati, 1989 (3-56)
15.0 Green Bay vs. New England, 1997 (6-90)
12.7 San Francisco vs. Denver, 1990 (3-38)

TOUCHDOWNS

Most Touchdowns, Game
None

KICKOFF RETURNS

Most Kickoff Returns, Game
9 Denver vs. San Francisco, 1990
8 San Diego vs. San Francisco, 1995
7 Oakland vs. Green Bay, 1968
Minnesota vs. Oakland, 1977
Cincinnati vs. San Francisco, 1982
Washington vs. L.A. Raiders, 1984
Miami vs. San Francisco, 1985
New England vs. Chicago, 1986

Fewest Kickoff Returns, Game
1 N.Y. Jets vs. Baltimore, 1969
L.A. Raiders vs. Washington, 1984
Washington vs. Buffalo, 1992
2 By seven teams

Most Kickoff Returns, Both Teams, Game
12 Denver (9) vs. San Francisco (3), 1990
San Diego (8) vs. San Francisco (4), 1995
11 Los Angeles (6) vs. Pittsburgh (5), 1980
Miami (7) vs. San Francisco (4), 1985
New England (7) vs. Chicago (4), 1986
Green Bay (6) vs. Denver (5), 1998
10 Oakland (7) vs. Green Bay (3), 1968
New England (6) vs. Green Bay (4), 1997

Fewest Kickoff Returns, Both Teams, Game
5 N.Y. Jets (1) vs. Baltimore (4), 1969
Miami (2) vs. Washington (3), 1973
Washington (1) vs. Buffalo (4), 1992
6 In three games

YARDS GAINED

Most Yards Gained, Game
244 San Diego vs. San Francisco, 1995
222 Miami vs. Washington, 1983
196 Denver vs. San Francisco, 1990

Fewest Yards Gained, Game
16 Washington vs. Buffalo, 1992
17 L.A. Raiders vs. Washington, 1984
25 N.Y. Jets vs. Baltimore, 1969

Most Yards Gained, Both Teams, Game
292 San Diego (244) vs. San Francisco (480, 1995
289 Green Bay (154) vs. New England (135), 1997
279 Miami (222) vs. Washington (57), 1983

Fewest Yards Gained, Both Teams, Game
78 Miami (33) vs. Washington (45), 1973
82 Pittsburgh (32) vs. Minnesota (50), 1975
92 San Francisco (40) vs. Cincinnati (52), 1982

AVERAGE GAIN

Highest Average, Game (3 returns)
44.0 Cincinnati vs. San Francisco, 1989 (3-132)
38.5 Green Bay vs. New England, 1997 (4-154)
37.0 Miami vs. Washington, 1983 (6-222)

TOUCHDOWNS

Most Touchdowns, Game
1 Miami vs. Washington, 1983
Cincinnati vs. San Francisco, 1989
San Diego vs. San Francisco, 1995
Green Bay vs. New England, 1997

PENALTIES

Most Penalties, Game
12 Dallas vs. Denver, 1978
10 Dallas vs. Baltimore, 1971
9 Dallas vs. Pittsburgh, 1979
Green Bay vs. Denver, 1998

Fewest Penalties, Game
0 Miami vs. Dallas, 1972
Pittsburgh vs. Dallas, 1976
Denver vs. San Francisco, 1990
1 Green Bay vs. Oakland, 1968
Miami vs. Minnesota, 1974; vs. San Francisco, 1985
Buffalo vs. Dallas, 1994
2 By six teams

Most Penalties, Both Teams, Game
20 Dallas (12) vs. Denver (8), 1978
16 Cincinnati (8) vs. San Francisco (8), 1982
Green Bay (9) vs. Denver (7), 1998
14 Dallas (10) vs. Baltimore (4), 1971
Dallas (9) vs. Pittsburgh (5), 1979

Fewest Penalties, Both Teams, Game
2 Pittsburgh (0) vs. Dallas (2), 1976
3 Miami (0) vs. Dallas (3), 1972
Miami (1) vs. San Francisco (2), 1985
4 Denver (0) vs. San Francisco (4), 1990

SUPER BOWL RECORDS

YARDS PENALIZED

Most Yards Penalized, Game

133 Dallas vs. Baltimore, 1971
122 Pittsburgh vs. Minnesota, 1975
94 Dallas vs. Denver, 1978

Fewest Yards Penalized, Game

0 Miami vs. Dallas, 1972
Pittsburgh vs. Dallas, 1976
Denver vs. San Francisco, 1990
4 Miami vs. Minnesota, 1974
10 Miami vs. San Francisco, 1985
San Francisco vs. Miami, 1985
Buffalo vs. Dallas, 1994

Most Yards Penalized, Both Teams, Game

164 Dallas (133) vs. Baltimore (31), 1971
154 Dallas (94) vs. Denver (60), 1978
140 Pittsburgh (122) vs. Minnesota (18), 1975

Fewest Yards Penalized, Both Teams, Game

15 Miami (0) vs. Dallas (15), 1972
20 Pittsburgh (0) vs. Dallas (20), 1976
Miami (10) vs. San Francisco (10), 1985
38 Denver (0) vs. San Francisco (38), 1990

FUMBLES

Most Fumbles, Game

8 Buffalo vs. Dallas, 1993
6 Dallas vs. Denver, 1978
Buffalo vs. Washington, 1992
5 Baltimore vs. Dallas, 1971

Fewest Fumbles, Game

0 By 15 teams

Most Fumbles, Both Teams, Game

12 Buffalo (8) vs. Dallas (4), 1993
10 Dallas (6) vs. Denver (4), 1978
8 Dallas (4) vs. Pittsburgh (4), 1976

Fewest Fumbles, Both Teams, Game

0 Los Angeles vs. Pittsburgh, 1980
Green Bay vs. New England, 1997
1 Oakland (0) vs. Minnesota (1), 1977
Oakland (0) vs. Philadelphia (1), 1981
Denver (0) vs. Washington (1), 1988
N.Y. Giants (0) vs. Buffalo (1), 1991
2 In five games

Most Fumbles Lost, Game

5 Buffalo vs. Dallas, 1993
4 Baltimore vs. Dallas, 1971
Denver vs. Dallas, 1978
New England vs. Chicago, 1986
2 In many games

Most Fumbles Lost, Both Teams, Game

7 Buffalo (5) vs. Dallas (2), 1993
6 Denver (4) vs. Dallas (2), 1978
New England (4) vs. Chicago (2), 1986
5 Baltimore (4) vs. Dallas (1), 1971

Fewest Fumbles Lost, Both Teams, Game

0 Green Bay vs. Kansas City, 1967
Dallas vs. Pittsburgh, 1976
Los Angeles vs. Pittsburgh, 1980
Denver vs. N.Y. Giants, 1987
Denver vs. Washington, 1988
Buffalo vs. N.Y. Giants, 1991
San Diego vs. San Francisco, 1995
Dallas vs. Pittsburgh, 1996
Green Bay vs. New England, 1997

Most Fumbles Recovered, Game

8 Dallas vs. Denver, 1978 (4 own, 4 opp.)
6 Dallas vs. Buffalo, 1993 (1 own, 5 opp.)
5 Chicago vs. New England, 1986 (1 own, 4 opp.)

TURNOVERS

(Number of times losing the ball on interceptions and fumbles.)

Most Turnovers, Game

9 Buffalo vs. Dallas, 1993
8 Denver vs. Dallas, 1978
7 Baltimore vs. Dallas, 1971

Fewest Turnovers, Game

0 Green Bay vs. Oakland, 1968
Miami vs. Minnesota, 1974
Pittsburgh vs. Dallas, 1976
Oakland vs. Minnesota, 1977; vs. Philadelphia, 1981
N.Y. Giants vs. Denver, 1987; vs. Buffalo, 1991
San Francisco vs. Denver, 1990; vs. San Diego, 1995
Buffalo vs. N.Y. Giants, 1991
Dallas vs. Pittsburgh, 1996
Green Bay vs. New England, 1997
1 By many teams

Most Turnovers, Both Teams, Game

11 Baltimore (7) vs. Dallas (4), 1971
Buffalo (9) vs. Dallas (2), 1993
10 Denver (8) vs. Dallas (2), 1978
8 New England (6) vs. Chicago (2), 1986

Fewest Turnovers, Both Teams, Game

0 Buffalo vs. N.Y. Giants, 1991
1 N.Y. Giants (0) vs. Denver (1), 1987
2 Green Bay (1) vs. Kansas City (1), 1967
Miami (0) vs. Minnesota (2), 1974
Cincinnati (1) vs. San Francisco (1), 1989

POSTSEASON GAME RECORDS

Compiled by Elias Sports Bureau

Throughout this all-time postseason record section, the following abbreviations are used to indicate various levels of postseason games:

SB Super Bowl (1966 to date)

AFC AFC Championship Game (1970 to date) or AFL Championship Game (1960-69)

NFC NFC Championship Game (1970 to date) or NFL Championship Game (1933-69)

AFC-D AFC Divisional Playoff Game (1970 to date), AFC Second-Round Playoff Game (1982), AFL Inter-Divisional Playoff Game (1969), or special playoff game to break tie for AFL Division Championship (1963, 1968)

NFC-D NFC Divisional Playoff Game (1970 to date), NFC Second-Round Playoff Game (1982), NFL Conference Championship Game (1967-69), or special playoff game to break tie for NFL Division or Conference Championship (1941, 1943, 1947, 1950, 1952, 1957, 1958, 1965)

AFC-FR AFC First-Round Playoff Game (1978 to date)

NFC-FR NFC First-Round Playoff Game (1978 to date)

POSTSEASON GAME COMPOSITE STANDINGS

	W	L	PCT.	PTS.	OP
Green Bay Packers	22	9	.710	745	528
Dallas Cowboys	32	19	.627	1254	932
San Francisco 49ers	23	14	.622	936	712
Washington Redskins*	21	14	.600	738	615
Oakland Raiders**	21	15	.583	855	659
Pittsburgh Steelers	21	15	.583	801	707
Denver Broncos	13	11	.542	518	604
Miami Dolphins	17	15	.531	700	650
Buffalo Bills	14	13	.519	648	612
Carolina Panthers	1	1	.500	39	47
Chicago Bears	14	14	.500	579	552
Indianapolis Colts***	10	10	.500	360	389
Jacksonville Jaguars	2	2	.500	83	116
New York Jets	5	6	.455	216	200
Philadelphia Eagles	9	11	.450	359	369
Detroit Lions	7	9	.438	352	377
New England Patriots#	7	9	.438	300	332
Seattle Seahawks	3	4	.429	128	139
New York Giants	14	19	.424	541	616
Kansas City Chiefs****	8	11	.421	301	384
Cincinnati Bengals	5	7	.417	246	257
Minnesota Vikings	14	20	.412	613	746
Tennessee Oilers†	9	13	.409	371	533
St. Louis Rams††	13	20	.394	501	697
San Diego Chargers†††	7	11	.389	332	428
Cleveland Browns	11	19	.367	596	692
Tampa Bay Buccaneers	2	4	.333	68	125
Atlanta Falcons	2	5	.286	139	181
Arizona Cardinals††††	1	4	.200	81	134
New Orleans Saints	0	4	.000	56	123

One game played when franchise was in Boston (lost 21-6).

***12 games played when franchise was in Los Angeles (won 6, lost 6, 268 points scored, 224 points allowed).*

****15 games played when franchise was in Baltimore (won 8, lost 7, 264 points scored, 262 points allowed).*

*****One game played when franchise was Dallas Texans (won 20-17).*

#Two games played when franchise was in Boston (won 26-8, lost 51-10).

†22 games played when franchise was in Houston (won 9, lost 13, 371 points scored, 533 points allowed).

††One game played when franchise was in Cleveland (won 15-14), 32 games played when franchise was in Los Angeles (won 12, lost 20, 486 points scored, 683 points allowed).

†††One game played when franchise was in Los Angeles (lost 24-16).

††††Two games played when franchise was in Chicago (won 28-21, lost 7-0), three games played when franchise was in St. Louis (lost 30-14, lost 35-23, lost 41-16).

INDIVIDUAL RECORDS

SERVICE

Most Games, Career

27 D.D. Lewis, Dallas (SB 5, NFC 9, NFC-D 12, NFC-FR 1)
26 Larry Cole, Dallas (SB 5, NFC 8, NFC-D 12, NFC-FR 1)
25 Charlie Waters, Dallas (SB 5, NFC 9, NFC-D 10, NFC-FR 1)

Most Games, Head Coach

36 Tom Landry, Dallas
Don Shula, Baltimore-Miami
24 Chuck Noll, Pittsburgh
22 Bud Grant, Minnesota

Most Games Won, Head Coach

20 Tom Landry, Dallas
19 Don Shula, Baltimore-Miami
16 Chuck Noll, Pittsburgh
Joe Gibbs, Washington

Most Games Lost, Head Coach

17 Don Shula, Baltimore-Miami
16 Tom Landry, Dallas
12 Bud Grant, Minnesota

SCORING

POINTS

Most Points, Career

120 Thurman Thomas, Buffalo, 19 games (20-td)
Emmitt Smith, Dallas, 15 games (20-td)
115 George Blanda, Chi. Bears-Houston-Oakland, 19 games (49-pat, 22-fg)
108 Jerry Rice, San Francisco, 21 games (18-td)

Most Points, Game

30 Ricky Watters, NFC-D:San Francisco vs. N.Y. Giants, 1993 (5-td)
19 Pat Harder, NFC-D: Detroit vs. Los Angeles, 1952 (2-td, 4-pat, 1-fg)
Paul Hornung, NFC: Green Bay vs. N.Y. Giants, 1961 (1-td, 4-pat, 3-fg)
18 By many players

Most Consecutive Games Scoring

19 George Blanda, Chi. Bears-Houston-Oakland, 1956-75
16 Norm Johnson, Seattle-Atlanta-Pittsburgh, 1983-97 (current)
15 Roy Gerela, Houston-Pittsburgh, 1969-78

TOUCHDOWNS

Most Touchdowns, Career

20 Thurman Thomas, Buffalo, 19 games (15-r, 5-p)
Emmitt Smith, Dallas, 15 games (18-r, 2-p)
18 Jerry Rice, San Francisco, 21 games (18-p)
17 Franco Harris, Pittsburgh, 19 games (16-r, 1-p)

Most Touchdowns, Game

5 Ricky Watters, NFC-D:San Francisco vs. N.Y. Giants, 1993 (5-r)
3 Andy Farkas, NFC-D: Washington vs. N.Y. Giants, 1943 (3-r)
Tom Fears, NFC-D: Los Angeles vs. Chi. Bears, 1950 (3-p)
Otto Graham, NFC: Cleveland vs. Detroit, 1954 (3-r)
Gary Collins, NFC: Cleveland vs. Baltimore, 1964 (3-p)
Craig Baynham, NFC-D: Dallas vs. Cleveland, 1967 (2-r, 1-p)
Fred Biletnikoff, AFC-D: Oakland vs. Kansas City, 1968 (3-p)
Tom Matte, NFC: Baltimore vs. Cleveland, 1968 (3-r)
Larry Schreiber, NFC-D: San Francisco vs. Dallas, 1972 (3-r)
Larry Csonka, AFC: Miami vs. Oakland, 1973 (3-r)
Franco Harris, AFC-D: Pittsburgh vs. Buffalo, 1974 (3-r)
Preston Pearson, NFC: Dallas vs. Los Angeles, 1975 (3-p)
Dave Casper, AFC-D: Oakland vs. Baltimore, 1977 (OT) (3-p)
Alvin Garrett, NFC-FR: Washington vs. Detroit, 1982 (3-p)
John Riggins, NFC-D: Washington vs. L.A. Rams, 1983 (3-r)
Roger Craig, SB: San Francisco vs. Miami, 1984 (1-r, 2-p)
Jerry Rice, NFC-D: San Francisco vs. Minnesota, 1988 (3-p)
Jerry Rice, SB: San Francisco vs. Denver, 1989 (3-p)
Kenneth Davis, AFC: Buffalo vs. L.A. Raiders, 1990 (3-r)
Andre Reed, AFC-FR: Buffalo vs. Houston, 1992 (OT) (3-p)
Sterling Sharpe, NFC-FR: Green Bay vs. Detroit, 1993 (3-p)
Napoleon McCallum, AFC-FR: L.A. Raiders vs. Denver, 1993 (3-r)
Thurman Thomas, AFC: Buffalo vs. Kansas City, 1993 (3-r)
William Floyd, NFC-D: San Francisco vs. Chicago, 1994 (3-r)
Ricky Watters, SB: San Francisco vs. San Diego, 1994 (1-r, 2-p)
Jerry Rice, SB: San Francisco vs. San Diego, 1994 (3-p)
Emmitt Smith, NFC: Dallas vs. Green Bay, 1995 (3-r)
Curtis Martin, AFC-D: New England vs. Pittsburgh, 1996 (3-r)
Terrell Davis, SB: Denver vs. Green Bay, 1997 (3-r)

Most Consecutive Games Scoring Touchdowns

8 John Stallworth, Pittsburgh, 1978-83
Thurman Thomas, Buffalo, 1992-96 (current)
Emmitt Smith, Dallas, 1993-96
7 John Riggins, Washington, 1982-84
Marcus Allen, L.A. Raiders, 1982-85
5 Duane Thomas, Dallas, 1970-71
Franco Harris, Pittsburgh, 1974-75
Franco Harris, Pittsburgh, 1977-79
James Lofton, Green Bay-Buffalo, 1982-90
Terrell Davis, Denver, 1996-97 (current)

POINTS AFTER TOUCHDOWN

Most (One-Point) Points After Touchdown, Career

49 George Blanda, Chi. Bears-Houston-Oakland, 19 games (49 att)
42 Mike Cofer, San Francisco, 12 games (46 att)
41 Rafael Septien, L.A. Rams-Dallas, 15 games (41 att)

Most (One-Point) Points After Touchdown, Game

8 Lou Groza, NFC: Cleveland vs. Detroit, 1954 (8 att)
Jim Martin, NFC: Detroit vs. Cleveland, 1957 (8 att)
George Blanda, AFC-D: Oakland vs. Houston, 1969 (8 att)

7 Danny Villanueva, NFC-D: Dallas vs. Cleveland, 1967 (7 att)
Raul Allegre, NFC-D: N.Y. Giants vs. San Francisco, 1986 (7 att)
Mike Cofer, SB: San Francisco vs. Denver, 1989 (8 att)
Lin Elliott, SB: Dallas vs. Buffalo, 1992 (7 att)
Doug Brien, SB: San Francisco vs. San Diego, 1994 (7 att)
Gary Anderson, NFC-FR: Philadelphia vs. Detroit, 1995 (7 att)
6 George Blair, AFC: San Diego vs. Boston, 1963 (6 att)
Mark Moseley, NFC-D: Washington vs. L.A. Rams, 1983 (6 att)
Uwe von Schamann, AFC: Miami vs. Pittsburgh, 1984 (6 att)
Ali Haji-Sheikh, SB: Washington vs. Denver, 1987 (6 att)
Scott Norwood, AFC: Buffalo vs. L.A. Raiders, 1990 (7 att)
Jeff Jaeger, AFC-FR: L.A. Raiders vs. Denver, 1993 (6 att)
Jason Elam, AFC-FR: Denver vs. Jacksonville, 1997 (6 att)

Most (Kicking) Points After Touchdown, No Misses, Career
49 George Blanda, Chi. Bears-Houston-Oakland, 19 games
41 Rafael Septien, L.A. Rams-Dallas, 14 games
36 Gary Anderson, Pittsburgh-Philadelphia-San Francisco, 15 games

Most Two-Point Conversions, Career
1 By many players

Most Two-Point Conversions, Game
1 By many players

FIELD GOALS

Most Field Goals Attempted, Career
39 George Blanda, Chi. Bears-Houston-Oakland, 19 games
31 Mark Moseley, Washington-Cleveland, 11 games
27 Gary Anderson, Pittsburgh-Philadelphia-San Francisco, 15 games

Most Field Goals Attempted, Game
6 George Blanda, AFC: Oakland vs. Houston, 1967
David Ray, NFC-D: Los Angeles vs. Dallas, 1973
Mark Moseley, AFC-D: Cleveland vs. N.Y. Jets, 1986 (OT)
Matt Bahr, NFC: N.Y. Giants vs. San Francisco, 1990
Steve Christie, AFC: Buffalo vs. Miami, 1992
5 By many players

Most Field Goals, Career
22 George Blanda, Chi. Bears-Houston-Oakland, 19 games
21 Matt Bahr, Pittsburgh-Cleveland-N.Y. Giants-New England, 14 games
Gary Anderson, Pittsburgh-Philadelphia-San Francisco, 15 games
20 Toni Fritsch, Dallas-Houston, 14 games
Steve Christie, Buffalo, 10 games
Norm Johnson, Seattle-Atlanta-Pittsburgh, 16 games

Most Field Goals, Game
5 Chuck Nelson, NFC-D: Minnesota vs. San Francisco, 1987
Matt Bahr, NFC: N.Y. Giants vs. San Francisco, 1990
Steve Christie, AFC: Buffalo vs. Miami, 1992
Brad Daluiso, NFC-FR: N.Y. Giants vs. Minnesota, 1997
4 Gino Cappelletti, AFC-D: Boston vs. Buffalo, 1963
George Blanda, AFC: Oakland vs. Houston, 1967
Don Chandler, SB: Green Bay vs. Oakland, 1967
Curt Knight, NFC: Washington vs. Dallas, 1972
George Blanda, AFC-D: Oakland vs. Pittsburgh, 1973
Ray Wersching, SB: San Francisco vs. Cincinnati, 1981
Tony Franklin, AFC-FR: New England vs. N.Y. Jets, 1985
Jess Atkinson, NFC-FR: Washington vs. L.A. Rams, 1986
Luis Zendejas, NFC-D: Philadelphia vs. Chicago, 1988
Gary Anderson, AFC-FR: Pittsburgh vs. Houston, 1989 (OT)
Norm Johnson, AFC-D: Pittsburgh vs. Buffalo, 1995
Chris Boniol, NFC-FR: Dallas vs. Minnesota, 1996
John Kasay, NFC-D: Carolina vs. Dallas, 1996
3 By many players

Most Consecutive Games Scoring Field Goals
13 Toni Fritsch, Dallas-Houston, 1972-79
9 Kevin Butler, Chicago, 1985-91
Scott Norwood, Buffalo, 1988-91
8 Mark Moseley, Washington-Cleveland, 1982-86
Rich Karlis, Denver-Minnesota, 1984-89
Steve Christie, Buffalo, 1993-95
Gary Anderson, Pittsburgh-Philadelphia, 1989-95

Most Consecutive Field Goals
16 Gary Anderson, Pittsburgh-Philadelphia, 1989-95
15 Rafael Septien, Dallas, 1978-82
9 Chuck Nelson, Minnesota, 1987
Steve Christie, Buffalo, 1993-95
Chris Boniol, Dallas, 1995-96 (current)

Longest Field Goal
58 Pete Stoyanovich, AFC-FR: Miami vs. Kansas City, 1990
54 Ed Murray, NFC-D: Detroit vs. San Francisco, 1983
Steve Christie, SB: Buffalo vs. Dallas, 1993
John Carney, AFC-FR: San Diego vs. Indianapolis, 1995
53 Al Del Greco, AFC-FR: Houston vs. N.Y. Jets, 1991

Highest Field Goal Percentage, Career (10 field goals)
90.9 Chuck Nelson, L.A. Rams-Minnesota, 6 games (11-10)
87.0 Steve Christie, Buffalo, 10 games (23-20)
86.7 Chris Boniol, Dallas, 7 games (15-13)

SAFETIES

Most Safeties, Game
1 Bill Willis, NFC-D: Cleveland vs. N.Y. Giants, 1950
Carl Eller, NFC-D: Minnesota vs. Los Angeles, 1969
George Andrie, NFC-D: Dallas vs. Detroit, 1970
Alan Page, NFC-D: Minnesota vs. Dallas, 1971
Dwight White, SB: Pittsburgh vs. Minnesota, 1974
Reggie Harrison, SB: Pittsburgh vs. Dallas, 1975
Jim Jensen, NFC-D: Dallas vs. Los Angeles, 1976
Ted Washington, AFC: Houston vs. Pittsburgh, 1978
Randy White, NFC-D: Dallas vs. Los Angeles, 1979
Henry Waechter, SB: Chicago vs. New England, 1985
Rulon Jones, AFC-FR: Denver vs. New England, 1986
George Martin, SB: N.Y. Giants vs. Denver, 1986
D.D. Hoggard, AFC: Cleveland vs. Denver, 1987
Bruce Smith, SB: Buffalo vs. N.Y. Giants, 1990
Reggie White, NFC-FR: Philadelphia vs. New Orleans, 1992
Willie Clay, NFC-FR: Detroit vs. Green Bay, 1994
Carnell Lake, AFC-D: Pittsburgh vs. Cleveland, 1994
Reuben Davis, AFC-D: San Diego vs. Miami, 1994

RUSHING

ATTEMPTS

Most Attempts, Career
400 Franco Harris, Pittsburgh, 19 games
327 Thurman Thomas, Buffalo, 19 games
318 Emmitt Smith, Dallas, 15 games

Most Attempts, Game
38 Ricky Bell, NFC-D: Tampa Bay vs. Philadelphia, 1979
John Riggins, SB: Washington vs. Miami, 1982
37 Lawrence McCutcheon, NFC-D: Los Angeles vs. St. Louis, 1975
John Riggins, NFC-D: Washington vs. Minnesota, 1982
36 John Riggins, NFC: Washington vs. Dallas, 1982
John Riggins, NFC: Washington vs. San Francisco, 1983

YARDS GAINED

Most Yards Gained, Career
1,556 Franco Harris, Pittsburgh, 19 games
1,413 Emmitt Smith, Dallas, 15 games
1,399 Thurman Thomas, Buffalo, 19 games

Most Yards Gained, Game
248 Eric Dickerson, NFC-D: L.A. Rams vs. Dallas, 1985
206 Keith Lincoln, AFC: San Diego vs. Boston, 1963
204 Timmy Smith, SB: Washington vs. Denver, 1987

Most Games, 100 or More Yards Rushing, Career
7 Emmitt Smith, Dallas, 15 games
6 John Riggins, Washington, 9 games
Thurman Thomas, Buffalo, 19 games
5 Franco Harris, Pittsburgh, 19 games
Marcus Allen, L.A. Raiders-Kansas City, 16 games

Most Consecutive Games, 100 or More Yards Rushing
6 John Riggins, Washington, 1982-83
4 Thurman Thomas, Buffalo, 1990-91
Terrell Davis, Denver, 1997 (current)
3 Larry Csonka, Miami, 1973-74
Franco Harris, Pittsburgh, 1974-75
Marcus Allen, L.A. Raiders, 1983
Emmitt Smith, Dallas, 1992

Longest Run From Scrimmage
80 Roger Craig, NFC-D: San Francisco vs. Minnesota, 1988 (TD)
78 Curtis Martin, AFC-D: New England vs. Pittsburgh, 1996 (TD)
74 Marcus Allen, SB: L.A. Raiders vs. Washington, 1983 (TD)

AVERAGE GAIN

Highest Average Gain, Career (100 attempts)
5.33 Terrell Davis, Denver, 5 games (126-672)
5.04 Marcus Allen, L.A. Raiders-Kansas City, 16 games (267-1,347)
4.89 Eric Dickerson, L.A. Rams-Indianapolis, 7 games (148-724)

Highest Average Gain, Game (10 attempts)
15.90 Elmer Angsman, NFC: Chi. Cardinals vs. Philadelphia, 1947 (10-159)
15.85 Keith Lincoln, AFC: San Diego vs. Boston, 1963 (13-206)
11.31 Zack Crockett, AFC-FR: Indianapolis vs. San Diego, 1995 (13-147)

TOUCHDOWNS

Most Touchdowns, Career
18 Emmitt Smith, Dallas, 15 games
16 Franco Harris, Pittsburgh, 19 games
15 Thurman Thomas, Buffalo, 19 games

Most Touchdowns, Game
5 Ricky Watters, NFC-D: San Francisco vs. N.Y. Giants, 1993
3 Andy Farkas, NFC-D: Washington vs. N.Y. Giants, 1943

Otto Graham, NFC: Cleveland vs. Detroit, 1954
Tom Matte, NFC: Baltimore vs. Cleveland, 1968
Larry Schreiber, NFC-D: San Francisco vs. Dallas, 1972
Larry Csonka, AFC: Miami vs. Oakland, 1973
Franco Harris, AFC-D: Pittsburgh vs. Buffalo, 1974
John Riggins, NFC-D: Washington vs. L.A. Rams, 1983
Kenneth Davis, AFC: Buffalo vs. L.A. Raiders, 1990
Napoleon McCallum, AFC-FR: L.A. Raiders vs. Denver, 1993
Thurman Thomas, AFC: Buffalo vs. Kansas City, 1993
William Floyd, NFC-D: San Francisco vs. Chicago, 1994
Emmitt Smith, NFC: Dallas vs. Green Bay, 1995
Curtis Martin, AFC-D: New England vs. Pittsburgh, 1996
Terrell Davis, SB: Denver vs. Green Bay, 1997

Most Consecutive Games Rushing for Touchdowns
8 Emmitt Smith, Dallas, 1993-96
7 John Riggins, Washington, 1982-84
Thurman Thomas, Buffalo, 1992-96 (current)
5 Franco Harris, Pittsburgh, 1974-75
Franco Harris, Pittsburgh, 1977-79
Terrell Davis, Denver, 1996-97 (current)

PASSING

PASSER RATING

Highest Passer Rating, Career (150 attempts)
104.8 Bart Starr, Green Bay, 10 games
96.0 Troy Aikman, Dallas, 14 games
95.6 Joe Montana, San Francisco-Kansas City, 23 games

ATTEMPTS

Most Passes Attempted, Career
734 Joe Montana, San Francisco-Kansas City, 23 games
565 John Elway, Denver, 19 games
561 Dan Marino, Miami, 14 games

Most Passes Attempted, Game
65 Steve Young, NFC-D: San Francisco vs. Green Bay, 1995
64 Bernie Kosar, AFC-D: Cleveland vs. N.Y. Jets, 1986 (OT)
Dan Marino, AFC-FR: Miami vs. Buffalo, 1995
58 Jim Kelly, SB: Buffalo vs. Washington, 1991

COMPLETIONS

Most Passes Completed, Career
460 Joe Montana, San Francisco-Kansas City, 23 games
322 Jim Kelly, Buffalo, 17 games
310 John Elway, Denver, 19 games

Most Passes Completed, Game
36 Warren Moon, AFC-FR: Houston vs. Buffalo, 1992 (OT)
33 Dan Fouts, AFC-D: San Diego vs. Miami, 1981 (OT)
Bernie Kosar, AFC-D: Cleveland vs. N.Y. Jets, 1986 (OT)
Dan Marino, AFC-FR: Miami vs. Buffalo, 1995
32 Neil Lomax, NFC-FR: St. Louis vs. Green Bay, 1982
Danny White, NFC-FR: Dallas vs. L.A. Rams, 1983
Warren Moon, AFC-D: Houston vs. Kansas City, 1993
Neil O'Donnell, AFC: Pittsburgh vs. San Diego, 1994
Steve Young, NFC-D: San Francisco vs. Green Bay, 1995

COMPLETION PERCENTAGE

Highest Completion Percentage, Career (150 attempts)
66.5 Troy Aikman, Dallas, 14 games (415-276)
66.3 Ken Anderson, Cincinnati, 6 games (166-110)
64.3 Warren Moon, Houston-Minnesota, 10 games (403-259)

Highest Completion Percentage, Game (15 completions)
88.0 Phil Simms, SB: N.Y. Giants vs. Denver, 1986 (25-22)
86.7 Joe Montana, NFC: San Francisco vs. L.A. Rams, 1989 (30-26)
84.2 David Woodley, AFC-FR: Miami vs. New England, 1982 (19-16)

YARDS GAINED

Most Yards Gained, Career
5,772 Joe Montana, San Francisco-Kansas City, 23 games
4,273 John Elway Denver, 19 games
3,863 Jim Kelly, Buffalo, 17 games

Most Yards Gained, Game
489 Bernie Kosar, AFC-D: Cleveland vs. N.Y. Jets, 1986 (OT)
433 Dan Fouts, AFC-D: San Diego vs. Miami, 1981 (OT)
422 Dan Marino, AFC-FR: Miami vs. Buffalo, 1995

Most Games, 300 or More Yards Passing, Career
6 Joe Montana, San Francisco-Kansas City, 23 games
5 Dan Fouts, San Diego, 7 games
4 Warren Moon, Houston-Minnesota, 10 games
Troy Aikman, Dallas, 14 games
Dan Marino, Miami, 14 games

Most Consecutive Games, 300 or More Yards Passing
4 Dan Fouts, San Diego, 1979-81
3 Jim Kelly, Buffalo, 1989-90
Warren Moon, Houston, 1991-93
2 Daryle Lamonica, Oakland, 1968
Ken Anderson, Cincinnati, 1981-82
Terry Bradshaw, Pittsburgh, 1979-82
Joe Montana, San Francisco, 1983-84
Dan Marino, Miami, 1984
Troy Aikman, Dallas, 1994
Steve Young, San Francisco, 1994-95

Longest Pass Completion
94 Troy Aikman (to Harper), NFC-D: Dallas vs. Green Bay, 1994 (TD)
93 Daryle Lamonica (to Dubenion), AFC-D: Buffalo vs. Boston, 1963 (TD)
88 George Blanda (to Cannon), AFC: Houston vs. L.A. Chargers, 1960 (TD)

AVERAGE GAIN

Highest Average Gain, Career (150 attempts)
8.45 Joe Theismann, Washington, 10 games (211-1,782)
8.43 Jim Plunkett, Oakland/L.A.Raiders, 10 games (272-2,293)
8.41 Terry Bradshaw, Pittsburgh, 19 games (456-3,833)

Highest Average Gain, Game (20 attempts)
14.71 Terry Bradshaw, SB: Pittsburgh vs. Los Angeles, 1979 (21-309)
13.33 Bob Waterfield, NFC-D: Los Angeles vs. Chi. Bears, 1950 (21-280)
13.16 Dan Marino, AFC: Miami vs. Pittsburgh, 1984 (32-421)

TOUCHDOWNS

Most Touchdown Passes, Career
45 Joe Montana, San Francisco-Kansas City, 23 games
30 Terry Bradshaw, Pittsburgh, 19 games
29 Dan Marino, Miami, 14 games

Most Touchdown Passes, Game
6 Daryle Lamonica, AFC-D: Oakland vs. Houston, 1969
Steve Young, SB: San Francisco vs. San Diego, 1994
5 Sid Luckman, NFC: Chi. Bears vs. Washington, 1943
Daryle Lamonica, AFC-D: Oakland vs. Kansas City, 1968
Joe Montana, SB: San Francisco vs. Denver, 1989
4 Otto Graham, NFC: Cleveland vs. Los Angeles, 1950
Tobin Rote, NFC: Detroit vs. Cleveland, 1957
Bart Starr, NFC: Green Bay vs. Dallas, 1966
Ken Stabler, AFC-D: Oakland vs. Miami, 1974
Roger Staubach, NFC: Dallas vs. Los Angeles, 1975
Terry Bradshaw, SB: Pittsburgh vs. Dallas, 1978
Don Strock, AFC-D: Miami vs. San Diego, 1981 (OT)
Lynn Dickey, NFC-FR: Green Bay vs. St. Louis, 1982
Dan Marino, AFC: Miami vs. Pittsburgh, 1984
Phil Simms, NFC-D: N.Y. Giants vs. San Francisco, 1986
Doug Williams, SB: Washington vs. Denver, 1987
Jim Kelly, AFC-D: Buffalo vs. Cleveland, 1989
Joe Montana, NFC-D: San Francisco vs. Minnesota, 1989
Warren Moon, AFC-FR: Houston vs. Buffalo, 1992 (OT)
Frank Reich, AFC-FR: Buffalo vs. Houston, 1992 (OT)
Troy Aikman, SB: Dallas vs. Buffalo, 1992

Most Consecutive Games, Touchdown Passes
13 Dan Marino, Miami, 1983-95
10 Ken Stabler, Oakland, 1973-77
Joe Montana, San Francisco-Kansas City, 1988-93
9 John Elway, Denver, 1984-89
Brett Favre, Green Bay, 1995-97 (current)

HAD INTERCEPTED

Lowest Percentage, Passes Had Intercepted, Career (150 attempts)
1.41 Bart Starr, Green Bay, 10 games (213-3)
1.99 Steve Young, San Francisco, 20 games (402-8)
2.15 Phil Simms, N.Y. Giants, 10 games (279-6)

Most Attempts Without Interception, Game
54 Neil O'Donnell, AFC: Pittsburgh vs. San Diego, 1994
48 Warren Moon, AFC-FR: Houston vs. Pittsburgh, 1989 (OT)
47 Daryle Lamonica, AFC: Oakland vs. N.Y. Jets, 1968

Most Passes Had Intercepted, Career
28 Jim Kelly, Buffalo, 17 games
26 Terry Bradshaw, Pittsburgh, 19 games
21 Joe Montana, San Francisco-Kansas City, 23 games

Most Passes Had Intercepted, Game
6 Frank Filchock, NFC: N.Y. Giants vs. Chi. Bears, 1946
Bobby Layne, NFC: Detroit vs. Cleveland, 1954
Norm Van Brocklin, NFC: Los Angeles vs. Cleveland, 1955
5 Frank Filchock, NFC: Washington vs. Chi. Bears, 1940
George Blanda, AFC: Houston vs. San Diego, 1961
George Blanda, AFC: Houston vs. Dall. Texans, 1962 (OT)
Y.A. Tittle, NFC: N.Y. Giants vs. Chicago, 1963
Mike Phipps, AFC-D: Cleveland vs. Miami, 1972
Dan Pastorini, AFC: Houston vs. Pittsburgh, 1978
Dan Fouts, AFC-D: San Diego vs. Houston, 1979
Tommy Kramer, NFC-D: Minnesota vs. Philadelphia, 1980
Dan Fouts, AFC-D: San Diego vs. Miami, 1982

Richard Todd, AFC: N.Y. Jets vs Miami, 1982
Gary Danielson, NFC-D: Detroit vs. San Francisco, 1983
Jay Schroeder, AFC: L.A. Raiders vs. Buffalo, 1990
4 By many players

PASS RECEIVING

RECEPTIONS

Most Receptions, Career
120 Jerry Rice, San Francisco, 21 games
83 Michael Irvin, Dallas, 15 games
80 Andre Reed, Buffalo, 19 games

Most Receptions, Game
13 Kellen Winslow, AFC-D: San Diego vs. Miami, 1981 (OT)
Thurman Thomas, AFC-D: Buffalo vs. Cleveland, 1989
Shannon Sharpe, AFC-FR: Denver vs. L.A. Raiders, 1993
12 Raymond Berry, NFC: Baltimore vs. N.Y. Giants, 1958
Michael Irvin, NFC: Dallas vs. San Francisco, 1994
11 Dante Lavelli, NFC: Cleveland vs. Los Angeles, 1950
Dan Ross, SB: Cincinnati vs. San Francisco, 1981
Franco Harris, AFC-FR: Pittsburgh vs. San Diego, 1982
Steve Watson, AFC-D: Denver vs. Pittsburgh, 1984
John L. Williams, AFC-D: Seattle vs. Cincinnati, 1988
Jerry Rice, SB: San Francisco vs. Cincinnati, 1988
Ernest Givins, AFC-FR: Houston vs. Pittsburgh, 1989 (OT)
Amp Lee, NFC-D: Minnesota vs. Chicago, 1994
Jay Novacek, NFC-D: Dallas vs. Green Bay, 1994
O.J. McDuffie, AFC-FR: Miami vs. Buffalo, 1995
Jerry Rice, NFC-C: San Francisco vs. Green Bay, 1995

Most Consecutive Games, Pass Receptions
22 Drew Pearson, Dallas, 1973-83
21 Jerry Rice, San Francisco, 1985-96 (current)
18 Paul Warfield, Cleveland-Miami, 1964-74
Cliff Branch, Oakland/L.A. Raiders, 1974-83

YARDS GAINED

Most Yards Gained, Career
1,742 Jerry Rice, San Francisco, 21 games
1,289 Cliff Branch, Oakland/L.A. Raiders, 22 games
1,283 Michael Irvin, Dallas, 15 games

Most Yards Gained, Game
227 Anthony Carter, NFC-D: Minnesota vs. San Francisco, 1987
215 Jerry Rice, SB: San Francisco vs. Cincinnati, 1988
198 Tom Fears, NFC-D: Los Angeles vs. Chi. Bears, 1950

Most Games, 100 or More Yards Receiving, Career
7 Jerry Rice, San Francisco, 21 games
6 Michael Irvin, Dallas, 13 games
5 John Stallworth, Pittsburgh, 18 games
Andre Reed, Buffalo, 19 games

Most Consecutive Games, 100 or More Yards Receiving, Career
3 Tom Fears, Los Angeles, 1950-51
Jerry Rice, San Francisco, 1988-89
2 By many players

Longest Reception
94 Alvin Harper (from Aikman), NFC-D: Dallas vs. Green Bay, 1994 (TD)
93 Elbert Dubenion (from Lamonica), AFC-D: Buffalo vs. Boston, 1963 (TD)
88 Billy Cannon (from Blanda), AFC: Houston vs. L.A. Chargers, 1960 (TD)

AVERAGE GAIN

Highest Average Gain, Career (20 receptions)
27.3 Alvin Harper, Dallas, 10 games (24-655)
23.7 Willie Gault, Chicago-L.A. Raiders, 12 games (21-497)
22.8 Harold Jackson, L.A. Rams-New England-Minnesota-Seattle, 14 games (24-548)

Highest Average Gain, Game (3 receptions)
46.3 Harold Jackson, NFC: Los Angeles vs. Minnesota, 1974 (3-139)
42.7 Billy Cannon, AFC: Houston vs. L.A. Chargers, 1960 (3-128)
42.0 Lenny Moore, NFC: Baltimore vs. N.Y. Giants, 1959 (3-126)

TOUCHDOWNS

Most Touchdowns, Career
18 Jerry Rice, San Francisco, 21 games
12 John Stallworth, Pittsburgh, 18 games
10 Fred Biletnikoff, Oakland, 19 games

Most Touchdowns, Game
3 Tom Fears, NFC-D: Los Angeles vs. Chi. Bears, 1950
Gary Collins, NFC: Cleveland vs. Baltimore, 1964
Fred Biletnikoff, AFC-D: Oakland vs. Kansas City, 1968
Preston Pearson, NFC: Dallas vs. Los Angeles, 1975
Dave Casper, AFC-D: Oakland vs. Baltimore, 1977 (OT)
Alvin Garrett, NFC-FR: Washington vs. Detroit, 1982
Jerry Rice, NFC-D: San Francisco vs. Minnesota, 1988
Jerry Rice, SB: San Francisco vs. Denver, 1989
Andre Reed, AFC-FR: Buffalo vs. Houston, 1992 (OT)
Sterling Sharpe, NFC-FR: Green Bay vs. Detroit, 1993
Jerry Rice, SB: San Francisco vs. San Diego, 1994

Most Consecutive Games, Touchdown Passes Caught
8 John Stallworth, Pittsburgh, 1978-83
5 James Lofton, Green Bay-Buffalo, 1982-90
4 Lynn Swann, Pittsburgh, 1978-79
Harold Carmichael, Philadelphia, 1978-80
Fred Solomon, San Francisco, 1983-84
Jerry Rice, San Francisco, 1988-89
John Taylor, San Francisco, 1988-89

INTERCEPTIONS BY

Most Interceptions, Career
9 Charlie Waters, Dallas, 25 games
Bill Simpson, Los Angeles-Buffalo, 11 games
Ronnie Lott, San Francisco-L.A. Raiders, 20 games
8 Lester Hayes, Oakland/L.A. Raiders, 13 games
7 Willie Brown, Oakland, 17 games
Dennis Thurman, Dallas, 14 games

Most Interceptions, Game
4 Vernon Perry, AFC-D: Houston vs. San Diego, 1979
3 Joe Laws, NFC: Green Bay vs. N.Y. Giants, 1944
Charlie Waters, NFC-D: Dallas vs. Chicago, 1977
Rod Martin, SB: Oakland vs. Philadelphia, 1980
Dennis Thurman, NFC-D: Dallas vs. Green Bay, 1982
A.J. Duhe, AFC: Miami vs. N.Y. Jets, 1982
2 By many players

Most Consecutive Games, Interceptions
3 Warren Lahr, Cleveland, 1950-51
Ken Gorgal, Cleveland, 1950-53
Joe Schmidt, Detroit, 1954-57
Emmitt Thomas, Kansas City, 1969
Mel Renfro, Dallas, 1970
Rick Volk, Baltimore, 1970-71
Mike Wagner, Pittsburgh, 1975-76
Randy Hughes, Dallas, 1977-78
Vernon Perry, Houston, 1979-80
Lester Hayes, Oakland, 1980
Gerald Small, Miami, 1982
Lester Hayes, L.A. Raiders, 1982-83
Fred Marion, New England, 1985
John Harris, Seattle-Minnesota, 1984-87
Felix Wright, Cleveland, 1987-88
Kurt Gouveia, Washington, 1991
Eric Davis, San Francisco, 1994
Deion Sanders, San Francisco-Dallas, 1994-95
Craig Newsome, Green Bay, 1996 (current)

YARDS GAINED

Most Yards Gained, Career
196 Willie Brown, Oakland, 17 games
187 Ronnie Lott, San Francisco-L.A.-Raiders, 20 games
160 George Teague, Green Bay-Dallas-Miami, 10 games

Most Yards Gained, Game
101 George Teague, NFC-FR: Green Bay vs. Detroit, 1993
98 Darrol Ray, AFC-FR: N.Y. Jets vs. Cincinnati, 1982
94 LeRoy Irvin, NFC-FR: L.A. Rams vs. Dallas, 1983

Longest Return
101 George Teague, NFC-FR: Green Bay vs. Detroit, 1993 (TD)
98 Darrol Ray, AFC-FR: N.Y. Jets vs. Cincinnati, 1982 (TD)
94 LeRoy Irvin, NFC-FR: L.A. Rams vs. Dallas, 1983

TOUCHDOWNS

Most Touchdowns, Career
3 Willie Brown, Oakland, 17 games
2 Lester Hayes, Oakland/L.A. Raiders, 13 games
Ronnie Lott, San Francisco-L.A. Raiders, 20 games
Darrell Green, Washington, 16 games
Melvin Jenkins, Seattle-Detroit, 5 games
George Teague, Green Bay-Dallas-Miami, 10 games

Most Touchdowns, Game
1 By many players

PUNTING

Most Punts, Career
111 Ray Guy, Oakland/L.A. Raiders, 22 games
84 Danny White, Dallas, 18 games
73 Mike Eischeid, Oakland-Minnesota, 14 games

Most Punts, Game
14 Dave Jennings, AFC-D: N.Y. Jets vs. Cleveland, 1986 (OT)
12 David Lee, AFC-D: Baltimore vs. Oakland, 1977 (OT)
11 Ken Strong, NFC: N.Y. Giants vs. Chi. Bears, 1933
Jim Norton, AFC: Houston vs. Oakland, 1967

Ode Burrell, AFC-D: Houston vs. Oakland, 1969
Dale Hatcher, NFC: L.A. Rams vs. Chicago, 1985

Longest Punt
76 Ed Danowski, NFC: N.Y. Giants vs. Detroit, 1935
Mike Horan, AFC: Denver vs. Buffalo, 1991
72 Charlie Conerly, NFC-D: N.Y. Giants vs. Cleveland, 1950
Yale Lary, NFC: Detroit vs. Cleveland, 1953
71 Ray Guy, AFC: Oakland vs. San Diego, 1980

AVERAGE YARDAGE

Highest Average, Career (25 punts)
44.5 Rich Camarillo, New England, 6 games (35-1,559)
44.4 Lee Johnson, Cleveland-Cincinnati, 7 games (28-1,244)
43.4 Jerrel Wilson, Kansas City-New England, 8 games (43-1,866)

Highest Average, Game (4 punts)
56.0 Ray Guy, AFC: Oakland vs. San Diego, 1980 (4-224)
52.5 Sammy Baugh, NFC: Washington vs. Chi. Bears, 1942 (6-315)
51.6 Lee Johnson, AFC-D: Cincinnati vs. L.A. Raiders, 1990 (5-258)

PUNT RETURNS

Most Punt Returns, Career
30 David Meggett, N.Y. Giants-New England, 11 games
25 Theo Bell, Pittsburgh-Tampa Bay, 10 games
21 Gerald McNeil, Cleveland-Houston, 8 games

Most Punt Returns, Game
7 Ron Gardin, AFC-D: Baltimore vs. Cincinnati, 1970
Carl Roaches, AFC-FR: Houston vs. Oakland, 1980
Gerald McNeil, AFC-D: Cleveland vs. N.Y. Jets, 1986 (OT)
Phil McConkey, NFC-D: N.Y. Giants vs. San Francisco, 1986
David Meggett, AFC-D: New England vs. Pittsburgh, 1996
6 George McAfee, NFC-D: Chi. Bears vs. Los Angeles, 1950
Eddie Brown, NFC-D: Washington vs. Minnesota, 1976
Theo Bell, AFC: Pittsburgh vs. Houston, 1978
Eddie Brown, NFC: Los Angeles vs. Tampa Bay, 1979
John Sciarra, NFC: Philadelphia vs. Dallas, 1980
Kurt Sohn, AFC: N.Y. Jets vs. Miami, 1982
Mike Nelms, SB: Washington vs. Miami, 1982
Anthony Carter, NFC-FR: Minnesota vs. New Orleans, 1987
Desmond Howard, SB: Green Bay vs.New England, 1996
5 By many players

YARDS GAINED

Most Yards Gained, Career
265 David Meggett, N.Y. Giants-New England, 11 games
259 Anthony Carter, Minnesota-Detroit, 9 games
221 Neal Colzie, Oakland-Miami-Tampa Bay, 10 games

Most Yards Gained, Game
143 Anthony Carter, NFC-FR: Minnesota vs. New Orleans, 1987
141 Bob Hayes, NFC-D: Dallas vs. Cleveland, 1967
117 Desmond Howard, NFC-D: Green Bay vs. San Francisco, 1996

Longest Return
84 Anthony Carter, NFC-FR: Minnesota vs. New Orleans, 1987 (TD)
81 Hugh Gallarneau, NFC-D: Chi. Bears vs. Green Bay, 1941 (TD)
79 Bosh Pritchard, NFC-D: Philadelphia vs. Pittsburgh, 1947 (TD)

AVERAGE YARDAGE

Highest Average, Career (10 returns)
15.3 Robert Brooks, Green Bay, 10 games (14-214)
15.2 Anthony Carter, Minnesota-Detroit, 9 games (17-259)
14.3 Antonio Freeman, Green Bay, 9 games (10-143)

Highest Average Gain, Game (3 returns)
47.0 Bob Hayes, NFC-D: Dallas vs. Cleveland, 1967 (3-141)
29.0 George (Butch) Byrd, AFC: Buffalo vs. San Diego, 1965 (3-87)
25.3 Bosh Pritchard, NFC-D: Philadelphia vs. Pittsburgh, 1947 (4-101)

TOUCHDOWNS

Most Touchdowns
1 Hugh Gallarneau, NFC-D: Chicago Bears vs. Green Bay, 1941
Bosh Pritchard, NFC-D: Philadelphia vs. Pittsburgh, 1947
Charley Trippi, NFC: Chicago Cardinals vs. Philadelphia, 1947
Verda (Vitamin T) Smith, NFC-D: Los Angeles vs. Detroit, 1952
George (Butch) Byrd, AFC: Buffalo vs. San Diego, 1965
Golden Richards, NFC: Dallas vs. Minnesota, 1973
Wes Chandler, AFC-D: San Diego vs. Miami, 1981 (OT)
Shaun Gayle, NFC-D: Chicago vs. N.Y. Giants, 1985
Anthony Carter, NFC-FR: Minnesota vs. New Orleans, 1987
Darrell Green, NFC-D: Washington vs. Chicago, 1987
Antonio Freeman, NFC-FR: Green Bay vs. Atlanta, 1995
Desmond Howard, NFC-D: Green Bay vs. San Francisco, 1996

KICKOFF RETURNS

Most Kickoff Returns, Career
29 Fulton Walker, Miami-L.A. Raiders, 10 games
23 Kevin Williams, Dallas, 10 games
22 Eric Metcalf, Cleveland-Atlanta, 5 games

Most Kickoff Returns, Game
8 Marc Logan, AFC-D: Miami vs. Buffalo, 1990
Andre Coleman, SB: San Diego vs. San Francisco, 1994
7 Don Bingham, NFC: Chi. Bears vs. N.Y. Giants, 1956
Reggie Brown, NFC-FR: Atlanta vs. Minnesota, 1982
David Verser, AFC-FR: Cincinnati vs. N.Y. Jets, 1982
Del Rodgers, NFC-D: Green Bay vs. Dallas, 1982
Henry Ellard, NFC-D: L.A. Rams vs. Washington, 1983
Stephen Starring, SB: New England vs. Chicago, 1985
Darick Holmes, AFC-D: Buffalo vs. Pittsburgh, 1995
Antonio Freeman, NFC: Green Bay vs. Dallas, 1995
6 By many players

YARDS GAINED

Most Yards Gained, Career
677 Fulton Walker, Miami-L.A. Raiders, 10 games
505 Kevin Williams, Dallas, 10 games
499 Eric Metcalf, Cleveland-Atlanta, 5 games

Most Yards Gained, Game
244 Andre Coleman, SB: San Diego vs. San Francisco, 1994
190 Fulton Walker, SB: Miami vs. Washington, 1982
170 Les (Speedy) Duncan, NFC-D: Washington vs. San Francisco, 1971

Longest Return
99 Desmond Howard, SB: Green Bay vs. New England, 1996 (TD)
98 Fulton Walker, SB: Miami vs. Washington, 1982 (TD)
Andre Coleman, SB: San Diego vs. San Francisco, 1994 (TD)
97 Vic Washington, NFC-D: San Francisco vs. Dallas, 1972 (TD)

AVERAGE YARDAGE

Highest Average, Career (10 returns)
30.1 Carl Garrett, Oakland, 5 games (16-481)
27.9 George Atkinson, Oakland, 16 games (12-335)
25.7 Nate Lewis, San Diego-Chicago, 4 games (11-283)

Highest Average, Game (3 returns)
56.7 Les (Speedy) Duncan, NFC-D: Washington vs. San Francisco, 1971 (3-170)
51.3 Ed Podolak, AFC-D: Kansas City vs. Miami, 1971 (OT) (3-154)
49.0 Les (Speedy) Duncan, AFC: San Diego vs. Buffalo, 1964 (3-147)

TOUCHDOWNS

Most Touchdowns
1 Vic Washington, NFC-D: San Francisco vs. Dallas, 1972
Nat Moore, AFC-D: Miami vs. Oakland, 1974
Marshall Johnson, AFC-D: Baltimore vs. Oakland, 1977 (OT)
Fulton Walker, SB: Miami vs. Washington, 1982
Stanford Jennings, SB: Cincinnati vs. San Francisco, 1988
Eric Metcalf, AFC-D: Cleveland vs. Buffalo, 1989
Andre Coleman, SB: San Diego vs. San Francisco, 1994
Desmond Howard, SB: Green Bay vs. New England, 1996
Chuck Levy, NFC: San Franisco vs. Green Bay, 1997

FUMBLES

Most Fumbles, Career
16 Warren Moon, Houston-Minnesota, 10 games
13 Tony Dorsett, Dallas, 17 games
John Elway, Denver, 19 games
10 Franco Harris, Pittsburgh, 19 games
Terry Bradshaw, Pittsburgh, 19 games
Roger Staubach, Dallas, 20 games
Jim Kelly, Buffalo, 17 games

Most Fumbles, Game
5 Warren Moon, AFC-D: Houston vs. Kansas City, 1993
4 Brian Sipe, AFC-D: Cleveland vs. Oakland, 1980
Randall Cunningham, NFC-FR: Minnesota vs. N.Y. Giants, 1997
3 By many players

RECOVERIES

Most Own Fumbles Recovered, Career
8 Warren Moon, Houston-Minnesota, 10 games
7 John Elway, Denver, 19 games
6 Jim Kelly, Buffalo, 17 games

Most Opponents' Fumbles Recovered, Career
4 Cliff Harris, Dallas, 21 games
Harvey Martin, Dallas, 22 games
Ted Hendricks, Baltimore-Oakland/L.A. Raiders, 21 games
Alvin Walton, Washington, 9 games
Monte Coleman, Washington, 21 games
3 Paul Krause, Minnesota, 19 games
Jack Lambert, Pittsburgh, 18 games
Fred Dryer, Los Angeles, 14 games
Charlie Waters, Dallas, 25 games
Jack Ham, Pittsburgh, 16 games

Mike Hegman, Dallas, 16 games
Tom Jackson, Denver, 10 games
Rich Milot, Washington, 13 games
Mike Singletary, Chicago, 12 games
Darryl Grant, Washington, 16 games
Wes Hopkins, Philadelphia, 3 games
Wilber Marshall, Chicago-Washington, 15 games
2 By many players

Most Fumbles Recovered, Game, Own and Opponents'
3 Jack Lambert, AFC: Pittsburgh vs. Oakland, 1975 (3 opp)
Ron Jaworski, NFC-FR: Philadelphia vs. N.Y. Giants, 1981 (3 own)
2 By many players

YARDS GAINED

Longest Return
93 Andy Russell, AFC-D: Pittsburgh vs. Baltimore, 1975 (opp, TD)
64 Leon Lett, SB: Dallas vs. Buffalo, 1992 (opp)
60 Mike Curtis, NFC-D: Baltimore vs. Minnesota, 1968 (opp, TD)
Hugh Green, NFC-FR: Tampa Bay vs. Dallas, 1982 (opp, TD)

TOUCHDOWNS

Most Touchdowns
1 By many players

COMBINED NET YARDS GAINED

Rushing, receiving, interception returns, punt returns, kickoff returns, and fumble returns.

ATTEMPTS

Most Attempts, Career
454 Franco Harris, Pittsburgh, 19 games
404 Thurman Thomas, Buffalo, 19 games
364 Emmitt Smith, Dallas, 15 games

Most Attempts, Game
40 Lawrence McCutcheon, NFC-D: Los Angeles vs. St. Louis, 1975
39 John Riggins, SB: Washington vs. Miami, 1982
Rodney Hampton, NFC-FR: N.Y. Giants vs. Minnesota, 1993
38 Ricky Bell, NFC-D: Tampa Bay vs. Philadelphia, 1979
Rob Carpenter, NFC-FR: N.Y. Giants vs. Philadelphia, 1981

YARDS GAINED

Most Yards Gained, Career
2,078 Thurman Thomas, Buffalo, 19 games
2,060 Franco Harris, Pittsburgh, 19 games
1,877 Marcus Allen, L.A. Raiders-Kansas City, 16 games

Most Yards Gained, Game
350 Ed Podolak, AFC-D: Kansas City vs. Miami, 1971 (OT)
329 Keith Lincoln, AFC: San Diego vs. Boston, 1963
285 Bob Hayes, NFC-D: Dallas vs. Cleveland, 1967

SACKS

Sacks have been compiled since 1982.

Most Sacks, Career
12 Bruce Smith, Buffalo, 18 games
Reggie White, Philadelphia-Green Bay, 18 games
11 Charles Haley, San Francisco-Dallas, 19 games
10.5 Richard Dent, Chicago-San Francisco-Indianapolis, 12 games

Most Sacks, Game
3.5 Rich Milot, NFC-D: Washington vs. Chicago, 1984
Richard Dent, NFC-D: Chicago vs. N.Y. Giants, 1985
3 Richard Dent, NFC-D: Chicago vs. Washington, 1984
Garin Veris, AFC-FR: New England vs. N.Y. Jets, 1985
Gary Jeter, NFC-D: L.A. Rams vs. Dallas, 1985
Carl Hairston, AFC-D: Cleveland vs. N.Y. Jets, 1986 (OT)
Charles Mann, NFC-D: Washington vs. Chicago, 1987
Kevin Greene, NFC-FR: L.A. Rams vs. Minnesota, 1988
Greg Townsend, AFC-D: L.A. Raiders vs. Cincinnati, 1990
Wilber Marshall, NFC: Washington vs. Detroit, 1991
Fred Stokes, NFC-FR: Washington vs. Minnesota, 1992
Pierce Holt, NFC-D: San Francisco vs. Washington, 1992
Tony Casillas, NFC: Dallas vs. San Francisco, 1992
Gerald Williams, AFC-FR: Pittsburgh vs. Kansas City, 1993
Chad Brown, AFC-FR: Pittsburgh vs. Indianapolis, 1996
Reggie White, SB: Green Bay vs. New England, 1996
Warren Sapp, NFC-D: Tampa Bay vs. Green Bay, 1997
2.5 Lyle Alzado, AFC-D: L.A. Raiders vs. Pittsburgh, 1983
Jacob Green, AFC-FR: Seattle vs. L.A. Raiders, 1984
Larry Roberts, NFC-D: San Francisco vs. Minnesota, 1988
Leslie O'Neal, AFC-FR: San Diego vs. Kansas City, 1992

TEAM RECORDS

GAMES, VICTORIES, DEFEATS

Most Seasons Participating in Postseason Games
24 Dallas, 1966-73, 1975-83, 1985, 1991-96
N.Y. Giants, 1933-35, 1938-39, 1941, 1943-44, 1946, 1950, 1956, 1958-59,1961-63, 1981, 1984-86, 1989-90, 1993, 1997
23 Cleveland, 1950-55, 1957-58, 1964-65, 1967-69, 1971-72, 1980, 1982, 1985-89, 1994
22 Cleveland/L.A. Rams, 1945, 1949-52, 1955, 1967, 1969, 1973-80, 1983-86, 1988-89

Most Consecutive Seasons Participating in Postseason Games
9 Dallas, 1975-83
8 Dallas, 1966-73
Pittsburgh, 1972-79
Los Angeles, 1973-80
San Francisco, 1983-90
7 Houston, 1987-93

Most Games
51 Dallas, 1966-73, 1975-83, 1985, 1991-96
37 San Francisco, 1957, 1970-72, 1981, 1983-90, 1992-97
36 Oakland/L.A. Raiders, 1967-70, 1973-77, 1980, 1982-85, 1990-91, 1993
Pittsburgh, 1947, 1972-79, 1982-84, 1989, 1992-97

Most Games Won
32 Dallas, 1967, 1970-73, 1975, 1977-78, 1980-82, 1991-96
23 San Francisco, 1970-71, 1981, 1983-84, 1988-90, 1992-94, 1996-97
22 Green Bay, 1936, 1939, 1944, 1961-62, 1965-67, 1982, 1993-97

Most Consecutive Games Won
9 Green Bay, 1961-62, 1965-67
7 Pittsburgh, 1974-76
San Francisco, 1988-90
Dallas, 1992-94
6 Miami, 1972-73
Pittsburgh, 1978-79
Washington, 1982-83

Most Games Lost
20 L.A. Rams, 1949-50, 1952, 1955, 1967, 1969, 1973-80, 1983-86, 1988-89
Minnesota, 1968-71, 1973-78, 1980, 1982, 1987-89, 1992-94,1996-97
19 Cleveland, 1951-53, 1957-58, 1965, 1967-69, 1971-72, 1980, 1982, 1985-89, 1994
Dallas, 1966-70, 1972-73, 1975-76, 1978-83, 1985, 1991, 1994, 1996
N.Y. Giants, 1933, 1935, 1939, 1941, 1943-44, 1946, 1950, 1958-59, 1961-63, 1981, 1984-85, 1989, 1993, 1997
15 Oakland/L.A. Raiders, 1967-70, 1972-75, 1977, 1982, 1984-85, 1990-91, 1993
Miami, 1970-71, 1974, 1978-79, 1981-85, 1990, 1992, 1994-95, 1997
Pittsburgh, 1947, 1972-73, 1976-77, 1982-84, 1989, 1992-97

Most Consecutive Games Lost
6 N.Y. Giants, 1939, 1941, 1943-44, 1946, 1950
Cleveland, 1969, 1971-72, 1980, 1982, 1985
Minnesota, 1988-89, 1992-94, 1996
5 N.Y. Giants, 1958-59, 1961-63
Los Angeles, 1952, 1955, 1967, 1969, 1973
Denver, 1977-79, 1983-84
Baltimore/Indianapolis, 1971, 1975-77, 1987
Philadelphia, 1980-81, 1988-90
Detroit, 1991, 1993-95, 1997 (current)
4 Washington, 1972-74, 1976
Miami, 1974, 1978-79, 1981
Chi. Cardinals/St. Louis, 1948, 1974-75, 1982 (current)
Boston/New England, 1963, 1976, 1978, 1982
New Orleans, 1987, 1990-92 (current)
Kansas City, 1993-95, 1997 (current)

SCORING

Most Points, Game
73 NFC: Chi. Bears vs. Washington, 1940
59 NFC: Detroit vs. Cleveland, 1957
58 NFC-FR: Philadelphia vs. Detroit, 1995

Most Points, Both Teams, Game
95 NFC-FR: Philadelphia (58) vs. Detroit (37), 1995
79 AFC-D: San Diego (41) vs. Miami (38), 1981 (OT)
AFC-FR: Buffalo (41) vs. Houston (38), 1992 (OT)
78 AFC-D: Buffalo (44) vs. Miami (34), 1990

Fewest Points, Both Teams, Game
5 NFC-D: Detroit (0) vs. Dallas (5), 1970
7 NFC: Chi. Cardinals (0) vs. Philadelphia (7), 1948
9 NFC: Tampa Bay (0) vs. Los Angeles (9), 1979

Largest Margin of Victory, Game
73 NFC: Chi. Bears vs. Washington, 1940 (73-0)
49 AFC-D: Oakland vs. Houston, 1969 (56-7)

48 AFC: Buffalo vs. L.A. Raiders, 1990 (51-3)

Most Points, Shutout Victory, Game

73 NFC: Chi. Bears vs. Washington, 1940
38 NFC-D: Dallas vs. Tampa Bay, 1981
37 NFC: Green Bay vs. N.Y. Giants, 1961

Most Points Overcome to Win Game

32 AFC-FR: Buffalo vs. Houston, 1992 (trailed 3-35, won 41-38) (OT)
20 NFC-D: Detroit vs. San Francisco, 1957 (trailed 7-27, won 31-27)
18 NFC-D: Dallas vs. San Francisco, 1972 (trailed 3-21, won 30-28)
AFC-D: Miami vs. Cleveland, 1985 (trailed 3-21, won 24-21)

Most Points, Each Half

1st: 41 AFC: Buffalo vs. L.A. Raiders, 1990
38 NFC-D: Washington vs. L.A. Rams, 1983
NFC-FR: Philadelphia vs. Detroit, 1995
35 NFC: Cleveland vs. Detroit, 1954
AFC-D: Oakland vs. Houston, 1969
SB: Washington vs. Denver, 1987
2nd: 45 NFC: Chi. Bears vs. Washington, 1940
35 AFC-FR: Buffalo vs. Houston, 1992
30 SB: N.Y. Giants vs. Denver, 1986
AFC: Cleveland vs. Denver, 1987
NFC-FR: Detroit vs. Philadelphia, 1995

Most Points, Each Quarter

1st: 28 AFC-D: Oakland vs. Houston, 1969
24 AFC-D: San Diego vs. Miami, 1981
21 NFC: Chi. Bears vs. Washington, 1940
AFC: San Diego vs. Boston, 1963
AFC-D: Oakland vs. Kansas City, 1968
AFC: Oakland vs. San Diego, 1980
AFC: Buffalo vs. L.A. Raiders, 1990
NFC: San Francisco vs. Dallas, 1994
2nd: 35 SB: Washington vs. Denver, 1987
31 NFC-FR: Philadelphia vs. Detroit, 1995
26 AFC-D: Pittsburgh vs. Buffalo, 1974
3rd: 28 AFC-FR: Buffalo vs. Houston, 1992
26 NFC: Chi. Bears vs. Washington, 1940
21 NFC-D: Dallas vs. Cleveland, 1967
NFC-D: Dallas vs. Tampa Bay, 1981
AFC-D: L.A. Raiders vs. Pittsburgh, 1983
SB: Chicago vs. New England, 1985
NFC-D: N.Y. Giants vs. San Francisco, 1986
AFC: Cleveland vs. Denver, 1987
AFC: Cleveland vs. Denver, 1989
4th: 27 NFC: N.Y. Giants vs. Chi. Bears, 1934
26 NFC-FR: Philadelphia vs. New Orleans, 1992
24 NFC: Baltimore vs. N.Y. Giants, 1959
OT: 6 NFC: Baltimore vs. N.Y. Giants, 1958
AFC-D: Oakland vs. Baltimore, 1977
NFC-D: L.A. Rams vs. N.Y. Giants, 1989

TOUCHDOWNS

Most Touchdowns, Game

11 NFC: Chi. Bears vs. Washington, 1940
8 NFC: Cleveland vs. Detroit, 1954
NFC: Detroit vs. Cleveland, 1957
AFC-D: Oakland vs. Houston, 1969
SB: San Francisco vs. Denver, 1989
7 AFC: San Diego vs. Boston, 1963
NFC-D: Dallas vs. Cleveland, 1967
NFC-D: N.Y. Giants vs. San Francisco, 1986
AFC: Buffalo vs. L.A. Raiders, 1990
SB: Dallas vs. Buffalo, 1992
SB: San Francisco vs. San Diego, 1994
NFC-FR: Philadelphia vs. Detroit, 1995

Most Touchdowns, Both Teams, Game

12 NFC-FR: Philadelphia (7) vs. Detroit (5), 1995
11 NFC: Chi. Bears (11) vs. Washington (0), 1940
10 NFC: Detroit (8) vs. Cleveland (2), 1957
AFC-D: Miami (5) vs. San Diego (5), 1981 (OT)
AFC: Miami (6) vs. Pittsburgh (4), 1984
AFC-FR: Buffalo (5) vs. Houston (5), 1992 (OT)
SB: San Francisco (7) vs. San Diego (3), 1994

Fewest Touchdowns, Both Teams, Game

0 NFC-D: N.Y. Giants vs. Cleveland, 1950
NFC-D: Dallas vs. Detroit, 1970
NFC: Los Angeles vs. Tampa Bay, 1979
1 NFC: Chi. Cardinals (0) vs. Philadelphia (1), 1948
NFC-D: Cleveland (0) vs. N.Y. Giants (1), 1958
AFC: San Diego (0) vs. Houston (1), 1961
AFC-D: N.Y. Jets (0) vs. Kansas City (1), 1969
NFC-D: Green Bay (0) vs. Washington (1), 1972
NFC-FR: New Orleans (0) vs. Chicago (1), 1990
NFC: N.Y. Giants (0) vs. San Francisco (1), 1990
AFC-FR: L.A. Raiders (0) vs. Kansas City (1), 1991
AFC-D: New England (0) vs. Pittsburgh (1), 1997
2 In many games

POINTS AFTER TOUCHDOWN

Most (One-Point) Points After Touchdown, Game

8 NFC: Cleveland vs. Detroit, 1954
NFC: Detroit vs. Cleveland, 1957
AFC-D: Oakland vs. Houston, 1969
7 NFC: Chi. Bears vs. Washington, 1940
NFC-D: Dallas vs. Cleveland, 1967
NFC-D: N.Y. Giants vs. San Francisco, 1986
SB: San Francisco vs. Denver, 1989
SB: Dallas vs. Buffalo, 1992
SB: San Francisco vs. San Diego, 1994
NFC-FR: Philadelphia vs. Detroit, 1995
6 AFC: San Diego vs. Boston, 1963
NFC-D: Washington vs. L.A. Rams, 1983
AFC: Miami vs. Pittsburgh, 1984
SB: Washington vs. Denver, 1987
AFC: Buffalo vs. L.A. Raiders, 1990
AFC-FR: L.A. Raiders vs. Denver, 1993
AFC-FR: Denver vs. Jacksonville, 1997

Most (One-Point) Points After Touchdown, Both Teams, Game

10 NFC: Detroit (8) vs. Cleveland (2), 1957
AFC-D: Miami (5) vs. San Diego (5), 1981 (OT)
AFC: Miami (6) vs. Pittsburgh (4), 1984
AFC-FR: Buffalo (5) vs. Houston (5), 1992 (OT)
NFC-FR: Philadelphia (7) vs. Detroit (3), 1995
9 In many games

Fewest (One-Point) Points After Touchdown, Both Teams, Game

0 NFC-D: N.Y. Giants vs. Cleveland, 1950
NFC-D: Dallas vs. Detroit, 1970
NFC: Los Angeles vs. Tampa Bay, 1979

Most Two-Point Conversions, Game

2 SB: San Diego vs. San Francisco, 1994
NFC-FR: Detroit vs. Philadelphia, 1995
1 By many teams

FIELD GOALS

Most Field Goals, Game

5 NFC-D: Minnesota vs. San Francisco, 1987
NFC: N.Y. Giants vs. San Francisco, 1990
AFC: Buffalo vs. Miami, 1992
NFC-FR: N.Y. Giants vs. Minnesota, 1997
4 AFC-D: Boston vs. Buffalo, 1963
AFC: Oakland vs. Houston, 1967
SB: Green Bay vs. Oakland, 1967
NFC: Washington vs. Dallas, 1972
AFC-D: Oakland vs. Pittsburgh, 1973
SB: San Francisco vs. Cincinnati, 1981
AFC-FR: New England vs. N.Y. Jets, 1985
NFC-FR: Washington vs. L.A. Rams, 1986
NFC-D: Philadelphia vs. Chicago, 1988
AFC-FR: Pittsburgh vs. Houston, 1989 (OT)
AFC-D: Pittsburgh vs. Buffalo, 1995
NFC-FR: Dallas vs. Minnesota, 1996
NFC-D: Carolina vs. Dallas, 1996
3 By many teams

Most Field Goals, Both Teams, Game

8 NFC-FR: N.Y. Giants (5) vs. Minnesota (3), 1997
7 AFC-FR: Pittsburgh (4) vs. Houston (3), 1989 (OT)
NFC: N.Y. Giants (5) vs. San Francisco (2), 1990
NFC-D: Carolina (4) vs. Dallas (3), 1996
6 NFC-D: Minnesota (5) vs. San Francisco (1), 1987
NFC-D: Philadelphia (4) vs. Chicago (2), 1988
AFC: Buffalo (5) vs. Miami (1), 1992

Most Field Goals Attempted, Game

6 AFC: Oakland vs. Houston, 1967
NFC-D: Los Angeles vs. Dallas, 1973
AFC-D: Cleveland vs. N.Y. Jets, 1986 (OT)
NFC: N.Y. Giants vs. San Francisco, 1990
AFC: Buffalo vs. Miami, 1992
5 By many teams

Most Field Goals Attempted, Both Teams, Game

9 NFC-D: Philadelphia (5) vs. Chicago (4), 1988
NFC-FR: N.Y. Giants (5) vs. Minnesota (4), 1997
8 NFC-D: Los Angeles (6) vs. Dallas (2), 1973
NFC-D: Detroit (5) vs. San Francisco (3), 1983
AFC-D: Cleveland (6) vs. N.Y. Jets (2), 1986 (OT)
NFC-D: Minnesota (5) vs. San Francisco (3), 1987
AFC-FR: Houston (4) vs. Pittsburgh (4), 1989 (OT)
NFC-FR: Chicago (4) vs. New Orleans (4), 1990

NFC: N.Y. Giants (6) vs. San Francisco (2), 1990
7 In many games

SAFETIES
Most Safeties, Game
1 By many teams
Most Safeties, Both Teams, Game
1 In many games

FIRST DOWNS
Most First Downs, Game
34 AFC-D: San Diego vs. Miami, 1981 (OT)
33 AFC-D: Cleveland vs. N.Y. Jets, 1986 (OT)
31 SB: San Francisco vs. Miami, 1984
NFC-D: San Francisco vs. Minnesota, 1997
Fewest First Downs, Game
6 NFC: N.Y. Giants vs. Green Bay, 1961
7 NFC: Green Bay vs. Boston, 1936
NFC-D: Pittsburgh vs. Philadelphia, 1947
NFC: Chi. Cardinals vs. Philadelphia, 1948
NFC: Los Angeles vs. Philadelphia, 1949
NFC-D: Cleveland vs. N.Y. Giants, 1958
AFC-D: Cincinnati vs. Baltimore, 1970
NFC-D: Detroit vs. Dallas, 1970
NFC: Tampa Bay vs. Los Angeles, 1979
8 By many teams
Most First Downs, Both Teams, Game
59 AFC-D: San Diego (34) vs. Miami (25), 1981 (OT)
55 AFC-FR: San Diego (29) vs. Pittsburgh (26), 1982
54 AFC-FR: Buffalo (28) vs. Miami (26), 1995
Fewest First Downs, Both Teams, Game
15 NFC: Green Bay (7) vs. Boston (8), 1936
19 NFC: N.Y. Giants (9) vs. Green Bay (10), 1939
NFC: Washington (9) vs. Chi. Bears (10), 1942
20 NFC-D: Cleveland (9) vs. N.Y. Giants (11), 1950

RUSHING
Most First Downs, Rushing, Game
19 NFC-FR: Dallas vs. Los Angeles, 1980
18 AFC-D: Miami vs. Cincinnati, 1973
AFC: Miami vs. Oakland, 1973
AFC-D: Pittsburgh vs. Buffalo, 1974
AFC-FR: Buffalo vs. Miami, 1995
AFC-FR: Denver vs. Jacksonville, 1997
17 AFC-D: Cincinnati vs. Seattle, 1988
AFC: Buffalo vs. Kansas City, 1993
Fewest First Downs, Rushing, Game
0 NFC: Los Angeles vs. Philadelphia, 1949
AFC-D: Buffalo vs. Boston, 1963
AFC: Oakland vs. Pittsburgh, 1974
NFC-FR: New Orleans vs. Minnesota, 1987
NFC: L.A. Rams vs. San Francisco, 1989
NFC-D: Chicago vs. N.Y. Giants, 1990
AFC-FR: Indianapolis vs. Pittsburgh, 1996
1 By many teams
Most First Downs, Rushing, Both Teams, Game
26 AFC: Buffalo (14) vs. L.A. Raiders (12), 1990
25 NFC-FR: Dallas (19) vs. Los Angeles (6), 1980
23 NFC: Cleveland (15) vs. Detroit (8), 1952
AFC-D: Miami (18) vs. Cincinnati (5), 1973
AFC-D: Pittsburgh (18) vs. Buffalo (5), 1974
AFC-FR: Buffalo (18) vs. Miami (5), 1995
Fewest First Downs, Rushing, Both Teams, Game
5 AFC-D: Buffalo (0) vs. Boston (5), 1963
6 NFC: Green Bay (2) vs. Boston (4), 1936
NFC-D: Baltimore (2) vs. Minnesota (4), 1968
AFC-D: Houston (1) vs. Oakland (5), 1969
AFC-FR: N.Y. Jets (1) vs. Houston (5), 1991
7 NFC-D: Washington (2) vs. N.Y. Giants (5), 1943
NFC: Baltimore (3) vs. N.Y. Giants (4), 1959
NFC: Washington (3) vs. Dallas (4), 1972
AFC-FR: N.Y. Jets (3) vs. Buffalo (4), 1981
NFC-D: Detroit (3) vs. Dallas (4), 1991
AFC-D: Kansas City (3) vs. Houston (4), 1993
NFC-FR: Detroit (1) vs. Green Bay (6), 1994
NFC-FR: Atlanta (1) vs. Green Bay (6), 1995
AFC-FR: New England (1) vs. Pittsburgh (6), 1997

PASSING
Most First Downs, Passing, Game
21 AFC-D: Miami vs. San Diego, 1981 (OT)
AFC-D: San Diego vs. Miami, 1981 (OT)
AFC-D: Cleveland vs. N.Y. Jets, 1986 (OT)
NFC-D: Philadelphia vs. Chicago, 1988
20 NFC-FR: Dallas vs. L.A. Rams, 1983
AFC-D: Buffalo vs. Cleveland, 1989
AFC-FR: Miami vs. Buffalo, 1995
NFC-FR: Detroit vs. Philadelphia, 1995
AFC-FR: San Diego vs. Indianapolis, 1995
19 NFC-FR: St. Louis vs. Green Bay, 1982
NFC-FR: Dallas vs. Tampa Bay, 1982
AFC-FR: Pittsburgh vs. San Diego, 1982
AFC-FR: San Diego vs. Pittsburgh, 1982
NFC: Dallas vs. Washington, 1982
NFC-D: Detroit vs. Dallas, 1991
AFC-FR: Kansas City vs. Pittsburgh, 1993 (OT)
Fewest First Downs, Passing, Game
0 NFC: Philadelphia vs. Chi. Cardinals, 1948
1 NFC-D: N.Y. Giants vs. Washington, 1943
NFC: Cleveland vs. Detroit, 1953
SB: Denver vs. Dallas, 1977
2 By many teams
Most First Downs, Passing, Both Teams, Game
42 AFC-D: Miami (21) vs. San Diego (21), 1981 (OT)
38 AFC-FR: Pittsburgh (19) vs. San Diego (19), 1982
34 NFC-FR: Washington (18) vs. San Francisco (16), 1990
AFC-FR: Kansas City (19) vs. Pittsburgh (15), 1993 (OT)
Fewest First Downs, Passing, Both Teams, Game
2 NFC: Philadelphia (0) vs. Chi. Cardinals (2), 1948
4 NFC-D: Cleveland (2) vs. N.Y. Giants (2), 1950
5 NFC: Detroit (2) vs. N.Y. Giants (3), 1935
NFC: Green Bay (2) vs. N.Y. Giants (3), 1939

PENALTY
Most First Downs, Penalty, Game
7 AFC-D: New England vs. Oakland, 1976
6 AFC-D: Cleveland vs. N.Y. Jets, 1986 (OT)
5 AFC-FR: Cleveland vs. L. A. Raiders, 1982
NFC-D: San Francisco vs. Minnesota, 1997
Most First Downs, Penalty, Both Teams, Game
9 AFC-D: New England (7) vs. Oakland (2), 1976
8 NFC-FR: Atlanta (4) vs. Minnesota (4), 1982
7 AFC-D: Baltimore (4) vs. Oakland (3), 1977 (OT)
AFC-FR: Denver (4) vs. L.A. Raiders (3), 1993
NFC-D: Dallas (4) vs. Carolina (3), 1996
AFC-D: Kansas City (4) vs. Denver (3), 1997

NET YARDS GAINED RUSHING AND PASSING
Most Yards Gained, Game
610 AFC: San Diego vs. Boston, 1963
602 SB: Washington vs. Denver, 1987
569 AFC: Miami vs. Pittsburgh, 1984
Fewest Yards Gained, Game
86 NFC-D: Cleveland vs. N.Y. Giants, 1958
99 NFC: Chi. Cardinals vs. Philadelphia, 1948
114 NFC-D: N.Y. Giants vs. Washington, 1943
Most Yards Gained, Both Teams, Game
1,038 AFC-FR: Buffalo (536) vs. Miami (502), 1995
1,036 AFC-D: San Diego (564) vs. Miami (472), 1981 (OT)
1,024 AFC: Miami (569) vs. Pittsburgh (455), 1984
Fewest Yards Gained, Both Teams, Game
331 NFC: Chi. Cardinals (99) vs. Philadelphia (232), 1948
332 NFC-D: N.Y. Giants (150) vs. Cleveland (182), 1950
336 NFC: Boston (116) vs. Green Bay (220), 1936

RUSHING
ATTEMPTS
Most Attempts, Game
65 NFC: Detroit vs. N.Y. Giants, 1935
61 NFC: Philadelphia vs. Los Angeles, 1949
59 AFC: New England vs. Miami, 1985
Fewest Attempts, Game
8 AFC-D: Miami vs. San Diego, 1994
9 SB: Miami vs. San Francisco, 1984
10 NFC: L.A. Rams vs. San Francisco, 1989
NFC-FR: Atlanta vs. Green Bay, 1995
Most Attempts, Both Teams, Game
109 NFC: Detroit (65) vs. N.Y. Giants (44), 1935
97 AFC-D: Baltimore (50) vs. Oakland (47), 1977 (OT)
91 NFC: Philadelphia (57) vs. Chi. Cardinals (34), 1948
Fewest Attempts, Both Teams, Game
32 AFC-D: Houston (14) vs. Kansas City (18), 1993
38 NFC-D: Detroit (16) vs. Dallas (22), 1991
39 NFC-FR: Atlanta (10) vs. Green Bay (29), 1995

YARDS GAINED
Most Yards Gained, Game
382 NFC: Chi. Bears vs. Washington, 1940
341 AFC-FR: Buffalo vs. Miami, 1995
338 NFC-FR: Dallas vs. Los Angeles, 1980
Fewest Yards Gained, Game
–4 NFC-FR: Detroit vs. Green Bay, 1994
7 AFC-D: Buffalo vs. Boston, 1963
SB: New England vs. Chicago, 1985
17 SB: Minnesota vs. Pittsburgh, 1974
Most Yards Gained, Both Teams, Game
430 NFC-FR: Dallas (338) vs. Los Angeles (92), 1980
426 NFC: Cleveland (227) vs. Detroit (199), 1952
411 AFC-FR: Buffalo (341) vs. Miami (70), 1995
Fewest Yards Gained, Both Teams, Game
77 NFC-FR: Detroit (–4) vs. Green Bay (81), 1994
90 AFC-D: Buffalo (7) vs. Boston (83), 1963
106 NFC: Boston (39) vs. Green Bay (67), 1936

AVERAGE GAIN
Highest Average Gain, Game
9.94 AFC: San Diego vs. Boston, 1963 (32-318)
9.29 NFC-D: Green Bay vs. Dallas, 1982 (17-158)
7.35 NFC-FR: Dallas vs. Los Angeles, 1980 (46-338)
Lowest Average Gain, Game
–0.27 NFC-FR: Detroit vs. Green Bay, 1994 (15-(–4))
0.58 AFC-D: Buffalo vs. Boston, 1963 (12-7)
0.64 SB: New England vs. Chicago, 1985 (11-7)

TOUCHDOWNS
Most Touchdowns, Game
7 NFC: Chi. Bears vs. Washington, 1940
6 NFC-D: San Francisco vs. N.Y. Giants, 1993
5 NFC: Cleveland vs. Detroit, 1954
NFC-D: San Francisco vs. Chicago, 1994
AFC-FR: Pittsburgh vs. Indianapolis, 1996
AFC-FR: Denver vs. Jacksonville, 1997
Most Touchdowns, Both Teams, Game
7 NFC: Chi. Bears (7) vs. Washington (0), 1940
6 NFC: Cleveland (5) vs. Detroit (1), 1954
NFC-D: San Francisco (6) vs. N.Y. Giants (0), 1993
NFC-D: San Francisco (5) vs. Chicago (1), 1994
AFC-FR: Denver (5) vs. Jacksonville (1), 1997
5 NFC: Chi. Cardinals (3) vs. Philadelphia (2), 1947
AFC: San Diego (4) vs. Boston (1), 1963
AFC-D: Cincinnati (3) vs. Buffalo (2), 1981
AFC-FR: Pittsburgh (5) vs. Indianapolis (0), 1996

PASSING
ATTEMPTS
Most Attempts, Game
66 AFC-FR: Miami vs. Buffalo, 1995
65 AFC-D: Cleveland vs. N.Y. Jets, 1986 (OT)
NFC-D: San Francisco vs. Green Bay, 1995
61 NFC-FR: Minnesota vs. Chicago, 1994
Fewest Attempts, Game
5 NFC: Detroit vs. N.Y. Giants, 1935
6 AFC: Miami vs. Oakland, 1973
7 SB: Miami vs. Minnesota, 1973
Most Attempts, Both Teams, Game
102 AFC-D: San Diego (54) vs. Miami (48), 1981 (OT)
96 AFC: N.Y. Jets (49) vs. Oakland (47), 1968
95 AFC-D: Cleveland (65) vs. N.Y. Jets (30), 1986 (OT)
Fewest Attempts, Both Teams, Game
18 NFC: Detroit (5) vs. N.Y. Giants (13), 1935
23 NFC: Chi. Cardinals (11) vs. Philadelphia (12), 1948
24 NFC-D: Cleveland (9) vs. N.Y. Giants (15), 1950

COMPLETIONS
Most Completions, Game
36 AFC-FR: Houston vs. Buffalo, 1992 (OT)
34 AFC-D: Cleveland vs. N.Y. Jets, 1986 (OT)
AFC-FR: Miami vs. Buffalo, 1995
33 AFC-D: San Diego vs. Miami, 1981 (OT)
NFC-FR: Minnesota vs. Chicago, 1994
Fewest Completions, Game
2 NFC: Detroit vs. N.Y. Giants, 1935
NFC: Philadelphia vs. Chi. Cardinals, 1948
3 NFC: N.Y. Giants vs. Chi. Bears, 1941
NFC: Green Bay vs. N.Y. Giants, 1944
NFC: Chi. Cardinals vs. Philadelphia, 1947
NFC: Chi. Cardinals vs. Philadelphia, 1948
NFC-D: Cleveland vs. N.Y. Giants, 1950
NFC-D: N.Y. Giants vs. Cleveland, 1950
NFC: Cleveland vs. Detroit, 1953
AFC: Miami vs. Oakland, 1973
4 NFC: N.Y. Giants vs. Detroit, 1935
NFC-D: N.Y. Giants vs. Washington, 1943
NFC-D: Pittsburgh vs. Philadelphia, 1947
NFC-D: Dallas vs. Detroit, 1970
AFC: Miami vs. Baltimore, 1971
SB: Miami vs. Washington, 1982
AFC-FR: Seattle vs. L.A. Raiders, 1984
Most Completions, Both Teams, Game
64 AFC-D: San Diego (33) vs. Miami (31), 1981 (OT)
57 AFC-FR: Houston (36) vs. Buffalo (21), 1992 (OT)
56 NFC-D: Dallas (28) vs. Green Bay (28), 1993
Fewest Completions, Both Teams, Game
5 NFC: Philadelphia (2) vs. Chi. Cardinals (3), 1948
6 NFC: Detroit (2) vs. N.Y. Giants (4), 1935
NFC-D: Cleveland (3) vs. N.Y. Giants (3), 1950
11 NFC: Green Bay (3) vs. N.Y. Giants (8), 1944
NFC-D: Dallas (4) vs. Detroit (7), 1970

COMPLETION PERCENTAGE
Highest Completion Percentage, Game (20 attempts)
88.0 SB: N.Y. Giants vs. Denver, 1986 (25-22)
87.1 NFC: San Francisco vs. L.A. Rams, 1989 (31-27)
80.0 NFC-D: Washington vs. L.A. Rams, 1983 (25-20)
Lowest Completion Percentage, Game (20 attempts)
18.5 NFC: Tampa Bay vs. Los Angeles, 1979 (27-5)
20.0 NFC-D: N.Y. Giants vs. Washington, 1943 (20-4)
25.8 NFC: Chi. Bears vs. Washington, 1937 (31-8)

YARDS GAINED
Most Yards Gained, Game
483 AFC-D: Cleveland vs. N.Y. Jets, 1986 (OT)
435 AFC: Miami vs. Pittsburgh, 1984
432 AFC-FR: Miami vs. Buffalo, 1995
Fewest Yards Gained, Game
3 NFC: Chi. Cardinals vs. Philadelphia, 1948
7 NFC: Philadelphia vs. Chi. Cardinals, 1948
9 NFC-D: N.Y. Giants vs. Cleveland, 1950
NFC: Cleveland vs. Detroit, 1953
Most Yards Gained, Both Teams, Game
809 AFC-D: San Diego (415) vs. Miami (394), 1981 (OT)
747 AFC: Miami (435) vs. Pittsburgh (312), 1984
666 AFC-D: Cleveland (483) vs. N.Y. Jets (183), 1986 (OT)
Fewest Yards Gained, Both Teams, Game
10 NFC: Chi. Cardinals (3) vs. Philadelphia (7), 1948
38 NFC-D: N.Y. Giants (9) vs. Cleveland (29), 1950
102 NFC-D: Dallas (22) vs. Detroit (80), 1970

TIMES SACKED
Most Times Sacked, Game
9 AFC: Kansas City vs. Buffalo, 1966
NFC: Chicago vs. San Francisco, 1984
AFC-D: N.Y. Jets vs. Cleveland, 1986 (OT)
AFC-D: Houston vs. Kansas City, 1993
8 NFC: Green Bay vs. Dallas, 1967
NFC: Minnesota vs. Washington, 1987
7 NFC-D: Dallas vs. Los Angeles, 1973
SB: Dallas vs. Pittsburgh, 1975
AFC-FR: Houston vs. Oakland, 1980
NFC-D: Washington vs. Chicago, 1984
SB: New England vs. Chicago, 1985
AFC-FR: Kansas City vs. San Diego, 1992
AFC-D: Pittsburgh vs. Buffalo, 1992
Most Times Sacked, Both Teams, Game
13 AFC: Kansas City (9) vs. Buffalo (4), 1966
AFC-D: N.Y. Jets (9) vs. Cleveland (4), 1986 (OT)
12 NFC-D: Dallas (7) vs. Los Angeles (5), 1973
NFC-D: Washington (7) vs. Chicago (5), 1984
NFC: Chicago (9) vs. San Francisco (3), 1984
AFC-FR: Kansas City (7) vs. San Diego (5), 1992
11 AFC-D: Houston (9) vs. Kansas City (2), 1993
Fewest Times Sacked, Both Teams, Game
0 AFC-D: Buffalo vs. Pittsburgh, 1974
AFC-FR: Pittsburgh vs. San Diego, 1982
AFC: Miami vs. Pittsburgh, 1984
AFC-D: Buffalo vs. Miami, 1990
AFC-D: Denver vs. Houston, 1991
AFC-FR: Buffalo vs. Miami, 1995
1 In many games

POSTSEASON GAME RECORDS

TOUCHDOWNS

Most Touchdowns, Game

6 AFC-D: Oakland vs. Houston, 1969
SB: San Francisco vs. San Diego, 1994
5 NFC: Chi. Bears vs. Washington, 1943
NFC: Detroit vs. Cleveland, 1957
AFC-D: Oakland vs. Kansas City, 1968
SB: San Francisco vs. Denver, 1989
4 By many teams

Most Touchdowns, Both Teams, Game

8 AFC-FR: Buffalo (4) vs. Houston (4), 1992 (OT)
7 NFC: Chi. Bears (5) vs. Washington (2), 1943
AFC-D: Oakland (6) vs. Houston (1), 1969
SB: Pittsburgh (4) vs. Dallas (3), 1978
AFC-D: Miami (4) vs. San Diego (3), 1981 (OT)
AFC: Miami (4) vs. Pittsburgh (3), 1984
AFC-D: Buffalo (4) vs. Cleveland (3), 1989
SB: San Francisco (6) vs. San Diego (1), 1994
NFC-FR: Detroit (4) vs. Philadelphia (3), 1995
6 NFC-FR: Green Bay (4) vs. St. Louis (2), 1982
AFC: Cleveland (3) vs. Denver (3), 1987
AFC-D: Buffalo (3) vs. Miami (3), 1990
AFC-FR: Denver (3) vs. L.A. Raiders (3), 1993

INTERCEPTIONS BY

Most Interceptions By, Game

8 NFC: Chi. Bears vs. Washington, 1940
7 NFC: Cleveland vs. Los Angeles, 1955
6 NFC: Green Bay vs. N.Y. Giants, 1939
NFC: Chi. Bears vs. N.Y. Giants, 1946
NFC: Cleveland vs. Detroit, 1954
AFC: San Diego vs. Houston, 1961
AFC: Buffalo vs. L.A. Raiders, 1990
NFC-FR: Philadelphia vs. Detroit, 1995

Most Interceptions By, Both Teams, Game

10 NFC: Cleveland (7) vs. Los Angeles (3), 1955
AFC: San Diego (6) vs. Houston (4), 1961
9 NFC: Green Bay (6) vs. N.Y. Giants (3), 1939
8 NFC: Chi. Bears (8) vs. Washington (0), 1940
NFC: Chi. Bears (6) vs. N.Y. Giants (2), 1946
NFC: Cleveland (6) vs. Detroit (2), 1954
AFC-FR: Buffalo (4) vs. N.Y. Jets (4), 1981
AFC: Miami (5) vs. N.Y. Jets (3), 1982

YARDS GAINED

Most Yards Gained, Game

138 AFC-FR: N.Y. Jets vs. Cincinnati, 1982
136 AFC: Dall. Texans vs. Houston, 1962 (OT)
130 NFC-D: Los Angeles vs. St. Louis, 1975

Most Yards Gained, Both Teams, Game

156 NFC: Green Bay (123) vs. N.Y. Giants (33), 1939
149 NFC: Cleveland (103) vs. Los Angeles (46), 1955
141 AFC-FR: Buffalo (79) vs. N.Y. Jets (62), 1981

TOUCHDOWNS

Most Touchdowns, Game

3 NFC: Chi. Bears vs. Washington, 1940
2 NFC-D: Los Angeles vs. St. Louis, 1975
NFC-FR: Philadelphia vs. Detroit, 1995
1 In many games

Most Touchdowns, Both Teams, Game

3 NFC: Chi. Bears (3) vs. Washington (0), 1940
2 NFC-D: Los Angeles (2) vs. St. Louis(0), 1975
NFC-D: Dallas (1) vs. Green Bay (1), 1982
NFC-D: Minnesota (1) vs. San Francisco (1), 1987
NFC-FR: Detroit (1) vs. Green Bay (1), 1993
NFC-FR: Philadelphia (2) vs. Detroit (0), 1995
AFC-FR: Buffalo (1) vs. Jacksonville (1), 1996
1 In many games

PUNTING

Most Punts, Game

14 AFC-D: N.Y. Jets vs. Cleveland, 1986 (OT)
13 NFC: N.Y. Giants vs. Chi. Bears, 1933
AFC-D: Baltimore vs. Oakland, 1977 (OT)
11 AFC: Houston vs. Oakland, 1967
AFC-D: Houston vs. Oakland, 1969
NFC: L.A. Rams vs. Chicago, 1985

Fewest Punts, Game

0 NFC-FR: St. Louis vs. Green Bay, 1982
AFC-FR: N.Y. Jets vs. Cincinnati, 1982
1 NFC-D: Cleveland vs. Dallas, 1969
AFC: Miami vs. Oakland, 1973
AFC-D: Oakland vs. Cincinnati, 1975
AFC-D: Pittsburgh vs. Baltimore, 1976
AFC: Pittsburgh vs. Houston, 1978
NFC-FR: Green Bay vs. St. Louis, 1982
AFC-FR: Miami vs. New England, 1982
AFC-FR: San Diego vs. Pittsburgh, 1982
AFC-D: Cleveland vs. Indianapolis, 1987
AFC-D: Buffalo vs. Miami, 1990
AFC-FR: L.A. Raiders vs. Kansas City, 1991
NFC-FR: Atlanta vs. New Orleans, 1991
NFC-FR: Chicago vs. Dallas, 1991
AFC-D: Houston vs. Denver, 1991
NFC: San Francisco vs. Dallas, 1992
NFC: Dallas vs. San Francisco, 1994
NFC-FR: Dallas vs. Minnesota, 1996
NFC-D: Carolina vs. Dallas, 1996
2 In many games

Most Punts, Both Teams, Game

23 NFC: N.Y. Giants (13) vs. Chi. Bears (10), 1933
22 AFC-D: N.Y. Jets (14) vs. Cleveland (8), 1986 (OT)
21 AFC-D: Baltimore (13) vs. Oakland (8), 1977 (OT)
NFC: L.A. Rams (11) vs. Chicago (10), 1985

Fewest Punts, Both Teams, Game

1 NFC-FR: St. Louis (0) vs. Green Bay (1), 1982
2 AFC-FR: N.Y. Jets (0) vs. Cincinnati (2), 1982
3 AFC: Miami (1) vs. Oakland (2), 1973
AFC-FR: San Diego (1) vs. Pittsburgh (2), 1982
AFC-D: Buffalo (1) vs. Miami (2), 1990
AFC-FR: L.A. Raiders (1) vs. Kansas City (2), 1991
AFC-D: Houston (1) vs. Denver (2), 1991
NFC-FR: Dallas (1) vs. Minnesota (2), 1996

AVERAGE YARDAGE

Highest Average, Punting, Game (4 punts)

56.0 AFC: Oakland vs. San Diego, 1980
52.5 NFC: Washington vs. Chi. Bears, 1942
51.6 AFC-D: Cincinnati vs. L.A. Raiders, 1990

Lowest Average, Punting, Game (4 punts)

24.9 NFC: Washington vs. Chi. Bears, 1937
25.3 AFC-FR: Pittsburgh vs. Houston, 1989
25.5 NFC: Green Bay vs. N.Y. Giants, 1962

PUNT RETURNS

Most Punt Returns, Game

8 NFC: Green Bay vs. N.Y. Giants, 1944
7 By many teams

Most Punt Returns, Both Teams, Game

13 AFC-FR: Houston (7) vs. Oakland (6), 1980
12 AFC-D: New England (7) vs. Pittsburgh (5), 1996
11 NFC: Green Bay (8) vs. N.Y. Giants (3), 1944
NFC-D: Green Bay (6) vs. Baltimore (5), 1965

Fewest Punt Returns, Both Teams, Game

0 NFC: Chi. Bears vs. N.Y. Giants, 1941
AFC: Boston vs. San Diego, 1963
NFC-FR: Green Bay vs. St. Louis, 1982
AFC-FR: Houston vs. N.Y. Jets, 1991
AFC-D: Denver vs. Houston, 1991
NFC-D: San Francisco vs. Washington, 1992
SB: Denver vs. Green Bay, 1997
1 In many games

YARDS GAINED

Most Yards Gained, Game

155 NFC-D: Dallas vs. Cleveland, 1967
150 NFC: Chi. Cardinals vs. Philadelphia, 1947
143 NFC-FR: Minnesota vs. New Orleans, 1987

Fewest Yards Gained, Game

–10 NFC: Green Bay vs. Cleveland, 1965
–9 NFC: Dallas vs. Green Bay, 1966
AFC-D: Kansas City vs. Oakland, 1968
–5 AFC-D: Miami vs. Oakland, 1970
NFC-D: San Francisco vs. Dallas, 1972
NFC: Dallas vs. Washington, 1972

Most Yards Gained, Both Teams, Game

166 NFC-D: Dallas (155) vs. Cleveland (11), 1967
160 NFC: Chi. Cardinals (150) vs. Philadelphia (10), 1947
146 NFC-D: Philadelphia (112) vs. Pittsburgh (34), 1947

Fewest Yards Gained, Both Teams, Game

–9 NFC: Dallas (–9) vs. Green Bay (0), 1966
–6 AFC-D: Miami (–5) vs. Oakland (–1), 1970
–3 NFC-D: San Francisco (–5) vs. Dallas (2), 1972

TOUCHDOWNS

Most Touchdowns, Game

1 By 12 teams

KICKOFF RETURNS

Most Kickoff Returns, Game

10 NFC-D: L.A. Rams vs. Washington, 1983
NFC-FR: Detroit vs. Philadelphia, 1995
9 NFC: Chi. Bears vs. N.Y. Giants, 1956
AFC: Boston vs. San Diego, 1963
AFC: Houston vs. Oakland, 1967
SB: Denver vs. San Francisco, 1989
AFC-D: Miami vs. Buffalo, 1990
AFC: L.A. Raiders vs. Buffalo, 1990
8 By many teams

Most Kickoff Returns, Both Teams, Game

15 AFC-D: Miami (9) vs. Buffalo (6), 1990
14 NFC-FR: Detroit (10) vs. Philadelphia (4), 1995
13 NFC-D: Green Bay (7) vs. Dallas (6), 1982

Fewest Kickoff Returns, Both Teams, Game

1 NFC: Green Bay (0) vs. Boston (1), 1936
AFC-FR: San Diego (0) vs. Kansas City (1), 1992
2 NFC-D: Los Angeles (0) vs. Chi. Bears (2), 1950
AFC: Houston (0) vs. San Diego (2), 1961
AFC-D: Oakland (1) vs. Pittsburgh (1), 1972
AFC-D: N.Y. Jets (0) vs. L.A. Raiders (2), 1982
AFC: Miami (1) vs. N.Y. Jets (1), 1982
NFC: N.Y. Giants (0) vs. Washington (2), 1986
3 In many games

YARDS GAINED

Most Yards Gained, Game

244 SB: San Diego vs. San Francisco, 1994
225 NFC: Washington vs. Chi. Bears, 1940
222 SB: Miami vs. Washington, 1982

Most Yards Gained, Both Teams, Game

379 AFC-D: Baltimore (193) vs. Oakland (186), 1977 (OT)
321 NFC-D: Dallas (173) vs. Green Bay (148), 1982
318 AFC-D: Miami (183) vs. Oakland (135), 1974

Fewest Yards Gained, Both Teams, Game

5 AFC-FR: San Diego (0) vs. Kansas City (5), 1992
15 NFC: N.Y. Giants (0) vs. Washington (15), 1986
31 NFC-D: Los Angeles (0) vs. Chi. Bears (31), 1950

TOUCHDOWNS

Most Touchdowns, Game

1 NFC-D: San Francisco vs. Dallas, 1972
AFC-D: Miami vs. Oakland, 1974
AFC-D: Baltimore vs. Oakland, 1977 (OT)
SB: Miami vs. Washington, 1982
SB: Cincinnati vs. San Francisco, 1988
AFC-D: Cleveland vs. Buffalo, 1989
SB: San Diego vs. San Francisco, 1994
SB: Green Bay vs. New England, 1996
NFC: San Francisco vs. Green Bay, 1997

PENALTIES

Most Penalties, Game

17 AFC-FR: L.A. Raiders vs. Denver, 1993
14 AFC-FR: Oakland vs. Houston, 1980
NFC-D: San Francisco vs. N.Y. Giants, 1981
13 AFC-FR: Houston vs. Cleveland, 1988
AFC-D: Houston vs. Denver, 1991

Fewest Penalties, Game

0 NFC: Philadelphia vs. Green Bay, 1960
NFC-D: Detroit vs. Dallas, 1970
AFC-D: Miami vs. Oakland, 1970
SB: Miami vs. Dallas, 1971
NFC-D: Washington vs. Minnesota, 1973
SB: Pittsburgh vs. Dallas, 1975
NFC: San Francisco vs. Chicago, 1988
SB: Denver vs. San Francisco, 1989
AFC-D: L.A. Raiders vs. Cincinnati, 1990
AFC-D: Miami vs. San Diego, 1992
1 By many teams

Most Penalties, Both Teams, Game

27 AFC-FR: L.A. Raiders (17) vs. Denver (10), 1993
22 AFC-FR: Oakland (14) vs. Houston (8), 1980
NFC-D: San Francisco (14) vs. N.Y. Giants (8), 1981
AFC-FR: Houston (13) vs. Cleveland (9), 1988
21 AFC-D: Oakland (11) vs. New England (10), 1976

Fewest Penalties, Both Teams, Game

1 AFC-D: L.A. Raiders (0) vs. Cincinnati (1), 1990
2 NFC: Washington (1) vs. Chi. Bears (1), 1937
NFC-D: Washington (0) vs. Minnesota (2), 1973
SB: Pittsburgh (0) vs. Dallas (2), 1975
3 AFC: Miami (1) vs. Baltimore (2), 1971
NFC: San Francisco (1) vs. Dallas (2), 1971
SB: Miami (0) vs. Dallas (3), 1971
AFC-D: Pittsburgh (1) vs. Oakland (2), 1972
AFC-D: Miami (1) vs. Cincinnati (2), 1973
SB: Miami (1) vs. San Francisco (2), 1984
NFC: San Francisco (0) vs. Chicago (3), 1988

YARDS PENALIZED

Most Yards Penalized, Game

145 NFC-D: San Francisco vs. N.Y. Giants, 1981
133 SB: Dallas vs. Baltimore, 1970
130 AFC-FR: L.A. Raiders vs. Denver, 1993

Fewest Yards Penalized, Game

0 By 10 teams

Most Yards Penalized, Both Teams, Game

227 AFC-FR: L.A. Raiders (130) vs. Denver (97), 1993
206 NFC-D: San Francisco (145) vs. N.Y. Giants (61), 1981
193 AFC-FR: Houston (118) vs. Cleveland (75), 1988

Fewest Yards Penalized, Both Teams, Game

5 AFC-D: L.A. Raiders (0) vs. Cincinnati (5), 1990
9 NFC-D: Washington (0) vs. Minnesota (9), 1973
15 SB: Miami (0) vs. Dallas (15), 1971

FUMBLES

Most Fumbles, Game

8 SB: Buffalo vs. Dallas, 1992
7 AFC-D: Houston vs. Kansas City, 1993
6 By 11 teams

Most Fumbles, Both Teams, Game

12 AFC: Houston (6) vs. Pittsburgh (6), 1978
SB: Buffalo (8) vs. Dallas (4), 1992
10 NFC: Chi. Bears (5) vs. N.Y. Giants (5), 1934
SB: Dallas (6) vs. Denver (4), 1977
9 NFC-D: San Francisco (6) vs. Detroit (3), 1957
NFC-D: San Francisco (5) vs. Dallas (4), 1972
NFC: Dallas (5) vs. Philadelphia (4), 1980

Most Fumbles Lost, Game

5 SB: Buffalo vs. Dallas, 1992
4 NFC: N.Y. Giants vs. Baltimore, 1958 (OT)
AFC: Kansas City vs. Oakland, 1969
SB: Baltimore vs. Dallas, 1970
AFC: Pittsburgh vs. Oakland, 1975
SB: Denver vs. Dallas, 1977
AFC: Houston vs. Pittsburgh, 1978
AFC: Miami vs. New England, 1985
SB: New England vs. Chicago, 1985
NFC-FR: L.A. Rams vs. Washington, 1986
NFC-FR: Minnesota vs. Dallas, 1996
3 By many teams

Fewest Fumbles, Both Teams, Game

0 NFC: Green Bay vs. Cleveland, 1965
AFC-D: Houston vs. San Diego, 1979
NFC-D: Dallas vs. Los Angeles, 1979
SB: Los Angeles vs. Pittsburgh, 1979
AFC-D: Buffalo vs. Cincinnati, 1981
NFC: Minnesota vs. Washington, 1987
NFC-D: San Francisco vs. Washington, 1990
NFC: Dallas vs. Green Bay, 1995
AFC-D: New England vs. Pittsburgh, 1996
SB: Green Bay vs. New England., 1996
1 In many games

RECOVERIES

Most Total Fumbles Recovered, Game

8 SB: Dallas vs. Denver, 1977 (4 own, 4 opp)
7 NFC: Chi. Bears vs. N.Y. Giants, 1934 (5 own, 2 opp)
NFC-D: San Francisco vs. Detroit, 1957 (4 own, 3 opp)
NFC-D: San Francisco vs. Dallas, 1972 (4 own, 3 opp)
AFC: Pittsburgh vs. Houston, 1978 (3 own, 4 opp)
6 AFC: Houston vs. San Diego, 1961 (4 own, 2 opp)
AFC-D: Cleveland vs. Baltimore, 1971 (4 own, 2 opp)
AFC-D: Cleveland vs. Oakland, 1980 (5 own, 1 opp)
NFC: Philadelphia vs. Dallas, 1980 (3 own, 3 opp)
SB: Dallas vs. Buffalo, 1992 (1 own, 5 opp)
NFC-D: Green Bay vs. San Francisco, 1996 (4 own, 2 opp)

Most Own Fumbles Recovered, Game

5 NFC: Chi. Bears vs. N.Y. Giants, 1934
AFC-D: Cleveland vs. Oakland, 1980
4 By many teams

TOUCHDOWNS

Most Touchdowns, Game

2 SB: Dallas vs. Buffalo, 1992

TURNOVERS

Numbers of times losing the ball on interceptions and fumbles.

Most Turnovers, Game

9 NFC: Washington vs. Chi. Bears, 1940
NFC: Detroit vs. Cleveland, 1954
AFC: Houston vs. Pittsburgh, 1978
SB: Buffalo vs. Dallas, 1992
8 NFC: N.Y. Giants vs. Chi. Bears, 1946
NFC: Los Angeles vs. Cleveland, 1955
NFC: Cleveland vs. Detroit, 1957
SB: Denver vs. Dallas, 1977
NFC-D: Minnesota vs. Philadelphia, 1980
7 In many games

Fewest Turnovers, Game

0 By many teams

Most Turnovers, Both Teams, Game

14 AFC: Houston (9) vs. Pittsburgh (5), 1978
13 NFC: Detroit (9) vs. Cleveland (4), 1954
AFC: Houston (7) vs. San Diego (6), 1961
12 AFC: Pittsburgh (7) vs. Oakland (5), 1975
Fewest Turnovers, Both Teams, Game
0 SB: Buffalo vs. N.Y. Giants, 1990
AFC-FR: Kansas City vs Pittsburgh, 1993 (OT)
NFC-FR: Detroit vs. Green Bay, 1994
AFC-FR:Denver vs. Jacksonville, 1996
1 AFC-D: Baltimore (0) vs. Cincinnati (1), 1970
AFC-D: Pittsburgh (0) vs. Buffalo (1), 1974
AFC: Oakland (0) vs. Pittsburgh (1), 1976
NFC-D: Minnesota (0) vs. Washington (1), 1982
NFC-D: Chicago (0) vs. N.Y. Giants (1), 1985
SB: N.Y. Giants (0) vs. Denver (1), 1986
NFC: Washington (0) vs. Minnesota (1), 1987
AFC-D: Cincinnati (0) vs. L.A. Raiders (1), 1990
NFC: N.Y. Giants (0) vs. San Francisco (1), 1990
NFC-FR: N.Y. Giants (0) vs. Minnesota (1), 1993
AFC-FR: L.A. Raiders (0) vs. Denver (1), 1993
NFC: Dallas (0) vs. San Francisco (1), 1993
AFC: Indianapolis (0) vs. Pittsburgh (1), 1995
NFC-D: San Francisco (0) vs. Minnesota (1), 1997
2 In many games

Includes records of AFC-NFC Pro Bowls, 1971-1998
Compiled by Elias Sports Bureau

INDIVIDUAL RECORDS

SERVICE

Most Games

10 Lawrence Taylor, N.Y. Giants, 1982-91
Ronnie Lott, San Francisco, 1982-85, 1987-91; L.A. Raiders 1992
Mike Singletary, Chicago, 1984-93
** Reggie White, Philadelphia, 1987-93; Green Bay, 1994, 1996-97
9 * Ken Houston, Houston, 1971-73; Washington, 1974-79
Joe Greene, Pittsburgh, 1971-77, 1979-80
Jack Lambert, Pittsburgh, 1976-84
Walter Payton, Chicago, 1977-81, 1984-87
Harry Carson, N.Y. Giants, 1979-80, 1982-88
Mike Webster, Pittsburgh, 1979-86, 1988
** Anthony Muñoz, Cincinnati, 1982-87, 1989-90, 1992
Randall McDaniel, Minnesota, 1990-98
Warren Moon, Houston, 1989-94; Minnesota 1995-96; Seattle 1998
Derrick Thomas, Kansas City, 1990-98
8 Tom Mack, Los Angeles, 1971-76, 1978-79
* Franco Harris, Pittsburgh, 1973-76, 1978-81
Lemar Parrish, Cincinnati, 1971-72, 1975-77; Washington, 1978, 1980-81
Art Shell, Oakland, 1973-79, 1981
Ted Hendricks, Baltimore, 1972-74; Green Bay, 1975; Oakland, 1981-82; L.A. Raiders, 1983-84
* John Hannah, New England, 1977, 1979-83, 1985-86
* Randy White, Dallas, 1978, 1980-86
James Lofton, Green Bay, 1979, 1981-86; Buffalo 1992
* Mike Munchak, Houston, 1985-86, 1988-93
Howie Long, L.A. Raiders, 1984-88, 1990, 1993-94
*** Jerry Rice, San Francisco, 1987-88, 1990-94, 1996
* Chris Doleman, Minnesota 1988-91, 1993-94; Atlanta 1996; San Francisco 1998
** Bruce Matthews, Houston, 1989-95, 1997
* Barry Sanders, Detroit, 1990-93, 1995-98

**Also selected, but did not play, in one additional game*
***Also selected, but did not play, in two additional games*
****Also selected, but did not play, in three additional games*

SCORING

POINTS

Most Points, Career

45 Morten Andersen, New Orleans, 1986-89, 1991, 1993; Atlanta, 1996 (15-pat, 10-fg)
30 Jan Stenerud, Kansas City, 1971-72, 1976; Minnesota, 1985 (6-pat, 8-fg)
26 Nick Lowery, Kansas City, 1982, 1991, 1993 (5 pat, 7 fg)

Most Points, Game

18 John Brockington, Green Bay, 1973 (3-td)
15 Garo Yepremian, Miami, 1974 (5-fg)
14 Jan Stenerud, Kansas City, 1972 (2-pat, 4-fg)

TOUCHDOWNS

Most Touchdowns, Career

3 John Brockington, Green Bay, 1972-74 (2-r, 1-p)
Earl Campbell, Houston, 1979-82, 1984 (3-r)
Chuck Muncie, New Orleans, 1980; San Diego, 1982-83 (3-r)
William Andrews, Atlanta, 1981-84 (1-r, 2-p)
Marcus Allen, L.A. Raiders, 1983, 1985-86, 1988; Kansas City, 1994 (2-r, 1-p)
Cris Carter, Minnesota, 1994-98 (3-p)
2 By 17 players

Most Touchdowns, Game

3 John Brockington, Green Bay, 1973 (2-r, 1-p)
2 Mel Renfro, Dallas, 1971 (2-ret)
Earl Campbell, Houston, 1980 (2-r)
Chuck Muncie, New Orleans, 1980 (2-r)
William Andrews, Atlanta, 1984 (2-p)
Herschel Walker, Dallas, 1989 (2-r)
Johnny Johnson, Phoenix, 1991 (2-r)
Eric Green, Pittsburgh, 1995 (2-p)

POINTS AFTER TOUCHDOWN

Most Points After Touchdown, Career

15 Morten Andersen, New Orleans, 1986-89, 1991, 1993; Atlanta, 1996 (15 att)
6 Chester Marcol, Green Bay, 1973, 1975 (6 att)
Mark Moseley, Washington, 1980, 1983 (7 att)
Ali Haji-Sheikh, N.Y. Giants, 1984 (6 att)
Jan Stenerud, Kansas City, 1971-72, 1976; Green Bay, 1985 (6 att)
5 Nick Lowery, Kansas City, 1982, 1991, 1993 (5 att)
John Carney, San Diego, 1995 (5 att)

Most Points After Touchdown, Game

6 Ali Haji-Sheikh, N.Y. Giants, 1984 (6 att)
5 John Carney, San Diego, 1995 (5 att)
4 Chester Marcol, Green Bay, 1973 (4 att)
Mark Moseley, Washington, 1980 (5 att)
Morten Andersen, New Orleans, 1986 (4 att), 1989 (4 att)

FIELD GOALS

Most Field Goals Attempted, Career

18 Morten Andersen, New Orleans, 1986-89, 1991, 1993; Atlanta, 1996
15 Jan Stenerud, Kansas City, 1971-72, 1976; Minnesota, 1985
10 Nick Lowery, Kansas City, 1982, 1991, 1993

Most Field Goals Attempted, Game

6 Jan Stenerud, Kansas City, 1972
Eddie Murray, Detroit, 1981
Mark Moseley, Washington, 1983
5 Garo Yepremian, Miami, 1974
4 Jan Stenerud, Kansas City, 1976
Nick Lowery, Kansas City, 1991, 1993
Morten Andersen, New Orleans, 1993
Cary Blanchard, Indianapolis, 1997
John Kasay, Carolina, 1997

Most Field Goals, Career

10 Morten Andersen, New Orleans, 1986-89, 1991, 1993; Atlanta, 1996
8 Jan Stenerud, Kansas City, 1971-72, 1976; Minnesota, 1985
7 Nick Lowery, Kansas City, 1982, 1991, 1993

Most Field Goals, Game

5 Garo Yepremian, Miami, 1974 (5 att)
4 Jan Stenerud, Kansas City, 1972 (6 att)
Eddie Murray, Detroit, 1981 (6 att)
3 Nick Lowery, Kansas City, 1991 (4 att)
Nick Lowery, Kansas City, 1993 (4 att)

Longest Field Goal

51 Morten Andersen, New Orleans, 1989
49 Fuad Reveiz, Minnesota, 1995
48 Jan Stenerud, Kansas City, 1972
Jeff Jaeger, L.A. Raiders, 1992
Mike Hollis, Jacksonville, 1998

SAFETIES

Most Safeties, Game

1 Art Still, Kansas City, 1983
Mark Gastineau, N.Y. Jets, 1985
Greg Townsend, L.A. Raiders, 1992

RUSHING

ATTEMPTS

Most Attempts, Career

81 Walter Payton, Chicago, 1977-81, 1984-87
68 O.J. Simpson, Buffalo, 1973-77
66 Barry Sanders, Detroit, 1990-93, 1995-98

Most Attempts, Game

19 O.J. Simpson, Buffalo, 1974
17 Marv Hubbard, Oakland, 1974
16 O.J. Simpson, Buffalo, 1973
Marcus Allen, L.A. Raiders, 1986

YARDS GAINED

Most Yards Gained, Career

368 Walter Payton, Chicago, 1977-81, 1984-87
356 O.J. Simpson, Buffalo, 1973-77
234 Chris Warren, Seattle, 1994-96

Most Yards Gained, Game

180 Marshall Faulk, Indianapolis, 1995
127 Chris Warren, Seattle, 1995
112 O. J. Simpson, Buffalo, 1973

Longest Run From Scrimmage

49 Marshall Faulk, Indianapolis, 1995 (TD)
41 Lawrence McCutcheon, Los Angeles, 1976
Natrone Means, San Diego, 1995
Marshall Faulk, Indianapolis, 1995
39 Chris Warren, Seattle, 1994

AVERAGE GAIN

Highest Average Gain, Career (20 attempts)

9.36 Chris Warren, Seattle, 1994-96, (25-234)
5.81 Marv Hubbard, Oakland, 1972-74 (36-209)
5.71 Wilbert Montgomery, Philadelphia, 1979-80 (21-120)

Highest Average Gain, Game (10 attempts)

13.85 Marshall Faulk, Indianapolis, 1995 (13-180)
9.07 Chris Warren, Seattle, 1995 (14-127)

7.00 O.J. Simpson, Buffalo, 1973 (16-112)
Ottis Anderson, St. Louis, 1981 (10-70)

TOUCHDOWNS

Most Touchdowns, Career

3 Earl Campbell, Houston, 1979-82, 1984
Chuck Muncie, New Orleans, 1980; San Diego, 1982-83
2 John Brockington, Green Bay, 1972-74
O.J. Simpson, Buffalo, 1973-77
Walter Payton, Chicago, 1977-81, 1984-87
Marcus Allen, L.A. Raiders, 1983, 1985-86, 1988; Kansas City, 1994
Herschel Walker, Dallas, 1988-89
Johnny Johnson, Phoenix, 1991
Barry Sanders, Detroit, 1990-93, 1995-98

Most Touchdowns, Game

2 John Brockington, Green Bay, 1973
Earl Campbell, Houston, 1980
Chuck Muncie, New Orleans, 1980
Herschel Walker, Dallas, 1989
Johnny Johnson, Phoenix, 1991

PASSING

ATTEMPTS

Most Attempts, Career

120 Dan Fouts, San Diego, 1980-84, 1986
90 Warren Moon, Houston, 1989-94; Minnesota, 1995-96; Seattle 1998
89 Steve Young, San Francisco, 1993-96, 1998

Most Attempts, Game

32 Bill Kenney, Kansas City, 1984
Steve Young, San Francisco, 1993
30 Dan Fouts, San Diego, 1983
28 Jim Hart, St. Louis, 1976

COMPLETIONS

Most Completions, Career

63 Dan Fouts, San Diego, 1980-84, 1986
45 Warren Moon, Houston, 1989-94; Minnesota, 1995-96; Seattle 1998
44 Bob Griese, Miami, 1971-72, 1974-75, 1977, 1979

Most Completions, Game

21 Joe Theismann, Washington, 1984
18 Steve Young, San Francisco, 1993
17 Dan Fouts, San Diego, 1983

COMPLETION PERCENTAGE

Highest Completion Percentage, Career (40 attempts)

68.9 Joe Theismann, Washington, 1983-84 (45-31)
64.4 Jim Kelly, Buffalo, 1988, 1991-92 (45-29)
58.9 Ken Anderson, Cincinnati, 1976-77, 1982-83 (56-33)

Highest Completion Percentage, Game (10 attempts)

90.0 Archie Manning, New Orleans, 1980 (10-9)
77.8 Joe Theismann, Washington, 1984 (27-21)
72.2 Jim Everett, L.A. Rams, 1991 (18-13)

YARDS GAINED

Most Yards Gained, Career

890 Dan Fouts, San Diego, 1980-84, 1986
579 Steve Young, San Francisco, 1993-96, 1998
554 Bob Griese, Miami, 1971-72, 1974-75, 1977, 1979

Most Yards Gained, Game

274 Dan Fouts, San Diego, 1983
242 Joe Theismann, Washington, 1984
236 Mark Brunell, Jacksonville, 1997

Longest Completion

93 Jeff Blake, Cincinnati (to Thigpen, Pittsburgh), 1996 (TD)
80 Mark Brunell, Jacksonville (to Brown, Oakland), 1997 (TD)
64 Dan Pastorini, Houston (to Burrough, Houston), 1976 (TD)

AVERAGE GAIN

Highest Average Gain, Career (40 attempts)

8.12 Brett Favre, Green Bay, 1993-94, 1996-97 (57-463)
8.02 Jim Kelly, Buffalo, 1988, 1991-92 (45-361)
7.91 Randall Cunningham, Philadelphia, 1989-91 (44-348)

Highest Average Gain, Game (10 attempts)

15.27 Randall Cunningham, Philadelphia, 1991 (11-168)
13.00 Brett Favre, Green Bay, 1997 (11-143)
11.40 Ken Anderson, Cincinnati, 1977 (10-114)

TOUCHDOWNS

Most Touchdowns, Career

4 Steve Young, San Francisco, 1993-96, 1998
3 Joe Theismann, Washington, 1983-84
Joe Montana, San Francisco, 1982, 1984-85, 1988
Phil Simms, N.Y. Giants, 1986
Jim Kelly, Buffalo, 1988, 1991-92
2 James Harris, Los Angeles, 1975
Mike Boryla, Philadelphia, 1976
Ken Anderson, Cincinnati, 1976-77, 1982-83
Bob Griese, Miami, 1971-72, 1974-75, 1977, 1979
Mark Rypien, Washington, 1990, 1992
John Elway, Denver, 1987-88, 1994-95
Brett Favre, Green Bay, 1993-94, 1996-97
Mark Brunell, Jacksonville, 1997-98

Most Touchdowns, Game

3 Joe Theismann, Washington, 1984
Phil Simms, N.Y. Giants, 1986
2 James Harris, Los Angeles, 1975
Mike Boryla, Philadelphia, 1976
Ken Anderson, Cincinnati, 1977
Jim Kelly, Buffalo, 1991
Mark Rypien, Washington, 1992
Steve Young, San Francisco, 1998

HAD INTERCEPTED

Most Passes Had Intercepted, Career

8 Dan Fouts, San Diego, 1980-84, 1986
6 Jim Hart, St. Louis, 1975-78
5 Ken Stabler, Oakland, 1974-75, 1978

Most Passes Had Intercepted, Game

5 Jim Hart, St. Louis, 1977
4 Ken Stabler, Oakland, 1974
3 Dan Fouts, San Diego, 1986
Mark Rypien, Washington, 1990
Steve Young, San Francisco, 1993
Jim Harbaugh, Indianapolis, 1996

Most Attempts, Without Interception, Game

27 Joe Theismann, Washington, 1984
Phil Simms, N.Y. Giants, 1986
26 John Brodie, San Francisco, 1971
Danny White, Dallas, 1983
22 Mark Brunell, Jacksonville, 1997

PERCENTAGE, PASSES HAD INTERCEPTED

Lowest Percentage, Passes Had Intercepted, Career (40 attempts)

0.00 Joe Theismann, Washington, 1983-84 (45-0)
2.13 Dave Krieg, Seattle, 1985, 1989-90 (47-1)
2.22 Jim Kelly, Buffalo, 1988, 1991-92 (45-1)

PASS RECEIVING

RECEPTIONS

Most Receptions, Career

28 Jerry Rice, San Francisco, 1987-88, 1990-94, 1996
23 Tim Brown, L.A. Raiders, 1989, 1992, 1994-95; Oakland 1996-98
18 Walter Payton, Chicago, 1977-81, 1984-87
Michael Irvin, Dallas, 1992-96

Most Receptions, Game

8 Steve Largent, Seattle, 1986
Michael Irvin, Dallas, 1992
Andre Rison, Atlanta, 1993
7 John Stallworth, Pittsburgh, 1983
Jerry Rice, San Francisco, 1992
Isaac Bruce, St. Louis, 1997
6 John Stallworth, Pittsburgh, 1980
Kellen Winslow, San Diego, 1982
Gary Clark, Washington, 1991
Keith Byars, Miami, 1994
Andre Rison, Atlanta, 1994
Jerry Rice, San Francisco, 1996

YARDS GAINED

Most Yards Gained, Career

408 Tim Brown, L.A. Raiders, 1989, 1992, 1994-95; Oakland, 1996-98
399 Jerry Rice, San Francisco, 1987-88, 1990-94, 1996
274 Michael Irvin, Dallas, 1992-96

Most Yards Gained, Game

137 Tim Brown, Oakland, 1997
129 Tim Brown, Oakland, 1998
125 Michael Irvin, Dallas, 1992

Longest Reception

93 Yancey Thigpen, Pittsburgh (from Blake, Cincinnati), 1996 (TD)
80 Tim Brown, Oakland (from Brunell, Jacksonville), 1997 (TD)
64 Ken Burrough, Houston (from Pastorini, Houston), 1976 (TD)

TOUCHDOWNS

Most Touchdowns, Career

3 Cris Carter, Minnesota, 1994-98
2 Mel Gray, St. Louis, 1975-78

Cliff Branch, Oakland, 1975-78
Terry Metcalf, St. Louis, 1975-76, 1978
Tony Hill, Dallas, 1979-80, 1986
William Andrews, Atlanta, 1981-84
James Lofton, Green Bay, 1979, 1981-86; Buffalo 1992
Jimmie Giles, Tampa Bay, 1981-83, 1986
Michael Irvin, Dallas, 1992-95
Eric Green, Pittsburgh, 1994-95
Jerry Rice, San Francisco, 1987-88, 1990-94, 1996

Most Touchdowns, Game
2 William Andrews, Atlanta, 1984
Eric Green, Pittsburgh, 1995

INTERCEPTIONS BY

Most Interceptions By, Career
4 Everson Walls, Dallas, 1982-84, 1986
3 Ken Houston, Houston, 1971-73; Washington, 1974-79
Jack Lambert, Pittsburgh, 1976-84
Ted Hendricks, Baltimore, 1972-74; Green Bay, 1975; Oakland, 1981-82; L.A. Raiders, 1983-84
Mike Haynes, New England, 1978-81, 1983; L.A. Raiders, 1985-87
Deion Sanders, Atlanta, 1992-94; San Francisco, 1995
2 By 11 players

Most Interceptions By, Game
2 Mel Blount, Pittsburgh, 1977
Everson Walls, Dallas, 1982, 1983
LeRoy Irvin, L.A. Rams, 1986
David Fulcher, Cincinnati, 1990

YARDS GAINED

Most Yards Gained, Career
77 Ted Hendricks, Baltimore, 1972-74; Green Bay, 1975; Oakland, 1981-82; L.A. Raiders, 1983-84
73 Rod Woodson, Pittsburgh, 1990-94
54 Ashley Ambrose, Cincinnati, 1997

Most Yards Gained, Game
73 Rod Woodson, Pittsburgh, 1994
65 Ted Hendricks, Baltimore, 1973
54 Ashley Ambrose, Cincinnati, 1997

Longest Gain
73 Rod Woodson, Pittsburgh, 1994 (lateral)
65 Ted Hendricks, Baltimore, 1973
54 Ashley Ambrose, Cincinnati, 1997 (TD)

TOUCHDOWNS

Most Touchdowns, Game
1 Bobby Bell, Kansas City, 1973
Nolan Cromwell, L.A. Rams, 1984
Joey Browner, Minnesota, 1986
Jerry Gray, L.A. Rams, 1990
Mike Johnson, Cleveland, 1990
Junior Seau, San Diego, 1993
Ken Harvey, Washington, 1996
Ashley Ambrose, Cincinnati, 1997

PUNTING

Most Punts, Career
33 Ray Guy, Oakland, 1974-79, 1981
23 Rohn Stark, Indianapolis, 1986-87, 1991, 1993
22 Reggie Roby, Miami, 1985, 1990; Washington, 1995

Most Punts, Game
10 Reggie Roby, Miami, 1985
9 Tom Wittum, San Francisco, 1974
Rohn Stark, Indianapolis, 1987
8 Jerrel Wilson, Kansas City, 1971
Tom Skladany, Detroit, 1982
Reggie Roby, Washington, 1995

Longest Punt
64 Tom Wittum, San Francisco, 1974
Darren Bennett, San Diego, 1996
61 Reggie Roby, Miami, 1985
Jeff Feagles, Arizona, 1996
Matt Turk, Washington, 1997
60 Ron Widby, Dallas, 1972
Reggie Roby, Washington, 1995

AVERAGE YARDAGE

Highest Average, Career (10 punts)
46.73 Reggie Roby, Miami, 1985, 1990; Washington, 1995 (22-1,028)
45.25 Jerrel Wilson, Kansas City, 1971-73 (16-724)
44.65 Rohn Stark, Indianapolis, 1986-87, 1991, 1993 (23-1,027)

Highest Average, Game (4 punts)
55.50 Darren Bennett, San Diego, 1996 (4-222)
50.13 Reggie Roby, Washington, 1995 (8-401)
49.57 Jim Arnold, Detroit, 1988 (7-347)

PUNT RETURNS

Most Punt Returns, Career
13 Rick Upchurch, Denver, 1977, 1979-80, 1983
11 Vai Sikahema, St. Louis, 1987-88
Eric Metcalf, Cleveland 1994-95; San Diego 1998
10 Mike Nelms, Washington, 1981-83

Most Punt Returns, Game
7 Vai Sikahema, St. Louis, 1987
6 Henry Ellard, L.A. Rams, 1985
Gerald McNeil, Cleveland, 1988
Eric Metcalf, Cleveland, 1995
5 Rick Upchurch, Denver, 1980
Mike Nelms, Washington, 1981
Carl Roaches, Houston, 1982
Johnny Bailey, Phoenix, 1993

Most Fair Catches, Game
2 Jerry Logan, Baltimore, 1971
Dick Anderson, Miami, 1974
Henry Ellard, L.A. Rams, 1985
Isaac Bruce, St. Louis, 1997

YARDS GAINED

Most Yards Gained, Career
183 Billy Johnson, Houston, 1976, 1978; Atlanta, 1984
138 Mel Renfro, Dallas, 1971-72, 1974
Rick Upchurch, Denver, 1977, 1979-80, 1983
135 Eric Metcalf, Cleveland, 1994-95; San Diego 1998

Most Yards Gained, Game
159 Billy Johnson, Houston, 1976
138 Mel Renfro, Dallas, 1971
117 Wally Henry, Philadelphia, 1980

Longest Punt Return
90 Billy Johnson, Houston, 1976 (TD)
86 Wally Henry, Philadelphia, 1980 (TD)
82 Mel Renfro, Dallas, 1971 (TD)

AVERAGE YARDAGE

Highest Average, Career (4 returns)
22.88 Billy Johnson, Houston, 1976, 1978; Atlanta, 1984 (8-183)
21.50 Tony Green, Washington, 1979 (4-86)
15.67 David Meggett, N.Y. Giants, 1990; New England, 1997

Highest Average, Game (3 returns)
39.75 Billy Johnson, Houston, 1976 (4-159)
39.00 Wally Henry, Philadelphia, 1980 (3-117)
21.50 Tony Green, Washington, 1979 (4-86)

TOUCHDOWNS

Most Touchdowns, Game
2 Mel Renfro, Dallas, 1971
1 Billy Johnson, Houston, 1976
Wally Henry, Philadelphia, 1980

KICKOFF RETURNS

Most Kickoff Returns, Career
14 Mel Gray, Detroit, 1991-92, 1995
11 Michael Bates, Carolina, 1997-98
Eric Metcalf, Cleveland, 1994-95; San Diego 1998
10 Rick Upchurch, Denver, 1977, 1979-80, 1983
Greg Pruitt, Cleveland, 1974-75, 1977-78; L.A. Raiders, 1984

Most Kickoff Returns, Game
7 Mel Gray, Detroit, 1995
6 Greg Pruitt, L.A. Raiders, 1984
David Meggett, New England, 1997
Michael Bates, Carolina, 1998
5 By six players

YARDS GAINED

Most Yards Gained, Career
309 Greg Pruitt, Cleveland, 1974-75, 1977-78; L.A. Raiders, 1984
294 Mel Gray, Detroit, 1991-92, 1995
274 Michael Bates, Carolina, 1997-98

Most Yards Gained, Game
192 Greg Pruitt, L.A. Raiders, 1984
175 Les (Speedy) Duncan, Washington, 1972
173 David Meggett, New England, 1997

Longest Kickoff Return
62 Greg Pruitt, L.A. Raiders, 1984
61 Eugene (Mercury) Morris, Miami, 1972
55 Ron Smith, Chicago, 1973

AFC-NFC PRO BOWL RECORDS

AVERAGE YARDAGE
Highest Average, Career (4 returns)
35.00 Les (Speedy) Duncan, Washington, 1972 (5-175)
31.25 Eugene (Mercury) Morris, Miami, 1972 (3-93)
30.90 Greg Pruitt, Cleveland, 1974-75, 1977-78; L.A. Raiders, 1984 (6-192)
Highest Average, Game (3 returns)
35.00 Les (Speedy) Duncan, Washington, 1972 (5-175)
32.00 Greg Pruitt, L.A. Raiders, 1984 (6-192)
31.00 Eugene (Mercury) Morris, Miami, 1972 (3-93)

TOUCHDOWNS
Most Touchdowns, Game
None

FUMBLES
Most Fumbles, Career
6 Dan Fouts, San Diego, 1980-84, 1986
4 Lawrence McCutcheon, Los Angeles, 1974-78
Franco Harris, Pittsburgh, 1973-76, 1978-81
Jay Schroeder, Washington, 1987
Vai Sikahema, St. Louis, 1987-88
3 O.J. Simpson, Buffalo, 1973-77
William Andrews, Atlanta, 1981-84
Joe Montana, San Francisco, 1982, 1984-85, 1988
Walter Payton, Chicago, 1977-81, 1984-87
Neil Lomax, St. Louis, 1985, 1988
Jim Kelly, Buffalo, 1988, 1991-92
Most Fumbles, Game
4 Jay Schroeder, Washington, 1987
3 Dan Fouts, San Diego, 1982
Vai Sikahema, St. Louis, 1987
2 By 12 players

RECOVERIES
Most Fumbles Recovered, Career
3 Harold Jackson, Philadelphia, 1973; Los Angeles, 1974, 1976, 1978 (3-own)
Dan Fouts, San Diego, 1980-84, 1986 (3-own)
Randy White, Dallas, 1978, 1980-86 (3-opp)
2 By many players
Most Fumbles Recovered, Game
2 Dick Anderson, Miami, 1974 (1-own, 1-opp)
Harold Jackson, Los Angeles, 1974 (2-own)
Dan Fouts, San Diego, 1982 (2-own)
Joey Browner, Minnesota, 1990 (2-opp)

YARDAGE
Longest Fumble Return
83 Art Still, Kansas City, 1985 (TD, opp)
51 Phil Villapiano, Oakland, 1974 (opp)
37 Sam Mills, New Orleans, 1988 (opp)

TOUCHDOWNS
Most Touchdowns, Game
1 Art Still, Kansas City, 1985
Keith Millard, Minnesota, 1990

SACKS
Sacks have been compiled since 1983.
Most Sacks, Career
9.5 Reggie White, Philadelphia, 1987-93; Green Bay, 1994
9 Howie Long, L.A. Raiders, 1984-88, 1990, 1993-1994
7.5 Bruce Smith, Buffalo, 1988-91, 1995-96, 1998
Most Sacks, Game
4 Mark Gastineau, N.Y. Jets, 1985
Reggie White, Philadelphia, 1987
3 Richard Dent, Chicago, 1985
Bruce Smith, Buffalo, 1991
2.5 Bruce Smith, Buffalo, 1998

TEAM RECORDS

SCORING
Most Points, Game
45 NFC, 1984
Fewest Points, Game
3 AFC, 1984, 1989, 1994
Most Points, Both Teams, Game
64 NFC (37) vs. AFC (27), 1980
Fewest Points, Both Teams, Game
16 NFC (6) vs. AFC (10), 1987

TOUCHDOWNS
Most Touchdowns, Game
6 NFC, 1984
Fewest Touchdowns, Game
0 AFC, 1971, 1974, 1984, 1989, 1994
NFC, 1987, 1988
Most Touchdowns, Both Teams, Game
8 AFC (4) vs. NFC (4), 1973
NFC (5) vs. AFC (3), 1980
Fewest Touchdowns, Both Teams, Game
1 AFC (0) vs. NFC (1), 1974
NFC (0) vs. AFC (1), 1987
NFC (0) vs. AFC (1), 1988

POINTS AFTER TOUCHDOWN
Most Points After Touchdown, Game
6 NFC, 1984
Most Points After Touchdown, Both Teams, Game
7 NFC (4) vs. AFC (3), 1973
NFC (4) vs. AFC (3), 1980
NFC (4) vs. AFC (3), 1986

FIELD GOALS
Most Field Goals Attempted, Game
6 AFC, 1972
NFC, 1981, 1983
Most Field Goals Attempted, Both Teams, Game
9 NFC (6) vs. AFC (3), 1983
Most Field Goals, Game
5 AFC, 1974
Most Field Goals, Both Teams, Game
7 AFC (5) vs. NFC (2), 1974

NET YARDS GAINED RUSHING AND PASSING
Most Yards Gained, Game
552 AFC, 1995
Fewest Yards Gained, Game
114 AFC, 1993
Most Yards Gained, Both Teams, Game
962 NFC (496) vs. AFC (466), 1997
Fewest Yards Gained, Both Teams, Game
424 AFC (202) vs. NFC (222), 1987

RUSHING
ATTEMPTS
Most Attempts, Game
50 AFC, 1974
Fewest Attempts, Game
14 AFC, 1994
Most Attempts, Both Teams, Game
80 AFC (50) vs. NFC (30), 1974
Fewest Attempts, Both Teams, Game
47 NFC (22) vs. AFC (25), 1996

YARDS GAINED
Most Yards Gained, Game
400 AFC, 1995
Fewest Yards Gained, Game
28 NFC, 1992
Most Yards Gained, Both Teams, Game
441 AFC (400) vs. NFC (41), 1995
Fewest Yards Gained, Both Teams, Game
131 NFC (28) vs. AFC (103), 1992

TOUCHDOWNS
Most Touchdowns, Game
3 NFC, 1989, 1991
AFC, 1995
Most Touchdowns, Both Teams, Game
4 AFC (2) vs. NFC (2), 1973
AFC (2) vs. NFC (2), 1980

PASSING
ATTEMPTS
Most Attempts, Game
55 NFC, 1993
Fewest Attempts, Game
17 NFC, 1972
Most Attempts, Both Teams, Game
94 AFC (50) vs. NFC (44), 1983
Fewest Attempts, Both Teams, Game
42 NFC (17) vs. AFC (25), 1972

COMPLETIONS
Most Completions, Game
32 NFC, 1993
Fewest Completions, Game
7 NFC, 1972, 1982
Most Completions, Both Teams, Game
55 AFC (31) vs. NFC (24), 1983
Fewest Completions, Both Teams, Game
18 NFC (7) vs. AFC (11), 1972

YARDS GAINED
Most Yards Gained, Game
387 AFC, 1983
Fewest Yards Gained, Game
42 NFC, 1982
Most Yards Gained, Both Teams, Game
735 AFC (369) vs. NFC (366), 1997
Fewest Yards Gained, Both Teams, Game
215 NFC (89) vs. AFC (126), 1972

TIMES SACKED
Most Times Sacked, Game
9 NFC, 1985
Fewest Times Sacked, Game
0 AFC, 1998
NFC, 1971, 1997
Most Times Sacked, Both Teams, Game
17 NFC (9) vs. AFC (8), 1985
Fewest Times Sacked, Both Teams, Game
1 NFC (0) vs. AFC (1), 1997

TOUCHDOWNS
Most Touchdowns, Game
4 NFC, 1984
Most Touchdowns, Both Teams, Game
5 NFC (3) vs. AFC (2), 1986

INTERCEPTIONS BY
Most Interceptions By, Game
6 AFC, 1977
Most Interceptions By, Both Teams, Game
7 AFC (6) vs. NFC (1), 1977

YARDS GAINED
Most Yards Gained, Game
103 AFC, 1994
Most Yards Gained, Both Teams, Game
116 AFC (103) vs. NFC (13), 1994

TOUCHDOWNS
Most Touchdowns, Game
1 AFC, 1973, 1990, 1993, 1997
NFC, 1984, 1986, 1990, 1996

PUNTING
Most Punts, Game
10 AFC, 1985
Fewest Punts, Game
0 NFC, 1989
Most Punts, Both Teams, Game
16 AFC (10) vs. NFC (6), 1985
Fewest Punts, Both Teams, Game
4 NFC (1) vs. AFC (3), 1992

PUNT RETURNS
Most Punt Returns, Game
7 NFC, 1985, 1987
AFC, 1995
Fewest Punt Returns, Game
0 AFC, 1984, 1989
Most Punt Returns, Both Teams, Game
11 NFC (7) vs. AFC (4), 1985
Fewest Punt Returns, Both Teams, Game
2 AFC (1) vs. NFC (1), 1996

YARDS GAINED
Most Yards Gained, Game
177 AFC, 1976
Fewest Yards Gained, Game
−1 NFC, 1991
Most Yards Gained, Both Teams, Game
263 AFC (177) vs. NFC (86), 1976
Fewest Yards Gained, Both Teams, Game
16 AFC (0) vs. NFC (16), 1984

TOUCHDOWNS
Most Touchdowns, Game
2 NFC, 1971

KICKOFF RETURNS
Most Kickoff Returns, Game
8 NFC, 1995
Fewest Kickoff Returns, Game
1 NFC, 1971, 1984, 1994
AFC, 1988, 1991
Most Kickoff Returns, Both Teams, Game
12 NFC (8) vs. AFC (4), 1995
Fewest Kickoff Returns, Both Teams, Game
5 NFC (2) vs. AFC (3), 1979
AFC (1) vs. NFC (4), 1988
NFC (2) vs. AFC (3), 1992
NFC (1) vs. AFC (4), 1994

YARDS GAINED
Most Yards Gained, Game
215 AFC, 1984
Fewest Yards Gained, Game
6 NFC, 1971
Most Yards Gained, Both Teams, Game
325 AFC (173) vs. NFC (152), 1997
Fewest Yards Gained, Both Teams, Game
99 NFC (48) vs. AFC (51), 1987

TOUCHDOWNS
Most Touchdowns, Game
None

FUMBLES
Most Fumbles, Game
10 NFC, 1974
Most Fumbles, Both Teams, Game
15 NFC (10) vs. AFC (5), 1974

RECOVERIES
Most Fumbles Recovered, Game
10 NFC, 1974 (6 own, 4 opp)
Most Fumbles Lost, Game
4 AFC, 1974, 1988
NFC, 1974

YARDS GAINED
Most Yards Gained, Game
87 AFC, 1985

TOUCHDOWNS
Most Touchdowns, Game
1 AFC, 1985
NFC, 1990

TURNOVERS
(Number of times losing the ball on interceptions and fumbles.)
Most Turnovers, Game
8 AFC, 1974
Fewest Turnovers, Game
0 AFC, 1991, 1997
NFC, 1991, 1995, 1996
Most Turnovers, Both Teams, Game
12 AFC (8) vs. NFC (4), 1974
Fewest Turnovers, Both Teams, Game
0 AFC vs. NFC, 1991

Rules

OFFICIALS

1998 NFL ROSTER OF OFFICIALS

Jerry Seeman, Senior Director of Officiating
Larry Upson, Supervisor of Officials **Al Hynes,** Supervisor of Officials
Mike Pereira, Supervisor of Officials **Ron DeSouza,** Supervisor of Officials

No.	Name	Position	College
115	Ancich, Hendi	Umpire	Harbor College
81	Anderson, Dave	Line Judge	Salem College
66	Anderson, Walt	Line Judge	Sam Houston State
108	Arthur, Gary	Line Judge	Wright State
34	Austin, Gerald	Referee	Western Carolina
22	Baetz, Paul	Field Judge	Heidelberg
91	Baker, Ken	Side Judge	Eastern Illinois
48	Balliet, Brian	Umpire	Lehigh
26	Baltz, Mark	Head Linesman	Ohio University
55	Barnes, Tom	Line Judge	Minnesota
56	Baynes, Ron	Line Judge	Auburn
32	Bergman, Jeff	Line Judge	Robert Morris
7	Blum, Ron	Referee	Marin College
18	Boston, Byron	Line Judge	Austin
110	Botchan, Ron	Umpire	Occidental
101	Boylston, Bob	Umpire	Alabama
31	Brown, Chad	Umpire	East Texas State
126	Carey, Don	Back Judge	U.C. Riverside
94	Carey, Mike	Referee	Santa Clara
39	Carlsen, Don	Side Judge	Cal State-Chico
63	Carollo, Bill	Referee	Wisconsin-Milwaukee
11	Carroll, Duke	Field Judge	Ithaca
41	Cheek, Boris	Field Judge	Morgan State
65	Coleman, Walt	Referee	Arkansas
99	Corrente, Tony	Referee	Cal State-Fullerton
71	Coukart, Ed	Umpire	Northwestern
61	Creed, Dick	Field Judge	Louisville
75	Daopoulos, Jim	Umpire	Kentucky
70	Dawson, Scott	Umpire	Virginia Tech
113	Dorkowski, Don	Back Judge	Cal State-Los Angeles
6	Dornan, Kirk	Back Judge	Central Washington
74	Duke, James	Umpire	Howard
89	Dunn, Neely	Side Judge	South Carolina State
57	Fiffick, Ed	Umpire	Marquette
47	Fincken, Tom	Side Judge	Kansas State
111	Frantz, Earnie	Head Linesman	No College
50	Gereb, Neil	Umpire	California
72	Gierke, Terry	Head Linesman	Portland State
19	Green, Scott	Back Judge	Delaware
23	Grier, Johnny	Referee	University of D.C.
96	Hakes, Don	Back Judge	Bradley
104	Hamer, Dale	Head Linesman	California, Pa.
105	Hantak, Dick	Referee	Southeast Missouri
125	Hayes, Laird	Side Judge	Princeton
54	Hayward, George	Head Linesman	Missouri Western
28	Hittner, Mark	Head Linesman	Pittsburg State
85	Hochuli, Ed	Referee	Texas-El Paso
114	Johnson, Tom	Head Linesman	Miami, Ohio
97	Jones, Nate	Side Judge	Lewis & Clark
106	Jury, Al	Field Judge	San Bernardino Valley
86	Kukar, Bernie	Referee	St. John's
120	Lane, Gary	Side Judge	Missouri
17	Lawing, Bob	Back Judge	North Carolina State
127	Leavy, Bill	Back Judge	San Jose State
130	Lewis, Darryll	Line Judge	Dartmouth
76	Liebsack, Ron	Side Judge	Regis
49	Look, Dean	Side Judge	Michigan State
98	Lovett, Bill	Field Judge	Maryland
59	Luckett, Phil	Referee	Texas-El Paso
102	Mack, Keven	Field Judge	Fort Valley State
92	Madsen, Carl	Umpire	Washington
107	Marinucci, Ron	Line Judge	Rowan State
9	Markbreit, Jerry	Referee	Illinois
38	Maurer, Bruce	Line Judge	Ohio State
77	McAulay, Terry	Side Judge	Louisiana State
95	McElwee, Bob	Referee	Navy
35	McGrath, Bob	Field Judge	Western Kentucky
64	McPeters, Lloyd	Field Judge	Oklahoma State
80	Millis, Timmie	Field Judge	Millsaps
117	Montgomery, Ben	Line Judge	Morehouse
60	Moore, Tommy	Side Judge	Stephen F. Austin
135	Morelli, Pete	Field Judge	St. Mary's
20	Nemmers, Larry	Referee	Upper Iowa
51	Orem, Dale	Line Judge	Louisville
46	Paganelli, Perry	Back Judge	Hope College
15	Patterson, Rick	Side Judge	Wofford
10	Phares, Ron	Line Judge	Virginia Tech
79	Pointer, Aaron	Head Linesman	Pacific Lutheran
5	Quirk, Jim	Umpire	Delaware
83	Reels, Richard	Back Judge	Chicago State
44	Rice, Jeff	Umpire	Northwestern
121	Rivers, Sanford	Head Linesman	Youngstown State
128	Rose, Larry	Side Judge	Florida
58	Saracino, Jim	Field Judge	Northern Colorado
21	Schleyer, John	Head Linesman	Millersville
122	Schmitz, Bill	Back Judge	Colorado State
109	Semon, Sid	Head Linesman	Southern California
118	Sifferman, Tom	Field Judge	Seattle
73	Skelton, Bobby	Back Judge	Alabama
30	Slaughter, Gary	Head Linesman	East Texas State
29	Slavin, Howard	Side Judge	Southern California
2	Smith, Billy	Back Judge	East Carolina
119	Spitler, Ron	Back Judge	Panhandle State
12	Spyksma, Bill	Line Judge	South Dakota
24	Stabile, Tom	Head Linesman	Slippery Rock
88	Steenson, Scott	Field Judge	North Texas
84	Steinkerchner, Mark	Line Judge	Akron
62	Stewart, Charles	Line Judge	Long Beach State
103	Stuart, Rex	Umpire	Appalachian State
4	Toole, Doug	Side Judge	Utah State
42	Triplette, Jeff	Back Judge	Wake Forest
93	Vaughan, Jack	Back Judge	Mississippi State
36	Veteri, Tony	Head Linesman	Manhattan College
25	Waggoner, Bob	Back Judge	Juniata College
100	Wagner, Bob	Umpire	Penn State
27	Warden, David	Field Judge	Oklahoma State
87	Weidner, Paul	Head Linesman	Cincinnati
123	White, Tom	Referee	Temple
8	Williams, Dale	Head Linesman	Cal State-Northridge
43	Wilson, James	Head Linesman	Eastern Kentucky
14	Winter, Ron	Referee	Michigan State
16	Wyant, David	Side Judge	Virginia
33	Zimmer, Steve	Field Judge	Hofstra

NUMERICAL ROSTER

No.	Name	Position
2	Billy Smith	BJ
4	Doug Toole	SJ
5	Jim Quirk	U
6	Kirk Dornan	BJ
7	Ron Blum	R
8	Dale Williams	HL
9	Jerry Markbreit	R
10	Ron Phares	LJ
11	Duke Carroll	FJ
12	Bill Spyksma	LJ
14	Ron Winter	R
15	Rick Patterson	SJ
16	David Wyant	SJ
17	Bob Lawing	BJ
18	Byron Boston	LJ
19	Scott Green	BJ
20	Larry Nemmers	R
21	John Schleyer	HL
22	Paul Baetz	FJ
23	Johnny Grier	R
24	Tom Stabile	HL
25	Bob Waggoner	BJ
26	Mark Baltz	HL
27	David Warden	FJ
28	Mark Hittner	HL
29	Howard Slavin	SJ
30	Gary Slaughter	HL
31	Chad Brown	U
32	Jeff Bergman	LJ
33	Steve Zimmer	FJ
34	Gerry Austin	R
35	Bob McGrath	FJ
36	Tony Veteri	HL
38	Bruce Maurer	LJ
39	Don Carlsen	SJ
41	Boris Cheek	FJ
42	Jeff Triplette	BJ
43	James Wilson	HL
44	Jeff Rice	U
46	Perry Paganelli	BJ
47	Tom Fincken	SJ
48	Brian Balliet	U
49	Dean Look	SJ
50	Neil Gereb	U
51	Dale Orem	LJ
54	George Hayward	HL
55	Tom Barnes	LJ
56	Ron Baynes	LJ
57	Ed Fiffick	U
58	Jim Saracino	FJ
59	Phil Luckett	R
60	Tommy Moore	SJ
61	Dick Creed	FJ
62	Charles Stewart	LJ
63	Bill Carollo	R
64	Lloyd McPeters	FJ
65	Walt Coleman	R
66	Walt Anderson	LJ
70	Scott Dawson	U
71	Ed Coukart	U
72	Terry Gierke	HL
73	Bobby Skelton	BJ
74	James Duke	U
75	Jim Daopoulos	U
76	Ron Liebsack	SJ
77	Terry McAulay	SJ
79	Aaron Pointer	HL
80	Timmie Millis	FJ
81	Dave Anderson	LJ
83	Richard Reels	BJ
84	Mark Steinkerchner	LJ
85	Ed Hochuli	R
86	Bernie Kukar	R
87	Paul Weidner	HL
88	Scott Steenson	FJ
89	Neely Dunn	SJ
91	Ken Baker	SJ
92	Carl Madsen	U
93	Jack Vaughan	BJ
94	Mike Carey	R
95	Bob McElwee	R
96	Don Hakes	BJ
97	Nate Jones	SJ
98	Bill Lovett	FJ
99	Tony Corrente	R
100	Bob Wagner	U
101	Bob Boylston	U
102	Keven Mack	FJ
103	Rex Stuart	U
104	Dale Hamer	HL
105	Dick Hantak	R
106	Al Jury	FJ
107	Ron Marinucci	LJ
108	Gary Arthur	LJ
109	Sid Semon	HL
110	Ron Botchan	U
111	Earnie Frantz	HL
113	Don Dorkowski	BJ
114	Tom Johnson	HL
115	Hendi Ancich	U
117	Ben Montgomery	LJ
118	Tom Sifferman	FJ
119	Ron Spitler	BJ
120	Gary Lane	SJ
121	Sanford Rivers	HL
122	Bill Schmitz	BJ
123	Tom White	R
125	Laird Hayes	SJ
126	Don Carey	BJ
127	Bill Leavy	BJ
128	Larry Rose	SJ
130	Darryll Lewis	LJ
135	Pete Morelli	FJ

1998 OFFICIALS AT A GLANCE

REFEREES

Gerry Austin, No. **34,** Western Carolina, president, leadership development group, 17th year.
Ron Blum, No. **7,** Marin College, professional golfer, 14th year.
Mike Carey, No. **94,** Santa Clara, owner, skiing accessories, 9th year.
Bill Carollo, No. **63,** Wisconsin-Milwaukee, marketing executive, 10th year.
Walt Coleman, No. **65,** Arkansas, president, dairy processor, 10th year.
Tony Corrente, No. **99,** Cal State-Fullerton, educator, 4th year.
Johnny Grier, No. **23,** University of D.C., planning engineer, 18th year.
Dick Hantak, No. **105,** Southeast Missouri, educator, 21st year.
Ed Hochuli, No. **85,** Texas-El Paso, attorney, 9th year.
Bernie Kukar, No. **86,** St. John's, sales representative, employees benefit plan, 15th year.
Phil Luckett, No. **59,** Texas-El Paso, computer program analyst, federal civil services, 8th year.
Jerry Markbreit, No. **9,** Illinois, corporate consultant, 23rd year.
Bob McElwee, No. **95,** Navy, owner, heavy construction firm, 23rd year.
Larry Nemmers, No. **20,** Upper Iowa, motivational speaker, 14th year.
Tom White, No. **123,** Temple, president, athletic sportswear, 10th year.
Ron Winter, No. **14,** Michigan State, university professor, 4th year.

UMPIRES

Hendi Ancich, No. **115,** Harbor, longshoreman, 17th year.
Brian Balliet, No. **48,** Lehigh, sales engineer, 2nd year.
Ron Botchan, No. **110,** Occidental, college professor, former AFL player, 19th year.
Bob Boylston, No. **101,** Alabama, stockbroker, 21st year.
Chad Brown, No. **31,** East Texas State, director, intramural/sports clubs, 7th year.
Ed Coukart, No. **71,** Northwestern, vice-president, commercial bank, 10th year.
Jim Daopoulos, No. **75,** Kentucky, mortgage broker, 10th year.
Scott Dawson, No. **70,** Virginia Tech, president/owner, commercial construction company, 4th year.
James Duke, No. **74,** Howard, regional manager, director of volunteer resources boys and girls clubs, 6th year.
Ed Fiffick, No. **57,** Marquette, podiatric physician, 20th year.
Neil Gereb, No. **50,** California, project manager, aircraft company, 18th year.
Carl Madsen, No. **92,** Washington, vice president of operations, 2nd year.
Jim Quirk, No. **5,** Delaware, senior vice-president, securities, 11th year.
Jeff Rice, No. **44,** Northwestern, attorney, 4th year.
Rex Stuart, No. **103,** Appalachian State, insurance agent, 15th year.
Bob Wagner, No. **100,** Penn State, executive director, cardiovascular institute, 14th year.

HEAD LINESMEN

Mark Baltz, No. **26,** Ohio University, manufacturer's representative, 10th year.
Earnie Frantz, No. **111,** no college, vice-president and manager, insurance company, 18th year.
Terry Gierke, No. **72,** Portland State, real estate broker, 18th year.
Dale Hamer, No. **104,** California Univ., Pa., consultant, 20th year.
George Hayward, No. **54,** Missouri Western, vice-president and manager, warehouse company, 8th year.
Mark Hittner, No. **28,** Pittsburg State, insurance sales, 2nd year.
Tom Johnson, No. **114,** Miami, Ohio, retired educator, president/owner, security company, 17th year.
Aaron Pointer, No. **79,** Pacific Lutheran, park department administrator, LOA, 12th year.
Sanford Rivers, No. **121,** Youngstown State, assistant vice-president, school administration, 10th year.
John Schleyer, No. **21,** Millersville, medical sales, 9th year.
Sid Semon, No. **109,** Southern California, physical educational consultant, 21st year.
Gary Slaughter, No. **30,** East Texas State, general manager, 3rd year.
Tom Stabile, No. **24,** Slippery Rock, secondary educational administrator, 4th year.
Tony Veteri, No. **36,** Manhattan, director of athletics, 7th year.
Paul Weidner, No. **87,** Cincinnati, marketing manager, 13th year.
Dale Williams, No. **8,** Cal State-Northridge, sports official, 19th year.
James Wilson, No. **43,** Eastern Kentucky, commercial truck marketing manager, 1st year.

LINE JUDGES

Dave Anderson, No. **81,** Salem, insurance executive, 15th year.
Walt Anderson, No. **66,** Sam Houston, dentist, orthodontics, 3rd year.
Gary Arthur, No. **108,** Wright State, commercial printing sales, 2nd year.
Tom Barnes, No. **55,** Minnesota, manufacturing representative, 13th year.
Ron Baynes, No. **56,** Auburn, school administrator, coach, 12th year.
Jeff Bergman, No. **32,** Robert Morris, president and chief executive officer, medical services, 7th year.
Byron Boston, No. **18,** Austin, tax consultant, 4th year.
Darryll Lewis, No. **130,** Dartmouth, associate professor, 2nd year.
Ron Marinucci, No. **107,** Glassboro State, vice president, novelty cone company, 2nd year.
Bruce Maurer, No. **38,** Ohio State, administrator/associate director, recreational sports, 12th year.
Ben Montgomery, No. **117,** Morehouse, school administrator, 17th year.
Dale Orem, No. **51,** Louisville, bank chairman of the board, 19th year.
Ron Phares, No. **10,** Virginia Tech, president, construction company, 14th year.
Bill Spyksma, No. **12,** South Dakota, commercial real estate, construction sales, 4th year.
Mark Steinkerchner, No. **84,** Akron, vice-president, 5th year.
Charles Stewart, No. **62,** Long Beach State, human services administrator, 7th year.

BACK JUDGES

Don Carey, No. **126,** California-Riverside, contract manager, 4th year.
Don Dorkowski, No. **113,** Cal State-Los Angeles, work experience coordinator, 13th year.
Kirk Dornan, No. **6,** Central Washington, industrial sales, 5th year.
Scott Green, No. **19,** Delaware, vice-president, government relations, 8th year.
Don Hakes, No. **96,** Bradley, retired educator, 22nd year.
Bob Lawing, No. **17,** North Carolina State, real estate management, 2nd year.
Bill Leavy, No. **127,** San Jose State, supervisor of officials, retired firefighter, 4th year.
Perry Paganelli, No. **46,** Hope College, high school administrator, 1st year.
Richard Reels, No. **83,** Chicago State, director of security, court services, 6th year.
Bill Schmitz, No. **122,** Colorado State, general sales manager, 10th year.
Bobby Skelton, No. **73,** Alabama, industrial representative, 14th year.
Billy Smith, No. **2,** East Carolina, federal government, 5th year.
Ron Spitler, No. **119,** Panhandle State, owner, service center, 17th year.
Jeff Triplette, No. **42,** Wake Forest, vice president, corporate accounts, 3rd year
Jack Vaughan, No. **93,** Mississippi State, marketing consultant, 22nd year.
Bob Waggoner, No. **25,** Juniata College, probation officer, 2nd year.

SIDE JUDGES

Ken Baker, No. **91,** Eastern Illinois, college educator, 8th year.
Don Carlsen, No. **39,** Cal State-Chico, assistant superintendent, county school, 10th year.
Neely Dunn, No. **89,** South Carolina State, principal, 4th year
Tom Fincken, No. **47,** Emporia State, retired educational administrator, 15th year.
Laird Hayes, No. **125,** Princeton, professor, physical education & athletics, 4th year.
Nate Jones, No. **97,** Lewis and Clark, high school principal, 22nd year.
Gary Lane, No. **120,** Missouri, owner hunting resort, former NFL player, 17th year.
Ron Liebsack, No. **76,** Regis, manager, telecommunications, 4th year.
Dean Look, No. **49,** Michigan State, consultant, medical manufacturing, former AFL player, 26th year.
Terry McAulay, No. **77,** Louisiana State, senior computer scientist, 1st year.
Tommy Moore, No. **60,** Stephen F. Austin, marketing, manufacturing representative, 7th year.
Rick Patterson, No. **15,** Wofford, banker, 3rd year.
Larry Rose, No. **128,** Florida, financial planner, 2nd year.
Howard Slavin, No. **29,** Southern California, attorney, 12th year.
Doug Toole, No. **4,** Utah State, physical therapist, 11th year.
David Wyant, No. **16,** Virginia, systems integration director, 8th year.

FIELD JUDGES

Paul Baetz, No. **22,** Heidelberg, financial consultant, 21st year.
Duke Carroll, No. **11,** Ithaca, president, insurance agency, 4th year.
Boris Cheek, No. **41,** Morgan State, director of operations and management, 3rd year.
Dick Creed, No. **61,** Louisville, real estate manager, 21st year.
Al Jury, No. **106,** San Bernardino Valley, state traffic officer, 21st year.
Bill Lovett, No. **98,** Maryland, managing partner, financial sales, 9th year.
Keven Mack, No. **102,** Ft. Valley State, economic development administrator, 2nd year.
Bob McGrath, No. **35,** Western Kentucky, sales representative, fund raiser, 6th year.
Lloyd McPeters, No. **64,** Oklahoma State, business insurance sales, 6th year.
Timmie Millis, No. **80,** Millsaps, financial investigative consultant, 10th year.
Pete Morelli, No. **135,** St. Mary's, high school principal, 2nd year.
Jim Saracino, No. **58,** Northern Colorado, secondary educator, 4th year.
Tom Sifferman, No. **118,** Seattle, manufacturer's representative, 13th year.
Scott Steenson, No. **88,** North Texas, commercial real estate broker, 8th year.
David Warden, No. **27,** Oklahoma State, dentist, 1st year.
Steven Zimmer, No. **33,** Hofstra, attorney, 2nd year.

OFFICIAL SIGNALS

1

TOUCHDOWN, FIELD GOAL, or SUCCESSFUL TRY
Both arms extended above head.

2

SAFETY
Palms together above head.

3

FIRST DOWN
Arm pointed toward defensive team's goal.

4

CROWD NOISE, DEAD BALL, or NEUTRAL ZONE ESTABLISHED
One arm above head with an open hand.
With fist closed: **Fourth Down.**

5

BALL ILLEGALLY TOUCHED, KICKED, or BATTED
Fingertips tap both shoulders.

6

TIME OUT
Hands crisscrossed above head.

Same signal followed by placing one hand on top of cap: **Referee's Time Out.**

Same signal followed by arm swung at side: **Touchback.**

7

NO TIME OUT or TIME IN WITH WHISTLE
Full arm circled to simulate moving clock.

8

DELAY OF GAME or EXCESS TIME OUT
Folded arms.

9

FALSE START, ILLEGAL FORMATION, or KICKOFF or SAFETY KICK OUT OF BOUNDS
Forearms rotated over and over in front of body.

10

PERSONAL FOUL
One wrist striking the other above head.

Same signal followed by swinging leg: **Roughing the Kicker.**

Same signal followed by raised arm swinging forward: **Roughing the Passer.**

Same signal followed by grasping face mask: **Major Face Mask.**

11

HOLDING
Grasping one wrist, the fist clenched, in front of chest.

12

ILLEGAL USE OF HANDS, ARMS, or BODY
Grasping one wrist, the hand open and facing forward, in front of chest.

13

PENALTY REFUSED, INCOMPLETE PASS, PLAY OVER, or MISSED FIELD GOAL or EXTRA POINT
Hands shifted in horizontal plane.

14

PASS JUGGLED INBOUNDS AND CAUGHT OUT OF BOUNDS
Hands up and down in front of chest (following incomplete pass signal).

15

ILLEGAL FORWARD PASS
One hand waved behind back followed by loss of down signal (23).

16

INTENTIONAL GROUNDING OF PASS
Parallel arms waved in a diagonal plane across body. Followed by loss of down signal (23).

OFFICIAL SIGNALS

17

INTERFERENCE WITH FORWARD PASS or FAIR CATCH
Hands open and extended forward from shoulders with hands vertical.

18

INVALID FAIR-CATCH SIGNAL
One hand waved above head.

19

INELIGIBLE RECEIVER or INELIGIBLE MEMBER OF KICKING TEAM DOWNFIELD
Right hand touching top of cap.

20

ILLEGAL CONTACT
One open hand extended forward.

21

OFFSIDE, ENCROACHMENT, or NEUTRAL ZONE INFRACTION
Hands on hips.

22

ILLEGAL MOTION AT SNAP
Horizontal arc with one hand.

23

LOSS OF DOWN
Both hands held behind head.

24

INTERLOCKING INTERFERENCE, PUSHING, or HELPING RUNNER
Pushing movement of hands to front with arms downward.

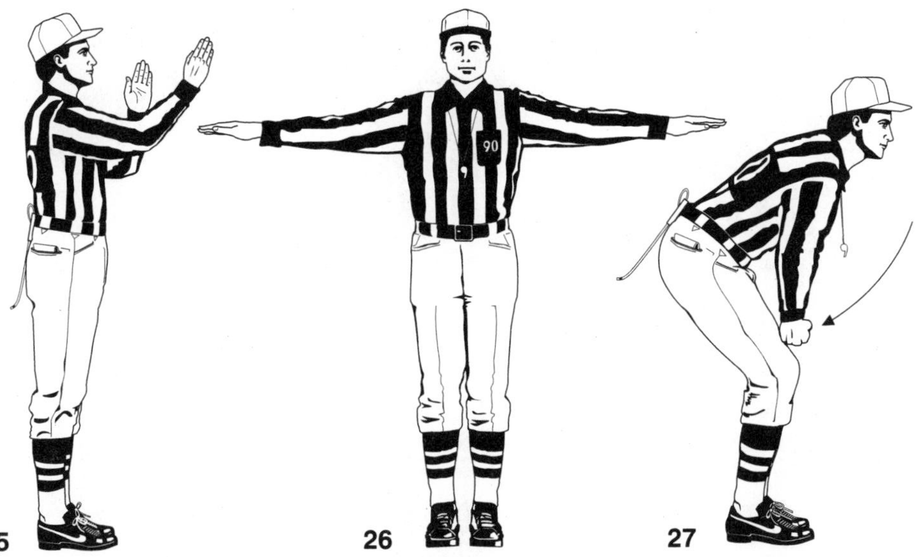

25

TOUCHING A FORWARD PASS or SCRIMMAGE KICK
Diagonal motion of one hand across another.

26

UNSPORTSMANLIKE CONDUCT
Arms outstretched, palms down.

27

ILLEGAL CUT
Hand striking front of thigh.
ILLEGAL BLOCK BELOW THE WAIST
One hand striking front of thigh preceded by personal-foul signal (10).
CHOP BLOCK
Both hands striking side of thighs preceded by personal-foul signal (10).
CLIPPING
One hand striking back of calf preceded by personal-foul signal (10).

28

ILLEGAL CRACKBACK
Strike of an open right hand against the right mid-thigh preceded by personal foul signal (10).

29

PLAYER DISQUALIFIED
Ejection signal.

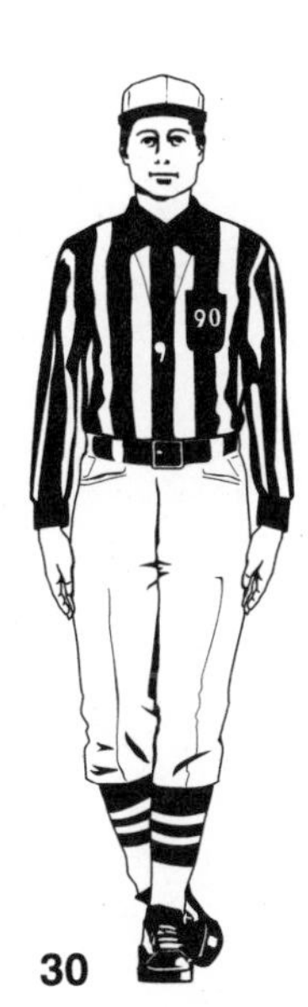

30

TRIPPING
Repeated action of right foot in back of left heel.

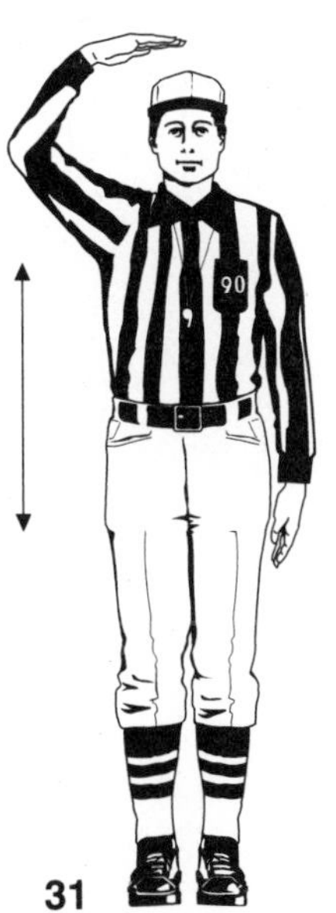

31

UNCATCHABLE FORWARD PASS
Palm of right hand held parallel to ground above head and moved back and forth.

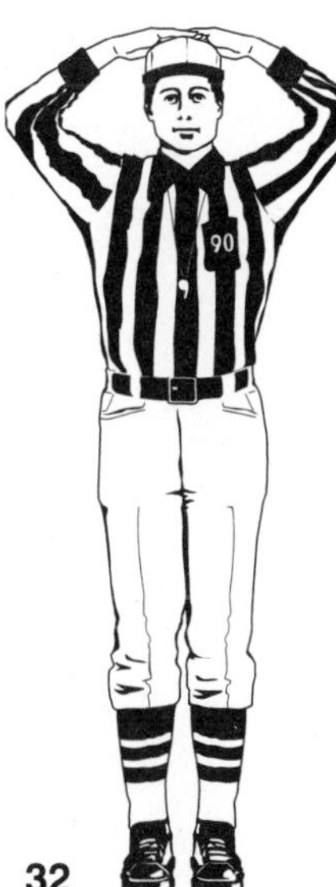

32

TWELVE MEN IN OFFENSIVE HUDDLE or TOO MANY MEN ON THE FIELD
Both hands on top of head.

33

FACE MASK
Grasping face mask with one hand.

34

ILLEGAL SHIFT
Horizontal arcs with two hands.

35

RESET PLAY CLOCK–25 SECONDS
Pump one arm vertically.

36

RESET PLAY CLOCK–40 SECONDS
Pump two arms vertically.

NFL DIGEST OF RULES

This Digest of Rules of the National Football League has been prepared to aid players, fans, and members of the press, radio, and television media in their understanding of the game.

It is not meant to be a substitute for the official rule book. In any case of conflict between these explanations and the official rules, the rules always have precedence.

In order to make it easier to coordinate the information in this digest, the topics discussed generally follow the order of the rule book.

OFFICIALS' JURISDICTIONS, POSITIONS, AND DUTIES

Referee—General oversight and control of game. Gives signals for all fouls and is final authority for rule interpretations. Takes a position in backfield 10 to 12 yards behind line of scrimmage, favors right side (if quarterback is right-handed passer). Determines legality of snap, observes deep back(s) for legal motion. On running play, observes quarterback during and after handoff, remains with him until action has cleared away, then proceeds downfield, checking on runner and contact behind him. When runner is downed, Referee determines forward progress from wing official and, if necessary, adjusts final position of ball.

On pass plays, drops back as quarterback begins to fade back, picks up legality of blocks by near linemen. Changes to complete concentration on quarterback as defenders approach. Primarily responsible to rule on possible roughing action on passer and if ball becomes loose, rules whether ball is free on a fumble or dead on an incomplete pass.

During kicking situations, Referee has primary responsibility to rule on kicker's actions and whether or not any subsequent contact by a defender is legal. The Referee will announce on the microphone when each period is ended.

Umpire—Primary responsibility to rule on players' equipment, as well as their conduct and actions on scrimmage line. Lines up approximately four to five yards downfield, varying position from in front of weakside tackle to strongside guard. Looks for possible false start by offensive linemen. Observes legality of contact by both offensive linemen while blocking and by defensive players while they attempt to ward off blockers. Is prepared to call rule infractions if they occur on offense or defense. Moves forward to line of scrimmage when pass play develops in order to insure that interior linemen do not move illegally downfield. If offensive linemen indicate screen pass is to be attempted, Umpire shifts his attention toward screen side, picks up potential receiver in order to insure that he will legally be permitted to run his pattern and continues to rule on action of blockers. Umpire is to assist in ruling on incomplete or trapped passes when ball is thrown overhead or short. On punt plays, Umpire positions himself opposite Referee in offensive backfield—5 yards from kicker and parallel.

Head Linesman—Primarily responsible for ruling on offside, encroachment, and actions pertaining to scrimmage line prior to or at snap. Keys on closest setback on his side of the field. On pass plays, Linesman is responsible to clear his receiver approximately seven yards downfield as he moves to a point five yards beyond the line. Linesman's secondary responsibility is to rule on any illegal action taken by defenders on any delay receiver moving downfield. Has full responsibility for ruling on sideline plays on his side, e.g., pass receiver or runner in or out of bounds. Together with Referee, Linesman is responsible for keeping track of number of downs and is in charge of mechanics of his chain crew in connection with its duties.

Linesman must be prepared to assist in determining forward progress by a runner on play directed toward middle or into his side zone. He, in turn, is to signal Referee or Umpire what forward point ball has reached. Linesman is also responsible to rule on legality of action involving any receiver who approaches his side zone. He is to call pass interference when the infraction occurs and is to rule on legality of blockers and defenders on plays involving ball carriers, whether it is entirely a running play, a combination pass and run, or a play involving a kick.

Line Judge—Straddles line of scrimmage on side of field opposite Linesman. Keeps time of game as a backup for clock operator. Along with Linesman is responsible for offside, encroachment, and actions pertaining to scrimmage line prior to or at snap. Line Judge keys on closest setback on his side of field. Line Judge is to observe his receiver until he moves at least seven yards downfield. He then moves toward backfield side, being especially alert to rule on any back in motion and on flight of ball when pass is made (he must rule whether forward or backward). Line Judge has primary responsibility to rule whether or not passer is behind or beyond line of scrimmage when pass is made. He also assists in observing actions by blockers and defenders who are on his side of field. After pass is thrown, Line Judge directs attention toward activities that occur in back of Umpire. During punting situations, Line Judge remains at line of scrimmage to be sure that only the end men move downfield until kick has been made. He also rules whether or not the kick crossed line and then observes action by members of the kicking team who are moving downfield to cover the kick. The Line Judge will advise the Referee when time has expired at the end of each period.

Field Judge—Operates on same side of field as Line Judge, 20 yards deep. Keys on wide receiver on his side. Concentrates on path of end or back, observing legality of his potential block(s) or of actions taken against him. Is prepared to rule from deep position on holding or illegal use of hands by end or back or on defensive infractions committed by player guarding him. Has primary responsibility to make decisions involving sideline on his side of field, e.g., pass receiver or runner in or out of bounds.

Field Judge makes decisions involving catching, recovery, or illegal touching of a loose ball beyond line of scrimmage; rules on plays involving pass receiver, including legality of catch or pass interference; assists in covering actions of runner, including blocks by teammates and that of defenders; calls clipping on punt returns; and, together with Back Judge, rules whether or not field goal attempts are successful.

Side Judge—Operates on same side of field as Linesman, 20 yards deep. Keys on wide receiver on his side. Concentrates on path of end or back, observing legality of his potential block(s) or of actions taken against him. Is prepared to rule from deep position on holding or illegal use of hands by end or back or on defensive infractions committed by player guarding him. Has primary responsibility to make decisions involving sideline on his side of field, e.g., pass receiver or runner in or out of bounds.

Side Judge makes decisions involving catching, recovery, or illegal touching of a loose ball beyond line of scrimmage; rules on plays involving pass receiver, including legality of catch or pass interference; assists in covering actions of runner, including blocks by teammates and that of defenders; and calls clipping on punt returns. On field goals and point after touchdown attempts, he becomes a double umpire.

Back Judge—Takes a position 25 yards downfield. In general, favors the tight end's side of field. Keys on tight end, concentrates on his path and observes legality of tight end's potential block(s) or of actions taken against him. Is prepared to rule from deep position on holding or illegal use of hands by end or back or on defensive infractions committed by player guarding him.

Back Judge times interval between plays on 40/25-second clock plus intermission between two periods of each half; makes decisions involving catching, recovery, or illegal touching of a loose ball beyond line of scrimmage; is responsible to rule on plays involving end line; calls pass interference, fair catch infractions, and clipping on kick returns; and, together with Field Judge, rules whether or not field goals and conversions are successful.

DEFINITIONS

1. **Chucking:** Warding off an opponent who is in front of a defender by contacting him with a quick extension of arm or arms, followed by the return of arm(s) to a flexed position, thereby breaking the original contact.
2. **Clipping:** Throwing the body across the back of an opponent's leg or hitting him from the back below the waist while moving up from behind unless the opponent is a runner or the action is in close line play.
3. **Close Line Play:** The area between the positions normally occupied by the offensive tackles, extending three yards on each side of the line of scrimmage.
4. **Crackback:** Eligible receivers who take or move to a position more than two yards outside the tackle may not block an opponent below the waist if they then move back inside to block.
5. **Dead Ball:** Ball not in play.
6. **Double Foul:** A foul by each team during the same down.
7. **Down:** The period of action that starts when the ball is put in play and ends when it is dead.
8. **Encroachment:** When a player enters the neutral zone and makes contact with an opponent before the ball is snapped.
9. **Fair Catch:** An unhindered catch of a kick by a member of the receiving team who must raise one arm a full length above his head while the kick is in flight.
10. **Foul:** Any violation of a playing rule.
11. **Free Kick:** A kickoff or safety kick. It may be a placekick, dropkick, or punt, except a punt may not be used on a kickoff following a touchdown, successful field goal, or to begin each half or overtime period. A tee cannot be used on a fair-catch or safety kick.
12. **Fumble:** The loss of possession of the ball.
13. **Game Clock:** Scoreboard game clock.
14. **Impetus:** The action of a player that gives momentum to the ball.
15. **Live Ball:** A ball legally free kicked or snapped. It continues in play until the down ends.
16. **Loose Ball:** A live ball not in possession of any player.
17. **Muff:** The touching of a loose ball by a player in an unsuccessful attempt to obtain possession.
18. **Neutral Zone:** The space the length of a ball between the two scrimmage lines. The offensive team and defensive team must remain behind their end of the ball.
    Exception: The offensive player who snaps the ball.
19. **Offside:** A player is offside when any part of his body is beyond his scrimmage or free kick line when the ball is snapped.
20. **Own Goal:** The goal a team is guarding.
21. **Play Clock:** 40/25 second clock.
22. **Pocket Area:** Applies from a point two yards outside of either offensive tackle and includes the tight end if he drops off the line of scrimmage to pass protect. Pocket extends longitudinally behind the line back to offensive team's own end line.
23. **Possession:** When a player controls the ball throughout the act of clearly touching both feet, or any other part of his body other than his hand(s), to the ground inbounds.
24. **Post-Possession Foul:** A foul by the receiving team that occurs after a ball is legally kicked from scrimmage prior to possession changing. The ball must cross the line of scrimmage and the receiving team must retain possession of the kicked ball.
25. **Punt:** A kick made when a player drops the ball and kicks it while it is in flight.
26. **Safety:** The situation in which the ball is dead on or behind a team's own goal if the impetus comes from a player on that team. Two points are scored for the opposing team.

DIGEST OF RULES

27. **Shift:** The movement of two or more offensive players at the same time before the snap.
28. **Striking:** The act of swinging, clubbing, or propelling the arm or forearm in contacting an opponent.
29. **Sudden Death:** The continuation of a tied game into sudden death overtime in which the team scoring first (by safety, field goal, or touchdown) wins.
30. **Touchback:** When a ball is dead on or behind a team's own goal line, provided the impetus came from an opponent and provided it is not a touchdown or a missed field goal.
31. **Touchdown:** When any part of the ball, legally in possession of a player inbounds, breaks the plane of the opponent's goal line, provided it is not a touchback.
32. **Unsportsmanlike Conduct:** Any act contrary to the generally understood principles of sportsmanship.

SUMMARY OF PENALTIES

Automatic First Down

1. Awarded to offensive team on all defensive fouls with these exceptions:
   (a) Offside.
   (b) Encroachment.
   (c) Delay of game.
   (d) Illegal substitution.
   (e) Excessive time out(s).
   (f) Incidental grasp of facemask.
   (g) Neutral zone infraction.
   (h) Running into the kicker.
   (i) More than 11 players on the field at the snap.

Five Yards

1. Defensive holding or illegal use of hands (automatic first down).
2. Delay of game on offense or defense.
3. Delay of kickoff.
4. Encroachment.
5. Excessive time out(s).
6. False start.
7. Illegal formation.
8. Illegal shift.
9. Illegal motion.
10. Illegal substitution.
11. First onside kickoff out of bounds between goal lines and not touched.
12. Invalid fair catch signal.
13. More than 11 players on the field at snap for either team.
14. Less than seven men on offensive line at snap.
15. Offside.
16. Failure to pause one second after shift or huddle.
17. Running into kicker.
18. More than one man in motion at snap.
19. Grasping facemask of the ball carrier or quarterback.
20. Player out of bounds at snap.
21. Ineligible member(s) of kicking team going beyond line of scrimmage before ball is kicked.
22. Illegal return.
23. Failure to report change of eligibility.
24. Neutral zone infraction.
25. Loss of team time out(s) or five-yard penalty on the defense for excessive crowd noise.
26. Ineligible player downfield during passing down.
27. Second forward pass behind the line.
28. Forward pass is first touched by eligible receiver who has gone out of bounds and returned.
29. Forward pass touches or is caught by an ineligible receiver on or behind line.
30. Forward pass thrown from behind line of scrimmage after ball once crossed the line.

10 Yards

1. Offensive pass interference.
2. Holding, illegal use of hands, arms, or body by offense.
3. Tripping by a member of either team.
4. Helping the runner.
5. Deliberately batting or punching a loose ball.
6. Deliberately kicking a loose ball.
7. Illegal block above the waist.

15 Yards

1. Chop block.
2. Clipping below the waist.
3. Fair catch interference.
4. Illegal crackback block by offense.
5. Piling on (automatic first down).
6. Roughing the kicker (automatic first down).
7. Roughing the passer (automatic first down).
8. Twisting, turning, or pulling an opponent by the facemask.
9. Unnecessary roughness.
10. Unsportsmanlike conduct.
11. Delay of game at start of either half.
12. Illegal low block.
13. A tackler using his helmet to butt, spear, or ram an opponent.
14. Any player who uses the top of his helmet unnecessarily.
15. A punter, placekicker, or holder who simulates being roughed by a defensive player.
16. A defender who takes a running start from beyond the line of scrimmage in an attempt to block a field goal or point after touchdown and lands on players at the line of scrimmage.

Five Yards and Loss of Down (Combination Penalty)

1. Forward pass thrown from beyond line of scrimmage.

10 Yards and Loss of Down (Combination Penalty)

1. Intentional grounding of forward pass (safety if passer is in own end zone). If foul occurs more than 10 yards behind line, play results in loss of down at spot of foul.

15 Yards and Loss of Coin Toss Option

1. Team's late arrival on the field prior to scheduled kickoff.
2. Captains not appearing for coin toss.

15 Yards (and disqualification if flagrant)

1. Striking opponent with fist.
2. Kicking or kneeing opponent.
3. Striking opponent on head or neck with forearm, elbow, or hands whether or not the initial contact is made below the neck area.
4. Roughing kicker.
5. Roughing passer.
6. Malicious unnecessary roughness.
7. Unsportsmanlike conduct.
8. Palpably unfair act. (Distance penalty determined by the Referee after consultation with other officials.)

15 Yards and Automatic Disqualification

1. Using a helmet (not worn) as a weapon.
2. Striking or purposely shoving a game official.

Suspension From Game For One Down

1. Illegal equipment. (Player may return after one down when legally equipped.)

Touchdown Awarded (Palpably Unfair Act)

1. When Referee determines a palpably unfair act deprived a team of a touchdown. (Example: Player comes off bench and tackles runner apparently en route to touchdown.)

FIELD

1. Sidelines and end lines are out of bounds. The goal line is actually in the end zone. A player with the ball in his possession scores when the ball is on, above, or over the goal line.
2. The field is rimmed by a white border, six feet wide, along the sidelines. All of this is out of bounds.
3. The hashmarks (inbound lines) are 70 feet, 9 inches from each sideline.
4. Goal posts must be single-standard type, offset from the end line and painted bright gold. The goal posts must be 18 feet, 6 inches wide and the top face of the crossbar must be 10 feet above the ground. Vertical posts extend at least 30 feet above the crossbar. A ribbon 4 inches by 42 inches long is to be attached to the top of each post. The actual goal is the plane extending indefinitely above the crossbar and between the outer edges of the posts.
5. The field is 360 feet long and 160 feet wide. The end zones are 30 feet deep. The line used in try-for-point plays is two yards out from the goal line.
6. Chain crew members and ball boys must be uniformly identifiable.
7. All clubs must use standardized sideline markers. Pylons must be used for goal line and end line markings.
8. End zone markings and club identification at 50 yard line must be approved by the Commissioner to avoid any confusion as to delineation of goal lines, sidelines, and end lines.

BALL

1. Thirty-six approved footballs will be used in games played outdoors (24 indoors).

COIN TOSS

1. The toss of coin will take place within three minutes of kickoff in center of field. The toss will be called by the visiting captain. The winner may choose one of two privileges and the loser gets the other:
   (a) Receive or kick
   (b) Goal his team will defend
2. Immediately prior to the start of the second half, the captains of both teams must inform the officials of their respective choices. The loser of the original coin toss gets first choice.

TIMING

1. The stadium game clock is official. In case it stops or is operating incorrectly, the Line Judge takes over the official timing on the field.
2. Each period is 15 minutes. The intermission between the periods is two minutes. Halftime is 12 minutes, unless otherwise specified.
3. On charged team time outs, the Field Judge starts watch and blows whistle after 1 minute 50 seconds, unless television does not utilize the time for commercial. In this case the length of the time out is reduced to 40 seconds.

4. The Referee will allow necessary time to attend to an injured player, or repair a legal player's equipment.
5. Each team is allowed three time outs each half.
6. Time between plays will be 40 seconds from the end of a given play until the snap of the ball for the next play, or a 25-second interval after certain administrative stoppages and game delays.
7. Clock will start running when ball is snapped following all changes of team possession.
8. With the exception of the last two minutes of the first half and the last five minutes of the second half, the game clock will be restarted following a kickoff return, a player going out of bounds on a play from scrimmage, or after declined penalties when appropriate on the referee's signal.
9. Consecutive team time outs can be taken by opposing teams but the length of the second time out will be reduced to 40 seconds.
10. When, in the judgment of the Referee, the level of crowd noise prevents the offense from hearing its signals, he can institute a series of procedures which can result in a loss of team time outs or a five-yard penalty against the defensive team.

SUDDEN DEATH

1. The sudden death system of determining the winner shall prevail when score is tied at the end of the regulation playing time of all NFL games. The team scoring first during overtime play shall be the winner and the game automatically ends upon any score (by safety, field goal, or touchdown) or when a score is awarded by Referee for a palpably unfair act.
2. At the end of regulation time the Referee will immediately toss coin at center of field in accordance with rules pertaining to the usual pregame toss. The captain of the visiting team will call the toss.
3. Following a three-minute intermission after the end of the regulation game, play will be continued in 15-minute periods or until there is a score. There is a two-minute intermission between subsequent periods. The teams change goals at the start of each period. Each team has three time outs per half and all general timing provisions apply as during a regular game. Disqualified players are not allowed to return.
   Exception: In preseason and regular season games there shall be a maximum of 15 minutes of sudden death with two time outs instead of three. General provisions that apply for the fourth quarter will prevail. Try not attempted if touchdown scored.

TIMING IN FINAL TWO MINUTES OF EACH HALF

1. On kickoff, clock does not start until the ball has been legally touched by player of either team in the field of play. (In all other cases, clock starts with kickoff.)
2. A team cannot buy an excess time out for a penalty. However, a fourth time out is allowed without penalty for an injured player, who must be removed immediately. A fifth time out or more is allowed for an injury and a five-yard penalty is assessed if the clock was running. Additionally, if the clock was running and the score is tied or the team in possession is losing, the ball cannot be put in play for at least 10 seconds on the fourth or more time out. The half or game can end while those 10 seconds are run off on the clock.
3. If the defensive team is behind in the score and commits a foul when it has no time outs left in the final 30 seconds of either half, the offensive team can decline the penalty for the foul and have the time on the clock expire.
4. Fouls that occur in the last five minutes of the fourth quarter as well as the last two minutes of the first half will result in the clock starting on the snap.

TRY

1. After a touchdown, the scoring team is allowed a try during one scrimmage down. The ball may be spotted anywhere between the inbounds lines, two or more yards from the goal line. The successful conversion counts one point by kick; two points for a successful conversion by touchdown; or one point for a safety.
2. The defensive team never can score on a try. As soon as defense gets possession or the kick is blocked or a touchdown is not scored, the try is over.
3. Any distance penalty for fouls committed by the defense that prevent the try from being attempted can be enforced on the succeeding try or succeeding kickoff. Any foul committed on a successful try will result in a distance penalty being assessed on the ensuing kickoff.
4. Only the fumbling player can recover and advance a fumble during a try.

PLAYERS-SUBSTITUTIONS

1. Each team is permitted 11 men on the field at the snap.
2. Unlimited substitution is permitted. However, players may enter the field only when the ball is dead. Players who have been substituted for are not permitted to linger on the field. Such lingering will be interpreted as unsportsmanlike conduct.
3. 12 men delayed in huddle—illegal substitution.
4. Players leaving the game must be out of bounds on their own side, clearing the field between the end lines, before a snap or free kick. If player crosses end line leaving field, it is delay of game (five-yard penalty).
5. Substitutes who remain in the game must move onto the field as far as the inside of the field numerals before moving to a wide position.
6. With the exception of the last two minutes of either half, the offensive team, while in the process of substitution or simulated substitution, is prohibited from rushing quickly to the line and snapping the ball with the obvious attempt to cause a defensive foul; i.e., too many men on the field.

KICKOFF

1. The kickoff shall be from the kicking team's 30-yard line at the start of each half and after a field goal and try-for-point. A kickoff is one type of free kick.
2. A one-inch tee may be used (no tee permitted for field goal or try attempt) on a kickoff. The ball is put in play by a placekick or dropkick.
3. If the kickoff clears the opponent's goal posts it is not a field goal.
4. A kickoff is illegal unless it travels 10 yards OR is touched by the receiving team. Once the ball is touched by the receiving team it is a free ball. Receivers may recover and advance. Kicking team may recover but NOT advance UNLESS receiver had possession and lost the ball.
5. When a kickoff goes out of bounds between the goal lines without being touched by the receiving team, the ball belongs to the receivers 30 yards from the spot of the kick or at the out-of-bounds spot unless the ball went out-of-bounds the first time an onside kick was attempted. In this case the kicking team is to be penalized five yards and the ball must be kicked again.
6. When a kickoff goes out of bounds between the goal lines and is touched last by receiving team, it is receiver's ball at out-of-bounds spot.

SAFETY

1. In addition to a kickoff, the other free kick is a kick after a safety (safety kick). A punt may be used (a punt may not be used on a kickoff).
2. On a safety kick, the team scored upon puts ball in play by a punt, dropkick, or placekick without tee. No score can be made on a free kick following a safety, even if a series of penalties places team in position. (A field goal can be scored only on a play from scrimmage or a free kick after a fair catch.)

FAIR CATCH KICK

1. After a fair catch, the receiving team has the option to put the ball in play by a snap or a fair catch kick (field goal attempt), with fair catch kick lines established ten yards apart. All general rules apply as for a field goal attempt from scrimmage. The clock starts when the ball is kicked. (No tee permitted.)

FIELD GOAL

1. All field goals attempted (kicker) and missed from beyond the 20-yard line will result in the defensive team taking possession of the ball at the spot of the kick. On any field goal attempted and missed where the spot of the kick is on or inside the 20-yard line, ball will revert to defensive team at the 20-yard line.

SAFETY

1. The important factor in a safety is impetus. Two points are scored for the opposing team when the ball is dead on or behind a team's own goal line if the impetus came from a player on that team.

Examples of Safety:

(a) Blocked punt goes out of kicking team's end zone. Impetus was provided by punting team. The block only changes direction of ball, not impetus.
(b) Ball carrier retreats from field of play into his own end zone and is downed. Ball carrier provides impetus.
(c) Offensive team commits a foul and spot of enforcement is behind its own goal line.
(d) Player on receiving team muffs punt and, trying to get ball, forces or illegally kicks (creating new impetus) it into end zone where it goes out of the end zone or is recovered by a member of the receiving team in the end zone.

Examples of Non-Safety:

(a) Player intercepts a pass with both feet inbounds in the field of play and his momentum carries him into his own end zone. Ball is put in play at spot of interception.
(b) Player intercepts a pass in his own end zone and is downed in the end zone, even after recovering in the end zone. Impetus came from passing team, not from defense. (Touchback)
(c) Player passes from behind his own goal line. Opponent bats down ball in end zone. (Incomplete pass)

MEASURING

1. The forward point of the ball is used when measuring.

POSITION OF PLAYERS AT SNAP

1. Offensive team must have at least seven players on line.
2. Offensive players, not on line, must be at least one yard back at snap. **(Exception:** player who takes snap.)
3. No interior lineman may move after taking or simulating a three-point stance.
4. No player of either team may invade neutral zone before snap.
5. No player of offensive team may charge or move, after assuming set position, in such manner as to lead defense to believe snap has started. No player of the defensive team within one yard of the line of scrimmage may make an abrupt movement in an attempt to cause the offense to false start.
6. If a player changes his eligibility, the Referee must alert the defensive captain after player has reported to him.
7. All players of offensive team must be stationary at snap, except one back who

may be in motion parallel to scrimmage line or backward (not forward).

8. After a shift or huddle all players on offensive team must come to an absolute stop for at least one second with no movement of hands, feet, head, or swaying of body.
9. Quarterbacks can be called for a false start penalty (five yards) if their actions are judged to be an obvious attempt to draw an opponent offside.

USE OF HANDS, ARMS, AND BODY

1. No player on offense may assist a runner except by blocking for him. There shall be no interlocking interference.
2. A runner may ward off opponents with his hands and arms but no other player on offense may use hands or arms to obstruct an opponent by grasping with hands, pushing, or encircling any part of his body during a block. Hands (open or closed) can be thrust forward to initially contact an opponent on or outside the opponent's frame, but the blocker must work to bring his hands on or inside the frame.
   Note: Pass blocking: Hand(s) thrust forward that slip outside the body of the defender will be legal if blocker worked to bring them back inside. Hand(s) or arm(s) that encircle a defender—i.e., hook an opponent—are to be considered illegal and officials are to call a foul for holding.
   Blocker cannot use his hands or arms to push from behind, hang onto, or encircle an opponent in a manner that restricts his movement as the play develops.
3. Hands cannot be thrust forward above the frame to contact an opponent on the neck, face or head.
   Note: The frame is defined as the part of the opponent's body below the neck that is presented to the blocker.
4. A defensive player may not tackle or hold an opponent other than a runner. Otherwise, he may use his hands, arms, or body only:
   (a) To defend or protect himself against an obstructing opponent.
   Exception: An eligible receiver is considered to be an obstructing opponent ONLY to a point five yards beyond the line of scrimmage unless the player who receives the snap clearly demonstrates no further intention to pass the ball. Within this five-yard zone, a defensive player may make contact with an eligible receiver that may be maintained as long as it is continuous and unbroken up until a point when the receiver is beyond the defender. The defensive player cannot use his hands or arms to push from behind, hang onto, or encircle an eligible receiver in a manner that restricts movement as the play develops. Beyond this five-yard limitation, a defender may use his hands or arms ONLY to defend or protect himself against impending contact caused by a receiver. In such reaction, the defender may not contact a receiver who attempts to take a path to evade him.
   (b) To push or pull opponent out of the way on line of scrimmage.
   (c) In actual attempt to get at or tackle runner.
   (d) To push or pull opponent out of the way in a legal attempt to recover a loose ball.
   (e) During a legal block on an opponent who is not an eligible pass receiver.
   (f) When legally blocking an eligible pass receiver above the waist.
   Exception: Eligible receivers lined up within two yards of the tackle, whether on or immediately behind the line, may be blocked below the waist at or behind the line of scrimmage. NO eligible receiver may be blocked below the waist after he goes beyond the line. (Illegal cut)
   Note: Once the quarterback hands off or pitches the ball to a back, or if the quarterback leaves the pocket area, the restrictions (illegal chuck, illegal cut) on the defensive team relative to the offensive receivers will end, provided the ball is not in the air.
5. A defensive player may not contact an opponent above the shoulders with the palm of his hand except to ward him off on the line. This exception is permitted only if it is not a repeated act against the same opponent during any one contact. In all other cases the palms may be used on head, neck, or face only to ward off or push an opponent in legal attempt to get at the ball.
6. Any offensive player who pretends to possess the ball or to whom a teammate pretends to give the ball may be tackled provided he is crossing his scrimmage line between the ends of a normal tight offensive line.
7. An offensive player who lines up more than two yards outside his own tackle or a player who, at the snap, is in a backfield position and subsequently takes a position more than two yards outside a tackle may not clip an opponent anywhere nor may he contact an opponent below the waist if the blocker is moving toward the ball and if contact is made within an area five yards on either side of the line.
8. A player of either team may block at any time provided it is not pass interference, fair catch interference, or unnecessary roughness.
9. A player may not bat or punch:
   (a) A loose ball (in field of play) toward his opponent's goal line or in any direction in either end zone.
   (b) A ball in player possession.
   Note: If there is any question as to whether a defender is stripping or batting a ball in player possession, the official(s) will rule the action as a legal act (stripping the ball).
   Exception: A forward or backward pass may be batted, tipped, or deflected in any direction at any time by either the offense or the defense.
   Note: A pass in flight that is controlled or caught may only be thrown backward, if it is thrown forward it is considered an illegal bat.
10. No player may deliberately kick any ball except as a punt, dropkick, or placekick.

FORWARD PASS

1. A forward pass may be touched or caught by any eligible receiver. All members of the defensive team are eligible. Eligible receivers on the offensive team are players on either end of line (other than center, guard, or tackle) or players at least one yard behind the line at the snap. A T-formation quarterback is not eligible to receive a forward pass during a play from scrimmage.
   Exception: T-formation quarterback becomes eligible if pass is previously touched by an eligible receiver.
2. An offensive team may make only one forward pass during each play from scrimmage (Loss of 5 yards).
3. The passer must be behind his line of scrimmage (Loss of down and five yards, enforced from the spot of pass).
4. Any eligible offensive player may catch a forward pass. If a pass is touched by one eligible offensive player and touched or caught by a second offensive player, pass completion is legal. Further, all offensive players become eligible once a pass is touched by an eligible receiver or any defensive player.
5. The rules concerning a forward pass and ineligible receivers:
   (a) If ball is touched accidentally by an ineligible receiver on or behind his line: loss of five yards.
   (b) If ineligible receiver is illegally downfield: loss of five yards.
   (c) If touched or caught (intentionally or accidentally) by ineligible receiver beyond the line: loss of 5 yards.
6. The player who first controls and continues to maintain control of a pass will be awarded the ball even though his opponent later establishes joint control of the ball.
7. Any forward pass becomes incomplete and ball is dead if:
   (a) Pass hits the ground or goes out of bounds.
   (b) Pass hits the goal post or the crossbar of either team.
   (c) Pass is caught by offensive player after touching ineligible receiver.
   (d) An illegal pass is caught by an offensive player.
8. A forward pass is complete when a receiver clearly possesses the pass and touches the ground with both feet inbounds while in possession of the ball. If a receiver would have landed inbounds with both feet but is carried or pushed out of bounds while maintaining possession of the ball, pass is complete at the out-of-bounds spot.
9. If an eligible receiver goes out of bounds accidentally or is legally forced out by a defender and returns to first touch and catch a pass, the play is regarded as an incomplete pass. Loss of 5 yards.
10. On a fourth down pass—when the offensive team is inside the opposition's 20-yard line—an incomplete pass results in a loss of down at the line of scrimmage.
11. If a personal foul is committed by the defense prior to the completion of a pass, the penalty is 15 yards from the spot where ball becomes dead.
12. If a personal foul is committed by the offense prior to the completion of a pass, the penalty is 15 yards from the previous line of scrimmage.

INTENTIONAL GROUNDING OF FORWARD PASS

1. Intentional grounding of a forward pass is a foul: loss of down and 10 yards from previous spot if passer is in the field of play or loss of down at the spot of the foul if it occurs more than 10 yards behind the line or safety if passer is in his own end zone when ball is released.
2. Intentional grounding will be called when a passer, facing an imminent loss of yardage due to pressure from the defense, throws a forward pass without a realistic chance of completion.
3. Intentional grounding will not be called when a passer, while out of the pocket and facing an imminent loss of yardage, throws a pass that lands at or beyond the line of scrimmage, even if no offensive player(s) have a realistic chance to catch the ball (including if the ball lands out of bounds over the sideline or end line).

PROTECTION OF PASSER

1. By interpretation, a pass begins when the passer—with possession of ball—starts to bring his hand forward. If ball strikes ground after this action has begun, play is ruled an incomplete pass. If passer loses control of ball prior to his bringing his hand forward, play is ruled a fumble.
2. No defensive player may run into a passer of a legal forward pass after the ball has left his hand (15 yards). The Referee must determine whether opponent had a reasonable chance to stop his momentum during an attempt to block the pass or tackle the passer while he still had the ball.
3. No defensive player who has an unrestricted path to the quarterback may hit him flagrantly in the area of the knee(s) when approaching in any direction.
4. Officials are to blow the play dead as soon as the quarterback is clearly in the grasp and control of any tackler, and his safety is in jeopardy.

PASS INTERFERENCE

1. There shall be no interference with a forward pass thrown from behind the line. The restriction for the passing team starts with the snap. The restriction on the defensive team starts when the ball leaves the passer's hand. Both restrictions end when the ball is touched by anyone.

2. The penalty for defensive pass interference is an automatic first down at the spot of the foul. If interference is in the end zone, it is first down for the offense on the defense's 1-yard line. If previous spot was inside the defense's 1-yard line, penalty is half the distance to the goal line.
3. The penalty for offensive pass interference is 10 yards from the previous spot.
4. It is pass interference by either team when any player movement beyond the offensive line significantly hinders the progress of an eligible player or such player's opportunity to catch the ball during a legal forward pass. When players are competing for position to make a play on the ball, any contact by hands, arms, or body shall be considered incidental unless prohibited. Prohibited conduct shall be when a player physically restricts or impedes the opponent in such a manner that is visually evident and materially affects the opponent's opportunity to gain position or retain his position to catch the ball. If a player has gained position, he shall not be considered to have impeded or restricted his opponent in a prohibited manner if all of his actions are a bona fide effort to go to and catch the ball. Provided an eligible player is not interfered with in such a manner, the following exceptions to pass interference will prevail:
   (a) If neither player is looking for the ball and there is incidental contact in the act of moving to the ball that does not materially affect the route of an eligible player, there is no interference. If there is any question whether the incidental contact materially affects the route, the ruling shall be no interference.
   Note: Inadvertent tripping is not a foul in this situation.
   (b) Any eligible player looking for and intent on playing the ball who initiates contact, however severe, while attempting to move to the spot of comple tion or interception will not be called for interference.
   (c) Any eligible player who makes contact, however severe, with one or more eligible players while looking for and making a genuine attempt to catch or bat a reachable ball, will not be called for interference.
   (d) It must be remembered that defensive players have as much right to the ball as offensive eligible receivers.
   (e) Pass interference by the defense is not to be called when the forward pass is clearly uncatchable.
   (f) Note: There is no defensive pass interference behind the line.

BACKWARD PASS

1. Any pass not forward is regarded as a backward pass. A pass parallel to the line is a backward pass. A runner may pass backward at any time. Any player on either team may catch the pass or recover the ball after it touches the ground.
2. A backward pass that strikes the ground can be recovered and advanced by either team.
3. A backward pass caught in the air can be advanced by either team.
4. A backward pass in flight may not be batted forward by an offensive player.

FUMBLE

1. The distinction between a fumble and a muff should be kept in mind in considering rules about fumbles. A fumble is the loss of player possession of the ball. A muff is the touching of a loose ball by a player in an unsuccessful attempt to obtain possession.
2. A fumble may be advanced by any player on either team regardless of whether recovered before or after ball hits the ground.
3. A fumble that goes forward and out of bounds will return to the fumbling team at the spot of the fumble unless the ball goes out of bounds in the opponent's end zone. In this case, it is a touchback.
4. On a play from scrimmage, if an offensive player fumbles anywhere on the field during fourth down, only the fumbling player is permitted to recover and/or advance the ball. If any player fumbles after the two-minute warning in a half, only the fumbling player is permitted to recover and/or advance the ball. If recovered by any other offensive player, the ball is dead at the spot of the fumble unless it is recovered behind the spot of the fumble. In that case, the ball is dead at the spot of recovery. Any defensive player may recover and/or advance any fumble at any time.

KICKS FROM SCRIMMAGE

1. Any kick from scrimmage must be made from behind the line to be legal.
2. Any punt or missed field goal that touches a goal post is dead.
3. During a kick from scrimmage, only the end men, as eligible receivers on the line of scrimmage at the time of the snap, are permitted to go beyond the line before the ball is kicked.
   Exception: An eligible receiver who, at the snap, is aligned or in motion behind the line and more than one yard outside the end man on his side of the line, clearly making him the outside receiver, replaces that end man as the player eligible to go downfield after the snap. All other members of the kicking team must remain at the line of scrimmage until the ball has been kicked.
4. Any punt that is blocked and does not cross the line of scrimmage can be recovered and advanced by either team. However, if offensive team recovers it must make the yardage necessary for its first down to retain possession if punt was on fourth down.
5. The kicking team may never advance its own kick even though legal recovery is made beyond the line of scrimmage. Possession only.
6. A member of the receiving team may not run into or rough a kicker who kicks from behind his line unless contact is:
   (a) Incidental to and after he had touched ball in flight.
   (b) Caused by kicker's own motions.
   (c) Occurs during a quick kick, or a kick made after a run, or after kicker recovers a loose ball. Ball is loose when kicker muffs snap or snap hits ground.
   (d) Defender is blocked into kicker.
   The penalty for running into the kicker is 5 yards. For roughing the kicker: 15 yards, an automatic first down and disqualification if flagrant.
7. If a member of the kicking team attempting to down the ball on or inside opponent's 5-yard line carries the ball into the end zone, it is a touchback.
8. Fouls during a punt are enforced from the previous spot (line of scrimmage).
   Exception: Illegal touching, illegal fair catch, invalid fair catch signal, and fouls by the receiving team during loose ball after ball is kicked.
9. While the ball is in the air or rolling on the ground following a punt or field goal attempt and receiving team commits a foul before gaining possession, receiving team will retain possession and will be penalized for its foul.
10. It will be illegal for a defensive player to jump or stand on any player, or be picked up by a teammate or to use a hand or hands on a teammate to gain additional height in an attempt to block a kick (Penalty: 15 yards, unsportsmanlike conduct).
11. A punted ball remains a kicked ball until it is declared dead or in possession of either team.
12. Any member of the punting team may down the ball anywhere in the field of play. However, it is illegal touching (Official's time out and receiver's ball at spot of illegal touching). This foul does not offset any foul by receivers during the down.
13. Defensive team may advance all kicks from scrimmage (including unsuccessful field goal) whether or not ball crosses defensive team's goal line. Rules pertaining to kicks from scrimmage apply until defensive team gains possession.

FAIR CATCH

1. The member of the receiving team must raise one arm a full length above his head and wave it from side to side while kick is in flight. (Failure to give proper sign: receivers' ball five yards behind spot of signal.) **Note:** It is legal for the receiver to shield his eyes from the sun by raising one hand no higher than the helmet.
2. No opponent may interfere with the fair catcher, the ball, or his path to the ball. Penalty: 15 yards from spot of foul and fair catch is awarded.
3. A player who signals for a fair catch is not required to catch the ball. However, if a player signals for a fair catch, he may not block or initiate contact with any player on the kicking team until the ball touches a player. Penalty: snap 15 yards behind spot of foul.
4. If ball hits ground or is touched by member of kicking team in flight, fair catch signal is off and all rules for a kicked ball apply.
5. Any undue advance by a fair catch receiver is delay of game. No specific distance is specified for undue advance as ball is dead at spot of catch. If player comes to a reasonable stop, no penalty. For violation, five yards.
6. If time expires while ball is in play and a fair catch is awarded, receiving team may choose to extend the period with one fair catch kick down. However, placekicker may not use tee.

FOUL ON LAST PLAY OF HALF OR GAME

1. On a foul by defense on last play of half or game, the down is replayed if penalty is accepted.
2. On a foul by the offense on last play of half or game, the down is not replayed and the play in which the foul is committed is nullified.
   Exception: Fair catch interference, foul following change of possession, illegal touching. No score by offense counts.

SPOT OF ENFORCEMENT OF FOUL

1. There are four basic spots at which a penalty for a foul is enforced:
   (a) Spot of foul: The spot where the foul is committed.
   (b) Previous spot: The spot where the ball was put in play.
   (c) Spot of snap, pass, fumble, return kick, or free kick: The spot where the act connected with the foul occurred.
   (d) Succeeding spot: The spot where the ball next would be put in play if no distance penalty were to be enforced.
   Exception: If foul occurs after a touchdown and before the whistle for a try-for-point, succeeding spot is spot of next kickoff.
2. All fouls committed by offensive team behind the line of scrimmage and in the field of play shall be penalized from the previous spot.
3. When spot of enforcement for fouls involving defensive holding or illegal use of hands by the defense is behind the line of scrimmage, any penalty yardage to be assessed on that play shall be measured from the line if the foul occurred beyond the line.

DOUBLE FOUL

1. If there is a double foul during a down in which there is a change of possession, the team last gaining possession may keep the ball unless its foul was committed prior to the change of possession.
2. If double foul occurs after a change of possession, the defensive team retains the ball at the spot of its foul or dead ball spot.
3. If one of the fouls of a double foul involves disqualification, that player must be removed, but no penalty yardage is to be assessed.

4. If the kickers foul during a kick before possession changes and the receivers foul after possession changes, the receivers will retain the ball after enforcement of its foul.

PENALTY ENFORCED ON FOLLOWING KICKOFF

1. When a team scores by touchdown, field goal, extra point, or safety and either team commits a personal foul, unsportsmanlike conduct, or obvious unfair act during the down, the penalty will be assessed on the following kickoff.

EMERGENCIES AND UNFAIR ACTS

Emergencies—Policy

The National Football League requires all League personnel, including game officials, League office employees, players, coaches, and other club employees to use best effort to see that each game—preseason, regular season, and postseason—is played to its conclusion. The League recognizes, however, that emergencies may arise that make a game's completion impossible or inadvisable. Such circumstances may include, but are not limited to, severely inclement weather, natural or manmade disaster, power failure, and spectator interference. Games should be suspended, cancelled, postponed, or terminated when circumstances exist such that comencement or continuation of play would pose a threat to the safety of participants or spectators.

Authority of Commissioner's Office

1. Authority to cancel, postpone, or terminate games is vested only in the Commissioner and the League President (other League office representatives and referees may suspend play temporarily; see point No. 3 under this section and point No. 1 under "Authority of Referee" below). The following definitions apply:
   - **Cancel.** To cancel a game is to nullify it either before or after it begins and to make no provision for rescheduling it or for including its score or other performance statistics in League records.
   - **Postpone.** To postpone a game is (a) to defer its starting time to a later date, or (b) to suspend it after play has begun and to make provision to resume at a later date with all scores and other performance statistics up to the point of postponement added to those achieved in the resumed portion of the game.
   - **Terminate.** To terminate a game is to end it short of a full 60 minutes of play, to record it officially as a completed game, and to make no provision to resume it at a later date. The Commissioner or League President may terminate a game in an emergency if, in his opinion, it is reasonable to project that its resumption (a) would not change its ultimate result or (b) would not adversely affect any other interteam competitive issue.
   - **Forfeit.** The Commissioner, (except in cases of disciplinary action; see last section on "Removing Team from Field"), League President, and their representatives, including referees, are not authorized unilaterally to declare forfeits. A forfeit occurs only when a game is not played because of the failure or refusal of *one* team to participate. In that event, the other team, if ready and willing to play, is the winner by a score of 2-0.
2. If an emergency arises that may require cancellation, postponement, or termination (see above), the highest ranking representative from the Commissioner's office working the game in a "control" capacity will consult with the Commissioner, League President, or game-day duty officer designated by the League (by telephone, if that person is not in attendance) concerning such decision. If circumstances warrant, the League representative should also attempt to consult with the weather bureau and with appropriate security personnel of the League, club, stadium, and local authorities. If no representative from the Commissioner's office is working the game in a "control" capacity, the referee will be in charge (see "Authority of Referee" below).
3. In circumstances where safety is of immediate concern, the Commissioner's-office representative may, after consulting with the referee, authorize a temporary suspension in play and, if warranted, removal of the participants from the playing field. The representative should be mindful of the safety of spectators, players, game officials, nonplayer personnel in the bench areas, and other field-level personnel such as photographers and cheerleaders.
4. If possible, the League-office representative should consult with authorized representatives of the two participating clubs before any decision involving cancellation, postponement, or termination is made by the Commissioner or League President.
5. If the Commissioner or League President decides to cancel, postpone, or terminate a game, his representative at the game or the game-day duty officer will then determine the method(s) for announcing such decision, e.g., by public-address announcement over referee's wireless microphone, by public-address announcement by home club, or by communication to radio, television, and other news media.

Authority of Referee

1. If a referee determines that an emergency warrants immediate removal of participants from the playing field for safety reasons, he may do so on his own authority. If, however, circumstances allow him the time, he must reach the highest ranking full-time League office representative working at the game in a "control" capacity or the game-day duty officer designated by the League (by telephone, if that person is not in attendance) and discuss the actual or potential emergency with such representative or duty officer. That representative or duty officer then will make the final decision on removal of participants from the field or obtain a decision from the Commissioner or League President.
2. If a referee removes participants from the playing field under No. 1 above, he may order them to their respective bench areas or to their locker rooms, whichever is appropriate in the circumstances.
3. After appropriate consultation under No. 1 above, the referee must advise the two participating head coaches of the nature of the emergency and the action contemplated (if the decision has not yet been reached) or of the final decision.
4. The referee must *not*, before a decision is reached, make an announcement on his microphone concerning the possibility of a cancellation, postponement, or termination unless instructed to do so by an appropriate representative of the Commissioner's office.
5. The referee must *not* discuss a forfeit with head coaches or club personnel and must *not* use that term over the referee's microphone (see definition of *forfeit* under No. 1 of "Authority of Commissioner's Office" above).
6. The referee must *not* assess an unsportsmanlike-conduct penalty on the home team for actions of fans that cause or contribute to an emergency.
7. The referee should be mindful of the safety of not only players and officials, but also of the spectators and other nonparticipants.
8. If an emergency involves spectator interference (for example, nonparticipants on the field or thrown objects), the referee immediately should contact the appropriate club or League representative for additional security assistance, including, if applicable, involvement of the League's security representative(s) assigned to the game.
9. The referee may order the resumption of play when he deems conditions safe for all concerned and, if circumstances warrant, after consultation with appropriate representatives of the Commissioner's office.
10. Under no circumstances is the referee authorized to cancel, postpone, terminate, or declare forfeiture of a game unilaterally.

Procedures for Starting and Resuming Games

Subject to the points of authority listed above, League personnel and referees will be guided by the following procedures for starting and resuming games that are affected by emergencies.

1. If, because of an emergency, a regular-season or postseason game is not started at its scheduled time and cannot be played at any later time that same day, the game nevertheless must be played on a subsequent date to be determined by the Commissioner.
2. If an emergency threatens to occur during the playing of a game (for example, an incoming tropical storm), the starting time of the game will not be moved to an earlier time unless there is clearly sufficient time to make an orderly change.
3. All games that are suspended temporarily and resumed on the same day, and all suspended games that are postponed to a later date, will be resumed at the point of suspension. On suspension, the referee will call timeout and make a record of the following: team possessing the ball, direction in which its offense was headed, position of the ball on the field, down, distance, period, time remaining in the period, and any other pertinent information required for an orderly and equitable resumption of play.
4. For regular-season postponements, the Commissioner will make every effort to set the game for no later than two days after its originally scheduled date and at the same site. If unable to schedule at the same site, he will select an appropriate alternative site. If it is impossible to schedule the game within two days after its original date, the Commissioner will attempt to schedule it on the Tuesday of the next calendar week. The Commissioner will keep in mind the potential for competitive inequities if one or both of the involved clubs has already been scheduled for a game close to the Tuesday of that week (for example, a Thursday game).
5. For postseason postponements, the Commissioner will make every effort to set the game as soon as possible after its originally scheduled date and at the same site. If unable to schedule at the same site, he will select an appropriate alternative site.
6. Whenever postponement is attributable to negligence by a club, the negligent club is responsible for all home club costs and expenses, including, subject to approval by the Commissioner, gate receipts and television-contract income. [See Section 19.11 (C) of the NFL Constitution and Bylaws.]
7. Each home club is strictly responsible for having the playing surface of its stadium well maintained and suitable for NFL play.

UNFAIR ACTS

Commissioner's Authority

The Commissioner has sole authority to investigate and to take appropriate disciplinary or corrective measures if any club action, nonparticipant interference, or emergency occurs in an NFL game which he deems so unfair or outside the accepted tactics encountered in professional football that such action has a major effect on the result of a game.

No Club Protests

The authority and measures provided for in this section (UNFAIR ACTS) do not constitute a protest machinery for NFL clubs to dispute the result of a game. The Commissioner will conduct an investigation under this section only to review an act or occurrence that he deems so unfair that the result of the game in question may be inequitable to one of the participating teams. The Commissioner will not apply his authority under this section when a club registers a complaint concerning judgmental errors or routine errors of omission by game officials. Games involving such complaints will continue to stand as completed.

Penalties for Unfair Acts

The Commissioner's powers under this section (UNFAIR ACTS) include the imposition of monetary fines and draft choice forfeitures, suspension of persons involved, and, if appropriate, the reversal of a game's result or the rescheduling of a game, either from the beginning or from the point at which the extraordinary act occurred. In the event of rescheduling a game, the Commissioner will be guided by the procedures specified above ("Procedures for Starting and Resuming Games" under EMERGENCIES). In all cases, the Commissioner will conduct a full investigation, including the opportunity for hearings, use of game videotape, and any other procedures he deems appropriate.

REMOVING TEAM FROM FIELD

No player, coach, or other person affiliated with a club may remove that club's team from the field during the playing of any game, including preseason, except at the direction of the referee. Any club violating this rule will be subject to disciplinary action by the Commissioner, including possible game forfeiture and sole liability for financial losses suffered by the opposing club and any other affected member clubs of the League. [See Section 9.1 (E) of the NFL Constitution and Bylaws.]

NATIONAL FOOTBALL LEAGUE, 1998

280 Park Avenue, New York, New York 10017 (212) 450-2000
NFL Internet Address: http://nfl.com

Commissioner: Paul Tagliabue
President: Neil Austrian

Executive Vice President-Labor Relations/Chairman NFLMC: Harold Henderson
Executive Vice President & League Counsel: Jeff Pash
Executive Vice President-League & Football Development: Roger Goodell
Chief Financial Officer: Tom Spock
Senior Vice President-Communications & Government Affairs: Joe Browne
Senior Vice President-Broadcasting & Network Television: Dennis Lewin
Senior Vice President-Football Operations: George Young

COMMUNICATIONS
Vice President of Public Relations: Greg Aiello
Director of International Public Affairs: Pete Abitante
Director of Media Services: Leslie Hammond
Director of Corporate Communications: Chris Widmaier

BROADCASTING
Vice President of Programming: John Collins
Director of Broadcasting Research: Joe Ferreira
Director of Broadcasting Services: Dick Maxwell

LEAGUE AND FOOTBALL DEVELOPMENT
Vice President of Club Administration & Stadium Management: Joe Ellis
Senior Director of Security: Milt Ahlerich
Senior Director of Officiating: Jerry Seeman
Director of Strategic Development: Neil Glat
Director of Game Operations: Peter Hadhazy
Director of Football Development: Gene Washington

SPECIAL EVENTS
Vice President of Special Events: Jim Steeg
Director of Special Events Operations: Don Renzulli
Director of Special Events Planning: Sue Robichek

MANAGEMENT COUNCIL
Senior Vice President-General Counsel: Dennis Curran
Senior Vice President-Labor Relations: Peter Ruocco
Vice President of Player & Employee Development: Lem Burnham
Senior Director of Player Personnel/ Football Operations: Joel Bussert
Director of Labor Relations: Lal Heneghan
Director of Compliance: Mike Keenan
Director of Player Programs: Guy Troupe
Director-Labor Administration & Information: John Jones

FINANCE AND ADMINISTRATION
Vice President-Law Enterprises, Broadcast & Finance: Frank Hawkins
Treasurer: Joe Siclare
Vice President-Internal Audit: Tom Sullivan
Controller: Peter Lops
Vice President of Systems & Information Processing: Mary Oliveti
Senior Director of Human Resources & Administration: John Buzzeo
Director of Business Planning: Dan Margoshes

NFL ENTERPRISES
President: Ron Bernard
Senior Vice President-International: Don Garber
Vice President-NFL Interactive: Ann Kirschner
Vice President-Marketing & Sales: Tola Murphy-Baran
Vice President-International TV Distribution: Anne Murray
Vice President-International Marketing: Doug Quinn
President, NFL Europe: Oliver Luck
CFO/Chief Administration Officer, NFL Europe: Ken Saunders
Managing Director, NFL Europe: Chris Heyne
Managing Director, NFL Europe: Bill Peterson

NFL FILMS
President: Steve Sabol
Senior Vice President-Finance & Operations: Barry Wolper
Vice President-Cinematography: Steve Andrich
Vice President-In Charge of Production: Jay Gerber
Vice President-Video Operations: Jeff Howard
Vice President-Production Director: Hal Lipman
Vice President-Editor-in-Chief: Bob Ryan
Vice President-Special Projects: Phil Tuckett

NFL PROPERTIES
President: Sara Levinson
Senior Vice President-Consumer Products: Jim Connelly
Senior Vice President-Business Affairs & General Counsel: Gary Gertzog
Senior Vice President-Marketing: Howard Handler
Senior Vice President-Club Services: Mark Holtzman
Senior Vice President-Corporate Sponsorships: Jim Schwebel
Vice President-Advertising & Design: Bruce Burke
Vice President-Finance: Ralph Carras
Vice President-Events: David Newman
Vice President-Corporate Sponsorship: Steve Phelps
Vice President-Publishing: John Wiebusch

NOTES

NOTES

NOTES

NOTES